Contemporary Authors

NEW REVISION SERIES

Contemporary

Authors

A Bio-Bibliographical Guide to
Current Writers in Fiction, General Nonfiction,
Poetry, Journalism, Drama, Motion Pictures,
Television, and Other Fields

ANN EVORY
LINDA METZGER
Editors

PETER M. GAREFFA
DEBORAH A. STRAUB
Associate Editors

NEW REVISION SERIES
volume **11**

GALE RESEARCH COMPANY • BOOK TOWER • DETROIT, MICHIGAN 48226

EDITORIAL STAFF

Christine Nasso, *General Editor, Contemporary Authors*

Ann Evory and Linda Metzger, *Editors, New Revision Series*

Peter M. Gareffa and Deborah A. Straub, *Associate Editors*

James G. Lesniak, Donna Olendorf, and Thomas Wiloch, *Senior Assistant Editors*

Candace Cloutier, Nancy Hebb, Kerry L. Lutz, Margaret Mazurkiewicz, Susan Salter,
Heidi A. Tietjen, Michaela Swart Wilson, and Robert T. Wilson, *Assistant Editors*

Fred Bornhauser, Jean W. Ross, and Walter W. Ross, *Interviewers*

Melissa J. Gaiownik, Timothy Marshall, and Mary Alice Rattenbury,
Editorial Assistants

Marian Walters and Debra G. Jones, *Contributing Editors*

Frederick G. Ruffner, *Publisher*   James M. Ethridge, *Editorial Director*

Copyright © 1963, 1964, 1965, 1966, 1967, 1968, 1969, 1970, 1971, 1972, 1973, 1974, 1975, 1976,
1977, 1978, 1979, 1981, 1982, 1984 by
GALE RESEARCH COMPANY

Library of Congress Catalog Card Number 81-640179
ISBN 0-8103-1940-3
ISSN 0275-7176

Authors and Media People
Featured in This Volume

Russell Baker—American journalist; author of the syndicated *New York Times* column "Observer" since 1962; recipient of two Pulitzer Prizes, one in 1979 for distinguished commentary and another in 1982 for his autobiography, *Growing Up*.

William Barrett—American philosopher, professor, and writer; his book *The Truants* chronicles his years with *Partisan Review* and discusses the ideas and personalities associated with that journal in the 1940s and 1950s; his other books, such as *What Is Existentialism?*, *Irrational Man*, and *Illusion of Technique*, cover the modern intellectual scene, existentialist philosophy, and Barrett's belief that a "deranged rationality" has overtaken Western society. (Sketch includes interview.)

Daniel Berrigan—American social activist, Roman Catholic priest, and author of nonfiction and poetry; known for his nonviolent protests against war and nuclear weapons; three of his books, *No One Walks Waters*, *Time without Number*, and *No Bars to Manhood*, have been nominated for National Book Awards; also author of autobiographical works, including the play *The Trial of the Catonsville Nine*.

Philip Berrigan—American social activist and former Roman Catholic priest; he has been arrested over forty times and has served at least three prison terms for his nonviolent protests against war and nuclear weapons; his views on these and other issues are covered in such books as *Widen the Prison Gates*, *Prison Journals of a Priest Revolutionary*, and *Of Beasts and Beastly Images*. (Sketch includes interview.)

Ben Bova—American science fiction writer, author of nonfiction, editor of anthologies, and former editor of *Analog* and *Omni* magazines; in his work he seeks scientific solutions to societal problems; among his writings are the novels *Exiled from Earth*, *Flight of the Exiles*, and *End of Exile* and the nonfiction books *The High Road* and *Vision of the Future*. (Sketch includes interview.)

Dee Brown—American librarian, professor, historian, and novelist; concentrating on the American West in both his novels and nonfiction, he consistently expresses outrage at the injustices inflicted upon the American Indian; his books include *Bury My Heart at Wounded Knee*, *Hear That Lonesome Whistle Blow*, *Creek Mary's Blood*, and *Killdeer Mountain*.

Rita Mae Brown—American novelist, essayist, and poet who first gained critical recognition in 1973 with her controversial autobiographical novel, *Rubyfruit Jungle;* also author of the novels *In Her Day*, *Six of One*, *Southern Discomfort*, and *Sudden Death*. (Sketch includes interview.)

Frederick Buechner—American minister, college instructor, novelist, short-story writer, and author of nonfiction; a Christian apologist, Buechner has been praised for the humor and sensitive characterizations in his novels, especially the tetralogy featuring Leo Bebb: *Lion Country*, *Open Heart*, *Love Feast*, and *Treasure Hunt*. (Sketch includes interview.)

Nigel Calder—British writer; his popular books and television documentaries cover such scientific topics as continental drift and changes in weather, recent discoveries in subatomic physics, and speculations on the future of the earth and humanity; author of *Eden Was No Garden*, *The Weather Machine*, *Einstein's Universe*, *Nuclear Nightmares*, and other related books.

Alan M. Dershowitz—American attorney and professor of law; known for taking on a number of controversial cases, usually because they involve interesting points of law; his book *The Best Defense* describes what he views as serious problems with the American judicial system, including frequent disregard of a defendant's constitutional and civil rights.

Mark Dintenfass—American professor and novelist who, according to Michael Mewshaw writing in the *New York Times Book Review*, possesses "an individual voice, a quirky vision and a vitality of language which is more than matched by his intelligence"; among his novels are *Make Yourself an Earthquake*, *The Case against Org*, and *Old World, New World*. (Sketch includes interview.)

Francine du Plessix Gray—French-born novelist, nonfiction writer, and editor and staff writer for journals; her widely reviewed autobiographical novel, *Lovers and Tyrants*, has been called a feminist fable about a woman freeing herself from her oppressors; also author of the novel *World Without End* and the nonfiction books *Divine Disobedience* and *Hawaii: The Sugar-Coated Fortress*. (Sketch includes interview.)

Sydney J. Harris—American journalist and author of "Strictly Speaking," a column syndicated to 200 newspapers worldwide; his collected work has appeared in such books as *The Best of Harris* and *Pieces of Eight*. (Sketch includes interview.)

Akira Iriye—Japanese-born professor of history and author; his book *Power and Culture*, which was nominated for a Pulitzer Prize in 1981, is a study of Japanese and American goals and motivations during World War II; also author of *Across the Pacific*, *The Cold War in Asia*, and *The Chinese and the Japanese*.

Menke Katz—Lithuanian-born American teacher, poet, short-story writer, and editor of the poetry journal *Bitterroot;* a proponent of unrhymed verse, Katz also stresses form and rhythm in his poetry, which includes the volumes *Land of Manna*, *Burning Village*, and numerous collections written in Yiddish; also author of the short-story collection *Forever and Ever and a Wednesday*. (Sketch includes interview.)

Judith Krantz—American author of the bestselling novels *Scruples*, *Princess Daisy*, and *Mistral's Daughter*, which have been described as fairy tales spun around beautiful people from wealthy backgrounds; former fashion editor and contributing writer to journals, including *Good Housekeeping* and *Cosmopolitan*.

Thomas S. Kuhn—American professor of the philosophy and history of science; his popular book, *The Structure of Scientific Revolutions*, notes that science undergoes radical shifts in thought that subsequently alter the nature of scientific research; also author of *The Essential Tension*, which was nominated for an American Book Award in 1980.

Bernard J. F. Lonergan—Canadian Roman Catholic priest, theology professor, and author of works on philosophy and theology; considered an authority on systematic and philosophical theology; among his works in English are *Insight: A Study of Human Understanding, Grace and Freedom, Method in Theology,* and *Philosophy of God, and Theology.*

Bobbie Ann Mason—American short-story writer and author of nonfiction; her collection *Shiloh and Other Stories* received the Ernest Hemingway Foundation Award in 1983 and was nominated for an American Book Award, National Book Critics Circle Award, and PEN/Faulkner Award; most of her stories, which often originally appeared in the *New Yorker,* are set in rural western Kentucky and vividly depict the region's social and physical geography.

Christopher Milne—British author and former bookshop owner; the son of A. A. Milne, he was portrayed as Christopher Robin in his father's "Winnie-the-Pooh" series; author of a work of philosophy, *The Hollow on the Hill,* and two autobiographies, *The Enchanted Places* and *The Path through the Trees.*

Frederik Pohl—American science fiction writer and editor; recipient of five Hugo Awards, two Nebula Awards, and, in 1979, an American Book Award; author or co-author of more than fifty books, among them *The Space Merchants, Gateway, JEM,* and his autobiography, *The Way the Future Was.* (Sketch includes interview.)

Albert Rosenfeld—American magazine editor, science writer, and author of books that explain biological and other scientific processes to the general reader; former science editor of *Life* and *Saturday Review;* his books include *The Second Genesis, Prolongevity,* and *Mind and Supermind.*

Joanna Russ—American professor and author of science fiction novels and short stories; *The Female Man, The Two of Them, On Strike against God,* and other of her works are written from a feminist perspective; in 1983 her novella "Souls" received Nebula and Hugo Awards.

Carl Sagan—American astronomer also known for his expertise in physics, biology, and exobiology; narrator and co-author of the Public Broadcasting System's popular television series "Cosmos"; his book *The Dragons of Eden,* although criticized by some for its highly speculative and fanciful material, received a Pulitzer Prize in 1978; two other books, *Cosmos* and *Broca's Brain,* were nominated for American Book Awards in 1981.

Flora Rheta Schreiber—American professor and writer; best known for her psychological profiles *Sybil* and *The Shoemaker.* (Sketch includes interview.)

Maurice Sendak—American writer and illustrator of children's books; his 1964 Caldecott Medal-winning book, *Where the Wild Things Are,* which depicts a small child's rage against his mother, was praised by many critics as being visionary and criticized by others as being unsuitable for children; nominated for an American Book Award in 1980 for *Higglety Pigglety Pop!* and recipient of this award in 1982 for *Outside over There.* (Sketch includes interview.)

Hedrick Smith—American *New York Times* correspondent who received a Pulitzer Prize for international reporting in 1974; former bureau chief in Moscow, Smith wrote the widely reviewed book *The Russians;* also co-author of *The Pentagon Papers* and *Reagan: The Man, the President.*

Ronald Story—American technical editor and nonfiction writer; in such works as *The Space Gods Revealed: A Close Look at the Theories of Erich von Daniken* and *Guardians of the Universe?,* he rebuts the theory that extraterrestrials visited the earth in the distant past; his other work includes *The Encyclopedia of UFOs* and *UFOs and the Limits of Science.*

Anne Tyler—American bestselling and award-winning novelist; in her novels she uses the family unit to portray the endurance of the human spirit; *Morgan's Passing* won the Janet Heidinger Kafka Prize and was nominated for a National Book Critics Circle Award and American Book Award; *Dinner at the Homesick Restaurant* received a PEN/Faulkner Award and was nominated for a Pulitzer Prize, American Book Award, and National Book Critics Circle Award.

Malcolm Weiss—American author of nonfiction books for children; *Man Explores the Sea, Storms, The Vitamin Puzzle,* and *Seeing through the Dark* were each named an Outstanding Science Trade Book for Children by the National Science Teachers Association.

Preface

The *Contemporary Authors New Revision Series* provides completely updated information on authors listed in earlier volumes of *Contemporary Authors*. Entries for active individual authors from *any* volume of *CA* may be included in a volume of the *New Revision Series*. The sketches appearing in *New Revision Series* Volume 11, for example, were selected from more than ten previously published *CA* volumes.

As always, the most recent *Contemporary Authors* cumulative index continues to be the user's guide to the location of an individual author's listing.

Compilation Methods

The editors make every effort to secure information directly from the authors. Copies of all sketches in selected *CA* volumes published several years ago are routinely sent to the authors at their last-known addresses. Authors mark material to be deleted or changed and insert any new personal data, new affiliations, new writings, new work in progress, new sidelights, and new biographical/critical sources. All author returns are assessed, more comprehensive research is done, if necessary, and those sketches requiring significant change are completely updated and published in the *New Revision Series*.

If, however, authors fail to reply, or if authors are now deceased, biographical dictionaries are checked for new information (a task made easier through the use of Gale's *Biography and Genealogy Master Index* and other volumes in the "Gale Biographical Index Series"), as are bibliographical sources such as *Cumulative Book Index* and *The National Union Catalog*. Using data from such sources, revision editors select and revise nonrespondents' entries that need substantial updating. Sketches not personally reviewed by the authors are marked with a dagger (†) to indicate that these listings have been revised from secondary sources believed to be reliable, but they have not been personally reviewed for this edition by the authors sketched.

In addition, reviews and articles in major periodicals, lists of prestigious awards, and, particularly, requests from *CA* users are monitored so that authors on whom new information is in demand can be identified and revised listings prepared promptly.

Comprehensive Revision

All listings in this volume have been revised and/or augmented in various ways, though the amount and type of change vary with the author. In many instances, sketches are totally rewritten, and the resulting *New Revision Series* entries are often considerably longer than the authors' previous listings. Revised entries include additions of or changes in such information as degrees, mailing addresses, literary agents, career items, career-related and civic activities, memberships, work in progress, and biographical/critical sources. They may also include the following:

1) Major new awards—Bobbie Ann Mason, Maurice Sendak, and Anne Tyler are only three of the numerous award-winning authors with updated entries in this volume. Bobbie Ann Mason's revised sketch, prepared by assistant editor Nancy Hebb, cites Mason's 1983 Ernest Hemingway Foundation Award for *Shiloh and Other Stories*, a collection that also received nominations for an American Book Award, National Book Critics Circle Award, and PEN/Faulkner Award. Maurice Sendak, the first American to be awarded the Hans Christian Andersen International Medal, has also received additional honors since his entry last appeared in *CA*, including an American Book Award in 1982 and the Laura Ingalls Wilder Award in 1983 for "a substantial and lasting contribution to children's literature." Novelist Anne Tyler comments in a letter to senior assistant editor Donna Olendorf, "It's funny . . . how little feeling I do have about awards and their impact—getting published at all seems the miracle"; nonetheless, between 1980 and 1983 recognition of her work included nominations for two American Book Awards, two National Book Critics Circle Awards, and a Pulitzer Prize.

2) Extensive bibliographical additions—Prior to his death, children's author and illustrator Gareth Adamson co-authored with his wife, Jean Adamson, over seventy-five books in their "Topsy and Tim" series; associate editor Deborah A. Straub has completed his bibliography by adding sixty of these titles to Adamson's updated sketch. Charles Keeping, another prolific children's author and illustrator, has written eight additional books and illustrated thirty-eight selections since his listing was last published in *CA*. And Frederik Pohl's already extensive bibliography has been augmented by senior assistant editor Thomas Wiloch to include the twenty books Pohl has written and nine new titles he has edited; the updated sketch also records fourteen previously unlisted pseudonyms.

3) Informative new sidelights—Numerous *CA* sketches contain sidelights, which provide personal dimensions to the listings, supply information about the critical reception the authors' works have received, or both. For example, in sidelights for French-born novelist, nonfiction writer, and former *New Yorker* staff writer Francine du Plessix Gray, assistant editor Heidi A. Tietjen aids the reader in understanding both Gray's themes and her motivations for writing. One response to Gray's two novels, *Lovers and Tyrants* and *World Without End,* is that they are too intellectual at points, particularly in regard to language. In the exclusive *CA* interview, Gray comments on this criticism: "I've lived in an academic world much of my life. I'm always eager to talk about Titian's iconography of the Resurrection or Pascal's theory of grace. That's the language I was brought up on, and you can't help being what you are. I might never have a very wide audience with such specialized novels, but one doesn't write for an audience. . . . One should only write what's in one's heart."

In contrast, Judith Krantz's bestselling books *Scruples, Princess Daisy,* and *Mistral's Daughter* have been criticized for their mass market appeal. Assistant editor Margaret Mazurkiewicz reports on the phenomenal success of Krantz's three novels, those personal experiences the author has drawn upon to write her books, and common elements in her work, as well as Krantz's reaction to her bestselling status. Krantz explains in the *Chicago Tribune:* "If you deal in the world of glamour, and that's my turf . . . then you're not taken seriously as a writer, and everyone focuses on how much money you make. . . . I chose my turf, [so] you can't complain when you get a little flack. . . . It may hurt a little . . . but you can't complain. You can't have it both ways."

Speculative, exuberant, entertaining, idiosyncratic—the characteristics that kept over 150 million viewers tuned to the television series "Cosmos" have also prompted some critics and fellow scientists to chastise astronomer Carl Sagan. His sidelights, prepared by assistant editor Susan Salter, trace Sagan's career from his early interest in science fiction and astronomy to his current status as one of modern science's most popular spokesmen.

These sketches, as well as others with sidelights compiled by *CA*'s editors, provide informative and enjoyable reading.

Writers of Special Interest

CA's editors make every effort to include in each *New Revision Series* volume a substantial number of revised entries on active authors and media people of special interest to *CA*'s readers. Since the *New Revision Series* also includes sketches on noteworthy deceased writers, a significant amount of work on the part of *CA*'s editors goes into the revision of entries on important deceased authors. Some of the prominent writers, both living and deceased, whose sketches are contained in this volume are noted in the list headed "Authors and Media People Featured in This Volume" immediately preceding the preface.

Exclusive Interviews

CA provides exclusive, primary information on certain authors in the form of interviews. Prepared specifically for *CA,* the never-before-published conversations presented in the section of the sketch headed *CA INTERVIEW* give *CA* users the opportunity to learn the authors' thoughts, in depth, about their craft. Subjects chosen for interviews are, the editors feel, authors who hold special interest for *CA*'s readers.

Authors and journalists in this volume whose sketches include interviews are William Barrett, Philip Berrigan, Ben Bova, Rita Mae Brown, Frederick Buechner, Mark Dintenfass, Francine du Plessix Gray, Sydney J. Harris, Menke Katz, Frederik Pohl, Flora Rheta Schreiber, and Maurice Sendak.

CA Numbering System

Occasionally questions arise about the *CA* numbering system. Despite numbers like "97-100" and "109," the entire *CA* series consists of only 47 physical volumes with the publication of *CA New Revision Series* Volume 11 in February, 1984. The following information notes changes in the numbering system, as well as in cover design, to help *CA* users better understand the organization of the entire *CA* series.

CA First Revisions	• 1-4R through 41-44R (11 books) *Cover:* Brown with black and gold trim. There will be no further *First Revisions* because revised entries are now being handled exclusively through the more efficient *New Revision Series* mentioned below.
CA Original Volumes	• 45-48 through 97-100 (14 books) *Cover:* Brown with black and gold trim. • 101 through 109 (9 books) *Cover:* Blue and black with orange bands. The same as previous *CA* original volumes but with a new, simplified numbering system and new cover design.
CA New Revision Series	• *CANR*-1 through *CANR*-11 (11 books) *Cover:* Blue and black with green bands. Includes only sketches requiring extensive change; **sketches are taken from any previously published *CA* volume.**
CA Permanent Series	• *CAP*-1 and *CAP*-2 (2 books) *Cover:* Brown with red and gold trim. There will be no further *Permanent Series* volumes because revised entries are now being handled exclusively through the more efficient *New Revision Series* mentioned above.

Retaining *CA* Volumes

As new volumes in the series are published, users often ask which *CA* volumes, if any, can be discarded. The chart following the preface is designed to assist users in keeping their collections as complete as possible. All volumes in the left column of the chart should be retained to have the most complete, up-to-date coverage possible; volumes in the right column can be discarded if the appropriate replacements are held.

Cumulative Index Should Always Be Consulted

The key to locating an individual author's listing is the *CA* cumulative index bound into the back of alternate original volumes (and available separately as an offprint). Since the *CA* cumulative index provides access to *all* entries in the *CA* series, the latest cumulative index should always be consulted to find the specific volume containing an author's original or most recently revised sketch.

Those authors whose entries appear in the *New Revision Series* are listed in the *CA* cumulative index with the designation **CANR-** in front of the specific volume number. For the convenience of those who do not have *New Revision Series* volumes, the cumulative index also notes the specific earlier volumes of *CA* in which the sketch appeared. Below is a sample index citation for an author whose revised sketch appears in a *New Revision Series* volume.

Vonnegut, Kurt, Jr. 1922- CANR-1
Earlier sketch in CA 3R
See also CLC 1, 2, 3, 4, 5, 8, 12, 22
See also AITN 1

For the most recent information on Vonnegut, users should refer to Volume 1 of the *New Revision Series,* as designated by "CANR-1"; if that volume is unavailable, refer to *CA* 1-4 First Revision, as indicated by "Earlier sketch in CA 3R," for his 1968 listing. (And if *CA* 1-4 First Revision is unavailable, refer to *CA* 3, published in 1963, for Vonnegut's original listing.)

Sketches not eligible for inclusion in a *New Revision Series* volume because the author or a revision editor has verified that no significant change is required will, of course, be available in previously published *CA* volumes. Users should always consult the most recent *CA* cumulative index to determine the location of these authors' entries.

For the convenience of *CA* users, the *CA* cumulative index also includes references to all entries in three related Gale series—*Contemporary Literary Criticism* (CLC), which is devoted entirely to current criticism of the works of today's novelists, poets, playwrights, short story writers, filmmakers, scriptwriters, and other creative writers, *Something about the Author* (SATA), a series of heavily illustrated sketches on authors and illustrators of books for young people, and *Authors in the News* (AITN), a compilation of news stories and feature articles from American newspapers and magazines covering writers and other members of the communications media.

As always, suggestions from users about any aspect of *CA* will be welcomed.

IF YOU HAVE:	YOU MAY DISCARD:
1-4 First Revision (1967)	1 (1962) 2 (1963) 3 (1963) 4 (1963)
5-8 First Revision (1969)	5-6 (1963) 7-8 (1963)
Both 9-12 First Revision (1974) AND *Contemporary Authors Permanent Series,* Volume 1 (1975)	9-10 (1964) 11-12 (1965)
Both 13-16 First Revision (1975) AND *Contemporary Authors Permanent Series,* Volumes 1 and 2 (1975, 1978)	13-14 (1965) 15-16 (1966)
Both 17-20 First Revision (1976) AND *Contemporary Authors Permanent Series,* Volumes 1 and 2 (1975, 1978)	17-18 (1967) 19-20 (1968)
Both 21-24 First Revision (1977) AND *Contemporary Authors Permanent Series,* Volumes 1 and 2 (1975, 1978)	21-22 (1969) 23-24 (1970)
Both 25-28 First Revision (1977) AND *Contemporary Authors Permanent Series,* Volume 2 (1978)	25-28 (1971)
Both 29-32 First Revision (1978) AND *Contemporary Authors Permanent Series,* Volume 2 (1978)	29-32 (1972)
Both 33-36 First Revision (1978) AND *Contemporary Authors Permanent Series,* Volume 2 (1978)	33-36 (1973)
37-40 First Revision (1979)	37-40 (1973)
41-44 First Revision (1979)	41-44 (1974)
45-48 (1974) 49-52 (1975) 53-56 (1975) 57-60 (1976) ↓ ↓ 109 (1983)	NONE: These volumes will not be super-seded by corresponding revised volumes. Individual entries from these and all other volumes appearing in the left column of this chart will be revised and included in the *New Revision Series.*
Volumes in the *Contemporary Authors New Revision Series*	NONE: The *New Revision Series* does not replace any single volume of *CA.* All volumes appearing in the left column of this chart must be retained to have information on all authors in the series.

Contemporary Authors

NEW REVISION SERIES

† Indicates that a listing has been revised from secondary sources believed to be reliable, but has not been personally reviewed for this edition by the author sketched.

ABBOTT, Carl (John) 1944-

PERSONAL: Born December 3, 1944, in Knoxville, Tenn.; son of Lyndon E. (a college professor) and Mildred (Schaeffer) Abbott; married Margery Post (a city planner), August 5, 1967. *Education:* Swarthmore College, B.A., 1966; University of Chicago, M.A., 1967, Ph.D., 1971. *Religion:* Society of Friends (Quaker). *Home:* 1830 Northeast Klickitat St., Portland, Ore. 97212. *Office:* School of Urban and Public Affairs, Portland State University, Portland, Ore. 97207.

CAREER: University of Denver, Denver, Colo., assistant professor of history, 1971-72; Old Dominion University, Norfolk, Va., assistant professor of history and urban studies, 1972-78; Portland State University, Portland, Ore., associate professor of history, 1978-79, associate professor of urban studies, 1979-83, professor of urban studies, 1983—. *Member:* American Historical Association, Organization of American Historians, Social Science History Association.

WRITINGS: The Human and Environmental Costs of American Growth, Forum Press, 1974; (editor and contributor) *Colonial Place, Norfolk: The Evolution of an Urban Neighborhood*, Institute of Government, University of Virginia, 1975; *Colorado: The History of the Centennial State*, Colorado Associated University Press, 1976, revised edition, 1982; *Boosters and Businessmen*, Greenwood Press, 1981; *The Great Extravaganza: Portland's Lewis and Clark Exposition*, Oregon Historical Society, 1981; *The New Urban America: Growth and Politics in Sunbelt Cities*, University of North Carolina Press, 1981; *Portland: Planning, Politics, and Growth in a Twentieth Century City*, University of Nebraska Press, 1983. Contributor of articles and reviews to national and regional magazines, history journals, and newspapers.

WORK IN PROGRESS: Urban America in the Modern Age: 1920-1980, for Harlan Davidson.

*   *   *

ABEL, Bob
  See ABEL, Robert

ABEL, Robert 1931-1981
  (Bob Abel)

PERSONAL: Born January 22, 1931, in Middletown, Conn.; died of cancer, December 21, 1981; son of Frank E. (an insurance agent) and Grace (Gordon) Abel; married wife, Carole (a literary agent), May 9, 1969; children: Douglas William, David Warren. *Education:* University of Connecticut, B.A., 1953; Boston University, B.S. (summa cum laude), 1956; graduate study at New School for Social Research, 1957-60. *Home:* 160 West 87th Street, New York, N.Y. 10024. *Agent:* Freya Manston Associates, Inc., 888 Seventh Ave., New York, N.Y. 10019. *Politics:* "Radical liberal." *Religion:* "To teach my children to be good and kind people."

CAREER: Free-lance writer. *Drug Trade News,* New York City, associate editor, 1956-59; *Ad-Lib,* New York City, editor-in-chief, 1961-62; *Realist,* New York City, managing editor, 1962-66; Dell Publishing Co., New York City, senior editor, 1968-72; Warner Books, New York City, executive editor, 1972-75. Consultant to Irwin Swann Collection of Caricature & Art, beginning 1974. *Military service:* U.S. Army, 1953-55. *Member:* American Society of Journalists and Authors; Upper West Side Made Redundant Editor's & Writer's Wednesday Luncheon Club (co-founder).

WRITINGS: (Editor with David Manning White) *The Funnies: An American Idiom*, Free Press of Glencoe, 1963; (editor under name Bob Abel) *The American Cartoon Album: An Anthology of Cartoon Humor, Published and Original, Reflecting the America Seen by Its Cartoonists*, Dodd, 1974; (under name Bob Abel) *The Book of Beer*, Regnery, 1976; (under name Bob Abel) *The Beer Book*, Quick Fox, 1981; (with Michael Valenti) *You Could Look It Up: The Best Quotations Past and Present, from the World of Sports*, Facts on File, 1983. Contributor to magazines and newspapers, including *New York Times, Playboy,* and *McCall's.* Contributing editor, *Cavalier,* 1967-70.

SIDELIGHTS: "I write satire on occasion," Robert Abel once told *CA,* "to prove that life is constantly imitating satire. Writing is painfully hard work—instant backaches, sudden needs for a cup of tea, et al—but there are lovely moments when the moon (I, a Night Person) is right or something, and it all comes out right—and those help—just barely, sometimes, make up for rewrites and late payment and all the other unpleasant business connected with the profession. . . . [These] problems come as no surprise to me [having been an editor,] but a bit more of sweet reasonableness on both sides would make for better work and more agreeable relationships.''

OBITUARIES: *New York Times*, December 30, 1981; *Publishers Weekly*, January 8, 1982.†

* * *

ADAIR, Ian 1942-

PERSONAL: Born December 20, 1942, in Scotland; son of John (a manager) and Isabell (a tracer; maiden name, Henderson) Adair; married Susan Ann Becraft, September 17, 1975; children: Kylie, Antony. *Education:* Educated at private academy in Scotland. *Home and office:* 20 Ashley Ter., Bideford, Devonshire, England.

CAREER: Children's entertainer, 1954—; magician and writer, 1960—. Partner in Supreme Magic Company Ltd. (theatrical suppliers), Bideford, Devonshire, England, 1965-73. Has also worked as a shoemaker, 1957, a television presenter, 1959, and a free-lance scriptwriter, 1960. Active in Round Table movement. *Member:* International Brotherhood of Magicians, Associated Wizards of the South (England; honorary vice-president), India Ring (Calcutta; honorary member), Magic Circle (London). *Awards, honors:* Invention awards from U.S. branch of International Brotherhood of Magicians, 1962, 1975, and 1976; gold medal from Magic Circle, 1974.

WRITINGS—Published by Supreme Magic Co. Ltd., except as indicated: *Adair's Ideas*, 1957, 3rd edition, 1970; *Entertaining Children*, 1960; *Magical Menu*, three volumes, 1960-63; *Encyclopaedia of Dove Magic*, four volumes, 1961-76; *Mental Magic*, 1962; *Dove Magic*, Part I, 1962, Part II, 1962; *Dove Magic Finale*, 1962; *Television Dove Magic*, 1963; *Illusions*, 1963; *My Card, Sir!*, 1963; *Twenty-One*, 1963; *Dove Magic Encore*, 1963; *Television Dove Steals*, 1964; *Doves in Magic*, 1964; *Doves from Silks*, 1964; *New Doves from Silks Methods*, 1964; *Dove Classics*, 1964.

Further Dove Classics, 1965; *More Modern Dove Classics*, 1965; *Stunners with Stamps*, 1965; *Television Card Manipulations*, 1966; *Classical Dove Secrets*, 1966; *Diary of a Dove Worker*, 1966; *Magic on the Wing*, 1966; *Cabaret Dove Act*, 1966; *A La Zombie Plus*, 1967; *Pot Pourri*, 1967; *Balloon-o-Dove*, 1967; *Spotlight on Doves*, 1967; *Watch the Birdie*, 1967; *Rainbow Dove Routines*, 1967; *Heads Off!*, 1967; *Tricks and Stunts with Rubber Doves*, 1967; *Magic with Doves*, 1968; *Dove Dexterity*, 1968; *Twin Dove Production*, 1968; *Magic with Latex Budgies*, 1968; *Paddle Antics*, 1969; *Television Puppet Magic*, 1969.

(Self-illustrated) *Conjuring As a Craft*, A. S. Barnes, 1970; (self-illustrated) *Party Planning and Entertainment*, A. S. Barnes, 1971; *Magic Step by Step*, Arco, 1972; *Papercrafts*, Arco, 1975; *Complete Guide to Conjuring*, A. S. Barnes, 1977; (with Heather Amery) *The Knowhow Book of Jokes and Tricks* (juvenile), Usborne Publishing, 1977; *The Complete Party Planner*, A. S. Barnes, 1978; (self-illustrated) *The Complete Guide to Card Conjuring*, A. S. Barnes, 1979.

Swindles: The Cheating Game, A. S. Barnes, 1980; *Mini Magic Book* (juvenile), Usborne Publishing, 1981; (ghost writer) Paul Daniels, *The Paul Daniels Magic Book*, Piccolo Books, 1981.

Author of ''Adair's Ideas'' and ''The Dove Column,'' monthly columns in *Magigram*. Contributor of more than three thousand articles to more than thirty-five magic journals in the United States and England.

WORK IN PROGRESS: *A Chance in a Lifetime*, and *Encyclopaedia of Dove Magic*, Volume V, both for Supreme Magic Co., Ltd.

SIDELIGHTS: Ian Adair writes: ''At the age of ten years I received a birthday present from my grandmother which completely changed my life. It was a toy box of conjuring tricks. Within a day I had learnt and perfected all and [gave] my first performance the following day, receiving praise from my friends who formed the audience. 'Conjuring' and 'magic' was to be my life, and not being content with the toy variety magic tricks which were available to anyone, I, now eleven years of age, invented my own. Entering a television talent show at eleven years of age, presenting a six-minute act, I won the major prize.

''Inventing magical principles and routines occupied most of my young life and at fourteen years, my first book was published. At sixteen years of age, although still inventing and writing, I became involved in television work, both local and national. When eighteen years of age, I was given my own television show. At twenty, I joined a thriving company, specialised in supplying original material for theatricals.

''During this time, my magical and novelty subject writings flourished, with books on puppetry, origami, [and] party planning techniques being published regularly by leading non-fiction publishers.

''Perhaps, one of my most pleasurable writing experiences has been that of compiling and writing, in collaboration with Heather Amery, *The Knowhow Book of Jokes and Tricks*. Printed in full colour with thousands of illustrations, we believe this to be the most comprehensive book, providing magic and secrets, by using the comic strip process.

''Inventing, lecturing, performing, writing, manufacturing, publishing, and promoting the craft to its fullness are my only interests. I live, eat, and sleep magic, just like the poet does with his words, the painter with his transformations to the canvas.

''I always make a point of presenting my own originations before an audience and do this by using television and stage. Making personal appearances on top BBC television shows, at leading cabaret venues, and more often, before groups of children at birthday, Christmas, and annual treat parties, is one way of ensuring that I learn the modern techniques which every performer can benefit from.''

* * *

ADAMS, Julian 1919-

PERSONAL: Born January 20, 1919, in California; son of Julian L. and Mary (Latham) Adams; married Ruth Metz; children: Gregory M. Thomas, Shirley McDonald. *Education:* University of California, A.B., 1939; San Francisco State College (now University), M.A., 1962. *Home:* 52 El Camino Real, Berkeley, Calif. 94705.

CAREER: Mare Island Navy Yard, Vallejo, Calif., administrative assistant, 1940-48; Richmond (Calif.) public schools, teacher and counselor, 1950-74; full-time writer, 1974—. *Military service:* U.S. Navy, 1946-48. *Member:* Journalism Education Association.

WRITINGS: (With Kenneth Stratton) *Press Time*, Prentice-Hall, 1963, 4th edition, 1984; *The Student Journalist and Mass Communication*, Richards Rosen, 1980; *Freedom and Ethics in the Press*, Richards Rosen, 1982.

*   *   *

ADAMSON, Gareth   1925-1982(?)

PERSONAL: Born May 10, 1925, in Liverpool, England; died c. 1982 in Cambridge, England; son of William John (a manufacturer) and Isobel (Hughes) Adamson; married Jean Elizabeth Bailey (a free-lance artist), October 5, 1957; children: Leo, Gabrielle, Kate. *Education:* Attended Edinburgh College of Art and Architecture, 1944-46; Goldsmiths' College, London, National Diploma in Design (illustration), 1951. *Politics:* Liberal. *Religion:* Roman Catholic. *Home:* 1 Bailiffgate, Alnwick, Northumberland, England. *Agent:* London Authors, 8 Upper Brook St., London W. 1, England.

CAREER: Hunt Partners Ltd. (packaging company), London, England, research designer, 1952-53; Cravens Advertising Ltd., Newcastle upon Tyne, England, creative chief, 1953-57; free-lance author and illustrator of children's books, 1957-82. *Awards, honors:* First prize from British Broadcasting Corporation and North East Association for the Arts, 1965, for a television play.

WRITINGS—Self-illustrated, except as indicated: *Neighbours in the Park*, illustrated by wife, Jean Adamson, Harrap, 1962; *Old Man up a Tree*, Abelard, 1963; *Mr. Budge Builds a House*, Brockhampton Press, 1963, Chilton, 1968; *Mr. Budge Buys a Car*, Brockhampton Press, 1965; (with J. Adamson) *The Ahmed Story*, Whiting, 1966; *Three Discontented Clowns*, Abelard, 1966; *Harold, the Happy Handyman*, Harvey House, 1968; (with J. Adamson) *Family Tree*, A. Whitman, 1968; *Machines at Home*, Lutterworth, 1969; *People at Home*, Lutterworth, 1972; (with J. Adamson) *Hop Like Me*, Chambers, 1973; *Wheels for the Road*, Dent, 1973.

"Topsy and Tim" series; all with J. Adamson; all published by Blackie & Son: *Topsy and Tim's Monday Book*, 1959, reprinted, 1977; *. . . Tuesday Book*, 1959, reprinted, 1977; *. . . Wednesday Book*, 1960, reprinted, 1977; *. . . Thursday Book*, 1960, reprinted, 1977; *. . . Friday Book*, 1961, reprinted, 1977; *. . . Saturday Book*, 1961, reprinted, 1977; *. . . Sunday Book*, 1962, reprinted, 1977; *. . . Foggy Day*, 1962; *Topsy and Tim at the Football Match*, 1963; *. . . Go Fishing*, 1963; *Topsy and Tim's Bonfire Night*, 1964; *. . . Snowy Day*, 1964; *Topsy and Tim Go on Holiday*, 1965; *. . . at the Seaside*, 1965; *. . . at the Zoo*, 1968.

Hullo, Topsy and Tim!, 1971; *Surprises for Topsy and Tim*, 1971; *Happy Days with Topsy and Tim*, 1971; *Topsy and Tim at School*, 1971; *. . . and Their Friends*, 1971; *. . . Go to Hospital*, 1971; *Topsy and Tim's Birthday Party*, 1971; *. . . Paddling Pool*, 1971; *Topsy and Tim Go Pony-Trekking*, 1972; *. . . Go Safely*, 1972; *Topsy and Tim's Ups and Downs*, 1973; *Topsy and Tim Learn to Swim*, 1973; *Safety First with Topsy and Tim*, 1973; *Topsy and Tim Go Hill-Walking*, 1973; *. . . Take No Risks*, 1973; *. . . Cross the Channel*, 1974; *. . . Go Sailing*, 1974; *. . . in Belgium*, 1974; *. . . in Holland*, 1974; *. . . Out and About*, 1974; *. . . Visit Europe*, 1974.

Topsy and Tim's New Brother, 1975; *Topsy and Tim Visit the Dentist*, 1975; *. . . Visit the Doctor*, 1975; *. . . at the Wedding*, 1976; *. . . Visit the Tower of London*, 1976; *Topsy and Tim's New School*, 1976; *. . . Pet Show*, 1976; *Topsy and Tim at the Circus*, 1977; *. . . Go Camping*, 1977; *. . . Go Shopping*,

1977; *. . . on the Farm*, 1977; *. . . at the Fairground*, 1978; *. . . at the Library*, 1978; *. . . at the Vet*, 1978; *. . . Choose a Puppy*, 1978; *. . . Meet the Monsters*, 1978; *Topsy and Tim's Picnic*, 1978; *. . . School Outing*, 1978; *. . . Sports Day*, 1978; *. . . Train Journey*, 1978; *. . . Caravan Holiday*, 1979; *Topsy and Tim at the Hairdresser*, 1979; *. . . Go in an Aeroplane*, 1979; *. . . Have a Barbecue*, 1979; *. . . Move House*, 1979; *. . . at the Fire Station*, 1979; *. . . at the Jumble Sale*, 1979; *. . . at the Pantomime*, 1979.

Seven Days with Topsy and Tim, 1980; *Topsy and Tim Can Print in Colour*, 1980; *. . . Can Sing and Play*, 1980; *. . . Can Garden*, 1980; *. . . Can Cook*, 1981; *. . . Can Look after Pets*, 1981; *. . . Can Play Party Games*, 1981; *. . . Go to Playschool*, 1981; *Topsy and Tim's Alphabet Frieze*, 1981; *. . . Birthday*, 1981; *. . . Country Day*, 1981; *. . . New Pet*, 1981; *Topsy and Tim Have Their Eyes Tested*, 1982.

Also author of a television play.

Illustrator: Charles Hatcher, *What Shape Is It?*, Brockhampton Press, 1963, Duell, Sloan & Pearce, 1966; Hatcher, *What Size Is It?*, Brockhampton Press, 1964, Duell, Sloan & Pearce, 1966.

SIDELIGHTS: Gareth Adamson's artistic interests included cartoon and animated puppet films (he and his wife Jean Adamson, devised a method of puppet animation they did not have time to develop) and architecture. The Adamsons lived in a house built in 1725 on the site of the old Baliff Gate, precisely ten paces from Alnwick Castle.

OBITUARIES: AB Bookman's Weekly, April 12, 1982.†

*   *   *

ADCOCK, Fleur   1934-

PERSONAL: Original name Kareen Fleur Adcock; name legally changed, 1982; born February 10, 1934, in Papakura, New Zealand; daughter of Cyril John (a professor of psychology) and Irene (Robinson) Adcock; married Alistair Campbell (a poet and civil servant), August, 1952 (divorced); married Barry Crump (a writer), February 9, 1962 (divorced); children: (first marriage) Gregory, Andrew. *Education:* Victoria University of Wellington, M.A. (with first class honors in classics), 1955. *Home:* 14 Lincoln Rd., London N.2, England.

CAREER: University of Otago, Dunedin, New Zealand, assistant lecturer, 1958, assistant librarian, 1959-61; Alexander Turnbull Library, Wellington, New Zealand, assistant librarian, 1962; Foreign and Commonwealth Office, London, England, assistant librarian, 1963-79; currently free-lance writer. Delivers talks on poetry for British Broadcasting Corp. *Awards, honors:* Wellington Festival Poetry Award, 1961; co-recipient of New Zealand State Literary Fund Award for Achievement, 1964; Buckland Award (New Zealand), 1968 and 1979; Jessie MacKay Prize (New Zealand), 1968; Cholmondeley Award, 1976.

WRITINGS—Poems: *The Eye of the Hurricane*, A. H. & A. W. Reed, 1964; *Tigers*, Oxford University Press, 1967; *High Tide in the Garden*, Oxford University Press, 1971; *The Scenic Route*, Oxford University Press, 1974; *The Inner Harbour*, Oxford University Press, 1979; *Selected Poems*, Oxford University Press, 1983.

Other: (Editor with A. Thwaite) *New Poetry*, Number 4, Hutchinson, 1978; (editor) *Oxford Book of Contemporary New Zealand Poetry*, Oxford University Press, 1981; (translator) *The*

Virgin and the Nightingale: Medieval Latin Poems, Bloodaxe Books, 1983.

Also author of several texts and libretti for musical works by composer Gillian Whitehead. Contributor of poems to literary journals and articles for children to *New Zealand School Journal.*

SIDELIGHTS: Much of Fleur Adcock's poetry is based upon the familiar and the domestic. A *Times Literary Supplement* critic comments in a review of *Tigers* that Adcock "makes a kind of suballegory out of the domestic context with occasional success" and that "the most rewarding verses" are those "addressed in a casually whimsical and yet pleasantly balanced way to children and animals." Writing about *High Tide in the Garden,* a *Times Literary Supplement* reviewer observes that Adcock's poems "have a well-bred, genteel air about them" as well as "an Eliotic trick of introducing the odd, fussily pedantic fact into their reflections ('a misty autumn Sunday, not unpopulated by birds')."

Despite her concern with the mundane, Adcock often introduces jarring images into her poetry. "There has been a quiet serendipity about Fleur Adcock's poetry in its more conventional moments: a casual, often very appealing, yet curiously unambitious assembling of sensations and observations," writes Alan Brownjohn in *Encounter.* "Then suddenly something angry, or nightmarish, or discomfiting leaps out." For example, in one poem the narrator has climbed into the hayloft only to encounter and to be pulled into an embrace with a decomposing woman. Another poem, "Against Coupling," speaks "in praise of the solitary act." However, the *Times Literary Supplement* reviewer of *High Tide in the Garden* speculates, "One can't entirely avoid the suspicion that the odd glimpse into chaos is briefly admitted into those elegantly wrought poems in order to confirm that there is, after all, a bit more to Miss Adcock's world than the garden, sons and cats of whom she fondly speaks." The *Times Literary Supplement* critic of *Tigers* suggests Adcock "is not a writer for the deeper matters, as some not-too-successful dream poems make clear."

Andrew Motion in *New Statesman* also acknowledges the duality of desire—to remain ordered and rational but to also delve into the fantastic—in Adcock's work. "Unillusioned self-knowledge is apparent in all her previous work," Motion states, "and *The Inner Harbour* develops it to a fine art. But this, paradoxically, is the book's weakness as well as its strength. What she calls 'The clogging multiplicity of things' is sometimes too absolutely ordered. It is almost as if she is shy of inexplicable or unruly elements in her nature and what she sees around her. Poems about dreams and the subconscious, for example, move quickly away from troublesome abstract speculation and seek comfort in the realm of reliable objects. As one might expect, she is well aware of this reductive tendency."

Peter Porter writing in the *Observer* finds Adcock's work admirable. "Poets are supposed to get better and better, so that when they really do, to report the fact seems little more than automatic praise," he comments in a review of *The Inner Harbour.* "In Fleur Adcock's case, the progress of her work has been into a warmer world of the affections, and never away from a classical detachment of style, which has always been hers to deploy. . . . She makes a virtue of the helplessness of words—in fact, throughout the book, her poems seem to rest on the page with a special lenient grace."

Adcock reads French, German, Italian, Latin, and Greek.

BIOGRAPHICAL/CRITICAL SOURCES: Times Literary Supplement, September 14, 1967, July 23, 1971, January 18, 1980; *New Statesman,* June 8, 1979; *Encounter,* August, 1979; *Observer,* September 9, 1979.

*   *   *

ADLER, Freda   1934-

PERSONAL: Born November 21, 1934, in Philadelphia, Pa.; daughter of David R. (an industrialist) and Lucia Green (DeWolfson) Schaffer; married Herbert M. Adler (a physician), June 18, 1955 (divorced, 1975); married Gerhard O.W. Mueller (chief of United Nations Crime Section), February 29, 1976; children: (first marriage) Mark, Jill, Nancy. *Education:* University of Pennsylvania, B.A., 1956, M.A., 1968, Ph.D., 1971. *Home:* 30 Waterside Plaza, Apt. 37J, New York, N.Y. 10010. *Office:* School of Criminal Justice, Rutgers University, 53 Washington St., Newark, N.J. 07102.

CAREER: Temple University, Philadelphia, Pa., instructor in psychiatry, 1971, research coordinator at Addiction Science Center, 1971-72; Medical College of Pennsylvania, Philadelphia, assistant professor of psychiatry and research director of Section on Drug and Alcohol Abuse, 1972-74; Rutgers University, Newark, N.J., associate professor, 1974-78, professor of criminal justice, 1978—. Member of faculty of National College of State Judiciary, 1973—, and of National College of Criminal Defense Lawyers and Public Defenders, 1976; visiting fellow at Yale University, 1976. Member of board of directors of Institute for the Continuous Study of Man, 1974—. Consultant to National Commission on Marijuana and Drug Abuse and the United Nations.

MEMBER: International Association of Penal Law, American Sociological Association, American Society of Criminology (executive counselor, 1971-72, 1974-75), University of Pennsylvania Alumnae Association (member of board of directors, 1974-77). *Awards, honors:* Herbert Bloch Award from American Society of Criminology, 1972; Ancient Order of Chamorri (Guam); Beccaria Medal from Deutsche Kriminologische Gesellschaft, 1979.

WRITINGS: (Editor with G.O.W. Mueller) *Politics, Crime and the International Scene: An Interamerican Focus,* North-South Center for Technical and Cultural Interchange, 1972; (with Arthur D. Moffett, Frederick B. Glaser, and others) *The Treatment of Drug Abuse in Pennsylvania,* Governor's Council on Drug and Alcohol Abuse, 1973; (contributor) William White, Jr. and Ronald F. Albano, editors, *North American Symposium on Drugs and Drug Abuse,* North American Publishing, 1974; (with Moffett, Glaser, and others) *A Systems Approach to Drug Treatment,* Dorrance, 1974; (with Moffett, Glaser, and Diana Horvitz) *Medical Lollipop, Junkie Insulin, Or What?: Patient and Staff Views of the Chemotherapy of Addiction,* Dorrance, 1974; *Sisters in Crime,* McGraw, 1975; (with Rita Simon) *The Criminology of Deviant Women,* Houghton, 1978.

The Incidence of Female Criminality in the Contemporary World, New York University Press, 1981; *Nations Not Obsessed with Crime,* Fred B. Rothman, 1983. Contributor to criminology, sociology, and psychiatry journals, law and medical journals, and *Washington Post.* Member of editorial board of *Criminology: An Inderdisciplinary Journal,* 1971-73; consulting editor of *Journal of Research in Crime and Delinquency,* 1977, and *Journal of Criminal Law and Criminology,* 1982—.

SIDELIGHTS: Freda Adler writes: "Several years ago while working for the government as an evaluator of drug and alcohol treatment centers it was part of my task to interview addicts in treatment. One of the important areas of concern was in each individual's arrest record. After studying hundreds of these profiles, I became aware that there was a change in the types of crime in which females were involved. No longer content with shoplifting and prostitution they were turning to crimes such as robbery and burglary. This realization led me to a three-year research study involving visits with inmates, administrators, police officers, judges, etc. These changing female crime patterns and their relationship to women's emancipation became the subject of *Sisters in Crime*. Since that time I have been studying female criminality and lecturing on the topic in many countries, including Mexico, Venezuela, Brazil, Canada, Switzerland, Germany, Finland, Poland, Hungary, Guam, Australia, Ivory Coast, and Saudi Arabia.''

AVOCATIONAL INTERESTS: Horseback riding, skiing, sailing.

* * *

ADLER, Warren 1927-

PERSONAL: Born December 16, 1927, in Brooklyn, N.Y.; son of Sol and Fritzie (Goldman) Adler; married Sonia Kline (a magazine editor); children: David Allen, Jonathan Robert, Michael Adam. *Education:* New York University, B.A., 1947; further study at New School for Social Research. *Home:* 3301 Woodbine St., Chevy Chase, Md. 20015. *Agent:* Peter Lampack, 551 Fifth Ave., New York, N.Y. 10017.

CAREER: Has worked for *New York Daily News;* former editor of *Queens Post*, Forest Hills, N.Y.; president of an advertising and public relations agency in Washington, D.C., 1959-78; writer. *Military service:* U.S. Army, Washington correspondent for Armed Forces Press Service, 1951-53. *Member:* Authors League of America, Authors Guild, National Press Club.

WRITINGS—Novels: *Options*, Whitman Publishing, 1974; *Banquet before Dawn*, Putnam, 1976; *The Henderson Equation*, Putnam, 1976; *Trans-Siberian Express*, Putnam, 1977; *The Sunset Gang*, Viking, 1978; *The Casanova Embrace*, Putnam, 1978; *Blood Ties*, Putnam, 1979; *Natural Enemies*, Pocket Books, 1980; *The War of the Roses*, Warner Books, 1981; *American Quartet*, Arbor House, 1982; *American Sextet*, Arbor House, 1983; *Random Hearts*, Macmillan, 1984.

WORK IN PROGRESS: A novel set in Venice.

BIOGRAPHICAL/CRITICAL SOURCES: New York Times Book Review, September 18, 1977, June 28, 1981, October 17, 1982, March 20, 1983; *Washington Post Book World*, April 11, 1982.

* * *

AFRICANO, Lillian 1935-

PERSONAL: Born June 7, 1935, in Paterson, N.J.; daughter of John and Nadwa (Gorab) Tabeek; married Arthur Africano (a physician), June 28, 1958 (divorced); children: David, Nina, Arthur. *Education:* Barnard College, B.A., 1957; Columbia University, graduate study, 1957-58. *Home and office:* 45 West 10th St., New York, N.Y. 10011. *Agent:* Elaine Markson Literary Agency, Inc., 44 Greenwich Ave., New York, N.Y. 10011.

CAREER: Teacher in Union City, N.J., 1957-59; *Villager*, New York City, theater critic and entertainment editor, 1970-75; *Acupuncture News Digest*, New York City, editor, 1975; author of syndicated column "Theatre U.S.A.," 1975; theater critic for *Asbury Park Press*, 1973-80; author of weekly column in *Woman's World;* author of monthly news column in *Forum*. Conducted exclusive interview with Egypt's former first lady, Jihan Sadat; also interviewed Tennessee Williams. *Member:* Outer Critic's Circle, Drama Desk (vice-president, 1974-75, secretary, 1975-77).

WRITINGS: The Businessman's Guide to the Middle East, Harper, 1977; (co-author) *The Doctor's Walking Book*, Ballantine, 1980; (ghost writer) *Faces in a Mirror*, Prentice-Hall, 1980; *Something Old, Something New*, Jove, 1983.

Contributor to syndicated column "One Woman's Voice"; contributor of articles to popular magazines and newspapers, including *National Review, Penthouse, Nation, Harper's Bazaar, Woman's Day, Reader's Digest, New York Times*, and *Christian Science Monitor*.

WORK IN PROGRESS: Two novels, one for Jove and one for Berkley; extensive research on recent economic developments in Arab countries; travel in the Middle East in connection with future writings.

AVOCATIONAL INTERESTS: Travel (Europe, the Caribbean, the Middle East—speaks Arabic).

* * *

AICHINGER, Peter 1933-

PERSONAL: Born July 13, 1933, in Cloverdale, British Columbia, Canada; son of Constantin Richard and Bridgit Eileen (Woods) von Aichinger; married Sigrid Hagemann (a secretary), November 4, 1972; children: Anne, John, Suzanne, Max. *Education:* Royal Military College, B.A., 1958; University of Toronto, B.A. (honors), 1959; University of Ottawa, M.A., 1963; University of Sussex, D.Phil., 1970. *Home:* 239 Kensington, Westmount, Quebec, Canada H3Z 2H1. *Office:* Department of English, College Militaire Royal, St. Jean, Quebec, Canada.

CAREER: College Militaire Royal, St. Jean, Quebec, lecturer, 1962-70, assistant professor, 1970-74, associate professor, 1974-79, professor of English, 1979—, chairman of department, 1973—. *Military service:* Canadian Army, Royal Horse Artillery, 1958-62; served in Germany, became lieutenant. *Member:* Association of Canadian University Teachers of English, Canadian Association of University Teachers, Canadian Historical Association, Shakespeare Association of America.

WRITINGS: The American Soldier in Fiction: A History of the American War Novel, 1880-1963, Iowa State University Press, 1975; *Earle Birney* (biography), Twayne, 1979; *At War with the Americans: The Journal of Claude de Lorimier*, Press Porcepic, 1981. Contributor to learned journals.

WORK IN PROGRESS: The Battle of Fort St. Jean, 1775.

* * *

AINSWORTH, Harriet
See CADELL, (Violet) Elizabeth

* * *

ALBRAND, Martha [a pseudonym] 1914-1981
(Katrin Holland, Christine Lambert)

PERSONAL: Name at birth Heidi Huberta Freybe; born September 8, 1914, in Rostock, Germany; died June 24, 1981, in

New York, N.Y.; came to United States in 1937, naturalized in 1947; daughter of Paul and Paula Freybe; married Joseph M. Loewengard, 1932 (deceased); married Sydney J. Lamon, March, 1957 (deceased). *Education:* Studied under private tutors and at schools in Italy, France, Switzerland, and England. *Religion:* Lutheran. *Home and office:* 953 Fifth Ave., New York, N.Y. 10021. *Agent:* Robert Lantz, The Lantz Office, Inc., 114 East 55th St., New York, N.Y. 10022.

CAREER: Writer. Began career as journalist in Europe and had first book published at age of seventeen. *Member:* P.E.N., Pen and Brush, Crime Writers' Association, National Book Committee (member of national board), American Academy of Achievement. *Awards, honors:* Le Grand Prix de Literature Policiers for *Desperate Moment;* honorary Ph.D., Colorado State Christian College, 1972.

WRITINGS—Under pseudonym Martha Albrand: *No Surrender* (also see below), Little, Brown, 1942; *Without Orders,* Little, Brown, 1943; *Endure No Longer,* Little, Brown, 1944; *None Shall Know,* Little, Brown, 1945; *Remembered Anger,* Little, Brown, 1946; *Whispering Hill,* Random House, 1947; *After Midnight,* Random House, 1948; *Wait for the Dawn,* Random House, 1950; *Desperate Moment,* Random House, 1951; *Challenge,* Random House, 1951; *The Hunted Woman* (Unicorn Mystery Book Club selection), Random House, 1952; *Nightmare in Copenhagen,* Random House, 1954; *The Mask of Alexander,* Random House, 1955; *The Liden Affair,* Random House, 1956; *The Story That Could Not Be Told,* Hodder & Stoughton, 1956; *The Obsession of Emmet Booth,* Random House, 1957; *A Day in Monte Carlo,* Random House, 1959.

Meet Me Tonight, Random House, 1960; (contributor) *Five Spy Novels* (includes *No Surrender*), Doubleday, 1962; *A Call from Austria,* Random House, 1963; *A Door Fell Shut,* New American Library, 1966; *Rhine Replica,* Random House, 1969; *Manhattan North,* Coward, 1971; *Zuerich/AZ 900* (Detective Book Club selection), Holt, 1974; *A Taste of Terror,* Putnam, 1976; *Final Encore,* St. Martin's, 1978; *Intermission,* Hodder & Stoughton, 1978.

Under pseudonym Katrin Holland: *Man spricht uber Jacqueline,* Ullstein, 1930; *Wie macht Man das Nur!* (juvenile novel), G. Stalling, 1930; *Unterwegs zu Alexander,* Ullstein, 1932; *Die silberne Wolke,* Ullstein, 1933, translation by June Head published as *The Silver Cloud,* Nicholson & Watson, 1936; *Girl Tumbles Out of the Sky,* Nicholson & Watson, 1934; *Babbett auf Gottes Gnaden,* Ullstein, 1934; *Das Frauenhaus,* Orell Fuessli, 1935; *Das Maedchen, das niemand mochte,* Ullstein, 1935; *Youth Breaks In,* Nicholson & Watson, 1935; *Sandro irrt sich,* Orell Fuessli, 1936; *Einsamer Himmel,* Orell Fuessli, 1938; *Carlotta Torresani,* Orell Fuessli, 1938; *Vierzehn Tage mit Edith,* Orell Fuessli, 1939; *Helene,* Orell Fuessli, 1940.

Under pseudonym Christine Lambert: *The Ball,* Atheneum, 1961; *A Sudden Woman,* Atheneum, 1964.

Contributor of short stories to *Ladies' Home Journal, Town and Country, Saturday Evening Post,* and other magazines.

SIDELIGHTS: Most of the Martha Albrand mystery stories ran as serials in the *Saturday Evening Post* before publication in book form. Many of them have been translated into German, Danish, Italian, French, Swedish, Arabic, and other languages. The film rights to both *The Sudden Woman* and *No Surrender* were sold. *Avocational interests:* Travel, dogs, gardening, fishing.

BIOGRAPHICAL/CRITICAL SOURCES: New York Times Book Review, June 22, 1947, February 9, 1964, July 31, 1966; *Saturday Evening Post,* December 30, 1950.

OBITUARIES: New York Times, June 26, 1981.†

*   *   *

ALCYONE
See KRISHNAMURTI, Jiddu

*   *   *

ALDEN, John R(ichard)   1908-

PERSONAL: Born January 23, 1908, in Grand Rapids, Mich.; son of Herman and Ida (Jonkmann) Alden; married Pearl B. Wells, December 22, 1934; children: Anne Maria. *Education:* University of Michigan, A.B., 1929, A.M., 1930, Ph.D., 1939.

CAREER: University of Michigan, Ann Arbor, Alfred H. Lloyd research fellow, 1939-40; Michigan State Normal College (now Eastern Michigan University), Ypsilanti, assistant professor of history, 1940-43; Bowling Green State University, Bowling Green, Ohio, assistant professor of history, 1943-45; University of Nebraska, Lincoln, assistant professor, 1945-47, associate professor, 1947-50, professor of history, 1950-55; Duke University, Durham, N.C., professor, 1955-63, James B. Duke Professor of History, beginning 1963. Visiting professor, University of Chicago, summer, 1949, University of Michigan, summers, 1950, 1954, Columbia University, summer, 1956; Walter Lynwood Fleming Lecturer, Louisiana State University, 1960; Commonwealth Fund Lecturer, University College, University of London, 1961.

MEMBER: Organization of American Historians, American Historical Association, Massachusetts Historical Society (corresponding member). *Awards, honors:* Beveridge Prize from American Historical Association, 1945; Johnson faculty research fellow, University of Nebraska, 1948; Guggenheim fellow, 1955-56; Mayflower Society Award, 1969, for *A History of the American Revolution;* American Philosophical Society research grant, 1974.

WRITINGS: John Stuart and the Southern Colonial Frontier: A Study of Indian Relations, War, Trade, and Land Problems in the Southern Wilderness, 1754-1775, University of Michigan Press, 1944, reprinted, Gordian, 1966; *General Gage in America: Being Principally a History of His Role in the American Revolution,* Louisiana State University Press, 1948; *General Charles Lee: Traitor or Patriot?,* Louisiana State University Press, 1951; (editor) Christopher Ward, *War of the Revolution,* Macmillan, 1952; *The American Revolution, 1775-1783,* Harper, 1954; *The South in the Revolution, 1763-1789,* Louisiana State University Press, 1957.

(With Alice Magenis) *A History of the United States,* American Book Co., 1960; *The First South,* Louisiana State University Press, 1961; *Rise of the American Republic,* Harper, 1963; *Pioneer America,* Knopf, 1966; *A History of the American Revolution,* Knopf, 1969 (published in England as *A History of the American Revolution: The British and the Loss of the Thirteen Colonies,* MacDonald, 1969); *Robert Dinwiddie: Servant of the Crown,* University Press of Virginia for Colonial Williamsburg, 1973; (editor) Bernhard Knollenberg, *Growth of the American Revolution,* Free Press, 1974; (with others) *1776,* edited by John Browning and Richard Morton, S. Stevens, 1976; *The Fleet Submarine in the U.S. Navy,* Naval Institute Press, 1979; (editor with Dennis C. Landis) *European*

Americana: A Chronological Guide to Works Printed in Europe Relating to the Americas, Readex Books, Volume I: *1493-1600,* 1980, Volume II: *1601-1650,* 1983.

Contributor of articles on the American Revolution to *World Book Encyclopedia, Encyclopaedia Britannica, Larousse Encyclopedia of Modern History, Encyclopedia Americana,* and other publications.

WORK IN PROGRESS: Additional volumes of *European Americana: A Chronological Guide to Works Printed in Europe Relating to the Americas,* covering the period up to the American Revolution.

SIDELIGHTS: John R. Alden and Dennis C. Landis's bibliographical study of European writings on America, *European Americana: A Chronological Guide to Works Printed in Europe Relating to the Americas,* contains more than 15,000 items, including works by Ben Jonson, Francis Bacon, Taylor the Water Poet, and Shakespeare. The bibliography takes a broad approach to its subject, covering factual and fictional writings from all European nations about both North and South America. Noting the narrower focuses of other bibliographies, David McKitterick, in a *Times Literary Supplement* review of Volume II: *1601-1650,* comments that in *European Americana* ''the geographical area has expanded, to encompass all the Americas, but the focus has shifted also, to include the impact of the New World as an idea as well as a geographical location and economic base: its absorption within the European intellectual, as well as material frame of reference. . . . Dozens of . . . imaginative writers . . . found cause to allude to it, sometimes in a contrived manner, as it was digested into the European consciousness. It is not the least important aspect of the approach taken by *European Americana* that it chronicles and describes this interplay between the Americas as a world for mental speculation and as a continent demanding exploration, trade and emigration, while at the same time working fundamental changes in Europe. . . . In these respects the period covered by this one [volume] is crucial.'' *European Americana,* says McKitterick, ''deserves the widest possible use.''

BIOGRAPHICAL/CRITICAL SOURCES: Robert W. Higgins, editor, *The Revolutionary War in the South—Power, Conflict, and Leadership: Essays in Honor of John Richard Alden,* Duke University Press, 1979; *Times Literary Supplement,* June 10, 1983.

*   *   *

ALLEN, Maury 1932-

PERSONAL: Born May 2, 1932; son of Harry and Frances (Leon) Allen; married Janet Kelly (a writer and public relations specialist), March 3, 1962; children: one daughter, one son. *Education:* City College (now City College of the City University of New York), B.A., 1953. *Politics:* Liberal Democrat. *Religion:* Hebrew. *Office:* New York Post, 210 South St., New York, N.Y. 10002.

CAREER: Worked on a newspaper in Seymour, Ind., and for *Sports Illustrated; New York Post,* New York, N.Y., sports writer, 1962—. *Military service:* U.S. Army, 1953-55.

WRITINGS: Ten Great Moments in Sports, Follett, 1960; (with Samuel Moody) *Reprieve from Hell,* Pageant, 1962; *Now Wait a Minute, Casey!,* Doubleday, 1965; *The Record Breakers,* Prentice-Hall, 1968; *The Incredible Mets,* Paperback Library, 1969; *Joe Namath's Sportin' Life,* Paperback Library, 1969.

(Editor) *Voices of Sport,* Grosset, 1971; (with Bo Belinsky) *Bo: Pitching and Wooing,* Dial, 1973; *Where Have You Gone, Joe DiMaggio?,* Dutton, 1975; *You Could Look It Up,* Times Books, 1977; *Damn Yankee,* Times Books, 1978; *Big Time Baseball,* Hart Publishing, 1979; *Mr. October,* Times Books, 1980; *Baseball's 100,* A & W Publishers, 1981. Also author of additional books on sports. Contributor to numerous periodicals, including *Sports Illustrated.*

SIDELIGHTS: Maury Allen writes: ''I grew up in Brooklyn, N.Y., wild about our baseball team, the Brooklyn Dodgers. I wanted to be a player but when I realized I wasn't big enough, strong enough or good enough, I turned to sports writing. I wrote for a high school paper and my college paper where I played on the football and baseball teams (we weren't very good) and then entered the Army. I wrote for an Army newspaper and returned to full time newspaper work in Seymour, Ind.

''I enjoyed writing and I enjoyed sports and I found that I could combine both and be a very lucky guy doing what I like and getting paid for it. I went from Seymour to Levittown, Pa., to *Sports Illustrated* magazine and then to the *Post* where I have covered every sport.

''I am a competitive tennis player, a swimmer, a three man basketball player with my son and his friends in our driveway and a skier. I enjoy writing sports as much today as I did when I started. I have written hundreds of magazine articles and some twenty books on sports and I never get tired of it.

''My wife is also a writer and public relations specialist and my daughter and son each enjoy writing as well as many other things including sports, theatre, and art.

''Writing is hard work and sometimes lonely but very rewarding. There is hardly any greater satisfaction in this life than seeing an empty page suddenly filled with your words. Writing is absolutely a beautiful way to make a living. It certainly beats real work.''

*   *   *

ALLEN, (Alexander) Richard 1929-

PERSONAL: Born February 10, 1929, in Vancouver, British Columbia, Canada; son of Harold Tuttle (a clergyman) and Ruby (a nurse; maiden name, Reilly) Allen; married Margaret Ritchie, July 14, 1951 (divorced, 1964); married Nettie Shewchuk, April 24, 1965; children: (second marriage) Daniel Richard, Philip Andrew. *Education:* Attended University of British Columbia, 1947-48, and 1949-50; University of Toronto, B.A. (with honors), 1956; University of Saskatchewan, M.A., 1961; Duke University, Ph.D., 1967. *Politics:* New Democratic Party. *Religion:* Protestant. *Home:* 85 Haddon Ave. N., Hamilton, Ontario, Canada L85 4A4. *Office:* Department of History, McMaster University, Hamilton, Ontario, Canada L8S 4L9.

CAREER: Elementary school teacher in public schools of Ottawa, Ontario, 1954-55, and Crystal Bay, Ontario, 1956-57; University of Saskatchewan, Saskatoon, general secretary of student Christian movement, 1957-61; University of Regina, Regina, Saskatchewan, special lecturer, 1964-67, assistant professor, 1967-70, associate professor of history, 1970-74, chairman of Canadian Plains Area Studies Program, 1967-70 and 1972-74; McMaster University, Hamilton, Ontario, associate professor, 1974-76, professor of history, 1976—. Elected member, Ontario Legislature, 1982. *Member:* Canadian Historical Association (council member, 1974-77), Social Science

Research Council (member of council, 1975-78). *Awards, honors:* Canada Council senior leave fellow, 1970-71 and 1978-79; research fellow, McGill University, 1978-79.

WRITINGS: The Social Passion; Religion and Social Reform in Canada, 1914-1928, University of Toronto Press, 1971; (editor) *A Region of the Mind: Interpreting the Western Canadian Plains,* Canadian Plains Studies Centre, 1973; (editor) *The Social Gospel in Canada* (conference papers), National Museum of Man, 1975; (contributor) Carl Berger and Ramsay Cook, editors, *The West and the Nation,* McClelland & Stewart, 1976; (editor) *Man and Nature on the Prairies,* Canadian Plains Studies Centre, 1977; (contributor) David R.E. Shephard and Andree Levesque, editors, *Norman Bethune: His Times and His Legacy,* Canadian Public Health Association, 1982. Contributor to history journals.

WORK IN PROGRESS: A biography of Salem Goldworth Bland.

*   *   *

ALLENDOERFER, Carl B(arnett) 1911-1974

PERSONAL: Born April 4, 1911, in Kansas City, Mo.; died September 29, 1974; buried in Kansas City, Mo.; son of Carl William (a banker) and Winifred (Barnett) Allendoerfer; married Dorothy Holbrook, June 26, 1937; children: Robert Duff, James Holbrook, William Barnett. *Education:* Haverford College, B.S., 1932; Oxford University, B.A., 1934, M.A., 1939; Princeton University, Ph.D., 1937. *Politics:* Republican. *Religion:* Protestant. *Home:* 4300 53rd Ave. N.E., Seattle, Wash. 98105. *Office:* University of Washington, Seattle, Wash. 98105.

CAREER: University of Wisconsin—Madison, instructor in mathematics, 1937-38; Haverford College, Haverford, Pa., instructor, 1938-39, assistant professor, 1939-42, associate professor, 1942-46, professor of mathematics, 1946-51; University of Washington, Seattle, professor of mathematics, 1951-74, executive officer of department, 1951-62. Fulbright lecturer at Cambridge University, 1957-58, and in Australia, 1963; visiting professor at New York University and Massachusetts Institute of Technology. Producer of films on mathematics. Member of Institute for Advanced Study, 1948-49; member of Commission on Mathematics, College Entrance Examination Board, 1955-59; member of Division on Mathematics, National Research Council, 1956-58, 1962-65. Consultant in operations research, U.S. Army and Navy, World War II; consulting editor in mathematics, Macmillan Co., beginning 1958.

MEMBER: Mathematical Association of America (president, 1959-60), American Association for the Advancement of Science (fellow), American Mathematical Society, National Council of Teachers of Mathematics, Society for Industrial and Applied Mathematics, Institute of Mathematical Statistics, Monday Club (Seattle), Phi Beta Kappa, Sigma Xi. *Awards, honors:* Rhodes scholar at Oxford University, 1934; Distinguished Service Award from Mathematical Association of America, 1972.

WRITINGS: (With C. O. Oakley) *Principles of Mathematics,* McGraw, 1955, 3rd edition, 1969; (with Oakley) *Fundamentals of Freshman Mathematics,* with instructor's manual, McGraw, 1959, 3rd edition, 1972; (editor) *Symposia in Pure Mathematics,* Volume III: *Differential Geometry,* American Mathematical Society, 1961; *Mathematics for Parents,* Macmillan, 1965; (with Oakley) *Fundamentals of College Algebra,* McGraw, 1967; (editor with others) *Fiftieth Anniversary Issue,* Mathematical Association of America, 1967; *Notes on Differ-*

ential Geometry, University of Washington, Department of Mathematics, 1968.

Calculus of Several Variables and Differential Manifolds, Macmillan, 1974; (with Oakley and Donald R. Kerr, Jr.) *Elementary Functions,* with instructor's manual, McGraw, 1976. Also author of *Principles of Arithmetic and Geometry,* 1971. Contributor to professional journals. Editor, *American Mathematical Monthly,* 1952-56.

AVOCATIONAL INTERESTS: Hiking and sailing.†

*   *   *

ALPERN, Andrew 1938-

PERSONAL: Born November 1, 1938, in New York, N.Y.; son of Dwight K. (a college professor, engineer, and mineralogist) and Grace (in public relations; maiden name, Michelman) Alpern. *Education:* Columbia University, B.Arch., 1964. *Home:* 315 Eighth Ave., New York, N.Y. 10001. *Office:* Coopers & Lybrand, 1251 Sixth Ave., New York, N.Y. 10020.

CAREER: Haines Lungberg Waehler (architectural firm), New York City, student trainee, 1959-61, architect, 1962-67; W. T. Grant (department store chain), New York City, architect, 1967-68; Saphier Lerner Schindler Environetics (space planning and design firm), New York City, project director, 1968-72; Environmental Research & Development, Inc. (planning, design, and real estate firm), New York City, vice-president and director of architecture, 1972-75; independent consulting architect, 1975-77; Hellmuth, Obata & Kassabaum, P.C. (architecture, engineering, and planning firm), New York City, project manager, 1977-78; Coopers & Lybrand (public accounting firm), New York City, director of real estate and planning, 1978—. Certified by National Council of Architectural Registration Boards, 1967; registered architect in New York, Pennsylvania, California, Washington, D.C., and West Virginia; licensed real estate salesman in New York. National arbitrator for American Arbitration Association, 1971—. Lecturer at the City College of the City University of New York and Institute for Architecture and Urban Studies. Institute of Applied Psychotherapy, member of advisory board, 1969-72, therapist in New York State drug abuse program, 1970-72.

MEMBER: American Institute of Architects, Society of Architectural Historians, National Trust for Historic Preservation, Association of Collegiate Schools of Architecture, New York State Association of Architects, Real Estate Board of New York, Architectural League of New York, Metropolitan Association of Urban Designers and Environmental Planners, New York Historical Society, Long Island Historical Society, Bronx County Historical Society, Municipal Art Society, Brownstone Revival Committee, Friends of Cast Iron Architecture. *Awards, honors:* Sc.D. from London College of Applied Science, 1971.

WRITINGS—Published by McGraw, except as indicated: *Apartments for the Affluent: A Historical Survey of Buildings in New York,* 1975; *Garret Ellis Winants: 1818-1890,* privately printed, 1976; *Alpern's Architectural Aphorisms,* 1979; *Handbook of Specialty Elements in Architecture,* 1980; *In the Manor Housed,* Metropolis, 1982; (with Seymour Durst) *Holdouts!,* 1983.

Editorial advisor and consultant to McGraw-Hill periodicals for architects. Editor-in-chief of *Legal Briefs for the Construction Industry,* 1975—.

WORK IN PROGRESS: Editing *Time-Saver Standards for Interior Architecture,* for McGraw; researching a history of architectural drawing instruments and their makers.

SIDELIGHTS: Andrew Alpern writes *CA:* "The practice of architecture encompasses science, technology, business, and art, and it is a wonderfully challenging and stimulating profession, but writing about architecture and buildings can reach a larger audience than mere construction. And through the written word (and copious illustrative material) the crucial, intimate, and often tempestuous interrelationships between architects, developers, and the world-at-large can be described. Buildings are stone and glass and steel, of course, but far more important, they represent physical manifestations of human needs. Perhaps the most important basic need after food and water, is enough of a shelter to call home."

Concerning the future of his profession, Alpern remarks: "My regular reporting of the legal entanglements of the construction industry has shown me that all involved—architects, engineers, contractors, and owners—must work more carefully and thoughtfully if they are to survive in our increasingly litigious society. This means that greater care must be given to the drafting of the contracts that form the basis of construction projects, and far greater care given to the professional planning and the actual construction work. It is no longer sufficient to rely on liability insurance, particularly since the premium cost has been escalating so significantly. With the media reporting the deaths of pedestrians hit by pieces of stonework falling from tall buildings, with scores crushed to death by a suspended hotel walkway that collapsed, and with death and widespread traffic disruption the result of a failed highway bridge, the awesome responsibility of design professionals becomes evident. Those professionals must shoulder that burden and walk ever more cautiously and carefully, mindful that their ultimate obligations are to the users of their architecture and engineering, and not to the owners who pay their fees."

*   *   *

AMARAL, Anthony   1930-1982

PERSONAL: Born August 19, 1930, in Yonkers, N.Y.; died June, 1982; son of Antone and Mae (Vitola) Amaral. *Education:* California State Polytechnic College (now University), B.S., 1960. *Home:* 201 North Roop, Carson City, Nev. 89701.

CAREER: Trainer of show horses, working at the Arabian horse ranch of the Kellogg Ranch in Pomona, Calif., before turning to writing; librarian at Ormsby Public Library, Carson City, Nev. *Military service:* U.S. Army, 1952-55; aide-de-camp to General Bruce C. Clarke; became first lieutenant.

WRITINGS: Comanche: The Horse That Survived the Custer Battle, Westernlore, 1961; *Movie Horses: Their Treatment and Training,* Bobbs-Merrill, 1967; *Will James: The Gilt-Edged Cowboy* (biography), Westernlore, 1967; *How to Train Your Horse: A Complete Guide to Making an Honest Horse,* Winchester Press, 1977; *Mustang: Life and Legends of Nevada's Wild Horses,* University of Nevada Press, 1977; *Will James: The Last Cowboy Legend,* University of Nevada Press, 1980; *Movie Horses: The Fascinating Techniques of Training,* Wilshire, 1982.

Contributor of about one hundred articles on horse subjects, and others on western Americana, to *Smithsonian, Western Horseman, True West, Frontier Times, Nevada,* and *Sports Afield;* contributor of short stories to *Point West* and *Fiction Magazine.*†

AMBRUS, Gyozo Laszlo   1935-
(Victor G. Ambrus)

PERSONAL: Born August 19, 1935, in Budapest, Hungary; son of Gyozo (a chemical engineer) and Iren (Toth) Ambrus; married Glenys R. Chapman (an illustrator), 1958; children: Mark, Sandor John. *Education:* Received early education in Hungary and attended Hungarian Academy of Fine Art for three years; Royal College of Art, London, England, Diploma A.R.C.A., 1959. *Politics:* Democrat. *Religion:* Roman Catholic. *Home:* 52 Crooksbury Rd., Farnham, Surrey, England.

CAREER: Author, artist, designer, and illustrator of books for children. Lecturer on illustration, West Surrey College of Art, Surrey, England, beginning 1964, and other universities. *Member:* Royal College of Art (associate member), Royal Society of Arts (fellow), Royal Society of Painters, Etchers, and Engravers (fellow). *Awards, honors:* Kate Greenaway Gold Medal for most distinguished work in illustration of a children's book, Library Association of Great Britain, 1964, for *The Three Poor Tailors,* and 1975, for *Horses in Battle* and *Mishka.*

WRITINGS—Under name Victor G. Ambrus; self-illustrated; published by Oxford University Press, except as indicated: *The Three Poor Tailors,* 1965, Harcourt, 1966; *Brave Soldier Janosh,* 1967; *The Little Cockerell,* 1968; *The Seven Skinny Goats,* 1969, Harcourt, 1970; *The Sultan's Bath,* Harcourt, 1972; *Hot Water for Boris,* 1972; *A Country Wedding,* 1973; *Horses in Battle,* 1975; *Mishka,* 1975; (adaptor) Brothers Grimm, *The Valiant Little Tailor,* 1980; (adaptor) *Dracula,* 1981; *Blackbeard,* 1981; *Dracula's Bedtime Storybook,* 1982; *Felix, Grandma and Mustapha Biscuit,* Morrow, 1983.

Illustrator of over 150 books, including: Ian Serraillier, *The Challenge of the Green Knight,* Oxford University Press, 1966; Helen Kay, *Henri's Hands for Pablo Picasso,* Abelard-Schuman, 1966; William Cowper, *The Diverting History of John Gilpin,* Abelard-Schuman, 1969; Robert J. Unstead, *Living in a Crusader Land,* A. & C. Black, 1971; Bonnie Highsmith, *Kodi's Mare,* Abelard-Schuman, 1973; Winifred Finlay, *Cap o' Rushes and Other Folk Tales,* Kaye & Ward, 1973; Alexander Cordell, *The Traitor Within,* Globe Books, 1975; Helen Griffiths, *Just a Dog,* Holiday House, 1975; *The Story of Britain,* A. & C. Black, 1976; Sir Bernard Miles, *Favorite Tales from Shakespeare,* Hamlyn, 1976; Miles, adaptor, *Robin Hood,* Rand McNally, 1978; Unstead, *The Life of Jesus,* Hamlyn, 1981; J. Riordan, *Tales of King Arthur,* Rand McNally, 1982; Riordan, *Tales from the Arabian Nights,* Rand McNally, 1983.

WORK IN PROGRESS: Illustrating *The Canterbury Tales,* for Oxford University Press.

SIDELIGHTS: Gyozo Laszlo Ambrus wrote *CA:* "Being an illustrator/author, story and pictures always go together when I am working on an idea for a book. And I am never too sure which comes first! I am also something of a split personality. When other authors stick to a certain line of books, I switch between subjects as far apart as the history of the Habsburg Empire and the comic strip frolics of Count Dracula.

"In many ways this is the most enjoyable thing about working on books—you never know what's going to occupy your drawing board next. In my days I have seen dinosaurs, sailing ships, romantic heroines, horses by the dozen, nursery rhyme characters, knights of King Arthur, Father Christmas—come and go in quick succession. Never a dull moment!

"To me the most rewarding experience as an author is to see a well-worn, dog-eared book of mine on the school library shelves—or to have a small child come up and say—'I know you—you are Dracula.'''

AVOCATIONAL INTERESTS: Military history (especially the Napoleonic wars), collecting arms, armor, and antique weapons, travel, old architecture, paintings.

*   *   *

AMBRUS, Victor G.
See AMBRUS, Gyozo Laszlo

*   *   *

AMES, Leslie
See RIGONI, Orlando (Joseph)

*   *   *

AMES, Mildred   1919-

PERSONAL: Born November 2, 1919, in Bridgeport, Conn.; daughter of Edward John and Amelia (Miller) Walsh; married William Ames (a technical writer), April 19, 1946. *Education:* Attended secondary school in Bridgeport, Conn. *Residence:* Palos Verdes Estates, Calif.

CAREER: Writer, 1965—. *Member:* Society of Children's Book Writers, Surfwriters Club (president, 1978-79), Southern California Council on Literature for Children and Young People.

WRITINGS: Shadows of Summers Past (young adult and adult), Bouregy, 1973; *The House of the Haunted Child* (young adult and adult), Bouregy, 1974; *Is There Life on a Plastic Planet?* (juvenile), Dutton, 1975; *Without Hats, Who Can Tell the Good Guys?* (juvenile), Dutton, 1976; *The Wonderful Box* (juvenile), Dutton, 1977; *What Are Friends For?* (juvenile), Scribner, 1978; *The Dancing Madness* (young adult), Delacorte, 1980; *Nicky and the Joyous Noise* (juvenile), Scribner, 1980; *Anna to the Infinite Power* (young adult), Scribner, 1981; *Philo Potts; or, The Helping Hand Strikes Again* (juvenile), Scribner, 1982; *The Silver Link, the Silken Tie* (young adult), Scribner, 1984. Contributor to *Young Miss* and *Cricket.*

WORK IN PROGRESS: Research on the early West.

SIDELIGHTS: Mildred Ames writes: "I wrote my first story at the age of eight or nine, a tearful melodrama. When the teacher read it in class, I thought it so achingly beautiful, I wanted to cry. Instead of admiration from my classmates, one little boy shot up and said, 'Well, I just don't believe she wrote it.'

"I have worked in a magic factory and in a five and ten, and learned that while there may be magic in a five and ten, there is none in a magic factory. I have sold hats, run an elevator, worked as a telephone operator, travelled for a chain of photography studios, and, as a clerical worker, worked for two aircraft plants, an air base, and an automobile dealer.

"I write for children because I share so many of their beliefs. Like them, I believe that there *can* be happy endings, that people *can* live happily ever after, and that if you wish hard enough and work hard enough, a dream can come true."

MEDIA ADAPTATIONS: A filmed version of *What Are Friends For?* appeared as an "Afterschool Special" on ABC-TV in March, 1980; *Anna to the Infinite Power* was filmed by Blue Marble Co., Inc., for release on cable television.

AMI, Ben
See ELIAV, Arie L(ova)

*   *   *

ANDERSEN, Doris   1909-

PERSONAL: Born February 6, 1909, in Tanana, Alaska; daughter of Edgar and Florence Maude (Walker) Crompton; married George C. Andersen, December 23, 1929; children: Deirdre (Mrs. W. J. McKechnie), Richard, David. *Education:* University of British Columbia, B.A., 1929; University of Washington, Seattle, B.S.L.S., 1930. *Home:* 1232 Esquimalt Ave., West Vancouver, British Columbia, Canada.

CAREER: Librarian with Seattle (Wash.) Public Library, 1929-30, and Ottawa (Ontario) Public Library, 1940-45; Vancouver (British Columbia) Public Library, branch head, 1956-74. *Awards, honors:* Runner-up for Canadian Association of Children's Librarians Best Children's Book Award in 1974, for *Slave of the Haida.*

WRITINGS: Blood Brothers (juvenile), St. Martin's, 1967; *Ways Harsh and Wild,* J. J. Douglas Ltd., 1973; *Slave of the Haida* (juvenile), Macmillan (Toronto), 1974; *Evergreen Islands,* Gray's Publishing, 1980; *The Columbia Is Coming!,* Gray's Publishing, 1982. Contributor to *Canadian Library* and *British Columbia Library Quarterly.*

SIDELIGHTS: Doris Andersen wrote to *CA:* "I enjoy the varied and extensive research needed for [my] fiction and nonfiction works, and try to show the problems of natives and white settlers from their many conflicting viewpoints as evinced in records of the eras covered. While I use action and suspense to engage interest, I hope to leave the reader with a heightened sensitivity to his environment, its people, and their past and present problems." *Blood Brothers* was translated into Norwegian.

MEDIA ADAPTATIONS: Blood Brothers was produced as a serial on CBS-Radio, 1982.

*   *   *

ANDERSON, Colena M(ichael)   1891-

PERSONAL: Born May 30, 1891, in Buffalo, N.Y.; daughter of Charles F. and Frances (Reppien) Michael; married Elam J. Anderson (a missionary to China and college president), July 3, 1916 (deceased); children: Frances (Mrs. Clarence S. Gulick), Victor, Elam. *Education:* Cornell University, B.A., 1914; University of Chicago, M.A., 1917; Claremont Graduate School, Ph.D., 1954. *Politics:* Republican. *Religion:* Christian. *Home:* 345 South Baker, McMinnville, Ore. 97128.

CAREER: Teacher, mainly of English, in Buffalo, N.Y., 1914-16, University of Shanghai, Shanghai, China, 1917-19, and Shanghai American School, 1928-29, 1931-32; Linfield College, McMinnville, Ore., associate professor of English and history, 1946-58, professor emeritus, 1958—, dean of women, 1952-58. *Member:* Phi Beta Kappa, Delta Kappa Gamma (president, 1952-54), Shakespeare Club (McMinnville).

WRITINGS: Handbook for Christian Writers, Zondervan, 1966; *Don't Put on Your Slippers Yet,* Zondervan, 1971; *Joy beyond Grief,* Zondervan, 1974; *Friendship's Bright Shinings,* Zondervan, 1976; *Primer of Chinese Art Symbols,* Oregon Lithoprint, 1980. Contributor of articles and stories to *Christian Herald* and denominational publications.

WORK IN PROGRESS: Rifts in the Sky, Come and Have Breakfast, and *Wood for His Fire,* all for Zondervan.

SIDELIGHTS: Colena M. Anderson told *CA:* "Soon after I could write the alphabet I discovered the charm of rhyming words: 'I sat on a mat and saw a cat eat a rat. The rat was fat.' Words, words—what fun! Years later at Cornell University in my senior year, I put some words together and won the Barnes-Shakespeare Prize for my essay 'The Infinite Variety of the Play *Antony and Cleopatra*' ($50.00).

"My purpose in writing: Beyond the nagging urge to get black on white, I trust that personal experiences may give comfort and strength, and I want to share my faith in the Trinity and in eternal life."

Don't Put On Your Slippers Yet has been translated into German and *Joy beyond Grief* has been translated into Spanish.

AVOCATIONAL INTERESTS: Reading, gardening, flower arrangement, and making personal greeting cards.

*   *   *

ANDERSON, Irvine H(enry)   1928-

PERSONAL: Born March 29, 1928, in Natchez, Miss.; son of Irvine Henry and Elizabeth Ogden (Reed) Anderson; married, 1950 (divorced, 1974); married Donna B. Denoon (a counselor), June 14, 1975; children: Emily, Grace; (stepdaughter) Mary. *Education:* Southwestern at Memphis, B.A., 1950; University of Cincinnati, M.A., 1968, Ph.D., 1973. *Politics:* Republican. *Religion:* Presbyterian. *Home:* 2619 Ardmore Ave., Cincinnati, Ohio 45237. *Office:* Aircraft Engine Group, General Electric Co., Cincinnati, Ohio 45215.

CAREER: Memphis International Center, Memphis, Tenn., associate director in foreign trade promotion, 1950-52; General Electric Co., New York, N.Y., in employee relations (worked in Syracuse, N.Y., Pittsfield, Mass., and Cincinnati, Ohio), 1956-67; University of Cincinnati, Cincinnati, instructor, 1970-73, assistant professor, 1973-76, associate professor of history, 1976-79; General Electric Co., Cincinnati, 1979—, currently manager of human resource development. Moderator of numerous television programs for "World Front" series in Cincinnati, 1974-76. *Military service:* U.S. Naval Reserve, active duty in Naval Air Intelligence, 1952-56; served in Pacific theater; became lieutenant commander.

MEMBER: International Studies Association, American Historical Association, Organization of American Historians, Society for Historians of American Foreign Relations. *Awards, honors:* Woodrow Wilson fellowship, summer, 1971; Louis Knott Koontz Award from *Pacific Historical Review,* 1976, for article on oil embargo to Japan; Thomas Newcomen Award from Newcomen Society and *Business History Review,* 1977, for *The Standard-Vacuum Oil Company and the United States East Asian Policy, 1933-1941.*

WRITINGS: The Standard-Vacuum Oil Company and the United States East Asian Policy, 1933-1941, Princeton University Press, 1975; *ARAMCO, the United States, and Saudi Arabia: A Study in the Dynamics of Foreign Oil Policy, 1933-1950,* Princeton University Press, 1981. Contributor of articles and reviews to history journals.

WORK IN PROGRESS: A theoretical work on international relations, based heavily on general systems theory.

SIDELIGHTS: Irvine H. Anderson writes *CA* that his "principal current interest is a theory of human systems and their dynamics. My general viewpoint has been heavily influenced by the work of Pierre Teilhard de Chardin."

*   *   *

ANDERSON, Madelyn Klein

PERSONAL: Born in New York, N.Y.; daughter of Max W. and Fannie (Siegel) Klein; married Douglas Ray Anderson (deceased); children: Justin Lee. *Education:* Hunter College (now Hunter College of the City University of New York), B.A., 1951; New York University, certificate in occupational therapy, 1958; Pratt Institute, M.L.S., 1974. *Home:* 80 North Moore St., New York, N.Y. 10013.

CAREER: Beth Israel Hospital, New York City, director of occupational therapy, 1959-63; New York Infirmary, New York City, director of occupational therapy, 1968-72; Julian Messner, Inc., New York City, senior editor, 1974-83; free-lance editor, 1983—. *Military service:* U.S. Army, Women's Medical Specialist Corps, 1954-55; became lieutenant. *Member:* Overseas Press Club, Beta Phi Mu.

WRITINGS: Iceberg Alley, Messner, 1976; *Sea Raids and Rescues: The United States Coast Guard,* McKay, 1979; *Counting on You: The U.S. Census,* Vanguard Press, 1980; *Oil in Troubled Waters: Cleaning Up Oil Spills,* Vanguard Press, 1983; *Greenland: Island at the Top of the World,* Dodd, 1983.

SIDELIGHTS: Madelyn Klein Anderson comments that the death of her husband in Vietnam "led to a drastic career change which in turn led to the development of my writing. I had travelled extensively as a military wife, but my most exciting trip was in connection with *Iceberg Alley,* when I traveled on a Coast Guard C130 to Newfoundland and Greenland. Travel and collecting rare books and antiques keep me busy—and broke—in between books."

*   *   *

ANDERSON, Margaret J(ean)   1931-

PERSONAL: Born December 24, 1931, in Gorebridge, Scotland; came to the United States in 1963; daughter of John A. (a clergyman) and Margaret (Reid) Hall; married Norman H. Anderson (a professor of entomology), September 15, 1956; children: Richard, Judy, Susan, Karen. *Education:* University of Edinburgh, B.Sc. (with honors), 1953. *Religion:* Presbyterian. *Home:* 1930 Northwest 29th Pl., Corvallis, Ore. 97330.

CAREER: Writer. East Malling Research Station, Kent, England, statistician, 1953-55; Canada Department of Agriculture, Summerland, British Columbia, entomologist, 1955-56; Oregon State University, Corvallis, statistician, 1956-57. *Member:* Society of Children's Book Writers.

AWARDS, HONORS: Writing competition award from Canadian Entomological Society, 1973, for "Making a Case for the Caddisfly"; *Exploring the Insect World* was named an outstanding science book for children by National Science Teachers Association and Children's Book Council, 1974; *To Nowhere and Back* was named outstanding book of the year by *New York Times Book Review,* 1975.

WRITINGS—All juveniles; published by Knopf, except as indicated: *Exploring the Insect World* (nonfiction), McGraw, 1974; *To Nowhere and Back* (fiction), 1975; (contributor) *Medley,* Houghton, 1976; *Exploring City Trees, and the Need for Urban Forest* (nonfiction), McGraw, 1976; *In the Keep of Time* (fiction; first book in trilogy), 1977; *Searching for Shona* (fiction), 1978; *In the Circle of Time* (fiction; second book in trilogy), 1979; (contributor) *Ranger Rick's Surprise Book*, National Wildlife Federation, 1979; *The Journey of the Shadow Bairns* (fiction), 1980; *Light in the Mountain* (fiction), 1982; *The Brain on Quartz Mountain* (fiction), 1982. Contributor to magazines, including *Nature and Science, Ranger Rick's Nature Magazine,* and *Instructor.*

WORK IN PROGRESS: Homecoming Song, Bigfoot on Quartz Mountain, and a book to complete the *In the Keep of Time/ Circle of Time* trilogy, all for Knopf.

SIDELIGHTS: Margaret J. Anderson told *CA:* "My writing—both fiction and nonfiction—reflects my interest in the environment. Time-slip fantasies become a vehicle for making children aware that we are connected to our past, and are making decisions now that will affect the future. Books for the young should leave room for hope, and also room for the reader's own response."

*   *   *

ANDERSON, Shirley Lord   1934-
(Shirley Lord)

PERSONAL: Born August 28, 1934, in London, England; came to the United States in 1971; daughter of Francis James (a company director) and Mabel (Williamson) Stringer; married Cyril Lord, January 17, 1960 (divorced December, 1973); married David Jean Anderson (a business consultant), August 3, 1974. *Education:* Attended secondary school in Essex, England. *Politics:* Conservative. *Religion:* Roman Catholic. *Office:* Vogue Magazine, 350 Madison Ave., New York, N.Y. 10017.

CAREER: London Star, London, England, woman's editor, 1960-61; *Evening Standard,* London, woman's editor, 1961-63; *Harper's Bazaar,* London and New York City, beauty and health editor, 1963-73; *Vogue,* New York City, beauty and health editor, 1973-75; Helena Rubinstein, New York City, vice-president for corporate relations, 1975-80; *Vogue,* director of special projects, 1980—. Professional tours in England and the United States include "Shirley Lord Show" and "Shirley Lord Beauty Breakfast." City commissioner for Craigavan, Northern Ireland.

WRITINGS—Under name Shirley Lord: *Small Beer at Claridge's* (autobiography), M. Joseph, 1968; *The Easy Way to Good Looks,* Crowell, 1976; *Golden Hill* (novel), Crown, 1982. Author of syndicated column, "Be Beautiful," Field Syndicate, 1975—. Woman's editor for London *Evening News,* 1963-67.

WORK IN PROGRESS: A series of twelve books on beauty, health, and psyche; a radio series on teenage beauty; a novel.

SIDELIGHTS: Shirley Lord's novel *Golden Hill,* set on the Caribbean island of Trinidad, tells the tale of a decades-old feud over the ownership of a large plantation there. According to Richard F. Shepard's review of the book in the *New York Times,* Lord "has an ability to tell a story that keeps you turning the pages. . . . She has a grasp of her subject that gives it all a ring of authenticity."

BIOGRAPHICAL/CRITICAL SOURCES: New York Times, October 21, 1982; *New York Times Book Review,* October 24, 1982; *Washington Post Book World,* December 5, 1982.

ANDRE, Evelyn M(arie)   1924-

PERSONAL: Born July 13, 1924, in Pennsylvania; daughter of J. Clyde (a carpenter)and Lillian (Haley) Andre. *Education:* Attended Adrian College, 1946-48; Capital University, B.A., 1950; Hartford Seminary, M.A., 1952. *Religion:* United Methodist. *Residence:* Nashville, Tenn. *Office:* United Methodist Publishing House, United Methodist Board of Discipleship, 201 Eighth Ave. S., Nashville, Tenn. 37203.

CAREER: Research assistant at Allegheny Ludlum Steel Corp., 1942-46; Court Street Methodist Church, Flint, Mich., director of Christian education, 1952-59; United Methodist Board of Discipleship, United Methodist Publishing House, Nashville, Tenn., editor of nursery materials, 1959—.

WRITINGS: Things We Like to Do (juvenile), Abingdon, 1969; (compiler with Jeneil Menefee) *Rejoice and Sing Praise* (juvenile songbook), Abingdon, 1977; (compiler with Margie McCarty) *I Can Teach Young Children* (teachers' manual), United Methodist Board of Discipleship, 1977; (compiler with Myron Brown) *Sing and Be Joyful* (juvenile songbook), Abingdon, 1979; *Places I Like to Be* (juvenile), Abingdon, 1980; *Bible Children Lived in Families,* Graded Press, 1980; *Jesus Grew and I Grow,* Graded Press, 1980; *Bible People Worked for God,* Graded Press, 1980.

SIDELIGHTS: Evelyn M. Andre writes *CA:* "I am the youngest in a family of eight children. I have always had a very great interest in young children. I started early caring for nieces and nephews.

"For close to twenty-five years, I have worked with or on behalf of very young children. And the more I work professionally for and with them, the more I realize the importance of the early years. Helping children feel good about themselves and know they are loved and valued as persons is a tremendously important task for adults who live or work with children.

"I'm 'Aunt Evie' to over fifty people who include my nineteen nieces and nephews and their children. As a member of a large, closely knit family, I've had many treasured times of helping children experience 'things we like to do, and places I like to be.'

"I would like to continue to work with children and other teachers in the church school, and in laboratory and leadership schools for church school teachers across the country."

AVOCATIONAL INTERESTS: Pastel and watercolor painting, golf, swimming, and singing in the church choir.

*   *   *

ANDREWS, Elton V.
See POHL, Frederik

*   *   *

ANDREWS, Peter   1931-

PERSONAL: Born May 23, 1931, in New York, N.Y.; son of Bert A. (a newspaperman) and Nadine (Wright) Andrews; married Marjorie Key, January 16, 1960; children: Regan. *Education:* Attended Hamilton College, 1950-51, and American Academy of Art, 1951-52. *Agent:* Scott Meredith Literary Agency, 845 Third Ave., New York, N.Y. 10022.

CAREER: United Press International (UPI), Washington, D.C., wire editor, Washington Capital News Service, 1958; national correspondent for Washington (D.C.) Bureau, Hearst Publications, 1958-63; *Newsweek,* New York, N.Y., associate editor, 1963; *Playboy,* Chicago, Ill., associate editor, 1964-66; *Reader's Digest,* Pleasantville, N.Y., senior editor, 1967-70; *Americana* magazine, editor, 1972—. Free-lance writer. *Member:* Authors Guild, Society of Magazine Writers, Overseas Press Club, National Press Club (Washington, D.C.). *Awards, honors:* Gavel Award from American Bar Association, 1972.

WRITINGS: (With father, Bert Andrews) *A Tragedy of History,* Robert B. Luce, 1962; *In Honored Glory: The Story of Arlington,* Putnam, 1966; *Sergeant York: Reluctant Hero,* Putnam, 1969; (editor) *Christmas in Germany,* World Book, 1974; *Christmas in Colonial and Early America,* World Book, 1975; *Pacific Northwest: A Guide to the Inns of Oregon, Washington, and British Columbia,* Holt, 1981; *The Southeast: A Guide to the Inns of Florida, Georgia, South Carolina, North Carolina, Virginia, and West Virginia,* Holt, 1982; *The Southwest: A Guide to the Inns of Arizona, New Mexico, and Texas,* Holt, 1982.

"Classic Country Inns of America" series, published by Holt in 1978: *Inns of New England and the Maritimes; . . . the Mid-Atlantic and the South; . . . the Pacific Coast and Southwest.*

"Country Inns of America" series; with George Allen and Tracy Ecclesine; published by Holt in 1980: *Country Inns of Upper New England; . . . Lower New England; . . . New York and Mid-Atlantic; . . . California.*

Also writer, producer, and narrator of television documentary film, "Street Crime in the Nation's Capital," for Metro Media Television. Contributor of articles and stories to *TV Guide, Playboy, Saturday Review, American Heritage, Coronet, Horizon,* and other periodicals.

SIDELIGHTS: Peter Andrews's first book, *A Tragedy of History,* is a firsthand account of the Alger Hiss affair. Although the original manuscript was written by his father, Bert Andrews (the *New York Herald Tribune* reporter credited with breaking the story concerning Whittaker Chambers's accusation of Alger Hiss's alleged involvement with the Communist Party), Peter Andrews completed the text and prepared it for publication after his father's death.

"What sets the Andrews story apart," explains John Tebbel in the *Saturday Review,* "is the 'inside' feeling it conveys, and to the professional reader, the picture it gives of a first-class reporter at work on the biggest story of his life." And J. L. Andrews writes in *Library Journal* that "for those familiar with the Hiss case, the author's personal experience will throw additional light on some of the principal participants, for those whose knowledge is sketchy, this book will give them the facts together with some honest and judicial appraisals."

BIOGRAPHICAL/CRITICAL SOURCES: Library Journal, September 15, 1962; *Saturday Review,* October 13, 1962; *New York Times Book Review,* October 14, 1962.†

*   *   *

ANTHONY, Geraldine C(ecilia)   1919-

PERSONAL: Born October 5, 1919, in Brooklyn, N.Y.; daughter of William (a pharmacist) and Agnes (Murphy) Anthony. *Education:* Attended Boston College, 1945-47; Mount St. Vincent University, B.A., 1951; St. John's University, New York, N.Y., M.A., 1956, Ph.D., 1963; post-doctoral study at Exeter College, Oxford, University of Minnesota, and Columbia University. *Home and office:* Department of English, Mount St.

Vincent University, 166 Bedford Highway, Halifax, Nova Scotia, Canada B3M 2J6.

CAREER: Member of Roman Catholic women's community, the Sisters of Charity, 1939—; junior high school teacher at Roman Catholic schools in Dorchester, Mass., 1942-48, Lowell, Mass., 1948-51, and Bellmore, N.Y., 1951-62; high school teacher of English in Halifax, Nova Scotia, 1963-65; Mount St. Vincent University, Halifax, assistant professor, 1965-71, associate professor, 1971-77, professor of English, 1977—, director of summer school, 1966-68, chairman of department, 1983—. Visiting professor at Hofstra University, summers, 1970-74. *Member:* Modern Language Association of America, Association for Canadian Theatre History (member of executive board), Association of Canadian and Quebecois Literature, Association of Canadian University Teachers of English. *Awards, honors:* Wall Street Journal fellow at University of Minnesota, 1965; Canada Council grants, 1975, 1976, 1977, and 1978 for research to complete *Gwen Pharis Ringwood;* British High Council grant, 1983.

WRITINGS: John Coulter, G. K. Hall, 1976; (editor) *Profiles in Canadian Drama,* three volumes, Gage, 1977; *Stage Voices,* Doubleday, 1978; *Gwen Pharis Ringwood,* G. K. Hall, 1981; (contributor) *Canadian Biographical Dictionary,* University of British Columbia Press, 1982. Also contributor to *Dictionary of Literary Biography* and *Canadian Book Review Annual.* Contributor to periodicals, including *Atlantis, Canadian Drama, Canadian Theatre Review, Canadian Library Journal, Cithara, World Literature, Canadian Children's Literature, Canadian Review of American Studies, Prairie Forum, Theatre History in Canada, Great Plains Quarterly,* and *Canadian Literature.* Member of editorial board of *Canadian Drama/L'Art Dramatique Canadien.*

WORK IN PROGRESS: A book on historical and political Canadian drama.

SIDELIGHTS: Geraldine C. Anthony told *CA* her interest in theatre "stemmed from my childhood in New York and my father's keen interest in the Broadway musicals. He stimulated me to a love of theatre that has become a passion, transferred from American to Canadian drama when I moved to Canada in 1963 and discovered that very little had been done in the way of dramatic literary criticism. Today many Canadian scholars are devoting more and more time to research in this field. I am happy to have been one of the first."

*   *   *

ANTROBUS, John   1933-

PERSONAL: Born July 2, 1933, in Aldershot, England; married Margaret McCormick, 1958; children: Daniel, Nicholas, Louise. *Education:* Attended King Edward VII Nautical College and Sandhurst Military Academy. *Home:* 13 Allfarthing Lane, London S.W. 18, England. *Agent:* Deborah Rogers Ltd., 5-11 Mortimer St., London W1N 7RH, England.

CAREER: Playwright, author of scripts for radio, television, and film, 1955—; theatre director and actor, 1963—; author of children's books. Directed and appeared in "You'll Come to Love Your Sperm Test," Hampstead Theatre, London, 1965, directed "The Bed-Sitting Room," with Spike Milligan, Mermaid Theatre, London, 1963, and acted in "An Evening with John Antrobus," London, 1969, and "The Contractor," London, 1970. *Military service:* British Merchant Navy, apprentice deck officer, 1950-52. British Army, East Surrey Regiment, 1952-55. *Awards, honors:* George Devine Award, 1970.

WRITINGS—Plays: (With Spike Milligan) *The Bed-Sitting Room* (first produced off the West End at Mermaid Theatre, January, 1963; produced on the West End at Duke of York's Theatre, 1963; revised version produced, 1966), Jack Hobbs, 1970; "Royal Commission Review," produced in London, 1964; "Cane of Honour," produced in London, 1965; "You'll Come to Love Your Sperm Test" (produced off the West End at Hampstead Theatre, 1965), published in *Plays and Players,* edited by Peter Roberts, Volumes 12 and 13, Hansom Books (London), 1965; *Trixie and Baba* (produced on the West End at Royal Court Theatre, August 21, 1968), Calder & Boyars, 1969; "Captain Oates' Left Sock," produced in London, 1969, produced on the West End at Royal Court Theatre, 1973; "An Evening with John Antrobus," produced in London, 1969.

Why Bournemouth? and Other Plays (contains "Why Bournemouth?," produced in London, 1968; "The Missing Links," televised, 1965; "An Apple a Day," televised, 1971), Calder & Boyars, 1970; "Stranger in a Cafeteria," produced in Edinburgh, 1971; "The Looneys," produced in Edinburgh at Edinburgh Traverse, 1971; "Crete and Sergeant Pepper," produced on the West End at Royal Court Theatre, May 24, 1972; "Mrs. Grabowski's Academy," produced on the West End at Royal Court Theatre, 1975; *Hitler in Liverpool and Other Plays* (contains "Hitler in Liverpool," produced, 1980), Riverrun Press, 1982.

Children's books: *The Boy with Illum: ~ted Measles,* Robson Books,1978; *Help! I Am a Prisoner in a Toothpaste Factory,* Robson Books, 1978.

Also author of plays, "Don't Feed the Fish," 1971; "The Dinosaurs, and Certain Humiliations," 1974, and "One Orange for the Baby," and screenplays, "Idle on Parade," 1960, (with others) "The Wrong Arm of the Law," 1963, "The Big Job," 1965, and "The Bed-Sitting Room" (adaptation of play by Antrobus and Milligan), 1970.

Author of television scripts for numerous series, including "The Army Game," "Bootsie and Snudge," "Early to Braden," and for individual shows. Radio scripts include the "Idiot Weekly" and "Goon Show" series.

*   *   *

ANVIC, Frank
See SHERMAN, Jory (Tecumseh)

*   *   *

APPLEBY, Joyce Oldham 1929-

PERSONAL: Born April 9, 1929, in Omaha, Neb.; daughter of Junius Graham and Edith (Cash) Oldham; children: Ann Lansburgh Bloxham, Mark Lansburgh, Frank Appleby. *Education:* Stanford University, B.A., 1950; University of California, Santa Barbara, M.A., 1959; Claremont Graduate School, Ph.D., 1966. *Home:* 615 Westholme Ave., Los Angeles, Calif. 90024. *Office:* Department of History, University of California, Los Angeles, Calif. 90024.

CAREER: San Diego State University, San Diego, Calif., assistant professor, 1967-70, associate professor, 1970-73, professor of American history, 1973-81, associate dean of College of Arts and Letters, 1974-75; University of California, Los Angeles, professor of history, 1981—. Visiting associate professor, University of California, Irvine, 1975-76; visiting professor, University of California, Los Angeles, 1978-79. Member of board of fellows, Claremont Graduate School, 1970-73;

fellow commoner, Churchill College, Cambridge University, 1977-78; summer fellow, Regional Economic History Research Center, Eleutherian Mills-Hagley Foundation, 1979; visiting fellow, St. Catherine's College, Oxford University, 1982. Institute of Early American History and Culture, member of council, 1980—, chairperson, 1983—. *Member:* American Historical Association (member of Chester Higby Prize committee, 1982; member of council, 1982-85), Organization of American Historians (member of program committee, 1982), American Antiquarian Society.

WRITINGS: (Editor) *Materialism and Morality in the American Past: Themes and Sources, 1600-1800,* Addison-Wesley, 1974; *Economic Thought and Ideology in Seventeenth-Century England,* Princeton University Press, 1978; (contributor) Margaret Jacob and James Jacob, editors, *The Origins of Anglo-American Radicalism,* Allen & Unwin, 1983; (contributor) Jack P. Green and J. R. Pole, editors, *Colonial British America: Essays in the New History of the Early Modern Era,* Johns Hopkins Press, 1983; *Capitalism and a New Social Order: The Republican Vision of the 1970s,* New York University Press, 1983.

Contributor to numerous journals, including *Journal of American History, Business History Review, Past and Present, American Quarterly,* and *Civil War History. William and Mary Quarterly,* member of editorial board, 1980-83, chairperson, 1981-83. Member of editorial board of *Intellectual History Group Newsletter,* 1981—, *Eighteenth-Century Studies,* 1982—, *Journal of the Early Republic,* 1982—, and *Encyclopedia of American Political History.*

*   *   *

ARKIN, Frieda 1917-

PERSONAL: Born September 4, 1917, in Brooklyn, N.Y.; daughter of Chaim (a merchant) and Anna (Gamsu) Weitzman; married; children: Thomas Edward, Constance Louise. *Education:* Attended Juilliard School of Music, 1936-37, and University of Missouri, 1937-38; University of Chicago, B.A., 1940; Columbia University, M.A., 1947. *Religion:* None. *Home:* One Winthrop St., Essex, Mass. 01929. *Agent:* A. L. Hart, Fox Chase Agency, Inc., 419 East 57th St., New York, N.Y. 10022.

CAREER: Writer. Lecturer in anthropology, Hofstra College (now Hofstra University), Hempstead, N.Y., summer, 1947; lecturer in physical anthropology, Hunter College (now Hunter College of the City University of New York), New York, N.Y., 1947-54.

WRITINGS: The Cook's Companion: Dictionary of Culinary Tips and Terms, Doubleday, 1968; *The Dorp* (novel), Dial, 1969; *Kitchen Wisdom,* Holt, 1977; *Soup Wisdom,* Holt, 1982; *More Kitchen Wisdom,* Holt, 1982.

Short stories have been anthologized in *Best American Short Stories 1962,* edited by Martha Foley and David Burnett, Houghton, 1962, and *Best American Short Stories 1964,* edited by Foley and Burnett, Houghton, 1964.

Contributor of short stories to numerous literary periodicals, including *Yale Review, New Mexico Quarterly, Colorado Quarterly, Kenyon Review, Georgia Review, Transatlantic Review,* and *Massachusetts Review.*

WORK IN PROGRESS: A novel; another cookbook; a garden book.

SIDELIGHTS: Frieda Arkin is the author of four books dealing with cooking tips and techniques. She offers *CA* this explanation of her feelings behind writing *The Cook's Companion: Dictionary of Culinary Tips and Terms, Kitchen Wisdom, Soup Wisdom,* and *More Kitchen Wisdom:* "The need to eat is, in part, what has driven me to writing. The joy of eating and a love of cooking is what has driven me to include cookbooks among my writings. Torn between the typewriter and the kitchen stove, I find that imagination is a common attribute of the proper employment of both."

Besides these four books on cooking, Arkin has also penned numerous short stories and a novel, *The Dorp.* Arkin's novel looks at the lives and trials of the citizens of Dorp, a small, rural town in upstate New York. "[Arkin] roams the Dorp, as it's colloquially known," explains Muriel Haynes in the *Saturday Review,* "as she would explore a museum rich in specimens . . . to garner an arbitrary selection of human foibles, quirks and crotchets. Her quarry is the endearing eccentricity that, in legend at least, comes to fullest ripening in the climate of the small town."

A number of critics have praised Arkin's novel for its delightful setting and characters. Pauline J. Earl declares in *Best Sellers:* "Frieda Arkin is amazing! She has taken a little town in upstate New York and written of it and its people in such explicit detail that the reader cannot help but feel he is vacationing there and visualizing the entire setting himself." Earl continues: "The people there are diverse and eccentric and Miss Arkin's pen portrays them all so vividly." B. J. Mitchell remarks in *Library Journal* that Arkin has a talent for making "each character [come] alive." And Martin Levin comments in the *New York Times Book Review* that "Arkin takes a delight in the humanity of her characters that gives her . . . first novel a refreshing point of view."

Arkin once shared with *CA* these thoughts related to writing fiction: "Thornton Wilder, during the fifteen years before his death, generously gave me much valuable critical advice. I am enormously indebted to him. I am indebted also to Martha Foley, a woman of astute literary judgment. I started writing fiction very late in life, at a time when most writers are at the peak of their powers. I run panting."

BIOGRAPHICAL/CRITICAL SOURCES: Library Journal, July, 1969; *New York Times Book Review,* August 24, 1969; *Saturday Review,* August 30, 1969; *New York Times,* September 2, 1969; *Best Sellers,* September 15, 1969.

*   *   *

ARMERDING, Hudson Taylor 1918-

PERSONAL: Born June 21, 1918, in Albuquerque, N.M.; son of Carl and Eva May (Taylor) Armerding; married Miriam Lucille Bailey, December 26, 1944; children: Carreen A., Hudson Taylor II, Paul Timothy, Miriam Ruth, Jonathan Edwards. *Education:* Wheaton College, Wheaton, Ill., A.B., 1941; Clark University, A.M., 1942; University of Chicago, Ph.D., 1948; Harvard University, postdoctoral study, 1949-50. *Politics:* Republican. *Home:* 29W780 Schick Rd., Bartlett, Ill. 60103. *Office:* Wheaton College, Wheaton, Ill. 60187.

CAREER: Ordained to Baptist ministry, 1951; Wheaton College, Wheaton, Ill., visiting instructor in social science, 1946-48; Gordon College, Wenham, Mass., professor of history, 1950-61, dean, 1951-61; Wheaton College, professor of history, 1961—, provost, 1963-65, president of college, 1965-82, president emeritus, 1982—. Minister in Brockton, Mass.,

1951-54. *Military service:* U.S. Naval Reserve, 1942-66; active duty, 1942-46; now commander (retired). *Member:* U.S. Naval Institute.

WRITINGS: Christian Patriotism, United Evangelical Action, 1966; *Academic Freedom in the Christian College,* United Evangelical Action, 1966; (editor) *Christianity and the World of Thought,* Moody, 1968; *Leadership,* Tyndale, 1978; *A Word to the Wise,* Tyndale, 1980. Contributor of articles on aspects of the Christian church to periodicals.

WORK IN PROGRESS: A book, *Jesus' Parables.*

*   *   *

ARMS, Johnson
See HALLIWELL, David (William)

*   *   *

ARMSTRONG, D(avid) M(alet) 1926-

PERSONAL: Born July 8, 1926, in Melbourne, Victoria, Australia; son of John Malet (a captain in the Royal Australian Navy) and Philippa Suzanne (Marett) Armstrong; married Madeleine Annette Haydon (a librarian and drama critic), March 3, 1950; married second wife, Jennifer Mary De B. Clark (a social worker), December 31, 1982. *Education:* University of Sydney, B.A., 1950; Exeter College, Oxford, B.Phil., 1954; University of Melbourne, Ph.D., 1960. *Politics:* "Liberal/Democratic, anti-Communist." *Religion:* Atheist. *Home:* 206 Glebe Point Rd., Glebe, Sydney, New South Wales 2037, Australia. *Office:* Philosophy Department, University of Sydney, Sydney, New South Wales 2006, Australia.

CAREER: University of London, Birkbeck College, London, England, assistant lecturer in philosophy, 1954-55; University of Melbourne, Melbourne, Victoria, Australia, 1956-63, began as lecturer, became senior lecturer in philosophy; University of Sydney, Sydney, New South Wales, Australia, Challis Professor of Philosophy, 1964—. Visiting assistant professor, Yale University, 1962; visiting professor, Stanford University, 1965, 1968, and University of Texas at Austin, 1980. *Military service:* Royal Australian Navy, 1945-46.

WRITINGS: Berkeley's Theory of Vision, Melbourne University Press, 1960; *Perception and the Physical World,* Humanities, 1961; *Bodily Sensations,* Humanities, 1962; *A Materialist Theory of the Mind,* Humanities, 1968; *Belief, Truth and Knowledge,* Cambridge University Press, 1972; *Universals and Scientific Realism,* Cambridge University Press, 1978; *What Is a Law of Nature?,* Cambridge University Press, 1983; (contributor) Radu J. Bogdan, editor, *Profiles,* Reidel Publishing, 1984. Contributor to journals in his field.

BIOGRAPHICAL/CRITICAL SOURCES: Radu J. Bogdan, editor, *Profiles,* Reidel Publishing, 1984.

*   *   *

ARNETT, Carroll 1927-
(Gogisgi)

PERSONAL: Born November 9, 1927, in Oklahoma City, Okla.; son of Herschel Warren (an accountant) and Ethel Mildred (Duckett) Arnett; married Claudia Wilson, August 19, 1964; children: Randall, Cassanda, Carlen. *Education:* Beloit College, B.A. (magna cum laude), 1951; University of Oklahoma, graduate study, 1953-55; University of Texas, M.A., 1958, and fifty hours graduate study beyond M.A. *Home:* 5586 Ten Mile Rd., Mecosta, Mich. 49332. *Office:* English Department, Central Michigan University, Mt. Pleasant, Mich. 48859.

CAREER: Instructor in English at Knox College, Galesberg, Ill., 1958-60, Stephens College, Columbia, Mo., 1960-64, Wittenberg University, Springfield, Ohio, 1964-68; Nasson College, Springvale, Me., assistant professor of English, 1968-70; Central Michigan University, Mt. Pleasant, professor of English, 1970—. Associate editor, Elizabeth Press, 1967—. Has given readings at numerous colleges, including Bucknell University, Bowling Green State University, Ohio State University, and State University of New York at Albany. Deer Clan Chief of Overhill Band, Cherokee Nation. *Military service:* U.S. Marine Corps, 1946-47. *Member:* Phi Beta Kappa. *Awards, honors:* National Endowment for the Arts fellowship in creative writing, 1974.

WRITINGS—Poetry; published by Elizabeth Press, except as indicated: *Then*, 1965; *The Intentions*, Ringading Editions, 1966; *Not Only That*, 1967; *Like a Wall*, 1969; *Through the Woods*, 1971; *Earlier*, 1972; *Come*, 1973; *Tsalagi*, 1976; *South Line*, 1979; *Rounds*, Cross-Cultural Communications Press, 1982.

Contributor to anthologies, including: *Of Poem*, Elizabeth Press, 1966; *Best Poems of 1966*, Pacific Books, 1967; *Poems for People*, Macmillan, 1968; *Poems of the Sixties*, J. Murray, 1970; *Another Eye*, Scott, Foresman, 1971; *. . . And Be Merry!*, Grossman, 1972; *My Music Bent*, Elizabeth Press, 1973; *Voices of the Rainbow: Contemporary Poems by American Indians*, Viking, 1975; *The First Skin around Me: Contemporary American Tribal Poetry*, Territorial Press, 1976; *The Remembered Earth: An Anthology of Contemporary Native American Literature*, University of New Mexico Press, 1980; (and editor with Peter Blue Cloud and others) *Coyote's Journal*, Book People, 1982.

Contributor of more than three hundred poems and stories, sometimes under Cherokee name Gogisgi, to magazines, including *Antioch Review*, *Beloit Poetry Journal*, *Cosmopolitan*, *Poetry*, and *Saturday Review*. Guest editor, *Beloit Poetry Journal*, 1979-80.

SIDELIGHTS: On poetry, Carroll Arnett told *CA:* "I write poems, when I can, because it seems sensible to do so and wasteful not to. A poem has a use insofar as it shows what it feels like to be alive or what a person does to himself or others by being alive. . . . No one writes well unless he's in love—with another person, an idea, language, himself. . . . When he writes in love, sometimes, with luck, what comes out is a poem."

On prose, Arnett explained to *CA:* "I write prose because it is the hardest thing I know, and I like to do hard things. I try to please people, a few of them, when I can, but pleasing is seldom an end in itself. More often it is a means of living—with or without people—and living is the most important thing."

BIOGRAPHICAL/CRITICAL SOURCES: Trace, 1966-67; *Poetry*, February, 1967; *Los Angeles Times Book Review*, January 23, 1983.

* * *

ARNOLD, Guy 1932-

PERSONAL: Born May 6, 1932, in Birkenhead, England; son of George Croft and Margaret Arnold. *Education:* Oxford University, M.A. (with honors), 1955. *Politics:* Radical. *Religion:* Agnostic. *Home:* 163 Seymour Pl., London W.1, England.

Agent: Gillon Aitken Ltd., 17 South Eaton Pl., London SW1W 9ER, England.

CAREER: Free-lance writer, lecturer, and traveler, 1955-58, 1960-61; teacher of English in Newmarket, Ontario, 1958-60; Ryerson Institute, Toronto, Ontario, lecturer in political geography, 1961-63; Government of Northern Rhodesia, consultant in youth services, 1963-64; Overseas Development Institute, London, England, researcher, 1965-66; writer and lecturer, 1966—. Director, Africa Bureau (London), 1968-72. *Military service:* British Army, 1951-52; became lieutenant. *Member:* Royal Institute of International Affairs.

WRITINGS: Longhouse and Jungle, Chatto & Windus, 1959; *Towards Peace and a Multiracial Commonwealth*, Chapman & Hall, 1964; *Economic Co-operation in the Commonwealth*, Pergamon, 1967; *Kenyatta and the Politics of Kenya*, Dent, 1974; *The Last Bunker*, Quartet, 1976; (with Ruth Weiss) *Strategic Highways of Africa*, Friedman, 1977; *Modern Nigeria*, Longman, 1977; *Britain's Oil*, Hamish Hamilton, 1978; *Aid in Africa*, Kogan Page, 1979; *Held Fast for England*, Hamish Hamilton, 1980; *The Unions*, Hamish Hamilton, 1981; *Modern Kenya*, Longman, 1981. Contributor to journals.

WORK IN PROGRESS: An Illustrated Atlas of the Commonwealth; British Brainwashing.

SIDELIGHTS: Guy Arnold led a scientific expedition to the interior of Borneo, 1955-56, collected folklore in Guiana among the Wapisiana Indians, and assisted in the establishment of the Canadian University Service Overseas.

* * *

ARNOLD, Leslie
See LAZARUS, A(rnold) L(eslie)

* * *

ARRE, John
See HOLT, John (Robert)

* * *

ASARE, Meshack (Yaw) 1945-

PERSONAL: Surname is pronounced *Ah*-suh-ree; born September 18, 1945, in Nyankumasi, Ghana; son of Joseph Kwaku (an accountant) and Adjoa (a trader; maiden name, Adoma) Asare; married Rose Tachie Menson (a bank clerk), 1969; children: Akosua (daughter), Kwajo (son), Kofi, Kwaku. *Education:* Attended University of Science and Technology, Kumasi, Ghana, University of Wisconsin, and School of Journalism and Television, Berkshire, England. *Politics:* "Universalism." *Religion:* Christian. *Home:* Block 424, R9, Sogeco Flats, Tema, Ghana. *Office address:* Educational Press & Manufacturers, Ltd., P.O. Box 9184, Airport, Accra, Ghana.

CAREER: Elementary school teacher in Tema, Ghana, 1966-68; Lincoln Community School, Accra, Ghana, teacher, 1969-79; Educational Press & Manufacturers, Ltd., Accra, art editor and illustrator, 1979—. Artist; has made sculptures for the government and for public buildings; illustrator and designer. *Member:* Ghana Association of Artists. *Awards, honors:* Ghana's National Book Award, 1980, for *Tawia Goes to Sea;* Noma Award for publishing in Africa, 1982, for *The Brassman's Secret*.

WRITINGS: (With others) *Ghana Welcomes You*, Valco, 1968; *Tawia Goes to Sea* (juvenile), Ghana Publishing, 1970, Panther

House, 1972; *Seeing the World,* Ghana Publishing, 1975; *The Brassman's Secret* (juvenile), Educational Press & Manufacturers, 1981.

Also author of playlets, "Ananse and Wisdom" and "The Outdooring," and of play, "The Hunter." Contributor of articles on Ghanian culture to magazines.

WORK IN PROGRESS: Nana and His Son, Meliga's Day, and *Komla's Call,* all juveniles, for Educational Press & Manufacturers.

SIDELIGHTS: Meshack Asare told *CA:* "Sometimes it is hard to tell what I am, but I like to think that I am an Artist. I feel that is a better way to think of myself, because then everything I am doing is art. . . . I sculpt and draw and design beautiful things. That is creativity. I enjoy doing those.

"But writing is different. My work in writing is very important to me. I consider writing to be a kind of construction; precisely, a kind of construction that bridges the gaps to reality—for even dreams and imagination are, in fact, reality. There are no dreams without images. Neither is there imagination without images. And, for that matter, no thought. Writing creates images. That is why it is so important. It creates images of time and life. Writing enables one to perceive the depth and roundness of civilization. It does not simply record it and enrich it.

"Who needs help in perceiving reality more than young people? The world is too complex to be perceived in its wholeness. . . . But there is a part of the world that is unchanging, unaffected and perhaps [permanent] in value. It is the warmth of knowing that there is something about you that the other person appreciates, something that everyone has a feeling for. It is a very exclusively human 'something' that universally communicates—and appeals. It is this 'something' that I try to write about."

*   *   *

ASTLEY, Thea (Beatrice May)   1925-

PERSONAL: Born August 25, 1925, in Brisbane, Queensland, Australia; daughter of Cecil and Eileen (Lindsay) Astley; married Edmund John Gregson, August 27, 1948; children: one son. *Education:* University of Queensland, graduated, 1947. *Home address:* P.O. Box 213, Kuranda, North Queensland, Australia 4872.

CAREER: Teacher of English in Queensland, Australia, 1944-48, and in New South Wales, Australia, 1948-67; Macquarie University, Sydney, senior tutor in department of English, beginning 1968, currently retired. *Awards, honors:* Commonwealth Literary Fund fellowships, 1961, 1964; Miles Franklin Awards, 1962, for *The Well-Dressed Explorer,* 1965, for *The Slow Natives,* 1973, for *The Acolyte;* Moomba Award, 1965, for *The Slow Natives;* Age Newspaper book-of-the-year award, 1975, for *A Kindness Cup.*

WRITINGS—Novels, except as indicated: *Girl with a Monkey,* Angus & Robertson, 1958; *A Descant for Gossips,* Angus & Robertson, 1960; *The Well-Dressed Explorer,* Angus & Robertson, 1962; *The Slow Natives,* Angus & Robertson, 1965, M. Evans, 1967; *A Boatload of Home Folk,* Angus & Robertson, 1968; (editor) *Coast to Coast, 1969-70* (short stories), Angus & Robertson, 1971; *The Acolyte,* Angus & Robertson, 1972; *A Kindness Cup,* Thomas Nelson, 1975; *Hunting the Wild Pineapple,* Thomas Nelson, 1979; *An Item from the Late News,* University of Queensland Press, 1982.

Short stories have appeared in anthologies, including *Coast to Coast,* Angus & Robertson, 1961, 1963, and 1965, and *Festival and Other Stories,* Wren (Melbourne, Australia), 1974. Contributor of poems to anthologies and periodicals.

SIDELIGHTS: Critics praise Thea Astley's ability to create true-to-life characters in her novels, especially in *The Slow Natives.* A *Time* reviewer writes: "The author's feminine eye and ear for . . . significant styles in decor, clothes, deportment and accent make her a lively social satirist. . . . She is . . . dealing with . . . a painfully recognizable family." William J. Lynch and Norman Horrocks also comment on the characters in the same novel. Lynch notes in *Best Sellers:* "Astley's novel is remarkable for its tight structure and its verbal economy. She manipulates and interweaves the lives of several pivotal characters without losing grip on any of them." Horrocks states in *Library Journal,* "The story gains its strength from . . . Astley's ability to record life-like dialogue and to make her characters interesting."

AVOCATIONAL INTERESTS: Music, friends, conversation.

BIOGRAPHICAL/CRITICAL SOURCES: Library Journal, September 1, 1967; *Time,* October 20, 1967; *Saturday Review,* November 4, 1967; *Best Sellers,* December 1, 1967; L. J. Blake, *Australian Writers,* Rigby, 1968; *Southerly 1* (Sydney), 1970.

*   *   *

ATHERTON, Pauline
See COCHRANE, Pauline A.

*   *   *

ATKESON, Ray A.   1907-

PERSONAL: Born February 13, 1907, in Grafton, Ill.; son of James M. (a farmer) and Danielle (Barber) Atkeson; married Mira E. Crane, June 14, 1930 (deceased); married Doris Schaffer, September 6, 1977; children: (first marriage) Eleanor J. Atkeson Schmeer. *Education:* Attended high school in Kansas City, Mo. *Politics:* Republican. *Religion:* Interdenominational. *Home and office:* 1675 Southwest Westwood Dr., Portland, Ore. 97201.

CAREER: Photo Art Commercial Studio, Portland, Ore., chief cameraman, 1929-46; free-lance photographer in Portland, 1946—. *Member:* Photographic Society of America, National Press Photographers Association, Audubon Society, Sierra Club, Nature Conservancy, 1000 Friends of Oregon, Mazama Club, Wy'east Climbers. *Awards, honors:* Named distinguished citizen by the governor of Oregon; Doctor of Fine Arts, Linfield College; Certificate of Special Recognition, Photographic Society of America; Aubrey R. Watzek Award, Lewis and Clark College; Distinguished Service Award, Western Oregon State College; Portland Beautification Association Award, for "capturing Oregon's beauty through photography."

WRITINGS—Self-illustrated: *Ski and Snow,* U.S. Camera, 1961; *Northwest Heritage: Cascade Range,* Charles H. Belding, 1969; *Pacific Coast,* Rand McNally, 1971; *Western Impressions,* Beautiful America Publishing, 1976; *Pacific Sea and Shore,* Writing Works, 1982.

Published by Graphic Arts Center: *Oregon,* 1968; *Washington,* 1969; *Oregon Coast,* 1972; *Washington II,* 1973; *Oregon II,* 1974; *Portrait of Oregon,* 1980; *Portrait of Washington,* 1980; *Portrait of California,* 1980.

Contributor of photographs to books by others. Contributor to photography, travel, and nature magazines.

WORK IN PROGRESS: Pacific Crest, a large-format picture book featuring photography of the Cascade Range and the Sierra Nevada Range, for Writing Works.

AVOCATIONAL INTERESTS: Environmental issues ("involving preservation of nature wherever possible").

*   *   *

ATKINSON, Anthony Barnes   1944-

PERSONAL: Born September 4, 1944, in Caerleon, England; son of Norman Joseph (a teacher) and Esther Muriel Atkinson; married Judith Mary Mandeville (a social worker), 1965; children: Richard, Sarah, Charles. *Education:* Churchill College, Cambridge, M.A., 1966. *Politics:* Socialist. *Residence:* Brightlingsea, Essex, England. *Agent:* Curtis Brown Ltd., 162-168 Regent St., London W1R 5TA, England. *Office:* London School of Economics and Political Science, University of London, Houghton St., Aldwych, London WC2A 2AE, England.

CAREER: Cambridge University, Cambridge, England, fellow of St. John's College, 1967-71; University of Essex, Colchester, England, professor of economics, 1971-76; University of London, London School of Economics and Political Science, London, England, professor of economics, 1976—. Chairman of Colchester Poverty Action Group, 1972-73. *Member:* Econometric Society (fellow).

WRITINGS: Poverty in Britain and the Reform of Social Security, Cambridge University Press, 1969; *Unequal Shares: Wealth in Britain,* Penguin, 1972; *The Tax Credit Scheme and the Redistribution of Income,* Institute of Fiscal Studies, 1973; (editor) *Wealth, Income, and Inequality,* Penguin, 1973; *The Economics of Inequality,* Oxford University Press, 1975; (with A. J. Harrison) *The Distribution of Wealth in Britain,* Cambridge University Press, 1977; (with J. E. Stiglitz) *Lectures on Public Economics,* McGraw, 1980; *Social Justice and Public Policy,* Harvester Press, 1982; (with A. K. Maynard and C. G. Trinder) *Parents and Children,* Heinemann, 1983. Editor of *Journal of Public Economics.*

WORK IN PROGRESS: Family Welfare and Government Policy, with M. A. King and N. H. Stern.

SIDELIGHTS: Anthony Barnes Atkinson told *CA* his "work on income and wealth tries to apply professional skills to important economic and social problems."

*   *   *

ATKINSON, John W(illiam)   1923-

PERSONAL: Born December 31, 1923, in Jersey City, N.J.; son of Frank Gray (a business executive) and Wilhelmina (Meyer) Atkinson; married Mary Jane Wanta, April 15, 1944; children: Ann Mina (Mrs. James R. Sawusch), David John, William Frank. *Education:* Wesleyan University, B.A. (with high distinction), 1947; University of Michigan, M.A., 1948, Ph.D., 1950. *Home:* 2363 Belgrade Notch, Ann Arbor, Mich. 48103. *Office:* Department of Psychology, University of Michigan, Ann Arbor, Mich. 48106.

CAREER: University of Michigan, Ann Arbor, instructor in psychology, 1948-49; Wesleyan University, Middletown, Conn.,

assistant professor of psychology, 1949-50; University of Michigan, assistant professor, 1950-55, associate professor, 1955-60, professor of psychology, 1960—, research associate of Survey Research Center, 1964-69. *Military service:* U.S. Army Air Forces, 1943-45; became second lieutenant. *Member:* American Psychological Association, American Association for the Advancement of Science, American Educational Research Association, American Association of University Professors. *Awards, honors:* Social Science Research Council faculty research fellow, 1952-55; Center for Advanced Study in the Behavioral Sciences fellow, 1955-56; Guggenheim fellow, 1960-61; U.S. Public Health Service special research fellow, 1969-70; American Academy of Arts and Sciences fellow, 1975; Distinguished Scientific Contribution Award, American Psychological Association, 1979.

WRITINGS: (With D. C. McClelland, R. A. Clark, and E. L. Lowell) *The Achievement Motive,* Appleton-Century-Crofts, 1953; (editor and contributor) *Motives in Fantasy, Action, and Society,* Van Nostrand, 1958; *An Introduction to Motivation,* Van Nostrand, 1964, revised edition (with David Birch), 1978; (editor with N. T. Feather and contributor) *A Theory of Achievement Motivation,* Wiley, 1966; (with Birch) *The Dynamics of Action,* Wiley, 1970; (editor with J. O. Raynor and contributor) *Motivation and Achievement,* V. W. Winston, 1974; (with Raynor) *Personality, Motivation, and Achievement,* Hemisphere Publishing, 1978; *Personality, Motivation, and Action,* Praeger, 1983.

*   *   *

AWAD, Elias M.   1934-

PERSONAL: Born October 6, 1934, in Latakia, Syria; son of Michael and Naifa Awad. *Education:* Geneva College (Beaver Falls, Pa.), B.S.B.A., 1956; University of Tulsa, M.B.A., 1958; New York University, graduate study, 1964; Northwestern University, M.A., 1968; University of Kentucky, D.B.A., 1975. *Religion:* Presbyterian.

CAREER: Aleppo College, Aleppo, Syria, business manager and instructor, 1958-59; Rochester Institute of Technology, College of Business, Rochester, N.Y., assistant professor of organization theory, 1960-65; DePaul University, Graduate School of Business, Chicago, Ill., assistant professor of management, 1967-75; Ball State University, College of Business, Muncie, Ind., George A. Ball Distinguished Professor of Management, 1975-77. *Member:* Academy of Management, American Economic Association, Data Processing Management Association, American Association of University Professors.

WRITINGS—All published by Prentice-Hall, except as indicated: *Business Data Processing,* 1965, 5th edition, 1980; *Automatic Data Processing: Principles and Procedures,* 1966, 3rd edition, 1973; *Problems and Exercises in Data Processing,* 1966; (editor) *Perspectives in Electronic Data Processing,* 1972; *Concepts in Business Data Processing,* 1975; *Issues in Business Data Processing,* 1975; *Introduction to Computers in Business,* 1977; *Systems Analysis and Design,* Irwin, 1979; (with Wayne F. Cascio) *Human Resources Management: An Information Systems Approach,* Reston, 1981.

AVOCATIONAL INTERESTS: Travel, camping, and photography.†

B

BAINS, Larry
  See SABIN, Louis

                *   *   *

BAKER, Russell (Wayne) 1925-

PERSONAL: Born August 14, 1925, in Loudoun County, Va.; son of Benjamin Rex and Lucy Elizabeth (Robinson) Baker; married Miriam Emily Nash, March 11, 1950; children: Kathleen Leland, Allen Nash, Michael Lee. *Education:* John Hopkins University, B.A., 1947. *Office:* New York Times, 229 West 43rd St., New York, N.Y. 10036.

CAREER: Baltimore Sun, Baltimore, Md., member of staff, 1947-53, London bureau chief, 1953-54; *New York Times,* member of Washington, D.C. bureau, 1954-62, author of column "Observer," 1962—, now based in New York, N.Y. *Military service:* U.S. Naval Reserve, 1943-45. *Awards, honors:* L.H.D. from Hamilton College, Princeton University, Wake Forest University, Johns Hopkins University, and Franklin Pierce College; LL.D., Union College; Frank Sullivan Memorial Award, 1976; George Polk Award for commentary, 1979; Pulitzer Prize, 1979, for distinguished commentary, and 1982, for *Growing Up.*

WRITINGS: (Author of text) *Washington: City, on the Potomac,* Arts, 1958; *An American in Washington,* Knopf, 1961; *No Cause for Panic* (collection of newspaper articles), Lippincott, 1964; *Baker's Dozen* (collection of newspaper articles), New York Times Co., 1964; *All Things Considered* (collection of newspaper articles), Lippincott, 1965; *Our Next President: The Incredible Story of What Happened in the 1968 Elections* (fiction), Atheneum, 1968.

Poor Russell's Almanac (collection of newspaper articles), Doubleday, 1972; *The Upside Down Man* (children's book), McGraw, 1977; *So This Is Depravity* (collection of newspaper articles), Congdon & Lattes, 1980; *Growing Up* (autobiography), Congdon & Weed, 1982; *The Rescue of Miss Yaskell and Other Ripe Dreams* (collection of newspaper articles), Condon & Weed, 1983.

Also co-author of musical play "Home Again," 1979. Contributor to periodicals, including *Saturday Evening Post, New York Times Magazine, Sports Illustrated, Ladies Home Journal, Holiday, Theatre Arts, Mademoiselle, Life, Look,* and *McCalls.*

SIDELIGHTS: "I didn't set out in life to be a humorist," Russell Baker once told Israel Shenker in the *New York Times Book Review.* "I set out in life to be a novelist, and I look like a novelist. Art Buchwald looks like a humorist. . . . I don't look like him and most of the time I don't even look like myself." Nevertheless, Baker is regarded today as one of America's most literate and successful humorists. His thrice-weekly "Observer" column has been running in the *New York Times* since 1962 and is syndicated to the more than 450 newspapers that subscribe to the *Times* News Service. He is also the recipient of two Pulitzer Prizes: the first in commentary, for ten columns published in 1979; the second in biography, for his bittersweet account of his early years, *Growing Up,* published in 1982.

Baker was born in rural Morrisville, Virginia, in 1925, "issued uneventfully into the governance of Calvin Coolidge," as he puts it in *Growing Up,* adding, "World War I was seven years past, the Russian revolution was eight years old, and the music on my grandmother's wind-up Victrola was 'Yes, We Have No Bananas.'" Baker's father, Benjamin, died at age 33, during the Depression, of diabetes. His mother, the stalwart Lucy Elizabeth Baker, after handing over her youngest child, Audrey, to more affluent relatives, began a new life with five-year-old Russell and his three-year-old sister, Doris, that included periods of residence in Virginia, New Jersey, and Baltimore, Maryland.

Baker began his newspaper career in 1947 as a reporter for the *Baltimore Sun,* eventually ending up in London, writing a spirited weekly series for that paper, "From a Window on Fleet Street." In 1954 he joined the *New York Times* staff in Washington, D.C. and covered the White House, State Department, politics and Congressional activities for the *Times* for eight years until, as he tells John Skow of *Time* magazine, "I just got bored. I had done enough reporting. I began to feel like Willy Loman in 'Death of a Salesman,' carrying that typewriter in one hand and that suitcase in the other and a dirty old raincoat into one more hotel lobby. It came to seem that this wasn't a worthy way for a grown man to spend his life. You have good seats, sure, but you're always on the sidelines. You're not making anything." The last straw came, Skow reports, one afternoon when Baker had spent several hours sitting on a hallway floor of the Senate Office Building, outside a closed meeting of the Armed Services Committee. "I began

31

to wonder," Baker says, "why, at the age of 37, I was wearing out my hams waiting for somebody to come out and lie to me."

Offered the "Observer" column by the *Times* as an incentive to stay at the paper, Baker accepted and soon produced his first piece, a farcical version of a John F. Kennedy press conference. He quickly established himself as an adroit political satirist and stayed in Washington throughout the Kennedy, Johnson, and Nixon administrations. By 1974, though, Baker felt he'd written all he could about politics and relocated to New York City. It was there that his articles expanded in subject matter; his 1979 Pulitzer Prize was for columns covering such topics as tax reform, trends, inflation, Norman Rockwell, fear, and the death of *New Times* magazine.

In his *Time* profile of Baker, Skow says that the columnist "walks the high wire between light humor and substantive comment, a balancing act so punishingly difficult that in the entire country there are not a dozen men and women who can be said to have the hang of the thing." "At his best," observes R. Z. Sheppard in his *Time* review of *Poor Russell's Almanac,* a collection of columns, "Baker fills his allotted space . . . with bizarre, often bleak fantasies about human foolishness. At his second best, he holds a funhouse mirror up to the nature of the consumer state. . . . Baker is a man of range, sensitive intellect and fertile imagination. He is also a fine stylist whose columns frequently unfurl to defend the language against corruption. . . . Russell Baker can then be best appreciated doing what a good humorist has always done: writing to preserve his sanity for at least one more day."

"I'm basically a guy with a yearning for the past," Baker told Thomas Chastain in a 1972 *Publishers Weekly* interview, "a time when things were better. Life was better when there were trains. It's probably a sign of the hardening of the mental arteries, this yearning for boyhood, the kind of thing I dislike when I hear it from other people." Ten years later the writer realized his need to connect with the past with his autobiography, *Growing Up.* Baker remarks in the book: "I wondered about the disconnections between children and parents that prevent them from knowing each other while there is still time. Children ought to know what went into their making, to know that life is a braided cord of humanity stretching up from time long gone. I thought that, when I am beyond explaining, they would want to know what the world was like when my mother was young and I was younger, and we two relics passed together through strange times."

Richard Lingeman, writing about *Growing Up* in the *New York Times Book Review,* comments that he "approached [the book] with high anticipation, expecting a heartening read about someone more miserable than I am. Alas, I was deeply disappointed. . . . This is not the kind of book one can put down with a contented sigh: 'that poor son of a bitch.' Instead of being a grim tale of drunken stepmothers and battered stepfathers, *Growing Up* is touching and funny, a hopeless muddle of sadness and laughter that bears a suspicious resemblance to real life." "This is not the dirt-poor South of easy fiction," offers *Los Angeles Times Book Review* critic Mary Lee Settle. She adds: "With sensuous grace, incisive recall and an evocation of daily language that is the poetry of the inarticulate, [Baker] recreates a place where there is dignity and ambition and an inflexible social and economic hierarchy run by women." Noting that "there are scenes as funny and as touching as Mark Twain's" and that the "acute simplicity of the scene of the father's death is a masterpiece," Settle concludes that *Growing*

Up is "a wondrous book, funny, sad and strong. Above all, it can make us see that the family cruelties we have suffered are often cultural and not personal—and that to recognize this is to begin to forgive."

According to Jonathan Yardley, writing in the *Washington Post Book World, Growing Up* is "a work as deeply rooted in what we know as the 'American experience' as anything [James] Thurber wrote; moreover, it leaves no doubt that Baker must not merely be compared with Thurber, as he has been in the past, but ranked with him as well." The author "has accomplished the memorialist's task: to find shape and meaning in his own life, and to make it interesting and pertinent to the reader. In lovely, haunting prose, he has told a story that is deeply in the American grain, one in which countless readers will find echoes of their own, yet in the end it is very much his own." Finally, *Detroit News* critic Leola Floren notes that "too often autobiographers exhibit an unfortunate compulsion to chronicle a thousand anecdotes, of which only a handful are either significant or interesting." But not Baker: his "timing is exquisite; he exits humbly into the wings with a smile and a wink at those of us pleading for encores. Bravo."

MEDIA ADAPTATIONS: One of Baker's columns, "How to Hypnotize Yourself into Forgetting the Vietnam War," was dramatized and filmed in 1971 by Eli Wallach for Public Broadcasting System's "The Great American Dream Machine."

BIOGRAPHICAL/CRITICAL SOURCES: Time, January 19, 1968, January 17, 1972, June 4, 1979, November 1, 1982; *Publishers Weekly,* January 24, 1972; *New York Times Book Review,* January 30, 1972, October 18, 1982; *Newsweek,* September 29, 1980, November 8, 1982; *Washington Post Book World,* October 5, 1980, October 3, 1982, October 9, 1983; *Los Angeles Times,* December 7, 1980; Russell Baker, *Growing Up,* Condon & Weed, 1982; *New York Times Magazine,* September 12, 1982; *New York Times,* October 6, 1982; *Los Angeles Times Book Review,* October 10, 1982; *Detroit News,* November 7, 1982; *People,* December 20, 1982.

—*Sketch by Susan Salter*

*   *   *

BAKKEN, Henry Harrison 1896-

PERSONAL: Born March 24, 1896, in Arena, Wis.; son of Halvor and Malla (Nelson) Bakken; married Clara K. Grimstad, September 2, 1922; children: Hugh R. (deceased), James F., David C., Haakon R. *Education:* University of Wisconsin—Madison, B.A., 1922, M.A., 1924; graduate study at Harvard University, 1929-30. *Home:* 2218 Chadbourne Ave., Madison, Wis. 53705.

CAREER: U.S. Department of Agriculture, Washington, D.C., economist in Cost of Marketing Division of Bureau of Agricultural Economics, 1922-23; University of Wisconsin—Madison, assistant agricultural economist, 1923-24, assistant professor, 1924-32, associate professor of agricultural economics, 1932-43; agricultural economist for Food Price Division of Office of Price Administration, 1943-44; Allied Control Commission of Foreign Economic Administration, Rome, Italy, price control officer, 1944-45; agricultural specialist in London, England, and Oslo, Norway, 1945; agricultural adviser in Field Service attached to American Embassy in Oslo, 1945-46; economic consultant to Headquarters of Supreme Commander of the Allied Powers in Japan, 1946-47; University of Wisconsin—Madison, associate professor, 1947-53, professor of agricultural economics, 1953-66, professor emeritus, 1966—.

University of Puerto Rico, research consultant to Experiment Station, 1953, lecturer at Extension Division, 1954; Smith-Mundt Exchange Professor at University of Chile, 1957; Fulbright lecturer in Finland and Norway, 1962-63. Owner and manager of Mimir Publishers. Member of Organization of American States agrarian reform team in Honduras and Puerto Rico, 1961; conducted research project in western Africa, 1967-69. Chairman of educational advisory committee of Chicago Board of Trade, 1960-63; economic consultant to Weitz-Hettelsater Engineers, 1964-65, 1968-69; consultant to Chicago Mercantile Exchange, 1965-70. *Military service:* U.S. Army, 1916-17.

MEMBER: American Economic Association, American Farm Economic Association, Royal Economic Association, Acacia, Masons, Shriners. *Awards, honors:* Life Professor, Universidad de Chile, 1957; Profesor Extraordinario, Universidad Catolica de Chile, 1957.

WRITINGS: (With Marvin A. Schaars) *The Economics of Cooperative Marketing*, McGraw, 1937; *Cooperation to the Finnish*, Mimir Publishers, 1939; (editor) *Pioneers in Dakota Territory*, Norwegian American Historical Association, 1942; (editor) *Cooperation behind the Iron Curtain*, Mimir Publishers, 1952; *Theory of Markets and Marketing*, Mimir Publishers, 1953; (with George Max Beal) *Fluid Milk Marketing*, Mimir Publishers, 1956; (with Elmer E. Zank) *Light and Power: Rates and Costs of Service in Wisconsin REA Cooperatives*, University of Wisconsin Press, 1959.

Futures Trading Seminar, Mimir Publishers, (with others) Volume I: *History and Development*, 1960, (editor) Volume II: *Environmental Factors*, 1963, (with others) Volume III: *A Commodity Market Forum for College Teachers of Economics*, 1966, (editor with others) Volume IV: *Futures Trading in Livestock: Origins and Concepts*, 1970; (with Holbrook Working, E. B. Harris, Gene Futrell, Roger Gray, Robert E. Schneider, and Don Paarlberg) *Informa Oficial de la Mision 105 de Asistencia Tecnica Directa a Honduras Sobre Reforma Agraria y Desarrollo Agricola* (title means "Official Report on Agrarian Reform for Honduras"), three volumes, Organization of American States, 1962; *Basic Concepts, Principles, and Practices of Cooperation*, Mimir Publishers, 1963; (with John Sharp, W. P. Mortenson, and John F. Heimovics) *Marketing and Storage Facilities for Selected Crops: Honduras*, Weitz-Hettelsater Engineers, 1965; (editor) *Marketing Grain: North Central Region-30*, Purdue University, 1968; (with Fernando Cavada, John C. White, Henry O. Heckman, and William S. Farris) *A Grain Stabilization Study of the Entente States and Ghana of West Africa*, Weitz-Hettelsater Engineers, 1969; *The Hills of Home: A Family History*, Mimir Publishers, 1976. Contributor to professional journals.

WORK IN PROGRESS: An autobiography.

*   *   *

BALSIGER, David W(ayne) 1945-
(David Wayne)

PERSONAL: Born December 14, 1945, in Monroe, Wis.; son of Leon C. (a real estate broker) and Dorothy May (a sales clerk; maiden name, Meythaler) Balsiger; married Janie Frances Lewis (an office administrator), September 26, 1969 (divorced, 1982); married Robyne Lynn Betzsold (a high school teacher) July 10, 1982; children: (first marriage) Lisa Atalie, Lori Faith. *Education:* Attended Pepperdine University, 1964-66, Cypress Junior College, 1966, Chapman College's World Campus Af-

loat, 1967-68, and International College in Copenhagen, 1968; National University, San Diego, Calif., B.A. 1977. *Religion:* Neo-Pentecostal. *Home:* 380 West Wilson St., F-101, Costa Mesa, Calif. 92627. *Office Address:* P.O. Box 10428, Costa Mesa, Calif. 92627.

CAREER: Bank of America, teller in Los Angeles, Santa Ana, and El Toro, Calif., 1964-66; *Anaheim Bulletin*, Anaheim, Calif., chief photographer and feature writer, 1968-69; *Money Doctor* (consumer magazine), Anaheim, publisher and editor, 1969-70; Walt Neil Associates (advertising and public relations agency), Anaheim, office manager, 1969-70; World Evangelism, San Diego, Calif., media director, 1970-72; Logos International (book publishers), Plainfield, N.J., director of marketing, 1972-74; Donald S. Smith Associates (advertising agency), Anaheim, vice-president, 1974-76; Schick Sunn Classic Productions, Inc., Los Angeles, director of research development, 1976-78; Balsiger Enterprises (business consulting and publishing firm), Santa Ana, owner, 1978-81; Donald S. Smith Associates, vice-president, 1982—.

Owner and operator of Master Media (marketing agency), San Diego, 1972; owner of Balsiger Literary Service (literary agency), Costa Mesa, Calif., 1974-78; president of Writeway Professional Literary Associates (talent and literary agency), Costa Mesa, 1978—. Researcher and technical advisor for various films and television programs, including "In Search of Noah's Ark," 1976, "The Lincoln Conspiracy," 1977, and "Beyond and Back," 1977, all based on the author's books of the same titles. Visiting professor, National University, San Diego, 1978-79. Assistant press agent for Ronald Reagan for Governor campaign, 1966; associate member of California Republican Central Committee, 1969-70; member of Orange County and San Diego World Affairs Councils, 1969-70; manager of James E. Johnson's campaign for U.S. Senate, 1974; Republican candidate for U.S. Congress, 1978. Member of board of directors of Chapman College's World Campus Afloat, 1967, and Chrisma Ministries, 1969-73.

MEMBER: International Association of Financial Planners, American Entrepreneurs Association, Republican Presidential Task Force (charter member), National University Alumni Association, Friends of the University of California Irvine Library, Religion in Media Association, Republican Associates of Orange County, Melodyland Christian Center, Hoag Memorial Hospital 552 Club.

AWARDS, HONORS: Leadership citation from alumni board of Pepperdine University, 1965; named "Writer of the Month" by *California Writer*, 1967; L.H.D. from Lincoln Memorial University for "outstanding Lincoln research," 1977; received Key to the City of Costa Mesa, Calif., for outstanding community service, 1977; George Washington Honor Medal from Freedoms Foundation, 1978, for The *Lincoln Conspiracy*, and 1979, for *Beyond Defeat;* National Religion in Media Association, Angel Award, 1979, for *Beyond Defeat*, Trophy Award, 1980, for *The Presidential Biblical Scoreboard*.

WRITINGS: (With Mike Warnke) *The Satan Seller* (biography), Logos International, 1972; *The Back Side of Satan*, Creation House, 1973; (with Don Musgraves) *One More Time* (biography), Bethany Fellowship, 1974; *Noah's Ark: I Touched It*, Logos International, 1974; (with Randy Bullock) *It's Good to Know* (biography), Mott Media, 1975; (with Charles E. Sellier, Jr.) *In Search of Noah's Ark*, Schick Sunn Classic Books, 1976; (with Sellier) *The Lincoln Conspiracy*, Schick Sunn Classic Books, 1977; (with James E. Johnson) *Beyond Defeat* (biography), Doubleday, 1978; (with Marvin Ford) *On *the Other Side,* Logos International, 1978; *The Presidential Biblical Scoreboard,* Biblical News Service, 1980.

Author, with others, of ''Balsiger's Mini Guide Books,'' a series on travel accomodations, resorts, restaurants, and amusement attractions in California; also author, with Barbara Lowe, of screenplay ''Mistah Abe.'' Foreign feature correspondent for magazines and southern California newspapers, covering numerous countries abroad. Contributor of articles and photographs, sometimes under pseudonym David Wayne, to magazines, including *Christian Bookseller, National Courier, National Star, Your Church, California Farmer,* and *Time.* News editor of *Logos Journal,* 1972-73.

WORK IN PROGRESS: A book on Jesse James; co-authoring a book entitled *Using Your Image to Get What You Want; Mistah Abe,* a nonfictional account of life with the Lincolns from 1850 to 1860 as told by their house servant (based on Balsiger's screenplay of the same title).

SIDELIGHTS: In 1974 David W. Balsiger spearheaded investigative efforts that resulted in a Grand Jury probe of the Orange County, Calif., Tax Assessor's Office. The Grand Jury eventually brought about criminal indictments and convictions against a congressman, local officials, and an officer of a large business congolomerate. In 1978 Balsiger ran as a Republican candidate for the 38th California Congressional District, losing by 979 votes. *Avocational interests:* hiking, camping, and ocean fishing.

BIOGRAPHICAL/CRITICAL SOURCES: California Writer, November, 1967; *Monroe Evening Times,* May 30, 1975; *Salt Lake Tribune,* September 18, 1977; *Los Angeles Times,* October 9, 1977; *San Clemente Sun Post,* April 10, 1978.

*   *   *

BANERJI, Ranan B(ihari) 1928-

PERSONAL: Surname is pronounced *Banner*-gee; born May 5, 1928, in Calcutta, India; came to United States in 1961, naturalized in 1969; son of Bijan Bihari (a professor) and Setabja (Chatterji) Banerji; married Purnima Purkayastha (a teacher), July 8, 1954; children: Anindita, Sunandita (daughters). *Education:* Patna University, B.Sc., 1947; University of Calcutta, M.S., 1949, D.Phil., 1956. *Politics:* Liberal. *Religion:* Quaker/Hindu. *Home:* 7612 Woodlawn Ave., Melrose Park, Pa. *Office:* Department of Computer Science, St. Joseph's University, Philadelphia, Pa. 19131.

CAREER: Pennsylvania State University, University Park, visiting assistant professor of engineering research, 1953-56; Indian Statistical Institute, Calcutta, senior maintenance engineer, computer section, 1956-58; Case Institute of Technology (now Case Western Reserve University), Cleveland, Ohio, research associate, 1958-59; University of New Brunswick, Fredericton, assistant professor of engineering, 1959-61; Case Western Reserve University, assistant professor, 1961-62, associate professor, 1963-67, professor of engineering, 1968-73; Temple University, Philadelphia, Pa., professor of computer science, 1973-82; St. Joseph's University, Philadelphia, Pa., professor of math and computer science, 1982—. *Member:* Institute of Electrical and Electronics Engineers, Association for Computing Machinery, Society for Industrial and Applied Mathematics, Mathematical Association of America, Pattern Recognition Society, Common Cause, American Civil Liberties Union, Sigma Xi.

WRITINGS: Theory of Problem Solving: An Approach to Artificial Intelligence, American Elsevier, 1969; (editor with M. D.

Mesarovic) *Theoretical Approaches to Non-Numerical Problem Solving* (proceedings of systems symposium), Springer-Verlag, 1970; *Artificial Intelligence: A Theoretical Approach,* North-Holland Publishing, 1979. Contributor to scientific journals. Editor, *Newsletter* of Association for Computing Machinery.

WORK IN PROGRESS: Research on complex information processing in computers.

SIDELIGHTS: ''Sometime early in one's scientific career,'' Ranan B. Banerji told *CA,* ''the motivation shifts from search for truth to search for personal glory. It is probably lucky for me that the latter search fell short of my expectation. The ego can hide truth very effectively—and deserves villification at a certain stage.

''Any goal pursued purely for its Truth (some call it 'the Glory of God') can be pursued without twisting up the psyche,'' the author adds. ''Success and failure take a new dimension of meaning.''

*   *   *

BANGERTER, Lowell A(llen) 1941-

PERSONAL: Born June 23, 1941, in Ogden, Utah; son of Alma H. (a civil servant) and Helen (Lone) Bangerter; married Judy Lee Pearson, September 16, 1964; children: Grant W., Stephen A., Carl W., Tamara Lynn, Janine Ann. *Education:* Stanford University, B.A., 1966, M.A., 1967; University of Illinois, Ph.D., 1970. *Religion:* Church of Jesus Christ of Latter-day Saints (Mormon). *Home:* 1114 Mitchell, Laramie, Wyo. 82070. *Office:* Department of Modern and Classical Languages, University of Wyoming, Box 3603 University Station, Laramie, Wyo. 82071.

CAREER: University of Wyoming, Laramie, assistant professor, 1970-76, associate professor, 1976-81, professor of German, 1981—, head of department of modern and classical languages, 1981—. *Member:* Modern Language Association of America, American Association of Teachers of German, Rocky Mountain Modern Language Association, Verband Deutschsprachiger Autoren in Amerika.

WRITINGS: Schiller and Hofmannsthal, Dos Continentes, 1974; *Hugo von Hofmannsthal,* Ungar, 1977; (contributor of translations of poetry by Johann Wolfgang von Goethe) Frederick Ungar, editor, *The Eternal Feminine,* Ungar, 1980; *The Bourgeois Proletarian: A Study of Anna Seghers,* Bouvier, 1980; *Lebensbilder,* Stoedtner, 1983; (contributor) Walton Beacham, editor, *Critical Survey of Long Fiction,* Salem Press, in press; (contributor) Beacham, editor, *Critical Survey of Poetry,* Salem Press, in press. Contributor to *Encyclopedia of World Literature in the Twentieth Century.* Contributor of articles and poems to language journals.

WORK IN PROGRESS: Translations of Austrian poetry for *Austria in Poetry and History,* for Ungar.

SIDELIGHTS: Lowell A. Bangerter writes that his ''interest in German language and literature was first aroused during my initial stay in Germany as an American Field Service exchange student in summer, 1958, and further stimulated during thirty months spent in Germany from 1961 to 1964, when I served as a missionary for the Church of Jesus Christ of Latter-day Saints. Language studies include German, French, Old Norse-Icelandic, Modern Danish, and Russian. . . . Most of my own poetry has been stimulated by the experience of the vast panorama of nature in the American West.''

BANTOCK, G(eoffrey) H(erman) 1914-

PERSONAL: Born October 12, 1914, in Blackpool, England; son of Herman Sutherland (a musician) and Annie (Bailey) Bantock; married Dorothy Jean Pick (a teacher), January 6, 1950. *Education:* Emmanuel College, Cambridge, B.A. (with honors), 1937, M.A., 1942. *Home:* The Old Rectory, 1807 Melton Rd., Rearsby, Leicester, England. *Office:* School of Education, University of Leicester, 21 University Rd., Leicester, England.

CAREER: English master in county school of Ealing, England, 1937-43; senior English master in county high school, Ilford, Essex, England, 1943-46; City of Leeds Training College, Leeds, England, lecturer in English, 1946-50; University of Leicester, Leicester, England, lecturer, 1950-54, reader, 1954-65, professor of education, 1965-75, professor emeritus, 1975—. Leverhulme research fellow, 1976-78.

WRITINGS: Freedom and Authority in Education, Faber, 1952, Humanities, 1966; *L. H. Myers: A Critical Study*, Leicester University Press and J. Cape, 1956.

Education in an Industrial Society, Faber, 1963, 2nd edition, 1973; *Education and Values*, Faber, 1965, Humanities, 1966; *Education, Culture and the Emotions*, Faber, 1967, Indiana University Press, 1968; *Culture, Industrialisation and Education*, Routledge & Kegan Paul, 1968, Humanities, 1969; *T. S. Eliot and Education*, Random House, 1969.

Dilemmas of the Curriculum, Martin Robertson, 1980; *Studies in the History of Educational Theory*, Allen & Unwin, Volume I: *Artifice and Nature*, 1980; *Parochialism of the Present*, Routledge & Kegan Paul, 1981. Contributor to education and literary journals.

WORK IN PROGRESS: Volume II of *Studies in the History of Educational Theory*.

SIDELIGHTS: In his collection of essays entitled *Parochialism of the Present* (1981), educator G. H. Bantock discusses various aspects of the theory and practice of education during the past decade. He believes that the current emphasis on knowledge that is quantifiable—or capable of being scientifically measured—is a mistaken one. Instead, he advocates a theory of education that is based on the humanities. Writing in the *Times Literary Supplement*, Denis Donoghue reports that "it is well to be reminded . . . that Renaissance humanism had a persuasive theory of education, and that it is still worthwhile." But he also wishes that Bantock "were not so certain of his certainties, or that that he did not assume that he has established them merely by taking them for granted. I wish, too, that he could find something, anything, in the modern experience which he could gather to himself for praise."

BIOGRAPHICAL/CRITICAL SOURCES: Times Literary Supplement, September 19, 1968, December 19, 1980, July 24, 1981.

*   *   *

BARBOUR, Douglas (Fleming) 1940-

PERSONAL: Born March 21, 1940, in Winnipeg, Manitoba, Canada; son of Harold Douglas (a fundraising executive) and Phyllis (Wilson) Barbour; married M. Sharon Nicoll, May 21, 1966. *Education:* Acadia University, B.A., 1962; Dalhousie University, M.A., 1964; Queen's University, Kingston, Ontario, Ph.D., 1976. *Politics:* "Anarchist (at heart)." *Residence:* Edmonton, Alberta, Canada. *Office:* Department of En-glish, University of Alberta, Edmonton, Alberta, Canada T6G 2E5.

CAREER: Alderwood Collegiate Institute, Toronto, Ontario, teacher of English, 1968-69; University of Alberta, Edmonton, assistant professor, 1969-77, associate professor, 1977-82, professor of English, 1982—. Member of editorial board of Ne West Press and Longspoon Press, 1980—. *Member:* Association of Canadian University Teachers, League of Canadian Poets (co-chairman, 1972-74).

WRITINGS—Poetry, except as indicated: *Land Fall*, Delta Books, 1971; *A Poem As Long As the Highway*, Quarry Press, 1971; *White*, Fiddlehead Books, 1972; *Song Book*, Talon Books, 1973; *He and She and*, Golden Dog Press, 1974; *Visions of My Grandfather*, Golden Dog Press, 1977; (editor) *The Story So Far Five* (short stories), Coach House Press, 1978; *Worlds Out of Words: The Science Fiction Novels of Samuel R. Delany* (criticism), Bran's Head Books, 1978; *Shore Lines*, Turnstone Press, 1979; *Vision/Sounding*, League of Canadian Poets, 1980; (with Stephen Scobie) *The Pirates of Pen's Chance*, Coach House Press, 1981; (editor with Scobie) *The Maple Laugh Forever: An Anthology of Canadian Comic Poetry*, Hurtig Press, 1981; (editor with Marni Stanley) *Writing Right: New Poetry by Canadian Women*, Longspoon Press, 1982; *The Harbingers*, Quarry Press, 1983. Author of "Canadian Poetry Chronicle," in *Dalhousie Review*, 1969-77, *West Coast Review*, 1977-82, and *Quarry*, 1983—. Member of editorial board of *Quarry*, 1965-68, *White Pelican*, 1972-76, and *Canadian Forum*, 1978-80.

WORK IN PROGRESS: Poetry.

SIDELIGHTS: Douglas Barbour told *CA*, "I share with those writers I most admire a sense of language as alive, as something which speaks out its own life rather than simply as a tool to be 'used'; the language shaped *by* desire gives shape *to* desire."

*   *   *

BARKER, Jane Valentine 1930-

PERSONAL: Born May 17, 1930, in Boulder, Colo.; daughter of John Burr (in hardware) and Roberta (Beckwith) Valentine; married Richard T. Barker, September 11, 1952; children: Richard Valentine, Bruce Thomas. *Education:* University of Colorado, B.A. *Religion:* Presbyterian. *Home and office:* 860 Sixth St., Boulder, Colo.

CAREER: Boulder Daily Camera, Boulder, Colo., columnist and feature writer, 1967-78; freelance writer, 1976—. *Member:* National Federation of Press Women, National Association of Bank Women, Society of Children's Book Writers, Western Writers of America, Colorado Authors' League, Colorado Press Women, Boulder Writers Club, Boulder Writers Workshop, University of Colorado Boulder Area Alumni Club (president, 1964).

WRITINGS—All published by Pruett: *Seventy-Six Historic Homes of Boulder*, 1976; *Historic Homes of Boulder County*, 1979.

All with Sybil Downing: *Mountain Treasures*, 1978; *Happy Harvest*, 1978; *Trappers and Traders*, 1979; *Mesas to Mountains*, 1979; *Adventures in the West*, 1979; *Magic, Mystery and Monsters*, 1979; *Building Up*, 1979; *Settling Down*, 1979; *Wagons and Rails*, 1980; *Beauty in the Rockies*, 1980; *Florence Rena Sabin: Pioneer Scientist*, 1981; *Martha Maxwell: Pioneer Naturalist*, 1982.

WORK IN PROGRESS: A sequel to *Seventy-Six Historic Homes of Boulder*, a history of the town and its pioneer families.

*   *   *

BARKER, Roger Garlock 1903-

PERSONAL: Born March 31, 1903, in Macksburg, Iowa; son of Guy (a farmer) and Cora (Garlock) Barker; married Louise Shedd, June 17, 1930; children: Celia Barker Lottridge, Jonathan Shedd, Lucy. *Education:* Stanford University, B.A., 1928, M.A., 1930, Ph.D., 1934. *Religion:* Presbyterian. *Residence:* Oskaloosa, Kan. 66066. *Office:* Midwest Psychological Field Station, Oskaloosa, Kan. 66066.

CAREER: Research associate at Stanford University, Stanford, Calif., 1934-36, University of Iowa, Iowa City, 1936-38; Harvard University, Cambridge, Mass., assistant professor of psychology, 1938-39; University of Illinois at Urbana-Champaign, assistant professor of psychology, 1939-42; Stanford University, Stanford, Calif., acting associate professor of psychology, 1942-46; Clark University, Worchester, Mass., G. Stanley Hall Professor of Genetic Psychology, 1946-47; University of Kansas, Lawrence, professor of psychology, 1947-72, professor emeritus, 1972—, chairman of department, 1947-51. Co-founder, Midwest Psychological Field Station, Oskaloosa, Kan., 1947. Summer professor at University of Oregon, Columbia University, University of Colorado, Stanford University, and University of California. National Research Council—National Academy of Sciences, member of Committee on Child Development, 1956-58, member of Committee on Primary Records in the Behavioral Sciences, 1957-61.

MEMBER: American Psychological Association (president, Division of Developmental Psychology, 1952-53; fellow), Society for Research in Child Development (president, 1957-59), Society for the Psychological Study of Social Issues, American Association for the Advancement of Science, Ecological Society of America, Society for General Systems Research, Society for Biological Rhythm, American Association of University Professors, Sigma Xi, Rotary International (Oskaloosa; president, 1960-61).

AWARDS, HONORS: Center for Advanced Study in the Behavioral Sciences fellow, 1957-58; U.S. Public Health Service career award, 1962; Kurt Lewin Award of Society for the Psychological Study of Social Issues, 1963; Research Career award of National Institute of Mental Health, 1963; distinguished contribution award from American Psychological Association, 1963; G. Stanley Hall Award, Division of Developmental Psychology, American Psychological Association, 1969.

WRITINGS: Frustration and Regression: An Experiment with Young Children, University of Iowa, 1941, reprinted, Arno, 1976; (with Jacob S. Kounin and Herbert F. Wright) *Viewpoints on Science and the Psychology of Motivation for Students of Child Psychology*, Stanford University Press, 1942; (editor with Kounin and Wright) *Child Behavior and Development: A Course of Representative Studies*, McGraw, 1943; (with Beatrice A. Wright, L. Meyerson, and Mollie R. Gonick) *Adjustment to Physical Handicap and Illness: A Survey of the Social Psychology of Physique and Disability*, Social Science Research Council, 1946, revised edition, 1953.

(With H. F. Wright and others) *Methods in Psychological Ecology: A Progress Report*, privately printed, 1950; (with H. F. Wright) *One Boy's Day: A Specimen Record of Behavior*, Harper, 1951, reprinted, Shoe String, 1966; (with H. F. Wright)

Midwest and Its Children: The Psychological Ecology of an American Town, Row, Peterson & Co., 1954.

(With Louise S. Barker, H. F. Wright, and Maxine Schoggen) *Specimen Records of American and English Children from the Midwest Psychological Field Station*, University of Kansas Press, 1961; (with Paul V. Gump and others) *Big School, Small School: Studies of the Effects of High School Size upon the Behavior and Experiences of Students*, Midwest Psychological Field Station, 1962, published as *Big School, Small School: High School Size and Student Behavior*, Stanford University Press, 1964; (editor and contributor) *The Stream of Behavior: Explorations of Its Structure and Content*, Appleton, 1963; *Ecological Psychology: Concepts and Methods for Studying the Environment of Human Behavior*, Stanford University Press, 1968.

(With Phil Schoggen) *Qualities of Community Life: Measurement of Environment and Behavior in an American and an English Town*, Jossey-Bass, 1973; *Habitats, Environments, and Human Behavior: Studies in Ecological Psychology and Eco-Behavioral Science*, Jossey-Bass, 1978.

Contributor: Q. McNelmar and Maude A. Merrill, editors, *Studies in Personality*, McGraw, 1942; W. Dennis, editor, *Readings in Child Psychology*, Prentice-Hall, 1951; J. H. Rohrer and M. Sherif, editors, *Psychology at the Crossroads*, Harper, 1951; R. Kuhlen and G. Thompson, editors, *Human Development*, Appleton, 1952; H. Brand, editor, *The Study of Personality*, Wiley, 1954; E. O. Wittkower and R. A. Cleghorn, editors, *Recent Developments in Psychosomatic Medicine*, Pitman (London), 1954; A. P. Coladarci, editor, *Educational Psychology: A Book of Readings*, Dryden Press, 1955; *Clinical Studies of Personality*, Harper, 1955; M. R. Jones, editor, *Nebraska Symposium on Motivation*, University of Nebraska Press, 1960; B. Kaplan, editor, *Studying Personality Cross-Culturally*, Row, Peterson & Co., 1961; *Handbook of Environmental Psychology*, Wiley, in press.

Also author with H. F. Wright, Louise S. Barker, and others of "Full Day Records" series, Midwest Social Psychology Field Station, 1951-52. Contributor to *Encyclopedia of Educational Research, Encyclopaedia Britannica*, and to pamphlets and bulletins. Contributor of several dozen articles to psychology, sociology, and education journals.

*   *   *

BARNARD, Ellsworth 1907-

PERSONAL: Born April 11, 1907, in Shelburne Falls, Mass.; son of David Thompson and Kate (Barnard) Barnard; married Mary Taylor, December 31, 1936. *Education:* University of Massachusetts, B.S., 1928; University of Minnesota, M.A., 1929, Ph.D., 1935. *Politics:* Independent Liberal. *Home:* 86 Leverett Rd., Amherst, Mass. 01002.

CAREER: University of Massachusetts, Amherst, instructor in English, 1930-33; University of Tampa, Tampa, Fla., assistant professor of English, 1936-37; Williams College, Williamstown, Mass., instructor in English, 1937-40; University of Wisconsin, Madison, lecturer in English, 1940-41; Alfred University, Alfred, N.Y., professor of English and head of department, 1941-50; University of Chicago, Chicago, Ill., lecturer in liberal arts, 1952-55; Bowdoin College, Brunswick, Me., visiting lecturer in English, 1955-57; Northern Michigan University, Marquette, associate professor, 1957-62, professor of English, 1962-68; University of Massachusetts, Amherst, visiting professor, 1968-69, professor of English, 1969-73, professor emeritus, 1973—.

MEMBER: Modern Language Association of America (member emeritus), American Association of University Professors (member emeritus), College English Association, National Council of Teachers of English. *Awards, honors:* L.H.D., University of Massachusetts, 1969.

WRITINGS: Shelley's Religion, University of Minnesota Press, 1937; (editor) *Shelley: Selected Poems, Essays, and Letters,* Odyssey, 1944; *Edwin Arlington Robinson: A Critical Study,* Macmillan, 1952.

Wendell Willkie: Fighter for Freedom, Northern Michigan University Press, 1966; (contributor) J. R. Bryer, editor, *Fifteen Modern American Authors,* Duke University Press, 1969; (editor and contributor) *Edwin Arlington Robinson: Centenary Essays,* University of Georgia Press, 1969; *English for Everybody,* Dinosaur Press, 1979; *A Hill Farm Boyhood,* Dinosaur Press, 1983.

Contributor to *Harper's, New York Times Magazine, Massachusetts Review,* and several other publications.

WORK IN PROGRESS: An autobiography.

SIDELIGHTS: Ellsworth Barnard told *CA:* "My first love was always teaching and my books were written mostly during summer vacations, or when I was out of a job, or when I took time off (at my own expense) near the end of a project. Not that I wish to downgrade my books. I wrote them because I wanted to, because I cared about the subjects and thought I had something new or significant to say about them. And if you care about the subject, you care—or ought to care—about the style; of which the great virtues, as I say in *English for Everybody,* seem to me to be clarity, naturalness, forcefulness, and beauty. You get a feeling for these through wide reading, especially of the classics of British and American literature. And then you simply work, no matter how long it takes, to get every word and sentence right. I suppose, too, that if over the years you devote your days and night to helping students to learn to write well, you learn something yourself."

AVOCATIONAL INTERESTS: Nature study, conservation, civil liberties.

*   *   *

BARNETT, Adam
   See FAST, Julius

*   *   *

BARRETT, Marvin   1920-

PERSONAL: Born May 6, 1920, in Des Moines, Iowa; son of Edwin Galbraith (a professor) and Esther (Kruidenier) Barrett; married Mary Ellin Berlin (a writer), October 14, 1952; children: Elizabeth, Irving, Mary Ellin, Katherine. *Education:* Harvard University, B.A., 1942; Drake University, M.A., 1976. *Politics:* Independent. *Religion:* Protestant. *Agent:* Russell & Volkening, Inc., 551 Fifth Ave., New York, N.Y. 10176.

CAREER: Time, New York City, contributing editor, 1948-52; free-lance writer, 1952-55; *Newsweek,* New York City, radio-television editor, 1955-59; *Show Business Illustrated,* New York City, executive editor, 1960; *Show,* New York City, editor, 1961-64; *Atlas,* New York City, editor, 1965-67; free-lance writer, 1967—; Columbia University, New York City,

faculty member of Graduate School of Journalism, 1968-83. *Military service:* U.S. Naval Reserve, active duty, 1942-46; became lieutenant. *Awards, honors:* Distinguished service award from Sigma Delta Chi, 1975, for *Moments of Truth?*

WRITINGS: The Jazz Age, Putnam, 1959; *The Years Between,* Little, Brown, 1961; *Meet Thomas Jefferson,* Random House, 1964; *Survey of Broadcast Journalism,* Grosset, 1969; *Year of Challenge, Year of Crisis,* Grosset, 1970; *State of Siege,* Grosset, 1971; *The Politics of Broadcasting,* Crowell, 1973; *Moments of Truth?,* Crowell, 1975; *The End of the Party,* Putnam, 1976; *Rich News, Poor News,* Crowell, 1977; (with Zachary Sklar) *The Eye of the Storm,* Lippincott, 1980; *Broadcast Journalism,* Everest House, 1982. Contributor to magazines.

*   *   *

BARRETT, William (Christopher)   1913-
   (Moses Brown)

PERSONAL: Born December 30, 1913, in New York, N.Y.; son of John Patrick (an engineer) and Delia (Connolly) Barrett; married Juliet Bigney, August 29, 1941 (died February 8, 1980); children: Susan, Michael. *Education:* City College (now City College of the City University of New York), A.B., 1933; Columbia University, A.M., Ph.D., 1938. *Home:* 34 Harwood Ave., North Tarrytown, N.Y. 10591.

CAREER: Instructor in philosophy at University of Illinois (now University of Illinois at Urbana-Champaign), Urbana, 1938-40, and Brown University, Providence, R.I., 1940-42; U.S. Department of State, vice consul in Rome, Italy, 1944-45; *Partisan Review,* New York City, associate editor, 1945-53; New York University, New York City, professor of philosophy, 1950-79; National Humanities Center, Research Triangle Park, N.C., Mellon fellow, beginning 1981; Pace University, New York City, distinguished professor, 1982—. *Military service:* Office of Strategic Services, World War II; served in Italy. *Member:* American Philosophical Association, Authors Guild, Authors League of America, Phi Beta Kappa. *Awards, honors:* Rockefeller Foundation fellow, 1946-47; Guggenheim fellow, 1975-76; National Endowment for the Humanities senior fellow, 1976-77.

WRITINGS: What Is Existentialism? (essay; also see below), Partisan Review, 1947; *Irrational Man: A Study in Existential Philosophy,* Doubleday-Anchor, 1958, reprinted, Greenwood Press, 1977; *What Is Existentialism?* (essays; contains "What Is Existentialism?" and "Heidegger: The Silent Power of the Possible"), Grove, 1964; (with Daniel Yankelovich) *Ego and Instinct: The Psychoanalytic View of Human Nature—Revised,* Random House, 1970; *Time of Need: Forms of Imagination in the Twentieth Century,* Harper, 1972; *The Illusion of Technique: A Search for Meaning in a Technological Civilization,* Doubleday-Anchor, 1978; *The Truants: Adventures among the Intellectuals,* Doubleday-Anchor, 1982.

Editor: (With D. T. Suzuki) *Zen Buddhism,* Doubleday, 1956; (with Henry David Aiken and author of introduction) *Philosophy in the Twentieth Century: An Anthology,* four volumes, Random House, 1962, published in three volumes as *Philosophy in the Twentieth Century,* Harper, 1971.

Contributor: Wilfred Healey Stone and Robert Hoopes, editors, *Form and Thought in Prose,* Ronald Press, 1954; Chandler Brossard, editor, *The Scene before You: A New Approach to American Culture,* Rinehart, 1955; George Bernard de Huszar, editor, *The Intellectuals: A Controversial Portrait,* Free Press of Glencoe, 1960.

Atlantic, literary reviewer, 1960—, author of column "Reader's Choice," 1961-64. Contributor, under pseudonym Moses Brown, of article on World War II in Italy to *Partisan Review;* contributor to other periodicals, including *Kenyon Review, Journal of Philosophy, American Mercury,* and *Commentary.*

WORK IN PROGRESS: Death of the Soul, a study of mind and psyche in modern philosophy.

SIDELIGHTS: "In no age of history has the intellectual been more influential upon human affairs than in the modern world," William Barrett observes in his book *The Truants,* and he speaks from experience. As an associate editor of *Partisan Review,* the literary and political bellwether of the 1940s and '50s, Barrett witnessed firsthand the shaping of postwar American culture. He not only worked with such prominent writers as Philip Rahv, William Phillips, Delmore Schwartz, Dwight Macdonald, Mary McCarthy, Hannah Arendt, Albert Camus, Sidney Hook, and Lionel Trilling, but he also helped introduce European existentialism to American readers. As a philosopher and literary critic, Barrett has written several acclaimed books on the modern intellectual scene, including a memoir and analysis of his *Partisan Review* days, *The Truants,* as well as a classic introduction to existentialism, *Irrational Man.* He has become one of America's best-known living philosophers, according to Quentin Lauer in *America,* because he "succeeds again and again in pinpointing the intellectual malaise of modernity."

Barrett first became interested in the world of ideas as a teenager, when he read Aristotle and realized the impact of the philosopher's thought on Western civilization. Years later, while studying for his doctorate in philosophy at Columbia University, he met Delmore Schwartz, the ill-fated poet and critic who would soon be hailed as the brightest new star in American letters. The two quickly became "spiritual brothers," Barrett recalls in *The Truants,* and when Schwartz was named an associate editor of *Partisan Review* in the winter of 1937-38, he introduced Barrett to the journal's editors, William Phillips and Philip Rahv. Barrett was awed by the men, he says in *The Truants,* because "they belonged to the great world outside the walls of the academy where I was still drudging for a degree. Theirs was the world of bohemia and the arts, of political movements and countermovements, bold and sweeping ideologies. . . . They were therefore beings invested in my eyes with a strange and mysterious glamor."

Partisan Review was founded in 1934 as an organ of the Communist Party, but by 1938 Rahv and Phillips had long broken with Stalinism and found the ideological mixture—a "purer" Marxism in politics and modernism in literature and the arts—that was to sustain them until the early 1960s. Like many young intellectuals in the 1930s who embraced Marxism and avant-garde culture, Barrett awaited each issue of the magazine with hope. *Partisan Review,* he writes, "marked the first appearance of an independent and literate Left in this country—something which we young people wanted badly to see but couldn't have created all by ourselves. It was particularly welcome to young teachers on campus, where the liberal members of the faculty were usually so thoroughly and subtly Stalinized that they didn't even know it."

Although he had been teaching philosophy at Brown University when the United States entered World War II, Barrett had little desire to return to academe after being discharged from the service. Determined to lead some sort of Bohemian existence if only for a while, he renewed his contact with Delmore Schwartz, who was by this time an editor of *Partisan Review,*

and rented a cold-water flat for $22 a month in New York's Greenwich Village. When Schwartz surprised him one day in 1945 with the news that he, Barrett, had been named an associate editor of the journal, Barrett was of course elated: *Partisan Review* was already emerging as "the very voice and soul of the New York intelligentsia," observes Pearl Bell in the *New Republic.* Yet, he was also startled and embarrassed by the news, because he and Schwartz had never even discussed the possibility of him joining the staff; moreover, he had only contributed two pieces to the magazine, one of them under the pseudonym Moses Brown.

Nevertheless, Barrett's familiarity with European intellectual movements, his knowledge of Italian, French, and German, and his ability to present abstract Continental philosophy in a lucid, non-technical style made him a valuable asset; for existentialism was the new philosophical movement that had just arrived from Europe, the new wave of painting soon to be called Abstract Expressionism was evolving, Marxism and socialism were topics of almost universal interest, and "nowhere were these issues more vigorously debated than in . . . *Partisan Review,* the . . . highly tuned seismograph of the intellectual climate," notes Michiko Kakutani of the *New York Times.*

Barrett quickly became the journal's chief exponent of existentialism and a steadfast critic of the American liberal establishment's Stalinist sentiments. He translated Hannah Arendt's important article "What Is *Existenz* Philosophy?" and lectured on the subject before gatherings of abstract expressionists and other avant-garde artists. In 1947, *Partisan Review* published his widely read essay *What Is Existentialism?,* which was, according to James Collins in *America,* "one of the earliest and most lucid presentations of French existentialism in English." The anti-Stalinism Barrett shared with the other *Partisan Review* editors arose from their belief that while liberty in its fullest sense could only be realized in a socialist system, Stalin had perverted the socialist ideal and created a criminal dictatorship. In his editorials, Barrett frequently castigated American liberals for their willingness to appease Stalin and for their blindness to the Soviet Union's totalitarian character.

During the eight years he was with *Partisan Review,* Barrett came to regard the intellectual circle surrounding him as both "a school and . . . a family," he says in the *New York Times.* But it was an unusual family, he notes, in that it was "full of divisions and squabbles," and discussions "were almost always carried on in a very raucous manner—one never said, 'I disagree with you'; one said, 'You're out of your mind.'" Moreover, despite the apparent intimacy of the group, Barrett remained somewhat of an outsider, as Mark Shechner explains in *Nation:* "A Gentile among Jews and a retiring existentialist among quarrelsome ex-Marxists, [Barrett] was a noncombatant in the struggles that regularly shook the office, struggles that, because they drew so deeply upon the Jewishness as well as the personal afflictions of the combatants, were not his own. He was an outsider who was permitted a privileged view of the turmoil within, the Horatio who survived to tell the story."

"As [*The Truants*] so clearly shows," adds Seymour Krim in the *Washington Post Book World,* "Barrett never tried to compete with the stars in the *Partisan Review* firmament. He had neither the aggressive self-confidence nor the flash; in fact, he was always the inquiring young philosopher, trying to see past the immediate editorial disputes . . . to the basic worth of people and issues. This quiet objectivity is what gives such spice and reality to the anecdotes he tells, and his stories of literary foolishness and feuding are little short of priceless."

The Truants, Barrett's memoir of his association with the journal, has been widely praised for its portraits of *Partisan Review* editors and contributors. Barry Gewen, for example, states in the *New Leader* that Barrett "has a great talent for character-portraiture, for searching out the root of people, what he calls their 'pietas.' His Mary McCarthy one remembers for her child-like playfulness, his [Lionel] Trilling for a quality of secular rationalism at once deep and limiting. But the finest portrait—and the center of the book—is that of Philip Rahv, the dominant figure at *Partisan Review* and Barrett's choice as the archetypal New York intellectual."

The portrait of Rahv "strikes me as quite the best thing in Mr. Barrett's book," exclaims Hilton Kramer in the *New York Times Book Review.* "Written with delicacy, precision and even at times a grim humor, it is not only an important contribution to intellectual history but a literary feat of no small distinction. Rahv was indeed a formidable personality of considerable influence, and Mr. Barrett has now succeeded in making his unusual story a permanent part of our literature." Gewen notes that although Barrett describes Rahv as "arrogant, rude, secretive, nihilistic, cowardly, [and] ruthless," Rahv nonetheless "emerges bigger than life, a large spirit whose failings prevented him from being a great man. I found this picture extremely moving, sadder even than Barrett's account of that unhappy individual, Delmore Schwartz."

A manic-depressive, Schwartz lost favor in the literary world as his mind and talent gradually deteriorated. Barrett, a devoted friend for many years, "feared being caught in the trap of derangement," says Pearl Bell in the *New Republic,* "and backed away [when Schwartz became violently manic]. Though he writes about Schwartz's self-destruction with painful candor, [Barrett] refuses to cheapen and falsify his friend's pathetic end with the currently fashionable notion that such poets as Schwartz, Sylvia Plath, and John Berryman were *poetes maudits,* the doomed victims of an 'alienating' society. As he sensibly observes, the troubles of these poets 'were so obviously deep-seated in the personality that neither of those abstract specters, Society or Poetry, can be invoked as culprits.'"

Christopher Lehmann-Haupt of the *New York Times* declares that Schwartz's "manic presence [in *The Truants*] is as powerful as it is in Saul Bellow's novel *Humboldt's Gift* and James Atlas's able biography of the poet-critic." But he maintains that there are equally "vivid portraits of . . . Rahv, Phillips, and [Edmund] Wilson, as well as Clement Greenberg, Dwight Macdonald, Hannah Arendt, Jean-Paul Sartre, Albert Camus, Jackson Pollock, Willem de Kooning—the list goes on and on."

Though the impressive sketches of people and places make *The Truants* read like a thoughtful novel, critics point out that the book is much more than a personal reminiscence. "It is also," says Kramer, "a penetrating analysis of the intellectual life of its period. And because our culture is still beset by so many of the illusions that were spawned and codified in the milieu that Mr. Barrett has set out to describe in this book, *The Truants* is very much a text for our time as well. The arguments it recounts, the positions it defines, the careers it retraces, the whole literary, artistic, and political ethos that is so cogently evoked in its pages—all of this turns out to contain a good deal of the intellectual debris that continues to litter the cultural scene today." Lehmann-Haupt believes that if Barrett's memoir "is read as widely as it deserves to be for the eloquence and power with which it dramatizes important ideas, then it may be all too evident to posterity how Mr. Barrett himself managed to shape America's future ideology."

Barrett now regards *Partisan Review's* effort to link together the values of radical politics and advanced art as a self-willed illusion. "The intellectual . . . has only to turn his mind in a certain direction and some unpleasant realities can disappear," he writes in *The Truants,* and he applies this observation to both bases of the journal's ideology. Though he defends the modernist vision in art for its attempt to come to terms with "the withdrawal of God," he nevertheless condemns the modernists' frequent disregard for standards, taste, tradition, and elemental feelings of human decency—a flaw that to some degree has endured in the arts. He also admits that, as the late Lionel Trilling had first suggested, the works of modern literature so revered by the journal's editors could not always be reconciled with their Marxist outlook. Innovators like T. S. Eliot, William Butler Yeats, and Ezra Pound were political reactionaries who abhorred the egalitarian ideals of socialism; moreover, by the 1940s these same artists had become the darlings of the bourgeoisie and their works had been absorbed into the classical canon.

Barrett's indictment of Marxism is more severe. The Marxist experience of the 1930s, he says, "was of something remote and distant—either intellectually in the intricacies of theory that didn't mesh with our actual life, or romantically remote in the deeds of socialist heroes in far-off lands. . . . We had inherited the experience of the '30s and thought we were doing enough simply to pass it on; but we were not radical enough to get to the root of its matter. . . . And in this sense we failed the decades that were to come. As the attitude of a liberal Marxism, vague enough to begin with, became even vaguer and more vaporous, it infected the whole of American liberalism; and it was to erupt again as the infantile Marxism of the '60s."

Barrett and his fellow editors "never once questioned the inherent loss of liberty that would occur in art and thought if their beloved 'socialism' ever came into being," explains Seymour Krim. "They were self-hypnotized utopians 'escaping for a while from the harshness of . . . practical reality,' hence the title of his book, *The Truants*—borrowed from an unwritten novel by Philip Rahv, and the perfect choice for the points Barrett wants to make. More, by searching for 'original and sweeping ideas,' the *Partisan Review* intellectuals conveniently forgot the number one condition for their own existences: the survival of the United States as 'a free nation in a world going increasingly totalitarian.'"

"Barrett's vote for common values has the ring of experience and reflection," states Mark Shechner, and so does his theme of the intellectual playing truant from reality; for Barrett left *Partisan Review* because he grew disillusioned with its "rarified, highbrow world," reports Michiko Kakutani of the *New York Times.* During the late 1940s, a sense of "gray emptiness" began to afflict him, and he recognized that his own immersion in the intellectual world had actually cut him off from the joys of ordinary life. "I realized my wife had a lot more insight into things than I had, even though she wasn't an intellectual," he told Kakutani. "I realized [that] I'd been a truant from my being—I'd been this snotty young man, abrasive and cocky about his intellectual powers—and that you can overintellectualize."

It was no accident that Barrett became aware at this time of the danger of overintellectualizing, since he was also deeply involved in the study of existentialism. "In the hands of Kierkegaard and Nietzsche," he says in the *New York Times,* "existentialism was originally a recoil from rampant rationality. And I began to realize that the great threat of the modern epoch was deranged rationality."

In several acclaimed works for the general reader, Barrett chronicles the development of this "deranged rationality" in Western civilization, warns of its dangers, and describes reactions to it. He explains in both *Irrational Man* and *The Illusion of Technique* that the seeds of "deranged rationality," of intellectual truancy from being, were sown when Western philosophy began. Plato and Aristotle, he points out, gave reason a unique function in the search for truth by detaching it from the mythic, religious, and poetic impulses with which it had formerly been mixed. From Greek philosophy, particularly Aristotle's invention of logic, came science and the dependence on increasingly abstract models to explain the world.

Beginning with the discoveries in the sixteenth and seventeenth centuries, modern science set up artificial concepts—ones not found in the everyday experiences of nature but in the mind itself—to measure and define natural phenomena. When Descartes transferred to philosophy the procedures on which science had already embarked and proposed that they be extended to all domains of human inquiry, the technological spirit was born and rationality became "deranged." The abstract techniques of science became recognized as the chief avenues to "truth," and "truth" itself became divorced from the experience of ordinary life.

"Since Descartes," writes Barrett in *The Illusion of Technique,* "we have been in the grip of a metaphysics of death that [Alfred North] Whitehead calls 'scientific materialism.' We understand the phenomena of life only as an assemblage of the lifeless. . . . We take the abstractions of our technical calculations to be ultimately concrete. Beneath our preoccupation with technique and apparatus, there is the prevalent metaphysical disposition to see things ultimately resolved into bits of brute matter pervading space, 'in a flux of configurations, senseless, valueless, purposeless.'"

"Barrett's narrative of the stages in [*The Illusion of Technique*] is highly speculative," notes James Atlas in *Time,* "but his hold on elusive ideas is so sure, his erudition so vast and effortless, that a coherent historical design gradually emerges." The abstract rationalism underlying technological civilization, according to Barrett, has severed man from nature, from his true being, thus producing the modern malaise of nihilism—the overwhelming intellectual and spiritual sense of meaninglessness. Because of his own conceptual constructions, technological man has cut himself off from the primitive and religious impulses of his being, and now confronts an alien and meaningless universe, a neutral realm over which he must seek mastery. Consequently, every object in the world, including man himself, has become impoverished of all qualities except those relevant to blind, technological purposes.

"A vast moral and conceptual vacuum has opened up," concludes Jane Larkin Crain in the *National Review,* "and Barrett sees it being filled with a technological spirit bent on molding human destiny in a variety of designs. Be it embodied in the utopian fantasies of B. F. Skinner, on the one hand, or in the naked brutalities of Marxism, on the other, this spirit is, at bottom, totalitarian. The attempt to realize one or another dream of social perfection threatens with violence those human possibilities that make life worth living at all."

Barrett insists, however, that the technological spirit need not have developed and therefore can be transcended. Existential-

ism in philosophy and modernism in art, he points out in *Irrational Man* and *Time of Need,* reflect the sense of crisis embodied in the rupture of man from nature, and challenge the abstract, oversimplified view of man in modern philosophy (philosophy since Descartes), behavioral psychology, Marxism, and other legacies of the technological spirit. Though the struggle with nihilism has resulted in much pessimism and an almost systematic destruction of forms in the arts, the two movements nevertheless re-inject the totality of individual existence—with all its mystery, guilt, fear, despair, and trembling—into art and thought.

Barrett's work on existentialism has led James Atlas to call him "our foremost chronicler" of the philosophy, and Philip Toynbee reports in the *Observer* that *Irrational Man,* published in 1958, is still "perhaps the best serious study of existentialism in the English language." Barrett has been widely praised for shattering the popular misconceptions of existentialism as simply "a postwar mood" or a peculiarly French phenomenon. Leslie Dewart, for example, writes in *Canadian Forum:* "Barrett conveys the . . . important truth that existentialism is not simply an interesting episode in the annals of recent academic fads, but the conceptualization and intellectualization of a culture-wide phenomenon, deeply rooted in the history of the Western mind, and sufficiently pervasive and powerful to warrant recognition as the philosophical type which manifests the thermonuclear age."

Indebted though he is to the existentialists, Barrett "is not just the academic propounder of other people's philosophies," notes Toynbee, but is "a true philosopher." In *The Illusion of Technique,* Barrett issues "his own passport to nature appreciation as never before," states Richard G. Hubler in the *Los Angeles Times Book Review.* "In a lucent style set with vigorous images, he affirms his allegiance to the world around him." Allen Lacy says in the *Chronicle Review* that Barrett "writes lucidly about the need for mystery [in our lives]. He describes, beautifully and elegantly, the need to recognize the claims of the silent and the wordless over our being. He argues rationally for the preservation of our freedom, for the maintenance of sufficient disorder in human existence, [because] it will always be a bit unpredictable."

The schizophrenia of our culture, Barrett concludes, can only be healed by returning to nature for the truth it conveys: "We forget that what we call mysticism was once a natural condition of mankind, and could be again if we let ourselves enter it. . . . We have only to be open to the world and it will pour its riches at our feet. Before this winter I had not known that the bark of a tree, caught in yellow sunlight, could be enough to restore a life."

AVOCATIONAL INTERESTS: Painting ("but find little time for it these days").

CA INTERVIEW

CA interviewed William Barrett April 30, 1982, in Chapel Hill, N.C. Barrett was finishing up a year's work at the National Humanities Center before returning to his home in Tarrytown, New York.

CA: An editor's note in The Illusion of Technique *says that your combination of knowledge "in technical philosophy and human interests" gives you your "unique quality as a leading contemporary thinker." Did that variety of interests make it difficult for you to settle on philosophy as a specialty?*

BARRETT: Before I went into philosophy, there was the question of whether my field would be mathematics or literature. It sort of fell in the middle. As a matter of fact, I'm very much interested in the technical and logical aspects of philosophy. I have a mathematical bent that goes a long way back. But apart from that, there is the other side of me, which rebels against the whole business—the poet, you might say. I really did see the conflict in civilization coming through this phase that started in the seventeenth century with a concentration on mathematics and technique and has gone on to become something quite curious. It feeds on itself. You step into a New York drugstore, sit at the counter for a Coke, and you hear two girls down the counter chatting in pseudo-Freudian vocabulary. I'm sure it adds nothing to their enlightenment about their particular emotional situation. It's an example of the buildup of a tremendous matrix of pseudo-exact terminology that affects us everywhere. At the same time we have suffered a loss of primitive and direct perceptions, feelings, intuitions.

CA: What thinkers had the greatest influence on you in the early stages of your education?

BARRETT: I came up through the usual academic curriculum, with an early exposure to modern philosophy. But I happened to know Greek, so I read Aristotle and Plato, Greek philosophy. I knew a little Latin, so I did medieval philosophy. And then I shifted into modern logic and other ''scientific'' areas of philosophy. I was young, intellectually eager, and was in the process of turning myself into an intellectual monster.

After World War II, coming back to New York and for a while stepping out of the academy (this was when I was an editor for the *Partisan Review*), I began to notice that something was happening to me. My cerebral self-possession suddenly exploded and there was all sorts of hell going on inside me. I was not able to sit still and write. I gradually realized that there was some point of view I was missing. Out of that came *Irrational Man*. I was really speaking to myself and against myself.

CA: So it wasn't a matter of having your whole attention caught up by one philosopher or branch of philosophy and being thus directed on a clear-cut path?

BARRETT: No, it was an organic development, and I can chart its steady subterranean flow only as I look back. At the time when my confusion was becoming obvious to me—I'm talking about 1946, '47, '48—Tolstoy and Dostoevski had an overwhelming impact on me because their message was precisely, as Tolstoy puts it, that he who remains within the intellect never comprehends life.

Those Russian writers were facing a kind of feverish situation of modernity as it was flowing into Russia from the West. I recently read a book about the Russian nihilists as they appeared in university life. They must have been very much like the hippies of the 1960s—different haircuts and manners and so on. That made an impact on me.

And there were things in my personal life, in dreams, that might have helped me, but I had no idea what these implied.

CA: Your writing, unlike that of many philosophers, has been very clear. Why don't more philosophers write clearly? Why do we have Kants and Hegels who are so obscure to us?

BARRETT: Kant is clear if you first learn to understand his terminology. But I don't know. Maybe the philosophers are

not thinking clearly. I have a disposition for saying it as simply and clearly as possible. Some people have praised me as a stylist, but I don't try to be one. I simply try to write as clearly as possible. I like to see the thought move.

I did a book with Henry D. Aiken, *Philosophy in the Twentieth Century,* and I remember his telling me (he just died recently), ''I admire what you're doing, but you drive me mad.'' He said that I wrote as if I had to be understood by the most uneducated reader.

CA: What are your writing habits? Do you rewrite a lot?

BARRETT: I've got very bad habits. I take three hours to pick my nose for every hour that I write. But when I write I just write it out. Sometimes I revise a little, but if it flows, it's OK. I tend to be nervous when it gets laborious because I know something's wrong. As a matter of fact, the book I'm working on has gotten laborious, probably because I'm not back in my old studio in Tarrytown. You get to be terribly dependent on your external condition. You get to be, in fact, a fuddy-duddy. I'm writing in longhand this time, and I don't like it. Usually I alternate between longhand and batting it out on an old portable typewriter—mainly the latter, using longhand just to ease off and then back to the typewriter. This time, because I can get the typing done at the Humanities Center, I'm writing it out in longhand. But it makes the flow a little too sedate.

CA: Young people are very much taken by the philosopher who lives his ideas, as Sartre did in fighting in the French Resistance during World War II. On the other hand, there's the ivory-tower philosopher. You seem to be one of the first kind. Would you comment on the difference between the two?

BARRETT: It's the difference between whether you're an organization man or a nonorganization man. Philosophy here in the United States is very much a departmentally organized matter. I've always stepped outside of that. I consider it my natural delinquency or something like that. I live my ideas in the sense that they're always gnawing at me. Sometimes I wish they would go away.

I don't really think Americans realize how thoroughly this process of academization has saturated our culture. Take the American Philosophical Association now as compared with when I attended some of the sessions as a youngster, and even read a paper there at a relatively early age. How comparatively informal, how much smaller and nonstructured it was! It's built itself up. But it's nothing compared with the Modern Language Association. Some years back there was this mammoth meeting of the MLA, which required two hotels in New York. I went there to attend a reception held by the French department, just for drinks and conversation with some aspiring young scholars. Well, there was a lot of talk about what they were working on, mainly tight, tidy little dissertations. I came away and said to a friend, ''You know, I had an awful impression. There was this vast body of the MLA, and there was the corpus of literature, and they were an army of termites eating into it.''

It's part of the stratification and organization of modern technical society. OK, you're going to get a dissertation, then you must become an expert in this tiny corner of the subject, though you had no intention of such narrow specialization when you started.

CA: In your own graduate-school days, did you have to resist becoming a termite?

BARRETT: No, the situation was different. Don't forget, it was quite early, the 1930s. I began my graduate work at nineteen, and I didn't think of it as graduate work that would lead to a degree and a job, as people do now. I'd just made some money as a ghostwriter. My father had died, and my mother said: "You can stay at home here and write. There's money." I was curious about philosophy. So I took a course, one thing led to another, and pretty soon I had all my credits for a Ph.D. Then I thought I might as well get the degree. But I didn't have my future mapped out the way graduate students do now. There were no jobs; you didn't think about that. I thought I'd probably end up teaching high-school English, and in fact, got a license to do that, but then I got another fellowship. It was much more informal then. The hierarchical stratification of the academic world has become much more intense in my lifetime.

When I was reading the Greek corpus (I knew Greek, as I said earlier), I almost became a scholar. What turned me off was this: I loved reading the original texts, but if you're going to produce articles, my God, you have to spend so much time on secondary sources. That wasn't interesting. And the fact is that scholarship has become largely a matter of manipulating secondary texts. Scholarship feeding on scholarship feeding on scholarship till the primary sources get lost.

CA: Both you and Walter Kaufmann deal with questions that the average person is interested in, such as what are we supposed to do with our lives? Why don't more philosophers address themselves to such basic questions?

BARRETT: Because they have to get academic promotion. They have to come up with something that will fit into the latest philosophical publications, something that will serve them well in the academic hierarchy. That shows you the corporate character of the philosophical enterprise.

CA: Is logical positivism still a very popular branch of philosophy?

BARRETT: No, because it has sort of disappeared, but it really is the ferment behind a lot of what is now called analytic philosophy. It's a kind of mental attitude that younger philosophers carry with them, often without being aware of it.

CA: In Irrational Man *you spoke of Americans as being not only nonintellectual but anti-intellectual. Do you still think that's true?*

BARRETT: Maybe not as much, but really I think they like to appear intellectual, to ape the products of intelligence, but not to go through the solitude and ardor of the thinker. In *The Truants* I didn't press the issue, but I did mention that intellectuals don't think, they *cerebrate*. There's quite a difference. You see two people talking together. Neither one is listening to what the other is saying; as one is talking, the other is thinking what he's going to say when it's his turn. There's no effort to absorb what the other one is saying, to let it sink in. And this is what's wrong in philosophy. There's too much spinning words without letting their meaning take hold of one.

CA: You said in your introduction to Zen Buddhism [*co-edited with D. T. Suzuki and published in 1956*] *that we Americans didn't know much about Zen Buddhism, partly because much of our idea of it came from Schopenhauer, who didn't understand it well because he was reading poor translations.* . . .

BARRETT: And also because he was reading his own thought into it, projecting his own particular pessimism.

CA: Do you think there's a lot in Zen Buddhism that could help us learn to live better lives?

BARRETT: Sure. I keep coming back to it in the need to revitalize something in Western culture. But I am being personal in what I say. And I should add that all my work has been in the nature of a personal search, a religious search. One interesting thing that's happened here is that I've formed a friendship with another fellow at the Humanities Center that I'd describe this way: it's like two men meeting in a whorehouse and finding out they came from the same hometown. It turns out that he isn't godless and I'm not godless; we're both searching. We're two oddballs. Every time we meet, we have a cocktail and toast to the greater glory of God.

CA: What about existentialism now? There was a lot of excitement over it back in the '50s and '60s, but we don't hear very much about it anymore.

BARRETT: No, because it's been absorbed. Now a course in existentialism is just another part of the philosophy curriculum. One of the fifty-seven varieties. The vocabulary is accessible and the ideas about it are batted around, but the point has been lost, that sense of naked self-confrontation that was behind it.

CA: You've been an editor and writer for Partisan Review, *you've done the book-review column for* Atlantic, *and you've contributed to other magazines such as the* Kenyon Review, American Mercury, *and* Commentary. *What periodicals do you consider important today?*

BARRETT: I haven't been following the magazines closely. I write for *Commentary,* but that's because on some important things (not all) I share its point of view. But my general impression of the magazine field is a great clamor of discordant voices. This is a period which seems to have no unity of mind, no intellectual center.

CA: In The Truants *you wrote about the New York intellectual establishment of the 1940s and '50s.*

BARRETT: It wasn't *establishment*. Now that I look back on the group, I'm going to pay them this due: there was not one bit of chichi. They were rude, they were solitary, they were themselves; Dwight Macdonald, Philip Rahv—no chichi. And that's the difference between the *Partisan Review* and the *New York Review*.

CA: Is there an influential New York intellectual establishment today?

BARRETT: No, but there are various intellectuals who are listened to by various people who have some kind of power. When it comes to something like politics and international policies, it's very funny to try to demarcate the lines along which intellectuals separate on clear intellectual grounds, because, I'm sorry to say, after all this time, politics is the most fuzzy portion of the human brain.

Take the business of political labels. People think in terms of them, and yet how deceiving these labels are. For example, I find I've been labeled as a conservative. In fact, I could describe myself as a radical liberal. Why? Because I think liberty is the primary value in a society. But if you're going to have liberty, genuine liberty, then you're going to have some conservative structures in your society. Kids have to grow up with some sense of moral behavior; you can't reinvent morality from generation to generation. Learning the traditions of civil behavior, how to accept the give and take of the democratic process, etc., etc.—these are things you can't just legislate on paper; they've got to become part of the habits of the people.

Liberty is the supreme political quality I'd want in a government, because if you have liberty you can really work for improvement within the framework of liberty. If you abolish liberty for the sake of some putative scheme of justice or equality and you say, "We're just rescinding liberty temporarily," you never get the liberty back, and you never get the justice. That seems to me one of the great historic lessons of our century. But some people, intellectuals mostly, refuse to learn from it. When they set their mind to it, intellectuals can be the most blinded people in the world. Truants, in fact.

CA: You said in The Truants *that you thought the James Atlas biography of Delmore Schwartz was remarkably sensitive. Would you comment further on it?*

BARRETT: I must say I was really astounded that Atlas dug out so many facts. He was the only person who had a feeling for Delmore. He had a few facts wrong, but that was understandable. It was not his fault. They were misreported.

CA: Was Delmore Schwartz a hard subject?

BARRETT: Yes, but in one sense clear-cut, because there's a thematic unity throughout his life: the self-destruction of a talented man. Delmore doomed himself. He had a deep religious yearning, and he couldn't fulfill it. He would have had psychological troubles anyway, but they wouldn't have been overwhelming. He didn't realize that religious aspect of himself was a part he just had to cling to. The Atlas book is very good.

CA: You said in a Partisan Review *article in 1976 that "anything that weakens the strength of the United States weakens the cause of liberty." Is the current administration doing enough to protect our strength?*

BARRETT: Well, Reagan's making some effort to build up defense. But Reagan is not a statesman. He's really just a very good local politician. And the situation is desperate. If I were president, I would proceed in an entirely different way with regard to foreign policy.

CA: Tougher?

BARRETT: Tougher and more appeasing. I would have launched an aggressive peace crusade. It is really awesome and awful and preposterous for the human race to be under this cloud of nuclear destruction. We should therefore propose gradual disarmament and control. But there is one and only one obstacle to this proposal, and that is the Soviet Union. What we want is frank, open international controls and inspections.

CA: Would it work?

BARRETT: The Russians would weasel in and out, but even if it didn't go through, it would be a tremendous propaganda coup with Western Europe, where they think of *us* as the destructive power and have for some time. Let's face it, the wind is from the East. We're in a period where socialistic rhetoric really holds the minds of the European people. That's one of the tragedies of our day. The West has no belief in itself, belief in freedom and liberty—in talking about it, yes, but not in giving up anything to protect it. By and large people are well fed and they're more affluent now than they ever were, so there are no particular goals. They can't have a world-historical imagination. Maybe we're reaching a turning point where what we have known as a liberal constitutional state, which came to exist at the end of the seventeenth century in England and was developed in the following centuries, may prove to have been one of the freaks in human history. It may be extinguished, and what humanity will know is totalitarianism. We tend to assume everything will go on as it has.

CA: Without our working at it?

BARRETT: Yes. I sound a little bit like Solzhenitsyn now, and I think he's right about motives. A civilization which loses its spiritual values can't stand up for something like liberty. This is why Vietnam was such a terrible war. I was against it from the start. The country wasn't ready for anything like that. It's too much of a demand on a comfort-loving country to defend its principles, which we may have to do.

CA: You've commented on the "cultural inflation" that we've undergone. You said we're "caught in a difficult period of transition, of reassessment and rediscovery of values." Do you think something positive will come of the reassessment?

BARRETT: It should. The potentialities are there. What we know as modernism has been operating now for a long time. It really began in the 1890s, and it's produced a body of works among which we can discriminate. I mean, there was experimentation and we can now distinguish where the experimentation was significant and where not. We can draw certain conclusions. For example, I think T. S. Eliot was absolutely right in saying that the experimentation that was significant always was traditional in some way. It was in tension with tradition, but it grew on the resources of tradition. Joyce, Eliot himself, Yeats, and Pound in literature, and then the painters—Picasso, Matisse, and so on. The early cubist painters in the 1910s and 1920s were working very deliberately against the traditional ordering of space, but they *respected* the tradition. And the tension against that tradition made the canvas more interesting because the tradition existed as its background.

Some of our young artists now have no traditional background to work against. Everything goes. There's an attitude of "It's new, let's try it." But that isn't what the earlier artists were doing. They were so saturated with tradition. Take Picasso. My God, he's like a one-man museum reincarnating the past, which is working both with him and against him.

CA: Would you like to talk about the book you're working on now?

BARRETT: I'm calling it *Death of the Soul.* It's a book that grew out of my teaching at New York University the last couple of years before I retired. It's about the fortunes of mind in modern philosophy from the seventeenth century to the present. Of course, it's the fortunes of our civilization at the same time, a civilization which becomes in some ways much more brilliant mentally, especially if you consider the structures of science and technology, but suddenly is unable to address the fact of mind and begins officially to depreciate it. The computer is one facet of it. It's created by the human mind, but suddenly is being used as a way to deflate the human mind. I'm just trying to carry this along and see where it will take me. It's a kind of analytical thematic history—the exploration of one theme in the development of the last three centuries, and the question of where it will leave us.

CA: And then a novel, maybe?

BARRETT: Yes, I'd like to write a novel. I'll have to get me a literary agent for it.

CA: You've never had an agent? I suppose you haven't needed one.

BARRETT: I thought I didn't at the start, but you really need one all the way along. Publishers are the enemy of writers. Edmund Wilson said to me, "No self-respecting writer should die without having taken at least two advances from publishers for work he never completes!"

BIOGRAPHICAL/CRITICAL SOURCES: William Barrett, *Irrational Man: A Study in Existential Philosophy,* Doubleday-Anchor, 1958; *Saturday Review,* September 6, 1958, February, 1982; *New York Times Book Review,* September 7, 1958, August 2, 1964, December 24, 1978, February 7, 1982; *New Republic,* October 27, 1958, October 14, 1972, October 14, 1978, March 17, 1982; *Nation,* December 6, 1958, May 11, 1970, February 27, 1982; *Commonweal,* December 26, 1958, June 8, 1979.

Newsweek, March 2, 1964, October 2, 1978, March 8, 1982; *America,* March 7, 1964, September 9, 1972, June 5, 1982; *Christian Science Monitor,* March 19, 1964; *New York Review of Books,* April 2, 1964, March 22, 1979; *Canadian Forum,* April, 1965.

Barrett, *Time of Need: Forms of Imagination in the Twentieth Century,* Harper, 1972; *Best Sellers,* August 1, 1972; *New York Times,* September 27, 1972, February 4, 1982, May 24, 1982; *Commentary,* December, 1972, June, 1974, September, 1974, March, 1976, September, 1976, November, 1976; *New Leader,* February 5, 1973, March 22, 1982; Barrett, *The Illusion of Technique: A Search for Meaning in a Technological Civilization,* Doubleday-Anchor, 1978; *Listener,* February 16, 1978; *Time,* September 4, 1978; *Chronicle Review,* November 13, 1978; *Chicago Tribune Book World,* December 10, 1978; *Los Angeles Times Book Review,* January 28, 1979, April 18, 1982; *National Review,* March 2, 1979, April 16, 1982; *Review of Metaphysics,* June, 1979; *Observer,* June 24, 1979; *Horizon,* September, 1979; *New Statesman,* September 28, 1979.

Contemporary Sociology, January, 1980; *Theology Today,* April, 1980; Barrett, *The Truants: Adventures among the Intellectuals,* Doubleday-Anchor, 1982; *Partisan Review,* Volume XLIX, number 3, 1982; *Washington Post Book World,* February 28, 1982.

—Sketch by James G. Lesniak

—Interview by Jean W. Ross and Walter W. Ross

*   *   *

BARRIO, Raymond   1921-

PERSONAL: Born August 27, 1921, in West Orange, N.J.; son of Saturnino and Angelita (Santos) Barrio; married Yolanda Sanchez, February 2, 1957; children: Angelita, Gabriel, Raymond, Jr., Andrea, Margarita. *Education:* Attended University of Southern California, 1941-43, and Yale University, 1943-44; University of California, Berkeley, B.A., 1947; Art Center College of Los Angeles, B.P.A., 1952. *Politics:* Humanist. *Religion:* Humanist. *Address:* P.O. Box 1076, Guerneville, Calif. 95446.

CAREER: Artist, art teacher, and writer. Former teacher of art in Los Angeles adult schools in Burbank, and Ventura College; art instructor at University of California, Santa Barbara, 1963-65, West Valley College, 1969-72, De Anza College, 1972, and Skyline College, 1972; currently teaching art history at Foothill College. Owner and operator of Ventura Press. Has exhibited art work at numerous showings. *Military service:* U.S. Army, 1943-46; served in Europe. *Awards, honors:* Creative Arts Institute faculty grant, University of California, 1964-65.

WRITINGS—All self-illustrated; all published by Ventura, except as indicated: *The Big Picture,* 1967; *Experiments in Modern Art,* Sterling, 1968; *Art: Seen,* 1968; *The Plum Plum Pickers,* 1969; *Selections from Walden,* 1970; *Prism/67,* 1970; *The Fisherman's Dwarf,* 1970; *Mexico's Art and Chicano Artists,* 1975; *The Devil's Apple Corps,* 1976. Contributor to anthologies. Contributor of weekly column, "Barrio's Political Estuary," to local and national periodicals; also contributor of articles to art magazines and fiction to literary quarterlies.

WORK IN PROGRESS: Two novels, *Carib Blue* and *Americus.*

SIDELIGHTS: When Raymond Barrio's novel *The Plum Plum Pickers* was turned down by every publishing house to which he offered it, he published it himself. In less than two years the "social and proletarian" novel, as Adorna Walia calls it in *Bilingual Journal,* was an underground classic and had sold more than 10,000 copies. At that point Harper & Row Publishers, Inc. took another look at Barrio's story of a Chicano migrant family and published it. Since then *The Plum Plum Pickers* has sold 22,000 copies and has been included in sixteen high school and college level anthologies. Barrio repurchased the rights to the book in 1976.

In examining the lives of Manuel Guttierrez, his family, and the other migrant workers, Barrio has given the reader "a study of the persistent exploitation of the stoopworkers, the migrant laborers in Santa Clara County," writes Walia. "Barrio has an unusually good understanding of the psychology of groveling foremen and managers who maintain their positions by oppressing those below them. He skillfully employs irony when he writes of the 'clear' consciences of Anglo executives and growers who sleep peacefully unaware of the misery of the migrants in their orchards because they leave the most sordid tasks to their Mexican overseers." Barrio, comments Linda Gray in the *Penninsula Bulletin,* "with uncompromising clarity, opens up the lives of these people for our eyes; their fears, hopes, stagnant misery and self-doubt." Adds Walia: "Barrio examines these marginal lives that are lived almost on a subterranean level. He understands the plight of the Chicanos."

In a particularly telling passage of *The Plum Plum Pickers* Barrio details the frustration the migrant worker feels: "The competition was not between pickers and growers, . . . it was between pickers. . . . Between the poor and the hungry, the desperate and the hunted, the slave and the slave, slob against slob, the depraved and himself. You were your own terrible boss. That was the cleverest part of the whole thing. The picker his own bone picker, his own willing built-in slave driver. Pick fast, pick hard, pick furious, pick, pick, pick. They didn't need straw bosses studying your neck to see if you kept bobbing up and down to keep your picking pace up. Like the barn-stupid chicken, you drove yourself to do it.''

The weight of *The Plum Plum Pickers* goes beyond its examination of the migrant life and becomes an indictment of the economic system that perpetuates the exploitation of the migrants, the Chicanos, and the illegal aliens who are often recruited to do the picking. ''*The Plum Plum Pickers* is both an ode to and a denunciation of California and the United States—an ode because California has some of the most fertile land in the world, and a denunciation because of the labor exploitation by the agricombines which perpetuate the migrant slavery,'' states Walia. ''Everyone gets rich from the fertile lands of California except the pickers. The corporation heads view the migrants as refuse.'' However, Gray notes, despite *The Plum Plum Pickers*'s strong indictment of the way in which migrant workers are treated and ''although deep with sadness, the book avoids moroseness through its fine satire of the local growers and politicians. A meeting of 'socially-conscious' corporation wives and a governor being dubbed 'Howlin' Mad' are good examples.''

Barrio is also praised for his skillful manipulation of language in *The Plum Plum Pickers*. ''Barrio's language is lyrical, a stream of consciousness that gathers poetic momentum through use of newscopy, graffiti, and excerpts from a government pamphlet of 'How to Pick Canning Tomatoes,''' says Gray. Walia considers ''the dialogues that imitate the speech of the migrant workers [to be] particularly effective, because of their black humor. As his workers speak, they often garble their words, and their malapropisms are humorous in an ironic way. Through dialogue, Barrio reveals the twisted thinking of landowners and company owners; their rationalizations and self-justifications. He apes the language of American politicians exposing them in all their hypocrisy.''

As evidenced in *The Plum Plum Pickers*, Barrio is concerned with inequalities he perceives in a capitalist system. In a letter to *CA* he said: ''Our modern America is suffering from a hideous disease called superaffluence. Mechanization, specialization, and modern technology are all linked together, eroding and destroying America's fine moral spirit. American multinational corporations conspire to drain all the resources they can rob from Third World countries, causing their misery, underdevelopment, and famine.

''Young writers coming through our schools see the tremendous production of great blockbuster million-dollar best sellers. Some use up great amounts of energy trying to figure out how to jump aboard that luscious circus wagon. It can be done, by a very few, but the price is devastating—the destruction of one's very soul.

''Young writers are the key to humanity's survival. As a lifelong teacher, artist, and writer, I do my best to persuade young people coming up to ignore the siren ululations of the money merchant, and to learn to listen to [their] own private drummer. To thine own self be true. Integrity above all. The most ignorant rural dweller can possess more integrity than the head of a great corporation—and often does. Therein lies the hope a young person needs to carry out his dreams, visions, ideals, and mission.

''To the question, 'What do you hope to achieve through the books you write?' my answer is: the salvation of humanity. Nothing less. I would hope that would serve as a role model for the idealistic young.''

The Plum Plum Pickers has been translated into German.

BIOGRAPHICAL/CRITICAL SOURCES: Raymond Barrio, *The Plum Plum Pickers*, Ventura, 1969; *Top of the News*, January, 1969; *Penninsula Bulletin*, December 11, 1976; *Bilingual Journal*, fall, 1982.

*   *   *

BARTH, Fredrik 1928-

PERSONAL: Born December 22, 1928, in Leipzig, Germany; son of Thomas Fredrik (a professor) and Randi (Thomassen) Barth; married Unni Wikan (an anthropologist), January 30, 1974. *Education:* University of Chicago, M.A., 1949; Cambridge University, Ph.D., 1957. *Home:* Roedkleivfaret 16, Oslo 3, Norway. *Office:* Ethnographic Museum, Frederiks Gt. 2B, Oslo 1, Norway.

CAREER: University of Bergen, Bergen, Norway, professor of social anthropology, 1961-72; University of Oslo, Oslo, Norway, professor of ethnography, 1973—. Visiting professor at Columbia University, 1961, University of Khartoum, 1963-64, and Yale University, 1972. Consultant to UNESCO, Food and Agriculture Organization, and United Nations Development Programme. *Member:* Royal Anthropological Institute of Great Britain (honorary fellow; life member), Norwegian Academy of Sciences, Danish Academy of Sciences, Association of Social Anthropologists of the Commonwealth, Phi Beta Kappa.

WRITINGS: Principles of Social Organization in Southern Kurdistan, University of Oslo Press, 1953; *Political Leadership among Swat Pathans*, Athlone Press, 1959; *Nomads of South Persia*, Little, Brown, 1961; *Ethnic Groups and Boundaries*, Allen & Unwin, 1969.

Ritual and Knowledge among the Baktaman of New Guinea, Yale University Press, 1975; *Scale and Social Organization*, Universitets Forlaget, 1978; *Selected Essays*, Routledge & Kegan Paul, Volume I: *Process and Form in Social Life*, 1981, Volume II: *Features of Person and Society in Swat*, 1981; *Sohar: Culture and Society in an Omani Town*, Johns Hopkins University Press, 1983. Contributor to numerous journals.

WORK IN PROGRESS: The Last Wali of Swat, a biography and history of the state of Swat and its ruler; field research in Indonesia aiming at the study of cultural variation and integration.

*   *   *

BASILE, Joseph 1912-

PERSONAL: Born May 7, 1912, in Brussels, Belgium; son of Augustin and Marie (Amato) Basile; married Betty Delmoitiez, May 25, 1951; children: Marina. *Education:* University of Brussels, Doctorate in Electrical Engineering, 1934. *Religion:* Roman Catholic. *Home:* 3 Avenue de Meise, Brussels, Belgium.

CAREER: Ateliers Basile S.A. (electrical manufacturing firm), Brussels, Belgium, general manager, 1935—; University of Louvain, Louvain, Belgium, professor of industrial design and social science for engineers, 1962—. Consular judge, Brussels Tribunal. President of economic committee, European Council for Electrical Appliances. Conducts workshops for multinational companies, including International Business Machines (IBM) International. *Member:* Cercle Royal Gaulois. *Awards, honors:* Commander, Order of St. Maurice and Lazare (Italy); Commander, Order of St. Sylvestre; Grand Officer, Order of Leopold II, and Chevalier, Order of the Crown (both Belgium).

WRITINGS: La Formation Culturelle des Cadres et des Dirigeants, Marabout, 1965, translation by Betty F. Adler published as *The Cultural Development of Managers, Executives, and Professionals,* Helicon, 1968; *Les Atouts de l'Europe,* Fayard, 1971; *Croissance 3: Les trois composants de notre future,* Gerard, 1972; *Les Sept Colonnes du Futur,* Renaissance du Livre, 1975; *Echeance 2000,* Renaissance du Livre, 1978; *Il se passe quelque chose du cote de Homme,* Renaissance du Livre, 1980; *Face ae l'Imprevisible,* Renaissance du Livre, 1982.

SIDELIGHTS: Joseph Basile explains to *CA* that in all his writings and speeches he "tries to conciliate and harmonize the three dimensions of human being: knowledge, behaviour, and interior sensibility." *Avocational interests:* Collecting books (many of which he custom-binds), painting, study of philosophy, literature, and history.

*   *   *

BASTIN, J(ohn) S(turgus)   1927-

PERSONAL: Born January 30, 1927, in Melbourne, Australia; son of William Henry and Dora (Wentman) Bastin; married Jane Margaret Andrews, June 22, 1949; married Rita Violet Elliott, July 7, 1966; children: (first marriage) Christopher, Jennifer; (second marriage) Mark, Marianne. *Education:* University of Melbourne, B.A. and M.A., 1950; University of Leiden, D.Litt., 1954; Oxford University, D.Phil., 1955. *Politics:* Conservative. *Religion:* Methodist. *Home:* Denstone, Berry Lane, Chorleywood, Hertfordshire, England. *Office:* School of Oriental and African Studies, University of London, Malet St., London WC1E 7HP, England.

CAREER: University of Queensland, Brisbane, Australia, lecturer in history, 1955-56; Australian National University, Canberra, fellow in Pacific history, 1956-59; University of Malaya, Kuala Lumpur, Federation of Malaya (now Malaysia), professor of history, 1959-63; University of London, School of Oriental and African Studies, London, England, reader in the modern history of Southeast Asia, 1963—. Fellow at Netherlands Institute for Advanced Studies, 1971-72; visiting professor at Flinders University of South Australia, 1975. *Member:* Royal Asiatic Society (Malaysian branch; honorary member).

WRITINGS: Raffles' Ideas on the Land Rent System in Java, Nijhoff, 1954; *Raffles in Java and Sumatra,* Clarendon Press, 1957; *Essays on Indonesian and Malayan History,* Eastern Universities Press (Singapore), 1961; *The British in West Sumatra, 1685-1825,* University of Malaya Press, 1965; (editor with Robin Winks) *Malaysia: Selected Historical Readings,* Oxford University Press (Kuala Lumpur), 1966; *The Emergence of Modern Southeast Asia,* Prentice-Hall, 1967; (with T. E. Smith) *Malaysia,* Oxford University Press, 1967; (with Harry J. Benda) *A History of Modern Southeast Asia,* Prentice-Hall, 1968, 2nd edition, 1977; *The Raffles Drawings,* Oxford University Press, 1978; (with P. Rohatgi) *Nineteenth Century Prints and Illustrated Books of Indonesia,* Spectrum, 1979; *Prints of Southeast Asia in the India Office Library,* H.M.S.O., 1979. General editor, "Oxford in Asia" historical reprint series. Contributor to history journals in the Netherlands, Singapore, Australia, and elsewhere.

WORK IN PROGRESS: Research on Sir Stamford Raffles and the study of natural history in Indonesia and Malaysia in the early nineteenth century.

BATES, Robert H(inrichs)   1942-

PERSONAL: Born December 5, 1942, in Brooklyn, N.Y.; son of David H. (a physician) and Lucy (Thomas) Bates; married Margaret Rouse (a college administrator), June 6, 1964; children: Elizabeth. *Education:* Haverford College, B.A. (summa cum laude), 1964; Massachusetts Institute of Technology, Ph.D., 1969. *Office:* Division of Social Sciences, California Institute of Technology, Pasadena, Calif. 91125.

CAREER: California Institute of Technology, Pasadena, assistant professor, 1969-76, associate professor of social sciences, 1976—. *Member:* American Political Science Association, African Studies Association, Phi Beta Kappa. *Awards, honors:* Recipient of fellowships from Woodrow Wilson National Fellowship Foundation, 1964-65, Center for International Studies at Massachusetts Institute of Technology, 1969, Social Science Research Council, 1969-70, National Institutes of Health, 1971-73, National Science Foundation, 1977-79 and 1983-84, and Social Science Research Council, 1983.

WRITINGS: Unions, Parties, and Political Development, Yale University Press, 1971; *Patterns of Uneven Development,* Graduate School of International Studies, University of Denver, 1974; *Rural Responses to Industrialization,* Yale University Press, 1976; (with Michael Lofchie) *Agricultural Development in Africa,* Praeger, 1980; *Markets and States in Tropical Africa: The Political Basis of Agricultural Policies,* University of California Press, 1981; *Essays on the Political Economy of Rural Africa,* Cambridge University Press, 1983. Contributor of chapters to books; contributor to political science and African studies journals.

WORK IN PROGRESS: Research on peasant politics, rural development, and agricultural development.

BIOGRAPHICAL/CRITICAL SOURCES: Times Literary Supplement, February 26, 1982.

*   *   *

BATTCOCK, Gregory   1938-1980

PERSONAL: Born July 2, 1938, in New York, N.Y.; died December 25, 1980, in San Juan, Puerto Rico; son of Gregory J.B. and Elizabeth B. Battcock. *Education:* Michigan State University, A.B.; Hunter College (now Hunter College of the City University of New York), M.A.; Academia de Belli Arti, Rome, certificate; New York University, doctorate in art history, 1979.

CAREER: Fairleigh Dickenson University, Teaneck Campus, Teaneck, N.J., associate professor of art history; William Paterson College, Wayne, N.J., professor of art history, beginning 1970. E. P. Dutton and Co., New York, N.Y., general editor, documents in modern criticism, 1973-76. Artist; work has been exhibited in New York City. Adjunct professor, New York University, beginning 1975. Member of board of trustees, Bronx Museum of the Arts. *Member:* International Air Transport Association.

WRITINGS—All published by Dutton: (Compiler) *Idea Art: A Critical Anthology,* 1973; (compiler) *New Ideas in Art Education: A Critical Anthology,* 1973; *Why Art: Casual Notes on the Aesthetics of the Immediate Past,* 1977.

Editor: *The New Art: A Critical Anthology,* 1965, revised edition, 1973; *The New American Cinema: A Critical Anthology,* 1967; *Minimal Art: A Critical Anthology,* 1968; *Super Realism: A Critical Anthology,* 1975; *New Artists Video: A Critical An-*

thology, 1978; *Breaking the Sound Barrier: A Critical Anthology of the New Music,* 1981.

New York correspondent, *Art and Artists;* correspondent, *Domus.* Contributor to *Film Culture, Soho News, Art in America, Projekt,* and to art education journals. Editor, *Arts* (magazine), beginning 1973.

WORK IN PROGRESS: A book on art theory; a book on narrative art.†

* * *

BAUER, Marion Dane 1938-

PERSONAL: Born November 20, 1938, in Oglesby, Ill.; daughter of Chester (a chemist) and Elsie (a kindergarten teacher; maiden name, Hempstead) Dane; married Ronald Bauer (an Episcopal priest), June 25, 1959; children: Peter Dane, Elisabeth Alison. *Education:* Student at La Salle-Peru-Oglesby Junior College, 1956-58, and University of Missouri, 1958-59; University of Oklahoma, B.A., 1962. *Politics:* Democrat. *Religion:* Episcopalian. *Home:* 13908 McGinty Rd., Minnetonka, Minn. 55343. *Agent:* Carol Mann Literary Agency, 168 Pacific St., Brooklyn, N.Y. 11201.

CAREER: High school English teacher in Waukesha, Wis., 1962-64; Hennepin Technical Center, Minneapolis, Minn., instructor in creative writing for adult education program, 1975-78; instructor at University of Minnesota Continuing Education for Women, 1978—, and Institute of Children's Literature, 1982—. *Member:* Authors Guild of Authors League of America, Society of Children's Book Writers. *Awards, honors:* *Foster Child* was selected as a Gold Kite Honor Book by the Society of Children's Book Writers, 1979.

WRITINGS—Novels for children, except as indicated; all published by Clarion Books: *Shelter from the Wind,* 1976; *Foster Child,* 1977; *Tangled Butterfly* (young adult novel), 1980; *Rain of Fire,* 1983.

WORK IN PROGRESS: Writing Fiction for Young People, a how-to book; a juvenile novel written in the first person about an adopted girl.

SIDELIGHTS: Marion Dane Bauer writes *CA:* "I write for children because there is a child in me who refuses to be subjugated into all the proper forms of adulthood. I write for children because such writing allows me to deal with all my old feeling issues in a context that approximates the original experience. I write for children because I figured, when I began, that if I wrote what was acceptable for children and managed to get published, I would still be acceptable to my parents and to my own children. I write for children because there is something in the inner workings of my brain which returns, always, to origins and to the form underlying form. I write for children because I like children, especially the twelve year olds I return to most often. They are so beautiful in that moment, so knowing and so innocent in the same breath. I write for children because I think children are important, not only for what they will be tomorrow—which is what they are usually trumpeted for—but for what they are today."

* * *

BAUER, Raymond A(ugustine) 1916-1977

PERSONAL: Born September 7, 1916, in Chicago, Ill.; died July 9, 1977, in Cambridge, Mass.; son of William Henry and Anna Barbara (Diedrich) Bauer; married Alice Haugh, June 12, 1941 (died, 1965); married Katharine Goldthwaite Dorr Clark, April 30, 1966; children: (first marriage) Linda Carol (Mrs. Donald H. Sibley). *Education:* Illinois Institute of Technology, student, 1936-38; Northwestern University, B.S. (with highest distinction), 1943; Harvard University, M.A., 1948, Ph.D., 1950. *Home:* 16 Highland St., Cambridge, Mass. 02138. *Office:* Harvard University, Graduate School of Business Administration, Boston, Mass. 02163.

CAREER: Crane Co., Chicago, Ill., chemical analyst, 1936-44; Harvard University, Cambridge, Mass., research assistant, 1947-48, Russian Research Center, fellow, 1948-50, lecturer in social psychology, and research associate, 1950-55; Massachusetts Institute of Technology, Cambridge, associate professor of social psychology, 1955-57; Harvard University, Graduate School of Business Administration, Boston, Mass., 1957-77, Ford Foundation visiting professor, 1957-60, professor, beginning 1960, became Joseph C. Wilson professor. Research associate, Center for International Studies, 1953-57; fellow, Center for Advanced Studies in Behavioral Sciences, 1955-56; member of the steering committee, National Advertising Review Board, 1972-74. Consultant, National Goals Research Staff, White House, 1969-70. *Military service:* U.S. Naval Reserve, 1944-46, Russian language officer, attained rank of lieutenant (junior grade).

MEMBER: American Academy of Arts and Sciences (fellow), American Psychological Association, Eastern Psychological Association, Massachusetts Psychological Association (president, 1964-66), American Sociological Society, American Marketing Association, American Association of Public Opinion Research (president, 1965-66), National Academy of Engineering, Phi Beta Kappa. *Awards, honors:* Co-winner of Woodrow Wilson Foundation Book Award, 1964, for *American Business and Public Policy: The Politics of Foreign Trade.*

WRITINGS: The New Man in Soviet Psychology, Harvard University Press, 1952; (with Edward Wasiolek) *Nine Soviet Portraits,* Wiley, 1955, reprinted, Greenwood Press, 1979; (with Alex Inkeles and Clyde Kluckhohn) *How the Soviet System Works: Cultural, Psychological, and Social Themes,* Harvard University Press, 1956; (with Inkeles) *The Soviet Citizen: Daily Life in A Totalitarian Society,* Harvard University Press, 1959.

(Editor) *Some Views on Soviet Psychology,* American Psychological Association, 1962, reprinted, Greenwood Press, 1975; (with Ithiel de Sola Pool and Lewis Anthony Dexter) *American Business and Public Policy: The Politics of Foreign Trade,* Atherton, 1963, 2nd edition, 1972; (editor) *Social Indicators,* M.I.T. Press, 1966; (editor with Kenneth J. Gergen) *The Study of Policy Formation,* Free Press, 1968; (with Stephen A. Greyser) *Advertising in America: The Consumer View,* Graduate School of Business Administration, Harvard University, 1968; (with Richard S. Rosenbloom and Laure Sharp) *Second-order Consequences: A Methodological Essay on the Impact of Technology,* M.I.T. Press, 1969.

(With Scott M. Cunningham) *Studies in the Negro Market,* Marketing Science Institute, 1970; (with Robert D. Buzzell and Stephen A. Greyser) *Presentations by Marketing Science Institute Associates to F.T.C. Hearings on Advertising,* Marketing Science Institute, 1971; (with Dan K. Fenn Jr.) *The Corporate Social Audit,* Russell Sage Foundation, 1972; (editor with Meinolf Dierkes) *Corporate Social Accounting,* Praeger, 1973; *The Obstinate Audience,* Atherton, 1976; (with Robert W. Ackerman) *Corporate Social Responsibility: Text and Cases,* Reston, 1976; (with Ackerman) *Corporate Social Responsiveness: The Modern Dilemma,* Reston, 1976.

Also author of technical reports for the Human Resources Research Institute, the Office of Economic Opportunity, and the Harvard Graduate School of Business Administration and Center for International Studies. Contributor to proceedings; also contributor to professional journals, including *Harvard Business Review, Journal of Social Issues,* and *Business and Society Review.*

OBITUARIES: New York Times, July 11, 1977.†

*   *   *

BAUS, Herbert M(ichael) 1914-

PERSONAL: Surname rhymes with "house"; born March 29, 1914, in Indianapolis, Ind.; son of Frank R. and Lenore (O'Connor) Baus; married Ruth Brumme, July 11, 1937 (divorced); married Helene Walther, December 23, 1952. *Education:* University of California, Los Angeles, A.B., 1936. *Politics:* Republican. *Home:* 549 Buenos Aires, San Clemente, Calif. 92672.

CAREER: Reporter for newspapers in Washington, D.C., and Los Angeles, Calif., 1933-37; Chamber of Commerce, Los Angeles, director of public relations, 1937-42; Downtown Business Men's Association, Los Angeles, general manager and promotion director, 1942-43; public relations counsel, Los Angeles, 1946-48; Baus & Ross (public relations consultants), Los Angeles, partner, 1948-69; restaurant critic, *Orange County Register,* 1977—. *Military service:* U.S. Army Air Forces, 1943-45.

WRITINGS: Publicity: How to Plan, Produce and Place It, Harper, 1942; *Public Relations at Work,* Harper, 1948; *Publicity in Action,* Harper, 1954; (with William B. Ross) *Politics Battle Plan,* Macmillan, 1968; *Expert's Crossword Puzzle Dictionary,* Doubleday, 1972; *How to Wine Your Way to Good Health,* Mason & Lipscomb, 1973; *Master Crossword Puzzle Dictionary,* Doubleday, 1981; *Best Restaurants of Orange County,* 101 Productions, 1982. Contributor to national magazines.

AVOCATIONAL INTERESTS: Chess, swimming, words, wine.

*   *   *

BAUSCH, William J. 1929-

PERSONAL: Born March 3, 1929, in Jamesburg, N.J.; son of Charles J. (a baker) and Colette (Perdoni) Bausch. *Education:* St. Mary's College of Maryland, A.B., 1951; St. Mary's Seminary and University, Baltimore, S.T.B., 1955. *Address:* Hwy. 34, Colts Neck, N.J. 07722.

CAREER: Roman Catholic priest. Parish priest and teacher in New Monmouth, Keyport, and Maple Shade, N.J., 1955-69; parish priest at St. Benedict's Church, Hazlet, N.J., 1969-73, and St. Mary's Church, Colts Neck, N.J., 1973—.

WRITINGS—Published by Fides: *A Boy's Sex Life* (juvenile), 1969; *It Is the Lord!: Sin and Confession Revisited,* 1970; *Renewal and the Middle Catholic,* 1971.

Published by Twenty Third Publications: *Pilgrim Church,* 1973, revised edition, 1977; *Positioning: Belief in the Mid Seventies,* 1975; *A New Look at the Sacraments,* 1977, revised edition, 1983; *The Christian Parish: Whispers of the Risen Christ,* 1980; *Traditions, Tensions, Transitions in Ministry,* 1982; *Storytelling: Imagination and Faith: Nathan's Legacy,* 1984. Contributor to Catholic journals.

BAXTER, Craig 1929-
(David Dunbar)

PERSONAL: Born February 16, 1929, in Elizabeth, N.J.; son of William James (an engineer) and Grace (Craig) Baxter; married Carol Alice Stuart, September 17, 1955; children: Craig, Louise Stuart. *Education:* University of Pennsylvania, B.S., 1951, M.A., 1954, Ph.D., 1967; studied Hindi and Urdu at Foreign Service Institute, 1960-61. *Religion:* Plymouth Brethren. *Home:* 1923 Moore St., Huntingdon, Pa. 16652. *Office:* Department of Political Science, Juniata College, Huntingdon, Pa. 16652.

CAREER: U.S. Department of State, Foreign Service officer, 1956-80, program officer for International Educational Exchange Service, 1956-58, vice-consul in Bombay, India, 1958-60, political officer in New Delhi, India, 1961-64, deputy principal officer and political officer in Lahore, Pakistan, 1965-68, analyst for India, 1968-69, senior political officer for Pakistan and Afghanistan, 1969-71, political counselor in Accra, Ghana, 1974-76, and Dhaka, Bangladesh, 1976-78, officer-in-charge of international scientific relations for the Near East, South Asia, and Africa, 1978-80; United States Military Academy, West Point, N.Y., visiting professor, 1971-74; Mount Vernon College, Washington, D.C., lecturer in South Asian studies, 1981; Juniata College, Huntingdon, Pa., visiting professor of political science and diplomat-in-residence, 1981—.

Member of Research Committee on the Punjab, 1965—, National Seminar on Pakistan and Bangladesh, Columbia University, 1969-74, Pakistan Studies Development Committee, 1969-75, 1979—, and Bengal Studies Conference, 1982—; cochairman of South Asia panel, National Council on Foreign Languages and International Studies, 1980-81. Adjunct lecturer in history and international relations, Northern Virginia Center, University of Virginia, 1969-71; lecturer at a number of other universities, including Harvard University, Columbia University, and University of Pennsylvania. Consultant to National Foreign Estimate Center, U.S. Department of State, United States Information Agency, American Institute of Indian Studies, Asia Foundation, and Asia Society. *Military service:* United States Army, 1952-54. *Member:* American Foreign Service Association, Association for Asian Studies, Middle East Institute.

WRITINGS: The Jana Sangh: A Biography of an Indian Political Party, University of Pennsylvania Press, 1969; *District Voting Trends in India: A Research Tool,* Columbia University Press, 1969; *Bangladesh: A Profile,* Westview, in press.

Contributor: Donald E. Smith, editor, *South Asian Politics and Religion,* Princeton University Press, 1966; John Stoessinger, editor, *Divided Nations in a Divided World,* McKay, 1974; J. Henry Korson, editor, *Contemporary Problems of Pakistan,* E. J. Brill, 1974; Maureen Patterson, editor, *South Asian Library Resources in North America,* Inter-Documentation, 1975; Myron Weiner and John Osgood Field, editors, *Electoral Politics in the Indian States,* Volume IV: *Party Systems and Cleavages,* Manohar (Delhi), 1975; W. Howard Wriggins, editor, *Pakistan in Transition,* University of Islamabad Press, 1975; Ralph Braibanti and others, editors, *Pakistan: The Long View,* Duke University Press, 1976; W. Eric Gustafson, editor, *Pakistan and Bangladesh: Bibliographic Essays in the Social Sciences,* University of Islamabad Press, 1976; Frederick L. Shiels, editor, *Ethnic Separatism and World Politics,* University Press of America, in press. Also contributor to *Yearbook on Inter-*

national Affairs, 1973 and 1974. Contributor of articles, sometimes under pseudonym David Dunbar, to professional journals, including *Asian Survey, Journal of Asian Studies, World Today,* and *Journal of Asian and African Studies.*

WORK IN PROGRESS: Works on South Asian history and politics.

*   *   *

BAXTER, Ian F. G.

OFFICE: Faculty of Law, University of Toronto, Toronto, Ontario, Canada.

CAREER: Osgoode Hall Law School, Toronto, Ontario, director of commercial law program, 1963-66; University of Toronto, Toronto, professor of law, 1966—. Visiting professor at University of Louvain, North Atlantic Treaty Organization (NATO), 1967, and at University of Bristol, 1975-76. Director of family law project, Ontario Law Reform Commission, 1965-68.

WRITINGS: (Editor with Ivan R. Feltham) *Export Practice,* Carswell, 1964; *Essays on Private Law: Foreign Law and Foreign Judgments,* University of Toronto Press, 1966; *Law of Banking and the Canadian Bank Act,* Carswell, 2nd edition, 1968, 3rd edition published as *Law of Banking,* 1981; *Marital Property,* Lawyers Cooperative, 1973; (editor with Mary Eberts) *The Child and the Courts,* Carswell, 1978. Contributor to *Encyclopaedia Britannica.*

*   *   *

BEALL, James Lee   1924-

PERSONAL: Born December 13, 1924, in Detroit, Mich.; son of Harry (a millwright) and Myrtle (a minister; maiden name, Monville) Beall; married Anne Broyles, July 3, 1946; children: James Lee, Jr., Analee, John Patrick. *Home:* 716 Balfour Rd., Grosse Pointe, Mich. 48230. *Office:* Bethesda Missionary Temple, 7616 East Nevada, Detroit, Mich. 48234.

CAREER: Bethesda Missionary Temple, Detroit, Mich., minister, 1947—, currently pastor. Lecturer. *Military service:* U.S. Navy, 1943-46. *Awards, honors:* Th.D., Pioneer Theological Seminary, 1954; D.D., National Bible College, 1956.

WRITINGS: The School of the Holy Spirit, Whitaker House, 1971; *Let Us Make Man,* Whitaker House, 1972; *Rise to Newness of Life,* Evangel, 1974; *The Adventure of Fasting,* Revell, 1974; *Strong in the Spirit,* Revell, 1975.

How to Achieve Security, Confidence and Peace, Logos International, 1980; *Laying the Foundation,* Logos International, 1980; *My Pastor, My Shepherd,* Logos International, 1981. Contributing editor, *Logos,* 1975—.

WORK IN PROGRESS: Mother Was a Preacher.

AVOCATIONAL INTERESTS: Golf, tennis, racquetball.

*   *   *

BEARDSLEY, Richard K(ing)   1918-1978

PERSONAL: Born December 16, 1918, in Cripple Creek, Colo.; died June 10, 1978, in Ann Arbor, Mich.; son of Earl Parson and Alice (Smith) Beardsley; married Grace Cornog, April 11, 1942; children: Elizabeth K., Kelcy A., Margaret B. *Education:* University of California, Berkeley, A.B., 1939, Ph.D.,

1947. *Politics:* Democrat. *Office:* Department of Anthropology, University of Michigan, Ann Arbor, Mich. 48104.

CAREER: University of Minnesota—Twin Cities, Minneapolis, instructor in anthropology, 1947; University of Michigan, Ann Arbor, instructor, 1947-48, assistant professor, 1948-53, associate professor, 1954-59, professor of anthropology, 1960-78, director of Center for Japanese Studies, 1961-64, 1973-74. *Military service:* U.S. Naval Reserve, 1942-46; became lieutenant.

MEMBER: American Association for the Advancement of Science (fellow), American Anthropological Association (fellow), Society for American Archaeology, Association for Asian Studies (director, 1961-64), Japanese Ethnological Society, Phi Beta Kappa, Sigma Xi.

AWARDS, HONORS: Faculty fellow from Center for Japanese Studies, University of Michigan, at Library of Congress, 1948; Social Science Research Council fellow in Japan, 1950; Ford Foundation research fellow in Japan, 1953-54, 1964-65, and 1970; Guggenheim fellow in Spain, 1958-59; Carnegie Corporation fellow in Japan, 1964-65; National Science Foundation grant for research in Japan, 1974-75.

WRITINGS: (With John B. Cornell and Edward Norbeck) *Bibliographic Materials in the Japanese Language on Far Eastern Archaeology and Ethnology,* University of Michigan Press, 1950; (with J. W. Hall and R. E. Ward) *Village Japan,* University of Chicago Press, 1959; *Field Guide to Japan,* National Academy of Sciences, National Research Council, 1959; (editor with R. J. Smith) *Japanese Culture: Its Development and Characteristics,* Aldine, 1962; (editor) *Studies on Economic Life in Japan,* University of Michigan Press, 1964; (with Hall) *Twelve Doors to Japan,* McGraw, 1965; *Studies in Japanese History and Politics,* University of Michigan Press, 1967; (compiler with Nakano Takashi) *Japanese Sociology and Social Anthropology: A Guide to Japanese Reference and Research Materials,* University of Michigan Press, 1970. Contributor to *American Antiquity, Far Eastern Quarterly,* and *American Anthropologist.*

WORK IN PROGRESS: A restudy of *Village Japan* and field research in Japan.

SIDELIGHTS: Richard K. Beardsley's *Village Japan* was "a major contribution to American scholarship on Japan and the Japanese," according to Hyman Kublin in *Social Education.* Writing in the *New York Herald Tribune Book Review,* Hugh Burton called the book "a masterful study of a Japanese farm community. [It is] by far the best and most complete study of a Japanese community in a Western language." Joseph Bram wrote in *Library Journal* that *Village Japan* "has no rival in thoroughness of documentation and should be viewed at this juncture as the best available study of rural Japan."

BIOGRAPHICAL/CRITICAL SOURCES: Library Journal, May 15, 1959; *Christian Science Monitor,* August 17, 1959; *New York Herald Tribune Book Review,* September 5, 1959; *Social Education,* November, 1959.

OBITUARIES: New York Times, June 11, 1978.†

*   *   *

BECK, Aaron T(emkin)   1921-

PERSONAL: Born July 18, 1921, in Providence, R.I.; son of Harry S. and Elizabeth (Temkin) Beck; married Phyllis Harriet Whitman (a lawyer), June 4, 1950; children: Roy, Judith, Daniel, Alice. *Education:* Brown University, A.B. (magna cum laude), 1942; Yale University, M.D., 1946. *Home:* 406 Wynmere Rd., Wynnewood, Pa. 19096. *Office:* 133 South 36th St., Room 602, Philadelphia, Pa. 19104.

CAREER: Rhode Island Hospital, Providence, intern, 1946, resident in pathology, 1947; Cushing Veterans Administration Hospital, Framingham, Mass., resident in neurology, 1948, resident in psychiatry, 1949-50; Austen Riggs Center, Stockbridge, Mass., fellow, 1950-52; University of Pennsylvania, Philadelphia, 1954—, assistant professor, 1956-67, associate professor, 1967-70, professor of psychiatry, 1970—; Philadelphia General Hospital, Philadelphia, chief of section in department of psychiatry, 1958—. Member of visiting staff, Institute of the Pennsylvania Hospital, 1956—; consultant, Veterans Administration Hospital, Philadelphia, 1967—. *Military service:* U.S. Army, 1943-46, 1952-54; became captain. *Member:* American Psychiatric Association, American Academy of Psychoanalysis, Philadelphia County Medical Society, Philadelphia Psychiatric Society, Phi Beta Kappa.

WRITINGS: Depression: Clinical, Experimental, and Theoretical Aspects, Harper, 1967; *Diagnosis and Management of Depression,* University of Pennsylvania, 1973; *Prediction of Suicide,* Charles Press, 1974; *Cognitive Therapy and the Emotional Disorders,* International Universities Press, 1976; *Cognitive Therapy of Depression,* Guilford Press, 1979; *Anxiety and Phobias: Cognitive Approaches,* Basic Books, 1983. Contributor of more than eighty articles to professional journals.

*   *   *

BECKER, Gary S(tanley)   1930-

PERSONAL: Born December 2, 1930, in Pottsville, Pa.; son of Louis W. and Anna (Siskind) Becker; married Doria Slote, 1955 (deceased); married Guity Nashat, 1979; children: (first marriage) Judith Sarah, Catherine Jean. *Education:* Princeton University, A.B. (summa cum laude), 1951; University of Chicago, A.M., 1953, Ph.D., 1955. *Home:* 1308 East 58th St., Chicago, Ill. 60637. *Office:* 1126 East 59th St., Department of Economics, University of Chicago, Chicago, Ill. 60637.

CAREER: University of Chicago, Chicago, Ill., assistant professor of economics, 1954-57; Columbia University, New York, N.Y., assistant professor, 1957-58, associate professor, 1958-60, professor of economics, 1960-68, Arthur Lehman Professor of Economics, 1968-69; University of Chicago, visiting professor, 1969-70, university professor of economics, 1970—. Research associate, Economics Research Center and National Opinion Research Center. *Member:* Union Internationale pour l'Etude Scientifique de la Population, National Academy of Sciences, American Economic Association, American Statistical Association, Econometric Society, American Academy of Arts and Sciences, National Academy of Education, Mont Pelerin Society, Phi Beta Kappa. *Awards, honors:* W. S. Woytinsky Award from University of Michigan, 1964, for *Human Capital;* John Bates Clark Medal from American Economic Association, 1967; professional achievement award from University of Chicago Alumni Association, 1968.

WRITINGS: Economics of Discrimination, University of Chicago Press, 1957, 2nd edition, 1971; *Human Capital: A Theoretical and Empirical Analysis with Special Reference to Education,* Columbia University Press, 1964, 2nd edition, 1975; *Human Capital and the Personal Distribution of Income: An Analytical Approach,* University of Michigan, 1967; *Economic Theory,* Knopf, 1971; (editor with William M. Landes) *Essays in the Economics of Crime and Punishment,* Columbia University Press, 1974; (with Gilbert Ghez) *The Allocation of Time and Goods over the Life Cycle,* Columbia University Press, 1975; *The Economic Approach to Human Behavior,* University of Chicago Press, 1976; *A Treatise on the Family,* Harvard University Press, 1981. Also editor of *Essays in Labor Economics in Honor of H. Gregg Lewis,* 1976.

WORK IN PROGRESS: A study of economics of political behavior; an analysis of intergenerational mobility.

*   *   *

BEER, Edith Lynn   1930-
(Edith Lynn Hornik)

PERSONAL: Born November 4, 1930, in Zurich, Switzerland; naturalized U.S. citizen; daughter of Simon (a tobacco manufacturer) and Rosa (Bruell) Beer; married Josef Bernard Hornik (a machine tool engineer), February 9, 1958 (divorced, 1979); children: Robert Bernard, Abigail. *Education:* Simmons College, B.S., 1953; University of Lausanne, graduate study, 1954. *Address:* 865 First Ave., No. 6D, New York, N.Y.; and Treescape, Cluster 4, Unit 9A, East Hampton, N.Y. 11937.

CAREER: Free-lance writer. Has lectured on literature and creative writing; has appeared on television and radio programs. *Member:* Overseas Press Club, Authors Guild of Authors League of America, American Society of Journalists and Authors.

WRITINGS: (Under name Edith Lynn Hornik) *You and Your Alcoholic Parent,* Association Press, 1974; (under name Edith Lynn Hornik) *The Drinking Woman,* Association Press, 1977; *Over a Thousand Financial Terms You Should Have at Your Fingertips before You Invest,* Monarch, 1983. Author of "The Young World" in *Scarsdale Inquirer, Riverdale Press,* and *Patent Trader,* all 1964-67. Contributor to magazines and newspapers in the United States and abroad, including *Young Miss, Ingenue, McCall's, Woman's Day, Co-Ed, Living for Young Homemakers, New York Times, Neue Zuercher Zeitung,* and *Berlin Tagesblatt.*

SIDELIGHTS: Edith Lynn Beer told *CA:* "I am very much aware of the World War II era and of our silent 1950's student days. Right after World War II due to family circumstances I lived part of each year in Europe and part in the U.S.A. As a woman I came to be aware of the Napoleonic law versus the English law. Living partly in Switzerland before women had the right to vote in that country I became deeply conscious of the subtle differences of the American society's view of women and the European's outlook. I came to see that religion has nothing to do with God but is only a reflection of the society and political atmosphere we live in."

*   *   *

BELFIELD, Eversley (Michael Gallimore)   1918-

PERSONAL: Born September 10, 1918, in London, England; son of Frederick Bruce (an officer, Royal Navy) and Diana Anwyl (Vernon) Belfield; married Felicity Ann Hellaby, July 8, 1950; children: Gervase, Clare, Stephen, Lucy, Dominic. *Education:* Pembroke College, Oxford, M.A. (with second class honors), 1948. *Politics:* Apolitical. *Religion:* Roman Catholic. *Residence:* Beauchamp, Sark, Channel Islands.

CAREER: University of Southampton, Southampton, England, 1950-79, became senior lecturer in Department of Adult Education, lecturing mainly on international relations, war studies, and military history to officers in British Army in southern England and at overseas stations in Germany, Malta, and Cyprus. *Military service:* British Army, Royal Artillery, air observation pilot, 1939-46; became captain; mentioned in dispatches.

WRITINGS: (With Major General J. H. Parham) *Unarmed into Battle,* Warren & Son, 1956; *The Annals of the Addington Family,* Warren & Son, 1959; (with Major General H. Essame) *The North-West Europe Campaign,* Gale & Polden, 1962; (with Essame) *The Battle for Normandy,* Batsford, 1965; *Sieges,* Batsford, 1967, published as *Defy and Endure: Great Sieges of Modern History,* Crowell-Collier, 1968; *Oudenarde 1708,* Knight, 1972; *The Boer War,* Cooper, 1975; (with Essame and General Sir Brian Horrocks) *Corps Commander,* Sidgwick & Jackson, 1977; *The Queen's Dragoon Guards,* Leo Cooper, 1978. Contributor to *History of the Second World War.*

WORK IN PROGRESS: A biography of the Third Lord Carrington, Marquis of Lincolnshire, "Governor of New South Wales, 1885-90, Lord Chamberlain, 1892-95, a member of Campbell-Bannerman's and Asquith's cabinets, hereditary Lord Great Chamberlain, and a close personal friend from boyhood of the Prince of Wales, later Edward VII''; a private edition of the author's poems; an autobiography.

SIDELIGHTS: "I am now retired and living very happily on Sark," Eversley Belfield told *CA:* "[Sark] is one of the smallest states both in size and population, but the proportion of its five hundred inhabitants who are in its Parliament (the Chief Pleas) and who are graduates must be about the largest in the world. The extreme contrast between the island's life in the busy tourist summer months and the relatively isolated winter months is most stimulating. But perhaps Sark's greatest asset is the elemental nature of life where the sea, the sun, and the air are always the dominant factors; this environment makes a writer respond to emotions that can be recollected in relative tranquility.''

The Battle for Normandy has appeared in a French edition.

*   *   *

BELFIGLIO, Valentine J(ohn)   1934-

PERSONAL: Surname is pronounced Bell-*feel*-yo; born May 8, 1934, in Troy, N.Y.; son of Edmond L. (a pharmacist) and Mildred (Sherwood) Belfiglio; married Jane M. Searles, May 27, 1957 (divorced, October, 1969); children: Valentine E. *Education:* Union University, Albany, N.Y., B.S., 1956; University of Oklahoma, M.A., 1967, Ph.D., 1970. *Politics:* Republican. *Religion:* Roman Catholic. *Home:* 2707 Douglas, Apt. 107, Dallas, Tex. 75219. *Office:* Department of History and Government, Texas Woman's University, Denton, Tex. 76204.

CAREER: U.S. Air Force, hospital unit training officer, 1959-67, leaving service as captain; University of Oklahoma, Norman, instructor in political science, 1967-70; Texas Woman's University, Denton, assistant professor, 1970-77, associate professor of history and government, 1977—. *Member:* International Studies Association, American Political Science Association, Mensa.

WRITINGS: The Essentials of American Foreign Policy, Kendall-Hunt, 1971; *The United States and World Peace,* McCutchan, 1971; *American Foreign Policy,* University Press of America, 1979, 2nd edition, 1983; *The Italian Experience in Texas,* Eakin (Austin, Texas), 1983.

Contributor to professional publications, including *Strategic Digest, Rocky Mountain Social Science Journal, Asian Survey, Asian Studies, International Studies,* and *International Problems,* and to newspapers.

WORK IN PROGRESS: The preparation of biographical sketches of prominent Italo-Texans for the revised version of *The Handbook of Texas,* for Texas State Historical Society.

SIDELIGHTS: Valentine J. Belfiglio told *CA:* "The broad masses of the people can be moved to immediate action by the power of the spoken word. But the power of the written word is more long-lasting and can inspire the opinion-shaping elite of society to act, centuries after the Angel of Death has embraced the author.'' *Avocational interests:* Gourmet cooking, bridge, golf, sailing, travel (Europe and the Orient).

*   *   *

BELL, Carolyn
See RIGONI, Orlando (Joseph)

*   *   *

BELVEDERE, Lee
See GRAYLAND, Valerie (Merle Spanner)

*   *   *

BELZ, Carl   1937-

PERSONAL: Born September 13, 1937, in Camden, N.J.; son of Irvin Carl (in sales) and Ella (Engler) Belz; married second wife, Barbara Vetter, June 17, 1968; children: (first marriage) Melissa, Gretchen. *Education:* Princeton University, B.A., 1959, M.F.A., 1962, Ph.D., 1963. *Home:* 85 Ridge Rd., Waban, Mass. 02168. *Agent:* Julian Bach, Jr., 3 East 48th St., New York, N.Y. 10017. *Office:* Rose Art Museum, Brandeis University, Waltham, Mass. 02154.

CAREER: University of Massachusetts, Amherst, teacher of art history, 1963-65; Mills College, Oakland, Calif., teacher of art history, 1965-68; Brandeis University, Waltham, Mass., teacher of art history, 1968-74, director of Rose Art Museum, 1974—.

WRITINGS: The Story of Rock (on folk art), Oxford University Press, 1969, 2nd edition, 1972; *Cezanne,* McGraw, 1974; *Frank Stella: Metallic Reliefs,* Rose Art Museum, 1979; *Helen Frankenthaler: The 1950s,* Rose Art Museum, 1981; *Charles Garabedian: Twenty Years of Work,* Rose Art Museum, 1983.

AVOCATIONAL INTERESTS: Tennis.

BIOGRAPHICAL/CRITICAL SOURCES: New York Times Book Review, November 9, 1969.

*   *   *

BEN-AMOS, Dan   1934-

PERSONAL: Born September 3, 1934, in Tel Aviv, Israel; came to the United States in 1961; son of Zalman (a construction worker) and Rivka (Feinzilber) Ben-Amos; married Paula D. Girschick (an anthropologist), 1960; children: Ilana (daughter), Ariel (son). *Education:* Hebrew University of Jerusalem, B.A., 1961; Indiana University, M.A., 1964, Ph.D., 1967. *Home:* 539 East Durham St., Philadelphia, Pa. 19119. *Office:* Folklore and Folklife Program, University of Pennsylvania, Philadelphia, Pa. 19174.

CAREER: University of California, Los Angeles, assistant professor of anthropology, 1966-67; University of Pennsylvania, Philadelphia, assistant professor, 1967-70, associate professor, 1970-77, professor of folklore and folklife, 1977—, acting chairman of folklore and folklife program, 1973-74, chairman, 1982-84. Assistant professor at Indiana University, summer, 1970. Intern of Midwest Universities Consortium for International Activities, with field research in Benin City, Nigeria, 1965-66. Member of joint committee on African studies of Social Science Research Council, 1976.

MEMBER: International African Institute, International Association for Semiotic Studies, World Union of Jewish Studies, American Folklore Society (fellow), American Anthropological Association (fellow), African Studies Association. *Awards, honors:* Annual prize from Israeli Society for Folk Narrative Research, 1958-59; honorable mention from Chicago Folklore Competition, 1967, for ''Narrative Forms in the Haggadah: Structural Analysis''; grants from National Science Foundation, 1968, 1970, National Institute of Mental Health, 1968, and African Studies Association, 1971; fellowships from American Council of Learned Societies, 1972-73, and Guggenheim Foundation, 1975-76; NEA Fellowship, 1980-81.

WRITINGS: (With Dov Noy) *Folktales of Israel,* University of Chicago Press, 1963; (editor with Jerome R. Mintz, and translator) *In Praise of the Baal Shem Tov,* Indiana University Press, 1970; (editor with Kenneth S. Goldstein) *Thrice-Told Tales: Folktales from Three Continents,* Hammermill Paper Co., 1970; (with Goldstein) *Folklore: Performance and Communication,* Mouton, 1975; (editor) *New Theories in Oral Literature: Literary Forms in Social Context,* Tel Aviv University, 1975; *Sweet Words: Storytelling Events in Benin,* Institute for the Study of Human Issues, 1975; (editor) *Folklore Genres,* University of Texas Press, 1976; *Folklore in Context: Essays,* South Asia Books, 1982.

Contributor: Richard M. Dorson, editor, *African Folklore,* Doubleday, 1972; Americo Paredes and Richard Bauman, editors, *Toward New Perspectives in Folklore,* University of Texas Press, 1972; Linda Degh, Henry Glassie, and Felix Oinas, editors, *Folklore Today: A Festschrift for Richard M. Dorson,* Research Center for Language and Semiotic Studies, and Indiana University, 1976; (author of introduction) Bin-Gorion, editor, *Mimekor Yisrael: Classical Jewish Folktales,* Indiana University Press, 1976; Dorson, editor, *Folklore in the Modern World,* Mouton, 1978; Bernth Lindfors, editor, *Forms of Folklore in Africa,* University of Texas Press, 1977; Venetia Newall, editor, *Folklore Studies in the Twentieth Century,* Rowman & Littlefield, 1980; Dov Noy and Frank Talmage, editors, *Studies in Jewish Folklore,* Association for Jewish Studies, 1980.

Past associate editor of ''Monographs in Folklore and Folklife,'' University of Pennsylvania; editor of ''Translations in Folklore Studies and Texts,'' Institute for the Study of Human Issues; co-editor of American Folklore Society publication series, 1973. Contributor of more than fifty articles and reviews to scholarly journals. Associate editor of *Research in African Literatures;* member of advisory board of *Genre.*

*   *   *

BENFORD, Timothy B(artholomew) 1941-

PERSONAL: Born May 29, 1941, in Jersey City, N.J.; son of Timothy Bartholomew (a businessman) and Margaret (Luzzu) Benford; married Marilyn Fabula, September 15, 1962; children: Susan, Timothy. *Education:* Attended Rutgers University, 1960-61. *Home:* 1464 Whippoorwill Way, Mountainside, N.J. 07092.

CAREER: Bayonne Times, Bayonne, N.J., 1959-65, began as printer's devil, became journeyman printer; Hudson County Publishing and Printing, Bayonne, owner and printer, 1965-67; *Travel Weekly,* New York City, night editor, 1967-75; Travel Trade Publications, New York City, managing editor, 1975-78; vice-president of three public relations agencies, Ruder, Finn & Rotman, Manning, Selvage & Lee, and M. Silver Associates, beginning 1978, specializing in travel industry accounts and destination tourism. Served as police commissioner and Borough Council member (two terms), Mountainside, New Jersey. United Way chairman. *Member:* North Jersey Press Association (former president, vice-president, secretary, and treasurer).

WRITINGS: The World War II Quiz & Fact Book, Harper, Volume I, 1982, Volume II, 1984; *Hitler's Daughter* (novel), Pinnacle Books, 1983. Contributor of articles on travel, antique cars, politics, coins, and crime to Associated Press sportswire, *Travel & Leisure, New York Post, Hartford Courant,* and other publications.

WORK IN PROGRESS: A nonfiction book on World War II and three proposals for novels under discussion with publishers.

SIDELIGHTS: Timothy B. Benford told *CA:* ''I didn't start out with any burning desire to be a writer. . . . I think it is because I eventually found success with my books that I was able to be successful in public relations. . . . I'm not pretending that my books are literary masterpieces or that I'm some sort of deep-thinking, pipe-smoking type. My writing is a hobby, if you will, the thing I do to unwind from the routine.

''I get asked quite often what I would suggest to aspiring writers. Simply this: writing isn't hard, getting published is. . . . If you are going to attempt a novel go the route of least resistance. Become familiar with what the public is buying, what editors want, and write your first book to those markets. Then, after you've been published, you may be able to convince some publisher to publish the great American novel that is churning itself inside you.''

AVOCATIONAL INTERESTS: ''Heavy interest in history, detail and trivia''; historical autographs, coins, antique automobiles (once owned a modest collection), politics, the space program, motor racing, and reading.

*   *   *

BENNETT, Jay 1912-

PERSONAL: Born December 24, 1912, in New York, N.Y.; son of Pincus Shapiro (a businessman) and Estelle Bennett; married Sally Stern, February 2, 1937; children: Steven Cullen, Randy Elliott. *Education:* Attended New York University. *Home:* 402 Ocean Parkway, Brooklyn, N.Y. 11218.

CAREER: Writer and lecturer. Has worked as a farmhand, factory worker, lifeguard, mailman, salesman, and senior editor of an encyclopedia. *Wartime service:* English features writer and editor, Office of War Information, 1942-45. *Member:* Mystery Writers of America, Dramatists Guild, Writers Guild of America, Authors League of America. *Awards, honors:* Edgar Allan Poe Award from Mystery Writers of America for best juvenile mystery novel, 1974, for *The Long Black Coat,* and 1975, for *The Dangling Witness.*

WRITINGS: Catacombs, Abelard-Schuman, 1959; Death Is a Silent Room, Abelard-Schuman, 1965; Murder Money, Fawcett, 1963; Deathman, Do Not Follow Me (juvenile mystery), Meredith Press, 1968; The Deadly Gift (juvenile mystery), Meredith Press, 1969; The Killing Tree (juvenile mystery), F. Watts, 1972; Masks: A Love Story, F. Watts, 1972; The Long Black Coat (juvenile mystery), Delacorte, 1973; Shadows Offstage, Nelson, 1974; The Dangling Witness (juvenile mystery), Delacorte, 1974; Say Hello to the Hit Man, Delacorte, 1976; The Birthday Murderer, Delacorte, 1977; The Pigeon, Methuen, 1980, Avon, 1981; The Executioner, Avon, 1982; Slowly, Slowly, I Raise the Gun, Avon, 1983; I Never Said I Loved You, Avon, 1984.

Plays: "No Hiding Place" (three-act), first produced in New York at President Theatre, November 10, 1949; "Lions after Slumber" (three-act), first produced in London at Unity Theatre, June 2, 1951.

Also author of radio scripts, including "Miracle before Christmas" and "The Wind and Stars Are Witness," broadcast on major networks; author of television scripts for "Alfred Hitchcock Presents," "Crime Syndicated," "Wide, Wide World," "Cameo Theater," and "Monodrama Theatre."

SIDELIGHTS: Jay Bennett told CA: "I always look for a central character and then let him find the story for me. In a way, I embark upon a voyage of discovery. I constantly find myself surprised at the revelations that come through the unconsciousness and onto the page. However, this must be kept in mind, I have spent many long years learning my craft of writing, particularly that of the suspense genre. So this knowledge always comes into play.

"As to writing for young adults, I have come to know them and they have come to know me. My work for them has been translated into fourteen languages. I am particularly well received in Sweden. I respect my readers. I am a totally committed writer when I work for them. I know of no other way to function in the young adult field."

*   *   *

BENTLEY, Nicolas Clerihew 1907-1978

PERSONAL: Born June 14, 1907, in London, England; died, August 14, 1978; son of Edmund Clerihew (a writer) and Violet (Boileau) Bentley; married Barbara Hastings, 1934; children: one daughter. Education: Attended University College School and Heatherly School of Art. Home: Old School, Downhead, Shepton Mallet, Somerset, England.

CAREER: Artist and writer; co-founder and director of Andre Deutsch Ltd. (publisher), 1951-78. In early career, performed as a circus clown for six weeks and appeared as an extra in a number of films; also worked in publicity department of Shell Oil Co. for three years in late 1920s. Member: Society of Industrial Artists and Designers (fellow), Garrick Club.

WRITINGS: Die? I Thought I'd Laugh: A Book of Pictures, Metheun, 1936; (self-illustrated) Ballet-Hoo, Transatlantic, 1937; Time of My Life (autobiography), Transatlantic, 1937; Gammon and Espionage, Cresset, 1938; (self-illustrated) Week-end Wants of a Guest: A Memorandum Book, Cobden-Sanderson, 1938; Week-end Worries of a Hostess: A Memorandum Book, Cobden-Sanderson, 1938; (self-illustrated) Le Sport, Ryerson Press, 1939; Second Thoughts on First Lines, and Other Poems, Ryerson Press, 1939; Animal, Vegetable, and South Kensington: A Book of Pictures, Metheun, 1940, Transatlantic, 1942; The Tongue-Tied Canary (thriller), M. Joseph, 1949.

The Floating Dutchman (thriller), M. Joseph, 1950, Panther, 1971; How Can You Bear to Be Human?, Deutsch, 1957, Dutton, 1958; A Version of the Truth (autobiography), Deutsch, 1960; Third Party Risk, Penguin, 1961; Book of Birds, Transatlantic, 1965; The Victorian Scene: A Picture Book of the Period, 1837-1901, New York Graphic Society, 1968.

(Self-illustrated) Don't Do-It-yourself: A Fantasy for Exporters, British National Export Council, 1970; Golden Sovereigns, and Some of Lesser Value: From Boadicea to Elizabeth II, Mitchell Beazley, 1970, Silver Jubilee edition published as Silver Sovereigns, and Some of Greater Value: From Boadicea to Elizabeth II, 1978; The Events of That Week, St. Martin's, 1972; Nicolas Bentley's Tales from Shakespeare, Mitchell Beazley, 1972, Simon & Schuster, 1973; Edwardian Album: A Photographic Excursion into a Lost Age of Innocence, Viking, 1974; Inside Information, Deutsch, 1974; The History of the Circus, M. Joseph, 1977. Also author of Pay Bed, 1976.

Editor: (With Leonard Russell) The English Comic Album, M. Joseph, 1948; Frederick Bason, Diary, Wingate, 1950; Evan Esar, Treasury of Humorous Comic Quotations, Phoenix House, 1951; The Pick of Punch (multi-volume work), Deutsch, 1955-57; A Choice of Ornaments, Deutsch, 1959; Bergen Evans, Comfortable Words, Random House, 1962; W. H. Russell, Dispatches from the Crimea, 1854-1856, Hill & Wang, 1976; (and author of introduction) The Shell Book of Motoring Humour, M. Joseph, 1976. Also editor of Images of Elsewhere, 1977.

Illustrator: George Mikes, Eureka!, Ekdoseis Galaxia, 1971; Hilaire Belloc, Cautionary Verses, Knopf, 1973; Lawrence Durrell, The Best of Antrobus, Faber, 1975; Tim Carew, How the Regiments Got Their Nicknames, Cooper, 1975; T. S. Eliot, Old Possum's Book of Practical Cats, Faber, 1975; Roy Fuller, Poor Roy, Deutsch, 1977; Rees Howell Gronow, Selections from "The Reminiscences of Captain Gronow," Folio Society, 1977; Humphry Berkeley, The Life and Death of Rochester Sneath: A Youthful Frivolity, Hamish Hamilton, 1980; Edmund Clerihew Bentley, The Complete Clerihews of E. Clerihew Bentley, Oxford University Press, 1981. Contributor of regular cartoon to Daily Mail in 1960s.

AVOCATIONAL INTERESTS: Music, looking at paintings, travel.

BIOGRAPHICAL/CRITICAL SOURCES: Nicolas Clerihew Bentley, Time of My Life, Transatlantic, 1937; Bentley, A Version of the Truth, Deutsch, 1960.

OBITUARIES: Publishers Weekly, September 18, 1978.†

*   *   *

BERDIE, Ralph F(reimuth) 1916-1974

PERSONAL: Born June 21, 1916, in Chicago, Ill.; died August 21, 1974; son of Sidney S. (a merchant) and Enid (Freimuth) Berdie; married Frances Strong (an administrative assistant), August 6, 1942; children: Phyllis (Mrs. Imre Somlai), Douglas, Carl. Education: University of Minnesota, B.A., 1938, M.A., 1939, Ph.D., 1942. Office: 408 Morrill Hall, University of Minnesota, Minneapolis, Minn. 55455.

CAREER: University of Minnesota—Twin Cities, Minneapolis, assistant to director of testing bureau, 1941-42; counselor and assistant professor of psychology, 1942-43; George Peabody College for Teachers, Nashville, Tenn., associate professor of psychology, 1946-47; University of Minnesota—Twin Cities, associate professor, 1947-49, professor of psychology,

1964-74, director of student life studies, 1965-71, coordinator of admissions, registration, and student records, beginning 1971. Visiting professor at Harvard University, 1949, University of California, Los Angeles, 1951, University of Montana, 1952, University of California, Berkeley, 1964, and Stanford University, 1967. Consultant to Veterans Administration. President, E. K. Strong Memorial Foundation. *Military service:* U.S. Naval Reserve, 1943-46; became lieutenant.

MEMBER: American Psychological Association (president of division of counseling, 1957), American Personnel and Guidance Association (member of executive council, 1963-66; president, 1970-71), American College Personnel Association (president, 1965-66), American Educational Research Association, Minnesota Psychological Association (executive secretary, 1947-50). *Awards, honors:* Fulbright scholarship, 1956-57; professional achievement award from American Board of Psychology, 1968.

WRITINGS: After High School—What?, University of Minnesota Press, 1954; (co-author) *Minnesota Counseling Inventory*, Psychological Corp., 1956; (with Layton and others) *Testing in Guidance and Counseling*, McGraw, 1964; (with A. Hood) *Decisions for Tomorrow*, University of Minnesota Press, 1965; *Revised Strong Vocational Interest Blank*, Stanford University, 1966; (with Bonifaco Pilapil) *Graduating Seniors' Satisfaction with the University*, University of Minnesota, 1968. Contributor of over two hundred articles to professional journals. Editor of *Journal of Counseling Psychology*, 1970-74.

WORK IN PROGRESS: Research on personality theory and vocational interests.†

*   *   *

BERKIN, Carol Ruth   1942-

PERSONAL: Born October 1, 1942, in Mobile, Ala.; daughter of Saul (a businessman) and Marian (a bookkeeper; maiden name, Goldreich) Berkin; married John Paull Harper (a dean of curriculum), June 21, 1970. *Education:* Barnard College, A.B., 1964; Columbia University, M.A., 1966, Ph.D., 1972. *Religion:* Jewish. *Home:* 118 West 79th St., Apt. 14B, New York, N.Y. 10024. *Office:* Department of History, Bernard M. Baruch College of the City University of New York, 17 Lexington Ave., New York, N.Y. 10010.

CAREER: Editorial assistant for "Papers of Alexander Hamilton," New York City, 1964; Hunter College of the City University of New York, New York City, lecturer in history, 1968; member of editorial staff for "Papers of John Jay," New York City, 1972; City University of New York, New York City, assistant professor, 1972-75, associate professor, 1975-81, professor of history at Bernard M. Baruch College, 1981—, member of university graduate faculty, 1982—.

MEMBER: American Antiquarian Society (fellow), American Historical Association, Organization of American Historians (member of bicentennial celebration committee, 1975—), Coordinating Committee for Women in the Historical Profession, Smithsonian Institution, Essex Institute, New York Historical Society, Columbia University Seminar in Early American History and Culture. *Awards, honors:* Bancroft Award from Bancroft Foundation and Columbia University, 1974, for doctoral dissertation on Jonathan Sewall; National Endowment for the Humanities grant, 1974; American Council of Learned Societies grant, 1975, study fellowship, 1978; City University of New York Research Foundation grant, 1975; American Association of University Women fellowship, 1978.

WRITINGS: Jonathan Sewall: Odyssey of an American Loyalist, Columbia University Press, 1974; *Within the Conjurer's Circle: Women in Colonial America* (pamphlet), General Learning Press, 1974; (editor with Mary Beth Norton) *Women of America: A History*, Houghton, 1979; (editor with Clara M. Lovett) *Women, War, and Revolution*, Holmes & Meier, 1980; *Land of Promise: A History of the United States*, Scott, Foresman, 1982.

WORK IN PROGRESS: Men in Crisis: The Loyalist Experience of the American Revolution, for Columbia University Press; *Moving On and Moving Out: Feminism and the American Woman, 1960-1984; A Concise History of American Women*, with Sara Evans, for Free Press.

SIDELIGHTS: Carol Ruth Berkin told *CA:* "My primary focus in my work has been to examine the personalities of men or women whose life style, ideology, or career patterns have placed them on the 'losing side' or out of the mainstream. Thus, the American Loyalists, for whom, in many ways, the world was turned upside down; thus, also, the study of American women who have always been outsiders as the 'second sex' in our history. Recently it has been noted that, 'while the patriots won the revolution, the Loyalists seem to be winning the bicentennial' because of the many sympathetic studies of these men and women in the 1960's and 70's. Perhaps with the new and exciting examination of women in our past, being done by so many able scholars today, it will also be said that women lost many struggles for equality, but they are winning a sense of their past."

*   *   *

BERMEL, Albert (Cyril)   1927-

PERSONAL: Surname is accented on last syllable; born December 20, 1927, in London, England; came to United States in 1955, naturalized in 1962; son of Harry (a shoe stall holder in an open-air market) and Rae (a partner in husband's business; maiden name, Sanders) Bermel; married Joyce Hartman (a magazine editor and writer), August 31, 1956; children: Neil, Derek. *Education:* London School of Economics and Political Science, B.Sc., 1951. *Politics:* "Nonpartisan egalitarian." *Religion:* Nonsectarian Jewish. *Home:* 5 Pershing Ave., New Rochelle, N.Y. 10801. *Agent:* Elaine Markson, Elaine Markson Literary Agency, 44 Greenwich Ave., New York, N.Y. 10011. *Office:* Department of Speech and Theatre, Herbert H. Lehman College of the City University of New York, Bronx, N.Y. 10468.

CAREER: Advertising and publicity copywriter in London, England, Montreal, Quebec, Toronto, Ontario, and New York City, 1951-56; free-lance writer in New York City, 1956-58; magazine and book editor in New York City, 1958-60, 1961-63; free-lance writer in New York City, 1963-66; Columbia University, New York City, associate professor of theatre, 1966-72; Herbert H. Lehman College of the City University of New York, Bronx, N.Y., associate professor, 1972-75, professor of theatre, 1975—. Visiting professor at Rutgers University, 1966-67, Juilliard School, 1971-72, and Columbia University, 1981-84. Adviser to several theatre companies. *Military service:* British Army, 1946-48; served in West Germany. *Member:* Authors League of America, Dramatists Guild, New Drama Forum. *Awards, honors:* Guggenheim fellow in playwriting, 1965-66; George Jean Nathan Award for best dramatic criticism published in 1973-74, for *New Leader* theatre reviews and book *Contradictory Characters: An Interpretation of the Modern Theatre.*

WRITINGS: (Editor) *The Genius of the French Theater,* New American Library, 1961; (editor and translator) *The Plays of Georges Courteline,* Theatre Arts, 1961; (translator and author of introduction) Pierre Corneille, *Horatius (Horace),* Chandler Publishing, 1962; (translator and author of introduction) *One-Act Comedies of Moliere,* World Publishing, 1964, 2nd edition, Ungar, 1975; *Contradictory Characters: An Interpretation of the Modern Theatre,* Dutton, 1973; (translator and author of notes) *Three Popular French Comedies,* Ungar, 1975; *Artaud's Theatre of Cruelty,* Taplinger, 1977; *Farce: A History from Aristophanes to Woody Allen,* Simon & Schuster, 1982; *Six One-Act Farces,* Oracle Press, 1982.

Plays; full-length: "One Leg over the Wrong Wall" (based on *The Song of Roland*), first produced in London at Royal Court Theatre, 1960; "Herod First," produced in London at Saville Theatre, 1965; "Thrombo," produced in New York City at Columbia Summer Theatre, 1968; "Family Weather," produced under title "The Terror of Suspension" in New York City at House Theatre, 1975. Also author of "Thank Harry Miner," "Backyard Utopias," and "Up and Up; or, Dr. and Mrs. Faustus; or, King and Queen Lear," as yet unproduced.

One-acts: "The Workout," first produced in London at Questors Theatre, 1963, and in New York City at New Theatre Workshop, 1967; "The Adjustment," first produced in Spoleto, Italy, at Theatre of Two Worlds, 1963; "The Recovery," first produced in Edinburgh at Traverse Theatre Club, 1965, produced in New York City at New Theatre Workshop, 1967; "The Seizure," "A Web," and "The Imp or Imps," first produced in New York at Assembly Theatre, 1970.

Translator and adaptor of plays by others for production, including Georges Courteline's "The Commissioner," Arthur Adamov's "Professor Taranne," Jean Cocteau's "The Infernal Machine," Albert Camus's "Caligula," Alfred Jarry's "Ubu Cocu," and four prose comedies by Moliere. Contributor of more than 200 essays and reviews to publications, including *The New Leader.*

SIDELIGHTS: Albert Bermel told *CA:* "I try to write on a fairly specialized topic, theatre, for a general audience, those hypothetical people, intelligent readers, in the belief that theatre is, by its nature, a popular art form that touches politics, economics, sociology, and other social sciences, as well as all the other arts, from painting to sculpture (and graffitti) to fiction, music, dance, mime, and conjuring.

"Of the plays I have written, I have junked at least twice as many plays as these, and hope to do so with many more. Edward Bond, a respected British playwright who acted in my first play, 'One Leg over the Wrong Wall,' said that he writes plays to avoid going mad. I believe I write plays to avoid going sane. Directors I have worked with will confirm this. Some years ago one play was done in a plushy, expensive staging which poisoned my feelings about the commercial theatre (they were none too friendly before that experience); since then I have tried to shun the horrors of bigness.

"As a playwright, translator, critic and teacher, I do everything in my desperately limited power to encourage students to re-make the impoverished American theatre in as many ways as they can, from the producing base on up."

In an article in *The Nation,* Fostre Hirsch comments on *Contradictory Characters: An Interpretation of the Modern Theatre,* Bermel's collection of drama criticism: "These are refreshing essays. Imposing a distinctive sensibility on the plays, Bermel has made them his own, and yet, writing in a brisk style that mixes high and low diction, that introduces the street into the library, Bermel is always accessible. That style, like his canny interpretations, is a challenge to safe academic criticism. . . . Bermel's central conviction is that good playwrights engage us and entertain us at the same time that they make us work. Bermel, a good critic, does the same."

According to Frederika Randall's review of *Farce: A History from Aristophanes to Woody Allen* in the *New York Times Book Review,* Bermel's 1982 critical work is both entertaining and thoughtful. "To call this bouncy encyclopedic book a work of enthusiasm would be to underestimate its antic approach," says Randall. "It races through the centuries of stage and film farce, putting its spin on everything from Moliere and Dada to Sid Caesar and Mickey Mouse, pausing briefly for whistle-stop commentaries on such questions as what defines farce as a genre and why the genre is not considered high art."

"Bermel seems to know everything about his subject," writes Harvey Mindess in a *Los Angeles Times Book Review* article, "and he relates it with grace and verve. . . . Highly informative, [*Farce*] is an excellent sourcebook for anyone engaged in theatrical production."

BIOGRAPHICAL/CRITICAL SOURCES: New Republic, August 11, 1973; *The Nation,* October 12, 1974; *New York Times Book Review,* April 11, 1982; *Los Angeles Times Book Review,* August 22, 1982.

*   *   *

BERRIGAN, Daniel 1921-

PERSONAL: Born May 9, 1921, in Virginia, Minn.; son of Thomas William (a railroad engineer and labor official) and Frieda (Fromhart) Berrigan. *Education:* St. Andrew on Hudson, B.A., 1946; Woodstock College, Baltimore, Md., M.A., 1952.

CAREER: Entered Order of Society of Jesus (Jesuits), 1939; ordained Roman Catholic priest, 1952. St. Peter's Preparatory School, Jersey City, N.J., teacher of French, English, and Latin, 1945-49; ministerial work in Europe, 1953-54; Brooklyn Preparatory School, Brooklyn, N.Y., instructor in French and theology, 1954-57; Lemoyne College, Syracuse, N.Y., associate professor of theology, 1957-62; sabbatical in Europe, 1962-63; *Jesuit Missions,* New York City, assistant editor, 1963-65; Cornell University, Ithaca, N.Y., associate director of United Religious Work, 1966-69; Woodstock College, New York City, professor of theology, beginning 1972; volunteer worker in cancer ward, Saint Rose's Hospital. Has taught at Union Seminary, Yale University, Columbia University, University of Manitoba, University of Detroit, Loyola University (New Orleans), College of New Rochelle, and the University of California, Berkeley.

Served as auxiliary military chaplain in Germany, 1954; religious director, Walter Farrell Guild, 1954-57; staff worker, Office of Economic Opportunity, Pueblo, Colo., summer, 1967; co-founder, Catholic Peace Fellowship. Visiting lecturer at various colleges and universities.

AWARDS, HONORS: Lamont Poetry Award, and National Book Award nomination, 1957, for *Time without Number;* National Book Award nomination, 1967, for *No One Walks Waters;* Frederick G. Melcher Book Award, Unitarian Universalist Association, 1970, for *The Trial of the Catonsville Nine, No Bars to Manhood,* and *Trial Poems: A Poet, a Painter;* National Book Award nomination, 1970, for *No Bars to Manhood;* Thomas More Award, 1971, for *The Dark Night of Resistance.*

WRITINGS: The Bride: Essays in the Church, Macmillan, 1959; *The Bow in the Cloud: Man's Covenant with God,* Coward, 1961; *The World Showed Me Its Heart* (pamphlet), National Sodality Service Center, 1966; *They Call Us Dead Men: Reflections on Life and Conscience,* Macmillan, 1966; *Consequences: Truth and . . . ,* Macmillan, 1967; *Go from Here: A Prison Diary,* Open Space Action Committee, 1968; (contributor) *Delivered into Resistance,* Advocate Press, 1969.

The Trial of the Catonsville Nine (one-act play; first produced in Los Angeles at Mark Taper Forum; produced Off-Broadway at Good Shepherd-Faith Church, February 4, 1971; produced on Broadway at Lyceum Theatre, June, 1971), Beacon Press, 1970; *No Bars to Manhood,* Doubleday, 1970; (author of introduction) Philip Berrigan, *Prison Journals of a Priest Revolutionary,* Holt, 1970; *The Dark Night of Resistance,* Doubleday, 1971; (with Robert Coles) *The Geography of Faith: Conversations between Daniel Berrigan, When Underground, and Robert Coles,* Beacon Press, 1971; *America Is Hard to Find* (contains letters from Danbury Prison and writings from underground), Doubleday, 1972; (with Lee Lockwood) *Absurd Convictions, Modest Hopes: Conversations after Prison with Lee Lockwood,* Random House, 1972; (author of foreword) Thich Nhat Hanh, *The Path of Return Continues the Journey,* Hoa Binh Press, 1972; *Contemplation and Resistance* (pamphlet), Hoa Binh Press, 1973; *Jesus Christ,* illustrations by Gregory Harris and Deborah Harris, Doubleday, 1973; *Lights On in the House of the Dead: A Prison Diary,* Doubleday, 1974; (with others) *Arabs and Jews: Possibility of Concord* (pamphlet), Association of Arab-American Graduates, 1974; (with Thich Nhat Hanh) *The Raft Is Not the Shore: Conversations toward a Buddhist/Christian Awareness,* Beacon Press, 1975.

A Book of Parables, Seabury, 1977; *The Words Our Savior Gave Us,* Templegate, 1978; *Uncommon Prayer: A Book of Psalms,* Seabury, 1978; *Beside the Sea of Glass: The Song of the Lamb,* Seabury, 1978; *The Discipline of the Mountain: Dante's 'Purgatorio' in a Nuclear World,* Seabury, 1979.

We Die before We Live: Talking with the Very Ill, Seabury, 1980; *Ten Commandments for the Long Haul,* Abingdon, 1981; *The Nightmare of God,* Sunburst Press, 1982; *Portraits—Of Those I Love,* Crossroad Publishing, 1982.

Poetry: *Time without Number,* Macmillan, 1957; *Encounters,* World Publishing, 1960, new edition, Associated Artists, 1965; *The World for Wedding Ring,* Macmillan, 1962; *No One Walks Waters,* Macmillan, 1966; *Love, Love at the End: Parables, Prayers, and Meditations,* Macmillan, 1968; *Night Flight to Hanoi: War Diary with 11 Poems,* Macmillan, 1968; *False Gods, Real Men: New Poems,* Macmillan, 1969.

Crime Trial, Impressions Workshop, 1970; (with Tom Lewis) *Trial Poems: A Poet, a Painter,* Beacon Press, 1970; *Selected Poetry of Daniel Berrigan S.J.,* Anchor-Doubleday, 1970; *Selected and New Poems,* Doubleday, 1973; *Prison Poems,* Unicorn Press, 1973; *Prison Poems,* Viking, 1974.

Poems anthologized in several volumes, including *From One Word,* Devin, 1950, *Anthology of Catholic Poets,* edited by Joyce Kilmer, with a new supplement by James Edward Tobin, Doubleday, 1955, *Sealed unto the Day,* Catholic Poetry Society of America, 1955, and *Twentieth-Century American Poetry,* edited by Conrad Aiken, Modern Library, 1963.

Recordings: "Berrigan Raps," Caedmon, 1972; "Not Letting Me Not Let Blood: Prison Poems," National Catholic Reporter, 1976.

SIDELIGHTS: Motivated by his radical interpretation of Roman Catholic doctrine, Daniel Berrigan has played a prominent role in the contemporary movements for peace, racial equality, and economic justice. His work as a Jesuit priest and as an author of nonfiction and poetry reflect his strong commitment to political and spiritual liberation.

During the Vietnam War, Berrigan came to national attention as one of the most active and outspoken opponents of the American role in Southeast Asia. He founded the national peace organization Clergy and Laity Concerned about Vietnam. He travelled with Howard Zinn to North Vietnam to escort three captured American pilots back home.

But Berrigan's most dramatic and important antiwar action took place in Catonsville, Maryland on May 17, 1968. On that day Berrigan, his brother Philip, also a priest, and seven other Roman Catholic activists went into a local draft board, seized hundreds of files concerning potential draftees, took the files outside, and burned the documents with homemade napalm. They then sat down and prayed until federal authorities came to arrest them. A note given to reporters shortly before the raid explained: "We destroy these draft records not only because they exploit our young men but because they represent misplaced power concentrated in the ruling class of America. . . . We confront the Catholic Church, other Christian bodies, and the synagogues of America with their silence and cowardice in the face of our country's crimes." Later, at his trial for his part in the raid, Berrigan stated: "I burned some paper because I was trying to say that the burning of children was unhuman and unbearable, and . . . a cry is the only response."

The Catonsville Nine, as the group of activists came to be known, were found guilty of destroying government property and sentenced to three years in jail. The Berrigan brothers and two other defendants decided to go underground rather than go to jail, and for several months Berrigan was the focus of a massive manhunt. After finally being captured on Block Island, R.I., on August 11, 1970, Berrigan served eighteen months of a reduced sentence in the federal prison in Danbury, Connecticut.

Berrigan sees his role as priest and social activist as inextricably linked. "For a priest to speak out on war ought to be no surprise," he once stated. "For him to be silent should be a surprise." He has explained his actions this way: "I've no stomach to come on as some sort of moral figure. I would really just like to awaken a bit of hope in people, because I have some. At least, I try to be a guy who has tried to be faithful to his conscience and life. . . . And, well, maybe we can all do that."

Several of Berrigan's books concern his experiences during the trial and subsequent prison term. One of these, *The Trial of the Catonsville Nine,* a courtroom drama, drew generally favorable reviews from critics, and enthusiasm from audiences. Clive Barnes calls the play "a wonderfully moving testament to nine consciences. It is radical, but not at all chic, and the sincerity of its sentiments reveals the simplicity of men with many fears but no doubts." Writing in her book *Plays, Politics, and Polemics,* Catharine Hughes says that *The Trial of the Catonsville Nine* "differs not only from most plays produced by that theatre of fact, but from most other courtroom dramas. It is more document than documentary, more personal testimony than play. . . . Yet it is surprisingly, even intensely, dramatic, more so than many more deliberately theatrical works."

Prison Poems was written during Berrigan's incarceration and contains poems on a variety of his prison observations and experiences. D. Keith Mano of *National Review* thinks the subject matter of the book is trivial: "Verses on: a tooth extraction, a visiting skunk, an anal search. Your average pickpocket has as much to say. . . . Jesus and Vietnam and Watergate are overwhelmed by peevish complaint." Another critic, Michael True of *New Republic,* judges the book to contain "the best poems of [Berrigan's] career, frequently brief lyrics, where the telling metaphor brings the events to life, tuned to the music of natural speech." True especially praises the poem "My Father," a 500-line work which he believes is "one of the most beautiful extended lyrics in contemporary poetry."

Berrigan is acknowledged by most critics as a skillful and profound poet; one who successfully blends art and protest. Edward Duff describes Berrigan as "a person of imaginative insight, a master of metaphor, a stylist of shining affirmation but, most significant, he is an artist of acute and resonant sensibility."

The book *Selected and New Poems* contains an overview of work from Berrigan's first book, the Lamont Poetry Award-winning *Time without Number,* through *Prison Poems.* Critics note a consistency of themes and concerns—particularly political concerns—in all of Berrigan's poems, but find a change in style from his early traditional work to tougher and more compact poems. "Those who see Berrigan as a developing poet," writes Alice Smith Haynes of the *Dictionary of Literary Biography,* "who merges his poetic voice with his actions understand him best." The reviewer for *Choice* believes that Berrigan's "earliest verse is closely allied to . . . such older poets as Emily Dickinson, G. M. Hopkins, and even Robert Frost. . . . In his later poetry he is much more open to experimentation in the use of alliteration, internal rhyme, and typography." "In the later poems," writes Fred Moramarco of *Western Humanities Review,* explaining the change in Berrigan's poetry, "artifice makes way for feeling as Berrigan poet, Berrigan priest, and Berrigan public conscience become one."

In recent years, Berrigan has focused his attention on nonfiction prose works on religious and political topics. In *The Raft Is Not the Shore,* for example, Berrigan and Buddhist monk Thich Nhat Hanh record their conversations about Jesus and Buddha, government, economics, war, prison, and death. Both men share a disenchantment with present society as well as a disillusionment with the alternatives that have arisen to it. D. J. O'Hanlan of *America* says that the two men "challenge us to create communities, countercultural islands of sanity, in which humanness can happen."

A similar collection of wide-ranging thoughts is found in *Ten Commandments for the Long Haul.* Berrigan "writes of his work in a cancer ward in New York City, of befriending some workers striking at a university for fair wages, of teaching in the Bronx, of being arrested at a Lockheed plant, of his time in the Danbury prison, [and] of his alliance in the works of peace with his brother, Philip," states Colman McCarthy of the *Washington Post.* "A tension runs through these pages. Berrigan is a citizen of fire. He writes with heat. He burns with hope."

We Die before We Live concerns Berrigan's volunteer work among terminally ill cancer patients. "It is a spiritual book," W. W. Benjamin of *Christian Century* believes, "albeit, not a religious one. Berrigan's vignettes of those in the process of dying are neither heroic nor maudlin, yet they are unique, graphic, and particular." S. J. Curley of *Library Journal* notices several "Anti-Pentagon and antibusiness digressions [which]

seem out of place" but finds that "Berrigan the poet makes us see the horror and beauty of human life and death."

The royalties from Berrigan's book *We Die before We Live* were donated to Saint Rose's Hospital, where for three years he did volunteer work. As "a member of the Society of Jesus," Barry Winningham writes in the *Los Angeles Times,* "he's committed to vows of poverty, chastity, and obedience. . . . When he says Mass or hears confession, it's always spontaneous, like his poetry, done while on the run." The cause of peace is still very much a part of his life, but Berrigan's peace efforts have turned to the antinuclear movement. In 1980, during a march at Livermore, California, which protested the arms race and the construction of nuclear weapons, Berrigan was one of twenty-two people arrested. On September 8, 1980, he was arrested at the General Electric plant in King of Prussia, Pa., for damaging three nuclear warheads under construction there. He is appealing his conviction in the case. Berrigan has also given classes in Christian nonviolence, counseled young men to defy draft registration, and urged resistance to nuclear arms. "It's important each person resist in terms of his own conscience," he told Winningham. "Peace is something that has to be *done,*" he once explained, "with your heart and your hands, like love."

MEDIA ADAPTATIONS: The Trial of the Catonsville Nine was filmed in 1972.

BIOGRAPHICAL/CRITICAL SOURCES—Books: Daniel Berrigan, *Go from Here: A Prison Diary,* Open Space Action Committee, 1968; Francine du Plessix Gray, *Divine Disobedience: Profiles in Catholic Radicalism,* Knopf, 1970; D. Berrigan and Robert Coles, *The Geography of Faith: Conversations between Daniel Berrigan, When Underground, and Robert Coles,* Beacon Press, 1971; William V. Casey and Philip Nobile, editors, *The Berrigans,* Praeger, 1971; William Stringfellow and Anthony Towne, *Suspect Tenderness: The Witness of the Berrigans,* Holt, 1971; D. Berrigan and Lee Lockwood, *Absurd Convictions, Modest Hopes: Conversations after Prison with Lee Lockwood,* Random House, 1972; Jack Nelson and Ronald J. Ostrow, *The FBI and the Berrigans: The Making of a Conspiracy,* Coward, 1972; Catharine Hughes, *Plays, Politics, and Polemics,* Drama Book Specialists, 1972; D. Berrigan, *Lights On in the House of the Dead: A Prison Diary,* Doubleday, 1974; Richard Curtis, *The Berrigan Brothers: The Story of Daniel and Philip Berrigan,* Hawthorn, 1974; *Contemporary Literary Criticism,* Volume IV, Gale, 1975; Anne Klejment, *The Berrigans: A Bibliography of Published Works by Daniel, Philip, and Elizabeth McAlister Berrigan,* Garland Publishing, 1979; *Dictionary of Literary Biography,* Volume V: *American Poets Since World War II,* Gale, 1980; Berrigan, *Ten Commandments for the Long Haul,* Abingdon, 1981.

Periodicals: *New Yorker,* April 9, 1966, March 14, 1970; *Poetry,* November, 1966, autumn, 1968; *New York Times Book Review,* July 28, 1968; *Newsweek,* October 14, 1968, February 22, 1971, February 7, 1972; *Nation,* November 18, 1968, May 4, 1970; *Carleton Miscellany,* fall, 1968; *Laurel Review,* Volume IX, number 1, 1969; *Saturday Review,* June 14, 1969; *Virginia Quarterly Review,* winter, 1969; *Christian Century,* May 20, 1970, June 24, 1970, April 7, 1971, December 19, 1973, July 20, 1977, October 12, 1977, February 18, 1981; *New Republic,* June 20, 1970, December 12, 1970, March 6, 1971, April 13, 1974; *New York Times,* August 12, 1970, January 31, 1971, February 8, 1971, May 30, 1971, June 16, 1971; *New York Review of Books,* November 7, 1970; *Washington Post,* December 18, 1970, August 18, 1971, August

13, 1981; *New York,* February 22, 1971; *Christian Science Monitor,* March 2, 1971; *Commonweal,* February 18, 1972, November 25, 1977, December 22, 1978; *Hudson Review,* summer, 1972; *Interpretations,* number 4, 1972; *Best Sellers,* October 1, 1972, September 15, 1973, October 1, 1973, March, 1976; *Publisher's Weekly,* July 23, 1973; *America,* September 15, 1973, December 13, 1975, September 30, 1978; *National Review,* November 9, 1973, March 1, 1974; *Choice,* February, 1974; *Thoreau Society Bulletin,* spring, 1974; *Sewanee Review,* spring, 1974; *Parnassus,* fall/winter, 1974; *Western Humanities Review,* winter, 1974; *Detroit News,* April 6, 1975; *Players,* fall/winter, 1975; *Los Angeles Times,* July 27, 1980; *Library Journal,* November 15, 1980.

—Sketch by Thomas Wiloch

*   *   *

BERRIGAN, Philip (Francis) 1923-

PERSONAL: Born October 5, 1923, in Two Harbors, Minn.; son of Thomas William (a railroad engineer and labor official) and Frieda (Fromhart) Berrigan; married Elizabeth McAlister (a former nun), 1969; children: three. *Education:* College of the Holy Cross, A.B., 1950; Loyola University, New Orleans, La., B.S., 1960; Xavier University, New Orleans, La., M.A., 1963. *Politics:* Independent (usually Democrat). *Home:* 1933 Park Ave., Baltimore, Md. 21217.

CAREER: Former Roman Catholic priest, member of St. Joseph's Society of the Sacred Heart (S.S.J.); ordained, 1955. Assistant pastor in Washington, D.C., 1955-56; St. Augustine High School, New Orleans, La., counselor, 1956-63; St. Joseph's Society of the Sacred Heart, New York, N.Y., director of promotion, 1963-64; Epiphany College, Newburgh, N.Y., instructor in English, 1964; St. Peter Claver Church, Baltimore, Md., curate, 1965-68. Active in antiwar movement, 1962—; frequent lecturer on Indochina, world hunger, the arms race, and Biblical perspectives on nonviolence; also involved in organizing small communities of nonviolent resistance to aspects of American militarism. *Military service:* U.S. Army, Artillery and Infantry, 1943-46; served in three European campaigns; became second lieutenant. *Member:* Catholic Peace Fellowship (co-founder; co-chairman).

WRITINGS: Berrigan: Dialogue with Doubt (pamphlet), Fellowship Publications, 1960; *No More Strangers* (essays), Macmillan, 1965; (contributor) John O'Connor, editor, *American Catholic Exodus,* Corpus Books, 1968; *A Punishment for Peace,* Macmillan, 1969; *Prison Journals of a Priest Revolutionary,* compiled and edited by Vincent McGee, with introduction by Daniel Berrigan, Holt, 1970; *Widen the Prison Gates: Writing from Jails, April, 1970-December, 1972,* Simon & Schuster, 1973; (author of foreword) Raymond J. Pontier, *On the Cutting Edge: Reflections of a Minister in Suburbia,* Exposition Press, 1978; *Of Beasts and Beastly Images: Essays under the Bomb,* Sunburst Press, 1978. Contributor of articles to *Commonweal, Jubilee, Catholic Worker, Interracial Review,* and other publications.

SIDELIGHTS: Antiwar activist Philip Berrigan has become known for his staging of symbolic acts of protest against the American military establishment. Inspired by a radical Catholicism, acquired during his years as a priest, Berrigan has taken part in many protests since the 1960s, all of them directed at ending what he sees as the dangerous and aggressive military policies of the United States. He has been arrested over forty times and has served at least three prison terms for his protest

activities. "It's much better to make a statement with one's life," Berrigan explains to *Newsweek,* "than with one's mouth."

In October of 1967, Berrigan captured national attention as one of several protesters who entered a Baltimore draft board office and poured blood on draft files in protest of the Vietnam War. This action was taken a step further the following year when Berrigan, his brother Daniel, and seven others entered a draft board office in Catonsville, Maryland, removed draft records from the office, and burned them with homemade napalm. In both instances the protesters waited quietly, praying, until the arrival of police and their subsequent arrest. A note given to reporters shortly before the Catonsville raid explained: "We destroy these draft records not only because they exploit our young men but because they represent misplaced power concentrated in the ruling class of America. . . . We confront the Catholic Church, other Christian bodies, and the synagogues of America with their silence and cowardice in the face of our country's crimes."

The Catonsville Nine, as the group of antiwar activists came to be known, were found guilty of destroying government property and sentenced to three years in jail. In January of 1970 Berrigan, his brother, and two other defendants went underground rather than serve their jail terms. Two weeks later, Berrigan was captured by the FBI while visiting a church in New York City. His brother was captured several months later.

Berrigan served his prison sentence at the Federal Penitentiary in Lewisberg, Pennsylvania, where, after the interception of his unauthorized correspondence with his wife and several other people, Berrigan once more found himself in trouble with the FBI. Authorities maintained that the intercepted letters showed that Berrigan, his wife Elizabeth, and five others had been conspiring to kidnap presidential advisor Henry Kissinger, to blow up the heating tunnels for government offices in Washington, D.C., and to commit twenty-one other criminal offences. At the subsequent trial of the Harrisburg Seven, the more flamboyant charges were dropped and Berrigan was found guilty of the lesser crime of smuggling letters from prison. In December of 1972 he was paroled.

Since his release from prison, Berrigan has continued his protests against the American military, turning his attention in recent years to the nuclear arms race in particular. "Fighting nuclear powers," Berrigan tells *New Times,* "is a matter of survival for this planet." In October of 1975, he was one of several people who threw blood on military aircraft at an exhibit in East Hartford, Connecticut. Although arrested for a short time, all the activists involved were released when it became clear that no damage had been done to the aircraft. In the spring of 1978, Berrigan was again arrested after participating in a "Die-In" at the Pentagon that involved smearing blood and ashes on the doors to the military building. The action, Berrigan explains in *New Times,* was "to offer a reminder of what nuclear war is going to look like." For his participation in this protest, Berrigan served six months in a federal prison. Other actions in which Berrigan has participated include the dumping of tons of rubbish at the Pentagon, protesting at the White House over alleged violations of the Paris Peace Accords, and the staging of sit-ins against the government's amnesty for draft resisters.

On September 9, 1980, Berrigan and other antinuclear protestors, calling themselves the Plowshares Eight, slipped into the General Electric factory in King of Prussia, Pennsylvania, and damaged several missile nose cones being constructed there. The protesters wielded hammers, striking the nose cones and "annointing" them with blood. "Civil disobedience," Berrigan writes in the *Progressive*, explaining the protest, "offers the hope of liberation, the hope of survival. . . . Who expects politicians, generals, and bomb makers to disarm? People must disarm the bombs. That's the only way it will happen." For his part in this protest, Berrigan has been sentenced to a three-to-ten-year prison term. He is appealing the sentence.

CA INTERVIEW

CA interviewed Philip Berrigan by telephone June 14, 1983, at his home in Baltimore.

CA: Your name became familiar to the public in the late 1960s when you and your brother Daniel Berrigan led raids to destroy draft board records in Baltimore and Catonsville, Maryland. For these acts you served more than three years in prison. What really inspired your revolutionary fervor, your willingness to put yourself at odds with church and state for the sake of your beliefs?

BERRIGAN: A lot of influence from some extraordinary people, I think, and a lot of help from friends. And acquaintance with the Scripture, continuing exposure to the Scripture and what it was really saying to us.

CA: One of your early causes and one in which you're still active is the fight for racial equality. In A Punishment for Peace *(1969) you wrote of "our racial impasse": "One can justify calling it 'impasse' because both sides have nearly irreconcilable views of the changes needed to reconcile differences and reduce tensions." How far have we come since you wrote that?*

BERRIGAN: I don't think we've come very far at all. It's impossible to gauge, but judging from the general situation of black Americans here in this country, or colored people around the world, it seems that the last twenty years have been a record of intransigence and resistance to racial equality. The plight of black Americans, just to give an example, is far worse now economically and by way of decent housing, education, and health care than it was in the early '60s.

CA: Don't you think some legal and actual gains have been made? In the job market, for instance, it could be argued that blacks hold more important positions now than they did in the late '60s. Is that misleading?

BERRIGAN: I think that's window dressing. In Chicago, seventy percent of black youth are unemployed. In Baltimore, the situation is extremely serious. We live in a largely black neighborhood, and the unemployment here is shocking. So, for rank-and-file blacks, I'm fairly convinced that nothing has changed. In fact, with the declining economy, the situation has probably regressed.

CA: Much of your work has been done in the cause of peace, but some confusion exists about your role in World War II. Written accounts of it differ. Would this be a good place to clear it up?

BERRIGAN: It was a matter of my being a callow youth, I suppose, and being highly influenced not only by our tradition within the Catholic church of serving honorably in the nation's wars, but also by the influence of my family. I had three older brothers who were involved in World War II. So I was eager

not only to go into the service, but also to fight in Europe. As it eventuated, I did not do that, even though I was commissioned overseas. I went over as an artilleryman and saw some action, insofar as artillerymen see action. While I was over there, I volunteered for the infantry and for training as an infantry platoon leader, went to officers' training school south of Paris, and was commissioned over there and then assigned to an infantry division. But I never saw a great deal of action, even though I was eager to. That was expressive of my mentality, and I had to unlearn it. I had to begin to understand, through reading and through talking with knowledgeable and very courageous people, that World War II solved nothing. The fifty million dead of World War II are expressive of its failure. So I began to seek options to war not only as a political institution, but also as a way of solving international conflict.

CA: In the late 1960s and early 1970s, we heard a lot about the New Catholic Left. Is there a sizeable active Catholic Left today?

BERRIGAN: It's not sizeable, but it's of very, very high quality. I think it's fair to state that the struggle against nuclear weapons has been led largely by radical Christians, and as far as my knowledge of the matter is concerned, over half of these are Catholic. I'm speaking of people who have done civil disobedience since 1975, who have faced the courts literally hundreds of times and have gone to jail for their abhorrence of war, particularly nuclear war. We work very commonly and very intensely with a network of Christian communities across the country, and it's these people who have catalyzed, if you will, the peace movement in the United States as it is today, who have given new expression to nonviolence and to nonviolent symbols, who are placing all sorts of new meanings on civil disobedience and making it much more acceptable as a way of holding the government to accountability, who have sparked the bishops to go as far as they have gone in taking a stand against nuclear war. So I would say the influence is disproportionate to the numbers; the numbers are of very high quality.

CA: How would you assess the church's performance in the area of human rights today?

BERRIGAN: Rather dismal, I would say. I try to understand that and be fair about it, but in the case of the Christian establishment, you're dealing with a mammoth bureaucracy, and perhaps the most cohesive form of that would be my own church, the Roman Catholic Church. It is global in scope. It has not only investments, but thousands upon thousands of trained personnel, and it has property all over the world. It is a huge enterprise to keep supported and to keep funded and to keep operational. Of course, all sorts of compromises with the world have to be made simply to keep it operational. And that's true, too, by and large, of the Christian establishment, of other churches, here in this country.

I keep reminding myself, just as a note of realism, that the Christian voice against nuclear weapons and the prospect of nuclear war was silent until about three years ago. Now, here we're speaking of a span of thirty-five years since the bombings of Hiroshima and Nagasaki. As Karl Barth, a great Protestant theologian, once said, the bomb has destroyed the faith of the church. He said that in 1953, because there was no voice then and Barth was appalled at the fact that there was no voice. And he tried to assess the caliber of the church in light of the fact that it was either ignorant of the threat of nuclear war or was frightened to engage this issue. So, even with the hope coming from the Catholic bishops and some stirring among the Western European hierarchy, the record over this span of time, almost four decades, has been a betrayal. And I don't hesitate to use that word in light of the fact that we're closer to nuclear war now than at any other time since the situation with Cuba in 1962—at least many thoughtful people think so, and that's my view.

CA: After your marriage and excommunication in 1973, you said, in an interview for Newsweek, *that you still considered yourself a Roman Catholic and a priest. That suggests a broader definition of priesthood. Would you comment on your feelings about priesthood and what you consider it to encompass?*

BERRIGAN: I should take on the notion of celibacy first of all. Both Elizabeth and myself not only honored this tradition and discipline for many decades, we honor people who practice it. But we say that it must be practiced voluntarily. It can't be a matter of course, a vow which in turn is a necessity for good standing within the church. That's what mandatory celibacy is within the Catholic church. And that, to us, is not only un-biblical, but it also offends against conscience and nonviolence. We've always maintained that since our marriage. We're all for celibacy, but we just insist that it has to be optional rather than mandatory.

In light of that, I suppose notions of the priesthood do change. I would consider it something reflected from the person of our Lord himself. He was king, prophet, and priest, and the priest is the mediator, but above all he focuses upon a central characteristic of the gospel which calls for the building of peace. That would mean being in the forefront in the struggle for justice, because it's one of the axioms of Christian theology that no peace is possible until there is first strict, definitive justice for especially the wretched of the earth, the offscouring and the crushed, the bombed and the starved. The very priesthood of Christians in general, let alone the professional priesthood, should be articulated by criteria like those. Without them, there's even a denial of sacramental life, just as Christians consistently deny their baptism by the fact that they refuse to live as Christ lived, or refuse to try seriously.

CA: Is there great psychological trauma for priests who leave the priesthood?

BERRIGAN: Yes, there is. I was speaking out in Minneapolis just recently, and I ran into a number of ex-priests out there. A lot of them had gone to work and gotten their doctorates and had gotten married and are now raising families. They were very eager to tell what a struggle it had been, and I could appreciate that. I think there are certain lapses in our training and, well, certain assumptions that are actually accepted by us which interfere with independence of judgment, conscience, real self-sufficiency, ability to take suffering and ostracism, and to take risks for principle. This was reflected in the lives of some of those very good people I encountered in the Minneapolis-St. Paul area. But the country is strewn with lives like those, and for the most part they are not of the use that they could be to the home and family or to the country at large.

CA: Is the church making any effort to put them to use in some different way so that their training is not wasted?

BERRIGAN: Only to a very, very limited extent. I know some American bishops have a great deal of compassion for ex-

priests and for their families, and beyond compassion, they have an understanding that here's a vast reservoir of potential that could be better utilized for the overall community as well as for the church. They're used as ministers, they're used as catechists, and they're used in justice-and-peace commissions to a degree, but by and large, no, they aren't used well. It's only an unusual bishop who'll do this.

CA: Do you think the church will ever admit women to the priesthood?

BERRIGAN: Not as long as this present pope is around, any more than you'll see any relaxing of mandatory celibacy as long as John Paul II is pontiff.

CA: How much lecturing are you doing now?

BERRIGAN: Well, in the last three months, I've done a great deal—so much, in fact, that it's kind of a blur. I've been gone from the community more than half the time, and that's particularly expensive for the community because we have our own work to do here, which involves organizing and working with a network of communities along the East Coast called the Atlantic Life Community. Sometimes that has to be sacrificed when one hits the road speaking, and I feel very poorly about that loss.

CA: Tell me about Jonah House, where you live in Baltimore with your family. It's usually referred to as a commune.

BERRIGAN: We call it a community, and we try to pattern it as well as we can after an early Christian community. When everyone is home, we have eight adults. There's one of our number in jail now, and there are several out on the road. Elizabeth and I have three children, so there's a total of eleven people in the household. We hold everything in common—we have only one bank account—and we share all aspects of our work, including child care and cooking. None of us carries any health insurance. We try to live in some spirit of faith and poverty, and it's very hard in this culture. We try to keep ourselves free for resistance and separation and imprisonment, whatever is necessary. In the last three years, I would say over half the community has been in jail all the time.

The community has participated heavily in what we call the Isaiah 2 actions (from the second chapter of Isaiah), or swords-into-plowshares witnesses; that is, the symbolic yet real damaging of first-strike nuclear weapons. A group called the Plowshares 8 started the process of disarmament at a General Electric plant in King of Prussia, Pennsylvania, on September 9, 1980. We damaged two Mark 12A first-strike reentry vehicles. For that I await a three-to-ten-year prison sentence, currently on appeal.

CA: Are you advocating complete disarmament?

BERRIGAN: Oh yes—in fact, the abolition of war. We're going to have to abolish war as well as disarm ourselves of nuclear weapons, for a whole variety of reasons.

CA: How do you respond to the general concern that other countries may not also disarm themselves, that we could be at their mercy?

BERRIGAN: The fact of the matter is that we're at the mercy of our weapons right now; folks usually don't know enough about the question to understand that. We're held hostage by these weapons, and we'll all die if they're ever used again. Now that can be accepted as some sort of intellectual statement or interesting assumption. But unless people understand it at gut level because they've invested some time in trying to imagine what nuclear war is, and they've gone deeply into the idiocy of forty times overkill of the Soviet Union, or they've done some homework into the real explosive power of the American arsenal, which is now about 800,000 Hiroshimas, there's no real understanding of the statement that we're being held hostage by these weapons. It's just rhetoric. But such is the case, and, in fact, it's been about twenty years that our respective societies have been holding each other hostage. And we could be killed not only by some official tantrum on the part of Reagan or some of the joint chiefs of staff, but by a miscalculation or by a fluke accident. The whole thing could go up like a match tomorrow.

So in light of all this, any move toward sanity and toward humanity is a gain. The problem of what other nations will do can be worked out, but if the United States were to disarm unilaterally tomorrow, the security of the people of this country—and these weapons are supposed to exist to insure our security—would be notably enhanced just by our action. Of course it isn't done because of the vested interests, because of the tremendous profits made by armaments makers and by their very powerful lobbies in Washington. It isn't done because people have not mobilized an equal voice.

CA: Are you doing any writing now that you'd like to mention?

BERRIGAN: Yes, I'm working on a book with Elizabeth right now. It's in the hands of a couple of publishers. Actually the manuscript is pretty well finished. But we've discovered in the last ten years that our writing is not very popular. We think it a matter of duty not only to try to be responsible ourselves, but also to call others to responsibility, and that doesn't make one popular as a writer.

CA: If you could go back twenty-five years, would you do anything differently?

BERRIGAN: I think probably I would. I often bemoan the fact that I've not been nonviolent enough, I've not been faithful enough. One makes some large mistakes with other people. I don't think that I've made any major mistakes tactically, but I've certainly made mistakes in that I've used other people and in some cases abused them because I didn't know enough about nonviolence or didn't have enough discipline myself. I regret very deeply some of those aspects of the struggle. But what we did strategically and tactically, I wouldn't take any of that back at all, including the time spent in prison, because it was the best that I could manage at the time. That's all that one can do.

CA: Is there anything more you'd like to say about your causes and concerns?

BERRIGAN: I think that anything I've said would be relatively useless and could be dismissed unless I said that there is no alternative to peace today. We have to prevent nuclear war. If we don't, in all likelihood we'll destroy the planet and the human family, and that would include, of course, the destruction of untold generations that would come from us. We have no right to do any of these things. We're caught in a kind of demonic bind today wherein we accept the assumptions and conclusions of a kind of mad leadership, whether it be Russian or our own, and conclude out of that that we can spend these astronomical sums on death, that we can poison the planet, that Reagan can have his MX missiles and his Tridents and all of the rest and that we're perfectly entitled and legally allowed to do these things. Of course we're neither legally allowed nor morally entitled to do any of them. Usually I try to say to Americans that the biggest business that all of us have is to raise a cry of outrage for justice and peace. First of all, our spirits depend upon this. We die inside if we don't. And secondly, the very fate of humankind might well rest upon our doing it. So one says it and then one allows people to make their own choices.

BIOGRAPHICAL/CRITICAL SOURCES—Books: Francine du Plessix Gray, *Divine Disobedience: Profiles in Catholic Radicalism,* Knopf, 1970; Philip Berrigan, *Prison Journals of a Priest Revolutionary,* Holt, 1970; William Stringfellow and Anthony Towne, *Suspect Tenderness: The Witness of the Berrigans,* Holt, 1971; William Van Etten Casey and Philip Nobile, editors, *Berrigans,* Praeger, 1971; Jack Nelson and Ronald J. Ostrow, *The FBI and the Berrigans: The Making of Conspiracy,* Coward, 1972; Berrigan, *Widen the Prison Gates: Writing from Jails, April, 1970-December, 1972,* Simon & Schuster, 1973; Richard Curtis, *The Berrigan Brothers: The Story of Daniel and Philip Berrigan,* Hawthorn, 1974; Anne Klejment, *The Berrigans: A Bibliography of Published Works by Daniel, Philip, and Elizabeth McAlister Berrigan,* Garland Publishing, 1979.

Periodicals: *Time,* June 7, 1968, May 4, 1970, February 14, 1972; *Commonweal,* August 22, 1969, September 27, 1974; *New Yorker,* March 14, 1970; *Newsweek,* May 4, 1970, March 22, 1971, August 13, 1973, April 15, 1974, September 5, 1977, March 26, 1979; *Christian Century,* May 20, 1970, October 21, 1970; *Atlantic,* August, 1970; *Harper,* August, 1970; *Washington Post,* May 30, 1973; *Village Voice,* December 20, 1973; *Saturday Review/World,* January 26, 1974; *New Times,* August 7, 1978; *Progressive,* May, 1981.

—Interview by Jean W. Ross

*   *   *

BESKOW, Bo 1906-
(Viktor Mall)

PERSONAL: Born February 13, 1906, in Djursholm, Sweden; son of Nathanael (a theologian involved in international peace work) and Elsa (a writer and artist) Beskow; married second wife, Greta Berge (a ceramic artist), 1955; children: (first marriage) two daughters; (second marriage) Maria, Susanna, Peter. *Education:* Attended Royal Academy of Fine Arts, Stockholm, 1923-26, Swedish Institute, Rome, 1927, Maison Watteau, 1929. *Politics:* World Federalist. *Home:* The Old Vicarage of Mogata, 61400 Soederkoeping, Sweden.

CAREER: Writer and artist. Among his murals are two at United Nations headquarters in New York; has done portraits of Swedish statesmen and other notables, among them John Steinbeck (portraits in 1937, 1946, 1957) and Dag Hammarskjoeld; his stained glass work is installed in cathedrals at Skara and Vaexjoe; has done stage design for Royal Opera and Royal Dramatic Theatre in Stockholm. *Member:* Swedish Authors Association, Swedish Artists Association. *Awards, honors:* Knight of the Northern Cross; Golden Plaque at Bratislava Biennial, 1969, for *Figge bygger snaekhus.*

WRITINGS: Trollsagor (children's book), Almqvist & Wiksell, 1924; *Bilsresan* (children's book), Ahlen & Akerlund, 1929; *Flyken till Portugal* (title means "Flight to Portugal"), Wahlstroem & Widstrand, 1934; (under pseudonym Viktor Mall) *Figge* (children's book), Gebers, 1945; *Och vattnet stod pa jorden*, Ragen & Sjoegren, 1978, English translation published as *Two by Two*, Bodley Head, 1980, Avon, 1981.

Published by Bonniers: *Janne i Rom* (title means "Janne in Rome"), 1929; *Ludde pa sjoebotten* (children's book), 1931; (under pseudonym Viktor Mall) *Pelle* (children's book), 1945; *Figge bygger snaekhus* (children's book; title means "Figge Builds a Shellhouse"), 1967; *Dag Hammarskjoeld: Ett portraett*, 1967, English edition, also by Beskow, published as *Dag Hammarskjoeld: Strictly Personal*, Doubleday, 1969; *Krokodilens middag* (semi-autobiographical essays; title means "Dinner for a Crocodile"), 1969; *Saang om Saldinien* (title means "Song of Sardinia"), 1971; *The Voice of Jacob*, 1980; *Jorden tycker om dig* (essays; title means "The Earth Loves You"), 1981; *Isebel* (title means "Jezebel"), 1982; *Samson*, 1983.

Contributor to journals.

SIDELIGHTS: Bo Beskow told *CA:* "I write when it is too dark to paint, at night or during the long winter months—grapple with words instead of colour and form.

"Writing and painting takes me into other worlds, other realities. An artist often walks in a no-man's-land between different realities—seeking his way in strange labyrinths—always in the hope of reaching the impossible. On my wanderings I meet many friends, painters, and philosophers from long, long ago—we recognize each other over time and space. I learned about alfresco painting and the Golden Rule from Piero della Francesca, and the 12th-century masters in Chartres helped me to the secret of making my own stained glass.

"When I wrote my four biblical novels, I lived with Noah, Jacob, Jezebel and Samson—on the overcrowded ark, in black tents on mountain camps, and on camelbacks over desert trails. Sometimes it is very hard to come back to the Swedish Well-Fare-State, to everyday life and its demands and duties. (I am a convinced Worldcitizen!)

"An artist is always on the run—on the way to something or in flight from something—often from himself. Working night and day has kept me from nothingness and despair through a long life. Maybe my work made me a bad husband and father, but it has kept me alive. I have learned to cope with deep depressions and momentary sense of failure—they make me try again!"

BIOGRAPHICAL/CRITICAL SOURCES: Bookbird, January, 1971; *Times Literary Supplement*, March 7, 1980.

*   *   *

BEYER, (Richard) Andrew 1943-

PERSONAL: Born November 17, 1943, in Carbondale, Ill.; son of Richard L. (a teacher) and Pauline (Sorgen) Beyer. *Education:* Attended Harvard University, 1961-66. *Home:* 2457 Tunlaw Rd. N.W., Washington, D.C. 20007. *Office:* Washington Post, 1150 15th St. N.W., Washington, D.C.

CAREER: Washington Post, Washington, D.C., reporter, 1966-69; sports columnist, *Washington Daily News*, Washington, D.C., 1969-72, *Washington Star*, Washington, D.C., 1972-79, and *Washington Post*, 1979—. *Military service:* U.S. Army, 1968-70.

WRITINGS: Picking Winners: A Horseplayer's Guide, Houghton, 1975; *My $50,000 Year at the Races*, Harcourt, 1978; *The Winning Horseplayer*, Houghton, 1983.

BIOGRAPHICAL/CRITICAL SOURCES: New Yorker, May 12, 1973.

*   *   *

BHUTTO, Zulfikar Ali 1928-1979

PERSONAL: Born January 5, 1928, in Larkana, Pakistan; executed by hanging April 4, 1979, in Rawalpindi, Pakistan; son of Shahnawaz Khan and Khurshid Bhutto; married Nusrat Ispahani, 1951; children: Benazir, Sanam Seema (daughters); Murtaza, Shahnawaz (sons). *Education:* University of California, Berkeley, B.A. (with honors), 1950; Christ Church, Oxford, M.A. (with honors), 1952. *Religion:* Islam. *Home:* Al-Murtaza, Bhutto Colony, Larkana, Pakistan.

CAREER: Called to Bar, Lincoln's Inn, London, 1953; University of Southampton, Highfield, Southampton, England, lecturer in international law, 1952-53; private practice of law, 1953-58; West Pakistan High Court, Karachi, attorney, 1953-58; Sind Muslim Law College, Karachi, teacher of constitutional law, 1956-58; Islamic Republic of Pakistan, Rawalpindi, Pakistan, minister of commerce, 1958-60, diplomat, 1959-66, minister of minority affairs, minister of national reconstruction and information, minister of fuel, power, and natural resources, and minister of Kashmir affairs, 1960-62, minister of industries and natural resources, 1962-63, interim minister of foreign affairs, 1962-63, minister of foreign affairs and atomic energy, 1963-66. Diplomatic career included heading delegations to the United States, 1959, Turkey, 1959-60, United Nations General Assembly, 1959-60, Soviet Union, 1960, Europe, 1961, Tehran Conference, 1963, and to Korea, People's Republic of China, Cyprus, and India.

Founder and chairman, Pakistan People's Party, 1967-77; arrested for fomenting disorder and imprisoned, November, 1968-February, 1969; Islamic Republic of Pakistan, deputy prime minister and foreign minister, 1970-71, chief martial law administrator, 1971-72, president, foreign minister, minister of defense, minister of interior affairs, and minister of provincial coordination, 1972-77, prime minister, 1973-77; arrested in military coup and imprisoned in Lahore, Pakistan, July, 1977-August, 1977, and rearrested for ordering the assassination of a political opponent and imprisoned in Rawalpindi, Pakistan, September, 1977-April, 1979; tried in military and civilian courts in Pakistan and ordered executed, April, 1979. *Awards, honors:* Hilal-i-Pakistan, 1964; LL.D., University of Sind, 1966; numerous foreign decorations.

WRITINGS: Peace-Keeping by the United Nations, Pakistan Publishing House (Karachi), 1967; *Political Situation in Pakistan*, Veshasher Prakashan, 1968, 2nd edition, Pakistan People's Party, 1969; *Pakistan and the Alliances*, Pakistan People's Party, 1969; *The Myth of Independence*, Oxford University Press, 1969; *Let the People Judge*, Pakistan People's Party, 1969; *The Great Tragedy*, Pakistan People's Party, 1971; *Thoughts on Some Aspects of Islam*, Sh. Muhammad Ashraf (Lahore), 1976; *The Third World: New Directions*, Quartet Books, 1977, published as *New Directions*, Namara Publications, 1980; *Mera Pakistan: Phansi ki kothri men likhi ga'i Zulfaqar Ali Bhutto ki akhri tahrir* (in Urdu), Bisvin Sadi Pablikeshanz, 1979; *Takhtah-yi dar par: Janab Bhutto ke savanih-i hayat ap biu ke uslub men* (in Urdu), Maktabah-yi Shankar (Lahore), 1979; *If I Am Assassinated*, Vikas Publishing House, 1979; *My Execution*, South Asia Books, 1980.

Collections of public statements: *Speeches Delivered by Zulfikar Ali Bhutto, Foreign Minister of Pakistan, before the Security Council in 1964*, Ministry of Foreign Affairs, Government of Pakistan, 1964; *Foreign Policy of Pakistan: A Compendium of Speeches Made in the National Assembly of Pakistan, 1962-64*, Pakistan Institute of International Affairs, 1964; *A South Asia View: A Collection of Speeches and Excerpts from Important Addresses Delivered in the United States by the Foreign Minister of Pakistan, Mr. Zulfikar Ali Bhutto, during the Years 1963 and 1964*, Embassy of Pakistan (Washington, D.C.), 1964; *The Quest for Peace: Selections from Speeches and Writings, 1963-65*, Pakistan Institute of International Affairs, 1966.

"I Have Kept My Pledge with God and Man": Collection of President Bhutto's Speeches, National Forum (Karachi), 1972; *Speeches and Statements, December 20, 1971-March 31, 1972*, Department of Films and Publications, Government of Pakistan, 1972; *Awakening the People: A Collection of Articles, Statements and Speeches*, Pakistan Publications, 1973; *Marching towards Democracy: A Collection of Articles, Statements and Speeches*, Pakistan Publications, 1973; *Reshaping Foreign Policy: A Collection of Articles, Statements and Speeches*, Pakistan Publications, 1973; *President of Pakistan Zulfikar Ali Bhutto: Interviews to the Press, December 20, 1971-August 13, 1973*, Ministry of Information and Broadcasting, Government of Pakistan, 1976; *Chairman Bhutto's Reply to General Zia's Second Statement in the Supreme Court*, Musawaat Press (Karachi), 1977. Also had speeches compiled in *Prime Minister Zulfikar Ali Bhutto: Speeches and Statements during Visit to the United States of America in September, 1973*, Ministry of Foreign Affairs, Government of Pakistan.

Also author of *The Pakistan Papers*, New Solidarity International Press Service, 1979 (these papers were written while Bhutto was imprisoned and were smuggled out).

SIDELIGHTS: Zulfikar Ali Bhutto, former president of the Islamic Republic of Pakistan, was summoned from his cell in a Rawalpindi jail in the early hours of April 4, 1979. Two hours later he was dead, hung for allegedly ordering the assassination of a political opponent five years before. According to *Time* and *Newsweek* accounts, Bhutto's last words were "Lord help me. I am innocent."

The political career of Zulfikar Bhutto was a dazzling one. Son of one of Pakistan's wealthy landowning families, Bhutto began his career as an American- and British-trained lawyer and professor of law. He entered Pakistani politics at the age of thirty when he was appointed minister of commerce in the conservative Ayub Khan government, becoming the youngest cabinet minister in Pakistan's history. He later assumed the portfolios of information and national reconstruction and of minority affairs.

Serving as interim foreign minister, Bhutto soon became known as a brilliant diplomat, negotiating agreements with the United States, the Soviet Union, the People's Republic of China, and Afghanistan. In 1963 he was formally named foreign minister and by 1965 was included in Ayub Khan's inner circle of advisors. As foreign minister, Bhutto gained respect as a tough and shrewd negotiator and a capable administrator.

However, Bhutto's politics began to lean increasingly toward the left. He supported a stronger alliance with Communist China, which he saw as a potential ally against India. When Bhutto publicly denounced Ayub Khan's pro-American policies during Pakistan's 1965 military dispute with India over Kashmir, he was ousted from the government.

Once again practicing law, Bhutto became an outspoken opponent of the Ayub Khan government and its foreign policies. In 1967 he formed the Pakistan People's Party—a political party that embraced a philosophy of "Islamic socialism" and which gained a broad base of support from the poor and unlanded classes. After anti-government riots erupted in 1968, Bhutto was arrested for fomenting disorder and was imprisoned. He was released from prison four months later and in that short time his stature among the common people had grown to immense proportions. When Ayub Khan was deposed in 1969 and general elections were held in 1970, Bhutto's Pakistan People's Party won a majority of West Pakistan's seats in the National Constituent Assembly.

The 1970 election was a crucial one for Pakistan. The Awami League political party swept the election for East Pakistan's seats in the Assembly. The Awami League leader, Sheik Mujibar Rahman, as head of the majority party, would then be appointed prime minister, and Bhutto, as leader of the largest minority, would become the powerless deputy prime minister. Realizing this, Bhutto called a boycott of the Pakistan People's Party of the Assembly and the election was then declared void. At this, Rahman—whose party had originally called for the autonomy of East Pakistan—began the clamor for East Pakistani independence. When the West Pakistanis tried to squelch the independence movement, the Indian army invaded East Pakistan to bolster the East Pakistani troops.

The war in Bangladesh—as East Pakistan became known—was a fierce and bloody one. World attention focused on the Pakistani civil war as journalists returned from Bangladesh with stories and photographs of thousands of starving refugees. Bhutto himself rose to international prominence during that debacle when, as a Pakistani delegate to the United Nations, he dramatically accused the U.N. Security Council of "legalizing aggression" with its refusal to call for a withdrawal of Indian forces from East Pakistan. Five days later, on December 20, 1971, an Indian ceasefire was signed, East Pakistan seceded from the Republic, and Bhutto became president of the Islamic Republic of Pakistan. He was officially sworn in four months later and in a power-retaining measure kept for himself the crucial portfolios of defense, foreign affairs, interior affairs, and provincial coordination.

As president, Bhutto promised sweeping reforms in Pakistan, including abolition of the death penalty, land reform, and an equalization of power within the country. In the first months of his rule he managed to restore a measure of self-respect to his war-weary and defeated countrymen. He also amazed the world by establishing diplomatic relations with the newly formed Bangladesh. However, after several years in power, allegations of corruption were raised against Bhutto, and Bhutto and his followers used increasingly rough tactics to quell opposition. The final crisis arose when the Pakistan People's Party was accused of rigging the election in order to win an overwhelming majority of the parliamentary seats. Soon after the dispute began, riots broke out in Pakistan's principle cities and several weeks later a group of army officers headed by Staff General Mohammad Zia ul-Haq overthrew Bhutto's government and placed Bhutto under arrest. Bhutto was later released and then rearrested when he was charged with ordering the political assassination of a political opponent. After being tried by a military tribunal and appealing his case to the Pakistan High Court, Bhutto was found guilty and condemned to death. News of his impending execution caused an outcry from many world leaders who pleaded on his behalf for a stay of execution. Bhutto's execution caused riots throughout Pakistan.

Bhutto's books mirrored his concerns with Third World solidarity and his resentment of interference from developed nations in the affairs of lesser developed countries. His most widely received book, *The Myth of Independence*, "is important because it sets out, with almost brutal clarity, a point of view which is held by statesmen in many other developing countries as well as in Pakistan," wrote a *Times Literary Supplement* reviewer. A critic in the *Annals of the American Academy* commented that in *The Myth of Independence* Bhutto "demonstrates an acute sensitivity to the concept of the balance of power. He attaches almost no importance to the role of ideology in international diplomacy which, in his judgment, only masks the forthright expression of national interest. . . . [His] prose, like his speech, is dramatic and passionate; the word 'confrontation' . . . comes easily to him."

BIOGRAPHICAL/CRITICAL SOURCES: Times Literary Supplement, May 22, 1969; *Annals of the American Academy*, November, 1969; *Choice*, December, 1969, April, 1978; *Political Science Quarterly*, March, 1971; *Time*, April 11, 1977, May 2, 1977, July 18, 1977, September 19, 1977, February 19, 1979; *Newsweek*, April 25, 1977, May 2, 1977, July 18, 1977, October 3, 1977, February 19, 1979; S. Kumar, *The New Pakistan*, Vikas Publishing House, 1978; *Nation*, April 29, 1978, August 19, 1978; *New Republic*, May 27, 1978; *Atlas*, December 1978; *MacLean's*, May 29, 1978, January 1, 1979, February 19, 1979; *National Review*, March 16, 1979; S. J. Burki, *Pakistan under Bhutto, 1971-1977*, St. Martin's, 1980; S. Tasser, *Bhutto: A Political Biography*, Vikas Publishing House, 1980.

OBITUARIES: Atlas, April 16, 1979; *New York Times*, April 4, 1979; *New Republic*, April 14, 1979; *Time*, April 16, 1979; *Newsweek*, April 16, 1979; *MacLean's*, April 16, 1979; *Nation*, April 21, 1979; *America*, April 21, 1979.†

—*Sketch by Heidi A. Tietjen*

*   *   *

BIEBER, Margarete   1879-1978

PERSONAL: Surname is pronounced Bee-ber; born July 31, 1879, in Schonau, Germany (now Preshowa, Poland); died February 25, 1978, in New Canaan, Conn.; came to the United States in 1934 "because of Hitler regime"; naturalized in 1940; daughter of Jacob (an industrialist) and Vally (Bukofzer) Bieber; children: (adopted) Ingeborg Christine (Mrs. William S. Sachs). *Education:* Attended Berlin University, 1901-04; Bonn University, Ph.D., 1907. *Politics:* "I vote for the best qualified person." *Religion:* "Old Catholic—Protestant Episcopal."

CAREER: German Archaeological Institute, Athens, Greece, assistant, 1910; assistant in museum in Kassel, Germany, 1913; Archaeological Institute, University of Berlin, Berlin, Germany, assistant, 1914; Justus-Lieg University, Giessen, Germany, lecturer, 1919, associate professor, 1923-31, professor of archaeology and director of seminar, 1931-33; Somerville College, Oxford, England, honorary fellow, 1933-34; Barnard College, New York City, lecturer, 1934-36; Columbia University, New York City, associate professor of fine arts and archaeology, 1936-48; Princeton University, Princeton, N.J., member of department of art, 1949-51; Columbia University, Institute of General Studies, New York City, special lecturer, 1948-56; affiliated with Associate University Seminars, department of classical civilization, 1960-74.

MEMBER: American Academy of Arts and Sciences (fellow), American Archaeological Society, German Archaeological Institute. *Awards, honors:* American Association of University Women, international fellowship, 1931-32; D.Litt., Columbia University, 1954; Honorary Senator, Giessen University, 1959; American Philosophical Society award; Red Cross medal; National Endowment for the Humanities fellowship, 1971; gold medal for achievement in archaeology, American Institute of Archaeology, 1974.

WRITINGS: Skenika, 75., Winckelmanns-Programm, 1915; *Katalog der Skulpturen in Kassel*, Marburg, 1916; *Die Denkmaeler zum Theaterwesen im Altertum*, Walter de Gruyter, 1920; *Griechische Kleidung*, Walter de Gruyter, 1928; *Entwicklungsgeschichte der griechischen Tracht*, Gebr. Mann, 1934, revised edition, 1966; *The History of the Greek and Roman Theatre*, Princeton University Press, 1939, revised edition, 1961.

Laocoon: The Influence of the Group since Its Rediscovery, Columbia University Press, 1942, revised edition, Wayne State University Press, 1966; (editor) *German Readings in the History and Theory of Fine Arts*, Part one, H. Bittner, 1946, 3rd edition published as *German Readings One: A Short Survey of Greek and Roman Art for Students of German and Fine Arts*, 1958; *The Sculpture of the Hellenistic Age*, Columbia University Press, 1955, revised edition, 1961, reprinted, Obol International, 1980; *Roman Men in Greek Himation*, Proceedings of American Philosophical Society, 1959.

The Copies of the Herculaneum Women, American Philosophical Society, 1962; *Alexander the Great in Greek and Roman Art*, Argonaut, 1964, reprinted, Obol International, 1979; *New Trends in the New Books on Ancient Art, 1958-1965*, [Cambridge, Mass.], 1965; *The Statue of Cybele in the J. Paul Getty Museum*, J. Paul Getty Museum, 1968; *Graeco-Roman Copies*, New York University Press, 1973; *Copies of Greek and Roman Art*, New York University Press, 1975; *The History of Greek, Etruscan, and Roman Clothing*, Thames & Hudson, 1975; *Ancient Copies: Contributions to the History of Greek and Roman Art*, New York University Press, 1977.

Also author of *A Bronze Statuette in Cincinnati and Its Place in the History of the Asklepios Type*, 1957. Contributor of over 300 articles to *American Journal of Archaeology, American Journal of Philology, Classical World*, and memorial volumes.

SIDELIGHTS: Margarete Bieber was an authority on Greek and Roman art, particularly Roman copies of Greek art, an area where many scholarly mistakes have been made. "These Roman copies," Bieber once told the *New York Times*, "have been used by scholars for almost 100 years for reconstructing Greek art. But the copies are not pure Greek sculpture—the Romans took Greek sculpture and transformed it into something new." *Ancient Copies: Contributions to the History of Greek and Roman Art*, Bieber's last book, is a clarification of the differences and similarities between Greek and Roman art. "This opus, monumental in format and content," wrote G. K. Rensch of *Library Journal*, "is the culmination of a lifetime of meticulous Germanic scholarship and dedicated research devoted to the study of Greek and Roman art."

BIOGRAPHICAL/CRITICAL SOURCES: Bibliography of the Works of Margarete Bieber, Columbia University Press, 1969; *New York Times*, May 22, 1971; *Archaeology*, April, 1975; *Library Journal*, September 1, 1977.

OBITUARIES: New York Times, February 25, 1978.†

BIEBUYCK, Daniel P. 1925-

PERSONAL: Born October 1, 1925, in Deinze, Belgium; son of Marcel G. and Bertha (Van Laere) Biebuyck; married Laure-Marie de Rycke, November 21, 1950; children: Brunhilde, Anne-Marie, Edwin, Hans, Jean-Christophe, Jean-Marie, Beatrice. *Education:* University of Ghent, B.A. (in classics), 1946, B.A. (in law), 1947, Licencie es Philosophie et Lettres, 1948, Ph.D., 1954; University of London, graduate study, 1948-49. *Home:* 271 West Main St., Newark, Del. 19711. *Office:* Department of Anthropology, University of Delaware, Newark, Del. 19711.

CAREER: Institut pour la Recherche Scientifique en Afrique Centrale, Kinshasa, Belgian Congo (now Zaire Republic), research fellow, 1949-57; Lovanium University of Kinshasa (now Universite Nationale du Zaire), Kinshasa, Zaire Republic, 1957-61, began as associate professor, became professor; University of Delaware, Newark, visiting professor, 1961-64; University of California, Los Angeles, professor of anthropology and curator of African collection, 1964-66; University of Delaware, H. Rodney Sharp Professor of Anthropology, 1966-74, H. Rodney Sharp Professor of Anthropology and Humanities, 1974—, chairman of anthropology department, 1969-72 and 1974-75, interim director of Black Studies. Visiting lecturer in anthropology, University of Liege, 1956-58; visiting professor of anthropology, University of London, 1960; visiting lecturer in anthropology and art history, Yale University, 1970-71 and 1976-77; adjunct professor of anthropology, New York University, 1971-72. Did field work on expeditions throughout the Congo, 1949-61, with intensive work among the Zoba, Bembe, Lega, and Nyanga. *Military service:* Belgian Army, 1954-56; became sergeant. *Member:* Academie Royale des Sciences d'Outre-Mer (Brussels), Institut des Civilisations Differentes (Brussels), Phi Kappa Phi, Phi Beta Kappa.

AWARDS, HONORS: Annual prize of Academie Royale des Sciences d'Outre-Mer, 1956, for *De Hond bij de Nyanga: Ritueel en sociologie;* Rockefeller Foundation fellowship, 1979-80; Guggenheim Memorial fellowship, 1980-81. Has received grants from numerous institutions, including African Studies Center of University of California, Los Angeles, 1965-67, Social Science Council, 1967-68, University of Delaware, 1968, J. T. Last/Teledyne, 1969-70, and National Endowment for the Humanities, 1971-73.

WRITINGS: De Hond bij de Nyanga: Ritueel en sociologie, Academie Royale des Sciences d'Outre-Mer, 1956; (with M. Douglas) *Congo Tribes and Parties,* Royal Anthropological Institute (London), 1961; *Les Mitamba: Systeme de mariages enchaines chez les Babembe,* Academie Royale des Sciences d'Outre-Mer, 1962; (editor) *African Agrarian Systems,* Oxford University Press, 1963; *Rights in Land and Its Resources among the Nyanga,* Academie Royale des Sciences d'Outre-Mer, 1966; (editor and translator with Kahombo C. Mateene) *The Mwindo Epic from the Banyanga,* University of California Press, 1969; (editor) *Tradition and Creativity in Tribal Art,* University of California Press, 1969; (with Mateene) *Anthologie de la litterature orale Nyanga,* Academie Royale des Sciences d'Outre-Mer, 1970; *Lega Culture: Art, Initiation, and Moral Philosophy among a Central African People,* University of California Press, 1973; *Symbolism and the Lega Stool,* ISHI Publications, 1977; *Hero and Chief: Epic Literature from the Banyanga (Zaire Republic),* University of California Press, 1978; *Statuary from the Pre-Bembe Hunters,* Musee Royal de l'Afrique Centrale (Belgium), 1981.

Contributor: W. H. Whiteley, editor, *A Selection of African Prose,* Volume I, Clarendon Press, 1964; Joseph Okpaku, editor, *New African Literature and the Arts,* Crowell, 1967; *Contributions to the Colloquium on the Function and Significance of Negro-African Art in the Life of the People and for the People,* Presence Africaine (Paris), 1971; D. Fraser and H. Cole, editors, *African Art and Leadership,* University of Wisconsin Press, 1972; N. Graburn, *Ethnic and Tourist Arts: Cultural Expressions from the Fourth World,* University of California Press, 1976; Peter Ucko, editor, *Form in Indigenous Art: Schematisation in the Art of Aboriginal Australia and Prehistoric Europe,* Australian Institute of Aboriginal Studies (Canberra), 1977; Felix J. Oinas, editor, *Heroic Epic and Saga: An Introduction to the World's Great Folk Epics,* Indiana University Press, 1978; G. Buccellati and C. Speroni, editors, *The Shape of the Past: Studies in Honor of Franklin D. Murphy,* University of California Press, 1981; M. H. Burssens, editor, *Liber Memorialis for Professor Vandenhoutte,* University of Ghent (Belgium), 1982.

Contributor to journals, including *Africa, African Arts, Man, Journal of American Folklore, American Anthropologist, Cultures et Developpement, Africa-Tervuren,* and *Research in African Literatures.*

WORK IN PROGRESS: The Arts of Central Africa, two volumes, University of California Press; *Headdresses from around the World,* to be published in Belgium; *An Annotated Bibliography of the Arts of Central Africa,* G. K. Hall.

SIDELIGHTS: Daniel P. Biebuyck speaks and reads Dutch, French, German, Latin, Portuguese, Swahili (Bantu), and three other Bantu languages of the Zaire Republic. He traveled widely while involved in field research in Africa, 1949-61. He has also traveled extensively in Europe and North America.

*   *   *

BIGSBY, C(hristopher) W(illiam) E(dgar) 1941-

PERSONAL: Born June 27, 1941, in Dundee, Scotland; son of Edgar Edward Leo and Ivy (Hopkins) Bigsby; married Pamela Lovelady, October 9, 1965; children: Gareth, Kirsten, Juliet, Ewan. *Education:* University of Sheffield, B.A., 1962, M.A., 1964; University of Nottingham, Ph.D., 1966. *Home:* 3 Church Farm, Colney, Norwich, Norfolk, England.

CAREER: University College of Wales, Aberystwyth, lecturer in American literature, 1966-69; University of East Anglia, Norwich, England, lecturer, 1969-73, senior lecturer in American literature, 1973—. Presenter on British Broadcasting Corp. (BBC) radio arts program, "Kaleidoscope." *Member:* British Association of American Studies.

WRITINGS: Confrontation and Commitment: A Study of Contemporary American Drama, 1959-1966, MacGibbon & Kee, 1967, University of Missouri Press, 1968; (editor) *Edward Albee,* Oliver & Boyd, 1969, Prentice-Hall, 1975; (editor) *The Black American Writer,* two volumes, Everett/Edwards, 1969.

(Editor) *Three Negro Plays,* Penguin, 1969; *Dada and Surrealism,* Methuen, 1972; (editor) *Superculture: American Popular Culture and Europe,* Elek, 1975; *Tom Stoppard,* Longman, 1976; *Approaches to Popular Culture,* Edward Arnold, 1976.

The Second Black Renaissance, Greenwood Press, 1980; (editor) *Contemporary English Drama,* Arnold, 1981; *Joe Orton,* Methuen, 1982; *A Critical Introduction to Twentieth-Century American Drama,* Cambridge University Press, 1982; (editor with Heide Ziegler) *The Liberal Tradition and the Radical Imagination*, Junction Books, 1982.

Contributor: Warren French, editor, *The Forties*, Everett/Edwards, 1969; French, editor, *The Fifties*, Everett/Edwards, 1970; Malcolm Bradbury, editor, *The American Novel and the Nineteen Twenties*, Edward Arnold, 1971; French, editor, *The Twenties*, Everett/Edwards, 1975.

Also author, with Malcolm Bradbury, of British Broadcasting Corp. (BBC)-TV plays, "The after Dinner Game" and "Stones"; also author of BBC-TV documentaries on John Steinbeck and Arthur Miller. Also author, with Bradbury, of BBC radio series "Patterson." General editor, with Bradbury, of "Contemporary Writers" series, Methuen.

SIDELIGHTS: C.W.E. Bigsby's *The Second Black Renaissance* is a "splendid book," according to William S. McFeely of the *Times Literary Supplement.* McFeely adds, "As intellectual history, this is work of the first order."

BIOGRAPHICAL/CRITICAL SOURCES: Times Literary Supplement, September 25, 1981, September 3, 1982.

* * *

BING, Elisabeth D. 1914-

PERSONAL: Born July 8, 1914, in Berlin, Germany; came to the United States in 1949; daughter of George Felix (an architect) and Kate (Born) Koenigsberger; married Fred M. Bing (in shipping), April 19, 1951; children: Peter. *Home:* 164 West 79th St., New York, N.Y. 10024.

CAREER: Mt. Sinai Hospital, New York City, member of staff of childbirth education program, 1952-60; Flower & Fifth Avenue Hospitals, New York City, instructor in childbirth education, 1960—. Assistant professor at New York Medical College, 1974—; gives private classes and public lectures on childbirth education. *Member:* American Society for Psychoprophylaxis in Obstetrics (co-founder).

WRITINGS: Six Practical Lessons for an Easier Childbirth, Grosset, 1967; (editor) *The Adventure of Birth: Experiences in the Lamaze Method of Prepared Childbirth*, Simon & Schuster, 1970; (with Gerald Barad) *A Birth in the Family*, Bantam, 1973; *Moving through Pregnancy*, Bobbs-Merrill, 1975; (with Tarvez Tucker) *Prepared Childbirth*, Tobey Publishing, 1975; (with Libby Colman) *Making Love during Pregnancy*, Bantam, 1977; *Having a Baby after 30*, Bantam, 1980; *Dear Elisabeth Bing, We've Had Our Baby*, Pocket Books, 1983; *The Elisabeth Bing Pregnancy Calendar*, Bantam, 1983; (with Karen Michele) *We Gave Birth Together*, Morrow, 1983.

SIDELIGHTS: Elisabeth D. Bing told *CA*, "I continue teaching in my own center for parents, and I seem to be continuing in my career as an author." She is responsible for the training record "Practice for Childbirth" and consultant for the record album "The Lamaze Experience."

* * *

BINGHAM, Charlotte (Mary Therese) 1942-

PERSONAL: Born June 29, 1942, in Haywards Heath, Sussex, England; daughter of John Michael Ward (seventh baron of Clanmorris; a writer of crime stories) and Madeleine (a writer; maiden name, Ebel) Bingham; married Terence Joseph Brady (an actor and writer), January 15, 1964; children: Candida, Matthew. *Education:* Attended Sorbonne, University of Paris,

1959-60. *Politics:* Liberal. *Religion:* Roman Catholic. *Home:* Hardway House, Brutow, Somerset, England. *Agent:* A. D. Peters & Co. Ltd., 10 Buckingham St., London WC2N 6BU, England.

CAREER: Playwright, novelist, and writer for television series. *Member:* Writers Guild of Great Britain.

WRITINGS: Coronet among the Weeds (autobiographical; also see below), Random House, 1963; *Lucinda* (novel), Heinemann, 1966; *Coronet among the Grass* (autobiographical; also see below), Heinemann, 1972; *No, Honestly!* (contains *Coronet among the Weeds* and *Coronet among the Grass*), Penguin, 1974; *Belgravia*, M. Joseph, 1983.

With husband, Terence Brady: *Rose's Story* (novel), Sphere Books, 1972, Pocket Books, 1975; *Victoria* (novel), W. H. Allen, 1972; *Victoria and Company* (novel), W. H. Allen, 1974; *Yes, Honestly*, Sphere Books, 1977. Also co-author with Brady of plays "One Two Sky's Blue," 1967, "Making the Party," 1973, and "Such a Small Word," 1973, and of radio play "The Victoria Line," 1971.

Scripts for television series; with Brady: "Take Three Girls," British Broadcasting Corp. (BBC-TV), 1968-71; "Upstairs, Downstairs," LWTV, 1971-73; "No, Honestly," LWTV, 1974-75; "One of the Family," Thames-TV, 1975; "Yes, Honestly," LWTV, 1975-76; "Plays for Today," BBC-TV, 1977; "Pig in the Middle," LWTV, 1980; "Nanny," BBC-TV, 1981-83. Also co-author with Brady of "Away from It All," "Thomas and Sarah," and "The Complete Lack of Charm of the Bourgeoisie." Creator of program "Oh, Madeline," ABC-TV, 1983.

Contributor to periodicals, including *Vogue, Harper's, Evening Standard,* and *Catholic Herald.*

WORK IN PROGRESS: A novel, *Country Life*, and a play, "A Dip before Breakfast," both with husband, Terence Brady.

SIDELIGHTS: Charlotte Bingham told *CA*: "I turned to writing at the age of eighteen because of an inability to master the arts of shorthand and typing. The resultant humorous book, *Coronet among the Weeds*, has been described as a book about being a debutante, which I no longer bother to deny, having too much regard for my royalties.

"Shortly after its publication I met and married Terence Brady, who put an end to any treasured thoughts of early retirement by lassoing me into partnership with him. Some of our television series have appeared in the United States, most notably our contributions to 'Upstairs, Downstairs' and 'No, Honestly,' which was based loosely upon *Coronet among the Grass*.''

* * *

BINGHAM, John (Michael Ward) 1908-

PERSONAL: Listed in some biographical and bibliographical sources under inherited title Baron John Michael Ward Bingham Clanmorris, or Lord Clanmorris; born November 3, 1908; son of Arthur Robert Maurice (sixth baron of Clanmorris) and Leila (Cloete) Bingham; married Madeleine Ebel (a writer), July 28, 1934; children: Simon, Charlotte (Mrs. Terence Brady). *Education:* Educated at Cheltenham College, Gloucestershire, England, and in France and Germany. *Religion:* Church of England. *Home:* 72 York Mansions, Prince of Wales Dr., London S.W.11, England. *Agent:* A. D. Peters & Co. Ltd., 10 Buckingham St., London WC2N 6BU, England.

CAREER: Seventh baron of Clanmorris, succeeding father to title, 1960. *Hull Daily Mail,* Hull, England, reporter, beginning 1931; later joined *Sunday Dispatch,* London, England, as reporter, picture-editor, then feature-writer; served with Control Commission in Germany during the 1940s; Ministry of Defence, London, civil servant, 1950—. *Military service:* British Army, Royal Engineers, 1939-40.

WRITINGS: My Name Is Michael Sibley, Dodd, 1952; *The Tender Poisoner,* Dodd, 1953 (published in England as *Five Roundabouts to Heaven,* Gollancz, 1953); *The Third Skin,* Dodd, 1954 (published in England as *The Third Skin: A Story of Crime,* Gollancz, 1954); *The Paton Street Case,* Gollancz, 1955, published as *Inspector Morgan's Dilemma,* Dodd, 1956; *Murder Off the Record,* Dodd, 1957 (published in England as *Marion,* Gollancz, 1958); *Murder Plan Six,* Gollancz, 1958, Dodd, 1959; *Night's Black Agent,* Dodd, 1961; *A Case of Libel,* Gollancz, 1963; *Fragment of Fear,* Gollancz, 1965, Dutton, 1966; *The Double Agent,* Gollancz, 1966, Dutton, 1967; *I Love, I Kill,* Gollancz, 1968; *Good Old Charlie,* Simon & Schuster, 1968.

Vulture in the Sun, Gollancz, 1971; *The Hunting Down of Peter Manuel, Glasgow Multiple Murderer,* Macmillan, 1973; *God's Defector: The Case of the Missing Priest,* Macmillan (London), 1976, published as *Ministry of Death,* Walker & Co., 1977; *Marriage Bureau Murders,* Macmillan, 1977; *Deadly Picnic,* Macmillan (London), 1980, State Mutual Book, 1982; *Brock,* Gollancz, 1981; *Brock and the Defector,* Doubleday, 1982.

SIDELIGHTS: Although John Bingham, seventh baron of Clanmorris, inherited a castle in Northern Ireland, he was not interested in "a feudal way of life" and hence disposed of the property; the castle became Bangor's Town Hall. *Media adaptations: Fragment of Fear* was filmed by Columbia in 1970.

AVOCATIONAL INTERESTS: Travel and gardening.

BIOGRAPHICAL/CRITICAL SOURCES: Books and Bookmen, March, 1968.

* * *

BINGHAM, Madeleine (Mary Ebel) 1912-
(Julia Mannering)

PERSONAL: Listed in some biographical sources under title Baroness Madeleine Mary Ebel Clanmorris; born February 1, 1912, in London, England; daughter of Clement Mary and Charlotte (Collins) Ebel; married John Michael Ward Bingham (seventh baron of Clanmorris; a writer of crime stories), July 28, 1934; children: Simon, Charlotte (Mrs. Terence Brady). *Education:* Educated in private schools in England and Belgium. *Religion:* Roman Catholic. *Home:* 72 York Mansions, Prince of Wales Dr., London S.W.11, England. *Agent:* A. D. Peters & Co. Ltd., 10 Buckingham St., London WC2N 6BU, England.

CAREER: Novelist, biographer, and playwright; formerly employed by *Times,* London, England.

WRITINGS: The Man from the Ministry (three-act comedy), Samuel French, 1947; (under pseudonym Julia Mannering) *The Passionate Poet: A Romantic Story Based upon Lord Byron's Loves and Adventures,* Museum Press, 1951; *Look to the Rose,* Museum Press, 1953; *Cheapest in the End,* Dodd, 1963; *Mary, Queen of Scots,* A. S. Barnes, 1969.

Scotland under Mary Stuart: An Account of Everyday Life, Allen & Unwin, 1971, St. Martin's, 1973; *Sheridan: The Track*

of a Comet, St. Martin's, 1972; *Masks and Facades: Sir John Vanbrugh, the Man in His Setting,* Allen & Unwin, 1974; *Peers and Plebs: Two Families in a Changing World* (autobiographical), Allen & Unwin, 1975; *Henry Irving: The Greatest Victorian Actor,* foreword by John Gielgud, Stein & Day, 1978 (published in England as *Henry Irving and the Victorian Theatre,* Allen & Unwin, 1978); *"The Great Lover": The Life and Art of Herbert Beerbohm Tree,* Atheneum, 1979; *Earls and Girls,* David & Charles, 1980 (published in England as *Earls and Girls: Dramas in High Society,* Hamish Hamilton, 1980); *Princess Lieven: Russian Intriguer,* David & Charles, 1982.

Also author of produced plays "In the Red" and "The Real McCoy." Contributor of short stories to periodicals, including *Harper's* and *Vanity Fair.*

SIDELIGHTS: Madeleine Bingham's *Henry Irving: The Greatest Victorian Actor* is "one of the best theatrical biographies of recent years," writes Jonathan Keates in the *New Statesman.* "Bingham, unsentimental and painstaking, convincingly argues the case for a life of monomaniacal devotion to a supremely ephemeral calling, and one which for better or worse, had turned a job into a profession." Robert Morley says in the *Times Literary Supplement* that Bingham "writes touchingly of . . . [Irving's] parting with Ellen Terry, of the happiness he found in the company of the last of his mistresses, . . . of his manager Bram Stoker, and of the extravagance and generosity with which he entertained his friends and his fellow actors, to whom he was always kindness and patience itself. I liked especially the story of how until far into the night he coached one of his supporting cast to deliver the single line with which he had entrusted him."

AVOCATIONAL INTERESTS: The theater, cooking, traveling.

BIOGRAPHICAL/CRITICAL SOURCES: Times Literary Supplement, March 19, 1976, May 5, 1978, September 5, 1980, March 18, 1983; *New Statesman,* April 7, 1978, March 2, 1979; *Times* (London), September 3, 1980; *Spectator,* August 29, 1982.

* * *

BIRD, Caroline 1915-

PERSONAL: Born April 15, 1915, in New York, N.Y.; daughter of Hobart S. (a lawyer) and Ida (Brattrud) Bird; married Edward A. Menuez, June 8, 1934 (divorced, 1945); married John Thomas Mahoney (a writer), January 5, 1957; children: (first marriage) Carol (Mrs. John Paul Barach); (second marriage) John Thomas, Jr. *Education:* Attended Vassar College, 1931-34; University of Toledo, B.A., 1938; University of Wisconsin—Madison, M.A., 1939. *Politics:* Democrat. *Religion:* Protestant. *Home:* 31 Sunrise Lane, Poughkeepsie, N.Y. 12603; and 60 Gramercy Park, New York, N.Y. 10010.

CAREER: Newsweek, New York City, researcher, 1942-43; *New York Journal of Commerce,* New York City, desk editor, 1943-44; *Fortune,* New York City, researcher, 1944-46; Dudley-Anderson-Yutzy (public relations firm), New York City, staff writer, 1947-68; Russell Sage College, Troy, N.Y., Froman Distinguished Professor, 1972-73. *Member:* Society of Magazine Writers (secretary, 1953), American Sociological Association, Women in Communications, Women's Equity Action League, National Organization for Women. *Awards, honors: The Invisible Scar* was named one of the best books of 1966 by the American Library Association.

WRITINGS—Published by McKay, except as indicated: *The Invisible Scar: The Great Depression and What It Did to American Life, from Then Until Now*, 1966; (with Sara Welles Briller) *Born Female: The High Cost of Keeping Women Down*, 1968, revised edition, 1970; *The Crowding Syndrome*, 1972; *Everything a Woman Needs to Know to Get Paid What She's Worth*, 1973, revised edition, Bantam, 1981; *The Case Against College*, 1975; *Enterprising Women: Their Contribution to the American Economy, 1776-1976*, Norton, 1976; *What Women Want*, Simon & Schuster, 1978; *The Two-Paycheck Marriage: How Women at Work Are Changing Life in America*, Rawson, Wade, 1979; *The Good Years: Your Life in the Twenty-First Century*, Norton, 1983.

SIDELIGHTS: Feminist writer Caroline Bird has focused her attention on women's roles in the business world. Her first book on the subject, *Born Female: The High Cost of Keeping Women Down*, is a detailed proof of job discrimination against women. Anne Bristein of *Book World* writes that Bird "is committed and convincing, proving point by point, patiently and painstakingly, with footnotes and heavy documentation, in category after category . . . that women are indeed kept down on the job, and that such discrimination is not inherently ridiculous but immoral." Bird "not only writes down all the things that women think but rarely say," Gloria Steinem writes in the *New York Times Book Review*, "she documents them. . . . The last chapter, 'The Case for Equality,' is a storehouse of strong opinions and suggested reforms. . . . Probably it should be sent to all the Presidential candidates just to shake up their thinking."

In *Everything a Woman Needs to Know to Get Paid What She's Worth*, Bird takes as given that many women are discriminated against in the workplace. She then offers tested methods women can use to improve their positions. "The recommendations," Cynthia Harrison of *Library Journal* writes, "are for those who want to best (rather than change) the system." June Goodwin of *Christian Science Monitor* finds that, like *Born Female*, *Everything a Woman Needs to Know* is a "highly serious, well-researched study of women's job plight. Using the old Socratic question-and-answer format, she teaches women how to get jobs, better jobs, better pay for their jobs, and how to fight the subtle and not so subtle pressures which would keep them down."

Bird turns her attention in *The Two-Paycheck Marriage* to the social effects of working women in America. As she states in the book, "Enough women are now earning enough money to change the terms of both family and work." To assess these changes, Bird "surveys a broad spectrum of working couples at all income levels," A. S. Kowler of *Library Journal* explains. Suzanne Fields of the *Washington Post Book World* writes that Bird "collates the sociological, psychological, and economic histories of the two-paycheck families; cool assessments of the child-care crisis, changing sex-and-power alignments, and child-bearing timetables; experiments of 'lifestyle pioneers' who are trying to balance demands of family and career, and a far-out feminist vision of the future." Writing in the *Journal of Marriage and Family*, M. M. Poloma concludes that the book is "a very readable introduction to the topic for the beginner and, at the same time, provides some creative insight into alternatives that have not yet been empirically explored by the social science researcher."

BIOGRAPHICAL/CRITICAL SOURCES: *New York Post*, March 4, 1966, August 31, 1968; *New York Times Book Review*, August 11, 1968; *Book World*, September 22, 1968; *Saturday Review*, November 2, 1968; *Detroit News*, March 26, 1971; *Gramercy Herald*, August 20, 1971; *Library Journal*, July, 1973, April 15, 1979; *Christian Science Monitor*, August 22, 1973; *Charlotte Observer*, January 28, 1974; *Today's Secretary*, March, 1974; *Los Angeles Times*, May 1, 1975; *Washington Post Book World*, April 29, 1979; *Journal of Marriage and Family*, February, 1980; *Washington Post*, July 15, 1983.

*   *   *

BIRMINGHAM, F(rederic) A(lexander)   1911-1982

PERSONAL: Born November 13, 1911, in New York, N.Y.; died of cancer, August 29, 1982, in Scranton, Pa.; son of John Francis and Louise (Westher) Birmingham; married Frances Atherton, November 8, 1941. *Education:* Dartmouth College, B.A., 1933. *Religion:* Episcopalian. *Residence:* Scranton, Pa.

CAREER: *Apparel Arts* (magazine), Eastern editor, 1935-36, consulting editor, beginning 1941; *Time*, New York City, editorial staff, 1936-37; author of cartoon-essay feature for Bell Syndicate and North American Newspaper Alliance, 1936-37; Ogden-Watney (publishers), New York City, editor, 1938-39; *Esquire*, New York City, sales promotion manager, 1941-43, managing editor, 1946-53, editor-in-chief, 1953-57; *Gentleman's Quarterly*, New York City, executive editor, 1947-57; fashion editor, *Playboy* 1957-58; editorial director, General Publishing Co., 1959-62; editor, *Cavalier*, 1963-66; *Reader's Digest*, Pleasantville, N.Y., special project editor, 1966-67; Status-Diplomat Magazines, New York City, editorial director, 1967-68; *Status Magazine*, New York City, editor, 1968-71; *Saturday Evening Post*, Indianapolis, Ind., managing editor, beginning 1971.

Member of board of directors, Curtis Publishing; president and executive editor, Third World News, beginning 1968. Lecturer at Radcliffe College, University of Missouri, Northwestern University, New York University, and City University of New York; adjunct professor of journalism, University of Scranton. Free-lance writer and lecturer, 1957-62. Senior editor, U.S. Office of War Information, 1942-43. *Military service:* U.S. Naval Reserve, 1943-46; became lieutenant commander. *Member:* Authors League of America, Overseas Press Club, Sigma Phi Epsilon, Alpha Iota Epsilon, Sigma Delta Phi.

WRITINGS: (Editor) *The Esquire Book of Etiquette*, Lippincott, 1953; (editor) *The Girls from Esquire*, Random House, 1953; *It Was Fun While It Lasted*, Lippincott, 1956; (editor and contributor) *The Esquire Drink Book*, Harper, 1956; (editor and contributor) *The Esquire Fashion Book*, Harper, 1957; *The Writer's Craft*, Hawthorn, 1958; *The Ivy League Today*, Crowell, 1961; *The Cookbook for Men*, Harper, 1961; *How to Succeed at Touch Football*, Harper, 1962; (with wife, Frances Birmingham) *The Wedding Book*, Harper, 1964.

The Saturday Evening Post Family Cookbook, Curtis Publishing, 1975; (with Charlotte Snyder Turgeon) *The Saturday Evening Post All-American Cookbook*, Curtis Publishing, 1976; (with Cory Servaas) *Fiber and Bran Better Health Cookbook*, Curtis Publishing, 1977; *John, the Man Who Would Be President*, edited by Thomas J. Synhorst, Curtis Publishing, 1979; *Ball Corporation: The First Century*, Curtis Publishing, 1980. Contributor of articles and short stories to magazines and newspapers in the United States and abroad.

AVOCATIONAL INTERESTS: Music, painting, sports.

OBITUARIES: *New York Times*, August 31, 1982.†

BIRO, B(alint) S(tephen) 1921-
(Val Biro)

PERSONAL: Val is Biro's translation of his Hungarian given name, Balint; surname is pronounced *Beer*-oh; born October 6, 1921, in Hungary; son of Balint (a lawyer) and Margaret (Gyulahazi) Biro; married Vivien Woolley, April 14, 1946; married Marie Louise Ellaway, 1970; children: (first marriage) Melissa. *Education:* Cistercian School, Budapest, Hungary, Baccaloreat, 1939; attended Central School of Arts and Crafts, London, England, 1939-42. *Politics:* Liberal Conservative. *Religion:* Roman Catholic. *Home and studio:* 95 High St., Amersham, Buckinghamshire, England.

CAREER: Production manager for Sylvan Press Ltd. and C. & J. Temple Ltd., 1945-48; art director, John Lehmann Ltd., 1948-53; free-lance artist and illustrator, 1953—; governor of Amersham College of Art and Design and Berkshire College of Art and Design. Designer of silver medals for collectors and of illustrations for engraving on glass. Urban district councillor, 1966-70. *Member:* Society of Industrial Artists and Designers (fellow).

WRITINGS—Under name Val Biro, except as indicated: *Discovering Chesham,* Shire Publications, 1968; *The Honest Thief: A Hungarian Folktale,* Hodder & Stoughton, 1972, Holiday House, 1973; *Hungarian Folk Tales,* Oxford University Press, 1980; *The Magic Doctor,* Oxford University Press, 1982; *Fables from Aesop,* Ginn, 1983.

"Gumdrop" series; published by Hodder & Stoughton, except as indicated; self-illustrated juveniles: *Gumdrop: The Adventures of a Vintage Car,* 1966, Follett, 1967; *Gumdrop and the Farmer's Friend,* 1967, Follett, 1968; . . . *on the Rally,* 1968, Follett, 1969; . . . *on the Move,* Follett, 1969; . . . *Goes to London,* 1971; . . . *Finds a Friend,* 1973; . . . *in Double Trouble,* 1975; . . . *and the Steamroller,* 1976; . . . *on the Brighton Run,* 1976; . . . *Posts a Letter,* 1976; . . . *Gets His Wings,* 1979; . . . *Finds a Ghost,* 1980; . . . *and the Secret Switches,* 1981; . . . *Makes a Start,* 1982; . . . *at Sea,* 1983. Also author of four "Little Gumdrop" books, 1982.

Illustrator: Enid Blyton, *Br'er Rabbit and the Alligator,* Knight Books, 1976; Blyton, *Br'er Rabbit Saves Br'er Terrapin,* Knight Books, 1976; E. W. Hildick, *The Case of the Nervous Schoolboy,* Hodder & Stoughton, 1976; John Denton, *Machines on the Farm,* Puffin, 1976; (under name B. S. Biro) Dora Thatcher, *Hovering with Henry,* Hodder & Stoughton, 1976; (under name B. S. Biro) Joan Drake, *Mr. Bubbus and the Railway Smugglers,* Hodder & Stoughton, 1976; (under name B. S. Biro) Jean Plaidy, *The Prince and the Quakeress,* Pan Books, 1976; Christina Hole, *British Folk Customs,* Hutchinson, 1976; Fanny Cradock, *The Sherlock Holmes Cook Book,* W. H. Allen, 1976; H.J.B. Peel, *Country Talk Again,* R. Hale, 1977; Norman J. Bull, *100 Bible Stories,* Hamlyn, 1980; Bull, *100 New Testament Stories,* Hamlyn, 1981; Blyton, *Bumblebee Stories,* four books, Hamlyn, 1981; *The St. Michael Book of Worzel Gummidge Stories,* Marks & Spencer, 1982; Kenneth Grahame, *Tales from 'The Wind in the Willows,'* Marks & Spencer, 1983.

Illustrator; all written by H. E. Todd; published by Hodder & Stoughton, except as indicated: *The Sick Cow,* 1976; *George, the Fire Engine,* 1976; *The Roundabout Horse,* 1978; *The Very, Very Long Dog,* Transworld Books, 1979; *The Crawly, Crawly Caterpillar,* Transworld Books, 1980; *The King of Beasts,* 1980; *Jungle Silver,* 1981; *The Tiny, Tiny Tadpole,* Transworld Books, 1981; *The Big Sneeze,* 1982.

WORK IN PROGRESS: More "Little Gumdrop" books; *Fables from Aesop; The Pied Piper of Hamelin; Adventures of Dilbert;* illustrating *The Scruffy, Scruffy Dog.*

SIDELIGHTS: Val Biro told *CA:* "Interest in vintage cars led to owning the original 'Gumdrop' (a 1926 tourer), which led to books for children about it." Biro travels mainly in England and Europe to sketch and paint.

*   *   *

BIRO, Val
See BIRO, B(alint) S(tephen)

*   *   *

BISSOONDOYAL, Basdeo 1906-

PERSONAL: Born April 15, 1906, in Riviere des Anguilles, Mauritius; son of Lutchuman (a job contractor) and Yashomatee (Oodit) Bissoondoyal; married Dowlutteea Sahjadah, August, 1940; children: Anupam (son), Rami (Mrs. Anil Saddul), Charudevi (Mrs. R. Deelchand), Aruna (Mrs. S. Harbans), Kunti (Mrs. K. Domah), Sanjna (daughters). *Education:* Attended schools in Mauritus, receiving Second Class Teacher's Certificate, 1924; Punjab University, B.A. (with honors), 1937; Calcutta University, M.A., 1939. *Religion:* Hindu. *Home and office:* 14 Sookdeo Bissoondoyal St., Port Louis, Mauritius.

CAREER: Primary teacher in Mauritius at Port Louis, 1922-26, and Saint Julien Village, Flacq, 1926-32; Gurukula University, Hardwar, India, served briefly on the faculty, 1935; writer. *Awards, honors:* Received distinction of Sahitya Vachasfrati from the Hindi Sahitya Sammelan, Allahabad, 1969.

WRITINGS: *Hindu Scriptures,* P. R. Macmillan, 1961; *Les Hindous et leurs Ecritures Sacrees,* Editions Adyar (Paris), 1965; *The Essence of the Vedas and Allied Scriptures,* Jaico (Bombay), 1966; *India in French Literature,* Luzac & Co., 1967; *The Truth about Mauritius,* Bhartiya Vidya Bhavan (Bombay), 1968; *Deux Indiens Illustres,* Editions Adyar, 1968; *L'Essence du vedisme,* Sri Aurobindo Ashram Press (Pondicherry), 1969.

The Message of the Four Vidas, Orient Longman (Delhi), 1972; *Le Rig Veda,* Sri Aurobindo Ashram Press, 1974; *Mahatma Gandhi: A New Approach,* Bhartiya Vidya Bhavan, 1975; *India in World Literature,* Luzac & Co., 1976; *Life in Greater India* (autobiography), Bhartiya Vidya Bhavan, 1983. Also contributor to *Moisson du Monde,* Book II, a French reader.

Translator into Hindi: Bernardin de Saint-Pierre, *Paul et Virginie,* Ledentu (Paris), 1956; Bernardin de Saint-Pierre, *La Chaumiere indienne,* Ledentu, 1959; *Le Cafe de Surat,* Ledentu, 1968. Contributor to *Contemporary Review* (London), *France-Asie/Asia* (Tokyo), *Lotus Bleu* (Paris), *Indo-Asian Culture* (Delhi), *Unesco Features* (Paris), *Calcutta Review, The Modern Review,* and *Indian Review.*

SIDELIGHTS: Cambridge University includes Basdeo Bissoondoyal's *Hindu Scriptures* on a recommended reading list for students studying advanced Hinduism. Cambridge University also requires instructors offering Hindi to use Bissoondoyal's translation of *Paul et Virginie* as a text.

BIOGRAPHICAL/CRITICAL SOURCES: Basdeo Bissoondoyal, *Life in Greater India* (autobiography), Bhartiya Vidya Bhavan, 1983.

BLACKLEDGE, Ethel H(ale)

PERSONAL: Born in Mount Vernon, Ky.; daughter of Wilburn and Allie (Allen) Hale; married Walter L. Blackledge (a professor), February 25, 1960; children: Walter L. Jr., Lawrence Allen. *Education:* Ohio State University, B.S., 1949; attended University of Oklahoma, 1949-51; University of Texas, M.Ed., 1959. *Religion:* Presbyterian. *Home:* 3620 Gary Ave., Alton, Ill. 62002.

CAREER: Former high school teacher in Ohio; worked for one year as secretary in Wiesbaden, Germany; University of Texas at Austin, lecturer, 1957-59; Southern Illinois University, Edwardsville Campus, Alton, lecturer, 1959-61.

WRITINGS: (With husband, Walter L. Blackledge) *Supervising Women Employees,* Dartnell, 1966; (with W. L. Blackledge and Helen J. Keily) *You and Your Job: Finding It, Getting It, and Keeping It,* South-Western, 1967; (with W. L. Blackledge) *The Job You Want: How to Get It,* South-Western, 1975, 3rd edition, 1983; *An Hour Is Forever* (novel), Avon, 1977; *The Fire* (novel), Sphere (London), 1978. Contributor to *Reader's Digest, Family Weekly,* and business education journals.

*   *   *

BLACKSTONE, William T(homas) 1931-

PERSONAL: Born December 8, 1931, in Augusta, Ga.; son of Thomas Watson and Katie (Curtis) Blackstone; married Norma Jean Tew, March 27, 1954; children: Lisa Brooks, Jeffrey. *Education:* Elon College, B.A., 1953; Duke University, M.A., 1955, Ph.D., 1957. *Home:* Barnett Shoals Rd., Athens, Ga. 30601. *Office:* Department of Philosophy, University of Georgia, Athens, Ga.

CAREER: Elon College, Elon College, N.C., associate professor of philosophy, 1957-58; University of Florida, Gainesville, assistant professor of philosophy, 1958-61; University of Georgia, Athens, associate professor, 1961-63, professor of philosophy and religion and head of department, 1963—, chairman of Division of Social Sciences. *Member:* International Association for Law and Social Philosophy (member of executive committee, 1975), American Philosophical Association (vice-president, 1960-61), Southern Society for Philosophy of Religion, Southern Society for Philosophy and Psychology (member of executive council, 1965-68), Southeastern Philosophy of Education Society (president, 1969), Georgia Philosophical Society (president, 1966-67). *Awards, honors:* Southern Society for Philosophy and Psychology annual award for 1958-59, 1959-60, 1960-61; Michael Award from University of Georgia, 1965.

WRITINGS: The Problem of Religious Knowledge, Prentice-Hall, 1963; *Francis Hutcheson and Contemporary Ethical Theory,* University of Georgia Press, 1965; *The Concept of Equality,* Burgess, 1969; *Ethics and Education,* University of Georgia Press, 1970; (editor) *Meaning and Existence,* Holt, 1971; *Political Philosophy,* Crowell, 1973; *Philosophy and Environmental Crisis,* University of Georgia Press, 1974; *Land Use: Dimensions for Decision Making,* Center for Continuing Education, University of Georgia, 1974; (with Robert Heslep) *Social Justice and Preferential Treatment: Women and Racial Minorities in Education and Business,* University of Georgia Press, 1977; (with Joel Feinberg and Tom Beauchamp) *Philosophy and the Human Conditions,* Prentice-Hall, 1980. Also author of *Religious Knowledge and Religion,* 1968. Contributor to numerous philosophy journals.

AVOCATIONAL INTERESTS: Tennis.†

*   *   *

BLAIR, Claude 1922-

PERSONAL: Born November 30, 1922, in Manchester, England; son of William Henry Murray (a businessman) and Lilian (Wearing) Blair; married Joan Drinkwater, February 23, 1952; children: William John. *Education:* University of Manchester, B.A. (with honors), 1950, M.A., 1963. *Politics:* Liberal. *Religion:* Anglican. *Home:* 90 Links Rd., Ashtead, Surrey KT1 2HW, England.

CAREER: Tower of London Armouries, London, England, assistant, 1951-56; Victoria and Albert Museum, London, assistant keeper in department of metalwork, 1956-66, deputy keeper, 1966-72, keeper, 1972-82, art consultant, 1983—. *Military service:* Royal Artillery, 1942-46; became captain. *Member:* Arms and Armour Society, Royal Archaeological Institute, Monumental Brass Society, Society of Genealogists, Danish Arms and Armour Society, German Arms and Costume Society, Polish Arms and Armour Society (honorary member), Lancashire and Cheshire Antiquarian Society, Society of Antiquaries of London (fellow), Accademia di San Marciano (Turin).

WRITINGS: European Armour, c. 1066-c. 1700, Batsford, 1958; *European and American Arms, c. 1100-1850,* Bonanza Books, 1962; *The Silvered Armour of Henry VIII in the Tower of London,* Ministry of Public Buildings and Works, 1965; *Pistols of the World,* Viking, 1968; *Three Presentation Swords in the Victoria and Albert Museum, and a Group of English Enamels,* Victoria and Albert Museum, 1972; *Arms, Armour and Base-Metalwork: The James A. de Rothschild Collection at Waddesdon Manor* (catalog), Office du Livre (Fribourg), 1974; (general editor and contributor) *History of Firearms,* Pollard, 1983.

Contributor to *Encyclopaedia Britannica* and *Encyclopedia of Firearms;* contributor of articles to *Connaissance des Arts, Antiquaries Journal, Connoisseur, Archaeological Journal, Metropolitan Museum Journal, Journal of the Arms and Armour Society,* and other publications. Honorary editor, *Journal of the Arms and Armour Society,* 1953-78.

WORK IN PROGRESS: Research on the history of English royal armor at Greenwich, on the history of English arms, and on the history of armor in general.

*   *   *

BLAIR, Edward P(ayson) 1910-

PERSONAL: Born December 23, 1910, in Woodburn, Ore.; son of Oscar Newton (a minister) and Bertha (Myers) Blair; married Vivian Elizabeth Krisel, 1934; children: Phyllis Marie (Mrs. George W. Belsey III), Sharon Louise (Mrs. Thomas H. Robinson). *Education:* Seattle Pacific College (now University), A.B., 1931; Biblical Seminary in New York (now New York Theological Seminary), S.T.B., 1934; American School of Oriental Research, Jerusalem, graduate study, 1935-36; Yale University, Ph.D., 1939. *Religion:* United Methodist. *Home:* 299 North Heather Dr., Camano Island, Wash. 98292.

CAREER: Seattle Pacific College (now University), Seattle, Wash., professor of Bible and dean of School of Religion, 1939-41; Biblical Seminary in New York (now New York Theological Seminary), New York, N.Y., professor of Old

Testament language and literature, 1941-42; Garrett Theological Seminary (now Garrett-Evangelical Theological Seminary), Evanston, Ill., professor, 1942-60, Harry R. Kendall Professor of New Testament Interpretation, 1960-71, adjunct professor of New Testament interpretation, 1971-75, professor emeritus, 1975—. Member of archeological expeditions at Anata, Palestine, 1935, Roman Jericho, 1951, Ostia, Italy, 1965, and Shechem, Israel, 1966 and 1968. Lecturer at conferences.

MEMBER: American Academy of Religion, National Association of Biblical Instructors, Society of Biblical Literature and Exegesis, Chicago Society of Biblical Research (president, 1952-53). *Awards, honors:* Citation of appreciation, Laymen's National Bible Committee, 1975, for *The Abingdon Bible Handbook;* named alumnus of the year, Seattle Pacific University, 1981.

WRITINGS—Published by Abingdon, except as indicated: *The Acts and Apocalyptic Literature,* 1946; *A Study of the Book of Acts,* 1951; *The Bible and You,* 1953; *Getting to Know the Bible,* 1956; *Jesus in the Gospel of Matthew,* 1960; (contributor) *Interpreter's Dictionary of the Bible,* 1962; *The Book of Deuteronomy, The Book of Joshua,* John Knox, 1964; (contributor) *The Layman's Bible Commentary,* John Knox, 1964; (contributor) *The Illustrated Family Encyclopedia of the Living Bible,* fourteen volumes, San Francisco Productions, 1967; *Leader's Guide to the Study of the Sermon on the Mount,* 1968; (contributor) *The Interpreter's One-Volume Commentary on the Bible,* 1971; *The Abingdon Bible Handbook,* 1975.

*   *   *

BLAKE, L(eslie) J(ames) 1913-
(James Lester, Peter Tabard)

PERSONAL: Born March 5, 1913, in Bendigo, Victoria, Australia; son of John Arthur (a construction foreman) and Alicia Anne (Taylor) Blake; married Shirley Jean Woodfine, April 16, 1938; children: Maureen Shirley (Mrs. Albert Chalmers), Michael Jon, Alisoun Elizabeth. *Education:* Melbourne Teachers' College, Trained Primary Teachers' Certificate, 1934; University of Melbourne, B.A., 1952, B.Ed., 1956, M.Ed., 1974. *Religion:* Church of England. *Home:* 4 Anton Ct., Karingal, Victoria 3199, Australia.

CAREER: Victoria Education Department, Melbourne, Australia, teacher in western Victoria schools, 1935-41, and Geelong schools, 1946-52, lecturer at Geelong Teachers' College, 1953-58, state inspector of schools, 1958-66, official historian, 1966-73; Victoria state historian, 1974-76. Lecturer at University of Melbourne, 1965, and throughout Australia. Chairman, State Education History Committee, 1966-73; chairman of education department, Centennial Celebration Committee, 1972-73; chairman, C. J. Dennis Commemorative Committee, 1975. Member, Preservation of Historic Places Committee, 1970-76, and History Advisory Council of Victoria, 1975. *Military service:* Australian Imperial Forces, 1942-46; served in Southwest Pacific. *Member:* International P.E.N. (vice-president, 1971-72), Australian College of Education (fellow), Australian Society of Authors, Fellowship of Australian Writers, Royal Historical Society of Victoria (fellow; president, 1966-71), Western Victorian Association of Historical Societies (president, 1963), Geelong Historical Society, Horsham District Historical Society (fellow; president, 1962-64). *Awards, honors:* Received Order of the British Empire, 1974.

WRITINGS: Teaching Social Studies, Whitcombe & Tombs, 1957, 3rd edition, 1964; *Shaw Neilson in the Wimmera,* Lowan

Shire, 1961; (editor) *Patterns in Poetry,* Angus & Robertson, 1962, 2nd edition, 1966; (with J. A. Cole) *Principles and Techniques of Teaching,* Whitcombe & Tombs, 1962, 3rd edition, 1965; (with K. Lovett) *Wimmera Shire Centenary,* Wimmera Shire, 1962, 4th edition, 1964; *Lost in the Bush,* Whitcombe & Tombs, 1964; *Australian Writers,* Tri-Ocean, 1968; *Richard Hale Budd,* privately printed, 1968.

Geelong Sketchbook, Rigby, 1971; *Gold Escort,* Hawthorn Press, 1971; (with Hugh Anderson) *John Shaw Neilson,* Rigby, 1972; *Wimmera: A Regional History,* Cypress, 1973; (general editor) *Vision and Realisation: A Centenary History of State Education in Victoria,* three volumes, Victoria Education Department, 1973; *Werribee Park,* Victoria Premier's Department, 1974; *Letters of Charles Joseph La Trobe,* Victoria Premier's Department, 1975; *Land of the Lowan: 100 Years in Nhill and the West Wimmera,* Nhill Historical Society, 1976; *Place Names of Victoria,* Rigby, 1976; *Pioneer Schools of Australia,* Rigby, 1976; *Gold Escorts in Australia,* Rigby, 1977; *The People of Colonial Australia,* Franklin Mint, 1978; *Covered Wagons in Australia,* Rigby, 1979; *Tales from Old Geelong,* Neptune Press, 1979, Book 2, 1983; *Peter Lalor: The Man from Eureka,* Neptune Press, 1979.

Young Nel, Neptune Press, 1980; *Tattyara: A History of Kaniva District,* Kaniva Shire, 1981; *Schools of the Tattyara,* Kaniva Shire, 1981; (editor) Ned Peters, *A Gold Digger's Diaries,* Neptune Press, 1981; (editor) Mary Read and Mary Spencer, *Aunt Spencer's Diaries,* Neptune Press, 1981; (with Hugh Anderson) *Green Days and Cherries,* Red Rooster Press, 1981; *Captain Dana and the Native Police,* Neptune Press, 1982.

Also author, under pseudonyms James Lester and Peter Tabard, of over 100 features and documentaries for Australian Broadcasting Commission and Radio Australia, 1952-61; also columnist for *Melbourne Herald* under pseudonym Peter Tabard, 1965-66. Contributor to *Australian Dictionary of Biography.* Contributor to magazines and newspapers. Member of advisory panel, *Medallic History of Australia,* 1971-78.

WORK IN PROGRESS: Golden Years of Buninyong; Overlander: The Mollison Papers; Banjo Paterson's Old Bush Songs; Oscar Asche; Old Eko; The Frontier File; Colonial Kaleidoscope.

SIDELIGHTS: L. J. Blake told *CA:* "In my writing I seek to fill some of the gaps in Australian historiography—aspects of biography, local, regional, and national history and geography. The increasing awareness of the contribution by so many Australians to world culture and achievement needs now to be reinforced by a greater recorded knowledge of the human environment—as distinct from the physical environment—which has given the impetus to such achievement."

MEDIA ADAPTATIONS: Blake's *Lost in the Bush* was filmed by AVEC in 1973.

*   *   *

BLAKE, Quentin 1932-

PERSONAL: Born December 16, 1932, in England. *Education:* Downing College, Cambridge, M.A., 1956. *Home:* Flat 8, 30 Bramham Gardens, London S.W.5, England. *Agent:* Georges Borchardt, Inc., 136 East 57th St., New York, N.Y. 10022; and A. P. Watt Ltd., 26-28 Bedford Row, London WC1R 4HL, England.

CAREER: Primarily an illustrator, drawing for *Punch* and other British magazines and illustrating children's and educational books. Royal College of Art, London, England, began as tutor in School of Graphic Design, currently head of Illustration Department. *Awards, honors:* Whitbread Literary Award, 1974, for *How Tom Beat Captain Najork and His Hired Sportsmen;* Hans Christian Andersen honor book for illustration, 1975, for *How Tom Beat Captain Najork and His Hired Sportsmen,* and 1980, for *Mr Magnolia;* Kate Greenaway Medal, 1980, for *Mr Magnolia.*

WRITINGS—Self-illustrated children's books: *Patrick,* J. Cape, 1968, Walck, 1969; *Jack and Nancy,* J. Cape, 1969; *Angelo,* J. Cape, 1970; *Snuff,* Lippincott, 1973; *Lester at the Seaside,* Collins Picture Lions, 1975; *Lester and the Unusual Pet,* Collins Picture Lions, 1975; (with John Yeoman) *Puffin Book of Improbable Records,* Puffin, 1975; *Mr Magnolia,* J. Cape, 1980; (with Yeoman) *Rumbelow's Dance,* Hamish Hamilton, 1982.

Illustrator: Ezo, *My Son-in-Law the Hippopotamus,* Abelard, 1962; Richard Schickel, *Gentle Knight,* Abelard, 1964; Edward Korel, *Listen and I'll Tell You,* Lippincott, 1964; Thomas L. Hirsch, *Puzzles for Pleasure and Leisure,* Abelard, 1966; Nils-Olof Franzen, *Agaton Sax and the Diamond Thieves,* Delacorte, 1967; Robert Tibber, *Aristide,* Dial, 1967; Helen J. Fletcher, *Put on Your Thinking Cap,* Abelard, 1968; Nathan Zimelman, *The First Elephant Comes to Ireland,* Follett, 1969; S. Forst, *Agaton Sax and the Scotland Yard Mystery,* Delacorte, 1969.

Thomas Corddry, *Kibby's Big Feat,* Follett, 1970; Forst, *Agaton Sax and the Incredible Max Brothers,* Delacorte, 1970; Fletcher, *Puzzles and Quizzles,* Abelard, 1971; Sid Fleischman, *McBroom's Wonderful One-Acre Farm,* Chatto & Windus, 1972; Joan Aiken, *Tales of Arabel's Raven,* J. Cape, 1974, published as *Arabel's Raven,* Doubleday, 1974; Dr. Seuss (pseudonym of Theodor Seuss Geisel), *Great Day for Up,* Random House, 1974; Russell Hoban, *How Tom Beat Captain Najork and His Hired Sportsmen,* Atheneum, 1974; Michael Rosen, *Mind Your Own Business,* S. J. Phillips, 1974; Bronnie Cunningham, *Puffin Joke Book,* Penguin, 1974; Hoban, *A Near Thing for Captain Najork,* Atheneum, 1975; Aiken, *Arabel and Mortimer,* J. Cape, 1980.

All by Rosemary Weir; published by Abelard: *Albert the Dragon,* 1961; *Albert the Dragon and the Centaur,* 1964; *Further Adventures of Albert the Dragon,* 1964.

All by Ennis Rees; published by Abelard: *Riddles, Riddles Everywhere,* 1964; *Pun Fun,* 1965; *Tiny Tall Tales,* 1967; *Gillygaloos and the Gollywhoppers: Tall Tales about Mythical Monsters,* 1969.

All by John Yeoman: *The Bear's Winter House,* World, 1969; *Alphabet Soup,* Faber (London), 1969, Follett, 1970; *The Bear's Water Picnic,* Blackie & Son, 1970, Macmillan, 1971; *Sixes and Sevens,* Blackie & Son, 1971, Macmillan, 1972; *Mouse Trouble,* Hamish Hamilton, 1972, Macmillan, 1973; *Beatrice and Vanessa,* Hamish Hamilton, 1974, Macmillan, 1975; *The Wild Washerwoman,* Greenwillow, 1979.

All by Roald Dahl; published by Knopf, except as indicated: *The Enormous Crocodile,* 1978; *The Twits,* 1980; *George's Marvellous Medicine,* 1982; *The BFG,* Farrar, Straus, 1982; *Roald Dahl's Revolting Rhymes,* 1983.

Also illustrator of *Boy Who Sprouted Antlers,* by Yeoman, published by Transatlantic, and of numerous other children's books.

SIDELIGHTS: Quentin Blake's award-winning *Mr Magnolia* is "economical, deceptively slapdash, glowing with colour,

. . . a delightful book," writes Vicki Feaver in the *Times Literary Supplement.* Blake has illustrated 150 books, most of them for children. Candida Lycett Green, commenting in another *Times Literary Supplement* review, calls the artist's style "sketchy and shambolic." She explains, "Mr Blake . . . doesn't need eyebrows on his characters, he just uses tiny dots for eyes and creates the most extraordinarily humorous expressions in an instant."

MEDIA ADAPTATIONS: Patrick was made into a film strip by Weston Woods.

BIOGRAPHICAL/CRITICAL SOURCES: New Statesman, October 31, 1969, November 9, 1973, November 21, 1980; *Spectator,* December 5, 1970, April 16, 1977; *New York Times Book Review,* November 3, 1974; *Signal,* January, 1975; *Graphis* (children's book edition), September, 1975; *Times Literary Supplement,* March 28, 1980, November 26, 1982; *Times Educational Supplement,* March 28, 1980, October 31, 1980.

*   *   *

BLANCHARD, Kendall A(llan)   1942-

PERSONAL: Born November 21, 1942, in Kankakee, Ill.; son of Craig Allan (a clergyman) and Lois (a professor of English; maiden name, Kendall) Blanchard; married Helen Martin, June, 1963 (divorced, 1972); married Kathy Arbeiter (a clinical psychologist), December, 1976; children: Jessie Sophia, Sarah Elizabeth. *Education:* Olivet Nazarene College, A.B., 1964; Vanderbilt University, M.Div., 1968; Southern Methodist University, M.A., 1970, Ph.D., 1971; Johns Hopkins University, postdoctoral study, 1976-77. *Home:* 1315 East Castle, L-1, Murfreesboro, Tenn. 37130. *Office:* Department of Sociology, Anthropology and Social Work, Middle Tennessee State University, Murfreesboro, Tenn. 37132.

CAREER: High school English teacher and basketball coach in Grant Park, Ill., 1964-65; Tennessee Securities, Nashville, Tenn., account executive, 1969; Middle Tennessee State University, Murfreesboro, assistant professor, 1971-75, associate professor, 1975-81, professor of anthropology, 1981—, chairman of department, 1978—. Visiting professor at University of Tennessee, 1972, Vanderbilt University, 1972, 1973, University of Western New Mexico, 1977, and University of Southern Mississippi, 1981.

MEMBER: American Anthropological Association (fellow), Association for the Anthropological Study of Play (president, 1983-84), American Ethnological Society, Tennessee Anthropological Association (member of board of directors, 1975-80). *Awards, honors:* Fellowship from National Endowment for the Humanities, 1976-77.

WRITINGS: The Ramah Navajos: The History of a Growing Sense of Community, Navajo Tribe, 1971; *The Economics of Sainthood: Religious Change among the Rimrock Navajos,* Associated University Presses, 1977; *The Mississippi Choctaws at Play: The Serious Side of Leisure,* University of Illinois Press, 1981; (with Alyce Cheska) *The Anthropology of Sport,* Bergin & Garvey, 1984; (editor) *The Many Faces of Play,* Leisure Press, 1984. Contributor to books and journals.

WORK IN PROGRESS: The Laotians Have Come to Tennessee: The Refugee Factor in the New South; Educating the Student Athlete.

SIDELIGHTS: Kendall Blanchard told *CA:* "When I was younger and less secure, I found solace in the assertion that anthropology was science. I dreamed of mathematical models, laws, and principles that would explain human nature. I wrote stilted prose to reinforce the aura of scientific respectability and scoffed at those like Oscar Lewis who dared to turn social facts into lively reading.

"Now, age has made me more secure. I talk less about models, science, and prediction, and more about feelings and understanding. Instead of sorting numbers and measuring responses, I search for words to capture that exotic smell or describe the mood of a foreign face. Oscar Lewis has become a hero, and I dream of writing an ethnography that reads like a novel."

*　*　*

BLAZIER, Kenneth D(ean) 1933-

PERSONAL: Born March 17, 1933, in Topeka, Kan.; son of Edwin B. and Hazel E. (Spencer) Blazier; married R. Elaine Kellogg (a nursery school director), August 25, 1956; children: Lynnette, Gregory, Kyle. *Education:* Ottawa University, Ottawa, Kan., B.A., 1955; American Baptist Seminary of the West, B.D., 1959. *Residence:* Norristown, Pa. *Office address:* Educational Ministries, American Baptist Churches, P.O. Box 851, Valley Forge, Pa. 19482.

CAREER: Pastor of Baptist churches in Hudson, N.Y., 1959-62, and Cazenovia, N.Y., 1962-66; American Baptist Churches, Valley Forge, Pa., director of department of educational planning services for Educational Ministries, 1966-82, director of department of adult ministries and administration, 1982—.

WRITINGS—All published by Judson: (With Joseph J. Hanson) *Launching the Church School Year,* 1972; (with Evelyn Huber) *Planning Christian Education in Your Church,* 1974; *Building an Effective Church School,* 1976; *A Growing Church School,* 1978; (editor) *The Teaching Church at Work,* 1980; *Workbook for Planning Christian Education,* 1983. Author of "Checklist for Administrators," a monthly column in *Baptist Leader.*

WORK IN PROGRESS: "Research on the Christian education of adults as change agents."

SIDELIGHTS: Kenneth D. Blazier writes *CA:* "My books have been part of my work as director of the department of educational planning services. This department was responsible for services (training and materials) for local church planners and administrators of Christian education. I plan to do similar writing in the field of adult ministry as director of the department of adult ministries and administration.

"I consider my active role as a volunteer leader in Calvary Baptist Church, Norristown, Pa., indispensable in my research and experimentation for my writings in the field of Christian education planning and administration. My involvement as trainer of local church educational leaders is also essential to my work."

*　*　*

BLISHEN, Edward 1920-

PERSONAL: Born April 29, 1920, in Whetstone, Middlesex, England; son of William George (a civil servant) and Elizabeth Ann (Pye) Blishen; married Nancy Smith, November 4, 1948; children: Jonathan Edward, Nicholas Martin. *Education:* Educated in England. *Home:* 12 Bartrams Lane, Hadley Wood, Barnet, England. *Agent:* Irene Josephy, 35 Craven St., Strand, London W.C. 2, England.

CAREER: Employed in London, England, and vicinity, as journalist, 1937-41, preparatory schoolmaster, 1946-49, and teacher

of English in secondary school, 1950-59; University of York, Heslington, England, part-time lecturer in department of education, 1963-65; free-lance writer, Barnet, England, 1965—. Conductor for thirteen years of British Broadcasting Corp. overseas program directed at young African writers; presenter of "World of Books" program, British Broadcasting Corp., 1973—. *Member:* P.E.N. (member of executive committee of English Center, 1962-66), Society of Authors. *Awards, honors:* Carnegie Award, Library Association, 1971, for *The God beneath the Sea;* Society of Authors travelling scholarship, 1979.

WRITINGS: Roaring Boys, Thames & Hudson, 1955; (editor) *Junior Pears Encyclopaedia,* Pelham Books, 1961, and annual revisions, 1962—; (editor) *Education Today,* BBC Publications, 1963; (editor) *Oxford Book of Poetry for Children,* Oxford University Press, 1963; *Town Story,* Anthony Blond, 1964; (editor) *Miscellany,* Oxford University Press, six volumes, 1964-69; (editor) *Come Reading* (anthology of prose for young readers), M. Joseph, 1968; *Hugh Lofting* (monograph), Bodley Head, 1968; (editor) *Encyclopaedia of Education,* Anthony Blond, 1969; *This Soft Lot,* Thames & Hudson, 1969; *The School That I'd Like,* Penguin, 1969.

(With Leon Garfield) *The God beneath the Sea,* Longmans, Green, 1970; *A Cackhanded War,* Thames & Hudson, 1972; (with Garfield) *The Golden Shadow,* Longman, 1973; *Uncommon Embrace,* Thames & Hudson, 1974; (editor) *The Thorny Paradise,* Kestrel, 1975; *Sorry, Dad,* Hamish Hamilton, 1978.

A Nest of Teachers, Hamish Hamilton, 1980; *Shaky Relations,* Hamish Hamilton, 1981; *Lizzie Pye,* Hamish Hamilton, 1982; *Donkey Work,* Hamish Hamilton, 1983.

SIDELIGHTS: Edward Blishen told *CA:* "I write in a curious form, a sort of false autobiography, for reasons I don't at all understand. They must spring, I guess, from whatever appetite has driven me to keep a diary since June 10, 1934. I take the facts provided by this diary and convert them into fictions: needing to rename even my wife, my children, and the town where I've always lived. I have this heretical feeling that life is an astoundingly able storyteller, and that the writer at best trails far behind. Look back over a long diary and you see that you have been living in hundreds of different simultaneous novels and thousands of short stories, some marvellously commonplace and some marvellously subtle, as well as having many other extraordinarily shapely scraps of experience. What I like to do has something of the kaleidoscope about it, I think: I shake up the fragments that compose some patch of time and see what pattern is made. I like to set myself cruel deadlines, getting as close as possible to the hopeless ideal that a book should be the product of a single uninterrupted effort.

"I am astonished when people assume that an autobiographer must be self-centered. I have the usual interest in myself, but when it comes to writing, count myself as one character among many, distinguished only by the specially large amount of deadly knowledge I have of him.

"In the end, I love work with words—jeweller's work—and also the toil of making books—laborer's work."

BIOGRAPHICAL/CRITICAL SOURCES: Times Literary Supplement, March 21, 1980, October 15, 1982; *Times* (London), July 2, 1981, September 1, 1983.

BLOM, Karl Arne 1946-
(Bo Lagevi)

PERSONAL: Born January 22, 1946, in Naessjoe, Sweden; son of Karl Axel (a hotel owner) and Ester (Skoeld) Blom; married Karin Ann-Marie Gyllen (a nurse), June 29, 1969; children: Karl Anders Bertil, Kristina Magdalena. *Education:* University of Lund, B.A., 1972. *Politics:* "Liberal, cosmopolitan, anti-Communist." *Religion:* Agnostic. *Home and office:* Smaaskolevaegen 22, S-223 67 Lund, Sweden. *Agent:* Lennart Sane, P.O. Box 25044, S-200 47 Malmoe 25, Sweden.

CAREER: Free-lance writer, 1970-75. *Member:* Union of Swedish Authors, Swedish Academy of Detection, Society of Detective Story Writers of Skane (honorary chairman), Mystery Writers of America, Crime Writers Association (England), Poe Club (Denmark). *Awards, honors:* Sherlock Award from *Expressen* (newspaper), 1974, for *The Moment of Truth.*

WRITINGS—In English translation: *Sanningens oegonblick,* AWE/Gebers, 1974, translation by Erik J. Friis published as *The Moment of Truth,* Harper, 1977; *Smartgransen,* AWE/ Gebers, 1978, translation by Joan Tate published as *The Limits of Pain,* Ram Publishing, 1979.

In Swedish; published by AWE/Gebers, except as indicated: *Naagon borde soerja* (title means "Somebody Should Mourn"), 1971; *Naagon aer skyldig* (title means "Somebody Is Guilty"), 1972; *Naagon slog tillbaka* (title means "Somebody Hit Back"), 1973; *Ett gammalt mord* (title means "An Old Murder"), Gleerups, 1974; (editor) *Brottpunkter* (title means "Murderous Points"), Lindqvist, 1975; *Vaaldets triumf* (title means "Triumph of Violence"), 1975; *Resan till ingenstans* (stories; title means "Journey into Nowhere"), Zindermans, 1975; *Lund,* Hermods, 1975.

(Editor) *Skaanska Brottstycken* (title means "Pieces of Crimes"), Bra Deckare, 1976; *Kortaste straaet* (title means "Second Best"), Lindqvist, 1976; *Noedhamm* (title means "Harbor of Refuge"), Lindqvist, 1976; *Lyckligt lottade* (title means "The Happy People"), 1976; (under pseudonym Bo Lagevi) *Allt vad du gjort mot naagon* (title means "All the Things You Did"), B. Wahlstroem, 1976; *Noedvaern* (novel; title means "Self-Defense"), Zinderman, 1977; *40° Kallti Solen* (stories; title means "40 Degrees Cold in the Sun"), Zindermans, 1977; *Frihetssoekarna* (title means "Searchers of Freedom"), 1977; (under pseudonym Bo Lagevi) *Utan personligt ansvar* (title means "Without Personal Responsibility"), B. Wahlstroem, 1977; *Det var en gang* (title means "Once upon a Time"), 1978; *Mannen i granden* (title means "The Man in the Alley"), 1979; *Bristningspunkten* (title means "The Breaking Point"), 1979.

Kvinnan pa bussen (title means "The Woman on the Bus"), 1980; *Nodvandigt Ont* (title means "Justified Evilness"), 1980; *Mordanglarna* (title means "The Murderous Angels"), 1981; *Med andra ogon* (title means "A Point of View"), 1981; *Nattboh* (title means "Nightbook"), 1982; *Ingenmansland* (title means "No Man's Land"), 1982; *Utragen* (title means "The Way Out"), 1983; *Aferresan* (title means "The Way Back"), 1983.

Translator into Swedish: Jack Higgins, *Bikten* (title means "A Prayer for the Dying"), Lindqvist, 1975; Emile Gaboriau, *Den lille mannen i Batignolles* (title means "The Little Man in Batignolles"), Lindqvist, 1975; Arthur Conan Doyle, *En studie i roett* (title means "A Study in Scarlet"), AWE/Gebers, 1977; Hanning Hjuler, *Raattorna* (title means "The Rats"), Bra Deckare, 1977; Doyle, *Minnena* (title means "The Memoirs

of Sherlock Holmes"), AWE/Gebers, 1977. Author of material for television series. Contributor of articles and stories to magazines.

SIDELIGHTS: Karl Arne Blom writes: "So far most of what I have written is crime novels . . . because this is the kind of novel by which you can best describe and try to analyze time, society, and human beings. I try to tell about our time—people as they are now and the problems people are facing in a Swedish so-called welfare society. My other novels and most of my short stories are efforts to describe the surrealistic and absurd realities of life.

"I regard the mystery genre as not inferior to so-called real literature. In my opinion a crime novel, a mystery, or whatever it happens to be, can be as good a book as any book of fiction. . . . A good mystery or crime novel is like an iceberg. You see what's on the surface and a lot of things are hidden.

"My first three books deal with crime and murder and violence. But the first one is also a book about how lonely people can be when they are apparently among many others. The second one is about the economic problems students are facing, and the third one is about unemployment among students with degrees. From there on I have dealt with the basic elements of violence among people, with violence in our time and how violence has become almost a natural way of expressing oneself."

In addition to English, Blom's books have been translated into German, Danish, Norwegian, Dutch, and Japanese.

BIOGRAPHICAL/CRITICAL SOURCES: New York Times Book Review, January 30, 1977.

*   *   *

BLOOM, Lillian D. 1920-

PERSONAL: Born July 17, 1920, in New York, N.Y.; daughter of Benjamin (an architect) and Frances (Eisenberg) Blumberg; married Edward A. Bloom (a college professor), June 17, 1947. *Education:* New York University, B.A., 1941, M.A., 1942; Yale University, Ph.D., 1946. *Home:* 82 Laurel Ave., Providence, R.I. 02906. *Office:* Department of English, Rhode Island College, Providence, R.I. 02908.

CAREER: University of Illinois (now University of Illinois at Urbana-Champaign), Urbana, instructor in English, 1945-46; Queens College (now Queens College of the City University of New York), New York, N.Y., instructor in English, 1946-47; University of Rhode Island, Kingston, assistant professor of English, 1947-51; Rhode Island College, Providence, 1956—, began as assistant professor, professor of English, 1964—. *Member:* Modern Language Association of America, American Association of University Professors, Phi Beta Kappa, Sigma Delta Omicron, Kappa Delta Pi. *Awards, honors:* American Council of Learned Societies grant, 1967-68; Huntington Library grant, 1976; Guggenheim fellow, 1977-78.

WRITINGS—With husband, Edward A. Bloom: *Willa Cather's Gift of Sympathy,* Southern Illinois University Press, 1962; (compiler) *The Variety of Fiction: A Critical Anthology,* Odyssey, 1969; (editor and author of introduction) Anthony Collins, *A Discourse Concerning Ridicule and Irony in Writing,* William Andrews Clark Memorial Library, 1970; *Joseph Addison's Sociable Animal: In the Market Place, on the Hustings, in the Pulpit,* Brown University Press, 1971; (editor) Fanny Burney, *Camilla,* Oxford University Press, 1972; (editor) *The Journals and Letters of Fanny Burney,* Volume VII: *1812-*

1814, Oxford University Press, 1978; *Satire's Persuasive Voice*, Cornell University Press, 1979; (editor) *Addison and Steele: The Critical Heritage*, Routledge & Kegan Paul, 1980. Contributor to scholarly journals.

WORK IN PROGRESS: The Letters of Mrs. Piozzi.

BIOGRAPHICAL/CRITICAL SOURCES: Times Literary Supplement, July 25, 1980.†

*   *   *

BLUM, Albert A(lexander) 1924-

PERSONAL: Born April 5, 1924, in New York, N.Y.; son of Morris (a businessman) and Estelle (Kaplan) Blum; married Roslyn Silver (an art consultant), January 16, 1949; children: Steven Ephraim, David Joshua. *Education:* City College (now City College of the City University of New York), B.S., 1947; Columbia University, M.A., 1948, Ph.D., 1953. *Home:* 5365 Feather River Dr., Stockton, Calif. 95207. *Office:* University of the Pacific, Stockton, Calif. 95211.

CAREER: Office of Chief of Military History, Washington, D.C., labor historian, 1951-53; National Industrial Conference Board, New York City, labor relations writer, 1955-57; New York University, New York City, assistant professor of industrial relations, 1957-58; Cornell University, Ithaca, N.Y., assistant professor of industrial relations, 1958-59; American University, Washington, D.C., associate professor of industrial relations, 1959-60; Michigan State University, East Lansing, 1960-74, began as associate professor, became professor of labor history and chairman of academic studies in the School of Labor and Industrial Relations and department of social science; University of Texas, Lyndon B. Johnson School of Public Affairs, Austin, professor, 1974-78; Illinois Institute of Technology, Stuart School of Business, Chicago, dean, 1978-82; University of the Pacific, Stockton, Calif., George Wilson Professor of International Management, 1983—.

Lecturer, Salzburg Seminar in American Studies, 1963. Research associate on study of civil-military relations, Twentieth Century Fund, 1953-54; member of visiting staff in automation unit, International Labour Office, Geneva, Switzerland, 1966-67. Labor arbitrator, American Arbitration Association; member of labor panel, Federal Mediation and Conciliation Service and Michigan Mediation Service. *Military service:* U.S. Army Air Forces, 1943-45; became sergeant. *Member:* Labor Historians, Industrial Relations Research Association, Phi Beta Kappa, Phi Alpha Theta, Kappa Delta Pi. *Awards, honors:* Recipient of grants from Social Science Research Council, Small Business Administration, Latin American Studies Center, and Center for Study of International Education.

WRITINGS: The Army and Industrial Deferment during World War II, Industrial College of the Armed Forces, 1955; (with J. Bambrick and Zagat) *Unionization among American Engineers*, National Industrial Conference Board, 1956; (co-author) *Labor Relations in the Atomic Energy Field*, National Industrial Conference Board, 1957.

An Annotated Bibliography of Industrial Relations and the Small Firm, New York State School of Industrial and Labor Relations, Cornell University, 1960; *Company Organization of Insurance Management*, American Management Association, 1961; (co-author) *Cases in Research Administration*, American University Press, 1961; (editor) *The Proper Climate for Labor Relations*, School of Labor and Industrial Relations, Michigan State University, 1962; *The Development of American Labor*,

Macmillan, 1963, published as *A History of the American Labor Movement*, American Historial Association, 1972; (editor with Solomon Barkin) *The Crisis in the American Trade-Union Movement*, [Philadelphia], 1963; (co-author) *Preparing for Collective Bargaining*, National Industrial Conference Board, 1963; *Management and the White Collar Union*, American Management Association, 1964.

(Editor with William Humbert Form) *Industrial Relations and Social Change in Latin America*, University of Florida Press, 1965; (co-editor) *Readings in Social Science: Problem of Power in American Society*, Michigan State University Press, 1967; *Drafted or Deferred: Practices Past and Present*, Bureau of Industrial Relations, University of Michigan, 1967; (editor) *L'Adaptation de la main d'oeuvre au progres technique*, three volumes, [Geneva], 1967-68; (editor) *Teacher Unions and Associations: A Comparative Study*, University of Illinois Press, 1969.

(With others) *White-Collar Workers*, Random House, 1971; (editor) *The Arts: Years of Development, Time of Decision*, Lyndon B. Johnson School of Public Affairs, University of Texas at Austin, 1976; (editor) *International Handbook of Industrial Relations: Contemporary Developments and Research*, Greenwood Press, 1981.

Contributor: *Problems of Competition and Economic Organization*, Michigan State University Press, 1952; *"Antioch Review" Anthology*, World Publishing, 1953; Harold Stein, editor, *American Civil-Military Decisions: A Book of Case Studies*, Twentieth Century Fund and University of Alabama Press, 1963; Arthur Ross, editor, *Poverty, Jobs, and Color*, Harcourt, 1966.

Editor of "Labor and Industrial Relations" series, Random House; general editor of "Masterworks in Industrial Relations" series, Southern Illinois University Press, 1969-72. Contributor to *Encyclopaedia Britannica* and *Collier's Encyclopedia*. Regular contributor to *Management Record* of National Industrial Conference Board, 1955-56; contributor of articles to professional journals. Editor, *Labor History*.

WORK IN PROGRESS: Evolution of Collective Bargaining among Federal Employees during Johnson Administration; comparative studies of public policy toward unemployment, industrial democracy, and strikes.

*   *   *

BOATENG, E(rnest) A(mano) 1920-

PERSONAL: Born November 30, 1920, in Aburi, Ghana; son of Christian Robert (a clergyman) and Adelaide (Asare) Boateng; married Evelyn K. Danso (a librarian), March 26, 1955; children: Akosua, Akua, Amanobea, Oduraa. *Education:* Attended Achimota College, Ghana; St. Peter's College, Oxford, M.A., 1953, M.Litt., 1954. *Religion:* Presbyterian. *Home:* 3 Aviation Rd., Airport Residential Area, Accra, Ghana.

CAREER: University of Ghana, Legon, Accra, lecturer, 1950-57, senior lecturer, 1958-61, professor of geography, 1961-73, dean of Faculty of Social Studies, 1961-69; University of Cape Coast, Cape Coast, Ghana, principal of University College, 1969-71, vice-chancellor of university, 1971-73; Environmental Protection Council, Accra, executive chairman, 1973-81; currently environmental and educational consultant. Visiting professor at University of Pittsburgh, 1966. Chairman of geography committee, Ghana Population Census, 1960; member of Planning Commission of Ghana, 1962-64; honorary director of Ghana National Atlas Project. Ghana representative, Scientific Council for Africa, and at international conferences, including thirty-first session of United Nations General Assembly, 1976.

MEMBER: Royal Geographical Society (London), Ghana Geographical Association (president, 1959-69), Ghana Academy of Sciences (president, 1972—), Royal Society of Arts (fellow). *Awards, honors:* Henry Oliver Becket Memorial Prize, 1949; Smuts Fellow at Cambridge University, 1965-66; Grand Medal of Ghana, 1967; Ghana Book Award, 1978; received D.Litt., 1979.

WRITINGS: A Geography of Ghana, Cambridge University Press, 1959, 2nd edition, 1966; (editor) *Ghana Junior Atlas,* Thomas Nelson, 1965, revised edition, International Publications Service, 1969; *West African Secondary School Atlas,* Thomas Nelson, 1968; *Independence and Nation Building in Africa,* Ghana Publishing Corp., 1973; *A Political Geography of Africa,* Cambridge University Press, 1978. Contributor to *Encyclopaedia Britannica,* 1961—, and to geography journals.

SIDELIGHTS: E. A. Boateng has a reading knowledge of French. He has traveled in the United States, most of Europe, the Soviet Union, Australia, India, and in several tropical African countries. *Avocational interests:* Photography, gardening, English literature, architecture, listening to classical music.

*   *   *

BOBER, Stanley   1932-

PERSONAL: Born January 13, 1932, in New York, N.Y.; son of Morris and Sylvia (Buckser) Bober; children: Sharon Leslie, Mitchell Stuart. *Education:* New York University, Ph.D., 1962. *Religion:* Jewish. *Home:* 1037 Firwood Dr., Pittsburgh, Pa. 15243. *Office:* Department of Economics, Duquesne University, Pittsburgh, Pa. 15219.

CAREER: Colby College, Waterville, Me., assistant professor of economics, 1960-64; Duquesne University, Pittsburgh, Pa., 1964—, began as associate professor, currently professor of economics.

WRITINGS: The Economics of Cycles and Growth, Wiley, 1968; *The Economics of Steady-State Growth,* University Press of America, 1976; *Capital, Distribution and Growth: A Look at Neo-Keynesian Economics,* University Press of America, 1980.

*   *   *

BOCK, Philip K.   1934-

PERSONAL: Born August 26, 1934, in New York, N.Y.; son of Eugene and Clara (Fleischman) Bock; married Barbara Lassig (an artist), July 30, 1976; children: (previous marriage) Marian F., Deborah J., Karen A. *Education:* Fresno State College (now California State University, Fresno), A.B., 1955; University of Chicago, M.A., 1956; Harvard University, Ph.D., 1962. *Politics:* Democrat. *Religion:* Jewish. *Home:* 303 Alamosa N.W., Albuquerque, N.M. 87107. *Office:* University of New Mexico, Albuquerque, N.M. 87131.

CAREER: PALL Corp., Glen Cove, N.Y., technical writer, 1960; University of New Mexico, Albuquerque, assistant professor, 1962-66, associate professor, 1966-71, professor of anthropology, 1971—. Visiting professor at Columbia University, Stanford University, and University Ibero-Americana. Consultant, Random House Dictionaries. *Military service:* U.S.

Air Force Reserve, 1956-57; became captain. *Member:* American Anthropological Association (fellow). *Awards, honors:* Woodrow Wilson fellowship; Harvard University fellowship; Danforth associate.

WRITINGS: (Editor) *Peasants in the Modern World,* University of New Mexico Press, 1968; *Modern Cultural Anthropology,* Knopf, 1969, 3rd edition, 1979; (editor) *Culture Shock,* Knopf, 1970; (contributor) *Handbook of American Indians,* Smithsonian Institution Press, 1978; *Continuities in Psychological Anthropology,* Freeman, 1980; *Shakespeare and Elizabethan Cultures,* Schocken, 1984. Also author of a monograph *The Micmac Indians of Restigouche,* National Museum of Canada bulletin, 1966. Contributor of numerous articles to scientific journals. Editor, *Journal of Anthropological Research,* 1982—.

WORK IN PROGRESS: The Formal Content of Ethnography, a monograph on social structure; several works for the theater, including a one-act play, "Malvolio's Revenge."

SIDELIGHTS: Philip K. Bock is also an amateur musician, a pianist and composer, and an amateur actor. In community theater he has performed leading roles in "Who's Afraid of Virginia Wolff" and "Talley's Folley."

Modern Cultural Anthropology has been translated into German, Spanish, Italian, and Japanese.

*   *   *

BOHN, Ralph C.   1930-

PERSONAL: Born February 19, 1930, in Detroit, Mich.; son of Carl N. (a carpenter) and Bertha (Abrams) Bohn; married Adella N. Stanul, September 2, 1950 (died July 8, 1975); married Jo Ann Olvera-Butler, February 19, 1977; children: Cheryl Ann, Jeffrey Ralph; stepchildren: Kathryn J., Kimberly O., Gregory E. *Education:* Wayne State University, B.S., 1951, M.A., 1954, Ed.D., 1957. *Religion:* Lutheran. *Home:* 15363 Robin Anne Lane, Monte Sereno, Calif. 95030. *Office:* Continuing Education, San Jose State University, San Jose, Calif. 95192.

CAREER: Detroit (Mich.) public schools, teacher of industrial arts, 1947-51, 1953-55; San Jose State University, San Jose, Calif., director of auto, safety, and driver education programs, 1955-61, chairman of department of industrial arts, 1961-69, associate dean of educational services, 1968-70, dean of continuing education, 1970—. Director of Inservice Education Program for Industrial Teachers, sponsored by U.S. Office of Education, 1966-69; director of National Driver Education Association's Institute for Advanced Study, summer, 1967.

Member of guest faculty, Colorado State College, summer, 1963, Arizona State University, summer, 1966, University of Puerto Rico, summers, 1967, 1974, Southern Illinois University, summer, 1970, Oregon State University, summer, 1971, Utah State University, summer, 1973, Virginia Polytechnic Institute, summer, 1973, and University of Idaho, summer, 1978. Has also participated in regional accreditation of various colleges and universities, including Portland State University, 1976, University of Guam, 1978, and California College of Podiatric Medicine, 1982.

Chairman, Board of Science and Human Values, Inc., 1967—; member of advisory committee for Quality of Life division of Far West Regional Laboratory, 1978—; member of special task force on contracts and off-campus instruction for Western Accreditation, 1976-82; member, California State Chamber of Commerce. Research consultant, United States Office of Education, American Institutes for Research, 1969—, Far West Regional Laboratory, 1971—. Also consultant to National Assessment of Educational Progress, 1967-79, and to Philco-Ford Corp. on educational matters, 1970-73. *Military service:* U.S. Coast Guard, active duty, 1951-53, inactive reserve, 1953—; present rank, captain.

MEMBER: American Council of Industrial Arts Teacher Education (past president), American Industrial Arts Association (past president), National Education Association, National Fluid Power Association, Association of Organizations for Teacher Education, Consortium of Professional Associations (member of board, 1967—), Western Association of Summer Session Administrators (past president), California Driver's Education Association, California State Employees Association (president, San Jose chapter, 1966-67), California Industrial Education Association, Lutheran Academy of Scholarship, Epsilon Pi Tau, Phi Delta Kappa, Rotary. *Awards, honors:* Service awards, American Vocational Association, 1966, 1967; Man-of-the-Year Award, American Council of Industrial Arts Teacher Education, 1967; SHIP's citations, California Industrial Education Association, and American Industrial Arts Association, both 1971.

WRITINGS: (Editor with Ralph Norman) *Graduate Programs in Industrial Arts,* McKnight & McKnight, 1961; (with G. Harold Silvius) *Organizing Course Materials for Industrial Education,* McKnight & McKnight, 1961, 2nd edition, McKnight Publishing, 1976; (with Marland Strasser, James Arron, and John Eales) *Fundamentals of Safety Education,* Macmillan, 1967, 3rd edition, 1981; (with Angus J. MacDonald) *Power: Mechanics of Energy Control,* McKnight & McKnight, 1970, 2nd edition, McKnight Publishing, 1983; (with MacDonald) *The McKnight Power Experiment,* McKnight & McKnight, 1970; (with Silvius) *Planning and Organizing Instruction,* McKnight & McKnight, 1974, 2nd edition, McKnight Publishing, 1976; (with Miller and MacDonald) *Power Mechanics,* McKnight Publishing, 1978.

Contributor of articles to various professional journals, including *Industrial Arts and Vocational Education, School Shop, Journal of Industrial Arts Education, American Vocational Journal, International Labor Journal, Continuum,* and *Visual Communication Journal.* Co-editor of yearbook of the American Council of Industrial Arts Teacher Education, 1961; editor, *Journal of Industrial Teacher Education,* 1962-64; industrial arts editor, *American Vocational Journal,* 1963-66; newsletter editor, *Western Association of Summer Session Administrators,* 1970-76.

WORK IN PROGRESS: Research into how institutions maintain program quality and assess student learning.

SIDELIGHTS: Ralph C. Bohn told *CA:* "Since I write at two levels—secondary school textbooks, and professional books and articles for educators and institutions of higher education— I have two separate goals.

"My 'fun' area is secondary school. My emphasis is on understanding. Young people need to understand the technology if they are to make intelligent decisions as adults. The recent revision of *Power: Mechanics of Energy Control* delves into the difficult concepts of pollution and the environment, nuclear power, and the use of fossil fuels. Rather than try[ing] to 'lead,' the emphasis is on understanding, so that they can lead more intelligently as adults.

"For educators and higher education, the emphasis is on improvement of what we're doing. The *Fiddler on the Roof* theme,

'Tradition,' best describes what must be modified in order to improve our educational system at all levels."

*   *   *

BOKSER, Ben Zion   1907-

PERSONAL: Born July 4, 1907, in Lubomi, Poland; came to United States in 1920; son of Elie Morris (a businessman) and Gittel (Katz) Bokser; married Kallia Halpern (a radio commentator), July 21, 1940; children: Miriam (Mrs. Wayne Caravella), Baruch. *Education:* City College (now City College of the City University of New York), B.A., 1928; Jewish Theological Seminary, rabbi, 1931; Columbia University, M.A., 1931, Ph.D., 1935. *Home:* 110-40 70th Ave., Forest Hills, N.Y. *Office:* 106-06 Queens Blvd., Forest Hills, N.Y.

CAREER: Rabbi of Jewish congregations in Bronx, N.Y., 1931-32, and Vancouver, British Columbia, 1932-33; Forest Hills Jewish Center, Forest Hills, N.Y., rabbi, 1934—. Adjunct professor at Queens College of the City University of New York, 1971—. Jewish Theological Seminary, visiting professor, 1952, lecturer, 1953—. Editor of radio program "Eternal Light" for Jewish Theological Seminary and National Broadcasting Corp., 1950. Member of Conference on Science, Philosophy, and Religion. *Military service:* U.S. Army, chaplain, 1944-46. *Member:* Phi Beta Kappa. *Awards, honors:* Frank and Ethel S. Cohen Award, 1964, for *Judaism: Profile of a Faith;* D.D. from Jewish Theological Seminary, 1964.

WRITINGS: Pharisaic Judaism in Transition, Bloch Publishing, 1935, reprinted, Arno 1973; *The Legacy of Maimonides,* Philosophical Library, 1950; *The Wisdom of the Talmud: A Thousand Years of Jewish Thought,* Philosophical Library, 1951; *From the World of the Cabbalah,* Philosophical Library, 1954; *The Gift of Life,* Abelard, 1956; *Judaism and the Modern Man,* Philosophical Library, 1957; (editor and translator) *Jewish High Holy Day Prayer Book,* Hebrew Publishing, 1957; (editor and translator) *Jewish Daily and Festival Prayer Book,* Hebrew Publishing, 1959.

Judaism: Profile of a Faith, Knopf, 1963; *Judaism and the Christian Predicament,* Knopf, 1966; *Jews, Judaism, and the State of Israel,* Herzl Press, 1973; (editor and translator) Moshe Silberg, *Talmudic Law and the Modern State,* Burning Bush Press, 1973; *The Gifts of Life and Love,* Hebrew Publishing, 1975; (editor and translator) *Abraham Isaac Kook: The Lights of Penitance, Lights of Holiness, the Moral Principles, Essays, Letters, and Poems,* Paulist Press, 1978; *The Jewish Mystical Tradition,* Pilgrim Press, 1981. Contributor to *Encyclopaedia Britannica* and *Encyclopedia Judaica.* Contributing editor of *Encyclopedia of Religion.*

WORK IN PROGRESS: A volume on the Talmud; an additional volume of translations of Rabbi Abraham Isaac Kook's writings.

SIDELIGHTS: Ben Zion Bokser is considered to be a knowledgeable and skillful writer on Judaism. It is perhaps Bokser's manner of presenting material in an interesting and simple manner that has led a number of reviewers to suggest that many of Bokser's studies make excellent introductions to specific aspects of Judaism. For instance, J. A. Maynard remarks in a review of *The Wisdom of the Talmud: A Thousand Years of Jewish Thought* in the *Churchman* that "this is the best introduction to the Talmud, both popular and sound, accurate and modern and easy to read, which is no mean virture." In the *Saturday Review* H. U. Ribalow writes that *The Wisdom of the Talmud* is "a popular introduction to the Talmud which is meant—as, indeed, the Talmud itself was meant—for the general reader.'' And of a later book, *Judaism: Profile of a Faith*, a critic for *Christian Century* believes that this book would be "useful as a first introduction [to] the basis of classic Jewish religious expressions of faith and life.''

In *Judaism and the Christian Predicament* Bokser displays the same interesting and informative writing style that has earned him the respect of many students of Jewish history and tradition for his earlier works. As Albert H. Friedlander states in a review of *Judaism and the Christian Predicament* in *Saturday Review:* "[Bokser's] previous works have displayed his competence in the Jewish field. And in the delineation of the nature of Hebrew scripture and rabbinic tradition Rabbi Bokser is at his best. Warmth and informed scholarship give a clear picture of Jewish tradition.''

BIOGRAPHICAL/CRITICAL SOURCES: New York Times, February 18, 1951; *Springfield Republican*, February 25, 1951; *Christian Century*, May 2, 1951, October 23, 1963; *Churchman*, April 1, 1952; *Saturday Review*, April 12, 1952, April 1, 1967; *New Republic*, May 6, 1967.

*   *   *

BONAPARTE, Felicia   1937-

PERSONAL: Born October 19, 1937, in Bucharest, Romania; daughter of Simon (a textile designer) and Anna (Weisman) Bonaparte. *Education:* New York University, B.A., 1959, Ph.D., 1970; Yale University, M.A., 1960. *Politics:* "Independent; usually vote Democratic.'' *Religion:* None. *Home:* 768 Hickory Hill Rd., Wyckoff, N.J. 07481. *Office:* Department of English, Graduate School and University Center, City University of New York, 33 West 42nd St., New York, N.Y. 10036.

CAREER: City College of the City University of New York, New York City, assistant professor of English, 1970-80; Graduate School and University Center of the City University of New York, New York City, professor of English, 1980—. *Member:* Modern Humanities Research Association, Modern Language Association of America, Jane Austen Society.

WRITINGS—All published by New York University Press: *Will and Destiny: Morality and Tragedy in George Eliot's Novels*, 1975; *The Triptych and the Cross: The Central Myths of George Eliot's Poetic Imagination*, 1979; *The Gypsy-Bachelor of Manchester: A Biography of Elizabeth Gaskell*, 1983.

WORK IN PROGRESS: The Christian, the Pagan, and the Primitive: The Mythological Worlds of George Eliot, Thomas Hardy, and D. H. Lawrence.

AVOCATIONAL INTERESTS: Philosophy, music, art.

*   *   *

BOND, Harold   1939-

PERSONAL: Born December 2, 1939, in Boston, Mass.; son of Khorin (a cook) and Ovsanna (Avakian) Bond (surname originally Bondjoukjian); married Ruth Thomason (a photograph historian under original family surname Thomasian), 1981. *Education:* Northeastern University, A.B., 1962; University of Iowa, M.F.A., 1967. *Home:* 11 Chestnut St., Melrose, Mass. 02176.

CAREER: Poet. Horizon House (magazine publishers), Dedham, Mass., production editor, 1962-65; Allyn & Bacon, Inc.

(textbook publishers), Boston, Mass., production editor, 1967-69; *Boston Globe*, Boston, copy editor, 1969-71. Instructor for poetry workshops at Cambridge Center for Adult Education, Cambridge, Mass., 1968—, for poets-in-the-schools programs in Massachusetts, 1971-74, 1977-79, and in New Hampshire, 1973-76, and for Boston's Model Cities higher education program, 1972. Has given readings from his works at American colleges and universities, and on radio programs in Boston and Iowa City. *Member:* Poets Who Teach (Massachusetts). *Awards, honors:* First prizes from Armenian Allied Arts Association of America poetry competitions, 1963, 1964, 1965, and from *Kansas City Star*, 1967, 1968; National Endowment for the Arts creative writing fellowship, 1976.

WRITINGS—Poems: (With Harry Barba and Leo Hamalian) *3x3*, Harian Press, 1969; *The Northern Wall*, Northeastern University Press, 1969; *Dancing on Water*, Cummington Press, 1970; *The Way It Happens to You*, Ararat Press, 1979.

Contributor to anthologies: *The Young American Poets*, edited by Paul Carroll, Follett, 1968; *Speaking for Ourselves: American Ethnic Writing*, edited by Lillian Faderman and Barbara Bradshaw, Scott, Foresman, 1969, 2nd edition, 1975; *The New Yorker Book of Poems*, Viking, 1969; *Ararat: A Decade of Armenian-American Writing*, edited by Jack Antreassian, Armenian General Benevolent Union of America, 1969.

Eleven Boston Poets, Harvard Advocate, 1970; *East Coast Poets*, edited by Ray Amorosi, Quixote Press, 1971; *Getting into Poetry*, edited by Morris Sweetkind, Holbrook, 1972; *New Voices in American Poetry*, edited by David Allan Evans, Winthrop Publishing, 1973; *Outside/Inside*, edited by Laurie Urbscheit and Jerrod Brumfield, Holt, 1973; *Shake the Kaleidoscope: A New Anthology of Modern Poetry*, edited by Milton Klonsky, Pocket Books, 1973; *Armenian-North American Poets: An Anthology*, edited by Lorne Shirinian, Manna Publishing, 1974.

The Blacksmith, edited by Gail Mazur, Blacksmith Press, 1975; *Poemmaking: Poets in Classrooms* (essays), edited by Ruth Whitman and Harriet Feinberg, Massachusetts Council of Teachers of English, 1975; *Writing a Poem*, edited by Florence Trefethen, Writer, 2nd edition (Bond was not associated with earlier edition), 1975; *Armenian-American Poets: A Bilingual Anthology*, edited by Garig Basmadjian, Armenian General Benevolent Union of America, 1976; *Traveling America with Today's Poets*, edited by David Kherdian, Macmillan, 1977; *I Sing the Song of Myself: Autobiographical Poems*, edited by Kherdian, Greenwillow, 1978.

The Aspect Anthology: A Ten-Year Retrospective, edited by Ed Hogan, Zephyr Press, 1981; *Anthology of Magazine Verse and Yearbook of American Poetry*, edited by Alan F. Pater, Monitor Book, 1981; *Poems: A Celebration*, edited by Carole Oles and Elinor Persky, Newton Free Library (Newton, Mass.), 1982.

Contributor of poems to national magazines, including *New Yorker, Harper's, Saturday Review*, and *New Republic*, and to literary journals, including *North American Review, Iowa Review, Ploughshares, Southern Poetry Review, Carleton Miscellany, Shenandoah, Choice, Sumac*, and *Beloit Poetry Journal. Ararat*, member of editorial board, 1968—, editor, 1969-70.

SIDELIGHTS: In an *American Literary Review* interview, Harold Bond offers this advice to beginning poets: "Love the language, love words. Read everything you can get your hands on. Don't be afraid to be influenced by the work of others. At the same time, work toward the development and refinement of a voice that is yours. Keep your mind open to all the many different possibilities of poetry. Eschew the obvious and facile. Don't get caught in the unproductive trap of explaining, defending or apologizing for your poems. Let the poems speak for themselves. If they don't—on some level or another—there's something wrong, and no amount of explanation is going to set them right.''

Bond also names some of the poets he admires: ''Yeats, Pound, Eliot, Cummings, Hart Crane, Stevens, Williams, Berryman, Roethke, Lowell—also Sylvia Plath, James Wright, Elizabeth Bishop, W. S. Merwin, Philip Levine, Galway Kinnell, Mark Strand. I admire, as well, the work of Pablo Neruda, Jose Garcia Lorca, Nazim Hikmet, Andrei Voznesensky and Baruir Sevag—an Armenian poet—internationally. This is not to say that I do not also admire and enjoy the work of other poets I have not named. In fact, I can't think of a poet in this century—one I have read, of course—who hasn't written something I have admired or enjoyed. I suppose that says something about the eclecticism of my tastes. What I think it also says is that I'd rather find something to like than something to dislike in a poet.''

BIOGRAPHICAL/CRITICAL SOURCES: American Literary Review, March, 1980.

* * *

BONDI, Joseph C. 1936-

PERSONAL: Born August 15, 1936, in Tampa, Fla.; son of Joseph C. (a teacher) and Virginia (Colie) Bondi; married Patsy Hammer (a teacher), August 6, 1960; children: Pamela Jo, Beth Jana, Bradley Joseph. *Education:* University of Florida, B.S., 1958, M.Ed., 1962, Ed.D., 1968. *Politics:* Democrat. *Religion:* Presbyterian. *Home:* 207 Bannockburn, Temple Terrace, Fla. 33617. *Office:* Department of Education, University of South Florida, Tampa, Fla. 33620.

CAREER: Hillsborough County (Fla.) Public Schools, teacher, administrator, and curriculum director, 1959-65; University of South Florida, Tampa, 1965—, began as assistant professor, currently professor of education, former chairman of department of curriculum and instruction. Elected mayor of Temple Terrace, Fla., 1974, re-elected, 1976. Member, Temple Terrace City Council, 1970-74; chairman of Tampa metropolitan council of governments. Chairman of State of Florida Middle School Committee; educational program consultant to schools throughout the United States. *Military service:* U.S. Naval Reserve, 1955-63. *Member:* Association for Supervision and Curriculum Development (member of board of directors and executive council; chairman of working group), National Middle School Association, American Educational Research Association, National Education Association, John Dewey Society, Florida Educational Research Association, Florida Association for Supervision and Curriculum Development (vice-president; president), Phi Delta Kappa, Kappa Delta Pi.

WRITINGS: (Editor with Glen Haas and Kimball Wiles) *Readings in Curriculum,* 2nd edition (Bondi was not associated with earlier edition), Allyn & Bacon, 1970; *Developing Middle Schools: A Guidebook,* MSS Information, 1972; (compiler with Haas and Jon Wiles) *Curriculum Planning: A New Approach,* Allyn & Bacon, 1974, 2nd edition, 1977; (with J. Wiles) *Curriculum Development: A Guide to Practice,* C. E. Merrill, 1979.

(With J. Wiles) *Supervision: A Guide to Practice,* C. E. Merrill, 1980; (with J. Wiles and David K. Wiles) *Practical Politics*

for School Administrators, Allyn & Bacon, 1981; (with J. Wiles) *The Essential Middle School,* C. E. Merrill, 1981; (with J. Wiles) *Principles of School Administration,* C. E. Merrill, 1983. Author of film script and study guide ''Profile of a Middle School.'' Contributor of articles to professional journals, including *Educational Leadership, Journal of Teacher Education, Middle School Journal, National Elementary School Principal,* and *Clearing House.*

WORK IN PROGRESS: With Jon Wiles, *The School Board Primer,* for Allyn & Bacon.

* * *

BONFANTE, Larissa

PERSONAL: Born in Naples, Italy; came to the United States in 1940, naturalized in 1952; daughter of Giuliano (a professor) and Vittoria Bonfante; married Peter Beach Warren, September, 1950 (divorced, August, 1962); married Leo Raditsa (a professor and writer), May 2, 1973; children: Alexandra Bonfante Warren. *Education:* Attended Radcliffe College and University of Rome; Barnard College, B.A.; University of Cincinnati, M.A.; Columbia University, Ph.D. *Home:* 50 Morningside Dr., New York, N.Y. 10025. *Office:* Department of Classics, New York University, 25 Waverly Pl., New York, N.Y. 10003.

CAREER: New York University, New York City, instructor, 1963-64, assistant professor, 1964-68, associate professor, 1968-78, professor of classics and chairman of department, 1978—. *Member:* Archaeological Institute of America (member of executive committee, 1982-84), Istituto di Studi Etruschi (foreign member), Phi Beta Kappa.

WRITINGS: (Translator) E. J. Bickerman, *Chronology of the Ancient World,* Thames & Hudson, 1968; (editor with Rolf Winkes) *Bibliography of the Works of Margarete Bieber for Her Ninetieth Birthday,* Columbia University Press, 1969; *Etruscan Dress,* Johns Hopkins University Press, 1975; (editor with Helga von Heintze) *In Memoriam Otto J. Brendel: Essays in Archaeology and the Humanities,* von Zabern (Mainz), 1976; (translator) *The Plays of Hratswitha of Gandersheim,* New York University Press, 1979; *Out of Etruria: Etruscan Influences North and South,* British Archaeological Reports, 1981; (contributor) *Women as Interpreters of the Visual Arts, 1820-1879,* Greenwood Press, 1981; (with father, Giuliano Bonfante) *The Etruscan Language: An Introduction,* New York University Press, 1983; (editor) *The Etruscans: Views and Aspects,* Wayne State University Press, in press.

* * *

BOOTH, Irwin
See HOCH, Edward D(entinger)

* * *

BORDIN, Ruth B(irgitta) 1917-

PERSONAL: Born November 11, 1917, in Litchfield, Minn.; daughter of Emil William (a merchant) and Martha (Linner) Anderson; married Edward Bordin (a psychologist), June 20, 1941; children: Martha (Mrs. Steven A. Hillyard), Charlotte (Mrs. Sung Piau Lin). *Education:* University of Minnesota, B.S., 1938, M.A., 1940. *Politics:* Democrat. *Religion:* Unitarian Universalist. *Home:* 1000 Aberdeen, Ann Arbor, Mich. 48104. *Office:* Bentley Historical Library, University of Michigan, Ann Arbor, Mich. 48109.

CAREER: University of Minnesota, Minneapolis, research assistant, 1945-46; Washington State University, Pullman, research associate, 1946-48; University of Michigan, Ann Arbor, research associate, 1956-57, assistant curator, 1957-60, curator of Michigan Historical Collections, 1960-65, research associate, 1965-67; Eastern Michigan University, Ypsilanti, lecturer in history, 1967-78; University of Michigan, Bentley Historical Library, research affiliate, 1978—. Dutch American Historical Society, consultant, 1966. *Member:* American Historical Association, Organization of American Historians, Phi Beta Kappa, Mortar Board.

WRITINGS: (Editor) L. V. McWhorter, *Hear Ye My Chiefs,* Caxton, 1952; (with Robert M. Warner) *The Manuscript Library,* Scarecrow, 1966; *The University of Michigan: A Pictorial History,* University of Michigan Press, 1967; *Woman and Temperance,* Temple University Press, 1981. Contributor to *Notable American Women.* Writer of radio scripts for "Footnote to History" program, 1963-64.

*   *   *

BOURNE, Kenneth   1930-

PERSONAL: Born March 17, 1930, in Wickford, Essex, England; son of Clarence Arthur (a master printer) and Doris (English) Bourne; married Eleanor Anne Wells (an advertising copywriter), January 1, 1955; children: Joanna, Henry. *Education:* University of Exeter, B.A. (with honors), 1951; London School of Economics and Political Science, Ph.D., 1955. *Home:* 15 Oakcroft Rd., London SE13 7ED, England. *Office:* Department of International History, London School of Economics and Political Science, University of London, London, England.

CAREER: University of London, Institute of Historical Research, London, England, research fellow in history, 1955-56; University of Reading, Reading, England, research fellow in history, 1956; University of London, London School of Economics and Political Science, assistant lecturer, 1957-59, lecturer, 1959-69, reader, 1969-76, professor of international history, 1976—. Associate member, George Washington University, Washington, D.C., 1961-62; visiting lecturer, University of California, Davis, 1966-67; visiting professor, University of Southern Mississippi, 1981 and 1983. Scaife Distinguished Visiting Lecturer, Kenyon College, fall, 1971; Kratter Professor, Stanford University, 1979; Griffin Lecturer, Stanford University, 1983; Albert Biever Memorial Lecturer, Loyola University, 1983. *Military service:* British Army, 1951-53; became sergeant. *Member:* Royal Historical Society (fellow).

AWARDS, HONORS: Fulbright grant and British Association for American Studies fellowship, 1961-62; Albert B. Corey Prize of the American and Canadian Historical Associations, 1967-69, for *Britain and the Balance of Power in North America 1815-1908.*

WRITINGS: (Editor with D. C. Watt) *Studies in International History: Presented to Professor W. N. Medlicott,* Archon Books, 1967; *Britain and the Balance of Power in North America 1815-1908,* University of California Press, 1967; *The Foreign Policy of Victorian England, 1830-1902,* Oxford University Press, 1970; *The Blackmailing of the Chancellor,* Lemon Tree Press, 1975; *The Letters of the Third Viscount Palmerston to Laurence and Elizabeth Sulivan, 1804-1863,* Royal Historical Society, 1979; *Palmerston: The Early Years, 1784-1841,* Macmillan, 1982.

WORK IN PROGRESS: A second volume on the life of Palmerston; an edition of the letters of Francis Horner; four hundred volumes of selections from the Foreign Office Confidential Print, for University Publications of America.

SIDELIGHTS: Kenneth Bourne is considered by many reviewers to be one of the more knowledgeable authors of books on British history. A critic for the *Times Literary Supplement* states that *The Foreign Policy of Victorian England, 1830-1902* is an "excellent book on the foreign policy of Victorian England." Zara Steiner remarks of this same book in *American Historical Review* that "the special value of [*The Foreign Policy of Victorian England, 1830-1902*] lies in Dr. Bourne's assimilation of the flood of new monographic work in this field. . . . Dr. Bourne excels in his description of Anglo-American relations. . . . This is an informative guide for the central decades of the Victorian period."

Of Bourne's *Palmerston: The Early Years* Norman Gash comments: "Bourne's book is in a class of its own for two reasons: the comprehensive foundation of archival material on which it is based, and the immense detail in which it is written. As far as one can tell, this will be the definitive life of Palmerston. . . . It marks an epoch in Palmerstonian historiography; it is also a scholarly achievement which will earn the admiration of fellow-historians." And a reviewer for *Choice* writes that this book is "brilliantly written and painstakingly researched. [*Palmerston: The Early Years*] is a fine biography in every sense. . . . All in all, Bourne has given us a model biography which must become the standard work on the subject."

BIOGRAPHICAL/CRITICAL SOURCES: Times Literary Supplement, December 28, 1967, January 8, 1971, October 22, 1982; *Choice,* July, 1968, May, 1971, September, 1982; *American Historical Review,* December, 1971.

*   *   *

BOVA, Ben(jamin William)   1932-

PERSONAL: Born November 8, 1932, in Philadelphia, Pa.; son of Benjamin Pasquale (a tailor) and Giove (Caporiccio) Bova; married Rosa Cucinotta, November 28, 1953 (divorced, 1974); married Barbara Berson Rose, June 28, 1974; children: (first marriage) Michael Francis, Regina Marie. *Education:* Temple University, B.S., 1954. *Religion:* Roman Catholic. *Home:* 32 Gramercy Park S., New York, N.Y. 10003. *Agent:* The Barbara Bova Literary Agency, 32 Gramercy Park S., New York, N.Y. 10003.

CAREER: Upper Darby News, Upper Darby, Pa., editor, 1953-56; Martin Aircraft Co., Baltimore, Md., technical editor on Vanguard project, 1956-58; Massachusetts Institute of Technology, Cambridge, screenwriter for Physical Science Study Committee, 1958-59; Avco-Everett Research Laboratory, Everett, Mass., marketing manager, 1960-71; Conde Nast Publishing Co., New York City, editor of *Analog,* 1971-78; Omni Publications International, New York City, editorial director and vice-president of *Omni,* 1978-82; science and technology consultant, "CBS Morning News" television show. Lecturer at universities and businesses. Science consultant to motion picture and television studios.

MEMBER: National Space Institute, Science Fiction Writers of America, P.E.N. International, American Association for the Advancement of Science, British Interplanetary Society (fellow), Free Space Society (honorary chairman), National Space Club, Nature Conservancy, New York Academy of Sciences, Explorers Club. *Awards, honors: The Milky Way Galaxy* and *The Fourth State of Matter* were named best science books of the year by the American Library Association; Hugo Award, World Science Fiction Convention, 1973-77, and 1979, for best editor; E. E. Smith Memorial Award, New England Science Fiction Society, 1974; named distinguished alumnus, Temple University, 1981; Balrog Award, 1983.

WRITINGS—Science fiction: The Star Conquerers, Winston, 1959; *Star Watchman*, Holt, 1964; *The Weathermakers*, Holt, 1967; *Out of the Sun*, Holt, 1968; *The Dueling Machine*, Holt, 1969; *Escape!*, Holt, 1970; *Exiled from Earth* (also see below), Dutton, 1971; (with George Lucas) *THX 1138*, Paperback Library, 1971; *Flight of Exiles* (also see below), Dutton, 1972; *As on a Darkling Plain*, Walker, 1972; *The Winds of Altair*, Dutton, 1973; *When the Sky Burned*, Walker, 1973; *Forward in Time* (short-story collection), Walker, 1973; (with Gordon R. Dickson) *Gremlins, Go Home!*, St. Martin's, 1974; *End of Exile* (also see below), Dutton, 1975; *The Starcrossed*, Chilton, 1975; *City of Darkness*, Scribner, 1976; *Millennium*, Random House, 1976; *The Multiple Man*, Bobbs-Merrill, 1976; *Colony*, Pocket Books, 1978; *Maxwell's Demons* (short-story collection), Baronet, 1978; *Kinsman*, Dial, 1979; *The Exiles Trilogy* (contains *Exiled from Earth*, *Flight of Exiles*, and *End of Exile*), Berkley, 1980; *Voyagers*, Doubleday, 1981; *Test of Fire*, Tor Books, 1982.

Nonfiction: *The Milky Way Galaxy: Man's Exploration of the Stars*, Holt, 1961; *Giants of the Animal World*, Whitman Publishing, 1962; *Reptiles since the World Began*, Whitman Publishing, 1964; *The Uses of Space*, Holt, 1965; *Magnets and Magnetism*, Whitman Publishing, 1966; *In Quest of Quasars: An Introduction to Stars and Starlike Objects*, Crowell, 1970; *Planets, Life, and LGM*, Addison-Wesley, 1970; *The Fourth State of Matter: Plasma Dynamics and Tomorrow's Technology*, St. Martin's, 1971; *The Amazing Laser*, Westminster Press, 1972; *The New Astronomies*, St. Martin's, 1972; *Starflight and Other Improbabilities*, Westminster Press, 1973; *Man Changes the Weather*, Addison-Wesley, 1973; (with Barbara Berson) *Survival Guide for the Suddenly Single*, St. Martin's, 1974; *The Weather Changes Man*, Addison-Wesley, 1974; *Workshops in Space*, Dutton, 1974; *Through Eyes of Wonder*, Addison-Wesley, 1975; *Science: Who Needs It?*, Westminster Press, 1975; *Notes to a Science Fiction Writer*, Scribner, 1975; *Viewpoint*, NESFA Press, 1977; (with Trudy E. Bell) *Closeup: New Worlds*, St. Martin's, 1977; *The Seeds of Tomorrow*, McKay, 1977; *The High Road*, Houghton, 1981; *Vision of the Future*, Abrams, 1982.

Editor: *The Many Worlds of SF*, Dutton, 1971; *SFWA Hall of Fame*, Volume II, Doubleday, 1973; *Analog 9*, Doubleday, 1973; *The Analog Science Fact Reader*, St. Martin's, 1974; *Analog Annual*, Pyramid Publications, 1976; *Analog Yearbook*, Baronet, 1978; *Best of Analog*, Baronet, 1978; (with Don Myrus) *The Best of Omni Science Fiction*, Omni Publications International, 1980; (with Don Myrus) *The Best of Omni Science Fiction*, four volumes, Omni Publications International, 1980-82.

SIDELIGHTS: Ben Bova, writes J. D. Brown in the *Dictionary of Literary Biography Yearbook: 1981*, "is a leading spokesman for expanded scientific research and the application of new technologies to solve present and future problems." Bova's science-fiction novels are set in the near future and detail the impact of high technology advances in solving the problems of present-day society. In his nonfiction science books, Bova explains the importance of recent scientific discoveries and the social effects these discoveries might have. And as editor of

Omni, he has presented both science fiction and science fact in a manner meant to enhance the role of technology in the betterment of the human condition.

Brown sees Bova's primary goal in all of his writing and editing to be convincing "the skeptical that proposed [scientific] research programs result in gains in knowledge which ultimately yield enormous practical benefits." Bova's *Workshops in Space*, for example, examines four outer space research stations and explains the beneficial information scientists have learned from using them. In *The Fourth State of Matter*, Bova discusses current scientific research into plasmas—which are neither solids, liquids, nor gases—and speculates on their possible uses in the future. A *Choice* reviewer finds the book "Outstanding! Popular treatments of science are difficult to do well and here is a thorough, readable, and reasonably accurate survey of plasmas. [Bova's] treatment of experiments [in the field] is most satisfying."

In his science-fiction novels, Bova dramatizes his interest in scientific solutions to societal problems, particularly the beneficial effects of space exploration on the whole of society. In his novel *Colony*, for example, Bova envisions a near future society in which three groups compete for power on a dangerously overcrowded Earth: a world government, a group of multinational corporations, and an underground terrorist organization. None of these groups has any solution to the pressing problem of overpopulation. "But the novel champions a fourth possibility," writes Brown, "a space vehicle constructed from lunar materials [and] large enough for millions of colonists in space orbit. The argument of the book is that . . . the key to Earth's survival is dispersal of its population throughout the solar system." Edward Wood of *Analog* finds the novel "a fast moving story that gives a very convincing picture of the future."

Speaking of *Colony* to Elton T. Elliott of *Science Fiction Review*, Bova emphasized the importance of space exploration: "One of the points that I am bringing out in . . . *Colony*, is that the [space] colonies, this concept of colonizing the solar system now, is incredibly important for many, many reasons. One of the most important reasons is we will have spread the home grounds of the human race to beyond this one planet. So if we do screw up this planet . . . there will still be a human race surviving elsewhere."

This idea is developed further in *The High Road*, Bova's nonfiction study of space exploration and its effects on Earth society. He states his thesis at the outset of the book: "For humankind to survive the plagues of overpopulation, environmental destruction, and war by the end of the century—we must expand into space." The building of permanent orbiting space colonies is especially recommended, as these colonies would be able to construct cheaply a myriad of vital products for the Earth, while relieving the problems of overpopulation by relocating large numbers of people to outer space. Critical reaction to the book has been generally favorable. John Adams of *School Library Journal* judges the book to be "a purposeful and fairly even-minded . . . study of important choices before us." Reuben Benumof of *Science Books and Films* finds it "a vigorous espousal of the benefits of a massive expansion of our present space program [which] will interest anyone who is concerned about alleviating the ills of society." "This is one of the most exciting and positive books to come out in years," Jack Kriwan of *National Review* believes. "It makes a compelling, practical case for America's expansion outward into the space frontier."

"I think that space flight offers perhaps the only opportunity we have," Bova told Elliott, "to solve the problems here on earth. [Few people] became colonists and settled the New World and yet the development of the New World changed the lives of every human being . . . all over the world. Very few human beings will go into space, and yet the things that they do there will change the lives of all the people who remain on earth. It has already changed our lives."

"Bova," Brown concludes, "has consistently pushed beyond formal restrictions and sought new forms to render in human terms the potential meaning and experience of science in the future, a bright, humane future, as opposed to the dark collapse of civilization which Bova regards as inevitable if we refuse to pursue fully all the new avenues of scientific research and technological application."

CA INTERVIEW

CA interviewed Ben Bova by phone February 2, 1982, at his *Omni* office in New York City.

CA: In your life's work you have extolled science as a "humanistic pursuit" and science fiction as "a bridge between science and art, between the engineers of technology and the poets of humanity." Did you become interested in science and science fiction at the same time, or did one interest precede and lead to the other?

BOVA: It happened at just about the same time, and mainly through the agency of the Fels Planetarium in Philadelphia, where I first got "turned on" to the universe.

CA: This was when you were very young?

BOVA: Yes, I was still in grammar school.

CA: How early did you start writing?

BOVA: I actually began professional writing in the tenth grade, if by professional you mean writing for publications. I started making up stories the first time I got caught with my hand in the cookie jar, but writing for other people to read started in the tenth grade, when I began to write for the school newspaper.

CA: You got a degree in journalism from Temple. Did you also take a lot of science courses there?

BOVA: No, not really. I took a sort of general science course that was required, but I always found science courses show you the wrong end of the telescope. Reading science fiction and reading the works of scientists written for the nonspecialist always excited me much more. You could learn to understand the principles easily enough, and it was great to see the results, to see the beauties of the final product, without going through the tedium of how they got there.

CA: Before you became an editor at Analog *and then* Omni, *you were a newspaperman, a marketing executive for Avco Everett Research Laboratory, a technical editor for Project Vanguard at the Martin Company, and a scriptwriter for instructional films. Did all of these jobs allow you to combine your writing and editing skills with your scientific interests?*

BOVA: Well, I have always considered myself a writer first, and all the other jobs were merely to support myself. I've been fortunate enough to find work where I not only supported myself but learned a lot and met the people that I wanted to write about. Yes, I was writing all along—very often without success, but writing steadily all the time.

CA: Through your own science fiction, your writing about science fiction, and your editing, you've been instrumental in promoting the genre to a more respectable critical position than it once held.

BOVA: I would debate that. I don't think I've been instrumental in promoting science fiction. Lots of other people have. What I've tried to do is write stories for people who don't ordinarily read science fiction and widen the audience that way.

CA: Do you feel that your work at Analog *and* Omni *has attracted readers who weren't especially interested in science fiction before?*

BOVA: I think it has. And you can see through the decades of the 1970s and '80s the growth of the public's interest in it. They don't always recognize what they're reading as science fiction. But stories that are definitely not about here and now are very, very popular, whether they're Robert Ludlum thrillers or "Star Wars" fantasies.

CA: Did you have anything to do with founding Science Fiction Research Associates?

BOVA: Not at all. I think Science Fiction Research Associates is almost a parasitical growth. It's a new ecological niche for untenured teachers to gain tenure, and most of them don't know as much about science fiction as the average twelve-year-old reader. I found this out through bitter experience. While there are many, many fine people in SFRA, most of the people teaching science fiction are little better than frauds. They not only don't know anything about the subject, they're rather proud of the fact that they don't know anything about it.

CA: Do you have mixed feelings about the increasing popularity of science fiction?

BOVA: Yes, yes. My basic problem is that I hate to see things categorized. It's such a categorized world already. To get a novel published nowadays, it has to fit into some marketing category. It's got to be a mystery or a romance or a science-fiction novel or a political novel, and what the book is in and of itself becomes less important than the cover that the publisher can wrap around it, the advertising slogans they can put on it. This is a terrible blow to the writer who wants people to appreciate what's inside the book, not what's outside it. Now, we get into this category called science fiction, and we begin as enthusiasts of this kind of story to try to get people to take it seriously. That's fine. But then when it grows into a sort of movement that says science fiction should have the same number of titles on the bookstand as any other field, or we must have professorships of science fiction, or there must be a world trade union of science-fiction writers, you begin to lose track of what you started out to do.

CA: Do you think people who don't read science fiction early in their lives are shut off from developing an interest in it later?

BOVA: I think not only are they shut off from developing an interest in science fiction, they are shut off from the real world. These are the people who pick up the newspaper every day and say, "How can this happen? Why are we in such a terrible fix?'' while their contemporaries who have been reading science fiction since childhood are quite aware of what's happening and why. They're powerless to do anything about it because there are not enough people who read science fiction to make a difference in the political arena. But at least those who have been reading science fiction are aware of the major forces and problem areas that impinge on the real world.

CA: Many people think of science-fiction fans as a weird lot of people who dress up in costumes at conventions. Is there as much dressing up as there used to be?

BOVA: The fans do dress up for science-fiction conventions. Chevrolet salesmen dress up for their conventions, too. I've seen both, and, frankly, I'll take the science-fiction conventions. They're much more intelligent, and they're safer. There's much less drinking and roughhousing. You have to remember that science-fiction conventions originated because there were so few people who enjoyed science fiction that they needed some social intercourse, and the conventions grew as a result.

CA: You've won six Hugo Awards for editing. What have you found to be the greatest problems as editor of Analog *and now* Omni?

BOVA: The most difficult problem is to get good short fiction that deals realistically with science and technology. And by good short fiction I mean stories as judged by all the criteria of any kind of fiction. Unfortunately, we now have more than one generation of writers coming on the scene who are interested in science fiction and have read science fiction since childhood, but have no other connection with science or technology. So they don't really know what they're doing. Many of them are very good writers, but they have no firsthand experience with the subject that they pretend to be writing about. As a result, what they're writing are merely pale imitations of the stories they enjoyed as children.

CA: Do you think the sciences are being taught inadequately in the secondary schools?

BOVA: The teaching of science is suffering the same way the teaching of reading is suffering. The reason is that we do not encourage the best people to go into teaching. For fifty years now teachers' colleges have been the refuge of the people who take education courses without knowing any other thing, without having any content to teach. If you want a really scathing report on the status of teachers' colleges, read the autobiography of Abraham Flexner, a man who devoted his entire life to teaching and to creating good education in this country. He was one of the founders of the Institute for Advanced Study in Princeton. And he said at the age of ninety in the year 1960 that teachers' colleges ''are absurd institutions'' and have only gotten where they are ''by wiring the state legislatures'' so that only people with diplomas can teach. It is sobering to realize that if Albert Einstein were alive and living at Princeton today, he would not be allowed to teach in a public school. He might be a terrible teacher, but the reason he would not be allowed to teach is that he doesn't have a teaching-school certificate.

CA: In your book Notes to a Science Fiction Writer, *originally published in 1975, you gave practical advice on the craftsmanship of writing good science-fiction stories. Did you get a lot of letters from people who read the book and tried to follow your advice?*

BOVA: Oh yes, I got lots of manuscripts with letters on top saying, ''I've read your book—now you've got to buy my story.''

CA: Did the book actually help some writers to do a better job?

BOVA: I think in a few cases, yes. But I've always found that the people who are going to be successful writers find out what they need to find out and go ahead and do it. And you could say the same in any field.

CA: Have you had trouble juggling your time so that you could do both editing and writing?

BOVA: Not until recently. As I said earlier, I've always thought of myself first as a writer, so normally I have no trouble at all juggling my time: first I write, and then everything else is fitted in. But what has happened in the past couple of years is that, both as a writer and as a member of the team here at *Omni,* I have become very active in the grass-roots movement for space, which is a lot like the environmental movement was twenty years ago. It requires a good deal of traveling and a good deal of politicking, and this is sort of a third full-time job.

CA: Are you getting the message across?

BOVA: We're beginning to. There is now a bipartisan caucus for space in the House of Representatives. We're beginning to make some political headway, which I think is very important.

CA: How does development of the space program relate to the national economy?

BOVA: The two go hand in hand. The technology developed in space has an immediate and powerful impact on the economy. *The High Road,* another book of mine that Houghton Mifflin published last year, examines the space effort and what it does for us on a day-to-day level. I've found, not only from my own research but from the work that economists have done, that investment in space has an incredibly beneficial effect on the economy. It lowers the inflation rate, increases productivity, makes real jobs, builds new industries. So it is no coincidence that when we cut the space program in the early '70s, the economy began to tailspin. As we begin to invest more in space and do more in space, we develop new industries that strengthen our economy.

CA: What publications besides Omni *should the layman read to keep up with scientific and technological development?*

BOVA: Depending on the depth he or she wants to get into, first of all there's a marvelous little weekly newsletter called *Science News,* which does a very good job of covering what's happening in the sciences. Then there's the *New Scientist,* a British weekly which goes into more detail. The American Association for the Advancement of Science publishes two monthly magazines. One is called *Science,* which has actual scientific-journal papers in various fields and frequently has some first-rate news about science. They also publish a magazine that almost competes with *Omni.* It's called *Science 82.* (The number changes each year; it started as *Science 80.*) It's a very nice piece of work and it complements *Omni* very well. If you want to get into real detail, there's the *Scientific American,* which even some specialists have trouble reading in fields outside their own. But it's a superb reference monthly. It's like getting a new issue of the encyclopedia every month. You just store them up for years.

CA: Were you involved in the production of "Omni: The New Frontier"?

BOVA: No. I gave a little advice, most of which was ignored. But it was produced by a team of television specialists who did their thing. They used *Omni* magazine and the people here mainly as departure points, as points of reference for information and background and ideas, and then went off and did things the way they must be done for TV. I reverse the situation and say, "Would I want these people coming in here and helping me put out the magazine?" And the answer is a clear no. So I think it's worked out very well. We've cooperated where it's beneficial to both sides.

CA: Do you think television is doing a good job of keeping people informed on science?

BOVA: Not at all. I think television covers science the way they cover the circus. You get a story once in a while, but between, when all the really important things are happening, they don't cover it at all. And when it comes to science fiction on television and in the films, they portray a very antiscience attitude. Whether you're talking about "Star Wars" or "The Time Bandits," somehow the scientist always comes out as either the useless, silly, foolish one or as the villain. "Time Bandits" is a marvelous show, but you'll find that the villain, the Devil, is interested in lasers and computers, while the *good* guy, God, is interested in flowers and shrubs. This is an attitude that pervades the motion-picture industry. They depend on science and technology; they make millions of dollars out of it. But they always portray the scientist as either an ineffectual fool or a downright villain, coldblooded and merciless. And that is deathly.

CA: It's that feeling that seems to exist among so many people that there's a dichotomy between the humanities and the sciences.

BOVA: It gets right down to what C. P. Snow described in *The Two Cultures.* And these people know very little of either. Film people in particular are so wrapped up in their own industry that there's very little spillover of knowledge into any other area. I have spent my life with scientists and writers and people in the arts and the technologies, and there are many, many more scientists who understand the *Bhagavad Gita* and poetry of many languages, who understand and appreciate ballet and opera and the arts in general, than there are so-called humanists who care about or understand the simplest kinds of science. C. P. Snow put it much better. He said, "If you go to a cocktail party and somebody asks you, 'What do you think of *Hamlet*?' and you say, 'I never heard of it,' you're regarded as a boor. But if you ask someone at the same cocktail party, 'What do you think of the second law of thermodynamics?' he will regard you as a boor for asking such a question." And to be ignorant of that is to be ignorant of the world.

CA: You've spoken out recently against teaching Creationism in the schools.

BOVA: I'm against teaching Creationism in biology classes. It is not biology. It was never intended to be biology, and it is not science. I have no objection to teaching it in a class of mythology or comparative religion or philosophy, whatever you like—even literature, because Genesis is a marvelous piece of literature that has come through several different languages. You can almost believe in God just by the miracle of having that beautiful poetry come through all those translations.

CA: Are you very concerned about the movement behind the effort to put Creationism in the schools, ban books, and exert a conservative influence in other basic ways?

BOVA: It worries me in that it's part of a whole effort more or less to return us to what could be construed as a religious conservative dictatorship. If you look at history, you see that one civilization after another has become the creature of the most conservative religious elements and then gone down the drain. This is what happened to the Roman Empire. This is what happened to Islam. It happened in England under the Protestant Reformation, when Cromwell got his hands on the government. Even in Massachusetts, the state I lived in for many years—the Puritans came there for religious freedom and immediately created a dictatorship that hanged Quakers. When a religious establishment gains control of the government, it very quickly establishes a dictatorship. And this is not what our countrymen have fought and died to create. We do have legal separation of church and state; in fact, that is the one thing that Thomas Jefferson apparently was proudest of accomplishing in his career. We don't kill people over religion in this country, and we could destroy everything that we have fought so hard and so long to maintain. The frightening thing is that these people have the best intentions in the world. They are so convinced that they are right and no one else is, that they're perfectly willing to hang you for it. As George Bernard Shaw said, "A fanatic who is willing to die for his faith is perfectly happy to kill *you* for it."

CA: What's given you the greatest satisfaction so far in your career?

BOVA: I think perhaps the greatest moment I've lived through was the first landing on the moon. This was truly a giant leap for the human race, and a historic moment by any measure. Hundreds of thousands of years from now, if there is still a human race writing history, this generation will be remembered for that event.

CA: In your own work, is there something you'd like to do that you haven't tried yet?

BOVA: Oh, constantly. I think any writer worth his salt is always trying to stretch his muscles and meet new challenges. One of the happiest moments of my life comes when a teacher or librarian or student comes up and says, "I read such-and-such a book of yours"—there's one book in particular, a children's book called *Escape!* that many librarians have told me about. It was written specifically for kids who don't like to read, and it's been very successful. Not only do I get more mail from that book than any other, but very often when I'm at a convention of librarians, they'll mob me and say, "Your book has gotten kids to begin reading who have never opened a book before." And that is a real thrill for me.

BIOGRAPHICAL/CRITICAL SOURCES: Christian Science Monitor, November 6, 1969, October 24, 1970; *Choice,* January, 1972; *Magazine of Fantasy and Science Fiction,* January, 1972, November, 1976, July, 1977; *Economist,* September 8, 1973; *New York Times Book Review,* November 10, 1974, March 7, 1976, April 11, 1976; *Children's Literature Review,*

Volume III, Gale, 1978; *Times Literary Supplement,* January 27, 1978; *Science Fiction Review,* September/October, 1978; *Analog,* March, 1979; *Washington Post Book World,* September 27, 1981; *Dictionary of Literary Biography Yearbook: 1981,* Gale, 1982; *School Library Journal,* February, 1982; *Science Books and Films,* March/April, 1982; *National Review,* May 14, 1982.

—*Sketch by Thomas Wiloch*
—*Interview by Jean W. Ross*

*   *   *

BOWSER, Eileen 1928-

PERSONAL: Born January 18, 1928, in Columbia Station, Ohio; daughter of Roy and Florence (Doyle) Putt; married William Patton Bowser, June 12, 1950. *Education:* Marietta College, B.A., 1950; University of North Carolina, M.A., 1953. *Office:* Department of Film, Museum of Modern Art, 11 West 53rd St., New York, N.Y. 10019.

CAREER: Museum of Modern Art, New York, N.Y., member of staff, 1953-55, secretary to curator of film department, 1955-57, research assistant, 1957-59, curatorial assistant, 1959-61, cataloger for D. W. Griffith Collection, 1961, curatorial assistant, 1961-65, assistant curator, 1965-69, associate curator, 1969-76, curator of film department, 1976—, member of archives advisory committee, 1971—. *Member:* Federation Internationale des Archives du Film (member of executive committee; vice-president, 1977—; president of documentation commission, 1972—).

WRITINGS: Carl Dreyer (monograph), Museum of Modern Art, 1964; (author of revision) Iris Barry, *D. W. Griffith: American Film Master* (monograph), Museum of Modern Art, 2nd edition, 1965; (editor and contributor) *Film Notes,* Museum of Modern Art, 1969; (editor and author of introduction) *Biograph Bulletins, 1908-1912,* Farrar, Straus, 1973; (contributor) Ted Perry, editor, *Performing Arts Resources,* Volume II, Drama Book Specialists, 1975; *David Wark Griffith,* Jugosovenska Kinoteka (Belgrade), 1979; (editor with John Kuiper and contributor) *A Handbook for Film Archives,* Federation Internationale des Archives du Film, 1980; (with Richard Griffith and Arthur Mayer) *The Movies,* 3rd edition, 1981; (contributor) Roger Holman, editor, *Cinema, 1900-1906,* Federation Internationale des Archives du Film, 1982.

Author of film series "D. W. Griffith," 1965, and "From the D. W. Griffith Collection," 1975; also author of "Films from the Archive" and "Recent Acquisitions." Contributor to professional journals.

WORK IN PROGRESS: The Slapstick Atlas.

*   *   *

BOYD, William Harland 1912-

PERSONAL: Born January 7, 1912, in Boise, Idaho; son of Harland D. and Cordelia (Crumley) Boyd; married Mary Kathryn Drake, June 25, 1939; children: Barbara A. Boyd Voltmer, William Harland, Jr., Kathryn Louise. *Education:* Riverside Junior College, A.A., 1933; University of California, Berkeley, B.A., 1935, M.A., 1936, Ph.D., 1942; graduate study at Fresno State College (now California State University, Fresno), Garrett Biblical Institute, Northwestern University, and University of California, Irvine. *Politics:* Republican. *Religion:* American Baptist. *Home:* 339 Cypress St., Bakersfield, Calif. 93304.

CAREER: High school teacher of history, music, and English in McArthur, Calif., 1937-38, Watsonville, Calif., 1941-42, and San Mateo, Calif., 1942-44; Trans-World Airlines, San Francisco, Calif., agent, 1944-46; Bakersfield College, Bakersfield, Calif., instructor, 1946-63, professor of social sciences, 1964-73, professor emeritus, 1973—, chairman of department, 1967-73. Fresno State College (now California State University, Fresno), instructor, summers, 1949-55, assistant professor, autumns, 1961-63, spring, 1965; adjunct lecturer at California State College, Bakersfield, 1972-73. Member of advisory committee of Kern County Museum, 1955-60; chairman of Fort Tejon Restoration Committee, 1952-55.

MEMBER: American Historical Association, Western History Association, California Historical Society, California Retired Teachers Association, Kern County Historical Society (past president), Tulare County Historical Society, Kern County Historical Records Commission, Friends of the Bancroft Library, Phi Alpha Theta. *Awards, honors:* Merit award from Kern County Board of Trade, 1960; commendatory resolutions from Kern County Board of Supervisors, 1976 and 1978.

WRITINGS—Published by Kern County Historical Society, except as indicated: *Land of Havilah, 1854-1874: The Story of Keyesville, Kernville, and Havilah, in the Kern River Country, California,* 1952; (with G. J. Rodgers) *San Joaquin Vignettes: The Reminiscences of Captain John Barker,* 1955; (with J. D. Stockton and Rodgers) *Spanish Trailblazers in the South San Joaquin,* 1957.

A Centennial Biography of Kern County, California, 1966; *A California Middle Border: The Kern River Country, 1772-1880,* Havilah Press, 1972; *A Climb through History: From Caliente to Mount Whitney in 1889,* Havilah Press, 1973; *Kern County Wayfarers, 1844-1881,* 1977.

Kern County Tall Tales, 1980; *The Shasta Route, 1863-1887,* Arno Press, 1981; (with John Ludeke and Marjorie Rump) *Inside Historic Kern,* 1982; *Stagecoach Heyday in the San Joaquin Valley, 1853-1876,* 1983. Contributor to *Encyclopaedia Britannica* and to history journals.

WORK IN PROGRESS: Continuing research on the history of Kern County, Calif., and the history of the San Joaquin Valley.

SIDELIGHTS: William Harland Boyd writes: "My interest in California local history began while I was a graduate student and part-time employee of the Bancroft Library at the University of California, Berkeley. My research in Kern County history began when I became a member of the history faculty at Bakersfield College. This interest has continued into my retirement years."

*   *   *

BOYER, Richard Lewis 1943-

PERSONAL: Born October 13, 1943, in Evanston, Ill.; son of Paul Frederick (an attorney) and Betty (Hatton) Boyer; married Elaine Edith Smudsky (a registered nurse), June 29, 1968; children: Clayton Paul, Thomas Edward. *Education:* Denison University, B.A., 1965; University of Iowa, M.F.A., 1968. *Politics:* Independent. *Religion:* Roman Catholic. *Agent:* Helen Rees, 308 Commonwealth Ave., Boston, Mass. 02116. *Office address:* Places Rated Partnership, P.O. Box 8040, Asheville, N.C. 22814.

CAREER: New Trier High School, Winnetka, Ill., English teacher, 1968-70; Little, Brown & Co. (publishers), Boston, Mass., textbook salesman, 1971-73, acquisitions editor in College Division, 1973-78; Places Rated Partnership, Asheville, N.C., founding partner, 1978—. Part-time lecturer in literature/communications department, University of North Carolina at Asheville. *Member:* Mystery Writers of America, Cox & Company of New England (Sherlock Holmes club). *Awards, honors:* Chicago Geographic Society publication award, 1981, for *Places Rated Almanac;* Edgar Award for best novel, Mystery Writers of America, 1982, for *Billingsgate Shoal.*

WRITINGS: The Giant Rat of Sumatra (novel), Warner Books, 1976; (with D. Savageau) *Places Rated Almanac,* Rand McNally, 1981; *Billingsgate Shoal,* Houghton, 1982.

WORK IN PROGRESS: Places Rated Retirement Guide and *Places Rated Almanac II,* both for Rand McNally; *The Penny Ferry,* a novel, for Houghton.

SIDELIGHTS: Richard Lewis Boyer writes that he began *The Giant Rat of Sumatra* in 1970. "From the time of its conception, it was to be a serious attempt to continue the Sherlockian saga much as Sir Arthur Conan Doyle would have written it were he still alive." Boyer continues: "After ten years of writing, I am finally almost a full-time writer, dividing my time between novels and nonfiction. My ultimate goal is to combine writing with a full-time teaching position at a college or university."

*   *   *

BRACE, Geoffrey (Arthur)   1930-

PERSONAL: Born February 18, 1930, in Bristol, England; son of Arthur Henry (a clerk) and Mabel (Hobbs) Brace; married Sylvia Jean Powell (a dressmaker), September 4, 1954; children: Nicholas Powell, Cynthia Nancy, Natalie Ann Mary. *Education:* Attended Sorbonne, University of Paris, 1949; University of Bristol, B.A., 1951; Royal Academy of Music (England), L.R.A.M., 1956. *Home:* 2 Ash Cottages, Fenny Bridges, Honiton, Devon, England.

CAREER: Director of music at schools in London, England, 1954-59, Cambridge, England, 1960-63, and Dorset, England, 1963-70; King's School, Ottery St. Mary, England, director of music, 1972—. Director of Mikrokosm (a youth singing group). *Military service:* Royal Navy, Russian interpreter, 1951-53; became sub-lieutenant. *Member:* Incorporated Society of Musicians, English Folk Dance and Song Society, Sing for Pleasure. *Awards, honors:* Schoolmaster Fellowship award, Clare College, Cambridge, 1985.

WRITINGS—Published by Cambridge University Press, except as indicated: *Something to Sing,* four volumes, 1963-68; *The Story of Music,* Ladybird Books, 1965; *Something to Play,* 1965; *Something to Sing at Assembly,* 1965; *Thirty-Five Songs from Thirty-Five Countries,* 1970; *Music and Nature,* 1976; *Music and You,* 1977; *Music and Civilization,* 1977; *Music and Musicians,* 1978.

Musical plays: "A Young Man's Fancy," first produced in Gillingham, England, at Gillingham School, July 11, 1972; "Aucassin and Nicolette," first produced in Ottery St. Mary, England, at King's School, July 10, 1975; "Patelin," first produced in Ottery St. Mary, at King's School, April 1, 1976; "Margarine," first produced in Ottery St. Mary, April 27, 1979; "Little Miss Mitty," first produced in Ottery St. Mary, April 21, 1982. Contributor to education and music journals.

WORK IN PROGRESS: A biography of soprano Nancy Storace; research on music education.

SIDELIGHTS: Geoffrey Brace writes: "I am particularly interested in promoting a non-elitist, irreverent if necessary, and socially non-divisive attitude to all aspects of the art and craft of music, musical 'ecumenicalism' and the accent on music-*making,* enjoyment of things because they are entertaining, not because they are 'clever' or 'noble,' and working like this with children so that they may be less pompous than their parents about music."

AVOCATIONAL INTERESTS: Musical holidays in Austria, directing amateur choirs and orchestras, chamber music, playing the cello, and folk dance.

*   *   *

BRAILSFORD, Frances
See WOSMEK, Frances

*   *   *

BRANCATO, Robin F(idler)   1936-

PERSONAL: Born March 19, 1936, in Reading, Pa.; daughter of W. Robert and Margretta (Neuroth) Fidler; married John J. Brancato (a teacher), December 17, 1960; children: Christopher Jay, Gregory Robert. *Education:* University of Pennsylvania, B.A., 1958; City College of the City University of New York, M.A., 1976. *Residence:* Teaneck, N.J.

CAREER: John Wiley & Sons, New York, N.Y., copy editor, 1959-61; Hackensack High School, Hackensack, N.J., teacher of English, journalism, and creative writing, 1967-79; part-time teacher, 1979—. *Awards, honors:* American Library Association Best Book award, 1977, for *Winning,* 1980, for *Come Alive at 505,* and 1982, for *Sweet Bells Jangled out of Tune.*

WRITINGS—All published by Knopf: *Don't Sit under the Apple Tree,* 1975; *Something Left to Lose,* 1976; *Winning,* 1977; *Blinded by the Light,* 1978; *Come Alive at 505,* 1980; *Sweet Bells Jangled out of Tune,* 1980; *Facing Up,* 1984.

SIDELIGHTS: Robin F. Brancato told *CA:* "I have wanted to write for as long as I can remember, but I didn't actually begin writing novels for young people until I had taught for a number of years and raised two sons. My books have included experiences of my own childhood *(Don't Sit under the Apple Tree),* dramatic events that touched my life as a teacher *(Winning),* and present concerns that won't leave me alone *(Facing Up).* I like the idea of writing stories that raise questions for readers to think about in terms of themselves. (Would life still be worth living if you lost movement in your body? How far should you go to influence a brother who has chosen to follow a belief you disapprove of? What would you do if a once-beloved grandmother lost touch with reality?) I write my books *to ask the questions,* not necessarily to provide all the answers. Above all, I hope that my readers will be carried along by the heart, spirit, and humor of the characters and will realize only after the fact that I've sneaked in a few important things to ponder."

MEDIA ADAPTATIONS: Blinded by the Light was made into a "Movie of the Week." It first aired on Columbia Broadcasting System stations in December, 1980.

BIOGRAPHICAL/CRITICAL SOURCES: New York Times Book Review, March 30, 1975, April 27, 1980; *Best Sellers,* December, 1977, March, 1979; *Newsweek,* December 18, 1978.

BRANDON, James Rodger 1927-

PERSONAL: Born April 10, 1927, in St. Paul, Minn.; married, 1961. *Education:* University of Wisconsin, Madison, Ph.B., 1948, M.S., 1949, Ph.D., 1955. *Office:* Department of Drama and Theatre, University of Hawaii, Honolulu, Hawaii 96822.

CAREER: University of Connecticut, Storrs, instructor in drama and speech, 1950; U.S. Information Agency, Washington, D.C., assistant cultural attache in Djakarta, 1955-56, radio officer, 1956-57, Japanese language officer in Tokyo, 1958-59, assistant cultural attache, 1959-61; Michigan State University, East Lansing, associate professor of drama, 1961-67, professor of Asian theater, 1967-68; University of Hawaii, Honolulu, professor of theater, 1968—. *Military service:* U.S. Army; became sergeant. *Member:* Asia Society, Japan Society, American Theatre Association.

AWARDS, HONORS: Ford Foundation research grant for Southeast Asia, 1963-64; Fulbright research grant, 1966-68 and 1983-84; National Endowment for the Humanities senior research fellowship, 1971-72; Regent's medal and award, 1977, for distinguished research; Japan Foundation grant, 1980; University of Hawaii award for distinctive merit, 1981-82.

WRITINGS: (Editor with Tamako Niwa) *Kabuki Plays,* Samuel French, 1966; *Theatre in Southeast Asia,* Harvard University Press, 1967.

(Editor and author of introduction) *On Thrones of Gold: Three Javanese Shadow Plays,* Harvard University Press, 1970; (editor and author of introduction) *The Performing Arts in Asia,* UNESCO, 1971; (editor and author of introduction) *Traditional Asian Plays,* Hill & Wang, 1972; (translator) *Kabuki: Five Classic Plays,* Harvard University Press, 1975; *Brandon's Guide to Theater in Asia,* University Press of Hawaii, 1976.

(Editor with Rachel Baumer) *Sanskrit Drama in Performance,* University Press of Hawaii, 1981; (editor and contributor) *Chushingura: Studies in Kabuki and the Puppet Theater,* University of Hawaii Press, 1982.

SIDELIGHTS: James Brandon's book *Theatre in Southeast Asia* is, according to Faubion Bowers in the *Village Voice,* "a masterpiece of knowledge. . . . It is a joy to be able to read some hard facts—and at times dry—lifted along by a truly felicitous style. . . . [This is] a superb survey of a fantastic and artistic part of the world."

BIOGRAPHICAL/CRITICAL SOURCES: Village Voice, March 21, 1968; *Books Abroad,* spring, 1968, spring, 1971; *Virginia Quarterly Review,* spring, 1968.

*   *   *

BRANDT, Keith
See SABIN, Louis

*   *   *

BRANNEN, Noah S(amuel) 1924-

PERSONAL: Born February 2, 1924, in Aspermont, Tex.; son of Calvin Ernest and Iva (Galoway) Brannen; married Ann Pruet (a missionary), May, 1950 (divorced, August 18, 1981); children: Christalyn, Sharon Jean, Mary Ann, Noah Samuel II. *Education:* Washburn University, A.B., 1944; Andover Newton Theological School, B.D., 1947; Southwestern Baptist Theological Seminary, Th.M., 1948; Yale Divinity School, graduate study, 1949; University of Michigan, Ph.D., 1966.

Office: International Christian University, 10-2, Osawa, 3-Chome, Mitaka-Shi, Tokyo, Japan.

CAREER: Missionary under appointment of American Baptist Foreign Mission Society; National Council of Churches, Center for Study of Japanese Religions, Kyoto, Japan, assistant director, 1963-65; International Christian University, Tokyo, Japan, 1966—, began as assistant professor, currently professor of language, linguistics, and literature; Japan Missionary Language Institute, Tokyo, curriculum coordinator, 1968-80. *Military service:* U.S. Navy, 1942-44. *Member:* International Institute for the Study of Religions (Tokyo), International House (Tokyo), Association for Asian Studies, Linguistic Society of America, Tokyo Linguistic Society, Asiatic Society.

WRITINGS: Soka Gakkai: Japan's Militant Buddhists, John Knox, 1968; *The Kinkafu Collection of Ancient Japanese Songs,* Sophia University, 1968; (compiler with Eldora Thorlin) *Everyday Japanese,* Weatherhill (Tokyo), 1969; *The Practical English-Japanese Dictionary,* Weatherhill, 1983.

Translator from the Japanese: (And author of foreword with William I. Elliott) *Festive Wine: Ancient Japanese Poems from the Kinkafu,* illustrated by Maki Haku, Walker & Co., 1969; (and author of foreword) Shiina Rinzo, *The Go-Between, and Other Stories,* Judson, 1970; (with Scott Baird) Yoichi Fijiwara, *The Sentence Structure of Japanese: Viewed in the Light of Dialectology,* University Press of Hawaii, 1973; (with Elliott) *Wind and Pines* (ancient poetry), Image Gallery, 1977.

Contributor: *New Writing in Japan,* Penguin, 1972; Bedell, Kobayashi, and Muraki, editors, *Explorations in Linguistics,* Kenkyusha (Tokyo), 1979; *Seisho hon'yaku kenkyu,* Japan Bible Society, 1980; *The Elek Book of Japanese Verse,* Elek, 1980; Keith Crim, editor, *The Abingdon Dictionary of Living Religions,* Abingdon, 1981; *Proceedings of the Japan Studies Center,* Japan Foundation, 1982.

Also author of five Japanese language texts entitled *Japanese by the Total Method,* 1975-76, 1979-80; author with E. A. Nida of *The Theory and Practice of Translation,* in Japanese. Also contributor of translation to *Hiroshima Jogakuln Daigaku Ronshu,* 1980; contributor to *Contemporary Religions* and *Japanese Religions;* contributor of linguistic articles in Japanese to *Kokugogaku;* contributor of translations from the Japanese and of book reviews to *Japan Christian Quarterly;* contributor of translation of story by Rinzo to *Transpacific.*

WORK IN PROGRESS: A book on translation theory and practice, with Haruhito Sawanobori; an anthology of ancient Japanese poetry, with Elliott; translations of and an introduction to the works of Shiina Rinzo, a post-war novelist and playwright.

SIDELIGHTS: Noah S. Brannen told *CA:* "When I first came to Japan in 1951, fresh out of Yale Divinity School, I was very idealistic. . . . [But] I had no illusions that the Japanese nation was eagerly waiting to hear what this green missionary had to say. . . . I wanted to associate with Japanese from every walk of life—to see what they had to say about life in general, and to see what Japanese Christians had to say about Christianity. . . . I felt that just possibly some great Japanese Christian theologian would have insights into the true Christian faith that had eluded theologians from the West.

"So . . . I began to look into some Japanese books on Christian theology. I talked with theologians. I talked with ministers. I talked with ordinary laymen. I was disillusioned. I felt that I was really not receiving new insights into Christianity which had grown from an indigenous faith in the soil of Japan, but rather that I was hearing the three B's—Barth, Brunner, and Bultmann—in Japanese translation.

"A few years later I met a man . . . not a theologian, but a writer, who seemed to be the answer to my quest. . . . After many talks with him and after immersing myself in his novels, plays, and essays, I think I have met a Japanese Christian with insight into his faith which could never have come to an American Christian."

BIOGRAPHICAL/CRITICAL SOURCES: Commonweal, June 6, 1969; *Virginia Quarterly Review*, summer, 1969; *Christian Century*, June 17, 1970.

*   *   *

BRATHWAITE, Edward (Kamau) 1930-

PERSONAL: Born May 11, 1930, in Bridgetown, Barbados; son of Hilton Edward and Beryl (Gill) Brathwaite; married Doris Welcome (a teacher and librarian), March 26, 1960; children: Michael. *Education:* Attended Harrison College, Barbados; Pembroke College, Cambridge, B.A. (honors in history), 1953, Diploma of Education, 1954; University of Sussex, D.Phil., 1968. *Office:* Department of History, University of the West Indies, Kingston 7, Jamaica.

CAREER: Education officer in Ghana, 1955-62; University of the West Indies, Kingston, Jamaica, extramural tutor on Saint Lucia (island), 1962-63, university lecturer, 1963-72, senior lecturer in history, 1972-82, professor of social and cultural history, 1982—. Plebiscite Officer for the United Nations in the Trans-Volta Togoland, 1956-57. *Member:* Caribbean Artists Movement (founding secretary, 1966—). *Awards, honors:* Arts Council of Great Britain bursary, 1967; Camden Arts Festival prize, 1967; Cholmondeley Award, 1970, for *Islands;* Guggenheim fellowship, 1972; City of Nairobi fellowship, 1972; Bussa Award, 1973; Casa de las Americas prize for poetry, 1976; Fulbright fellow, 1982.

WRITINGS: (Editor) *Iouanaloa: Recent Writing from St. Lucia*, Department of Extra Mural Studies, University of West Indies, 1963; *Four Plays for Primary Schools* (first produced in Saltpond, Ghana, 1961), Longmans, Green, 1964; *Odale's Choice* (play; produced in Saltpond and Accra, Ghana, 1962), Evans Brothers, 1967; *Rights of Passage* (poetry), Oxford University Press, 1967; *Masks* (poetry), Oxford University Press, 1968; (editor and coauthor) *The People Who Came*, three volumes, Longman, 1968-72; *Islands* (poetry), Oxford University Press, 1969; *Panda No. 349*, Roy Institute for the Blind (London), 1969; *Alan Bold, Edward Brathwaite, Edwin Morgan* (collection of poetry), Penguin, 1969.

Folk Culture of the Slaves in Jamaica, New Beacon, 1970; *The Development of Creole Society in Jamaica, 1770-1820*, Clarendon Press, 1971; *The Arrivants: A New World Trilogy* (contains *Rights of Passage, Masks,* and *Islands*), Oxford University Press, 1973; *Caribbean Man in Space and Time*, Savacou (Mona, Jamaica), 1974; *Contradictory Omens: Cultural Diversity and Integration in the Caribbean*, Savacou, 1974; *Other Exiles*, Oxford University Press, 1975; *Black and Blues*, Casa de las Americas, 1976; *Mother Poem*, Oxford University Press, 1977.

Sun Poem, Oxford University Press, 1982; *Third World Poems*, Longman, 1983; *History of the Voice: The Development of Nation-Language in English-Speaking Caribbean Poetry*, New Beacon, 1983.

Recordings; all by Argo: "The Poet Speaks 10," 1968; "Rights of Passage," 1969; "Masks," 1972; "Islands," 1973.

Contributor to *Bim* and other periodicals. Editor, *Savacou* (magazine), 1970—.

SIDELIGHTS: Edward Brathwaite's poetry collections *Rights of Passage, Masks,* and *Islands* constitute an autobiographical trilogy that examines a Caribbean Negro's search for identity. The volumes trace Brathwaite's initial encounter with white culture, his journey to Africa in search of a racial self-image, and his eventual return to his Caribbean homeland. Laurence Lieberman writes in *Poetry:* "[Brathwaite] has been able to invent a hybrid prosody which, combining jazz/folk rhythms with English-speaking meters, captures the authenticity of primitive African rituals." "In general," writes Hayden Carruth in the *Hudson Review,* "[Brathwaite] has been remarkably successful in reproducing black speech patterns, both African and Caribbean, in English syntax, using the standard techniques of contemporary poetry, and he has been equally successful in suggesting to an international audience the cultural identities and attitudes of his own people."

BIOGRAPHICAL/CRITICAL SOURCES: Times Literary Supplement, February 16, 1967, November 14, 1975, February 18, 1983; *New Statesman*, April 7, 1967; *Books and Bookmen*, May, 1967; *Saturday Review*, October 14, 1967; *Virginia Quarterly Review*, autumn, 1968, spring, 1970; *Poetry*, April, 1969, May, 1971; *Book World*, November 3, 1968; *Books*, January, 1970; *Critical Quarterly*, summer, 1970; *Caribbean Studies*, January, 1971; *Caribbean Quarterly*, June, 1973; *Hudson Review*, summer, 1974; *Caribbean Writers*, Three Continents Press, 1979; *Contemporary Literary Criticism*, Volume XI, Gale, 1979.

*   *   *

BRATHWAITE, Errol (Freeman) 1924-

PERSONAL: Born April 3, 1924, in Clive, New Zealand; son of Jack Lister and Dorathea Beatrice (Anstis) Brathwaite; married Alison Irene Whyte, March 20, 1948; children: Michael John, Pamela Ann. *Education:* Attended secondary schools in New Zealand. *Religion:* Church of England. *Home:* 12 Fulton Ave., Christchurch 1, New Zealand.

CAREER: New Zealand Railways, Napier, cadet, 1940-42, 1945; Rehabilitation Department, King Country, Tekuiti, New Zealand, farm trainee (shepherd), 1946-47; New Zealand Broadcasting Corp., Christchurch, advertising copywriter, 1959-62; Dobbs, Wiggins-McCann, Erikson, Christchurch, advertising copywriter, 1962-67; Carlton-Carruthers du Chateau, Christchurch, advertising copywriter, 1968-72, manager, 1972—. *Military service:* New Zealand Army, Wellington Regiment, 1942-43, New Zealand Signals, 1955-58, Royal New Zealand Air Force, 1943-45, 1947-55, airgunner in No. 3 Bomber Reconnaissance Squadron, 1943-45; received Pacific Star, Empire War Medal, and New Zealand War Medal.

MEMBER: International P.E.N., Brevet Club. *Awards, honors:* Winner of centennial novel contest sponsored by *Otago Daily Times*, 1961, and New Zealand Literary Fund Award, 1962, both for *An Affair of Men.*

WRITINGS: Fear in the Night (novel), Caxton Press, 1959; *An Affair of Men* (novel), Collins, 1961, St. Martin's, 1962; *Long Way Home* (novel), Caxton Press, 1963; *The Flying Fish* (novel; first volume of trilogy), Collins, 1963, Tri-Ocean, 1969; *The Needle's Eye* (novel; second volume of trilogy), Collins,

1965, Tri-Ocean, 1969; *The Evil Day* (novel; third volume of trilogy), Collins, 1967, Tri-Ocean, 1969; *The Companion Guide to the North Island of New Zealand,* Collins, 1969.

The Companion Guide to the South Island of New Zealand, Collins, 1971; *New Zealand and Its People,* Government Printer (New Zealand), 1973; *The Beauty of New Zealand,* Golden Press, 1973; *The Flame Box* (fairy tale fantasy), Collins, 1976; *Historic New Zealand,* Kowhai Press, 1980; *New Zealand,* Kowhai Press, 1980; *Sixty Red Nightcaps,* David Bateman, 1980; *The Beauty of Waikato: Bay of Plenty,* Kowhai Press, 1980; *The Beauty of the North Island,* Kowhai Press, 1981; *The Companion Guide to Westland,* Collins, 1981; *The Beauty of the South Island,* Kowhai Press, 1982; *The Companion Guide to Otago, Southland, and Stewart Island,* Collins, 1982; *Just Looking,* David Bateman, 1982.

Author of *A Definitive History of the Royal New Zealand Air Force,* and *A History of BP (New Zealand) Limited;* also author of numerous radio plays and radio play adaptations, including "Long Way Home," "The Needle's Eye," and "An Affair of Men" (all based on his novels of the same titles), "Holes in the Air," "Shape Up or Ship Out," and "The Soapstone."

WORK IN PROGRESS: Four novels, one of which is tentatively entitled *The Dragon's Teeth.*

SIDELIGHTS: Errol Brathwaite told *CA:* "I write from a deep compulsion, and also from—fortunately—a great love of storytelling. If I have a principal theme, it is probably warfare, partly because of its dramatic possibilities, and partly because I regard life itself as a conflict between good and evil. As in total war, there is no escape from it, for anyone, and we each have to take sides or get caught, helpless, in the middle.

"I do not, however, use my work as a platform from which to preach. I simply tell my story with what realism and truth I can, and permit my readers to draw their own conclusions from whatever is revealed in the action. (I owe them that courtesy). . . . Writing is still to me, like life itself, an adventure. Perhaps, after all, I am rather like a child in a candy shop, with a penny in my fist, surveying an endless selection of delights."

AVOCATIONAL INTERESTS: Aviation, military history.

* * *

BRENNER, Yehojachin Simon 1926-

PERSONAL: Born December 24, 1926, in Berlin, Germany; son of Abraham (a headmaster) and Rosel (Hilb) Brenner; married Nancy Golomb (a historian, mathematician, and statistician), March 27, 1955; children: Eli (son), Yael (daughter). *Education:* Attended University of Basel; Hebrew University of Jerusalem, M.A. (history), 1956; University of London, M.A. (price history), 1962. *Politics:* "Liberal—not member of any party." *Religion:* Jewish. *Home:* Mozartlaan 23, Bilthoven JL 3723, Netherlands. *Office:* Department of Social Sciences, State University of Utrecht, Utrecht, Netherlands.

CAREER: University of Maryland, European Extension, lecturer in economics, 1960-62; University College of Cape Coast, Ghana, West Africa, head of economics department and senior lecturer in economic development, 1962-67; Institute of Social Studies, The Hague, Netherlands, professor and deputy chairman of economic planning, 1967-69; Middle East Technical University, Ankara, Turkey, professor of economics, 1969-72; State University of Utrecht, Utrecht, Netherlands, professor of

economics, 1972—. *Military service:* Israeli Armed Forces, 1948.

WRITINGS: Theories of Economic Development and Growth, Praeger, 1966; *A Short History of Economic Progress,* Augustus M. Kelley, 1969; *Agriculture and the Economic Development of Low Income Countries,* Mouton, 1971; *An Introduction to Economics,* Middle East Technical University Press, 1972; *Looking into the Seeds of Time,* van Gorcum (Assen), 1979; *Bezuiningen is Geen Werk,* Uitgeverij Intermediair (Amsterdam), 1981; (contributor) E. Kedourie, editor, *Palestine and Israel,* Frank Cass, 1982.

WORK IN PROGRESS: Structural Adjustments in Industrially Advanced Countries.

* * *

BRIDGERS, Sue Ellen 1942-

PERSONAL: Born September 20, 1942, in Greenville, N.C.; daughter of Wayland L. (a farmer) and Elizabeth (Abbott) Hunsucker; married Ben Oshel Bridgers (an attorney), March 17, 1963; children: Elizabeth Abbott, Jane Bennett, Sean Mackenzie. *Education:* Western Carolina University, B.A., 1976. *Home:* 64 Savannah Dr., Sylva, N.C. 28779. *Office address:* P.O. Box 248, Sylva, N.C. 28779.

CAREER: Writer, 1970—. *Awards, honors:* Boston Globe-Horn Book Award for fiction, Christopher Award, named to American Library Association list of best books for young adults, all 1979, and American Book Award nomination, 1981, all for *All Together Now;* American Book Award nomination, 1983, for *Notes for Another Life.*

WRITINGS—Novels; all published by Knopf: *Home before Dark,* 1976; *All Together Now,* 1979; *Notes for Another Life,* 1981. Contributor of stories to magazines, including *Redbook, Ingenue, Carolina Quarterly,* and *Mountain Living.*

WORK IN PROGRESS: Sara Will, a novel about sisters.

SIDELIGHTS: Sue Ellen Bridgers once told *CA:* "My writing seems to find its expression in nostalgia. My personal childhood experiences and the setting of a small southern town combine with a sense of the inevitable loss of that way of life. I feel very close to my roots when I'm working, as if the writing itself, although not autobiographical, is taking me back in time and is revealing some of the complexities of what seems to be a simple agrarian way of life. I am also interested in family relationships, especially the tradition of the southern woman's two faces—gentility and power—as portrayed in a domestic setting."

Since young people figure so prominently in Bridgers's examinations of family relationships, Bridgers is generally classified as a writer for young adults. Many critics, however, find that her novels appeal to readers of all ages. *Washington Post Book World* reviewer Katherine Paterson, for example, describes Bridgers's first novel, *Home before Dark,* as a book "for people like me, who want above all a really good story with characters they can care deeply for." And although one of the characters in *All Together Now* is a twelve-year-old girl spending the summer with her grandparents in a small town in North Carolina, Paterson points out that the novel "is not about emerging adolescence." Joyce Milton describes the book in the *New York Times Book Review* as a story about "good-hearted people in the process of discovering that love also takes perseverance." Bridgers's third novel, *Notes for Another Life,* discusses more sensitive subject matter, including mental illness, divorce, and attempted suicide. In a *Washington Post Book World* review of the work, Doris Betts maintains that "unlike many who write for young adults, Sue Ellen Bridgers affirms the earned sweetness of life without ever pretending it has a cream center or sugar coating."

BIOGRAPHICAL/CRITICAL SOURCES: New York Times Book Review, November 14, 1976, April 29, 1979, November 2, 1980, November 15, 1981; *New York Times,* December 4, 1979; *Washington Post Book World,* May 13, 1979, November 9, 1980, November 8, 1981, November 7, 1982; *Contemporary Literary Criticism,* Volume XXVI, Gale, 1983.

* * *

BRILLIANT, Ashleigh 1933-

PERSONAL: Born December 9, 1933, in London, England; son of Victor (a British civil servant) and Amelia (Adler) Brilliant; married Dorothy Tucker (vice-president of family business), June 28, 1968. *Education:* University of London, B.A., 1955; Claremont Graduate School, M.A., 1957; University of California, Berkeley, Ph.D., 1964. *Home and office:* 117 W. Valerio St., Santa Barbara, Calif. 93101.

CAREER: Edgware Gazette, Edgware, Middlesex, England, foreign correspondent, 1951; Central Oregon Community College, Bend, professor of history, 1964-65; Chapman College, Orange, Calif., professor of history, 1965-67; Brilliant Enterprises (publishers), Santa Barbara, Calif., founder and president, 1967—. Writer and cartoonist. Columnist and reporter for *Midtown Record,* San Francisco, Calif., 1967-69. Professor of history at Santa Barbara Community College, 1973-74.

MEMBER: International Platform Association, National Association of Television Arts and Sciences, Newspaper Comics Council, Northern California Cartoonists, Group against Smoking Pollution (GASP), Human Understanding of Sound and Hearing (HUSH). *Awards, honors:* United Nations population cartoon competition runner up, 1976.

WRITINGS: Unpoemed Titles, C.O.C. Press, 1965; *The Haight-Ashbury Songbook,* H-B Publications, 1967; *Pot Shots,* Brilliant Enterprises, 1968; *I May Not Be Totally Perfect But Parts of Me Are Excellent,* Woodbridge Press, 1979; *I Have Abandoned My Search for Truth and Am Now Looking for a Good Fantasy,* Woodbridge Press, 1980; *Appreciate Me Now and Avoid the Rush,* Woodbridge Press, 1981. Also author of column, "Trash from Ash," appearing in *San Francisco Midtown Record,* 1967-69, and of feature panel cartoon, "Pot Shots," syndicated to more than thirty newspapers, including *Chicago Tribune* and *Detroit Free Press.*

SIDELIGHTS: Ashleigh Brilliant, who says he prefers to think of himself as a "philosopher-prophet-poet rather than a cartoonist," is best known for his widely syndicated captioned drawings. The success of his "Pot Shots," as they are called, began as an unexpected result of Brilliant's first painting exhibit. While only a few of the paintings were sold, their odd titles aroused much attention. "Soon," Brilliant recalls, "I was making lists of titles for pictures I had not yet painted."

Brilliant, who admits that he would like to win the Nobel Prize, finds parallels between his "Pot Shots" and Japanese Haiku poems. Both, he feels, illustrate a way to "reduce literature to its pure essential." He describes "Pot Shots" as "very concise descriptions of reality," and thinks that they are simultaneously simple and complex. He explains: "It's however you choose to interpret it—like a poem. And that's what I'd

like to win the Nobel Prize in Literature for—for creating a new genre of poetry."

BIOGRAPHICAL/CRITICAL SOURCES: New Zealand Herald, March 31, 1973; *Chicago Tribune Book World,* January 11, 1981.

* * *

BRINKLEY, William (Clark) 1917-

PERSONAL: Born September 10, 1917, in Custer, Okla.; son of Daniel Squire (a minister) and Ruth (Clark) Brinkley. *Education:* Attended William Jewell College, 1936-37; University of Oklahoma, B.A., 1940; attended Yale School of Drama, 1961-1962. *Home:* 500 Wichita, No. 79, McAllen, Tex. 78501. *Agent:* The Sterling Lord Agency, Inc., 660 Madison Ave., New York, N.Y. 10021.

CAREER: Daily Oklahoman, Oklahoma City, Okla., reporter, 1940-41; *Washington Post,* Washington, D.C., reporter, 1941-42, 1949-51; *Life,* New York, N.Y., Washington correspondent, assistant editor, and staff writer, 1951-58; free-lance writer, 1958—. *Military service:* U.S. Navy, 1942-46; served chiefly in Mediterranean and Pacific; became lieutenant. *Member:* National Press Club (Washington), Overseas Press Club (New York), Phi Beta Kappa.

WRITINGS: Quicksand (novel), Dutton, 1948; (with Sister Cecilia) *The Deliverance of Sister Cecilia,* Farrar, Straus, 1954; *Don't Go near the Water* (novel), Random House, 1956; *The Fun House* (novel), Random House, 1961; *The Two Susans* (novel), Random House, 1962; *The Ninety and Nine* (novel), Doubleday, 1966; *Breakpoint* (novel), Morrow, 1978; *Peeper: A Comedy* (novel), Viking, 1981.

SIDELIGHTS: William Brinkley's *Peeper: A Comedy* is "a gentle pastoral comedy about a way of life and a geographical setting, the lushly fertile Rio Grande Valley," according to David Guy in the *Washington Post Book World.* Guy adds: "Probably *Peeper*—because it is largely a light comedy, and because William Brinkley's *Don't Go near the Water* was a best seller—will be considered commercial, yet it has virtues that many a literary novelist would do well to imitate: immaculate construction, a swift and vivid style, a wealth of descriptive detail. Brinkley is particularly adept at the concise portrayal of a wide range of characters."

MEDIA ADAPTATIONS: Don't Go near the Water was filmed under the same title by Metro-Goldwyn-Mayer in 1957. The movie grossed $4,500,000 and ranked among the ten best pictures of the year in *Film Daily*'s poll.

BIOGRAPHICAL/CRITICAL SOURCES: Washington Post Book World, June 15, 1978, December 20, 1981.

* * *

BROCK, Van(dall) K(line) 1932-

PERSONAL: Born October 31, 1932, in Boston, Ga.; son of William Arthur (a farmer) and Gladys (a teacher; maiden name, Lewis) Brock; married Frances Ragsdale (a writer and editor), August 3, 1961; children: Geoffrey Arthur, Brantley Ragsdale. *Education:* Attended Florida State University, 1949-50, and Georgia Institute of Technology, 1950-51; Emory University, B.A., 1954, graduate study, summer, 1959; Garrett Theological Seminary, graduate study, 1954-56; University of Iowa, M.A., 1963, M.F.A., 1964, Ph.D., 1970. *Politics:* Democrat. *Religion:* "Unaffiliated." *Home:* 2302 Amelia Cir., Tallahassee, Fla. 32304. *Office:* Department of English, Florida State University, Tallahassee, Fla. 32306.

CAREER: Emerson House (Chicago Commons), Chicago, Ill., group worker, 1954-55; Evanston Children's Home, Evanston, Ill., recreational counselor, 1955-56; Emory University, Atlanta, Ga., librarian, 1958-60; Street & Newsboys Club, Houston, Tex., director, 1960-61; Fulton County Juvenile Court, Atlanta, Ga., intake officer, 1961-62; University of Iowa, Iowa City, instructor in English, 1963-64; Oglethorpe College, Atlanta, Ga., assistant professor of English, 1964-68; University of Iowa, instructor in English, 1968-70; Florida State University, Tallahassee, assistant professor, 1970-75, associate professor, 1975-78, professor of English, 1978—, co-director of writing program, 1981—. Founder and director of Anhinga Press, 1974—. Recreational counselor for Atlanta's Young Men's Christian Association (YMCA), 1961-62; coordinator of Tallahassee's poets-in-the-schools program, 1972-74, and poets-in-the-prisons programs (for all Florida), 1974—; founder and director of Apalachee Poetry Center, 1973—. *Military service:* Air National Guard, 1957-59. U.S. Air Force Reserve, 1959-63.

MEMBER: College English Association, National Council of Teachers of English, South Atlantic Modern Language Association, Associated Writing Programs, Florida College English Association, Florida Council of Teachers of English.

AWARDS, HONORS: First prize from Kansas City Poetry Contest, 1964, for "The Horses"; Borestone Mountain poetry award, 1965, for "The Seabirds," and 1972, for "Peter's Complaint"; Georgia Writers Association prizes, all 1967, for "The Daydream," Reeves Lyric Award for "For One Who Is," Maywood Prize for "Complexity of Landscapes," first prize in Best Poems Contest for "Dead Man Creek," and first prize in best article contest for "The Place of the Writer in the Modern World"; first prize from Florida Poetry Contests, 1977; Florida Creative Writing fellowship, 1977-78; Rockefeller fellowship, 1977-78.

WRITINGS: Final Belief (poems), Back Door Press, 1972; (editor) *Lime Tree Prism: Poems by Children,* Apalachee Poetry Center, 1973; (editor) *A Spot of Purple Is Deaf: Children's Poems,* Anhinga Press, 1974; (editor) *The Space behind the Clock: Poems from Florida Prisons,* Anhinga Press, 1975; (editor) *Cafe at St. Marks: The Apalachee Poets,* Anhinga Press, 1975; *Spelunking* (poems), New Collage Press, 1977; *Weighing the Penalties* (poems), Burnt Hickory Press, 1978; *The Hard Essential Landscape* (poems), University Presses of Florida, 1980; (contributor) Jack Tharpe, editor, *Elvis: Images and Fancies,* University Press of Mississippi, 1980; *The Window* (poems), Chase Avenue Press, 1981.

Work has appeared in numerous anthologies, including: *Southern Writing in the Sixties: Poetry,* edited by John Carrington and Miller Williams, Louisiana State University Press, 1969; *New Voices in American Poetry,* edited by David Allan Evans, Winthrop Publishing, 1973; *New Southern Poets,* edited by Guy Owen, University of North Carolina Press, 1975; *Contemporary Southern Poetry,* edited by Owen, Louisiana State University Press, 1980.

Reporter for *Wilmington Morning Star,* 1960. Contributor of articles and poems to literary journals, including *New Yorker, Southern Review, Sewanee Review,* and *Yale Review.* Special editor of Tallahassee poets section of *Apalachee Quarterly,* 1975; poetry editor of *National Forum: Phi Kappa Phi Journal,* 1978—; editorial advisor of *Sun Dog,* 1979—.

WORK IN PROGRESS: Poetry collections, *The Locust Angel Elegies, Sand-dollars, Islands, Marriages, Mountains, Cities,* and *The Elvis Poems;* a novel, *The View;* nonfiction, *The Narcissist as Hero in American Culture;* literary criticism, *The Practice of Poetry.*

SIDELIGHTS: Van K. Brock writes: "I find myself increasingly concerned with the problem of suffering and the need for a joy in and a love of life through which suffering can be transcended and the perception of evil can be endured without evasion and without emotional and intellectual oppression. I firmly believe that we must be able to look without flinching, and without becoming desensitized, at the pervasive existence of evil, injustice, and suffering. But our awareness must not overcome; we must find cause for the celebration of existence, and without complacency."

AVOCATIONAL INTERESTS: Travel.

BIOGRAPHICAL/CRITICAL SOURCES: Florida Flambeau, September 13, 1973, July 30, 1979, May 2, 1980; *Tallahassee Democrat,* December 16, 1973, March 9, 1980; *New Look,* October 15, 1977; *North American Review,* December, 1980; *Sun-Times* (Chicago), December 21, 1980; *National Forum,* spring, 1981; *New Letters,* summer, 1981.

*   *   *

BRONSON, Lynn
See LAMPMAN, Evelyn Sibley

*   *   *

BROOKS, D(avid) P.   1915-

PERSONAL: Born February 15, 1915, in Shelby, N.C.; son of George E. (a farmer) and Aquilla (Scruggs) Brooks; married Fan Bost; children: Susan (Mrs. James L. Pike), Rebekah, Jane (Mrs. Jeffrey Sanders), Polly. *Education:* Wake Forest University, B.A., 1939; Southern Baptist Theological Seminary, Th.M., 1942. *Home:* 2712 Western Hills Dr., Nashville, Tenn. 37214. *Office:* Department of Religion, Belmont College, Nashville, Tenn. 37203.

CAREER: Clergyman of Southern Baptist Church; Baptist Sunday School Board, Nashville, Tenn., editor of *Adult Bible Study* and *Advanced Bible Study,* 1960-80; Belmont College, Nashville, part-time professor of religion, 1982—.

WRITINGS: (Contributor) O. T. Binkley, editor, *How to Study the Bible,* Convention Press, 1969; *The Bible: How to Understand and Teach It,* Broadman, 1969; *Dealing with Death: A Christian Perspective,* Broadman, 1974; (contributor) *Working with Adults in Sunday School,* Convention Press, 1974; (contributor) *Teaching Adults in Sunday School,* Convention Press, 1976; *Free to Be Christian,* Broadman, 1981. Contributor to *The Sunday School at Work* (annual), Convention Press, 1966, 1968; also contributor to religious teaching periodicals.

SIDELIGHTS: D. P. Brooks told *CA:* "The prophetic urge is the driving force in my writing. Certain things need to be said, and I feel compelled to write. Intense emotion is the precondition to powerful writing. Deep caring overcomes the reluctance to undergo the stress of crafting the word of concern."

*   *   *

BROOKS, Patricia   1926-

PERSONAL: Born December 17, 1926, in Chicago, Ill.; daughter of Robert C. and Mable (Harrington) Kersten; married Lester James Brooks (a writer), September 10, 1950; children: Lester James III, Jonathan, Christopher. *Education:* Vassar College, B.A., 1947; University of Minnesota, M.A., 1947-48; graduate study, University of London, 1949. *Politics:* Democratic. *Home and office:* 43 Marshall Ridge Rd., New Canaan, Conn. 06840.

CAREER: KGCU Radio, Mandan, N.D., copywriter and announcer, 1948-49; WLEE Radio, Richmond, Va., copywriter, 1949-50; Borden Co., New York, N.Y., scriptwriter for radio program, 1950-51; *Weekly Women's Magazine* and *Manila Times,* Manila, Philippines, feature writer, 1951-53; free-lance writer. Lecturer at Ateneo de Manila Graduate School, Manila, 1953; lecturer to women's clubs and other groups on art, travel, food, and American history, 1967—. *Member:* Society of Magazine Writers, Society of American Travel Writers. *Awards, honors:* Award from Philippine Tourist and Travel Association for best travel article of 1966; *Venture* magazine's Critic's Choice Award, 1967.

WRITINGS: (With Poppy Cannon) *The President's Cookbook,* Funk, 1968; *The Philippines: Wonderland of Many Cultures* (for grades eight to twelve), Dodd, 1968; *Meals That Can Wait,* Funk, 1970; (with husband, Lester Brooks) *How to Buy Property Abroad,* Doubleday, 1974; (with L. Brooks) *How to Buy a Condominium,* Stein & Day, 1975; *Best Restaurants New England,* 101 Productions, 1980; (with L. Brooks) *Fisher Guide to Spain and Portugal,* New American Library, 1983; *Best Restaurants Southern New England,* 101 Productions, 1983.

Contributor to numerous periodicals, including *Saturday Review, McCall's, Reader's Digest, New York Times, Vogue, Cosmopolitan,* and *Cuisine.*

SIDELIGHTS: Patricia Brooks has visited every continent except Australia, specializing particularly in travel in the Far East, Spain, and Turkey. Her writing specialties include food, travel, art, and features. *Avocational interests:* Archaeology, anthropology, politics.

*   *   *

BROTHERSTON, James Gordon   1939-

PERSONAL: Born August 5, 1939, in England; son of Thomas Percy and Ada Isabel (Smith) Brotherston; married Gisela Langsdorff, July 13, 1962; children: Isabel, Jenny, Lucy, Katie. *Education:* University of Leeds, B.A. (with first class honors), 1961; Cambridge University, Ph.D., 1965. *Home:* 2 The Dale, Wivenhoe, Essex, England. *Office:* Department of Literature, University of Essex, Colchester, Essex, England.

CAREER: University of London, King's College, London, England, assistant lecturer in department of Spanish, 1964-65; University of Essex, Colchester, England, lecturer, 1965-68, senior lecturer, 1968-73, reader, 1973-78, professor of literature, 1978—, chairman of department, 1972-75, dean of School of Comparative Studies, 1976-79, director of M.A. Schemes in Theory and Practice of Literary Translation, 1960—, and Native American Studies, 1979—. Visiting professor at University of Iowa, Iowa City, 1968-69, and University of British Columbia, 1975; external examiner, lecturer, and assessor for appointments at several universities. Tutor and advisor, National Extension College, 1964-68. Editor of Latin American Division, Pergamon Press Ltd., 1965—.

MEMBER: International Association of Hispanists, International Association of Americanists (member of national committee, 1981-82), Society for Latin American Studies, Royal Anthropological Institute, European Association of Americanists, Association of Hispanists of Great Britain and Northern Ireland, Midwest Modern Language Association. *Awards, honors:* Spanish Government scholarship to Curso superior de filologia espanola, Santander, 1964; grants from Astor Foundation and University of Essex Research Endowment Fund for research in six Latin American countries, 1966; Alexander von Humboldt fellowship for research in Berlin and Hamburg on American Indian literature, 1970-71; American Philosophical Society grant, 1972; Nuffield Foundation grant for research on ancient Mexican literature and art, 1975-76.

WRITINGS: (Editor and author of introduction and notes) Jose Enrique Rodo, *Ariel,* Cambridge University Press, 1967; (editor and author of introduction and notes with Mario Vargas Llosa) *Seven Stories from Spanish America,* Pergamon, 1967, 2nd edition, 1973; *Manuel Machado: A Revolution,* Cambridge University Press, 1968; *Spanish American Modernista Poets: A Critical Anthology,* Pergamon, 1968; (editor and translator with Edward Dorn) *Our Word: Guerilla Poems from Latin America,* Grossman, 1968; (translator with Dorn) Jose Emilio Pacheco, *Tree between Two Walls,* Black Sparrow Press, 1968.

(Translator) Reinaldo Arenas, *Hallucinations,* J. Cape, 1971; *Latin American Poetry: Origins and Presence,* Cambridge University Press, 1975; (editor and translator with Dorn) Cesar Vallejo, *Selected Poems,* Penguin, 1976; (editor and author of introduction with Peter Hulme) Jose Luis Borges, *Ficciones,* Harrap, 1976; *The Emergence of the Latin American Novel,* Cambridge University Press, 1977; *Image of the New World: The American Continent Portrayed in Native Texts,* Thames & Hudson, 1979; *The Other America: Native Artifacts from the New World,* Museum of Mankind, 1982; *A Key to the Mesoamerican Reckoning of Time,* British Museum, 1982. Also editor, with Anthony Aveni, of *Calendars in Mesoamerica and Tahuanhinsuyu,* Oxford University Press.

Contributor: N. Glendinning, editor, *Essays in Modern Spanish Literature and Art,* Tamesis Books, 1972; N. Hammond, editor, *Mesoamerican Archeology: New Approaches,* University of Texas Press, 1974; Hammond and Gordon Willey, editors, *Maya Archeology and Ethnohistory,* University of Texas Press, 1979; F. Barker and others, editors, *1936: The Politics of Modernism,* [Colchester], 1979; R. Cavendish, editor, *Mythology: An Illustrated Encyclopaedia,* [London], 1980; Barker and others, editors, *1642: Literature and Power in the Seventeenth Century,* [Colchester], 1981; Barker and others, editors, *1789: Reading Writing Revolution,* [Colchester], 1982; A. F. Aveni, editor, *Archeoastronomy in the New World,* Cambridge University Press, 1982; Anna Balakian, editor, *The Symbolist Movement in Literature in European Languages,* [New York], 1982. Also contributor to *Indians and Americans,* edited by Jacqueline Fear, *Encyclopaedia of Latin America and the Caribbean,* edited by Harold Blakemore and Simon Collier, and, with Oriana Baddeley, *Legends of the World,* edited by R. Cavendish, 1982.

Contributor of translations: *Short Stories in Spanish,* Penguin, 1966; *Latin American Writing Today,* Penguin, 1967; *Writers in the New Cuba,* Penguin, 1967; *Penguin Book of Socialist Verse,* Penguin, 1972; *Poetry of the Committed Individual,* Penguin, 1973; *East German Poetry,* Dutton, 1973; *Words and Beyond,* Lexington, 1973; *Ernesto Cardenal: Selected Poems,* Penguin, 1976; Gunner Harding and Anselm Hollo, editors, *Modern Swedish Poetry in Translation,* University of Minnesota, 1979.

Contributor of articles and reviews to periodicals, including *Times Literary Supplement, Cambridge Review, Bulletin of Hispanic Studies, Books Abroad,* and *Indiana;* contributor of translations to *Seneca Review, Poetry Review, Evergreen Review,* and other journals.

*   *   *

BROWN, Dee (Alexander)   1908-

PERSONAL: Born February 28, 1908, in Louisiana; son of Daniel Alexander and Lula (Cranford) Brown; married Sara Baird Stroud, 1934; children: James Mitchell, Linda. *Education:* Attended Arkansas State Teachers College (now University of Central Arkansas); George Washington University, B.L.S., 1937; University of Illinois, M.S., 1952.

CAREER: U.S. Department of Agriculture, Washington, D.C., library assistant, 1934-42; U.S. War Department, Washington, D.C., technical librarian, 1945-48; University of Illinois at Urbana-Champaign, librarian of agriculture, 1948-72, professor, 1962-72. *Military service:* U.S. Army, 1942-45. *Member:* Authors Guild, Western Writers of America, Organization of American Historians.

WRITINGS: Wave High the Banner (novel based on life of Davy Crockett), Macrae Smith, 1942; (with Martin F. Schmitt) *Fighting Indians of the West,* Scribner, 1948.

(With Schmitt) *Trail Driving Days,* Scribner, 1952; *Grierson's Raid,* University of Illinois Press, 1954; (with Schmitt) *The Settlers' West,* Scribner, 1955; *Yellowhorse* (novel), Houghton, 1956; *The Gentle Tamers: Women of the Old Wild West,* Putnam, 1958; *Cavalry Scout* (novel), Permabooks, 1958; *The Bold Cavaliers: Morgan's Second Kentucky Cavalry Raiders,* Lippincott, 1959.

They Went Thataway (satirical novel), Putnam, 1960; (editor) *Pawnee, Blackfoot and Cheyenne,* Scribner, 1961; *Fort Phil Kearny: An American Saga,* Putnam, 1962 (published in England as *The Fetterman Massacre,* Barrie & Jenkins, 1972); *The Galvanized Yankees,* University of Illinois Press, 1963; *Showdown at Little Big Horn* (juvenile), Putnam, 1964; *The Girl from Fort Wicked* (novel), Doubleday, 1964; *The Year of the Century: 1876,* Scribner, 1966; *Action at Beecher Island,* Doubleday, 1967.

Bury My Heart at Wounded Knee: An Indian History of the American West, Holt, 1970, abridged edition for children by Amy Erlich published as *Wounded Knee: An Indian History of the American West,* Holt, 1974; *Andrew Jackson and the Battle of New Orleans,* Putnam, 1972; *Tales of the Warrior Ants,* Putnam, 1973; *The Westerners,* Holt, 1974; *Hear That Lonesome Whistle Blow: Railroads in the West,* Holt, 1977; *Teepee Tales of the American Indians,* Holt, 1979; *Creek Mary's Blood* (novel), Holt, 1980; *The American Spa,* Rose Publishing (Little Rock), 1982; *Killdeer Mountain* (novel), Holt, 1983.

Editor, "Rural America" series, Scholarly Resources, 1973. Contributor of articles to *American History Illustrated.* Editor, *Agricultural History,* 1956-58.

SIDELIGHTS: The American West of the nineteenth century figures prominently in the writings of historian and novelist Dee Brown. His bestseller *Bury My Heart at Wounded Knee: An Indian History of the American West,* for example, chronicles the settling of the West during the nineteenth century from the viewpoint of the American Indians. In his novels *Creek Mary's Blood* and *Killdeer Mountain,* Brown dramatizes events and characters from western history, while his many nonfiction

works concern such subjects as the building of the railroads, the massacre at Little Big Horn, and women settlers of the old West. In all of his work, Brown has shown a consistent compassion for the American Indians and moral outrage at the injustices they have suffered.

Brown's interest in Indians stems from his childhood in Arkansas where, he tells an interviewer for *Publishers Weekly,* "there were quite a few Indians around, people with mixed blood, and at the beginning, I swallowed all the old myths. When I began to travel and meet more Indians I began wondering, Why do people think of them as such villains?" The question spurred Brown to investigate Indians on his own, reading everything he could on their history and culture. This interest led in time to his writing about the American West. Three of his early books, *Fighting Indians of the West, Trail Driving Days,* and *The Settlers' West,* were coauthored with Martin F. Schmitt and were based on historic photographs the two men discovered in the National Archives. Writing their text around these previously unpublished photographs, Brown and Schmitt succeeded in presenting pictorial histories of three great western subjects that had never been seen before.

After writing a score of books about the Old West, Brown embarked upon perhaps his most ambitious and successful historical work, *Bury My Heart at Wounded Knee,* a book that chronicles the settling of the West based on eyewitness reports from the Indians who lived there. Brown's reason for writing the book, explains Peter Farb of the *New York Review of Books,* lies in his belief that "whites have for long had the exclusive use of history and that it is now time to present, with sympathy rather than critically, the red side of the story."

"The Indians," writes Helen McNeil of *New Statesman* in her review of *Bury My Heart,* "knew exactly what was being done to them." Brown uses quotes from the Indians themselves to present their history of the period. The book, according to J. W. Stevenson of *Library Journal,* "based largely upon primary source material such as treaty council records, pictographic and translated autobiographical accounts of Indian participants in the events, and contemporary newspaper and magazine interviews, [is an] extensively researched history." N. Scott Momaday, in his review of the book for the *New York Times Book Review,* agrees with this assessment. *Bury My Heart at Wounded Knee,* he states, is "a compelling history of the American West, distinguished not because it is . . . an Indian history . . . but because it is so carefully documented and designed." As Brown told an interviewer for *Publishers Weekly,* "I had a document for everything in the book."

The uniquely Indian viewpoint of the book was achieved not only through the extensive use of the Indians' own words, but also by the use of the Indian names for the white historical figures of the period. General Custer, for example, was called "Hard Backsides" by the Indians, and is so referred to in the book. When the names are "consistently used," writes R. A. Mohl of *Best Sellers,* "these become creative and effective literary devices which force the reader, almost without his knowing it, into the position of the defeated, retreating Indian."

Although *Bury My Heart at Wounded Knee* took him over two years to write in his free time, Brown managed to keep a consistently Indian perspective throughout the whole book. Speaking to Anne Courtmanche-Ellis for the *Wilson Library Bulletin,* Brown explains how he did it: "I would tell myself every night, 'I'm a very, very old Indian, and I'm remembering the past. And I'm looking toward the Atlantic Ocean.' And I always kept that viewpoint every night. That's all I did.''

The importance of the book to the field of western history is noted by several reviewers. ''Brown,'' Farb relates, ''dispels any illusions that may still exist that the Indian wars were civilization's mission or manifest destiny; the Indian wars are shown to be the dirty murders they were. . . . *Bury My Heart* is an extremely ambitious and readable attempt to write a different kind of history of white conquest of the West: from the point of view of the victims, using their words whenever possible.'' McNeil judges the book to be ''a deliberately revisionist history [that tells] the story of the Plains Indians from an amalgamated Indian viewpoint, so that the westward march of the civilized white men, 'like maggots,' according to a Sioux commentator, appears as a barbaric rout of established Indian culture.'' *Bury My Heart*, Cecil Eby of *Book World* writes, ''will undoubtedly chart the course of other 'revisionist' historical books dealing with the Old West.''

Bury My Heart became a nationwide bestseller, gaining the number one spot on the country's bestselling books list and selling well over one million copies. But Brown claims the best compliment he ever received for the book came from an old Indian friend who told him: ''You didn't write that book. Only an Indian could have written that book! . . . Every time I read a page, I think: That's the way I feel.''

In *Hear That Lonesome Whistle Blow*, Brown approached the ruthless settling of the West from a different perspective, writing the history of the building of the western railroads. The book turned out to be an expose of the treacherous dealings of the railroad companies, although Brown claims, ''I didn't start out to write an expose.'' Union Pacific was so upset with Brown's manuscript that they denied him access to their company library for further research.

Hear That Lonesome Whistle Blow, writes Margo Jefferson, ''is a fast-moving narrative of ambition, greed and conflict that takes in the high-finance railroad moguls, bribing congressmen and future Presidents with lucrative stocks and bonds in exchange for enormous land grants and construction privileges; the waves of Irish and Chinese immigrants building the railroads . . . ; the Plains Indians fighting railroad workers to hold onto the land that the government was either cheating them out of or driving them off.'' Philip French of *New Statesman* agrees but believes that ''the constant emphasis on shoddy deals serves not merely to qualify almost out of existence the epic nature of the undertaking, but to deny a true complexity to the events and a full humanity to the participants.'' But Winifred Farrant Bevilacqua of the *Dictionary of Literary Biography* describes the book as ''an engaging reconstruction of the drama surrounding the advent of the iron horse and a case against the railroads.''

In his fiction, Brown dramatizes many of the historical themes he presents in his nonfiction, creating stories from the actual historical conditions of the nineteenth century. *Creek Mary's Blood*, for instance, is based on an Indian woman in Georgia who organized an attack on British-held Savannah during the American Revolutionary War. The novel tells her story and that of her descendants as they are pushed farther and farther west by the expanding frontier. Brown told Judy Klemesrud of the *New York Times*: ''I tried to make the historical events as accurate as possible, but I did make some changes for dramatic effect. That's something you never do in nonfiction, and I felt guilty about it.''

Despite its fictional liberties, the novel accurately describes Indian life of the nineteenth century while chronicling the lives of one Indian family on their westward trek. Interspersed with their story are chapters about events of the time that affected all Indians. ''In this absorbing historical romance,'' Bevilacqua states, ''Brown skillfully blends fact with fiction but falters in his attempt to confer on his characters an authentic Indian perspective.'' But Joseph McClellan of the *Washington Post Book World* thinks otherwise: ''Using fictional characters against a carefully researched historical background, [Brown] combines the attractions of both genres. The major incidents of his story are true, but by inventing fictional participants he is able to give the events a human dimension lacking in the historic record.''

''The dominant themes of *Creek Mary's Blood*,'' explains Mary Anne Norman of *The Lone Star Book Review*, ''are the displacement of the Indians and the treachery of the U.S. government in its dealings with the Indians.'' Through the misfortunes of Creek Mary's family, Brown outlines the fate of all Indians during the course of the nineteenth century. Creek Mary's two husbands, McClellan points out, symbolize the two ways that Indians sought to deal with the white settlers. Her first husband was an English colonist, ''who is related thematically to the effort at accommodation and assimilation,'' McClellan writes. Her second husband was a Cherokee warrior, ''a leader of the resistance to white encroachment.'' ''Both ways of coping,'' McClellan concludes, ''ultimately proved futile, and in his novel's epic length Dee Brown has leisure to examine the modes of futility in assimilation and in resistance.''

Although concerned with the same themes as his earlier works, Brown's novel *Killdeer Mountain* is a stylistic departure from his previous writings. It is told in a disjointed narrative structure that presents a number of conflicting versions of the same basic story. Reviewing the book for the *Chicago Tribune Book World*, Robert Gish claims that it is ''perhaps [Brown's] most intriguing book to date.'' Told by a newspaper reporter who is unraveling the true story of Major Charles Rawley, an Indian fighter and military hero, the novel contains the differing accounts of a number of people who knew and worked with him. The reporter's attempts to make sense of the ambiguities and contradictions in the stories, and his efforts to discover the truth concerning the major's heroism and supposed death, turn the novel into a kind of mystery story. ''The world we view,'' Brown states in the novel, ''is a complex mirror that tricks us with false images so that what we believe to have happened . . . may or may not have taken place.'' ''We gradually acquire,'' writes Michael A. Schwartz of the *Detroit News*, ''a complex tangled web of evidence resting upon a shadow. Brown makes the various guises that Major Rawley assumes seem quite real, and in Rawley's manifestations we discover the ambiguous nature of this country's westward expansion.''

The strongest aspect of the book, several critics claim, lies in Brown's narrative ability, which makes adventurous scenes come alive, while the weakest aspect is his use of dialogue. ''Brown's gift for strong narrative,'' Jonathan Coleman of the *New York Times Book Review* believes, ''far outweighs his skill at writing dialogue, which, at times, hurts his novel by trivializing it.'' In similar terms, C. C. Loomis writes in the *Washington Post Book World*: ''Brown is at his best narrating adventurous episodes within the novel. . . . But most readers want vivid characters in novels as well as vivid narration, and here . . . Brown has only limited success. . . . [His] dialogue is artificial; it flattens his characters.'' Brown's narrative strength was best used, Schwartz relates, in a scene involving the massacre of Sioux Indians which "shows Brown's mastery as a storyteller and his thorough understanding of these times. . . . It is rendered with such intensity that it becomes a brutally realistic portrait of the Indian wars."

In book after book, Brown has examined the history of the settling of the West and presented the hardships and triumphs of this vast undertaking. He has particularly drawn attention to "the destruction of ancient Indian cultures," Bevilacqua states, "and investigated other aspects of the toll exacted by the nation's western expansion. . . . He has always been recognized as a tireless researcher and a gifted raconteur who narrates his stories in an informative and entertaining manner."

Brown's books have been published in over twenty languages, including Latvian, Russian, and Icelandic.

MEDIA ADAPTATIONS: Bury My Heart at Wounded Knee has been optioned for a television production.

BIOGRAPHICAL/CRITICAL SOURCES: New York Times Book Review, May 3, 1942, March 7, 1971, May 15, 1977, April 13, 1980, April 27, 1980, May 25, 1980, April 26, 1981, June 5, 1983; *American Historical Review*, April, 1955; *Journal of American History*, November, 1966.

Library Journal, December 15, 1970; *Atlantic*, February, 1971; *Time*, February 1, 1971; *Newsweek*, February 1, 1971, May 23, 1977, March 28, 1983; *Christian Century*, February 3, 1971; *New Yorker*, February 13, 1971; *Book World*, February 28, 1971; *Best Sellers*, March 1, 1971; *National Review*, March 9, 1971; *Life*, April 2, 1971; *Publishers Weekly*, April 19, 1971, March 21, 1980; *New York Post*, April 22, 1971; *Catholic World*, August, 1971; *Village Voice*, August 5, 1971, June 27, 1977; *New Statesman*, October 1, 1971, September 30, 1977; *Economist*, October 2, 1971, September 10, 1977; *New York Review of Books*, December 16, 1971; *Pacific Historical Review*, November, 1972; *Guardian*, September 21, 1974; *New Republic*, December 14, 1974; *American West*, March, 1975; *New York Times*, December 3, 1976, April 13, 1980; *Christian Science Monitor*, June 21, 1977; *Times Literary Supplement*, December 16, 1977; *Wilson Library Bulletin*, March, 1978.

Chicago Tribune Book World, March 2, 1980, March 13, 1983; *Washington Post Book World*, March 16, 1980, March 14, 1983; *Lone Star Book Review*, April, 1980; *New York*, April 7, 1980; *Dictionary of Literary Biography Yearbook: 1980*, Gale, 1981; *Contemporary Literary Criticism*, Volume XVIII, Gale, 1981; *Los Angeles Times Book Review*, April 3, 1983; *Detroit News*, July 13, 1983.

—*Sketch by Thomas Wiloch*

*   *   *

BROWN, John Arthur 1914-

PERSONAL: Born August 28, 1914, in Burlington, Wash.; son of Marcus and Bernice (Sawyer) Brown; married Mary Rae Hansen, August 19, 1939; children: Janet. *Education:* Attended Mount Vernon Junior College, Mount Vernon, Wash., 1932-33, Seattle Pacific College, 1933-35; University of Washington, Seattle, B.A., 1938, M.A., 1942. *Home:* 1325 South Hills Dr., Wenatchee, Wash. 98801.

CAREER: Wenatchee Valley College, Wenatchee, Wash., 1946—, began as instructor, became professor of history, professor emeritus, 1976—, dean of men, 1948-52. Member of Chelan County Public Utility District Historical Advisory

Committee, 1961—, and of North Central Washington Museum Association, 1970—. *Member:* Washington State Historical Society.

WRITINGS—With Robert H. Ruby; published by University of Oklahoma Press, except as indicated: *Half-Sun on the Columbia*, 1965; *The Spokane Indians: Children of the Sun*, 1970; *The Cayuse Indians: Imperial Tribesmen of Old Oregon*, 1972; *Ferryboats of the Columbia River*, Superior, 1974; *Myron Eells and the Puget Sound Indians*, Superior, 1976; *The Chinook Indians: Traders of the Lower Columbia River*, 1976; *Indians of the Pacific Northwest: A History*, 1981; *Guidebook to Pacific Northwest Indian Tribes*, in press. Contributor to educational journals.

WORK IN PROGRESS: Dreamer Indian Movement of the Pacific Northwest, for University of Oklahoma Press.

AVOCATIONAL INTERESTS: Archaeology, particularly in the Columbia River area.

*   *   *

BROWN, John Russell 1923-

PERSONAL: Born September 15, 1923, in Bristol, England; son of Russell Alan (a butcher) and Olive Helen (Golding) Brown; married Hilary Sue Baker (a potter), April, 1961; children: Alice Amelia, Sophia Clemence, Jasper James Mallord. *Education:* Keble College, Oxford, B.A., 1949, B.Litt., 1952; University of Birmingham, Ph.D., 1960. *Office:* Department of Theatre Arts, State University of New York, Stony Brook, N.Y., 11794; and National Theatre, South Bank, London SE1, England.

CAREER: University of Birmingham, Birmingham, England, 1955-71, began as lecturer, became senior lecturer in English literature, 1955-63, professor of drama and theater arts and head of department, 1963-71; University of Sussex, Falmer, Brighton, Sussex, England, professor of English, 1971-82; State University of New York at Stony Brook, professor, 1982—. Reynolds Lecturer, University of Colorado, 1957; Folger Library fellow, Washington, D.C., 1957, 1963; Mellon Professor of Drama, Carnegie Institute (now Carnegie-Mellon University), 1964; Jones Lecturer, University of Liverpool, 1972; Robb Lecturer, University of Auckland, 1979. Visiting professor, University of Zurich, Switzerland, 1970-71; university lecturer, University of Toronto, 1971. Director, Orbit Theatre Company, 1971—; associate director, National Theatre, 1973—. Theatre Museum, London, England, member of advisory council, 1975—, chairman, 1980—. Member of the drama panel of the Arts Council of Great Britain, 1978-82; member of advisory council of Victoria and Albert Museum, 1980—. *Military service:* Royal Navy, 1942-46; became sub-lieutenant.

WRITINGS: (Editor) Shakespeare, *The Merchant of Venice*, Methuen, 1955; *Shakespeare and His Comedies*, Methuen, 1957, 2nd edition, Barnes & Noble, 1962; (editor) John Webster, *The White Devil*, Methuen, 1960; *Shakespeare: The Tragedy of Macbeth*, Edward Arnold, 1962; (editor) Webster, *The Duchess of Malfi*, Methuen, 1965; (editor) Shakespeare, *Henry V*, New American Library, 1965; *Shakespeare's Plays in Performance*, Edward Arnold, 1966, St. Martin's, 1967; *Effective Theatre*, Heinemann, 1969.

Shakespeare's Dramatic Style, Heinemann, 1970; *Theatre Language*, Allen Lane, 1972; *Free Shakespeare*, Heinemann, 1974; *Shakespeare in Performance: An Introduction through Six Major Plays*, Harcourt, 1976; *Discovering Shakespeare*, Macmillan, 1982; *Shakespeare and His Theatre*, Kestrel Books, 1982; *A Short Guide to Modern British Drama*, Heinemann, 1982. General editor, ''Stratford-upon-Avon Studies'' and ''Stratford-upon-Avon Library.''

WORK IN PROGRESS: New Prefaces to Shakespeare, for Batsford.

*   *   *

BROWN, Moses
   See BARRETT, William (Christopher)

*   *   *

BROWN, R(eginald) Allen   1924-

PERSONAL: Born January 19, 1924, in Ipswich, Suffolk, England; son of William and Gladys (Willis) Brown; married Patricia Hindmarch, 1952; children: Philippa Jane, Giles Patrick. *Education:* Oxford University, B.A., 1948, M.A., 1949, D.Phil., 1953; University of Manchester, postgraduate study, 1950-51. *Politics:* Conservative. *Religion:* Anglican. *Home:* Low Farm, Uggeshall, Beccles, Suffolk, England. *Office:* Department of History, King's College, University of London, London WC2R 2LS, England.

CAREER: Public Record Office, London, England, assistant keeper, 1951-59; University of London, King's College, London, lecturer in medieval history, 1959-65, reader in history, 1965—. *Military service:* British Army, King's Dragoon Guards, 1943-46; became lieutenant. *Member:* Royal Historical Society (fellow), Society of Antiquaries (fellow), Pipe Roll Society (member of council), Royal Archaeological Institute, Society for Medieval Archaeology, Suffolk Record Society (member of council).

WRITINGS: English Medieval Castles, Batsford, 1954, Simmons-Boardman, 1961, revised edition published as *English Castles*, Batsford, 1962, 3rd revised edition, 1976; *Castles*, Batsford, 1954, reprinted, Blandford, 1980, Sterling, 1981; (editor) *Memorandum Roll 10 John*, Pipe Roll Society, 1957, reprinted, Kraus Reprint, 1974; *East Anglia*, Batsford, 1957; (contributor) *Studies Presented to Sir Hilary Jenkinson*, Oxford University Press, 1957; (contributor) *A Medieval Miscellany for Doris Mary Stenton*, Pipe Roll Society, 1962; *The Middle Ages*, H.M.S.O., 1963; (with H. M. Colvin and A. J. Taylor) *The History of the King's Works*, Volumes I and II, H.M.S.O., 1963; (editor) *Pipe Roll 17 John*, Pipe Roll Society, 1965; *The Normans and the Norman Conquest*, Constable, 1968, Crowell, 1969, new edition, Constable, 1973.

The Origins of Modern Europe: The Medieval Heritage of Western Civilization, Constable, 1972, Crowell, 1973; *Origins of English Feudalism*, Barnes & Noble, 1973; (editor) *Battle Conference on Anglo-Norman Studies*, two volumes, Boydell, 1979-80.

Booklets: *The History and Origin of Horse Brasses: The Symbolic Reasons for Many of the Designs*, [London], 1963; *Orford Castle* (official guide), H.M.S.O., 1964; *Dover Castle* (official guide), H.M.S.O., 1966, 2nd edition, 1974; *Rochester Castle* (official guide), H.M.S.O., 1969; (compiler) *One Hundred Horse Drawn Carriages*, Quartilles, 1974; *Castle Rising: Norfolk* (official guide), H.M.S.O., 1978.

Contributor of articles and reviews to professional journals. Editor, Public Record Office, 1959—.†

BROWN, Richard Maxwell   1927-

PERSONAL: Born July 26, 1927, in Mobridge, S.D.; son of John Floyd and Norma Lena (McClary) Brown; married Estella Dee Cutler, January 25, 1951; children: Brooks, Laura Jean. *Education:* Reed College, B.A., 1952; Harvard University, A.M., 1955, Ph.D., 1959. *Politics:* Democrat. *Office:* Department of History, University of Oregon, Eugene, Ore. 97403.

CAREER: Harvard University, Center for the Study of History and Liberty in America, Cambridge, Mass., resident fellow, 1959-60; Rutgers University, New Brunswick, N.J., assistant professor, 1960-64, associate professor of history, 1964-67; College of William and Mary, Williamsburg, Va., professor of history, 1967-77; University of Oregon, Department of History, Eugene, Beekman Professor of History, 1977—, head of department, 1980—. Consultant to National Commission on the Causes and Prevention of Violence, 1968-69; member of council, Institute of Early American History and Culture, 1969-72. *Military service:* U.S. Army, 1946-48; became sergeant.

MEMBER: American Historical Association, Organization of American Historians, American Association of University Professors, Southern Historical Association (program chairman, 1974), Western Historical Association, South Carolina Historical Society, Virginia Historical Society, Phi Beta Kappa. *Awards, honors:* Award of Merit, American Association for State and Local History, for *The South Carolina Regulators*; William and Mary Phi Beta Kappa Faculty Award for the Advancement of Scholarship, 1970.

WRITINGS: The South Carolina Regulators, Harvard University Press, 1963; (contributor) John A. Carroll, editor, *Reflections of Western Historians*, University of Arizona Press, 1969; (contributor) Hugh D. Graham and Ted R. Gurr, editors, *The History of Violence in America*, Praeger, 1969, revised edition, Sage, 1979.

(Contributor) Thomas Rose, editor, *Violence in America*, Random House, 1970; (editor) *American Violence*, Prentice-Hall, 1970; (editor with A. G. Olson) *Anglo-American Political Relations, 1675-1775*, Rutgers University Press, 1970; (contributor) Donald Fleming and Bernard Bailyn, editors, *Law in American History*, Little, Brown, 1972; (contributor) Stephen G. Kurtz and James Hutson, editors, *Essays on the American Revolution*, University of North Carolina Press, 1973; *Strain of Violence: Historical Studies of American Violence and Vigilantism*, Oxford University Press, 1975; (co-editor and contributor) *Tradition, Conflict and Modernization: Perspectives on the American Revolution*, Academic Press, 1977.

Perspectives on the American South, Gordon & Breach, 1981.

Also contributor to *Reader's Encyclopedia of the American West*, Crowell, 1977. Member of editorial board, *William and Mary Quarterly*, 1970-71.

WORK IN PROGRESS: Books on colonial South Carolina and the prosopography of the South Carolina Regulators.†

*   *   *

BROWN, Rita Mae   1944-

PERSONAL: Born November 28, 1944, in Hanover, Pa.; adopted daughter of Ralph and Julia (Buckingham) Brown. *Education:* Attended University of Florida; New York University, B.A., 1968; New York School of Visual Arts, cinematography certificate, 1968; Institute for Policy Studies, Washington, D.C., Ph.D., 1973. *Residence:* Charlottesville, Va. *Agent:* Julian

Bach Literary Agency, Inc., 747 Third Ave., New York, N.Y. 10017.

CAREER: Writer. Sterling Publishing, New York, N.Y., photo editor, 1969-70; Federal City College, Washington, D.C., lecturer in sociology, 1970-71; Institute for Policy Studies, Washington, D.C., fellow, 1971-73; Goddard College, Plainfield, Vt., visiting member of faculty in feminist studies, beginning 1973. Member of board of directors of Sagaris, a feminist school. *Awards, honors:* Shared in Writers Guild of America award, 1983, for television special "I Love Liberty."

WRITINGS: (Translator) *Hrotsvitra: Six Medieval Latin Plays,* New York University Press, 1971; *The Hand That Cradles the Rock* (poems), New York University Press, 1971; *Rubyfruit Jungle* (novel; also see below), Daughters, Inc., 1973; *Songs to a Handsome Woman* (poems), Diana Press, 1973; *In Her Day* (novel), Daughters, Inc., 1976; *A Plain Brown Rapper* (essays), Diana Press, 1976; *Six of One* (novel), Harper, 1978; *Southern Discomfort* (novel), Harper, 1982; *Sudden Death* (novel), Bantam, 1983.

Also author or co-author of eight screenplays, including "Rubyfruit Jungle" (based on novel of same title), and "Slumber Party Massacre"; contributor to script of television special "I Love Liberty," ABC-TV, 1982.

WORK IN PROGRESS: A novel.

SIDELIGHTS: With the 1973 publication of her "exuberantly raunchy" autobiographical novel *Rubyfruit Jungle,* Rita Mae Brown joined the ranks of those in the forefront of the feminist and gay rights movements. Described by *Ms.* reviewer Marilyn Webb as "an inspiring, bravado adventure story of a female Huck Finn named Molly Bolt," *Rubyfruit Jungle* was at first rejected by editors at the major New York publishing companies due to what they believed to be its lack of mass-market appeal. Eventually published by the small feminist firm Daughters, Inc., it sold an unexpected 70,000 copies. The book's popularity soon brought it to the attention of Bantam Books, which acquired the rights to *Rubyfruit Jungle* in 1977 and printed an additional 300,000 copies. Total sales of the novel now number more than one million.

As Webb's comment suggests, *Rubyfruit Jungle* is told in a picaresque, Mark Twain-like fashion, an observation shared by *New Boston Review* critic Shelly Temchin Henze. "Imagine, if you will, Tom Sawyer, only smarter; Huckleberry Finn, only foul-mouthed, female, and lesbian, and you have an idea of Molly Bolt," writes Henze. Though some have adopted *Rubyfruit Jungle* as "a symbol of a movement, a sisterly struggle," the critic continues, the plot of the book is basically that of the "classic American success story." Explains Henze: "*Rubyfruit Jungle* is not about revolution, nor even particularly about feminism. It is about standing on your own two feet, creaming the competition, looking out for Number One." The truly original part of the novel, maintains the critic, is Brown's perspective. "While American heroes may occasionally be women, they may not be lesbian. Or if they are, they had better be discreet or at least miserable. Not Molly. She is lusty and lewd and pursues sex with relentless gusto."

Village Voice reviewer Bertha Harris has a few reservations about the authenticity of Brown's portrayal of lesbian life. "Much of Molly's world seems a cardboard stage set lighted to reveal only Molly's virtues and those characteristics which mark her as the 'exceptional' lesbian," remarks Harris. Nevertheless, Harris goes on to state, "it is exactly this quality of *Rubyfruit Jungle* which makes it exemplary (for women) of its

kind: an American primitive, whose predecessors have dealt only with male heroes. Although Molly Bolt is not a real woman, she is at least the first real *image* of a heroine in the noble savage, leatherstocking, true-blue bullfighting tradition in this country's literature."

Another *Village Voice* critic, Terry Curtis Fox, views *Rubyfruit Jungle* in a somewhat different light. Like Henze, Fox finds that Brown relies on a well-known theme for her novel; namely, "sensitive member of outside group heads toward American society and lives to tell the tale." Since this portrayal of resilience and triumph in the face of adversity is so familiar and appealing, maintains the reviewer, "you don't have to be gay or female to identify with Molly Bolt—she is one of the outsiders many of us believe ourselves to be." Furthermore, says Fox, Brown "can laugh at herself as well as at others, and make us laugh, too."

Acutely aware of the fact that humor is a quality seldom found in books dealing with homosexual life, Brown attaches special importance to her ability to make readers laugh, regarding it as a means of overcoming offensive stereotypes. "Most lesbians are thought to be ugly, neurotic and self-destructive and I just am not," she explains in a *New York Times* article. "There's no way they can pass me off that way. I'm not passing myself off as gorgeous, and a bastion of sanity, but I'm certainly not like those gay stereotypes of the miserable lesbian, the poor woman who couldn't get a man and eventually commits suicide. . . . I'm funny. Funny people are dangerous. They knock down barriers. It's hard to hate people when they're funny. I try to be like Flip Wilson, who helped a lot of white people understand blacks through humor. One way or another, I'll make 'em laugh, too."

The novel *Six of One* was Brown's second major breakthrough into the mass-market arena. Based once again on the author's own life as well as on the lives of her grandmother, mother, and aunt, *Six of One* (like *Rubyfruit Jungle*) attempts to make its point through ribald humor and an emphasis on the poor and uneducated as sources of practical wisdom. The story chronicles the events in a half-Northern, half-Southern, Pennsylvania-Maryland border town from 1909 to 1980 (focusing on the years between 1911 and 1921) as viewed through the eyes of a colorful assortment of female residents. John Fludas of the *Saturday Review*, noting that *Six of One* is a "bright and worthy successor" to *Rubyfruit Jungle*, writes that Brown "explores the town's cultural psychology like an American Evelyn Waugh, finding dignity and beauty without bypassing the zany and the corrupt. . . . If at times the comedy veers toward slapstick, and if there are spots when the prose just grazes the beauty of the human moment . . . , the novel loses none of its warmth."

Both Eliot Fremont-Smith and Richard Boeth feel that Brown could have done a better job with her material. Commenting in the *Village Voice,* for example, Fremont-Smith admits that *Six of One* "does have a winning cheerfulness," but concludes that "it's mostly just garrulous. . . . As a novel, it doesn't go anywhere; there's no driving edge; and the chatter dissipates. And as a polemical history (the secret and superior dynamics of female relationships), it gives off constant little backfires." *Newsweek* critic Boeth is even less impressed. He states: "It is a major sadness to report that Brown has made her women [in *Six of One*] not only boring but false. . . . Her only verbal tool is the josh—speech that is not quite witty, sly, wry, sardonic, ironic or even, God help us, clever, but only self-consciously breezy. . . . These aren't human beings talking; it's 310 pages of 'Gilligan's Island.'"

Henze also finds fault with Brown's characterization, remarking that the author peoples an otherwise "surprisingly accepting, even celebratory portrait of down-home America" with men and women who exhibit "the simplicity of heroes of a Western." Continues the critic: "Time progresses, measured off in days and years [in *Six of One*], but the characters do not: the two old biddies at the center of the narrative trade off the same scatological insults at seventy as at six; [another personage] acquires political insight but no emotional depth."

In her *New York Arts Journal* review of *Six of One*, Liz Mednick attributes these characterization problems to Brown's determination "to show how wise, witty, wonderful and cute women really are. Her silent competitor in this game is the masculine standard; her method, systematic oneupmanship. The women in *Six of One* buzz around like furies trying to out-curse, out-class, out-wit, out-smart, out-shout, out-smoke, out-drink, out-read, out-think, out-lech, out-number and outrage every man, dead or alive, in history. Needless to say, ambition frequently leads the author to extremes. . . . As if to insure her success, Brown makes her men as flat as the paper on which they're scrawled. The problem with her men is not even so much that they lack dimension as that they don't quite qualify as male." In short, concludes Mednick, *Six of One* "is less a novel than a wordy costume the author wears to parade herself before her faceless audience. Her heroines are presented not for inspection but as subjects for whom the narrative implicitly demands admiration."

Washington Post Book World reviewer Cynthia Macdonald, on the other hand, cites *Six of One* as evidence of a welcome change in women's literature. She writes: "The vision of women we have usually gotten from women novelists is of pain and struggle or pain and passivity; it is seldom joyous and passionate, and almost never funny. And what humor there was has been of the suffering, self-deprecating New York Jewish stand-up comedian type. *Six of One* by Rita Mae Brown is joyous, passionate and funny. What a pleasure! . . . In spite of its spacious time span, this is no historical novel. . . . [It] clicks between the present and the past neatly and precisely. . . . I believe that Brown uses a kind of revisionist history to support her conviction that what was seen in the first half of the 20th century as the life of women was only what was on the surface, not what was underneath. She opens the seams to give us her vision of what was really there. We are shown not the seamy side of life, but a body ready for anything, especially celebration."

Responding to criticism that women of the early 1900s could not possibly have been as liberated, not to mention as raucous, as they are depicted in the novel, Brown told Leonore Fleischer in a *Washington Post Book World* interview: "I grew up with these two almost mythical figures around me, my mother and my aunt, who didn't give a rat's a—— what anybody thought. They'd say anything to anybody, and they did as they damn well pleased. We were so poor, who cares what poor people do? Literature is predominantly written by middle-class people for middle-class people and their lives were real different. As a girl, I never saw a woman knuckle under to a man, or a man to a woman, for that matter. . . . The people closest to me were all very dominating characters. The men weren't weak, but somehow the women . . . were the ones you paid attention to."

Though it, too, focuses on the difficulties straight and gay women face in a hypocritical and judgmental society, Brown's novel *Sudden Death* represents what the author herself terms "a stylistic first for me." Written in an uncharacteristically plain and direct manner, *Sudden Death* examines the "often vicious and cold-blooded" world of professional women's tennis; many readers assume that it more or less chronicles Brown's experiences and observations during her involvement with star player Martina Navratilova. As Brown sees it, however, the book is much more than that: it is the fulfillment of a promise to a dying friend, sportswriter Judy Lacy, who had always wanted to write a novel against the background of women's tennis. Just prior to her death from a brain tumor in 1980, Lacy extracted a reluctant promise from Brown to write such a novel, even though Brown "didn't think sports were a strong enough metaphor for literature." "'[Judy] tricked me into writing it," explained the author to Fleischer in a *Publishers Weekly* column. "She knew me well enough to know how I'd feel about my promise, that it would be a deathbed promise. . . . I thought about her all the time I was writing it. It was strange to be using material that you felt belonged to somebody else. It's really Judy's book.''

For the most part, critics agree that *Sudden Death* has few of the qualities that make *Rubyfruit Jungle* and *Six of One* so entertaining. In the *Chicago Tribune Book World*, for instance, John Blades notes that despite the inclusion of "intriguing sidelights on how [tennis] has been commercialized and corrupted by sponsors, promoters and greedy players," *Sudden Death* "lacks the wit and vitality that might have made it good, unwholesome fun. Brown seems preoccupied here with extraliterary affairs; less interested in telling a story than in settling old scores."

Anne Chamberlin has a similar reaction to the novel, commenting in the *Washington Post*: "If you thought Nora Ephron's *Heartburn* had cornered the market on true heartbreak, thinly veiled, make room for *Sudden Death*. . . . Don't get mad; get even, as the saying goes, and this novel should bring the score to deuce. It not only chops the stars of women's professional tennis down to size; it tackles the whole pro tennis establishment. . . . Having reduced that tableau to rubble, Brown turns her guns on America's intolerance of lesbians. That's a lot of targets for one bombing run, and all 241 acerbic pages of *Sudden Death* are jammed with as disagreeable a bunch of people doing mean things to each other as you are likely to meet at one time."

"I would like to be able to report without qualification that this novel is a smash, an ace," states *Los Angeles Times Book Review* critic Kay Mills in her article on *Sudden Death*. "But that would be like calling a ball a winner just because you admired the way someone played yesterday." Though Mills does point out that "Brown is devastating to the hype, the fashion shows, [and] the product pimping that now accompany women's tennis," she believes that the protagonist is characterized so flatly "that one is devoid of sympathy for her when a jealous rival seeks to break her."

In short, concludes Elisabeth Jakab in the *New York Times Book Review*, Brown "is not at her best here. The world of tennis does not seem to be congenial terrain for her, and her usually natural and easy style seems cramped. The novel tends to read like the casebook of an anthropologist stranded in the midst of a disappointingly boring tribe. She does what she can, but there's just not that much to work with. In *Sudden Death* we can almost hear the pieces of the plot clanking into their proper slots."

Brown, who says she does not read reviews of her books, is nevertheless aware of the kinds of remarks critics are making about *Sudden Death,* to which she responds: "I don't care; it doesn't matter at all; and anyway, I'm already on the next book. . . . I wrote this because Judy asked me to. . . . I learned a lot, but I can't wait to get back on my own territory."

Despite her commitment to depicting gay women in a positive light, Brown balks at being labeled a "lesbian writer." In a *Publishers Weekly* interview, she states: "Calling me a lesbian writer is like calling Baldwin a black writer. I say no; he is not: he is a great writer and that is that. I don't understand people who say Baldwin writes about 'the black experience'— as if it is so different from 'the white experience' that the two aren't even parallel. That is so insulting . . . and I really hate it."

In an essay written for the *Publishers Weekly* column "My Say," Brown elaborates on her opposition to the use of such labels. "Classifying fiction by the race, sex or sex preference of the author is a discreet form of censorship," she maintains. "Americans buy books by convicted rapists, murderers and Watergate conspirators because those books are placed on the bestseller shelf, right out in front where people can see them. Yet novels by people who are not safely white or resolutely heterosexual are on the back shelves, out of sight. It's the back of the bus all over again. Is this not a form of censorship? Are we not being told that some novels are more 'American' than others? That some writers are true artists, while the rest of us are 'spokespersons' for our group? What group? A fiction writer owes allegiance to the English language only. With that precious, explosive tool the writer must tell the *emotional* truth. And the truth surely encompasses the fact that we Americans are female and male; white, brown, black, yellow and red; young, old and in-between; rich and poor; straight and gay; smart and stupid. . . . On the page all humans really are created equal. All stories are important. All lives are worthy of concern and description. . . . Incarcerating authors into types is an act of treason against literature and, worse, an assault on the human heart." Therefore, concludes Brown in the *Publishers Weekly* interview, "next time anybody calls me a lesbian writer I'm going to knock their teeth in. I'm a writer and I'm a woman and I'm from the South and I'm alive, and that is that."

CA INTERVIEW

Rita Mae Brown answered *CA*'s questions by mail in February, 1983.

CA: Your characters have a spicy way with words. Was their kind of colorful language a part of your own growing up and perhaps an early impetus to write?

BROWN: Yes. My parents and kin did not suffer the rigors of a higher miseducation; therefore, their language owed more to Anglo-Saxon than it did to Latin.

CA: Although you first attracted widespread attention with the novel Rubyfruit Jungle, *in 1973, you'd had poetry published earlier. Reviewing* The Hand That Cradles the Rock *(1971) in the* Hudson Review, *William H. Pritchard wrote: "Rita Mae Brown is the daughter of Matthew Arnold and Elizabeth Barrett Browning, and has successfully revived the Victorian tradition in American verse." Were you consciously influenced by the Victorian period or by any specific writers that you can pinpoint?*

BROWN: Mr. Pritchard gave that nice quote? I don't know because I never read reviews. The only Victorian whom I like,

truly, is Charles Dickens. Those writers who have most influenced me are Aristophanes, Euripides, and Mark Twain. When I doubt, I return, always, to Athens, fifth century B.C. My next stop-off point is Rome, roughly 33 B.C.

CA: Did you aspire to write poetry, or were you working on both poetry and fiction at the same time?

BROWN: I aspired to write anything. To me, as long as it's on the page, I'm happy. Makes no difference to me if it's an epic poem or a one-liner.

CA: Rubyfruit Jungle *got you tagged as a "lesbian writer," a label you've resented for its narrowness. Do you feel your subsequent novels have enlarged the reading public's concept of your work?*

BROWN: Yes.

CA: Do you think writing that deals with homosexuality gets fair critical treatment generally?

BROWN: Absolutely not.

CA: You were quite actively involved in the women's liberation movement in its earlier days and in the struggle for gay rights, though you advocated the separation of the two movements. Where do you think both stand now? What's been accomplished, and what's the next step?

BROWN: The women's liberation movement got sidetracked by legislative illusions. If it doesn't wake up it will be as relevant as hula hoops. What has been accomplished is cultural awareness. That's wonderful, but I myself prefer political power. The next step is to get serious and stop focusing on "women's issues," which is exactly where our enemies want us. We need to fight like hell over food, clothing, shelter, and nuclear disarmament. We need women leading those fights, not sitting before Senate subcommittees haggling over abortion. The right wing is making mincemeat out of us precisely because they do not stay on one issue only. They develop a program; they have an answer for every issue and they go out and fight for it.

The gay movement is slightly more successful in terms of actual power because it is a male movement and men have so much more money than women. A woman still makes 59¢ to a man's $1.00. Furthermore, many gay men do not have families to support, so they have much more money available for their own purposes.

CA: Are you presently involved in either movement?

BROWN: I'm not a street organizer anymore, if that's what you mean. I belong to groups and send in my dues, which I suspect pleases them—although, when pissed, I do not send in my dues.

CA: What writers do you enjoy reading, aside from those you mentioned earlier?

BROWN: Horace, Terence, Eudora Welty, Alice Walker, Barbara Tuchman. It's hard to answer since I read so much and so often.

CA: In your teaching and lecturing, what advice have you given aspiring writers?

BROWN: Don't expect those near and dear to you to understand what you are doing and don't expect to make any money at this. Fewer than three hundred Americans make a living from writing. This excludes journalism, but that's not literature.

CA: Do you find it harder, more distracting, to work in California than in Charlottesville?

BROWN: I can work anywhere but I can't live anywhere. I can only live in Charlottesville, Virginia. Whenever I go to the West Coast for long periods of time, it's because I have business there. It's fine out there; I just happen to know where I belong.

CA: Does your work benefit somehow from the periodic change of scene?

BROWN: Never.

CA: Recently you've worked with Norman Lear on the television special ''I Love Liberty'' and have done the script for Roger Corman's movie ''Slumber Party Massacre.'' Are there more screenplays and television scripts in the near future?

BROWN: Yes, but I take those jobs as they come. It's not at all like writing novels.

CA: Is there still a chance that Rubyfruit Jungle *will become a movie? And what about* Sudden Death?

BROWN: Beats me. I need $125,000 to buy back the option to *Rubyfruit Jungle,* and I don't have that kind of cash. As for *Sudden Death,* there is no way to tell if it has a chance as a movie. Normally, sport movies do poorly at the box office.

CA: Are you happy with your work and your recognition at this point?

BROWN: Yes, but I rarely think about it because I'm thinking about the book I'm currently working on. I figure if you sit on your laurels, you get a fat ass.

CA: Is there anything you'd like to try that's completely different from your previous work?

BROWN: I want to write a play, and I will do that in my forties. That's the only form I have not tried—well, that and epic poetry, but no one does epic poetry anymore. Or let's just say no one does it well.

BIOGRAPHICAL/CRITICAL SOURCES: Ms., March, 1974, June, 1974, April, 1977; *Village Voice,* September 12, 1977, October 9, 1978; *New York Times,* September 26, 1977; *Saturday Review,* September 30, 1978; *Publishers Weekly,* October 2, 1978, February 18, 1983, July 15, 1983; *Newsweek,* October 2, 1978; *Washington Post Book World,* October 15, 1978; *New York Arts Journal,* November-December, 1978; *Maclean's,* November 13, 1978; *Christian Science Monitor,* November 22, 1978; *Best Sellers,* February, 1979, May, 1982; *New Boston Review,* April-May, 1979; *Times Literary Supplement,* December 7, 1979; *Contemporary Literary Criticism,* Volume XVIII, Gale, 1981; *Los Angeles Times,* March 10, 1982; *New York Times Book Review,* March 21, 1982, June 19, 1983; *People,* April 26, 1982; *Nation,* June 19, 1982; *Chicago Tribune Book World,* July 4, 1982, July 3, 1983; *Detroit News,* May 8, 1983; *Detroit Free Press,* May 15, 1983;

Los Angeles Times Book Review, May 22, 1983; *Washington Post,* May 31, 1983.

—Sketch by Deborah A. Straub

—Interview by Jean W. Ross

*　　*　　*

BROWN, Sanborn C(onner)   1913-1981

PERSONAL: Born January 19, 1913, in Beirut, Lebanon, of American parents; died November 28, 1981, in Henniker, N.H.; son of Julius Arthur (a professor) and Helen (Conner) Brown; married Lois Wright, June 21, 1940; children: Peter M., Stanley W., Prudence E. Nagel. *Education:* Dartmouth College, A.B., 1935, M.A., 1937; Massachusetts Institute of Technology, Ph.D., 1944. *Residence:* Henniker, N.H. *Office:* Massachusetts Institute of Technology, 77 Massachusetts Ave., Cambridge, Mass. 02139.

CAREER: Massachusetts Institute of Technology, Cambridge, instructor, 1941-45, assistant professor, 1945-49, associate professor, 1949-62, professor of physics, 1962-75, professor emeritus, 1975-81, associate dean of Graduate School, 1963-75. Technical adviser to U.S. delegation, United Nations International Conference on Peaceful Uses of Atomic Energy, Geneva, 1958; U.S. delegate to International Atomic Energy Agency Conference on Plasma Physics and Controlled Thermonuclear Fusion, Salzburg, 1961; member of Research Advisory Committee on Fluid Mechanics, National Aeronautics and Space Administration, 1963-65. Member of U.S. national committee, International Union of Pure and Applied Physics and president of Union's Commission on Physics Education; member of Interunion Commission on the Teaching of Science, International Council of Scientific Unions. Lexington (Mass.) School Committee, member 1958-64, chairman, 1961-64. *Wartime service:* Civilian staff scientist, Office of Scientific Research and Development, 1941-44.

MEMBER: American Physical Society (fellow; chairman of division of electron physics, 1951-52), American Association for the Advancement of Science (fellow), American Association of Physics Teachers (treasurer, 1955-62), American Academy of Arts and Sciences (fellow; secretary, beginning 1964), History of Science Society, Royal Institution of Great Britain, National Science Teachers Association, Conference Board of Associated Research Councils, Phi Beta Kappa, Sigma Xi (national lecturer, 1961).

AWARDS, HONORS: Distinguished service citation, American Association of Physics Teachers, 1962; Guggenheim fellow, 1968-69.

WRITINGS: Basic Data of Plasma Physics, Technology Press and Wiley, 1959, revised edition, 1961, second edition published as *Basic Data of Plasma Physics 1966,* M.I.T. Press, 1967; (editor with Norman Clarke) *International Education in Physics,* Technology Press and Wiley, 1960; *Count Rumford, Physicist Extraordinary,* Anchor Books, 1962, reprinted, Greenwood Press, 1979; (with Norman Clarke and Jayme Tiomno) *Why Teach Physics?,* M.I.T. Press, 1964.

The Education of a Physicist, M.I.T. Press, 1966; (with J. Charles Ingraham) *Plasma Diagnostics,* M.I.T., Research Laboratory of Electronics, 1966; *Introduction to Electrical Discharges in Gases,* Wiley, 1966; (editor) Benjamin Thompson, Count Rumford, *Count Rumford on the Nature of Heat,* Pergamon, 1967; (editor) *Electrons, Ions and Waves: Selected Works of William Phelps Allis,* M.I.T. Press, 1967; (editor)

Thompson, Count Rumford, *Collected Works of Count Rumford*, Belknap Press, Volume I: *The Nature of Heat*, 1968, Volume II: *Practical Applications of Heat*, 1969, Volume III: *Devices and Techniques*, 1969, Volume IV: *Light and Armament*, 1970, Volume V: *Public Institutions*, 1970.

(Editor with Brian B. Schwartz) *Scientific Manpower: Dilemma for Graduate Education*, M.I.T. Press, 1971; (with F. J. Kedves and E. J. Wenham) *Teaching Physics: An Insoluble Task?*, M.I.T. Press, 1971; (editor) *Changing Careers in Science and Engineering*, M.I.T. Press, 1972; *Physics Fifty Years Later*, National Academy of Sciences, 1973; (with Leonard M. Rieser) *Natural Philosophy at Dartmouth: From Surveyors' Chains to the Pressure of Light*, University of New England, 1974.

(Editor with Alexandra Oleson) *The Pursuit of Knowledge in the Early American Republic: American Scientific and Learned Societies from Colonial Times to the Civil War*, Johns Hopkins University Press, 1976; *Wines and Beers of Old New England: A How-To-Do-It History*, University Press of New England, 1978; *Electron Molecule Scattering*, Wiley Interscience, 1980; *Benjamin Thompson, Count Rumford*, M.I.T. Press, 1981.

Also author of *Directions and Forms for the Computation of Preliminary Orbits from Three or Four Observations*, with C. Haskins, 1937, and *Basic Data of Electrical Discharges*, with William Phelps Allis, M.I.T., Research Laboratory of Electronics, 4th edition, 1958.

Contributor to physics journals.

SIDELIGHTS: Basic Data of Plasma Physics was published in the Soviet Union in an unauthorized translation, 1961.

OBITUARIES: New York Times, December 2, 1981.†

* * *

BROWNE, Ray B(roadus) 1922-

PERSONAL: Born January 15, 1922, in Millport, Ala.; son of Garfield (a banker) and Anne Nola (Trull) Browne; married second wife, Alice Matthews, August 1, 1965; children: (first marriage) Glenn, Kevin; (second marriage) Alicia. *Education:* University of Alabama, A.B., 1943; Columbia University, M.A., 1947; University of California, Los Angeles, Ph.D., 1956. *Home:* 210 North Grove, Bowling Green, Ohio 43402. *Office:* Department of Popular Culture, Bowling Green State University, Bowling Green, Ohio 43402.

CAREER: Instructor in English at University of Nebraska, Lincoln, 1947-50, and University of Maryland, College Park, 1956-60; Purdue University, Lafayette, Ind., assistant professor, 1960-63, associate professor of American literature, 1963-67; Bowling Green State University, Bowling Green, Ohio, professor of English, 1967—. Visiting professor, University of Maryland, 1975-76. *Military service:* U.S. Army, Field Artillery, 1943-46; became sergeant. *Member:* Modern Language Association of America, Melville Society, Popular Culture Association (founder, 1970; secretary-treasurer), American Culture Association (founder, 1977; secretary-treasurer).

WRITINGS: Folk Beliefs and Practices from Alabama, University of California Press, 1958; *Melville's Drive to Humanism*, Purdue University Studies, 1971; *Popular Abstracts*, Popular Press, Bowling Green State University, 1978. Also author of *Heroes in American Culture* and *Tabus and Tabuism in Popular Culture*, both published by Popular Press, Bowling Green State University.

Editor; published by Popular Press, Bowling Green State University, except as indicated: *The Burke-Paine Controversy: Text and Criticism*, Harcourt, 1963; (with William John Roscelli and Richard Loftus) *The Celtic Cross: Studies in Irish Culture and Literature*, Purdue University Studies, 1964; John Williams, *The Indian Doctor: Frontier Pharmacology*, Indiana Historical Society, 1964; (with Martin Light) *Critical Approaches to American Literature*, Crowell, 1965; (with others) *New Voices in American Studies*, Purdue University Studies, 1966; (with others) *Frontiers of American Culture*, Purdue University Studies, 1968; *Themes and Directions in American Literature*, Purdue University Studies, 1969; *Mark Twain's Quarrel with Heaven: "Captain Stormfield's Visit to Heaven" and Other Sketches*, College and University Press, 1969; (with Ronald J. Ambrosetti) *Popular Culture and Curricula*, 1969, 2nd edition, 1972; (with others) *Challenges in American Culture*, 1969.

(With Marshall Fishwick) *Icons of Popular Culture*, 1970, 2nd edition, 1972; (with Russell Blaine Nye) *Crises on Campus*, 1970; (with B. D. Owens) *Teach In: Viability of Change*, 1971; (with David Madden) *The Popular Culture Explosion*, William C. Brown, 1972; (with Fishwick and Michael Marsden) *Heroes of Popular Culture*, 1972; *Popular Culture and the Expanding Consciousness*, Wiley, 1973.

Lincoln Lore: Lincoln in the Contemporary Popular Mind, 1975; (and compiler) *A Night with the Hants and Other Alabama Folk Experiences*, 1976; (with Larry N. Landrum and Pat Browne) *Dimensions of Detective Fiction*, 1976; (with Fishwick) *Icons of America*, 1978; *The Alabama Folk Lyric: A Study in Origins and Media of Dissemination*, 1979; *Rituals and Ceremonies in Popular Culture*, 1980; *Objects of Special Devotion: Fetishism in Popular Culture*, 1982; (with Fishwick) *The Hero in Transition*, 1983; (with Gary Hoppenstand) *The Defective Detective*, 1983.

Editor, *Journal of Popular Culture, Journal of American Culture*, and *Journal of Regional Cultures*.

* * *

BRUCKER, Roger W(arren) 1929-
(Warren Rogers)

PERSONAL: Born July 27, 1929, in Shelby, Ohio; son of Franklin Henry and Marian Jane (a social worker; maiden name, Love) Brucker; married Joan Wagner, 1951 (divorced, 1981); married Lynn Weller (an electrical engineer), 1983; children: (first marriage) Thomas Alan, Ellen, Jane Corson, Emily Lenore. *Education:* Oberlin College, B.A., 1951. *Politics:* Democrat. *Religion:* Christian. *Home:* 21 Murray Hill Dr., Dayton, Ohio 45403. *Agent:* International Creative Management, 40 West 57th St., New York, N.Y. 10019. *Office address:* Odiorne Industrial Advertising, P.O. Box 280, Yellow Springs, Ohio 45387.

CAREER: Odiorne Industrial Advertising, Yellow Springs, Ohio, account executive, 1955-71, president, 1971—. Adjunct assistant professor at Wright State University, 1975—. Chairman of Yellow Springs Planning Commission, 1964-70, and Board of Zoning Appeals, 1970—. Member of board of directors of Cave Research Foundation, 1957-81; member of editorial board of Cave Books. *Military service:* U.S. Air Force, 1951-55; became staff sergeant. *Member:* National Speleological Society (honorary life fellow; governor, 1954-56), Academy of Marketing Science (fellow), Central Ohio Industrial Marketers (president, 1968), Engineers Club of Dayton.

WRITINGS: (With Joe Lawrence, Jr.) *The Caves Beyond,* Funk, 1955, Zephyrus Press, 1975; *Film Planning and Production,* U.S. Air Force, 1956; (with Richard A. Watson) *The Longest Cave,* Knopf, 1976; (with Robert K. Murray) *Trapped!,* Putnam, 1979.

Author of libretto for opera *The Proposal,* Mills Music, 1955; also author of film scripts for U.S. Air Force. Contributor of articles to marketing and advertising journals, and to speleological journals. Editor of *National Speleological Bulletin,* 1956-58.

WORK IN PROGRESS: A biography of Stephen Bishop; a chapter to be included in *Hydrology of the Central Kentucky Karst,* edited by William B. White; marketing and advertising research.

SIDELIGHTS: An advertising executive currently involved in marketing research, Roger W. Brucker is a caver by avocation. He describes himself to *CA* as "a storyteller, whether writing about caves or marketing." His second book on caving, *The Longest Cave,* is a narrative co-authored with Richard A. Watson that relates the history of the Flint Ridge/Mammoth Cave system in Kentucky and the search for the link that established the network as the longest in the world. *New York Times* reviewer George Vecsey writes that the book "contains generous amounts of photographs, maps, drawings of caving techniques and an appendix of caving terms and history."

In addition to factual information, *The Longest Cave* also details the folklore of the Flint Ridge system, including the story of Floyd Collins, who is credited with the discovery of Great Crystal Cave beneath the Flint Ridge in 1917. Collins attracted national news coverage in 1925 when he became trapped under the network in a landslide. For fifteen days the country followed news reports of rescuers' futile attempts to free him. After his death, Collins's body was displayed in a glass-topped coffin in Great Crystal Cave, and for years tourists paid to view it. Although no longer on display, the coffin is still in the cave, and according to Brucker and Watson, some cavers have reported hearing the voice of Collins's ghost.

Despite the extensive public attention and popular folklore generated by the Collins story, it was not until the 1950s that explorers began proceeding through the Flint Ridge with the assumption that it could eventually be linked to the adjacent Mammoth Cave. Brucker and Watson participated in these early expeditions, and in 1972, they worked with the group that finally established the connection when team member Pat Crowther was the first to squeeze through a point now called the Tight Spot. *Time* reviewer John Skow writes, "When she and her skinny companions popped like corks through the Tight Spot and moved on into Mammoth Cave, the provable length of the great limestone entrails became 144.4 miles." Unfortunately Brucker was unable to squeeze through the Tight Spot, so technically he was not present at the linkup.

According to Skow, however, *The Longest Cave* is "a splendid armchair challenge properly made, properly obsessive. . . . The sensation of being trapped in Mother Earth's vermiform appendix is persuasively real, and the impulse to run gasping into the open air is strong."

BIOGRAPHICAL/CRITICAL SOURCES: Roger W. Brucker and Richard A. Watson, *The Longest Cave,* Knopf, 1976; *Time,* August 16, 1976; *New York Times,* August 21, 1976; *New Yorker,* September 6, 1976.

BRYAN, J(oseph) III 1904-

PERSONAL: Born April 30, 1904, in Richmond, Va.; son of Joseph St. George and Emily Page (Kemp) Bryan; married Jacqueline de la Grandiere, 1960; children: St. George II (deceased), Joan (Mrs. Peter Gates), Courtland. *Education:* Princeton University, A.B., 1927. *Religion:* Episcopalian. *Home:* Brook Hill, Richmond, Va.

CAREER: Reporter and editorial writer, *News Leader,* Richmond, Va., and *Chicago Journal,* Chicago, Ill., 1928-31; associate editor, *Parade,* 1931-32; managing editor, *Town and Country,* 1933-37; associate editor, *Saturday Evening Post,* 1937-40; free-lance writer, 1940—. Fellow and former trustee, Virginia Museum of Fine Arts. *Military service:* U.S. Army Reserve, 1927-37; became first lieutenant; U.S. Naval Reserve, 1942-53; became lieutenant commander; U.S. Air Force Reserve, 1953-64; became colonel. *Member:* Virginia Historical Society, Society of the Cincinnati, Commonwealth Club (Richmond, Va.), Buck's Club (London), Ivy Club (Princeton), Racquet and Tennis Club (New York City).

WRITINGS: (With Philip Reed) *Mission beyond Darkness,* Duell, Sloan & Pearce, 1945; (with William F. Halsey) *Admiral Halsey's Story,* Whittlesey House, 1947; *Aircraft Carrier,* Ballantine, 1954, reprinted, Bantam, 1982; *The World's Greatest Showman: The Life of P. T. Barnum* (juvenile), Random House, 1956; *The Sword over the Mantel,* McGraw, 1960; *The Merry Madmen of 52nd Street* (booklet), Whittet & Shepperson, 1968; (with Charles J.V. Murphy) *The Windsor Story,* Morrow, 1979. Contributor of more than 100 articles to popular magazines, including *Reader's Digest, McCall's,* and *Holiday.*

SIDELIGHTS: *The Windsor Story* is a dual biography of the Duke and Duchess of Windsor. Authors J. Bryan III and Charles J.V. Murphy portray the royal couple in sometimes unflattering terms, going behind their public image of marital bliss to the true nature of their relationship. The couple's life together, according to Jean Strouse of *Newsweek,* is "a nasty, pathetic tale of selfishness, greed, weakness, and ineptitude."

In 1936, the Duke of Windsor, then King Edward VIII of England, renounced his throne because the woman he wished to marry, American divorcee Wallis Simpson, could not be named his queen. His was the shortest reign—eleven months—of any English king in over 500 years. At the time, according to the *Newsweek* article, H. L. Mencken described his abdication as "the greatest news story since the Resurrection." *The Windsor Story* primarily concentrates on the lives of the royal couple after the abdication, when they became the leading figures in cafe society. "The couple," writes a reviewer for the *New Yorker,* "appear to have lived lives compounded of frivolity and grievance, extravagance and meanness."

There are several scandalous incidents related by Bryan and Murphy to support their contention that the Windsors were not as happily married as they were often depicted. The Duchess's affair with a millionaire playboy, the Duke's sometimes ambivalent sexual orientation, and the couple's shameless use of other people's money are all examined in sensational detail, much of it supplied by their former servants and friends. But the most damning evidence of marital strife seems, to the authors, to lie in what they see as the Duchess's domination of the Duke. "[The Duke] was waiting for the woman who would dominate him," they write. "He was happiest under a despot." The Duke, writes Strouse, "never stopped worshipping his Duchess, and she never stopped punishing him." "Although the king traded his crown for the woman he insisted he could not live without,'' Nancy Naglin of the *Chicago Tribune Book World* states, ''in both life and love, she conspired to make him the most miserable of men.'' As Anthony Howard of the *New York Times Book Review* puts it, ''One undoubtedly became a monster and the other in no time was translated into her creature.''

Bryan and Murphy also shed light on some of the reasons for the Duke's failure to be given any government work after his abdication, emphasizing his ambivalence toward Nazism as a major factor. During a visit to Germany just before World War II, the Duke was warmly greeted by government officials and was seen to give Nazi salutes in public. After the war began, the Nazis offered to set up the Duke as King once they had conquered England, an offer to which the Duke apparently kept himself open. The Duke's ineffective performance during his brief stint as ambassador to the Bahamas also reflected badly on his judgement and abilities. As ambassador, his administration was marred by an openly racist attitude, while the Windsors' frequent trips to jet-setter vacation spots abroad left him little time to deal with problems of state.

Although John Richardson of the *New York Review of Books* describes *The Windsor Story* as ''a geyser of dirt and hot air,'' and Elizabeth Wheeler of the *Los Angeles Times Book Review* finds that ''the authors don't present a lot of evidence for this portrait aside from their own observations, the comments of other Windsor friends who disliked the duke and duchess, and a few pretty shaky suppositions,'' other critics found the book, for all its scandal, to be well-researched and fascinating. ''The authors,'' the *New Yorker* critic believes, ''succeed in making [the Windsors] continuously interesting . . . partly by shrewd reporting and partly by furnishing a first-rate background, which offers a history of social change in Western society.'' Eve Auchincloss of the *Washington Post Book World* states, ''One would have to be insensible to read the appalling but fair-minded story [Bryan and Murphy] so skillfully tell without gloating fascination.''

BIOGRAPHICAL/CRITICAL SOURCES: J. Bryan III and Charles J. V. Murphy, *The Windsor Story*, Morrow, 1979; *Village Voice*, September 17, 1979; *New York Times Book Review*, October 28, 1979; *New Yorker*, November 5, 1979; *Washington Post Book World*, November 11, 1979; *Los Angeles Times Book Review*, November 11, 1979; *Newsweek*, December 3, 1979; *Chicago Tribune Book World*, December 9, 1979; *Times Literary Supplement*, January 4, 1980; *New York Review of Books*, February 21, 1980.

* * *

BRYANS, Robert Harbinson   1928-
   (Robin Bryans, Robert Harbinson; pseudonym:
   Donald Cameron)

PERSONAL: Born April 24, 1928, in Belfast, Northern Ireland; son of Robert (a window cleaner) and Georgina (Bell) Bryans. *Education:* Attended state school in Belfast, Northern Ireland. *Home:* Welkin Cottage, 39 Falmer Rd., Rottingdean, Brighton, Sussex BN2 7DA, England.

CAREER: Belfast Harbour Commission, Belfast, Northern Ireland, cabin boy, 1942; Barry Bible Depot, Barry, Wales, ship colporteur, 1944-45; Adelaide College, Ilfracombe, England, house master, 1946-47; Clayesmore School, Blandford, England, house master, 1947-48; Ogilvie Mills, Edmonton, Alberta, Canada, stockkeeper, 1948-49; Shawnigan Lake School, Vancouver Island, Canada, house master, 1949-50; Forestry

Commission, Oban, Scotland, shepherd, 1950; British Council, lecturer in Venezuela, 1955. Writer. *Member:* India Club (London).

WRITINGS—Under name Robin Bryans; published by Faber, except as indicated: *Gateway to the Khyber*, R. Hale, 1959; *Madeira: Pearl of the Atlantic*, R. Hale, 1959; *Summer Saga: A Journey in Iceland*, 1960; *Danish Episode*, 1961; *Fanfare for Brazil*, 1962; *The Azores*, 1963; *Ulster: A Journey through the Six Counties*, 1964; *Lucio* (novel), 1964; *Morocco: Land of the Farthest West*, 1965; *Malta and Gozo*, 1966; *Trinidad and Tobago: Isles of the Immortelles*, 1967; (editor) *Best True Adventure Stories*, 1967; *Crete*, 1969.

Under pseudonym Donald Cameron: *The Field of Sighing: A Highland Boyhood*, Longmans, 1966.

Under name Robert Harbinson; all published by Faber: *No Surrender: An Ulster Childhood*, 1960; *Song of Erne*, 1960; *Tattoo Lily* (fiction), 1961; *Up Spake the Cabin Boy*, 1961; *The Far World, and Other Stories*, 1962; *The Protege*, 1963.

Also author of scripts for British Broadcasting Corp. and ITV. Contributor to *Listener, Guardian, Irish Press*, and other periodicals.†

* * *

BRYANS, Robin
   See BRYANS, Robert Harbinson

* * *

BRYANT, Edward (Albert)   1928-

PERSONAL: Born July 23, 1928, in Lenoir, N.C.; son of Edmond Henry and Shelton Emmaline (Robbins) Bryant; married Tamara Thompson, May 28, 1965; children: Adam Edmond, Mary Emmaline. *Education:* University of North Carolina at Chapel Hill, B.A., 1950, M.A., 1954; graduate study at North Carolina State College of Agriculture and Engineering (now University of North Carolina at Raleigh), 1956, and Columbia University, 1958. *Home:* 1400 Marron Circle, N.E., Albuquerque, N.M. 87112. *Office:* Art Museum, University of New Mexico, Albuquerque, N.M. 87131.

CAREER: Brooklyn Museum, Brooklyn, N.Y., fellow, 1957-58; Wadsworth Atheneum (art museum), Hartford, Conn., general curator, 1959-61; Whitney Museum of Modern Art, New York, N.Y., associate curator, 1961-65; University of Kentucky Art Gallery, Lexington, director, 1965-68; Colgate University, Hamilton, N.Y., professor of fine arts and director of Picker Art Gallery, 1968-80; University of New Mexico, Albuquerque, N.M., professor of art and director of art museum, 1980—. Painter; works have been exhibited in national and regional shows. *Awards, honors:* Fulbright scholar, University of Pisa, 1954-55; Brooklyn Museum travel grant to Italy, 1958-59; National Endowment for the Arts research grant, 1964.

WRITINGS: (With Frieda Tenenbaum) *African Sculpture*, Brooklyn Museum, 1958; (with Lloyd Goodrich) *Forty Artists under Forty, from the Collection of the Whitney Museum of American Art*, Praeger, 1962; *Recent Paintings by Jack Tworkov*, Yale Art Gallery, 1963; (with Marcello Venturoli) *Sarai Sherman*, Edizioni Penelope, 1963; *Jack Tworkov*, Praeger, 1964; (author of introduction) *Robert Broderson: 32 Drawings*, Duke University Press, 1964; *Viewpoints 7: Painters of the Land and Sky*, Widtman Press, 1972; *Pennell's New York Etchings: Ninety-One Prints*, Dover, 1981. Also author of correspondence course in art history, Bureau of Correspondence Instruction, University of North Carolina, 1958, and of art exhibition catalogs. Contributor of articles on artists and art history to periodicals.

WORK IN PROGRESS: A book on 19th-century American cemetery sculpture; an autobiography.

*   *   *

BUCKMAN, Peter   1941-

PERSONAL: Born August 18, 1941, in Amersham, England; son of Bernard (a businessman) and Irene (a barrister; maiden name, Amiel) Buckman; married Rosemary Waeny (a literary agent), December 12, 1969; children: Jessica, Sasha. *Education:* Attended Sorbonne, University of Paris, 1959; Balliol College, Oxford, M.A., 1962. *Home:* Ryman's Cottage, Little Tew, Oxfordshire, England. *Agent:* Fraser & Dunlop Scripts Ltd., 91 Regent St., London W1R 8RU, England.

CAREER: Writer. Penguin Books Ltd., Harmondsworth, Middlesex, England, member of editorial board, 1962-64; New American Library, Inc., New York City, member of editorial board, 1964-65; McGraw-Hill, Inc., New York City, European editor, 1966-68.

WRITINGS: The Limits of Protest, Bobbs-Merrill, 1970; *Playground,* Macmillan, 1973; *Education without Schools,* Souvenir Press, 1973; *Lafayette,* Paddington Press, 1977; *Let's Dance,* Paddington Press, 1978; *The Rothschild Conversion,* Secker & Warburg, 1979.

Plays: "All Together Now," first produced in Leicester, England, 1979, produced in London, 1980; "Daucray Country" (television play), produced by British Broadcasting Corp., 1981; (adapter) "Tristram Shandy" (radio play), produced by British Broadcasting Corp., 1982.

Contributor of television reviews to *Listener,* 1974-80; contributor of book reviews to newspapers, including *Nation* and *Times.* Advisory editor of *Paris Review,* 1965-69, and *Ramparts,* 1966-69.

WORK IN PROGRESS: All for Love, an essay on soap operas, commissioned by Secker & Warburg; a radio script on Virginia Woolf, commissioned by British Broadcasting Corp.; *Orlando;* a one-man play on Oscar Wilde, commissioned by Peter Egan; a musical with composer Edward Gregson; a children's book with artist Penelope Rippon; plays for stage, radio, and television.

*   *   *

BUECHNER, (Carl) Frederick   1926-

PERSONAL: Born July 11, 1926, in New York, N.Y.; son of Carl Frederick and Katherine (Kuhn) Buechner; married Judith Friedrike Merck, April 7, 1956; children: Katherine, Dinah, Sharman. *Education:* Princeton University, A.B., 1948; Union Theological Seminary, B.D., 1958. *Residence:* Rupert, Vt. *Mailing address:* Box 1160, Pawlet, Vt. 05761. *Agent:* Lucy Kroll Agency, 390 West End Ave., New York, N.Y. 10024.

CAREER: Lawrenceville School, Lawrenceville, N.J., teacher of English, 1948-53; East Harlem Protestant Parish, New York, N.Y., head of employment clinic, 1954-58; ordained minister of the United Presbyterian Church, 1958; Phillips Exeter Academy, Exeter, N.H., chairman of department of religion, 1958-60, school minister, 1960-67; writer, 1967—. Instructor in

creative writing, New York University, summers, 1953, 1954. William Belden Nobel Lecturer, Harvard University, 1969; Russell Lecturer, Tufts University, 1971; Lyman Beecher Lecturer, Divinity School, Yale University, 1976; Harris Lecturer, Bangor Seminary, 1979; Zabriskie Lecturer, Virginia Theological Seminary, 1982. Guest preacher and lecturer. Trustee, Barlow School, 1965-71. *Military service:* U.S. Army, 1944-46. *Member:* National Council of Churches, Council for Religion in Independent Schools (regional chairman, 1959-63), Foundation for Arts, Religion, and Culture, Presbytery of Northern New England, P.E.N., Authors Guild, Authors League of America, Century Association. *Awards, honors:* O. Henry Memorial Award, 1955, for short story "The Tiger"; Richard and Hinda Rosenthal Award, 1959, for *The Return of Ansel Gibbs,* National Book Award nomination, 1971, for *Lion Country;* Pulitzer Prize nomination, 1980, for *Godric;* D.D. from Virginia Theological Seminary, 1982.

WRITINGS—Novels; published by Atheneum, except as indicated: *A Long Day's Dying,* Knopf, 1950; *The Seasons' Difference,* Knopf, 1953; *The Return of Ansel Gibbs,* Knopf, 1958; *The Final Beast,* 1965, reprinted, Harper, 1982; *The Entrance to Porlock,* 1970; *Lion Country* (also see below), 1971; *Open Heart* (also see below), 1972; *Love Feast* (also see below), 1974; *Treasure Hunt* (also see below), 1977; *The Book of Bebb* (contains *Lion Country, Open Heart, Love Feast,* and *Treasure Hunt*), 1979; *Godric,* 1980.

Non-fiction: *The Magnificent Defeat* (meditations), Seabury, 1966; *The Hungering Dark* (meditations), Seabury, 1969; *The Alphabet of Grace* (theological and autobiographical essays), Seabury, 1970; *Wishful Thinking: A Theological ABC,* Harper, 1973; *The Faces of Jesus,* Simon & Schuster, 1974; *Telling the Truth: The Gospel as Tragedy, Comedy, and Fairy Tale,* Harper, 1977; *Peculiar Treasures: A Biblical Who's Who,* Harper, 1979; *The Sacred Journey* (autobiography), Atheneum, 1982; *Now and Then* (autobiography), Atheneum, 1983.

Short stories have been anthologized in *Prize Stories 1955: The O. Henry Awards,* edited by Paul Engle and Hansford Martin, Doubleday, 1955. Contributor to periodicals, including *Poetry* and *Lawrenceville Literary Magazine.*

SIDELIGHTS: Two years after graduating from Princeton University, Frederick Buechner published his first novel, *A Long Day's Dying.* "[This novel] is a strikingly fine first novel, and it seems entirely safe to say that its publication will . . . introduce a new American novelist of the greatest promise and the greatest talent," declares C. W. Weinberger in the *San Francisco Chronicle.* "In strict accuracy, it is not proper to refer to Mr. Buechner as being a novelist of great promise, for he has already arrived in superlative fashion."

Buechner's *A Long Day's Dying* is generally considered to be an unusually sensitive and insightful study of the relationships formed between the book's six characters. "Buechner has written a perceptive and often astringently witty study of subtle human relationships and delicate tensions," states C. J. Rolo in a review published in *Atlantic,* "a book which continually reaches for the emotional meanings of the moment." And David Daiches writes in the *New York Times* that "this first novel by a young man of twenty-three is a remarkable piece of work. There is a quality of civilized perception here, a sensitive and plastic handling of English prose and an ability to penetrate to the evanescent core of a human situation."

Buechner's second novel, *The Seasons' Difference,* was not greeted with the same degree of enthusiasm as *A Long Day's*

Dying. For example, Oliver La Farge points out in *Saturday Review* that *"The Seasons' Difference* starts with promise. Again and again it looks as if the promise were going to be fulfilled. There are moments when it lights up brightly, and one thinks, at last he has hit his stride—but always, somehow, the light goes out again. It is one of those most tantalizing of all things in writing—a near miss." H. L. Roth writes in *Library Journal* that Buechner's "emphasis is less on plot than on the development of atmosphere but even that emphasis seems to get lost in an arty attempt at developing a feeling of mysticism."

However, Tangye Lean finds Buechner's book "brilliant and closely knit both in its rather overloaded descriptive power and its invention." Writing in *Spectator* Lean remarks that *"The Seasons' Difference* may be recommended as one of the most distinguished novels that has recently come out of America." And a critic for *U.S. Quarterly Review* believes "the arresting quality of this sensitively and elaborately written novel lies in the delineation of its characters, especially the children, and of their interrelations: adult to adult, child to adult, and child to child." Nevertheless, reasons Horace Gregory in the *New York Herald Tribune Book Review*, "Buechner probably needs more time to complete his own vision of the world that is glimpsed in certain descriptive passages of [*The Seasons' Difference*]. . . . The promise of his first book is still awaiting its fulfillment."

Critics were more impressed with Buechner's third novel. "In *The Return of Ansel Gibbs*, Buechner makes a more decisive departure from his earlier manner," Ihab Hassan comments in *Radical Innocence: Studies in the Contemporary American Novel*. "The book is reasonably forthright; its material, though rich in moral ambiguities, is topical rather than mythic, dramatic more than allusive." A reviewer for *Atlantic* believes that this book "is quite a departure from [Buechner's] two previous novels, which were open to the charge of preciosity. Now the style is less ornate, the plot straightforward." Richard McLaughlin remarks in *Springfield Republican* that Buechner's earlier novels "established him as a writer with a distinguished style but a rather narrow range of interests. In [*The Return of Ansel Gibbs*] he explores, with his usual subtlety and feeling for language and moods, a wider, more public domain."

Writing for *Saturday Review*, A. C. Spectorsky declares that "there is a quality of distinction about Frederick Buechner's [*The Return of Ansel Gibbs*] which might best be compared to the gleam of hand-polished old silver. . . . There is about his work some of the charming cultivation of the best of Marquand, and Cozzens's capacity to make each incident—however casual or trivial in appearance—emerge as meaningful and illuminating."

In 1958, the same year *The Return of Ansel Gibbs* was published, Buechner was ordained a minister of the United Presbyterian Church. For the next several years Buechner performed the duties of school minister at Phillips Exeter Academy while continuing to write his novels. As Elizabeth Janeway explains in the *New York Times:* "Part of Frederick Buechner is a writer of imagination and insight. Part of him is a . . . man with a Christian mission so strong that he . . . decided to enter the Presbyterian ministry. There is no reason why the two shouldn't combine to write excellent and powerful novels."

Not all critics share Janeway's contention that the ministry and the writing of novels is a likely and acceptable combination. A reviewer for *Publishers Weekly* observes that "to a certain number of critics and reviewers . . . there is something disconcerting about a minister who can write a novel . . . containing some vivid sex scenes and a four-letter word or two." Buechner, however, sees no conflict with being a minister and a novelist. He explains in a *Publishers Weekly* interview: "Writing *is* a kind of ministry." Buechner elaborates further to *CA:* "As a preacher I am trying to do many of the same things I do as a writer. In both I am trying to explore what I believe life is all about, to get people to stop and listen a little to the mystery of their own lives. The process of telling a story is something like religion if only in the sense of suggesting that life itself has a plot and leads to a conclusion that makes some kind of sense."

Buechner's first literary work written after his ordination was *The Final Beast*. Published five years after *The Return of Ansel Gibbs, The Final Beast* displayed a shift in theme that a number of critics, including Gerald Weales, believed would be a preoccupation in future Buechner novels. In the *Reporter*, Weales describes the theme as "the possibility of spiritual rebirth." And a *Choice* reviewer feels this book marks the beginning of Buechner's "concern with religious belief and the religious life." Charles Dollen remarks in *Best Sellers:* "Despite what might sound like heavy drama in the plot, this [book] is a joyous one and its fictional people are searching for, and finding, real happiness. . . . This is a deeply religious book without the slightest hint of [piety] or sentimentalism."

In 1971, Buechner published *Lion Country*, the first book of a tetralogy that also includes *Open Heart, Love Feast*, and *Treasure Hunt*. Eight years later these four novels were published in one volume entitled *The Book of Bebb*. This tetralogy traces the activities and relationships of Leo Bebb, a former Bible salesman, founder of the Church of Holy Love, Inc. and of the Open Heart Church, and president of the Gospel Faith College, a religious diploma mill. Buechner did not originally intend to write a follow-up to *Lion Country*. He explains how the series evolved in his introduction to *The Book of Bebb:* "When I wrote the last sentence of *Lion Country*, I thought I had finished with [the characters in the series] for good but soon found out that they were not finished with me. And so it was with the succeeding volumes, at the end of each of which I rang the curtain down only to find that, after a brief intermission, they'd rung it up again."

With few exceptions critics view the Bebb series to be Buechner's best work. One such reviewer, Christopher Lehmann-Haupt, writes in the *New York Times:* "You smile to think how Frederick Buechner keeps getting better with each new novel, for where he was gently amusing in *Lion Country*, he is funny *and* profound in *Open Heart*." While numerous elements have been cited as reasons for the popularity of these four novels, most critics agree that much of the credit belongs to Buechner's presentation of thought-provoking ideas in a witty manner. A reviewer for the *Times Literary Supplement* believes that Buechner maintains "a strange, serene balancing act which blends successfully . . . satirical talent and the moral purpose." And writing in *Publishers Weekly*, a critic notes that the way Buechner "writes is special and engaging—serious, comic, with a kind of reverent irreverence for his people and their lives. [He has an] amused and amusing view." Another reviewer for *Publishers Weekly* holds *Lion Country* up as a perfect example of a "human comedy of complexity and persuasion." And a *Virginia Quarterly Review* writer remarks: "Urbane, arcane, intelligent, low-keyed comedy is rare enough in these parlous times, but [*Lion Country*] is a choice example certain to appeal to a variety of tastes."

Many reviewers have noted that Buechner's comical sense is especially evident in his handling of religious matters. "This may sound like slapstick [to] suggest that although Mr. Buechner takes bows toward religion he is really more interested in laughs," suggests Michael Mewshaw in the *New York Times Book Review,* "but throughout the [tetralogy] he is most serious when he is funny, and he has found an inevitable and instructive confusion between wheat and chaff. As the Bible warns, one can't be cut away without injuring the other." And in a review of *Open Heart,* John Skow observes in *Time:* "It is something of a mystery how Buechner has produced a live, warm, wise comic novel. And yet that is exactly what, in all shifty-eyed innocence, he has done. . . . [He] seems to have found an acceptable way to deal with religious mysteries in fiction."

Many critics agree with Skow that Buechner seems to have mastered a technique for dealing with theological subjects in an entertaining fashion. A reviewer for the *Times Literary Supplement* points out: "The fine lucidity of Mr. Buechner's prose, the pure verve of his humour, the grisly authenticity of his characters and settings make this highly elusive, indeed almost deliquescent brand of Christian Philosophy seem not unpalatable but actually convincing." Lehmann-Haupt writes in the *New York Times* that Buechner's "contrast between the serious and the absurd serves to underline the meaning of both *Love Feast* and the [tetralogy] as a whole: to wit, the message of Jesus Christ may emanate from strange places indeed, but it is the message that matters, not the messenger."

Cynthia Ozick believes that the reason the religious messages seem to fit so well into Buechner's novels is that to the author "sacredness lurks effortlessly (it is pointless to grope after it) nearly everywhere; it singles us out." As Buechner himself writes in *The Hungering Dark:* "There is no place or time so lowly and earthbound but that holiness can be there too. And this means that we are never safe, that there is no place where we can hide from God, no place where we are safe from his power . . . to recreate the human heart because it is . . . just where we least expect him where he comes most fully."

"Life is . . . what Buechner is writing about," says Jonathan Yardley in the *Washington Post Book World.* "Beneath all the antics of Leo Bebb and those who surround him there is a continuing celebration of life and the interrelation of lives. Buechner's people may at first glance seem caricatures, but their robustness is merely humanity magnified." And Thomas Howard remarks in the *New York Times Book Review* that "[Buechner's] vision, then, is that of the poet—the Christian poet. He has articulated what he sees with a freshness and clarity and energy that hails our stultified imaginations."

Another factor that contributes to the success of these novels is Buechner's skill at characterization. "What makes [the Leo Bebb novels] succeed is Buechner's deft placing of all these characters," explains Roger Sale in *Hudson Review,* "keeping them funny or impossible when seen from a distance, then making them briefly very moving when suddenly seen from close up." P. A. Doyle states in *Best Sellers* that Buechner "grasps each figure firmly and forces it to concrete life. A type of Flannery O'Connor vibrant vividness pervades Bebb . . . and the other principals causing them to pop out most fully alive from the novel[s]." And Sale, writing in another issue of *Hudson Review,* singles out Buechner's treatment of the main character, Leo Bebb, and comments: "The word about Bebb is simple—he lights up every page on which he appears, making each one a joy to read and to anticipate, and of all the characters in American literature, only Hemingway's Bill Gorton rivals him in that respect."

Buechner's skillful use of characters does not end with the Bebb series of novels. Numerous reviewers have cited Buechner's following novel, *Godric,* as still another example of how an effective characterization enriches Buechner's novels. In *Godric,* Buechner tells the story of a twelfth-century Anglo-Saxon saint. Francine Cardman illustrates in *Commonweal:* "Peddler, merchant seaman, pilgrim and perhaps pirate, ultimately hermit; roguist, conniving, irascible, repentant, gentle, fierce: Godric is compelling in his struggle for sanctity. Buechner's retelling draws reader/listener into the world of his words, a world and language so strangely and strongly evocative they would seem to be Godric's own." Noel Perrin comments in the *Washington Post Book World* that "the old saint [Godric] is so real that it's hard to remember this is a novel. . . . I can think of only one other book like this: Thomas Mann's *The Holy Sinner.* That's the story, taken from medieval legend, of another carnal saint."

In addition to his novels, Buechner has also written a number of works of nonfiction, including two collections of meditations, several religious studies, and autobiographies. Critics have noted that these books are similar in many ways to Buechner's novels. As Edmund Fuller notes in the *New York Times Book Review:* "The same stylistic power, subtlety and originality that have distinguished his novels, from *A Long Day's Dying* to *Open Heart,* lift *Wishful Thinking* far above commonplace religion books nearly to the level of C. S. Lewis's *Screwtape Letters.* An artist is at work here in the vineyard of theology, an able aphorist with a natural gift for gnomics, a wit with wisdom." Reviewing *The Alphabet of Grace,* Thomas Howard writes in the *New York Times Book Review* that Buechner "takes the common, mundane experiences of daily life and reflects on them. . . . What he does with his material is what the poets do with theirs: he surprises and delights (and—very softly—teaches) us by giving some shape to apparently random experience by uttering it."

"Novelist Buechner writes about as well as anyone we know of, when it comes to Christian themes today," declares a reviewer for *Christian Century.* In an article on *The Alphabet of Grace,* M. M. Shideler observes in another issue of *Christian Century* that "Buechner's style is by turns meditative, narrative and anecdotal. His manner is honest, sensitive and direct." And N. K. Burger observes in the *New York Times Book Review* that in *The Magnificent Defeat* (Buechner's first book of meditations) Buechner "combines high writing skill with a profound understanding of Christian essentials." Tony Stoneburner writes in *Christian Century* that Buechner's collections of meditations "grant relative value to the world, distinguish Christianity and morality, argue the propriety of poetry for discourse about mystery." Commenting on Buechner's second collection, *The Hungering Dark,* Fuller states in the *New York Times Book Review* that "the touches that distinguish [this book] spring from the fact that in addition to Buechner's role as Presbyterian minister and sometime chaplain . . . , he is also one of the better literary talents of his generation. . . . He has artistic as well as pastoral insights into the human soul and also some distinction of style." Reviewing *Telling the Truth: The Gospel as Tragedy, Comedy, and Fairy Tale,* Richard Sistek points out that "this is the kind of book that asks for reflection, creativity, and response. With continually changing times and a church in transition, human experience and creativity are sorely needed to make sense out of change, and move forward with hope. The author has challenged me."

Perhaps nowhere else does the reader achieve a real understanding of Buechner, the author and minister, than in his autobiographies. In his introduction to *The Sacred Journey* Buechner writes: "What I propose to do now is to try listening to my life as a whole, or at least to certain key moments of the first half of my life thus far, for whatever of meaning, of holiness, of God, there may be in it to hear. My assumption is that the story of any one of us is in some measure the story of us all." A *Publishers Weekly* reviewer writes that in *The Sacred Journey*, Buechner "exemplifies his conviction that God speaks to us not just through sounds but 'through events in all their complexity and variety, through the harmonies and disharmonies and counterpoint of all that happens.'"

Reynolds Price remarks in the *New York Times Book Review* that in *The Sacred Journey*, Buechner "isolates and recreates a few powerfully charged incidents ranging from his early childhood to the time of his decision to enter the ministry." "The heart of this book," Julian N. Hart believes, "is a series of encounters for which 'epiphany,' overworked though it may be, is entirely appropriate." Hart writes in the *Washington Post Book World* that "the persistent core metaphor is 'journey'; in his case a life-process defined, not merely punctuated, by revelations of what he comes to acknowledge of divine goodness and power."

Buechner's sequel to *The Sacred Journey, Now and Then*, "picks up where the first book ends, with the author's experience of having his life turned upside down while listening to a George Buttrick sermon," writes Marjorie Casebier McCoy in *Christian Century*. "Part I covers Buechner's years at Union Theological Seminary, where he encountered the theologians and biblical scholars who became his mentors. . . . In Part II Buechner recalls his nine years as a minister and teacher of religion at Phillips Exeter Academy, trying to be an apologist for Christianity against its 'cultured despisers' by presenting the faith 'as appealingly, honestly, relevantly and skillfully as I could.' . . . Part III begins with Buechner's move to Vermont in 1967, chronicles his struggle to minister through full-time writing and speaking, and provides insights into the development of his subsequent novels and nonfiction."

In all of his writings—the collections of meditations, autobiographical studies, as well as fiction—Buechner has proven to many his ability to successfully maintain a literary career that reflects his dual roles as author and minister. Concludes Max L. Autrey in the *Dictionary of Literary Biography Yearbook*: "Early appraisals of Buechner's work have proved accurate. After producing ten novels and volumes of nonfictional writings, he has demonstrated his right to be listed among such contemporary writers as Mailer, Ellison, Updike, and Barth. Although his literary appeal has been primarily to the intelligentsia, he is now widely recognized as a brilliant, inspirational writer and an original voice."

A collection of Buechner's manuscripts has been established at Princeton University.

CA INTERVIEW

CA interviewed Frederick Buechner by telephone on March 23, 1983, at his home in Rupert, Vermont.

CA: You seem happy to be called a Christian writer, and indeed your books are fairly bursting with the promise and possibility of life open to God's grace. But does the label "Christian writer" have negative effects as well as positive? Has it limited your audience in any way?

BUECHNER: I think it has because people may think of it as suggesting that I write propaganda, which I don't. I think of being a Christian writer in the sense that a black man may think of himself as a black writer or a woman of being a woman writer. It's the form my work takes and the context I write out of. It's not in my mind a sinister title at all.

CA: Does your mail from readers indicate that some of them are attracted to your nonfiction by first reading your fiction, and vice versa?

BUECHNER: I don't know which category people start with, but what pleases me is that more and more of my mail indicates that people have read both the fiction and the nonfiction. Five years ago, on the contrary, I got the feeling that I had two separate audiences altogether, neither aware of the existence of the other.

CA: In your novels, grace is often visited on the least likely and seemingly least deserving characters, such as Leo Bebb, while others hang back or for some reason fall short of receiving it. What are you saying about grace, and why some people get it and others don't?

BUECHNER: I think the ones who get it are the ones who are open to the possibility of it, who sense an inner emptiness that needs to be filled. It's the ones who think they already have grace as a possession, as theirs by right almost, who are apt to miss the real thing when it comes their way.

CA: Your first novel, A Long Day's Dying *(1950), elicited critical comparisons with the fiction of Henry James and Marcel Proust. Later your fiction became earthier, funnier, freer. Can you say what caused that change?*

BUECHNER: In that ancient first novel, begun while I was a senior in college, I was writing in a way for a creative writing class, and I was very much on my best literary behavior in it—trying to get everything right, to show off everything I'd learned, to impress Teacher. Later on, through my work both as a teacher myself and as a preacher later still, I thought of myself much more as writing for a live audience, and little by little that loosened me up considerably. You can't teach or preach in the kind of labyrinthine language I indulged myself in in *A Long Day's Dying*. You'd be laughed off the podium. So my sentences got much shorter and more colloquial. I learned to take many more risks, both stylistically and in terms of content. After a while I reached the point where I even dared trying to be funny from time to time.

CA: Bebb came out of your unconscious, you've said, as a gift, triggered by something you saw in a magazine in a barber shop. Was there a great deal of work in refining the character and in creating the other characters that inhabit the Bebb books?

BUECHNER: There's always a lot of work, of course, but looking back on the Bebb books—*Lion Country* especially—I'm struck by how much of them seemed to come very much as a gift from somewhere. The characters in particular seemed to emerge more or less intact and full of life from wherever it is such things emerge from. It was a matter much less of refining them, as book followed book, than of simply watching them, fascinated, as the refinements appeared.

CA: Did you meet people through your earlier work in a Harlem mission who became characters later in your books?

BUECHNER: Several minor characters in *The Return of Ansel Gibbs* had counterparts, as I remember it, in East Harlem, or were at least composite sketches. And in *Now and Then*, the second of my two autobiographical volumes, I speak at some length about an elderly alcoholic I found a job for there. Otherwise I can't think of anybody.

CA: And Dr. James Muilenburg?

BUECHNER: I knew Dr. Muilenburg not in East Harlem but at Union Theological Seminary, and it is true that the character of Kuykendall in *Ansel Gibbs* is a partial portrait of that extraordinary man.

CA: You studied at Union Theological Seminary in the mid-'50s, an extremely exciting time because Reinhold Niebuhr and Paul Tillich were there, among other fine teachers and theologians, and Martin Buber came to speak during that time. One doesn't hear of such interesting figures in theology today. Is that kind of intellectual excitement missing?

BUECHNER: I'm probably not in a better position than you are to comment on that, being away from the seminary, but that is my impression. I don't know anybody now who could pack the wallop those men did. They had such stature, such an aura about them. They were on the cover of *Time;* they advised presidents; they wrote vast, eloquent, dramatic works. I don't think there are men like that today—at least none that I know about. We hear more about the spellbinders, like Jerry Falwell and Oral Roberts.

CA: You've described the skepticism of the young students you had at Phillips Exeter when you organized and taught the religion program there. Do you have any feeling about how young people today compare with them in their attitude toward religion?

BUECHNER: I think that for a variety of reasons the young of today are much more receptive to and interested in religion than they were when I started out at Exeter in 1958. Who knows why? I think that drugs, the Buddhist craze, the interest in various forms of meditation all tended to open them up to the possibility at least of a reality beyond the reality of time and space. I think also that the activism of the '60s and of course the whole Vietnam issue made them much more receptive to the essentially religious questions of meaning, purpose, and value. When it comes to institutionalized religion in general and the church in particular, I think the young are as full of skepticism as they ever were, but religion in itself and as an approach to the mysteries of life and death seems to me to be much more viable for them than it was for their counterparts twenty-five years ago.

CA: Have your students and your own daughters had any direct bearing on what you've written?

BUECHNER: To ask about the influence of my daughters on my work is like asking about the influence of my life on my work. In both cases, it is both enormous and very hard to pin down. I can answer more easily about my students. Insofar as I am a Christian apologist, it is still very much their kind of doubt, skepticism, sophistication, and honesty that I find myself addressing.

CA: Dreams and the unconscious play an important part in your work, both for you in creating the work, and for your characters. Have you been much influenced by the work of Carl Jung?

BUECHNER: Somebody once made a distinction between being intellectual and being bookish. I am not an intellectual. I *am* bookish. I have read a lot of Jung, but in the way of a bookish person rather than an intellectual—I never could have systematized it, and I haven't really remembered it in an organized way. But it has had a great influence on me, as other people I've read have in the same way.

CA: In your writing, grace is often associated with humor. Would you comment on that relationship?

BUECHNER: When Sarah and Abraham were told by God that they were going to produce a child in their nineties, the Bible tells us that they both burst into fits of laughter. Grace always comes as a joyous surprise like that, and joy and surprise are where some of our best laughter comes from always.

CA: There is sometimes an element of slapstick in your books. Could it be related to some of the movies you loved as a child, which you mentioned in the preface to Now and Then?

BUECHNER: I heard somebody on the West Coast lecturing about my books the other day, and she said among other things that, in them, even the ridiculous, the farcical, the obscene are somehow redeemed. It pleases me very much to think that maybe that's true. That although Leo Bebb is in some ways a very comic figure, he is also a saint, a very comic saint. Just where the movies of my childhood come into this I'm not sure, but I'm sure they come in somewhere.

CA: As literary influences you've talked about reading the Oz books early, and about C. S. Lewis and Graham Greene and King Lear. *Mythology too figures in your work. Are there newer writers whose work you enjoy reading?*

BUECHNER: I enjoy Robertson Davies, his Deptford trilogy especially, and the best of Annie Dillard, and D. M. Thomas's *The White Hotel*. But my real love—though scarcely a "newer" writer—is Anthony Trollope. My wife and I started reading him aloud about five years ago, especially on long car journeys, and among novelists there is no writer I love and admire as much. It was Tolstoy, I believe, who wrote somewhere, "I am overwhelmed by his genius." He had reason to be, I think, and so do we all.

CA: Your first book brought instant recognition; you won the O. Henry Award for a short story later, then the Richard and Hinda Rosenthal Award for The Return of Ansel Gibbs. *How do you feel about such public affirmation for writers?*

BUECHNER: It's very nice. There's nothing a writer wants more than readers, and you always hope such affirmation will lead to increasing your audience. Lately I don't win prizes, though; I just get nominated for them. *Lion Country* was nominated for the National Book Award and *Godric* was nominated for the Pulitzer Prize. The main reason I wish they'd won is just so I'd be more apt to find my books in drugstores and airports and railway stations. Most of what you find there is such ghastly trash.

CA: You said Godric came to you easily, like Bebb: he all but jumped out at you from the Penguin Dictionary of Saints *and became the subject of your tenth and favorite novel. How did you work out the language you used in that book to convey the patterns of speech and life in medieval England?*

BUECHNER: I can tell you certain things about how I did it. In an effort to make it sound authentic, I decided to remove from my vocabulary all Latin derivatives, because Godric in fact would not have been apt to know them. And I was very iambic in a way that I thought might suggest the cadences of medieval speech and legend. But what's surprising about this book was how it came with great ease, though I really did very little research and knew only a little about that period in history. I found myself describing things I'd never seen, using words that in some cases I had to look up to make sure they meant what I thought they meant. Perhaps I'd come across them somewhere once and forgotten. I don't want to sound spooky about it, but it really made me feel in touch with something other than my own creativity, however one wants to explain that. After all, there was a Godric, and he was called a saint; and as I said in *Now and Then*, I believe he may have had something to do with my finding him and with how I wrote the book.

CA: In writing the two recent volumes of autobiography, The Sacred Journey *(1982) and* Now and Then *(1983), you subjected yourself to the ordeal of the quest that you've sent so many of your characters on. Was it harder to trace the patterns and clues of your own life than to map out the fictional journeys of your characters?*

BUECHNER: On the whole, I would say that it was easier. The memories were there, and I simply had to go back and wend my way through them. I didn't have to *invent* anything, as with fiction. Most of the pain that some of my sadder memories cost me was a pain that I had already felt and come to terms with before I got around to writing the memories down, so in that sense too the autobiographical quest wasn't especially hard.

CA: Do you paint, or continue to enjoy art in some way as you did in your student days?

BUECHNER: I don't paint, but I do still enjoy art. I was in the National Gallery in Washington the other day and was so absorbed, so enthralled, by some of the paintings I saw—especially a room full of seventeenth-century ones—that there were a few moments when I almost felt that I was in danger of being actually transported out of the real world into the world that the paintings made seem even realer still.

CA: Writing became your ministry, you've said, but you also continue to preach and lecture. How much speaking are you doing now?

BUECHNER: I've just got enough books in print now and I'm just popular enough so that I get probably four or five invitations a week to speak somewhere. Obviously if I accepted one hundredth of them, I would be doing nothing else. I've accepted more in the last year and a half than I ever have before, with the result that I've written nothing since *Now and Then*. As of right now I have one more thing that I'm signed up to do, and then I'm not going to take on any more for at least another year until I get, I hope, another novel done.

CA: Has there been any talk of movies based on the novels?

BUECHNER: Occasionally. The most serious talk now is about a miniseries based on the Bebb books, to be done by public television. It's in the early stages; they've got a scriptwriter and a couple of stations that are willing to finance at least the writing of the script.

CA: How do you relax in the hours that you're not writing or speaking?

BUECHNER: We play tennis, we go riding (we live in the country), we go to movies—nothing startling. I love reading, and I love books—not just reading or writing them, but *having* them on the shelves, so I spend a lot of time in used-book stores.

CA: Is there work planned or in progress that you'd like to talk about?

BUECHNER: Over the last few years I've collected a number of fairly short pieces that I think could be a book and I'm trying to write an introduction to that now. But what I really want to write is a novel. I don't want to talk about it specifically, but I have a very strong feeling for what it's going to be about. You never really know, of course, if it's going to work out; I've made several false starts toward novels in the past few years. But so much goes on in the subconscious before the actual writing, and a lot of work has taken place there toward this book, so I hope that when I start writing it down it will come glittering up out of the depths.

BIOGRAPHICAL/CRITICAL SOURCES—Books: John W. Aldridge, *After the Lost Generation*, McGraw, 1951; Ihab Hassan, *Radical Innocence: Studies in the Contemporary American Novel*, Princeton University Press, 1961; Frederick Buechner, *The Hungering Dark*, Seabury, 1969; Buechner, *The Alphabet of Grace*, Seabury, 1970; *Contemporary Literary Criticism*, Gale, Volume II, 1974, Volume IV, 1975, Volume VI, 1976, Volume IX, 1978; Buechner, *The Book of Bebb*, Atheneum, 1979; *Dictionary of Literary Biography Yearbook: 1980*, Gale, 1981; Buechner, *The Sacred Journey*, Atheneum, 1982; Buechner, *Now and Then*, Atheneum, 1983.

Periodicals: *New York Times*, January 8, 1950, February 16, 1958, May 19, 1972, September 25, 1974; *San Francisco Chronicle*, January 22, 1950; *Atlantic*, February, 1950, March, 1958, September, 1979, December, 1980; *Library Journal*, January 1, 1952, April 15, 1979; *New York Herald Tribune Book Review*, January 13, 1952; *Saturday Review*, January 19, 1952; *U.S. Quarterly Book Review*, June, 1952; *Spectator*, July 25, 1952; *Springfield Republican*, May 11, 1958; *Best Sellers*, February 1, 1965, March 1, 1971, February, 1978, December, 1980, June, 1982; *Reporter*, September 9, 1965; *Christian Century*, February 9, 1966, April 1, 1970, September 19, 1973, October 13, 1982, March 23, 1983; *New York Times Book Review*, February 20, 1966, March 2, 1969, December 6, 1970, February 14, 1971, June 11, 1972, May 13, 1973, September 22, 1974, October 30, 1977, November 23, 1980, April 11, 1982.

Publishers Weekly, December 28, 1970, March 29, 1971, June 27, 1977, February 12, 1982; *Newsweek*, February 22, 1971, November 10, 1980; *Time*, April 12, 1971, July 3, 1972; *Virginia Quarterly Review*, summer, 1971, autumn, 1972; *Commonweal*, July, 1971, February 26, 1982; *Choice*, September, 1971, June, 1978; *Washington Post Book World*, May 28, 1972, November 3, 1974, November 9, 1980, June 6, 1982; *New York Review of Books*, July 20, 1972; *Saturday Review of the Society*, July 29, 1972; *Hudson Review*, winter, 1972-73, winter, 1974-75; *Times Literary Supplement*, December

29, 1972, May 23, 1975, May 12, 1978, June 13, 1981; *Books and Bookmen*, March, 1973; *America*, April 14, 1973, December 14, 1974; *Saturday Review/World*, October 5, 1974; *New Yorker*, October 21, 1974; *National Review*, December 20, 1974; *New Republic*, January 25, 1975, September 17, 1977.

—*Sketch by Margaret Mazurkiewicz*
—*Interview by Jean W. Ross*

*   *   *

BUESCHEL, Richard M. 1926-

PERSONAL: Surname is pronounced Bush-ell; born December 26, 1926, in Chicago, Ill.; son of Martin W. and Helen (Kernacs) Bueschel; married Helen Snyder, November 24, 1951; children: Stacey Brooks, Megan Conley. *Education:* Wright Junior College, Chicago, Ill., A.Sc., 1949; Illinois College, Jacksonville, B.A., 1951. *Home:* 414 North Prospect Manor, Mount Prospect, Ill. 60056. *Office:* c/o Zylke & Affiliates, Inc., 3703 West Lake Ave., Glenview, Ill. 60025.

CAREER: Wilson Sporting Goods, Chicago, Ill., advertising assistant, 1951-52; Wallace, Ferry, Hanly & Co. (advertising), Chicago, copy-contact, 1952-54; Erwin Wasey & Co. (advertising), Chicago, copywriter, 1954-57; Erwin Wasey, Ruthrauff & Ryan, Chicago, account executive, 1957-58; Waldie & Briggs, Inc. (advertising), Chicago, 1959-75, president, 1967-75; Ladd/Wells/Presba Advertising, Inc., senior vice-president and creative director, 1975-79; Zylke & Affiliates, Inc., Glenview, Ill., affiliate, creative supervisor, 1979—. Consultant on Oriental aviation to Twentieth Century-Fox, and on popular culture and coin machines to Smithsonian Institution. *Military service:* U.S. Army Air Forces, Ninth Air Force Aviation Engineers, 1945-46. *Member:* Business and Professional Advertising Association (president of Chicago chapter, 1968-69), Authors Guild.

WRITINGS: Japanese Aircraft Camouflage and Markings, Aero, 1966; *Japanese Code Names*, Aero, 1966; *Communist Chinese Airpower*, Praeger, 1968; *Japanese Army and Navy Aircraft*, AeroFile, 1976; *Aircam Japanese Fighters*, eight volumes, Osprey, 1970-71; *Aircam Japanese Bombers*, four volumes, Osprey, 1972-73; *Japanese Army Aircraft*, AeroFile, 1976.

Published by Coin Slot Books: *Guide to Collectible Slot Machines*, four volumes, 1978-83; *Guide to Collectible Trade Stimulators*, three volumes, 1979-83; *Coin Slot Guide*, forty volumes, 1979-83; (with Steve Gronowski) *Guide to Collectible Arcade Machines*, 1983. Historical editor, *Coin Slot Magazine*, 1974—. Consultant on Oriental aviation to *American Heritage*, 1966-74.

WORK IN PROGRESS: Japanese Aircraft in Color; Lemons, Cherries, and Bell-Fruit Gum; Rolling Mountain, a history of the Ferris wheel, for Vestal Press; research on the battle of El Caney of the Spanish-American War.

SIDELIGHTS: Richard M. Bueschel told *CA:* "To find the unfindable, and to publish the unknown—that's the direction of my research and writing. The search is the thing, and the ability to share these findings with a ready reading audience is a joy unto itself. My areas are popular culture and American industrial growth. Both are forgotten subjects, and the surface has barely been tapped. Yet all are of unusual and general interest. And there's room for as many writers as are interested. We can't really understand our present if we don't know our past. It's fun to find out, and exciting to share."

BULL, Peter (Cecil) 1912-

PERSONAL: Born March 21, 1912, in London, England; son of Sir William (a politician and lawyer) and Lilian Hestxher (Brandon) Bull. *Education:* Attended Winchester College in England and University of Tours in France; studied acting under Elsie Fogerty and at Central School of Drama. *Politics:* Liberal. *Religion:* Protestant. *Home:* 149 King's Rd., London SW3, England.

CAREER: Journalist in England, 1930-33; actor, 1933—, occasional producer, and writer. Made first appearance on the London stage in "If I Were You," 1933, his film debut in "The Silent Voice," 1934, and first New York appearance in "Escape Me Never," 1935; subsequently played in five more London productions before the war, and opened and managed the Perranporth Summer Theatre, 1936-39; resumed his producing role with a provincial tour of "Cage Me a Peacock," 1946, then played in "The Lady's Not for Burning," 1948, "Under the Sycamore Tree," 1952, "Second Best Bed," 1953, "The Man with Expensive Tastes," 1953, "The Dark Is Light Enough," 1954, "Waiting for Godot," 1955, "The Restless Heart," 1957, "Man of Distinction," 1957, "Luther," 1961, and "Pickwick," 1963; came to New York in "The Lady's Not for Burning," 1950, "Luther," 1964, "Pickwick," 1965, and "Black Comedy," 1967.

Motion pictures include "Oliver Twist," United Artists, 1951, "The African Queen," United Artists, 1951, "The Captain's Paradise," United Artists, 1953, "The Old Dark House," Universal, 1963, "Tom Jones," United Artists, 1963, "Doctor Strangelove," Columbia, 1964, "Doctor Doolittle," 1967, "Lock Up Your Daughters," Columbia, 1969, "Alice in Wonderland," 1971, "Joseph Andrews," 1977, and "The Tempest," 1979. Also actor in television plays in England and member of television panels; in the United States he has been on the Johnny Carson, Merv Griffin, Dick Cavett, and Tom Snyder television shows. Has devised a one-man show called "An Evening of Bull" which he took on tour throughout the United States and Britain. *Military service:* Royal Naval Volunteer Reserve, 1940-46; became lieutenant commander; received Distinguished Service Cross, 1945.

WRITINGS—Published by P. Davies, except as indicated: *To Sea in a Sieve*, 1956; *Bulls in the Meadows*, 1957; *I Know the Face But—*, 1959; *Not on Your Telly!*, 1962; *I Say, Look Here!*, 1965; *It Isn't All Greek to Me*, 1967; *Bear with Me: The Teddy Bear—A Symposium*, Hutchinson, 1969, published as *Teddy Bear Book*, Random House, 1970; *Life Is a Cucumber*, 1972.

"Bully Bear" series; published by Bull & Irving: *Bully Bear Goes to a Wedding*, c. 1982; . . . *to a Rally*, c. 1982; . . . *Punk*, c. 1982; . . . *to Hollywood*, c. 1982; . . . *to Australia*, c. 1983; . . . *to Harrods*, c. 1983. Also author of *Dr. Bully Bear*.

Contributor to *Punch, New York Times, Harper's Bazaar*, and *After Dark*.

WORK IN PROGRESS: Additional "Bully Bear" books for children.

SIDELIGHTS: Peter Bull spends part of every year on a small Greek island in a house he built himself, presumably with his family of fourteen Teddy bears also in residence (all of his bears, he claims, get into a foul temper when he is away from them). To gather data on Teddy companions of other adults for his *Teddy Bear Book,* Bull ran a front page ad in the London *Times* and made a plea on television for bear lovers to come forward. According to *Time,* he found that the late Donald Campbell set new speed records with his Teddy, Mr. Woppitt, riding along, actress Samantha Eggar took hers to her wedding, the King of Thailand has taken his on state visits, and mountaineer Walter Bonnati climbed the Matterhorn with a Teddy in his knapsack. He also found that stuffed friends do not stay lost for long. Of the 250 Teddy bears left on London buses each year, almost all are claimed.

BIOGRAPHICAL/CRITICAL SOURCES: Time, December 5, 1969.

*   *   *

BULLOCK, Paul 1924-

PERSONAL: Born November 6, 1924, in Pasadena, Calif.; son of Paul (a bookkeeper) and Eleanor (Galloway) Bullock; married Constance Strickland (a librarian), June, 1962. *Education:* Occidental College, B.A., 1948, M.A., 1949; University of California, Los Angeles, graduate study, 1948-50. *Politics:* Democrat. *Religion:* None. *Home:* 640 The Village, No. 117, Redondo Beach, Calif. 90277. *Office:* Institute of Industrial Relations, University of California, Los Angeles, Calif. 90024.

CAREER: El Camino College, Los Angeles, Calif., instructor in economics, 1949-50; Occidental College, Los Angeles, instructor in economics, 1950-51; Wage Stabilization Board, Los Angeles Region, Los Angeles, wage analyst, 1951-53; University of California, Los Angeles, research economist, Institute of Industrial Relations, 1953—. Consultant to McCone Commission, 1965, and Kerner Commission, 1967. Chairman of New Careers Task Force, Los Angeles County Commission on Delinquency and Crime, 1968-70; member of board of directors, Central City Community Mental Health Center. Member of Los Angeles City Training and Job Development Advisory Board and the advisory committee of the Historic Southern Tenant Farmers Union. *Military service:* U.S. Army, 1943-46. *Member:* Industrial Relations Research Association, Associaton for Evolutionary Economics, National Committee for Full Employment, Los Angeles Urban League, Los Angeles City Private Industry Council, Phi Beta Kappa, Pi Gamma Mu.

WRITINGS: Standards of Wage Determination, Institute of Industrial Relations, University of California, 1960; *Merit Employment,* Institute of Industrial Relations, University of California, 1960; *Equal Opportunity in Employment,* Institute of Industrial Relations, University of California, 1965; (with Fred H. Schmidt and Robert Singleton) *Hard-Core Unemployment and Poverty in Los Angeles,* U.S. Government Printing Office, 1965; (contributor) Irving Howe and Jeremy Larner, editors, *Poverty: Views from the Left,* Morrow, 1968; (editor and contributor) *Watts: The Aftermath, by the People of Watts,* Grove, 1969.

(Contributor) John H. Burma, editor, *Mexican-American Problems in the United States: A Reader,* Harper, 1970; *Aspiration vs. Opportunity: "Careers" in the Inner City,* University of Michigan Press, 1973; (editor and contributor) *A Full Employment Policy for America,* Institute of Industrial Relations, University of California, 1974; (editor and contributor) *Goals for Full Employment,* Institute of Industrial Relations, University of California, 1976; *Creative Careers: Minorities in the Arts,* Institute of Industrial Relations, University of California, 1977; *Jerry Voorhis: The Idealist as Politician,* privately printed, 1978; (editor) *Directory of Organizations in*

Greater Los Angeles, Institute of Industrial Relations, University of California, 1979; (co-author) *The Arts in the Economic Life of the City,* American Council for the Arts, 1979.

CETA at the Crossroads: Employment Policy and Politics, Institute of Industrial Relations, University of California, 1981; *Building California: The Story of the Carpenter's Union,* Institute of Industrial Relations, University of California, 1982. Contributor of articles to *New Republic, Progressive, Journal of Negro Education,* and other journals.

WORK IN PROGRESS: Policy studies in youth employment and training.

SIDELIGHTS: Paul Bullock told *CA:* "I believe that, above all, writing is the art of communication. Writing which does not communicate to the intended reader is bad writing, regardless of how 'poetic' or 'literary' it may seem. I have three basic rules for good writing: 1) Know exactly what you want to say before you start; 2) Say it as briefly, directly, and simply as possible; and 3) Then shut up. Too many books are no more than overblown essays, written by someone who, for professional or other reasons, has to produce a book.

"I also believe that economics remains a social science, dealing with human relationships which cannot be reduced to 'natural' or 'mathematical' laws. Pure objectivity is impossible to attain. Consciously or unconsciously, we are the prisoners of our values and experiences, and our task as writers in the field is to acknowledge our value norms and not pretend that they do not exist. The effort of some economists to sell economics as a mathematical science is either phony or self-deceiving."

*   *   *

BULLOUGH, Bonnie 1927-

PERSONAL: Born January 5, 1927, in Delta, Utah; daughter of Ruth Uckerman; married Vern L. Bullough (a college professor), August 2, 1947; children: David (deceased), James, Steven, Susan, Robert. *Education:* University of Utah, R.N., 1947; Youngstown State University, B.S., 1957; University of California, Los Angeles, M.S. (nursing), 1962, M.A. (sociology), 1965, Ph.D., 1968, postdoctoral study, 1970-74. *Home:* 590 Le Brun Rd., Amherst, N.Y. 14226. *Office:* School of Nursing, State University of New York at Buffalo, Buffalo, N.Y. 14214.

CAREER: Santa Rosa General Hospital, Santa Rosa, Calif., nurse, 1947-48; Salt Lake General Hospital, Salt Lake City, Utah, operating room head nurse, 1948-51; University of Chicago Clinics, Chicago, Ill., operating room nurse, 1951-52; City of Chicago, field nurse for health department, 1952-54; Youngstown State University, Youngstown, Ohio, part-time instructor in nursing, 1956-59; Northridge Hospital, Northridge, Calif., part-time nurse, 1959-61; Cairo University, Higher Institute of Nursing, Cairo, Egypt, Fulbright lecturer in nursing, 1966-67; San Fernando Valley State College (now California State University, Northridge), part-time instructor in sociology, 1967-68; University of California, Los Angeles, assistant professor, 1968-72, associate professor of nursing, 1972-75; California State University, Long Beach, associate director of pediatric nurse practitioner program, 1971-75, chairperson of primary care section, 1972-74, professor of nursing and coordinator of graduate nursing program, 1975-79; State University of New York at Buffalo, dean of School of Nursing, 1980—. Certified family nurse practitioner.

MEMBER: American Nurses Association (member of local board of directors, 1973-74), American Public Health Association, National Association of Pediatric Nurse Practitioners and Associates. *Awards, honors:* Award from Los Angeles Nursing Fund, 1976; American Academy of Nursing fellow; recipient of grants from National Center for Health Services, Research, and Development, 1970-72, and W. K. Kellogg Foundation, 1975-79.

WRITINGS: Social Psychological Barriers to Housing Desegregation, Center for Real Estate Research and Urban Economics, University of California, Berkeley, 1969; (contributor) Saleem A. Farag, editor, *Selected Papers on Health Issues in California,* State of California, 1971; (contributor) Judith Lorber and Eliot Friedson, editors, *Medical Men and Their Work,* Aldine-Atherton, 1972; (editor and contributor) *The Law and the Expanding Nursing Role,* Appleton-Century-Crofts, 1975, 2nd edition, 1980; (editor) *The Management of Common Human Miseries: A Text for Primary Care Practitioners,* Springer Publishing Co., 1979.

With husband, Vern Bullough: *What Color Are Your Germs?* (pamphlet), Committee to End Discrimination in Chicago Medical Institutions, 1954; *The Emergence of Modern Nursing,* Macmillan, 1964, 2nd edition, 1969; (editors) *Issues in Nursing,* Springer Publishing Co., 1966; (editors) *New Directions for Nurses,* Springer Publishing Co., 1971; *Poverty, Ethnic Identity, and Health Care,* Appleton-Century-Crofts, 1972; (editors) *The Subordinate Sex: A History of Attitudes toward Women,* University of Illinois Press, 1973; *Sin, Sickness, and Sanity: A History of Sexual Attitudes,* New American Library, 1977; (editors) *Expanding Horizons in Nursing,* Springer Publishing Co., 1977; *Prostitution: An Illustrated Social History,* Crown, 1978; *The Care of the Sick,* Neale Watson, 1978; *Nursing: An Historical Bibliography,* Garland Publishing, 1981; *Health Care for the Other Americans,* Appleton-Century-Crofts, 1982; (editors with Mary Claire Soukup) *Nursing Issues and Strategies for the Eighties,* Springer Publishing Co., 1983.

Contributor of chapters to other books. Contributor of more than fifty-eight articles to professional journals.

WORK IN PROGRESS: With husband, Vern Bullough, *History and Politics of Nursing,* for Appleton-Century-Crofts; research on state nurse practice acts, particularly as they relate to nurse practitioners; a bibliography of issues in nursing; research on the use of Kegel exercises to treat stress incontinence.

SIDELIGHTS: Bonnie Bullough writes: "I consider this an exciting time to be involved in nursing. The role of the nurse is in a period of rapid change as nurses take on more responsibility in acute, long term, and primary care. This means that the education of nurses must necessarily be strengthened. Since social change of this proportion is always somewhat painful, the profession is also beset by many problems, and problems, if they are not overwhelming, can be interesting."

*   *   *

BULLOUGH, Vern (LeRoy) 1928-

PERSONAL: Born July 24, 1928, in Salt Lake City, Utah; son of David Vernon (a tool and die maker) and Augusta (Rueckert) Bullough; married Bonnie Uckerman (a nurse and teacher), August 2, 1947; children: David (deceased), James, Steven, Susan, Robert. *Education:* University of Utah, B.A., 1951; University of Chicago, M.A., 1951, Ph.D., 1954; California State University, Long Beach, R.N., 1980. *Home:* 590 Le Brun Rd., Amherst, N.Y. 14226. *Office:* State University of New York College at Buffalo, 1300 Elmwood Ave., Buffalo, N.Y. 14222.

CAREER: Youngstown University, Youngstown, Ohio, assistant professor of history, 1954-59; California State University, Northridge, 1959-80, began as associate professor, became professor of history; State University of New York College at Buffalo, dean of natural and social sciences, 1980—. Lecturer, California College of Medicine, Los Angeles; visiting lecturer, School of Public Health, University of California, Los Angeles, and University of Southern California; Morris Fishbein Lecturer, University of Chicago, 1970; Beaumont Lecturer, University of Vermont, 1975; adjunct professor of nursing and history, State University of New York at Buffalo. Member of southern California board, American Civil Liberties Union; member of Los Angeles Building Commission, 1975-78. *Military service:* U.S. Army, Army Security Agency, 1946-48.

MEMBER: International Society for Comparative Study of Civilizations, American Historical Association, American Association for Advancement of Science, Mediaeval Academy, Renaissance Society, American Association for History of Medicine, History of Technology Society, American Sociological Association, History of Science Society, Society for the Scientific Study of Sex (president, 1981-83). *Awards, honors:* Newberry fellowship; Huntington Library fellowship; recipient of grants from American Philosophical Society, National Science Foundation, U.S. Department of Education, and Erickson Educational Foundation; named outstanding professor, California State Universities and Colleges, 1969; President's Award, California State University, 1978; Distinguished Humanist Award, 1979; Founders Award, Center for Sex Research, 1980.

WRITINGS: The History of Prostitution, University Books, 1964; *The Development of Medicine as a Profession: The Contribution of the Medieval University to Modern Medicine,* S. Karger, 1966; *Man in Western Civilization,* Holt, 1970; *The Scientific Revolution,* Holt, 1970; (with Raoul Naroll and Frada Naroll) *Military Deterrence in History: A Statistical Survey,* State University of New York Press, 1971; *Sex, Society, and History,* Neale Watson, 1976; *Sexual Variance in Society and History,* Wiley, 1976; (with Barett Elcano) *Bibliography of Prostitution,* Garland Publishing, 1978; (with others) *Annotated Bibliography of Homosexuality,* Garland Publishing, 1977; *Homosexuality: A History,* New American Library, 1979; (editor) *The Frontiers of Sex Research,* Prometheus Books, 1979; (with James Brundage) *Sexual Practice and the Medieval Church,* Prometheus Books, 1982.

With wife, Bonnie Bullough: *What Color Are Your Germs?* (pamphlet), Committee to End Discrimination in Chicago Medical Institutions, 1954; *The Emergence of Modern Nursing,* Macmillan, 1964, 2nd edition, 1969; (editors) *Issues in Nursing,* Springer Publishing Co., 1966; (editors) *New Directions for Nurses,* Springer Publishing Co., 1971; *Poverty, Ethnic Identity, and Health Care,* Appleton-Century-Crofts, 1972; (editors) *The Subordinate Sex: A History of Attitudes toward Women,* University of Illinois Press, 1973; *Sin, Sickness, and Sanity: A History of Sexual Attitudes,* New American Library, 1977; (editors) *Expanding Horizons in Nursing,* Springer Publishing Co., 1977; *Prostitution: An Illustrated Social History,* Crown, 1978; *The Care of the Sick,* Neale Watson, 1978; *Nursing: An Historical Bibliography,* Garland Publishing, 1981; *Health Care for the Other Americans,* Appleton-Century-Crofts, 1982; (editors with Mary Claire Soukup) *Nursing Issues and Strategies for the Eighties,* Springer Publishing Co., 1983.

Contributor of chapters to about twenty-five books. Contributor of articles to *Nation, Saturday Review, Progressive, New Leader, Free Inquiry,* and numerous other publications.

WORK IN PROGRESS: With wife, Bonnie Bullough, *History and Politics of Nursing,* for Appleton-Century-Crofts; books on achievement, sex research, and biohistory.

*   *   *

BUNING, Sietze
See WIERSMA, Stanley M(arvin)

*   *   *

BURBY, Raymond J(oseph) III   1942-

PERSONAL: Born June 26, 1942, in Los Angeles, Calif.; son of Raymond Joseph (a sales manager) and Barbara (in community service; maiden name, Del Pino) Burby; married Nannie Harbour (an editorial assistant), December 27, 1965; children: Barbara Derina, Raymond Joseph IV. *Education:* Attended University of Washington, 1960-62; George Washington University, A.B., 1964; University of North Carolina at Chapel Hill, M.R.P., 1966, Ph.D., 1969. *Home:* 315 Granville Rd., Chapel Hill, N.C. 27514. *Office:* Center for Urban and Regional Studies, University of North Carolina at Chapel Hill, 067A Hickerson House, Chapel Hill, N.C. 27514.

CAREER: University of North Carolina at Chapel Hill, assistant professor of planning, 1969-72, research associate of Center for Urban and Regional Studies, 1968-72, senior research associate, 1972-76, assistant director of research, 1976—. Chairman of Chapel Hill Parks and Recreation Commission, 1981-82; president of North Carolina Land Use Congress, 1982-83; member of Governor's Solar Law Task Force, 1982-83. Consultant to U.S. Air Force, 1976, and Wayne Community College, 1977-78. *Member:* American Planning Association (president of North Carolina chapter, 1982-83), Regional Science Association, Southern Regional Science Association (member of executive council, 1982—).

WRITINGS: Lake-Oriented Subdivisions in North Carolina: Decision Factors and Policy Implications for Urban Growth Patterns—Developer Decisions (monograph), Center for Urban and Regional Studies, University of North Carolina at Chapel Hill, 1967; *Planning and Politics: Toward a Model of Planning-Related Policy Outputs in American Local Government,* Center for Urban and Regional Studies, University of North Carolina at Chapel Hill, 1968.

(Editor with Shirley F. Weiss and Edward J. Kaiser) *New Community Development: Planning Process, Implementation, and Emerging Social Concerns,* two volumes, Center for Urban and Regional Studies, University of North Carolina at Chapel Hill, 1971; (with Wiess and Thomas G. Donnelly) *Multipurpose Reservoirs and Urban Development,* Center for Urban and Regional Studies, University of North Carolina at Chapel Hill, 1972; (with Weiss and Robert B. Zehner) *Evaluation of New Communities: Selected Preliminary Findings,* Center for Urban and Regional Studies, University of North Carolina at Chapel Hill, 1974; (contributor) Daniel H. Carson, editor, *Man-Environment Interactions: Evaluations and Applications,* Halsted, 1975; (with Weiss) *New Communities, U.S.A.,* Lexington Books, 1976; *Recreation and Leisure in New Communities,* Ballinger, 1976; (with N. H. Loewenthal) *Health Care in New Communities,* Ballinger, 1976; (with Donnelly) *Schools in New Communities,* Ballinger, 1977; (contributor with Weiss and others) Roland L. Warren, editor, *New Perspectives on the American Community,* 3rd edition, Rand McNally, 1977; (editor with A. Fleming Bell) *Energy and the Community,* Ballinger, 1978.

(Contributor with Kaiser and Mary Ellen Marsden) Joel Werth, editor, *Energy in the Cities Symposium,* American Planning Association, 1980; (editor with Marsden) *Energy and Housing: Consumer and Builder Perspectives,* Oelgeschlager, Gunn & Hain, 1980; (contributor with Kaiser and Marsden) Robert W. Burchell and David Listokin, editors, *Energy and Land Use,* Center for Urban Policy Research, Rutgers University, 1982; (with Kaiser, Todd L. Miller, and David H. Moreau) *Drinking Water Supplies: Protection through Watershed Management,* Ann Arbor Science Publishers, 1983.

Editor of "New Community Research Series," Ballinger, 1976. Contributor to *Proceedings of the 1979 National Conference on Technology for Energy Conservation;* contributor to professional journals. Manuscript reviewer for *Journal of Leisure Research,* 1964—; *Journal of the American Planning Association,* book review editor, 1979-83, co-editor, 1983—.

WORK IN PROGRESS: Energy and Human Settlement; Second Home Communities and Recreational Land Development; Development and Utilization of Flood Plains.

*   *   *

BURGESS, Robert F(orrest)   1927-

PERSONAL: Born November 30, 1927, in Grand Rapids, Mich.; son of Forrest L. (a watchmaker) and D. LaVerne (Brown) Burgess; married Julia A. Scarborough, June 22, 1956. *Education:* Attended Grand Rapids Junior College, 1945-46, and University of Neuchatel, Neuchatel, Switzerland, 1948-49; Michigan State University, A.B., 1951. *Residence:* Chattahoochee, Fla. *Agent:* Paul R. Reynolds, Inc., 12 East 41st St., New York, N.Y. 10017.

CAREER: Former railroad section hand, truck driver, seaman on the Great Lakes, lineman, laboratory technician, maintenance man painting high tension wire towers, member of surveying crew, and magazine editor; free-lance writer and photographer for national outdoor magazines here and abroad, 1953—. *Military service:* U.S. Army, 1946-48; served with Ski Troops in Italy.

WRITINGS: International Diner's Phrase Book, Museum Press, 1965; *The Mystery of Mound Key* (juvenile), World Publishing, 1966; *A Time for Tigers* (juvenile), World Publishing, 1968; *Where Condors Fly* (teen book), World Publishing, 1969.

The Sharks (nonfiction), Doubleday, 1970; *Sinkings, Salvages and Shipwrecks* (nonfiction), American Heritage Press, 1970; *Life in a Coral Reef,* Crowell-Collier, 1972; *Ships beneath the Sea: A History of Subs and Submersibles* (nonfiction), McGraw, 1975; *The Cave Divers* (nonfiction), Dodd, 1976; *Gold, Galleons and Archaeology,* Bobbs-Merrill, 1976; *They Found Treasures,* Dodd, 1977; (with William R. Royal) *The Man Who Rode Sharks,* Dodd, 1978.

Man: 12,000 Years Under the Sea, A History of Underwater Archaeology, Dodd, 1980; *Secret Languages of the Sea,* Dodd, 1981; *Florida's Golden Galleons: The Search for the 1715 Spanish Treasure Fleet,* Florida Classics Library, 1982.

WORK IN PROGRESS: A book with the working title of *The Trailerable Sailboat Handbook.*

SIDELIGHTS: Robert F. Burgess has written a number of books examining underwater exploration and adventure. Many reviewers note that these books appeal to both the beginning student and to the person reading for adventure and entertainment. For instance, in a review of *The Cave Divers* published in the *Christian Science Monitor,* W. W. Smith remarks that "Burgess has written a highly readable and exciting book about the adventures of brave divers who ventured into sunken caves. . . . This book has enough technical background to interest the diver and spelunker, yet enough suspense and fresh insight to interest the casual reader." And of the same book L. E. Logan comments in *Library Journal,* "This book is highly recommended reading for all scuba divers, cave divers, and anyone else who has an interest in the development of underwater paleontology and archaeology."

Another one of Burgess's books, *Man: 12,000 Years Under the Sea, A History of Underwater Archaeology,* is described by a reviewer for *Choice* as "the best popular account yet of underwater archaeology." And J. D. Suleiman writes in *Library Journal* that this book is "written in language that is understandable to the layperson [and] is particularly valuable for the amount of detail given on new technologies and methods."

AVOCATIONAL INTERESTS: Skindiving, sailing, underwater photography, and shark fishing.

BIOGRAPHICAL/CRITICAL SOURCES: Library Journal, October 1, 1975, April 15, 1977, July, 1980; *Christian Science Monitor,* June 9, 1976; *School Library Journal,* December, 1977; *Choice,* February, 1981; *Science Books and Films,* September/October, 1981.

*   *   *

BURKHALTER, Barton R.   1938-

PERSONAL: Born July 22, 1938, in Toledo, Ohio; son of Robert Richard and Mary Louise (Barton) Burkhalter; married Eliana Godoy; children: Eric Nasset, Genevieve Divin. *Education:* University of Michigan, B.S.E. in Engineering Mathematics and B.S.E. in Engineering Mechanics, 1961, M.S.E., 1962, Ph.D., 1964. *Office:* Zana International, Inc., 2605 Camino del Rio S., San Diego, Calif.

CAREER: University of Michigan, Ann Arbor, instructor in department of industrial engineering, 1961-62, lecturer on management sciences in department of library science, 1964-69, lecturer on public management in department of political science, 1968-69, adjunct professor of urban and regional planning, 1971-77; currently affiliated with Zana International, San Diego, Calif. Community Systems Foundation (non-profit research and engineering firm), co-founder and member, 1963—, president, 1963-73; CSF Ltd. (consulting firm to health care industry), chairman, 1973-75, senior scientist, 1975-76. Research professor of family and community medicine, University of Arizona, 1979—. Consultant to President's Commission on Income Maintenance, 1968, and nutrition planning committee, U.S. Agency for International Development, 1973—; member of steering committee, Health, Education and Welfare Conference on the Cost of Health Care Facilities, 1968. Chairman, Summer Science Camp, 1967—.

MEMBER: American Association for the Advancement of Science, Operations Research Society of America, American Public Health Association, Hospital Management Society.

WRITINGS: (Editor) *Systems Analysis in a University Library,* Scarecrow, 1968; *Investigations of Rapidly-Changing Papago Tribal Health Programs,* Papago Tribe (Sells, Ariz.), 1979. Author of reports on management improvement for governmental units, public institutions, and trade conferences. Contributor to journals. Founder and editor, *Nutrition Planning,* 1976-80.

WORK IN PROGRESS: Value Issues in the Conduct of Science in American Indian Communities; Reliability of Health Care Quality Assessment Methods; Cost-Effectiveness of Lighting Systems.

*   *   *

BURKHOLZ, Herbert   1932-
(John Luckless, a joint pseudonym)

PERSONAL: Born December 9, 1932, in New York, N.Y.; son of Sidney and Eva (Margolin) Burkholz; married Yvonne Schwartz, December 9, 1948 (divorced, 1962); married Susan Blaine, November 1, 1962; children: (first marriage) Howard, Matthew. *Education:* New York University, A.B., 1950. *Agent:* J.C.A. Literary Agency, Inc., 242 West 27th St., New York, N.Y. 10001.

CAREER: Writer. Former insurance broker, editor, ski instructor, bartender, and book reviewer; College of William and Mary, Williamsburg, Va., visiting professor and writer-in-residence, 1975-76; Hofstra University, Hempstead, N.Y., lecturer, 1977-78. *Member:* P.E.N. International.

WRITINGS: Sister Bear (novel), Simon & Schuster, 1969; (with Clifford Irving) *Spy: History of Modern Espionage,* Macmillan, 1969; *The Spanish Soldier* (novel), Charterhouse, 1973; *Mulligan's Seed* (novel), Harcourt, 1975; (with Irving) *The Death Freak* (novel), Summit Books, 1978, published under joint pseudonym John Luckless, M. Joseph, 1979, published under real names, Sphere Books, 1979; (with Irving) *The Sleeping Spy* (novel), Atheneum, 1983; *The Snow Gods* (novel), Poseidon Books, 1984. Contributor of short stories to numerous magazines.

SIDELIGHTS: "[Herbert] Burkholz is a writer of considerable skill and more than considerable versatility," comments L. J. Davis in the *Washington Post Book World.* Known for his inventiveness and humor, the author chooses themes ranging from incest, in *Sister Bear,* to international intrigue in *The Sleeping Spy.*

Davis describes Burkholz's widely reviewed work *The Spanish Soldier* as an "extraordinarily ingenious, refreshingly intricate, and beautifully worked out" novel. The book's central character, Matthew Mendelsohn, lives two lives: that of a widowed ex-politician from New York who resides with his beautiful mistress on a Spanish island and that of the title's "Spanish soldier." The latter existence is purely one of imagination— a fantasy life where Mendelsohn is variously a Carlist soldier in the 1835 Spanish civil war, a member of the Abraham Lincoln Brigade in 1939, or an Israeli intelligence officer in the 1970s. Writes Davis, "Whatever [Mendelsohn's] identity of the moment, in the realms of both fantasy and reality, he is searching ceaselessly for the Unholy Grail, the battered pewter cup Judas drank from at the Last Supper." While "this may sound like a lot of romantic hokum . . . *The Spanish Soldier* is considerably more than that," Davis contends.

Sara Blackburn, however, notes in her *New York Times Book Review* article that she "had the eerie feeling . . . that the author is a writer of talent who, somehow lacking material, has settled for concerns considerably beneath either his skills or his real interests." Calling *The Spanish Soldier* "well-written," Blackburn nonetheless feels its central character is a shallow, decadent person, a fact that "seems to go unrecognized by the author, . . . [and that] just doesn't mesh with Burkholz's very apparent abilities at character, dimension, humor and setting." "Yet," maintains Davis, "even in its flaws

The Spanish Soldier is . . . an achievement of considerable proportions and much more than passing interest. It is a well-wrought novel boldly conceived and boldly executed, with a breadth and audacity of vision that is all too rare.''

AVOCATIONAL INTERESTS: Sailing and skin diving.

BIOGRAPHICAL/CRITICAL SOURCES: Times Literary Supplement, January 29, 1970; *New York Times Book Review,* January 28, 1973, February 13, 1983; *Washington Post Book World,* March 18, 1973.

* * *

BURNS, William A. 1909-

PERSONAL: Born October 7, 1909, in New York, N.Y.; son of William A. and Florence (Willis) Burns; married Adelaide Jordan, October 7, 1955. *Education:* Manhattan College, A.B., 1934; Columbia University, M.A., 1937, Ed.D., 1949. *Office:* Florence Museum, 558 Spruce St., Florence, S.C. 29501.

CAREER: Field director, Occupational Adjustment Study, 1939-40; American Museum of Natural History, New York, N.Y., 1940-62, associate curator of department of education and assistant chairman of department, 1945-51, assistant to director and membership secretary, 1951-62; Witte Museum, San Antonio, Tex., director, 1961-70; San Diego Natural History Museum, San Diego, Calif., executive director and secretary of board, 1970-73; Florence Museum, Florence, S.C., director, 1975—. Chairman, San Deigo County Cultural Heritage Commission; member of several historical and cultural committees, including Florence Historical Preservation Committee, New York Mayor's Golden Jubilee Commission, and Creative Educational Resources Council. Trustee, Metropolitan Educational Television Association, New York, 1957-62, American Red Cross, and other organizations. Consultant or member of advisory boards of other museums in the United States, including Gay Head Museum and Nimitz Museum. *Military service:* U.S. Army, 1943-46; served in Southwest Pacific and Australia; became first lieutenant.

MEMBER: International Council of Museums, American Association of Museums (member of council, 1950-53), Science Directors Association, Association of Science Museum Directors (president), National Speleological Society, Rocks and Minerals Society, Chamber Music Society, Mexican-American Art Council, Mountains-Plains Museum Conference, Texas Museums Conference, Texas Art Museums Conference (member of survey commission), Florence Heritage Foundation, San Antonio Conservation Society, San Antonio Art Guild, Trinity University Library Council, Kappa Delta Pi, Gamma Theta Upsilon, Rotary Club, Jazz Society Club, Torch Club, Alamo Club, Press Club, Argyle Club, Shell Club, Manuscript Club. *Awards, honors:* Paul Harris fellow, Rotary Club, 1981.

WRITINGS: A World Full of Homes, McGraw, 1954; *Horses and Their Ancestors,* McGraw, 1955; *Man and His Tools,* McGraw, 1956; *Exploring for Fun: A Young Explorer's Handbook,* Dutton, 1961; (with Frank Debenham) *Illustrated World Geography,* McGraw, 1960; (editor and contributor) *Natural History of the Southwest,* F. Watts, 1960; (with Edwin Harris Colbert) *Digging for Dinosaurs,* new edition, Childrens Press, 1967; *Your Future in Museums,* Rosen Press, 1967; *Noise and Man,* J. Murray, 1968, Lippincott, 1969; *Teenagers and Museums,* Rosen, 1973; *Enjoying the Arts: Museums* (young adult), Rosen, 1974.

Former editor, ''Man and Nature Publications,'' American Museum of Natural History. Contributor to *Museum Registration Methods;* co-editor of *Illustrated World Geography.* Conductor of column ''Witte Museum Question Box,'' carried in San Antonio newspapers. Contributor to museum periodicals and to *Field and Stream, Air Force Journal,* and *Rotarian.* Editor, *Natural History of the Southwest* and *Witte Museum Quarterly,* 1963-70.

WORK IN PROGRESS: A novel.

SIDELIGHTS: William A. Burns is competent in Dutch, French, Spanish, German, Afrikaans, and Flemish; he knows a little Japanese and Russian. *Avocational interests:* Anthropology, world travel, fishing, breeding fancy guppies, making antique furniture; collecting brass, copper, and pewter clocks; writing detective stories for friends (not for publication).†

* * *

BUROW, Daniel R(obert) 1931-

PERSONAL: Born April 26, 1931, in Kodai Kanal, India; son of Ralph Julius (a minister) and N. Ruth (Everett) Burow; married Marcia Caverly, May 26, 1958; children: Mark, Paul, Elizabeth. *Education:* Concordia Collegiate Institute, Bronxville, N.Y., A.A., 1951; Concordia Theological Seminary, St. Louis, Mo., B.A., 1953, B.D., 1969; St. Louis University, graduate study, 1971. *Home:* 3123 East 51st St., Minneapolis, Minn. 55417. *Office:* 16515 Luther Way, Eden Prairie, Minn. 55344.

CAREER: Minister of Lutheran Church; pastor of churches in Orlando, Fla., 1957-64, and Augusta, Ga., 1964-67; Lutheran Church, Missouri Synod, Board of Parish Education, St. Louis, Mo., editor, 1967-75; American Lutheran Church, Division for Life and Mission in the Congregation, Minneapolis, Minn., director for children's ministries, 1975-77; Augsburg Publishing House, Minneapolis, editor of curricular materials, 1977-82; Immanuel Lutheran Church, Eden Prairie, Minn., minister, 1982—.

WRITINGS—Published by Concordia, except as indicated: *I Meet God through the Strangest People,* 1970; (with Estelle Griffen) *Joyfully Alive,* 1971; (with Dorothy Hoyer) *Alive Together,* 1971; (with Marian Baden) *Always Alive,* 1972; *Maker of Heros,* Lutheran Television, 1973; *Sound of the Bugle* (juvenile novel), 1973; *Plattertales* (juvenile short story collection, with phonograph record), 1974; (with Carol Greene) *The Little Christian's Songbook,* 1975; *'Til Morning Breaks,* Lutheran Television, 1975; *A Peek at the Promise,* 1975; *Hail to Our Promised King,* 1975; *A Peek inside God's Heart,* 1976; *The Spirit Moves,* 1976; *When Jesus Was Born,* Augsburg, 1983.

Also author of religious education filmstrips and kindergarten story books. Contributor to magazines. Editor, *My Devotions,* 1967-69, *Concordia Pulpit,* 1977 and 1979; assistant editor, *His People,* 1967-69.

WORK IN PROGRESS: A book, tentatively entitled *Persons in Discipleship,* for Augsburg.

SIDELIGHTS: I Meet God through the Strangest People has been translated into German and published in Germany.

* * *

BURT, John J. 1934-

PERSONAL: Born September 3, 1934, in Enfield, N.C.; son of Johnny Joseph (a farmer) and Pearl (Nevellie) Burt; married

Ann Gillett (a teacher), December 28, 1956; children: Emelia, Keith, Joe. *Education:* Duke University, A.B., 1956; University of North Carolina, M.Ed., 1957; University of Oregon, M.S., 1960, Ed.D., 1962. *Office:* Department of Health Education, PERH Bldg., Valley Dr. Suite 2387, University of Maryland, College Park, Md. 20742.

CAREER: Former member of faculty at Temple University, Philadelphia, Pa., and professor at University of Toledo, Toledo, Ohio; currently professor of health education and chairman of department at University of Maryland, College Park. *Member:* Association for the Advancement of Health Education (president).

WRITINGS: (With Benjamin Miller) *Good Health,* Saunders, 1966; (with Linda A. Brower) *Education for Sexuality: Concepts and Programs for Teaching,* illustrated by James C. Brower, Saunders, 1970, 3rd edition (with Linda A. Brower Meeks), 1984, abridged and revised edition published as *Toward a Healthy Sexuality,* 1973; *Personal Health Behavior in Today's Society,* Saunders, 1972; (with Meeks and Shron Pottebaum) *Toward a Healthy Life Style,* Wadsworth, 1980.

SIDELIGHTS: Education for Sexuality has been translated into French, Spanish, Italian and Japanese.

*   *   *

BURTCHAELL, James Tunstead   1934-

PERSONAL: Born March 31, 1934, in Portland, Ore.; son of James Tunstead, Jr. (an executive) and Marion Margaret (Murphy) Burtchaell. *Education:* University of Notre Dame, A.B., 1956; Pontifical Gregorian University, Rome, Italy, S.T.B., 1958; Catholic University of America, S.T.L., 1960; Ecole Biblique et Archeologique Francaise de Jerusalem, graduate study, 1961-63; Pontifical Biblical Commission, Rome, S.S.B., 1961, S.S.L., 1964; Cambridge University, Ph.D., 1966. *Office:* Department of Theology, University of Notre Dame, Notre Dame, Ind. 46556.

CAREER: Ordained Roman Catholic priest of Congregation of Holy Cross (C.S.C.), 1960; University of Notre Dame, Notre Dame, Ind., assistant professor, 1966-69, associate professor, 1969-75, professor of theology, 1975—, chairman of department, 1968-70, provost, fellow, and trustee, 1970-77. S. A. Cook Bye Fellow at Gonville and Caius College, Cambridge University, 1965-66. Member of advisory council, Danforth Foundation, 1971-74; member of commission on higher education, North Central Accrediting Association, 1972-75; member of overseers' committee to visit Harvard University Divinity School, 1975-81. Member of board of visitors, Vanderbilt University Divinity School, 1971-81; member of board of directors, East Asia History of Science, Inc., 1980—.

MEMBER: American Academy of Religion (member of executive committee, 1969-74; vice-president, 1969; president, 1970), Catholic Theological Society of America, Society of Biblical Literature, Catholic Biblical Association, Society for Values in Higher Education, Council on the Study of Religion (chairman of constituting committee, 1969-70), American Council of Learned Societies, American Association of University Professors (member of executive committee, 1967-70), Association of Catholic Colleges and Universities, Association of American Colleges, North Central Association of Colleges and Secondary Schools, Phi Beta Kappa, Phi Delta Kappa. *Awards, honors:* D.H.L. from St. Mary's College of California, 1974, and Rose-Hulman Institute of Technology, 1976.

WRITINGS: Catholic Theories of Biblical Inspiration since 1810, Cambridge University Press, 1969; *Philemon's Problem: The Daily Dilemma of the Christian,* Life in Christ, 1973; (editor) *Marriage among Christians: A Curious Tradition,* Ave Maria Press, 1977; *Abortion Parley,* Andrews & McMeel, 1980; (editor) *Rachel Weeping, and Other Essays on Abortion,* Andrews & McMccl, 1982.

Contributor: *Cambridge Sermons in Christian Unity,* Oldbourne, 1966; Andrew Bauer, editor, *The Debate on Birth Control,* Hawthorne, 1969; Paul T. Jersild and Dale A. Johnson, editors, *Moral Issues and Christian Response,* Holt, 1971; Peter Foote, John Hill, Laurence Kelly, John McCudden, and Theodore Stone, editors, *Church: Vatican II's Dogmatic Constitution on the Church,* Holt, 1969; Willis W. Bartlett, editor, *Evolving Religious Careers,* Center for Applied Research in the Apostolate, 1970; Claude Welch, editor, *Religion in the Undergraduate Curriculum: An Analysis and Interpretation,* Association of American Colleges, 1972; Ninia Smart, John Clayton, Steven Katz, and Patrick Sherry, editors, *Religious Thought in the Nineteenth Century,* Cambridge University Press, 1981.

Also author of tape cassette, "Bread and Salt: A Cassette Catechism," 1978. Contributor to *Ann Landers Encyclopedia A to Z,* 1978. Also contributor of book reviews and articles to *Commonweal, America, Christian Century,* and numerous other journals.

WORK IN PROGRESS: "Studies on the history of office in the earliest Christian Church."

SIDELIGHTS: Writing on James Tunstead Burtchaell's *Rachel Weeping, and Other Essays on Abortion,* Lisa Mitchell notes in the *Los Angeles Times Book Review* that this book "is a searing, impeccable documentation—awesome in detail and scope, stunning in intelligence and stylistic grace. Burtchaell exposes misinformation from abortion advocates, presents firsthand accounts of abortion-related experiences by women and men, draws analogies between abortion and slavery, abortion and infanticide."

BIOGRAPHICAL/CRITICAL SOURCES: Los Angeles Times Book Review, September 19, 1982.

*   *   *

BURTT, George   1914-

PERSONAL: Born May 18, 1914, in Vancouver, British Columbia, Canada; son of George Keyes (an accountant) and Josephine (a teacher; maiden name, Woolson) Burtt; married Dorothy Smith, September 23, 1937 (divorced, 1950); married Marian Zametkin (a scientific research worker and teacher), June 3, 1950 (divorced, 1976); married Marian G. Simpson (a psychologist and author), January 29, 1977; children: (first marriage) Gregory, Marcia (Mrs. Richard Challacombe), Jonathan, Portia (Mrs. Robert Jennings); (second marriage) Jennifer Ellen (Mme. Jacques Lauruol). *Education:* Attended public schools. *Politics:* Republican. *Home:* 935 Talcott St., Sedro-Woolley, Wash. 98284.

CAREER: Worked as ad layout man for newspapers in Washington, D.C., 1935-41; The Ad Shop, Harrisonburg, Va., owner, 1939-41; employed as art director, account executive, creative director at advertising agencies in Philadelphia, Washington, and Baltimore, 1944-48; Western Stove Co., Culver City, Calif., advertising manager, 1948-52; George Burtt Advertising, Hollywood, Calif., owner, 1952-59; Enyart & Rose Advertising

Agency, Los Angeles, Calif., creative director, 1959-69; Vector Community Church, Hollywood, pastor, 1967-78. Owner, Creative Service Office, 1969-78. *Member:* International Mensa (area vice-chairman, 1966-67), Hollywood Radio and Television Society (honorary life member; managing director, 1952-59), Authors Guild, Authors League of America.

WRITINGS: Vector Handbook, Adams Press, 1967; *Putting Yourself Across with the Art of Graphic Persuasion,* Parker Publishing, 1972; *Psychographics in Personal Growth* (monograph), Vector Counseling Institute, 1972; *Stop Crying at Your Own Movies: How to Solve Personal Problems and Open Your Life to Its Full Potential Using the Vector Method,* Nelson Hall, 1975; *The Explicated Tao,* Vector Counseling Institute, 1978; *The Barter Way to Beat Inflation,* Everest House, 1980.

SIDELIGHTS: George Burtt is the creator of a "system of viewing human nature which makes it possible by conversation or self-examination to eliminate unwanted behavior patterns. This is a highly effective counseling modality; but more important, as a life-growth adjunct it helps keep from creating new problems the equivalent of the old ones."

*   *   *

BUTLER, Robert Albert 1934-

PERSONAL: Born July 1, 1934, in Thomaston, Ga.; son of Reginald Alton (a textile engineer) and Martha (a musician; maiden name, Smith) Butler; married Alicia Suarez (a Spanish teacher), July 18, 1964; children: Martha Rose, Anthony Alfredo. *Education:* University of North Carolina, Chapel Hill, A.B., 1958, M.A.T., 1966; Duke University, M.A.T., 1961; Columbia Pacific University, Ph.D., 1980. *Religion:* Methodist. *Home:* 211 Edgewood Dr., Louisburg, N.C. 27549. *Office:* Department of Sociology, Louisburg College, Louisburg, N.C. 27549.

CAREER: Louisburg College, Louisburg, N.C., professor of sociology, 1962—. *Military service:* U.S.Army, 1954-56. *Member:* North Carolina Council for Albert Schweitzer International Prizes, Kappa Delta Pi, Beta Phi Gamma, Alpha Tau Omega.

WRITINGS: Sociology: An Individualized Course, Westinghouse Learning Corp., 1971, revised edition, 1975; *Handbook of Practical Writing,* McGraw, 1978; *Sociology: A Basic Course,* Cambridge Book Co., 1979.

SIDELIGHTS: Robert Albert Butler has traveled extensively in Europe and South America. *Avocational Interests:* Classical music, sports, senior citizens, travel.

*   *   *

BUTLER, William E(lliott II) 1939-

PERSONAL: Born October 20, 1939, in Minneapolis, Minn.; son of William Elliott (a public accountant) and Maxine (Elmberg) Butler; married Darlene Mae Johnson (an economist), September 2, 1961; children: William Elliott III, Bradley Newman. *Education:* Hibbing State Junior College (now Hibbing Community College), A.A., 1959; American University, B.A., 1961; Johns Hopkins University, M.A., 1963, Ph.D., 1970; Harvard University, J.D., 1966. *Religion:* Protestant. *Home:* 9 Lyndale Ave., London NW2 2QD, England. *Office:* Faculty of Laws, University College, University of London, 4-8 Endsleigh Gardens, London WC1, England.

CAREER: Member of Bar of U.S. District Court and U.S. Court of Appeals for District of Columbia; member of Bar of

U.S. Supreme Court. Johns Hopkins University, Washington Center of Foreign Policy Research, Washington, D.C., research assistant in international relations, 1966-68; Catholic University of America, Washington, D.C., lecturer in international law, 1967-68; Harvard University, Cambridge, Mass., research associate in law and associate of Russian Research Center, 1968-70; University of London, University College, London, England, reader, 1970-76, professor of comparative law, 1976—, dean of Faculty of Laws, 1977-79, director of Centre for the Study of Socialist Legal Systems, 1982—. Guest senior scholar, Department of International Law, Faculty of Laws, Moscow State University, U.S.-U.S.S.R. cultural exchange agreement, 1971-72, 1981; guest scholar, Institute of State and Law, U.S.S.R. Academy of Sciences, Anglo-Soviet cultural exchange agreement, 1976, 1980, 1982, and Mongolian Academy of Sciences, 1979. Member, first British lawyers' delegation to China, 1979-80; vice-chairman, Council of the School of Slavonic and East European Studies, University of London, 1982—.

MEMBER: International Law Association, International Academy of Comparative Law, American Society of International Law, American Bar Association (committee member on Soviet law), American Association for the Advancement of Slavic Studies, American Foreign Law Association, British Institute of International and Comparative Law, National Association for Soviet and East European Studies, Society of Public Teachers of Law, United Kingdom National Committee for Comparative Law, Bookplate Society (secretary, 1978—), Private Libraries Association (secretary), Bibliographical Society (secretary), Anglo-Mongolian Society (secretary), Cosmos Club. *Awards, honors:* LL.D., University of London, 1979.

WRITINGS: (Editor and translator) *Russian Family Law,* Hazen, 1965; (editor with Vaclav Mostecky, and contributor) *Soviet Legal Bibliography,* Harvard Law School Library, 1965; (editor) *Writings on Soviet Law and Soviet International Law,* Harvard Law School Library, 1966; (editor and translator) *Customs Code of the USSR,* Hazen, 1966; *The Law of Soviet Territorial Waters: A Case Study of Maritime Legislation and Practice,* Praeger, 1967; (with David W. Wainhouse, Bernhard G. Bechhoefer, Anne P. Simons, and Arnold Wolfers) *Alternative Methods for Dealing with Breaches of Arms Control Agreements,* five volumes, U.S. Arms Control and Disarmament Agency, 1968.

(Co-editor and translator) *The Merchant Shipping Code of the U.S.S.R. (1968),* Johns Hopkins Press, 1970; *The Soviet Union and the Law of the Sea,* Johns Hopkins Press, 1971; (editor) *Microfiche Project on Russian-Soviet Law,* Inter Documentation Co. (Leiden), 1972; (editor and author of introduction) P. P. Shafirov, *A Discourse Concerning the Just Causes of the War between Sweden and Russia: 1700-1721,* Oceana, 1973; (editor with Donald D. Barry and George Ginsburgs, and contributor) *Contemporary Soviet Law: Essays in Honor of John N. Hazard,* Martinus Nijhoff, 1974.

(Translator and author of introduction) G. I. Tunkin, *Theory of International Law,* Harvard University Press, 1975; (compiler and editor) *Russian and Soviet Law: An Annotated Catalogue of Reference Works, Legislation, Court Reports, Serials, and Monographs on Russian and Soviet Law (Including International Law),* Inter Documentation Co., 1976; (with J. N. Hazard and P. B. Maggs) *The Soviet Legal System,* 3rd edition, Oceana, 1977; (editor and contributor) *Russian Law: Historical and Political Perspectives,* A. W. Sijthoff, 1977; *Northeast Arctic Passage,* A. W. Sijthoff, 1978; (editor and translator)

A Source Book on Socialist International Organizations, A. W. Sijthoff, 1978; (compiler and translator) *The Soviet Legal System: Legislation and Documentation,* Oceana, 1978; (editor, compiler, and translator) *Collected Legislation of the U.S.S.R. and Constituent Union Republics,* seven volumes, Oceana, 1979—.

(Editor and contributor) *International Law in Comparative Perspective,* A. W. Sijthoff, 1980; (editor and compiler) *Soviet Commercial and Maritime Arbitration,* Oceana, 1980; (editor) *Law in the Mongolian People's Republic: Mongolian Law on Microfiche,* Inter Documentation Co., 1980; *The Mongolian Legal System,* Martinus Nijhoff, 1982; *Commercial, Business and Trade Laws: The Soviet Union and Mongolia,* Oceana, 1982; (editor and author of introduction) *Anglo-Polish Legal Essays,* Transnational, 1982; (editor) *Microfiche Project on Public International Law,* Inter Documentation Co., 1982; (editor and contributor) *The Legal System on the Chinese Soviet Republic, 1931-1934,* Transnational, 1983; (editor) *Mongolian-English-Russian Dictionary of Legal Terms and Concepts,* Martinus Nijhoff, 1983. Also author of *Contemporary Soviet Bookplate Design,* 1982.

Contributor: L. M. Alexander, editor, *The Law of the Sea: The United Nations and Ocean Management,* University of Rhode Island, 1971; M. Cherif Bassiouni and V. P. Nanda, editors, *A Treatise on International Criminal Law,* C. C Thomas, 1973; M. MacGwire, editor, *Soviet Naval Developments: Context and Capability,* Praeger, 1973; F.J.M. Feldbrugge, editor, *Encyclopedia of Soviet Law,* A. W. Sijthoff, 1973; M. A. Kaplan, editor, *Great Issues of International Politics: The International System and National Policy,* 2nd edition (Butler was not associated with 1st edition), Aldine, 1974; G. T. Yates and J. H. Young, editors, *Limits to National Jurisdiction over the Sea,* University of Virginia Press, 1974; J. N. Moore, editor, *Law and Civil War in the Modern World,* Johns Hopkins Press, 1974.

Feldbrugge, editor, *Codification in the Communist World,* A. W. Sijthoff, 1975; J. Nowak, editor, *Environmental Law: International and Comparative Aspects,* Oceana, 1976; *Pinner's World Unfair Competition Law,* A. W. Sijthoff, 1978-79; A. G. Cross, editor, *Anglo-Russian Relations in the Eighteenth Century,* O.R.P., 1979; D. Barry and others, editors, *Soviet Law after Stalin,* A. W. Sijthoff, 1979; W. B. Simons, editor, *The Soviet Codes of Law,* A. W. Sijthoff, 1980; Feldbrugge and Simons, editors, *Perspectives on Soviet Law for the 1980s,* Martinus Nijhoff, 1982; T. A. Clingan, editor, *Law of the Sea: State Practice in Zones of Special Jurisdiction,* University of Hawaii, 1982; *Hommage a Rene Dekkers,* Bruylant, 1982.

Editor and translator, *Vignettes of Bookplate Collecting in Leningrad,* 1981, and *The Graphic Work of A. I. Kalishnikov,* 1982; also editor, *Collected Works on Socialist Legal Systems on Microfiche,* 1981. Editor, "Legal Systems of the World" series, Butterworth & Co. Contributor of over three hundred articles, translations, and reviews to journals, including *International Legal Materials* and *Soviet Statutes and Decisions.*

Harvard International Law Journal, editor, 1965-66, member of editorial advisory committee, 1983—; *Soviet Statutes and Decisions,* editor, 1969-76, member of editorial board, 1977—; editor, *Bookplate Journal,* 1983—; contributing editor, *International Journal of Politics,* 1969—; member of editorial board, *Earth Law,* 1975-77; editorial advisor, *International Legal Materials,* 1982—.

WORK IN PROGRESS: Russian international legal history; the systematization of Soviet law; selected documents on socialist

international organizations; Russian and Soviet legal history; socialist legal systems; international and comparative law; history of Russian bookplates.

SIDELIGHTS: William E. Butler told *CA* that he "has travelled in the Soviet Union on more than twenty occasions since 1960 and was the first Western jurist ever to undertake legal research in Mongolia during 1979."

* * *

BUTTERICK, George F. 1942-

PERSONAL: Born October 7, 1942, in Yonkers, N.Y.; son of George W. (a factory worker) and Kathleen (a clerk; maiden name, Byrnes) Butterick; married Colette Marie Hetzel (a painter), June 19, 1965; children: George Adam, Aaron. *Education:* Manhattan College, B.A. (with honors), 1964; State University of New York at Buffalo, Ph.D., 1970. *Home:* 194 North St., Willimantic, Conn. 06226. *Office:* Literary Archives, University of Connecticut Library, Storrs, Conn. 06268.

CAREER: Wilson College, Chambersburg, Pa., instructor, 1968-69, assistant professor of English, 1969-70; University of Connecticut, Storrs, assistant professor, 1970-72, lecturer in English, 1972—, curator of Literary Manuscripts, 1972—.

WRITINGS: The Norse (poems), Institute of Further Studies, 1973; *Reading Genesis by the Light of a Comet* (poems), Ziesing Brothers, 1976; *A Guide to the Maximus Poems of Charles Olson,* University of California Press, 1978, revised edition, 1980; *Rune Power* (poems), Tin Man, 1983; *Editing the Maximus Poems,* University of Connecticut Library, in press.

Editor: (With Albert Glover) *A Bibliography of Works by Charles Olson,* Phoenix Book Shop, 1967; Charles Olson, *Poetry and Truth: The Beloit Lectures and Poems,* Four Seasons Foundation, 1970; Olson, *Additional Prose,* Four Seasons Foundation, 1974; (with Charles Boer) Olson, *The Maximus Poems, Volume Three,* Grossman, 1975; Olson, *The Post Office,* Grey Fox Press, 1975; Vincent Ferrini, *Selected Poems,* University of Connecticut Library, 1976; Olson, *The Fiery Hunt and Other Plays,* Four Seasons Foundation, 1977; Olson, *Muthologos: Collected Lectures and Interviews,* Four Seasons Foundation, 1978-79; *Charles Olson and Robert Creeley: The Complete Correspondence,* five volumes, Black Sparrow Press, 1980; (with Donald Allen) *The Postmoderns,* Grove Press, 1982; Olson, *The Maximus Poems,* University of California Press, 1983.

Contributor of essays and reviews to numerous periodicals, including *American Literature, Chicago Review, Credences, Iowa Review, New England Quarterly,* and *Sagetrieb.*

Co-editor of *Audit,* 1966-68; editor of *Olson: The Journal of the Charles Olson Archives,* 1974-78; contributing editor of *Magazine of Further Studies,* 1968-70, and *Athanor,* 1970-75.

WORK IN PROGRESS: Poems, including a collection called *The Three-Percent Stranger;* editing more writings of Charles Olson, including his collected papers.

AVOCATIONAL INTERESTS: Distance running.

BIOGRAPHICAL/CRITICAL SOURCES: Times Literary Supplement, December 14, 1979; *Los Angeles Times Book Review,* May 10, 1981, September 4, 1983.

* * *

BYE, Beryl (Joyce Rayment) 1926-

PERSONAL: Born August 4, 1926, in Maidavale, England;

daughter of Leonard and Olive (Stanbridge) Cotterell; married Denis Robert Bye (a civil service executive), August 9, 1945; children: Roger, Susan, Catherine, Andrew. *Education:* Wolsey Hall, Oxford, external study, 1967-68. *Religion:* Church of England. *Home:* The Old Coach House, Lye Lane, Cleeve Hill, Cheltenham, Gloucestershire, England.

CAREER: Free-lance writer, 1960—.

WRITINGS: Three's Company, Scripture Union, 1961; *Wharf Street,* Kingfisher Books, 1962; *Prayers at Breakfast,* Lutterworth, 1964; *A Christian's Guide to Teaching Our Children the Christian Faith,* Hodder & Stoughton, 1965, Moody, 1966; *Please God,* Church Pastoral Aid Society, 1966; *About God,* Church Pastoral Aid Society, 1967; *Nobody's Pony,* Lutterworth, 1967; *Looking into Life,* Lutterworth, 1967; *Jesus Said: Parables and Prayers for Children,* Church Pastoral Aid Society, 1968; *Pony for Sale,* Lutterworth, 1969; *Learning from Life,* Lutterworth, 1969; *Jesus at Work,* Church Pastoral Aid Society, 1969.

Start the Day Well, Lutterworth, 1970; *Beryl Bye's Prayers for All Seasons for Women's Meetings,* Lutterworth, 1971; *People Like Us,* Church Pastoral Aid Society, 1971; *More People Like Us,* Church Pastoral Aid Society, 1972; *To Be Continued,* Church Pastoral Aid Society, 1972; *Belle's Bridle,* Lutterworth, 1973; *Following Jesus,* Church Pastoral Aid Society, 1974; *Family Prayers,* Scripture Union, 1975; *What about Lifestyle?,* Paternoster Press, 1977; *Time for Jesus,* Kings Way Publications, 1980.

SIDELIGHTS: Beryl Bye told *CA:* "I write from a compulsion to share my views—not always religious ones, and a desire to make people laugh at themselves, and see above and beyond the present materialistic age." *Avocational interests:* Riding, walking, swimming, conservation, donkey driving, and goatkeeping.

*   *   *

BYRD, C. L.
    See ROSENKRANTZ, Linda

C

CABLE, Mary 1920-

PERSONAL: Born January 24, 1920, in Cleveland, Ohio; daughter of Robert Winthrop (an engineer) and Elizabeth (a painter; maiden name, Southwick) Pratt; married Arthur Goodrich Cable, May 25, 1949; children: Cassandra Southwick. *Education:* Barnard College, A.B., 1941; also studied at Cas'Alta School, Florence, Italy, 1939. *Home:* 1810 Calle de Sebastian (J2), Santa Fe, N.M. 87501. *Agent:* Harriet Wasserman Literary Agency, 230 East 48th St., New York, N.Y. 10017.

CAREER: Member of editorial staff of *New Yorker,* New York City, 1944-49, *Harper's Bazaar,* New York City, 1949-51, and American Heritage Publishing Co., Inc., New York City, 1963-65. *Awards, honors:* Grants from the National Endowment for the Arts, 1977, and the National Endowment for the Humanities, 1978; Louisiana Library Association Award, 1980, for *Lost New Orleans.*

WRITINGS: Dream Castles, Viking, 1966; (with the editors of *American Heritage) American Manners and Morals,* American Heritage Press, 1969; *The Avenue of the Presidents,* Houghton, 1969; *Black Odyssey: The Case of the Slave Ship Amistad,* Viking, 1971; (with the editors of Newsweek Books) *El Escorial,* Newsweek, 1971; *The Little Darlings: A History of Childrearing in America,* Scribner, 1975; *Lost New Orleans,* Houghton, 1980; *Avery's Knot,* Putnam, 1981.

Contributor of short stories and articles to *New Yorker, Horizon, Harper's Bazaar, Atlantic, American Heritage, Vogue,* and other periodicals.

SIDELIGHTS: Mary Cable's fact-based novel, *Avery's Knot,* re-creates the case of Sarah Maria Cornell, a twenty-nine-year-old millworker who, on a December morning in 1832, was found beaten and hanging from a stake in a Rhode Island field. Her accused murderer was the Reverend Mr. Ephraim Avery, a Methodist minister who apparently killed her to hide the fact that she was pregnant with his child. When Avery was brought to trial in Bristol, R.I., according to Edith McNulty's review of the book in the *Washington Post,* "he denied the crime in a few words and then, with eloquent sanctimony, put the dead girl on trial. She was a known fornicator, he said, and afflicted with a foul disease. The court absolved him."

As a profile of the treatment and the rights of women in nineteenth-century America, *Avery's Knot,* says McNulty, "brings

their condition into a sharp focus that has the impact of revelation. Sarah Cornell's life is a case history of what can happen to a woman in a society totally dominated by men. . . . A modern woman, accustomed to the comparative freedom of the 20th century, reads Sarah's story with some of the emotions blacks must feel when they read about slave days, and in addition recognizes the ancestors of ideas that are alive today as we debate abortion, ERA and other aspects of women's place in society. In bringing Sarah Cornell back to life, Mary Cable has awakened a troubling ghost." The reviewer concludes: "If Sarah has a message for us, it may be a warning never to allow one group of people to have total power over another group, and to guard against those who seek to blame victims in order to absolve the perpetrators of crime."

BIOGRAPHICAL/CRITICAL SOURCES: New York Times Book Review, August 24, 1969, January 16, 1982; *New Yorker,* July 28, 1975, November 24, 1980; *Washington Post,* November 6, 1981.

* * *

CACHIA, Pierre J. E. 1921-

PERSONAL: Surname is pronounced Ka-*Kee*-ah; born April 30, 1921, in Faiyum, Egypt; son of Francois (a bank official) and Anna (Axler) Cachia; married Phyllis Barbara Oyston, March 21, 1953; children: Susan Margaret, Philip Greville, Helen Frances. *Education:* American University at Cairo, B.A. (with distinction), 1942; University of Edinburgh, Ph.D., 1951. *Politics:* "Floating voter." *Religion:* Methodist. *Home:* 456 Riverside Dr., New York, N.Y. 10027. *Office:* 608 Kent Hall, Columbia University, New York, N.Y. 10027.

CAREER: American University at Cairo, Cairo, Egypt, teacher of English, 1945-48; University of Edinburgh, Edinburgh, Scotland, assistant lecturer, 1950-51, lecturer, 1951-65, senior lecturer, 1965-69, reader in department of Arabic, 1969-75; Columbia University, New York, N.Y., professor of Arabic, 1975—. *Military service:* British 8th Army, 1942-45; became sergeant; received Africa Star. *Member:* American Oriental Society, Middle East Studies Association, American Association of Teachers of Arabic, Union of Maltese Writers (corresponding member).

WRITINGS: Taha Husayn: His Place in the Egyptian Literary Renaissance, Luzac, 1956; (editor) Eutychius of Alexandria,

Kitab al-Burhan (title means "The Book of the Demonstration"), Corpus Scriptorum Christianorum Orientalium (Louvain), Volume I, 1960, Volume II, 1961; (with W. Montgomery Watt) *Islamic Spain,* Edinburgh University Press, 1965, published as *History of Islamic Spain,* Anchor Books, 1967.

The Monitor: A Dictionary of Arabic Grammatical Terms, Longman, 1973; (contributor) B. Parekh, editor, *Colour, Culture and Consciousness,* Allen & Unwin, 1974; (contributor) R. C. Ostle, editor, *Studies in Modern Arabic Literature,* Aris & Phillips, 1975; (contributor) Roger Allen, editor, *In the Eye of the Beholder,* Bibliotheca Islamica, 1978; (editor with A. T. Welch and contributor) *Islam: Past Influence and Present Challenge,* Edinburgh University Press, 1979.

Contributor to *Encyclopaedia Britannica, Encyclopedia Americana, Dictionary of Oriental Literature, Encyclopaedia of Islam,* and *Chambers' Encyclopedia.* Contributor of articles to *Maltese Folklore Review, Journal of the American Oriental Society, University of Toronto Quarterly, Journal of Semitic Studies,* and other journals. Co-founder and joint editor, *Journal of Arabic Literature.*

WORK IN PROGRESS: Modern Egyptian Narrative Ballads, comprising a number of ballads transcribed and translated, and an introductory study; *The Arch-Rhetorician,* a handbook of Arabic tropes.

SIDELIGHTS: Pierre J. E. Cachia told *CA* that as a child he "spoke French, it being the only language [my] Maltese father and Russian mother had in common." He adds that he has tried to "break away from Orientalist tradition by treating Arabic literature as *literature,* and not as a repository of philological material."

BIOGRAPHICAL/CRITICAL SOURCES: L-Orizzont, March 26, 1968.

*   *   *

CADELL, (Violet) Elizabeth 1903-
(Harriet Ainsworth)

PERSONAL: Born November 10, 1903, in Calcutta, India; daughter of Frederick Reginald (a colonial officer) and Elizabeth (Lynch) Vandyke; married Henry Dunlop Raymond Mallock Cadell (a banker), 1928 (deceased); children: one son, one daughter. *Politics:* Conservative. *Religion:* Church of England. *Residence:* Portugal.

CAREER: Novelist.

WRITINGS—All novels: *My Dear Aunt Flora,* R. Hale, 1946; *Last Straw for Harriet,* Morrow, 1947 (published in England as *Fishy, Said the Admiral,* R. Hale, 1948); *River Lodge,* R. Hale, 1948; *Gay Pursuit,* Morrow, 1948, published as *The Marrying Kind,* Morrow, 1980; *Iris in Winter,* Morrow, 1949.

Brimstone in the Garden, Morrow, 1950; *Sun in the Morning* (for young readers; Catholic Children's Book Club selection), Morrow, 1950, abridged edition, University of London Press, 1963; *The Greenwood Shady,* Hodder & Stoughton, 1951; *Enter Mrs. Belchamber,* Morrow, 1951 (published in England as *The Frenchman and the Lady,* Hodder & Stoughton, 1952); *Men and Angels,* Hodder & Stoughton, 1952; *Crystal Clear,* Morrow, 1953 (published in England as *Journey's Eve,* Hodder & Stoughton, 1953); *Spring Green,* Hodder & Stoughton, 1953, reprinted, White Lion, 1973; *The Cuckoo in Spring,* Morrow, 1954, reprinted, Corgi, 1973; *Money to Burn,* Hodder & Stoughton, 1954, Morrow, 1955, reprinted, White Lion, 1973;

Around the Rugged Rock, Morrow, 1954 (published in England as *The Gentlemen Go By,* Hodder & Stoughton, 1964).

The Lark Shall Sing, Morrow, 1955; (under pseudonym Harriet Ainsworth) *Consider the Lilies,* Hodder & Stoughton, 1955, published under name Elizabeth Cadell, White Lion, 1974; *The Blue Sky of Spring,* Hodder & Stoughton, 1956, reprinted, Coronet, 1973; *I Love a Lass,* Morrow, 1956; *Bridal Array,* Hodder & Stoughton, 1957, reprinted, Corgi, 1973; *Shadows on the Water,* Morrow, 1958; *The Green Empress,* Hodder & Stoughton, 1958, reprinted, Corgi, 1973; *Sugar Candy Cottage,* Hodder & Stoughton, 1958; *Alice, Where Art Thou?,* Hodder & Stoughton, 1959.

The Yellow Brick Road, Morrow, 1960, reprinted, White Lion, 1973; *Honey for Tea,* Hodder & Stoughton, 1961, Morrow, 1962; *Six Impossible Things,* Morrow, 1961; *The Toy Sword,* Morrow, 1962 (published in England as *Language of the Heart,* Hodder & Stoughton, 1962); *Letter to My Love,* Hodder & Stoughton, 1963; *Mixed Marriage: The Diary of a Portuguese Bride,* Hodder & Stoughton, 1963; (under pseudonym Harriet Ainsworth) *Death among Friends,* Hodder & Stoughton, 1964; *Come Be My Guest,* Morrow, 1964 (published in England as *Be My Guest,* Hodder & Stoughton, 1964).

Canary Yellow, Morrow, 1965; *The Corner Shop,* Hodder & Stoughton, 1966, Morrow, 1967; *The Fox from His Lair,* Morrow, 1966; *The Stratton Story,* Hodder & Stoughton, 1967; *Mrs. Westerby Changes Course,* Morrow, 1968; *The Golden Collar,* Morrow, 1969.

The Friendly Air, Hodder & Stoughton, 1970, Morrow, 1971; *The Past Tense of Love,* Morrow, 1970; *Home for the Wedding,* Morrow, 1971; *Royal Summons,* Morrow, 1973; *Deck with Flowers,* Morrow, 1974; *The Haymaker,* Hodder & Stoughton, 1974.

The Fledgling, Morrow, 1975; *Game in Diamonds,* Morrow, 1976; *Parson's House,* Morrow, 1977; *The Round Dozen,* Morrow, 1978; *River Lodge,* R. Hale, 1978; *Return Match,* Morrow, 1979; *Family Gathering,* R. Hale, 1979; *Any Two Can Play,* Morrow, 1981; *A Lion in the Way,* Morrow, 1982.

SIDELIGHTS: Raised in India, Elizabeth Cadell was educated in England and has traveled often to Ireland. As a widow she discovered her talent for writing and has since produced a prodigious number of light, romantic novels.†

*   *   *

CAIRNS, David 1904-

PERSONAL: Born June 11, 1904, in Ayton, Berwickshire, Scotland; son of David S. (a minister) and Helen Wilson Cairns; married Rosemary Russell, 1947; children: Elisabeth Mary, John Alexander. *Education:* Balliol College, Oxford, B.A., 1928, M.A., 1938; attended University of Aberdeen, 1928-31, University of Zurich, 1932-33, and University of Montpelier, 1933-34. *Home:* 29 Viewfield Gardens, Aberdeen AB1 7XN, Scotland.

CAREER: Ordained minister of Church of Scotland, 1935; Bridge of Allan, Scotland, minister, 1935-40; Oxford University, Oxford, England, secretary of Student Christian Movement, 1945-47; Christ's College, Aberdeen, Scotland, professor of practical theology, 1948-72, professor emeritus, 1972—. Kerr Lecturer, University of Glasgow, 1948; visiting professor, Columbia Seminary, Decatur, Ga., 1961; Cunningham Lecturer, University of Edinburgh, 1965; reader in systematic theology, University of Aberdeen, 1965-72. Member of Faith and

Order Commission, World Council of Churches, 1958-68. *Military service:* British Army, 1940-45; chaplain. *Awards, honors:* D.D., University of Edinburgh, 1953.

WRITINGS: The Image of God in Man, Philosophical Library, 1953, revised and enlarged edition, Fontana Press, 1973; *A Gospel without Myth? Bultmann's Challenge to the Preacher,* S.C.M. Press, 1960; *In Remembrance of Me: Aspects of the Lord's Supper,* Bles, 1967; *God up There?: A Study in Divine Transcendence,* Westminster Press, 1968; (editor) *Worship Now: A Collection of Services and Prayers for Public Worship,* St. Andrew Press, 1972; (compiler and editor) D. S. Cairns, *A System of Christian Doctrine,* St. Andrew Press, 1979.

Translator from the German: Paul Althaus, *The So-Called Kerygma and the Historical Jesus,* Oliver & Boyd, 1959; Joachim Jeremias, *Infant Baptism in the First Four Centuries,* S.C.M. Press, 1960; Heinrich Emil Brunner, *God and Man in 1936,* S.C.M. Press, 1963; Brunner, *Christian Dogmatics,* Volume III, Lutterworth, 1963; (with A. W. Loos) Brunner, *Truth as Encounter,* S.C.M. Press, 1964; Helmut Gollwitzer, *Rich Christian and Poor Lazarus,* Macmillan, 1970; Gollwitzer, *The Christian Faith and the Marxist Criticism of Religion,* St. Andrew Press, 1975; Gollwitzer, *The Way to Life,* T & T Clark, 1982; Gollwitzer, *Introduction to Protestant Theology,* Westminster Press, 1982; Annemarie Ohler, *Categories in the Old Testament,* Clark, 1983. Contributor to *Scottish Journal of Theology, Religious Studies,* and to other periodicals.

WORK IN PROGRESS: A continuation of theological work and translation.

AVOCATIONAL INTERESTS: Watercolor painting.

*   *   *

CALDER, Nigel (David Ritchie) 1931-

PERSONAL: Born December 2, 1931, in London, England; son of (Peter) Ritchie (Lord Ritchie-Calder; a writer) and Mabel (McKail) Calder; married Elisabeth Palmer (a research assistant), May 22, 1954; children: Sarah, Penelope, Simon, Jonathan, Katharine. *Education:* Attended Merchant Taylors' School; Sidney Sussex College, Cambridge, B.A., 1954, M.A., 1957. *Home and office:* 8 The Chase, Furnace Green, Crawley, Sussex, England. *Agent:* Elisabeth Calder, 8 The Chase, Furnace Green, Crawley, Sussex, England.

CAREER: Writer. Mullard Research Laboratories, Redhill, Surrey, England, research physicist, 1954-56; *New Scientist,* London, England, staff writer, 1956-60, science editor, 1960-62, editor, 1962-66. *Military service:* British Army, 1950-51; became lieutenant. *Member:* Association of British Science writers (chairman, 1962-64), Cruising Association (London; vice-president). *Awards, honors:* UNESCO Kalinga Prize for the popularization of science, 1972.

WRITINGS: Electricity Grows Up, Phoenix House, 1958; *Robots,* Roy, 1958; *Radio Astronomy,* Roy, 1959, revised edition, Phoenix House, 1964; (editor) *The World in 1984,* Penguin, 1965; *The Environment Game,* Secker & Warburg, 1967, published as *Eden Was No Garden: An Inquiry into the Environment of Man,* Holt, 1967; (editor) *Unless Peace Comes: A Scientific Forecast of New Weapons,* Viking, 1968; *Technopolis: Social Control of the Uses of Science,* MacGibbon & Kee, 1969, Simon & Schuster, 1970; *Violent Universe: An Eyewitness Account of the New Astronomy,* BBC Publications, 1969, Viking, 1970.

Living Tomorrow, Penguin, 1970; *The Mind of Man,* Viking, 1970; *Restless Earth,* Viking, 1972; *The Life Game,* BBC Publications, 1973, Viking, 1974; (editor) *Nature in the Round,* Weidenfeld & Nicolson, 1973, Viking, 1974; *The Weather Machine: How Our Weather Works and Why It Is Changing,* BBC Publications, 1974, Viking, 1975; *The Human Conspiracy,* Viking, 1976; *The Key to the Universe,* Viking, 1977; *Spaceships of the Mind,* Viking, 1978; *Einstein's Universe,* Viking, 1979; *Nuclear Nightmares: An Investigation into Possible Wars,* BBC Publications, 1979, Viking, 1980; *The Comet Is Coming!: The Feverish Legacy of Mr. Halley,* BBC Publications, 1980, Viking, 1981; *Time-Scale,* Viking, 1983; *1984 and After,* Viking, 1983.

Television documentaries; produced by British Broadcasting Corp., some in conjunction with Public Broadcasting System: "Russia: Beneath the Sputniks," 1967; "The World in a Box," 1968; "The Violent Universe," 1969; "The Mind of Man," 1970; "The Restless Earth," 1972; "The Life Game," 1973; "The Weather Machine," 1974; "The Human Conspiracy," 1975; "The Key to the Universe," 1977; "The Whole Universe Show," 1977; "Spaceships of the Mind," 1978; "Einstein's Universe," 1979; "Nuclear Nightmares," 1979; "The Comet Is Coming!," 1981.

Science correspondent, *New Statesman,* 1959-62, 1966-71. Contributor to science journals in England and the United States.

WORK IN PROGRESS: Books, for Viking.

SIDELIGHTS: Nigel Calder has gained a reputation as a writer of popular works on scientific topics. Calder's books, often published as companion pieces to his television documentaries, cover a wide range of subject matter, including the continental drift, the human mind, and recent discoveries in subatomic physics. In several of his books he speculates on the future and on humanity's place in a changing world.

In *Eden Was No Garden: An Inquiry into the Environment of Man,* for example, Calder examines the problem of providing food for a rapidly growing earth population. He proposes that large-scale factory food production, not traditional agricultural methods, is the best way to supply food in the future and discusses how new technology would aid the preservation of the environment. R. C. Cowen, in a *Christian Science Monitor* review, says, "Perhaps the book will appeal as a review of today's scientific and technical developments as they bear on man's basic problems." *Library Journal* critic Harold Bloomquist praises Calder's offering of a "full-blown Utopian vision of what the world might be; . . . truthfully, it looks pretty good."

Calder's interest in the future is not limited to earthly matters. His book *Spaceships of the Mind* explores the possibilities of outer space colonization. He includes a study of physicist Gerard O'Neill, who is working on a space superstructure capable of housing its own atmosphere, environment, and populace. "Calder's book is on the borderline between science and fantasy, but no matter," writes Martin Gardner in the *New York Review of Books,* "Calder knows his science, and between discussions of outrageous plans there are solid facts about the universe, and informed speculation about the awesome possibilities that lie ahead as population pressures and energy needs propel us into what O'Neill calls the High Frontier."

Two of Calder's books, *Unless Peace Comes: A Scientific Forecast of New Weapons* and *Nuclear Nightmares: An Investigation into Possible Wars,* focus on what he perceives to be an immediate threat to the future of humanity. *Unless Peace*

Comes, which Calder edited, contains the thoughts of fifteen scientists from around the world who predict the warfare that may result unless nations can resolve their conflicts peacefully. *Nation* critic John Gliedman finds the book "rather conservative in its approach. . . . No attention is given to the future technology of guerilla war and counter insurgency. And yet, even with these important omissions, the book illuminates perhaps the greatest of the many ironies of the arms race: that it often feeds upon breakthroughs in civilian fields." In a *New York Times Book Review* article, D. S. Greenberg says that the scientists' contributions "are clearly intended to shock and appall. The intention is achieved, not through raucous prophecy and admonition, but rather through a fairly detached, even-toned recitation of technically attainable possibilities for conducting wars of the next decade, and, equally important, the political tensions that may be created simply because of the existence of unfamiliar and potentially devastating means of warfare."

Calder's concern with atomic warfare is continued in *Nuclear Nightmares.* In this book, the author lists four circumstances—"nightmares"—that might trigger nuclear war: worldwide nuclear arms proliferation, imperfections of command systems, escalation of a conflict in Europe, and the fear of one superpower that the other is about to attempt a disabling first strike. "Calder's particular and enviable talent is for turning abstruse technicalities into everyday language, without damage to the subtlety of the specialists' language," comments John Keegan in *New Republic.* "He demonstrates it once again here and, after reading the book, no layman will be able to take refuge in the comforting belief that he doesn't understand the issues." Keegan continues: "Proliferation is, in the author's view, a problem which the superpowers still could solve between themselves, by forbidding nuclear testing of any sort and making life impossible for states that broke the ban. . . . Inevitably his conclusion has a utopian ring. But what appeal against the apparently inexorable tightening of the nuclear collar around all of our throats has not? At least critics will not be able to accuse him of mere hand-wringing. He knows the facts almost as well as those whose daily round it is to deal with them. He has concrete suggestions to make for setting limits on a trend which no sane person can wish to see continue."

Published during the centenary year of the birth of Albert Einstein, Calder's *Einstein's Universe* interprets the physicist's theories for the non-specialist reader. However, some critics find the work still too specialized for its intended audience. For instance, *Chicago Tribune Book World* reviewer Guy Murchie notes that while the author "explains all these [theories], and without using academic or technological jargon, . . . not many of us will be able to comprehend how 'all physical processes' are 'governed by the speed of light' or will accept without challenge that 'incest among the gravitons produces the curvature of space.'" *Village Voice* critic Eliot Fremont-Smith comments on Calder's simplified approach to Einstein's theory of relativity: "The trouble is that at crucial points it isn't simple at all; it's horrendously complex, convoluted, and contradictory. This makes one fret—not so much over the difficulties of relativity as over the accumulating evidence that, as a layman, one isn't measuring up." According to Edmund Fuller's review in the *Wall Street Journal,* however, the author "is a singularly lucid writer with a gift for the memorable metaphors which, for the general reader, must take the place of the physicist's equations."

Among Calder's other books dealing with natural science are *The Weather Machine: How Our Weather Works and Why It Is Changing* and *The Comet Is Coming!: The Feverish Legacy of Mr. Halley.* In *The Weather Machine,* the author discusses how changes in climate can affect everything from literature (a particularly wet, gloomy summer influenced Mary Shelley's writing of the gothic classic *Frankenstein*) to politics (an overly hot summer in 1788 shriveled the grain crops in France, causing bread riots in 1789 and, ultimately, the French Revolution). But, more alarmingly, Calder reports, recent climactic studies indicate a new ice age is imminent—which is "ominous for the human species," as the author puts it. "So, unless [scientists] do something fast," concludes Christopher Lehmann-Haupt in the *New York Times,* "it looks like falling temperatures, severe draught, and woolly mammoths. Thanks to his elegantly diagramed book with its chilly forecast, Mr. Calder has me worrying about the weather for a change."

The phenomenon of Halley's comet is explored in Calder's 1981 book, *The Comet Is Coming!* The comet, which appears once every seventy-six years, has historically induced suicide, human sacrifice, and predictions of Armageddon. "In addition to the army of soothsayers and astrologers who heretofore have interpreted it for us," writes Michael Collins in the *Washington Post Book World,* "Halley is preceded by a first-rate PR man. At T minus five years, Nigel Calder . . . has put together a potpourri of fact and fancy, a fascinating compendium of all we would ask about comets, if we only knew the right questions." Both Collins and *New Republic* reviewer Katha Pollitt note that Calder himself takes a dim view of the fervor caused by the comet; Pollitt remarks that "it's not [the comet's] fault that human beings are superstitious and prone to paranoia," and she praises Calder's "wealth of fascinating comet lore."

AVOCATIONAL INTERESTS: Sailing.

BIOGRAPHICAL/CRITICAL SOURCES: Library Journal, June 1, 1967; *Christian Science Monitor,* June 22, 1967; *New York Times Book Review,* July 28, 1968, March 11, 1979, November 23, 1980; *Nation,* October 28, 1968; *Scientific American,* May, 1971, July, 1972; *Natural History,* August/September, 1972; Nigel Calder, *The Weather Machine: How Our Weather Works and Why It Is Changing,* BBC Publications, 1974, Viking, 1975; *New York Times,* April 17, 1975, March 12, 1979; *Saturday Review,* June 14, 1975; *Listener,* April 8, 1976; *New York Review of Books,* September 29, 1977, November 23, 1978; *New Republic,* January 7, 1978, September 27, 1980, September 23, 1981; Calder, *Einstein's Universe,* Viking, 1979; *Chicago Tribune Book World,* March 11, 1979; *Village Voice,* March 19, 1979; *Wall Street Journal,* March 19, 1979; *Washington Post Book World,* March 25, 1979, May 10, 1981; Calder, *The Comet Is Coming!: The Feverish Legacy of Mr. Halley,* BBC Publications, 1980, Viking, 1981; *New Statesman,* February 29, 1980; *Los Angeles Times Book Review,* September 21, 1980; *Atlantic,* June, 1981.

—*Sketch by Susan Salter*

*   *   *

CALDER, Robert
   See MUNDIS, Jerrold

*   *   *

CALIN, William (Compaine) 1936-

PERSONAL: Surname is pronounced *Kale*-in; born April 4, 1936, in Newington, Conn.; son of Jack and Nettie (Compaine) Calin; married Francoise Geffroy, January 5, 1971. *Education:* Studied in France, 1955-56; Yale University, B.A., 1957, Ph.D.,

1960. *Home:* 2849 Central Blvd., Eugene, Ore. 97403. *Office:* Department of Romance Languages, University of Oregon, Eugene, Ore.

CAREER: Dartmouth College, Hanover, N.H., instructor, 1960-62, assistant professor of French, 1962-63; Stanford University, Stanford, Calif., assistant professor, 1964-65, associate professor, 1965-70, professor of French, 1970-73; University of Oregon, Eugene, professor of French, 1973—, chairman of department of Romance languages, 1976-78. *Member:* Modern Language Association of America, Societe Rencesvals. *Awards, honors:* Guggenheim fellowship and American Council of Learned Societies grants, both 1963-64; Gilbert Chinard First Literary Prize, 1981; Fulbright award, 1982; Canada Federation in the Humanities grant, 1982.

WRITINGS: The Old French Epic of Revolt, Droz (Geneva), 1962; (editor with Michel Benamou) *Aux Portes du Poeme,* Macmillan, 1964; *The Epic Quest: Studies in Four Old French Chansons de Geste,* Johns Hopkins Press, 1966; (editor) *La Chanson de Roland,* Appleton, 1968.

(Editor) *A Poet at the Fountain: Essays on the Narrative Verse of Guillaume de Machaut,* University Press of Kentucky, 1974; *Crown, Cross and "Fleur-de-lis": An Essay on Pierre Le Moyne's Baroque Epic "Saint Louis,"* Stanford University Press, 1977; *A Muse for Heroes: Nine Centuries of the Epic in France,* University of Toronto Press, 1983. Contributor to journals.

WORK IN PROGRESS: A book on the theory of French poetry; a book on the French literary tradition and medieval English literature.

*   *   *

CALVERT, Peter (Anthony Richard) 1936-

PERSONAL: Born November 19, 1936, in Islandmagee, Northern Ireland; son of Raymond and Irene (Earls) Calvert; married Diana Elizabeth Farrow, September 4, 1962; children: Simon, Katharine. *Education:* Queen's College, Cambridge, B.A., 1960, M.A. and Ph.D., 1964; University of Michigan, A.M., 1961. *Home:* 8 Pewsey Pl., Southampton SO1 2RX, England. *Office:* Department of Politics, University of Southampton, Southampton SO9 5NH, England.

CAREER: Brookings Institution, Washington, D.C., visiting scholar, 1963; University of Southampton, Southampton, England, lecturer, 1964-71, senior lecturer, 1971-74, reader in politics, 1974—. Visiting lecturer in history, University of California, Santa Barbara, summer, 1966; research fellow, Charles Warren Center for Studies in American History, Harvard University, 1969-70. Member, Cambridge City Council, 1962-64. *Military service:* British Army, 1955-57; served in Malaya.

MEMBER: Political Studies Association, British Association for American Studies, Society for Latin American Studies, Royal Historical Society (fellow). *Awards, honors:* Fulbright travel grant, 1960-61; Avery and Jule Hopwood Award in drama, University of Michigan, summer, 1961; William Waldorf Astor Foundation grant for research in Mexico, 1966; American Studies fellowship, American Council of Learned Societies, 1969-70.

WRITINGS: The Mexican Revolution, 1910-1914: The Diplomacy of Anglo-American Conflict, Cambridge University Press, 1968; *Latin America: Internal Conflict and International Peace,* St. Martin's, 1969; *Revolution,* Praeger, 1970; *A Study of Rev-*

olution, Clarendon Press, 1970; *Mexico,* Praeger, 1973; *The Mexicans: How They Live and Work,* Praeger, 1975; *Emiliano Zapata,* Hispanic Council, 1979; *The Concept of Class: An Historical Introduction,* Hutchinson, 1982; *The Falklands Crisis: The Rights and Wrongs,* St. Martin's, 1982; *Politics, Power and Revolution: A Comparative Analysis of Contemporary Government,* St. Martin's, 1983; *Boundary Disputes in Latin America,* Institute for the Study of Conflict, 1983.

WORK IN PROGRESS: A book on revolution and international politics; a study of Guatemala.

SIDELIGHTS: Peter Calvert's *The Concept of Class: An Historical Introduction* is "a welcome guide to the changing uses of 'class' as a social and political concept," according to Geoffrey Sampson in the *Times Literary Supplement.* He continues: "Originally the word referred to legally established divisions of Roman society. . . . The word *classe* was first applied to contemporary society by French economists of the physiocratic school in the 1750s, and Calvert sees this usage as a by-product of the eighteenth-century interest in the classification of biological species. At that time the plant and animal kingdoms were still perceived in terms of a Great Chain of Being stretching linearly from lower to higher. . . . This, perhaps, is why we inherit a notion of 'class' that encourages men to envy those they see as located 'higher' on the social ladder, rather than to feel thankful that the progressive division of labour has offered them a more attractive range of life-options than were available to their forefathers." Calvert concludes the book, says Sampson, "by urging that 'class' is a prime candidate for verbal euthanasia."

BIOGRAPHICAL/CRITICAL SOURCES: Times Literary Supplement, March 4, 1983, May 13, 1983.

*   *   *

CAMERON, Donald
See BRYANS, Robert Harbinson

*   *   *

CAMPBELL, David A(itken) 1927-

PERSONAL: Born August 14, 1927, in Kirkcudbrightshire, Scotland; son of Walter (a station master) and Isabella Ferguson (Aitken) Campbell; married Cynthia Dutton, August 23, 1956; children: Alison, Helen, Fiona. *Education:* University of Glasgow, M.A. (with first class honors), 1948; Jesus College, Oxford, Classical Moderations (with first class honors), 1951, B.A., 1953, M.A., 1967. *Politics:* Left-wing. *Religion:* Episcopal. *Office:* Department of Classics, University of Victoria, Victoria, British Columbia, Canada V8W 2Y2.

CAREER: University of Bristol, Bristol, England, assistant lecturer, 1953-58, lecturer, 1958-68, senior lecturer, 1968-71; University of Victoria, Victoria, British Columbia, professor of classics, 1971—. Visiting assistant professor, University of Toronto, 1959-60; visiting professor, University of Texas, 1969-70. External examiner, University of London, 1968, and University of Sheffield, 1968. *Military service:* Royal Air Force, pilot officer, 1948-49. *Member:* Hellenic Society, American Philological Association, Joint Association of Classical Teachers, Classical Association, Classical Association of Canada.

WRITINGS: (Editor) *More Essays in Greek History and Literature,* Basil Blackwell, 1962; (editor) *Greek Lyric Poetry: A Selection of Early Greek Lyric, Elegiac and Iambic Poetry,* Macmillan (London), 1967, St. Martin's, 1968; *Greek Lyric,*

Volume I, Harvard University Press, 1982; *The Golden Lyre: The Themes of the Greek Lyric Poets,* Duckworth, 1983. Contributor to classical journals.

WORK IN PROGRESS: Further work in Greek lyric poetry.

AVOCATIONAL INTERESTS: Travel, tennis, squash, walking.

BIOGRAPHICAL/CRITICAL SOURCES: Times Literary Supplement, June 10, 1983.

* * *

CAMPBELL, Peter (Walter) 1926-

PERSONAL: Born June 17, 1926, in Poole, Dorsetshire, England; son of Walter Howard (a clerk) and Lillian (Locke) Campbell. *Education:* New College, Oxford, B.A., 1947, M.A., 1951; Nuffield College, Oxford, research student, 1947-49. *Office:* University of Reading, Whiteknights Park, Reading RG6 2AA, England.

CAREER: University of Manchester, Manchester, England, assistant lecturer, 1949-52, lecturer in government, 1952-60; University of Reading, Reading, England, professor of political economy, 1960-64, professor of politics, 1964—. Visiting lecturer, Victoria University of Wellington, 1954. Vice-chairman of Reading and District Council for Social Service, 1965-71; member of board of Social Sciences Council for National Academic Awards, 1969-78; member of social sciences subcommittee, University Grants Committee, 1973-78; member of academic advisory council, University College, Buckingham, England. *Member:* Institute of Electoral Research (chairman, 1959-65), Political Studies Association (secretary, 1955-58), British Association for American Studies, Hansard Society (councilor, 1962-77).

WRITINGS: (Editor) Walter Theimer, *Encyclopaedia of World Politics,* Faber, 1950; *French Electoral Systems and Elections,* Faber, 1958, 2nd edition, 1965; (with Brian Chapman) *Constitution of the Fifth Republic,* Basil Blackwell, 1958; *Homosexuality in Britain: A Conservative Perspective,* Conservative Group for Homosexual Equality, 1983. Contributor to political science journals. Editor, *Political Studies,* 1963-69.

WORK IN PROGRESS: Research on the state and higher education in Britain since 1962; political writing on sexual law reform.

SIDELIGHTS: Peter Campbell told *CA:* "Having spent a good deal of time in the period 1968-83 as a member of British government advisory and executive bodies concerned with higher education and research, I am now engaged in research on the state and higher education in Britain. I am also writing on a very different theme: the need to reform the law so that homosexuals are treated as the ordinary people they are instead of being treated as second-class citizens subjected to discriminatory laws and practices which violate their human rights."

* * *

CAMPOLO, Anthony, Jr. 1935-

PERSONAL: Born February 25, 1935, in Philadelphia, Pa.; son of Anthony (a radio repairman) and Mary (Piccirelli) Campolo; married Margaret Davidson, June 7, 1958; children: Lisa Davidson, Bart Anthony. *Education:* Eastern Baptist College (now Eastern College), B.A., 1956; University of Pennsylvania, graduate study, 1958-59; Eastern Baptist Theological Seminary, Th.M. and B.D., both 1960; Temple University,

Ph.D., 1968. *Office:* Department of Sociology, Eastern College, St. Davids, Pa. 19087.

CAREER: Ordained Baptist minister, 1959. Pastor of Baptist Churches in Jacobstown and Chesterfield, N.J., 1957-61, and of American Baptist church in King of Prussia, Pa., 1961-65; Eastern College, St. Davids, Pa., associate professor, 1965-73, professor of sociology, 1973—, chairman of department, 1966—, chairman of youth ministries, 1982—. Visiting associate professor at University of Pennsylvania, 1966-75; visiting lecturer at Eastern Baptist Theological Seminary, 1968-73. Executive director of Youth Guidance of Southeastern Pennsylvania. Staff member of WCAU-Television; host of television programs; has appeared on "Good Morning America." Democratic candidate for U.S. Congress, 1976. *Member:* American Baptist Sociological Association, Evangelical Association for the Promotion of Education (founder and president).

WRITINGS: A Denomination Looks at Itself, Judson, 1971; *The Success Fantasy,* Victor Books, 1982; *A Reasonable Faith: Responding to Secularism,* Word Books, 1983; *The Power Delusion,* Victor Books, 1983; *Ideas for Social Action,* Youth Specialities, 1983. Contributor to periodicals, including *Watchman-Examiner, Foundations,* and *Observer.*

WORK IN PROGRESS: Intellectuals Christians Must Take Seriously, for Word Books.

SIDELIGHTS: "The most important aspect of my ministry is the challenging of young people to participate in missionary work for Jesus Christ," Anthony Campolo told *CA.* "Much of this is done by encouraging their participation in the projects of the Evangelical Association for the Promotion of Education, which operates out of my offices at Eastern College. Many Eastern students are directly involved in missions in Third World countries and in the city of Philadelphia. Other volunteers are recruited when I travel to churches, and to other college and seminary campuses across the country."

* * *

CANARY, Robert H(ughes) 1939-

PERSONAL: Born February 1, 1939, in Providence, R.I.; son of Richard Lee (a teacher) and Marjorie (Hughes) Canary; married Margaret Anne Cook (a teacher), June 12, 1961; children: Richard Douglas, Linda Anne. *Education:* Denison University, B.A., 1960; University of Chicago, M.A., 1962, Ph.D., 1963. *Politics:* Democrat. *Religion:* Protestant. *Home:* 420 Carlton Dr., Racine, Wis. 53402. *Office:* University of Wisconsin—Parkside, Box 2000, Kenosha, Wis. 53141.

CAREER: San Diego State College (now University), San Diego, Calif., assistant professor of English, 1963-66; Grinnell College, Grinnell, Iowa, assistant professor of English, 1966-68; University of Hawaii, Honolulu, associate professor of English, 1968-70; University of Wisconsin—Parkside, Kenosha, associate professor, 1970-74, professor of English, 1974—, chairman of Humanities Division, 1976-79, 1982—. Visiting summer professor at Hofstra University, 1967, and University of Michigan, 1968. Songwriter; compositions include "To Catch the Blues," 1967, and "To Anthony Hecht," 1968.

WRITINGS: William Dunlap, Twayne, 1970; *George Bancroft,* Twayne, 1974; *The Cabell Scene,* Revisionist Press, 1977; *William Faulkner: A Study Guide,* University of Wisconsin Extension, 1978; (co-editor) *The Writing of History,* University of Wisconsin, 1978; *Robert Graves,* Twayne, 1980; *T. S. Eliot:*

The Poet and the Critics, American Library Association, 1982. Contributor to literature journals. Co-editor, *Clio.*

WORK IN PROGRESS: A book of criticism, *The Pleasure of Cumulative Form;* a farce, *The Werewolf Effect.*

SIDELIGHTS: Robert Canary told *CA,* "I have spent much of my time in academic administration lately, and I find it almost as good as straightening up my study or looking for a better word processing program as a way of putting off the actual work of writing."

*   *   *

CANDELARIA, Nash   1928-

PERSONAL: Born May 7, 1928, in Los Angeles, Calif.; son of Ignacio N. (a railway mail clerk) and Flora (Rivera) Candelaria; married Doranne Godwin (a fashion designer), November 27, 1955; children: David, Alex. *Education:* University of California, Los Angeles, B.S., 1948. *Politics:* "I usually seem to vote for the person who doesn't get elected." *Religion:* "Non-church-going monotheistic and cultural Christian." *Home and office:* 1295 Wilson St., Palo Alto, Calif. 94301.

CAREER: Don Baxter, Inc. (pharmaceutical firm), Glendale, Calif., chemist, 1948-52; *Atomics International,* Downey, Calif., technical editor, 1953-54; Beckman Instruments, Fullerton, Calif., promotion supervisor, 1954-59; Northrup-Nortronics, Anaheim, Calif., in marketing communications, 1959-65; Hixon & Jorgensen Advertising, Los Angeles, Calif., account executive, 1965-67; Varian Associates, Inc. (in scientific instruments), Palo Alto, Calif., advertising manager, 1967-82; freelance writer, 1982—. *Military service:* U.S. Air Force, 1952-53; became second lieutenant. *Awards, honors: Not by the Sword* was a finalist in the Western Writers of America Spur Award competition, 1982, and received the Before Columbus Foundation American Book Award, 1983.

WRITINGS: Memories of the Alhambra (novel), Cibola Press, 1977; (contributor) Gary D. Keller and Francisco Jimenez, editors, *Hispanics in the United States: An Anthology of Creative Literature,* Bilingual Press, Volume I, 1980, Volume II, 1982; *Not by the Sword* (novel), Bilingual Press, 1982; (contributor) Nicholas Kanellos, editor, *A Decade of Hispanic Literature: An Anniversary Anthology,* Arte Publico, 1982; *Inheritance of Strangers* (novel), Bilingual Press, 1984. Contributor of short stories to *Bilingual Review;* contributor to *Science.* Editor of *VIA.*

WORK IN PROGRESS: A novel, tentatively entitled *Sandcastles,* about science, business, academia, and the price scientists pay for success.

SIDELIGHTS: Nash Candelaria writes: "*Memories of the Alhambra* is about the Chicano heritage myth of being descendants of conquistadors, the unsolvable dilemma of Hispanics from the state of New Mexico who acknowledge their European heritage and may not accept their American Indian heritage. . . . *Not by the Sword* is a look at the Mexican War (1846-48) from the point-of-view of New Mexicans, who became Americans by conquest. *Inheritance of Strangers,* a sequel to *Not by the Sword,* looks at the aftermath of the Mexican War forty years later, and the problems of assimilation; it focuses on the futility of revenge and the difficulty of forgiveness by a conquered people. *Sandcastles* is a contemporary middle-class novel about science with a Spanish surname protagonist.

"I am a descendant of one of the founding families of Albuquerque, New Mexico, and an ancestor, Juan, authored a history of New Mexico in 1776. Although I was born in California, I consider myself a New Mexican by heritage and sympathy. My writing is primarily about Hispanic-Americans, trying, through fiction, to present some of their stories to a wider audience that may only be aware of them as a 'silent minority.'"

AVOCATIONAL INTERESTS: The arts and family, reading, and the stock market.

*   *   *

CANDY, Edward
See NEVILLE, B(arbara) Alison (Boodson)

*   *   *

CARDUS, Neville   1889-1975

PERSONAL: Born April 2, 1889, in Manchester, England; died February 28, 1975, in London, England; married Edith Honorine King, 1921 (died, 1968). *Education:* Attended free lectures at University of Manchester, 1904-1912. *Home:* 112 Bickenhall Mansions, Baker Street, London W.1, England.

CAREER: Shrewsbury School, Manchester, England, assistant cricket coach and secretary to the headmaster, 1912-1916; *Manchester Guardian,* Manchester, reporter, music writer, and cricket correspondent, 1916-27, music critic, 1927-40; *Morning Herald,* Sydney, Australia, music critic and cricket writer, 1941-47; *Sunday Times,* London, England, staff member, 1948-49; *Manchester Guardian,* Manchester, music critic, 1951-75. *Member:* National Liberal Club, Garrick Club. *Awards, honors:* Wagner Medal from City of Bayreuth, 1963; Commander of the British Empire, 1964; Knighted by Queen Elizabeth II, 1967; International Press Club special award, 1970.

WRITINGS: A Cricketer's Book, G. Richards, 1922; *Days in the Sun: A Cricketer's Journal,* G. Richards, 1924, new edition, Hart-Davis, 1948; (editor) Samuel Langford, *Musical Criticisms,* Oxford University Press, 1929; *The Summer Game: A Cricketer's Journal,* Cayme Press, 1929, new edition, Hart-Davis, 1948; *Cricket,* Longmans, Green, 1930, new edition, 1949; *Good Days: A Book of Cricket,* J. Cape, 1934, new edition, Hart-Davis, 1948; (contributor) Thomas Moult, editor, *Bat and Ball,* Arthur Baker, 1935; (author of introduction) Wilhelm Mueller, *Die schonen Muellerin, Schubert,* Die schonen Muellerin Society (London), 1935; *Australian Summer,* J. Cape, 1937, new edition, Hart-Davis, 1949.

Music for Pleasure, Angus & Robertson, 1942; *Ten Composers,* J. Cape, 1945, enlarged edition published as *A Composers Eleven,* J. Cape, 1958, published as *Composers Eleven,* Braziller, 1959; *English Cricket,* Collins, 1945; *Autobiography,* Collins, 1947, 3rd edition, 1961, reprinted, 1975; *The Essential Neville Cardus,* edited by Rupert Hart-Davis, J. Cape, 1949, revised edition published as *Cardus on Cricket: A Selection from the Cricket Writings of Sir Neville Cardus,* edited and introduced by Hart-Davis, Souvenir Press, 1977; *Second Innings* (autobiography), Collins, 1950; *Cricket All the Year,* Collins, 1952; (editor and contributor) *Kathleen Ferrier: A Memoir,* Hamish Hamilton, 1954, Putnam, 1955, 3rd edition, Hamish Hamilton, 1969; *Close of a Play,* Collins, 1956; *Talking of Music,* Macmillan, 1957, reprinted, Greenwood Press, 1975.

Sir Thomas Beecham: A Memoir, Collins, 1961; *The Playfair Cardus,* Dickens Press, 1963; *Gustav Mahler: His Mind and*

His Music, St. Martin's, 1965; *The Delights of Music: A Critic's Choice*, Gollancz, 1966; (compiler with John Arlott) *The Noblest Game: A Book of Fine Cricket Prints*, Harrap, 1969; *Full Score*, Cassell, 1970; (author of foreword) Robin Daniels, *Blackpool Football: The Official Club History*, Hale, 1972; Margaret Hughes, editor, *What Is Music?*, illustrated by Richard Hook, White Lion, 1977.

Published by Souvenir Press: *Cardus in the Covers*, 1978; *Play Resumed with Cardus*, 1979; *A Fourth Innings with Cardus*, 1981; *The Roses Matches, 1919-1939*, 1983.

SIDELIGHTS: As both a music critic and one of England's leading authorities on cricket, Neville Cardus "richly fulfilled his two-fold ambition," according to his *London Times* obituary. The article noted: "He had no formal training in either field. The start of cricket for him was bowling for hours at a bucket, shielded by a broad piece of wood. Music came to him naturally and gave him his first chance of getting into print. . . . A versatile all-round journalist, Cardus delighted in commenting on the contrast he had known in the social scene over the years. He could talk as well as he wrote and was as welcome in exalted music circles as among cricketers in a pub. No compliment pleased him more than that he had made many people wish they had actually been at a cricket match or actually attended a concert. He wrote on cricket as a cricketer; on music as a listener."

Neville Cardus was raised in the slums of Manchester by an aunt who he said "joined the oldest of professions and became an ornament of it." He never knew his parents. Cardus spent his youth working at odd jobs instead of attending school. He once said: "I am a terribly uneducated man. I took a terrible lot of risks. I suppose now I would have been given a grant and probably would have gone to university and I would probably never have known as much as I know now."

AVOCATIONAL INTERESTS: Walking, conversation, and "anything not in the form of a game or sport."

BIOGRAPHICAL/CRITICAL SOURCES: Neville Cardus, *Autobiography*, Collins, 1947, 3rd edition, 1961, reprinted, 1975; Cardus, *Second Innings* (autobiography), Collins, 1950; *Times Literary Supplement*, November 6, 1969, November 20, 1970, June 26, 1981, May 20, 1983; Robin Daniels, *Conversations with Cardus*, foreword by Yehudi Menuhin, Gollancz, 1976.

OBITUARIES: New York Times, March 1, 1975; *London Times*, March 1, 1975; *AB Bookman's Weekly*, March 17, 1975.†

*   *   *

CARNEGIE, Raymond Alexander 1920-
(Sacha Carnegie)

PERSONAL: Born July 9, 1920, in Edinburgh, Scotland; married Patricia Dawson, April 17, 1943; married second wife, The Countess of Erroll, November 27, 1964; children: (first marriage) Alexandra, Susan; (second marriage) Jocelyn. *Education:* Attended Eton College, 1933-37. *Religion:* Church of England. *Home:* Crimonmogate, Lonmay, Aberdeenshire, Scotland. *Agent:* John Johnson, Clerkenwell House, 45-47 Clerkenwell Green, London EC1R OHT, England.

CAREER: British Army, Scots Guards, regular officer, 1940-52, became major; served in Italy and Malaya; mentioned in dispatches during World War II. Writer. *Member:* P.E.N. (London).

WRITINGS—Under name Sacha Carnegie; published by P. Davies, except as indicated: *Noble Purpose*, 1954; *Sunset in the East*, 1955; *Holiday from Life: A Scandinavian Interlude*, 1957; *The Devil and the Deep*, Appleton, 1957; *Pigs I Have Known*, 1958; *The Lion and Francis Conway*, 1958; *Red Dust of Africa*, 1959; *The Dark Night*, 1960; *The Deerslayers*, 1961; *The Golden Years*, 1962; *A Dash of Russia*, 1966, International Publications Service, 1967; *The Guardian*, Dodd, 1966; *The Banners of Love*, 1968, published as *Scarlet Banners of Love*, Dodd, 1968; *Banners of War*, Dodd, 1970; *Banners of Power*, 1972, published as *Kasia and the Empress*, Dodd, 1973; *Banners of Courage*, 1976; *Banners of Revolt*, 1977; *The Colonel*, Magnum, 1979. Contributor to *Scotsman, Field, Country Life, Sunday Times*, and other publications.

WORK IN PROGRESS: A series of novels with background in eastern Europe and Russia in the eighteenth century.

SIDELIGHTS: Raymond Alexander Carnegie told *CA:* "As was the case with many young men, I was launched into real adult life very swiftly indeed by the harsh impact of war. I began to write for the first time while helpless in the overcrowded ward of a military hospital in Italy. In any overcrowded ward of any hospital you learn a lot—or you should—but in a place surrounded by the badly broken bodies of other men, some brave, some not so brave, you learn just that little bit more—the bit that is worth remembering."

*   *   *

CARNEGIE, Sacha
See CARNEGIE, Raymond Alexander

*   *   *

CARO, Francis G(eorge) 1936-

PERSONAL: Born September 28, 1936, in Milwaukee, Wis.; son of Walter (an engineer) and Elizabeth (Voss) Caro; married Carol Bauer (a librarian), December 28, 1965; children: Paul, David. *Education:* Marquette University, B.S., 1958; University of Minnesota, Ph.D., 1962. *Politics:* Democrat. *Home:* 262 Farrington Ave., North Tarrytown, N.Y. 10591. *Office:* Community Service Society, 105 East 22nd St., New York, N.Y. 10010.

CAREER: Community Studies, Inc., Kansas City, Mo., research associate, 1962-64; Community Progress, Inc., New Haven, Conn., research associate, 1964-65; Marquette University, Milwaukee, Wis., assistant professor of sociology, 1965-67; University of Colorado, Boulder, associate professor of sociology, 1967-70; Brandeis University, Waltham, Mass., associate professor of social welfare, 1970-74; Community Service Society, New York, N.Y., director of Institute for Social Welfare Research, 1974—. *Member:* American Sociological Association, Society for the Study of Social Problems, Gerontological Society, Evaluation Research Society.

WRITINGS: (Editor) *Readings in Evaluation Research*, Russell Sage, 1970, 2nd edition, 1977; (co-author) *Family Care of the Elderly*, Heath, 1981; (contributor) E. M. Goldberg and N. Connelly, *Evaluative Research in Social Care*, Heinemann, 1982; (co-author) *Revisiting the Default Debtor*, Community Service Society of New York, 1983; (contributor) H. E. Freeman and others, *Applied Sociology*, Jossey-Bass, 1983.

Contributor to gerontology and evaluation research journals.

WORK IN PROGRESS: A book on major study of impact of publicly-funded home care programs for the elderly.

CARPENTIER (y VALMONT), Alejo   1904-1980
(Jacqueline)

PERSONAL: Born December 26, 1904, in Havana, Cuba; died April 24, 1980, in Paris, France, after a long illness; son of Jorge Julian Carpentier y Valmont (an architect); married Andrea Esteban. *Education:* Attended Universidad de Habana. *Home:* Apartado 6153, Havana, Cuba. *Office:* Embassy of Cuba, 3 rue Scribe, Paris 4e, France.

CAREER: Journalist, editor, educator, musicologist, and author. Worked as a commercial journalist in Havana, Cuba, 1921-24; *Cartels* (magazine), Havana, editor-in-chief, 1924-28; Foniric Studios, Paris, France, director and producer of spoken arts programs and recordings, 1928-39; CMZ radio, Havana, writer and producer, 1939-41; Conservatorio Nacional, Havana, professor of history of music, 1941-43; traveled in Haiti, Europe, the United States and South America in self-imposed exile from his native Cuba, 1943-59; Cuban Publishing House, Havana, director, 1960-67; Embassy of Cuba, Paris, cultural attache, beginning 1966. *Awards, honors:* Prix du Meilleur Livre Etranger (France), 1956, for *The Lost Steps (Los pasos perdidos);* Cino del duca Prize, 1975; Prix Medici, 1979.

WRITINGS—Novels, except as indicated: *Poemes des Antilles* (poetry), [Paris], 1929; *Ecue-yambo-o,* [Paris], 1933, reprinted, Editorial Xanadu (Buenos Aires), 1968; *La musica en Cuba* (music history), Fondo de cultura economica (Mexico), 1946, reprinted, Editorial Letras Cubanas (Havana), 1979; *El reino de este mundo,* originally published in 1949, Organizacion Continental de los Festivales del Libro (Havana), c. 1958, 7th edition, Seix Barral (Barcelona), 1978, translation by Harriet de Onis published as *The Kingdom of This World,* Knopf, 1957; *Los pasos perdidos,* Ibero Americana de Publicaciones (Mexico), 1953, enlarged edition, Editorial de Arte y Literatura (Havana), 1976, translation by de Onis published as *The Lost Steps,* Knopf, 1956, new edition with introduction by J. B. Priestly, Knopf, 1967.

El acoso, Editorial Losada (Buenos Aires), 1956, new edition with introduction by Mercedes Rein, Biblioteca de Marcha (Montevideo), 1972; *Guerra del tiempo: Tres Relatos y una novela,* Compania General de Ediciones, 1958, translation by Frances Partridge published as *The War of Time,* Knopf, 1970; *El siglo de las luces,* Compania General de Ediciones (Mexico), 1962, 8th edition, Seix Barral, 1979, translation by John Sturrock published as *Explosion in a Cathedral,* Little, Brown, 1963; *El camino de Santiago* (short story), Editorial Galerna (Buenos Aires), 1967; *Tientos y diferencias,* Arca (Montevideo), 1967, 3rd enlarged edition, 1973; *Literatura y conciencia politica en America Latina* (essays), edited by A. Corazon, [Madrid], 1969.

(Author of text) *La ciudad de las columnas* (architectural study of Havana; photographs by Paolo Gasparini), Editorial Lumen (Barcelona), 1970; *Viaje a la semilla y otros relatos* (short stories), Editorial Nascimento (Santiago), 1971; *El derecho de asilo; dibujos de Marcel Berges,* Editorial Lumen, 1972; *Los convidados de plata,* Sandino (Montevideo), 1972; *Concierto barroco: Novela,* Siglo XXI Editores (Mexico), 1974, 8th edition, Siglo Veintiuno Editores (Mexico), 1979; *El recurso del metodo: Novela,* Editorial Arte y Literatura (Havana), 1974, 16th edition, Siglo Veintiuno Editores, 1978, translation by Partridge published as *Reasons of State,* Knopf, 1976; *Novelas*

y relatos, Union de Escritores y Artistas de Cuba (Havana), 1974; *Cuentos cubanos,* Laia (Barcelona), 1974.

America Latina en su musica, UNESCO (Havana), 1975; *Letra y solfa,* Sintesis Dosmil (Caracas), 1975; *El acoso* [and] *El derecho de asilo* (collection), Editora Latina (Buenos Aires), 1975; *Cronicas* (collection of articles), Editorial Arte y Literatura, 1975; *Dos novelas* (contains *El reino de este mundo* and *El acoso*), Editorial Arte y Literatura, 1976; *Razon de ser: Conferencias,* Ediciones del Rectorado (Caracas), 1976; *Vision de America* (essays), Ediciones Nemont (Buenos Aires), 1976; *Cuentos,* Editorial Arte y Literatura, 1977; *Bajo el signo de La Cibeles: Cronicas sobre Espana y los espanols, 1925-1937,* Editorial Nuestra Cultura (Madrid), 1979; *La consagracion de la primavera: Novela,* Siglo Veintiuno de Espana (Madrid), 1979, 5th edition, 1979; *El arpa y la sombra,* Siglo Veintiuno Editores, 1979, 2nd edition, Siglo XXI Editores, 1979; *El adjetivo y sus arrugas,* Editorial Galerna, 1980; *La novela latinoamericana en visperas de un nuevo siglo y otros ensayos* (essays), Siglo Veintiuno Editores, 1981.

Author of oratorio, "La Passion noire," first performed in Paris in the 1920s. Also author of librettas; author of two sound recordings, both produced by Casa de las Americas, "Alejo Carpentier narraciones" (cassette), and "Alejo Carpentier lee sus narraciones." Former columnist for *El Nationale* (Caracas). Contributor of articles on politics, literature, and musicology to numerous publications, including *Revolutions Surrealist.* Former editor, under pseudonym Jacqueline, of fashion section of Havana publication; former editor, *Iman* (Paris).

SIDELIGHTS: Although considered a major literary force in his native Latin America, Cuban Alejo Carpentier did not achieve widespread recognition with the American reading public. His prose examines historico-political factors as they relate to Latin American life and cultural development. In his writing, "Carpentier searches for the marvelous buried beneath the surface of Latin American consciousness, where African drums still beat and Indian amulets rule; in depths where Europe is only a vague memory of a future still to come," asserted Roberto Gonzalez Echevarria in his *Alejo Carpentier: The Pilgrim at Home.* Echevarria continued: "On the one hand, Carpentier maintains that the baroque nature of Latin American literature stems from the necessity to name for the first time realities that are outside the mainstream of Western culture. On the other, he states that what characterizes Latin American reality is its stylelessness, which results from its being an amalgam of styles from many cultural traditions and epochs: Indian, African, European, Neoclassical, Modern, etc."

Carpentier's relative obscurity in the United States may have been related to the broad spectrum of knowledge he displayed in his writing, according to critics. Commented Gene H. Bell in the *New Boston Review:* "Out of a dozen or so major [South American] authors (Borges and Garcia Marquez are the best-known here), Alejo Carpentier remains the one least recognized in these parts. . . . Some readers may be put off by Carpentier's displays of learning, an encyclopedism that ranges over anthropology, history, geography, botany, zoology, music, folk and classical, the arts, visual and culinary, and countless forgotten novels and verse—in all an erudition easily rivaling that of Borges." Yet despite Carpentier's immense scholarship, Bell perceived a universal quality in the author's writing, noting, "Precisely because of . . . national differences, however, Carpentier's novel[s] (like those of Fuentes or Garcia Marquez) can furnish already interested Americans more insight into the social dislocations of the Southern continent than many a Yankee Poli Sci professor could."

Most critics familiar with Carpentier's work applauded the scholarly qualities that Bell enumerated, yet others criticized these very elements. The *New York Times Book Review*'s Alexander Coleman commented that Carpentier's early books were "often pretty heavy going, what with their tiresome philosophizing and heavily laid-on historical panoplies." Alan Cheuse concurred in *Review,* observing that some "readers may have decided that indeed the reasons for Carpentier's failure to capture an audience here are the same reasons put forth by the earliest reviewers: that his fiction is too 'erudite,' that he is more a 'cultural historian' than a novelist, . . . or that he is a 'tiresome philosophizer.'" However, Paul West remarked, also in *Review,* that "Carpentier is a master of both detail and mass, of both fixity and flux." West continued, "He can not only describe: he can describe what no-one has seen; and, best, he seems to have the hypothetical gift of suggesting, as he describes."

Carpentier's writing encompasses numerous styles and techniques. The *New York Review of Books*'s Michael Wood remarked that Carpentier "is interested not in myth but in history, and his method is to plunge us circumstantially into an earlier period, before, during, and after the First World War." Cheuse noted: "Intelligence and erudition are certainly present . . . in Carpentier's fiction. But so are sex, violence, political uproar, war, revolution, voyages of exploration, naturalist extravaganzas, settings ranging from ancient Greece to contemporary New York City, and characters running the gamut from the simple Haitian protagonist of *The Kingdom of This World* to the worldly wise, word-weary Head of State [in *Reasons of State*], . . . all of this comprising a complex but highly variegated and appealing fictional matrix."

Carpentier's themes often illustrate an awareness of broad social issues. Bell noted in the *New Boston Review* that "Carpentier's fiction regularly depicts individuals swept—often against their wishes—into the larger social struggle; they thereby become participants in history and embody the conflicts of their times." Echevarria asserted that "the plot in Carpentier's stories always moves from exile and fragmentation toward return and restoration, and the overall movement of each text is away from literature into immediacy." Echevarria further explained the historical relevance of Carpentier's themes: "The persistence of the structure and thematics of fall and redemption, of exile and return, of individual consciousness and collective conscience, stems from a constant return to the source of modern Latin American self-awareness."

Many critics found *Reasons of State* and *The Lost Steps* among Carpentier's best efforts. *Reasons of State (El recurso del metodo)* deals with a Francophile South American dictator attempting to rule the fictitious Nueva Cordoba from his Paris home, periodically returning to his country to control revolutionary outbreaks. Bell stated, "This is no drama of the individual soul, but an imaginative evocation of the material and cultural forces of history." He added: "*Reasons of State* is not a psychological study in tyranny. . . . Carpentier rather places the Dictator (who is actually something of a cultural-historical caricature) within a broader global process, shows how the petty brutalities of South American politics ultimately interlock with European and, later, U.S. interests."

Reviewers saw *Reasons of State* as a departure in style from earlier Carpentier books. The *New York Times Book Review*'s Coleman commented: "*Reasons of State* is something different—a jocular view of imaginative idealism, repressive power and burgeoning revolution, all done with breezy panache. Once

again Carpentier has shown how canny and adept a practitioner he can be in mediating between the many realms which his own life has touched upon." Bell concurred, noting that the novel "exhibits a new lightness of touch, a wry and rollicking humor."

Carpentier's *The Lost Steps (Los pasos perdidos)* "is considered his masterpiece," wrote Ruth Mathewson in the *New Leader.* The novel, which contains autobiographical elements, "represents an attempt at unification and synthesis, if only because it is centered on a continuous and reflexive narrative presence," suggested author Echevarria. Like his other novels which deal with historical analysis, *The Lost Steps* also exhibits historical aspects. Gregory Rabassa observed in the *Saturday Review* that "Carpentier digs into the past: it almost seems as if he cannot get away from it, even in his novel *The Lost Steps,* which is contemporary in time but is really a search for origins—the origin first of music and then of the whole concept of civilization."

In an overall summation of Carpentier's work, Echevarria stated, "History is the main topic in Carpentier's fiction, and the history he deals with—the history of the Caribbean—is one of beginnings or foundations." Echevarria concluded that, "In a sense, as in *The Lost Steps,* Carpentier's entire literary enterprise issues from the desire to seize upon that moment of origination from which history and the history of the self begin simultaneously—a moment from which both language and history will start, thus the foundation of a symbolic code devoid of temporal or spatial gaps."

BIOGRAPHICAL/CRITICAL SOURCES: Books Abroad, spring, 1959; *PMLA,* spring, 1963; E. Rodriguez Monegal, *Narradores de esta America,* Alfa (Montevideo), 1963; Luis Harss and Barbara Dohmann, *Into the Mainstream,* Harper, 1967; *Studies in Short Fiction,* winter, 1971; *UNESCO Courier,* January, 1972, June, 1973; *Sentata aniversario de Alejo Carpentier,* La Habana, 1975.

New York Times Book Review, May 2, 1976; *New Statesman,* May 28, 1976; *Saturday Review,* May 29, 1976; *New Leader,* July 5, 1976; *New Boston Review,* fall, 1976; *Review,* fall, 1976; *New York Review of Books,* December 9, 1976; Roberto Gonzalez Echevarria, *Alejo Carpentier: The Pilgrim at Home,* Cornell University Press, 1977; *Contemporary Literary Criticism,* Gale, Volume VIII, 1978, Volume XI, 1979.

OBITUARIES: New York Times, April 26, 1980; *Times* (London), April 26, 1980.†

—*Sketch by Michaela Swart Wilson*

*   *   *

CARPOZI, George, Jr. 1920-

PERSONAL: Born November 25, 1920, in New York, N.Y.; son of George John (a restaurateur) and Julie (Camber) Carpozi; married Chrysanthe Haranis, June 26, 1949; children: Julie, Elaine, George III, Harriette, Chrysanthe, James. *Education:* Attended New York University, 1940-43, 1946-47, and Dartmouth College, 1943. *Home:* 47 Roundtree Dr., Melville, N.Y. 11747. *Agent:* The Foley Agency, 34 East 38th St., New York, N.Y. 10016.

CAREER: New York Times, New York City, sports copy boy, 1946-47; Standard News Association, New York City, 1948-53, became assistant city editor; *Bronx Press Review,* Bronx, N.Y., assistant editor, 1949-53; *New York Journal-American,* New York City, 1953-65, became chief assistant city editor;

New York Post, New York City, reporter-writer, 1965—. *Military service:* U.S. Marine Corps, 1943-46; served in Pacific; became staff sergeant. *Member:* New York City Press Club.

AWARDS, HONORS: New York City Newspaper Reporters Association Gold Typewriter Award for helping in the capture of city's "Mad Bomber"; Hearst Newspapers awards for writing achievement; New York City Uniformed Firemen's Association award for excellence in reporting; National Police Officers Association public service award.

WRITINGS: The Brigitte Bardot Story, Belmont Books, 1961; *Clark Gable,* Pyramid Books, 1962; *Let's Twist,* Pyramid Books, 1962; *The Agony of Marilyn Monroe,* World Distributors, 1962; *Vince Edwards,* Belmont Books, 1962; (with Pierre J. Huss) *Red Spies in the UN,* Coward, 1965; *The Hidden Side of Jacqueline Kennedy,* Pyramid Books, 1967; *Red Spies in Washington,* Trident, 1968; *Jackie and Ari: For Love or Money?,* Lancer, 1968; *Three Mothers: Their Life Stories,* Macfadden, 1968.

The Gary Cooper Story, Arlington House, 1970; *The Johnny Cash Story,* Pyramid Publications, 1970; *The John Wayne Story,* Arlington House, 1972; *Ordeal by Trial: The Alice Crimmins Case,* Walker & Co., 1972; (with Anne-Marie Stein) *Three Picassos before Breakfast: The Story of an Art Forger's Wife,* Hawthorn Books, 1973; *Marilyn Monroe: "Her Own Story,"* Universal-Award House, 1973; *Red Spies in the U.S.,* Arlington House, 1973; *The Carol Burnett Story,* Warner Paperback, 1975; *Cher,* Berkley, 1975; *Son of Sam: The .44-Caliber Killer,* Manor, 1977; (with Will Balsamo) *Always Kill a Brother,* Dell, 1977; *The Fabulous Life of Bing Crosby,* Manor, 1977; *Sunstrike,* Pinnacle Books, 1978; *Andrew Young: The Impossible Man,* Manor, 1978; *The Gangland Killers,* Manor, 1979; *The Suicide Cults,* Manor, 1979; (with Daniel J. Chiodo) *The Velvet Jungle,* Playboy Press, 1979; (compiler and contributor) Ayatollah Ruhollah Khomeini, *Islamic Government,* Manor, 1979; *Frank Sinatra: Is This Man Mafia?,* Woodhill, 1979; *John Lennon: Death of a Dream,* Manor, 1981.

"Great Crimes of the Century" series; all published by Woodhill: *Great Crimes of the Century, Number 1,* 1979; . . . , *Number 2,* 1979; . . . , *Number 3,* 1979; . . . , *Number 4,* 1979; . . . : *The Senseless Slayers, Number 5,* 1979; . . . : *The Weird Murderers, Number 6,* 1979; . . . : *The Savage Killers, Number 7,* 1980; . . . : *Murderers Leave Clues, Number 8,* 1980.

"That's Hollywood" series; all published by Woodhill: *That's Hollywood: The Matinee Idols,* 1978; . . . : *The Love Goddesses,* 1978; . . . : *The Magnificent Entertainers,* 1978; . . . : *The Great Ladies of Hollywood,* 1978; . . . : *The Distinguished Performers,* 1979; . . . : *The Colossal Cowboys,* 1980.

Contributor of stories to magazines, including *Photoplay, True Detective, Master Detective, Impact, Pageant, Ladies Home Journal, Reader's Digest,* and *Us.*

SIDELIGHTS: George Carpozi, Jr. wrote a number of exposes on insurance rackets, phony clinics, and police shakedowns for the *New York Journal-American* and covered the burning of the carrier "Bennington," the sinking of the "Andrea Doria," and the Harlem riots of the summer of 1964. Besides helping in the capture of New York's "Mad Bomber," he uncloaked the British spy, Jack Kroger, as a former Bronx resident (real name, Morris "Unc" Cohen).

Carpozi was a middle- and long-distance runner for New York University and Dartmouth University; he ran on the New York

University two-mile relay team that won the national championship in Madison Square Garden, 1943.

AVOCATIONAL INTERESTS: Home improvement (laid fifteen thousand bricks for a patio), gardening, astronomy, photography.

BIOGRAPHICAL/CRITICAL SOURCES: Editor and Publisher, June 18, 1960; *New York Times Book Review,* April 5, 1981.

*　　*　　*

CARVAJAL, Ricardo
See MENESES, Enrique

*　　*　　*

CASSITY, (Allen) Turner 1929-

PERSONAL: Born January 12, 1929, in Jackson, Miss.; son of Allen Davenport and Dorothy (Turner) Cassity. *Education:* Millsaps College, B.A., 1951; Stanford University, M.A., 1952; Columbia University, M.S., 1956. *Politics:* "I am by investment, temperament, and conviction a burgher." *Home:* 510-J East Ponce de Leon Ave., Decatur, Ga. 30030. *Office:* Emory University Library, Atlanta, Ga. 30322.

CAREER: Jackson Municipal Library, Jackson, Miss., assistant librarian, 1957-58; Transvaal Provincial Library, Pretoria, South Africa, assistant librarian, 1959-61; Emory University Library, Atlanta, Ga., chief of serials and binding department, 1962—. *Military service:* U.S. Army, 1952-54. *Awards, honors:* Blumenthal-Leviton-Blonder Prize for poetry, 1966.

WRITINGS: Watchboy, What of the Night? (poetry), Wesleyan University Press, 1966; *Steeplejacks in Babel,* Godine, 1973; *Silver Out of Shanghi: A Scenario for Josef von Sternberg, Featuring Wicked Nobles, a Depraved Religious Wayfoong, Princess Ida, the China Clipper, and Resurrection Lily, with a Supporting Cast of Old Hands, Merchant Seamen, Sikhs, Imperial Marines, and Persons in Blue* (poetry), Planet Mongo Press (Atlanta), 1973; *Yellow for Peril, Black for Beautiful: Poems and a Play,* Braziller, 1975; *The Defense of the Sugar Islands: A Recruiting Post,* Symposium Press, 1979. Contributor of poems to *Poetry, Kenyon Review,* and other publications.

SIDELIGHTS: A stark and oftentimes satiric poet, Turner Cassity is noted for his tightly structured verse. "His is an art by exclusion; his poems are what remains after the completion of a rigorous economizing exercise," Richard Johnson observes in *Parnassus.* Writing in the *Sewanee Review,* Paul Ramsey describes the verse of *Steeplejacks in Babel* as "traditional in meter, tight yet ragged," while the *Southern Review* critic Francis Golfing believes the poems of *Yellow for Peril, Black for Beautiful* "bring to mind the surrealistic acrobatics of Cocteau or Picabia." Jerome J. McGann deems Cassity a "limited poet," but notes in *Poetry* that "he recognizes perfectly what his words and lines can do, and he performs candidly within his range."

BIOGRAPHICAL/CRITICAL SOURCES: Sewanee Review, spring, 1974; *Parnassus,* fall/winter, 1974; *Poetry,* October, 1974; *Contemporary Literary Criticism,* Volume VI, Gale, 1976; *Southern Review,* winter, 1978.†

*　　*　　*

CASTELLANETA, Carlo 1930-

PERSONAL: Born February 8, 1930, in Milan, Italy; son of

Michele and Teresa (Ruffini) Castellaneta; married Catarina Zaina, May 18, 1980. *Education:* Attended public high school. *Home:* Via Muratori 29, Milan, Italy.

CAREER: Journalist; currently works for newspaper *Il Giorno,* Milan, Italy.

WRITINGS—Novels, except as indicated; published by Rizzoli, except as indicated: *Viaggio col padre,* Mondadori, 1958, translation published as *Journey with Father,* MacDonald & Co., 1962; *Una lunga rabbia,* Feltrinelli, 1961; *Villa di delizia* (title means "Villa of Delights"), 1965; *Gli incantesimi,* 1968, translation by George Kay published as *Until the Next Enchantment,* Chatto & Windus, 1970; *L'opera completa del Perugino,* 1969.

La dolce compagna, 1970, translation by Sebastian Roberts published as *This Gentle Companion,* Chatto & Windus, 1971; *L'opera completa di Hayez,* 1971; *La Paloma,* 1972; *Tante storie* (short stories), 1973; *Storia di Milano,* 1975; *Notti e nebbie,* 1975; *Da un capo all' altro della citta* (short stories), 1977; *Progetti di allegria,* 1978; *Professione poliziotto,* 1978; *Anni beati,* 1979.

Dizionario dei sentimenti, 1980; *Una citta per due,* 1981; *Un'infanzia italiana,* 1981; *Ombre,* 1982; *Effusioni,* 1982; *Questioni di cuore,* 1983.

Contributor of short stories to newspapers; writer and illustrator of reports, from Senegal, Gibraltar, Spain, and Andorra for *Le vie del mondo* and *Atlas Histoire,* and from Brazil, Cuba, Togo, and the Philippines for *Weekend;* translator of French-language poets, including Leopold Sedar Senghor.

WORK IN PROGRESS: Questa primavera, collected short stories.

*   *   *

CATOIR, John T. 1931-

PERSONAL: Surname is pronounced Ca-*toor;* born September 8, 1931, in New York, N.Y.; son of John T. (an accountant) and Catherine (Caslin) Catoir. *Education:* Fordham University, B.S., 1953; Immaculate Conception Seminary, S.T.B., 1960; Catholic University of America, J.C.D., 1964. *Office:* The Christophers, 12 East 48th St., New York, N.Y. 10017.

CAREER: Ordained Roman Catholic priest, 1960; Diocese of Paterson, N.J., 1965—, currently director of The Christophers and co-host of "Christopher Closeup" television program. Lecturer on spirituality, individual responsibility, and communications in marriage. *Military service:* U.S. Army, 1953-54. *Member:* Canon Law Society of America, Association of Church Personnel Administrators (president, 1975-77), UNDA-USA, Catholic Press Association of the United States and Canada.

WRITINGS: A Brief History of the Catholic Church in New Jersey, New Jersey Press, 1965; (with Jose de Vink) *The Challenge of Love: Practical Advice for Married Couples and Those Planning Marriage,* Hawthorn, 1969; *We Dare to Believe,* Franciscan Herald, 1972; *The Way People Pray,* Paulist/Newman, 1974; *Enjoy the Lord,* Christopher Books, 1978; *That Your Joy May Be Full,* Christopher Books, 1982. Author of syndicated weekly and daily newspaper columns. Contributor to *New Catholic Encyclopedia, Commonweal, America, Marriage Magazine,* and other publications.

CATZ, Max
See GLASER, Milton

*   *   *

CAVELL, Stanley (Louis) 1926-

PERSONAL: Born September, 1926, in Atlanta, Ga.; son of Irving H. and Fannie (Segal) Goldstein; married Marcia Schmid, July, 1955 (divorced January, 1963); married Cathleen Cohen, June, 1967; children: Rachel Lee, Benjamin William. *Education:* University of California, Berkeley, A.B., 1947; University of California, Los Angeles, graduate study, 1948-51; Harvard University, Ph.D., 1961. *Office:* Emerson Hall, Harvard University, Cambridge, Mass. 02138.

CAREER: Harvard University, Cambridge, Mass., junior fellow of Society of Fellows, 1953-56; University of California, Berkeley, assistant professor of philosophy, 1956-62; Institute for Advanced Studies, Princeton, N.J., fellow, 1962-63; Harvard University, Walter M. Cabot Professor of Aesthetics and General Theory of Value, 1963—.

WRITINGS: Must We Mean What We Say? A Book of Essays, Scribner, 1969; *The World Viewed: Reflections on the Ontology of Film,* Viking, 1971; *The Senses of Walden,* Viking, 1972, published as *The Senses of Walden: An Expanded Edition,* North Point Press, 1981; *The Claim of Reason: Wittgenstein, Skepticism, Morality, and Tragedy,* Oxford University Press, 1979; *Pursuits of Happiness: The Hollywood Comedy of Remarriage,* Harvard University Press, 1981.

SIDELIGHTS: Reviewing Stanley Cavell's *The Claim of Reason: Wittgenstein, Skepticism, Morality, and Tragedy,* Anthony Kenny writes in the *Times Literary Supplement* that Cavell "possesses the rare ability to present Wittgenstein's thought in a manner that is philosophically accurate while making an immediate imaginative impact." Kenny admires the author's writing ability, but concludes, "Despite Cavell's philosophical and literary gifts his book as it stands is a misshapen amalgam of ill-assorted parts." In a similar opinion, Jonathan Lear comments in *New York Times Book Review,* "While much of the book is charming, there is much that is overwritten and self-conscious."

J. Hoberman claims that in *Pursuits of Happiness: The Hollywood Comedy of Remarriage* "Cavell's language is refreshingly jargon-free, albeit chewy." Hoberman, writing in the *Village Voice Literary Supplement,* adds, "Cavell's insights (many of them brilliant) would be more persuasive were they better grounded." Yet *Times Literary Supplement* critic S. S. Prawer observes that Cavell "has a sure eye and ear for thematically important ideas and objects in the films discussed" and concludes that the work illustrates "with gratifying clarity that in academic film-criticism the structuralist and semiotic game is decidedly not the only one in town."

BIOGRAPHICAL/CRITICAL SOURCES: New York Times Book Review, December 2, 1979; *Los Angeles Times Book Review,* March 9, 1980; *Times Literary Supplement,* April 18, 1980, February 26, 1982; *Washington Post Book World,* July 19, 1981; *New York Times,* February 9, 1982; *Village Voice Literary Supplement,* March, 1982.

*   *   *

CAVERHILL, Nicholas
See KIRK-GREENE, Anthony (Hamilton Millard)

CHANCE, Stephen
   See TURNER, Philip

*   *   *

CHANDLER, David (Geoffrey) 1934-

PERSONAL: Born January 15, 1934, in England; son of Geoffrey Edmund (a clergyman) and Joyce Mary (Ridsdale) Chandler; married Gillian Dixon (a part-time indexer), February 18,
1961; children: Paul Geoffrey, John Roger, Mark David. *Education:* Keble College, Oxford, B.A. (with second class honors), 1955, Diploma of Education, 1956, M.A., 1960. *Politics:*
Conservative. *Religion:* Church of England. *Home:* ''Hind-
ford,'' Monteagle Lane, Yateley, near Camberley, Surrey, England. *Office:* Department of War Studies and International
Affairs, Royal Military Academy Sandhurst, Camberley, Surrey, England.

CAREER: Royal Military Academy Sandhurst, Camberley,
Surrey, England, lecturer in politics and modern history, 1960-
61, lecturer, 1961-64, senior lecturer in military history, 1964-
70, deputy head of department, 1970-80, head of department
of war studies and international affairs, 1980—. Visiting professor, Ohio State University, 1970; visiting lecturer, Naval
War College, 1974. *Military service:* British Army, 1957-60;
seconded to Nigerian Military Forces; became captain. *Member:* International Commission of Military History (international vice-president, 1975—), Royal Historical Society (fellow), Royal Geographical Society (fellow), Society for Army
Historical Research (council member), Society of Cavaliers,
Royal Masonic Society.

WRITINGS: (Contributor) C. Falls, editor, *Great Military Battles,* Weidenfeld & Nicolson, 1965; (editor) *A Traveller's Guide
to the Battlefields of Europe,* two volumes, Hugh Evelyn, 1965,
Chilton, 1966; *The Campaigns of Napoleon,* Macmillan, 1966;
(contributor) Brian Bond, editor, *Victorian Military Campaigns,* Hutchinson, 1967; (contributor) *History of the Second
World War,* Purnell & Sons, 1967; (editor) Robert Parker and
Comte de Merode-Westerloo, *The Marlborough Wars,* Shoe
String, 1968.

(Contributor) *New Cambridge Modern History,* Cambridge
University Press, 1971; *Marlborough as Military Commander,*
Scribner, 1973, new edition, 1979; *Napoleon,* Saturday Review Press, 1974; *Art of Warfare on Land,* Hamlyn, 1974; *Art
of War in the Age of Marlborough,* Batsford, 1976; *A Dictionary of the Napoleonic Wars,* Macmillan, 1979.

An Atlas of Military Strategy, 1618-1878, Free Press, 1980;
Waterloo: The Hundred Days, Macmillan, 1980. Contributor
to military and historical journals.

WORK IN PROGRESS: A life of Field-Marshal ''Jumbo'' Wil-
son, for publication by Collins; an edited version of the *Hunter
Journal* (Marlburian period), for publication by the Society of
Army Historical Research.

SIDELIGHTS: David Chandler has made lecture tours to British
bases in the Mediterranean, Far East, Germany, and to universities and other institutions in the United States. He has also
made battlefield tours to Flanders, northern Italy, Belgium,
Germany, the United States, and France. *Avocational interests:*
Sailing, war games, model ship construction, gardening, camping.

*BIOGRAPHICAL/CRITICAL SOURCES: St. Louis Post-Dis-
patch,* December 17, 1967; *Guardian* (London), December 21,
1981.

*   *   *

CHANEY, Jill 1932-

PERSONAL: Born June 5, 1932, in Hertfordshire, England;
daughter of Walter Sidney (a barrister) and Barbara (Webb)
Chaney; married Walter Francis Leeming (a chartered civil
engineer), August 26, 1960; children: Catherine Frances, Matthew John. *Education:* Attended private schools in England,
and Waterperry Horticultural School, 1949-51. *Home:* White
Cottage, Berks Hill, Chorleywood, Hertfordshire, England.

CAREER: Author. Worked as a gardener in London, England,
1951-61, mainly at an old people's home operated by the Jewish Board of Guardians. Director of Chorleywood Bookshop.
Member: Royal Horticultural Society, Zoological Society, National Trust.

WRITINGS—All published by Dobson, except as noted: *On
Primrose Hill* (juvenile), Methuen, 1961; *Half a Candle* (youth
novel), 1968, Crown, 1969.

A Penny for the Guy (juvenile), 1970; *Mottram Park* (youth
novel), 1971; *Christopher's Dig* (juvenile), 1972; *Return to
Mottram Park* (youth novel), 1974; *Taking the Woffle to Peb-
blecombe-on-Sea* (juvenile), 1974; *Christopher's Find* (juvenile), 1975; *Woffle R.A.* (juvenile), 1976; *The Buttercup Field*
(youth novel), 1976; *Canary Yellow* (youth novel), 1977; *Angel
Face* (youth novel), 1978; *Vectis Diary* (youth novel), 1979.
Also contributor of short stories to periodicals.

WORK IN PROGRESS: A book for children.

*   *   *

CHANT, Barry (Mostyn) 1938-

PERSONAL: Born October 23, 1938, in Adelaide, South Australia; son of James Oswald (a teacher) and Vera (Penno) Chant;
married Vanessa Bennett, January 23, 1960; children: Rebekah, Michael, Clinton. *Education:* University of Adelaide,
B.A. (with honors), 1959, diploma in education, 1962; Melbourne College of Divinity, B.D., 1968. *Home and office:* The
House of Tabor, 84 Northgate St., Unley Park, South Australia
5061.

CAREER: Teacher of English, history, and social studies in
secondary school in Murray Bridge, South Australia, 1960-63;
ordained to ministry, 1961; pastor of Pentecostal church in
Adelaide, South Australia, 1964-75; Crusade Bible College,
Adelaide, dean, 1964—; House of Tabor (Christian education
center), Unley Park, South Australia, director, 1979—. Partner
of Luke Publications, 1974—; chairman of Christian Revival
Crusade (South Australia), 1974-81.

WRITINGS—Published by Crusade Publications, except as in-
dicated: *Upon Dry Ground,* 1969, published as *Your Pocket
Guide to the Power of God,* 1975, published as *Your Guide to
God's Power,* House of Tabor, 1981; *Fact or Fantasy,* 1970;
The Secret Is Out, 1971.

Published by Luke Publications: *Heart of Fire: The Story of
Australian Pentecostalism,* 1974, revised edition, 1976; *Spindles of the Dusty Range* (children's stories), 1975; *Straight
Talk about Sex,* 1976; *Spindles and Eagles,* 1976; *Spindles and
the Wombat,* 1978.

Published by House of Tabor: *Spindles and the Orphan*, 1980; *Miracle of Calvary*, 1980; (with Fred Grice) *Spindles and the Lamb* (stage musical), 1982; *Spindles and the Children*, 1983; *Straight Talk about Marriage*, 1983.

Associate editor and feature writer, *Impact* (formerly *Revivalist*), 1964—.

WORK IN PROGRESS: A revision of *Heart of Fire;* lyrics and music for a new "Spindles" musical.

SIDELIGHTS: Barry Chant told *CA:* "I am an incurable writer. Indeed, it is only in the last twelve months that I finally forced myself to use a dictating machine for correspondence. Prior to that, I even typed all of my own letters. I seem to find it easier to crystallize my thinking and to be accurate when I put words on paper. But it is not just that. I guess I am also an incurable communicator.

"I like to teach. I find that ignorance, misunderstanding or prejudice are problems which really aggravate me. Other people are aggravated by other things. It seems to me, however, that when people think properly and when their ideas are clear, that many other problems are automatically solved. I see this especially in regard to the Scriptures. When people really know and understand the Bible, the rest of their lives begin to become whole. So, I write with this in mind."

*   *   *

CHAPMAN, Marie M(anire)   1917-

PERSONAL: Born December 12, 1917, in Buhl, Idaho; daughter of John Leonard (a newspaper editor) and Emma (Rodman) Manire; married Kenneth Arthur Chapman (a pastor and college teacher), August 6, 1941; children: John Arthur, Fran Chapman Osburn, Ramona, Daniel K. *Education:* Kinman Business University, secretarial diploma, 1935; attended Moody Bible Institute, 1939-41; Lynchburg Baptist College, B.S., 1973. *Religion:* Independent Baptist. *Home:* 2909 Center St., Lynchburg, Va. 24501.

CAREER: Oakville Courier, Oakville, Wash., reporter and compositor, 1935-39; Bible Institute Colportage Association (now Moody Press), Chicago, Ill., secretary, 1939-41; *Pacific Builder and Engineer*, Seattle, Wash., circulation manager, 1940; *Daily News Journal*, Murfreesboro, Tenn., feature writer and proofreader, 1952-58; Baptist Sunday School Board, Nashville, Tenn., editorial assistant, 1958-64; Lynchburg Baptist College, Lynchburg, Va., administrative assistant, 1971-73, instructor in Christian education and journalism, 1971—; freelance editor. Piano teacher.

WRITINGS: Practical Methods for Sunday School Teachers, Zondervan, 1962; *Yelling for Help,* Moody, 1972; *Teaching Aids,* Gospel Promotions, 1973; *Disciples Lessons: Primary,* Gospel Promotions, 1973; *Christian Journalism,* Faithlift Ministries, 1974; *Reachout in Writing,* privately printed, 1974; *Successful Teaching Ideas,* Standard Publishing, 1975; *Puppet Animals Tell Bible Stories,* Accent Books, 1977; *Fun with Bible Geography,* Accent Books, 1980.

WORK IN PROGRESS: Jesus Questions Teachers; A Word for Today (meditations based on a single word).

*   *   *

CHENOWETH, Vida S.   1928-

PERSONAL: Surname is pronounced *Chen*-o-weth; born Oc-tober 18, 1928, in Enid, Okla.; daughter of Louis A. (owner of a music company) and Velma R. (Warrick) Chenoweth. *Education:* William Woods College, A.A., 1949; Northwestern University, B.M., 1951; American Conservatory of Music, Chicago, Ill., M.M., 1953; further study at University of Oklahoma, summers of 1961, 1962, 1964, and at Asbury Theological Seminary, 1963; University of Auckland, Ph.D., 1974. *Home:* 3302 West Oklahoma, Enid, Okla. 73701.

CAREER: Concert marimbist, New York, N.Y., 1954-64, playing in recitals, as soloist with symphony orchestras, and as recording artist; ethnomusicologist and Bible translator in New Guinea, 1965-77; Wheaton College, Wheaton, Ill., currently professor of ethnomusicology. Advisor in marimba to National Federation of Music Clubs, 1957-64; international consultant in ethnomusicology to Summer Institute of Linguistics. *Member:* International Folk Music Council, Society for Ethnomusicology. *Awards, honors:* First place for marimba, Chicagoland Music Festival, 1948; Fulbright scholarship, 1957.

WRITINGS: The Marimbas of Guatemala, University of Kentucky Press, 1963; *Melodic Perception and Analysis,* Summer Institute of Linguistics, 1972, 2nd edition, 1974; *The Usarufas and Their Music,* Summer Institute of Linguistics, 1977. Also author of *The Music of the Usarufas,* two volumes, 1974, *A Catalog of Musical Instruments of Papua New Guinea,* 1980, and *A Music Primer for the Eastern Highlands,* 1981. Contributor to *Ethnomusicology, Bible Translator, Practical Anthropology, American Anthropologist, Percussive Arts,* and *Oceania.*

*   *   *

CHERNAIK, Judith   1934-

PERSONAL: Born October 24, 1934, in New York, N.Y.; daughter of Reuben and Gertrude (Lapidus) Sheffield; married Warren Lewis Chernaik (a lecturer in English), September 2, 1956; children: Laura Rose, David Jacob, Sara Elizabeth. *Education:* Cornell University, B.A., 1955; Yale University, Ph.D., 1964. *Home:* 124 Mansfield Rd., London N.W.3, England. *Agent:* Wendy Weil, Julian Bach Literary Agency, Inc., 747 Third Ave., New York, N.Y. 10017.

CAREER: Columbia University, New York, N.Y., lecturer in English, 1963-65; Tufts University, Medford, Mass., assistant professor of English, 1965-69; writing and research, 1969-74; University of London, London, England, lecturer in English, 1974-75. *Awards, honors:* Radcliffe Institute fellowship, 1966-68; American Council of Learned Societies fellowship, 1972-73.

WRITINGS: The Lyrics of Shelley, Case Western Reserve University Press, 1972; *Double Fault* (novel), Putnam, 1975; *The Daughter: A Novel Based on the Life of Eleanor Marx,* Harper, 1979. Contributor of articles and reviews to magazines including *Atlantic, Saturday Review, Times Literary Supplement,* and *London Magazine* and to newspapers.

WORK IN PROGRESS: A biography of Clara Schumann, for Knopf; *Queen Leah,* a novel.

SIDELIGHTS: In *The Daughter: A Novel Based on the Life of Eleanor Marx,* Judith Chernaik re-creates the last fifteen years of Karl Marx's youngest daughter, focussing on her life with fellow socialist and "free thinker" Edward Aveling, a relationship which ended with Eleanor's suicide in 1898 at age forty. The author "respects, admires, [and] pities her extraordinary, admirable, lovable heroine,'' writes Saul Maloff in the *New York Times Book Review,* ''and she respects the public life [Eleanor] lived, always staying faithfully within the general limits of the known.'' Chernaik's interest, according to *Times Literary Supplement* critic Jennifer Uglow, ''is in Eleanor Marx not as mover of historical forces but as their victim, not as inspired speaker and tireless committee worker, but as 'Tussy,' 'the daughter.''' Uglow continues: ''Growing in resonance throughout the novel is the similarity between [Karl] and Aveling, which Eleanor senses in the blending of faces in her dreams. . . . She comes to see all relationships, whether sexual, political or evolutionary, as governed not by consent but by 'necessity': 'The weak gave themselves up to the protection of the strong and the strong used the weak to extend their power and domain.'''

''At times the dialogue has the tone of a primer in sexual politics and socialism,'' Uglow concludes, ''but the presentation of a heroine dragged by tides of ideas as well as emotions makes [*The Daughter*] an extraordinary novel. By virtue of her imaginative sympathy and formal virtuosity, Judith Chernaik succeeds to a remarkable degree in shaping untidy lives into suggestive oppositions and exemplars.''

AVOCATIONAL INTERESTS: Music.

BIOGRAPHICAL/CRITICAL SOURCES: Judith Chernaik, *The Daughter: A Novel Based on the Life of Eleanor Marx,* Harper, 1979; *New York Times Book Review,* April 15, 1979; *Observer,* February 15, 1981; *Times Literary Supplement,* March 20, 1981.

*   *   *

CHERRY, C. Conrad 1937-

PERSONAL: Born March 31, 1937, in Kerens, Tex.; son of Charles C. and Laura (Owens) Cherry; married Mary Ella Bigony, August 22, 1959; children: Kevin, Diane. *Education:* McMurry College, B.A., 1958; Drew University, B.D., 1961, Ph.D., 1965. *Home:* 9 Brittany Lane, Chico, Calif. 95926. *Office address:* 101 Salem, Box 2268, Chico, Calif. 95927.

CAREER: Pennsylvania State University, University Park, 1964-81, began as assistant professor, became professor of religious studies; currently director, Scholars' Press. *Member:* American Society of Church History, American Academy of Religion, Society for Values in Higher Education. *Awards, honors:* *American Quarterly* Award, 1969; Society for Religion in Higher Education fellow, 1970-71.

WRITINGS: The Theology of Jonathan Edwards: A Reappraisal, Anchor Books, 1966; (editor with John Fenton) *Religion in the Public Domain,* Center for Continuing Liberal Education, Pennsylvania State University, 1966; *God's New Israel,* Prentice-Hall, 1971; *Nature and Religious Imagination,* Fortress, 1980.

*   *   *

CHI, Madeleine 1930-

PERSONAL: Born April 16, 1930, in Shanghai, China; came to United States in 1952, naturalized citizen in 1975; daughter of Matthew (an importer) and Agnes (Jung) Chi. *Education:* Manhattanville College, B.A., 1955, M.A., 1960; Fordham University, Ph.D., 1968; Columbia University, certificate from East Asian Institute (M.A. equivalent), 1971. *Religion:* Roman Catholic. *Office:* Department of History, Graduate School, Fu-jen Catholic University, Hsinchuang, Taipei, Taiwan 242.

CAREER: International School of the Sacred Heart, Tokyo, Japan, teacher, 1959-62; Sacred Heart College, Taipei, Taiwan, president, 1967-68; Manhattanville College, Purchase, N.Y., professor of history, 1969-78, director of East Asian studies program, 1971-78; member of staff, Historical Office, U.S. Department of State, 1978-81; Fu-jen Catholic University, Taipei, Taiwan, member of faculty, department of history, 1982—. Co-chairperson of seminar on modern China, Columbia University, 1975-76. *Member:* American Historical Association. *Awards, honors:* Awards from National Humanities Faculty, 1972, 1973; grants from Social Science Research Council, 1972-73, and American Philosophical Society, 1975.

WRITINGS: China Diplomacy, 1914-1918, Harvard University Press, 1970; *Ts'ao Ju-lin (1876-1966): His Japanese Connections,* Princeton University Press, 1980; *The 1911 Revolution and Women Intelligentsia in China,* Academia Sinica (Taipei), 1983. Contributor to *Encyclopedia of Japan.* Contributor of articles to professional journals.

WORK IN PROGRESS: Research on European diplomatic history and the nineteenth century.

AVOCATIONAL INTERESTS: Photography and painting.

*   *   *

CHIGNON, Niles
See LINGEMAN, Richard R(oberts)

*   *   *

CHILDRESS, James Franklin 1940-

PERSONAL: Born October 4, 1940, in Mt. Airy, N.C.; son of Roscoe Franklin (a salesman) and Zella (a teacher; maiden name, Wagoner) Childress; married Georgia Harrell (a teacher), December 21, 1958; children: Albert Franklin and James Frederic (twins). *Education:* Guilford College, B.A., 1962; Yale University, B.D. (cum laude), 1965, M.A., 1967, Ph.D., 1968. *Religion:* Society of Friends. *Home:* 1819 Rugby Rd., Charlottesville, Va. 22903. *Office:* Department of Religious Studies, University of Virginia, Charlottesville, Va. 22903.

CAREER: University of Virginia, Charlottesville, assistant professor, 1968-71, associate professor, 1971-75, professor of religious studies, 1975, acting chairman of department, 1970-71, chairman, 1972-75; Georgetown University, Kennedy Institute, Center for Bioethics, Washington, D.C., Joseph P. Kennedy Senior Professor of Christian Ethics, 1975-79; University of Virginia, professor of religious studies, 1979-81, professor of religious studies and medical education, 1981-83, Commonwealth Professor of Religious Studies and Medical Education, 1983—. Adjunct professor of Christian ethics at Union Theological Seminary, Richmond, Va., 1969; visiting professor of ethics and society at University of Chicago Divinity School, 1977; visiting professor of religion at Princeton University, 1978.

MEMBER: Society for Values in Higher Education, American Society of Christian Ethics (member of board of directors, 1972-76), American Academy of Religion, American Society for Social and Political Philosophy, American Theological Society, Society for Health and Human Values, Institute of Society, Ethics and Life Sciences (fellow), Duodecim, Inter-University Seminar on Armed Forces and Society. *Awards, honors:* American Council of Learned Societies study fellowship, 1972-73; Harvard University fellowship in law and religion, 1972-73; Huntington Library research award, summer, 1974.

WRITINGS: (Editor with David Harned) *Secularization and the Protestant Prospect,* Westminster, 1970; *Civil Disobedience and Political Obligation: A Study in Christian Social Ethics,* Yale University Press, 1971; (with Tom L. Beauchamp) *Principles of Biomedical Ethics,* Oxford University Press, 1979, 2nd edition, 1983; *Priorities in Biomedical Ethics,* Westminster, 1981; *Moral Responsibility in Conflicts: Essays on Non-violence, War and Conscience,* Louisiana State University Press, 1982; *Who Should Decide?: Paternalism in Health Care,* Oxford University Press, 1982.

Contributor: Claude A. Frazier, editor, *Should Doctors Play God?,* Broadman, 1971; Richard W. Wertz, editor, *Readings on Ethical and Social Issues in Bio-Medicine,* Prentice-Hall, 1973; Robert Veatch and Roy Branson, editors, *Ethics and Health Care,* Ballinger, 1976; Furman Stough and Urban Holmes, editors, *Realities and Visions,* Seabury, 1976; Tom Shannon, editor, *Readings in Bioethics,* Paulist Press, 1976, 2nd edition, 1981; Stanley J. Reiser and others, editors, *Ethics in Medicine: Historical Perspectives and Contemporary Concerns,* M.I.T. Press, 1977; *HEW Secretary's Task Force on the Compensation of Injured Research Subjects: Appendix A,* National Institutes of Health, 1977; Tom L. Beauchamp and LeRoy Walters, editors, *Contemporary Issues in Bioethics,* Dickenson, 1978, 2nd edition, 1982; Bertram Bandman and Elsie Bandman, editors, *Bioethics and Human Rights,* Little, Brown, 1978; Louis W. Hodges, editor, *Social Responsibility: Journalism, Law, Medicine,* Washington and Lee University, Volume IV, 1978, Volume VIII, 1982; Steven E. Rhoads, editor, *Valuing Life: The Public Policy Dilemmas,* Westview, 1979; Ronald Munson, editor, *Intervention and Reflection: Basic Issues in Medical Ethics,* Wadsworth, 1979, 2nd edition, 1983; Michael S. Pritchard and Wade L. Robison, editors, *Philosophical Issues in Medical Ethics,* Humana Press, 1979; Veatch, editor, *Life Span: The Hastings Center Report on Values and Life Extending Technology,* Harper, 1979.

Shannon, editor, *War or Peace?: The Search for New Answers,* Orbis, 1980; Virginia Abernethy, editor, *Frontiers in Medical Ethics: Applications in a Medical Setting,* Ballinger, 1980; Donald W. Shriver, editor, *Religious Studies and Medicine,* University of Pittsburgh Press, 1980; Thomas Mappes and Jane Zembaty, editors, *Biomedical Ethics,* McGraw, 1981; Michael H. Shapiro and Roy G. Spece, Jr., editors, *Bioethics and Law,* West Publishing, 1981; Earl E. Shelp, editor, *Justice and Health Care,* Reidel, 1981; John A. Downey, Georgia Reidel, and Austin H. Kutscher, editors, *Bereavement of Physical Disability: Recommitment to Life, Health and Function,* Arno, 1981; Shelp, editor, *Beneficence and Health Care,* Reidel, 1982; Constance C. Conrad, editor, *Biomedical Ethics: Unique Issues for Preventive Medicine,* American College of Preventive Medicine, 1982; Natalie Abrams and Michael D. Buckner, editors, *Medical Ethics: A Clinical Textbook and Reference for the Health Care Professions,* M.I.T. Press, 1983.

Also author of pamphlet, "Civil Disobedience and Trust," 1975. Editor of "Studies in Religious Ethics" monograph series for American Academy of Religion. Contributor to *Encyclopedia of Bioethics,* 1978; contributor of articles and reviews to numerous journals. *Journal of Religious Ethics,* associate editor, 1975, co-editor, 1978-81; member of editorial board, *Bioethics Digest,* 1977-78, *Journal of Health, Politics, Policy, and Law,* 1981—, *Journal of Medicine and Philosophy,* 1982—, and *Bioethics Reporter,* 1982—.

WORK IN PROGRESS: A Dictionary of Christian Ethics, second edition, for Westminster; co-editing *Readings in Bioethics*

for Prentice-Hall; co-editing *Religious Ethics and Moral Problems.*

*   *   *

CHURCHILL, E(lmer) Richard 1937-

PERSONAL: Born May 25, 1937, in Greeley, Colo.; son of Emery Roy and Olive (Whitteker) Churchill; married Linda Ruler (a junior high school teacher), August 18, 1961; children: Eric Richard, Robert Sean. *Education:* Colorado State College (now University of Northern Colorado), A.B., 1959, M.A., 1962. *Home:* 25890 WCR 53, Kersey, Colo. 80644.

CAREER: Public library employee in Greeley, Colo., for ten years; Park Elementary School, Greeley, fifth grade teacher, beginning 1959; Maplewood Middle School, Greeley, librarian, 1974—. Co-owner of Timberline Books, beginning 1971. *Military service:* Colorado Air National Guard, 1961-67.

WRITINGS: (With Edward H. Blair) *Games and Puzzles for Family Leisure,* Abingdon, 1965; *Everybody Came to Leadville,* Timberline, 1971; *The McCartys: They Rode with Butch Cassidy,* Timberline, 1972; *Colorado Quiz Bag,* Timberline, 1973; *Doc Holliday, Bat Masterson, and Wyatt Earp: Their Colorado Careers,* Timberline, 1974; *Math Duplicator Masters for Basic Math,* J. Weston Walch, 1974; *One Hundred and One Shaggy Dog Stories,* Scholastic Book Services, 1975; (compiler) *The Six-Million Dollar Cucumber: Riddles and Fun for Children,* F. Watts, 1976; (with sons, Eric Churchill and Sean Churchill) *Holiday Hulabaloo!: Facts, Jokes, and Riddles,* F. Watts, 1977; *The Timberline Books,* eight volumes, Pruett, 1981; *New Puzzles,* Scholastic Book Services, 1981; *Bet I Can,* Sterling, 1982.

With wife, Linda R. Churchill: (And with E. H. Blair) *Fun with American History,* Abingdon, 1966; (and with E. H. Blair and Kay K. Blair) *Fun with American Literature,* Abingdon, 1968; *Short Lessons in World History,* J. Weston Walch, 1971; *Puzzle It Out,* Scholastic Book Services, 1971; *How Our Nation Became Great,* J. Weston Walch, 1971; *Community Civics Case Book,* J. Weston Walch, 1973; *Enriched Social Studies Teaching through the Use of Games and Activities,* Fearon, 1973; *Puzzles and Quizzes,* Scholastic Book Services, 1973; *American History Activity Reader,* J. Weston Walch, 1974; *Puzzles and Games for Concepts and Inquiry,* Allyn & Bacon, 1974; *World History Activity Reader,* J. Weston Walch, 1975; *Casebook on Marriage and the Family,* J. Weston Walch, 1975; *Family Health Casebook,* J. Weston Walch, 1975; *Hidden Word Puzzles,* Scholastic Book Services, 1975; *You and the Law,* J. Weston Walch, 1976; *Twentieth-Century Europe Activity Reader,* J. Weston Walch, 1976; *Middle Ages Activity Reader,* J. Weston Walch, 1977; *Hidden Word Puzzles 2,* Scholastic Book Services, 1977; *Bionic Banana,* F. Watts, 1979.

Also author of more than one hundred other books, activity readers, and duplicator packages for J. Weston Walch, including *Understanding Our Economy, Supernatural Reader, Musicians Activity Reader, Artists Activity Reader, World Geography Puzzles, Vocabulary Boosters, State Puzzles, Spanish Puzzles,* and *Latin American Map Studies.*

*   *   *

CHURCHILL, Linda R. 1938-

PERSONAL: Born September 26, 1938, in Evanston, Ill.; daughter of Orville Vinton (a realtor) and Ruth Jane (Markham) Ruler; married E. Richard Churchill (a teacher), August 18,

1961; children: Eric Richard, Robert Sean. *Education:* Attended Colorado State University, 1956-58; Colorado State College (now University of Northern Colorado), A.B., 1961, M.A., 1962. *Religion:* Episcopalian. *Home:* 25890 WCR 53, Kersey, Colo. 80644.

CAREER: Greeley Public Library, Greeley, Colo. assistant, 1958-61; Greeley (Colo.) public schools, history teacher, 1961—. Co-owner of Timberline Books, beginning 1971.

WRITINGS—All with husband, E. Richard Churchill: (And with Edward H. Blair) *Fun with American History,* Abingdon, 1966; (and with E. H. Blair, and Kay K. Blair) *Fun with American Literature,* Abingdon, 1968; *Puzzle It Out,* Scholastic Book Services, 1971; *Short Lessons in World History,* J. Weston Walch, 1971; *How Our Nation Became Great,* J. Weston Walch, 1971; *Community Civics Case Book,* J. Weston Walch, 1973; *Enriched Social Studies Teaching through the Use of Games and Activities,* Fearon, 1973; *Puzzles and Quizzes,* Scholastic Book Services, 1973; *American History Activity Reader,* J. Weston Walch, 1974; *Puzzles and Games for Concepts and Inquiry,* Allyn & Bacon, 1974; *World History Activity Reader,* J. Weston Walch, 1975; *Casebook on Marriage and the Family,* J. Weston Walch, 1975; *Family Health Casebook,* J. Weston Walch, 1975; *Hidden Word Puzzles,* Scholastic Book Services, 1975; *You and the Law,* J. Weston Walch, 1976; *Twentieth-Century Europe Activity Reader,* J. Weston Walch, 1976; *Hidden Word Puzzles 2,* Scholastic Book Services, 1977; *Middle Ages Activity Reader,* J. Weston Walch, 1977; *Bionic Banana,* F. Watts, 1979.†

* * *

CIEPLAK, Tadeusz N(owak) 1918-

PERSONAL: Born October 7, 1918, in Tarnopol, Poland; immigrated to the United States in 1957, naturalized in 1963; son of Antoni (a farmer) and Agnieszka (Pszeniczna) Cieplak; married Irena Kondraciuk (a nurse), June 19, 1948; children: Bozena M. Dobrzynska (stepdaughter). *Education:* Attended Lvov and Warsaw universities, 1936-39; Oxford University, B.C.L., 1946; McGill University, LL.M., 1955, Ph.D., 1962. *Home:* 372 Burns St., Forest Hills, N.Y. 11375. *Office:* Department of Government and Politics, St. John's University, Grand Central & Utopia Parkways, Jamaica, N.Y. 11439.

CAREER: International Peasant Union, New York, N.Y., secretary to the president, 1957-61; San Francisco State College (now University), San Francisco, Calif., assistant professor of political science, 1961-63; Pennsylvania State University, University Park, assistant professor of political science, 1963-64; Alliance College, Cambridge Springs, Pa., associate professor of political science, 1964-65; St. John's University, Jamaica, N.Y., associate professor of political science, 1965—. Foreign service officer of Polish Government-in-Exile, serving in the Soviet Union, Turkey, and Portugal, 1941-45. Host of "Conference Call" on WABC-Radio, 1975—.

MEMBER: International Platform Association, American Political Science Association, American Association for the Advancement of Slavic Studies, Polish Institute of Arts and Sciences in America, Center for the Study of Democratic Institutions, Kosciuszko Foundation, Delta Tau Kappa (life member).

WRITINGS: (Editor and contributor) *Poland since 1956: Readings and Essays,* Twayne, 1972; (contributor) Ivan Volgyes, editor, *The Peasantry of Eastern Europe, Volume II: 20th Century Developments,* Pergamon, 1979; (contributor) Vincent McHale, editor, *Political Parties of Europe,* Greenwood Press,

1983; *Sorel and European Radicalism* (monograph), Sadhna Prakashan (Meerut, India), 1984; (editor) Wojciech Solalski, *Evolution of the Polish Populist Movement since Its Origin to 1939,* Sadhna Prakashan, in press. Contributor to academic journals.

WORK IN PROGRESS: Rural Solidarity, 1980-1981 (monograph), for Sadhna Prakashan.

SIDELIGHTS: Tadeusz N. Cieplak writes: "After the war, I felt that I should complement my war-time experiences with graduate studies in law and politics so that I could become an effective college teacher and writer. A concerted, dynamic, and creative cooperation of the Free World, in the political, economic, and intellectual realms, should decidedly tilt the scales in favor of democracy before the end of the century."

* * *

CIRCUS, Anthony
See HOCH, Edward D(entinger)

* * *

CIVILLE, John R(aphael) 1940-

PERSONAL: Born July 8, 1940, in Athens, Ohio; son of George P. (a government employee) and Mary (a teacher; maiden name, Guerra) Civille. *Education:* Athenaeum of Ohio, A.B., 1962; Xavier University, Cincinnati, Ohio, M.Ed., 1965; Alfonsiana, S.T.D., 1972. *Politics:* Democrat. *Home and office:* 6104 Desmond St., Cincinnati, Ohio 45227.

CAREER: Ordained diocesan Roman Catholic priest. Associate pastor of Roman Catholic church in Cincinnati, Ohio, 1966-69; Mount St. Mary's Seminary, Cincinnati, assistant professor of moral theology, 1972-82; St. Anthony Church, Cincinnati, pastor, 1978—. Assistant professor at Xavier University, 1974—; assistant adjunct professor at University of Dayton, 1979—. Director of World Justice and Peace Commission of the Archdiocese of Cincinnati, 1973-79. Chaplain of Sisters of St. Ursula, Cincinnati, 1974-76. *Member:* American Society of Christian Ethics, Catholic Theological Association of America.

WRITINGS: Tanzania and Nyerere, Orbis, 1976; (co-author) *Principles of Catholic Theology,* Alba House, 1981.

WORK IN PROGRESS: Research on Tanzania's UJAMAA socialism.

SIDELIGHTS: John R. Civille has studied in Rome, East Africa, and South America, and visited more than sixty countries. He told *CA:* "I have a great interest in social justice and in trying to understand what that means in practice, especially concerning international questions. I feel that my experiences from living in Africa and South America have given me more sensitivity to the problems people of the Third World face, as well as a greater realization of their struggle for economic advancement. I [have used] these insights in my teaching of social ethics and in my World Justice and Peace Commission work to stress the interdependence of the human family."

* * *

CLARE, Ellen
See SINCLAIR, Olga

* * *

CLARK, LaVerne Harrell 1929-

PERSONAL: Born June 6, 1929, in Smithville, Tex.; daughter of James Boyce (a railway engineer) and Belle (Bunte) Harrell; married L. D. Clark (a professor and writer), September 15, 1951. *Education:* Texas Woman's University, B.A., 1950; Columbia University, courses in creative writing, and graduate study, 1951-54; University of Arizona, M.A., 1962. *Home and office:* 4690 North Campbell Ave., Tucson, Ariz. 85718.

CAREER: Fort Worth Press, Fort Worth, Tex., reporter and librarian, 1950-51; Columbia University Press, New York City, employee in sales-advertising department, 1951-53; Episcopal Diocese of New York, New York City, assistant in promotion-news department, 1958-59; University of Arizona, Tucson, director of Poetry Center, 1962-66; writer, photographer, and lecturer, 1966—. *Member:* National League of American Pen Women, Westerners International, Western Writers of America, Society of Southwestern Authors, Theta Sigma Phi, Kappa Alpha Mu, Pi Lambda Theta.

AWARDS, HONORS: American Philosophical Society grant, 1967, 1969, for research in Spain; first place folklore prize, University of Chicago, 1967, and national second place in nonfiction, Biennial Letters Contest, National League of American Pen Women, 1968, both for *They Sang for Horses: The Impact of the Horse on Navajo and Apache Folklore;* named Distinguished Alumna, Texas Woman's University, 1973; Creative Writer of the Year, National League of American Pen Women, Tucson branch, 1977; recipient of nine additional Biennial awards, National League of American Pen Women, for various projects.

WRITINGS: They Sang for Horses: The Impact of the Horse on Navajo and Apache Folklore, University of Arizona Press, 1966; (editor) *The Face of Poetry: 101 Poets in Two Significant Decades,* illustrated with photographs by Clark, Gallimaufry Press, 1976; *Re-Visiting the Plains Indian Country of Mari Sandoz,* illustrated with photographs by Clark, Blue Cloud Quarterly, 1977; *Focus 101,* illustrated with photographs by Clark, Heidelberg Graphics, 1979.

Contributor: Austin E. Fife and J. Golden Taylor, editors, *The Western Folklore Conference: Selected Papers,* Utah State University Press, 1964; Kenneth Donelson, editor, *Southwestern Literature and Culture in the English Classroom,* Arizona State University, 1971; Karl Kopp, Jane Kopp, and Bart Lanier Stafford III, editors, *Southwest: A Contemporary Anthology,* Red Earth Press, 1977.

Contributor of photographs: L. D. Clark, *Dark Night of the Body: D. H. Lawrence's "The Plumed Serpent,"* University of Texas Press, 1964; Clark, *The Minoan Distance: The Symbolism of Travel in D. H. Lawrence,* University of Arizona Press, 1980; Robert B. Partlow, Jr. and Harry T. Moore, editors, *D. H. Lawrence: The Man Who Lived,* Southern Illinois University Press, 1980.

Contributor of articles and photographs to periodicals, including *American Scandinavian Review, Arizona and the West, Journal of Popular Culture, Phantasm, American Indian Quarterly,* and *Bits and Pieces.*

SIDELIGHTS: LaVerne Harrell Clark told *CA:* "I consider myself primarily a folklorist and a fiction writer. Mythology is the mirror of mankind, but so I think is the true fiction; for it, like the enduring myths and legends, transcends the factuality of a certain time or place or people thus bringing a universality to the sharing of each man's truth. Thus I write actually to share my discoveries, reactions, and feelings with my most sought-after companion, the reader. Therefore whether I'm recounting some Navajo and Apache tales, or forming my own fiction about the lives of people in some small Texas town, I hope to share the tone and texture and truth of what I have seen and felt, and thus to arouse a feeling of recognition and reflection in those who read my words.

"I work whenever I can, and as a busy wife of another writer, as long as I can. But always alone, and always on a number of very differing projects: Indian and Spanish folklore, short stories, and photography of literary personages, as well as of writers' lives and trails. Always with anxiety to get one of several projects done well, and another begun. However, my life is such that I have never been able to plan it carefully, nor to keep any day-to-day unbending schedule; still I admire those who can do so and never cease to try to organize my own creative impulses in this way. I feel I am cursed by Andrew Marvell's lines: 'But at my back I always hear / Time's winged chariot scurrying near.' But in bad times, the words of C. Day Lewis about the rise and flow and tide of writers do *cheer* me, for I realize that he has shared with me his truth: that despite the dry times all writers know, the productive ones do come."

BIOGRAPHICAL/CRITICAL SOURCES: The Western Folklore Conference: Selected Papers, Monograph Series of the Utah State University Press, Volume XI, Number 3, June, 1964; *Coda,* September/October, 1977.

*   *   *

CLARK, Leroy D.

PERSONAL: Married Christine Philpot (an attorney), July 14, 1964; children: Chad, Kimani. *Education:* City College of the City of New York (now City College of the City University of New York), B.A., 1956; New York University, graduate study, 1956-58; Columbia University, LL.B., 1961. *Home:* 4636 South 34th St., Arlington, Va. 22206. *Office:* School of Law, Catholic University, Washington, D.C. 20064.

CAREER: State of New York, Attorney General's Office, New York City, staff counsel, 1961-62; National Association for the Advancement of Colored People, Legal Defense and Educational Fund, New York City, assistant counsel and head of civil litigation, 1962-68; New York University, New York City, professor of law, 1968-79; Equal Employment Opportunity Commission, Washington, D.C., general counsel, 1979-81; currently affiliated with Catholic University, Washington, D.C. Member of board of directors of Commission on Juvenile Justice Standards of Institute for Judicial Administration and American Bar Association. *Member:* American Arbitration Association, National Conference of Black Lawyers, Society of American Law Teachers, Phi Beta Kappa. *Awards, honors:* American Bar Association award for "contribution to public understanding of the law."

WRITINGS: (Contributor) Allan C. Ornstein, editor, *Educating the Disadvantaged,* Volume I, AMS Press, 1968; (contributor) *When the Marching Stopped: An Analysis of Black Issues in the '70's,* National Urban League, 1973; (contributor) *Minority Opportunities in Law for Blacks, Puerto Ricans, and Chicanos,* Law Journal Press, 1974; *The Grand Jury: The Use and Abuse of Political Power,* Quadrangle, 1975; (with Arthur Smith, Jr. and Charles B. Craver) *Employment Discrimination Law: Cases and Materials,* 2nd edition (Clark not associated with previous edition), Bobbs-Merrill, 1982. Contributor to professional journals.

CLARK, Samuel Delbert 1910-

PERSONAL: Born February 24, 1910, in Lloydminster, Alberta, Canada; son of Samuel David (a farmer) and Mary Alice (Curry) Clark; married Rosemary J. Landry, December 26, 1939; children: Ellen Margaret, Samuel David, William Edmond. *Education:* University of Saskatchewan, B.A., 1930, M.A., 1931; London School of Economics and Political Science, graduate study, 1932-33; McGill University, M.A., 1935; University of Toronto, Ph.D., 1938. *Home:* 9 Lamont Ave., Agincourt, Ontario, Canada M1S 1A8.

CAREER: University of Manitoba, Winnipeg, lecturer in sociology, 1937-38; University of Toronto, Toronto, Ontario, 1938—, became professor of sociology, 1953-76, professor emeritus, 1976—, chairman of department, 1963-69. McCulloch Professor, Dalhousie University, 1972-74. Visiting professor, University of California, Berkeley, 1960-61, University of Guelph, 1976-78, Lakehead University, 1978-80, Tsukuba University, 1980, and University of Edinborough, 1980-81.

MEMBER: Royal Society of Canada (president, 1975-76), Canadian Association of Sociology and Anthropology (honorary president), American Sociological Association, American Academy of Arts and Sciences (honorary foreign member).

AWARDS, HONORS: Guggenheim fellowship, 1944-45; Tyrell medal, Royal Society of Canada, 1960; officer, Order of Canada, 1978; honorary degrees from University of Calgary, St. Mary's University, Dalhousie University, and Lakehead University.

WRITINGS—Published by University of Toronto Press, except as indicated: *The Canadian Manufacturers' Association: A Study in Collective Bargaining and Political Pressure,* 1939; *Social Development of Canada,* 1942; *Church and Sect in Canada,* 1948; *Movements of Political Protest in Canada, 1660-1840,* 1959; *The Developing Canadian Community,* 1963, revised edition, 1969; *The Suburban Society,* 1968; *The Canadian Society in Historical Perspective,* McGraw-Hill/Ryerson, 1976; *The New Urban Poor,* McGraw-Hill/Ryerson, 1978.

WORK IN PROGRESS: Social Change in Canada since the Second World War.

*   *   *

CLARKE, Mary Washington 1913-

PERSONAL: Born February 4, 1913, in Scarbro, W.Va.; daughter of William Calvin (a teacher and public school administrator) and Dulcie (Bragg) Washington; married Kenneth Wendell Clarke (a college professor), August 25, 1960; stepchildren: Suzanne (Mrs. Larry Ellis). *Education:* Marshall College (now University), A.B., 1933; West Virginia University, M.A., 1936; University of Pennsylvania, Ph.D., 1960. *Politics:* Republican. *Religion:* Protestant. *Home:* 26250 Omar Dr., Fort Bragg, Calif. 95437.

CAREER: High school teacher of journalism and creative writing in Oak Hill, W.Va., 1935-44; American Red Cross, Brooklyn, N.Y., family caseworker, 1944-46; Marshall College (now University), Huntington, W.Va., instructor, 1946-49, associate professor, 1949-53, associate professor of English, 1953-54; Indiana State College (now Indiana University of Pennsylvania), Indiana, Pa., associate professor of English, 1954-

58; Chico State College (now California State University, Chico), assistant professor of English, 1958-60; Western Kentucky University, Bowling Green, associate professor, 1964-67, professor of English and folklore, 1967-75, professor emeritus, 1975—. Held short-term positions as editorial worker for Doubleday, Doran, 1944, Huntington *Herald-Advertiser,* 1946, University of Nevada, 1960, and Indiana University Southeastern Campus, Jeffersonville, 1962-64. *Awards, honors:* Chicago Folklore Contest, 1968, second place; distinguished service award, Western Kentucky University, 1969; National Endowment for the Humanities grants, 1969-70, 1970-71.

WRITINGS: (With husband, Kenneth W. Clarke) *Introducing Folklore,* Holt, 1963; (editor with K. W. Clarke) *A Folklore Reader,* A. S. Barnes, 1965; (compiler with K. W. Clarke) *A Concise Dictionary of Folklore,* Kentucky Folklore Society, 1965, revised edition, 1971; *Jesse Stuart's Kentucky,* McGraw, 1968.

The Harvest and the Reapers: Oral Traditions of Kentucky, University Press of Kentucky, 1974; (compiler with Charles S. Guthrie) *Twenty Year Index to the Kentucky Folklore Record,* Kentucky Folklore Society, 1975; (contributor) Lionel D. Wyld, editor, *American Civilization: An Introduction to Research and Bibliography,* Everett/Edwards, 1975; *Kentucky Quilts and Their Makers,* Kentucky Bicentennial Bookshelf, 1976; (editor with J. R. LeMaster) *Jesse Stuart: Essays on His Work,* University Press of Kentucky, 1977. Contributor to folklore journals. Co-editor, *Kentucky Folklore Record* (quarterly), 1965-70, and compiler of annual bibliographies of folklore of the state.

WORK IN PROGRESS: With husband Kenneth W. Clarke, an illustrated study of northern California water towers and tank houses.

SIDELIGHTS: Mary Washington Clarke wrote *CA:* "Although my published work has been incidental to my career as a teacher, I never pass up an opportunity to reiterate the age-old dicta for beginning writers to write of what they really know and—be the impulse toward creative expression or to record information—exert the discipline to *get it right.* My writing had journalistic beginnings, growing out of a lifelong involvement with traditional materials, an interest that spilled over into public programs, graduate studies, teaching career, avocational activities including the writing of articles and books."

AVOCATIONAL INTERESTS: Outdoor life, music, folk arts.

*   *   *

CLAYTON, John J(acob) 1935-

PERSONAL: Born January 5, 1935, in New York, N.Y.; son of Charles (an executive) and Leah (Kaufman) Clayton; married Marilyn Hirsch (an educational consultant), July 31, 1956 (divorced, 1974); married Marlynn Krebs (a teacher; divorced, 1983); children: (first marriage) Laura Sharon, Joshua Benjamin; (second marriage) Sasha. *Education:* Columbia University, A.B. (with honors), 1956; New York University, M.A., 1959; Indiana University, further graduate study, 1959-62, Ph.D., 1966. *Office:* Department of English, University of Massachusetts, Amherst, Mass.

CAREER: University of Victoria, Victoria, British Columbia, instructor in English, 1962-63; University of Maryland, Overseas Division, lecturer to servicemen in Europe, 1963-64; Boston University, Boston, Mass., assistant professor of humanities, 1964-69; University of Massachusetts, Amherst, 1969—, began as associate professor, professor of English, 1975—. Summer teaching at University of British Columbia and California State University, Hayward.

WRITINGS: Saul Bellow: In Defense of Man, Indiana University Press, 1968, 2nd edition, 1979; *What Are Friends For?* (novel), Little, Brown, 1979; *Bodies of the Rich* (short stories), University of Illinois Press, 1983.

Contributor of articles to *Journal of Esthetic Education, American Review, Massachusetts Review, Journal of Aesthetic Education,* and *Pagean,* and short fiction to *Antioch Review* and other literary journals.

WORK IN PROGRESS: A novel, *Eternal Youth.*

SIDELIGHTS: In John J. Clayton's novel *What Are Friends For?,* Sid, a young Harvard graduate tired of superficial relationships, embarks upon a relationship with Joan, a thirty-eight-year-old mother of four. Joan, according to Anatole Broyard of the *New York Times,* hopes to "separate the man from the boy in Sid by introducing him to the particular." Sid, Broyard continues, "is like a long, lost brother. We are glad to see him, to find ourselves back inside human nature. He invites us to step in and make ourselves at home in his perplexity."

Commenting on *What Are Friends For?* in the *New York Times Book Review,* Daphne Merkin feels the book "is not without glimmerings of talent, despite its generally unconvincing characters (Joan, in particular, seems to be a composite assembled from various articles on the 'new' female) and irritatingly polarized conception of the world (Bad Guys sell out; Good Guys strum their guitars)." Merkin concludes that if Clayton "were to let some of his perceptions grow up a little, [he] might arrive at the maturity that eludes his characters." And Broyard notes that although the author "lets his poise slip every now and then and loses the esthetic distance between his characters and himself," it's "not as off-putting as it sounds. Not at all, in fact. Sid's mistakes are youthful, sometimes even definitive, and there is something appealingly sincere about his empirical approach to reality. So many people seem to look for bypasses these days."

BIOGRAPHICAL/CRITICAL SOURCES: New York Times, April 14, 1979; *New York Times Book Review,* July 8, 1979.

*   *   *

CLAYTON, Keith (M.) 1928-

PERSONAL: Born September 25, 1928, in London, England; son of Edgar Francis and Constance (Clark) Clayton; married former wife, 1952; married Jennifer Haschak, 1974; children: (first marriage) Richard, Jill, Michael, Ian. *Education:* University of Sheffield, B.Sc., 1949, M.Sc., 1951; University of London, Ph.D., 1958. *Home:* Well Close, Pound Lane, Norwich NR7 0UA, England. *Office:* University of East Anglia, Norwich NR4 7TJ, England.

CAREER: State University of New York at Binghamton, professor of geography, 1960-62; University of London, London School of Economics and Political Science, London, England, reader in geography, 1962-67; University of East Anglia, Norwich, England, dean of environmental sciences, 1967-71, professor of environmental sciences, 1972—. Director, Geo Books and *Geo Abstracts.*

WRITINGS: The Earth's Crust, Aldus Books, 1966, published as *The Crust of the Earth,* Natural History Press, 1967; (editor

with I. B. Kormoss) *Oxford Regional Economic Atlas: Western Europe,* Clarendon Press, Cartographic Department, 1971; (editor) *Pollution Abatement,* David & Charles, 1973; (with Allan Straw) *Eastern and Central England,* Methuen, 1979; *Coastal Geomorphology,* Macmillan, 1979. Editor, "Geomorphology" series, Oliver & Boyd and Longman, including Cliff Ollier's *Weathering,* 1969; editor, *Geo Abstracts A.*

WORK IN PROGRESS: Coastal Hazards, for Longman.

*   *   *

CLEGG, Stewart (Roger) 1947-

PERSONAL: Born September 4, 1947, in Bradford, England; son of Willie (a sales representative) and Joyce Sylvia (Rogers) Clegg; married Caroline Lynne Bowker (a teacher), August 7, 1971; children: Jonathan James. *Education:* University of Aston, B.Sc. (with honors), 1971; University of Bradford, Ph.D., 1974. *Politics:* Social democrat ("in the European mould, rather than the British SDP sense"). *Religion:* None. *Agent:* A. D. Peters & Co., 10 Buckingham St., London W.C.2, England. *Office:* School of Humanities, Griffith University, Nathan, Brisbane, Queensland 4111, Australia.

CAREER: Lecturer for Faculty of Business and Professional Studies, Trent Polytechnic, 1974-75; University of Bradford, Bradford, England, research fellow of European Group for Organization Studies at Management Centre, 1975-77; Griffith University, Brisbane, Australia, reader in sociology, 1977—. *Member:* Australian and Pacific Researchers in Organization Studies, European Group for Organization Studies, British Sociological Association of Australia and New Zealand.

WRITINGS: Power, Rule and Domination: A Critical and Empirical Understanding of Power in Sociological Theory and Organizational Life, Routledge & Kegan Paul, 1975; (editor with David Dunkerley) *Critical Issues in Organizations,* Routledge & Kegan Paul, 1977; *The Theory of Power and Organization,* Routledge & Kegan Paul, 1979; (with Dunkerley) *Organization, Class and Control,* Routledge & Kegan Paul, 1980; (editor with Geoff Dow and Paul Boreham) *Politics, the State and Recession,* St. Martin's, 1983; (with Dow and Boreham) *Class, Politics and the Economy: The Politics and Organization of Class Structure,* Wheatsheaf, 1984. Contributor to professional journals. Editor of *Australian and New Zealand Journal of Sociology* and of *Organization Studies.*

WORK IN PROGRESS: Research on the class structure of Australia in comparative perspective; cross-cultural research.

SIDELIGHTS: Stewart Clegg told *CA:* "Older now, more uncertain about most things except very close private things, I find that my conception of my writing as political has changed enormously. I still write about political issues but I doubt that I entertain any illusions about that activity amounting to or contributing towards politics. Hence, writing these days is a wholly secularized, wholly de-enchanted pastime. It feels more comfortable in some ways, even if more routinized."

*   *   *

CLEMENTS, John 1916-

PERSONAL: Born July 23, 1916, in Wilkes-Barre, Pa.; son of Dillon F. (a businessman) and Lynn (Hershberger) Clements; married Gladys Johnston (a secretary); children: Lynn Clements Burleson, Daphne Clements Firestone, Allan. *Education:* Attended University of Minnesota. *Politics:* Independent. *Re-*

ligion: Methodist. *Home:* 6140 Spring Valley, Dallas, Tex. 75240. *Office:* Political Research, Inc., 16850 Dallas Parkway, Dallas, Tex. 75248.

CAREER: Writer, researcher, and lecturer. Writer for Mc-Graw-Hill Book Co. in New York City; board chairperson of McCullers Press, Inc.; Political Research, Inc., Dallas, Tex., founder, board chairperson, and chief executive officer, 1968—.

WRITINGS: Taylors Encyclopedia of Government Officials, Political Research, Inc., 1967, 9th edition, 1983; *Clements' Encyclopedia of World Governments,* Political Research Inc., 1974, 5th edition, 1982; *Chronology of the United States,* McGraw, 1975; *The United Kingdom/The Commonwealth of Nations: A Directory of Governments,* Political Research, Inc., 1979.

WORK IN PROGRESS: The Story of Tegoland.

SIDELIGHTS: John Clements writes that he has served as special analyst to two U.S. presidents and to other federal and state officials.

*   *   *

CLEVERLEY FORD, D(ouglas) W(illiam) 1914-

PERSONAL: Born March 4, 1914, in Sheringham, England; son of Arthur James (a clerk) and Mildred (Cleverley) Ford; married Olga Mary Gilbart-Smith, June 28, 1939. *Education:* London College of Divinity, A.L.C.D. (with first class honors), 1936; University of London, B.D., 1937, M.Th., 1941. *Home:* Rastrevor, Lingfield, Surrey RH7 6BZ, England.

CAREER: Ordained priest of Church of England in St. Paul's Cathedral, London, England, 1937; tutor at London College of Divinity, London, 1937-39; curate of Bridlington, Yorkshire, England, 1939-42; vicar of Holy Trinity, Hampstead, London, 1942-55; vicar of Holy Trinity, South Kensington, London, 1955-74; senior chaplain to the Archbishop of Canterbury, 1975-80; Six Preacher of Canterbury Cathedral, 1982—. Chaplain to Queen Elizabeth II, 1973—. Honorary director, College of Preachers, 1960-73; rural dean of Westminster, 1965-74; prebendary of St. Paul's Cathedral, 1968, currently prebendary emeritus; provincial canon of York, 1969—. Chairman of Queen Alexandra's House, Kensington Gore, 1966-74. Member of governing body, Westminster City School and United Westminster Schools, 1965-74. *Member:* British and Foreign Bible Society (life governor), Church's Ministry among the Jews. *Awards, honors:* Queen's Jubilee Medal, 1977.

WRITINGS: Why We Believe in Jesus Christ, Lutterworth, 1950; *A Key to Genesis,* S.P.C.K., 1951; *An Expository Preacher's Notebook,* Harper, 1960; *A Theological Preacher's Notebook,* Hodder & Stoughton, 1962; (co-author) *The Churchman's Companion,* Hodder & Stoughton, 1964; *A Pastoral Preacher's Notebook,* Hodder & Stoughton, 1965; *A Reading of St. Luke's Gospel,* Lippincott, 1967; *Preaching Today,* S.P.C.K., 1969; *The Ministry of the Word,* Eerdmans, 1979.

Published by Mowbray: *Preaching at the Parish Communion,* 1967; *Preaching at the Parish Communion: On the Epistles,* 1968; *Preaching at the Parish Communion: The Saints Days,* 1969; *Preaching through the Christian Year,* 1971; *Praying through the Christian Year,* 1973; *Have You Anything to Declare?,* 1973; *Preaching at the Parish Communion Series 3,* 1975; *Preaching on the Special Occasions,* 1975, Volume II, 1982; *New Preaching on the Old Testament,* 1976; *New Preaching from the New Testament,* 1977; *Preaching through*

the Acts of the Apostles, 1980; *More Preaching from the New Testament,* 1982; *More Preaching from the Old Testament,* 1983; *Preaching through the Psalms,* 1984.

Contributor to *Expository Times* (Edinburgh) and *Church Times* (London).

SIDELIGHTS: D. W. Cleverley Ford has working knowledge of German, French, and Italian. *Avocational interests:* Music, the arts, European travel, gardening and carpentry at his house in the country.

BIOGRAPHICAL/CRITICAL SOURCES: Church Times, January 4, 1963.

*   *   *

CLIFFORD, Martin 1910-
(Paul Roger Kenian)

PERSONAL: Born March 10, 1910; son of Georgi and Goldie (Kliefferd) Clifford; married Sarah Pryzant (a writer), May 2, 1939 (deceased); children: Kenneth Ian, Paul Ralph, Jerrold Roger. *Education:* City College (now City College of the City University of New York), B.Sc., 1939. *Politics:* Conservative.

CAREER: Engineer, Sperry Gyroscope Co., 1945-50; Gernsback Library, Inc., New York, N.Y., vice-president, 1950-65; writer.

WRITINGS: (Editor) *Television Technotes,* Radcraft, 1952; (editor) *Radio and TV Hints,* Radcraft, 1952; (editor) *High-Fidelity: Design, Construction, Measurements,* Gernsback, 1953; (with Bruno Zucconi) *Probes,* Gernsback, 1955, revised edition published as *Probes for Test Instruments,* 1968.

(Editor with others) *Hints and Kinks for TV, Radio, Audio,* Gernsback, 1961; *Transistors: How to Test Them [and] How to Build All-Transistor Test Equipment,* Gernsback, 1961; (under pseudonym Paul Roger Kenian) *Basic Transistor Course,* Gernsback, 1962; (with L. C. Lane) *Our Texas Heritage,* Waterview Publishing, 1964; *Electronics Data Handbook,* Gernsback, 1965, 2nd edition, TAB Books, 1972; *Color TV Repair,* Gernsback, 1965; *Diodes,* M. W. Lads, 1966; *The Volt-Ohm Milliammeter,* M. W. Lads, 1966; *Basic Alternating Current,* M. W. Lads, 1966; *How to Read Circuit Diagrams,* M. W. Lads, 1966; (under pseudonym Paul Roger Kenian) *Basic Electronics Math,* M. W. Lads, 1966; *Handbook of Transistor Circuits,* M. W. Lads, 1966; *The Oscilloscope,* M. W. Lads, 1966; *The Vacuum Tube Voltmeter,* M. W. Lads, 1966; *Elements of Electronics,* M. W. Lads, 1966; *How to Use and Enjoy Your Tape Recorder,* M. W. Lads, 1966; *Practical Radio,* M. W. Lads, 1966; *Learn Electronics in 5 Minutes, 37 Seconds,* M. W. Lads, 1966; (editor) *Test Instruments for Electronics,* Gernsback, 1966; *Psychology for Daily Living,* Waterview Publishing, 1967; *Your Tape Recorder,* Elpa, 1968; *How to Use Your VOM, VTVM, and Oscilloscope,* G/L Tab Books, 1968; *You and the World of Science,* National School of Home Study, 1969.

Computer Programming Course, Programming and System Institute, 1970; *Handbook of Electronic Tables,* 2nd edition (Clifford was not associated with earlier edition), TAB Books, 1972, 4th edition published as *Master Handbook of Electronic Tables,* 1983; *Electrical Mathematics at Work,* General Learning Corp., 1972; *Understanding High Fidelity,* Drake, 1972; *Basic Electricity and Beginning Electronics,* TAB Books, 1973; *Security: How to Protect Yourself, Your Home, Your Office, and Your Car,* Drake, 1974; *Encyclopedia of Home Wiring and Electricity,* Drake, 1974; *The Encyclopedia of Household*

Plumbing, Drake, 1975; (with wife Sarah Clifford) *Mind-benders,* three volumes, Drake, 1975; (with son Jerrold R. Clifford) *Modern Electronics Math,* TAB Books, 1976; *Microphones,* TAB Books, 1977.

Basic Drafting, TAB Books, 1980; *The Complete Guide to Car Audio,* Sams, 1981; *The Complete Guide to Security,* Sams, 1982; *The Complete Guide to High Fidelity,* Sams, 1982; *Master Handbook of Household Repairs,* TAB Books, 1982; *The Complete Guide to Video,* Sams, 1983.

Also author of correspondence courses in radio, electronics, television, drafting, and computer programming. Ghostwriter of several books. Contributor to newspapers and magazines.

WORK IN PROGRESS: The Video Encyclopedia: Satellite TV.

SIDELIGHTS: Martin Clifford wrote *CA:* "It isn't difficult to become a published author of books provided you are willing to follow a few guidelines. It is much easier to publish non-fiction than fiction. Select any subject in which you are interested, but do not start by writing a manuscript. Instead, find as many magazines as you can on your chosen topic and, using the contents pages, make a list of the material covered. You will soon realize that some segments of your chosen subject have not been written about—and those should be the topics on which you should concentrate. Naturally, you must make yourself as knowledgeable as you can.

"Following this approach, you should be able to get articles published. No one says it is easy, but it can be done. By the time you have three or more of these in print, you will have more than just a few book ideas. Select a non-fiction book publisher (get some help from your local reference librarian) and, armed with your articles, you will be in a good position to represent your book ideas.

"Can it really be done this way? I should know, for I have had more than fifty books published on topics as diverse as plumbing, electricity, science, electronics, high fidelity, video, psychology, history, and mathematics."

*   *   *

CLIFFORD, Sarah   1916-1976

PERSONAL: Born February 10, 1916, in Zaromb, Poland; died November 18, 1976; daughter of Morris and Rebecca (Edel) Pryzant; married Martin Clifford (a professional writer), May 2, 1939; children: Kenneth Ian, Paul Ralph, Jerrold Roger.

WRITINGS: Jacob and His Wives, M. W. Lads, 1968; *Polygamy in Hebron,* Curtis Books, 1971; *Adam and His Women,* Curtis Books, 1972; (with husband Martin Clifford) *Mindbenders,* three volumes, Drake, 1975.

SIDELIGHTS: Sarah Clifford and her husband traveled a dozen times to Israel, Turkey, and Greece to do research in museums and study ancient cultures.

[Sketch reviewed by husband, Martin Clifford]

*   *   *

CLOKE, Richard   1916-

PERSONAL: Born January 23, 1916, in Seattle, Wash.; son of Harold E. (an army officer) and Alice Bird (Findley) Cloke; married Shirley Jane Rodecker (a teacher); children: Kenneth, William. *Education:* Attended University of Virginia; University of California, B.A., 1940; graduate study at California State University, Northridge. *Office:* Kent Publications, 18301 Halsted St., Northridge, Calif. 91324.

CAREER: Writer. Kent School, Northridge, Calif., principal, 1965-78; Kent Publications, Northridge, president, 1973—. Has worked variously as auto worker, pile driver operator, shipwright, carpenter, poultry rancher, electronics technician in a television factory, account executive at KDUO-FM Radio in Los Angeles, Calif., and teacher.

WRITINGS—All published by Kent Publications: *Mister Pistol-John* (Western novel), 1976; *Vector Lee* (science fiction spy novel), 1977; *Jerry the Put* (gangster novel), 1978; *My Pal Al* (World War I novel), 1978; *Yvar, Prince of Rus* (historical novel), 1981; *Liberty Boys and Belles* (historical novel), 1982; *Earth Ovum* (poem), 1982. Contributor of poems to small literary magazines. Editor of *San Fernando Poetry Journal.*

WORK IN PROGRESS: A sequel to *My Pal Al.*

*   *   *

CLUBBE, John   1938-

PERSONAL: Born February 21, 1938, in New York, N.Y.; son of John and Gabrielle (Boiteux) Clubbe. *Education:* Columbia University, B.A., 1959, M.A., 1960, Ph.D., 1965; attended University of Paris, Sorbonne, 1960-61. *Office:* English Department, University of Kentucky, Lexington, Ky. 40506.

CAREER: Part-time lecturer in English at Columbia University, New York City, 1962-63, and City University of New York, New York City, 1963-65; University of Munster, Munster, Germany, lecturer in English, 1965-66; Duke University, Durham, N.C., assistant professor, 1966-70, associate professor of English, 1970-76; University of Kentucky, Lexington, professor of English, 1976—. *Member:* Modern Language Association of America, South Atlantic Modern Language Association, Keats-Shelley Association, American Byron Society (founding member; chairman, 1976—). *Awards, honors:* National Endowment for the Humanities fellowship, 1971-72, 1983-84; Guggenheim fellowship, 1975-76.

WRITINGS: Victorian Forerunner: The Later Career of Thomas Hood, Duke University Press, 1968; (editor) *Selected Poems of Thomas Hood,* Harvard University Press, 1970; (assistant editor) *The Letters of Thomas and Jane Welsh Carlyle, 1812-1828,* Duke University Press, Volumes I-IV, 1970, (associate editor) Volumes V-VII, 1977, Volumes VIII-IX, 1981; *Two Reminiscences of Thomas Carlyle,* Duke University Press, 1974; (co-editor) *Nineteenth Century Literary Perspectives,* Duke University Press, 1974; *Carlyle and His Contemporaries,* Duke University Press, 1976; *Froude's Life of Carlyle,* Ohio State University Press, 1979; (co-author) *Byron et la Suisse,* Droz, 1982; (co-author) *English Romanticism: The Grounds of Belief,* Macmillan, 1983; (contributor) *The English Romantic Poets: A Review of Research and Criticism,* Modern Language Association, 1984.

WORK IN PROGRESS: Byron in Switzerland, a biographical and critical study; a critical biography of J. A. Froude and an edition of his letters.

SIDELIGHTS: "There are certain books that one could go on writing and talking about for days, whether read in their own time or years following initial publication," writes Kay Dick in the *London Times.* "Their power to pleasure, intellect and imagination, to engage memory, to stimulate partisanship and controversy makes them classic. In biography, *Froude's Life of Carlyle* is as outstanding a work of art as Lockhart's Scott and Boswell's Johnson. Professor John Clubbe's abridged edition gives a renewal of life to this extraordinarily vivid and tantalizing masterpiece.''

BIOGRAPHICAL/CRITICAL SOURCES: London Times, February 25, 1980.

*   *   *

COALE, Samuel Chase   1943-

PERSONAL: Born July 26, 1943, in Hartford, Conn.; son of Samuel Chase (a photographer) and Harriet (Kimberly) Coale; married Gray Emory, June 24, 1972. *Education:* Trinity College, Hartford, Conn., B.A., 1965; Brown University, M.A. and Ph.D., both 1970. *Office:* Department of English, Wheaton College, Norton, Mass. 02766.

CAREER: Wheaton College, Norton, Mass., instructor, 1968-71, assistant professor, 1971-76, associate professor, 1976-81, professor of American literature, 1981—. Attended Poznan Summer Seminar, Poznan, Poland, 1977, 1978, and 1979. Member of board of directors, Trinity Square Repertory Theatre, Looking Glass Theatre, and Rhode Island Dane Repertory Theatre. Member of Rhode Island Bicentennial Commission. *Member:* Modern Language Association of America, English-Speaking Union (president, 1975—), Phi Beta Kappa. *Awards, honors:* Ford Foundation summer grants, 1970, 1971; grants for study in England, 1970, 1972; Fulbright fellowship in Greece, 1976-77; elected Knight of Mark Twain for book *John Cheever;* named outstanding young man, 1978, U.S. Jaycees; National Endowment for the Humanities fellowship, 1981-82.

WRITINGS: (Contributor) Committee on the Frost Centennial of University of Southern Mississippi English Department, editors, *Frost: Centennial Essays,* University Press of Mississippi, 1975; *John Cheever,* Ungar, 1977; *Anthony Burgess,* Ungar, 1982. Contributor of articles and reviews to literature journals. Book reviewer, *Providence Journal;* theatre and film reviewer, *East Side* (Providence, R.I.) and *Newport: This Week.*

WORK IN PROGRESS: In Hawthorne's Shadow: The Romance in American Fiction; Open Spaces, a mystery novel; ''Rogues and Redeemers,'' a play.

SIDELIGHTS: ''[Anthony] Burgess' improbable history and his wide shelf of work,'' writes Charles Champlin in the *Los Angeles Times Book Review,* ''have been set forth and analyzed with admirable succinctness by Samuel Coale [in *Anthony Burgess*]. Enriched by some extended conversations with Burgess, [the book] is a swift but clarifying view of what appears to be the major theme of Burgess' work—the ceaseless contending of good and evil (with no more than temporary victories on either side) in a Manichaean world.''

Speaking of his writing, Coale told *CA:* ''I like alternating between fiction and nonfiction, between novels and articles on contemporary writers. Travelling recently to India, Pakistan, and Sweden has opened other possibilities. I'm now writing reviews, interviews, and articles for newspapers and magazines in Sweden, Greece, Poland, and India. It's great fun to see yourself in print in a language totally alien to your own. Writing remains compulsive and incessant. I couldn't get through a day without it. I work every day at any odd moment. It requires self-discipline and daily 'slog'. Just don't stop!''

BIOGRAPHICAL/CRITICAL SOURCES: Los Angeles Times Book Review, January 10, 1982.

COCHRANE, Pauline A.   1929-
(Pauline Atherton)

PERSONAL: Born December 2, 1929, in Berwyn, Ill.; daughter of John and Ann (Jakovich) Blazina; married Glynn Cochrane. *Education:* Illinois College, A.B., 1951; Rosary College, M.A., 1954; graduate study at University of Chicago, 1955-70. *Home:* 2 Bishop's Glen, Fayetteville, N.Y. 13066. *Office:* School of Information Studies, Syracuse University, Syracuse, N.Y. 13210.

CAREER: Chicago Teachers College (now Chicago State University), Chicago, Ill., acting reference librarian, 1956-58, assistant professor of library science, 1958-61; Field Enterprises Educational Corp., Chicago, cross reference editor of *World Book Encyclopedia,* 1958-59; American Institute of Physics, New York, N.Y., associate director of documentation, 1961-66; Syracuse University, Syracuse, N.Y., professor of library science, 1966—. Consulting librarian, Rodfei Zedek Congressional Library, Chicago, 1960-61; consultant, *World Book Encyclopedia,* 1960-72; consultant to UNESCO, National Library of Medicine, Library of Congress, H. W. Wilson Co., Online Computer Library Center, Inc., and others. *Member:* American Library Association, American Society for Information Science, Phi Beta Kappa.

WRITINGS—Under name Pauline Atherton, except as indicated: (Editor) *Classification Research,* Munksgard, 1965; (with Kenneth H. Cook and Jeffrey Katzer) *Free Text Retrieval Evaluation,* Syracuse University, 1972; *Humanization of Knowledge in the Social Sciences: A Symposium,* School of Library Science, Syracuse University, 1972; *Putting Knowledge to Work,* Vikas (Delhi), 1973; *Guidelines for the Organization of Training Courses, Workshops and Seminars in Scientific and Technical Information and Documentation,* UNESCO, 1975; *Handbook for Information Systems and Services,* UNESCO, 1977; (with Roger W. Christian) *Librarians and Online Services,* Knowledge Industry Publications, 1977; (director) *Books Are for Use: Final Report of the Subject Access Project to the Council on Library Resources,* School of Information Studies, Syracuse University, 1978; (under name Pauline Cochrane, with Charles T. Meadow) *Basics of Online Searching,* Wiley, 1981. Also author of pamphlets; editor of newsletter and of two series for Syracuse University School of Library Science, 1972 and 1974. Contributor of articles and book reviews to professional journals.

WORK IN PROGRESS: A book on online subject access.

*   *   *

COCHRANE, Willard W(esley)   1914-

PERSONAL: Born May 15, 1914, in Fresno, Calif.; son of Willard W. (a rancher) and Clare A. (Chambers) Cochrane; married Mary Herget, August 23, 1942; children: W. Wesley, Stephen A., James M., Timothy S. *Education:* University of California, B.S., 1937; Montana State University, M.S., 1938; Harvard University, M.P.A., 1942, Ph.D., 1945. *Politics:* Democrat. *Religion:* Protestant. *Home:* 12860 Shake Ridge Rd., Sutter Creek, Calif. 95685.

CAREER: U.S. Government, Washington, D.C., economist for Farm Credit Administration, 1939-41, War Food Administration, 1943, and Bureau of Agricultural Economics, U.S. Department of Agriculture, 1943-47; United Nations Food and

Agricultural Organization, Washington, D.C., economist, 1947-48, member of U.S. Mission to Siam, 1948; Pennsylvania State University, University Park, associate professor, 1948-49, professor of agricultural economics, 1950-51; University of Minnesota, Minneapolis, professor of agricultural economics, 1951-61; U.S. Department of Agriculture, Washington, D.C., director of agricultural economics and economic adviser to Secretary of Agriculture, 1961-64; University of Minnesota, St. Paul, professor of agricultural economics, 1964-81, dean of international programs, 1965-70. Visiting professor at University of Wisconsin, summer, 1951, and University of Chicago, 1958-59. Consultant to Commodity Credit Corp., 1964-68, to Agency for International Development on food problems of India, 1964-65, to United Nations Food and Agriculture Organization, 1965-68, and to Ministry of Agriculture, Saudi Arabia, 1973-74; Ford Foundation consultant to India's Ministry of Food and Agriculture, 1967 and 1970, to Thailand, 1970, and to the Philippines, 1973. *Military service:* U.S. Naval Reserve, active duty as ensign, 1942-43.

MEMBER: American Agricultural Economic Association (vice-president, 1954-55; president, 1959-60; fellow), American Academy of Political and Social Science. *Awards, honors:* Distinguished Service Award, U.S. Department of Agriculture, 1964; LL.D., Montana State University, 1967.

WRITINGS: (With Walter W. Wilcox) *Economics of American Agriculture,* Prentice-Hall, 1951, 3rd edition, 1974; (with Carolyn Shaw) *Economics of Consumption,* McGraw, 1956; *Farm Prices: Myth and Reality,* University of Minnesota Press, 1958; *The City Man's Guide to the Farm Problem,* University of Minnesota Press, 1965; *The World Food Problem,* Crowell, 1969; *Agricultural Development Planning: Economic Concepts, Procedures, and Political Process,* Praeger, 1974; (with Mary E. Ryan) *American Farm Policy, 1948-1973,* University of Minnesota Press, 1976; *The Development of American Agriculture: A Historical Analysis,* University of Minnesota Press, 1979. Author of more than one hundred articles, reviews, and bulletins, including the prize-winning article "Farm Price Gyrations—An Aggregate Hypothesis" in *Journal of Farm Economics,* 1947.

SIDELIGHTS: Willard W. Cochrane has made many trips to India on technical assistance projects, and traveled extensively in Latin America and South and Southeast Asia. *Avocational interests:* History of the exploration of the Rocky Mountains; camping and fishing in the Rocky Mountains and High Sierras; raising, driving, and riding Morgan horses.

*   *   *

COERR, Eleanor (Beatrice) 1922-
(Eleanor B. Hicks, Eleanor Page)

PERSONAL: Surname rhymes with "more"; born May 29, 1922, in Kamsack, Saskatchewan, Canada; daughter of William Thomas (a druggist) and Mabel (Selig) Page; married Wymberley De Renne Coerr (a career diplomat and U.S. ambassador to South American countries), June 10, 1965. *Education:* Attended University of Saskatchewan; Kadel Airbrush School, Chicago, Ill., graduate, 1945; American University, B.Z., 1969; University of Maryland, M.L.S., 1971. *Home:* 1360 Josselyn Canyon, No. 34, Monterey, Calif. 93940.

CAREER: Writer. Editorial posts with *Advertiser-Journal,* Montgomery, Ala., 1953-58, and *Manila Times,* Manila, Republic of the Philippines, 1958-60; editor for U.S. Information Service, Taipei, Taiwan; Voice of America, Washington, D.C.,

contributing editor, 1963-65; Davis Memorial Library, Bethesda, Md., librarian, 1971-72. Lecturer and visiting author to schools, organizations, and reading councils in the United States and other countries. *Awards, honors:* West Australia Book Award and OMAR Award, both 1982, for *Sadako and the Thousand Paper Cranes.*

WRITINGS—All juveniles: (Under name Eleanor Page; self-illustrated) *Snoopy,* Institute of Applied Art, 1945; (under name Eleanor B. Hicks; self-illustrated) *Circus Day in Japan,* Tuttle, 1954, 2nd edition, 1958; (self-illustrated) *The Mystery of the Golden Cat,* Tuttle, 1968; *Twenty-Five Dragons,* Follett, 1971; *The Big Balloon Race,* Harper, 1981; *The Bellringer and the Pirates,* Harper, 1983.

All published by Putnam: *Biography of a Giant Panda,* 1974; *Biography of a Kangaroo,* 1976; *The Mixed-Up Mystery Smell,* 1976; *Biography of Jane Goodall,* 1976; *Sadako and the Thousand Paper Cranes,* 1977; *Waza Wins at Windy Gulch,* 1977; *Gigi, A Baby Whale,* 1980.

Contributor of features to the *Monterey Peninsula Herald* and other newspapers. Editor of *CAT Bulletin* (travel magazine), 1958-60.

WORK IN PROGRESS: The Josefina Story Quilt; In the Tiger's Mouth; To Fall from a Star.

SIDELIGHTS: Sadako and the Thousand Paper Cranes has been translated into Swedish and German.

*   *   *

COGHILL, Nevill (Henry Kendall Aylmer) 1899-1980

PERSONAL: Born April 19, 1899, in Skibbereen, Cork County, Eire (now Republic of Ireland); died November 6, 1980, in Cheltenham, England; son of Sir Egerton Bushe (a painter) and Hildegarde (Somerville) Coghill; married Elspeth Nora Harley (an author and translator), 1927 (divorced, 1933); children: Carol (Mrs. Robert Martin). *Education:* Exeter College, Oxford, B.A., 1922, M.A., 1926. *Religion:* Church of England. *Home:* Savran House, Aylburton, near Lydney, Gloucestershire, England. *Agent:* Innes Rose, John Farquharson Ltd., Bell House, 8 Bell Yard, London WC2A 2JU, England.

CAREER: Oxford University, Oxford, England, research fellow of Exeter College, 1924, official fellow, tutor in English literature, and librarian of Exeter College, 1925-57, Merton Professor of English Literature, 1957-66. Senior member of Oxford University Dramatic Society, 1934-66; founder of Oxford University Experimental Theatre Club, 1935; curator of Oxford University Theatre. Director and producer of plays by Milton, Shakespeare, Marlowe, and others, in Oxford and London, beginning 1930. Gresham Professor of Rhetoric at Mercer's Company, London, 1948. Governor of Shakespeare Memorial Theatre, Stratford, 1956. *Military service:* British Army, Royal Field Artillery, 1918-19; served on Salonika front; became second lieutenant.

MEMBER: Royal Society of English Literature (fellow), English Association (president, 1970-71), Poetry Society (president, 1964-68), Travellers' Club. *Awards, honors:* D.Litt., Williams College, 1966; LL.D., St. Andrews College, 1971.

WRITINGS: The Pardon of Piers Plowman (Sir Israel Gollancz Memorial Lecture), Folcroft, 1945, reprinted, Arden Library, 1978; *The Poet Chaucer,* Oxford University Press, 1949, 2nd edition, 1967; *Geoffrey Chaucer,* Longmans, Green, 1956, revised edition, 1969; *Geoffrey Chaucer,* bound with *Sir Thomas Malory,* by M. C. Bradbrook, University of Nebraska Press, 1963; *Shakespeare's Professional Skills* (Clark Lecture for 1959), Cambridge University Press, 1964; (author of introduction) William Langland, *The Vision of Piers Plowman,* translated into modern English by Henry W. Wells, Greenwood Press, 1968; *The Tragedy of Romeo and Juliet,* Pan Books, 1971.

Translator into modern English: Langland, *Visions from Piers Plowman,* Phoenix House, 1949, reprinted, Oxford University Press, 1970; Geoffrey Chaucer, *The Canterbury Tales* (also see below), Penguin, 1951, revised edition, 1975; Chaucer, *Troilus and Criseyde,* Penguin, 1971.

Editor: T. S. Eliot, *Murder in the Cathedral,* Faber, 1965; (and author of introduction and commentary) Eliot, *The Family Reunion,* Faber, 1970; *A Choice of Chaucer's Verse,* Faber, 1972; *T. S. Eliot's "The Cocktail Party,"* Faber, 1974.

Editor with Christopher Tolkien: Chaucer, *The Pardoner's Tale,* Harrap, 1958, new edition, 1976; Chaucer, *The Nun's Priest's Tale,* Harrap, 1959, new edition, 1975; Chaucer, *The Man of Law's Tale,* Harrap, 1960.

Plays: (With Martin Starkie) "Canterbury Tales" (based on Chaucer's book of the same title), first produced in London at the Phoenix Theatre, 1968, produced on Broadway in 1969.

Also author with Glynne Wickham of *The Masque of Hope,* 1948, and of screenplay adaptation for film "Doctor Faustus," produced by Columbia, 1968.

WORK IN PROGRESS: Writing on Elizabethan drama and on twentieth-century drama, especially English.

SIDELIGHTS: Nevill Coghill was a scholar of Middle English whose translation of *The Canterbury Tales* dispelled "the difficulties of Chaucer for a rising generation of students of English literature," reported the *London Times.* In addition to his academic pursuits, Coghill involved himself in the theatre. Together he and Martin Starkie adapted *The Canterbury Tales* into a musical stage version that was so successful it played at London's Phoenix Theatre for five years and enjoyed runs in New York, Europe, and Australia as well. According to the *London Times,* the many open air productions Coghill produced and directed "seemed to hint at a new art form. He married the art of the theatre to those of gardener and architect. The changing beauties of a park or garden as evening darkened qualified the words and the movements of the actors. . . . Among other things, he was credited with giving Richard Burton his first part."

AVOCATIONAL INTERESTS: Music.

BIOGRAPHICAL/CRITICAL SOURCES: New York Times, December 5, 1979, February 13, 1980.

OBITUARIES: London Times, November 10, 1980; *Time,* November 24, 1980.†

*   *   *

COLEMAN, Evelyn Scherabon
    See FIRCHOW, Evelyn Scherabon

*   *   *

COLEMAN, Marion (Reeves) Moore   1900-

PERSONAL: Born March 10, 1900, in Brooklyn, N.Y.; daughter of David Halsey (a bookkeeper) and Elizabeth Shaw (Mer-

rill) Moore; married Arthur Prudden Coleman (former president of Alliance College), 1922 (deceased). *Education:* New York College for Teachers (now State University of New York at Albany), B.A., 1920. *Politics:* Democrat. *Religion:* Congregational. *Home:* Manzano del Sol, Apt. 432, 5201 Roma Ave. N.E., Albuquerque, N.M. 87108.

CAREER: Writer. Alliance College, Alliance, Pa., lecturer in comparative cultures, 1950-62. *Awards, honors:* Chevalier of Polonia Restituta, 1963; Polish P.E.N. of Warsaw award, 1973.

WRITINGS: (With husband, Arthur Prudden Coleman) *The Polish Insurrection of 1863,* Bayard Press, 1934; (editor) *The Polish Land,* Columbia University Press, 1943, revised edition published as *The Polish Land: A Journey through Poland from the Vistula to the Poet's Land of the Eastern Border,* Cherry Hill, 1974; (editor) *The Wayside Willow,* Columbia University Press, 1945.

Young Mickiewicz, Alliance College Press, 1956; (compiler) *Polish Literature in English Translation, 960-1960, A Bibliography,* Cherry Hill, 1963; (with A. P. Coleman) *Wanderers Twain, Modjeska and Sienkiewicz: A View from California,* Cherry Hill, 1964; *A World Remembered,* Cherry Hill, 1965; *Mazeppa on the American Stage,* Cherry Hill, 1966; (editor) Helena Modjeska, *Letters to Emilia: Record of a Friendship,* translated by Michael Kwapiszewski, Cherry Hill, 1967; *Fair Rosalind: The American Career of Helena Modjeska,* Cherry Hill, 1969.

The Man on the Moon: The Story of Pan Twardowski, Cherry Hill, 1971; *A Brigand, Two Queens, and a Prankster,* Cherry Hill, 1972; (editor) Henryk Sienkiewicz, *Western Septet: Seven Stories of the American West,* new edition, Alliance College, 1973; *Vistula Voyage: Lore of the Polish Mother of Waters,* Cherry Hill, 1974; *Zosia and Thaddeus, or an Ancient Feud Ended,* Cherry Hill, 1974; (compiler) *The Cheshire Academy: The First Twelve Decades, 1794-1919,* Cherry Hill, 1976; *Our Other World: A Polish Scrapbook,* Cherry Hill, 1978; *Our Town: Cheshire, Connecticut, 1780-1980,* Cherry Hill, 1980.

Translator from the Polish: (With A. P. Coleman) Juliusz Slowacki, *Mary Stuart: A Romantic Drama,* Electric City Press, 1937, reprinted, Greenwood, 1978; Roman Dyboski, *Seven Years in Russia and Siberia, 1914-1921,* Cherry Hill, 1971.

Also author of *Journey into Another World,* three volumes, Cherry Hill. Contributor of articles to journals, including *Perspectives.* Editor, American Association of Teachers of Slavic and East European Languages, 1943-48, *Alliance Journal* (Alliance College), 1951-60, and *Polish Folklore,* 1956-62.

SIDELIGHTS: Marion Moore Coleman became interested in the Slavs, especially the Poles, after her marriage to Dr. Arthur Coleman. Since then, she has learned to read Polish and has made several trips to Poland and Eastern Europe besides visiting Slavic settlements in the United States.

*   *   *

COLLINS, David R(aymond)   1940-

PERSONAL: Born February 29, 1940, in Marshalltown, Iowa; son of Raymond A. (an educator) and Mary Elizabeth (Brecht) Collins. *Education:* Western Illinois University, B.S., 1962, M.S., 1966. *Politics:* Democrat. *Religion:* Roman Catholic. *Home:* 3403 45th St., Moline, Ill. 61265. *Office:* Department of English, Moline Senior High School, 3600 23rd Ave., Moline, Ill. 61265.

CAREER: Teacher of English in Moline, Ill., at Woodrow Wilson Junior High School, 1962-83, and Moline Senior High School, 1983—. President, Friends of the Moline Public Library, 1965-67. *Member:* National Education Association (life member), Children's Reading Roundtable, Society of Children's Book Writers, Authors Guild, Authors League of America, Juvenile Forum (president, 1975—), Writers' Studio (president, 1968-72), Mississippi Valley Writers Conference (founder; director, 1974—), Illinois Education Association, Illinois Congress of Parents and Teachers (life member), Illinois State Historical Society (life member), Blackhawk Division of Teachers of English (president, 1967-68), Quad City Writers Club, Quad City Arts Council, Phi Delta Kappa, Kappa Delta Pi, Delta Sigma Pi.

AWARDS, HONORS: Outstanding Juvenile Writer Award, Indiana University, 1970; Judson College Writing Award, 1971; Writer of the Year Awards, Writers' Studio, 1971, and Quad City Writers Club, 1972; Western Illinois University Alumni Achievement Award, 1973; Junior Literary Guild Award, 1981; Midwest Writing Award, 1982; Gold Key Award, 1983; Catholic Press Writing Award, 1983.

WRITINGS—Juveniles: *Kim Soo and His Tortoise,* Lion Press, 1970; *Great American Nurses,* Messner, 1971; *Walt Disney's Surprise Christmas Present,* Broadman, 1971; *Linda Richards: First American Trained Nurse,* Garrard, 1973; *Harry S. Truman: People's President,* Garrard, 1975; *Football Running Backs: Three Ground Gainers,* Garrard, 1976; *Abraham Lincoln,* Mott Media, 1976; *Illinois Women: Born to Serve,* DeSaulniers, 1976; *Joshua Poole Hated School,* Broadman, 1976; *George Washington Carver,* Mott Media, 1977; *A Spirit of Giving,* Broadman, 1978; *Charles Lindbergh: Hero Pilot,* Garrard, 1978; *If I Could, I Would,* Garrard, 1979.

Joshua Poole and Sunrise, Broadman, 1980; *The Wonderful Story of Jesus,* Concordia, 1980; *The One Bad Thing about Birthdays,* Harcourt, 1981; *Joshua Poole and the Special Flowers,* Broadman, 1981; *George Meany: Mr. Labor,* St. Anthony Messenger Press, 1981; *Dorothy Day: Catholic Worker,* St. Anthony Messenger Press, 1981; *Thomas Merton: Monk with a Mission,* St. Anthony Messenger Press, 1982; *Francis Scott Key,* Mott Media, 1982; (with Evelyn Witter) *Notable Illinois Women,* Quest Publishing, 1982; *Johnny Appleseed,* Mott Media, 1983; *Florence Nightingale,* Mott Media, 1983; *Clara Barton,* Mott Media, 1984; *The Special Guest,* Broadman, 1984. Contributor to periodicals, including *Plays, Modern Woodman, Junior Discoveries, Catholic Boy, Vista,* and *Catholic Miss.*

WORK IN PROGRESS: Research on great American doctors, for a collective biography.

SIDELIGHTS: David R. Collins told *CA* this about writing for children: "Children are curious, their minds open and flexible. A child is eager to enjoy new adventures. Anyone choosing to write for young readers faces an exciting challenge and a great responsibility. He must remember that his words and ideas may have a lasting effect on his reader's imagination, personality, even his entire character. Young readers deserve the best in reading.

"Why did I decide to write for children? Probably because some of my best childhood adventures were discovered in books. . . . I owe a tremendous debt to the realm of children's literature. Perhaps if I can offer something worthwhile to young readers, part of that debt will be repaid."

COLLINS, Marjorie A(nn)   1930-

PERSONAL: Born December 29, 1930, in Attleboro, Mass.; daughter of Harry M. (a gladiola grower) and Muriel (Bessom) Collins. *Education:* Providence-Barrington Bible College (now Barrington College), B.A., 1952; graduate study at Columbia Bible College, 1979-80. *Religion:* Protestant. *Home:* 543 Woodfire Way, Casselberry, Fla. 32707.

CAREER: Missionary in Pakistan for International Christian Fellowship, 1954-58; Barrington College, Barrington, R.I., secretary of department of education, 1959-60; Bethlehem Baptist Church, Springfield, Mass., secretary and director of Christian education, 1960-61; World Radio Missionary Fellowship, Inc., Miami, Fla., administrative assistant and personnel secretary, 1961-68; Boston University, School of Nursing, Boston, Mass., executive secretary to dean, 1968-69; Children's Hospital Medical Center, Boston, Mass., executive secretary to chief of endocrine division, 1969-70; University of Miami, School of Medicine, Coral Gables, Fla., administrative supervisor in department of otolaryngology, 1970-71; free-lance Christian writer, 1971—; Ocean, Inc. (Organization of Continuing Education for American Nurses), Pine Lake, Ga., began as executive secretary, 1975, director of public relations in Columbia, S.C., 1980-82; Columbia Bible College, administrative assistant to the president and teacher of creative writing, 1977-80. Visiting professor at Columbia Bible College, 1975.

WRITINGS: Manual for Missionaries on Furlough, William Carey Library, 1972, revised edition, 1978; *Manual for Accepted Missionary Candidates,* William Carey Library, 1972, revised edition, 1978; *Search the Bible Quizzes,* Moody, 1974; *Search the Gospels and Acts,* Moody, 1974; *Who Cares about the Missionary?,* Moody, 1974; *Dedication: What It's All About,* Bethany Fellowship, 1976; *Search the Books of Poetry,* Moody, 1976; *Search the Old Testament Law and History,* Moody, 1976; *To Know Him and to Make Him Known,* Columbia Bible College, 1978; *Guidelines for Planning and Executing an OCEAN-Sponsored Workshop,* OCEAN, Inc., 1980; *Bible Quizzes on Bible Themes,* Standard, 1983.

Contributor of weekly devotional column to *Laconia News,* 1973-75. Contributor of more than three hundred articles to religious periodicals.

WORK IN PROGRESS: Adult Education in the Sunday School; a novel, *Darkest Before Dawn;* a nonfiction book on aspects of loneliness.

AVOCATIONAL INTERESTS: Stamp collecting, travel (North, Central, and South America, Europe, Asia, and Africa).

*   *   *

COLOMBO, John Robert   1936-

PERSONAL: Born March 24, 1936, in Kitchener, Ontario, Canada; son of J. A. and Irene (Nicholson) Colombo; married Ruth Brown (a teacher); children: Jonathan, Catherine, Theodore. *Education:* Attended Waterloo College, Waterloo, Ontario, 1956-57; University of Toronto, B.A. (with honors), 1959, graduate study, 1959-60. *Home:* 42 Dell Park Ave., Toronto, Ontario, Canada M6B 2T6.

CAREER: University of Toronto Press, Toronto, Ontario, editorial assistant, 1959-60; Ryerson Press, Toronto, assistant editor, 1960-63; McClelland & Stewart, Toronto, advisory editor and editor-at-large, 1964-70. Occasional instructor at At-kinson College, York University. Has given poetry readings throughout Canada and in New York and London. Member of advisory arts panel, Canada Council; representative for Ca-nadian poetry, Commonwealth Arts Festival, Cardiff and London, 1965; advisor, Ontario Arts Council. *Member:* League of Canadian Poets (provisional coordinator), P.E.N. (Canada), Arts and Letters Club.

AWARDS, HONORS: Centennial Medal, 1967; Canada Council grant, 1967; certificate of merit, Ontario Library Association; cited for best paperback of the year, Periodical Distributors of Canada; named Esteemed Knight of Mark Twain; recipient of Order of Cyril and Methodius (first class).

WRITINGS: (Editor) *The Varsity Chapbook,* Ryerson, 1959; (editor with Jacques Godbout) *Poesis 64/Poetry 64,* Ryerson and Editions du Jour, 1963; *The Mackenzie Poems,* Swan Publishing, 1966; *The Great Wall of China,* Delat Montreal, 1966; *Abracadabra,* McClelland & Stewart, 1967; (editor with Raymond Souster) *Shapes and Sounds: Poems of W.W.E. Ross,* Longmans, Green (Canada), 1968; *John Toronto,* Oberon Press, 1969.

Neo Poems, Sono Nis Press, 1970; *How Do I Love Thee?,* Hurtig Publishers, 1970; *Translations from the English* (poems), PMA, 1974; *The Sad Truths* (poems), PMA, 1974; *Mostly Monsters,* Hounslow, 1977; *Variable Cloudiness* (poems), Hounslow, 1977; *Private Parts* (poems), Hounslow, 1978; *The Great Cities of Antiquity* (poems), Hounslow, 1979; *Other Canadas,* McGraw-Hill Ryerson, 1979; (co-editor) *CDN SF&F,* Hounslow, 1979; *Colombo's Book of Marvels,* NC Press, 1979.

Friendly Aliens, Hounslow, 1981; *Not to Be Taken at Night,* Lester & Orpen Dennys, 1981; *Blackwood's Books,* Hounslow, 1981; *Selected Poems,* Black Moss Press, 1982; (editor) *Windigo: An Anthology of Fact and Fantastic Fiction,* Western Producer Prairie Books, 1982.

Compiler: *Colombo's Canadian Quotations,* Hurtig Publishers, 1974; *Colombo's Little Book of Canadian Proverbs, Graffiti, Limericks & Other Vital Matters,* Hurtig Publishers, 1975; *Colombo's Concise Canadian Quotations,* Hurtig Publishers, 1976; *Colombo's Canadian References,* Oxford, 1976; *The Poets of Canada,* Hurtig Publishers, 1978; *Colombo's Book of Canada,* Hurtig Publishers, 1978; *Colombo's Names and Nicknames,* NC Press, 1979; *Colombo's Hollywood,* Collins, 1979, published as *Popcorn in Paradise,* Holt, 1980; *The Canada Colouring Book,* Hounslow, 1980; *222 Canadian Jokes,* Highway, 1981.

Translator; published by Hounslow, except as indicated: Robert Zend, *From Zero to One,* Sono Nis Press, 1973; (with Nikola Roussanoff) *Under the Eaves of a Forgotten Village: Sixty Poems from Contemporary Bulgaria,* 1975; (with Roussanoff) *The Balkan Range: A Bulgarian Reader,* 1976; (with Roussanoff) Lyubomir Levchev, *The Left-Handed One,* 1977; George Faludy, *East and West,* 1978; (with Roussanoff) Andrei Germanov, *Remember Me Well,* 1978; (with Roussanoff) Dora Gabe, *Depths,* 1978; Waclaw Iwaniuk, *Dark Times,* 1979; Ewa Lipska, *Such Times,* 1981; Pavel Javor, *Far from You,* 1981; *Poems of the Inuit,* Oberon, 1981; *Selected Translations,* Black Moss Press, 1982.

Also author of *Songs of the Indians,* 1983, and of plays and documentaries for Canadian Broadcasting Corp. Contributor of articles, art criticism, and reviews to periodicals. Member of editorial board, *Tamarack Review,* 1960-82.

SIDELIGHTS: John Robert Colombo has been a guest of the Writers' Unions of Russia, Romania, and Bulgaria.

BIOGRAPHICAL/CRITICAL SOURCES: Times Literary Supplement, May 13, 1983.

* * *

CONNELLY, Thomas L(awrence) 1938-

PERSONAL: Born February 14, 1938, in Nashville, Tenn.; son of Fred Marlin (a certified public accountant) and Mildred Inez Connelly. *Education:* David Lipscomb College, B.A., 1959; Rice University, M.A., 1961, Ph.D., 1963. *Office:* Department of History, University of South Carolina, Columbia, S.C. 20208.

CAREER: Presbyterian College, Clinton, S.C., professor of history and head of department, 1963-64; Mississippi State University, State College, assistant professor, 1964-66, associate professor of history, 1966-69; University of South Carolina, Columbia, associate professor, 1969-71, professor of history, 1971—.

AWARDS, HONORS: John Gardner Award, Rice University, 1963; John T. Moore Award, Tennessee Historical Society, 1964; American Philosophical Society research grant, 1965; Mississippi State University Development Foundation research grants, 1965-66, 1967; Jules Landry Award, Louisiana State University Press, 1971; Jefferson Davis Award, Museum of the Confederacy, 1971, 1973; Russell Award, 1971; Fletcher Pratt Award, New York City Civil War Roundtable, 1972.

WRITINGS: Will Success Spoil Jeff Davis?: The Last Book about the Civil War, illustrated by Campbell Grant, McGraw, 1963; *Army of the Heartland: The Army of Tennessee, 1861-1862,* Louisiana State University Press, 1967; *Discovering the Appalachians,* Stackpole, 1968; *Autumn of Glory: The Army of Tennessee, 1862-1865,* Louisiana State University Press, 1971; (with Archer Jones) *The Politics of Command: Factions and Ideas in Confederate Strategy,* Louisiana State University Press, 1973; *The Marble Man: Robert E. Lee and His Image in American Society,* Knopf, 1977; *Civil War Tennessee: Battles and Leaders,* University of Tennessee Press, 1979; (with Barbara Bellows) *God and General Longstreet: The Lost Cause and the Southern Mind,* Louisiana State University Press, 1982; *Will Campbell and the Soul of the South,* Continuum, 1982. Contributor to historical journals. Member of board of advisory editors, *Civil War History* and *The Papers of Jefferson Davis.*

SIDELIGHTS: Historian Thomas L. Connelly is noted for his profiles of the Civil War South, including his study of Robert E. Lee. In *The Marble Man: Robert E. Lee and His Image in American Society,* the author examines the way Lee's image has evolved from that of a defeated Southern general to a national hero of mythic proportions. As Connelly writes in the preface: "In the Reconstruction era, Lee's image offered the South explanations for both secession and defeat. In the heyday of romantic Southern letters during the 1890's, the image became the ultimate proof of the superiority of Southern life and Anglo-Saxon supremacy. To the American mind of 1900, torn between intense national pride and fear of a new value system being introduced by industrial growth, the Lee image provided a sense of nationalism and the value of individual character. During the Depression of the 1930's, Lee was the Virginia cavalier for those who sought escape in a romantic portrayal of the war. . . . And to the American mind of the 1960's, which groped for meaning and purpose in the war, Lee became the hero of the middle class."

The author's exploration of the man behind the myth has garnered some critical attention. John Leonard, reviewing *The Marble Man* in the *New York Times,* comments that the "trouble with [the book] is that it doesn't tell us much we didn't already know about Lee or the hydraulics of American hero-worship. It is the book's large ambitions that sink what might have been a perfectly respectable account of how the Virginians stole Civil War historiography from the rest of the South—the 'cotton South'—and sanitized themselves." William S. McFeely, however, finds that Connelly "has written a stimulating study of how popular images of a hero are created not only by sculptors but by other legend-makers, like historians, who exploit the need for such myths." Writing in *Times Literary Supplement,* McFeely continues: "Connelly has brought us closer to the Robert E. Lee his contemporaries knew. They saw him as mortal and we wonder how they evaluated the man who surrendered the Army of Northern Virginia on April 9, 1865."

According to C. Vann Woodward, in the *New York Times Book Review,* Connelly depicts "an extremely complicated Lee, tormented by failure and frustration, tortured by feelings of inadequacy, self-doubt, self-pity, and fear of disgrace." Commenting on Connelly's analysis of the historic meeting of Lee and Ulysses S. Grant at Appomattox, Woodward states: "Both protagonists brought a record and self-image of prewar failure. On this the author has some interesting if speculative views about the relation of frustration and guilt to aggressiveness. He suggests that lack of success and vast reputations to uphold made both Lee and Grant less fearful of failure, more willing to take risks, more aggressive and audacious." The reviewer concludes: "This book reopens the case of Robert E. Lee, the Marble Man. Never again can he be successfully represented as 'a gentleman of simple soul.' Fierce resistance is to be expected, for there are heavy investments involved. But the complexities are now revealed and there will be no avoiding them."

BIOGRAPHICAL/CRITICAL SOURCES: Nashville Tennessean Sunday Magazine, May 5, 1957; *Houston Post,* October 8, 1961; *State and Columbia Record,* December 8, 1963; *New York Times Book Review,* March 14, 1971, April 3, 1977; *Virginia Quarterly Review,* autumn, 1973, summer, 1977; Thomas L. Connelly, *The Marble Man: Robert E. Lee and His Image in American Society,* Knopf, 1977; *New York Times,* April 2, 1977; *America,* May 7, 1977; *Times Literary Supplement,* November 4, 1977; *Journal of Southern History,* February, 1978; *Los Angeles Times Book Review,* August 29, 1982.

*   *   *

CONSIDINE, Douglas M(axwell) 1915-

PERSONAL: Born May 24, 1915, in Norwalk, Ohio; son of Benjamin Maxwell (a business executive) and May Louise Considine; married Glenna Louise Taylor (a registered nurse), August 14, 1940; children: Glenn Douglas. *Education:* Case Western Reserve University, B.S., 1937. *Residence:* Columbus, Ga.

CAREER: Registered professional engineer in state of California. D. W. Haering & Co. (chemicals), Chicago, Ill., director of research, 1937-40; Honeywell, Inc., Philadelphia, Pa., manager of Market Extension Division, 1940-54; P. R. Mallory & Co. (electronic and metallurgical products), Indianapolis, Ind., manager of marketing, 1954-57; Hughes Aircraft Co. (defense systems), Culver City, Calif., manager of advanced control engineering, 1957-69; writer, 1969—. Former consultant to Beckman Instruments, General Signal Corp.,

Varian Associates, and Dun & Bradstreet. *Member:* American Association for the Advancement of Science (fellow), Instrument Society of America (fellow), American Institute of Chemical Engineers (senior member).

WRITINGS: Van Nostrand's Scientific Encyclopedia, Van Nostrand, 1938, 6th edition, 1982; *Industrial Weighing,* Reinhold, 1948; *Process Instruments and Controls Handbook,* McGraw, 1958, 3rd edition, 1983; *Handbook of Applied Instrumentation,* McGraw, 1964; *Encyclopedia of Instrumentation and Control,* McGraw, 1973; *Chemical and Process Technology Encyclopedia,* McGraw, 1974; *Encyclopaedie Naturwissenschaft und Technik,* five volumes, Verlag Moderne Industrie, 1976-82; *Energy Technology Handbook,* McGraw, 1977; *Foods and Food Production Encyclopedia,* Van Nostrand, 1982; *Encyclopedia of Chemistry,* Van Nostrand, 1983. Contributor of more than seventy articles on management sciences, instrumentation, and automation to magazines.

SIDELIGHTS: Douglas M. Considine told *CA* that his special areas of professional interest are instrumentation and control systems engineering, energy and environmental systems, food production and food processing analyses and systems, and chemical and photochemical process engineering. He holds U.S. patents for thermocouples, flowmeters, protecting tubes and control systems, and is co-inventor of a laser fabric cutter used in garment and textile industries. During World War II, Considine was active in the development of automatic control systems for synthetic rubber and aviation gasoline plants.

*   *   *

COPPER, John Franklin 1940-

PERSONAL: Born October 30, 1940, in Omaha, Neb.; son of Russell B. (a businessman) and Ina (Townsend) Copper; married Athena Chen, December 7, 1966; children: Harrison Blair, Elizabeth Allison, Anne Devona. *Education:* University of Nebraska, B.A., 1961; University of Hawaii, M.A., 1965; University of South Carolina, Ph.D., 1975. *Home:* 9314 Christopher St., Fairfax, Va. 22031. *Office:* Asian Studies Center, Heritage Foundation, 214 Massachusetts Ave. N.E., Washington, D.C. 20002.

CAREER: U.S. Department of Defense, San Francisco, Calif., research analyst, 1965-67; College of Notre Dame, Belmont, Calif., instructor in political science, 1967-68; Tamkang College of Arts and Sciences, Taipei, Taiwan, associate professor of political science, 1968-69, 1971; University of Maryland, Far East Division, Tokyo, Japan, lecturer in government and politics, 1971-76; Stanford University, Stanford, Calif., research fellow at Hoover Institution on War, Revolution and Peace, 1976-77; Southwestern University, Memphis, Tenn., associate professor in department of international studies, 1977-83; Heritage Foundation, Washington, D.C., director of Asian Studies Center, 1983—. *Military service:* U.S. Air Force Reserve, 1962-68.

MEMBER: International Studies Association, American Political Science Association, Association of Asian Studies, East-West Center Alumni Association, American Association for Chinese Studies (member of board of directors, 1983—), Mensa. *Awards, honors:* Publication awards from University of Maryland's Far East Division, 1972-75 for articles, and 1976, for *China's Foreign Aid: An Instrument of Peking's Foreign Policy;* Clarence Bay Foundation award for outstanding research and creativity, 1981, for *China's Global Role: An Analysis of China's National Power Capabilities in the Context of an Evolving International System.*

WRITINGS: (Translator with Sun Li-feng) Lawrence J. Peter and Raymond Hull, *Pi-teh Yuan-li* (title means "The Peter Principle"), Prometheus Books, 1971; (translator with Sun Li-feng and Chen Hui-Guang) Peter, *Pi-teh Ling-fang* (title means "The Peter Prescription"), Prometheus Books, 1975; *China's Foreign Aid: An Instrument of Peking's Foreign Policy*, Heath, 1976; (with William R. Kinter) *A Matter of Two Chinas: The China-Taiwan Issue in U.S. Foreign Policy*, Foreign Policy Research Institute, 1979; *China's Global Role: An Analysis of China's National Power Capabilities in the Context of an Evolving International System*, Hoover Institution Press, 1980; (editor with Daniel S. Papp) *Communist Nations Military Assistance*, Westview, 1983.

Also author of monographs; contributor of chapters to ten books. Contributor of more than forty articles and reviews to Asian studies journals and to *Current Scene, Japan Times,* and *Bangkok Post.*

WORK IN PROGRESS: Taiwan's Elections: Progress in Democratization and Political Development.

SIDELIGHTS: John Franklin Copper told *CA:* "In the present world, all important problems have political implications. Hence, politics is the master science. The study of international politics and Asia are the most challenging part of the field. Moreover, the U.S. has fought all of its wars in my generation in Asia. The next major war, if there is one, will be in Asia, and the U.S. will be involved. Alternatively, the foundation for world peace lies in America's relationship with nations of the Western Pacific."

*   *   *

CORCORAN, Barbara 1911-
(Paige Dixon, Gail Hamilton)

PERSONAL: Born April 12, 1911, in Hamilton, Mass.; daughter of John Gilbert (a physician) and Anna (Tuck) Corcoran. *Education:* Wellesley College, B.A., 1933; University of Montana, M.A., 1955. *Politics:* Democrat. *Religion:* Episcopalian. *Home address:* P.O. Box 4394, Missoula, Mont. 59806.

CAREER: Celebrity Service, Hollywood, Calif., researcher, 1945-53; Station KGVO, Missoula, Mont., copywriter, 1953-54; University of Kentucky, Covington, instructor in English, 1956-57; Columbia Broadcasting System, Hollywood, Calif., researcher, 1957-59; Marlboro School, Los Angeles, Calif., teacher of English, 1959-60; University of Colorado, Boulder, instructor in English, 1960-65; Palomar College, San Marcos, Calif., instructor in English, 1965-69; full-time writer, 1969—. *Member:* Authors League of America, Society of Children's Book Writers.

AWARDS, HONORS: Samuel French Award for original play, 1955; *The Long Journey* was named a Child Study Association children's book of the year, 1970; William Allen White Children's Book Award, 1972, for *Sasha, My Friend;* Pacific Northwest Book Sellers' Award, and National Science Teachers' Award, both 1975.

WRITINGS—For young people; published by Atheneum, except as indicated: *Sam,* 1967; (with Jeanne Dixon and Bradford Angier) *The Ghost of Spirit River,* 1968; *Sasha, My Friend,* 1969; *A Row of Tigers,* 1969.

The Long Journey, 1970; (with Angier) *A Star to the North* (Junior Literary Guild Selection), Thomas Nelson, 1970; *The Lifestyle of Robie Tuckerman,* Thomas Nelson, 1971; *This Is a Recording,* 1971; *A Trick of Light* (Junior Literary Guild

Selection), 1972; *Don't Slam the Door when You Go,* 1972; *All the Summer Voices,* 1973; *The Winds of Time,* 1973; *A Dance to Still Music,* 1974; *Meet Me at Tamerlane's Tomb,* 1975; *The Clown,* 1975, published as *I Wish You Love,* Scholastic Book Services, 1977; *Axe-Time, Sword-Time,* 1976; *Make No Sound,* 1977; *Faraway Island,* 1977; *Hey, That's My Soul You're Stomping On,* 1977; (with Angier) *Ask for Love, and They Give You Rice Pudding,* Houghton, 1977; *Me and You and a Dog Named Blue,* 1979; *Rising Damp,* 1979.

Person in the Potting Shed, 1980; *You're Allegro Dead,* 1981; *Making It,* Little, Brown, 1981; *The Call of the Heart,* Ballantine, 1981; *Abigail,* Ballantine, 1981; *Beloved Enemy,* Ballantine, 1981; *Love Is Not Enough,* Ballantine, 1981; *A Husband for Gail,* Ballantine, 1981; *Song for Two Voices,* Ballantine, 1981; *Abbie in Love,* Ballantine, 1981; *By the Silvery Moon,* Ballantine, 1981; *Child of the Morning,* 1982; *A Watery Grave,* 1982; *Which Witch Is Which?,* 1983.

Under pseudonym Paige Dixon: *Lion on the Mountain,* 1972; *Silver Wolf,* 1973; *The Young Grizzly,* 1973; *Promises to Keep,* 1974; *May I Cross Your Golden River?,* 1975; *Cabin in the Sky,* 1976; *The Search for Charlie,* 1976; *Pimm's Cup for Everybody,* 1976; *Summer of the White Goat,* 1977; *The Mustang and Other Stories,* 1978; *The Loner,* 1979; *Skipper,* 1979; *Walk My Way,* 1980.

Under pseudonym Gail Hamilton: *Titania's Lodestone,* 1975; *A Candle to the Devil,* 1976; *Love Comes to Eunice K. O'Herlihy,* 1977.

Contributor of short stories to *Woman's Day,* short stories and a novel to *Redbook,* and a novel to *American Girl* and *Good Housekeeping.*

WORK IN PROGRESS: Other books for young people.

SIDELIGHTS: Barbara Corcoran's young adult novels often center on adolescents who suffer a handicap. Some suffer from a physical defect, such as deafness, a learning disability, or a terminal disease; others endure a social or emotional stigma, such as shyness, being a member of a minority group, having eccentric parents, or being from a broken family. In the end of these highly moralistic novels, the protagonists have usually learned to come to grips with their situation. For instance, Margaret in *A Dance to Still Music* is "newly deaf, . . . [and] still struggling against the unfamiliar isolation of her condition and against the label 'handicapped,'" writes a *Kirkus Reviews* critic. "For the hearing person, Margaret is a reliable guide to the problems of a handicap that is less well understood—and often less sympathetically treated—than blindness. And as always, Corcoran's gentle, supportive solutions have a convincing grace that compensates for their circumscribed reality." In *Hey, That's My Soul You're Stomping On* Rachel goes to live with her grandparents until her parents decide if they are to divorce. "[Through] the quiet wisdom of her grandparents and her observations of the other elderly vacationers at the comfortable but unfashionable Palm Springs resort motel, [Rachel] acquires a tolerance for human failings and the understanding that concern for one's parents, however burdensome it may sometimes be, is not lightly dismissed," notes Mary Burns in *Horn Book Magazine.*

Corcoran's books are also praised for their style. Writing about *May I Cross Your Golden River?,* Georgess McHargue observes in *New York Times Book Review:* "What makes the book worth reading is the warm and careful drawing of the Phillips family, particularly the four brothers. Their jokes are funny, their horseplay and self-mockery ring true, and in the end their lives and relationships are more important and moving than the drama of death.'' In a review of *A Star to the North* Gwen Liv comments in *In Review: Canadian Books for Children* that Corcoran's ''style is fluent, clear, mild and more reserved than outgoing. There is little exaggeration, few words stronger than necessary, and no melodramatic writing. It is like a cup of good tea served straight without cream or sugar. The flavor and aroma may not be too strong, but they certainly linger on, and on, and on.''

BIOGRAPHICAL/CRITICAL SOURCES: In Review: Canadian Books for Children, summer, 1971; *Kirkus Reviews,* July 15, 1974; *New York Times Book Review,* January 4, 1976; *Horn Book Magazine,* June, 1978; *Contemporary Literary Criticism,* Volume XVII, Gale, 1981.

*   *   *

CORDER, Eric
See MUNDIS, Jerrold

*   *   *

CORDIS, Lonny
See DONSON, Cyril

*   *   *

COREY, Dorothy

PERSONAL: Born in Rush Lake, Saskatchewan, Canada; married Edward Corey (an engineer; deceased); children: Richard, Jan Sebastian. *Education:* Attended school in Nebraska. *Home:* 16654 Parthenia St., Sepulveda, Calif. 91343.

CAREER: Writer. Active in a cooperative nursery school, Parent/Teacher Association; leader in Girl Scouts of America. *Member:* Society of Children's Book Writers (charter member).

WRITINGS—All children's books; published by Albert Whitman, except as indicated: *You Go Away,* 1975; *No Company Was Coming to Samuel's House/No llegaban invitados a la casa de Samuel* (in English and Spanish; translation by Marguerite Arguedas Baker), Blaine Ethridge, 1976; *Tomorrow You Can,* 1977; *Pepe's Private Christmas,* Parents Magazine Press, 1978; *Everybody Takes Turns,* 1980; *We All Share,* 1980. Also author of *You Can Depend on Santa.* Contributor of short stories to numerous magazines, including *Humpty Dumpty.*

WORK IN PROGRESS: More picture books for children.

SIDELIGHTS: Dorothy Corey writes: ''I made my first sale when I was ten years old. A large garage in Omaha was having a slogan contest. I entered and won fourth prize—a generous two hundred-fifty dollars worth of parts and labor at the garage!

''I wrote many extra-curricular skits during the seventh and eighth grades and I sometimes think I did my best writing in the eighth grade. I didn't write again until, as a teen-ager, I published some verse and Rebecca Caudill encouraged me to continue my writing.

''When I read to my first child I decided to write for children. I made a brief start. Then I moved to the country and had so much outdoor work and another child that I didn't get back to juvenile manuscripts for many years.

''In the meantime I fell into the clutches of the local Parent/Teacher Association and I spent years preparing skits and pro-

grams for them (they always needed one more) when I could have had books of my own. After all, memories are not very permanent.

''I wish I could say that I was imaginative enough to make up plots and situations, but all my manuscripts, published and unpublished, grew out of things that really happened. My child left the door open for Santa Claus so I wrote *Pepe's Private Christmas.* My niece received a bike with one wheel so I wrote *You Can Depend on Santa.*

''My concept books grow from my own experiences and the suggestions of a panel of nursery school teachers I am fortunate to have as friends. A bilingual teacher told me there was no material about a Spanish Thanksgiving. Everything was American turkey and her pupils could not relate to it. So I wrote the bilingual *No Company Was Coming to Samuel's House.*

''In nursery school we used to tell the children that 'maybe tomorrow' they would be able to go down the slide and do all kinds of grown-up things, so I wrote *Tomorrow You Can. You Go Away* was inspired by seeing Glo Coalson's 'On Mother's Lap,' but it drew upon many departures. Nursery school teachers have found *You Go Away* especially useful.''

AVOCATIONAL INTERESTS: Music.

*   *   *

CORNELL, James (Clayton, Jr.) 1938-

PERSONAL: Born September 25, 1938, in Niagara Falls, N.Y.; son of James C. (an accountant) and Mary Elizabeth (Linick) Cornell; married Carole Fusaro (an ethnologist), September 8, 1962; children: Jennifer. *Education:* Hamilton College, B.A., 1960; Boston University, M.S., 1968. *Residence:* Boston, Mass. *Office:* Harvard-Smithsonian Center for Astrophysics, 60 Garden St., Cambridge, Mass. 02138.

CAREER: Worcester Telegram & Gazette, Worcester, Mass., promotion and feature writer and editor of in-house publication, 1960-62; Rust Craft Publishers, Dedham, Mass., public relations and advertising copywriter, 1963; Harvard-Smithsonian Center for Astrophysics, Cambridge, Mass., public information officer for Smithsonian Astrophysical Observatory, 1963-71, manager of publications department, 1971—. Instructor, Cambridge Center for Adult Education, 1969, and Boston University, 1971; lecturer in science communications, Suffolk University, 1976—. *Military service:* Massachusetts Army National Guard, broadcast media specialist, 1964-69. *Member:* International Science Writers Association (secretary-treasurer, 1979-83; president, 1983—), National Association of Science Writers, Mystery Writers of America, Authors League of America, Authors Guild. *Awards, honors:* Gold ''Cindy'' award from Information Film Producers Association, 1979, for script ''Mirrors on the Universe: The MMT Story.''

WRITINGS: The People Get the Credit, Spiegel, Inc., 1965; (editor with John Surowiecki) *Pulse of the Planet,* Crown, 1972; *It Happened Last Year,* Macmillan, 1974; *Nature at Its Strangest: True Stories from the Files of the Smithsonian Institution's Center for Short-Lived Phenomena* (juvenile), Sterling, 1974; (editor with E. Nelson Hayes) *Man and Cosmos,* Norton, 1975; *The Great International Disaster Book,* Scribner, 1976; (contributor) *The Smithsonian Experience,* Smithsonian Institution Press, 1977; *Lost Lands and Forgotten People* (juvenile), Sterling, 1978; *The First Stargazers: An Introduction to the Origins of Astronomy,* Scribner, 1981; (with Alan Lightman) *Revealing the Universe: Prediction and Proof in Astronomy*, MIT Press, 1982; (with Paul Gorenstein) *Astronomy from Space: Sputnik to Space Telescopes*, MIT Press, 1983.

Published by Scholastic Book Services: *Strange, Sudden, and Unexpected*, 1972; *Mythical Monsters*, 1973; *Fakes, Frauds, and Phonies*, 1973; *Unbelievable . . . But True!*, 1974; *Catastrophe, Calamity, and Cataclysm*, 1975, published as *Terror in Paradise*, 1978; *Where Did They Go?*, 1976; *The Monster of Loch Ness*, 1977; *Where Did They Come From?*, 1978; *Very Strange People*, 1980.

Also author of film script "Mirrors on the Universe: The MMT Story"; contributor to several volumes prepared by Sociological Resources for the Social Studies, edited by Helen MacGill Hughes, Allyn & Bacon, 1967-71. Book reviewer, *Quincy Patriot-Ledger*, 1970—; author of columns "Science Hot Line," *Science World*, 1970-75, and "Science," *Boston Sunday Globe*, 1977-79. Contributor of science and travel articles to newspapers and magazines. *Beacon Hill News*, executive editor, 1965-68, contributing editor, 1968-70; editor, International Science Writers Association *Newsletter;* member of editorial advisory board, *Harvard Magazine*.

WORK IN PROGRESS: A book on "official" nomenclature in science; research on Mexican pottery and the Pre-Columbian Tarascan culture; a mystery novel.

SIDELIGHTS: James Cornell told *CA:* "I consider myself primarily a journalist who happens to write books about natural science topics. My motivation is simply to share with others my fascination and sense of wonder about the natural world, including both its extraordinary physical phenomena and the diverse human cultures that have evolved to cope with these processes of nature."

One field in particular has been a favorite of Cornell's since the early 1960s, when scientists first theorized that the massive structures at Stonehenge had been arranged to serve as an astronomical observatory. The scientists arrived at their conclusion after analyzing the placement of the stones and comparing them to the positions of the rising and setting sun and moon during the time it is believed the monument was erected. This blend of archeology and astronomy led to the emergence of the modern science of archeoastronomy, the subject of Cornell's book *The First Stargazers*.

According to a *New York Times Book Review* critic, *The First Stargazers* is "a lively summary of some of the most interesting work in archeoastronomy. Although [it] is not always as carefully crafted as one might wish . . . it is enlivened by descriptions of the sites [the author] has visited. . . . His grasp of the subject is firm, his research unimpeachable, and his bibliography will aid those who want to investigate archeoastronomy in greater depth."

John R. Kalafut has a similar opinion of *The First Stargazers*. As he comments in a *Best Sellers* review: "Cornell's book represents a fine introduction to a fascinating subject. He has traveled to many of the sites himself, so the writing rings of personal experience. Anyone who is familiar with his excellent books on science for young adults will recognize a master expositor at work again."

BIOGRAPHICAL/CRITICAL SOURCES: New York Times Book Review, July 19, 1981; *Best Sellers*, September, 1981.

*   *   *

CORNMAN, James W(elton)   1929-1978

PERSONAL: Born August 16, 1929, in Philadelphia, Pa.; died

May 31, 1978, in an automobile accident; son of Ralph Miller (a manufacturer) and Rose (Scharfe) Cornman; married Elizabeth Marie Pedrotty (a volunteer worker), February 2, 1955; children: Deborah, Julie, Diane, Elizabeth. *Education:* Dartmouth College, B.A., 1956; Brown University, M.A., 1957, Ph.D., 1960. *Politics:* Democrat. *Religion:* Atheist. *Home:* 201 Walnut Ave., Wayne, Pa. 19087. *Office:* Department of Philosophy, University of Pennsylvania, Philadelphia, Pa. 19174.

CAREER: Ohio State University, Columbus, instructor in philosophy, 1960-63; University of Rochester, Rochester, N.Y., assistant professor, 1963-65, associate professor of philosophy, 1965-67; University of Pennsylvania, Philadelphia, associate professor, 1967-69, professor of philosophy, 1969-78, chairman of department, 1970-72. Member of board of directors of Radnor, Pa., Better Chance Program. *Member:* American Philosophical Association, Philosophy of Science Association. *Awards, honors:* Andrew Mellon fellowship, 1965-66; National Science Foundation grant, 1968-70; American Council of Learned Societies fellowship, 1970-71; Guggenheim fellowship, 1974-75.

WRITINGS: Metaphysics, Reference, and Language, Yale University Press, 1966; (with Keith Lehrer) *Philosophical Problems and Arguments*, Macmillan, 1968, 3rd edition, 1982; *Materialism and Sensations*, Yale University Press, 1971; *Perception, Common Sense, and Science*, Yale University Press, 1975; *Skepticism, Justification and Explanation*, D. Reidel Publishing, 1980. Contributor of about forty articles to philosophy journals, including *The Journal of Philosophy* and *Nous*.

SIDELIGHTS: Cornman once told *CA:* "My primary philosophical goal has long been to complete a comprehensive philosophical theory of man, the world around him, his perception and knowledge of that world, and the place of ethics and art in the resulting metaphysical and epistemological world view. Thus far I have tried to develop and justify a metaphysical theory that is a unification of the common sense view of man and the world with the scientific view that so many thinkers (such as Galileo, Newton, Descartes, and Locke) have thought requires the rejection of our common sense view. I believe that this reconciliation of science and common sense opens the way for a fuller understanding and more judicious balancing of the scientific world view and the humanistic, artistic construals of man and his world. I am currently finishing work on an epistemological theory, and have begun to develop a theory of moral obligation. Work in aesthetics lies somewhere in the future."†

*   *   *

COTTON, John   1925-

PERSONAL: Born March 7, 1925, in London, England; son of Arthur Edmund (a structural engineer) and Florence (Mandy) Cotton; married Peggy Midson (a secretary), December, 1948; children: Toby, Bevis. *Education:* University of London, B.A. (with honors), 1956. *Home:* 37 Lombardy Dr., Berkhamsted, Hertfordshire HP4 2LQ, England.

CAREER: Middlesex Education Authority, England, teacher of English, 1947-57; Southall Grammar Technical School, England, head of English department, 1957-63; Highfield Comprehensive School, Hemel Hempstead, England, headmaster, 1963—. Tutor for the Arvon Foundation, Tarleigh Barton, Devon; member of literature panel, Eastern Arts. *Military service:* Royal Naval Commandos, 1942-46; served in the Far

East. *Member:* National Poetry Society (member of council; chairman of council, 1973-75, and 1977). *Awards, honors:* Publication award from Arts Council of Great Britain, 1971, for *Old Movies and Other Poems;* Page scholarship from English Speaking Union, 1975.

WRITINGS—Poetry: *Fourteen Poems,* Priapus, 1967; *Outside the Gates of Eden and Other Poems,* Taurus Press, 1969; *Ampurias,* Priapus, 1969; *Old Movies and Other Poems,* Chatto & Windus, 1971; *The Wilderness,* Priapus, 1971; *Columbus on St. Dominica,* Sceptre Press, 1972; *Photographs,* Sycamore Press, 1973; *A Sycamore Press Broadsheet,* Sycamore Press, 1973; *British Poetry since 1965: A Selected List,* National Book League, 1973; *Kilroy Was Here* (Poetry Book Society selection), Chatto & Windus, 1974; *Places,* Priapus, 1975; *Day Books,* Priapus, 1981; *Catullus at Sirmione,* Priapus, 1982.

Contributor to anthologies: *Holding Your Eight Hands,* edited by Edward Lucie-Smith, Doubleday, 1969; *Children of Albion,* edited by Michael Horovitz, Penguin, 1969; *Best Science Fiction, 1972,* edited by Harry Harrison and Brian Aldiss, Putnam, 1972; *New Poetry,* Hutchinson, Number 1, 1975, Number 2, 1976, Number 3, 1977, Number 7, 1981, Number 8, 1982, Number 9, 1983; *Over the Bridge,* edited by John Loveday, Kestrel Books, 1981. Also contributor to P.E.N. poetry annuals, 1965, 1967, 1974, and 1975.

Editor of *Priapus,* 1962-72, and *Private Library,* 1970-80; advisory editor for *Contemporary Poets of the English Language.*

WORK IN PROGRESS: The Nightward, a collection of poems.

BIOGRAPHICAL/CRITICAL SOURCES: Poetry Book Society Bulletin 69, summer, 1971; *Stand,* Volume XIV, number 1, 1972; *Teacher,* May, 1973; *Hertfordshire Countryside,* July, 1973; *Poetry Book Society Bulletin 84,* spring, 1975.

* * *

COURT, Wesli 1940-

PERSONAL: Born April 1, 1940, in Oswego, N.Y.; son of Putnam and Suella (Larsen) Court. *Education:* Attended school in Oswego, N.Y. *Address:* P.O. Box 161, Dresden, Me. 04342. *Office:* Mathom Bookshop and Bindery, Blinn Hill Rd., Dresden, Me. 04342.

CAREER: Longshoreman and seaman on the Great Lakes, 1956-77; writer, beginning 1965; Mathom Bookshop and Bindery, Dresden, Me., owner, 1979—. Contributing editor for Mathom Publishing Co., 1977—. *Awards, honors:* World Order of Narrative Poets Traditional Forms Contest, first prize, three second prizes, two honorable mentions, 1983.

WRITINGS—Poetry, except as indicated: (Contributor) Lewis Turco, editor, *Poetry: An Introduction through Writing,* Reston, 1973; *Courses in Lambents,* Mathom, 1977; *Murgatroyd and Mabel* (juvenile), Mathom, 1978; *Curses and Laments,* Song Magazine Press, 1978; (contributor) David R. Pichaske, editor, *Beowulf to Beatles and Beyond,* Macmillan, 1981; (contributor) X. J. Kennedy, editor, *Tygers of Wrath,* University of Georgia Press, 1981; (contributor) Miller Williams, editor, *Patterns of Poetry,* Louisiana State University Press, in press. Also author of "The Airs of Wales" (modern versions of Medieval Welsh poems), Temple University *Poetry Newsletter* special chapbook edition, 1981. Contributor of poems, translations, articles and reviews to *American Weave, Arts Journal, Cimarron Review, Iowa Review, New York Quarterly,* and *Phantasm.*

WORK IN PROGRESS: Ancient Music (modern versions of Medieval Welsh, Irish, and Anglo-Saxon poems); *The Meadows of Deja-Vu* (poems).

SIDELIGHTS: Wesli Court writes: "I am now proprietor of the Mathom Bookshop and Bindery in Maine. My shop specializes in antiquarian books, signed moderns and first editions, scholarly books, and general browsing—a compatible occupation for a writer. It is also an outlet for Mathom Publishing Company, which issues work about Upstate New York and books by Upstate authors."

* * *

COWLEY, (Cassia) Joy 1936-

PERSONAL: Born August 7, 1936; daughter of Peter (a builder) and Cassia (Gedge) Summers; married Malcolm Mason (an accountant and writer), c.1970; children: (previous marriage) Sharon, Edward, Judith, James. *Education:* Attended Girls' High School in Palmerston North, Wellington, New Zealand. *Politics:* None. *Religion:* Catholic. *Home:* 29 Everest St., Khandallah, Wellington, New Zealand.

CAREER: Pharmacists' apprentice in New Zealand, 1953-56, and farmer's wife, 1956-67; full-time writer, 1967—. *Awards, honors:* New Zealand Buckland Literary Award, 1970, for *Man of Straw;* New Zealand literary achievement award, 1980; Children's Book of the Year award, 1983.

WRITINGS—Published by Doubleday, except as indicated: *Nest in a Falling Tree* (novel), 1967; *The Duck in the Gun* (children's book), illustrations by Edward Sorel, 1968; *Man of Straw,* 1970; *Of Men and Angels* (novel), 1973; *The Mandrake Root* (novel), 1975; (contributor) *New Zealand Short Stories,* Volume III, Oxford University Press, 1975; *The Growing Season,* 1978; *The Silent Ones* (children's book), Knopf, 1981.

Stories have appeared in New Zealand literary periodicals and school readers; writer of radio scripts for New Zealand Broadcasting Corp. Co-author of the Story Box Reading Programme.

WORK IN PROGRESS: A novel, *Tigers and Horses;* children's book, *Bow Down, Shadrach.*

SIDELIGHTS: Joy Cowley told *CA* that she is "increasingly concerned with writing for young people learning to read and those with reading problems. [I use] humour, quirkiness of language, rhythm, alliteration, to aid [a] child's discovery of the pleasure of the written word." Cowley also believes that "most reading problems stem from lack of confidence, and high-interest language is needed to break through self-consciousness: children cannot be tense while they are laughing."

MEDIA ADAPTATIONS: Nest in a Falling Tree was adapted by Roald Dahl into the film "The Night Digger."

AVOCATIONAL INTERESTS: Spinning, fishing, "and other soothing pastimes."

BIOGRAPHICAL/CRITICAL SOURCES: New York Times Book Review, August 13, 1967; *Best Sellers,* August 15, 1967, September 15, 1970; *Observer Review,* October 22, 1967; *New Statesman,* October 27, 1967; *Listener,* January 4, 1968.

* * *

COX, Richard 1931-

PERSONAL: Born March 8, 1931, in Winchester, England; son of Hubert Eustace (an engineer) and Joan (Thornton) Cox;

married Caroline Jennings, October, 1963; children: Lorna Katherine, Ralph Pelham, Jeremy Philip. *Education:* St. Catherine's College, Oxford, second class honors in English language and literature, 1955. *Politics:* Conservative. *Religion:* Church of England. *Agent:* Curtis Brown, Ltd., 1 Craven Hill, London W2 3EW, England. *Office:* 11 Victoria St., Aldesney C.1, England.

CAREER: Colman, Prentis & Varley (advertising agency), London, England, advertising executive, 1957-59; *Sunday Times,* London, staff foreign correspondent, 1961-64, with foreign office, 1964-66; *Daily Telegraph,* London, correspondent, 1966-73; Thornton Cox Ltd., and Brassey's Publishers, London, managing director, 1974-78; writer. Radio and television commentator on African and British Commonwealth affairs, British Broadcasting Corp.; temporary African correspondent, Westinghouse Broadcasting Corp. Private pilot. Chelsea borough councillor, 1962-65. *Military service:* British Army, Royal Artillery, 1949-51; became reserve major. Royal Air Force Volunteer Reserve, 1951-56. *Member:* Army and Navy Club, Freemen, Guild of Air Pilots and Navigators.

WRITINGS: Pan-Africanism in Practice, Oxford University Press, 1964; *Kenyatta's Country,* Hutchinson, 1965, Praeger, 1966; (editor) *Institute of Directors Guide to Europe,* Thornton Cox, 1968, 2nd edition, 1970; *Operation Sea Lion,* Thornton Cox, 1975; *Sam 7,* Hutchinson, 1976, Reader's Digest Press, 1977; *The Botticelli Madonna,* McGraw, 1978; *The KGB Directive,* Viking, 1981. Also editor of "Thorton Cox Traveller's Guides."

SIDELIGHTS: Richard Cox's thriller-detective novels—*Sam 7, The Botticelli Madonna,* and *The KGB Directive*—are noted for their meticulous attention to detail. For example, Newgate Callendar comments in *New York Times Book Review:* "It is not the story alone, good as it is, that is the main interest of *The Botticelli Madonna.* Without slowing down the plot, Mr. Cox goes into great detail about what happens when a great painting surfaces: the legalities of the situation, the way a strapped art concern goes about financing the painting, the way a good art historian thinks, the wheeling and dealing between seller and buyer, the problem of authentication, the dealings with an auction house, the hesitation and deficiencies of a so-called 'expert' and the search for the provenance of the painting."

Hubert Saal, referring to *The KGB Directive* in *New York Times Book Review,* considers Cox's "grasp of the book's diverse background" to be "formidable. He seems to know the Soviet spy apparatus in London and is able to trace it all the way back to Moscow, and his portrayal of the K.G.B. is convincing. He knows his unions too, right down to the musicians union, which has one member at Western Aircraft to handle the single piece of piano wire used in manufacturing the 207. Moreover, he is most persuasive in describing the way the 207 is manufactured, as well as where and how it is sabotaged. Norris is a first-class villain, clever and ruthless. Donaldson, plodding and indefatigable, is the very symbol of British perseverance. These characters and the exciting context invest this book with the climate of frightening reality."

Other critics, however, find Cox's extensive use of detail not just meticulous but sometimes tedious. In a *Library Journal* review of *Sam 7,* a critic calls the book "a rather long disaster-terrorist thriller, padded out by a great deal of corroborative detail which could have been cut in half." However, continues the critic, "in spite of all the relentlessly meticulous detail,

this one is still exciting, and may do well in spite of the English background."

AVOCATIONAL INTERESTS: Flying, studying art and architecture, and traveling.

BIOGRAPHICAL/CRITICAL SOURCES: Publishers Weekly, January 31, 1977, September 25, 1981; *Library Journal,* April 1, 1977; *New York Times Book Review,* June 24, 1979, January 24, 1982.

*   *   *

CRABBE, Buster
  See CRABBE, Clarence Linden

*   *   *

CRABBE, Clarence Linden   1908-1983
  (Buster Crabbe)

PERSONAL: Born February 7, 1908, in Oakland, Calif.; died April 23, 1983, in Scottsdale, Ariz.; son of Edward and Agnes (McNamara) Crabbe; married Adah Virginia Held, April 13, 1933; children: Susan Ann Fletcher, Caren, Cullen. *Education:* University of Southern California, B.A., 1932. *Politics:* Republican. *Religion:* Episcopal. *Home:* 11216 North 74th Street, Scottsdale, Ariz. 85260. *Agent:* Ventura Associates, 40 East 49th Street, New York, N.Y. 10017.

CAREER: Signed as actor by Paramount Pictures, Hollywood, Calif., after winning 400-meter race in 1932 Olympics; appeared in motion pictures for Paramount Pictures, Universal Studios, and Producers Releasing Corporation, the most notable of which include "Tarzan the Fearless," 1933, "King of the Jungle," 1933, "Nevada," 1936, "Flash Gordon's Trip to Mars," 1938, "Mars Attacks the World," 1938, "Buck Rogers," 1939, "Queen of Broadway," 1943, "Last of the Redmen," 1947, "Caged Fury," 1948, "Gunfighters of Abilene," 1959, "Arizona Raiders," 1965, and in the "Buck Rogers," "Flash Gordon," and "Billy the Kid" serials in the 1930's and 1940's; appeared in lead role in "Captain Gallant of the French Foreign Legion" television series syndicated by National Broadcasting Company (NBC), 1955-61; The Concord, Kiamesha Lake, N.Y., director of water sports, 1951-69; Cascade Industries, Edison, N.J., vice-president, beginning 1956. Lecturer. *Member:* Sigma Chi. *Awards, honors:* Elected to Swimming Hall of Fame, 1965.

WRITINGS—Under name Buster Crabbe: *Energistics: The Simple Shape-Up Exercise Plan,* Playboy Press, 1976; (with Raphael Cilento) *Buster Crabbe's Arthritis Exercise Book,* Simon & Schuster, 1980.

WORK IN PROGRESS: A book about Hollywood, *From the Outside Looking In.*

SIDELIGHTS: "There [is] a certain irony in [Buster Crabbe's] death coming on a Saturday," wrote Jerry Belcher in the *Los Angeles Times,* "for as the most celebrated of cliff-hanger serial heroes, Crabbe had escaped fictional deaths on the screen virtually every Saturday afternoon for decades." The record-setting swimmer and 1932 Olympic gold medalist was working in a California clothing store when he was tested by Paramount. "They . . . gave us G-strings, then took some pictures," the paper noted Crabbe as saying. "Then they had us all throw a spear and pick up a papier-mache rock. About three days after the Olympics they called me back. I finally got the part [of Lion Man in 'King of the Jungle,' 1933]. It paid $100 a week, which was a lot more than I was making at the clothing store."

Crabbe also appeared as the screen's seventh Tarzan in the 1933 movie "Tarzan the Fearless," a film the star himself described, according to the *Washington Post,* as "the worst Tarzan movie ever made. . . . We had only two animals, a retired elephant and a toothless lion." But "there were a lot of good fights, so the kids liked it." It was the film serials, beginning in the 1930s, however, that earned Crabbe his greatest acclaim. He played such dashing characters as Billy the Kid, Buck Rogers, and television's Captain Gallant of the French Foreign Legion, but his most famous role was that of Flash Gordon. The four-year, forty-episode series found Crabbe's golden-haired hero exploring outer space with romantic interest Dale Arden and engaging in constant battle with Ming the Merciless. While Crabbe never had much regard for his dramatic ability ("Some say that my acting rose to the point of incompetence and then leveled off," he once said, according to the *Los Angeles Times*), *Washington Post* writer Christian Williams thought differently. According to Williams, Crabbe "was not an actor, but a light source. His Flash Gordon was at all times a hawk-nosed, bare-chested American Olympic Swimmer pitted against Ming the Merciless. You would not want an actor to go up against Ming, anyhow."

His later years saw Crabbe as a successful businessman and lecturer. A hearty and active man up until his death, he was the author of two books on exercise for the elderly, *Energistics: The Simple Shape-Up Exercise Plan* and *Buster Crabbe's Arthritis Exercise Book.*

BIOGRAPHICAL/CRITICAL SOURCES: Washington Post, April 25, 1983.

OBITUARIES: Los Angeles Times, April 24, 1983; *Washington Post,* April 24, 1983; *Chicago Tribune,* April 25, 1983; *New York Times,* April 25, 1983; *Newsweek,* May 2, 1983; *Time,* May 2, 1983; *Rolling Stone,* June 9, 1983.†

*   *   *

CRAFT, Maurice 1932-

PERSONAL: Born May 4, 1932, in London, England; son of Jack (an upholsterer) and Polly (Lewis) Craft; married Alma Sampson (a national coordinator for multicultural education), May 19, 1957; children: Anna, Naomi. *Education:* University of London, B.Sc.Econ., 1953, Academic Diploma in Education, 1959; University of Dublin, H.Dip.Ed., 1956; University of Liverpool, Ph.D., 1972. *Office:* School of Education, University of Nottingham, Nottingham NG7 2RD, England.

CAREER: High school teacher in London, England, 1956-60; Edge Hill College of Education, Ormskirk, Lancashire, England, principal lecturer in sociology and head of department, 1960-67; University of Exeter, Exeter, Devon, England, senior lecturer in School of Education, 1967-73; La Trobe University, Melbourne, Australia, professor of education and chairman of Centre for the Study of Urban Education, 1973-75; University of London, London, Goldsmiths' Professor of Education at Institute of Education, 1976-80; University of Nottingham, Nottingham, England, professor of education, chairman of School of Education, and pro-vice-chancellor, 1980—.

Member of British delegation to European Economic Community Colloquia on Ethnic Minority Education, 1979, 1982; chairman of East Midlands Regional Consultative Group on Teacher Education, 1980—; United Kingdom delegate to Council of Europe seminars on the intercultural training of teachers, 1981-83. Consultant to Devonshire County Council, 1970-72, Australian Federal Poverty Commission, 1974-75, Social Sci-

ence Research Council, 1974—, Association of Commonwealth Universities, 1976, 1979, Council for National Academic Awards, 1978—, House of Commons Home Affairs Committee, 1981, British Government Committee on the Education of Children from Ethnic Minority Groups, 1982-83, and other organizations. *Military service:* British Army, Royal Army Ordnance Corps, 1953-55; served in Suez Canal Zone; became second lieutenant.

MEMBER: British Sociological Association, Association of Teachers in Colleges and Departments of Education (past member of national executive committee; founder and chairman of sociology section, 1967-69). *Awards, honors:* Research grants from Social Science Research Council, 1966-72, 1974-76, Government of the Commonwealth of Australia, 1974-75, and Japan Foundation, 1975.

WRITINGS: (Chief editor) *Linking Home and School,* Longmans, Green, 1967, revised edition, 1972; (editor with H. Lytton) *Guidance and Counselling in British Schools,* Edward Arnold, 1969, revised edition, 1974; (editor) *Family Class and Education: A Reader,* Longmans, Green, 1970; *Urban Education: A Dublin Case Study,* The Open University, 1974; *School Welfare Provision in Australia,* Australian Government Public Service, 1976; (editor) *Teaching in a Multicultural Society,* Falmer Press, 1981; *Education for Diversity,* University of Nottingham, 1982; (with M. Atkins) *Training Teachers of Ethnic Minority Community Languages,* University of Nottingham, 1983; *Education in a Plural Society,* Falmer Press, 1984; *Change in Teacher Education,* Holt-Saunders, 1984.

Contributor: W. H. Pedley, editor, *Education and Social Work,* Pergamon, 1967; W. Taylor, editor, *Towards a Policy for the Education of Teachers,* Butterworth, 1969; J. W. Tibble, editor, *The Future of Teacher Education,* Routledge & Kegan Paul, 1971; R. Jackson, editor, *Careers Guidance: Practice and Problems,* Edward Arnold, 1973; S. J. Eggleston, editor, *Contemporary Research in the Sociology of Education,* Methuen, 1974; R. E. Best, editor, *Perspectives on Pastoral Care,* Heinemann, 1979; M. O'Mahony, editor, *Young People, School and Society in Ireland,* Mental Health Association of Ireland, 1981; L. Cohen, editor, *Educational Research and Development in Britain, 1970-80,* NFER-Nelson, 1982.

Joint general editor of "Aspects of Modern Sociology" series, Longman, 1965—; editor of "Education in a Multicultural Society" series, Batsford, 1981. Contributor to numerous professional journals. Member of management committee of *Sociology of Education Abstracts;* member of editorial board of *Journal of Multilingual and Multicultural Development* and *Multicultural Education Abstracts.*

WORK IN PROGRESS: Directing a national project in multicultural teacher education.

AVOCATIONAL INTERESTS: Music, walking.

*   *   *

CRAIG, Elizabeth (Josephine) 1883-1980

PERSONAL: Born February 16, 1883, in Addiewell, West Lothian, Scotland; died June 7, 1980; daughter of John Adam (a clergyman) and Katherine (Nicholl) Craig; married Arthur E. Mann (a war correspondent), December 29, 1919 (died, 1973). *Education:* Attended George Watson's Ladies' College and Forfar Academy. *Home:* Withyfield, Green Lane, Farnham Common, Buckinghamshire, England. *Agent:* E. P. Lewin, E.P.S. Lewin and Partners, 7 Chelsea Embankment, London

S.W.3, England; and Innes Rose, John Farquharson Ltd., Bell House, 8 Bell Yard, London WC2A 2JU, England.

CAREER: Woman's page editor and reporter in Scotland, 1912-15, in London, England, 1915-18; editor of *Woman's Life,* 1915-18; cookery editor of *Woman's Journal,* 1927-59; also free-lance columnist, interviewer, and feature writer. Lecturer, British Ministry of Agriculture and Ministry of Food, throughout World War II. Consultant on food products. *Member:* P.E.N., Royal Society of Arts (fellow), Food and Cookery Association (fellow), Institute of Hygiene, Dame de la Chaine des Rotisseurs, Chevaliere de l'Ordre des Coteaux (de Champagne), Women's Press Club, Circle of Wine Writers, Wine and Food Society, Royal Horticultural Society. *Awards, honors:* Member, Order of the British Empire, 1980.

WRITINGS: (Editor) *The Stage Favourites' Cook Book,* Hutchinson, 1924; *Cooking with Elizabeth Craig,* Collins, 1932, new edition, 1961; (editor) *New Standard Cookery Illustrated,* Oldhams Press, 1932; *Entertaining with Elizabeth Craig,* Collins, 1933; (with Andre Simon) *Madeira: Wine, Cakes and Sauce,* Constable, 1933; *Elizabeth Craig's Economical Cookery,* Collins, 1934, revised edition, 1940; *Elizabeth Craig's Standard Recipes,* Collins, 1934; *Wine in the Kitchen,* Transatlantic, 1934; *Elizabeth Craig's Everyday Cookery,* Collins, 1935; *Elizabeth Craig's Family Cookery,* Collins, 1935; *Cookery Illustrated and Household Management,* Oldhams Press, 1936; *Bubble and Squeak,* Chapman & Hall, 1936; *The Housewives Monthly Calender,* Chapman & Hall, 1936; *Keeping House with Elizabeth Craig: A New Guide to Planning and Running Your Home,* Collins, 1936; (editor) *278 Tested Recipes,* Clerke & Cockeran, 1936; *Woman, Wine and a Saucepan,* Chapman & Hall, 1936; *The Way to a Good Table: Electric Cookery,* British Electrical Development Association, 1937; *Gardening,* Collins, 1937; *Housekeeping,* Collins, 1937; *Needlecraft,* Collins, 1937; *1500 Everyday Menus,* Collins, 1937; *1000 Household Hints,* Collins, 1937; *Cookery,* Collins, 1937; *Enquire Within: The Happy Housewife,* Collins, 1938; *Simple Gardening,* Collins, 1938; *Simple Housekeeping,* Collins, 1938.

Cooking in War-Time, Collins, 1940; *Gardening with Elizabeth Craig: A Complete Guide to All Aspects of Gardening in War-Time,* Collins, 1940; *Elizabeth Craig's Household Library,* six volumes (includes *Gardening, Housekeeping, Needlecraft, 1000 Household Hints, Cookery, 1500 Everyday Menus*), Collins, 1940; *Cooking for Today,* Woman's Journal, 1948; *Court Favourites: Recipes from Royal Kitchens,* British Book Centre, 1953; *Waterless Cooking,* Milbro Products, 1953; *Beer and Vittels,* Museum Press, 1955; *The Scottish Cookery Book,* Deutsch, 1956, new edition, Corgi, 1980; *Instructions to Young Cooks,* Museum Press, 1957, Sportshelf, 1958, 2nd edition, Museum Press, 1960; *Collins Family Cookery,* Collins, 1957, revised edition, 1971; *The Elizabeth Craig Complete Family Cookery,* Educational Book Co., 1957; *Scandinavian Cooking,* Deutsch, 1958; *A Cook's Guide to Wine,* Constable, 1959.

Cottage Cheese and Yogurt, Jenkins, 1960; (editor) Thora H. Campbell, *The Potluck Cookery Book,* revised edition, Oliver & Boyd, 1962; *Banana Dishes,* Wehman, 1962; (editor) Victor Bennett and Cecil Kahman, *Around the World in a Salad Bowl,* revised edition, Oliver & Boyd, 1963; *Cook Continentale,* Oliver & Boyd, 1965, International Publications Service, 1966; *What's Cooking in Scotland,* Rand McNally, 1965; *The Art of Irish Cooking,* Ward, Lock, 1969; *The Business Woman's Cook Book,* Pelham Book, 1970; (editor) *The Penguin Salad Book,* Penguin, 1972; *Elizabeth Craig's Hotch Potch,* Collins, 1978.

Also author of *Practical Gardening,* 1952, and *Wartime Housekeeping.*

Contributor to *Scottish Annual, Jewish Chronicle Supplement, Doctor on Holiday, House and Garden, Wine Magazine, Scottish Field, People's Friend,* and other periodicals, and to most national newspapers in Great Britain and some in United States. Former cookery editor, *Woman's Journal, Woman's Pictorial,* and *Mother and Home.*

WORK IN PROGRESS: Traditional English Cookery, for Ward, Lock.

SIDELIGHTS: An avid gardener, Elizabeth Craig traveled all over Europe, the United States, Canada, and North Africa, gathering material for articles on food, wine, and travel.

OBITUARIES: London Times, June 11, 1980; *New York Times,* June 12, 1980.†

*   *   *

CRAIN, Jeff
See MENESES, Enrique

*   *   *

CRATTY, Bryant J. 1929-

PERSONAL: Born November 9, 1929, in Baltimore, Md.; married Barbara Lutomski, June, 1960 (divorced); married Madeleine Lundin, June 28, 1969 (divorced); married Jraneide De Oliviera, December 13, 1981; children: (first marriage) Darren. *Education:* University of California, Los Angeles, B.S., 1952, M.S., 1955, Ed.D., 1961; Pomona College, graduate study, 1952-53. *Home:* 10827 Savona Dr., Los Angeles, Calif. 90024. *Office:* Department of Kinesiology, University of California, Los Angeles, Calif. 90024.

CAREER: Campbell Hall School, North Hollywood, Calif., instructor, 1950; Pomona College, Pomona, Calif., swimming and water polo coach, 1952-57; Pomona (Calif.) public schools, high school teacher of physical education and mathematics, 1955-58; University of California, Los Angeles, assistant professor, 1961-65, associate professor, 1965-69, professor of kinesiology, 1969—, director of perceptual-motor learning laboratory, 1963—. Lecturer at Baylor University Medical Center, 1965; consultant to Research Bureau, U.S. Department of Education, and to Joseph P. Kennedy, Jr. Foundation.

MEMBER: International Society for Psychology and Sport, American Association for Health, Physical Education and Recreation (president of national kinesiology council, 1967), College Physical Education Association, North American Society for the Study of Psychology and Physical Acitvity (president), French Society of Sports Psychology (honorary member), California Association for Health, Physical Education and Recreation, Phi Epsilon Kappa. *Awards, honors:* U.S. Public Health Service study grant to National Institute of Neurological Diseases and Blindness, 1964-66; National Science Foundation grant, 1966-68; U.S. Department of Education grant, 1968-70.

WRITINGS: Movement Behavior and Motor Learning, Lea & Febiger, 1964, 3rd edition, 1975; *Developmental Sequences of Perceptual-Motor Tasks for Neurologically Handicapped and Retarded Children,* Educational Activities, 1967; *Social Dimensions of Physical Activity,* Prentice-Hall, 1967; *Psychology and Physical Activity,* Prentice-Hall, 1968; (editor with Roscoe C. Brown, and contributor) *New Perspectives of Man in Action,*

Prentice-Hall, 1968; *Moving and Learning: 50 Games for Children with Learning Difficulties,* Educational Activities, 1968; *Perceptual-Motor Behavior and Educational Processes,* C. C Thomas, 1969; (with Sister Margaret Mary Martin) *Perceptual-Motor Efficiency in Children,* Lea & Febiger, 1969; *Motor Activity and the Education of Retardates,* Lea & Febiger, 1969, 2nd edition, 1975; (with R. S. Hutton) *Experiments in Movement Behavior and Motor Learning,* Lea & Febiger, 1969.

(With Miroslav Vanek) *Psychology and the Superior Athlete,* Macmillan, 1970; *Perceptual and Motor Development of Infants and Children,* Macmillan, 1970, 2nd edition, Prentice-Hall, 1979; *Educational Implications of Movement Experiences,* Seattle Special Child Publications, 1970; *Motor Activity, Movement Behavior and the Education of Children,* C. C Thomas, 1970; *Active Learning,* Prentice-Hall, 1971; *Movement and Spatial Awareness in Blind Children and Youth,* C. C Thomas, 1970; *Career Potentials in Physical Activity,* Prentice-Hall, 1972; *Physical Expressions of Intelligence,* Prentice-Hall, 1973; *Teaching Motor Skills,* Prentice-Hall, 1973; *Psychomotor Behavior in Education and Sports: Selected Papers,* C. C Thomas, 1974; *Children and Youth in Competitive Sport,* Educational Activities, 1974; *Psychology in Contemporary Sport: Guidelines for Coaches and Athletes,* Prentice-Hall, 1974, 2nd edition, 1983; *Educational Games for the Physically Handicapped,* Love Publishing, 1974; *Remedial Motor Activity for Children,* Lea & Febiger, 1975; *Intelligence in Action,* Prentice-Hall, 1975; *Teaching about Human Behavior via Active Games,* Prentice-Hall, 1976; (with Jean Stabenow) *Speech and Language Problems in Children,* Love Publishing, 1978.

Adapted Physical Education for Handicapped Children and Youth, Love Publishing, 1980; *Social Psychological of Athletics,* Prentice-Hall, 1980; *Psychological Preparation and Athletic Excellence,* Mouvement, 1984; (with Robert Piggott) *Student Projects in Sport Psychology,* Mouvement, 1984.

Contributor: William Johnson, editor, *The Science and Medicine of Exercise and Sport,* Macmillan, 1967; Jerome Hellmuth, editor, *Learning Disorders,* Volume III, Seattle Special Child Publications, 1968; Paul Pearson, *Physical Therapy Services for Mentally Retarded,* C. C Thomas, 1968. Also contributor to Gilbert Schiffmen amd Darrel Carter, editors, *Multidisciplinary Approaches to Learning Disorders,* Wiley, and to *Encyclopaedia Britannica.*

Author or co-author of five research monographs, including *The Body-Image of Blind Children,* published by American Foundation for the Blind, 1968; also author of *Coding Games,* 1981. Other writings include mobility and motor tests, four recordings issued by Educational Activities, and about forty research articles. Review editor, *Research Quarterly, International Journal of Sports Psychology,* and *Journal of Motor Behavior.*

SIDELIGHTS: Bryant J. Cratty's books have been translated into Chinese, Portuguese, Japanese, Italian, Dutch, and German.

*   *   *

CRIMMINS, James Custis   1935-

PERSONAL: Born January 13, 1935, in Palo Alto, Calif.; son of Edward Custis (a businessman) and Naneen (Burnap) Crimmins; married Marcy Tench, February 18, 1962; married Jennifer Leahy, December 16, 1978; children: (first marriage) Ethan Custis, Samantha Olmstead, Page Tench, Tory Roberts; (second marriage) Courtney Leahy. *Education:* Princeton Uni-

versity, A.B., 1956. *Home:* 17 East 89th St., New York, N.Y. 10028. *Office:* Business Times, Inc., 727 Eleventh Ave., New York, N.Y. 10019.

CAREER: Curtis Publishing, Indianapolis, Ind., creative director, 1956-60; *Newsweek,* New York City, special projects director, 1960-67; *Harper's,* New York City, associate publisher and vice-president, 1967-72; chairman and founder, Playback Associates, 1972-80; senior vice-president and director, Reeves Communications Corp., 1977-80; Business Times, Inc., New York City, currently president and editor-in-chief.

WRITINGS: Nicholas, The Boy Who Wanted to Be Santa Claus, Lippincott, 1962; (with Peter A. Derow) *Successful Publishing on the Campus,* Newsweek, Inc., 1968; (with John Bunyan) *Television and Management: The Manager's Guide to Video,* Knowledge Industries, 1977; (with Bunyan and N. Kyri Watson) *Practical Video: The Manager's Guide to Applications,* Knowledge Publications, 1978; (with H. B. Darrach, L. L. Larison Cudmore, and Gerald Jonas) "The Search for Solutions" (film series), distributed by Playback Associates, 1979; (with Mary Keil) *Enterprise in the Non-Profit Sector,* Rockefeller Brothers Fund and Partners for Livable Places, 1983.

WORK IN PROGRESS: "The Challenge of the Unknown," a film series to be shown in fall of 1984.

*   *   *

CROOKENDEN, Napier   1915-

PERSONAL: Born August 31, 1915, in Chester, England; son of Arthur (a colonel in the British Army) and Dorothy (Rowlandson) Crookenden; married Patricia Nassau Kindersley, August 3, 1948; children: James Napier, Elisabeth Jane (Mrs. T. C. Wilson), Charles Stephen Napier, Catherine Nancy. *Education:* Attended Royal Military College, 1934-35. *Religion:* Church of England. *Home:* Twin Furs, Four Elms, Edenbridge, Kent, England.

CAREER: British Army, career officer, 1935-72, retiring as lieutenant general; commissioned to Cheshire Regiment, 1935, Sixth Airlanding Brigade, 1943-44; commanding officer of Ninth Battalion Parachute Regiment, 1944-46; general staff officer to director of operations in Malaya, 1952-54; commander of Sixteenth Parachute Brigade, 1960-61; at Imperial Defence College, 1962; director of Land/Air Warfare for Ministry of Defence, 1964-66; commandant of Royal Military College of Science in Shrivenham, 1967-69; colonel of Cheshire Regiment, 1969-71; commander-in-chief of Western Command, 1969-72. Colonel commandant of Prince of Wales Division, 1971-74; lieutenant of Tower of London, 1975-81. Member of board of trustees of Imperial War Museum, 1973-83.

MEMBER: Soldiers', Sailors', and Airmen's Families Association (chairman, 1974—), Ski Club of Great Britain, Army and Navy Club. *Awards, honors:* Distinguished Service Order, 1945; officer of Order of the British Empire, 1954; Knight Commander of the Bath, 1970; deputy lieutenant, county of Kent.

WRITINGS: Drop Zone Normandy, Scribner, 1976; *Airborne at War,* Ian Allan, 1977; *Battle of the Bulge,* Ian Allan, 1979.

SIDELIGHTS: Napier Crookenden writes: "I know America well, and having fought alongside American airborne troops, I find my work on the history of our combined operations stimulating. I speak French and German and find equal interest in my researches into World War II battles.''

*   *   *

CROSBY, Jeremiah
  See CROSBY, Michael (Hugh)

*   *   *

CROSBY, Michael (Hugh) 1940-
  (Jeremiah Crosby)

PERSONAL: Born February 16, 1940, in Fond du lac, Wis.; son of Hugh John (an insurance man) and Blanche (Bouser) Crosby. *Education:* Attended St. Lawrence College, Mount Calvary, Wis.; Capuchin Seminary of St. Mary, Crown Point, Ind., B.A., 1963; graduate study, University of Wisconsin—Milwaukee, 1974. *Office:* Justice and Peace Center, 1016 North Ninth St., Milwaukee, Wis. 53233.

CAREER: Ordained Roman Catholic priest of Capuchin order (O.F.M. Cap.), 1966. Member, executive committee, Milwaukee Archdiocese Priest Senate, 1972—, chairman, committee on justice and peace, 1972—; coordinator, Corporate Responsibility Action Group of Milwaukee, 1973—; member, executive committee of governing board, Interfaith Center on Corporate Responsibility, New York, N.Y., 1975—. Charter member, Milwaukee Forum, 1971, first vice-president, 1976.

WRITINGS: (Under pseudonym Jeremiah Crosby) *Bearing Witness: The Place of the Franciscan Family in the Church,* Franciscan Herald, 1966; *The Call and the Answer,* Franciscan Herald, 1969; *Franciscan Charism: A Sociological Investigation,* Franciscan Publishers, 1969; *Thy Will Be Done: Praying the Our Father as a Subversive Activity,* Orbis, 1977; *The Spirituality of the Beatitudes: Matthew's Challenge for First World Christians,* Orbis, 1981.

Contributor to *New Catholic Encyclopedia, America, Emmanuel, Bible Today,* and other periodicals. Past editor, *Round Table of Franciscan Research.*

WORK IN PROGRESS: A book developing a theology of vocation.

SIDELIGHTS: Michael Crosby is competent in Latin and knows some Italian and Spanish.†

*   *   *

CROUT, George C(lement) 1917-

PERSONAL: Born February 10, 1917, in Middletown, Ohio; son of Ebert (a policeman) and Myrtle M. (a teacher; maiden name, Williamson) Crout. *Education:* Miami University, Oxford, Ohio, B.S., 1938, M.A., 1941, M.E., 1948, Specialist in Ed., 1955; additional graduate study at Bowling Green State University, 1962, Appalachian State University, 1963, University of Michigan, 1964, and George Peabody College for Teachers (now George Peabody College for Teachers of Vanderbilt University), 1965. *Politics:* Independent. *Religion:* Methodist. *Home:* 48-A Miami Dr., Monroe, Ohio 45050.

CAREER: Free-lance writer. Middletown (Ohio) public schools, teacher, 1938-42 and 1946-48, principal of elementary schools, 1948-75. Instructor in Evening College, Miami University, Oxford, Ohio, 1946-47. *Military service:* U.S. Army Air Forces, 1942-45; served in Pacific theater; became staff sergeant; received six battle stars. *Member:* National Education Associa-

tion, American Association for State and Local History, National Association of Elementary School Principals, Ohio Education Association, Ohio Department of Elementary School Principals, Ohio Historical Society, Canal Society of Ohio, Butler County Historical Society, Middletown Historical Society (trustee; curator of canal museum), Phi Beta Kappa, American Legion. *Awards, honors:* American Educators Medal of Freedoms Foundation.

WRITINGS—Children's books, except as indicated: *Stories of Our School Community,* illustrations by Herbert W. Fall, Perry Printing Co., 1960, 5th edition, 1977; *Middletown U.S.A.: All American City* (adult), edited by Wilfred D. Vorhis, Perry Printing Co., 1960; (with Edith McCall) *Where the Ohio Flows,* Benefic, 1960; *Ohio Caravan* (poems), Perry Printing Co., 1961; *Seven Lives of Johnny B. Free,* Denison, 1961; *Middletown Diary* (adult), privately printed, 1965; *Lincoln's Littlest Soldier,* Denison, 1969; *Lucky Cloverleaf of the 4-H,* Denison, 1971; (with McCall) *You and Ohio,* Benefic, 1971; *Middletown Landmarks* (adult), Perry Printing Co., 1974; *You and Dayton,* News Publishing Co., 1976; *Old Middletown* (adult), KGI Printing Co., 1976; *Ohio: Its People and Culture,* Denison, 1977; *Miami Valley Vignettes,* URS Printing, 1982; *History of Butler County,* Windsor Books, 1984.

Plays for children; all published by Eldridge Publishing Co.: *Do It Yourself Christmas Plays,* 1960; *Little Star Lost,* 1960; *The Tinsel Fairy,* 1964; *Santa's Christmas Satellite,* 1970.

Author of radio scripts. Contributor to journals and newspapers.

WORK IN PROGRESS: Jungle Air Force, a story of World War II; *Other Days in Ohio.*

SIDELIGHTS: George C. Crout wrote *CA:* ''Each book represents basic historical research utilizing previously unpublished manuscript material, presented simply for the young reader. An underlying theme is explored that may provide a young person with background in solving a problem he may face. *The Seven Lives of Johnny B. Free* shows how life has changed for youth searching for economic independence, while *Ohio: Its People and Culture* explores planning a career today in a state with a diverse culture, made up of many ethnic groups. Local and regional history is presented against a backdrop of national events, for American culture is a composite of its many localities.

''A knowledge of one's own area creates a feeling of belonging to a very special part of America. It enriches one's life, being aware of the people who came before and the landmarks that played a part in a community's development. This all adds depth and meaning to life. This is what I have attempted to do in the trilogy just completed—covering the city, county, and the valley.''

AVOCATIONAL INTERESTS: Gardening, lecturing, collecting historical items.

*   *   *

CULLINAN, Elizabeth 1933-

PERSONAL: Born June 7, 1933, in New York, N.Y.; daughter of Cornelius G. and Irene (O'Connell) Cullinan. *Education:* Marymount College, B.A., 1954. *Religion:* Roman Catholic. *Residence:* New York, N.Y.

CAREER: Writer. *New Yorker,* New York, N.Y., secretary and typist, intermittently, 1955-64; lived in Dublin, Ireland,

1961-62, returned to New York for several months, and went back to Dublin for two more years. Taught at University of Iowa, University of Massachusetts, and Fordham University. *Awards, honors:* Houghton Mifflin literary fellowship, 1969, and New Writers Award, Great Lakes Colleges Association, 1970, both for *House of Gold;* National Endowment for the Arts grant, 1974; Carnegie Fund grant, 1978.

WRITINGS: *House of Gold* (novel), Houghton, 1969; *The Time of Adam* (short stories), Houghton, 1971; *Yellow Roses* (short stories), Viking, 1977; (contributor) *The Best Irish Short Stories, Number 3,* edited by David Marcus, Paul Elek, 1978; (contributor) *The Best American Short Stories, 1978,* edited by Ted Solotaroff and Shannon Ravenel, Houghton, 1978; *A Change of Scene* (novel), Norton, 1982. Contributor of short stories to the *New Yorker.*

SIDELIGHTS: In her writing, Elizabeth Cullinan explores the trivial and commonplace in the face of larger themes. Although her characters are usually Irish-American, and, in the words of Muriel Haynes in *Saturday Review,* "people who in their ordinary, less-than-spiritual lives, happen to have been born Catholics," Cullinan's concerns are universal. Celia Betsky comments in *Saturday Review* that in the short-story collection *Yellow Roses,* for example, "Cullinan offers up the universal elements of parochialism and turns descriptions of death and ritual into acts of insight."

Most reviewers also agree that a narrow Catholicism is prominent in Cullinan's highly acclaimed novel *House of Gold,* but John Leonard points out in the *New York Times* that the book is a novel about an "American family lost in the thickets of self-deception." The story of the death of Julia Devlin, a formidable Irish-American Roman Catholic matriarch, the novel chronicles events that occur one humid summer day as the Devlins gather at Julia's home. Devlin lies upstairs in a coma, "a being on the verge of nothingness who still manages to hold all in her powerful sway," writes Richard M. Elman in the *New York Times Book Review.*

According to Edward Weeks in the *Atlantic,* Cullinan's observant descriptions "re-create Mrs. Devlin's illusion, which she imposed upon her children, that home was a special place of consecration." The home, a dilapidated house decorated in gold and filled with religious pictures and statuettes, is described by Maeve Brennan in the *New Yorker* as "a shanty-Irish dream of lace-curtain grandeur come true[,] . . . where a lithograph of the flaming, engorged Sacred Heart of Jesus is more real than any words Christ ever uttered. What the house actually is is a tabernacle for the rabidly devout motherhood of Julia Devlin."

This religiosity is also apparent in the short-story collection *The Time of Adam.* As Joyce Carol Oates observes in the *New York Times Book Review,* Cullinan's Roman Catholic Church "operates not so much as an institution dedicated to the enrichment of its members' lives, but as a kind of diversion for them, an excuse for the curtailment of their instincts." According to Haynes, the author's "preoccupation is with the frailties that corrode the virtue of Catholic truth, the total of those venial sins that betray its grace: self-righteousness, snobbery, passivity, the substitution of ritual and habit for engagement with life. . . . At her best she transcends the parochial limits of her chosen milieu, and stretches it to nonsectarian human dimension."

Cullinan's concerns in *House of Gold,* for example, are larger than the book's domestic setting. The novel's theme, comments

Sister Mary Rose Weir in *Best Sellers,* is of "one of life's inevitable facts—the stark reality of death. The theme of death serves as a catalyst to bring to a head some of the small dramas of an Irish-American Catholic family of the old style." In the opinion of a *Times Literary Supplement* reviewer, "the effect . . . of this wonderfully controlled and intelligent novel is to make one question most of the values which most families find necessary to uphold and hand on in order to convince themselves they are unique and united."

House of Gold has also been praised for its profusion of finely wrought detail. "What is so strangely impressive about this . . . novel," Elman points out, "is its complete dedication to the ordinary, to sensation, event, process, detail." Weir agrees, maintaining that Cullinan knows "the art of using the ordinary things of life to produce an extraordinary effect. . . . Each gesture betrays some sort of feeling; each glance some expectation or disappointment." "The details of domestic pain," writes Leonard, are "unflinchingly perceived and remorselessly recorded."

Detail is an important part of Cullinan's other works as well. The novel *A Change of Scene,* for instance, tells the story of a young Irish-American woman, still in the process of defining herself, who lives briefly in Dublin during the 1960s. According to Lois Decker O'Neill in *Washington Post Book World,* Cullinan "evokes this Dublin with emotion and an authenticity of detail that brings to life a city as far removed as is Joyce's Dublin of 1904 from the present scruffy reality." The author's talent for depicting ordinary detail is also evident in her shorter fiction. Writing in *Newsweek,* Margo Jefferson finds that in *Yellow Roses,* Cullinan "delineates [circumstances] with precision, gravity and grace—the small happenings of a day, the arc of a life, the demands of temperament, background and necessity." Cullinan "is always intelligent, precise and skillful," comments Oates, "turning out stories of near-faultless craftsmanship, quite satisfied to leave the world of passion, violence and chaos to other contemporaries, who may very well be working with less challenging subjects. It takes immense skill, after all, to deal with trivia and escape becoming trivial."

BIOGRAPHICAL/CRITICAL SOURCES: *New York Times,* January 13, 1970, April 7, 1977; *New York Times Book Review,* January 18, 1970, February 7, 1971, April 17, 1977; *Atlantic,* February, 1970; *Best Sellers,* February 1, 1970, February 1, 1971, July, 1982; *Christian Science Monitor,* February 5, 1970, January 28, 1971; *New Yorker,* February 14, 1970, May 17, 1982; *America,* February 21, 1970, April 19, 1971; *Commonweal,* March 20, 1970, January 22, 1971, August 19, 1977; *Critic,* May, 1970, May, 1971; *Book World,* February 7, 1971; *Times Literary Supplement,* February 19, 1971; *Saturday Review,* February 27, 1971, April 16, 1977, May, 1982; *Newsweek,* May 16, 1977; *Los Angeles Times,* June 10, 1982; *Washington Post Book World,* July 28, 1982.

—*Sketch by Candace Cloutier*

*   *   *

CULSHAW, John (Royds)   1924-1980

PERSONAL: Born May 28, 1924, in Southport, Lancashire, England; died April 27, 1980, in London, England; son of Percy Ellis and Doris (Crowther) Culshaw. *Education:* Educated at King George V School, Southport, England. *Home:* 16 Arlington Ave., London N1, England.

CAREER: Decca Record Co. Ltd., London, England, chief producer of classical recordings, 1956-67; British Broadcasting

Corp., London, director of television music, 1967-75; free-lance author and television producer, beginning 1975. Frequent broadcasting commentator for the Metropolitan Opera performances. Broadcaster on musical topics for British Broadcasting Corp. prior to joining the staff; occasional lecturer for extra-mural departments of University of London and Oxford University. *Military service:* Royal Navy, Fleet Air Arm, 1942-46; became lieutenant. *Awards, honors:* Co-recipient of Nicolai Medal presented by Vienna Philharmonic Orchestra, 1959, and Schalk Medal, 1967; Order of the British Empire, 1966, for services to music.

WRITINGS: Sergei Rachmaninov, Oxford University Press, 1948; *The Concerto,* Parrish, 1949, reprinted, Greenwood Press, 1979; *The Sons of Brutus* (novel), Secker & Warburg, 1950; *A Century of Music,* Dobson, 1951; *A Place of Stone* (novel), Secker & Warburg, 1952; *Ring Resounding: The Stirring Account of How Wagner's "Der Ring des Nibelungen" Was Recorded for the First Time,* Viking, 1967; *Reflections on Wagner's "Ring,"* Viking, 1976; *Wagner: The Man and His Music,* Dutton, 1978; *Putting the Record Straight: The Autobiography of John Culshaw,* Secker & Warburg, 1981, Viking, 1982.

Contributor to *Encyclopaedia Britannica Book of the Year,* 1948-53, and to *High Fidelity, Saturday Review, Gramophone,* and other periodicals.

SIDELIGHTS: "When John Culshaw became Decca's senior [record] producer in 1956, the gramophone was at its second turning point within a decade," Richard Osborne wrote in a *Times Literary Supplement* review of Culshaw's posthumously-published autobiography *Putting the Record Straight.* "The long playing record had rather anonymously evolved, but it was Culshaw and his team who first recognized the creative possibilities of stereophonic sound." Among the notable projects undertaken by Culshaw and his team of sound engineers was a recording of Wagner's "Ring" cycle in Vienna, which began in 1958 and took seven years to complete.

Putting the Record Straight chronicles Culshaw's career at Decca and contains the author's impressions of the many renowned classical artists he had worked with. "As a source of often brutal anecdotes about distinguished musicians," remarked Osborne, "[the book] will be eagerly perused. [It] is given coherence, though, not by its scabrous table-talk but by the sense it gives of a man at odds with an enervatingly conservative management which tolerated a revolution and its own growing international prestige while steadfastly laying the foundation of its own eventual destruction. . . . By a strange wrench of fate," Osborne concluded, "Decca and Culshaw died about the same time. That once proud label is now under foreign control."

AVOCATIONAL INTERESTS: Flying (Culshaw was a licensed pilot).

BIOGRAPHICAL/CRITICAL SOURCES: New York Times Book Review, April 1, 1979; John Culshaw, *Putting the Record Straight: The Autobiography of John Culshaw,* Secker & Warburg, 1981, Viking, 1982; *Punch,* January 27, 1982; *London Review of Books,* February 4, 1982; *Times Literary Supplement,* February 26, 1982; *Washington Post Book World,* March 14, 1982; *New York Review of Books,* May 13, 1982.

OBITUARIES: New York Times, April 29, 1980; *Washington Post,* April 29, 1980; *London Times,* April 29, 1980; *Chicago Tribune,* April 29, 1980; *Time,* May 12, 1980.†

CUMMING, Patricia (Arens) 1932-

PERSONAL: Born September 7, 1932, in New York, N.Y.; daughter of Egmont (an industrial designer) and Camille Davied (an editor and writer) Arens; married Edward Chandler Cumming, July 7, 1954 (deceased); children: Julie, Susanna. *Education:* Radcliffe College, B.A., 1954; Middlebury College, M.A., 1956. *Address:* Box 251, Adamsville, R.I. 02801.

CAREER: Theatre Company of Boston, Boston, Mass., co-producer, 1964-65; *Daedalus,* Cambridge, Mass., editorial associate, 1966-69; Massachusetts Institute of Technology, Cambridge, instructor, 1969-72, assistant professor, 1972-77, associate professor of humanities, 1977-79. Lecturer, College of Public and Community Service, University of Massachusetts—Boston, 1978; held Language and Thinking Workshop, Bard College, summer, 1981. *Member:* Phi Beta Kappa.

WRITINGS: Afterwards (poetry), Alice James Books, 1974; (with others) *Free Writing: A Group Approach,* Hayden, 1976; *Letter to an Outlying Province,* Alice James Books, 1976.

Plays: "The Triangle," first produced in Boston at Image Theatre, 1963; "After Us the Deluge" (three-act), first produced in Kingston at University of Rhode Island Summer Theatre Festival, 1968; "The Hoax" (one-act), first produced in Boston at the Theatre Company of Boston, 1973.

Contributor to anthologies: *Best Poems of 1972: Borestone Mountain Poetry Awards of 1973,* edited by Lionel Stevenson and others, Pacific Books, 1973; *Working Women: Stories and Poems,* edited by Nancy Hoffman and Florence Howe, Feminist Press, 1978; *By Women: An Anthology of Literature,* edited by Linda Kirschner and Marcia Folsom, Houghton, 1976. Contributor to literary journals, including *Kayak, Shenandoah,* and *Hanging Loose.*

WORK IN PROGRESS: A poetry collection, tentatively entitled *Portraits, Notes and Occasional Poems;* a novel, tentatively entitled *Scenes from Family Life.*

SIDELIGHTS: Patricia Cumming tells *CA* that she is now living in the country, writing, editing, and gardening.

*   *   *

CUNLIFFE, John Arthur 1933-

PERSONAL: Born June 16, 1933, in Colne, England; married Sylvia Thompson (a musician); children: Julian Edward. *Education:* North-Western Polytechnic, fellow of Library Association, 1957; Charlotte Mason College, teaching qualification, 1975. *Home:* Flat 2, 7 The Beeches, Manchester M20 8PQ, England.

CAREER: Currently deputy head, Crawcroft Park School, Manchester, England. *Member:* Society of Authors, National Union of Teachers.

WRITINGS—All published by Deutsch: *The Adventures of Lord Pip,* 1970; *The Giant Who Stole the World,* 1971; *Riddles and Rhymes and Rigmaroles,* 1971; *The Giant Who Swallowed the Wind,* 1972; *The Story of Giant Kippernose,* 1972; *The Great Dragon Competition,* 1973; *The King's Birthday Cake,* 1973; *Small Monkey Tales,* 1974; *The Farmer, the Rooks, and the Cherry Tree,* 1975; *Giant Brog and the Motorway,* 1975; *Sara's Giant and the Upside-Down House,* 1980; *Mr. Gosling and the Runaway Chair,* 1981; *Giant Kippernose and Other Stories,* 1981.

"Farmer Barnes" series; published by Deutsch, except as indicated: *Farmer Barnes Buys a Pig,* 1964, Lion Press, 1969; *. . . and Bluebell,* 1966; *. . . at the County Show,* 1966, published as *Farmer Barnes at the County Fair,* Lion Press, 1970; *. . . and the Goats,* 1971; *. . . Goes Fishing,* 1972; *. . . and the Snow Picnic,* 1974; *. . . Fells a Tree,* 1981.

Also author of "Postman Pat and His Black and White Cat," a BBC television series. Contributor to *Children's Book Review.*

BIOGRAPHICAL/CRITICAL SOURCES: Times Literary Supplement, December 6, 1974.

* * *

CUSACK, (Ellen) Dymphna   1902-198(?)

PERSONAL: Born September 22, 1902, in Wyalong, New South Wales, Australia; deceased; daughter of James (a sheep farmer) and Beatrice (Crowley) Cusack; married Norman Randolph Freehill (a journalist and writer). *Education:* Attended St. Ursalas College, 1917-20; University of Sydney, B.A. (with honors), 1925, diploma of education, 1925. *Politics:* Progressive. *Address:* c/o Clients' Mail Department, Bank of New South Wales, Head Office, George St., Sydney, New South Wales, Australia. *Agent:* Madame Odette Arnaud, 11 rue de Teheran, Paris, France.

CAREER: Writer. Department of Education, New South Wales, Australia, high school teacher, 1926-43. Lecturer in extramural university studies, 1942-43. Lecturer and broadcaster. *Member:* Society of Authors (England), Fellowship of Australian Writers (vice-president, 1949-61), P.E.N. *Awards, honors:* West Australian drama prizes, 1942, for "Morning Sacrifice," and 1943, for "Comets Soon Pass"; Playwrights' Advisory Board drama prizes, 1945, for "Shoulder the Sky," and 1946, for "Stand Still Time"; *Sydney Daily Telegraph* novel award, 1948, for *Come in Spinner!;* Coronation Medal for services to Australian literature, 1953; British Arts Council Award, for "The Golden Girls"; Commonwealth literary fellowship, for *Southern Steel.*

WRITINGS: Jungfrau (novel), Bulletin Publishing (Sydney), 1936; (with Miles Franklin) *Pioneers on Parade,* Angus & Robertson, 1939; (with Florence James) *Come in Spinner!,* Morrow, 1951; *Say No to Death,* Heinemann, 1951, reprinted, Angus & Robertson, 1967, published as *The Sun in My Hands,* Morrow, 1952; *Southern Steel,* Constable, 1953; *The Sun in Exile,* Constable, 1955; *Chinese Women Speak* (travelbook), Angus & Robertson, 1958; *Heatwave in Berlin,* Heinemann, 1961; *Picnic Races,* Heinemann, 1962, reprinted, Hutchinson Publishing Group, 1978; *Holidays among the Russians* (travelbook), Heinemann, 1964; *Black Lightning* (novel), Heinemann, 1964; (with James) *Four Winds and a Family,* new edition, Lansdowne, 1965; (with T. Inglis Moore and Barrie Ovendeu) *Mary Gilmore: A Tribute,* Australian Book Society, 1965; *Ilyria Reborn* (travelbook about Albania), Heinemann, 1966; *The Sun Is Not Enough,* Heinemann, 1967; *The Half-Burnt Tree,* Heinemann, 1969; *A Bough in Hell,* Heinemann, 1971; (with husband, Norman Freehill) *Dymphna Cusack* (autobiography), Thomas Nelson, 1975. Also author of *Nurse No Long Grief,* 1978, and *The Triple Concerto,* 1979.

Plays: *Red Sky at Morning* (three-act), Melbourne University Press and Oxford University Press, 1942; *Three Australian Three-Act Plays* (includes "Comets Soon Pass," "Shoulder the Sky," and "Morning Sacrifice"), Australasian Publishing Co., 1950; *The Golden Girls* (three-act), Baker, 1955, reprinted, 1970. Also author of British and Australian sound or television productions, "Stand Still Time," "Exit," and "Pacific Paradise."

SIDELIGHTS: Dymphna Cusack's novels and plays have been translated for publication or production in thirty-one countries. She spoke French, Italian, German, Chinese, and some Russian, and traveled throughout Australia, in China, Southeast Asia, Europe, Panama, the Caribbean, and Egypt.

MEDIA ADAPTATIONS: Heatwave in Berlin was adapted for a British Broadcasting Corp. series; *The Sun in Exile* was adapted for an Australian Broadcasting Commission presentation.†

D

DACHS, David   1922-1980
(Dave Stanley)

PERSONAL: Born January 23, 1922, in Brooklyn, N.Y.; died January, 1980; son of Morris (a garment worker) and Ethel (a dress shop owner; maiden name, Krieg) Dachs; married Julie Mandel (a songwriter), June, 1951; children: Joshua. *Education:* Attended City College (now City College of the City University of New York), 1941. *Politics:* Independent. *Home and office:* 6923 Loubet St., Forest Hills, N.Y. 11375.

CAREER: Broadcast Music Inc. (BMI), New York City, radio scriptwriter, 1954-55; feature writer for North American Newspaper Alliance (NANA), 1957-58; Pope Publications, New York City, reporter for *Drug and Cosmetic Industry* and *Beauty Fashion* magazines, 1959-60; Caedmon Records, New York City, director of public relations, 1961-64; American Guild of Authors and Composers (AGAC), New York City, director of public relations, 1965-68; writer, 1968-80. Free-lance publicist. *Member:* American Guild of Authors and Composers, National Academy of Recording Arts and Sciences.

WRITINGS: Straw Hat: Guide to Summer Theatres, Musical Tents, and Shakespeare Festivals, Frank Productions, 1957; *Anything Goes: The World of Popular Music,* Bobbs-Merrill, 1964; *Inside Pop: America's Top Ten Groups,* Scholastic Book Services, 1968; *American Pop,* Scholastic Book Services, Book I, 1969, Book II, 1970; *Inside Pop 2,* Scholastic Book Services, 1970; *Pop/Rock Question and Answer Book,* Scholastic Book Services, 1971; *Encyclopedia of Pop and Rock,* Scholastic Book Services, 1972; *TV's Top Comedians* (profiles and notes), Scholastic Book Services, 1973; *Tops in TV* (portraits of television personalities), Grosset & Dunlap, 1974; *John Denver* (biography), Pyramid Books, 1976; *Pop Rock, Question and Answer Book II,* Scholastic Book Services, 1977; *TV Jokes,* Scholastic Book Services, 1978; *Rock's Biggest Ten,* Scholastic Book Services, 1979; *One Hundred Pop/Rock Stars,* Scholastic Book Services, 1980.

Under pseudonym Dave Stanley: (With Jack Gaver) *There's Laughter in the Air* (comedy radio anthology), Greenberg, 1945; *A Treasury of Sports Humor* (short stories and essays), Lantern Press, 1946; (editor with Stan Lomax) *Treasury of Baseball Humor,* Lantern Press, 1950; (with George Ross) *The Golfer's Own Book* (essays and articles), Lantern Press, 1955; (with

Ronald C. Hill) *Rails in the Northwest: A Contemporary Glimpse,* Colorado Railroad Museum, 1978.

Also author of *Blazing Couches* (satirical novel). Author of books for several unproduced musicals, including "Miss Seedless Raisin" and "Expense Account." Contributor to magazines, including *Saturday Review, Redbook, Saga, High Fidelity, Down Beat, Family Weekly,* and *Variety.*

WORK IN PROGRESS: The books for two musicals.

SIDELIGHTS: David Dachs told *CA* he had an "ambivalent love-hate relationship with pop culture. I enjoy pop music (mostly show music and jazz), theatre, comedy (on TV, movies, theatre). I'm concerned with cultural impact of pop and how mass taste is manipulated. Having been a press agent, I know how cultural products are pushed. However, good products are also promoted by skillful PR as schlock (Bernstein records, the Met, good films) so taste and seasoning yardsticks become more crucial. My feelings find their way (sometimes) into my work, particularly in *Anything Goes: The World of Popular Music,* which I am quite proud of. . . .

"About hype: PR is a neutral tool used to sell everything from politicians to pop. It can sell the Met, good films, as well as schlock. But it can be particularly powerful in pop because most of the record-buyers and those who go to pop concerts (the life-support system of the music business) are 11-18, the impressionable years.

"Call it hype, call it legitimate public relations, call it taste manipulation—today's pop is full of it—and there's more of it than ever before. With so much money to be made on records, on concerts, and from TV, the battle for mere exposure grows more fierce. Consequently more press agents are hired, more full-page ads are taken in pop-minded media (*Rolling Stone, The Village Voice,* etc.). Specialists in disc jockey promotion criss-cross the land daily seeking airplay. Payola is not unknown either, as government trials in Newark, N.J. have shown.

"While hype cannot create pop stars and groups automatically (groups promoted lavishly often fail) hype leaves an imprint. People's critical faculties are softened up. Generally speaking more dollars are spent on what is commercial than what is creative.

"One of the biggest villains in my songbook is formula radio where hits and popstars are made. In its pursuit of profit, radio stations pick an audience target, and then tailor an approach. Often this leads to musical segregation: stations playing one kind of music, hard-rock, soft rock, middle of the road, country music, classical music, or Top 40 (which is based on *Billboard* charts or *Record World* charts, plus samplings of record shop sales).

"A good station should play a little of everything—show music (Broadway and Hollywood musicals), jazz, rock and roll, country, contemporary folk, Tin Pan Alley, middle of the road. Where are the stations of this sort? Practially nonexistent. So the pop audience, mostly young people, are push-overs for the latest hype-sensation, since they have little musical knowledge of the great traditions of popular music. Their ears, minds, and tastes are programmed by the stations they listen to, to a certain sound.

"Ask the average teen record buyer if he knows the works of Gershwin ('Who's he?'), Richard Rodgers, Stephen Sondheim, Burton Lane, E. Y. Harburg, Larry Hart, Frank Loesser, Irving Berlin, Fats Waller, Duke Ellington, Harold Arlen. You'll get a glazed look. Most kids today do not know their musical 'roots.'

"Millions of poor teen-agers are being hurt by the airwaves (ostensibly owned by the people) as are the adults. Adults who enjoy jazz, swing, the big bands, and Broadway theatre music can't abide much of today's pop. There are those in the record business who recognize this.

"About cultural impact: Pop is the most pervasive cultural force among young people. It influences what music they listen to, as well as manners, fashions, speech, courtship, sexual behaviour. It is unmistakably true that certain pop figures and groups have popularized and glamourized the taking of hard and soft drugs.

"Pop is also getting increasingly sexual with blue lyrics, lp's of girls experiencing an orgasm, and songs like 'The More You Do It,' 'It's All Right to Make Love on the First Night,' and 'Shake Your Body.' Reverend Jesse Jackson traces the rise in illegitimate births and abortions to milieu fashioned by pop.

"Of course, the picture isn't all bleak. A lot of material today is less dreamy, more realistic. There are songs celebrating brotherhood, the joys of nature, the processes of growing up. Protest songs aren't banned. There's more black music on, but a lot of 'soul' is monotonous, repetitious, and sugared-up, typical of the worst of Tin Pan Alley of yesteryear. (Incidentally, a lot of black-oriented stations will not play white artists.) And on the positive side, too, there are fine songs that do come along such as 'Feelings,' and good story-songs such as Harry Chapin's portrait of a high-intensity disc jockey, called 'W O L D.'"

AVOCATIONAL INTERESTS: Pop culture, politics, travel, walking, and good talk with friends.†

*   *   *

DAGG, Anne Innis   1933-

PERSONAL: Born January 25, 1933, in Toronto, Ontario, Canada; daughter of Harold Adams (a professor) and Mary (a writer; maiden name, Quayle) Innis; married Ian Ralph Dagg (a professor), August 22, 1957; children: Hugh Eric, Ian Innis, Mary Christine. *Education:* University of Toronto, B.A., 1955, M.A., 1956; University of Waterloo, Ph.D., 1967. *Home:* 81

Albert St., Waterloo, Ontario, Canada. *Office:* University of Waterloo, Waterloo, Ontario, Canada N2L 3G1.

CAREER: Waterloo Lutheran University, Waterloo, Ontario, lecturer in biology, 1962-65; University of Guelph, Guelph, Ontario, assistant professor of zoology, 1967-72; free-lance biology writer and researcher, 1972—; University of Waterloo, Waterloo, integrated studies resource person, 1978—. *Member:* Canadian Society of Environmental Biologists (member of board of directors, 1977-80), American Society of Mammalogy, Writer's Union of Canada (member of national council, 1981-82). *Awards, honors:* Named one of Canada's top female biologists by the National Museums of Canada, 1975, for International Women's Year.

WRITINGS: (With C. A. Campbell) *Mammals of Waterloo and South Wellington Counties,* Otter Press, 1972; *Canadian Wildlife and Man,* McClelland & Stewart, 1974; *Mammals of Ontario,* Otter Press, 1974; (with J. B. Foster) *The Giraffe: Its Biology, Behavior, and Ecology,* Van Nostrand, 1976, revised edition, Robert E. Krieger, 1981; *Wildlife Management in Europe,* Otter Press, 1977; *Running, Walking, and Jumping: The Science of Locomotion,* Taylor & Francis, 1977; *Camel Quest,* York Publishing, 1978; *A Reference Book of Urban Ecology,* Otter Press, 1981; (with H. Gauthier-Pilters) *The Camel: Its Evolution, Ecology, Behavior and Relationship to Man,* University of Chicago Press, 1981; *Harems and Other Horrors: Sexual Bias in Behavioral Biology,* Otter Press, 1983.

WORK IN PROGRESS: Researching a book, tentatively entitled *Spoilers,* about scientific work that has been shown to be wrong because of incorrect assumptions on the part of the original scientists. ("A great deal of research is rendered invalid because those doing it have not appreciated all possible parameters involved.")

SIDELIGHTS: Anne Innis Dagg writes: "Academic books on biology usually have a fairly limited market, so I often wonder why I keep writing them. My main reason is to try and share my wonder at the incredible complexity of animals and the ecosystems they live in. I hope that if more people understand such relationships, there will be a better chance that they will work to prevent the extermination of any species from the earth."

*   *   *

DANIELL, Jere Rogers   1932-

PERSONAL: Born November 28, 1932, in Millinocket, Me.; son of Warren F. (an engineer) and Mary (Holway) Daniell; married Sally Wellborn, December 17, 1955; married Elena Lillie (a leather worker), July 17, 1969; children: (first marriage) Douglas, Alexander, Matthew; stepchildren: Breena, Clifford. *Education:* Dartmouth College, A.B., 1955; Harvard University, M.A., 1961, Ph.D., 1964. *Home:* 11 Barrymore Rd., Hanover, N.H. 03755. *Office:* Reed Hall, Dartmouth College, Hanover, N.H. 03755.

CAREER: Dartmouth College, Hanover, N.H., assistant professor, 1964-69, associate professor, 1969-74, professor of history, 1974—, chairman of department, 1979-83, director, Dartmouth College Oral History Project, 1975—. Trustee, New Hampshire Historical Society, 1979—. *Military service:* U.S. Navy, 1955-58; became lieutenant junior grade. *Member:* National Humanities Faculty, Organization of American Historians, Colonial Society of Massachusetts. *Awards, honors:* American Association of State and Local History research grant, 1968.

WRITINGS: Experiment in Republicanism: New Hampshire Politics and the American Revolution, 1741-1794, Harvard University Press, 1970; (contributor) Lawrence Leber, editor, *The Colonial Legacy,* Harper, 1973; (contributor) *Dictionary of Canadian Biography,* University of Toronto Press, 1974; (contributor) *Years of Revolution,* Profiles Publishing, 1976; *Colonial New Hampshire: A History,* KTO Press, 1981.

Contributor to *William and Mary Quarterly, American Historical Review,* and other publications. Member of editorial board, University Press of New England, 1970-72, 1978—; member of publications committee, *Historical New Hampshire,* 1971—.

WORK IN PROGRESS: A book on small-town New England.

*   *   *

DANK, Milton 1920-

PERSONAL: Born September 12, 1920, in Philadelphia, Pa.; son of Charles (a barber) and Olga (Olessker) Dank; married Naomi Rand (a hospital administrator), March 18, 1954; children: Gloria, Joan. *Education:* University of Pennsylvania, B.A., 1947, Ph.D., 1953. *Politics:* "Unenthusiastic Democrat." *Religion:* "Diabolist (lapsed)." *Home:* 1022 Serpentine Ln., Wyncote, Pa. 19095.

CAREER: Writer. Owens-Illinois Glass, Toledo, Ohio, research physicist, 1953-56; General Electric (Aerospace), King of Prussia, Pa., research manager, 1958-72; research consultant in thermonuclear fusion power, laser applications, and space vehicle vulnerability, 1972—. *Military service:* U.S. Army Air Forces, 1940-45; became first lieutenant. *Member:* American Physical Society, National World War II Glider Pilots Association, Authors Guild, Authors League of America.

WRITINGS: The French Against the French, Lippincott, 1974; *The Glider Gang,* Lippincott, 1977; *The Dangerous Game,* Lippincott, 1977; *Game's End,* Lippincott, 1979; *Khaki Wings,* Delacorte, 1980; *Red Flight Two,* Delacorte, 1981; *The Computer Caper,* Delacorte, 1983; *A UFO Has Landed,* Delacorte, 1983; *Albert Einstein,* F. Watts, 1983.

WORK IN PROGRESS: The Gestapo in France: The Case of Klaus Barbie.

SIDELIGHTS: Milton Dank told *CA* that most of his books have been "derived from my wartime experiences. *The French Against the French* and *The Dangerous Game* were based on my study of the behavior of the French under the German occupation. As squadron translator and liaison officer, I found the French civilians most reluctant to talk of the fifty months during which the Nazis occupied France.

"*The Glider Gang* is a tribute to the Allied glider pilots, my comrades-in-arm. They flew in fragile canvas and wood motorless craft at low altitudes over enemy guns, and brought in jeeps, howitzers and antitank guns to the paratroopers. Their casualties were high, as much from poor planning and faulty intelligence as from enemy resistance. They wore no parachutes because their passengers wore none. I thought it was wrong that their story should go untold.

"In my next book, I am going back to the theme that fascinated me while researching my first book: the permissible limits of collaboration under a foreign military occupation."

*   *   *

DAUENHAUER, Richard L(eonard) 1942-

PERSONAL: Born April 10, 1942, in Syracuse, N.Y.; son of Leonard G. (a teacher) and Jane (Grier) Dauenhauer; married Sandra Dudley, 1965 (divorced, 1972); married Nora Marks Florendo, November 28, 1973; stepchildren: Leonora Florendo, Carmella Tapacio, Lorenzo Florendo, Adela Ransom. *Education:* Syracuse University, B.A., 1964; University of Texas, M.A., 1966; Helsinki University, graduate study, 1966-67; University of Wisconsin—Madison, Ph.D., 1975. *Home:* 4801 Canterbury Way, Anchorage, Alaska 99503. *Office:* Alaska Pacific University, Anchorage, Alaska 99504.

CAREER: Alaska Methodist University, Anchorage, assistant professor of comparative literature, 1969-75; Alaska Native Education Board, Anchorage, education specialist, 1974-76; staff associate, Alaska Native Foundation, 1976-78; consultant and free-lance writer, 1978-80; Alaska Pacific University, Anchorage, associate professor of humanities, 1980—.

Teacher, Sheldon Jackson College, summers, 1972-74, and University of Alaska, summer, 1975. Tlingit researcher for Alaska Native Language Center at University of Alaska, 1972-73; language arts specialist for Alaska Bilingual Education Center of Alaska Native Education Board, 1974-75. Has conducted field research in southeast Alaska, the Yukon Territory, and in Eskimo and Athapaskan areas. Charter member, Tlingit Readers, Inc. *Member:* American Folklore Society. *Awards, honors:* Woodrow Wilson fellowship, 1964-65; Fulbright fellowship, 1966-67; named humanist of the year, 1980; named Poet Laureate of Alaska, 1981.

WRITINGS: (Translator with others) Goeran Sonnevi, *On the War: A Bilingual Pamphlet of Poems from the Swedish,* Third Coast Press, 1968; *Tlingit Spelling Book,* Tlingit Readers, Inc., 1974; *Folklore Handbook for Bilingual Classrooms,* Alaska Native Education Board, 1975; *Koyukon Riddles,* Alaska Native Education Board, 1975; (editor with W. Philip Binham, and contributor) *Snow in May: An Anthology of Modern Finnish Writing, 1945-1972,* Fairleigh Dickinson University Press, 1978; *Glacier Bay Concerto,* Alaska Pacific University Press, 1980; *Phrenologies: Poems, 1970-1972,* Thorp Springs Press, 1981.

Translations have been anthologized in *Probes: An Introduction to Poetry,* edited by William K. Harlan, Macmillan, 1973, and *Pushcart Prize VI: Best of the Small Presses,* Pushcart Press, 1978.

Contributor to *Encyclopedia of World Literature in the Twentieth Century.* Contributor of about eighty poems, translations, and articles to literary journals and little magazines, including *Quixote, Beloit Poetry Journal, Hyperion, Poet Lore, Literary Review,* and *Raven.* Guest editor of *Literary Review,* autumn, 1970.

WORK IN PROGRESS: Translating modern German, Russian, Finnish and Swedish poems, classical and medieval Greek poems, and Tlingit Indian material; several collections of poetry.

SIDELIGHTS: Richard Dauenhauer writes: "I am probably best known for my translations. I can speak German, Russian, and Finnish, and I can read over one dozen languages to varying degrees. I disagree with many scholars, but with few poets, in my belief that translation is a discipline of creative writing rather than of scholarship, although scholarship is involved, and although each translation is in a very real sense an act of literary criticism and commentary as well as an act of poetry. . . . It's exciting to find that the dusty poets of antiquity are not so dusty after all. There was nothing dull about their vision. When we translate, we are not revitalizing Rouphinos, Meleagros, Sappho, or any other poet: we are revitalizing ourselves."

AVOCATIONAL INTERESTS: Outdoor activity (hiking, camping, canoeing, fishing, cross country skiing), fencing (sabre and epee), photography, model railroads (N gauge), choir singing.

*   *   *

DAVIDSON, H(ilda) R(oderick) Ellis   1914-
(Hilda Roderick Ellis)

PERSONAL: Born October 1, 1914, in Bebington, Cheshire, England; daughter of Henry Roderick (a stationer) and Millie (Cheesman) Ellis; married Richard Robertson Davidson (a research scientist), December 27, 1943; children: Hilary, Richard Neil Roderick. *Education:* Newnham College, Cambridge, M.A., 1939, Ph.D., 1940. *Politics:* Liberal. *Religion:* Church of England.

CAREER: University of London, London, England, assistant lecturer in English, Royal Holloway College, 1939-44, part-time lecturer in English, Birkbeck College, 1945-54, lecturer in extramural department, 1942-54; Cambridge University, Lucy Cavendish College, Cambridge, England, research fellow, 1968-71, lecturer, 1971—. *Member:* Society of Antiquaries of London (fellow), Folklore Society (council member). *Awards, honors:* Leverhulme research award for work in Soviet Union, 1964.

WRITINGS: (Under name Hilda Roderick Ellis) *The Road to Hel: A Study of the Conception of the Dead in Old Norse Literature,* Cambridge University Press, 1943, reprinted, Greenwood Press, 1968; *The Golden Age of Northumbria,* Longmans, Green, 1958; *The Sword in Anglo-Saxon England,* Clarendon Press, 1961; *Gods and Myths of Northern Europe,* Pelican Books, 1965, published as *Gods and Myths of the Viking Age,* Crown, 1981; (contributor) Joan Cadogan Lancaster, *Godiva of Coventry,* Coventry Corp., 1967; *Pagan Scandinavia,* Praeger, 1967; (with G. N. Garmonsway and Jacqueline Simpson) *Beowulf and Its Analogues,* Dent, 1968; *Scandinavian Mythology,* Hamlyn, 1969; (with Peter Gelling) *The Chariot of the Sun,* Praeger, 1969.

(Editor) *The Journey to the Other World: Papers from the Exeter Conference, 1971,* Rowman & Littlefield, 1975; *The Viking Road to Byzantium,* Allen & Unwin, 1976; *Symbols of Power,* Brewer, 1977; *Patterns of Folklore,* Rowman & Littlefield, 1978; (editor) *Gesta Danorum: The History of the Danes, Books I-IX,* translated by Peter Fisher, Rowman & Littlefield, Volume I: *Saxo Grammaticus: English Text,* 1979, Volume II: *Saxo Grammaticus: Commentary,* 1980; (editor with W. M. Russell) *The Folklore of Ghosts,* Brewer, 1982.

Contributor to *Encyclopaedia Britannica,* and to *Antiquity, Folklore, Arms and Armour,* and other journals.

SIDELIGHTS: H. R. Ellis Davidson has reading knowledge of Anglo-Saxon, early Norse, Norwegian, Swedish, Danish, Icelandic, Russian, Latin, and German.

BIOGRAPHICAL/CRITICAL SOURCES: Times Literary Supplement, January 29, 1982.†

*   *   *

DAVIS, Grant Miller   1937-

PERSONAL: Born May 26, 1937, in Tuscaloosa, Ala.; son of Theoren Wilburn (a bus driver) and Mary (Craton) Davis; married Susan Bridgens Riden, February 17, 1966; children: Susan Louise, Grant II. *Education:* Georgia State College (now University), B.B.A., 1963; University of Alabama, M.A., 1966, Ph.D., 1968. *Religion:* Episcopal. *Home:* 2217 Juneway Ter., Fayetteville, Ark. 72701. *Office:* Center for Transportation Research, University of Arkansas, Fayetteville, Ark. 72701.

CAREER: Manager of traffic, Mason & Dixon Line, Inc., 1958-60; Ford Motor Co., Atlanta, Ga., manager of inbound freight distribution, 1961-65; University of Alabama, University, research associate in economics, 1965-66, instructor in finance, 1966-68; Arizona State University, Tempe, assistant dean, 1968-70; Auburn University, Auburn, Ala., associate professor, 1970-72; University of Arkansas, Fayetteville, Oren Harris Professor of Transportation and director of Center for Transportation Research, 1972—. Consultant, Vertico Manufacturing Co., Inc., 1968-71, Sperry-Rand Corp., 1968—, Arrow Trucking Co., Inc., 1970—. *Military service:* U.S. Army, 1955-58. *Member:* Association of Interstate Commerce Commission Practitioners, American Society of Traffic and Transportation, Society of Logistics Engineers, American Economic Association, American Marketing Association, Beta Gamma Sigma.

WRITINGS: The Department of Transportation, Heath, 1970; (with Stephen W. Brown) *Logistics Management,* Lexington Books, 1974; (with Charles S. Sherwood) *Rate Bureaus and Antitrust Conflicts in Transportation: Public Policy Issues,* Praeger, 1975; (with Martin T. Farris and Jack J. Holder, Jr.) *Management of Transportation Carriers,* Praeger, 1975.

(Editor) *Transportation Regulation: A Pragmatic Assessment,* Interstate, 1976; (with John E. Dillard, Jr.) *Increasing Motor Carrier Productivity: An Empirical Analysis,* Praeger, 1977; (with Eugene Shepard) *Motor Carrier Rate Structures,* Praeger, 1978; *Collective Ratemaking in the Motor Carrier Industry,* Interstate Publishers, 1980; *Motor Carrier Economics, Regulation, and Operations,* University Press of America, 1981; (with Dillard) *Physical Logistics Management,* University Press of America, 1983.

Contributor to *Alabama Business, Transportation Journal, Quarterly Review of Economics and Business, Journal of Purchasing, Arizona Business Bulletin, Public Logistics Review, Journal of Economic Issues,* and other professional journals and newspapers. Transportation and logistics editor, Praeger Publishers, 1977-79.

*   *   *

DAVIS, L(awrence) J(ames)   1940-

PERSONAL: Born July 2, 1940, in Seattle, Wash.; son of Maurice Nelson and Eula Jane (Randall) Davis; married Barbara Frances Ball (a social worker), September 21, 1961; children: Jeremy Randall, Gabriel Sprague, Barbara Victoria, Tina Rose. *Education:* Stanford University, A.B., 1962; Columbia University, graduate study, 1962. *Politics:* Democratic. *Home:* 138A Dean St., Brooklyn, N.Y. 11217. *Agent:* Sterling Lord, Sterling Lord Agency, 660 Madison Ave., New York, N.Y. 10021.

CAREER: Restoration Realty, Brooklyn, N.Y., salesman, 1966-69; Sterling Wine and Liquor Co., Brooklyn, morning manager, 1969-70; University of Rochester, Rochester, N.Y., Writers' Workshop, faculty member, 1970-73, and program director, 1974—, university instructor, summers, 1974-78. Lecturer, New York University, 1972-75; instructor, Hofstra University, 1972-75. Boerum Hill Association, chairman of community planning committee, 1965-66, vice-president, 1968-71; chairman, United Neighborhood Playground Committee;

member, Mayor's Task Force for South Brooklyn. *Military service:* Idaho Air National Guard, 1957-59. U.S. Army Reserve, 1959-64; became sergeant. *Awards, honors:* Wallace Stegner fellowship in creative writing at Stanford University, 1964-65; Guggenheim fellowship, 1975-76; Gerald Loeb Award for distinguished business and financial journalism, 1982.

WRITINGS—Novels, except as indicated: *Whence All But He Had Fled,* Viking, 1968; *Cowboys Don't Cry,* Viking, 1969; *A Meaningful Life,* Viking, 1971; *Walking Small,* Braziller, 1974; *Bad Money* (nonfiction), St. Martin's, 1982; *Christina Onassis: A Modern Greek Tragedy* (biography), Empire Books, 1983. Columnist, *Penthouse,* 1972, *National Observer,* 1974-78. Contributor of articles and reviews to newspapers and periodicals. Contributing editor, *Harper's,* 1980-82.

WORK IN PROGRESS: A Study of the SEC, for publication by St. Martin's.

SIDELIGHTS: L. J. Davis writes about banking and finance in his book *Bad Money.* R. C. Longworth asserts in the *Chicago Tribune Book World* that "Davis is a prize-winning financial reporter who understands the system he writes about: unlike most financial reporters, he writes in straight-forward prose." In the *Washington Post Book World,* Robert Lekachman describes the book as "exceedingly well-written and researched" and concludes, "Among popular financial and business writers, L. J. Davis belongs in the company of Adam Smith and Anthony Sampson—the best in the trade."

L. J. Davis told *CA:* "My principal interests, outside of writing, are in community planning, inter-ethnic relations, and Victorian architecture. I love Brooklyn and Manhattan, hate the Bronx and Queens, and am cool to Staten Island. I am fond of French and East Indian food, the street life of the Lower East Side, and Italian grocery stores with cheese.

"I used to think that the writing of fiction was high art and that nonfiction was hackwork, a mug's game; I was wrong about that. The trouble with *Harper's,* Lewis Lapham said recently, was that we always predicted everything too soon: the fall of the Shah, the debt crisis in the Third World, the collapse of the OPEC pricing structure. Still, there's a certain amount of satisfaction in the realization that the world is a knowable place, that mysterious forces are not at work, and nothing happens in a vacuum. We may have rung our tocsins too soon, but it was better than never having rung them at all."

BIOGRAPHICAL/CRITICAL SOURCES: Books, January, 1968; *New York Times Book Review,* January 14, 1968, June 15, 1969; *Book World,* March 24, 1968, June 22, 1969; *New Leader,* April 22, 1969; *Washington Post Book World,* October 17, 1982; *Los Angeles Times Book Review,* December 12, 1982; *Chicago Tribune Book World,* January 16, 1983.

*   *   *

DAVIS, Morris 1933-

PERSONAL: Born October 9, 1933, in Boston, Mass.; son of Hyman William (an accountant) and Mary (Goldstein) Davis; married Ruth Miller, June 21, 1958; children: Jonathan Miller, Melissa Anne, William Atticus. *Education:* Harvard University, A.B. (cum laude), 1954; Princeton University, A.M. and Ph.D., both 1958. *Politics:* Democrat. *Religion:* Jewish. *Home:* 3 Burnett Circle, Urbana, Ill. 61801. *Office:* Department of Political Science, University of Illinois at Urbana-Champaign, 361 Lincoln Hall, Urbana, Ill. 61801.

CAREER: Princeton University, Princeton, N.J., research assistant at Center for International Studies, 1958; University of Wisconsin—Madison, instructor in political science, 1958-59; Dalhousie University, Halifax, Nova Scotia, assistant professor of political science, 1960-62; Tulane University, New Orleans, La., assistant professor, 1962-64, associate professor of political science, 1964-65; University of Illinois at Urbana-Champaign, associate professor, 1965-68, professor of political science, 1968—. Visiting professor at Dalhousie University, summer, 1971. *Member:* Peace Science Society (International), National Academy of Sciences (member of committee on international disaster assistance, 1977-79), Association for Canadian Studies in the United States.

AWARDS, HONORS: Social Science Research Council training fellowship in Iceland, Norway, and England, 1959-60; grants from Canada Council, summer, 1961, Atlantic Provinces Studies of Social Science Research Council of Canada, 1962, 1963, 1965, U.S. Public Health Service, 1964-67, Midwest Universities Consortium for International Activities, summer, 1970, and National Science Foundation, 1971-74; Guggenheim fellowship, 1967-68; Ford Foundation fellowship in England, Switzerland, and Nigeria, 1969-70; Isaak Walton Killam senior fellowship from Dalhousie University, 1972-73; Institute for the Study of World Politics fellowship, 1977.

WRITINGS: Iceland Extends Its Fisheries Limits: A Political Analysis, Allen & Unwin, 1963; (with M. G. Weinbaum) *Metropolitan Decision Processes: An Analysis of Case Studies,* Rand McNally, 1969; (with J. F. Krauter) *The Other Canadians: Profiles of Six Minorities,* Methuen, 1971; *Civil Wars and the Politics of International Relief,* Praeger, 1975; *Interpreters for Nigeria: The Third World and International Public Relations,* University of Illinois Press, 1977; (with Krauter) *Minority Canadians: Ethnic Groups,* Methuen, 1978.

Contributor: John Meisel, editor, *Papers on the 1962 Election,* University of Toronto Press, 1964; J. C. Courtney, editor, *Voting in Canada,* Prentice-Hall (Canada), 1967; Richard Rose, editor, *Studies in British Politics,* St. Martin's, 1966; Arend Lijphart, editor, *Politics in Europe,* Prentice-Hall, 1969; R. Schwartz and J. Skolnick, editors, *Society and the Legal Order,* Basic Books, 1970; J. C. Pierce and R. A. Pride, editors, *Cross-National Micro-Analysis,* Sage Publications, 1972; L. Bickman and T. Henchy, editors, *Beyond the Laboratory,* McGraw, 1972; I. Davis, editor, *Disasters and the Small Dwelling,* Pergamon, 1978. Contributor to *World Book Encyclopedia* and to professional journals.

WORK IN PROGRESS: Research on international relief for man-made disasters "and on correlates and scenarios of disaster situations"; studies of political aspects of Plato's and Aristotle's philosophy.

*   *   *

DAVISSON, William I. 1929-

PERSONAL: Born January 27, 1929, in Tacoma, Wash.; son of Ralph F. and Florence (Davis) Davisson; married Deloris Jungert, June, 1955; children: Michael C., Margaret A., Sandra D., Joanna L. *Education:* College of Puget Sound (now University of Puget Sound), B.A., 1953, M.A., 1954; Cornell University, Ph.D., 1961. *Office:* Department of Economics, University of Notre Dame, Notre Dame, Ind. 46556.

CAREER: Eastern Montana College of Education (now Eastern Montana College), Billings, assistant professor of economics, 1957-59; Whittier College, Whittier, Calif., assistant professor of economics, 1959-60; Sacramento State College (now California State University, Sacramento), Sacramento, Calif., associate professor of economics, 1960-66; University of Notre Dame, Notre Dame, Ind., professor of economics, 1966—. Consultant to Bellwood Door Co., 1959, California State Department of Finance, 1960-61, Loyalty Savings and Loan Association, 1962, and California State Senate, 1963-64. *Military service:* U.S. Army, 1951-53; served in Japan.

WRITINGS: (With John G. Ranlett) *An Introduction to Microeconomic Theory,* Harcourt, 1965; *Essex County Price (Wealth) Trends,* Essex Institute and Historical College, 1967; *The Historian and the Computer,* Essex Institute and Historical College, 1968.

Information Processing: Applications in the Social Behavioral Sciences, Plenum, 1970; (with James E. Harper) *European Economic History,* Appleton, 1972; *Computer-assisted Instruction in Economic Education: A Case Study,* University of Notre Dame Press, 1976; (with John J. Uhran) *A Primer for NDTRAN: A Systems Dynamics Interpreter,* University of Notre Dame Press, 1977.

Author of monographs; contributor to professional journals.

WORK IN PROGRESS: Research in computer programming and computer application to economic growth and development.

*   *   *

DAWE, (Donald) Bruce 1930-

PERSONAL: Born February 15, 1930, in Geelong, Australia; son of Alfred (a laborer) and Mary Ann (Hamilton) Dawe; married Gloria Desley, January 1, 1964; children: Brian, Jamie, Katrina, Melissa. *Education:* University of Queensland, B.A., 1969, M.A., 1975, Ph.D., 1980; University of New England, Litt. B., 1973. *Religion:* Roman Catholic. *Home:* 30 Cumming St., Toowoomba, Queensland, Australia 4350. *Office:* School of Arts, Institute of Advanced Education, Darling Heights, Toowoomba, Queensland, Australia 4350.

CAREER: Has worked as a laborer, postman, and gardener; Institute of Advanced Education, Toowoomba, Australia, lecturer in literature, 1971—. *Military service:* Royal Australian Air Force, 1959-68; became sergeant. *Awards, honors:* Myer Award for poetry, 1966, for *A Need of Similiar Name,* and 1969, for *An Eye for a Tooth;* Ampol Arts Award for Creative Literature, 1967; Dame Mary Gilmore Medal, 1971, for *Condolences of the Season;* Grace Leven Poetry Prize, 1978, and Braille Book of the Year award, 1979, both for *Sometimes Gladness: Collected Poems, 1954-1978;* Patrick White Literary Award for contribution to Australian poetry, 1980.

WRITINGS—Poems, except as indicated: *No Fixed Address,* Cheshire (Melbourne), 1962; *A Need of Similiar Name,* Cheshire, 1965; *An Eye for a Tooth,* Cheshire, 1968; *Beyond the Subdivision,* Cheshire, 1969; *Heat-Wave,* Sweeny Reed (Melbourne), 1970; *Condolences of the Season,* Cheshire, 1971; *Bruce Dawe Reads from His Own Work,* University of Queensland Press, 1971; (editor) *Dimensions,* McGraw, 1974; *Just a Dugong at Twilight,* Cheshire, 1975; *Sometimes Gladness: Collected Poems, 1954-1978,* Longman Cheshire, 1979, revised edition published as *Sometimes Gladness: Collected Poems, 1954-1982,* 1983; *Over Here, Harv! and Other Stories,* Penguin, 1983.

WORK IN PROGRESS: The Elephant's Kindness and Other Essays.

SIDELIGHTS: Bruce Dawe writes: "One of the reasons why the use of various verse forms may help me to capture something of the evanescence of the contemporary Australian idiom is that the use of various traditional rhyme-forms and some metrical regularity together with elements of the contemporary scene and idiom provide a 'mix' of past and present in an acceptable form overall."

In response to *CA*'s question as to how he chose the dramatic monologue as one of his major poetic forms, Dawe said: "I never *consciously* chose the dramatic monologue form—it just occurred as a form frequently enough to confirm its possibilities. I am sure this is the general way things happen—forms choose us."

"Regional poetry," Dawe continued, "is not (as in the United States) a very obvious and characteristic kind of poetry here, Australian society being culturally and linguistically far more homogeneous than American—urban and rural are the significant 'regions' rather than Southwest, West, Midwest, East, etc. This is one of our greatest losses, I feel, artistically."

BIOGRAPHICAL/CRITICAL SOURCES: Ian Victor Hansen, editor, *Bruce Dawe: The Man down the Street,* Victorian Association for the Teaching of English, 1972; Basil Shaw, editor, *Times and Seasons: An Introduction to Bruce Dawe,* Chesire, 1973; K. L. Goodwin, *Selected Poems of Bruce Dawe,* Longman York Press, 1983.

*   *   *

DEAK, Istvan 1926-

PERSONAL: Born May 11, 1926, in Szekesfehervar, Hungary; came to United States in 1956, naturalized in 1962; son of Istvan (an engineer) and Anna (Timar) Deak; married Gloria Alfano (a free-lance editor and writer), July 4, 1959; children: Eva. *Education:* Studied at University of Budapest, 1945-48, and Sorbonne, University of Paris, 1949-51; Columbia University, M.A., 1958, Ph.D., 1964. *Home:* 410 Riverside Dr., New York, N.Y. 10025. *Office:* 1229 International Affairs Bldg., Columbia University, New York, N.Y. 10025.

CAREER: Smith College, Northampton, Mass., instructor in history, 1962-63; Columbia University, New York, N.Y., instructor, 1963-64, assistant professor, 1964-67, associate professor, 1967-71, professor of history, 1971—, director of Institute on East Central Europe, 1967-78. Member of Institute for Advanced Study, 1981. *Member:* American Association for the Advancement of Slavic Studies, American Association of University Professors, Habsburg History Association, Conference Group for Central European History. *Awards, honors:* Guggenheim fellowship, 1970-71; Lionel Trilling Book Award from Columbia University, 1977, for *The Lawful Revolution: Louis Kossuth and the Hungarians, 1848-1849.*

WRITINGS: (Contributor) Hans Rogger and Eugen Weber, editors, *The European Right,* University of California Press, 1965; *Weimar Germany's Left-Wing Intellectuals: A Political History of the Weltbuehne and Its Circle,* University of California Press, 1968.

(Contributor) Ivan Volgyes, editor, *Hungary in Revolution, 1918-1919,* University of Nebraska Press, 1971; (editor with Sylva Sinanian and Peter C. Ludz) *Eastern Europe in the 1970's,* Praeger, 1972; (editor with Allan Mitchell) *Everyman in Europe: Essays in Social History,* two volumes, Prentice-Hall, 1974, 2nd edition, 1981; (contributor) *Situations revolutionnaires en Europe, 1917-1922,* University of Montreal, 1977;

The Lawful Revolution: Louis Kossuth and the Hungarians, 1848-1849, Columbia University Press, 1979.

(Contributor) *German Realism of the Twenties,* Minneapolis Institute of Arts, 1980; (contributor) Jaroslaw Pelenski, editor, *The American and European Revolutions, 1776-1848,* University of Iowa Press, 1980. Contributor to the *Slavonic and East European Review, Austrian History Yearbook, Oesterreichische Osthefte, East Central Europe, New York Review of Books,* and other journals.

*   *   *

DEATON, John (Graydon) 1939-

PERSONAL: Born August 19, 1939, in Houston, Tex,; son of Charles F. (an automobile mechanic) and Frances (a beautician; maiden name, Kimberlin) Deaton; married Miriam Ann Garrett (a teacher), August 26, 1960; children: Roger, Stephen, Lara, Jennie. *Education:* Attended Texas A & M University, 1957-58; University of Texas, B.A., 1960, M.D., 1963. *Home and office:* 3917 Sierra Dr., Austin, Tex. 78731.

CAREER: Memorial Medical Center, Corpus Christi, Tex., intern, 1963-64; University of Texas Medical Branch at Galveston, resident in internal medicine, 1964-66, fellow in hematology research, 1966-67; University of Wisconsin—Madison, fellow in immunology, 1969-70; Texas Department of Mental Health and Mental Retardation, Austin, staff physician and medical director at Denton State School and Mexia State School, 1970-71; University of Texas at Austin, visiting lecturer and assistant professor of human physiology, 1972-73; free-lance writer, 1973—. Diplomate of American Board of Internal Medicine. *Military service:* U.S. Air Force, Medical Corps, 1967-69; became captain. *Member:* Phi Beta Kappa, Alpha Omega Alpha.

WRITINGS: Markets for the Medical Author, Warren Green, 1971; *New Parts for Old: The Age of Organ Transplants,* Franklin Publishing, 1974; *Woman's Day Book of Family Medical Questions,* Random House, 1979. Free-lance editor of over 600 articles for medical journals.

WORK IN PROGRESS: A novel.

SIDELIGHTS: John Deaton comments: "I became a writer because I love it. I have never done as well at it as I hoped or expected, and I doubt I ever will. But on the good days, when words and ideas grow and live and *are,* I am happier than at any other time. The joy is that it's always there (if you can find it). The heartache is that you cannot share it or convey it to others (even if you try). It's lonely and it is self-indulgent, but it seems to beat straitjackets, drugs, immorality and peanut butter. And, for the most part, it is lovely. (Wherever you are, Ernest, are you listening?)"

AVOCATIONAL INTERESTS: Working around the home, listening to records, watching movies on HBO, "reading, reading, and reading."

*   *   *

DEFFNER, Donald L(ouis) 1924-

PERSONAL: Born March 12, 1924, in Wichita, Kan.; son of Louis H. (a clergyman) and Rose May (Kreitzer) Deffner; married Corinne C. Clasen, January 30, 1949; children: David Louis, Deborah Kathleen, Carol Rose, Christina Corinne. *Education:* Concordia Seminary, St. Louis, Mo., B.A., 1945, B.D., 1947; University of Michigan, M.A., 1946; University

of California, Berkeley, Ph.D., 1957; Pacific Lutheran Theological Seminary, Th.M., 1962. *Home:* 49 Corliss Dr., Moraga, Calif. 94556. *Office:* Department of Christian Education, Pacific Lutheran Theological Seminary, 2770 Marin, Berkeley, Calif. 94708.

CAREER: Ordained minister of Lutheran Church-Missouri Synod, 1947; University of California, Berkeley, campus pastor, 1947-59; Concordia Seminary, St. Louis, Mo., professor of religious education, 1959-69, chairman of department of practical theology, 1964-69; Pacific Lutheran Theological Seminary, Berkeley, professor of Christian education and homiletics, 1969—. Assistant pastor, Immanuel Lutheran Church, Danville, Calif., 1975—. Guest professor at Concordia Theological Seminary, Springfield, Ill., 1963-69, Concordia Seminary, St. Louis, Mo., 1972 and 1973, and Christ College Irvine, 1976; visiting associate professor of education, University of Missouri, 1967; professor of Christian education, Graduate Theological Union, 1969—; fellow of Case Study Institute, Cambridge, Mass., 1974—. Lutheran Church-Missouri Synod, chairman of Commission on College and University Work and of Concordia Commission Leadership Training Committee; Religion-in-Life-Week speaker on college campuses in the West and Midwest; conductor of adult education retreats and of continuing education courses for pastors, 1973—. Advisor to Office of Chief of Chaplains, 1967.

MEMBER: Association of Seminary Professors in Practical Fields, Religious Education Association, Lutheran Academy for Scholarship, Lutheran Education Association, Lutheran Society for Worship, Music and the Arts, Gamma Delta.

WRITINGS—Published by Concordia, except as indicated: (With W. H. Fields, Ronald Goerss, and Edward Wessling) *Meditations for College Students,* 1961; (editor and contributor) *Toward Adult Christian Education: A Symposium,* Lutheran Education Association, 1962; *Christ on Campus: Meditations for College Life,* 1965; *Bold Ones on Campus: A Call for Christian Commitment,* 1973; *You Say You're Depressed?: How God Helps You Overcome Anxieties,* Abingdon, 1976; *The Best of Your Life Is the Rest of Your Life,* Abingdon, 1977; *The Real Word for the Real World,* 1977; (with Richard Andersen) *For Example: Illustrations for Contemporary Preaching,* Volume I, 1977; *Bound to Be Free: The Quest for Inner Freedom,* Morse Press, 1981; *You Promised Me, God!: God's Promises to the Christian,* 1981; *Come Closer to Me, God!,* 1982; *I Hear Two Voices, God!: Struggling with Temptation,* 1983; *Please Talk to Me, God!,* 1983.

Also author of *Preaching Repentance to Forgiveness: A Homiletics Textbook* and *Message to Saecula: A Science Fiction Novelette for Youth.* Contributor of articles and discussion guides to *Campus Pastor's Workbook, Concordia Commentator,* and other periodicals. Editor of California and Nevada edition of *Lutheran Witness,* 1951-54.

WORK IN PROGRESS: A Doubter's Diary: Objections to Christianity; Reaching the Educated Adult; Telling Is Not Teaching; Case Studies on Problems in the Parish for the Laity; Volume II of *For Example: Illustrations for Contemporary Preaching; Sometimes I Wonder: An Author's Scrapbook; Conversations with the Creator; Diverse Cultures but One Gospel.*

BIOGRAPHICAL/CRITICAL SOURCES: Concordia Journal, January, 1982.

DEMPSEY, Hugh Aylmer   1929-

PERSONAL: Born November 7, 1929, in Edgerton, Alberta, Canada; son of Otto L. and Lily (Sharp) Dempsey; married Pauline S. Gladstone, September 30, 1953; children: L. James, Louise, John, Leah, Lois. *Education:* Educated in primary and secondary schools in Edmonton, Alberta. *Religion:* Anglican. *Home:* 95 Holmwood Ave. N.W., Calgary, Alberta, Canada T2K 2G7. *Office:* Glenbow Museum, 130 Ninth Ave. S.E., Calgary, Alberta, Canada T2G 0P3.

CAREER: Edmonton Bulletin, Edmonton, Alberta, reporter and editor, 1949-51; Government of Alberta, Edmonton, publicity writer, 1951-56; Glenbow Foundation, Calgary, Alberta, archivist, 1956-67; Glenbow-Alberta Institute, Calgary, technical director, 1967-70, director of history, 1970-80; Glenbow Museum, Calgary, assistant director, collections, 1980—. Lecturer at Canadian universities. Association director of Calgary Exhibition and Stampede, 1958—; member of Alberta Records Publication Board, and of Historic Sites Board of Alberta, 1981—.

MEMBER: Canadian Historical Association (chairperson of archives section, 1961-62), Canadian Museums Association (executive member, 1968-70), Indian-Eskimo Association of Canada (executive member, 1960-65), Champlain Society (member of council, 1972-74), Historical Society of Alberta (executive member, 1952—; vice-president, 1955-56; president, 1956-57), Indian Association of Alberta, Fort Calgary Preservation Society (executive member, 1969-75), Kainai Chieftainship. *Awards, honors:* Annual award from Historical Society of Alberta, 1963; Alberta Achievement Award, 1974, 1975; D.U.C. from University of Calgary, 1974; Order of Canada, 1975; Alberta Non-Fiction Award, 1975, for *The Best of Bob Edwards.*

WRITINGS: Historic Sites of Alberta, Government of Alberta, 1952; (editor) *The Big Chief of the Prairies* (on Father Lacombe), Palm Publishers, 1953; *Historic Sites of Alberta,* Alberta Government Travel Bureau, 1966; (editor) Thomas Edmund Wilson, *Trailblazer of the Canadian Rockies,* Glenbow-Alberta Institute, 1972; *Crowfoot: Chief of the Blackfeet,* University of Oklahoma Press, 1972; *A History of Rocky Mountain House,* Department of Indian Affairs and Northern Development (Ottawa), 1973; *William Parker, Mounted Policeman,* Hurtig, 1973; (editor) *A Winter at Fort Macleod,* McClelland & Stewart, 1974; (editor) *Men in Scarlet,* McClelland & Stewart, 1974; (editor) *The Best of Bob Edwards,* Hurtig, 1975.

(Editor) *The Wit and Wisdom of Bob Edwards,* Hurtig, 1976; (editor) Robert Terrill Rundle, *The Rundle Journals, 1840-1848,* Historical Society of Alberta, 1977; *Charcoal's World,* Western Producer Prairie Books, 1978; *Indian Tribes of Alberta* (monograph), Glenbow-Alberta Institute, 1978; *Hutterites: The Hutterite Diamond Jubilee,* Glenbow-Alberta Institute, 1978; (editor and author of introduction) *My Tribe, the Crees,* Glenbow Museum, 1979; *Red Crow, Warrior Chief,* University of Nebraska Press, 1980; (editor) *The Best from Alberta History,* Western Producer Prairie Books, 1981; *Christmas in the West,* Western Producer Prairie Books, 1982; *History in Their Blood,* Douglas & MacIntyre, 1982.

Former author of column "Tawasi," in the daily *Edmonton Bulletin.* Contributor to national and international journals, including *Journal of American Folklore, Plains Anthropologist,* and *Journal of the Washington Academy of Science.* Editor of *Canadian Archivist,* 1963-66; associate editor of *Alberta History,* 1953-58, editor, 1958—; Northern and Canadian editor of *Montana Magazine of History.*

WORK IN PROGRESS: Big Bear and His Mission; James Gladstone: Senator in Buckskins.

SIDELIGHTS: While associated with the Government of Alberta, Hugh Aylmer Dempsey was responsible for historical work, including a historic highway sign program and historic sites research. His interest in history developed alongside his work with and research on Canadian Indians. His wife is a Blood Indian and in 1967 Dempsey was made an honorary Blood chief. Beginning with work for the Indian Association of Alberta, he assisted attempts to organize locals on Blackfoot and Peigan Reserves. Much of his writing concerns the Indian tribes of Alberta. He directed the documentary film "Okan, Sun Dance of the Blackfoot" and served as consultant for "West to the Mountains."

*   *   *

DENTINGER, Stephen
See HOCH, Edward D(entinger)

*   *   *

DENVER, Walt
See SHERMAN, Jory (Tecumseh)

*   *   *

DERSHOWITZ, Alan M.   1938-

PERSONAL: Born September 1, 1938, in Brooklyn, N.Y.; son of Harry (a store owner) and Claire (Ringel) Dershowitz; divorced; children: Elon Marc, Jamin Seth. *Education:* Brooklyn College (now Brooklyn College of the City University of New York), B.A., 1959; Yale University, LL.B., 1962. *Religion:* Jewish. *Office:* Law School, Harvard University, Cambridge, Mass. 02138.

CAREER: Admitted to the Bar, 1962; practicing civil liberties lawyer, 1962—; Harvard University, Law School, Cambridge, Mass., assistant professor, 1964-67, professor of law, 1967—. Consultant, National Institute of Mental Health. *Member:* American Civil Liberties Union, Phi Beta Kappa, Order of Coif. *Awards, honors:* Guggenheim fellowship.

WRITINGS: (With Jay Katz and others) *Psychoanalysis, Psychiatry and the Law,* Free Press of Glencoe, 1967; (with Joseph Goldstein and Richard Schwartz) *Criminal Law: Theory and Process,* Free Press, 1974; *The Best Defense,* Random House, 1982.

WORK IN PROGRESS: How to Reduce Violent Crime by 25 Percent (Without Curtailing Civil Liberties).

SIDELIGHTS: Alan Dershowitz, the youngest tenured professor in the history of Harvard Law School, is "the attorney of last resort for the desperate and despised, counselor for lost causes and forlorn hopes," writes Elaine Kendall in the *Los Angeles Times. The Best Defense* is Dershowitz's account of many of the cases he has undertaken as an appellate defense attorney, cases which were lost at the trial stage but which he agreed to appeal because no one else would take them or because they involved interesting points in law.

Dershowitz has built his reputation on the defense of a number of notorious clients. Among them are Jewish Defense League terrorist Sheldon Seigel, who set a bomb that killed an innocent young woman; nursing home owner Rabbi Bernard Bergman, called "the meanest man in New York" by the press; porno film star Harry Reems; the Tison brothers, who helped their father escape from prison and were with him when he later murdered an entire family; Stanford professor H. Bruce Franklin, faced with dismissal because his communist politics led him to incite students to wage "a people's war" against the university; and corrupt defense lawyer Edmund Rosner, the U.S. Attorney's Office's "public enemy number one" whose trial formed the basis for the film "The Prince of the City." Other clients have included Anatoly Shcharansky and other Soviet dissidents, nude bathers on a Cape Cod beach, trial lawyer F. Lee Bailey, and former CIA agent Frank Snepp, who refused to submit his book manuscript to the Agency for approval.

"This is more than a book by a lawyer about his cases," writes David S. Tatel in *Washington Post Book World*. "It is an articulate defense of many fundamental principles that are under attack in our country today. . . . Dershowitz's book is a compelling answer to those who . . . seek to dilute the Bill of Rights. It is particularly persuasive because his arguments emanate from courtrooms where constitutional principles are transformed from inspiring words to life and death realities." And indeed, in *The Best Defense* Dershowitz demonstrates that he is deeply committed to protecting the civil liberties of all citizens; many of his cases challenge the constitutionality of certain laws or procedures or question police and prosecution methods in obtaining the original conviction. "*The Best Defense* is a labor of love for the law by a man who has lost some of his illusions but kept his faith intact," writes Kendall. "He believes that the adversary process, allowing a defendant to challenge the government, is the foundation of American liberty; he is prepared to fight for that cause whenever and however it seems jeopardized. If some of our cherished preconceptions about the legal system are casualties of that battle, the system itself will not only survive but be strengthened by his efforts."

Dershowitz readily admits that most of his clients are guilty—as are those of any defense attorney—but argues, "One of the surest ways of undercutting the independence of defense attorneys is to question the propriety of their representing the guilty. Those who argue that defense attorneys should limit their representation to the innocent, or indeed to any specific group or category, open the door to a system where the government decides who is, and who is not, entitled to a defense."

"The basic dilemma presented by *The Best Defense* is the propriety of a lawyer's using every legal devise he can think of to get off a man who he knows to be guilty," comments Joseph W. Bishop, Jr. in *Commentary*. For example, Dershowitz was horrified that Sheldon Seigel was freed because of government misconduct in gathering evidence against the Jewish Defense League, but he says, quoting former Chief Justice Oliver Wendell Holmes, "It is a lesser evil that some criminals should escape than that the government should play an ignoble role." In the case of the Tison brothers, Dershowitz questioned the legality of sentencing someone to death for a murder he did not actually commit. The defense of Harry Reems, H. Bruce Franklin, Frank Snepp, and the nude bathers was, for Dershowitz, a defense of the Bill of Rights. It is clear that Dershowitz believes, says Bishop, that "the first person a good advocate convinces is himself, and what he convinces himself of is that his client may be a criminal but that he is not guilty of the crime with which he is charged or at least he is being treated unfairly."

While questioning the actual magnitude of the accusations Dershowitz levels against the government, the courts, and the

prosecution, *New Leader* contributing critic Barry Gewen concedes that the case histories Dershowitz presents are "immensely readable, thought-provoking, often troubling," and acknowledges that "perhaps there are no satisfactory answers . . . in many of the . . . cases included in *The Best Defense* where public safety is set against civil liberties. Bringing such ethical conundrums to the general attention could be the book's greatest virtue." John Greenya observes in the *Detroit News* that "Dershowitz writes well enough so his passion for his clients and their legal predicaments comes through loud and clear. One can feel the 'last resort' desperation that must always be at one's back, and not just in capital cases. Dershowitz is successful in doing something much more difficult than portraying the human drama: he makes the *law* exciting, the intellectual wrestling that embodies the best advocacy confrontation, especially on the appellate level."

A basic contention of Dershowitz's is that there are serious problems with the American judicial system, stemming from, among other things, prosecutorial and magisterial disregard for the constitutional rights and civil liberties of the defendant and from the frequent collusion between prosecution and the judges. The justice system, Dershowitz contends, is "corrupt to its core." Noting a number of the harsh charges Dershowitz makes in *The Best Defense, New York Times Book Review* contributor Tom Goldstein remarks: "These are all serious charges—charges that may have some truth to them but that ultimately are not sustained in *The Best Defense*. Time and again, Dershowitz draws large dark inferences from little evidence. . . . The failure of *The Best Defense* is that too many of Alan Dershowitz's conclusions are simply not documented. A book that relies so heavily on the credibility of its author must display an intellectual rigor that is missing in Dershowitz's passionate portrayal of his cases and clients."

Writing in the *Nation*, David Bruck states, "The 'real assessment of the American justice system' which Dershowitz promises in his introduction is not to be found in *The Best Defense*. Dershowitz rails against the hypocrisy or incompetence of the judges who have ruled against him and his clients over the years, but the readers looking for an analysis of why the courts are the way they are will have to look elsewhere." Graham Hughes in a *New York Review of Books* essay admits that "it is healthy that someone should write frankly about [the injustices and corruptions in the court system], but from a Harvard law professor we may rightly expect more than a set of exciting tales from the war zone. After being stirred by Dershowitz's exploits and shocked at the villainy of prosecutors and judges we ought to be offered a larger analysis of legal institutions and perhaps proposals for reform. Such professorial detachment is surprisingly lacking in this book."

Bruck also questions Dershowitz's underlying assumption "that the determination of guilt and innocence should always take second place to the legal demands and moral concerns of the criminal justice system itself. Dershowitz's complaint is that the courts subscribe to this principle in theory while routinely violating it in practice. He's right. . . . But I suspect that for most Americans . . . the real question is whether the principle is worth preserving. This is the principle, after all, which frees criminals on 'technicalities,' which prevents the murder weapon from being introduced as evidence if the police violated the murderer's privacy in securing it, which puts the rights of the defendant far above those of the victim. That this litany is a staple of right-wing rhetoric makes it no less true. It really does describe aspects of the criminal justice system when it works the way Dershowitz says it's supposed to, and the system's tacit refusal to live up to this ideal will surely not upset everyone as much as it does him. If he thinks it should, he ought to explain why.''

On the other hand, *Commentary* critic Joseph W. Bishop, Jr. supports Dershowitz's attempts to uphold Constitutional principles even if it sometimes means freeing a guilty man. Without such a fight, says Bishop in concurrence with Dershowitz, the United States will have Soviet-style justice. ''Dershowitz has seen too much of that (he has been active in the Soviet Jewry Legal Defense Project) to think that the unjust acquittal of some criminals is too high a price to pay to avoid Communist justice,'' Bishop concludes.

BIOGRAPHICAL/CRITICAL SOURCES: Alan Dershowitz, *The Best Defense,* Random House, 1982; *Washington Post Book World,* June 6, 1982; *New York Times Book Review,* June 13, 1982; *Los Angeles Times,* June 15, 1982; *New York Review of Books,* June 24, 1982; *New Leader,* July 12-26, 1982; *Nation,* August 7-14, 1982; *Detroit News,* August 29, 1982; *Commentary,* October, 1982; *Chicago Tribune Book World,* June 19, 1983.

—*Sketch by Heidi A. Tietjen*

*   *   *

DeVOS, George A(lphonse)   1922-

PERSONAL: Born July 25, 1922, in Detroit, Mich.; married Winifred Olsen (a psychiatric social worker), May 4, 1944; married Suzanne Lake (a singer); children: Laurie, Eric, Susan, Michael. *Education:* University of Chicago, B.A., 1946, M.A., 1948, Ph.D., 1951. *Office:* Department of Anthropology, University of California, Berkeley, Calif. 94720.

CAREER: Michael Reese Hospital, Chicago, Ill., research associate in psychology, 1950-51; Elgin State Hospital, Elgin, Ill., chief psychologist, 1951-53; Nagoya National University, Nagoya, Japan, Fulbright research fellow, 1953-55; University of Michigan, Ann Arbor, assistant professor of psychology and director of Ford Foundation's Japanese Personality and Culture Research Project, 1955-57; University of California, Berkeley, associate professor of social welfare, 1957-65, professor of anthropology, 1965—, chairman of Center for Japanese and Korean Studies, 1965-68, associate research psychologist and director of comparative research on delinquency, Institute of Human Development, 1960-68, research associate, Institute of Personality Assessment and Research, 1969-70. Research fellow of National Institute for Training Research on Delinquency, French Ministry of Justice, Vaucresson, France, 1963-64; visiting professor of anthropology and research psychologist, University of Hawaii, 1966-67; consultant on family planning research, Korean Institute of the Behavioral Sciences, Seoul, Korea, 1970-71; principal investigator, National Science Foundation Project, The Korean Minority in Japan, 1974-75. *Military service:* U.S. Army, 1943-46. *Member:* American Psychological Association, American Anthropological Association. *Awards, honors:* Fulbright, Ford Foundation, and National Institute for Mental Health research grants.

WRITINGS: (With Hiroshi Wagatsuma) *Japan's Invisible Race: Caste in Culture and Personality,* University of California Press, 1966; *American Japanese Intercultural Marriages,* Chinese Association for Folklore (Taipei), 1973; *Socialization for Achievement: Essays on the Cultural Psychology of the Japanese,* University of California Press, 1973; (with William Wetherall) *Japan's Minorities,* Minority Rights Group (London), 1974; (editor with Lola Romanucci-Ross) *Ethnic Identity:*

Cultural Continuities and Change, Mayfield, 1975, 2nd edition, University of Chicago Press, 1982; (editor) *Responses to Change,* Van Nostrand, 1975; (with Changsoo Lee) *Koreans in Japan: Ethnic Conflict and Accommodation,* University of California Press, 1981; (with Hiroshi Wagatsuma) *Heritage of Endurance,* University of California Press, 1982.

Contributor: Yehudi A. Cohen, editor, *Social Structure and Personality,* Holt, 1961; Francis L.K. Hsu, editor, *Psychological Anthropology,* Dorsey, 1961; Robert J. Smith and Richard K. Beardsley, editors, *Japanese Culture: Its Development and Characteristics,* Aldine, 1962; Mildred B. Kantor, editor, *Mobility and Mental Health,* C. C Thomas, 1965; Bernard E. Segal, editor, *Racial and Ethnic Relations,* Crowell, 1966; Staten W. Webster, editor, *The Disadvantaged Learner,* Chandler Publishing, 1966; R. P. Dore, editor, *Aspects of Social Change in Modern Japan,* Princeton University Press, 1967; H.L.P. Resnick, editor, *Suicidal Behaviors: Diagnosis and Management,* Little, Brown, 1968; Edward Norbeck, Douglass Price-Williams, and William M. McCord, editors, *Personality: An Interdisciplinary Appraisal,* Holt, 1968; Joseph C. Finney, editor, *Culture Change, Mental Health, and Poverty,* University of Kentucky Press, 1969.

Georgene H. Seward and Robert C. Williams, editor, *Sex Roles in Changing Society,* Random House, 1970; Minako Kurokawa, editor, *Minority Responses,* Random House, 1970; Nevitt Sanford and Craig Comstock, editors, *Sanctions for Evil,* Jossey-Bass, 1971; Norman R. Yetman and C. Hoy Steele, editors, *Majority and Minority,* Allyn & Bacon, 1971; William P. Lebra, editor, *Transcultural Research in Mental Health,* University of Hawaii Press, 1972; Ben Whitaker, editor, *The Fourth World Victims of Group Oppression,* Sidgwick & Jackson, 1972; Takie Sugiyama Lebra and William Lebra, editors, *Japanese Culture and Behavior,* University Press of Hawaii, 1974; William P. Lebra, editor, *Youth, Socialization and Mental Health,* University Press of Hawaii, 1974; Irwin Scheiner, editor, *Modern Japan: An Interpretive Anthology,* Macmillan, 1974; *Modern Japanese Organization and Decision Making,* University of California Press, 1975. Contributor of articles and reviews to psychology and anthropology journals.

*   *   *

DeWOLF, Rose (Doris)   1934-

PERSONAL: Born July 18, 1934, in Reading, Pa.; daughter of Lewis Marcus (a merchant) and Pauline (Hirshout) DeWolf; married Bernard Ingster (a management consultant), September 30, 1967; children: Carole. *Education:* Temple University, B.S., 1956. *Home:* 2226 Lombard St., Philadelphia, Pa. 19146. *Office:* *Philadelphia Daily News,* 400 North Broad St., Philadelphia, Pa. 19101.

CAREER: *Daily Intelligencer,* Doylestown, Pa., writer, 1956-60; *Camden Courier-Post,* Camden, N.J., writer, 1960-61; *Philadelphia Inquirer,* Philadelphia, Pa., columnist, 1961-68; *Philadelphia Bulletin,* Philadelphia, columnist, 1969-82; *Philadelphia Daily News,* Philadelphia, writer, 1982—. Free-lance magazine writer. Television interviewer, WFIL-TV, Philadelphia, 1968-69, and WCAU-TV, Philadelphia, 1976—; commentator, KYW-TV, Philadelphia, 1971; lecturer.

WRITINGS: *The Bonds of Acrimony,* Lippincott, 1970; (with Joel Moldorsky) *The Best Defense,* Macmillan, 1975; *How to Raise Your Man,* F. Watts, 1983.

DEYNEKA, Anita 1943-

PERSONAL: Born July 7, 1943, in Seattle, Wash.; daughter of Frank Howard and Ada (McIntosh) Marson; married Peter Deyneka, Jr. (a director of a mission organization), June 15, 1968. *Education:* Attended Wenatchee Valley College, 1961-63; Seattle Pacific College, B.A. (summa cum laude), 1966; Mundelein College, M.A., 1982. *Religion:* Evangelical Protestant. *Home:* 1263 Casa Solana, Wheaton, Ill. 60187. *Office address:* Slavic Gospel Association, P.O. Box 1122, Wheaton, Ill. 60187.

CAREER: Overseas Radio and Television, Taipei, Taiwan, missionary, spring, 1966; high school English teacher in Wenatchee, Wash., 1966-68; Slavic Gospel Association, Wheaton, Ill., publications administrator, 1968—. Instructor, Institute of Slavic Studies, 1980—. Clerk-typist for U.S. Forest Service, summers, 1963-67. *Member:* Evangelical Press Association, National Religious Broadcasters, Society for the Study of Religion and Communism, Outstanding Young Women of America.

WRITINGS—All published by David Cook; for children: *Tanya and the Borderguard*, 1973; *Fire!*, 1974; *Alexi's Secret Mission*, 1975; *Alexi and the Mountain Treasure*, 1979.

For adults: (With husband, Peter Deyneka, Jr.) *Christians in the Shadow of the Kremlin*, 1974; *A Song in Siberia*, 1977. Contributor to religious periodicals, including *New Oxford Review, Christianity Today, Christian Herald, Moody Monthly*, and *Sparks.*

WORK IN PROGRESS: A biography of Russian ballerina Luba Bershadskaya.

SIDELIGHTS: Anita Deyneka's travels have taken her to the Far East, South America, Central America, the Soviet Union, and eastern and western Europe. Many of her books have been translated into foreign languages, including German, Spanish, Finnish, and Dutch.

* * *

DIARA, Schavi M(ali) 1948-

PERSONAL: Name is pronounced Sha-*vee* Ma-*lee* Dee-*are*-ra; born April 30, 1948, in Detroit, Mich.; daughter of William Earl (a mechanical engineer) and Margaret Ruis (Walton) Ross. *Education:* Wayne State University, B.A., 1970, M.A., 1976. *Politics:* "Pan-Africanism." *Religion:* Islam. *Residence:* Detroit, Mich. *Office:* Department of English, Wayne State University, Detroit, Mich. 48202; and Creative Educational Concepts, Inc., P.O. Box 02542, Detroit, Mich. 48202.

CAREER: High school teacher of English and life science in the public schools of Highland Park, Mich., 1970-71; Wayne State University, Detroit, Mich., instructor in English and social studies, 1971-72; Wayne County Community College, Detroit, instructor in English, 1972-73; Roeper City and Country School, Bloomfield Hills, Mich., teacher of English, 1973-77; Wayne State University, 1977—, began as instructor, currently professor of English and Afro-American studies. Director of Diara Institute, 1977—; owner of Creative Educational Concepts, Inc. *Member:* National Council of Teachers of English, Association for Study of Afro-American Life and History, Animal Protection Institute of America, Pan African Congress, Mid-Western Association of Black Professional Women,

Michigan Council of Teachers of English, Michigan Poetry Society, Phi Delta Kappa.

WRITINGS: Growing Together (poetry), Agascha Productions, 1972; *Legacy* (anthology of poems, essays, and short stories), Agascha Productions, 1975; *Song for My Father* (novella), Agascha Productions, 1975; *Glistening Reflections: A Summary of the Harlem Renaissance*, Exposition Press, 1984.

SIDELIGHTS: Schavi M. Diara writes: "I feel that it is imperative that Black people recognize their African heritage, take pride in it, relate to it, and begin to move in ways that will cause others to respect [them] and see [them] as equals rather than lesser-men." Her long-range goal is to establish a private college-preparatory secondary school which places emphasis on African and African-American studies.

* * *

DIENES, C(harles) Thomas 1940-

PERSONAL: Born January 9, 1940, in Chicago, Ill.; son of Walter N. (a teacher) and Florence (Weiskaar) Dienes; married Peggy Clements (a teacher), August 14, 1965; children: Kimberly. *Education:* Loyola University, Chicago, Ill., B.S., 1961; Northwestern University, J.D. (cum laude), 1964, Ph.D., 1968. *Home:* 11806 Charen Lane, Potomac, Md. 20854. *Office:* National Law Center, George Washington University, 720 20th St. N.W., Washington, D.C. 20052.

CAREER: Admitted to Illinois Bar, 1964; University of Houston, Houston, Tex., assistant professor of law, 1967-70, and political science, 1969-70; American University, Washington, D.C., associate professor, 1970-73, professor of law and government, 1973-79; George Washington University, Washington, D.C., professor of law, 1980—. Visiting assistant professor, Indiana University, summer, 1970; instructor, Bar Review, Inc., 1971—; visiting professor of law, Cornell University, 1978-79; member of faculty, San Diego International and Comparative Law Institute in Guadalajara, Mexico, and Dublin, Ireland, summers, 1980, 1982, 1983. Reviewer of proposals for National Science Foundation, 1972—.

MEMBER: Law and Society Association, American Political Science Association, American Civil Liberties Union, Association of American Law Schools (Section on Education Law), Society of American Law Teachers, Order of Coif.

WRITINGS: (Editor with others) *Welfare Law Handbook*, National Institute for Education in the Law and Poverty, 1968; *Law, Politics, and Birth Control*, University of Illinois Press, 1972; (with Jerome Barron) *Constitutional Law: Principles and Policy, Cases and Materials*, Bobbs-Merrill, 1975, 2nd edition, Mitchie, 1982; (with Barron) *Handbook of True Speech and Free Press*, Little, Brown, 1979; (with David Aaronson and Michael Musheno) *Decriminalization of Public Drunkenness: Tracing the Implementation of a Public Policy*, National Institute of Justice, U.S. Department of Justice, 1982; (with Barron) *Constitutional Law*, West's Black Letter Series, 1983; (with Barron) *Nutshell on Constitutional Law*, West, 1984. Contributor of articles and reviews to law journals.

* * *

DINTENFASS, Mark 1941-

PERSONAL: Born November 15, 1941, in New York, N.Y.; son of Sidney (a cutter) and Gerri (Berger) Dintenfass; married Phyllis Schulman (a teacher), June 10, 1962. *Education:* Columbia University, B.A., 1963, M.A., 1964; University of Iowa, M.F.A., 1968. *Home:* 738 East Eldorado St., Appleton, Wis. 54911. *Agent:* Mitch Douglas, International Creative Management, 40 West 57th St., New York, N.Y. 10019. *Office:* Main Hall, Lawrence University, Appleton, Wis. 54911.

CAREER: U.S. Peace Corps, teacher at Haile Selassie I University, Addis Ababa, Ethiopia, 1964-66; Lawrence University, Appleton, Wis., associate professor of English, 1968—.

WRITINGS—Novels, except as indicated: (Editor and adaptor) Phyllis Dintenfass, *How to Adapt and Use Reading Materials: A Teacher's Guide* (nonfiction), Oxford University Press, 1967; *Make Yourself an Earthquake,* Little, Brown, 1969; *The Case against Org,* Little, Brown, 1970; *Figure 8,* Simon & Schuster, 1973; *Montgomery Street,* Harper, 1978; *Old World, New World,* Morrow, 1982.

WORK IN PROGRESS: A novel.

SIDELIGHTS: In a 1969 *Library Journal* article, Mark Dintenfass described himself as "a sort of tourist with a sharp eye for the doubleness of things, the sad and ludicrous spectacle, the chaotically disciplined march of events. I do not march: I only write. As honestly as I can, of course; as well as I can, of course. There is nothing special about that and there is nothing special about me." According to *New York Times Book Review* critic Michael Mewshaw, however, there is something special about Dintenfass: he is an "original" with "an individual voice, a quirky vision and a vitality of language which is more than matched by his intelligence. Perhaps it is this last gift which is most impressive. Ideas flash from Dintenfass's prose, yet never blind one to character or action."

The novelist first came to critical attention with *Make Yourself an Earthquake* and *The Case against Org.* Both books are set, as are his later ones, in New York City; both feature as protagonist an "outsider" who doesn't fit into New York's accepted lifestyle. *Make Yourself an Earthquake* tells the story of Solomon Leab, an aging Jewish schoolteacher whose attempts to recapture his youth involve him in campus riots, pot smoking, banana-peel smoking, and forays into African culture. The novel, says Harry Roskolenko in the *New York Times Book Review,* "full of pertinent realism, has some offhand symbols one does not always penetrate. But there are enough clues in this zany melange of literary manners and myths for a real put-down, especially in its Yiddish-dervish nuances. For the author has everything that a good writer needs: style, wit, economy, fantasy—and he can spin like a top with his equipment."

In *The Case against Org* the obese George Nathan Blomberg ("Org"), separated from his wife and living with his nagging mother on Manhattan's Upper West Side, declares his liberation through his fat—"Listen, one must choose to be obese: it is an act of courage"—and is controlled by his "orgone," described as "a vital energy held to pervade nature, and to be accumulable for use by the human body by sitting in a specially designed box." In a *New York Times Book Review* article, Steven Kroll compares the two books and finds elements of James Joyce in the author's style: "[*Make Yourself an Earthquake*] had its Joycean mannerisms. [*The Case against Org*] has only the Joycean exuberance, but in both Leab and Org there is more than a passing dependence on [Joyce's] randy, timorous, gluttonous Leopold Bloom." And although Kroll feels that "Org's not big enough (as a character) to make [*The Case against Org*] an important book," he finds the novel "boisterous, buoyant, vital, funny, and more than a little sad. Org lives."

Dintenfass's next novel, *Figure 8,* is a tale of adultery and seduction centering on Michael Silversmith, a silversmith, whose wife has left him for a third-rate poet. Through a complex series of events, Silversmith eventually becomes the lover of the poet's daughter, thus completing the "figure eight" of the book's title. "The reader has to swallow the sort of coincidence that we expect in Dickens, not in a contemporary novel," writes Anatole Broyard of the *New York Times.* "Somehow, though, this is not disturbing. When an author gets you on his side, as Mr. Dintenfass does in *Figure 8,* you allow him all sorts of liberties."

The narrator of *Montgomery Street,* Stephen Mandreg, is a successful film director embarking on an autobiographical movie about his youth on the streets of Brooklyn. Herbert Gold, writing in the *New York Times Book Review,* contends that "nothing is developed" in *Montgomery Street.* Gold remarks: "Yes, there are fugues, repetitions, circlings about themes. There is evident intelligence and sincerity and verbal energy. But there's the rub: *verbal* energy. We need more energies than that." And while *Christian Science Monitor* critic David Sterritt finds the novel "a winning book," nevertheless "its muted tone and familiar aphorisms get wearying. A few flashes of color and a little bold music on the soundtrack might have worked wonders."

On the other hand, W. R. Evans thinks the book "captures the universal qualities of growing up—the childish fears, the sense of limited freedom, the first awareness of sex." Evans continues in *Best Sellers:* "*Montgomery Street* is an affectionate, nostalgic, but unsentimental work that touches home. The writer's unadorned, unpretentious style effectively portrays the inner being of life itself. The process of creation, as well as the successful tale of adolescents growing up, makes this book a winner."

"Come, meet the family," invites Dintenfass in the opening of his novel *Old World, New World.* The family is the Liebers, whom the book follows through seventy years, from their life in turn-of-the-century Poland through their immigration to and assimilation in Brooklyn. A key conflict revolves around the Lieber elders; Sophie, who strives to adopt all the values of her new homeland, and Jacob, who yearns for the contentment he knew in Poland. Daphne Merkin, in the *New York Times Book Review,* calls *Old World, New World* "a family saga to do the genre proud, a novel to bring critics and fans together. . . . Mark Dintenfass's energetic yet careful prose conveys both the story of a particular family and the swelling life that extends beyond it. Behind the chorus of groans and shouts of the Liebers at love and war, there is another tune distantly heard, in a minor key, which suggests what the Liebers might have been—grander, wiser, kinder. This implicit narrative fleshes out their lives so effectively that by the end we feel we know not only the characters themselves but their dreams for themselves. I couldn't get enough of them."

CA INTERVIEW

CA interviewed Mark Dintenfass by telephone June 14, 1983, in London, where he was spending a year at the London Center of Lawrence University.

CA: Your fiction has a strong New York flavor and primarily New York settings. Does your interest in being a writer go back to your childhood there?

DINTENFASS: My interest in being a writer started when I was in college. It's not so much that growing up in New York made me a writer; it's that, when I decided to be a writer, it seemed to me that New York was my subject.

CA: You got an M.A. degree in drama from Columbia, I noticed. Had you thought about acting, or writing plays?

DINTENFASS: I'd thought about drama criticism first, and then later about writing plays, but I decided pretty early on not to write plays, because the thought of other people mucking around with my work turned me off. I like the fact that with a novel I'm in control of the outcome; if you write a play, six other egos want to push in on you and take over your act.

CA: Was your first novel, Make Yourself an Earthquake *(1969), written entirely at the University of Iowa's Writers' Workshop while you were working on your M.F.A. there, or had you begun it during your years with the Peace Corps in Ethiopia?*

DINTENFASS: I actually began it at Iowa. It was one of the nice things that came out of going to Iowa. It took me about eighteen months to write it.

CA: How was the Writers' Workshop most helpful to you?

DINTENFASS: It gave me two years of free space—I think that's really what it amounted to. I had been in Africa and wanted to write and got admitted to the workshop. I fell in there with Richard Yates, whom I owe a lot to. He's a remarkable man. He taught me, among other things, to write about life, about people who cry and bleed, rather than about abstract ideas, and that is one of the things I owe to him. I think I was too academically oriented, having gone to graduate school and taught at the university level before I met him.

Iowa really amounted to two years to put up or shut up, and I was one of the lucky ones who managed to accomplish something. I sold that book fairly early in its making, which certainly helped a lot in terms of getting it finished. It was only half done when I sold it. Selling that first novel was of course a great breakthrough; after that I could begin to think, Hey, maybe I really am a writer.

CA: How do teaching and writing work together for you? Is it a struggle to do both, or does one help the other?

DINTENFASS: I think the answer to that is both. As opposed to other ways of making a living, teaching is nice because I have more time for my writing than I would if I worked in a regular nine-to-five job, obviously. And being able to turn your thoughts to something other than your writing when you're not writing—having something worth turning them to, as you do being in the classroom with young students—and having students, especially in my writing courses, to stimulate me a little bit certainly is a plus. On the other hand, all those complaints people have about academe being a somewhat closed and sheltered environment are true enough. But I've been lucky enough to get out and see the world a bit—for example, having this year in London.

CA: Are you teaching there?

DINTENFASS: I have taught for six of the months I've been here.

CA: Do you teach literature as well as creative writing?

DINTENFASS: Yes. Since Lawrence is a small school, I get to do a variety of things. I've taught American literature, British

literature, modern drama, and a film course, as well as a basic freshman course, and my fiction-writing courses.

CA: How are you best able to help students in the fiction-writing courses?

DINTENFASS: I try to do what was done for me at Iowa, and also at Columbia, where I had a teacher whose philosophy of teaching writing was to leave people alone and let them find their own way—to make space, as I said about my experience at Iowa. I don't set assignments of any specific sort. I tell them I can't really teach them how to write, and I'm certainly not going to make them into writers, in three months or six months or even a year; I tell them that if they are talented and lucky, and are willing to invest about ten years of their lives, they can learn for themselves how to write.

I do insist, though, that the students take each other seriously as beginning writers. Actually, I hope that a large percentage of my students decide after a course or two that they're *not* very interested in writing, because I think that's a healthy thing to learn when you're young. You know, a lot of people dream of writing, but when it comes to actually sitting down and having to write, many of them find that the dream of writing and the actual doing it are two very different things. So I think among the other things a writing course can do is give people a chance to live that dream and find out whether they really want to do it or not. If not, they can go on and do something practical with their lives.

CA: What kind of writing schedule do you keep?

DINTENFASS: I try to write in the morning, five days a week, and keep my classes in the afternoon.

CA: Do you ever get a vacation from writing?

DINTENFASS: I take breaks from it, and between books I often take as much as six months when I'm not trying to write every day, but spending time taking notes and letting the new book take shape in my head.

CA: Writing about Figure 8 *in the* New York Times Book Review *(September 15, 1974), Michael Mewshaw compared you to John Barth and Thomas McGuane. David Sterritt, reviewing* Montgomery Street *in the* Christian Science Monitor *(May 12, 1978), compared the structure of that book with James Joyce's* Ulysses. *What writers do you think have been definite influences on your own work?*

DINTENFASS: I've done a bit of book reviewing myself, and I know that one of the functions of a book review is to label the product. And one easy, though I think not very useful, way of labeling a *new* product, a writer that lots of people haven't heard of, is to compare him to famous writers. I think Michael's review was a wonderful review—I wish they were all that good—but I'm not sure the comparisons were really very apt ones. One reviewer of *Make Yourself an Earthquake* compared me to Saul Bellow, and I'm not sure that was very apt either. He meant that we were both Jewish intellectual writers; that's about it. So I don't really like the comparisons, and I'm not even sure I want to talk about influences. Hemingway once answered a similar question by naming every worthwhile writer he had ever read, starting with Aeschylus. I am sympathetic to that approach, and I suspect my list might be considerably longer than his.

I'm perfectly happy, though, to talk about writers I admire. One of the troubles with teaching literature is that you end up teaching writers you think are important to teach, but they may not be your favorite writers, and there are writers you like a lot whom you may not want to teach. So I have a little trouble sorting out those writers I would, so to speak, take to bed on a cold night and those writers I feel I am obligated to share with my students; those are often two different categories. Certainly, though, at or near the top of my list of relatively recent writers would be Nabokov, Singer, and Márquez, whom I admire a lot, and Richard Yates, who I think is a very underrated writer. But there are writers I *would* take to bed to read on a cold night, or have spent a lot of time with, who might not be great writers, or writers you would want to teach in a literature class. I like Rex Stout. I'm not a great lover of detective stories—I don't like Agatha Christie, for example—but I think Rex Stout has real style and real flair, and to me style and flair are very important.

CA: In Figure 8 *you wrote about Michael Silversmith, a silversmith, with lots of good silversmithing details and metaphors. Have you done silversmithing yourself?*

DINTENFASS: Yes, I have. At Iowa they have the wonderful theory that writers should go out and experiment with something nonverbal, so the program requires that you do a second art of some sort. I chose metalwork, silversmithing, for the heck of it—well, actually because my wife wanted to do it! I'm not very good at it, but I did learn enough to be able to go on doing it. I have enough equipment now in my basement at home so that occasionally I can go down and make something. I certainly learned enough to have a feel for what it would be like to be a really good silversmith, though I'm not. That's the source of Michael Silversmith.

CA: There seemed to be too much emotion in those descriptions to have come from just research.

DINTENFASS: I don't believe in research, a la James Michener. There might be a small point or two in a book that I'd want to check, but I'm not a researcher; I don't believe you can write real fiction by researching. I know that's a kind of heresy in the American marketplace today, but for me writing is a matter of taking the things you've experienced and lived, and transforming them into some stylish and elegant form. Researching isn't living, and it seldom leads to elegance; it's a different part of the mentality altogether.

There's something a lot of readers don't know: Fiction is words, and good fiction is words well used. I think that when you compare the average bestseller list with what people who spend their lives dealing with fiction *know* is good, there's obviously a large discrepancy. That's the reason I feel so strongly about the matter of research, for example. Fiction isn't facts, and fiction isn't the inside dope on the Mafia, the automobile business, or outer space; fiction is a sequence of enchanted words. What a writer does is to make that sequence as perfect and enchanting as he can. That's what it's all about, as far as I'm concerned.

CA: You dedicated Old World, New World *to your parents. How much does the family history in that novel relate to your own family?*

DINTENFASS: I'd say about fifty percent, though I don't think I'd want to say which fifty percent! My parents were long due

for a dedication. My first book had been dedicated to Richard Yates and to George Nobbe, my professor at Columbia who did such a lot for me. The second book was dedicated to my wife, and by the time I wrote my third and fourth books, I had kids to dedicate them to. So my parents had been waiting all those years. But also, *Old World, New World* is a book that I had actually kept in the back of my head for a good ten years or more. It's a lot bigger than the earlier works, not only in terms of the number of words, but in terms of the whole conception. It's dedicated to my parents as parents in the sense that their generation made my generation, and the business of generations is very important in that book.

CA: There were so many separate but interwoven stories in the book, it must have been hard to keep track of them in the writing.

DINTENFASS: Sure it was hard. That's why I enjoyed doing it. I used index cards and wrote, not the stories so much, but lines, sentences, images, for different characters. Then, putting the index cards together in different ways, I was able to thread the various things through. It was a little bit like juggling, and I feel quite good about what I was able to do with the narrative line. That, as much as what the stories were about, was the fun of writing the book.

CA: After five published novels, would you say writing has become easier in any way, or does it become more difficult as you go?

DINTENFASS: If anything, it gets harder. When you write the first couple of books, you don't know how hard it is, really. One thing that happens to a writer is that he becomes, inevitably, more conscious of what he's done, and more conscious of how hard it is to go on doing it, and more conscious of the kinds of things he wants to be able to do. I think in a way it's like playing baseball. A twenty-year-old plays sort of by instinct. If he manages to keep playing, by the time he's forty he can't trust his instincts or his body anymore, so he has to trust his smarts. He becomes an "old pro." There's something a little like that involved in writing a number of books. I'm now into a new book, which I've recently sold, although it's far from completion, and it's giving me the dickens of a time.

CA: Will it be like the others much, or is it too early to talk about it?

DINTENFASS: I'd rather not talk about it, though I will say this: Though there are a lot of similarities in all my books, one of the things I consciously try to do is make each one different. In that sense certainly this one will be different from all the others. Otherwise there would be no point doing it.

CA: Is there any kind of writing you'd like to try that you haven't done?

DINTENFASS: I have done other kinds of writing besides novels. In fact, I've done many kinds of writing, but so far I've only been successful—at least in terms of getting published—with the novels. I've done two screenplays, both of which went the rounds and had some encouragement, but the nature of the movie industry is such that there are probably 300 screenplays written for every one that gets made, and the one that gets made isn't necessarily the most interesting one.

When I was younger I wrote poetry, and of course I've written short stories, one of which has been published. But the short-story market is a difficult one, and I don't really have the touch of a short-story writer. I'm a putter-inner, I guess, by temperament, and short-story writers are taker-outers. I've even done a play or two, though it was some time ago, and I've shied away from writing plays for the reason I've mentioned before. I even did ghostwriting for a fellow for a couple of summers while I was in college. In fact, I think that's part of what made me disciplined as a writer—writing for a penny a word, grinding out word after word after word. The visible works of mine are the novels, but there's a lot of invisible work in my drawers, in boxes in the basement, in closets.

CA: Maybe some of it will resurface.

DINTENFASS: Most of it probably should stay invisible! A lot of it is very bad, I think—especially the stuff I wrote ten or fifteen years ago. When very famous writers die, people start pulling out of the closets all of those things the writers purposely put *in* the closets. I'm not sure that's fair; I think it's a kind of invasion of their privacy. James Joyce wrote a lot of bad poetry and other stuff when he was young. The fact that he was a supreme genius when he wrote *Ulysses* doesn't mean we have to have a look at all the garbage he wrote while he was learning how to write.

CA: Any long-range plans or goals for the future that you'd like to talk about?

DINTENFASS: I'm anxious to get rid of the book I'm working on now, because I have an even larger one in mind, something rather ambitious. I think I've worked that way. As I've said, *Old World, New World* sat in the back of my mind while I was writing *Figure 8* and *Montgomery Street*. Big books like that have a long gestation period, and the one that's gestating now may come after the one I'm finishing or maybe two or three books down the line, but it's nice to know that it's there. It's a good feeling to have something you can turn to when everything else is not working out, and dream it a little at a time.

BIOGRAPHICAL/CRITICAL SOURCES: Library Journal, February 1, 1969; *New York Times Book Review,* March 30, 1969, November 15, 1970, September 15, 1974, April 30, 1978, February 28, 1982; Mark Dintenfass, *The Case against Org,* Little, Brown, 1970; *New York Times,* August 19, 1974; *Christian Science Monitor,* May 12, 1978; *Best Sellers,* June, 1978; Dintenfass, *Old World, New World,* Morrow, 1982; *Chicago Tribune Book World,* June 20, 1982.

—*Sketch by Susan Salter*
—*Interview by Jean W. Ross*

*   *   *

DIXON, Paige
    See CORCORAN, Barbara

*   *   *

DMYTRYSHYN, Basil   1925-

PERSONAL: Born January 14, 1925, in Poland; naturalized U.S. citizen; married Virginia Roehl, July 16, 1949; children: Sonia, Tania. *Education:* University of Arkansas, B.A., 1950, M.A., 1951; University of California, Berkeley, Ph.D., 1955. *Politics:* Democrat. *Home:* 11300 Southwest 92nd Ave., Portland, Ore. 97223. *Office:* Department of History, Portland State University, Portland, Ore. 97207.

CAREER: University of California, Berkeley, research associate, 1955-56; Portland State University, Portland, Ore., assistant professor, 1956-59, associate professor, 1959-64, professor of history, 1964—. Visiting professor at University of Illinois, 1964-65, and Harvard University, summer, 1971. Conductor of college credit course in history on both Oregon educational television and commercial television. *Member:* American Historical Association, American Association for the Advancement of Slavic Studies, Canadian Association of Slavicists. *Awards, honors:* Fulbright fellowship for research in Germany, 1967-68.

WRITINGS: Moscow and the Ukraine, 1918-53, Bookman Associates, 1956; (translator with John M. Letiche and Richard Pierce) *A History of Russian Economic Thought,* University of California Press, 1964; *USSR: A Concise History,* Scribner, 1965, 3rd edition, 1978; (editor) *Medieval Russia: A Source Book, 900-1700,* Holt, 1967, 2nd edition, Dryden, 1973; (editor) *Imperial Russia: A Source Book, 1700-1917,* Holt, 1967, 2nd edition, Dryden, 1974; (author of introduction) Fedir Savchenko, *Zabrona ukrainstva tysiacha visimsot simdesiat shostyi r* (title means "The Supression of the Ukrainian Activities in 1876"), W. Fink (Munich), 1970; (editor) *Modernization of Russia under Peter I and Catherine II,* Wiley, 1974; *A History of Russia,* Prentice-Hall, 1977; (editor with E.A.P. Crownhart-Vaughan) *The End of Russian America: Captain P. N. Golovin's Last Report, 1862,* Oregon Historical Society, 1979. Contributor to professional journals in United States, Canada, and Germany.

WORK IN PROGRESS: Research in Russian expansion to the Pacific, mercantilist thought, and the impact of Adam Smith on Russia.

SIDELIGHTS: Basil Dmytryshyn speaks German, Russian, Czechoslovak, and Ukrainian. He also reads French and Church Slavonic.

*   *   *

DOBRIN, Arnold   1928-

PERSONAL: Born June 6, 1928, in Omaha, Neb.; son of Ralph and Ethel (Abrahamson) Dobrin; married Norma Zane Chaplain (a sociologist), June 29, 1956 (divorced); children: Adam, Brian. *Education:* Studied at Chouinard Art Institute, at Academie de la Grande Chaumiere, Paris, France, and at New York University. *Address:* c/o Cash, 1333 North Stanley Ave., Apt. 17, Los Angeles, Calif. 90046.

CAREER: Free-lance art director and designer, 1948-52; staff designer for Metro-Goldwyn-Mayer and then for Twentieth Century-Fox Studios, 1952-56; free-lance art director and designer, 1956-62; writer, 1962—. *Member:* P.E.N. *Awards, honors:* Fellow at MacDowell Colony in Peterborough, N.H.

*WRITINGS—*Youth books; most are self-illustrated: *Little Monk and the Tiger,* Coward, 1965; *Taro and the Sea Turtles,* Coward, 1966; *Carmello's Cat: The Story of a Roman Christmas,* Coward, 1967; *Aaron Copland: His Life and Times,* Crowell, 1967; *The Snow Fox,* Coward, 1968; *Italy: Modern Renaissance,* Thomas Nelson, 1968; *Marshes and Marsh Life,* Coward, 1969.

Igor Stravinsky: His Life and Times, Crowell, 1970; *Gerbils,* Lothrop, 1970; *Ireland: The Edge of Europe,* Thomas Nelson, 1970; *Scat!,* Four Winds Press, 1970; *The New Life: The Mexican Americans Today,* Dodd, 1971; *To Katmandu,* Crowell, 1971; *Voices of Joy, Voices of Freedom,* Coward, 1972; *Jo-*

sephina's 'Magination,' Four Winds Press, 1973; *Vincent Van Gogh,* Warne, 1973; *Jillions of Gerbils,* Lothrop, 1973; *Going to Moscow,* Four Winds Press, 1973; *Careers in Recreation,* Lothrop, 1974; *A Life in Israel: The Story of Golda Meir,* Dodd, 1974.

Irish: The Story of a Girl and Her Horse, Walker & Co., 1976; *Gilly Gilhooley,* Crown, 1976; *The Peter Rabbit Natural Foods Cookbook,* Warne, 1977; *Make a Witch, Make a Goblin: A Book of Halloween Crafts,* Four Winds Press, 1978. Contributor of travel articles to publications.

SIDELIGHTS: Arnold Dobrin lived in Japan in 1957 and in Rome in 1962-64; he travels abroad annually.

*   *   *

DOHRENWEND, Barbara Snell   1927-1982

PERSONAL: Born March 26, 1927, in New York, N.Y.; died June 28, 1982; daughter of Foster D. and Cornelia (Tyler) Snell; married Bruce P. Dohrenwend (a professor), September 21, 1951. *Education:* Wellesley College, B.A., 1947; Columbia University, M.A., 1948, Ph.D., 1954. *Address:* 1270 Fifth Ave., New York, N.Y. 10029. *Office:* Department of Psychology, City College of the City University of New York, New York, N.Y. 10031.

CAREER: University of Michigan, Ann Arbor, research assistant in social psychology, 1949-51; Cornell University, Ithaca, N.Y., research associate, 1952-57; New York University, New York City, research assistant professor, 1958-61; City College of the City University of New York, New York City, lecturer, 1961-64, assistant professor, 1964-68, associate professor, 1969-72, professor of psychology, beginning 1972. Lecturer, Columbia University, beginning 1972. Has served on several research groups. Consultant, Population Council, 1967-69, and Community Relations Bureau, New York City Fire Dept., 1968-71.

MEMBER: American Psychological Association (president of Division of Community Psychology, 1976-77), American Sociological Association, American Association for Public Opinion Research, American Public Health Association, American Association for the Advancement of Science, Society for the Psychological Study of Social Issues, Sigma Xi. *Awards, honors:* National Institute of Mental Health grants, 1966-68, 1973-74; National Science Foundation grant, 1970-71.

WRITINGS: (With S. A. Richardson and D. Klein) *Interviewing: Its Forms and Functions,* Basic Books, 1965; (with husband, Bruce P. Dohrenwend) *Social Status and Psychological Disorder: A Causal Inquiry,* Wiley, 1969; (editor with B. P. Dohrenwend) *Stressful Life Events: Their Nature and Effects,* Wiley, 1974; (editor with B. P. Dohrenwend) *Stressful Life Events and Their Contexts,* Watson, 1981; (editor with David F. Ricks) *Origins of Psychopathology: Problems in Research and Public Policy,* Cambridge University Press, 1983. Contributor to psychology journals.

WORK IN PROGRESS: Further research on the relation of social status to psychological disorder and on the methodology of research interviewing.

OBITUARIES: *New York Times,* July 2, 1982.†

DOMANSKA, Janina

PERSONAL: Born in Warsaw, Poland; came to U.S. in 1952, naturalized citizen, 1964; daughter of Wladyslaw (an engineer) and Jadwiga (a writer, maiden name, Muszynska) Domanski; married Jerzy Laskowski (a writer), December 22, 1953. *Education:* Academy of Fine Arts, Warsaw, Poland, diploma, 1939. *Home and office:* 3 Sweetcake Mountain Road, New Fairfield, Conn.

CAREER: Artist and illustrator. Lived in Italy, 1946-51, teaching at Academy of Fine Arts, Rome, and exhibiting at art shows and galleries, including Roman Foundation of Fine Arts Show and the International Exposition Biennale, in Genoa, both 1951; came to United States in 1952, and worked as textile designer, 1952-56; exhibited at Studio 3 and Kew Gardens, both New York City, 1959, and at one-man shows in the New York area, including three exhibitions at Lynn Kottler Galleries. Returned to exhibit work in Poland, 1972. Paintings owned by Warsaw's Museum of Modern Art and private galleries in Rome, Italy.

AWARDS, HONORS: *The Golden Seed* was exhibited in the American Institute of Graphic Arts Children's Book Show, 1962, and received first place certificate from the Printing Industries of Metropolitan New York, 1963; *The Coconut Thieves* was a prize book in the *New York Herald Tribune* Children's Book Festival, 1964, was listed as a notable children's book of 1964 by the American Library Association, and was exhibited in the American Institute of Graphic Arts Children's Book Show, 1964; *If All the Seas Were One Sea* was listed as a notable children's book of 1971 by the American Library Association, and was an Honor Book for the Caldecott Medal, 1972.

WRITINGS—All self-illustrated: (Translator from the Polish) Maria Konopnicka, *The Golden Seed,* adapted by Catharine Fournier, Scribner, 1962; (translator from the Polish) *The Coconut Thieves,* adapted by Catharine Fournier, Scribner, 1964; (adapter) *Why So Much Noise?,* Harper, 1964; *Palmiero and the Orge,* Macmillan, 1967; *Look, There Is a Turtle Flying,* Macmillan, 1968; (adapter) *The Turnip,* Macmillan, 1969; *Marilka,* Macmillan, 1970; *If All the Seas Were One Sea,* Macmillan, 1971; *I Saw a Ship A-Sailing* (Junior Literary Guild selection), Macmillan, 1972; (adapter) *Little Red Hen,* Macmillan, 1973; *What Do You See?,* Macmillan, 1974; (adapter from the Polish Christmas carole) *Din Dan Don, It's Christmas,* Greenwillow, 1975; *Spring Is,* Greenwillow, 1976; (adapter from an African folktale) *The Tortoise and the Tree,* Greenwillow, 1978; *King Krakus and the Dragon,* Greenwillow, 1979; (adapter from the Russian folktale) *A Scythe, a Rooster, and a Cat,* Greenwillow, 1981; *Marek, the Little Fool,* Greenwillow, 1982.

Illustrator: Alma R. Reck, *Clocks Tell the Time,* Scribner, 1960; Dorothy Kunhardt, *Gas Station Gus,* Harper, 1961; Natalie Savage Carlson, *Song of the Lop-Eared Mule,* Harper, 1961; Astrid Lindgren, *Mischievous Meg,* Viking, 1962; Aileen Fisher, *I Like Weather,* Crowell, 1963; Mara Kay, *In Place of Katia,* Scribner, 1963; Sally P. Johnson, *Harper Book of Princes,* Harper, 1964; Ruth Tooze, *Nikkos of the Pink Pelican,* Viking, 1964; Babette Deutsch and Avram Yarmolinsky, editors, *More Tales of Faraway Folk,* Harper, 1964; Deutsch and Yarmolinsky, *Steel Flea,* Harper, 1964; Bernice Kohn, *Light,* Coward, 1965; Dorothy Hogue, *The Black Heart of Indri,* Scribner, 1966; Eric P. Kelly, *Trumpeter of Krakow,* Macmillan, 1966; Jerzy Laskowski, *The Dragon Liked Smoked Fish,* Seabury, 1967; Laskowski, *Master of the Royal Cats,* Seabury, 1967; Elizabeth Coatsworth, *Under the Green Willow,* Macmillan,

1971; Edward Lear, *Whizz!*, Macmillan, 1973; *The Fifth Day* (anthology of poems for children), edited by Mary Q. Steele, Greenwillow, 1978; Jacob and Wilhelm Grimm, *The Bremen Town Musicians*, translation from the German by Elizabeth Shub, Greenwillow, 1980. Also illustrator of other childrens books. Drawings have appeared in *Harper's, Reporter,* and other magazines.

SIDELIGHTS: After the Nazi invasion of Poland, Janina Domanska was imprisoned in a concentration camp but was released when a Polish doctor claimed she was his relative in order to have her paint portraits of his family.

BIOGRAPHICAL/CRITICAL SOURCES: Hartford Courant, June 2, 1974; *Authors in the News,* Volume I, Gale, 1976.†

*   *   *

DONALDSON, Scott   1928-

PERSONAL: Born November 11, 1928, in Minneapolis, Minn.; son of Frank A. (a manufacturer) and Ruth E. (Chase) Donaldson; married Winifred M. Davis, December 27, 1953 (died July 28, 1954); married Janet K. Mikelson, April 12, 1958 (divorced, February, 1982); married Vivian Breckenridge, March 5, 1982; children: (second marriage) Matthew Chase, Stephen Scott, Andrew Wilson. *Education:* Yale University, B.A., 1951; University of Minnesota, M.A., 1952, Ph.D., 1966. *Home:* 100 Winsterfax, Williamsburg, Va. 23185. *Office:* College of William and Mary, Williamsburg, Va. 23185.

CAREER: Minneapolis Star, Minneapolis, Minn., reporter, 1956-58; *Bloomington Sun-Suburbanite,* Bloomington, Minn., editor-publisher, 1959-63; University of Minnesota, Minneapolis, instructor in humanities and American literature, 1963-66; College of William and Mary, Williamsburg, Va., 1966—, began as associate professor, currently professor of American literature. Fulbright lecturer in Turku, Finland, 1970-71; visiting professor, University of Leeds, Leeds, England, 1972-73; visiting fellow, Princeton University, 1978; Fulbright senior lecturer, Milan, Italy, 1979; fellow, MacDowell Colony, 1980-81; research fellow, Villa Serbelloni, Italy, 1982. *Military service:* U.S. Army, 1953-56. *Member:* American Studies Association, Modern Language Association of America, Organization of American Historians, Fulbright Alumni Association, Sigma Delta Chi.

WRITINGS: The Making of a Suburb, Bloomington (Minn.) Historical Society, 1964; *The Suburban Myth,* Columbia University Press, 1969.

Poet in America: Winfield Townley Scott, University of Texas Press, 1972; *By Force of Will: The Life and Art of Ernest Hemingway,* Viking, 1977; (with Ann Massa) *American Literature: Nineteenth and Early Twentieth Centuries,* Barnes & Noble, 1978; (editor) Jack Kerouac, *On the Road,* Viking, 1979; (contributor) *American Writers,* Supplement I, Part I, Scribner, 1979.

(Contributor) *American Literary Scholarship: 1980,* Duke University, 1982; (contributor) *American Literary Scholarship: 1981,* Duke University, 1983; *Fool for Love: F. Scott Fitzgerald,* Congdon & Weed, 1983; (editor) *Critical Essays on "The Great Gatsby,"* G. K. Hall, 1983-84; (editor) Harold Frederic, *The Damnation of Theron Ware,* Viking, 1984. Contributor to *Sewanee Review, American Literature, Modern Fiction Studies,* and other journals.

WORK IN PROGRESS: A critical biography of John Cheever.

SIDELIGHTS: "My principal interest is in the American experience," Scott Donaldson writes, "particularly as it finds shape and is expressed in the nation's literature."

BIOGRAPHICAL/CRITICAL SOURCES: New York Times, April 19, 1977; *New York Times Book Review,* April 24, 1977.

*   *   *

DONSON, Cyril   1919-
   (Lonny Cordis, Via Hartford, Russ Kidd, Anita Mackin)

PERSONAL: Born May 26, 1919, in Mexborough, Yorkshire, England; son of Ernest (a coal miner) and Ada (Wagstaffe) Donson; married Dorothy Denham (a teacher), May 23, 1942; children: Valerie Norma Noble. *Education:* Educated at Bristol College, Loughborough College, and University of Nottingham; received Teacher's Certificates in psychology and education, and Diploma of Loughborough College, 1950. *Politics:* Liberal. *Religion:* Nonconformist. *Home and office:* 24 Eaton Close, Hartford, Huntingdonshire, England.

CAREER: Newspaper journalist in England, 1941-43; schoolmaster, 1944-62, intermittently deputy headmaster and head of handicraft department in a bilateral school; public relations officer for a short period in 1964; writer. *Military service:* Royal Air Force, 1936-40. *Member:* Royal Society of Arts, Crime Writers' Association, Western Writers. *Awards, honors:* Nominated for Tom Gallon Trust Award as best short-story writer.

WRITINGS—Published by R. Hale, except as indicated: (With Armand Georges) *Lonelyland: A Panorama of Loneliness, from Childhood to the "Sunset Years,"* [and] *Bedsitterland: One-room Living; A Contribution towards a Greater Understanding and Awareness of the Loneliness Scene and the Problems of the Lonely,* Bala Press, 1967; *Born in Space,* 1968; *The Perspective Process,* 1969; *Tritonastra: Planet of the Gargantua,* 1969; *Draco the Dragon* (horror novel), New English Library, 1974; *Make Your Own Wooden Toys,* Arrow, 1975; *Guide to Authors,* Venton, 1976; *Ghost Town Marshall,* 1982; *Battle for Bear Head Creek,* 1982; *The Man from Wyoming,* 1982; *Banner's Back from Boothill,* 1983; *Vengeance Ride to Mesa,* 1983; *Town Tamer from Texas,* 1983; *Trouble Brand,* 1984; *Borrowed Badge,* 1984; *The Merciless Marshall,* 1984. Also author of three crossword puzzle books.

Under pseudonym Russ Kidd; all published by Ward, Lock: *Brannan of the Bar B,* 1964; *Thunder at Bushwhack,* 1965, Arcadia House, 1967; *Jinx Ranch,* 1966; *Gun Law at Concho Creek,* 1966; *Throw a Tall Shadow,* 1967; *Fight for Circle C,* 1967; *Dead Man's Colts,* 1968. Writer of romantic short stories for women under pseudonym Via Hartford and other short stories under pseudonyms Lonny Cordis and Anita Mackin. Past editor of various county magazines.

SIDELIGHTS: Cyril Donson told *CA:* "I presently write to make a living. But were this not necessary I would still be a compulsive writer, as I have been since the age of fourteen years.

"Present day trends in 'literature' I largely deprecate. As I see it, writing today has been desecrated to come down to the general level of human morals, standards, etc. But I do believe, and have always done, that a writer can say what he wants to say in any kind of wrapping, be it of the highest quality or closer to the gutter.

"My advice to aspiring writers would be simply . . . DON'T. There is no lonelier, more difficult occupation. If the would-be writer still persists, I would then warn him or her to watch out for the sharks, ever ready to cream off profit from the author's creative skill. My own experience has sadly included the copyright in one book ignored by a publisher, my work being sold without my knowledge by agents abroad, being left unpaid for work ordered by agents abroad (including some in America). And there is little protection against this."

*   *   *

DOODY, Margaret (Anne)   1939-

PERSONAL: Born September 21, 1939, in St. John, New Brunswick, Canada; daughter of Hubert (an Anglican clergyman) and Anne (a social worker; maiden name, Cornwall) Doody. *Education:* Dalhousie University, B.A. (with honors), 1960; Lady Margaret Hall, Oxford, B.A. (with first class honors), 1962, D.Phil., 1968. *Politics:* "Much the same as Dr. Johnson's." *Religion:* Anglican. *Residence:* Princeton, N.J. *Office:* Department of English, McCosh 22, Princeton University, Princeton, N.J. 08544.

CAREER: University of Victoria, Victoria, British Columbia, instructor, 1962-64, assistant professor of English, 1968-69; University of Wales, University College, Swansea, lecturer in English, 1969-76; University of California, Berkeley, visiting associate professor, 1976-77, associate professor of English, 1977-80; Princeton University, Princeton, N.J., professor of English, 1980—. *Member:* Modern Language Association (on eighteenth-century panel). *Awards, honors:* Guggenheim fellow, 1978; American Philosophical Society research grant, 1982.

WRITINGS: A Natural Passion: A Study of the Novels of Samuel Richardson, Clarendon Press, 1974; *Aristotle Detective* (novel), Bodley Head, 1978, Harper, 1980; *The Alchemists* (novel), Bodley Head, 1980; (contributor) Ricks and Michaels, editors, *The State of the Language,* University of California Press, 1980; (author of introduction) Samuel Richardson, *Pamela,* edited by Peter Sabor, Penguin, 1981; (contributor) Martin and Mullen, editors, *No Alternative: The Prayer Book Controversy,* Basil Blackwell, 1981.

Also co-author with Florian Stuber of Act I of "Clarissa: A Theater Work" (based on Richardson's novel *Clarissa*), first produced in Directors' Lab, Circle Rep., New York, N.Y., 1983. Contributor to *Times Literary Supplement.* Advisor, *Studies in English Literature.*

WORK IN PROGRESS: Bread of Independence: The Working Woman in Eighteenth-Century Fiction; Augustan Poetry, for Cambridge University Press; *Fanny Burney: The Achievement of an Eighteenth-Century Woman; Aristotle and Poetic Justice,* another detective novel; *Bath Cats,* a children's book; completing, with Stuber, "Clarissa: A Theater Work," a dramatization of Richardson's novel.

SIDELIGHTS: Margaret Doody told *CA:* "I find that the academic life and the writing of detective stories mesh quite nicely. I look forward to escaping from the eighteenth century from time to time (it seems so very modern to me) and going back to ancient Greece with Aristotle, my Sherlock Holmes. A recent venture into drama has convinced me that I want to stay there. I have several plans for plays, but first Florian Stuber and I must complete our dramatization of Richardson's *Clarissa*—a monumental undertaking, and totally rewarding. I am very grateful for the chance of working with professional actors under the aegis of Circle Rep Directors' Lab in May, 1983."

Aristotle Detective has been translated into Italian, French, and German.

AVOCATIONAL INTERESTS: Detective stories, children's books, theatre, travel.

BIOGRAPHICAL/CRITICAL SOURCES: Times Literary Supplement, November 10, 1978, April 25, 1980.

*   *   *

DOULIS, Thomas   1931-

PERSONAL: Born December 31, 1931, in Vandergrift, Pa.; son of John and Argiro (Stradis) Doulis; married Nancy Ritter (a mathematics teacher), July 8, 1962; children: John Randolph, Dion Argent. *Education:* La Salle College, B.A., 1955; Stanford University, M.A., 1963. *Religion:* Greek Orthodox. *Home:* 2236 Northeast Regents Dr., Portland, Ore. 97212. *Agent:* Gunther Stuhlmann, P.O. Box 276, Becket, Mass. 01223. *Office:* Department of English, Portland State University, Portland, Ore. 97207.

CAREER: Friends' Select School, Philadelphia, Pa., teacher of American literature, 1960-62; Philadelphia College of Art, Philadelphia, assistant professor, 1962-68; Fulbright Foundation resident in Athens, Greece, 1968-70, and Exeter College, Oxford University, 1970-72; Portland State University, Portland, Ore., 1972—, began as associate professor, currently professor of English and creative writing. *Military service:* U.S. Army, 1957-59. *Member:* American Association of University Professors, Modern Greek Studies Association, McDowell Colonists. *Awards, honors:* American Council of Learned Societies grant, 1980-81.

WRITINGS: Path for Our Valor (novel), Simon & Schuster, 1963; *The Quarries of Sicily* (novel), Crown, 1969; *George Theotokas* (biography), Twayne, 1975; *Disaster and Fiction: The Impact of the Asia Minor Disaster of 1922 on Modern Greek Fiction,* University of California Press, 1977; *A Surge to the Sea: The Greeks in Oregon,* Jack Lockie Associates, 1977; *Landmarks of Our Past: The First Twenty-five Years of the Greek Orthodoxy Community of Oregon,* Gann Publishing, 1983.

Also author of *Moments of Grace.* Translator of Greek verse and poetry. Contributor of numerous articles to various encyclopedias. Contributor of short stories, poetry, and reviews to *Four Quarters, Athene, Virginia Quarterly Review, Hellenic Journal,* and other periodicals; also contributor of numerous articles on Greek literature to *Northwest Review, American Scholar, Chicago Review, Popular Culture Quarterly,* and other journals.

WORK IN PROGRESS: Generations of Leaves, a fictional trilogy about the Americanization of a Greek family that spans the twentieth century; *Precursors,* a critical analysis of nineteenth-century Greek fiction.

SIDELIGHTS: In a review of Thomas Doulis's *The Quarries of Sicily,* Fred Rotondaro states in *Best Sellers* that this "is an excellent novel that tells an interesting story of interesting people, that comments on several aspects of contemporary life, including man's ability to face the unknown world." R. F. Cayton remarks in *Library Journal* that in this novel Doulis "writes with passion and maturity, and his characters are finely done, humanly flawed, and understandable." And a critic for the *Virginia Quarterly Review* comments that *The Quarries of Sicily* is "an intelligently presented, pleasantly literate narrative."

Of his work in progress, Doulis explained to *CA:* "In many respects, *Generations of Leaves* will be the major effort of the present decade for me, since it will demand my researching the American reality from the era before the First World War to the 1980s. Volume I . . . has required my being familiar with the generation of the immigrant working class whose members established families, businesses, tightly-knit ethnic communities, and churches in the new land. Volume II will demand familiarity with the American-born generation that came of age in time for World War II, returned to a post-war society that abandoned the old cities and moved to the suburbs, taking with them their intelligence and vitality. Volume III, finally, will treat the fully American generation which, while trying to identify with an ethnic past they can no longer understand, confront a world as dangerous as ever with a sense that they represent a great nation in disarray after the Vietnam experience that has divided them from their parents' generation."

BIOGRAPHICAL/CRITICAL SOURCES: Book World, July 6, 1969; *Best Sellers,* July 15, 1969; *Library Journal,* October 1, 1969; *Carleton Miscellany,* winter, 1970; *Virginia Quarterly Review,* winter, 1970.

*   *   *

DOWN, Goldie (Malvern)   1918-

PERSONAL: Born June 26, 1918, in Sydney, Australia; daughter of Herbert William (an insurance inspector) and Violet Marie (Knox) Scarr; married David Kyrle Down (a clergyman), September 8, 1946; children: Kendall, Glenda, Michele, Teddy, Richley, another daughter (adopted). *Education:* Attended Avondale College (New South Wales, Australia), 1940-42. *Home:* 2 Neridah Ave., Mount Colah 2079, Australia.

CAREER: Secretary in Australia, 1943-44; Seventh-Day Adventist missionary with her husband, in India, 1953-73; teacher of creative writing to adult students, principally at government evening colleges, 1976—; free-lance writer. *Awards, honors:* Second prize in *Write Now* competition, Review & Herald, for *Fear Was the Pursuer.*

WRITINGS—Published by Review & Herald: *Missionary to Calcutta,* 1958; *Their Kind of Courage,* 1973; *Kerri and Company,* 1978; *You Never Can Tell When You May Meet a Leopard,* 1980; *Fear Was the Pursuer,* 1981; *Missionaries Don't Cry,* 1981; *Like Fire in His Veins,* 1982; *We Gotta Tell Them, Edie,* 1982.

Published by Southern Publishing: *Twenty-One Thousand Miles of Adventure,* 1964; *God Plucked a Violet,* 1968; *If I Have Twelve Sons,* 1968; *No Forty Hour Week,* 1977; *More Lives Than a Cat,* 1979.

Contributor of numerous stories and articles to church and health periodicals.

WORK IN PROGRESS: Research for a report on one hundred years of progress in the work for the children and youth of the Seventh-Day Adventist Church in Australasia, to be incorporated in a book published to mark the centenary.

SIDELIGHTS: Goldie Down told *CA* that three of the five Down children completed their entire twelve years of schooling in India by correspondence, with her help, before they returned to Australia to do college work. Three times the entire family travelled overland by jeep and trailer from India through the Middle East, and twice on to Europe and England. In addition to their own five children, the Downs have an adopted Indian daughter. Down claims to be a compulsive writer and writes solely for her own pleasure, hoping that those who read her writings may also be entertained, instructed, or amused by her efforts. She explained that her writings are all truth, not fiction.

*   *   *

DOYLE, Charles (Desmond)   1928-   (Mike Doyle)

PERSONAL: Born October 18, 1928, in Birmingham, England; son of Charles and Mary (Carroll) Doyle; married Helen Merlyn Lopdell, November 26, 1952 (deceased); married Doran Ross Smithells, July 28, 1959; children: (second marriage) Aaron William, Patrick Haakon, Kegan Ross, Mary Elizabeth Katharine. *Education:* Victoria University College, University of New Zealand (now Victoria University of Wellington), B.A., 1956, M.A. (honors), 1958; Wellington Teachers' College, Diploma of Teaching, 1955; University of Auckland, Ph.D., 1968. *Politics:* "Socialist anarchist." *Religion:* Catholic. *Home:* 759 Helvetia Crescent, Victoria, British Columbia, Canada. *Office:* Department of English, University of Victoria, Victoria, British Columbia, Canada.

CAREER: University of Auckland, Auckland, New Zealand, lecturer, 1961-66, senior lecturer in English and American literature, 1966-68; University of Victoria, Victoria, British Columbia, associate professor, 1968-76, professor of English and American literature, 1976—. Visiting fellow in American studies, Yale University, 1967-68. *Military service:* Royal Navy. *Member:* League of Canadian Poets, Canadian Union of Writers, Canadian Association of University Teachers. *Awards, honors:* UNESCO creative artist's fellowship, 1959; American Council of Learned Societies fellow at Yale University, 1967-68; Canada Council grants, 1971, 1972, fellowship, 1974-75.

WRITINGS—Poetry: *A Splinter of Glass: Poems, 1951-56,* Pegasus, 1956; (with James K. Baxter, Louis Johnson, and Kendrick Smithyman) *The Night Shift: Poems on Aspects of Love,* Capricorn Press, 1957; *Distances: Poems, 1956-61,* Paul's Book Arcade (Auckland), 1963; *Messages for Herod,* Collins, 1965; *A Sense of Place,* Wai-te-Ata Press, 1965; *Earth Meditations: 2,* Alldritt, 1968; *Noah,* Soft Press, 1970; (under pseudonym Mike Doyle) *Abandoned Sofa,* Soft Press, 1971; (under pseudonym Mike Doyle) *Earth Meditations: One to Five,* Coach House Press, 1971; (under pseudonym Mike Doyle) *Earth Shot,* Exeter Books, 1972; (under pseudonym Mike Doyle) *Preparing for the Ark,* Weed/Flower Press, 1973; (under pseudonym Mike Doyle) *Planes,* Seripress, 1975; (under pseudonym Mike Doyle) *Stone-dancer,* Oxford University Press, 1976; (under pseudonym Mike Doyle) *A Steady Hand,* Porcupine's Quill, Auckland University Press, 1983.

Nonfiction: (Editor) *Recent Poetry in New Zealand,* Collins, 1965; *Small Prophets and Quick Returns: Reflections on New Zealand Poetry,* New Zealand Publishing Society, 1966; *R.A.K. Mason,* Twayne, 1970; *James K. Baxter,* Twayne, 1976; (editor) *William Carlos Williams: The Critical Heritage,* Routledge & Kegan Paul, 1980; *William Carlos Williams and the American Poem,* Macmillan, 1982.

Poetry represented in nine anthologies, including: *Twentieth Century New Zealand Poetry,* edited by Vincent O'Sullivan, Oxford University Press, 1970; *Contemporary Poetry of British Columbia,* edited by J. M. Yates, Sono Nis, 1970; *New Zealand Poetry: An Introduction,* edited by F. M. McKay, New Zealand University Press, 1970. Contributor of poetry to periodicals, and critical essays to professional journals.

WORK IN PROGRESS: A biographical study of Richard Aldington; a study of Wallace Stevens.

SIDELIGHTS: Charles Doyle wrote *CA:* "Unless we can bring about multilateral armaments control in the very near future, nothing else is going to matter." *Avocational interests:* Modern American poetry, mythology, ethnopoetics, Jung, Taoism.

*   *   *

DOYLE, Mike
    See DOYLE, Charles (Desmond)

*   *   *

DRAKE, George Randolph   1938-

PERSONAL: Born March 27, 1938, in Trenton, N.J.; son of Edward H. (an administrator for New Jersey state highway department) and Catharine (Hunt) Drake; married Mary J. Margerum (a speech therapist), October 1, 1960; children: Natalie J., Jeffrey E., Paul R. *Education:* Attended Bucknell University, 1956-58; Temple University, A.E.T., 1961; University of Baltimore, B.S., 1969. *Home and office:* 503 Raven Rock Ct., Parkton, Md. 21120.

CAREER: Martin-Marietta Corp., Baltimore, Md., technical writer and instructor for Gemini Space Program, 1961-67; AAI Corp., Cockeysville, Md., publications and training manager, 1969-74; free-lance writer, 1974—. Consultant to business, industry, and government. *Member:* American Society for Training and Development (member of board of directors, 1976-77).

WRITINGS—Published by Reston, except as indicated: *Everyone's Book of Hand and Small Power Tools,* 1974; *The Complete Handbook of Power Tools,* 1975; *The Repair and Maintenance of Small Gasoline Engines,* 1976; *The Repair and Servicing of Small Appliances,* 1977; *Weatherizing Your Home,* 1978; *Routercraft,* Black & Decker, 1979; *Small Gasoline Engines: Maintenance, Troubleshooting, and Repair,* 1981; *The Rotary Hobby Shop Handbook,* Black & Decker, 1982. Author of technical manuals. Contributor to popular magazines, including *Popular Science, Woman's World, Swimming World,* and *Yachting.*

WORK IN PROGRESS: Owner's manuals, for Black & Decker; technical manuals, for various firms, including Bendix Corp., Amstar Corp., and Gould, Inc.

SIDELIGHTS: George Randolph Drake describes his writing briefly, "My concerns (and hence written materials) are for the do-it-yourselfer—the detailed step by step how-to-do-it-yourself for self-satisfaction and dollar savings." *Avocational interests:* Woodworking, photography, amateur radio, sailing, swimming (Red Cross swimming instructor), computer programming.

*   *   *

DROIT, Michel (Arnould Arthur)   1923-

PERSONAL: Born January 23, 1923, in Vincennes, France; son of Jean (an artist) and Suzanne (Plisson) Droit; married Janine Bazin, January 20, 1947; children: Corinne, Eric. *Education:* University of Paris, Faculte des Lettres, Licence es Lettres, 1944; Ecole Libre des Sciences Politiques, diploma, 1944. *Address:* 76 rue Spontini, 75116 Paris, France.

CAREER: War correspondent with French Army and U.S. Army, 1944-45; reporter for newspapers, radio, and television in Paris,

France, 1944-56; foreign affairs commentator for French television, 1956-60; editor-in-chief of television news service "Tribunes et debats," Radio Diffusion-Television Francaise, 1960-61; *Le Figaro litteraire,* Paris, editor-in-chief, 1961-71; *Le Figaro,* Paris, management advisor, 1971—. Producer of television programs "A propos," 1962-74, and "Ces Annees la," 1975. Advisory editor, La Librairie Plon, 1968. Chairman, Safaris de la Ouandjia-Vakaga, Central African Republic. *Member:* International P.E.N., Academie Francaise, Association des Grands Reporters Francais, Societe des Auteurs Dramatiques, Maison de la Chasse et de la Nature, Comite Francais des Grandes Chasses, Association des Chasseurs Professionnels d'Afrique Francophone.

AWARDS, HONORS: Croix de Guerre; Medaille Militaire, Chevalier de la Legion d'Honneur; Officier de l'Ordre National du Merite; Prix Max Barthou, 1955, for *Plus rien au monde;* Prix Carlos de Lazerme, 1961, and Grand Prix Rhodanian de Litterature, both for *La Camargue;* Grand Prix du Roman de l'Academie Francaise, 1964, for *Le Retour;* Prix Edmond-Michelet, 1972, for filmscript of documentary "Un Francais libre"; Prix Malherbe, 1975, for *La Coupe est pleine.*

WRITINGS: De Lattre, Marechal de France, P. Horay, 1952; *Chez les mangeurs d'hommes: Cinquante annees de luttes apostoliques en Papouasie,* Table Ronde, 1952; *Jours et nuits d'Amerique,* Nizet, 1952; *Andre Maurois,* Editions Universitaires, 1953, 2nd edition, 1958; *Plus rien au monde* (novel), Ferenczi, 1954, published as *L'Ecorche,* Julliard, 1968; *Visas pour l'Amerique du Sud,* Gallimard, 1956; *Pueblo* (novel), Julliard, 1957, translation by Edward Hyams published under same title, Eyre & Spottiswoode, 1959; *J'ai vu vivre le japon,* Fayard, 1958; *Panoramas mexicains,* Fayard, 1960; *La Camargue,* Arthaud, 1961, translation by Ernest Heimann and Adair Heimann published as *Camargue,* Rand McNally, 1963; (editor) *Michel Droit presente le Japon vu par Michel Hetier,* G. Victor, 1964; *Le Retour* (novel), Julliard, 1964, translation by Olwyn Hughes published as *The Return,* Deutsch, 1966; *Le Temps des hommes,* Julliard, Volume I: *Les Compagnons de la foret noire* (novel), 1966, Volume II: *L'Orient perdu* (nonfiction), 1969, Volume III: *La Ville blanche,* 1973, Volume IV: *La Mort du connetable,* 1976; *A propos,* R. Solar, 1967.

Hambourg, P. Cailler, 1970; *L'Homme du destin: Charles de Gaulle,* Larrieu-Bonnel, 1972, Volume I: *La Resistance,* Volume II: *La Liberation,* Volume III: *Le Retour,* Volume IV: *L'Achevement,* Volume V: *Documents et archives;* (author of introduction) *XXIVe Salon du dessin et de la peinture a l'eau: Grand Palais des Champs-Elysees, du 17 mai au 16 juin 1974* (exhibition catalog), Imprimerie Municipale (Paris), 1974; *La Coupe est pleine,* Editions France-Empire, 1975; (author of introduction) *Michel Ciry,* Ides et Calendes, 1977; *Les Feux du crepuscule:Journal, 1968-1969-1970,* Plon, 1977; *Les Clartes du jour: Journal, 1963-1964-1965,* Plon, 1978.

Also author of a collection of short stories, *La Fille de l'ancre bleue,* of radio and television scripts, including "Les Roses de septembre" (adapted from the work of Andre Maurois), "Les Pelouses de Bagatelle" (adapted from the work of Pulman), and "De tres chers amis" (adapted from the work of R. Rose), and of a documentary film script on the life of Charles de Gaulle, "Un Francais libre."

WORK IN PROGRESS: Several novels.

SIDELIGHTS: Michel Droit is the only journalist to have interviewed Charles de Gaulle on television. His conversations with the late French general and president occurred in December, 1965, June, 1968, and April, 1969. *Avocational interests:* Travel, big game hunting, skin-diving, judo, karate, jazz music, collecting paintings and exotic objects.

*   *   *

DUIGNAN, Peter   1926-

PERSONAL: Surname is pronounced Deg-nan; born August 6, 1926, in San Francisco, Calif.; son of Peter James (a fireman) and Delia (Conway) Duignan; married Francis Helen Sharpe, August 13, 1949; children: one son, five daughters. *Education:* University of San Francisco, B.S. (cum laude), 1951; Stanford University, M.A., 1953, Ph.D., 1960. *Religion:* Roman Catholic. *Home:* 939 Casanueva, Stanford, Calif. *Office:* Hoover Institution on War, Revolution and Peace, Stanford University, Stanford, Calif. 94305.

CAREER: Stanford University, Stanford, Calif., instructor in Western civilization, 1957-60, curator of African Collection, Hoover Institution on War, Revolution and Peace, 1959—, research associate of Hoover Institution on War, Revolution and Peace, 1962-65, director of African program, 1965—, coordinator of international studies, 1980—. *Military service:* U.S. Army, 1944-46; served in South Pacific; received Combat Infantry Badge. *Member:* American Civil Liberties Union, National Association for the Advancement of Colored People, American Historical Association, American Political Science Association, African Studies Association, Bibliographical Society of America. *Awards, honors:* Ford Foundation fellow in Africa, 1958-59; Rockefeller Foundation international fellowship, 1963-64; Guggenheim fellowship, 1973.

WRITINGS: (With Lewis H. Gann) *White Settlers in Tropical Africa,* Penguin, 1962, reprinted, Greenwood Press, 1977; (contributor) Rogers and Frantz, editors, *Racial Themes in Southern Rhodesia,* Yale University Press, 1962; (with Clarence C. Clendenen) *The United States and the Slave Trade, 1619-1865,* Hoover Institution Press, 1963, reprinted, Greenwood Press, 1978; (with Kenneth Glazier) *A Checklist of African Serials, Based on the Hoover Institution and Stanford University Libraries,* Hoover Institution, 1963; (co-author) *Americans in Africa: A Preliminary Guide to American Missionary Archives and Library Manuscript Collections on Africa,* Hoover Institution, 1963; (co-author) *Americans in Black Africa up to 1865,* Hoover Institution, 1964; (with C. C. Clendenen) *Americans in Africa: 1865-1900,* Stanford University, 1966; *Handbook of American Resources for African Studies,* Stanford University, 1967; (with Gann) *Burden of Empire: An Appraisal of Western Colonialism in Africa South of the Sahara,* Praeger, 1967.

(With others) *African and Middle East Collections: A Survey of Holdings at the Hoover Institution on War, Revolution and Peace,* Hoover Institution, 1971; (with others) *Africa South of the Sahara: A Bibliography for Undergraduate Libraries,* Bro-Dart Publishing, 1971; (with Gann) *Africa and the World: An Introduction to the History of Sub-Saharan Africa from Antiquity to 1840,* Chandler Publishing, 1972; (with Gann) *Africa: The Land and the People,* Chandler Publishing, 1972; (with Gann) *The Rulers of German Africa: 1884-1914,* Stanford University Press, 1977; (with Gann) *The Rulers of British Africa, 1870-1914,* Stanford University Press, 1978; (with Gann) *South Africa: War, Revolution, or Peace?,* Hoover Institution Press, 1978, published as *The Stability of South Africa, or Why South Africa Will Survive,* 1980, new edition published as *Why South Africa Will Survive: A Historical Analysis,* St. Martin's, 1981;

(with Gann) *The Rulers of Belgian Africa, 1884-1914,* Princeton University Press, 1979; (with Gann) *Africa South of the Sahara: The Challenge to Western Security,* Hoover Institution Press, 1981; (with Gann) *The Middle East and North Africa: The Challenge to Western Security,* Hoover Institution Press, 1981.

Editor: *Colonialism in Africa, 1870-1960,* Cambridge University Press, Volume I: *The History and Politics of Colonialism, 1870-1914,* 1969, Volume II: *The History and Politics of Colonialism, 1914-1960,* 1970, Volume V: *A Bibliographical Guide to Colonialism in Sub-Saharan Africa,* 1974, Volume IV: *The Economics of Colonialism,* 1975; (and compiler with Helen F. Conover) *Guide to Research and Reference Works on Sub-Saharan Africa,* Hoover Institution, 1971; (with Gann) *African Proconsuls: European Governors in Africa,* Free Press, 1978; (with Alvin Rabushka) *The United States in the 1980s,* Hoover Institution Press, 1980, abridged edition, Addison-Wesley, 1980.

Contributor to *American Anthropologist, National Review, New Leader,* and to political science journals. Editor of *American and Canadian Publications on Africa* (annual), 1961—, of *Africana Newsletter* (quarterly), 1962-64, and of *African Studies Bulletin,* 1965—.

SIDELIGHTS: The United States in the 1980s, edited by Peter Duignan and Alvin Rabushka, "read[s] as if [it] were a series of position papers written for Ronald Reagan," states Arthur S. Miller in *Washington Post Book World.* A collection of essays on economics, labor, foreign policy, national defense, energy, taxes, health care, housing, arms control, the welfare system, and the military published by the conservative Hoover Institution on War, Revolution and Peace at Stanford University, *The United States in the 1980s* defines the problems of the current system and states plans to remedy them.

Published during the 1980 presidential campaign, the book's concurrence with Ronald Reagan's conservative fiscal and political ideology has not gone unremarked. John Dombrink in the *Progressive* writes that *The United States in the 1980s* "will probably rest on the Oval Office bookshelves like a copy of the *Physician's Desk Reference* in a doctor's office." Andrew Hacker in the *New York Review of Books* comments that the volume "can . . . be read as a ten-year plan for [Ronald Reagan's] presidency and beyond. Its thirty-three contributors include expected figures like Milton Friedman and Edward Teller, as well as Martin Anderson, now of the White House staff, and Murray Weidenbaum, the new chairman of the Council of Economic Advisors, whose advice will have a hearing in administration circles." An *Economist* critic suggests that "the reader who glances down [*The United States in the 1980s*'s] table of contents is likely to conclude that this vast volume contains the distilled advice of America's right-of-centre academics to the hoped for Republican presidents of the 1980s."

According to Miller, the underlying premise of *The United States in the 1980s* is that "the next decade will be, as the Hoover volume puts it, 'a harsher, more exacting, and more perilous age.' . . . Hoover's . . . experts believe that Adam Smith economics will help us 'save more than we spend, work more than we play, and spend more on defense and less on welfare.'" In Hacker's opinion, what the authors in *The United States in the 1980s* "propose, to put it simply, is that capitalism be given a chance to show what it can do. . . . [It] opens with the ('reputed') statement of Thomas Jefferson about how the best government governs least. In fact, its position is stalwartly Hamiltonian, although the father of American capitalism is not mentioned once in its 868 pages." For example, Hacker continues, "the Hoover authors would have business regain its pride of place among the nation's institutions, with those at its helm our foremost citizens. Others will understand that business must have a generous latitude to serve us at its best, and that competition rather than controls can give the country what it wants. 'The price mechanism,' the editors tell us, 'is the most efficient means by which to prevent environmental deterioration.' It is also in business's self-interest to ensure the safety of its personnel and products."

The authors of *The United States in the 1980s* advocate a decrease in government regulation, an increase in military spending because, they say, the Soviet Union is a greater threat than most Americans have been led to believe, and the abolishment of the welfare system except for those who are genuinely disabled, thus encouraging others to work, to succeed, to save, and to invest. Milton and Rose Friedman suggest a constitutional amendment establishing a "full-fledged laissez-faire economy," says Miller. Thomas Moore writes in the book that "private sector incentives, following the dictates of Adam Smith's invisible hand, will provide energy at the cost of finding and developing it." In the end, writes Dombrink in the *Progressive*, the contributors to *The United States in the 1980s* maintain that "in this decade . . . America faces serious political, economic, and military problems whose resolution will determine whether we enter the Twenty-first Century as a second-rate economic and military power or remain a guiding light of the 'free world.' To achieve the latter, the contributors argue, this country must reverse its thinking and resolve problems that are the result of misguided government activism in economic matters and a softening of the national will on foreign policy issues."

However, the *Economist* reviewer points out, a number of the solutions suggested in *The United States in the 1980s* conflict with others stated in the volume. "Essays that are actually consecutive contradict each other, giving a putative president a wide range of choice," the critic says. For example, one writer advocates the cessation of foreign grants, arguing that they are costly and useless, while another author views aid to the third world as beneficial to the truly poor and in America's "enlightened self interest." The critic also notes that there is "a striking dissonance" between the call for governmental limitation in domestic matters and the advocacy of increased military spending and the buildup of military strength that dominates the sections on U.S. foreign policy. Furthermore, the *Economist* writer notes, while "most of the essays are temperate and accomplished," it is also "disappointing in a book of this kind . . . [to find] the absence of any advice for dealing with America's fundamental economic problems: falling productivity, inflation and recession. . . . It seems that, rather than set the subjects to be dealt with, the editors (who changed in midstream) chose a group of experts and gave them their head."

Andrew Hacker in the *New York Review of Books* notes another contradiction in *The United States in the 1980s*. "The phrase that recurs throughout [the book] is 'individual freedom,'" he says. "This is not construed as the right to stage a demonstration or make a seditious speech. Rather it means the freedom to make as much money as you can, to keep virtually the entire amount, to spend it as you choose, and run your business as you will. One consequence may be that the rich will get even richer. However, this will benefit society, for dollars accruing to the well-to-do end up invested in economic ventures." Miller observes that "while denying that they want a 'garrison state,' their recommendations constitute precisely that."

The greatest benefit of publishing *The United States in the 1980s,* says Miller, is that "in implicitly asking Americans to think seriously about the 1980s (and beyond), the several authors have rendered a singular service. Not that such thought will come easily—or even at all. A nation of avowed pragmatists, we have a history of not recognizing problems until they become crises—until, that is, it is usually too late to mount a rational response." Dombrink concludes in his *Progressive* essay: "The contributors to this volume are not pessimists but activists, and the book represents a blueprint for the decade. The Hoover fellows represent a 'serious conservatism,' and they promise to have a lasting influence in the 1980s. They address fundamental questions that will not soon be resolved. The answers they provide are not inimical to ruling-class interests. They call for slight and only tactical changes in our major institutions, implying that any loss of legitimacy by these institutions is largely undeserved. And their work is of a high quality; they marshal evidence as well as emotion."

BIOGRAPHICAL/CRITICAL SOURCES: Peter Duignan and Alvin Rabushka, editors, *The United States in the 1980s,* Hoover Institution Press, 1980, abridged edition, Addison-Wesley, 1980; *Washington Post Book World,* May 25, 1980; *Economist,* July 19, 1980; *Progressive,* October, 1980; *New York Review of Books,* April 30, 1981.

—*Sketch by Heidi A. Tietjen*

*　　　*　　　*

DUKE, Charles (Richard) 1940-

PERSONAL: Born July 6, 1940, in West Stewartstown, N.H.; son of George T. and Evelyn (Murray) Duke; married Jonquelyn R. Simpson (a teacher), May 20, 1973; married second wife, Leona Blum, June 1, 1983. *Education:* Plymouth State College, B.Ed., 1962; Middlebury College, M.A., 1968; Duke University, Ph.D., 1972. *Home address:* P.O. Box 1043, Murray, Ky. 42071. *Office:* Department of English, Murray State University, Murray, Ky. 42071.

CAREER: High school English teacher and department chairman in Sunapee, N.H., 1962-68; Plymouth State College, Plymouth, N.H., instructor, 1968-72, assistant professor, 1972-73, associate professor of English, 1973-78; Murray State University, Murray, Ky., associate professor, 1978-81, professor of English, 1981—. Director of West Kentucky Writing Project.

MEMBER: International Reading Association, Association for Supervision and Curriculum Development, National Council of Teachers of English, American Association of University Professors, Modern Language Association of America, Conference on English Education, Association of Teachers of Advanced Composition, Council of Writing Program Administrators, Adolescent Literature Assembly, New England Association of Teachers of English (member of advisory board, 1973-74; publicity chairman, 1974-75; president-elect, 1976-77; president, 1977-78), Midwest Regional Conference on Teaching English in the Two Year College, Kentucky Philological Association, Kentucky Council of Teachers of English (vice-president, 1979-80; president, 1980-81), New Hampshire Association of Teachers of English (vice-president, 1971; president, 1973-77).

WRITINGS: (Editor) *Granite State Writers,* New Hampshire Association of Teachers of English, 1972; *Creative Dramatics and English Teaching,* National Council of Teachers of English, 1974; (contributor) R. Baird Shuman, editor, *Creative*

Approaches to the Teaching of English: Secondary, F. E. Peacock, 1974; *Teaching Fundamental English Today,* J. Weston Walch, 1976; (contributor) Shuman, editor, *Educational Drama for Today's Schools,* Scarecrow, 1978; *Teaching Literature Today,* J. Weston Walch, 1979.

(Contributor) Shuman, editor, *English for the 80's,* National Education Association, 1980; *Writing through Sequence: A Process Approach,* Little, Brown, 1983; (editor with Sally Jacobsen) *Reading and Writing Poetry: Successful Approaches for the Student and Teacher,* Oryx Press, 1983. Contributor of articles and reviews to English language journals. Editor of *Exercise Exchange.*

WORK IN PROGRESS: A book dealing with the teaching of English language skills; editing a collection of articles on the teaching of writing; researching a composition textbook for students.

SIDELIGHTS: Charles Duke told *CA:* "I find that my writing is almost always a direct product of my teaching interests; the books I have done thus far have grown out of classroom experiences and needs. My writing is addressed to definite audiences—the practicing teacher and students—and I derive a good deal of satisfaction from being able to translate theory into practical applications which can be of use to others."

AVOCATIONAL INTERESTS: Camping, fast European cars.

*   *   *

DUNBAR, David
   See BAXTER, Craig

*   *   *

DUNN, Jerry G.   1916-

PERSONAL: Born June 30, 1916, in Dayton, Ohio. *Education:* Attended Ohio Wesleyan University, Northwestern University, and Newspaper Institute of America. *Office address:* 1445 27th Ave., No. 8, Lewiston, Idaho 83901.

CAREER: A former advertising and public relations executive, Dunn says he "hit the alcoholic skids and came to his senses at the end of a two-year drunk when he picked up a Bible in a Texas prison cell"; following his release from prison, he worked for newspapers until entering the ministry; ordained Baptist minister; served a church in Union, Neb.; Open Door Mission, Omaha, Neb., director of public relations and rehabilitation, 1955-68; People's City Mission, Lincoln, Neb., executive director, 1968-80; lecturer and consultant, International Union of Gospel Missions, 1980; Warner Avenue Alliance Church, Lewiston, Idaho, associate pastor, 1981—. Lecturer at University of Nebraska School of Medicine, and for religious, civic, and other groups; conducts weekly half-hour television program "Slices from the Bread of Life" on Station KFAB, Omaha. Member of board of directors and executive committee of Lincoln Council on Alcoholism and Drugs; chairman of Comprehensive Alcoholic Planning Committee for Lancaster County, Neb.; vice-president of Better Lincoln Committee; member of Region IV Mental Health Planning Committee; vice-president in charge of education for Nebraska Council on Alcohol Education, Inc.

MEMBER: International Union of Gospel Missions (past president), Agency Executives Association of Lincoln Community Services, Lincoln Evangelical Minister's Fellowship (president), Omaha Press Club (honorary member), Rotary Inter-

national. *Awards, honors:* Service to Mankind Award, Sertoma Club, 1959; Good Neighbor Award, National Conference of Christians and Jews, 1962; Omaha Lion's Club public service award, 1965; Citizen of Year Award, Concord Club, 1965; Doulos (servant to community) Award, Lincoln Fellowship of Churches, 1975.

WRITINGS: God Is for the Alcoholic, Moody, 1965; *Alcoholic Victorious,* Moody, 1969; *Yeah, Why Not Try God?,* Light and Life Evangel, 1971; *The Christian in a Drinking Society,* Good News Broadcasting Association, 1974; *What Will You Have to Drink?,* Horizon House, 1980. Contributor to periodicals.

*   *   *

DUNN, John (Montfort)   1940-

PERSONAL: Born September 9, 1940, in Fulmer, England; son of Henry G. M. (an Army officer) and Catherine M. (Kinloch) Dunn; married Susan Fyvel, 1965 (divorced, 1973); married Judy Pace (a research psychologist), 1973. *Education:* Kings College, Cambridge, B.A. (with first class honors), 1962. *Politics:* "Democratic socialist." *Home:* 31 Station Rd., Swavesey, Cambridge CB4 5QJ, England. *Office:* Department of History and Politics, Kings College, Cambridge University, Cambridge CB2 1ST, England.

CAREER: Cambridge University, Cambridge, England, fellow of Jesus College, 1965-66, fellow and director of studies at Kings College, 1966—, lecturer in political science, 1972-77, reader in politics, 1977—. Visiting lecturer at University of Ghana, 1968-69; Cecil H. and Ida Green Visiting Professor at University of British Columbia, 1977; visiting professor at University of Bombay, 1979, and Tokyo Metropolitan University, 1983. *Member:* Political Studies Association of the United Kingdom, Past and Present Society, American Society for Political and Legal Philosophy.

WRITINGS—Published by Cambridge University Press, except as indicated: *The Political Thought of John Locke,* 1969; *Modern Revolutions: An Introduction to the Analysis of a Political Phenomenon,* 1972; (with A. F. Robertson) *Dependence and Opportunity: Political Change in Ahafo,* 1973; (editor) *West African States: Failure and Promise,* 1978; *Western Political Theory in the Face of the Future,* 1979; *Political Obligation in Its Historical Context,* 1980; *Locke,* Oxford University Press, 1984. Also author of *The Politics of Socialism,* 1984.

Contributor: John Yolton, editor, *John Locke: Problems and Perspectives,* Cambridge University Press, 1969; David Martin, editor, *Anarchy and Culture: The Problem of the Contemporary University,* Columbia University Press, 1969; Eric Homberger, William Janeway, and Simon Schama, editors, *The Cambridge Mind,* J. Cape, 1970; Gordon J. Schochet, editor, *Life, Liberty, and Property: Essays on Locke's Political Ideas,* Wadsworth, 1971; Peter Laslett, W. G. Runciman, and Quentin Skinner, editors, *Philosophy, Politics and Society,* fourth series, Blackwell, 1972; Dennis Austin and Robin Luckham, editors, *Politicians and Soldiers in Ghana 1966-1972,* F. Cass, 1975.

W. H. Morris-Jones, editor, *The Making of Politicians: Studies from Africa and Asia,* Athlone Press, 1976; C. Hookway and P. Pettit, editors, *Action and Interpretation: Studies in the Philosophy of Social Science,* Cambridge University Press, 1978; R. Brandt, editor, *John Locke: Symposium Wolfenbuettel 1979,* W. de Gruyter, 1981; Christopher Lloyd, editor, *Social Theory and Political Practice,* Oxford University Press, 1983. Contributor to journals of history, political studies, and philosophy, and to *Listener, London Review of Books,* and other periodicals.

WORK IN PROGRESS: Research for books on the political theory of post-colonial states, the development of the concept of revolution, and the fundamentals of political analysis.

SIDELIGHTS: John Dunn wrote: "All of my work is concerned with the effort to develop a less grossly inadequate understanding of the political realities of most of the world today than is at present provided either by American political science or sociology or by the self-conscious heirs of the social and political theories of Karl Marx."

*   *   *

DUNNE, Philip   1908-

PERSONAL: Born February 11, 1908, in New York, N.Y.; son of Finley Peter (a humorist) and Margaret (Abbott) Dunne; married Amanda Duff, July 15, 1939; children: Miranda, Philippa, Jessica. *Education:* Attended Middlesex School, 1920-25, and Harvard University, 1925-29. *Home:* 24708 Pacific Coast Hwy., Malibu, Calif. 90265.

CAREER: Twentieth Century-Fox Film Corp., and other studios, writer, producer, and director of films, beginning 1933. Director of "In Love and War," 1958, "Wild in the Country," 1961, and "Lisa," 1962; producer and director of "Prince of Players," 1955, all Twentieth Century-Fox Film Corp. U.S. Office of War Information, Overseas Branch, chief of production in Motion Picture Bureau, 1942-45. Member, Committee to Defend America by Aiding the Allies, and of Americans for a Democratic Society; co-founder, Committee for the First Amendment. Radio commentator of "In the Public Interest," 1983.

MEMBER: Screen Writers Guild (co-founder), Writers Guild of America, West (former vice-president), Academy of Motion Picture Arts and Sciences (former governor). *Awards, honors:* Academy Award nominations for best screenplay, 1942, for "How Green Was My Valley," and best story and screenplay, 1952, for "David and Bathsheba"; Laurel Award of Writers Guild of America, 1962; Valentine Davies Award, Writers Guild of America, 1974.

WRITINGS: (Editor and author of introduction and commentary) Finley Peter Dunne, *Mr. Dooley Remembers,* Little, Brown, 1963; *Take Two: A Life in Movies and Politics,* McGraw, 1980. Also author of stage play, "Mr. Dooly's America," 1976.

Screenplays: (With Dan Totheroh and Rowland V. Lee) "The Count of Monte Cristo," United Artists, 1934; (with Ralph Spence) "Student Tour" (original story by George Seaton, Arthur Bloch, and Samuel Marx), Metro-Goldwyn-Mayer, 1934; (with Ralph Block) "The Melody Lingers On" (based on the novel by Lowell Brentano), Reliance Productions, 1935; "Last of the Mohicans" (based on the novel by James Fenimore Cooper), United Artists, 1936; (author of screen story with Finley Peter Dunne, Jr.) "Breezing Home," screenplay by Charles Grayson, Universal, 1937; "Lancer Spy" (based on the novel by Marthe McKenna), Fox, 1937; (with Julien Josephson and Sam Duncan) "Suez," Fox, 1938; (with Josephson) "Stanley and Livingstone," Fox, 1939; (with Josephson) "The Rains Came" (based on the novel by Louis Bromfield), Fox, 1939; (with John Taintor Foote) "Swanee River" (based on the life and career of Stephen Foster), Fox, 1939.

(With Roland Brown, Samuel G. Engel and Hal Long) "Johnny Apollo," Fox, 1940; "How Green Was My Valley" (based on the novel by Richard Llewellyn), Fox, 1941; "Son of Fury" (based on the novel *Benjamin Blake* by Edison Marshall), Fox, 1942; "The Late George Apley" (based on the novel by J. P. Marquand and the play by Marquand and George S. Kaufman), Fox, 1947; (with Ring Lardner, Jr.) "Forever Amber" (based on the novel by Kathleen Winsor), Fox, 1947; "The Ghost and Mrs. Muir" (based on the novel *The Ghost of Captain Gregg and Mrs. Muir* by R. A. Dick), Fox, 1947; "Escape" (based on the play by John Galsworthy), Fox, 1948; "The Luck of the Irish" (based on the novel by Guy and Constance Jones), Fox, 1948; (with Dudley Nichols) "Pinky" (based on the novel by Cid Ricketts Summer), Fox, 1949.

"David and Bathsheba," Fox, 1951; (with Arthur Caesar) "Anne of the Indies" (based on a short story by Herbert Ravenal Sass), Fox, 1951; (with Michael Blankfort) "Lydia Bailey" (based on the novel by Kenneth Roberts), Fox, 1952; (and producer) "Way of a Gaucho" (based on the novel by Herbert Childs), Fox, 1952; "The Robe" (based on the novel by Lloyd C. Douglas), Fox, 1953; "Demetrius and the Gladiators" (based on a character from Lloyd C. Douglas's *The Robe*), Fox, 1954; (with Casey Robinson) "The Egyptian" (based on the novel by Mika Waltari), Fox, 1954; (and producer-director) "The View from Pompey's Head" (based on the novel by Hamilton Basso), Fox, 1955; (and director) "Hilda Crane" (based on the play by Samuel Raphaelson), Fox, 1956; (and director) "Three Brave Men" (based on Pulitzer Prize newspaper articles by Anthony Lewis), Fox, 1957; (and director) "Ten North Frederick" (based on the novel by John O'Hara), Fox, 1958; (with Edith Sommer; and director) "Blue Denim" (based on the play by James Leo Herlihy and William Noble), Fox, 1959.

(And director) "The Agony and the Ecstasy" (based on the novel by Irving Stone), Fox, 1965; (with W. H. Menger; and director) "Blindfold" (based on the novel by Lucille Fletcher), Universal, 1966.

Author of newspaper articles, syndicated by Network News, Inc. Contributor of short stories and articles to *New Yorker, Atlantic,* and other magazines.

SIDELIGHTS: In his thirty-five years in the film industry, Philip Dunne has written or directed many notable movies, including "How Green Was My Valley," "The Robe," and "Ten North Frederick." He also weathered the Communist "witch hunts" and blacklists of the fifties and appeared as a character witness at the trial of Dalton Trumbo, Jr., one of the "Hollywood Ten." In his autobiography *Take Two: A Life in Movies and Politics* Dunne reflects on the era when "we [Americans] desecrated our democracy, made national heroes of petty tyrants and snitches."

A staunch liberal, Dunne clashed with Hollywood's industry leaders throughout his career. During the "witch hunt" years Dunne "fought the blacklist tenaciously, and only cooperated with it to the extent that he helped provide a process by which blacklistees could come in and out of the cold should their consciences and desire for work so dictate," as Bruce Cook remarks in his *Chicago Tribune Book World* review of *Take Two.* The author's memoirs "remind us . . . of the honored place once held by liberal political values and liberal delusions," according to *Nation* critic Larry Ceplair. *Washington Post* writer Thomas Weiner adds: "His involvement with the convoluted politics of [the fifties] arose simply out of his principles of civil libertarianism. For his seemingly aloof attitude, he was vilified by both the right and the left. The way Dunne describes it, that stance sounds like the only sane one in Hollywood during those deranged days.''

While Ceplair notes that the author ''savagely criticizes 'revisionist' historians (by which he means those who have elevated the blacklistees to heroic stature),'' the critic finds Dunne ''a revisionist historian himself. He writes of the Hollywood Ten: 'They were not the warriors in [the conflict over civil liberties]—though they fought bravely if confusedly in their own defense—but [were] simply the battlefield over which others fought for the rights of all Americans supposedly guaranteed by our Constitution.'''

''Dunne's book is constructed more or less like a three-act play,'' comments Wiener. ''In Act One, we have the young writer coming to Hollywood, working his way into the good graces of such legends as [producer Darryl F.] Zanuck and [director] John Ford. . . . In Act Two, the storm clouds of the inquisitions and blacklists move in. In Act Three, the clouds part briefly, as the veteran writer becomes a producer and director, although with less success and happiness than in Act One.''

BIOGRAPHICAL/CRITICAL SOURCES: Philip Dunne, *Take Two: A Life in Movies and Politics*, McGraw, 1980; *Washington Post*, September 2, 1980; *Nation*, October 4, 1980; *Los Angeles Times Book Review*, November 16, 1980; *Chicago Tribune Book World*, December 14, 1980.

* * *

DUPONT, Paul
     See FREWIN, Leslie Ronald

* * *

DURAN, Manuel E.   1925-

PERSONAL: Born March 28, 1925, in Barcelona, Spain; naturalized U.S. citizen, 1955; married Gloria Diana Bradley (a writer), May 28, 1949; children: Alex, Phillip. *Education:* National University of Mexico, B.A. (cum laude), 1943, M.A. (cum laude), 1950, Doctor of Law, 1950; Princeton University, Ph.D., 1953. *Home:* 889 Indian Hill Rd., Orange, Conn. *Office:* 493 College St., Yale University, New Haven, Conn. 06520.

CAREER: National University of Mexico, Mexico City, instructor, 1950-51; Smith College, Northampton, Mass., assistant professor, 1954-59, associate professor of Spanish, 1959; Yale University, New Haven, Conn., associate professor, 1959-66, professor of Spanish, 1966—. *Member:* Modern Language Association of America. *Awards, honors:* Guggenheim fellow, 1963-64; Commander, Order of Queen Isabella, 1981.

WRITINGS: Puente, National University of Mexico, 1946; *Las deudas publicas y el derecho internacional*, National University of Mexico, 1950; *El Superrealismo en la poesia espanola contemporanea*, National University of Mexico, 1952; *Ciutat i figures*, [Mexico City], 1952; (translator) Karl Manheim, *Liberted, poder y planificacion democratica*, Fondo de Cultura Economica (Mexico City), 1953; *Ciudad Asediada*, Fondo de Cultura Economica (Mexico City), 1954; *Metodo Cortina, Revisado*, 1957; *La Paloma Azul* (poems), Tezontle, 1959.

La ambiguedad en el Quijote, University of Verz Cruz Press, 1960; (compiler) *Antologia de la poesia italiana*, Mexico Editorial Universitaria, 1961; (editor) *Lorca* (critical anthology), Prentice-Hall, 1962; (contributor) R. Kostelanetz, editor, *On

Contemporary Literature, Avon, 1964; (with F. Alvarez) *Voces espanolas de hoy*, Harcourt, 1965; *El lugar del hombre* (poems), University of Mexico, 1965; (contributor) *Collected Studies in Honor of Americo Castro's Eightieth Year*, Boars Hill, Oxford, 1965; (editor with wife, Gloria Duran) Ana Maria Matute, *Doce historias de la Artamila*, Harcourt, 1965; *Ortega y Gasset, sus mejores paginas*, Prentice-Hall, 1966; (editor with Agusti Bartra) *Panorama de la literatura espanola* (anthology), Harcourt, 1967.

Genio y figura de Amado Nervo, Eudeba (Buenos Aires), 1970; *Luis de Leon*, Twayne, 1971; *Cervantes*, Twayne, 1974; *Marques de Santillana, Poesias completas*, Editorial Castalia (Madrid), 1975; *Rafael Alberti*, Taurus Ediciones (Madrid), 1975; (with R. Gonzalez) *Calderon de la Barca*, Editorial Gredos (Madrid), 1976; (with G. Duran) *El mundo del mas alla*, Harcourt, 1976; (with G. Duran) *Autorretratos y espejos*, Prentice-Hall, 1977; *Quevedo*, EDAF (Madrid), 1978; *El lago de los signos* (poems), [Mexico], 1978; (with G. Duran and C. Karry) *Spoken Spanish for Students and Travellers*, Heath, 1978.

El tres es siempre magico (poems), Universidad Nacional Autonoma de Mexico, 1981; (with Margery Safir) *Earth Tones: The Poetry of Pablo Neruda*, Indiana University Press, 1981; (with G. Duran) *Vivir Hoy*, 2nd edition, Harcourt, 1981. Also author, with N. Corles-Rivas, of *Graded Spanish Reader*, Lexington. Contributor of more than 120 articles, essays, poems, and reviews to professional publications.

BIOGRAPHICAL/CRITICAL SOURCES: Times Literary Supplement, October 16, 1981.

* * *

DUVOISIN, Roger Antoine   1904-1980

PERSONAL: Born August 28, 1904, in Geneva, Switzerland; came to United States, 1927; naturalized, 1938; died June 30, 1980, of a heart attack in Morristown, N.J.; son of Jacques J. (an architect) and Judith (More) Duvoisin; married Louise Fatio (a writer of juvenile books), July 25, 1925; children: Roger, Jacques. *Education:* Attended College Moderne and Ecole des Arts et Metiers, 1917-24, both Geneva, Switzerland. *Address:* P.O. Box 116, Peapack-Gladstone, N.J. 07934.

CAREER: Manager of pottery, Ferney-Voltaire, France, 1924-26; designer of scenery for Geneva Opera and other stage productions in Geneva, Switzerland, 1926-27; textile designer in Lyons and Paris, France, 1927, and in United States for Mallenson Silk Co., 1927-31; magazine and book advertising illustrator, New York, N.Y., beginning 1929; author and illustrator of children's books, 1932-80.

AWARDS, HONORS: Bronze Medal, Paris Exhibition of Potteries of Ferney, 1925; work selected to exhibit in Fifty Best Books of the Year shows, American Institute of Graphic Art, 1933, 1938, 1939, 1945-50, 1953-62, and 1965-68, and included on Nine Best Childrens Books of the Year list of the American Library Association, 1937, and *New York Times's* Ten Best Books lists, 1952, 1954, 1955, 1961, 1965, and 1966; first prize, *New York Herald Tribune* Children's Spring Book Festival Award, 1945, for *They Put Out to Sea: The Story of the Map*, and 1952; Caldecott Medal for best illustrated book for children, 1948, for *White Snow, Bright Snow;* first prize for juvenile book, West German Republic, 1956, for *The Happy Lion* and *The Happy Lion in Africa;* Society of Illustrators Award, 1961; Bicentennial Award for distinguished work in children's literature, Rutgers University, 1966; runner up, Hans

Christian Andersen International Children's Book Medal, International Board on Books for Young People, 1968; awards from University of Southern Mississippi, 1971, and University of Minnesota, 1976; Children's Book Award, New York Academy of Science, 1975, for *See What I Am;* honorary doctorate of letters, Kean State College.

WRITINGS—Self-illustrated: *A Little Boy Was Drawing,* Scribner, 1932; *Donkey-Donkey: The Troubles of a Silly Little Donkey,* Whitman, 1933, new edition published as *Donkey-Donkey,* Grosset, 1940, reprinted, Parents Magazine Press, 1968; *All Aboard!,* Grosset, 1935; *And There Was America,* Knopf, 1938; *The Christmas Cake in Search of Its Owner,* American Artists Group, 1941; *The Three Sneezes, and Other Swiss Tales,* Knopf, 1941 (published in England as *Fairy Tales from Switzerland: The Three Sneezes and Other Swiss Tales,* Muller, 1958); *They Put Out to Sea: The Story of the Map,* Knopf, 1943, new edition, University of London Press, 1959; *The Christmas Whale,* Knopf, 1945; *Chanticleer, the Real Story of This Famous Rooster,* Grosset, 1947; *The Four Corners of the World,* Knopf, 1948.

Petunia, Knopf, 1950, reprinted, Random House, 1973, sound recording, Caedmon, 1973; *Petunia and the Song,* Knopf, 1951; *A for the Ark,* Lothrop, 1952; *Petunia's Christmas,* Knopf, 1952; *Petunia Takes a Trip,* Knopf, 1953, reprinted, 1974; *Easter Treat,* Knopf, 1954; *Two Lonely Ducks: A Counting Book,* Knopf, 1955; *One Thousand Christmas Beards,* Knopf, 1955; *The House of Four Seasons,* Lothrop, 1956; *Petunia, Beware!,* Knopf, 1958.

Day and Night, Knopf, 1960; *Veronica,* Knopf, 1961; *The Happy Hunter,* Lothrop, 1961; *Our Veronica Goes to Petunia's Farm,* Knopf, 1962 (published in England as *Veronica Goes to Petunia's Farm,* Bodley Head, 1963); *Spring Snow,* Knopf, 1963; *Lonely Veronica,* Knopf, 1963; *Veronica's Smile,* Knopf, 1964; *Petunia, I Love You,* Knopf, 1965; *The Missing Milkman,* Knopf, 1967; *What Is Right for Tulip,* Knopf, 1969.

Veronica and the Birthday Present, Knopf, 1971; *The Crocodile in the Tree,* Bodley Head, 1972, Knopf, 1973; *Jasmine,* Knopf, 1973; *See What I Am,* Lothrop, 1974; (with wife, Louise Fatio) *Marc and Pixie, and the Walls in Mrs. Jones's Garden,* McGraw, 1975; *Petunia's Treasure,* Knopf, 1975; *Periwinkle,* Knopf, 1976; *Crocus,* Knopf, 1977; *Snowy and Woody,* Knopf, 1979.

Illustrator: Daniel Defoe, *The Life and Adventures of Robinson Crusoe,* F. Watts, 1946; Alvin R. Tresselt, *White Snow, Bright Snow,* Lothrop, 1947; Tresselt, *Johnny Maple-Leaf,* Lothrop, 1948; Walter Retan, *The Steam Shovel That Wouldn't Eat Dirt,* Aladdin Books, 1948; Tresselt, *Sun Up,* Lothrop, 1949; Tresselt, *"Hi, Mr. Robin!,"* Lothrop, 1950; Frederic Attwood, *Vavache, the Cow Who Painted Pictures,* Aladdin Books, 1950;

Mabel Watts, *Dozens of Cousins,* Whittlesey House, 1950; Jack Tworkov, *The Camel Who Took a Walk,* Aladdin Books, 1951; Tresselt, *Autumn Harvest,* Lothrop, 1951; Gian Carlo Menotti, *Amahl and the Night Visitors,* Whittlesey House, 1952; Tresselt, *Follow the Wind,* Lothrop, 1953; Tresselt, *I Saw the Sea Come In,* Lothrop, 1954; Tresselt, *Wake Up, Farm!,* Lothrop, 1955; Tresselt, *Wake Up, City!,* Lothrop, 1957; Mary Calhoun, *Houn' Dog,* Morrow, 1959; Pedro Antonio de Alarcon, *The Three-cornered Hat,* Plantin Press, 1959.

Tresselt, *Timothy Robbins Climbs the Mountain,* Lothrop, 1960; Tresselt, *Under the Trees and through the Grass,* Lothrop, 1962; Aesopus, *The Miller, His Sons, and Their Donkey,* Whittlesey House, 1962, French translation by Duvoisin published as *Le Meunier, sons fils, et l'ane,* Whittlesey House, 1962; Tresselt, *Hide and Seek Fog,* Lothrop, 1965; Adelaide Holl, *The Rain Puddle,* Bodley Head, 1965; Dean Frye, *Days of Sunshine, Days of Rain,* McGraw, 1965; Jean B. Showalter, *Around the Corner,* Doubleday, 1966; William Lipkind, *Nubber Bear,* Harcourt, 1966; Tresselt, *The World in the Candy Egg,* Lothrop, 1967; William Jay Smith, compiler, *Poems from France,* Cromwell, 1967; Holl, *The Remarkable Egg,* Lothrop, 1968; Berniece Freschet, *The Old Bullfrog,* Scribner, 1968; Mona Dayton, *Earth and Sky,* Harper, 1969.

Tresselt, *The Beaver Pond,* Lothrop, 1970; Freschet, *The Web in the Grass,* Scribner, 1972; Pat Ross, *What Ever Happened to the Baxter Place?,* Pantheon, 1976; Mirra Ginsburg, *Which Is the Best Place?,* Macmillan, 1976; Tresselt, *What Did You Leave Behind?,* Lothrop, 1978; Janice, *Mr. and Mrs. Button's Wonderful Watchdogs,* Lothrop, 1978.

Written by wife, L. Fatio: *The Christmas Forest,* Aladdin Books, 1950; *Anna, the Horse,* Aladdin Books, 1951; *The Happy Lion,* Whittlesey House, 1954; *The Happy Lion in Africa,* Whittlesey House, 1955; *The Happy Lion Roars,* Whittlesey House, 1957; *A Doll for Marie,* Whittlesey House, 1957; *The Three Happy Lions,* Whittlesey House, 1959; *The Happy Lion's Quest,* Whittlesey House, 1961; *The Happy Lion and the Bear,* Whittlesey House, 1964; *The Happy Lion's Vacation,* McGraw, 1967; *The Happy Lion's Treasure,* McGraw, 1971; *Hector Penguin,* McGraw, 1973; *The Happy Lion's Rabbits,* McGraw, 1973; *Hector and Christina,* McGraw, 1977; *The Happy Lioness,* McGraw, 1980.

Also illustrator of about 100 other children's books by various authors. Contributor to *New Yorker,* 1934-80, and to juvenile and book magazines.

AVOCATIONAL INTERESTS: Reading, music, gardening, painting, and travel abroad.

OBITUARIES: New York Times, July 3, 1980; *Publishers Weekly,* July 25, 1980.†

E

EARNSHAW, Brian 1929-

PERSONAL: Born December 26, 1929, in Wrexham, Wales; son of Eric and Annie (Barker) Earnshaw. *Education:* Cambridge University, B.A., 1952, M.A., 1955; University of Bristol, Certificate in Education, 1957; University of London, Diploma of Education, 1970; University of Warwick, Ph.D., 1983. *Politics:* "Smugly patriotic since Mrs. Thatcher arrived." *Religion:* Church of England. *Home and office:* St. Paul's College, Cheltenham, Gloucestershire, England. *Agent:* Jonathan Clowes Ltd., 19 Jeffrey's Place, London NW1 9PP, England.

CAREER: "Taught English at a poor public school, a good grammar school, and a charming comprehensive school," 1952-65; currently teacher of creative writing at St. Paul's College, Cheltenham, England. Warden, Pembrokeshire National Park, 1963-65.

WRITINGS: And Mistress Pursuing, Hodder & Stoughton, 1966; *At St. David's a Year* (poems), Hodder & Stoughton, 1968; *Planet in the Eye of Time* (science fiction), Hodder & Stoughton, 1968.

"Dragonfall Five" series: *Dragonfall Five and the Space Cowboys,* Methuen Children's Books, 1972, Lothrop, 1975; . . . *and the Royal Beast,* Lothrop, 1972; . . . *and the Empty Planet,* Lothrop, 1973; . . . *and the Hijackers,* Methuen Children's Books, 1974; . . . *and the Master Mind,* Methuen Children's Books, 1975; . . . *and the Superhorse,* Methuen Children's Books, 1977; . . . *and the Haunted Planet,* Methuen Children's Books, 1979.

WORK IN PROGRESS: A new series of children's science fiction; a study of the influence of Germany on the English Romantic Movement, entitled *The German Mania.*

SIDELIGHTS: Brian Earnshaw told *CA:* "It is not easy to understand what matters in what I write. I spent years, off and on, writing a 'masterwork' novel with strong autobiographical undertone. Now I think it a blessing that publishers turned it down. On the other hand, a science fiction series which I began in three books written in three weeks still rolls the money in and still seems fresh, witty, and unpretentious when I reread it. So I'm going all out for my lost adolescence now and am writing a science fiction [book] about a pop group.

"Americans don't like my books as much as the Japanese because they're not violent enough for American tastes and American publishers are frightened of books about tensions between two races on one planet. I can understand this, but it still smells of brainwashing."

BIOGRAPHICAL/CRITICAL SOURCES: Punch, March 27, 1968.

*   *   *

EDBERG, Rolf 1912-

PERSONAL: Born March 14, 1912, in Lysvik, Sweden; married Astrid Persson, 1937; children: Joergen, Ranveig Jacobsson, Birgitta. *Home:* Hagtornsgatan 3, 652 30 Karlstad, Sweden.

CAREER: Oskarshamns Nyheter, Oskarshamm, Sweden, chief editor, 1934-37; *Oestgoeten,* Linkoeping, Sweden, chief editor, 1938-44; *Ny Tid,* Gothenburg, Sweden, chief editor, 1945-56; Swedish ambassador to Norway, 1956-67; governor of Swedish province of Vaarmland, 1967-77. Member of Swedish Parliament, 1940-44 and 1948-56. Delegate to Council of Europe, 1949-52, United Nations, 1952-55, 1957, 1960-61, Northern Council, 1953-56, and Disarmament Conference, 1961-65.

MEMBER: Swedish Press Club (president, 1951-53), Swedish Association of Writers, Pen Club, Swedish Association of Biologists, Swedish Royal Academy of Sciences, Swedish Society for Anthropology and Geography. *Awards, honors:* Socrates Prize, 1972, from School of Adult Education; gold medal, 1974, from Royal Swedish Academy of Science; Doctor Honoris Causa, 1974, from University of Gothenburg; gold medal, 1976, from Geographical-Anthropological Society; Selma Lagerloef's Prize, 1976; Dag Hammarskjoeld Medal, 1978; King's Medal, 1981.

WRITINGS: Nansen, european: En studie i vilja och god-vilja (title means "Nansen, the European: A Study in Will and Good Will"), Tiden, 1961; *Spillran av ett moln,* Norstedt, 1966, translation by Sven Aahman published as *On the Shred of a Cloud: Notes in a Travel Book,* University of Alabama Press, 1969, same translation published as *On the Shred of a Cloud: Reflections on Man and His Environment,* Harper, 1971; *Vid traedets fot,* Norstedt, 1971, translation by David Mel Paul and Margareta Paul published as *At the Foot of the Tree: A Wanderer's Musings before the Fall,* University of Alabama

Press, 1974; *Ett hus i kosmos* (title means "A House in the Cosmos"), Esselte Studium, 1974.

Dalens Ande, Norstedt, 1976, translation by Keith Bradfield published as *The Dream of Kilimanjaro*, Pantheon, 1979; *Skuggor oever Savannen* (title means "Shadows across the Savannah"), Bra Boecker & Trevi, 1977; *De glittrande vattnens land* (title means "The Land of Glittering Waters"), Bra Boecker & Norstedts, 1980; (editor) *Haer aer ve hemma* (title means "This Is Our Home"), Bra Boecker & Norstedts, 1982; (editor) *Vaart hotade hem* (title means "Our Threatened Home"), Bra Boecker & Norstedts, 1983.

Also author of *Ge dem en chans* (title means "Give Them a Chance"), 1939, *I morgon Norden* (title means "Tomorrow Nordic"), 1944, *Demokratisk linje* (title means "Democratic Line"), 1948, *Femte etappen* (title means "The Fifth Stage"), 1949, *Oeppna grindarna* (title means "Open the Gates"), 1952, and *Paa jordens villkor* (title means "On Earth's Terms"), 1974.

WORK IN PROGRESS: Droppar av vatten, droppar av aar (title means "Drops of Water, Drops of Years").

SIDELIGHTS: Rolf Edberg writes to *CA:* "I grew up in a fresh and beautiful countryside and very early I got in contact with the science of evolution, which started a lifelong interest in natural sciences. The first book about man's condition was created in order to disentangle my own meditating threads and to put man's moment on earth in a bigger continuity. We have in our constantly greedy searching acquired an ever increasing richness in knowledge of details and have been forced into an even harder specialization. However, nature is interaction, not separation. What we have to do today is to place our varying knowledge under a unifying comprehensive view giving us a vision of our destiny. My ambition as a layman has been to arrive at such a comprehensive view.

"The scientific literature—especially in the environmental field—published in the United States has given me great inspiration in my work. Europe has a lot to learn from the American research which is the most advanced in the world. But I believe that America, highly urbanized, has some to learn from the Scandinavian people with their natural love of nature.

"And that is the way it ought to be: that we learn from each other's research, thinking, and experience."

BIOGRAPHICAL/CRITICAL SOURCES: Chicago Tribune Book World, May 20, 1979.

* * *

EDMONDSON, G. C. 1922-
(Garry C. Edmondson; pseudonyms: Kelly P. Gast, J. B. Masterson, Mario Murphy)

PERSONAL: Original name, Jose Mario Garry Ordonez Edmondson y Cotton; born October 11, 1922, in the United States (some biographical sources cite birthplace as Hermosa de Rascuachitlan, Tabasco, Mexico); son of William J. Edmondson and Edith Cotton; married Carmen Medrano Paez; children: two sons, two daughters. *Education:* "Damn little; Percussion U." *Home:* 12328 Rockcrest, Lakeside, Calif. 92040. *Agent:* Robert P. Mills, Ltd., 333 Fifth Ave., New York, N.Y. 10016.

CAREER: Writer. Blacksmith and weapons maker. *Military service:* U.S. Marine Corps, 1942-46. *Member:* Science Fiction Writers of America, Western Writers of America.

WRITINGS: Novels, except as indicated; published by Doubleday, except as indicated: *The Ship That Sailed the Time Stream* [and] *Stranger Than You Think,* Ace Books, 1965; *Chapayeca,* 1971, published as *Blue Face,* Daw Books, 1972; *T.H.E.M.,* 1974; *The Aluminum Man,* Berkley, 1975; (under pseudonym Kelly P. Gast) *Dil Dies Hard,* 1975; (under pseudonym Kelly P. Gast) *Murphy's Trail,* 1976; (under pseudonym Kelly P. Gast) *The Long North Trail,* 1976; (under name Garry C. Edmondson; with Leroy A. Scheck) *Practical Welding* (nonfiction), Bruce, 1976; *Le Livre noir d'haute cuisine* (dictionary), Bookmaker, 1977; (under pseudonym Kelly P. Gast) *Last Stage from Opal,* 1978; (under pseudonym Kelly P. Gast) *Murder at Magpie Flats,* 1978; (with T. J. Roybal) *The Basic Book of Home Maintenance and Repair* (nonfiction), American Technical Society, 1979; (under pseudonym Kelly P. Gast) *Paddy,* 1979; (under pseudonym J. B. Masterson) *Rudge,* 1979; (with Richard Little) *Diesel Mechanics: An Introduction* (nonfiction), Wadsworth, 1982. Also author of *The Man Who Corrupted the Earth* and *To Sail the Century Sea,* both for Ace, and of more than forty other novels under various pseudonyms.

WORK IN PROGRESS: A western novel, a science fiction novel, and a historical novel set in Ireland, Iceland, Finland ca. 1000 A.D.

SIDELIGHTS: G. C. Edmondson is one of the few remaining blacksmiths in the United States. He speaks Spanish, Portuguese, Italian, French, and German "in descending scale of fluency."

* * *

EDMONDSON, Garry C.
See EDMONDSON, G. C.

* * *

ELDRIDGE, J(ohn) E. T. 1936-

PERSONAL: Born May 17, 1936, in Southampton, England. *Education:* University of Leicester, B.S., 1957, M.A., 1959. *Office:* Department of Sociology, Adam Smith Bldg., University of Glasgow, Glasgow G12 8QQ, Scotland.

CAREER: University of York, Heslington, England, lecturer, 1964-67, senior lecturer in sociology, 1967-69; University of Bradford, Bradford, England, professor of sociology, 1969-72; University of Glasgow, Glasgow, Scotland, professor of sociology, 1972—. *Member:* British Sociological Association (chairperson, 1975-77; president, 1979-81), British Universities Industrial Relations Association, International Industrial Relations Association.

WRITINGS: Industrial Disputes: Essays in the Sociology of Industrial Relations, Humanities, 1968; *Max Weber: The Interpretation of Social Reality,* M. Joseph, 1970; *Sociology and Industrial Life,* M. Joseph, 1971; (with A. D. Crombie) *A Sociology of Organizations,* Allen & Unwin, 1975; (co-author) *Bad News,* Routledge & Kegan Paul, 1976; (co-author) *More Bad News,* Routledge & Kegan Paul, 1980; *Recent British Sociology,* Macmillan, 1980; *C. Wright Mills,* Tavistock, 1983. Contributor to sociology journals.

WORK IN PROGRESS: Media Coverage of Defence and Disarmament Issues.

* * *

ELIAV, Arie L(ova) 1921-
(Ben Ami)

PERSONAL: Born November 21, 1921, in Moscow, U.S.S.R.;

immigrated to Israel in 1924; son of Joseph and Matilda Eliav; married Tania Zvi, October 12, 1947; children: Zvi, Ofra, Eyal. *Education:* Attended University of Reading and Cambridge University, both 1953; Hebrew University of Jerusalem, diploma (cum laude), 1959. *Home:* 3 Karl Netter St., Tel Aviv, Israel. *Office:* International Center for Peace in the Middle East, 107 Hahashmonaim St., Tel-Aviv 67011, Israel.

CAREER: Israeli government official in Settlement Department, Ministry of Agriculture, and Ministry of Finance, 1949-53; instructor in immigrants' village of Moshav Nevatim, 1954; first director of Lachish regional project, 1955-57, Arad and Chazvin projects, 1960-63; Israeli Embassy, Moscow, U.S.S.R., first secretary, 1958-60; head of Israeli aid and rehabilitation team to earthquake stricken Ghazvin region of Iran, 1962-64; Mapai Organization Department, head and member of the Knesset (Israeli Parliament), 1965-79; deputy minister of Commerce and Industry, 1966-67, Immigration and Absorption, 1968-70; Labor Party, Tel Aviv, Israel, secretary general, 1970-72; Center for International Affairs, Harvard University, Cambridge, Mass., lecturer and fellow, 1979-80; scholar-in-residence, American Jewish Committee of Greater Boston, 1979-80; adult education teacher in Or-Akiva, Israel, 1980-81; Tel Hai Regional College, Galilee, Israel, teacher, 1981-82; International Center for Peace in the Middle East, Tel-Aviv, chairman of board of trustees, 1982—.

Member of mission on behalf of Beit Hillel to the United States, 1964, and mission to Mullah Mustafa Barzani (head of Kurdish national movement), 1966; represented Israel at Council of Europe in Strasbourg, 1965-73; head of Israeli aid mission to earthquake stricken Managua, Nicaragua, 1973; participated in talks with Palestinian-Arab leaders in Paris, 1976-77; chairman of Sheli (Israeli Peace movement), 1977-79; negotiated exchange of Israeli prisoners of war (Lebanese War), 1982-83. Served as emergency room volunteer at Hadassah Hospital, Tel-Aviv, 1974-75. *Military service:* Served in Hagana (Jewish underground defense organization), 1936-40. British Army, served in artillery and engineering united during World War II. Served in Mossad illegal immigration operations, 1945-47. Israeli Defense Forces, 1948-49; became lieutenant colonel; commanded during Sinai campaign. *Awards, honors:* Ussishkin Prize for Zionist literature (Jerusalem), 1966; Dr. Bruno Kreisky Prize for peace (Vienna), 1979; Love of Israel Prize (Jerusalem), 1983.

WRITINGS: Some Observations on Regional Planning Practice, Tahal, 1964; (under pseudonym Ben Ami) *Ben ha-patish veha-magal,* Am Oved Publishers, 1965, translation published as *Between Hammer and Sickle,* Jewish Publication Society of America, 1967, revised edition, New American Library, 1969; (with Galia Yardeni) *Sipurah shel sefinat ma'pilim* (title means "The Story of an 'Illegal' Immigrants Ship"), World Zionist Organization, 1965; *Ha-Sefinah Ulu'ah Seporo shel Artor,* Am Oved Publishers, 1967, translation by Israel I. Taslitt published as *The Voyage of the Ulua,* Funk, 1969; *Ye'adim hadashim le-Yisrael,* Lewin-Epstein, 1969, translation published as *New Targets for Israel,* Jerusalem Post Publications, 1969, 3rd Hebrew edition, Lewin-Epstein, 1971.

Kefitsat ha-derekh, Am Oved Publishers, 1970, translation by Dov Chaikin published as *No Time for History: A Pioneer Story,* Sabra Books, 1970; *Erets ha-tsvi,* Am Oved Publishers, 1972, translation by Judith Yalon published as *Land of the Hart: Israelis, Arabs, the Territories, and a Vision of the Future,* Jewish Publication Society of America, 1974; *Ha-Ruah lo yikah* (title means "The Wind Shall Not Carry Them Away"),

Am Oved Publishers, 1974; *Shalom,* Massadah, 1975, translation by Misha Louvish published as *Shalom: Peace in Jewish Tradition,* Massadah, 1977; *Sulam Yisrael* (title means "Israel's Ladder"), Zemora Bitan Modan, 1977.

An Entire World (in Hebrew), Am Oved Publishers, 1980; *Rings* (in Hebrew), Am Oved Publishers, 1983. Also author of *Ba-yam, be-derekh mahteret,* 1964. Contributor to periodicals in Israel and abroad.

SIDELIGHTS: Arie L. Eliav served as commander of the rescue ship "Ulua" which carried two thousand Jewish refugees from Europe to Palestine. He participated in the Sinai Campaign, and in the rescue evacuation of Jews from Port Said. After bringing thousands of refugees into Israel, he continued thereafter to help them adjust to their new homes. His books, which have also been translated into French and Spanish, reflect his ongoing concern for the Jewish immigrants and for the country which they have helped to shape.

BIOGRAPHICAL/CRITICAL SOURCES: Washington Post, May 31, 1969; *Christian Science Monitor,* August 19, 1969; *Time,* January 26, 1970.

*   *   *

ELLIS, Hilda Roderick
      See DAVIDSON, H(ilda) R(oderick) Ellis

*   *   *

ELSEN, Albert E(dward)   1927-

PERSONAL: Born October 11, 1927, in New York, N.Y.; son of Albert (a lawyer) and Julia (Huseman) Elsen; married Patricia Morgan Kline, July 7, 1951; children: Matthew, Nancy, Katherine. *Education:* Columbia University, B.A. (with distinction), 1949, M.A., 1951, Ph.D., 1955. *Politics:* Democratic. *Home:* 723 Alvarado Row, Stanford, Calif. 94305. *Office:* Department of Art, Stanford University, Stanford, Calif. 94305.

CAREER: Carleton College, Northfield, Minn., 1952-58, began as instructor, became assistant professor of history of art; Indiana University at Bloomington, associate professor, 1958-63, professor of history of art, 1964-68; Stanford University, Stanford, Calif., professor of art history, 1968—. Visiting professor at Stanford University, 1963-64. Brandeis Poses Lecturer; lecturer on art at various institutions, including Metropolitan Museum of Art, Museum of Modern Art, Philadelphia Museum of Art, S. R. Guggenheim Museum, Cambridge University, and Courtauld Institute of Art, University of London. Taught educational television program, "Images of Man in Modern Art," 1958; art commentator for television station KQED in San Francisco, Calif. Helped organize art exhibitions for Museum of Modern Art, 1963, Baltimore Museum, 1969, National Gallery of Art, the Guggenheim Museum, and London's Hayward Gallery. Member of committee on advanced placement in art history, Educational Testing Service; founder of committee for the development of art in negro colleges, 1970—. Consultant to U.S. Office of Education, 1965-66; adviser to Kinsey Institute for Sex Research, 1966-68. *Military service:* U.S. Army, 1946-47; 752nd Tank Batallion in Italy; became sergeant major.

MEMBER: American Association of University Professors, College Art Association of America (member of board of directors, 1966-70; secretary and chairman of committee on public policy, 1970-72; vice-president and chairman of professional practices committee, beginning 1972; president, 1974-76), Authors Guild, Authors League of America. *Awards, honors:* Fulbright fellow, 1949-50; grant-in-aid for research on Rodin from American Council of Learned Societies, 1952 and 1960; Clark Foundation research grant for work on second Rodin book, and to assist in assembling Rodin show, 1962; Guggenheim fellowship for research in the origins and development of modern sculpture, 1966-67; National Endowment for the Humanities, senior fellow, 1973-74.

WRITINGS: Rodin's Gates of Hell, University of Minnesota Press, 1960; *Purposes of Art: An Introduction to the History and Appreciation of Art,* Holt, 1962, 4th edition, 1981; *Problem Book to Accompany Purposes of Art,* Holt, 1962, 2nd edition, 1968; *Rodin,* Museum of Modern Art, 1963; (editor) *Auguste Rodin: Readings on His Life and Work,* Prentice-Hall, 1965; *Rodin's the Walking Man,* Smith College Museum of Art, 1966; *The Partial Figure in Modern Sculpture, from Rodin to 1969,* Baltimore Museum, 1969.

Seymour Lipton, Abrams, 1970; *Arp-Rodin: Catalogue of an Exhibition Held at the Feingarten Galleries, Los Angeles, March 2 to April 10, 1971,* [Los Angeles], 1971; (with J. Kirk T. Varnedoe) *The Drawings of Rodin,* Praeger, 1971; *The Sculpture of Henri Matisse,* Abrams, c. 1972; *Paul Jenkins,* Abrams, 1973; (author of introductory essay) *Pioneers of Modern Sculpture: Catalogue of an Exhibition Held at the Hayward Gallery, London, 20 July - 23 September, 1973,* Arts Council of Great Britain, 1973; *Origins of Modern Sculpture: Pioneers and Premises,* Braziller, 1974; (with John Henry Merryman) *Law, Ethics, and the Visual Arts,* Matthew Bender, 1979; *Other Realities: Modern European Sculpture, 1918-1945,* Braziller, 1979.

In Rodin's Studio: A Photographic Record of Sculpture in the Making, Cornell University Press, 1980; (editor) *Rodin Rediscovered,* New York Graphic Society, 1981.

Also editor of *Handbook for the Development of Art in Small Colleges.* Contributor of articles on art to various magazines, including *Magazine of Art, Art Journal, Burlington Magazine, Art International, Art Forum,* and *Studio International.*

SIDELIGHTS: Albert E. Elsen, an art historian, told *CA* that the most important influence on his career was a doctoral study with Meyer Schapiro at Columbia University. "His writings as well as those of Sidney Geist and Leo Steinberg have been crucial to my own," he said. Elsen calls his text *Purposes of Art: An Introduction to the History and Appreciation of Art* "a topical approach to art history, meant to counter the linear chronological approach prevalent in this country." His research in modern sculpture, as seen in *The Partial Figure in Modern Sculpture, from Rodin to 1969* deals with what he calls "ideas and premises of modern art rather than styles, movements and national groupings."

In his 1974 publication *The Origins of Modern Sculpture,* Elsen gives readers "a rigorous critical account of the development of modern European sculpture during the crucial years 1890-1918," the *Times Literary Supplement* reviewer reports, adding that "not the least of the merits of Elsen's book is his refusal to accept glib generalizations." And, writing in the *New York Times Book Review,* Raymond A. Sokolov praises Elsen's 1980 publication *In Rodin's Studio: A Photographic Record of Sculpture in the Making,* "Elsen, a Rodin specialist at Stanford University, edited this quite fabulous album and shows, in an introductory essay and in notes to the plates, how the pictures relate to Rodin's life and to the creation of the statues they depict."

BIOGRAPHICAL/CRITICAL SOURCES: Times Literary Supplement, March 23, 1973, April 25, 1975, November 14, 1980; *New York Times Book Review,* May 18, 1980.†

*   *   *

EMERY, Edwin 1914-

PERSONAL: Born May 14, 1914, in California; son of William E. (a rancher) and Laura A. (Miller) Emery; married Mary M. McNevin, December 28, 1935; children: Michael, Laurel, Alison. *Education:* University of California, Berkeley, B.A., 1935, Ph.D., 1943. *Politics:* Democrat. *Home:* 2524 Seabury Ave., Minneapolis, Minn. 55406. *Office:* School of Journalism, University of Minnesota, Minneapolis, Minn. 55455.

CAREER: San Francisco Examiner, San Francisco, Calif., reporter, 1935; *California Monthly,* Berkeley, managing editor, 1936-43; United Press, San Francisco, Calif., correspondent and bureau chief, 1943-45, on war desk, 1944-45; University of Minnesota, Minneapolis, member of faculty, 1945-54, professor of journalism, 1954—. Taught and lectured in Taiwan and Spain, 1972-73, and in Singapore, 1979-80.

MEMBER: International Press Institute, International Association for Mass Communication Research, National Conference of Editorial Writers, Public Relations Society of America (president of Minnesota chapter), Association for Education in Journalism (president, 1974-75), Phi Beta Kappa, Sigma Delta Chi. *Awards, honors:* National research awards from Sigma Delta Chi, 1950, 1954; Guggenheim fellowship, 1959-60; Social Science Research Council grant, 1960; Bleyer award, Association for Education in Journalism, 1980, for historical research; national journalism teacher of the year award, Sigma Delta Chi, 1980.

WRITINGS: History of the American Newspaper Publishers Association, University of Minnesota Press, 1950; (with E. H. Ford) *Highlights in the History of the American Press,* University of Minnesota Press, 1954; *The Press and America,* Prentice-Hall, 1954, 5th edition (with son Michael Emery), 1984; (with W. K. Agee and P. H. Ault) *Introduction to Mass Communications,* Harper, 1960, 7th edition, 1982; *The Story of America as Reported by Its Newspapers, 1690-1970,* Simon & Schuster, 1965; (with M. Emery and R. S. Schuneman) *America's Front Page News, 1690-1970,* Doubleday, 1971; (with Agee and Ault) *Perspectives on Mass Communications,* Harper, 1982; (with Agee and Ault) *Reporting and Writing the News,* Harper, 1983.

Editorial writer for *St. Paul Pioneer Press,* summers, 1946-53; editor of *Journalism Quarterly,* 1964-73.

WORK IN PROGRESS: International news flow and media research project, including teaching and lecturing in Beijing, China, 1984-85.

*   *   *

EMMERICK, R(onald) E(ric) 1937-

PERSONAL: Born March 9, 1937, in Sydney, New South Wales, Australia; son of Eric Steward (a builder) and Myrtle (Smith) Emmerick; married Margaret Ann Frohnsdorf, July 4, 1962; children: Paul Ronald, Catherine Ann, Veronica Jane. *Education:* University of Sydney, B.A. (with first class honors), 1959; St. John's College, Cambridge, B.A., 1961, M.A. and Ph.D., 1965. *Home:* Waidmannsring 7, 2085 Quickborn, West Germany. *Office:* Seminar for the History and Culture of the Near East, University of Hamburg, Rothenbaumchaussee 36, 2 Hamburg 13, West Germany.

CAREER: University of London, School of Oriental and African Studies, London, England, lecturer in Iranian studies, 1964-71; University of Hamburg, Seminar for the History and Culture of the Near East, Hamburg, West Germany, professor, 1971—. Visiting associate professor of Old and Middle Iranian, University of Chicago, 1967-68. Research fellow, St. John's College, Cambridge University, 1964-67. *Member:* Royal Asiatic Society, Philological Society (council member, 1968-71), Societe Asiatique, Deutsche Morgenlaendische Gesellschaft.

WRITINGS: Tibetan Texts Concerning Khotan, Oxford University Press, 1967; *Saka Grammatical Studies,* Oxford University Press, 1968; (editor and translator) *The Book of Zambasta, a Khotanese Poem on Buddhism,* Oxford University Press, 1968; *The Khotanese Surangamasamadhisutra,* Oxford University Press, 1970; *The Sutra of Golden Light,* Luzac (London), 1970; *Saka Documents,* Lund, Humphries, Volume V, 1971, Volume VI, 1973; *A Guide to the Literature of Khotan,* The Reiyukai Library (Tokyo), 1979; *The Siddhasara of Ravigupta,* F. Steiner Verlag, Volume I: *The Sanskrit Text,* 1980, Volume II: *The Tibetan Version with Facing English Translation,* 1982; (with P. O. Skjaervo) *Studies in the Vocabulary of Khotanese I,* Austrian Academy of Sciences, 1982. Contributor to learned journals.

*   *   *

EMSLIE, M. L.
  See SIMPSON, Myrtle L(illias)

*   *   *

EPSTEIN, William   1912-

PERSONAL: Born July 10, 1912, in Calgary, Alberta, Canada; came to the United States in 1946; son of Harry Louis (a merchant) and Masha Bella (Geffen) Epstein; married Edna Frances Hyman, September 22, 1946; children: Mark Gil. *Education:* University of Alberta, B.A. (with first class honors), 1933, LL.B. (with first class honors), 1935; London School of Economics and Political Science, graduate study, 1937-38. *Home:* 400 East 58th St., New York, N.Y. 10022. *Office:* United Nations Institute for Training and Research, 801 United Nations Plaza, New York, N.Y. 10017.

CAREER: Called to the Bar of Alberta, 1936; private practice of law in Calgary, Alberta, 1935-42; United Nations Secretariat, New York, N.Y., acting head of Middle East section, 1946-50, senior political officer in Palestine, 1948, director of Disarmament Division, 1950-73, chairman of staff committee, 1949-50, secretary of Disarmament Commission, 1952-73. Special fellow of United Nations Institute for Training and Research, 1973—; senior research associate, School of International Affairs, Carleton University, 1979—. Represented United Nations Secretary General on various disarmament committees, including five-power sub-committee on disarmament in London, 1954-57, conference on discontinuance of nuclear tests in Geneva, 1960, ten nation committee on disarmament in Geneva, 1960, eighteen nation committee on disarmament, and conference of the committee on disarmament, both in Geneva, both 1962-73. Helped prepare a report on chemical and biological weapons, 1968-69, and a report on a comprehensive nuclear test ban, 1980, both for the United Nations.

Visiting professor, University of Victoria, 1974-78, and Carleton University, 1977-78; Cecil H. and Ida Greene Visiting Professor, University of British Columbia, 1975; Killam Visiting Scholar, University of Calgary, 1978-79; special lecturer, United Nations program of fellowships in disarmament, 1979—; visiting lecturer, University of Lethbridge, 1980, and regents lecturer, University of California, 1981. Has also lectured and conducted seminars on nuclear disarmament at various other institutions in the United States, Canada, and Europe. Member of Canadian Institute of International Affairs, Canadian Peace Research Institute, Canadian Arms Control Seminar, North American Council of International Peace Academy, Council on Foreign Relations (New York), 1977-78, Canadian delegation to the United Nations General Assembly, 1978-81, and to first and second special sessions on disarmament, 1978 and 1982; member-at-large, General Assembly of Canadian Social Science Federation, 1979-80.

Consultant to commission for denuclearization of Latin America, 1965-67; special consultant to United Nations Secretary General, 1973—, and consultant on disarmament and arms control to Canadian government, 1978—; member of advisory board, Disarmament Times, 1978—. *Military service:* Canadian Army, 1942-45; became captain.

MEMBER: Alberta Law Society (non-practicing), Arms Control Association. *Awards, honors:* LL.D., University of Calgary, 1971; Rockefeller Foundation fellowship, 1973-75; Order of the Aztec Eagle (Mexico), 1976; Rolex Award for Enterprise (Geneva), 1978; Peace Hero Award of the World Federalists of Canada, 1978.

WRITINGS: (Editor) *The United Nations and Disarmament, 1945-1970,* United Nations, 1971; *Disarmament: Twenty-Five Years of Effort,* Canadian Institute of International Affairs, 1971; *The Last Chance: Nuclear Proliferation and Arms Control,* Free Press, 1976; (editor with Toshiyuki Toyoda) *A New Design for Nuclear Disarmament,* Pugwash Conferences on Science and World Affairs, 1977; (editor with B. T. Feld) *New Directions in Disarmament,* Praeger, 1981; (editor with Lucy Webster) *We Can Avert a Nuclear War,* O. G. & H. Publishers, 1983; *The Prevention of Nuclear War: A United Nations Perspective,* United Nations Institute for Training and Research, 1983.

Contributor: Carlo Schaerf and Frank Barnaby, editors, *Disarmament and Arms Control,* Gordon & Breach, 1972; A.M.J. Hyatt, editor, *Dreadnought to Polaris,* Copp Clark, 1973; David Carlton and Schaerf, editors, *The Dynamics of the Arms Race,* Croom Helm, 1975; Anne Marks, editor, *NPT: Paradoxes and Problems,* Arms Control Association, Carnegie Endowment for International Peace, 1975; Robert F. Scagel, editor, *Mankind's Future in the Pacific: Special Lectures of the Thirteenth Pacific Science Congress,* University of British Columbia Press, 1976; A. M. Chayes and W. Bennett Lewis, editors, *International Arrangements for Nuclear Fuel Cycle Facilities,* Ballinger, 1977; Joseph I. Coffey, editor, *Nuclear Proliferation: Prospects, Problems and Proposals,* American Academy of Political and Social Science, 1977; Carlton and Schaerf, editors, *Arms Control and Technological Innovation,* Croom Helm, 1977; F. Griffiths and J. C. Polanyi, editors, *The Danger of Nuclear War,* University of Toronto Press, 1979; Hans Gunter Brauch and Duncan L. Clarke, editors, *Decision-Making for Arms Limitation in the 1980s,* Ballinger, 1982.

Also contributor to proceedings of the International School of Disarmament and Arms Control, 1966, to the conference of the Canadian Council of International Law, 1977, and to proceedings of numerous Pugwash conferences. Contributor to the annals of the American Academy of Political and Social Science, 1977. Contributor to international journals, popular magazines, including *Scientific American, Survival, Saturday Review, Bulletin of Atomic Scientists* and *World Today,* and to newspapers.

WORK IN PROGRESS: Disarmament Negotiations.

AVOCATIONAL INTERESTS: Walking, reading, sculpting, art.

BIOGRAPHICAL/CRITICAL SOURCES: Week End, August 9, 1975; *Monday,* October 11, 1976.

*   *   *

EPTON, Nina C(onsuelo)

PERSONAL: Born in London, England; daughter of Robert (an interior architect) and Matilde (deBark) Epton. *Education:* Attended Lycee Racine; Sorbonne, Licence-es-Lettres, 1939. *Home and office:* Blue Gates, 58 Vale Rd., Seaford, Sussex, England.

CAREER: Writer. British Broadcasting Corp., in charge of French-Canadian section, 1943-56. *Member:* Women's Council of Great Britain, National Book League, International P.E.N. (London branch). *Awards, honors:* Star of Republic of Tunisia, presented by President Bourguiba for services rendered, by writing, before the emergence of the independent republic; Daha de la Orden del Merito Civil, for her books on Spain.

WRITINGS: Journey under the Crescent Moon, Gollancz, 1949; *Oasis Kingdom: The Libyan Story,* Jarrolds, 1951; *Islands of the Sunbird* (travel), Jarrolds, 1953; *The Valley of Pyrene,* Cassell, 1954; *Grapes and Granite,* Cassell, 1955; *The Palace and the Jungle,* Oldbourne, 1956; *The Golden Sword* (biography of Sir Stamford Raffles), Oldbourne, 1956; *Navarre: The Flea between Two Monkeys,* Cassell, 1957; *Saints and Sorcerers: A Moroccan Journey* (travel), Cassell, 1958; *Love and the French,* Cassell, 1959.

Love and the English, Cassell, 1960, Collier, 1963; *Love and the Spanish,* Cassell, 1961; *Milord and Milady,* Oldbourne, 1962; *Seaweed for Breakfast* (travel), Dodd, 1963; *Madrid,* Dodd, 1964; *Spain's Magic Coast, from the Mino to the Bidassoa: A Personal Guidebook,* Weidenfeld & Nicolson, 1966; (with Stewart Wavell and Audrey Butt) *Trances,* Allen & Unwin, 1966, Dutton, 1967; *Andalusia,* Weidenfeld & Nicolson, 1968; *Spanish Fiestas: Including Romerias, Excluding Bullfights,* A. S. Barnes, 1968.

Victoria and Her Daughters, Norton, 1971; *The Spanish Mousetrap: Napoleon and the Court of Spain,* Macdonald & Co., 1973; *The Burning Heart: A Novel Based on the Life of Jane Digby, Lady Ellenborough,* Macdonald & Jane's, 1974; *Magic and Mystics of Java,* Octagon Press (London), 1974; *Cat Manners and Mysteries,* M. Joseph, 1974; *Josephine: The Empress and Her Children,* Norton, 1975; *Dora Bell's Village Cats,* M. Joseph, 1977.

SIDELIGHTS: Born of a Scottish father and Spanish mother ("and, I suspect, Moorish blood from the Middle Ages"), and reared in France, Nina C. Epton has long "been fascinated by international and racial relationships, by turns amused and horrified by human prejudices. I love the beauties of creation—hence my cottage by the sea—and have begun to sketch to illustrate some of my travel books. I love to grow flowers and feed wild birds and yet be near the theatre-concert-literary-gossip of the capital. I am interested in science, although not mechanically-minded, hate cars and shall never own one. I walk whenever I can, in places where cars cannot get to. . . . On the whole, an optimist."†

*   *   *

ERICKSON, Carolly   1943-

PERSONAL: Born April 12, 1943, in Los Angeles, Calif.; daughter of Roland L. and Louise (Kiger) Bliss; children: Hal. *Education:* University of Washington, Seattle, double B.A., 1963; Columbia University, M.A., 1964, Ph.D., 1969. *Residence:* Berkeley, Calif. *Agent:* Lynn Nesbit, International Creative Management, 40 West 57th St., New York, N.Y. 10019.

CAREER: Barnard College, New York, N.Y., lecturer in history, 1964-66; San Fernando Valley State College (now California State University, Northridge), Northridge, Calif., instructor in history, 1966-67; Mills College, Oakland, Calif., assistant professor of medieval history, 1967-70; full-time writer, 1970—. Lecturer at Brooklyn College of the City University of New York, 1965-66. *Member:* Mediaeval Academy of America, American Historical Association, Medieval Association of the Pacific, West Coast Association of Women Historians, Phi Beta Kappa.

WRITINGS: The Records of Medieval Europe, Doubleday, 1971; *The Medieval Vision* (History Book Club selection), Oxford University Press, 1976; *Bloody Mary* (Book of the Month Club featured alternate), Doubleday, 1978; *Civilization and Society in the West,* Scott, Foresman, 1978; *Great Harry* (Book of the Month Club featured alternate; History Book Club main selection), Summit Books, 1980; *The First Elizabeth* (Book of the Month Club featured alternate; History Book Club selection), Summit Books, 1983; *Mistress Anne,* Summit Books, 1984.

Contributor of articles to periodicals; reviewer for *Los Angeles Times.*

WORK IN PROGRESS: The Age of Opulence, a popular history of Regency England and the first book of a trilogy, for Viking; pseudonymous fiction.

SIDELIGHTS: In 1975, medieval scholar Carolly Erickson began an exploration of Tudor England that has led to four popular biographies. The lives of Mary Tudor, Henry VIII, Elizabeth I, and the ill-fated Anne Boleyn (whose biography is scheduled for release in 1984) are explored in her books. Erickson brings to her studies both historical expertise and narrative talent, along with an eye for relevant detail. The result, according to several reviewers, is history that engages like fiction. As Edward White puts it in his review of *The First Elizabeth* for the *Los Angeles Times Book Review:* "Those familiar with Elizabethan life and times will find no fresh discoveries and few surprises. What they, and everyone else, will applaud is a masterpiece of narrative, a story so absorbing that it is as hard to put down as a fine novel."

Reader response to Erickson's approach has been enthusiastic, and nearly half-a-million copies of her books have been sold worldwide. Her first biography, *Bloody Mary* (1977), examines the life of Henry VIII's eldest daughter, Mary Tudor. A staunch Catholic who was bastardized by an Act of Parliament to facilitate her father's remarriage, Mary tried to restore the Roman faith to England during her short reign. Though she married a Catholic prince from Spain, her campaign failed. Furthermore, her role in the burning of 300 Protestant resisters was recorded in John Foxe's *Book of Martyrs,* and this widely read document contributed to her unpopularity. In Erickson's book, the queen is reevaluated, and John Kenyon reports that the study "tries to do full justice to her." Writing in the *Washington Post Book World,* he goes on to say: "Erickson's great strength is that she deals fully with Mary's life before her accession; indeed, her five-year reign is for once set in proper proportion, occupying less than a quarter of the book. Without venturing into amateur psychology, she exposes and analyzes the tensions created by an upbringing which was irrational and unnatural even for a princess of royal blood."

While Paul Johnson also finds Erickson's portrayal of Mary praiseworthy, he misses what he refers to in the *New York Times Book Review* as "the important structural changes in the historical picture of the reign. . . . What I should like in short," he adds, "are the historical nuts and bolts which made up the machinery of the Marian restoration, and these Miss Erickson cannot, or does not, give us. Instead we have a well-organized, readable and sympathetic portrait of a sad and lonely lady."

In *Great Harry* (1980), Erickson shifts her focus from daughter to father, making Henry VIII the subject of her second biography. Remembered largely for his gluttonous appetites and his procession of wives, Henry was a man of many faces and a difficult character to assess. But, "in this splendid biography, Carolly Erickson does what is most difficult with a legendary figure," Robert Kirsch reports. "She convinces us to suspend judgement of the caricature, the mythic royal satyr, the gouty old monster, to allow us to experience the life as lived," he writes in the *Los Angeles Times Book Review.*

A popular account intended for the general reader, the book "does not pretend to say anything new, but it tells the old story forcefully and well," the *Times Literary Supplement* reviewer observes. And writing in the *New York Times Book Review,* Christopher Hibbert expresses a similar view. Erickson "disclaims any intention of arriving at a fresh assessment of the reign or of detailing the political accomplishments of Henry or his ministers. But she has written an admirable biography, graphic, judicious, carefully researched, skillfully constructed and full of those telling details that are an essential ingredient of the narrator's art."

Similar in approach to *Great Harry,* Erickson's *The First Elizabeth* (1983) "deemphasizes the public events of Elizabeth's reign in favor of the neglected years before it, and paints in rich detail the queen's daily life instead of the foreign and domestic intrigues that cluttered her reign," Mark Caldwell reports in the *Village Voice.* As always, Erickson draws her information from cited sources, using as dialogue only those conversations which have been verified. She is careful, as well, not to impose twentieth-century thoughts on Renaissance characters, as she explains to Leah Garchik in a *San Francisco Chronicle* interview: "It would be very easy to go over the cliff into feminist polemics. But I try to write from the subject's perspective." Garchik adds that "Erickson never speculates about what Elizabeth might have been thinking, nor imposes insights of modern psychological thinking. Every hint of personality is drawn from a specified document."

Because Erickson emphasizes Elizabeth the woman rather than Elizabeth the policymaker, the reader glimpses a more human monarch than is usually portrayed. Erickson's "Virgin Queen" is not only vain and conniving, she is an overtly sexual creature who uses her single status to protect her power. "If you were married," the Scots envoy Melville reportedly told the monarch, "you would be but queen of England; and now you are both king and queen." Here, as in earlier works, Erickson sets the queen's actions against a Renaissance background in which

everything from the sanitary conditions at Hampton Court to the philosophical biases of the queen's childhood teachers are revealed. "These scenes give Erickson's work a wonderful sense of depth and texture," reports Alida Becker in the *Philadelphia Inquirer.* "And they build on each other until, at the close of the book, the aged but already legendary 'Virgin Queen' has been rendered an intensely human, even poignant figure."

Though critical response to Erickson's work, both in the United States and abroad, has been largely favorable, her private approach occasionally draws fire. *Washington Post Book World* contributing reviewer Thomas Flanagan complains that Erickson does not "relate her great personages to their historical moments and to the political, economic and cultural worlds in which they moved." Instead, she is "content with the simply picturesque. But Elizabeth, if presented without a deep surrounding background of the Elizabethan world, is a cardboard figure, no matter how skillful the coloring." And echoing this sentiment, Maureen Quilligan writes in the *New York Times Book Review* that while sacrificing "clarity of critical analysis for ease and drama of narration may be a legitimate choice in a popular biography," we are never told "exactly how this royal brat evolved into Gloriana who kept a nation at peace and enthralled."

Despite her objections, Quilligan concludes: "While we await her next book, a much-needed study of Elizabeth's mother, Anne Boleyn—a real victim of the sexual scandals her brilliant daughter escaped, and a subject Miss Erickson's sensitivity to sexual and political nuance should well serve—we can appreciate this vivid and eminently readable portrait of history's favorite Tudor. If the roses have been painted in slightly more lurid colors than before, we may also better understand the political necessity of some of the thorns."

Several of Erickson's biographies have been translated into Italian, Spanish, and French.

BIOGRAPHICAL/CRITICAL SOURCES: New York Times Book Review, January 15, 1978, June 29, 1980, April 3, 1983; *Washington Post Book World,* February 12, 1978, March 29, 1983; *Los Angeles Times Book Review,* May 25, 1980, March 27, 1983; *Times Literary Supplement,* September 12, 1980; *Philadelphia Inquirer,* April 3, 1983; *Village Voice,* April 19, 1983; *San Francisco Chronicle,* May 29, 1983.

—*Sketch by Donna Olendorf*

*   *   *

ESMAN, Aaron H(irsh) 1924-

PERSONAL: Born December 9, 1924, in Pittsburgh, Pa.; son of Mayer G. (a merchant) and Hermoine (Bernstein) Esman; married Rosa Mencher (an art dealer); children: Susanna (Mrs. Peter Singer), Marjorie, Abigail. *Education:* Cornell University, B.A., 1944, M.D., 1947; attended New York Psychoanalytic Institute, 1954-61. *Home:* 115 East 86th St., New York, N.Y. 10028. *Office:* 525 East 68th St., New York, N.Y. 10021; and Department of Psychiatry, Medical College, Cornell University, New York, N.Y.

CAREER: Psychiatrist in private practice, 1954—. Senior assistant surgeon, New York Public Health Service, 1952-54; psychiatrist-in-charge of children's service, Bellevue Hospital, 1957-59; Jewish Board of Guardians, director of training, 1961-70, chief psychiatrist, 1970-79; Cornell University, Medical College, New York, N.Y., professor of clinical psychiatry, 1979—. *Member:* American Psychoanalytic Association,

American Psychiatric Association, American Academy of Child Psychiatry, New York Psychoanalytic Society (secretary, 1973-75).

WRITINGS—Editor; published by International Universities Press, except as indicated: *New Frontiers in Child Guidance,* 1958; (with W. Muensterberger) *Psychoanalytic Study of Society,* Volumes IV-VI (Esman was not associated with earlier volumes), 1972-74, Volume VII, Yale University Press, 1975; *Psychology of Adolescence,* 1975; *The Psychiatric Treatment of Adolescents,* 1982. Contributor to professional journals.

WORK IN PROGRESS: Two contributions to journals, one on the "stimulus barrier" and the other on the assessment of adolescent psychopathology; research for a work on the psychology of creativity.

AVOCATIONAL INTERESTS: Art, art history, and archaeology.

*   *   *

EVEREST, Allan S(eymour)   1913-

PERSONAL: Born October 9, 1913, in South Shaftsbury, Vt.; son of Charles Seymour (a merchant) and Clara (Hawkins) Everest; married Elsie Hathaway Lewis, October 10, 1942; children: Martha Everest Lockwood. *Education:* University of Vermont, Ph.D., 1936; Columbia University, M.A., 1937, Ph.B., 1948. *Home:* 26 South Catherine St., Plattsburgh, N.Y. 12901. *Office:* Department of History, State University of New York College, Plattsburgh, N.Y. 12901.

CAREER: Green Mountain Junior College, Poultney, Vt., instructor in social science, 1938-41; State University of New York College at Plattsburgh, professor of American history, 1947—. *Military service:* U.S. Army Air Forces, 1941-46; became captain. *Member:* New York State Historical Association, Vermont Historical Society, Clinton County Historical Association (former president), Phi Beta Kappa, Pi Gamma Mu.

WRITINGS: Morgenthau, the New Deal and Silver: A Story of Pressure Politics, King's Crown Press, 1950; *British Objectives at the Battle of Plattsburgh,* Moorsfield Press, 1960; (editor) David Sherwood Kellogg, *Recollections of Clinton County and the Battle of Plattsburgh, 1800-1840,* Clinton County Historical Association, 1964; *Pioneer Homes of Clinton County, 1790-1820,* Clinton County Historical Association, 1966.

(Editor) Kellogg, *A Doctor at All Hours: A Private Journal of a Small-Town Doctor's Varied Life, 1886-1909,* Greene, 1970; *Our North Country Heritage: Architecture Worth Saving in Clinton and Essex Counties,* Tundra Books, 1972; (editor) Charles Carroll, *The Journal of Charles Carroll of Carrollton,* Champlain-Upper Hudson Bicentennial Committee, 1976; *Moses Hazen and the Canadian Refugees in the American Revolution,* Syracuse University Press, 1976; *Rum across the Border: The Prohibition Era in Northern New York,* Syracuse University Press, 1978; *Henry Delord and His Family,* George Little Press, 1979; *The War of 1812 in the Champlain Valley,* Syracuse University Press, 1981.

WORK IN PROGRESS: A History of Plattsburgh, New York.

SIDELIGHTS: Allan S. Everest has traveled extensively in the British Isles, Western Europe, and Canada and has twice taught at English universities.

EVERITT, Alan (Milner)   1926-

PERSONAL: Born August 17, 1926, in Sevenoaks, Kent, England; son of Robert Arthur and Grace (Milner) Everitt. *Education:* University of St. Andrews, M.A., 1951; University of London, Ph.D., 1957. *Home:* Fieldedge, Kimcote, Lutterworth, England. *Office:* Department of English Local History, University of Leicester, Leicester, England.

CAREER: University of Leicester, Leicester, England, research assistant in agrarian history, 1957-59, research fellow in urban history, 1960-65, lecturer in English local history, 1965-68, Hatton Professor and head of English local history department, 1968-82, professor emeritus, 1982—. Member, Council for Name Studies; trustee, Marc Fitch Fund. *Member:* Historical Association, Council for Tutors in Regional and Local History (president, 1982-83), Economic History Society, Past and Present Society, British Agricultural History Society, Kent Archaeological Society, Leicestershire Archaeological Society, Leicestershire Local History Council (vice-president, 1970—).

WRITINGS: The County Committee of Kent in the Civil War, Leicester University Press, 1957; *Suffolk and the Great Rebellion, 1640-1660,* Suffolk Records Society, 1960; *The Community of Kent and the Great Rebellion, 1640-1660,* Leicester University Press, 1966; *Change in the Provinces: The Seventeenth Century,* Leicester University Press, 1969; *The Local Community and the Great Rebellion,* Historical Association, 1969.

New Avenues in English Local History (lecture), Leicester University Press, 1970; *Ways and Means in Local History,* National Council of Social Service for the Standing Conference for Local History, 1971; *The Pattern of Rural Dissent: The Nineteenth Century,* Leicester University Press, 1972; (editor) *Perspectives in English Urban History,* Macmillan, 1973; (with E. Margery Tranter) *English Local History at Leicester, 1948-1978,* University of Leicester, Department of English Local History, 1981.

Contributor: Joan Thirsk, editor, *The Agrarian History of England, 1500-1640,* Cambridge University Press, 1967; A. E. Brown, editor, *The Growth of Leicester,* Leicester University Press, 1970; T. G. Cook, editor, *Local Studies and the History of Education,* Methuen, 1972; H. J. Dyos, editor, *Urban History Yearbook,* Leicester University Press, 1974; C. W. Chalklin and M. A. Havinden, editors, *Rural Change and Urban Growth, 1500-1800,* Longman, 1974; Jack Simmons, editor, *English County Historians,* E. P. Publishing, 1978; R. L. Greenall, editor, *Philip Doddridge, Nonconformity, and Northampton,* University of Leicester, Department of Adult Education, 1981.

WORK IN PROGRESS: Studies in Northampton evangelicalism, 1700-1850, the market town in English history, and early English settlement; three books, *The Making of the Kentish Landscape,* for Hodder & Stoughton, *The Grass Roots of History,* for Penguin, and *Continuity and Colonization: the Evolution of Kentish Settlement,* for Leicester University Press.

SIDELIGHTS: Alan Everitt states his historical studies are concentrated on the origins of English society (circa 500 to 1300) and on the period between 1530 and 1880, when the "cast of thought of English people was more conditioned by local environment than by national events and politics." He adds: "[I] believe deeply that history is an art as well as a science. . . . Exploring the past is like exploring another country."

AVOCATIONAL INTERESTS: Walking, music.

EYCK, Frank 1921-

PERSONAL: Born July 13, 1921, in Berlin, Germany; son of Erich (a historian) and Hedwig (Kosterlitz) Eyck; married Rosemarie Schmidt, December 10, 1955; children: Andrew, George. *Education:* Worcester College, Oxford, B.A., 1949, M.A., 1954; St. Antony's College, Oxford, B.Litt., 1958. *Religion:* Lutheran. *Office:* Department of History, University of Calgary, Calgary, Alberta, Canada T2N 1N4.

CAREER: British Broadcasting Corp., London, England, member of news editorial staff, 1949-56; St. Antony's College, Oxford, England, research fellow, 1956-58; University of Liverpool, Liverpool, England, temporary assistant lecturer in modern history, 1958-59; University of Exeter, Exeter, England, lecturer in modern European history, 1959-68; University of Calgary, Calgary, Alberta, professor of history, 1968—. Vice-chairman, Council of the Inter-University Centre of Post-Graduate Studies, Dubrovnik, Yugoslavia, 1974-79. *Military service:* British Army, 1940-46; became staff sergeant. *Member:* Canadian Historical Association, Royal Historical Society (fellow), Royal Commonwealth Society (fellow), London Library.

WRITINGS: The Prince Consort, Chatto & Windus, 1959; *The Frankfurt Parliament, 1848-1849,* Macmillan, 1968; (editor) *The Revolutions of 1848-49,* Oliver & Boyd, 1972; (editor) Frederick Hertz, *The German Public Mind in the Nineteenth Century,* Allen & Unwin, 1975; *G. P. Gooch: A Study in History and Politics,* Macmillan, 1982.

Contributor: W. Laqueur and G. L. Mosse, editors, *Historians in Politics,* Sage Publications, 1974; W. Kloetzer, editor, *Ideen und Strukturen der deutschen Revolution 1848,* Verlag Dr. Waldemar Kramer, 1974; Mosse and others, editors, *Revolution and Evolution: 1848 in German-Jewish History,* J.C.B. Mohr, 1981; T.H.E. Travers and C. I. Archer, editors, *Men at War: Politics, Technology, and Innovation in the Twentieth Century,* Precedent Publishing, 1982.

WORK IN PROGRESS: A study of the relationship between religion and politics in Germany during the nineteenth century.

SIDELIGHTS: Historian Frank Eyck's lengthy study of Britain's G. P. Gooch, *G. P. Gooch: A Study in History and Politics,* is considered a definitive work. ''No one else could have done the job with such exemplary patience and persistence,'' observes the *Times Literary Supplement* reviewer, who adds that, ''in all probability, Eyck on Gooch will have few competitors in the future.'' In a review for the *Economist,* Paul Kennedy observes that Gooch's ''was a long and interesting life, reflecting many changes in scholarship and politics, and Professor Eyck has captured it admirably in this well-written . . . biography.''

Two of Eyck's books, *The Prince Consort* and *The Frankfurt Parliament,* have been translated into German.

BIOGRAPHICAL/CRITICAL SOURCES: Economist, May 1, 1982; *Times Literary Supplement,* July 30, 1982.

F

FAHY, Christopher 1937-

PERSONAL: Surname is pronounced Fay; born November 15, 1937, in Philadelphia, Pa.; son of William J. (a teacher) and Dorothy (a teacher; maiden name, Kitsch) Fahy; married Davene Sernoff (a school administrator), January 25, 1960; children: Gregory, Benjamin. *Education:* Temple University, B.A., 1959, M.A., 1962. *Politics:* "Declining." *Religion:* "Stable." *Residence:* Tenants Harbor, Me. 04860.

CAREER: Speech therapist in public schools in New Jersey, 1961-62; Bancroft School, Haddonfield, N.J., speech therapist, 1962-65, director of speech clinic and coordinator of clinical services, 1967-72; free-lance writer, 1972—. Vice-president of Friends of Jackson Library, 1975—, and Memorial Library League, 1982-83; coordinator of Service Social International Disabled Children's Program, Knox and Lincoln Counties, Me., 1979-81; member of literature advisory panel, Maine State Commission on the Arts and Humanities, 1983-84. *Member:* International Society for General Semantics, American Speech and Hearing Association, Authors Guild, Authors League of America.

WRITINGS: The Compost Heap (novel), Outerbridge & Dienstfrey, 1970; *Home Remedies* (on home repair), Scribner, 1975; (contributor) David Kherdian, editor, *Travelling America with Today's Poets* (anthology), Macmillan, 1977; *Greengroundtown* (short stories), Puckerbrush Press, 1978; *The End Beginning* (poetry), Red Earth, 1978; *Nightflyer* (novel), Jove, 1982. Contributor of stories and poems to literary journals, including *Beloit Poetry Journal, Gallery, Twilight Zone,* and *Transatlantic Review.*

WORK IN PROGRESS: Dark Harvest, a fantasy suspense novel; *The Broken Seed,* and *Bear at Forty-two,* both novels.

SIDELIGHTS: Christopher Fahy comments: "The earth and the brain are equal magic. Words are the plants of the mind. We have to tend our gardens lovingly but leave some stones. Nothing but bones remain when we're done, but hell, have fun." *Avocational interests:* Fixing old houses, gardening.

*   *   *

FARNDALE, W(illiam) A(rthur) J(ames) 1916-

PERSONAL: Born January 24, 1916, in Birtley, County Dur-
ham, England; son of William Edward (a Methodist minister, lecturer, and writer) and Florence (Price) Farndale; married Audrey Hogg, July 21, 1940; children: Wendy Elizabeth, Michael James. *Education:* University of London, B.Com., 1945, Ph.D., 1961. *Politics:* Liberal. *Religion:* Methodist. *Home:* 58 Ravenswood Ave., West Wickham, Kent, England. *Office:* Ravenswood Publications, Ltd., P.O. Box 24, 205 Croydon Rd., Beckenham BR3 3AL, Kent, England; and London Association for Health Services, Polytechnic of Central London, 311 Regent St., London W.1., England.

CAREER: Called to the bar, London, England, 1947. Employed in various insurance offices in Grimsby and Lincoln, England, 1932-39; University of London, London School of Economics and Political Science, London, England, administration posts, 1945-48; deputy house governor and secretary to the board of governors of Bethlehem Royal Hospital, Beckenham and Maudsley Hospital, London, 1948-62; Polytechnic of the South Bank, London, principal lecturer in health service administration and law, 1962-81. Arbitrator. Director of Ravenswood Publications Ltd.; founder and trustee of Ravenswood Charitable Trust; founder, trustee, and honorary director, London Association for Health Services Studies, and London Health Services Studies Trust, Polytechnic of Central London, 1981—. Local (lay) preacher of Methodist Church. Delegate to International Hospital Federation conferences in Portugal, Paris, and Chicago. *Military service:* British Army, Royal Army Ordnance Corps, 1939-45, with final assignment on General Staff, War Office, London; became major; received four medals, including African Star.

MEMBER: European Association for Health Service Studies, Royal Society of Health (fellow), Institute of Health Service Administrators (fellow), Royal Institute of Health and Hygiene, Royal Society of Medicine, Conservative Medical Society (member of executive committee), Medico Legal Society, Association of Law Teachers, Chartered Insurance Institute (fellow), Chartered Institute of Arbitrators (fellow), British Academy of Forensic Science, Independent Publishers Guild.

WRITINGS—Published by Pergamon, except as indicated: *The Day Hospital Movement in Great Britain,* 1961; (editor with Hugh Freeman) *Trends in the Mental Health Services,* 1963; (editor) *Trends in the National Health Service,* 1964; (editor) *Trends in Social Welfare,* 1965; (editor with James Leicester) *Trends in Services for Youth,* 1967; (editor with Freeman) *New*

Aspects of the Mental Health Services, 1967; (contributor) G. O'Gorman, editor, *Modern Trends in Mental Health,* Butterworth & Co., 1968; *Medical Negligence: Legal Case Studies,* White, 1969; (editor with A. T. Elder) *Trends in Environmental Health Technology,* 1971.

Published by Ravenswood Publications: *Law of Human Transplants and Bequest of Bodies,* 1970; *Health Services Travelogue: Northern Ireland, Holland, Denmark and the United States,* 1972; (with E. C. Larman) *Legal Liability for Claims Arising from Hospital Treatment,* 1973; *French Hospitals and Medical Care Services,* 1975; (editor) *Aspects of Health Service Law,* 1981; (editor and contributor) *West German Hospitals and European Medical Care Service,* 1983.

Author of three pamphlets on hospital laundry services, 1966-68. General editor, "Health Service Management Law" series, published by Ravenswood Publications, 1971—; former general editor, "Modern Legal Outlines" series, published by Pergamon. Also general editor for a series of books on law and practice for health service management, published by Ravenswood Publications.

SIDELIGHTS: W.A.J. Farndale told *CA:* "I set up Ravenswood Charitable Trust as a medical and educational charity in 1971, at the same time as I formed a separate company—Ravenswood Publications—to publish some of my research and for health service law, medical, nursing and administrative publications. When I set these up, I wanted to serve staff and students with whom I have been associated for a number of years, especially those in hospital health and social services, and lecturers in further and higher education, such as Polytechnics, which does not appear to attract prize funds, research funds, and travel funds to the same extent as universities.

"I know from experience how useful short visits to other establishments, both in Britain and abroad, can be, and how difficult it is for such visits for study purposes to be fully subsidised by public funds or grants. I hope that both Ravenswood Charitable Trust and the London Health Services Studies Trust will go some way towards assisting students, staff, and lecturers to widen their experiences for the benefit of the health and social services."

AVOCATIONAL INTERESTS: Gardening, golf, reading.

*   *   *

FARRIS, Martin T(heodore) 1925-

PERSONAL: Born November 5, 1925, in Spokane, Wash.; son of Jacob B. (an editor, publisher, and insurance agent) and Edith (Gunderson) Farris; married Rhoda F. Harrington, August 20, 1948; children: Christine Zenobi, Lynn, Elizabeth Louise, Martin Theodore II. *Education:* Attended Montana State University, 1943; University of Montana, B.A. (with honors), 1949, M.A., 1950; Ohio State University, Ph.D., 1957. *Religion:* Episcopalian. *Home:* 6108 East Vernon, Scottsdale, Ariz. 85257. *Office:* College of Business Administration, Arizona State University, Tempe, Ariz. 85287.

CAREER: Ohio State University, Columbus, instructor in economics, 1955-57; Arizona State University, Tempe, assistant professor, 1957-59, associate professor, 1959-62, professor of economics, 1962-73, chairman of department, 1967-69, professor of transportation, 1973—, assistant director of bureau of business and economic research, 1964-66. University of Hawaii, visiting professor, 1969-70, visiting scholar, 1979. Consultant to business and government agencies. *Military ser-*

vice: U.S. Army, Signal Corps, 1944-46; received two battle stars and Philippine Liberation Medal with Bronze Star.

MEMBER: American Economic Association, American Society of Traffic and Transportation (member of board of examiners, 1962-74), Association of Interstate Commerce Commission Practitioners, Transportation Research Forum, Western Economic Association (member of executive committee, 1966-69), Phoenix Traffic Club (president, 1960), Delta Nu Alpha (president, 1967-68), Phi Kappa Phi, Beta Gamma Sigma, Omicron Delta Epsilon, Delta Sigma Pi, Sigma Phi Epsilon.

WRITINGS: (Contributor) P. A. Kolb and Otis Lipstreu, editors, *New Concepts and Current Issues in Public Utility Regulation,* Peerless Publishing, 1963; (with Grant M. Davis and Jack V. Holder, Jr.) *Management of Transportation Carriers,* Praeger, 1975; (with Forrest E. Harding) *Passenger Transportation,* Prentice-Hall, 1976; (with H. David Bess) *U.S. Maritime Policy: History and Prospects,* Praeger, 1981; (with Steve Hoppel) *Managerial Economics,* Addison-Wesley, 1984.

All published by Houghton: (With Roy J. Sampson) *Domestic Transportation: Practice, Theory, and Policy,* 1966, 5th edition, 1984; (editor with Paul T. McElhiney) *Modern Transportation: Selected Readings,* 1967, 2nd edition, 1973; (with Sampson) *Public Utilities: Regulation, Management, and Ownership,* 1973.

Contributor of about 130 articles and reviews to journals.

SIDELIGHTS: Martin T. Farris writes *CA:* "When I write articles and scholarly monographs, my audience is small—mostly academic colleagues and graduate students. I'm not sure how much impact my ideas carry here, but most do recognize my name. But when I write textbooks, my audience is very large—and the impact of my ideas falls on thousands—but none remember my name! Frankly, I'm not sure which is more important—so I continue to do both!"

*   *   *

FAST, Julius 1919-
(Adam Barnett)

PERSONAL: Born April 17, 1919, in New York, N.Y.; son of Barnett A. (a pattern maker) and Ida (Miller) Fast; married Barbara Hewitt Sher (a novelist), June 8, 1946; children: Jennifer, Melissa, Timothy H. *Education:* New York University, B.A., 1942. *Home address:* P.O. Box 81, Southbury, Conn. 06488. *Agent:* Robert P. Mills, 333 Fifth Ave., New York, N.Y. 10016.

CAREER: Smith, Kline & French (drugs), Philadelphia, Pa., writer, 1952-54; Purdue Frederick (drugs), New York City, research associate, 1954-61; *Medical News,* New York City, feature editor, 1961-62; *Medical World News,* New York City, editor and writer, 1962-63; *Ob-Gyn Observer,* New York City, editor, 1963-75. *Military service:* U.S. Army, 1943-46; became staff sergeant. *Awards, honors:* Edgar Allan Poe Award of Mystery Writers of America for best first mystery novel, 1946, for *Watchful at Night.*

WRITINGS: (Editor) *Out of This World,* Penguin, 1944; *Watchful at Night,* Farrar & Rinehart, 1945; *Bright Face of Danger,* Rinehart, 1946; *Walk in Shadow,* Rinehart, 1947, published as *Down through the Night,* Fawcett, 1956; *A Model for Murder,* Rinehart, 1956; *Street of Fear,* Rinehart, 1958.

(Self-illustrated) *Blueprint for Life: The Story of Modern Genetics,* St. Martin's, 1964; *What You Should Know about Hu-*

man Sexual Responses, Putnam, 1966; *The Beatles: The Real Story,* Putnam, 1968; *How to Stop Smoking and Lose Weight,* National Education Association, 1969; *League of Grey-Eyed Women,* Lippincott, 1969.

Body Language, M. Evans, 1970; *You and Your Feet,* St. Martin's, 1970; *The New Sexual Fulfillment,* Berkley Publishing, 1972; *The Incompatibility of Men and Women,* M. Evans, 1971; *Bisexual Living,* M. Evans, 1975; *The Pleasure Book,* Stein & Day, 1975; *Creative Coping,* Morrow, 1976; *The Body Language of Sex, Power, and Aggression,* M. Evans, 1976; *Psyching Up,* Stein & Day, 1978; *Weather Language,* Wyden Books, 1979.

Body Politics, Tower, 1980; *The Body Book,* Tower, 1981; *Ladies Man,* St. Martins, 1983; *Sexual Chemistry,* M. Evans, 1983.

Under pseudonym Adam Barnett: (With Larry Alexander) *Iron Cradle,* Crowell, 1954; *Doctor Harry: The Story of Dr. Harry Lorber,* Crowell, 1958.

SIDELIGHTS: H. S. Resnik of *Saturday Review* writes of Julius Fast's *Body Language:* "Although he pays far too much homage to other people's studies and published papers, Fast does make some interesting points about the ways in which people's bodies communicate their feelings and needs. . . . His book is actually a crash course in sensitivity, and some people can probably benefit from reading it."

Reviewing *The Incompatibility of Men and Women* for *Best Sellers,* Joseph Szuhay states that Fast "has presented an authoritative how-to-do-it course on incompatibility. . . . Basically the research cited may be a beginning of a scientific basis for the theoretical relationship between aggression, fear, and sexuality in man. . . . The book offers us a good, hard look at the sexual equality which according to all research cited is greatly misapprehended. The final section on marriage presents a plea to all readers to focus on what in our concept a male-female relationship should be, and how this concept should be answered. . . . The book should be recommended reading for all adults, married or not, for it provides an interesting understanding of human relationships at the most important levels. It no doubt could provide building blocks for better relationships for couples on the brink of separation or divorce."

BIOGRAPHICAL/CRITICAL SOURCES: Best Sellers, June 1, 1970, December 1, 1971; *Newsweek,* June 22, 1970; *Saturday Review,* July 25, 1970; *New York Times Book Review,* October 25, 1970; *American Journal of Public Health,* April, 1972.

*   *   *

FATCHEN, Max   1920-

PERSONAL: Born August 3, 1920, in Adelaide, South Australia; son of Cecil William (a farmer) and Isabel (Ridgway) Fatchen; married Jean Wohlers (a teacher), May 15, 1942; children: Winsome Genevieve, Michael John, Timothy James. *Education:* Attended schools in South Australia. *Religion:* Uniting Church of Australia. *Residence:* Smithfield, South Australia. *Agent:* John Johnson, Clerkenwell House, 45-47 Clerkenwell Green, London EC1R 0HT, England. *Office address:* c/o *Advertiser,* 121 King William St., Adelaide, South Australia.

CAREER: Adelaide News and *Sunday Mail,* Adelaide, South Australia, journalist and special writer, 1946-55; *Advertiser,* Adelaide, special writer, 1955-71, literary editor, 1971-82, special writer, 1982—. *Military service:* Royal Australian Air

Force, World War II. *Awards, honors: The River Kings* received a commendation and *The Spirit Wind* received a high commendation in annual book-of-the-year awards of Australian Children's Book Council; made member of Order of Australia for services to journalism and literature, 1980.

WRITINGS—Juveniles: The River Kings, Methuen, 1966, St. Martin's, 1968; *Conquest of the River,* Methuen, 1970; *The Spirit Wind,* Methuen, 1973; *Chase through the Night,* Methuen, 1976; *The Time Wave,* Methuen, 1978; *Songs for My Dog* (verse), Kestrel Books, 1980; *Closer to the Stars,* Methuen, 1981; *Wry Rhymes for Troublesome Times,* Kestrel Books, 1983. Contributor of light verse to *Denver Post.*

SIDELIGHTS: Max Fatchen, who has made two trips to the United States for the *Advertiser,* is "very fond of America and Americans," and has "warm links with Denver and the *Denver Post.*" He explains that his light verse first found its way into the *Post* through a long friendship with that newspaper's former cartoonist, Pulitzer Prize-winner Pat Oliphant, who began his career on the Adelaide *Advertiser* illustrating Fatchen's lighter pieces.

"I have a great interest in rivers," Fatchen writes, "and know the Murray [on which *The River Kings* is based] intimately. My forays into the Australian Outback have included a mapping expedition with Army surveyors and Naval support group to the Gulf of Carpentaria and Arnhem Land—a wild and remote area. . . . [I] have also travelled on mailman's truck on Birdsville Track, one of Australia's loneliest trails, landed on many offshore islands on the Australian coast, and travelled with trains supplying settlers on outback lines such as the trans-Australia line."

MEDIA ADAPTATIONS: Chase through the Night has been filmed for the Australian Broadcasting Corporation.

*   *   *

FAULKNER, Virginia (Louise)   1913-1980

PERSONAL: Born March 1, 1913, in Lincoln, Neb.; died September 15, 1980; buried in Lincoln, Neb.; daughter of Edwin Jerome and Leah (Meyer) Faulkner. *Education:* Attended University of Nebraska, 1928-30, Moxley School, Rome, 1930-31, and Radcliffe College, 1932-33. *Politics:* Republican. *Religion:* Presbyterian. *Home:* 721 South 14th St., Lincoln, Neb. 68508. *Office:* University of Nebraska Press, 901 North 17th St., Lincoln, Neb. 68588.

CAREER: Washington Post, Washington, D.C., special writer, 1933-34; *Town and Country,* New York, N.Y., assistant editor, 1934-35; Metro-Goldwyn-Mayer, Culver City, Calif., screenwriter, 1935-38; free-lance writer, 1938-56; University of Nebraska, Lincoln, assistant editor, 1956-59, editor-in-chief, 1959-80; University of Nebraska, Lincoln, associate professor, 1969-71, professor of English, 1971-80. Member of board of governors, Willa Cather Pioneer Memorial, 1960-80. *Member:* Modern Language Association of America, Alpha Phi.

WRITINGS: Friends and Romans, Simon & Schuster, 1934; *The Barbarians,* Simon & Schuster, 1935; *My Hey-Day,* Duell, Sloan & Pearce, 1940; (compiler and editor) *Roundup: A Nebraska Reader,* University of Nebraska Press, 1957, reprinted, 1975; (editor) *Hostiles and Friendlies: Mari Sandoz's Selected Short Writings,* University of Nebraska Press, 1959; (editor) *Willa Cather's Collected Short Fiction, 1892-1912,* University of Nebraska Press, 1965, revised edition, 1970; (editor) *Sandhill Sundays and Other Recollections by Mari Sandoz,* University of Nebraska Press, 1970; (editor with Bernice Slote) *The Art of Willa Cather,* University of Nebraska Press, 1974; (editor with Frederick C. Luebke) *Vision and Refuge: Essays on the Literature of the Great Plains,* University of Nebraska Press, 1982.

Also author of *Out to the Wind,* with Robert Readell, 1979; author of book and lyrics of a two-act musical comedy, "That Does It," with Dana Suesse, 1943; co-author of "Maiden Voyage," a screenplay produced by Metro-Goldwyn-Mayer, 1938. Contributor of sketches and lyrics to two-act review "All in Fun," first produced in New York at Majestic Theatre, December 26, 1939, and to three-act play, "It Takes Two," with Suesse, first produced in New York at Biltmore Theater, February 3, 1946. Contributor to national magazines and scholarly publications, including *Saturday Evening Post, College English,* and *Cosmopolitan.* Associate editor, *Prairie Schooner,* 1962-80.†

*   *   *

FELLOWS, Jay 1940-

PERSONAL: Born April 17, 1940, in New York, N.Y.; son of Otis Edward (a professor) and Frances (Young) Fellows. *Education:* Harvard University, B.A. (magna cum laude), 1962; Columbia University, Ph.D., 1969. *Politics:* None. *Religion:* None. *Home:* 560 Riverside Dr., New York, N.Y. 10027. *Office:* Cooper Union, New York, N.Y. 10003.

CAREER: Fiction writer and free-lance editor, 1969-72; Herbert H. Lehman College of the City University of New York, Bronx, N.Y., adjunct assistant professor of English, 1972-81; Cooper Union, New York, N.Y., Melon Adjunct Professor of Literature, 1977 and 1981—. *Awards, honors:* Guggenheim fellow, 1981 and 1982.

WRITINGS: The Failing Distance: The Autobiographical Impulse in John Ruskin, Johns Hopkins Press, 1975; *Ruskin's Maze: Mastery and Madness in His Art,* Princeton University Press, 1981.

WORK IN PROGRESS: A book concerning Walter Pater on landscape and time; a book on literary forgeries.

AVOCATIONAL INTERESTS: Running with his Borzoi.

BIOGRAPHICAL/CRITICAL SOURCES: Virginia Quarterly Review, spring, 1982; *Times Literary Supplement,* March 12, 1982; *Burlington Magazine,* September, 1982; *New York Review of Books,* March 31, 1983.

*   *   *

FENSCH, Thomas 1943-
(Lander Moore)

PERSONAL: Born November 29, 1943, in Ashland, Ohio; son of Edwin A. Fensch (an educator) and stepson of Flossie (Hoover) Fensch; married Jean Robinson, December 27, 1977; stepchildren: Bill, Susan, LynnMarie. *Education:* Ashland College, B.A., 1965; University of Iowa, M.A., 1967, additional graduate study, 1967-70; Syracuse University, Ph.D., 1977. *Home:* 11705 Blackhawk Dr., Austin, Tex. 78759. *Office:* Department of Journalism, University of Texas, Austin, Tex. 78712.

CAREER: Writer and educator. Shippensburg State College, Shippensburg, Pa., associate professor of English and journalism, 1970-71; Ohio State University, Columbus, instructor

in journalism, 1971-73; University of Texas at Austin, associate professor of journalism, 1977—. *Member:* Authors Guild, Authors League of America, American Society of Journalists and Authors, Mensa. *Awards, honors:* Received honorable mention in *Story, the Yearbook of Discovery,* 1968, 1970; Book of the Year in Biography award, Martha Kinney Cooper Ohioana Library Association, 1980, for *Steinbeck and Corvici;* honorable mention, Texas Institute of Letters, 1980, for *Steinbeck and Corvici.*

WRITINGS—Nonfiction: *The Lions and the Lambs* (illustrated with his own photographs), A. S. Barnes, 1970; *Alice in Acidland,* A. S. Barnes, 1970; *Films on the Campus* (illustrated with his own photographs), A. S. Barnes, 1970; *Smokeys, Truckers, C.B. Radios and You,* Fawcett, 1976; *Steinbeck and Corvici: The Story of a Friendship,* Paul Eriksson, 1979; *Skydiving,* Anderson-World, 1980. Frequent contributor to magazines under pseudonym Lander Moore.

WORK IN PROGRESS: Additional books of nonfiction.

SIDELIGHTS: Thomas Fensch told *CA:* "When I was young, I recall reading and keeping great stacks of *Time, Newsweek, Life,* and other magazines. I wondered then who the people were who knew *secrets,* who knew things before I did—later I discovered they were reporters and editors and writers. I wanted to be someone who *knew the secrets*—who knew facts and stories—before anyone else did. Writing nonfiction is one of the most satisfying preoccupations in the world: dealing with real people, their fears, hopes, dreams, lives. As a writer and college educator, it is satisfying to know the secrets about people and to pass on the techniques of nonfiction writing to young writers."

AVOCATIONAL INTERESTS: Skydiving.

BIOGRAPHICAL/CRITICAL SOURCES: Des Moines Register, March 30, 1969; *Chicago Tribune Book World,* August 19, 1979; *Los Angeles Times,* August 24, 1979; *New York Times,* August 31, 1979; *Washington Post Book World,* September 16, 1979; *New York Times Book Review,* December 16, 1979.

*   *   *

FERLITA, Ernest (Charles) 1927-

PERSONAL: Born December 1, 1927, in Tampa, Fla.; son of Giuseppe R. (a macaroni manufacturer) and Vicenta (Ficarrotta) Ferlita. *Education:* Spring Hill College, B.S., 1950; St. Louis University, M.A., 1964; Yale University, D.F.A., 1969. *Home and office:* Department of Drama and Speech, Loyola University, New Orleans, La. 70118.

CAREER: Entered Order of Society of Jesus (Jesuits), 1950, ordained Roman Catholic priest, 1962; high school teacher in New Orleans, La., 1956-59; Spring Hill College, Mobile, Ala., instructor in English and speech, 1964-65; Loyola University, New Orleans, La., professor of drama and chairman of department of drama and speech, 1969—. Member of board of directors, Loyola University, 1970-75, chairman of board, 1972-75. *Military service:* U.S. Army, Medical Corps, 1946-47; became sergeant.

WRITINGS: The Hills Send off Echoes (one-act play), Baker's Plays, 1962; "The Ballad of John Ogilvie" (three-act play), first produced Off-Broadway at Blackfriars' Theatre, October 9, 1968; *New Fire* (play), Baker's Plays, 1968; *The Theatre of Pilgrimage,* Sheed, 1971; (with John R. May) *Film Odyssey,* Paulist/Newman, 1976; (with May) *The Parables of Lina Wert-*

muller, Paulist/Newman, 1977; *The Way of the River: A Book of Scriptural Meditations,* Paulist/Newman, 1977; (with May and others) *Religion in Film,* University of Tennessee, 1983; *Gospel Journey,* Winston Press, 1983. Contributor to *Drama Critique* and *New Orleans Review.*

SIDELIGHTS: Ernest Ferlita told *CA,* "Both as teacher and writer, I am very interested in the dialectic between religion and drama."

*   *   *

FERRACUTI, Franco 1927-

PERSONAL: Born April 1, 1927, in Montottone, Italy; son of Vasco and Antonietta (Berdini) Ferracuti; married Mirella Garutti, January 26, 1955; children: Stefano and Daniele (sons). *Education:* University of Rome, M.D. (cum laude), 1951, Diploma in Forensic Medicine, 1955, Diploma in Criminal Anthropology, 1960. *Home:* Via G. Marchi 3, Rome 00161, Italy.

CAREER: University of Rome Hospitals, Rome, Italy, intern, 1951; licensed to practice medicine, 1952; University of Rome, Rome, assistant in Institute of Psychology, 1951-56, 1966-73, instructor in Postgraduate Training School in Penal Law, 1952-66, assistant in Institute of Criminal Anthropology, 1957-66, professor of criminal anthropology in School of Law, 1966-73, professor of criminological medicine and forensic psychiatry in Medical School, 1973—.

Carabinieri Officers Training School, Rome, instructor, 1955-62, 1966-81; University of Wisconsin, research associate in Psychiatric Institute, 1954; University of Puerto Rico, visiting professor of psychology, 1956-57, research professor, and later director of research and training program in criminology of Social Science Research Center, 1959-67; University of Modena, School of Law, professor of criminal anthropology, 1961-63; New York University, School of Law, instructor in juvenile delinquency, 1963-64. Instituto Nazionale di Osservazione, Rome, psychologist, 1952-74; United Nations, social affairs officer, 1963-64; Council of Europe, member of criminological scientific council, 1965-68. Consultant to United Nations Social Defence Research Institute, Rome, 1968-73.

MEMBER: International Society for Criminology (member of scientific council, 1967-69), Societa Italiana di Psicologia, Societa Romana di Medicina Legale a delle Assicurazioni, Society for Projective Techniques, American Psychological Association, International Association of Applied Psychology, National Council on Crime and Delinquency (Italian correspondent, 1962-80), American Sociological Association (associate member), Italian Social Sciences Association (national counselor, 1962-65).

AWARDS, HONORS: Scholarships from Italian League for the Control of Tumors to study psychological aspects of terminal cancer cases, 1952, 1953; Rotary Club scholarship to study penal institutions and psychiatric clinics for criminals in Sweden, 1952; Fulbright travel grant to study at University of Wisconsin, 1954; National Institute of Mental Health research grant, 1963; American Society for Criminology award, 1974.

WRITINGS: Appunti di psicologia giudiziaria (text in forensic psychology), Tipografia Ufficiali Carabinieri, 1959; (with M. E. Wolfgang) *Il comportamento violento: Moderno studio criminologico,* Giuffre, 1966, translation published as *The Subculture of Violence,* Tavistock Publications, 1967; (with others) *Delinquents and Nondelinquents in the Puerto Rican Slum Culture,* Ohio State University Press, 1975.

(With S. Dinitz and A. Piperno) *Deterioramento mentale da detenzione,* Italian Ministry of Justice, 1976, translation published as *Mental Deterioration in Prison,* Center for the Study of Crime and Delinquency, Ohio State University, 1976; (with M. L. Solivetti) *La pornografia nei mezzi di comunicazione di massa con particolare riguardo alla televisione* (title means "Pornography in Mass-Media, with Particular Reference to Television"), RAI (Rome), 1977; (editor with Wolfgang) *Criminological Diagnosis: An International Perspective,* two volumes, Lexington Books, 1983.

Contributor: E. S. Shneidman and N. C. Farberow, editors, *Corso per analisti di mercato,* Giuffre, 1955; *Clues to Suicide,* Blakiston Co., 1957; *Il Corso di perfezionamento per Uditori Giudiziari,* Giuffre, 1959; *Principi di criminologia clinica e psichiatria forense,* Istituto di Medicina Sociale, 1960; G. Mueller, editor, *Essays in Criminal Science,* Sweet & Maxwell, 1961; B. Di Tullio, *Principi di criminologia clinica,* Instituto di Medicina Sociale, 1963; Daniel Glaser, editor, *Handbook for Criminology,* Random House, 1975.

Bibliographies: (With S. P. Fragola and F. Gioggi) *Bibliografia criminologica italiana, 1955-1964,* Giuffre, 1965; *Intelligenza e criminalita,* Giuffre, 1966; (with A. Hess and G. Keh Fang Hess) *Il delinquente giovane adulto,* Giuffre, 1967; (with M. Fontanesi, I. Melup, and G. Minervina) *Bibliografia sui delinquenti anormali psichici,* Mantellate, 1967.

Translator into Italian: Lean Radzinowicz, *In Search of Criminology,* Giuffre, 1964; (with G. Tartaglione) Eleanor Glueck and Sheldon Glueck, *Physique and Delinquency,* Editrice Universitaria (Florence), 1965; (with wife, Mirella Ferracuti) B. B. Burgemeister, *Psychological Techniques in Neurological Diagnosis,* O.S. (Florence), 1967. Also translator of ten psychology texts and their manuals published by O.S.

Co-author of report, "Replication of 'Unraveling Juvenile Delinquency' in Puerto Rico," Harvard University, 1966. Contributor of over one hundred and sixty articles on psychology and criminology, and about one hundred reviews in the same fields, to professional journals. Editor, *Quaderni di Criminologia Clinica,* Ministry of Justice (Rome), 1959-80; member of scientific board, *Excerpta Criminologica,* 1960-67; editorial consultant, *Journal of Criminal Law, Criminology and Police Science,* 1965—; member of advisory board, *British Journal of Criminology,* 1965—.

*   *   *

FERRER, Aldo 1927-

PERSONAL: Born April 15, 1927, in Buenos Aires, Argentina; son of Antonio and Isabel (Agretti) Ferrer; married Susanna Lustig (a physician and psychoanalyst), December 23, 1958; children: Carmen, Amparo, Lucinda. *Education:* University of Buenos Aires, Dr.Econ., 1949. *Home:* Libertador 1750, Buenos Aires, Argentina.

CAREER: United Nations Secretariat, New York, N.Y., economist, 1950-53; Argentine Embassy, London, England, economic counselor, 1956-57; Province of Buenos Aires, Buenos Aires, Argentina, minister of economics, 1958-60; University of Buenos Aires, Buenos Aires, professor of economics, 1963-66; National Government of Argentina, Buenos Aires, minister of works and public services, 1970, minister of economy and labour, 1970-71. Member of panel of experts, Inter-American Committee of Alliance for Progress, 1967-70; executive secretary, Latin American Social Science Council, 1967-70. *Member:* National Academy of Economic Sciences of Argentina.

WRITINGS: El Estado y el desarrollo economico, Editorial Raigal, 1956; *La economia argentina: Las etapas de su desarrollo y problemas actuales,* Fondo de Cultura Economica Mexico, 1963, 15th edition, 1982, translation by Marjory M. Urquidi published as *The Argentine Economy,* University of California Press, 1967; *Industrialization in Argentina and Australia: A Comparative Study,* Centro de Investigaciones Economicas, Instituto Torcuatodi Tilla, 1966.

Desarrollo sin dependencia, Quadrante Latino, 1974; *Tecnologia y politica economica en America Latina,* [Buenos Aires], 1974; *Economia internacional contemporanea: Texto para latinoamericanos,* Fondo de Cultura Economica, 1976; *Crisis y alternativas de la politica economica argentina,* Fondo de Cultura Economica, 1977, 2nd edition, 1981; (contributor) *America Latina y el sistema internacional,* Montvideo Centro Latinoamericano de Economia Humana, 1979.

La posguena, El Cid Editor, 1982; *Puede Argentina pagar su deuda externa?,* El Cid Editor, 1982; *Nacionalismo y orden constitucional,* Fondo de Cultura Economica, 2nd edition, 1983. Also author of numerous published papers.

*　　*　　*

FERRIS, Timothy 1944-

PERSONAL: Born August 29, 1944, in Miami, Fla.; son of Thomas A. (a publicist) and Jean (a literary critic; maiden name, Baird) Ferris. *Education:* Northwestern University, B.S., 1966, graduate study, 1966-67. *Home:* 1741 Ivar St., Hollywood, Calif. 90028. *Agent:* Owen Laster, William Morris Agency, 1350 Avenue of the Americas, New York, N.Y. 10019. *Office:* School of Journalism, University of Southern California, Los Angeles, Calif. 90089.

CAREER: United Press International, New York City, reporter, 1967-69; *New York Post,* New York City, reporter, 1969-71; *Rolling Stone,* New York City, associate editor, 1971-73, contributing editor, 1973-80; University of Southern California, Los Angeles, associate professor of journalism, 1982—. Professor at Brooklyn College of the City University of New York, 1974-82. Among his journalistic assignments were the Democratic and Republican national conventions in 1972, and the Viking landing on Mars in 1976. *Awards, honors: Galaxies* was nominated for an American Book Award in science, 1981.

WRITINGS: The Red Limit: The Search for the Edge of the Universe, Morrow, 1977; *Galaxies,* Sierra Club Books, 1980. Contributor to national magazines, including *Harper's, Playboy, Esquire, New Republic,* and *New York Times Magazine.*

WORK IN PROGRESS: Coming of Age in the Milky Way, a history of human concepts of space, time, and natural law; *Journalism: An Introduction,* a textbook, with Bruce Porter.

SIDELIGHTS: An experienced science writer specializing in astronomy, Timothy Ferris writes about the cosmos in terms the layman can understand. "A lot of what I do consists of pointing out that there is more to the world than this world, and more to this world than we know," he told *CA.* "This idea got hold of me years ago, and never let go. It is *my* author."

In his 1980 publication, *Galaxies,* Ferris takes the reader on an imaginary starship that travels from Earth to the edge of the universe. "When Timothy Ferris extends an invitation to join him on a guided tour of the universe, you would be wise to accept," notes George Alexander in the *Los Angeles Times Book Review.* The book is "at once a linear, visual, historical,

futurist, cultural and philosophical journey to forever, as good books on astronomy ought to be," says contributing *New York Times* book reviewer Richard Severo. "It is easy to read because the author insists on being as incisive as he is imaginative. He gives us the data we need to appreciate the premise, but we are not inundated by numbers that would be, at the least, intimidating, and frequently speculative."

In his review of *Galaxies* for *Saturday Review,* Isaac Asimov deems the lavishly illustrated text "a very good candidate for the most beautiful book in the world. . . . In outsize opulence, it spreads its photographs over a square foot and more. . . . The captions are concise and clear," Asimov continues, "and Ferris's running commentary could stand on its own as an essay designed to give the reader a dramatic overview of the universe." Notes the *Village Voice*'s Eliot Fremont-Smith, "One wades into it not knowing quite what to expect and leery of romantics, and is enthralled."

BIOGRAPHICAL/CRITICAL SOURCES: New York Times, March 12, 1979, August 26, 1982; *New York Times Book Review,* July 15, 1979, January 25, 1981, July 11, 1982; *Saturday Review,* December, 1980; *Village Voice,* December 3, 1980; *Los Angeles Times Book Review,* December 14, 1980.

*　　*　　*

FEUCHTWANGER, E(dgar) J(oseph) 1924-

PERSONAL: Born September 28, 1924, in Munich, Germany; son of Ludwig (a publisher) and Erna (Rheinstrom) Feuchtwanger; married Primrose Essame, June 2, 1962; children: Antonia, Adrian, Judith. *Education:* Magdalene College, Cambridge, B.A., 1947, M.A., 1950; University of Southampton, Ph.D., 1958. *Home:* Highfield House, Dean, Sparsholt, Winchester SO21 2LP, England. *Office:* Department of Adult Education, University of Southampton, Southampton SO9 5NH, England.

CAREER: University of Southampton, Southampton, England, lecturer in extra-mural studies, 1949-63, senior lecturer, 1966-73, reader in history, 1973—, deputy director of extra-mural studies, 1963—. *Member:* International Institute for Strategic Studies, Royal Historical Society (fellow).

WRITINGS: Disraeli, Democracy, and the Tory Party, Clarendon Press, 1968; *Prussia: Myth and Reality,* Regnery, 1970; (editor) *Upheaval and Continuity: A Century of German History,* University of Pittsburgh Press, 1973; *Gladstone,* St. Martin's, 1975; (editor with John Erickson) *Soviet Military Power and Performance: A Symposium,* Macmillan, 1977.

(Editor with Richard Bessel) *Social Change and Political Development in Weimar Germany,* Barnes & Noble, 1981; (editor with Peter Nailor) *The Soviet Union and the Third World,* Macmillan, 1981; (contributor) *Preussen-Ploetz,* Verlag Ploetz (Freiburg), 1983; *The New History of England,* Harvard University Press, Volume IX: *Democracy and Empire, Britain 1865-1914,* 1984.

WORK IN PROGRESS: Research on the decline of organised liberal parties in Britain and Germany, circa 1890-1935.

SIDELIGHTS: E. J. Feuchtwanger comments briefly that his main interests are English and German political history of the nineteenth and twentieth centuries, and that subsidiary interests include contemporary international relations and strategic studies. Some of his books have been published in German.

BIOGRAPHICAL/CRITICAL SOURCES: *Spectator*, August 30, 1968; *Times Literary Supplement*, April 16, 1970, November 21, 1975; *New Statesman*, August 8, 1975.

* * *

FIAROTTA, Noel
  See FICAROTTA, Noel

* * *

FIAROTTA, Phyllis
  See FICAROTTA, Phyllis

* * *

FICAROTTA, Noel 1944-
  (Noel Fiarotta)

PERSONAL: Born March 13, 1944, in Meriden, Conn.; son of Anthony (an engineer) and Santa (a secretary; maiden name, Lentini) Ficarotta; married Beatriz Esteban (a teacher). *Education:* Jersey City State College, B.A., 1966; Fairleigh Dickinson University, M.A., 1973. *Politics:* "Depends on who and what." *Religion:* "I believe in God." *Home and office address:* Brook Way, Llewellyn Park, West Orange, N.J. 07052.

CAREER: Language arts teacher in elementary school in East Orange, N.J., 1967-74; King Features Syndicate, New York City, editor of column "Leisure Craftsman," 1972—. Professional singer, 1962-68; director of A. Harry Moore Camp, 1972-74; participant in Fabric Arts Show, New York City, 1983. Costume designer for the Yard Dance Company; co-owner of Culinary Design, a cooking/catering business.

WRITINGS—Editor and contributor; all by sister Phyllis Ficarotta; all published by Bantam: *A Hundred One Gifts You Can Make at Home*, 1968; *Sewing without a Pattern*, 1969; *A Hundred One Children's Gifts You Can Make at Home*, 1970; *Children's Parties*, 1971; *Making It with Leather and Beads*, 1971; *Sewing Tricks*, 1971; *How to Make Stuffed Animals*, 1973; *The Complete Treasury of Decorative Craft*, 1973.

Editor, under name Noel Fiarotta: Phyllis Fiarotta, *Phyllis Fiarotta's Nostalgia Crafts Book*, Workman Publishing, 1974.

With Phyllis Ficarotta, under names Noel and Phyllis Fiarotta; published by Workman Publishing, except as indicated: *Sticks and Stones and Ice Cream Cones: The Craft Book for Children*, 1973; *Snips and Snails and Walnut Whales: Nature Crafts for Children*, 1975; *Pin It, Tack It, Hang It*, 1975; *The You and Me Heritage Tree: Children's Crafts from Twenty-one American Traditions*, 1976; *Be What You Want to Be*, 1977; *Confetti*, 1978; *Zippers, Snaps and Flaps*, Van Nostrand, 1983.

Also author of *A Very Eggciting Craft Book*, 1980.

WORK IN PROGRESS: A cookbook for novice cooks, revolving around the theatre.

SIDELIGHTS: Noel Ficarotta told *CA:* "Living is that once in a lifetime opportunity to do everything you really want to do, and so be it with my life. I started writing at the ripe old age of ten, nothing too fancy, just childhood thoughts set to adult situations. Adolescence got the better of this shortlived literary career and the corner candy store replaced the bedroom desk, a pretzel stick took the place of my pencil.

"Caught up in the times, of rock and roll, bebop, customized cars, high school dances, and hanging out, music became my main interest. Everyone wanted to become a rock and roll star, and I was there waiting in line. I headed several rock and roll and folk groups, through my high school and college years, with many minor successes: several TV appearances, the college circuit, the Bitter End, and a couple of not-so-unsuccessful records. I even tried producing records, owned a record company called Felicia Records. The music field was getting too crowded and I was looking forward to a new career, as an English teacher.

"I taught English in an experimental school in East Orange, N.J. My main concern was teaching the writing skills to grades five through eight, in a little red school house atmosphere. Students were encouraged to undertake a yearly project: to write a novel, collection of poems, essays, etc. and through their writings they would learn what language arts is all about. The experiment lasted six years, and was replaced by traditional teaching. During the summers I worked at a camp for the physically handicapped and the mentally retarded, and eventually directed the camp for two years. The A. Harry Moore Camp really pointed out the beauty of life. My teaching experiences gave me a good foundation for preparing children's craft books.

"My future plans may possibly include a TV show for children (craft oriented): writing, directing, performing, and producing. I guess I will continue to try to keep quite active and doing it all before my name is added to the dead file with the epitaph, 'He did all he possibly could!'"

* * *

FICAROTTA, Phyllis 1942-
  (Phyllis Fiarotta)

PERSONAL: Born August 21, 1942, in Meriden, Conn.; daughter of Anthony (an engineer) and Santa (a secretary; maiden name, Lentini) Ficarotta. *Education:* Attended Newark School of Fine and Industrial Arts, 1960-63. *Politics:* Democrat. *Religion:* Roman Catholic. *Home and office address:* Brook Way, Llewellyn Park, West Orange, N.J. 07052.

CAREER: Good Housekeeping, New York City, associate art director, 1965-71; King Features Syndicate, New York City, author and illustrator of column "The Leisure Craftsman," 1972—. Assistant art director for Pharmaceutical Advertising, 1963-65. Assistant stage manager for International Ladies' Garment Workers' Union Theatre. Guest and demonstrator on more than a hundred television and radio programs. Spokesperson for Ivory Soap 100-year birthday soap-carving contest; also involved in Elmers' Glue contests.

WRITINGS—Self-illustrated; edited by brother, Noel Ficarotta; published by Bantam, except as indicated: *A Hundred One Gifts You Can Make at Home*, 1968; *Sewing without a Pattern*, 1969; *A Hundred One Children's Gifts You Can Make at Home*, 1970; *Children's Parties*, 1971; *Making It with Leather and Beads*, 1971; *Sewing Tricks*, 1971; *How to Make Stuffed Animals*, 1973; *The Complete Treasury of the Decorative Craft*, 1973; (under name Phyllis Fiarotta) *Phyllis Fiarotta's Nostalgia Crafts Book*, Workman Publishing, 1974.

Self-illustrated books, with Noel Ficarotta, under names Noel and Phyllis Fiarotta; published by Workman Publishing, except as indicated: *Sticks and Stones and Ice Cream Cones: The Craft Book for Children*, 1973; *Snips and Snails and Walnut Whales: Nature Crafts for Children*, 1975; *Pin It, Tack It, Hang It*, 1975; *The You and Me Heritage Tree: Children's Crafts from Twenty-one American Traditions*, 1976; *Be What You Want to*

Be, 1977; *Confetti,* 1978; *Zippers, Snaps and Flaps,* Van Nostrand, 1983.

Contributor to popular magazines, including *Woman's Day, Family Circle,* and *Essence.* Art editor of *Good Housekeeping Family Christmas Book,* 1963-65. Illustrator of children's stories for Western Publishing.

WORK IN PROGRESS: "Between craft books, sneaking in my first novel."

SIDELIGHTS: Phyllis Ficarotta told *CA:* "Although I was born in Connecticut and presently live in New Jersey, I will be eternally a New Yorker. I have an intense love affair with this, the greatest city in the world.

"I have a passion for everything that is connected with my precious life, and I reject very little.

"My philosophy of life was summed up by Fred Flintstone of cartoon fame, saying, as he emptied a quart of milk on the floor, 'I laugh at spilt milk.'

"My extreme loves, my mother, father, brother, tacos, Mexican trees of life, opera, my house, landscaping, colors, and *The Grinch That Stole Christmas* keep me busy. My extreme dislike, DYING."

*   *   *

FIEDLER, Jean(nette Feldman)

PERSONAL: Born in Pittsburgh, Pa.; daughter of Harry (a businessman) and Dina (Diness) Feldman; married Milton Moss, September 2, 1945 (divorced); married Harold Fiedler (a painter), July 5, 1949; children: Judith (Mrs. Elliot Glass), Joan (Mrs. Jim Mele). *Education:* University of Pittsburgh, B.A., 1945, teaching certificate, 1947; graduate study at New York University, 1955-57, and New School for Social Research, 1960-61. *Politics:* Democrat. *Home:* 69-23 Bell Blvd., Bayside, N.Y. 11364.

CAREER: Children's Aid Society, Pittsburgh, Pa., social worker, 1945; high school teacher of English in Pittsburgh, 1946-48; Gimbel's Department Store, Pittsburgh, copywriter, 1948; Brooklyn Public Library, Brooklyn, N.Y., librarian, 1949-50; free-lance writer and editor in New York City, 1950—; substitute teacher in New York City high schools, 1961—; librarian in private high school in Queens, N.Y., 1967-77. City University of New York, teacher of juvenile writing at Queens College, 1964, teacher of creative writing at Queensborough Community College, 1975-82; teacher of creative writing in Bayside, N.Y., 1964-67. Reader for Harcourt Brace Jovanovich Publishing Co., 1978-82; instructor, Institute of Children's Literature, 1978—. *Member:* Mystery Writers of America, P.E.N., Society of Children's Book Writers, Forum of Writers for Young People, Authors League of America.

WRITINGS—Juvenile and young adult books, except as indicated: *The Green Thumb Story,* Holiday House, 1952; *Big Brother Danny,* Holiday House, 1953; *Teddy and the Ice Cream Man,* Abelard, 1957; (with Carol Reuter) *The Last Year,* McKay, 1962; *A Yardstick for Jessica,* McKay, 1964; *Jill's Story,* McKay, 1965; *Great American Heroes,* Hart Publishing, 1966; *Call Me Juanita,* McKay, 1968; *In Any Spring,* McKay, 1969; *A Break in the Circle,* McKay, 1971; *Atone with Evil* (gothic novel), Bantam, 1976; *The Year the World Was out of Step with Jancy Fried,* Harcourt, 1981; (with Jim Mele) *Isaac Asimov,* Ungar, 1982.

Picture books; published by Whitman Publishing, except as indicated: *Lassie: The Sandbar Rescue,* 1965; *Lassie and the Deer Mystery,* 1966; *My Special House,* 1966; *New Brother, New Sister,* Western Publishing, 1966; *My Special Day,* 1967; *Gentle Ben and the Pesky Puppy,* 1969; *Daktari: Judy and the Kitten,* 1969; *I Know What a Farm Is,* 1969; *Betty, the Ballerina,* 1970.

Contributor: *Golden Prize and Other Stories about Horses,* Whitman Publishing, 1965; *Here, Boy,* Whitman Publishing, 1966; *Round the Corner,* Macmillan, 1966; *Free and Easy,* Macmillan, 1974. Also contributor to *Critical Encounters* and *The Bedside, Bathtub, and Armchair Companion to Agatha Christie,* both published by Unger.

Author of two filmstrips, "Reading Perception," Audiovisual Instructional Devices, 1975, and "And Then What Happened?," Prentice-Hall Media, 1976. Contributor of stories and articles to magazines.

WORK IN PROGRESS: An adult thriller.

SIDELIGHTS: Jean Fiedler told *CA:* "A trip to Mexico was responsible for two books, *Atone with Evil* and *Call Me Juanita.* San Cristobal de las Casas struck me as an ideal locale for a suspense novel—*Atone with Evil* was the result. My growing up in Pittsburgh, exposure to classical music, living with parents who were readers and who encouraged me in my writing—all helped my career."

Jill's Story and *A Yardstick for Jessica* have been published in German; *My Special Day* has been published in French.

AVOCATIONAL INTERESTS: Music, travel, transcendental meditation.

BIOGRAPHICAL/CRITICAL SOURCES: Best Sellers, April 1, 1969; *Commonweal,* May 23, 1969.

*   *   *

FIENNES, Richard
See TWISLETON-WYKEHAM-FIENNES, Richard Nathaniel

*   *   *

FIGGINS, Ross 1936-

PERSONAL: Born March 10, 1936, in Plainfield, N.J.; son of Albert F. (in advertising) and Frances (MacAlvanah) Figgins; married Jacque Weiss (a professor), August 1, 1974 (died, 1982). *Education:* Los Angeles Valley College, A.A., 1958; California State University, Northridge, B.A., 1961, M.A., 1962; University of Illinois at Urbana-Champaign, M.A., 1965; University of Southern California, Ph.D., 1972. *Home:* 567 South Albertson, Covina, Calif. 91723. *Office:* Department of Communication Arts, 1/310, California State Polytechnic University, Pomona, Calif. 91768.

CAREER: California State Polytechnic University, Pomona, 1965—, currently professor in department of communication arts and chairperson of department. Adjunct professor, University of Southern California, 1976-80. Assistant director, Institute of Multidisciplinary Studies, 1973; member of board of directors, Community Health Projects, 1981—. Institute of Advanced Systems Studies, management coordinator, 1974, emeritus fellow. Manuscript editor and reviewer of textbooks for Harper & Row, Richard D. Irwin, Prentice-Hall, Wadsworth, and John Wiley & Sons. Consultant and speaker on business and organizational communication. *Military service:* U.S. Army Reserve, 1958-65. *Member:* International Association of Business Communication, Academy of American Poets, American Haiku Society, National Council of College Publications Advisers, Speech Association of America, National Collegiate Players, American Business Communication Association, University of Southern California Alumni Association, Blue Key (charter faculty adviser), Sigma Delta Chi, Sigma Chi.

AWARDS, HONORS: Arizona State Poetry Society National Haiku Contest, first place awards, 1972, for ''Gnarled Oak,'' and 1976, for ''Dark Bamboo''; Japan and California Yukuharu Haiku Society award, 1976, for ''Walking with the Wind''; award for best feature story and general excellence from Union Teacher Press Association, 1976, for editing *United Professors of California Advocate;* received first place awards and recognitions in contests sponsored by *Modern Haiku, Haiku Highlights, Dragonfly, Bonsai, Haiku West,* and *Portals.*

WRITINGS: Techniques of Job Search, Canfield, 1976; *Untitled Haiku Anthology,* Raindrop Press, 1977; (with Frank Higgins) *American Haiku,* Raindrop Press, 1979; *The Job Game,* Prentice-Hall, 1980; (with C. Glenn Pearce and Steven Golen) *Principles of Business Communication: Theory, Application, and Technology,* Wiley, 1984; (with Pearce and Golen) *Business Communication Basics: Applications and Technology,* Wiley, 1984; (with Golen and Larry Smeltzer) *Cases and Readings in Business Communication,* Wiley, 1984; (with Pearce and Golen) *Business Report Writing,* Wiley, 1984.

Contributor to anthologies: *I Am Talking about Revolution,* Harper Square (Chicago), 1973; *Haiku,* Washington Poet's Association, 1974; *Haiku,* Paco Press (Lynwood, Wash.), 1975; *Anthology of the Western World Haiku Society,* J & C Transcripts, 1976.

Contributor of book reviews, columns, editorials, recipes, and poems to magazines and newspapers, including *New Orleans Review of Literature, Denver Post, Patterson's California Beverage Journal,* and *Sunset.* Editor of *United Professors of California Advocate,* 1975-78; associate editor and columnist for *All about Beer,* 1980—.

WORK IN PROGRESS: Interpersonal Communication in Business, for Wiley; *Whistle Belly Vengeance,* a historical beer drink book; *Tales from a Bolsa,* an unpublished collection of Mexican ghost stories.

*   *   *

FIRCHOW, Evelyn Scherabon 1932-
(Evelyn Scherabon Coleman)

PERSONAL: Born November 29, 1932, in Vienna, Austria; naturalized U.S. citizen; daughter of Raimund (a government official) and Hildegard (Nickl) Scherabon; married Peter E. Firchow; children: Felicitas Giselle, Pamina Maria. *Education:* Attended University of Vienna, 1950-51; University of Texas, B.A., 1956; University of Manitoba, M.A., 1957; attended University of Munich, 1960-61; Harvard University, Ph.D., 1963. *Office:* German Department, University of Minnesota, Minneapolis, Minn. 55455.

CAREER: Balmoral Hall School, Winnipeg, Manitoba, teacher of mathematics, 1953-55; University of Maryland Overseas Branch, Munich, Germany, lecturer, 1961; University of Wisconsin—Madison, 1962-65, began as instructor, became assistant professor of German; University of Minnesota, Min-

neapolis, associate professor, 1965-69, professor of Germanic philology, 1969—. Guest professor, University of Florida, 1973; Fulbright research professor, University of Iceland, 1980; visiting research professor, National Cheng Kung University, Tainan, Taiwan, 1982-83.

MEMBER: Modern Language Association of America (member of executive committee of German I, 1970-73; member of Delegate Assembly, 1970-72; chairman, Medieval German Division, 1979), American Association of Teachers of German, American Association of University Professors, Mediaeval Academy of America, Internationale Vereinigung der Germanisten, International Comparative Literature Association, Modern Humanities Research Association, Association for Literary and Linguistic Computing, Society for the Advancement of Scandinavian Study, Midwest Modern Language Association, German-American Society, Lambda Alpha Phi.

AWARDS, HONORS: Fulbright scholar, University of Texas at Austin, 1951-52; Alexander von Humboldt-Stiftung fellow in Germany, 1960-61, 1974, 1981; Fulbright-Hays fellow at University of Iceland, 1967-68; MacMillan Travel grant for research in Iceland, 1969; Institute for Advanced Studies (Edinburgh) grant for research in Scotland, 1973-74; numerous grants from the University of Wisconsin and University of Minnesota for research.

WRITINGS—Under name Evelyn Scherabon Coleman: (Editor with Werner Betz and Kenneth Northcott, and contributor) *Taylor Starck—Festschrift,* Mouton & Co., 1964; (contributor) F. A. Raven, W. K. Legner, and J. C. King, editors, *Germanic Studies in Honor of Edward Henry Sehrt,* University of Miami Press, 1968; *Stimmen aus dem Studenglas: Deutsche Gedichte und Lieder,* Prentice-Hall, 1968; (translator and author of introduction) *Einhard: Vita Karoli Magni, Das Leben Karls des Grossen,* [Stuttgart], 1968, translation under name Evelyn Scherabon Firchow with E. H. Zeydel published as *Einhard: The Life of Charlemagne (Vita Karoli Magni): The Latin Text with a New English Translation, Introduction, Notes and Illustrations,* University of Miami Press, 1972, 2nd edition of German version, [Stuttgart], 1981.

Under name Evelyn Scherabon Firchow: (Author of introduction and notes) W. L. van Helten, *Die altostniederfraenkischen Psalmenfragmente: Die Lipsius' schen Glossen und die altsuedmittelfraenkischen Psalmenfragmente,* Johnson Reprint, 1969; (editor with others) *Studies by Einar Haugen,* Mouton & Co., 1972; (editor with others) *Studies for Einar Haugen,* Mouton & Co., 1972; (author of introduction) Eduard Sievers, *Die Murbacher Hymnen,* Johnson Reprint, 1972; (editor with Karl Van D'Elden) *Was Deutsche lesen: Modern German Short Stories,* McGraw, 1973; (editor with others) *Deutung und Bedeutung: Studies in German and Comparative Literature,* Mouton & Co., 1973; (editor and translator) *Icelandic Short Stories,* Twayne, 1974; (translator and editor with husband Peter E. Firchow) *East German Short Stories,* Twayne, 1979; (editor with Kaaren E. Grimstad) *The Old Icelandic Elucidarius,* MS Institute, University of Iceland, 1983.

Contributor to *Dictionnaire international des termes litteraires* and *The Medieval Dictionary.* Contributor of numerous articles and reviews to professional journals.

WORK IN PROGRESS: An analysis of the language of Notker III's translation of Aristotle's *De interpretatione* with the help of a computer.

SIDELIGHTS: Evelyn Scherabon Firchow is competent in French, Spanish, Latin, and Modern Icelandic. *Avocational interests:* Travel, music, cooking.

FISHER, John H(urt) 1919-

PERSONAL: Born October 26, 1919, in Lexington, Ky.; son of C. Bascom (a teacher) and Franke (Sheddan) Fisher; married Jane Elizabeth Law, February 21, 1942; children: Janice Carol, John Craig, Judith Law. *Education:* Maryville College, B.A., 1940; University of Pennsylvania, M.A., 1942, Ph.D., 1945. *Home:* 505 Scenic Dr., Knoxville, Tenn. 37919. *Office:* McClung Tower, University of Tennessee, Knoxville, Tenn. 37916.

CAREER: University of Pennsylvania, Philadelphia, instructor in English, 1942-45; New York University, New York, N.Y., instructor, 1945-48, assistant professor of English, 1948-55; Duke University, Durham, N.C., associate professor, 1955-58, professor of English, 1958-60; Indiana University at Bloomington, professor of English, 1960-62; New York University, professor of English, 1962-72; University of Tennessee, Knoxville, John C. Hodges Professor of English, 1972—, head of department, 1976-78. Summer instructor at Yale University, 1944; lecturer at University of Southern California, 1955, and University of Michigan, 1956. Consultant to U.S. Office of Education, 1962-64; member of U.S. Commission to UNESCO, 1962-68.

MEMBER: Modern Language Association of America (treasurer, 1952-55; executive secretary, 1961-71; president, 1974), National Council of Teachers of English, Linguistic Society of America, Mediaeval Academy of America, New Chaucer Society (president, 1982; executive director, 1982—). *Awards, honors:* L.H.D., Loyola University of Chicago, 1970; Litt.D., Middlebury College, 1970; National Endowment for the Humanities senior fellowship, 1975-76; University of Tennessee Chancellor's Research Scholar, 1980.

WRITINGS: (Editor) *Tretyse of Love,* Oxford University Press, 1951; (co-author) *The College Teaching of English,* Appleton-Century-Crofts, 1965; *John Gower, Moral Philosopher and Friend of Chaucer,* New York University Press, 1965; (editor) *The Medieval Literature of Western Europe: A Review of Research,* New York University Press, 1966; (with D. Bornstein) *In Forme of Speche Is Chaunge,* Prentice-Hall, 1974; (editor) *The Complete Poetry and Prose of Geoffrey Chaucer,* Holt, 1977; (contributor) Beryl Rowland, editor, *Companion to Chaucer Studies,* Oxford University Press, 1979; (contributor) Joseph Gibaldi, editor, *Approaches to Teaching Chaucer,* Modern Language Association of America, 1980; (contributor) Donald Rose, editor, *New Perspectives in Chaucer Criticism,* Pilgrim Books, 1981. Contributor to *Speculum.* Editor, *PMLA,* 1963-71.

WORK IN PROGRESS: Research in medieval studies and in English linguistics.

*   *   *

FISHMAN, Lew 1939-

PERSONAL: Born June 20, 1939, in Albany, N.Y.; son of Phillip (a drycleaner and tailor) and Ann (a clerk; maiden name, Bellin) Fishman; married Joanne Alessandroni, November 28, 1964; children: David, Lee. *Education:* Rutgers University, B.A., 1964; University of Suffolk, graduate study in law, 1966-67. *Home:* 22 Vista Way, Port Washington, N.Y. 11050. *Office:* Golf Magazine, 380 Madison Ave., New York, N.Y.

CAREER: Sports writer and sports editor for daily newspapers on the East Coast, including *Baltimore Sun, Albany Times-Union,* and *New York Post,* 1962-71; *Long Island Press,* Jamaica, N.Y., sports writer, 1971-77; *Golf Magazine,* New York, N.Y., 1977—, currently executive editor. Has worked as public relations representative for Madison Square Garden and as business manager of Peninsula Astro Baseball Club. *Member:* Golf Writers of America, New York Press Club.

WRITINGS: New York Mets: Miracle at Shea, Prentice-Hall, 1974; *The New York Knicks: Pride of Gotham,* Prentice-Hall, 1974; *Shortcuts to Better Golf,* Harper, 1979.

*   *   *

FISK, Nicholas 1923-

PERSONAL: Born October 14, 1923, in London, England; married Dorothy Antoinette, 1949; children: Moyra and Nicola (twins), Steven, Christopher. *Education:* Educated in private secondary school in Sussex, England. *Home:* 59 Elstree Rd., Bushey Heath, Hertfordshire WD2 3QX, England. *Agent:* Laura Cecil, 17 Alwyne Villas, Canonbury, London N1, England.

CAREER: Writer and illustrator. Percy Lund, Humphries & Co. (printers/publishers), London, England, former head of creative group. Has worked as actor, publisher, and musician. *Military service:* Royal Air Force. *Member:* Savile Club.

WRITINGS: Cars, Parrish, 1963; *Making Music,* Crescendo, 1966; *Richthofen the Red Baron,* Coward, 1968; *Lindbergh the Lone Flier* (juvenile), Coward, 1968; (contributor of photographs) Eric Fenby, *Menuhin's House of Music,* Praeger, 1970; *Grinny* (juvenile science fiction), Heinemann, 1973, Thomas Nelson, 1974; *Der Ballon,* Junior Press (Germany), 1974; (with Carol Barker) *Emma Borrows a Cup of Sugar* (juvenile), Heinemann, 1974; *Little Green Spacemen,* Heinemann, 1974.

(Contributor) Edward Blishen, editor, *The Thorny Paradise* (juvenile anthology), Kestrel, 1975; *The Witches of Wimmering,* Pelham Books, 1976; *Time Trap,* Gollancz, 1976; *Wheelie in the Stars,* Heinemann, 1976; *Escape from Splatterbang,* Pelham Books, 1977, Macmillan (New York), 1978, published as *Flamers,* Knight, 1979; *Antigrav,* Kestrel, 1978; *Monster Maker,* Macmillan, 1980; *The Starstormer Saga,* Knight, 1980; *A Rag, a Bone and a Hank of Hair,* Kestrel, 1980; *Robot Revolt,* Pelham Books, 1981; *Sweets from a Stranger and Other SF Stories,* Kestrel, 1982.

Published by Hamish Hamilton, except as indicated: *Look at Cars* (self-illustrated juvenile), 1959, revised edition, Panther, 1970; (illustrator) Philip Joubert, *Look at Aircraft,* 1960; *Look at Newspapers* (juvenile), 1962; *The Young Man's Guide to Advertising,* 1963; *The Bouncers* (self-illustrated), 1964; *The Fast Green Car,* 1965; *There's Something on the Roof,* 1966; *Space Hostages* (juvenile), 1967, Macmillan (New York), 1969; *Trillions* (juvenile), 1971, Pantheon, 1973; *High Way Home,* 1973; (illustrator) W. Mayne, *Skiffy,* 1973.

General editor of "Hamish Hamilton Monographs," Hamish Hamilton, 1964; contributor to "Take Part" series, Ward Lock, 1977. Contributor to *Pears Junior Encyclopedia;* contributor of articles and science fiction stories to magazines.

WORK IN PROGRESS: Children's novels; television scripts.

SIDELIGHTS: Nicholas Fisk told *CA:* "I cannot escape the buzzword 'communications.' [While] my main interest lies in writing books for children, I am also an illustrator and photographer and often an impresario of adult printed works. But children come first. They have wide, generous minds. They are quick to accept and master a computer or a new skill, and, similarly, quick to accept such premises as domestic robots, dual existences, alien worlds, [or] a viciously inclined teddy-bear. Children no longer form a separate tribe. They live among adults and share adult amusements and preoccupations. They are separated only by size, experience, and power to command. So I like my readers, and like the tautness and pace of children's books. Of course I write for TV, but books are what matter to me, so books are my main products.''

"Nicholas Fisk keeps his readers guessing," writes a *Times Literary Supplement* reviewer. "All one can forecast with confidence is that his next [book] will be stimulating and startlingly original." Gillian Cross, writing in the same periodical, states that Fisk "has a gift for combining the fantastic with the down-to-earth. In books like *Grinny* and *Trillions*, the interest comes not merely from the central events, but also from the effect of those events on recognizable characters."

Similarly, another *Times Literary Supplement* critic comments on the tale of *Grinny*, a metal and plastic alien who invades an ordinary middle-class household: "[While] the materials of the story . . . are commonplace, the treatment [is] startlingly original and in parts downright nasty. . . . Fisk—a master in this genre—makes the fantasy of his invention horribly real by putting it into an everyday contemporary setting."

BIOGRAPHICAL/CRITICAL SOURCES: Times Literary Supplement, April 6, 1973, June 15, 1973, December 10, 1976, July 7, 1978; Edward Blishen, editor, *The Thorny Paradise*, Pelham Books, 1975.

*   *   *

FITTER, Richard Sidney Richmond   1913-

PERSONAL: Born March 1, 1913, in London, England; son of Sidney Harry (a produce broker) and Dorothy Isacke (Pound) Fitter; married Alice Mary Stewart Park (an editor), 1938; children: Jenny Elizabeth (Mrs. Alexander Graham), Julian Richmond, Alastair Hugh. *Education:* London School of Economics and Political Science, B.Sc. Econ., 1933. *Home:* Drifts, Chinnor Hill, Oxford OX9 4BS, England.

CAREER: Writer and naturalist. Member of research staff, Political and Economic Planning, 1936-40, Mass-Observation, 1940-42; member of operational research section, Coastal Command, 1942-45; editor of *London Naturalist*, 1942-46; secretary of Wildlife Conservation Special Committee, Hobhouse Committee on National Parks, 1945-46; assistant editor of *Countryman*, 1946-59; open air correspondent for *Observer*, 1958-66; director of intelligence unit, Council for Nature, 1959-63; editor of *Kingfisher*, 1965-72.

MEMBER: International Union for the Conservation of Nature (member of Survival Service Commission, 1963; chairman of steering committee), World Wildlife Fund, United Kingdom (trustee, 1977-83), Fauna Preservation Society (honorary secretary, 1964-80; vice-chairman, 1980-83; chairman, 1983—), British Trust for Ornithology, Royal Society for the Protection of Birds, Berkshire, Buckinghamshire, and Oxfordshire Naturalists' Trust, Zoological Society of London (fellow), Athenaeum Club.

WRITINGS: The Starling Roosts of the London Area, London Naturalist, 1943; (with E. R. Parrinder) *A Check-List of the Birds of the London Area*, London Naturalist, 1944; *London's Natural History: The New Naturalist, a Survey of British Natural History*, Collins, 1945; *Bird-Watching in London*, Royal Society for the Protection of Birds, 1948; *London's Birds*, Collins, 1949.

(Editor) *British Birds in Colour*, Odhams, 1951; *Home Counties*, Collins, 1951; *The Pocket Guide to British Birds*, Collins, 1952, Dodd, 1953, revised edition published as *Collins Pocket Guide to British Birds*, Collins, 1966, 3rd edition, 1970; (with Job Edward Lousley) *The Natural History of the City*, Corporation of London, 1953; *Birds of Town and Village*, Collins, 1953; *The Starling*, School-Aid Department, Daily Mail, 1953; (with Guy Charteris) *The Pocket Guide to Nests and Eggs*, Collins, 1954, revised edition published as *The Collins Pocket Guide to Nests and Eggs*, 1968; (with David McClintock) *The Pocket Guide to Wild Flowers*, Collins, 1956; *Fontana Bird Guide*, Collins, 1956; *Fontana Wild Flower Guide*, Collins, 1957; (editor with H. N. Southern) Marie N. Stephens, *The Natural History of the Otter*, University Federation for Animal Welfare (London), 1957; *Your Book of Bird Watching* (juvenile), Transatlantic, 1958; *The Ark in Our Midst: The Story of the Introduced Animals of Britain: Birds, Beasts, Reptiles, Amphibians, Fishes*, Collins, 1959; *Six Great Naturalists: White, Linnaeus, Waterton, Audubon, Fabre, Huxley*, Hamish Hamilton, 1959.

(Editor) *The Countryman Nature Book: An Anthology from the Countryman*, Brockhampton Press, 1960; *Your Book about Wild Flowers* (juvenile), Faber, 1960; *Collins Guide to Birdwatching*, Collins, 1963, 2nd edition, 1970; *Fitter's Rural Rides: The Observer Illustrated Map-Guide to the Countryside*, Observer, 1963; *Wildlife in Britain*, Gannon, 1963; *Wildlife and Death*, Newman Neame, 1964; *British Wildlife: Rarities and Introductions*, Kay, 1966; (with wife, Maisie Fitter) *The Penguin Dictionary of British Natural History*, Penguin, 1967, Barnes & Noble, 1968, revised edition, A. & C. Black, 1968; *Vanishing Wild Animals of the World*, F. Watts, 1968.

(With Hermann Heinzel and J.L.F. Parslow) *The Birds of Britain and Europe with North Africa and the Middle East*, Lippincott, 1972, 2nd edition, Collins, 1974; *Finding Wild Flowers*, Collins, 1972; (author of introduction) *BBONT: The First Ten Years, 1959-1969*, Berkshire, Buckinghamshire, and Oxfordshire Naturalists' Trust, 1973; (contributor) Alan Aldridge, *The Butterfly Ball and the Grasshopper's Feast*, J. Cape, 1973; (with son, Alastair Fitter) *The Wild Flowers of Britain and Northern Europe*, Scribner, 1974; (with Sir Peter Scott) *The Penitent Butchers*, Collins, 1978; (with Marjorie Blamey) *Handguide to the Wild Flowers of Britain and Europe*, Collins, 1979.

Wild Flowers, Collins, 1980; (with A. Fitter) *The Complete Guide to British Wildlife*, Collins, 1981; (editor with Eric Robinson) *John Clare's Birds*, Oxford University Press, 1982; (with A. Fitter) *Collins Guide to the Countryside*, Collins, 1984; (with A. Fitter) *The Grasses, Sedges, Rushes and Fens of Britain and Northern Europe*, Collins, 1984.

AVOCATIONAL INTERESTS: Observing wild life and human life, exploring new habitats, reading.

*   *   *

FITTING, Melvin (Chris)   1942-

PERSONAL: Born January 24, 1942, in Troy, N.Y.; son of Chris and Helen (Van Denburg) Fitting; married Greer Russell, January 17, 1971 (divorced, 1983). *Education:* Rensselaer Polytechnic Institute, B.S., 1963; Yeshiva University, M.A. and Ph.D., 1968. *Home:* 11 Kings Lane, Montrose, N.Y. 10548. *Office:* Herbert H. Lehman College of the City University of New York, Bronx, N.Y. 10468.

CAREER: Herbert H. Lehman College of the City University of New York, Bronx, N.Y., 1968—, began as assistant professor, currently professor of mathematics. *Member:* American Mathematical Society, Association for Symbolic Logic.

WRITINGS: *Intuitionistic Logic Model Theory and Forcing,* North Holland Publishing, 1969; (with wife, Greer Fitting) *In Praise of Simple Things,* McKay, 1975; *Fundamentals of Generalized Recursion Theory,* North Holland Publishing, 1981; *Proof Methods for Modal and Intuitionistic Logics,* D. Reidel, 1983. Contributor to *Journal of Symbolic Logic, Notre Dame Journal of Formal Logic, Theoria,* and *West Coast Review.*

WORK IN PROGRESS: Researching modal logic and recursion theory.

* * *

FitzGERALD, C(harles) P(atrick) 1902-

PERSONAL: Born March 5, 1902, in London, England; son of Johannes (a medical doctor) and Cecilia (Fitz-Patrick) Sauer; married Pamela Sara Knollys, February 15, 1941; children: Nicola (Mrs. Jonathan Dawson), Mirabel (Mrs. Mark Ward), Anthea. *Education:* Attended School of Oriental and African Studies, 1927-30. *Politics:* "Not a member of any party." *Home:* 82 Gloucester Ter., London W2 3HH, England.

CAREER: Author of books on Chinese history, anthropology, and current affairs. Lived in China most of the time from 1923 to 1939, and then again from 1946-50 as representative of the British Council in northern China; Australian National University, Canberra, Australian Capital Territory, reader in Oriental studies, 1951-54, professor of Far Eastern history, 1954-69, professor emeritus, 1969—, visiting fellow, department of international relations, 1968-69. *Member:* Savile Club (London). *Awards, honors:* Leverhulme fellowship for anthropological research in China, 1936-39; D.Litt. from Australian National University, 1968.

WRITINGS: *Son of Heaven: A Biography of Li Shih-Min, Founder of the T'ang Dynasty,* Cambridge University Press, 1933, reprinted, AMS Press, 1971; *China: A Short Cultural History,* Cresset, 1935, 4th edition, Barrie & Jenkins, 1976; *The Tower of Five Glories: A Study of the Min Chia of Ta Li,* Cresset, 1941, Hyperion Press, 1973; (with George Yeh) *Introducing China,* Pitman, 1948.

Revolution in China, Cresset, 1952, revised edition published as *The Birth of Communist China,* Praeger, 1966; *The Empress Wu,* F. W. Cheshire, 1955, 2nd edition, Cresset, 1968; *Flood Tide in China,* Cresset, 1958; *Finding Out about Imperial China,* Muller, 1961; *The Chinese View of Their Place in the World,* Oxford University Press, 1964, 4th edition, 1969; *The Third China: The Chinese Communities in South-East Asia,* F. W. Cheshire, 1965; *Barbarian Beds: The Origin of the Chair in China,* Cresset, 1965, A. S. Barnes, 1966; *A Concise History of East Asia,* Praeger, 1966; *The China Giant: Perspective on Communist China,* Scott, Foresman, 1967; *China and the Future of Southeast Asia,* Australian Institute of International Affairs, 1968; (editor with Norman Kotker and others) *The Horizon History of China,* American Heritage Publishing, 1969; *China's Revolution Twenty Years After,* D. B. Young, 1969.

Communism Takes China: How the Revolution Went Red, American Heritage Press, 1971; *Changing Directions of Chinese Foreign Policy,* Australian Institute of International Affairs, 1971; *The Southern Expansion of the Chinese People,* Praeger,

1972; *China: A World So Changed,* Thomas Nelson, 1972; *China and Southeast Asia since 1945,* Longman, 1974; *Mao Tsetung and China,* Holmes & Meier, 1976, revised edition, Penguin, 1977; *Ancient China,* Elsevier-Phaidon, 1978; (with Keith Buchanan and Colin A. Ronan) *China,* Crown, 1981; *Why China?,* Australian National University Press, 1984. Contributor to numerous journals in his field.

SIDELIGHTS: C. P. FitzGerald is one of the world's leading experts on Chinese history. Born in London, England, FitzGerald spent almost twenty years of his life studying and working in China. His books are generally regarded as accurate, well-written, and interesting to both the scholar and the layman. For example, Hyman Kublin writes in *Library Journal* that "there are few historians of East Asia today who write as forcefully and gracefully as [FitzGerald] does."

FitzGerald's first major book, *China: A Short Cultural History,* quickly brought him to the attention of many international students of Chinese history. Originally published in 1935, this book has been revised four times, with each volume receiving the kind of praise A. L. Kroeber bestows on the third edition in *American Anthropologist.* Remarks Kroeber: "This volume is written with perspicacity of insight, understanding, and balance, and is extremely readable. [*China: A Short Cultural History*] was admirable in 1935 and is as admirable [today]." A reviewer for *Manchester Guardian* also finds *China: A Short Cultural History* praiseworthy. The critic states: "This is a perfectly admirable book which in [a] comparatively short space . . . contrives to give a just account of the developments of over 3,000 years. In spite of the vastness of the subject it is no mere outline." And C. D. Gower comments in *American Sociological Review* that this "book is excellently written and well illustrated. It is also remarkably free from errors."

Reviewing *China: A Short Cultural History* for *Saturday Review of Literature,* K. S. Latourette feels, however, that "in some ways, Mr. FitzGerald's work is a distinct disappointment. . . . The book has some excellencies, but is by no means comprehensive of the best scholarship on things Chinese." K. A. Wittfogel of *American Historical Review* takes exception to Latourette's remarks: "In a pioneer work like this, limitations should not be overemphasized. Both the author and the editor are to be congratulated on their attempt to get away from a type of history in which history actually remains a meager by-product of philology."

Chen Shou-Yi writes in *Pacific Affairs* that the greatest merit of *China: A Short Cultural History* "is that it is entirely free of all national and racial biases and prejudices and seeks only to present a history of Chinese culture as seen by a citizen of the world. It does not condemn the Chinese for what they are and have been. It does not justify the British Empire to satisfy chauvinistic desires. It will correct many wrong impressions and dispel many misunderstandings on the part of lay readers in the Western world." In short, comments H. P. Linton in *Library Journal,* this work "will continue to be used as an authoritative, reliable guide to the cultural history of China from pre-history times to rule under the Manchus."

Another of FitzGerald's books to command much international attention is *Revolution in China.* "[This] book is one of the best which has been written on the Communist stage of the Chinese Revolution," declares Latourette in *Saturday Review.* "[FitzGerald] combines scholarship, time perspective, and first-hand observation as he seeks to interpret recent events." A *Times Literary Supplement* critic remarks that "it is rare to find a book on so complex a subject in which theory is so clearly related to practice. For some time it is bound to remain the standard work on the Chinese Communist Revolution." Reviewing the same book for *Spectator,* J.M.D. Pringle believes that it "should be read and pondered by everyone concerned with political developments in the Far East today. It has the stamp of a clear, logical and penetrating mind." And E. O. Reischauer explains in the *New York Herald Tribune Book Review* that FitzGerald's *Revolution in China* is "an account enlived in parts by firsthand reporting and studded with stimulating, if not always convincing, interpretations."

Writing about another of FitzGerald's works, *The Southern Expansion of the Chinese People,* a *Times Literary Supplement* reviewer comments: "Once inside this learned, fluently written and absorbing book . . . we are reminded of the unique nature of China's evolution and why it has given birth to attitudes and to behavior that the sterotyped patterns of a Western mind can make little sense of." And Francis Hope remarks in *New Statesman,* "FitzGerald has done a service to sanity as well as to scholarship by his brief survey of the past, present, and possible futures of China's southern expansion."

In addition to praising FitzGerald's books for their insight and sensitivity, reviewers have marveled at the exceptional illustrations that accompany many of his studies. "*China* is stunningly attractive, with excellent reproductions," C. W. Hayford writes in *Library Journal.* A reviewer for *Choice* remarks that *The Horizon History of China* is "a masterwork even among the superb produce of its makers. The illustrations . . . are carefully chosen and richly executed." And Richard Edwards writes in *Saturday Review* of *The Horizon History of China:* "Pictorially this is magnificent journalism. Worlds are revealed in an absolutely first-rate and imaginative selection of material."

In the same article Edwards seems to summarize the feelings of many who read and enjoy FitzGerald's work. Observes the critic: "FitzGerald writes in an expected lively fashion. Events, anecdote, custom and ideas unfold with interest and ease. There is admiration for the past and a just attempt within the scope of such a general book to evaluate its importance. There is also clear sympathy for the present and an understanding of the necessity for that revolutionary change which has so tragically produced a case of overshock among so many who cannot for China equate the facts of tradition with the compelling demands of the modern world."

BIOGRAPHICAL/CRITICAL SOURCES: Manchester Guardian, January 14, 1936; *Pacific Affairs,* September, 1936, winter, 1972/73; *Saturday Review of Literature,* February 19, 1938; *American Sociological Review,* October, 1938; *American Historical Review,* October, 1938; *Library Journal,* May 15, 1951, July, 1966, February 1, 1970, January 15, 1982; *American Anthropologist,* July, 1951; *Spectator,* August 15, 1952; *Christian Science Monitor,* August 18, 1952; *New York Herald Tribune Book Review,* August 24, 1952; *Saturday Review,* September 6, 1952, December 6, 1969; *Times Literary Supplement,* September 12, 1952, June 16, 1972, March 1, 1974; *New York Times Book Review,* April 24, 1966; *Choice,* May, 1970, November, 1976, April, 1982; *New Statesman,* March 17, 1972; *New York Review of Books,* April 1, 1982.

—*Sketch by Margaret Mazurkiewicz*

FLAVELL, John H(urley) 1928-

PERSONAL: Born August 9, 1928, in Rockland, Mass.; son of Paul I. (an engineer) and Anne (O'Brien) Flavell; married Eleanor R. Wood, July 24, 1954; children: Elizabeth, James. *Education:* Northeastern University, A.B., 1951; Clark University, M.A., 1952, Ph.D., 1955; additional study at Sorbonne, University of Paris, 1963-64. *Home:* 41 Pearce Mitchell Pl., Stanford, Calif. 94305. *Office:* Department of Psychology, Stanford University, Stanford, Calif. 94305

CAREER: University of Rochester, Rochester, N.Y., clinical associate, 1955-56, assistant professor, 1956-60, associate professor of psychology, 1960-65; University of Minnesota, Minneapolis, professor of psychology, Institute of Child Development, 1965-76; Stanford University, Stanford, Calif., professor of psychology, 1976—. *Military service:* U.S. Army, 1946-47. *Member:* American Psychological Association, Society for Research in Child Development.

WRITINGS: The Developmental Psychology of Jean Piaget, Van Nostrand, 1963; *The Development of Role-Taking and Communication Skills in Children,* Wiley, 1968; (editor with David Elkind) *Studies in Cognitive Development: Essays in Honor of Jean Piaget,* Oxford University Press, 1969.

(With Mary Anne Kreutzer) *An Interview Study of Children's Knowledge About Memory,* University of Chicago Press, 1975; *Cognitive Development,* Prentice-Hall, 1977; (editor with Lee Ross) *Social Cognitive Development: Frontiers and Possible Futures,* Cambridge University Press, 1981. Contributor to developmental psychology journals.

AVOCATIONAL INTERESTS: Golf, bicycle riding, and travel in general.

*   *   *

FLEISHMAN, Edwin A(lan) 1927-

PERSONAL: Born March 10, 1927, in New York, N.Y.; son of Harry E. and Sera (Weinblatt) Fleishman; married Pauline S. Utman, February 6, 1949; children: Jeffrey B., Alan R. *Education:* Loyola College, Baltimore, Md., B.S., 1945; University of Maryland, M.A., 1949; Ohio State University, Ph.D., 1951. *Home:* 8201 Woodhaven Blvd., Bethesda, Md. 20134.

CAREER: U.S. Air Force, Skill Components Research Laboratory, San Antonio, Tex., director, 1951-56; Yale University, New Haven, Conn., professor of industrial administration and psychology, 1957-63; American Institutes for Research, Washington, D.C., senior vice-president and director of Washington office, 1963-75; president, Advanced Research Resources Organization, 1976—. Visiting professor, Israel Institute of Technology, 1962-63, University of California, Irvine, 1975-76. Consultant to Army Surgeon General's Office and Office of Naval Research; member of advisory panel on social science, Office of Secretary of Defense. *Military service:* U.S. Navy, 1945-46.

MEMBER: International Association of Applied Psychology (president, 1974-82), American Psychological Association (president, division of industrial and organizational psychology, 1973-74, division of engineering psychology, 1977-78, and division of evaluation and measurement, 1978-79), American Association for the Advancement of Science, Psychometric Society, Sigma Xi, Cosmos Club (Washington, D.C.). *Awards, honors:* Guggenheim fellow, 1962-63; Franklin V. Taylor award of Society of Engineering Psychologists, 1974, for distinguished contributions; distinguished scientific award,

American Psychological Association, 1980, for the application of psychology; honorary doctorate, University of Edinburgh, 1982; professional practice award, Society of Industrial and Organizational Psychology, 1983.

WRITINGS: (With E. F. Harris and H. E. Burtt) *Leadership and Supervision in Industry,* Ohio State University, 1955; (with R. M. Gagne) *Psychology and Human Performance: An Introduction to Psychology,* Holt, 1959; *Manual for Administering the Leadership Opinion Questionnaire,* Science Research Associates, 1960, supplement, 1963; (editor) *Studies in Personnel and Industrial Psychology,* Dorsey, 1961, 2nd revised edition, 1974; *The Structure and Measurement of Physical Fitness,* with *Examiner's Manual* and *Performance Record,* Prentice-Hall, 1964; (with A. S. Glickman, C. P. Hahn, and B. Barth) *Top Management Development and Succession,* Macmillan, 1968.

(With J. C. Hunt) *Current Developments in the Study of Leadership,* Southern Illinois University Press, 1973; (with M. D. Dunnette) *Human Performance and Productivity: Human Capability Assessment,* Erlbaum, 1982; (with W. C. Howell) *Human Performance and Productivity: Information Processing and Decision Making,* Erlbaum, 1982; (with E. A. Allvisi) *Human Performance and Productivity: Stress and Performance Effectiveness,* Erlbaum, 1982; (with M. K. Quaintance and L. A. Broedling) *Taxonomies of Human Performance: The Description of Human Tasks,* Academic Press, 1983.

Contributor: M. L. Blum, editor, *Readings in Experimental Industrial Psychology,* Prentice-Hall, 1952; R. M. Stogdill, editor, *Aspects of Leadership Organization,* Personnel Research Board, Ohio State University, 1953; Stogdill and A. E. Coons, editors, *Leader Behavior: Its Description and Measurement,* Bureau of Business Research, Ohio State University, 1957; C. G. Browne and T. S. Cohn, editors, *The Study of Leadership,* Interstate, 1958; J. G. Miller and L. Uhr, editors, *Drugs and Behavior,* Wiley, 1960; *Some Views on Soviet Psychology,* American Psychological Association, 1962; R. Glaser, editor, *Training Research and Education,* University of Pittsburgh Press, 1962; R. A. Sutermeister, editor, *People and Productivity,* McGraw, 1963; E. A. Bilodeau, editor, *The Acquisition of Skill,* Academic Press, 1966; R. M. Gagne, editor, *Learning and Individual Differences,* C. E. Merrill, 1966.

R. N. Singer, editor, *The Psychomotor Domain,* Lea & Febiger, 1972; W. T. Singleton and P. Spingeon, editors, *Measurement of Human Resources,* Halsted, 1975.

Author of technical and research reports for U.S. Air Force and Navy. Contributor to *International Encyclopedia of the Social Sciences,* 1967, *Encyclopedia of Educational Research,* 4th edition, 1968, *Annual Review of Psychology,* 1969, and *International Encyclopedia of Neurology, Psychiatry, Psychoanalysis, and Psychology,* 1976. Contributor of more than 100 articles to professional publications. Editor in chief, *Journal of Applied Psychology,* 1971-76; associate editor of *Personnel Psychology, Organizational Behavior and Human Performance,* and *Journal of Motor Behavior.*

*   *   *

FLETCHER, Colin   1922-

PERSONAL: Born March 14, 1922, in Cardiff, Wales; became United States citizen in 1974; son of Herbert Reginald and Margaret Elizabeth (Williams) Fletcher; married twice (both marriages ending in divorce). *Education:* Attended West Buckland School, North Devon, England, 1934-39. *Residence:* California. *Agent:* Carl D. Brandt, Brandt & Brandt Literary Agents, Inc., 1501 Broadway, New York, N.Y. 10036.

CAREER: Writer. Immigrated to Kenya in 1947, working first as a manufacturer's representative in Nairobi, then as a manager of a hotel in Kitale, 1947-48; farmed near Nakuru, Kenya, 1948-52; road builder on a tea estate near Inyanga, Southern Rhodesia (now Zimbabwe), 1952-53; returned to England briefly before crossing the Atlantic as a herdsman for a planeload of cattle; prospected and helped lay out roads for a mining company in western Canada during the summers, 1953-56, and spent the winters writing; moved to California where he was head janitor at Polyclinic Hospital in San Francisco, 1957-58, and a department store Santa Claus. Member of Solar Lobby and Center for Law in the Public Interest. *Military service:* Royal Marines, commandos, 1940-47; became captain.

MEMBER: Wilderness Society, National Audubon Society, Sierra Club, Nature Conservancy, Common Cause, Friends of the Earth, East African Wild Life Society, Save the Redwoods League, Planning and Conservation League, Zero Population Growth, Environmental Defense Fund, Friends of the Sea Otter, U.S. Tennis Association, Cousteau Society, Fund for Peace, Union of Concerned Scientists, Trustees for Alaska, Natural Resources Defense Fund.

WRITINGS: *The Thousand-Mile Summer: In Desert and High Sierra,* Howell-North, 1964, reprinted, 1982; *The Man Who Walked through Time,* Knopf, 1968; *The Complete Walker: The Joys and Techniques of Hiking and Backpacking,* Knopf, 1969, revised edition published as *The New Complete Walker,* 1974; *The Winds of Mara,* Knopf, 1973; *The Man from the Cave,* Knopf, 1982. Contributor to *Reader's Digest, Field and Stream,* and other magazines in the United States, Canada, Britain, and Africa.

WORK IN PROGRESS: A third, revised edition of *The Complete Walker;* a book on wilderness walking and the mind; a novel about discipline and freedom.

SIDELIGHTS: Colin Fletcher, describing himself as a "semi-professional bum," made a trip from London to Vancouver in 1953 on a fare of ten dollars, hitchhiking from New York to Toronto, and driving a new car west. In 1958, he made a six-month thousand-mile walk from Mexico to Oregon, and in 1963, a two-month solitary foot trip through the Grand Canyon.

In 1968, as he was hiking in the Nevada desert, Fletcher discovered a cave once inhabited by a turn-of-the-century prospector. This discovery led Fletcher to a ten-year exploration of the prospector's life, and to reconstruct his personality in the book *The Man from the Cave.*

Carol Van Strom writes in a *Washington Post Book World* review that *The Man from the Cave* is a "touching biography of a man whose greatest gift to earth was the little harm he caused it. . . . In this tale of 'an ordinary man who was far from ordinary,' Colin Fletcher has written a far from ordinary book. To a culture obsessed with youth and achievement, *The Man from the Cave* brings affirmation of age, memory and the benign defiance of a man true to his own wavering star. . . . [This book is] a work of art, a triumph, a monument to the unique spark of humanity Fletcher intuitively recognized in a wild desert cave."

Fletcher speaks Swahili. *The New Complete Walker* has been translated into Japanese.

BIOGRAPHICAL/CRITICAL SOURCES: Authors in the News, Volume I, Gale, 1974; *Washington Post Book World,* April 10, 1981; *New York Times Book Review,* June 7, 1981.

FLETCHER, Joseph (Francis III) 1905-

PERSONAL: Born April 10, 1905, in Newark, N.J.; son of Joseph Francis II (a businessman) and Julia (Davis) Fletcher; married Forrest Hatfield (a poet), September 5, 1928; children: Joseph Francis IV, Jane Elizabeth (Mrs. Robert J. Geniesse). *Education:* West Virginia University, A.B., 1925; Yale University, graduate study, 1928-30; Berkeley Divinity School, B.D., 1929; University of London, S.T.D., 1932. *Politics:* Independent. *Home:* 52 Van Ness Rd., Belmont, Mass. 02178. *Office:* Box 368, Medical School, University of Virginia, Charlottesville, Va. 22903.

CAREER: Ordained minister of Protestant Episcopal Church, 1929; St. Peter's Church, London, England, curate, 1930-32; St. Mary's Junior College, Raleigh, N.C., lecturer and chaplain, 1932-35; Graduate School of Applied Religion, Cincinnati, Ohio, dean, 1936-44; St. Paul's Cathedral, Cincinnati, dean, 1936-40; University of Cincinnati, Cincinnati, lecturer in labor history and Bible literature, 1939-43; Episcopal Theological School, Cambridge, Mass., professor of pastoral theology and Christian ethics, 1944-70; University of Virginia, Charlottesville, visiting professor of medical ethics, 1970-77. Supervisor, Episcopal Summer Training Program, West Indies, 1955; Lilly Visiting Professor, International Christian University, Tokyo, Japan, 1963-64; visiting professor, University of Texas at Houston, 1973-79. Lecturer, Harvard Divinity School, 1964-65, and at University of St. Andrews, summer, 1966; visiting fellow, Cambridge University, 1967-68. Director of National Religion and Labor Foundation, Musser Seminar of Harvard Business School, and Institute of Pastoral Care.

MEMBER: Association for the Study of Abortion (vice-president), Association for Voluntary Sterilization, American Society of Christian Ethics, Institute of Society, Ethics and Life Sciences (fellow), Soviet-American Friendship Society, Planned Parenthood Federation, Episcopal League for Social Action, Alpha Omega Alpha (honorary fellow). *Awards, honors:* Humanist of the Year, Southern Medical Association, 1974.

WRITINGS: The Church and Industry, Longmans, Green, 1930; *Christianity and Property,* Westminster, 1948; *Morals and Medicine,* Princeton University Press, 1954; *William Temple: 20th Century Christian,* Seabury, 1963; *Situation Ethics,* Westminster, 1966; *Moral Responsibility,* Westminster, 1967; (with Harvey Cox) *The Situation Ethics Debate,* Westminster, 1968; (with T. A. Wassmer) *Hello Lovers! An Introduction to Situation Ethics,* Corpus Books, 1970; *The Ethics of Genetic Control,* Doubleday, 1974; *Humanhood: Essays in Biomedical Ethics,* Prometheus, 1979.

Contributor to *Encyclopedia of Religious Knowledge,* 1955, *Die Religion in Geschichte und Gegenwart,* 1956, and to *Encyclopedia of Bioethics,* 1978. Associate editor, *Christendom,* 1935-47, *Witness,* 1935-71, *Anglican Theological Review,* 1936-48, *Journal of Pastoral Care,* 1947-57, *Churchman,* 1963—, *International Journal,* and *Science, Medicine, and Man.*

WORK IN PROGRESS: Conscience and Consequences.

AVOCATIONAL INTERESTS: Reading; salt water fishing, photography, and motor travel.

SIDELIGHTS: "Critical studies of problems about good and evil and right and wrong," Joseph Fletcher told *CA,* "get close to our feelings as well as the reasoning we do about them, but as a moral philosopher I like to think that how I write is as important as what I write. It may seem naive to most of the writers in *Contemporary Authors,* but the fact is that as I write I imagine that I'm *talking.* Talking to somebody who is not only intelligent but truly interested. I am confident that the practice works, at least for me. Since nearly everybody is interested in ethical questions, matters of value and moral judgment, my subject itself helps me. I am also aware, of course, that the constant use of 'real life' cases adds to readability."

*   *   *

FLEUR, Paul
See POHL, Frederik

*   *   *

FLEXNER, Stuart Berg 1928-

PERSONAL: Born March 22, 1928, in Jacksonville, Ill.; son of David and Gertrude (Berg) Flexner; married Doris Harcomb; children: two. *Education:* University of Louisville, A.B., 1948, M.A., 1949; Cornell University, three years postgraduate study. *Office:* Random House, Inc., 201 East 50th St., New York, N.Y. 10022.

CAREER: Cornell University, Ithaca, N.Y., instructor, 1949-52; editor, mainly for Macmillan Co. (publishers), New York City, 1954-58; bookseller, editor, and publisher, Mexico City, Mexico, 1959-64; Random House, Inc. (publishers), New York City, editor, 1964—. Lexicographer. *Member:* National Council of Teachers of English, Dictionary Society of North America.

WRITINGS: (Editor with Harold Wentworth) *Dictionary of American Slang,* Crowell, 1960, revised edition, 1967; *How to Increase Your Word Power,* Reader's Digest Association, 1971; *The Family Word Finder,* Reader's Digest Association, 1975; *I Hear America Talking: An Illustrated History of American Words and Phrases,* Simon & Schuster, 1977; *Listening to America: An Illustrated History of Words and Phrases from Our Lively and Splendid Past,* Simon & Schuster, 1982.

Also editor of various editions of *The Random House Dictionary of the English Language,* Random House. Contributor of short stories, poetry, and articles to magazines.

WORK IN PROGRESS: Books on the American language; a novel.

SIDELIGHTS: "In American slang, *can* has meant a toilet since 1900, a jail since 1910, a cheap car since 1929, and the buttocks since 1930. *To can* has meant to fire a person from a job (1885) or expel him from school (1905) and *can it* has meant stop or shut up since 1906." Passages like this are characteristic of Stuart Berg Flexner's works dealing with the American language. In his books *I Hear America Talking: An Illustrated History of American Words and Phrases* and *Listening to America: An Illustrated History of Words and Phrases from Our Lively and Splendid Past,* Flexner catalogs the vocabulary of the United States, noting derivations, obscure meanings, and slang usages. As the author comments in his introduction to *Listening to America,* he records "the voices of the people, from Wall Street brokers, movie stars, advertising men, Philadelphia lawyers, and labor leaders through baseball and football players, golfers, boxers, smokers and drinkers, housewives, firemen, cab drivers, telephone operators, pirates, mailmen and waiters and waitresses to hippies, prostitutes, and the Mafia."

Critics generally agree that Flexner's books work successfully on several levels. Malcom Boyd, for instance, writing about *Listening to America* in the *Los Angeles Times*, finds that book "fascinating . . . in different ways. It's a reference work to be used on demand. It's social history to be picked up and read in segments, informative in endless surprising ways. Finally, it's simply fun to read." The author, according to *New York Times Book Review* critic William Cole, "unlike [other linguists], is not prescriptive. To sink into the vernacular, he could care less if you misuse 'hopefully.' He's not a grammarian but a derivation detective; he shows us how our society has changed old words and brought new ones in." And in a *New York Times Book Review* article about *I Hear America Talking*, William Safire calls Flexner "the foremost scholar of the colloquial" and his work "a masterpiece of cultural history, excitingly laid out and illustrated, infused with the passion and color of the real world of words."

Flexner is fluent in Spanish and has a lexicographer's knowledge of German, Anglo-Saxon, and other languages.

BIOGRAPHICAL/CRITICAL SOURCES: New York Times, November 26, 1976; *New York Times Book Review,* December 12, 1976, January 16, 1983; Stuart Berg Flexner, *Listening to America: An Illustrated History of Words and Phrases from Our Lively and Splendid Past,* Simon & Schuster, 1982; *Los Angeles Times,* November 26, 1982; *Washington Post Book World,* December 5, 1982.

* * *

FOLEY, Gerald (Patrick) 1936-

PERSONAL: Born March 1, 1936, in Derry, Northern Ireland; son of Edward Daniel (an auditor) and Kathleen (McIvor) Foley; married Lanna McCarthy (a teacher), October 3, 1961; children: Kathleen Jane, Conor Gerald. *Education:* University College, Cork, Ireland, Bachelor of Engineering (with honors), 1957; University of Leeds, postgraduate diploma in concrete technology, 1959. *Home:* 12 Whitehall Gardens, London W4 3LT, England. *Office:* Earthscan, International Institute for Environment and Development, 10 Percy St., London W1P 0DR, England.

CAREER: Electricity Supply Board, Dublin, Ireland, engineer, 1957-58; Harris & Sutherland (consulting engineers), London, England, design engineer, 1959-62; J. Jarvis & Sons (building contractors), London, site engineer, 1962-64; Harris & Sutherland, section leader, 1964-66; Indulex Engineering, London, technical services manager, 1966-67; Building Design Partnership, London, senior design engineer and associate, 1967-71; Architectural Association School of Architecture, London, senior lecturer and director of Postgraduate Energy Programme, 1971-78; International Institute for Environment and Development, London, senior fellow and head of Earthscan Energy Information Programme, 1978—. Project manager, conference organizer, and consultant for numerous international studies and forums concerned with the role of selected renewable technologies in developing countries, 1977—. Part-time lecturer at School of Architecture, Cambridge University, 1971-72; senior visiting research fellow at Beijer Institute, Royal Swedish Academy of Sciences, Stockholm, Sweden; has presented papers and lectured at professional conferences and seminars. *Member:* Institution of Civil Engineers.

WRITINGS: The Energy Question, Penguin, 1976, 2nd edition, 1981; (co-editor) *Nuclear or Not: Choices for Our Energy Future,* Heinemann Educational, 1978; (contributor) *Atlas of Earth Resources,* Mitchell Beazley, 1979; *A Low Energy Strategy for the United Kingdom,* Sciences Reviews, 1979; *Coal: Bridge to the Future,* Ballinger, 1980; (contributor) *The European Transition from Oil,* Academic Press, 1981; (co-editor and contributor) *Energy in the Transition from Rural Subsistence,* Westview Press, 1982; (co-author) *Biomass Gasification for Developing Countries,* Earthscan, 1983; (contributor) *Energy Options,* Wiley, 1983. Contributor of numerous articles and reviews to periodicals and design journals, including *Washington Post, Ecologist, Built Environment, Building Design, New Civil Engineer,* and *Architectural Design.*

WORK IN PROGRESS: Research on energy strategies for educational buildings, effects of energy constraints on future traffic levels, and social and political implications of future energy policies; evaluation studies concerning energy use in developing countries, including community forestry, charcoal, and cooking stoves.

SIDELIGHTS: Gerald Foley says that since abandoning professional engineering, he has become increasingly convinced that "industrial society is entering a period of great change during which its ability to sustain and extend its liberal institutions will be tested to the limit. Many of its problems will arise from the changing patterns of energy supply and availability. If we are to avoid a future which is poor, brutish, and oppressed, we must work to devise strategies for the preservation and enhancement of what is good in the society we have created. I am a pessimist about what can be done, but prepared to be cheerful about it.

"My engineering training impels me to use simple numbers to describe some of the economic and energy variables with which we are dealing; but I believe strongly that our problems and their potential answers are social and political rather than technological. My writing is not directed towards producing deterministic models of what must be, but towards an illumination of the range of choice which exists within the boundaries of what can be."

* * *

FORD, Daniel (Francis) 1931-

PERSONAL: Born November 2, 1931, in Arlington, Mass.; son of Joseph Patrick (a carpenter) and Anne (Crowley) Ford; married Sarah Lansing Paine (an editor), 1967; children: Katharine. *Education:* University of New Hampshire, B.A. (summa cum laude), 1954; University of Manchester, Manchester, England, graduate study, 1954-55. *Politics:* "Fiscal conservative, environmental liberal." *Home and office:* Shankhassick Farm, Durham Point Rd., Durham, N.H. 03824.

CAREER: Overseas Weekly, Frankfurt, Germany, reporter, 1958; *New Hampshire Profiles,* Portsmouth, N.H., associate editor, 1959-60; University of New Hampshire, Durham, publications editor, 1961-68; writer. Editorial consultant, National Institute of Justice, 1975—. *Military service:* U.S. Army, Psychological Warfare, 1956-57; served overseas in France. *Awards, honors:* Fulbright scholar in England, 1954-55; Stern magazine writer's grant to visit South Vietnam and write series for *Nation,* 1964.

WRITINGS: Now Comes Theodora (novel), Doubleday, 1965; *Incident at Muc Wa* (novel), Doubleday, 1967, published as *Go Tell the Spartans,* Jove, 1979; (editor) Robert Carter, *Carter's Coast of New England* (travel), New Hampshire Publishing, 1969; *The High Country Illuminator* (novel), Doubleday, 1971; *The Country Northward* (travel), New Hampshire Publishing, 1976. Also author, with Sally Ford, of ski touring guides to New Hampshire and Vermont. Contributor of articles to *Nation, New Republic, Backpacker, Skiing,* and *Country Journal.*

WORK IN PROGRESS: *Michael's War,* "a novel set during the Anglo-Irish conflict of 1916-1923 and based on my father's experiences as a young man."

SIDELIGHTS: Daniel Ford told *CA* that his "main source of income is editorial work for government and other agencies" but his "main interest is writing novels and magazine articles." *Incident at Muc Wa* has been published in England and Holland.

MEDIA ADAPTATIONS: *Incident at Muc Wa* was filmed in 1978 as "Go Tell the Spartans" by Avco Embassy Pictures. ("Watching it was one of the great moments of my life, a major prompt to return to writing fiction after a long interlude in journalism and editorial work.")

AVOCATIONAL INTERESTS: Wilderness travel (especially on skis), working on his house and farm.

*   *   *

FORD, Nick Aaron   1904-1982

PERSONAL: Born August 4, 1904, in Ridgeway, S.C.; died July 17, 1982, in Baltimore, Md.; son of Nick A. and Carrie Ford; married Janie Etheridge, September 8, 1927; married Ola Scroggins Tatum (a college teacher), June 4, 1968; children: (first marriage) Leonard Aaron. *Education:* Benedict College, A.B., 1926; University of Iowa, M.A., 1934, Ph.D., 1945. *Politics:* Democrat. *Religion:* Protestant. *Home:* 919 East 43rd St., Baltimore, Md. 21212. *Office:* Coppin State College, Baltimore, Md. 21216; and Brookings Institution, 1755 Massachusetts Ave., Washington, D.C.

CAREER: Schofield Normal School, Aiken, S.C., principal, 1926-28; Florida Normal and Industrial Institute (now Florida Memorial College), Miami, instructor in English, 1929-36; St. Philips Junior College, San Antonio, Tex., dean of faculty, 1936; Langston University, Langston, Okla., associate professor of English, 1937-44; Morgan State College, Baltimore, Md., professor of English and chairman of department, 1945-73, Alain Locke Professor of Black Studies, 1973-74; Coppin State College, Union Graduate School, Baltimore, professor and director of Center for Minority Students, 1974-82. Member of conference on college composition and communication. Consultant, U.S. Office of Education, 1964-66.

MEMBER: National Council of Teachers of English (member of board of directors, 1964-67), Modern Language Association of America, Association of Departments of English, College English Association (president, 1960-62), Langston Hughes Society, Middle Atlantic Writers Association. *Awards, honors:* National Endowment for the Humanities grant, 1970-72.

WRITINGS: *The Contemporary Negro Novel,* Meador Press, 1936; *Songs From the Dark* (poems), Meador Press, 1940; (editor with H. L. Faggett) *Best Short Stories by Afro-American Writers,* Meador Press, 1950, published as *Baltimore Afro-American: Best Short Stories by Afro-American Writers, 1925-1950,* Kraus Reprint Co., 1977; (with Waters E. Turpin) *Basic Skills for Better Writing,* Putnam, 1959, 2nd edition, 1962; (editor) *Language in Uniform: A Reader on Propaganda,* Odyssey, 1967; *American Culture in Literature,* Rand McNally, 1967; (with Turpin) *Extending Horizons: A Freshman College Reader,* Random House, 1969.

(Editor) *Black Insights: Significant Literature by Black Americans, 1870 to Present,* Ginn, 1971; *Black Studies: Threat or Challenge?,* Kennikat, 1973; *Seeking a Newer World: Memoirs of a Black American Teacher,* Todd & Honeywell, 1982. Contributor to professional journals.†

*   *   *

FORD, Richard   1944-

PERSONAL: Born February 16, 1944, in Jackson, Miss.; son of Parker Carrol (a salesman) and Edna (Akin) Ford; married Kristina Hensley (a research professor), 1968. *Agent:* Amanda Urban, International Creative Management, 40 West 57th St., New York, N.Y. 10016.

CAREER: Writer, 1976—. *Member:* Writers Guild (East), P.E.N. *Awards, honors:* University of Michigan Society of Fellows, 1971-74; Guggenheim fellow, 1977-78; National Endowment for the Arts fellow, 1979-80.

WRITINGS: *A Piece of My Heart* (novel), Harper, 1976; *The Ultimate Good Luck* (novel), Houghton, 1981; (contributor) L. Rust Hills, editor, *Fifty Great Years of Esquire Fiction,* Viking, 1983. Also author of a screenplay. Contributor of stories, articles, and reviews to magazines.

WORK IN PROGRESS: A novel, *The Sportswriter,* for Simon & Schuster.

SIDELIGHTS: Richard Ford's novel *The Ultimate Good Luck* is "a page-turner of the first order, felicitously rendered in a prose style rare in contemporary fiction," according to Raymond Carver in the *Chicago Tribune Book World.* The book follows the quest of Harry Quinn and his girlfriend, Rae, who are in Mexico trying to get Rae's brother out of an Oaxaca prison, where he has been jailed for drug dealing. "Ford's sense of place is extraordinary," states *Newsweek* critic Walter Clemons. "His Oaxaca, perpetually strung with Christmas lights and wire-mesh bells . . . is a tourist town under military law. Terrorists bomb a Baskin-Robbins ice-cream store. . . . Quinn the bystander, who just wanted to get in and get out, is drawn into a labyrinth of betrayals, double deals and murder."

In a *New York Times Book Review* article, C.D.B. Bryan finds that the author "keeps the crucial distance in his writing" and that his prose "has a taut cinematic quality that permits him to record the color, the architecture, the movement, the violence occuring in front of him with the Cyclopean detachment of a wide-angle lens affixed to a camera on an exploratory spacecraft landing on an alien planet. It is a style that bathes his story with the same hot, flat, mercilessly white light that scorches Mexico, and it captures exactly that disquieting sense of menace one often feels lurking there just off the road."

"On a deeper level," says Carver, "the book is a meditation on love and comportment between two ordinary but 'marginal' people, Rae and Quinn." Clemons expresses "dissatisfaction" at the way Ford portrays these characters (like "laboratory animals in a demonstration that Quinn's belief in living without attachments is an insufficient code") but feels that *The Ultimate Good Luck* is the "work of a formidably talented novelist." And Carver, calling Ford "a masterful writer," feels the book "belongs alongside Malcolm Lowry's *Under the Volcano* and Graham Greene's *The Power and the Glory.* I can't give this novel higher marks."

BIOGRAPHICAL/CRITICAL SOURCES: *Chicago Tribune Book World,* April 19, 1981; *Newsweek,* May 11, 1981; *New York Times Book Review,* May 31, 1981.

FORTMAN, Edmund J. 1901-

PERSONAL: Born July 21, 1901, in Chicago, Ill.; son of Fred and Louise (Smith) Fortman. *Education:* Loyola University, Chicago, Ill., A.B., 1922; St. Louis University, M.A., 1927; Gregorian University, S.T.D., 1937. *Politics:* Democrat. *Home and office:* Jesuit Retreat House, P.O. Box 268, Barrington, Ill. 60010.

CAREER: Roman Catholic priest, member of Society of Jesus; Bellarmine School of Theology (formerly West Baden College, West Baden Springs, Ind.), North Aurora, Ill., professor of dogmatic theology, beginning 1939.

WRITINGS: (Editor) *The Theology of Man and Grace*, M. M. Bruce, 1966; (editor) *The Theology of God*, M. M. Bruce, 1968; *The Triune God: A Historical Study of the Doctrine of the Trinity*, Westminster, 1971; *Everlasting Life after Death*, Alba House, 1976.

SIDELIGHTS: The Theology of God has been published in Spanish.

*　　*　　*

FOX, Connie
See FOX, Hugh (Bernard, Jr.)

*　　*　　*

FOX, G(eoffrey) P. 1938-

PERSONAL: Born April 20, 1938, in Manchester, England; son of Frederick Platts (a furnishing consultant) and Marjorie (Percival) Fox; married Sara Hughes (a clinical nursing tutor), September 2, 1961; children: Jane, Alison. *Education:* Oxford University, M.A.; Associate of the Drama Board (Education), 1974. *Home:* 4A, Thornton Hill, Exeter, Devon, England.

CAREER: Manchester Grammar School, Manchester, England, teacher, 1961-69; University of Exeter, School of Education, Exeter, England, senior lecturer, 1969—. Tutor in extramural department, University of Manchester. Exchange teacher, Newton High School, Newton, Mass., 1966-67; master teacher, Harvard-Newton Summer School, 1967-72; visiting professor and lecturer at universities in the United States, Australia, and Canada. External examiner for Oxford and Cambridge Universities, University of Southampton, University of London, and North London Polytechnic. *Military service:* Royal Air Force, 1956-58; became senior aircraftsman.

WRITINGS: (With Brian A. Phythian) *Starting Points*, English Universities Press, 1967; *Shakespeare's "Winter's Tale,"* Basil Blackwell, 1967; (contributor) Phythian, editor, *Considering Poetry: An Approach to Criticism*, English Universities Press, 1970; *Writers, Critics and Children* (collection of articles), Heinemann, 1976; (contributor) John L. Foster, editor, *Reluctant to Read?*, Ward, Lock, 1977; (contributor) *Twentieth Century Children's Writers*, Macmillan, 1978; (contributor) *Le Livre dans la vie quotidienne de l'enfant*, UNICEF, 1979; (co-editor) *Responses to Children's Literature*, K. G. Saur, 1979. General editor, "Cascades" series of fiction for young people, for Collins. Contributor of articles and reviews to journals.

AVOCATIONAL INTERESTS: Sport, walking, travel, collecting children's books.

FOX, Hugh (Bernard, Jr.) 1932-
(Connie Fox)

PERSONAL: Born February 12, 1932, in Chicago, Ill.; son of Hugh Bernard (a physician) and Helen M. (Mangan) Fox; married Lucia Alicia Ungaro (a Peruvian poet and critic), June 9, 1957 (divorced, 1969); married Nona W. Werner (a professor and writer), June, 1970; children: (first marriage) Hugh B. III, Cecilia, Marcella; (second marriage) Margaret, Alexandra, Christopher. *Education:* Loyola University, Chicago, B.A., 1954, M.A., 1955; University of Illinois, Ph.D., 1958. *Politics:* None. *Religion:* None. *Office:* Department of American Thought and Language, Michigan State University, East Lansing, Mich. 48823.

CAREER: Loyola University of Los Angeles (now Loyola Marymount University), Los Angeles, Calif., professor of American literature, 1958-68; Michigan State University, East Lansing, professor of American thought and language, 1968—. U.S. Information Service lecturer throughout Latin America, 1958—; Fulbright professor in Mexico, 1961, in Caracas, Venezuela, 1964-66, and in Brazil at Federal University of Santa Catarina, 1978-80. *Member:* Committee of Small Magazine Editors and Publishers (member of board of directors, 1968-76). *Awards, honors:* John Carter Brown Library magazines grant, 1968; Organization of American States research grant, 1969-70, for study in Buenos Aires.

WRITINGS: America Today (lectures), [Caracas], 1965; *Problems of Our Time* (essays), [Caracas], 1966; *A Night with Hugh Fox* (three one-act plays), [Caracas], 1966; *Henry James: A Critical Introduction*, J. Westburg (Conesville, Iowa), 1968; *Countdown on an Empty Streetcar* (novel), Abyss Publications, 1969; *Charles Bukowski: A Critical and Bibliographical Study*, Abyss Publications, 1969; (editor with Sam Cornish) *The Living Underground: An Anthology of Contemporary American Poetry*, Ghost Dance, 1969, revised edition (sole editor), Whitston Publishing, 1973; *Gnosis Knows Best: A Radiography of the North American Subconsciousness* (novella), [East Lansing], 1969.

The Living Underground: A Critical Overview, Whitston Publishing, 1970; *The Omega Scriptures*, Ghost Dance, 1971; *Peeple* (short stories), Dustbooks, 1972; *The Gods of the Cataclysm: A Revolutionary Investigation of Man and His Gods before and after the Great Cataclysm* (anthropology), Harper's Magazine Press, 1976; *The Invisibles* (novel), The Smith, 1976; *The Face of Guy Lombardo* (short stories), Fault, 1976; *Happy Deathday*, edited by John Bennett, Vagabond, 1977; (editor) *First Fire* (anthology of Amerindian poetry), Doubleday-Anchor, 1978; *Honeymoon/Mom* (novel), December Press, 1978; *The Poetry of Charles Potts* (criticism), Dustbooks, 1979; *Leviathan* (novel), Carpenter Press, 1981; *The Guernica Cycle: The Year Franco Died* (diary), Cherry Valley, 1983.

Poetry: *Soul-Catcher Songs*, Ediciones de la Frontera, 1967, 2nd edition, 1968; *Eye into Now*, Ediciones de la Frontera, 1967; *Apotheosis of Olde Towne*, Fat Frog Press, 1968; *Glyphs*, Fat Frog Press, 1969; *The Permeable Man*, Black Sun Press, 1969; *Son of Camelot Meets the Wolf Man*, Quixote Press, 1969; *Waca*, Ghost Dance, 1975; *Almazora 42*, Laughing Bear Press, 1982.

Under pseudonym Connie Fox; poetry, except as indicated: *Blood Cocoon*, Zahir, 1980; *The Dream of the Black Topaze Chamber*, Ghost Pony Press, 1983; *Nachthymnen*, Mudborn, in press. Author of play "The Schoenbrunn Monologues," published in special issue of *Dramatika*, fall, 1981, and of unpublished novel version of *The Dream of the Black Topaze Chamber*.

Also author of novel *Sketches toward the Definition of a False Brazilian Messiah*, chapters of which have been published in *Story*, *Mississippi Mud*, and *Gargoyle*, three essays that appeared as a special issue of *Camels Coming*, and a critical study of Lyn Lifshin, for Whitston Publishing. Author of several screenplays, including "The Laundromat." Unpublished works include novels *Shaman* and *Mandala*, prose piece *Dialogue*, and play "Voices." Editor, "Ghost Dance Portfolio" series, 1968—.

Contributor of poetry, criticism, fiction, and articles on cultural history to periodicals, including *Transatlantic Review*, *Tri-Quarterly*, *Pan American Review*, *Prairie Schooner*, *Western Humanities Review*, *Trace*, *Western World Review*, *Choice*, *College English*, *West Coast Review*, *Ole*, and *Fragments*. Founder and editor, *Ghost Dance: The International Quarterly of Experimental Poetry*.

WORK IN PROGRESS: The Voyage to the House of the Sun, "anti-diffusionist book on Amerindian myth, linking it to Old World cultures"; *The Night before Christmas*, "novel about my family in Kansas—more memoir than fiction."

SIDELIGHTS: Hugh Fox writes *CA:* "The most 'releasing' experiences I've had in recent years were trips to Spain (1975-76) and Brazil (1978-80). While in Spain I fell under the influence of contemporary Spanish authors like Juan Bennett and Camilo Jose Cela. When I came back [I] did three essays that came out as a special issue of *Camels Coming*. While in Spain, I wrote a non-stop diary, *The Guernica Cycle: The Year Franco Died*. I also did some poetry in Spain that came out recently as *Almazora 42* (my address in Valencia). When I came back to the States in 1976, I went into a fit of depression and wrote a whole book of death-meditations that John Bennett excerpted from to produce *Happy Deathday*.

"The Brazil trip activated everything. I fell in love with Brazilian *Modernismo*, especially the work of Oswald de Andrade, his 'mural novels,' which triggered my own novel *Sketches toward the Definition of a False Brazilian Messiah* . . . and my first novel as Connie Fox, *The Dream of the Black Topaze Chamber*. I also did a volume of poems on the same theme—namely the contrast between a 'chamber'/middle-class isolation and the poverty of the Third World outside—and gave it the [same title]. I found Brazil itself a huge experiment, romantic, surrealistic, magic, a complicated syncretic blend of the African, the Portuguese, the Indian. Never stopped writing.

"I suppose Brazil also allowed my feminine persona to escape. I wrote *Blood Cocoon* when I was first down there, then a novel exploring role in relation to ambience, the psyche in its psycho-kinesthetic 'sheath.' Title—*Shaman*. Also drew heavily from my twenty-seven years of research into Amerindian anthropology.

"Back in the U.S. (1980), I did a full-length critical study of Lyn Lifshin and started doing novel after novel. For years I'd experimented around with fringe-intelligibility. Now I wanted to . . . use all the experimental resources I'd learned in twenty years of avant-garde reading at the service of pure story. Produced *Dialogue*, based on the life of Blythe Ayne, poet, belly-dancer, sociologist. Nothing happens but TALK. It's like reading a movie. Then two plays, "The Schoenbrunn Monologues" and "Voices," the former a one-and-a-half-hour monologue

spoken by a seventy-five-year-old Viennese actress and the latter just white- or black-face actors defining themselves in a void. Then I wrote a novel to precede my already-published double-volume *Honeymoon/Mom*. It's called *Mandala* and catches the hero when he's eighteen, a young Dante looking for a Beatrice. After I finish *The Night before Christmas*, I'm going to do a novel vaguely based on the life of Harry Smith (*The* Smith), kind of a latter-day *Citizen Kane/The Last Tycoon*.

"Through this whole thing, of course, I keep working on Amerindian anthropology. . . . It's this critical work that keeps me intellectually honest."

BIOGRAPHICAL/CRITICAL SOURCES: Cumberland Journal, spring, 1981.

*   *   *

FOX, William Price (Jr.)   1926-

PERSONAL: Born April 9, 1926, in Waukegan, Ill. *Education:* University of South Carolina, B.A., 1950. *Agent:* Lynn Nesbit, International Creative Management, 40 West 57th St., New York, N.Y. 10019.

CAREER: Full-time writer. Packaging salesman in New York, N.Y.; University of Iowa, Iowa City, teacher at Writers Workshop, 1968-72, instructor in journalism, 1974-76; University of South Carolina, Columbia, writer-in-residence, beginning 1976. *Military service:* U.S. Army Air Forces, 1943-46; became lieutenant.

WRITINGS: Southern Fried (short stories; also see below), Gold Medal Books, 1962; *Dr. Golf*, Lippincott, 1963; *Moonshine Light, Moonshine Bright*, Lippincott, 1967; *Southern Fried Plus Six* (contains "Southern Fried" and other stories), Lippincott, 1968; *Ruby Red*, Lippincott, 1971; *Dixiana Moon*, Viking, 1981; *Chitlin Strut*, Peachtree Press, 1983.

Screenplays: "Off We Go," Paramount, 1968; "Cold Turkey," Paramount, 1970. Also author of "Southern Fried" (based on his book of the same title), Twentieth Century Fox, "The Great Southern Amusement Company," and a television screenplay "Fast Nerves" for American Playhouse, WNET-TV, New York City.

Contributor of short stories and articles to *Saturday Evening Post*, *Holiday*, *Sports Illustrated*, *Harper's*, and *West Magazine* of *Los Angeles Times*.

WORK IN PROGRESS: A novel; articles for *Travel and Leisure*, *Esquire*, *Golf Digest*, and *Southern Living*.

SIDELIGHTS: A novelist and short-story writer who grew up in South Carolina, William Price Fox captures the humorous side of southern living in his books. Critics say his eye for detail coupled with his ear for regional dialect and his story-teller's instincts make his writing lively and fun to read. *Southern Fried*, his 1962 collection of short stories, remains his best-known work but his later titles have also been commercially successful, and his 1981 novel, *Dixiana Moon*, was enthusiastically endorsed by such respected fellow writers as John D. Macdonald and Kurt Vonnegut. Notwithstanding this success, Fox has not received much critical recognition. As George Garrett explains in the *Dictionary of Literary Biography Yearbook 1981*, "the support of neither readers, writers, nor even the regional book reviewers in his native South . . . has been able to give Fox the kind of national recognition that he seems justly to deserve."

One reason his books have not attracted more critical attention is "because his works contain few of those nuggets of obscurity that inspire critical articles," Carol Johnston writes in the *Dictionary of Literary Biography*. "His characters are clearly drawn and his plots are unobscured. He is that most misunderstood of contemporary writers, a traditional storyteller, and his tales resound with humor and moonshine instead of perplexity and dilemma."

A high school dropout from a bootlegging family, Fox tried his hand at several occupations before stumbling onto writing at age thirty-four. By that time, he had already completed a tour of duty in the Air Force, returned to South Carolina to finish his schooling, and settled into a career as a packaging salesman in New York. One day he was sitting at the White Horse Bar with Bill Manville, a friend of his and a writer for the *Village Voice*. Manville, who had a hangover and felt unable to meet an approaching deadline, asked Fox if he would do an article in his place. Fox agreed, producing a humorous story called "Moncks Corner." It ran on the first page.

The article attracted the attention of Knox Burger, an editor at Gold Medal (a division of Fawcett), and he asked if Fox were interested in writing more stories for a book. He was, for reasons which he explained to Matthew J. Bruccoli in *Conversations with Writers I*: "I think a lot of the motivation there was I always read stories. . . . I read a lot of short stories, and I've always noticed that the authors would get to a confrontation scene where there is any action or physical fighting going on, and they would veer away from it, or they would handle it in such a way where you knew they were faking. . . . I'm very competitive anyway, and I knew I could handle stuff that had action in it. I had never seen enough of it in fiction or nonfiction. . . . I got the offer from Knox, and then Knox began sending stuff around to the magazines. And the magazines began calling. The *Post* called and *Harper's* and *Sports Illustrated*. So I got into them very quickly. In '62 I was writing for all those magazines, all at once."

Nonetheless, Fox held on to his job in sales. "I figured . . . this isn't going to last because I really wasn't a writer," he told Bruccoli. And, thinking one opportunity was all he would have, Fox filled the book that would be named *Southern Fried* with what he calls "virtuoso stuff"—monologue, dialogue, black humor, repetition—in short, whatever he wanted to do. Much to his surprise, the book, which had been printed only in soft cover because of its regionalism—was a national success that launched Fox's writing career.

Since that time, Fox has published a second book of stories (*Southern Fried Plus Six*) as well as four novels. He has also returned to Columbia, South Carolina, his childhood home. George Garrett finds this relocation significant for "even when dealing with characters who are in many details distinctly different from himself, Fox tends to draw directly from the capital of his own experience to invest imaginary figures with the breath of life."

Fox's ability to make his characters "something more than the stereotypical sum of their parts" is what distinguishes Fox's fiction from that of many other modern writers, according to Garrett. "What we are talking about here is unusual dimensionality of character, of characterization in the classic and dramatic sense—classic in that the author is equally involved, or equally disengaged if you prefer, with each and all of the characters. . . . The kind of story Fox likes to write simply will not work if the characters are merely puppets manipulated by huge invisible social and economic forces. These forces

may or may not exist, like ghosts and other psychic phenomenon. But his characters must at least preserve the freedom allowed by Boethius in *The Consolation of Philosophy*. That is, they perceive themselves to be both free and responsible and try to act accordingly."

Writing in *Best Sellers*, William A. C. Francis notes that Fox's characters "are of the lower class: moonshiners, laborers, razor fighters, short order cooks, gamblers, poolroom loafers, hustlers, and the like. They are never portrayed bitterly. Rather, they are treated warmly and fondly." A case in point is Ruby Jean Jamison, the aspiring young country and western singer whose quest for fame and fortune is depicted in *Ruby Red*. Ruby is a sexy unscrupulous creature—a hustler whose talent is questionable, but she has what Carol Johnston calls "a belief in her own ability to create the future and like [earlier Fox protagonists,] her success is dependent on her country ingenuity and persistence."

Despite her authenticity, Ruby creates a problem for those critics who believe that she and some of her fictive cohorts are developed more for their own sake than for the good of the story as a whole. Nor is it just some of the characters' antics that strike these critics as superfluous. Many of the vignettes of Southern life are also gratuitous, they maintain. "Fox gets caught up in some Columbia stories at the expense of the narrative, and he still delights in 'characters' whether they move with the story or across it. His cast includes Agnes McCoy, Ruby Jean Jamison, Virgil Hooper Haynes, Preacher Roebuck Alexander, Spider Harold Hornsby, Jimmy Lee Rideout, Raymond La Mer, Hoover Joe Hooks, Ferlin Stover Peterson, Thelma Jean Hooker, and Mary Lou Tyler—enough to give any writer problems," William Koon writes in the *Georgia Review*. Notes the *New York Times*'s Christopher Lehmann-Haupt, "If Mr. Fox knows any detail that might tell you just a bit more about Nashville and environs, he'll work it in whether it belongs to his story or not. And that's basically the trouble with *Ruby Red*. It's as much an insider's guide to the C & W industry as it is the tale of how Ruby Jean Jamison and Agnes McCoy . . . scrap, connive, hustle, bite and scratch their ways to success." What could have been "a fine book trails into overlong nothingness," a *Publishers Weekly* critic maintains.

The book's loose structure reflects Fox's unorthodox method of composition. "I don't plan stuff and that's one of my real problems," he told Bruccoli. "I don't plan anything. I do plan basically, but not really. I try to keep my options completely open, and that's a good thing and a terrible thing, and you can just waste your life doing it. But *Ruby Red*, now was—that book was going to be about my uncle, Martin Luther Fox. He's called Spider in the book. I was going to write a book about him. He's an incredible character. I wrote at least 300 pages about him, then I introduced Ruby. Then about a hundred pages later I realized that she was better than he was. So I got rid of all his stuff and went with her. . . . I have no trouble cranking up, ever. But I try to keep myself open and not plot it, because I find my best characters come out of people that just kind of walk on, you know. And then I let them stay for a while and see how it feels. This is the kind of thing most people would plan in books, I guess. I guess that's why they write more books than I do."

Despite *Ruby Red*'s limitations, William Koon concludes that with that book the short-story-writer-turned-novelist "seems to have gotten the upper hand on his new genre, to have learned to aim his mobs of characters and his good episodes in one direction. And I think we can anticipate the complete success of the novelist as well as that of his character."

BIOGRAPHICAL/CRITICAL SOURCES—Books: Matthew J. Bruccoli, *Conversations with Writers I*, Gale, 1977; *Dictionary of Literary Biography*, Volume II: *American Novelists since World War II*, Gale, 1978; *Dictionary of Literary Biography Yearbook 1981*, Gale, 1982; *Contemporary Literary Criticism*, Volume XXII, Gale, 1982.

Periodicals: *Publishers Weekly*, March 15, 1971, January 2, 1981; *New York Times*, June 1, 1971; *Best Sellers*, July 1, 1971; *Georgia Review*, winter, 1973; *New York Times Book Review*, February 15, 1981; *Los Angeles Times*, March 10, 1981; *Washington Post Book World*, April 5, 1981; *Village Voice*, June 10-16, 1981.

—*Sketch by Donna Olendorf*

* * *

FREEDLAND, Michael 1934-

PERSONAL: Born December 18, 1934, in London, England; son of David (a sales manager) and Lily (Mindel) Freedland; married Sara Hockerman (a secretary), July 3, 1960; children: Fiona Anne, Danielle Ruth, Jonathan Saul. *Education:* National Council for Training of Journalists, proficiency certificate, 1955. *Religion:* Jewish. *Home and office:* 35 Hartfield Ave., Elstree, Hertfordshire WD6 3JB, England.

CAREER: Luton News, Luton, England, journalist, 1951-60; *Daily Sketch*, London, England, journalist, 1960-61; British Broadcasting Corp., London, executive producer and presenter of radio show "You Don't Have to Be Jewish," 1971—. Member of board of deputies of British Jews, 1969-72.

WRITINGS: Jolson, Stein & Day, 1972; *Irving Berlin*, Stein & Day, 1974; *Cagney*, Stein & Day, 1975; *Fred Astaire*, W. H. Allen, 1976, Grosset, 1978; *Sophie: The Story of Sophie Tucker*, Woburn Press, 1976; *The Two Lives of Errol Flynn*, Morrow, 1978; *Gregory Peck*, Morrow, 1980; *Jerome Kern*, Stein & Day, 1981; *Maurice Chevalier*, Morrow, 1982; *There's No Answer to That*, Arthur Barker, 1982; *Peter O'Toole*, St. Martin's, 1983. Contributor to *Times* (London), *Evening Standard*, and national magazines.

WORK IN PROGRESS: Two biographies and a study of the Jewish contribution to show business.

* * *

FRENCH, Richard (De Land) 1947-

PERSONAL: Born February 25, 1947, in Montreal, Quebec, Canada; son of John Kenneth (an engineer) and Clare Erina (a teacher; maiden name, Richardson) French; married Diane Louise Boivin (a public servant); children: Elizabeth Menard (stepdaughter). *Education:* Attended Dartmouth College, 1964-65; University of British Columbia, B.Sc., 1968; Oxford University, D.Phil., 1974. *Office:* Assemblee Nationale du Quebec, Suite 230-A, Quebec, Quebec, Canada G1A 1A4.

CAREER: Princeton University, Princeton, N.J., visiting research fellow in history and philosophy of science, 1970-71, lecturer and assistant professor of history, 1971-72; Ministry of State for Science and Technology, Ottawa, Ontario, assistant science adviser, 1972-73; Science Council of Canada, Ottawa, science adviser, 1973-74; Government of Canada, Privy Council Office, Ottawa, assistant director of machinery of government, 1974-77; McGill University, Montreal, Quebec, associate professor of management, 1977-81; member of National Assembly of Quebec for Westmount, 1981—. *Awards, honors:* Woodrow Wilson fellowship, 1968; Rhodes scholarship, 1968.

WRITINGS: (With Peter Aucoin) *Knowledge, Power, and Public Policy*, Science Council of Canada, 1974; *Antivivisection and Medical Science in Victorian Society*, Princeton University Press, 1975; (with Andre Beliveau) *The R.C.M.P. and the Management of National Security*, Institute for Research on Public Policy, 1979; *How Ottawa Decides*, James Lorimer, 1980. Contributor to professional journals.

SIDELIGHTS: Richard French lists his interests as "the social and political problems raised by science and medicine; public decision-making on technically complex issues; planning in government; policy analysis in government; management of information and knowledge in the public sector; and political sociology of public service."

* * *

FRESCHET, Berniece (Louise Speck) 1927-

PERSONAL: Born August 4, 1927, in Miles City, Mont.; daughter of Paul Vernon and Rose (Zigele) Speck; married Ferruccio Freschet (a high school dean of boys and assistant principal), January 26, 1952; children: Leslie Ann, Gina Marie, Dinah Sue, Maria Theresa, Frankie Paul. *Education:* Attended University of Montana, 1946-48.

CAREER: Author of children's books. *Awards, honors:* Irma Simonton Black Award from Bank Street College of Education, 1974, for *Bear Mouse;* Children's Science Book Award from New York Academy of Science, 1974, for *The Web in the Grass*.

WRITINGS: Young Eagle, Scribner, 1965; *Kangaroo Red*, Scribner, 1966; *The Little Woodcock*, Scribner, 1966; *The Old Bullfrog*, Scribner, 1968; *The Owl and the Prairie Dog*, Scribner, 1969; *Beaver on the Sawtooth*, Crowell, 1969.

The Flight of the Snow Goose, Crown, 1970; *The Jumping Mouse*, Crowell, 1970; *Turtle Pond*, Scribner, 1971; *The Web in the Grass*, Scribner, 1972; *The Ants Go Marching*, Scribner, 1973; *Bear Mouse*, Scribner, 1973; *Pronghorn on the Powder River*, Crowell, 1973; *Skunk Baby*, Crowell, 1973; *Year on Muskrat Marsh*, Scribner, 1974; *The Park, the Park*, Ginn, 1974; *Wufu: The Story of a Little Brown Bat*, Putnam, 1975; *Grizzly Bear*, Scribner, 1975; *Lizard Lying in the Sun*, Scribner, 1975; *Bernard Sees the World*, Scribner, 1976; *Biography of a Buzzard*, Putnam, 1976; *Little Black Bear Goes for a Walk*, Scribner, 1977; *Elephant and Friends*, Scribner, 1977; *The Happy Dromedary*, Scribner, 1977; *Possum Baby*, Putnam, 1978; *Porcupine Baby*, Putnam, 1978; *Bernard of Scotland Yard*, Scribner, 1978; *Moose Baby*, Putnam, 1979; *The Watersnake*, Scribner, 1979; *Five Fat Raccoons*, Scribner, 1980; *Where's Henrietta's Hen?*, Putnam, 1980; *Bernard and the Catnip Caper*, Scribner, 1981; *Black Bear Baby*, Putnam, 1981.

SIDELIGHTS: Berniece Freschet once told *CA* she "began writing because after ten straight years of diapers and dishes I needed a new outlook. My husband encouraged me . . . , and with a great deal of luck and help, I finally had a book accepted."

AVOCATIONAL INTERESTS: Music, reading, camping, and traveling.†

FRETHEIM, Terence E(rling)   1936-

PERSONAL: Born January 27, 1936, in Decorah, Iowa; son of Erling Hartvig (a minister) and Marie (Langseth) Fretheim; married Faith Luzum (an elementary school teacher), August 5, 1956; children: Tanya, Andrea. *Education:* Luther College, B.A., 1956; Luther Theological Seminary, B.D., 1960; graduate study at University of Durham, 1960-61; Princeton Theological Seminary, Th.D., 1967. *Home:* 2256 Hendon Ave., St. Paul, Minn. 55018. *Office:* Luther Theological Seminary, 2375 West Como Ave., St. Paul, Minn. 55108.

CAREER: Lutheran clergyman and theologian. Augsburg College, Minneapolis, Minn., instructor, 1961-63; Princeton Theological Seminary, Princeton, N.J., instructor in Old Testament, 1966-67; Augsburg College, assistant professor of religion, 1967-68; Luther Theological Seminary, St. Paul, Minn., assistant professor, 1968-71, associate professor, 1971-78, professor of Old Testament and dean of academic affairs, 1978—. Minister, Dennison Lutheran Church, Dennison, Minn., 1968-71. *Member:* Society of Biblical Literature, American Lutheran Church Clergy. *Awards, honors:* Fulbright scholar at University of Durham, 1960-61; Fredrik Schiotz Award, Air Association of Lutherans.

WRITINGS: Creation, Fall and Flood: Studies in Genesis 1-11, Augsburg, 1969; *Our Old Testament Heritage,* Augsburg, Volume I, 1970, Volume II, 1971; *The Message of Jonah,* Augsburg, 1977; *Deuteronomic History,* Abingdon, 1983; *The Suffering of God,* Fortress, 1984. Contributor to theology journals.

*   *   *

FREUDENTHAL, Hans   1905-

PERSONAL: Born September 17, 1905, in Luckenwalde, Germany; son of Joseph and Elsbeth (Ehmann) Freudenthal; married Susanna Johanna Catharina Lutter, July 20, 1932; children: Jedidja, Matthijs, Thomas, Mirjam. *Education:* University of Berlin, Ph.D., 1930. *Home:* Franz Schubertstraat 44, Utrecht, Netherlands.

CAREER: Jahrbuch Fortschritte der Mathematik, Berlin, Germany, assistant, 1930; University of Amsterdam, Mathematical Institute, Amsterdam, Netherlands, assistant, 1931-37, conservator, 1937-46; State University of Utrecht, Mathematical Institute, Utrecht, Netherlands, professor, 1946-76, director of institute curriculum development in mathematics, 1971-76. Lecturer at American universities. President, International Committee on Mathematical Instruction. *Member:* Royal Netherlands Academy of Sciences, American Mathematical Society. *Awards, honors:* D.Sc., Humboldt University in Berlin; Ph.D. from Erlangen University, Free University, Brussels, York University, and University of Amsterdam.

WRITINGS: Oktaven, Ausnahmegruppen, Oktavengeometric, [Utrecht], 1951, 2nd edition, 1960; *Inleiding tot het denken van Albert Einstein,* Assen, 1952; *Waarschijnly ikheid en statistiek,* Bohn, 1957, translation published as *Probability and Statistics,* Elsevier, 1965; *Logique mathematique appliquee,* Gauthier-Villars (Paris), 1958; (editor) *Report on Methods of Initiation into Geometry,* J. B. Wolters, 1958; *Lie Groups and Foundations of Geometry,* University of New Brunswick, 1959.

(Compiler) *Lincos, Design of a Language for Cosmic Intercourse,* North-Holland Publishing, 1960; *Lie Groups: Mathematics S-283,* Associated Students' Store, University of California, 1960; *Exacte Logica,* Bohn, 1961, translation published

as *The Language of Logic,* Elsevier, 1966; *Lie Groups,* Department of Mathematics, Yale University, 1961; (editor) *The Concept and the Role of the Model in Mathematics and Natural and Social Sciences,* Gordon & Breach, 1961; (editor) *Colloquium on Algebraic and Topological Foundations of Geometry, Utrecht, 1959,* Pergamon, 1962; (editor) *Report on the Relations between Arithmetic and Algebra in Mathematical Education up to the Age of 15 Years,* J. B. Wolters, 1962; *De Eerste Ontmoeting tussen de Wiskunde en de Sociale Wetenschappen,* [Brussels], 1966; *Mathematics Observed,* translation by Stephen Rudolfer and I. N. Baker, McGraw, 1967, original German version published as *Mathematik in Wissenschaft und Alltag,* Kindler Verlag, 1968; (with H. de Vries) *Linear Lie Groups,* Academic Press, 1969.

Vijfentwintig jaar Wiskundige ideenen methoden, Math. Centrum., 1972; *Mathematics as an Educational Task,* Reidel, 1973; (editor) L.E.J. Brower, *Collected Works II,* North-Holland Publishing, 1976; *Weeding and Sowing: Preface to a Science of Mathematics Education,* Reidel, 1978, 2nd edition, 1980; (editor) *Raumtheorie,* Wissenschaftliche Buchgesellschaft, 1978.

Fiabilite, validite, pertinence: Criteres sur la recherche de l'enseignement mathematique, Journees didactiques, 1980. Also author of fiction printed in Dutch. Editor-in-chief of *Educational Studies in Mathematics,* nine volumes, Reidel, 1968-79, and *Geometricae Dedicata,* 1972.

SIDELIGHTS: Hans Freudenthal told *CA:* "Although my writings extend from poetry to mathematics, from formal publications to informal letters, from fiction to fact-finding reports, I have pursued both rigor and art in all of them even when I knew it was unfeasible. Neither as a speaker nor as a writer do I master any language as well as I would like or even as others would expect me to. The worst is the one I invented myself, and the worst but that one is English, which is the easiest language to be written at a low level and the most difficult for high aspirations to be satisfied. I started publishing at the age of thirteen; now sixty-five years later my pace is still accelerating. I doubt whether anybody ever took such a pleasure in reading my work as I did in writing it. Fortunately nobody is obliged to read all I am writing, and nobody remembers any substantial part of my writings—myself included. If I will ever be remembered, I will be so as the one who is not worth being remembered."

*   *   *

FREWIN, Leslie Ronald   1917-
(Paul Dupont, Mark Nicholls)

PERSONAL: Born August 8, 1917, in Westminster, London, England; son of William Sydney and Anne (Dorland-Cumberland) Frewin; married June Fox (a company director), April 14, 1948 (divorced, 1976); married Susan Nicholls, 1977; children: Michael Leslie Pirie-Frewin, Colin Anthony. *Education:* Attended St. Stephen's College (London, England). *Home:* Hope House, Westleigh, Instow, North Devonshire, England. *Office:* Leslie Frewin Publishers Ltd., 5 Goodwin's Court, St. Martin's Lane, London WC2N 4LL, England.

CAREER: Trained for theater with impresario J. Wyndham Pemberton; joined Gainsborough Pictures Ltd. (film production), then Gaumont British Pictures, Production Facilities Ltd. (films); worked for Walt Disney on loan-out, Twentieth Century-Fox, John Huston, and many others, variously in production, writing, and advertising fields. Chairman, Leslie Frewin

Organization Ltd., White Lodge Books Ltd., and Leslie Frewin Publishers Ltd. (publishers), London, England; partner in Terence Verity Associates (architects and design consultants). Chairman, member of council, honorary chief archivist, The Lord's Taverners. *Military service:* British Army, Infantry, World War II.

MEMBER: National Playing Field Association (former president), British Association of Industrial Editors, Institute of Directors (fellow), Institute of Public Relations, French and Italian Chambers of Commerce, National Sporting Club, British Sportsmen's Club, Forty Club, Authors Club, Landsdowne Club, Royal Automobile Club.

WRITINGS: Battledress Ballads, W. H. Allen, 1943; *I Did Not Hear the Laughter,* Wren Books, 1948; *The Legends of Rob Roy MacGregor,* Rylee, 1948, published as *The Highland Rogue: The Legends of Rob Roy MacGregor,* Frewin, 1968; *Blond Venus,* MacGibbon & Kee, 1955, revised edition published as *Dietrich: The Story of a Star,* Stein & Day, 1967.

(With preface by The Duke of Edinburgh) *The Boundary Book,* Macdonald, 1962; (with preface by Graham Greene) *The Cafe Royal Story,* Hutchinson, 1962; (editor) *The Poetry of Cricket,* Macdonald, 1964; (editor) *Cricket Bag,* Macdonald, 1965; (editor under pseudonym Paul Dupont) *Across a Crowded Room,* Nelson, 1965; (editor) *Parnassus near Piccadilly,* Frewin, 1965, *Soccer,* 1966; (editor) *The Best of Cricket's Fiction,* Macdonald, 1966; (compiler) *The Spy Trade,* Frewin, 1966; (editor) *The Saturday Men,* Macdonald, 1967; (editor) *The Royal Silver Anniversary Book, 1947-1972,* Frewin, 1972; (compiler) *Immortal Jester: A Treasury of the Great Good Humour of Sir Winston Churchill, 1874-1965,* Frewin, 1973; (compiler) *More Wit of Prince Philip,* Frewin, 1974; *The Importance of Being Oscar (Wilde),* St. Martin's, 1981.

Writer-producer of "Film Festival," "Story of a Star," and other television productions for British Broadcasting Corp.; "Your Name in Print," "Pick of the Week," and other broadcasts for radio. Editor, *Focus Magazine.*

WORK IN PROGRESS: Sarabande for a Voice from the Past, a novel.

*   *   *

FRIES, Fritz Rudolf 1935-

PERSONAL: Born May 19, 1935, in Bilbao, Spain; son of Friedrich (a merchant) and Amparo (Schulze-Manteola) Fries; married Marianne Wellinghausen, December 30, 1960 (divorced, 1981); children: Milena, Michael, Robert, Daniel. *Education:* University of Leipzig, Diplom-Philologe, 1958. *Home:* Johannesstrasse 51/52, 1273 Petershagen/Berlin, East Germany.

CAREER: Interpreter and translator in Leipzig, Germany, 1958-60; German Academy of Science, Berlin, Germany, scientific assistant in Hispanic section, 1960-66; full-time writer and translator, 1966—. Author-in-residence, St. John's College, Stanford University, and in San Francisco, Nashville, and New York. *Awards, honors:* Heinrich-Mann-Preis, Academy of Arts (Berlin), 1979.

WRITINGS: (Contributor) *Neue Beitraege zur Literatur der Aufklaerung,* Ruetten & Loening, 1964; *Der Weg nach Oobliadooh* (novel), Suhrkamp Verlag, 1966, translation by Leila Vennewitz published as *The Road to Oobliadooh,* McGraw, 1968; (editor with Carlos Rincon and K. H. Barck) *Metamorphose der Nelke: Moderne spanische Lyrik,* Reclam, 1968; *Der*

Fernsehkrieg (short-story collection; title means "The Television War"), Mitteldeutscher Verlag, 1969, revised edition, Hinstorff Verlag, 1975; *Seestucke,* Hinstorff Verlag, 1973; *Das Luft-Schiff* (novel), Hinstorff Verlag, 1974; *Verbannung und Sieg des Ritters Cid aus Bivar* (juvenile), Kinderbuch-Verlag, 1979; *Alle meine Hotel Leben,* Aufbau Verlag, 1980; *Alexanders neue Welten* (novel), Aufbau Verlag, 1982.

Translator from the Spanish, except as indicated: Celestina, *Tragikomoedie von Calisto und Melibea,* Dieterich, 1959; B. Perez Galdos, *Misericordia,* Dieterich, 1962; Miguel de Cervantes, *Die Zwischenspiele,* Insel, 1967; Estabanillo Gonzalez, *Sein Leben und seine Taten aufgeschrieben von ihm selbst,* Reclam, 1967; L. Otero, *Schaler Whisky,* Volk & Welt, 1967; Calderon de la Barca, *Komoedie der Eifersucht,* Wossilus Buehnenverlag, 1968; A. Pareja Diezcanseco, *Offiziere und Senoras,* Volk & Welt, 1968; Juan Bosch, *Der Pentagonismus,* Rowohlt, 1969; Calderon de la Barca, *Dame Kobold,* Henschelverlag, 1969; (translator from the French) Armand Gatti, *General Francos Leidenswege,* Fischer, 1969; Julio Cortazar, *Das Feur aller Feur,* Suhrkamp Verlag, 1975; Miguel Delibes, *Fuenf Stunden mit Mario,* Aufbau Verlag, 1976; Cortazar, *Rayuela,* Suhrkamp Verlag, 1981.

Translator and adaptor for the stage, Tirso de Molina, *Don Gil von den gruenen Hosen,* Henschelverlag, 1968, and Antonio Buero Vallejo, *Die Stiftung,* Henschelverlag, 1975. Also author of epilogues to editions of books by Cervantes, Alfred de Vigny, Clarin, Salas Barbadillo, Maria de Zayas, and E. Gonzalez. Contributor to *Jahrbuch fuer Literatur, Anthologie der neueren DDR-Literatur,* and to other German periodicals.

WORK IN PROGRESS: Two novels, one on contemporary life in East Germany; short stories; a book of travels; radio and television plays.

SIDELIGHTS: Fritz Rudolf Fries told *CA:* "Important to my writing is the division of Germany. I guess, literarily, there are influences on my first writings from the American 'beat scene' (Jack Kerouac) and jazz of the forties and fifties. Today, I think an author must write about himself and his circumstances, geographical and political, to contribute to a man's world."

Fries has travelled to numerous countries, including the United States, the Soviet Union, France, Poland, Cuba, Bulgaria, and Albania.

BIOGRAPHICAL/CRITICAL SOURCES: Time, January 10, 1969.

*   *   *

FRITSCH, Bruno 1926-

PERSONAL: Born July 24, 1926, in Prague, Czechoslovakia; son of Josef (a civil servant) and Rosa Fritsch; married Jadwiga Przybyl, October 23, 1953; children: Martin, Caroline. *Education:* University of Basel, Dr.rer.pol., 1952, habilitation, 1958; attended University of Prague, 1964, and Harvard University. *Home:* Aussichtsstrasse 13, Herrliberg 8704, Switzerland. *Office:* Eidgenoessiche Technische Hochschule-Institut fuer Wirtschaftsforschung, Zurich 8092, Switzerland.

CAREER: Basel Center for Economic and Financial Research, Basel, Switzerland, director, 1958; University of Karlsruhe, Karlsruhe, Germany, professor of economics, 1959-63; University of Heidelberg, South Asia Institute, Heidelberg, Germany, professor of economics, 1963-65; Swiss Federal Institute of Technology, Zurich, professor of economics, 1965—.

Visiting instructor, College of Europe, 1960-69, Harvard University, summers, 1963-74, and Australian National University, 1971. Advisor to various governments, missions in Asia, and Latin America.

MEMBER: World Future Studies Federation, Swiss Future Studies Association (president), Swiss Economic Association, Swiss Association for Environmental Protection, American Economic Association, German Economic Association. *Awards, honors:* Institute for Advanced Studies fellow, Berlin, 1982-83.

WRITINGS—In English: (With others) *World Trade Flows,* Polygraphischer Verlag, 1971; (editor with others) *Problems of World Modeling: Political and Social Implications,* Ballinger, 1977.

In English translation: *Wachstumsbegrenzung als Machtinstrument,* Deutsche Verlag (Stuttgart), 1974, translation by Claire E. Reade published as *Growth Limitation and Political Power,* Ballinger, 1976; *Wir werden ueberleben,* Olzog, 1981, translation by Fritsch and Karl W. Deutsch to be published as *We Shall Survive,* in preparation.

In German: *Die Geld-und Kredittheorie von Karl Marx: Eine Darstellung und kritische Wuerdigung* (title means "Karl Marx's Theory of Money and Loanable Funds"), Polygraphischer Verlag, 1954; (translator from the English) K. William Kapp, *Volkswirtschaftliche Kosten der Privatwirtschaft* (title means "The Social Costs of Private Enterprise"), Polygraphischer Verlag, 1958; *Geschichte und Theorie ser amerikanischen Stabilisierungspolitik, 1933-1939/1946-1953* (title means "History and Theory of American Stabilization Policy, 1933-1939/1946-1953"), Polygraphischer Verlag, 1959; (editor) *Entwicklungslaender* (title means "Developing Countries"), Kiepenheuer & Witsch, 1968.

(Contributor) Gerhard Kocher, editor, *Zukunftsforschung in der Schweiz* (title means "Further Research in Switzerland"), Paul Haupt, 1970; *Die Vierte Welt: Modell einer neuen Wirklichkeit* (title means "The Fourth World: The Model of a New Reality"), Deutsche Verlag, 1970; *Bildung, Luxus oder Ueberlebenschance?* (title means "General Education: Luxury or Chance for Survival?"), Artemis, 1973; (editor with Deutsch) *Zur Theorie der Vereinfachung: Reduktion von Komplexitaet in der Dalenverarbeitung fuer Weltmodelle* (title means "On the Theory of Simplification: Reduction of Complexity in Data Processing for World Models"), Athenaeum, 1980.

WORK IN PROGRESS: Research on global modeling, the future of the world system, global energy models, the relationship between industrial and less-developed countries, and the future of the international system.

*   *   *

FROST, Carol 1948-

PERSONAL: Born February 28, 1948, in Massachusetts; daughter of William Arthur and Renee (Fellner) Perrins; married Richard Frost (a poet and college professor), August 21, 1969; children: Daniel Adam, Joel Richard. *Education:* Attended Sorbonne, University of Paris, 1967; State University of New York College at Oneonta, B.A., 1970; Syracuse University, M.A., 1978. *Home address:* R.D. 2, Box 73, Otego, N.Y. 13825.

CAREER: Poet. Founder and administrator of Oneonta Children's School (an "alternative-to-public-school"), 1971-74; visiting poet, Syracuse University, fall, 1979; teacher, Hartwick College, 1981—. *Awards, honors:* Bread Loaf scholarship, summer, 1976; Borestone Mountain Poetry Award, 1976, for "A Woman with Her Plants Talking"; sole honorable mention, Elliston Prize, 1978; Yaddo residencies, 1978, 1980, 1982; Margaret Bridgeman fellowship, Bread Loaf Writers Conference, summer, 1979; National Endowment for the Arts fellowship, 1981-82.

WRITINGS—All poetry: The Salt Lesson (chapbook), Graywolf Press, 1976; *Liar's Dice,* Ithaca House, 1978; *Cold Frame* (chapbook), Owl Creek Press, 1982; *The Fearful Child,* Ithaca House, 1983.

Represented in anthologies, including *Borestone Mountain Poetry Awards: Best Poems of 1976,* 1976, *Syracuse Poems,* 1976, 1977, and *The Ardis Anthology of New American Poetry,* 1977. Contributor of about 125 poems to literary journals, including *Antioch Review, Shenandoah, Beloit Poetry Journal, Poetry Miscellany, Kenyon Review, American Poetry Review, Antaeus,* and *Prairie Schooner.*

WORK IN PROGRESS: A new manuscript of poems.

SIDELIGHTS: Carol Frost writes: "After starting college I tried to find what would satisfy and provoke me. To that end I studied French literature and art at the Sorbonne, trained with the Pan American flat-water kayak team, learned photography well enough to place some of my photographs in art shows in New York, married and had two children, and traveled for three years, learning German and some Greek, in Austria, Italy, East and West Germany, England, Yugoslavia, Hungary, Lebanon, Greece, the Bahamas, France, Mexico, and from Texas to Maine.

"Satisfied as I have been in my travels, no territory or endeavor seems more provocative than sitting in a room with the scrappy beginnings of a poem, not knowing if the fragments will ever be wholly a poem; not knowing, yet still willing to empty myself of a pleasing, conscious order or emotion, a set morality or voice. Then, in the chamber that is the unfixed imagination or at sea with the imagination, off charts, to discover what will suffice, what will shine in the eye and resolve for the ear. Not to be comforted by the usual or the unusual until it is right, right for the poem, and then to savor it and take it.

"The essential part of a poem isn't in its subject or mode but in its reverberations, the inward arabesque of emotion and notation; and my particular concern has been not to write poems about this or that locality, in jargon or embroidered by simpleness, but to try to give the reader a sense of human truth and natural wonder based on little particulars, actual or imagined, which accumulate, treating each emotional instance as a palpable mystery which can with very great care be described, and each time finding in words the illumination which both clarifies reality and gnaws at its edges."

*   *   *

FROST, Lawrence A(ugust) 1907-

PERSONAL: Born May 1, 1907, in Ann Arbor, Mich.; son of Elvin Rinehart (a podiatrist) and Selema (a musician; maiden name, Teufel) Frost; married Ethel Duby, September 1, 1932; children: Jill Thel (Mrs. William Merke). *Education:* Attended Illinois College of Podiatry and University of Toledo; Ohio College of Podiatric Medicine, D.S.C., 1929. *Religion:* Presbyterian. *Home:* 211 Cranbrook Blvd., Monroe, Mich. 48161.

CAREER: Podiatrist in Monroe, Mich., 1929-79. Diplomate of American Board of Foot Surgery; president of Michigan Board of Registration in Podiatry, 1944-50. Member of Advisory Committee, Center for the History of Foot Care, Pennsylvania College of Podiatric Medicine. Instructor of postgraduate foot surgery at Ohio College of Podiatric Medicine and the Illinois College of Podiatry. Member of Monroe City Commission, 1956-57; vice-president of Michigan Municipal League, 1960; mayor of Monroe, 1960-64; vice-chairman of Monroe County Board of Supervisors, 1962; member of Monroe County Planning Commission, 1964-75 (chairman, 1972-75), and Monroe County Historical Commission (Custer curator, 1950-70; chairman, 1967-69; Custer curator emeritus, 1981).

MEMBER: American Podiatry Association (historian), American College of Foot Surgeons (fellow; president, 1950-52), Company of Military Historians (fellow), Council on America's Military Past (member of board of directors, 1974-77), First Cavalry Division Association (life member), Little Big Horn Associates (member of board of directors, 1967—), Michigan State Podiatry Association (president, 1935-37), Michigan State Historical Society (member of board of trustees, 1950-52), Monroe County Historical Society (president, 1948-50, 1966, 1973). *Awards, honors:* Gran Prix diploma and medal from City of Paris, France, in international foot research competition, 1952, for a new surgical technique for in-grown toenails; D.Litt. from Ohio College of Podiatric Medicine, 1968; Ohioana Book Award from Ohioana Library Association, 1970, for *The Thomas A. Edison Album;* Liberty Bell Award, Monroe County Bar Association, 1981.

WRITINGS: The Custer Album, Superior, 1964; *The U.S. Grant Album,* Superior, 1966; *The Phil Sheridan Album,* Superior, 1968; *The Court-Martial of General George Armstrong Custer,* University of Oklahoma Press, 1968; *The Thomas A. Edison Album,* Superior, 1969; *General Custer's Libbie,* Superior, 1976; (editor with John M. Carroll) *Private Theodore Ewert's Diary of the Black Hills Expedition of 1874,* CRI Books, 1976; *With Custer in '74,* Brigham Young University Press, 1979; *Addressing the Custer Story,* Gary Owen Publishers, 1980; *Some Observations on the Yellowstone Expedition of 1873,* Arthur H. Clark, 1981; *Custer Legends,* Bowling Green University Press, 1981.

WORK IN PROGRESS: General Custer's Horses; The Custer Statue Story; Military Duty on the Yellowstone.

SIDELIGHTS: Lawrence A. Frost's *The Custer Album* has been translated into Italian. He writes *CA:* ''It has been my fate to live in a town steeped in Custer lore. Since Monroe is General Custer's hometown, it abounds with Custer legends. Here, as elsewhere, people delight in repeating and believing the sensational stories about him. Though many of these legends are based on the truth, a great number are exaggerations or untruths. Others are figments of the imagination. Many wonder why I concentrate my writing and research on the life of a soldier when there is so much source material about statesmen like Lincoln. I have a ready answer. Lincoln didn't live here.''

*   *   *

FRUCHTENBAUM, Arnold G(enekovich)   1943-

PERSONAL: Born September 26, 1943, in Tobolsk, Siberia, Russia; son of Henry (a photographer) and Adele (Suppes) Fruchtenbaum; married Mary Ann Morrow, June 29, 1968. *Education:* Attended Shelton College, 1962-65; Cedarville College, B.A., 1966; Hebrew University of Jerusalem, graduate study, 1966-67; Dallas Theological Seminary, Th.M., 1971; New York University, doctoral candidate. *Religion:* ''Hebrew-Christian.'' *Address:* Ariel Ministries, P.O. Box 13266, San Antonio, Tex. 78213.

CAREER: American Board of Missions to the Jews, Dallas, Tex., minister, 1967-71, teacher at Messianic Assembly in Jerusalem, Israel, 1971-73, Englewood Cliffs, N.J., editor, 1973-75; Christian Jew Foundation, San Antonio, Tex., associate director, 1976-77; Ariel Ministries, San Antonio, director, 1977—.

WRITINGS: Hebrew Christianity: Its Theology, History, and Philosophy, Baker Book, 1974; *Jesus Was a Jew,* Broadman Press, 1975; *The Footsteps of the Messiah: A Study of the Sequence of Prophetic Events,* Ariel Press, 1982. Editor of *Chosen People,* 1973-75.

WORK IN PROGRESS: Biblical Love Making, for Ariel Press.

SIDELIGHTS: Arnold G. Fruchtenbaum is anxious to make the position of the Hebrew Christian known in the Jewish community. He ultimately hopes to immigrate to Israel and set up a school of Hebrew Christianity.

G

GABEL, Medard 1946-

PERSONAL: Born January 24, 1946, in Evanston, Ill.; son of Medard Anthony (a banker) and Dorothy (a teacher; maiden name, Wenthe) Gabel. *Education:* Attended University of Illinois, 1965-66; Southern Illinois University, B.A., 1972; International College, Los Angeles, Calif., Ph.D., 1977. *Residence:* Media, Pa. *Office:* Cornucopia Project, Rodale Press, Inc., 33 East Minor St., Emmaus, Pa. 18049.

CAREER: R. Buckminster Fuller, Philadelphia, Pa., research associate and archivist, beginning 1969; Rodale Press, Emmaus, Pa., currently director of Cornucopia Project. Co-director, Earth Metabolic Design, Inc., beginning 1972; member of board of directors, Upland Hills Ecological Awareness Center, 1975—; director, World Game. Consultant to Office of the Environment, 1980, and Agency for International Development, 1983, both U.S. Department of State, and to Governor's Energy Council, Commonwealth of Pennsylvania, 1981. *Member:* World Future Society, Society for International Development, American Association for the Advancement of Science.

WRITINGS: Energy, Earth, and Everyone, Straight Arrow Books, 1975; (with Howard Brown and Robert Cook) *Environmental Design Science Primer,* Earth Metabolic Design, Inc., 1975; *Ho-Ping: Food for Everyone,* Doubleday-Anchor, 1979; (co-author) *Empty Breadbasket: The Coming Challenge to America's Food Supply and What You Can Do About It,* Rodale Press, 1982.

WORK IN PROGRESS: A novel on "decentralizing the power structure," tentatively entitled *Whyld People.*

SIDELIGHTS: Medard Gabel writes: "The world has more than four and a half billion people. At least half of these people have inadequate food, shelter, clothing, health care, education, employment, recreational opportunities, and access to decision making that affects their lives. Oftentimes the world is a great place to visit but not to live in. It can be greatly improved. There are enough resources on the earth for everyone. We know how to take care of everyone on earth at a standard of living higher than anyone currently enjoys. My books (so far) have shown how this could come about."

GAIL, Marzieh

PERSONAL: Born in Boston, Mass.; daughter of Ali-Kuli (a diplomat, Baha'i scholar, and art collector) and Florence (Breed) Khan; married Howard L. Carpenter, July 29, 1929 (died November 24, 1935); married Harold E. Gail (a researcher), October 3, 1939. *Education:* Attended Vassar College, 1926, and Mills College, 1927; Stanford University, B.A. (summa cum laude), 1930; University of California, Berkeley, M.A., 1932. *Religion:* Baha'i. *Home:* 1601 Sacramento St., No. 14, San Francisco, Calif. 94109.

CAREER: Writer. Chairperson of Baha'i Unity of East and West Committee, Teheran, Iran, 1934, Baha'i Assembly, Nice, France, 1955-56, Baha'i Assembly, Salzburg, Austria, 1957-63, and Austrian National Baha'i Assembly, Vienna, 1963. *Member:* Phi Beta Kappa.

WRITINGS: (Translator from the Persian) Baha'u'llah, *The Seven Valleys and the Four Valleys,* Baha'i Publishing Trust, 1945; *Persia and the Victorians,* Allen & Unwin, 1951; *Six Lessons on Islam,* Baha'i Publishing Trust, 1953; *Baha'i Glossary,* Baha'i Publishing Trust, 1955; (translator from the Persian) 'Abdu'l-Baha, *The Secret of Divine Civilization,* Baha'i Publishing Trust, 1957; *The Sheltering Branch,* Ronald, 1959.

Avignon in Flower, Houghton, 1965; *The Three Popes,* Simon & Schuster, 1969; *Life in the Renaissance,* Random House, 1969; (translator from the Persian) 'Abdu'l-Baha, *Memorials of the Faithful,* Baha'i Publishing Trust, 1971; *Dawn Over Mount Hira,* Ronald, 1976; (contributing translator from the Persian and Arabic) *Selections from the Writings of 'Abdu'l-Baha,* Baha'i World Centre (Israel), 1978.

Khanum, Ronald, 1981; (contributing translator from the Persian) *Bahiyyih Khanum,* Baha'i World Centre, 1981; (translator from the Persian) *My Memories of Baha'u'llah,* Kalimat Press (Los Angeles), 1982; *Other People, Other Places,* Ronald, 1982.

WORK IN PROGRESS: A book about the troubadours in the twelfth century; gathering material for a biography of her father, Ali-Kuli Khan; translating Persian classics.

SIDELIGHTS: Marzieh Gail, whose father was chief diplomatic representative to the United States from Persia during the Roosevelt, Taft, and Wilson administrations, writes that as a child, she accompanied him to diplomatic posts around the world. She has made three pilgrimages to the Baha'i World Centre in Haifa, Israel, during the lifetime of the Guardian, Shoghi Effendi. Gail is fluent in French, German, and Persian.

BIOGRAPHICAL/CRITICAL SOURCES: Best Sellers, September 1, 1969; *New Leader,* September 29, 1969.

* * *

GALENSON, Walter 1914-

PERSONAL: Born December 5, 1914, in New York, N.Y.; son of Louis P. (a certified public accountant) and Libby (Mishell) Galenson; married Marjorie Spector (a professor), June 27, 1940; children: Emily, Alice, David. *Education:* Columbia University, A.B., 1934, Ph.D., 1940. *Home:* 104 Homestead Circle, Ithaca, N.Y. 14850. *Office:* School of Industrial and Labor Relations, Cornell University, Ithaca, N.Y. 14850.

CAREER: Hunter College (now Hunter College of the City University of New York), New York, N.Y., assistant professor of economics, 1938-41; economist with U.S. Office of Strategic Services, 1942-44, and U.S. Foreign Service, 1944-46; Harvard University, Cambridge, Mass., assistant professor of economics, 1946-51; University of California, Berkeley, professor of economics, 1951-66; Cornell University, Ithaca, N.Y., professor of economics, 1966—. *Member:* Association for Comparative Economic Studies. *Awards, honors:* Fulbright fellow, 1950; Guggenheim fellow, 1954-55.

WRITINGS: Rival Unionism in the United States, American Council on Public Affairs, 1940, reprinted, Russell & Russell, 1966; *Labor in Norway,* Harvard University Press, 1949, reprinted, Russell & Russell, 1970.

Unemployment Compensation in Massachusetts, State of Massachusetts, 1950; *The Danish System of Labor Relations,* Harvard University Press, 1952; (editor) *Comparative Labor Movements,* Prentice-Hall, 1952; *Labor Productivity in Soviet and American Industry,* Columbia University Press, 1955; (editor) *Labor and Economic Development,* Wiley, 1959.

The CIO Challenge to the AFL, Harvard University Press, 1960; (with S. M. Lipset) *Labor and Trade Unionism: An Interdisciplinary Reader,* Wiley, 1960; *Trade Union Democracy in Western Europe,* University of California Press, 1961; (editor) *Labor in Developing Economies,* University of California Press, 1962; (with F. G. Pyatt) *The Quality of Labor and Its Impact on Economic Development,* International Labour Office, 1964; *A Primer on Employment and Wages,* Random House, 1966; (editor with Alexander Eckstein and T. C. Liu) *Economic Trends in Communist China,* Aldine, 1968; (with Nai-Ruenn Chen) *The Chinese Economy under Communism,* Aldine, 1969.

The Labor Force and Labor Problems, Fontana, 1975; *Labor in the Twentieth Century,* Academic Press, 1978; *Economic Growth and Structural Change in Taiwan,* Cornell University Press, 1979.

The International Labor Organization, University of Wisconsin Press, 1981; *The United Brotherhood of Carpenters,* Harvard University Press, 1983. Contributor to economics journals.

SIDELIGHTS: Many of Walter Galenson's books have been translated into Danish, Russian, Japanese, and Spanish. He is competent in Russian, Dano-Norwegian, and French.

GALLAGHER, Patricia

PERSONAL: Born in Lockhart, Tex.; daughter of Frank (in construction business) and Martha (Rhody) Bienek; married James D. Gallagher (a television engineer; died, 1966); children: James C. *Education:* Attended Trinity University, San Antonio, Tex., 1951. *Residence:* San Antonio, Tex. *Agent:* Scott Meredith Literary Agency, Inc., 845 Third Ave., New York, N.Y. 10022.

CAREER: Writer, 1949—. Limited operator for KTSA-Radio, 1950-51; has appeared on television and radio programs in Texas.

WRITINGS—Novels; published by Avon, except as indicated: *The Sons and the Daughters,* Messner, 1961; *Answer to Heaven,* 1964; *The Fires of Brimstone,* 1966; *Shannon,* 1967; *Shadows of Passion,* 1971; *Summer of Sighs,* 1971; *The Thicket,* 1974; *Castles in the Air,* 1976; *Mystic Rose,* 1977; *No Greater Love,* 1979; *All for Love,* 1981; *Echoes and Embers,* 1983.

WORK IN PROGRESS: More novels.

SIDELIGHTS: Patricia Gallagher writes *CA:* "I've been interested in writing since childhood, wrote short stories in high school, and walked three miles each way to the Public Library. 'Making it' was a long hard struggle, writing on a small portable on my kitchen table between the chores of housewife and mother, and often late at night when my family was asleep, and the kitchen was the quietest place in the house." Her books have been published in French, German, Spanish, Portuguese, Dutch, Danish, Swedish, and Norwegian.

AVOCATIONAL INTERESTS: Travel, reading.

BIOGRAPHICAL/CRITICAL SOURCES: San Antonio News, March 11, 1961; *Dallas News,* April 16, 1961, May 27, 1976; *Houston Post,* April 1, 1962, June 1, 1976; *Dallas Times-Herald,* March 25, 1962; *San Antonio Light,* May 23, 1976; *San Antonio Magazine,* October, 1976.

* * *

GALLUP, Donald (Clifford) 1913-

PERSONAL: Born May 12, 1913, in Sterling, Conn.; son of Carl Daniel (a lumberman) and Lottie (Stanton) Gallup. *Education:* Yale University, B.A., 1934, Ph.D., 1939. *Home:* 216 Bishop St., New Haven, Conn. 06511.

CAREER: Southern Methodist University, Dallas, Tex., instructor in English, 1937-41; Yale University, New Haven, Conn., assistant professor of bibliography, curator of Yale Collection of American Literature, and fellow of Jonathan Edwards College, 1947-80. *Military service:* U.S. Army, 1941-46; became lieutenant colonel; received Croix de Guerre. *Member:* Bibliographical Society of America, Elizabethan Club (Yale), Grolier Club and Yale Club (both New York). *Awards, honors:* Guggenheim fellowships, 1961, 1968-69; Litt.D., Colby College, 1972.

WRITINGS: (Compiled with Robert Bartlett Haas) *A Catalogue of the Published and Unpublished Writings of Gertrude Stein,* Yale University Library, 1941, reprinted, Folcroft Library Editions, 1974; *T. S. Eliot: A Bibliography,* Faber, 1952, Harcourt, 1953, revised edition, 1969; (editor) *The Flowers of Friendship: Letters Written to Gertrude Stein,* Knopf, 1953.

(Editor) Eugene O'Neill, *Inscriptions,* Yale University Library, 1960; *Ezra Pound: A Bibliography,* Hart-Davis, 1963, revised edition, University Press of Virginia, 1983; (editor) O'Neill, *More Stately Mansions,* Yale University Press, 1964; (editor) Gertrude Stein, *Fernhurst, Q.E.D., and Other Early Writings,* Liveright, 1971; (editor) Thornton Wilder, *American Characteristics and Other Essays,* Harper, 1979.

(Editor) O'Neill, *Poems, 1912-1944,* Ticknor & Fields, 1980; *Work Diary,* Yale Library, 1981; *The Calms of Capricorn,* Ticknor & Fields, 1982; (editor) Kathryn Hulme, *Of Chickens and Plums,* Yale Library, 1982.

Editor, *Yale University Library Gazette,* 1947-80.

WORK IN PROGRESS: A study of the cycle plays of Eugene O'Neill; editions of the journals of Thornton Wilder and the letters of Gertrude Stein.

SIDELIGHTS: As curator of the Beinecke Library Collection of American Literature at Yale, Donald Gallup's interests went "beyond the conservation of books to the conservation of literature," the *New York Times* reports. "He . . . prepared definitive bibliographies—an ordering and tidying of the clutter that creeps into the printed record of any major author—for T. S. Eliot, [Ezra] Pound, and Gertrude Stein."

According to the *Times Literary Supplement,* Gallup's bibliography of Pound "has been frequently cited as the model bibliography of a modern author," while the 1952 edition of his Eliot bibliography was "at once acclaimed for its thoroughness and clarity." When the latter was revised to reflect the effect of a Nobel Prize on the author's literary standing and to meet the increasingly sophisticated demands of Eliot scholars, the *Times Literary Supplement* proclaimed the resulting edition "one of the classics of its type."

AVOCATIONAL INTERESTS: Book-collecting (T. S. Eliot, Ezra Pound, Gertrude Stein, Edward Lear).

BIOGRAPHICAL/CRITICAL SOURCES: Times Literary Supplement, March 7, 1969, May 3, 1970, March 20, 1981; *New York Times,* April 24, 1980.

*   *   *

GAMMAGE, Allen Z. 1917-

PERSONAL: Born May 27, 1917, in Cale, Ark.; son of Charles Floyd (a farmer) and Effie Ann (Jobe) Gammage; married Selma Ann Ulmer (an account clerk), December 17, 1955. *Education:* Tarleton State College (now University), A.Sc., 1935; University of Texas, B.A., 1938, M.S., 1945, Ph.D., 1958. *Politics:* Democrat. *Religion:* Baptist. *Office:* Department of Criminal Justice, California State University, 6000 J St., Sacramento, Calif. 95819.

CAREER: University of Texas (now University of Texas at Austin), Austin, instructor in government, 1945-48; Louisiana Polytechnic Institute (now Louisiana Tech University), Ruston, La., assistant professor of political science, 1948-50; California State University, Sacramento, Calif., assistant professor, 1952-56, associate professor, 1956-66, professor of criminal justice, 1966—. *Military service:* U.S. Army, 1942-43, became captain. *Member:* American Society of Criminology, American Society for Public Administrators, International Association of Chiefs of Police.

WRITINGS: Basic Police Report Writing, C. C Thomas, 1961, 2nd edition, with study guide, 1974; *Your Future in Law Enforcement,* Rosen, 1961, revised edition, Arco, 1971; *Police Training in the United States,* C. C Thomas, 1963; (with David L. Jorgenson and Eleanor M. Jorgenson) *Alcoholism, Skid Row,*

and the Police, C. C Thomas, 1972; (with Stanley L. Sachs) *Police Unions,* C. C Thomas, 1972; (with Charles F. Hemphill, Jr.) *Basic Criminal Law,* with study guide, McGraw, 1974, 2nd edition, 1979.†

*   *   *

GAMST, Frederick C(harles) 1936-

PERSONAL: Born May 24, 1936, in New York, N.Y.; son of Rangvald Julius and Aida (Durante) Gamst; married Marilou Swanson, January 28, 1961; children: Nicole Christina. *Education:* Pasadena City College, A.A., 1959; University of California, Los Angeles, A.B. (with highest honors), 1961; University of California, Berkeley, Ph.D., 1967. *Politics:* Democrat. *Religion:* None. *Home:* 73 Forest Ave., Cohasset, Mass. 02025. *Office:* Department of Anthropology, University of Massachusetts, Boston, Mass. 02125.

CAREER: Railroad engineman, 1955-61; Rice University, Houston, Tex., instructor, 1966-67, assistant professor, 1967-71, associate professor of anthropology, 1971-75, associate of Lovett College, 1967-75; University of Massachusetts, Boston, professor of anthropology, 1975—, chairman of department, 1975-78, associate provost for graduate studies, 1978-83. *Military service:* U.S. Army Reserve, 1955-63; became sergeant. *Member:* American Anthropological Association (fellow), Royal Anthropological Institute (fellow), Society for Applied Anthropology (fellow), American Association for the Advancement of Science (fellow), American Ethnological Society, Railway Fuel and Operating Officers Association, American Association of Railroad Superintendents, Sigma Xi, Pi Gamma Mu.

AWARDS, HONORS: Woodrow Wilson national fellowship, 1961-62; Ford Foundation foreign area fellowship, 1962-63; Social Science Research Council and American Council of Learned Societies fellowships for field research in Ethiopia, 1963-64, 1964-65, 1966; Rice University grant-in-aid for research in Ethiopia, summer, 1967; Center for Research in Social Change and Economic Development grants-in-aid for research in Ethiopia, Rice University, summers, 1968 and 1969; National Science Foundation grant for research on railroad enginemen, 1970-71; National Institute of Mental Health grant for research on railroads, 1972-74.

WRITINGS: The Qemant: A Pagan-Hebraic Peasantry of Ethiopia, Holt, 1969; *Peasants in Complex Society,* Holt, 1974; (editor) *Studies in Cultural Anthropology,* Rice University Studies, 1975; (editor with Edward Norbeck) *Ideas of Culture: Sources and Uses,* Holt, 1976; *The Hoghead: An Industrial Ethnology of the Locomotive Engineer,* Holt, 1980; (contributor) Eric Ross, editor, *Behind the Myths of Culture,* Academic Press, 1980; (contributor) Richard Weekes, editor, *Muslim Peoples: A World Ethnographic Survey,* Greenwood Press, 1984.

Contributor to professional journals in America, Germany, and Ethiopia, and to *Trains* and *Railroad* (magazines).

WORK IN PROGRESS: Articles and a book based on research on railroad operations; articles on Ethiopian studies.

SIDELIGHTS: Frederick C. Gamst told *CA:* "An ethnologist writes with reference to the native's, or insider's, viewpoint whether discussing Ethiopian hippopotamus hunters or American locomotive engineers."

GARNER, Wendell R(ichard) 1921-

PERSONAL: Born January 21, 1921, in Buffalo, N.Y.; son of Richard Charles (a minister) and Lena (Cole) Garner; married Barbara Ward, February 18, 1944; children: Deborah Ann, Peter Ward, Elinor Elizabeth. *Education:* Franklin and Marshall College, A.B., 1942; Harvard University, A.M., 1943, Ph.D., 1946. *Office:* Department of Psychology, Yale University, New Haven, Conn. 06520.

CAREER: Johns Hopkins University, Baltimore, Md., 1946-67, began as instructor, became professor of psychology, chairman of department, 1954-67; Yale University, New Haven, Conn., James Rowland Angell Professor of Psychology, 1967—. *Member:* American Psychological Association, Eastern Psychological Association, Acoustical Society of America, Psychometric Society, Society of Experimental Psychologists, American Association for the Advancement of Science.

WRITINGS: (With Chapanis and Morgan) *Applied Experimental Psychology,* Wiley, 1949; *Uncertainty and Structure as Psychological Concepts,* Wiley 1962; (contributor) F. A. Geldard, editor, *Communication Processes,* Pergamon Press, 1965; (with E. Cook) *Percentage Baseball,* MIT Press, 1966; (contributor) H. Helson and W. Bevan, editors, *Theories and Data in Psychology,* Van Nostrand, 1967; (with Shiro Imai) *Structure in Perceptual Classification,* Psychonomic Press, 1968; (contributor) J. C. Mancuso, editor, *Readings for a Cognitive Theory of Personality,* Holt, 1970; *The Processing of Information and Structure,* L. Erlbaum Associates, 1974.

Contributor to proceedings. Contributor of articles to *American Psychologist, Perception and Psychophysics, Psychology Review,* and other journals.

* * *

GASCON, The
See MILLER, F(rederick) W(alter) G(ascoyne)

* * *

GASKELL, Jane 1941-

PERSONAL: Born July 7, 1941, in Grange-over-Sands, Lancashire, England; daughter of Andrew Gaskell (a watercolor painter) and Edith (a teacher; maiden name, Hackett) Denvil; married Gerald Lynch (a lorry driver), May 10, 1963 (divorced, 1968); children: Lucy Emma. *Education:* Educated at home by parents. *Politics:* "Rather conservative." *Office:* Daily Mail, Northcliffe House, Tudor St., London EC4, England.

CAREER: Journalist and novelist. Former theater usherette in London, England, reader for *Argosy,* and feature writer for *Daily Express,* London; *Daily Mail,* London, feature writer, 1965—. *Awards, honors:* Runner-up, John Llewellyn Rhys Memorial Prize, for *Attic Summer;* Somerset Maugham Award, 1971, for *A Sweet, Sweet Summer.*

WRITINGS—Novels; published by Hodder & Stoughton, except as indicated: *Strange Evil,* Hutchinson, 1957, Dutton, 1958, reprinted, Pocket Books, 1979; *King's Daughter,* Hutchinson, 1958, Pocket Books, 1979; *Attic Summer,* 1962; *The Serpent,* 1963, St. Martin's, 1977; *The Shiny Narrow Grin,* 1964; *Atlan* (sequel to *The Serpent*), 1965, St. Martin's, 1978; *The Fabulous Heroine,* 1965; *All Neat in Black Stockings* (also see below), 1966, State Mutual Book, 1981; *The City,* 1966,

Pocket Books, 1979; *A Sweet, Sweet Summer,* 1969, St. Martin's, 1972; *Summer Coming,* 1972; *Some Summer Lands,* St. Martin's, 1979. Also author of *The Dragon,* c. 1963, reprinted, St. Martin's, 1977.

Screenplays: (With Hugh Whitemore) "All Neat in Black Stockings" (based on Gaskell's novel of the same title), National General, 1969.

* * *

GAST, Kelly P.
See EDMONDSON, G. C.

* * *

GAULT, Frank 1926-1982

PERSONAL: Born August 14, 1926, in Cameroon, West Africa; died 1982; son of Frank M. (a clergyman) and Josephine (a teacher; maiden name, Maxwell) Gault; married Clare Solberg (a teacher), August 12, 1950; children: Marsha, Bryan, Davison. *Education:* Northwestern University, B.S., 1949. *Religion:* Protestant. *Home:* 148 High Tor Dr., Watchung, N.J. 07060.

CAREER: Buick Motor Division, Chicago, Ill., assistant distributor, 1949-51; Waller Buick, Chicago, salesman, 1951-54; Handy & Harman (in precious metals), New York City, advertising manager, 1955-64; free-lance promotion writer in New York City, 1965-76; free-lance writer, 1976-82. Democratic committeeman in Watchung, N.J.; member of Watchung Volunteer Fire Co. *Military service:* U.S. Army, 1945-46. *Member:* Authors Guild, Authors League of America. *Awards, honors:* Lucky Four-Leaf Clover Award, 1978, for children's fiction.

WRITINGS—Juveniles; all with wife, Clare Gault: *Norman Plays Second Base,* Scholastic Book Services, 1973; *How to Be a Good Baseball Player,* Scholastic Book Services, 1973; *Four Stars from the World of Sports: Henry Aaron, Roger Staubach, Kareem Abdul Jabbar, Bobby Orr,* Walker & Co., 1973; *The Home Run Kings, Babe Ruth, Henry Aaron,* Walker & Co., 1974; *The Day the Stars Played the Monsters,* Scholastic Book Services, 1974; *How to Be a Good Football Player,* Scholastic Book Services, 1974.

Norman Joins the Football Team, Scholastic Book Services, 1976; *Norman Plays Ice Hockey,* Scholastic Book Services, 1976; *Pele, the King of Soccer,* Walker & Co., 1976; *Stories from the Olympics: From 776 B.C. to Now,* Walker & Co., 1976; *The Harlem Globetrotters and Basketball's Funniest Games,* Walker & Co., 1976; *The Cartoon Book of Sports,* Scholastic Book Services, 1977; *How to Be a Good Basketball Player,* Scholastic Book Services, 1977; *Norman Plays Basketball,* Scholastic Book Services, 1977; *A Super Fullback for the Superbowl,* Scholastic Book Services, 1977; (with Grace McCalley) *The Red White and Blue Songbook,* Scholastic Book Services, 1977; *How to Be a Good Soccer Player,* Scholastic Book Services, 1978.

Norman Plays Soccer, Scholastic Book Services, 1981; *The Miracle Halfback,* Scholastic Book Services, 1982.

SIDELIGHTS: Frank Gault told *CA:* "Our books encourage youngsters to read. Strong interests in the subjects plus easy-to-read texts help get kids into the habit at an early age that reaps educational rewards for life."†

GEISMAR, L(udwig) L(eo) 1921-

PERSONAL: Born February 25, 1921, in Mannheim, Germany; son of Heinrich (a salesman) and Lina Geismar; married Shirley Ann Cooperman (an editor), September 18, 1948; children: Lavah Greenman, Deborah, Aviva. *Education:* University of Minnesota, B.A. (cum laude), 1947, M.A., 1950; Hebrew University of Jerusalem, Ph.D., 1956. *Religion:* Jewish. *Home:* 347 Valentine St., Highland Park, N.J. 08904. *Office:* Graduate School of Social Work, Rutgers University, New Brunswick, N.J. 08903.

CAREER: Ministry of Social Welfare, Jerusalem, Israel, co-ordinator of social research, 1954-56; Family Centered Project, St. Paul, Minn., director, 1956-59; Rutgers University, New Brunswick, N.J., associate professor, 1959-62, professor of social work and sociology, 1962—, director of Rutgers University Social Work Research Center. Visiting professor and director of a cross-national family study, University of Melbourne, 1975-76. Lecturer at Columbia University School of Social Work, summers, 1963-66, 1968, and at Brandeis University, University of Sydney, University of New South Wales, and Flinders University. Project director of a cross-national family study in Stockholm, 1969-73. Member of review team in Mediterranean countries, United Nations, 1955; member of Social Welfare Administration grant review panel, U.S. Department of Health, Education, and Welfare, 1963. Member of Raritan Valley Community Welfare Council, 1960-62, and Middlesex County Mental Health Board, 1962-64. Consultant, Area Development Project, Vancouver, 1962-67. *Military service:* U.S. Army, 1942-45; served in North Africa and Europe; became sergeant.

MEMBER: American Sociological Association (fellow), National Association of Social Workers, Council on Social Work Education (member of accreditation commission, 1965—), National Council on Family Relations, Society for the Study of Social Problems, American Association of University Professors. *Awards, honors:* Research grants from U.S. Department of Health, Education, and Welfare, Ford Foundation, Buckland Foundation (Australia), Victorian Family Council (Australia), U.S. Social and Rehabilitation Service, National Institute of Mental Health, New Haven Foundation, Tri-Centennial Fund of the Bank of Sweden, Rutgers Research Council, and Australian Department of Social Security.

WRITINGS: Community Organization in Israel, Israel Ministry of Social Welfare, 1955; (with Michael La Sorte) *Understanding the Multi-Problem Family: A Conceptual Analysis and Exploration in Identification,* Association Press, 1964; (with Jane Krisberg) *The Forgotten Neighborhood: Site of an Early Skirmish in the War on Poverty,* Scarecrow, 1967; *Preventive Intervention in Social Work,* Scarecrow, 1968; *Family and Community Functioning,* Scarecrow, 1971, revised edition, 1980; (with Bruce Lagey and others) *Early Supports for Family Life,* Scarecrow, 1972; *555 Families: A Social Psychological Study of Young Families in Transition,* Transaction Books, 1973; (with wife, Shirley Geismar) *Families in an Urban Mold,* Pergamon, 1979.

All published by Family Centered Project (St. Paul, Minn.): *Family Centered Project,*1957; *Report on a Check List Survey,* 1957; (with Beverly Ayres) *Families in Trouble,* 1958; (with Ayres) *Patterns of Change in Problem Families,* 1959; (with Ayres) *Measuring Family Functioning,* 1960.

Contributor: *The Social Welfare Forum 1960,* Columbia University Press, 1960; Ellen B. Hill, editor, *Ricerche Applicate Al Servizio Sociale Negli Stati Uniti,* Instituto Per Gli Studi De Servizio Sociale (Rome), 1964; (with Lagey) *Social Welfare Practice 1965,* Columbia University Press, 1965; Gordon E. Brown, editor, *The Multi-Problem Dilemma,* Scarecrow, 1968; Hadden and Borgatta, editors, *Marriage and the Family,* F. E. Peacock, 1969; Edward J. Mullen and James R. Dumpson, editors, *Evaluation of Social Intervention,* Jossey-Bass, 1972. Contributor to professional journals.

Member of editorial committee, *Social Casework,* 1964-65.

*   *   *

GEIWITZ, P(eter) James 1938-

PERSONAL: Surname is pronounced *Guy*-wits; born June 9, 1938, in Minneota, Minn.; son of Peter H. (a hardware dealer) and Hansina (a teacher; maiden name, Johanson) Geiwitz; married Judith Haefele, 1963 (divorced); married Roberta Klatzky, 1972; children: (first marriage) Charles Paul. *Education:* St. Olaf College, B.A., 1960; University of Michigan, Ph.D., 1964. *Home and office:* 1122 Olive St., Santa Barbara, Calif. 93101.

CAREER: Operated his own business, the Gopher Stamp Co., at age fourteen, worked as a garage mechanic and on a road crew to pay for his education, and wrote sports and political columns for a local newspaper; University of Michigan, Ann Arbor, instructor in psychology, 1964; Stanford University, Stanford, Calif., assistant professor of psychology, 1965-69; free-lance writer, 1969—; University of California, Santa Barbara, lecturer in psychology, 1971-72. *Member:* Gerontological Society, Society for the Psychological Study of Social Issues, Phi Beta Kappa.

WRITINGS: Non-Freudian Personality Theories, Brooks/Cole, 1969; (with P. Mussen, M. Rosenzweig, and others) *Psychology: An Introduction,* Heath, 1973, 2nd edition, 1977, abridged edition, 1979; *Looking at Ourselves,* Little, Brown, 1976, 2nd edition, 1980; (with M. Moursund) *Approaches to Personality,* Brooks/Cole, 1979; (with Mussen, J. Conger, and J. Kagan) *Psychological Development,* Harper, 1979; (with K. W. Schaie) *Adult Development and Aging,* Little, Brown, 1982; (with Schaie) *Readings in Adult Development and Aging,* Little, Brown, 1982. Contributor to professional journals.

WORK IN PROGRESS: An introductory textbook in psychology.

SIDELIGHTS: "Of all the problems a textbook writer faces," writes P. James Geiwitz, "the most annoying and intractable is that of the sexist generic pronouns. It is no longer acceptable to use the masculine forms when referring to a person who can be either male or female. But no generally applicable alternative has emerged—'he or she,' 'he/she,' pluralizing, singular 'they,' etc. I believe we must create a new pronoun, but I have no clear vision of what it should be."

*   *   *

GERTZ, Elmer 1906-

PERSONAL: Born September 14, 1906, in Chicago, Ill.; son of Morris (a merchant) and Grace (Grossman) Gertz; married Ceretta Samuels, August 16, 1931 (died, 1958); married Mamie Laitchin Friedman, June 21, 1959; children: (first marriage) Theodore Gerson, Margery Ann (Mrs. Henry R. Hechtman); (stepson) Jack M. Friedman. *Education:* University of Chicago, Ph.D., 1928, J.D., 1930. *Politics:* Independent Democrat. *Religion:* Jewish. *Home:* 6249 North Albany Ave., Chicago, Ill. 60659. *Office:* John Marshall Law School, 315 South Plymouth Ct., Chicago, Ill. 60604.

CAREER: Admitted to Illinois bar, 1930; McInerney, Epstein, & Arvey (law firm), Chicago, Ill., associate, 1930-44; attorney in private practice in Chicago, 1941—; Gertz & Giampietro (law firm), Chicago, partner, 1973-76. Active in civic and community activities in Chicago for more than four decades, serving as president of Public Housing Association, 1943-49, legislative chairman of Mayor's Emergency Housing Committee, 1946-48, member of Mayor's Housing Action Committee, 1949-51; president of Greater Chicago Council of the American Jewish Congress, 1959-63, and president of Adult Education Council of Greater Chicago, 1965-69; elected delegate, Illinois Constitutional Convention, 1969, and chairman of Bill of Rights Committee and Convention, 1969-70; professor, John Marshall Law School, 1970—; member of board of trustees, Bellefaire and City of Hope; member of board of directors, Jackson Park Hospital; director, Blind Services Association.

MEMBER: American Bar Association, American Judicature Society, Federal Bar Association, Illinois State Bar Association, Chicago Bar Association (chairman of legal education committee and civil rights committee), First Amendment Lawyers Association (president), Appellate Lawyers Association, Decalogue Society of Lawyers (president, 1954-55), Civil War Round Table of Chicago (a founder; president, 1952-53; honorary life member), Society of Midland Authors, Friends of Literature, Shaw Society of Chicago (founder; president, 1956-61), Chicago Literary Club (president), Cliff Dwellers (Chicago), City Club (Chicago), Caxton Club.

AWARDS, HONORS: Decalogue Society of Lawyers Award of Merit, 1949; citations from Illinois Division of American Civil Liberties Union, 1963, from University of Chicago Alumni Association, for public service, and from Roosevelt University, Society of Midland Authors, American Jewish Congress, and Chicago Council against Discrimination; State of Israel's Prime Minister's Medal, 1972.

WRITINGS: (With A. I. Tobin) *Frank Harris: A Study in Black and White*, Mendelsohn, 1931, reprinted, Haskell, 1970; *The People vs. the Chicago Tribune*, Union for Democratic Action, 1942; *American Ghettos*, American Jewish Congress, 1946.

(Contributor) *Henry Miller and the Critics*, Southern Illinois University Press, 1963; *A Handful of Clients*, Follett, 1965; *Books and Their Right to Live*, University of Kansas Library, 1965; *Moment of Madness: The People vs. Jack Ruby*, Follett, 1968; (author of preface) Earl R. Hutchison, *"Tropic of Cancer" on Trial*, Grove, 1968.

(Contributor) David G. Clark and Hutchison, *Mass Media and the Law: Freedom and Restraint*, Wiley, 1970; *For the First Hours of Tomorrow: The New Illinois Bill of Rights*, University of Illinois Press, 1972; (contributor) Alan S. Gratch and Virginia H. Ubik, *Ballots for Change: New Suffrage and Amending Articles for Illinois*, University of Illinois Press, 1974; *To Life* (memoirs), McGraw, 1974; (editor) *The Short Stories of Frank Harris*, Southern Illinois University Press, 1975; (editor with Felice F. Lewis) *Henry Miller: Years of Trial and Triumph, 1962-1964: The Correspondence of Henry Miller and Elmer Gertz*, Southern Illinois University Press, 1978; *Odyssey of a Barbarian: The Biography of George Sylvester Viereck*, Pro-

metheus, 1979; (with Joe Pisciotte) *Charter for a New Age: An Inside View of the Sixth Illinois Constitutional Convention*, University of Illinois Press, 1980.

Author of radio plays, including "Mrs. Bixby Gets a Letter," 1942, and "Second Inaugural." Contributor to *Encyclopaedia Britannica, Junior Britannica, Encyclopedia Judaica,* and *American People's Encyclopedia.* Contributor of articles to periodicals, including *Nation, Progressive, Public Opinion Quarterly, American Mercury,* and *Journal of the Illinois State Historical Society.*

WORK IN PROGRESS: A guide to estate planning for laymen, with son, Theodore Gerson, and Robert Garro; a book about Samuel Witwer, president of the Sixth Illinois Constitutional Convention, with Edward Gilbreth; a book about the libel case of Elmer Gertz versus Robert Welch.

SIDELIGHTS: Elmer Gertz, a lawyer, law professor, and writer, told *CA* he has participated in "some of the celebrated cases of the day: the freeing of Nathan Leopold, the setting aside of the death sentence of Jack Ruby, [and] many censorship cases, including those involving [Henry Miller's] *Tropic of Cancer,* a landmark libel case that has caused the Supreme Court to modify the law in that area."

Gertz also writes that in 1981 he was sent by the National Conference on Soviet Jewry to meet with the dissidents—"This was probably the most emotion-laden experience of my life."

BIOGRAPHICAL/CRITICAL SOURCES: Elmer Gertz, *To Life* (memoirs), McGraw, 1974; *Chicago Tribune Book World,* May 20, 1979.

*   *   *

GIBBONS, Brian 1938-

PERSONAL: Born October 8, 1938. *Education:* Cambridge University, M.A., Ph.D., the latter in 1965. *Office:* Englisches Seminar, Universitat Zurich, Plattenstrasse 47, CH8032 Zurich, Switzerland.

CAREER: University of York, Heslington, Yorkshire, England, 1965-81, began as lecturer, became senior lecturer in English; University of Leeds, Leeds, England, professor of English literature, 1981-83; University of Zurich, Zurich, Switzerland, professor of English literature, 1983—.

WRITINGS: (Editor) Cyril Tourneur, *The Revenger's Tragedy,* Hill & Wang, 1967; *Jacobean City Comedy: A Study of Satiric Plays by Jonson, Marston and Middleton,* Harvard University Press, 1968, 2nd edition, Methuen, 1980; (editor) William Congreve, *The Way of the World,* Norton, 1976. Also editor of an edition of *Romeo and Juliet,* 1980. General editor of "New Mermaid" series for Norton; contributor to *Year's Work in English Studies,* 1971-81, and to *Shakespeare Survey.* Contributor of reviews and articles to various scholarly journals and reviews, including *Modern Language Review, Review of English Studies,* and *Times Higher Education Supplement.*

WORK IN PROGRESS: A book on dramatic monologue; an edition of Shakespeare's *Measure for Measure;* general editor of *New Cambridge Shakespeare.*

*   *   *

GIBBS, James A.
See GIBBS, James Atwood

GIBBS, James Atwood 1922-
(James A. Gibbs, Jim Gibbs)

PERSONAL: Born January 17, 1922, in Seattle, Wash.; son of A. James (in investments) and Vera (Smith) Gibbs; married Cherie Lola Norman, May 26, 1950; children: Debbie Ann Gibbs Pedrick. *Education:* Attended University of Washington, Seattle. *Politics:* Independent. *Religion:* Baptist. *Address:* Cleft of the Rock Lighthouse, P.O. Box 93, Yachats, Ore. 97498.

CAREER: Marine Digest, Seattle, Wash., assistant editor, 1948-55, editor, 1959-72; G.E.B. Properties, Seattle, partner, 1964—. *Military service:* U.S. Coast Guard, 1942-46. *Member:* Puget Sound Maritime Historical Society (co-founder; charter member). *Awards, honors:* Twelve Anchor Award from the Port of Seattle, 1954-72; award of merit from Seattle Historical Society, 1955, for *Sentinels of the North Pacific: The Story of Pacific Coast Lighthouses and Lightships.*

WRITINGS: Pacific Graveyard: A Narrative of the Ships Lost Where the Columbia River Meets the Pacific Ocean, Binford & Mort, 1950, 3rd edition (under name James A. Gibbs), 1964; *Tillamook Light,* Binford & Mort, 1953; *Sentinels of the North Pacific: The Story of Pacific Coast Lighthouses and Lightships,* Binford & Mort, 1955; *Shipwrecks of the Pacific Coast,* Binford & Mort, 1957; (with Joe Williamson) *Maritime Memories of Puget Sound,* Superior, 1977.

Under name James A. Gibbs: *Shipwrecks off Juan de Fuca,* Binford & Mort, 1968; *Tillamook Light: A True Narrative of Oregon's Tillamook Rock Lighthouse,* Binford & Mort, 1979.

Under name Jim Gibbs: *West Coast Windjammers in Story and Pictures,* Superior, 1968; *Pacific Square-Riggers: Pictorial History of the Great Windships of Yesteryear,* Superior, 1969; *The Unusual Side of the Sea: A Slop Chest of Sea Lore,* Windward Publishing, 1971; *Disaster Log of Ships,* Superior, 1971; *West Coast Lighthouses: A Pictorial History of the Guiding Lights of the Sea,* Superior, 1974; *Shipwrecks in Paradise,* Superior, 1977; *Oregon's Salty Coast,* Superior, 1978; *Sentinels of Solitude: West Coast Lighthouses,* Graphic Arts Center, 1981.

WORK IN PROGRESS: Where the Columbia River Meets the Sea; The Other Captain Bligh.

SIDELIGHTS: James Atwood Gibbs told *CA:* "One should write about the things he enjoys most, then, even if nobody else likes his work, he feels satisfied. If people enjoy his work, he's doubly satisfied. Everything comes from the good Lord and to him all basic credit must go for any works. Without him one has a missing ingredient."

*   *   *

GIBBS, Jim
See GIBBS, James Atwood

*   *   *

GIBNEY, Frank (Bray) 1924-

PERSONAL: Born September 21, 1924, in Scranton, Pa.; son of Joseph James (a restauranteur) and Edna (Wetter) Gibney; married Harriet Cochran Suydam, November, 1957 (divorced, 1972); married Hiroko Doi, October 5, 1972; children: Alex, Margot, Frank, Jr., James, Thomas, Elise, Josephine. *Edu-* *cation:* Yale University, B.A., 1945. *Politics:* Democrat. *Religion:* Roman Catholic. *Home:* 1901 East Las Tunas Rd., Santa Barbara, Calif. 93103. *Office: Encyclopaedia Britannica,* 310 South Michigan Ave., Chicago, Ill. 60604.

CAREER: Time, New York City, foreign correspondent, 1947-54; *Newsweek,* New York City, senior features editor, 1954-57; *Life,* New York City, editorial writer and staff writer, 1957-61; *Show,* New York City, publisher, 1961-64; *Encyclopaedia Britannica,* Chicago, Ill., president in Japan, 1966-69, vice-president in Asia-Pacific region, 1969-71, president of TBS Britannica, 1969-75, vice-president of planning and development (in Chicago), 1976-79, vice chairman of board of editors, 1976—, vice chairman of company, 1983—; Pacific Basin Institute, Santa Barbara, Calif., president, 1980—. Presidential speech writer for Democratic National Committee, 1964. *Military service:* U.S. Naval Reserve, active duty, 1942-46; became lieutenant.

MEMBER: Council on Foreign Relations, Japan Society, America-Japan Society, Overseas Press Club (vice-president, 1958-61), Century Association, Foreign Correspondents Club (Tokyo; vice-president, 1970-71), Chicago Council on Foreign Relations, Arts Club (Chicago), Tavern Club (Chicago), Tokyo Club, Yale Club of New York City. *Awards, honors:* Order of the Rising Sun, third class (Japan), 1976; Christopher Award from the Christopher Society, 1976, for *Japan: The Fragile Superpower.*

WRITINGS: Five Gentlemen of Japan, Farrar, Straus, 1953; *The Frozen Revolution,* Farrar, Straus, 1959; (with Peter Deriabin) *The Secret World,* Doubleday, 1960; *The Operators,* Harper, 1960; *The Khrushchev Pattern,* Duell, Sloan & Pierce, 1962; *The Reluctant Space-Farers,* New American Library, 1965; (editor) *The Penkovskiy Papers,* Doubleday, 1966; *Japan: The Fragile Superpower,* Norton, 1976; *Miracle by Design: The Real Reasons behind Japan's Economic Successes,* Times Books, 1983. Contributor to popular magazines, including *Harper's, Foreign Affairs,* and *Atlantic Monthly.*

SIDELIGHTS: Frank Gibney's books on the business philosophy and culture of Japan are based on his many years of experience as a publishing executive in that country. In *Japan: The Fragile Superpower* the author examines, according to *Time* reviewer Jerrold Schecter, "Japan's deep-rooted psychological dependence on the U.S. [which is,] in fact, . . . an extension into the realm of international relations of a chain of dependence and corresponding obligation between the younger, poorer and weaker and the old, rich and more powerful that runs from top to bottom in Japanese life. As Gibney compares and contrasts the two countries, he reflects on how our own industrial superpower—individualistic, given to philosophical absolutes and brusque manners—might profit from the example of a reluctant world power that is group-oriented, philosophically relativist and almost piously polite." "Gibney makes some familiar but fascinating sociological observations of Japanese society," says Margo Jefferson in her *Newsweek* article about the book. "He describes the tension between Japan's assimilation of foreign influences . . . and its urge to maintain its insularity and ancient traditions." Japan is "still a society in which individual initiative is subordinated to consensus and to the elaborate system of hierarchy in family and office alike," Jefferson continues, "and Gibney describes the Japanese need . . . for *amae,* or extreme dependence, which can cause a parent to indulge a child indefinitely or prevent an employer from firing an inept worker."

Japan's paternalistic culture is reflected in its business philosophy, as Gibney notes in *Miracle by Design: The Real Reasons behind Japan's Economic Successes*. The author explains that the country's industrial leaders believe "that long-term investment in people—which includes training them, partly educating them, and developing them within a company" is as important to that company as the development of new factories and technologies. In this way, Gibney remarks, the leaders have "made the company into a village. And in so doing they have not only given the worker a sense of belonging, they have also given the company a constituency that speaks up for it: its own workers." "Here we come to the nub of Gibney's thesis, which is a perceptive, serious and challenging one," comments Eliot Janeway in the *Los Angeles Times Book Review*. "The incumbents of America's executive suites, he warns us . . . are 'still living in the era of Adam Smith, Marx and mass production, where people are one thing and the investments of capitalists are another.' The Japanese achievement is based on the rejection of the approach common to Smith and Marx of treating labor as a commodity subject to the vagaries of the market."

BIOGRAPHICAL/CRITICAL SOURCES: Time, April 21, 1975; *Newsweek,* April 28, 1975; *New York Review of Books,* July 17, 1975; Frank Gibney, *Miracle by Design: The Real Reasons behind Japan's Economic Successes,* Times Books, 1983; *Washington Post Book World,* January 9, 1983; *Los Angeles Times Book Review,* February 13, 1983.

*   *   *

GILES, Elizabeth
See HOLT, John (Robert)

*   *   *

GILES, Raymond
See HOLT, John (Robert)

*   *   *

GILPIN, Alan 1924-

PERSONAL: Born August 20, 1924, in Whitley Bay, Northumberland, England; son of George and Clara M. (Dobeson) Gilpin; married Sheila Margaret Humphries, April 3, 1954; children: Elizabeth Mary, Alan Stuart, David Anthony. *Education:* Attended Rutherford College of Technology, 1940-43, 1947-49; University of London, B.Sc. (with honors), 1953; University of Queensland, Ph.D., 1974. *Office:* Office of Commissioners of Inquiry, 291 George St., Sydney, New South Wales 2000, Australia.

CAREER: County Borough of Wallasey, Cheshire, England, chief public health inspector, 1958-61; Central Electricity Generating Board, London, England, planning engineer, 1961-65; Queensland State Government, Brisbane, Australia, director of air pollution control, 1965-72; Environment Protection Authority, Victoria, Australia, chairman, 1972-74; Department of Environment, Housing and Community Development, Canberra, Australia, director of Natural Resources branch, 1974-77; assistant director of environmental control, New South Wales State Pollution Control Commission, 1977—. Part-time lecturer at University of Queensland; occasional lecturer at University of Sydney. Chartered engineer, United Kingdom, 1972. *Military service:* British Army, 1943-47; served in Middle East. *Member:* Institute of Energy (United Kingdom), Royal

Society of Arts (fellow), St. Paul's College Union (University of Sydney).

WRITINGS: Control of Air Pollution, Butterworth & Co., 1963; *Dictionary of Economic Terms,* Butterworth & Co., 1965, 5th edition, 1983; *Dictionary of Fuel Technology,* Philosophical Library, 1969; *Air Pollution,* University of Queensland Press, 1971; *Dictionary of Environmental Terms,* University of Queensland Press, 1976; *Environment Policy in Australia,* University of Queensland Press, 1980; *The Australian Environment: Twelve Controversial Issues,* Macmillan, 1981; *Dictionary of Energy Technology,* Butterworth & Co., 1982. General editor, "Australian Environment" series, University of Queensland Press, 1972—.

WORK IN PROGRESS: The Human Environment: The World since Stockholm.

AVOCATIONAL INTERESTS: Bushwalking.

*   *   *

GINSBURG, Mirra

PERSONAL: Born in Bobruisk, Minsk, Russia; daughter of Joseph and Bronia (Geier) Ginsburg. *Education:* Attended schools in Russia, Latvia, Canada, and the United States. *Home and office:* 150 West 96th St., New York, N.Y. 10025.

CAREER: Free-lance writer, editor, and translator from Russian and Yiddish. *Member:* P.E.N. *Awards, honors:* National Translation Center grant, 1967; Lewis Carroll Shelf Award, 1972, for *The Diary of Nina Kosterina;* Mildred L. Batchelder nomination, 1973, for *The Kaha Bird: Tales from Central Asia,* and 1974, for *The White Ship;* Children's Book Showcase Title, 1973, for *The Chick and the Duckling;* Guggenheim fellow, 1975-76.

WRITINGS: The Strongest One of All, Greenwillow, 1977; *The Striding Slippers,* Macmillan, 1978; *Little Rystu,* Greenwillow, 1978; *Ookie-Spooky,* Crown, 1979; *Kitten from One to Ten,* Crown, 1980; *The Little Magic Stove,* Coward, 1982; *The Sun Is Down behind the Hill,* Greenwillow, 1982; *Across the Stream,* Greenwillow, 1982.

Editor and translator: *The Fatal Eggs and Other Soviet Satire,* Macmillan, 1965; *The Dragon: Fifteen Stories by Yevgeny Zamyatin,* Random House, 1966; *The Last Door to Aiya: Anthology of Soviet Science Fiction,* S. G. Phillips, 1968; *The Fox and the Hare* (picture book), Crown, 1969; *The Master of the Winds: Folk Tales from Siberia,* Crown, 1970; *Three Rolls and One Doughnut: Fables from Russia,* Dial, 1970; *A Soviet Heretic: Essays by Yevgeny Zamyatin,* University of Chicago Press, 1970; *The Ultimate Threshold: Anthology of Soviet Science Fiction,* Holt, 1970; *The Kaha Bird: Tales from Central Asia,* Crown, 1971; *The Lazies: Folk Tales from Russia,* Macmillan, 1973; *One Trick Too Many: Tales about Foxes,* Dial, 1973; *How Wilka Went to Sea: Folk Tales from West of the Urals,* Crown, 1974; *The Air of Mars* (anthology), Macmillan, 1976; *Pampalche of the Silver Teeth,* Crown, 1976; Kirill Bulychev, *Alice* (science fiction), Macmillan, 1977.

Translator: Roman Goul, *Azef,* Doubleday, 1962; Vera Alexandrovna, *A History of Soviet Literature,* Doubleday, 1963; Mikhail Bulgakov, *The Master and Margarita,* Grove, 1967; Bulgakov, *Heart of a Dog,* Grove, 1968; *The Diary of Nina Kosterina* (young adult), Crown, 1968; Bulgakov, *Flight* (play), Grove, 1969; Bulgakov, *The Life of Monsieur Moliere,* Funk, 1970; Yevgeny Zamyatin, *We* (novel), Viking, 1972; Chingiz Aitmatov, *The White Ship,* Crown, 1972; Vladimir Grigor'-

evich Suteev, *The Chick and the Duckling*, Macmillan, 1972; Suteev, *The Three Kittens*, Crown, 1973; Lydia Obukhova, *Daughter of Night* (science fiction), Macmillan, 1974; Fyodor Dostoyevsky, *Notes from Underground*, Bantam, 1974; Audrey Platanov, *The Foundation Pit*, Dutton, 1975.

Adapter: Suteev, *What Kind of Bird Is That?*, Crown, 1973; Suteev, *Mushroom in the Rain*, Macmillan, 1974; *The Proud Maiden, Tungak, and the Sun*, Macmillan, 1974; *How the Sun Was Brought Back to the Sky*, Macmillan, 1974; Pyotr Dudochkin, *Which Is the Best Place?*, Macmillan, 1976; *The Two Greedy Bears*, Macmillan, 1976; *The Fisherman's Son*, Greenwillow, 1979; *The Night It Rained Pancakes*, Greenwillow, 1979; *The Twelve Clever Brothers and Other Fools: Folktales from Russia*, Lippincott, 1979; *Good Morning, Chick*, Greenwillow, 1980; *Where Does the Sun Go at Night?*, Greenwillow, 1980.

Also translator of stories by Isaac Bashevis Singer, Alexey Remizov, Isaac Babel, and Zoshchenko, for various anthologies, collections and periodicals; co-translator of Isaac Babel's play, "Sunset," produced in 1966 and 1972.

SIDELIGHTS: Mirra Ginsburg writes: "I have loved folktales since childhood, and have gone on collecting them and delighting in them ever since. I place folktales among the greatest works of literature. To me they are a distillation of man's deepest experience into poetry, wisdom, truth, sadness, and laughter."

Many of Ginsburg's books have been translated into various languages, including Japanese, Swedish, Afrikaans, Portugese, and Danish.

AVOCATIONAL INTERESTS: Poetry, cats (big and little), birds, early music, early and primitive art.

*   *   *

GLASER, Milton 1929-
(Max Catz)

PERSONAL: Born June 26, 1929, in New York, N.Y.; son of Eugene and Eleanor (Bergman) Glaser; married Shirley Girton, August 13, 1957. *Education:* Cooper Union, graduate, 1951; also studied at Academy of Fine Arts, Bologna, Italy. *Religion:* Hebrew.

CAREER: Artist and illustrator; Push-Pin Studios, Inc., New York City, founder and partner, 1954-74; president, Milton Glaser, Inc. (design studio), 1974—. Design director, *New York* (magazine), 1968-77; vice-president and design director, *Village Voice*, 1975-77. Member of faculty of School of Visual Arts. *Member:* American Institute of Graphic Arts (vice-president), Alliance Graphique International. *Awards, honors:* Fulbright scholarship to Bologna, Italy; Gold Medal from Society of Illustrators; Gold Medal from Art Directors Club; St. Gaudens Medal from Cooper Union; Medal Award from American Institute of Graphic Arts, 1972; honorary D.F.A. from Minneapolis Institute of Art.

WRITINGS: (With wife, Shirley Glaser) *If Apples Had Teeth*, Knopf, 1960; (with Jerome Snyder) *The Underground Gourmet*, Simon & Schuster, 1968, 3rd edition published as *The All New Underground Gourmet*, 1977; *Graphic Design*, Overlook Press, 1973; (with Snyder) *The Underground Gourmet Cookbook*, edited by Joyce Zonana, Simon & Schuster, 1975; (with Lally Weymouth) *America in 1876*, Random House, 1976; (self-illustrated) *The Milton Glaser Posterbook*, Harmony Books, 1977. Editor with Burton Wolf and James Beard

of "The Great Cook's Library" series, Random House, 1977-78.

Illustrator: Alvin Tresselt, *The Smallest Elephant in the World*, Knopf, 1959; Conrad Aiken, *Cats and Bats and Things with Wings* (poetry), Atheneum, 1965; Gian Carlo Menotti, *Help, Help, The Gobolinks*, adapted by Leigh Dean, McGraw, 1970; George Mendoza, *Fish in the Sky*, Doubleday, 1971; (with Seymour Chwast and Barry Zaid) Ormonde DeKay, Jr., translator, *Rimes de la Mere Ole*, Little, Brown, 1971; *Asimov's Illustrated Don Juan*, Doubleday, 1972.

WORK IN PROGRESS: Mirror of Your Mind.

SIDELIGHTS: Milton Glaser writes *CA:* "There is a mystique about children's books as being a place for adventure and creativity, for taking risks, for extending the possibilities of defining what a children's book can be. But in fact the criteria are the usual: How similar is a new title to other successes, how significant is the author's name already, how closely does it cling to the established formulas.

"Statistically there are never a great number of good people doing anything at one time. But in some ways the level of achievement was once higher. A lot of the older books look better, and those of one hundred years ago look better than those of twenty-five years ago, even over and above the value they have accrued with nostalgia. The old techniques were more difficult to master and required a higher technical competence; they tended to weed out the mediocre and the dilettantes. Today's easy photomechanical processes provide less resistance."

BIOGRAPHICAL/CRITICAL SOURCES: Graphis, July, 1962; *Industrial Design*, July, 1962; *Idea*, October, 1964.

*   *   *

GODDARD, Donald 1934-

PERSONAL: Born April 16, 1934, in Cortland, N.Y.; son of Don Gay (a newspaperman) and Adele (Letcher) Goddard. *Education:* Princeton University, A.B., 1956. *Politics:* Independent. *Address:* 425 West Broadway, New York, N.Y. 10012.

CAREER: Writer of books on art. American Archives of World Art, New York City, editor, 1958-65; McGraw-Hill Book Co., New York City, editor, 1966-68; director, Editorial Photocolor Archives, 1968-74; *ARTnews*, managing editor, 1974-78, contributing editor, 1978—; senior writer, New York Zoological Society, 1981—.

WRITINGS: (Editor) *American Library Compendium and Index of World Art*, American Archives of World Art, 1961; *Lecture Notes for the Study of Art History*, American Archives of World Art, 1961—; *Tschacbasov*, American Archives of World Art, 1964; (editor) *Ad Reinhardt*, Abrams, 1979.

(With Robert Farber) *Moods*, Amphoto, 1980; (editor) *Olitski*, Abrams, 1980; (with Farber) *The Professional Fashion Photographer*, Amphoto, 1981; (with John Walker and others) *Harry Jackson, Forty Years of His Work, 1941-1981: Forty Years of His Art*, Wyoming Foundry Studios, 1981; (with Larry Pointer) *Harry Jackson*, Abrams, 1981; (editor) *Yves Klein*, Abrams, 1982; *Watercolors and Drawings of the French Impressionists and Their Parisian Contemporaries*, Abrams, 1982.

Editor of *The McGraw-Hill Dictionary of Art*, 1969, and *Encyclopedia of Painting*, Crown, 1970.

WORK IN PROGRESS: Writing on contemporary art.

GODFREY, (William) Dave 1938-

PERSONAL: Born August 9, 1938, in Winnipeg, Manitoba, Canada; son of Richmond (a lawyer) and Marguerite (a teacher; maiden name, Hutcheson) Godfrey; married Ellen Swartz, 1963; children: Jonathan, Rebecca, Samuel. *Education:* Attended Harvard University, 1957, and University of Toronto, 1957-58; University of Iowa, B.A., 1960, M.F.A., 1963, Ph.D., 1966; Stanford University, M.A., 1963; attended University of Chicago, 1965. *Home:* 4355 Gordon Head Rd., Victoria, British Columbia, Canada U8N 3Y4. *Office:* Press Porcepic Ltd., 235 Market Square, Victoria, British Columbia, Canada U8W 3C6.

CAREER: Adisadel College, Cape Coast, Ghana, lecturer in African literature and English and acting head of department, 1963-65; University of Toronto, Trinity College, Toronto, Ontario, assistant professor of English, 1966-68, 1969-74, writer-in-residence at Erindale College, 1973-74; York University, Downsview, Ontario, visiting professor of English, 1974-75; University of Toronto, Trinity College, visiting professor of English, 1975-76, coordinator of Canadian literature minor program; York University, associate professor of humanities, 1976-77; University of Victoria, Victoria, British Columbia, head of creative writing department, 1977-82. Editor, Press Porcepic Ltd., Victoria, 1972—. Co-founder, editor, and president of House of Anansi, 1966-70; senior editor of New Press, 1969-73.

MEMBER: Association of Canadian Publishers (president, 1972-73), Association for the Export of Canadian Books (founding director, 1972—). *Awards, honors:* President's medals from University of Western Ontario, 1964, for story "Gossip: The Birds That Flew, the Birds That Fell," and 1966, for article "Letter from Africa to an American Negro" and story "The Hard-Headed Collector"; Canada Council grants, 1965 and 1968-69; Governor-General's award, 1970, for *The New Ancestors.*

WRITINGS: Death Goes Better with Coca-Cola (stories), House of Anansi Press, 1967, 3rd edition, 1976; (editor with Bill McWhinney) *Man Deserves Man: CUSO in Developing Countries,* Ryerson, 1967; *The New Ancestors* (novel), New Press, 1970; (editor with Mel Watkins) *Gordon to Watkins to You—A Documentary: The Battle for Control of Our Economy,* New Press, 1970; (with Robert Fulford and Abe Rotstein) *Read Canadian: A Book about Canadian Books,* Lewis & Samuel James, 1972; *I Ching Kanada,* Press Porcepic, 1976; *Dark Must Yield,* Press Porcepic, 1978; *Gutenberg Two,* Press Porcepic, 1979; *The Telidon Book,* Press Porcepic, 1981, Reston, 1982; *Elements of CAL,* Reston, 1982.

Contributor to anthologies, including *Great Canadian Short Stories,* edited by Alec Lucas, Dell, 1971, *Power Corrupted,* edited by A. Rotstein, New Press, 1971, and *Canadian Anthology,* edited by Carl F. Klink and Reginald Watters, Gage, 1976. Contributor of twenty short stories and of articles and reviews to periodicals, including *Tamarack Review, Canadian Literature, Saturday Night, Impulse,* and *Canadian Forum.* General editor of "Canadian Writers," New Canadian Library, 1968-72. Editor of *Canadian Poetry Annual,* 1976—. Fiction editor of *Canadian Forum,* 1971-72; editor of *Porcepic,* 1972—.

WORK IN PROGRESS: Two novels; another collection of stories.

SIDELIGHTS: Dave Godfrey told *CA:* "I am most interested in that portion of literature where myth meets social realities; literary dogma concerning the purity of fantasy or of realism does not interest me. The Canadian environment has influenced me greatly although I write mainly about people from cultures other than my own. A good part of my twenties was spent traveling about the U.S. and Africa. I strive for great complexity in my writing because that is how I find life; I do not believe the writer has the duty to simplify or interpret life for his readers; his major tasks are to be as intelligent as possible and to take flights of imagination into bodies, minds and situations other than his own."

BIOGRAPHICAL/CRITICAL SOURCES: Saturday Night, June, 1968; *Ellipse,* autumn, 1970; *Mysterious East,* December, 1970; *Canadian Forum,* March, 1968, October, 1968, February, 1969, April, 1971; *Nation,* September 6, 1971.

*   *   *

GOEDICKE, Patricia (McKenna) 1931-
(Patricia McKenna, Patricia Robinson)

PERSONAL: Born June 21, 1931, in Boston, Mass.; daughter of John Bernard (a psychiatrist) and Helen (Mulvey) McKenna; married Victor Goedicke (a professor), September 12, 1956 (divorced, 1968); married Leonard Wallace Robinson (a writer), June 3, 1971. *Education:* Middlebury College, Middlebury, Vt., B.A. (cum laude), 1953; studied under W. H. Auden at Young Men's Hebrew Association, New York City, 1955; Ohio University, M.A. in creative writing and poetry, 1965. *Home address:* 310 McLeod Ave., Missoula, Mont. 59801. *Office:* Department of English, University of Montana, Missoula, Mont. 59812.

CAREER: Harcourt, Brace & World (publishers), New York City, editorial assistant, 1953-54; T. Y. Crowell (publishers), New York City, editorial assistant, 1955-56; co-editor, *Page* (poetry broadsheet), 1961-66; Ohio University, Athens, instructor in English, 1963-68; reader-writer for Book-of-the-Month Club, 1968-69; Hunter College of the City University of New York, New York City, lecturer in English, 1969-71; Instituto Allende, Guanajuato, Mexico, associate professor of creative writing, 1972-79; Sarah Lawrence College, Bronxville, N.Y., guest faculty member in the writing program, 1980-81; University of Montana, Missoula, visiting poet-in-residence, 1981-83, associate professor of English, 1983—. Has given readings of her poetry at colleges and universities, including State University of New York College at Brockport, Columbia University, New York University, Dartmouth College, Kalamazoo College, Washington University, Lake Forest College, San Francisco State University, Queens College of the City University of New York, and University of Alaska. Panel member, Ohio Poetry Association annual meeting, 1974. *Member:* P.E.N., Academy of American Poets, Associated Writing Programs, Phi Beta Kappa.

AWARDS, HONORS: Emily Clark Balch Poetry Contest second prize and National Endowment for the Arts award, both 1968, for her poem "You Could Pick It Up"; National Endowment for the Arts creative writing fellowship, 1976-77; Coordinating Council of Literary Magazines prize, 1976, for poem "Lost"; Duncan Frazier Prize from *Loon,* fall, 1976; William Carlos Williams Prize for poetry from *New Letters,* spring, 1977; *Quarterly West* Prize for poetry, 1977; Pushcart Prize, 1977.

WRITINGS: Between Oceans (poems), Harcourt, 1968; *For the Four Corners* (poems), Ithaca House, 1976; *The Trail That*

Turns on Itself (poems), Ithaca House, 1978; *The Dog That Was Barking Yesterday* (poems), Lynx, 1980; *Crossing the Same River* (poems), University of Massachusetts Press, 1980; *The Wind of Our Going* (poems), Copper Canyon Press, 1984.

Work represented in many anthologies, including: *The American Literary Anthology,* Volume III, Viking, 1970; *And Be Merry,* edited by William Cole, Grossman, 1972; *Psyche: The Feminine Poetic Consciousness,* Dell, 1975; *The Ardis Anthology of New American Poetry,* edited by David Rigsbee, Ardis, 1976; *The Pushcart Prize, II: Best of the Small Presses,* edited by Bill Henderson, Pushcart, 1978; *Tangled Vines,* Beacon Press, 1978; *The Treasury of American Poetry,* Doubleday, 1978; *A Geography of Poets,* Bantam, 1979; *Editor's Choice,* Spirit That Moves Us, 1980; *Of Silence and Solitude,* Beacon Press, 1982. Contributor to periodicals, including *New Yorker, American Poetry Review, Antioch Review, Saturday Review, Nation,* and *Harper's.*

SIDELIGHTS: Patricia Goedicke's poetry is described in the *Times Literary Supplement* by David Kirby as "intensely emotional, intensely physical." According to Peter Schjeldahl in the *New York Times Book Review,* she "bears down hard on the language, frequently producing exact ambiguities of phrasing that are startling and funny." *Harper's* reviewer Hayden Carruth concludes that Goedicke's poems "have a hard truthful ring, like parables of survival."

BIOGRAPHICAL/CRITICAL SOURCES: Southern Humanities Review, fall, 1971; *Modern Poetry Studies,* winter, 1976; *Chicago Sun-Times,* July 9, 1978; *New York Times Book Review,* December 17, 1978; *Los Angeles Times Book Review,* April 27, 1980; *Times Literary Supplement,* June 13, 1980; *Harper's,* December, 1980.

*   *   *

GOGISGI
See ARNETT, Carroll

*   *   *

GOLDBERG, E(lliott) Marshall 1930-

PERSONAL: Born December 19, 1930, in North Adams, Mass.; son of Jack and Ida (Lenhoff) Goldberg; children: five. *Education:* University of Rochester, A.B. (with high honors), 1952; Tufts University, M.D., 1956. *Agent:* Mel Berger, William Morris Agency, 1350 Avenue of the Americas, New York, N.Y. 10019. *Office:* Hurley Medical Center, Flint, Mich. 48502.

CAREER: District of Columbia Hospital, Washington, intern, 1956-57; Memorial Hospital, Worcester, Mass., resident, 1960-61; University Hospitals, Madison, Wis., resident, 1962-63; Wayne State University, Detroit, Mich., assistant professor of medicine, 1964-65; Michigan State University, East Lansing, assistant professor, 1966-68, associate professor, 1968, professor of medicine, 1973—; Hurley Hospital, Flint, Mich., chief of medicine, 1970—. Research associate in endocrinology at St. Vincent's Hospital, Worcester, Mass., 1960; endocrine fellow at University of Wisconsin, 1961-62. Diplomate of American Board of Internal Medicine; licensed in Massachusetts, Wisconsin, and Michigan. Book editor for Physicians' Radio Network; health expert for "Canada A.M." on Canadian Television (CTV). Member of board of directors of Medgar Evers Foundation. *Military service:* U.S. Army, Medical Corps, 1957-59; served in France; became captain.

MEMBER: American College of Physicians (fellow), Endocrine Society, American Federation of Clinical Research,

American Diabetes Association, Royal College of Physicians (associate), Massachusetts Medical Society, Michigan Medical Society, Michigan Association for Medical Education (president, 1972-75), Genesee County Medical Society. *Awards, honors:* National Institutes of Health research grant, 1963-64; Humanitarian Award from National Association for the Advancement of Colored People, 1974.

WRITINGS—Novels: *The Karamanov Equations,* World Publishing Co., 1972; *The Anatomy Lesson,* Putnam, 1974; *Critical List* (also see below), Bantam, 1978; *Skeletons* (also see below), Bantam, 1979; (with Kenneth Kay) *Disposable People,* Tower, 1979; *Nerve,* Coward, 1981.

Screenplay adaptations; produced by National Broadcasting Company, Inc.: "Critical List," 1978; "Skeletons," 1978. Contributor of articles to medical journals and popular magazines, including *Ladies Home Journal, Parade, TV Guide, Detroit,* and *Medical World News.*

WORK IN PROGRESS: Natural Killers, a novel.

*   *   *

GOLDEMBERG, Isaac 1945-

PERSONAL: Born November 15, 1945, in Chepen, Peru; came to the United States in 1964; son of Isaac (a merchant) and Bertila (a merchant; maiden name, Bay) Goldemberg; married Mona Stern, December 19, 1963 (separated); children: David, Dina. *Education:* City College of the City University of New York, B.A. (magna cum laude), 1968; New York University, graduate study, 1968—. *Home:* 515 West 110th St., New York, N.Y. 10025.

CAREER: Writer. Worked in a kibbutz in Israel, 1962-63; insurance salesman in Barcelona, Spain, 1963; New York Public Library, New York City, clerk in Jewish Division, 1965-66; Grolier, Inc., New York City, Spanish editor, 1968-69; American Book Co., New York City, Spanish editor, 1969; New York University, New York City, lecturer in Spanish, 1970-75. Writer-in-residence at Center for Inter-American Relations, 1981. *Member:* Phi Beta Kappa.

WRITINGS: Tiempo de silencio (poems; title means "Time for Silence"), Coleccion de Poesia Hispanoamericana, 1969; (with Jose Kozer) *De Chepen a la Habana* (poems; title means "From Chepen to Havana"), Editorial Bayu-Menorah, 1973; *The Fragmented Life of Don Jacobo Lerner* (novel), Persea Books, 1976; *Hombre de paso/Just Passing Through* (poems), bilingual edition, Ediciones del Norte, 1981; *Tiempo al Tiempo: o: La Conversion* (novel), Ediciones del Norte, 1983, published as *The Conversion,* Persea Books, 1983. Contributor to Spanish- and English-language journals, including *Present Tense, Nimrod,* and *Mundo Nuevo.*

WORK IN PROGRESS: An anthology of Latin American fiction by writers living in New York; an anthology of Latin American Jewish writers; a book of poems.

SIDELIGHTS: Isaac Goldemberg writes: "I am a Peruvian of Jewish, Russian, English, Italian, Spanish, and Indian descent. I traveled to Israel in 1962. Then I moved to Barcelona, where I spent a year in medical school. I decided (age eighteen) I wanted to be a writer and quit medical school. I settled in New York. Prior to my return to Peru (for the first time in fifteen years) in 1976, I wrote *The Fragmented Life of Don Jacobo Lerner,* an attempt at reconstructing my own past and that of the Peruvian Jewish community at large.

"Even though my work deals mainly with the Jewish experience in Peru, the burdens of exile and spiritual rootlessness, I am also concerned with Peruvian life as a whole, particularly that of provincial Peru, marked by narrowness and claustrophobia. This is the world depicted in my first novel, where I attempted to draw the life of the Jewish immigrant as a tragic and heroic parody of the legend of the Wandering Jew."

Frank Macshane comments on *The Fragmented Life of Don Jacobo Lerner* in an article for the *New York Times Book Review*, writing that the world depicted by Goldemberg "is a nightmare world of frustrated hopes, of narrowness and claustrophobia where no one can afford to be generous and where people become insane and destructive. Goldemberg allows his characters to tell their own stories and interrupts these private narratives with notices, documents and newspaper headlines to give a sense of the public dimension of the life of these exiles. This technique also insures that the novel . . . remains refreshingly free of the exotic trimmings that are often associated with Latin American fiction: it is a moving exploration of the human condition."

Margo Jefferson writes in a *Newsweek* review that Goldemberg "shows with great perception how history, belief and myth can burden people with more contradictions than they can bear. This insight, joined to well-observed details . . . makes this novel a wonderfully promising debut for a gifted writer."

BIOGRAPHICAL/CRITICAL SOURCES: New Yorker, April 4, 1977; *Newsweek*, May 9, 1977; *New York Times*, May 18, 1977; *New York Times Book Review*, June 12, 1977; *Times Literary Supplement*, March 10, 1978; *Village Voice Literary Supplement*, May, 1982.

*   *   *

GOLDSTEIN, David   1933-

PERSONAL: Born January 31, 1933, in London, England; son of Nathan (a textile manager) and Sarah (Malwartz) Goldstein; married Berenice Phillips, August 26, 1956; children: Joshua, Daniel, Benjamin. *Education:* St. Edmund Hall, Oxford, B.A. (honors in English), 1956; University College, London, B.A. (honors in Hebrew), 1959, M.A., 1962, Ph.D., 1967. *Home:* 56 Creighton Ave., Muswell Hill, London N10 1NT, England. *Office:* Hebrew Books and Manuscripts, British Library, 14 Store St., London WC1, England.

CAREER: South London Liberal Jewish Synagogue, London, England, rabbi, 1959-64; Liberal Jewish Synagogue, London, associate rabbi, 1964-81; British Library, London, curator of Hebrew Books and Manuscripts, 1975—. Lecturer, Leo Baeck College, London, 1966—. *Member:* Jewish Historical Society, Society for Jewish Study, Eurasia Society.

WRITINGS: (Editor and translator) *Hebrew Poems from Spain*, Routledge & Kegan Paul, 1965, Schocken, 1966; (editor and translator) *The Jewish Poets of Spain*, Penguin, 1971; (contributor) E. G. Parrinder, editor, *Man and His Gods: Encyclopedia of the World's Religions*, Hamlyn, 1971; (contributor) H. A. Guy, editor, *Our Religions*, Dent, 1973; *The Religion of the Jews*, Open University Press, 1979; *Jewish Folklore and Legend*, Hamlyn, 1980.

WORK IN PROGRESS: Editing *Commentary to the Pentateuch*, by Immanuel ben Solomon of Rome; translating *Anthology of the Zohar* and *Biblical Hebrew Poetry*.

SIDELIGHTS: David Goldstein is competent in French, Italian, classical Latin and Greek. *Avocational interests:* Cricket, music, reading poetry, philately.

GOMPERTZ, Rolf   1927-

PERSONAL: Born December 29, 1927, in Krefeld, Germany; son of Oscar (a business executive) and Selma (Selle) Herrmann; married Carol Brown (a teaching assistant), April 28, 1957; children: Ron, Nancy, Philip. *Education:* University of California, Los Angeles, B.A., 1951, M.A., 1953. *Politics:* Democrat. *Religion:* Jewish. *Home:* 6516 Ben Avenue, North Hollywood, Calif. 91606. *Office:* NBC, 3000 West Alameda Ave., Burbank, Calif. 91523.

CAREER: Torrance Press, Torrance, Calif., editor, 1953-57; National Broadcasting Co., Inc. (NBC), Burbank, Calif., publicist, 1957—; University of California, Los Angeles, instructor in media, 1974—. *Military service:* U.S. Army, Quartermaster Intelligence, 1946-48. *Member:* Writers Guild of America, Publicists Guild of America, Public Relations Society of America, Phi Beta Kappa.

WRITINGS—Published by WorDoctor, except as indicated: (Contributor) A. H. Hoffnung, editor, *For Love of Torah*, Jonathan David, 1970; *My Jewish Brother Jesus*, 1977; *Publicity Handbook for Radio and Television*, Tab Books, 1977; *Sparks of Spirit: A Handbook for Personal Happiness*, 1983; *A Celebration of Life with Menachem*, 1983; *The Messiah of Midtown Park*, 1983.

Author with Mel Epstein of documentary film "The Spark"; author of forty-eight radio dramas for "Heartbeat Theater." Contributor to *Jewish Spectator* and other periodicals.

WORK IN PROGRESS: Screenplays, "The Messiah of Midtown Park" (based on his book of the same title), "Messiah" (based on *My Jewish Brother Jesus*), "Tough Love," "Widow," "Love and Marriage," and "The Mid-Life Crisis of Lee Spangler."

SIDELIGHTS: "I consider myself a writer," Rolf Gompertz told *CA*, "and, as such, believe in being able to handle various forms and various subjects, including commercial needs, journalistic assignments, public relations writing, and literary work. My love, obviously, is 'soul' writing. In this respect, I have been intrigued with the messianic theme since college days. Virtually all my serious writing deals with this."

*   *   *

GOOD, Edwin M(arshall)   1928-

PERSONAL: Born April 23, 1928, in Bibia, Cameroun, West Africa; son of Albert Irwin (a missionary) and Mary (Middlemiss) Good; married Janice Sundquist, July 26, 1952; children: Brian Christopher, Lawrence Marshall, John Alexander. *Education:* Westminster College, New Wilmington, Pa., B.A., 1949; Princeton Theological Seminary, additional study, 1949-51; Union Theological Seminary, New York, N.Y., M.Div., 1953; Columbia University, Ph.D., 1958; Stanford University, M.A., 1974. *Politics:* Democratic. *Home:* 827 Sonoma Ter., Stanford, Calif. 94305. *Office:* Stanford University, Stanford, Calif. 94305.

CAREER: Princeton University, Princeton, N.J., instructor in Old Testament, 1954-55; Union Theological Seminary, New York, N.Y., instructor in Old Testament, 1955-56; Stanford University, Stanford, Calif., assistant professor, 1956-61, associate professor of religion and Hebrew, 1970, professor of religious studies, 1970—. *Member:* Society for Values in Higher

Education, Society of Biblical Literature, American Academy of Religion, American Association of University Professors, Uppsala Exegetical Society (Sweden).

WRITINGS: You Shall Be My People: Books of Covenant and Law, Westminster, 1959; *Irony in the Old Testament,* Westminster, 1965, 2nd edition, Almond Press, 1981; *Hosea and the Jacob Tradition,* Vetus Testamentum, 1966; *The Composition of Hosea,* Svensk Exegetisk Arsbok, 1966; *Job and the Literary Task: A Response,* Garland Soundings, 1973; *Giraffes, Black Dragon and Other Pianos: A Technological History from Christofori to Modern Concert Grand,* Stanford University Press, 1982.

Editor "Westminster Guides to the Bible" series. Contributor to *Interpreter's Dictionary of the Bible, Annotated New English Bible,* and to religion and education journals.

WORK IN PROGRESS: A literary study of the Book of Job.

AVOCATIONAL INTERESTS: Music, especially piano and chamber music.

*   *   *

GORDON, Ian A(listair) 1908-

PERSONAL: Born July 30, 1908, in Edinburgh, Scotland; son of Alexander R. and Isobel (McLean) Gordon; married Mary Ann McLean Fullarton (a university lecturer), July 15, 1936; children: Elizabeth (Mrs. A. J. Gurr), Alistair, Frances (Mrs. M. Waddle), Catherine (Mrs. A. Levine). *Education:* University of Edinburgh, M.A. (honors in classics), 1930, M.A. (honors in English), 1932, Ph.D., 1936. *Home:* 91 Messines Rd., Wellington, New Zealand.

CAREER: University of Edinburgh, Edinburgh, Scotland, assistant lecturer in English language and literature, 1932-36; Victoria University of Wellington, Wellington, New Zealand, professor of English language and literature, 1937-74, professor emeritus, 1974—, dean of Faculty of Arts, 1944-47, 1952, 1957-61; University of Edinburgh, research fellow, 1974-75; University of Leeds, Leeds, Yorkshire, England, visiting fellow in Commonwealth literature, 1975. Vice-chancellor, University of New Zealand, 1947-52. Visiting professor at King's College, University of London, 1954, University of Edinburgh, 1962, University of the South Pacific, Fiji Islands, 1972, and University of Waikato, 1980. Former chairman, New Zealand Literary Fund. *Military service:* New Zealand Army Education Service, World War II; became honorary major.

MEMBER: Australasian Universities Language and Literature Association, Association for Scottish Literary Studies, Aorangi Ski Club (past president). *Awards, honors:* L.L.D., University of Bristol, 1948; Litt.D., University of New Zealand, 1961; Commander, Order of the British Empire, 1971; D.Univ., University of Stirling, 1975.

WRITINGS: John Skelton, Poet Laureate, Oxford University Press, 1943, Octagon, 1970; (contributor) *The University and the Community,* [Wellington], 1946; *The Teaching of English,* New Zealand Council for Educational Research, 1947, Oxford University Press, 1950; *English Prose Technique,* New Zealand University Press, 1948, 4th edition, A. H. & A. W. Reed, 1972; *Katherine Mansfield,* Longmans, Green, 1954, revised edition, 1963, University of Nebraska Press, 1964; (with others) *Government Printing Office Style Book,* Government Printer (Wellington), 1958, 4th edition, 1976; *The Movement of English Prose,* Longmans, Green, 1966, University of Indiana

Press, 1967; *John Galt: The Life of a Writer,* Oliver & Boyd, 1972; *A Word in Your Ear,* Heinemann, 1980.

Editor: *William Shenstone's Miscellany, 1759-1763,* Clarendon Press, 1952; (and author of introduction and notes) John Galt, *The Entail,* Oxford University Press, 1970; (and author of introduction and notes) Galt, *The Provost,* Oxford University Press, 1973; (and author of introduction and notes) *Undiscovered Country: The New Zealand Stories of Katherine Mansfield,* Longman, 1974; (and author of introduction and notes) Galt, *The Member,* Scottish Academic Press, 1975; (and author of introduction and notes) Galt, *The Last of the Lairds,* Scottish Academic Press, 1976; (and author of introduction and notes) Galt, *Selected Short Stories,* Scottish Academic Press, 1978; (and author of introduction and notes) Katherine Mansfield, *The Urewera Notebook,* Oxford University Press, 1979; *Collins Concise English Dictionary* (New Zealand edition), Collins, 1982; *Word Finder: The New Zealand Thesaurus,* Reader's Digest Press, 1983.

Also author of adaptation of *A Word in Your Ear* for Television New Zealand, 1982. Author of seven studies published by New Zealand Department of Education. Contributor to *Edinburgh Essays on Scots Literature,* 1933, *Essays in Literature,* 1936, and to encyclopedias. Author of weekly language column, *New Zealand Listener.* Contributor to journals and newspapers, including *Times Literary Supplement, New Zealand Science Review, Listener, Library,* and *Linguistic Review.* Sub-editor, *Scottish National Dictionary,* 1930-36; editor, *New Zealand New Writing,* 1943-45.

SIDELIGHTS: Ian A. Gordon's book on Katherine Mansfield has also been published in Japanese and Italian. His *Movement of English Prose* has been published in Japanese.

*   *   *

GORDON, John (William) 1925-

PERSONAL: Born November 19, 1925, in Jarrow, England; son of Norman (a teacher) and Margaret (Revely) Gordon; married Sylvia Ellen Young, January 9, 1954; children: Sally, Robert. *Education:* Educated in Jarrow and Wisbech, England. *Home:* 99 George Borrow Rd., Norwich, Norfolk NR4 7HU, England. *Office:* Eastern Daily Press, Norwich, Norfolk, England.

CAREER: Isle of Ely and Wisbech Advertiser, Wisbech, England, reporter, 1947-49, sub-editor, 1949-51; *Bury Free Press,* Bury St. Edmunds, Suffolk, England, 1951-58, began as chief reporter, became sub-editor; *Western Evening Herald,* Plymouth, England, sub-editor, 1958-62; *Eastern Evening News,* Norwich, England, columnist and sub-editor, 1962-73; *Eastern Daily Press,* Norwich, sub-editor, 1973—. *Military service:* Royal Navy, 1943-47.

WRITINGS—Children's books: *The Giant under the Snow,* Hutchinson, 1968, Harper, 1970.

The House on the Brink, Hutchinson, 1970, Harper, 1971, revised edition, Patrick Hardy Books, 1983; *The Ghost on the Hill,* Kestrel, 1976; *The Waterfall Box,* Kestrel, 1978; *The Spitfire Grave and Other Stories,* Kestrel, 1979; *The Edge of the World,* Patrick Hardy Books, 1983, Atheneum, 1983.

Contributor: M. R. Hodgkin, editor, *Young Winter's Tales,* Macmillan, Number 2, 1971, Number 4, 1973, Number 6, 1975; Edward Blishen, editor, *The Thorny Paradise,* Kestrel, 1975; Jean Russell, editor, *The Methuen Book of Strange Tales,* Methuen, 1980; Deborah Shine, editor, *Ghost Stories,* Octopus, 1980; Shine, editor, *Detective Stories,* Octopus, 1980; A. Smith and F. Mann, editors, *Englishcraft,* University Tutorial Press, 1981; Aidan Chambers, editor, *Ghost after Ghost,* Kestrel, 1982. Work represented in numerous anthologies. Contributor of articles and stories to periodicals.

WORK IN PROGRESS: A collection of ghost stories.

SIDELIGHTS: John Gordon wrote *CA:* "Stories are dreams in disguise. There are dreams hidden in all my stories. They are necessary, but they must remain hidden because they are mine and mean nothing to anybody else. The stories that surround them are meant to make you have similar dreams, your *own* dreams, which will again be secret. Stories are a way of sharing secrets too deep to mention.

"It is because I have to share this kind of feeling with other people that I write stories. And a story, no matter how strange the events in it, must be largely a matter of fact. So the places are real. I was brought up in the Fen Country of England, the eastern part that was once all marshes (or fens), but is now fields of rich black earth that stretch away as flat as the sea from horizon to horizon. It is a place full of stories already. There was a giant killer called Hickathrift; nearer the coast a ghost dog called Old Shuck pads the roads at night; King John is said to have lost his Crown Jewels in the marsh and people still dig for them. I use the places I know. The people become real to me as I write.

"I said I use dreams. Dreams reach into strange areas. *The House on the Brink* is a kind of ghost story and it led me into one of the strangest experiences I have had. The house of the title is an actual old house on the brink of an actual river. The 'ghost', a stump of wood that may be a body, is found in the mud of the river and it exerts a powerful influence over the woman who lives in the house.

"I invented everything except the house and the river, and I had not been in the house for fifteen years when I wrote the book and did not revisit it until after the book was published. When I did so I discovered a part of the garden I had not known existed. It was to one side, behind a wall, and stretched away a considerable distance from the house. In the farthest part of it, on the far side of a lawn and almost in the trees, stood a stump. It was very much the shape of the stump I had described in the book but when I went closer I discovered it was stone and not wood. However, at the blunt, rounded top, which in the story contains a skull, there was carved, very faintly and almost worn away by time, the face of a man.

"Everything fitted so close to my story I went back to the house, which is a showplace open to visitors, and asked about the stump. The custodian told me that it was the shaft of an ancient stone cross that had once stood in the road behind the house, and that seemed to be the end of the matter. She did not know me nor the story I had written, but then she said, 'About a century ago they dredged that old stump from the mud of the river outside.'

"The fens, as I said, are full of stories."

*   *   *

GOTTESMAN, S. D.
See POHL, Frederik

*   *   *

GOUGH, Barry Morton 1938-

PERSONAL: Born September 17, 1938, in Victoria, British

Columbia, Canada; son of John (an educator and historian) and Dorothy (a pianist; maiden name, Mouncy) Gough; married second wife Marilyn Joy Morris, December 11, 1981; children: (first marriage) Melinda, Jason. *Education:* University of British Columbia, B.Ed., 1962; University of Montana, M.A., 1966; Kings College, London, Ph.D., 1969. *Religion:* United Church of Canada. *Home:* 37 Ahrens St. W., Kitchener, Ontario, Canada N2H 4B6. *Office:* Department of History, Wilfrid Laurier University, Waterloo, Ontario, Canada N2L 3C5.

CAREER: Western Washington University, Bellingham, lecturer, 1968-69, assistant professor, 1969-71, associate professor of history, 1972, founder of Canadian Studies Program, 1970; Wilfrid Laurier University, Waterloo, Ontario, associate professor, 1972-78, professor of history, 1978—, founder of Canadian Studies Program, 1974. Adjunct professor at University of Waterloo, 1973-78; visiting professor at University of Victoria, 1972, Duke University, 1974, University of Maine, 1978, 1979, Simon Fraser University, 1980-81, and University of British Columbia, 1981. Has lectured in the United States on Canadian-American relations. *Military service:* Royal Canadian Air Force Reserve, 1956.

MEMBER: Conference on British Studies, American Historical Association, North American Society for Oceanic History (secretary), Canadian Institute for International Affairs (past president), Canadian Historical Association, Champlain Society. *Awards, honors:* Social Science Council-Canada Council publishing award, 1971, for *The Royal Navy and the Northwest Coast of North America, 1810-1914;* Leon and Thea Koerner research grant, 1974; Canada Council leave fellowship, 1977-78; John Lyman Award for Oceanic History, 1980; Royal Historical Society fellowship, 1980; European Community visiting fellowship, 1981.

WRITINGS: The Royal Navy and the Northwest Coast of North America, 1810-1914: A Study of British Maritime Ascendancy, University of British Columbia Press, 1971; *To the Pacific and Arctic with Beechey,* Cambridge University Press, 1973; *Canada,* Prentice-Hall, 1975; (editor) *Search for the Visible Past,* Wilfrid Laurier University Press, 1975; *Distant Dominion: Britain and the Northwest Coast of North America, 1579-1809,* University of British Columbia Press, 1980; (contributor) *The Discoverers,* McGraw, 1980. Contributor to journals. Corresponding editor of *British Studies Intelligencer,* 1971—; *Albion,* associate editor, 1968-69, managing editor, 1969-72, editor, 1972—.

WORK IN PROGRESS: Research on British maritime authority and Northwest Coast Indians in the nineteenth century; research on the relationship of technology to the British Empire in the nineteenth and twentieth centuries, on Canada in the Commonwealth, and on race relations in the British Empire and Commonwealth.

SIDELIGHTS: Barry Morton Gough tells *CA:* "I write on the themes of Canada and the sea. Living hard by the pervasive power of the United States, Canadians have scarcely given much attention to the oceans over which they travelled to get to their new homeland. To my way of thinking, Canada owes its existence to the interplay of land and sea. I started with the least known aspect of Canadian maritime history—British Columbia—and I hope to complete the whole continental cycle from the Pacific to the Arctic to the Atlantic and to the Great Lakes. My fellow historians can write about the miseries of the human condition, or they can press forward with recondite and largely illiterate econometric studies. But I still prefer to think of history as literature in which narrative coupled with analysis still has a place. History ought to be a good read."

AVOCATIONAL INTERESTS: Travel (has travelled widely in Canada, the United States, New Zealand, and Europe).

*   *   *

GOUGH, Catherine
See MULGAN, Catherine

*   *   *

GRAHAM, Otis L., Jr. 1935-

PERSONAL: Born June 24, 1935, in Little Rock, Ark.; son of Otis L. (a clergyman) and Lois (Patterson) Graham; married Delores Elliott; children: Ann, Wade. *Education:* Yale University, B.A., 1957; Columbia University, M.A., 1961, Ph.D., 1966. *Office:* University of North Carolina, Chapel Hill, N.C. 27514.

CAREER: University of California, Santa Barbara, associate professor of history, 1966-80; University of North Carolina at Chapel Hill, distinguished university professor, 1980—. *Military service:* U.S. Marine Corps, 1957-60; served in Hawaii; became captain. *Member:* American Historical Association, Organization of American Historians.

WRITINGS: An Encore for Reform: The Old Progressives and the New Deal, Oxford University Press, 1967; *The Great Campaigns: Reform and War in America,* Prentice-Hall, 1971; (editor) *From Roosevelt to Roosevelt,* Appleton, 1971; (editor) *The New Deal: The Critical Issues,* Little, Brown, 1971; *Toward a Planned Society: From Roosevelt to Nixon,* Oxford University Press, 1976.

WORK IN PROGRESS: A history of growth and growth politics in the United States since 1945.

*   *   *

GRAY, Captain Bill
See GRAY, William Bittle

*   *   *

GRAY, Francine du Plessix 1930-

PERSONAL: Born September 25, 1930, in France; came to United States in 1941; daughter of Bertrand (a diplomat) and Tatiana (Iacovleff) du Plessix; married Cleve Gray (a painter), April 23, 1957; children: Thaddeus, Luke. *Education:* Attended Bryn Mawr College, 1948-50, and Black Mountain College, summers, 1951-52; Barnard College, B.A., 1952. *Politics:* Democrat. *Religion:* Roman Catholic. *Home:* Greystones, Cornwall Bridge, Conn. 06754. *Agent:* Georges Borchardt, Inc., 136 East 57th St., New York, N.Y. 10022.

CAREER: United Press International, New York City, reporter at night desk, 1952-54; *Realities* (magazine), Paris, France, editorial assistant for French edition, 1954-55; free-lance writer, 1955—; *Art in America,* New York City, book editor, 1964-66; *New Yorker,* New York City, staff writer, beginning 1968. Distinguished visiting professor at City College of the City University of New York, spring, 1975; visiting lecturer at Saybrook College, Yale University, 1981; adjunct professor, School of Fine Arts, Columbia University, 1983—. Judge of 1974 National Book Award in philosophy and religion. At-

tended Soviet-American Writers' Workshop in Batumin, U.S.S.R., 1979.

MEMBER: International P.E.N., Authors Guild, Authors League of America. *Awards, honors:* Putnam Creative Writing Award from Barnard College, 1952; National Catholic Book Award from Catholic Press Association, 1971, for *Divine Disobedience: Profiles in Catholic Radicalism;* Front Page Award from Newswomen's Club of New York, 1972, for *Hawaii: The Sugar-Coated Fortress;* LL.D. from City University of New York, 1981.

WRITINGS: Divine Disobedience: Profiles in Catholic Radicalism, Knopf, 1970; *Hawaii: The Sugar-Coated Fortress,* Random House, 1972; *Lovers and Tyrants* (novel), Simon & Schuster, 1976; *World Without End* (novel), Simon & Schuster, 1981.

Contributor of articles, stories, and reviews to periodicals, including *Vogue, New Yorker, Saturday Review, New York Review of Books, New York Times Book Review,* and *New Republic.*

WORK IN PROGRESS: October Blood, a novel.

SIDELIGHTS: In 1976 *New Yorker* columnist Francine du Plessix Gray published *Lovers and Tyrants,* a book Caryl Rivers describes in *Ms.* as being "as rich in its texture as the lace tablecloths women of my grandmother's generation used to crochet." The novel, a startling and often touching autobiographical *bildungsroman,* gained the attention of many critics. "Every woman's first novel about her own break-through into adulthood is significant—liberation of any kind is significant—but Francine du Plessix Gray has created, in hers, something memorable," comments Kathleen Cushman in the *National Observer.* "To the cathartic throes of autobiography she has added a good dose each of humor, irony, and skill; *Lovers and Tyrants* transcends its limited possibilities as a book about Woman Oppressed and crosses into the realm of art."

The eight parts of this novel of "ascent and liberation," as Joan Peters calls it in the *Nation,* describe various periods in the life of Stephanie, the heroine. It begins with her childhood in Paris as the daughter of a Russian mother and an aristocratic French father who wanted her to be a boy. She is raised by a hypochondriac governess and her childhood, she writes in the opening lines of the book, was "muted, opaque, and drab, the color of gruel and of woolen gaiters, its noises muted and monotonous as a sleeper's pulse. . . . My temperature was taken twice a day, my head was perpetually wrapped in some woolen muffler or gauze veiling. I was scrubbed, spruced, buffed, combed, polished, year round, like a first communicant." After her father's death in the Resistance, Stephanie and her mother move to New York where Stephanie attends a fancy boarding school. Later, a young adult, she returns to France to visit her relatives and has an affair with a French prince who describes himself as "style incarnate." Nearing thirty, she marries an architect, bears two sons, and continues her career as a journalist. She feels confined and dissatisfied in her marriage and leaves to tour the Southwest, writing about bizarre religious cults and taking up with a twenty-five-year-old homosexual who longs to be both a bisexual and a photographer and who continuously begs Stephanie to feed him. The theme of the novel, as Stephanie points out, is the tyranny of love: "Every woman's life is a series of exorcisms from the spells of different oppressors: nurses, lovers, husbands, gurus, parents, children, myths of the good life. The most tyrannical despots can be the ones who love us the most."

That theme, Gray acknowledges, came from experiences in her own life. In an essay for the *New York Times Book Review*, Gray writes that her late start in writing fiction was partially due to fear of disapproval from her father—even though he had died when she was eleven. *Lovers and Tyrants* grew out of her frustration as a young wife and mother. "I was married and had two children," Gray stated in the *New York Times Book Review* "The Making of an Author" column, "and since I live deep in the country and in relative solitude, encompassed by domestic duties, the journal [that I kept] became increasingly voluminous, angry, introspective. The nomad, denied flight and forced to turn inward, was beginning to explode. One day when I was 33, after I'd cooked and smiled for a bevy of weekend guests whom I never wished to see again, I felt an immense void, a great powerlessness, the deepest loneliness I'd ever known. I wept for some hours, took out a notebook, started rewriting one of the three stories that had won me my Barnard prize. It was the one about my governess. . . . It was to become, 12 years and two books of nonfiction later, the first chapter for *Lovers and Tyrants*. The process of finishing that book was as complex and lengthy as it was painful."

"There is something very French—Cartesian—in the orderly, rigid pattern that Francine's novel imposes on the random richness of Stephanie's life," remarks Audrey Foote in *Washington Post Book World*. "It is convenient, too; Gray herself has compared it to stringing beads. Once the themes are established, Stephanie-Francine is absolved of all problems of plot construction, free to proceed methodically yet meaningfully through the heroine's life, devoting every stage, every chapter to the unmasking of another 'jailer.' *Lovers and Tyrants* is an apt and total title; the book is a litany of oppressors, a rosary of named identities." It is that process of naming her oppressors that is central to Stephanie's story, for, to her, that is the way to liberation. "We must name the identities of each jailer before we can crawl on toward the next stage of freedom," Stephanie writes in her journal. "To herself, and to me," says Peters, "Stephanie is simply a person trying to acknowledge and accommodate the forces that have acted on her and which remain a part of her."

The process of naming her oppressors and liberating herself from them (and from the strangling memories of past 'jailers') forms the crux of *Lovers and Tyrants*. But it is not only a personal liberation that Stephanie seeks. She views her situation as part of the historical oppression of women. When she leaves her husband and takes to the road, she says that she rebels "for all women, because we are killing each other in our doll's houses." Her ultimate desire, she tells the reader, is "to be free, to be a boy, to be God." Comments Rivers in *Ms.*: "[Stephanie] sees dropping out as the prelude to rebirth. She will be Kerouac, Dean; she will infringe on male territory. . . . *Lovers and Tyrants* may be a classic in a new genre of literature—the woman as wanderer, seeker of truth. . . . To take this journey with her is to confront not only the questions of love and freedom, but those of death and immortality and existence as well." Sara Sanborn considers the novel to be a feminist fable. "The theme of this novel," Sanborn writes in *Saturday Review*, "[is] the perpetual seduction of women by those who will offer tenderness and authority, the feminine materials of feminine transcendence."

The first three-fourths of the novel—the first-person sections describing her childhood, her return to France, and her marriage—is widely praised for its wit, fine writing, and evocative detail. "The author has no trouble persuading the reader that

there was once a small girl in Paris named Stephanie," says *Time*'s Timothy Foote, as he notes the similarities between Stephanie's life and that of her creator's (the French and Russian parentage, the immigration to New York, the private schools, the fling in Paris, the career as a journalist, an artistic husband, two sons, even, notes Foote, the same high cheekbones and large eyes). "Stephanie's remembrance of things past flashes with literary style and wit. Remarkable siblings, and sexual suitors are summoned up, often in hilarious detail, though they are mostly kept frozen at the edge of caricature by Stephanie's satiric perceptions." These early sections of the novel, writes Julian Moynahan in the *New York Times Book Review*, "are crammed with unforgettably drawn characters, rich emotion and complex social portraiture. In counterpoint they bring out contrasted aspects of French life that are both immemorial and contemporary, and that perhaps only a cultural 'amphibian' like Mrs. du Plessix Gray would clearly see." Joan Peters in *Nation* deems "the depiction of Stephanie's relationship with Paul . . . as complex a portrait of love and marriage as I have seen in recent novels."

While critical opinion of the beginning sections of *Lovers and Tyrants* is overwhelmingly favorable, reviews of the last chapters tend to be negative. Michael Wood, for example, in his *New York Review of Books* article calls the final chapters of *Lovers and Tyrants* "truly lamentable," citing sloppy writing and a final section that "has expanded too far into fantasy" as his reasons for such harsh criticism. "There is a great deal that goes on in the eighth, last, longest, and presumably climactic chapter of *Lovers and Tyrants*," Christopher Lehmann-Haupt comments in the *New York Times*. "There is abundant activity. . . . There is sex. . . . But nowhere in that concluding chapter is it possible to find anything to rouse the reader from his intensifying somnolence. Nowhere is there an interesting unanswered question about the plot or the heroine's development. Nowhere is there activity or thought that one hasn't long since been able to predict. Nowhere is there articulation of Stephanie's problem that we haven't heard uttered before. ('God, I hate puritanism, wasp puritanism, all kinds. Do you realize it's puritanism got us into Vietnam?') Nowhere is there surprise. And that is why *Lovers and Tyrants*, for all the wit and thrust of its prose, is finally so exasperating. The drone of its intelligence ultimately bores."

Village Voice book editor Eliot Fremont-Smith also finds *Lovers and Tyrants* intelligent but at the same time lacking because of that intelligence. "I think something more basic is wrong," he remarks, referring to the abrupt change in the book's tone in the last sections, "and it has to do with intelligence and class. And tone. And tonyness. *Lovers and Tyrants* is nothing if not wonderfully intelligent. For much of the novel, the intelligence is presumed and shared; the reader is in really interesting company, and feels there by right of respectful invitation, and is so honored. But toward the end, the intelligence—not so much of Stephanie or her witty companion, but of the *book*—turns into something else, a sort of shrill IQ mongering. Intellectual references from the very best places are tossed around like Frisbees; it becomes a contest, and a rather exclusionary one, with the reader on the sidelines. This subverts, first, credibility. (Such *constant* smartness, such unflagging articulation of sensibility, such *memories*! Don't they ever say Stekel when they mean Ferenczi? Don't they ever get tired?) It subverts, second, a sense of caring. A defensive reaction, but that's what happens when one feels snubbed, or made the fool. In the end, *Lovers and Tyrants* seems more crass than Class; there is an unpleasant aftertaste of having been unexpectedly and for no deserving reason, insulted. This is inelegant.''

Credibility is also seen as a problem by other reviewers of *Lover and Tyrants*. A major criticism of the novel is that, in the end, the story is not believable. ''There is so much in this book to admire that I wish I could believe Stephanie's story. I don't,'' says Sara Sanborn in *Saturday Review*. ''Stephanie seems twice-born, her sensibility as narrator formed more by other writers, from Henry James to Kate Millet, than by the events recounted, which also have their haunting familiarity. I don't believe for one minute that Stephanie really has two children: in twenty years the chief effect they have on her is to supply her with wise-child sayings. Finally, I don't believe in Stephanie's unvarying superiority. Even in her bad moments, she is more thoughtful, sensitive, and self-perceptive, more humorous, open, and finally free than anyone she encounters. The other characters seem to have their existence only to further her self-exploration.'' *Newsweek* reviewer Peter S. Prescott also agrees: ''For three-quarters of its route, *Lovers and Tyrants* is a remarkably convincing, even exhilarating performance. [However,] toward the end, in a long section in the third person, I sensed the author striking poses, lecturing us a bit to emphasize points already amply developed, introducing two characters—a radical Jesuit and a homosexual youth—who are not as engaging as I suspect the author means them to be.''

Time's Timothy Foote questions Stephanie's credibility as a character and narrator because, he says, ''Stephanie's cries rise to heaven like those of De Sade's Justine, a girl one recollects, with far more justification for complaint.'' At the point Stephanie leaves her husband (who, Foote mentions, is a ''fine husband, a kind man, a devoted father'') and goes on the road, ''Mrs. Gray abruptly switches from the first-person 'I' narrative form that has preserved whatever degree of credibility the story maintains. Stephanie in the third-person, Stephanie as 'she,' makes fairly ludicrous fiction. . . . This is an age that has learned any grievance must be accepted as both genuine and significant if the public weeping and wailing are long and loud enough. It would therefore be wise to take seriously Mrs. Gray's passionate meditation on the tyranny of love. Not as a novel, though.'' In the end, Michael Wood in *New York Review of Books* finds that ''this hitherto solid and patient novel has expanded too far into fantasy, and has lost even the truth of seriously entertained wishes.''

Concomitant to the lack of credibility that Stephanie suffers is what is perceived by some critics as her inability to reconcile her feminist beliefs with her actions. Writing in the *Nation*, Joan Peters observes that ''one of the problems with *Lovers and Tyrants* is that not all the contradictions are accounted for or, it seems, planned for. Among the most perplexing of these is the tension between Stephanie's feminist analysis of her life and her persistent identification with men. On the one hand, she is quite strong in her analysis of how confining it is to be a woman, how discrimination operates, how few models women have, etc. . . . On the other hand, the actual record of Stephanie's life is a Freudian's delight and a feminist's nightmare. Again and again Stephanie realizes that she wants to be a boy.'' Peters then points out contradictions that belie Stephanie's words: ''[her] need to be with men, her desire to be a boy, the absence of female friends, the Henry Milleresque sexual descriptions, her assumption that it is because Mishka couldn't love men that she was so cruel.'' Moynahan calls Stephanie ''the unsatisfactory representation or symbol of modern woman in the throes of an unprecedented process of liberation.'' Earlier in his article, Moynahan had questioned the value of Stephanie's

liberation, noting that despite her access to almost every pleasure desired and freedom from most worries, Stephanie slips ''into madness out of a conviction that her freedom is obstructed.''

Audrey Foote in *Washington Post Book World* says, ''Gray writes with such passion, grace and wit, and her themes are so fashionable, that the reader is swept along in sympathetic credulity until he begins to scrutinize these tyrants.'' Stephanie's tyrants—governess, family, husband, lovers, friends—Foote points out, are hardly that, loving and indulging Stephanie in any way they can. Continues Foote: ''Surely none of these 'lovers' in the wide sense she intends, can seriously be classified as 'tyrants.' . . . *Enfin*, there is only one clue that her obsession with tyranny is not pure paranoia: the sex scenes. . . . They are significant in showing that Stephanie, so heroic if quixotic in defiance of imagined oppression, is, alas, a sexual masochist. 'He ordered,' 'she asked permission,' 'he commanded'—she *chooses* these dominating lovers, and her compliance, her collaboration explains her conviction: 'Our enslavers segregate us into zoos, with our full consent.' Speak for yourself, Stephanie! Thus finally the provocative title and grand design of this novel turn out to be based on little more than a retrogressive sexual taste, a dreary and dubious cliche. . . . She is in search of freedom—to do what? What does she want? What do women want? Francine never quite tells us about Stephanie (does *she* know?)''

Despite reservations about *Lovers and Tyrants,* most critics have, in the end, judged it favorably. Peters concludes that in spite of the book's limitations, ''what *Lovers and Tyrants* does do, and does beautifully, is exploit the limited strength of the autobiographical genre. Gray presents a fascinating, intelligent woman whose personal contradictions concerning tradition, freedom, sex, culture, and religion shed light on the larger society in a way that is sometimes inadvertant, more often artistically controlled.'' Michael Wood concedes that *Lovers and Tyrants* ''is an absorbing and intelligent book, if a little too icy to be really likeable.'' Finally, the *Village Voice*'s Fremont-Smith observes: ''*Lovers and Tyrants* has all sorts of problems and gets tiresomely narcissistic and irritating; still, it is one of the very truly interesting and stimulating—one wants to argue with it and about it—books I've read all year. . . . If Gray's book burns a bit, and it does, that should suggest fire as well as ice at its core.''

World Without End, Gray's second novel, is also noted for its sensitivity and intelligence. The story of three lifelong friends who reunite in middle age to tour Russia and, hopefully, to ''learn how to live the last third of our lives,'' *World Without End* is ''an ambitious novel about love and friendship, faith and doubt, liberty and license,'' comments Judith Gies in *Saturday Review*. D. M. Thomas, writing in the *Washington Post Book World*, considers *World Without End* to be ''clearly the work of a richly talented writer. . . . The book is struggling with an important subject: the conflict within each of us between the psychological hungers symbolized by America and Russia—individualism and brotherhood, anarchy and order. It is no small achievement to have explored interestingly one of the most crucial dilemmas of our age.''

Doris Grumbach in *Commonweal* calls *World Without End* ''a prime entry in the novel of intelligence. It is just that: the lives [Gray] tells about ring with authenticity for their times and their place.'' It is the novel's ''intelligence''—its lengthy discourses on a variety of subjects and the articulate growing self-awareness of its characters—that holds the attention of many of its reviewers. The *New York Times*'s John Leonard notes the ''lyric excess'' of the characters's musings, but believes that Gray ''has chosen to satirize the art, the religion and the politics of the last 35 years'' through characters Sophie, Claire, and Edmund. ''[Gray] has also chosen to forgive the creatures of her satire,'' says Leonard. ''They are more disappointed in themselves than readers will be in them as characters.''

For other critics, the intellectual discussions in *World Without End* are a hindrance to an appreciation of the novel. ''Anyone not conversant with the intellectual and esthetic upheavals in American art and politics over the last 30 years ought not attempt to read this novel,'' suggests Henrietta Epstein in the *Detroit News*, ''for these concerns, along with those of friendship and love, are at the heart of Francine du Plessix Gray's work.'' *Newsweek* reviewer Annalyn Swan concurs with Leonard that ''some of this is obviously satire'' and says that ''when Gray is not trying to be wry, or brilliant, she can be wonderful.'' Swan concludes that Gray, ''like many social critics who cross the line into fiction, . . . has not yet mastered the difference between show and tell, between writing fiction that lives and using fiction as a forum for ideas. What she aspires to here is a highbrow critique of art and society in the last twenty years. What she has written is a novel that strives too hard to impress. The prose is full of bad breathiness, the characters suffer from terminal solipsism, and the social criticism is often as cliched as the attitudes it attacks.''

Esquire columnist James Wolcott also comments on Gray's satiric designs: ''Tripping through *World Without End*, I kept telling myself that the book might be a spoofy lark—a Harlequin romance for art majors—but I have a lurking suspicion that Gray is serious. After all, the novel's theme—the pull and persistence of friendship—is buttressed by quotations from Catullus and from Roland Barthes, and floating through the text are the sort of flowery phrases only a tremulously sincere epicurean would use.'' *Commentary*'s Pearl K. Bell is also highly critical of Gray's second novel. ''Francine Gray's sententious dialogue about love and death and self-fulfillment does not blind us to the poverty of thought in what seems to have been conceived as a novel of ideas,'' the critic contends. ''*World Without End* is not a novel of ideas, it is an adolescent daydream, an orgy of pseudo-intellectual posturing, a midnight bull session in a college dorm.''

Grumbach finds that a distance is placed between the reader and the characters because of the intense intellectualism of the novel. She asserts that ''despite the impressive and always accurate documentation of place (Edmund's visit to the Hermitage and the art he looks at there consumes five dense pages) and the character, social movements, parental backgrounds, lovers, husbands, visits with each other, letters and postcards [the three friends] exchange for all those years, do we ever feel *close* to these people? Curiously, not really. They are so detailed and cerebral, their talk is so elevated and informed, we know so many *facts* about their milieus that, somehow, passion is smothered.'' But, other critics disagree. Reynolds Price in the *New York Times Book Review*, for instance, finds that in *World Without End*, Gray ''displays the one indispensable gift in a novelist—she generates slowly and authoritatively a mixed set of entirely credible human beings who shunt back and forth through credible time and are altered by the trip. Ample, generous and mature, the book is stocked with the goods a novel best provides.''

The *New York Times*'s Leonard also finds the book—and the characters in it—touching. ''The reader chooses sides,'' he

writes. ''In this novel about Renaissance art and Puritanism, about Anglican convents and academic departments of art, about friendship and that televised soap opera 'General Hospital,' about lust and literature and missing fathers and saints full of greed and pride and envy—in this popcorn-popper of ideas, in which Edmund is the tourist of art, Claire the tourist of suffering and Sophie the tourist of everything, we are blessed with real people in the middle of an important argument about art and religion and sexuality. We are persuaded. . . . I chose Sophie to root for. It's been a long time in novels since I was a fan. Mrs. Gray tells us that 'Orpheus dismembered will continue to sing, his head floating down our rivers.' A real friend will either scoop up the head or hit it with a stick. Mrs. Gray scoops and sings.''

AVOCATIONAL INTERESTS: Tennis, gardening, cooking Provencal food.

CA INTERVIEW

CA interviewed Francine du Plessix Gray by phone on November 2, 1982, at her home in Cornwall Bridge, Connecticut.

CA: Like Sophie Ross in your second novel, World Without End, *you are a woman of many interests and talents. Does writing allow you to channel more of them than other careers might have done—theology and architecture, for example, which you considered; or painting and criticism, which you did for five years?*

GRAY: It's certainly channeled a greater variety of my gluttonously varied interests than any other career might have. When I write about an art historian who started as a painter, like the Edmund of *World Without End*, I write from first-hand experience. On the other hand, such wide-ranging passions can have their drawback: one's experience of diverse fields has been so intimate that one tends to delve into certain vocational problems, as I did with Edmund's, in a way which is too specialized for much of the reading public. I remember a very funny review in my local paper (The *New Milford Times*, circulation of about 3000). Lead sentence: ''The trouble with Francine Gray's last novel is that its language is just too darn hifalutin'.'' I've lived in a rather academic world much of my life. I'm always eager to talk about Titian's iconography of the Resurrection or Pascal's theory of grace. That's the language I was brought up on, and you can't help being what you are. I might never have a very wide audience with such specialized novels, but one doesn't write for an audience—I think that's an odious idea. One should only write what's in one's heart, and in *World Without End* my heart was with people who've had very varied careers: nomadic journalist—Sophie; painter and art critic—Edmund; political activist—Claire. It was great fun for me to write about their vocations in detail because I know them each so deeply. It may be less fun for the reader!

CA: In a recent essay in the New York Times Book Review *(September 12, 1982), you described the ''joy and liberation'' you found in learning English when you came to this country at the age of eleven with your mother. Was this a major factor in your desire to write?*

GRAY: I think it eventually was. The challenge of a new language in one's adolescence! Think of Conrad—he was eighteen or nineteen when he learned English. Learning a language beyond the nursery years turns you into both a soldier and a lover. In that *Times* interview I stressed the erotic part of it, the new language as a lover to be conquered. But there's also the soldierly aspect of the conquest: if you don't keep very careful order within that regiment of words while you're waging your battle with it, you're risking mutiny. You tend to be more meticulous about a new language than people who take it for granted.

I liked to write in high school, but I was always so devoid of ideas for fiction. I have a basically uninventive mind. It's fundamentally more analytic. Throughout my college years I didn't put high value on the excellence with which I was performing in criticism, or in the essay form. At that time I was still under the spell of the obnoxious myth that the only "creative writing" is either fiction or poetry. I wasn't writing in those forms, so I didn't value my writing. That's another issue I pointed to in the *New York Times Book Review* article: the terrible value judgment we used to make about certain literary genres being more creative than others has been very harmful to young aspiring writers.

CA: Your work has followed an interesting progression: years of keeping a journal; simultaneously, reporting on a wide variety of topics, some of which were of great personal interest to you; finally the autobiographical and fictional writing that represented a difficult psychological breakthrough. Looking at this progression, one senses that your writing may have been a search for identity. Is that close to the mark?

GRAY: That search is at the heart of many authors' work, don't you think? What are Proust's twenty volumes but a search for identity, a quest for naming himself? Yet careers vary vastly. *Naming* myself is probably much more central to my writing than to that of Anne Tyler, say, who can put herself into the shell of an invented character at a moment's notice and produce marvelous novels every two years. I know nothing about her background, but I imagine Anne Tyler found her own identity very early. This essential wisdom was denied me for some decades.

My self-knowledge was belated by the fact that my parents, whom I adored, belonged to a world in which I was a total misfit—the international jet-set crowd, the high-fashion world. It's a milieu which confused me for years. I looked on it with an almost schizophrenic ambivalence—both seduced by it because it was my parents' reality and repelled by its tyrannical frivolity. I tried working in it for two years in the 1950s (as a fashion reporter in Paris, another of my serendipitous activities!) and it damn nearly destroyed me; it drove me to spend some months in a Swiss sanatorium. After that near breakdown it took several years to pick up the pieces of me, so the process of naming myself didn't begin until my late twenties, didn't crystalize until my late thirties. It's significant that my first published book dealt with values diametrically opposed to the world I had to escape from as a young woman—the ascetic, self-sacrificial social activism of the Catholic left.

CA: That book, Divine Disobedience: Profiles in Catholic Radicalism *(1970), followed your return to the Catholic Church at a time when it was becoming more attuned to human needs and problems. How much of the spirit of that time do you think remains in the church today?*

GRAY: It remains dissenting in a very different way. On the widest social level, it may have found one of its finest fruitions in the stand the Catholic bishops are presently evolving against nuclear war. That's quite unprecedented; in the '60s American

bishops tended to follow whatever hawkish lines the government was taking. And I think the Catholic left, which I wrote about in *Divine Disobedience,* laid the groundwork for that flowering of dissenting, pacifist opinion which in the past year is reaching to the highest echelons of the American church. I had written that book because I found great irony in the fact that the American Catholic community had traditionally been the most politically *conservative* sector of American society, while a minority of them, the Berrigans among them, were engaging in our society's most *radical* actions. I think we're now seeing the fruits of those acts of conscience.

CA: Your fictional voice was hushed by your father when you were nine, then again years later at Black Mountain College by the poet Charles Olson, who said, "You're writing pure junk." Eleven years, two children, and two books later, the voice resurfaced. Were the nonfiction and the painting and the domesticity all part of an effort to rechannel the fictional energy?

GRAY: The gift of painting was very real. Robert Motherwell, whom I met at Black Mountain in 1951 and who became a good friend, is very ambivalent about my choice of vocation, very candid about it. He appreciates my writing, but he says I really had it as a painter also. Painting was not a pastime to relieve excess energy. I was good at it and I was very serious. Even as a child I had a terrific gift for realistic drawing, the way other children have perfect pitch in music. I wanted to use the gift. I loved to paint as much as I loved to write, and I was torn between the two for a long time. So in my case the seething energy of a potential writer was not being temporarily diverted into painting; I was suffering a genuine and painful cleavage within a rather schizophrenic personality who was half writer, half painter.

CA: In the introduction to Divine Disobedience, *you credited William Maxwell, William Shawn, Judith Jones, and Robert Silvers for having given you "the confidence to be a writer." How closely have you worked with your editors?*

GRAY: I love authority; I love to work closely with editors. William Maxwell and William Shawn of the *New Yorker* accepted and assigned important pieces before anyone else did. To them I have eternal gratitude. The last pieces I did for Bob Silvers in the *New York Review of Books* were on Clare Boothe Luce and on the Moonie cult, and in each case that meant two or three hours of work on the phone with Bob. Back in the '60s, when I was reporting frequently for the *New York Review,* I'd attend such events as the Nixon Inaugural. I'd literally get off the plane back home on Sunday, type out a thirty-page text by Thursday; Bob Silvers would send out a messenger to pick it up in Connecticut, he and Barbara Epstein would read it through, and we'd have a three-hour phone session on Friday to take out the kinks. It would be in print the following week. So I've worked on that kind of tight deadline, and although it tends to destroy me, I rather enjoy that war of nerves. . . .

Since I published *Divine Disobedience* I met the woman who's edited my last two books, Alice Mayhew at Simon and Schuster. That's by far the closest editorial relationship I've ever had; it's also a close woman-to-woman friendship, which makes it all very different. I'll show Alice a novel some two or three times while it's in progress. After a book is finished, we get together for a weekend and go over the manuscript page by page. I love suggestions; I love being corrected and improved. I'll remain a perennial student until the day I die. Little I write has meaning or value to me until it resonates with the understanding of a person whose judgment I totally trust.

CA: Both your fiction and nonfiction are concerned in part with the oppression of women. More than one of your fictional characters dream of being expected to cook for fourteen and there's no food in the house. Early in Lovers and Tyrants *Stephanie says, "I shall never cease to marvel at the way we beg for love and tyranny." Do you think women are becoming psychologically freer from oppression as we are becoming more liberated in fact?*

GRAY: I certainly think the generation growing up now is. When I look at my students at Yale or at my sons' girl friends, I find these young women more liberated from that desire to please, that *damned* desire to please, which plagued women for millenia. We were like poodles, all ribboned and prettied up, sitting up on our hind legs saying, "Bowwow! I love you! Look how pretty I am! I want my candy, my reward!" We were saying that to the world as well as to the men and the children in our lives. Just think of the way we used to dress, even in the early '60s: the bouffant skirts and ruby-red lipstick and mascara and waistcinchers. Though less restrictive, that waistcincher, like any corset, was rather analogous to the footbinding of Chinese females, a symbol of submission and oppression. It's appalling to think that we only liberated ourselves some twenty years ago from those symbols! The way we tortured our bodies to subserviently charm the world! Terrifying!

CA: In your commencement address to the 1980 graduating class at Bryn Mawr College, you said, "I believe that the Women's Movement that surfaced in America shortly after mid-century was in some part caused by the fact that women's lives had been more severely deritualized—and therefore made more meaningless—than at any other time in human history." Do you think we're handling that deficiency by returning to the old rituals or replacing them with new ones?

GRAY: That's a difficult issue. One of the great problems in the lives of women with full-time jobs is finding time to keep the rituals alive. A matrix of most good manners, for example, the ritual of leisurely dining with one's children: how do you observe it if you're a lawyer kept out late at night on a long court case, or a doctor, or a member of many other professions which allow your children to run berserk on peanut butter and television? It's a very real problem; rituals are time-consuming. Compromises are possible; we can choose a branch of our vocation that's less prone to emergencies, specialize in allergies rather than pediatrics, in corporation law rather than trial law. We may have to make such adjustments; we might never achieve the full latitude of choice offered to men. I grieve at these restrictions.

CA: Are you teaching at all now?

GRAY: No. I taught at Yale in the summer of '81, and I'll probably teach at Columbia in the autumn of '83. I don't like to teach more than a semester a year. I've enjoyed the short, intensive workshops I've done at Berkeley, Iowa, Indiana. But I'm such a slow, tortured writer that if I taught full-time I might never get anything published.

CA: You participated in a 1979 Soviet-American writers' workshop in Russia. Was that your first trip to Russia?

GRAY: No, I'd been twice before—first in '76 with my husband, and then in '78 with Rose Styron, one of the three women to whom *World Without End* is dedicated. We traveled with our two sons, who were then nineteen and had been through twelve years of school together, a most moving and hilarious trip. But I had a much more extensive insight into the Russian mind when I traveled as the guest of the Union of Soviet Writers.

CA: You've named Milan Kundera, Italo Calvino, Guenter Grass, and Salman Rushdie as favorite foreign contemporary writers. What about American ones?

GRAY: I like Bellow very much, especially late Bellow, *Herzog.* I love the short fiction of William Gass, perhaps more than anything else being written in the United States today. I'm more passionate about Gass's *In the Heart of the Heart of the Country* than about any other contemporary American fiction I can think of. I tend to have rather underground tastes. Among younger writers I admire those who are not yet as fully recognized as they should be—Jayne Anne Phillips, who wrote *Black Tickets;* Mark Helprin, *Ellis Island;* Walter Abish, *How German Is It;* Joy Williams's extraordinary new collection *Taking Care.* Such books often get nominated for prizes, thank God, but they seldom become bestsellers. These are texts which constantly startle and surprise me by their insights and have a highly innovative approach to the texture, the skin of prose, which are some of the aspects of literature I value the most.

CA: Do you write on a rigid schedule?

GRAY: I work roughly from about eleven to six, on rare best days from ten to six-thirty, which obviously doesn't mean I'm writing all that time. There's the research and the endless drafts of rewriting and refitting of parts and laborious cabinet-making which take up ninety-nine percent of the working day. I'm not an early-morning worker—I don't trust myself in the early morning. I feel logy, I tend to sleep very badly, I wake up in a bad mood. Also, I like to get all the household thinking out of the way before I start working: letters written, bills paid, invitations accepted or refused, friends soothed, children counseled, pregnant mothers calmed, cats and dogs fed—all the business of friendship and nurturing, which is very important to me, put safely behind me by ten-thirty or so and then my mind is free. I often feel I spend too much time being polite to ever be a first-rate writer, but that's part of the courtly European tradition in which I grew up, and which I don't intend to shed off. My best working hours are really in the late afternoon. If I started earlier in the morning and stopped earlier, I would miss out on my most fruitful period. I've realized over the years that subconsciously I reserve my strength for the afternoon span—from four to seven, when I'm really cooking on all four burners. But then by seven it's time to stop and feed a husband . . . and I don't like to work after dinner. I can pencil copy then, but anything more arduous keeps me from sleeping.

CA: Is there something you'd like to write, or write about, that you haven't done yet?

GRAY: I always seem to have a character in search of God in my novels. I have that kind of protagonist again in the novel I'm presently finishing. I've become interested in the lives of men who've worked in the priesthood and have left it, in the particular psychological traumas of that turn of vocation. This prevailing search may have something to do with my father's early death—search for the Father, search for God, part of the same problem.

As for the future: I'll always remain a social activist, and I'm impatient to write about some of the innumerable injustices in our society, be it our neglect of prisons, our indifference to the aged, our mishandling of the mentally ill. I probably have to do it in nonfiction form. I'm ready to write another *Divine Disobedience* of sorts. I'm rather fed up with reading and writing about my own kind, which is the reality dealt with by most contemporary fiction.

BIOGRAPHICAL/CRITICAL SOURCES: New York Times Book Review, May 31, 1970, October 17, 1976, May 24, 1981, September 12, 1982; *Saturday Review,* June 13, 1970, October 30, 1976, May 1981; *New Republic,* June 27, 1970; *Nation,* February 1, 1971, November 20, 1976; *Listener,* February 25, 1971, June 2, 1977; *Books and Bookmen,* March, 1971; Francine du Plessix Gray, *Lovers and Tyrants,* Simon & Schuster, 1976; *Washington Post Book World,* August 29, 1976, October 24, 1976, May 24, 1981; *New York Times,* October 8, 1976, September 15, 1979, May 19, 1981, August 20, 1981; *Newsweek,* October 11, 1976, June 22, 1981; *Wall Street Journal,* October 25, 1976, June 1, 1981; *Harpers,* November, 1976; *Ms.,* November, 1976, July, 1981; *Time,* November 1, 1976; *New York Review of Books,* November 11, 1976; *National Review,* November 12, 1976; *Village Voice,* November 22, 1976; *National Observer,* December 18, 1976; *Times Literary Supplement,* May 20, 1977; Gray, *World Without End,* Simon & Schuster, 1981; *Commonweal,* May 22, 1981; *Chicago Tribune Book World,* May 31, 1981, August 15, 1982; *Esquire,* June, 1981; *Commentary,* August, 1981; *Progressive,* November, 1981; *Detroit News,* December 16, 1981; *Contemporary Literary Criticism,* Volume XXII, Gale, 1982.

—*Sketch by Heidi A. Tietjen*
—*Interview by Jean W. Ross*

*   *   *

GRAY, Nicholas Stuart   1922-1981

PERSONAL: Born October 23, 1922, in Scotland; died March 17, 1981, in London, England; son of William Stuart and Lenore May (Johnson) Gray. *Education:* Educated at "various private grammar schools, names forgotten. No degrees, as never tried for any, and probably wouldn't have got them if had done so." *Politics:* None. *Religion:* None. *Home:* 20 Perrins Walk, Hampstead, London N.W.3, England; Castle House, Castle St., Bampton, Devonshire, England; and Langamull, Calgary, Isle of Mull, Scotland. *Agent:* Samuel French, Inc., 25 West 45th St., New York, N.Y. 10036; and Lawrence Fitch, 113 Wardour St., London W1V 4EH, England.

CAREER: Playwright, novelist, actor, stage director, and illustrator. Had his first play produced professionally when he was seventeen; actor and director in repertory in London theaters and throughout England; directed many of his plays, and appeared in some, including "New Clothes for the Emperor," "The Imperial Nightingale," "The Tinder-Box," "The Marvellous Story of Puss in Boots," "The Wrong Side of the Moon," and "The Princess and the Swineherd"; also played Hamlet, Richard II, and Iago in "Othello," at the Malvern Festival Theatre. *Member:* P.E.N., Societe des Auteurs (Paris).

WRITINGS—Fiction: Over the Hills to Fabylon, Oxford University Press, 1954; *Down in the Cellar,* Dobson, 1961; *The Seventh Swan,* Dobson, 1962; *The Stone Cage,* Dobson, 1963; *Grimbold's Other World* (Junior Literary Guild selection), Fa-

ber, 1963, Meridith, 1972; *The Apple Stone* (Junior Literary Guild selection), Dobson, 1965, Meridith, 1968; *Mainly in Moonlight,* Faber, 1965, published as *Mainly in Moonlight: Ten Stories of Sorcery and the Supernatural,* Meridith, 1967; *The Boys; or, Cats with Everything,* Meridith, 1969; *The Further Adventures of Puss in Boots,* Faber, 1971; *The Edge of Evening,* Faber, 1976; *Killer's Cookbook,* Dobson, 1976; *A Wind from Nowhere,* Faber, 1978; *The Wardens of the Weir,* Dobson, 1978; *The Garland of Filigree,* Dobson, 1979.

Plays; published by Oxford University Press, except as indicated: *Beauty and the Beast,* 1951; *The Princess and the Swineherd,* 1952; *The Tinder-Box,* 1952; *The Hunters and the Henwife,* 1953; *The Marvellous Story of Puss in Boots,* 1955; *The Imperial Nightingale,* 1956; *New Clothes for the Emperor,* 1957; *The Other Cinderella,* 1958; *The Seventh Swan,* Dobson, 1962; *The Stone Cage,* Dobson, 1963; *Gawain and the Green Knight,* Dobson, 1967; *New Lamps for Old,* Dobson, 1967. Also author of television plays.

OBITUARIES: Times (London), March 20, 1981.†

*   *   *

GRAY, William Bittle   1891-1974
(Captain Bill Gray)

PERSONAL: Born 1891 in Lima, Pa.; died March 4, 1974; son of William Smith and Annie (Bittle) Gray; married Sarah Githens, 1921 (deceased). *Home:* 2451 Burkell Ave., Miami, Fla. 33129. *Office:* Miami Seaquarium, Virginia Key, Miami, Fla.

CAREER: Left school at sixteen to work as a fisherman off the New Jersey coast. His continuing interest in fish led him to Florida, where he eventually began collecting live specimens for the salt water aquarium he built on his own pier. From 1955, he was director of collections and exhibits of the Miami Seaquarium, Miami Beach, Fla. He also directed several expeditions into the Pacific for scientific and museum purposes, including the Leon Mandel Expedition sponsored by Field Museum, Chicago, Ill., and the George Vanderbilt Expedition, sponsored by the Academy of Natural Sciences, Philadelphia, Pa. *Military service:* U.S. Coast Guard, five years. *Member:* Explorers Club (New York), Surf Club and LaGorce Country Club (both Miami).

WRITINGS: Creatures of the Sea, Funk, 1960; *Porpoise Tales,* A. S. Barnes, 1964; *Fish Tales and Ocean Oddballs,* A. S. Barnes, 1970; *Flipper the Star,* E. A. Seeman, 1973; *Friendly Porpoises,* A. S. Barnes, 1974. Contributor of numerous short stories to periodicals.

SIDELIGHTS: William Bittle Gray was responsible for catching Miami Seaquarium's 10,000 sea creatures. A number of newly-identified fish have been named for him. *Avocational interests:* Biology and natural history.†

*   *   *

GRAYLAND, Eugene C(harles)   1916-1976

PERSONAL: Born June 21, 1916, in Wellington, New Zealand; died December 7, 1976; son of Charles Henry and Anne (Mawhinney) Grayland; married Valerie Merle Spanner (an author), November 13, 1948. *Education:* Attended New Zealand schools. *Religion:* Anglican. *Home:* 4031 Great North Rd., Kelston, Auckland, New Zealand.

CAREER: Reporter or sub-editor for newspapers in Hastings, Auckland, New Plymouth, and Palmerston North, New Zealand, 1947-53; chief-of-staff of magazine group, *Newsview, Better Business, Women's Choice,* Auckland, New Zealand, 1953-54; *Auckland Star,* Auckland, education and science reporter, 1954-64, medical and science reporter, 1964-75; editor, *Auricle,* 1974-76. *Military service:* New Zealand Army, four years; served mostly with War History and Archives Branch. *Member:* New Zealand Journalists' Association, Auckland Institute and Museum, Royal Society of New Zealand, New Zealand Association of Scientists (associate), Medical Journalists' Association (Great Britain), Bookpeople.

WRITINGS: Private Presses: Their Contributions to Literature and Typography, Colenso Press, 1947; *The Newspaper Morgue,* Colenso Press, 1947; *The Value of Newspaper Sources for Historical and Other Research,* Colenso Press, 1947; *Special Uses of Press Clippings Material,* Colenso Press, 1949; *Research as an Aid to Writing,* Colenso Press, 1949; *The Newspaper Reference Library and the Filing and Uses of Clippings,* Colenso Press, 1950; *There Was Danger on the Line: Stories of Disastrous Train Smashes,* Belvedere Books, 1954; *New Zealand Disasters,* A. H. & A. W. Reed, 1957, 3rd edition, 1963.

(With J.C.M. Cresswell) *Auckland, Queen City of New Zealand,* A. H. & A. W. Reed, 1961; *Coasts of Treachery,* A. H. & A. W. Reed, 1963; (with wife, Valerie Grayland) *Coromandel Coast,* A. H. & A. W. Reed, 1965, revised edition, 1968; *Famous New Zealanders,* Whitcombe & Tombs, 1968; *Unusual Newspapers of New Zealand and Australia,* Colenso Press, 1969; (with V. Grayland) *Historic Coromandel,* A. H. & A. W. Reed, 1969; (with V. Grayland) *Tarawera,* Hodder & Stoughton, 1971; *More Famous New Zealanders,* Whitcombe & Tombs, 1971; *More New Zealand Disasters,* A. H. & A. W. Reed, 1979. Also author of *Christianity Comes to New Zealand,* 1964. Contributor to many medical journals, including *Medical News, Medical Tribune,* and *Medical Post.* Joint editor, *Hearing News,* beginning 1969.

WORK IN PROGRESS: Several feature and travel books on New Zealand subjects.†

* * *

GRAYLAND, V. Merle
See GRAYLAND, Valerie (Merle Spanner)

* * *

GRAYLAND, Valerie (Merle Spanner)
(V. Merle Grayland; pseudonyms: Lee Belvedere, Valerie Subond)

PERSONAL: Born in Thames, New Zealand; daughter of Jens Koeford (a farmer) and Eva (Howe) Spanner; married Eugene Charles Grayland (a journalist), November 13, 1948 (died December 7, 1976); married David Alan Duthie, May 14, 1979. *Education:* Attended Seddon Memorial Technical College, Auckland, New Zealand. *Home:* 4031 Great North Rd., Kelston, Auckland, New Zealand.

CAREER: Office worker until 1948; free-lance writer, 1948—.

WRITINGS—Children's books: The First Strawberry, Colenso Press, 1954; *John and Hoani,* Blackie & Son, 1962; *Early One Morning,* Rand McNally, 1963; *Baby Sister,* Rand McNally, 1964.

Nonfiction; with first husband, Eugene C. Grayland: *Coromandel Coast,* A. H. & A. W. Reed, 1965, revised edition,

1968; *Historic Coromandel,* A. H. & A. W. Reed, 1969; *Tarawera,* Hodder & Stoughton, 1971.

Under name V. Merle Grayland; novels; published by R. Hale: *The Dead Men of Eden,* 1962; *Night of the Reaper,* 1963; *The Grave Digger's Apprentice,* 1964; *Jest of Darkness,* 1965.

Under pseudonym Lee Belvedere; novels; published by Bouregy: *Farewell to a Valley,* 1971; *Meet a Dark Stranger,* 1971; *Thunder Beach,* 1972; *Fringe of Heaven,* 1972; *The Smiling House,* 1973; *Return to Moon Bay,* 1973.

Under pseudonym Valerie Subond; novels: *The Heights of Havenrest,* Beagle Books, 1972; *The House over Hell Valley,* Beagle Books, 1974; *House at Haunted Inlet,* Bouregy, 1978.

Short stories anthologized in *White Robin Storybook,* Longacre Press, 1960, and *Lucky Dip,* edited by Barbara Ker Wilson, Angus & Robertson, 1970. Contributor of short stories and articles to magazines in New Zealand and Australia.

WORK IN PROGRESS: The Birds and the Boys; Find Lottie Varden, a novel.

* * *

GREEN, Paul E(dgar) 1927-

PERSONAL: Born April 4, 1927, in Glenolden, Pa.; son of Joseph (a law book dealer) and Lucy Mae (Gordy) Green; married Elizabeth Ann Weamer; children: three. *Education:* University of Pennsylvania, A.B., 1950, A.M., 1953, Ph.D., 1961. *Office:* Department of Marketing, Wharton School, Suite 1450, Dietrich Hall, University of Pennsylvania, Philadelphia, Pa. 19104.

CAREER: Sun Oil Co., Philadelphia, Pa., statistician, 1950-53; Lukens Steel Co., Coatesville, Pa., commercial research analyst, 1953-54; University of Pennsylvania, Wharton School, Philadelphia, instructor in statistics, 1954-55; Lukens Steel Co., supervisor of operations research group and senior market analyst, 1955-58; E. I. duPont de Nemours & Co., Wilmington, Del., market planning consultant, 1958-62; University of Pennsylvania, Wharton School, deputy director of Management Science Center and associate professor, 1962-65, professor, 1965-71, S. S. Kresge Professor of Marketing, 1971—. Guest lecturer at more than seventy colleges and universities in the United States and abroad, including University of Delaware, Massachusetts Institute of Technology, Stanford University, University of Tel Aviv, University of London, University of Leiden, University of Grenoble, and University of Paris. Chairman of Institute of Management Sciences' College on Marketing, 1970-71. Member of advisory council, Association for Consumer Behavior, 1970-74; member of Census Advisory Committee, 1980-83.

MEMBER: American Association for the Advancement of Science, American Marketing Association (member of local executive council, 1965-67, 1968-69, and local board of directors, 1976-77), Operations Research Society of America, Institute of Management Sciences, American Institute of Decision Sciences (fellow, 1981), Society of Multivariate Experimental Psychology, American Statistical Association (fellow, 1980), Psychometric Society, Association of Consumer Behavior (member of advisory council, 1970-74). *Awards, honors:* Award from Alpha Kappa Psi, 1963, for "Bayesian Decision Theory in Pricing Strategy," and 1981, for "A General Approach to Optimal Product Design via Conjoint Analysis"; silver medal from J. Walter Thompson Agency, 1970, for "Advertisement Perception and Evaluation: An Application of Multidimensional Scaling''; honorable mention in research design contest sponsored by American Marketing Association, 1971, for ''On the Measurement of Judgmental Responses to Multi-Attribute Stimuli''; first prize in research design competition sponsored by American Psychological Association, 1972; Parlin Award from American Marketing Association, 1977; Paul D. Converse Award in marketing theory, 1978.

WRITINGS: (With Wroe Alderson) *Planning and Problem Solving in Marketing,* Irwin, 1964; (with D. S. Tull) *Research for Marketing Decisions,* Prentice-Hall, 1966, 4th edition, 1978; (with P. T. FitzRoy and P. J. Robinson) *Experiments on the Value of Information in Simulated Marketing Environments* (monograph), Allyn & Bacon, 1967; (with R. E. Frank) *A Manager's Guide to Marketing Research: Survey of Recent Developments,* Wiley, 1967; (with Frank) *Quantitative Methods in Marketing Analysis,* Prentice-Hall, 1967.

(With F. J. Carmone) *Multidimensional Scaling and Related Techniques in Marketing Analysis,* Allyn & Bacon, 1970; (with V. R. Rao) *Applied Multidimensional Scaling,* Holt, 1972; (with Yoram Wind) *Multi-Attribute Decisions in Marketing,* Holt, 1973; (editor with Martin Christopher) *Brand Positioning,* EJM Publishers (London), 1973; *Mathematical Tools for Applied Multivariate Analysis,* Academic Press, 1976; *Analyzing Multivariate Data,* Dryden, 1978.

Contributor: Wroe Alderson and Stanley Shapiro, editors, *Marketing and the Computer,* Prentice-Hall, 1963; Alderson, Shapiro, and Cox, editors, *Theory in Marketing,* Irwin, 1964; Peter Langhoff, editor, *Models, Measurement, and Marketing,* Prentice-Hall, 1964; Michael Halbert, editor, *The Nature and Sources of Marketing Theory,* McGraw, 1965; Patrick Robinson, editor, *Promotional Decision-Making: Practice and Theory,* McGraw, 1965.

J. W. Newman, editor, *On Knowing the Consumer,* Wiley, 1966; George Fisk, editor, *The Psychology of Management Decision,* C.W.K. Gleerup, 1967; Frank Bass, Charles King, and Edgar Pessemier, editors, *Applications of the Sciences in Marketing,* Wiley, 1967; P. J. Robinson and C. L. Hinkle, editors, *Sales Promotion Analysis: Some Applications of Quantitative Techniques,* Allyn & Bacon, 1967; Almarin Phillips, editor, *Pricing Theories and Policies,* University of Pennsylvania Press, 1968; Montrose Sommers and Jerome Kernan, editors, *Explorations in Consumer Behavior,* University of Texas Press, 1968; Irving Crespi, editor, *Attitude Research on the Rocks,* American Marketing Association, 1968.

Fisk, editor, *Essays in Marketing Theory,* Allyn & Bacon, 1971; King, editor, *Attitude Research Reaches New Heights,* American Marketing Association, 1971; R. N. Shepard, A. Romney and Sara Nerlove, editors, *Multidimensional Scaling,* Academic Press, 1972; W. D. Wells, editor, *Life Styles and Psychoanalysis,* American Marketing Association, 1973; *Studies in Multiple Criterion Decision Making,* University of South Carolina Press, 1973; J. N. Sheth, editor, *Multivariate Procedures in Marketing,* American Marketing Association. 1975.

Sheth, editor, *Research for Marketing,* Jai Press, 1977; Wind and Marshall Greenberg, editors, *Moving Ahead with Attitude Research,* American Marketing Association, 1977; (with J. D. Carroll and S. M. Goldberg) Wind, editor, *Product Policy: Concepts, Methods, and Strategies,* Addison-Wesley, 1981; (with Carroll) Wind, V. Mahajan, and R. Cardoza, editors, *New Product Forecasting: Models and Applications,* Lexington Books, 1981; (with Wind) *Encyclopedia of the Statistical Sciences,* McGraw, 1983; (with Carroll, S. M. Goldberg, P. K.

Kedia, and W. S. DeSarbo) Wind, editor, *Advances in Product and Marketing Strategy,* Jai Press, 1983.

Co-editor of a marketing series, Holt, 1967—. Contributor to *Handbook of Marketing Management, Handbook of Marketing Research,* and *Marketing Handbook.* Contributor of more than a hundred articles to technical journals. Member of editorial board of *Journal of Marketing Research,* 1965—, *Journal of Consumer Research,* 1973—, *Journal of Business Research,* 1973—, *Journal of Marketing,* 1978—, *Journal of the Market Research Society,* 1981—, and *Marketing Science;* referee for *Psychometrika, Journal of the Operations Research Society, Management Science,* and *Decision Sciences.*

WORK IN PROGRESS: Research on multi-attribute choice theory in marketing.

*   *   *

GREENLEE, James W(allace)   1933-

PERSONAL: Born November 25, 1933, in Chicago, Ill.; son of Robert P. (an electrician) and Eleanor (Burbank) Greenlee; married Nancy Pool (a teacher), June 8, 1955; children: Edward, Andrew, Kenneth, Aaron. *Education:* University of Illinois, B.A., 1956, M.A., 1962, Ph.D., 1967. *Politics:* Democrat. *Home:* 1057 Diamond St., San Diego, Calif. 92109. *Office:* Megatek Corp., San Diego, Calif. 92121.

CAREER: High school teacher of French in Miranda, Calif., 1959-60; University of Illinois at Urbana-Champaign, instructor in French, 1965-66; California Institute of Technology, Pasadena, instructor, 1966, assistant professor of French, 1967-73; Northern Illinois University, DeKalb, associate professor of French, 1973-80; Megatek Corp., San Diego, Calif., senior editor, 1981—. Operator of an editorial consulting service in San Diego. Member of DeKalb County Democratic Party's central committee and precinct committeeman, 1976-79. *Military service:* U.S. Army, counterintelligence agent, 1956-59; served in France.

MEMBER: Modern Language Association of America, American Association of Teachers of French, San Diego Independent Scholars (co-founder; vice-president, 1982—). *Awards, honors:* Fulbright grant for research at Institut de Professeurs de Francais a l'Etranger, 1962-63; Mellon Fund grant, 1968; Old Dominion Fund grant, summer, 1968; National Endowment for the Humanities grant, 1970-71.

WRITINGS: Malraux's Heroes and History, Northern Illinois University Press, 1975; *Glossary of Computer Graphics,* Megatek, 1983. Also adapter and translator of Pierre Le Rouzic, *Un prenom pour la vie,* Bantam. Contributor to language, literature, and computer journals, and to travel publications.

WORK IN PROGRESS: Amica Gallia, a history-travelogue on France using ''annaliste'' interpretation; *Treating Mental Illness,* with Rodrigo Munoz.

SIDELIGHTS: James W. Greenlee writes: ''I am particularly interested in investigating the individual's role in history. My first book treated Malraux's attempts to make history a surrogate religion. My current work focuses on history associated with significant historical sites in France. I am an acknowledged Francophile, spend as much time as possible in Paris.''

*   *   *

GREGOR, Arthur   1923-

PERSONAL: Born November 18, 1923, in Vienna, Austria;

came to United States c. 1938; surname legally changed; son of Benjamin and Regine (Reiss) Goldenberg. *Education:* Newark College of Engineering, B.S., 1945. *Religion:* Jewish. *Home:* 131 West 78th St., New York, N.Y. 10024. *Office:* Department of English, Hofstra University, Hempstead, N.Y. 11550.

CAREER: Electronic Transformer Corp., New York City, engineer, 1947-54; Whitney Publications, New York City, technical editor, 1956-61; Macmillan Co. (publishers), New York City, senior editor, 1962-70; California State University, Hayward, visiting professor, 1972-73; Hofstra University, Hempstead, N.Y., professor of English, 1974—. Has given poetry readings at Guggenheim Museum under the auspices of the Academy of American Poets, at Poetry Center in New York, at New York University, Bard College, Princeton University, University of Illinois, Brown University, University of California, for other groups, and over radio and television. *Member:* Authors League of America, P.E.N. *Awards, honors:* First Appearance Prize of *Poetry* Magazine, 1947; first prize for play, "Fire," in University of Illinois competition, 1952.

WRITINGS: "Fire" (play), first produced in Urbana at University of Illinois Arts Festival, 1952; *Octavian Shooting Targets* (poems), Dodd, 1954; *The Little Elephant* (children's book), Harper, 1956; *Declensions of a Refrain* (poems), Dodd, 1957; *1 2 3 4 5* (verses for children), Lippincott, 1957; *Animal Babies* (children's book), Harper, 1958; *Basic Movements* (poems), Gyre Press (limited edition), 1966; *Figure in the Door* (poems), Doubleday, 1968; *A Bed by the Sea* (poems), Doubleday, 1970; *Selected Poems,* Doubleday, 1971; *The Past Now: New Poems,* Doubleday, 1975; *Embodiment and Other Poems,* Sheep Meadow Press, 1982; *A Longing in the Land: Memoir of a Quest,* Schocken, 1983.

Contributor: Alfredo Rizzardi, editor, *Poesia Americana del Dopoguerra,* [Milan], 1960; Horace Gregory and Marya Zaturenska, editors, *The Crystal Cabinet,* Holt, 1962; *125th Anniversary Anthology,* Dodd, 1964; Horace Gregory and Marya Zaturenska, editors, *The Silver Swan,* Holt, 1966; *The American Judaism Reader,* Abelard, 1966; *Best Poems of 1966,* Pacific Books, 1967; *Best Poems of 1969,* Pacific Books, 1969; Hayden Carruth, editor, *The Voice That Is Great Within Us,* Bantam, 1969.

The New Yorker Anthology of Poems, Viking, 1970; *The New York Times Book of Verse,* Macmillan, 1970; Louis Kronenberger, editor, *Atlantic Brief Lives,* Little, Brown, 1971; C. F. Main and Peter J. Seng, editors, *Poems,* Wadsworth, 1973; Stanley and Gillespie, editors, *The Treehouse,* Winthrop, 1974; Jean Garrigue, editor, *Love's Aspects,* Doubleday, 1975; Nancy Sullivan, editor, *The Treasury of American Poetry,* Doubleday, 1978; Edward Field, editor, *A Geography of Poets,* Bantam, 1979; Schwartz and Rudolf, editors, *Voices within the Ark,* Avon, 1980; David Ray, editor, *A to Z,* Swallow Press, 1981.

Contributor to periodicals, including *New Yorker, Commentary, New York Times, Esquire, Harper's* and *Sewanee Review.*

SIDELIGHTS: "We are refreshed to find a mystical poet who still speaks to us about his experience with assurance of candor and simplicity," writes Hayden Carruth. In his *Nation* review of Arthur Gregor's *Basic Movements* he states: "For [the poet], metaphor remains all of poetry; . . . no direct re-creation of mystical intuition is possible. Hence most of his failures are poems in which he succumbs to the risk of metaphor and crosses over entirely into symbolism, the manipulation of 'objective correlatives,' while his successes are poems in which he lets

his objects speak for themselves. Or perhaps we should say, more accurately, that his successes come from the times when his dream, his vision, has presented itself in sufficiently concrete terms. Given the abstractness of the human mind, such occasions are bound to be rare.''

Gregor is often noted for the introspective quality of his poetry; he has been compared to Rainer Maria Rilke and Hugo von Hofmannsthal. In the *Yale Review,* Laurence Lieberman suggests that Gregor has "evolved a poetic manner that serves as a frictionless conveyor for his thought. Ideas in the poems are as inseparable from the style of their expression as wave from water, wind from air. Because Gregor's work is more a poetry of ideas than we are accustomed to reading today, it is easy enough to make the mistake of dismissing him as merely a philosopher-in-verse. But these poems are not doctrinaire; rather, they employ ideas as one of many elements in the service of projecting an inner luminosity of being. Philosophy is subordinate to the stream of intensely devotional feeling running throughout most of the poems.''

The poetry in Gregor's *A Bed by the Sea,* according to *Sewanee Review* critic H. T. Kirby-Smith, Jr., "appears to be a record of a kind of voyage of the soul—which coincides with a good deal of actual travel. In the course of his meditations, Gregor seems to be considering the question of where to live, in the mind as well as in the world, and he entertains alternatives which are all escapes of one kind or another. . . . Travel poems are, of course, perfect vehicles for such meditations. Much of the charm of travel is its endless superficiality, the emotional relief of knowing nothing whatever of the lives of the persons one encounters.''

The Past Now: New Poems has elicited praise from critics Philip Dacey and Josephine Jacobsen. Dacey, writing in *Prairie Schooner,* notes that Gregor is "famous for his expression of the tension in man created by the opposing lures of the postlapsarian world and the absolute world of Otherness." Dacey calls *The Past Now* "a gripping, dramatic record of a man living between the two outposts of hope and despair" and thinks the poet's work "is the unimpugnable testimony of a pilgrim." "In Gregor's work, the past is never the past," comments Jacobsen in *Nation.* "It is alive in every aspect of the poem. The danger for poetry which has a strong spiritual force at its center is that the poems may become remote from the immediate and tangible. Gregor's most impressive accomplishment is his ability to make the spiritual intensely apprehended by the senses.''

BIOGRAPHICAL/CRITICAL SOURCES: Arthur Gregor, *Basic Movements,* Gyre Press (limited edition), 1966; *Nation,* November 6, 1967, May 15, 1972, October 9, 1976; *Choice,* April, 1968; *Commonweal,* June 21, 1968; *Hudson Review,* summer, 1968, spring, 1978; *Yale Review,* summer, 1968; *Poetry,* October, 1968, January, 1973; *New York Times,* December 11, 1971; *Modern Poetry Studies,* Volume II, number 5, 1971; *Sewanee Review,* summer, 1972; *Prairie Schooner,* winter, 1972, winter, 1976; *Spirit,* spring/summer, 1975; *Contemporary Literary Criticism,* Volume IX, Gale, 1978; *Washington Post Book World,* August 24, 1983.

*   *   *

GREGOR, Lee
See POHL, Frederik

GREGORIOS, Paulos Mar 1922-
(T. Paul Verghese)

PERSONAL: Original name Thadikkal Paul Verghese; name legally changed on becoming bishop in Syrian Orthodox Church, 1975; born August 9, 1922, in Tripunithura, India; son of Thadikkal Piely and Aley (Piely) Verghese. *Education:* Goshen College, B.A., 1952; Princeton Theological Seminary, S.T.M., 1960; additional study at Oxford University, 1960-61, and Gregory of Nyssa Institute, Muenster, Germany; Serampore University, D.Th., 1975. *Address:* Orthodox Theological Seminary, P.O. Box 98, Kottayam, Kerala 686002, India; and St. Gregorios Orthodox Church, B-2 Janakpuri, New Delhi 110058, India.

CAREER: Malabar Mail, Malabar, India, staff reporter, 1938-42; Indian Posts and Telegraphs, Travancore and Cochin, staff member, 1942-45, associate secretary, 1945-47; Ethiopian Ministry of Education, Addis Ababa, teacher, 1947-50; general secretary of Orthodox Student Movement of India, 1955-57; member of personal staff of Emperor Haile Sellasie of Ethiopia, 1956-59; ordained priest of Syrian Orthodox Church in India, 1961, became bishop, 1975, and later Metropolitan of Delhi; World Council of Churches, Geneva, Switzerland, associate general secretary and director of Division of Ecumenical Action, 1962-67; Orthodox Theological Seminary, Kottayam, Kerala, India, principal, 1967—. Honorary lecturer at Union Christian College, 1954-56, University College of Addis Ababa, 1956-59, and Leningrad Theological Academy; Hein Memorial Lecturer in the United States, 1968; Mary Louise Illif Distinguished Visiting Lecturer in Denver, Colo., 1978; Dudley Lecturer at Harvard University, 1979; distinguished visiting professor at College of Wooster, 1981; has lectured at numerous universities throughout the world.

Observer of Second Vatican Council, 1963-65; member of Joint Working Group, Roman Catholic Church-World Council of Churches, 1963-75; World Council of Churches, leader of delegation to UNESCO, 1966, and to Heads of African States, 1968, member of Faith and Order Commission, 1968-75, member of central and executive committees, chairman of World Conference on Faith, Science, and the Future, 1979, president, 1983—; secretary for inter-church relations and member of standing committee, Orthodox Episcopal Synod; chairman of Federated Faculty for Research in Religion and Culture, Kerala, and of Oriental Orthodox Curriculum Committee; organizer and chairman of inter-faith conferences and symposia. Advisor to Ethiopian Ministry of Education, 1957-59.

MEMBER: International Society for Metaphysics, International Society for Neoplatonic Studies, International Biographical Association (fellow), Association of Humanist Psychologists, Christian Peace Conference (vice-president), Societas Liturgica (founder), Gregory of Nyssa Society, Comparative Education Society in Europe, Association of Christian Philosophers of India, Indian Institute of World Culture, India International Centre, Indian Philosophical Congress, Indo-Soviet Cultural Society, Indo-Cuba Friendship Society, All India Peace and Solidarity Organization, Kerala Philosophical Congress, Pro Oriente, Serampore University Council.

AWARDS, HONORS: Certificate of merit from *Dictionary of International Biography,* for "distinguished service and inspired leadership of the World Church"; member of Order of St. Vladimir, Soviet Union, and Order of St. Mary Magdalene, Poland; D.Th. from Leningrad Theological Academy, Lu-

theran Theological Academy, Budapest, Hungary, Jan Hus Faculty, Prague, Czechoslovakia, and Comenius Faculty, Prague.

WRITINGS: The Quest for Certainty, Sophia Publications, 1975; (editor and contributor) *Burning Issues,* Sophia Publications, 1977; (editor and contributor) *Science and Our Future,* Christian Literature Society, 1978; *The Human Presence: An Orthodox View of Nature,* World Council of Churches, 1978; *Truth without Tradition?,* Sri Venkateswara University, 1978; (editor and contributor) *Faith, Science, and the Future,* World Council of Churches, 1978; *Science for Sane Societies,* Christian Literature Society, 1980; *Cosmic Man: The Divine Presence,* Sophia Publications, 1980; (editor and contributor) *Does Chalcedon Divide or Unite?: Towards Convergence in Orthodox Christology,* World Council of Churches, 1981; *The Orthodox Church in India: An Overview,* Sophia Publications, 1982.

Under name T. Paul Verghese: (Editor) *Education and the Nature of Man,* World Council of Churches, 1965; (co-editor) *Report of Conversations between Oriental Orthodox and Eastern Orthodox Theologians,* Greek Orthodox Theological Review, 1965; *The Joy of Freedom: Eastern Worship and Modern Man,* John Knox, 1967; *The Gospel of the Kingdom,* Christian Literature Society, 1968; *Be Still and Know* (nine addresses and meditations), Christian Literature Society, 1971; *Freedom of Man: An Inquiry into Some Roots of the Tension between Freedom and Authority in Our Society,* Westminster, 1972; (editor and contributor) *Koptisches Christentum: Die Orthodoxen Kirchen Agyptens und Athiopiens,* Evangelisches Verlagswerk, 1973; *Die Syrischen Kirchen in Indien,* Evangelisches Verlagswerk, 1974; *Freedom and Authority,* Christian Literature Society, 1974. Also author of *Pretres et Pasleurs,* 1968.

Contributor of hundreds of articles to periodicals. Editor, *Journal of Christian Colleges in India, Star of the East,* and *Purohitan.*

SIDELIGHTS: Paulos Mar Gregorios is competent in French, Greek, Hebrew, and Aramaic.

*   *   *

GROSS, Martin (Arnold) 1934-

PERSONAL: Born June 23, 1934, in New York, N.Y. *Education:* Hunter College (now Hunter College of the City University of New York), B.A., 1956.

CAREER: Advertising copywriter.

WRITINGS: Feature Writer's Passport to the Travel Market, Gross, 1959; (with Ted Sennett) *Are You Sure You're Kosher?,* Paul Eriksson, 1964; *The Nostalgia Quiz Book,* Arlington House, 1969.

The Nostalgic Quiz Book #2, Arlington House, 1974; *The Nostalgic Quiz Book #3,* New American Library, 1976; *The Official Movie Trivia Quiz Book #2,* New American Library, 1978.†

*   *   *

GUEST, Barbara 1920-

PERSONAL: Born September 6, 1920, in Wilmington, N.C.; daughter of James Harvey and Ann (Hetzel) Pinson; married Lord Stephen Haden-Guest, 1949 (divorced, 1954); married Trumbull Higgins (a military historian), August, 1954; children: (first marriage) Hadley; (second marriage) Jonathan van Lennep. *Education:* Attended University of California, Los Angeles; University of California, Berkeley, B.A., 1943. *Home:* 116 Meeting House Lane, Southampton, N.Y. 11968.

CAREER: Writer and painter. *Art News,* New York, N.Y., associate editor, 1951-54. *Member:* P.E.N., Poetry Society of America (member of board of governors, 1983-84). *Awards, honors:* Yaddo fellowship, 1958; Longview Award, Longview Foundation, 1960, for *The Location of Things;* National Endowment for the Arts fellow, 1980.

WRITINGS: The Location of Things (poems), Tibor de Nagy Press, 1960; (with B. H. Friedman) *Robert Goodnough, Painter,* Musee de Poche, 1962; *Poems: The Location of Things, Archaics, The Open Skies,* Doubleday, 1963; *The Blue Stairs* (poems), Corinth Books, 1968; (with Shiela Isham) *I Ching: Poems and Lithographs,* Mourlot, 1969; *Moscow Mansions* (poems), Viking, 1973; *The Countess from Minneapolis* (poems), Burning Deck, 1976; *Seeking Air* (novel), Black Sparrow Press, 1978; *The Turner Losses* (poems), Mansfield Press (Montreal), 1980; *Biography* (poems), Burning Deck, 1981; *Quilts* (poems), Vehicle Editions, 1981.

Plays: "The Ladies Choice," produced in New York at Artists Theatre, 1953; "The Office," produced in New York at Cafe Chino, 1961; "Port," produced in New York at American Theatre for Poets, 1965.

WORK IN PROGRESS: Herself Defined: The Poet H. D. and Her World, for Doubleday.

SIDELIGHTS: Barbara Guest told *CA* that her interest in painting strongly affects her poetry. Anthony Manousos describes this influence in the *Dictionary of Literary Biography:* "Guest's poetry may be viewed as the logical extension of Imagism into abstract expressionism. Avoiding traditional metrics and forms, her poems are verbal collages that juxtapose objects, shapes, colors, and experiences in striking and often disconcerting ways. . . . Given this preoccupation with verbal elements as objects that can be arranged to dazzle, astonish, and move the reader in their own right, it is not surprising that many of her poems ultimately are concerned with the process of composition, the act of imaginative transformation through language."

Also reflected in her work, indicates Guest, is her interest in overseas travel. Manousos confirms that, "although her poetry tends to be urbane, cosmopolitan, and refined, it also suggests the psychological dislocations and restless imagination of the perpetual traveler." He concludes: "Guest's poetry will continue to make its presence felt among those who are moved by the play of language for its own sake. She seems serenely confident in her calling, willing to go her own way despite the fads and political pressures of her age."

BIOGRAPHICAL/CRITICAL SOURCES: Poetry, March, 1969, April, 1974; *Virginia Quarterly Review,* winter, 1969; *American Book Review,* summer, 1978; *The New Fiction,* Kennikat Press, 1978; *Washington Post Book World,* April 16, 1978; *Dictionary of Literary Biography,* Volume V, Gale, 1980.

*   *   *

GUINTHER, John 1927-

PERSONAL: Born April 3, 1927, in Reading, Pa.; son of Earl (a bookkeeper) and Mary Guinther; married Elaine McCabe, September 3, 1954 (deceased); children: Carol. *Education:* Kutztown State Teachers College (now Kutztown State Col-

lege), B.S., 1948. *Home:* 2528 Lombard, Philadelphia, Pa. 19146. *Office:* 1420 Walnut St., Suite 1420, Philadelphia, Pa. 19102.

CAREER: Writer. Previously held various jobs ranging from raising show dogs to selling advertising. Instructor in investigative journalism at Charles Morris Price School, Philadelphia, 1977—; visiting professor at Temple University, 1974, 1976, 1977, 1982, 1983. Active in early civil rights movement in Washington, D.C., late 1940s and early 1950s; active in political reform movements in Philadelphia, Pa., 1950s until 1971; co-founder of New Democratic Coalition, Philadelphia, 1968-69.

AWARDS, HONORS: Robert F. Kennedy Memorial Award from Robert F. Kennedy Foundation, 1973, for best magazine article of the year on the problems of the disadvantaged American, for "The Only Good Indian"; four Silver Gavel Awards from American Bar Association, 1974-80, for articles on justice system; best magazine article award from Sigma Delta Chi, 1975, for two-part study on investigative grand juries; Gerald Loeb Award for distinguished writing on business and finance from Loeb Memorial Foundation, 1976, for article, "Don't Worry, It's Only Money."

WRITINGS: Moralists and Managers: Public Interest Movements in America, Doubleday, 1976; *The Malpractitioners,* Doubleday, 1978; *Winning Your Personal Injury Suit,* Doubleday, 1980; *Philadelphia: A Dream for the Keeping* (history), Continental Heritage, 1982. Author of documentary scripts for WCAU/CBS Television. Contributor of more than 100 articles to newspapers and magazines. Contributing editor of *Philadelphia.*

WORK IN PROGRESS: A social history of American revolutionary period.

*   *   *

GUTHRIE, William Keith Chambers 1906-1981

PERSONAL: Born August 1, 1906, in London, England, died May 17, 1981; son of Charles Jameson and Catherine Guthrie; married Adele Marion Ogilvy, June 10, 1933; children: Robert, Anne (deceased). *Education:* Trinity College, Cambridge, B.A., 1928, M.A., 1931. *Home:* 3 Roman Hill, Barton, Cambridge CB3 7AX, England.

CAREER: Member of research expeditions of the American Society for Archaeological Research in Asia Minor, 1929, 1930, 1932; Cambridge University, Cambridge, England, fellow of Peterhouse, 1930, 1932-57, university proctor, 1936-37, public orator of the university, 1939-57, P. M. Laurence Reader in Classics, 1947-53, Laurence Professor of Ancient Philosophy, 1957-73, master of Downing College, 1957-72. Messenger Lecturer at Cornell University, 1957; James B. Duke Visiting Professor of Philosophy at Duke University, 1966; Raymond Visiting Professor of Classics at State University of New York, Buffalo, 1974. *Military service:* British Army, Intelligence Corps, 1941-45; became temporary major.

MEMBER: Classical Association (president, 1967-68), British Academy (fellow). *Awards, honors:* Honorary fellow of Peterhouse, Cambridge, 1957, and Downing College, Cambridge, 1972; D.Litt. from University of Melbourne, 1957, and University of Sheffield, 1967; Litt.D. from Cambridge University, 1959.

WRITINGS: (With William Calder and W. H. Buckler) *Monumenta Asiae Minoris Antiqua,* Volume IV, Manchester University Press, 1933; *Orpheus and Greek Religion: A Study of the Orphic Movement,* Methuen, 1935, revised edition, Methuen, 1957, Norton, 1967; (editor and translator) *Aristotle De Caelo,* Harvard University Press, 1939.

The Greeks and Their Gods, Methuen, 1950, Beacon Press, 1951; *The Greek Philosophers from Thales to Aristotle,* Methuen, 1950, reprinted, Harper, 1975; (editor and contributor) F. M. Cornford, *The Unwritten Philosophy and Other Essays,* Cambridge University Press, 1950, reprinted, 1967; *Greek Philosophy: The Hub and the Spokes,* Cambridge University Press, 1953; *Myth and Reason,* London School of Economics and Political Science, University of London, 1953; *In the Beginning: Some Greek Views on the Origins of Life and the Early State of Man,* Cornell University Press, 1956; (translator) Plato, *Protagoras and Meno,* Penguin, 1956; (contributor) *Recherches sur la tradition platonicienne* (title means "Investigation of the Platonic Tradition"), Entretiens Hardt, 1957; *Socrates and Plato,* University of Queensland Press, 1958.

(With B. A. Van Gronigen) *Tradition and Personal Achievement in Classical Antiquity,* Athlone Press, 1960; *A History of Greek Philosophy,* Cambridge University Press, Volume I: *The Early Presocratics and the Pythagoreans,* 1962, Volume II: *The Presocratic Tradition from Parmenides to Democritus,* 1965, Volume III: *The Fifth Century Enlightenment,* 1969 (also published separately; see below), Volume IV: *Plato: The Man and His Dialogues, Earlier Period,* 1975, Volume V: *The Later Plato and the Academy,* 1978, Volume VI: *Aristotle: An Encounter,* 1981; *Twentieth Century Approaches to Plato,* Princeton University Press for University of Cincinnati, 1967.

Socrates (first half of *The Fifth Century Enlightenment*), Cambridge University Press, 1971; *The Sophists* (second half of *The Fifth Century Enlightenment*), Cambridge University Press, 1971; (translator) Malcolm Brown, *Plato's Meno, with Essays,* Bobbs-Merrill, 1971.

Contributor to *Cambridge Ancient History.* Contributor to professional journals.

SIDELIGHTS: William Keith Chambers Guthrie, historian of Greek philosophy and professor at Cambridge University, was the author of several scholarly works on ancient Greek tradition and was noted in particular for his six-volume series *A History of Greek Philosophy.* "His forte was the exposition in books and lectures of the systems of the ancients and of the evidence for them," according to his *London Times* obituary. "[He] was the master of an usually lucid and persuasive style, both in speech and writing, and all that he said or wrote was marked by sobriety of judgment, ample knowledge, and complete absence of flamboyance."

Times Literary Supplement critic J. L. Ackrell recalled Guthrie's writing style in a review of Volume VI of *A History of Greek Philosophy.* "In a preface to the first volume [the author] listed the qualities and powers which the ideal writer of a large-scale history of Greek philosophy would need, and he modestly disclaimed their possession," wrote Ackrell. "[Guthrie] has in fact displayed them in large measure. Moreover, his history has been free of the two commonest weaknesses of multi-volumed professorial tractates, dullness and dogmatism: he has always been interesting, and he has always kept the argument open and made it clear that the truth is difficult to discover. A final conspicuous feature of the *History* is its good temper: Guthrie is appreciative of the work of others, and courteous even when in strong disagreement."

Towards the end of the sixth volume of *A History of Greek Philosophy,* Guthrie quoted Aristotle, who, discussing logic, said: "If, when you look at it, this discipline appears to you in pretty good shape . . . when compared with other subjects which have grown up over the generations, then the only thing left for all of you who have followed the lectures is to pardon any omissions—and be heartily grateful for what has been discovered." "The writing of a multi-volumed history of Greek philosophy in English," concluded Ackrill, "is, like the invention of logic, an unusual achievement. Any omissions will be certainly pardoned; and generations of students will be heartily grateful for Professor Guthrie's *magnum opus.*"

BIOGRAPHICAL/CRITICAL SOURCES: Times Literary Supplement, April 30, 1970, December 12, 1975, August 25, 1978, November 6, 1981; William Keith Chambers Guthrie, *A History of Greek Philosophy,* Volume VI: *Aristotle: An Encounter,* Cambridge University Press, 1981.

OBITUARIES: London Times, May 18, 1981.†

H

H.M.S.
See KIRK-GREENE, Anthony (Hamilton Millard)

*   *   *

HAHNER, June E(dith) 1940-

PERSONAL: Born July 8, 1940, in New York, N.Y.; daughter of Fred (a businessman) and Edith (Konrad) Hahner. *Education:* Earlham College, A.B., 1961; Cornell University, M.A., 1963, Ph.D., 1966. *Office:* Department of History, State University of New York at Albany, 1400 Washington Ave., Albany, N.Y. 12222.

CAREER: Texas Technological University (now Texas Tech University), Lubbock, assistant professor of history, 1966-68; lecturer in Peace Corps training programs for Latin America, 1966; State University of New York at Albany, professor of history, 1968—, first director, Women's Studies Program. Has lectured on the subject of Brazilian women at universities in Brazil and Japan. *Member:* American Historical Association, Conference on Latin American History, Latin American Studies Association, Conference Group on Modern Portugal, New York State Latin Americanists, Coordinating Committee on Women in the Historical Profession, Conference Group in Women's History, New England Council of Latin American Studies.

AWARDS, HONORS: Organization of American States fellowship for research in Brazil, 1963, 1970; American Philosophical Society grant for research in Brazil, 1968, 1970; State University of New York Foundation grant for research in Brazil, 1969, 1970, 1971, 1974; National Endowment for the Humanities grant, 1971, 1982-83; Calouste Gulbenkian Foundation grant for research in Portugal, 1977; Fulbright Commission research and teaching award (Brazil), 1980.

WRITINGS: Civilian-Military Relations in Brazil, 1889-1898, University of South Carolina Press, 1969; (editor) *Women in Latin American History: Their Lives and Views,* University of California at Los Angeles Latin American Center, 1976, revised edition, 1981; (editor) *A Mulher Brasileira,* Editora Civilizacao Brasileira, 1978; *A Mulher Brasileira e Suas Lutas Sociais e Politicas, 1850-1937,* Editora Brasiliense, 1981. Contributor to journals in the United States and Brazil. Area editor, *Modern Brazilian;* member of editorial board, *The Americas,* 1974—.

WORK IN PROGRESS: A book on urban groups and politics in late nineteenth-century and early twentieth-century Brazil.

SIDELIGHTS: June E. Hahner is fluent in Portuguese and Spanish. She has spent extended periods in Colombia and Brazil and has traveled extensively throughout most of Latin America.

*   *   *

HALLINAN, P(atrick) K(enneth) 1944-

PERSONAL: Born November 1, 1944, in Los Angeles, Calif.; son of Kenneth Frank (a salesman) and Marguerite (Rommel) Hallinan; children: Kenneth P., Michael T. *Education:* Attended University of California, Berkeley, 1962, Foothill College, 1963-65, and California State University, Northridge, 1969. *Politics:* Republican. *Home:* 630 Law St., San Diego, Calif. 92109.

CAREER: J. C. Penney & Co., Saratoga, Calif., sporting goods manager, 1967-69; Lockheed Aircraft Corp., Burbank, Calif., project scheduler, 1969-72; Attal, Champion & Associates Advertising, San Diego, Calif., copy writer, 1973-74; Rohr Industries (aerospace manufacturing), Chula Vista, Calif., expediter, 1974-76; writer, 1976-77; marketing communications manager, Topaz, Inc., 1977—.

WRITINGS—All self-illustrated children's books; published by Children's Press, except as indicated: *How Really Great to Walk This Way,* 1972; *The Looking Book,* 1973; *We're Very Good Friends, My Brother and I,* 1973; *Just Being Alone,* 1976; *That's What a Friend Is,* 1977; *I'm Glad to Be Me,* 1977; *Where's Michael?,* 1978; *I'm Thankful Each Day,* Ideals Publishing, 1980; *Just Open a Book,* 1980.

WORK IN PROGRESS: God's Here, I Know, a self-illustrated children's book for Ideals Publishing.

SIDELIGHTS: P. K. Hallinan writes *CA:* "From the very first time I ever attempted to write and illustrate for children, I was fascinated by children's incredible animation. I also felt strongly that a children's book should be completely honest; that the value presented not be masked behind impossible, imaginary creatures. For this reason, I never write about talking animals or dancing refrigerators. I state the truth as well as I can and then try to capture the spirit of it with my cartoons. And then, if my kids laugh at my manuscript, I figure I'm doing okay."

HALLIWELL, David (William) 1936-
(Johnson Arms)

PERSONAL: Born July 31, 1936, in Brighouse, Yorkshire, England; son of Herbert (a managing director of a textile firm) and Ethel (Spencer) Halliwell. *Education:* Attended Huddersfield College of Art, 1953-59; Royal Academy of Dramatic Art, diploma, 1961. *Politics:* Libertarian Socialist. *Home:* 28 Chepstow Court, Chepstow Crescent, London W11 3ED, England. *Agent:* Phil Kelvin, Goodwin Associates, 19 London St., London W2 1HL, England.

CAREER: Actor in Nottingham, England, 1962, Stoke-on-Trent, England, 1962-63, and London, England, 1963-67; Quipu Productions, London, co-founder and director, 1966-76; director of plays in London at New Arts Theatre, 1966-67, at Little Theatre, 1971-73, at Bankside Globe Theatre, 1974, and at New End Theatre, 1975; director for productions of other managements, in Edinburgh, Scotland, at Traverse Theatre, 1971, in London for National Theatre at Young Vic Theatre, 1975, at Royal Court, 1976-77, at Kingston Overground Theatre, 1978, and in Sheffield, England, at Sheffield Crucible, 1978; director at Old Red Lion, 1982. Visiting fellow, University of Reading, 1970; resident dramatist, Royal Court, 1976-77, Hampstead Theatre, 1978-79. Interviewer for Thames Television "Question '68" show, 1968. *Member:* Equity, Writers Guild of Great Britain (member of radio committee, 1982—), Theatre Writers Union (member of negotiating team, 1976-82), Dramatists Club, Alibi Club. *Awards, honors:* Named most promising playwright by *Evening Standard,* 1966, for *Little Malcolm and His Struggle against the Eunuchs;* John Whiting Award, 1978, for "Prejudice" (later retitled "Creatures of Another Kind").

WRITINGS—Plays: *Hail Scrawdyke* (produced in New York, 1966), Grove, 1966 (published in England as *Little Malcolm and His Struggle against the Eunuchs* [produced in London at Unity Theatre, March 30, 1965], Samuel French, 1966); *A Discussion,* Faber, 1968.

Muck from Three Angles, Faber, 1970; *K. D. Dufford Hears K. D. Dufford Ask K. D. Dufford How K. D. Dufford'll Make K. D. Dufford* (first produced in London at Lambda Theatre, 1969), Faber, 1970; *A Who's Who of Flapland and Other Plays,* Faber, 1971; "An Amour, and a Feast" (first produced in London at Little Theatre, January, 1972), published in *Fun Art Bus Book,* Methuen, 1971; "Meriel the Ghost Girl" (first produced as a television play, 1976, produced at Old Red Lion, 1982), published in *The Mind Beyond* (anthology), Penguin, 1976; *The House,* Methuen, 1979. Also author, under pseudonym Johnson Arms, of *They Travelled by Tube* (biographies of notable people who moved by means of London's Underground), Butterworth.

Unpublished plays: (With David Calderisi) "The Experiment," first produced in London at New Arts Theatre, January 16, 1967; "The Girl Who Didn't Like Answers," first produced in London at Mercury Theatre, June 29, 1971; "A Last Belch for the Great Auk," first produced at Mercury Theatre, 1971; "Bleats from a Brighouse Pleasureground," first produced at Little Theatre, 1972; "Janitress Thrilled by a Prehensile Penis," first produced at Little Theatre, 1972; "An Altercation," first produced in London at the Covent Garden Street Festival, 1973; "The Freckled Bum" (first play of quartet), first produced in London at Bankside Globe Theatre, 1974;

"Minyip" (second play of quartet), first produced in London at Bankside Globe Theatre, 1974.

"Progs" (third play of quartet), first produced at British Drama League, 1975; "A Process of Elimination" (final play of quartet), first produced at the Howff, 1975; "Prejudice" (later retitled "Creatures of Another Kind"), first produced in Sheffield at Sheffield Crucible, 1978; "A Rite Kwik Metal Tata," first produced in Sheffield at Sheffield Crucible, 1979; "Was It Her?," first produced at Old Red Lion, 1982.

Also author of television plays, including "A Plastic Mac in Winter," 1963, "Cock, Hen and Courting Pit," 1966, "Triptych of Bathroom Users," 1972, "Blur and Blank via Checkheaton," 1972, "Triple Exposure," 1972, "Steps Back," 1972, "Daft Mam Blues," 1976, "Pigmented Patter," 1976, "Treewomen of Jagden Crag," 1976, and "There's a Car Park in Witherton." Also author of radio plays, "Spongehenge," 1982, and "Grandad's House," for British Broadcasting Corp.

WORK IN PROGRESS: A play for Harlech Television, "a conjectural psychology of and psychological conjecture about George Orwell."

SIDELIGHTS: David Halliwell told *CA:* "A very basic motivating factor in my career has been a compulsion to surpass other people in some way (accompanied by a compulsion to be inferior to them). When I was an art student, I realised I had no chance of surpassing other students as a graphic artist, and so I turned to the theatre, writing and acting in revue sketches. I work out the overall framework of a play in my head before I write a single word. This often takes longer than the writing. Then I write numerous drafts, each one a development on its predecessor, until I have a producible text. I revise this text during rehearsal.

"I like to direct my own plays in the theatre, and I believe that the writing and directing of a play are both parts of the same task, given that the playwright is an experienced director. The opinion that a playwright is incapable of . . . directing his or her own work is a prejudice, an artificial separation not found in any other medium. In addition to directing my own plays, I have directed plays by Pinter, Shaw, Tony Connor, and Brian Friel, amongst others. I perform in my own plays and those of other playwrights. . . .

"My advice to aspiring dramatists is: listen to people talking wherever you are. My own main interest as a playwright is the psychology underlying behaviour. I have been influenced by many people. By other writers, including Sean O'Casey, D. H. Lawrence, George Orwell, James Joyce, Norman Mailer, Samuel Beckett, Harold Pinter, and Sigmund Freud, but more by artists in other disciplines, including Charles Chaplin, George Burns, Bix Beiderbeck, Tommy Ladnier, Charles Parker, and Charles Mingus."

MEDIA ADAPTATIONS: Hail Scrawdyke was used as the basis for the film, "The Movement," in 1970.

BIOGRAPHICAL/CRITICAL SOURCES: New Statesman, September 26, 1969; *Plays and Players,* October, 1970; *Time Out,* November, 1981; *City Limits,* November, 1981; *Event,* November, 1981.

*   *   *

HAM, Wayne 1938-

PERSONAL: Born May 13, 1938, in Toronto, Ontario, Canada; son of Albert F. and Edna (Dempster) Ham; married Marliene

Miller, December 24, 1959; children: Terry Russell, Brian Neal. *Education:* Graceland College, B.A., 1959; Brigham Young University, M.A., 1961; College of the Siskiyous, graduate study, 1962; St. Paul's School of Theology, M.Div., 1969; Central Missouri State College (now University), teaching certificate, 1970; University of Florida, Ph.D., 1977. *Religion:* Reorganized Church of Jesus Christ of Latter Day Saints. *Home address:* Box 1059, Independence, Mo. 64051.

CAREER: High school teacher of Spanish, German, and Latin in Dunsmuir, Calif., 1961-62; University of Valle, Cali, Colombia, assistant professor of English, 1962-63; Reorganized Church of Jesus Christ of Latter Day Saints, Independence, Mo., member of department of religious education, 1963-70; Florida School System, Sumter County, supervisor, 1970-80; Temple School, Independence, Mo., administrator, 1980-82; Reorganized Church of Jesus Christ of Latter Day Saints, program services director, 1982—.

WRITINGS—All published by Herald House: *Enriching Your New Testament Studies,* 1966; *Man's Living Religions,* 1967; *Call to Covenant,* 1970; *Publish Glad Tidings,* 1970; *Yesterday's Horizons,* 1975; *More than Burnt Offerings,* 1978.

*   *   *

HAMILTON, Gail
See CORCORAN, Barbara

*   *   *

HAMLEY, Dennis 1935-

PERSONAL: Born October 14, 1935, in Crockham Hill, Kent, England; son of Charles Richard (a post office engineer) and Doris May (Payne) Hamley; married Agnes Moylan (a nurse), August 6, 1965; children: Peter Richard John, Mary Elizabeth Carmel. *Education:* Jesus College, Cambridge, M.A., 1959; University of Bristol, P.G.C.E., 1960; University of Manchester, diploma in advanced studies in education, 1965; University of Leicester, Ph.D. *Politics:* "Generally leftward inclined. But hating Communism, despairing of Labour Party and not impressed with Social Democratic Party, wondering how one can take the political process seriously anymore." *Religion:* "Lapsed Anglican, but still with Christian belief." *Home:* "Hillside," 2 King's Rd., Hertfordshire SG13 7EY, England. *Office:* Education Department, County Hall, Hertfordshire SG13 8DF, England.

CAREER: English master at grammar and secondary modern schools in England, 1960-67; Milton Keynes College of Education, Bletchley, Milton Keynes, England, lecturer, 1967-69, senior lecturer in English, 1969-78; Hertfordshire Local Education Authority, Hertfordshire, England, county adviser for English and drama, 1978—. Counselor and tutor for Open University, 1971-78. *Military service:* Royal Air Force, 1954-56. *Member:* Society of Authors (chairman, educational writers group, beginning 1983), National Association of Educational Inspectors and Advisers.

WRITINGS: Three Towneley Plays (adapted into modern English), Heinemann, 1963; *Pageants of Despair* (novel for children; also see below), S. G. Phillips, 1974; (with Colin Field) *Fiction in the Middle School,* Batsford, 1975; *Very Far from Here* (novel for juveniles), Deutsch, 1976, Granada, 1979; *Landings,* Deutsch, 1979, Granada, 1981; (contributor) Jean Russell, editor, *The Methuen Book of Sinister Stories,* Methuen, 1982.

Adaptor into English texts; all written by Gian Paolo Ceserani; all published by Kestral: *The Travels of Columbus,* 1979; *The Travels of Livingstone,* 1979; *The Travels of Marco Polo,* 1980; *The Travels of Captain Cook,* 1980.

Author of two radio plays, "Pageants of Despair" (based on his novel of the same title), and "Court Jester," both for BBC-Radio, both 1979. Also author of "Julius Caesar, Study Guide and Cassette," Argo Records, 1980. Reviewer for *School Librarian.*

WORK IN PROGRESS: A book of nine ghost stories tentatively entitled *The Shirt off a Hanged Man's Back,* for Deutsch; *The Fourth Plane at the Fly-Past,* a children's novel.

SIDELIGHTS: Dennis Hamley writes that he has "always loved the art of narrative, but for many years as a listener, not a teller—until I started to write for myself, when I discovered that the end of a story is implicit in its beginning. If you begin it, you will end it. You don't always see the destination at the start of the journey, but you'll get there all right. This to me is now a simple fact which only writing as a sort of act of faith taught me. Not realizing it delayed my start as a writer of stories for many years because, try as I would—and I thought one had to—I could never work out a story before I started writing it.

"My own children, Peter and Mary, have always been helpful and assiduous critics. They've given advice I ignore at my peril, suggestions I always use, on occasions have changed the course of stories for me—always correctly. They—and a marvelous editor at Andre Deutsch—have been very good for me."

AVOCATIONAL INTERESTS: Music, railways, watching football, drama, camping, motoring.

*   *   *

HAMMER, Richard 1928-

PERSONAL: Born March 22, 1928, in Hartford, Conn.; son of Morris Harry and Mildred (Chaimson) Hammer; married Nina Ullman, November 27, 1955; married Arlene Nadel (an actress), November 24, 1970; children: (first marriage) Joshua I., Anthony G.; (second marriage) Allison R. (deceased), Emily C. *Education:* Syracuse University, A.B., 1950; Trinity College, Hartford, Conn., M.A., 1951; Columbia University, graduate study, 1951-53. *Politics:* Democrat. *Religion:* Jewish. *Agent:* Barna Ostertag, 501 Fifth Ave., New York, N.Y. 10017.

CAREER: National Broadcasting Co., New York City, news assistant, 1952-53; *Barron's Weekly,* New York City, associate editor, 1954-59; *Fortune,* New York City, associate editor, 1959-63; *New York Times,* New York City, member of editorial staff, 1963-72. *Member:* Authors League of America, P.E.N. American Center, Writers Guild of America East. *Awards, honors:* Academy Award for Best Documentary Short Subject, 1971, for "Interviews with My Lai Veterans"; nominated for National Book Award and Pulitzer Prize, 1972; Edgar Allan Poe Award, 1983, for *The Vatican Connection.*

WRITINGS—Nonfiction, except as indicated: *Between Life and Death,* Macmillan, 1969; *One Morning in the War: The Tragedy at Son My,* Coward-McCann, 1970; *The Court Martial of Lieutenant Calley,* Coward, 1971; (with Martin A. Gosch) *The Last Testament of Lucky Luciano,* Little, Brown, 1973.

Playboy's Illustrated History of Organized Crime, Playboy Press, 1975, Volume I: *Gangland U.S.A.: The Making of the Mob,* Volume II: *Hoodlum Empire: The Survival of the Syn-*

dicate; An End to Summer (novel), Carlyle Books, 1979; *Mr. Jacobson's War* (novel), Harcourt, 1981; *The Vatican Connection,* Holt, 1982.

Author-narrator of film, ''Interviews with My Lai Veterans''; author of screenplays and film treatments, including ''The Vatican Connection'' (based on his book of the same title), ''The Shadow Government,'' and ''Organized Crime.'' Contributor to periodicals, including *Playboy, New York Times Magazine, Harper's,* and *Nation.*

SIDELIGHTS: Richard Hammer's books have been translated into numerous languages, including Japanese, German, French, Italian, Dutch, and Spanish.

BIOGRAPHICAL/CRITICAL SOURCES: Washington Post Book World, November 7, 1982.

*   *   *

HANDEL, Gerald 1924-

PERSONAL: Born August 8, 1924, in Cleveland, Ohio; son of Louis and Pearl (Seidman) Handel; married Ruth Doman, February 5, 1956; children: Jonathan, Michael. *Education:* University of Chicago, A.B., 1947, A.M., 1951, Ph.D., 1962; additional graduate study at Michael Reese Hospital. *Office:* City College of the City University of New York, New York, N.Y. 10031.

CAREER: University of Chicago, Chicago, Ill., research associate and instructor, 1952-56; Social Research, Inc., Chicago, research associate, 1956-62, assistant director, 1962-65, vice-president, 1965-66; Center for Urban Education, New York City, senior research psychologist, 1966-67; City University of New York, City College and Graduate School, New York City, associate professor, 1967-72, professor of sociology, 1973—. *Member:* American Sociological Association, American Psychological Association, Eastern Sociological Society.

WRITINGS: (With Robert Hess) *Family Worlds,* University of Chicago Press, 1959; (with Lee Rainwater and Richard Coleman) *Workingman's Wife: Her Personality, World and Life Style,* Oceana, 1959; (editor) *The Psychosocial Interior of the Family,* Aldine, 1967, 2nd edition, 1972; (with Frederick Elkin) *The Child and Society: The Process of Socialization,* Random House, 1972, 3rd edition, 1978; *Social Welfare in Western Society,* Random House, 1982; (editor with Vernon Boggs and Sylvia F. Fava), *The Apple Sliced: Sociological Studies of New York City,* J. F. Bergin Publishers, 1983. Contributor to professional journals.

*   *   *

HANFORD, Lloyd D(avid) 1901-1979

PERSONAL: Born June 29, 1901, in San Francisco, Calif.; died in 1979; son of Albert J. (a merchant) and Blanche (Coblentz) Hirschfeld; married Elise Phillips, February 11, 1926. *Education:* University of California, Berkeley, A.B. *Office:* 47 Kearny St., San Francisco, Calif. 94108.

CAREER: Realtor; president, Property Management Company; consultant, San Francisco Redevelopment Agency for South of Market; former chairman of San Francisco Citizens Participation Committee for Urban Renewal. *Military service:* U.S. Army, Chemical Corps, 1940-42; became captain.

MEMBER: National Association of Real Estate Boards (member of board of directors, beginning 1959), Institute of Real

Estate Management (president, 1958), National Institute of Real Estate Brokers, American Society of Real Estate Counsellors, California Real Estate Association (member of board of directors, 1958-64), San Francisco Real Estate Board (president, 1954), San Francisco Chamber of Commerce, San Francisco Building Owners and Managers Association, Lambda Alpha.

WRITINGS—Published by Institute of Real Estate Management, except as indicated: (Co-author) *Investment Properties,* University of California Press, 1952; (co-author) *The Management Office: How to Operate It,* 1957; *Development and Management of Investment Property,* 1964, 3rd edition published as *Analysis and Management of Investment Property,* 1970; *Investing in Real Estate,* 1966; *The Economics of Apartment Construction* (monograph), National Association of Home Builders, 1969; *The Real Estate Dollar,* 1969; *Feasibility Study Guidelines,* 1972; *The Property Management Process,* 1972. Contributor to *Journal of Property Management* and to appraisal journals.

AVOCATIONAL INTERESTS: Fishing (both stream and deep sea) in Canada, California, Hawaii, Florida.†

*   *   *

HANKINS, Norman E(lijah) 1935-

PERSONAL: Born May 15, 1935, in Greeneville, Tenn.; son of Charles Alexander (a farmer) and Helen Irene Hankins; married Marilyn A. Wampler (a teacher), December 18, 1970. *Education:* Tusculum College, B.S., 1958; East Tennessee State University, M.A., 1962; University of Tennessee, Ed.D., 1964. *Home:* 306 College St., Jonesboro, Tenn. 37659. *Office:* Department of Human Development and Learning, East Tennessee State University, Box 18940A, Johnson City, Tenn. 37601.

CAREER: Memphis State University, Memphis, Tenn., assistant professor of psychology, 1964-65; East Tennessee State University, Johnson City, assistant professor, 1965-67, associate professor, 1967-73, professor of psychology, 1973—. *Military service:* U.S. Army Reserve, 1958-64. *Member:* American Personnel and Guidance Association, American Rehabilitation Counselors Association, National Education Association, Tennessee Education Association.

WRITINGS: Psychology for Contemporary Education, C. E. Merrill, 1973; *How to Become the Person You Want to Be,* Nelson-Hall, 1979; (with Roger Bailey) *Psychology of Effective Living,* Brooks/Cole, 1980.

*   *   *

HANNAM, Charles 1925-

PERSONAL: Born July 26, 1925, in Essen, Germany. *Education:* Cambridge University, B.A., 1951, M.A., 1961. *Office:* School of Education, University of Bristol, Bristol BS8 1JA, England.

CAREER: Teacher in secondary schools in England, 1951-59; University of Bristol, Bristol, England, member of faculty, 1959—, senior lecturer in education, 1973—. *Military service:* British Army 1943-47; served in India and Burma.

WRITINGS: (Contributor) M. Ballard, editor, *New Movements in the Study and Teaching of History,* Temple Smith, 1970; (with Pat Smyth and Norman Stephenson) *Young Teachers and Reluctant Learners,* Penguin, 1971; *Parents and Mentally Handicapped Children,* Penguin, 1974, 2nd edition, 1980; (with

Smyth and Stephenson) *The First Year of Teaching,* Penguin, 1975; *A Boy in Your Situation,* Harper, 1977; *Almost an Englishman,* Deutsch, 1979. Contributor to journals.

WORK IN PROGRESS: A study of childhood; working with children who have difficulty in adjusting to schools; small groups, communication, and learning.

SIDELIGHTS: Parents and Mentally Handicapped Children has been translated into seven languages.

* * *

HANNAVY, John Michael 1946-

PERSONAL: Born April 30, 1946, in Edinburgh, Scotland; married. *Education:* Attended University of Manchester Institute of Science and Technology, 1963-66. *Office:* Wigan College of Technology, Wigan, England.

CAREER: Wigan College of Technology, Wigan, England, photographic historian and lecturer in photography, 1969—. Researcher for photo-historical exhibitions, 1974—; broadcaster on photographic history, 1977—. *Member:* Royal Photographic Society (fellow), Institute of Incorporated Photographers (fellow), Master Photographers Association of Great Britain (fellow).

WRITINGS: Prospect of Scotland, Bartholomew, 1974; *Roger Fenton of Crimble Hall* (biography), Godine, 1976; *Masters of Victorian Photography,* Holmes & Meier, 1976; *Fox Talbot: Father of Modern Photography,* Shire Publications, 1977; *Pictures of Wigan,* Wigantech, 1978; *The Victorian Professional Photographer,* Shire Publications, 1979; *Thomas Keith's Scotland,* Canongate, 1981; *A Moment in Time,* 3rd Eye/Interbook, 1983; *Maypole: Diary of a Colliery Disaster,* Wigantech, 1983. Also author of a four-part documentary series on the history of Scotland and Scottish photography over the past one hundred years, broadcast on British television. Contributor to *Photographer, Photo Technique,* and other periodicals. Editor, *Master Photographer.*

WORK IN PROGRESS: Research for a major study of the Waxed Paper Process of the 1950s; a television film exploring the history of photography as propaganda.

SIDELIGHTS: John Michael Hannavy told *CA* that his "full and varied career" includes working on his books, operating as a professional photographer in architecture and landscape, lecturing at Wigan College, and editing *Master Photographer.* He adds that he "is currently becoming increasingly involved in using historic photography as a visual resource rather than simply a collectible antique."

* * *

HARBINSON, Robert
See BRYANS, Robert Harbinson

* * *

HARDGRAVE, Robert L(ewis), Jr. 1939-

PERSONAL: Born February 6, 1939, in Greensburg, Pa.; son of Robert L. (a cattle rancher) and Orlene (Pirtle) Hardgrave. *Education:* University of Texas, B.A., 1960; University of Chicago, M.A., 1960, Ph.D., 1966. *Office:* Department of Government, University of Texas, Austin, Tex. 78712.

CAREER: Oberlin College, Oberlin, Ohio, assistant professor of government, 1966-67; University of Texas at Austin, 1967—,

began as associate professor, currently professor of government. Consultant to U.S. Department of State, 1982-83. *Member:* American Political Science Association, Association for Asian Studies, Phi Beta Kappa. *Awards, honors:* Rotary International fellowship for research in India, 1960-61; Foreign Area fellowship to India, 1964-66; Ford faculty research grant to India, 1969-70; American Institute of Indian Studies grant, 1974 and 1982.

WRITINGS: The Dravidian Movement, Popular Prakashan (Bombay), 1965; *The Nadars of Tamilnad: The Political Culture of a Community in Change,* University of California Press, 1969; (with James A. Bill) *Comparative Politics: The Quest for Theory,* C. E. Merrill, 1973; (with Santiago Hinojosa) *The Politics of Bilingual Education,* Swift Publishing, 1975; *India: Government and Politics in a Developing Nation,* Harcourt, 1970, 3rd edition, 1980; *Essays in the Political Sociology of South India,* Usha (New Delhi), 1979; *American Government,* Harcourt, in press.

Contributor: Donald E. Smith, editor, *South Asian Politics and Religion,* Princeton University Press, 1966; N. Murugesa Mudaliar, editor, *The Justice Party: Golden Jubilee Commemoration Volume,* [Madras], 1968; Rajni Kothari, editor, *Caste in Indian Politics,* Allied (Bombay), 1969. Contributor to professional journals.

WORK IN PROGRESS: Research on international politics of South Asia.

SIDELIGHTS: The Nadars of Tamilnad: The Political Culture of a Community in Change has been translated into the Tamil.

* * *

HARMAN, Jeanne Perkins 1919-

PERSONAL: Born July 27, 1919, in Baxter Springs, Kan.; daughter of Enoch (a mining engineer) and Maude (Himes) Perkins; married Harry E. Harman III (a writer), March 27, 1949. *Education:* Smith College, B.A. (magna cum laude), 1939. *Politics:* Independent. *Religion;* Episcopalian. *Home and office:* 3105 Country Club Dr., Valdosta, Ga. 31602.

CAREER: New York Herald Tribune, New York City, reporter, 1940-41; *Hearst* (magazine), New York City, editor, 1941-42; *Life,* New York City, editor and writer, 1942-49; Time, Inc., New York City, correspondent, 1951-68; full-time writer, 1968—. Instructor at University of Miami, 1953-54; journalism instructor at Emory University, 1983. Correspondent for McGraw-Hill News Service and *New York Times,* both 1955-1968. Assignments have included interviews with Nelson Rockefeller, Franklin D. Roosevelt, Lauren Bacall, Emily Post, and Mary Martin. *Member:* International Platform Association, Society of American Travel Writers, Overseas Press Club, Dixie Council of Authors and Journalists, Phi Beta Kappa.

WRITINGS: The Love Junk (travel book; Travel Book Club Book-of-the-Month selection), Appleton-Century-Crofts, 1951; *Such Is Life* (Literary Guild outstanding selection), Crowell, 1956; *The Virgins: Magic Islands,* Appleton-Century-Crofts, 1961; (editor with husband, Harry E. Harman III) *Fielding's Guide to the Caribbean, Including the Bahamas,* Fielding, 1968, 9th edition published as *Fielding's Guide to the Caribbean, plus the Bahamas,* 1977; (with H. E. Harman) *Harman's Official Guide to Cruise Ships,* Simon & Schuster, 1972; *Hilton Head Report,* National Research Group, 1973; *St. Simons/Sea Island Report,* National Research Group, 1983.

Contributor to *Encyclopedia Americana.* Author of syndicated travel articles for Los Angeles Times Mirror Syndicate, Cox and Gannett Newspapers, and *Toronto Star;* contributor to popular magazines, including *Gourmet, Sports Illustrated, Life,* and *Business Week.* Founder, editor, and publisher of *Here's How: Your Guide to St. Thomas,* 1957-68.

WORK IN PROGRESS: A guide to eating out in America; a travel guide to the Southeast.

SIDELIGHTS: Jeanne Perkins Harman writes *CA:* "I was something of a grind at Smith, worked hard at my political science major, was rewarded accordingly with Phi Beta Kappa grades in all subjects except the only English course I took, Creative Writing, in which I earned an inglorious C. The professor added the cheery comment that how anyone who had had the opportunities of growing up in the South Pacific, traveling to interesting places, and meeting fascinating people as the child of a mining engineer could be such a crashing bore on paper was beyond her comprehension.

"First efforts in the journalistic world were no more auspicious. When John Shaw Billings, a classical Southern gentleman of the old school with supertraditional ideas about women, promoted me from researcher to being the first bylined woman writer on a very chauvinistic *Life* staff, he hastened to explain, 'I'm not making you a writer because you can write; only because you don't cry.' And [he] proceeded to try to teach me to write.

"How successful his efforts were remains open to question. This incomparably able editor and teacher did, however, provide me with a craft (not an art), that has not only made me an agreeable living all my adult life, but an exciting and fulfilling one as well.

"As one who is living proof of the fact that you don't have to have talent to become a writer, I urge anyone who feels the slightest inclination in that direction to Go For It: rich you may never be. But stimulated, informed, diverted, amused, and seldom bored? More than likely."

BIOGRAPHICAL/CRITICAL SOURCES: Newsweek, February 17, 1975; *Miami Herald,* May 18, 1975; *Philadelphia Inquirer,* July 13, 1975; *Florida Times Union,* October 19, 1975.

*   *   *

HARRINGTON, Harold David   1903-1981

PERSONAL: Born March 14, 1903, in De Motte, Ind.; died January 22, 1981, in Fort Collins, Colo.; son of Charles G. and Alma (Hilton) Harrington; married Edith Jirsa, August 17, 1933. *Education:* Northern Iowa University, B.S., 1928; University of Iowa, Ph.D., 1933.

CAREER: Teacher in Iowa schools, 1927-34; Colorado State University, Fort Collins, assistant professor, 1935-39; Chicago Teachers College (now Chicago State University), Chicago, Ill., professor of biology, 1939-43; Colorado State University, associate professor, 1943-54, professor of botany, 1954-68, professor emeritus, 1968-81. *Member:* American Society of Plant Taxonomists, Sigma Xi.

WRITINGS: (With L. W. Durrell) *Colorado Ferns and Fern Allies: Pteridophyta,* Colorado Agricultural Research Foundation, Colorado Agricultural and Mechanical College, 1950; *Manual of the Plants of Colorado, for the Identification of the Ferns and Flowering Plants of the State,* Sage Books, 1954, 2nd edition, University Microfilms, 1964; *How to Identify Plants,*

Sage Books, 1957; *Edible Native Plants of the Rocky Mountains,* University of New Mexico Press, 1967; *Western Edible Wild Plants,* University of New Mexico Press, 1972; *How to Identify Grasses and Grasslike Plants (Sedges and Rushes),* illustrated by Ann Steely, Robin Hause, and Janet Klein, Swallow Press, 1977.†

[Sketch reviewed by wife, Edith Harrington]

*   *   *

HARRIS, Sydney J(ustin)   1917-

PERSONAL: Born September 14, 1917, in London, England; brought to United States in 1922; married Grace Miller (divorced, 1951); married Patricia Roche, 1953; children: Carolyn (deceased), Michael, Barbara, David, Lindsay. *Education:* Attended University of Chicago and Central College, Chicago, Ill. *Office: Chicago Sun-Times,* 401 North Wabash Ave., Chicago, Ill. 60611.

CAREER: Worked various jobs on *Chicago Herald-Examiner* and *Chicago Daily Times,* Chicago, Ill., 1934-36; *Beacon* (magazine), Chicago, editor, 1937-38; City of Chicago, Chicago, member of staff of public relations department and legal division, 1939-41; *Chicago Daily News,* Chicago, reporter and feature writer, 1941-44, author of column, "Strictly Personal," 1944-78, drama critic, beginning 1945; *Chicago Sun-Times,* Chicago, author of column "Strictly Personal," currently syndicated by Field Enterprises, Inc. to about two hundred newspapers in the United States, Canada, and South America, 1978—. Director, Hickory Humanities Forum, 1980—. Visiting scholar, Lenoir-Rhyne College; instructor, University of Chicago, 1946—; summer faculty member, Aspen Institute for Humanistic Studies; trustee, Francis W. Parker School, Chicago; lecturer.

MEMBER: Associates for the Institute for Psychoanalysis in Chicago (vice-president), Sigma Delta Chi, Arts Club, Headline Club, Press Club. *Awards, honors:* Ferguson Award, Friends of Literature, 1958; Brotherhood Award, National Conference of Christians and Jews, 1968; LL.D., Villa Maria College; Litt.D., Frances Schimer College; D.L.A., Lenoir-Rhyne College; Freedom of the Press Award, American Civil Liberties Union, 1980; elected to Chicago Journalism Hall of Fame, Chicago Press Club, 1982.

WRITINGS—Published by Houghton, except as indicated: *Strictly Personal,* Regnery, 1953; *A Majority of One,* 1957; *Last Things First,* 1961; *On the Contrary,* 1964; *Leaving the Surface,* 1968; *For the Time Being,* 1972; *The Authentic Person: Dealing with Dilemma,* Argus Communications, 1972; *Winners and Losers,* Argus Communications, 1973; *The Best of Harris,* 1975; *Would You Believe . . .?,* Argus Communications, 1979; *Pieces of Eight,* 1982. Member of usage panel, *American Heritage Dictionary.*

SIDELIGHTS: "Columnist Sydney J. Harris is so right about absolutely everything," begins an editorial in the *Long Beach Press Telegram.* "He is so reasonable behind that mustache. He has clear blue eyes, undoubtedly, and he never screams at the kids." This may well be the impression of Harris shared by the millions of readers who follow his column, "Strictly Personal," syndicated to some 200 newspapers worldwide.

Although he never finished college, Harris (who has since been awarded three honorary doctorate degrees) founded the opinion magazine *Beacon* at age twenty; Saul Bellow was an assistant editor. Harris has also worked as a reporter, feature writer, and drama critic for various Chicago newspapers, including the *Herald-Examiner*, the *Daily News*, and the *Daily Times*, forerunner of the *Chicago Sun-Times*, where he is now based. According to Gene Schroeder, writing in the *Omaha World Herald*, Harris, who has been producing five eight-paragraph columns per week since 1944, has been called a "perfect master of the short essay form."

In writing "Strictly Personal" Harris muses upon society and human nature, often touching on such controversial subjects as religion, politics, sexual mores, and intelligence. *Sun-Times Book Week* reviewer William Karp feels that "taken as a whole, Harris's essays, written with verve, are worthy products of a mind endowed with powers of perception and objectivity—and one does not have to agree with him down the line to say this." The columnist is also known for his witty and insightful aphorisms and his aversion to long-windedness. "As a solidly hit baseball smashes a plate-glass window," writes David B. Whitaker in the *Louisville Times*, "Sydney J. Harris shatters the so-called communication barrier. He has an astonishing ability to express his thoughts in concise, pinpointed terms." In a *Washington Post* review of *Pieces of Eight*, one of Harris's many collections of columns, Robert W. Smith offers some examples of the author's philosophy: "Two are needed for oneness. . . . The loser gains more than the winner because the loser learns most from the experience. . . . The adult is not satisfied with riches, fame, or honor, because only the satisfaction of our earliest emotional needs, those of a child, gratify us over a long period."

Smith states: "To read [Harris] is to breathe again the air of Martin Buber and his meeting ground, of G. K. Chesterton the laughing Christian, and especially of Alain (Emile Chartier), the French philosopher whose *propos*, little 'remarks' of 500-600 words, made him a national treasure." *Chicago Daily News* critic Elmer Gertz also compares Harris to a social commentator of another age: "Like Harris, [George Bernard] Shaw was tempted to disbelieve everything that was too readily taken to be true. And he chose simple (but not too simple) language to drive home his preachments about our uncertain existence on this planet Earth." Gertz concludes, "Without being a Shaw or a Voltaire or a Pascal, this man Harris—who is generally himself even when he borrows the thoughts of others—has served a unique purpose in the journalism of our community and, happily, many other communities."

AVOCATIONAL INTERESTS: Tennis, chess.

CA INTERVIEW

CA interviewed Sydney J. Harris by telephone on December 3, 1982, at his office in Chicago, Ill.

CA: You did various newspaper jobs and some work for the city of Chicago before you settled into writing the column "Strictly Personal," which is what you're best known for now. With your range of interests, how did you decide on doing primarily the column?

HARRIS: I wanted something that did not restrict me physically or mentally. I could write the column at home or abroad, wherever I was. Also, I decided it wouldn't be topical so I didn't have to write right on top of the news. I could write many weeks ahead and then go away and take a rest somewhere. It was for my own comfort and convenience, although I pretended otherwise!

CA: Do you work several columns ahead of schedule?

HARRIS: I write at least one a day and sometimes two or three a day, and I'm always eight to ten weeks ahead, so I can afford to get ill or get drunk or beat my wife and go to jail and not have a break. I haven't missed a column in thirty-eight years.

CA: Some of the opinions you expressed early in "Strictly Personal" provoked angry response. Do you recall any of those pieces?

HARRIS: No, but controversial ones usually center around politics, which I don't write too much about. I can't recall specific ones. In fact, I can't remember the one I wrote yesterday. I discharge them in order to get them out of my gullet and get something new in.

CA: How much mail do you get from readers?

HARRIS: Maybe 200 to 300 letters a week. That's not a lot, considering the column appears in almost 200 newspapers.

CA: Do you try to respond to all of it?

HARRIS: Yes, we answer everything. My secretary answers the insulting mail and I answer the flattering mail.

CA: How does the general columnist compare with the editorial cartoonist or the political writer? What does he owe his readers?

HARRIS: I don't think of owing my readers anything. It sounds very egotistic, but I really write for myself. I feel that if I please myself, I can only hope it will please adult readers. Once you start thinking about the readers, you're an entertainer. You're looking for applause or trying to generate controversy; you're not writing as honestly as you might. I try not to think about the reader. If something I'm writing doesn't please me, I throw it away.

CA: You never write with the idea of changing anyone's opinion?

HARRIS: I would like people to agree with me, but what I want to do more than anything else is get them to think. If I can change their opinion, so much the better, but that's not my prime purpose. I try to stimulate them to think logically and honestly, and I feel that if they do, most of them will come to pretty much the same conclusions I do.

CA: You've also been a drama critic . . .

HARRIS: I did drama criticism for thirty years. I was the drama critic for the old *Chicago Daily News*.

CA: Do you keep up with drama now?

HARRIS: Oh yes. I just went to see "Nicholas Nickleby" the other night—the other day and night and day and night, I mean.

CA: Yes, it does go on and on, doesn't it? Some drama critics are pretty gloomy about theater now. What do you think?

HARRIS: Well, you know they call theater the Fabulous Invalid; it's always about to die but it never does. I think it's right to be somewhat gloomy about it, but theater has great powers of recuperation. They used to say the difference between the people in Berlin and the people in Vienna was that in Berlin the situation was always serious but never critical;

in Vienna the situation was always critical but never serious. I suppose that's the way I feel about the theater.

CA: You're said to be a voracious reader, and you've taught Great Books at the University of Chicago. Were you an early reader?

HARRIS: Yes. I began reading when I was a very little boy. I can't remember when I didn't read. And I can't remember when I didn't write, either. I began writing when I was about eight, and nobody ever told me to stop, so I never did.

CA: What do you most enjoy reading currently?

HARRIS: I enjoy reading theology. I read it for recreation and for information. You see, I love mysteries, and I consider that the greatest mystery in the world. I've been trying to unravel it most of my life—with no particular success.

CA: What theologians are you reading?

HARRIS: Barth, Bultmann, Teilhard, the modern existentialists. I don't read the old fundamentalists, because I think they have nothing to tell me. I enjoy the modern biblical researchers; I read a lot of exegesis. I find it fascinating.

CA: Is there any contemporary fiction you like?

HARRIS: I don't read fiction very much. I'm not temperamentally attuned to it. If a novel comes out and eight or ten years later my intellectual friends are still discussing it, I'll pick it up and read it. I let time winnow them out for me. I don't read new novels at all; they're mostly a waste of time.

CA: You've won several honorary degrees and awards, including the 1968 Brotherhood Award of the National Conference of Christians and Jews, and the 1980 Freedom of Press Award of the American Civil Liberties Union. Is there one award that stands out, that's meant more to you than the others?

HARRIS: Last year I was elected to the Journalism Hall of Fame in Chicago, which includes people like Carl Sandburg, Eugene Field, and Ben Hecht. I think I was prouder of that in a way because it reflected the judgment of my peers on the collective body of my work. I'll tell you the truth: although I appreciate them all, a lot of organizations will give awards to people more for the sake of getting publicity than to honor the recipients. Some of those things are flak.

CA: Many newspapers have been in trouble in recent years, some fatally. Do you think newspapers will have to make fundamental changes to stay alive?

HARRIS: I don't know. I'm very bad at predicting the future. I think they're in trouble not because of their quality but because of demographics almost beyond their control. The *Chicago Daily News* was the best paper in Chicago and one of the best in the country. It went down largely because it was an afternoon paper. If it had been a morning paper, it would have survived. Our readers moved out to the suburbs, then they stopped taking the train and started driving to and from work. We were also hurt by the evening news on television; people would come home at six and plunk down and watch that instead of reading the paper.

CA: In an essay entitled ''Science Can't Give Us Everything,'' collected in your 1968 book, Leaving the Surface, *you stressed the need for well-rounded people above the need for ''better-trained technicians.'' With the developments in computer technology since that time, and the important roles they've begun to play in business, we seem to have even more well-trained technicians who lack a grounding in the humanities. Where is it leading us?*

HARRIS: We do have more, but there are more complaints, too, that these people can't read and write and think, can't conceptualize. I think these technical people need to be supervised by people with a liberal education, and I think they will *have* to be, eventually. We have so many computer foul-ups because they don't know anything except their own little jobs. Computers are changing rapidly. If technicians can't change with them, they'll become as obsolescent as the old textile workers.

CA: You've been a member of the usage panel of the American Heritage Dictionary, *but you've also written editorially in defense of slang. Is there a contradiction there?*

HARRIS: No. Slang vitalizes a language, keeps it alive. What I'm against is the use of nonce words and ungrammatical usage. What we have to do, as T. S. Eliot said long ago, is maintain a steady control over the language so that it neither petrifies nor changes too fast. On the one hand it becomes a stilted and dead language; but if we let it change without control, then it runs riot and our communication is ruined. I'm not a stuffy old fellow who wants the language to be frozen. I would like it to change with order—not without order. I'm a member of the extreme center!

CA: You've lived and worked in Chicago for most of your life. After years of playing second fiddle to New York City, Chicago seems to be coming into an increased pride in its own assets and accomplishments. Is that the general feeling among Chicagoans you know?

HARRIS: I suppose so. A little pride, but also a little disgust at the way the city is run. Chicago gets things done, but not without slipping a few bucks under the table. I'm a bit ambivalent about it, although I enjoy the city very much. I would prefer to live in New York if I had unlimited funds and could have a penthouse apartment and a car and a driver and not have all the angst that people have there; short of that, it's easier and better to live in Chicago on a lesser income. You still get to do a lot, really. It seems to me to be an optimum between living in a small town and living in a big city.

CA: You manage to do an amazing number of things in addition to your writing. You were for years vice-president of the Associates for the Institute for Psychoanalysis in Chicago, and now you're involved in some relatively new work in North Carolina. Tell me about that.

HARRIS: For the last couple of years I've been laughingly called a visiting scholar at Lenoir-Rhyne College in Hickory, North Carolina. I go down there about once a month to lecture and strut about importantly. I'm also director of the Hickory Humanities Forum that we have at Wildacres, near Ashville, every spring. It's sponsored by Lenoir-Rhyne. About a hundred people attend, and I have people like Clifton Fadiman and Jacques Barzun to lead the discussion of Great Books. We read, talk, have a chamber music concert, show a film—it's a general celebration of the humanities, which I enjoy very much.

CA: Are you doing any other lecturing or teaching?

HARRIS: From September through May I lecture once or twice a week; I talk at colleges all over the country. That's how I got this Lenoir-Rhyne job; I was there a couple of times and they decided they wanted to be stuck with me for a while.

CA: Are there future writing projects or other plans you'd like to talk about?

HARRIS: No. Writing a column five days a week is pretty taxing. Every four years we collect the best columns and do a book. I have no ambition to write a magnum opus or anything like that. I know my place!

BIOGRAPHICAL/CRITICAL SOURCES: Nashville Banner, May 24, 1968; *Chicago Sun-Times Book Week,* June 2, 1968; *Louisville Times,* July 2, 1968; *Long Beach Press Telegram,* August 15, 1973; *Chicago Daily News,* November 15-16, 1975; *Chicago Sun-Times,* December 7, 1975; Sydney J. Harris, *Pieces of Eight,* Houghton, 1982; *Washington Post,* October 15, 1982; *Houston Post,* November 14, 1982; *Omaha World Herald,* December 19, 1982.

—*Interview by Jean W. Ross*

*   *   *

HARRIS, (Theodore) Wilson   1921-

PERSONAL: Born March 24, 1921, in New Amsterdam, British Guiana (now Guyana); immigrated to England, 1959; son of Theodore Wilson (an insurer and underwriter) and Millicent Josephine (Glasford) Harris; married Margaret Nimmo Burns (a writer), April 2, 1959. *Education:* Queen's College, Georgetown, Guyana, 1934-39; studied land surveying and geomorphology under government auspices, 1939-42. *Residence:* London, England. *Address:* c/o Faber and Faber, 3 Queen Square, London W.C. 1, England.

CAREER: British Guiana Government, government surveyor, 1942-54, senior surveyor, 1955-58; full-time writer in London, England, 1959—. Visiting lecturer, State University of New York at Buffalo, 1970, Yale University, 1979; guest lecturer, Mysore University (India), 1978; writer-in-residence, University of West Indies, 1970, University of Toronto, 1970, and Newcastle University, 1979; visiting professor, University of Texas at Austin, 1972, 1981-82, 1983, and University of Aarhus, 1973. Delegate, UNESCO Symposium on Caribbean Literature in Cuba, 1968, National Identity Conference in Australia, 1968. *Awards, honors:* English Arts Council grants, 1968 and 1970; Commonwealth fellow at University of Leeds, 1971; Guggenheim fellow, 1972-73; Henfield writing fellow at University of East Anglia, 1974; Southern Arts fellow, Salisbury, 1976.

WRITINGS—Novels; all published by Faber: *Palace of the Peacock* (Book I of the "Guiana Quartet"), 1960; *The Far Journey of Oudin* (Book II of the "Guiana Quartet"), 1961; *The Whole Armour* (Book III of the "Guiana Quartet"), 1962; *The Secret Ladder* (Book IV of the "Guiana Quartet"), 1963; *Heartland,* 1964; *The Eye of the Scarecrow,* 1965; *The Waiting Room,* 1967; *Tumatumari,* 1968; *Ascent to Omai,* 1970; *Black Marsden,* 1972; *Companions of the Day and Night,* 1975; *Da Silva da Silva's Cultivated Wilderness,* 1977; *Genesis of the*

Clowns, 1977; *The Tree of the Sun,* 1978; *The Angel at the Gate,* 1982.

Poetry: *Fetish,* privately printed (Georgetown, Guyana), 1951; *Eternity to Season,* privately printed (Georgetown, Guyana), 1954.

Nonfiction: *Tradition and the West Indian Novel,* New Beacon, 1965; *Tradition, the Writer and Society,* New Beacon, 1967; *Explorations* (essays), Dangeroo Press (Denmark), 1981; *The Womb of Space,* Greenwood Press, 1983.

Short stories: *The Sleepers of Roraima,* Faber, 1970; *The Age of the Rainmakers,* Faber, 1971.

Contributor to anthology *Caribbean Rhythms: The Emerging English Literature of the West Indies,* edited by J. T. Livingston, Washington Square Press, 1974.

SIDELIGHTS: Wilson Harris's novels are notable for the author's imaginative use of language. In a review of *Ascent to Omai,* a *Times Literary Supplement* critic compares Harris's narrative style to poetry, warning that "no reader should attempt Mr. Harris's novels unless he is willing to work at them," adding that perhaps the book is better suited to "a line-by-line commentary rather than a review." In another *Times Literary Supplement* article, Shirley Chew writes of *The Tree of the Sun:* "One cannot deny that Wilson Harris's powers of invention are vigourous and fertile, . . . nor can one deny that, bristling in the intricate criss-cross of 'parallel and estranged expeditions' which form the structure of the novel, are important ideas and themes. . . . [But] *The Tree of the Sun* neither captivates nor moves . . . because Wilson Harris has failed to rise to some of the more common expectations one brings to the reading of a novel."

However, *Times Literary Supplement* critics Louis James and J. P. Durix find the author's novels somewhat more rewarding. In a review of *Companions of the Day and Night,* for example, James states, "The novels of Wilson Harris . . . form one ongoing whole. Each work is individual; yet the whole sequence can be seen as a continuous, ever-widening exploration of civilization and creative art." And Durix, writing about *The Angel at the Gate,* finds that in the author's work "patterns collide, merge and are transformed into other designs. [His] dense style and meticulous construction, his attention to visual and rhythmic effects, are matched by an inventiveness which few contemporary novelists can equal."

Commenting on the craft of writing, Harris told *CA:* "A summary of motivations by a writer is inevitably an unfinished statement since with each imaginative work a new discovery arises that alerts one to intuitive and implicit dimensions, in previous novels, that acquire a new significance and bearing on future work. It is as if each novel is another step in a drama of consciousness or unpredictable creative potential in the past and in the future.

"I think all this bears on a vision of community as a capacity for evolving insight and deepseated change. The nature of freedom is complex, subtle, and demanding of unceasing responsibility to that still unfathomable 'muse' (however apparently archaic that expression may sound) in a world that is susceptible to polarisations, tyrannies and monoliths that are as frightful and dangerous today as they have ever been in the history of cultures and civilisations."

Harris's manuscripts are collected at University of the West Indies, University of Texas at Austin, and Indiana University at Bloomington.

BIOGRAPHICAL/CRITICAL SOURCES: Louis James, editor, *The Islands In Between,* Oxford University Press, 1968; Gerald Moore, *Chosen Tongue,* Longman, 1969; *Journal of Commonwealth Literature,* July, 1969, June, 1971, April, 1975; *Times Literary Supplement,* May 21, 1970, October 10, 1975, May 19, 1978, October 15, 1982; *Language and Literature,* autumn, 1971; *Literary Half-Yearly,* January, 1972; Ivan Van Sertima, *Enigma of Values,* Dangaroo Press (Aarhus, Denmark), 1975; John Fletcher, *Commonwealth Literature and the Modern World,* Didier (Brussels), 1975; Michael Gilkes, *Wilson Harris and the Caribbean Novel,* Longman, 1975; Hena Maes-Jelinek, *The Naked Design,* Dangaroo Press, 1976; Wilson Harris, *The Tree of the Sun,* Faber, 1978; Maes-Jelinek, *Wilson Harris,* Twayne, 1982; *Contemporary Literary Criticism,* Volume XXV, Gale, 1983.

*   *   *

HARRISON, Randall P(aul)   1929-

PERSONAL: Born February 3, 1929, in Eau Claire, Wis.; son of Randall Joseph and Catherine (an educator; maiden name, Paul) Harrison; married Elizabeth Halsted (a journalist), October 1, 1955 (divorced May 19, 1972). *Education:* University of Wisconsin—Madison, B.S., 1950; Michigan State University, Ph.D., 1964. *Home:* 9 Ethel Lane, Mill Valley, Calif. 94941. *Agent:* Michael Larsen/Elizabeth Pomada, 1029 Jones St., San Francisco, Calif. 94109. *Office address:* P.O. Box 22541, San Francisco, Calif. 94122.

CAREER: United Press, reporter in Pierre, S.D., and Chicago, Ill., 1950-51; WKOW-Television, Madison, Wis., news editor and art director, 1953-54; McGraw-Hill Book Co., New York, N.Y., magazine editor, 1954-56; Jam Handy Organization, Detroit, Mich., motion picture writer, 1956-59; Michigan State University, East Lansing, instructor, 1963-64, assistant professor, 1964-68, associate professor, 1968-73, professor of communication, 1973-77; free-lance writer, 1977—. University of California, San Francisco, visiting professor, 1970-71, research psychologist and adjunct professor, 1974—. Writer for Motion, Inc., 1953-54; director of Communication Press. *Military service:* U.S. Air Force, 1951-53; became captain. *Member:* International Communication Association (fellow), American Psychological Association, Society of Western Artists.

WRITINGS: Beyond Words: An Introduction to Nonverbal Communication, Prentice-Hall, 1974; *How to Cut Your Water Use in Half and Still Stay Sane and Sanitary,* Communication Press, 1977; *The Cartoon: Communication to the Quick,* Sage Publications, 1981; (editor with J. M. Wiemann) *Nonverbal Interaction,* Sage Publications, 1983; *Formulas for Fund Raisers,* Public Service Materials, 1983.

Contributor to *Handbook of Communication* and *Joy of Knowledge Encyclopedia.* Member of editorial board of *Journal of Communication, Communication Yearbook,* and *Annual Review of Communication Research.*

WORK IN PROGRESS: A collection of cartoons; a book on international nonverbal communication.

SIDELIGHTS: Randall P. Harrison comments: "A central concern is information and communication. I see these as major issues of our age, providing both challenges and opportunities."

HART, John   1948-

PERSONAL: Born June 18, 1948, in Berkeley, Calif.; son of Lawrence (a teacher and writer) and Jeanne (a writer, under pseudonym Jeanne McGahey; maiden name, Brown) Hart. *Education:* Princeton University, A.B., 1970. *Politics:* Independent. *Religion:* None. *Home address:* c/o 13 Jefferson Ave., San Rafael, Calif. 94903.

CAREER: Free-lance writer. *Pacific Sun,* Mill Valley, Calif., writer on environment and planning, 1970-73; teacher for Lawrence Hart Seminars, 1981—; associate editor of *the poetry LETTER,* 1982—. *Member:* Sierra Club, Wilderness Society, American Alpine Club, Poets and Writers, Inc. *Awards, honors:* James D. Phelan Award from San Francisco Foundation, 1970, for an unpublished manuscript of poetry; merit award from California chapter of American Institute of Planners, 1972, for articles on planning.

WRITINGS: (Contributor) David Walker and Rowan Rowntree, editors, *Tomales Bay Environmental Study,* Conservation Foundation, 1973; *Hiking the Bigfoot Country: The Wildlands of Northern California and Southern Oregon,* Sierra Club, 1975; (contributor) Randall W. Scott, editor, *Management and Control of Growth,* Urban Land Institute, 1975; *Walking Softly in the Wilderness: The Sierra Club Guide to Backpacking,* Sierra Club, 1977, 2nd edition, 1984; *The Climbers,* University of Pittsburgh Press, 1978; *San Francisco's Wilderness Next Door,* Presidio Press, 1979; *Hiking the Great Basin: The High Desert Country of California, Oregon, Nevada, and Utah,* Sierra Club, 1981.

Work has been anthologized in *Accent on Barlow,* edited by Lawrence Hart, privately printed, 1962; *Mark in Time,* edited by Nick Harvey, Glide Publications, 1971; *Poems One Line and Longer,* edited by William Cole, Grossman, 1973. Contributor of articles, poems, and translations to numerous periodicals, including *Western American Literature, Cry California, Works, Ishmael, Pacific Sun,* and *Sierra Club Bulletin.* Member of editorial staff, *California Land,* 1975, *Endangered Harvest,* 1980, and *California 2000: The Next Frontier,* 1982. Script consultant for television documentary film, "The Wild Places."

WORK IN PROGRESS: Research for a book on the poetry of the Wagner librettos; *Storm Camp,* poems; research for a book on his father, Lawrence Hart, the poetry seminars he has conducted since 1935, the poets who have developed their talents there, and the role his "Activist Movement" has played in American Literature.

SIDELIGHTS: John Hart writes: "I find this an odd time in which to be writing poetry. The condition of that art, in America in the 1980s, can hardly fail to distress anyone anxious to do good and disciplined work. To be sure, poetry is popular as never before; more than that, it is subsidized as never before. But this climate, apparently so favorable, actually seems to promote a poetry so slack and trivial that it scarcely counts as poetry at all.

"Thirty years ago there were at least five major American poets alive. Today there is not one. Historians will, I think, look back on this period as one of drought in poetry—a period in which the growth of the art progressed, as it were, underground, while work of little importance commanded the chief rewards and set the admired style.

"If such unfavorable climates had not been recorded before, in the literature of other languages and in the other arts, the present situation would be even more disheartening than it is."

The Sierra Club Guide to Backpacking has been published in Japan.

AVOCATIONAL INTERESTS: Wilderness travel and climbing, winter mountaineering, European travel, opera and theatre, the politics of wilderness preservation.

* * *

HARTFORD, Via
See DONSON, Cyril

* * *

HARTLEY, Robert F(rank) 1927-

PERSONAL: Born December 15, 1927, in Beaver Falls, Pa.; son of Frank H. (a merchant) and Eleanor (Theis) Hartley; married Dorothy Mayou, June 30, 1962; children: Constance, Matthew. *Education:* Drake University, B.B.A., 1949; University of Minnesota, M.B.A., 1962, Ph.D., 1967. *Home:* 17405 South Woodland Rd., Shaker Heights, Ohio 44120. *Office:* Department of Marketing, Cleveland State University, Cleveland, Ohio 44115.

CAREER: Management employee for national department store chains, 1949-59; Dayton Corp., Minneapolis, Minn., in merchandise management, 1959-63; University of Minnesota, Minneapolis, instructor in marketing, 1963-65; George Washington University, Washington, D.C., assistant professor, 1965-69, associate professor of marketing, 1969-72; Cleveland State University, Cleveland, Ohio, professor of marketing, 1972—. *Member:* American Marketing Association, Case Research Association, Southern Marketing Association, Midwest Business Administration Association.

WRITINGS: Marketing Management and Social Change, International Textbook Co., 1972; *Retailing: Challenge and Opportunity,* Houghton, 1975, 3rd edition, 1984; *Marketing for Responsive Management,* Dun Donnelly, 1976; *Marketing Mistakes,* Grid Publishing, 1976, 2nd edition, 1980; *Sales Management,* Houghton, 1979; (co-author) *Essentials of Marketing Research,* PennWell, 1983; *Management Mistakes,* Grid Publishing, 1983; *Marketing Fundamentals,* Harper, 1983. Contributor to business and marketing journals.

WORK IN PROGRESS: A book on classic marketing successes, for Grid Publishing.

SIDELIGHTS: Robert F. Hartley writes: "I have attempted in my writings, aimed primarily at the college market, to blend the practical with the conceptual. An underlying theme in all my books has been the desirability of business to be responsive to the needs and dictums of society and the environment, rather than strictly corporate short-term self-interest."

* * *

HART-SMITH, William 1911-

PERSONAL: Born November 23, 1911, in Tunbridge Wells, Kent, England; son of George May Coleridge (a banker) and Florence (Gomez) Hart-Smith; married Mary Wynn, October 17, 1939 (divorced, 1943); married Patricia Ann McBeath (an astrologer), January 8, 1949; children: (second marriage) Katherine, Christopher, Julian. *Education:* Had short periods of

formal schooling in Scotland and England, and one year of high school in Auckland, New Zealand. *Politics:* Democracy ("after extreme swing to Communism in Australia before, during, and shortly after World War II"). *Religion:* "Sufi influences, a 'natural' mystic." *Office:* 17 Raeben Ave., Takapuna, Auckland, New Zealand.

CAREER: Radio mechanic in Auckland, New Zealand (where he operated one of the earliest "ham" radio stations), and Sydney and Hobart, Australia, 1927-41; free-lance journalist and radio copywriter, Sydney, 1939-46; Radio Station 2CH, Sydney, copywriter and announcer, 1941-45; Australian Broadcasting Commission, Sydney, air publicity officer, 1945-46; University of Canterbury, Christchurch, New Zealand, tutor-organizer in adult education department, 1948-55; Charles Kidd & Co. Pty. Ltd. (mail order business), North Sydney, New South Wales, Australia, art director, 1955-66. Writer-in-residence and creative writing instructor, University of Western Australia. Lecturer on poetry and on the culture and mythology of Australian aborigines; has given numerous public poetry readings. *Military service:* Australian Imperial Forces, 1941-43; became sergeant. *Member:* Poetry Society of Australia (president, 1963-64; vice-president, 1964—), Jindyworobak Club (Australia; president, 1939-55). *Awards, honors:* Crouch Memorial Medal for best book of poems (Australia), 1959, for *Poems of Discovery;* Grace Leven Prize for best book of poems (Australia), 1966, for *The Talking Clothes.*

WRITINGS—Poetry, except as indicated: *Columbus Goes West,* Georgian House (Melbourne) with Jindyworobak Club, 1943; *Harvest,* Georgian House with Jindyworobak Club, 1945; *The Unceasing Ground,* Angus & Robertson, 1946; *Christopher Columbus, a Sequence,* Caxton Publishing Co. (Christchurch, New Zealand), 1948; *On the Level,* Timaru Herald (New Zealand), 1950; *Poems in Doggerel,* Handcraft Press (Wellington, New Zealand), 1955; *Poems of Discovery,* Angus & Robertson, 1959.

(Contributor) *Voyager Poems,* Jacaranda Press (Brisbane, Australia), 1960; *The Talking Clothes,* Angus & Robertson, 1966; (author of foreword) Leslie Horsphol, *Transubstantiation and Other Poems,* F. P. Leonard (Sydney), 1967; (with Judith Wright and Randolph Stow) *Poetry from Australia,* compiled by Howard Sergeant, Pergamon, 1969; *Minipoems,* Western Australian Institute of Technology (Perth), 1976; (with Mary Morris) *Let Me Learn the Steps,* Fremantle Art Centre Press, 1977; *Selected Poems, 1942-82,* Angus & Robertson, 1983. Author of a book on graphology, privately printed. Contributor to poetry anthologies, books of verse for schools, and periodicals, including *Quadrant* (Sydney) and *Artlook* (Western Australia). Reviewer, *New Zealand Listener, Sydney Bulletin,* and other periodicals.

WORK IN PROGRESS: Poetry ("endeavoring to perfect technique"); work on his bibliography.

SIDELIGHTS: William Hart-Smith, who received only six and one-half years of formal schooling, told *CA:* "I went across to Australia from New Zealand in 1936 to see what my father was up to, taking with me a swatch of extremely romantic and immature poems of which one only ('The Poplar') had been published in N.Z. [New Zealand] (*Auckland Star*). In Sydney I met Marion Griffin, wife of Walter Burley Griffin; she was an anthroposophist living with other followers of the ideas of Dr. Rudolph Steiner in a Griffin home at Castle Crag. I was asked to join the open air theatre, having had some experience with the Children's Theatre in Sydney. She kindly read some of my poetry. The result was an elucidation coupled with a warning, and my first public poetry reading.

"War was coming. I married Mary Wynn and went to live in a Griffin-type house. Ever since those days I've been true to one love only: poetry. Conscience made me enlist in the A.I.F., and I was discharged in W.A. [Western Australia] with a cerebral hemorrhage. Didn't realise it at the time, but it was a busted aneurysm on the left lobe. My hasty marriage, too, went bust. I coped, tried in all sorts of ways to earn a living. One of my highs was an appointment as tutor-organiser for the Adult Education department in N.Z. when I ran for home in 1946. I married again, in Timaru, and had three lovely children to Patsy McBeath.

"In 1955 I had another brain bleed, this time on the right side. This time I died for a few seconds: a wonderful experience. After a year of convalescence, and further life experience, I left my wife and hurried back to my spiritual home, Australia, with a N.Z. lass. My wife and children followed, but I was still searching for a poet, or someone who could live with one. I found her in another lass, a pianist from W.A. with whom I went to live. A boy child joined us; we went back to Western Australia. There my life was centred on poet friends, and the W.A. Institute of Technology and the University of W.A. I taught creative writing, was writer-in-residence at University for a given period. Darn me if *both* danger spots in my head didn't leak on me! My de facto (33 years younger) and I parted amicably.

"Once again I scurred back to N.Z. where I now live with a wise little lass (now a wise little lady of 68) I had to part from in 1936. My odd and persistent 'jumps' both backwards and forwards in time happen no longer; my eyesight is bad. Mrs. Griffin's warnings have come true. On my shelves I have two large lever files with hundreds of poems, all in alphabetical order, but in their original artistic disorder. These I work on when I feel inclined and send to *Quadrant* [the Australian monthly literary journal]. Where I once read 'vastly' (and acquired an education), I now read selectively and am rapidly finding out that I really know nothing at all."

About his religious beliefs, Hart-Smith writes that he's currently interested in "the shaping effect of animism, etc., of the Australian Aborigines plus 'Sufism,' thanks to Gurdjieff and Ouspensky, and Idries Shah's book, *Sufism*."

AVOCATIONAL INTERESTS: Collector of New South Wales Cowrie shells (discovered a new species which was named after him, "Notadusta hartsmithi"); graphology; philately.

*   *   *

HASLAM, Gerald W. 1937-

PERSONAL: Born March 18, 1937, in Bakersfield, Calif.; son of Fred M. (an oil worker) and Lorraine (Johnson) Haslam; married Janice E. Pettichord, July 1, 1961; children: Frederick, Alexandra, Garth, Simone, Carlos. *Education:* San Francisco State College (now University), A.B., 1963, M.A., 1965; Washington State University, additional study, 1965-66; Union Graduate School, Ph.D., 1980. *Home:* 1100 G St., Petaluma, Calif. 94952. *Office:* Sonoma State University, 1801 East Cotati Ave., Rohnert Park, Calif. 94928.

CAREER: Before and during his college years, Haslam worked as a roustabout in oilfields, picked, plowed, irrigated, and packed crops in the San Joaquin Valley, and was employed in stores, banks, and shops; San Francisco State College (now

University), San Francisco, Calif., instructor in English, 1966-67; Sonoma State University, Rohnert Park, Calif., professor of English, 1967—. *Military service:* U.S. Army, 1958-60. *Member:* College Language Association, National Council of Teachers of English, Western Literature Association (vice-president, 1982; president-elect, 1983-84), California Teachers Association, California Association of Teachers of English, Sierra Club, Trout Unlimited, Valley of the Moon Track Club, Napa Valley Runners' Club, Little Hills Striders. *Awards, honors: Arizona Quarterly* nonfiction award, 1969, for "The Subtle Thread"; General Semantics Foundation grant; Joseph Henry Jackson Award, 1970, for *Okies*.

WRITINGS: (Editor) *Forgotten Pages of American Literature*, Houghton, 1970; *William Eastlake*, Steck, 1970; *The Language of the Oilfields*, Old Adobe Press, 1972; *Okies: Selected Stories*, New West Publications, 1973, revised and enlarged edition, Peregrine Smith, 1975; (editor) *Western Writings*, University of New Mexico Press, 1974; *Jack Schaefer*, Boise State College Western Writers, 1976; *Masks: A Novel*, Old Adobe Press, 1976; (editor with James D. Houston) *California Heartland*, Capra, 1978; *The Wages of Sin*, Duck Down Press, 1980; *Hawk Flights: Visions of the West*, Seven Buffaloes Press, 1983.

Contributor to anthologies, including *The Far Side of the Storm*, edited by Gary Elder, Holmgangers, 1975, *Father Me Home Wind*, and *American Ethnic Stories*. General editor, "Western American Writers" series, Everett/Edwards. Contributor to *Arizona Quarterly, College English, Western American Literature, Negro American Literature Forum, The Nation, American History Illustrated, New Society, Southwest Review, Mother Jones*, and other journals; has had many short stories and poems published. Former production editor, *ETC: A Review of General Semantics.* Editor, *Ecolit.*

WORK IN PROGRESS: Co-editing *Literary History of the American West*, for T.C.U. Press; *The Man Who Cultivated Fire and Other Stories; In the War Zone*, a novel; "most attention being given to short stories, with continued forays into interpretive journalism."

SIDELIGHTS: Gerald Haslam told *CA:* "Most of my time and energy goes to the crafting of short stories, the large majority of which are set in the American West. I hope to achieve universality through original presentation of the particular, and to expand regional vistas and perceptions in the process.

"I was raised in a richly varied area—California's San Joaquin Valley—where oral tale-telling was a fine art. I was a good listener and I still am. Since no one ever told me a novel, I have always considered the story, not its longer counterpart, to be fiction's most natural and apotheotic expression. It is a continuing source of both wonder and satisfaction to me that I have evolved into a storyteller.

"Perhaps because I came to writing directly from the oral tradition, I've never yearned to be an *Author*, although I'm certainly pleased to see my work in print. No, for me the act of writing is the most important thing, experiencing the emergence of a new reality. Like love, it remains an enduring thrill. I can't wait to face the typewriter each morning. I'm always amazed at what's in there."

AVOCATIONAL INTERESTS: Backpacking, flyfishing, competitive running, cycling.

HAUSER, Hillary 1944-

PERSONAL: Born September 4, 1944, in California; daughter of Carl Richard and Mabel (Hensel) Hauser. *Education:* University of Washington, Seattle, B.A., 1966. *Home and office:* 1655 Fernald Point Lane, Santa Barbara, Calif. 93108.

CAREER: TV Guide, Los Angeles, Calif., local editor, 1966-67, national programmer, 1967-68; *Skin Diver,* Los Angeles, Calif., assistant editor, 1968-71; *Ocean Science News,* Washington, D.C., West Coast editor, 1971—; free-lance writer, 1971—; *Santa Barbara News-Press,* Santa Barbara, Calif., reporter, 1981—. Member of Harbor Commission of Avalon, Catalina Island, 1971-72. Technical consultant for television films "Shark Kill" and "Trapped beneath the Sea." *Awards, honors:* Winner of *Redbook* adventure writing contest, 1978.

WRITINGS: (Associate editor) *Ski World,* Peterson, 1973; (associate editor) Corky Fowler, *Skiing Techniques,* Peterson, 1973; *Women in Sports: Scuba Diving,* Harvey House, 1976; *The Living World of the Reef,* Walker & Co., 1978; *Book of Fishes,* Photographic Book Co. (New York), 1984. Author of monthly features "Fish of the Month" and "News Briefs" in *Skin Diver,* 1968—. Contributor to diving magazines, *Westways, Caballero, Western's World, National Geographic, Reader's Digest,* and *Submarin* (Germany). West Coast editor of *Coastal Zone Management,* 1971-75.

WORK IN PROGRESS: Heart of a Sourdough, a tale of the Alaska gold rush of 1900.

SIDELIGHTS: Hillary Hauser writes: "Dr. Carleton Ray . . . said some time ago that the marine revolution is on the way—to take place alongside the agricultural and industrial revolutions. As people turn their heads, minds, hearts to the sea—I hope to help them enlarge their concept of the ocean, by writing about the animals, the life, the underwater activities, about being in the sea."

*　　*　　*

HAUSMANN, Winifred 1922-
(Winifred Wilkinson)

PERSONAL: Born September 1, 1922, in Atlanta, Ga.; daughter of Boyce Taylor (an insurance representative) and Ruby (a voice teacher; maiden name, Gaffney) Wilkinson; married George Rowe Hausmann (a Unity minister), December 19, 1965. *Education:* Agnes Scott College, B.A., 1946; Unity Training School, Lee's Summit, Mo., graduate, 1958. *Home:* 11298 Heath Rd., Chesterland, Ohio 44026. *Office:* Unity Center of Cleveland, 2653 South Taylor Rd., Cleveland Heights, Ohio 44118.

CAREER: Ordained Unity minister, 1959; Unity Church, Little Rock, Ark., minister, 1957-58; Unity Center of Cleveland, Cleveland Heights, Ohio, minister, 1958-66, co-minister with husband, George Rowe Hausmann, 1966—. Association of Unity Churches, member of board of directors, 1965-67; Great Lakes Unity Regional Conference, secretary, 1966-67. Affiliated with U.S. Office of Censorship and U.S. Army Signal Corps, 1941-44; publicity and promotion worker for *Atlanta Journal* and International News Service, 1946-48. Writer and narrator of "Focus on Living" (five-minute weekday radio program), WCLV-FM, 1964-68, WBKC-AM, 1969-70, and WABQ-AM, 1979-82.

WRITINGS: (Under name Winifred Wilkinson) *Focus on Living,* Unity Books, 1967; (under name Winifred Wilkinson) *Miracle Power for Today,* Doubleday, 1969; *Your God-Given Potential,* Unity Books, 1978; *How to Live Life Victoriously,* Unity Books, 1982.

SIDELIGHTS: Winifred Hausmann told *CA:* "I believe that we all have greater potentiality than we have ever begun to express. The whole purpose of my work as a Unity minister and as an author is to help others . . . develop, as one of my books puts it, their 'God-given potential.' I am dedicated to the Unity proposition that God is good and God is all, and that all things are possible as we learn the spiritual laws and co-operate with them."

*　　*　　*

HAVERKAMP-BEGEMANN, Egbert 1923-

PERSONAL: Born March 6, 1923, in Naarden, Netherlands. *Education:* University of Amsterdam, M.A., 1947, M. Phil., 1949; University of Utrecht, Ph.D., 1958. *Office:* Department of History of Art, Yale University, Box 2009, New Haven, Conn. 06608.

CAREER: Museum Boymans-van Beuningen, Rotterdam, Netherlands, curator, 1950-58; Harvard University, Cambridge, Mass., lecturer, 1959-60; Yale University, New Haven, Conn., assistant professor, 1960-65, associate professor, 1965—, curator of prints, 1960-64, curator of drawings and prints, 1964—.

WRITINGS: William Buytewech, Hertzberger (Amsterdam), 1959; (with Standish D. Lawder and Charles W. Talbot) *Drawings from the Clark Art Institute,* two volumes, Yale University Press, 1964; *Hercules Seghers* (booklet), J. M. Meulenhoff (Amsterdam), 1968; (author of introduction) *Rembrandt in the National Gallery of Art, Washington, D.C.,* H. K. Press, 1969; *Rembrandt after Three Hundred Years,* Art Institute of Chicago, 1969; (with Madzy Rood-De Boer) *Kinderbescherming en gezondheidszorg,* Nationale Federatie voor Kinderbescherming, 1969.

(With Anne-Marie Logan) *European Drawings and Watercolors in the Yale University Art Gallery: 1500-1900,* two volumes, Yale University Press, 1970; *The Achilles Series,* Phaidon, 1975; (editor) *Wadsworth Atheneum Paintings,* Atheneum, 1978; (with others) *Small Paintings of the Masters,* three volumes, Shorewood Fine Art, 1980; *Rembrandt: The Nightwatch,* Princeton University Press, 1982. Also author of catalog, with John Gordon, *Gabor Peterdi,* 1964. Co-editor, *Master Drawings,* 1963—; member of editorial board, *Art Bulletin,* 1965—.†

*　　*　　*

HAWKINS, Brett W(illiam) 1937-

PERSONAL: Born September 15, 1937, in Buffalo, N.Y.; son of Ralph Charles and Irma (Rowley) Hawkins; married Linda Knuth, November 30, 1974; children: (first marriage) Brett William, Jr. *Education:* University of Rochester, A.B., 1959; Vanderbilt University, M.A., 1962, Ph.D., 1964. *Politics:* Republican. *Religion:* Christian Scientist. *Home:* 3730 North Morris, Shorewood, Wis. 53211. *Office address:* Department of Political Science, University of Wisconsin, P.O. Box 413, Milwaukee, Wis. 53201.

CAREER: Washington and Lee University, Lexington, Va., assistant professor of political science, 1963-65; University of

Georgia, Athens, assistant professor, 1965-68, associate professor of political science, 1968-70; University of Wisconsin—Milwaukee, associate professor, 1970-71, professor of political science, 1971—. *Member:* American Society for Public Administration, Phi Beta Kappa.

WRITINGS: Nashville Metro, Vanderbilt University Press, 1966; (editor with Thomas R. Dye) *Politics in the Metropolis,* C. E. Merrill, 1967, 2nd edition, 1971; (editor with Robert Lorinskas) *The Ethnic Factor in American Politics,* C. E. Merrill, 1970; *Politics and Urban Policies,* Bobbs-Merrill, 1971; (with Richard D. Bingham and F. Ted Hebert) *The Politics of Raising State and Local Revenue,* Praeger, 1978; (with Bingham, John Frendreis, and Mary Le Blanc) *Professional Associations and Municipal Innovation,* University of Wisconsin Press, 1981. Contributor of numerous articles to professional journals.

* * *

HAWLEY, Donald Thomas 1923-
(Robert McDermott)

PERSONAL: Born March 13, 1923, in St. Paul, Minn.; son of Donald Dewey (a dentist) and Ruth Lucille (Thomas) Hawley; married Helen Weston Beasley, July 9, 1946 (divorced, 1980); married Anita Mae Broder, 1981; children: (first marriage) Cassandra June, Craig Scott, Shareen Renee. *Education:* Union College, Lincoln, Neb., B.A., 1950. *Home:* 24414 University, Loma Linda, Calif. 92354. *Office address:* Box 904, Loma Linda, Calif. 92354.

CAREER: Ordained Seventh-Day Adventist minister, 1955; Nebraska Book and Bible House, Lincoln, assistant manager, 1950-51; pastor of Seventh-day Adventist churches in Nebraska, 1951-56; Seventh-day Adventist Hospital, Karachi, Pakistan, chaplain, 1956-61; Hinsdale Sanitarium and Hospital, Hinsdale, Ill., director of public relations, 1961-63; Michigan Conference of Seventh-day Adventists, Lansing, director of communications, 1963-66; Greater New York Conference of Seventh-day Adventists, New York, N.Y., director of communications, 1966-71; *Life and Health,* Washington, D.C., managing editor, 1972-75, editor, 1975-77; director of public relations and development, "It Is Written" television program, Thousand Oaks, Calif., 1977-80; free-lance writer, 1980—. *Military service:* U.S. Navy, 1943-46; served in the South Pacific.

WRITINGS: Pakistan Zindabad!, Pacific Press Publishing Association, 1961; *From Gangs to God,* Review & Herald, 1973; *Getting It All Together,* Review & Herald, 1974; *Come Alive!: Feel Fit—Live Longer,* Review & Herald, 1975; (under pseudonym Robert McDermott) *Hypnosis: Is It for You?,* Pacific Press Publishing, 1982. Contributor to magazines.

WORK IN PROGRESS: A book on the history of medicine.

SIDELIGHTS: Over 400,000 copies of Donald Thomas Hawley's books, which have appeared in several foreign editions, have been sold. *Avocational interests:* Ham radio, caving.

* * *

HEALY, Sean D(esmond) 1927-

PERSONAL: Born May 15, 1927, in London, England; son of Christopher Francis (an administrator) and Mabelle (Kitts) Healy; married Patricia Abrahams (an American-born artist), December 27, 1967. *Education:* Pembroke College, Cambridge, B.A., 1950, M.A., 1956; University of London, Postgraduate Cer-

tificate of Education, 1956; Rutgers University, Ed.D., 1979. *Religion:* Catholic. *Home:* 423 Forest Dr., Union, N.J. 07083. *Office:* Kean College of New Jersey, Union, N.J. 07083.

CAREER: Schoolmaster, 1956—; chairman of history department at a school in Stevenage, England, 1964-69; Kean College of New Jersey, Union, 1969—, began as assistant professor at the Educational Foundation, currently associate professor of educational policy. Healys' Graphic Ark (contemporary religious graphic design studio), co-founder with wife, craftsman in dalles de verre, typographer and printer. *Member:* American Federation of Teachers, Alternate Education Association, American Printing History Association, Phi Delta Kappa. *Awards, honors:* Kean College Alumni Teacher of 1978 Award.

WRITINGS: Town Life (young adult book), Batsford, 1968; *Ideas for Teaching History,* Batsford, 1974; *Boredom, Self and Culture,* Fairleigh Dickinson University Press, 1984.

WORK IN PROGRESS: A book on Brendan the Navigator.

SIDELIGHTS: Sean D. Healy explains that Healys' Graphic Ark, which he founded with his wife, is a "contemporary religious graphic design studio dedicated to providing thinking Christians with symbols and images offering an alternative to the kitsch and schlock that have to such a large extent usurped the field. We are dedicated to couching the words of Christ, the prophets, and saints in forms that speak to today's world and especially to a younger generation nurtured on the materialistic brilliance of Madison Avenue."

* * *

HEBERT, Jacques 1923-

PERSONAL: Surname pronounced Hay-bear; born June 21, 1923, in Montreal, Quebec, Canada; son of Louis-Philippe (a doctor) and Denise (Saint-Onge) Hebert; married Therese DesJardins, October 20, 1951; children: Michel, Pascale, Isabelle, Bruno, Sophie. *Education:* Attended College Sainte-Marie, Montreal, and University St. Dunstan, Charlottetown; Ecole Des Hautes Etudes Commerciales de Montreal, license en sciences commerciales. *Home:* 3480, Prud-homme, Montreal, Quebec, Canada H4A 3H4. *Office:* Canada World Youth, 4824 Cote des Neiges, Montreal, Quebec, Canada H3V 1G4.

CAREER: Editions de l'Homme, Montreal, Quebec, founder, 1958; Editions du Jour, Montreal, founder, president, and director general, 1961-74; Canada World Youth, Montreal, founder and president, 1971—. Founder and president, Katimavik, 1976—. Commissioner, Canadian Radio Television Commission, 1971-78. Co-chairman, Federal Cultural Review Committee, 1981-82. Order of Canada, officer, 1979, senator, 1983.

WRITINGS: Autour des trois Ameriques, Beauchemin, 1948; *Autour de l'Afreque,* Fides, 1950; *Aicha l'Africaine* (stories), Fides, 1950; *Aventure autour du Monde,* Fides, 1952; *Nouvelle aventure en Afrique,* Fides, 1953; *Coffin etait innocent,* Editions de l'Homme, 1958; *Scandale a Bordeaux,* Editions de l'Homme, 1959; (with Pierre Elliott Trudeau) *Deux innocents en Chine rouge,* Editions de l'Homme, 1960, translation published as *Two Innocents in Red China,* Oxford University Press (Toronto), 1968; *J'accuse les assassins de Coffin,* Editions du Jour, 1963, translation published as *I Accuse the Assassins of Coffin,* 1964; *Trois jours en prison,* Club du Livre du Quebec, 1965; *Les Ecoeurants* (novel), Editions du Jour, 1966; *The Temple on the River* (novel), Harvest House, 1967; *Ah! mes Aieux!,* Editions du Jour, 1968.

Obscenite et Liberte, Editions du Jour, 1970; *Blablabla du bout de monde,* Editions du Jour, 1971; *The World Is Round,* McClelland & Stewart, 1976; *Have Them Build a Tower Together,* McClelland & Stewart, 1979; (with Maurice F. Strong) *The Great Building-Bee,* General Publishing, 1980; *L'Affaire Coffin,* Domino, 1980, translation published as *The Coffin Affair,* General Publishing, 1982.

SIDELIGHTS: The World Is Round, Have Them Build a Tower Together, and *The Great Building-Bee* have been published in French.

*   *   *

HENDERSON, Richard I(van)   1926-

PERSONAL: Born January 4, 1926, in Altoona, Pa.; son of Edgar M. and Augusta (Pasekoff) Henderson; married Jean Simonton, August 10, 1970. *Education:* U.S. Naval Academy, B.S., 1948; University of Miami, Coral Cables, Fla., M.B.A., 1967; Georgia State University, Ph.D., 1970. *Residence:* Norcross, Ga. *Office:* Department of Management, Georgia State University, University Plaza, Atlanta, Ga. 30303.

CAREER: Saf-T-Bak, Inc., Altoona, Pa., plant manager, 1949-50, 1953-55; Needle Trade Industry, plant manager in Hawaii, Japan, Hong Kong, and the Philippines, 1955-58; Bertrand Frank Associates, New York, N.Y., management consultant, 1958; Saf-T-Bak, Inc., sales manager and senior salesman for southern states, 1959-67; University of Miami, Coral Gables, Fla., lecturer in management, 1967-68; Middle Tennessee State University, Murfreesboro, assistant professor of management, 1970-71; Georgia State University, Atlanta, assistant professor, 1971-75, associate professor, 1975-80, professor of management, 1980—. Director of middle-management courses at University of Miami, 1967-73; management and planning consultant, 1967—; compensation and performance appraisal consultant, 1972—. *Military service:* U.S. Navy, 1943-49, 1950-53; became lieutenant senior grade. *Member:* Academy of Management, American Compensation Association, Southern Management Association.

WRITINGS: Toward a Faculty Self-Appraisal System (monograph), Bureau of Business and Economic Research, Georgia State University, 1969; (with Joseph L. Reina) *In-Service Training Aid* (monograph), Tennessee Nursing Association, 1972; (with Waino W. Suojanen) *The Operating Manager: An Integrative Approach,* with workbook (with W. Michael Field and Gary L. Swallow), Prentice-Hall, 1974; *Job Descriptions: Critical Documents, Versatile Tools* (monograph), AMACOM, 1976; *Compensation Management: Rewarding Performance in the Modern Organization,* Reston, 1976, 3rd edition, 1982; (with Stephen C. Carlson and Robert O. Wilson) *COMP-$-MAN* (workbook), Reston, 1976; *Performance Appraisal: Theory to Practice,* Reston, 1980, 2nd edition, 1984; *Influencing Employee Behavior at Work* (monograph), College of Business Administration, Georgia State University, 1982. Contributor of articles and reviews to management and economic journals, and to *Modern Nursing Home.*

WORK IN PROGRESS: Research on compensation practices in American organizations, executive compensation, the productivity of American organizations, and quality of work life.

*   *   *

HENRY, David Lee
See HILL, R. Lance

HIAT, Elchik
See KATZ, Menke

*   *   *

HICKS, Eleanor B.
See COERR, Eleanor (Beatrice)

*   *   *

HIEBEL, Friedrich   1903-

PERSONAL: Given name listed in some sources as Frederick; born February 10, 1903, in Vienna, Austria; naturalized U.S. citizen, 1945; son of Gustav and Adele (von Goldberger-Buda) Hiebel; married Beulah Emmet, June 24, 1945; children: Benedict Thomas, Margaret Sophia. *Education:* Attended University of Jena, 1924-25, and University of Goettingen, 1925-26; University of Vienna, Ph.D., 1928. *Religion:* Catholic. *Home:* Luzernestrasse 14, CH 4143 Dornach, Switzerland. *Office:* Goetheanum College, Freie Hochschule fuer Geisteswissenschaft, CH 4143 Dornach, Switzerland.

CAREER: Teacher at Waldorfschool, Stuttgart, Germany; Princeton University, Princeton, N.J., instructor in German literature, 1945-46; Upsala College, East Orange, N.J., associate professor of German and chairman of department, 1946-47; Rutgers University, New Brunswick, N.J., assistant professor of German, 1947-53; Wagner College, Staten Island, N.Y., associate professor, 1953-56, professor of German, 1956-63; Goetheanum College, Dornach, Switzerland, professor, head of literature section, and dean of College, 1963—, publisher and editor of weekly periodical, *Das Goetheanum,* 1966—. Wayne State University, resident director of junior year at University of Freiberg, 1962-62. *Member:* Modern Language Association of America, P.E.N. (Switzerland), Schweizerischer Schriftsteller Verein.

WRITINGS: Paulus und die Erkenntnislehre der Freiheit (title means "St. Paul and the Philosophy of Freedom"), Rudolf Geering Verlag, 1946, 2nd edition, Goetheanum Buecherei, 1959; *The Gospel of Hellas: The Mission of Ancient Greece and the Advent of Christ,* Anthroposophic Press (New York), 1948.

Novalis: Der Dichter der blauen Blume (title means "Novalis: The Poet of the Blue Flower"), Francke Verlag, 1951, revised edition published as *Novalis: Deutscher Dichter, europaeischer Denker, christlicher Seher,* 1972, translation published as *Novalis: German Poet, European Thinker, Christian Mystic,* University of North Carolina Press, 1954, revised edition, 1959; *Goethe,* Francke Verlag, 1951; *Die Botschaft von Hellas: Von der griechischen Seele zum christlichen Geist* (title means "The Gospel of Hellas"), Francke Verlag, 1953, 2nd edition, 1963; *Christian Morgenstern: Wende und Aufbruch unseres Jahrhunderts* (title means "Christian Morgenstern: Turning Point of Our Century"), Francke Verlag, 1957; *Bibelfunde und Zeitgewissen: Die Schiftrollen vom Toten Meer im Lichte der Christologie Rudolf Steiners* (title means "The Qumran Texts"), Rudolf Geering Verlag, 1959.

Albert Steffen: Die Dichtung als schoene Wissenschaft (title means "Albert Steffen: Poetry and Belles Lettres"), Francke Verlag, 1960; *Goethe: Die Erhoehung des Menschen; Perspektiven einer morphologischen Lebensschau* (title means "Goethe: Perspectives of a Morphological Biography"), Francke

Verlag, 1961; (editor with others) *Alpha und Omega: Sprachbetrachtungen* (title means "Alpha and Omega: Reflections about Language"), Philosophisch-Anthroposophischer Verlag, 1963; (editor with others) *Himmelskind und Adamsbotschaft: Kunstgeschichtliche Menschheitsmotive im besonderen Zusammenhang mit Michelangelos Sixtinischer Decke* (title means "Heavenly Childhood and Adam's Message: In Connection with Michelangelo's Sistine Ceiling"), Philosophisch-Anthroposophischer Verlag, 1964; *Rudolf Steiner in Geistesgang des Abendlandes* (title means "Rudolf Steiner in the Evolution of the Occident"), Francke Verlag, 1965.

Biographick und Essayistik (title means "Biography and Essay"), Francke Verlag, 1970; *Campanella: Der Sucher nach dem Sonnenstaat; Geschichte eines Schicksals* (novel; title means "Campanella: The Seeker for the Sun"), Verlag Freies Geistesleben, 1972; *Seneca: Drama*, [Stuttgart], 1974; *Der Tod des Aristoteles* (novel; title means "The Death of Aristotle"), Verlag Freies Geistesleben, 1977; *Im stillstand der Stunden* (poems), [Dornach], 1978; *Goethe und die Schweiz* (essays), Philosophisch-Anthroposophischer Verlag, 1982.

* * *

HILL, Dave
See HILL, David Charles

* * *

HILL, David Charles 1936-
(Dave Hill)

PERSONAL: Born October 6, 1936, in Minneapolis, Minn.; son of Charles W. (a wanderer) and Joyce (Hansen) Hill. *Education:* Attended about thirty elementary schools in Minnesota, Oregon, and Washington; earned high school diploma and some college credits by correspondence. *Politics:* "Apathetic—no choice, as I see it." *Religion:* Christian Existentialist.

CAREER: Full-time free-lance writer. *Member:* Minneapolis Writers Workshop.

WRITINGS: Juvenile books, except as indicated; under name Dave Hill, except as indicated: *Big Bible Puzzle Book*, Bethany Fellowship, 1965; *Ramon's World*, Herald Press, 1965; *Welfare Kid*, Herald Press, 1966; *Secret of the Star* (picture book), Concordia, 1966; (under name David Charles Hill) *They Met the Master* (adult), Augsburg, 1967; *The Boy Who Gave His Lunch Away*, Concordia, 1967; *The Walls Came Tumbling Down*, Concordia, 1967; *The Most Wonderful King*, Concordia, 1968; (under name David Charles Hill) *Messengers of the King*, Augsburg, 1968; (editor with Hugh Scott) *Softball Hall of Famers*, Amateur Softball Association, 1976; (with Nick Seitz) *Teed Off*, Prentice-Hall, 1977; *Invader*, Jove Publications, 1981. Stories included in teenage anthologies. Regular contributor to denominational magazines.

SIDELIGHTS: David Charles Hill once told *CA:* "I write for money, have no other interest, skill, or abilities. [I] have spent large part of my life in various jails for criminal activity of a trivial nature. [I] do have some knowledge of Chippewa Indian language." Hill calls himself an expert on the world of small-time criminals.†

* * *

HILL, Harold E(verett) 1905-

PERSONAL: Born December 10, 1905, in Manchester, N.H.; son of Arthur and Luella (Manley) Hill; married Ruth Gaertner, August 8, 1928; children: Linda Anne. *Education:* Pratt Institute, E.E., 1926. *Politics:* "Kingdom of God." *Religion:* "King's Kid." *Residence:* Severna Park, Md. *Office address:* P.O. Box 8655, Baltimore, Md. 21240.

CAREER: R. A. Lister Co., Dursley, England, chief engineer and vice president of U.S. operations, 1927-46; Curtis Engine and Equipment Co., Baltimore, Md., vice-president, 1946-51, president, 1951-73, advisor, 1973—. *Member:* International Christian Leadership, Full Gospel Business Men's Fellowship International, Christian Business Men's Committees, Propeller Club of the United States.

WRITINGS—Published by Logos International, except as indicated: *How to Live Like a King's Kid*, 1975; (with Irene Harrell) *How Did It All Begin?: From Goo to You by Way of the Zoo*, 1976, revised edition, 1984; *How to Be a Winner*, 1976; *How to Live in High Victory*, 1977; *Instant Answers for King's Kids*, 1978, published as *Bible Answers for King's Kids*, Revell, 1983; *How to Flip Your Flab Forever*, 1979; *How to Live the Bible Like a King's Kid*, Revell, 1980; *God's in Charge Here*, Revell, 1982.

WORK IN PROGRESS: "A practical book on money management on the theme 'How to Make Your Money Behave,' . . . combining the best money-management principles of the secular world with the Spiritual Laws of Prosperity as given by God in the Bible"; a book "on the theme 'I'm Not *That* Bad . . . I Can Take It or Leave It,' . . . based on my own lengthy and hefty bout with the heavy drug Alcohol."

SIDELIGHTS: Harold E. Hill told *CA:* "After having spent a half century seeking REALITY to life in such things as religion, philosophy, monetary successes, scientific achievement, active hobbies, and worldly pleasures, I finally found the answer through a personal, first-hand hookup with the Head Man of the Universe, whose name is Jesus Christ and who IS total and complete satisfaction. My books are factual reports on how my life under God's management has worked out these past twenty-nine years since meeting Jesus as my personal Counsellor, Guide, Consultant and Friend. All Boredom, Depression, Anxiety, and GUILT are GONE!"

Hill states that his book *How Did It All Begin?: From Goo to You by Way of the Zoo* contains "valuable scientific data and a comprehensive Bibliography . . . helpful to readers planning on a career in science" and says that the book's "evidence for Evolution and Creation gives the reader an opportunity to form his own unbiased opinion as to whether we got here by way of a reeking, itching, banana-burbing Babboon baying at the moon in a vermin-infested jungle; or whether a loving Heavenly Father really did create us in His image and after His own Likeness."

Hill also told *CA* that he "invented the Ground Energizer used for starting airplane engines on the ground," which was "an important contribution to winning World War II."

* * *

HILL, R. Lance 1943-
(David Lee Henry)

PERSONAL: Born May 1, 1943, in Canada; married Darlene Moroz, 1971. *Education:* Graduated from high school in Toronto, Ontario. *Politics:* "Apolitical." *Religion:* "None." *Agent:* Curtis Brown Ltd., 575 Madison Ave., New York, N.Y. 10022.

CAREER: Writer. Former professional automobile race driver and engine builder. *Member:* Writers Guild of America. *Awards, honors:* "Harry Tracy" was Canada's official entry in 1982 Manila Film Festival and was nominated for seven Canadian Genie Awards, 1983.

WRITINGS: Nails, Lester & Orpen, 1974; *King of White Lady* (Book-of-the-Month Club selection), Putnam, 1975; *The Evil That Men Do* (Book-of-the-Month Club selection), Times Books, 1978.

Screenplays: "Harry Tracy," filmed by Desperado Productions, 1981, released by Quartet Films, 1983; "The Evil That Men Do" (based on his book of the same title), ITC Productions, 1983.

WORK IN PROGRESS: A film adaptation of Tom Stoppard's play "Night and Day."

SIDELIGHTS: Nails has been translated into Spanish and Portuguese; *King of White Lady* and *The Evil That Men Do* have been translated into Italian.

* * *

HINKEMEYER, Michael T(homas) 1940-
(Vanessa Royall)

PERSONAL: Born October 18, 1940, in St. Cloud, Minn.; son of Ralph Stephen (a farmer) and Melania Ann (Kuhn) Hinkemeyer; married Arlene Dingilian, August 5, 1967; children: Ellen Lara, Jonathan Edward. *Education:* St. John's University, Collegeville, Minn., A.B., 1962; Northwestern University, M.A.T., 1966, Ph.D., 1971. *Politics:* Democrat. *Religion:* None. *Home:* 35 Cove Dr., Manhasset, N.Y. 11030. *Agent:* Writer's House, Inc., 21 West 26th St., New York, N.Y. 10010.

CAREER: Writer. Montgomery Ward, St. Paul, Minn., management trainee, 1964-65; high school teacher in Glend Head, N.Y., 1966-67; Northwestern University, Evanston, Ill., instructor in education, 1967-69; St. Mary's College, Notre Dame, Ind., assistant professor of education, 1969-71; Queens College of the City University of New York, Flushing, N.Y., associate professor of education, 1971-76. *Military service:* U.S. Army, 1962-64; served in Europe; became first lieutenant. *Member:* Authors Guild, Authors League of America, Mystery Writers of America. *Awards, honors:* Harvard Prize for Special Education, 1966.

WRITINGS: The Dark Below (suspense novel), Fawcett, 1974, published as *Sea Cliff,* Pocket Books, 1979; *Summer Solstice* (suspense novel), Putnam, 1976; *The Fields of Eden* (mystery novel), Putnam, 1977; *The Creator* (suspense novel), Pinnacle, 1978; *The Harbinger* (suspense novel), Pocket Books, 1980; *Lilac Night* (suspense novel), Crown, 1981; *A Time to Reap* (mystery novel), St. Martin's, 1984.

All under pseudonym Vanessa Royall; all historical romances; all published by Dell: *Flames of Desire,* 1978; *Come Faith, Come Fire,* 1979; *Firebrand's Woman,* 1980; *Wild Wind Westward,* 1982; *Seize the Dawn,* 1983.

WORK IN PROGRESS: A historical romance, tentatively entitled *The Passionate and the Proud,* for Dell; *The Big Three,* "a contemporary novel dealing with changes in the lives of three men and their women against a backdrop of American history from 1963 to the present."

SIDELIGHTS: Michael T. Hinkemeyer told *CA:* "If there is any particular truth that I have been able to divine in the writing

business, it is this: learn as much, and have as many experiences, as you can. These are the things you put in your personal 'writer's bank.' The more you have deposited there, the more you can draw upon. Little did I know, ten years ago, that all my years of studying history would make me 'Vanessa Royall,' historical romance novelist. But I am glad of it. . . . It is heartening that, even in America, someone with a Ph.D. can have a little success."

Hinkemeyer's works, which have sold almost three million copies, have been translated into eight languages.

* * *

HIRSCH, Ernest A(lbert) 1924-1977

PERSONAL: Born January 8, 1924, in Stuttgart, Germany; naturalized United States citizen, 1940; died, 1977; son of Eugene (a wine dealer) and Fanny (Wormser) Hirsch. *Education:* Queens College (now Queens College of the City University of New York), B.A., 1948; Menninger Foundation, School of Psychology, certificate, 1950, certificate in clinical psychology, 1955; University of Kansas, Ph.D., 1952. *Politics:* Democrat. *Religion:* Jewish. *Home:* 3601 Huntoon, Topeka, Kan. 66604. *Office:* Menninger Foundation, Box 829, Topeka, Kan. 66601.

CAREER: Winter Veterans Administration Hospital, Topeka, Kan., clinical psychologist, 1952-54; Menninger Foundation, Topeka, postdoctoral fellow in child psychology, 1954-55, chief psychologist, Children's Service, 1956-62, senior research psychologist and member of faculty of School of Clinical Psychology, beginning 1962. Associate member, Topeka Institute for Psychoanalysis, beginning 1959. *Military service:* U.S. Army, 1942-46; became technical sergeant. *Member:* American Psychological Association (fellow), American Orthopsychiatric Association (fellow), Kansas Psychological Association (fellow), Topeka Psychoanalytic Society (associate member).

WRITINGS: (Contributor) L. A. Pennington and Irwin A. Berg, editors, *An Introduction to Clinical Psychology,* 2nd edition, Ronald, 1954; (contributor) J. E. Simmons, *Disturbed Children,* Jossey-Bass, 1969; (with Frank Petroni) *Two, Four, Six, Eight: When You Gonna Integrate?,* Behaviorial Publications, 1970; *The Troubled Adolescent: As He Emerges in Psychological Tests,* International Universities Press, 1970; *Starting Over: The Autobiographical Account of a Psychologist's Experience with Multiple Sclerosis,* foreword by Karl A. Menninger, Christopher, 1977; *Joy, Woe, Hope and Fear: Thoughts about the Life of the Young and Old, the Free and Imprisoned,* University Press of America, 1982.

Contributor to medical journals. Member of editorial board, *Psychotherapy: Theory, Research and Practice.*†

* * *

HIRSCH, William Randolph
See LINGEMAN, Richard R(oberts)

* * *

HO, Ping-ti 1917-

PERSONAL: Born September 1, 1917, in Tientsin, Hopei, China; naturalized U.S. citizen in 1982; son of Shou-ch'uan Ho (a judge) and Yun-lan Chang; married Ching-lo Shao, July 3, 1940; children: Sidney K'o-yueh, Bartlet K'o-chun. *Edu-*

cation: National Tsing-hua University, Peking, China, B.A., 1938; Columbia University, Ph.D., 1952. *Home:* 4741 South Woodlawn Ave., Chicago, Ill. 60615. *Office:* Department of History, University of Chicago, Chicago, Ill. 60637.

CAREER: National Tsinghua University, K'un-ming, China, instructor in history, 1939-45; University of British Columbia, Vancouver, instructor, 1948-52, assistant professor, 1952-56, associate professor, 1956-60, professor of history and Asian studies, 1960-63; University of Chicago, Chicago, Ill., professor of Chinese history and institutions, 1963-65, James Westfall Thompson Professor of History, 1965—. Member of Council of Sino-American Cooperation in Humanities and Social Sciences, 1966-69. *Member:* Association of Asian Studies (president, 1975-76), American Academy of Arts and Sciences (fellow), National Association of Chinese-Americans (vice-president, 1977—). *Awards, honors:* L.L.D., Chinese University of Hong Kong, 1975; L.H.D., Lawrence University, 1978.

WRITINGS: (Translator) *Ten Classical Chinese Poems,* [Montreal], 1958; *Studies on the Population of China, 1368-1953,* Harvard University Press, 1959; *The Ladder of Success in Imperial China: Aspects of Social Mobility, 1368-1911,* Columbia University Press, 1962; *Chung-kuo hio-kuan shih-lun* (title means "History of Landsmannschaften in China"), [Taipei], 1966; (editor with Tang Tsou) *China in Crisis: China's Heritage and the Communist Political System,* University of Chicago Press, 1968; *Huang-t'u yu Chung-kuo nung-yeh ti ch'i-yuan* (title means "The Loess and the Origins of Chinese Agriculture"), Chinese University of Hong Kong Press, 1969; *The Cradle of the East: An Inquiry into the Indigenous Origins of Techniques and Ideas of Neolithic and Early Historic China, 5000-1000 B.C.,* University of Chicago Press, 1975; (contributor) Charles A. Reed, editor, *Origins of Agriculture,* Mouton, 1977.

Contributor to *Proceedings of the 1959 Annual Spring Meeting of the American Ethnological Society,* and to *Proceedings of the Twenty-fifth International Congress of Orientalists,* 1963. Contributor to academic journals.

SIDELIGHTS: Studies on the Population of China, 1368-1953 and *The Ladder of Success in Imperial China: Aspects of Social Mobility, 1368-1911* have been translated into Italian.

*   *   *

HOCH, Edward D(entinger)   1930-
(Irwin Booth, Anthony Circus, Stephen Dentinger, Pat McMahon, Mister X, R. L. Stevens)

PERSONAL: Surname rhymes with "coke"; born February 22, 1930, in Rochester, N.Y.; son of Earl G. (a banker) and Alice (Dentinger) Hoch; married Patricia McMahon, June 5, 1957. *Education:* Attended University of Rochester, 1947-49. *Politics:* Liberal Republican. *Religion:* Roman Catholic. *Home:* 2941 Lake Ave., Rochester, N.Y. 14612.

CAREER: Rochester Public Library, Rochester, N.Y., researcher, 1949-50, member of board of trustees, 1982—; Pocket Books, Inc., New York, N.Y., staff member in adjustments department, 1952-54; Hutchins Advertising Co., Rochester, copy writer, 1954-68; full-time author, 1968—. *Military service:* U.S. Army, Military Police, 1950-52. *Member:* Mystery Writers of America (president, 1982-83), Authors Guild, Authors League of America, Science Fiction Writers of America. *Awards, honors:* Edgar Allan Poe ("Edgar") Award of Mys-

tery Writers of America for best mystery short story of 1967, for "The Oblong Room."

WRITINGS: The Shattered Raven, Lancer, 1969; *The Transvection Machine,* Walker & Co., 1971; *The Judges of Hades,* Leisure Books, 1971; *The Spy and the Thief,* Davis Publications, 1971; *City of Brass,* Leisure Books, 1971; *The Fellowship of the Hand,* Walker & Co., 1973; *The Frankenstein Factory,* Warner Books, 1975; *The Thefts of Nick Velvet,* Mysterious Press, 1978; *The Monkey's Clue* [and] *The Stolen Sapphire* (juvenile), Grosset, 1978.

Editor: *Dear Dead Days,* Walker & Co., 1973; *Best Detective Stories of the Year—1976-1981,* Dutton, 1976-81; *All But Impossible!,* Ticknor & Fields, 1981; *The Year's Best Mystery and Suspense Stories—1982-1984,* Walker, 1982-84. Contributor of more than six hundred short stories to periodicals, including *Antaeus, Argosy, Ellery Queen's Mystery Magazine,* and *Alfred Hitchcock's Mystery Magazine;* some of the stories have appeared under one of his six pseudonyms.

MEDIA ADAPTATIONS: Fourteen of Edward D. Hoch's stories have been adapted for television, including three for the NBC-TV series "McMillan and Wife."

AVOCATIONAL INTERESTS: The contemporary motion picture as an art form.

BIOGRAPHICAL/CRITICAL SOURCES: New York Times Book Review, June 29, 1968, March 11, 1973; *Rochester Democrat and Chronicle,* September 7, 1969; *Writer,* April, 1974; *Ellery Queen's Mystery Magazine,* August, 1976.

*   *   *

HODGES, Doris M(arjorie)   1915-
(Charlotte Hunt)

PERSONAL: Born April 28, 1915, in Bristol, England; daughter of Charles George and Christine (Lintern) Hodges. *Education:* Attended a girls' school in Bristol, England. *Home:* Romadene, 5 St. Andrews Rd., Blackwell, near Bristol, England. *Office:* Medical Library, Barrow Psychiatric Hospital, Barrow Gurney, near Bristol, England.

CAREER: Barrow Psychiatric Hospital, Barrow Gurney, near Bristol, England, medical librarian, 1958—. Lecturer on writing for profit, North Bristol Evening Institute. *Member:* Society of Authors, Society of Women Journalists.

WRITINGS—Under pseudonym Charlotte Hunt; published by Ace Books, except as indicated: *Healing Stones,* Pyramid Publishers (Hiawatha, Iowa), 1961; *The Gilded Sarcophagus,* 1967; *The Cup of Thanatos,* 1968; *The Lotus Vellum,* 1970; *The Thirteenth Treasure,* 1972; *Gemini Revenged,* 1973; *A Touch of Myrrh,* 1973; *Chambered Tomb,* 1974; *Tremayne's Wife,* 1974; *Wreath for Jenny's Grave,* 1975.

Under name Doris M. Hodges: *Healing Gems,* Venton, 1972; *Crossfire,* New Playwrights' Network, 1975; *Writing for Profit,* New Horizon Books, 1979; *Story of Hymns,* Kingsmead Press, 1979; *Writing for Profit Two,* New Horizon Books, 1983.

Also author of *Trewornan Water* and *Heart's Journey,* both published by Millington Books. Author of articles and short stories about the occult.

WORK IN PROGRESS: Wind from the West, a historical book for children about the Monmouth Rebellion.

HOFFMAN, William M(oses) 1939-

PERSONAL: Born April 12, 1939, in New York, N.Y.; son of Morton and Johanna (Papiermeister) Hoffman. *Education:* City College (now City College of the City University of New York), B.A. (cum laude), 1960. *Home:* 199 Prince St., New York, N.Y. 10012. *Agent:* Helen Merrill, 337 West 22nd St., New York, N.Y. 10011.

CAREER: Playwright, poet, and editor. Barnes & Noble (book publishers), New York City, editorial assistant, 1960-61; Hill & Wang (book publishers), New York City, assistant editor, 1961-67, associate editor and drama editor, 1967-68, editor of "New American Plays Series," 1968-71; Hofstra University, Hempstead, N.Y., Star Adjunct Professor in Playwriting, 1980. Has directed plays. Founder and director, Wolf Company, 1968—. Artist-in-residence, Lincoln Center Student Program, 1971-72, Changing Scene, 1972; playwright-in-residence, American Conservatory Theatre (San Francisco), 1978, La Mama Experimental Theatre Club (New York City), 1978-79. Lecturer, Eugene O'Neill Foundation, 1971; visiting lecturer, University of Massachusetts, 1973. Member of board of directors, Orion Repertory Company, 1975—. Drama adviser, Cable Arts Foundation, 1973; playwriting consultant, CAPS Program of New York State Council on the Arts, 1975-77, and Massachusetts Arts and Humanities Foundation, 1978.

MEMBER: American Society of Composers, Authors, and Publishers (ASCAP), P.E.N., New York Theatre Strategy (founding member), Phi Beta Kappa. *Awards, honors:* MacDowell fellowship, 1971; Carnegie Fund for Authors grant, 1972; P.E.N. American Center grant, 1972; Guggenheim fellowship, 1974-75; National Endowment for the Arts, librettist's grant, 1975-76, creative writing fellowship, 1976-77; Metropolitan Opera commission for libretto for centennial season, 1983-84.

WRITINGS—Plays: "Thank You, Miss Victoria" (one-act), first produced Off-Broadway at Martinique Theatre, 1965; "Saturday Night at the Movies" (one-act), first produced Off-Broadway at Cafe Cino, 1965; *Good Night, I Love You* (one-act; first produced at Cafe Cino, 1966), Breakthrough Press, 1974; "Spring Play" (two-act), first produced Off-Broadway at La Mama Experimental Theatre Club, 1967; "Incantation" (one-act), first produced at La Mama Experimental Theatre Club, 1967; "Three Masked Dances" (two-act), first produced at La Mama Experimental Theatre Club, 1967; "Uptight" (musical; three-act), first produced Off-Off-Broadway at Old Reliable Theatre, 1968; "XXXXX" (long one-act), first produced at La Mama Experimental Theatre Club, 1969, produced in London, England, as "Nativity Play," 1970.

"Luna" (one-act), first produced at Old Reliable Theatre, 1970; "A Quick Nut Bread to Make Your Mouth Water" (long one-act), first produced at Old Reliable Theatre, 1970; "From Fool to Hanged Man" (dance play), first produced in New York, N.Y., at Clark Center, 1972; "The Children's Crusade" (dance play), first produced at Clark Center, 1972; "I Love Ya, Ya Big Ape" (one-act), first produced at University of Massachusetts, 1973; "Gilles de Rais" (three-act), first produced Off-Broadway at Gate Theatre, 1975.

"Cornbury" (staged reading), first produced Off-Broadway at Public Theatre, 1976; "Shoe Palace Murray," first produced in San Francisco at American Conservatory Theatre, 1978; "Gulliver's Travels" (musical), first produced at La Mama Experimental Theatre Club, 1978; "A Book of Etiquette" (musical), first produced at La Mama Experimental Theatre Club, 1978.

Other writings: *The Cloisters* (song cycle), music by John Corigliano, G. Schirmer, 1968; (editor and contributor) *New American Plays,* Hill & Wang, Volume II, 1968, Volume III, 1970, Volume IV, 1971; (editor) *31 New American Poets,* Hill & Wang, 1970; *Fine Frenzy* (poems), McGraw, 1972; (author of lyrics) *Wedding Song,* G. Schirmer, 1979.

Author of television scripts, including "Notes from the New World: Louis Moreau Gottschalk," Columbia Broadcasting System, Inc. (CBS-TV), 1976, "Pink Panther's Magic Music Hall," 1977, "The Last Days of Stephen Foster," CBS-TV, 1977, and "Whistler: Five Portraits," CBS-TV, 1978. Also author of scripts for WNET, 1976-77; also author of motion picture and radio scripts.

Plays represented in anthologies, including: *M.E.A.L.,* edited by Peter Fusco, Hunter College of the City University of New York, 1970; *Now: Theater der Erfahrung,* edited by Jens Heilmeyer and Pia Frolich, M. Dumont Schauberg (Cologne), 1971; *More Plays from Off-Off-Broadway,* edited by Michael Smith, Bobbs-Merrill, 1973; *Spontaneous Combustion,* edited by Rochelle Owens, Winter House, 1973; *The Off-Off-Broadway Book,* edited by Albert Poland and Bruce Mailman, Bobbs-Merrill, 1973; *Gay Plays: The First Collection,* Avon, 1979.

Also author of play criticism. Contributor to *Dramatics.* Literary adviser, *Scripts,* 1971-74.

SIDELIGHTS: William M. Hoffman's "XXXXX," a one-act play about the life of Jesus, is "beautiful," according to Marvin Pletzke in *Show Business.* Pletzke explains that Hoffman "evokes our senses to an awareness of color and smell and sound—the full experience of being alive." Jon Carlson of the *Village Voice* also admires the play, commenting, "Most of the credit . . . goes to William Hoffman for the writing and directing of this charming play, which has more insights than its casual and light-hearted appearance would imply."

BIOGRAPHICAL/CRITICAL SOURCES: Village Voice, August 14, 1969; *Show Business,* August 16, 1969, July 11, 1970; *Changes,* March, 1971.

*   *   *

HOLENSTEIN, Elmar 1937-

PERSONAL: Born January 7, 1937, in St. Gallen, Switzerland; son of Adolf and Johanna (Fuerer) Holenstein; married Kae Ito (a psychologist), December 1, 1981. *Education:* Attended University of Louvain, Belgium, 1964-67, Ph.D., 1970; graduate study at University of Heidelberg, 1967-69, and University of Zurich, 1969-71. *Home:* Hustadtring 139, D 4630 Bochum, West Germany. *Office:* Institut fuer Philosophie, Ruhr-Universitaet, D 4630 Bochum, West Germany.

CAREER: Husserl Archives, Louvain, Belgium, scientific collaborator, 1971-73; University of Cologne, Cologne, Germany, scientific collaborator, 1975-77; University of Zurich, Zurich, Switzerland, lecturer, 1976-77; Ruhr-Universitaet, Bochum, West Germany, professor, 1977—. Fellow, Japan Foundation, 1983-84. *Member:* Allgemeine Gesellschaft fuer Philosophie in Deutschland, Deutsche Gesellschaft fuer Phaenomenologische Forschung, Deutsche Gesellschaft fuer Semiotik. *Awards, honors:* Bourse Burrus from Swiss National Foundation for Scientific Research, 1974.

WRITINGS—In English translation: *Roman Jakobsons phae-nomenologischer Strukturalismus*, Suhrkamp (Frankfurt), 1975, translation by Cathrine Schelbert and Tarcisius Schelbert published as *Roman Jakobson's Approach to Language*, Indiana University Press, 1976.

In German: *Phaenomenologie der Assoziation* (title means "Phenomenology of Association"), Nijhoff (The Hague), 1972; (editor) *Edmund Husserl: Logische Untersuchungen I* (title means "Logical Investigations I"), Nijhoff, 1975; (editor) *Roman Jakobson: Hoelderlin-Klee-Brecht*, Suhrkamp, 1976; *Linguistik, Semiotik, Hermeneutik*, Suhrkamp, 1976; (editor with Tarcisius Schelbert) *Roman Jakobson: Poetik*, Suhrkamp, 1979; *Von der Hintergehbarkeit der Sprache*, Suhrkamp, 1980.

WORK IN PROGRESS: Research in philosophy of language (universals) and in philosophy of mind (relationship between mind and body and between knowledge and language).

*   *   *

HOLLAND, Katrin
    See ALBRAND, Martha

*   *   *

HOLLI, Melvin G(eorge)   1933-

PERSONAL: Born February 22, 1933, in Ishpeming, Mich.; son of Walfred M. (a welder) and Sylvia (Erickson) Holli; married Betsy Biggar (a clinic dietitian), August 12, 1961; children: Susan J., Steven E. *Education:* Northern Michigan University, B.A., 1957; University of Michigan, M.A., 1958, Ph.D., 1966. *Religion:* Lutheran. *Home:* 1311 Ashland Ave., River Forest, Ill. 60305. *Office:* Department of History, University of Illinois at Chicago Circle, Chicago, Ill. 60680.

CAREER: University of Michigan, Ann Arbor, curator of historical collections, 1963-64; University of Illinois at Chicago Circle, Chicago, associate professor of history, 1965—. *Member:* American Historical Association, Organization of American Historians. *Awards, honors:* Woodrow Wilson fellowship, 1957-58; National Endowment for the Humanities fellowship, 1969-70; Society of Midland Authors prize for best history, 1981, for *Ethnic Chicago.*

WRITINGS: *Reform in Detroit: Hazen S. Pingree and Urban Politics*, Oxford University Press, 1969; (author of new introduction) Tom L. Johnson, *My Story*, University of Washington Press, 1971; *Detroit: Fur Trading Post to Industrial Metropolis, 1701-1976*, New Viewpoints, 1976; (with P. Jones) *Ethnic Frontier*, Eerdmans, 1977; *Ethnic Chicago*, Eerdmans, 1981; (editor with Jones) *Biographical Dictionary of American Mayors, 1820-1980*, Greenwood Press, 1982.

WORK IN PROGRESS: A study of political decision-making in the American city, 1865-1920.

*   *   *

HOLLINGSHEAD, (Ronald) Kyle   1941-

PERSONAL: Born July 29, 1941, in Baird, Tex.; son of Olaf M. (a groceryman) and Pearlie (Gillit) Hollingshead; married Maxine Lee Valentino, December 28, 1981. *Education:* Texas Technological College (now Texas Tech University), student, 1959-61. *Politics:* Democrat. *Religion:* Methodist. *Home:* 4225 53rd St., Lubbock, Tex. 79413.

CAREER: Partner in H & H Food Market, 1961-68, and 4th St. Laundry, 1968—, both in Lubbock, Tex. *Member:* Western Writers of America.

WRITINGS—All novels; all published by Ace Books: *Echo of a Texas Rifle*, 1967; *The Franklin Raid*, 1968; *Ransome's Debt*, 1970; *Ransome's Move*, 1971; *Ransome's Army*, 1974; *The Man on the Blood Bay*, 1977; *Across the Border*, 1978.

WORK IN PROGRESS: Science fiction and fantasy novels.

AVOCATIONAL INTERESTS: Collecting and reading books, golf.

*   *   *

HOLMES, Colin   1938-

PERSONAL: Born August 8, 1938, in South Normanton, Derbyshire, England; son of Oswald and Grace Mary (Watson) Holmes; married Joyce Bagnall (a civil servant), August 23, 1962; children: one daughter. *Education:* University of Nottingham, B.A., 1960, Certificate in Education, 1962, M.A., 1964. *Home:* 59 Marsh House Rd., Sheffield S11 95Q, Yorkshire, England. *Office:* Department of Economic and Social History, University of Sheffield, Sheffield S10 2TN, Yorkshire, England.

CAREER: University of Sheffield, Sheffield, England, lecturer, 1963-72, senior lecturer, 1972-80, reader in economic and social history, 1980—. *Member:* Economic History Society.

WRITINGS: (With Sidney Pollard) *Documents of European Economic History*, Volume I: *The Process of Industrialization, 1760-1870*, Edward Arnold, 1968, St. Martin's, 1969; *Industrial Power and National Rivalry*, Edward Arnold, 1972; *The End of Old Europe*, Edward Arnold, 1973; (with B. J. Elliott) *World Society*, Hulton, 1973; *Immigrants and Minorities in British Society*, Allen & Unwin, 1976; (with Pollard) *Essays in the Economic and Social History of South Yorkshire*, South Yorkshire Chamber of Commerce, 1976; *Anti-Semitism in British Society, 1876-1939*, Edward Arnold, 1979; *Immigration into Britain, 1870-1982*, Macmillan, 1984. Co-editor, *Immigrants and Minorities.*

AVOCATIONAL INTERESTS: The cinema.

*   *   *

HOLMES, Paul Carter   1926-

PERSONAL: Born September 10, 1926, in Niagara Falls, N.Y.; son of Frederick Greenwood and Helen Louise (Carter) Holmes. *Education:* Santa Rosa Junior College, A.A., 1955; University of California, Berkeley, B.A., 1957; San Francisco State College (now University), M.A., 1964. *Politics:* Democrat. *Religion:* Episcopalian. *Home:* 2011 Los Angeles Ave., Berkeley, Calif. 94707. *Office:* Department of English, College of San Mateo, 1700 Whillsdale, San Mateo, Calif. 94402.

CAREER: San Leandro (Calif.) Unified School District, teacher of English and reading, 1959-62; College of San Mateo, San Mateo, Calif., 1964—, began as instructor in English and reading, currently instructor in reading and supervisor of reading program. *Military service:* U.S. Army, 1950-52. *Member:* International Reading Association, American Association of University Professors, American Federation of Teachers, National Council of Teachers of English, Western College Reading Association, California Teachers Association, Northern California College Teachers of Reading.

WRITINGS: (With Anita J. Lehman) *A Parade of Lines,* Canfield Press, 1971; *Phonics Guidelines,* Kendall/Hunt, 1980; (with Henry Cordes) *Going Places,* College of San Mateo, 1982.

All published by Harper: (With Lehman) *Keys to Understanding: Receiving and Sending the Essay,* 1968, 2nd edition, 1974; (with Lehman) *Keys to Understanding: Receiving and Sending the Poem,* 1969; *Keys to Understanding: Receiving and Sending Drama,* 1970; (with Harry Souza) *The Touch of a Poet,* 1975; (with Lehman) *The Challenge of Conflict* (short story anthology), 1976.

WORK IN PROGRESS: Vocabulary materials.

*   *   *

HOLST, Johan J(oergen)   1937-

PERSONAL: Born November 29, 1937, in Oslo, Norway; son of Nils Oluf (in marine insurance) and Ester (Salvesen) Holst; married Judith Ann Perry, March 20, 1960; children: Haldis Margrete, Kerstin Elisabet, Johan Joergen, Jr., Katerina Andrea. *Education:* Columbia University, A.B., 1960; University of Oslo, Magistergrad, 1965. *Politics:* Social Democrat. *Home:* Midtskogvien 22, N-2020 Skedsmo, Norway. *Office address:* Norwegian Institute of International Affairs, P.O. Box 8159-Dep, Oslo-1, Norway.

CAREER: Harvard University, Cambridge, Mass., research associate, Center for International Affairs, 1962-63; Norwegian Defense Research Establishment, Kjeller, Norway, senior researcher, 1963-67; Hudson Institute, Croton, N.Y., senior member of professional staff, 1967-69; Norwegian Institute of International Affairs, Oslo, Norway, director of research, 1969-76; Norwegian Ministry of Defence, Oslo, 1976-79, began as under secretary of state, became state secretary; Norwegian Ministry of Foreign Affairs, Oslo, state secretary, 1979-81; Norwegian Institute of International Affairs, director, 1981—.

President, Norwegian European Movement; member, foreign policy council of Norwegian Labor party. Member, Trilateral Commission; member of the council, Centre for European Policy Studies; member of steering group, European Security Study; member of council executive committee, International Institute for Strategic Studies; member of board of directors, Institute for East-West Security Studies. *Military service:* Royal Norwegian Army, 1956-58; became sergeant. *Member:* World Future Society, Oslo Military Society.

WRITINGS: Norsk Sikkerhetspolitikk i Strategisk Perspektiv, two volumes, Norwegian Institute of International Affairs, 1967; (co-author) *Future of the Oceans,* Trilateral Commission, 1976; *Var Forararspolitikk,* Tiohn, 1978.

Editor: (With William Schneider, Jr.) *Why ABM?: Policy Issues in the Missile Defense Controversy,* Pergamon, 1969; *Security, Order, and the Bomb,* Oslo University Press, 1972; (with John Sanness) *Hvorfor JA ti EF,* JA ti EF, aksjonen, 1972; (with Valter Angell) *EF-Norges Vei?,* Oslo University Press, 1972; *Five Roads to Nordic Security,* Oslo University Press, 1973; *Norge og Rustningskontroll i Europa,* Dreyer, 1974; *Norsk Utennkspolitisk Arbok 1973,* NUP, 1974.

Norsk Utennkspolitisk Arbok 1974, NUP, 1975; *Oljen i sikkerhetspolitikken,* DNAK, 1975; (with Christopher Bertram) *New Strategic Factors in the North Atlantic,* Oslo University Press, 1977; (with Clive Norlich) *Beyond Nuclear Deterrence: New Arms, New Aims,* Crane, Russak, 1977. Contributor to

political science journals in the United States and Europe. Editor, *Cooperation and Conflict,* 1970-75.

AVOCATIONAL INTERESTS: Modern literature, classical music, philately.

BIOGRAPHICAL/CRITICAL SOURCES: National Review, July 29, 1969.

*   *   *

HOLSTI, Ole R(udolf)   1933-

PERSONAL: Born August 7, 1933, in Geneva, Switzerland; became American citizen, 1954; son of Rudolf W. (a diplomat) and Liisa (Franssila) Holsti; married Ann Wood, September 20, 1953; children: Eric Lynn, Maija. *Education:* Stanford University, B.A., 1954, Ph.D., 1962; Wesleyan University, Middletown, Conn., M.A.T., 1956. *Home:* 608 Croom Ct., Chapel Hill, N.C. 27514. *Office:* Department of Political Science, Duke University, Durham, N.C. 27706.

CAREER: Stanford University, Stanford, Calif., instructor, 1962-63, acting assistant professor, 1963-65, assistant professor of political science, 1965-67, research coordinator and associate director of Studies in International Conflict and Integration, 1962-67; University of British Columbia, Vancouver, associate professor, 1967-71, professor of political science, 1971-74; Duke University, Durham, N.C., George V. Allen Professor of Political Science, 1974—, chairman of department, 1978—; University of California, Davis, professor of political science, 1978-79. Member of advisory board, University Press of America, 1976—. *Military service:* U.S. Army, 1956-58. U.S. Army Reserve, 1954-56, 1958-62; became staff sergeant.

MEMBER: International Institute of Strategic Studies (London), Peace Science Society (southern section president, 1975-77), International Studies Association (western president, 1969-70; southern president, 1975-76; president, 1979-80), American Political Science Association (council member, 1982-85), Western Political Science Association (executive council member, 1971-74), Inter-university Consortium for Political Research, Fleet Feet Running Club, Carolina Godiva Track Club, Duke Master Runners, Phi Beta Kappa.

AWARDS, HONORS: Owen D. Young Fellowship, General Electric Foundation, 1960-61; research fellowship, Haynes Foundation, 1961-62; Canada Council, research grant, 1969, leave fellowship, 1970-71; fellowship, Center for Advanced Study in the Behavioral Sciences, 1972-73; faculty research fellowship, Ford Foundation, 1972-73; research grants, National Science Foundation, 1975-77, 1979-81, 1983-85; Best Published Paper award, *International Studies Quarterly,* 1979-81, for "The Three Headed Eagle"; Guggenheim fellowship, 1981-82.

WRITINGS: (With Robert C. North, M. George Zaninovich, and Dina A. Zinnes) *Content Analysis: A Handbook with Application for the Study of International Crisis,* Northwestern University Press, 1963; (with David J. Findlay and Richard R. Fagen) *Enemies in Politics,* Rand McNally, 1967; *Content Analysis for the Social Sciences and Humanities,* Addison-Wesley, 1969; (with George Gerbner, Klaus Krippendorff, Philip J. Stone and William Paisley) *The Analysis of Communication Content,* Wiley, 1969.

Crisis, Escalation, War, McGill-Queens University Press, 1972; (with Terrence Hopmann and John D. Sullivan) *Unity and Disintegration in International Alliances,* Wiley, 1973; (with Alexander L. George and Randolph M. Siverson) *Change in the International System,* Westview, 1980; (with James M. Rosenau) *American Leadership in World Affairs: The Breakdown of Consensus,* Allen & Unwin, 1984.

Contributor: *The Grand Design,* University of Southern California Press, 1964; Davis B. Bobrow, editor, *Components of Defence Policy,* Rand McNally, 1965; *Computers for the Humanities,* Yale University Press, 1965; Elton B. McNeil, editor, *The Nature of Human Conflict,* Prentice-Hall, 1965; Stone, editor, *The General Inquirer: A Computer Approach to Content Analysis in the Behavioral Sciences,* M.I.T. Press, 1966; (with North) Richard Merritt and Stein Rokkan, editors, *Comparing Nations,* Yale University Press, 1966.

John C. Farrell and Asa P. Smith, editors, *Image and Reality in World Politics,* Columbia University Press, 1967; Edmund A. Bowles, editor, *Computers in Humanistic Research,* Prentice-Hall, 1967; K. J. Holsti, *International Politics: A Framework for Analysis,* Prentice-Hall, 1967, 4th edition, 1982; (with North and Richard A. Brody) J. David Singer, editor, *Quantitative International Politics: Insights and Evidence,* Free Press, 1967; Peter Toma and Andrew Gyorgy, editors, *Basic Issues in International Relations,* Allyn & Bacon, 1967; John H. Bunzel, editor, *Issues of American Public Policy,* Prentice-Hall, 2nd edition, 1968; Louis Kriesberg, editor, *Social Process in International Relations,* Wiley, 1968; Bobrow and Judah L. Schwartz, editors, *Computers and the Policy Making Communities,* Prentice-Hall, 1968; Gardner Lindzey and Elliot Aronson, editors, *The Handbook of Social Psychology,* Addison-Wesley, 2nd edition, 1968.

Charles F. Hermann, editor, *Foreign Policy Crisis: A Simulation Analysis,* Bobbs-Merrill, 1969; John E. Mueller, editor, *Approaches to Measurement in International Relations,* Appleton-Century-Crofts, 1969; Richard C. Snyder and Dean Pruitt, editors, *Theory and Research on the Causes of War,* Prentice-Hall, 1969; Jan F. Triska, editor, *Communist Party-States: International and Comparative Studies,* Bobbs-Merrill, 1969; *The World Communist System: International and Comparative Studies,* Bobbs-Merrill, 1969; Rosenau, editor, *International Politics and Foreign Policy,* Free Press, 2nd edition, 1969; Rosenau, editor, *Linkage Politics: Essays on the Convergence of National and International Systems,* Free Press, 1969.

Naomi Rosenbaum, editor, *Readings in International Political Behavior,* Prentice-Hall, 1970; George Cole, John H. Kessel, and Robert G. Seddig, editors, *Micropolitics,* Holt, 1970; Leroy Graymer, editor, *Systems and Actors in International Politics,* Chandler & Sharp, 1971; William D. Coplin and Charles W. Kegley, editors, *A Multi-Method Introduction to International Politics,* Markham, 1971; Samuel A. Kirkpatrick and Lawrence K. Pettit, editors, *The Social Psychology of Political Life,* Duxbury, 1972; Ivo D. Duchacek, editor, *Discord and Harmony,* Holt, 1972; Hermann, editor, *International Crises: Insights from Behavioral Research,* Free Press, 1972; Hermann, editor, *International Crises,* Free Press, 1973; Cornelius P. Cotter, editor, *Political Science Annual,* Volume VI, Bobbs-Merrill, 1975.

Robert Axelrod, editor, *The Structure of Decision,* Princeton University Press, 1976; I. William Zartman, editor, *The 50% Solution: How to Bargain Successfully with Hijackers, Strikers, Bosses, Oil Magnates, Arabs, Russians, and Other Worthy Opponents in This Modern World,* Anchor Books, 1976; Rosenau, editor, *In Search of Global Patterns,* Free Press, 1976; Rosenau, Kenneth Thompson, and Gavin Boyd, editors, *World Politics,* Free Press, 1976; (with North and Nazli Choucri) Francis W. Hoole and Zinnes, editors, *Quantitative Interna-*

tional Politics: An Appraisal, Praeger, 1976; Donald Freeman, editor, *Political Science: History, Scope and Methods,* Free Press, 1977; G. Matthew Bonham and Michael J. Shapiro, editors, *Thought and Action in Foreign Policy,* Birkhauser Verlag, 1977; Daniel Heradstveit and Ove Narvasen, editors, *Decision-Making Research: Some Recent Developments,* Norwegian Institute of International Affairs, 1977.

C. F. Smart and W. T. Stanbury, editors, *Studies on Crisis Management,* Butterworths, 1978; David W. Orr and Marvin Soroos, editors, *The Global Predicament: Ecological Perspectives on World Order,* University of North Carolina Press, 1979; G. W. Keeton and C. Schwarzenberger, editors, *The Year Book of World Affairs,* London Institute of World Affairs, 1979; Paul Gordon Lauren, editor, *Diplomacy: New Approaches in History, Theory, and Policy,* Free Press, 1979; Charles W. Kegley, Jr. and Patrick T. McGowan, editors, *Challenges to America: United States Foreign Policy in the 1980s,* Sage Publications, 1979.

Richard A. Falk and Samuel S. Kim, editors, *The War System: An Interdisciplinary Approach,* Westview, 1980; Ellen Boneparth, editor, *Women, Power, and Policy,* Pergamon, 1982; Crister Jonsson, editor, *Cognitive Dynamics and International Politics,* Pinter, 1982; Kegley and E. R. Wittkopf, editors, *The Sources of American Foreign Policy,* St. Martin's, 1983.

Contributor to "Peace Research Society Papers," 1964-65; contributor of articles and reviews to professional journals. Associate editor, *Journal of Conflict Resolution,* 1969-72, *International Studies Quarterly,* 1970-75, and *Western Political Quarterly,* 1970-79; member of board of editors, *International Studies Quarterly,* 1967-70 and 1975-80, *Computer Studies in the Humanities and Verbal Behavior,* 1968-76, *American Journal of Political Science,* 1975-80, and *International Interaction,* 1980—.

WORK IN PROGRESS: Articles and a book on "post-Vietnam divisions on foreign policy among American leaders," supported by a National Science Foundation grant.

*   *   *

HOLT, John (Robert) 1926-
(John Arre, Elizabeth Giles, Raymond Giles)

PERSONAL: Born September 24, 1926; son of Harold Griffith (an Episcopal priest) and Helen (Ritter) Holt; married Margaret Stone, May 7, 1955; children: Helen Margaret, Carol Elizabeth. *Education:* University of Illinois, B.A., 1951. *Agent:* Henry Morrison, Inc., 58 West 10th St., New York, N.Y. 10011.

CAREER: Free-lance writer. National Association of Educational Broadcasters, Washington, D.C., manager of NAEB Network; Scott Meredith Literary Agency, Inc., New York City, beginning 1960, became manager of foreign department; former editor, Lancer Books, New York City. *Military service:* U.S. Army.

WRITINGS—Under pseudonym Raymond Giles, except as indicated: *Night of the Warlock,* Paperback Library, 1968; *Night of the Vampire,* Avon, 1969; *Sabrehill,* Fawcett, 1974; *Rogue Black,* Fawcett, 1974; *Dark Master,* Fawcett, 1975; (under pseudonym John Arre) *Message to My Daughter* (novelization of television play), Pyramid Publications, 1975; *Slaves of Sabrehill,* Fawcett, 1975; *Rebels of Sabrehill,* Fawcett, 1977; *Storm over Sabrehill,* Fawcett, 1978; *Hellcat of Sabrehill,* Fawcett, 1982. Also author of gothic novels under pseudonym

Elizabeth Giles. Has done considerable ghostwriting, and script for "U.S. Steel Hour." Contributor to several anthologies and to *Ellery Queen's Mystery Magazine* and *Alfred Hitchcock's Mystery Magazine.*

SIDELIGHTS: John Holt told *CA:* "Aside from making a living at this racket, my only wish is now and then to make the magic work."

*   *   *

HOMANS, Peter   1930-

PERSONAL: Born June 24, 1930, in New York, N.Y.; married Celia Ann Edwards (an associate director, National Opinion Research Center); children: Jennifer, Patricia, Elizabeth. *Education:* Princeton University, A.B., 1952; Protestant Episcopal Theological Seminary in Virginia, B.D., 1957; University of Chicago, M.A., 1962, Ph.D., 1964. *Office:* Divinity School, University of Chicago, Chicago, Ill. 60637.

CAREER: Institute for Juvenile Research, Chicago, Ill., supervisor of residential treatment for children, 1961-62; University of Toronto, Trinity College, Toronto, Ontario, instructor in department of religion, 1962-64; Hartford Seminary Foundation, Hartford, Conn., assistant professor of theology and psychology, 1964-65; University of Chicago, Divinity School, Chicago, associate professor, 1965-78, professor of religion and psychological studies, 1978—. *Member:* American Psychological Association, American Academy of Religion, Society for Values in Higher Education.

WRITINGS: (Editor) *The Dialogue between Theology and Psychology,* University of Chicago Press, 1968; *Theology After Freud: An Interpretive Inquiry,* Bobbs-Merrill, 1970; (editor and contributor) *Childhood and Selfhood: Essays on Tradition, Religion and Modernity in the Thought of Erik H. Erikson,* Bucknell University Press, 1978; *Jung in Context: Modernity and the Making of a Psychology,* University of Chicago Press, 1979.

WORK IN PROGRESS: A book on the psychoanalytic interpretation of Western religious traditions.

SIDELIGHTS: Peter Homans writes *CA:* "Religion is like politics: Everyone has an opinion about it, and considers his/her opinion to be the final word. My writing is, for this reason, as frustrating as it is challenging, for I attempt a comprehensive, objective theory of religion, one which believer and unbeliever alike can tolerate."

*   *   *

HOOBLER, Dorothy

PERSONAL: Born in Philadelphia, Pa.; daughter of Frederick and Eleanor (Bystrom) Law; married Thomas Hoobler (a writer and editor), December 18, 1971; children: Ellen Marie. *Education:* Wells College, A.B., 1963; New York University, M.A., 1971. *Home:* 320 West 83rd St., Apt. 6-C, New York, N.Y. 10024. *Agent:* Virginia Barber Literary Agency, Inc., 353 West 21st St., New York, N.Y. 10011.

CAREER: Has worked as an editor and genealogist; free-lance writer, 1973—.

WRITINGS—All with husband, Thomas Hoobler: *Frontier Diary,* Macmillan, 1974; *Margaret Mead: A Life in Science,* Macmillan, 1974; *House Plants,* Grosset, 1975; *Vegetable Gardening and Cooking,* Grosset, 1975; *Pruning,* Grosset, 1975;

An Album of World War I, F. Watts, 1976; *The Year in Bloom,* Bantam, 1977; *Photographing History: The Career of Mathew Brady,* Putnam, 1977; *An Album of World War II,* F. Watts, 1977; *The Trenches: Fighting on the Western Front in World War I,* Putnam, 1978; *Photographing the Frontier,* Putnam, 1980; *U.S.-China Relations since World War II,* F. Watts, 1981; *An Album of the Seventies,* F. Watts, 1981; *The Social Security System,* F. Watts, 1982; *The Voyages of Captain Cook,* Putnam, 1983.

WORK IN PROGRESS: Chinese Lives, a historical work for young adults, with T. Hoobler.

AVOCATIONAL INTERESTS: Oriental, American, and European medieval history, music, photography, gardening, and travel.

*   *   *

HOOBLER, Thomas

PERSONAL: Born in Cincinnati, Ohio; son of John T. (a printer) and Jane Frances (Pachoud) Hoobler; married Dorothy Law (a writer), December 18, 1971; children: Ellen Marie. *Education:* University of Notre Dame, A.B., 1964; attended University of Iowa, Writer's Workshop, 1965. *Home:* 320 West 83rd St., Apt. 6-C, New York, N.Y. 10024. *Agent:* Virginia Barber Literary Agency, Inc., 353 West 21st St., New York, N.Y. 10011.

CAREER: Worked in various positions at private schools in Cincinnati, Ohio, including teacher of English and photography, audio-visual coordinator, and basketball coach, 1965-70; trade magazine editor, 1971-76; free-lance writer and editor, 1976—.

WRITINGS—With wife, Dorothy Hoobler, except as indicated: *Frontier Diary,* Macmillan, 1974; *Margaret Mead: A Life in Science,* Macmillan, 1974; *House Plants,* Grosset, 1975; *Vegetable Gardening and Cooking,* Grosset, 1975; *Pruning,* Grosset, 1975; *An Album of World War I,* F. Watts, 1976; *The Year in Bloom,* Bantam, 1977; *Photographing History: The Career of Mathew Brady,* Putnam, 1977; *An Album of World War II,* F. Watts, 1977; *The Trenches: Fighting on the Western Front in World War I,* Putnam, 1978; (with Burt Wetanson) *The Hunters,* Doubleday, 1978; *Photographing the Frontier,* Putnam, 1980; *U.S.-China Relations since World War II,* F. Watts, 1981; *An Album of the Seventies,* F. Watts, 1981; *The Social Security System,* F. Watts, 1982; *The Voyages of Captain Cook,* Putnam, 1983; (with Wetanson) *The Treasure Hunters,* Playboy Press, 1983.

WORK IN PROGRESS: The House, an adult novel; *Chinese Lives,* a historical work for young adults, with D. Hoobler.

AVOCATIONAL INTERESTS: Oriental, American, and European medieval history, music, photography, gardening, and travel.

*   *   *

HORNIK, Edith Lynn
See BEER, Edith Lynn

*   *   *

HOSOKAWA, Bill
See HOSOKAWA, William K.

HOSOKAWA, William K.   1915-
(Bill Hosokawa)

PERSONAL: Born January 30, 1915, in Seattle, Wash.; son of Setsugo and Kimiyo (Omura) Hosokawa; married Alice Tokuko Miyake, August 28, 1938; children: Michael C., Susan (Mrs. Warren Boatright), Peter E., Christie (Mrs. Lloyd C. Harveson). *Education:* University of Washington, B.A., 1937. *Politics:* Independent. *Religion:* "Protestant preference." *Home:* 140 South Upham Ct., Denver, Colo. 80226.

CAREER: Writer for *Singapore Herald,* Singapore, 1938-40, and *Shanghai Times and Far Eastern Review,* Shanghai, China, 1940-41; *Des Moines Register,* Des Moines, Iowa, editor, 1943-46; *Denver Post,* Denver, Colo., associate editor, 1946-83. *Member:* American Association of Sunday and Feature Editors (president, 1956), American Association of Newspaper Editors, Denver Press Club. *Awards, honors:* Western Heritage Award from Cowboy Hall of Fame, 1966; named Outstanding Colorado Journalist by University of Colorado School of Journalism, 1967; named Outstanding Journalist by the Colorado chapter of Sigma Delta Chi, 1976.

WRITINGS—Under name Bill Hosokawa; published by Morrow, except as indicated: *Nisei: The Quiet Americans,* 1969; (with Jim Yoshida) *The Two Worlds of Jim Yoshida,* 1972; *Thunder in the Rockies: The Incredible "Denver Post,"* 1976; *Thirty-five Years in the Frying Pan,* McGraw, 1978; (with Robert A. Wilson) *East to America: A History of the Japanese in the United States,* 1980; *JACL in Quest of Justice,* 1982.

SIDELIGHTS: In *East to America: A History of the Japanese in the United States,* William K. Hosokawa and Robert A. Wilson "show how Japanese-Americans have overcome stiff odds to make vital contributions to the United States," writes John K. Roth in the *Los Angeles Times Book Review.* The authors report, for instance, that after 1907 Japanese entry into the United States was restricted and then prohibited altogether for nearly thirty years by the Immigration Act of 1924. Moreover, first-generation arrivals—the Issei—had no access to citizenship via naturalization; being neither white nor black, they were excluded by legal interpretations based on racial criteria. Roth believes the book deserves plaudits, for it "meets the need for a scholarly overview of a minority too little studied."

Hosokawa's *Nisei: The Quiet Americans* reconstructs the history of the Nisei, the second-generation Japanese immigrants. American citizens by birth, many were forcibly removed to "relocation centers" in the wake of hysteria following Pearl Harbor. In the *New York Times Book Review,* Gladwin Hill calls the book "an absorbing chronicle of this important slice of history," noting that Hosokawa "went through the evacuation experience, yet remarkably eschews first-person commentary entirely and covers the subject with . . . detachment."

BIOGRAPHICAL/CRITICAL SOURCES: Saturday Review, November 15, 1969; *New York Times Book Review,* December 21, 1969; *Detroit News,* August 27, 1972; *Los Angeles Times Book Review,* August 24, 1980.

*   *   *

HOUCK, John W(illiam)   1931-

PERSONAL: Born April 16, 1931, in Beloit, Wis.; son of Walter and Gertrude (Coakley) Houck; married Mary Dooley, December 27, 1955; children: Christopher, Monica, Gregory.

Education: University of Notre Dame, A.B., J.D.; University of North Carolina, M.B.A.; Harvard University, LL.M. *Office:* College of Business Administration, University of Notre Dame, Notre Dame, Ind. 46556.

CAREER: University of Notre Dame, College of Business Administration, Notre Dame, Ind., began as instructor, currently professor of management and co-director of Notre Dame Center for Ethics and Religious Values in Business. Luce Foundation Lecturer, Wake Forest University, 1983. President, St. Joseph County Mental Health Association; member of board of directors, South Bend Urban League, 1960-62; president, Catholic Interracial Council, 1962. *Member:* American Association of University Professors (member of panel of consultants, 1967—). *Awards, honors:* Ford Foundation summer fellowship, 1961; Danforth teacher's fellowship, 1962-63.

WRITINGS: (Editor with Edward Manier) *Academic Freedom and the Catholic University,* Fides, 1967; (editor) *Outdoor Advertising: History and Regulation,* University of Notre Dame Press, 1969; (editor with William Heisler) *A Matter of Dignity: Inquiries into the Humanization of Work,* University of Notre Dame Press, 1977; (with Oliver F. Williams) *Full-Value: Cases in Christian Business Ethics,* Harper, 1979; (editor with Williams) *The Judeo-Christian Vision and the Modern Corporation,* University of Notre Dame Press, 1982; (editor with Williams) *Co-Creation and Capitalism: John Paul II's Laborem Exerceus,* University Press of America, 1983.

Contributor to *St. Louis Times-Democrat, Review of Politics, Notre Dame Magazine, Sign,* and other publications.

SIDELIGHTS: John W. Houck told *CA:* "My writings and editing seek to build conceptual bridges between business, business studies, and the humanities. In addition, I work to strengthen the religious perspective and contribution to business leadership and decision-making by building a body of literature which takes these issues seriously."

*   *   *

HOWARD, Constance (Mildred)   1910-

PERSONAL: Born December 8, 1910, in Northampton, England; daughter of Arthur (a teacher) and Mildred (Abbott) Howard; married Harold Wilson Parker, December 15, 1945; children: Charlotte (Mrs. Peter Busby). *Education:* Royal College of Art, A.R.C.A., 1934. *Home:* 43 Cambridge Rd. S., Chiswick, London W4 3DA, England.

CAREER: Professional embroiderer, 1947—. University of London, Goldsmiths College, part-time lecturer in School of Art, 1947-59, senior lecturer, 1959-73, principal lecturer, 1973-75. Member of British Craft Centre and of advisory committee to London College of Fashion. *Member:* Art Workers Guild, Society of Designer Craftsmen (fellow; member of council), Embroiderers Guild (member of council). *Awards, honors:* Member of Order of the British Empire; honorary fellow of College of Crafts.

WRITINGS: Design for Embroidery from Traditional English Sources, Batsford, 1956; *Inspiration for Embroidery,* Batsford, 1966; *Embroidery and Colour,* Van Nostrand, 1976; *The History of Embroidery in the Twentieth Century,* Reinhold, 1977; (editor) *Textile Crafts,* Scribner, 1978; *The Constance Howard Book of Stitches,* Batsford, 1980; *Twentieth-Century Embroidery in Great Britain,* Batsford, Volume I, 1982, Volume II, 1983, Volume III, in press. Contributor to magazines.

SIDELIGHTS: Constance Howard was trained as a wood engraver and book illustrator from 1931 to 1934. Now her embroidery is often commissioned, and she lectures on the subject in England, the United States, and Canada.

BIOGRAPHICAL/CRITICAL SOURCES: Embroidery, summer, 1973.

* * *

HOWARD, Warren F.
  See POHL, Frederik

* * *

HOWELL, Roger (Jr.) 1936-

PERSONAL: Born July 3, 1936, in Baltimore, Md.; son of Roger (a university dean and professor of law) and Katherine (Clifford) Howell; married Marcia Lunt, June 11, 1966 (divorced, 1976); children: Tracy Walker, Ian Christopher. *Education:* Bowdoin College, A.B. (summa cum laude), 1958; St. John's College, Oxford, B.A., 1960, M.A. (first class honors), 1964, D.Phil., 1964; Johns Hopkins University, graduate study, 1960-61. *Politics:* Republican. *Religion:* Episcopalian. *Home:* 16 Cleaveland St., Brunswick, Me. 04011.

CAREER: Oxford University, St. John's College, Oxford, England, research fellow and tutor in Honour School of Modern History, 1961-64, junior dean of arts, 1962-64; Bowdoin College, Brunswick, Me., assistant professor, 1964-66, associate professor, 1966-68, professor of history, 1968—, chairman of department, 1967-68, 1982—, acting dean of the college, 1967-68, president, 1969-78. Visiting professor, University of Maine, 1967-68. Member of Maine State and New England Rhodes Scholarship Selection Committees.

MEMBER: American Historical Association, Conference on British Studies, Renaissance Society of America, Economic History Society, Royal Historical Society (fellow), Historical Association (Great Britain), Royal Anthropological Institute of Great Britain and Ireland (fellow), Scottish History Society, Societe d'Etude du Dix-septieme Siecle, Past and Present Society, Society of Antiquaries (Newcastle), Stubbs Society (Oxford), New England Conference on British Studies (executive secretary, 1967-69), Anglo-American Associates (executive committee member, 1974—), Century Association, Phi Beta Kappa, St. Botolph Club, Oxford and Cambridge University Club, London Scottish Football Club.

AWARDS, HONORS: Rhodes Scholarship, 1958-60; LL.D. from Colby College and from Nasson College, 1970; L.H.D., University of Maine, 1971; Litt.D., Bowdoin College, 1978.

WRITINGS: (Editor) *Prescott: The Conquest of Mexico,* Twayne, 1966; *Newcastle upon Tyne and the Puritan Revolution,* Clarendon Press, 1967; *Sir Philip Sidney: The Shepherd Knight,* Little, Brown, 1968; *The Constitutional and Intellectual Origins of the English Revolution,* Forum Press, 1975; *Crowell,* Little, Brown, 1977; *Monopoly on the Tyne, 1650-58,* Society of Antiquaries, 1978.

Contributor of articles and reviews to *History Today, Archaeologia Aeliana, Canadian Journal of History,* and numerous other periodicals in his field. Editor, *British Studies Monitor,* 1969-81; co-editor, *Erasmus,* 1975-80.

WORK IN PROGRESS: The Image of Oliver Cromwell, 1660-1899 (book-length study); a study of urban politics in the English revolution.

AVOCATIONAL INTERESTS: Rugby football (former member of Oxford City Rugby Club), tennis, pre-Columbian archaeology.

BIOGRAPHICAL/CRITICAL SOURCES: Baltimore Sunday Sun Magazine, April 19, 1959.

* * *

HUCKLEBERRY, E(vermont) R(obbins) 1894-

PERSONAL: Born June 4, 1894, in Decatur County, Ind.; son of John F. (a Baptist clergyman) and Ella (Robbins) Huckleberry; married Florence Barker, September 3, 1917 (died, 1979); children: Robert, Neel I., Carole (Mrs. Robert Morton). *Education:* Attended Baylor University, 1912-14; University of Chicago, S.B., 1917; Rush Medical College (now Rush University), M.D., 1921. *Politics:* Republican. *Religion:* Baptist. *Home:* 2375 Sheridan Rd., Salt Lake City, Utah.

CAREER: Los Angeles County Hospital, Los Angeles, Calif., intern, 1921-22; Oregon State Board of Health, Portland, engaged in educational work related to venereal disease, 1922-23; country doctor in Tillamook, Ore., 1923-46, McMinnville, Ore., 1946-48, and Umitilla, Ore., 1948-50; industrial physician in Lark, Utah, 1951-63. General council of American Baptist Convention, member, 1966-72, member of executive committee, 1970-71. *Military service:* U.S. Army, 1917-18; served in Oregon State Guard; became captain. *Member:* American Medical Association, Utah State Medical Society, Masons, Lions.

WRITINGS: The Adventures of Doctor Huckleberry: Tillamook, Oregon, Oregon Historical Society, 1970; *How to Make Your Own Wooden Jewelry,* TAB Books, 1979; *234 Wooden Wall-Decoration Projects,* TAB Books, 1981.

SIDELIGHTS: Describing his first book, E. R. Huckleberry writes: "I wanted to leave a record of a good life-style that is no more. It was intended only for family and friends, but an interested friend asked that it be submitted to the Historical Society." *Avocational interests:* Woodcarving and whittling, making jewelry, building play equipment for church schools.

BIOGRAPHICAL/CRITICAL SOURCES: American Baptist, October, 1972; *Skaggs Drug Centers,* January, 1974; *Deseret News,* March 6, 1975.

* * *

HUGHES, Charles L(loyd) 1933-

PERSONAL: Born December 18, 1933, in Dallas, Tex.; son of Charles Lloyd (an auditor) and Euna (Hogan) Hughes; married Kayren Frahm, July 10, 1954; children: Michelle, Patrice, Scott. *Education:* Southern Methodist University, A.B., 1955, M.A., 1956; University of Houston, Ph.D., 1959. *Home:* 13410 Mill Grove Lane, Dallas, Tex. 75240.

CAREER: Member of management development staff, International Business Machines Corp. (I.B.M.), New York, N.Y., 1959-64; Texas Instruments, Inc., Dallas, Tex., industrial psychologist, 1964-67, components group personnel director, 1967-69, director of corporation industrial relations, 1969-71, director of corporation personnel, 1971-72, director of personnel and organization development, beginning 1972. Instructor in psychology, Southern Methodist University, Dallas, Tex., 1964-67. *Member:* American Psychological Association, Dallas Psychological Association (president). *Awards, honors:* McKinsey Award, McKinsey Foundation and Academy Management, 1965.

WRITINGS—Published by Executive Enterprises Publications, except as indicated: *Goal Setting—Key to Individual and Organizational Effectiveness*, American Management Association, 1965; *Making Unions Necessary*, 1976; *Making Unions Unnecessary*, 1976; (with Alfred T. DeMaria) *Managing to Stay Non-Union*, 1979; *A Guide to Texas Title Insurance*, Gulf Publishing, 1983. Contributor to personnel journals.

WORK IN PROGRESS: New Styles of Supervision.†

*   *   *

HULL, Raymond 1919-

PERSONAL: Born February 27, 1919, in Shaftesbury, England; son of Edgar John (a clergyman) and May (Coates) Hull. *Education:* Attended Berkhamsted School, Hertfordshire, England. *Politics:* "Libertarian conservative, believing in individual responsibility and minimal government intervention in the lives of citizens." *Religion:* None. *Home:* Suite 1703, 1200 Alberni St., Vancouver, British Columbia, Canada V6E 1A6.

CAREER: Writer. Has worked as farm and construction laborer, fruit picker, janitor, puppeteer, artists' model, church organist, folksinger, radio broadcaster, and civil servant. Spends three months each year lecturing in U.S. and Canada. *Member:* Canadian Authors Association.

WRITINGS: (With Stanley F. Anderson) *The Art of Making Wine*, Longmans, Green, 1968; *How to Get What You Want*, Funk, 1969; *Profitable Playwriting*, Funk, 1969; (with Laurence J. Peter) *The Peter Principle—Why Things Always Go Wrong*, Morrow, 1969; *Writing for Money in Canada*, Longmans, Green, 1969.

(Editor) *Tales of a Pioneer Surveyor*, Longmans, Green, 1970; (with Anderson) *The Art of Making Beer*, Longman, 1971; *Successful Public Speaking*, Arco, 1971; (with Jack Sleight) *The Home Book of Smoke Cooking*, Stackpole, 1971; (with Sleight) *Gastown's Gassy Jack*, Soules, 1971; *Man's Best Fiend*, Hippocrene, 1972; (with Rose Naumann) *The Off-Loom Weaving Book*, Scribner, 1973; (with G. Soules and C. Soules) *Vancouver's Past*, Soules, 1974; (with Ida Larden) *The Off-Wheel Pottery Book*, Scribner, 1975; (with Anderson) *The Advanced Winemaker's Practical Guide*, Longman, 1975; (with H. J. Ruebsaat) *The Male Climacteric*, Hawthorn, 1975; (with Anthony J. Gargrave) *How to Win an Election*, Macmillan, 1979.

How to Write How-to Books and Articles, Writer's Digest, 1981; *How to Write a Play*, Writer's Digest, 1983.

Television plays; all produced by British Broadcasting Corp.: "Roast Pig," 1958; "Punch's Opera," 1958; "The Emperor's New Clothes," 1958; "Rhymes and Reasons," 1958; "Asses' Ears," 1958; "The Magician's Nephew," 1959; "Little House on the Prairie," 1959; "Fools and Funny Fellows," 1959; "The Quality of Mercy," 1961.

Stage Plays: "The Quality of Mercy," produced in Vancouver, British Columbia, at Vancouver Little Theatre, 1959; "Bless This House," produced at Vancouver Little Theatre, 1960; "To Reason Why," produced at Vancouver Little Theatre, 1960; "The Washing Machine," produced at Vancouver Little Theatre, 1960; "Wedded to a Villain," produced in Vancouver, British Columbia, at Vancouver Arts Club, 1960; "Beastly Cinderella," produced at Vancouver Arts Club, 1960; "A Little Organization," produced in British Columbia by Emerald

Players, 1961; "The Drunkard," produced in British Columbia by Gastown Players, 1962; "The Bunker," produced in British Columbia by United Jewish Peoples Organization, 1963.

"Son of the Drunkard," produced in British Columbia by Gastown Players, 1965; "The Tenderfoot," produced in British Columbia by John Wright Productions, 1965; *Sweeney Todd, the Demon Barber of Fleet Street* (one-act, first produced at Barkerville Historic Park, British Columbia, 1976), Pioneer Drama Service, 1980.

Also author of radio scripts. Translator of several of Moliere's plays from the French. Contributor of articles, poems, and reviews to magazines and newspapers.

WORK IN PROGRESS: Six books and a musical comedy.

AVOCATIONAL INTERESTS: Playing guitar, chess, psychical research.

*   *   *

HUNT, Charlotte
See HODGES, Doris M(arjorie)

*   *   *

HURLBUT, Cornelius S(earle), Jr. 1906-

PERSONAL: Born June 30, 1906, in Springfield, Mass.; son of Cornelius Searle (a dentist) and Marion (Adams) Hurlbut; married Anne Dawson, June 18, 1932 (died, 1954); married Margaret Richards Carver, October 27, 1956; children: (first marriage) Cornelius Searle IV, Patricia Anne (Mrs. John L. Williams), Marcus Dawson. *Education:* Antioch College, A.B., 1929; Harvard University, M.A., 1932, Ph.D., 1933. *Home:* 51 Clifton St., Belmont, Mass. 02178. *Office:* Harvard University, 24 Oxford St., Cambridge, Mass. 02138.

CAREER: Harvard University, Cambridge, Mass., instructor in petrography, 1933-34, instructor in mineralogy, 1935-40, associate professor, 1941-53, professor of mineralogy, 1954—. Vice-president, Cambridge Thermionic Corp. *Member:* Mineralogical Society of America (president, 1963), Geological Society of America (fellow), American Academy of Arts and Sciences, Mineralogical Society of Great Britain, Mineralogical Society of Canada, Society of Economic Geologists, Association of Geology Teachers, Geochemical Society, Geological Society of South Africa. *Awards, honors:* Neil Miner Award from American Association of Geology Teachers for excellence in teaching.

WRITINGS: (Reviser) *Dana's Manual of Mineralogy*, 15th edition, Wiley, 1941, 19th edition (with Cornelis Klein), 1977; *Minerals and How to Study Them*, Wiley, 1949; (with Henry E. Wenden) *The Changing Science of Mineralogy*, Heath, 1964; *Minerals and Man*, Random House, 1968; (editor) *The Planet We Live On: An Illustrated Encyclopedia of the Earth Sciences*, Abrams, 1978; (with George Switzer) *Gemology*, Wiley, 1979. Regular contributor to *American Mineralogist*.

WORK IN PROGRESS: Researching borate minerals of Argentina; rewriting *Manual of Mineralogy*.

SIDELIGHTS: Cornelius S. Hurlbut's principal expeditions to study and collect minerals include three in southern Africa and three in Argentina.

I

INCH, Morris Alton 1925-

PERSONAL: Born October 21, 1925, in Wytopitlock, Me.; son of Clarence S. and Blanche (Mix) Inch; married Joan Parker (a secretary), December 16, 1950; children: Deborah, Lois, Thomas, Joel, Mark. *Education:* Houghton College, A.B., 1949; Gordon Divinity School, M.Div., 1951; Boston University, Ph.D., 1955. *Home:* 201 West Lincoln, Wheaton, Ill. 60187. *Office:* Department of Biblical, Religious, and Archeological Studies, Wheaton College, Wheaton, Ill. 60187.

CAREER: Pastor of Baptist churches in Massachusetts, 1951-60; Gordon College, Wenham, Mass., member of faculty, 1955-62, administrator, 1960-62; Wheaton College, Wheaton, Ill., professor of theology, 1962—, chairman of department of biblical, religious, and archeological studies, 1964-65, 1969—. *Member:* Evangelical Theological Society, College Theological Society.

WRITINGS: Psychology in the Psalms, Word, 1969; *Christianity without Walls,* Creation House, 1972; *Paced by God,* Word, 1973; *Celebrating Jesus as Lord,* Moody, 1975; (editor with Schultz) *Interpreting the Word of God,* Moody, 1976; *Understanding Biblical Prophecy,* Harper, 1977; *The Evangelical Heritage,* Westminster, 1978; *My Servant Job,* Baker, 1979; (general editor) *The Literature and Meaning of Scripture,* Baker, 1981; *Doing Theology across Cultures,* Baker, 1982; (editor with Youngblood) *The Living and Active Word of God,* Eisenbrauns, 1983. Contributor to symposia and periodicals.

SIDELIGHTS: Morris Alton Inch wrote to *CA:* "My purpose in writing has generally been to address some issue being faced by my students. It likewise rises out of a Christian perspective on life and tends to have both confessional and apologetic implications."

*   *   *

IRIYE, Akira 1934-

PERSONAL: Surname is pronounced *Ee*-ree-ai; born October 20, 1934, in Tokyo, Japan; son of Keishiro (a teacher) and Naoko (Tsukamoto) Iriye; married Mitsuko Maeda, May 14, 1960; children: Keiko and Masumi (daughters). *Education:* Haverford College, B.A., 1957; Harvard University, Ph.D., 1961. *Office:* Department of History, University of Chicago, Chicago, Ill. 60637.

CAREER: Harvard University, Cambridge, Mass., instructor, 1961-64, lecturer in history, 1964-66; University of California, Santa Cruz, assistant professor of history, 1966-68; University of Rochester, Rochester, N.Y., associate professor of history, 1968-69; University of Chicago, Chicago, Ill., associate professor, 1969-71, professor of history, 1971-83, distinguished service professor of history, 1983—, chairman of department, 1979—. *Member:* American Historical Association, Organization of American Historians, Society for Historians of American Foreign Relations (president, 1978). *Awards, honors:* Runner-up for Pulitzer Prize in history, 1981, for *Power and Culture: The Japanese-American War, 1941-1945.*

WRITINGS: After Imperialism, Harvard University Press, 1965; *Bei-Chu kankei no imeiji,* Japan Institute of International Affairs, 1965; *Nihon no gaiko,* Chuokoronsha, 1966; *Across the Pacific: An Inner History of American-East Relations,* Harcourt, 1967; (editor) *U.S. Policy toward China,* Little, Brown, 1968; *Pacific Estrangement,* Harvard University Press, 1972; *The Cold War in Asia,* Prentice-Hall. 1974; (editor) *Mutual Images,* Harvard University Press, 1975; *From Nationalism to Internationalism: U.S. Foreign Policy to 1914,* Routledge & Kegan Paul, 1977; (co-editor) *The Origins of the Cold War in Asia,* University of Tokyo Press, 1977; *Nichi-Bei senso,* Chuokoronsha, 1978; (editor) *The Chinese and the Japanese: Essays in Political and Cultural Interactions,* Princeton University Press, 1980; *Power and Culture: The Japanese-American War, 1941-1945,* Harvard University Press, 1981.

WORK IN PROGRESS: The Origins of World War II; Cultural Foundations of War and Peace.

SIDELIGHTS: Akira Iriye's *Power and Culture: The Japanese-American War, 1941-1945,* runner-up for the 1981 Pulitzer Prize in history, is a unique study of both Japanese and American thought, motivation, and goals during World War II. Gordon Daniels, in a *Times Literary Supplement* review, states that the 1948 International Military Tribunal for the Far East found a number of Japan's wartime leaders guilty of waging an aggressive war, and to most of the world at the time, "militarism" and "ultranationalism" were simple but satisfactory explanations for that country's actions. But since that time, Daniels notes, the historical view of the war in the Pacific has gradually changed: "In Japan painstaking research challenged the Tribunal's . . . simplicities, while in the United States the Vietnam war stimulated a radical reinterpretation of Asia's

273

past. This movement to reinterpret Japanese war history has reached an impressive new pinnacle with Akira Iriye's *Power and Culture: The Japanese-American War, 1941-1945.* This imaginative new study contrasts Japan's ideology of a new order in East Asia with the untidy complexities of wartime politics.''

John Toland, himself a Pulitzer-Prize-winning historian for a book on wartime Japan *(The Rising Sun: The Decline and Fall of the Japanese Empire, 1936-1945),* finds that the World War II Japanese ''shared many similarities with Americans, striking parallels which have been relatively unexplored in postwar studies. It is fortunate that Akira Iriye has finally brought forward a thoughtful and independent reassessment of the Japanese-American war from the perspectives of both combatants.'' Most important among these similarities, writes Toland in the *Washington Post Book World,* is the meaning that the two countries attached to the war; he explains Iriye's assertion that ''the war for both nations was a search for international stability, not a struggle for power, and that throughout the hostilities influential Japanese . . . shared with the Roosevelt administration a Wilsonian dream of international cooperation; and that in the latter stage of the war, Japanese leaders, including Tojo, were actively planning a cooperative world structure very much like that being considered in Washington.''

Daniels feels that ''perhaps Iriye's book errs in abstracting ideas too far from the destruction which surrounded Japanese reflection'' and that ''relations between diplomats and soldiers might have been more fully explored.'' He believes ''the Pacific War still demands research and reinterpretation, but Professor Iriye reminds us that it was a short interlude in a longer struggle for understanding and peace.'' Toland disagrees with Iriye's statement that Japan's military leaders and their civilian supporters were the primary cause of the conflict, believing instead that ''America must share the blame for starting the war.'' But in the end Toland concludes: ''This is an excellent, meaty book, blessed with original research. Iriye has delved resourcefully into official Japanese archives as well as recently declassified U.S. documents; and the result is a refreshingly welcome appraisal of the wartime relationship between Japan and America.''

BIOGRAPHICAL/CRITICAL SOURCES: Washington Post Book World, May 17, 1981; *Times Literary Supplement,* October 30, 1981.

ISENBERG, Irwin M.   1931-1979

PERSONAL: Born September 30, 1931, in Boston, Mass.; died August 3, 1979; son of Harry (a salesman) and Emma (Slate) Isenberg; married Milda Rutelionis (a social worker), March 20, 1956; children: Errol, Brenda. *Education:* Boston University, A.B., 1953; Harvard University, A.M., 1955. *Home:* 129 West 94th St., New York, N.Y. 10025. *Office:* United Nations Development Programme, 866 United Nations Plaza, New York, N.Y. 10017.

CAREER: Scholastic Magazines, New York City, writer, 1959-62; Foreign Policy Association, New York City, senior editor, 1962-66; United Nations, New York City, special assistant, beginning 1966.

WRITINGS—Published by H. W. Wilson, except as indicated: (Co-author) *Understanding Foreign Aid,* Foreign Policy Association, 1963; *The Soviet Satellites of Eastern Europe: An Introduction to the Geography, History, Peoples, and Problems of the Soviet-Dominated Nations of Eastern Europe,* Scholastic Book Services, 1963, revised edition published as *Eastern Europe—The Soviet Satellites and Other European Communist States: An Introduction to the Geography, History, Peoples, and Problems of the Communist-Dominated Lands of Eastern Europe,* 1968; (editor) *The Drive against Illiteracy,* 1964; *Caesar,* American Heritage, 1964; (co-author) *Making Foreign Policy in a Nuclear Age,* Foreign Policy Association, 1965; (editor) *Ferment in Eastern Europe,* 1965; (editor) *The Russian-Chinese Rift: Its Impact on World Affairs,* 1966; (editor) *France under De Gaulle,* 1967; (editor) *The City in Crisis,* 1968; (editor) *The Developing Nations: Poverty and Progress,* 1969.

(Editor) *The Outlook for Western Europe,* 1970; (editor) *Japan: Asian Power,* 1971; *Indian Subcontinent,* Scholastic Book Services, 1972; (editor) *China: New Force in World Affairs,* 1972; (editor) *The Nations of the Indian Subcontinent,* 1974; (editor) *South America: Problems and Prospects,* 1975; (editor) *The Arab World,* 1976; (editor) *The Death Penalty,* 1977.†

J

JACKSON, Anthony 1926-

PERSONAL: Born September 4, 1926, in London, England; son of Jack Zelechin and Esther (Plotkin) Jackson; married Sarah Sherman (an artist), August 28, 1949; children: Timothy, Melanie. *Education:* City of London Polytechnic, diploma in architecture, 1950. *Politics:* Social Democrat. *Religion:* Jewish. *Home:* 1411 Edward St., Halifax, Nova Scotia, Canada B3H 3H5. *Office:* School of Architecture, Technical University of Nova Scotia, Halifax, Nova Scotia, Canada B3J 2X4.

CAREER: Design Research Unit, London, England, designer, 1950-51; School of Architecture, Southend-on-Sea, England, assistant lecturer in architecture, 1951-56; Canadian Government Exhibition Commission, Ottawa, Ontario, designer, 1957-59; *Canadian Architect,* Toronto, Ontario, technical editor, 1959-61, managing editor, 1961-62; Technical University of Nova Scotia, Halifax, associate professor, 1963-73, professor of architecture, 1973—. *Military service:* British Army, 1945-48; served in India. *Member:* Royal Architectural Institute of Canada, Nova Scotia Association of Architects.

WRITINGS: The Politics of Architecture: A History of Modern Architecture in Britain, Architectural Press, 1970; *A Place Called Home: A History of Low-Cost Housing in Manhattan,* M.I.T. Press, 1976; *The Democratization of Canadian Architecture,* Tech Press, 1978; *The Future of Canadian Architecture,* Tech Press, 1979; *Space in Canadian Architecture,* Tech Press, 1981. Contributor to architecture journals.

WORK IN PROGRESS: The Sociology of Architecture: A Canadian Perspective; "Our Home and Native Land/Terre de nos aieux," a film on Canadian architecture.

SIDELIGHTS: Anthony Jackson writes: "Architects are given the right to practice as a profession by society through its laws. In return for this trust, our final responsibility is to the people who live in the environment that we design, not necessarily to those who pay for it. Architects are not technicians giving their clients anything they want to buy but human beings looking for a better way of life. As such they deal with values rather than facts. These are what I write about—to insist upon their importance, clarify their role, and to advocate those in which I believe."

JACKSON, Joseph 1924-

PERSONAL: Born August 21, 1924, in London, England; son of Samuel and Hetty Jackson; married Marjorie Henrietta Lyons (a barrister), August 10, 1952; married Margaret Booth (a high court judge), August 25, 1982; children: Louise Melanie, Madeleine Annette, Samantha Jane. *Education:* Cambridge University, B.A., 1945, LL.B., 1946, M.A., 1948; Middle Temple, Barrister-at-Law, 1947; University of London, LL.M., 1949. *Office:* 1 Mitre Court Buildings, Temple, London E.C.4, England.

CAREER: Barrister-at-law, London, England, 1947—. Queen's Counsel, 1967. Lecturer, primarily on legal subjects, in England and to bar associations abroad.

WRITINGS: (Editor) Ronald H. Graveson, *Examination Note-Book of the English Legal System,* 2nd edition (Jackson not associated with earlier edition), Sweet & Maxwell, 1951; *The Law Relating to the Formation and Annulment of Marriage, and Allied Matters, in English Domestic and Private International Law,* Sweet & Maxwell, 1951, 2nd edition published as *The Formation and Annulment of Marriage,* Butterworth & Co., 1969; (editor) *English Legal History in a Nutshell,* Sweet & Maxwell, 1951, 2nd edition, 1955.

(Editor with others) William Rayden, *Practice and Law in the Divorce Division of the High Court of Justice and on Appeal Therefrom,* Butterworth & Co., 6th edition (with F. C. Ottway), including supplements, 1953, 7th edition (with D. H. Colgate), including supplement, 1958, supplements to 8th edition (with C. F. Turner), 1960, 9th edition (with Turner and D. R. Ellison) published as *Rayden's Practice and Law of Divorce,* includes supplement, 1964, 10th edition (with R. B. Rowe and Margaret Booth), including supplements, 1967, 11th edition, 1971, 13th edition published as *Law and Practice in Divorce and Family Matters,* 1979.

(With M. Booth) *Matrimonial Finance and Taxation,* Butterworth & Co., 1972, 3rd edition, 1980; (editor with W. Clarke Hall and A.C.L. Morrison) *Law Relating to Children and Young Persons,* Butterworth & Co., 9th edition, 1977, 1st supplement, 1979, 2nd supplement, 1981.

Also author of *Divorce in Halsbury's Laws of England* and *Husband and Wife and Infants.* Contributor to *Atkins Ency-*

clopaedia of Court Forms and *Encyclopaedia Britannica.* Contributor of articles to *Cambridge Law Journal, Guardian Gazette, Punch, Modern Law Journal,* and other periodicals.

WORK IN PROGRESS: Further work on marriage and divorce law.

*   *   *

JACOBS, Jerry 1932-

PERSONAL: Born July 5, 1932, in New York, N.Y.; son of Alex and Sarah (Rosen) Jacobs. *Education:* University of California, Los Angeles, B.A., 1959, Ph.D., 1967. *Residence:* Syracuse, N.Y. *Office:* Department of Sociology, Syracuse University, Syracuse, N.Y. 13210.

CAREER: University of Southern California, School of Medicine, Los Angeles, research associate, 1964-67; University of California, San Francisco Medical Center, San Francisco, assistant professor of medical sociology, 1967-69; University of California, Riverside, assistant professor of sociology, 1969-72; Syracuse University, Syracuse, N.Y., professor of sociology, 1972—. *Member:* American Sociological Association, Alpha Kappa Delta.

WRITINGS: The Search for Help: A Study of the Retarded Child in the Community, Brunner, 1969; *Adolescent Suicide,* Wiley, 1971; (editor) *Getting By: Studies in Marginal Living,* Little, Brown, 1972; (editor) *Deviance: Field Studies and Self-Disclosures,* Mayfield, 1974; *Fun City: An Ethnographic Study of a Retirement Community,* Holt, 1974; *Older Persons and Retirement Communities: Case Studies in Social Gerontology,* C. C Thomas, 1975; (with Howard Schwartz) *Qualitative Sociology,* Free Press, 1979; (editor) *Mental Retardation: A Phenomenological Approach,* C. C Thomas, 1980; *In the Best Interest of the Child: Evaluating Assessment Center,* Pergamon, 1982; (editor) *The Moral Justification of Suicide,* C. C Thomas, 1982; *Social Problems through Social Theory,* Cap & Gown Press, 1983.

Contributor: Simon Dinitz and others, editors, *Deviance: Studies in the Process of Stigmatization and Societal Reaction,* Oxford University Press, 1969; Jack Douglas, editor, *Deviance and Respectability: The Social Construction of Moral Meanings,* Basic Books, 1970; Douglas, editor, *Introduction to Sociology: Situations and Structures,* Free Press, 1973; Roy Bryce-LaPorte, editor, *Alienation and Contemporary Society,* Praeger, 1976; Cary S. Kart and Barbara Manard, editors, *Aging in America,* Alfred Publishing, 1976. Contributor to sociology and psychiatry journals.

SIDELIGHTS: Adolescent Suicide has been translated into German.

*   *   *

JACQUELINE
See CARPENTIER (y VALMONT), Alejo

*   *   *

JENNINGS, Robert E(dward) 1931-

PERSONAL: Born in 1931, in Southampton, N.Y.; son of Robert Rikeman and Mildred (Squires) Jennings; married Audrey L. Atkinson, 1954; children: Nancy Elizabeth, Richard Edward. *Education:* State University of New York at Albany, B.A. (cum laude), 1956, M.A., 1957, Ed.D., 1966. *Politics:*

"Yes." *Religion:* "Occasionally." *Home:* 230 Capen Blvd., Buffalo, N.Y. 14226. *Office:* Department of Educational Organization, Administration, and Policy Studies, State University of New York at Buffalo, Buffalo, N.Y. 14214.

CAREER: Reading specialist in public schools in Greene County, N.Y., 1957-61; administrative intern in public school in Chatham, N.Y., 1962-63; assistant to the provost, State University of New York, 1963-66; U.S. Department of Health, Education, and Welfare, Washington, D.C., Office of Education fellow, 1966-67; State University of New York at Buffalo, assistant professor, 1967-73, associate professor, 1973-80, professor of education, 1980—, acting chairman of department, 1981, assistant dean of faculty of educational studies, 1967-69. Research assistant of Capital Area School Development Association (Albany), 1961-63; instructor for in-service training program for target area school staffs in Buffalo, 1969-70; visiting lecturer, University of Keele, 1973-74; visiting fellow, Sheffield City Polytechnic. Legislative chairman of Albany District Board of New York State Congress of Parents and Teachers, 1963-64; member of board of directors of Buffalo Community Education Council, 1967-71. *Military service:* U.S. Navy, 1948-52.

MEMBER: American Association of University Professors, American Educational Research Association. *Awards, honors:* Grants from Western New York School Development Council, 1968-69, U.S. Office of Education, 1968-70, National Science Foundation, 1969-70, and U.S. Department of Agriculture, 1978; senior research fellow, Leverhulme Trust (London), 1978-79.

WRITINGS: Alternative Roles and Inter-Agency Relationships of State Education Agencies in Comprehensive Statewide Planning (monograph), Improving State Leadership in Education Project (Denver, Colo.), 1971; (with Mike M. Milstein) *Educational Policy-Making and the State Legislature: The New York Experience,* Praeger, 1973; (contributor) Milstein and James A. Belasco, editors, *Educational Administration and the Behavioral Sciences: A Systems Perspective,* Allyn & Bacon, 1973; (with Milstein and James A. Conway) *Understanding Communities,* Prentice-Hall, 1974.

Education and Politics: Policy-Making in Local Education Authorities, Batsford, 1977; *Corporateness and Education: Changing Power Relationships in Local Government* (monograph), Sheffield City Polytechnic, 1980; (contributor) G. Baron, editor, *The Politics of School Government,* Pergamon, 1981; *Education and Politics: Going Corporate in Local Education Authorities,* Gower Publishing, 1983. Contributor of articles and reviews to education journals. Editor of *Bulletin of the Politics of Education,* a newsletter of a special interest group in the American Educational Research Association, 1970-71.

SIDELIGHTS: Robert E. Jennings told *CA:* "Much of my writing effort has been directed toward making research findings useful for both professionals and laymen interested in politics and education. My point of view has come to reflect Elliot's statement that education is too important to be left to the educators."

*   *   *

JEREMIAS, Joachim 1900-

PERSONAL: Born September 20, 1900, in Dresden, Germany (now Dresden, East Germany); son of Friedrich and Annaliese (Fortsch) Jeremias; married Gertrud von der Heide, 1932; children: Isolde Jeremias Mack, Gert, Jorg. *Education:* University of Leipzig, Dr. phil., 1922, Lic. theol., 1923. *Office:* Department of Theology, University of Goettingen, Wilhelmsplatz 1, 3400 Goettingen, West Germany.

CAREER: University of Leipzig, Leipzig, Germany (now Leipzig, East Germany), privatdozent, 1925-28; University of Berlin, Berlin, Germany, professor, 1928-29; University of Greifswald, Greifswald, Germany (now Greifswald, East Germany), professor of New Testament, 1929-35; University of Goettingen, Goettingen, West Germany, professor of New Testament, beginning 1935. *Member:* Studiorum Novi Testamenti Societas (president, 1955-56), Akademie der Wissenschaften (Goettingen), Koninklijke Nederlandse Akademie van Wetenschappen. *Awards, honors:* D. theol., University of Leipzig, 1929; D.D., University of St. Andrews, 1955; Teol. Dr., University of Uppsala, 1957; Burkitt Medal for Biblical Studies, British Academy, 1958; D.D., Oxford University, 1963.

WRITINGS: Jerusalem zur Zeit Jesu: Kulturgeschichtliche Untersuchung zur neutestamentlichen Zeitgeschichte, E. Pfeiffer, 1923, 3rd edition, Vandenhoeck & Ruprecht, 1962, translation by F. H. Cave and C. H. Cave published as *Jerusalem in the Time of Jesus: An Investigation into the Economic and Social Conditions during the New Testament Period,* Fortress, 1969 (published in England as *Jerusalem in the Time of Jesus,* S.C.M. Press, 1969, 3rd edition, 1975); *Golgotha,* E. Pfeiffer, 1926.

Die Passahfeier der Samaritaner, und ihre Bedeutung fuer das Verstaendnis der alttestamentlichen Passahueberlieferung, A. Toepelmann, 1932; *Die Abendmahlsworte Jesu,* Vandenhoeck & Ruprecht, 1935, 4th edition, 1967, translation of 2nd edition by Arnold Ehrhardt published as *The Eucharistic Words of Jesus,* Macmillan, 1955, translation of 3rd edition by Norman Perrin, Scribner, 1966.

Die Gleichnisse Jesu, Swingli Verlag, 1947, 8th edition, Vandenhoeck & Ruprecht, 1970, translation by S. H. Hooke published as *The Parables of Jesus,* S.C.M. Press, 1954, Scribner, 1955, 3rd revised edition, S.C.M. Press, 1972, abridged edition published as *Die Gleichnisse Jesu: Kurausgabe,* Siebenstern Taschenburg Verlag, 1965, translation by Frank Clarke published as *Rediscovering the Parables,* Scribner, 1966; *Unbekannte Jesusworte,* Zwingli Verlag, 1948, 3rd edition (with Otfried Hofius), Guetersloher Verlagshaus, 1963, translation by Reginald H. Fuller published as *Unknown Sayings of Jesus,* Macmillan, 1957, revised edition, S.P.C.K., 1964.

Jesu Verheissung fuer die Voelker, Kohlhammer, 1956, translation by Hooke published as *Jesus' Promise to the Nations,* Allenson, 1958, reprinted, Fortress, 1982; (with Kurt Adolph) *Rabbinischer Index,* Beck, 1956; *Heiligengraeber in Jesu Umwelt: Eine Untersuchung zur Volksreligion der Zeit Jesu,* Vandenhoeck & Ruprecht, 1958; *Die Kindertaufe in den ersten view Jahrhunderten,* Vandenhoeck & Ruprecht, 1958, translation by David Cairns published as *Infant Baptism in the First Four Centuries,* Westminster, 1960.

(Editor with Adolph) *Verzeichnis der Schriftgelehrten* [and] *Geographisches Register,* Beck, 1961; *Nochmals: Die Anfaenge der Kindertaufe* (a reply to *Die Saeuglingstaufe im neuen Testament und in der alten Kirche,* by Kurt Aland), C. Kaiser, 1962, translation by Dorothea M. Barton published as *The Origins of Infant Baptism: A Further Study in Reply to Kurt Aland,* Allenson, 1963; *Der Opfertod Jesu Christi,* Calver Verlag, 1963, 2nd edition, 1966; (translator and author of commentary with Hermann Strathmann) *Die Briefe an Timotheus und Titus* [and] *Der Brief an die Hebraer,* Vandenhoeck &

Ruprecht, 1963; *The Central Message of the New Testament* (lectures), Scribner, 1965, reprinted, Fortress, 1981; *Abba: Studien zur neutestamentlichen Theologie und Zeitgeschichte,* Vandenhoeck & Ruprecht, 1966, translation of one section by Christoph Burchard and John Reumann published as *The Prayers of Jesus,* Allenson, 1967; *Jesu Botschaft vom Vater,* Calwer Verlag, 1967.

Neutestamentliche Theologie, Volume I: *Die Verkuendigung Jesu,* Verlagshaus G. Mohr, 1971, translation by John Bowden published as *New Testament Theology,* Volume I: *The Proclamation of Jesus,* Scribner, 1971; *Jesus und seine Botshcraft,* Calver Verlag, 1976; *Die Sprache des Lukasevangeliums,* Vandenhoeck & Ruprecht, 1980.

SIDELIGHTS: In *The Prayers of Jesus,* Joachim Jeremias ''attempts to bring us once again into hearing distance of the 'very voice' of Jesus of Nazareth,'' writes M. Eugene Boring in *Encounter.* ''Time and again [Jeremias] seems to succeed: 'abba,' 'amen,' the words of institution at the Last Supper. Does he thereby *prove* anything? No, he readily admits. That Jesus introduced a radically new linguistic phenomenon in the way he used *abba* and *amen* is significant theologically only if Jesus Himself is significant theologically. . . . But for those who hold the presupposition (faith in God's act in Jesus), such illumination of the meaning of the words of the historical Jesus is not only stimulating and theologically significant, but positively edifying.''

BIOGRAPHICAL/CRITICAL SOURCES: Walther Eltester, editor, *Judentum, Urchristentum, Kirche: Festschrift fuer Joachim Jeremias,* A. Toepelmann, 1960, 2nd edition, 1964; Edward Lohse, Christoph Burchard, and Berndt Schaller, editors, *Der Ruf Jesu und die Antwort der Gemeinde* (festschrift), Vandenhoeck & Ruprecht, 1970.†

*   *   *

JOHNSON, James H(enry)   1930-

PERSONAL: Born November 19, 1930, in Coleraine, Northern Ireland; son of James William and Martha Moore (Linton) Johnson; married Jean McKane (a teacher), March 31, 1956; children: Ruth, Kathleen, David, Owen. *Education:* Queen's University of Belfast, B.A. (with honors), 1953; University of Wisconsin, M.A., 1954; University of London, Ph.D., 1961. *Home:* Coach House, Wyreside Hall, Dolphinholme, near Lancaster LA2 9DH, England. *Office:* Department of Geography, University of Lancaster, Bailrigg, Lancaster LA1 4YR, England.

CAREER: University of London, University College, London, England, assistant lecturer, 1954-57, lecturer, 1957-65, university reader in geography, 1965-74; University of Lancaster, Lancaster, England, professor of geography and head of department, 1974—; principal, Lansdale College, 1982—. *Member:* Institute of British Geographers, Geographical Association, Royal Geographical Society (fellow), Geographical Society of Ireland, Association of American Geographers, Regional Studies Association, Ulster Archaeological Society, Economic History Society.

WRITINGS: Urban Geography: An Introductory Analysis, Pergamon, 1967; (editor with R. U. Cooke) *Trends in Geography: An Introductory Survey,* Pergamon, 1969; (co-author) *Housing and the Migration of Labour in England and Wales,* Saxon House, 1974; (co-author) *An Advanced Geography of the British Isles,* Hulton Educational Publications, 1974; (editor) *Sub-*

urban Growth: Geographical Processes at the Edge of the Western City, Wiley, 1974; *Urbanisation,* Macmillan (London), 1980; (editor with C. G. Pooley) *The Structure of Nineteenth-Century Cities,* St. Martin's, 1982. Contributor to geography journals and journals in related subjects.

WORK IN PROGRESS: Research on aspects of the geography of nineteenth-century Ireland; population migration in Britain.

SIDELIGHTS: James H. Johnson told *CA:* "As well as undertaking research and scholarship, I feel that it is the responsibility of an academic to communicate to more people than his immediate colleagues. Most of the books that I have been associated with have had that aim. The style I struggle to produce values clarity and simplicity rather than slickness and pomposity; and I never fail to be impressed by the personal satisfaction that follows from unravelling often unnecessarily complex ideas in order to make them accessible to a broader audience."

*   *   *

JOHNSTON, A(aron) Montgomery 1915-

PERSONAL: Born December 26, 1915, in Harrisonburg, Va.; son of James Chapman (a professor and author) and Althea (a professor; maiden name, Loose) Johnston; married Pauline Brown (a teacher), November 20, 1941; children: James, John, Jane, Joseph. *Education:* Columbia University, B.S., M.A., 1939; University of Exeter, graduate study, 1936-37; University of Chicago, Ph.D., 1948. *Politics:* Democrat. *Religion:* Episcopalian. *Home:* 118 Herron Dr., Knoxville, Tenn. 37919.

CAREER: University of Tennessee, Knoxville, assistant professor, 1948-51, associate professor, 1951-56, professor of education, 1956-80. Visiting professor at Pennsylvania State University, University of Maine, and San Jose State College (now University). Spent three months observing open curriculum schools in Britain, 1973. *Military service:* U.S. Army, 1942-46; became captain; received Bronze Star. *Member:* National Geneology Society, American Rose Society, Ascension Recorder Ensemble, Common Cause.

WRITINGS: The Relationship of Various Factors to Democratic and Autocratic Classroom Practices, University of Chicago Press, 1948; *Arithmetic in Tennessee: A Study of Teaching Practices Grades 1-8,* University of Tennessee, 1960; (editor with John U. Michaelis) *The Social Sciences: Foundations of the Social Studies,* Allyn & Bacon, 1965; (editor) *Priorities for Schools in Tennessee,* University of Tennessee Press, 1965; (with Paul C. Burns) *Research in Elementary School Curriculum,* Allyn & Bacon, 1970; *School Celebrations: Teaching Practices Related to Celebration of Special Events,* University of Tennessee Press, 1979; *Ancestors and Descendents of James and Althea (Loose) Johnston, and Allied Families,* A. M. Johnston Publishing, 1983. Contributor to education journals.

SIDELIGHTS: A. Montgomery Johnston told *CA:* "Every family needs to be recorded in some fashion for the benefit of living and future generations. The oral transmission of family history appears to be decreasing, perhaps due to lack of sufficient meaningful contacts between generations and to the mobility and fragmentation of the family, and perhaps also due to the competition of television, radio, and faster paced life styles. Consequently, a published record that can be shared broadly over time and geography with the many elements of the larger family seems to be needed for each member. A greater sense of family, a heightened pride in family, more of a feel for the breadth and scope of our current family and its activities and a keener feeling that we have blood ties to many living persons with whom we have mutual interests, and deeper appreciation of our ancestoral roots and of the vitality of the oncoming generation are purposes a family history and geneology might serve."

AVOCATIONAL INTERESTS: Tennis, stamps, coins, travel, music, crafts, politics.

*   *   *

JOHNSTON, Basil H. 1929-

PERSONAL: Born July 13, 1929, in Parry Island, Ontario, Canada; son of Rufus Francis and Mary (Lafreniere) Johnston; married Lucie Bella Desroches, July 29, 1959; children: Miriam Gladys, Elizabeth Louise, Geoffery Lawrence. *Education:* Loyola College, Montreal, Quebec, graduated (cum laude), 1954; Ontario College of Education, secondary school teaching certificate, 1962. *Politics:* "Apolitical." *Home:* 253 Ashlar Rd., Richmond Hill, Ontario, Canada. *Office:* Royal Ontario Museum, 100 Queens Park, Toronto, Ontario, Canada.

CAREER: History teacher in secondary school, Toronto, Ontario, 1962-69; Royal Ontario Museum, Toronto, lecturer in North, Central, and South American history, 1969-72, member of ethnology department, 1972—. Night school teacher of English, 1965-70; lecturer in Indian culture. Vice-president of Canadian Indian Centre of Toronto, 1963-69; secretary of Indian consultations with Canadian Government, 1968; committee member of Indian Hall of Fame, 1968-70. *Member:* Indian Eskimo Association, Toronto Indian Club (president, 1957). *Awards, honors:* Samuel J. Fels literary award from Coordinating Council of Literary Magazines, 1976.

WRITINGS: Ojibway Heritage, Columbia University Press, 1976; *Moose Meat and Wild Rice,* McClelland & Stewart, 1978; *How the Birds Got Their Colors,* Kids Can Press, 1978; *Ojibway Language Course Outline,* Indian Affairs Branch, Canadian Department of Indian Affairs and Northern Development, 1979; *Ojibway Language Lexicon for Beginners and Others,* Indian Affairs Branch, Canadian Department of Indian Affairs and Northern Development, 1979; *Tales Our Elders Told,* Royal Ontario Museum, 1981; *Ojibway Ceremonies,* McClelland & Stewart, 1983.

Contributor: *The Only Good Indian,* New Press, 1970; *Travel Ontario,* New Press, 1971; *Teacher's Manual for History,* Ginn, 1972; *Read Canadian,* James Lewis & Samuel, 1972; *Starting Points in Reading,* Ginn, 1974. Also contributor to *Dictionary of Canadian Biography.* Contributor of stories, essays, articles, and poems to educational readers, literary magazines, and newspapers.

Translator of brochures and travel guides into Ojibway. Guest editor of *Tawow,* publication of Indian Affairs Branch of Canadian Department of Indian Affairs and Northern Development.

*   *   *

JOHNSTON, Leonard 1920-

PERSONAL: Born March 11, 1920, in County Durham, England. *Education:* Attended Ushaw College, Durham, England, 1932-45, University of Louvain, 1947-50, Biblical Institute, Rome, Italy, 1950-51. *Religion:* Roman Catholic.

CAREER: Ushaw College, Durham, England, lecturer in Biblical studies, 1951-66; Mary Ward College of Education, Keyworth, England, lecturer in religious studies, beginning 1967.

WRITINGS: (Translator) F. Van Steenbergen, Aristotle in the West, Nauwelaerts, 1955; Witnesses to God, Sheed & Ward (London), 1960, Paulist Press, 1964; (with Aiden Pickering) Before Our Lord, Darton, 1962; (editor with Pickering) A Harmony of the Gospels in the Knox Translation, Burns & Oates, 1962, Sheed & Ward (New York), 1963; A History of Israel, Sheed & Ward (London and New York), 1964.

The God of Our Fathers: Israel's Account of Her Origins, Paulist Press, 1965; The Word and the Flesh: John 1-13, Longman & Todd, 1969; (Old Testament editor) A New Catholic Commentary on Holy Scripture, new and revised edition (Johnston was not associated with 1st edition), Thomas Nelson, 1969; (with Michael Smith) Psalms and Wisdom, edited by Laurence Bright, A.C.T.A. Foundation, 1972; Teaching the Faith: A Guide to the Modern Presentation of Traditional Catholic Belief, Sheed & Ward (London), 1974; God Made the World, Incorporated Catholic Truth Society, 1975. Contributor to religious journals.†

*   *   *

JONES, Bob
  See JONES, Robert Reynolds, Jr.

*   *   *

JONES, G(eorge) William   1931-

PERSONAL: Born February 26, 1931, in Austin, Tex.; son of George Willis (a church business administrator) and Mary (Patterson) Jones; married Frances Joanne Baggett, May 29, 1954 (divorced, 1975); married Barbara Lanctot Hamilton, May 30, 1980; children: (first marriage) Christopher Shaw, David Whitefield. Education: Southern Methodist University, B.A., 1951, M.Th. (Perkins School of Theology), 1956; Syracuse University, Ph.D., 1971. Home: 6882 Avalon, Dallas, Tex. 75214. Office: Division of Video and Cinema, Southern Methodist University, Dallas, Tex. 75275.

CAREER: Keitz & Herndon Film Co., Dallas, Tex., writer and salesman, 1952-53; Tyler Street Methodist Church, Dallas, minister to youth, 1953-56; pastor in Justin, Tex., 1956-58, and Grand Prairie, Tex., 1958-63; Casa View Methodist Church, Dallas, minister of education, 1963-65; Southern Methodist University, Dallas, assistant professor, 1965-70, professor of video and cinema, 1970—. Director of Southwest Film/Video Archive, 1969—, and U.S.A. Film Festival, 1970-81. Moderator of Dallas Youth Film Forum, 1966-68; film reviewer for KGRA-TV (Public Broadcasting System), 1981-82. Appointed by President Johnson as member of Commission on Obscenity and Pornography, 1968-70. Consultant on use of screen media in education to film companies, church organizations, industries, and military. Military service: U.S. Air Force, 1951-52.

MEMBER: Methodist Association for Study and Training (chairman of board of directors, 1966), Sex Information and Education Council of U.S. (member of executive board, 1972-76), Texas Commission on Arts and Humanities, Texas Film Commission, Lambda Chi Alpha.

WRITINGS: Dialogue with the World, Encyclopaedia Britannica, 1966; Sunday Night at the Movies, John Knox, 1967;

The Innovator, and Other Modern Parables, Abingdon, 1969; Relationship of Screen-Mediated Violence to Anti-Social Behavior, Syracuse University Press, 1971; Landing Right-Side Up in TV and Film, Abington, 1973; To the Crowds in Parables, Argus, 1981; Sten Survives: In the Jungle, E-Heart Press, in press. Author of column for Vision Magazine, 1979-81, and Parkway Magazine, 1982—. Reviewer for Southwest Review, 1964-65. Contributor of more than forty articles to magazines and journals.

*   *   *

JONES, John Paul, Jr.   1912-

PERSONAL: Born March 3, 1912, in Micanopy, Fla.; son of John Paul and Lorna Doone (McCredie) Jones; married Marion Antoinette Pecot, January 29, 1938; children: John Paul III, Judy (Mrs. Thomas Joel Glenn), Letty Kay (Mrs. Oscar Rayneri). Education: University of Florida, B.A.J., 1937; University of Wisconsin—Madison, M.A.J., 1939. Politics: Democrat. Religion: Methodist. Home and office: 6000 Northwest 17th Pl., Gainesville, Fla. 32605.

CAREER: University of Florida, Gainesville, instructor in journalism, 1937-38; University of Illinois (now University of Illinois at Urbana-Champaign), Urbana, instructor, 1939-43, assistant professor of journalism, 1946-48; University of Florida, associate professor, 1948-51, professor of journalism, 1951—, dean of College of Journalism and Communications, 1968-76, dean emeritus, 1976—; North Florida Publishing Co., Gainesville, president, and editor and publisher of Guide to North Florida Living, 1981—. Military service: U.S. Navy, 1943-46; became lieutenant.

MEMBER: American Association of Schools and Departments of Journalism (vice-president, 1975-76), Newspaper Association Managers (past president; past vice-president; past member of board of directors), National Newspaper Association (past member of board of directors), Florida Magazine Association (life member), Florida Press Association (life member; secretary-manager, 1952-68), Kappa Tau Alpha (president, 1967-69), Kiwanis International (past lieutenant governor of Florida district; past president of local chapter).

WRITINGS: (With L. R. Campbell) Effective News Reporting, Macmillan, 1942; (with Campbell) News Beat, Macmillan, 1949; The Modern Reporter's Handbook, Rinehart, 1949; (with Donald Brown) Radio and Television News, Rinehart, 1954; Gathering and Writing the News: A Reporter's Complete Guide to Techniques and Ethics of News Reporting, Nelson-Hall, 1976; St. Augustine and Other Poems, Old Mariner's Press (Gainesville), 1976; Plain of Dura and Other Poems, Christopher, 1979; The Ithaca Sojourners, Old Mariner's Press, 1980. Editor of Florida Press, 1957-68.

WORK IN PROGRESS: William McKinley and the Press; Ink in the Sand: The First Fifty Years of the Florida Press Association, 1879-1929; Gold Braid, on his experiences in World War II; The Florida Boys on the Suwannee River, the first book in a series of stories for young people, pointing out geographical points of interest in Florida; Magazine and Feature Writing.

SIDELIGHTS: John Paul Jones, Jr. writes: "My entire career has been in the teaching of journalism, with intense interest in the teaching of journalistic writing. I have always had a strong motivation toward helping young people develop concepts of professionalism and responsibility.

"Now, I hope to spend as much time as possible in more creative writing of my own, such as poetry, novels, fact articles, landscape photography, and research into the history of Florida, with emphasis on specific areas."

*   *   *

JONES, Robert Reynolds, Jr. 1911-
(Bob Jones)

PERSONAL: Born October 19, 1911, in Montgomery, Ala.; son of Robert Reynolds (an educator) and Mary Gaston (Stollenwerck) Jones; married Fannie May Holmes, June 1, 1938; children: Robert Reynolds III, Jon Edward, Joy Estelle (Mrs. Gerald William Jordan). *Education:* Bob Jones College (now University), B.A., 1930; University of Pittsburgh, M.A., 1932; additional graduate study at University of Chicago, University of Alabama, 1930, and Northwestern University, 1936. *Politics:* Conservative. *Religion:* Independent Baptist. *Home and office:* Bob Jones University, Greenville, S.C. 29614.

CAREER: Bob Jones University, Greenville, S.C., acting president, 1932-47, president, 1947-71, chairman of board of trustees, 1964—, chancellor, 1971—. Shakespearean actor and lecturer; actor in religious films. Chairman, International Committee of Biblical Fundamentalists; chairman of board, Gospel Fellowship Association; member of board, Mideast Baptist Mission; member of boards of reference, Indiana Baptist College and Maranatha Baptist Mission. Associate trustee, San Francisco Baptist Theological Seminary. Colonel, Governor's Staffs of South Carolina, Tennessee, and Alabama. Member of board of advisors, Gospel Projects, Inc. *Member:* International Cultural Society of Korea. *Awards, honors:* Litt.D. from Asbury College, 1935, and Chung-ang University (Korea), 1972; L.H.D., John Brown University, 1941; LL.D., Houghton College, 1943; D.D., Northwestern Schools (Minneapolis), 1959; S.T.D., Midwestern Bible College, 1974.

WRITINGS—All under name Bob Jones; published by Bob Jones University Press, except as indicated: *All Fulness Dwells,* Loizeaux, 1942; *How to Improve Your Preaching,* Revell, 1945; *As the Small Rain,* Zondervan, 1945; *Inspirational and Devotional Verse,* Zondervan, 1946; *Wine of Morning* (novel), Van Kampen Press, 1950; *Showers upon the Grass,* Zondervan, 1951.

Revealed Religion (study of the art of Benjamin West), 1963; *Ancient Truths for Modern Days,* Sword of the Lord, 1963; *Fundamentals of Faith,* 1964; (contributor) R. Campbell, editor, *Spectrum of Protestant Beliefs,* Bruce Publishing, 1968; *Prologue, a Drama of John Hus,* 1968; (with father Bob Jones, Sr. and son Bob Jones III) *Heritage of Faith,* 1973; *Old Testament Sermons* (four volumes), 1973; *Rhyme and Reason,* 1981. Author of weekly syndicated article, "A Look at the Book." Contributor to periodicals. Editor, *FAITH for the Family Magazine.*

SIDELIGHTS: Bob Jones told *CA:* "I regard my writing as a part of the ministry to which I believe God has called me. Traveling constantly as the Chancellor of Bob Jones University, as a preacher of the Gospel, and in visiting foreign mission fields around the world, I have to do my writing quite largely on the move—on airplanes and in hotel rooms. I am sure my literary style has been formed largely by the early reading of the great classics of literature, both English and French, which I have read vociferously since I was a young boy. Since a large share of our 'liberal' writers are concerned with revolutionary propaganda, I feel it imperative that a Christian writer be care-

ful always to present the Biblical viewpoint, whether he is dealing with poetry, fiction, sermons, or editorials."

AVOCATIONAL INTERESTS: Art history and art collecting.

*   *   *

JONSEN, Albert R(upert) 1931-

PERSONAL: Born April 4, 1931, in San Francisco, Calif.; son of Albert R. (an advertising executive) and Helen (Sweigert) Jonsen. *Education:* Gonzaga University, B.A. and M.A., 1956; Santa Clara University, S.T.M., 1963; Yale University, Ph.D., 1967. *Politics:* Democrat. *Home:* 2356 North Point, San Francisco, Calif. 94123. *Office:* Division of Medical Ethics, School of Medicine, University of California, 1326 Third Ave., San Francisco, Calif. 94147.

CAREER: Roman Catholic priest, member of Society of Jesus (S.J.), 1949-76. University of San Francisco, San Francisco, Calif., associate professor of ethics and moral theology, 1967-72, president of the University, 1969-72; University of California, San Francisco, School of Medicine, professor of ethics in medicine and chief of Division of Medical Ethics, 1973—. Director, American Society of Law and Medicine. Member, Institute of Medicine, National Academy of Sciences. Fellow, Institute for Society, Ethics, and the Life Sciences. Commissioner, National Commission for Protection of Human Subjects of Biomedical and Behavioral Research, 1974-78. Affiliated with President's Commission for Study of Ethical Problems in Medicine and in Biomedical and Behavioral Research, 1979-83. *Member:* Society for Christian Ethics, Society for Health and Human Values.

WRITINGS: Responsibility in Modern Religious Ethics, Corpus Books, 1968; *Patterns in Moral Behavior,* Corpus Books, 1969; *Christian Decision and Action,* Bruce Publishing, 1970; *Ethics of Newborn Intensive Care,* University of California, 1973; *Clinical Ethics,* Macmillan, 1983.

Associate editor, *Encyclopedia of Bioethics.* Contributor to *America, Thought, Modern Schoolman, Religious Education, Sciences Ecclesiastiques, Hastings Report, New England Journal of Medicine, Journal of the American Medical Association,* and other journals.

WORK IN PROGRESS: Articles on medical ethics for *Encyclopedia of Bioethics;* a bioethics text.

*   *   *

JUDD, Cyril
See POHL, Frederik

*   *   *

JUPP, James 1932-

PERSONAL: Born August 23, 1932, in Croydon, England; son of James Thomas (a Merchant Navy officer) and Florence C. (McCone) Jupp. *Education:* London School of Economics and Political Science, B.Sc., 1953, M.Sc., 1956, Ph.D., 1975. *Politics:* Labour Party. *Religion:* None. *Home:* 5 Wisdom Place, Hughes, Canberra, Australia. *Office:* Politics Discipline, Canberra College of Advanced Education, Belconnen, Australian Capital Territory 2616, Australia.

CAREER: University of Melbourne, Melbourne, Victoria, Australia, lecturer in politics, 1957-66; University of York,

York, England, senior lecturer in politics, 1966-76; University of Waterloo, Waterloo, Ontario, professor of political science, 1976-78; Canberra College of Advanced Education, Canberra, Australia, principal lecturer in politics, 1978—. *Member:* Australasian Political Studies Association, Federation of College Academics, Australian Institute of International Affairs, Australian Asian Studies Association.

WRITINGS: Australian Party Politics, Melbourne University Press, 1964, 2nd edition, 1968; *Arrivals and Departures,* Cheshire-Lansdowne, 1966; *Political Parties,* Humanities, 1968; *Sri Lanka: Third World Democracy,* Cass & Co., 1978; *The Radical Left in Britain, 1931-1941,* Cass & Co., 1982; *Party Politics: Australia, 1966-1981,* Allen & Unwin, 1982; (editor) *Ethnic Politics in Australia,* Allen & Unwin, 1983. Contributor to numerous academic and political science journals. Editor, *Dissent* (Melbourne), 1961-63.

K

KAPLAN, Edward 1946-

PERSONAL: Born March 1, 1946, in New Jersey; son of Philip (a salesman) and Leah (a jewelry manager; maiden name, Melnick) Kaplan; married Marcia Berman, May 11, 1969 (divorced, 1977). *Education:* Temple University, B.A., 1969, M.A., 1972; Gratz College, teaching certificate, 1973. *Religion:* Jewish. *Home and office:* 56 Main St., Millburn, N.J. 07041.

CAREER: Association for Jewish Children, Philadelphia, Pa., director of residences, 1971-73; Jewish Memorial Center, Altoona, Pa., executive director, 1973-75; B'nai B'rith, Millburn, N.J., regional director for northern New Jersey, 1975—. Instructor at Temple University. Has given performance oriented poetry readings at Walt Whitman International Poetry Center, St. Clement's Poetry Festival, Hammerjack's, and Ziesing Brothers' Book Emporium. Visual poems exhibited at A Hole in the Sky Gallery, Grover City, Calif., 1982, and in "The Magic Show," presented by the Santa Barbara Contemporary Arts Forum, Santa Barbara, Calif., 1982-83. Member of board of directors of Blair County Day Care, 1973-75, Union County Council on Alcoholism, 1976, and Ad Hoc Committee of the National Conference on Mixed Marriage. Attended special mission to Israel, 1973.

MEMBER: National Conference of Jewish Communal Service, Artist and Writers for Peace in the Middle East, Academy of American Poets, B'nai B'rith Century Club. *Awards, honors:* Award of merit from United Jewish Appeal, 1974; citation from northern New Jersey Council of B'nai B'rith, 1976; New Jersey State Council on the Arts poetry grant fellowship, 1982-83.

WRITINGS—Poetry: *Alvin,* Triton Press, 1976; *Baja,* Fleetwood Art Studio, 1976; *Hard Acts,* Triton/Hankshaw Press, 1977; *Book of Ghosts,* Hankshaw Press, 1977; *Landing Blue,* Small Press Collective, 1977; *Pancratium,* Swamp Press, 1978; *Zero Station,* Stone Country, 1979; *Seraphics,* Avalon Editions, 1980; *Mechos,* Gleniffer Press, 1982; *Pancratia,* Swamp Press, 1983; *Virgin Birth,* Cedarshouse Press, 1983.

Poems represented in *Red Hand Book II,* 1980. Contributor of poems to over two hundred literary journals, including *Sulfur, Adz, Alph Null, Parallax,* and *Smoke Signals.* Contributor of reviews and essays to various periodicals, including *Newsart, Stony Hills, Cumberland, Menu, De-evolutionary Times,* and

Parallax. Co-founder and co-editor of *Sapiens;* founding editor of *Rising Sun Monthly;* editor of *Dirt,* 1983.

WORK IN PROGRESS: "*All the Love Poems Ever Written,* a long poem for several voices, possibly theatric, but a book as well; *Scroll,* a long poem trance, a kind of extra-human instance, a spell; *Table of the Permanent,* a big collection of poems already ten years in the fires; a special compilation of letters and correspondence, called *Transversations;* a series of audio tapes."

SIDELIGHTS: Edward Kaplan writes *CA* that he "started with Charles Olson and fascinations with sound, the shakespeares of resonance in human voice manifested first with him and the likes of equals, Dylan Thomas, Rimbaud and rock 'n roll music. Which converged in graduate school as studies in zen and oriental science, amerikan literary parallel in Ginsberg. Wrote poems to be separate things of themselves. Want poetry to be as beautiful to look at as people; very much taken with spacing on the page. Have been considered a Language Poet, though no school has fully opened their doors to me; private secluded poet, work through the mail system more than any other kind of community. Hearing poems remains incantory.

"Continue to work in a variety of forms. Most usual is the tightfisted stanza, broken, truncated, descending down white page. Prose poems offer wider fields of vision to play in. Long poems, from seven to twenty pages, seem now the right amount of room. Try to hinge the poem on personal process. This process of human impermanence is recorded phenomenally in poetry: all life can be an allowance which commands originality to subvert and reveal sublime thought, for carrying accounts of meaning no one can be sure of. Thus, I contest ordinary laws. Poems of mine do that before they're all done."

*   *   *

KAREN, Ruth 1922-

PERSONAL: Born February 18, 1922, in Germany; came to United States in 1940, naturalized in 1946; daughter of David (an attorney) and Paula (Freudenthal) Karpf; married S. Alexander Hagai (a management sciences consultant), March, 1962. *Education:* Attended Hebrew University of Jerusalem and University of London; New School for Social Research, graduate. *Politics:* Democrat. *Home:* 360 East 55th St., PHC, New York,

N.Y. 10022. *Agent:* Curtis Brown Ltd., 575 Madison Ave., New York, N.Y. 10022.

CAREER: War, foreign, and United Nations correspondent for *Reporter, Toronto Star,* and World Wide Press, 1947-62; full-time writer, 1962-66; Business International Corp., New York, N.Y., senior editor of Latin America division, 1966-71, senior editor of Asia/Africa division, 1972-74, managing editor, 1974-75, editor, 1975-76, vice-president, corporate public policy division, 1976-81, vice-president, global issue systems, and director, corporate public policy division, 1982—. *Wartime service:* War correspondent with British Army, with assimilated rank of lieutenant colonel, 1947-48, and with U.S. Army, with assimilated rank of major, 1952-53. *Member:* Overseas Press Club of America.

WRITINGS: The Land and People of Central America, Lippincott, 1965, revised edition, Harper, 1972; *Neighbors in a New World: The Organization of American States,* World Publishing, 1966; *The Seven Worlds of Peru,* Funk, 1968.

Hello, Guatemala, Norton, 1970; *Song of the Quail: The Wondrous World of the Maya,* Four Winds Press, 1972; *Brazil Today: A Case Study in Developmental Economics that Worked,* Getulio Vargas Foundation, 1974; *Kingdom of the Sun: The Inca, Empire Builders of the Americas,* Four Winds Press, 1975; *Feathered Serpent, the Rise and Fall of the Aztecs,* Four Winds Press, 1979.

Questionable Practices (a novel), Harper, 1980.

WORK IN PROGRESS: Towards an Unlimited Future: Mankind Can Manage, a book based on brainstorming sessions with eighty-three business leaders around the world.

SIDELIGHTS: "Having completed the trilogy on the great pre-Columbian civilizations, an unfinished piece of business connected with my job stirred my conscience and my passions," Ruth Karen told *CA.* "In the course of a study on 'Questionable Corporate Payments Abroad' involving lengthy sessions with some fifty multinational corporations in the United States, Europe, Japan, and the Middle East, I found that the vital and stirring aspects of this global problem were emotional and moral rather than operational and financial. This prompted, or more accurately propelled, me into telling the story in a novel, *Questionable Practices,* which also depicts the high drama and adventure of international business."

Writing in the *Los Angeles Times,* Mark Matousek describes the book as an "important and timely novel," concluding that "as a work of fiction and an unconstrued revelation of common, contemptible corporate amoralism, *Questionable Practices* is a courageous and vital success."

Ruth Karen offers the following advice to aspiring writers, "Write about what you know that engages your conscience and your passion."

BIOGRAPHICAL/CRITICAL SOURCES: Publishers Weekly, February 1, 1980; *Library Journal,* April 15, 1980; *Los Angeles Times,* May 1, 1980.

*   *   *

KARPAT, Kemal H(asim) 1925-

PERSONAL: Born February 15, 1925, in Tulca, Romania; came to the United States in 1951; son of Hashim H. and Zubeyda (Cavush) Omer; married, 1962 (divorced, 1967). *Education:* Attended Teacher's College, Mejidie, Romania, 1942; University of Istanbul, LL.B., 1948; University of Washing-

ton, M.A., 1950; New York University, Ph.D., 1957. *Office:* Department of History, 3211 Humanities Building, 455 North Park St., University of Wisconsin—Madison, Madison, Wis. 53706.

CAREER: Attorney in Istanbul, Turkey, 1948; United Nations Secretariat, New York City, staff member of social research department, 1952-53; Montana State University, Missoula, assistant professor, 1957-58, associate professor of history, 1959-62; New York University, New York City, assistant professor, 1962-64, associate professor of history, 1964-67; University of Wisconsin—Madison, professor of history, 1967-79, Distinguished Professor of History, 1979—, chairman of Middle East Studies Program, 1967—. Middle East Technical University, chairman of public administration, 1958-59, visiting professor, 1968-72; visiting associate professor at Robert College, Istanbul, and School of Political Science, Ankara, Turkey, 1962; visiting lecturer at School of Advanced International Studies, Johns Hopkins University, 1967; research associate at Center for International Studies, Princeton University, 1972. Trustee, Institute of Mediterranean Affairs, 1967-71; member of board of governors, Institute of Turkish Studies. Organizer and director of Social Science Research Council conference in Turkey, 1965; area director of Peace Corps training program at New York University, 1966. Consultant to National Endowment for the Humanities, 1975-80. *Military service:* Turkish Armed Forces, 1953-55; became second lieutenant.

MEMBER: International Political Science Association, Middle East Studies Association of North America (founding member; fellow; member of board of directors, 1970-72), American Historical Association, American Political Science Association, American Oriental Society, American Association for the Advancement of Slavic Studies, American Association for South European Studies, Bulgarian Studies Association, Romanian Studies Association, Turkish Studies Association (president, 1971-74), American-Turkish Society (vice-president, 1967-71), Middle East Institute (fellow), Royal Asiatic Society.

AWARDS, HONORS: Rockefeller Foundation grant, 1960; fellow at Harvard University, 1960; Social Science Research Council grants, 1961 and 1980; postdoctoral study grants from the state of Wisconsin, 1968, 1975, and 1978; grants from University of Wisconsin—Madison Graduate School, 1968, 1971, 1975, and 1980; American Association of Learned Societies awards, 1974, 1980, and 1982.

WRITINGS: Turkey's Politics: The Transition to a Multi-Party System, Princeton University Press, 1959; *Turk demokrasi tarihi* (title means "History of Turkish Democracy"), [Istanbul], 1967; *Political and Social Thought in the Contemporary Middle East,* Praeger, 1968, revised edition, 1982; *The Middle East and North Africa,* Harcourt, 1969.

Cagdas Turk edebiyatinda sesyal konular (title means "Social Topics in Turkish Literature"), Varlik Yayinevi, 1971; *Social Change and Politics in Turkey,* Brill (Leiden), 1973; *An Inquiry into the Social Foundations of Nationalism in the Ottoman State: From Social Estates to Classes, from Millets to Nations,* Center for International Studies, Princeton University, 1973; *Gecekondu uzerine* (title means "On the Squatter Settlements"), Middle East Technical University, 1973; (editor and contributor) *The Ottoman State and Its Place in World History,* Brill (Leiden), 1974; (editor and contributor) *Turkey's Foreign Policy in Transition 1950-1974,* Brill (Leiden), 1975; *The Gecekondu: Rural Migration and Urbanization in Turkey,* Cambridge University Press, 1976; *Ottoman Population in 1830-1914,* University of Wisconsin Press, 1984.

Contributor: Robert E. Ward and Dankwart A. Rustow, editors, *Political Modernization in Japan and Turkey,* Princeton University Press, 1964; Benjamin Rivlin and Joseph Szylowicz, editors, *The Contemporary Middle East: Tradition and Innovation,* Random House, 1966; William Polk and Richard Chambers, editors, *The Beginnings of Modernization in the Middle East,* University of Chicago Press, 1968.

P. M. Holt, Ann K. Lambton, and Bernard Lewis, editors, *The Cambridge History of Islam,* Cambridge University Press, 1970; Ibrahim Abu-Lughod and Baha-Abu Laban, editors, *Settler Regimes in Africa and the Arab World,* Madina, 1974; E. D. Akarli and Gabriel Ben-Dor, editors, *Political Participation in Turkey,* Bogazici University (Istanbul), 1975; *Structures Sociale et Developpement Culturel des Villes Sud-Est Europeenes et Adriatiques,* Association Internationale d'Etudes du Sud-Est Europeen, 1975; C.A.O. van Nieuwenhuijze, editor, *Commoners, Climbers, and Notables: A Sampler of Studies on Social Ranking in the Middle East,* Brill (Leiden), 1977; William O. McCagg, Jr. and Brian D. Silver, editors, *Soviet Asian Ethnic Frontiers,* Pergamon, 1979.

Die Berliner Kongress Von 1878, F. Steiner Verlag, 1982; Benjamin Braude and Lewis, editors, *Christians and Jews in the Ottoman Empire: The Functioning of a Plural Society,* Holmes & Meier, 1982. Contributor to *Proceedings of the First International Conference of South East European Studies,* 1969; contributor of numerous articles and reviews to political science and international studies journals, including *Western Political Quarterly, World Politics, Journal of Contemporary History, Middle East Journal, Middle East Forum, American Historical Review, International Journal of Middle East Studies,* and *Reviews in European History.* Editor, *International Journal of Turkish Studies.*

WORK IN PROGRESS: A history of modern Turkey; a book on literature and social change.

SIDELIGHTS: Kemal H. Karpat told *CA:* "My interest in literature and in writing has been nourished basically by my direct contact, in my childhood days, with Turkish and Romanian folklore and the literature written in these languages. However, from the very start I developed a critical attitude toward literature. The society in which I was growing up regarded literature as a means of self-expression and amusement, whereas I was trained by my Muslim culture to regard society as a whole with all its parts and activities well integrated and functioning around certain societal goals. In other words, I found the segmented and almost contradictory relationship between society and literature, advocated by some writers, unacceptable.

"The search for understanding society led me to the study of politics and social science, with history acquiring increasing importance as the record of total human experience. However, my studies led me to a very painful and personal experience. I discovered that the West had placed me in a special category on the basis of my ethnic origin, religion, and background. In the eyes of the Western people, I belonged to a different world which had been condemned in advance as uncreative and even inferior. I discovered to my great chagrin that my beloved writers—with whom I became emotionally identified and to whom I owed much for my development as a sensitive, socially and politically alert human being—were used as symbols of Western superiority rather than the common heritage of all mankind. Thus, Dickens appeared as an Englishman who could see the social evils in his society as no others, especially non-Westerners, could. Balzac and Hugo became the symbols of

French uniqueness, while Tolstoy was the symbol of Russian genius and messianism. In these circumstances I, the Turk, appeared as the *bete noire* of history, on whom all the 'civilized' nations discharged their prejudice. My Muslim culture was depicted as stemming from a non-revealed religion (Islam), while the West drew the essence of its culture from a revealed, and by implication divine and superior, source.

"Events in the non-Western societies, including the one to which I was identified by origin and background, were described to occur under the whimsical impulse of oppressive and corrupt tyrants. In the West, decisions were supposedly made rationally by humanitarian, civic-minded, well-educated leaders.

"I read all this, first with interest and amusement and then with growing indignation. The memories of beautiful folktales of humanity, tenderness, and compassion I had read in my childhood and which lay dormant in my subconscious began to awaken and arise to a new level. I began thinking that the literary masterpieces of the West which helped to mature my intellect defended the idea that all people were born equal— that differences in education, living standards, etc., resulted from objective conditions rather than inherent superior or inferior human characteristics. In this light I began to look into the history and culture of the Middle East people. There I discovered literary figures, thinkers, and artists whose depth of feeling and sharpness of intellect were equal, if not superior, to the West's.

"I have devoted considerable time and energy to the history and cultures of the Middle East in order to bring forth the value of their contribution to the civilization of all mankind. Although the forms of Western and non-Western culture and history differ, their human essence is the same. I believe that the Western idea of inherent superiority was artificially contrived in order to justify colonialism and imperialism and that this ugly period in history is rapidly approaching its end. The message of my work is to point out the originality and importance of the periphery, so that we can build, in common, a strong center belonging to all of us regardless of our ethnic, linguistic, racial, and religious differences."

                              *   *   *

KATTAN, Naim   1928-

PERSONAL: Born August 26, 1928, in Bagdad, Iraq; immigrated to Canada in 1954, naturalized in 1959; son of Nessim and Hela (Saleh) Kattan; married Gaetane Laniel (an actress), July 12, 1961; children: Emmanuel. *Education:* Attended University of Bagdad, 1944-47, and Sorbonne, University of Paris, 1947-52. *Religion:* Jewish. *Home:* 4803 Mira Rd., Montreal, Quebec, Canada. *Office:* 255 Albert, Ottawa, Ontario, Canada.

CAREER: Nouveau Journal, Montreal, Quebec, commentator on international affairs, 1961-62; Laval University, Quebec, Quebec, instructor in Middle Eastern affairs, 1962; Commission on Bilingualism, Ottawa, Ontario, writer, 1964-67; Canada Council, Ottawa, head of writing and publication section, 1967—. Member of board, Place des Arts, 1964—. *Member:* Royal Society of Canada, Academic Canadienne Francaise, Order of Canada (officer). *Awards, honors:* France Canada Award, 1971, for *Le reel et le theatral;* I. J. Segal literary award, 1976.

WRITINGS: Le reel et le theatral (critical essays), Editions HMH (Montreal), 1970, translation by Alan Brown published as *Reality and Theatre,* Anansi, 1972; *Ecrivains des Ameriques* (critical essays), Editions HMH, Volume I: *Les Etats Unis*, 1972, Volume II: *Le Canada Anglais*, 1976, Volume III: *L'Amerique latine*, 1980; *La discretion*, l'Avant-Scene (Paris), 1973; *Dans le Desert*, Lemeac (Montreal), 1974; *La discretion, La neige, Le trajet, Les Protagonistes*, Lemeac, 1974; *Adieu Babylone* (novel), Editions La Presse, 1976, translation by Sheila Fischman published as *Farewell Babylon*, McClelland & Stewart, 1976, Taplinger, 1980; *La Traversee*, Editions HMH, 1976; *Les Fruits Arraches* (novel), Editions HMH, 1977; *La memoire et la promesse* (essay), Editions HMH, 1978.

Le Sable de l'ile, Editions HMH, 1981; *Le desir et le pouvoir* (essay), Editions HMH, 1983; *La fiancee promise* (novel), Editions HMH, 1983. Author of "Litterature Etrangere" column for *Le Devoir*, 1962—. Contributor to *Les lettres nouvelles, La Quinzaine Litteraire, Tamarack Review*, and *Canadian Literature*. Director and editor of *Le Bulletin du Cercle Juif*, 1954-67.

WORK IN PROGRESS: La reprise; La fortune du passager, a novel; *Le repos et l'oubli*, an essay.

*   *   *

KATZ, Menke   1906-
(Elchik Hiat)

PERSONAL: Born June 7, 1906, in Michalishek, Lithuania; brought to United States in 1920, naturalized in 1925; son of Heershe David (an operator of ice and coal business) and Badane (Gubersky) Katz; married Chaske Bliacher, 1926; married second wife, Ruth Feldman (a teacher), July 30, 1950; children: (first marriage) Troim Handler, Noah (deceased); (second marriage) Heershe Dovid. *Education:* Attended Columbia University, 1924-26, University of Southern California, 1926-27, and Brooklyn College (now Brooklyn College of the City University of New York), 1946-48. *Residence:* Spring Glen, N.Y. 12483. *Office address:* Blythebourne Station, P.O. Box 51, Brooklyn, N.Y. 11219.

CAREER: Teacher of Jewish studies in New York, N.Y., 1936-45, 1947-54, 1956-59, in Philadelphia, Pa., 1945-46, simultaneously in Washington, D.C., and Baltimore, Md., 1946-47, in Safad, Israel, 1954-56, 1959-60, on Long Island, N.Y., 1960-65, in Jackson Heights, N.Y., 1966-69; *Bitterroot* (poetry magazine), Brooklyn, N.Y., editor-in-chief, 1962—. Lecturer on poetry, cabala, and Jewish history at various institutions, including Long Island University, 1972, Grove City College, 1975-76, University of Evansville, 1978, 1981, Wells College, 1981, and Bates College, 1982. *Awards, honors:* Honorary poet laureate, United Poets Laureate International, 1967; Stephen Vincent Benet Award for poetry, 1969 and 1973; distinguished service citation, World Poetry Society, 1972.

WRITINGS—Poetry, in Yiddish: Drei Shwester (title means "Three Sisters"), [Milwaukee], 1932; *Der Mentch in Togn* (title means "Dawning Man"), [New York], 1935; *Brenendik Shtetl* (title means "Burning Village"), two volumes, [New York], 1938; *Es Hut dos Vort Mine Bubeh Moina* (title means "My Grandmother Myrna Speaks"), [New York], 1939; *Tsu Dertsayln een Fraydn* (title means "A Story to Be Told in Happier Days"), [New York], 1941; *Der Pusheter Cholem* (title means "The Simple Dream"), [New York], 1947; *Inmitn Tog* (title means "Midday"), [New York], 1954; *Tsfat* (title means "Safad"), [Tel Aviv, Israel], 1979.

Poetry, except as indicated, in English: *Land of Manna*, Windfall Press, 1965; *Rockrose*, Smith-Horizon Press, 1970; *Burning Village*, Smith-Horizon Press, 1972; *Forever and Ever and a Wednesday* (short stories), The Smith, 1980; (with Harry Smith) *Two Friends*, State of Culture (New York), 1981.

Has translated the Hebrew writings of Rashi into English and Yiddish. Contributor, occasionally under pseudonym Elchik Hiat, to *Atlantic, Bitterroot, New York Times, Sewanee Review, Canadian Poetry, Commentary, South and West, Prairie Schooner*, and others. Poetry editor, *Meer*, 1944-47.

WORK IN PROGRESS: A Rainbow or Two; Two Friends, Volume II, written with Harry Smith; another book of poems.

SIDELIGHTS: As the editor of *Bitterroot*, Menke Katz has sought poetry that he calls "just, genuine and beautiful" and has for the most part eschewed the verse of those he considers "ultra 'modernists' with little or no talent" and those who rhyme their lines. Though he concedes that a rhymed poem can be great, he writes in *Poet Lore*: "It is about time to leave the rhyme (where it belongs) in the nursery, forever and ever. . . . The rhymeless poem may free the poet to create work of greater vision rich with the melody, rhythm, harmony of his own talent." He decidedly prefers a "tongue . . . unpolished as a wound" that allows him to "ride a word—free and rimeless as a tempest." He calls himself "a Yiddish poet" and "a doomed troubadour."

Though his first seven books appeared in Yiddish, Katz began writing poems in English for local newspapers at the age of fifteen. Of his first book of English poetry, *Land of Manna*, Bob Roberts writes in the *Normal News*: "*Manna*'s crowning achievement, perhaps its messianic triumph, lies in its highly unique and personalized optimism, sensitively and eloquently expressed by a poet, Menke Katz, who courageously and persistently defies the fatalistic trends in contemporary writing. . . . Katz has woven for the reader a tapestry of many colors and textures and has combined in his ornate, living fabric the strands of fibers that link us to the past as well as to the future." Writing in the *Prairie Schooner*, Patrick Callahan deems *Land of Manna* "a fascinating book for those who enjoy modern poetry, but who at times find modern poets too tossed about by the ideological currents of the day, too often without an anchor in locale or tradition. Katz founds his poems on his remembrances on a varied personal history, and on his knowledge of Jewish lore and scripture."

"Katz' solution to the human dilemma," observes Fred Cogswell in the *Fiddlehead*, "is to establish a well-defined sense of one's own identity, to organize that sense into a value system out of reaction to both personal experience and learning, and then, within the limits of that system, to allow the myth-making capacities of the imagination spurred by love and/or hate to remould the world until it becomes a part of the self."

Concludes Roberts, "Menke Katz, the universal poet, possesses the power to touch all the senses and his work will endure as long as there is civilization to read it."

CA INTERVIEW

CA interviewed Menke Katz by mail in February, 1983.

CA: Between 1932 and 1981, you published fourteen books: nine books of poetry in Yiddish and four in English, but only one book of prose.

MENKE: Yes. The fourth book of poems, *Two Friends* was co-authored by my publisher, my friend, Harry Smith. My only book of prose is *Forever and Ever and a Wednesday* (1980), in English. It is a book of stories about the village of

Michalishek, Lithuania, where my forefathers lived, laughed, and cried hundreds of years.

CA: Burning Village came out in 1970. Is it an exact English translation of your third book in Yiddish, Brenendik Shtetl?

MENKE: Burning Village is not a translation of my two Yiddish books of poems *Brenendik Shtetl*. It is another book of poems about the war-torn village of Michalishek. My poems have been translated into a number of languages; in book-form: Hebrew, Greek, Japanese, Kannada (a language in India), French, Italian. Other translations of my poems appeared in Chinese, Esperanto, German, Hungarian, Russian, Ibo, Korean, Lithuanian, Polish, Portuguese, Rumanian, Spanish, Swahili, Swedish, Shona, and Tagalog.

CA: What is interesting about this English version, presumably your own, is that many of the poems are composed in traditional fixed forms—tanka, sonnet, ballade, chant royal—often labeled as such. I wonder whether the original Yiddish poems were also in these precise forms?

MENKE: Yes. I experiment with various forms also in Yiddish, but not as much as in English.

CA: In the same vein, it is noticeable that you have a propensity to write in shaped stanzas—sometimes called hieroglyphic stanzas. Were you aware of George Herbert, the seventeenth-century English poet who employed similar devices? What, for you, are the advantages of such patterns on the printed page?

MENKE: My forms were not at all influenced by the seventeenth-century poet and Anglican priest George Herbert. His forms are many, more than one hundred. He sometimes abandons the stanza and uses free rhapsodic forms as in "The Collar." We find in his poems tetrameters, dimeters, pentameters, trimeters. He binds his unequal lines with strong rhymes. However, he could not have influenced me. I dislike many of his forced lines—for instance, "I him sought" in his poem "Redemption." There he sacrificed the flow of the language because he wanted to rhyme *sought* with *bought*.

Concerning the advantages of my forms, I learned form from the drum dancer whom I saw dancing on the crooked alleys of my Lithuanian village of Michalishek and again on the streets of the East Side of New York City. He danced while beating the drumhead with a beater, expressing all his love for rhythm. He sometimes began slowly, let us say with one or two syllables; when he reached the peak, about fifteen syllables, he resembled a whirlwind. It sounded as if it were a call for battle or to remind us that Messiah is here, time to wake the dead.

There were no rhymes in his dance. I am still very far from reaching the wild rhythms of the drum dancer, but I did make a start. I feel that I free the forms of stoic rigidity when I begin a rhymeless sonnet with a two-beat iambic first line and end with a fifteen-beat trochaic last line, or conversely begin with a fifteen-beat trochaic line and end with a two-beat iambic line. My chant royal consists of five stanzas of eleven lines, each followed by an envoi, but it is unrhymed, unrefrained.

Except for some of my early poems in English, as in my book *Land of Manna*, I don't use any rhymes at all. In Yiddish I rarely use full rhymes. Many poets are still not weary of conventional rhyme, still not gorged with hemstitch of all sorts of artificial verse. I think the natural melodies of the poem are wondrous without the help of the rhyme. The rhyme singsonged

long enough through the ages. Even such classic poets as Gray, Blake, Thompson, Browning, Meredith, the great masters of the rhyme, would probably now consider it a relic, the remains of a glorious past. Shelley and Browning might now have been less proud of their successful employment of terza rima. It was much easier for W. E. Henley to write a traditional villanelle than for Walt Whitman to open rhymeless roads of democracy.

It matters little whether poets use identical rhyme, near-rhyme, vowel, masculine, feminine, or leonine rhyme (after Leo of St. Victor, who used the internal rhyme in his elegiacs). The true music of the poem is in the metaphor, in the passion, the zeal which keeps the lines intense. Poets long ago had chosen the assonance which disturbs a bit the monotony by letting the consonants disagree.

John Milton wrote in the seventeenth century: "Rhyme is the invention of a barbarous age to set off wretched matter and lame meter." Henry Wadsworth Longfellow compared the rhyme to "a prisoner dancing to the music of his chains." Ben Jonson wrote "A Fit of Rhyme Against Rhyme": "He that first invented thee / may his joints tormented be / Cramped forever."

Of course, trite or great poetry may be in all schools and genres with or without rhyme. I believe in modern fervent poetry which does not deny the effect of the great classics. The modern, the symbolic, the romantic may blend into each other to influence the poet blessed with talent, no matter what the subject or style may be: dreamborn or actual, nearby or metaphysical.

Rhyme is being driven out of the poetry of the twentieth century. The atomic bomb of Hiroshima did not fall in rhymes. No true poet of future centuries will let himself be fettered to rhyme schemes. The rhymeless poet is free to create greater work with the melody, rhythm, harmony of his own visions.

I am against the ultramodern poets who threw out not only rhyme but also poetry. While fighting against cliches and all forms of traditional poetry, these presumptuous pseudopoets are themselves huge, modern cliches. Unlike medieval alchemists who changed base metals into gold, they transmute gold into tin.

CA: You came to America from Lithuania when you were fourteen. Presumably Yiddish was your primary tongue. Did you think, even after you had mastered English, that you could do your best work in Yiddish?

MENKE: Yiddish was and always will be my primary language. Let others say if my best work is in Yiddish or in English.

CA: Writers are usually conscious of their prospective audience. If this is so for you, what effect is there on your work written for the more limited number of people who read Yiddish? What feelings do you have about this?

MENKE: I don't think any true poet would write in another language only because a more limited number of people read the poems in his or her mother tongue. Every poet should be more concerned with the quality of the readers than the quantity. Of course, it is hardly possible to achieve both.

CA: Obviously for many years you have composed poems in English and, in your capacity as editor-in-chief of the poetry journal Bitterroot, *encouraged the writing of English poetry. Do you still sometimes write in Yiddish?*

MENKE: Yes, I also write in Yiddish as much as in English. When I am deeply involved in a poem, in the exciting moments of inspiration I am sometimes not aware whether I write in Yiddish or in English. I am often so overanxious to enhance the richness, the vividness, the depth of the line, that there is hardly any mind left to think in what language I write.

CA: Not too many poets, even if they are bilingual, write poetry in two languages. (Of course in the older days of classical education some English masters wrote also in Latin—and Milton even ventured Italian as well.) What do you think is the special nature of poetry which makes this so? And what has been your own experience working in two languages?

MENKE: I think and dream in Yiddish. Yiddish is my first and last love. No matter how many books of poetry I may yet write in English (a new 200-page book of poems in English is already in the hands of my publisher), I would always like to be known as a Yiddish poet. My love for Yiddish is so inherent in me that it seems to me my mother tongue is hidden subconsciously within or beyond every line of my English poems.

CA: What do you look for among the contributors to Bitterroot? *What kind of alternative do you attempt to make it to the other periodicals publishing poetry?*

MENKE: As editor of *Bitterroot* during the twenty-one years of its existence, I have constantly inspired unknown, promising poets of all ethnic groups. I conducted workshops in poetry at Napanoch and Greenhaven jails. We published a special prison issue. We do not insult poets by sending printed rejection slips. The poet always receives a personal warm reply.

I discourage stereotyped forms in poetry which leave no individual mark. I try to encourage poets to seek their own identity through original poetry, realistic or fantastic, close to earth or cabalistic. Many poets who publish their work in *Bitterroot* see it as a palm in a desert.

CA: Getting back to Burning Village, *your best known book, would you care to comment on your intentions when you conceived it—or did it just grow? It has a wonderful unity in its variety. Would you illuminate its cultural and historical background, and whatever else ties it together?*

MENKE: I'm delighted you think *Burning Village* has a wonderful unity in its variety. It grew on me since my early childhood. I was a war child. My father was in the United States. My mother was left with five little children. We all have gone through the horrors of war: hunger, disease, death. (My youngest brother is the only one born in the United States.) Of course it is harder to write a book of longer narrative poems than short lyrics. Poe in "The Poetic Principle" is against long poems. Such French symbolists as Baudelaire, Mallarme, and Valery were disciples of Poe. I think a poorly written short poem is long, an inspiring long poem is short.

The background of *Burning Village* is Michalishek, a tiny island surrounded by the Viliya River. It seems to me now we actually lived in a legend. The villagers were so much in love with stories that when my aunt Beilke entertained the folks with her endless tales, on Pig Street, many closed their so-called businesses to listen to the champion storyteller, to see pennies fall from heaven.

My aunt Beilke contradicted the rabbi in almost everything we children learned "in chayder" through the long winter days, from nine in the morning until long after sunset, when every child returned home with a lit candle in a crude homemade lantern. For instance, judging by the stories of my aunt Beilke, it was not easy for God to create the world. When God ordered all the waters to unite so that land could be formed, the rivers refused to give up their identity. Rahob, the king of the rivers, fought God. When God sent little sands to cover the rivers so that land could be formed, the waves laughed: look whom he's sending against us, mighty waves—little sands! After many wars between God and the rivers he finally scattered Mount Svir into grains of sand, defeated the rivers, and was able to form land. (Svir was a neighboring village with a mountain which was punished for trying to climb to the throne of God.)

When we children saw the moon we all believed my aunt Beilke that the moon once upon a time had as much light as the sun but the moon demanded of God that the sun be given less light so the moon could be greater than the sun. This angered God. He punished the moon, made its light much smaller than the sun's. The moon complained that the punishment was too severe, that it might perish of so much loneliness, wandering all alone through the skies. Hence God said to the moon: I will give you the stars to keep you company.

My aunt Beilke told us legends about every animal in the village. I shall mention here only the sheep which came to God with a complaint that anyone could easily kill it. The sheep asked God for protection. God said: I will give you horns to stab, claws to scratch your enemies; but the sheep refused. It wanted to be only a kind child of God. Finally, God promised to give the sheep wool so that people could use it and in return protect the sheep against all enemies. As a vegetarian all my life I disagreed with my aunt Beilke. I knew even as a little child that man is not a guardian of the sheep but its killer.

CA: I like the characters who recur in these poems—Amy the Sorceress and Itche the Convert, Colonel Mendele and his love Bloomele, the children of Pig Street. Did they also take shape out of your life?

MENKE: Yes. They are like true legends. I have written about them in detail in my book of stories, *Forever and Ever and a Wednesday.*

CA: And of course Elchik, who has your own original name and must be some manifestation of yourself in the surely very autobiographical book of poems. What about Elchik? Is he the same as Menke—who also has your name? And if so, why the use of both names? Are they different aspects of yourself?

MENKE: No, Elchik is not Menke. Elchik, my oldest brother, died at seventeen during the war. I have written much about him. He is one of the main characters in *Burning Village*, also in *Forever and Ever and a Wednesday*. He influenced my poems very much, always has been, always will be a great inspiration to me. When I wrote the last chapter of *Burning Village*, "From Elchik's Love Diary" (a diary which my brother Elchik wrote in a cold, lonely barrack), I spent a part of the winter, all alone, in the woods, a bit like Henry Thoreau, to feel Elchik's loneliness, to try to rethink his last thoughts before he died.

CA: You seem to write very much from your own experience—as, say, Berryman and Lowell do, and Stevens and Eliot do not. What are your ideas about how themes rooted in a given locus become universal in import?

MENKE: I think all poets write on subjects which interest them most. I write mostly on themes closest to my heart, on people I know best. I have been very much influenced by two worlds: my tiny village of Michalishek, where my cradle stood, and by the other extreme—New York City, where I lived most of my life. In my poetry the village of Michalishek seems bigger than New York. Michalishek was destroyed by the Nazis; left is only the dream. Who can measure the distance of a dream?

CA: The Yale critic Harold Bloom, reviewing Voices Within the Ark, *an anthology of modern Jewish poets, raised some interesting questions about such categorizations, too complicated to sum up here. But I would like to ask you whether you think there is such a thing as modern Jewish poetry, and if so, what it is that distinguishes it from other modern poetry?*

MENKE: Of course there is modern Jewish poetry. Jewish poetry may be in Yiddish, Hebrew, English, Ladino (Judezmo), or any other language used by Jews throughout time and space in their tragic history. I think Jewish poetry can be written best in Yiddish, spoken by Jews about a thousand years. Forever modern are such Yiddish poets as Mani Leib, Leivick, Rolnick, Moishe Leib Halpern, Zisha Landeh, Reuven Eisland. They called themselves ''Di Yunge''—The Young. They came after the old: Winchevsky, Bovshever, Edelshtad. Interesting, it is not easy to find Jewish poets who write in English as great as those who write in Yiddish, but the reasons cannot be answered here.

CA: I gather from what I know about Two Friends, *the book of poetical dialectic co-authored by you and Harry Smith, that your interest lies not only in* de rerum natura *but in the nature of poetry as well. Could we conclude by hearing your notions about the nature of poetry—that is, poetics?*

MENKE: Concerning *Two Friends*, I think it is best to answer your question by quoting a few lines of the long essay by Buddy Burniske published in the *Arts Journal* (Asheville, North Carolina), December, 1981: ''Menke Katz and Harry Smith are friends. Though they have much in common—poetry, literary magazines, mysticism and mortality—they have friendship to keep them apart, as only friendship can. For it is their freindship which makes them 'reach common ground by very different approaches,' as Smith notes in the first poem of . . . *Two Friends. Two Friends* is the continuation of a literary discourse that Smith and Katz began with *L'Chaims* over a decade ago.''

I will conclude with a bit of poetics. I am fascinated by such rhythms as the ascending iamb and anapest or the descending trochee and dactyl. When I listen in spring to the rivulet across the road from our forest house rushing over mountains and dales I hear it babbling endless repetitions in iamb: O Spring is here. In autumn I hear the busy rivulet announcing in trochee: Autumn, Autumn, where is Summer?

I hear people at a wedding walk in iamb. I hear mourners at funerals speak in trochee. I threw a stone over a mountain, the stone rushed its way up in iamb: success, success. I heard the stone grumble on its way down: failure, failure, or in Yiddish: oy vay, oy vay.

I observed the disappointed steps of a girl leaving her boyfriend after a last good-bye. Even her thoughts seemed to descend in trochee. I saw a girl leaving her lover, who promised to love her to the end of time, walking as through Lord Byron's poem: ''She walks in beauty like the night.''

BIOGRAPHICAL/CRITICAL SOURCES: Piggott Banner (Arkansas), March 12, 1965; *Poet Lore*, autumn, 1965, summer, 1966, autumn, 1973; *Normal News*, September 29, 1966; *Prairie Schooner*, fall, 1966, spring, 1971; *Fiddlehead*, winter, 1966; *South and West*, winter, 1966; *Midwest Quarterly*, spring, 1970, spring, 1973, summer, 1980; *Greenfield Review*, fall, 1970; *Library Journal*, December 15, 1980; *Arts Journal*, December, 1981.

—Interview by Fred Bornhauser

*   *   *

KATZ, Mort 1925-

PERSONAL: Born May 27, 1925, in Brooklyn, N.Y.; son of Morris (in real estate) and Sophie (Guttman) Katz; married Ellen Loeb (a doctor of medicine), July 18, 1964. *Education:* Sarah Lawrence College, B.A., 1949; Columbia University, M.S.S.W., 1952. *Religion:* Judaism. *Home:* 4318 Briar Creek Lane, Dallas, Tex. 75214. *Office:* Mort Katz—Family Counseling, One North Park East, Suite 320, Dallas, Tex. 75231.

CAREER: Dallas State Mental Health Clinic, Dallas, Tex., social psychotherapist, 1962-69; private practice in social psychotherapy, Dallas, 1969—. Consultant therapist at Center Hospital for Alcoholism, Dallas, 1972-74; trainer at Suicide Prevention Center, Dallas, 1974—. *Military service:* U.S. Army, Medical Corps, 1943-46; served in Pacific theater. *Member:* American Orthopsychiatric Association (fellow), Academy of Certified Social Workers, Family Therapy Association of Texas (president, 1969-70), Texas Society for Social Psychotherapy.

WRITINGS: The Marriage Survival Kit: A Daily Guide to Happier Marriage, Farnsworth Publishing 1975; (with Beverly Coon) *When Everyone Else Is Merry Merry and Happy and I Don't Feel So Pretty Good . . . , What Can I Do?,* Family Development Center (Dallas), 1980; *Living Together: A Complete Guide to Personal Relationships,* Farnsworth Publishing, 1982.

WORK IN PROGRESS: A book on interpersonal relationships.

SIDELIGHTS: Mort Katz told *CA* that he became a psychotherapist because he saw a need and had convictions that he could help individuals with specific problems in contemporary society. One of the major goals in his work is ''to create simple tools for the average person to help him understand better his own feelings and the feelings of others, and to help him achieve more satisfying relationships—with himself, his family, on the job, and in society in general.''

AVOCATIONAL INTERESTS: Travel, horseback riding, sailing.

BIOGRAPHICAL/CRITICAL SOURCES: Fort Worth Star-Telegram, August 27, 1972.

*   *   *

KATZ, Robert 1933-

PERSONAL: Born June 27, 1933, in Brooklyn, N.Y.; son of Sidney and Helen (Holland) Katz; married Beverly Gerstel, September 22, 1957; children: Stephen Lee, Jonathan Howard. *Education:* Attended Brooklyn College (now Brooklyn College of the City University of New York), 1951-53. *Residence:* Rome, Italy. *Agent:* Literistic Ltd., 32 West 40th St., New York, N.Y. 10018.

CAREER: United Hias Service, New York City, writer and photographer, 1953-57; American Cancer Society, New York

City, writer, 1958-63; United Nations, New York City and Rome, Italy, writer, 1963; free-lance writer, 1963—. *Awards, honors:* Guggenheim fellowship in literature, 1970-71; Pulitzer Prize nomination, 1981, for *Days of Wrath: The Ordeal of Aldo Moro, the Kidnapping, the Execution, the Aftermath.*

WRITINGS: Death in Rome, Macmillan, 1967; *Black Sabbath: A Journey through a Crime against Humanity,* Macmillan, 1969; *The Fall of the House of Savoy,* Macmillan, 1971 (published in England as *The Fall of the House of Savoy: A Study in the Relevance of the Commonplace or the Vulgarity of History,* Allen & Unwin, 1972); *A Giant in the Earth,* Stein & Day, 1973; *The Cassandra Crossing,* Ballantine, 1976; *Ziggurat,* Houghton, 1977; *The Spoils of Ararat: A Novel,* Houghton, 1978; *Days of Wrath: The Ordeal of Aldo Moro, the Kidnapping, the Execution, the Aftermath,* Doubleday, 1980 (published in England as *Days of Wrath: The Public Agony of Aldo Moro,* Granada, 1980).

Author of screenplays "Massacre in Rome" (based on his book *Death in Rome*), 1973, "The Cassandra Crossing" (based on his book of the same title), 1977, "La Pelle," 1981, "The Salamander," 1983, and "Kamikaze," 1983; author of sound recording "The Great Population Explosion Hoax," Pacifica Tape Library, 1973.

WORK IN PROGRESS: A biography of German filmmaker Rainer Werner Fassbinder, for Random House.

SIDELIGHTS: About Robert Katz's *Days of Wrath: The Ordeal of Aldo Moro, the Kidnapping, the Execution, the Aftermath,* Caroline Moorehead of the *Times Literary Supplement* asserts, "It is a skilful book in which the arts of a thriller writer are combined with the critical curiosity of a reporter." She comments on the book's authenticity: "Where *Days of Wrath* is fascinating is in its detail; names, places, protagonists, phone calls, the long saga of political and private manipulation that went into this full-blown Italian theatre of terrorism." Godfrey Hodgson of the *Washington Post Book World* observes that "anyone who can be moved by the pity and terror of a modern tragedy, will want to read this original and passionately heart-felt book."

Yet some reviewers challenge Katz's conclusions in the work. Flora Lewis writes in the *New York Times* that "it is an exciting and tragic story Mr. Katz tells, but it is made repugnant for me by his judgments." Lewis concludes: "Above all, the book reflects the moral morass of our time. It is interesting, but not illuminating."

Katz encountered legal difficulties with the release of the film "Massacre in Rome," based on his best-seller *Death in Rome.* The book aroused international religious and political controversy; the film brought the controversy to court, culminating in a two-year criminal trial. Katz was ultimately convicted and sentenced to fourteen months in prison for defaming the memory of Pope Pius XII. The case is under appeal.

BIOGRAPHICAL/CRITICAL SOURCES: New York Times Book Review, August 31, 1969, June 12, 1977, August 6, 1978, May 18, 1980; *Times Literary Supplement,* January 1, 1970, July 11, 1980; *Los Angeles Times,* May 23, 1980; *Washington Post Book World,* May 27, 1980.

*   *   *

KAUFFMAN, Donald T(homas) 1920-

PERSONAL: Born February 13, 1920, in Plattsburgh, N.Y.; son of Daniel C. (a minister) and Jane (Brant) Kauffman;

married Jeanne Thompson, July 8, 1950; children: Cynthia, Nancy, Elizabeth, Karen, Harold. *Education:* Houghton College, A.B., 1941; Westminster Theological Seminary, Th.B. and Th.M., 1945; additional study at Union Theological Seminary, New York, N.Y., Syracuse University, and Columbia University. *Home:* Atchison Cove, Sherman, Conn. 06784. *Office:* Foundation for Christian Living, Pawling, N.Y. 12564.

CAREER: Presbyterian minister, serving various churches, 1945-58; Fleming H. Revell Co. (publishers), Westwood, N.J., managing editor, 1958-68; Christian Herald Family Bookshelf (book club), New York, N.Y., editor, 1969-74; Inspirational Book Service (book sales corporation), and Good Reading Club (book club), both Pawling, N.Y., editor and director, 1974-76; Foundation for Christian Living (publishers and distributor), managing editor, 1977—. President, Donald T. Kauffman, Inc., 1981—. Member, Presbytery of the Hudson, Presbyterian Church, 1980—.

WRITINGS—Published by Revell, except as noted: *Dictionary of Religious Terms,* 1967.

Editor: *Favorite Inspirational Poems,* 1960; *The Gist of the Lesson* (annual), 1960-67; *The Treasury of Religious Verse,* 1962; *A Treasury of Great Prayers,* 1964; *With Love to Mother,* 1964; *America in Verse,* Pyramid Books, 1968; *Favorite Christian Poems,* 1969; *For Instance,* Doubleday, 1970; (and compiler) *And the Greatest of These Is Love,* 1980; (and compiler) *Mothers Are a Gift of Love,* 1980.

Contributor to *Creative Help for Daily Living.* Also contributor to *Woman's Day, St. Anthony's Messenger, Church Management, New Century Leader, Christianity Today, Comprehensive Bible Study, Adult Teacher's Guild,* and *Quiet Hour.*

WORK IN PROGRESS: Help Yourself to Miracles; Letters for the 21st Century.

SIDELIGHTS: Donald T. Kauffman told *CA:* "During the last half of my life I intend to write books, fiction and nonfiction, that reflect something of the light of the Eternal dimension within the frustrations and irrationalities of this three-dimensional world." *Avocational interests:* Chess, hiking, music, jogging, sailing.

*   *   *

KAYSEN, Carl 1920-

PERSONAL: Born March 5, 1920, in Philadelphia, Pa.; son of Samuel and Elizabeth (Resnick) Kaysen; married Annette Neutra, September 13, 1940; children: Susanna Neutra, Laura Neutra. *Education:* University of Pennsylvania, A.B. (with highest honors in economics), 1940; graduate study at Columbia University, 1940-42; Harvard University, M.A., 1947, Ph.D., 1954. *Office:* Program in Science Technology and Society, Massachusetts Institute of Technology, Cambridge, Mass. 02139.

CAREER: National Bureau of Economic Research, New York, N.Y., member of financial research project staff, 1940-42; U.S. Office of Strategic Services, Washington, D.C., economist, 1942-43; Harvard University, Cambridge, Mass., assistant professor, 1950-55, associate professor, 1955-57, professor of economics, 1957-66, Lucius N. Littauer Professor of Political Economy, 1964-66, associate dean, Graduate School of Public Administration, 1960-66; Institute for Advanced Study, Princeton, N.J., director, 1966-76, professor, 1966-77; Massachusetts Institute of Technology, Cambridge, David W. Skinner Professor of Political Economy, 1977—, director of Program in Science Technology and Society, 1981—. Lecturer at London School of Economics and Political Science, 1956; Haynes Lecturer, California Institute of Technology, 1966; Stafford Little Lecturer, Princeton University, 1968; Oliver Wendell Holmes Lecturer, Harvard Law School, 1969; Paley Lecturer, Hebrew University, Jerusalem, Israel, 1970; Godkin Lecturer, Harvard University, 1976.

Clerk to Judge E. E. Wyzanski, U.S. District Court, 1950-52; deputy special assistant to President Kennedy for national security affairs, 1961-63; special consultant to the President, beginning 1963; chairman of President's Task Force on Foreign Economic Policy, 1964; member of Carnegie Commission on Higher Education, 1968—; vice-chairman and director of research, Sloan Commission on Government and Higher Education, 1977-79. Life trustee, University of Pennsylvania; trustee, German Marshall Fund and Russell Sage Foundation; director, Polaroid Corp. and United Parcel Service. *Military service:* U.S. Army Air Forces, Intelligence, 1943-45; served in Europe; became captain.

MEMBER: American Economic Association, American Academy of Arts and Sciences, American Philosophical Society, Econometric Society, Phi Beta Kappa, Century Club (New York City). *Awards, honors:* Fulbright research scholar, London School of Economics and Political Science, University of London, 1955-56; Guggenheim fellow, 1955-56; Ford Foundation fellow in Greece, 1959-60.

WRITINGS: "*United States v. United Shoe Machinery Corporation*"*: An Economic Analysis of an Anti-Trust Case,* Harvard University Press, 1956; (with F. K. Sutton, W. E. Harris, and J. Tobin) *The American Business Creed,* Harvard University Press, 1956; (with Donald F. Turner) *Anti-Trust Policy: An Economic and Legal Analysis,* Harvard University Press, 1959; (with Franklin M. Fisher) *The Demand for Electricity in the United States,* North-Holland, 1962; *The Higher Learning: The Universities and the Public,* Princeton University Press, 1969; (editor) *Content and Context: Essays on College Education,* McGraw, 1973; (with William Tavoulareas) *A Debate on "A Time to Choose,"* Ballinger, 1977; (editor) *Program for Renewed Partnership: A Report,* Ballinger, 1980.

Contributor: E. S. Mason, editor, *The Corporation in the Modern Economy,* Harvard University Press, 1960; H. Arndt, editor, *Die Konzentration in der Wirtschaft,* Dunker and Humboldt, 1960; Seymour E. Harris, editor, *Higher Education in the United States,* Harvard University Press, 1960. Contributor of articles and book reviews to *World Politics, New Republic,* and other scholarly journals in America and abroad. Member of editorial board, *American Scholar* and *Foreign Affairs.*†

*   *   *

KEARNS, Lionel   1937-

PERSONAL: Born February 16, 1937, in Nelson, British Columbia, Canada; son of Frank (a game warden and writer) and Dorothy (Welch) Kearns; married Dolly Revati Maharaj (a teacher), June, 1960 (divorced, 1976); children: Frank, Shakuntala, Liam. *Education:* University of British Columbia, B.A., 1961, M.A., 1964; additional study at School of Oriental and African Studies, University of London, 1964-65. *Home:* 1616 Charles St., Vancouver, British Columbia, Canada V5L 2T3. *Office:* Simon Fraser University, Burnaby, British Columbia, Canada.

CAREER: Prior to 1961, worked as waiter, laborer, peat-worker, truck driver, and at other jobs; University of British Columbia,

Vancouver, teaching assistant and lecturer in English, 1961-64; Simon Fraser University, Burnaby, British Columbia, assistant professor, 1966—. Writer-in-residence at Concordia University, 1982-83. *Awards, honors:* Canada Council fellowship, 1964-65, 1965-66; Canada Council Arts Award, 1973.

WRITINGS: Songs of Circumstance (poems in stacked verse), Tish Press, 1963; *Pointing,* Ryerson Press, 1967; *By the Light of the Silvery McLune: Media Parables, Poems, Signs, Gestures and Other Assaults on the Interface,* Daylight Press, 1969; *About Time,* Prince George, 1974; *Practicing up to Be Human,* Coach House Press (Toronto), 1978; *Loops and Chains: Selected Poems,* Talon Books, 1982; *Convergences I,* Coach House Press, 1982.

Creator with Gordan Payne of animated film/poems, "The Birth of God," 1973, and "Negotiating a New Canadian Constitution," National Film Board of Canada, 1974.

WORK IN PROGRESS: A musical based on the life of Carl Jung.

SIDELIGHTS: "[Lionel] Kearns believes day to day experience in the world gives one identity," explains Roy Geiger in *Buck.* "Poems are a way of experiencing and a way of bridging alienation. Rather than detaching himself," Geiger concludes, "[Kearns] attaches himself to society through poems, which are his identifying marks in the world."

Kearns believes his principal influences are Norbert Weiner, Buckminster Fuller, Kenneth Boulding, and Stafford Beer. He has traveled and lived in Mexico, Great Britain, and the West Indies, and considers that his principal occupation is "being human."

BIOGRAPHICAL/CRITICAL SOURCES: Delta, number 19, October, 1962, number 25, November, 1965; *Canadian Literature,* spring, 1964; *Kulchur,* number 15, autumn, 1964, number 20, winter, 1965-66; *Poetry* (Chicago), September, 1964; *Quarry,* spring, 1966; *Parallel,* March-April, 1966; *Canadian Forum,* January, 1969; *Buck,* spring, 1980.

*   *   *

KEENAN, Deborah (Anne)   1950-

PERSONAL: Born December 5, 1950, in Minneapolis, Minn.; daughter of Clifford A. (a chemical engineer) and Virginia (an English teacher; maiden name, Wells) Bowman; married J. Michael Keenan (a professor of English), September 19, 1970; married Stephen M. Seidel, July 23, 1983; children: (first marriage) Brendan, Molly. *Education:* Macalester College, B.A., 1973. *Home:* 1168 Laurel Ave., St. Paul, Minn. 55104.

CAREER: Poet-in-residence at a private school in St. Paul, Minn., beginning 1975; director of programming for COMPAS (a statewide arts organization), 1981-83.

WRITINGS: On Stage: The Beatles, Creative Education Press, 1976; *On Stage: Barbra Streisand,* Creative Education Press, 1976; *Household Wounds* (poetry), New Rivers Press, 1981; *One Angel Then* (poetry), Midnight Paper Sales Press, 1981. Contributor of poems to literary magazines, including *Pequod* and *New England Review of Literature.*

WORK IN PROGRESS: A third collection of poetry; essays on twentieth-century novels; memoirs.

SIDELIGHTS: Deborah Keenan told *CA* she writes "because it is difficult, necessary, and because the process keeps me sane.'' *Avocational interests:* Travel (Scotland, Greece), rock and roll, gardening, the subject of grace.

* * *

KEEPING, Charles 1924-

PERSONAL: Born September 22, 1924, in London, England; son of Charles (a professional boxer, under name Charles Clark, and newspaperman) and Eliza Ann (Trodd) Keeping; married Renate Meyer (an artist and illustrator), September 20, 1952; children: Jonathan, Vicki, Sean, Frank. *Education:* London Polytechnic, London, England, 1949-52, received National Diploma in Design, 1952. *Politics:* ''Individualist.'' *Religion:* None. *Home:* 16 Church Rd., Shortlands, Bromley BR2 OHP, England. *Agent:* B. L. Kearley Ltd., 59 George St., London W.1, England. *Office:* Camberwell School of Art and Crafts, London, England.

CAREER: Apprenticed to printing trade at age of fourteen; after war service, worked as engineer and rent collector before starting full-time art studies in 1949; London Polytechnic, London, England, teacher of lithography, 1956-63; Croydon College of Art, Croydon, England, visiting lecturer in drawing, 1963-78; Camberwell School of Art and Crafts, London, teacher of illustration, 1979—. Book illustrator, advertising artist, and designer of wall murals, posters, and book jackets. Lithographs exhibited in London, Italy, Australia, and United States, including International Exhibition of Lithography at Cincinnati, 1958; prints in many collections, including the Victoria and Albert Museum, London. *Military service:* Royal Navy, telegraphist, 1942-46.

AWARDS, HONORS: Certificate of Merit, Library Association, for *Shaun and the Carthorse;* Certificate of Merit, Leipzig Book Fair, for *Black Dolly: The Story of a Junk Cart Pony;* Kate Greenaway Medal, Library Association, 1968, for illustrations in *Charley, Charlotte and the Golden Canary,* and 1982, for *The Highwayman,* and runner-up, 1971, for illustrations in *The God Beneath the Sea;* Francis Williams Memorial Bequest Prize, 1972, for *Tinker, Tailor: Folk Song Tales,* and 1976, for *The Wildman;* honorable mention, Bratislava Biennial, 1974, for *The Spider's Web,* and Golden Apple Award, Bratislava, 1976, for *The Railway Passage;* Hans Christian Andersen International Children's Book Medal runner-up, 1974.

WRITINGS—Books for children, self-illustrated: *Shaun and the Carthorse,* F. Watts, 1966; *Molly o' the Moors: The Story of a Pony,* World Publishing, 1966 (published in England as *Black Dolly: The Story of a Junk Cart Pony,* Brockhampton Press, 1966); *Charley, Charlotte and the Golden Canary,* Oxford University Press, 1966, F. Watts, 1967; *Alfie Finds the Other Side of the World,* F. Watts, 1968 (published in England as *Alfie and the Ferryboat,* Oxford University Press, 1968); (compiler) *Tinker, Tailor: Folk Song Tales,* Brockhampton Press, 1968; (reteller) *The Christmas Story,* F. Watts, 1969 (published in England as *The Christmas Story as Told on "Play School,"* B.B.C. Publications, 1969); *Joseph's Yard,* Oxford University Press, 1969, F. Watts, 1970.

Through the Window, F. Watts, 1970; *The Garden Shed,* Oxford University Press, 1971; *The Spider's Web,* Oxford University Press, 1972; *Richard,* Oxford University Press, 1973; *The Nanny Goat and the Fierce Dog,* Abelard, 1973; (compiler of words and music) *Cockney Ding Dong,* Kestrel Books, 1973; *The Railway Passage,* Oxford University Press, 1974; *The Wasteground Circus,* Oxford University Press, 1975; *Inter-*

City, Oxford University Press, 1977; *River,* Oxford University Press, 1978; *Willie's Fire Engine,* Oxford University Press, 1980; *The Highwayman,* Oxford University Press, 1981; *Beowulf,* Oxford University Press, 1982.

Illustrator: Nicholas Stuart Gray, *Over the Hills to Babylon,* Oxford University Press, 1954, Hawthorn, 1970; Rosemary Sutcliff, *The Silver Branch,* Oxford University Press, 1957, Walck, 1958; Sutcliff, *Warrior Scarlet,* Walck, 1958; Sutcliff, *The Lantern-Bearers,* Walck, 1959.

Sutcliff, *Knight's Fee,* Oxford University Press, 1960, Walck, 1961; John Stewart Murphy, *Roads,* Oxford University Press, 1960; Murphy, *Canals,* Oxford University Press, 1961; Sutcliff, *Beowulf,* Bodley Head, 1961, Dutton, 1962; Ruth Chandler, *Three Trumpets,* Abelard, 1962; Kenneth Grahame, *The Golden Age* [and] *Dream Days,* Bodley Head, 1962, Dufour, 1965; Barbara Leonie Picard, *Lost John,* Oxford University Press, 1962, Criterion, 1963; Murphy, *Dams,* Oxford University Press, 1963; Clare Compton, *Harriet and the Cherry Pie,* Bodley Head, 1963; E. M. Almedingen, *The Knights of the Golden Table,* Bodley Head, 1963, Lippincott, 1964; Paul Berna, *Flood Warning,* Pantheon, 1963; Mollie Hunter, *Patrick Kentigern Keenan,* Blackie & Son, 1963, published as *The Smartest Man in Ireland,* Funk, 1965; James Holding, *The King's Contest and Other North African Tales,* Abelard, 1964; Murphy, *Railways,* Oxford University Press, 1964; Henry Treece, *The Last of the Vikings,* Brockhampton Press, 1964, published as *The Last Viking,* Pantheon, 1966; Hunter, *The Kelpie's Pearls,* Blackie & Son, 1964, Funk, 1966; Almedingen, *The Treasure of Seigfried,* Bodley Head, 1964, Lippincott, 1965.

Murphy, *Wells,* Oxford University Press, 1965; Gray, *The Apple Stone,* Dobson, 1965, Hawthorn, 1969; Alan Garner, *Elidor,* Collins, 1965; Henry Daniel-Rops, *The Life of Our Lord,* Hawthorn, 1965; Sutcliff, *Heroes and History,* Putnam, 1965; Treece, *Splintered Sword,* Brockhampton Press, 1965, Duell, Sloan & Pearce, 1966; Kevin Crossley-Holland, *King Horn,* Macmillan (London), 1965, Dutton, 1966; Walter Macken, *Island of the Great Yellow Ox,* Macmillan (London), 1966; Erich Maria Remarque, *All Quiet on the Western Front,* translation by A. W. Wheen, Folio Society, 1966; Holding, *The Sky-Eater and Other South Sea Tales,* Abelard, 1966; James Reeves, *The Cold Flame,* Hamish Hamilton, 1967, Meredith, 1969; Treece, *Swords from the North,* Pantheon, 1967; Gray, *Mainly in Moonlight: Ten Stories of Sorcery and the Supernatural,* Hawthorn, 1967; Treece, *The Dream-Time,* Brockhampton Press, 1967, Hawthorn, 1968; Kenneth McLeish, *The Story of Aeneas,* Longmans, Green, 1968; Richard Potts, *The Haunted Mine,* Lutterworth, 1968; Reeves, compiler, *An Anthology of Free Verse,* Basil Blackwell, 1968; Walter Macken, *The Flight of the Doves,* Macmillan, 1968; Holding, *Poko and the Golden Demon,* Abelard, 1968; Reeves, *The Cold Flame,* Meredith Press, 1969; Margaret Jessy Miller, editor, *Knights, Beasts and Wonders: Tales and Legends from Mediaeval Britain,* David White, 1969; Roger Lancelyn Green, reteller, *The Tale of Ancient Israel,* Dent, 1969, Dutton, 1970.

Lee Cooper, *Five Fables from France,* Abelard, 1970; Leon Garfield and Edward Blishen, *The God Beneath the Sea,* Kestrel Books, 1970, Pantheon, 1971; P. L. Travers, *Friend Monkey,* Harcourt, 1971; William Cole, compiler, *The Poet's Tales: A New Book of Story Poems,* World Publishing, 1971; Fedor Dostoevski, *The Idiot,* Folio Society, 1971; Mary Francis Shura, *The Valley of the Frost Giants,* Lothrop, 1971; Treece, *The Invaders: Three Stories,* Crowell, 1972; Robert Newman, *The*

Twelve Labours of Hercules, Crowell, 1972; Roger Squire, *Wizards and Wampum: Legends of the Iroquois,* Abelard, 1972; Garfield and Blishen, *The Golden Shadow,* Kestrel Books, 1972, Pantheon, 1973; Ursula Synge, *Weland: Smith of the Gods,* Bodley Head, 1972, S. G. Phillips, 1973; Montague Rhodes James, *Ghost Stories of M. R. James,* Folio Society, 1973; Sutcliff, *The Capricorn Bracelet,* Oxford University Press, 1973; Cooper, *The Strange Feathery Beast, and Other French Fables,* Carousel, 1973; Helen L. Hoke, *Weirdies: A Horrifying Concatenation of the Super-Sur-Real or Almost or Not-Quite Real,* Franklin Watts (London), 1973, published as *Weirdies, Weirdies, Weirdies: A Horrifying Concatenation of the Super-Sur-Real or Almost Not-Quite Real,* F. Watts (New York), 1975; Hoke, *Monsters, Monsters, Monsters,* F. Watts, 1974; Lewis Jones, *The Birds, and Other Stories,* Longman, 1974; Eric Allen, *The Latchkey Children,* Oxford University Press, 1974; Travers, *About the Sleeping Beauty,* McGraw, 1975; Robert Swindells, *When Darkness Comes,* Morrow, 1975; Crossley-Holland, *The Wildman,* Deutsch, 1976.

Also illustrator of Charles Dickens's *Pickwick Papers, Great Expectations, Our Mutual Friend, Edwin Drood, David Copperfield,* and *Hard Times,* and of Victor Hugo's *Les Miserables,* for the Folio Society.

SIDELIGHTS: Charles Keeping's maternal ancestors were seafarers, and his paternal, London street traders. He was born in Lambeth Walk in South London, grew up in the docks and market area, and his work is mainly concerned with the people in the work streets of London.

Jessica Jenkins, writing in *Books,* views *Joseph's Yard* as "a recreation of the myth of Adonis in a bleak backyard. There is no question of finding an alternative to its impact in words and no point in considering the words on their own. With a brief text and a combination of resist-work techniques (wax and scratch, wax and watercolor, water and waterproof ink), Charles Keeping creates page after page of visual stimulus and an extraordinary range and depth of emotion. . . . To most children *Joseph's Yard* will probably and rightly be just one more book: one from which they will absorb as much visual and emotional experience as they are ready for."

In a *Books* review, Anne Wood writes that in *Through the Window* Charles Keeping draws "upon the background of his own childhood, he seeks to show the effect of a child's closeness to a particular environment upon his developing understanding of some of the texture of life. Here the child views everything in a frame of heavy net so that the scene is widened or narrowed or even swirled as he moves and is moved by the violence of the action. . . . Keeping sets out the truth about feelings in the uncompromising context of his wonderfully beautiful art, and we owe him a debt for his courage in widening the scope of the picture book in this way."

AVOCATIONAL INTERESTS: Walking, good conversation over a pint of beer in a pub, modern jazz, and folksinging.

MEDIA ADAPTATIONS: Charley, Charlotte and the Golden Canary, Alfie Finds the Other Side of the World, and *Through the Window* were made into filmstrips by Weston Woods.

BIOGRAPHICAL/CRITICAL SOURCES: Illustrators of Children's Books: 1957-1966, Horn Book, 1968; *Books,* March, 1970, November, 1970; *Horn Book,* October, 1974; Wintle and Fisher, *The Pied Pipers,* Paddington Press, 1975.

KEITH, W(illiam) J(ohn)   1934-

PERSONAL: Born May 9, 1934, in London, England; son of William Henry (a clerk) and Elna Mary (Harpham) Keith; married Hiroko Teresa Sato, December 3, 1965. *Education:* Cambridge University, B.A., 1958; University of Toronto, M.A., 1959, Ph.D., 1961, F.R.S.C., 1979. *Home:* 142 Hilton Ave., Toronto, Ontario, Canada M5R 3E9. *Office:* Department of English, University College, University of Toronto, Toronto, Ontario, Canada M5S 1A1.

CAREER: McMaster University, Hamilton, Ontario, lecturer, 1961-62, assistant professor of English, 1962-66; University of Toronto, University College, Toronto, Ontario, associate professor, 1966-72, professor of English, 1972—.

WRITINGS—Published by University of Toronto Press, except as indicated: *Richard Jefferies: A Critical Study,* 1965; *Charles G. D. Roberts,* Copp Clark, 1969; *Rural Tradition: A Study of the Nonfiction Prose Writers of the English Countryside,* 1974; (editor) Charles G. D. Roberts, *Selected Poetry and Critical Prose,* 1974; *The Poetry of Nature: Rural Perspectives in Poetry from Wordsworth to the Present,* 1980; (editor with B. Z. Shek) *The Arts in Canada: The Last Fifty Years,* 1980; *Epic Fiction: The Art of Rudy Wiebe,* University of Alberta Press, 1981; (editor) *A Voice in the Land: Essays by and about Rudy Wiebe,* NeWest Press (Alberta), 1983.

* * *

KELLER, Fred S(immons)   1899-

PERSONAL: Born January 2, 1899, in Rural Grove, N.Y.; son of Vrooman Barney (a salesman) and Minnie (Simmons) Keller; married Frances Scholl, 1936; children: Anne Simmons (Mrs. Thomas C. Cline), John Vanderveer. *Education:* Tufts College (now University), B.S., 1926; Harvard University, M.A., 1928, Ph.D., 1931. *Home:* 820 Emory Dr., Chapel Hill, N.C. 27514. *Office:* Department of Psychology, University of North Carolina, Chapel Hill, N.C. 27514.

CAREER: Tufts College (now University), Medford, Mass., instructor in psychology, 1926-28; Colgate University, Hamilton, N.Y., instructor in psychology, 1931-38; Columbia University, New York, N.Y., instructor, 1938-41, assistant professor, 1941-46, associate professor, 1946-50, professor of psychology, 1950-64, professor emeritus, 1964—; Arizona State University, Tempe, professor of psychology, 1964-67; Institute for Behavioral Research, Silver Spring, Md., visiting scientist, 1967-68; Western Michigan University, Kalamazoo, visiting professor, 1968-70, adjunct professor, 1970-73, distinguished adjunct professor of psychology, 1973-74; Georgetown University, Washington, D.C., distinguished visiting scholar, 1974, distinguished visiting psychologist, 1974-76; writer, 1976—; University of North Carolina at Chapel Hill, adjunct research professor of psychology, 1980—.

Summer professor at University of California, Los Angeles, 1948; Fulbright-Hays Professor at University of Sao Paulo, 1961; professor at University of Brasilia, 1964; Cecil H. and Ida Green Honors Professor at Texas Christian University, autumn, 1973. Chairman of board of directors of Independent Learning Systems, 1970-71; member of board of directors of Individual Learning Systems, 1971-72; member of board of trustees of Cambridge Center for Behavioral Studies, 1982—. Participated in the film "Skinner and Behavior Change," Research Press, 1972. *Military service:* U.S. Army, American Expeditionary Forces, 1918-19; became sergeant.

MEMBER: American Psychological Association (fellow), American Association for the Advancement of Science (fellow), Eastern Psychological Association, (fellow; president, 1956-57).

AWARDS, HONORS: Received award from Society of Experimental Psychologists, 1947; certificate of merit from President Harry Truman, 1948; awards from American Psychological Association, 1974, for teaching, and 1976, for contributions to psychology; medal and diploma from Ministry of Labor of Brazil, 1979, for work as a pioneer psychologist. Academic: Sc.D. from C. W. Post Center of Long Island University, 1972, and Colgate University, 1976; D.H.L. from Institute for Behavioral Research, 1976.

WRITINGS: The Definition of Psychology, Appleton, 1937, revised edition, 1973; (with W. N. Schoenfeld) *Principles of Psychology,* Appleton, 1950; *Learning: Reinforcement Theory,* Random House, 1954, revised edition, 1969; (with J. G. Sherman) *The Keller Plan Handbook,* W. R. Benjamin, 1974, revised edition published as *The PSI Handbook: Essays on Personalized Instruction,* TRI Publications, 1982; (editor with Emilio Ribes-Inesto) *Behavior Modification: Applications to Education,* Academic Press, 1974; (editor) *History of Psychology: A PSI Companion* (readings), Scholars' Press, 1975; *Summers and Sabbaticals,* Research Press, 1977; *Pedagogue's Progress,* TRI Publications, 1982.

Also co-author of scripts for filmstrips "Together," Appleton, 1972, and "Keller on PSI," School of Communications, University of Texas, 1975. Contributor of numerous articles to professional journals.

WORK IN PROGRESS: An autobiography.

SIDELIGHTS: Fred S. Keller explains to *CA:* "The book that was most important to my career was B. F. Skinner's *Behavior of Organisms* (1938). This is reflected in my own writings and is responsible for what success I may have had as a teacher and an educational reformer. My major interest has been in animal learning, human training, and teaching."

BIOGRAPHICAL/CRITICAL SOURCES: American Psychologist, January, 1977.

* * *

KELLNER, Bruce 1930-

PERSONAL: Born March 17, 1930, in Indianapolis, Ind.; son of Gordon (an insurance executive) and Lillian (Zumbrunn) Kellner; married Margaret Wilcox, December 28, 1961; children: Hans Carl, Kate Hein. *Education:* Colorado College, B.A., 1955; University of Iowa, M.F.A., 1958. *Politics:* Democrat. *Religion:* None. *Home:* 514 North School Lane, Lancaster, Pa. 17603. *Office:* Department of English, Millersville University, Millersville, Pa. 17551.

CAREER: Coe College, Cedar Rapids, Iowa, assistant professor of English, 1955-60; Hartwick College, Oneonta, N.Y., assistant professor of English and drama director, 1960-69; Millersville University, Millersville, Pa., professor of English, 1969—. *Military service:* U.S. Navy, 1951-54. *Member:* Modern Language Association of America, American Association of University Professors, Alpha Psi Omega, Pi Delta Kappa, Kappa Sigma.

WRITINGS: Carl Van Vechten and the Irreverent Decades, University of Oklahoma Press, 1968; (editor) *"Keep A-Inchin' Along": Selected Writings of Carl Van Vechten ut Black Arts and Letters,* Greenwood Press, 1979; *A Bibliography of the Work of Carl Van Vechten,* Greenwood Press, 1980. Also author of *The Harlem Renaissance: An Historical Dictionary for the Era,* 1984, and of essays and articles on modern Irish poetry, obscure literary figures, and bibliography.

Contributor: James Vinson, editor, *Great Writers of the English Language,* Scribner, 1979; A. Walton Litz, editor, *American Writers,* Scribner, 1981; George Walsh and others, editors, *Contemporary Photographers,* St. Martin's, 1982.

WORK IN PROGRESS: An edition of Carl Van Vechten's letters; a biography of Ralph Barton; a selection of Carl Van Vechten's uncollected musical and literary criticism; *The Bookshelf Onstage,* a textbook with scripts for reader's theatre.

SIDELIGHTS: "Like Joanne Trautmann, who may have coined the phrase to describe herself when she was editing Virginia Woolf's letters, I am a 'footnote fetishist,'" Bruce Kellner told *CA.* "My natural habitat is the library, but I care passionately about language and believe that scholarly writing can be as handsomely constructed as other literary forms. Craft and art are not the especial possessions of poetry and fiction. Regardless of the form, however, I believe that craft must precede art. Our greatest critics, like our greatest poets, have always known that."

BIOGRAPHICAL/CRITICAL SOURCES: New York Times Book Review, February 16, 1969; *Variety,* March 26, 1969.

* * *

KELLY, George A. 1916-

PERSONAL: Born September 17, 1916, in New York, N.Y. *Education:* Catholic University of America, M.A., 1943, Ph.D., 1946. *Office:* St. John's University, Grand Central and Utopia Parkways, Jamaica, N.Y. 11439.

CAREER: Ordained Roman Catholic priest, 1942, elevated to right reverend monsignor, 1964. Parish priest, 1945-59; Archdiocese of New York, New York, N.Y., director of Family Life Bureau, 1955, secretary for education, 1966-70; St. John's University, Jamaica, N.Y., John A. Flynn Professor of Contemporary Catholic Problems, 1970—, director, Institute for Advanced Studies in Catholic Doctrine, 1975—. Member of Papal Birth Control Commission, 1965. Lecturer at St. Joseph's Seminary, Yonkers, N.Y., 1946-49, and Catholic University of America, 1952. Associate chaplain for Catholic Trade Unionists Association, 1945-52; conductor of Family Life Institutes, U.S. Army and U.S. Air Force, 1960-61; member of advisory board, National Catholic Welfare Conference, 1965.

MEMBER: American Association of University Professors, American Sociological Association, Association for the Sociology of Religion, American Catholic Historical Association, American Catholic Theological Society, American Catholic Sociological Society, Fellowship of Catholic Scholars (executive secretary, 1976-81), National Catholic Education Association. *Awards, honors:* Cardinal Wright Award, Friends of the Fellowship of Catholic Scholars, 1979, for *The Battle for the American Church.*

WRITINGS: Catholics and the Practice of Faith, 1946; *Primer on the Taft-Hartley Act,* Christopher, 1948; *The Story of St. Monica's Parish,* Monica Press, 1954; *Catholic Marriage*

Manual, Random House, 1958; *Catholic Family Handbook*, Random House, 1959.

Catholic Youth's Guide to Life and Love, Random House, 1960; *Overpopulation—A Catholic View*, Paulist Press, 1960; *Catholic Guide to Expectant Motherhood*, Random House, 1961; *Dating for Young Catholics*, Doubleday, 1963; *Birth Control and Catholics*, Doubleday, 1963; *Your Child and Sex*, Random House, 1964; *Who Is My Neighbor?*, Random House, 1966; *The Christian Role in Today's Society*, Random House, 1966; *Catholics and the Practice of the Faith*, St. John's University Press, Volume I: *Catholic Youth*, 1967, Volume II: *Catholic Parents*, 1971.

Why Should the Catholic University Survive?, St. John's University Press, 1975; *The Political Struggle of Active Homosexuals to Gain Social Acceptance* (monograph), Franciscan Herald Press, 1976; *The Catholic Church and the American Poor*, Alba House, 1976; *Sacrament of Penance and Reconciliation*, Franciscan Herald Press, 1976; *Who Should Run the Catholic Church?*, Our Sunday Visitor, 1976; *The Battle for the American Church*, Doubleday, 1979; *The Crisis of Authority*, Regnery-Gateway, 1980.

Editor; published by Daughters of St. Paul, except as indicated: *Government Aid to Nonpublic Schools: Yes or No?*, St. John's University Press, 1972; *The Parish*, St. John's University Press, 1973; *The Sacrament of Penance in Our Time*, 1976; *The Sacrament of the Eucharist in Our Time*, 1978; *The Teaching Church in Our Time*, 1978; *Human Sexuality in Our Time*, 1979; *Catechetical Instruction and the Catholic Faithful*, 1982.

Contributor to *Catholic Digest, Homiletic and Pastoral Review*, and other periodicals.

SIDELIGHTS: George A. Kelly opens his book *The Battle for the American Church* by stating: "A guerilla-type warfare is going on inside the Church and its outcome is clearly doubtful. The Pope and the Roman Curia are fending off with mixed success the attacks of their theologians who, in the name of scholarship, demand more radical accommodation with Protestant and secular thought. The issues at stake are the correctness of Catholic doctrine and the survival of the Catholic Church as a significant influence in the life of her own communicants." In a *Washington Post* review of the book, Colman McCarthy comments that although he doesn't agree with Kelly's thesis, he nevertheless "enjoyed nearly every page of [the author's work]. His intelligence is forceful and he is able to be angry without being mean. He loves his church and thrives on its teachings, ancient and modern."

BIOGRAPHICAL/CRITICAL SOURCES: George A. Kelly, *The Battle for the American Church*, Doubleday, 1979; *Washington Post*, October 5, 1979.

*   *   *

KELLY, Rosalie (Ruth)

PERSONAL: Born in Grand Rapids, Mich.; daughter of Charles (a builder) and Emmeline (Barth) Schley; married Gleason Kelly (an accountant), May 18, 1944; children: Nancy, Meredith (Mrs. Philip Lewis), William. *Education:* Attended Oregon State University, 1939-40. *Home:* 246 Orchard Rd., Orinda, Calif. 94563. *Agent:* Ruth Cantor, 156 Fifth Ave., New York, N.Y. 10010.

CAREER: Worked as secretary and clerk in private industry, 1940-42, and for U.S. Department of the Interior, 1950-52.

WRITINGS: The Great Toozy Takeover (juvenile), Putnam, 1975; (contributor) Theodore Clymer and others, editors, *Measure Me, Sky*, Ginn, 1979; *Addie's Year* (young adult), Beaufort Book Co., 1981. Contributor of short stories to literary magazines.

WORK IN PROGRESS: Love Jane and *Robins of Kirkleigh*, both juveniles; *Savage*, a suspense novel.

SIDELIGHTS: Rosalie Kelly tells *CA*: "I started to write soon after we moved to the San Francisco Bay Area in 1968. Author Sonia Levitin had organized a creative writing class conveniently located nearby, and my husband, tired of hearing me talk writing without doing much about it, suggested I enroll.

"Since our children were grown—why not? Thus I abandoned the scattergun method and began a disciplined program: A minimum of a thousand words per day, three to four hours at the typewriter. My first book for children, *The Great Toozy Takeover*, resulted from my work during this period, so I have little patience with those who claim such classes are a waste of time. Being naturally competitive may have helped, too.

"My second novel, *Addie's Year*, a book for young adults, was written after I began teaching the writing class I'd attended as a student. There are benefits attached to teaching, and I'm happy to have had the chance to receive them, but there are also losses in time and energy, so this is my final year as a teacher.

"Meanwhile, my agent suggested that *The Great Toozy Takeover* might be suitable for television, so a 'treatment' I wrote is now making the rounds. Whether anything will come of this I have no idea, but it was fun to try something different."

Kelly writes that she and her husband enjoy traveling, and she hopes to set one of her future works in Yorkshire, England. "It would be nice to use the Bay Area as a setting," she indicates, "but for some reason I have to be away from a place for a time before I can write about it. Both my books have dealt with the midwest during the 1920's; now I am almost ready to place one in Oregon where we lived for many years—almost, but not quite. Maybe next year."

*   *   *

KENIAN, Paul Roger
See CLIFFORD, Martin

*   *   *

KENT, Stella
See PHILLIPS, Stella

*   *   *

KESSNER, Thomas   1946-

PERSONAL: Born December 20, 1946, in Germany; came to the United States in 1950, naturalized citizen, 1958; son of Eugene (a laborer) and Livia (Farkas) Kessner; married Rachel Roth, December 17, 1967; children: Joseph, Hadassah, Sara, Aryeh, Meir, David. *Education:* Brooklyn College of the City University of New York, B.A. (magna cum laude), 1967; Columbia University, M.A., 1968, Ph.D., 1975. *Home:* 1312 54th St., Brooklyn, N.Y. 11219. *Office:* Department of History, Kingsborough Community College, Manhattan Beach, Brooklyn, N.Y. 11235.

CAREER: City University of New York, New York City, adjunct lecturer of world history at Brooklyn College, 1969,

Kingsborough Community College and the Graduate School and University Center, 1971—, began as instructor, currently associate professor of history, associate director of graduate program in history and humanities, 1980-83. Member of faculty at New School for Social Research, 1976, and New York University Graduate School; adjunct associate professor of history at Brooklyn College of the City University of New York, 1980; lecturer at numerous conferences. Associate member of University Seminar on the City, Columbia University, 1976—; director of Fiorello H. La Guardia Archives, La Guardia Community College, 1982-83. Reader for Oxford University Press, Prentice-Hall International, Inc., and Temple University Press, 1978-79. Consultant in immigrant history to Drew University doctoral program, 1978; administrative consultant to Research Foundation on Jewish Immigration, 1979. *Member:* Organization of American Historians, Social Science History Association, Phi Beta Kappa, Alpha Sigma Lambda.

AWARDS, HONORS: Research grants from National Foundation for Jewish Culture, 1974, National Endowment for the Humanities, 1976, and American Council of Learned Societies, 1976 and 1977; National Endowment for the Humanities junior fellow, 1976, and fellow, 1979 and 1983; Memorial Foundation for Jewish Culture fellow, 1977-78; PSC-BHE Award, City University of New York, 1977-79 and 1980-81; research award from Kingsborough Community College of the City University of New York, 1978.

WRITINGS: The Golden Door: Italian and Jewish Immigrant Mobility in New York City, 1880-1915, Oxford University Press, 1977; (with Betty Caroli) *Ethnic Heritage: A Teacher's Manual,* New York Board of Education District 22, 1979; (editor with Robert Hirt) *Issues in Teaching the Holocaust: A Guide,* Yeshiva University Press, 1981; (with Caroli) *Today's Immigrants, Their Stories: A New Look at the Newest Americans,* Oxford University Press, 1981; (contributor) Diane Ravitch and Ronald Goodenow, editors, *Educating an Urban People,* Teacher's College Press, 1981; (contributor) Alexander Callow, editor, *American Urban History,* Oxford University Press, 1982; (contributor) David Berger, editor, *The Legacy of Jewish Migration,* Columbia University Press, 1983.

Member of editorial board, ''The Heritage of Modern European Jewry'' series, Yeshiva University; consultant on American Jewish history for *Harvard Encyclopedia of American Ethnic Groups,* edited by Stephan Thernstrom, 1980. Contributor to *Proceedings of the Eighth World Congress of Jewish Studies,* 1982; contributor of articles and reviews to periodicals, including *Journal of Ethnic History, American Jewish History, Journal of American History, New York History, Jewish Journal of Sociology,* and *International Migration Review.*

WORK IN PROGRESS: Fiorello La Guardia and the Making of Modern New York, for McGraw.

SIDELIGHTS: ''While my purpose in writing *The Golden Door* and *Today's Immigrants, Their Stories* was to explore the broad process of the immigrant experience, my present work focuses on a man I find endlessly fascinating,'' Thomas Kessner told *CA.* ''Fiorello La Guardia was a child of immigrant parents who grew up in the western United States, where he learned to demand his rights and to be sensitive to the slights visited upon others. He cultivated a fierce resentment against privilege and corruption. He became the first Italian-American to be elected to Congress and in that body committed himself to many good fights. It never bothered him that he was in a minority; indeed he was quite comfortable in his iconoclasm. He had an affection and real concern for the underprivileged.

''In the midst of the Depression he was elected mayor of New York City, and the city would never be the same. He cleaned out corruption and brought this most difficult of cities into modernity. He showed what a leader committed to honest and efficient government could do. At the same time, he was a driven, ambitious man whose story is punctuated with private grief and public frustration.

''The challenge in writing his biography is to render the temper of the times and his impact on these times faithfully, to show what he could and could not do, to understand what he did and why, and to make the reader care enough to ask the same questions.''

BIOGRAPHICAL/CRITICAL SOURCES: New York Times Book Review, November 1, 1981.

*   *   *

KEVLES, Bettyann 1938-

PERSONAL: Born August 20, 1938, in New York, N.Y.; daughter of David Marshal (a lawyer) and Sondra (a theatrical producer; maiden name, Alosoroff) Holtzmann; married Daniel Jerome Kevles (a historian), May 18, 1961; children: Beth, Jonathan. *Education:* Vassar College, B.A., 1959; Columbia University, M.A., 1961. *Home:* 575 La Loma Rd., Pasadena, Calif. 91105.

CAREER: Sunbeam, Northridge, Calif., editor and writer, 1967-69; Westridge School, Pasadena, Calif., instructor in history, 1970-76. *Awards, honors:* Best older juvenile award from New York Academy of Science, 1977, for *Watching the Wild Apes.*

WRITINGS: Watching the Wild Apes, Dutton, 1976; *Thinking Gorillas,* Dutton, 1980; *Listening In,* Scholastic Book Services, 1981.

Science fiction and spy stories represented in anthologies, including *Cassandra Rises: Science Fiction by Women,* edited by Alice Lawrance, Doubleday, 1978. Also author of column for the *Los Angeles Times.*

WORK IN PROGRESS: Females of the Species, an exploration of some animal behavior.

SIDELIGHTS: Bettyann Kevles explains to *CA:* ''Animal behavior has led me to a broader interest in science.''

*   *   *

KIDD, Russ
See DONSON, Cyril

*   *   *

KIEFER, Irene 1926-

PERSONAL: Born November 1, 1926, in Red Lodge, Mont.; daughter of John (a grocer) and Madalene (Giachino) Giovanini; married David Kiefer (a science journalist), April 9, 1955; children: Timothy, Katherine. *Education:* Montana State University, B.S. (with honors), 1948. *Home:* 6917 Ayr Lane, Bethesda, Md. 20817.

CAREER: DuPont Co., chemist in Waynesboro, Va., 1948-50, and Wilmington, Del., 1950-51; *Chemical Engineering News,* Washington, D.C., assistant editor, 1952-57; free-lance writer, 1964—. Editorial consultant to National Science Foundation, U.S. Department of Energy, and U.S. Environmental Protection Agency. *Awards, honors: Underground Furnaces:*

The Story of Geothermal Energy was named an outstanding science book for children by the National Science Teachers Association-Children's Book Council Joint Committee; Outstanding Science Book for Children Award, National Science Teachers Association-Children's Book Council Joint Committee, 1981, for *Poisoned Land: The Problem of Hazardous Wastes,* and 1982, for *Nuclear Energy at the Crossroads.*

WRITINGS—Juveniles: *Underground Furnaces: The Story of Geothermal Energy,* Morrow, 1976; *Global Jigsaw Puzzle: The Story of Continental Drift,* Atheneum, 1978; *Energy for America,* Atheneum, 1978; *Poisoned Land: The Problem of Hazardous Wastes,* Atheneum, 1981; *Nuclear Energy at the Crossroads,* Atheneum, 1982.

Also author of public information booklets for U.S. Environmental Protection Agency. Contributor to periodicals, including *Smithsonian, Washingtonian, Maryland, Travel,* and *Mosaic.*

WORK IN PROGRESS: Publications for the "superfund" program of the Environmental Protection Agency.

SIDELIGHTS: Irene Kiefer writes: "Modern society is becoming increasingly specialized, making it imperative that specialists know how to communicate outside their own narrow fields. This is especially true in science, where public funds are frequently involved. If science is to continue to receive public support, it must be presented in a form the layman can understand. This desire to explain science motivates my writing, and led me quite naturally to children's books."

*   *   *

KIERNAN, (E.) V(ictor) G(ordon) 1913-

PERSONAL: Born September 4, 1913, in Manchester, England; son of J. E. Kiernan. *Education:* Trinity College, Cambridge, B.A., 1934, M.A., 1937. *Politics:* Socialist (independent). *Religion:* None. *Home:* 27 Nelson St., Edinburgh EH3 6LJ, Scotland. *Office:* Department of History, University of Edinburgh, 50 George Sq., Edinburgh, Scotland.

CAREER: Cambridge University, Cambridge, England, fellow of Trinity College, 1937-39, 1946-48; University of Edinburgh, Edinburgh, Scotland, lecturer, 1948-64, reader, 1964-70, professor of history, beginning 1970, currently professor emeritus.

WRITINGS: British Diplomacy in China, 1880-1885, Cambridge University Press, 1939, published with a new foreword as *British Diplomacy in China, 1880 to 1885,* Octagon, 1970; *Metcalfe's Mission to Lahore, 1808-1809,* Panjab Record Office, 1943; *The Revolution of 1854 in Spanish History,* Clarendon Press, 1966; *The Lords of Human Kind: Black Man, Yellow Man and White Man in an Age of Empire,* Little, Brown, 1969 (published in England as *The Lords of Human Kind: European Attitudes towards the Outside World in the Imperial Age,* Weidenfeld & Nicolson, 1969); *Marxism and Imperialism,* Edward Arnold, 1974, St. Martin's, 1975; *America: The New Imperialism,* Zed Press, 1978; *State and Society in Europe, 1550-1650,* Basil Blackwell, 1980; *European Empires from Conquest to Collapse,* Fontana, 1982.

Translator: *Poems from Iqbal,* Kutub (Bombay), 1947; Faiz Ahmed Faiz, *Poems,* People's Publishing House (Delhi), 1958; (and author of introduction) Faiz, *Poems by Faiz,* Allen & Unwin, 1971.

Contributor of articles and reviews on history and literary history to periodicals.

WORK IN PROGRESS: Religion and History and *Duelling in Social History.*

SIDELIGHTS: V. G. Kiernan lived for a number of years in India.

BIOGRAPHICAL/CRITICAL SOURCES: Times Literary Supplement, March 13, 1981.

*   *   *

KILBOURN, William (Morley) 1926-

PERSONAL: Born December 18, 1926, in Toronto, Ontario, Canada; son of Kenneth and Mary Rae (Fawcett) Kilbourn; married Mary Elizabeth Sawyer, September 10, 1949; children: Nicholas, Timothy, Michael, Philippa, Hilary. *Education:* University of Toronto, B.A., 1948; Harvard University, A.M., 1949, Ph.D., 1957; Oxford University, M.A., 1954. *Religion:* Anglican. *Office:* 66 Collier St., 12C, Toronto, Ontario, Canada.

CAREER: McMaster University, Hamilton, Ontario, 1951-53, 1955-62, began as lecturer, became associate professor of history; York University, Toronto, Ontario, professor of history and humanities, 1962—, chairman of Humanities Division, 1962-67. Alderman for city of Toronto, 1970-76; member of the Metropolitan Toronto Council, 1973-76. Executive member of the Canada Council, 1979—; chairman of the Toronto Arts Council. Planner, writer, and host-interviewer for films and television and radio documentaries on politics, the arts, the Common Market, town planning, the church, and other topics; drama critic on Canadian Broadcasting Corp. weekly panel, "Views on the Shows"; has done other broadcasting in Canada and on American educational network.

MEMBER: Royal Society of Canada (fellow). *Awards, honors:* President's Medal for biography, University of British Columbia, 1957, for *The Firebrand;* A. B. Corey Prize, American and Canadian Historical Association, 1980, for *C. D. Howe: A Biography.*

WRITINGS: The Firebrand: William Lyon Mackenzie and the Rebellion in Upper Canada, Clarke, Irwin, 1956.

The Elements Combined, Clarke, Irwin, 1960; (contributor) Bissell and others, editors, *The Literary History of Canada,* University of Toronto Press, 1965; (editor) *The Restless Church* (collection of commissioned articles), Lippincott, 1966; *The Making of the Nation,* McClelland & Stewart, 1966, revised edition, 1973; (contributor) *The Canadians,* Macmillan, 1967; (author of introduction) Cornell, Trudel, and others, *Unity in Diversity,* Holt, 1967; *Religion in Canada,* McClelland & Stewart, 1968.

Pipeline: Trans-Canada and the Great Debate, Clarke, Irwin, 1970; (editor) *Canada: A Guide to the Peaceable Kingdom* (anthology), Macmillan, 1971; (editor) *The Toronto Book* (anthology), Macmillan, 1975; *Toronto,* McClelland, 1979; *C. D. Howe: A Biography,* McClelland, 1979.

*   *   *

KING, C(lyde) Richard 1924-

PERSONAL: Born January 14, 1924, in Gorman, Tex.; son of Clyde Stewart and Alice (Neill) King. *Education:* John Tarleton Agricultural College (now Tarleton State University), A.S., 1941; University of Oklahoma, B.A., 1948, M.A., 1949; Baylor University, Ph.D., 1962. *Religion:* Methodist. *Home and office:* 830 Alexander Rd., Stephenville, Tex. 76401.

CAREER: Mary Hardin-Baylor College (now University of Mary Hardin-Baylor), Belton, Tex., instructor in journalism and director of news service, 1949; John Tarleton Agricultural College (now Tarleton State University), Stephenville, Tex., instructor in English, 1950; East Texas State Teachers College (now East Texas State University), Commerce, instructor in journalism and director of news service, 1950-55; University of Texas at Austin, assistant professor, 1956-63, associate professor, 1963-70, professor of journalism, 1970—. News and feature editor for *Stephenville Empire-Tribune;* former business manager of "Journalism Monographs" for Association for Education in Journalism. President of board of directors, Stephenville Historical House Museum. *Military service:* U.S. Army, 1943-46; served in European theater; received four Bronze Stars. *Member:* International Association of Business Communicators, Texas State Historical Association, West Texas Historical Association, Masons (Scottish Rite), Sigma Delta Chi.

WRITINGS: Ghost Towns of Texas, Naylor, 1953; *Manana with Memories,* Von Boeckman-Jones, 1964; *Wagons East,* Department of Journalism, University of Texas, 1965; *Watchmen on the Walls,* Department of Journalism, University of Texas, 1967; *Letters from Fort Sill, 1886-1887,* Encino Press, 1971; *Victorian Lady on the Texas Frontier,* University of Oklahoma Press, 1972; *Susanna Dickinson: Messenger of the Alamo,* Shoal Creek Publications, 1976; *A Birthday in Texas,* Shoal Creek Publications, 1980; *Fred Gipson: Before "Old Yeller,"* Eakius, 1980; *The Lady Cannoneer,* Eakins, 1981. Author of "Northside Kitchen," a column in *Northside News,* 1966—. Contributor to magazines and newspapers.

WORK IN PROGRESS: A biography of James Clinton Neill of the Alamo; a revision of *Ghost Towns of Texas.*

SIDELIGHTS: C. Richard King writes: "My interest in Texas also takes the form of collecting Texana: books, papers, artifacts. I'm also interested in the genealogy of the Neill, Honea, Stewart, Bailey, and King families."

*   *   *

KIRK, H(enry) David 1918-

PERSONAL: Born March 15, 1918, in Duesseldorf, Germany (now West Germany); son of Simon (a manufacturer) and Anna C. (Simson) Kirk; married Ruth Vail (a psychologist), August 30, 1942 (divorced, 1973); married Beve Cherin-Tansey (a counselor), August 22, 1977; children: (first marriage) Peter, Frances, Deborah, William. *Education:* City College (now City College of the City University of New York), B.S. (cum laude), 1948; Cornell University, M.A., 1950, Ph.D., 1953. *Home:* 756 Harding Lane, Brentwood Bay, British Columbia, Canada V0S 1A0. *Office:* Department of Sociology, University of Waterloo, Waterloo, Ontario, Canada N2L 3G1.

CAREER: Cortland State Teachers College (now State University of New York College at Cortland), Cortland, N.Y., assistant professor of sociology, 1953-54; McGill University, Montreal, Quebec, associate professor of sociology, 1954-64; University of Waterloo, Waterloo, Ontario, professor of sociology, 1964—. Adjunct professor, law faculty, University of Victoria. Visiting professor at Whittier College, 1959-61, Los Angeles State College (now California State University, Los Angeles), 1961, and Temple University, 1968; summer visiting professor at Allegheny College and faculty research fellow, Community Studies, Inc., Kansas City, Mo., both 1961; Hilda Lewis Memorial Lecturer, London, England, 1969. Re-

search director, Royal Commission on the Status of Women in Canada, 1967. Consultant to Mental Hygiene Institute of Montreal.

MEMBER: International Sociological Association, American Sociological Association, Canadian Association of Anthropology and Sociology, Americans for a Safe Israel (member of academic advisory board). *Awards, honors:* U.S. Public Health Service fellow, 1951-53.

WRITINGS: Shared Fate: A Theory of Adoption and Mental Health, Free Press of Glencoe, 1964, revised edition published as *Shared Fate: A Theory and Method of Adoptive Relationships,* Ben-Simon Publications, 1984; *The Friendly Perversion—Quakers as Reconcilers: Good People and Dirty Work,* Americans for a Safe Israel, 1979; *Adoptive Kinship: A Modern Institution in Need of Reform,* Butterworth (Toronto), 1981, new and enlarged edition, Ben-Simon Publications, 1984. Contributor to sociology, social work, and law journals.

WORK IN PROGRESS: Research, with Murray Fraser, on several aspects of adoption law.

SIDELIGHTS: A German-born Jew educated in Germany, England, and the United States, H. David Kirk told *CA:* "My own early career as a refugee has imprinted its theme on my outlook and interests. When, after World War II, I obtained a university education, it was in part to wrestle with the questions of our era. I think I became a historically oriented sociologist in that mode: with a principal interest in the study of social change and the impact of drastic change on institutions, social relations, and human identity. In that context I have studied and taught minority group relations and have given much of my time to the investigation of adoptive kinship patterns, for these, in microcosm, demonstrate the ubiquity of social and personal changes in modern society. Similarly, I have had an interest in the history and sociology of modern anti-Semitism, with special reference to the churches."

*   *   *

KIRK-GREENE, Anthony (Hamilton Millard) 1925-
(Anthony H. M. Kirk-Greene; pseudonyms: Nicholas Caverhill, H.M.S., P.L.K., Yerima Yola)

PERSONAL: Born May 16, 1925, in Tunbridge Wells, England; son of Leslie (a civil engineer) and Helen (Millard) Kirk-Greene; married Helen Margaret Sellar, April 22, 1967. *Education:* Clare College, Cambridge, B.A. (with first class honors), 1949; graduate study at Cambridge University, 1955-56, Northwestern University and University of California, Los Angeles, 1958-59, and Edinburgh University, 1965-66. *Home:* 34 Davenant Rd., Oxford, England. *Office:* St. Antony's College, Oxford University, Oxford OX1 2JD, England.

CAREER: British Colonial Administrative Service, Northern Nigeria, district officer, 1950-57; Institute of Administration, Zaria, Nigeria, senior lecturer in government, 1957-60; Ahmadu Bello University, Zaria, associate professor of government and head of department, 1961-66; Oxford University, St. Antony's College, Oxford, England, senior research fellow in African studies, 1967-81, University Lecturer in the Modern History of Africa, 1982—, director of Oxford Colonial Records and Research Project, 1980—. Visiting professor at Syracuse University, 1961, University of California, Los Angeles, 1962, 1963, 1967, and 1968, University of Paris, 1971, 1973, and 1975, and Scandinavian Institute of African Studies, 1974; visiting fellow at Clare College, Cambridge University, 1967, and Hoover Institution on War, Revolution, and Peace, 1975; Hans Wolff Memorial Lecturer at University of Indiana, 1973; scholar-in-residence, Trent University, 1975. Consultant to Kenya Government, 1961, East African Staff College, 1969 and 1970, East African Community, 1972, and African Association for Public Administration and Management, 1975. *Military service:* Royal Warwickshire Regiment, 1943-44. Indian Army, 8th Punjab Regiment, 1944-47; became captain.

MEMBER: International African Institute, African Studies Association (council member, 1966-69 and 1975-78), Royal African Society, Hawks Club, Oxford and Cambridge United University Club. *Awards, honors:* M.A., Cambridge University, 1954, Oxford University, 1967; Harkness fellowship, 1958-59; member of Order of the British Empire, 1963; Canada Council fellowship, 1975.

WRITINGS: This Is Northern Nigeria: Background to an Invitation, Government Printer of Northern Nigeria (Kaduna), 1956; *Maiduguri and the Capitals of Bornu,* bilingual edition, Northern Regional Literature Agency (Zaria, Nigeria), 1958; *Adamawa, Past and Present: An Historical Approach to the Development of a Northern Cameroons Province,* Oxford University Press for the International African Insitute, 1958, new edition, Humanities, 1969; (with Caroline Sassoon) *The Cattle People of Nigeria,* Oxford University Press, 1959.

(With Sassoon) *The Niger,* Oxford University Press, 1961; *Barth's Travels in Nigeria,* Oxford University Press, 1962; *The Principles of Native Administration in Nigeria: Selected Documents, 1900-1947,* Oxford University Press, 1965; (with Sidney Hogben) *The Emirates of Northern Nigeria,* Oxford University Press, 1966; (compiler and translator) *Hausa ba dabo ba ne: A Collection of 500 Proverbs,* Oxford University Press, 1966; (with Yahaya Aliyu) *A Modern Hausa Reader,* McKay, 1967; (editor) *Lugard and the Amalgamation of Nigeria: A Documentary Record,* Cass, 1968.

(Translator with Paul Newman) *West African Travels and Adventures: Two Autobiographical Narratives from Northern Nigeria,* Yale University Press, 1971; *Crisis and Conflict in Nigeria: A Documentary Sourcebook,* two volumes, Oxford University Press, 1971; (editor and author of introduction and preface) *Gazetteers of the Northern Provinces of Nigeria,* revised edition, Volume I: *The Hausa Emirates,* Volume II: *The Eastern Kingdoms,* Volume III: *The Central Kingdoms,* Volume IV: *The Highland Chieftaincies,* Cass, 1972; (with Charles Kraft) *Teach Yourself Hausa,* University of London Press, 1973; *Mutumin Kirkii: The Concept of the Good Man in Hausa* (monograph), University of Indiana, 1974; *The Genesis of the Nigerian Civil War* (monograph), University of Uppsala, 1975; (with Pauline Ryan) *Faces North: Some Peoples of Nigeria,* Pitkin Publications, 1975; (editor) *The Transfer of Power: The African Administrator in the Age of Decolonization,* Oxford University Press, 1978.

A Biographical Dictionary of the British Colonial Governor, Volume I: *Africa,* Hoover Institution, 1980; *"Stay by Your Radios": Documentation for a Study of Military Government in Tropical Africa,* University of Leiden Press, 1981; (with Douglas Rimmer) *Nigeria since 1970: A Political and Economic Outline,* Holmes & Meier, 1981; (editor) *West Africa Portraits: A Biographical Dictionary of West African Personalities, 1947-1977,* Biblio Distribution, 1983; *African Administrators in Action,* revised edition, Biblio Distribution, 1983; *The Sudan Political Service: A Profile in the Sociology of Empire,* Oxford University Press, in press.

Contributor: Donald C. Stone, editor, *Education and Public Administration,* International Institute of Administrative Sciences, 1963; James S. Coleman, editor, *Education and Political Development,* Princeton University Press, 1965; L. Franklin Blitz, editor, *The Politics and Administration of Nigeria,* Praeger, 1966; H. Schiffers, editor, *Heinrich Barth Festschrift,* Steiner (Hamburg), 1967; Arnold Rivkin, editor, *Nations by Design,* Doubleday, 1968; John Spencer, editor, *The English Language in West Africa,* Longman, 1968.

Robert Rotberg, editor, *African Explorers and Exploration,* Harvard University Press, 1971; C. Fyfe and G. Shepperson, editors, *The Exploration of Africa in the Eighteenth and Nineteenth Centuries,* Edinburgh University, 1972; K. Ingham, editor, *Foreign Relations of African States,* Butterworth & Co., 1974; A. Adedeji and C. Baker, editors, *Education and Research in Public Administration in Africa,* Hutchinson, 1974; Adedeji and G. Hyden, editors, *Developing Research on African Administration,* [Nairobi], 1975; Fyfe, editor, *African Studies since 1945,* Longman, 1976; L. H. Gann and Peter Duignan, editors, *African Proconsuls: European Governors in Africa,* Hoover Institution, 1978; D. K. Fieldhouse and A. F. Madden, *Oxford and Empire,* Croom Helm, 1982; Prosser Gifford and W. Roger Louis, editors, *The Transfer of Power in Africa: Decolonization 1940-1960,* Yale University Press, 1982.

Author of introduction: C. J. Orr, *The Making of Northern Nigeria,* 2nd edition, Cass, 1965; Heinrich Barth, *Travels and Discoveries in North and Central Africa,* centenary edition, Barnes & Noble, 1965; Sonia Graham, *Government and Mission Education in Northern Nigeria,* Ibadan University Press, 1966; P. A. Benton, *The Languages and People of Bornu,* Cass, 1968; Barth, *The Vocabularies of Central African Languages,* Cass, 1970; Frederick Lugard, *Political Memoranda,* Cass, 1971; J. A. Burdon, *History of the Emirates of Northern Nigeria,* Gregg, 1973.

Also author of pamphlets and research papers on African languages, history, and governmental institutions. General editor of "Studies in African History" series, Methuen, 1971—; co-editor of "Colonial History Series," Hoover Institution, 1975—. Contributor of several hundred articles and reviews to African and historical journals. Editorial advisor, *Journal of African Administration,* 1957-67, *African Affairs,* 1975—, and *Culture et Developpement,* 1976—.

WORK IN PROGRESS: A history of the British Colonial Administrative Service; the political history of modern Nigeria; documents on decolonization.

BIOGRAPHICAL/CRITICAL SOURCES: Times (London), June 11, 1981; *Times Literary Supplement,* September 25, 1981.

*   *   *

KIRK-GREENE, Anthony H. M.
  See KIRK-GREENE, Anthony (Hamilton Millard)

*   *   *

KLAASSEN, Leo(nardus) H(endrik) 1920-

PERSONAL: Born June 21, 1920, in Rotterdam, Netherlands; son of Cornelis Hendrik Leonardus (an administrator) and Alida (Bakker) Klaassen; married Maria Ablinger, June 19, 1957; children: Marianne Elizabeth, Hendrik Leonardus. *Education:* Netherlands School of Economics, M.A., 1946, Ph.D., 1959. *Home:* Joost Banckertsplaats 133, Rotterdam, Netherlands. *Of-*

fice: Netherlands Economic Institute, Pieter de Hoochweg 118, Rotterdam, Netherlands.

CAREER: Economic Technological Institute, Rotterdam, Netherlands, research fellow, 1943-45; Netherlands Economic Institute, Rotterdam, research fellow, 1945-51, chief of research, 1951-59, director, 1959-68, president, 1968—; Erasmus University, Netherlands School of Economics, Rotterdam, lecturer, 1951-59, professor, 1959—. Visiting professor, University of California, Los Angeles, 1962, 1966.

Supervisor of studies on economic development of Curacao, 1960-68, on the economic consequences of the Euphrates Dam in Syria, 1964, on mineral development possibilities in Turkey, 1964, on economic evaluation of the Jordan Valley irrigation project in Jordan, 1967-68, on national transportation in the Netherlands, 1967—, on regional development in Algecia, Spain, on the industry in the Ruhr Area, 1969—, and on the national accounts and the administrative structure of the Netherlands Antilles, 1973—; member of transportation or survey teams in Niger and Dahomey (now Republic of Benin), 1961-62, Finland, 1964-65, Korea, 1965-68 and 1968-70, Cameroon and Central African Republic, 1967-69, Nigeria, 1970, and Iran, 1971; trustee for regional development study of Malaysia, 1967-69; director of study on the development potentials of Clyde area in Scotland, 1971-73. Member of Common Market Committee on Capital-coefficients and Investment Forecasts, and of Government of Netherlands Committee on the Profitability of Infrastructural Investments. Member of selection committee of the August Loesch Honour Ring.

Consultant to World Bank on transport study in Zambia, 1964, to NEDECO transportation mission to Brazil, 1965-67, to Iranian Government on city planning of Tehran, 1967-68, to Portuguese Government on industrialization policies and on amenity planning, 1968—, to Spanish government, 1973-74, to Institute of Land Reform, Wageningen, and to Netherlands Ministries of Transport, Agriculture, Communication, Health and Environment, and Finance.

MEMBER: World Academy of Art and Science (fellow), American Geographic Society (fellow), Econometric Society, Society for Statistics, Netherlands Demographic Association, Regional Science Association (vice-president of Philadelphia branch, 1972). *Awards, honors:* Medal of honor, University of Gdansk; honorary doctorate, University of Poznan and University of Lodz; Knight of the Order of the Dutch Lion; Golden Badge of the Order of Merit, Polish People's Republic.

WRITINGS: (With D. H. van Dongen Torman and L. M. Koyck) *Hoofdlijnen van de Sociaal-Economische Ontwikkeling der Gemunte Amersfoort van 1900-1970* (title means "The Development of the City of Amersfoort 1900-1970"), H. E. Stenfert Kroese, 1949.

(With J. Tinbergen and E. H. Mulder) *Observations on the Planned Provision of Nitrogen Fertilizers for the World*, H. E. Stenfert Kroese, 1956; (with A. de Klerk) *De Verwarming van de Volkswoning* (title means "Heating of Low Rent Houses"), H. E. Stenfert Kroese, 1959; (with W. C. Kroft, W. M. van Liefland, and D. Zuiderhoek) *Deventer, Stad van 250,000 inwoners* (title means "Deventer, City of 250,000"), A. E. Kluwer, 1959; *Richtlijnen voor het toegepast economisch onderzoek* (title means "Principles of Economic Research"), H. E. Stenfert Kroese, 1959.

(With E. H. van den Poll) *Economische Aspecten van de Wegenbouw* (title means "Economic Aspects of Road Construction"), Het Nederlandse Wegencongres, 1960; (contributor)

J. L. Mey, editor, *Depreciation and Replacement Policy*, North-Holland Publishing, 1961; (with others) *Capital Formation for Housing in Latin America*, Pan American Union, 1963.

(With others) *Area Redevelopment Policy in Great Britain and the Countries of the Common Market*, U.S. Department of Commerce, 1965; *Area Economic and Social Redevelopment*, Organization for Economic Co-operation and Development, 1965; (co-author) *Energie in Perspectief* Steenkolen Handels-Vereniging, 1966; *Kurzfristige Sozialloesungen contra langfristige Regionalpolitik* (title means "Short-term Social Solutions and Longrun Regional Policy") [Hamburg], 1966; *Methods of Selecting Industries for Depressed Areas: An Introduction to Feasibility Studies*, Organization for Economic Co-operation and Development, 1967; *Social Amenities in Area Economic Growth: An Analysis of Methods of Defining Needs for Local Social Amenities*, Organization for Economic Co-operation and Development, 1967; (with van den Poll) *Lineamenti della politica economica nei Paesi Bassi* (title means "Economic Policy in the Netherlands"), Instituto per gli Studi Sullo Sviluppo Economico e il Progresso Tecnico, [Rome], 1968; (with others) *Theory and Practice in Transport Economics*, European Conference of Ministers of Transport, 1969.

(With others) *The Future of European Ports*, College of Europe, 1970; (co-author and editor) *Regionale economie* (title means "Regional Economics"), Noordhoff, 1972; (with others) *Growth Poles*, United National Research Institute for Social Development, 1972; *The Impact of Changes in Society on the Demand for Passenger and Freight Transport*, European Conference of Ministers of Transport, 1973; (editor with J. R. Zuidema) *Economie dezer dagen* (title means "Economics of These Days"), University Press of Rotterdam, 1973; (with Paul Drewe) *Migration Policy in Europe: A Comparative Study*, Lexington books, 1973; (with G. Rehn and A. Bernfeld) *Manpower in Germany*, Organization for Economic Co-operation and Development, 1974; (with Jean J. P. Paelinck) *Integration of Socio-Economic and Physical Planning*, Rotterdam University Press, 1974; (with A.C.P. Verster and T. H. Botterweg) *Kosten-Batenanalyse in Regionaal Perspectief*, H. D. Tjeenk Willink, 1974.

(With J.A.M. Heijke and C. J. Offereins) *Naar een arbeidmarktmodel*, H. D. Tjeenk Willink, 1975; (with Paelinck) *Spatial Econometrics*, Saxon House, 1979; (with Paelinck and S. Wagenaar) *Spatial Systems: An Introduction*, Saxon House, 1979.

(With Norbert Vanhove) *Regional Policy: A European Approach*, Allanheld, Osmun, 1980; (editor with W.T.M. Molle and Paelinck) *The Dynamics of Urban Development: Proceedings of an International Conference Held on the Occasion of the Fiftieth Anniversary of the Netherlands Economic Institute in Rotterdam, September 4, 1979*, St. Martin's, 1981; (with J. A. Bourdrez and J. Volmuller) *Transport and Reurbanization*, Lexington Books, 1981.

Also author of *The Influence of Centralization on the Future*, 1970, *Amenity and Recreation in High Density Zones*, 1971, *Energy Conservation: Ways and Means*, 1974, *The Quality of Life in European Cities*, 1974, *Urban Europe*, and numerous books and pamphlets on economy, regional development, and society, in Russian, German, Dutch, French, Italian, Spanish, and Polish.

WORK IN PROGRESS: Several studies in regional economics and development programming.

KLEIN, Daniel Martin 1939-

PERSONAL: Born April 20, 1939, in Wilmington, Del.; son of David Xavier (a chemist) and Sophia (a teacher; maiden name, Posner) Klein; married Freke Quirine Vuijst, 1976. *Education:* Harvard University, A.B., 1961. *Religion:* Jewish. *Home address:* Box 80A, R.D. 1, Great Barrington, Mass. 01230. *Agent:* Mel Berger, William Morris Agency, 1350 Avenue of the Americas, New York, N.Y. 10019.

CAREER: Social worker and welfare worker in New York, N.Y., 1962-63; high school teacher in Boiceville, N.Y., 1963-64; television writer in New York, N.Y., 1963-65; free-lance writer, 1965—.

WRITINGS: Everything You Wanted to Know about Marijuana, Tower, 1972; *Seven Perfect Marriages That Failed,* Stein & Day, 1975; *Embryo,* Doubleday, 1981; *Wavelengths,* Doubleday, 1982. Contributor of articles and stories to magazines, including *Realist, Saturday Evening Post, McCall's, Eye, Cavalier,* and *Nation.*

WORK IN PROGRESS: Magic Time, a novel for Doubleday.

SIDELIGHTS: Daniel Martin Klein writes: "Somehow it took me until I was forty to write a novel and here I am forty-three, at work on my third and actually making a living doing exactly what I've always wanted to do."

BIOGRAPHICAL/CRITICAL SOURCES: New York Times Book Review, February 8, 1981; *Los Angeles Times Book Review,* October 10, 1982.

*   *   *

KNIGHT, Wallace E(dward) 1926-

PERSONAL: Born February 4, 1926, in Charleston, W.Va.; son of Clarence H. and Ednah (Thomas) Knight; married Betty Howery, August 16, 1950; children: John Sydney, Stephen Howery, Leslie Harriett, Stuart Edward. *Education:* West Virginia Wesleyan College, A.B., 1949; Ohio University, M.A., 1950. *Politics:* Democrat. *Religion:* Protestant. *Home:* 121 Mount Savage Dr., Ashland, Ky. 41101. *Office:* W. Page Pitt School of Journalism, Marshall University, Huntington, W.Va. 25701.

CAREER: Charleston Gazette, Charleston, W.Va., reporter and business editor, 1950-55; Ashland Oil, Inc., Ashland, Ky., held various public relations posts, 1955-81; Marshall University, W. Page Pitt School of Journalism, Huntington, W.Va., associate professor of journalism, 1982—. *Military service:* U.S. Army, Third Armored Division, 1944-46; served in Europe; became sergeant. *Member:* Public Relations Society of America, Authors Guild.

WRITINGS: The Way We Went (fiction), Great Books Foundation, 1976; *Lightstruck* (novel), Atlantic Monthly Press, 1979.

Also author of book length narrative poem "Out of Wilderness," published in *River Cities Monthly,* 1980. Work has been anthologized in *Best American Short Stories of 1973,* edited by Martha Foley, Houghton, 1973. Contributor of articles, short stories, and poems to *Atlantic Monthly* and to various periodicals.

WORK IN PROGRESS: A Dead Duck, a novel.

SIDELIGHTS: Wallace E. Knight's novel *Lightstruck* relates the changes in the lives of several citizens of a small town after they witness the appearance of a mysterious, bright light in the sky. Joseph McLellan explains in the *Washington Post Book World* that Knight's "intricate, often beautifully written novel traces the diverse ways in which each of these people interpret what they have seen, how the experience affects them, and what they finally learn about the experience and themselves." Writing in *Library Journal* Joyce W. Smothers states, "Through the characters' individual interpretations of this phenomenon, the author skillfully illuminates their personalities [and] how the small-minded and the poor in spirit can diminish the things they don't understand."

Knight shared his background with *CA:* "My former employment as an oil company public relations manager involved responsibility for an extensive publications program; this left very little time for writing 'for fun.' However, beginning in 1972 I decided to write one evening a week. Most of the short stories I've written have sold, and I'm now concentrating on novels."

BIOGRAPHICAL/CRITICAL SOURCES: Kirkus Reviews, December 1, 1978; *Publishers Weekly,* December 11, 1978; *Library Journal,* January 1, 1979; *Washington Post Book World,* March 8, 1979.

*   *   *

KNOTTS, Howard (Clayton, Jr.) 1922-

PERSONAL: Born October 13, 1922, in Springfield, Ill.; son of Howard Clayton (a lawyer) and Charlotte (Sterling) Knotts; married Ilse-Margret Vogel (a writer and artist), June 1, 1959. *Education:* Attended Knox College, 1940-43; Art Institute of Chicago, B.F.A. (honors), 1949. *Home and office address:* Duell Rd., Bangall, N.Y. 12506.

CAREER: Artist and writer. Paintings exhibited in major museums across the United States, and are in collections at Phillips Gallery and Joseph Hirshhorn Museum, both Washington, D.C., and University of California Art Museum, Berkeley, Calif. *Military service:* U.S. Army Air Forces, 1946-49. *Awards, honors: The Winter Cat* was named best juvenile book of the year by Friends of American Writers, 1972.

WRITINGS—Self-illustrated juveniles: *The Winter Cat,* Harper, 1972; *Follow the Brook,* Harper, 1975; *The Lost Christmas,* Harcourt, 1978; *Great-Grandfather, the Baby, and Me,* Atheneum, 1978; *The Summer Cat,* Harper, 1981.

Illustrator: Willis Barnstone, *A Day in the Country,* Harper, 1971; May Sarton, *Punch's Secret,* Harper, 1974; Charlotte Zolotow, *When the Wind Stops,* Harper, 1975; Eve Bunting, *Winter's Coming,* Harcourt, 1977; Bunting, *The Big Red Barn,* Harcourt, 1979; Bunting, *Goose Dinner,* Harcourt, 1981.

WORK IN PROGRESS: Illustrating *Wings,* by wife, Ilse-Margret Vogel.

SIDELIGHTS: Howard Knotts told *CA,* "I am an artist (painter) who gradually became an author-illustrator of children's books because of my wife's activity in this field and because of an apparently natural enthusiasm and affinity for the genre."

*   *   *

KNUDSON, Danny (Alan) 1940-

PERSONAL: Born September 28, 1940, in Dunedin, New Zealand; son of George Allan (an electrical engineer) and Jean (McAra) Knudson; married Julie Ellen Smellie, May 11, 1963;

children: Deborah Julie, Carol Jean, Claire Ellen. *Education:* University of Otago, B.A., 1966, diploma in education, 1967, M.A., 1974, advanced diploma of teaching, 1974. *Home:* 79 Centennial, Wakari, Dunedin, New Zealand. *Office:* George Street Normal School, George St., Dunedin, New Zealand.

CAREER: Teacher in elementary school in Dunedin, New Zealand, 1962-65; organizing teacher for gifted children in Otago, New Zealand, 1966; area organizer of special classes in schools in Otago and Southland, New Zealand, 1967; Green Island School, Dunedin, New Zealand, deputy principal, 1973-77; Reid Park School, Mosgiel, South Island, New Zealand, principal, 1978-80; Fairfield School, Otago, principal, 1980-81; George Street Normal School, Dunedin, principal, 1982—. Lecturer at Dunedin Teacher's College, 1974 and 1976. Member of New Zealand Educational Institute's yearbook committee, Otago Education Board and of the executive committee of the New Zealand College of Education. New Zealand gymnastic awards examiner, 1972—.

MEMBER: Intercontinental Biographical Association (fellow), New Zealand Educational Institute (associate; Otago president, 1975), New Zealand Council for Educational Research Electoral College, Otago Institute for Educational Research (president, 1976-77), Otago School Sports Association (member of executive committee, 1974), Otago Early Settlers' Association.

WRITINGS: The Story of Wakatipu, Whitcombe & Tombs, 1968; *The Road to Skippers,* A. H. & A. W. Reed, 1974, distributed in the United States as *Goldfields Wonderland: The Road to Skippers,* Tuttle, 1975; *Goldtown School,* New Zealand Educational Institute, 1975; *Standard V, 1892: A School Day,* Longman Paul, 1981. Also editor of *The Creative Arts,* the yearbook of the New Zealand Educational Institute. Contributor to educational journals.

WORK IN PROGRESS: Homework? Homework!; developing aspects of language teaching in the primary schools; using his own programmed instruction material and scrambled textbooks in his teaching.

SIDELIGHTS: Danny Knudson writes: "New Zealand is a young country, having been settled by white colonists only a hundred thirty-four years ago, but it can be justly proud of its limited history which is crowded with colourful and exciting developments. Books which record aspects of our past way of life make a fitting contribution to an understanding of the nation's heritage. At the most specific level, a physical feature such as a hillside hut, is all the more significant and memorable when it is known to have unusual associations with past events."

AVOCATIONAL INTERESTS: Coaching children's sports (especially athletics and gymnastics), horse racing, veteran athletics, and square dancing.

*   *   *

KOBAL, John 1943-

PERSONAL: Born May 30, 1943, in Ottawa, Ontario, Canada; son of John and Paula Kobal. *Education:* Attended schools in Canada and Germany. *Home and office:* 38 Drayton Ct., Drayton Gardens, London SW10 9RH, England.

CAREER: Actor, 1959-64; British Broadcasting Corp., London, England, broadcaster, 1964-68; director, Kobal Collection. Lecturer on films and free-lance writer.

WRITINGS: (With Raymond Durgnat) *Greta Garbo,* Studio Vista, 1966; *Dietrich,* Studio Vista, 1967; (editor) Daniel C.

Blum, *A New Pictorial History of the Talkies,* revised edition (Kobal was not associated with previous edition), Putnam, 1968 (published in England as *A Pictorial History of the Talkies,* Spring Books, 1968), 2nd revised edition, 1973 (published in England as *A Pictorial History of the Talkies,* Spring Books, 1973).

Gotta Sing, Gotta Dance: A Pictorial History of Film Musicals, Hamlyn, 1970; *Gods and Goddesses of the Movies,* Crescent, 1973; *Romance and the Cinema,* Studio Vista, 1973; (editor and compiler) *Fifty Years of Movie Posters,* Hamlyn, 1973; *Marilyn Monroe: A Life on Film,* Hamlyn, 1974; (compiler with Peter Cargin) *Fifty Super Stars,* Hamlyn, 1974; *Hollywood Glamor Portraits: 145 Photos of Stars, 1926-1949,* Dover, 1976; *Movie-Star Portraits of the Forties: 163 Glamour Photos,* Dover, 1977; *Rita Hayworth: The Time, the Place, and the Woman,* Norton, 1978.

Film-Star Portraits of the Fifties, Dover, 1980; *The Art of the Great Hollywood Portrait Photographers, 1925-1940,* Knopf, 1980; *Hollywood Color Portraits,* Morrow, 1981; *Great Film Stills of the German Silent Era,* Dover, 1981; (with A. V. Wilson) *Foyer Pleasure,* Aurum, 1982; *Gotta Sing, Gotta Dance II: A History of Movie Musicals,* Hamlyn, 1983.

Contributor to *Vogue, Paris Match, Esquire,* and other magazines.

SIDELIGHTS: John Kobal's *The Art of the Great Hollywood Portrait Photographers, 1925-1940* is an examination of the publicity photographs used by film stars to create and promote their glamorous personal images. "The gorgeous photographs [in this book]," Lisa Mitchell of the *Los Angeles Times Book Review* writes, "are more than 150 breath-taking time capsules of Hollywood gods and goddesses at their mystical perfection."

These publicity photos, Kobal argues, are extremely important to the creation of a star's image. "Kobal," Anne Hollander of the *New York Times Book Review* states, "goes as far as to suggest that the acknowledged power of a star's looks depends on still images rather than motion pictures." Kobal, Hollander explains, compares the movie close-up, "a method especially designed to 'glamorize' movie stars—to enhance their personal magic," to the studio publicity photos. "The studio photographer's business," she states, "was to fix just such visions of unique beauty [as are found in movie close-ups] that could transcend films even while promoting them." "These images," Kobal writes in his book, "belong to an experience. The finest among them create an emotional empathy akin to that found in a bar of music, a line of poetry, or a canvas filled with color."

"Kobal's text," Mitchell judges, "is richly rounded with his own insights and there are quotations about the photographic sessions from some of the photographers and the stars." Andrew Hislip of the *Times Literary Supplement* calls the book "authoritative" and "beautifully produced." Mitchell concludes that *The Art of the Great Hollywood Portrait Photographers* is "an extraordinary record."

BIOGRAPHICAL/CRITICAL SOURCES: Times Literary Supplement, December 16, 1965, January 2, 1981; *New York Times Book Review,* November 9, 1980, December 6, 1981; *Los Angeles Times Book Review,* November 30, 1980; *Chicago Tribune Book World,* December 7, 1980, December 5, 1982.

*   *   *

KOCH, Thilo 1920-

PERSONAL: Born September 20, 1920, in Canena, Halle,

Germany (now East Germany); son of Friedrich Wilhelm and Helene (Krumbach) Koch; married Susanne Gaertner, May 22, 1944; children: Bettina, Thilo Cornelius. *Education:* Attended University of Berlin, 1939-40 and 1946-49. *Religion:* Lutheran. *Home:* 7201 Hausen ob Verena, West Germany.

CAREER: Journalist and writer; head of Berlin studio, North West German Radio, 1954-60; Washington correspondent for German Television, West German Radio, and *Die Zeit* (weekly), 1960-64; writer and television producer for NDR, ARD, and Studio Hamburg, 1964-82; editor-in-chief, *ARAL-Journal,* 1976—. *Military service:* German Army, 1939-45. *Member:* P.E.N.

WRITINGS: Stille und Klang (poems), Pontes, 1947; *Eine Jugend war das Opfer* (novel), Pontes, 1947; *Zwischen Grunewald und Brandenburger Tor,* Langen-Mueller, 1956; *Gottfried Benn* (biography), Langen-Mueller, 1957; *Berliner Luftballons,* Langen-Mueller, 1958; *Casanova* (essay), Langen-Mueller, 1959; *Literatur und Journalismus* (pamphlet), Cotta, 1959; (editor) *Portraets deutsch-juedischer: Geschichte,* DuMont Schauberg, 1961; *Zwischentoene: Ein Skizzenbuch,* Ullstein, 1963; *Tagebuch aus Washington,* three volumes, Wegner, 1963-64; *Wohin des Wegs, Deutschland?,* Kindler, 1965; *Briefe aus Kraehwinkel,* Nannen/Wegner, Volume I, 1965, Volume II, 1967; *Kaempfer fuer eine neue Welt: John F. Kennedy, Martin Luther King, Robert F. Kennedy,* Bucher, 1968, translation published as *Fighters for a New World: John F. Kennedy, Martin Luther King, Robert F. Kennedy,* Putnam, 1969; *Fuenf Jahre des Entscheidung,* Athenaion, 1969.

Auf dem Schachbrett der Sowjetunion: Die DDR, Wegner, 1970; (contributor) Hannelore Frank, editor, *15 x Sonntag,* Kreuz, 1970; *Die Goldener Zwanziger Jahre: Portraet eines Jahrzehnts,* Athenaion, 1970; *Aehnlichkeit mit lebenden Personen ist beabsichtigt,* Wegner, 1970; *Interview mit Sudamerika,* Deutsche Verlags-Anstalt, 1971; *Deutschland war teilbar: Die fuenfziger Jahre,* Deutsche Verlags-Anstalt, 1972; *Berlin: Teils, teils* (in German and English), illustrated with photographs by Ludwig Windstosser, Deutsche Verlags-Anstalt, 1972; *Nordamerika: Texte, Bilder, Dokumente,* K. Desch, 1972; (with Heinz Maegerlein) *Olympia 1972,* W. Limpert Verlag, 1972; *Reporter Report,* Heidelberg Ueberreuter, 1973; (editor) *Europa persoenlich: Erlebnisse und Betrachtungen deutscher P.E.N.-Autoren,* Erdmann, 1973; *Jugend wohin,* Bruckmann, 1973; *Piktogramm der Spiele/Pictogram of the Games,* Bruckmann, 1973; *Die Zehn Gebote Heute,* Volume I: *Gebote 1-4,* Verlag Prosportakuchin, 1973; *Hundert Jahre und ein Tag,* Boellhoff, 1975; (editor) *Was die Menschheit bewegt,* Verlag Prosportakuchin, 1977; (editor) *Die Zukunft unserer Kinder,* Verlag Prosportakuchin, 1979.

Ein Jubilaeum des Wissens: 175 Jahre Brockhaus, F. A. Brockhaus, 1980; (editor) *Freiheit, die ich meine,* Verlag Prosportakuchin, 1981; *Unser Mann in. . . ,* Arena, 1981.

Also author of 150 television documentaries. Columnist for Zeitungskette BRD, 1964—.

*   *   *

KOLYER, John (McNaughton)   1933-

PERSONAL: Born June 30, 1933, in East Williston, N.Y.; son of John (a salesman) and Mildred (a teacher; maiden name, McNaughton) Kolyer; married in 1970, 1972, 1974 (unmarried at present); children: Scott M., Paul F., Craig D., Jeffrey J. *Education:* Hofstra College (now University), B.A., 1955; University of Pennsylvania, Ph.D., 1960. *Home:* Apt. 311,

885 Sea Gull Lane, Newport Beach, Calif. 92663. *Office:* Autonetics Division, Rockwell International Corp., 3370 Miraloma Ave., Anaheim, Calif. 92803.

CAREER: Olin Mathieson Chemical Corp., Port Jefferson, N.Y., technician working on pesticides, 1955-56; FMC Corp., Princeton, N.J., research chemist, 1960-62; Thompson Chemical Co., Hebronville, Mass., research chemist, 1962-63; Allied Chemical Corp., Morristown, N.J., technical supervisor, 1962-72, senior research chemist in plastics division, 1964-65, group leader, 1965-67; Rockwell International Corp., Anaheim, Calif., member of technical staff in solar energy research, 1973—. Member of Lepidoptera Foundation, 1965—. *Member:* Poetry Society of America, American Chemical Society, Lepidoptera Society. *Awards, honors:* Poetry prizes from regional organizations.

WRITINGS—Published by Sangreal Press: *Dissections* (drawings), 1978; *The Romance of Narcissa Drek,* 1978; *The Octopus Returns* (poems), 1978; *Songs to a Mustached Moon* (poems), 1978; *Hell on Earth and Other Tales,* 1979; *Two Returns,* 1979; *The Arimathean Scrolls,* 1979; *In the Image* (play), 1979; *A Cargo from Mytilene* (poems), 1980; *Brief Biography of a Failure* (autobiography), 1980; *The Cynic's Tarot* (drawings), 1981; *Dharna* (play), 1981; *The Wings of the Morning,* 1981; *Cleaning the Slate,* 1981; *A Glass of Sand,* 1982; *Something Is Wrong* (drawings), 1983.

Published by Branden Press: *My Last Mistress,* 1972; *Ares and the Dove,* 1973; *Sonnets from Hell,* 1973; *Blasphemies with Paradise Judged,* 1974; *Dragon's Kisses,* 1975; *Neptune Taming a Seahorse,* 1975; *A Ballet of Brokers,* 1976; *The Garden of Mars,* 1976; *The Birds of Buna,* 1976; *The Black Calla,* 1977; *Odin's Other Eye,* 1977; *Drawings and Sculpture,* 1977.

Also author of technical material in the fields of chemistry, entomology, and ballistics.

WORK IN PROGRESS: A novella and a book of drawings.

SIDELIGHTS: A research chemist who holds fourteen U.S. patents on plastics, John Kolyer is also a poet, novelist, and playwright. He told *CA:* "Perhaps it's best to be commercial—Shakespeare was commercial—but I'm not. I prefer to be, or rather I can't help but be, idiosyncratic. At present I'm concerned not with publication ('not the business of poets,' Emily Dickinson) but with completing a large *oeuvre.* This consumes all my time and energy; a book of drawings, for example, can take years to finish. In the meantime, I give my books to universities. The University of California at Irvine has all of them in its special collections department."

*   *   *

KOPPETT, Leonard   1923-

PERSONAL: Born September 15, 1923, in Moscow, U.S.S.R.; son of David and Marie (Dvoretskaya) Kopeliovitch; married Suzanne Silberstein, April 24, 1964; children: Katherine, David. *Education:* Columbia University, B.A., 1946. *Politics:* Democrat. *Religon:* Jewish. *Office: Peninsula Times Tribune,* 245 Lytton Ave., Palo Alto, Calif. 94301.

CAREER: Sports reporter in New York, N.Y., for *New York Herald Tribune,* 1947-54, *New York Post,* 1954-63, and *New York Times,* 1963-78; free-lance columnist, 1978—; *Peninsula Times Tribune,* Palo Alto, Calif., executive sports editor, 1980-81, editor, 1982—. Columnist, *Sporting News,* 1966-81; teacher of sports journalism, Stanford University, 1977—. *Military service:* U.S. Army, 1943-45. *Member:* Authors Guild, Authors League of America, Baseball Writers Association, Professional Football Writers of America.

WRITINGS: A Thinking Man's Guide to Baseball, Dutton, 1967; *Twenty-four Seconds to Shoot*, Macmillan, 1968; *New York Mets*, Macmillan, 1970; *Championship N.B.A.*, Dial, 1971; *The New York Times Guide to Spectator Sports*, Quadrangle, 1971; *The Essence of the Game Is Deception*, Little, Brown, 1973; *All about Baseball*, Quadrangle, 1973; *The New York Times at the Super Bowl*, Quadrangle, 1974; *Sports Illusion, Sports Reality*, Houghton, 1981.

SIDELIGHTS: In *Sports Illusion, Sports Reality*, Leonard Koppett examines the world of sports in relation to the political and social conditions that exist in the world today. The "illusion," says Koppett, has been promoted by the sports establishment and accepted by fans who "believed that sports represented one of the glories of American democracy. They considered competitiveness, team loyalty, preoccupation with success, insistence on fair play, and physical exertion to be basic virtues of free enterprise, traditional family morality, and the Puritan ethic." And syndicated *Washington Post* columnist Colman McCarthy asks, "So what? . . . What's wrong with any of that? Nothing, if it were the reality. But Koppett is writing about sports *illusion*. The large value of his analysis is in his point that efforts to understand sports are worthwhile if they go beyond 'accepting superficial myths.' It's necessary to 'deal accurately with how things work, because understanding how we operate can tell us what we are.'"

Thus Koppett embarks upon what *Sports Illustrated* writer Art Hill calls "a detailed study of big-money spectator sports from every conceivable angle." The book begins with an in-depth look at sports finance, a section that Hill says is not very startling, "but it's all solid information." Then the author goes into "an examination of sports journalism, which should be instructive to any young reporter and a few old ones—especially the chapters on reporting techniques and sportswriting ethics." In a segment of the book entitled "Cultural Interaction," Koppett expounds on the notion of "sports-think," defined by Hill as "the American tendency to make analogies between the playing field and the real world." Koppett cautions against this kind of thinking: "In sports, of course, victory in the contest is an end in itself; there is nothing beyond it, except the next game or the next season. So a sports-loving culture, steeped in sports-think, starts to follow the contest for [political] power in contest terms, rather than in terms of what the winner will do later."

Philip Maddocks, in a *Christian Science Monitor* review, states that in the process of clarifying "the position of sports in American society, Mr. Koppett raises many valid objections to sports at an amateur level." Koppett says that our present view of amateurism evolved from the time in Victorian England when "gentlemen" did not work for pay, and they especially disdained the idea of receiving money for playing sports. This attitude, he maintains, has spawned a system that is obviously hypocritical and even a "poison" to sports today. Hill explains: "To Koppett, an amateur is someone who jogs or plays weekend softball. In his view, it's not only misleading but also insulting to call someone who has spent his or her life perfecting a skill—the miler who holds the world record, for example— an amateur." Koppett's solution: Abolish our present code of amateur athletics. He feels that if the Olympic Games, for instance, are to remain an amateur contest, then the athletes would not be paid; but their former "professionalism"—the fact that they had, at some time in the past, been paid to

compete—should not affect their eligibility for the Olympics. Likewise, the sham of college amateurism would be eliminated. He believes it is absurd to confer amateur status on players who are compensated with athletic scholarships worth thousands of dollars.

As a result of the controversial opinions expressed in *Sports Illusion, Sports Reality*, writes McCarthy, "there won't be any half-time shows for Len Koppett, nor is he likely to rate even a syllable from the many sports toadies who pass for journalists on the local evening news programs. Koppett's cheering section will be the small group that values athletic play apart from attendance figures, salaries and won-loss percentages. It's been a while since I've read a book on sports as tempered with reasoned judgments and well-written analysis as this."

BIOGRAPHICAL/CRITICAL SOURCES: Washington Post, October 30, 1981; *Sports Illustrated*, December 28, 1981; *Christian Science Monitor*, December 30, 1981; Leonard Koppett, *Sports Illusion, Sports Reality*, Houghton, 1982.

*   *   *

KOREN, Edward 1935-

PERSONAL: Born December 13, 1935, in New York, N.Y.; son of Harry L. (a dentist) and Elizabeth (Sorkin) Koren; married Miriam Siegmeister (an editor), April 22, 1961 (divorced); children: Nathaniel, Alexandra. *Education:* Columbia University, B.A., 1957; Pratt Institute, M.F.A., 1964. *Office: New Yorker* Magazine, 25 West 43rd St., New York, N.Y. 10036.

CAREER: Writer, sculptor, painter, print maker, illustrator, and cartoonist. Former advertising manager for Columbia University Press and rewrite man for a trade journal; *New Yorker* magazine, New York, N.Y., cartoonist, 1962—; Brown University, Providence, R.I., associate professor, 1969-77, adjunct associate professor of art, 1977—. Work has been exhibited at Terry Dintinfass Gallery, 1975, 1977, and 1979. *Awards, honors:* Guggenheim fellow, 1970.

WRITINGS—Self-illustrated: Don't Talk to Strange Bears (juvenile), Simon & Schuster, 1969; *Behind the Wheel* (juvenile), Holt, 1972; *Do You Want to Talk about It?*, Pantheon, 1976; *Are You Happy?*, Pantheon, 1980; *Well, THERE'S Your Problem*, Pantheon, 1980; *The Penguin Edward Koren*, Penguin, 1982; *Caution: Small Ensembles*, Pantheon, 1983.

Illustrator: (Contributor) *The Gordon of Sesame Street Storybook*, Random 1972; Delia Ephron, *How to Eat Like a Child; and Other Lessons in Not Being a Grown-up*, Viking, 1978; Ephron, *Teenage Romance*, Viking, 1981. Editor-in-chief, *Columbia Jester*, 1957.

SIDELIGHTS: Described by *Newsweek*'s Walter Clemons as "the best of the younger *New Yorker* cartoonists," Edward Koren is noted for his drawings of fuzzy creatures (animal and human) whose comments on middle-aged, middle-class life are tinged with satire and whimsy. Koren extracts humor from a variety of seemingly ordinary situations. In one cartoon, for instance, an early-morning glance in the bathroom mirror is met with the ominous message, "TIME HAS NOT BEEN KIND TO YOU." In another, a mechanic peers under the hood of a car to determine the source of a particular problem and finds a woolly monster grinning back at him. In short, notes a *New York Times Book Review* critic, Koren's world "is a warm, fine-tuned place where academic civility and furry, lovable monstrosity continue to mix on terms of equality."

BIOGRAPHICAL/CRITICAL SOURCES: Newsweek, December 13, 1976; *New York Times Book Review,* September 4, 1977, December 14, 1980; *Chicago Tribune Book World,* December 7, 1980; *Time,* December 8, 1980.

*   *   *

KORINETS, Iurii Iosifovich
See KORINETZ, Yuri (Iosifovich)

*   *   *

KORINETZ, Yuri (Iosifovich) 1923-
(Iurii Iosifovich Korinets)

PERSONAL: Born January 14, 1923, in Moscow, Union of Soviet Socialist Republics; son of Josef (a diplomat) and Elly (Nagel) Korinetz; married Natalia Burlova (a translator), 1964; children: Ekaterina, Yuri. *Education:* Attended Art School, Samarkand, Soviet Central Asia, 1948-51, and A. M. Gorky Institute of Literature, Moscow, 1953-57. *Home:* 125319 Krasnoarmeyskaya 21 kw. 108, Moscow, Union of Soviet Socialist Republics. *Agent:* VAAP-Bolshaya Bronnaya G-A 103104, Moscow, Union of Soviet Socialist Republics.

CAREER: Writer. *Member:* Union of U.S.S.R. Writers, Union of the Soviet Societies of Friendship and Cultural Relations with Foreign Countries. *Awards, honors:* First prize in U.S.S.R. Children's Book Competition dedicated to Lenin's Centenary, 1968, for *Tam, Vdali, ze Rekoi; Dort weit hinter dem Fluss,* the German translation of *Tam, Vdali, ze Rekoi,* was runner-up for the German prize for best youth book, 1973, and the Italian edition was named one of the best youth books of 1973 in Italy; books selected among the best of the year for inclusion in UNESCO International Youth Library, 1972, 1973, and 1974.

WRITINGS: Cybota Subbota v Ponedelnik (title means "Saturday in Monday"; selected verses and poems), Detskaya Literatura (Moscow), 1966; *Tam, Vdali ze Rekoi* (youth novel), Detskaya Literatura, 1967, translation by Anthea Bell based on German edition and published as *There, Far Beyond the River,* J. Philip O'Hara, 1973; (translator into Russian) James Kruess, *Govoriashchaia mashina (Die Sprechmaschine),* Detskaya Literatura, 1969.

Chetyre Sestry (title means "Four Sisters"; selected verses and poems), Detskaya Literatura, 1970; *Privet ot Vernera* (title means "Greeting from Verner"; youth novel), Detskaya Literatura, 1972; *Volodiny Bratya* (title means "Volodya's Brothers"; youth novel), Detskaya Literatura, 1975; *The Smart Horse* (youth novel), Detskaya Literatura, 1976; *Meister Mischa und seine Freunde* (juvenile), Parabel Verlag (Munich), 1978; (translator) Otfried Preubler, *Three Tales,* Detskaya Literatura, 1979.

Das ganze Leben und ein Tag, Beltz und Gelberg (Weinheim), 1980; *Selected Novels and Verses,* two volumes, Detskaya Literatura, 1982; *Das Kochbuch vom Onkel Juri die besten Rezepte aus der uissischen Kuche,* Mosaik Verlag, 1982.

Also author of radio plays for children and contributor to Soviet children's magazines.

WORK IN PROGRESS: Over the Krals Mountains, a youth novel for Detskaya Literatura.

SIDELIGHTS: Yuri Korinetz's prize winning novel *There, Far Beyond the River* tells the story of Misha, a young Russian boy who "learns about the past, and about his place in the

present" from his Uncle Porfiri, writes a critic for the *Times Literary Supplement.* Uncle Porfiri, "whose abilities as hunter, fisherman, storyteller, and revolutionary are both infinitely fascinating and apparently endless," according to Mary M. Burns of *Horn Book Magazine,* imparts his ideals to his nephew during their fishing and camping trips in the Russian wilderness. The book is, C.E.J. Smith of *School Librarian* states, "a study of a remarkable man pursuing an ideal through several decades of Russian politics. It is the story of a boy's growth in knowledge and awareness of human values." "The book is beautifully written . . . ," Konstantin Bazarov of *Books and Bookmen* believes. "Beyond that it is also the story of a boy coming to terms with new experiences and acquiring a sense of values."

Although Misha narrates the novel, "Uncle Porfiri—indulgent, wise, and humorous—dominates the story and commands the reader's attention," Burns writes. "The boy narrator," the *Times Literary Supplement* critic believes, "has no grafted adult characteristics; he is all boy. . . . Porfiri and the other adult characters are all seen through the boy's eyes and so legitimately seem rather larger than life." Bazarov finds Uncle Porfiri "a magnificent and tremendously vital figure."

Korinetz's evocations of the natural beauty of the wilderness have been particularly praised. *There, Far Beyond the River* has "a vivid feel of place and time with its graphic descriptions of brooding northern landscapes of forests and rivers," Bazarov writes. The book is, Smith maintains, "a hymn of praise to the outdoor life, the beauty of wilderness, the joy of self-reliance, the warmth of friendship." "Misha's story," Burns concludes, "is a celebration of living and an exploration of life's meaning."

Yuri Korinetz wrote to *CA:* "At the age of fifteen I wrote my first story. From that time on my dream was to be a writer or a painter (I had visited Moscow art school at that time). My present interests besides writing are hi-fi stereophonic, fishing, traveling, and watercolor painting."

There, Far Beyond the River has been published in England and translated into ten languages, including Norwegian, Czech, Swedish, Italian, French, and Dutch. *Privet ot Vernera* and *Volodiny Bratya* have been published in German editions.

BIOGRAPHICAL/CRITICAL SOURCES: Times Literary Supplement, September 28, 1973; *Books and Bookmen,* October, 1973; *Listener,* November, 1973; *School Librarian,* December, 1973; *Horn Book Magazine,* April, 1974; *Growing Point,* September, 1977, July, 1978; *Times Educational Supplement,* December 30, 1977, May 19, 1978; *Children's Literature Review,* Volume IV, Gale, 1982.

*   *   *

KOVACH, Bill 1932-

PERSONAL: Born September 16, 1932, in Tenn.; son of John and Olga (Sicos) Kovach; married Lynne Marie Stamm, January 15, 1956; children: Theresa, David, Charles, John. *Education:* Attended University of Miami, 1957-58; East Tennessee State University, B.S., 1959. *Religion:* Episcopalian. *Home:* 5504 Park St., Chevy Chase, Md. 20815. *Office:* 1000 Connecticut Ave., Washington, D.C. 20036.

CAREER: Johnson City Press-Chronicle, Johnson City, Tenn., reporter, 1959-61; *Nashville Tennessean,* Nashville, reporter, 1961-68; *New York Times,* New York, N.Y., reporter, 1968-69, Albany bureau chief, 1969-71, Boston bureau chief, 1971-

73, Washington news editor, 1973-76, deputy national editor, 1976-79, Washington bureau chief, 1979—. Notable assignments include coverage of the civil rights movement in the South, the antiwar movement, occupation of Wounded Knee, presidential campaigns of 1964, 1968, and 1972, and President Ford's trip to China, 1975. Eugene Pulliam Lecturer, Ball State University, 1982. *Military service:* U.S. Navy, 1951-52. *Member:* National Press Foundation (member of board of directors, 1983—). *Awards, honors:* New York State Bar award, Stanford professional journalism fellow, and National Science Foundation fellow.

WRITINGS: The Battle of Nashville, Nashville Press, 1965; (contributor) *Assignment America,* Quadrangle Books, 1974. Contributor to *New Republic, Reporter,* and *Field and Stream.*

AVOCATIONAL INTERESTS: Woodworking, travel, photography, painting in water colors.

* * *

KRAF, Elaine 1946-

PERSONAL: Born February 21, 1946, in New York; daughter of Harry (a judge) and Lena (a teacher; maiden name, Rosenfeld) Kraf; married, 1979. *Education:* Hunter College of the City University of New York, A.B., 1965; Queens College of the City University of New York, M.A. (special education), 1978; also attended Pennsylvania Academy of Fine Arts. *Religion:* Jewish. *Residence:* Maspeth, N.Y.

CAREER: Writer. Preschool and kindergarten teacher in New York City, 1965-67, substitute teacher of retarded and handicapped children, 1968; Research and Rehabilitation Center for Retarded Adults, New York City, teacher, 1970; Brooklyn Developmental Center, Brooklyn, N.Y., teacher of profoundly retarded, 1978-79; United Cerebral Palsy, Queens, N.Y., teacher of profoundly retarded, 1979-82. One-woman exhibitions of her box-collages held at Ward-Nasse Gallery, Soho, 1976 and 1978. Has taught art classes. *Member:* International P.E.N. *Awards, honors:* National Endowment for the Arts award, 1970, for story "Westward and Up a Mountain"; Yaddo Colony fellowships, 1971, 1973, 1976; Breadloaf Conference fellowship, 1971; MacDowell Colony fellowship, 1972; National Endowment for the Arts grant, 1982-83.

WRITINGS—Novels: *I Am Clarence,* Doubleday, 1969; *The House of Madelaine,* Doubleday, 1971; *Find Him!,* Fiction Collective, 1977; *The Princess of 72nd Street,* New Directions, 1979.

Work has been anthologized in *The American Literary Anthology,* edited by George Plimpton and Peter Ardery, Viking, 1970; *The Stonewall Book of Short Fictions,* edited by Kent Dixon and Robert Coover, Stone Wall Press, 1973; *Bitches and Sad Ladies,* edited by Pat Rotter, Harper, 1975; *New Directions 31,* edited by James Laughlin, New Directions, 1975; *Statements 2,* edited by J. Baumbach and Peter Spielberg, Fiction Collective, 1977. Contributor to *Quarterly Review* and *Fiction* magazine.

WORK IN PROGRESS: A novel, *The Final Delusions of Cinderella Korn.*

SIDELIGHTS: Elaine Kraf's interest in the arts, especially in poetry, is apparent in her novels. Shane Steven, for example, notes the poetic influence in Kraf's narrative style. In the *New York Times Book Review* he comments: "The rhythm of words, the precision of phrase, the art of metaphor, the joy of correspondence: it's all here. . . . When a novelist tells a good

story well, it becomes a good novel. When a novelist uses words as if they were a sacred love, what he writes becomes poetry. Elaine Kraf is a poet."

Martin Altman writes similarly of a "poetic reality" in Kraf's *I Am Clarence.* Altman states in *Dictionary of Literary Biography Yearbook,* "All of [Kraf's] writing is lyrical, rhythmic, and concerned with color." In two of her books, Kraf's characters themselves are poets, and she includes two of their poems in the text of these novels.

Commenting on her own writing, the novelist told *CA:* "I am interested in many arts—study dance, have exhibited my art. My writing reflects interest in color, music, new form. For me to regard a novel as a work of art, its language must be poetic or original. My writing is influenced by musical composition, choreography, and painting—not by reading."

BIOGRAPHICAL/CRITICAL SOURCES: New York Times Book Review, November 2, 1969; *Publishers Weekly,* August 20, 1979; *Library Journal,* October 1, 1979; *Dictionary of Literary Biography Yearbook: 1981,* Gale, 1982.

* * *

KRAHN, Fernando 1935-

PERSONAL: Born January 4, 1935, in Santiago, Chile; son of Otto (a lawyer) and Laura (a singer; maiden name, Parada) Krahn; married Maria de la Luz Uribe (a writer), February, 1966; children: Fernanda, Santiago, Matias. *Education:* Attended Catholic University, Santiago, 1952-55, and University of Chile, 1954-62. *Home:* San Guadencio 23, Sitges, Spain. *Agent:* Harriet Wasserman Literary Agency, 230 East 48th St., New York, N.Y. 10017.

CAREER: Writer and illustrator of children's books and cartoonist for magazines, 1962—; currently cartoonist for *Internacional Herald Tribune,* Paris, France, *Die Zeit,* Hamburg, West Germany, and *Tages Anzeiger,* Zurich, Switzerland. *Awards, honors:* Guggenheim fellowship for film animation experiments, 1972-73; "Apeles Mestres" award for children's books (Spain), 1982.

WRITINGS—Juveniles, except as indicated; self-illustrated: *The Self-Made Snowman,* Lippincott, 1975; *Little Love Story,* Lippincott, 1976; *The Family Minus,* Parent's Magazine Press, 1977; *A Funny Friend from Heaven,* Lippincott, 1977; *The Biggest Christmas Tree on Earth,* Atlantic-Little, Brown, 1978; *The Great Ape: Being the True Version of the Famous Saga of Adventure and Friendship Newly Discovered,* Viking, 1978; *The Family Minus's Summer House,* Parent's Magazine Press, 1980; *Here Comes Alex Pumpernickel!,* Atlantic-Little, Brown, 1981; *Sleep Tight Alex Pumpernickel!,* Atlantic-Little, Brown, 1982; *The Creepy Thing,* Clarion, 1982; *The Secret in the Dungeon,* Clarion, 1983; *Mr. Top,* Morrow, 1983.

Published by Delacorte: *Journeys of Sebastian,* 1968; *Hildegarde and Maximilian,* 1970; *How Santa Claus Had a Long and Difficult Journey Delivering His Presents,* 1971; *What Is a Man?,* 1972; *Sebastian and the Mushroom,* 1976.

Published by Dutton: *The Possible Worlds of Fernando Krahn* (collection of cartoons), 1965; *Gustavus and Stop,* 1968; *The Flying Saucer Full of Spaghetti,* 1970; *April Fools,* 1974; *Who's Seen the Scissors?,* 1975; *The Mystery of the Giant Footprints,* 1977; *Catch That Cat!,* 1978; *Robot-Bot-Bot,* 1979; *Arthur's Adventure in the Abandoned House,* 1981.

Illustrator and co-author: (With Carol Newman) *Strella's Children,* Atheneum, 1967; (with Alastair Reid) *Uncle Timothy's*

Traviata, Delacorte, 1967; (with wife, Maria Krahn) *The First Peko-Neko Bird,* Simon & Schuster, 1969; (with M. Krahn) *The Life of Numbers,* Simon & Schuster, 1971.

Illustrator: Jan Wahl, *The Furious Flycycle,* Delacorte, 1968; Fred Gardner, *The Lioness Who Made Deals,* Norton, 1969; Wahl, *Abe Lincoln's Beard,* Delacorte, 1971; Wahl, *Lorenzo Bear and Company,* Putnam, 1971; Wahl, *S.O.S. Bobomobile!; or, The Further Adventures of Melvin Spitznagle and Professor Mickimecki,* Delacorte, 1973; Wahl, *Mooga, Mega, Mekki,* J. Philip O'Hara, 1974; Miriam Chaikin, *Hardlucky,* Lippincott, 1975; Walt Whitman, *I Hear America Singing,* Delacorte, 1975; Yuri Suhl, *Simon Boom Gets a Letter,* Four Winds, 1976; *They've Discovered a Head in the Box of the Bread* (collection of limericks), Crowell, 1978; William Jay Smith, *Laughing Time,* Delacorte, 1980; Jill Tomlinson, *Hilda the Hen Who Wouldn't Give Up,* Harcourt, 1980; Sonia Levitin, *Nobody Stole the Pie,* Harcourt, 1980.

Contributor to magazines and newspapers in the United States, France, Germany, and England, including *Esquire, Horizon, New Yorker, Reporter, Show, Evergreen, Atlantic, Gourmet, Sky, National Lampoon,* and *Playboy.*

SIDELIGHTS: Fernando Krahn's books for children have been translated into German, Norwegian, Swedish, and Danish.

BIOGRAPHICAL/CRITICAL SOURCES: Children's Literature Review, Volume III, Gale, 1978.

*　　*　　*

KRAMMER, Arnold Paul 1941-

PERSONAL: Born August 15, 1941, in Chicago, Ill.; son of David and Eva (Vas) Krammer; married Rhoda Miriam Nudelman, June 19, 1968 (divorced, 1980); children: Adam. *Education:* University of Wisconsin—Madison, B.S., 1963, M.S., 1965, Ph.D., 1970; University of Vienna, diploma, 1964. *Religion:* Jewish. *Home:* 1613 Moss Glenn Cir., College Station, Tex. 77840. *Office:* Department of History, Texas A & M University, College Station, Tex. 77843.

CAREER: Rockford College, Rockford, Ill., assistant professor of history, 1970-74; Texas A & M University, College Station, associate professor, 1974-79, professor of history, 1979—, principal investigator on German Documents Retrieval Project, Center for Energy and Mineral Resources, 1975—. Visiting professor at Rice University, 1980, 1982. Has presented numerous radio and television lectures throughout the United States; testified before Congress, 1977. Consultant to Nebraska Educational Television Network, 1978, and Greenwich Film Co. *Member:* Society for Historians of American Foreign Relations, American Historical Association, American Committee of Historians of the Second World War, National Institute on the Holocaust, Phi Alpha Theta.

AWARDS, HONORS: American Council of Learned Societies grant, 1972, 1975, 1980; American Philosophical Society grant, 1973, 1976, 1979; National Endowment for the Humanities research grant, 1975; *The Forgotten Friendship: Israel and the Soviet Bloc, 1947-1953* was named "book of the year" by Jewish Book Council of the Jewish Welfare Board in 1975; Congressional Award, Missouri House of Representatives, 1980, for research on German synthetic fuel; National Science Foundation research grant, 1982.

WRITINGS: (Contributor) Walid Khalidi, editor, *From Haven to Conquest,* Institute for Palestine Studies, 1971; *The Forgotten Friendship: Israel and the Soviet Bloc, 1947-1953,* Uni-

versity of Illinois Press, 1974; *Nazi Prisoners of War in America,* Stein & Day, 1979; *PW-Gefangen in Amerika: Die umfassende Darstellung uber die US-Kriegsgefangenschaft von 400000 deutschen Soldaten,* Motobuch-Verlag (Stuttgart), 1981; (contributor) L. J. Perelman and others, editors, *Energy Transitions: Long-Term Perspectives,* American Association for the Advancement of Science, 1981; (contributor) Ronald H. Bailey, editor, *Prisoners of War,* Time-Life, 1981; (contributor) Samuel R. Williamson, Jr. and Peter Pastor, editors, *War and Society in East Central Europe,* Volume V, Columbia University Press, 1981.

Contributor to *Proceedings of the American Society for Engineering Education,* 1982; contributor of articles and reviews to more than forty history and technical journals. Editorial consultant to *Southwestern Historical Quarterly* and *German Studies Review.*

WORK IN PROGRESS: Prisoner of War Art in the U.S.; Splendid Isolation: Axis Diplomats at the Greenbriar; The History of the Palestine Police, 1920-1948.

SIDELIGHTS: Arnold Paul Krammer told *CA:* "I was born and raised in a Hungarian household where European history and its languages and customs were as vivid as Chicago's North Side beyond the window. Surviving the rigors of Chicago's public school systems, I pursued the study of history first as a student, and now as a teacher, and [I] try to present history with a storyteller's verve and a scholar's care.

"My research has taken me through Europe and the Soviet Union, as well as the Middle East; from the Arab-Israeli War of 1967, to the Russian invasion of Czechoslovakia in August of 1968. It was my love of adventure and my resentment toward midwestern winters, however, which ultimately brought me to Texas."

As the principal investigator on the German Documents Retrieval Project at the Center for Energy and Mineral Resources at Texas A & M University, Krammer is in the process of analyzing nearly 173 tons of captured World War II German industrial records on synthetic fuel for possible use by the American energy industry.

BIOGRAPHICAL/CRITICAL SOURCES: Time, April 18, 1977; *Newsweek,* July 4, 1977; *Christian Science Monitor,* July 26, 1977.

*　　*　　*

KRANTZ, Judith 1927-

PERSONAL: Born January 9, 1927, in New York, N.Y.; daughter of Jack D. (an advertising executive) and Mary (an attorney; maiden name, Braeger) Tarcher; married Stephen Krantz (an independent film producer and author); children: Nicholas, Anthony. *Education:* Wellesley College, B.A., 1948. *Residence:* Beverly Hills, Calif. *Agent:* Morton Janklow, 598 Madison Ave., New York, N.Y. 10022. *Mailing address:* c/o Stephen Krantz Productions, Inc., 9601 Wilshire Blvd., Suite 343, Beverly Hills, Calif. 90210.

CAREER: Novelist. Fashion publicist in Paris, France, 1948-49; *Good Housekeeping,* New York City, fashion editor, 1949-56; contributing writer, *McCall's,* 1956-59, and *Ladies Home Journal,* 1959-71; contributing West Coast editor, *Cosmopolitan,* 1971-79.

WRITINGS—Novels; published by Crown: Scruples, 1978; *Princess Daisy,* 1980; *Mistral's Daughter* (Doubleday Book Club selection; Literary Guild dual selection), 1982.

SIDELIGHTS: "I'm living proof that you can never do anything until you try," Judith Krantz has maintained on numerous occasions since the publication of her first novel, *Scruples.* Before she achieved such phenomenal success as an author, Krantz worked as a fashion editor for *Good Housekeeping,* then became a free-lance journalist after the birth of her eldest son. It wasn't until a number of years later, at the age of fifty-one, that she published *Scruples,* her first work of fiction since her college days. Cynthia Gorney notes in an interview with Krantz published in the *Washington Post:* "There had been one short-story writing class, in her sophomore year at Wellesley, but the professor gave her a B, so she dumped fiction writing." According to Gorney, Krantz "understood herself to be a journalist" during her years as a freelancer. "Journalists have notebooks," Krantz explains. "Journalists have tape recorders. I thought if I tried to do something from my imagination, there wasn't anything there. I didn't realize I had an imagination until I wrote *Scruples.*"

Krantz was encouraged to try writing fiction by her husband, independent film producer and author Stephen Krantz, who for years remarked that his wife had such an exceptional talent for description and a real eye for detail that she had to be a natural-born novelist. Krantz agrees with his assessment, stating in the *Washington Post:* "I'm a stickler for detail. I don't know if anybody doing the so-called commercial fiction researches as thoroughly as I do. . . . I try to create characters who are a little bit larger than life."

After her youngest son graduated from high school, Krantz began working on a novel, writing six and a half hours a day, five days a week. After nine months *Scruples* was completed. "I truly enjoy writing," the author revealed to Jill Gerston of the *Philadelphia Inquirer.* "If I didn't, I could never close myself in my room for . . . almost a year." Krantz then asked family friend and lawyer Morton L. Janklow to read the manuscript. Janklow says he knew immediately that *Scruples* was destined to be a bestseller, and he agreed to serve as Krantz's literary agent. Although *Scruples* was at first rejected by an editor at Simon & Schuster, Crown Publishers eventually purchased the hardcover rights and released it in March of 1978. Four months later the novel became the number one bestseller, according to the *New York Times,* and remained on its bestseller list for almost one year.

Because *Scruples* sold more than 220,000 copies in hardcover and more than three million in paperback, there was much interest in Krantz's second novel, *Princess Daisy.* In September, 1979, six months before the hardcover edition was scheduled to appear in bookstores, Bantam Books purchased the paperback rights to *Princess Daisy* for an advance of $3,208,875, which was then the highest price ever paid for the reprint rights to a work of fiction. The sale ended what the *New York Times* describes as "a fourteen and a half hour auction that involved eight of the nine leading paperback [publishing] houses."

The purchase of reprint rights to *Princess Daisy* for such a huge sum of money triggered discussions concerning the high fees paid to successful authors for their work. According to Tony Chiu in the *New York Times,* "the sale [of *Princess Daisy*] renewed criticism among some publishing executives of the growing practice of investing in 'blockbuster' properties to the possible detriment of less commercial authors." Chiu goes on to state that one publishing executive "estimated the sum Bantam paid for the Krantz book could have obtained the reprint rights to sixty books not in the blockbuster category."

Replying to these objections, Marc Jaffe, then president and publisher of Bantam Books, stated according to *Publishers Weekly* that this point of view is "an accountant's, not an editor's way of looking at publishing. . . . Bantam is in the business of publishing all across the spectrum of reader interest—books for young readers, reference works, translations, general nonfiction, novels of all kinds. We are also in the blockbuster business. We hope to continue to acquire blockbusters we're excited about at whatever the cost. We will also continue to acquire all the other kinds of books we publish."

Furthermore, Jaffe explains to Tom Zito of the *Washington Post, Princess Daisy* is the type of book that can really help publishing instead of injuring it: "This is a book that will pull people into the bookstores. . . . There's nothing like a big best seller to pull the industry along." And Krantz's former editor at Crown, Larry Freundlich, states in the *New York Times* that "it's intellectual purblindness to think that if you give one author three million, you're taking it from someone else. That amount of money should not be considered anything other than investment capital—no publisher will pay it unless he is more than reasonably certain that it can be earned back. Judy Krantz writes subtly about love, and pointedly about merchandising. She's a remarkably good novelist speaking to the center of America's venal interest."

Krantz's ability to "pull people into the bookstores" amazes people in the publishing industry and disturbs many of her outspoken critics. Her "ability to tap a readership" (in the words of a *New York Times* writer) has led many to compare her to the late Jacqueline Susann, author of such books as *Valley of the Dolls, Once Is Not Enough,* and *The Love Machine.* Grace Glueck writes in the *New York Times Book Review* that "philosophically, Mrs. Krantz is an absolutist of the Susann persuasion. A painting is a masterpiece, or nothing; a woman is a beauty, or nobody; sex has to be the sun and the moon and the stars."

Krantz's interest in and talent for promoting her books has also been compared to Susann's. "She's very wise in the ways of publicity, just as Jacqueline Susann was," observes Kay Sexton, a vice-president of B. Dalton Bookseller, in *New York Times Magazine.* And in the same article, Howard Kaminsky, editor-in-chief of Warner Books (the paperback publisher of *Scruples*), remarks, "Both as promoters and novelists, Jackie and Judy are in the same tradition."

In order to publicize her first novel, Krantz spearheaded an extensive, $50,000 promotional campaign that included touring the country from coast-to-coast autographing copies of her novel at bookstores and appearing on television and radio talk shows. "It turned out that I was a natural on television," Krantz says in an interview with Claudia Dreyfus for *Newsday*'s *LI* magazine. "I discovered that I had a quality that communicates itself on camera. Eventually, there came a time with *Scruples* when, instead of [our] running after publicity, it came to us." Krantz has given the promotion of *Princess Daisy* and *Mistral's Daughter* the same dedication.

All three of Krantz's novels have been classified as "riches-to-near-rags-to-riches Cinderella stories" or fairy tales spun around beautiful people from wealthy backgrounds living exciting lives. Or, as Natalie Gittelson states in the *New York Times Magazine,* Krantz's books are "marked by mass-appeal preoccupation with sex, fame, and power." Another characteristic her books have in common is that all of her heroines are strong, independent, and powerful survivors. The daughter of an advertising executive father and lawyer mother, Krantz told Stella Dong of *Publishers Weekly* that in her family ''it was understood that when a girl grows up she gets a job. . . . I could never write about a woman who didn't work. I couldn't feel emotionally involved.''

Scruples, for instance, is the story of Billy Ikehorn Orsini, a member of an aristocratic but impoverished Boston family. The reader is introduced to a neglected and overweight Billy who is transformed into a beautiful, slim young woman after a year's stay in Paris. Returning to America, she finds a job and marries a multimillionaire. They live happily until Billy's husband suffers a stroke. After her husband's death, Billy opens and manages a successful and glamorous boutique she names Scruples. Billy finds ultimate personal happiness when she meets and marries Vito Orsini, a movie producer. Calling *Scruples* a ''raunchy, behind-the-scenes look at the world of fashion, retailing, and movie production,'' Barbara Nelson writes in *Library Journal* that ''Krantz has a real talent for juggling her fascinating subplots and bringing them to a happy ending.'' Nora Johnson notes in the *New York Times Book Review* that ''power is what this book is all about, and the fascination with power is why it is . . . hard to put down. Like porn, power hypnotizes by its apparent ability to exist apart from emotionality; that its price is the ability to feel doesn't become apparent until later, when those who have it wonder why there is still something wrong.''

Robert Friedman maintains in the *New York Post* that *Scruples* contains more information about the world of fashion and gives the reader a much closer view of Hollywood ''than you'd find in a dozen manuals.'' The world of fashion is an area that Krantz knows well. As she told *Los Angeles Times* reporter Pat Nation: ''I didn't really have to research it. Fashion is one of the things I have always been interested in. A lot of my friends are retailers. I like to talk to sales people in the stores. I had been living and shopping in Beverly Hills for six years with the eye of a New Yorker.''

In an interview with Herbert Mitgang for the *New York Times Book Review,* Krantz gives her own view of *Scruples:* ''My novel gives women a big bubble bath. It's a chocolate eclair. It's the kind of novel people love. I loved it myself. I love writing fiction. I write about 10,000 words a week. I discovered, to my surprise, that I'm very competitive. My book is great fantasy. But I haven't got a single multiple-orgasm sex scene in it.''

Princess Daisy, Krantz's second novel, chronicles the adventures of Marguerite Alexandrovna (Daisy) Valensky, the daughter of a White Russian prince and an American actress. At an early age Daisy begins guarding a family secret—a retarded sister who is hidden from the public. At fifteen she is taken advantage of by her half-brother and loses her fortune. After pulling herself together, Daisy rises through the ranks to achieve a successful and powerful career position in television advertising. Her life is complete when she finds the man of her dreams.

The reviewers seem to regard *Princess Daisy* in the same manner as they did *Scruples*—as light-weight entertainment. In her review of *Princess Daisy* published in *Washington Post Book World,* Barbara Mertz states: ''This is, of course, a genre novel, in the same sense that gothics, westerns and mysteries are genre novels. The literary style is on a par with that of a fairly well written detective story, the plot makes a gothic novelist's fantasies pale into stark realism.'' M. A. Pradt writes in *Library Journal:* ''Preordained to be a major best seller, *Princess Daisy* is also a rewarding read with a memorable heroine. . . . Tolstoy Krantz isn't, yet this tale has vivid settings, credible char-

acters, and careful plotting.'' ''Judith Krantz knows exactly what she's doing and does it well,'' declares Jean Strouse in *Newsweek.* ''This novel is verbal popcorn—light, addictive, not exactly nourishing but not really bad for you either. . . . There's something refreshing in pure sell. Pass the popcorn.'' And Charlotte Curtis remarks in the *New York Times Book Review:* ''It is fantasy, not reality, that Mrs. Krantz is after, and she's good at it. . . . Krantz writes in a florid, effusive and exclamatory style, punctuated by scenic catalogues. She knows the rules by which the rich, beautiful and powerful play, and she articulates them effectively.'' John Leonard also attributes *Princess Daisy*'s success to Krantz's thorough acquaintance with the allure of clothes, food, and sex. ''We want what we can't have or be,'' he notes. ''*Princess Daisy* is ridiculous, but I enjoyed it. It has a sort of despotic allure.''

Comparing her second novel to her first, Krantz tells Stella Dong of *Publishers Weekly:* ''I expect *Princess Daisy* to attract a much wider audience than did *Scruples.* Daisy is a more well-rounded and lovable character than Billy Ikehorn. She's steadfast, loyal, hardworking—and not a rich woman.'' Another difference between the two novels is that while some reviewers criticize *Scruples* for its sexual explicitness (which some critics feel borders on soft-core pornography), few critics find *Princess Daisy* objectionable. ''*Princess Daisy* is much less sexually explicit,'' Krantz explains in the *Los Angeles Times.* ''It's more erotic in a strange way but sex is much less important. You know, when I was writing *Scruples* I had no agent, no publisher. I was sitting there writing away, not dreaming that lots of people would be reading the sexual fantasies that I was putting down on paper. I think if I had known, I might have censored myself a little bit, but knowing this time that they would be reading, I certainly made sure that it would not offend anyone. On the other hand, it will not disappoint anyone, from the erotic point of view.''

Krantz's third novel, *Mistral's Daughter,* is the story of three beautiful women (Maggy Lunel, her daughter Teddy, and her granddaughter Fauve) and their relationship with a French artist named Julien Mistral. Describing *Mistral's Daughter* in *Library Journal,* Michele Leber writes: ''Another Krantz confection—romance, high fashion, and heroines as gorgeous as they are talented—all suffused with the atmosphere of southern France, with touches of the Paris art scene. . . . It's an appealing fantasy world—sex is always euphemistically romantic, tragedy (untimely death, deception) never overwhelming. A first-rate divertissement.'' Anatole Broyard notes in the *New York Times:* ''I began reading *Mistral's Daughter* as you read a story that is not necessarily a work of art, but which offers a certain pleasure. . . . And on that level Judith Krantz's third novel works pretty well.'' And Merle Rubin remarks in the *Los Angeles Times* that ''whatever its faults, *Mistral's Daughter* is less exploitative than many other mass-market novels. Romance, sex and glamour are used to entice the reader, but there is no gratuitous violence. There is little if any gratuitous sex and the content is believable.''

After the publication of *Mistral's Daughter,* Krantz told Penny Perrick of the London *Times* that she realizes her novels are not Pulitzer Prize material. ''If [they] were, I'd think something terrible had happened. I know perfectly well that I'm not a literary writer, I just write the way it comes naturally. For lack of another word it is storytelling.'' On this same theme Krantz explains to Pat Nation of the *Los Angeles Times:* ''I'm a storyteller. . . . If I can't be a Doris Lessing or Iris Murdoch, it doesn't depress me. What I do is entertainment and I do it as well as I can.''

Larry Freundlich, Krantz's former editor, remarks in the *New York Times Magazine*: "Judy's writing has the same attraction as *People* magazine. You learn about the lives of men and women. She answers all the burning questions you never dared ask. . . . It would make Judy's work grotesque to burden it with attempts at profundity and truth. She doesn't vulgarize her story by trying to make subtle points that don't exist." Krantz explains further in the *Chicago Tribune*: "If you deal in the world of glamour, and that's my turf . . . then you're not taken seriously as a writer, and everyone focuses on how much money you make. But I want to make something very plain—I'm not complaining. Because I chose my turf, and you can't complain when you get a little flack and you knew to expect it. It may hurt a little . . . but you can't complain. You can't have it both ways."

As Helen Gurley Brown, a long-time friend of Krantz's and editor of *Cosmopolitan* magazine, observes in the *New York Times Magazine*: "So many people act as if it's easy to write like Judy; as if they could do it, too, if only they would denigrate themselves. They're insane with jealousy! The most difficult thing in the world is to make things simple enough, and enticing enough, to cause readers to turn the page."

MEDIA ADAPTATIONS: Scruples was produced as a three-part, six-hour television miniseries on CBS-TV in February, 1980; *Princess Daisy* was produced as a two-part, four-hour television miniseries on NBC-TV in November, 1983; the film rights to *Mistral's Daughter* have been sold to CBS-TV.

BIOGRAPHICAL/CRITICAL SOURCES: Publishers Weekly, January 16, 1978, September 24, 1979, January 11, 1980, July 17, 1981, October 15, 1982; *Library Journal,* March 1, 1978, February 15, 1980, November 15, 1982; *New York Post,* March 3, 1978; *Washington Post,* March 3, 1978, September 14, 1979, February 26, 1980; *New York Times Book Review,* March 19, 1978, March 2, 1980, January 2, 1983; *Los Angeles Times,* May 19, 1978, September 25, 1979, November 26, 1982; *People,* June 26, 1978, October 1, 1979, October 18, 1982, December 13, 1982; *New York Times,* September 14, 1979, January 30, 1980, March 2, 1980, December 8, 1982; *Detroit News,* September 30, 1979, February 10, 1980, November 6, 1983.

Washington Post Book World, January 27, 1980; *Newsweek,* February 18, 1980; *Time,* February 18, 1980; *Village Voice,* February 18, 1980; *Chicago Sun Times,* February 25, 1980; *New York Times Magazine,* March 2, 1980; *Chicago Tribune,* March 9, 1980; *Booklist,* April 1, 1980; *Philadelphia Inquirer,* May 19, 1980; *LI,* July 6, 1980; *New Yorker,* October 13, 1980; London *Times,* May 13, 1983; *Detroit Free Press,* November 6, 1983.†

—*Sketch by Margaret Mazurkiewicz*

* * *

KRANZBERG, Melvin 1917-

PERSONAL: Born November 22, 1917, in St. Louis, Mo.; son of Samuel (a businessman) and Rose (Fitter) Kranzberg; married Nancy Lee Fox, 1943 (divorced, 1955); married Eva Mannering, 1956; married Adelaide H. Waltz, 1962; married Dolores Campen, 1972 (died, 1981); children: (first marriage) Steven J., John F. *Education:* Amherst College, A.B., 1938; Harvard University, M.A., 1939, Ph.D., 1942; graduate study at several other universities, including University of Paris, 1945. *Home:* 4850 Kendall Ct. N.E., Atlanta, Ga. 30342.

Office: Department of Social Sciences, Georgia Institute of Technology, Atlanta, Ga. 30332.

CAREER: U.S. Office of Price Administration, Washington, D.C., administrative assistant, 1942; Harvard University, Cambridge, Mass., instructor in history, 1946; Stevens Institute of Technology, Hoboken, N.J., instructor in history, 1946-47; Amherst College, Amherst, Mass., assistant professor of history, 1947-52; Case Institute of Technology (now Case Western Reserve University), Cleveland, Ohio, associate professor, 1952-59, professor of history, 1959-72; Georgia Institute of Technology, Atlanta, Callaway Professor of the History of Technology, 1972—. Sigma Xi national lecturer, 1966-67, bicentennial lecturer, 1974-75; Harris Lecturer, Northwestern University, 1970; Mellon Lecturer, Lehigh University, 1975; U.S. Information Agency lecturer in India, 1975, Southeast Asia, 1976, Africa, 1980, and West Germany, 1982; Zarem Lecturer, Harvey Mudd College, 1976; Bicentennial lecturer, Oak Ridge National Laboratory, 1976; Centennial lecturer, Texas A & M University, 1976; Taft Lecturer, University of Cincinnati, 1980; Phi Beta Kappa Associates lecturer, 1982—.

Member of Columbia University Seminar on Technology and Social Change, 1963-75, and of visitors committee, Vanderbilt University School of Engineering, 1970-80; National Aeronautics and Space Administration, member of historical advisory committee, 1964-78, chairman, 1966-68; vice-president of International Commission on the History of Technology, 1968—; National Science Foundation, chairman of advisory panel for Division of Policy Research and Analysis, and Division of Science Resources Studies, 1971-73; co-chairman of Brooklyn Bridge Centennial Symposium, 1983. *Military service:* U.S. Army, Military Intelligence, 1943-46; became master sergeant; received Bronze Star Medal, Combat Infantry Badge, and three battle stars.

MEMBER: International Union of the History and Philosophy of Science (chairman of U.S. international commission, 1971-73), Society for the History of Technology (secretary, 1959-74; vice-president, 1981-82; president, 1983-84), American Association for the Advancement of Science (vice-president, 1966; chairman of Section L, 1966, 1979; chairman of committee on Science, Engineering, and Public Policy, 1978-81), American Historical Association (chairman of Congressional fellowships committee), American Society for Engineering Education (chairman of humanistic-social division, 1957), Society for French Historical Studies (vice-president, 1959), Sigma Xi (member of national board of directors, 1970-77; national president, 1979-80).

AWARDS, HONORS: L.H.D., Denison University, 1967, and Amherst College, 1983; Leonardo da Vinci Medal, Society for the History of Technology, 1967; Litt.D., Newark College of Engineering (now New Jersey Institute of Technology), 1968, and Northern Michigan University, 1972; Apollo Achievement Award, National Aeronautics and Space Administration, 1970; special recognition award, American Industrial Arts Association, 1978; Roe Medal, American Society of Mechanical Engineers, 1980; Jabotinsky Centennial Medal, State of Israel, 1980; Energy Education Award, Academy for Educational Development, 1980, for *Energy and the Way We Live;* D.Eng., Worcester Polytechnic Institute, 1981.

WRITINGS: The Siege of Paris, 1870-71, Cornell University Press, 1951, reprinted, Greenwood Press, 1970; (editor) *1848: A Turning Point?,* Heath, 1959; (editor with Carroll W. Pursell, Jr.) *Technology in Western Civilization,* two volumes, Oxford University Press, 1967; (editor with William H. Davenport)

Technology and Culture: An Anthology, Schocken, 1972; (with Joseph Geis) *By the Sweat of Thy Brow: Work in the Western World* (Fortune Book Club alternate selection), Putnam, 1975; (with Patrick Kelly) *Technological Innovation: A Critical Review of Current Knowledge,* San Francisco Press, 1978; (with Timothy A. Hall) *Energy and the Way We Live,* Boyd & Fraser, 1980; (editor) *Ethics in an Age of Pervasive Technology,* Westview, 1980. Contributor to encyclopedias and professional journals. Editor, *Technology and Culture,* 1958-81.

WORK IN PROGRESS: Research on innovations and on technology-society relations.

SIDELIGHTS: Volume I of *Technology in Western Civilization* has been translated into Spanish, Volume II into Japanese. *Technology and Culture* has been translated into Arabic and Spanish, and *By the Sweat of Thy Brow* into Italian.

BIOGRAPHICAL/CRITICAL SOURCES: Culture Technique, Number 10, 1983.

* * *

KRASILOVSKY, Phyllis   1926-

PERSONAL: Born August 28, 1926, in Brooklyn, N.Y.; daughter of Richard and Florence Manning; married William Krasilovsky (an attorney and author), September 14, 1947; children: Alexis, Jessica, Margaret, Peter. *Education:* Attended Brooklyn College (now Brooklyn College of the City University of New York), 1944-47, and Cornell University, 1949-50. *Home:* 1177 Hardscrabble Rd., Chappaqua, N.Y. 10514.

CAREER: Writer of children's books. Marymount College, Tarrytown, N.Y., teacher of children's literature, 1969-70; teacher of creative writing, Katonah Library, 1970-72.

WRITINGS—Juveniles; published by Doubleday: The Man Who Didn't Wash Dishes, 1953; *The Very Little Girl,* 1955; *The Cow Who Fell in the Canal,* 1957; *The Very Little Boy,* 1964; *The Girl Who Was a Cowboy,* 1965; *The Very Tall Little Girl,* 1969; *The Man Who Tried to Save Time,* 1979; *The Man Who Entered a Contest,* 1980; *The First Tulips in Holland,* 1982.

Other juvenile books: *Scaredy Cat,* Macmillan, 1960; *Benny's Flag,* World Publishing, 1960; *Susan Sometimes,* Macmillan, 1962; *The Shy Little Girl,* Houghton, 1971; *Popular Girls Club,* Simon & Schuster, 1973; *L. C. Is the Greatest,* Thomas Nelson, 1975.

Contributor of travel articles to numerous periodicals including *Travel, Saturday Evening Post, Cosmopolitan, Washington Post, Boston Globe, San Diego Union, New York Times,* and various women's magazines. Travel editor, *Westchester* and *Long Island* (magazines), 1975—.

WORK IN PROGRESS: Several picture-books; an adult novel.

BIOGRAPHICAL/CRITICAL SOURCES: New York Times Book Review, March 8, 1981, April 25, 1982.

* * *

KRASSNER, Paul   1932-
(Rumpleforeskin)

PERSONAL: Born April 9, 1932; son of Michael E. (a printer) and Ida (Garlock) Krassner; married Jeanne Johnson, June 30, 1963 (divorced, June 30, 1966); children: Holly. *Education:* Attended City College of New York (now City College of the City University of New York), four years. *Politics:* "Inde-

pendent Dupe." *Religion:* "Zen Bastard." *Address:* Box 14667, San Francisco, Calif. 94114.

CAREER: Former writer for *Mad* magazine and "The Steve Allen Show"; *The Independent* (newspaper), New York City, managing editor, 1954-58; *The Realist* (magazine), New York City, founder and editor, 1958-74; editor, *Hustler* (magazine), 1978; head writer of Home Box Office television special on the presidential election, 1980; nightclub comedian; columnist for *Oui* (magazine). Co-founder, Youth International Party (Yippies), 1968. Ordained minister, Universal Life Church. *Member:* American Civil Liberties Union. *Awards, honors:* Playboy Award, 1972, for article "Thomas Eagleton Seagull"; Feminist Party Media Workshop Award, 1974, for editing *The Realist.*

WRITINGS: Impolite Interviews, Lyle Stuart, 1961; (author of introduction) R. Crumb, *Head Comix,* Viking, 1968; *How a Satirical Editor Became a Yippie Conspirator in Ten Easy Years,* Putnam, 1971; (editor) Lenny Bruce, *How to Talk Dirty and Influence People,* Playboy Press, 1972; *Tales of Tongue Fu,* And/Or Press, 1981; *The Winner of the Slow Bicycle Race* (autobiography), St. Martin, 1984. Also editor, with Ken Kesey, of *The Last Supplement to the Whole Earth Catalog.* Author of syndicated column "Rumpleforeskin." Contributor of articles to *Co-Evolution Quarterly, Playboy, Rolling Stone, National Lampoon, Playgirl, Mother Jones, Village Voice,* and other publications. Contributing editor, *Playboy* and *High Times.*

SIDELIGHTS: There is general agreement on the statement, once made by *Books,* that Paul Krassner, former editor of the country's most popular underground magazine, "is rapidly becoming America's best-known iconoclast and, to many, a humorist who will fill the void left by Lenny Bruce's death." Speaking of Krassner, Groucho Marx said in 1971: "I predict in time he will wind up as the only live Lenny Bruce." Bruce, Krassner's idol, "was part of everything he indicted," says Krassner, as indeed *The Realist* was. Krassner refused to sell *The Realist,* which he founded with about $2,000, to any corporation, discouraging interested parties by showing them his most offensive issues.

Perhaps *the* most offensive issue of this irregularly published magazine carried the sections allegedly left out of William Manchester's *The Death of a President.* These sections dealt with an alleged sexual act between President Lyndon Johnson and the body of President John Kennedy shortly after Kennedy's assassination. Incredibly, a great many readers believed *The Realist's* account. Why did Krassner publish it? "I got sort of a perverse satisfaction from getting subscription cancellations because you know you're still hitting raw nerves," he said at the time. "And we just got a letter from someone saying, 'I didn't think the Manchester stuff was so bad, but this! Cancel my subscription!' And he circles the part about making fun of the humane slaughter of Jews." The Manchester story was simply another put-on with a purpose. These put-ons were so common with *The Realist* that a competing magazine, striving for a similar tone, once ran Krassner's obituary.

Krassner once described *The Realist* as a magazine of "free thought, criticism, and satire." It was, he added, "a personal chronology of the things I've been involved in: war protest, censorship, obscenity, psychedelics, and the stage it's currently at is revolution, more or less. But it's grown and changed because it's an extension of my personality which has grown and changed." He insists that he is not a crusader: "I just want to do it. . . . The theory comes after the practice."

The Realist, writes Jan Herman of the *Los Angeles Times,* "sallied forth with the deepest, darkest, most cynical belly laughs ever to appear between magazine covers. Paul Krassner, its left-wing, anarchist editor, held nothing sacrosanct. [It] was the prototypical voice of the counterculture."

Krassner told John Stickney: "If I had one thing to tell everybody, it would be: do it now. Take up music, read a book, proposition a girl—but do it now. We know we are all sentenced to death. People cannot become prisoners of guilts and fears. They should cling to each moment and take what enjoyment they can from it. I do not mean reckless, hedonistic pleasure. There just should not be a dichotomy between doing and being, spirit and flesh, pleasure and principles, work and play, orgasm and love."

"I read *The Realist,*" Krassner's father once told *Books,* "but I don't subscribe. Paul sends it to us. I don't understand it. All those big words. And I think he goes too far. Why is it necessary to use so many four-letter words? We never cursed in this house." His mother, who relates how her son the violinist, at the age of six, was the youngest soloist to ever play at Carnegie Hall, doesn't read *The Realist,* but she tolerantly admits that Paul "was always a nonconformist. Even when he was a tiny baby he would stand in the play pen on our lawn and grunt at the kids on their way to school."

Krassner now makes his living as a nightclub comedian and is, he told *CA,* "working on a novel about a controversial comedian inspired by Lenny Bruce. As a standup comedian I have been developing material on stage which gets put into the mouth of my fictional comic. This is somewhat schizophrenic as I find myself resenting this imaginary character who is stealing my material. I may have to publish this book myself, since the protagonist uses real names of public figures for his onstage fantasies. I am most influenced these days by J. D. Salinger, who says that he is not writing for publication any more because what he has to say is too personal. I am more curious about that than about stuff that gets published."

BIOGRAPHICAL/CRITICAL SOURCES: Newsweek, August 3, 1964; *Books,* April, 1967, February, 1968; *Fifth Estate* (Detroit), February 15, 1968; *Avant Garde,* May, 1968; *Life,* July, 1968, October 4, 1968; *Chicago Literary Review,* January, 1969; *Saturday Night,* July, 1969; *Los Angeles Times,* November 28, 1982.

*   *   *

KRAUS, Richard G(ordon)   1923-

PERSONAL: Born October 21, 1923, in New York, N.Y.; son of David (an attorney) and Ethel (Gordon) Kraus; married Anne Ripley (a ceramist), June 3, 1950; children: Lisa, Andrew. *Education:* City College (now City College of the City University of New York), B.A., 1942; Columbia University, M.A., Ed.D. *Office:* Department of Recreation, Temple University, Broad and Montgomery, Philadelphia, Pa. 19122.

CAREER: Editor of children's magazines for Fawcett Publications and Parents Institute, 1943-48; part-time recreation leader or dance teacher for Young Women's Christian Association, community recreation departments, hospitals, and schools, beginning 1943; affiliated with Columbia University, Teachers College, New York City, 1949-69; affiliated with Herbert H. Lehman College of City University of New York, New York City, 1969-77; affiliated with Temple University, Philadelphia, Pa., 1978—. Director of dance and recreation workshops in many states.

MEMBER: American Association for Health, Physical Education and Recreation (chairman of commission on research and evaluation; head of recreation division, Eastern district). *Awards, honors:* Distinguished Fellow Award, Society of Parks and Recreation Educators, 1979; National Literary Award, National Recreation and Park Association, 1983.

WRITINGS: Square Dances of Today, Ronald, 1950; *Recreation Leader's Handbook,* McGraw, 1955; *Play Activities of Boys and Girls,* McGraw, 1957.

Family Book of Games, McGraw, 1960; (with Dave Garroway) *Fun on Wheels,* McGraw, 1960; *Folk Dancing: A Guide for Schools, Colleges, and Recreation Groups,* Macmillan, 1962; *Recreation and the Schools,* Macmillan, 1964; (with Lola Sadlo) *Beginning Social Dance,* Wadsworth, 1964; *A Pocket Guide of Folk and Square Dances and Singing Games for the Elementary School,* Prentice-Hall, 1966; *Recreation Today: Program Planning and Leadership,* Prentice-Hall, 1966, 2nd edition, Goodyear, 1977; *Public Recreation and the Negro: A Study of Participation and Administrative Practices,* Center for Urban Education, 1968; (with Sarah Chapman), *A History of the Dance in Art and Education,* Prentice-Hall, 1969, 2nd edition, 1981.

Recreation and Leisure in Modern Society, Prentice-Hall and Goodyear, 1971, 2nd edition, Goodyear, 1978; *Urban Parks and Recreation: Challenges of the 1970s,* Community Council of Greater New York, 1972; (with Joseph E. Curtis) *Creative Administration in Recreation and Parks,* Mosby, 1973, 3rd edition published as *Creative Management in Recreation and Parks,* 1982; *Therapeutic Recreation Service: Principles and Practices,* Saunders, 1973, 2nd edition, 1978; (with Barbara Bates) *Recreation Leadership and Supervision: Guidelines for Professional Development,* Saunders, 1975, 2nd edition, 1981; *Social Recreation: A Group Dynamics Approach,* Mosby, 1979.

(With Margery Scanlin) *Introduction to Camp Counseling,* Prentice-Hall, 1983.

*   *   *

KRISHNAMURTI, Jiddu   1895-
(Alcyone)

PERSONAL: Born May 22, 1895, in Madanapalle, India; adopted son of Annie Besant (president of the Theosophical Society). *Education:* Educated privately in England. *Office address:* Krishnamurti Foundation of America, P.O. Box 219, Ojai, Calif. 93023; and Krishnamurti Foundation Trust Ltd., 24 Southend Rd., Beckenham, Kent BR3 1SD, England.

CAREER: Founder and head of Order of the Star in the East, 1911-29; lecturer and writer, 1929—; Krishnamurti Foundation of America, Ojai, Calif., and Krishnamurti Foundation Trust Ltd., Kent, England, president of board of directors, 1969—. Summer lecturer at Ommen, Holland, 1924-39, Saanen, Switzerland, 1961—, and Brockwood Park, Hampshire, England, 1969—. Founder of Oak Grove School, Ojai, Calif., and Brockwood Park School, Hampshire, England.

WRITINGS: (Under pseudonym Alcyone) *At the Feet of the Master,* Rajput Press, 1911, reprinted, Theosophical Publishing, 1970; (under pseudonym Alcyone) *Education as Service,* Rajput Press, 1912; *Self-Preparation,* Order of the Star in the East, 1926; *The Kingdom of Happiness,* Boni & Liveright, 1927; *Life in Freedom,* Liveright, 1928; *The Pool of Wisdom, Who Brings the Truth, By What Authority,* and *Three Poems,* Star Publishing Trust, 1928; *The Immortal Friend,* Liveright,

1928; *The Song of Life*, Liveright, 1931; *The Cloth of Gold: A Dance-Drama in Verse with a Dream-Epilogue*, Tuttle, 1951; *Talks and Dialogues*, Avon, 1968; *Meditations, 1969*, Krishnamurti Foundation, 1969; *The Flight of the Eagle*, Servire Publishers, 1971; *The Impossible Question*, Gollancz, 1972, Harper, 1973; *Tradition and Revolution*, edited by Pupul Jayakar and Sunandra Patwardhan, Fernhill, 1973; *Early Writings of J. Krishnamurti*, Krishna Press, 1974.

Published by Harper: *Education and the Significance of Life*, 1953; *The First and Last Freedom*, foreword by Aldous Huxley, 1954; *Commentaries on Living*, edited by D. Rajagopal, Volume I, 1956, Volume II, 1958, Volume III, 1960; *Life Ahead*, edited by Rajagopal, 1963; *Think on These Things*, edited by Rajagopal, 1964; *Freedom from the Known*, 1969; *The Only Revolution*, edited by Mary Lutyens, 1970; *The Penguin Krishnamurti Reader*, compiled by Lutyens, 1970; *The Urgency of Change*, edited by Lutyens, 1971; *You Are the World*, 1972; *Beyond Violence*, 1973; *The Awakening of Intelligence*, 1974; *Beginnings of Learning*, 1975; *Krishnamurti's Notebook*, 1976; *Truth and Actuality: Conversations on Science and Consciousness*, 1977; *Krishnamurti on Education*, 1977; *The Wholeness of Life*, 1978; *Meditations*, 1979; *Explorations into Insight*, 1980; *From Darkness to Light—Poems and Parables: The Collected Works of Krishnamurti*, 1980; *Letters to the Schools*, 1981; *Krishnamurti's Journal*, 1982.

Also author of *Australian Talks*, 1970. Talks and discussions have been published by Star Publishing Trust and by Krishnamurti Foundation.

SIDELIGHTS: Jiddu Krishnamurti's books have been published in most languages; videotapes and audiotapes of his discussions have been distributed worldwide by Krishnamurti Foundation.

BIOGRAPHICAL/CRITICAL SOURCES: Emily Luytens, *Candles in the Sun*, Lippincott, 1954; Mary Luytens, *To Be Young: Some Chapters of Autobiography*, Hart-Davis, 1956; Chaman Lal Nahal, *A Conversation with J. Krishnamurti*, Arya Book Depot (New Delhi), 1965; John E. Coleman, *The Quiet Mind*, Harper, 1971; *Time*, June 7, 1971; James Webb, *The Occult Underground*, Library Press, 1974; S. Weeraperuma, *Bibliography of the Life and Teachings of J. Krishnamurti*, E. J. Brill (Leiden, Netherlands), 1974; M. Luytens, *The Years of Awakening*, Farrar, Straus, 1975.

* * *

KUHN, Thomas S(amuel) 1922-

PERSONAL: Born July 18, 1922, in Cincinnati, Ohio; son of Samuel L. (an industrial engineer) and Minette (Stroock) Kuhn; married Kathryn Louise Muhs, November 27, 1948 (divorced September, 1978); children: Sarah, Elizabeth, Nathaniel Stroock. *Education:* Harvard University, S.B. (summa cum laude in physics), 1943, A.M., 1946, Ph.D., 1949. *Home:* 175 Commonwealth Ave., Boston, Mass. 02116. *Office address:* Department of Linguistics and Philosophy, Massachusetts Institute of Technology, 20D-213, Cambridge, Mass. 02139.

CAREER: U.S. Office of Scientific Research and Development, civilian employee at Harvard University, Cambridge, Mass., 1943-44, and in Europe, 1944-45; Harvard University, junior fellow, 1948-51, instructor, 1951-52, assistant professor of general education and history of science, 1952-56; University of California, Berkeley, assistant professor of history and philosophy, 1956-58, associate professor, 1958-61, professor of history of science, 1961-64; Princeton University, Princeton,

N.J., professor of history of science, 1964-68, M. Taylor Pyne Professor of the History of Science, 1968-79; Massachusetts Institute of Technology, Cambridge, professor of philosophy and history of science, 1979—. Director of project, Sources of History for Quantum Physics, sponsored by the American Physical Society and American Philosophical Society, 1961-64; member of Institute for Advanced Study, 1972-79.

MEMBER: American Academy of Arts and Sciences, History of Science Society (president), American Philosophical Society, American Historical Association, Social Science Research Council (member of board of directors, 1964-66), National Academy of Sciences, American Association for the Advancement of Science, Academie Internationale d'Histoire des Sciences (membre effectif), Phi Beta Kappa, Sigma Xi.

AWARDS, HONORS: Guggenheim fellow, 1954-55; Center for Advanced Study in the Behavioral Sciences fellow, 1958-59; LL.D., University of Notre Dame, 1973; Howard T. Behrman Award, Princeton University, 1977; American Book Award nomination, 1980, for *The Essential Tension: Selected Studies in Scientific Tradition and Change*.

WRITINGS: The Copernican Revolution: Planetary Astronomy in the Development of Western Thought, Harvard University Press, 1957, 2nd edition, 1959; *The Structure of Scientific Revolutions*, University of Chicago Press, 1962, 2nd edition, 1964, reprinted, 1982; (with J. L. Heilbron, P. L. Forman, and Lini Allen) *Sources for History of Quantum Physics*, American Philosophical Society, 1967; *The Essential Tension: Selected Studies in Scientific Tradition and Change*, University of Chicago Press, 1977; *Black-Body Theory and the Quantum Discontinuity, 1894-1912*, Oxford University Press, 1978.

Contributor: I. B. Cohen, editor, *Isaac Newton's Papers and Letters on Natural Philosophy*, Harvard University Press, 1958; Marshall Clagett, editor, *Critical Problems in the History of Science*, University of Wisconsin Press, 1959; Harry Woolf, editor, *Quantification: A History of Measurement in the Natural and Social Sciences*, Bobbs-Merrill, 1961; B. Barber and W. Hirsch, editors, *The Sociology of Science*, Free Press of Glencoe, 1961; C. W. Taylor and F. Barron, editors, *Scientific Creativity: Its Recognition and Development*, Wiley, 1963; A. C. Crombie, editor, *Scientific Change*, Basic Books, 1963; Cohen and R. Taton, editors, *Melanges Alexandre Koyre*, Volume II: *L'Aventure de l'esprit*, Hermann, 1964.

Member of board of editors, *Dictionary of Scientific Biography*, 1964—. Contributor to *Encyclopedia of the Social Sciences*, 1968; also contributor to *Isis*, *Science*, and to symposium volumes.

WORK IN PROGRESS: Research in the history of quantum physics and in philosophy of scientific development.

SIDELIGHTS: Thomas S. Kuhn's first exposure to the history of science came as an assistant to James B. Conant in a course designed to present science to non-scientists. He states that he was attracted to this field "by the great difference between the image of science provided by historical study, on the one hand, and by scientific training or philosophy of science, on the other."

In *The Structure of Scientific Revolutions*, Kuhn writes that the conventional view of progress in science bears almost no relation to how science actually progresses. According to the conventional view, scientists construct theories from firm, neutral facts, test their theories against new data, and gradually—over years and centuries—accommodate new evidence. Kuhn maintains that what really happens is that some prevailing view of nature undergoes a radical ''paradigm shift,'' a revolution in thought comparable to one in politics. Such a change alters the kinds of experiments scientists perform, the instruments they use, the form of questions they ask, even the types of problems considered important. Isaac Newton and Albert Einstein are only two of the scientists cited by Kuhn as having ushered in major paradigm shifts.

Judging by academic standards, *The Structure of Scientific Revolutions* has been extremely popular and influential, reports Robert Kanigel in the *Los Angeles Times Book Review.* Kanigel says that when the book first appeared in 1962, it ''almost overnight changed how many scientists imagined science worked. [It has since] sold almost 600,000 copies. Each year, hundreds of scholarly treatises cite it. One publisher came out with a collection of essays devoted exclusively to issues it raised. And while, narrowly speaking, the book deals only with the physical sciences, its ideas are, as one critic has put it, 'so seductive' that scholars in economics, political science and sociology have applied them to their own fields.''

BIOGRAPHICAL/CRITICAL SOURCES: Los Angeles Times Book Review, December 19, 1982.

*   *   *

KUPER, Leo 1908-

PERSONAL: Born November 24, 1908, in Johannesburg, South Africa; son of Morris (a merchant) and Pesha Kuper; married Hilda Beemer (a professor of anthropology), January 14, 1934; children: Jenny, Mary. *Education:* University of the Witwatersrand, B.A. (with honors), 1928, LL.B., 1930; University of North Carolina (now University of North Carolina at Chapel Hill), M.A., 1949; University of Birmingham, Birmingham, England, Ph.D., 1952. *Politics:* Liberal. *Religion:* Jewish. *Home:* 1282 Warner Ave., Los Angeles, Calif. 90024. *Office:* Department of Sociology, University of California, Los Angeles, Calif. 90024.

CAREER: Practiced law, 1931-40; University of Natal, Durban, South Africa, professor of sociology and social work, and dean of the Faculty of Social Science, 1952-61; University of California, Los Angeles, 1961—, began as professor of sociology, currently professor emeritus, director of African Studies Center, 1968-72. Organizing secretary, National War Memorial Health Foundation, 1946-49; Liberal Party executive, 1954-60. *Military service:* South African Army, 1940-45; became lieutenant. *Member:* International Sociological Association, American Sociological Association, African Studies Association. *Awards, honors:* Herskovits Book Award, 1966, for *An African Bourgeoisie;* Spivak fellowship, American Sociological Association, 1978, for contributions to the study of group relations.

WRITINGS: (Editor) *Living in Towns,* Cresset, 1952; *Passive Resistance in South Africa,* Yale University Press, 1957; (with Hilstan Watts and Ronald Davies) *Durban: A Study in Racial Ecology,* Columbia University Press, 1958; *College Brew* (satirical novel), privately printed, 1960; *An African Bourgeoisie,* Yale University Press, 1965; (editor with wife, Hilda Kuper) *African Law: Adaptation and Development,* University of California Press, 1966; (editor with M. G. Smith) *Pluralism in Africa,* University of California Press, 1969; *Race, Class and Power,* Duckworth, 1974; *The Pity of It All,* University of Minnesota Press, 1978; *Genocide: Its Political Use in the Twentieth Century,* Penguin (London), 1981, Yale University Press, 1982.

WORK IN PROGRESS: International Action against Genocide.

SIDELIGHTS: Leo Kuper's *Genocide: Its Political Use in the Twentieth Century* is ''a useful study of the subject, with extensive historical detail in an analytical framework,'' writes Telford Taylor in the *New York Times Book Review.* ''The author is a specialist in African studies, and his accounts of 'genocidal massacres' in Rwanda, Burundi, Nigeria, and the Sudan are vivid and apparently authentic. . . . The analytical portions are more impressive from a psychological than a legal standpoint, especially in discussing the social and political situations that stimulate genocidal behavior (colonization, decolonization, change of governments, racial and religious 'pluralism') and the mental processes by which perpetrators of genocide justify their conduct to themselves.''

Genocide represents the ''climax of a concern which Leo Kuper has pursued over many years and in many different books,'' notes Michael Banton in the *Times Literary Supplement,* and ''from his studies, Kuper concludes that despite its responsibility for the Convention on Genocide, the [United Nations] responds with indifference, if not condonation, to evidence of [genocide].'' The reason, as Kuper sees it, is that several of the sovereign states making up the UN fear that enforcement of the Convention might lead to encroachment on national sovereignty.

Though Kuper admits the UN has prevented some political situations from deteriorating into genocide, he nevertheless calls for an international penal code with a court to rule on accusations, as well as the establishment of a UN High Commissioner for Human Rights who could visit threatened populations and prepare reports. Kuper's recommendations and his tenacity lead Banton to conclude: ''Leo Kuper has been more successful than others in discerning lessons in these horrid episodes. . . . If there were a peace prize for sociologists, it should be awarded to him.''

BIOGRAPHICAL/CRITICAL SOURCES: Times Literary Supplement, February 7, 1975, July 2, 1982; *New York Times Book Review,* March 28, 1982.

*   *   *

KURLAND, Michael (Joseph) 1938-
(Jennifer Plum)

PERSONAL: Born March 1, 1938, in New York, N.Y.; son of Jack (a manufacturer) and Stephanie (a dress designer; maiden name, Yacht) Kurland. *Education:* Attended Hiram College, 1955-56, University of Maryland, 1959-60, foreign study in Germany, 1960-61, and Columbia University, 1963-64. *Politics:* Whig. *Religion:* Secular Humanist. *Residence:* New York, N.Y. *Agent:* Richard Curtis Associates, 340 East 66th St., New York, N.Y. 10021.

CAREER: Full-time writer, 1963—. High school English teacher in Ojai, Calif., 1968; managing editor, *Crawdaddy Magazine,* 1969. Occasional director of plays for Squirrel Hill Theatre, 1972—. *Military service:* U.S. Army, Intelligence, 1958-62.

MEMBER: Authors Guild, Authors League of America, Mystery Writers of America, Science Fiction Writers of America, Institute for Twenty-First Century Studies, Baker Street Irregulars. *Awards, honors:* Edgar scroll from Mystery Writers of America, 1971, for *A Plague of Spies,* and 1979, for *The Infernal Device;* American Book Award nomination, 1979, for *The Infernal Device.*

WRITINGS—All fiction: (Under pseudonym Jennifer Plum) *The Secret of Benjamin Square,* Lancer Books, 1972; *The Whenabouts of Burr,* DAW Books, 1975; *Pluribus,* Doubleday, 1975; *Tomorrow Knight,* DAW Books, 1976; *The Princes of Earth,* Thomas Nelson, 1978; *The Infernal Device,* New American Library, 1978; *The Last President,* William Morrow, 1980; (with H. Beam Piper) *Death by Gaslight,* New American Library, 1982.

Published by Pyramid Publications: (With Chester Anderson) *Ten Years to Doomsday,* 1964; *Mission: Third Force,* 1967; *Mission: Tank War,* 1968; *A Plague of Spies,* 1969; *The Unicorn Girl,* 1969; *Transmission Error,* 1971.

Author of editorials for *National Examiner,* 1966, and of "Impropa-Ganda" column in *Berkeley Barb,* 1967. Contributor to *Worlds of Tomorrow.*

WORK IN PROGRESS: A Victorian suspense-detective novel, tentatively entitled *The Murder Trust.*

SIDELIGHTS: Michael Kurland notes: "*The Unicorn Girl* is part of a unique trilogy, the middlework of a linked three-book opus with three different authors. The first [is] *The Butterfly Kid* by Chester Anderson, and the third [is] *The Probability Pad* by T. A. Waters."

AVOCATIONAL INTERESTS: Politics, bear baiting, barn storming, lighter-than-air craft, carnivals, vaudeville, science fiction incunabula.

KUSHEL, Gerald 1930-

PERSONAL: Surname rhymes with "bushel"; born July 18, 1930, in Trenton, N.J.; son of Ben (a businessman) and Bella (Gordon) Kushel; married Selma Plaxsun (a teacher), April 14, 1957; children: Joan, Lynne. *Education:* Rider College, B.S., 1952; Columbia University, M.A., 1957, Ed.D., 1966. *Home:* 10 Earl Rd., Melville, N.Y. *Office:* C. W. Post Center, Long Island University, Brookville, N.Y.

CAREER: Teaneck (N.J.) public schools, district director of guidance, 1957-61, 1966-67; Long Island University, C. W. Post Center, Brookville, N.Y., professor of counselor education, 1967—; president, Execupower Associates, Inc., 1982—. Trainer with American Management Association, 1979—. *Military service:* U.S. Navy, 1952-54. *Member:* American Personnel and Guidance Association, American Association of Marriage and Family Counselors, Long Island Personnel and Guidance Association.

WRITINGS: Discord in Teacher-Counselor Relations, Prentice-Hall, 1967; *Fact and Folklore,* Wiley, 1974; *Centering,* New York Times Co., 1979; *The Fully Effective Executive,* Contemporary Books, 1982.

AVOCATIONAL INTERESTS: Oil painting, tennis, travel.

L

LABARGE, Margaret Wade 1916-

PERSONAL: Born July 18, 1916, in New York, N.Y.; daughter of Alfred Byers and Helena (Mein) Wade; married Raymond C. Labarge (deputy minister of National Revenue, Canada), June 20, 1940 (died, 1972); children: Claire, Suzanne, Charles, Paul. *Education:* Radcliffe College, B.A., 1937; St. Anne's College, Oxford, B.Litt., 1939. *Religion:* Roman Catholic. *Home:* 312-211 Wurtemburg, Ottawa, Ontario, Canada K1N 8R4. *Agent:* Curtis Brown Academic, Ltd., 1 Craven Hill, London W2 3EP, England; and John Cushman Associates, 25 West 43rd St., New York, N.Y. 10036.

CAREER: University of Ottawa, Notre Dame College, Ottawa, Ontario, lecturer in history, 1940-42, 1950-51, 1953-58; Carleton University, Ottawa, lecturer in history, 1952-53, 1960-62; St. Vincent's Hospital, Ottawa, director, 1969-81, chairman of board of governors, 1977-79. Public representative, Board of Canadian Nurses Association, 1980-83. Chairman of hospital advisory board, Ottawa-Carleton Regional District Health Council. Member of board of directors, Rehabilitation Institute. *Member:* Mediaeval Academy of America, Phi Beta Kappa. *Awards, honors:* D.Litt., Carleton University, 1976; Order of Canada, 1982; Bene Merenti Medal, 1982.

WRITINGS: Simon de Montfort, Eyre & Spottiswoode, 1962, Norton, 1963; *A Baronial Household of the Thirteenth Century,* Eyre & Spottiswoode, 1965, Barnes & Noble, 1966; *Saint Louis: The Life of Louis IX of France,* Little, Brown, 1968; (contributor) R. Pernoud, editor, *Le Siecle de Saint Louis,* Hachette, 1970; *Court, Church, and Castle,* National Gallery of Canada, 1972; *Henry V: The Cautious Conqueror,* Secker & Warburg, 1975, Stein & Day, 1976; *Gascony: England's First Colony,* Hamish Hamilton, 1980; *Medieval Travellers: The Rich and Restless,* Hamish Hamilton, 1982, Norton, 1983. Contributor to *History Today, Commonweal,* and *Parliamentary Affairs;* also has reviewed books on radio.

WORK IN PROGRESS: A study of women's activities in the Middle Ages, for Hamish Hamilton.

SIDELIGHTS: Of Margaret Wade Labarge's *Medieval Travellers: The Rich and Restless,* the *Times Literary Supplement* reviewer says: "Mrs. Labarge's is an enjoyable, undemanding book, chatty and anecdotal, which suggests few general conclusions. It is filled with the kind of picturesque detail which her subjects would have thought unimportant. At the same time

it is a book which could not have been written without a very thorough knowledge of the scattered sources for the domestic life of the aristocracy of the late Middle Ages."

BIOGRAPHICAL/CRITICAL SOURCES: Economist, October 4, 1975; *History Today,* November, 1975; *Speculum,* October, 1981; *Times Literary Supplement,* February 18, 1983; *Los Angeles Times Book Review,* May 1, 1983.

*   *   *

LACEY, W(alter) K(irkpatrick) 1921-

PERSONAL: Born May 25, 1921, in Glasgow, Scotland; son of Walter Roland (a minister of religion) and Ellen (Paterson) Lacey; married Iris Olive Watson, March 20, 1954; children: Alastair, Jonathan (deceased), Roger, Sebastian. *Education:* St. Catharine's College, Cambridge, B.A., 1947, M.A., 1949. *Politics:* "I belong to no political party; I always vote." *Religion:* Church of England. *Home:* 33 Nihill Crescent, Mission Bay, Auckland 5, New Zealand. *Office:* Faculty of Arts, University of Auckland, Auckland, New Zealand.

CAREER: Assistant lecturer in classics at Durham College, Durham, England, and tutor at Hatfield College, Durham, 1949-51; Cambridge University, Cambridge, England, fellow and director of studies in classics at St. Catharine's College, 1951-68, assistant university lecturer, 1955-60, university lecturer in classics, 1960-68; University of Auckland, Auckland, New Zealand, professor of classics, 1969—, dean of Faculty of Arts, 1974-77. Member of education committee, Cambridgeshire and Isle of Ely County Council, 1965-67. *Military service:* British Army, 1941-42; commissioned into Indian Army, 1942-46; became major. *Member:* Roman Society (council member, 1961-65), Hellenic Society, New Zealand Linguistic Society, Joint Association of Classical Teachers (council member, 1965-68), Classical Association of Auckland (council member, 1969—; president, 1980-81), New Zealand Association of Classical Teachers, New Zealand Association of Language Teachers, Australasian Universities Languages and Literature Association, Cambridge Philological Society (treasurer and council member, 1955-63).

WRITINGS: (Reviser) *Cicero's Correspondence: An Easy Selection,* 2nd edition, Cornell University Press, 1962; *The Family in Classical Greece,* Cornell University Press, 1968, revised edition, Auckland University Press, 1980; (translator with

B.W.G. Wilson) Cicero, *Res Publica: Roman Politics and Society,* Oxford University Press, 1970; *Cicero and the End of the Roman Republic,* Hodder & Stoughton, 1978; *Students' Materials and Teachers' Guides for Athenian Democracy,* University of Otago, 1980; *Roman Politics,* University of Otago, 1980; *Roman Social Life,* University of Otago, 1980. Contributor to classical journals.

WORK IN PROGRESS: Augustan Essays; The Roman Family; edition of Cicero's *Second Philippic* for publication by Aris & Phillips.

*   *   *

LADD, Everett Carll, Jr.   1937-

PERSONAL: Born September 24, 1937, in Saco, Me.; son of Everett Carll and Agnes (Macmillan) Ladd; married Cynthia Northway, June 13, 1959; children: Carll, Corina, Melissa, Benjamin. *Education:* Bates College, A.B. (magna cum laude), 1959; Cornell University, Ph.D., 1964. *Politics:* Independent. *Religion:* Protestant. *Address:* 86 Ball Hill Rd., Storrs, Conn. 06268. *Office:* Roper Center for Public Opinion Research, University of Connecticut, Storrs, Conn. 06268.

CAREER: Cornell University, Ithaca, N.Y., assistant dean for public affairs, 1963-64; University of Connecticut, Storrs, assistant professor, 1964-67, associate professor, 1967-69, professor of political science, 1969—, director of Institute for Social Inquiry, 1968-77, executive director and president of the Roper Center for Public Opinion Research, 1977—. Visiting professor of political science, Yale University, 1973; lecturer at numerous colleges and universities, including Harvard University, Virginia Commonwealth University, Stanford University, Connecticut College, and Nichols College. Research fellow at Center for International Studies, Harvard University, 1969-75; visiting fellow at Hoover Institution, 1976-77 and 1979-80; adjunct scholar of American Enterprise Institute of Public Policy Research, 1978—; fellow at Center for Advanced Study in the Behavioral Sciences, 1979-80. Member of committee on faculty research grants, Social Science Research Council, 1967-71; Inter-University Consortium for Political and Social Research, official representative, 1967—, member of executive council, 1975-77; chairman, University of Connecticut Research Council, 1975-76. Editorial advisor in the social sciences, W. W. Norton, 1977—. Special consultant to Carnegie Commission on Higher Education, 1969-72, and to Connecticut General Assembly, 1970-71.

MEMBER: American Political Science Association, American Association for the Advancement of Science, American Sociological Association, American Association for Public Opinion Research, National Council on Public Polls, Academy of Political Science, New England Political Science Association (president, 1982-83), Connecticut Academy of Arts and Sciences, Phi Beta Kappa, Delta Sigma Rho, Pi Sigma Alpha.

AWARDS, HONORS: Woodrow Wilson fellow, 1959-60; Ford research fellow in the social sciences, 1969-70; Guggenheim fellow, 1971-72; Rockefeller Foundation fellow, 1976-77. Recipient of grants from Social Science Research Council, 1966-67, National Science Foundation, 1966-68, 1976-78, and 1978-79, National Municipal League, 1966-69, Carnegie Commission for Higher Education, 1969-72, Connecticut Research Commission, 1970-72, American Enterprise Institute for Public Policy Research, 1972 and 1976-78, National Institute of Education, 1973-76, Spencer Foundation, 1974-77, Earhart Foundation, 1975-77, Carnegie Corporation, 1976-78, Na-

tional Oceanic and Atmospheric Administration, 1976-79, Smith Richardson Foundation, 1976-80, Scaife Family Charitable Trust, 1977-80, Sloan Foundation, 1978-80, Exxon Education Foundation, 1979-80, Institute for Educational Affairs, 1981-82, and Stamford Foundation, 1982.

WRITINGS: Negro Political Leadership in the South, Cornell University Press, 1966; (contributor) Harry Bailey, editor, *Negro Politics in America,* C. E. Merrill, 1967; *Ideology in America: Change and Response in a City, a Suburb, and a Small Town,* Cornell University Press, 1969, revised edition, Norton, 1972; *American Political Parties: Social Change and Political Response,* Norton, 1970; (with S. M. Lipset) *Professors, Unions, and American Higher Education,* Carnegie Commission on Higher Education, 1973; (with Lipset) *Academics, Politics, and the 1972 Election,* American Enterprise Institute for Public Policy Research, 1973; (with C. D. Hadley) *Political Parties and Political Issues: Patterns in Differentiation since the New Deal,* Sage Publications, 1973.

(With Lipset) *The Divided Academy: Professors and Politics,* McGraw, 1975; (with Hadley) *Transformations of the American Party System: Political Coalitions from the New Deal to the 1970's,* Norton, 1975, revised edition, 1978; *Where Have All the Voters Gone?: The Fracturing of America's Political Parties,* Norton, 1978, revised edition, 1982; *The American Polity: The United States in Historical, Cross-National, and Societal Perspective,* Norton, 1983.

Contributor of articles to magazines and journals, including *Nation, Yale Review, South Atlantic Quarterly, Science, Massachusetts Review,* and *Journal of the History of Ideas. Public Opinion,* consulting editor, 1977-83, senior editor, 1983—. Member of editorial board, *Public Opinion Quarterly,* 1976-82, *Political Behavior,* 1978—, *Politics and Behavior,* 1978—, *Polity,* 1980—, and *Micropolitics,* 1980—; member of editorial advisory board, *Political Science Quarterly.*

*   *   *

LAGEVI, Bo
See BLOM, Karl Arne

*   *   *

LAI, T'ien-Ch'ang   1921-

PERSONAL: Born in 1921, in Hong Kong; son of Chi-Hsi (a professor) and Cheong (Fung-Ying) Lai; married Flora Wan-Fong (a teacher); children: Ross, Miranda. *Education:* University of Hong Kong, B.A., 1942, M.A., 1956; University of Manchester, Dip. Ad. Ed., 1962. *Home:* Residence 3D, Starview Discovery Bay, Lantau, Hong Kong. *Office:* Extra-Mural Department, Chinese University of Hong Kong, 67 Chatham Rd., Kowloon, Hong Kong.

CAREER: Chinese Embassy, London, England, secretary, 1946-50; director of Chung On Trading, Hong Kong, 1950-54; University of Hong Kong, Hong Kong, tutor in English, 1955-56, lecturer in extra-mural department, 1957-65; Chinese University of Hong Kong, Kowloon, director of extra-mural studies, 1965—. Member of International Congress of University Adult Education. *Member:* Rotary International.

WRITINGS: (Editor and translator) *Selected Chinese Sayings,* University Book Store, University of Hong Kong, 1960, 3rd edition, 1966; *Ch'i Pai Shih* (abridged autobiography of Ch'i Pai Shih), University of Washington Press, 1973; *Three Contemporary Chinese Painters: Chang Da-chien, Ting Yin-yung,*

Ch'eng Shih-fa, University of Washington Press, 1975; *Chinese Seals,* University of Washington Press, 1976; *Chinese Food for Thought,* Hong Kong Book Centre, 1978; *A Wild Swan's Trail: Travels of a Mandarin,* Hong Kong Book Centre, 1978; *Animals of the Chinese Zodiac,* Hong Kong Book Centre, 1979; (with Robert Mok) *Jade Flute: The Story of Chinese Music,* Hong Kong Book Centre, 1981; *Brushwork in Chinese Landscape Painting,* Chung Hwa Book Co. and Swindon Book Co., 1983; *To the Yellow Springs: The Chinese View of Death,* Kelly & Walsh and Joint Publishing Co., 1983.

Published by Swindon Book Co., except as indicated: (With Jen Tai) *Love Poetry from the Chinese,* 1968; (editor and translator) *Chinese Couplets,* 1969; (editor) Husein Rofe, *Things Chinese,* 1971; (translator with Y. T. Kwong) *Chinese Poetry,* 1972; *The Eight Immortals,* 1972; (translator) *More Chinese Sayings* (bilingual text), 1972; *A Chinese Book of Friendship,* 1973; *Chinese Calligraphy: Its Mystic Beauty,* 1973, published as *Chinese Calligraphy: An Introduction,* University of Washington Press, 1975; *Chinese Painting: Its Mystic Essence,* 1974; *Pa ta shan jen: Chinese Monk-Painter,* 1974; *Treasures of a Chinese Studio,* 1976; *Mountain Love Songs,* 1976; *Noble Fragrance,* 1977; (editor with Joyce Hsia) *Hong Kong: Images on Shifting Waters,* 1977; *Chinese Decorated Letter-paper,* 1978; *Visiting China: A Cultural Guide,* 1979; *Huang Bin Hong,* 1980; *Chinese Characters,* 1980.

Published by Kelly & Walsh: (With Kwong) *Chinese Proverbs,* 1970; *A Scholar in Imperial China,* 1970; *T'ang Yin, Poet/Painter, 1470-1524,* 1971; *Kweilin: China's Most Scenic Spot,* 1976; *Chinese Motifs in Modern Art,* 1977; (with Monica Lai) *The Young Cowherd and Other Poems,* 1978; (with Lai) *Rhapsodic Essays from the Chinese,* 1979; (editor) *The Consort of Peace,* 1980.

SIDELIGHTS: T'ien-Ch'ang Lai writes, ''I believe that introduction of Chinese culture (and therefore *values*) is vital to the world's welfare, particularly at a time of rampant materialism.''

*   *   *

LAMBERT, Christine
  See ALBRAND, Martha

*   *   *

LAMONT, Corliss   1902-

PERSONAL: Born March 28, 1902, in Englewood, N.J.; son of Thomas William and Florence (Corliss) Lamont; married Margaret H. Irish, 1928; married second wife, Helen Boyden (an economist), August 3, 1962; children: (first marriage) Margaret H. (Mrs. J. David Heap), Florence P. (Mrs. Ralph Antonides), Hayes C., Anne S. (Mrs. George Jafferis). *Education:* Harvard University, A.B. (magna cum laude), 1924; New College, Oxford, graduate study, 1924-25; Columbia University, Ph.D., 1932. *Politics:* Independent. *Home and office:* 315 West 106th St., New York, N.Y. 10025.

CAREER: Writer. Instructor in philosophy at Columbia University, New York City, 1928-32, at New School for Social Research, New York City, 1940-42; lecturer on contemporary Russian civilization at Cornell University, Ithaca, N.Y., 1943; conductor of social studies workshop on Soviet Russia at Graduate School of Education, Harvard University, Cambridge, Mass., 1944, and School of General Studies, Columbia University, 1947-59; seminar associate, Columbia University,

1971—. Candidate for U.S. Senate, American Labor Party, 1952, Independent Socialist Party, 1958. Chairman of Congress of American-Soviet Friendship, 1942, National Council of American-Soviet Friendship, 1943-46; indicted for contempt of Congress (McCarthy hearings), 1953, but dismissal of indictment upheld by U.S. Appeals Court, 1956; Bill of Rights Fund, co-founder, 1954, chairman, 1954-69; chairperson of National Emergency Civil Liberties Committee, 1963—; vice-president, Poetry Society of America, 1973-74.

MEMBER: American Philosophical Association, American Humanist Association, Academy of Political Science, American Civil Liberties Union (member of board, 1932-54), National Association for the Advancement of Colored People, United Nations Association of the U.S.A., Columbia Faculty Club, Harvard Club of New York City, Clan Lamont Society (Scotland), Phi Beta Kappa. *Awards, honors:* New York City Teachers Union Annual Award, 1955.

WRITINGS: Issues of Immortality: A Study in Implications, Henry Holt, 1932; (with Margaret Lamont) *Russia Day by Day: A Travel Diary,* Covici, Friede, 1933; *The Illusion of Immortality,* Putnam, 1935, 4th revised edition, Ungar, 1965; *You Might Like Socialism: A Way of Life for Modern Man,* Modern Age Books, 1939; *Soviet Russia versus Nazi Germany: A Study in Contrasts,* American Council on Soviet Relations, 1941; *Soviet Russia and the Post-war World,* National Council of American-Soviet Friendship, 1943; *The Peoples of the Soviet Union,* Harcourt, 1946; *Humanism as a Philosophy,* Philosophical Library, 1949, published as *The Philosophy of Humanism,* 1957, 6th revised edition, Ungar, 1982.

The Independent Mind: Essays of a Humanist Philosopher, Horizon, 1951; *Soviet Civilization,* Philosophical Library, 1952, 2nd edition, 1955; *Freedom Is as Freedom Does: Civil Liberties Today,* Horizon, 1956; *The Crime against Cuba,* Basic Pamphlets, 1961; *The Enduring Impact of George Santayana,* Basic Pamphlets, 1964; *Freedom of Choice Affirmed,* Horizon, 1967; *Remembering John Masefield,* Fairleigh Dickinson University Press, 1971; *Lovers Credo,* Barnes, 1972; *Voice in the Wilderness,* Prometheus, 1974; *Yes to Life: Memoirs of Corliss Lamont,* Horizon, 1981.

Editor: *Man Answers Death: An Anthology of Poetry,* Putnam, 1936, 2nd enlarged edition, Philosophical Library, 1952; (with Mary Redmer) James T. Farrell and others, *Dialogue on John Dewey,* Horizon, 1959; (with Mary Redmer) James Gutmann and others, *Dialogue on George Santayana,* Horizon, 1959; *Albert Rhys Williams, Sept. 28, 1883-Feb. 27, 1962, in Memoriam,* Horizon, 1962; Thomas Lamont and others, *The Thomas Lamont Family,* Horizon, 1962; (and author of introduction) *The Trial of Elizabeth Gurley Flynn by the American Civil Liberties Union,* Horizon, 1968; *The Thomas Lamonts in America,* Barnes, 1971; (with nephew, Lansing Lamont) *Letters of John Masefield to Florence Lamont,* Columbia University Press, 1980.

Also author of ''Basic Pamphlet'' series on contemporary issues, 1957—, including *My Trip around the World,* 1960, *My First Sixty Years,* 1962, and *Adventures in Civil Liberties,* 1977.

SIDELIGHTS: Corliss Lamont, the son of noted financier Thomas William Lamont, has long associated himself with socialism and is the author of several books centering on the political and social culture of the Soviet Union. An early effort is his 1933 book *Russia Day by Day: A Travel Diary,* the account of six weeks' travel in the Soviet Union by Lamont and his

LAMONT

CONTEMPORARY AUTHORS • New Revision Series, Volume 11

wife, co-author Margaret Lamont. The work "tells nothing new to people who read the current accounts in magazines and newspapers," according to Helen Mears in *Survey Graphic*. "But as a human document it is priceless." The Lamonts, Mears contends, "being intelligent and scrupulously honest, . . . trembled lest their known bias [in favor of Russian society] should influence their judgements. For that reason they tell the bitter with the sweet, they balance every advantage with its disadvantage, they weed the picture carefully of any exuberance, and the result is devastatingly devoid of any sense of humanity."

Russia Day by Day was greeted with measured praise by *Nation* critic W. H. Chamberlin, who writes that because the authors "were so obviously enjoying the manifold sights and impressions and discussion topics of what they regard as 'the new world of the twentieth century,' . . . they are somewhat jauntily willing and even eager to learn and credit the ever-ready official excuses for this or that obvious failing." However, notes Chamberlin, "one admires their philosophic good nature in the face of nocturnal insects on Volga boats and of mired buses on the steppes of the North Caucasus, and feels that they would have been agreeable travel companions on the somewhat strenuous tour of Russia."

AVOCATIONAL INTERESTS: Tennis, skiing, hiking, and the movies.

BIOGRAPHICAL/CRITICAL SOURCES: Corliss Lamont and Margaret Lamont, *Russia Day by Day: A Travel Diary*, Covici, Friede, 1933; *Survey Graphic*, August, 1933; *Nation*, August 30, 1933; Philip Wittenberg, editor, *Lamont Case: History of a Congressional Investigation*, introduction by Horace M. Kallen, Horizon, 1957; *Los Angeles Times*, February 11, 1980; *Times Literary Supplement*, February 15, 1980; C. Lamont, *Yes to Life: Memoirs of Corliss Lamont*, Horizon, 1981.

* * *

LAMONT, Lansing 1930-

PERSONAL: Born March 13, 1930, in New York, N.Y.; son of Thomas Stilwell (a banker) and Elinor (Miner) Lamont; married Ada Jung, September 18, 1954; children: Douglas, Elisabeth, Virginia, Thomas S. II. *Education:* Harvard University, A.B., 1952; Columbia University, M.S. (honors), 1958. *Politics:* Independent. *Religion:* Episcopal. *Home:* 133 East 80th St., New York, N.Y. 10021. *Office:* 680 Park Ave., New York, N.Y. 10021.

CAREER: Washington Star, Washington, D.C., reporter, 1958-59; Congressional correspondent for *Worcester Gazette*, Worcester, Mass., and other New England dailies, 1959-60; *Time*, New York, N.Y., congressional and national correspondent with Washington bureau, 1961-68, deputy chief of London bureau, 1969-71, chief Canadian correspondent and Ottawa bureau chief, 1971-73, United Nations bureau chief and world affairs writer, 1973-74; free-lance writer, 1975-80; director, Canadian Affairs Forum, Americas Society, 1981—. *Military service:* U.S. Army, 1954-57; became first lieutenant. *Member:* National Press Club. *Awards, honors: Day of Trinity* was among 250 best American books, 1961-65, chosen by American Booksellers Association for presentation to White House library.

WRITINGS: Day of Trinity (Literary Guild alternate selection), Atheneum, 1965; *Campus Shock: A Firsthand Report on College Life Today*, Dutton, 1979; (editor with uncle, Corliss La-

mont) *Letters of John Masefield to Florence Lamont*, Columbia University Press, 1980.

SIDELIGHTS: Lansing Lamont's book *Campus Shock: A Firsthand Report on College Life Today* is "a grim and thought-provoking account of the lives of quiet (and sometimes frantic) desperation being played out against the ivy-covered backdrop of America's finest colleges and universities," according to John Rabb in the *Washington Post Book World*. Lamont surveyed students at twelve American colleges and universities, including eight Ivy League schools on the East Coast, in compiling his work. He describes many of today's students as "unhappy, beset by tension, trapped in insecurity and frustration," and his reports often focus on the prevalent cheating, vandalism, and even rape that occurs at these institutions. However, "it's clear that he intends the shock to produce change, not cheap thrills," says *Ms.* reviewer Charla Gabert. "[Lamont] is adept at charting the spiraling trap students are caught in: a shrinking job market and cynicism about social change that compel more students to choose traditional, lucrative professions."

Rabb notes the author's acknowledgement that "he is not an educator or an administrator; indeed, his book is presented from a refreshingly unpretentious point of view. Rather, his concerns and suggestions are (or should be) those of all parents of college-age students: that their children be given the option to attend school in an atmosphere that is as free from undue pressure and expectation as possible. This, Lamont feels, is the only way to shed a fresh, new light on the dark side of college life." *Campus Shock*, concludes Jeff Greenfield in the *New York Times Book Review*, "is a useful corrective to the 'thank-God-the-raucous-60's-are-over' approach of other accounts."

BIOGRAPHICAL/CRITICAL SOURCES: Lansing Lamont, *Campus Shock: A Firsthand Report on College Life Today*, Dutton, 1979; *New York Times Book Review*, April 29, 1979; *Time*, July 2, 1979; *Washington Post Book World*, August 12, 1979; *Ms.*, September, 1979; *Los Angeles Times*, February 11, 1980; *Times Literary Supplement*, February 15, 1980.

* * *

LAMPMAN, Evelyn Sibley 1907-1980
(Lynn Bronson)

PERSONAL: Born April 18, 1907, in Dallas, Ore.; died of cancer, June 13, 1980, in Portland, Ore.; daughter of Joseph E. and Harriet (Bronson) Sibley; married Herbert Sheldon Lampman, May 12, 1934 (died June, 1943); children: Linda Sibley Lampman McIsaac, Anne Hathaway Lampman Knutson. *Education:* Oregon State University, B.S., 1929. *Religion:* Episcopalian.

CAREER: Radio Station KEX, Portland, Ore., continuity writer, 1929-34, continuity chief, 1937-45; Radio Station KGW, Portland, educational director, 1945-52; full-time writer of children's books, 1952-80. *Member:* Delta Delta Delta. *Awards, honors:* Award from Committee on Art of Democratic Living, 1949, for *Treasure Mountain;* two Jean Hersholt Awards for radio script writing; Dorothy Canfield Fisher Memorial Children's Book Award, 1962, for *City under the Back Steps;* Western Writers of America Spur Award, 1968, for *Half-Breed*, and 1971, for *Cayuse Courage;* Children's Book Showcase Award, 1977, for *The Potlatch Family*.

WRITINGS—Juveniles; published by Doubleday, except as indicated: *Crazy Creek*, 1948; *Treasure Mountain*, 1949; *The*

318

Bounces of Cynthiann', 1950; *Elder Brother*, 1951; *Captain Apple's Ghost*, 1952; *Tree Wagon*, 1953; *Witch Doctor's Son*, 1954; *The Shy Stegosaurus of Cricket Creek*, 1955; *Navaho Sister*, 1956; *Rusty's Space Ship*, 1957; *Rock Hounds*, 1958; *Special Year*, 1959.

City under the Back Steps, 1960; *Princess of Fort Vancouver*, 1962; *Shy Stegosaurus at Indian Springs*, 1962; *Mrs. Updaisy*, 1963; *Temple of the Sun: A Boy Fights for Montezuma*, 1964; *Wheels West*, 1965; *The Tilted Sombrero*, 1966; *Half-Breed*, 1967; *The Bandit of Mok Hill*, 1969; *Cayuse Courage*, Harcourt, 1970; *Once upon the Little Big Horn*, Crowell, 1971; *The Year of Small Shadow*, Harcourt, 1971; *Go up the Road*, Atheneum, 1972; *Rattlesnake Cave*, Atheneum, 1974; *White Captives*, Atheneum, 1975; *The Potlatch Family*, Atheneum, 1976; *Bargain Bride*, Atheneum, 1977; *Squaw Man's Son*, Atheneum, 1978; *Three Knocks on the Wall*, Atheneum, 1980.

Under pseudonym Lynn Bronson: *Timberland Adventure*, Lippincott, 1950; *Coyote Kid*, Lippincott, 1951; *Rogue's Valley*, Lippincott, 1952; *The Runaway*, Lippincott, 1953; *Darcy's Harvest*, Doubleday, 1956; *Popular Girl*, Doubleday, 1957.

Also author of adult book, *Of Mikes and Men*, a fictionalized account of Lampman's early experiences as a writer for Portland radio stations.

SIDELIGHTS: A granddaughter of pioneers who arrived in Oregon by covered wagons, Evelyn Sibley Lampman based many of her books on stories handed down through her family. Several of her works deal with the persecution and cultural conflict experienced by Native Americans in the West.

OBITUARIES: New York Times, June 14, 1980; *Washington Post*, June 16, 1980.†

* * *

LAND, Myrick (Ebben) 1922-

PERSONAL: Born February 25, 1922, in Shreveport, La.; son of James Arthur and Mary Edna (Fancher) Land; married Barbara Neblett, 1949; children: Robert Arthur, Jacquelyn Myrick. *Education:* University of California, Los Angeles, B.A., 1945; Columbia University, M.S. in Journalism, 1946. *Office:* Department of Journalism, University of Nevada—Reno, Reno, Nev. 89557. *Agent:* Sterling Lord Agency, 660 Madison Ave., New York, N.Y. 10021.

CAREER: American National Red Cross, Washington, D.C., director of information in Europe and North Africa, 1949-52; Scholastic Magazines, New York City, editor 1952-55; *This Week*, New York City, assistant editor, 1955-59; *Look*, New York City, senior editor, 1959-66, assistant managing editor, 1967-71; University of Queensland, Brisbane, Australia, senior lecturer in journalism, 1972-76; University of Nevada—Reno, assistant professor of journalism, 1976-79; University of Wisconsin—Oshkosh, associate professor of journalism, 1979-81; University of Nevada—Reno, associate professor of journalism, 1982—. *Military service:* U.S. Army Air Forces, 1942-43. *Member:* Authors Guild, Columbia Journalism Alumni (president, 1963-65). *Awards, honors:* Pulitzer traveling fellowship, 1946-47; nomination from Mystery Writers of America as author of one of the three best first mysteries of the year, 1969.

WRITINGS: Search the Dark Woods (novel), Funk, 1955, published as *The Search*, Dell, 1959; *The Fine Art of Literary Mayhem*, Holt, 1963, revised edition, Lexikos, 1983; (with wife, Barbara Land, and Robert L. Oswald) *Lee: A Portrait*

of Lee Harvey Oswald by His Brother, Coward, 1967; *Quicksand*, Harper, 1969; *Last Flight*, Norton, 1975; *The Dream Buyers*, Norton, 1980; *Writing for Magazines*, Random House, 1984.

Juvenile books with wife, B. Land: *Jungle Oil*, Coward, 1957; *The Changing South*, Coward, 1959; *The Quest of Isaac Newton*, Doubleday, 1961.

Contributor of some two hundred articles to *Look, This Week, New York Times Magazine, Cosmopolitan, Script, Coronet*, and other periodicals.

WORK IN PROGRESS: Beyond the Sea, a novel set in Australia during the convict period; "At the Beach House," a suspense play; *Point Danger*, a suspense novel.

AVOCATIONAL INTERESTS: Painting, traveling.

* * *

LANDMAN, David 1917-

PERSONAL: Born October 24, 1917, in Philadelphia, Pa.; son of Isaac (a rabbi) and Beatrice (a social worker; maiden name, Eschner) Landman; married Joan Klein, September 1, 1946 (deceased); married Hedy Backlin (a museum director), December 30, 1964; children: Alicia, Michael Isaac. *Education:* Brown University, A.B. (magna cum laude), 1939; graduate study at Yale University, summer, 1954; Columbia University, M.A., 1963. *Religion:* Jewish. *Home and office:* 40 East Cedar St., Apt. 20-C, Chicago, Ill. 60611.

CAREER: Springfield Union, Springfield, Mass., reporter, 1939; *Universal Jewish Encyclopedia*, New York City, associate editor, 1939-41; *Look at America*, New York City, writer, 1945-46; free-lance writer, 1946-59; Cooper Union, New York City, assistant to the president, 1959-63; Princeton University, Princeton, N.J., associate director of development, 1963-69; Harvard University, Harvard Business School, Cambridge, Mass., director of public information, 1969-73; Pathfinder Fund, Boston, Mass., director of public affairs, 1973-77; University of Illinois, Urbana and Chicago, director of public information, 1977-79, editor of *Medical Center Alumni News*, 1979-82, editor for special projects, 1982-83; free-lance writer, 1983—. Lecturer at Boston University, 1973-76. Hamilton-Madison House (settlement house), member of board of directors, 1949-69, vice-president of board of directors, 1960-64. *Military service:* U.S. Army, Infantry, 1941-45; became major; received Bronze Star Medal.

MEMBER: American Society of Journalists and Authors (chairman of Midwest chapter, 1983—), Council for the Support and Advancement of Education, Asia Society, Phi Beta Kappa. *Awards, honors:* Ford Foundation fellowship, Indonesia, 1955-56.

WRITINGS: (With wife, Joan Landman) *Where to Ski*, Houghton, 1949; (contributor) Terry Morris, editor, *Prose by Professionals*, Doubleday, 1961; (editor with Johnson E. Fairchild) *America Faces the Nuclear Age*, Sheridan House, 1961; (editor with others) *Population: Theory and Policy*, University of Illinois, 1982. Contributor to professional journals and popular magazines, including *Redbook, True, Collier's, New Republic, Coronet, Pageant*, and *Nation's Business*.

SIDELIGHTS: David Landman writes: "I consider myself to be a professional writer and communicator who for almost two decades has dedicated himself to communicating for non-profit institutions, usually colleges and universities. Whether these institutions flourish or flounder depends in large part on whether their story is heard, understood, and believed—by their several publics.''

*   *   *

LANGER, Lawrence L(ee) 1929-

PERSONAL: Born June 20, 1929, in New York, N.Y.; son of Irving and Esther (Strauss) Langer; married Sondra Weinstein (an educator), February 21, 1951; children: Andrew, Ellen. *Education:* City College (now of the City University of New York), B.A., 1951; Harvard University, A.M., 1952, Ph.D., 1961. *Home:* 249 Adams Ave., West Newton, Mass. 02165. *Office:* Department of English, Simmons College, 300 Fenway, Boston, Mass. 02115.

CAREER: University of Connecticut, Storrs, instructor in English, 1957-58; Simmons College, Boston, Mass., instructor, 1958-61, assistant professor, 1961-66, associate professor, 1966-72, professor, 1972-76, alumnae professor of English, 1976—. Fulbright lecturer at University of Graz, 1963-64. Program associate in interdisciplinary studies at Institute for Services to Education. *Member:* P.E.N. American Center, Modern Language Association of America, American Association of University Professors, Phi Beta Kappa. *Awards, honors:* National Endowment for the Humanities fellowship for independent study and research, 1978-79.

WRITINGS: The Holocaust and the Literary Imagination, Yale University Press, 1975; *The Age of Atrocity: Death in Modern Literature,* Beacon Press, 1978; (contributor) Alvin Rosenfeld and Irving Greenberg, editors, *Confronting the Holocaust: The Impact of Elie Wiesel,* Indiana University Press, 1978; (contributor) Henry Friedlander and Sybil Milton, editors, *Holocaust: Ideology, Bureaucracy, and Genocide,* Kraus International Publications, 1981; *Versions of Survival: The Holocaust and the Human Spirit,* State University of New York Press, 1982; (contributor) Sarah Blacher Cohen, editor, *From Hester Street to Hollywood: The Jewish-American Stage and Screen,* University of Indiana Press, 1983.

WORK IN PROGRESS: Heroic Discontent: From Manfred to Moses Herzog.

BIOGRAPHICAL/CRITICAL SOURCES: Los Angeles Times Book Review, March 7, 1982.

*   *   *

LASKY, Kathryn 1944-

PERSONAL: Born June 24, 1944, in Indianapolis, Ind.; daughter of Marven and Hortense Lasky; married Christopher Knight (a photographer and filmmaker), May 30, 1971; children: Maxwell, Meribah. *Education:* University of Michigan, B.A., 1966; graduate study at Wheelock College. *Home:* 7 Scott St., Cambridge, Mass. *Agent:* Sheldon Fogelman, 10 East 40th St., New York, N.Y.

CAREER: Writer. *Awards, honors:* National Jewish Book Award from Jewish Welfare Board Book Council, 1982, for *The Night Journey; Boston Globe-Horn Book* Award, for *The Weaver's Gift.*

WRITINGS—All juveniles: *Agatha's Alphabet,* Rand McNally, 1975; *I Have Four Names for My Grandfather,* illustrated with photographs by husband, Christopher Knight, Little, Brown, 1976; *Tugboats Never Sleep,* illustrated with photographs by Knight, Little, Brown, 1977; *Tall Ships,* illustrated with pho-

tographs by Knight, Scribner, 1978; *My Island Grandma,* Warne, 1979; *The Weaver's Gift,* illustrated with photographs by Knight, Warne, 1981; *The Night Journey,* Warne, 1981; *Jem's Island,* Scribner, 1982; *Sugaring Time,* illustrated with photographs by Knight, Macmillan, 1983; *Beyond the Divide,* Macmillan, 1983. Contributor to *Sail.*

SIDELIGHTS: Kathryn Lasky told *CA:* ''When I was growing up I was always thinking up stories—whether I wrote them down or not didn't seem to matter. I was a compulsive story maker. I was fiercely private about these early stories—never really sharing them with anybody. I always wanted to be a writer, but on the other hand it seemed to lack a certain legitimacy as a profession. It was enjoyable, not reliable, and you were your own boss. This all seemed funny. It was only when I began to share my writing with my parents (and much later my husband) and sensed their responsiveness that I began to think that it was o.k. to want to be a writer. One of the greatest things about my experiences in writing recently is that my husband has illustrated many of my books with his photographs.''

*   *   *

LAVOND, Paul Dennis
See POHL, Frederik

*   *   *

LAWRENCE, R(onald) D(ouglas) 1921-

PERSONAL: Born September 12, 1921, in Vigo, Spain; son of Thomas Edward and Esther (Rodriguez) Lawrence; married Joan Frances Gray, September 18, 1962 (died June 7, 1969); married Sharon Janet Frise (a teacher), December 16, 1973. *Education:* Educated at private school in Barcelona, Spain, and by a private tutor. *Politics:* None. *Religion:* None. *Home and office address:* RR1, Norland, Ontario, Canada K0M 2L0. *Agent:* Wallace & Sheil Agency, Inc., 177 East 70th St., New York, N.Y. 10021.

CAREER: Writer. *Daily Mirror,* London, England, journalist, 1945-54; trapper, logger, and cattle farmer on homestead in northern Ontario, 1954-57; *Free Press,* Winnipeg, Manitoba, night editor, 1957-61; *Telegram,* Toronto, Ontario, worked as reporter, entertainment and financial editor, and publisher of affiliate suburban weekly newspaper, 1960-70. *Military service:* British Army, Military Intelligence, Tank Corps, 1939-44. *Member:* American Society of Mammalogists, Writers Union of Canada, Mark Twain Society (honorary member). *Awards, honors:* Frank H. Kortright awards from Toronto Sportsman's Show, 1967 and 1968, for writing on conservation.

WRITINGS: Wildlife in Canada, M. Joseph, 1966; *The Place in the Forest,* M. Joseph, 1967; *Where the Water Lilies Grow,* M. Joseph, 1968; *The Poison Makers,* Thomas Nelson, 1968; *Maple Syrup,* Thomas Nelson, 1970; *Cry Wild,* Thomas Nelson, 1970; *Wildlife in North America: Mammals,* Chilton, 1974; *Wildlife in North America: Birds,* Chilton, 1974; *Paddy: A Naturalist's Story of an Orphan Beaver Rescued, Adopted and Observed,* Knopf, 1976, condensed edition, Reader's Digest Press, 1978; *The North Runner,* Holt, 1979, condensed edition, Reader's Digest Press, 1979; *Secret Go the Wolves,* Holt, 1980, condensed edition, Reader's Digest Press, 1982; *The Zoo That Never Was,* Holt, 1981; *Voyage of the Stella,* Holt, 1982; *The Ghost Walker,* Holt, 1983; *Canada's National Parks,* Collins, 1983. Contributor to proceedings of Myrin Institute, 1980.

WORK IN PROGRESS: A layman's guide to the biology of sharks; a novel dealing with Communist pressures on the United States from bases in Canada; a book examining the wildlife of Canada and the United States, and the measures employed by governmental wildlife agencies of both nations to ensure their conservation.

SIDELIGHTS: R. D. Lawrence told *CA:* "The single most potent motive force is my consuming interest in living things, from mouse to man, and it was on this subject that I wrote a diary of wildlife seen which I later expanded into my first book, *Wildlife in Canada.*

"I began writing about nature as a child; I explored nature as a child, but perhaps the greatest influence in my life, and writings, comes from Thoreau. At fourteen I read *Walden* and was deeply impressed by one of Thoreau's sentences: 'In wildness is the preservation of the world.'

"Over the years I have received, and continue to receive, thousands of letters from readers of my work; this is the greatest stimulation that I obtain from my writings. The knowledge that so many people share my passion for life lived in mutual respect and toleration keeps me elevated during those times (which are now occurring with greater frequency) when the insanity of man's politics begins to debase and depress me."

A *New York Times Book Review* critic writes that Lawrence's book *The North Runner,* a memoir of his experiences living with a wolf in northern Ontario, contains "sensitive moments, quietly and richly described. . . . Lawrence reveals not a little of his own honesty and also offers insight into the psychology of the lone human."

Lawrence's books have been translated into thirteen languages and have been published in sixteen countries.

BIOGRAPHICAL/CRITICAL SOURCES: New York Times Book Review, July 24, 1977, July 22, 1979; *Washington Post Book World,* April 17, 1979.

*   *   *

LAX, Robert 1915-

PERSONAL: Born November 30, 1915, in Olean, N.Y.; son of Sigmund (a clothier) and Betty (Hotchner) Lax. *Education:* Columbia University, B.A., 1938. *Politics:* Democrat. *Religion:* Roman Catholic. *Residence:* Olean, N.Y. *Address:* c/o Marcia Kelly, 70 Riverside Dr., New York, N.Y. 10024.

CAREER: New Yorker, New York City, member of editorial staff, 1941-42; University of North Carolina at Chapel Hill, instructor in English, 1943-44; *Time,* New York City, film critic, 1945-46; Samuel Goldwyn Studio, Hollywood, Calif., script writer, 1946-48; Connecticut College for Women (now Connecticut College), New London, instructor in English and comparative literature, 1948-49; *Jubilee* (magazine), New York City, 1953-67, began as executive editor, became roving editor; free-lance writer, 1967—. *Awards, honors:* National Council on the Arts award, 1969.

WRITINGS—Poetry, except as indicated; published by Journeyman Books, except as indicated; illustrated with drawings by Emil Antonucci, except as indicated: *The Circus of the Sun,* 1959, new edition with facing translations in German, French, and Spanish published as *Circus,* photographs by Bernhard Moosbrugger, Pendo Verlag (Zurich), 1981; *New Poems,* 1962; *3 or 4 Poems about the Sea,* 1966; *Thought,* 1966; *Sea Poems,* Wild Hawthorn Press (Scotland), 1967; *Three Poems,* 1969.

Tree, 1970; *Homage to Wiggenstein,* [Kalymnos], 1970; *Able Charlie Baker Dance,* Tarasque Press, 1971; *Another Red Red Blue Poem,* 1971; *Black and White,* 1971; *An Evening at Webster Hall,* 1971; *A Guide for the Perplexed,* 1971; *A Moment,* 1971; *Mostly Blue,* 1971; *WASSER, WASSER, WATER, WATER, EAU,* photographs by Moosbrugger, Pendo Verlag, 1974; *Color Poems,* 1976; *Color,* Exempla Editione (Florence), 1977; *A Catch of Anti-Letters* (correspondence with Thomas Merton), drawings by Merton, Sheed Andrews, 1978; *Selected Poems,* Joe Di Maggio & X-Press (London), 1978; *Mythoi* (title means "Fables"), translated from original English manuscript into Greek by Moschos Lagouvardos, [Salonika], 1980; *Ten Poems,* Patmos Press, 1981; *Episodes,* Pendo Verlag, 1983; *Tiger, Whole, the Way,* Furthermore Press (Lyndonville, Vt.), 1983.

Contributor to anthologies, including: *Concrete Poetry,* edited by Stephen Bann, Secker & Warburg, 1967; *Thirty-one New American Poets,* edited by Ron Schrieber, Hill & Wang, 1969; *American Literary Anthology,* edited by George Plimpton and others, Viking, 1970; *Imaged Words and Worded Images,* edited by Richard Kostelanetz, Outerbridge & Dienstfrey, 1970; *Expanded Poetry,* edited by Emmett Williams, Simon & Schuster, 1970; *TAU/MA 7,* edited by Claudio Parmiggiani, [Bologna], 1981. Contributor of poems to numerous periodicals.

WORK IN PROGRESS: "A poem-journal or journal poem, and abstract poems."

SIDELIGHTS: "Most of my books to date," writes Robert Lax, "have been published by other poets, or by graphic artists who have discovered the work in small press editions in America, Europe, or Australia, and have undertaken to do small editions of their own, designing and illustrating them, each according to his own ideas. The results have been most gratifying: a series of often slim, inexpensive but life-breathing books, warmly conceived and lovingly designed. They go out of print almost as fast as they come into it, but each is beautiful while it lasts.

"The first of these artists to produce my work, and the most prodigious, is Emil Antonucci, the publisher of Journeyman Books. He has designed and published at least twenty-five of my books, large and small, and has produced three or four short films in black and white and in color based on poems he had already published. [Among the films are 'New Film,' 'Shorts,' and 'Red & Blue.'] Maurizio Nannucci—poet, artist, and demiurge in Florence—has designed and published other of my books and produced a cassette of my readings, [*Sea and Sky*]. Bernhard Moosbrugger, an outstanding Swiss photographer and publisher of Pendo Verlag, Zurich, has designed and illustrated several of my books (in English, with German translation) and has still others in the works." Other artists and poets who have been instrumental in getting Lax's work published, broadcast, or filmed include John Ashbery, Thomas Merton, Mark Van Doren, Theodore Weiss, Richard Kostelanetz, Thomas A. Clark, Stephen Bann, Mario Diacono, Jiri Valoch and Ernesto Cardenal.

Lax has recorded his poems for the Lamont Poetry Room at Harvard University. In 1968, a double issue of *Voyages* was devoted to his work.

BIOGRAPHICAL/CRITICAL SOURCES: Art International, January 20, 1971.

LAZARUS, A(rnold) L(eslie)   1914-
(Leslie Arnold, A. L. Leslie)

PERSONAL: Born February 20, 1914, in Revere, Mass.; son of Benjamin (a merchant) and Bessie (Winston) Lazarus; married Keo Felker (a writer of children's books), July 24, 1938; children: Karie (Mrs. John Block Friedman), Dianne (Mrs. James Runnels), Jonathan, Peter. *Education:* Attended College of William and Mary, 1931; University of Michigan, B.A., 1935; University of California, Los Angeles, M.A., 1941, Ph.D., 1957. *Home:* 945 Ward Dr., No. 69, Santa Barbara, Calif. 93111.

CAREER: Instructor in English, foreign languages, and Latin in Santa Barbara County, Calif. 1944-45; Chaffey Junior College (now Chaffey Community College), Ontario, Calif., instructor in English and Latin, 1945-47; Santa Monica Public Schools, Santa Monica, Calif., instructor in English, 1947-53; Santa Monica City College (now Santa Monica College), Santa Monica, instructor in English, 1953-58; Los Angeles State College of Applied Arts and Sciences (now California State University, Los Angeles), Los Angeles, Calif., lecturer in English education, 1958-59; University of Texas at Austin, associate professor of English, 1959-62; Purdue University, Lafayette, Ind., professor of English and education, beginning 1962, director of English Curriculum Center, beginning 1963. Member of English Commission, College Entrance Examination Board, 1962-64; chief Midwest judge, Book-of-the-Month-Club Writing Fellowships, 1967-70. *Military service:* U.S. Army, Special Services, 1942-44.

MEMBER: National Council of Teachers of English (member of executive board, Conference on English Education), Modern Language Association of America, Poetry Society of America, Tippecanoe County (Indiana) Historical Society, Phi Beta Kappa.

AWARDS, HONORS: Ford Foundation fellow, 1954; Indiana Sesquicentennial poetry prize, 1967; Purdue Research Foundation grant for tour of most imaginative schools in England, Switzerland, and the Scandinavian countries, 1968; Best Teacher Award, Purdue University School of Humanities, 1974; Kemper McComb Award, Indiana Teachers of English, 1976.

WRITINGS: Your English Helper, Globe Books, 1950; (editor) Francis Parkman, *Oregon Trail* (school edition), Globe Books, 1953; (editor with Robert Frier) *Adventures in Modern Literature,* 4th edition, Harcourt, 1956, 6th edition (with Robert Lowell and others), 1970; (contributor) *Foundations of Education,* Wiley, 1963; *An Integrated Curriculum in Literature, Language, and Composition,* Purdue Research Foundation, 1967; (with Rozanne Knudson) *Selected Objectives for the English Language Arts,* Houghton, 1967; (contributor) *The New Book of Knowledge,* Grolier, 1967; (contributor) *College English,* Harcourt, 1968, new edition, 1978; (general editor) *Project English Study Units,* National Text Co., 1969.

Entertainments & Valedictions (poetry), Windfall Press, 1970; (with Andrew MacLeish and H. Wendell Smith) *A Glossary to Literature and Language,* Grosset, 1970; (with J. N. Hook and others) *Performance Objectives for High School English,* Ronald, 1971; (with others) *A Suit of Four* (poetry), Purdue University Press, 1973; *The Indiana Experience,* Indiana University Press, 1977; (with Victor H. Jones) *Beyond Graustark,* Kennikat, 1981; (with Smith) *A Glossary of Literature and Composition,* National Council of Teachers of English, 1983.

Author with Louis Zahner and others, of "English Language" series, Harcourt, 1967; author of fiction under pseudonyms Leslie Arnold and A. L. Leslie. Contributor to numerous periodicals, including *Saturday Review, New Republic, Quarterly Review of Literature, Prairie Schooner, American Poetry Review,* and *Christian Century. Quartet* (magazine of the arts), editor, 1962-69, poetry editor, 1969-73.

WORK IN PROGRESS: The Best of George Barr McCutcheon: A Reader; The Best of George Jean Nathan: A Reader; Some Light (collection of light verse).

SIDELIGHTS: A. L. Lazarus is competent in classical Greek and Latin, German, French, Spanish, and Italian. He writes that his viewpoint is "Humanist—as reflected in the magazine *Quartet,* [which is] 'dedicated to the integrity of the individual.'" *Avocational interests:* Travel ("Europe—especially England, France, and Scandinavia").

*   *   *

LAZARUS, Mell   1927-
(Mell)

PERSONAL: Born May 3, 1927, in New York, N.Y.; son of Sidney and Frances (Mushkin) Lazarus; married Eileen Hortense Israel, June 19, 1949; children: Marjorie, Susan, Catherine. *Education:* Educated in public schools in New York, N.Y. *Office:* Field Newspaper Syndicate, 401 North Wabash Avenue, Chicago, Ill. 60611.

CAREER: Cartoonist of comic strips "Miss Peach," 1957—, and "Momma," 1970—, both published by Field Newspaper Syndicate, Chicago, Ill. *Military service:* U.S. Naval Reserve, 1945. U.S. Air Force Reserve, 1951-54. *Member:* National Cartoonists Society (chairman of membership committee, 1965), Newspaper Comics Council, Writers Guild of America, Overseas Press Club, President's People-to-People Committee. *Awards, honors:* Named Humor Strip Cartoonist of the Year by the National Cartoonists Society, 1973 and 1979.

WRITINGS: (Under name Mell) *Miss Peach,* Prentice-Hall, 1960; *Miss Peach, Are These Your Children?,* Dial, 1964; *The Boss Is Crazy, Too: The Story of a Boy and His Dog of a Boss* (novel), Dial, 1964; *Dear Mr. ASPCA,* Taplinger, 1965; *Please Pass the P's and Q's,* World, 1967; (with B. Hazen) *Please Protect the Porcupine,* World, 1967.

Miss Peach Again, Grosset, 1972; *Momma,* Dell, 1972; *Francine, Your Face Would Stop a Clock,* afterword by Ann Landers, Sheed & Ward, 1975; *The Momma Treasury,* foreword by mother, Frances Lazarus, Sheed Andrews, 1978; *The Phantom Momma Strikes Again!,* Bantam, 1981; *Miss Peach,* Bantam, 1981; *Miss Peach Two,* Bantam, 1981; *Arthur, Isn't the Atmosphere Polluted Enough?,* Bantam, 1981; *I'll See You in My Dreams, At Least,* Bantam, 1981.

Plays: "Everybody into the Lake," "Elliman's Fly," "Lifetime Eggeream," 1969-70. Also author of scripts for special television programs "Turkey Day Pageant" and "Annual Heart Throb Ball."†

*   *   *

LEA, Joan
See NEUFELD, John (Arthur)

*   *   *

LEAB, Daniel Josef   1936-

PERSONAL: Born August 29, 1936, in Berlin, Germany; son

of Leo (a salesman) and Herta (Marcus) Leab; married Katharine Kyes (an editor), August 17, 1964; children: Abigail Elizabeth, Constance Martha, Marcus Rogers. *Education:* Columbia University, B.A., 1957, M.A., 1961, Ph.D., 1969; Harvard University, additional study, 1957-58. *Religion:* Jewish. *Home address:* P.O. Box 216, Washington, Conn. 06793. *Agent:* Wallace, Aitken & Shiel, 177 East 70th St., New York, N.Y. 10021. *Office:* Department of History, Seton Hall University, South Orange, N.J. 07079; and P.O. Box 216, Washington, Conn. 06793.

CAREER: Columbia University, New York, N.Y., instructor, 1966-68, assistant professor of history, 1969-74, associate dean of Columbia College, 1969-71, assistant dean of faculties, 1971, special assistant to executive vice-president, 1973-74; Seton Hall University, South Orange, N.J., associate professor, 1974-79, professor of history, 1979—, director of American studies, 1974-79. Director, Bancroft Parkman Corp., 1973—. Lecturer, graduate seminar in American studies, Falkenstein, West Germany, 1970, 1972, 1975. *Member:* American Historical Association, Organization of American Historians, American Association of University Professors, Century Club, Grolier Club. *Awards, honors:* Lawrence Chamberlain fellowship, 1973; Fulbright-Hays fellowship, 1977; National Endowment for the Humanities fellowship, 1981.

WRITINGS: (Contributor) A.J.P. Taylor, editor, *History of the Twentieth Century,* Purnell & Sons, 1969; *A Union of Individuals: The Formation of the American Newspaper Guild, 1933-36,* Columbia University Press, 1970; (contributor) Richard B. Morris and Graham W. Irwin, editors, *Harper Encyclopedia of the Modern World: A Concise Reference History from 1760 to the Present,* Harper, 1970; *From Sambo to Superspade: The Black Motion Picture Experience,* Houghton, 1975; (with wife, Katharine Leab) *The Auction Companion,* Harper, 1981; (with Maurice Neufeld and Dorothy Swanson) *American Working Class History: A Bibliography,* Bowker, 1983.

Contributor to *Monthly Labor Review, Gazette: International Journal for Mass Communications Studies, Labor History, Cultural Affairs, Midcontinent American Studies Journal, Journalism Quarterly, Columbia Journalism Review,* and *New England Quarterly.* Editor, *Labor History,* 1974—, and *American Book Prices Current,* 1974—. Editor, American history, *Columbia Encyclopedia,* 3rd edition, 1960-63; *Columbia Journalism Review,* assistant editor, 1963-66, research associate, 1967-69, contributing editor, 1971—; contributing editor, *Atlas World Press Review,* 1973—.

SIDELIGHTS: Daniel Josef and Katharine Kyes Leab's *The Auction Companion,* according to *Times Literary Supplement* critic Geoffrey Naylor, "has a good deal of useful advice for the novice on how to buy and how to sell, when to bid in person, or through an agent, or through the desk. . . . It is not just the tyro buyer, [however,] who will find the *Companion* helpful. It will be particularly useful even for experienced international purchasers for the up-to-date information it gives on local and national tax complications, and on export restrictions." Naylor concludes that the authors "convey their carefully prepared information with an engaging patter, and without being too jokey about it show that buying at auction, or merely frequenting the rooms as an informed browser, can be Fun."

"My interests professionally are based on my personal interests," Leab told *CA.* "These stem from work done as a graduate student, as a free-lance writer, and as a professional historian and teacher. If anything underlies my writing, research,

and other professional activities, it is that reasonable men can get together."

BIOGRAPHICAL/CRITICAL SOURCES: New York Times Book Review, November 9, 1975; *Times Literary Supplement,* January 9, 1976, January 1, 1982.

*   *   *

LECHT, Leonard A. 1920-

PERSONAL: Born October 16, 1920, in Providence, R.I.; son of Harry (a meat packer) and Sarah (Finkle) Lecht; married Jane A. Gillespie (a writer and editor), September 15, 1950; children: David Jonathan. *Education:* University of Minnesota, B.A., 1942; Columbia University, Ph.D., 1953. *Home:* 625 Main St., New York, N.Y. 10044.

CAREER: Columbia University, New York City, lecturer in economics, 1947-49; University of Texas, Main University (now University of Texas at Austin), Austin, assistant professor of economics, 1949-53; Carleton College, Northfield, Minn., assistant professor of economics, 1953-54; Long Island University, Brooklyn, N.Y., associate professor, 1954-56, professor of economics and sociology, 1956-63, chairman of department, 1954-63; National Planning Association, Washington, D.C., director of national goals project, 1963-67, director of Center for Priority Analysis, 1967-74; Conference Board, New York City, director of special project research, 1974-80; economic consultant, 1980—. Adjunct professor at City University of New York, 1982—. Consultant on merger of New York Central and Pennsylvania railroads, 1962-63, and to a number of government agencies and private groups concerned with manpower, education, and planning. *Military service:* U.S. Army, 1943-45. *Member:* American Economic Association, Industrial Relations Research Association, American Statistical Association, Phi Beta Kappa.

WRITINGS: Experience under Railway Labor Legislation, Columbia University Press, 1956; *The Dollar Cost of Our National Goals,* National Planning Association, 1965; *Goals, Priorities and Dollars: The Next Decade,* Macmillan, 1966; *Manpower Needs for National Goals in the 1970s,* Praeger, 1969; *Dollars for National Goals: Looking Ahead to 1981,* Wiley, 1974; *Evaluating Vocational Education Policies and Plans for the 1970s,* Praeger, 1974; *Changes in Occupational Characteristics,* Conference Board, 1976; *Occupational Choices and Training Needs: Prospects for the 1980s,* Praeger, 1977. Contributor to economic journals.

*   *   *

LEE, Dennis (Beynon) 1939-

PERSONAL: Born August 31, 1939, in Toronto, Ontario, Canada; son of Walter and Louise (Garbutt) Lee; married Donna Youngblut, June 24, 1962 (divorced); children: two daughters, one son. *Education:* University of Toronto, B.A., 1962, M.A., 1964. *Address:* c/o House of Anansi Press, 35 Britain St., Toronto, Ontario, Canada M5A 1R7.

CAREER: Writer. University of Toronto, Victoria College, Toronto, Ontario, lecturer in English, 1964-67; Rochdale College (experimental institution), Toronto, self-described "resource person," 1967-69; House of Anansi Press, Toronto, co-founder and editor, 1967-72. Editorial consultant, Macmillan of Canada, 1973-78; poetry editor, McClelland & Stewart, 1981—. Lyricist for television series "Fraggle Rock," 1982—.

AWARDS, HONORS: Governor-General's Award for Poetry, 1972, for *Civil Elegies;* Independent Order of Daughters of the Empire award, 1974; Canadian Association of Children's Librarians, Best Book Medals, 1974 and 1977, and English Medal, 1975, for *Alligator Pie;* named to Hans Christian Andersen Honour List and recipient of Canadian Library Association award, both 1976, both for *Alligator Pie.*

WRITINGS: Kingdom of Absence (poetry), House of Anansi, 1967; *Civil Elegies* (poetry), House of Anansi, 1968, revised edition published as *Civil Elegies and Other Poems,* 1972; (co-editor) *The University Game* (essays), House of Anansi, 1968; (editor) *T. O. Now: The Young Toronto Poets* (poetry), House of Anansi, 1968; *Wiggle to the Laundromat* (children's poetry), New Press, 1970; *Alligator Pie* (children's poetry), Macmillan (Toronto), 1974, Houghton, 1975; *Nicholas Knock and Other People* (children's poetry), Macmillan (Toronto), 1974, Houghton, 1975.

The Death of Harold Ladoo (poetry), Kanchenjunga Press, 1976; *Savage Fields: An Essay in Cosmology and Literature,* House of Anansi, 1977; *Garbage Delight* (children's poetry), Macmillan (Toronto), 1977, Houghton, 1978; *The Ordinary Bath* (juvenile), McClelland & Stewart, 1977; *Jelly Belly* (children's poetry), Macmillan, 1983; *Cadence, Country, Silence* (essays), McClelland & Stewart, in press. Also author of a collection of poetry, *The Gods,* 1979; co-editor of two high school poetry anthologies.

SIDELIGHTS: Canadian author Dennis Lee, commenting on his work in a speech delivered at the 1975 Loughborough Conference in Toronto and reprinted in *Canadian Children's Literature,* examined the way his attitude toward children's verse evolved. Contemplating Mother Goose as an adult and parent, he made an important personal discovery. Explained the poet in his speech: "The nursery rhymes I love . . . are necessarily exotic. . . . But they were in no way exotic to the people who first devised them and chanted them. . . . The air of far-off charm and simpler pastoral life which now hangs over Mother Goose was in no way a part of those rhymes' initial existence. . . . The people who told nursery rhymes for centuries would be totally boggled if they could suddenly experience them the way children do here and now, as a collection of references to things they never see or do, to places they have never heard of and may never visit, told in words they will sometimes meet only in those verses."

Convinced that "the imagination leads always and only to the holy city of elsewhere," Lee decided to build his imaginary "city" from the language of familiar objects—elements of contemporary life made extraordinary by their unique use and sound in verse. Maintaining that "you are poorer if you never find your own time and place speaking words of their own," he believes the "fire hydrants and hockey sticks and T-4 slips" of today are just as remote to very young children as curds and whey. Thus, he says, "to look for living nursery rhymes in the hockey-sticks and the high-rises that [children know] first-hand [is not] to go on a chauvinistic trip, nor to wallow in a fad of trendy relevence. It [is] nothing but a rediscovery of what Mother Goose [has been] about for centuries."

Lee's poetic narratives, tongue-twisters, and riddles have been compared to the nonsense verse of Lewis Carroll and A. A. Milne. Lee, however, emphasizes the here-and-now objects of daily life in his work—things children may or may not recognize. Canadian places, history, politics, and colloquial diction, as well as purely invented words, all play a part in the pieces, which the poet says are "never calculated for the read-

ing level of a specific age group." Many critics feel the readability and repeatability of the poems—rather than "references to things they never see or do, to places they have never heard of"—are what fascinate young children. As Betsy English writes in *In Review: Canadian Books for Children,* the strong rhythms, rhymes, and other sound devices in Lee's work produce "a sense of gaiety, an appeal that shouts for reading aloud."

"I used to know what constitutes a good kid's poem," Lee muses, "and now that I write and read them aloud all the time, I don't. At least not the way I used to." While he finds it important to "get in touch with one of [the children within himself] and then follow his nose, going wherever the child's interests lead," he also emphasizes control. "I'm quite unwilling to surrender any of the adult's prerogatives; . . . the thing has to be written well," he contends. "This involves using the instinct of the child and the craft of the adult." The author focuses not on past works, but on poems that are waiting to be written. Assessing *Alligator Pie* and *Nicholas Knock and Other People,* Lee concludes: "I'm anything but satisfied. Not so much because of what is in the books, but because of what isn't. . . . I think: there are terrors, and joys, and states of daily despair and amazement which I was barely making passes at here. How could I take this as anything but a first flirtation?"

BIOGRAPHICAL/CRITICAL SOURCES: Fiddlehead, spring, 1968, March-April, 1969; *Canadian Forum,* March, 1968; *Saturday Night,* July, 1968, August, 1969; *In Review: Canadian Books for Children,* spring, 1971, winter, 1975; Sheila Egoff, *The Republic of Childhood: A Critical Guide to Canadian Children's Literature,* Oxford University Press, 1975; *Canadian Children's Literature,* Number IV, 1976; *Children's Literature Review,* Volume III, Gale, 1978; *Descant,* winter, 1982.

*   *   *

LEE, Hahn-Been 1921-

PERSONAL: Born February 9, 1921, in Korea; son of Sung-Chong (a farmer) and Sung-yo (Han) Lee; married Chung-Hay Ryu, October 28, 1955; children: Wonshik (George), Sonni (Susy). *Education:* Seoul National University, B.A., 1949, Ph.D., 1967; Harvard University, M.B.A., 1951. *Religion:* Presbyterian. *Home:* Samho Apt. Ra-801, 724 Bangbe Dong, Kangnam Ku, Seoul, South Korea.

CAREER: Government of South Korea, Seoul, budget director, 1958-61, vice-minister of finance, 1961; Korean ambassador to Switzerland, 1962-65; University of Hawaii, East-West Center, Honolulu, senior specialist, 1965-66; Seoul National University, Graduate School of Public Administration, Seoul, dean and professor, 1966-70; University of Hawaii, East-West Technology Institute, director, 1970-72; Soong Jun University, Seoul, president, 1973-76; Ajou Institute of Technology, Suwon, Korea, president, 1977-79; writer. Deputy prime minister and minister of Economic Planning Board, Government of Korea, 1979-80.

Chairman of board, Korea Advanced Institute of Science and Technology, 1981-82. Member of board, Asian Institute of Technology (Bangkok), 1973—. Visiting professor, Yonsei University Graduate School, 1981—. Member of Administrative Reform Commission, Republic of Korea, and Aspen Institute for Humanistic Studies, 1980—. Conference moderator, Pacific Conference on Urban Growth, 1967; seminar leader, Asian Workshop on Higher Education, 1969. Fellow, Woodrow Wilson International Center for Scholars, 1982-83.

MEMBER: Korean Association for Public Administration (founding member), Eastern Regional Organization for Public Administration (chairman of development administration group, 1966-70; vice-chairman of council, 1968-70), Korean Society for Future Studies (founder). *Awards, honors:* Republic of Korea, honor of Diplomatic Service Merit, order of Heungin, and honor of Educational Merit, order of Moran.

WRITINGS: The Way a Small Country Lives: The Case of Switzerland, Dong-A Publishing, 1965; *Korea: Time, Change, and Administration,* East-West Center Publications, 1968; *A Handbook on Development Administration Curriculum,* International Institute of Administrative Sciences (Brussels), 1969; (contributor) Edward W. Weidner, editor, *Development Administration in Asia,* Duke University Press, 1969; (contributor) Dwight Waldo, editor, *Development Administration: Temporal Aspects,* Duke University Press, 1969; *Theory and Strategy of National Development,* Pagyongsa, 1969.

(Editor with Abelardo G. Samonte) *Administrative Reforms in Asia,* Eropa (Manila), 1970; *Creativity and Innovation,* Samwha Publishing, 1973; *A Window Looking into the Future,* Jungwoo Sa, 1978; *The Road to the Future,* Saemteo Sa, 1980; *An Optique of Future Perfect,* Voice Sa, 1982; *Future, Innovation and Development,* Panmem Book Co. (Seoul), 1982.

*   *   *

LEFEBVRE, Henri   1901-

PERSONAL: Born June 16, 1901, in Hagetmau, Landes, France; son of Rene (a Ministry of Finance official) and Jeanne (Darracq) Lefebvre; married second wife, 1981; children: (first marriage) Pierre, Joel, Roland, Janine, Olivier, Armelle. *Education:* Lycee Louis le Grand, baccalaureat, 1917; Faculte des Lettres d'Aix en Provence, licence de philosophie, 1919; University of Paris, Sorbonne, diplome d'etudes superieures de philosophie, 1920, Doctorat d'Etat, 1959. *Home:* 30 rue Rambuteau, Paris III, France.

CAREER: Professeur, 1930-40; member of French Resistance, 1940-43; reinstated as artistic director of Radiodiffusion Francais (French radio-broadcasting), Toulouse, France, 1944-49; Centre National de la Recherche Scientifique, Paris, France, director of research, 1949-61; University of Strasbourg, Strasbourg, France, professor of sociology, 1962-65; affiliated with University of Paris-Nanterre, Nanterre, France, 1965-73. Member of Comite de Redaction, La Nouvelle Critique, 1949-57. *Awards, honors:* Prix des Critiques, 1959, for *La Somme et le reste.*

WRITINGS: Le Nationalisme contre les nations, Editions Sociales Internationales, 1937 (seized in November, 1939); *Hitler au pouvoir: Bilan de cinq annees de fascisme en Allemagne,* Bureau d'Editions (Paris), 1938 (withdrawn from sale by suppression of publisher, 1939); *Nietzsche,* Editions Sociales Internationales, 1939 (withdrawn from sale by suppression of publisher); *Le Materialisme dialectique,* Alcan, 1939 (placed on the "Otto" list of forbidden books and destroyed by Nazi authorities during the occupation), 5th edition, 1964, translation by John Sturrock published as *Dialectical Materialism,* J. Cape, 1968.

L'Existentialisme, Editions du Sagittaire (Paris), 1946; *Logique formelle et logique dialectique,* Editions Sociales Internationales (Paris), 1947; *Critique de la vie quotidienne: Introduction,* Grasset, 1947, 3rd edition, Editions l'Arche (Paris), 1981; *Descartes,* Editeurs Francais Reunis (Paris), 1947; *Marx et la liberte,* Editions des Trois Collines (Geneva), 1947; *Le Marx-*

isme, Presses Universitaires de France, 1947, 19th edition, 1982; *Pour connaitre le pensee de Marx,* Editions Bordas (Paris), Volume I, 1949, Volume II, 1954; *Diderot,* Editeurs Francais Reunis, 1949.

Contribution a l'esthetique, Editions Sociales Internationales, 1953; *Musset dramaturge,* Editions l'Arche, 1953, revised edition, 1970; *Rabelais,* Editeurs Francais Reunis, 1955; *Pignon,* Editions Falaise (Paris), 1956; *Pour connaitre la pensee de Lenine,* Editions Bordas, 1957; *Les Problemes actuels du marxisme,* Presses Universitaires de France, 1958, 3rd edition, 1963; *La Somme et le reste,* Editions la Nef de Paris, 1959.

Introduction a la modernite, Editions de Minuit, 1962; *La Vallee de Campan: Etude de sociologie rurale,* Presses Universitaires de France, 1964; *La Proclamation de la Commune,* Gallimard, 1965; *Metaphilosophie,* Editions de Minuit, 1965; *Les Pyrenees,* Editions Rencontres (Lausanne), 1965; *Marx sociologue,* Presses Universitaires de France, 1966, translation by Norbert Guterman published as *The Sociology of Marx,* Pantheon, 1968; *Le Langage et la societe,* Gallimard, 1966; *Position: Contre les technocrates,* Gontheir Editeur, 1967, new edition published as *Vers le cybernanthrope,* 1971; *Le Droit a la ville,* Editions Anthropos, Volume I, 1968, Volume II: *Espace et politique,* 1972, Volume III, 1977; *La Vie quotidienne dans le monde contemporain,* Gallimard, 1968, translation by Sacha Rabinovitch published as *Everyday Life in the Modern World,* Harper, 1971; *L'Irruption de Nanterre au sommet,* Editions Anthropos, 1968, translation by Alfred Ehrenfeld published as *The Explosion: Marxism and the French Revolution,* Monthly Review Press, 1969; *Marx,* Presses Universitaires de France, 1969.

Le Manifeste differentialiste, Gallimard, 1970; *La Fin de l'histoire,* Editions de Minuit, 1970; *La Revolution urbaine,* Gallimard, 1970; *Du rural a l'urbain,* Editions Anthropos, 1970; *Au-dela de structuralisme,* Feuilles, 1970; *Trois Textes pour le theatre,* Editions Anthropos, 1972; *La Pensee marxiste et la ville,* Edition Casterman, 1972; *La Survie du capitalisme,* Editions Anthropos, 1973, translation by Frank Bryant published as *The Survival of Capitalism: Reproduction of the Relations of Production,* St. Martin's, 1976; (with Pierre Fougeyrollas) *Le Jeu de Kostas Axelos,* Edition Fata Morgana, 1973; *La Production de l'espace,* Editions Anthropos, 1974; *Le Temps des meprises,* Editions Stock, 1975; *L'Ideologie structuraliste,* Editions de Seuil, 1975; *Hegel, Marx, Nietzsche ou le royaume des ombres,* Editions Casterman, 1975; *De l'Etat,* four volumes, Union Generale d'editions, 1975-78; (with Catherine Regulier) *La Revolution n'est plus ce qu'elle etait,* Editions Libres Hallier, 1978.

La Presence et l'Absence, Editions Casterman, 1980; *Une Pensee devenue Monde,* Edition Fayard, 1980.

Editor and author of introductions with C. Norbert Guterman; all published by Gallimard: *Oeuvres choisies de Karl Marx,* 1934, new edition in two volumes, 1964; *La Conscience mystifiee,* 1936; *Morceaux choisis de Hegel,* 1938; *Cahiers de Lenine sur la dialectique de Hegel,* 1938 (placed on the "Otto" list of forbidden books and destroyed by Nazi authorities during the occupation), new edition, 1967.

Contributor of numerous articles to scientific and other publications, such as *Le Monde* and *France-Observateur.*

WORK IN PROGRESS: Qu'est ce que Penser?; Introduction a la Rythmanalyse, with Regulier.

SIDELIGHTS: Henri Lefebvre's interest in Karl Marx has led to several important books illuminating the thought and writings of the German philosopher. Of his book, *The Sociology of Marx,* a *Choice* reviewer states: "Translation of this seminal work, particularly in view of the current interest in Marxism as a frame for thought rather than a fixed ideology, is a noteworthy event for scholars whatever their philosophical proclivities. Lefebvre argues that characterization of Marxism as 'economic determinism' is a partial analysis based on failure to distinguish between the work of Marx as a critic of capitalism and the work of Marx as a student of human relations over the course of history."

Lefebvre has traveled to Canada, the United States, Japan, Venezuela, Colombia, Chile, and most European countries, often as guest lecturer at universities.

BIOGRAPHICAL/CRITICAL SOURCES: New York Times Book Review, May 19, 1968; *Choice,* October, 1968; *Books and Bookmen,* February, 1969.

* * *

LEFEBVRE d'ARGENCE, Rene-Yvon 1928-

PERSONAL: Born August 21, 1928, in Plouescat, France; raised in France, Syria, and Vietnam; son of Marc (a general and a mayor) and Andree (Thierry) Lefebvre d'Argence; married Ritva Anneli Pelanne, September 7, 1955; children: Chantal, Yann, Luc. *Education:* Attended Ecole Nationale des Langues Orientales Vivantes, 1950-52; Sorbonne, University of Paris, License-es Lettres, 1952; additional study at Pembroke College, Cambridge. *Religion:* Roman Catholic. *Home:* 16 Midhill, Mill Valley, Calif. 94941. *Office:* Avery Brundage Collection, Asian Art Museum of San Francisco, Golden Gate Park, San Francisco, Calif. 94118.

CAREER: Museum director at Ecole Francaise d'Extreme-Orient, Vietnam, 1954-56; Cernuschi Museum, Paris, France, curator, 1956-59; French Government scholar in Taiwan, 1959-61; University of California, Berkeley, professor of Asian art history, 1962-65; M. H. de Young Museum, San Francisco, Calif., director of Avery Brundage Collection, 1964-69; Asian Art Museum of San Francisco, San Francisco, director and chief curator, 1969—. Founder and board member, Ecole Francaise of San Francisco, 1967—; French-American Bilingual School, San Francisco, president, 1976-79, executive vice-president, 1979—; founder, board member, and vice-president, Chinese-American Bilingual School, 1981—. Member of advisory committee, Society for Asian Art, 1964; member of San Francisco-Osaka Sister City Committee, 1980—, San Francisco-Seoul Sister City Committee, 1980—, San Francisco-Shanghai Sister City Committee, 1980—, advisory council of Marin Cultural Center, 1981—, and of executive board, Institute of Sino-American Studies, 1981—; trustee, Asian Art Foundation, 1979—. *Military service:* Served with the Free French Army in Indo-China during World War II; received Medaille de la Reconnaissance Francaise. *Member:* Sociedad Asiatic de la Argentina (corresponding member).

AWARDS, HONORS: Chevalier de l'Etoile du Nort, Government of Sweden, 1968; Order of Merit, Avery Brundage Foundation, 1968; honorary doctorate, Chinese Academy, Taiwan, 1969; Chevalier de l'Order National du Merite, Government of France, 1970.

WRITINGS: Les Ceramiques a base chocolatee, Ecole Francaise d'Extreme-Orient, 1958; *Ancient Chinese Bronzes in the Avery Brundage Collection: A Selection of Vessels, Weapons, Bells, Belthooks, Mirrors, and Various Artifacts from the Shang to the T'ang Dynasty, Including a Group of Gold and Silver Wares,* Diablo Press, 1966; *Chinese Ceramics in the Avery Brundage Collection: A Selection of Containers, Pillows, Figurines, and Models from the Neolithic Period to Modern Times,* M. H. de Young Museum Society, 1967; *Chinese Treasures from the Avery Brundage Collection,* Asia Society, 1968; (author of introduction) *Selected Works of World Art: Avery Brundage Collection* (exhibition catalogue), Comite Organizador de los Juegos de la XIX Olimpiada, 1968; *Indian and Southeast Asian Stone Sculptures from the Avery Brundage Collection,* Pasadena Art Museum, 1969.

Chang Dai-chien: A Retrospective Exhibition, Illustrating a Selection of Fifty-four Works Painted by the Master from 1928 to 1970, Kodansha, 1972; *Chinese Jades in the Avery Brundage Collection: A Selection of Religious Symbols, Insignia of Rank, Ceremonial Weapons, Pendants, Ornaments, Figurines, Miniature Mountains and Containers from the Neolithic Period to Modern Times,* M. H. de Young Museum Society, 1972; *The Hans Popper Collection of Oriental Art: A Selection of One Hundred Thirty-One Chinese Ancient Bronzes, Sculptures, Ceramics, and Korean Celadons,* Kodansha, 1973; (with Diana Turner, Fred A. Cline, Alexander C. Soper, and others) *Chinese, Korean, and Japanese Sculpture: The Avery Brundage Collection, Asian Art Museum of San Francisco,* Kodansha, 1974; (editor and author of introduction) *Asian Art: Museum and University Collections in the San Francisco Bay Area,* Allanheld & Schram, 1978.

Also author of *A Decade of Collecting,* 1976, *Bronze Vessels of Ancient China in the Avery Brundage Collection,* 1977, and *Five Thousand Years of Korean Art,* 1979. Contributor to journals in France, Asia, and the United States.

WORK IN PROGRESS: Ancient Chinese Bronzes in the Avery Brundage Collection, Volume I; *Atlas of Lin-an Fu: Capital of Sung China.*

SIDELIGHTS: Rene-Yvon Lefebvre d'Argence told *CA:* "Being in charge of one of the major collections of Oriental art in the world, I regard it as one of my prime responsibilities to make this collection accessible to as many people as possible. This can only be achieved through an intensive program of publication.

"Raised and partly trained in the Far East, I know Chinese, Japanese, and Vietnamese. I am also fluent in French and Finnish."

* * *

LEISTER, Mary 1917-

PERSONAL: Surname is pronounced *Lye*-ster; born October 4, 1917, in Brackenridge, Pa.; daughter of W. Clare and Martha (Nolf) McFarland; married Robert E. Leister (an electronics engineer), June 4, 1942 (divorced, 1978). *Education:* Attended Johns Hopkins University. *Residence:* Sykesville, Md.

CAREER: Writer and lecturer. Has worked as a stenographer and volunteer elementary school teacher. *Member:* International Wildlife Association, National Wildlife Association, National Audubon Society, Natural History Association, Environmental Defense Fund, Maryland Ornithological Society.

WRITINGS: The Silent Concert (juvenile), Bobbs-Merrill, 1970; (contributor) *From Falcons to Forests,* Harper, 1973; *Wildlings* (adult nonfiction), Stemmer House, 1976; *Flying Fur, Fin, and Scale: Strange Animals that Swoop and Soar,* Stemmer House, 1977; (contributor) *Patterns,* Laidlaw Brothers, 1978; *Wee Green Witch,* Stemmer House, 1978; *Seasons of Heron*

Pond (adult nonfiction), Stemmer House, 1981. Author of columns in *Baltimore Sunday Sun*, 1972—, and "Read Aloud Nature Story," in *Humpty Dumpty*, 1976-79. Contributor of stories, articles, and poems to nature and children's magazines, including *Ranger Rick, Boys' Life, Jack and Jill, National Wildlife*, and *American Forests*.

WORK IN PROGRESS: Children's books, mainly concerned with nature and wildlife.

SIDELIGHTS: Mary Leister writes: "With a deep belief in the inter-relatedness, the oneness, of all life—and believing that, possibly, everything is alive—I write of animals, and plants, and weather, and water, and earth that others may learn to love all those things that share our small planet, and accord them the right to grow and to be. I realize that this is a closed system, that one species must prey upon another, that all life lives upon life, but it should be done respectfully and not wantonly. However, mostly my writing is light and happy and makes creatures interesting to humans because of the out-of-the-ordinary observations I have been permitted to make."

AVOCATIONAL INTERESTS: Camping, hiking, traveling, reading, gardening, dogs, cats, public speaking, good conversation.

BIOGRAPHICAL/CRITICAL SOURCES: Baltimore Sunday Sun, June 20, 1976; *Valley News Dispatch,* July 27, 1976; *New York Times,* August 7, 1976; *National Wildlife Federation Conservation News,* September 15, 1976; *Detroit Free Press,* October 24, 1976.

*   *   *

LENT, Blair
(Ernest Small)

PERSONAL: Born in Boston, Mass.; son of Stanley Blair (an electrical engineer) and Hazel (Small) Lent. *Education:* Boston Museum School, graduate (with honors), 1953; studied art in Switzerland and Italy, 1953-54.

CAREER: Container Corp. of America, Medford, Mass., assistant art director, 1954-56; Bresnick Advertising Co., Boston, Mass., creative designer, 1957-61; professional artist and author and illustrator of children's books. Work has been exhibited at Boston Arts Festival, 1953, 1955-57, Boston Printmaker's Show, 1955-61, 1963, Institute of Contemporary Art, 1955, American Institute of Graphic Arts shows, 1964, 1967, Illustrations for Children, University Art Gallery, Albany, N.Y., 1972, Contemporary American Illustrators of Children's Books, Rutgers University, 1974-75, Museum of Fine Arts, Boston, 1977, Brattleboro Museum, 1980, and University of Connecticut, 1982; has had one-man shows of silk screen prints and oils in Provincetown, Mass., 1961, and collage and oils in New York City, 1962; also one-man show, The Work of Blair Lent for Picture Books, Wiggin Gallery, Boston, 1970. *Military service:* U.S. Army Reserve Engineers.

AWARDS, HONORS: Cummings Memorial traveling scholarship, 1953-54, and Clarissa Barlett traveling scholarship, 1967-68, both from Boston Museum of Fine Arts; *Pistachio* and *The Wave* were included on American Institute of Graphic Arts list of best children's books, 1963-64, *John Tabor's Ride* and *Baba Yaga*, 1965-66, *From King Boggen's Hall to Nothing-at-All* and *Why the Sun and the Moon Live in the Sky*, 1967-68, and *The Funny Little Woman*, 1974-75; *The Wave* was named one of the ten best illustrated books of the year, *New York Times*, 1964, received silver medal for illustration

and design, Bienal Internacional du Livro e Arte Grafica, San Paulo, Brazil, 1965, and was runner-up for Caldecott Medal, 1965.

Baba Yaga was an honor book at *New York Herald Tribune*'s Children's Book Festival, 1966; included on the *New York Times* list of the year's best juveniles are *Baba Yaga, John Tabor's Ride*, and *Why the Sun and the Moon Live in the Sky*, 1966, *The Little Match Girl*, 1968, and *The Funny Little Woman*, 1972; *Boston Globe* Horn Book citation, 1968, for *Tikki Tikki Tembo;* runner-up for Caldecott Medal, 1969, for *Why the Sun and the Moon Live in the Sky*, and 1971, for *The Angry Moon;* Caldecott Medal, 1973, for *The Funny Little Woman;* bronze medal, Biennale of Illustration, 1969, for *From King Boggen's Hall to Nothing-at-All;* Hans Christian Andersen honor book, 1973, for *The Funny Little Woman;* Nakawori Prize, Tokyo, Japan, 1975, for *Why the Sun and the Moon Live in the Sky;* nominee, American Book Award for children's paperback, 1982, for *The Angry Moon*.

WRITINGS—Self-illustrated: *Pistachio* (Junior Literary Guild selection), Little, Brown, 1963; *John Tabor's Ride*, Little, Brown, 1966; (pseudonym, Ernest Small, used for author's credit; illustrations by Blair Lent) *Baba Yaga*, Houghton, 1966; (compiler) *From King Boggen's Hall to Nothing-at-All* (poetry), Little, Brown, 1967; *Bayberry Bluff*, Houghton, 1984; *A Boston Fantasy*, Dutton, 1984.

Illustrator: *The Wave* (adapted by Margaret Hodges from Lafcadio Hearn), Houghton, 1964; Olga Economakis, *Oasis of the Stars*, Coward, 1965; Franklyn M. Branley, *The Christmas Sky*, Crowell-Collier, 1966; Arlene Mosel, *Tikki Tikki Tembo*, Holt, 1968; Elphinstone Dayrell, *Why the Sun and the Moon Live in the Sky*, Houghton, 1968; Hans Christian Andersen, *The Little Match Girl*, Houghton, 1968; Jan Wahl, *May Horses*, Delacorte, 1969; William Sleator, *The Angry Moon*, Little, Brown, 1970; Arlene Mosel, *The Funny Little Woman*, Dutton, 1972; Kornei Chukovsky, *The Telephone*, Seymour Lawrence, 1976; Aileen Fisher, *I Stood upon a Mountain*, Crowell, 1976.

Contributor to *Horn Book, Wilson Library Bulletin*, and *Publishers Weekly.* Cover designs have appeared on *Atlantic* and *Boston Magazine.* Adapted Elphinstone Dayrell's *Why the Sun and the Moon Live in the Sky* into animated film, 1970, distributed by A.C.I. Films.

SIDELIGHTS: Blair Lent used his second Boston Museum scholarship for six months travel in Russia. He states: "I sketched the old, but rapidly modernizing cities and villages, and studied local folklore. I have always been fascinated with the vast plains, the birch forest, and the wooden villages of Russia."

Lent has built himself a studio on the edge of a pond on his land in northeast Connecticut.

BIOGRAPHICAL/CRITICAL SOURCES: Francis Brow, *Collage*, Pitman, 1963; Lee Bennet Hopkins, *Books Are by People*, Citation Press, 1969; *Horn Book*, August, 1973; Lee Kingman, *Newbery and Caldecott Medal Books, 1966-1975*, Horn Book, 1975; Barbara Bader, *American Picture Books from Noah's Ark to The Beast Within*, Macmillan, 1976; Kingman, *The Illustrator's Notebook*, Horn Book, 1978.

*   *   *

LEON-PORTILLA, Miguel 1926-

PERSONAL: Born February 22, 1926, in Mexico City, Mexico; son of Miguel Leon-Ortiz and Luisa Portilla; married Ascension Hennandez Trivino (a historian), May 2, 1965. *Education:*

Loyola University of Los Angeles (now Loyola Marymount University), B.A., 1948, M.A., 1952; National University of Mexico, Ph.D., 1956. *Home:* Alberto Zamora 103, Coyoscan, Mexico City, District Federal 21, Mexico.

CAREER: Mexico City College (now University of the Americas), Mexico City, Mexico, professor of ancient Mexican history, 1954-57; National University of Mexico, Mexico City, professor of ancient Mexican history, 1957—, director of Institute of Historical Research, 1963—. Lecturer at universities in the United States, Israel, and Europe; distinguished lecturer at the seventy-fourth meeting of the American Anthropological Association, 1974. Member of council, Institute of Different Civilizations, Brussels, 1959—; Inter-American Indian Institute, secretary general, 1955-60, director, 1960-66; secretary general of thirty-fifth International Congress of Americanists, 1962. *Member:* Royal Spanish Academy of History, Royal Spanish Academy of the Language, Societe des Americanistes de Paris.

AWARDS, HONORS: Prize Elias Sourazky, bestowed by Mexican Secretary of Education, 1966; Guggenheim fellow, 1970; Fulbright fellow, 1976-77; Commendatore de la Republica Italiana, 1977; Serra Award, 1978; D.H.L. honoris causa, Southern Methodist University, 1980; Mexican National Prize in history and the social sciences, 1981.

WRITINGS—In English: *Voyages of Francisco De Ortega: California, 1632-1636,* Dawson's Book Shop, 1973; (with Edward H. Spicer) *Aztecs and Navajos: A Reflection on the Right of Not Being Engulfed* [and] *Indian Identity versus Assimilation* (the former by Leon-Portilla, the latter by Spicer), Weatherhead Foundation, 1975; (editor and author of foreword, introduction, and notes) *Native Mesoamerican Spirituality: Ancient Myths, Discourses, Stories, Doctrines, Hymns, Poems from the Aztec, Yucatec, Quiche-Maya, and Other Sacred Traditions,* Paulist Press, 1980.

In English translation: *La Filosofia Nahuatl: Estudiada en sus Fuentes,* Inter-American Indian Institute, 1956, 4th edition, Institute of Historical Research, National University of Mexico, 1974, translation by Jack Emory Davis published as *Aztec Thought and Culture: A Study of the Ancient Nahuatl Mind,* University of Oklahoma Press, 1963; (editor and author of introduction and notes) *Vision de los Vencidos: Relaciones indigenas de la conquista,* National University of Mexico, 1959, 5th edition, 1971, translation by Lysander Kemp published as *The Broken Spears: The Aztec Account of the Conquest of Mexico,* Beacon Press, 1962.

Los Antiguos Mexicanos a traves de sus Cronicas y Cantares, Fondo de Cultura Economica, 1961, 3rd edition, 1970, translation published as *The Ancient Mexicans,* Rutgers University Press, 1968; (contributor) *Estudios de historia de la filosofia en Mexico,* National University of Mexico, 1963, 2nd edition, 1973, translation by A. Robert Caponigri published as *Major Trends in Mexican Philosophy,* University of Notre Dame Press, 1966; *Las Literaturas Precolombinas de Mexico,* Editorial Pormaca, 1964, translation by Leon-Portilla and Grace Lobanov published as *Pre-Columbian Literature of Mexico,* University of Oklahoma Press, 1969.

In Spanish: (Compiler) *Indices de America indigena y Boletin indigenista,* fourteen volumes, Inter-American Indian Institute, 1954; (with Salvador Mateo) *Catalogo de los codices indigenas del Mexico antiguo,* [Mexico City], 1957; *Siete ensayos sobre cultura Nahuatl,* National University of Mexico, 1958; (translator and author of introduction) Bernardino de Sahagun, *Ritos,*

sacerdotes y atavios de los dioses, Institute of Historical Research, National University of Mexico, 1958.

Imagen del Mexico antiguo, University of Buenos Aires Press, 1963; *Historia documental de Mexico,* Institute of Historical Research, National University of Mexico, 1964, 2nd edition, 1974; *El reverso de la Conquista: Relaciones Aztecas, Mayas e Incas,* Editorial J. Mortiz, 1964, 2nd edition, 1970; *Trece Poestas del Mundo Azteca,* Institute of Historical Research, National University of Mexico, 1968, 2nd edition, 1975; *Quetzalcoatl,* Fondo de Cultura Economica, 1968.

(Editor and author of introduction and notes) Jaime Bravo, Juan de Ugarte, and Clemente Guillen, *Nueva entrada y establecimiento en el puerto de La Paz, 1720,* National University of Mexico, 1970; (compiler) *De Teotihuacan a los Aztecas: Antologia de fuentes e interpretaciones historicas,* Institute of Historical Research, National University of Mexico, 1971; (author of introduction) Andres de Olmos, *Arte para aprender la lengua Mexicana,* Levy, 1972; *Nezahualcoyotl: Poesia y pensamiento, 1402-1472,* Gobierno del Estado de Mexico, 1972; *Religion de los Nicaraos: Analisis y comparacion de tradicionos culturales nahuas,* Institute of Historical Research, National University of Mexico, 1972; *Tiempo y realidad en el Pensamiento Maya: Ensayo de acercamiento,* foreword by J. Eric S. Thompson, Institute of Historical Research, National University of Mexico, 1973; *Microhistoria de la Ciudad de Mexico,* Secretary of Works and Services, Department of the Federal District (Mexico City), 1974.

Culturas en Peligro, Alianza Editorial, 1976; *La Mineria en Mexico: Estudios sobre su desarrollo historico,* National University of Mexico, 1978; *Mexico-Tenochtitlan: Su Espacio y tiempo sagrados,* National Institute of Anthropology and History, 1978; *Los Manifesto en Nahuatl de Emiliano Zapata,* Institute of Historical Research, National University of Mexico, 1978; (editor, translator, and author of introduction) *Literatura del Mexico antiguo: Los Textos en lengua Nahuatl,* Biblioteca Ayacucho, 1978; *Los Olmecas en Chalco-Amaquemecan: Un Testimonio de Sahagun aprovechado por Chimalpahin,* Centro de Estudios Bernardino de Sahagun, 1980.

Also author of *El Templo Mayor de Mexico,* 1982. Contributor to periodicals in Mexico, Belgium, France, and the United States, including *Evergreen Review, Current Anthropology, Americas,* and *America Indigena.*

WORK IN PROGRESS: A study "that includes indigenous testimonies on the sixteenth-century Spanish-Aztec religious confrontation; a work on the lives and productions of twenty pre-Columbian Aztec poets."

SIDELIGHTS: Miguel Leon-Portilla writes that his "main concern has been to present in a humanistic way the rich heritage of the history, art, and literature of ancient Mexico." *La Filosofia Nahuatl* was published in Moscow in 1961, and *Vision de los Vencidos* has appeared in German, French, and Italian. Leon-Portilla is fluent in English, French, German, Italian, and Aztec; his travels cover most countries of the Americas, and many in Europe and the Far East.

BIOGRAPHICAL/CRITICAL SOURCES: American Indigena, October, 1966.

* * *

LESLIE, A. L.
    See LAZARUS, A(rnold) L(eslie)

LESTER, James
    See BLAKE, L(eslie) J(ames)

*   *   *

LEVINE, Isaac Don   1892-1981

PERSONAL: Born February 1, 1892, in Mozyr, Russia (now U.S.S.R.); came to United States in 1911; died February 15, 1981, in Venice, Fla.; son of Don and Sarah (Maloff) Levine; married Mary Leavitt; married second wife, Ruth Newman, December 14, 1936; children: (first marriage) Robert Don. *Education:* Educated at schools in Russia and Kansas City, Mo. *Residence:* Waldorf, Md. 20601.

CAREER: Kansas City Star, Kansas City, Mo., contributor of special articles, 1914; *New York Tribune,* New York City, foreign news editor, 1917; foreign correspondent for *Chicago Daily News,* Chicago, Ill., 1919-21 and for Hearst Newspaper Syndicate, 1922-24; Book League of America (first paperback book club), New York City, managing editor, 1928-29; *Plain Talk* (monthly review), New York City, editor, 1946-50; ''Radio Free Europe,'' Munich, West Germany, European director, 1951-52; writer and tobacco farmer in Waldorf, Md., 1952-81. Honorary member of staff and faculty of the U.S. Army Command and General Staff College, Ft. Leavenworth, Kan. Radio Liberty Committee, trustee, beginning, 1951. *Member:* Overseas Press Club (founder member). *Awards, honors:* Freedoms Foundation Award, 1950.

WRITINGS: The Russian Revolution, Harper, 1917; *The Resurrected Nations,* Stokes, 1918; (with M. Botchkareva) *Yashka,* Stokes, 1919; (editor) *Letters from the Kaiser to the Czar,* Stokes, 1920; *The Man Lenin,* Seltzer, 1924; (compiler) *Letters from Russian Prisons,* Boni, 1924; *Stalin,* Cosmopolitan, 1931; (with V. Zenzinov) *The Road to Oblivion,* McBride, 1931; *Red Smoke,* McBride, 1932; (editor) Jan Valtin, *Out of the Night,* Alliance, 1941; *Mitchell: Pioneer of Air Power,* Duell, Sloan & Pearce, 1943, reprinted, Arno, 1971; *Stalin's Great Secret,* Coward, 1956; *The Mind of an Assassin,* Farrar, Straus, 1959, reprinted, Greenwood Press, 1979; *I Rediscover Russia,* Duell, Sloan & Pearce, 1964; *Intervention,* McKay, 1969; *Eyewitness to History: Memoirs and Reflections of a Foreign Correspondent for Half a Century* (autobiography), Hawthorn Books, 1973; (editor) *Plain Talk: An Anthology from the Leading Anti-Communist Magazine of the Forties,* Arlington House, 1976; *Hands Off the Panama Canal,* Monticello Books, 1976.

Also author with Oksana Kosenkina, Russian school teacher detained by Soviet agents against her will, of her story. Editor, Macaulay ''Drama Library,'' 1927. Writer of motion picture script, ''Jack London''; translator with H. Alsberg of play, ''Princess Turandot,'' 1925, produced by Provincetown Playhouse. Correspondent on special assignments for *Life.*

BIOGRAPHICAL/CRITICAL SOURCES: Isaac Don Levine, *I Rediscover Russia,* Duell, Sloan & Pearce, 1964; Levine, *Eyewitness to History: Memoirs and Reflections of a Foreign Correspondent for Half a Century* (autobiography), Hawthorn Books, 1973.

OBITUARIES: New York Times, February 17, 1981; *Chicago Tribune,* February 17, 1981; *Washington Post,* February 17, 1981.†

*   *   *

LEVINE, Robert M.   1941-

PERSONAL: Born March 26, 1941, in New York, N.Y. *Ed-*

ucation: Colgate University, B.A., 1962; Princeton University, M.A., 1966, Ph.D., 1967. *Office:* Department of History, University of Miami, Coral Gables, Fla. 33124.

CAREER: State University of New York at Stony Brook, assistant professor, 1966-71, associate professor, 1971-76, professor of history, 1976-81; University of Miami, Coral Gables, Fla., professor of history, 1981—. Chairman of committee on Brazilian studies, Conference on Latin American History, 1970-71, and Latin American Seminar, Columbia University, 1972-73; senior Fulbright-Hays lecturer in Brazil, 1973. *Member:* American Historical Association, Latin American Studies Association, Association of Brazilianists, Conference on Latin American History, Phi Beta Kappa.

WRITINGS: Brazil: Field Guide to Research in the Social Sciences, Institute of Latin American Studies, Columbia University, 1967; *The Vargas Regime,* Columbia University Press, 1970; *Pernambuco in the Brazilian Federation,* Stanford University Press, 1978. Also author of other publications on Brazilian political history.

WORK IN PROGRESS: Research on Brazilian regionalism and race relations; a social history of Latin America.

*   *   *

LEWIS, Jean   1924-

PERSONAL: Born June 2, 1924, in Shanghai, China, of American parents; daughter of David and Nettie Craig (Lambuth) Lewis. *Education:* Tutored at home. *Politics:* Republican. *Religion:* Protestant. *Home:* 321 Avenue C, New York, N.Y. 10009.

CAREER: Writer of children's books. Actress and singer in radio, television, and theater, mainly in New York City, 1940-53; program director of American Theatre Wing's Hospital Committee, New York City, 1947-51; executive director of Volunteer Service Photographers, New York City, 1953—. Writer of sales promotion and continuity for women's television shows.

WRITINGS—All children's books: Pebbles Flintstone, Artists & Writers Press, 1963; *Bamm-Bamm and Pebbles Flintstone,* Artists & Writers Press, 1963; *The Flintstones Meet the Gruesomes,* Golden Press, 1965; *Jane and the Mandarin's Secret,* Hawthorn, 1970; *Hot Dog,* Grosset, 1971; *Dr. Leo's Pet Patients,* American Heritage Press, 1971.

Published by Whitman Publishing: *Touche Turtle and the Fire Dog,* 1963; *The Flintstones at the Circus,* 1963; *Boo Boo Bear and the V.I.V.,* 1965; *The Flintstones's Picnic Panic,* 1965; (contributor) *Golden Prize, and Other Stories about Horses,* 1965, revised edition, 1972; *Hoppity Hooper versus Skippity Snooper,* 1966; *Alvin and the Chipmunks and the Deep Sea Blues,* 1966; *The Road Runner and the Bird Watchers,* 1968; *Frankenstein, Jr. and the Devilish Double,* 1968; *Tom and Jerry Scairdy Cat,* 1969; *Tom and Jerry under the Big Top,* 1969.

Published by Western Publishing: *Gumby and Pokey to the Rescue,* 1969; *H. R. Pufnstuf,* 1970; *Wacky Witch and the Royal Birthday,* 1971; *Wacky Witch and the Mystery of the King's Gold,* 1973; *Lassie and the Busy Morning,* 1973; *Nancy and Sluggo and the Big Surprise,* 1974; *Scooby Doo and the Pirate Treasure,* 1974; *Bullwinkle's Casserole,* 1975; *Bugs Bunny: Too Many Carrots,* 1976; *Mickey Mouse and the Pet Show,* 1976; *Benji, the Detective,* 1978; *Donald Duck in It's*

Play Time, 1980; *Around the Year with Pooh,* 1980; *Little Golden Book: Dogs,* in press.

Published by Rand McNally: *Kathi and Hash San and the Case of Measles,* 1972; *The Sleeping Tree Mystery,* 1975; *Hong Kong Phooey and the Fortune Cookie Caper,* 1975; *Scooby Doo and the Haunted Dog House,* 1975; *Scooby Doo and the Mystery Monster,* 1975; *Santa's Runaway Elf,* 1977; *Mumbley to the Rescue,* 1977.

Adapter: *Swiss Family Robinson,* Artists & Writers Press, 1961; *The Tortoise and the Hare,* Whitman Publishing, 1963; *The Jungle Book,* Golden Press, 1967; *Old Yeller,* Golden Press, 1968; *The Absent-Minded Professor,* Golden Press, 1968; *Chitty Chitty Bang Bang,* Golden Press, 1968.

Contributor to periodicals, including *Professional Photographer* and *Human Services.*

WORK IN PROGRESS: The Teddy Bear Book, for Grosset; *The Big Apple Treasure Dig,* young adult fiction; *The Gift,* a fantasy adventure set in China; *The Kyoto Cat,* written in the style of a Japanese fairy tale; *The Temple Summer,* young adult fiction set in China during the Boxer Rebellion of 1900; *I Remember Amah,* memoirs of her childhood in China.

AVOCATIONAL INTERESTS: Animals, particularly cats.

*   *   *

LEXAU, Joan M.
(Joan L. Nodset)

PERSONAL: Surname is pronounced Lex-o; born in St. Paul, Minn., daughter of Ole H. and Anne (Haas) Lexau. *Education:* Took special courses at College of St. Thomas and College of St. Catherine in St. Paul, Minn., and at New School for Social Research. *Politics:* Independent. *Religion:* Catholic. *Residence:* New York.

CAREER: Worked for short periods as department store saleswoman, library clerk, and bookkeeper, in St. Paul, Minn., and as kitchen girl in a Montana resort; *Catholic Digest,* St. Paul, editorial secretary, 1953-55; *Glass Packer* (trade magazine), New York City, advertising production manager, 1955-56; *Catholic News,* New York City, reporter, 1956-57; Religious News Service, New York City, free-lance correspondent, 1957; Harper & Row Publishers, Inc., New York City, production-liaison work on children's books, 1957-61; full-time free-lance writer, mostly for young people, 1961—. *Member:* Society of Children's Book Writers, Mystery Writers of America. *Awards, honors:* Child Study Association of America Children's Book Award, 1962, for *The Trouble with Terry;* Charlie May Simon Children's Book Award, for *Striped Ice Cream; The Spider Makes a Web* was named an American Library Association Outstanding Science Book.

WRITINGS—For young people, except as indicated: *Cathy Is Company,* Dial, 1961; *Olaf Reads,* Dial, 1961, Initial Teaching Alphabet edition published as *Oelaf Reedz,* Scholastic Book Services, 1965; *Millicent's Ghost,* Dial, 1962; *The Trouble with Terry,* Dial, 1962; *Olaf Is Late,* Dial, 1963; *That's Good, That's Bad,* Dial, 1963; *Jose's Christmas Secret,* Dial, 1963, revised edition for younger readers published as *The Christmas Secret,* Scholastic Book Services, 1973; *Benjie,* Dial, 1964; *Maria,* Dial, 1964; (editor) *Convent Life* (adult anthology), Dial, 1964; *I Should Have Stayed in Bed,* Harper, 1965; *More Beautiful than Flowers,* Lippincott, 1966; *The Homework Caper,* Harper, 1966; *Kite Over Tenth Avenue,* Doubleday, 1967; *Finders Keepers, Losers Weepers,* Lippincott, 1967; *Every*

Day a Dragon, Harper, 1967; *Three Wishes for Abner,* Ginn, 1967; *Striped Ice Cream,* Lippincott, 1968; *The Rooftop Mystery,* Harper, 1968; *A House So Big,* Harper, 1968; *Archimedes Takes a Bath,* Crowell, 1969; *Crocodile and Hen,* Harper, 1969.

It All Began with a Drip, Drip, Drip, McCall, 1970; *Benjie on His Own,* Dial, 1970; *Me Day,* Dial, 1971; *T for Tommy,* Garrard, 1971; *That's Just Fine and Who-o-o Did It?,* Garrard, 1971; *Emily and the Klunky Baby and the Next-Door Dog,* Dial, 1972; (adaptor) *The Tail of the Mouse,* Ginn, 1974; *I'll Tell on You,* Dutton, 1979; *I Hate Red Rover,* Dutton, 1979; *The Spider Makes a Web,* Scholastic Book Services, 1979.

(Adaptor) *Jack and the Beanstalk* (Random House Student Book Club selection), Random House, 1980; *Mean Jean,* Houghton, 1981; *Strawberry Shortcake and Sad Mister Sun,* Parker Brothers, 1983.

Under pseudonym Joan L. Nodset: *Who Took the Farmer's Hat?,* Harper, 1963; *Go Away, Dog,* Harper, 1963; *Where Do You Go When You Run Away?,* Bobbs-Merrill, 1964; *Come Here, Cat,* Harper, 1973.

Also author of other stories for children's textbooks. Contributor of articles about children's books and poetry to adult periodicals.

WORK IN PROGRESS: Come! Sit! Stay!; The Poison Ivy Case and *The Dogfood Caper,* both for Dial.

SIDELIGHTS: Joan M. Lexau writes *CA:* "As far as my memory goes back, I wanted to be a writer. As a child I wrote what I saw around me in my mind but I put very little on paper. Then, when I was working for Harper & Row, I suddenly realized that it would be even more enjoyable to write books myself than to work on other writer's books. So I did. Of course, it took me a couple years of hard work to finally write a publishable manuscript.

"I get ideas from my own past or from what I see or read or hear—I'm always on the lookout for ideas. I even dream them. A book I [wrote] called *Benjie on His Own* began as a dream that I was writing a new book about Benjie. I simply expanded the plot from the dream, which was an incident very similar to one that happened to me as a child, when I realized I didn't know the way home from school alone."

AVOCATIONAL INTERESTS: Organic gardening, photography, reading mysteries and nonfiction.

BIOGRAPHICAL/CRITICAL SOURCES: Lee Bennett Hopkins, *Books Are by People,* Citation Press, 1969.

*   *   *

LILLY, Doris   1926-

PERSONAL: Born December 26, 1926, in South Pasadena, Calif.; daughter of Otto and Edith (Humphries) Lilly. *Education:* Attended public schools in Santa Monica, Calif. *Home:* 150 East 69th St., New York, N.Y. 10021.

CAREER: Has been employed as film actress under contract to Cecil B. De Mille, beauty editor of *Town and Country,* and press agent; society columnist for *New York Post* for eight years, and columnist for *Daily Mirror.* Regular guest on "Merv Griffin Show"; panelist on other television programs; currently starring in her own nightly gossip show for WPIX-TV in New York.

WRITINGS: How to Marry a Millionaire, Putnam, 1951; *How to Make Love in Five Languages,* Bobbs-Merrill, 1965; *Those Fabulous Greeks: Onassis, Niarchos and Livanos,* Cowles, 1970; (with Robin Moore) *Glamour Girl,* Woodhill, 1977; *How to Marry a Billionaire,* Delacorte, 1984. Gossip columnist, McNault Syndicate. Also author of film scripts for De Sica. Contributor to *McCall's, Ladies' Home Journal,* and *Cosmopolitan.*

SIDELIGHTS: Doris Lilly told *CA:* "If it were true money grew on trees, all my friends would be married to apes."

*   *   *

LINDARS, Barnabas 1923-

PERSONAL: Name originally Frederick Chevallier Lindars; born June 11, 1923, in Leighton Buzzard, Bedfordshire, England; son of Walter St. John (a clergyman) and Rose (Chevallier) Lindars. *Education:* St. John's College, Cambridge, B.A. (with honors), 1944, M.A., 1947; Westcott House, Cambridge, theological study, 1946-48. *Home:* Hulme Hall, Oxford Place, Manchester M14 5RR, England. *Office:* Faculty of Theology, Victoria University of Manchester, Manchester M13 9PL, England.

CAREER: Ordained Anglican priest, 1948; curate in Pallion, Sunderland, England, 1948-52; became member of Society of Saint Francis, taking the name of Barnabas, 1952; Cambridge University, Cambridge, England, assistant lecturer, 1961-66, lecturer in Old Testament studies, 1966-78, fellow and dean of Jesus College, 1976-78; Victoria University of Manchester, Manchester, England, Rylands Professor of Biblical Criticism and Exegesis, 1978—. *Military service:* British Army, Intelligence Corps, 1944-45; became lieutenant. *Member:* Studiorum Novi Testamenti Societas (assistant secretary, 1962-76), Society for Old Testament Study. *Awards, honors:* B.D. from Cambridge University, 1961, for *New Testament Apologetic;* D.D. from Cambridge University.

WRITINGS: (Contributor) F. L. Cross, editor, *Studies in the Fourth Gospel,* Mowbray, 1957; *New Testament Apologetic,* Westminster, 1961; (contributor) C.F.D. Moule, editor, *Miracles,* Mowbray, 1965; (editor with P. R. Ackroyd and contributor) *Words and Meanings,* Cambridge University Press, 1968; (editor) *Church without Walls,* Society for Promoting Christian Knowledge, 1968.

Behind the Fourth Gospel, Society for Promoting Christian Knowledge, 1971; *The Gospel of John,* Oliphants, 1972; (editor with S. S. Smalley and contributor) *Christ and Spirit in the New Testament,* Cambridge University Press, 1974; (contributor) G. R. Dunstan, editor, *Duty and Discernment,* Society for Promoting Christian Knowledge, 1975; (contributor) J. A. Emerton, editor, *Studies in the Historical Books of the Old Testament,* E. J. Brill, 1979; (contributor) M. Sanker, editor, *Their Lord and Ours,* Society for Promoting Christian Knowledge, 1982; *Jesus Son of Man,* Society for Promoting Christian Knowledge, 1983. Contributor to magazines and theological journals.

WORK IN PROGRESS: Commentary on Judges for *The International Critical Commentaries,* for T. & T. Clark.

SIDELIGHTS: Barnabas Lindars told *CA:* "As a follower of Saint Francis of Asissi teaching biblical criticism in a great university, I stand at a point of tension for faith today: how can the gospel of Jesus Christ be retained when the Bible is subjected to searching critical and historical analysis? I believe

that the search for truth at the scholarly level is not opposed to the religious call, but an essential part of the pursuit of the vision of God and his will for mankind."

Behind the Fourth Gospel has been translated into French and Spanish.

*   *   *

LINDBERG, David C. 1935-

PERSONAL: Born November 15, 1935, in Minneapolis, Minn.; son of Milton B. (a clergyman) and Elizabeth (a writer; maiden name, MacKinney) Lindberg; married E. Greta Johnson (a secondary school teacher), June 20, 1959; children: Christin Lisa, Erik David. *Education:* Wheaton College, Wheaton, Ill., B.S. (magna cum laude), 1957; Northwestern University, M.S., 1959; Indiana University, Ph.D., 1965. *Home:* 5038 Marathon Dr., Madison, Wis. 53705. *Office:* H. C. White Hall, University of Wisconsin, Madison, Wis. 53706.

CAREER: University of Michigan, Ann Arbor, assistant professor of history, 1965-67; University of Wisconsin—Madison, assistant professor, 1967-69, associate professor, 1969-72, professor of history of science, 1972-82, Evjue-Bascom Professor of the History of Science and Integrated Liberal Studies, 1982—, member of Institute for Research in the Humanities, 1975. Member of Institute for Advanced Study, 1970-71. *Member:* History of Science Society, Mediaeval Academy of America, Renaissance Society of America. *Awards, honors:* Guggenheim fellowship, 1977-78.

WRITINGS: John Pecham and the Science of Optics, University of Wisconsin Press, 1970; *A Catalogue of Medieval and Renaissance Optical Manuscripts,* Pontifical Institute of Mediaeval Studies, 1975; *Theories of Vision from al-Kindi to Kepler,* University of Chicago Press, 1976; (editor) *Science in the Middle Ages,* University of Chicago Press, 1978; *Roger Bacon's Philosophy of Nature,* Clarendon Press, 1983; *Studies in the History of Medieval Optics,* Variorum, 1983.

WORK IN PROGRESS: A book on the history of the relations between Christianity and science, edited with Ronald L. Numbers; research on early modern optics.

*   *   *

LINDE, Gunnel 1924-

PERSONAL: Born October 14, 1924, in Stockholm, Sweden; daughter of Gunnar E. and Liv (Nordenstrom) Af Geijerstam; married Einar Linde (a television producer), January 6, 1949; children: Liv, Vysse Gunnel, Sunniva (all daughters). *Education:* Attended Anders Beckmans Reklamskola, Stockholm, 1943-44, and Stockholms Konstskola, 1953. *Home:* Grindavagen 9, Waxholm, Sweden. *Office:* Sveriges Televisions AB, Oxenstiernsgatan 2, Stockholm, Sweden.

CAREER: Journalist with newspapers in Katrineholm, Linkoping, Halsingborg, Sweden, 1945-47, and with Roster i Radio, Stockholm, Sweden, 1948-49; Sveriges Radio, Stockholm, producer of radio programs for children, 1957-63, and television programs for children, 1964—. *Member:* Sveriges Foerfattarfoerbund, Svenska Journalistfoerbund, Publicistklubben, Sveriges Dramatikerfoerbund, Samfundet Visans Vanner, Stim Foereningen TV-Producenterna, Foereningen Idun, Foereningen Barnens Raetti Samhaellet (BRIS), International Society for Prevention of Child Abuse and Neglect.

AWARDS, HONORS: Diploma of Merit (as runner-up), International Hans Christian Andersen Award, 1964, for *Till av-*

entyrs i Skorstensgrand; Nils Holgersson Award, 1965, for *Den vita stenen;* the translation of *Den vita stenen, The White Stone,* was chosen by the American Library Association as one of the notable children's books of 1966; Foerfatterfondens premium, 1970; Club 100 prize, and *Expressen* (newspaper) prize, 1974, both for the best family television program of the year, "The White Stone"; Astrid Lindgren prize, 1978; Natur och Kultur culture prize, 1979.

WRITINGS—Published by Albert Bonniers, except as indicated: *Osynliga klubben och honshusbaten,* 1958; *Tacka vet jag Skorstensgrand,* 1959, translation by Lise Soemme McKinnon published as *Chimney Top Lane,* Harcourt, 1965; *Lurituri,* 1959; *Osynliga klubben och kungliga spoket,* 1960, translation by Anne Parker published as *The Invisible League and the Royal Ghost,* Harcourt, 1970; *Lurituri reser bort,* 1961; *Till aventyrs i Skorstensgrand,* 1962; *Froken Ensam Hemma aker gungstol,* 1963; *Den vita stenen,* 1964, translation by Richard Winston and Clara Winston published as *The White Stone,* Harcourt, 1966; *Med Lill-Klas i Kappsacken,* 1965, translation by Parker published as *Pony Surprise,* Harcourt, 1968.

Den olydiga ballongen, 1966; *I Eviga skogen,* International Book Production, 1966; *I Evasjams land,* 1967; *Evasjam och Nalle,* 1968; *Evasjam och Lua,* 1968; *Pellepennan och suddagumman,* Sveriges Radios Foerlag, 1968; *Pellepennan och suddagumman och kluddabarnen,* Sveriges Radios Foerlag, 1969; *Loejliga familjerna,* 1971; *Jag aer en varulvsunge,* 1972; *Om man misstaenker barnmisshandel-vad goer man?,* Almaenna Barnhuset, 1975; *Mamm-och pappsagor,* 1976; *Om livet aer dig kaert,* 1977; *Lita pa det ovaentade,* 1979; *Dingo, rymmare utan fasttagare,* 1981; *Foresta laeseboken,* Almquist & Wiksells Foerlag, 1982.

Author of radio scripts, including features for adults and children, dramatizations, and serials; also author of more than 100 television plays, mainly for children and families. Has had eight recordings issued by Decca, Barben, Warner Bros., and others, 1958-65. Author of an opera, "Frooken Ensam Hemma," for the Royal Swedish Opera, 1969-70.

WORK IN PROGRESS: Two books for Albert Bonniers; a television film and cinema film based on *Pony Surprise.*

SIDELIGHTS: In addition to the English translations, some of Gunnel Linde's books have been published in Danish, Finnish, Norwegian, German, French, Czech, Spanish, Polish, Yugoslavian, Dutch, and Japanese.

*   *   *

LINDSAY, Jack 1900-
(Peter Meadows, Richard Preston)

PERSONAL: Born October 20, 1900, in Melbourne, Australia; son of Norman Alfred William (an artist and writer) and Kathleen (Parkinson) Lindsay; married Meta Waterdrinker (an art potter), June 30, 1958; children: Philip Jan, Helen Marietta. *Education:* University of Queensland, B.A. (with first class honors in classics). *Politics:* Communist. *Home:* Castle Hedingham, Queen St., Halstead, Essex, England.

CAREER: Vision (quarterly), Sydney, Australia, co-editor, 1922-23; Fanfrolico Press, London, England, editor and operator, 1927-30, concurrently co-editor of *London Aphrodite* (periodical), 1928-29; *Arena* (periodical), London, co-editor, 1949-51; writer, poet, editor, and translator. *Military service:* British Army, 1941-45; served in Royal Signal Corps, 1941-43, detailed to War Office as script writer, 1943-45.

MEMBER: Royal Society of Literature (fellow), Ancient Monuments Society (fellow), Egyptian Exploration Society, Roman and Hellenic Societies, Essex and Suffolk Archaeological Societies. *Awards, honors:* Golden Medal of Australian Literary Society, 1962; Znak Pocheta (a Soviet Order for translating Russian poetry); D.Litt., University of Queensland.

WRITINGS—Nonfiction: (Contributor) William Blake, *Poetical Sketches,* edited by E. H. Partridge, Scholartis Press, 1927; *William Blake: Creative Will and the Poetic Image,* Fanfrolico, 1927, 2nd edition, enlarged, 1929, Haskell House, 1971; *Dionysos: Nietzsche contra Nietzsche* (essay in lyrical philosophy), Fanfrolico, 1928.

A Retrospect of the Fanfrolico Press, Simpkin Marshall, 1931; *The Romans,* A. & C. Black, 1935; *Marc Antony: His World and His Contemporaries,* Routledge, 1936, Dutton, 1937; *The Anatomy of Spirit: An Inquiry into the Origins of Religious Emotion,* Methuen, 1937; *John Bunyan, Maker of Myths* (biography), Methuen, 1937, Augustus M. Kelley, 1969; *England, My England,* Fore Publications, 1939; *A Short History of Culture,* Gollancz, 1939, revised edition, Studio Books, 1962, published as *A Short History of Culture, from Prehistory to the Renaissance,* Citadel, 1962.

Mulk Raj Anand (critical essay), Hind Kitabs Ltd. (Bombay), 1948, 2nd revised edition published as *The Elephant and the Lotus: A Study of the Novels of Mulk Raj Anand,* Kutub Popular (Bombay), 1965; *Song of a Falling World: Culture During the Break-up of the Roman Empire, A.D. 350-600,* Dakers, 1948; *Marxism and Contemporary Science; or, The Fullness of Life,* Dobson, 1949.

Charles Dickens: A Biographical and Critical Study, Philosophical Library, 1950; *A World Ahead: Journal of a Soviet Journey,* Fore Publications, 1950; (compiler and author of introduction) Leslie Hurry, *Paintings and Drawings,* Grey Walls Press, 1950; (author of introduction) Dame Edith Sitwell, *Facade, and Other Poems, 1920-1935,* Duckworth, 1950; (reviser and author of introduction) Zaharia Stancu, *Barefoot,* Fore Publications, 1951; *Byzantium into Europe: The Story of Byzantium as the First Europe, 326-1204 A.D., and Its Further Contribution till 1435 A.D.,* Fernhill, 1952; (with Maurice Conforth) *Rumanian Summer: A View of the Rumanian People's Republic,* Lawrence & Wishart, 1953; *Civil War in England* (account of the Civil War of 1642-49), Muller, 1954, Barnes & Noble, 1967.

After the Thirties: The Novel in Britain and Its Future, Lawrence & Wishart, 1956; *George Meredith: His Life and Work,* John Lane, 1956, reprinted, Kraus Reprint, 1973; *The Romans Were Here: The Roman Period in Britain and Its Place in Our History,* Muller, 1956, Barnes & Noble, 1969; *Arthur and His Times: Britain in the Dark Ages,* Muller, 1958, Barnes & Noble, 1966; *The Discovery of Britain* (guide to archaeology), Merlin Press, 1958; *Life Rarely Tells* (first in an autobiographical trilogy), Bodley Head, 1958; *1764: The Hurlyburly of Daily Life Exemplified in One Year of the 18th Century,* Muller, 1959.

Death of the Hero (study of French painting from David to Delacroix), Studio, 1960; *The Roaring Twenties* (second in the autobiographical trilogy), Bodley Head, 1960; *The Writing on the Wall: An Account of Pompeii in its Last Days,* Muller, 1960, Dufour, 1964; *Fanfrolico, and After* (last in the autobiographical trilogy), Bodley Head, 1962; *Our Celtic Heritage* (juvenile), Dufour, 1962; *Daily Life in Roman Egypt,* Muller, 1963; *Masks and Faces,* Muller, 1963; *Nine Days' Hero: Wat Tyler* (biography), Dobson, 1964; (contributor) Mervyn Levy, editor, *The Paintings of D. H. Lawrence,* Viking, 1964.

The Clashing Rocks: A Study of Early Greek Religion and Culture and the Origins of Drama, Chapman & Hall, 1965; *Leisure and Pleasure in Roman Egypt,* Miller, 1965, Barnes & Noble, 1966; *Our Anglo-Saxon Heritage* (juvenile), Dufour, 1965; *J.M.W. Turner: His Life and Work* (critical biography), New York Graphic Society, 1966, new edition published as *Turner,* Panther, 1973, Academy Chicago, 1981; *Our Roman Heritage* (juvenile), Dufour, 1967; Richard Friedenthal, editor, *The Ancient World: Manners and Morals,* Putnam, 1968; *Meetings with Poets: Memories of Dylan Thomas, Edith Sitwell, Louis Aragon, Paul Eluard, Tristan Tzara,* Muller, 1968, Ungar, 1969; *Men and Gods on the Roman Nile,* Barnes & Noble, 1968; *Cezanne: His Life and Art,* New York Graphic Society, 1969.

The Origin of Alchemy in Graeco-Roman Egypt, Barnes & Noble, 1970; *The Origins of Astrology,* Barnes & Noble, 1971; *Cleopatra,* Coward, 1971; *Life of Courbet: His Life and Art,* 1973, published as *Gustave Courbet: His Life and Art,* State Mutual Book, 1981; *Helen of Troy: Woman and Goddess,* Rowman & Littlefield, 1974; *Normans and Their World,* Hart-Davis, 1974; *Blast Power and Ballistics: Concepts of Force and Energy in the Ancient World,* Muller, 1974; *William Morris: His Life and Work,* Constable, 1975, Taplinger, 1979; *The Troubadours and Their World,* Muller, 1976; *Decay and Renewal* (literary criticism), Lawrence & Wishart, 1976; *William Hogarth: His Life and His World,* Hart-Davis, 1977, published as *William Hogarth: His Art and His World,* Taplinger, 1979; *The Monster City: Defoe's London,* St. Martin's, 1978; *William Blake: His Life and Work,* Constable, 1978, Braziller, 1979; *Thomas Gainsborough: His Life and Art,* Universe, 1981; *The Crisis in Marxism,* B & N Imports, 1981.

Fiction; historical novels, except as indicated: *Cressida's First Lover: A Tale of Ancient Greece* (fantasy novel), John Lane, 1931, R. Long & R. R. Smith, 1932; *Rome for Sale* (first in Rome trilogy), foreword by Colin Still, Harper, 1934; *Caesar Is Dead* (second in Rome trilogy), Nicholson & Watson, 1934.

Despoiling Venus, Nicholson & Watson, 1935; *Last Days with Cleopatra* (last in Rome trilogy), Nicholson & Watson, 1935; *Runaway* (boys' novel), Oxford University Press, 1935; *Storm at Sea* (novella), wood engravings by John Farleigh, Golden Cockerel Press, 1935; *Adam of a New World* (novel about Giordano Bruno), Nicholson & Watson, 1936; *Come Home at Last* (short stories), Nicholson & Watson, 1936; *The Wanderings of Wenamen, 1115-1114, B.C.,* Nicholson & Watson, 1936; *Rebels of the Goldfields* (boys' novel), Lawrence & Wishart, 1936; (under pseudonym Richard Preston) *Shadow and Flame* (contemporary novel), Chapman & Hall, 1936; *Sue Verney,* Nicholson & Watson, 1937; (under pseudonym Richard Preston) *End of Cornwall* (contemporary novel), J. Cape, 1937, Vanguard, 1938; *The Invaders,* Oxford University Press, 1938; *1649: A Novel of a Year,* Methuen, 1938; *To Arms! A Story of Ancient Gaul* (boys' novel), Oxford Press University, 1938; *Brief Light: A Novel of Catullus,* Methuen, 1939; *Lost Birthright,* Methuen, 1939.

Hannibaal Takes a Hand, Dakers, 1941; *Light in Italy,* Gollancz, 1941; *The Stormy Violence,* Dakers, 1941; *The Dons Sight Devon* (boys' novel), Oxford University Press, 1942; *We Shall Return: A Novel of Dunkirk and the French Campaign,* Dakers, 1942; *Beyond Terror: A Novel of the Battle of Crete,* Dakers, 1943.

The Barriers Are Down: A Tale of the Collapse of a Civilisation, Gollancz, 1945; *Hullo Stranger* (contemporary novel), Dakers, 1945; *Time to Live* (contemporary novel), Dakers, 1946; *The Subtle Knot* (contemporary novel), Dakers, 1947; *Men of Forty-Eight,* Methuen, 1948.

Fires in Smithfield: A Novel of Mary Tudor's Days, John Lane, 1950; *The Passionate Pastoral,* John Lane, 1951; *Betrayed Spring* (contemporary novel), John Lane, 1953; *Rising Tide* (contemporary novel), John Lane, 1953; *The Moment of Choice* (contemporary novel), John Lane, 1955; *The Great Oak: A Story of 1549,* Bodley Head, 1957; *A Local Habitation* (contemporary novel), John Lane, 1957.

The Revolt of the Sons (contemporary novel), Muller, 1960; *All on the Never-Never* (contemporary novel), Muller, 1961, reprinted, State Mutual Book, 1981; *The Way the Ball Bounces* (contemporary novel), Muller, 1962; *Choice of Times* (contemporary novel), Muller, 1964; *Thunder Underground: A Story of Nero's Rome,* Muller, 1965.

Poetry: *Fauns and Ladies,* Kirtley (Sidney), 1923; (contributor) Philip Lindsay, *Morgan in Jamaica,* includes poem panegyrical by J. Lindsay, Fanfrolico, 1930; *The Passionate Neatherd,* Fanfrolico, 1930; *Into Action: The Battle of Dieppe,* Dakers, 1942; *Second Front,* Dakers, 1944; *Clue of Darkness,* Dakers, 1949; *Peace Is Our Answer,* linocuts by Noel Counihan, Collets Holdings, 1950; *Three Letters to Nikolai Tikhonov,* Fore Publications, 1950; *Three Elegies,* Myriad Press, 1957; *Faces and Places,* Basilike (Toronto), 1974.

Plays: *Helen Comes of Age* (three verse plays), Fanfrolico, 1927; *Marino Faliero* (tragedy in verse), Fanfrolico, 1927; *Hereward,* Fanfrolico, 1930; "Robin of England," first produced, 1944; "The Whole Armour of God," first produced, 1944; (with B. Coombes) "Face of Coal," first produced at Scala Theatre, London, England, 1946; (adapter) "Lysistrata," first produced, 1948. Author of other plays, and writer of scripts for documentary and educational films.

Editor: (With K. Slessor) *Poetry in Australia,* Vision Press (Sydney), 1923; (with Peter Warlock) Sir John Harington, *The Metamorphosis of Ajax,* Fanfrolico, 1927; *Loving Mad Tom* (Bedlamite verses of the 16th and 17th centuries), foreword by Robert Graves, musical transcriptions by Peter Warlock, Fanfrolico, 1927, A. M. Kelley, 1970; (under pseudonym Peter Meadows) Robert Herrick, *Delighted Earth* (selection from "Hesperides"), Fanfrolico, 1927; *The Parlement of Pratlers* (Elizabethan dialogues and monologues), translated by John Eliot, Fanfrolico, 1928; *Inspiration* (anthology), Fanfrolico, 1928; *Letters of Philip Stanhope, Second Earl of Chesterfield,* Fanfrolico, 1930; (with Edgell Rickword) *A Handbook of Freedom: A Record of English Democracy through Twelve Centuries* (anthology), International Publishers, 1939, published as *Spokesmen for Liberty,* Lawrence & Wishart, 1941.

Giuliano the Magnificent (adaptation of unpublished drama by Dorothy Johnson), Dakers, 1940; (with Maurice Carpenter and Honor Arundel) *New Lyrical Ballads,* Editions Poetry, 1945; *Anvil: Life and the Arts* (miscellany), Meridian Books, 1947; Robert Herrick, *Selected Poems,* includes essay by Lindsay, British Book Centre, 1948; (and author of introduction) William Morris, *Selected Poems,* Grey Walls Press, 1948.

J.M.W. Turner, The Sunset Ship (collected poems), includes essay by Lindsay, Evelyn, 1966; (and author of introduction)

Joseph Priestley, *Autobiography: Memoirs Written by Him-self—An Account of Further Discoveries in the Air,* Adams & Dart, 1970, Fairleigh Dickinson University Press, 1971; Jack London, *People of the Abyss,* Journeyman Press, 1977; Jane Harrison, *Ancient Art and Ritual,* Moonraker Press, 1978. Also editor of "New Development Series," Bodley Head, 1947-48, and co-editor, with Randall Swingler, of "Key Poet Series," Alan Swallow, 1951.

Translator: Aristophanes, *Lysistrata,* Fanfrolico, 1926; (and editor) *The Complete Works of Petronius Arbiter* (comprising *The Satyricon* and poems), Fanfrolico, 1927, revised edition, including introduction by Lindsay, published as *The Satyricon and Poems,* Elek Books, 1960; *Propertius in Love* (verse), Fanfrolico, 1927; *A Homage to Sappho* (poems, embodying translations of the fragments), Fanfrolico, 1928; *The Complete Poetry of Gaius Catullus,* includes essay by Lindsay, Fanfrolico, 1929, new translation, with introduction and commentary by Lindsay, published as *Catullus: The Complete Poems,* Sylvan Press, 1948; *The Mimiambs of Herondas* (verse), foreword by Brian Penton, Fanfrolico, 1929; Theocritos, *The Complete Poems,* introduction by Edward Hutton, Fanfrolico, 1929; *Women in Parliament* (Aristophanes' *Ecclesiazusae*), foreword by Rickword, Fanfrolico, 1929.

D. M. Ausonius, *Patchwork Quilt* (selected poems), Fanfrolico, 1930; *Homer's Hymns to Aphrodite,* Fanfrolico, 1930; *Sulpicia's Garland* (Roman poems), McKee, 1930; Lucius Apuleius, *The Golden Ass,* Limited Editions Club (New York), 1932, revised edition, Indiana University Press, 1962; *I Am a Roman,* Mathews & Marrot, 1934; *Medieval Latin Poets* (verse), Mathews & Marrot, 1934.

Longus, *Daphnis and Chloe,* includes critical essay by Lindsay, Daimon Press, 1948; (with Stephen Jolly) Vitezslav Nezval, *Song of Peace,* Fore Publications, 1951; Adam Mickiewicz, *Poems,* Sylvan Press, 1957; (also editor and author of introduction) *Russian Poetry, 1917-1955,* Bodley Head, 1957, reprinted, Greenwood Press, 1978; Asclepiades, *The Loves of Asklepiades,* Myriad Press, 1959.

(And compiler) *Modern Russian Poetry,* Vista Books, 1960; (and editor) *Ribaldry of Greece* (anthology), Bestseller Library, 1961, published as *Ribaldry of Ancient Greece: An Intimate Portrait of Greeks in Love,* Ungar, 1965; (and editor) *Ribaldry of Rome* (anthology), Bestseller Library, 1961, published as *Ribaldry of Ancient Rome: An Intimate Portrait of Romans in Love,* Ungar, 1965; (and author of introduction) Giordano Bruno, *Cause, Principle and Unity,* Daimon Press, 1962, International Publishers, 1964, reprinted, Greenwood Press, 1976; Eleonore Bille-de Mot, *The Age of Akhenaton,* Cory, Adams & Mackay, 1967; Euripides, *Iphigeneia in Aulis, Hecuba, Electra, Orestes* (four plays), Mermaid Theatre, 1967; Gotthold Ephraim Lessing, *Nathan and the Wise,* Mermaid Theatre, 1967; (and author of introduction) Tefkros Anthias, *Greece, I Keep My Vigil for You,* Anthias Publications, 1968; Alexander Blok, *The Twelve and the Scythians,* Lawrence Hill, 1982.

Booklets: *Perspective for Poetry,* Fore Publications, 1944; *British Achievement in Art and Music,* Pilot Press, 1945; *William Morris, Writer* (lecture given at Caxton Hall, London, November 14, 1958), William Morris Society, 1961. Also author of unpublished book, "The Starfish Road; or, The Poet as Revolutionary," a study of modern poetry in relation to the Industrial Revolution. Contributor to numerous periodicals, including *Life and Letters, Adam, British Ally, New Directions,* and *Horizon.*

WORK IN PROGRESS: An introduction to *Life of V. G. Childe,* by Sally Greene, for Moonraker Press; *Collected Poems,* for J.M.W. Borg.

SIDELIGHTS: Jack Lindsay is known as an extremely prolific novelist, poet, social and literary critic, verse dramatist, biographer, classical scholar, and translator. He has participated in many of the European literary trends of the past half-century, among them the fine-press movement in London during the late twenties, the French Resistance of the early thirties, mass-declamation poetry in England in the late thirties, and post-war experimental drama techniques, which he used later in documentary films and radio scripts. Since World War II he has turned to the contemporary social scene and a series of analyses of the British way of life, while continuing his work in the area of pure scholarship, linking European with ancient history in critical studies such as his *Byzantium into Europe,* published in 1952. His personal acquaintance with Dylan Thomas and Dame Edith Sitwell is well documented in *Meetings with Poets.* The third section of the book concentrates on the French Resistance poets, Eluard, Aragon, and Tzara in particular.

Lindsay ventured into the realm of the artist and art critic with his biographies of Turner and Cezanne. Clement Greenberg comments on *J.M.W. Turner: His Life and Work* in *Book Week:* "The insights here, such as they are, seem to me to be dulled by a tincture of pedestrian Marxism or, less often, of routine Freudianism. . . . [Lindsay] fares even worse as an art critic. Turner's pictures are put through the 'parallels-and-diagonals, verticals-and-horizontals' hopper that constituted advanced pictorial analysis 30 years ago. . . . But when he is not an art critic and not an interpreter, [Lindsay] is a scrupulous scholar and sets straight many facts about Turner." *New York Review of Books* critic Francis Haskell also feels that this "very readable biography does make of [Turner] (for the first time) a credible human being. The task is unusually difficult, for the contradictory elements in his life were more compartmentalized in him than they are in most men."

A *Times Literary Supplement* reviewer remarks that in *Cezanne: His Life and Art* "we are given a highly romanticized and often contradictory account of the moral, intellectual and professional attitudes which the author thinks can be attributed to the Cezanne of his imagining." However, J. R. Mellow of the *New York Times Book Review* believes that this kind of treatment adds a great deal to biographies of historical figures who, like Cezanne, left few records of a personal nature. "The Cezanne which Jack Lindsay . . . presents is not exactly a new man, but he is a fully realized figure, complex and contradictory. . . . The wealth of personal and literary associations that Lindsay brings to his discussions of the subject-matter of Cezanne's paintings . . . gives his book solidity and weight."

In *William Blake: His Life and Work,* Lindsay states of his subject, "I do not write as someone interested in Blake from the outside, but as someone for whom he has been a vitally formative influence throughout life." The author's intellectual analysis of Blake's work elicits this reaction from *New Statesman* critic Peter Conrad: "The best contemporary criticism can do in defence of Blake's visionary extrapolations is to treat them as a form of the higher astrology, inventions whose symmetry is nonsensical rather than fearful and to pardon him . . . for having on occasion written well. But for Mr. Lindsay, Blake remains a philosopher, his work an anticipatory synthesis of Nietzsche's metaphysical self-transformation and Marx's political self-betterment." Conrad concludes that by "intellectually aggrandising Blake . . . Lindsay has actually diminished him, because he slights that mystical ingenuousness which is Blake's most endearing and perplexing quality.''

However, Martin Butlin finds that Lindsay ''has all the advantages of the outsider with few of the disadvantages.'' Writing about *William Blake* in *Spectator*, Butlin finds that the author ''displays a remarkably comprehensive appreciation of the various forces, intellectual, social and political, that affected Blake's development. He acknowledges a particular debt to David Erdman's establishment of Blake as a political thinker, and his own beliefs enable him to see Blake in some ways as a forerunner of Hegel and Marx, but he never allows this to distort his account. . . . Lindsay will not please every school of Blake criticism—indeed, it would be amazing, and worrying, if he did—but his summary of Blake's thought is the most convincing yet published.'' This view is shared by *Los Angeles Times* reviewer Robert Kirsch, who states that in Lindsay's book ''Blake is placed in terms of his influence and effect . . . more credibly than in any other I have read. Part of this is achieved by critical scholarship, particularly an examination of the sources of anecdotes and information on Blake.'' Kirsch further suggests that ''for those who have had difficulty lending themselves to Blake's symbolic creations, Lindsay is perhaps the best guide so far.''

''I originally conceived myself as a poet and nothing else,'' Lindsay told *CA*, ''with Keats, Shelley, Blake, Donne, Shakespeare, Aristophanes, Theocritos, [and] Catullus as my guides.'' He continued: ''At the same time, through Plato, Blake, Coleridge, Neitzsche, [and] Croce, I was seeking a dialectic which would throw light on the secret of creative activity of novelists (Dickens, Balzac, and Dostoevsky most affected me). In 1926 I came to England and till 1930 directed the Fanfrolico Press, as editor and typographer, attempting to invade the English scene with what we called the Australian Renaissance (mainly based on the work and ideas of my father, Norman Lindsay). As I hand-set and hand-printed several books, including some of my own, I was following in the track of another of my heroes, William Morris.

''In 1930-31, with the breakdown of the fine presses through the economic depression, I went to the West Country, mainly Cornwall, and lived in extreme hardship, seeking to find a new way forward in my work and ideas. At last I broke through with the historical novel, in a trilogy set in the world of Julius Caesar [*Rome for Sale, Caesar Is Dead*, and *Last Days with Cleopatra*]. As I put it later in an essay: 'I had seen experience as always flowing in to the point of poetic activity where it was transformed into the image. Now, seeking a basis in history, in social existence, I had to turn the process inside-out. The problem presented itself to me as that of writing a novel set in the period of Catullus. I had translated his poems and explored them for all their meanings, which meant, first the comprehension of the poet's inner life, then the working-outwards to realise as thoroughly as possible the impacts upon him from people and from his society in general as it moved into the matured revolutionary crisis under Caesar.'

''In Greek tragedy . . . the vital structure of initiation ritual and experience found its developed artistic expression: the conflict of two deeply opposed forces, a disaster or death (sacrifice), an account of the disaster or death, a lament, a discovery (called by Aristotle the moment of recognition), and a theophany (rebirth or resurrection). There . . . the relation of art-form and ritual structure was clear; in the full working-out of culture it became even more complex, but still remained central, I believe.''

''Since the early 1930s I have worked in a large number of forms, ranging from novels, contemporary and historical, to cultural anthropology and direct history, biographies of writers and artists, literary and artistic criticism, the history of science, philosophy, and so on; but I believe that there is a common method in all of my works, the quest for the structure and significance of development in human beings, in the individual and in society. The attempt to understand the past leads into the attempt to understand the present, to grasp the formative forces at work in our world and the future which they imply— not in any dogmatic way, but with all due allowance for the elements of unpredictability and the complexity of the human condition.''

In 1944 Martin Browne and his Pilgrim Players performed a poetic documentary, written by Lindsay, in churches all over England; this concerned the Christian Resistance to Hitler and was entitled ''The Whole Armour of God.'' Lindsay reports that his books have been widely translated; over one million copies of his novels have been printed in the Soviet Union.

AVOCATIONAL INTERESTS: Archaeology, bricklaying, tree-planting.

BIOGRAPHICAL/CRITICAL SOURCES: Colin Arthur Roderick, *Twenty Australian Novelists*, Angus & Robertson, 1947; Jack Lindsay, *Life Rarely Tells*, Bodley Head, 1958; Alick West, *Mountain in the Sunlight: Studies in Conflict and Unity*, Lawrence & Wishart, 1958; Lindsay, *The Roaring Twenties*, Bodley Head, 1960; Lindsay, *Fanfrolico, and After*, Bodley Head, 1962; *Book Week*, September 11, 1966; *New York Review of Books*, December 1, 1966; *Times Literary Supplement*, August 31, 1967, October 16, 1969, July 16, 1970, November 30, 1973, January 25, 1974, October 3, 1975, May 22, 1981; *London Magazine*, May, 1968; *Books and Bookmen*, June, 1968, March, 1971; *Economist*, November 9, 1968; *New York Times Book Review*, October 12, 1969, June 24, 1979; *Spectator*, September 16, 1978; *New Statesman*, November 3, 1978; *Los Angeles Times*, July 16, 1979; *Commentary*, October, 1979.

*   *   *

LINDSAY, Jean 1926-

PERSONAL: Born August 29, 1926, in Derby, England; daughter of William (an engineer) and May (Bennett) Forrest; married David Lindsay (a university teacher), October 17, 1959; children: Cora, John. *Education:* London School of Economics and Political Science, B.Sc., 1951, M.Sc., 1957; University of Aberdeen, Ph.D., 1962. *Home:* Llwydmor, Upper Garth Rd., Bangor, Gwynedd LL57 2SS, Wales.

CAREER: Teacher in Derby, England, 1946-59; University of Aberdeen, Aberdeen, Scotland, assistant lecturer in economic history, 1960; Queen's University of Belfast, Belfast, Northern Ireland, tutor in social and economic history, 1964-66; John Bright School, Llandudno, Wales, head of history department, 1979—. *Member:* Economic History Society.

WRITINGS: The Canals of Scotland, Augustus M. Kelley, 1968; *A History of the North Wales Slate Industry*, David & Charles, 1974; *The Scottish Poor Law*, Stockwell, 1976; *The Trent and Mersey Canal*, David & Charles, 1979. Contributor to *Derbyshire Archaeological Journal, Derbyshire Countryside*, and other journals.

WORK IN PROGRESS: A book, *The Penrhyan Dispute, 1900-1903*.

SIDELIGHTS: Jean Lindsay told *CA* that the main motivating factor in her writing has been "a desire to record social and economic history." Initially interested in "places which had caught [her] imagination in childhood," the author says she hopes to "inspire people with a sense of the reality of the past, and to awaken curiosity and a belief in historical research." Lindsay adds, "I think aspiring writers of any kind need integrity and imagination and determination."

*   *   *

LING, Dwight L(eroy) 1923-

PERSONAL: Born October 9, 1923, in Johnstown, Pa.; son of Leroy V. and Nellie (Cypher) Ling; married Phyllis May Cooper, June 8, 1946; children: Douglas, Gregory, Angela. *Education:* Pennsylvania State University, B.A., 1948, M.A., 1949; University of Illinois, Ph.D., 1955. *Politics:* Democrat. *Religion:* Methodist. *Home:* 107 Rathbone Rd., Marietta, Ohio 45750. *Office:* Office of the Provost and Dean, Marietta College, Marietta, Ohio.

CAREER: Centre College of Kentucky, Danville, assistant professor of history, 1949-52; DePauw University, Greencastle, Ind., instructor, 1955-56, assistant professor, 1956-59, associate professor, 1959-65, professor of history and assistant dean, 1965-72; Rollins College, Winter Park, Fla., provost, beginning 1972; Marietta College, Marietta, Ohio, currently provost and dean of the college. Fulbright lecturer and researcher in the Netherlands, 1976. *Military service:* U.S. Army, 1943-46. *Member:* American Historical Association, Middle East Institute, Middle East Studies Association, American Association of University Administrators.

WRITINGS: Tunisia from Protectorate to Republic, Indiana University Press, 1967; *Morocco and Tunisia: A Comparative History,* University Press of America, 1979. Contributor of articles and reviews to historical journals.

SIDELIGHTS: Dwight L. Ling traveled and studied in Tunisia, 1963 and 1967, and in Morocco, 1970.

*   *   *

LING, Trevor 1920-

PERSONAL: Born February 17, 1920, in London, England; son of Albert Oswald and Emma Frances (Meachen) Ling; married Mary Evelyn Inkster (a high school teacher), August 6, 1949 (died October, 1973); married Jeanne Openshaw, June 15, 1978; children: Elspeth Mary, Stephanie Ruth Margaret, Catherine Judith Rosmarie. *Education:* Oxford University, B.A., 1949, M.A., 1953, B.D., 1957; University of London, Ph.D., 1960. *Politics:* Socialist. *Religion:* Church of England. *Office:* University of Manchester, Manchester M13 9PL, England.

CAREER: Baptist minister in England, 1949-59; University of Nottingham, Nottingham, England, university lecturer, 1951-53; University of Rangoon, Rangoon, Burma, chaplain and lecturer, 1960-62; University of Leeds, Leeds, England, lecturer, 1963-66, senior lecturer, 1967-70, professor of comparative religion, 1970-73; University of Manchester, Manchester, England, professor of comparative religion, 1973—. Visiting professor, Visvabharti University, India, 1978-79. Conducted research in Thailand and Ceylon, 1968. *Military service:* British Army, 1939-46; became warrant officer; received Burma Star.

MEMBER: International Association for the History of Religion, International Union for the Scientific Study of Popula-

tion, Royal Asiatic Society, Royal Anthropological Institute (fellow), Royal Society for India, Pakistan, and Ceylon, British Sociological Association. *Awards, honors:* B. S. Law Prize for Pali Buddhist studies, School of Oriental and African Studies, University of London, 1961.

WRITINGS: The Significance of Satan, S.P.C.K., 1961; *Buddhism and the Mythology of Evil,* Allen & Unwin, 1962; *Prophetic Religion,* St. Martin's, 1966; *Buddha, Marx, and God,* St. Martin's, 1966; *History of Religion—East and West,* St. Martin's, 1968.

The Buddha: Buddhist Civilization in India and Ceylon, Maurice Temple Smith, 1973; *Religious Change and the Secular State,* K. P. Bagchi & Co., 1978; *Buddhism, Imperialism and War: Burma and Thailand in Modern History,* Allen & Unwin, 1979; *Karl Marx and Religion: In Europe and India,* Macmillan, 1980; *Buddhist Revival in India: Aspects of the Sociology of Buddhism,* Macmillan, 1980; *The Buddha's Philosophy of Man: Early Indian Buddhist Dialogues,* Dent, 1981; *A Dictionary of Buddhism: Indian and South-East Asian,* K. P. Bagchi & Co., 1981.

Contributor: *Buddhist Studies in Honour of I. B. Horner,* Reidel (Holland), 1974; A. K. Narain, editor, *Studies in Pali and Buddhism,* B. R. Publishing, 1979; *History and Society: Essays in Honour of Nihar Ranjan Ray,* [Calcutta], 1978; Kenneth P. Jameson and Charles K. Wilber, editors, *Religious Values and Development,* Oxford University Press, 1980; Dale Rieper, editor, *Asian Philosophy Today,* Gordon & Breach, 1981.

WORK IN PROGRESS: Across Religious Frontiers: Experience and Theory in the Study of Religion; Buddhist Nationalism and Human Community.

SIDELIGHTS: Trevor Ling, who cites writer Max Weber as his strongest influence, is competent in Latin, Greek, Pali, French, Hindi, and Bengali. His books have been published in German, Dutch, Spanish, Japanese, Sinhalese, and Thai.

BIOGRAPHICAL/CRITICAL SOURCES: Journal of the International Association of Buddhist Studies, Volume III, number 2, 1980; *Tablet,* December 14, 1981; *Religious Studies,* June, 1982.

*   *   *

LINGEMAN, Richard R(oberts) 1931-
(Niles Chignon; William Randolph Hirsch, a joint pseudonym)

PERSONAL: Born January 2, 1931, in Crawfordsville, Ind.; son of Byron Newton and Vera (Spencer) Lingeman; married Anthea Nicholson (a graphic designer), April 3, 1965. *Education:* Haverford College, B.A., 1953; also studied law at Yale University and did graduate work at Columbia University. *Office: Nation,* 72 Fifth Ave., New York, N.Y. 10011.

CAREER: Monocle (magazine), New York City, co-founder and executive editor, beginning 1962; *New York Times Book Review,* New York City, associate editor and columnist, 1969-78; *Nation,* New York City, executive editor, 1978—. Public relations consultant to Peace Corps. *Military service:* U.S. Army, 1953-56.

WRITINGS: (Editor with Victor Navasky) *The Monocle Peep Show,* Bantam, 1965; (under pseudonym Niles Chignon) *The Camp Follower's Guide,* Avon, 1965; (with Marvin Kitman under joint pseudonym William Randolph Hirsch) *The Red Chinese Air Force Diet, Exercise, and Sex Book,* Stein & Day,

1967; *Drugs from A to Z*, McGraw, 1969, revised edition, 1974; *Don't You Know There's a War On: The American Home Front, 1941-45*, Putnam, 1970; *Small Town America: A Narrative History, 1620-The Present*, Putnam, 1980. Contributor to periodicals, including *New York Times Book Review, Der Spiegel, Esquire, Playboy, World, Nation*, and *New Republic*. Editor, *Outsider's Newsletter*.

WORK IN PROGRESS: A biography of Theodore Dreiser, for Putnam.

SIDELIGHTS: "In American folklore," writes Stephen Darst in *Commonweal*, "the small town is either Eden or Zenith and one of the considerable accomplishments of Richard Lingeman's *Small Town America* is that his portrait is balanced, whole and unburdened by either hostility or sentimentality in its pursuit of the reality behind the twin myths." Lingeman's book is both a comprehensive survey and a critical analysis of American small town life. According to John Leonard of the *New York Times*, the work is "grand social history. It sweeps to generalization and stoops to anecdote. It is full of idealism and flimflam, corn and greed, sod and technology. It takes us from the usual New England theocracy of white churches and green commons to the frontier outposts of the Northwest territories of Ohio, Indiana and Illinois; from the homesteads and prairie junctions of the Great Plains to the mining camps of California and Colorado; from the plantation to the mill town to the trading post to the company store to the tourist trap. Small, it tells us, has seldom been beautiful, although it always wanted to be."

In reviewing *Small Town America*, some critics make special mention of the author's extensive research. Nicholas Lemann suggests that perhaps Lingeman has incorporated too much of what he learned into his book. Lemann remarks in *New Republic* that the author "has read virtually every word ever written by a sociologist, historian, novelist, or poet on the subject [of small town life], and done a solid job of putting it all together. The only drawback to his research is that its total reliance on secondary sources makes him a prisoner of what's in the library; when there's a *Babbitt* or a *Middletown* to draw from the book works, and when there isn't it gets bogged down in a mass of the small details of social history, such as the contents of shelves in frontier stores." *New York Times Book Review* critic Evan Connell finds the author has done his research "so conscientiously and thoroughly that nobody else will attempt a similar book. Whatever you might conceivably want to know about American small towns is here; . . . everything you might care about is here. Everything and considerably more. The magnitude of Mr. Lingeman's research is not just impressive, it is appalling. The bibliography lists some 300 sources."

Some critics question whether all this detail contributes to an overall understanding of Lingeman's subject. Michael Zuckerman, in a *Nation* article, feels that "for all the pages he devotes to all these aspects of the past, Lingeman never allows his history to intrude importantly on his conceptions of those little communities. His concern is with the residues of the towns in the American mind, not with their realities on the ground. From his first sentence, he deals in 'memory' more than in anything substantial. To his last line, he dwells on 'dreams' more than on anything mundane." *Small Town America* "fairly bursts with interesting material," writes *Washington Post Book World* reviewer Noel Perrin, "but if you really want to *understand* American small towns, you would do better to read something like Truman Capote's *In Cold Blood*, which captures

the western-open form, or James Gould Cozzen's novel *By Love Possessed*, which captures the eastern-inward variety. This book documents and describes, but it never captures anything."

Reviewers Robert R. Harris and Walter Clemons, however, find more to praise in the book. According to Harris's *Village Voice* article, "Interspersed throughout and concentrated in two chapters is, in effect, another book, an absorbing and authoritative examination of the creative writers who blew the whistle on small-town hypocrisy—e.g., Sinclair Lewis (*Main Street*), Sherwood Anderson (*Winesburg, Ohio*), Edgar Lee Masters (*Spoon River Anthology*). It is in these sections that Lingeman seems most at home, and where his analysis is most penetrating. It could be argued that he should have written just this second book of literary commentary; he has enough material. But he has seen (rightly, I think) that careful consideration of these novels and poems needs the underpinning history he supplies. He wisely views these creative works as social history intricately bound up with 'factual' small-town realities." And Clemons, writing about *Small Town America* in *Newsweek*, states that Lingeman's "most original stroke is his broadening investigation into areas we don't usually consider part of this story. He has a witty chapter on the opening of the Northwest Territory after the American Revolution, when solid towns like Marietta, Ohio—named after Marie Antoinette, considered a patroness of the American cause—sprang up alongside doomed, speculative bubbles like Gallipolis, populated by an untried band of French 'small craftsmen—jewelers, wigmakers, woodcarvers, coachmakers, gilders.'" Clemons concludes that *Small Town America* is a "finely detailed, first-rate social history."

BIOGRAPHICAL/CRITICAL SOURCES: Richard Lingeman, *Small Town America: A Narrative History, 1620-The Present*, Putnam, 1980; *New York Times*, June 13, 1980; *Washington Post World*, June 13, 1980; *New York Times Book Review*, July 6, 1980; *Newsweek*, July 28, 1980; *Nation*, August 30-September 6, 1980; *New Republic*, August 30, 1980; *Village Voice*, September 17-23, 1980; *Commonweal*, October 9, 1981.

*   *   *

LIROFF, Richard A(lan) 1948-

PERSONAL: Born June 21, 1948, in Brooklyn, N.Y.; son of Jacob S. (an attorney) and Ruth (an attorney) Liroff. *Education:* Brandeis University, B.A. (cum laude), 1969; Northwestern University, M.A., 1970, Ph.D., 1976. *Office:* Conservation Foundation, 1717 Massachusetts Ave. N.W., Washington, D.C. 20036.

CAREER: Environmental Law Institute, Washington, D.C., project associate, 1973-78; Conservation Foundation, Washington D.C., senior associate, 1979—. Member of policy board of environmental impact assessment project, Institute of Ecology, 1974. Brookings Institution, guest scholar, 1971, research fellow, 1972. Consultant to National Academy of Sciences, National Science Foundation, and U.S. Army Corps of Engineers. *Member:* Brandeis University Alumni Association (member of national executive board, 1973-75, 1979-80; vice-president, 1983-85), Washington Area Bicyclist Association (co-founder and member of board of directors, 1972-74). *Awards, honors:* Woodrow Wilson fellow, 1971.

WRITINGS: (Contributor) Leslie L. Roos, editor, *The Politics of Ecosuicide*, Holt, 1971; (contributor) Stuart Nagel, editor, *Environmental Politics*, Praeger, 1974; (contributor) Khristine

Hall and others, editors, *Enforcement of Federal and State Water Pollution Controls,* Environmental Law Institute, 1975; *A National Policy for the Environment: NEPA and Its Aftermath,* Indiana University Press 1976; *Air Pollution Offsets: Trading, Selling, and Banking,* Conservation Foundation, 1980; (co-author) *Protecting Open Space: Land Use Control in the Adirondack Park,* Ballinger, 1981; (co-editor) *Cost-Benefit Analysis and Environmental Regulations: Politics, Ethics, and Methods,* Conservation Foundation, 1982. Contributor to *Natural Resources Journal, Environmental Law Reporter, Journal of the American Planning Association, Policy Studies Journal,* and other scholarly journals.

*   *   *

LLOYD, Peter C(utt) 1927-

PERSONAL: Born June 7, 1927, in Bournemouth, England; son of Sidney and Gladys (Figg) Lloyd; married Barbara Bloom (a lecturer in social psychology at University of Sussex), July 4, 1964; children: Rachel Ann, David Ayodeji Justin. *Education:* New College, Oxford, B.A., 1948, B.Sc., 1952, D.Phil., 1958. *Home:* 50 Woodland Dr., Hove, Sussex BN3 6DL, England. *Office:* School of Social Sciences, University of Sussex, Brighton, England.

CAREER: West African Institute of Social and Economic Research, Ibadan, Nigeria, research fellow, 1949-56; Western Nigerian Ministry of Lands, Ibadan, lands research officer, 1956-59; University of Ibadan, Ibadan, Nigeria, lecturer, 1959-62, senior lecturer in sociology, 1962-64; University of Birmingham, Birmingham, England, senior lecturer, 1964-66, reader in sociology, 1966-67; University of Sussex, Brighton, England, reader, 1967-78, professor of social anthropology, 1978—. *Member:* Association of Social Anthropologists of the British Commonwealth (honorary secretary, 1967-71). *Awards, honors:* Amaury Talbot Prize, 1962, for *Yoruba Land Law,* 1967, for *Africa in Social Change: Changing Traditional Societies in the Modern World,* and 1974, for *Power and Independence.*

WRITINGS: Yoruba Land Law, Oxford University Press, 1962; (editor) *The New Elites of Tropical Africa,* Oxford University Press, 1966; *Africa in Social Change: Changing Traditional Societies in the Modern World,* Penguin, 1967, Praeger, 1969; (editor with A. Mabogunje and B. Awe) *The City of Ibadan,* Cambridge University Press, 1967.

Classes, Crises, and Coups, McGibbon & Kee, 1971, Paladin, 1972; *Power and Independence,* Routledge & Kegan Paul, 1974; *Slums of Hope?,* Penguin, 1979; *The "Young Towns" of Lima,* Cambridge University Press, 1980; *A Third World Proletariat?,* Allen & Unwin, 1981. Contributor to journals.

WORK IN PROGRESS: Research in Third World shanty towns and on community action.

BIOGRAPHICAL/CRITICAL SOURCES: Times Literary Supplement, February 8, 1968.

*   *   *

LOCKE, Elsie 1912-

PERSONAL: Born August 17, 1912, in Hamilton, New Zealand; daughter of William John (a builder) and Ellen (Bryan) Farrelly; married John Gibson Locke (a meat worker); children: Donald Bryan, Keith James, Maire Frances, Alison Gwyneth. *Education:* University of Auckland, B.A., 1932. *Politics:* No

political affiliation. *Religion:* Agnostic-humanist. *Home:* 392 Oxford Ter., Christchurch 1, New Zealand.

CAREER: Has worked in libraries in New Zealand and in a number of other occupations; began to write "seriously and systematically" only after her children were grown enough to allow her the time and freedom from distractions. *Awards, honors:* Katherine Mansfield Award, 1959, for essay "Looking for Answers," published in *Landfall,* December, 1958.

WRITINGS: The Runaway Settlers (juvenile historical novel), J. Cape, 1965, Dutton, 1966; *The End of the Harbour* (juvenile historical novel), J. Cape, 1968; *Maori King and British Queen,* Hulton Educational, Round the World Histories, 1974; *Look under the Leaves* (juvenile ecological picture book), Pumpkin Press (Christchurch, New Zealand), 1975; *Moko's Hideout* (New Zealand animal stories), Whitcoulls (Christchurch), 1976; (with Ken Dawson) *The Boy with the Snowglass Hair* (juvenile adventure novel), Whitcoulls, 1976; *Explorer Zach* (juvenile novel), Pumpkin Press, 1978; *The Gaoler* (adult history), Dunmore Press, 1978; (contributor) Dorothy Butler, editor, *The Magpies Said* (juvenile anthology), Kestrel, 1980; *Student at the Gates* (personal experience), Whitcoulls, 1981; *Journey under Warning* (juvenile historical novel), Oxford University Press, 1983; *The Kauri and the Willow,* Government Printer (New Zealand), in press.

Also author of a juvenile historical novel, and of radio scripts, articles, and poems.

SIDELIGHTS: Of European descent from early New Zealand settlers on both sides of her family, Elsie Locke told *CA* that she is "also very interested in the Maori (Polynesian) side of New Zealand life, and the human relationship with the earth and all it bears." She adds: "Children are to be enjoyed, their individuality respected, their imaginations cherished; and writing for them is a privilege and a pleasure. To defend their world from the threat of nuclear and/or ecological disaster, and to secure a fully human life for those now deprived, are aims I share with millions of others; but I am optimistic and not solemn in my writings. I would like all children to enjoy their childhood as much as I did mine."

*   *   *

LONERGAN, Bernard J(oseph) F(rancis) 1904-

PERSONAL: Born December 17, 1904, in Buckingham, Quebec, Canada; son of Gerald Joseph (a surveyor) and Josephine Helen (Wood) Lonergan. *Education:* Attended Loyola College, Montreal, Quebec, 1920-22, Ignatius College, 1922-26, and Heythrop College (now of University of London), 1926-30; University of London, B.A., 1930; Pontifical Gregorian University, S.T.L., 1937, S.T.D., 1945. *Office:* Jesuit Community, Boston College, Chestnut Hill, Mass. 02167.

CAREER: Entered Society of Jesus (Jesuits), 1922, ordained Roman Catholic priest, 1936; L'Immaculee Conception, Montreal, Quebec, extraordinary professor, 1940-42, ordinary professor of theology, 1942-47; Jesuit Seminary, Toronto, Ontario, ordinary professor of theology, 1947-53; Pontifical Gregorian University, Rome, Italy, ordinary professor of theology, 1953-65; Regis College, Willowdale, Ontario, research professor of theology, 1965-75; Boston College, Chestnut Hill, Mass., visiting distinguished professor of theology, 1975—. Stillman Professor at Harvard University Divinity School, 1971-72. Peritus of Second Vatican Council; member of International Theological Commission, 1969-74; consultor of Secretariat for Non-Believers, 1973-78.

Spellman Award, Catholic Theological Society of America, 1949; Aquinas Medal, American Catholic Philosophical Association, 1970; Companion of the Order of Canada, 1970; John Courtney Murray Award, Catholic Theological Society of America, 1973; Aquinas Award, Aquinas College, 1974. Honorary doctorates from St. Mary's University (Halifax), 1964; Holy Cross College (Worcester, Mass.) and University of St. Michael's (Toronto), 1969; Marquette University and Boston College, 1970; Catholic University of America, University of Notre Dame, Fordham University, and University of Santa Clara, 1971; St. Joseph's College (Philadelphia) and St. Louis University, 1972; Wilfred Laurier University, 1973; and University of Chicago, 1974.

WRITINGS: De Constitutione Christi Ontologica et Psychologica (title means "Systematic Theology of the Incarnation"), Pontifical Gregorian University Press, 1956, supplement, 1964; *Divinarum Personarum Conceptionem Analogicam*, Pontifical Gregorian University Press, 1957; *Insight: A Study of Human Understanding*, Philosophical Library, 1957, 4th edition, Harper, 1978; *De Deo Trino* (title means "On the Trinity"), Volume I: *Pars Dogmatica*, Pontifical Gregorian University Press, 1959, translation by Conn O'Donovan published as *The Way to Nicea: The Dialectical Development of Trinitarian Theology*, Westminster, 1976, Volume II: *Pars Analytica*, Pontifical Gregorian University Press, 1961, 3rd edition, 1964.

De Verbo Incarnato (title means "On the Incarnation"), Pontifical Gregorian University Press, 1961, 3rd edition, 1964; *Collection* (essays on philosophy and theology), edited by Frederick E. Crowe, Herder & Herder, 1967; *Verbum: Word and Idea in Aquinas* (essays originally published in *Theological Studies*, 1946-49), edited by David B. Burrell, University of Notre Dame Press, 1967.

Grazia e Liberta: La Grazia Operante nel Pensiero di S. Tommaso (originally published in four installments in *Theological Studies*, 1941-42), Pontifical Gregorian University Press, 1970, translation published as *Grace and Freedom: Operative Grace in the Thought of St. Thomas Aquinas*, edited by J. Patout Burns, introduction by Crowe, Herder & Herder, 1971; *Doctrinal Pluralism*, Marquette University Press, 1971; *Method in Theology*, Herder & Herder, 1972, 2nd edition, 1973; *Philosophy of God, and Theology: The Relationship between Philosophy of God and the Functional Specialty, Systematics*, Darton, Longman & Todd, 1973, Westminster, 1974; *Introducing the Thought of Bernard Lonergan* (contains three essays originally published in *Collection*, "Cognitional Structure," "Existenz and Aggiornamento," and "Dimensions of Meaning"), Darton, Longman & Todd, 1973; *A Second Collection*, Darton, Longman & Todd, 1974, Westminster, 1975; *Bernard Lonergan: Three Lectures*, edited by R. Eric O'Connor, Thomas More Institute for Adult Education (Montreal), 1975; *Theologie im Pluralismus Heutiger Kulturen*, Herder (Freiburg im Breisgau), 1975; *Understanding and Being: An Introduction and Companion to "Insight,"* edited by Elizabeth A. Morelli and Mark D. Morelli, Edwin Mellen, 1980.

Contributor: Christopher F. Mooney, editor, *The Presence and Absence of God*, Fordham University Press, 1969; *Foundations of Theology*, University of Notre Dame Press, 1970; J. Papin, editor, *The Pilgrim People*, Villanova University Press, 1970; R. Laflamme and M. Gervais, editors, *Le Christ hier, aujourd'hui, et demain*, Laval University Press, 1976; T. A. Dunne and J. M. Laporte, editors, *Trinification of the World: A Festschrift in Honour of F. E. Crowe*, Regis College Press, 1978; Fred Lawrence, editor, *Lonergan Workshop I*, Scholars

Press, 1978. Contributor to *Proceedings* of American Catholic Philosophy Association and to periodicals, including *Studies in Religion, Journal of Religion,* and *Cultural Hermeneutics.*

SIDELIGHTS: Bernard J. F. Lonergan "is a philosopher's philosopher and a theologian's theologian," writes the late Kenneth Rexroth in *The Elastic Retort*, "[though] even the well-informed public has scarcely heard of him." Described as a naturally shy man who seems indifferent to when, if ever, his writings reach publication, Lonergan ranks as one of the foremost Roman Catholic thinkers in the area of systematic and philosophical theology. In appropriating the best of secular knowledge into a higher Christian synthesis, he has "closed a seven-century gap in Catholic thought," says Michael Novak in *Commonweal*, "[and] given Catholic theology both scientific and historical consciousness." Yet, Lonergan's influence has spread far beyond religious circles, due primarily to his work *Insight*, which "has become a philosophic classic comparable in scope to [David] Hume's *Inquiry Concerning Human Understanding,*" notes a *Newsweek* reporter. Lonergan's attempt to provide "an understanding of understanding," according to *Time*, has led many intellectuals to consider him "the finest philosophic thinker of the twentieth century."

After entering the Society of Jesus in 1922, Lonergan studied philosophy at the Jesuit's Heythrop College in England and theology at Rome's Pontifical Gregorian University. When he began instructing seminarians in theology, he found it impossible to teach the subject properly without first establishing an underlying philosophy; to do that, however, required a consideration of the fundamental question "What does it mean to know?" Lonergan's studies in epistemology initially led him to rediscover the introspective psychological data out of which Thomas Aquinas elaborated his insights into Church doctrine. Recognizing that theology had not kept pace with man's intellectual evolution, Lonergan gradually expanded the focus of his inquiry to include other fields of knowledge: mathematics, the natural sciences, the arts. His research into man's knowing process culminated in *Insight*, a work acclaimed by secular and religious thinkers alike for its all-embracing theory of knowledge.

"With that boldness characteristic of genius," exclaims a *Newsweek* reviewer, "Lonergan has set out [in *Insight*] to do for the twentieth century what even Aquinas could not do for the thirteenth: provide an 'understanding of understanding' that can illuminate not only the broad outline of all accumulated knowledge but also reveal an 'invariant pattern' for further developments in human understanding." A *Time* writer states that Lonergan's "viewpoint is inherited from Aristotle and Aquinas, but has been expanded by Kant and Freud. Using a vocabulary uniquely his own, he has written a general field theory of the mind—the origin and nature of human insight, how it relates to its various forms of expression, whether in the formulas of the physicist, the work pictures of the poet, [or] the concepts of the philosopher."

Lonergan's theory is immensely valuable in an age where specialization often stifles interdisciplinary communication, observes the *Time* writer: "*Insight* . . . spells out the possibility of a transcultural philosophy that would allow thinkers from different traditions . . . to understand one another by paying attention first to each other's basic cognitional activity: how one unifies data, why he does so in a particular fashion. To understand someone else, says Lonergan, a thinker must first understand how his own awareness of reality has been historically and psychologically conditioned by preconceptions."

Lonergan insists that all real human knowledge is "self-appropriation"—a claim that "reveals an unexpected kinship with Oriental paths to enlightenment," according to the *Newsweek* reporter. "Yet, like Anglo-Saxon empiricists, [Lonergan] requires validation for judgments and, like the classical European metaphysicians, he insists that reality is ultimately intelligible. To those who would learn from him, he counsels Socratically: learn from your own consciousness, not from my [book].''

In focusing on the personal, dynamic aspects of understanding, Lonergan borrows from the phenomenologists, particularly the German philosopher Edmund Husserl. Adopting Husserl's idea of "horizon"—the vastness or narrowness of the world a man perceives based on his environment, his loves and fears, his interests and prejudices—Lonergan maintains that understanding changes with perspective and the understander himself must change as he approaches each new horizon. A *Time* reviewer summarizes the theory this way: "A man can alter his horizon by recognizing it as a limitation on his ability to know—indeed, as a limitation on the very questions that he must ask in order to know. He can open himself to information from outside his horizon, use that information to formulate new questions, and continue to grow. By thus transcending his limitations, a man undergoes 'conversion,' which may be moral, intellectual, social or religious. In Lonergan's approach. . . , the ultimate horizon is an openness to an experience of God.''

Prior to *Insight* (his first book in English), Lonergan wrote primarily in Latin and for scholarly journals; his reputation therefore rested for many years on the convictions of his peers and a scattering of essays. *Insight*, published in 1957, did little to alter this situation at first because of the book's technical nature and language. But by 1970, Lonergan's work had become so influential that seventy-seven of the world's best minds—critics and admirers, Protestants, Roman Catholics, and agnostics—gathered at St. Leo College in Florida to offer him a "living festschrift." Such distinguished participants as British philosopher Elizabeth Anscombe, poet Kenneth Rexroth, Protestant theologian Langdon Gilkey, and U.S. Senator Eugene McCarthy critiqued Lonergan's ideas, often comparing him with such thinkers as John Dewey and Ludwig Wittgenstein. "As everyone who took part and even the most cynical observers from the press recognized," Rexroth later noted, "[the conference] was a landmark.''

Despite the acclaim awarded him, Lonergan has received his share of negative criticism. Some non-Catholic thinkers grappling with the same issues are repelled by his unfashionably Thomistic starting point. Doctrinaire Thomists, on the other hand, are bothered by his unconventional revision of Aquinas—especially by the notion of "moving horizons," which contrasts sharply with the traditional position that knowledge is absolute. And Michael Novak, a lay theologian who studied under Lonergan at the Pontifical Gregorian University, claims that he "has not yet carried theology to an adequate political consciousness, nor to an adequate theoretical understanding of action and experience." Novak believes that Lonergan's theory, thematized largely in the context of science, "does not provide a good model for the horizon of daily human understanding, and not even for the horizon of theoretical, highly thematized understanding that is directed toward culture, politics, and personal history.''

Lonergan's work, however, ultimately commands respect. "I used to read Jacques Maritain or Etienne Gilson to find out what Roman Catholic intellectuals were thinking," Langdon Gilkey says in *Newsweek*. "Now I read Father Lonergan to

find out what *I* am thinking." Novak writes that among major thinkers, Lonergan "is unparalleled for his emphasis on the sheer *experience* of having insights, reaching concrete judgments, making decisions. . . . He has taken the subjective side of Western thought (Pascal, Blake, Kierkegaard, Nietzsche, etc.) and made its power apparent *inside* the inmost citadels of the objective side of Western thought (Aquinas, Leibniz, Kant, Newton, Hume, Russell, etc.). He has given the word 'empirical' a subjective meaning, and altered our understanding both of 'objectivity' and 'subjectivity.''' "Lonergan has become a true 'philosopher of culture,''' concludes a *Time* reporter. "In his grasp of the process of understanding that underlies every science, he is the twentieth century counterpart of a Renaissance man.''

BIOGRAPHICAL/CRITICAL SOURCES: Bernard J. F. Lonergan, *Insight: A Study of Human Understanding,* Philosophical Library, 1957; *Social Studies,* April, 1958; *Times Literary Supplement,* April 4, 1958; *Continuum,* Volume II, number 3, 1964; *Time,* January 22, 1965, April 20, 1970; *America,* July 1, 1967, March 21, 1970, February 12, 1972, August 5, 1972; *Critic,* August, 1967; *Foundations of Theology,* University of Notre Dame Press, 1970; David Tracy, *Achievement of Bernard Lonergan,* Herder & Herder, 1970; *Newsweek,* April 20, 1970; *Commonweal,* May 29, 1970, February 23, 1973, July 4, 1975; *Christian Century,* June 24, 1970, September 16, 1970; McShane, editor, *Papers from Lonergan Congress,* University of Notre Dame Press, Volume I, 1971, Volume II, 1972; Kenneth Rexroth, *The Elastic Retort: Essays in Literature and Ideas,* Seabury, 1973; Frederick E. Crowe, *The Lonergan Enterprise,* Cowley, 1980; McShane, *Lonergan's Challenge to the University and the Economy,* University Press of America, 1980; Matthew Lamb, editor, *Creativity and Method: In Honor of Bernard Lonergan,* Marquette University Press, 1981.

—*Sketch by James G. Lesniak*

*   *   *

LORD, Shirley
See ANDERSON, Shirley Lord

*   *   *

LORTZ, Richard 1917-1980

PERSONAL: Born January 13, 1917, in New York, N.Y.; died November 5, 1980, in New York, N.Y.; divorced; children: one. *Education:* Attended Columbia University. *Home:* 545 Beach 133rd St., Belle Harbor, Long Island, N.Y. 11694. *Agent:* Don Congdon, Harold Matson Co., Inc., 22 East 40th St., New York, N.Y. 10016. *Office:* 322 West 88th St., New York, N.Y. 10024.

CAREER: Novelist and playwright, beginning 1954; Hoffman Publications, New York City, successively managing editor and editor of various business magazines, 1954-65; *Industrial Photography* and *Audio-Visual Communications,* New York City, managing editor, 1965-71. Artist; had work exhibited in several one-man and group shows. *Military service:* U.S. Army; became sergeant. *Awards, honors:* St. Gaudens Medal for fine draftsmanship, 1948; Hallmark International Art Award for painting, 1952; Stanley Drama Award, 1970, for play "Three Sons.''

WRITINGS—Novels: *A Crowd of Voices,* Bobbs-Merrill, 1958; *A Summer in Spain,* P. Davies, 1961, published as *The Valdepenas,* Second Chance Press, 1980; *Children of the Night,* Dell, 1974; *The Betrothed,* Dell, 1975; *Lovers Living, Lovers*

Dead, Dell, 1977; *Bereavements*, Permanent Press, 1980; *Dracula's Children*, Permanent Press, 1981.

Plays: "A Journey with Strangers" (three-act; later titled "Martin Doyle"), first produced Off-Broadway at Greenwich Mews Theatre, 1958; "The Others" (two-act), first produced in Leatherhead, England, 1967, produced on the West End at Strand Theatre, 1968, produced as "Voices" on Broadway at Ethel Barrymore Theatre, 1972 (also see below); *Of Sons and Brothers: A Play* (two-act; first produced as "Three Sons" in Staten Island, N.Y., at Wagner College, 1970; produced in New York by Circle Theatre Repertory Company, 1974; later titled "Prodigal"), Studio Duplicating Service, 1970; "The Juniper Tree" (two-act), first produced Off-Off-Broadway by the Splinters Company, 1972; *Voices* [and] *The Widow* (both one-act), Performance Publishing, 1974. Also author of plays "Recent Bestiaries" (two one-acts), "Big Rock Candy," and "The Dream," produced in Philadelphia, Pa., at Forest Theatre.

Author of television plays, all produced in the late 1950s, "Mr. Nobody," "The Kiss-Off," "The Bet," "The Others," "Vacancy for Death," "M Is for Murder," "The Key," "Circle of Doom," and other dramas for series, including "Studio One," "Suspense," "The Web," and "Danger." Also author of radio dramas. Contributor of stories to magazines, including *Esquire, Story, New Story* (Paris), *Virginia Quarterly Review, Review of Literature, Tiger's Eye on Arts and Letters, Liberty,* and *Scholastic Voice.*

WORK IN PROGRESS: Two novels, *Strangers in Cameroon* and *Ramon.*

SIDELIGHTS: In 1961, Richard Lortz published a novel, *A Summer in Spain,* which met with critical, but not commercial, success. Almost twenty years later, the book was re-released under the title *The Valdepenas.* In a *New York Times* review of the novel, Anatole Broyard remarked: "It is easy to see why *The Valdepenas* was neglected in its first time out, because it is merely well written. It has no grand symptomatology, no identifiable pretensions. Its story consists of interesting and well-realized characters behaving according to the dictates of their needs and desires." And a *New Yorker* critic hoped that "this time around [the book] will be more widely enjoyed for its whimsy and panache."

MEDIA ADAPTATIONS: "The Others" has been produced as a television play in London, England, and Toronto, Ontario; the play was also adapted into a film, "Voices," in 1974.

BIOGRAPHICAL/CRITICAL SOURCES: New York Times, January 31, 1980; *New Yorker,* March 17, 1980.

OBITUARIES: New York Times, November 11, 1980; *Publishers Weekly,* December 5, 1980; *AB Bookman's Weekly,* December 15, 1980.†

*   *   *

LOVE, Sandra (Weller) 1940-

PERSONAL: Born March 28, 1940, in Louisville, Ky.; daughter of Carroll Dane (a businessman) and Alma (a teacher; maiden name, Hoffmann) Weller; married Joseph Daniel Love, August 19, 1961 (divorced, 1972); married Samuel W. Young (a businessman), June 3, 1975; children: (first marriage) Lisa Carroll, Linda Elizabeth; (second marriage) Michael Lloyd, Ellen Campbell (stepchildren). *Education:* Purdue University, B.S., 1961; University of Louisville, M.A., 1964. *Home:* 135 North Walnut St., Yellow Springs, Ohio 45387. *Agent:* Roberta Pryor,

International Creative Management, Inc., 40 West 57th St., New York, N.Y. 10019.

CAREER: Teacher of English, department chairman, and supervisor of student teachers in public schools in Louisville, Ky., 1961-66; University of Georgia, Extension, Warner Robins, instructor in English, 1967-68; *Dayton Journal Herald,* Dayton, Ohio, reporter, 1971-72; Wright State University, Dayton, instructor in English, 1972-75; writer, 1975—. Visiting lecturer in children's literature, Antioch College, Yellow Springs, Ohio, 1983. *Member:* Authors Guild, Authors League of America, Society of Children's Book Writers, Martha Kinney Cooper Ohioana Library Association, Yellow Springs Library Association, Yellow Springs Writers Group. *Awards, honors:* Elizabeth Enright Award from Indiana Writers Conference, 1972, for story "Sunday Morning, Winter Morning"; Society of Children's Book Writers award, 1980, and Ohio Arts Council award, 1981, both for *Dive for the Sun.*

WRITINGS—All juveniles: *But What About Me?,* Harcourt, 1976; *Melissa's Medley,* Harcourt, 1978; *Crossing Over,* Lothrup, 1981; *Dive for the Sun,* Houghton, 1982.

WORK IN PROGRESS: Discovery Mountain, a novel for young people.

SIDELIGHTS: Sandra Love told *CA:* "I write to capture the special moments in life, the times that change one's viewpoint permanently. I write for children because they like the simplicity of language and immediacy of plot that help me explore life.

"In my stories I focus on a central problem that I know and care about. In *But What About Me?* Lucy is frightened by her mother's going to work—she feels it is desertion. When Lucy faces the problems and solves them, she becomes a different, stronger person. In my second book, Melissa has to come to terms with priorities—for her, it is complicated by the fact that she is a competitive swimmer. In *Crossing Over,* Megan tangles with two conflicts: living with a father she no longer knows well, and studying at a military academy not designed for women. Kris Ramsey, in *Dive for the Sun,* is a young man headed into crisis. He can neither transform his own loss and fear nor cope with his father's search for a lost Spanish galleon until he encounters a dream world of his own.

"More generally, I write to make order out of chaos. If fiction fights its way to a small triumph, even though it is linked to a limited time, place, and character, something good happens. I see women changing, too, and as we do, we alter the world around us. I want to show this growing consciousness."

AVOCATIONAL INTERESTS: Gardening, photography, swimming (also teaches swimming), sailing, scuba diving.

*   *   *

LOVEGROVE, Philip
See RAY, John (Philip)

*   *   *

LOWENS, Irving 1916-

PERSONAL: First syllable of surname rhymes with "row"; born August 19, 1916, in New York, N.Y.; son of Harry and Hedwig (Abramovich) Lowens; married Violet Elen Halper (a music librarian), July 30, 1939; married Margery Louise Morgan, February 1, 1969. *Education:* Columbia University, B.S. in Music, 1939; University of Maryland, M.A., 1957, graduate study, 1957-59. *Home:* 5511 North Charles St., Baltimore, Md. 21210. *Office:* Peabody Institute, Johns Hopkins University, 1 East Mount Vernon Pl., Baltimore, Md. 21202.

CAREER: Washington Star, Washington, D.C., contributing music critic, 1953-61, principal music critic, 1961-78; Johns Hopkins University, Peabody Institute, Baltimore, Md., dean, 1978—. Library of Congress, reference librarian for sound recordings, 1959-61, assistant head of reference section, 1962-66. Lecturer at colleges and universities, including Dunbarton College, 1958-59, Yale University, University of Michigan, Ohio State University, and University of Southern California; senior research fellow and visiting professor at Institute for Studies in American Music, Brooklyn College of the City University of New York, 1975-76. Acting chairman of organizational committee, Musical Arts Research and Development Institute, 1965. Member of advisory board, Inter-American Institute for Musical Research, Tulane University, 1961-76, Oral History of Music in America Project, City University of New York, 1974—, and Terrace Theater, Kennedy Center for the Performing Arts, 1979—; trustee, Robert D. Lehman Foundation, 1964-66, and Inter-American Music and Arts Festivals Foundation, 1976—; member of board of directors, American Music Center, 1966-72, and People-to-People Music Committee, 1973—; member of board of governors, WJHU-FM, 1978—. Consultant to Moravian Music Foundation, 1956—, and to Juilliard Repertory Project, 1965.

MEMBER: International Musicological Society, International Association of Music Libraries, American Musicological Society (member of national council; member-at-large of executive board, 1965), Music Library Association (member of executive board, 1962-64; vice-president, 1964-65; president, 1965-66), Music Critics Association (treasurer, 1962-69; vice-president, 1969-71; president, 1971-75; member of executive board, 1975-77), Society for Ethnomusicology, American Studies Association, Inter-American Association of Music Critics (vice-president, 1973—), American Antiquarian Society (fellow), American Folklore Society, Bibliographical Society of America, College Music Society, Hymn Society of America, American Association of University Professors, Manuscript Society, American Liszt Society (member of advisory board, 1977—), Sonneck Society (chairman pro tem, 1974-75; president, 1975—), Cosmos Club (Washington, D.C.), Johns Hopkins Faculty Club (Baltimore).

AWARDS, HONORS: First recipient of Moramus Award, Moravian Music Foundation, 1960, for distinguished service to American music; American Council of Learned Societies and Rockefeller Foundation travel grants to International Musicological Congresses in Germany, 1962, Austria, 1964, and Romania, 1967; U.S. Department of State travel grant to Venezuela, 1968, and Greece and Cyprus, 1970; American Council of Learned Societies grant; National Endowment for the Arts research grant, 1969; American Society of Composers, Authors, and Publishers-Deems Taylor Award, 1973 and 1977, for best newspaper articles on music.

WRITINGS: The Hartford Harmony: A Selection of American Hymns from the Late Eighteenth and Early Nineteenth Centuries, Hartford Seminary Foundation, 1953; (with Vincent Silliman) *We Sing of Life: Songs for Children, Young People, Adults,* Starr King Press, 1955; *Music and Musicians in Early America,* Norton, 1964; (author of preface) *Lectures on the History and Art of Music: The Louis Charles Elson Memorial Lectures at the Library of Congress,* facsimile edition, Da Capo Press, 1968; (author of introduction) Edward MacDowell, *Crit-*

ical and Historical Essays, edited by W. J. Baltzell, facsimile edition, Da Capo Press, 1969.

A Bibliography of Songsters Printed in America before 1821, American Antiquarian Society, 1976; *Music in America and American Music: Two Views of the Scene,* Institute for Studies in American Music, Brooklyn College of the City University of New York, 1978; *Hadyn in America,* Information Coordinators, 1980.

Editor: John Tufts, *Introduction to the Singing of Psalm-Tunes,* facsimile edition, Musical Americana, 1954; Benjamin Carr, *Federal Overture,* facsimile edition, Musical Americana, 1957; *The American Harmony* (recording), Washington Records, 1961; John Wyeth, *Repository of Sacred Music, Part Second,* facsimile edition, Da Capo Press, 1964; O. G. Sonneck and W. T. Upton, *A Bibliography of Early Secular American Music,* facsimile edition, Da Capo Press, 1964.

Also author of *Opera and Sonic Collage* and *Beatrix Cenci;* compiler of editions of early American music published by E. B. Marks Music Corp. and G. Schirmer. Original songs and choruses published by G. Schirmer and Willis Music Co., and in *Musicology.* Contributor of articles and reviews to music journals and other periodicals. Chairman of board of directors, *American Musical Digest,* 1967-70.

WORK IN PROGRESS: Source Readings in American Music History; A History of American Music.

SIDELIGHTS: Irving Lowens is fluent in German, competent in French, Italian, and Spanish, and has reading knowledge of Romanian. *Avocational interests:* Chess, subminiature photography, collecting musical Americana and stamps about music.†

*   *   *

LOXTON, (Charles) Howard 1934-

PERSONAL: Surname originally Loxston; born July 10, 1934, in Birmingham, England; son of Percy (a clerk) and Florence (Howard) Loxston. *Education:* Attended Birmingham Theatre School, 1949-51. *Address:* 21 Alma St., London NW5 3DJ, England.

CAREER: Editor and author. Performer and stage director, working in theater, films, and television in England, 1950-58; director of Jackdaw Publications, London, England, 1964-71. Served on Arts Council Working Party investigating the Obscene Publication Acts, 1968-69. *Member:* National Union of Journalists (chairman).

WRITINGS: (Editor) *Dogs, Dogs, Dogs,* Paul Hamlyn, 1962; *Railways,* Paul Hamlyn, 1962, revised edition, 1970; *Pompeii and Herculaneum,* Spring Books, 1966; *The Beauty of Cats,* Ward Lock, 1972; *The Beauty of Big Cats,* Ward Lock, 1973; *All Colour Book of Kittens,* Octopus Books, 1974; *Caring for Your Cat,* Arco, 1975; *Guide to the Cats of the World,* Phaidon Press, 1975; *In Search of Cats,* Excalibur Books, 1976; *Pilgrimage to Canterbury,* David & Charles, 1978; *Train Your Human,* David & Charles, 1979; *Cats,* Sundial, 1979; *Spotters Guide to Cats,* Usborne, 1980; *Cats,* Ward Lock, 1981, Granada, 1983; (editor) *How to Hold a Crocodile,* Ballantine, 1981. Contributor to encyclopedias, and to story collections for children. Editor of *Viewpoint* (magazine about television), 1956-58.

Compiler; all published by Jackdaw Publications: *The Battle of Agincourt: A Collection of Contemporary Documents,* 1966;

(with Lawrence E. Tanner and Nicholas H. MacMichael) *Westminister Abbey: A Collection of Contemporary Documents*, 1967; (and designer with Michael Rand and Len Deighton) *The Assassination of President Kennedy*, 1970; *Christmas: A Collection of Documents*, 1970; *The Murder of Thomas Beckett: A Collection of Contemporary Documents*, 1971; *Shakespeare's Theatre*, 1972.

WORK IN PROGRESS: Historical and topographical projects; a feline anthology; a study of the relationships between animals and Man.

*   *   *

LUCAS, J(ohn) R(andolph) 1929-

PERSONAL: Born June 18, 1929, in London, England; son of Egbert de Grey (a clergyman) and Joan Mary (Randolph) Lucas; married Helen Morar Portal, June 17, 1961; children: Edward de Grey, Helen Mary, Richard Henry, Deborah Joan. *Education:* Balliol College, Oxford, B.A. (first class honours), 1951. *Religion:* Church of England. *Home:* Postmaster's Hall, Merton St., Oxford OX1 4JE, England. *Office:* Merton College, Oxford University, Oxford, England.

CAREER: Fellow of Merton College, Oxford University, Oxford, England, 1953-56, and Corpus Christi College, Cambridge University, Cambridge, England, 1956-59; University of Leeds, Leeds, England, Leverhulme fellow in philosophy of science, 1959-60; Oxford University, Merton College, fellow, 1960—. Proctor Visiting Fellow, Princeton University, 1957-58; Gifford Lecturer, University of Edinburgh, 1971-73. Oxford Consumer Group, chairman, 1961-63, 1966-67, vice-chairman, 1963-66. *Awards, honors:* John Locke Prize, Oxford University, 1952.

WRITINGS: The Principles of Politics, Clarendon Press, 1966; *The Concept of Probability*, Clarendon Press, 1970; *The Freedom of the Will*, Clarendon Press, 1970; (with A.J.P. Kenny, H. C. Longuet-Higgins, and C. H. Waddington) *The Nature of Mind*, University of Edinburgh Press, 1972; (with Kenny, Longuet-Higgins, and Waddington) *The Development of Mind*, University of Edinburgh Press, 1973; *A Treatise on Time and Space*, Methuen, 1973; *Democracy and Participation*, Penguin, 1976; *Essays on Freedom and Grace*, S.P.C.K., 1976; *On Justice*, Clarendon Press, 1980; *Space, Time and Causality*, Clarendon Press, 1983.

Contributor: B. G. Mitchell, editor, *Faith and Logic*, Macmillan, 1957; R. J. Butler, editor, *Analytical Philosophy*, Barnes & Noble, 1962; Kenneth M. Sayre and Frederick J. Crosson, editors, *Modeling of Mind*, University of Notre Dame Press, 1964; Alan R. Anderson, editor, *Minds and Machines*, Prentice-Hall, 1964; R. S. Summers, *Essays in Legal Philosophy*, Oxford University Press, 1968; Hugo A. Bedau, editor, *Justice and Equality*, Prentice-Hall, 1971; Richard E. Flathman, editor, *Concepts in Social and Political Philosophy*, Macmillan, 1973; Bryan R. Wilson, editor, *Education, Equality and Society*, Allen & Unwin, 1975; J. Rachels, editor, *Moral Problems*, Harper, 1975; Mary Briody Mahowald, editor, *Philosophy of Woman*, Hacket, 1978.

WORK IN PROGRESS: An Introduction to the Philosophy of Mathematics; Morality and Scepticism; Moods and Tenses: An Essay on Modal and Tense Logic; Freedom and Foreknowledge.

BIOGRAPHICAL/CRITICAL SOURCES: Yale Review, autumn, 1967; *Times Literary Supplement*, September 12, 1980.

LUCE, William (Aubert) 1931-

PERSONAL: Born October 16, 1931, in Portland, Ore.; son of Darrel (a merchant) and Elenora (a Christian Science practitioner; maiden name, Kuul) Luce. *Education:* Attended Boston University, University of Washington, Seattle, and Lewis and Clark College. *Home and office address:* Penmaen Press, RD 2, Box 145, Great Barrington, Mass. 01230. *Agent:* Gilbert Parker, William Morris Agency, 1350 Avenue of the Americas, New York, N.Y. 10019.

CAREER: Church organist and composer of church music, 1948-66; writer, 1966—; currently affiliated with Penmaen Press, Great Barrington, Mass. Christian Science practitioner, 1954-66. Singer; has performed with Norman Luboff Choir, Ray Charles Singers, Roger Wagner Chorale, Gregg Smith Singers, and on the "Julie London Show"; has also performed with national singing tours, and on television programs and recordings.

MEMBER: American Society of Composers, Authors and Publishers, National Federation of Poets, California State Poetry Society. *Awards, honors:* Award from Chicago Poets' Club, 1973, for "Odyssey Sonnets"; award from New England Book Show, 1982, for *World Alone*.

WRITINGS: Catalogue of Sacred Songs, Carl Fischer, 1962; *Spring Song and Other Poems*, Ritchie, 1963; *The Belle of Amherst* (one-woman two-act play; first produced in Seattle, Wash., at Moore Theatre, February 25, 1976; produced on Broadway at Longacre Theatre, April 28, 1976), Houghton, 1976; (and illustrator) *Tygers of Wrath*, University of Georgia Press, 1981; *Toward the Light: Wood Engravings by Michael McCurdy*, introduction and commentary by McCurdy, Porcupine's Quill, 1982; (and illustrator) *World Alone*, privately printed, 1982; (and illustrator) *The Best Christmas Tree Ever*, David R. Godine, 1984.

Also author of plays "Caruso," "Bronte," and "Zelda," and musicals "Sayonara" and "Peg." Author of screenplay "The Last Days of Patton." Contributor to literary journals, including *California State Poetry Quarterly*, and to newspapers.

WORK IN PROGRESS: A new play on the life of Lillian Hellman.

SIDELIGHTS: William Luce writes: "*The Belle of Amherst* is my first play. It is the culmination of years of interest in poetry—first motivated by the influence of a high school English teacher." Julie Harris has appeared both on Broadway and on tour in the play based on the life of Emily Dickinson, and she won her fifth Tony Award for her performance.

Referring to his publishing career, Luce told *CA:* "My preoccupation is with the entire book. I am a publisher of contemporary fiction, poetry, and translation—and I design and print these special editions myself. My work as a wood engraver has appeared in many publications and a book of my prints was published in 1982. The large press is beginning to pay attention now to the small press, and R. R. Bowker's premier issue [of] *Small Press* will feature Penmaen Press."

Several songs composed by Luce have been recorded by Doris Day, including "Let No Walls Divide," "Be a Child at Christmas Time," "Be Still and Know," and "The Prodigal Son."

AVOCATIONAL INTERESTS: Piano, geneology.

BIOGRAPHICAL/CRITICAL SOURCES: Oregonian, February 25, 1976; *Rocky Mountain News,* March 5, 1976; *Christian Science Monitor,* April 22, 1976; *Washington Post,* September 24, 1976.

* * *

LUCHINS, Abraham S(amuel)   1914-

PERSONAL: Surname is pronounced *Loo*-kins; born March 8, 1914, in Brooklyn, N.Y.; son of Moriss A. (a carpenter) and Anne E. (Yampolsky) Luchins; married Edith Hirsch (a professor of mathematics), October 10, 1942; children: David, Daniel, Jeremy, Anne, Joseph. *Education:* Brooklyn College (now of the City University of New York), B.A. (cum laude), 1935; Columbia University, M.A., 1936; graduate study at New School for Social Research, 1937-42; New York University, Ph.D., 1939. *Politics:* None. *Religion;* Jewish. *Residence:* Albany, N.Y. *Office:* Department of Psychology, State University of New York at Albany, Albany, N.Y. 12203.

CAREER: Psychology teacher, New York City Board of Education adult education project, 1935-39; Yeshiva College (now University), New York City, instructor, 1940-42, assistant professor of psychology, 1942-49, chairman of department, 1946-49, director of guidance, 1949; McGill University, Montreal, Quebec, associate professor of psychology in charge of social clinical program, 1949-55; University of Oregon, Eugene, associate professor of psychology, 1955-58; University of Miami, Coral Gables, Fla., professor of psychology, 1958-62; State University of New York at Albany, professor of psychology, 1962—. Research assistant to Max Wertheimer, 1939-43. Diplomate of American Board of Professional Psychology. Clinical psychologist and director of clinical psychology training at Veterans Administration Regional Office in New York City, 1947-49. Consultant to Veterans Administration, 1955-65, and to Touro College, 1974—. *Military service:* U.S. Army, 1943-46; became first lieutenant in field. *Member:* American Psychological Association (fellow), Psychonomic Society, Educational Research Association. *Awards, honors:* Named Danforth Associate, with wife, Edith H. Luchins, 1980-86.

WRITINGS: Mechanization in Problem Solving: The Effect of Einstellung, American Psychological Association, 1942; *The Study of a Mental Hospital: A Functional Approach to the Training of the Psychologist,* Oregon State Hospital, 1956; (with wife, Edith Hirsch Luchins) *Rigidity of Behavior: A Variational Approach to the Effect of Einstellung,* University of Oregon Books, 1959; *A Functional Approach to Training in Clinical Psychology via Study of a Mental Hospital,* C. C Thomas, 1959.

(With Lewis Aumack and Harold R. Dickman) *Manual of Group Therapy,* Psychology Service, Veterans Administration Hospital (Roseburg, Ore.), 1960; *Group Therapy: A Guide,* Random House, 1964; (with E. H. Luchins) *Logical Foundations of Mathematics for Behavioral Scientists,* Holt, 1965; (contributor) Samual M. Seltzer, editor, *Einstellung Tests of Rigidity,* Craig Colony School and Hospital, 1966; (with E. H. Luchins) *The Search for Factors That Extremize the Autokinetic Effect,* Faculty-Student Association, State University of New York at Albany, 1969; *Wertheimer's Seminars in Perception,* six volumes, Bucknell University Press, 1970-75; (contributor with E. H. Luchins) *Psychological Investigations,* Tbilisi (Russia), 1973; *Wertheimer's Seminars on Character and Personality,* four volumes, Bucknell University Press, 1975-77; (contributor with E. H. Luchins) P. N. Johnson-Laird and P. C. Wason, editors, *Thinking: Readings in Cognitive Science,*

Cambridge University Press, 1978; (contributor with E. H. Luchins) Lynn H. Fox and others, editors, *Women and the Mathematical Mystique,* Johns Hopkins University Press, 1980.

"Wertheimer's Seminars Revisited" series, with E. H. Luchins; published by Faculty-Student Association, State University of New York at Albany, except as indicated: *Wertheimer's Seminars Revisited: Problem Solving and Thinking,* three volumes, 1970; . . . : *Value, Social Influences and Power* (also see below), 1971; . . . : *Problems in Social Psychology* (also see below), 1972; . . . : *Problems in Perception,* Volume I, 1972, Volumes II-III, 1973, Volume IV, 1974, Volume V, 1975; . . . : *Expression of Personality and Memory for Impressions,* 1978; *Revisiting Wertheimer's Seminars* (contains revised editions of *Wertheimer's Seminars Revisited: Value, Social Influences and Power* and *Wertheimer's Seminars Revisited: Problems in Social Psychology*), Bucknell University Press, 1978; *Wertheimer's Seminars Revisited: Impressions and Conceptions of Personality,* 1979; . . . : *Character, Personality and the Social Order,* three volumes, 1980.

Contributor of more than one hundred twenty-five articles to journals in his field.

WORK IN PROGRESS: A biography of Max Wertheimer; editing Wertheimer's letters to Albert Einstein; continuing research on topics related to Wertheimer's seminars, especially the experimental outgrowths in the published monographs; a joint psychology-mathematic project, with wife, Edith H. Luchins, for producing books on logic and thinking.

* * *

LUCHINS, Edith H(irsch)   1921-

PERSONAL: Surname is pronounced *Loo*-kins; born December 21, 1921, in Poland; daughter of Max (a businessman, writer, and actor) and Leah (Kravetsky) Hirsch; married Abraham S. Luchins (a professor of psychology), October 10, 1942; children: David, Daniel, Jeremy, Anne, Joseph. *Education:* Brooklyn College (now Brooklyn College of the City University of New York), B.A. (cum laude), 1942; New York University, M.S., 1944, further study, 1944-46; University of Oregon, Ph.D., 1957. *Religion:* Hebrew. *Residence:* Albany, N.Y. *Office:* Department of Mathematical Sciences, Rensselaer Polytechnic Institute, Troy, N.Y. 12181.

CAREER: Sperry Gyroscope Co., Long Island, N.Y., government inspector, 1942-43; Brooklyn College (now Brooklyn College of the City University of New York), instructor in mathematics, 1944-46, 1948-49; University of Miami, Coral Gables, Fla., research associate and associate professor, department of mathematics, 1959-62; Rensselaer Polytechnic Institute, Troy, N.Y., associate professor, 1962-70, professor of mathematics, 1970—. *Member:* American Mathematical Society, Mathematical Association of America, American Association for the Advancement of Science, American Education Research Association (member, joint committee on women, 1980-83), American Association of University Professors, Sigma Xi, Pi Mu Epsilon. *Awards, honors:* New York State fellowship, American Association of University Women, 1958-59, for research in mathematics; named Danforth Associate, with husband, Abraham S. Luchins, 1980-86; American Association for the Advancement of Science fellowship, 1982.

WRITINGS—With husband, Abraham S. Luchins, except as indicated: *Rigidity of Behavior: A Variational Approach to the Effect of Einstellung,* University of Oregon Books, 1959; *Logical Foundations of Mathematics for Behavioral Scientists,* Holt,

1965; (with V. L. Parsegian and others) *Mathematical Supplement to Introduction to Natural Science,* Part I: *The Physical Sciences,* Academic Press, 1965; *The Search for Factors That Extremize the Autokinetic Effect,* Faculty-Student Association, State University of New York at Albany, 1969; (contributors) *Psychological Investigations,* Tbilisi (Russia), 1973; (contributors) P. N. Johnson-Laird and P. C. Wason, editors, *Thinking: Readings in Cognitive Science,* Cambridge University Press, 1978; (contributors) Lynn H. Fox and others, editors, *Women and the Mathematical Mystique,* Johns Hopkins University Press, 1980.

"Wertheimer's Seminars Revisited" series; published by Faculty-Student Association, State University of New York at Albany, except as indicated: *Wertheimer's Seminars Revisited: Problem Solving and Thinking,* three volumes, 1970; . . . : *Value, Social Influences and Power* (also see below), 1971; . . . :*Problems in Social Psychology* (also see below), 1972; . . . :*Problems in Perception,* Volume I, 1972, Volumes II-III, 1973, Volume IV, 1974, Volume V, 1975; . . . : *Expression of Personality and Memory for Impressions,* 1978; *Revisiting Wertheimer's Seminars* (contains revised editions of *Wertheimer's Seminars Revisited: Value, Social Influences and Power* and *Wertheimer's Seminars Revisited: Problems in Social Psychology),* Bucknell University Press, 1978; *Wertheimer's Seminars Revisited: Impressions and Conceptions of Personality,* 1979; . . . : *Character, Personality and the Social Order,* three volumes, 1980.

WORK IN PROGRESS: A joint psychology-mathematic project, with husband, Abraham S. Luchins, for producing books on logic and thinking; using computer graphics to improve spatial skills in pre-college mathematics.

SIDELIGHTS: Edith H. Luchins told *CA:* "Much of my current writing is concerned with what can be done to encourage more women to pursue studies and careers in mathematics. Another focus is the application of psychology to mathematics and vice-versa."

*   *   *

LUCKLESS, John
See BURKHOLZ, Herbert

*   *   *

LUTTWAK, Edward N(icholae)   1942-

PERSONAL: Surname is pronounced Loo-twack; born November 4, 1942, in Arad, Rumania; son of Joseph (a businessman) and Clara (Baruch) Luttwak. *Education:* Attended schools in Palermo and Milan, Italy, 1949-55, and Carmel College in England; London School of Economics and Political Science, B.Sc. (Econ.), 1964. *Politics:* Social-democrat. *Religion:* Jewish. *Office:* Center for Strategic and International Studies, Georgetown University, Washington, D.C. 20057.

CAREER: Worked in Eastern Europe for CBS-TV, 1964-65; University of Bath, Bath, England, lecturer, 1965-67; Walter J. Levy, London, England, oil consultant, 1967-68; strategic consultant, Washington, D.C., 1969; Middle East Study Group, Jerusalem, Israel, deputy director, 1970-72; Washington Center of Foreign Policy Research, Washington, D.C., associate director, 1972-75; Georgetown University, Center for Strategic and International Studies, Washington, D.C., senior fellow, 1976—.

WRITINGS: Coup D'Etat—A Practical Handbook, Allen Lane, 1968, Knopf, 1969; *A Dictionary of Modern War,* Harper,

1971; *The Strategic Balance 1972,* Library Press, 1972; *The Political Uses of Sea Power,* Johns Hopkins Press, 1974; *The US-USSR Nuclear Weapons Balance,* Sage, 1974; (with Dan Horowitz) *The Israeli Army,* Harper, 1975; *Strategic Power: Military Capabilities and Political Utility,* Sage, 1976; *The Grand Strategy of the Roman Empire: From the First Century A.D. to the Third,* Johns Hopkins University Press, 1976; (editor with Herbert Block and contributor) *The Economic and Military Balance between East and West, 1951-1978,* American Bar Association, 1978; (with R. G. Weinland) *Sea Power in the Mediterranean,* Sage, 1979; *Strategy and Politics: Collected Essays,* Transaction Books, 1980; *The Grand Strategy of the Soviet Union,* St. Martin's, 1983.

Contributor: Louis Henkin, editor, *World Politics and the Jewish Condition,* Quadrangle, 1972; Ray S. Cline, *World Power Assessment,* Center for Strategic and International Studies, Georgetown University, 1975; M. Cherif Bassiouni, editor, *Issues in the Mediterranean,* Chicago Council on Foreign Relations, 1975; Diana Reisch, editor, *Energy: Demand vs. Supply,* Wilson, 1975; Louis Williams, editor, *Military Aspects of the Israeli-Arab Conflict,* University Publishing Projects, 1975; Robert Kilmarx, *Soviet-United States Naval Balance,* Center for Strategic and International Studies, Georgetown University, 1975; Walter Slocombe, *Controlling Strategic Nuclear Weapons,* Foreign Policy Association, 1975.

Eugene Rostow, editor, *The Middle East: Critical Choices for the United States,* Westview, 1976; *Forum on the U.S. and East Asia,* number 7, Asia and the World Forum, 1977; Conquest, Draper, and others, *Defending America,* Basic Books, 1977; Donald C. Daniel, editor, *International Perceptions of the Superpower Military Balance,* Praeger, 1978; *Glimpses of Tibet Today,* Information Office of His Holiness the Dalai Lama (New Delhi), 1978; W. Scott-Thompson, editor, *The Third World: Premises of U.S. Policy,* Institute for Contemporary Studies, 1978; Martin F. Herz, editor, *Decline of the West? George Kennan and His Critics,* Ethics and Public Policy Center, Georgetown University, 1978; *Perceptions: Relationships between the United States and the Soviet Union,* Committee on Foreign Relations, 1979.

Scott-Thompson, editor, *National Security in the 1980s: From Weakness to Strength,* Institute for Contemporary Studies (San Francisco), 1980; *The Future of Strategic Deterence,* Part I, International Institute for Strategic Studies (London), 1980; *Struggling for Change in Mainland China: Challenges and Implications,* Institute of International Relations (Taipei), 1980; Kenneth A. Myers, editor, *NATO: The Next Thirty Years,* Center for Strategic and International Studies, 1980; *Elazer Papers—2,* Elazer Memorial Association and Tel Aviv University, 1980; Jeffrey G. Barlow, editor, *Reforming the Military,* Heritage Foundation, 1980; Philip S. Wronenberg, editor, *Planning U.S. Security,* National Security Affairs Institute, National Defense University, 1981; Douglas Stuart and William Tow, editors, *China, the Soviet Union, and the West,* Westview, 1982.

Also author of several research papers and contributor to conferences and proceedings. Contributor to periodicals, including *Esquire, Times Literary Supplement, Commentary, Survival,* and *International Security.*

WORK IN PROGRESS: A Time to Change: Reforming the American Armed Forces.

SIDELIGHTS: For his study *The Grand Strategy of the Roman Empire: From the First Century A.D. to the Third,* Edward N.

Luttwak drew partly upon his expertise in the fields of modern military and political issues. E. Badian, in the *New York Review of Books*, admires the author's foray into early Roman history: "[Luttwak] provides reassuring demonstration of the fact that, in our depressingly fragmented scholarly world, an outsider, trained in a totally different field, but trained in rigorous thought and endowed with controlled creative imagination, can lovingly steep himself in the mass of technical publications with their minutiae of fact and reasoned conjecture produced by 'the archaeologists, epigraphists, numismatists, and textual critics' (as he, tongue half in cheek, describes modern historians of Rome)—and come up with a fascinating scholarly synthesis that teaches them how they ought to be doing their job."

"Diehard classicists may remain skeptical, may doubt the existence of a grand strategy at all and raise their eyebrows whenever Luttwak uses a jargon more familiar to people working in institutes for modern strategic studies than to scholars accustomed to learned journals in classical philology," states *New Republic* critic Z. Yavetz. "Those who have difficulty understanding Luttwak's terminology in phrases like 'the input and output of the system are finally equated' should start reading the book with his appendix on power and force: 'definitions and implications.' But no classicist will find it easy to contradict [the author's] basic assumption that the Romans had no need of a Clausewitz [the Russian army officer noted for his books on war strategy] to subject their military energies to the discipline of political goals, and that without the knowledge of 'systems analysis' they were capable of designing a large and complex security system."

Badian contends that "Luttwak has done scholarship an immense service by propounding and carefully documenting these stimulating ideas. Every page brings detailed insights into the working of Roman military organization, in strategy and tactics, which, even when not wholly original, draw together and unify what is fragmented in obscure canons of strategic interpretation in terms of rigid categories of peace and war, offense and defense, that have beset Roman (indeed, all ancient) history. A century after Theodor Mommsen first provided the ancient Romans with their treatise on public law, Luttwak has now provided them with the comprehensive theoretical treatment of their strategy and foreign policy. Roman statesmen and commanders, on the whole devoid of the gift for either acute analysis or bold synthesis, would have been equally puzzled by both. They were given to proceeding by practical experience and precedent as recorded and remembered; and the powerful individual, Republican noble or emperor, had full freedom to mold tradition to his personality."

Coup D'Etat—A Practical Handbook has been published in several languages, including Dutch, Swedish, and Arabic. Some of Luttwak's other books have been published in Spanish, Italian, and Chinese.

BIOGRAPHICAL/CRITICAL SOURCES: New Statesman, December 6, 1968; *Spectator,* December 13, 1968; *New Yorker,* July 19, 1969; *New Republic,* November 15, 1975, May 21, 1977; Edward Luttwak, *The Grand Strategy of the Roman Empire: From the First Century A.D. to the Third,* Johns Hopkins University Press, 1976; *Times Literary Supplement,* February 20, 1976, February 10, 1978, August 26, 1983; *New York Review of Books,* June 23, 1977.

* * *

LYNCH, Owen M(artin) 1931-

PERSONAL: Born January 4, 1931, in New York, N.Y.; son of John Sylvester and Mary E. (O'Neill) Lynch. *Education:* Fordham University, A.B., 1956; Columbia University, Ph.D., 1966. *Politics:* None. *Religion:* None. *Office:* Department of Anthropology, New York University, New York, N.Y. 10003.

CAREER: State University of New York at Binghamton, 1966-73, began as assistant professor, became associate professor of anthropology; New York University, New York, N.Y., Charles F. Noyes Professor of Urban Anthropology, 1974—. *Member:* American Anthropological Association (fellow), American Ethnological Association, Royal Anthropological Institute of Great Britain and Ireland, Association for Asian Studies. *Awards, honors:* American Council of Learned Societies research grant, 1970; American Institute of Indian Studies grants, 1970 and 1980.

WRITINGS: (Contributor) *India and Ceylon: Unity and Diversity,* Oxford University Press, 1967; *The Politics of Untouchability: Social Mobility and Social Change in a City of India,* Columbia University Press, 1969; (contributor) J. M. Mahar, editor, *The Untouchables in Contemporary India,* University of Arizona Press, 1972; (contributor) *Aspects of Political Mobilization in South Asia,* Syracuse University Press, 1976; (contributor) Kenneth David, editor, *The New Wind: Changing Identities in South Asia,* Aldine, 1977.

(Contributor) Walter Zenner and George Gmelch, editors, *City Life: Reader in Urban Ethnography,* St. Martin's, 1980; (contributor) E. Adamson Hoebel, Richard Currier, and Susan Kaiser, editors, *Crisis in Anthropology: View from Spring Hill, 1980,* Garland STPM Press, 1982; (author of foreword) Yvonne Arterburn, *The Loom of Interdependence,* Hindustan Publishing, 1982; (author of foreword) Barbara Joshi, *Democracy in Search of Equality: Untouchable Politics and Indian Social Change,* Hindustan Publishing, 1982; (editor and author of introduction) *Culture and Community in Europe: Essays in Honor of Conrad M. Arensberg,* Hindustan Publishing, 1983. Contributor to professional journals.

WORK IN PROGRESS: A study of "pilgrimage in Braj, the birthplace of Lord Krishna."

M

MACKIN, Anita
   See DONSON, Cyril

      *   *   *

MACKSEY, Kenneth J. 1923-
   (Major K. J. Macksey)

PERSONAL: Born July 1, 1923, in Epsom, Surrey, England; son of Henry George and Alice (Nightingall) Macksey; married Joan Little, June 22, 1946; children: Susan, Andrew. *Education:* Received army schooling at Royal Military College, Sandhurst, 1943-44, and British Army Staff College, 1956. *Religion:* Church of England. *Home and office:* Whatley Mill, Beaminster, Dorset, England. *Agent:* Watson Little, Ltd., Suite 8, 26 Charing Cross Rd., London WC2H 0DG, England.

CAREER: Writer. British Army, Royal Tank Regiment, 1941-68, retired as major; Purnell's *History of the Second World War* (weekly series), and *History of the First World War,* London, England, deputy editor, 1968-70. *Member:* Royal United Services Institute, Savage Club (London). *Awards, honors*—Military: Military Cross. Literary: George Knight Clowes military essay prize, 1956, 1958.

WRITINGS: To the Green Fields Beyond, Royal Tank Regiment, 1965; *The Shadow of Vimy Ridge,* Kimber & Co., 1965; *Armoured Crusader: A Biography of Major-General Sir Percy Hobart,* Hutchinson, 1967; *Afrika Korps,* Ballantine, 1968; (under name Major K. J. Macksey) *Panzer Division: The Mailed Fist,* Ballantine, 1968; *The Crucible of Power: The Fight for Tunisia,* Hutchinson, 1969.

Tank Force: Allied Armor in World War II, Ballantine, 1970; *Tank: A History of Armoured Fighting Vehicles,* Macdonald, 1970; *Tank Warfare: A History of Tanks in Battle,* Hart-Davis, 1971; *Beda Fomm,* Ballantine, 1971; *Vimy Ridge,* Ballantine, 1972; *The Guinness Guide to Tank Facts and Feats,* Guinness Superlatives, 1972; *The Guinness History of Land Warfare,* Guinness Superlatives, 1973; *Battle,* Macdonald & Jane's, 1974; *The Partisans of Europe,* Hart-Davis, 1975; (co-author) *The Guinness History of Sea Warfare,* Guinness Superlatives, 1975; (co-author) *The Guinness Guide to Feminine Achievements,* Guinness Superlatives, 1975; *Guderian: Panzer General,* Macdonald & Jane's, 1975.

The Guinness History of Air Warfare, Guinness Superlatives, 1976; *The Guinness Book of 1952,* Guinness Superlatives, 1976;

The Guinness Book of 1953, Guinness Superlatives, 1977; *The Guinness Book of 1954,* Guinness Superlatives, 1978; *Kesselring: The Making of the Luftwaffe,* Batsford, 1978; *Rommel: Campaigns and Battles,* Arms & Armour Press, 1979; *The Tanks, 1945-1975,* Arms & Armour Press, 1979; *Invasion,* Arms & Armour Press, 1980; *The Tank Pioneers,* Jane's Publishing, 1981; *History of the RAC, 1914-1975,* Newtown Publications, 1983. Contributor to military journals.

      *   *   *

MACKSEY, Major K. J.
   See MACKSEY, Kenneth J.

      *   *   *

MacMANUS, Yvonne 1931-

PERSONAL: Born March 18, 1931, in Los Angeles, Calif. *Office:* MS./smiths, 31-M Clapboard Ridge Rd., Danbury, Conn. 06810; and Timely Books, P.O. Box 267, New Milford, Conn. 06776.

CAREER: For more than twenty years, worked in editorial positions for book publishers on the East and West coasts, including Dell Publishing Co., Bobbs-Merrill Co., Brandon House, Avon Books, and Fawcett; free-lance writer and editorial consultant; currently co-owner, MS./smiths (editorial consultants), Danbury, Conn., and co-publisher, Timely Books, New Milford, Conn. *Member:* Authors Guild, Authors League of America.

WRITINGS: Love Is a Dirty Word, Award Books, 1965 (published in England as *Better Luck Elsewhere,* Odhams, 1977); *The Reunion,* Award Books, 1965; *With Fate Conspire,* Dell, 1974; *Bequeath Them No Tumbled House,* Doubleday, 1977; *The Presence,* Pinnacle Books, 1982; *You Can Write a Romance and Get It Published!,* Pocket Books, 1983. Also author of more than twenty novels under undisclosed pseudonyms. Contributor of numerous articles to magazines.

SIDELIGHTS: Yvonne MacManus told *CA:* "The best advice I can give to any budding author is: Get a job until your accountant informs you that, because of taxes, you can't afford to make any more money. Writing is one of the most frustrating, infuriating, insane careers anyone can undertake. It is also immensely rewarding (psychologically) and an opportunity to express yourself without someone interrupting your thoughts. The two greatest requirements for survival are a strong stomach and an Olympian sense of humor; without these traits, you'll despair more than rejoice.''

*   *   *

MAHAJAN, Vidya Dhar   1913-

PERSONAL: Born September 1, 1913, in Punjab, India; son of Hari Ram and Sulakhni (Devi) Mahajan; married Savitri (a school principal), April 13, 1945; children: Mridula, Sucheta, Ajaya. *Education:* Punjab University, Lahore, M.A. (history), 1936, M.A. (politics), 1937, Ph.D., 1945; University of Delhi, LL.B., 1948. *Religion:* Hindu. *Home and office:* D-805, New Friends Colony, New Delhi 65, India.

CAREER: Punjab University College, New Delhi, India, teacher of history and politics to M.A. candidates, 1950-60; Supreme Court of India, New Delhi, advocate, 1960—. Part-time lecturer in law, University of Delhi, 1962-67. *Member:* Indian Law Association (New Delhi; secretary), Cultural League of India (secretary), Servants of People Society (New Delhi), Constitution Club, Indian Council of World Affairs, Bar Association of India, International Law Association, Delhi Welfare Society (president), Delhi Pradesh Mahajan Sabha (president), Sulakhani Devi Mahajan Trust (founder and president), Hari Ram Mahajan Trust (founder and president).

WRITINGS: Essays in Municipal Administration in the Punjab, foreword by Beni Prasad, Doaba House (Lahore), c. 1943; *The General Clauses Act,* Eastern Book Co. (Lucknow), 1952, 3rd edition, 1968; *Commentaries on Indian Sale of Goods Act: Act III of 1930,* Eastern Book Co., 1953, supplement, 1956; *Recent Political Thought,* Premier, 1953, 6th edition, S. Chand, 1982; *The Law Relating to Sales Tax in Delhi,* Eastern Book Co., 1954; (with R. R. Sethi) *Constitutional History of India,* 2nd edition, S. Chand, 1954, 11th edition, 1982; (with Sethi) *Indian Constitution and Administration,* S. Chand, 1954.

English Constitutional Law, Eastern Book Co., 1955, 3rd edition, 1962; *The Constitution of India,* Eastern Book Co., 1955, 9th edition, 1982; *Principles of Civics,* Modern Publications, 1955; *International Law,* Eastern Book Co., 1956, 4th edition, 1963; (with Sethi) *Mughal Rule in India,* 3rd edition, S. Chand, 1957, 13th edition, 1982; *India since 1956,* 3rd edition, S. Chand, 1958, 14th edition, 1983; (with B. K. Gahrana) *Select Modern Governments,* 3rd edition, S. Chand, 1958, 14th edition, 1983.

Ancient India, S. Chand, 1960, 9th edition, 1979; (with wife, Savitri Mahajan) *The Muslim Rule in India,* S. Chand, 1962, 7th edition, 1981; *The Nationalist Movement in India and Its Leaders,* S. Chand, 1962; (with B. M. Lalwani and Y. N. Deodhar) *Political and Cultural History of Ancient India,* S. Chand, 1962; (with S. Mahajan) *The Sultanate of Delhi,* S. Chand, 1962, 6th edition, 1981; *Principles of Jurisprudence,* 2nd edition, Eastern Book Co., 1962, 4th edition published as *Principles of Jurisprudence and Legal Theory,* 1980; (with S. Mahajan) *British Rule in India and After,* 6th edition, S. Chand, 1964, 11th edition, 1974; *International Politics since 1900,* 2nd edition, S. Chand, 1964, 3rd edition, 1968.

The Constitution of Pakistan, revised edition, Munawar Book Depot, 1965, 2nd revised edition, S. Chand, 1969; *Early History of India,* S. Chand, 1965; *England since 1688,* 6th edition, S. Chand, 1965, revised edition, 1976; *England under the Tudors and Stuarts,* S. Chand, 1966; *Chief Justice P. B. Gajendragadkar,* S. Chand, 1966; *History of Modern Europe*

since 1789, 4th edition, S. Chand, 1966, 9th edition, 1983; *Chief Justice K. Subba: Defender of Liberties,* S. Chand, 1967; *Chief Justice Mehr Chand Mahajan: The Biography of the Great Jurist,* Eastern Book Co., 1969.

Fifty Years of Modern India, 1919-1969, S. Chand, 1970, 2nd edition published as *Fifty-five Years of Modern India, 1919-1974,* 1975; *History of India from the Beginning to 1526,* S. Chand, 1970, 3rd edition, 1976; *Principles of Political Science,* S. Chand, 1970, 3rd edition, 1981; *International Law,* 5th edition, Eastern Book Co., 1974; *Select Foreign Governments,* S. Chand, 1975; *Leaders of the Nationalist Movement,* Sterling (New Delhi), 1975; *International Politics,* S. Chand, 1976; *The Nationalist Movement in India,* Sterling, 1976, 2nd edition, 1981; *The British Constitution,* S. Chand, 1977; *England since 1485,* 4th edition, S. Chand, 1978; *Early History of India,* S. Chand, 1979.

Commentary on the General Clauses Act, 5th edition, Eastern Book Co., 1980; *International Relations since 1900,* 6th edition, S. Chand, 1982; *History of Great Britain,* 2nd edition, S. Chand, 1982; *Modern Indian History from 1707 up to Date,* S. Chand, 1983; *History of Modern India, 1919-1974,* two volumes, S. Chand, 1983; *Advanced History of India,* 2nd edition, S. Chand, 1983; *Constitutional Law of India,* Eastern Book Co., 1983; *Modern Indian Political Thought,* S. Chand, 1984.

SIDELIGHTS: ''I write as I feel inspired to write,'' Vidya Dhar Mahajan told *CA*. ''I write because I want to carry my message to the readers. I find personal satisfaction only when I write something. I do not find the same satisfaction when preparing and arguing cases in courts.''

*   *   *

MAHESHWARI, Shriram   1931-

PERSONAL: Born November 27, 1931, in India; son of Muniraj Maheshwari; married May 30, 1955, wife's name, Bimla; children: Manjula (daughter), Rajiv (son), Sanjiv (son), Anjula (daughter), Manish (son). *Education:* D.A.V. College, Kanpur, India, B.A., M.A. (economics), M.A. (political science); University of Delhi, Ph.D., 1965; University of Pennsylvania, M.G.A., 1964. *Religion:* Hinduism. *Office:* Indian Institute of Public Administration, New Delhi, India.

CAREER: Agra University, Agra, India, lecturer, 1955-61; University of Delhi, Indian School of Public Administration, New Delhi, India, reader in public administration, 1965-73; Indian Institute of Public Administration, New Delhi, professor of political science and public administration, 1973—. Affiliated with Institute of Developing Economies, Tokyo, Japan. *Member:* Indian Public Administration Association (secretary-cum-treasurer).

WRITINGS: (With A. Avasthi) *Public Administration,* Lakshmi Narain Agarwal, 1962, 7th edition, 1974; *The General Election in India,* Chaitanya Publishing House, 1963; *Indian Administration,* Orient Longman, 1968, 2nd edition, 1974; *The Evolution of Indian Administration,* Lakshmi Narain Agarwal, 1970; *Local Government in India,* Orient Longman, 1971; *Government through Consultation,* Indian Institute of Public Administration, 1972; *The Administrative Reforms Commission,* Lakshmi Narain Agarwal, 1972; (editor) *The Study of Public Administration,* Lakshmi Narain Agarwal, 1974; *Civil Service in Great Britain,* Concept Publishing, 1976; *President's Rule in India,* Macmillan (India), 1977; *Indian Parliamentary Sys-*

tem, Lakshmi Narain Agarwal, 1981; *Electoral Politics in the National Metropolis,* Ritu Publishers, 1982.

Also author of *Administrative Reforms in India* and *Open Government in India,* both published by Macmillan.

*   *   *

MALL, Viktor
See BESKOW, Bo

*   *   *

MANDELL, Maurice I(ra) 1925-

PERSONAL: Born October 23, 1925, in New York, N.Y.; son of Benjamin David and Myn (Lester) Mandell; married Natalie Gould, July 29, 1956; children: David Gould, Lisa Rose. *Education:* New York University, B.S., 1947; Syracuse University, M.B.A., 1949; Indiana University, D.B.A., 1953. *Home and office:* 3815 Countryside Lane, Sarasota, Fla. 33583.

CAREER: Syracuse University, Syracuse, N.Y., instructor in marketing, 1948-50; Western Reserve University (now Case Western Reserve University), Cleveland, Ohio, assistant professor of marketing, 1951-53; Bowling Green State University, Bowling Green, Ohio, associate professor, 1953-61, professor of marketing, 1961-81, chairman of department, 1965-81; writer, lecturer, and consultant in the fields of marketing and advertising, 1981—. Visiting professor, University of Oklahoma, 1955, Indiana University, 1979, University of South Florida, 1981-82, and Florida International University, 1982; Fulbright lecturer in Finland, 1956-57; Ford Foundation consultant, Dacca University, 1967. *Member:* American Marketing Association, American Academy of Advertising, Theta Chi, Alpha Delta Sigma, Delta Pi Epsilon, Beta Gamma Sigma, Omicron Delta Kappa.

WRITINGS: Advertising, Prentice-Hall, 1968, 3rd edition, 1980; (editor with Larry J. Rosenberg) *Marketing,* 2nd edition (Mandell was not associated with earlier edition), Prentice-Hall, 1981.

WORK IN PROGRESS: A 4th edition of *Advertising;* sole editor of 3rd edition of *Marketing.*

*   *   *

MANNERING, Julia
See BINGHAM, Madeleine (Mary Ebel)

*   *   *

MANSFIELD, Roger (Ernest) 1939-

PERSONAL: Born November 27, 1939, in Cambridge, England; son of Ernest Walter (an engineer) and Ruby May (Welch) Mansfield; married Patricia Lawrence, May 26, 1962 (divorced, December 28, 1979); married Frances Williams, March 7, 1982; children: (first marriage) Kim and Kerry (daughters), Conrad. *Education:* City of Worcester Training College, Teachers Certificate, 1960; Torrens College of Advanced Education, diploma in teaching, 1974; Salisbury College of Advanced Education, graduate diploma in educational technology, 1977. *Politics:* None. *Religion:* Atheist. *Home:* 100 Cambridge Terrace, Malvern, South Australia, Australia 5061.

CAREER: Taught briefly in 1958 before entering training college; Inner London Education Authority, London, England, teacher of English, 1960-69; program director for ETV (edu-

cational television) Service, 1969-71; Department of Further Education, South Australia, lecturer, 1971—.

WRITINGS: "The Art of English: General Course" series, five books for students eleven-to-fifteen, Schofield & Sims, 1965-68, revised edition, 1971-72, new edition, 1983-85; *Tranfer English* (handbook), Oxford University Press, 1980.

Editor: (With Isobel Armstrong) *Every Man Will Shout* (anthology of modern poetry, including poetry by children), Oxford University Press, 1964; (with Tony Murray) *Fantasy, Fiction and Fact* (anthology of modern prose), Blackie & Sons, 1965; *Subjects of Enquiry* (modern short stories), Blackie & Sons, 1967; *The Starlit Corridor* (science fiction stories and poems), Pergamon, 1968; (with Keith Newson) *Contrast I* (short stories of Bill Naughton and Liam O'Flaherty), Pergamon, 1968; *Contrast II* (short stories of Dorothy Parker and Saki), Pergamon, 1969.

Contrast III (short stories of Alan Sillitoe and Angus Wilson), Pergamon, 1970; John Wyndham, *The Kraken Wakes,* school edition, Longman, 1971; *The Storytellers I* (short stories), Schofield & Sims, 1971; *The Storytellers II* (short stories), Schofield & Sims, 1971; (with Deborah McCulloch) *See What I Say* (anthology of modern poetry, including poetry by children), Oxford University Press, 1975; (with Armstrong) *A Sudden Line* (anthology of modern poetry, including poetry by children), Oxford University Press, 1976; *The Playmakers I* (short modern plays), Schofield & Sims, 1976; *The Playmakers II* (short modern plays), Schofield & Sims, 1976; *Short Stories I* (short stories for young readers), Schofield & Sims, 1977; *Short Stories II* (short stories for young readers), Schofield & Sims, 1977; *Short Stories III* (short stories for young readers), Schofield & Sims, 1977; *Poetry Allsorts 1, 2, 3* (poetry anthologies for young children; with teacher's guide), Rigby Education, 1981.

Also author of scripts for Thames Television (educational). Contributor to *Use of English* and *Forum.*

SIDELIGHTS: Roger Mansfield told *CA:* "To write a good educational text—one that transforms the complicated into the simple, reduces the long-winded to the concise, and reveals the relevance in the apparently removed—is as demanding, I think, as writing a novel, play, or poem. Perhaps even more so. After all, how many twentieth-century educational works have really excited students or caught the imagination of the general public? Not many. And you can't blame that entirely on lack of interest. The quality of the offerings must have something to do with it. Anyway, I'm an educational writer and proud of it, because of the challenge involved."

*   *   *

MARAINI, Dacia 1936-

PERSONAL: Born November 13, 1936, in Florence, Italy; daughter of Fosco (an Orientalist) and Topazia (Alliata) Maraini; married Lucio Pozzi (divorced). *Home:* Via Beccaria 18, Rome, Italy.

CAREER: Writer. Film director of "Conjugal Love," 1970.

AWARDS, HONORS: Prix Formentor, 1962, for *L'Eta del malessera;* Premio Saint Vincent, 1972; Premio Riccione, 1978; Premio Arta Terme, 1983.

WRITINGS—Novels, except as indicated: *La Vacanza,* Lerici (Milan), 1962, translation by Stuart Hood published as *The Holiday,* Weidenfeld & Nicolson, 1966; *L'Eta del malessera,*

Einaudi (Torino), 1963, translation by Frances Frenaye published as *The Age of Malaise,* Grove, 1963 (published in England as *The Age of Discontent,* Weidenfeld & Nicolson, 1963); *A Memoria,* Bompiani, 1967; *Mio Marito* (short stories), Bompiani, 1968; *Memorie di una Ladra,* Bompiani, 1972, translation published as *Memories of a Female Thief,* Weidenfeld & Nicolson, 1973; *Donna in Guerra,* Einaudi, 1975; *Lettere a Marina,* Bompiani, 1981.

Poetry: *Crudelte All' Aria Aperta,* Feltrinelli, 1966; *Donne Mie,* Einaudi, 1974; *Mangiami Pure,* Einaudi, 1978; *Dimenticato di dimenticare,* Einaudi, 1983.

Plays: *Ricatto a Teatro,* Einaudi, 1970; *Viva L'Italia,* Einaudi, 1973; *Dialogo di una Prostituta col Cliente* (first produced at Teatro Alberico in Rome), Images, 1975; *I Sogni di Clitennestra* (first produced at Teatro Tendra, Prato), Bompiani, 1981; *Maria Stuarda* (produced in Holland by Publieketheatre and in Spain by Teatro Espanol de Madrid), Bompiani, 1981. Also author of "La Famiglia Normale" (one-act play), 1967, and of "Recitation," first produced at Teatro Centouno, 1969.

Screenplays: (With Piera Degli Esposti and Marco Ferreri) "The Story of Piera," Faso Film S.R.L., T. Films, Sara Films, and Ascot, 1983.

WORK IN PROGRESS: Il Treno per Helsinki, a novel, for Einaudi.

SIDELIGHTS: Dacia Maraini has traveled widely in Africa, Finland, and Russia, and lived eight years in Japan. *Memorie di una Ladra* and *Donna in Guerra,* as well as several of her plays, have been translated into French.

BIOGRAPHICAL/CRITICAL SOURCES: Variety, March 26, 1969, June 24, 1970, July 8, 1970.

* * *

MARGOLIES, Edward   1925-

PERSONAL: Born December 19, 1925, in Boston, Mass.; son of Jacob and Bessie (Freidson) Margolies; married Claire Norman (a researcher and high school language teacher), June 30, 1958; children: Jacob, Peter, William. *Education:* Brown University, B.A., 1950; New York University, M.A., 1959, Ph.D., 1964. *Home:* 141 East Third St., New York, N.Y. 10009. *Agent:* Gunther Stuhlmann, P.O. Box 276, Becket, Mass. 01223. *Office:* Department of English, College of Staten Island of the City University of New York, 715 Ocean Ter., Staten Island, N.Y. 10301.

CAREER: Elementary and high school teacher of English in the public and private schools of New York, N.Y., 1952-59; College of Staten Island of the City University of New York, Staten Island, N.Y., 1959—, began as instructor, professor of English and American studies, 1968—. Also affiliated with University of Nijmegen, Holland, 1977, and University of Paris, 1979; Fulbright senior lecturer, 1977. *Military service:* U.S. Army, 1944-46. *Member:* Modern Language Association of America, American Studies Association, Popular Culture Association, American Civil Liberties Union, Phi Beta Kappa. *Awards, honors:* American Council of Learned Societies fellow, 1965.

WRITINGS: Native Sons: A Critical Study of Twentieth-Century Negro-American Authors, Lippincott, 1968; *The Art of Richard Wright,* Southern Illinois University Press, 1969; (editor) *A Native Sons Reader,* Lippincott, 1970; (with others) *The Black Writer in Africa and the Americas,* Hennessey &

Ingalls, 1973; (with others) *Dimensions of Detective Fiction,* Popular Press, 1976; (with David Bakish) *Afro-American Fiction, 1853-1976,* Gale, 1979; *Which Way Did He Go?: The Private Eye in Dashiell Hammett, Raymond Chandler, Chester Hines, and Ross Macdonald,* Holmes & Meir, 1982.

Also author of a pamphlet, *Antebellum Slave Narratives: Their Place in American Literary History,* Harper, 1975. Contributor to journals in his field.

WORK IN PROGRESS: Co-editing *The Letters of Richard Wright;* a book on American literature, popular culture, and American values.

SIDELIGHTS: In a *Saturday Review* article on Edward Margolies's *Native Sons: A Critical Study of Twentieth-Century Negro-American Authors,* Charles R. Larson expresses surprise that the author chooses to profile only a handful of the many contemporary black authors available to him. Larson notes that "simply by making these choices, Margolies is telling us something about his attitudes toward the current state of black American writing. Yet his concern with quality instead of quantity is clearly what raises his work above those of many of his predecessors." The reviewer concludes: "Margolies reminds us . . . of the vitally important part the Negro has played in the growth of American literature. Over and over he tells us that these writers are worth reading, not simply because we can learn something from them about Negroes but because we might also learn something from them about literature."

BIOGRAPHICAL/CRITICAL SOURCES: Saturday Review, November 30, 1968; *Ramparts,* October, 1969; *American Literature,* October, 1982.

* * *

MARGOLIUS, Sidney (Senier)   1911-1980

PERSONAL: Born May 3, 1911, in Perth Amboy, N.J.; died January 30, 1980, in Roslyn, N.Y.; son of Max (a businessman) and Helen (Senier) Margolius; married Esther Papert, November 14, 1942; children: Richard. *Education:* Rutgers University, Litt.B., 1934. *Home:* 74 Davis Rd., Port Washington, N.Y.

CAREER: Worked for United Press, New York City, 1934-35; *Market Observer,* New York City, editor, 1936-37; *Retailing,* New York City, associate editor, 1937-40; *PM,* New York City, consumer editor, 1940-42, 1945-48; full-time freelance writer, beginning 1948. Member of President's Consumer Advisory Council; director of Metropolitan New York Consumer Council; member of New York State Consumer Advisory Committee, and Nassau County, N.Y., Consumer Advisory Council. Served on National Commission on Product Safety, 1968-70. Trustee of Consumers Union, 1951-60. Lecturer. Consultant to International Cooperation Administration, and to U.S. Government. *Military service:* U.S. Army, 1942-45. *Member:* American Council for Consumer Interests.

AWARDS, HONORS: Special Service award, International Labor Press Association; Community Service award, New York City Central Labor Council, 1962; Media award, Family Service Association, 1968, for developing public interest of family needs; Consumer Federation of America award; Distinguished Service award, New York Consumer Assembly, 1968; Community Service award, National Council of Senior Citizens, 1969; Leadership award, Consumer Federation of America, 1972; National Press Award for best consumer book, 1973, for *Health Foods: Facts and Fakes;* also recipient of awards from Major Appliance Action Panel and Association of Home Appliance Manufacturing.

WRITINGS: How to Buy More for Your Money, Modern Age Books, 1942, revised edition published as *The Consumer's Guide to Better Buying,* Pocket Books, 1972; *The Fresh Start: Plain Facts about Small Business,* B. Ackermann, 1946; *It's Your Money: Come and Get It,* Fawcett, 1951; *First National Tax and Budget Guide, 1954,* Whiteside & W. Morrow, 1953; *Your Guide to Financial Security,* New American Library, 1955.

Better Homes and Gardens Money Management for Your Family, Meredith, 1962; *Planning for College,* Avon, 1965; *How to Make the Most of Your Money,* Appleton, 1966, second revised edition, Hawthorn Books, 1972; *The Innocent Consumer vs. the Exploiters,* Trident, 1967; *Adulthood for Beginners,* Macmillan, 1968; *The New Adult Guide to Independent Living,* Macmillan, 1968; *Your Personal Guide to Successful Retirement: The Complete, Step-by-Step Handbook of Retirement Planning,* Random House, 1969; *The Great American Food Hoax,* Walker & Co., 1971; *The Innocent Investor* [and] *The Shaky Ground Floor,* Trident, 1971; *Health Foods: Facts and Fakes,* Walker & Co., 1973; *Your Money's Worth: Consumer Tips to Economy,* Union Label Department, International Ladies' Garment Workers' Union, 1978.

Also author of fifteen public affairs pamphlets. Contributor of articles to magazines.

SIDELIGHTS: The Consumer's Guide to Better Buying is used as a college and high school textbook and has had a total sale in excess of 800,000 copies.

BIOGRAPHICAL/CRITICAL SOURCES: Harper's, November, 1967; *Book World,* December 17, 1967; *New York Times Book Review,* December 31, 1967; *Christian Science Monitor,* January 15, 1968.

OBITUARIES: New York Times, February 1, 1980; *Time,* February 11, 1980.

[Sketch verified by wife, Esther Margolius]

*   *   *

MARINER, Scott
   See POHL, Frederik

*   *   *

MARLOWE, Derek   1938-

PERSONAL: Born May 21, 1938, in London, England; son of Frederick William (an electrician) and Helene (Alexandroupolos) Marlowe; married Sukie Phipps, 1968; children: three sons and two daughters. *Education:* Attended Cardinal Vaughan School, 1949-57, University of London, 1957-60. *Politics:* Socialist. *Religion:* Humanist. *Home:* 8 Holland Park Rd., London W. 14, England. *Agent:* Tim Corrie, Fraser & Dunlop Scripts, Ltd., 91 Regent St., London W1R 8RU, England.

CAREER: Full-time writer. *Awards, honors:* Foyle Award, best play of 1961-62, for "The Scarecrow"; Writers Guild award and Emmy award, both 1972, for television writing.

WRITINGS: A Dandy in Aspic (also see below), Putnam, 1966; *Memoirs of a Venus Lackey,* Viking, 1968; *A Single Summer with L.B.: The Summer of 1816,* J. Cape, 1969, published as *A Single Summer with Lord B.,* Viking, 1970; *Echoes of Celandine,* Viking, 1970, published as *The Disappearance,* Penguin,

1978; *Do You Remember England?,* Viking, 1972; *Somebody's Sister,* Viking, 1974; *Nightshade,* Weidenfeld & Nicolson, 1975, Viking, 1976; *The Rich Boy from Chicago,* Weidenfeld & Nicolson, 1980; *Nancy Astor, the Lady from Virginia: A Novel* (also see below), Weidenfeld & Nicolson, 1982.

Plays: (Adapter) "The Seven Who Were Hanged," produced in Edinburgh, Scotland, 1961, produced in London as "The Scarecrow," 1964; (adapter) "The Lower Depths," produced in London, 1962; "How Disaster Struck the Harvest," produced in London, 1964; "How I Assumed the Role of a Popular Dandy for Purposes of Seduction and Other Base Matters," produced in London, 1965.

Author of screenplays "A Dandy in Aspic," produced in 1968, "A Single Summer," 1979, and "The Knight," 1979. Also author of television scripts for "Requiem for Modigliani," 1970, "The Search for the Nile," 1971, "The Knight," 1978, "Nancy Astor," 1982, "Jamaica Inn," 1983, and "A Married Man," 1983.

SIDELIGHTS: Although Derek Marlowe's novels range from the romantic (*A Single Summer with L.B.*) to the biographical (*Nancy Astor*), he is best known as an author of espionage thrillers. *A Dandy in Aspic,* for instance, is the story of a Russian spy in Britain who wants to quit but is not allowed to do so. The novel was favorably received by Guy Davenport in *National Review:* "Marlowe is an accomplished master of the [spy novel], and before one is halfway through his Byzantine plot anything at all has become plausible. . . . Only the most serious duties will keep a reader from going all the way to the end once he's hooked around page three."

Marlowe's books have generally met with mixed critical opinion. *Spectator* critic Mary Hope, reviewing *The Rich Boy from Chicago,* says the author "bursts with good, romantic ideas, but he can't somehow allow himself to be carried along with them; there has to be bitterness, dust and ashes, so that in the long run what remains is a desperately unfocused parade of too many characters, none of them properly internalized or thought through." Peter Prince, on the other hand, has praise for the thriller *Somebody's Sister.* Prince notes in *New Statesman* that the novel "is carefully constructed not as an attempt (surely foredoomed) to match [Raymond] Chandler at his own game, but rather to offer a kind of realistic critique of the whole school of romantic/idealistic detective fiction as exemplified by the Philip Marlowe series. Which is a very different and much more promising enterprise."

MEDIA ADAPTATIONS: The Disappearance was filmed and released under that title by World Northal Corporation in 1981.

BIOGRAPHICAL/CRITICAL SOURCES: National Review, October 4, 1966; *Book Week,* October 30, 1966; *New Statesman,* November 8, 1974, January 23, 1976; *Listener,* February 14, 1980; *Spectator,* March 15, 1980; *Punch,* March 10, 1982.

*   *   *

MARSH, Andrew
   See O'DONOVAN, John

*   *   *

MARSH, Mary Val   1925-

PERSONAL: Born April 28, 1925, in Uniontown, Pa.; daughter of Roy William (an osteopathic physician) and Mary (a teacher; maiden name, Hickman) Marsh; married Dwight Ellsworth

Twist (a school superintendent), August 4, 1962; stepchildren: Barbara (Mrs. Roger A. Williams), Charles Russell. *Education:* University of California, Los Angeles, B.A., 1946; Claremont Graduate School, M.A., 1953. *Politics:* Republican. *Religion:* Presbyterian. *Home:* 879 Rosecrans St., San Diego, Calif. 92106.

CAREER: Elementary school teacher in Redlands, Calif., 1946-48; curriculum consultant for San Bernadino County Department of Education, Calif., 1948-52, music coordinator, 1952-59; music supervisor for public schools in Beverly Hills, Calif., 1959-62; San Diego State University, San Diego, Calif., part-time lecturer in music education, 1963-73; free-lance writer, music arranger, and consultant in music education, 1973—. Faculty member at University of Redlands, Claremont Graduate School and University Center, and Idyllwild School of Music and the Arts; director of music education workshops in the United States and Canada. Member of Music Educators National Conference-Ford Foundation "Contemporary Music Project" Committee, San Diego, 1963-65; supervisor of local "Opera Participation Project for Youth," 1971-75; member of board of directors of Civic Youth Orchestra, 1976—.

MEMBER: International Society for Music Education, Music Educators National Conference (life member), California Music Educators Association (life member), Sigma Alpha Iota, Delta Kappa Gamma, Pi Lambda Theta, P.E.O. Sisterhood.

WRITINGS: Choruses and Carols (for unchanged voices), Summy-Birchard, 1964; *Here a Song, There a Song* (for elementary and junior high school choruses), Shawnee Press, 1969; *Explore and Discover Music: Creative Approaches to Music Education in Elementary, Middle, and Junior High Schools,* Macmillan, 1970; (with Carroll Rinehart and Edith Savage) *The Spectrum of Music* (textbook series for elementary grades), Macmillan, 1974-75, 1978-79, 1983.

Choral compositions and arrangements, published by Alfred Publishing: *Aardvarks on the Ark,* 1978; *Singin' a Song,* 1980; *Watah Come a Me Eye,* 1982; *I'd Rather Be Sailing,* 1982; *Linstead Market,* 1983.

Contributor to *Music Educators Journal.* Editor, *CMEA News,* 1978-82, and *Soundings,* 1982—.

WORK IN PROGRESS: Choral arranging and composing; textbook and professional book revision.

SIDELIGHTS: Mary Val Marsh writes: "I am committed to the belief that arts education is essential to improving the quality of life for all, and that without a commitment to the arts, a culture will gradually deteriorate. Only as children and youth encounter the arts in meaningful situations will they develop aesthetic sensitivity. As a specialist in music education, I believe that *creating music* is one of the most effective means of learning about music and of developing a continuing interest in it. This belief led me a number of years ago to organize an experimental creative music class, which subsequently led to my writing of *Explore and Discover Music.*"

*   *   *

MARTIN, Ann Bodenhamer   1927-

PERSONAL: Born October 24, 1927, in El Dorado, Ark.; daughter of R. C. (in insurance and real estate) and Jewel (Little) Bodenhamer; married Ken D. Elliott, July 25, 1953 (died, 1969); married James E. Martin (divorced); children: (first marriage) Richard Clinton, Mark Andrew. *Education:* Attended Lindenwood College and University of Arkansas.

Home and office: 2424 North Tustin, A-1, Santa Ana, Calif. 92705. *Agent:* JET Literary Associates, Inc., 124 East 84th St., Suite 4A, New York, N.Y. 10028.

CAREER: KELD-Radio, El Dorado, Ark., disc jockey, 1948-50; KSJB-Radio, Minot, N.D., disc jockey, 1950-52; WWEZ-Radio, New Orleans, La., disc jockey, also in public relations, programming, production, and promotion, 1952-56; WJMR-Television, New Orleans, in special programming, 1956-60; WWL-Television, New Orleans, presented "Hospitality House" and "Ann Elliott Show," also in special programming, public relations, and promotion, 1960-64; WNOE-Radio, New Orleans, free-lance disc jockey, also in special programming, public relations, and promotion, 1964-67; KTVE-TV, El Dorado, presented "Today in the Ark-La-Miss," 1967-68; WILZ-Radio, St. Petersburg, Fla., in special programming, public relations, and promotion, 1968-72; writer, 1972—.

Conducted "A Man and a Woman" and "The Ann Martin Show," on WILZ-Radio; worked for various radio and television stations in North Dakota, 1950-52, and Louisiana, 1952-60; wrote, produced, and hosted "Action People" and "Exploration of the Occult," originating from the Queen Mary, Long Beach, Calif., 1974-78. Ordained New Thought minister, 1976. Docent, Broward Community College, 1974-77. Founder and executive director, Manava Bharati Heritage International School for homeless children, 1981—. Interim minister, Unity of St. Croix, U.S. Virgin Islands, 1982. Fashion model, 1950-70; fashion show narrator and coordinator, 1956—; teacher of modeling, 1970—. *Member:* New Thought Alliance, World Fellowship of Religions (India), National Speakers Association. *Awards, honors:* "Ann Elliott Show" was named outstanding local television show by *Broadcasting,* 1962, and named most promising new television show by *TV Guide,* 1962; honorary doctorate from Southeastern University, 1978.

WRITINGS: Calico Families (poems), Pelican, 1976; *Build a Better You—Starting Now,* Showcase, 1980; *Metabionics: Mystic Power of the Mind,* Prentice-Hall, 1981; *Pathways to Self-improvement Using a Cassette Recorder,* Professional Publications, 1983.

Author of scripts and commercials for television and radio, including "Some Gold of Your Own" and "The Motorcycle Madonna," both on WILZ-Radio. Contributor to magazines, including *Science of Mind, Modern Maturity, Floridian, Spiritual India,* and *Executive Magazine.* Associate editor, *Money Tree,* 1977-81.

WORK IN PROGRESS: The Radioman, a science fiction novel; *No Place for A Baptist,* memories of New Orleans during the 1950's; *Metaphysical Whispers from Universal Mind,* poems; *Cry of the Sandpiper,* a novel; *The Ministers,* a novel; *Honeysucklers,* memories of her brother; *A Study in Angels; Earthbeat to Ecstasy* and *Written on My Heart,* contemporary romances under an undisclosed pseudonym.

SIDELIGHTS: Ann Bodenhamer Martin writes: "Thank God I'm a writer! Not a Hemingway, of course, nor any of those others who had such a dynamic impact on my life, yet seem to forever remain shadowy figures on the road extending into projected eternity . . . ahead . . . always ahead. But thank God for that kind of mind, that driving need to examine, dissect, analyze, explore and the accompanying need to express, however ineptly. Sometimes the thoughts are incomplete, or seem to come full circle back to point of origin. Others seem to scatter wildly or run pell-mell into inexhaustible space, like the red helium-filled balloons of my childhood which disappeared from sight once I lost hold on the string! . . . I wonder if we writers—as a breed—feel more pain, more pleasure, more self-doubt? Or does it just seem so as in our openness we deliberately invite in, and nourish, every myth and monster, every wood nymph and watersprite, every demi-god and demon? There's no way, I know, of being clear about that, but there is one thing I do know for certain: with words we wield great power. . . . We could do so much more to build a better world if we sought fame and fortune less, and cared not a whit for popularity or being understood, but instead directed our words toward building magnificent images of beauty and love and peace and the beneficence of the Universe. To wit: Reporters have free rein in reinforcing the negatives as long as we creative writers abdicate our royal right to renew and refresh reasons for optimism.''

*   *   *

MARTIN, Cort
See SHERMAN, Jory (Tecumseh)

*   *   *

MARTIN, (Basil) Kingsley   1897-1969

PERSONAL: Born December 2, 1897, in Pershore, England; died February 16, 1969, in Cairo, Egypt; son of D. Basil (a Unitarian minister) and Alice (Turberville) Martin. *Education:* Attended Hereford Cathedral School and Mill Hill; Magdalene College, Cambridge, M.A. (with first class honors), 1921; Princeton University, M.A., 1923. *Politics:* Socialist. *Religion:* Humanist. *Home:* Hilltop, Rodmell, Lewes, Sussex, England. *Agent:* A. D. Peters, 10 Buckingham, London WC2N 6BU, England. *Office:* New Statesman, 10 Great Turnstile, London W.C. 1, England.

CAREER: London School of Economics and Political Science, London, England, lecturer, 1924-28; *Manchester Guardian* (now *Guardian*), Manchester, England, member of editorial staff, 1928-30; *New Statesman,* London, editor, 1930-60, editorial consultant, 1962-69. *Wartime service:* Friends Ambulance Unit, 1916-19. *Member:* Savile Club (London).

WRITINGS: The Triumph of Lord Palmerston: A Study of Public Opinion in England before the Crimean War, Allen & Unwin, 1924, revised edition, Hutchinson, 1963; *The British Public and General Strike,* Hogarth, 1927; *French Liberal Thought in the Eighteenth Century: A Study of Political Ideas from Bayle to Condorcet,* Little, Brown, 1929, 2nd revised edition published as *The Rise of French Liberal Thought: A Study of Political Ideas from Bayle to Condorcet,* edited by J. P. Mayer, New York University Press, 1954, reprinted, Greenwood, 1980, 3rd edition, under original title, Harper, 1963; (with David Low) *Low's Russian Sketch Book,* Gollancz, 1932; *The Magic of Monarchy,* Knopf, 1937; *Fascism, Democracy and the Press,* New Statesman, 1938.

100,000,000 Allies—If We Choose, Gollancz, 1940, published as *How to Win the War,* Knopf, 1941; *Propaganda's Harvest,* Routledge, 1941; *What Is Britain Telling the World,* Routledge, 1941; *Truth and the Public,* Watts, 1945; *The Press the Public Wants,* Hogarth, 1947; (contributor) Cyril Edwin Mitchinson Joad, editor, *Shaw and Society: An Anthology and a Symposium,* Odhams, 1953, reprinted, Norwood Editions, 1978; *Harold Laski: A Memoir,* Viking, 1953; *War, History, and Human Nature,* Asia Publishing House, 1959.

Critic's London Diary: From the New Statesman, 1931-1956, Secker & Warburg, 1960; *The Magic of the British Monarchy,*

Little, Brown, 1962 (published in England as *The Crown and the Establishment,* Hutchinson, 1962, revised edition, Penguin in association with Hutchinson, 1965); (with others) *Objection to Humanism,* Constable, 1963; *Father Figures: A First Volume of Autobiography, 1897-1931,* Hutchinson, 1966, published as *Father Figures: The Evolution of an Editor, 1897-1931,* Regnery, 1970; *Editor: A Second Volume of Autobiography, 1931-1945,* Hutchinson, 1968, published as *Editor: New Statesman Years, 1931-1945,* Regnery, 1970; *Kingsley Martin: Portrait and Self-Portrait,* Barrie & Jenkins, 1969.

Contributor of articles on many subjects to *Punch, Encounter, Sunday Times, Atlantic Monthly, New Republic,* and other journals in England, United States, and India. *Political Quarterly,* co-founder, 1929, editor, 1929-31.

SIDELIGHTS: During his thirty-year editorship of the *New Statesman,* Kingsley Martin transformed the periodical from ''an insignificant left-wing weekly'' to ''Britain's foremost intellectual forum,'' *Time* magazine reported. Circulation increased from 15,000 in 1931 to 90,000 in 1945, and even advertising flourished. According to *Nation* contributor Alexander Werth, Martin's column ''London Diary'' was ''the most brilliant journalism in England—witty, well written and enormously readable.''

''One of the secrets of his success at the *New Statesman,''* noted Maurice Cranston in *London Magazine,* ''was to make it a literary as well as political paper, and however much the political pages might champion the cause of the working class multitude, the critical pages upheld the fastidious and fiercely anti-democratic standards of Bloomsbury.'' In fact, ''the standard of literary criticism under him was so high that it drew people who loathed its politics,'' the *London Times* reported.

Martin recalled fifteen years of the magazine's political history in *Editor: A Second Volume of Autobiography, 1931-45.* Writing in *Punch,* Kenneth Allsop described the era as ''the darkness-at-noon period of the National Government and hunger-marches, of the Spanish war and the dictators' ascension, of Munich and the Blitz—and of socialism's agonising over the terminal choice between pacifism and fascism.'' He went on to say that ''the strength of Mr. Martin's chronicle is the engaging candour with which he lets the record stand. . . . Faithfully on the file are the misjudgements, waverings and disenchantments of an honest journalist trying, from week to week, to hew to a navigational line of sanity and decency through conditions of poor visibility and bad turbulence.''

Malcolm Muggeridge believed that ''in a way, autobiography is a misnomer for *Editor;* it tells us very little about its author's personal life.'' But he and other critics also acknowledged that Martin's life was probably more externalized than most. As Muggeridge noted in the *Observer Review,* ''At each Station of the Cross of our time—the depression, the Spanish Civil War, Munich, the Nazi-Soviet Pact—he . . . stood to beat his breast and offer up his prayer, and then pushed eagerly, even joyously, on to the next.''

BIOGRAPHICAL/CRITICAL SOURCES: Spectator, November 18, 1960; *Newsweek,* November 27, 1961; Edward Hyams, *New Statesman,* Longmans, Green, 1963; *Observer Review,* March 31, 1968; *Listener,* April 4, 1968; *Punch,* April 24, 1968; *Books and Bookmen,* May, 1968; *London Magazine,* May, 1968; *Nation,* March 10, 1969.

OBITUARIES: London Times, February 18, 1969; *New York Times,* February 18, 1969; *Observer Review,* February 23, 1969; *Time,* February 28, 1969; *Newsweek,* March 3, 1969.†

MARTON, Beryl M(itchell)   1922-

PERSONAL: Born July 27, 1922, in Montreal, Quebec, Canada; came to the United States in 1953, naturalized citizen in 1957; daughter of Charles S. (a salesman) and Marie Blanche (Kilpin) Mitchell; married Mort N. Marton (an innkeeper), March 29, 1953 (divorced, 1979); children: Bruce Eric, Stewart David. *Education:* Attended secondary school in Montreal, Quebec. *Politics:* Democrat. *Address:* c/o Hawk, Billings Rd., Plymouth, Vt. 05056.

CAREER: Yorktown Gourmet Cooking School, Yorktown Heights, N.Y., director and instructor, 1963-70; Fundador Lodge, South Londonderry, Vt., co-owner and chef, 1971-77, instructor in gourmet cooking, summers, 1971-77, served as food consultant, demonstrator, and director of cooking programs for various firms dealing in culinary equipment and services, 1977-82; Hawk Mountain Corp. Cooking School, Pittsfield, Vt., director and coordinator, 1983—. Media spokesperson for Ruder, Finn & Rotman, New York City, 1977-81; guest chef at University Club, New York City, 1980; free-lance stylist for cookbook photography, 1980-81; guest on television and radio programs, often for R. T. French Co. *Awards, honors:* National Tastemaker Award from R. T. French Co., 1974, for *Diet for One, Dinner for All.*

WRITINGS: The Complete Book of Salads (Cooking and Crafts Club selection), Random House, 1968; *Diet for One, Dinner for All* (Literary Guild selection), Western Publishing, 1974; *Out of the Garden, into the Kitchen,* McKay, 1977; *The Coupon Saver's Cookbook,* Crown, 1980. Author of "Diary of a Cook," a monthly column in *Yorktowner,* 1967-70, *Window of Vermont,* 1975-78, and *Stratton Mountain News,* 1975-82. Food editor of *Window of Vermont.*

WORK IN PROGRESS: A cookbook based on cooking school curriculum.

SIDELIGHTS: Beryl M. Marton told *CA:* "Of all my many interests and diversifications, I find writing the most rewarding. I only wish I could get away from the technicalities of writing cookbooks and food columns and do something I consider more productive in a cultural and literary sense." *Avocational interests:* Making quilted wall-hangings of New England scenes, batik, needle-point, ceramics, leather-tooling, and sewing.

BIOGRAPHICAL/CRITICAL SOURCES: New York Times, March 9, 1972.

*   *   *

MARTY, Myron A.   1932-

PERSONAL: Born April 10, 1932, in West Point, Neb.; son of Emil A. (a teacher) and Louise (Wuerdemann) Marty; married Shirley Lee Plunk, July 31, 1954; children: Miriam Lee, Timothy David, Elizabeth Jane, Jason Charles. *Education:* Concordia Teachers College, River Forest, Ill., B.S.Ed., 1954; Washington University, St. Louis, Mo., M.A.Ed., 1960; St. Louis University, M.A., 1965; Ph.D., 1967. *Politics:* Democrat. *Religion:* Lutheran. *Home:* 7308 Statecrest Dr., Annandale, Va. 22003. *Office:* National Endowment for the Humanities, 1100 Pennsylvania Ave., Washington, D.C. 20506.

CAREER: Elementary teacher in Fort Wayne, Ind., 1954-57; teacher of history in secondary schools, St. Louis, Mo., 1957-65; Florissant Valley Community College, St. Louis, Mo.,

assistant professor, 1966-69, associate professor, 1969-72, professor, 1972-80, chairman of Social Science Division, 1967-75; National Endowment for the Humanities, Division of Education Programs, Washington, D.C., deputy director, 1980, 1982—, acting director, 1981-82. Summer instructor, Washington University, 1968; adjunct professor, University of Missouri at St. Louis, fall, 1976. Consultant and evaluator, Commission on Institutions of Higher Education of the North Central Association, 1969-80. Member of Missouri State Advisory Committee, U.S. Commission on Civil Rights, 1974-79.

MEMBER: Organization of American Historians, American Historical Association, American Society of Church History, Society for History Education, Community College Social Science Association, American Studies Association, National Trust for Historic Preservation, Sixteenth Century Studies Conference, American Association for State and Local History, National Book Critics Circle, Phi Beta Kappa. *Awards, honors:* National Endowment for the Humanities fellow, 1972-73; Newberry Library fellow, 1979.

WRITINGS: Faiths in Conflict: Christianity and Communism, Concordia, 1966; *Lutherans and Roman Catholicism: The Changing Conflict, 1917-1963,* University of Notre Dame Press, 1968; (with H. Theodore Finkelston) *Retracing Our Steps: Studies in Documents from the American Past,* two volumes, Canfield Press, 1972; (editor and contributor) *Responding to New Missions: New Directions for Community Colleges,* Jossey-Bass, 1978; (with David Kyvig) *Your Family History: A Handbook for Research and Writing,* Harlan Davidson, 1978; (with Kyvig) *Nearby History: Exploring the Past around You,* American Association for State and Local History, 1982. Contributor of articles to *Christian Century, History Teacher, Social Studies, Community College Humanities Review,* and *Social Education.*

*   *   *

MASON, Bobbie Ann   1940-

PERSONAL: Born May 1, 1940, in Mayfield, Ky.; daughter of Wilburn A. (a dairy farmer) and Christie (Lee) Mason; married Roger B. Rawlings (a magazine editor and writer), April 12, 1969. *Education:* University of Kentucky, B.A., 1962; State University of New York at Binghamton, M.A., 1966; University of Connecticut, Ph.D., 1972. *Agent:* Amanda Urban, International Creative Management, 40 West 57th St., New York, N.Y. 10019.

CAREER: Writer. *Mayfield Messenger,* Mayfield, Ky., writer, 1960; Ideal Publishing Co., New York, N.Y., writer for magazines, including *Movie Stars, Movie Life,* and *T.V. Star Parade,* 1962-63; Mansfield State College, Mansfield, Pa., assistant professor of English, 1972-79.

AWARDS, HONORS: National Book Critics Circle Award nomination and American Book Award nomination, both 1982, P.E.N.-Faulkner Award for fiction nomination and Ernest Hemingway Foundation Award, both 1983, all for *Shiloh and Other Stories;* National Endowment for the Arts fellowship, 1983; Pennsylvania Arts Council grant, 1983; Guggenheim fellowship, 1984.

WRITINGS: Nabokov's Garden: A Nature Guide to Ada, Ardis, 1974; *The Girl Sleuth: A Feminist Guide to the Bobbsey Twins, Nancy Drew, and Their Sisters,* Feminist Press, 1975; (contributor) Hortense Calisher and Shannon Ravenel, editors, *Best American Short Stories, 1981,* Houghton, 1981; *Shiloh and Other Stories,* Harper, 1982; (contributor) Anne Tyler and Ravenel, editors, *Best American Short Stories, 1983*, Houghton, 1983; (contributor) Bill Henderson, editor, *The Pushcart Prize: Best of the Small Presses*, Volume VIII, Pushcart, 1983. Contributor of short stories to numerous magazines, including *New Yorker, Atlantic,* and *Redbook;* frequent contributor to "The Talk of the Town" column, *New Yorker.*

WORK IN PROGRESS: Short stories and a novel.

SIDELIGHTS: Shiloh and Other Stories, Bobbie Ann Mason's first volume of fiction, established her reputation as a rising young voice in Southern literature. "To say that she is a 'new' writer is to give entirely the wrong impression, for there is nothing unformed or merely promising about her," emphasizes Anne Tyler in the *New Republic.* "She is a full-fledged master of the short story." Most of the sixteen works in *Shiloh* originally appeared in the *New Yorker,* the *Atlantic,* or other national magazines, a fact surprising to several critics who, like Anatole Broyard in the *New York Times Book Review,* label Mason's work "a regional literature that describes people and places almost unimaginably different from ourselves and the big cities in which we live." Explains David Quammen in another *New York Times Book Review* piece: "Miss Mason writes almost exclusively about working-class and farm people coping with their muted frustrations in western Kentucky (south of Paducah, not far from Kentucky Lake, if that helps you), and the gap to be bridged empathically between her readership and her characters [is] therefore formidable. But formidable also is Miss Mason's talent, and her craftsmanship."

Most critics attribute Mason's success to her vivid evocation of a region's physical and social geography. Hers is "the same world George Jones and Tammy Wynette sing about," reports Gene Lyons in *Newsweek,* "but without the sentimentality. As often as not . . . it's a matter of town—paved roads, indoor plumbing, and above all, TV—having come to the boondocks with the force of an unimagined social revolution." Here, people still dip snuff, catch mites from cleaning hen houses, and travel the fleamarket circuit selling hound dogs and knives. But they are just as likely to play video games, smoke marijuana, read best-sellers or watch Phil Donahue on television, and study physics when they go off to college. It is, reviewers note, a world in transition, with the old South fast becoming the new. Comments Suzanne Freeman in *Washington Post Book World,* "Mason's characters are just trying not to get lost in the shuffle."

Although these people may seem "stranger and more remote than the inhabitants of any French, Italian, or Spanish village," as Broyard maintains in the *New York Times,* most critics agree that they never become mere caricatures. "Mason never assumes her characters are ignorant," Freeman writes. "She lets us see the humor in their situations, but she knows better than to set them up as fools." They may refer to a Dachshund as a "datsun dog" or repeat "I reckon" and "I declare," but Mason's people do not fit the Hollywood image of backwoods hillbillies content to let the rest of the world pass by. Tyler notes that "they have an earnest faith in progress; they are as quick to absorb new brand names as foreigners trying to learn the language of a strange country they've found themselves in. . . . It is especially poignant that the characters . . . are trying to deal with changes most of us already take for granted."

Mason explores intensely personal events that lead to the individuals' acceptance of something new or the rejection—or loss—of something old. These adjustments in the characters' lives, sometimes subtle but at other times nothing less than revelatory, reflect a general uneasiness that pervades the cul-

tural landscape. The forces of change and alienation are no less frightening because they are universal or unavoidable. "Loss and deprivation, the disappointment of pathetically modest hopes, are the themes Bobbie Ann Mason works and reworks," states Quammen. "She portrays the disquieted lives of men and women not blessed with much money or education or luck, but cursed with enough sensitivity and imagination to suffer regrets."

Individuals contend with senile grandparents and dying dogs, suspected breast tumors, disability, divorce, and disillusioned retirement. They contemplate their assets and accomplishments only to suspect that they have overlooked, or been overlooked by, a better life. In the book's title story "Shiloh," for instance, Norma Jean lifts weights to develop her pectorals, takes night school courses, and experiments with what her husband, Leroy, considers to be exotic foods—lasagna and tacos. Norma Jean buys a book of sixties tunes and teaches herself to play them on the electric organ. "I didn't like these old songs back then, but I have this crazy feeling I missed something," she explains. Even those who move physically beyond the region are left disoriented by rapid change. "You educated me," a wife tells her northern husband. "I used to be so out of it. One day I was listening to Hank Williams and shelling corn for the chickens and the next day I was expected to know what wines went with what."

In many of the stories, love fails to offer stability. Rather than providing something dependable and static, relationships serve to magnify both the isolation and the transience of these characters' lives. Children leave home to enter the world of the more highly educated. Women escape, temporarily, their household roles (and in some cases their housebound husbands) to experience new ideas, new interests, or new lovers. Men go off to find work or look for a new home in a strange city. When thrown together again, couples find themselves distanced emotionally and intellectually. Leroy, a truck driver confined to his home by an injured leg, dreams of building a log cabin for Norma Jean, but a log cabin is the last thing college-student Norma Jean desires. In "The Ocean," Bill and Imogene retire, buy a camper, and travel to Florida via Nashville, where thirty-five years earlier they spent time as newlyweds. Bill cannot, Freeman tells us, see any connection between his bride and the now old Imogene or between life on the farm and his wayfaring life in the luxury camper.

Examining individuals' reactions to relationships allows the author to define the parts played by men and women in this shifting society. "Mason has an unwavering bead on the relationship between instincts and individual longings," writes R. Z. Sheppard in *Time.* "Her women have ambitions but never get too far from the nest; her men have domestic moments but spend a lot of time on wheels." Broyard concurs, calling the men "sometimes silent and transient, as if their only language was a language of place-names." Adds a *Chicago Tribune Book World* critic: "More often than not it is the men who act on their impulses, lighting out for the territory in search of a fresh start or adventure. Left behind with a child to support or a farm to maintain, the women can only fantasize about such liberation. This is not to say that Mason's women are helpless, without resources. Often, the men are terrified of their wives' or girlfriends' power and newfound resolve." One of Mason's wives, realizing that her husband actually fears all members of her sex, is "so sick and heavy with her power over him that she wants to cry."

In the *New York Times Book Review,* Broyard contends that these husbands, wives, and children "exist in a psychological rather than a physical environment, one that has been gutted—like an abandoned building—by the movement of American life. They fall between categories, occupy a place between nostalgia and apprehension. . . . They live, without history or politics, a life more like a linoleum than a tapestry.'' Other critics, while noting Mason's ability to evoke psychological states, emphasize her skill at depicting the material details of her ''linoleum'' world. Tyler points out that readers know precisely what dishes constitute the characters' meals, what clothes hang in their closets, and what craft projects fill their spare time. Mason intones the brand names that are infiltrating her characters' vocabularies, showing, for example, an irate female's choice of a ''Corning Ware Petite Pan'' to throw at an offending male. The exact titles of soap operas and popular songs, note several reviewers, provide an aural backdrop for Mason's own emotional dramas. Likewise, her characters' voices, according to Tyler, ''ring through our living rooms.''

Freeman, however, cites Mason's use of colloquialisms as one of the book's few problems. ''A couple of the stories have promising starts and clunky, disappointing endings,'' she writes. ''And, here and there throughout the stories, Mason has overdone the country talk.'' Yet in the final analysis, ''Mason has a vision and she makes us see it too—it is a glimpse straight into the heart of her characters' lives,'' Freeman proclaims. ''In true short-story tradition, [her] insights and epiphanies are spring-loaded,'' adds Sheppard. ''Mason rarely says more than is necessary to convey what Hemingway called 'the real thing, the sequence of motion and fact which made the emotion.' '' The *Chicago Tribune Book World* critic concludes, ''[Mason] is a writer of immense sensitivity, a true seer; technically, in terms of the making of sentences, she is a near virtuoso.''

BIOGRAPHICAL/CRITICAL SOURCES: Washington Post, February 5, 1976; Bobbie Ann Mason, *Shiloh and Other Stories,* Harper, 1982; *Washington Post Book World,* October 31, 1982; *Village Voice Literary Supplement,* November, 1982; *New Republic,* November 1, 1982; *Newsweek,* November 15, 1982; *New York Times Book Review,* November 21, 1982, December 19, 1982; *New York Times,* November 23, 1982; *Time,* January 3, 1983; *Chicago Tribune Book World,* January 23, 1983; *Chicago Tribune,* January 23, 1983; *Times* (London), August 11, 1983; *Times Literary Supplement,* August 12, 1983.

—Sketch by Nancy Hebb

*   *   *

MASON, Ernst
   See POHL, Frederik

*   *   *

MASTERSON, J. B.
   See EDMONDSON, G. C.

*   *   *

MAY, Derwent (James)   1930-

PERSONAL: Born April 29, 1930, in Eastbourne, England; son of Herbert and Nellie (Newton) May; married Jolanta Sypniewska, September 22, 1961; children: Orlando James, Miranda Izabella. *Education:* Lincoln College, Oxford, B.A., 1952, M.A., 1956. *Home:* 201 Albany St., London N.W. 1, England. *Office: Listener,* Broadcasting House, London W.1, England.

CAREER: Continental Daily Mail, Paris, France, drama critic, 1952-53; lecturer in English at University of Indonesia, Dja-

karta, 1955-58, and at University of Lodz and University of Warsaw in Poland, 1959-63; *Times Literary Supplement,* London, England, leader-writer and poetry editor, 1963-65; *Listener,* London, literary editor, 1965—. Member of literature advisory panel, Arts Council of Great Britain, 1967-70.

WRITINGS: (Editor with James Price) *Oxford Poetry 1952,* Basil Blackwell, 1952; *The Professionals* (novel), Chatto & Windus, 1964, David White, 1968; (editor) *Good Talk: An Anthology from BBC Radio,* Gollancz, 1968, Taplinger, 1969; *Dear Parson* (novel), Chatto & Windus, 1969; (editor) *Good Talk, 2,* Gollancz, 1969, Taplinger, 1970; *The Laughter in Djakarta* (novel), Chatto & Windus, 1973; *A Revenger's Comedy* (novel), Chatto & Windus, 1979; (editor) *The Music of What Happens: Poems, 1965-1980,* B.B.C. Publications, 1981; *Proust,* Oxford University Press, 1983; *The Times Nature Diary,* Robson, 1983.

Contributor of critical articles to *Essays in Criticism, Times Literary Supplement,* and other periodicals.

WORK IN PROGRESS: A volume of short stories.

BIOGRAPHICAL/CRITICAL SOURCES: Times Literary Supplement, May 29, 1981, May 27, 1983; *Punch,* June 24, 1981.

*   *   *

MBITI, John S(amuel)   1931-

PERSONAL: Born November 30, 1931, in Kitui, Kenya; married Verena Siegenthaler (a social worker and teacher), May 15, 1965; children: Samuel Kyeni, Maria Mwende, Esther Mwikali, Anna Kavata. *Education:* Makerere University College, University of East Africa (now Makerere University), B.A., 1953; Barrington College, A.B., 1956, Th.B., 1957; Cambridge University, Ph.D., 1963. *Home and office:* Einschlagweg 11, CH 3400 Burgdorf, Switzerland.

CAREER: Anglican priest. Teacher Training College, Kangundo, Kenya, teacher, 1957-59; Selly Oak Colleges, Birmingham, England, visiting William Paton Lecturer, 1959-60; St. Michael's Church, St. Albans, England, curate, 1963-64; Makerere University, Kampala, Uganda, 1964-74, began as lecturer in New Testament and African religions and philosophy, became professor of theology and comparative religion, and head of department; Ecumenical Institute, Bossey, Geneva, Switzerland, director and professor, 1974-80; parish minister in Burgdorf, Switzerland, 1981—. Visiting lecturer, University of Hamburg, 1966-67; Harry Emerson Fosdick Visiting Professor, Union Theological Seminary, New York, N.Y., 1972-73; part-time professor at University of Bern, 1983—. *Member:* Studiorum Novi Testamenti Societas. *Awards, honors:* L.H.D., Barrington College, 1973.

WRITINGS: Mutunga na Ngewa Yake, Thomas Nelson, 1954; (translator into Kikamba) Robert Louis Stevenson, *Treasure Island,* East African Literature Bureau, 1954; *English-Kamba Vocabulary,* East African Literature Bureau, 1959; (editor) *Akamba Stories* (collection of folktales), Oxford University Press, 1966; *African Religions and Philosophy,* Praeger, 1969; *Poems of Nature and Faith,* East African Publishing House, 1969.

Concepts of God in Africa, Praeger, 1970; *New Testament Eschatology in an African Background: A Study of the Encounter between New Testament Theology and African Traditional Concepts,* Oxford University Press, 1971; *The Crisis of Mission in Africa,* Uganda Church Press (Kampala), 1971; *The Voice of Nine Bible Trees,* Uganda Church Press, 1973;

Love and Marriage in Africa, Longman, 1973; *Death and the Hereafter in the Light of Christianity and African Religion*, Makerere University Printery, 1974; *Introduction to African Religion*, Praeger, 1975; *The Prayers of African Religion*, S.P.C.K., 1975, Orbis, 1976; (editor) *Confessing Christ in Different Cultures*, Ecumenical Institute (Bossey, Switzerland), 1977; (editor) *African and Asian Contributions to Contemporary Theology*, Ecumenical Institute, 1977.

Also author of *Bible and Theology in African Christianity*, 1984; editor of *Indigenous Theology and the Universal Church*, 1979, and *Christian and Jewish Dialogue on Man*, 1980. Contributor of poems and articles to anthologies and periodicals in Europe, Africa, India, Japan, and the United States.

SIDELIGHTS: John S. Mbiti speaks Kikamba, Swahili, Gikuyu, French, and German. He reads New Testament Greek and a little Old Testament Hebrew.

* * *

McCANN, Edson
    See POHL, Frederik

* * *

McCREIGH, James
    See POHL, Frederik

* * *

McDEARMON, Kay

PERSONAL: Born in San Francisco, Calif.; daughter of John (an engineer) and Mary (Gavin) Healy; married James R. McDearmon (a college professor), July 26, 1954. *Education:* University of California, Berkeley, B.A. *Home:* 2160 Julie, Turlock, Calif. 95380.

CAREER: High school teacher in Oakland, Calif., 1948-51; high school teacher of business education in Lafayette, Calif., 1951-54; writer, 1955—. *Member:* Toastmasters. *Awards, honors:* All of McDearmon's books about animals have been named outstanding science books for children by National Science Teachers Association.

WRITINGS—All for children; all published by Dodd: *A Day in the Life of a Sea Otter* (Junior Literary Guild selection), 1973; *The Walrus: Giant of the Arctic Ice*, 1974; *Mahalia: Gospel Singer*, 1976; *Polar Bear*, 1976; *Cougar*, 1977; *Gorillas*, 1979; *Foxes*, 1980; *Rocky Mountain Bighorns*, 1981; *Orangutans*, 1983. Contributor of about twenty-five articles to magazines, including *Cricket*.

WORK IN PROGRESS: Biographies; animal books.

SIDELIGHTS: Kay McDearmon told *CA:* "I have always liked to write; in fact, in high school I often wrote two themes when only one was required. In college I worked on the university daily. I am interested primarily in people; did a bit of 'Roots' study on a three-week trip to Ireland. I do considerable talking to groups—children and adults. This I really enjoy."

AVOCATIONAL INTERESTS: Travel.

* * *

McDERMOTT, Robert
    See HAWLEY, Donald Thomas

McDOUGALL, Joyce 1926-

PERSONAL: Born April 26, 1926, in Dunedin, New Zealand; daughter of Harold (a manufacturer) and Lilian (Blackler) Carrington; married James McDougall, 1941; married second husband, Sidney Stewart (a psychoanalyst), 1966; children: (first marriage) Martin John, Rohan (Mrs. Joseph Collier). *Education:* University of Otago, D.Ed., 1946; trained as a psychoanalyst in London and Paris, 1950-60. *Home:* 60 Rue Quincampoix, 75004 Paris, France.

CAREER: Psychoanalyst in Paris, France; training analyst at psychoanalytical children's clinic, Institut Claparede, 1960-72; Paris Psychoanalytical Institute, Paris, lecturer, training and supervising analyst, 1964—. *Member:* International Psychoanalytic Association, Paris Psychoanalytic Society.

WRITINGS: (With Serge Lebovici) *Un Cas de psychose infantile*, Presses Universitaires de France, 1960, translation and revision by McDougall published as *Dialogue with Sammy: A Psycho-analytical Contribution to the Understanding of Child Psychosis*, edited by Martin James, International Universities Press, 1969; (with J. Chassequet and others) *La Sexualite feminine*, Payot (Paris), 1965, translation published as *Female Sexuality: New Psychoanalytic Views*, University of Michigan Press, 1970.

(Contributor) *La Sexualite Perverse*, Payot, 1972; *Plaidoyer pour une certaine anormalite*, Gallimard, 1978, translation published as *Plea for a Measure of Abnormality*, International Universities Press, 1980; (contributor) *Sexual Deviators*, Oxford University Press, 1979; *Countertransference*, Jason Aronson, 1979; (contributor) *Ten Years of Psychoanalysis in France*, International Universities Press, 1980; *Theatres du Je*, Gallimard (Paris), 1982.

WORK IN PROGRESS: On-going research into the psychoanalytic process.

AVOCATIONAL INTERESTS: Joyce McDougall has two retreats, a Normandy farm house with flowers, vegetables, chickens, and rabbits, and a cottage in a small fishing village in Andalusia.

* * *

McFAGUE, Sallie 1933-
    (Sallie McFague TeSelle)

PERSONAL: Born May 25, 1933, in Quincy, Mass.; daughter of Maurice Graeme and Jessie (Reid) McFague; children: Elizabeth, John. *Education:* Smith College, B.A., 1955; Yale University, B.D., 1959, Ph.D., 1964. *Politics:* Democrat. *Religion:* Methodist. *Home:* 3703 Meadowbrook Ave., Nashville, Tenn. 37205. *Office:* Vanderbilt University, Nashville, Tenn. 37203.

CAREER: Yale University, Divinity School, New Haven, Conn., lecturer in Christianity and contemporary culture, 1963-65; Vanderbilt University, Nashville, Tenn., currently professor of theology and former dean of Divinity School. *Member:* American Academy of Religion, Society for Values in Higher Education, Phi Beta Kappa.

WRITINGS—Under name Sallie McFague TeSelle, except as indicated: *Literature and the Christian Life*, Yale University Press, 1966; (editor) *The Family, Communes, and Utopian Societies*, Harper, 1971; (editor) *The Rediscovery of Ethnicity*,

Harper, 1973; *Speaking in Parables: A Study in Metaphor and Theology,* Fortress, 1975; (under name Sallie McFague) *Metaphorical Theology: Models of God in Religious Language,* Fortress, 1982. Editor, *Soundings: A Journal of Interdisciplinary Studies,* 1967-75.

*   *   *

McGREEVEY, William Paul   1938-

PERSONAL: Born April 14, 1938, in Greenville, Ohio; son of Paul H. (an engineer) and Aletha M. (a teacher; maiden name, Myers) McGreevey; children: Sean Robb, Alicia Ireys. *Education:* Ohio State University, B.A. (with high distinction), 1960; Massachusetts Institute of Technology, Ph.D., 1964. *Home:* 2911 P St. N.W., Washington, D.C. 20007. *Office:* World Bank, 1818 H St. N.W., Washington, D.C. 20433.

CAREER: University of Oregon, Eugene, assistant professor of economics, 1964-65; University of California, Berkeley, assistant professor of history, 1965-71, Center for Latin American Studies, research associate and acting chairman, 1965-71, chairman, 1966-69; Organization of American States, Washington, D.C., senior economist in department of economic affairs, 1971-72; Smithsonian Institution, Washington, D.C., staff social scientist with Interdisciplinary Communications Program, 1972-76; consulting economist and writer, 1976-77; Battelle Memorial Institute, Washington, D.C., program director, 1977-80; World Bank, Washington, D.C., senior economist, 1980—.

Economist with Alliance for Progress, 1962; director of migration research group in Colombia, 1965; co-director of Social Science Research Council-American Council of Learned Societies Latin American studies project, 1967-69; member of panel on Latin America for World Press, 1967-71. Member of board of directors of International Center for Research on Women. Consultant to Agency for International Development.

MEMBER: American Economic Association, Conference of Latin American Historians, Latin American Studies Association, American Historical Association, Econometric Society.

WRITINGS: An Economic History of Colombia, 1845-1930, Cambridge University Press, 1971; (contributor) Richard M. Morse, editor, *The Urban Development of Latin America,* Stanford University Press, 1971; (contributor) Jacob Price and Val Lorin, editors, *The Dimensions of the Past,* Yale University Press, 1972; (with Nancy Birdsall) *The Policy Relevance of Recent Social Research on Fertility* (monograph), Smithsonian Institution, 1974; (editor) *Third-World Poverty: Strategies for Measuring Development Progress,* Lexington Books, 1980; (editor with M. Buvinic) *Women and Poverty in the Third World,* Johns Hopkins University Press, 1983. Contributor to academic journals.

WORK IN PROGRESS: Population Growth and Development Policy.

*   *   *

McGUIGAN, Dorothy Gies   1914-1982

PERSONAL: Surname is pronounced McKwigen; born November 12, 1914, in Ann Arbor, Mich.; died October 28, 1982; daughter of Charles George (a businessman) and Jennie (a scholar; maiden name, Sturman) Gies; married Bernard Joseph McGuigan, August 3, 1946 (deceased); children: Michael John, Cathleen Mary. *Education:* University of Michigan, A.B. (cum

laude), 1936; Columbia University, M.A., 1939; King's College, London, graduate study, 1937-38. *Politics:* Democrat. *Religion:* Episcopalian. *Home:* 470 Rock Creek Dr., Ann Arbor, Mich. 48104. *Office:* Center for Continuing Education of Women, University of Michigan, 330 Thompson St., Ann Arbor, Mich. 48109.

CAREER: Macmillan Publishing Co., Inc., New York, N.Y., member of sales promotion staff, 1938-43; Jack Starr Hunt News Agency, Mexico City, Mexico, feature writer, 1943-44; American Red Cross, staff assistant in England and Germany, 1944-46; *Stars and Stripes,* feature writer in Germany, 1946-49; *Weekend Magazine,* feature writer in Germany, 1955-56; University of Michigan, Ann Arbor, School of Business Administration, instructor in English, 1956-58, 1963-66, Center for Continuing Education of Women, program director and editor, beginning 1970, lecturer in English, beginning 1974. *Member:* Authors Guild, Authors League of America, Mortarboard, Womens Research Club of the University of Michigan, Phi Beta Kappa (president, University of Michigan chapter, 1973-74). *Awards, honors:* Five Avery and Jule Hopwood Awards at University of Michigan, 1934-36, for poetry, essay, and novel; Regent's citation for distinguished achievement, University of Michigan, 1975.

WRITINGS—Published by Center for the Continuing Education of Women, University of Michigan, except as indicated: *The Habsburgs,* Doubleday, 1966; *A Dangerous Experiment,* 1970; (editor) *A Sampler of Women's Studies,* 1973; (editor) *New Research on Women at the University of Michigan,* 1974; *Metternich and the Duchess,* Doubleday, 1975; (editor) *New Research on Women and Sex Roles at the University of Michigan,* 1976; (editor) Berenice A. Carroll, and others, *The Role of Women in Conflict and Peace: Papers,* 1977; (editor) *Changing Family, Changing Workplace: New Research,* 1980.

WORK IN PROGRESS: English Women in the Literary Trades; a history of women's education; a biography of Isabella of Spain.

SIDELIGHTS: The Habsburgs has been published in German, French, Spanish, Dutch, and Yugoslav.†

*   *   *

McHUGH, Heather   1948-

PERSONAL: Born August 20, 1948, in California; daughter of John Laurence (a marine biologist) and Eileen Francesca (Smallwood) McHugh. *Education:* Radcliffe College, B.A., 1970; University of Denver, M.A., 1972. *Politics:* Independent. *Religion:* Pantheism. *Office:* Department of English, State University of New York at Binghamton, Binghamton, N.Y. 13901.

CAREER: Antioch College, Yellow Springs, Ohio, visiting lecturer in English, 1971-72; Stephens College, Columbia, Mo., instructor in English and poet-in-residence, 1974-76; State University of New York at Binghamton, associate professor of English, 1976—. Visiting appointments at Columbia University, University of California, and University of Washington; affiliated with M.F.A. writing program, Warren Wilson College. *Member:* Associated Writing Programs (member, board of directors, 1980-83).

AWARDS, HONORS: Fellow of Cummington Community for the Arts, 1970, and Provincetown Fine Arts Work Center, 1972; prize from Academy of American Poets, 1972, for "In the Third Person"; Macdowell Colony fellowships, 1973, 1974,

1976; National Endowment for the Arts grant, 1974, 1981; winner of New Poetry Series Competition, 1976, for *Dangers*.

WRITINGS—Poetry: (Contributor) Daniel Halber, editor, *American Poetry Anthology*, Avon, 1976; *Dangers*, Houghton, 1977; (contributor) David Rigsbee, editor, *Ardis Anthology of New American Poetry*, Ardis, 1977; *A World of Difference*, Houghton, 1981; (translator) *D'Apres Tout: Poems by Jean Follain*, Princeton University Press, 1981. Contributor of poems to magazines, including *New Yorker, Harper's Atlantic, Antaeus*, and *Antioch Review*.

WORK IN PROGRESS: More poems.

SIDELIGHTS: "Heather McHugh is likable," writes Alfred Corn of the poet's first collection, *Dangers*, in the *New York Times Book Review*. "The virtues—and weaknesses—of her first book are: personality, energy, and immediacy." Although Corn feels that "too often McHugh's winning brashness hardens into brass," nonetheless he says the poet "writes ingeniously, playing with syntax and words as the gifted do." Referring to *A World of Difference* in the *New York Times Book Review*, Hugh Seidman concludes: "In general, Heather McHugh writes terse, well-wrought, often ironic poems. She manipulates language to produce resonances of meaning without necessarily creating a psychological depth that might justify her insights and conclusions."

AVOCATIONAL INTERESTS: Rhythm and blues, shooting pool, the state of Maine.

BIOGRAPHICAL/CRITICAL SOURCES: New York Times Book Review, July 3, 1977, September 13, 1981.

* * *

McKEE, Alexander (Paul Charrier)   1918-

PERSONAL: Born July 25, 1918, in Ipswich, Suffolk, England; son of Alexander Gray (a surgeon-commander, Royal Navy) and Dorothy (Charrier) McKee; married Ilse Heimerdinger (a writer), February 23, 1952; children: Alexander Michael, Monica Elizabeth, Thomas Paul Gray, Cornelia Barbara, Gabriela Christine. *Education:* Privately educated in England and abroad. *Politics:* "Never voted." *Religion:* Church of Scotland (Presbyterian). *Home and office:* Lorelei, 41 St. Thomas Ave., Hayling Island, Hampshire, England.

CAREER: Soloed at fifteen, received pilot's license two years later, and started selling stories on flying to British aviation magazines at eighteen; served in British Army, 1942-52, becoming a sergeant, and writer, producer, and broadcaster for the Forces Radio Station in Hamburg, Germany, 1948-52; continued writing ("it was hard getting established") in England and eventually divided his time between free-lance features for British Broadcasting Corp. and editing *Conveyor*, the house magazine of a coal and oil company group; now concentrating on books, but occasionally writes television scripts and does broadcasting for Southern Television (south of England) and TWW (West England and Wales). *Member:* British Sub-Aqua Club. *Awards, honors:* Award for best feature script, Writers Guild of Great Britain, 1970, for "The Dark Page."

WRITINGS: The Coal-Scuttle Brigade, Souvenir Press, 1957, abridged edition, New English Library, 1973; *Black Saturday: The Tragedy of the Royal Oak*, Souvenir Press, 1959, reprinted, Hamlyn, 1978, published as *Black Saturday*, Holt, 1960; *Strike from the Sky: The Story of the Battle of Britain*, Souvenir Press, 1960, Little, Brown, 1961, published as *Strike from the Sky: The Battle of Britain Story*, New English Library, 1978; *The*

Golden Wreck: The True Story of a Great Maritime Disaster (Book Society choice), Souvenir Press, 1961, published as *The Golden Wreck*, Morrow, 1962, reprinted, New English Library, 1977; *The Truth about the Mutiny on the Bounty*, Mayflower Books, 1961, published as *H.M.S. Bounty*, Morrow, 1962; *The Friendless Sky: The Story of Air Combat in World War I*, Souvenir Press, 1962, Morrow, 1964; (contributor) James F. Sunderman, editor, *World War II in the Air: Europe*, F. Watts, 1963; (contributor) Don Congden, editor, *Combat: The War with Germany*, Dell, 1963; *From Merciless Invaders: An Eye-Witness Account of the Spanish Armada*, Souvenir Press, 1963, Norton, 1964; *Caen: Anvil of Victory*, Souvenir Press, 1964, published as *Last Round against Rommel: Battle of the Normandy Bridgehead*, New American Library, 1966; *Gordon of Khartoum*, Mayflower Books, 1965, Lancer Books, 1966.

Vimy Ridge, Souvenir Press, 1966, published as *The Battle of Vimy Ridge*, Stein & Day, 1967; *Farming the Sea: First Steps into Inner Space*, Souvenir Press, 1967, Crowell, 1969; *History under the Sea*, Hutchinson, 1968, Dutton, 1969; *The Race for the Rhine Bridges: 1940, 1944, 1945*, Stein & Day, 1971; *King Henry VIII's Mary Rose*, Souvenir Press, 1973, Stein & Day, 1974; *Death Raft: The Human Drama of the Medusa Shipwreck*, Souvenir Press, 1975, Scribner, 1977.

The Queen's Corsair: Drake's Journey of Circumnavigation, Souvenir Press, 1978, published as *The Queen's Corsair*, Stein & Day, 1979; *Ice Crash*, Souvenir Press, 1978, published as *Ice Crash: Disaster in the Antarctic*, St. Martin's, 1980; *Great Mysteries of Aviation*, Stein & Day, 1982; *How We Found the Mary Rose*, St. Martin's, 1983.

Also author of "The Dark Page" (radio script).

Contributor to British and Canadian service journals and newspapers in World War II; more recently contributor to *Triton, Diver, New York Times, Radio Times, Yachts and Yachting*, and other publications.

SIDELIGHTS: Alexander McKee's forte has been documentary writing in various forms since 1948, something of a discipline for a man who likes to recall that he broadcast a radio commentary while flying a jet fighter near the speed of sound, and who likes to prowl undersea wrecks ("it fascinates me"). He is noted for his book *Death Raft: The Human Drama of the Medusa Shipwreck*, an exploration of the 1816 disaster which claimed hundreds of lives. *Newsweek* reviewer Walter Clemons calls the book a "beautifully built . . . account of the original disaster [that] opens out into a study of the ensuing cover-up and widening political scandal, which deeply embarrassed the French Government." Clemons concludes: "Instead of exploiting the Medusa episode as a unique horror story, McKee searches out the paradigmatic elements of human behavior under stress. This is a first-rate piece of work."

McKee writes of his criterion for choosing a story: "One in which ordinary (or for that matter, extraordinary) people are involved in some drama or event in which we really see what they are made of. . . . A number of my books, such as those on the 'Bounty' or the 'Royal Oak,' involve getting to know a small number of people simultaneously pitchforked into a crisis.

"The other type of book which I write, the campaign history, is a different form. There can obviously be no unity of time and place. The attraction for me lies in finding the reactions of many men (and some women) engaged in these great events."

One of the campaign histories, *Strike from the Sky*, was published almost simultaneously in four countries, and has since

359

been brought out by two other London publishers. *H.M.S. Bounty* has been published in foreign-language editions and a French edition of *From Merciless Invaders* has been issued.

McKee says he would like to do more writing on his undersea research, but admits that it has not been remunerative "apart from the sale of the odd article or photograph." For five years he has been handling the explorations of a priory church and village submerged in fourteenth-century floods. Most of his work has been local to the English Channel, but he went on an expedition to the Tyrrhenian Sea in Italy in 1962, and explored six Greek, Roman and Etruscan wrecks plus a Spanish galleon.

In October, 1982, McKee supervised the successful excavation of the ship *Mary Rose,* which had sunk near the harbour at Portsmouth, England, in 1545. The project, which McKee had been working on since 1965, yielded many valuable artifacts from the Tudor period, including bows and arrows, shoes, medical supplies, and even heavily-preserved food. The author chronicles his participation in the excavation in *How We Found the Mary Rose,* described by *Washington Post Book World* critic Matthew Schudel as an "adventure-filled [book that is] all the more appealing because [McKee] is an amateur who pursues his dreams in spite of what scholars and experts might say. The world needs more like him."

BIOGRAPHICAL/CRITICAL SOURCES: Times Literary Supplement, January 19, 1967; *Books and Bookmen,* April, 1968; *Washington Post Book World,* January 16, 1977, September 11, 1983; *Newsweek,* January 31, 1977; *New Yorker,* February 14, 1977.†

*   *   *

McKENNA, Patricia
See GOEDICKE, Patricia (McKenna)

*   *   *

McMAHON, Pat
See HOCH, Edward D(entinger)

*   *   *

McNALL, Scott G(rant)   1941-

PERSONAL: Born January 16, 1941, in New Ulm, Minn.; son of Everett Herman (a farmer) and Dorothy Grant (a schoolteacher; maiden name, Brown) McNall; married Sally Anne Allen (a college professor), October 30, 1960; children: Miles Allen, Amy Ellen. *Education:* Portland State College (now University), B.A., 1962; University of Oregon, Ph.D., 1965. *Politics:* Independent. *Religion:* Protestant. *Home:* 3026 Riverview Rd., Lawrence, Kan. 66044. *Office:* Department of Sociology, University of Kansas, Lawrence, Kan. 66044.

CAREER: University of Oregon, Eugene, instructor in sociology, 1964-65; University of Minnesota, Minneapolis, assistant professor of sociology, 1965-70; Arizona State University, Tempe, associate professor of sociology, 1970-76; University of Kansas, Lawrence, professor of sociology and chairman of department, 1976—. Fulbright lecturer, Pierce College, Athens, Greece, 1968-69; Fulbright scholar, University of Waikato, New Zealand, 1983. *Member:* Midwest Sociological Society (president, 1982-83).

WRITINGS: (Editor) *Sociological Perspective: Introductory Readings,* Little, Brown, 1968, 4th edition, 1977; *The Socio-*

logical Experience: A Modern Introduction to Sociology, Little, Brown, 1969, 3rd edition, 1977; *The Greek Peasant,* American Sociological Association, 1974; *Career of a Radical Rightist,* Kennikat, 1975; *Social Problems Today,* Little, Brown, 1975; (editor) *Theoretical Perspectives in Sociology,* St. Martin's, 1979; (editor) *Current Perspectives in Social Theory,* Jai Press, Volume I, 1980, Volume II, 1981, Volume III, 1982; (editor) *Political Economy: A Critique of American Society,* Scott, Foresman, 1981; (with wife, Sally A. McNall) *Plains Families: Exploring Sociology through Social History,* St. Martin's, 1983.

*   *   *

McNALLY, Robert E(dward)   1917-1978

PERSONAL: Born December 24, 1917, in New York, N.Y.; died December 21, 1978; son of Louis J. and Margaret C. (Dolan) McNally. *Education:* Georgetown University, A.B., 1942; Woodstock College, S.T.L., 1950; Catholic University of America, M.A., 1952; University of Munich, Dr.Phil. (summa cum laude), 1957. *Home and office:* Fordham University, Bronx, N.Y. 10458.

CAREER: Roman Catholic priest of Society of Jesus (Jesuits). Woodstock College, Woodstock, Md., professor of church history, 1957-66; Fordham University, Bronx, N.Y., professor of historical theology, beginning 1966. Guest professor, Georgetown University, 1958-59, George Washington University, 1961-62; professor of Catholic studies, Brown University, 1965-66. *Member:* Mediaeval Academy of America, American Catholic Historical Association, Society of Church History. *Awards, honors:* D.H.L., Salve Regina College, 1967; American Council of Learned Societies grant-in-aid.

WRITINGS: Der irische Liber de Numeris: Eine Quellenanalyse des pseudo-Isidorischen Liber de Numeris, [Munich], 1957; *The Bible in the Early Middle Ages,* Newman, 1959; *The Reform of the Church: Crisis and Criticism in Historical Perspective,* Herder & Herder, 1963; *The Unreformed Church,* Sheed, 1965; (editor and contributor) *Old Ireland,* Gill & Son, 1965; (editor with John C. Olin and James D. Smart) *Luther, Erasmus, and the Reformation: A Catholic-Protestant Reappraisal,* Fordham University Press, 1969; (editor) *Scriptores Hiberniae Minores Corpus Christianorum,* [Turnhout, Belgium], 1973; (with Robert M. Grant and George H. Tavard) *Perspectives on Scripture and Tradition: Essays,* Fides, 1976. Also author of *The Council of Trent and the Vernacular Bible,* 1966, and *The Ninety-Five Theses of Martin Luther: 1517-1967,* 1967.

Contributor: Isidoriana, [Leon, Spain], 1961; *Reformers in Profile,* Fortress Press, 1967; R. A. Schroth, editor, *Jesuit Spirit in a Time of Change,* Newman, 1968. Contributor to *Encyclopaedia Britannica, Catholic Encyclopedia for School and Home,* and *Encyclopedia International;* also contributor of more than thirty articles to theology journals and religion periodicals.

WORK IN PROGRESS: A history of the Bible in the Middle Ages.†

*   *   *

MEADOR, Roy   1929-

PERSONAL: Born April 23, 1929, in Cordell, Okla.; son of Walter Raymond (a carpenter) and Gladys (in politics; maiden name, Reed) Meador. *Education:* University of Southern California, A.B., 1951; Columbia University, M.A., 1972. *Politics:* "Reduce Human Suffering." *Religion:* "Questioning?" *Address:* P.O. Box 2045, Ann Arbor, Mich. 48106.

CAREER: Pfizer, Inc., New York City, advertising and technical writer, 1960-72; Gelman Instrument Co., Ann Arbor, Mich., advertising and technical writer, 1972-78; writer of publications for National Aeronautics and Space Administration (NASA), U.S. Department of Energy, and the State of Michigan, 1978-81; free-lance writer, 1981—. Member of editorial advisory board of Ann Arbor Science Publishers. *Military service:* U.S. Navy, 1951-54; served in Korea; became lieutenant. *Member:* National Guild of Bookworkers, Ann Arbor Bookbinders Guild.

WRITINGS—Published by Ann Arbor Science Publishers, except as indicated: *Future Energies,* 1974; *Franklin: Revolutionary Scientist,* 1975; (editor with Howard Gordon) *Perspectives on the Energy Crisis* (two volumes), 1977; (with Bruce Watkins) *Technology and Human Values,* 1977; *Future Energy Alternatives,* 1978.

Cogeneration and District Heating, 1981; (contributor) *Analog Yearbook II,* Ace Books, 1981. Contributor to numerous periodicals, including *Newsday, Christian Science Monitor, New York Times, Smithsonian, Ovation,* and *True West.*

WORK IN PROGRESS: Manual on Technical Writing; Energy Frontiers; Technical Writing Doesn't Have to Be Dull; How to Propose: Science and Art of Winning Proposals; Benjamin Franklin Reappraised; The Automobile and Frontier America; a critical biography of H. M. Tomlinson.

SIDELIGHTS: Roy Meador writes *CA:* "Having a book published and then another, confirmed what I saw hazily at fifteen, that for me no other activity will do except writing. In my future writing I want to understand and help others understand the challenge, the perils, and the beauty of our strange world and stranger lives. I want to write about what is going on in science to threaten us and enrich us. If my mind hides in caves for false safety, I want to leave the caves and help others leave. I hope through writing to contribute what I can in preserving a world worth living in and maybe even a human race to live here beyond the twentieth century. If I find anything true to say, I want to say it. If I find anything both true and funny to say, I want to shout it. We need a good laugh.

"Keeping hope alive is a perennial occupational obligation of the writer who must cope with subjects that don't jell, rejection slips, publications that forget their promises to pay, and the constant lack of sufficient time to develop ideas fully in the course of days that are never long enough. Since hope is the perpetual need and yearning of mankind, the writer, as one of the walking wounded, is a veteran uniquely trained by his professional life to help others master the mystery of continuing to hope. I hope in my future writing to help others remember how to hope."

Meador goes on to explain his vocational interests thus: "Personalizing, explaining, defanging, and demystifying technology; doing what I can to keep reading alive in the age of picture boxes; learning and writing about energy for greater public awareness; exploring neglected corridors of history, science, literature, and writing about them."

AVOCATIONAL INTERESTS: Reading, the Arizona desert, book collecting, walking in New York City, bookbinding, music.

MEADOWS, Peter
See LINDSAY, Jack

*   *   *

MEAGHER, John C.   1935-

PERSONAL: Surname is pronounced *Mah*-her; born March 23, 1935, in St. Louis, Mo.; son of John Ford (a broker) and Eleanor (Ackerman) Meagher; married Sheila McMahon Cary, August 9, 1958 (divorced, 1982); children: Mary, Kathleen, Margaret, Sean, Michael. *Education:* University of Notre Dame, B.A., 1956; Princeton University, M.A., 1958, Ph.D. (English), 1962; University of London, Ph.D. (English), 1961; McMaster University, Ph.D. (religion), 1975. *Religion:* Catholic. *Home:* 19 Orley Ave., Toronto, Ontario, Canada. *Office:* St. Michael's College, Toronto, Ontario, Canada M5S IJ4.

CAREER: University of Notre Dame, Notre Dame, Ind., assistant professor of English, 1961-66; University of Toronto, St. Michael's College, Toronto, Ontario, associate professor, 1966-70, professor of English, 1970—, special lecturer in religious studies, beginning 1970, professor of theology, 1973—. Director of Institute of Christian Thought, 1973-80. *Member:* Malone Society, Canadian Association of University Teachers, Canadian Society for the Study of Religion, Canadian Society for Biblical Studies, American Academy of Religion (president, 1977), Society of Biblical Literature, Society for Values in Higher Education, Association of Marshall Scholars and Alumni.

AWARDS, HONORS: Woodrow Wilson fellowship, 1956; Danforth fellowship, 1956; Marshall scholarship for study at University of London, 1959; Cross Disciplinary fellowship for study at University of Paris and Institut Catholique, 1965; Canada Council leave fellowship, 1972-73; Social Systems and Human Resources Council leave fellowship, 1980-81.

WRITINGS: (Editor) *The Downfall of Robert Earl of Huntingdon,* Malone Society, 1965; *Method and Meaning in Jonson's Masques,* University of Notre Dame Press, 1966; (editor) *The Death of Robert Earl of Huntingdon,* Malone Society, 1967; *Toward a Moral Theory of Idioms,* Soundings, 1971; (contributor) *Shakespeare 1971,* University of Toronto, 1972; *The Gathering of the Ungifted,* Herder & Herder, 1972; *The Way of the Word: The Beginning and the Establishing of Christian Understanding,* Seabury, 1975; *Clumsy Construction in Mark's Gospel: A Critique of Form and Redaktionsgeschichte,* E. Mellen, 1979; *Five Gospels,* Winston Press, 1983.

WORK IN PROGRESS: Tudor and Stuart entertainments; first-century theology; constructive theology; Renaissance drama (English).

*   *   *

MEARES, Ainslie Dixon   1910-

PERSONAL: Born March 10, 1910, in Melbourne, Victoria, Australia; son of Albert George and Eva (Ham) Meares; married Bonnie Byrne, 1934; children: Russell, Garda (Mrs. Charles Langley), Sylvia (Mrs. Peter Black). *Education:* University of Melbourne, B.Agr.Sc., 1934, M.B. and B.S., 1940, D.P.M., 1947, M.D., 1948. *Home and office:* 99 Spring St., Melbourne, Victoria 3000, Australia.

CAREER: Psychiatrist in private practice in Melbourne, Australia, 1946-73; currently practicing as a non-medical consultant in mental relaxation. *Military service:* Australian Army

Medical Corps, 1941-45; became captain. *Member:* International Society for Clinical and Experimental Hypnosis (past president), Australian Medical Association, British Medical Association, American Psychiatric Association, Royal Medico-Psychologist Association, Australian and New Zealand College of Psychiatrists, American Ontoanalytical Association, American Society for Clinical and Experimental Hypnosis, Medico-Legal Society of Victoria (president, 1975-76), Australian Club, Melbourne Club, Athenaeum Club.

WRITINGS: Medical Interview: A Study of Clinically Significant Inter-Personal Reactions, C. C Thomas, 1957; *Hypnography: A Study in the Therapeutic Use of Hypnotic Painting,* C. C Thomas, 1957; *Marriage and Personality,* C. C Thomas, 1958; *The Introvert,* C. C Thomas, 1958; *The Door of Serenity,* Faber & Faber, 1958.

Shapes of Sanity, C. C Thomas, 1960; *A System of Medical Hypnosis,* Saunders, 1960; *Management of the Anxious Patient,* Saunders, 1963; *Relief without Drugs,* Doubleday, 1967; *Where Magic Lies,* Hawthorn, 1968; *Student Problems and a Guide to Study,* Hawthorn, 1969; *Strange Places and Simple Truths,* Souvenir Press, 1969.

The Way Up, Souvenir Press, 1970; *Dialogue with Youth,* Fontana, 1973; *The New Woman,* Fontana, 1974; *Why Be Old?,* Fontana, 1975.

Published by Hill of Content: *From the Quiet Place,* 1976; *Cancer—Another Way?,* 1977; *The Wealth Within,* 1978; *The Hidden Powers of Leadership,* 1978; *Dialogue on Meditation,* 1979; *Thoughts,* 1980; *Prayer and Beyond,* 1981.

Also author of *Let's Be Human,* Fontana. Contributor of more than one hundred papers to medical journals, relating to the use of medical hypnosis and to the psychological treatment of cancer by intensive meditation. Associate editor, *Australian and New Zealand Journal of Psychiatry,* 1967-69; member of editorial board, *Existential Psychiatry.*

SIDELIGHTS: Ainslie Meares has traveled widely in the East, studying aspects of Eastern mysticism including Yoga, Zen, and fire-walking. He has also made a study of witch doctors in East Africa.

*   *   *

MEDINA, Jeremy T(yler)   1942-

PERSONAL: Born August 1, 1942, in Orange, N.J.; son of Standish F. and Hope T. (Kiesewetter) Medina; married Jacquelyn N. Savoie, July 2, 1966; children: Carolyn Tracy, Kristin Hillyer, Jocelyn Tyler. *Education:* Princeton University, A.B., 1964; Middlebury College, M.A., 1966; University of Pennsylvania, Ph.D., 1970. *Home:* 13 Stryker Lane, Clinton, N.Y. 13323; and Box 159, Westhampton, N.Y. 11977 (summer). *Office:* Department of Romance Languages, Hamilton College, Clinton, N.Y. 13323.

CAREER: Teacher of Spanish at a private school in Andover, Mass., 1964-65; University of Pennsylvania, Philadelphia, instructor in Spanish, 1967; Hamilton College, Clinton, N.Y., instructor, 1968-70, assistant professor, 1970-75, associate professor, 1975-82, professor of Spanish, 1982—, founder and general director of year-in-Spain program. *Member:* Modern Language Association of America, American Association of Teachers of Spanish and Portuguese, American Association of University Professors.

WRITINGS: Introduction to Spanish Literature: An Analytical Approach, Harper, 1974; *Spanish Realism: The Theory and*

Practice of a Concept in the Nineteenth Century, Jose Porrua Publications, 1979.

Contributor; published by Salem Press; in press: *Leopoldo Alas (Clarin); Vicente Blasco Ibanez; Benito Perez Glados; Emilia Pardo Bazan; The Spanish Realistic Novel.*

Contributor to Romance language and Spanish studies journals, including *Hispania, Romance Notes,* and *Hispanic Journal.*

WORK IN PROGRESS: The Valencian Novels of Vicente Blasco Ibanez.

*   *   *

MEDVED, Michael   1948-

PERSONAL: Born October 3, 1948, in Philadelphia, Pa.; son of David Bernard (a physicist) and Renate (a chemist; maiden name, Hirsch) Medved; married Nancy Herman (a writer and researcher), August 5, 1972. *Education:* Yale University, B.A., 1969, graduate study, 1969-70; San Francisco State University, M.A., 1974. *Politics:* "A fan of *Commentary* magazine." *Religion:* "Traditional Judaism." *Office:* 610 South Venice Blvd., No. 4904, Venice, Calif. 90291. *Agent:* Arthur Pine Associates, 1780 Broadway, New York, N.Y. 10019.

CAREER: Teacher in Hebrew day school in New Haven, Conn., 1969-70; speechwriter for congressional and presidential campaigns, 1970-72; Anrick, Inc. (advertising agency), Oakland, Calif., creative director and advertising copywriter, 1972-74; free-lance writer and lecturer, 1974—. Movie reviewer for cable television station WTBS and Cable News Network, 1981—.

WRITINGS: (With David Wallechinsky) *What Really Happened to the Class of '65?,* Random House, 1976; *The Shadow Presidents: The Secret History of the Chief Executives and Their Top Aides,* Times Books, 1979; (with brother, Harry Medved) *The Golden Turkey Awards: The Worst Achievements in Hollywood History,* Putnam-Perigee, 1980; *Hospital: The Hidden Lives of a Medical Center Staff,* Simon & Schuster, 1983; (with H. Medved) *The Hollywood Hall of Shame,* Putnam-Perigee, 1984.

WORK IN PROGRESS: A book about the Rolling Stones, tentatively entitled *Satisfaction,* for McGraw.

SIDELIGHTS: Michael Medved told *CA* that the variety of subject matter in his books "give[s] clear indication of my diverse interests and reflect[s] my reluctance to specialize in one specific area." The author is perhaps best known for his bestseller *What Really Happened to the Class of '65?,* a revealing ten-years-after look at some of the students referred to in a *Time* cover story as the "smarter, subtler and more sophisticated kids . . . pouring into and out of more expert, exacting and experimental schools." Interviews by Medved and co-author David Wallechinsky, themselves members of the Palisades (California) High School class of 1965, reveal how, for example, the student voted "Most Likely to Succeed" became a masseur, how a classmate described by *Time* as a "near genius" ended up a devotee of the John Birch Society, and how the most popular boy committed suicide.

"The results of Mr. Medved's and Mr. Wallechinsky's explorations should not shock anyone sobered up from the intoxication with youth of the 1960s," writes Christopher Lehmann-Haupt in the *New York Times.* The reviewer finds *What Really Happened to the Class of '65?* "extremely engaging. Partly this [is] because the authors do such a good job of dramatizing their subjects' lives with skillfully edited autobiographical statements and shrewdly arranged cross-references, . . . [or] maybe it's just that what with high school having been such a miserably ill-shaped and ill-defined time for most of us, it's just gratifying to bear witness to all the coalescing and defining. . . . So it's all the more to the credit of [the authors] that they have made a group of strangers interesting to look at then and now.'' According to *Commonweal* critic Ed McConville, Medved and Wallechinsky exercise, ''for the most part, a wise forbearance from the facile analyses and gauche generalizations which characterize so much of the writing on the subject. They record the stories of individual members of the generation, told in their own words. These profiles imply some of the common characteristics of our generation, without slighting its complexity and variety.'' McConville further notes that the book's value ''lies not so much in its own insights or conclusions as in the sober stock-taking and self-realization it cannot help but trigger in younger readers. More than anything, it is a book about the process of learning our own limitations, both as individuals and as a collective political and cultural force.''

In *The Shadow Presidents: The Secret History of the Chief Executives and Their Top Aides,* Medved explores the role of presidential advisors through twenty-two administrations—from Abraham Lincoln's to Jimmy Carter's. ''It is a readable, well-researched book, good popular history,'' comments Patrick Anderson in the *Washington Post Book World,* ''but my main reaction to it is a sense that we have tended in recent years to overrate, overexamine and overglamorize the men around our presidents.'' ''While there are some mild surprises here and there,'' writes Elaine Kendall, ''*The Shadow Presidents* is a cautious book, occasionally suggestive but generally restrained and even respectful. Revisionist historians may find it disappointingly mild.'' Kendall, reporting in the *Los Angeles Times Book Review,* finds that ''instead of the unrelieved chronicle of scurrility we've been led to expect, *The Shadow Presidents* is often inadvertently moving and affecting. Medved seems most comfortable when he is discussing the men he admires, faltering only when he attempts to be insinuating and ominously speculative.''

In a *New York Times Book Review* article, Richard Reeves calls the book ''a buffet of fascinating anecdotes and information about the background of the men—the former private secretaries, the private detective, the advertising man, the sand-and-gravel salesman—who worked their way into Presidential confidences.'' However, Reeves notes, ''I'm not sure most readers will care that, for instance, Richard Cheney was a competent assistant to Gerald Ford, that he got Mr. Ford to appointments on time and straightened out the paperwork and backbiting in that confused Administration. Most of the 22 assistants really were shadows, and the proof is that after they left the White House they became relatively inconsequential people, known primarily for what they used to be.''

The inspiration for Medved's book *Hospital: The Hidden Lives of a Medical Center Staff* came through ''a close friend who happened to be an obstetrician/gynecologist [and] had a nervous breakdown,'' explains the author to a *Chicago Tribune Magazine* reporter. ''He was wandering naked along the freeway and had to be committed to a psychiatric ward. Two hours after he was released he was back delivering babies, doing abortions, and performing hysterectomies. We had dinner a few weeks later and I said, 'Doesn't it feel strange to have to pretend to be the invulnerable doctor when you have so much

personal turmoil?' And he said, 'No. The hospital is full of crazy docs.''' ·

Part of Medved's research for *Hospital* led the author to spend a year at a California medical center, observing procedures and conducting interviews with twenty-eight hospital employees, including an intern, a radiologist, a plastic surgeon, a maid, and the head of the morgue. The results of the interviews elicited this reaction from William A. Nolen, himself a surgeon, in the *Washington Post Book World:* ''If you are one of the many who have complete faith in hospitals and prefer to surrender all responsibility to the hospital staff, then it might be best if you didn't read Michael Medved's book. It is going to disillusion you. Once you've read it, you will probably never again feel completely at ease in a hospital.'' The work ''reads sometimes like 28 characters in search of a plot and sometimes like one collective voice talking to a psychotherapist,'' according to *Time* critic R. Z. Sheppard. ''Details of depression, marital misery and frustration abound. . . . [The subjects] are also quick to see their own worst traits in colleagues: selfishness, excessive competitiveness and arrogance. This is particularly true when the doctors were formerly husband and wife.''

The author ''may not have intended that his book be regarded as an expose,'' writes Nolen, ''but I can assure him that that is exactly what it is. Perhaps not in the pejorative sense, but certainly in the sense that it exposes the hospital more completely than it ever has been. And Medved may not consider his book a critique of the medical profession, but it is one; certainly the doctors and nurses in this book will not be confused with the dedicated professionals who used to appear in the Dr. Kildare films.'' Nolen sums up that *Hospital* is ''a fascinating book; I think it is an honest book . . . but I also found it depressing. Some readers are going to learn from Medved's book a lot more about hospitals than they really want to know.''

''The hospital is a prison here; an addiction,'' remarks Carolyn See of the *Los Angeles Times.* ''People drowning in anomie, battling with death, and viciously turning on each other. . . . Just as the premise of *Hospital* is simple but profound, the problems besetting these people are easy to list but impossible to solve. How do I balance my work and my life? How do I find love—and keep it? How can I love? How can I keep my feelings for the patients I'm supposed to help from degenerating into hatred and contempt? Loneliness, isolation, piercing sadness pervade this book. How incredibly weird, these people who work in Medved's hospital. But how valiant.''

Medved concluded to *CA* that a variety of book topics ''helps keep me interested in my own work, and I have always believed it is harder to hit a moving target. Ironically, perhaps, one subject—traditional Judaism—which engages a huge amount of my time and energy has so far escaped my attention as a writer. I believe it was [Somerset] Maugham who suggested it was impossible to write about a love affair before it has ended, and certainly my personal involvement in Jewish community affairs is still in full flower. I am the president and co-founder of a traditional congregation near the beach in Venice, and over the past five years we have met with considerable success in creating a closeknit community of observant Jews in this unlikely locale.''

MEDIA ADAPTATIONS: What Really Happened to the Class of '65? was adapted into a television series and broadcast in 1977.

BIOGRAPHICAL/CRITICAL SOURCES: Time, January 29, 1965, January 24, 1983; Michael Medved and David Wallechinsky, *What Really Happened to the Class of '65?*, Random House, 1976; *New York Times*, September 8, 1976; *New York Times Book Review*, October 3, 1976, September 23, 1979; *New Yorker*, October 25, 1976; *Commonweal*, January 21, 1977; *New Statesman*, September 8, 1978; *Washington Post Book World*, September 9, 1979, January 2, 1983; *Los Angeles Times Book Review*, November 4, 1979; *Cincinnati Enquirer*, December 16, 1979; *Los Angeles Times*, December 28, 1982; *Chicago Tribune Magazine*, February 13, 1983.

—*Sketch by Susan Salter*

*   *   *

MELL
See LAZARUS, Mell

*   *   *

MELLEN, Joan   1941-

PERSONAL: Born September 7, 1941, in New York, N.Y.; daughter of Louis (a lawyer) and Norma (Wieder) Spivack. *Education:* Hunter College of the City University of New York, B.A., 1962; Graduate School and University Center of the City University of New York, M.A., 1964, Ph.D., 1968. *Home address:* P.O. Box 359, Pennington, N.J. 08534. *Agent:* Berenice Hoffman Literary Agency, 215 West 75th St., New York, N.Y. 10023. *Office:* Department of English, Temple University, Philadelphia, Pa. 19122.

CAREER: Temple University, Philadelphia, Pa., assistant professor, 1967-73, associate professor, 1973-76, professor of English, 1977—. Lecturer. Consultant to Oxford University Press and Pantheon Books. *Member:* Phi Beta Kappa. *Awards, honors:* Mainichi Shimbun award and study tour of Japan, 1972; National Endowment for the Humanities summer stipend, 1976.

WRITINGS: A Film Guide to the Battle of Algiers, Indiana University Press, 1973; *Marilyn Monroe*, Pyramid Publications, 1973; *Women and Their Sexuality in the New Film*, Horizon Press, 1974; *Voices from the Japanese Cinema*, Liveright, 1975; *The Waves at Genji's Door: Japan through Its Cinema*, Pantheon, 1976; *Big Bad Wolves: Masculinity in the American Film*, Pantheon, 1978; (editor) *The World of Luis Bunuel*, Oxford University Press, 1980; *Natural Tendencies: A Novel*, Dial, 1981; *Privilege: The Enigma of Sasha Bruce*, Dial, 1982.

Contributor: *Japan and the Japanese*, Japan Publications, 1973; Gerald R. Barrett and Thomas L. Erskine, editors, *From Fiction to Film: The Rocking-Horse Winner*, Dickenson, 1974; E. Bradford Burns, editor, *Latin American Cinema: Film and History*, University of California at Los Angeles Latin American Center, 1975; Stuart M. Kaminsky, editor, *Ingmar Bergman: Essays in Criticism*, Oxford University Press, 1975; Donald Richie, editor, *The Films of Akira Kurosawa*, revised edition, University of California Press, 1983.

Member of editorial board, *Quarterly Review of Film Studies*, 1975—; consultant to *Antioch Review*.

SIDELIGHTS: Joan Mellen has written a variety of books dealing with the cinema, including two works that explore the way movies portray the sexes. The first, *Women and Their Sexuality in the New Film*, examines the depiction of women as "flawed creatures" and analyzes films from political and social standpoints. In a *Washington Post* review of the book, Larry McMurtry calls Mellen "an extremely well-informed critic, . . . neither

politically nor cinematically naive." McMurtry finds *Women and Their Sexuality in the New Film* "easily the best of the several recent books about the treatment of women in films; it is so good, indeed, that practically the only mark that can be scored against it is a small, tactical mark—to wit, that [Mellen] restates her basic point so often that she somewhat blunts its effectiveness." And although *New York Times Book Review* critic Jane Wilson remarks that the author "watches her movies from a position so far to the left of the screen that it is difficult to see how she can get an undistorted picture," the reviewer feels that Mellen "does arrive at an interesting explanation of the raw deal women have been getting in the movies. She attempts an answer, unlike [other critics] who content themselves with getting together an indictment."

In *Big Bad Wolves: Masculinity in the American Film* Mellen offers a consideration of "the stereotype of the self-controlled, invulnerable, stoical hero" that has been sustained through six generations of film history. The author asserts that this traditional masculine image was developed by Hollywood producers intent upon affirming male superiority. One critic who does not share Mellen's view is Mark Crispin Miller. Reviewing *Big Bad Wolves* in *Nation*, Miller contends that "something like a feminist critical method has been hastily applied to something like a survey of American film. . . . [The author] promotes the conspiracy theory of popular culture, insisting that movies dictate attitudes dreamt up by evil tycoons. According to this notion, Hollywood does not reflect widespread feelings but manufactures concepts for consumption by the ignorant, who then suffer. Rather than seek to determine the cultural foundation of extant preconceptions, Mellen looks for somebody to blame them on."

Peter Brunette, on the other hand, thinks the author has "a richly provocative work" in *Big Bad Wolves*. Writing in the *Chronicle of Higher Education*, Brunette comments, "Mellen marches us patiently through the decades of American cinema, trying to isolate the central masculine images in each." Brunette does have some criticisms: "This arrangement is not wholly satisfactory because the quirks and bumps, advances and regressions, of cinematic (or any other) history rarely follow neat chronological lines. Another difficulty is that the widely varying demands of countless film genres . . . are impossible to reconcile, especially by decade, and resist easy homogenization under a set of all-encompassing generalizations." However, the critic concludes, "rarely is a book responsible for so many nods of surprised assent, and in spite of all my complaints, I enjoyed every word of *Big Bad Wolves*." The book "bristles with new insights and shows muted signs of anger," according to John Fludas in *Saturday Review*. "[Mellen] writes intelligently of the changing values in American culture and of the political and psychological factors that helped create the masculine mystique. And she can treat film as an art without any tiresome critic's jargon."

In addition to her books of film comment, Mellen has published a novel, *Natural Tendencies*, and a nonfiction work, *Privilege: The Enigma of Sasha Bruce*. In the latter book the author examines the life of Alexandra ("Sasha") Bruce, the daughter of ambassador David K. E. Bruce, and recounts the events which led to her shooting death in 1975. "How could Sasha Bruce, endowed with wit, intelligence, money, and status, come to inhabit such a dark and destructive world?," asks Suzanne Fields in the *Washington Post Book World*. Fields continues: "Inevitably, Joan Mellen raises more questions about the barren nature of Sasha's life than she answers, and her inventory of Sasha's cash exchanges tends to pall. But her story is a compelling one, her telling of it lively and ambitious. She asks the right questions and does not pander to the prurient wrong ones.''

BIOGRAPHICAL/CRITICAL SOURCES: Joan Mellen, *Women and Their Sexuality in the New Film,* Horizon Press, 1974; *Washington Post,* February 18, 1974; *New York Times Book Review,* March 24, 1974, October 10, 1982; *Nation,* February 15, 1975, April 22, 1978; *New York Review of Books,* June 12, 1975; Mellen, *Big Bad Wolves: Masculinity in the American Film,* Pantheon, 1978; *Saturday Review,* January 21, 1978; *Psychology Today,* February, 1978; *Atlantic,* March, 1978; *Commonweal,* May 12, 1978; *Chronicle of Higher Education,* May 22, 1978; *Film Comment,* July-August, 1978; *Observer,* December 10, 1978; *Washington Post Book World,* October 24, 1982.

*   *   *

MENDEL, Werner M(ax)   1927-

PERSONAL: Born June 11, 1927; son of Herbert I. (an attorney) and Edith (Frankel) Mendel; children: Carl, Dirk. *Education:* University of California, Los Angeles, B.A., 1948; Stanford University, M.A., 1949, M.D., 1953; Southern California Psychoanalytic Institute, graduate, 1964.

CAREER: Psychiatrist, certified by American Board of Psychiatry and Neurology, 1959. Menninger School of Psychiatry, Topeka, Kan., fellow, 1955-57; Metropolitan State Hospital, Norwalk, Calif., staff psychiatrist and director of pilot rehabilitation project for chronic schizophrenics, 1957-58, director of outpatient services, 1958-60; University of Southern California, School of Medicine, Los Angeles, clinical instructor, 1958-60, assistant professor, 1960-64, associate professor, 1964-67, professor of psychiatry, 1967-82; Los Angeles County General Hospital, Psychiatric Division, Los Angeles, member of attending staff, 1960-82, clinical director of Adult Inpatient Services, 1965-67; captain of sailing ship ''Freedom 5,'' 1982—. Instructor, Southern California Psychoanalytic Institute, 1965-82. Consultant to California State Department of Mental Hygiene, 1960-82, and to mental health committee of American Academy of General Practice, 1963-66. Special project director, Basic Books, Inc., 1966-69.

MEMBER: American Medical Association, American Psychiatric Association (fellow), American Association of Medical Colleges, American Psychoanalytic Association, California Medical Association (secretary of section on psychiatry and neurology, 1964-66, and chairman, 1966-67), Southern California Psychoanalytic Institute, Southern California Psychiatric Society, Southern California Institute of Psychoanalysis, Los Angeles County Medical Association.

WRITINGS: (Co-translator) *Existence,* Basic Books, 1958; (with G. Green) *Therapeutic Management of Psychological Illness: The Theory and Practice of Supportive Care,* Basic Books, 1967; (editor with P. Solomon and contributor) *The Psychiatric Consultation,* Grune, 1968; (contributor) *Comprehensive Mental Health,* University of Wisconsin Press, 1968; (editor) *A Celebration of Laughter,* Mara Books, 1970; (with Arthur Burton and others) *Schizophrenia as a Life Style,* Springer Publishing, 1974; (contributor) *Twelve Therapists: How They Live and Actualize Themselves,* Jossey-Bass, 1974; *Supportive Care: Theory and Technique,* Mara Books, 1975; *Schizophrenia: The Experience and Its Treatment,* Jossey-Bass, 1979.

Contributor to *Current Psychiatric Therapies,* 1964, 1966, 1974, and to medical journals. Editor-in-chief, Mara Books; member

of advisory board, *International Encyclopaedia of Neurology, Psychiatry, Psychoanalysis, and Psychology;* member of book review staff, *American Journal of Psychotherapy.*

SIDELIGHTS: Werner M. Mendel told *CA:* ''Life is too long and too rich to spend it all in one activity. I want to look at life from many points of view, so at age 55 I terminated my career as a research scientist in psychiatry to spend the next five years as captain of a sailing vessel circumnavigating the globe. At age 60 I will make another change, this time to view the world as a General Practitioner of medicine providing primary health care as the only physician in town in a small northern California coastal community. These changes provide a different focus on the same issues and problems facing mankind. The question remains: how does one best live a life?''

*   *   *

MENDELSOHN, Everett (Irwin)   1931-

PERSONAL: Born October 28, 1931, in Yonkers, N.Y.; son of Morris H. and May (Albert) Mendelsohn; married Mary B. Anderson, September 13, 1974; children: (previous marriage) Daniel L., Sarah E., Joanna M.; stepchildren: Jesse Marshall Wallace. *Education:* Antioch College, A.B., 1953; Harvard University, Ph.D., 1960. *Home:* 26 Walker St., Cambridge, Mass. 02138. *Office:* Harvard University, Science Center 235, Cambridge, Mass. 02138.

CAREER: Harvard University, Cambridge, Mass., assistant professor, 1960-65, associate professor, 1965-69, professor of history of science, 1969—, chairman of department, 1971-78. Director of research group on bio-medical sciences. Conducted university program on technology and society, Harvard University, 1966-68. Vice-president, International Council for Science Policy Studies, 1980—; chairman, Harvard-Radcliffe Child Care Council. Member of board of directors, Institute for Defense and Disarmament Studies, 1980—. Chairman of executive committee, American Friends Service Committee; trustee, Cambridge Friends School.

MEMBER: International Academy of the History of Medicine, Academie International d'Historie des Sciences, History of Science Society (council member), American Association for the Advancement of Science (fellow; council member, 1961-62; vice-president, chairman, section L), American Academy of Arts and Sciences (fellow). *Awards, honors:* Bowdoin Prize, 1957; D.H.L., Rhode Island College, 1977; Churchhill College, Cambridge University, overseas fellow.

WRITINGS: (Editor with I. B. Cohen and H. M. Jones) *Treasury of Scientific Prose: A Nineteenth-Century Anthology,* Little, Brown, 1963; *Heat and Life: The Development of the Theory of Animal Heat,* Harvard University Press, 1964; (editor) *Human Aspects of Biomedical Innovation,* Harvard University Press, 1971; (editor with Arnold Thackray) *Science and Values: Patterns of Tradition and Change,* Humanities, 1974; (editor with Marjorie Grene) *Topics in the Philosophy of Biology,* D. Reidel, 1976; (editor with Peter Weingart and Richard Whitley) *The Social Production of Scientific Knowledge,* Reidel, 1977; (editor with Yehuda Elkana) *Sciences and Cultures: Anthropological and Historical Studies of the Sciences,* Reidel, 1981; *A Compassionate Peace: A Future of the Middle East,* Hill & Wang, 1982.

Member of editorial board, *Science,* 1965-70, *Social Studies of Science,* 1970-82, *Ethics in Science and Medicine,* 1973-81, *Philosophy and Medicine,* 1974—, *Sociology of Sciences,*

1976—, *Social Sciences and Medicine*, 1981—. Editor, *Journal of the History of Biology*, 1967—.

*   *   *

MENDELSON, Edward 1946-

PERSONAL: Born March 15, 1946, in New York; son of Ralph (a lawyer and teacher) and Grace (a teacher; maiden name, Stein) Mendelson. *Education:* University of Rochester, B.A., 1966; Johns Hopkins University, Ph.D., 1969. *Home:* 39 Claremont Ave., Apt. 31, New York, N.Y. 10027. *Office:* Department of English, 602 Philosophy Hall, Columbia University, New York, N.Y. 10027.

CAREER: Yale University, New Haven, Conn., assistant professor, 1969-75, associate professor of English, 1975-79; Columbia University, New York, N.Y., visiting associate professor, 1979-80, associate professor, 1980-83, professor of English and comparative literature, 1983—. Visiting associate professor at Harvard University, 1977-78. *Awards, honors:* National Book Critics Circle award nomination in criticism, 1981, for *Early Auden*.

WRITINGS: (With B. C. Bloomfield) *W. H. Auden: A Bibliography*, University Press of Virginia, 1972; (editor) *W. H. Auden, Collected Poems*, Random House, 1976; (editor with Michael Seidel) *Homer to Brecht: The European Epic and Dramatic Traditions*, Yale University Press, 1977; (editor) *The English Auden*, Random House, 1977; (editor) *Thomas Pynchon: A Collection of Critical Essays*, Prentice-Hall, 1978; (editor) *Auden, Selected Poems*, Random House, 1978; *Early Auden*, Viking, 1981.

Contributor: Robert Shaw, editor, *American Poetry since 1960*, Carcanet, 1973; Kenneth Baldwin and David Kirby, editors, *Individual and Community*, Duke University Press, 1975; Stephen Spender, editor, *W. H. Auden: A Tribute*, Macmillan, 1975; George Levine and David Leverenz, editors, *Mindful Pleasures: Essays on Thomas Pynchon*, Little, Brown, 1976. Also contributor to *The Absolute Sound*. Contributor to magazines, including *New Statesman, Yale Review, Times Literary Supplement, London Review of Books, Harvard English Studies,* and *New Republic,* and to professional journals in his field.

WORK IN PROGRESS: A study of W. H. Auden's later work; a critical study of Thomas Pynchon.

SIDELIGHTS: "The current literary business has few practitioners more assiduous than . . . Edward Mendelson, W. H. Auden's extremely intelligent executor, bibliographer, editor, and critic," writes Paul Fussell in the *New Republic.* Of the several books Mendelson has written about the renowned poet, essayist, and playwright, perhaps the most widely reviewed to date is his critical biography *Early Auden.* According to Fussell, the book, "virtually an intellectual history of the 1930s with Auden at its center, is rich and suggestive in its generalizations, resourceful in its scholarship, and precise in its readings of Auden's work. And it is discriminating: Mendelson recognizes immediately when Auden writes badly and speculates on the reasons, usually Auden's taking a position not fully understood or believed, or allowing himself to camp up serious things."

In analyzing the life and career of Auden up until about 1942, Mendelson "nails his colors to the mast," says *Newsweek* reviewer Walter Clemons. "In [the author's] view, Auden's brilliant, curtly obscure, incohesive early work was that of the first poet to absorb the fragmented modernism of Eliot and

Pound and then to move beyond it to the humbler ideal of the civil poet, user of traditional forms . . . and plain truth-teller to fellow citizens." In a *Nation* review of *Early Auden,* Robert B. Shaw notes Mendelson's reaction to "Auden's indebtedness to the authors he drew upon in forming his voice and point of view—Hardy, Yeats, Eliot, Lawrence, Marx, Freud . . . and so on." Shaw states that Mendelson "has managed to give a reasonably full account of these eclectic borrowings without getting snarled in a web of cross-reference. He does this, no doubt, by focusing not so much on the ideas themselves as on their concrete presentation in Auden's poems. He gives the reader a map of Auden's imaginative landscape, plotting the positions and relationships of its key images." "Some of the most exciting passages in *Early Auden,*" declares Christopher Lehmann-Haupt of the *New York Times,* "attempt to define the links between literary Modernism and the tradition of Romanticism—a thesis that the author develops not just to keep his critical muscles in tone, but rather to explain, among other things, the inner contradictions of Auden's early historical poems."

One critic who does not concur with the author's consideration of his subject is Denis Donoghue. In a *New York Times Book Review* article, Donoghue calls *Early Auden* "an odd book. Professor Mendelson claims that Auden 'became the most inclusive poet of the twentieth century, its most technically skilled, and its most truthful.' The claim is loosely worded: Before it could make sense, virtually every adjective would have to be expounded, the necessary qualifications taken into account, judicious comparisons made. But in any case the claim is effectively refuted by the book itself. The dominant impression enforced by . . . Mendelson is that Auden's moral and intellectual vanity kept him at every moment of his early life excited and bewildered, able to talk loud but not to think straight. Going through the early poems and plays, [the author] finds, mostly, incoherence, contradiction, extravagance. Indeed, while he mocks those critics who thought of Auden as a permanent undergraduate, a glittering adolescent, he goes far toward proving them right."

Stuart Hampshire, writing in the *New York Review of Books,* feels that Mendelson "dwells rather heavily on the undeniable inadequacies and inconsistencies of Auden's thought as that of a poet of the left and an occasional advocate of social revolution," during his early years. Hampshire says that Mendelson "will not let him off the charge of having at this stage no firm and thought-out position, no solid basis for the continuing moralizing in his verse." Yet, the critic notes, "Auden loved aphorisms and epigrams, his own and those of others, which he very successfully anthologized; and his aphorisms and epigrams naturally tend to carry a moral punch as general reflections on life, as he wove them into his verse."

America critic James Finn Cotter finds Mendelson "no blind worshipper of the poet[;] he points out contradictions when they occur, even within the same works, and he calls doggerel just that. He supposes some factual familiarity with Auden's life, but he does illuminate critical moments in his spiritual development with some felicitous quotations." While the author's book, according to Jeffery Meyers in *Commonweal,* "is not as original as those of his predecessors Monroe Spears (1963) and John Fuller (1970)—he is sound rather than brilliant—and his rather relentless exposition of scores of complex poems makes difficult reading, . . . his interpretations are backed with the authority of personal conversations, manuscripts and unpublished letters that cast new light on Auden's intellect, ideas, and intentions." "Indeed, so detailed is Professor Mendelson's text," observes Lehmann-Haupt, "so precise is his reading of Auden's work and so complex are the ties he establishes between the work and the poet's psychology, politics and esthetics, that I wish I'd had time to go through *Early Auden* with all the time in the world. Its highest rewards appear to depend on a first-hand familiarity with Auden's poems, plays, and essays. Because the author could only afford to quote fragments of these, the ideal way to read him would be with Auden's complete works at hand." In conclusion, Fussell sees Edward Mendelson as a "civic critic, whose means and whose voice—learned, rational, measured, calm, sympathetic—are beautifully appropriate to the task at hand."

BIOGRAPHICAL/CRITICAL SOURCES: Edward Mendelson, *Early Auden,* Viking, 1981; *New Republic,* August 1, 1981; *New York Times,* August 4, 1981; *Nation,* August 8, 1981; *New York Times Book Review,* August 9, 1981; *New York Review of Books,* August 13, 1981; *Washington Post Book World,* September 13, 1981; *Newsweek,* September 28, 1981; *America,* October 17, 1981; *Commonweal,* November 6, 1981; *Times Literary Supplement,* December 11, 1981.

—*Sketch by Susan Salter*

*   *   *

MENESES, Enrique 1929-
(Ricardo Carvajal, Jeff Crain)

PERSONAL: Surname is pronounced Me-*ness*-es; born October 21, 1929, in Madrid, Spain; son of Enrique (a writer) and Carmen (Miniaty) Meneses; married Barbara Montgomery (a journalist), July 26, 1963; children: Barbara. *Education:* Received primary and secondary education at schools in France, Portugal, and Spain; Instituto San Isidro, Madrid, Bachillerato, 1949; studied law at University of Salamanca, 1949-50, and law and journalism at University of Madrid, 1950-51. *Politics:* Independent. *Religion:* "Non-practicing Roman Catholic." *Home:* Calle Ginzo de Limia 53, Madrid-34, Spain. *Office:* Television Espanola, Prado del Rey, Madrid-24, Spain.

CAREER: Reader's Digest, circulation manager for Iberian Edition, 1951-53; Prensa Intercontinental, Paris, France, correspondent in Madrid, Spain, 1954; *Informaciones* (daily newspaper), Madrid, correspondent in Cairo, Egypt, 1955; *Paris-Match* (magazine) and Europe Number One (radio station), Paris, correspondent in Cairo, 1956-57, Havana, Cuba, 1957-58, Cairo, 1958-59, and New Delhi, India, 1959-60; Delta Press, Paris, managing editor, 1961-62; correspondent in New York City for *Blanco y Negro* (Madrid weekly magazine), Rex Features (London agency), and Dalmas (Paris news agency), 1962-63; Life Editorial Services, New York City, representative in Madrid, 1964—; Spanish National Television Network, Madrid, editor-in-chief of monthly news hour, "A Toda Plana," 1964-65; Fotopress (feature agency), Madrid, editor, 1964—; Lumefa Publishing Co., Madrid, general manager, 1966-72; *Cosmopolis* (monthly news magazine), Madrid, managing editor, 1968—. Staff journalist of "Los Reporters," Spanish weekly television news program, 1973-77; affiliated with television consumer's program, 1981, and "Robinson," an adventure series, 1982; also affiliated with radio series "Los Aventureros," 1982. Circulation advisor, *Iberian Sun* (English-language daily newspaper), Madrid, 1968. *Military service:* Spanish Army, 1950-51. *Member:* Overseas Press Club of America, Real Automobile Club of Spain.

WRITINGS: Fidel Castro, A. Aguado, 1966, Taplinger, 1968; *Nasser: El Ultimo faraon* (title means "Nasser, the Last of the

Pharaohs"), Prensa Espanola, 1968; (with others) *How I Got That Story,* Dutton, 1968; *Seso y Sexo* (title means "Sex and Brains"), Campus, 1979; *Escrito en Carne* (title means "Written on Flesh"), Planeta, 1979. Also author of *Naked Witchcraft,* 1975. Author of magazine articles under pseudonyms Ricardo Carvajal and Jeff Crain.

Editor of Spanish editions of *Lui* (Paris), 1977, and *Playboy,* 1980.

WORK IN PROGRESS: Escrito en Aire (title means "Written on the Air"), a second part to *Escrito en Carne.*

SIDELIGHTS: Fidel Castro is "not specifically a character analysis of Castro, but simply a well-compressed and readable account of the Cuban revolution from its beginning to the end," according to an *Observer Review* writer. Enrique Meneses spent a year with Castro and his handful of rebels in the days before Batista was ousted. The author states that his biographies are not traditional, explaining that he has "placed less emphasis on chronological detail than on the place occupied by Castro and Nasser within the political, historical, socio-economic and moral circumstances affecting their lives." He is convinced that "man is a Product of his Environment and his own personal drive." *Fidel Castro* was also published in England and in German and Japanese translations.

Meneses is a lover of the arts "in what spare time I have," and paints in both oil and watercolor. In 1956 he organized and took part in an overland expedition through Africa from Cairo to Capetown, and in 1960 formed a second expedition to the region of Bankatti on the Indian-Nepal frontier. In 1983 Meneses embarked with a film crew on a three-month trip from Madrid to Zaire and Cairo, for a television series on Africa.

BIOGRAPHICAL/CRITICAL SOURCES: Observer Review, June 30, 1968.

*   *   *

MENON, R(amakrishna) Rabindranath 1927-

PERSONAL: Born June 13, 1927, in Perumpavoor, India; son of K. Ramakrishna (a lawyer) and Seetha (Radha Devi) Menon; married December 14, 1950; wife's name, Syamala; children: Surendra and Balachandra (sons), Latha (daughter). *Education:* University of Kerala, B.Sc. (with first class honors), 1947; Indian Institute of Science, Bangalore, D.I.I.Sc. (with first class honors), 1950. *Politics:* None. *Home:* Eanchakkal House, Vallakkadavoo, Trivandrum-8, Kerala, India. *Office:* Bihar State Industrial Development Corp., Bandar Bagicha, Patna, India.

CAREER: Indian Government, Administrative Service, served as income tax officer, 1951-58, sub-divisional magistrate and collector in Bihar, 1959-61, director of evaluation for department of planning in Bihar, 1961-63, deputy commissioner in South Kanara, 1963-64, managing director of Board of Mineral Development in Bangalore, 1964-66, director of treasuries in Karnataka, 1966, managing director of sugar factory in Hiriyoor, 1966, controller of civil supplies in Mysore, 1966-67, managing director of Government Electric Factory in Bangalore, 1967-68, joint secretary in departments of public works and finance, 1968-69, chairman of Marine Products Export Promotion Council, 1970-71, chairman of Coir Board, 1970-76; secretary, ombudsman in Bihar, 1976-78; Hindustan Latex Ltd., Trivandrum, India, chairman and managing director, 1978-81; Administrative Training Institute and Bihar Institute of Rural Development, Ranchi, India, training commissioner and director, 1981-83; Bihar State Industrial Development Corp., Patna, India, chairman and managing director, 1983—. Member of Indian Institute of Metals, 1956; incorporated accountant, 1958. Member of governing body, All India Shippers Council, 1971-76, Indian Council of Arbitration, 1972-76; chairman of experts panel, Export Inspection Council of India, 1973-76.

MEMBER: World Poetry Society (regent), Poetry Society of England. *Awards, honors:* Gold medal and poet laureate crown from United Poet Laureate International of the Philippines, 1971; Litt.D., University of Asia, 1973; D.Litt., Academicia Pax Mundi, 1975.

WRITINGS—All poetry; published by Writers Workshop (Calcutta), except as indicated: *Ode to Parted Love and Other Poems,* Jaico (Bombay), 1958; *Dasavatara and Other Poems,* 1967; *Seventy-Seven,* 1971; *Straws in the Wind,* 1974; *Gananjali* (Malayalam poetry), National Book Stall (Kottayam, India), 1974; *Shadows in the Sun,* 1975; *Grass in the Garden,* 1978; *Heart on a Shoe-String,* 1978; *Pebbles on the Shore,* 1981. Poetry editor, *Adam and Eve* magazine, 1972-75.

WORK IN PROGRESS: Pulse from the Eighties.

SIDELIGHTS: R. Rabindranath Menon told *CA:* "Poetry is my hobby, not any laboured attempt, yet I consider that every piece must pass through a process of careful polishing. As a matter of fact, I don't publish any poem until at least six months have elapsed since its original birth, and during that interval I come to it again and again working on it and improving upon it. There is no motivation of profit. I don't seek fame either. Not that I am against either, but true poetry should have no motivation except that of pure pleasure—'pleasure' in its enlarged sense—and this includes the enjoyment of others also.

"I can't remember any particular circumstance as having been the cause of my becoming a poet. My father taught me Sanscrit at an early age, and this gave me a wonderful reservoir of words with which to express in my own mother-tongue, which is related to Sanscrit. But later I veered round to English in which I find even a greater facility of expression. This changeover was probably caused by my having to live away from Kerala (the home of Malayalam), and transact English alone in an all-India career. I believe that a poet should use the language which he can wield with the maximum facility, and this need not be his mother-tongue, as in my case. I am a bilingual poet, but I don't believe in translation for poetry, for poetry is untranslatable expression."

*   *   *

MERRICK, Gordon 1916-

PERSONAL: Born August 3, 1916, in Cynwyd, Pa.; son of King Rodney (an investment broker) and Mary (Gordon) Merrick. *Education:* Princeton University, B.A., 1939. *Home:* Le Clos Vorin, Tricqueville, 27500 Pont-Audemer, France.

CAREER: An actor, 1938-41, appeared in New York company of "The Man Who Came to Dinner," 1939-40; a journalist, 1941-44, with the *Washington Star, Baltimore Evening Sun, PM, New York Post;* author. *Wartime service:* Office of Strategic Services in France, 1944-45; civilian employee, rank equaling captain.

WRITINGS—All novels: *The Strumpet Wind,* Morrow, 1947; *The Demon of Moon,* Messner, 1954; *The Vallency Tradition,* Messner, 1955 (published in England as *Between Darkness and Day,* R. Hale, 1957); *The Hot Season,* Morrow, 1957

(published in England as *The Eye of One,* R. Hale, 1959); *The Lord Won't Mind,* Geis, 1970; *One for the Gods,* Geis, 1971; *Forth Into Light,* Avon, 1974; *An Idd for Others,* Avon, 1977; *The Quirk,* Avon, 1978; *Now Let's Talk About Music,* Avon, 1981; *Perfect Freedom,* Avon, 1982.

Contributor of book reviews and articles to *New Republic, Ikonos,* and other periodicals. Author of television script adapted from James Purdy's *The Nephew.*

WORK IN PROGRESS: A novel; several television projects.

SIDELIGHTS: Gordon Merrick speaks French and Greek and divides his residence between those two countries. His first three novels have been published in French.

*   *   *

MERTZ, Barbara (Gross) 1927-
(Barbara Michaels, Elizabeth Peters)

PERSONAL: Born September 29, 1927, in Canton, Ill.; daughter of Earl D. (a printer) and Grace (a teacher; maiden name, Tregellas) Gross; married Richard R. Mertz (a professor of history), June 18, 1950 (divorced, 1968); children: Elizabeth Ellen, Peter William. *Education:* University of Chicago, Ph.B., 1947, M.A., 1950, Ph.D., 1952.

CAREER: Historian and writer. *Member:* Egypt Exploration Society, American Research Council in Egypt, Society for the Study of Egyptian Antiquities, American Association of University Women, Critics Circle, Authors Guild, Authors League of America, Mystery Writers of America, National Organization for Women.

WRITINGS—Published by Coward: *Temples, Tombs, and Hieroglyphs: The Story of Egyptology,* 1964; *Red Land, Black Land: The World of the Ancient Egyptians,* 1966; (with Richard R. Mertz) *Two Thousand Years in Rome,* 1968.

Under pseudonym Barbara Michaels; all novels; published by Dodd, except as indicated: *The Master of Blacktower,* Appleton, 1966; *Sons of the Wolf,* Meredith Press, 1967; *Ammie, Come Home,* Meredith Press, 1969; *Dark on the Other Side,* 1970; *Crying Child,* 1971; *Greygallows,* 1972; *Witch,* 1973; *House of Many Shadows,* 1974; *The Sea King's Daughter,* 1975; *Patriot's Dream,* 1976; *Wings of the Falcon,* 1977; *Wait for What Will Come,* 1978; *Walker in Shadows,* 1979; *The Wizard's Daughter,* 1980; *Someone in the House,* 1981; *Black Rainbow,* Congdon & Weed, 1982.

Under pseudonym Elizabeth Peters; all novels; published by Dodd, except as indicated: *The Jackal's Head,* Meredith Press, 1968; *The Camelot Caper,* Meredith Press, 1969; *The Dead Sea Cipher,* 1970; *The Night of 400 Rabbits,* 1971; *The Seventh Sinner,* 1972; *Borrower of the Night,* 1973; *The Murders of Richard III,* 1974; *Crocodile on the Sandbank,* 1975; *Legend in Green Velvet,* 1976; *Devil-May-Care,* 1977; *Street of the Five Moons,* 1978; *Summer of the Dragon,* 1979; *The Love Talker,* 1980; *The Curse of the Pharohs,* 1981; *The Copenhagen Connection,* Congdon & Lattes, 1982.

WORK IN PROGRESS: Contributing, under pseudonym Barbara Michaels, to *Tales of the Uncanny,* for Reader's Digest Press.

SIDELIGHTS: Barbara Mertz is the author of several popular Gothic romances, written under the pseudonyms Barbara Michaels and Elizabeth Peters. In an interview for the book *Love's Leading Ladies,* Mertz described some stylistic differences in the books she writes under the two pseudonyms: "Michaels does interject humor, because I think this is an important element in pacing a suspense story—if Shakespeare did it, it's good enough for me. However, . . . with the Peters books I can let myself go, indulge in crazy plot devices and silly puns, and in general have a good time with the plot. Michaels is more inclined to write of the supernatural. In this sense, the Michaels books are more like the true Gothics, which were heavy with mystic atmosphere.''

Mertz told *CA:* ''Like Dorothy Parker I hate writing and love having written. I earn my living as a writer, so obviously money is an important consideration, but I also derive enormous pleasure from the letters I receive. My readers are a bright, energetic lot; many are budding authors and several have gone on to publish books and articles.'' Mertz also commented that ''like Alfred Hitchcock I appear in most of my books, usually as the peculiar old lady.''

AVOCATIONAL INTERESTS: Reading, needlework, cats, music, football.

BIOGRAPHICAL/CRITICAL SOURCES: Publishers Weekly, October 9, 1978; *Washington Post Book World,* January 6, 1980; *Times Literary Supplement,* July 10, 1981; Kathryn Falk, *Love's Leading Ladies,* Pinnacle Books, 1982.

*   *   *

MICHAELS, Barbara
See MERTZ, Barbara (Gross)

*   *   *

MILES, (Mary) Patricia   1930-

PERSONAL: Born September 8, 1930, in Lancashire, England; daughter of Robert (a businessman) and Bridget (a teacher and writer; maiden name, Clancy) Storey; married Francis George Miles (a company executive), October 17, 1953; children: Patrick, Siobhan, Hugh. *Education:* Somerville College, Oxford, B.A. (with honors), 1953, M.A., 1956. *Politics:* ''No real insight: constantly fluctuating.'' *Home:* Windrush, Rabley Heath, Welwyn, Hertfordshire AL6 9UF, England. *Agent:* Curtis Brown Group Ltd., 162-168 Regent St., London W1R 5TA, England; and Harold Ober Associates, Inc., 40 East 49th St., New York, N.Y. 10017.

CAREER: Writer. Oxford University Press, London, England, reader of Latin and Greek books, 1953-54; Latin teacher in girls' schools in Kent, England, 1958-60, and 1963-65; Nobel Comprehensive School, Stevenage, England, teacher of French, English, and Latin, 1967-76. *Awards, honors: The Gods in Winter* was chosen for the Hans Christian Andersen list, 1980.

WRITINGS: Nobody's Child (for children and adults), Dutton, 1975; *If I Survive* (for children and adults), Hamish Hamilton, 1976; *The Gods in Winter* (juvenile humor/fantasy), Dutton, 1978; *A Disturbing Influence* (for adolescents), Lothrop, 1979; *Louther Hall* (for adolescents), Hamish Hamilton, 1981; *The Mind Pirates* (juvenile science fiction), Hamish Hamilton, 1983. Also co-author of *Sing, Sailor, Sing,* World's Work. Author of material for British Broadcasting Corp. Contributor of articles and stories to magazines and newspapers.

WORK IN PROGRESS: ''Various stories and full-length books.''

SIDELIGHTS: Patricia Miles told *CA:* ''My background is half English, half Irish, and wholly ambitious. My grandfather leapt fully grown from the murk of Manchester with a copy of *Self-Help* in his hand and founded a food business to which he

fettered all his family. My father worked all his life in it, doggedly, though with distaste. My mother came from a small farm in Tipperary. . . . I myself was the archetypal provincial scholarship girl, cramming a four-year Greek course into six months in the effort to get into Oxford, which I did.

''How to reconcile all this determined striving with the free-wheeling inventiveness which is a good part of writing! The truth is, I'm a dreamer; I always was. The practicality and endeavour have been superimposed, for which I'm profoundly grateful—to realise any dream you've got to wake up.

''My dream is to provide satisfying entertainment. More precisely: to make the past come alive for children, with humor if possible, and to use language with vigor.

''I don't have a defined philosophy, though I do feel strongly that the ordinary business of living makes demands which many people meet gallantly: life is full of unsung heroes. My own life is easy enough at present; I teach occasionally and sometimes work as a guide in a stately home—we live twenty-odd miles from London in an ancient stretch of countryside.

''In 1978, I accompanied my husband on a year's business assignment in Tokyo, Japan. On the way there and back we managed to visit Bangkok, Hong Kong, Hawaii, Mexico City, and also San Francisco, Washington, New York, and Swarthmore, Pa. . . . What a very great pleasure!''

AVOCATIONAL INTERESTS: Gardening, travel in France, Scandinavia, and Italy.

*   *   *

MILHOUSE, Paul W(illiam)   1910-

PERSONAL: Born August 31, 1910, in St. Francisville, Ill.; son of Willis Cleveland (a merchant) and Carrie (Pence) Milhouse; married Mary Frances Noblitt, June 29, 1932; children: Mary Catherine (Mrs. Ronald L. Hauswald), Pauline Joyce (Mrs. Arthur Vermillion), David. *Education:* Indiana Central College, A.B., 1932; American Theological Seminary (no longer in existence), B.D., 1937, Th.D., 1945. *Home:* 2213 Northwest 56th Ter., Oklahoma City, Okla. 73112. *Office:* Oklahoma City University, Oklahoma City, Okla. 73106.

CAREER: Pastor in Birds, Ill., 1928-29; ordained to ministry of United Brethren Church, 1931; pastor in Elliott, Ill., 1932-37, Olney, Ill., 1937-41, and Decatur, Ill., 1941-51; *Telescope-Messenger,* Harrisburg, Pa., associate editor, 1951-59; Evangelical United Brethren Church, executive secretary of Council of Administration, Dayton, Ohio, 1959-60, bishop of Kansas City, Mo., 1960-68; United Methodist Church (formed by union of Evangelical United Brethren Church and The Methodist Church, 1968), bishop of Oklahoma City, Okla., 1968-80; Oklahoma City University, Oklahoma City, bishop-in-residence, 1980—. Former member of General Assembly of World Council of Churches and National Council of Churches. *Awards, honors:* D.D. from Indiana Central College, 1950, and Southern Methodist University, 1969; H.L.D., Westmar College, 1965; S.T.D., Oklahoma City University, 1969.

WRITINGS: Enlisting and Developing Church Leaders, Warner Press, 1945; *Come unto Me,* Otterbein Press, 1946; *Except the Lord Build the House,* Evangelical Press (Harrisburg), 1949; *Doorways to Spiritual Living,* Otterbein Press, 1950; *Christian Worship in Symbol and Ritual,* Evangelical Press, 1953; *Lift up Your Eyes,* Otterbein Press, 1956; *Laymen in the Church,* Warner Press, 1957; *At Life's Crossroads,* Warner Press, 1959.

(Editor) *Facing Frontiers,* Otterbein Press, 1960; *Philip William Otterbein,* Upper Room, 1968; *Nineteen Bishops of the Evangelical United Brethren Church,* Parthenon Press, 1974; *History and Theological Roots of United Methodists,* Cowan, 1980; *Organizing for Effective Ministry,* Cowan, 1980. Also author of a series of historical articles for United Methodist Church Paper. Contributor to church periodicals.

WORK IN PROGRESS: Oklahoma City University History.

*   *   *

MILLAR, Jeff(ery Lynn)   1942-

PERSONAL: Born July 10, 1942, in Pasadena, Tex.; son of Daniel Lynn Millar and Betty (Shove) Millar Coons; divorced. *Education:* University of Texas, B.A., 1964. *Politics:* "Vague." *Home:* 1301 Spring Oaks Circle, Houston, Tex. 77055. *Office:* Houston Chronicle, 801 Texas Ave., Houston, Tex. 77002.

CAREER: Houston Chronicle, Houston, Tex., film critic, 1965—, columnist, 1972—; author of the comic strip "Tank McNamara," syndicated by Universal Press Syndicate to about 250 newspapers, 1974—.

WRITINGS: Private Sector (novel), Dial, 1979.

Cartoon books, all with Bill Hinds; published by Sheed Andrews, except as indicated: *Tank McNamara,* Grossett, 1975; *And I'm Tank McNamara with the Norts Spews,* 1975; *Shoot, Tank, Shoot!,* 1976; *If I Quit Baseball, Will You Still Love Me?,* 1976; *God Intended Blond Boys to Be Quarterbacks,* 1977; *The Tank McNamara Chronicles,* 1978; *Another Day, Another 11,247.63 Dollars,* 1983. Also author of "Mighty Moose and the Quarterback Kid," a screenplay for ABC-TV.

BIOGRAPHICAL/CRITICAL SOURCES: Cartoonists Profile, June, 1975; *U.S. News and World Report,* June 9, 1975; *Kansas City Star,* January 16, 1976; *Washington Post,* January 25, 1976.

*   *   *

MILLARD, A(lan) R(alph)   1937-

PERSONAL: Born December 1, 1937, in Harrow, England; son of Ralph Walter and Joyce (Chapman) Millard; married Margaret Louise Sibley, September 12, 1964; children: Clare Louise, Stephen Dudley, Jonathan Ralph. *Education:* Magdalen College, Oxford, B.A., 1959, M.A., 1963; School of Oriental and African Studies, M.Phil., 1967. *Religion:* Protestant. *Home:* 21 Riverside Rd., West Kirby, Wirral, Merseyside, England. *Office:* School of Archaeology and Oriental Studies, University of Liverpool, Liverpool, England.

CAREER: British Museum, London, England, temporary assistant keeper in department of western Asiatic antiquities, 1961-63; Tyndale Library, Cambridge, England, librarian, 1963-70; University of Liverpool, Liverpool, England, Rankin Lecturer, 1970-76, Rankin Senior Lecturer in Hebrew and Ancient Semitic Languages, 1976—. Participated in excavations at Tell Rifa'at, Syria, 1960, Petra, Jordan, 1960, Nimrud, Iraq, 1961, and Tell Nebi Mend, Syria, 1975, 1976, 1977, and 1979. *Member:* Society for Old Testament Study, Society of Antiquaries of London (fellow).

WRITINGS: (With W. G. Lambert) *Cuneiform Texts from Babylonian Tablets,* Volume XLVI, British Museum, 1965; *Catalogue of the Cuneiform Tablets in the Kouyunjik Collection, Second Supplement,* British Museum, 1968; (with Lambert)

Atra-hasis: The Babylonian Story of the Flood, Clarendon Press, 1969; (advisory editor and contributor) D. S. Alexander, editor, *Eerdmans Handbook to the Bible,* Eerdmans, 1973 (published in England as *The Lion Handbook to the Bible,* Lion Publishing, 1973).

The Bible B.C.: What Can Archaeology Prove?, Inter-Varsity Press, 1977, Presbyterian & Reformed, 1982; (consulting editor and contributor) P. Alexander, editor, *Eerdmans Encyclopedia of the Bible,* Eerdmans, 1978 (published in England as *The Lion Encyclopedia of the Bible,* Lion Publishing, 1978); (consulting editor and contributor) J. D. Douglas, editor, *The Illustrated Bible Dictionary,* Tyndale, 1980; (editor with D. J. Wiseman and contributor) *Essays on the Patriarchal Narratives,* Inter-Varsity Press, 1980, Eisenbraun's, 1983; (with A. Abou Assaf and Pierre Bordreuil) *La Statue de Tell Felcherye et son inscription bilingue assyro-arameenne,* A.D.P.F. (Paris), 1982.

WORK IN PROGRESS: An edition of *The Assyrian Eponym Lists.*

SIDELIGHTS: The Bible B.C.: What Can Archaeology Prove? has been translated into Danish, Afrikaans, German, and Dutch.

*   *   *

MILLER, Arthur S(elwyn)   1917-

PERSONAL: Born March 4, 1917, in Oregon; son of Dallas D. and Irene Miller; married Dagmar Meister (an executive secretary), October 29, 1948. *Education:* Willamette University, A.B., 1938; Stanford University, LL.B., 1949; Yale University, J.S.D., 1959. *Home:* 1106 Fleming St., Key West, Fla. 33040.

CAREER: George Washington University, Washington, D.C., assistant professor of law, 1950-53; Emory University, Atlanta, Ga., assistant professor, 1953-55, associate professor, 1955-57, professor of law, 1957-61; George Washington University, professor of law, 1961-78, professor emeritus, 1978—. Lecturer at Brookings Institution, 1962—; associate fellow of Institute for Policy Studies, 1963; Leo Goodwin, Sr., Distinguished Visiting Professor of Law, Nova University, 1982-83. Chief consultant to U.S. Senate Select Committee on Presidential Campaign Activities, 1973-74; chairman of board of advisors, Public Law Institute, Nova University Law Center. *Military service:* U.S. Army, 1941-46. U.S. Air Force, 1950-53. U.S. Air Force Reserve, 1953-77; became colonel. *Member:* Association of Evolutionary Economics, Federation of American Scientists, American Society of Political and Legal Philosophy. *Awards, honors:* Guggenheim fellow, 1957-58; Ford Foundation fellow, 1960-61; grant from Columbia University, 1967-68.

WRITINGS: Racial Discrimination and Private Education, University of North Carolina Press, 1957; *The Supreme Court and American Capitalism,* Free Press, 1968; *The Supreme Court and the Living Constitution,* Lerner Law Book, 1969; *The Modern Corporate State: Private Governments and the American Constitution,* Greenwood Press, 1976; *Presidential Power,* West Publishing, 1977; *The Supreme Court: Myth and Reality,* Greenwood Press, 1978; *Social Change and Fundamental Law,* Greenwood Press, 1979; *Democratic Dictatorship: The Emergent Constitution of Control,* Greenwood Press, 1981; *Toward Increased Judicial Activism: The Political Role of the Supreme Court,* Greenwood Press, 1982.

Contributor of more than 100 articles to law journals, newspapers, and popular magazines, including *Progressive* and *Nation.*

WORK IN PROGRESS: Writing a biography of federal judge J. Skelly Wright, editing a volume of Wright's nonjudicial writings, and editing a book on nuclear weapons and law, all for Greenwood Press.

SIDELIGHTS: Arthur S. Miller writes: "I write because I think. I think because I have to and it is something to do. I write on such topics as interest me, principally on public law and politics. The urge to write can be (and is) a terrible curse. One should hesitate these days to perpetrate another book. But one does it because one must."

BIOGRAPHICAL/CRITICAL SOURCES: Washington Post Book World, August 15, 1976.

*   *   *

MILLER, Barbara S(toler)   1940-

PERSONAL: Born August 8, 1940, in New York, N.Y.; daughter of Louis O. (a business executive) and Sara (Cracken) Stoler; married James R. Miller (a neurologist), August 13, 1960; children: Gwenn Allison. *Education:* Barnard College, A.B. (magna cum laude), 1962; Columbia University, M.A., 1964; University of Pennsylvania, Ph.D. (with distinction), 1968. *Office:* Department of Oriental Studies, Barnard College, Columbia University, New York, N.Y. 10027.

CAREER: Columbia University, Barnard College, New York, N.Y., assistant professor, 1968-72, associate professor, 1972-77, professor of Oriental studies, 1977—, chairman of department, 1972-74, 1979-81.

Member of Joint Committee on South Asia, American Council of Learned Societies-Social Science Research Council, 1982-85. Director of a summer seminar for college teachers, National Endowment for the Humanities, 1981. Member of publication board, Columbia University Press, 1973-79; faculty representative, Barnard College Board of Trustees, 1976-79; member of committee on academic priorities, Columbia University, 1978-79; member of governing board, Columbia University Society of Fellows in the Humanities, 1978—; co-chairperson, Barnard Studies in the Humanities, 1978—; member of university committee on general education, 1978-81; member of executive committee, Southern Asia Institute, Columbia, 1979—. Member of advisory committee, Princeton University Press, 1980—; member of advisory council on archaeology, anthropology, and related disciplines, Smithsonian Institution, 1983-85. *Member:* P.E.N. (member of translation committee), American Oriental Society (director-at-large), Association for Asian Studies, American Numismatic Society, Phi Beta Kappa.

AWARDS, HONORS: Avery and Jule Hopwood Award for writing, University of Michigan, 1959; Institute of Indian Studies, senior fellow, 1974-75, 1981-82, travel grant, summer, 1977; Guggenheim fellow, 1974-75; Mellon fellow, 1976; National Council of Women award, 1979, for work in higher education; Social Science Research Council, South Asia fellow, 1981-82. Also recipient of a number of grants or stipends from American Association of University Women, 1965-66, National Endowment for the Humanities, summer, 1971, American Philosophical Society, summer, 1971, American Council of Learned Societies, 1973 and 1978, and Smithsonian Institution, 1981.

WRITINGS—Published by Columbia University Press, except as indicated: (Translator from the Sanskrit) D. D. Kosambi, editor, *Bhartrihari: Poems,* 1967; (editor and translator from the Sanskrit) *Phantasies of a Love-Thief: The Caurapancasika Attributed to Bilhana,* 1970; (with Leonard Gordan) *A Syllabus of Indian Civilization,* 1971; (contributor) Jaroslav Prusek, editor, *The Dictionary of Oriental Literatures,* Basic Books, 1973; (editor and translator from the Sanskrit) *Love Song of the Dark Lord: Jayedeva's Gitagovinda,* Oxford University Press, 1977; *The Hermit and the Love-Thief: Sanskrit Poems of Bhartrihari and Bilhana,* 1978; (translator from the Spanish) Agueda Pizzaro, *Sombraventadora/Shadowinnower,* 1979.

(Editor and author of biographical essay) *Exploring India's Sacred Art: Selected Papers of Stella Kramrisch,* University of Pennsylvania Press, 1983; (contributor) *Essays in Gupta Culture,* Motilal Banarsidas (Delhi, India), 1983; (editor and translator from the Sanskrit) *Kalidasa: Plays of Love,* 1984. Also contributor to *The Divine Consort,* 1982. Contributor to numerous journals. Guest editor, *Journal of South Asian Literature,* 1971. Member of editorial board, *Translations from the Oriental Classics,* Columbia University Press, 1975—.

WORK IN PROGRESS: A translation and study, *The Birth of Siva's Son: Kalidasa's Kumarasanibhava;* a novel, *A Nest of Mothers;* editorial work, with Mildred Archer, on William Archer's *The Wedding of the Scribes: Kayastha Marriage Songs of Shahabad Bihar;* studies of text and image in Indian art, focusing on coins, painting, and poetry.

SIDELIGHTS: Barbara S. Miller told *CA:* "My close rereading of works of American and European literature in the context of Asian works has stimulated me to return to a major preoccupation of my student years: the writing of poetry and fiction. I am currently at work on a novel, tentatively entitled *A Nest of Mothers.* In it I am examining the relationships among an orphaned young Russian woman, her brother (an air force pilot 'lost' in the Himalayan foothills while flying a transport plane from India to China in 1944), her two aunts (one a poet, the other a physician), and her foster mother (an eccentric collector of Oriental art). The characters are modeled on various members of my family, partly based on diaries, poems, letters, and other documents that have recently come into my possession.

"I feel that the novel is the most appropriate form in which to express the range of my ideas about the 'encounter' with Asia. Rather than conflicting with my scholarly work, the long and highly disciplined sessions of analyzing my fictional characters are helping me to 'flesh out' the personalities of the elusive kings, priests, and poets of ancient India."

Miller is competent in French, Spanish, Hindi, Sanskrit, Pali, and Prakrits. She has traveled extensively in India and also in other parts of Asia, Europe, South America, and Africa.

*   *   *

MILLER, Ella May   1915-

PERSONAL: Born May 22, 1915, in Harper, Kan.; daughter of Reuben M. (a farmer and preacher) and Lucinda Ella (Neuhauser) Weaver; married Samuel E. Miller (a clergyman and professor of Spanish), June 10, 1941; children: Samuel Ernest, John David, Martin Robert, Jeanne Susan. *Education:* Goshen College, B.A. and Th.B., 1941. *Home:* 1218 Dogwood Dr., Harrisonburg, Va. 22801.

CAREER: Mennonite missionary to Argentina, 1941-52; Mennonite Broadcasts, Inc., Harrisonburg, Va., conductor of homemakers program, "Heart to Heart," 1958-77. *Member:* American Mothers Committee, Inc. (Virginia chapter).

WRITINGS: Ella May's Favorite Recipes, Mennonite Broadcasts, 1965; *I Am a Woman,* Moody, 1967; *A Woman in Her Home,* Moody, 1968; *Hints for Homemakers,* Herald, 1973; *Happiness Is Homemaking,* Moody, 1974; *The Joy of Housekeeping,* Revell, 1975; *I Am a Mother,* Moody, 1976; *The Peacemakers,* Revell, 1977. Miller's radio messages have been printed in leaflet form. Contributor to Mennonite periodicals.

BIOGRAPHICAL/CRITICAL SOURCES: Under the Southern Cross, Mennonite Publishing House, 1943; *The Touch of God,* Herald, 1965; *God Healed Me,* Herald, 1974.

*   *   *

MILLER, F(rederick) W(alter) G(ascoyne)   1904-
(The Gascon)

PERSONAL: Born September 19, 1904, in Hastings, New Zealand; son of Walter McNair and Caroline (Gascoyne) Miller; married Ngaire Malcolm, September 11, 1928; children: John, Elizabeth, Judith Miller Crosswell, Mary Miller Gray, Natalie Miller Jaceglav. *Education:* Educated in New Zealand schools until seventeen. *Religion:* Methodist. *Home:* 156 Venus St., Invercargill, New Zealand.

CAREER: Otago Daily Times, Dunedin, New Zealand, journalist, 1922-28; Christchurch Press (publishing house), Christchurch, New Zealand, journalist, 1928-32; gold miner in Clutha River valley and neighborhood, 1932-37; *Southland Daily News,* Invercargill, New Zealand, feature writer, 1945-68; *Southland Times,* Invercargill, staff member, 1968-73. Former member, State Literary Grants Advisory Committee; former member and past chairman, Invercargill Licensing Trust. *Military service:* Home service during World War II; became sergeant. *Member:* New Zealand Journalist's Union (life member), Lions Club, Freemasons. *Awards, honors:* Officer, Order of the British Empire; Civic Award, Invercargill Host Lions Club.

WRITINGS: Gold in the River, A. H. & A. W. Reed, 1946, 2nd edition, 1969; *Golden Days of Lake County,* Whitcombe & Tombs, 1949, 5th edition, 1973; *West to the Fiords,* Whitcombe & Tombs, 1954, 2nd revised edition, Whitcoulls, 1975; *Beyond the Blue Mountains,* Whitcombe & Tombs, 1954, 2nd edition, 1976; *History of Waikaia,* Waikaia Historical Committee, 1966; *Ink on My Fingers,* A. H. & A. W. Reed, 1967, Tri-Ocean, 1968.

Historic Central Otago, A. H. & A. W. Reed, 1970; *Historic Wakatipu,* A. H. & A. W. Reed, 1970; *The Story of the Kingston Flyer,* Whitcombe & Tombs, 1975; *Cromwell,* Craig-McKenzie, 1976; *King of Counties, a History of the Southland County Council,* Southland County Council, 1977. Also author of *Hokonui, the School and the People,* 1982, and *Lodge Victoria 147, the First Hundred Years,* 1983. Under pseudonym, The Gascon, wrote daily column, "The Day's Darg," in *Southland Daily News* for twenty years; has written daily verse for local newspapers since 1944.

SIDELIGHTS: F.W.G. Miller told *CA:* "The writing of regional histories has always been my prime interest because it brings the past to life and penetrates the curtain of time—especially in a young country like New Zealand whose past is not so remote. The story of settlement, of the gold discoveries, and of the establishment of a way of life in a new land with farms, schools, churches, and other institutions gives the av-

erage New Zealander a deeper appreciation of his heritage. Five years of gold mining provided the material for my first book—and set the course for my succession of regional histories. When I began researching my first history, my wife Ngaire set a room apart for my writing, but I was so inured to family life that I could not stand the solitude and moved my typewriter and script back to the living room table where family come and go and there is constant movement. But now my problem is that my wife will persist in using my office as a living room and my desk as a dining room table which I have to clear at meal times. There's nothing in life that's perfect."

*   *   *

MILLER, Herbert E(lmer)   1914-

PERSONAL: Born August 11, 1914, in DeWitt, Iowa; son of Elmer Joseph and Marian (Briggs) Miller; married Lenore Snitkey, July 1, 1938; children: Barbara Ruth. *Education:* University of Iowa, B.A., 1936, M.A., 1937; University of Minnesota, Ph.D., 1944. *Home:* 12 South Stratford Dr., Athens, Ga. 30605. *Office:* School of Accounting, University of Georgia, Athens, Ga. 30601.

CAREER: Simpson College, Indianola, Iowa, instructor, 1937-38; University of Minnesota, Minneapolis, 1938-46, began as instructor, became assistant professor; University of Michigan, Ann Arbor, 1946-61, began as associate professor, became professor; Michigan State University, East Lansing, professor of accounting and finance, 1961-70; Arthur Andersen & Co., Chicago, Ill., partner, 1970-78; University of Georgia, Athens, professor and director of School of Accounting, 1978—. Visiting professor at University of Iowa, 1945, Stanford University, 1960, 1962, 1965, University of Hawaii, 1964, and Georgia State University, 1970. Worked at various times as staff accountant for Arthur Andersen & Co., Chicago, Ill., and Touche Ross, Bailey & Smart, Detroit, Mich.

MEMBER: American Institute of Certified Public Accountants (director, 1968-70), American Accounting Association (vice-president, 1958; president, 1965-66), Iowa Society of Certified Public Accountants, Illinois Society of Certified Public Accountants, Georgia Society of Certified Public Accountants, Beta Gamma Sigma, Beta Alpha Psi (national president, 1961-62), Acacia, Union League Club (Chicago). *Awards, honors:* Elijah Watt Sells Gold Medal Award, 1945; Paton Medal, 1946; named Outstanding Educator of the Year, 1977, Accountant of the Year, 1978, and Distinguished Lecturer, 1981, by American Accounting Association; American Institute of Certified Public Accountants Gold Medal, 1981.

WRITINGS—Published by Prentice-Hall: (Editor and contributor) *C.P.A. Review Manual,* 1951, 3rd edition published as *CPA Review Manual,* 1966, 5th edition (with George C. Mead), 1979; (with Harry Anson Finney) *Principles of Accounting,* intermediate level, 4th edition (Miller was not associated with earlier editions), 1951, 7th edition (with James A. Gentry, Jr. and Glenn L. Johnson) published as *Finney and Miller's Principles of Accounting: Intermediate,* 1974; (with Finney) *Principles of Accounting,* advanced level, 4th edition (Miller was not associated with earlier editions), 1952, 6th edition (with Gentry and Johnson) published as *Finney and Miller's Principles of Accounting: Advanced,* 1971; (with Finney) *Principles of Accounting,* introductory level, 4th edition (Miller was not associated with earlier editions), 1953, 7th edition (with Gentry and Johnson) published as *Finney and Miller's Principles of Accounting: Introductory,* 1970, 8th edition, 1980.

(With Finney) *The Accounting Process* (programmed adaptation of *Principles of Accounting,* introductory level, 6th edition), 1963; (with Finney) *Principles of Financial Accounting: A Conceptual Approach,* 1968. Contributor of articles to journals, including *Accounting Review* and *Journal of Accountancy.*

* * *

MILLER, Warren E. 1924-

PERSONAL: Born March 26, 1924, in Hawarden, Iowa; son of John C. (an educator) and Mildred O. (Lien) Miller; married Ruth S. Jones, May 9, 1981; children: (previous marriage) Jeffrey, Jennifer. *Education:* University of Oregon, B.S., 1948, M.S., 1950; Syracuse University, D.S.S., 1954. *Religion:* Unitarian Universalist. *Home:* 8814 North 86th St., Scottsdale, Ariz. 85258. *Office:* Department of Political Science, Arizona State University, Tempe, Ariz. 85281.

CAREER: University of Michigan, Institute for Social Research, Survey Research Center, Ann Arbor, assistant study director, 1951-53, study director, 1953-56, research associate, 1956-58, program director, 1959-68, research coordinator, Political Behavior Program, 1968-70; University of California, Berkeley, assistant professor of political science, 1954-56; University of Michigan, assistant professor, 1956-58, associate professor, 1958-63, professor of political science, 1963-80, Arthur W. Bromage Professor of Political Science, 1981, adjunct professor, 1981—, Institute for Social Research, executive director, Inter-University Consortium for Political and Social Research, 1962-70, program director, Center for Political Studies, 1970-81, director, Social Science Data Archive, 1971-75; Arizona State University, Tempe, professor of political science, 1982—. Visiting professor of political science at University of Tilburg, 1973, University of Geneva, 1973, European University Institute, 1979, and Arizona State University, 1981. Consultant, President's Commission on Registration and Voting Participation, 1963-64; principal investigator, National Election Studies, 1977—. *Military service:* U.S. Army Air Forces, 1943-46.

MEMBER: American Political Science Association (president, 1979-80), Social Science History Association (president, 1979-80), International Political Science Association, Society for the Psychological Study of Social Issues, Midwest Political Science Association. *Awards, honors:* Fellow, Center for Advanced Study in the Behavioral Sciences, 1961-62; honorary doctorate, University of Goeteborg, 1972; distinguished alumnus award, Syracuse University, 1974; fellow, American Academy of Arts and Sciences, 1977; distinguished faculty achievement award, University of Michigan, 1977.

WRITINGS: (With Angus Campbell and Gerald Gurin) *The Voter Decides,* Row, Peterson & Co., 1954; (with Campbell, P. Converse, and D. Stokes) *The American Voter,* Wiley, 1960; (with Campbell, Converse, and Stokes) *Elections and the Political Order,* Wiley, 1966; (with T. E. Levitin) *Leadership and Change: Presidential Elections from 1952-1976,* Winthrop, 1977; (with others) *The American National Election Studies Data Sourcebook, 1952-1976,* Harvard University Press, 1980.

Contributor: *Twenty-Eighth Yearbook,* National Council for the Social Studies, 1958; *American Government Annual, 1960-61,* Holt, 1960; E. Allardt and Y. Littunenm, editors, *Cleavages, Ideologies, and Party Systems,* [Helsinki], 1964; E. Bowles, editor, *Computers in Humanistic Research,* Prentice-Hall, 1967;

James N. Rosenau, editor, *Domestic Sources of Foreign Policy,* Free Press, 1967; Mattei Dogon and Stein Rokkan, editors, *Quantitative Ecological Analysis in the Social Sciences,* MIT Press, 1969; Allardt and Rokkan, editors, *Mass Politics: Studies in Political Sociology,* Free Press, 1970; Edward C. Dreyer and Walter A. Rosenbaum, editors, *Political Opinion and Behavior: Essays and Studies,* 2nd edition, Wadsworth, 1970; *Party Identification and Beyond,* Wiley, 1976; *Congressional Elections,* Volume 6, Sage Publications, 1981.

Contributor of articles to *American Political Science Review, Scientific American, Public Opinion, Editor and Publisher,* and other publications.

* * *

MILNE, Christopher (Robin) 1920-

PERSONAL: Born August 21, 1920, in London, England; son of A(lan) A. (author of "Winnie the Pooh" series) and Dorothy (de Selincourt) Milne; married Lesley de Selincourt, July 24, 1948; children: Clare. *Education:* Trinity College, Cambridge, B.A. (with honours), 1947. *Home:* Embridge Forge, Dartmouth, Devon, England. *Agent:* Curtis Brown Ltd., 575 Madison Ave., New York, N.Y. 10022.

CAREER: Harbour Bookshop, Dartmouth, England, owner, 1951-81; writer. *Military service:* British Army, Royal Engineers, 1941-46; served in the Middle East and Italy; became lieutenant.

WRITINGS: The Enchanted Places (autobiography), Methuen, 1974, Dutton, 1975; *The Path through the Trees* (autobiography), Dutton, 1979; *The Hollow on the Hill: The Search for a Personal Philosophy,* Methuen, 1982.

SIDELIGHTS: "Practically everybody's heard of Christopher Robin and his friend 'Winnie-the-Pooh,'" writes Nancy Mills in the *Detroit News Magazine.* "He's the little boy who was immortalized in A. A. Milne's imaginative Pooh Bear tales, first published in 1924. What most people don't know is that Christopher Robin grew up." As Christopher Milne, the author of two autobiographies and a book of philosophy, he reflects on his public life as a literary figure of great renown, and on his private life as a bookseller, husband, and father who champions the preservation of the environment from his secluded home in Devon, England.

Milne's first book, *The Enchanted Places,* delves into his early years and his relationship, often strained, with his parents. Milne's mother, Dorothy de Selincourt (of England's distinguished de Selincourt family), made no secret of the fact that she had wanted a baby girl called Rosemary, and as a result Christopher Robin spent his first eight years with long hair and somewhat unboyish clothes. "I remained a boy," Milne remarks in the book. "But only just. I was one of her few failures." Milne told *CA* that his relationship with his celebrated father was rather closer, "with a shared love of cricket, golf, mathematics and crossword puzzles. [I] even came to share [my] father's unsuspected agnosticism—something which often surprises those who have misinterpreted [his] well-known poem 'Vespers' ('Hush! Hush! Whisper who dares? Christopher Robin is saying his prayers.') And [we] both were haunted in later life by ['Christopher Robin's'] world wide fame."

In a *Time* review of *The Enchanted Places,* Timothy Foote suggests that the book is as much about A. A. Milne as about his son. Foote states: "*Enchanted Places* is eloquent about the joys of countryside, the felicities of light verse. Milne writes with wit and humane perception about his later relationship with his father. In a space hardly larger than a Pooh book, he has, in fact, unobtrusively condensed a mini-memoir, a portrait of A. A. Milne, a bittersweet study of a literary celebrity in the '20s and something very like an annotated *Winnie-the-Pooh*. It is pure HUNNY all the way to the bottom of the jar.''

The Path through the Trees, Milne's second autobiography, takes the author from age nineteen, when he yearns to be a World War II combat soldier, through adulthood and the opening of his Harbour Bookshop in the small town of Dartmouth. Roy Fuller, in a *Listener* article, notes the author's ''constant inclination to chamfer off the edges of experience, more in a dreamy, self-centered manner than as a way of romanticising things.'' Fuller continues: ''Those with special concerns—fellow-warriors, booksellers, teachers—may find their own bits, so to speak, quite absorbing. Moreover, [Milne] philosophises and observes nature, if not with great profundity, certainly in a fashion appealing to many. It cannot be said that he comes out as a particularly likeable fellow, but one must admire him. He had courage, though not constitutionally courageous.'' In the *New York Times Book Review*, Moira Hodgson calls *The Path through the Trees* ''a sad book. It is not a book about grand passion, great ambition or even eccentric behavior. . . . [It] is not the 'success story' characteristic of most autobiographies. It is the account of the way in which a gentle, shy and kindly man survived worldwide notoriety. Mr. Milne leaves Pooh behind and takes his reader on a country walk—because it is here, in the countryside, that he can turn away from the complexities of the past to the simplicity of the present.''

Milne's great respect for nature and his questioning of Christianity have culminated in his book *The Hollow on the Hill: The Search for a Personal Philosophy*. In this work the author expounds on the need to recognize nature as a supreme life force and urges the preservation of the environment. For Milne, writes an *Economist* reviewer, ''Christianity is ultimately destructive, because its emphasis on heaven encourages its adherents to treat the world as a camp site, and because its insistence on the supremacy of man over the other animals is destroying the balance of nature.'' Brian Sibley, writing about *The Hollow on the Hill* in the *Listener*, is skeptical about Milne's personal philosophy: ''[He] can offer few credentials for speaking on such matters other than the questing curiosity of Everyman, and he is constantly trying to be fair and reasonable and inoffensive, while at the same time attempting to give his essentially after-dinner philosophies an authoritative—even scientific—tone.'' Sibley labels the author's dogma ''a kind of ecological pantheism [that is] probably the oldest religious concept in the world. When he says—and I don't doubt him for a moment—that he has 'an intense and burning love of the natural world,' . . . I can't help thinking he is closer to Adam the gardener or David the harpist than he perhaps realizes.''

As an author, Christopher Milne inevitably finds himself compared to his father. He tells Nancy Mills: ''I was very easily influenced by my father. He never wanted me to and I never dared to enter his particular field—writing—either as a competitor or even as a friendly companion of his. This was his field and he didn't want me there. I didn't ever want to measure myself alongside him, but to some extent I suppose I've had to. It's all right now he's dead. It doesn't really matter whether I succeed. . . . I've now ventured onto his field briefly and I'm happy that it's worked.''

BIOGRAPHICAL/CRITICAL SOURCES: Christopher Milne, *The Enchanted Places*, Methuen, 1974, Dutton, 1975; *New*

Statesman, January 17, 1975; *Time*, June 23, 1975; *Authors in the News*, Volume II, Gale, 1976; *Detroit News Magazine*, April 25, 1976; Milne, *The Path through the Trees*, Dutton, 1979; *Washington Post Book World*, August 26, 1979; *New York Times Book Review*, September 2, 1979; *Listener*, September 27, 1979, August 19, 1982; *Virginia Quarterly Review*, winter, 1980; Milne, *The Hollow on the Hill: The Search for a Personal Philosophy*, Methuen, 1982; *Economist*, September 4, 1982.

—*Sketch by Susan Salter*

*   *   *

MINER, Caroline Eyring   1907-

PERSONAL: Born December 14, 1907, in Colonia Juarez, Mexico; daughter of Edward C. (a cattleman) and Caroline C. (Romney) Eyring; married Glen Bryant Miner (a teacher and statistician), May 20, 1931; children: Caroline (Mrs. Edward E. Morgan), Bryant Albert, Rosemary (Mrs. D. Clayton Fairbourn), Edward Glen, Henry Lee, Camilla Virginia (Mrs. George D. Smith), Joseph Kay, Steven Eyring. *Education:* Brigham Young University, A.B., 1929; Utah State University, M.S., 1943; additional summer study at University of Hawaii, University of Alaska, and University of California, Berkeley. *Religion:* Church of Jesus Christ of Latter-day Saints. *Home:* 2415 St. Mary's Dr., Salt Lake City, Utah 84108.

CAREER: Teacher, primarily of English, in Pima, Ariz., 1927-28, Safford, Ariz., 1929-31, Logan, Utah, 1939-43, Riverton, Utah, 1947-49, and Salt Lake City, Utah, 1946-47; University of Utah, Salt Lake City, instructor in English, 1949-50; Salt Lake City (Utah) public schools, teacher of English at secondary level, 1952-73.

MEMBER: National League of American Pen Women (president of Salt Lake City chapter, 1968-70; state president, 1970-72), League of Utah Writers (vice-president, 1974 and 1976; president, 1975), Utah Mothers Association (president, 1973-75), Reynolds Literary Club (president, 1956-66), Delta Kappa Gamma. *Awards, honors:* Distinguished service award, Brigham Young University, 1962; named Kiwanis Teacher of 1963; Utah Mother of the Year, 1973; American Cancer Society award, Utah division, 1983.

WRITINGS—Published by Publishers Press, except as indicated: (Co-author) *If I Were in My Teens*, Bookcraft, 1955; *Earthbound No Longer* (poetry), 1961; *As A Great Tree* (biography), 1962; *Life Story of Edward Christian Eyring*, 1966; *Lasso the Sunrise* (poetry), 1976; *Miles Romney and Elisabeth Gaskell*, 1978.

Published by Deseret: *To Warm the Heart* (stories and essays), 1961; *Building a Home to Last Forever* (religious book), 1962; *There's Always Mother* (poetry and prose), 1968; *Facts and Fancies* (biography), 1976; *Camilla*, 1980; *Joy*, 1980; *A Legacy Remembered: 1914-1970*, 1982.

Contributor of more than one hundred poems and essays to magazines.

SIDELIGHTS: Caroline Eyring Miner traveled around the world in 1955. Since then she has visited South and Central America, Russia (with a party of students), Alaska, the South Pacific, the Caribbean, Finland, Africa, China, Spain, Turkey, Israel, and the Galapagos Islands. She has also camped around the United States and in Mexico and Canada. *Avocational interests:* Reading, gardening, oil painting, genealogy.

MINGAY, G(ordon) E(dmund) 1923-

PERSONAL: Both syllables of surname are accented equally; born June 20, 1923, in Long Eaton, Derbyshire, England; son of William Edmund (a naval officer) and Florence (Tuckwood) Mingay; married Mavis Tippen, January 20, 1945. *Education:* University of Nottingham, B.A., 1952, Ph.D., 1958. *Office:* University of Kent at Canterbury, Canterbury, Kent, England.

CAREER: Woolwich Polytechnic, London, England, lecturer in economics, 1953-56; London School of Economics and Political Science, University of London, London, England, lecturer in economic history, 1957-65; University of Kent at Canterbury, Canterbury, Kent, England, reader in economic history, 1965-68, professor of agrarian history, 1968—. Visiting professor at University of Wisconsin, 1962-63, University of British Columbia, 1964, University of Montana, 1966, University of Nebraska, 1969, Western Washington State College (now Western Washington University), 1971, and University of Auckland, 1973. *Military service:* Royal Naval Volunteer Reserve, 1942-47; became lieutenant. *Member:* Economic History Society, Economic History Association, British Agricultural History Society, Agriculture History Society (United States).

WRITINGS: English Landed Society in the Eighteenth Century, Routledge & Kegan Paul, 1963; (with J. D. Chambers) *The Agricultural Revolution, 1750-1880,* Batsford, 1966; (author of introduction) Gonner, *Common Land and Inclosure,* 2nd edition, Cass & Co., 1966; (editor with E. L. Jones) *Land, Labor, and Population in the Industrial Revolution,* Edward Arnold, 1967; *Enclosure and the Small Farmer in the Age of the Industrial Revolution,* Macmillan, 1968.

(With Philip S. Bagwell) *Britain and America: A Study of Economic Change, 1850-1939,* Routledge & Kegan Paul, 1970; *Fifteen Years On: The B.E.T. Group, 1956-1971,* British Electric Traction Co., 1973; *The Gentry,* Longman, 1975; *Arthur Young and His Times,* Macmillan, 1975; *Georgian London,* Batsford, 1975; *Rural Life in Victorian England,* Heinemann, 1976; *The Agricultural Revolution,* Black, 1977; (author of introduction) Hammond, *Village Labourer,* Longman, 1978; (editor) *The Victorian Countryside,* Routledge & Kegan Paul, 1981; *Mrs. Hurst Dancing,* Gollancz, 1981.

Contributor to economic and agricultural history journals. Appointed editor, *Agricultural History Review,* 1972—.

AVOCATIONAL INTERESTS: Adult education, opera.

BIOGRAPHICAL/CRITICAL SOURCES: Times Literary Supplement, August 21, 1981, January 22, 1982.

*   *   *

MISTER X
See HOCH, Edward D(entinger)

*   *   *

MITCHELL, G(eoffrey) Duncan 1921-

PERSONAL: Born June 5, 1921, in England; son of George H. and Helen (Grimshaw) Mitchell; married Margaret Miller (a physician); children: Jeremy, Catherine. *Education:* University of London, B.Sc. (with honors), 1949. *Religion:* Church of England. *Office:* Institute of Population Studies, Hoopern House, University of Exeter, 101 Pennsylvania Rd., Exeter, Devon, England.

CAREER: University of Exeter, Exeter, England, professor of sociology and research fellow in population studies. Chairman, Devon Community Housing Society. *Military service:* Royal Air Force, 1941-46; became flight lieutenant; received Order of the British Empire. *Member:* Royal Anthropological Institute (fellow).

WRITINGS: Sociology: A Study of Social Systems, University Tutorial Press, 1959, 2nd edition, 1970; *A Hundred Years of Sociology,* Aldine, 1968; *A Dictionary of Sociology,* Aldine, 1968; *Sociological Questions,* University of Exeter, 1969; (editor) *Sociology: An Outline for the Intending Student,* Humanities, 1970; *A New Dictionary of Sociology,* Routledge & Kegan Paul, 1979; (with R. Snowden) *The Artificial Family,* Allen & Unwin, 1981; (with R. Snowden and E. Snowden) *Artificial Reproduction: A Social Investigation,* Allen & Unwin, 1983.

WORK IN PROGRESS: Sociology of artificial reproduction; the history of sociology.

*   *   *

MITCHUM, Hank
See SHERMAN, Jory (Tecumseh)

*   *   *

MONET, Jacques 1930-

PERSONAL: Born January 26, 1930, in Saint-Jean, Quebec, Canada. *Education:* University of Montreal, B.A., 1955; College de l'Immaculee Conception, Ph.L., 1956, Th.L., 1967; University of Toronto, M.A., 1961, Ph.D., 1964. *Office:* Regis College, Toronto School of Theology, University of Toronto, 15 St. Mary St., Toronto, Ontario, Canada M4Y 2R5.

CAREER: Entered Society of Jesus (Jesuits; S.J.), 1949, ordained Roman Catholic priest, 1966; Loyola College, Montreal, Quebec, sessional lecturer in history, 1964-67; University of Toronto, Toronto, Ontario, assistant professor of history, 1968-69; University of Ottawa, Ottawa, Ontario, associate professor, 1969-81, professor of history, 1981-82, chairman of department, 1972-77; University of Toronto, Toronto School of Theology, president of Regis College, 1982—. Research officer to the governor general of Canada, 1977-78; special advisor on cultural policy to the secretary of state of Ottawa, 1978-79. Member of Huronia Historical Development Council, 1971-76, of research policy committee of Social Science Federation of Canada, 1976—, and of Stamp Advisory Council, Canada Post, 1978—. Chairman of academic council, Jesuit Fathers of Upper Canada, 1973-79; member of formation council, Upper Canada Province of the Society of Jesus, 1979—. *Member:* Royal Society of Canada, Canadian Historical Association (French language secretary, 1969-74; president, 1975-76), Canadian Catholic Historical Association (member of council, 1977-79).

WRITINGS: The Last Cannon Shot: A Study of French Canadian Nationalism, University of Toronto Press, 1969; *The Canadian Crown,* Clarke, Irwin, 1979; *Jules Leger,* La Presse, 1982.

Contributor: *Man's Search for Values,* Gage, 1966; W. L. Morton, editor, *The Shield of Achilles,* Macmillan, 1968; J. M. Bumsted, editor, *Documentary Problems in Canadian History,* Irwin-Dorsey, 1969; M. Hamelin, editor, *The Political Ideas of the Prime Ministers of Canada,* University of Ottawa Press, 1969; J.M.S. Careless, editor, *Colonists and Canadiens,* Macmillan, 1971; C. McFarland, editor, *Canada: The Annual*

Handbook of Present Conditions and Recent Progress, Statistics Canada, 1975; R. Cook and C. Berger, editors, *The West and the Nation: Essays in Honour of W. L. Morton,* McClelland & Stewart, 1976.

Also contributor to *Dictionary of Canadian Biography* and *Encyclopaedia Britannica.* Contributor of articles to numerous journals, including *Canadian Historical Review, Culture,* and *Revue du Centre d'Etudes du Quebec.*

*   *   *

MONTELL, William Lynwood   1931-

PERSONAL: Born February 18, 1931, in Tompkinsville, Ky.; son of Willie G. (a vocational supervisor) and Hazel (Chapman) Montell; married Ruth Evelyn Jackson (a teacher), December 31, 1951 (divorced, July 11, 1979); children: Monisa Elaine Wright, William Brad. *Education:* Andrew Jackson Business University, business certificate, 1949; attended Campbellsville College, 1955-56, and University of Kentucky, 1956-57; Western Kentucky State College (now Western Kentucky University), A.B., 1960; Indiana University, M.A., 1963, Ph.D., 1964. *Religion:* Baptist. *Office:* Center for Intercultural and Folk Studies, Western Kentucky University, Bowling Green, Ky. 42101.

CAREER: High school teacher in Temple Hill, Ky., 1958-59; Campbellsville College, Campbellsville, Ky., assistant professor, 1963-64, associate professor of history and chairman of the department of social science, 1964-66, professor of history and dean of academic affairs, 1966-69; Western Kentucky University, Bowling Green, Ky., associate professor of history and folklore, assistant dean of Potter College of Liberal Arts, and coordinator of Center for Intercultural and Folk Studies, 1969-71, professor of history, 1971-78, professor of folklore and director of Center for Intercultural and Folk Studies, 1971—. Member, Kentucky Oral History Commission; member, Education Commission of the Southern Baptist Convention, 1969-76. Consultant to numerous organizations, including schools, museums, private agencies, and media production groups. *Military service:* U.S. Navy, 1951-55. U.S. Naval Reserve, 1955-59.

MEMBER: International Society for Folk Narrative Research, Oral History Association, Pioneer America Society, American Folklore Society, Society for Ethnology and Folklore, South Atlantic Modern Language Association, Kentucky Folklore Society (president, 1966-70), Kentucky Folklife Foundation (vice-president), John Edwards Memorial Foundation.

WRITINGS: The Saga of Coe Ridge: A Study in Oral History, University of Tennessee Press, 1970; *Monroe County History, 1820-1970,* Monroe County Press, 1970; (contributor) Wayland D. Hand, editor, *American Folk Legend,* University of California Press, 1971; *Ghosts along the Cumberland: Deathlore in the Kentucky Foothills,* University of Tennessee Press, 1975; (editor) *Monroe County Folklife,* Monroe County Press, 1975; *Folk Medicine of the Mammoth Cave Region,* Monroe County Press, 1976; (with Michael Morse) *Kentucky Folk Architecture,* University Press of Kentucky, 1976.

(Contributor) Lutz Niethammer, editor, *Lebenserfahrung und Kollectives Gedachtnis die "Oral History,"* Syndikat, 1980; *From Memory to History: Using Oral Sources in Local Historical Research,* American Association for State and Local History, 1981; *Don't Go Up Kettle Creek: Verbal Legacy from the Upper Cumberland,* University of Tennessee Press, 1983;

(contributor) Hand, editor, *American Folk Custom,* University of California Press, 1984.

Contributor to numerous journals, including *International Folklore Review, Kentucky Folklore Record, Mountain Life and Work, Register of the Kentucky Historical Society, Journal of American Folklore,* and *Southern Folklore Quarterly.*

WORK IN PROGRESS: Two books, tentatively entitled *Interpersonal Violence in the Upper Cumberland* and *The Death of a Culture in the Arkansas Ozarks.*

SIDELIGHTS: William Lynwood Montell's field research activities include recording historical legends from blacks and whites living along the Cumberland River in Tennessee and Kentucky, and making surveys of folk architectural forms in the Southern states. In another research project he asks, "Why did people of the Upper Cumberland use violence as a means of settling disputes? Why do people still like to talk about these events?"

Montell told *CA:* "In all of my writings I make every effort to tell the story of the people—the grass roots residents whose names never get into 'typical' history books. Additionally, I try to write in a style which these people can read and appreciate. My books are scholarly, but they are not above the heads of the people who provide me with their historical recollections."

*   *   *

MOORE, Lander
See FENSCH, Thomas

*   *   *

MOORE, Robert (Samuel)   1936-

PERSONAL: Born June 3, 1936, in Bekenham, Kent, England; son of Douglas Kenneth (a telephone engineer) and Kathleen (Murphy) Moore; married Lindy Ruth Parker, 1969; children: one son, one daughter. *Education:* University of Hull, B.A., 1964; University of Durham, Ph.D., 1973. *Politics:* Socialist. *Religion:* Methodist. *Home:* 72 Tillydrone Ave., Aberdeen AB2 2TN, Scotland. *Office:* Department of Sociology, King's College, University of Aberdeen, Aberdeen AB9 2TY, Scotland.

CAREER: Royal Navy, 1953-61, left service as lieutenant; University of Durham, Durham, England, lecturer in sociology, 1965-70; University of Aberdeen, Aberdeen, Scotland, senior lecturer, 1970-75, reader, 1975-76, professor of sociology, 1976—. *Member:* British Sociological Association (chairperson, 1981-83), British Association for the Advancement of Science (secretary of sociology section, 1968-70; member of council, 1969—; recorder, 1971-76).

WRITINGS: (With John Rex) *Race, Community and Conflict,* Oxford University Press, for Institute of Race Relations, 1967, revised edition, 1973; *Pitmen, Preachers and Politics,* Cambridge University Press, 1974; *Racism and Black Resistance in Britain,* Pluto Press, 1975; (with Tina Wallace) *Slamming the Door: The Administration of Immigration Control,* Martin Robertson, 1975; *The Social Impact of Oil: The Case of Peterhead,* Routledge & Kegan Paul, 1982.

Contributor: R. Hooper, editor, *Colour in Britain,* British Broadcasting Corp., 1965; Bruce Douglass, editor, *Reflections on Protest,* John Knox, 1967; Lewis Donnelly, editor, *Justice First,* Sheed, 1969; Paul de Berker, editor, *Interactions,* Cassirer, 1970; *Max Weber and Modern Sociology*, Routledge & Kegan Paul, 1971; *Majority and Minority*, Allyn & Bacon, 1975; *Working Class Images of Society*, Routledge & Kegan Paul, 1975.

R. Scase, editor, *Cleavage and Constraint: Studies in Industrial Society*, Allen & Unwin, 1976; C. Bell and H. Newby, editors, *Knowledge for Whom: Doing Sociological Research*, Allen & Unwin, 1976; G. Littlejohn and others, editors, *Power and the State*, Croom Helm, 1978; H. Willmer, editor, *Christian Faith and Political Hopes: A Reply to E. R. Norman*, Epworth Press, 1979; F. H. Buttel and Newby, editors, *The Rural Sociology of the Advanced Societies*, Allanheld, Osmun, 1980; R. Passler and D. Shapiro, editors, *The Social Impact of Oil in Scotland*, Gower, 1980; *Energy in the Balance*, British Association for the Advancement of Science, 1980; M. Harloe, editor, *New Perspectives in Urban Change and Conflict*, Heinemann, 1981.

Contributor to *New Society, Advancement of Science, Newsletter* of Institute of Race Relations, *British Journal of Sociology*, and other journals. Editor, *Sage Race Relations Abstract*, 1974-77; member of editorial board, *Sociology*, 1981—.

WORK IN PROGRESS: Research on migrant workers in north and northeast Scotland in connection with North Sea oil exploration and development; writing introductory text on racism in the United Kingdom.

BIOGRAPHICAL/CRITICAL SOURCES: Times Literary Supplement, April 13, 1967, September 10, 1982.

*   *   *

MORRIS, Ivan (Ira Esme)   1925-1976

PERSONAL: Born November 29, 1925, in London, England; died July 19, 1976, in Bologna, Italy; son of Ira Victor (a writer) and Edita (a writer; maiden name deToll) Morris; married three times. *Education:* Harvard University, B.A. (magna cum laude), 1946; University of London, Ph.D., 1951. *Religion:* Church of England. *Home:* 173 Riverside Dr., New York, N.Y. 10024. *Agent:* Georges Borchhardt, 136 East 57th St., New York, N.Y. 10022. *Office:* Department of East Asian Languages and Cultures, Columbia University, New York, N.Y. 10027.

CAREER: British Broadcasting Corp., London, England, news editor, 1951-52; British Foreign Office, London, senior research assistant, 1953-56; lived in Japan, 1956-59; Columbia University, New York, N.Y., associate professor, 1960-66, professor of Japanese history, 1966-76, chairman of department of East Asian languages and cultures, 1966-69. Amnesty International, member of executive committee, London, co-founder of American section, 1966, general secretary in United States, chairman of American section, 1973-76. *Military service:* U.S. Navy Intelligence, during World War II; became lieutenant junior grade. *Member:* Royal Asiatic Society, Royal Institute of International Affairs, Association of Teachers of Japanese (chairman, 1962-65), Association for Asian Studies, Asiatic Society of Japan.

AWARDS, HONORS: Royal Institute of International Affairs, London travelling grant, 1956; D.Lit., University of London, 1964; Duff Cooper Memorial Prize, 1965, for *The World of the Shining Prince: Court Life in Ancient Japan.*

WRITINGS: Nationalism and the Right Wing in Japan: A Study of Post-War Trends, Oxford University Press, 1960; *Japan*, Cambridge University Press, 1960; *The World of the Shining Prince: Court Life in Ancient Japan*, Knopf, 1964, reprinted, Putnam, 1981; *Selected List of Bungo and Other Forms Found in Japanese Literature until c. 1330*, privately printed, 1965; *Dictionary of Selected Forms in Classical Japanese Literature*, Columbia University Press, 1966, *Corrigenda, Addenda, Substituenda*, 1970; *The Riverside Puzzles*, Walker & Co., 1969 (published in England as *The Pillow Book Puzzles*, Bodley Head, 1969).

The Lonely Monk and Other Puzzles, Bodley Head, 1970, Little, Brown, 1971; (with Herbert Paul Varley and Nobuko Morris) *The Samurai*, Weidenfeld & Nicolson, 1970, Delacorte, 1971; *The Tale of Genji Scroll*, Kodansha International, 1971; *Foul Play and Other Puzzles*, Bodley Head, 1972, Vintage, 1974; *The Nobility of Failure: Tragic Heroes in the History of Japan*, Holt, 1975.

Translator: (To the French, with Rosenblum and Beerblock) *Les Portes de l'enfer: Suivie d'autres nouvelles choisies*, Stock (Paris), 1957; Ooka Shohei, *Fires on the Plain*, Knopf, 1957, reprinted, Greenwood, 1978; Yukio Mishima, *The Temple of the Golden Pavilion*, Knopf, 1959, reprinted, Putnam, 1981; Jiro Osaragi, *The Journey*, Knopf, 1960; Sugawara Takasue no Musume, *As I Crossed a Bridge of Dreams: Recollections of a Woman in Eleventh Century Japan*, Dial, 1971.

Editor: (With Paul C. Blum) *Comprehensive Index: A Classified List Followed by Author and Subject Indexes, of Papers Appearing in the Transactions, 1872-1957*, Asiatic Society of Japan, 1958, Tuttle, 1959; (and translator with others, and author of introduction) *Modern Japanese Stories*, Tuttle, 1961, reprinted, 1977; (and translator) Saikaku Ihara, *The Life of an Amorous Woman, and Other Writings*, New Directions, 1963; (and translator) Masao Maruyama, *Thought and Behaviour in Modern Japanese Politics*, Oxford University Press, 1963; (and author of introduction) *Japan 1931-1945: Militarism, Fascism, Japanism?*, Heath, 1963; (and translator) Sei Shonagon, *The Pillow Book of Sei Shonagon*, two volumes, Columbia University Press, 1967; (and author of preface) *Madly Singing in the Mountains: An Appreciation and Anthology of Arthur Waley*, Walker & Co., 1970. Drama critic, *Vogue.*

WORK IN PROGRESS: Japan in the Seventeenth Century; a book about the life and work of Muryaki Shikabu.

SIDELIGHTS: Ivan Morris was "an indefatigable interpreter of East to West," wrote D. J. Enright in *New York Review of Books.* In his widely acclaimed book *The Nobility of Failure: Tragic Heroes in the History of Japan*, Morris explained a national trait of the Japanese that he claimed is one of the most incomprehensible to Westerners: the desire to die—often needlessly and by one's own hand—in order to preserve the purity of the nation.

"Ivan Morris has hit upon a brilliant method of introducing even the most reluctant reader to a foreign culture: he approaches Japanese history thematically and selectively by tracing through myth and fact the peculiar nature of Japan's tragic heroes, stressing the similarity of their noble, futile efforts over the course of seventeen centuries," commented *Newsweek*'s Peter S. Prescott. "'In the mystique of Japanese heroism,' Morris writes, 'nothing succeeds like failure.' That about sums it up: throughout history the Japanese hero has chosen the losing side and cherished defeat."

Examining the lives and deaths of Japanese heroes in ten chapters—beginning with the nearly mythical Prince Yamoto Takeru in the fourth century and ending with the kamakaze pilots of World War II—Morris revealed "a deeper concern for the

Japanese *attitude* toward these men than for the literal truth of their sometimes murky careers," wrote David Brudnoy in *New Republic*. The careers of these heroes, Brudnoy pointed out, "reflect a dominant national consciousness teaching that in defeat is found real victory and virtue." Prescott described the characteristics of the heroes in *The Nobility of Failure* in this way: "Typically, the hero is a brilliant warrior who, in time of strife, supports his Emperor or the conservative faction. For a while his prowess leads him to victory in a succession of epic battles, but in time his sincerity, the purity of motive that marks him as a hero will clash with the corrupt pragmatism of the real world and he will recognize that a tragic fate awaits him. Believing that the manner of his death will validate his life, that 'nobility in the face of a certain defeat proclaims the magnificent tragedy of life,' he will write a few farewell haiku before committing hara-kiri, secure in the knowledge that he will be remembered as a hero by his nation. Typically, he is done in by his impracticality and political innocence—weaknesses that are—to the Japanese, admirable qualities."

The underlying premise of *The Nobility of Failure* is that the Japanese tradition of the failed hero is one that is alien to Western societies. "Morris argues that the Japanese hero is distinguished from his Western counterpart by a certain genius for failure and that he is revered and loved precisely for his capacity to encounter failure with an unflinching sincerity of purpose and profound contempt for the material consequences of his resolve," commented Roger Scruton in *Times Literary Supplement*. However, several other critics questioned whether or not the tragic Japanese hero is really so different than many of the men admired in Western culture, such as Roland, Don Quixote, General George Custer, or Robert E. Lee. "It is a pity that Morris has not offered a detailed argument to support his contention [that Japanese heroes are radically different from those in the West]," stated Gordon Graham Dowling in *Nation*, "for the reverse appears to be nearer the truth. It would seem that Japan, alone among non-Western cultures, shares exclusively with the West that variety of romanticism which glorifies the failed hero. . . . In fact, if any generalized difference is detectable, it might be said that the failure which characterizes the Western hero, from Achilles and the protagonists of the Greek tragedies to Hamlet, is most often an interior collapse rather than an external defeat."

The Nobility of Failure was admired for its unique approach to Japanese history. "I can't imagine a better introduction to Japanese culture than the one *The Nobility of* Failure provides," remarked Christopher Lehmann-Haupt in *New York Times*. "Professor Morris manages to highlight the crucial events that have shaped the island empire." Robert Jay Lifton stated in *New York Times Book Review* that "each chapter illuminates important subterranean byways of Japanese history, and no reader can finish the book without having greatly expanded his knowledge of this strangely impressive nation. Moreover, Morris wears his considerable scholarship lightly, writes lucidly, always in a comparative spirit (rather than seeing Japan as a self-enclosed exotic entity) and provides detailed notes that in themselves offer a remarkable body of information and associations."

AVOCATIONAL INTERESTS: Chess and playing the tenor recorder.

BIOGRAPHICAL/CRITICAL SOURCES: Observer Review, December 10, 1967; *Listener,* December 14, 1967, November 26, 1970; *Punch,* January 24, 1968; *Virginia Quarterly Review,* summer, 1968; *Hudson Review,* autumn, 1968; *Christian Sci-*

ence Monitor, July 14, 1970; *New York Times*, June 11, 1971, October 6, 1975; *Newsweek*, September 8, 1975; *New York Review of Books,* September 18, 1975; *New York Times Book Review*, September 28, 1975; *Nation*, November 1, 1975; *New Republic,* December 20, 1975; *Times Literary Supplement,* January 16, 1976.

OBITUARIES: New York Times, July 21, 1976; *Publishers Weekly,* August 16, 1976.†

*   *   *

MORRIS, Jerrold 1911-

PERSONAL: Born January 22, 1911, in London, England; son of John (a hat manufacturer) and Hilda (Erb) Morris; married Vivian Fay, October 13, 1944; children: John. *Education:* Attended Ashton Preparatory School, Kent, England, and The London Polytechnic; took extension courses in art history at University of London. *Home:* 235 St. Clair Ave. W., Toronto, Ontario, Canada. *Office address:* Morris Gallery, P.O. Box 250, Station Q, Toronto, Ontario, Canada M4T 2M1.

CAREER: Acton Educational Committee, Acton, England, school liaison officer, 1932-34; school art teacher in England, 1932-34; Van Enden Gold Mines, Dutch Guiana, surveyor, 1935-39; Vancouver Art Gallery, Vancouver, British Columbia, curator, 1948-56; San Francisco Museum of Art, San Francisco, Calif., chief curator, 1956-57; Laing Galleries, Toronto, Ontario, manager, 1958-62; Morris Gallery, Toronto, managing director, 1962—. *Military service:* Royal Canadian Air Force, 1940-46; became squadron leader; received Distinguished Flying Cross and bar. *Member:* Association of Art Museum Directors, Western Association of Art Museum Directors (president, 1935-55).

WRITINGS: On the Enjoyment of Modern Art, McClelland & Stewart, 1965, New York Graphic Society, 1968; *The Nude in Canadian Painting*, New Press (Toronto), 1972; *Canadian Artists and Airmen, 1940-45*, Morris Gallery (Toronto), 1974; *Adrift on Course*, Hawthorn Art Press, 1978; *100 Years of Canadian Drawing*, Methuen, 1980.

*   *   *

MORRIS-JONES, W(yndraeth) H(umphreys) 1918-

PERSONAL: Born August 1, 1918, in Carmarthen, South Wales; son of William James and Annie Mary (Morris) Jones; married Graziella Genre, 1953; children: two daughters, one son. *Education:* London School of Economics and Political Science, B.Sc., (with honors), 1938; Christ's College, Cambridge, research scholar, 1940. *Home:* 95 Ridgway, London S.W. 19, England. *Office:* Institute of Commonwealth Studies, University of London, 27 Russell Sq., London W.C.1, England.

CAREER: University of London, London School of Economics and Political Science, London, England, lecturer in political science, 1946-55; University of Durham, Durham, England, professor of political theory and institutions, 1955-65; University of London, Institute of Commonwealth Studies, director, 1966—. Constitutional advisor to Viceroy of India, 1947. Visiting professor at Indian School of International Studies, New Delhi, 1960, University of Chicago, 1962, and University of California, Berkeley, 1964-65. *Military service:* Indian Army, 1941-46; became lieutenant-colonel. *Member:* Political Studies Association of the United Kingdom. *Awards, honors:* Rockefeller traveling fellow, 1954, 1960, and 1966-67.

WRITINGS: Parliament in India, Longmans, Green, 1957; *Government and Politics of India,* Hutchinson, 1964, Doubleday, 1967, 3rd edition, Hutchinson, 1971; (with Biplab Dasgupta) *Patterns and Trends in Indian Politics,* Allied Publishers (Bombay), 1975; *The Making of Politicians,* Athlone Press, 1978; *Politics, Mainly Indian,* Longman, 1978; (editor) *From Rhodesia to Zimbabwe,* Cass, 1980. Contributor to political science journals.

WORK IN PROGRESS: Research on legislatures in new states.

AVOCATIONAL INTERESTS: Motoring, gardening, walking, tennis, music.

BIOGRAPHICAL/CRITICAL SOURCES: Journal of Politics, August, 1978; *Times Literary Supplement,* December 5, 1980.

*   *   *

MOULTON, Eugene R(ussell)   1916-1981

PERSONAL: Born March 18, 1916, in Mogadore, Ohio; died October 18, 1981; son of Leon R. and Della (Meadows) Moulton; married Lillian Foote, May 10, 1941; children: Jeanne Rae, Joanne Mae, Russell Eugene, Jaime Patrick. *Education:* Attended Kent State University, 1940-41; Western Reserve University (now Case Western Reserve University), B.A., 1947, M.A., 1948, Ph.D., 1953. *Politics:* Democrat. *Religion:* Protestant.

CAREER: Porcelain Steel Co., Cleveland, Ohio, personnel manager, 1944-46; Carroll College, Waukesha, Wis., associate professor of speech and chairman of department, 1949-52; University of Redlands, Redlands, Calif., professor of speech and chairman of department, 1952-68; Madison College, Harrisonburg, Va., professor of speech and chairman of department of speech and drama, 1968-70; Eastern Montana College, Billings, professor of speech and communications, beginning 1970, chairman of division of humanities, 1970-75, and department of speech communication and theatre arts, beginning 1975.

Consultant on creativity, California State Department of Education; member of summer faculty, State University of New York at Buffalo. Member of leadership council, National Creative Education Foundation. Consultant, Lockheed Propulsion Co.; member of speaker's bureau, National Association of Manufacturers. *Military service:* U.S. Army Air Forces, pilot, 1941-44. *Member:* Speech Association of America, American Forensic Association, Western Speech Association, Pacific Forensic Association (executive secretary, 1962-65), Pi Kappa Delta (province governor, 1954-58).

WRITINGS: Newton D. Baker, Western Reserve University Press, 1954; *Fundamentals of Speech,* Nichols Publishing, 1958, revised edition, 1963; *The Dynamics of Debate,* Harcourt, 1966; *The New Interpersonal Communication: Ideas, Their Origination, Organization, and Presentation,* Burgess, 1975; (coauthor) *How to Create a Speech,* Kendall/Hunt, 1976; (with McDonald W. Held) *Communication: A Creative Process,* Burgess, 1976. Also author of "Three Billion Dollar Computer between Your Ears" (taped lecture), McGraw, 1967. Contributor to speech journals.†

*   *   *

MOUNT, (William Robert) Ferdinand   1939-

PERSONAL: Born July 2, 1939, in London, England; son of Robert Francis and Lady Julia (Pakenham) Mount. *Education:*

Attended Eton College and University of Vienna; Christ Church, Oxford, B.A. (with first class honors), 1961. *Politics:* Conservative. *Religion:* Anglican. *Home:* 17 Ripplevale Grove, London N. 1, England.

CAREER: Sunday Telegraph, London, England, editorial assistant, 1961; Conservative Party, London, officer in research department, and secretary to Parliamentary committees on health, social security, and Home Office affairs, 1962-65, assistant, Selwyn Lloyd inquiry into Conservative Party organization, 1964-65; *Daily Sketch,* London, leader writer and columnist, 1965-67; *National Review,* New York, N.Y., editor, 1967; *Daily Mail,* London, chief leader writer, 1968-73; free-lance journalist and novelist, 1973—; *Spectator,* London, political editor, 1977-82; British Prime Minister's staff, London, head of policy unit, 1982—.

WRITINGS: Very Like a Whale (novel), Weybright & Talley, 1967; *The Theatre of Politics,* Schocken, 1973; *The Man Who Rode Ampersand* (novel), Chatto & Windus, 1975; *The Clique* (novel), Chatto & Windus, 1978; *The Subversive Family: An Alternative History of Love and Marriage,* J. Cape, 1982. Contributor to periodicals and newspapers.

BIOGRAPHICAL/CRITICAL SOURCES: Times Literary Supplement, August 27, 1982.

*   *   *

MUCHA, Jiri   1915-

PERSONAL: Born March 12, 1915, in Prague, Czechoslovakia; son of Alphonse Maria (an art noveau artist) and Maria (Chytilova) Mucha; married Vitezslava Kapralova (a composer), April 26, 1940; married second wife, Geraldine Thomson (a composer), July 5, 1941; children: (second marriage) John. *Education:* Attended Charles University, 1934-39. *Religion:* Protestant. *Home:* Hradcanske namesti 6, Prague 1, Czechoslovakia. *Agent:* Dilia, Vysehradska 28, Prague 2, Czechoslovakia; and A. P. Watt & Son, 26/28 Bedford Row, London WC1R 4HL, England.

CAREER: British Broadcasting Corp. correspondent in North Africa, Middle East, Southeast Asia, and Northwestern Europe during the later years of World War II; writer in Prague, Czechoslovakia, 1946-51; arrested for alleged espionage and imprisoned, 1951-54; writer and translator in Prague, 1954—. *Military service:* French Army, 1939, served in Czech Division; evacuated to Britain, 1940; Royal Air Force, 1943-45, served as flight lieutenant. *Member:* P.E.N., Garrick Club (London). *Awards, honors:* Order of Merit; Mlada Fronta Award, 1966, for *Cerny a bily New York;* Memorial Medal, 1968; Ph.D., Dundee University, 1969.

WRITINGS: Most (title means "The Bridge"), Lofox, 1943; *The Problems of Lieutenant Knap* (short-story collection), Hogarth Press, 1945; *Ohen proti ohni* (war diary; title means "Fire Braves Fire"), Sfinx (Prague), 1947; *Sklenena Stena* (title means "The Glass Wall"), Prace, 1948; *Spalena Setba,* Melantrich, 1948, translation published as *The Scorched Crop,* Hogarth Press, 1949; *Valka Pokracuje* (title means "The War Continues"), Knihovna Lidovych Novin, 1949; *Cim zraje cas* (title means "Maturing and Time"), Ceskoslovensky Spisovatel, 1958.

Provdepodobna tvar (novel; title means "Probable Face"), Ceskoslovensky Spisovatel, 1963; *Cerny a bily New York* (title means "Black and White New York"), Mlada Fronta, 1965; *Alphonse Mucha: His Life and Art,* Heinemann, 1966; *Al-*

phonse Mucha: The Master of Art Nouveau, Hamlyn, 1966; *Living and Partly Living* (prison diary), translated from the original Czech by Ewald Osers, Hogarth Press, 1967, McGraw, 1968; *Studene Slunce,* Ceskoslovensky Spisovatel, 1968; *Kankan se svatozari* (title means "Cancan with a Halo"), Obelisk, 1968; *Marieta v noci* (title means "Marieta by Night"), Ceskoslovensky Spisovatel, 1969; (with Marina Henderson and Aaron Scharf) *Mucha,* Academy Editions, 1971; (with Henderson) *The Graphic Works of Alphonse Mucha,* Academy Editions, 1973; *Alfons Mucha,* Mlada Fronta, 1982. Also author of *The Permanent Garden* and *Lloyd's Head.*

Contributor: John Lehmann, *The Face of War Britain,* [London], 1946; Desmond Hawkins and Donald Boyd, editors, *Invasion,* Sfinx, 1947; *Klaus Mann zum Gedaechtnis,* Querido Verlag, 1950; Cecil Woolf and John Bagguley, editors, *Authors Take Sides on Vietnam,* Owen, 1967; Marianne Alexandre, editor, *Viva Che!,* Lorrimer Publishing, 1968; A. J. Liehm, *Generation,* [Paris], 1969; B. S. Johnson, editor, *You Always Remember the First Time,* Quartet Books, 1975. Also contributor to *New Writing* by Lehmann.

Translator of books into Czech; all published by Statni Nakladatelstvi Krasne Literatury: Jack Lindsay, *The Betrayed Spring,* 1956; Norman Mailer, *The Naked and the Dead,* 1957; Sinclair Lewis, *The Man Who Knew Coolidge,* 1957; Kingsley Amis, *Lucky Jim,* 1959.

Also author of produced plays: "Zlaty vek," 1948; "Broucci ve fraku," 1960; "Tanec mezi stiny," 1966. Also author of filmscripts, including "Roztrzka," "Povoden," "Prvna a posledni," "Vanice," "Kral kralu," "Kohout plasi smrt," "Thirty-nine in the Shade," and "Prazske noci."

Also translator of plays into Czech: Edward Albee, *The Zoo Story;* Samuel Beckett, *Happy Days;* William Gibson, *Two for the Seesaw;* Frank Gillroy, *Who Will Save the Ploughboy;* Doris Lessing, *Play with a Tiger;* Brendan Behan, *The Hostage;* Keith Waterhouse and Willis Hall, *Billy Liar, The Long and the Short and the Tall;* Arnold Wesker, *Roots* (Orbis, 1961), and *Kitchen;* Monty Norman, Julian More, and David Heneker, *Irma La Douce;* Wolf Mankowitz, More, Heneker, and Norman, *Expresso Bongo;* Mankowitz and Norman, *Belle; or The Ballad of Dr. Crippen;* Mankowitz, Norman, and Heneker, *Make Me an Offer;* John Osborne and Anthony Creighton, *Epitaph for George Dillon;* Peter Shaffer, *The Private Eye, Royal Hunt of the Sun;* Noel Coward, *Nude with Violin;* Patrick Hamilton, *Gas Light;* Norman and More, *The Perils of Scobie Prilt;* Arthur Miller, *A Memory of Two Mondays;* Shelagh Delaney, *Taste of Honey;* Robert Bolt, *A Man for All Seasons* (Orbis, 1963); Peter Ustinov, *Photo Finish, Half Way Up the Tree,* and *The Unknown Soldier and His Wife.*

Regular contributor to *Literarni Listy* (Czechoslovak weekly), 1968—, and *Nation;* also contributor to *New York Review of Books.*

SIDELIGHTS: Jiri Mucha was one of a group of young writers who helped launch the publication *Daylight* in London in the early days of World War II. He was sentenced to prison in Czechoslovakia for espionage for a term of six years in 1951. He served half of the sentence and recorded his thoughts and experiences in a prison diary, *Living and Partly Living.* He wrote the book secretly in prison with pencil stubs by the light of a lamp that he had to dig up and then bury again every day.

Mucha told *CA:* "Even though my books made usually several editions with over 100,000 copies and were translated into various languages, I would have written more, had I not been most of my life prevented from publishing. On the other hand, this saved me probably from publishing a lot of nonsense. Hence—you never know what is good for you."

BIOGRAPHICAL/CRITICAL SOURCES: *London Tribune,* December 14, 1945; *Spectator,* December 14, 1945; *Narodni Osvobozeni* (Prague), September 15, 1946; *Kultura* (Prague), December 8, 1946; *Lidova Kultura* (Prague), February 5, 1947; *Mlada Fronta* (Prague), February 26, 1947; *Vyvoj* (Prague), July 16, 1947; *Lud* (Bratislava), January 1, 1950; *Observer,* February 2, 1950; *Kulturni Politika,* September 9, 1950; Jiri Mucha, *Living and Partly Living* (prison diary), translated from the original Czech by Ewald Osers, Hogarth Press, 1967, McGraw, 1968; *Observer Reviews,* April 23, 1967; *Month* (London), May, 1967; *Times Literary Supplement,* June 22, 1967; *Canadian Forum,* August, 1968; *New York Times,* January 13, 1969, February 16, 1969; *Tvorba,* July 7, 1970; Mucha, Marina Henderson, and Aaron Scharf, *Mucha,* Academy Editions, 1971.

* * *

MULGAN, Catherine 1931-
(Catherine Gough)

PERSONAL: Born May 29, 1931, in Bristol, England; daughter of John Weidhofft (a historian) and Margaret (Rintoul) Gough; married Philip Anthony Mulgan (a publisher), January 10, 1953; children: Clare, Felicity, Geoffrey. *Education:* Newnham College, Cambridge, historical tripos, honors, 1952. *Home:* 51 Wood Lane, Highgate, London, England.

CAREER: Royal Ballet School, London, England, history teacher, 1953-55; Henrietta Barnett School, London, history teacher, 1967-77; history teacher, South Hampstead High School, 1977—.

WRITINGS: (Under name Catherine Gough) *Boyhoods of Great Composers* (juvenile), illustrated by Edward Ardizzone, Walck, Book I, 1960, Book II, 1963; *London: An Illustrated History,* Edward Arnold, 1979. Contributor to *Ideas.*

AVOCATIONAL INTERESTS: Music (plays piano and viola, is member of an amateur orchestra, and sings in a choir).

* * *

MULLIGAN, Hugh A. 1925-

PERSONAL: Born March 23, 1925; son of John J. and Jeanette (Wilton) Mulligan; married Brigid Murphy, January 14, 1948. *Education:* Attended Cathedral College, Brooklyn, N.Y., 1942-44; Marlboro College, B.A. (summa cum laude), 1948; Harvard University, M.A. (English literature), 1951; Boston University, M.S. (journalism), 1951. *Religion:* Roman Catholic. *Home:* 50 Crest Rd., Ridgefield, Conn. 06877.

CAREER: Associated Press, special correspondent, 1951—; has traveled in and reported from 104 countries on all continents; coverage has included such major news events as the missile shots, President Kennedy's trip to Ireland and his assassination and funeral, national political conventions, the Vietnam War, 1965-72, the Arab-Israel Wars of 1967 and 1973, the Cyprus conflict, President Nixon's 1972 trip to China, the 1981 British royal wedding, two papal conclaves, and papal trips to Africa, Mexico, Ireland, Central America, Poland, and the U.S.A. *Military service:* U.S. Army Infantry, World War II; served in European theater. *Member:* Overseas Press Club (member of board of governors), Authors League, American Irish Historical Society, Players, Dutch Treat Club.

AWARDS, HONORS: Short story award, *Tomorrow,* 1948; short story award, *Ellery Queen's Mystery Magazine,* 1949; American Newspaper Publishers Association Gold Medal, 1951; Headliners Award, 1963, 1967; Overseas Press Club award for best foreign reporting, 1967; Sigma Delta Chi award for best foreign reporting, 1971; Associated Press Managing Editors Best Reporting award, 1972, 1978; D.Hu.L., Marlboro College, 1973; Distinguished Alumni, Boston University School of Public Communication, 1983.

WRITINGS: (Contributor) H. Hoke, editor, *The Family Book of Humor,* Hanover House, 1957; (with Saul Pett, Sid Moody, and Tom Henshaw) *The Torch Is Passed: The Associated Press Story of the Death of a President,* Associated Press, 1964; (editor) *The World in 1964* (news yearbook), Associated Press, 1964; *No Place to Die: The Agony of Vietnam,* Morrow, 1967; (with John Barbour, Jules Loh, and Moody) *Lighting out of Israel,* Prentice-Hall, 1967; (contributor) D. Brown, editor, *How I Got That Story* (anthology), Dutton, 1967; *Writing from the Front Row Seats* (about reporting), Simon & Schuster, 1971; *Best Sports Stories, 1980,* Dutton, 1980; *Best Sports Stories, 1982,* Dutton, 1982.

*   *   *

MUNDIS, Jerrold 1941-
(Robert Calder, Eric Corder)

PERSONAL: Born March 3, 1941, in Chicago, Ill.; son of James M. (a business executive) and Dolores M. (an art teacher; maiden name, Hank) Mundis; married second wife, Hester Siegel (a novelist), March, 1966 (divorced, October, 1983); children: Shepard Siegel, Jesse Max. *Education:* Attended Beloit College, 1959-61; New York University, B.A., 1963. *Politics:* "Troubled." *Religion:* "None." *Agent:* Richard Curtis Associates, 164 East 64th St., New York, N.Y. 10021.

CAREER: "Various brief odd jobs following college, including a year's stint as a literary agent"; full-time writer, 1966—.

WRITINGS: (With Robert Leonard) *King of the Ice Cream Mountain* (juvenile one-act play; first produced by Wisconsin Bureau of Arts and Lectures, 1961), Dramatic Publishing, 1968; *The Guard Dog* (nonfiction), McKay, 1970; *Gerhardt's Children* (novel; Book-of-the-Month Club selection), Atheneum, 1976; (editor) *The Dog Book,* Arbor House, 1983; *The Retreat,* Warner Books, 1984.

Under pseudonym Robert Calder: *The Dogs,* Delacorte, 1976; *Best Offer,* Jove Books, 1981.

Under pseudonym Eric Corder: *Slave,* Pocket Books, 1967; *The Long Tattoo,* Pocket Books, 1968; *Slave Ship,* McKay, 1969; *Prelude to Civil War* (nonfiction), Crowell, 1970; *Hellbottom,* Pocket Books, 1972; *The Bite,* Dell, 1975; *Savage Rite,* Pocket Books, 1976; *Shame and Glory,* Pocket Books, 1978.

Contributor of stories and articles to *American Heritage, Harper's, New York,* and *New Worlds.*

BIOGRAPHICAL/CRITICAL SOURCES: New York Times, August 9, 1976.

*   *   *

MUNN, H(arold) Warner 1903-1981

PERSONAL: Born November 5, 1903, in Athol, Mass.; died January 10, 1981; son of Edward Emerson (a painter) and Jessica (Lemon) Munn; married Malvena Bodway, January 14, 1930; children: John Warner, James Edward, Gerald Douglas, Robin Shawn. *Education:* Attended public schools in Athol, Mass. *Politics:* Democrat. *Religion:* Lutheran. *Home:* 5019 North Vassault, Tacoma, Wash. 98407.

CAREER: Worked as salesman, truck driver, deck hand, brakeman for New York Central Railroad, tool maker and foundry man for L. S. Starrett Co., Athol, Mass., and assistant manager of F. W. Woolworth store, Athol, Mass.; Buffelen Woodworking Co., Tacoma, Wash., rip saw operator and planer, beginning 1958; Stoker-Lad Heating Co., Tacoma, office manager, beginning 1969. Free-lance writer. *Wartime service:* Massachusetts State Guard, 1940-42. *Member:* Tacoma Writers Club. *Awards, honors:* Henry Broderick Play Award, Pacific Northwest Writers Conference, 1970; Clark Ashton Smith Poetry Award, 1977.

WRITINGS: (Contributor) *By Daylight Only,* Selwyn & Blount, 1928; *The Werewolf of Ponkert,* Grandon, 1958, reprinted, Centaur, 1976; (contributor) *More Macabre,* Ace Books, 1961; *The King of the World's Edge,* Ace Books, 1966; *The Ship from Atlantis* (bound with *The Stolen Sun* by Emil Petaja), Ace Books, 1967; *Christmas Comes to the Little House,* Almar Press, 1974; *Merlin's Ring,* Ballantine, 1974; *The Banner of Joan* (poems), Grandon, 1975; *To All Amis: 1975 Season's Greetings* (poems), privately printed, 1975; *Season's Greetings with Spooky Poems,* privately printed, 1976; *Merlin's Godson,* Ballantine, 1976; *The Lost Legion,* Doubleday, 1979; *The Book of Munn, or "A Recipe for Roast Camel"* (poems), Outre House, 1979; *Tales of the Werewolf Clan,* Donald M. Grant, Volume I: *In the Tomb of the Bishop,* 1979, Volume II: *The Master Goes Home,* 1980.

Contributor of stories and poems to *Weird Tales, Unknown, Whispers,* and other publications. Editor, *Tacoma Writers Club Newsletter,* 1966, and 1967-68.

SIDELIGHTS: H. Warner Munn once explained to *CA* how he wrote his fantasy and horror stories: "I like to take an obscure fact as a foundation and base upon it fantastic situations and plots." *Avocational interests:* Witchcraft and demonology, folklore, curiosa of all kinds, autobiographies, poetry, ancient history.

BIOGRAPHICAL/CRITICAL SOURCES: New York Times Book Review, September 8, 1974; *Fantasy Newsletter,* April, 1981.

OBITUARIES: Fantasy Newsletter, March, 1981.†

*   *   *

MUNRO, John M(urchinson) 1932-

PERSONAL: Born August 29, 1932, in Wallasey, England; son of Duncan M. (an engineer) and Edith Mary Doris (Smith) Munro; married H. Ingrid B. Lipp, August 10, 1956; children: Karen Christine, Peter Duncan, Stephen Hans, Kirsten Caroline. *Education:* University of Durham, B.A., 1955; Washington University, St. Louis, Mo., Ph.D., 1960. *Politics:* "Uncommitted." *Religion:* None. *Home:* AUB Avenue de Francais, Apt. 804, Beirut, Lebanon; and Prastio-Evdemou, Cyprus. *Office:* Department of English, American University of Beirut, Beirut, Lebanon.

CAREER: Washington University, St. Louis, Mo., part-time instructor in English, 1956-60; University of North Carolina at Chapel Hill, instructor in English, 1960-63; University of Toronto, Toronto, Ontario, assistant professor of English, 1963-65; American University of Beirut, Beirut, Lebanon, associate professor, 1965-68, professor of English, 1968—, associate dean, 1970-73. Professor at Lebanese University, 1967-80. English-language broadcaster for Radio Kuwait, Radio Libya, Radio Tunis, and Radio Qatar. Free-lance journalist. *Awards, honors:* United Nations Day Award from Government of the Philippines, 1967, for organizing Kahlil Gibran International Festival; Lebanese World Union Award, 1967, for service to Lebanese culture.

WRITINGS: (With Charles Edge and T. Y. Greet) *Worlds of Fiction,* Houghton, 1964; *English Poetry in Transition,* Pegasus, 1968; *Arthur Symons,* Twayne, 1969; *Decadent Poetry of the 1890's,* American University of Beirut, 1970; *Royal Aquarium: Failure of a Victorian Compromise,* American University of Beirut, 1971; *Selected Poems of Theo Marzials,* American University of Beirut, 1974; *James Elroy Flecker,* Twayne, 1976; *A Mutual Concern,* Caravan Books, 1977; *The Nairn Way: Desert Bus to Baghdad,* Caravan Books, 1980; *Adnan the Dreamer,* Oxford University Press, 1981; *The Road to Jerusalem,* Oxford University Press, 1981. Also author of *The Story of Modern Cyprus.* Beirut correspondent for *Middle East, Middle East Times, Middle East Agribusiness,* and other periodicals. Contributor to English literature and education journals.

WORK IN PROGRESS: Selected Letters of Arthur Symons, with Karl Beckson.

SIDELIGHTS: John M. Munro writes: "I was jogging along quite happily in my academic career until I decided to go to Lebanon as a visiting professor for a couple of years. Once in Lebanon I stayed. This was partly because Lebanon was a splendid place to live, and partly because I became fascinated by Middle Eastern culture. After almost twenty years I am still in Lebanon—even though it is no longer the place it was when I arrived—and for better or for worse I feel tied to a country where I have spent most of my working life.

"I remember the country in its prime, and I have witnessed its decline; as a journalist I have tried to convey as accurately as I can various aspects of Lebanese life during the period I have lived here. Meanwhile I have continued my career as an academician, and while I have endeavored to maintain my professorial integrity, I must confess to an interest in Middle Eastern culture and a desire to write about it, which sometimes surpasses my enthusiasm for the more conventional concerns of a professor of English literature."

* * *

MURPHY, Mario
   See EDMONDSON, G. C.

* * *

MURPHY, Thomas Basil, Jr.   1935-
   (Tom Murphy)

PERSONAL: Born October 12, 1935, in Wallingford, Conn.; son of Thomas Basil (a physician) and Margaret Louise (a registered nurse; maiden name, Fitzgerald) Murphy. *Education:* Harvard University, A.B., 1957. *Agent:* Writer's House, 21 West 26th St., New York, N.Y. 10010. *Office:* Bozell & Jacobs, Inc., One Dag Hammarskjold Plaza, New York, N.Y. 10017.

CAREER: Vice-president and creative supervisor, J. Walter Thompson, Co., 1961-72; vice-president and creative supervisor, de Garmo, Inc., 1972-73; associate creative supervisor,

William Esty, Co., 1973-74; Bozell & Jacobs, Inc., New York City, vice-president and creative supervisor, 1974—. Registered dealer in Oriental and Western art and antiquities. *Military service:* U.S. Army, intelligence analyst, 1957-60; served in Berlin.

WRITINGS—Under name Tom Murphy: *Sky High,* Putnam, 1977; *Ballet!,* New American Library, 1977; *Aspen Incident,* New American Library, 1978; *Lily Cigar,* New American Library, 1979; *Auction!,* New American Library, 1981; *The Panther Throne,* New American Library, 1982.

WORK IN PROGRESS: A romantic novel set in contemporary New York.

SIDELIGHTS: Thomas Murphy told *CA:* "I write for fun, in the hope of entertaining people. My books contain no planned political, religious, or other moral or aesthetic message, nor do I aspire to re-create written English."

* * *

MURPHY, Tom
   See MURPHY, Thomas Basil, Jr.

* * *

MURRAY, Les(lie) A(llan)   1938-

PERSONAL: Born 1938, in Nabiac, New South Wales, Australia; son of Cecil Allan (a dairy farmer) and Miriam Pauline (Arnall) Murray; married Valerie Gina Maria Morelli, 1962; children: five. *Education:* Attended University of Sydney. *Politics:* "Anti-colonial, Boeotian as opposed to Athenian, anti-totalitarian, fiercely egalitarian and anti-mandarin." *Religion:* Catholic by conversion. *Home:* 27 Edgar St., Chatswood, New South Wales 2067, Australia.

CAREER: Australian National University, Institute of Advanced Studies, Canberra, translator of scholarly and technical material from western European languages, 1963-67; research in folklore, history, and language in Great Britain, 1967-68; officer in Prime Minister's Department, 1970-71; free-lance writer, 1971—. Has given poetry readings, lectures, talks in theaters, schools, and universities in Australia, Britain, Europe, and the United States. *Military service:* Royal Australian Naval Reserve, 1960-61. *Member:* Australian Society of Authors, Australian Translators' Association. *Awards, honors:* Grace Leven Prize for best book of verse published in Australia, joint winner, 1965, sole winner, 1980; Cook Bi-Centenary Prize for Poetry, 1970; shared National Book Award, 1974; C. J. Dennis Memorial Prize, 1976; shared Mattara Prize, 1981.

WRITINGS—Published by Angus & Robertson, except as indicated: (With Geoffrey J. Lehmann) *The Ilex Tree* (poetry), Australian National University Press, 1965; (translator from the German) Troubetzkoy, *An Introduction to the Techniques of Phonological Description,* Nijhoff, 1967; *The Weatherboard Cathedral* (poetry), 1969; *Poems against Economics,* 1972; *Lunch and Counter Lunch* (poetry), 1974; *The Vernacular Republic* (poetry), 1975, published as *The Vernacular Republic: Poems, 1961-1981,* Persea Books, 1982, expanded and updated edition, Angus & Robertson, 1982; *Ethnic Radio* (poetry), 1978; *The Peasant Mandarin* (prose articles and essays), University of Queensland Press, 1978; *The Boys Who Stole the Funeral* (verse novel), 1980. Acting editor, *Poetry Australia,* 1973-79.

SIDELIGHTS: "Of all the poets now writing in Australia Les A. Murray is probably the most Australian and probably also the best," claims Fleur Adcock in the *Times Literary Supplement*. About Murray's techniques, Adcock notes: "He is a highly sophisticated user of language, and there is nothing archaic or limited about his stylistic range or his handling of tones and forms. He is a linguist . . . with an enthusiastic appetite for words and a joyfully profligate energy in using them." The reviewer concludes that Murray's "generous, witty, good-tempered poems are immensely likeable . . . ; and his combination of clear-headed fact-facing with a transcending optimism leaves a good taste in the mouth."

Murray told *CA* that he has a "vital interest in giving utterance and form to hitherto unexpressed elements of Australian mind and character. Somewhat vain about technical skill. Am inclined to be celebratory in intention and baroque in method. Seek post-Galileo universes. Chief sources of inspiration: Australian landscape, folklore, history, war, technology, deserts also important. Metaphysical more often than social; I like poetry partly because it isn't exclusively tied to the human. One may write about trees, mountains, the future, the heavens, because it is understood that one is also writing about the human whatever the ostensible subject. This belief suits me."

AVOCATIONAL INTERESTS: Geography, regional studies, landscape, farming, mythology, animals, plants, fine machinery, tall tales, driving through beautiful country.

BIOGRAPHICAL/CRITICAL SOURCES: Times Literary Supplement, July 30, 1982.

*   *   *

MUSGROVE, Philip 1940-

PERSONAL: Born September 4, 1940, in Dallas, Tex.; son of Gordan Bass (an accountant) and Retha (a psychologist; maiden name, Anthony) Musgrove; married Zina Pisarko; children: Antonina. *Education:* Haverford College, B.A., 1962; Princeton University, M.P.A., 1964; Massachusetts Institute of Technology, Ph.D., 1974. *Office:* Pan American Health Organization, 525 23rd St. N.W., Washington, D.C. 20037.

CAREER: Brookings Institution, Washington, D.C., research associate in economics, 1964-68, 1971-80, consultant, 1968-70; affiliated with World Bank, 1981; affiliated with Pan American Health Organization, Washington, D.C., 1982—. Adjunct professor, American University, 1968—.

WRITINGS: (With Joseph Grunwald) *Natural Resources in Latin American Development*, Johns Hopkins Press, 1970; *The General Theory of Gerrymandering: Professional Papers in American Politics*, Sage Publications, 1977; *Income and Spending of Urban Families in Latin America*, Brookings Institution, 1978; (with Adele Shapanka) *Income and Demographic Effects on the Structure of Consumer Expenditure in the U.S., 1975-2025*, Resources for the Future, 1982; (editor) *Ingreso, Desigualdad y Pobreza en America Latina*, Estudios Conjuntos sobre Integracion Economica Latinoamerica Program, 1983.

Contributor: *Energy and U.S. Foreign Policy*, Ballinger, 1974; *Latin America's New Internationalism*, Praeger, 1976; *Patterns in Household Demand and Saving*, Oxford University Press, 1977; *Natural Resources, Uncertainty, Dynamics and Trade*, Academic Press, 1977; *Financiamiento de la Educacion en America Latina*, Fondo de Cultura Economica, 1978; *Consumption and Income Distribution in Latin America*, Organization of American States, 1980; *The Collection and Analysis of Economic and Consumer Behavior Data*, University of Illinois, 1983.

Also contributor to proceedings of the American Institute of Mining, Metallurgical and Petroleum Engineers, 1971. Contributor of articles to professional journals, including *Journal of Political Economy, Review of Economics and Statistics, Review of Income and Wealth, American Economic Review, Latin American Research Review*, and *Journal of Health Economics*.

WORK IN PROGRESS: Evaluation of food transfer and food subsidy programs for poor consumers in Brazil; survey of health care needs and use of health facilities in Peru; determinants of food consumption in the Dominican Republic.

N

NAMIOKA, Lensey 1929-

PERSONAL: Born June 14, 1929, in Peking, China; daughter of Yuen Ren (a linguist) and Buwei (a physician and writer; maiden name, Yang) Chao; married Isaac Namioka (a mathematician), September 9, 1957; children: Aki, Michi (daughters). *Education:* Attended Radcliffe College, 1947-49; University of California, Berkeley, B.A., 1951, M.A., 1952. *Home:* 2047 23rd Ave. E., Seattle, Wash. 98112. *Agent:* Patricia Lewis, 450 Seventh Ave., Room 602, New York, N.Y. 10001.

CAREER: Wells College, Aurora, N.Y., instructor in mathematics, 1957-58; Cornell University, Ithaca, N.Y., instructor in mathematics, 1958-61; broadcasting monitor for Japan Broadcasting Corp., 1969—. Translator for American Mathematical Society, 1958-66. *Member:* Seattle Free Lances.

WRITINGS: (Translator) Buwei Y. Chao, *How to Order and Eat in Chinese*, Vintage, 1974; *The Samurai and the Long-Nosed Devils*, McKay, 1976; *White Serpent Castle*, McKay, 1976; *Japan: A Traveler's Companion*, Vanguard, 1979; *Valley of Broken Cherry Trees*, Delacorte, 1980; *Village of the Vampire Cat*, Delacorte, 1981; *Who's Hu?*, Vanguard, 1981. Contributor of travel and humor articles to magazines and newspapers.

WORK IN PROGRESS: Komiya; Phantom of the Huang-Lung Mountains.

SIDELIGHTS: Lensey Namioka writes: "For my writings I draw heavily on my Chinese cultural heritage and on my husband's Japanese cultural heritage. My involvement with Japan started before my marriage, since my mother spent many years in Japan. My long years of training in mathematics had little influence on my writing, except for an urge to economy."

AVOCATIONAL INTERESTS: Music ("prefer to make it myself badly than to hear it performed superbly").

BIOGRAPHICAL/CRITICAL SOURCES: Chicago Tribune Book World, July 5, 1981.

* * *

NAREMORE, James 1941-

PERSONAL: Born April 7, 1941, in Shreveport, La.; son of James Lawrence and Grace (Killian) Naremore; married Rita Chandler (a professor), May 19, 1963; children: James Law-

rence. *Education:* Louisiana State University, B.A., 1963, M.A., 1965; University of Wisconsin, Ph.D., 1970. *Home:* 321 East 14th St., No. B-4, Bloomington, Ind. 47401. *Office:* Department of English, Indiana University, Bloomington, Ind. 47401.

CAREER: Indiana University, Bloomington, assistant professor, 1970-74, associate professor, 1974-78, professor of English and comparative literature, 1978—, director of film studies, 1979, 1982. Visiting professor, University of Hamburg, West Germany, 1980-81. *Member:* Modern Language Association of America, American Film Institute.

WRITINGS: The World without a Self: Virginia Woolf and the Novel, Yale University Press, 1973; *Filmguide to Psycho*, Indiana University Press, 1973; *The Magic World of Orson Welles*, Oxford University Press, 1979.

Films: (And co-director) "A Nickel for the Movies," Indiana University Audio Visual Center, 1983.

Contributor: William Schutte, editor, *Twentieth Century Interpretations of Portraits of the Artist*, Prentice-Hall, 1970; Ronald Gottesman, editor, *Focus on Orson Welles*, Prentice-Hall, 1976; Bernard Benstock, editor, *Approaches to Portraits of the Artist*, University of Pittsburg Press, 1977; Ralph Freedman, editor, *Virginia Woolf: Revaluation and Continuity*, University of California Press, 1980.

Also contributor of articles to professional journals.

WORK IN PROGRESS: A book on performance in American cinema.

SIDELIGHTS: James Naremore's book *The Magic World of Orson Welles* is "the best that I know about Welles," Stanley Kauffmann writes in the *Times Literary Supplement*. "Naremore has seen the persistence of some impulses and characteristics in Welles, as well as some changes. He makes a credible connection between Welles's childhood and the fact that throughout his career 'one finds the same theme recurring—weakling fathers . . . being set off against strong, dominating women, and the legal structure . . . being undermined by sexual passion.' He makes legitimately much of the fact that the child and adolescent Welles delighted to alter his face and horrify people. . . . Indeed, he sees, throughout Welles's life, the contrast between the liberal humanism of a man formed politically under the New Deal . . . and his passion for power, indicated in boyhood by his fascination with magic tricks.''

BIOGRAPHICAL/CRITICAL SOURCES: New York Times Book Review, July 23, 1978; Times Literary Supplement, November 10, 1978.

*   *   *

NEARING, Helen K(nothe)   1904-

PERSONAL: Born February 23, 1904, in New York, N.Y.; daughter of Frank K. (a businessman) and Maria (Obreen) Knothe; married Scott Nearing (a writer), December 12, 1947 (died August 24, 1983). Education: Studied violin privately at home and abroad. Home: Harborside, Me. 04642.

CAREER: Writer. Worked as secretary of Social Science Institute. With husband, Scott Nearing, farmed organically on homesteads in Vermont and Maine, beginning 1932.

WRITINGS—With husband, Scott Nearing, except as indicated: The Maple Sugar Book: Being a Plain, Practical Account of the Art of Sugaring Designed to Promote an Acquaintance with the Ancient as Well as the Modern Practice, Together with Remarks on Pioneering as a Way of Living in the Twentieth Century, John Day, 1950, published as The Maple Sugar Book: Together with Remarks on Pioneering as a Way of Living in the Twentieth Century, Schocken, 1971; Living the Good Life: Being a Plain, Practical Account of a Twenty Year Project on a Self-Subsistent Homestead in Vermont, Together with Remarks on How to Live Sanely and Simply in a Troubled World, Social Science Institute (Harborside, Me.), 1954, published as Living the Good Life: How to Live Sanely and Simply in a Troubled World, introduction by Paul Goodman, Schocken, 1970; USA Today: Reporting Extensive Journeys and First-Hand Observations, Social Science Institute, 1955; The Brave New World (on travels in U.S.S.R. and China), Social Science Institute, 1958; Socialists around the World, Monthly Review Press, 1958.

Building and Using Our Sun-Heated Greenhouse: Grow Vegetables All Year-Round, Garden Way Press, 1977; (sole author) The Good Life Album of Helen and Scott Nearing, Dutton, 1974; Continuing the Good Life: Half a Century of Homesteading, Schocken, 1979; (sole author) Wise Words on the Good Life: An Anthology of Quotations, Schocken, 1980; (sole author) Simple Food for the Good Life: An Alternative Cook Book, Delacorte, 1980; (sole author) Our Home Made of Stone: Building in Our 70's and 90's, Down East, 1983. Also author with husband of pamphlet, Our Right to Travel, Social Science Institute, 1959.

SIDELIGHTS: "Helen and Scott Nearing are the great-grandparents of the current back-to-the-land movement, having abandoned the city in 1932 for a rural life based on self-reliance, good health and a minimum of cash," writes Vic Sussman in Washington Post Book World. An aspiring concert violinist when she met her future husband in the 1930s, Helen K. Nearing quickly adapted to a strict rural regimen the Nearings labeled "the good life." With her husband, the author documented their lifestyle in such books as Living the Good Life: How to Live Sanely and Simply in a Troubled World, Continuing the Good Life: Half a Century of Homesteading, Building and Using Our Sun-Heated Greenhouse: Grow Vegetables All Year-Round, and The Maple Sugar Book: Together with Remarks on Pioneering as a Way of Living in the Twentieth Century. As sole author of four additional works, Helen K. Nearing has also presented pictorial and philosophical sketches on the good life, a book on Simple Food for the Good Life, and a volume detailing the construction of their home.

Explaining her latest book, Our Home Made of Stone: Building in Our 70's and 90's, the author told CA: "It might be interesting to note that two old-agers took upon ourselves to build a two-story stone house from the ground up. The project took three summers (more, in clearing the site and putting in roads and a stone outhouse and storage-workshop). Over a hundred photographs detail the building from toe to top. Singularly apt quotations from ancient and modern sources caption the photos." (For more information on Helen K. Nearing, see the "Sidelights" section for her husband, Scott Nearing.)

BIOGRAPHICAL/CRITICAL SOURCES: New Republic, September 5, 1970, May 15, 1971, February 5, 1972, June 16, 1979; Newsweek, September 14, 1970, August 29, 1983; Harper's, November, 1970; Boston Globe, November 1, 1970; Chicago Tribune, November 26, 1970; Best Sellers, December 1, 1970; Time, January 18, 1971, April 28, 1971; Washington Post, June 3, 1971; Saturday Review, November 27, 1971; New York Times Book Review, May 6, 1979, February 17, 1980; Washington Post Book World, May 6, 1979, April 20, 1980; Christian Science Monitor, January 8, 1981.

*   *   *

NEARING, Scott   1883-1983

PERSONAL: Born August 6, 1883, in Morris Run, Pa.; died August 24, 1983, in Harborside, Me.; son of Louis (a merchant) and Minnie (Zabriskie) Nearing; married Nellie Marguerite Seeds, June 10, 1908 (died, 1946); married Helen Knothe (secretary of Social Science Institute and writer), December 12, 1947. Education: University of Pennsylvania, law student, 1901-02, B.S., 1905, Ph.D., 1909; Temple University, B.Oratory, 1905. Politics: Socialist-Communist. Religion: "To live superbly." Home and office: Harborside, Me. 04642.

CAREER: Writer. Pennsylvania Child Labor Commission, Philadelphia, secretary, 1905-07; University of Pennsylvania, Wharton School, Philadelphia, instructor, 1906-14, assistant professor of economics, 1914-15; Swarthmore College, Swarthmore, Pa., instructor in economics, 1908-13; University of Toledo, Toledo, Ohio, professor of social science and dean of College of Arts and Science, 1915-17. Lecturer, Rand School of Social Science, 1916; chairman, Social Science Institute, 1953. Chairman, People's Council of America, 1917-18; Socialist candidate for U.S. Congress, 1919; speaker, debated Clarence Darrow during nationwide tour; defendant with American Socialist Society in civil liberties trial, charged with obstructing recruiting in armed forces, held in U.S. District Court, New York, 1919. With wife, Helen K. Nearing, farmed organically on homesteads in Vermont and Maine, beginning 1932. Awards, honors: Honorary professor emeritus of economics from the Wharton School, University of Pennsylvania, 1973.

WRITINGS: (With F. D. Watson) Economics, Macmillan, 1908; Wages in the United States, 1908-1910, Macmillan, 1911; The Solution of the Child Labor Problem, Moffat, Yard, 1911; Social Adjustment (doctoral thesis), Macmillan, 1911; The Super Race: An American Problem, Huebsch, 1912; (with first wife, Nellie M.S. Nearing) Woman and Social Progress: A Discussion of the Biologic, Domestic, Industrial and Social Possibilities of American Women, Macmillan, 1912; Social Religion: An Interpretation of Christianity in Terms of Modern Life, Macmillan, 1913; Social Sanity, Moffat, Yard, 1913; Financing the Wage-Earner's Family, Huebsch, 1913; Reducing the Cost of Living, G. W. Jacobs, 1914; Income: An Examination of the Returns for Services Rendered and from Property Owned *in the United States*, Macmillan, 1915; *Anthracite: An Instance of Natural Resource Monopoly*, John C. Winston, 1915; *The New Education: A Review of Progressive Educational Movements of the Day* (collection of articles originally prepared for *Ladies' Home Journal*), Row, Peterson, 1915, reprinted, Arno, 1969; *Poverty and Riches: A Study of the Industrial Regime*, John C. Winston, 1916; (with Jessie Field) *Community Civics*, Macmillan, 1916; *Work and Pay*, Rand School of Social Science, 1917; *The Menace of Militarism*, Rand School of Social Science, 1917.

The American Empire, Rand School of Social Science, 1921; *The Next Step: A Plan for Economic World Federation*, privately printed, 1922; (with Bertrand A. Russell) *Debate between Scott Nearing and Bertrand Russell*, League for Public Discussion, 1924; (with Joseph Freeman) *Dollar Diplomacy: A Study in American Imperialism*, Viking, 1925, reprinted, Arno, 1970; *Educational Frontiers: A Book about Simon Nelson Patten and Other Teachers*, Seltzer, 1925; *The British General Strike*, Vanguard, 1926; *Education in Soviet Russia*, International Publishers, 1926; (with Jack Hardy) *Economic Organization of the Soviet Union*, Vanguard, 1927; *Where Is Civilization Going?*, Vanguard, 1927; *Whither China? An Economic Interpretation of Recent Events in the Far East*, International Publishers, 1927; *Black America*, Vanguard, 1929, reprinted with new introduction by the author, Schocken, 1969.

The Twilight of Empire: An Economic Interpretation of Imperialist Cycles, Vanguard, 1930; *War: Organized Destruction and Mass Murder by Civilized Nations*, Vanguard, 1931; *Free Born* (novel), Urquhart Press, 1932; *Must We Starve?*, Vanguard, 1932; *Fascism*, privately printed, 1933; *Europe-West, East*, privately printed, 1935; *United World: The Road to International Peace*, Open Road Press, 1944; *The Soviet Union as a World Power*, Island Workshop Press, 1945; *The Tragedy of Empire*, Island Workshop Press, 1945; *Democracy Is Not Enough*, Island Workshop Press, 1945; *War or Peace?*, Island Workshop Press, 1946.

Economics for the Power Age, John Day, 1952; *Man's Search for the Good Life*, Social Science Institute, 1954; *Freedom: Promise and Menace*, Social Science Institute, 1961; *Socialism in Practice: The Transformation of Eastern Europe*, New Century Publishers, 1962; *The Conscience of a Radical*, Social Science Institute, 1965; *The Making of a Radical: A Political Autobiography*, Harper, 1972; *Civilization and Beyond: Learning from History*, Social Science Institute, 1975.

With wife, Helen K. Nearing: *The Maple Sugar Book: Being a Plain, Practical Account of the Art of Sugaring Designed to Promote an Acquaintance with the Ancient as Well as the Modern Practice, Together with Remarks on Pioneering as a Way of Living in the Twentieth Century*, John Day, 1950, published as *The Maple Sugar Book: Together with Remarks on Pioneering as a Way of Living in the Twentieth Century*, Schocken, 1971; *Living the Good Life: Being a Plain, Practical Account of a Twenty Year Project on a Self-Subsistent Homestead in Vermont, Together with Remarks on How to Live Sanely and Simply in a Troubled World*, Social Science Institute (Harborside, Me.), 1954, published as *Living the Good Life: How to Live Sanely and Simply in a Troubled World*, introduction by Paul Goodman, Schocken, 1970; *USA Today: Reporting Extensive Journeys and First-Hand Observations*, Social Science Institute, 1955; *The Brave New World* (on travels in U.S.S.R. and China), Social Science Institute, 1958; *Socialists around the World*, Monthly Review Press, 1958; *Building and Using Our Sun-Heated Greenhouse: Grow Vegetables*

All Year-Round, Garden Way Press, 1977; *Continuing the Good Life: Half a Century of Homesteading*, Schocken, 1979.

Booklets and pamphlets, published by Rand School of Social Science or Nearing Affiliates, except as indicated: *Women in American Industry*, American Baptist Publication Society, 1915; *The Germs of War*, National Rip-Saw Publishing, 1916; *The Great Madness: A Victory for the American Plutocracy*, 1917; *Work and Pay*, 1917; *The Coal Question*, 1918; *Labor and the League of Nations*, 1919; *Debs Decision*, 1919; *A Nation Divided*, Socialist Party, 1920; *Europe in Revolution*, 1920; *Europe and the Next War*, 1920; *The One Big Union of Business*, 1920; *The New Slavery*, Socialist Party, 1920; *Irrepressible America*, League for Industrial Democracy, 1922; *Oil and the Germs of War*, 1923; *Russia Turns East: The Triumph of Soviet Diplomacy in Asia*, 1926; *World Labor Unity*, 1926; *Glimpses of the Soviet Republic*, 1926; *British Labor Bids for Power*, 1926; *Stopping a War: The Fight of the French Workers against the Moroccan Campaign of 1925*, 1926.

"To Promote the General Welfare," 1954; (with H. K. Nearing) *Our Right to Travel*, Social Science Institute, 1959; *Soviet Education: What Does It Offer to America?*, 1959; *Cuba and Latin America: Eyewitness Report on the Continental Congress for Solidarity with Cuba*, 1963; *Economic Crisis in the United States*, 1961; and others.

Also author of newsletter, "World Events, Interpreted by Scott Nearing," 1944-54.

SIDELIGHTS: Scott Nearing, according to Glenn Fowler in the *New York Times*, once defined himself by saying: "I have been a Socialist for a long time but I am not a Marxist. Just a tough U.S.A. radical." Dedicated to the ideas and ideals he felt were right, Nearing promoted social reforms well before they became popular causes. Explains Jerry Buckley in *Newsweek*: "As early as 1912 Nearing had written about women and social progress; in 1929, about discrimination against blacks in America. Once an economics professor at the University of Pennsylvania, he had been fired for speaking out against child labor, though fifty-eight years later the university would honor him as professor emeritus." Refusing to soften his outspoken criticism of what he saw as a "dying social order," Nearing found it increasingly difficult to get, and keep, teaching jobs. In 1932 with his future wife, Helen Knothe, he opted to abandon the urban intellectual society of New York for a simpler existence in rural Vermont.

"If one were to pick a single person to represent the counterculture, it would not be a young Californian living in a hollow redwood tree, or a Columbia dropout now part of an urban commune," Noel Perrin claims in the *New York Times Book Review*. "It would be a . . . man named Scott Nearing. But one would immediately have to add his wife, Helen." Together, the Nearings developed a philosophy of living which they called "the good life." Perrin points out that, unlike Americans who enjoyed the ever-increasing ease provided by labor-saving devices and money, the Nearings felt "the good life" meant a "steady expenditure of labor and a degree of simplicity that would have sent the average Spartan screaming off to Athens or Sybaris." Each day they followed a "'four-four-four formula': Four hours on gardening or similar work providing 'the basic essentials of living normal, healthful, serviceful lives.' Four hours of professional activity—Scott [wrote] fifty books on economics and homesteading, six of them with Helen. And four hours 'dedicated to fulfilling our obligations and responsibilities as members of the human race,'" as Vic Sussman reports in the *Washington Post Book World*.

Farming organically without the help of machinery or power tools, the authors by necessity became expert homesteaders. They scythed meadows, constructed walls and buildings, dug a pond (16,000 wheelbarrow loads of dirt moved by the Nearings and their helpers), and learned to tap maple syrup (their one "cash crop" in Vermont). The first twenty years of their subsistence farming are documented in *Living the Good Life: Being a Plain, Practical Account of a Twenty Year Project on a Self-Subsistent Homestead in Vermont, Together with Remarks on How to Live Sanely and Simply in a Troubled World.* Called "one of the great documents of the back-to-the-land movement" by Perrin, the work first appeared in 1954. Reprinted sixteen years later, it offered both practical and spiritual guidance to a new generation of Americans who were looking for "the good life" on rural farms and communes.

In the early 1950s, construction of the Stratton Mountain Ski Area on a nearby slope convinced the Nearings that, although home for two decades, their "Forest Farm" was no longer conducive to their isolated, intense lifestyle. They moved to Maine and, with Scott in his late sixties and Helen approaching fifty, began again. Their life became even more austere. Their vegetarian diets were simplified. They constructed stone buildings, including their two-story farmhouse. And they continued to write about their experiences. Published in 1979, *Continuing the Good Life: Half a Century of Homesteading* takes up their story where *Living the Good Life* left off. Other how-to works, including the jointly-authored *Building and Using Our Sun-Heated Greenhouse: Grow Vegetables All Year-Round* and Helen's *Simple Food for the Good Life: An Alternative Cook Book,* offer not only practical suggestions, but also emphasize philosophical ideals.

Reviewing a reprint of the Nearings' first homesteading book, *The Maple Sugar Book: Being a Plain, Practical Account of the Art of Sugaring Designed to Promote an Acquaintance with the Ancient as Well as the Modern Practice, Together with Remarks on Pioneering as a Way of Living in the Twentieth Century,* Peter Caws writes in *New Republic,* "The *real* subject of this book is not the practice of maple sugaring at all, but the practice of a certain kind of life." Other reviewers feel the Nearings' entire body of homesteading work teaches readers not how-to-do-it but how to live. Sussman calls the authors "stewards of the mind and soul as well as the body."

One of Scott Nearing's last public appearances was as a "witness" in the motion picture *Reds,* the story of radical journalist John Reed. Buckley explains that Nearing and Reed "met in Greenwich Village around 1915, when Nearing was considered as radical as the wild journalist Reed." When Scott Nearing celebrated his one-hundredth birthday, just eighteen days before his death on August 24, 1983, neighborhood children and elders came to the party bearing a banner with a picture of a man chopping wood and the words, "The world is a better place for 100 years of Scott Nearing." Says Helen in a *Newsweek* interview, "There were plenty of people who loved him. . . . Scott grew up in a very conservative family. In a decent world he would have been a conservative. But this isn't one. Life made him a radical."

BIOGRAPHICAL/CRITICAL SOURCES: The Trial of Scott Nearing and the American Socialist Party, Rand School of Social Science, 1919, reprinted, Da Capo, 1970; *New Republic,* September 5, 1970, May 15, 1971, February 5, 1972, June 16, 1979; *Harper's,* November, 1970; *Time,* January 18, 1971; *Saturday Review,* November 27, 1971; Scott Nearing, *The Making of a Radical: A Political Autobiography,* Harper, 1972;

Choice, July, 1972; *Newsweek,* September 14, 1972, August 29, 1983; *Washington Post Book World,* May 6, 1979; *New York Times Book Review,* May 6, 1979, February 17, 1980.

OBITUARIES: New York Times, August 25, 1983; *Los Angeles Times,* August 25, 1983; *Washington Post,* August 25, 1983; *Chicago Tribune,* August 26, 1983.

[Sketch reviewed by wife, Helen K. Nearing]

—*Sketch by Nancy Hebb*

*   *   *

NELSON, Esther L.   1928-

PERSONAL: Born September 9, 1928, in New York, N.Y.; daughter of Rubin (a fabric cutter) and Freda (a nurse; maiden name, Seligman) Nelson; married Leon Sokolsky (an art teacher), November 18, 1949; children: Mara, Risa. *Education:* Brooklyn College (now Brooklyn College of the City University of New York), B.A., 1949; New York University, M.A., 1951; also attended New School for Social Research and Bank Street College of Education. *Home:* 3605 Sedgwick Ave., Bronx, N.Y. 10463. *Office address:* Dimension Five, P.O. Box 185, Kingsbridge Station, Bronx, N.Y. 10463.

CAREER: Knollwood School, Elmsford, N.Y., dance teacher, 1953-56; Scarsdale Dance Inc., Scarsdale, N.Y., dance teacher, 1953-70; Fieldston School, Riverdale, N.Y., dance teacher, 1958-63; Dimension Five (record company), Bronx, N.Y., partner, 1963—. Lecturer at Brooklyn College of the City University of New York, Shippensburg College, and Millersville State College. Has conducted dance and music workshops for teachers. Has performed on records for children. Member of Dance Library (Israel). *Member:* American Dance Guild, American Alliance for Health, Physical Education and Recreation (Dance Division). *Awards, honors:* "Dance, Sing and Listen Again" was named one of the best children's recordings of 1979 by the American Library Association.

WRITINGS—All published by Sterling: *Dancing Games for Children of All Ages,* 1973; *Movement Games for Children of All Ages,* 1975; *Musical Games for Children of All Ages,* 1976; *Singing and Dancing Games for the Very Young,* 1977; *Holiday Singing and Dancing Games,* 1980; *The Silly Songbook,* 1981; *The Funny Songbook,* 1984.

Co-author of material for children's records: "Dance, Sing and Listen," "Dance, Sing and Listen Again," "Dance, Sing and Listen Again and Again," "The Way Out Record for Children," "The Electronic Record for Children," "Together," "Dance to the Music," "Funky Doodle," and "Ebenezer Electric."

Contributor to *Dance* and *Day Care.*

WORK IN PROGRESS: Records to accompany books already published.

SIDELIGHTS: Esther Nelson writes: "I have always loved and been involved with music and dance, and so it was natural for me to continue into adulthood and to get a masters degree in dance education. My branching into the fields of recording and books came both times from parents of children in my dance classes. One mother said that her child loved class so much, and she couldn't wait to come back from week to week, so wasn't there anything we could do that she could take into her home. That was how our record company started. Bruce Haack and I made our first record with borrowed money and a nine-dollar mike. That was all the equipment we had at the time.

Now we have a totally equipped sound studio where we record, and have to date sold more than eighty thousand of our children's music and dance participation records to schools and libraries all over the country, and in foreign countries as well.''

AVOCATIONAL INTERESTS: Yoga (''the Alexander Technique, different body and mind investigations''), international travel.

BIOGRAPHICAL/CRITICAL SOURCES: White Plains Reporter Dispatch, February 9, 1974; *Patent Trader,* September 11, 1976.

* * *

NEUFELD, John (Arthur) 1938-
(Joan Lea)

PERSONAL: Born December 14, 1938, in Chicago, Ill.; son of Leonard Carl (a manufacturer) and Rhoda (Padway) Neufeld. *Education:* Yale University, B.A., 1960. *Residence:* Los Angeles, Calif. *Agent:* Arthur Pine, 1780 Broadway, New York, N.Y. 10019.

CAREER: Writer and editor. Staff member, Golden Press. *Awards, honors: Edgar Allan* was named an American Library Association notable book.

WRITINGS: Edgar Allan (juvenile), S. G. Phillips, 1968; *Lisa, Bright and Dark* (juvenile; also see below), S. G. Phillips, 1969; *Touching,* S. G. Phillips, 1970; *Sleep Two, Three, Four!,* Harper, 1971; *For All the Wrong Reasons,* Norton, 1973; *You Think I'd Go around Making These Things Up?* (juvenile), Random House, 1973; *Freddy's Book,* Random House, 1973; *Sunday Father,* New American Library, 1975; (under pseudonym Joan Lea) *Trading Up,* Atheneum, 1975; *The Fun of It,* Putnam, 1977; *A Small Civil War,* Fawcett/Ballantine, 1982; *Sharelle,* New American Library, 1983; *Rolling the Stone,* New American Library, 1984.

Also author of television scripts ''Lisa, Bright and Dark'' (based on book of the same title), NBC-TV, ''Death Sentence'' and ''You Lie So Deep, My Love,'' both ABC-TV.

SIDELIGHTS: John Neufeld's young-adult novels often focus on social issues, as in *Edgar Allan,* in which a black child is adopted into a white minister's family. *New York Times Book Review* critic Richard Horchler suggests that *Edgar Allan* ''is not a novel about prejudice or race relations or brotherhood. . . . It is about parents and children, young people, and older people, about love and failure, loss and discovery, coming to terms with oneself and others, . . . and therefore about what it means to be a human being.''

Touching tells the story of teenager Harry Walsh and his relationship with his stepsister, Twink, who has cerebral palsy. The book is ''less a novel than a personified tract, written in a distracting patchwork narrative style and featuring two-dimensional supporting characters,'' according to Jean C. Thomson in *School Library Journal.* However, in his *English Journal* review of *Touching,* John W. Conner finds the novel has ''tightly structured style and sparse but brilliant language. The author often breaks his account at the point when a reader can imagine eloquently for himself. . . . And I think an adolescent reader may understand himself better because he has met Harry Walsh.''

MEDIA ADAPTATIONS: Freddy's Book has been optioned for a television production.

BIOGRAPHICAL/CRITICAL SOURCES: New York Times Book Review, November 3, 1968; *Saturday Review,* January 18,

1969; *School Library Journal,* November, 1970; *English Journal,* December, 1970; *Contemporary Literary Criticism,* Volume XVII, Gale, 1981; *ALAN Review,* spring, 1983.

* * *

NEVILLE, B(arbara) Alison (Boodson) 1925-
(Edward Candy)

PERSONAL: Born August 22, 1925, in London, England; daughter of Hyman and Elizabeth (Dawe) Boodson; married Joseph Godfrey Neville (a retired children's psychiatrist), July 1, 1946; children: Jeremy, Tom, Paul, Lucy, Sarah. *Education:* University College, London, and University College Hospital Medical School, M.B. and B.S., 1948, D.C.H., 1950. *Politics:* ''None to speak of.'' *Religion:* Humanist. *Home:* 2 Mile End Rd., Norwich, England. *Agent:* John Farquharson Ltd., Bell House, 8 Bell Yard, London WC2A 2JU, England; and Anthony Sheil Associates Ltd., 2-3 Morwell St., London WC1B 3AR, England.

CAREER: Novelist. Has held resident posts in electroencephalography in various hospitals in England. *Awards, honors:* Arts Council award, 1968.

WRITINGS—All novels under pseudonym Edward Candy; published by Gollancz, except as indicated: *Which Doctor,* Rinehart, 1953; *Bones of Contention,* 1954, reprinted, Doubleday, 1983; *The Graver Tribe,* 1958; *A Lady's Hand,* 1960; *A Season of Discord,* 1964; *Strokes of Havoc,* 1966; *Parents' Day,* 1967; *Doctor Amadeus,* 1969; *Word for Murder, Perhaps,* 1971; *Scene Changing,* 1977; *Voices of Children,* David & Charles, 1980.

WORK IN PROGRESS: Making Amends, a book of autobiographical sketches; an anthology for conservationists, tentatively entitled *Imperilled Garlands.*

SIDELIGHTS: B. Alison Neville told *CA:* ''Since 1970 I have, like most of my generation, I suspect, suffered a prolonged disillusionment with political and apparently humanitarian action. My two last novels are, I fear, books of despair. *Scene Changing* is about the trading in of a mundane, insignificant private life for public adulation, and the likely cost of such an exchange. *Voices of Children* suggests that private romantic fantasy and utopian dreams may be totally inappropriate and even destructive once translated into social action. At the moment, rather than sadden my readers any further, I'm compiling an anthology of nature poems, writing poems of my own (for the first time since adolescence), and planning some short stories.''

AVOCATIONAL INTERESTS: Reading, music, friends.

BIOGRAPHICAL/CRITICAL SOURCES: Times Literary Supplement, July 15, 1977, January 25, 1980; *Washington Post Book World,* August 21, 1983.

* * *

NEVILLE, Robert C(ummings) 1939-

PERSONAL: Born May 1, 1939, in St. Louis, Mo.; son of Richard Perry (a chemist) and Rose (Cummings) Neville; married Elizabeth Egan (an artist and teacher), June 8, 1963; children: Gwendolyn (deceased), Naomi, Leonora. *Education:* Yale University, B.A., 1960, M.A., 1962, Ph.D., 1963. *Home:* 49 Harbor Circle, Centerport, N.Y. 11721. *Office:* 2355 Melville Library, State University of New York, Stony Brook, N.Y. 11794.

CAREER: Ordained minister of United Methodist Church. Yale University, New Haven, Conn., instructor in philosophy, 1963-65; Wesleyan University, Middletown, Conn., visiting instructor, 1964-65, assistant professor of philosophy, 1966-67; Fordham University, Bronx, N.Y., assistant professor, 1965-68, associate professor of philosophy, 1968-71; State University of New York College at Purchase, associate professor, 1971-74, professor of philosophy, 1974-77; State University of New York at Stony Brook, professor of philosophy and religious studies, 1977—, dean of humanities and fine arts, 1982—. Director of Stony Brook Center for Religious Studies, 1978-82. *Member:* American Philosophical Association, American Theological Society, American Academy of Religion, Metaphysical Society of America, Society for the Study of Process Philosophy, Institute of Society, Ethics and the Life Sciences (fellow).

WRITINGS: God the Creator: On the Transcendence and Presence of God, University of Chicago Press, 1968; *The Cosmology of Freedom,* Yale University, 1974; (editor with Willard Gaylin and Joel Meister) *Operating on the Mind,* Basic Books, 1975; (co-editor) *Encyclopedia of Bioethics,* Free Press, 1977; *Soldier, Sage, Saint,* Fordham University Press, 1978; *Creativity and God,* Seabury, 1980; *Reconstruction of Thinking,* State University of New York Press, 1981; *The Tao and the Daimon,* State University of New York Press, 1982.

Contributor of articles and reviews to *Journal* of the American Medical Association, *Man and World, Review of Metaphysics,* and other journals.

WORK IN PROGRESS: A Systematic Metaphysical System Based on Axiology.

BIOGRAPHICAL/CRITICAL SOURCES: Christian Century, June 5, 1968; *Theological Studies,* Volume XXX, number 1, 1969; *Southern Journal of Philosophy,* Volume X, number 1, 1972.

*   *   *

NICHOLLS, Mark
    See FREWIN, Leslie Ronald

*   *   *

NIST, John (Albert)   1925-1981

PERSONAL: Born November 27, 1925, in Chicago, Ill.; died June 18, 1981, in Naples, Italy; son of Albert Charles (a livestock buyer) and Margaret T. (Rice) Nist; married Joan Irene Stidham, June 17, 1950 (divorced September 26, 1971); married Maria Grazia Cimmino, December 16, 1971; children: Brian Thomas, Brice Robert, Brent Philip, Blair William, Chiara Ann. *Education:* DePauw University, A.B., 1949; Indiana University, M.A., 1950, Ph.D., 1952. *Politics:* Democrat/Independent. *Religion:* Roman Catholic. *Home:* 624 Seminole St., Auburn, Ala. 36830. *Office:* Department of English, Auburn University, Auburn, Ala. 36830.

CAREER: Eastern Michigan University, Ypsilanti, assistant professor, 1952-55, associate professor of English, 1955-61; University of Brazil, Rio de Janeiro, research fellow, 1961-62; University of Arizona, Tucson, visiting professor of English, 1962-63; Austin College, Sherman, Tex., Shoap Professor of English and chairman of department, 1963-66; Auburn University, Auburn, Ala., professor of English, beginning 1966. Fulbright lecturer, University of Sao Paulo, 1958-59, and University of Rome, 1970-71. Linguistics consultant, Al-

abama Department of Education, beginning 1967. *Military service:* U.S. Naval Reserve, active duty, 1944-46; received two battle stars.

MEMBER: Modern Language Association of America, National Council of Teachers of English, Conference on College Composition and Communication, Linguistics Society of America. *Awards, honors:* Social Science Research Council fellowship to Brazil, 1961-62; Machado de Assis Medal, Brazilian Academy of Letters, 1964.

WRITINGS: The Structure and Texture of "Beowulf," University of Sao Paulo, 1959, reprinted, Norwood, 1977; *Fui Crucificado,* Editora Anhambi (Sao Paulo), 1960; (editor and translator) *Modern Brazilian Poetry,* Indiana University Press, 1962; (translator and editor) Carlos Drummond de Andrade, *In the Middle of the Road: Selected Poems of Carlos Drummond de Andrade,* University of Arizona Press, 1965; *A Structural History of English,* St. Martin's, 1966; *The Modernist Movement in Brazil: A Literary Study,* University of Texas Press, 1967; *Speaking into Writing: A Guide to English Composition,* St. Martin's, 1969; (editor) *Style in English,* Bobbs-Merrill, 1969.

Handicapped English: The Language of the Socially Disadvantaged, C. C Thomas, 1974; *Among the Pyramids and Other Poems,* Northwood Institute Press, 1977; *Love Songs for Marisa,* Northwood Institute Press, 1978; *The Garden of Love,* Pteranodon Poetry Series, 1981. Also author of *Phonological Aspects of Modern English,* 1978. Contributor to *Encyclopedia of Education,* 1971; also contributor of more than two hundred articles, essays, poems, and reviews to a score of journals in America, Latin America, and Europe.

SIDELIGHTS: John Nist once told *CA:* "Motivated by the two central attributes of all esthetic activity: the drive for permanence and the desire to achieve an infinite reiterability." He was competent in Greek, Latin, Portuguese, Spanish, French, German, and Old and Middle English. *Avocational interests:* Travel, hiking, swimming, and experimenting with words.

[Sketch reviewed by wife, Maria C. Nist]

*   *   *

NODSET, Joan L.
    See LEXAU, Joan M.

*   *   *

NUTTALL, A(nthony) D(avid)   1937-

PERSONAL: Born April 25, 1937, in Hereford, England; son of Kenneth (a schoolmaster) and Hilda (Addison) Nuttall; married May Donagh, July 1, 1960; children: William James, Mary Addison. *Education:* Merton College, Oxford, B.A., 1959, M.A., 1962, B.Litt., 1963. *Politics:* None. *Religion:* None. *Home:* 35 Kensington Pl., Brighton, Sussex, England. *Office:* Arts Building, University of Sussex, Falmer, near Brighton, Sussex, England.

CAREER: Oxford University, Oxford, England, research and teaching, 1959-62; University of Sussex, Brighton, England, member of faculty, 1963—.

WRITINGS: William Shakespeare: The Winter's Tale, Edward Arnold, 1966; *Two Concepts of Allegory: A Study of Shakespeare's "The Tempest" and the Logic of Allegorical Expression,* Barnes & Noble, 1967; (editor with D. Bush) John Milton, *The Minor Poems in English,* Macmillan (London), 1972;

A Common Sky: Philosophy and the Literary Imagination, University of California Press, 1974; *Dostoevsky's "Crime and Punishment": Murder as Philosophic Experiment,* Scottish Academic Press for Sussex University Press, 1978; *Overheard by God: Fiction and Prayer in Herbert, Milton, Dante and St. John,* Methuen, 1980; *A New Mimesis,* Methuen, 1983.

Also author of *Pope's Essay on Man;* author, with Arthur Raleigh Humphreys, of phonotape, "Coriolanus," BFA Educational Media, 1972. Contributor to *Critical Quarterly, Review of English Studies,* and other publications.

SIDELIGHTS: A. D. Nuttall told *CA:* "The only language I speak easily is English, but I enjoy reading Latin verse (especially Horace). Am interested primarily in the connection between the study of literature and the study of philosophy. Have in addition a less articulate passion for the art and architecture of Italy."

BIOGRAPHICAL/CRITICAL SOURCES: Criticism, winter, 1969; *Times Literary Supplement,* April 24, 1981.

O

O'CONNELL, Jeffrey 1928-

PERSONAL: Born September 28, 1928, in Worcester, Mass.; son of Thomas Joseph (a realtor) and Mary (Carroll) O'Connell; married Virginia A. Kearns, November 26, 1960; children: Mara, Devin. *Education:* Dartmouth College, B.A. (cum laude), 1951; Harvard University, LL.B., 1954. *Politics:* Democrat. *Religion:* Roman Catholic. *Home:* 4 Oak Circle, Charlottesville, Va. 22901. *Office:* University of Virginia Law School, Charlottesville, Va. 22901.

CAREER: Tufts University, Medford, Mass., instructor in speech, 1953-54; admitted to Massachusetts Bar, 1954, and practiced with Sherburne, Powers & Needham, Boston, Mass., 1954-57; Hale & Dorr (law firm), Boston, associate, 1958-59; University of Iowa, College of Law, Iowa City, assistant professor, 1959-62, associate professor of law, 1962-63; University of Illinois at Urbana-Champaign, Law School, associate professor, 1964-65, professor of law, 1965-79; University of Virginia, Law School, Charlottesville, John Allan Love Professor of Law, 1980—. Associate director of auto claims study, Harvard University, 1963-64; visiting summer professor at Northwestern University, 1963, University of Michigan, 1966, 1975, Southern Methodist University, 1972, Oxford University, 1973, 1979, and University of Washington, 1979. Member of board of directors, Consumers Union, 1970-76; member of educational advisory board, Guggenheim Foundation, 1975—. Member, National Highway Safety Advisory Committee, 1967-70. *Military service:* U.S. Air Force, 1955-58; became first lieutenant. *Awards, honors:* Guggenheim fellowship, 1972, 1979.

WRITINGS: (With R. E. Keeton) *Basic Protection for the Traffic Victim,* Little, Brown, 1965; (with Arthur Myers) *Safety Last: An Indictment of the Auto Insurance Industry,* Random House, 1966; (with Keeton) *After Cars Crash: The Need for Legal and Insurance Reform,* Irwin, 1967; (editor with Keeton and J. McCord) *Crisis in Car Insurance,* University of Illinois Press, 1968; (with Wallace H. Wilson) *Car Insurance and Consumer Desires,* University of Illinois Press, 1969.

The Injury Industry: And the Remedy of No-Fault Insurance, Commerce Clearing House, 1971; (with Rita James Simon) *Payment for Pain and Suffering: Who Wants What, When and Why,* Insurors Press, 1972; *Ending Insult to Injury: No-Fault Insurance for Products and Services,* University of Illinois

Press, 1975; (with Roger Henderson) *Tort Law: No-Fault and Beyond,* Matthew Bender, 1975; *The Lawsuit Lottery: Only the Lawyers Win,* Free Press, 1979.

*   *   *

O'CONNOR, A(nthony) M(ichael) 1939-

PERSONAL: Born June 5, 1939, in London, England; son of John Louis and Marjorie (Atkinson) O'Connor; married Angela Mary Templeman, January 1, 1964; children: one son, one daughter. *Education:* Cambridge University, B.A., 1960, Ph.D., 1963. *Office:* Department of Geography, University College, University of London, London WC1E 6BT, England.

CAREER: Makerere University College, Kampala, Uganda, lecturer in geography, 1963-67; University of London, University College, London, England, lecturer in geography, 1967—. University of Ibadan, Ibadan, Nigeria, visiting lecturer, 1967, visiting senior lecturer, 1972-73; University of Sierra Leone, Sierra Leone, West Africa, visiting professor and head of geography department, 1974-75; University of Dar es Salaam, Tanzania, visiting lecturer, 1979. Member of Council on African Studies in Europe. *Member:* Institute of British Geographers, African Studies Association of the United Kingdom.

WRITINGS: Railways and Development in Uganda, Oxford University Press, 1965; *An Economic Geography of East Africa,* Praeger, 1966, 2nd edition, Bell, 1971; *The Geography of Tropical African Development,* Pergamon, 1971, 2nd edition, 1978; *Urbanization in Tropical Africa: Annotated Bibliography,* G. K. Hall, 1981; *The African City,* Hutchinson, 1983. Contributor to *Everyman's Encyclopaedia, Atlas of Uganda,* and to journals.

*   *   *

O'CONNOR, Mark 1945-

PERSONAL: Born March 19, 1945, in Melbourne, Australia; son of Kevin J. (a magistrate) and Elaine (a journalist; maiden name, Riordan) O'Connor. *Education:* University of Melbourne, B.A. (with first class honors), 1965. *Politics:* "Humanist." *Religion:* "Biologist." *Home address:* c/o 8 Ailsa Ave., East Malvern, Victoria 3145, Australia; and c/o Fred Goldsworthy, Humanities, Riverina C.A.E., P.O. Box 508,

Wagga Wagga, New South Wales 2650, Australia. *Agent:* Tim Curnow, Curtis Brown Ltd., 85 William St., Paddington, Sydney, Australia.

CAREER: University of Western Australia, Perth, lecturer in English, 1966; Australian National University, Canberra, lecturer in English, 1967-68; writer, 1968—. Writer in residence, James Cook University, 1983. *Member:* Australian Society of Authors (Australian Capital Territory state vice-president), Australian Capital Territory Fellowship of Australian Authors (vice-president, 1973-74). *Awards, honors:* International prize from *Poetry Australia,* 1973, for "Flight Poem," and 1975, for "Turtle Hatching"; Marten Bequest travelling scholarship for poetry, 1976; Shell Prize for poetry, 1979; Commonwealth Short Story Prize, 1979; Kenneth Allsop Memorial Prize for prose, 1980; John Shaw Nielson Poetry Prize, 1981.

WRITINGS: Reef Poems, University of Queensland Press, 1976; *The Eating Tree* (poetry), Angus & Robertson, 1980; *The Fiesta of Men* (poetry), Hale & Iremonger, 1983; *Modern Australian Styles* (criticism), James Cook University (Townsville, Queensland, Australia), 1983; *Words on Paper* (theory), James Cook University, 1983. Contributor of articles and stories to periodicals.

Plays: "Cure of the Ring" (one-act), first produced in Canberra, Australia, at Street Theatre Locations, March, 1973; "Reft" (one-act), first produced in Canberra at Act IV Festival, August, 1974; "Dillion" (four-act), first produced in Melbourne, Australia, at Melbourne Theatre, August, 1974; "Scenes" (four-act), first produced in Canberra at Australian National University, September, 1976.

WORK IN PROGRESS: A book on Europe, entitled *Journey to the Northern Antipodes;* poetry.

SIDELIGHTS: Mark O'Connor writes that he has "a particular interest in biology, ecology, conservation, and islands. A strong anti-populationist. Have spent much time on the Great Barrier Reef, and have spent two years traveling around Mediterranean islands."

AVOCATIONAL INTERESTS: Diving, gardening.

* * *

O'DONOVAN, John 1921-
(Andrew Marsh)

PERSONAL: Born January 29, 1921, in Dublin, Ireland; son of Simon Christopher (a chemist) and Anna Maria (Purcell) O'Donovan; married Veronica Patricia Morris, January 29, 1949; children: Anne, Hilary. *Education:* Educated at National Library of Ireland. *Politics:* Socialist. *Religion:* Humanist. *Home:* 21 Barnhill Ave., Dalkey, County Dublin, Ireland; and Slievecorragh, Hollywood, County Wicklow, Ireland.

CAREER: Clerk in Ireland, 1938-41, 1945-46; Royal Victoria Hospital, Belfast, Northern Ireland, member of auxiliary fire service, 1942-45; *Radio Review,* Dublin, Ireland, music critic and deputy editor, 1947-50; *Sunday Press,* Dublin, features editor, 1952; *Irish Press,* Dublin, assistant chief sub editor, 1954-55; *Evening Press,* Dublin, chief sub editor and deputy editor, 1955-60; Royal Irish Academy of Music, governor, 1960-64, vice-president (with life tenure), beginning 1964, now senior vice-president; free-lance writer and broadcaster. *Member:* Irish Georgian Society, Society of Irish Playwrights, Royal Society of Antiquaries of Ireland, Kildare Archaeological Society, Old Dublin Society.

WRITINGS: Shaw and the Charlatan Genius, Oxford University Press, 1965; *The Shaws of Synge Street* (three-act play), Proscenium Press, 1966; (contributor of two-act play) Robert Hogan, editor, *Seven Irish Plays, 1946-1964,* University of Minnesota Press, 1967; (contributor) Michael Holroyd, editor, *The Genius of Shaw,* Rainbird Publishing Group, 1980; *Wheels and Deals: A History of the Irish Motor Industry,* Gill & Macmillan, 1983; *Bernard Shaw: A Biography Incorporating New Material,* Gill & Macmillan, 1983; *A Social History of Dublin,* Gill & Macmillan, 1984. Editor and presenter of "Dear Sir or Madam," a radio feature which has been running for over twenty years; author of radio plays, talks, features, and television documentaries. Prolific contributor to magazines and newspapers.

BIOGRAPHICAL/CRITICAL SOURCES: Robert Hogan, *After the Irish Renaissance,* University of Minnesota Press, 1967.

* * *

OEHMKE, T(homas) H(arold) 1947-

PERSONAL: Surname is pronounced *Em*-kee; born November 13, 1947, in Detroit, Mich.; son of Harold Warren (an attorney) and Elizabeth (a legal assistant; maiden name, Ryerse) Oehmke; married Carol Bukrey, June 14, 1968 (divorced March 25, 1975); children: Theodore, Jason. *Education:* Attended University of Madrid, summer, 1965; Wayne State University, Ph.B., 1969, J.D., 1973; graduate study at Michigan State University, 1970. *Politics:* Independent. *Religion:* Agnostic. *Home:* 13548 Tacoma Ave., Detroit, Mich. 48205. *Office:* 639 Beaubien, Detroit, Mich. 48226.

CAREER: St. Edward Elementary School, Detroit, Mich., teacher, 1967-69; Stephenson High School, Stephenson, Mich., teacher of English and Spanish, 1969-70; Employers Association of Detroit, Detroit, director of training and senior research analyst, 1970-73; admitted to bar of the State of Michigan, 1973; Oehmke Legal Associates, P.C. (law firm), Detroit, attorney and managing partner, 1973—. Political economist and project director, New Detroit, Inc., 1973-79; publisher, American Law Research Institute (law book publishing company), 1978—. Instructor, Macomb County Community College, 1973-74; has conducted seminars and lectured on various topics concerning law, business and labor, 1972—. Has appeared on Detroit television shows.

Member of Governor's Commission on Worker's Disability Compensation, 1974-75, Governor's Michigan Economic Action Council, 1975-76, Wayne County Business and Commercial Development Council, 1975-77, Governor's State Fair Planning Commission, 1977, and American Arbitration Association's Commercial Panel of Arbitrators; representative, Mayor's Overall Economic Development Plan Committee, 1978-79; Americans for Democratic Action, Michigan Chapter, member, 1976-79, chairman, vice-chairman, and treasurer, and treasurer of Political Action Committee, 1976-79; member of corporate/foundation relations committee, Wayne State Fund, 1979—; treasurer of candidate committee, Citizens for Feuer, 1982—; member of board of directors, Accounting Aid Society of Detroit, 1983—. Advisor to Student Code Committee of Federal Court Monitoring Commission, 1982—.

MEMBER: American Bar Association, American Arbitration Association, National Defense Executive Reserve, Wayne State University Alumni Association (member of board of directors, 1983-86).

WRITINGS: *Sex Discrimination in Employment,* Trends Publishing, 1974; *Michigan Incorporation Manual,* Michigan Law Research Institute, 1976; (co-author) *Michigan Appeals Manual,* 2nd edition, American Law Research Institute, 1979; (editor) *Michigan Divorce Manual,* 2nd edition, American Law Research Institute, 1979; *The Civil Litigation Manual,* American Law Research Institute, 1980; (author of annual supplements) Schmidt and Cavitch, *Michigan Corporation Law,* Matthew Bender, 1981, 1982, 1983, 1984; (editor) Hermann Hesse, *Poetry of Siddhartha,* Labyrinth, 1981; (co-author) *Commercial Arbitration Manual,* Matthew Bender, 1983. Also author of published papers, "An Analysis of Compulsory Arbitration of Labor Disputes in Michigan's Police and Fire Departments Under 312 PA 1969," 1971, and "Complete Guide to the Affirmative Action Program," 1973, both for Employers Association of Detroit. Has also had a number of law cases published. Contributor of articles to *Menominee County Journal* and *Michigan Bar Journal,* a short story to *Detroit Magazine,* and poetry to *Poet.*

SIDELIGHTS: T. H. Oehmke told *CA:* "There is but one way to become a good writer and that is—to write. Historically, authors have practiced the craft by the use of diaries, journals, and correspondence with friends. My approach, because of a hectic business schedule, has been to practice the craft by writing professional literature. While the English language is replete with well-crafted examples of literary prose, no doubt, there is a paucity of well-written professional literature within the classic disciplines: law, medicine, engineering, and the like.

"Never did I wish to be a starving author. The sacrifice in writing the great American novel or the classic stageplay was too great for the laurel bequeathed. The thought of being a noble author, incarcerated in an attic studio writing eternal literature while ostracized socially, was not enticing. Consequently, I conceive of myself as an author who practices law to make a living. For esthetic pleasure and intellectual reward, I may compose poetry, children's literature, or adult fiction; however, to practice the craft (while staving off starvation), I have elected to write legal literature. But what contribution can I make to legal literature while I practice the craft?

"With every author of, admittedly, less than classic stature, there seems to be the need to find [his or her] niche. Dr. Seuss found his. John Irving discovered his. Shel Silverstein discovered his. And the litany could continue. The niche I have chosen to practice the craft while awaiting the opportunity to compose the great American novel, has been legal practice manuals. Indeed, that is a niche.

"No one has written the comprehensive set of law office practice manuals which routinize those types of things which attorneys do that do not require the unique and individual creation on a client by client basis. In other words, some standard, formatted, universal approach can offer good law in many circumstances. My books have included law practice manuals touching in the areas of civil litigation, divorce, incorporation, and appellate law. Certainly, I would prefer to be writing those plays which someday may succeed the stature of George Bernard Shaw, with all humility and respect. Yet, that is impossible in terms of time demand to accomplish seeing that my competing goals include enjoying life, raising two sons, and engaging in the daily advocacy and clash of opponent upon opponent in the courtroom arena.

"Practice the craft? That is precisely what is afforded when writing law practice manuals. I am practicing the craft of ex-pressing ideas through writing, albeit in a professional communication. While it is much less eternal to be considered a great writer of legal books than it is to be considered a great writer, crafting professional literature offers that practice which is essential to [becoming], someday, a better writer.

"So, my advice for the aspiring writers who cannot find a publisher for their epic poetry, their great American novel, or their classic stageplay: I would advise that you continue plotting in those good directions; meanwhile, however, take every opportunity, including professional writing, to practice the craft!"

AVOCATIONAL INTERESTS: Jogging.

* * *

OFFER, Daniel 1930-

PERSONAL: Born December 24, 1930, in Berlin, Germany; son of Walter Hirsch (a physician) and Ilse (Meyer) Offer; married Judith Lynn Baskin (a research assistant), July 2, 1961 (died, 1976); married Marjorie Kaiz, August 19, 1979; children: Raphael, Tamar, Susan. *Education:* University of Rochester, B.A., 1953; University of Chicago, M.D., 1957. *Religion:* Jewish. *Home:* 1270 Ashbury St., Winnetka, Ill. 60093. *Office:* Michael Reese Hospital and Medical Center, 2959 South Cottage Grove Ave., Chicago, Ill. 60616.

CAREER: University of Illinois Research and Educational Hospital, Urbana, Ill., intern, 1958; Michael Reese Hospital and Medical Center, Institute for Psychosomatic and Psychiatric Research and Training, Chicago, Ill., resident, 1961-64, associate director, 1964-74, co-chairman of Psychiatric Institute, 1974-77, chairman of department of psychiatry, 1977—. Consultant for Illinois Department of Mental Health. *Military service:* Israeli Army, 1948-50.

MEMBER: American Society for Adolescent Psychiatry (president, 1972-73), Illinois Psychiatric Society (chairman of membership committee, 1965-66), Chicago Society for Adolescent Psychiatry (secretary-treasurer, 1964-67; president, 1968-69), Institute of Medicine (fellow). *Awards, honors:* Center for Advanced Study of Education fellow.

WRITINGS: (With M. Sabshin) *Normality: Theoretical and Clinical Concepts of Mental Health,* Basic Books, 1966; (with Sabshin) *The Psychological World of the Teenager: A Study of Normal Adolescent Boys,* Basic Books, 1969.

(Editor with J. F. Masterson) *Teaching and Learning Adolescent Psychiatry,* C. C Thomas, 1971; (editor with D. X. Freedman) *Modern Psychiatry and Clinical Research: Essays in Honor of Roy R. Grinker, Sr.,* Basic Books, 1972; (with wife, Judith Offer) *From Teenage to Young Manhood,* Basic Books, 1975; (with R. C. Marohn and E. Ostrov) *The Psychological World of the Juvenile Delinquent,* Basic Books, 1979; (with Ostrov and K. I. Howard) *The Adolescent: A Psychological Self-Portrait,* Basic Books, 1981. Editor-in-chief, *Journal of Youth and Adolescence.*

AVOCATIONAL INTERESTS: Music, fishing.

* * *

OKUN, Arthur M. 1928-1980

PERSONAL: Born November 28, 1928, in Jersey City, N.J.; died March 23, 1980, in Washington, D.C.; son of Louis and Rose (Cantor) Okun; married Suzanne Grossman, July 1, 1951; children: Lewis Edward, Matthew James, Steven John. *Education:* Columbia University, A.B., 1949, Ph.D., 1956.

CAREER: Yale University, New Haven, Conn., instructor, 1952-56, assistant professor, 1956-60, associate professor, 1960-63, professor of economics, 1963-67, staff member of Cowles Foundation for Research in Economics, 1956-57; Council of Economic Advisers, Washington, D.C., staff economist, 1961-62, member of council, 1964-68, chairman, 1968-69; Brookings Institution, Washington, D.C., senior fellow, 1969-80. Consultant, Donaldson, Lufkin & Jenrette, beginning 1969, and American Security & Trust Company, beginning 1970. *Member:* American Statistical Association (fellow), American Academy of Arts and Sciences (fellow), Econometric Society (fellow), American Economic Association (vice-president, 1972), Phi Beta Kappa. *Awards, honors:* M.A., Yale University, 1963; Medal for Excellence, Columbia University, 1968; McKinsey Foundation Book Award, 1970, for *The Political Economy of Prosperity*.

WRITINGS—Published by Brookings Institution, except as indicated: (Editor and author of introduction) *The Battle against Unemployment: An Introduction to a Current Issue of Public Policy*, Norton, 1965, 3rd edition (with Martin Bailey), 1982; (with Henry M. Fowler and Milton Gilbert) *Inflation: The Problems It Creates and the Policies It Requires*, New York University Press, 1970; *The Political Economy of Prosperity*, 1970; *Rules and Roles for Fiscal and Monetary Policy*, 1971; *Political Economy: Some Lessons of Recent Experience*, 1972; *Equality and Efficiency: The Big Tradeoff*, 1975; (editor with George L. Perry) *Curing Chronic Inflation*, 1978; *Prices and Quantities: A Macroeconomic Analysis*, 1981.

Contributor to journals. Co-editor, *Brookings Papers on Economic Activity*, beginning 1970. Editor, *Yale Economic Essays*, 1963-64.

SIDELIGHTS: Economist Arthur M. Okun was widely known for his formulation of Okun's Law, which provides the mathematical relationship between the rate of unemployment and the gross national product (GNP). According to this law, the unemployment rate drops one percent for every three percent rise in the GNP. Okun's Law is now widely used in economic analysis and forecasting.

OBITUARIES: Washington Post, March 24, 1980; *New York Times*, March 24, 1980; *Chicago Tribune*, March 25, 1980; *Times* (London), March 25, 1980; *Newsweek*, April 7, 1980; *Time*, April 7, 1980.†

*   *   *

OLSEN, Edward G(ustave) 1908-

PERSONAL: Born March 26, 1908, in Portland, Ore.; son of Gustav Adolph (a merchant) and Emma (Bush) Olsen; married Faith Theresa Elliott, June 25, 1931 (died, 1947); married Pauline Walsh (a teacher), September 11, 1948; children: (first marriage) Marvin Elliott, Marica Evelyn (Mrs. Edward Kolar); (second marriage) Douglas Walsh. *Education:* Pacific University, A.B., 1930; Columbia University, M.A., 1932, Ed.D., 1937; Union Theological Seminary, B.D., 1933. *Politics:* Independent. *Religion:* Unitarian. *Home:* 317 Memory Lane, Brookings, Ore. 97415.

CAREER: Colgate University, Hamilton, N.Y., instructor in education and acting chairman of the department, 1936-41; Russell Sage College, Troy, N.Y., associate professor of education and director of School of Education, 1941-45; Office of Washington State Superintendent of Public Instruction, director of school and community relations, 1945-50; University of Texas, Austin, associate professor of educational adminis-

tration, 1950-51; National Conference of Christians and Jews, Chicago, Ill., director of education, 1951-66; California State University at Hayward, professor of education, 1966-73, professor emeritus, 1973—. Visiting professor at Georgia State Teachers College, University of Washington, College of William and Mary, Western Washington State College (now Western Washington University), University of Maine, and Stanford University. Fulbright lecturer at University College of Rhodesia and Nyasaland, 1958. President, Council on Human Relations, Park Ridge, Ill., 1963-65; executive secretary, Washington State Coordinating Council for UNESCO; director of several workshops on community resources and human relations.

MEMBER: National Education Association (life), National Community Education Association, City Club (Chicago; member of board of governors, 1955-62; vice-president, 1960), Kappa Delta Pi, Phi Delta Kappa, Blue Key Club, Rotary Club. *Awards, honors:* Thomas H. Wright Award of City of Chicago for work in human relations education, 1957; distinguished service award, National Community School Education Association, 1969; life membership award, National Community Education Association, 1979.

WRITINGS: (Editor and compiler) *School and Community*, Prentice-Hall, 1945, revised edition, 1954; (editor) *School and Community Programs*, Prentice-Hall, 1949; (editor) *The Modern Community School*, Appleton, 1953; (editor) *The School and Community Reader: Education in Perspective*, Macmillan, 1963; *One Moment in Time: The Ancestry and Life Records of Edward Gustave Olsen*, Photolith (Portland, Ore.), 1976; (with Phillip A. Clark) *Life-Centering Education*, Pendell, 1977; *Then till Now in Brookings-Harbor: A Social History of the Chetco Community Area*, Rotary Club of Brookings, Ore., 1979. Contributor to professional journals.

SIDELIGHTS: Edward G. Olsen told *CA* that his philosophy of education developed through more than forty-three years of research, teaching and writing: "The goal of Education should be to improve the quality of human living, both as individuals and in group life on this planet. The school curriculum must be centered in the enduring life concerns of humankind, oriented to the future yet ever aware of the relevant past in relation to present human needs."

School and Community has been published in Spanish and Japanese.

BIOGRAPHICAL/CRITICAL SOURCES: Edward G. Olsen, *One Moment in Time: The Ancestry and Life Records of Edward Gustave Olsen*, Photolith (Portland, Ore.), 1976.

*   *   *

OPTON, Edward M., Jr. 1936-

PERSONAL: Born June 12, 1936, in New York, N.Y.; son of Edward M. and Carolyn (Brown) Opton; married, March 23, 1963. *Education:* Yale University, B.A., 1957; Duke University, Ph.D., 1964; University of California, Berkeley, J.D., 1977. *Office:* Office of the General Counsel, University of California, 2200 University Ave., Berkeley, Calif. 94720.

CAREER: North Carolina College at Durham (now North Carolina Central University), visiting instructor in psychology, 1962-63; University of California, Berkeley, assistant research psychologist, 1963-66, associate research psychologist and lecturer, 1966-69; The Wright Institute, Berkeley, senior research psychologist and associate dean of Graduate School, 1969-77;

Morrison & Foerster (law firm), San Francisco, Calif., attorney, 1977-81; University of California, Berkeley, assistant counsel, 1981—. Lecturer in psychology at San Francisco State College (now San Francisco State University), 1965. *Member:* American Psychological Association, Society for Psychophysiological Research, American Bar Association, Bar Association of San Francisco.

WRITINGS: (Contributor) C. D. Spielberger, editor, *Anxiety and Behavior*, Academic Press, 1966; (editor with R. S. Lazarus) *Personality* (readings), Penguin, 1967; (contributor) *Advances in Psychological Assessment*, Science and Behavior Books, 1968; (with Alan Scheflin) *The Mind Manipulators*, Paddington, 1978. Contributor to *Psychosomatic Medicine, Journal of Gerontology, Psychophysiology*, and other journals.

*　　*　　*

OSGOOD, Don(ald W.) 1930-

PERSONAL: Born November 15, 1930, in Brookdale, N.Y.; son of Dennis Wright (a minister) and Clara (Parker) Osgood; married Joan Timpson (a musician), June 10, 1952; children: Kevin, Jeff, Drew, Trevor. *Education:* Attended Houghton College, Centenary College, University of Maryland, Long Island University, and C. W. Post College (now C. W. Post College of Long Island University). *Religion:* Christian. *Home:* Buck Hill Lane, Pound Ridge, N.Y. 10576. *Office:* IBM Corp., Management Development Center, Old Orchard Rd., Armonk, N.Y. 10504.

CAREER: Linotype setter, 1949-50; International Business Machines Corp. (IBM), Kingston, N.Y., staff member in personnel department, 1956-60, manager of Personnel Board and Benefits Administration, Bethesda, Md., 1961-62, personnel representative at Federal Systems Center, Bethesda, 1963-64, manager for management development at Federal Systems Center, Washington, D.C., 1965-67, founder and program manager-director of Southeast Management School, Warrenton, Va., 1967-68, program manager at Management School in Glen Cove, N.Y., and Sands Point, N.Y., 1969-72, district personnel manager and program manager for management development in Data Processing Division, Kansas City, Kan., 1972, program manager of personnel planning at World Trade Corp., New York City, 1973, program manager of education in Systems Development and Systems Communications Divisions, White Plains, N.Y., beginning 1974, became program manager of Community Executive Programs, White Plains, program manager and curriculum development manager for Management Development Center, Armonk, N.Y., 1983—.

Executive director of Career Performance Group; director of Management Strategies International. Management consultant; has appeared on national television and radio talk shows; has spoken before corporate groups and professional organizations. Adjunct instructor at Marymount College; visiting faculty member at American Management Association. Co-founder of Aspen Hill Wesleyan Church, Rockville, Md.; president of Onteora Council for Release Time Christian Education. Member of advisory boards of New York City Bowery Mission and Children's Home. *Military service:* U.S. Air Force, 1951-55. *Member:* American Society for Training and Development. *Awards, honors:* IBM outstanding contribution award, 1970, for conducting management education.

WRITINGS: The Family and the Corporation Man, Harper, 1975; *Pressure Points: The Christian's Response to Stress*, Christian Herald, 1978, revised edition published as *Pressure*

Points: How to Deal with Stress, 1980; *Thirty Days to a Less Stressful You*, Christian Herald, 1980; *The Back Country Church: There Is Spirit in Our History*, privately printed, 1982. Contributor to *Personnel*.

AVOCATIONAL INTERESTS: Sailing, swimming, camping, jogging, reading.

*　　*　　*

OSMAN, Jack D(ouglas) 1943-

PERSONAL: Born January 26, 1943, in Philadelphia, Pa.; son of William Henry and Eva Mae (Given) Osman; married Beverly Kelly, August 22, 1981; children: (previous marriage) Scott Allen, Brooks Douglas. *Education:* West Chester State College, B.S., 1965; University of Maryland, M.A., 1967; Ohio State University, Ph.D., 1971. *Home:* 201 Wilden Ave., Towson, Md. 21204. *Office:* Department of Health Science, Towson State University, Baltimore, Md. 21204.

CAREER: High school teacher of health education in Washington, D.C., 1967-69; Ohio State University, Columbus, instructor in health education, 1969-71; Towson State University, Baltimore, Md., associate professor, 1971-77, professor of health science, 1977—. President, Fat Control, Inc. Associate of Sex Information and Education Council of the United States. *Member:* Association for the Advancement of Health Education, American School Health Association (fellow), American Association of Sex Educators and Counselors, Nutrition Today Society, Society for Nutrition Education, Maryland Association for Higher Education.

WRITINGS: (Contributor) Howard Kirschenbaum and Sidney B. Simon, editors, *Readings in Values Clarification*, Winston Press, 1973; (with Clint E. Bruess) *Nutrition Teaching Manual for Allied Health Workers in India*, Johns Hopkins University, 1973; *Thin from Within*, Hart Publishing, 1976, vegetarian edition, Review & Herald, 1981; *American Medical Joggers Association Runner's Daily Diary*, American Medical Joggers Association, 1979; *The Fat Control Program*, Fat Control, Inc., 1982.

Also author of 6 filmstrips on nutrition and weight control, Photo Lab. Contributor to *Journal of School Health, Health Education, Nutrition News, Instructor*, and other publications.

SIDELIGHTS: Jack D. Osman writes: "After spending four-and-a-half years in high school (during which time I flunked English three times), I realized that I didn't enjoy learning and desired to join the teaching force and do my part to change education from within. I believe that an effective educator entertains through subject matter, enabling learning to 'sneak' into one's head."

AVOCATIONAL INTERESTS: Photography, developing multimedia presentations, fitness (jogging, cycling, walking), camping, "learning and living life to its fullest; playing the guitar and composing health and spiritual songs."

*　　*　　*

OTTO, Wayne (R.) 1931-

PERSONAL: Born October 22, 1931, in Fremont, Wis.; son of Henry F. (a mechanic) and Edna (Wohlt) Otto; married Shirley Bergen (an administrative assistant), October 13, 1953 (divorced, 1978); children: Eleni. *Education:* Wisconsin State College at River Falls (now University of Wisconsin—River Falls), B.S., 1953; University of Wisconsin, M.S., 1958, Ph.D.,

1961. *Politics:* Independent. *Religion:* Eclectic. *Home:* 4161 Cherokee Dr., Madison, Wis. 53711. *Office:* Department of Curriculum and Instruction, University of Wisconsin, 225 North Mills St., Madison, Wis. 53706.

CAREER: University of Oregon, Eugene, assistant professor of education, 1961-64; University of Georgia, Athens, associate professor of education, 1964-65; University of Wisconsin—Madison, professor of education, 1965—, associate director, 1975-76, and co-director, 1976-80, of Research and Development Center. Senior researcher, Institute for Research on Teaching, Michigan State University, 1976-80. *Military service:* U.S. Marine Corps, 1953-55; became sergeant. *Member:* International Reading Association, National Reading Conference, American Educational Research Association, American Reading Forum.

WRITINGS: (With Richard J. Smith) *Corrective and Remedial Teaching,* Houghton, 1966, third edition, 1980; (with David Ford) *Teaching Adults to Read,* Houghton, 1967; (with Karl Koenke) *Remedial Teaching,* Houghton, 1969; (with Smith) *Administering the School Reading Program,* Houghton, 1970; *Focused Reading Instruction,* Addison-Wesley, 1975; *New Linguistic Readers,* Bobbs-Merrill, 1975; *Speedway: The Action Way to Speed Read,* HyCite, 1975, revised edition, 1980.

(With Robert D. Chester) *Objective Based Reading,* Addison-Wesley, 1976; (editor with others) *Reading Problems: A Multidisciplinary Approach,* Addison-Wesley, 1977; *DELTA: An Adaptation of the Wisconsin Design for Disabled Readers,* 1977; (with others) *Steck-Vaughn Adult Reading: A Sequential Program,* Steck, 1978; (with Smith and Lee Hanson) *The School Reading Program,* Houghton, 1978; (with Robert Rude and Dixie Spiegel) *How to Teach Reading,* Addison-Wesley, 1979; (editor with Sandra White) *Reading Expository Material,* Academic Press, 1982. Also author of *Wisconsin Design for Reading Skill Development,* National Computer Systems, 1971-77. Executive editor, *Journal of Educational Research.*

WORK IN PROGRESS: With Eunice Askov, *Corrective Reading in the Classroom,* for Bobbs-Merrill.

P

P.L.K.
   See KIRK-GREENE, Anthony (Hamilton Millard)

* * *

PAGE, Eleanor
   See COERR, Eleanor (Beatrice)

* * *

PANNENBERG, Wolfhart (Ulrich) 1928-

PERSONAL: Born October 2, 1928, in Stettin, Germany (now Szczecin, Poland); son of Kurt Bernhard Siegfried (a customs officer) and Irmgard (Kersten) Pannenberg; married Hilke Schuette, May 3, 1954. *Education:* Attended Universities of Berlin, Goettingen, Basel, and Heidelberg, 1947-53; University of Heidelberg, Dr. theol., 1953. *Home:* 8 Sudetenstrasse, Graefelfing, Germany 8032. *Office:* University of Munich, 3 Schellingstrasse, Munich, Germany 8000.

CAREER: Professor of systematic theology at University of Heidelberg, Heidelberg, Germany, 1955-58, Kirchliche Hochschule Wuppertal, Wuppertal, Germany, 1958-61, University of Mainz, Mainz, Germany, 1961-67, and University of Munich, Munich, Germany, 1967—. Visiting professor at University of Chicago, 1963, Harvard University, 1966-67, ₂ ₂ Claremont School of Theology, 1967 and 1975. *Member:* Bavarian Academy of Science. *Awards, honors:* D.D. theol., University of Glasgow, 1972, University of Manchester, 1977, and University of Dublin, 1979.

WRITINGS: Die Praedestinationslehre des Duns Skotus, Vandenhoeck & Ruprecht, 1954; (editor with Rolf Rendtorff and others) *Offenbarung als Geschichte,* Vandenhoeck & Reprecht, 1961, 5th edition, 1982, translation by David Granskou published as *Revelation as History,* Macmillan, 1969; *Was ist der Mensch?: Die Anthropologie der Gegenwart im Lichte der Theologie,* Vandenhoeck & Ruprecht, 1962, translation published as *What Is Man?,* Fortress, 1970; (editor with Wilfried Joest) *Dogma und Denkstrukturen,* Vandenhoeck & Ruprecht, 1963; *Grundzuege der Christologie,* Guetersloher Verlagshaus Gerd Mohn, 1964, translation by Lewis L. Wilkins and Duane A. Priebe published as *Jesus: God and Man,* Westminster, 1968; *Grundfragen Systematischer Theologie,* Vandenhoeck & Ruprecht, Volume I, 1967, Volume II, 1980, translation by

George Kehm published as *Basic Questions in Theology,* Fortress, Volume I, 1970, Volume II, 1971; *Theology and the Kingdom of God,* Westminster, 1969.

(With Avery Dulles and Carl E. Braaten) *Spirit, Faith, and Church,* Westminster, 1970; (with A.M.K. Mueller) *Erwaegungen Zur Theologie der Natur,* Guetersloher Verlagshaus Gerd Mohn, 1970; *Thesen Zur Theologie der Kirche,* Claudius, 1970; *Das Glaubensbekenntnis,* Siebenstern, 1972; translation by Margaret Kohl published as *The Apostles' Creed in the Light of Today's Questions,* Westminster, 1972; *Gottesgedanke und Menschliche Freiheit,* Vandenhoeck & Ruprecht, 1972, translation by R. H. Wilson published as *The Idea of God and Human Freedom,* Westminster, 1972; *Wissenschafts theorie und Theologie,* Suhrkamp, 1973, translation by Francis McDonagh published as *Theology and Philosophy of Science,* Westminster, 1976; *Human Nature, Election, and History,* Westminster, 1977; *Ethik und Ekklesiologie,* Vandenhoeck & Ruprecht, 1977, translation by Keith Crim published in two volumes, Westminster, Volume I: *Ethics,* 1981, Volume II: *The Church,* 1983.

Theological Issues in Christian Spirituality, Westminster, 1983; (contributor) *Anthropologie in Theologisher Perspective,* Vandenhoeck & Ruprecht, 1983. Contributor to anthologies. Co-editor of *Kerygma und Dogma.*

BIOGRAPHICAL/CRITICAL SOURCES: James M. Robinson and John B. Cobb, editors, *New Frontiers in Theology,* Harper, 1967; Carl E. Braaten, *History and Hermeneutics,* Westminster, 1967; *Christian Century,* March 19, 1969; *Encounter,* summer, 1969; Ignace Berten, *Die Theologie Wolfhart Pannenberg,* Claudius, 1970, translation by E. Frank Tupper published as *The Theology of Wolfhart Pannenberg,* Westminster, 1973; Allan D. Galloway, *Wolfhart Pannenberg,* Allen & Unwin, 1973.

* * *

PAREEK, Udai (Narain) 1925-

PERSONAL: Born January 21, 1925, in Jaipur, India; son of Vijailal and Gaindi Pareek; married Rama Sharma, May 13, 1945; children: Sushama, Surabhi, Anagat. *Education:* St. John's College, Agra, India, B.A., 1944; Teachers Training College, Ajmer, India, B.T., 1945; Calcutta University, M.A., 1950; Agra University, M.A., 1952; University of Delhi, Ph.D.,

397

1956. *Home:* Mohalla Madara, Chaukri Topkhana Desh, Jaipur, India. *Office:* Indian Institute of Management, Ahmedabad 380015, India.

CAREER: Teachers Training School, Jaipur, India, teacher of psychology, 1945-48; Teachers Training College, Bikaner, India, lecturer in psychology, 1953-54; Delhi School of Social Work, Delhi, India, lecturer in psychology, 1954-55; National Institute of Basic Education, New Delhi, India, psychologist, 1956-62; Indian Agricultural Research Institute, New Delhi, psychologist, 1962-64; Small Industry Extension Training Institute, Hyderabad, India, director of extension education, 1964-66; University of North Carolina at Chapel Hill, visiting associate professor of psychology, 1966-68; National Institute of Health Administration and Education, New Delhi, professor of social sciences, 1968-70; University of Udaipur, Udaipur, India, director of School of Basic Sciences and Humanities and dean of faculty of social sciences, 1970-73; Indian Institute of Management, Ahmedabad, India, Larsen and Toubro Professor of Organisational Behaviour, 1973—.

Member of the governing board, Centre for Entrepreneurship Development, National Institute of Motivational and Institutional Development, and Learning Systems; member of advisory committee, Family Planning Foundation of India and Survey of Research in Psychology of the Indian Council of Social Science Research. *Member:* Indian Psychological Association, American Psychological Association, American Sociological Association, Psychometric Society, Society for the Psychological Study of Social Issues, National Training Laboratories (fellow), Madras Psychological Association, Andhra Pradesh Psychological Association (president, 1964-66). *Awards, honors:* Escorts Award, 1981, for *Designing and Managing Human Resource Systems.*

WRITINGS: Developmental Patterns in Reaction to Frustration, Asia Publishing House (Bombay), 1964; (with S. R. Mittal) *A Guide to the Literature of Research Methodology in Behavioural Sciences,* Behavioural Sciences Centre (Delhi), 1965; (editor) *Studies in Rural Leadership,* Behavioural Sciences Centre, 1966; *Behavioural Science Research in India: A Directory, 1925-1965,* Acharan Sahkar, 1966; *A Guide to Indian Behavioural Science Periodicals,* Behavioural Sciences Centre, 1966; (with Rolf P. Lynton) *Training for Development,* Irwin, 1967; (with S. R. Devi and Saul Rosenzweig) *Manual of the Indian Adaptation of the Adult Form of the Rosenzweig P. F. Study,* Roopa Psychological Corp., 1968; (with Willis H. Griffin) *The Process of Planned Change in Education,* Somaiya, 1969.

Foreign Behavioural Research on India: A Directory of Research and Researchers, Acharan Sahkar, 1970; (with T. V. Rao) *A Status Study on Population Research in India,* Volume I, McGraw, 1974; (with Rao) *Handbook of Psychological and Social Instruments,* Samashti, 1974; (with Y. P. Singh and D. R. Arora) *Diffusion of an Interdiscipline,* Bookhive, 1974; (with Rao and Ravi Matthai) *Institution Building in Education and Research: From Stagnation to Self-Renewal,* All India Management Association, 1977; (with Rao) *Performance Appraisal and Review: Trainer's Manual, Operating Manual, and Skills Workbook,* Learning Systems, 1978; (with Rao) *Developing Entrepreneurship,* Learning Systems, 1978.

Survey of Psychological Research in India, 1971-1976, Popular Prakashan, Part 1, 1980, Part 2, 1982; (with Rao) *Designing and Managing Human Resource Systems,* Oxford University Press, 1981; *Beyond Management: Essays on the Processes of Institution Building,* Oxford University Press, 1981; (with Rao

and D. M. Pestonjee) *Behavioural Processes in Organisations,* Oxford University Press, 1981; (with Rao) *Developing Motivation through Experiencing,* Oxford University Press, 1982; (with Rao) *Handbook for Trainees in Educational Management,* UNESCO Regional Office for Education in Asia and the Pacific, 1981; (with Somnath Chattopadhyay) *Managing Organisational Change,* Oxford University Press, 1982; *Managing Conflict and Collaboration,* Oxford University Press, 1982; *Education and Rural Development in Asia,* Oxford University Press, 1982; *Role Stress Scales,* Navin Publishers, 1982; *Role Pics: Coping with Role Stress,* Navin Publishers, 1982; *The Internal Manager,* Navin Publishers, 1983; *Influence Styles,* Navin Publishers, 1983; *Readings in Human Processes,* Navin Publishers, 1983.

Contributor: Charni P. Sinha, editor, *Consultants and Consulting Styles,* Vision Books, 1979; Harry C. Triandis and John W. Berry, editors, *Handbook of Cross-Cultural Psychology,* Volume II, Allyn & Bacon, 1980; J. W. Pfeiffer and J. E. Jones, editors, *The 1980 Annual Handbook for Group Facilitators,* University Associates, 1980; R. S. Dwivedi, editor, *Manpower Management,* Prentice-Hall (India), 1980; J. E. Jones and J. W. Pfeiffer, editors, *The 1981 Annual for Group Facilitators,* University Associates, 1981; Dwivedi, editor, *Dynamics of Human Behaviour at Work,* Oxford University Press, 1981; Pfeiffer and L. D. Goodstein, editors, *The 1982 Annual for Facilitators, Trainers, and Consultants,* University Associates, 1982.

Editor, *Indian Psychological Abstracts* and *Manas.* Member of editorial board, *Psychologie, Managerial Psychology, Group and Organization Studies, Psychological Panorama,* and *New Trends in Education.*

*   *   *

PARK, Jordan
See POHL, Frederik

*   *   *

PARKER, Dorothy Mills

PERSONAL: Born in Jacksonville, Fla.; daughter of George Wiley and Lidie V. (Clark) Mills; married Robert Wallace Parker (divorced). *Education:* Attended Florida State University and American University. *Politics:* Democrat. *Religion:* Episcopalian.

CAREER: St. Columba's Episcopal Church, Washington, D.C., parish and press secretary, 1959-70; Wesley Theological Seminary, Washington, D.C., academic secretary to the dean, 1970-81. Member, Episcopal Diocese of Washington, Department of Information, 1965-66. *Member:* National Society of Colonial Dames of America, National Cathedral Association, English-Speaking Union, Washington Cathedral Choral Society (former member of board of directors and press officer), Junior League of Washington (former member board of directors).

WRITINGS: (Compiler and editor) *Lee Chronicle: Studies of the Early Generations of the Lees of Virginia,* New York University Press, 1957; *The Prayer Book Issue,* Prayer Book Society, 1978; *In Praise of Music,* Washington Cathedral, 1982. Washington correspondent, *American Church News,* 1958-70, and *Living Church,* 1968—. Columnist, *Georgetowner,* 1956-57. Contributor to *Cathedral Age, Washington Evening Star, Washington Post,* and other publications.

WORK IN PROGRESS: Tracts, stories, and articles for Episcopal publications.

SIDELIGHTS: Motivated by "the plea of Episcopal lay people for an exposition they could understand," Dorothy Mills Parker wrote *The Prayer Book Issue*, an examination of this controversy. *Avocational interests:* Music (especially Renaissance and Baroque), heraldry, illuminated manuscripts, antiques, English history.

* * *

PARKER, Lois M(ay) 1912-

PERSONAL: Born April 18, 1912, in Nebraska; daughter of William A. (a field man for a beet sugar company) and Mamie (a teacher; maiden name, Durnin) Nelson; married William Allen Parker (a rancher), December 25, 1935 (deceased); children: Joan Parker Yeatts, George, Ellen Parker Dietel, William Allen, Jr. *Education:* Attended Scottsbluff Junior College, 1929-30, and Hastings College, 1930-31; St. Luke's Hospital School of Nursing, R.N., 1934; graduate study at Oregon Medical School (now Oregon Health Sciences University), 1954, and Walla Walla College, 1965-67. *Religion:* Seventh-day Adventist. *Home:* 704 Southeast Date Ave., College Place, Wash. 99324.

CAREER: Free-lance writer. St. Luke's Hospital, Denver, Colo., night ward supervisor, 1935; St. Valentine's Hospital, Wendell, Idaho, night nurse, 1941; Lake City General Hospital, Coeur d'Alene, Idaho, night nurse, 1950-53; public health nurse in Coeur d'Alene, 1953-55; Community Hospital, Bonners Ferry, Idaho, night nurse, 1956-64; Tri-Cities Junior Academy, Pasco, Wash., teacher of English, 1966-68. *Awards, honors:* Best juvenile manuscript of the year award from Review & Herald, 1958, for *Yellow Cat of Cottonwood Creek*.

WRITINGS—For young people, except as indicated; published by Review & Herald, except as indicated: *Brave Heart*, 1958; *Yellow Cat of Cottonwood Creek*, 1959, reprinted, 1976; *Quack-Quack and Duck-Duck*, 1961; (with Gerald R. Nash) *Investment, the Miracle Offering* (adult), Pacific Press Publishing Association, 1965; *A New Friend for Kelly*, 1966; *Once Upon a Summer*, 1970; *Thee, Patience* (on the first Quakers in Rhode Island), edited by Bobbie J. Van Dolson, illustrations by Vick Taylor, 1974; *Princess of the Two Lands* (on the Exodus from the Egyptian point of view), illustrations by Bill Meyers, Southern Publishing, 1975; *Duncan, Son of Malcolm*, Southern Publishing, 1977; *Brothers of the Longhouse*, edited by Thomas A. Davis, illustrations by Terry Crews, 1979; *They of Rome*, Southern Publishing, 1980; *Crusader Conspiracy*, 1983; *Miracle at Jamestown*, 1984. Contributor of more than one hundred poems and articles to adult and juvenile church publications, and to *Life and Health*.

SIDELIGHTS: Lois M. Parker writes: "I started writing for my own entertainment, and for my children, who loved 'ancestor stories,' ranch and animal adventures, and nursing experiences. [The] last two provided most of the material for [my] shorter published material. I have written mostly family history, or fictionalized history for children and young adults. Have always enjoyed history so much it seems a shame that many young people think it dull. Hence I try to show that it is made of real people, exciting, and very much related to us."

AVOCATIONAL INTERESTS: Travel (including England), birdwatching, living in her small cabin in the woods.

* * *

PARMET, Herbert S. 1929-

PERSONAL: Surname is accented on second syllable; born September 28, 1929, in New York, N.Y.; son of Isaac and Fanny (Scharf) Parmet; married John Kronish (a public school teacher), September 12, 1948; children: Wendy Ellen. *Education:* Oswego State Teachers College (now State University of New York College at Oswego), B.A., 1951; Queens College (now Queens College of the City University of New York), M.A., 1957; Columbia University, graduate study, 1957-62. *Politics:* Democrat. *Home:* 18-40 211th St., Bayside, N.Y. 11360. *Office:* Department of History, Queensborough Community College, Bayside, N.Y. 11364.

CAREER: Teacher in North Babylon, N.Y., 1951-54; Mineola High School, Mineola, N.Y., teacher, 1954-68, chairman of department of social studies, 1961-68; Queensborough Community College, Bayside, N.Y., assistant professor, 1968-73, associate professor, 1973-75, professor, 1975-83, distinguished professor of history, 1983—. Part-time instructor, Fairleigh Dickinson University, 1958-64. *Military service:* U.S. Army, 1952-54. *Member:* Academy of Political Science.

WRITINGS: (With Marie B. Hecht) *Aaron Burr: Portrait of an Ambitious Man*, Macmillan, 1967; (with Hecht) *Never Again: A President Runs for a Third Term*, Macmillan, 1968; (contributor) James Moran, editor, *Our Presidents*, Macmillan, 1969.

Eisenhower and the American Crusades, Macmillan, 1972; (contributor) Frank Merli and Theodore Wilson, editors, *Makers of American Diplomacy*, Scribner, 1974; (contributor) Philip Dolce and George Skau, editors, *The Presidency*, Scribner, 1976; *The Democratic Umbrella: The Years after FDR*, Macmillan, 1976; *Jack: The Struggles of John F. Kennedy*, Dial, 1980; *J.F.K.: The Presidency of John F. Kennedy*, Dial, 1982.

Contributor to *New York Times Book Review*, *Chicago Tribune*, *American Historical Review*, *Newsday*, *New York Historical Society Quarterly*, and other publications.

SIDELIGHTS: The life of John F. Kennedy is chronicled in Herbert S. Parmet's *Jack: The Struggles of John F. Kennedy*, which covers the period up until the 1960 presidential election, and *J.F.K.: The Presidency of John F. Kennedy*, which covers his years as president. Reviewing *Jack* for the *New York Review of Books*, Ronald Steel calls it "a serious and scrupulously researched work [that] for the first time puts the Kennedy story into perspective." Steve Neal of the *Chicago Tribune Book World* finds *J.F.K.* "a balanced and comprehensive study that contains more than a few surprises."

The many books written about Kennedy can be divided into three phases, Neal contends. The first phase of books were by those who admired Kennedy, the second by those who faulted him, and "with his painstaking research, Parmet has launched the third phase of Kennedy studies, which will do much to shape history's verdict on J.F.K." Parmet's unbiased approach to Kennedy's life and achievements is applauded by Richard J. Margolis of the *New York Times Book Review*. "Parmet," he writes, "strikes a nice balance between romance and revision, between Camelot and the realities of Kennedy's 1,000 days in office." Steel explains that "a straightforward biography of the sort Parmet has done, without the gee-whizzes or the axe-grinding of earlier works on the subject, is a welcome relief."

Several critics point out that the primary strength of Parmet's biographies lies in the firsthand sources that he was able to utilize. "He has unearthed schoolmates and Navy friends who have not been interviewed before," writes Priscilla Johnson McMillan of the *Chicago Tribune Book World*, "has mined new information from earlier sources, and has made impressive use of oral history and other archives in the John F. Kennedy Library.'' ''Although Kennedy has been the subject of hundreds of books,'' Neal states, ''Parmet's treatment is fuller and richer because he has had more access to primary source material than earlier scholars.'' Jim Miller of *Newsweek* believes that ''the flavor of the era comes through vividly in a wealth of anecdotes, many culled from firsthand interviews and 'oral histories.''' McMillan praises Parmet's ''meticulous piling up of sources, allowing findings to emerge more or less as they will. . . . Precisely because of his restraint in making judgments, his conclusions carry all the more weight.''

The picture of Kennedy that emerges from Parmet's two books is of ''a finely tuned politician—young, glamorous, brilliant—who disappointed the expectations that he was so good at arousing,'' according to Margolis. Neal appraises Kennedy much the same way. ''Kennedy,'' he writes, ''will be remembered as an inspiring chief executive who promised much but delivered little [and yet,] with style and eloquence, the young president seemed to give the nation a sense of purpose that had been lacking since World War II.'' Neal points out, too, that because of his many health problems, Kennedy lived in almost constant pain, and ''for living with pain throughout his presidency,'' he concludes, ''Parmet also demonstrates that Kennedy was a real-life profile in courage.''

BIOGRAPHICAL/CRITICAL SOURCES: New York Times Book Review, October 22, 1972, July 11, 1976, July 27, 1980, April 17, 1983; *National Review*, May 28, 1976; *New Republic*, June 7, 1980; *Chicago Tribune Book World*, July 6, 1980, April 3, 1983; *Newsweek*, July 14, 1980, April 4, 1983; *New York Review of Books*, August 14, 1980; *Los Angeles Times Book Review*, April 17, 1983.

*   *   *

PASSEL, Anne W(onders)   1918-
(Anne Wonders)

PERSONAL: Born September 12, 1918, in Baltimore, Md.; daughter of Darcy V. (a lawyer) and Hazel (Miller) Wonders; married Howard B. Passel (a professor and artist), August 22, 1942; children: Paul H., Jonathan C. *Education:* Mount Holyoke College, A.B. (cum laude), 1940; University of the Pacific, M.A., 1964, Ph.D., 1967. *Office:* Department of English, California State College, 9001 Stockdale Hwy., Bakersfield, Calif. 93309.

CAREER: Former writer and editor for *Evening Post*, Charleston, S.C., *Philadelphia Inquirer*, Philadelphia, Pa., *Junior League* (magazine), McGraw-Hill, Inc., and Robbins Publishing Co.; former advertising copywriter in San Diego, Calif., and Washington, D.C.; University of the Pacific, Stockton, Calif., instructor, 1966-67, assistant professor of English, 1967-69; Fresno State College (now California State University, Fresno), Bakersfield Center, Bakersfield, Calif., associate professor of English, 1969-70; California State College, Bakersfield, associate professor, 1970-72, professor of English, 1972—. *Member:* National League of American Pen Women, Bronte Society (England), Phi Kappa Phi.

WRITINGS: Poems 68, Crafton Press, 1968; *Jane Eyre by Charlotte Bronte* (book notes), Barnes & Noble, 1969; *Poems 77*, Crafton Press, 1977; *Your Words: Public and Private*, University Press of America, 1977, 2nd edition, 1981; *The Learning Poets*, University Press of America, 1977; *April Seventeenth and Other Poems*, Atheneum, 1978; *Charlotte and*

Emily Bronte: An Annotated Bibliography, Garland Publishing, 1979; *Writing with Confidence*, Reprographics, 1980; *Sojourn in Paris and Other Stories*, Crafton Press, 1981; (editor) *Saturday Mornings*, Reprographics, 1981. Also author of *Poems 83*, 1983. Work represented in anthologies, including *Valley Light*, Poet and Printer Press, 1978, and *Nineteenth and Chester*, 1983. Contributor, sometimes under name Anne Wonders, of poems and reviews to small magazines.

WORK IN PROGRESS: Two novels, *Up Cycle* and *Impostors Just the Same;* two movie scripts for television, ''No Third Way'' and ''Wrong Man in the Picture.''

SIDELIGHTS: Anne W. Passel told *CA:* ''I am influenced and affected by the people I watch and listen to, especially those whose creative activity keeps them alive. For the last fifteen years, with rewarding regularity, I have been dealing with the basics of creativity in workshops for young poets and upcoming novelists. Every time I listen to students and other productive adults as they talk about what they hope to do in their writing, I find myself becoming a better writer. I hope this interchange never stops.''

*   *   *

PATTILLO, James W(ilson)   1937-

PERSONAL: Born April 17, 1937, in Robstown, Tex.; son of Reuben Terry (a grocer) and Ruby (Englert) Pattillo; married Susan Ann Tower, December 3, 1966; children: Kenneth, Teri, Tony. *Education:* St. Edward's University, B.S., 1958; Texas Technological College (now Texas Tech University), M.B.A., 1959; Louisiana State University, Ph.D., 1963. *Politics:* Independent. *Religion:* Roman Catholic. *Home:* 51199 Deer Path Dr., Granger, Ind.

CAREER: University of Southern California, Los Angeles, assistant professor, 1962-65, associate professor of accounting, 1965-67; Louisiana State University, Baton Rouge, 1967-74, began as associate professor, became professor of accounting and director of graduate studies of College of Business Administration; University of Notre Dame, Notre Dame, Ind., Peat Marwick Mitchell Professor of Accounting, 1974-78; Crowe, Chizek & Co., South Bend, Ind., manager, 1978-81; currently professor of accounting at Indiana University at South Bend. Staff accountant, Ernst & Ernst, Los Angeles, 1963-67. Certified public accountant in Texas, 1962, California, 1967, Indiana, 1975, and Michigan, 1983. Certified management accountant, 1975. *Member:* American Institute of Certified Public Accountants, National Association of Accountants, American Accounting Association, Institute of Internal Auditors, Financial Executives Institute, Institute of Management Accounting, Indiana CPA Society.

WRITINGS: Foundation of Financial Accounting, Louisiana State University Press, 1965; *A Guide to Accounting Instruction: Concepts and Practices*, American Accounting Association, 1968; (with Bruce Joplin) *Effective Accounting Reports*, Prentice-Hall, 1969; *Materiality in Financial Reporting*, Financial Executives Foundation, 1975; *Advanced Accounting*, Houghton, 1978; *Quality Control and Peer Review*, Wiley, 1983. Contributor to professional journals.

*   *   *

PAULSEN, Wolfgang   1910-

PERSONAL: Born September 21, 1910, in Duesseldorf, Germany; came to United States in 1938; son of Hans (a physician) and Luise (Hunaeus) Paulsen; married Herta Schindler, June 18, 1938; children: Judith. *Education:* Studied at Universities of Tuebingen, Bonn, Berlin, Leipzig, and Berne, 1930-34; University of Berne, Ph.D., 1934. *Home:* 49 Maplewood Dr., Amherst, Mass. 01002. *Office:* Department of Germanic Languages, University of Massachusetts, Amherst, Mass. 01002.

CAREER: Assistant lecturer at University of Durham, Durham, England, 1935-37, and University of Reading, Reading, England, 1937-38; assistant professor of modern languages at Southwestern College, Memphis, Tenn., 1938-43, and of German at University of Iowa, Iowa City, 1943-47; Smith College, Northampton, Mass., associate professor of German, 1947-53; State University of New York at Albany, assistant professor of German, 1953; University of Connecticut, Storrs, professor of German, 1954-66; University of Massachusetts, Amherst, professor of German, 1966—, head of department of Germanic languages, 1966-71. *Member:* Modern Language Association of America, American Association of Teachers of German, Schiller Gesellschaft.

WRITINGS: Expressionismus und Aktivismus, [Bern], 1935; (editor with Arno Schirokauer, and contributor) *Corona: Studies in Philology, In Celebration of the Eightieth Birthday of Samuel Singer,* Duke University Press, 1941; (with Fred L. Fehling) *Elementary German,* American Book Co., 1947, 3rd edition (with Fehling, A. Reh, and S. Bauchinger), Van Nostrand, 1971; (editor with Fehling) *Vagabunden,* Holt, 1950; (editor) Werner Bergengruen, *Der spanische Rosenstock— Schneider und sein Obelisk,* Norton, 1957.

Georg Kaiser, Max Niemeyer [Tuebingen], 1960; *"Die Ahnfrau": Zu Grillparzers frueher Dramatik,* Max Niemeyer, 1962; (editor and author of introduction and critical notes) Bonaventura, *Nachtwachen,* Reclam Verlag (Stuttgart), 1964; (editor) Franz Grillparzer, *Die Juedin von Toledo,* Reclam Verlag, 1966; (with S. J. Kapolowitt) *German Review Grammar,* Ronald, 1970; *Christoph Martin Wieland: Der Mensch und sein Werk in psychologischen Perspektiven,* Francke Verlag, 1975; *Eichendorff und sein Taugenichts: Die innere Problematik des Dichters in seinem Werk,* Francke Verlag, 1976; *Johann Elias Schlegel und die Komoedie,* Francke Verlag, 1977; *Der Expressionismus in der deutschen Literatur: Eine historische Darstellung Die Gruendlagen, Die Gatlungen,* Peter Lang Verlag (Bern/Frankfurt), 1982.

Also author of *Versuch ueber Rolf Bongs: Der Schriftsteller als Dichter,* Blaeschke Verlag (Darmstadt), *Wielands Aristipp als Roman,* K. Thomae, 1973, and *Versuch ueber Rolf Bongs: der Schriftsteller als Dichter,* Blaeschke, 1973. Also editor of and contributor to twelve volumes of conference proceedings, *Amherster Kolloquiem zur modernen deutschen Literatur,* Lothar Stiehm Verlag and Francke Verlag, beginning 1967. Contributor of about thirty articles to journals in America, Germany, and England. Co-editor and regular contributor, *Universitas* and *Germanistik* (German periodicals); editor of "Franco-German Studies: A Current Bibliography," in *Bulletin of Bibliography,* 1948-57.

*   *   *

PAYNE, Alma Smith
See RALSTON, Alma (Smith Payne)

*   *   *

PEARSON, Scott Roberts   1938-

PERSONAL: Born March 13, 1938, in Madison, Wis.; son of Carlyle Roberts (a physician and surgeon) and Edith Hope (Smith) Pearson; married Sandra Carol Anderson, September 12, 1962; children: Sarah Roberts, Elizabeth Hovden. *Education:* University of Wisconsin, B.S., 1961; University of Grenoble, Diploma, 1964; Johns Hopkins School of Advanced International Studies, M.A., 1965; Harvard University, Ph.D., 1969. *Home:* 691 Mirada Ave., Stanford, Calif. 94305. *Office:* Food Research Institute, Stanford University, Stanford, Calif. 94305.

CAREER: U.S. Peace Corps, teacher of African history and geography at Sokoto Training College, Sokoto, Nigeria, 1961-63; Stanford University, Food Research Institute, Stanford, Calif., assistant professor, 1968-74, associate professor, 1974-80, professor of economics, 1980—, associate director, 1977—. Staff economist, Commission on International Trade and Investment Policy, Washington, D.C., 1970-71. Consultant at intervals, U.S. Agency for International Development, 1965—, and International Bank for Reconstruction and Development, 1971—. *Military service:* U.S. Army Reserve, 1956-64.

MEMBER: American Economic Association, American Agricultural Economics Association, African Studies Association, Association for the Advancement of Agricultural Sciences in Africa, American Academy of Political and Social Science, Royal Economic Society, Phi Beta Kappa. *Awards, honors:* Research grant from Social Science Research Council and American Council of Learned Societies, 1971-72.

WRITINGS: Petroleum and the Nigerian Economy, Stanford University Press, 1970; (with John Cownie and others) *Commodity Exports and African Economic Development,* Heath, 1974; (with J. Dirck Stryker, Charles P. Humphreys, and others) *Rice in West Africa: Policy and Economics,* Stanford University Press, 1981; (with C. Peter Timmer and Walter P. Falcon) *Food Policy Analysis,* Johns Hopkins University Press, 1983; (with Falcon, William O. Jones, and others) *The Cassava Economy of Java,* Stanford University Press, in press.

Contributor: John D. Montgomery and Arthur Smithies, editors, *Public Policy,* Harvard University Press, 1966; Carl K. Eicher and Carl Leidholm, editors, *Growth and Development of the Nigerian Economy,* Michigan State University Press, 1970; E. W. Erickson and Leonard Waverman, editors, *The Energy Question,* University of Toronto Press, 1974.

Also contributor to journals in his field.

WORK IN PROGRESS: Research on the effects of Portuguese accession to the European Economic Community on Portuguese agriculture.

*   *   *

PELL, Arthur R.   1920-

PERSONAL: Born January 22, 1920, in New York, N.Y.; son of Harry and Rae (Meyers) Pell; married Erica Frost (a music teacher), May 19, 1946; children: Douglas, Hilary. *Education:* New York University, B.A., 1939, M.A., 1944; Cornell University, Professional Diploma, 1943; California Coast University, Ph.D., 1977. *Home and office:* 111 Dietz St., Hempstead, N.Y. 11550.

CAREER: Eagle Electric Manufacturing Co., Long Island, N.Y., personnel manager, 1946-50; North Atlantic Construction Co., New York City, personnel manager, 1950-53; Harper Associates (personnel consultants), New York City, vice-president, 1953-73; consultant in human resources management in Long Island, 1975—. Professor of management in evening classes,

City College of the City University of New York, 1947-67. Adjunct professor of management, New York University, 1960-81, and St. John's University, 1971-77. *Military service:* U.S. Army, 1942-46; became warrant officer. *Member:* American Society for Personnel Administration, American Society for Training and Development, National Association of Personnel Consultants.

WRITINGS: Placing Salesmen, Impact Publishers, 1963; (with Walter Patterson) *Fire Officers Guide to Leadership,* privately printed, 1963; *Placing Executives,* Impact Publishers, 1964; *Police Leadership,* C. C Thomas, 1967; (with Maxwell Harper) *How to Get the Job You Want after Forty,* Pilot Books, 1967; *Recruiting and Selecting Personnel,* Simon & Schuster, 1969.

(With Harper) *Starting and Managing an Employment Agency,* U.S. Small Business Administration, 1971; *Advancing Your Career* (home study program), Management Games Institute, 1971; *Recruiting, Training and Motivating Volunteer Workers,* Pilot Books, 1973; *Interviewing and Selecting Sales, Advertising and Marketing Personnel,* Personnel Publications, 1974, revised edition, 1981; *Be a Better Employment Interviewer,* Personnel Publications, 1974, revised edition, 1976; (with Wilma Rogalin) *Women's Guide to Management Positions,* Simon & Schuster, 1975; (with Albert Furbay) *The College Student Guide to Career Planning,* Simon & Schuster, 1975; *Managing through People,* Simon & Schuster, 1975; *Choosing a College Major: Business,* McKay, 1978; *Enrich Your Life the Dale Carnegie Way,* Dale Carnegie & Associates, 1979.

Interviewing and Selecting Engineering and Computer Personnel, Personnel Publications, 1980; (editor) Dale Carnegie, *How to Win Friends and Influence People,* revised edition (Pell was not associated with previous edition), Simon & Schuster, 1981; (with George Sadek) *Resumes for Engineers,* Simon & Schuster, 1982; *Interviewing and Selecting Financial and Data Processing Personnel,* Personnel Publications, 1982; *How to Sell Yourself on an Interview,* Simon & Schuster, 1982.

Also author of "Career Aid Pamphlets" series for Personnel Publications. Contributor of more than one hundred articles to trade and professional magazines, including syndicated newspaper series, "When Your Husband Loses His Job," 1971; columnist on personnel subjects, *Placement.*

WORK IN PROGRESS: Resumes for Computer Professionals, for Simon & Schuster; *Motivational Salesmanship,* for Dale Carnegie & Associates.

*   *   *

PELLETIER, Kenneth R.   1946-

PERSONAL: Born April 27, 1946, in New Hampshire; son of Roger N. (a designer) and Lucy B. Pelletier. *Education:* University of California, Berkeley, A.B., 1969, Ph.D., 1974; graduate study at University of Pennsylvania, 1969, and C. G. Jung Institute, Zurich, Switzerland, 1971-72. *Home:* 2259 Mastlands Dr., Piedmont, Calif. 94611. *Agent:* Robert Briggs Associates, P.O. Box 9, Mill Valley, Calif. 94941. *Office:* University of California, School of Medicine, 400 Parnassus Ave., A 405, San Francisco, Calif. 94143.

CAREER: University of California, Berkeley, intern in psychology clinic, 1971-74; San Francisco Veterans Administration Hospital, San Francisco, Calif., intern in department of psychiatry, 1973-74; Everett A. Gladman Memorial Hospital, Oakland, Calif., clinical psychologist, 1974—; University of California, School of Medicine, San Francisco, department of

psychiatry and Langley Porter Neuropsychiatric Institute, clinical instructor, 1974-78, assistant clinical professor, 1978—, department of medicine, assistant clinical professor, 1982—; Psychosomatic Medicine Clinic, Berkeley, director, 1976-81.

Licensed clinical psychologist in State of California, 1976—; registrant of Council for the National Register of Health Service Providers in Psychology, 1976—; certified biofeedback practitioner in the State of California, 1977—; registered provider for California State Psychological Health Plan, 1979—; certified biofeedback practitioner, Biofeedback Certification Institute of America, Biofeedback Society of America, 1979—. Assistant research psychologist at Langley Porter Neuropsychiatric Institute, School of Medicine, University of California, San Francisco, 1972-77 and 1974-76; research and clinical practice have been the subject of numerous national television programs, including the "Today" show, "Good Morning America," several segments of "ABC World News," and the award-winning British Broadcasting Corporation series "The Long Search." Program coordinator and instructor of psychology, psychiatry, and postgraduate medicine at University of California Extension Division, 1971—; program coordinator at Esalen Institute, Big Sur, 1971—; director of Institute for the Study of Consciousness, Berkeley, 1974-76; visiting assistant professor in department of public health, University of California, Berkeley, 1980—. Director of California Health and Medical Foundation, 1976—.

Member of board of directors of Center for Integral Medicine, University of California, Los Angeles, 1974—; member of professional advisory board of National Health Services, Inc., 1976—; member of advisory board of East-West Academy of Healing Arts, 1976—; member of Psychosocial Rehabilitation Committee, Northern California Cancer Program, 1976—; member of board of advisors, American Institute of Stress, 1981—, and Health Headways Foundation, 1982—; member of board of Institute for the Advancement of Health. Member of board of directors of Golden Gate National Recreation Area, United States Department of Interior, 1976-79; member of California Governor's Council on Wellness and Physical Fitness, 1980. Clinical consultant to research projects in departments of cardiology and psychiatry, School of Medicine, University of California, San Francisco, and the department of public health, University of California, Berkeley, both 1976-79; clinical consultant to research project at the Acupuncture Clinic in the department of anesthesiology, School of Medicine, University of California, Los Angeles, 1976-82; consultant to National Heart, Lung and Blood Institute, U.S. Department of Health and Human Services, 1979—; advisor to the National Institute of Mental Health, the Canadian Ministry of Health, and to many major corporations in the design of employee health programs.

MEMBER: American Association for the Advancement of Science, American Psychological Association (member of task force on Health Promotion and Prevention, 1981—), Academy of Psychosomatic Medicine, Society for Psychophysiological Research, Biofeedback Society of America, Association for Transpersonal Psychology, Association for Humanistic Psychology, American Holistic Medical Association (founding professional member, 1981—), The Society of Behavioral Medicine, American Association of Fitness Directors in Business and Industry, Western Psychological Association, Biofeedback Society of California (member of board of directors, 1974-76), Phi Beta Kappa. *Awards, honors:* Woodrow Wilson fellowship, 1969; recipient of grants from John E. Fetzer Foundation, 1974-75, Aletheia Foundation, 1974-75, Taylor Foundation, 1979-80, Dextra, Baldwin & McGonagle Foundation, 1980-82, Mary Minneapolis Foundation, 1980—, B. Crocker Foundation, 1981—, and Mott Foundation, 1981—.

WRITINGS—Published by Delacorte, except as indicated: (With C. Garfield) *Consciousness: East and West*, Harper, 1976; *Mind As Healer, Mind As Slayer: A Holistic Approach to Preventing Stress Disorders*, 1977; *Toward a Science of Consciousness*, 1978; *Holistic Medicine: From Stress to Optimum Health*, 1979; *Longevity: Fulfilling Our Biological Potential*, 1981; *Healthy People in Unhealthy Places: Stress and Fitness at Work*, 1983.

Contributor: Demetri Kanellakos and Jerome Lukas, editors, *The Psychobiology of Transcendental Meditation*, W. R. Benjamin, 1974; P. G. Zimbardo and F. L. Ruch, editors, *Psychology and Life*, Scott, Foresman, 1975; L. Domash, J. Farrow, and David Orme-Johnson, editors, *Scientific Research on Transcendental Meditation: Collected Papers*, Maharishi International University Press, 1976; (with A. E. Gladman and T. H. Mikuriya) *Handbook of Physiological Feedback*, Autogenic Systems, 1976; Gay Hendricks and James Fadiman, editors, *Transpersonal Education*, Prentice-Hall, 1976; Kenneth Blum, editor, *Social Psychology*, Basic Books, 1977; Dolores Krieger, editor, *The Persistent Reality*, Quest Books, 1977; Zimbardo and C. Maslach, editors, *Psychology for Our Times: Readings*, 2nd edition, Scott, Foresman, 1977; Orme-Johnson, editor, *Scientific Research on the Transcendental Meditation Program*, Volume I, MIU Press, 1977; Garfield, editor, *Stress and Survival: The Emotional Realities of Life-Threatening Illness*, Mosby, 1979; (author of introduction) D. Saltoon, *The Common Book of Consciousness*, Chronicle Books, 1979; (with E. Peper and B. Tandy) E. Peper, S. Ancoli, and M. Quinn, editors, *Mind/Body Integrations: Essential Readings in Biofeedback*, Plenum, 1979.

C. F. Wilson and D. L. Hall, editors, *Stress Management for Educators*, U.S. Department of Education, 1980; A. Hastings, Fadiman, and J. S. Gordon, editors, *Holistic Medicine: An Annotated Bibliography*, National Institute of Mental Health, 1980, published as *Health for the Whole Person*, Westview, 1980; K. Blum, J. Cull, and G. G. Meyer, editors, *Folk Healing and Herbal Medicine*, C. C Thomas, 1981; Bresler, J. Gordon, and D. Jaffe, editors, *Body, Mind, and Health: Toward an Integral Medicine*, National Institute of Mental Health, 1981; (author of introduction) C. F. Wilson and D. L. Hall, *Preventing Burnout in Education*, Wright Publishing Group, 1981; J. Manuso, editor, *Occupational Clinical Psychology*, Praeger, 1982; D. H. Shapiro, Jr., and R. N. Walsh, editors, *The Art and Science of Meditation: A Reader*, Aldine, 1982.

Contributor to *Collier's Encyclopedia*, Macmillan, 1977; contributor to University of California School of Medicine *Extension Division Catalog*, 1976; contributor to proceedings of biofeedback societies, including Biofeedback Research Society, 1974, 1975, and 1976, and Biofeedback Society of America, 1977. Contributor of over 100 articles on behavioral medicine, clinical biofeedback, and neurophysiology to professional journals, including *Journal of Biofeedback*, *Journal of Altered States of Consciousness*, *Journal of Contemporary Psychotherapy*, *Journal of Holistic Health*, *Journal of Humanistic Psychology*, *Western Journal of Medicine*, and *American Journal of Clinical Biofeedback*. Member of editorial board, *American Journal of Clinical Biofeedback* and *Journal of Mind and Behavior*, 1978—; associate editor, *Medical Self-Care*, 1979—; member of editorial board, *Journal of Holistic Medicine*, 1981—.

AVOCATIONAL INTERESTS: Sailing, tennis, horseback riding, foreign travel (Europe, North Africa, Mexico, and Canada).

BIOGRAPHICAL/CRITICAL SOURCES: Washington Post Book World, October 4, 1981.

*   *   *

PERL, Susan   1922-1983

PERSONAL: Born September 8, 1922, in Vienna, Austria; died of cancer, June 27, 1983; daughter of Norbert (an accountant) and Marie (Bargl) Perlman. *Education:* Attended state and art schools in Vienna, Austria. *Politics:* Democrat. *Religion:* "Metaphysic, New Thought." *Residence:* New York, N.Y.

CAREER: Advertising artist and illustrator of books and magazines. *Member:* Friends of Animals, Greenwich Village Humane Society, Save a Cat Club. *Awards, honors:* New York Art Directors Show awards; Palma d'Oro Award for international cartoonists, Italy, 1965.

WRITINGS: (Self-illustrated) *The Sex Life of the American Female*, Stein & Day, 1964.

Illustrator: Irmengarde Eberle, *The Favorite Place* (Junior Literary Guild selection), F. Watts, 1957; Marion Conger, *Who Has Seen the Wind*, Abingdon, 1959; A. A. Milne, *Once on a Time*, New York Graphic Society, 1962; Hubert I. Bermont, *Psychoanalysis Is a Great Big Help!*, Stein & Day, 1963; Clement Moore, *The Night before Christmas*, Dell, 1963; Sara Murphey, *Bing-Bang Pig*, Follett, 1964; Ruth S. Radlauer, *Stein, the Great Retriever*, Bobbs-Merrill, 1964; Ralph Underwood, *Tell Me Another Joke*, Grosset, 1964; Norah Smaridge, *Watch Out!*, Abingdon, 1965; E. H. MacPherson, *The Wonderful Whistle*, Putnam, 1965.

Johanna Johnston, *The Story of the Barber of Seville*, Putnam, 1966; Bill Adler, editor, *Letters to Smokey the Bear*, Wonder-Treasure Books, 1966; Smaridge, *What a Silly Thing to Do*, Abingdon, 1967; Alice T. Gilbreath, *Beginning-To-Read Riddles and Jokes*, Follett, 1967; John Greenway, *Don't Talk to My Horse*, Silver Burdett, 1968; Harold S. Longman, *What's behind the Word*, Coward, 1968; Herb Valen, *The Boy Who Could Enter Paintings*, Little, Brown, 1968; William Wise, *Sir Howard the Coward*, Putnam, 1968; Beth Goff, *Where Is Daddy?: The Story of a Divorce*, Beacon Press, 1969; Dan Greenburg, *Jumbo the Boy and Arnold the Elephant*, Bobbs-Merrill, 1969; Susanne Kirtland, *Easy Answers to Hard Questions*, Grosset, 1969; Patrick McGivern, *The Ultimate Auto*, Putnam, 1969; Lilian Moore, *Too Many Bozos*, Western, 1969.

Barbara Klimowicz, *The Word-Birds of Davy McFifer*, Abingdon, 1970; Kornei Ivanovich Chukovskii, *Telephone*, translated and adapted by Marguerita Rudolph, Bobbs-Merrill, 1971; Margaret Gabel, *Sparrows Don't Drop Candy Wrappers*, Dodd, 1971; Betty F. Horvath, *Small Paul and the Bully of Morgan Court*, Ginn, 1971; Rudolph, *Sharp and Shiny*, McGraw, 1971; Solveig P. Russell, *Motherly Smith and Brother Bimbo*, Abingdon, 1971; Myra Scovel, *The Happiest Summer*, Harper, 1971; Martha L. Moffett, *A Flower Pot Is Not a Hat*, Dutton, 1972; Joel Rothman, *I Can Be Anything You Can Be*, Scroll Press, 1973; Patrick Mayers, *Lost Bear, Found Bear*, Albert Whitman, 1973; Smaridge, *You Know Better Than That*, Abingdon, 1973; Leslie McGuire, *You: How Your Body Works*, Platt, 1974; Joyce Richards, *How Come . . .? Easy Answers to Hard Questions*, Platt, 1975; Paul Showers, *The Moon Walker*, Doubleday, 1975.

Richards, *More Easy Answers,* Platt, 1977; Showers, *A Book of Scary Things,* Doubleday, 1977; McGuire, *Susan Perl's Human Body Book,* Platt, 1977; June Dutton, *Hope Is a Handful of Dreams,* Determined Productions, 1978; Greenway, *Tales from the United States,* Silver Burdett, 1979; Peter Robinson, *Susan Perl's Color Wheel,* Platt, 1979.

Also author, with Monica Bailey, of *Susan Perl's Park Peeple,* and, with June Dutton, of *Faith, Hope, and Charity,* both illustrated by Perl, both published by Determined Publications; also illustrator of *The Traveling Woman,* by Dena Kaye, *Games to Play in the Car,* by Michael Harwood, *The Weekenders,* by Max Gunther, *Games Christians Play: An Irreverent Guide to Religion without Tears,* by Judi Culbertson and Patt Bard, *Phyllis Diller's Housekeeping Hints,* and *Phyllis Diller's Marriage Manual.* Author of filmstrip adaptation of *I Can Be Anything You Can Be,* distributed by Doubleday Multimedia; creator of television commercial cartoons "The Health-Tex Kids." Contributor of drawings to *New York Times.*

AVOCATIONAL INTERESTS: Children, animals, travel, religion, metaphysics, and psychology.

OBITUARIES: New York Times, June 30, 1983; *Publishers Weekly,* July 29, 1983.†

*   *   *

PERRIN, (Horace) Norman   1920-1976

PERSONAL: Born November 29, 1920, in Willingborough, Northamptonshire, England; died in 1976; came to United States in 1956; naturalized U.S. citizen; son of Horace (a factory worker) and Dorothy May (Healey) Perrin; married Rosemary Watson, July 2, 1949. *Education:* University of Manchester, B.A., 1949; University of London, B.D., 1952, M.Th., 1955; Kirchliche Hochschule, Berlin, Germany, graduate study, 1956-57; University of Gottingen, D.Theol., 1959. *Politics:* Liberal Democrat. *Home:* 6019 South Ingleside, Chicago, Ill. 60637. *Office:* Divinity School, University of Chicago, 5801 Ellis Ave., Chicago, Ill. 60637.

CAREER: Ordained minister of Baptist Union of Great Britain and Northern Ireland, 1949, serving churches in London, England, and Swansea, South Wales, 1949-56; Emory University, Chandler School of Theology, Atlanta, Ga., assistant professor, 1959-62, associate professor of New Testament, 1962-64; University of Chicago, Divinity School, Chicago, Ill., associate professor of New Testament, 1964-76. *Military service:* Royal Air Force, 1940-45. *Member:* American Association of University Professors, Society of Biblical Literature, Studiorum Novi Testamenti Societas. *Awards, honors:* Christian Research Foundation Award, 1966; Guggenheim memorial fellowship, 1968-69.

WRITINGS: The Kingdom of God in the Teaching of Jesus, Westminster, 1963; *Rediscovering the Teaching of Jesus,* Harper, 1967; *The Promise of Bultmann,* Lippincott, 1969; *What Is Redaction Criticism?,* Fortress, 1969; *A Modern Pilgrimage in New Testament Christology,* Fortress, 1974; *The New Testament: An Introduction,* Harcourt, 1974; *Jesus and the Language of the Kingdom: Symbol and Metaphor in New Testament Interpretation,* Fortress, 1976; *The Resurrection According to Matthew, Mark, and Luke,* Fortress, 1977.

Translator of works of J. Jeremias: *The Lord's Prayer in Modern Research,* Expositiory Times, 1959-60; *The Sermon on the Mount,* Athlone Press, 1961; *The Question of the Historical Jesus,* Facet Books, 1964; *The Eucharistic Words of Jesus,* revised edition, Westminster, 1966.

Contributor of articles and reviews to theological journals.

AVOCATIONAL INTERESTS: Cricket, chess, travel.†

*   *   *

PETERS, Elizabeth
See MERTZ, Barbara (Gross)

*   *   *

PETERSON, William S(amuel)   1939-

PERSONAL: Born June 14, 1939, in Black River Falls, Wis.; son of Bert S. and Juanita (Thompson) Peterson; married Eileen J. Lester, June 5, 1961; children: Heather E., Glenn E. *Education:* Walla Walla College, B.A. (cum laude), 1961; University of Wisconsin, M.A., 1962; Northwestern University, Ph.D., 1968. *Office:* Department of English, University of Maryland, College Park, Md. 20742.

CAREER: Andrews University, Berrien Springs, Mich., instructor, 1962-64, 1966-67, assistant professor, 1967-70, associate professor of English, 1970-71; University of Maryland, College Park, associate professor, 1971-76, professor of English, 1976—. *Member:* Modern Language Association of America, Lewis Carroll Society of North America, Browning Institute (member, board of directors), William Morris Society, Printing Historical Society, American Printing History Association.

AWARDS, HONORS: Grants from American Council of Learned Societies, 1969, and Newberry Library, 1970, both for research on Mrs. Humphry Ward; grants from Huntington Library, 1973, University of Maryland General Research Board, 1974, American Philosophical Society, 1974, and National Endowment for the Humanities, 1977, all for research on Robert Browning; grants from University of Maryland, 1981, and Guggenheim Foundation, 1981-82, both for research on the Kelmscott Press.

WRITINGS: Interrogating the Oracle: A History of the London Browning Society, Ohio University Press, 1970; *Robert and Elizabeth Barrett Browning: An Annotated Bibliography, 1951-1970,* Browning Institute, 1974; *Victorian Heretic: Mrs. Humphry Ward's "Robert Elsmere,"* Leicester University Press, 1976; (editor) Elizabeth Barrett Browning, *Sonnets from the Portuguese: A Facsimile Edition of the British Library Manuscript,* Barre, 1977; (editor) *Browning's Trumpeter: The Correspondence of Robert Browning and Frederick J. Furnivall, 1872-1879,* Decatur House, 1979; (editor) William Morris, *The Ideal Book: Essays and Lectures on the Arts of the Book,* University of California Press, 1982; *A Bibliography of the Kelmscott Press,* Oxford University Press, 1984.

Contributor of articles to *Bulletin of the New York Public Library, Times Literary Supplement, Papers of the Bibliographical Society of America, Printing History,* and other publications. Editor, *Browning Institute Studies.*

WORK IN PROGRESS: A history of the Kelmscott Press.

*   *   *

PHILLIPS, Stella   1927-
(Stella Kent)

PERSONAL: Born December 26, 1927, in Plymouth, Devonshire, England; daughter of George (a chief petty officer, Royal Navy) and Edith Mary (Robb) Temp; married Victor Leonard Phillips, December 10, 1953; children: S. John Victor,

D. Amanda Clare. *Education:* University of Birmingham, Associateship of Library Association, 1952. *Religion:* Church of England. *Home:* 33 Bishopton Ave., Stockton, Cleveland, England.

CAREER: Shropshire County Library, Shropshire, England, library assistant, 1944-53; Walker Technical College, Wellington, Shropshire, England, librarian, 1960-63. *Member:* Library Association, Crime Writers Association, Romantic Novelists Association.

WRITINGS—Under pseudonym Stella Kent; published by R. Hale: *The Cautious Heart,* 1980; *All Her Lovely Companions,* 1981.

Detective stories; published by R. Hale, except as indicated: *Down to Death,* 1967; *The Hidden Wrath,* 1968, Walker & Co., 1982; *Death in Arcady,* 1969; *Death Makes the Scene,* 1970; *Death in Sheep's Clothing,* 1971, Walker & Co., 1983; *Yet She Must Die,* 1973; *Dear Brother, Here Departed,* 1975. Contributor of stories to periodicals.

*   *   *

PHILP, Richard Nilson 1943-

PERSONAL: Born July 7, 1943, in Plainfield, N.J.; son of Lester Perry and Gladys Emma Linea (Nilson) Philp. *Education:* University of North Carolina, Chapel Hill, B.A. (cum laude), 1965; Yale University, M.F.A., 1968. *Politics:* Registered Democrat. *Religion:* Episcopalian. *Home:* R.D. 3, Box 82, Route 385, Catskill, N.Y. 12414; and The Towers, Apt. 22, 33-15 80th St., Jackson Heights, N.Y. 11372. *Office:* Dance Magazine, 33 West 60th St., New York, N.Y. 10019.

CAREER: Critics Choice, New York City, associate editor 1968-70; *Dance* Magazine, New York City, managing editor, 1970—. Associate editor of *After Dark,* 1970-74; executive editor, Dancebooks, 1978-83. Episcopalian vestryman, 1980-83. *Member:* Catskill Writers Group, Greene County Historical Society (founder, 1978), Sigma Delta Chi. *Awards, honors:* Award from Society of Publication Designers, 1974, in recognition of work at *Dance* Magazine.

WRITINGS: Move to Learn, Temple University Press, 1977; *Danseur: The Male in Ballet,* McGraw, 1977; (editor and contributor) *Memoirs of a Dancer: Shadows, Dreams, Memories,* Dance Horizons, 1979; (editor) Giora Manor, *The Gospel According to Dance,* Dancebooks/St. Martin's, 1980; *American Choreographers,* Doubleday, 1984.

Plays: "Sydney," first produced in Chapel Hill, N.C., 1964; "The Anniversary," first produced in Chapel Hill, 1965; "The Birdcage," first produced in Durham, N.C., 1965; "Dabney," first produced in Chapel Hill, 1965; "Priscilla," first produced in New Haven, Conn., 1965; "The Camel Question," first produced in New Haven, 1966; "Thrush," first produced in New Haven, 1966; "Winter Fire," first produced in New Haven, 1967; "Guests," first produced in New Haven, 1968, revised for Louisiana Arts Council, 1971; (translator and adapter) Eugene Labiche, "Gladiator's Thirty Millions," first produced in New York City at Institute for Advanced Studies in Theatre Arts, 1970.

Author of column, "The Broadway Scene," in *After Dark,* 1970-74, and of a column about dance in the theater, in *Dance* Magazine, 1974—. Contributor to *New York Times;* contributor of reviews and features to *Dance* Magazine.

WORK IN PROGRESS: Death Dance, a mystery thriller; a television documentary on Ted Shawn, produced by REBO Associates.

SIDELIGHTS: Richard Nilson Philp writes that he moved from "an academic theater background to professional journalism in dance and theater." He said "Of all the performing arts, I have a particular fascination with dance—the richest, by far—especially with its history. I have been very fortunate as a writer to be able to work in an area I love so much." *Avocational interests:* Painting, music (violin and piano), gardening (upstate).

*   *   *

PICANO, Felice 1944-

PERSONAL: Born February 22, 1944, in New York, N.Y.; son of Phillip (a grocer) and Ann (Del Santo) Picano. *Education:* Queens College of the City University of New York, B.A., 1964. *Residence:* New York, N.Y. *Agent:* Jane Berkey, Jane Rotrosen Agency, 226 East 32nd St., New York, N.Y. 10016.

CAREER: New York City Department of Welfare, New York City, social worker, 1964-66; *Art Direction,* New York City, assistant editor, 1966-68; Doubleday Bookstore, New York City, assistant manager, 1969-70; free-lance writer, 1970-72; Rizzoli's Bookstore, New York City, assistant manager and buyer, 1972-74; free-lance writer, 1974—; founder and publisher of the Sea Horse Press Ltd., 1977—; co-founder and co-publisher of the Gay Presses of New York, 1980—. Instructor of fiction writing classes, YMCA West Side Y Writers Voice Workshop, 1982—.

WRITINGS—Novels, except as indicated: *Smart As the Devil,* Arbor House, 1975; *Eyes,* Arbor House, 1976; *The Mesmerist,* Delacorte, 1977; *The Deformity Lover and Other Poems* (poetry), Sea Horse Press, 1978; *The Lure,* Delacorte, 1979; (editor) *A True Likeness: An Anthology of Lesbian and Gay Writing Today* (anthology), Sea Horse Press, 1980; *Late in the Season,* Delacorte, 1981; *An Asian Minor: The True Story of Ganymede* (novella), Sea Horse Press, 1981; *Slashed to Ribbons in Defense of Love and Other Stories* (short stories), Gay Presses of New York, 1983; *House of Cards,* Delacorte, 1984.

Contributor to anthologies: *New Terrors, Number 2,* edited by Campbell, Pan Books (England), 1978; *Orgasms of Light,* edited by Leland, Gay Sunshine, 1979; *Aphrodisiac: Fiction from Christopher Street,* edited by Denneny, Coward, 1980; *Masters of Modern Horror,* edited by Coffey, Coward, 1981; *On the Line,* edited by Young, Crossing Press, 1982; *Getting from Here to There: Writing and Reading Poetry,* edited by F. Grossman, Boynton/Cook, 1982; *The Christopher Street Reader,* edited by Ortleb and Denneny, Coward, 1983; *The Penguin Book of Homosexual Verse,* edited by Stephen Coote, Penguin, 1983; *The Male Muse, Number 2,* edited by Young, Crossing Press, 1983.

Contributor of articles, poems, stories, and reviews to periodicals, including *OUT, Mouth of the Dragon, Islander, Cumberland Review, Connecticut Poetry Review, Cream City Review, Cats Eye, Gay Sunshine, New York Native, Soho Weekly News, New Dawn, Twilight Zone, Advocate, Christopher Street, Blueboy,* and *Drummer.* Books editor, *New York Native,* 1980-83.

WORK IN PROGRESS: Window Elegies, a poetry collection; *Looking Glass Lives,* a novel illustrated by Ron Fowler; *The Cashmere Coat,* a novel.

SIDELIGHTS: Several of Felice Picano's works have been translated into French, Japanese, Spanish, and Portuguese. He describes his writing to *CA:* "In my poetry I am keeping a sort of notebook of fragmentary experiences and understandings. In the past, this meant a polarization of subject matter: poems dealing either with perceptions gathered from the world of nature as revealed in Big Sur or Fire Island; or poems dealing with contemporary aspects of urban life and characters: portraits of epileptics, deformity lovers, obscene phone callers, etc. Of late, however, my poetry has become more autobiographical—though not at all confessional, integrating interior and exterior worlds. And forms have changed from lyric and monologic to more experimental structures such as self-interviews, imaginary dialogues, and letters to unknown persons.

"In fiction I write about the possible rather than the actual, and so I suppose, 'Romances' in Hawthorne's sense of the word, even with 'realistic' settings, characters, and actions. My novels, novellas, and short stories deal with ordinary individuals who are suddenly thrust into extraordinary situations and relationships which test their very existence. Unusual perceptions and abilities, extrasensory powers, and psychological aberrations become tools and weapons in conflicts of mental and emotional control. Previous behavioral patterns are inadequate for such situations and must be changed to enable evolved awareness and survival, or they destroy their possessor. Thus, perspective is of the utmost importance in my fiction, both for structure and meaning. I am dedicated to experimenting with new and old points of view, which seem to have progressed little since the pioneering work of Henry James and James Joyce."

BIOGRAPHICAL/CRITICAL SOURCES: New York Times Book Review, December 2, 1979; *Village Voice,* December 24, 1979.

*   *   *

PIENKOWSKI, Jan 1936-

PERSONAL: Born August 8, 1936, in Warsaw, Poland; son of Jerzy Dominik and Wanda (a chemist; maiden name, Garlicka) Pienkowski. *Education:* King's College, Cambridge, B.A., 1957, M.A., 1961. *Politics:* None. *Religion:* Catholic. *Home:* 45 Lonsdale Rd., London S.W.13, England. *Office:* Gallery Five, 14 Ogle St., London W1P 7LG, England.

CAREER: J. Walter Thompson (advertising agency), London, England, art director, 1957-59; William Collins Sons & Co. (publisher), London, art director in publicity, 1959-60; *Time and Tide,* London, art editor, 1960-61; Gallery Five, London, art director, 1961-78, consultant art director, 1978—. Consultant on mechanical books, Walker Books Ltd. *Member:* Society of Authors. *Awards, honors:* Kate Greenaway Award, 1971, for *The Kingdom Under the Sea and Other Stories,* and 1979, for *Haunted House.*

WRITINGS—Self-illustrated children's books: *Numbers,* Harvey House, 1975; *Colours,* Harvey House, 1975; *Shapes,* Harvey House, 1975; *Sizes,* Harvey House, 1975; *Homes,* Heinemann, 1979; *Weather,* Heinemann, 1979; *Haunted House,* Heinemann, 1979; *A. B. C.,* Heinemann, 1980; *Time,* Heinemann, 1980; (with Anne Carter) *Dinner-Time,* Gallery Five, 1980; (with Helen Nicoll) *Quest for the Gloop,* Heinemann, 1980; *Robot,* Heinemann, 1981; *Gossip,* Gallery Five, 1983.

"Meg and Mog" series; with Nicoll: *Meg and Mog,* Heinemann, 1972, Atheneum, 1973, revised edition, Heinemann, 1977; *Meg's Eggs,* Heinemann, 1972, Atheneum, 1973, revised edition, Heinemann, 1977; *Meg on the Moon,* Heine-

mann, 1973; *Meg at Sea,* Heinemann. 1973, revised edition, Heinemann, 1979; *Meg's Car,* Heinemann, 1975; *Meg's Castle,* Heinemann, 1975; *Mog's Mumps,* Heinemann, 1976; *Meg's Veg,* Heinemann, 1976; *Meg and Mog Birthday Book,* Heinemann, 1979; *Mog at the Zoo,* Heinemann, 1982.

Illustrator: Nancy and John Langstaff, *Jim Along, Josie,* Harcourt, 1970; Jessie Gertrude Townsend, *Annie, Bridget and Charlie: An A.B.C. for Children of Rhymes,* Pantheon, 1967; Joan Aiken, *A Necklace of Raindrops and Other Stories,* Doubleday, 1967, revised edition, 1972; Edith Brill, *The Golden Bird,* F. Watts, 1970; Aiken, *The Kingdom Under the Sea and Other Stories,* J. Cape, 1971, revised edition, 1975; Agnes Szudek, *The Amber Mountain,* Hutchinson, 1976; Dinah Starkey, *Ghosts and Bogles,* Good Reading, 1978; Aiken, *A Tale of a One Way Street,* J. Cape, 1978.

"Jan Pienkowski Fairy Tale Library" series; illustrator; published by Heinemann: Brothers Grimm, *Jack and the Beanstalk,* 1977; Brothers Grimm, *Snow White,* 1977; Brothers Grimm, *Sleeping Beauty,* 1977; Charles Perrault, *Puss in Boots,* 1977; Perrault, *Cinderella,* 1977.

Graphic illustrator for "Watch!," a British Broadcasting Corp. television series, 1969-71; created design for "Meg and Mog Show," Arts Theatre, London, 1982 and 1983, and for "Chips' Comic" television show.

WORK IN PROGRESS: Two new titles in the "Meg and Mog" series.

SIDELIGHTS: Jan Pienkowski told *CA:* "I had no formal art school training but went to Cambridge University to read classics and English literature. It was there that I began designing: plays, posters, and greeting cards for friends which led to the formation of Gallery Five. . . . Book illustration came later. The silhouette technique evolved out of my first book with Joan Aiken. . . . I began to experiment with 'marble' backgrounds sometimes producing marvellously unexpected results. It may be that my work harks back to Polish background; the two-dimensional approach I use is characteristic of that part of the world. The 'Meg and Mog' books are in a completely different style, with bold black line on vibrant flat colour, again rooted in the Polish ethnic artistic tradition. What I particularly enjoy about them is the opportunity to use the devices of the strip cartoon, with its merits of impact and economy. Words and pictures are completely integrated, and the kids seem to enjoy them. 'Mechanical books [, books which have moving parts,] have been a new departure into cut paper, another east European tradition. The pop-up book enables the child to put on a 'show' for [his] family and friends and introduces participation into the world of picture books."

*   *   *

PIRTLE, Caleb (Jackson) III 1941-

PERSONAL: Born December 30, 1941, in Kilgore, Tex.; son of Caleb Jackson, Jr. (an oil field worker) and Mary Eunice (Price) Pirtle; married Linda Sue Greer (a legal secretary), August 31, 1963; children: Joshua Jackson. *Education:* Kilgore College, A.A., 1961; University of Texas, B.J., 1963. *Home:* 129 Chieftan, Waxahachie, Tex. 75165. *Office:* Calan Enterprises, Waxahachie, Tex. 75165.

CAREER: Plainfield Daily Herald, Plainview, Tex., reporter, 1963; *Fort Worth Star-Telegram,* Fort Worth, Tex., feature writer, 1963-65; Texas Tourist Development Agency, Austin, press chief, 1965-68; *Southern Living,* Birmingham, Ala., travel editor, 1968—; Crawford, Pirtle & Lynn, Waxahachie, Tex., partner, 1977-83; Calan Enterprises, Waxahachie, partner, 1983—. *Member:* Society of American Travel Writers (past vice-president of Central States chapter), Discover America Travel Organizations.

AWARDS, HONORS: Award from Southwest Journalism Forum, 1963, for feature writing; William Randolph Hearst Award, 1963; feature writing award from Texas Associated Press, 1964, and from Texas Headliners, 1964; awards from Discover America Travel Organizations, 1969, 1971, 1973, for magazine coverage of travel; named headliner of the year by local chapter of Texas Women's Press Association, 1975; award from Southeastern Library Association, 1973, for *Callaway Gardens: The Unending Season*, and 1975, for *XIT: The American Cowboy*.

WRITINGS: (With Gerald Crawford) *Callaway Gardens: The Unending Season*, Oxmore, 1973; *XIT: The American Cowboy*, Oxmore, 1975; (with Texas Cowboy Artists Association) *American Cowboy*, Oxmoor, 1977; *The Grandest Day*, Opryland, 1979; *Fort Worth: The Civilized West*, Continental Heritage, 1980; *M.L.M.: A Shortcut to Financial Freedom*, Synergetic Publishing, 1982; *This Great Land*, Rand McNally, 1983. Contributor to magazines, including *Westward, Travel and Leisure, Travel, Sky, Holiday Inn Companion*, and *Rotarian*.

WORK IN PROGRESS: Texas: Its Lore and Its Lure, an artbook, with Dallas artist Donald F. Mitchell.

SIDELIGHTS: Caleb Pirtle III told *CA* that some of his writing assignments have included interviews with former President Lyndon Johnson, former vice-president John Nance Garner, governor John Connally, the world's strongest man, country-western performers Tom T. Hall, Minnie Pearl, Porter Waggoner, Dolly Parton, Jimmy Driftwood, Dottie West, and Jerry Clower, the world champion tobacco spitter, the world champion muleshoe pitcher, champion cowboys, and professional golfers and tennis players.

He comments: "I believe in people. And I'm convinced that what happens is not nearly as important as the people who make it happen. And that has been my approach to travel writing. Most simply tell you where to go, how to get there, and how much it's going to cost. I like to add a new dimension. I like to tell you the kind of people you're going to meet when you get there. And these include tobacco spitters, muleshoe pitchers, story tellers, chili cookers, domino players, and guitar pickers. I've been fortunate enough to travel throughout the United States, Mexico, Europe and Russia. And when I get home I find I remember the people I've talked with long after I've forgotten the sights I've seen. I write for one reason. I'm curious and like to find out what's going on. . . . Then I can't wait to tell someone."

*   *   *

PLANTINGA, Alvin C.   1932-

PERSONAL: Born November 15, 1932, in Ann Arbor, Mich.; son of Cornelius A. (a professor) and Lettie (Bossenbroeck) Plantinga; married Kathleen De Boer, June 16, 1955; children: Carl, Jane, Harry, Ann. *Education:* Calvin College, A.B., 1954; University of Michigan, A.M., 1955; Yale University, Ph.D., 1958. *Religion:* Protestant. *Home:* 50505 Hollyhock Rd., South Bend, Ind. 46637. *Office:* Department of Philosophy, University of Notre Dame, Notre Dame, Ind. 46556.

CAREER: Yale University, New Haven, Conn., instructor in philosophy, 1957-58; Wayne State University, Detroit, Mich.,

instructor, 1958-60, assistant professor, 1960-62, associate professor of philosophy, 1962-63; Calvin College, Grand Rapids, Mich., associate professor, 1963-64, professor of philosophy, 1965-82; University of Notre Dame, Notre Dame, Ind., John A. O'Brien Professor of Philosophy, 1982—. Visiting lecturer at University of Illinois, 1960, and Harvard University, 1964-65; visiting professor at University of Michigan, 1967, University of California, Los Angeles, 1972, and University of Arizona, 1979-80; adjunct professor, University of Notre Dame, 1974. *Member:* American Philosophical Association (president of Western Division, 1981-82), American Academy of Arts and Sciences, Society for Christian Philosophers.

AWARDS, HONORS: Woodrow Wilson fellow, 1954-55; E. Harris Harbison Award for distinguished teaching, 1968; Center for Advanced Study in the Behavioral Sciences fellow, 1968-69; Guggenheim fellow, 1971-72; visiting fellow at Balliol College, Oxford University, 1975-76; National Endowment for the Humanities fellow, 1975-76; D.D., Glasgow University, 1982.

WRITINGS: (Editor) *Faith and Philosophy*, Eerdmans, 1964; (editor) *The Ontological Argument*, Doubleday, 1965; *God and Other Minds: A Study of the Rational Justification of Belief in God*, Cornell University Press, 1967; *The Nature of Necessity*, Oxford University Press, 1974; *God, Freedom, and Evil*, Harper, 1974; *Does God Have a Nature?*, Marquette University Press, 1980. Contributor to philosophy and metaphysics journals.

WORK IN PROGRESS: Philosophy of religion, epistemology and metaphysics; philosophy of science; semantics of modal logic.

AVOCATIONAL INTERESTS: Mountain climbing and hiking, mainly in the Cascades of Washington and the Grand Tetons of Wyoming.

*   *   *

PLATT, Kin   1911-

PERSONAL: Born December 8, 1911, in New York, N.Y.; divorced; children: Christopher. *Agent:* Marilyn Marlow, Curtis Brown, 575 Madison Ave., New York, N.Y. 10022.

CAREER: Cartoonist and writer. New York Herald Tribune Syndicate, New York, N.Y., cartoonist (writer and illustrator) of comic strip, "Mr. and Mrs.," 1947-63, and "The Duke and the Duchess," 1950-54. Sometime theatrical caricaturist for New York newspapers, including *Village Voice*, and for *Los Angeles Times. Military service:* U.S. Army Air Forces, Air Transport Command, 1943-46; served in China-Burma-India theater; received Bronze Star. *Member:* Writers Guild of America, Mystery Writers of America, National Cartoonist Society. *Awards, honors:* Edgar Award, Mystery Writers of America, 1967, for *Sinbad and Me;* Southern California Council on Literature for Children and Young People award for fiction, 1974, for *Chloris and the Creeps*.

WRITINGS: The Blue Man (juvenile), Harper, 1961; *Big Max* (juvenile), Harper, 1965; *Sinbad and Me* (juvenile), Chilton, 1966; *The Boy Who Could Make Himself Disappear*, Chilton, 1968; *Mystery of the Witch Who Wouldn't*, Chilton, 1969.

The Pushbutton Butterfly, Random House, 1970; *The Kissing Gourami*, Random House, 1970; *Hey, Dummy*, Chilton, 1971; *Dead As They Come*, Random House, 1972; *The Princess Stakes Murder*, Random House, 1973; *Chloris and the Creeps*, Chilton, 1973; *The Giant Kill*, Random House, 1974; *Match*

Point for Murder, Random House, 1975; *Headman,* Greenwillow, 1975; *Chloris and the Freaks,* Bradbury, 1975.

The Body Beautiful Murder, Random House, 1976; *The Terrible Love Life of Dudley Cornflower,* Bradbury, 1976; *The Doomsday Gang,* Greenwillow, 1977; *Big Max in the Mystery of the Missing Moose,* Harper, 1977; *Run for Your Life,* F. Watts, 1977; *The Screwball King Murder,* Random House, 1978; *Chloris and the Weirdos,* Bradbury, 1978; *Dracula, Go Home,* F. Watts, 1979.

The Ghost of Hellsfire Street, Delacorte, 1980; *Flames Going Out,* Methuen, 1980; *The Ape Inside Me,* Crowell, 1980; *Brogg's Brain,* Crowell, 1981; *Frank and Stein and Me,* F. Watts, 1982; *Crocker,* Lippincott, 1983.

Editor; all published by Pendulum Press: Jack London, *The Call of the Wild,* 1973; Robert Louis Stevenson, *Dr. Jekyl and Mr. Hyde,* 1973; Arthur Conan Doyle, *The Great Adventures of Sherlock Holmes,* 1974; Stevenson, *Kidnapped,* 1974.

*MEDIA ADAPTATIONS: * Kin Platt's novel *The Boy Who Could Make Himself Disappear* was filmed under the title "Baxter" in 1973.

BIOGRAPHICAL/CRITICAL SOURCES: New York Times Book Review, February 1, 1981; *Contemporary Literary Criticism,* Volume XXVI, 1983.

*   *   *

PLUM, Jennifer
    See KURLAND, Michael (Joseph)

*   *   *

PLUMSTEAD, A(rthur) William 1933-

*PERSONAL: * Born March 27, 1933, in Toronto, Ontario, Canada; son of Arthur Noyes and Lila (Somerville) Plumstead; married Nicoll Cleary, August 27, 1955; children: Bryan, Peggy, David. *Education: * University of Western Ontario, B.A., 1955; University of Rochester, M.A., 1957, Ph.D., 1960. *Home: * Island 658, Lake Temagami, Ontario, Canada POH 2HO. *Office: * Department of English, Laurentian University, Sudbury, Ontario, Canada.

*CAREER: * University of Saskatchewan, Saskatoon, instructor, 1959-61, assistant professor, 1961-64; University of Minnesota, Minneapolis, assistant professor, 1964-67, associate professor, 1964-68; University of Massachusetts, Amherst, associate professor, 1968-71, professor of English, 1971-75; Laurentian University, Sudbury, Ontario, adjunct professor of English, 1981—.

*WRITINGS: * (Editor and author of introductions) *The Wall and the Garden: Selected Massachusetts Election Sermons, 1670-1775,* University of Minnesota Press, 1968; (editor) *Journals and Miscellaneous Notebooks of Ralph Waldo Emerson,* Harvard University Press, Volume VII (with Harrison Hayford), 1969, Volume XI (with William Gilman), 1975; (New England editor) *American Literary Manuscripts,* University of Georgia Press, 1977.

*WORK IN PROGRESS: * A history of the sketch in America, 1780-1860.

*SIDELIGHTS: * A. William Plumstead tells *CA: * "I seem to think most of the writing I still have to do when furthest from the academic world, especially when on or beside the lake I

love so much, Temagami. But I'm also running a marina, so the writing is less frequent."

*   *   *

PLUTCHIK, Robert 1927-

*PERSONAL: * Born October 21, 1927, in Brooklyn, N.Y.; son of Leon (in clothing industry) and Libby (Solow) Plutchik; married Anita Freyberg, July 1, 1962; children: Lisa Robin, Lori Jill, Roy Elliot. *Education: * City College (now City College of the City University of New York), B.S., 1949; Columbia University, M.A., 1950, Ph.D., 1952. *Home: * 1131 North Ave., New Rochelle, N.Y. 10804. *Office: * Department of Psychiatry, Albert Einstein College of Medicine, Bronx, N.Y. 10461.

*CAREER: * Hofstra University, Hempstead, Long Island, N.Y., associate professor of psychology, 1951-67; Columbia University, College of Physicians and Surgeons, New York, N.Y., associate research scientist in department of psychiatry, 1967-68; Bronx State Hospital, Bronx, N.Y., director of evaluation research program, 1968-71; Albert Einstein College of Medicine, Bronx, 1971—, began as director of clinical research unit, department of psychiatry, currently professor of psychiatry and psychology. Special fellow, National Institute of Mental Health, Bethesda, Md., 1961-63. *Member: * American Psychological Association (fellow), Sigma Xi.

WRITINGS: Small Group Discussion in Orientation and Teaching, Putnam, 1959; *The Emotions: Facts, Theories and a New Model,* Random House, 1962; *Foundations of Experimental Research,* Harper, 1968, 3rd edition, 1982; *Emotion: A Psychoevolutionary Synthesis,* Harper, 1980; (editor and contributor) *Theories of Emotion,* Academic Press, 1980. Poetry included in *National Poetry Anthology.* Contributor of articles on emotion to *World Book Encyclopedia, Academic American Encyclopedia, Blackwell's Encyclopedic Dictionary of Psychology,* and *International Encyclopedia of Neurology, Psychiatry,* and *Psychoanalysis and Psychology;* contributor to numerous psychology journals.

*AVOCATIONAL INTERESTS: * Sculpturing in wood, etching.

*   *   *

PLYMELL, Charles 1935-

*PERSONAL: * Born April 26, 1935, in Holcomb, Kan.; son of Fred Douglass and Audrey (Sipe) Plymell; married Pamela Beach, September 3, 1966. *Education: * Attended Wichita State University, 1955-61; Johns Hopkins University, M.A., 1970. *Politics: * None. *Religion: * None. *Home: * 2314 Georgian Woods Place, Silver Spring, Md. 20902. *Office: * Cherry Valley Editions, Box 303, Cherry Valley, N.Y. 13320.

*CAREER: * Writer, artist, and animated film maker. Publisher of magazines *Poet's Corner* and *Mikrokosmos,* 1959, *Now,* 1963-65, *The Last Times,* 1967, and *Bulletin from Nothing.* Cherry Valley Editions, Cherry Valley, N.Y., editor and publisher, 1974—. Instructor in English at colleges and universities in Washington, D.C., Virginia, and Maryland. Graphic arts teacher in Connecticut, 1972-73; Poet-in-the-schools in Pennsylvania, Virginia, Delaware, and New York, 1974-78. Has given poetry readings; panelist, lecturer, and guest editor at several professional meetings. Presenter at Meeting of Popular Culture Association and American Cultural Association. Judge, Honors Tournament, Montgomery County Forensic League, 1982. Consultant to New York State Council on the Arts.

AWARDS, HONORS: National Book Award nomination, 1972; general support grants from Coordination Council of Literary Magazines, 1974-78, National Education Association, 1976-79, 1981, and New York State Council on the Arts, 1977, 1979-81; named most promising poet, *World Book,* 1976.

WRITINGS: (Editor) Roxie Powell, *Dreams of Straw,* privately printed, 1963; *Apocalypse Rose,* introduction by Allen Ginsberg, D. Haselwood, 1966; *Neon Poems,* Atom Mind Publications, 1970; *The Last of the Moccasins,* City Lights, 1971; *Over the Stage of Kansas,* Telephone Books, 1972; *The Trashing of America Phase I,* The Unspeakable Visions of the Individual, 1973; *The Trashing of America,* Kulchur Foundations, 1975; *Blue Orchid Numero Uno,* Telephone Books, 1975; *In Memory of My Father,* Cherry Valley, 1977; *Are You a Kid?,* Cherry Valley, 1977; *Panik in Dodge City,* Expanded Media, 1981.

Contributor to anthologies: *Mark in Time: Poets and Poetry,* New Glide, 1971; *And the Roses Race around Her Name,* Stonehill, 1975; *Turpentin on the Rocks,* Maro Verlag (Augsburg, West Germany), 1978; *A Quois Bon,* Le Soleil Noir (Paris), 1978; *On Turtle's Back: A Biogeographic Anthology of New York,* White Pine, 1978. Contributor to journals. Guest editor, *Grist Magazine,* 1967; contributing editor, *Nola Express,* 1969; editor, *Coldspring Journal,* 1974-78, and *Northeast Rising Sun,* 1976-80.

WORK IN PROGRESS: The Great Western Turnpike.

SIDELIGHTS: According to Brown Miller, writing in the *Dictionary of Literary Biography,* poet Charles Plymell "is associated with Beat Generation writers for several reasons: he lived with Allen Ginsberg and Neal Cassady in San Francisco in the early 1960s; he admired and was influenced by much of the Beat writing; his work was published in Beat journals and by Lawrence Ferlinghetti's City Lights Books. As an editor and publisher he has, in turn, published many Beat figures, such as Ginsberg, William S. Burroughs, and Herbert Huncke." "On the other hand," Miller continues, "it is important to recognize some of the differences between Plymell and the Beats: he is quite a bit younger than the main Beat writers; he has lived in the Haight-Ashbury district of San Francisco under what he calls 'Hippie Movement conditions'; and he has in recent years been moving away from Beat influences, often criticizing what he considers bad writing and corrupt politics from some Beats who continue writing today."

"Plymell's primary concerns in his writing," says Miller, "are the need to live honestly and to see through the many shams he perceives in today's world, as well as the need to be sensitive to and enraptured by the beauty of the physical world. The poetic image, for him, is the key to a vision that gives meaning and pleasure to life, even in the midst of harsh realities."

BIOGRAPHICAL/CRITICAL SOURCES: Dictionary of Literary Biography, Volume XVI: *The Beats: Literary Bohemians in Postwar America,* Gale, 1983.

*   *   *

POHL, Frederik   1919-
   (Elton V. Andrews, Paul Fleur, Warren F. Howard, Ernst Mason, James McCreigh; S. D. Gottesman, Lee Gregor, Cyril Judd, Paul Dennis Lavond, Scott Mariner, Edson McCann, Jordan Park, Charles Satterfield, Dirk Wilson, joint pseudonyms)

PERSONAL: Born November 26, 1919, in New York, N.Y.; son of Fred George (a salesman) and Anna Jane (Mason) Pohl; married Doris Baumgardt (divorced, 1944); married Dorothy Louise LesTina (divorced, 1947); married Judith Merril (divorced, 1952); married Carol M. Ulf, September 15, 1952 (divorced, 1981); children: Ann (Mrs. Walter Weary), Karen (Mrs. Robert Dixon), Frederik III (deceased), Frederik IV, Kathy. *Education:* Attended public schools in Brooklyn, N.Y., "dropped out in senior year." *Politics:* Democrat. *Religion:* Unitarian. *Home and office:* 320 East 22nd St., New York, N.Y. 10010. *Agent:* Curtis Brown, Ltd., 575 Madison Ave., New York, N.Y. 10022.

CAREER: Popular Publications, New York City, editor, 1939-43; Popular Science Publishing Co., New York City, editor in book department and assistant circulation manager, 1946-49; literary agent, 1946-53; free-lance writer, 1953-60; *Galaxy* Magazine, New York City, editor, 1961-69; Ace Books, New York City, executive editor, 1971-72; Bantam Books, New York City, science fiction editor, 1973-79.

Staff lecturer, American Management Association, 1966-69; cultural exchange lecturer in science fiction for U.S. Department of State in Yugoslavia, Romania, and the Soviet Union, 1974; also lecturer at more than two hundred colleges in the United States, Canada, and abroad; represented United States at international literary conferences in England, Italy, Brazil, Canada, and Japan. Has appeared on more than four hundred radio and television programs in nine countries. County committeeman, Democratic Party, Monmouth City, N.J., 1956-69; trustee, The Harbour School, Red Bank, N.J., 1972-75, and First Unitarian Church of Monmouth City, 1973-75. *Military service:* U.S. Army Air Forces, 1943-45; received seven battle stars.

MEMBER: Science Fiction Writers of America (president, 1974-76), British Interplanetary Society, American Astronautical Society, World SF (president, 1980-82), Authors Guild (member of council, 1975—), American Association for the Advancement of Science (fellow, 1982), World Future Society, American Civil Liberties Union (trustee, Monmouth County, N.J., 1968-71), New York Academy of Sciences.

AWARDS, HONORS: Edward E. Smith Award, 1966; Hugo Award, World Science Fiction Convention, 1966, 1967, and 1968, for best editor, 1974, for short story, "The Meeting," and 1978, for best novel, *Gateway;* H. G. Wells Award, 1975; Nebula Award, Science Fiction Writers of America, 1977, for best novel, *Man Plus,* and 1978, for best novel, *Gateway;* John W. Campbell Award, 1978, for *Gateway;* American Book Award, 1979, for *JEM;* Popular Culture Association annual award, 1982.

WRITINGS—Science fiction, except as indicated; published by Ballantine, except as indicated: (Under pseudonym James McCreigh) *Danger Moon,* American Science Fiction (Sydney), 1953; (with Lester del Rey under joint pseudonym Edson McCann) *Preferred Risk,* Simon & Schuster, 1955; *Alternating Currents* (short stories), 1956; *Edge of the City* (novel based on screenplay by Robert Alan Aurthur), 1957; *Slave Ship,* 1957; *Tomorrow Times Seven: Science Fiction Stories,* 1959.

The Man Who Ate the World, 1960; *Drunkard's Walk,* 1960; *Turn Left at Thursday: Three Novelettes and Three Stories,* 1961; *The Abominable Earthman,* 1963; *The Case against Tomorrow: Science Fiction Short Stories,* 1965; *A Plague of Pythons,* 1965; *The Frederik Pohl Omnibus,* Gollancz, 1966; *Digits and Dastards,* 1966; *The Age of the Pussyfoot,* 1969.

Day Million (short stories), 1970; *Practical Politics, 1972* (nonfiction), 1971; *The Gold at the Starbow's End,* 1972; (with

Carol Pohl) *Jupiter*, 1973; *The Best of Frederik Pohl*, introduction by Lester del Rey, Doubleday, 1975; *The Early Pohl*, Doubleday, 1976; *Man Plus*, Random House, 1976; *Gateway*, St. Martin's, 1977; *The Way the Future Was: A Memoir*, 1978; *JEM*, St. Martin's, 1979.

Beyond the Blue Event Horizon, 1980; *Syzgy*, Bantam, 1981; *The Cool War*, 1981; *Planets Three*, Berkley, 1982; *Bipohl, Two Novels: Drunkard's Walk and The Age of the Pussyfoot*, 1982; *Starburst*, 1982; *Starbow*, 1982; (author of introduction) *New Visions: A Collection of Modern Science Fiction Art*, Doubleday, 1982; *Midas World*, St. Martin's, 1983.

With Cyril M. Kornbluth: (Under joint pseudonym Cyril Judd) *Gunner Cade*, Simon & Schuster, 1952; (under joint pseudonym Cyril Judd) *Outpost Mars*, Abelard Press, 1952; *The Space Merchants*, 1953, 2nd edition, 1981; *Search the Sky*, 1954; *Gladiator-at-Law*, 1955; *A Town Is Drowning*, 1955; *Presidential Year*, 1956; (under joint pseudonym Jordan Park) *Sorority House*, Lion Press, 1956; (under joint pseudonym Jordan Park) *The Man of Cold Rages*, Pyramid Publications, 1958; *Wolfbane*, 1959, reprinted, Garland Publishing, 1975; *The Wonder Effect*, 1962.

With Jack Williamson: *Undersea Quest*, Gnome Press, 1954; *Undersea Fleet*, Gnome Press, 1956; *Undersea City*, Gnome Press, 1958; *The Reefs of Space*, 1964; *Starchild*, 1965; *Rogue Star*, 1969; *Farthest Star: The Saga of Cuckoo*, 1975; *The Starchild Trilogy*, Paperback Library, 1977.

Editor: *Beyond the End of Time*, Permabooks, 1952; *Star Science Fiction Stories*, 1953; *Star Short Novels*, 1954; *Assignment in Tomorrow: An Anthology*, Hanover House, 1954.

Star of Stars, Doubleday, 1960; *The Expert Dreamer*, Doubleday, 1962; *Time Waits for Winthrop*, Doubleday, 1962; *The Best Science Fiction from "Worlds of If" Magazine*, Galaxy Publishing Corp., 1964; *The Seventh Galaxy Reader*, Doubleday, 1964; *Star Fourteen*, Whiting & Wheaton, 1966; *The If Reader of Science Fiction*, Doubleday, 1966; *The Tenth Galaxy Reader*, Doubleday, 1967, published as *Door to Anywhere*, Modern Literary Editions, 1967; *The Eleventh Galaxy Reader*, Doubleday, 1969.

Nightmare Age, 1970; *Best Science Fiction for 1972*, Ace Books, 1973; (with Carol Pohl) *Science Fiction: The Great Years*, Ace Books, 1973; *The Science Fiction Roll of Honor*, Random House, 1975; *Science Fiction Discoveries*, Bantam, 1976; *Science Fiction of the Forties*, Avon, 1978.

Galaxy Magazine: Thirty Years of Innovative Science Fiction, Playboy Press, 1980; *Nebula Winners Fourteen*, Harper, 1980; *The Great Science Fiction Series*, Harper, 1980; *Frederik Pohl's Favorite Stories: Four Decades as a Science Fiction Editor*, Putnam, 1981; (with son, Frederik Pohl IV) *Science Fiction: Studies in Film*, Ace Books, 1981.

Contributor: Harlan Ellison, editor, *Dangerous Visions*, Doubleday, 1967; Damon Knight, editor, *Orbit 11*, Putnam, 1972. Contributor, sometimes under pseudonyms, to *Galaxy, Worlds of Fantasy, Science Fiction Quarterly, Rogue, Impulse, Astonishing, Imagination, If, Beyond, Playboy, Infinity*, and other magazines.

SIDELIGHTS: "Like all the other great men in SF," writes Algis Budrys in the *Magazine of Fantasy and Science Fiction*, "Frederik Pohl is idiosyncratic, essentially self-made, and brilliant. Unlike many of the others, he has an extremely broad range of interests and education." As both an author and editor Pohl has been, Robert Scholes and Eric S. Rabkin assert in

Science Fiction: History, Science, Vision, "one of few men to make a genuine impact on the science fiction field."

In the 1950s, Pohl wrote a number of influential books with the late C. M. Kornbluth in which they "pioneered and excelled in a completely new kind of science fiction," writes Charles Platt in *Dream Makers: The Uncommon People Who Write Science Fiction*. "They invented and played with 'Sociological SF'—alternate futures here on Earth, exaggerating and satirizing real-life social forces and trends." The best of these collaborations was *The Space Merchants*, a satirical look at a world ruled by advertising; the book was inspired by Pohl's own short stint in an advertising agency. In this world, "exploitation of resources, pollution of environment, and overpopulation are all rampant," Scholes and Rabkin point out, "while the advertisers use every device of behavior control including addictive substances in the products. . . . The beauty of [the book] is that it manages to be absurd and at the same time frighteningly close to the way that many people actually think. . . . The lightness of touch and consistency of imagination make it a true classic of science fiction." "This novel is the single work most mentioned when Pohl's fiction is discussed," Stephen H. Goldman of the *Dictionary of Literary Biography* explains. "It is on every critic's list of science fiction classics and has never been out of print since its first appearance. . . . While Pohl and Kornbluth produced other highly readable novels . . . , *The Space Merchants* remains their single greatest achievement."

As editor of *Galaxy* and later with Bantam Books, Pohl was a strong supporter of the 'new wave' in science fiction. This was a movement by some writers to incorporate literary techniques from mainstream literature into science fiction, while eliminating what they saw as the genre's cliches. Ironically, Pohl came under fire from some of these writers for being too conservative. "I *published* the majority of 'new-wave' writers," Pohl told Charles Platt. "It wasn't the stories I objected to, it was the snottiness of the proponents. . . . The thing that the 'new wave' did that I treasure was to shake up old dinosaurs, like Isaac [Asimov], and for that matter me . . . , and show them that you do not really have to construct a story according to the 1930s pulp or Hollywood standards."

Some of the new wave's influence can be seen in Pohl's prize-winning novel *Gateway*, the story of the discovery of an ancient spaceport of the Heechee, a long-dead civilization. Each spaceship found at the port is operable, but so highly advanced that the propulsion system and the destination for which it is programmed are incomprehensible to humans. A few brave adventurers dare to travel in the ships in a kind of lottery system. "Occasionally," writes Goldman, "one of the Heechee ships lands at a site that is filled with undiscovered artifacts, and the human riders share in the financial rewards these discoveries can bring." At other times, the adventurers never return, or return dead. "The story . . . ," Mark Rose of the *New Republic* finds, "conveys a vivid sense of the pathos and absurdity of human ignorance in attempting to exploit a barely understood universe." Patrick Parrinder of the *Times Literary Supplement* agrees: "The novel is remarkable for its portrayal of human explorers rushing into space in a mood of abject fear and greed, in machines they cannot understand or control."

The story of the spaceport and its hazardous explorations is interspersed with seriocomic scenes involving a guilt-ridden adventurer—one who made a fortune during a trip on which he was forced to abandon the woman he loves—and his computer psychoanalyst. "Pohl's touch is always light and sure,"

Rose comments, "and, indeed, parts of the novel are extremely funny." Goldman notes that in *Gateway* "Pohl has finally balanced the demands of an imaginative world and the presentation of a highly complex character. . . . This balance has led to his most successful novel thus far." In *Gateway*, Roz Kaveney of *Books and Bookmen* believes, Pohl "successfully combined wit and humanity in a novel of character. [The result is] a highly competent, darkly witty entertainment." Other critics found the computer psychoanalyst a particularly believable character. "What makes this book so intriguing," Peter Ackroyd of *Spectator* writes, "is not its occasional satire and consistent good humor, but the fact that Pohl has managed to convey the insistent presence of the non-human, a presence which may indeed haunt our future."

Pohl's next novel, *JEM*, also won critical praise. Set in the near future when the Earth has been divided into three camps—People, Fuel, and Food—the novel details the story of three bands of human colonists on another planet. When there is a war and a resulting social breakdown on Earth, the colony is suddenly independent and "must then find a way to reconcile its divisions, both among the colonists and between the colonists and the three excellently depicted native sapient species, if it is to survive," writes Tom Easton of the *Magazine of Fantasy and Science Fiction*. Gerald Jonas of the *New York Times Book Review* compares *JEM* to *The Space Merchants* because "*JEM* is also social satire—but without the humor." "It is essentially a political allegory," Alex de Jonge of *Spectator* observes, "describing the struggle between the world's three blocs . . . each attempting to colonize a planet."

The colonization of Jem repeats some mistakes made on Earth. "With systematic, undeviating logic," writes Budrys, "Pohl depicts the consequent rape of Jem. As each of the expeditions struggles to do its best, there are moments of hope, and moments of triumph. But they are all no more than peaks on a downhill slope. The ending of it all is so genuinely sad that one realizes abruptly how rarely SF evokes pure sorrow, and how profound Pohl's vision was in conceiving of this story." Russell Lord of the *Christian Science Monitor* found it is Pohl's "basically poetic imagination that elevates this novel to a high position among the author's works."

Joseph McClellan of the *Washington Post Book World* offers an insight into what has made Pohl's writing among the best in the science fiction field. "Pohl's work," McClellan writes, "offers science fiction at its best: basic human problems . . . woven deftly into an intricate plot; pure adventure happening to believable (if not deeply drawn) characters in surroundings almost beyond the borders of imagination; and at the end, when other questions have been laid to rest, the posing of a new question as unfathomable as time and space themselves."

CA INTERVIEW

CA interviewed Frederik Pohl by phone on November 30, 1982, at his home in New York City.

CA: Back in the Depression days when you were discovering science fiction and becoming a part of fandom, people were attracted to it for two reasons, you've said: "One is that science fiction was a way out of a bad place; the other, that it was a window on a better one." After fifty years of involvement in the genre—as fan, writer, agent, and editor—do you still see it that way?

POHL: Yes, I do, though the grimy landscape of the Depression has changed. The world is more exciting now, and maybe

a little more scary, but it does not seem to have that soul-deadening hopelessness that a lot of people felt during the Depression. They may worry a great deal about nuclear war or damage to the environment or any of a thousand other things, but they're worried about tangible things; it's not that there's no prospect of change in view. Science fiction is very good at describing for us what the future might be like, good or bad. And that, of course, is the first step to doing something about it. First you have to know what's possible, and then you start thinking about how to make it happen.

CA: For the most part, people seem to be attracted to science fiction early or not at all. Do you have any thoughts on this?

POHL: I think it's true. There are fairly few people I know who read science fiction who didn't begin before they were twenty, and a great many began when they were ten or twelve. Possibly it has to do with the fact that very young people are more willing to stretch their imagination. Once you form the habit, it's easy to keep doing it. But if you've never formed it, it's hard to start at forty or fifty.

CA: You were a member of the Brooklyn Science Fiction League, which was the first chapter of the Science Fiction League, started by Wonder Stories. Do small, local-level fan groups still form an important part of fandom?

POHL: Not so much. The place of the local clubs has been taken over by the conventions, of which there are hundreds every year. Some of those early clubs do exist; in fact, there are a couple that have met regularly since the 1930s—one in Philadelphia and one in Los Angeles. But I think mostly where local clubs exist today, they exist primarily for the purpose of putting on an annual convention.

CA: Do you attend a lot of the conventions?

POHL: Many more than makes any sense at all. I go to about twenty a year. That is a lot but still only a tiny fraction of the available ones. The science fiction magazine *Locus* lists over three hundred a year in the United States alone, and that doesn't include all of them. There are sometimes four or five conventions on the same weekend.

CA: You and many other science fiction writers acknowledge a great debt to your fellows. Are you still as close a lot as you used to be?

POHL: We're close in the sense that a family is close. There are disagreements among us, as there are in families, and there are some members of the family who aren't speaking to others. But it is almost a blood relationship. It's a community. And it's worldwide, not just in the United States. I've been in countries where I not only didn't speak the language but didn't even *know* anybody who spoke the language and have found people much like the people I associate with here. I've found this in Eastern Europe, in Japan, in Latin America.

CA: This seems to be more the case in science fiction than in other genres.

POHL: I think so. There is no other kind of writing, with the possible exception of poetry, that has the same sort of devoted audience that science fiction has. People who read poetry do tend to want to discuss it with other people who read poetry, but you don't find that with people who read bestsellers, and certainly not with people who read things like mysteries and Westerns.

CA: As a literary agent, you represented Isaac Asimov, C. M. Kornbluth, and many other writers in your field.

POHL: More than half the top ones in the country.

CA: How big a role do agents play in science fiction, especially with newcomers?

POHL: With newcomers, almost no role at all. It's of little use to an agent to take on a newcomer; he can't hope to make a profit on a writer who has not already shown a capacity to make money. A few agents will do it out of an innate sense of good fellowship, but most won't even look at a new writer. And it's not a great deal of help for the writer anyway, because the agent probably can do very little to get his first stories published. He possibly could if he used all his influence, but he isn't likely to do that unless he's personally committed, and he's not likely to let himself get personally committed.

An agent is absolutely indispensable, however, for a writer who finds himself signing book contracts that he doesn't understand. Any writer who sells a book should have an agent, unless he knows an awful lot about it himself. At that point it's not too hard to get one, but before that it's very difficult.

CA: How does the beginner get started, then?

POHL: He writes stories, and he mails them off to somebody who might buy them, and he keeps on doing that until either somebody *does* buy them or he begins to get the message.

CA: That sounds like your advice in The Early Pohl *on how to become a writer: "You write. That is, you put words on paper until you have completed one or more stories. There is simply no other way to do it."*

POHL: That's the only real difference between writers and other people: writers write. Other people may talk about it. Writers do it.

CA: Do you think the process can be helped along by classes, workshops, readings?

POHL: Anything that adds to a person's knowledge of the world or the skills involved in getting along with it is helpful. I'm not at all sure that a course in short-story writing is more valuable than, say, a course in sociology or history. I'd be inclined to doubt it. There are some writers who have taken creative writing courses and believe that they were helped a lot by them. Most writers, I think, learn it for themselves. The best thing in that area is not so much taking a course but participating in a workshop. The idea of being taught how to write is almost a contradiction because the only thing any writer has is his own individual view of the universe, and nobody else can teach him what that is. But to be in a workshop environment and discuss your work with other people who are writing can be very illuminating.

CA: Your various pen names and collaborations must have made you a difficult subject for bibliographers. Do you get a lot of queries from people trying to figure out what you've done?

POHL: I don't think there is a complete bibliography, but then the stuff that's left out probably deserves to be left out. There

are maybe a dozen books I edited that don't appear in any bibliography because my name never appeared on them. They were done for *Popular Science* when I was working there as an editor and afterward on a free-lance basis. They're on subjects like how to trap a moose or build a log cabin or make a radio set in a frying pan—home-workshop and outdoor-sports things.

I do get some queries from people. I refer them to whatever I can think of that might provide the answers, like my autobiography. There is a bibliography about to be published. I'm looking forward to that, because it'll answer a lot of my own questions.

CA: You don't have a complete list yourself?

POHL: No. Certainly not of all the various editions. I don't even know what all the editions were, because some of them were pirated.

CA: You've collaborated with C. M. Kornbluth and Jack Williamson on several books, and with Lester del Rey on one, Preferred Risk, *which you've said was a difficult collaboration . . .*

POHL: *Difficult* is the mildest word for it. It very nearly destroyed a close and long-term friendship.

CA: Have any of the collaborations been easy, from a working standpoint?

POHL: Writing is never terribly easy, but there are times when it goes with less strain than other times. With Cyril Kornbluth it was relatively strain-free. It was nice to be able to rely on somebody else to do half the work. With Kornbluth it actually worked out just about that way: I would write four pages, then he would write four pages, turn about, until we had the rough skeleton of a book finished. Of course the books were rewritten after that first draft—patched together, smoothed out, and generally neatened up—but structurally they were complete. I've never been able to do that with anybody else.

A collaboration is like a marriage: it's very hard if the two people in the combination are working at cross-purposes. That was the trouble with Lester and myself. He had one way of writing and I had quite a different one, and they did not ever blend. It wasn't a matter of style or the nature of the manuscript we were working on, it was just the way we went about putting words on paper.

CA: Gateway *(1977) won the Nebula Award, the John W. Campbell Award, and the Hugo. Do you consider it your best novel?*

POHL: I consider it my best novel that's far enough in the past for me to view at all objectively. I'm not sure whether ten years from now I will like it better than some of the others I have published or am about to publish. But I'll stand on it. I don't think I'll ever do a great deal better. There are some books I've published that I don't even like, but I'm very fond of *Gateway*.

CA: With your son Frederik IV you wrote Science Fiction Studies in Film *(1981), which grew partly out of your childhood love for movies. In fact, you saw "Death Takes a Holiday" and "Things To Come" something like twenty times or more, you noted. Are there current movies you like as much?*

POHL: There's no imaginable movie that I'd want to see twenty times anymore—this is a different world. Still, I think there are better movies coming out now than either of those. As a matter of fact, ''Death Takes a Holiday'' is a pretty puerile and soapy movie. I saw it on television a few months ago, and I was embarrassed to have liked it so much. ''Things To Come'' is different. It's stodgy and it has a lot of technical flaws; if it were being done today it would be quite different. But I still think it is a milestone in the history of film, and not just science fiction but film in general. It's one of the first films ever made that regarded the audience as capable of thought.

CA: How do you feel about the reviewing and critical writing on science fiction?

POHL: I try not to pay any attention to it. It's not that I'm not interested in what people say, but rather that I probably take it too seriously. If I get a bad review from someone in whom I have confidence, it depresses me a lot. If I get a good one, it makes me want to take the reviewer on a Caribbean cruise. The other day I saw a review of a book of mine done by a reviewer I'd always thought disliked me. It was a glowing review, and my conscience has been bothering me ever since for having thought so poorly of this obviously intelligent and astute person!

CA: What do you think of the teaching of science fiction in colleges and universities?

POHL: I had grave doubts about it at first; I feared it. My own school experience was almost all negative. I would have preferred to be left out of school and just given a library card when I was nine years old, because most of what I know I learned from reading books on my own rather than in school. I didn't start school until the fourth grade, and I dropped out as soon as I legally could. Some things are better taught than learned independently, but I don't think any of them are the things usually found in the school curriculum. I don't think I learned anything about history, ever, in any school course, and I've learned a great deal about it since then just by trying to piece together the various isolated events I knew something about. And science is hard to teach in school because the most interesting parts of it change almost weekly. The areas where big, important things are happening, such as molecular biology, are hard to keep up with, and there's no hope that a school course can, especially at the high school or undergraduate level.

But as to teaching science fiction, I have pretty much been converted. It's not an altogether bad thing. It may even be a good thing. I was most worried that it would be taught by people who didn't know anything about it. Indeed that did happen quite a lot. But a great many of the people who were members of the same fan clubs I was twenty or more years ago, and who had discovered science fiction when they were ten years old, have gone on to get degrees and get teaching jobs, and they're teaching science fiction. They've loved it all their lives, so they teach it from that perspective, and I think they're able to communicate some of that feeling to their students. Still, I'm a little skeptical of teaching literature in any form, because there's so much of what I think is called the intentional thought fallacy, the need of the teacher to say what the writer intended. The writer himself may not really know what he intended, and probably it's nothing like what the teacher thinks.

CA: You've talked on college campuses, on radio and television, and in places as far away as Russia. Do you still do a lot of it?

POHL: Not as much as I used to. It does take me away from what I want to do. I do some writing every day, no matter where I am—even on a lecture tour, a publicity tour, a vacation—because it's the only way I know to avoid the terrible problem of writer's block. I cut it down into manipulable fragments, four pages a day. But lecturing does distract me, and I do get tired of the sound of my own voice. What I have done is eliminate some kinds of lecturing. I used to do quite a lot of it for management groups, trade associations, civic and church groups. I do almost none of that now. I do speak at universities when a suitable opportunity presents itself; I spoke at Princeton a week ago and at Cambridge, in England, last month.

CA: Do you enjoy the college audience a lot?

POHL: A lot. I think I would speak every day if I could have the right kind of audience. College undergraduates and science fiction fans are very quick. I don't really have to explain things too carefully, because they readily grasp what I'm saying. I like that. It becomes more of a dialogue than a lecture.

CA: Do you have favorite contemporary writers?

POHL: I do, but mostly they change from day to day. There are some long-term favorites whose work I have admired: Norman Mailer is one; Nevil Shute was one until he died. There are some mystery writers I like very much. I have an incurable need to do a certain amount of reading each day, and I don't always want to read something difficult, so I tend to read mysteries by John D. MacDonald and Nicolas Freeling and Ed McBain.

CA: Isn't music very important to you also?

POHL: Symphonic music is a great enthusiasm of mine. I'm very fond of the romantic violin concerto, anything from about 1800 to 1945 or so. More recent music I don't like particularly, with some exceptions. The era before the big band has produced a lot of marvelous compositions, but they're not as much fun for me to listen to as that 100-piece orchestra, especially with a violin playing a solo in front of it.

CA: You've written about how much you love New York City and have recently moved back there after living in New Jersey for several years. Do you find New York somehow more stimulating to your work?

POHL: It is in a way, but I can't really define the way. I don't make a great deal of use of it—I mean, it has all these museums and the Metropolitan Opera and Carnegie Hall and Lincoln Center, and I've managed to use all of them with the same frequency I did when I lived in New Jersey. But there's something in the atmosphere, I think, that makes me feel more stimulated, and I'm not sure what it is. It could be just the noise! It's hard to sink into torpor in New York City, particularly where I live, which is in an area that has twelve major hospitals within a few blocks. There are sirens going by all the time. And I like knowing I can go out at any hour of the day or night and find the grocery store and movie theaters open, which is not always true in the suburbs.

CA: In The Way the Future Was *you alluded to some ''perfectly lousy New Yorkerish stories about Army life'' that are still hidden away. Are your readers likely to get something from you that's different from what you've been doing?*

POHL: It's possible. I have a couple of science fiction novels on contract which I've almost finished. I hope to have them both out of my hair within the next three or four months, and I've been thinking about what I want to do next. I'm toying with the idea of writing something that is not science fiction. There are some possibilities: one is a mainstream novel that I've been thinking about on and off for a while, and one is a revision of a book of mine called *Practical Politics,* which is not science fiction or fiction at all, but a how-to-do-it manual of party politics. I'm not sure what I'll do, but these ideas are stirring around in my head. I think perhaps I should not write as many science fiction novels as I have in the past couple of years; perhaps I saturate the market.

CA: But you still consider science fiction important, don't you?

POHL: I do attach a considerable importance to it. It's not simply a hobby, a kind of escape reading like detective stories. I think it does indeed stimulate the imagination and help people retain that youthful naivete that allows them to stretch their minds now and then. I have spent some time in future studies. I have been a member of the World Future Society since it began and have attended most of its world general meetings; I've lectured on the subject and even taught a course in it at the University of Kansas. A very desirable trait that doesn't exist in many people is the time-binding sense, the willingness to contemplate the future and consider what the options are, and I think science fiction does a very good job of encouraging that.

BIOGRAPHICAL/CRITICAL SOURCES—Books: Kingsley Amis, *New Maps of Hell: A Survey of Science Fiction,* Harcourt, 1960; Brian Aldiss, *Billion Year Spree: The History of Science Fiction,* Doubleday, 1973; Robert Scholes and Eric S. Rabkin, *Science Fiction: History, Science, Vision,* Oxford University Press, 1977; Paul A. Carter, *The Creation of Tomorrow: Fifty Years of Magazine Science Fiction,* Columbia University Press, 1977; Paul Walker, *Speaking of Science Fiction: The Paul Walker Interviews,* Luna Press, 1978; Frederik Pohl, *The Way the Future Was: A Memoir,* Ballantine, 1978; Charles Platt, *Dream Makers: The Uncommon People Who Write Science Fiction,* Berkley, 1980; *Contemporary Literary Criticism,* Volume XVIII, Gale, 1981; *Dictionary of Literary Biography,* Volume VIII: *Twentieth Century American Science Fiction Writers,* Gale, 1981.

Periodicals: *Times Literary Supplement,* January 14, 1977, January 27, 1978, May 14, 1983; *Analog,* February, 1977, January, 1979, December, 1979, May, 1980; *New York Times Book Review,* March 27, 1977, May 20, 1979; *New Statesman,* April 15, 1977; *New Republic,* November 26, 1977; *Spectator,* January 28, 1978; *Magazine of Fantasy and Science Fiction,* March, 1978, September, 1979; *Publishers Weekly,* July 31, 1978; *Christian Science Monitor,* June 20, 1979; *Books and Bookmen,* November, 1979; *Washington Post Book World,* March 14, 1980, November 23, 1980, July 25, 1982; *New York Times,* September 7, 1983.

—*Sketch by Thomas Wiloch*

—*Interview by Jean W. Ross*

*   *   *

POLA
See WATSON, Pauline

POMPIAN, Richard O(wen) 1935-

PERSONAL: Born July 17, 1935, in Chicago, Ill.; son of Bertram Edwin (a swimming-pool builder) and Molly (Pumpian) Pompian; married Rita Beyers (an assistant professor in English at Pace University), December 20, 1970. *Education:* University of Michigan, A.B. and Certificate in Journalism, 1958, Internship Certificate in Advertising, 1961; New York University, M.B.A. (with distinction), 1965, Certificate in Graphics, 1967, Certificate in Television, 1968, Certificate in Computer Programming and Systems, 1970; further graduate study in psychology at New School for Social Research, 1965 and 1968-69; University of Texas at Austin, doctoral candidate in business and organizational communication, 1982—; additional studies in musicianship and private studies in voice. *Home:* 300 Riverside Dr., New York, N.Y. 10025. *Office:* Department of Communication Arts, St. John's University, Jamaica, N.Y. 11439.

CAREER: Dancer-Fitzgerald-Sample, Inc., New York City, advertising copywriter, 1960-68; Davis, Mayer & Joyce, Englewood, N.J., advertising consultant, 1968-69; Mitchell Barkett Advertising, Inc., New York City, vice-president, 1970; Pompian Advertising, Inc., New York City, president, 1970—; St. John's University, Jamaica, N.Y., adjunct assistant professor, 1979-80, assistant professor of communication arts, 1980—. Lecturer in advanced writing, Pace University, 1974; adjunct lecturer in communications, Marymount Manhattan College, and adjunct lecturer in media studies, Fordham University, 1979-80. Consultant in writing to American Telephone and Telegraph Co., IBM Corp., and Chase Manhattan Bank, 1976—; consultant and writer for other advertising agencies in New York City. *Military service:* U.S. Army, 1958-60; became first lieutenant. *Member:* American Association for the Advancement of Science, American Business Communication Association, American Association of University Professors, National Association of Television Arts and Sciences, Sigma Delta Chi. *Awards, honors:* National Endowment for the Arts grant, 1979.

WRITINGS: Advertising (juvenile), F. Watts, 1970; (editor) *The Rhythm Book* (music textbook), Associated Music Publishers, 1971; (author of introduction and glossary) *Buyer's Book of American Crafts,* American Crafts Enterprises, 1979; *Writing for Professionals,* Pompians/Training Consultants, 1981. Also contributing editor of *Africa and the Arab World,* Sadlier. Editor, *Northeast Gazette,* 1976-80.

WORK IN PROGRESS: Research and writing on business communication relative to other writing crafts and to psycholinguistics.

SIDELIGHTS: Richard O. Pompian told *CA:* ''I am a 'commercial writer' in most every sense, including the literal: a writer of advertising commercials. I produce mass and organizational communications, both information and persuasive, for business sponsorship and for business and general audiences. Thus, my creativity is less artistically and more pragmatically oriented: gaining attention and interest, communicating quickly and credibly, and causing desired action. My current interest is administrative communication (letters, reports, proposals, etc.). Here I find journalistic techniques useful in facilitating quick reading of routine material. Similarly, advertising techniques—many borrowed from the arts—facilitate comprehension of the unknown and dramatization of the familiar. I teach many of these techniques to business students and business writers.''

AVOCATIONAL INTERESTS: Music, photography, graphics, psychology, language, psycholinguistics.

*   *   *

PORTEN, Bezalel   1931-

PERSONAL: Born February 14, 1931, in Philadelphia, Pa.; son of Bernard (a merchant) and Dora (Goldman) Porten; married Deborah Blaker (a teacher), October 21, 1956; children: Joshua Joel, Avrum David, Gavriel Hanan, Naomi Hannah. Education: Temple University, B.A., 1952; Columbia University, M.A., 1954, Ph.D., 1964; Jewish Theological Seminary of America, M.H.L. and Rabbi, 1957. Home: 28 Efrata, Jerusalem, Israel 93384. Office: Department of Jewish History, Hebrew University of Jerusalem, Jerusalem, Israel.

CAREER: Jewish Theological Seminary of America, Teachers Institute, New York, N.Y., instructor, 1958; College of Jewish Studies, Chicago, Ill., lecturer, 1958-60, assistant professor of Bible, 1962-64; Roosevelt University, Chicago, lecturer in history, 1963-64; University of California, Berkeley, visiting assistant professor of Bible, 1964-65; University of California, Davis, assistant professor, 1965-68, associate professor of Hebrew and Bible, 1968-69; Hebrew University of Jerusalem, Jerusalem, Israel, teaching fellow, 1969-72, senior lecturer, 1972-83, associate professor, 1983—.

Teaching fellow, Haifa University, 1968-72; visiting associate professor, York University, Toronto, Canada, 1975-76; senior fellow, University of Pennsylvania, 1979-81. Participant in archaeological excavations at Gezer and Arad, Israel, summer, 1967; examined and photographed Aramaic papyri in museums and libraries in Brooklyn, Cambridge, Oxford, London, Paris, Strassburg, Goettingen, East and West Berlin, Turin, Padua, Florence, Rome, Cairo, and Jerusalem; first scholar from Israel after signing of Camp David Accords to do research in Egypt, October, 1978. Member: American Schools of Oriental Research, Israel Exploration Society, Rabbinical Assembly of America, Society of Biblical Literature.

AWARDS, HONORS: Lena Socolow grant for study and travel in Israel, 1960-61; National Foundation for Jewish Culture grant, 1961-62; Fuerstenberg Award, University of Chicago, 1963-64; summer faculty fellowship, University of California, Davis, 1967; research grant, University of California, Los Angeles, Near Eastern Center, 1968-70; National Endowment for the Humanities fellowship, 1979-80; American Council of Learned Societies grant-in-aid, 1979-80; American Philosophical Society grant-in-aid, shared with J. Tigay, 1980-81; American Research Center in Egypt research fellowship, 1980-81.

WRITINGS: Archives from Elephantine: The Life of an Ancient Jewish Military Colony, University of California Press, 1968; (with J. C. Greenfield) Jews of Elephantine and Arameans of Syene (Fifth Century B.C.E.): Fifty Aramaic Texts with Hebrew and English Translations, Hebrew University of Jerusalem, 1974; (with J. C. Greenfield) The Bisutun Inscription of Darius the Great: Aramaic Version, Corpus Inscriptionum Iranicarum, Part I, Volume V, Texts I (London), 1982. Contributor of articles and reviews to scholarly journals.

WORK IN PROGRESS: Preparation of a corpus of Aramaic texts; research on narrative techniques in the Old Testament.

POWELL, G. Bingham, Jr.   1942-

PERSONAL: Born February 8, 1942, in Salem, Ore.; son of G. Bingham (a savings officer) and Gretchen (Spencer) Powell; married V. Patricia Lee, August 23, 1963 (divorced, 1974); married Lynda L. Watts, June 5, 1975; children: (first marriage) Elizabeth, Suzanne, Katrin; (second marriage) Eleanor. Education: Princeton University, B.A. (magna cum laude), 1963; Stanford University, M.A., 1964, Ph.D., 1968. Office: Department of Political Science, University of Rochester, Rochester, N.Y. 14627.

CAREER: University of California, Berkeley, assistant professor of political science, 1968-70; University of Rochester, Rochester, N.Y., assistant professor, 1970-73, associate professor, 1973-79, professor of political science, 1979—. Visiting professor, University of North Carolina at Chapel Hill, 1982-83. Has delivered professional papers at meetings of the American Political Science Association and at other national and international conferences. Chairman of Samuel Beer prize committee for British Politics Group, 1981-82. Member: American Political Science Association (chairman of section on teaching political science, 1971; member of Woodrow Wilson Prize committee, 1973; chairman of section on comparative political behavior, 1983), Phi Beta Kappa. Awards, honors: Social Science Research Council fellow, 1967-68, Guggenheim fellow, 1983-84; grants from Institute of International Studies, Berkley, 1969-70, and from National Science Foundation, 1971-73; Woodrow Wilson Foundation Award, American Political Science Association, 1983, for best book published in the United States during 1982 on government, politics, or international affairs, for Contemporary Democracies.

WRITINGS: (With Gabriel A. Almond) Comparative Politics: A Developmental Approach, Little, Brown, 1966; Social Fragmentation and Political Hostility: An Austrian Case Study, Stanford University Press, 1970; (with Almond) Comparative Politics: System, Process, and Policy, Little, Brown, 1977; (editor with Almond) Comparative Politics Today, 2nd edition (Powell was not associated with earlier edition), Little, Brown, 1980; Contemporary Democracies: Participation, Stability and Violence, Harvard University Press, 1982.

Contributor: Almond, Scott Flanigan, and Robert Mundt, editors, Crisis, Choice and Change, Little, Brown, 1973; (with Lynda W. Powell) Sidney Verba and Lucien W. Pye, editors, The Citizen and Politics, Greylock, 1976; Richard Rose, editor, Electoral Participation: A Comparative Perspective, Sage Publications, 1980; William T. Bluhm, editor, The Paradigm Problem in Political Science, Carolina Academic Press, 1982; Almond, M. Chodorow, and R. H. Pierce, editors, Progress and Its Discontents, University of California Press, 1982.

Contributor of articles to American Political Science Review, American Journal of Political Science, Comparative Politics, and International Political Science Review, and of book reviews to American Journal of Sociology, and Contemporary Sociology. Member of editorial board, Midwest Journal of Political Science, 1973-75, and American Journal of Political Science, 1979-81.

WORK IN PROGRESS: A book on extremist political parties, their origin, definition, and support bases, as well as the role they play in contemporary democracies; a research project on the factors leading voters to defect from support of government incumbents.

SIDELIGHTS: Comparative Politics: A Developmental Approach has been translated into Dutch, French, German, Italian, Korean, and Spanish; *Comparative Politics: System, Process and Policy* has been translated into French.

*   *   *

PRESTON, Lee E.   1930-

PERSONAL: Born July 28, 1930, in Dallas, Tex.; son of Lee E. and Cecil (Degan) Preston; married Patricia Leahy, January 27, 1958; children: Katherine, James, Mary Jane. *Education:* Vanderbilt University, B.A., 1951; Harvard University, M.A., 1953, Ph.D., 1958. *Home:* 7015 Hunter Lane, Hyattsville, Md. 20782. *Office:* Center for Business and Public Policy, University of Maryland, College Park, Md. 20782.

CAREER: University of California, Berkeley, assistant professor, 1958-62, associate professor, 1962-66, professor of business administration, 1966-69, associate dean, School of Business Administration, 1967-69; State University of New York at Buffalo, Melvin H. Baker Professor of American Enterprise, 1969-79, director, Center for Policy Studies, 1973-79; University of Maryland, College Park, professor and director, Center for Business and Public Policy, 1979—. Member of White House Task Force on Anti-Trust Policy, 1967-68. Consultant to various government agencies, private firms, law firms, and public bodies. *Military service:* U.S. Army, 1954-56. *Member:* American Economic Association, Academy of Management. *Awards, honors:* Western Farm Economics Association annual research award, 1961, 1966.

WRITINGS: (With James S. Duesenberry) *Cases and Problems in Economics,* Prentice-Hall, 1960; *Exploration for Non-Ferrous Metals: An Economic Analysis,* Resources for the Future, Inc., 1960; (editor) *Managing the Independent Business,* Prentice-Hall, 1962; *Profits, Competition and Rules of Thumb in Retail Food Pricing,* Institute of Business and Economic Research, University of California, 1963; (with others) *Competition and Price Behavior in the British Columbia Petroleum Industry,* Stanford Research Institute, 1964; (with Norman R. Collins) *Studies in a Simulated Market,* Institute of Business

and Economic Research, University of California, 1966; (with Paul E. Nelson) *Price Merchandising in Food Retailing: A Case Study,* Institute of Business and Economic Research, University of California, 1966; (editor) *Social Issues in Marketing,* Scott, Foresman, 1968; (with Collins) *Concentration and Price-Cost Margins in Manufacturing Industries,* University of California Press, 1968; *Consumer Good Marketing in a Developing Economy: The Case of Greece,* Center for Economic Research and Planning (Athens), 1968.

Markets and Marketing: An Orientation, Scott, Foresman, 1970; *Trade Patterns in the Middle East,* American Enterprise Institute, 1970; *The Industry and Enterprise Structure of the U.S. Economy,* General Learning Press, 1971; (with James E. Post) *Private Management and Public Policy,* Prentice-Hall, 1975; (editor) *Research in Corporate Social Performance and Policy,* Jai Press, Volume I, 1978, Volume II, 1980, Volume III, 1981, Volume IV, 1982, Volume V, 1983.

Contributor: C. J. Friedich and J. K. Galbraith, editors, *Public Policy,* Graduate School of Public Administration, Harvard University, 1954; Moyer and Hollander, editors, *Markets and Marketing in Developing Economies,* Irwin, 1968; J. F. Weston, editor, *Public Policy toward Mergers,* Goodyear Publishing, 1969; Louis P. Bucklin, editor, *Vertical Marketing Systems,* Scott, Foresman, 1970; J. Fred Weston and Stanley I. Ornstein, editors, *The Impact of Large Firms on the U.S. Economy,* Heath, 1973; Fred C. Allvine, editor, *Public Policy and Marketing Practices,* American Marketing Association, 1973; J. W. McGuire, editor, *Contemporary Management: Issues and Viewpoints,* Prentice-Hall, 1975. Contributor of articles, research reports, and reviews to journals in his field.

Member of editorial review board, *Journal of Industrial Economics, Industrial Organization Review, Academy of Management Journal,* and *Journal of Reprints for Antitrust Law and Economics.*

*   *   *

PRESTON, Richard
See LINDSAY, Jack

R

RADER, Dotson 1942-

PERSONAL: Born July 25, 1942, in Minnesota; son of Paul Carlyle (a preacher) and Lois (an organist; maiden name, Schacht) Rader. *Education:* Attended Columbia University, 1963-68. *Politics:* Democratic Socialist. *Home:* 4560 Province Lane, Princeton, N.J. 08540. *Agent:* Morton L. Janklow, 598 Madison Ave., New York, N.Y. 10022. *Office: Parade* Magazine, 750 Third Ave., New York, N.Y. 10017.

CAREER: Writer. Editor of *Defiance* magazine, 1969-71; *Evergreen Review,* New York City, contributing editor, 1969-71; *New Politics,* New York City, editorial consultant, 1971—; *Esquire* magazine, New York City, contributing editor, 1972-80; *Parade* magazine, New York City, national correspondent, 1980-82, contributing editor, 1982—. Honorary ambassador, West Virginia, 1982. Co-chairman, Peoples Coalition for Peace and Justice; chairman, Humanitas; traveler, Students for a Democratic Society. Consultant to National Committee for Literary Arts at Lincoln Center, 1980—. *Member:* P.E.N., Authors League, War Resisters League. *Awards, honors:* Odyssey Institute Award for Journalism, 1982.

WRITINGS: I Ain't Marchin' Anymore! (memoir), McKay, 1969; *Government Inspected Meat* (novel), McKay, 1970; *Blood Dues* (memoir), Knopf, 1973; *The Dream's on Me* (novel), Putnam, 1975; *Miracle* (novel), Random House, 1978; *Beau Monde* (novel), Random House, 1981. Also author of screenplay "The Bronze Lily," 1975.

WORK IN PROGRESS: A biography of Tennessee Williams.

BIOGRAPHICAL/CRITICAL SOURCES: New York Times Book Review, May 21, 1978; *Chicago Tribune Book World,* May 24, 1981.

* * *

RAEF, Laura (Gladys) C(auble)

PERSONAL: Born in Walnut Grove, Mo.; daughter of William Arthur (a construction worker) and Edna May (Fox) Cauble; married William Raef (a businessman); children: Sharon Ann. *Education:* Burge Hospital School of Nursing, R.N., 1934; attended College of San Mateo, and San Francisco State College (now University), 1956-58. *Politics:* Republican. *Religion:* Christian Scientist. *Home and office:* 965 San Marcos Cir., Mountain View, Calif. 94040.

CAREER: Writer. Metropolitan Life Insurance Co., San Francisco, Calif., industrial nurse, 1948-57. *Member:* California's Writers' Club (Berkeley; past president; program chairman). *Awards, honors:* Jack London Award from California Writers' Club, for exemplary service as a member.

WRITINGS—Published by Bouregy, except as indicated: *Symphony in the Sky,* 1970; *Nurse in the News,* 1970; *Nurse in Fashion,* 1972; *Nurse Jan and the Legacy,* 1974; *Miracle at Seaside,* 1975; *Waikiki Nurse,* 1976; *Trade Winds over Kokio,* Manor, 1979; *Target for Terror,* 1979; *Dangerous Designs,* 1981; *Under a Florida Moon,* 1984; *Dr. Tris: Cartoonist,* 1984. Also author of *Cave Diving Romance.* Contributor of feature articles to *Christian Science Monitor* and children's and women's stories to various newspapers and magazines.

WORK IN PROGRESS: A young adult novel, *The Canyon Curse.*

SIDELIGHTS: Laura C. Raef writes: "The question most often asked of me is, 'where do you get your ideas?' To me, this is one of the easiest things about writing. Ideas are everywhere. Sometimes, they spring from an off-hand phrase of a friend. Other times, an article in the newspaper hints at an idea. At times, ideas come to me 'out of the blue.' *But an idea must grab me,* if it's going to supply enough material for a novel. It must start the juices pumping in both my head and my heart. It must keep 'nagging' me until I listen . . . enough to start putting it on paper.

"Recently, while flying to Florida, I was skimming through the flight magazine and ran across an article that intrigued me to no end. It was on cave diving (not scuba) in Florida. This opened up a whole new world to me, and I have completed a novel with that background. My heroine is a cave diving instructor. The completed manuscript is out now to a publisher for consideration."

* * *

RALSTON, Alma (Smith Payne)
(Alma Smith Payne)

PERSONAL: Born in Oakland, Calif.; daughter of Robert Russell (a businessman) and Neva (Palmer) Smith; married James W. Chambers, October 10, 1924 (divorced, 1937); married Buford Burke Payne, September 26, 1947 (died, 1959); married William Robertson Ralston, February 12, 1967 (died, 1969); children: (first marriage) Robert Warner Chambers, James W. Chambers, Jr.; stepchildren: Richard Montague Payne, Margaret Payne Ferris, William R. Ralston, Jr., Donald Ralston. *Education:* University of California, A.B., 1922, M.A., 1936. *Residence:* Walnut Creek, Calif.

CAREER: California Department of Education, San Francisco, northern California supervisor of emergency education program in nursery schools, 1936-40; Berkeley (Calif.) public schools, supervisor of nursery schools, parent education and child care centers, 1940-47; University of California Extension, Berkeley, lecturer, 1941-43; Diablo Valley College, Pleasant Hill, Calif., instructor in journalism and creative writing, beginning 1971.

Member of board of directors, California Heart Association; past president and member of board of directors, Alameda County Heart Association; president of Friends of California Libraries, 1966. *Member:* National League of American Pen Women (president of Piedmont Oakland branch, beginning 1974), Phi Beta Kappa, Theta Sigma Phi, California Writers Club (first vice-president). *Awards, honors:* Received California Heart Association bronze medallion, 1960, and silver medallions, 1964 and 1966, for nutrition work and for participation in the fight against heart disease.

WRITINGS—All under name Alma Smith Payne: (With Dorothy Callahan) *The Low Sodium Cook Book,* Little, Brown, 1953, 2nd edition published as *The Low Sodium, Fat-Controlled Cookbook,* 1960, 4th edition published as *The Fat and Sodium Control Cookbook,* 1975; (with Callahan) *The Great Nutrition Puzzle,* Scribner, 1956; (with Callahan) *Young America's Cookbook,* Scribner, 1959; (with son, Robert Warner Chambers) *From Cell to Test Tube,* Scribner, 1960; *Discoverer of the Unseen World: Biography of Antoni van Leeuwenhoek,* World Publishing, 1966; *Partners in Science,* World Publishing, 1968; *Jinglebells and Pastry Shells,* World Publishing, 1968; *Pressure Cooking,* Nitty Gritty Productions, 1977; *The Baby Food Book,* Little, Brown, 1977.

AVOCATIONAL INTERESTS: Grandchildren, the arts, travel, reading, and experimenting with foods.†

*   *   *

RAUCH, Irmengard   1933-

PERSONAL: Born April 17, 1933, in Dayton, Ohio; daughter of Konrad (an electronics research engineer) and Elsa (Knott) Rauch; married Gerald F. Carr (a professor); children: Christopher, Gregory. *Education:* University of Dayton, B.S., 1955; Ohio State University, M.A., 1957; University of Michigan, Ph.D., 1962; also studied at National University of Mexico and University of Munich. *Office:* University of California, Berkeley, Calif. 94720.

CAREER: University of Wisconsin—Madison, 1962-66, began as instructor, became assistant professor of Germanic linguistics; University of Pittsburgh, Pittsburgh, Pa., associate professor of Germanic linguistics, 1966-68; University of Illinois at Urbana-Champaign, associate professor, 1968-72, professor of Germanic linguistics, 1972-82; University of California, Berkeley, professor of Germanic linguistics, 1982—.

MEMBER: American Association of Teachers of German, Linguistic Society of America, Modern Language Association of America, Societas Linguistica Europaea, International Linguistic Association, International Phonetics Association, Se-

miotic Society of America, American Name Society, Alpha Sigma Tau, Delta Phi Alpha.

AWARDS, HONORS: Fulbright fellow in Munich, Germany, 1957-58; University of Wisconsin research grant, 1966; National Science Foundation and Linguistic Society of America travel grant, 1972; National Endowment for the Humanities grant, 1978; Guggenheim fellowship, 1982-83.

WRITINGS: The Old High German Dipthongization, Mouton & Co., 1967; (editor with C. T. Scott) *Approaches in Linguistic Methodology,* University of Wisconsin Press, 1967; (editor with J. Eichhoff) *Der Heliand,* Wissenschaftliche Buchgesellschaft, 1973; (editor with Gerald F. Carr) *Linguistic Method: The Herbert Penzl Festschrift,* Peter de Ridder Press, 1979; *The Signifying Animal: The Grammar of Language and Experience,* Indiana University Press, 1980. Contributor to *Linguistics, Monatshefte, Lingua, Indogermanische,* and other journals.

WORK IN PROGRESS: Several books in linguistics.

SIDELIGHTS: Irmengard Rauch is competent in several modern European and classical languages.

*   *   *

RAVIELLI, Anthony   1916-

PERSONAL: Born July 1, 1916, in New York, N.Y.; son of Peter (a sculptor) and Letizia (Cacacce) Ravielli; married Georgia Ann Weber, May 3, 1954; children: Jane, Ellen, Anthony, Jr. *Education:* Attended Cooper Union, 1932-35, and Art Students League, 1936. *Home and office:* 79 Lolly Lane, Stamford, Conn. 06903.

CAREER: Frances Buente Advertising Agency, New York, N.Y., assistant art director, 1932-34; art director, Superior Litho Co., 1934-37, and Otto Freund Studios, 1937-42, both New York. Illustrator of adult and children's books; exhibited with American Institute of Graphic Arts (A.I.G.A.) Children's Book Show, New York, 1955-57, and other shows; represented in permanent collections of National Club, Augusta, Ga., Officers Club, Governors Island, N.Y., and Fort Niagara, Niagara Falls, N.Y. *Military service:* U.S. Army, 1942-45. *Member:* Authors League of America. *Awards, honors:* A.I.G.A. Children's Book Show award, 1955-57.

WRITINGS—All self-illustrated juveniles: *Wonders of the Human Body,* Viking, 1954; *An Adventure in Geometry,* Viking, 1957 (published in England as *An Adventure with Shapes,* Phoenix House, 1960); *The World Is Round,* Viking, 1963; *The Rise and Fall of the Dinosaurs,* Parents' Magazine Press, 1963; *Elephants, the Last of the Land Giants,* Parents' Magazine Press, 1965; *From Fins to Hands: An Adventure in Evolution,* Viking, 1968; *What Is Bowling?,* Atheneum, 1975; *What Is Golf?,* Atheneum, 1976; *What Is Tennis?,* Atheneum, 1977; *What Are Street Games?,* Atheneum, 1978.

Illustrator: Kate Shippen, *Men, Microscopes and Living Things,* Viking, 1955; Ben Hogan and Herbert Warren Wind, *Five Lessons: The Modern Fundamentals of Golf,* A. S. Barnes, 1957; Don Carter, *Ten Secrets of Bowling,* Viking, 1958; Sybil Sutton-Vane, *The Story of Eyes,* Viking, 1958; Charles Robert Darwin, *Voyage of the Beagle,* abridged and edited by Millicent E. Selsam, Harper, 1959; Martin Gardner, *Relativity for the Million,* Macmillan, 1962; Isaac Asimov, *The Human Body,* Houghton, 1963; Asimov, *The Human Brain,* Houghton, 1963; H. Chandler Elliott, *The Shape of Intelligence,* Scribner, 1969;

Robert T. Jones, *Bobby Jones on the Basic Golf Swing*, Doubleday, 1969.

Dick Aultman, *Square-to-Square Golf Swing*, Golf Digest, 1970; Navin Sullivan, *Controls in Your Body*, Lippincott, 1971; John Jacobs and Ken Bowden, *Practical Golf*, Quadrangle, 1972; Carl Lohren and Larry Dennis, *One Move to Better Golf*, Quadrangle, 1975; Aultman and Bowden, *The Methods of Golf's Masters*, Coward, 1975; Byron Nelson and Dennis, *Shape Your Swing the Modern Way*, Simon & Schuster, 1976; Memmler, *The Human Body in Health and Disease*, Lippincott, 1977; Memmler, *Structure and Function of the Human Body*, Lippincott, 1977, updated edition, 1983; Paul Runyon, *The Short Way to Lower Scoring*, Simon & Schuster, 1979; Aultman, *Better Golf in Six Swings*, Simon & Schuster, 1982; Tom Watson, *Getting Up and Down*, Random House, 1983.

WORK IN PROGRESS: Evolution of the Human Brain; Speed.

SIDELIGHTS: Anthony Ravielli told *CA:* "All of my juvenile books evolved from the myriad questions my nieces, nephews, and my own children asked during their formative years. My answers invariably were carefully researched and illuminated with countless sketches to clarify subjects which, to them, seemed puzzling and mysterious." When the author showed these sketches to May Masee of the Viking Press, she encouraged him, he says, "to organize this material into children's books so that other young, inquiring minds might share this information. Needless to say," the author concludes, "in the course of my research my own interests expanded and preferences formed. So it is not surprising that over the years I have poured all of my efforts into those areas which fascinate me the most—Science and Sports."

AVOCATIONAL INTERESTS: Paleontology, photography, golf, woodworking.

BIOGRAPHICAL/CRITICAL SOURCES: David Harris Russell, Mary Agnella Gunn, and others, *The Ginn Basic Reading Program, Junior High-School Series: Achievement Through Reading*, Ginn, 1965; Henry Thompson Fillmer and others, *Composition Through Literature*, American Book Co., 1967; Diana Klemin, *The Illustrated Book: Its Art and Craft*, C. N. Potter, 1970.

*   *   *

RAY, John (Philip)   1929-
(Philip Lovegrove)

PERSONAL: Born May 5, 1929, in London, England; son of John Albert (a railwayman) and Grace (Lovegrove) Ray; married Mary Creese, March 31, 1951; children: Susan, Margaret, Jennifer. *Education:* Attended Goldsmith's College, London, 1946-48, and City Literary Institute (as extramural student), 1951-55. *Religion:* Church of England. *Home:* Cherrytrees, 10 Exeter Close, Tonbridge, Kent, England.

CAREER: Schoolmaster and teacher of history and other subjects in British schools, 1948—, currently deputy headmaster of Hugh Christie School, Tonbridge, Kent. *Military service:* British Army, national service. *Member:* Historical Association, Society of Authors, Crime Writers Association.

WRITINGS: (Under pseudonym Philip Lovegrove) *The Von Stahmer Jigsaw* (novel), Cassell, 1980.

All textbooks for ages 11-18, published by Heinemann: *The History of Flight*, 1968; *Britain and the Modern World*, 1969; (with wife, Mary D. Ray) *The Victorian Age*, 1969; *A History*

of Britain's Modern Transport, 1969; *A History of the Railways*, 1969; *Hitler and Mussolini*, 1970; *Roosevelt and Kennedy*, 1970; *Lloyd George and Churchill*, 1970; *Britain Between the Wars*, 1975; *The First World War*, 1975; *The Second World War*, 1977; *Discovery and Exploration*, 1980.

Textbooks for ages 11-18: *A History of the Motor Car*, Pergamon, 1966; *A History of Britain, 1900-1939*, Pergamon, 1966; *The Place of Women*, Thomas Nelson, 1971; *The Growth of Schools*, Thomas Nelson, 1972; *Headline History: Nineteenth Century*, Dent, 1972; *Headline History: Twentieth Century*, Dent, 1973; *British Agriculture*, Thomas Nelson, 1973; *Cars*, A. & C. Black, 1973; *Inventors and Scientists*, Thomas Nelson, 1974; *Headline History to 1485*, Evans Brothers, 1976; *Headline History: Tudor and Stuart*, Evans Brothers, 1976; *Headline History: The Eighteenth Century*, Evans Brothers, 1976.

WORK IN PROGRESS: Britain and the Wider World Since 1945, The World Since 1900, and *Flight in the 20th Century*, all educational books; *The Rosen Secret* and *Glos*, both fiction.

AVOCATIONAL INTERESTS: The novels of Graham Greene, cricket, brass rubbing, boxing, old cars, and drinking rum.

*   *   *

READ, Leonard Edward   1898-1983

PERSONAL: Born September 26, 1898, in Hubbardston, Mich.; died May 14, 1983, in Irvington-on-Hudson, N.Y.; son of Orville Baker (a farmer) and Ada (Sturgis) Read; married Gladys Emily Cobb, July 15, 1920; children: Leonard Edward, James Baker. *Education:* Ferris Institute (now Ferris State College), graduate, 1917. *Politics:* Republican. *Religion:* Congregationalist. *Home:* Hillside, Irvington-on-Hudson, N.Y. *Office:* Foundation for Economic Education, Irvington-on-Hudson, N.Y.

CAREER: Ann Arbor Produce Co., Ann Arbor, Mich., president, 1919-25; Chamber of Commerce executive in Burlingame, Calif., 1927, and Palo Alto, Calif., 1928; U.S. Chamber of Commerce, assistant manager, Western Division, Seattle, Wash., 1929-32, manager, 1932-39; Los Angeles Chamber of Commerce, Los Angeles, Calif., manager, 1939-45; National Industrial Conference Board, New York, N.Y., executive vice-president, 1945-46; Foundation for Economic Education, Inc., Irvington-on-Hudson, N.Y., president, 1946-83.

Lecturer and conductor of seminars throughout the United States, Sweden, Canada, Japan, and in South and Central America. *Military service:* U.S. Air Service, American Expeditionary Forces, 1917-19; survivor of torpedoed "Tuscania." *Member:* American Economic Association, Canadian Club of New York, St. Andrew's Golf Club. *Awards, honors:* Litt.D., Grove City College.

WRITINGS—Published by Foundation for Economic Education, except as indicated: *Romance of Reality*, Dodd, 1937; *Pattern for Revolt*, privately printed, 1945; *Students of Liberty*, 1950; *Outlook for Freedom*, 1951; *Government: An Ideal Concept*, 1954; *Why Not Try Freedom?*, Centro de Estudios sobre la Libertad, 1958.

Elements of Libertarian Leadership, 1962; *Anything That's Peaceful*, 1964; *The Free Market and Its Enemy*, 1965; *Deeper Than You Think*, 1967; *Accent on the Right*, 1968; *The Coming Aristocracy*, 1969; *Let Freedom Reign*, 1969.

Talking to Myself, 1970; *Then Truth Will Out*, 1971; *To Free or Freeze*, 1972; *Meditations on Freedom*, 1972; *Instead of*

Violence: The Case for the Non-coercive Society, O. R. Bramble (Lansing), 1973; *Who's Listening?*, 1973; *Having My Way*, 1974; *The Free Man's Almanac*, 1974; *Castles in the Air*, 1975; *The Love of Liberty*, 1975.

ABC's of Freedom, 1976; *Comes the Dawn*, 1976; *Awake for Freedom's Sake*, 1977; *Vision*, 1978; *Liberty: Legacy of Truth*, 1978; *The Freedom Freeway*, 1979.

Seeds of Progress, 1980; *Thoughts Rule the World*, 1981; *How Do We Know?*, 1981; *The Path of Duty*, 1982.

OBITUARIES: *New York Times*, May 16, 1983; *Chicago Tribune*, May 17, 1983; *Los Angeles Times*, May 19, 1983.†

*   *   *

REDDING, Robert Hull   1919-

PERSONAL: Born December 3, 1919, in Honolulu, Hawaii; married Grace Feeny, July 14, 1956. *Home:* 391 West Spruce, Sequim, Wash. 98382.

CAREER: Resident of Alaska for forty-nine years, living in every geographical area except the Aleutians, and working at a wide variety of jobs; supply officer for the Alaska State Department of Public Works until 1977. *Military service:* U.S. Army Air Forces, 1942-46; became sergeant. *Member:* Pioneers of Alaska. *Awards, honors:* First prize for nonfiction, League of Alaska Writers, 1965; prizes in poetry, juvenile writing, and fiction, League of Alaska Writers, 1966.

WRITINGS: The Partners (western novel), Doubleday, 1981; *Boeing, Planemaker to the World* (nonfiction), Bison Books, 1983.

Juveniles: *Aluk: An Alaskan Caribou*, Doubleday, 1967; *Mara: An Alaskan Weasel*, Doubleday, 1968; *North to the Wilderness: The Story of an Alaskan Boy* (autobiographical), Doubleday, 1970; *The Alaska Pipeline*, Children's Press, 1980; *The Girl from Limbo*, Fawcett, 1981. Stories, articles, and poems have been published in youth magazines and adult periodicals.

WORK IN PROGRESS: Two romantic novels; a collection of stories about the Suchatna country of Alaska; a series of adventure stories based on Alaskan history just prior to the Klondike gold rush of 1898; research on life in Alaska during the 1930s.

*   *   *

REES, David   1928-

PERSONAL: Born October 15, 1928, in Swansea, Wales. *Education:* University College of Swansea, University of Wales, B.A. (with honors), 1952. *Address:* 103 Vivian Rd., Sketty, Swansea, Wales.

CAREER: Writer. *Spectator*, London, England, staff member, beginning 1963, literary editor, 1964-67.

WRITINGS: Korea: The Limited War, St. Martin's, 1964; *The Age of Containment: The Cold War, 1945-1965*, St. Martin's, 1967; *The New Pressures from North Korea*, Current Affairs Research Services Centre (London), 1970; *Harry Dexter White: A Study in Paradox*, Coward, 1973; *Rhys Davies*, University of Wales Press, 1975; (editor) *A Gower Anthology*, C. Davies, 1977.

All published by Institute for the Study of Conflict (London): *North Korea's Growth as a Subversive Centre*, 1972; *Southern Europe: NATO's Crumbling Flank*, 1975; *North Korea: Un-*

dermining the Truce, 1976; *Soviet Strategic Penetration of Africa*, 1976; *Soviet Sea Power: The Covert Support Fleet*, 1977; *Vietnam Since Liberation: Hanoi's Revolutionary Strategy*, 1977; *The Two Koreas in Conflict: A Comparative Study*, 1978. Contributor to journals.

AVOCATIONAL INTERESTS: Walking.

BIOGRAPHICAL/CRITICAL SOURCES: Christian Science Monitor, October 19, 1967.†

*   *   *

REEVES, Bruce Douglas   1940-

PERSONAL: Born August 27, 1940, in Salt Lake City, Utah; son of Paul Sylvester (a tilesetter) and Florence (Hyler) Reeves; married Sherrill McPhee (a librarian), September 29, 1964; children: Simone Patricia. *Education:* Attended San Jose State College (now University), 1958-61, and University of California, Berkeley, 1963-64. *Politics:* Democrat. *Religion:* Agnostic. *Residence:* Berkeley, Calif.

CAREER: Writer. Has worked for San Jose Public Library, San Jose, Calif., and Bancroft Library, University of California, Berkeley, and as a magazine editor. Also a "serious painter, working primarily in oils and watercolor, as well as in ink and pastel. Specialize in portraits and what might be called psychological paintings (always of human beings)." *Awards, honors:* Third place short fiction award, *Runner's World* magazine, for "The Challenge."

WRITINGS—Novels: *The Night Action*, New American Library, 1966; *Man on Fire*, Pyramid Books, 1970; *Street Smarts*, Beaufort Book Co., 1981. Has written television plays for the Television Repertory Theatre of San Francisco, 1973-74. Also author of books under undisclosed pseudonyms. Contributor to *Masterplots of World Literature*, *McGill's Literary Annual*, and *One for the Road*, an anthology for young adults. Contributor of essays, articles, and stories to periodicals, including *Playboy*, *Pulpsmith*, *Express*, *California Living*, *Journal of Applied Management*, and *Franchising Today*.

WORK IN PROGRESS: North Beach, a book of short stories; *The Movie Freak*, *Weekend*, *Running Out of Time*, and *The Househusband*, novels; "Revenge," "The Wedding Party," and "Nautilis," plays.

SIDELIGHTS: Bruce Douglas Reeves told *CA:* "My writing career has been divided between novels, short stories, nonfiction articles and literary criticism, and drama. My fiction deals with human beings in conflict in, and sometimes with, contemporary society. My articles range in subject matter from how to succeed in the literary marketplace, to business and banking, to pornographic movie making."

MEDIA ADAPTATIONS: Film rights to *The Night Action* have been bought by Warner Brothers Pictures.

AVOCATIONAL INTERESTS: Collecting art, painting, travel.

*   *   *

REID, John Calvin

PERSONAL: Born in Charlotte, N.C.; son of John Calvin and Ximena (Hunter) Reid; married Charlotte Boyce Orr, November 15, 1935. *Education:* Erskine College, B.A., 1922; Pittsburgh Theological Seminary, Th.M., 1926; graduate study at University of Edinburgh and Oxford University, 1928; Southern Baptist Theological Seminary, Ph.D., 1930. *Home:* 1827 Senate St., Columbia, S.C. 29201.

CAREER: Presbyterian clergyman. Minister in Louisville, Ky., 1926-29, Butler, Pa., 1930-39, Columbus, Ga., 1940-45, and Pittsburgh, Pa., 1945-67; Presbyterian Church, Hilton Head Island, S.C., minister, 1967-72. Interim supply minister at First Presbyterian Church, Albuquerque, N.M., 1967, Grosse Pointe Memorial United Presbyterian Church, Grosse Pointe Farms, Mich., 1968, Menlo Park United Presbyterian Church, Menlo Park, Calif., 1973, Memorial Drive Presbyterian Church, Houston, Tex., 1974, Walnut Creek Presbyterian Church, Walnut Creek, Calif., 1976, Eastminster Presbyterian Church, Columbia, S.C., 1977, First Presbyterian Church, Aiken, S.C., 1978, Shandon Presbyterian Church, Columbia, 1979, Winter Park Presbyterian Church, Orlando, Fla., 1980, First Presbyterian Church, Orlando, 1981, Second Presbyterian Church, Memphis, Tenn., 1982, and First Presbyterian Church, Delray Beach, Fla., 1983. Vice-moderator, United Presbyterian Church, 1985, moderator of Pittsburgh Presbytery, 1966. Lecturer under auspices of United Presbyterian Church in the United States, Egypt, Spain, Iran, and Lebanon, 1965. *Awards, honors:* D.D. from Muskingham College and Tarkio College; Algernon Sydney Sullivan Award from Erskine College, 1979.

WRITINGS: Birdlife in Wington, Eerdmans, 1940, reprinted, 1979; *Reserves of the Soul,* John Knox, 1942; *Parables from Nature,* Eerdmans, 1945; *On toward the Goal,* John Knox, 1949; *We Knew Jesus,* Eerdmans, 1954; *We Wrote the Gospels,* Eerdmans, 1960; *Prayer Pilgrimage,* Cokesbury, 1963; *War of the Birds* (juvenile), Eerdmans, 1963; *Surprise for Dr. Retriever* (juvenile), Eerdmans, 1963; *Frisky Finds a Treasure* (juvenile), Eerdmans, 1963; *We Spoke for God,* Eerdmans, 1967; *The Marriage Covenant,* John Knox, 1967; *B.C.: A Digest of the Old Testament,* Regal Books (Glendale), 1971; *His Story,* Word, Inc., 1971, revised edition, 1973; *Psalms to Live By,* Regal Books, 1972; *Proverbs to Live By,* Regal Books, 1972; *Living Prayers,* Regal Books, 1974; *Come Be My Guest,* Regal Books, 1975; *Blessed Are They That Mourn,* Regal Books, 1975; *Green Fields of Promise,* Master's Press, 1978; *Secrets from Field and Forest,* Tyndale, 1979; *My Favorite Old Testament Stories,* Beka Books, 1980; *Thirty Favorite Bible Stories,* Standard Publishing, 1982.

SIDELIGHTS: John Calvin Reid told *CA:* "My interest in writing children's books goes back to the beginning of my ministry and my strong conviction that there should be something special for them in every church service, as well as for adults. . . . In all churches that I have served, it has been my custom to invite the children to come down to the front of the sanctuary and sit with me on the steps and help me 'tell the story.'"

*   *   *

REVELL, J(ohn) R(obert) S(tephen)   1920-
(Jack Revell)

PERSONAL: Born April 15, 1920, in Tunbridge Wells, Kent, England; son of Clifford Walter (a shopkeeper) and Edith (Wren) Revell; married Patricia M. B. Hiatt, February 23, 1946; children: Barbara, Alison, David John. *Education:* London School of Economics and Political Science, B.Sc., 1950; Cambridge University, M.A., 1960.

CAREER: Cambridge University, Cambridge, England, senior research officer in department of applied economics, 1957-68, fellow and senior tutor of Fitzwilliam College, 1965-68; Uni-

versity College of North Wales, Bangor, professor of economics, 1969-83; Institute of European Finance, Bangor, Wales, director, 1973—. *Military service:* British Army, 1940-46; became staff sergeant. *Member:* Royal Economic Society, Societe Universitaire Europeenne de Recherche Financiere.

WRITINGS: (With John Moyle) *The Owners of Quoted Ordinary Shares: A Survey for 1963,* Chapman & Hall, 1966; *The Wealth of the Nation: The National Balance Sheet of the United Kingdom, 1957-1961,* Cambridge University Press, 1967; *Changes in British Banking: The Growth of a Secondary Banking System,* Hill, Samuel & Co., 1968.

The British Financial System, Macmillan, 1973; (with C. R. Tomkins) *Personal Wealth and Finance in Wales,* Welsh Office, 1974; *Flexibility in Housing Finance,* Organization for Economic Cooperation and Development, 1975; *Solvency and Regulation of Banks,* University of Wales Press, 1975; *Savings Flows in Europe,* Financial Times, 1976; *Inflation and Financial Institutions,* Financial Times, 1979.

Costs and Margins in Banking, Organization for Economic Cooperation and Development, 1980; *A Study of the Spanish Banking System,* Banco de Vizcaya, 1980; *Banking and Electronic Fund Transfers,* Organization for Economic Cooperation and Development, 1983.

WORK IN PROGRESS: Research on the future shape of the British financial system; research on the structure of financial systems and the operation of financial institutions.

*   *   *

REVELL, Jack
See REVELL, J(ohn) R(obert) S(tephen)

*   *   *

RICHARDS, Arlene Kramer   1935-

PERSONAL: Born June 24, 1935, in New York, N.Y.; daughter of Emanuel and Edith (Burstein) Kramer; married Arnold David Richards (a psychoanalyst), March 21, 1953; children: Stephen Louis, Rebecca Dawn, Tamar Beth. *Education:* University of Chicago, A.B., 1953; graduate study at Brooklyn College (now of the City University of New York), 1955-56, and Washburn University, 1960-61; Columbia University, M.A., 1965, Ed.D., 1969. *Home:* 50 East 89th St., New York, N.Y. 10028. *Office:* 40 East 89th St., New York, N.Y. 10028.

CAREER: Substitute teacher in public schools in New York City, 1956-60; Washburn University, Topeka, Kan., instructor in reading and study skills, 1961-63; Richard Bland College, Petersburg, Va., instructor in reading and study skills, 1963-64; Columbia University, Teachers College, New York City, assistant supervisor of Reading Clinic, 1965-67; Center for Urban Education, New York City, tester, 1967; Centenary College for Women (now Centenary College), Hackettstown, N.J., instructor in reading and study skills, 1967-68; Columbia University, Teachers College, associate project director at Center for Research and Education in American Liberties, 1968-70, instructor in educational psychology, 1969-70; New York University, New York City, adjunct assistant professor, 1970-71, associate professor of psychology, 1970-71; psychologist with private practice in New York City, 1971—. Remedial therapist at Northside Center for Child Development, 1967-69; educational therapist at Mount Sinai Hospital, 1971-72; consultant to White House Conference on Children and Youth. *Member:* American Psychological Association, Institute for

Psychoanalytic Training and Research, New York Freudian Society.

WRITINGS: (Contributor) John P. DeCecco, editor, *The New Educational Psychology: A Book of Readings,* Holt, 1970; (contributor) DeCecco, editor, *Introduction to Educational Psychology,* CRM Books, 1972; (contributor) DeCecco, editor, *The Regeneration of the School,* Holt, 1972; (with De-Cecco) *Growing Pains: Uses of High School Conflict,* Aberdeen Press, 1974; (with Irene Willis) *How to Get It Together When Your Parents Are Coming Apart,* McKay, 1976; (with Willis) *Boyfriends, Girlfriends, Just Friends,* Atheneum, 1978; (with Paula Kernberg) *Good Vibrations,* Scholastic Book Services, 1979; (with Willis) *Leaving Home,* Atheneum, 1980; (with Willis) *Under Eighteen and Pregnant: What to Do if It Happens to You or Someone You Know,* Morrow, 1983.

Published by Center for Research and Education in American Liberties, Teachers College, Columbia University: *Learning to Participate by Taking Part in Learning,* 1969; *A Cross-Sectional Study of Schools in Four Communities,* 1969; *Moral Development in Adolescence,* 1970; *Civic Education: Urban and Suburban,* 1970; *Schools with Black Students,* 1970.

Contributor to *Standard Reference Encyclopedia* and to psychology, psychiatry, and sociology journals.

SIDELIGHTS: Arlene Kramer Richards told *CA:* "I am interested in the interaction between cognition and affects; between thought and feeling. While my most current research and thinking has to do with adolescents and their development, I have always been interested in how people of all ages work out their views of the world to correspond with their feelings. The despondent person picks out sombre interests, pursues difficult or impossible tasks, chooses to do what can give little satisfaction. The optimistic one finds easier jobs, more fun, more friends. In my current writing, I am attempting to help adolescents find ways of coping with their world. In my practise as a psychologist, I try to help patients shed their guilt and shame so that they are no longer despondent and can allow themselves satisfaction."

AVOCATIONAL INTERESTS: Bicycling, poetry, swimming, sailing.

*   *   *

RICHARDS, Guy   1905-1979

PERSONAL: Born May 18, 1905, in New York, N.Y.; died January 3, 1979, in New York, N.Y.; son of Guy (a banker) and Alice Lydia (Reese) Richards; married first wife, June 21, 1932 (divorced July 8, 1938); married Mary Spence Francis, August 26, 1940; children: Antonia (Mrs. Graham Judson), Pamela (Mrs. J. G. Smit). *Education:* Yale University, Ph.B., 1927. *Politics:* Republican. *Religion:* Episcopalian. *Home and office:* 340 East 57th St., New York, N.Y. 10022.

CAREER: Member of Whitney South Sea Expedition to New Guinea and Solomon Islands for American Museum of Natural History, 1927; worked as reporter for *New York Sun,* Newhouse Newspapers, and *New York Daily News,* all New York City; *New York Journal-American,* New York City, began as reporter and feature writer, became city editor; *World Journal Tribune,* New York City, became investigative reporter and assistant city editor. Member of board of trustees, Graham Home for Children. *Military service:* U.S. Marine Corps, 1942-44; became major; served in Pacific Theatre. U.S. Marine Corps Reserve; became lieutenant colonel.

MEMBER: American Museum of Natural History (associate member), First Marine Division, U.S. Naval Institute (associate member), Sheffield Historical Society, Century Club. *Awards, honors:* Received two Page One Awards from New York Newspaper Guild; Order of Silurians prize; Correction Officers' Benevolent Association special award; Free Assembly of Captive European Nations award.

WRITINGS: Two Rubles to Times Square (novel), Duell, Sloan & Pearce, 1956 (published in England as *Brother Bear,* M. Joseph, 1957); *Imperial Agent: The Goleniewski-Romanov Case* (nonfiction), Devin-Adair, 1966; *The Hunt for the Czar,* Doubleday, 1970; *The Rescue of the Romanovs: Newly Discovered Documents Reveal How Czar Nicholas II and the Russian Imperial Family Escaped,* Devin-Adair, 1975; *The Salekov Kill,* Fawcett, 1981.

Contributor of more than one hundred fifty articles to *Life, Liberty, Marine Corps Gazette, Leatherneck, Adventure,* and other periodicals.

WORK IN PROGRESS: A history of the Polish underground as a source of intelligence help to the West.

BIOGRAPHICAL/CRITICAL SOURCES: Best Sellers, November 15, 1967; *Spectator,* March 20, 1971.

OBITUARIES: New York Times, January 5, 1979.†

*   *   *

RICHARDS, Todd
See SUTPHEN, Richard Charles

*   *   *

RICHARDSON, Elmo (R.)   1930-

PERSONAL: Born April 6, 1930, in Chicago, Ill.; son of Ray Alphonso and Irene (Presley) Richardson. *Education:* University of Illinois, A.B. and M.A., 1952; University of California, Los Angeles, Ph.D., 1958. *Office:* Historians' Services of the Northwest, 730 North 71st St., Seattle, Wash. 98103.

CAREER: University of Kansas, Lawrence, instructor in history, 1957-60; Washington State University, Pullman, assistant professor, 1961-64, associate professor of history, 1964-72; Center for the Study of Popular Education and Recreation, Delaware Water Gap National Recreational Area, New Jersey, director, beginning 1972; assistant to state of Washington archivist, 1973-74; University of Kansas, visiting professor, 1975-76; Forest History Society, Inc., Santa Cruz, Calif., senior research associate, 1976-80; Historians' Services of the Northwest, Seattle, Wash., public historian, 1981—. Visiting professor at University of Washington, 1964-65, Northwestern University, 1969-70, and University of New Mexico, summer, 1976. History projects director, American Indian Resource Organization, 1981-82; has done work for U.S. Bureau of Land Management, U.S. Bureau of Indian Affairs, and U.S. Forest Service. Consultant to corporations and non-profit organizations. Editorial consultant to several university presses. *Member:* Forest History Society.

WRITINGS: (Compiler) *The Papers of Cornelius Cole and the Cole Family,* University of California (Los Angeles) Library, 1956; (co-author) *John Palmer Usher: Lincoln's Secretary of the Interior,* University of Kansas Press, 1960; *The Politics of Conservation: Crusades and Controversies, 1897-1913,* University of California Press, 1962; *Dams, Parks and Politics: Resource Development and Preservation in the Truman-Eisen-*

hower Era, University Press of Kentucky, 1973; *The Presidency of Dwight D. Eisenhower,* Regents Press of Kansas, 1979; *BLM's Billion-Dollar Checkerboard: Managing the O and C Lands,* U.S. Government Printing Office, 1980; *David T. Mason, Forestry Advocate: His Role in the Application of Sustained Yield Management to Private and Public Forest Lands,* Forest History Society, 1983. Also co-author of history of the Quinault Indian Reservation Forest, 1976, and author of histories of Willamette National Forest, 1981, and San Carlos Apache Indian Reservation Forest, 1982. Contributor of articles and reviews to historical journals on the subject of federal land and resources management and preservation.

SIDELIGHTS: "Although the subject of public land and resource policies is significant in itself," writes Elmo Richardson, "I have particularly emphasized the role of personalities and politics in that subject. My concern for the frequent gap that exists between intentions and accomplishments constitutes the basis for my assessment of men in history and in my own experiences. I am therefore particularly interested in those adventures which provide the opportunity for human encounters: teaching young people, traveling to places with an overlay of several cultures (i.e., the Caribbean), and maintaining a vigorous body, mind, and spirit with which to pursue my work and recreation."

AVOCATIONAL INTERESTS: Creative arts, overseas travel, fiction, metaphysics, camping, gardening.

* * *

RIGONI, Orlando (Joseph) 1897-
(Carolyn Bell, James Wesley; Leslie Ames, a joint pseudonym)

PERSONAL: Born December 27, 1897, in Mercur, Utah; son of Christian Joseph (a contractor) and Emma (Elseman) Rigoni; married Carolyn Broadhurst, July 16, 1946 (deceased); married Stella Marie Gandolfo, July 28, 1972; children: Patricia Margaret Rigoni Epperly, Orlando Patrick. *Education:* Attended high school and business college in Salt Lake City, Utah. *Politics:* Democrat. *Religion:* Realist. *Home and office:* 2900 Dogwood Ave., Morro Bay, Calif. 93442.

CAREER: Has worked in railroading, construction, mining, and business, including a term as forest clerk in the forest service; currently realtor and writer. *Military service:* U.S. Army and Navy.

WRITINGS: Brand of the Bow, Arcadia House, 1965; *Twisted Trails,* Arcadia House, 1965; *Massacre Ranch,* Arcadia House, 1966; *Showdown at Skelton Flat,* Arcadia House, 1967; *Six-Gun Song,* Arcadia House, 1967; *Ambuscade,* Arcadia House, 1968; *A Nickel's Worth of Lead,* Arcadia House, 1968; *The Pikabo Stage,* Arcadia House, 1968; *Headstone for a Trail Boss,* Arcadia House, 1969; *Close Shave at Pozo,* Lenox Hill, 1970; *Hunger Range,* Lenox Hill, 1970; *Drove Rider,* Lenox Hill, 1971; *Guns of Folly,* Lenox Hill, 1971; *Bullet Breed,* Lenox Hill, 1972 (published in England as *Brand of the Bullet,* R. Hale, 1972); *The Big Brand,* Crown, 1972; *Muskeg Marshal,* Lenox Hill, 1973; *Brand X,* Lenox Hill, 1974; *Western Vengeance,* Woodhill, 1977. Also author of *Western Justice,* Manor Books, and *Four Graves to Jericho,* Lenox Hill.

Under pseudonym Leslie Ames: (With W.E.D. Ross) *Bride of Donnybrook,* Arcadia House, 1966; *Journey to Romance,* R. Hale, 1966; *The Angry Wind,* Arcadia House, 1967; (with Ross) *The Hungry Sea,* Arcadia House, 1967; (with Ross) *The Hidden Chapel,* Arcadia House, 1967; (with Ross) *The Hill of Ashes,* Arcadia House, 1968; *To Shadow Our Love,* R. Hale, 1968; *Sinister Love,* R. Hale, 1968; *Castle on the Island,* Arcadia House, 1969; (with Ross) *King's Castle,* Lenox Hill, 1970; *Wind over the Citadel,* Lenox Hill, 1971; *The Phantom Bride,* Lenox Hill, 1972. Also author of *The House of Haddon,* Lenox Hill.

Under pseudonym Carolyn Bell: *House of Clay,* Lenox Hill, 1971; *Delivery,* Lame Johnny, 1980.

Under pseudonym James Wesley; all published by Bouregy: *Showdown in Mesa Bend,* 1972; *Maverick Marshall,* 1974; *Diamond Range,* 1975; *Showdown at the MB Ranch,* 1976; *Trouble at the Lazy K,* 1978; *Showdown at Eureka,* 1978; *The Guns of Redemption,* 1978; *Dead Man's Trail,* 1979; *Canyon Showdown,* 1981. Also author of *Texas Justice* and *Trail to Boothill,* Bouregy.

Contributor of 1,000 short stories to magazines.

WORK IN PROGRESS: Guns of Tranquility, House of Wroth, The Devout Agnostic, a nonfiction book about writing.

SIDELIGHTS: Orlando Rigoni told *CA:* "As one can see by my birthdate, I am no neophyte in the writing profession. I became addicted fifty years ago, to escape reality by involving myself in the personalities of characters of my own creation. A writer of books must not only create the story, but must be the casting director, the producer, the stage director, the scene setter, and the characters. He must cry with the ingenue, fall in love with his heroine, defy and defend like the hero, scheme and plot with the villain, and in the end bring it all together in a surprising conclusion that will be plausible and satisfying to the reader."

* * *

RINDER, Walter (Murray) 1934-

PERSONAL: Born June 3, 1934, in Chicago, Ill.; son of Samuel Murray (a salesman and businessman) and Geneta (Tamblyn) Rinder. *Education:* Attended North San Antonio Junior College, 1952-54. *Home and office address:* Mercurius Productions, P.O. Box 96, Brightwood, Ore. 97011.

CAREER: Writer and photographer. Has designed and produced posters, parchments, greeting cards, books, and a record album. *Military service:* U.S. Army, 1954-56.

WRITINGS—All published by Celestial Arts: *Love Is an Attitude,* 1970; *This Time Called Life,* 1971; *Spectrum of Love,* 1973; *Follow Your Heart,* 1973; *The Humanness of You,* two volumes, 1973-74; *Love Is My Reason,* 1975; *Will You Share with Me?,* 1975; *Where Will I Be Tomorrow?,* 1976; *Friends and Lovers,* 1978; *A Promise of Change,* 1979; *Forever Us,* 1981.

WORK IN PROGRESS: Our Renaissance, a color photographic essay of the male, accompanied by prose; *The Best of Walter Rinder,* an anthology; *Tomorrow Is Here,* "a continuation of the awarenesses shared in *Where Will I Be Tomorrow?*"; a series of children's stories for adults.

SIDELIGHTS: Walter Rinder writes *CA* that, through his creative ability, he wishes to share with all people, contribute to their well-being, and help them to achieve a balance between the body and the spirit. He is involved in social change and is interested in expanding attitudes towards all types of loving relationships. According to Rinder, "Loving is a way of life, rather than the traditional search for only one person in a lifetime commitment." He writes that he hopes someday to create a community of people "where difference is a positive force to build upon, and loving is the path toward that goal." He believes that "where there is an absence of fear, loving has room to grow."

* * *

RIORDAN, James 1936-

PERSONAL: Born October 10, 1936, in Portsmouth, England; son of William (an engineer) and Kathleen (a cleaner; maiden name, Smith) Brown; married Annick Vercaigne, July 4, 1959 (divorced, 1964); married Rashida Davletshina (a teacher), July 1, 1965; children: Tania, Nadine, Sean, Nathalie, Catherine. *Education:* University of Birmingham, B.S., 1959, Ph.D., 1975; University of London, certificate in education, 1960; University of Moscow, diploma in political science, 1962. *Politics:* Marxist. *Religion:* Atheist. *Home:* 15 Bankfield Dr., Shipley, West Yorkshire, England. *Office:* Modern Languages Centre, University of Bradford, Bradford, West Yorkshire BD7 1DP, England.

CAREER: British Railways, Portsmouth, England, clerk, 1956-57; translator in Moscow, Soviet Union, 1963-65; Portsmouth Polytechnic, Portsmouth, lecturer in Russian, 1965-69; University of Bradford, Bradford, England, 1971—, began as lecturer, currently reader in Russian studies. *Military service:* Royal Air Force, 1954-56; served in Berlin; served as British Olympic attache at Moscow Olympic Games, 1980.

WRITINGS: The Mistress of the Copper Mountain, Muller, 1974; (with Eileen Colwell) *Little Grey Neck,* Addison-Wesley, 1975; *Russian Tales,* Viking, Volume I: *Tales from Central Russia,* 1976, Volume II: *Tales from Tartary,* 1978; *Sport in Soviet Society: Development of Sport and Physical Education in Russia and the U.S.S.R.,* Cambridge University Press, 1977; *Sport under Communism,* Queen's University Press, 1978; *Soviet Sport Background to the Olympics,* Washington Mews Books, 1980; *The Boy Who Turned into a Goat,* Macmillan, 1983; *Petrushka and Other Tales from the Ballet,* Stodder & Houghton, 1984; *The Woman in the Moon and Other Feminist Tales,* Hutchinson, 1984.

Published by Hamlyn: *A World of Folktales,* 1980; *Tales of King Arthur,* 1980; *A World of Fairy Tales,* 1981; *Tales of the Arabian Nights,* 1982; *The Little Humpback Horse,* 1983; *A World of Myths and Legends,* 1985.

WORK IN PROGRESS: Folktales of the British Isles and *Sports Medicine in the U.S.S.R. and the German Democratic Republic.*

SIDELIGHTS: James Riordan told *CA:* "My writing on folk tales is based on a personal acquaintance with the people and the land. For example, with the Russian tales I lived, worked, and journeyed in Russia for five years, visiting thirteen of the fifteen republics, gathering folktale material. For my Tartar tales, I spent several months in Soviet Tartary in the homes of friends and relations of my Tartar wife Rashida. And for my Siberian tales, I spent two months during 1977 travelling in Siberia. My writing on Soviet sport is based on membership in the Moscow Spartak Sports Club for five years, 1961-65."

* * *

RIVES, Stanley G(ene) 1930-

PERSONAL: Born September 27, 1930, in Decatur, Ill.; son of James and Frances Bunker (Haverfield) Rives; married Sandra Belt, December 28, 1957; children: Jacqueline, Joseph. *Education:* Attended Northwestern University, 1948-49, Ph.D., 1963; Illinois State University, B.S., 1952, M.S., 1955. *Home:* 2308 Andover Pl., Charleston, Ill. 61920. *Office:* Provost and Vice-President for Academic Affairs, Eastern Illinois University, Charleston, Ill. 61920.

CAREER: Instructor in speech at West Virginia University, Morgantown, 1955-56, and Northwestern University, Evanston, Ill., 1956-58; Illinois State University, Normal, assistant professor, 1958-63, associate professor, 1963-67, professor of information science, 1967-80, dean of Undergraduate Instruction, 1972-80; Eastern Illinois University, Charleston, provost and vice-president for academic affairs and professor of speech communication, 1981—. Visiting professor, University of Hawaii, Honolulu, 1963-64. Member of board of directors, National Debate Tournament. *Military service:* U.S. Army, 1952-54.

MEMBER: Speech Association of America (member of legislative assembly, 1966-70), American Forensic Association, American Association for Higher Education, American Association of University Professors, Central States Speech Association, Midwest Forensic Association (president, 1961-63), Illinois Speech and Theatre Association.

WRITINGS: (With Donald Klopf) *Individual Speaking Contests: Preparation for Participation,* Burgess, 1967; (with Gene A. Budig) *Academic Quicksand: Some Trends and Issues in Higher Education,* Professional Educators Publications, 1973; *Fundamentals of Oral Interpretation,* Eichosa (Tokyo), 1981. Contributor to *Journal of the American Forensic Association.*

* * *

RIVKIN, Allen (Erwin) 1903-

PERSONAL: Born November 20, 1903, in Hayward, Wis.; son of Samuel Richard (a merchant) and Rose (Rosenberg) Rivkin; married Laura Hornickel (a writer, under pseudonym Laura Kerr), November 8, 1952; children: Caroline (Mrs. Philip Saltzman). *Education:* University of Minnesota, B.A., 1925. *Politics:* Democrat. *Religion:* Jewish. *Residence:* Los Angeles, Calif.

CAREER: Writer, 1925—. Has also worked as a newspaper man, publicity man, and advertising man. Television producer (produced the series "Troubleshooters," 1958-59); founder and president of Motion Picture Industry Council, 1951-52; liaison representative of American Bar Association, 1963—; director of Jewish Film Advisory Committee, 1963—; secretary of Writers-Producers Pension Fund, 1965-66; treasurer of Writers Guild Foundation, 1966—. Chairman of U.S. delegation to Cannes Film Festival, 1962; vice-president of Hollywood Guilds Festival Committee, 1962-63. National director of Democratic National Committee (performing arts division), 1948-52; public relations director of Democratic National Convention, 1960. Director of Hollywood for Roosevelt, 1936-44, Hollywood for Truman, 1948, Hollywood for Stevenson, 1952-56, and Hollywood for Kennedy, 1960. *Wartime service:* U.S. War Department, head motion picture officer in Special Services Division, 1942-44.

MEMBER: International Writers Guild (co-founder, 1963), Dramatists Guild, Academy of Motion Picture Arts and Sciences, Writers Guild of America (founder of West branch; vice-president, 1954; director of public relations, 1962—), Screen Writers Guild (founder; member of board of directors; president, 1960-62), West Side Riding and Asthma Club, Sigma Alpha Mu. *Awards, honors:* American Academy of Motion Picture Arts and Sciences award nomination, Box Office Blue Ribbon award, and *Look* and *Photoplay* magazine awards, all 1948, all for "The Farmer's Daughter"; Books and Authors Seventh Annual Award, 1954, for "Timberjack"; Valentine Davies Award from Writers Guild of America, 1963, for community service; Morgan Cox Award from Writers Guild of America, 1972, for guild service.

WRITINGS: (With Leonard Spigelgass) *I Wasn't Born Yesterday: An Anonymous Autobiography*, Macauley, 1935; (with wife, Laura Kerr) *Hello, Hollywood: A Book about the Movies by the People Who Make Them*, Doubleday, 1962; (editor) *Who Wrote the Movie . . . And What Else Did He Write?*, Academy of Motion Picture Arts and Sciences, 1970.

Screenplays: "Radio Patrol," Universal, 1932; "70,000 Witnesses," Paramount, 1932; "Night World," Universal, 1932; "Is My Face Red?" (also see below), RKO, 1932; "Madison Square Garden," Paramount, 1932; "The Devil Is Driving," Paramount, 1932; "Headline Shooter," RKO, 1933; "Picture Snatcher," Warner Bros., 1933; "The Girl in 419," Paramount, 1933; "Melody Cruise," RKO, 1933; "Meet the Baron," Metro-Goldwyn-Mayer, 1933; "Dancing Lady," Metro-Goldwyn-Mayer, 1934; "Cheating Cheaters," Universal, 1934; "Our Little Girl," Fox, 1935; "Black Sheep," Fox, 1935; "Bad Boy," Fox, 1935; "Your Uncle Dudley," Fox, 1935.

"Champagne Charlie," Fox, 1936; "Half Angel," Fox, 1936; "Love under Fire," Fox, 1937; "This Is My Affair," Fox, 1937; "Straight, Place and Show," Twentieth Century-Fox, 1938; "It Could Happen to You," Twentieth Century-Fox, 1939; "Let Us Live," Columbia, 1939; "Behind the News," RKO, 1940; "Typhoon," Paramount, 1940.

"Dancing on a Dime," Paramount, 1941; "Singapore Woman," Warner Bros., 1941; "Highway West," Warner Bros., 1941; "Joe Smith, American," Metro-Goldwyn-Mayer, 1942; "Sunday Punch," Metro-Goldwyn-Mayer, 1942; "The Kid Glove Killer," Metro-Goldwyn-Mayer, 1942.

"The Thrill of Brazil," Columbia, 1946; "Till the End of Time," RKO, 1946; "Dead Reckoning," Columbia, 1947; "The Guilt of Janet Ames," Columbia, 1947; (with Kerr) "The Farmer's Daughter," RKO, 1947; (with Kerr) "My Dream Is Yours," Warner Bros., 1948; "Tension," Metro-Goldwyn-Mayer, 1949; (with Kerr) "Grounds for Marriage," Metro-Goldwyn-Mayer, 1950.

"Gambling House," RKO, 1951; "The Strip," Metro-Goldwyn-Mayer, 1951; (with Kerr) "Battle Circus," Metro-Goldwyn-Mayer, 1954; "Timberjack," Republic, 1954; "Prisoner of War," Metro-Goldwyn-Mayer, 1954; "The Eternal Sea," Republic, 1954; "The Man from Texas," Republic, 1955.

"Girls on the Loose," Universal-International, 1957; "Live Fast, Die Young," Universal-International, 1957; "Big Operator," Metro-Goldwyn-Mayer, 1959; (and co-producer) "Mister," Guggenheim, 1961; "I Thought I'd Die Laughing," Leonard Filed Productions, 1964.

Author of plays "Knock on Wood," first produced on Broadway at Cort Theatre, May 28, 1935, and "Is My Face Red?" (based on his screenplay of the same title). Also author of television scripts. Editor, *Writers Guild West Newsletter*, 1965—, and *Writers Guild Directory*.

WORK IN PROGRESS: Hollywood Is No Laughing Matter.

ROBBINS, Keith (Gilbert) 1940-

PERSONAL: Born April 9, 1940, in Bristol, England; son of Gilbert Henry John (a cashier) and Mary (Carpenter) Robbins; married Janet Thomson, August 24, 1963; children: Paul John Gilbert, Daniel Henry Keith, Lucy Helen, Adam Edward Ivo. *Education:* Magdalen College, Oxford, B.A., 1961; St. Antony's College, Oxford, D.Phil., 1964. *Politics:* Conservative. *Religion:* Baptist. *Home:* 15 Hamilton Dr., Glasgow G12 8DN, Scotland. *Office:* Department of Modern History, University of Glasgow, Glasgow G12 8QQ, Scotland.

CAREER: University of York, Heslington, York, England, lecturer in history, 1963-71; University College of North Wales, Bangor, professor of history, 1971-79; University of Glasgow, Glasgow, Scotland, professor of modern history, 1980—. *Member:* British Association of Contemporary Historians, Royal Historical Society (fellow), Ecclesiastical History Society (president, 1980-81). *Awards, honors: Munich, 1938* was "highly commended" in Winston Churchill Prize competition, 1968.

WRITINGS: Munich, 1938, Cassell, 1968; *Sir Edward Grey: A Biography of Lord Grey of Fallodon*, Cassell, 1971; (contributor) Herbert van Thal, editor, *The Prime Ministers*, Volume II: *From Lord John Russell to Edward Heath*, Allen & Unwin, 1975; *The Abolition of War: The Peace Movement in Britain, 1914-1919*, University of Wales Press, 1976; *John Bright*, Routledge & Kegan Paul, 1979; *The Eclipse of a Great Power: Modern Britain 1870-1975*, Longman, 1983.

Contributor to *International Affairs, Historical Journal, Journal of Ecclesiastical History, Slavonic and East European Review, Journal of Imperial and Commonwealth History*, and *Journal of Contemporary History*. Editor, *History*, 1977—.

WORK IN PROGRESS: A bibliography of writings on British history since 1914.

BIOGRAPHICAL/CRITICAL SOURCES: Observer, May 26, 1968, June 6, 1971; *Statesman*, June 14, 1968; *New Statesman*, June 4, 1971; *Times Literary Supplement*, November 23, 1979, April 15, 1983.

*   *   *

ROBINSON, Patricia
See GOEDICKE, Patricia (McKenna)

*   *   *

ROBINSON, Spider 1948-
(B. D. Wyatt)

PERSONAL: Born November 24, 1948, in New York, N.Y.; son of Charles Vincent (a salesman) and Evelyn (a secretary; maiden name, Meade) Robinson; married Jeanne Rubbicco (a dancer, dance teacher, and writer), July, 1975; children: Luanna Mountainborne. *Education:* State University of New York at Stony Brook, B.A., 1972; attended State University of New York College at Plattsburgh and Le Moyne College. *Politics:* "None whatever." *Religion:* "Pantheist/Humanist." *Home and office:* Tottering-on-the-Brink, 1663 Henry St., Halifax, Nova Scotia, Canada B3H 3K4. *Agent:* Kirby McCauley, 425 Park Ave. S., New York, N.Y. 10016.

CAREER: Long Island Commercial Review, Syosset, N.Y., realty editor, 1972-73; science fiction writer, 1973—. Chairman of the board of directors, Dance Advance Association. *Member:* Writers Federation of Nova Scotia (chairman, executive council). *Awards, honors:* John W. Campbell Award, 1974, for short story "The Guy with the Eyes"; Hugo Award, World Science Fiction Convention, 1976, for best novella, "By Any Other Name," 1977, for best novella, "Stardance," and 1983, for best short story, "Melancholy Elephants"; Nebula Award, Science Fiction Writers of America, 1977, for best novella, "Stardance"; *Locus* (magazine) Award, 1976, for best critic, and 1977, for best novella, "Stardance"; E. E. Smith Memorial Award, 1977; Pat Terry Memorial Award, 1977.

WRITINGS—Science fiction novels, except as indicated: *Telempath*, Berkley, 1976; *Callahan's Crosstime Saloon* (story collection), Ace Books, 1977; (with wife, Jeanne Robinson) *Stardance*, Dial, 1978; *Antinomy* (story collection), Dell, 1980; (editor) *The Best of All Possible Worlds* (anthology), Ace Books, 1980; *Time Travelers Strictly Cash* (story collection), Ace Books, 1981; *Mindkiller*, Holt, 1982.

Contributor: Roy Torgeson, editor, *Chrysalis 4*, Kensington, 1979; George R.R. Martin, editor, *New Voices 2*, Harcourt, 1979.

Work appears in anthologies, including: *Analog Annual*, edited by Ben Bova, Pyramid Publications, 1976; *The Best of Galaxy*, Volume III, edited by Jim Baen, Award Books, 1976.

Author of "Galaxy Bookshelf" column, *Galaxy*, 1974-77. Contributor of short stories and novellas, sometimes under pseudonym B. D. Wyatt, to *Analog, Fantastic, Vertex, Cosmos, Galaxy*, and other magazines. Contributing editor, *Galaxy*, 1974-77. Book reviewer, *Destinies*, 1977-79, and *Analog*, 1978-80.

SIDELIGHTS: Spider Robinson told *CA:* "Many SF writers have eloquently indicted mankind. I intend to spend my life presenting the case for the defense. I believe that shared pain is lessened, shared joy increased; I further maintain that to be a specific formula for saving the world. I find doom-crying (like all forms of despair) to be a cop-out, a personal irresponsibility the world can no longer afford."

Reviewing the novel *Mindkiller* for the *New York Times Book Review*, Gerald Jonas writes: "If I didn't think it understated his achievement, I'd nominate Spider Robinson, on the basis of this book, as the new Robert Heinlein. Like Mr. Heinlein in his prime, Mr. Robinson writes in a crisp, tightly controlled prose about a future that is recognizably descended from today's world yet provocatively altered—and he writes with such authority that you find yourself accepting his projection as *the* future."

BIOGRAPHICAL/CRITICAL SOURCES: Fourth Estate, June 16, 1976; *Analog*, March, 1977; *Algol*, winter, 1977-78; *Maclean's*, May 14, 1979; *Best Sellers*, June, 1979; *Village Voice*, September 17, 1979; *Magazine of Fantasy and Science Fiction*, October, 1979; *New York Times Book Review*, August 29, 1982; *Washington Post Book World*, August 29, 1982.

*　　*　　*

ROGERS, Alan 1933-

PERSONAL: Born February 25, 1933, in Wallington, Surrey, England; son of E. W. (a local preacher) and Edith (Cuthbert) Rogers; married Marjorie Dawe (a musician), August 1, 1958; children: Malcolm D., Katherine Hilary. *Education:* University of Nottingham, B.A., 1954, M.A., 1956, Certificate of Education, 1957, Ph.D., 1966. *Religion:* Church of England.

Office: Centre for Continuing Education, Magee University College, New University of Ulster, Londonderry, North Ireland.

CAREER: School teacher and part-time university teacher, 1957-59; University of Nottingham, Department of Adult Education, Nottingham, England, lecturer, 1959-65, senior lecturer, 1965-77, reader in history, 1977-79; New University of Ulster, Magee University College, Londonderry, North Ireland, professor of continuing education and director of Institute of Continuing Education, 1979—. Member of Heritage Education Group. *Member:* Royal Historical Society (fellow), Society of Antiquaries (fellow).

WRITINGS: (Editor) *The Making of Stamford*, Leicester University Press, 1965; (editor) *Stability and Change: Some Aspects of North and South Rauceby in the Nineteenth Century*, Department of Adult Education, University of Nottingham, 1969; *History of Lincolnshire*, Darwin Finlayson, 1970; *Medieval Buildings of Stamford*, Department of Adult Education, University of Nottingham, 1970; *This Was Their World: Approaches to Local History*, B.B.C. Publications, 1972, 2nd edition published as *Approaches to Local History*, Longman, 1977; (editor) *Approaches to Nottingham's History*, Department of Adult Education, University of Nottingham, 1972; (with John S. Hartley) *The Religious Foundations of Medieval Stamford*, Department of Adult Education, University of Nottingham, 1974; (editor with Trevor Rowley) *Landscapes and Documents*, Bedford Square Press for the Standing Conference for Local History, 1974; (editor) *Southwell Minster after the Civil Wars: A Study Paper*, Department of Adult Education, University of Nottingham, 1974.

(Editor) *The Spirit and the Form: Essays in Adult Education by and in Honour of Professor Harold Wiltshire*, Department of Adult Education, University of Nottingham, 1976; (editor) *Group Projects in Local History*, Dawson, 1977; *Knowledge and the People*, Magee University College, New University of Ulster, 1981; (editor) *Coming into Line*, Centre for Local History, University of Nottingham, 1982; (with Brian Groombridge and others) *The Universities and Continuing Education*, New University of Ulster Institute of Continuing Education, Magee University College, 1982. Contributor to historical journals. Editor, *Bulletin of Local History, East Midlands Region*, 1966-78.

WORK IN PROGRESS: A book on Stamford.

*　　*　　*

ROGERS, Warren
See BRUCKER, Roger W(arren)

*　　*　　*

ROONEY, David Douglas 1924-

PERSONAL: Born May 17, 1924, in London, England; son of Douglas and Violet (Broadbridge) Rooney; married E. Muriel Coutts, August 18, 1948; children: Kathryn, Keith. *Education:* Oxford University, M.A., B.Litt. *Religion:* Church of England. *Home:* 23 Black Horse Lane, Swavesey, Cambridge, England.

CAREER: Campbell College, Belfast, Northern Ireland, senior history master, 1954-60; Royal Military Academy, Sandhurst, England, senior lecturer, 1960-64; King's School (operated by British Families Education Service for children of British military and other services in Germany), Gutersloh, Germany, headmaster, 1964-72; Neale Wade School, March, Cambridge, England, headmaster, 1972-77; The Village College, Swavesey, Cambridge, warden, 1977—. *Military service:* British Army, 1944-47; served in India and West Africa; became staff captain.

WRITINGS: (With E. Halladay) *Building of Modern Africa*, Harrap, 1965, 2nd edition, 1967; *The Story of the Commonwealth*, Pergamon, 1967; *Stilwell*, Ballantine, 1971; *Sir Charles Arden-Clarke*, Rex Collings, 1982.

AVOCATIONAL INTERESTS: Tennis, swimming, bridge, gardening.

*   *   *

ROSENBLUM, Leonard A.   1936-

PERSONAL: Born May 18, 1936, in Brooklyn, N.Y.; son of Samuel A. and Mae (Kotkin) Rosenblum; married Marie B. Lopresti, September 8, 1956; children: Gianine Denice, Douglas Samuel. *Education:* Brooklyn College (now Brooklyn College of the City University of New York), B.A., 1956, M.A., 1958; University of Wisconsin—Madison, Ph.D., 1961. *Home:* 900 East 19th St., Brooklyn, N.Y. 11230. *Office:* Department of Psychiatry, State University of New York Downstate Medical Center, 450 Clarkson Ave., Brooklyn, N.Y. 11203.

CAREER: State University of New York Downstate Medical Center, Brooklyn, N.Y., professor in department of psychiatry, 1961—. *Member:* International Primatological Society, International Society for Developmental Psychobiology (president, 1980), American Psychobiology Association (member of executive committee of division six, 1981-84), American Psychological Association, National Institute of Mental Health, Sigma Xi. *Awards, honors:* Research Scientist Award (level II) from National Institute of Mental Health.

*WRITINGS—*Editor: (With R. W. Cooper) *The Squirrel Monkey*, Academic Press, 1968; *Primate Behavior: Developments in Field and Laboratory Research*, Academic Press, Volume I, 1970, Volume II, 1971, Volume III, 1973, Volume IV, 1975; (with M. Lewis) *The Effect of the Infant on Its Caregiver*, Wiley, 1974; (with Lewis) *The Origins of Fear*, Wiley, 1974; (with Lewis) *Peer Relations and Friendship*, Wiley, 1975; (with Lewis) *Interaction, Conversation and the Development of Language*, Wiley, 1974; (with Lewis) *The Development of Affect*, Plenum, 1978; (with Lewis) *The Uncommon Child*, Plenum, 1981; (with C. Coe) *The Handbook of Squirrel Monkey Research*, Plenum, 1983; (with H. F. Harlow and S. Suomi) *The Social Behavior of Primates*, Academic Press, in press; (with H. Moltz) *Symbiosis in Parent-Young Interactions*, Plenum, in press.

Contributor to journals in his field. Editor, *Brain, Behavior and Evolution, Archives of Sexual Behavior;* consultant reviewer, National Science Foundation and National Institute of Child Health and Human Development.

WORK IN PROGRESS: Research on the effects of environmental demand on social behavior and mother-infant relations in primates; research on the relationship of size to thermoregulation and parent-offspring relations in primates; studies of male sexual dysfunction.

SIDELIGHTS: Leonard A. Rosenblum writes: "I am attempting to learn more about the biological basis of human behavior and its development through the study of non-human primates. Such research, while not providing the answers to man's problems, helps to order the priorities with which we seek to tackle problems at the human level by suggesting the evolutionary background to particular areas of behavioral development."

*   *   *

ROSENFELD, Albert (Hyman)   1920-

PERSONAL: Born May 31, 1920, in Philadelphia, Pa.; son of Samuel and Annie (Zeiffert) Rosenfeld; married Lillian Elizabeth Snow (a librarian), August 24, 1948; children: Robert, Shana. *Education:* New Mexico State University, B.A., 1950. *Politics:* Democrat. *Religion:* Jewish. *Home:* 25 Davenport Ave., New Rochelle, N.Y. 10805. *Agent:* Ann Elmo, 60 East 42nd St., New York, N.Y. 10017. *Office:* March of Dimes Birth Defects Foundation, 1275 Mamaroneck Ave., White Plains, N.Y. 10605.

CAREER: Acting bureau chief and correspondent for Time, Inc., based in Las Cruces, N.M., 1948-50, and Santa Fe, N.M., 1950-58; *Life* Magazine, New York City, worked on news desk, 1956-57, writer, 1957-58, science editor, 1958-69; *Family Health*, New York City, managing editor, 1970-71; *Saturday Review*, New York City, science editor, 1973-81. Medical editor, Time-Life Video and Time-Life Broadcast, 1971-72. Adjunct professor of biophilosophy, Drexel University, 1971-74; senior research associate in contemporary ethics, Manhattanville College, 1972-73; adjunct assistant professor of human biological chemistry and genetics, University of Texas at Galveston, 1973—. Science interviewer for CBS's "Summer Semester," 1975. Consultant, March of Dimes Birth Defects Foundation, 1973—. Editorial consultant, Time-Life Books, 1972-73; consulting science editor, Knopf Publishing Co., 1972-74. *Military service:* U.S. Army, European theater of operations, 1942-45.

MEMBER: Council for the Advancement of Science Writing (president, 1968, 1970, 1974), National Association of Science Writers, American Medical Writers Association, American Society of Law and Medicine, Institute for Society, Ethics and the Life Sciences, Authors Guild, Smithsonian Associates, American Museum of Natural History, Sigma Delta Chi.

AWARDS, HONORS: Aviation-Space Writers Association award, 1964; Distinguished Alumnus Award, New Mexico State University, 1965; American Association for the Advancement of Science-Westinghouse Writing Award, 1966; Albert Lasker Award for Distinguished Service to the Handicapped, Rehabilitation Institute, 1967; D.Lett., New Mexico State University, 1970; Claude Bernard Science Journalism Award, National Society for Medical Research, 1975; Jesse H. Neal Editorial Achievement Award, American Business Press, Inc., 1976; National Magazine award, 1976; James T. Grady Medal for Interpreting Chemistry to the Public, American Chemical Society, 1981; Janusz Korczak Literary Award, B'nai B'rith Anti-Defamation League, 1982.

WRITINGS: The Quintessence of Irving Langmuir, Pergamon, 1962, published as *Man of Physics: Irving Langmuir*, 1966; *The Second Genesis: The Coming Control of Life*, Prentice-Hall, 1969; *Prolongevity*, Knopf, 1976; (editor) *Mind and Supermind*, Holt, 1978; (with G. W. Kliman) *Responsible Parenthood*, Holt, 1981. Contributor of articles to popular and professional journals, including *Harper's, Commentary*, and *Smithsonian.* Consulting editor, *Physician's World*, 1972-74; contributing editor, *Geo*, 1978-81, *Prime Time*, 1979-81, *Science Digest*, 1979-80, and *Science*, 1980—.

WORK IN PROGRESS: Further research on scientific, biomedical subjects, and related topics, for books and articles.

SIDELIGHTS: Albert Rosenfeld, "one of the nation's most competent reporters of science," according to H. Jack Geiger in *New York Times Book Review,* has made a career of explaining biological and scientific processes to the layperson. In *The Second Genesis: The Coming Control of Life,* for example, Rosenfeld "supplies a readable, mostly sympathetic account of work in progress on artificial insemination, genetic sex determination, isolation of genetic defects, laboratory growth of embryos, and divers other efforts at genetic manipulation," writes M. Stanton Evans in *National Review.* In *Prolongevity,* Rosenfeld seeks to inform the reader of recent medical discoveries concerning the aging process. "For anyone who wants to understand what is now known about the biology of aging, there are no better accounts [than the ones in *Prolongevity*]," says Geiger. Alex Comfort in *Washington Post Book World* notes that *Prolongevity* "gives almost every floatable theory of the mechanism which causes physical strength to decline with age, and mortality to increase. He follows this with a racy and well-researched account of what is being done about these mechanisms, both by way of comprehension and interference."

Speaking about his work as a science writer in his acceptance speech for the James T. Grady Medal for Interpreting Chemistry to the Public, Rosenfeld told members of the American Chemical Society: "I have often had people tell me how they avoid 'cold' science for fear that it will spoil things for them—a beautiful sunset, for example. Why 'analyze it out of existence,' why destroy the mystery and wonder of it all, by studying the optical principles involved, by measuring and calculating the precise degree of diffraction and diffusion, how the lightwaves impinge upon the retina of the eye—and so on. To me, this doesn't destroy the beauty or wonder of a sunset in the least. To understand, in a very dim way, that this phenomenon we admire is the result of the fact that the earth and sun are aligned in a certain way at a certain time of day, and that the angle at which the lightwaves come through the atmosphere when it's in a given state, and how it's recorded on our optical receptors and sent on to the perceiving brain . . . *that's* what a sunset is made of! The science of it only renders it yet more marvelous, and certainly doesn't do away with the mystery.

"And to begin to know a little something about our bodies, and our cells, and our molecules and the language in which they speak to one another—what a fantastic turn-on! I think most science journalists are fascinated with science per se. And the fascination seems to enhance their appreciation of life's other aspects as well. I know a lot of science journalists, and—as is also the case with scientists—I know very few who are bored. They may be unhappy with the size of their paychecks, or with the space their editors give them for their stories, but they aren't bored. Perhaps that's why I find them, on the average, such good company.

"I think [science writers] have another function to serve—and that is as critics of science. Whether it's the space program, cancer research, health policy, funding priorities, nuclear waste disposal, you-name-it—we can't simply rely on taking the word of our favorite expert—especially in areas where there is no unanimity or even consensus among the experts and this is more often the case than not. Here again, we must do some independent homework, make at least tentative judgments, and be prepared to make the appropriate noises where we feel they should be made. We certainly should be careful about abusing this privilege; I should hate to see some major research program have to close down, like a Broadway show, because one of us didn't give it a good review. We've got to be careful and

responsible critics, and naturally we risk making mistakes—but it's a function I think we can't afford to neglect.

"If we are critics of science, I think we also need to be critics *for* science, as distinct from slavish advocates. Science is often attacked mindlessly from a number of sources, for all the wrong reasons; scientists are unfairly made the villains and science the scapegoat. I think part of our job in promoting the public understanding of science is to see that people really do understand it.

"Science journalists cannot hope to do their job, of course, unless the people they work for believe it to be important—or at least half as interesting as, say, sports, so that it merits regular coverage. . . . We should try, too, to reach other creative people—the artists, novelists, poets, playwrights who have largely seen science as wicked, dehumanizing, and destructive. Science can be all those things, of course; or at least the *use* we make of it can be all those things. But the use we make of it—or choose not to make of it—is up to all of us; and science is also one of the most potent tools available for solving the problems into which our misuse of it has led us.

"I have a great sense of mission about science writing. There are few jobs in the world more fascinating or more potentially exciting in both the subject matter and the people they deal with; and, in its importance to the world, I can't think of many occupations that surpass it. But let's tackle it with gusto and good humor. We can be serious without being solemn-high in our approach. We should strive to keep our touch as light as the subject matter will allow, so as not to impose a burden on our readers—like a sermon that must somehow be got through if they are to prove their virtue.

"We have the opportunity to enhance the quality of people's lives—and, remember, the people include presidents, congressmen, and media gatekeepers (and their wives, who perhaps read more than they do)—in at least two ways: and if we think of them as goals, the first goal is to enhance their personal pleasure. The second is to enhance their understanding of the world, and by dispelling, to some degree, the sense of confusion and helplessness, arm them with the means to exert some influence on policy matters. I firmly believe that our route to the second goal will be rendered much easier if we first achieve the first [goal]."

AVOCATIONAL INTERESTS: Hiking, swimming, jogging, tennis, dancing, yoga.

BIOGRAPHICAL/CRITICAL SOURCES: New York Times, June 11, 1969; *Washington Post Book World,* October 10, 1976; *New York Times Book Review,* November 28, 1976; *National Review,* March 18, 1977.

*   *   *

ROSENKRANTZ, Linda   1934-
(C. L. Byrd)

PERSONAL: Born May 26, 1934, in New York, N.Y.; daughter of Samuel Herbert (a manufacturer) and Frances (Sillman) Rosenkrantz; married Christopher Finch, 1973. *Education:* University of Michigan, B.A., 1955. *Politics:* Liberal. *Home:* 321 West 12th St., New York, N.Y. 10014.

CAREER: Parke-Bernet Galleries, New York, N.Y., member of public relations staff, 1956-67; editor of *Auction* (magazine), 1967-72.

WRITINGS: Talk (novel), Putnam, 1968; (with husband, Christopher Finch) *Gone Hollywood* (nonfiction), Doubleday, 1979;

(under pseudonym C. L. Byrd) *SoHo*, Doubleday, 1981. Author of monthly column on the art market in *Arts*, 1966-67.

BIOGRAPHICAL/CRITICAL SOURCES: Books, September, 1967, June, 1968; *Book World*, June 2, 1968; *Nation*, July 22, 1968; *New Republic*, August 17, 1968; *New York Times Book Review*, November 3, 1968.

*   *   *

ROSENTHAL, Bernard G(ordon)   1922-

PERSONAL: Born February 3, 1922, in Chicago, Ill.; son of Benjamin J. and Sonia (Gordon) Rosenthal; married Judith Straka, September 22, 1957; children: Amy, Mark. *Education:* Northwestern University, B.S. (with distinction), 1942; Princeton University, M.A., 1943, Ph.D., 1944. *Home:* 801 Hinman Ave., Evanston, Ill. 60616. *Office:* Forest Institute of Professional Psychology, Des Plaines, Ill.

CAREER: Princeton University, Princeton, N.J., instructor in psychology, 1947-48; University of Chicago, Chicago, Ill., assistant professor of psychology, 1948-54; Harvard University, Cambridge, Mass., lecturer and research associate in psychology, 1957-60; Illinois Institute of Technology, Chicago, professor of social psychology, 1964-78; Forest Institute of Professional Psychology, Des Plaines, Ill., currently professor of psychology and director of research. Consultant in research study, Chicago State Hospital, Chicago, 1955-56; co-chairman of Greater Boston Committee for a Sane Nuclear Policy, 1959-60; chairman of Greater Illinois Faculty Committee on Vietnam, 1965-66. *Wartime service:* U.S. War Department, Morale Services Division, 1944-45. *Member:* American Psychological Association, American Association for Humanistic Psychology (midwestern regional chairman, 1966-68), American Association of University Professors, Phi Beta Kappa, Sigma Xi, Princeton Club of Chicago.

WRITINGS: Images of Man, Basic Books, 1971; (contributor) Blank and Gottsegen, editors, *Confrontation: Encounters in Self and Inter-Personal Relations*, Macmillan, 1971; *Von der Armut der Psychologie: Und wie ihr Abzuhelfen ware*, Ernst Klett Verlag (Stuttgart), 1974; *The Development of Self-Identification in Relation to Attitudes towards the Self in the Chippewa Indians*, Genetic Psychology Monographs, 1974; (contributor) Back, editor, *In Search for Community: Encounter Groups and Social Change*, Westview, 1978; (contributor) *Drug Dependence and Alcoholism*, Plenum, 1981; *Crowding Behavior and the Future*, Irvington, 1983.

Author of thirty scientific papers. *Human Context* (an international journal), co-editor, 1968-76, executive editor of American editorial board.

WORK IN PROGRESS: The Psychology of Courage; studies and research papers on various social psychological subjects, including the effect of size on behavior of groups, a system of conceptual and empirical designs for studies of the effects of crowding on behavior and affect, the development of attitudes toward money in rich and poor children; a book, tentatively entitled *Social and Psychological Conditions for the Optimization of Human Behavior;* a paper entitled "Humanistic and Middle-Class Psychology, Social-Economic Reality and Social Change."

AVOCATIONAL INTERESTS: Tennis, music, walking, manual construction and labor, swimming; travel in Europe, North Africa, Central America.

ROSS, James F(rancis)   1931-

PERSONAL: Born October 8, 1931, in Providence, R.I.; married Kathleen M. Fallon, 1956; children: four. *Education:* Catholic University of America, A.B., 1953, A.M., 1954; Brown University, Ph.D., 1958; University of Pennsylvania, J.D., 1975. *Home:* 4807 Springfield Ave., Philadelphia, Pa. 19143. *Office:* Department of Philosophy, University of Pennsylvania, Philadelphia, Pa. 19104.

CAREER: Providence Redevelopment Agency, Providence, R.I., staff consultant, 1957-60; University of Michigan, Ann Arbor, instructor in philosophy, 1959-61; University of Pennsylvania, Philadelphia, assistant professor, 1962-65, associate professor, 1965-68, professor of philosophy, 1968—, chairman of department, 1965-70, 1981—; admitted to Pennsylvania Bar, 1975. Visiting lecturer, Johns Hopkins University, 1964; visiting professor, Brown University, 1977. Member of Institute for Advanced Study, Princeton, N.J., 1975-76; associate, Cambridge University, 1982-83.

MEMBER: American Philosophical Association, American Theological Society, Society for Values in Higher Education. *Awards, honors:* Christian R. and Mary F. Lindback Foundation Award for distinguished teaching, University of Pennsylvania; award for distinguished scholarship, Catholic University of America, 1972; National Endowment for the Humanities fellowship, 1975-76; Guggenheim fellowship, 1982-83.

WRITINGS: (Translator, editor, and author of introduction) Francisco Suarez, *On Formal and Universal Unity*, Marquette University Press, 1965; (translator) Paul Grenet, *Le Thomism*, Harper, 1967; *Introduction to the Philosophy of Religion*, Macmillan, 1967; *Philosophical Theology*, Bobbs-Merrill, 1967, 2nd edition, Hackett, 1980; (editor) *Studies in Medieval Philosophy*, Greenwood Press, 1971; *Portraying Analogy*, Cambridge University Press, 1982; *Creation* (lecture), Notre Dame University Press, in press.

WORK IN PROGRESS: Embodied Consciousness: An Evolutionary Account.

*   *   *

ROSSE, Ian
See STRAKER, J(ohn) F(oster)

*   *   *

ROUSSEAU, George Sebastian   1941-

PERSONAL: Born February 23, 1941, in New York, N.Y.; son of Hyman Victoire (a social welfare worker) and Esther (Zacuto) Rousseau. *Education:* Amherst College, B.A., 1962; Princeton University, M.A., 1964, Ph.D., 1966; University of London, postdoctoral study, 1967. *Home:* 2424 Castilian Dr., Los Angeles, Calif. 90068. *Office:* Department of English, University of California, 405 Hilgaard Ave., Los Angeles, Calif. 90024.

CAREER: Harvard University, Cambridge, Mass., instructor in English, 1966-68; University of California, Los Angeles, professor of English, 1968—, professor of eighteenth-century studies, 1975—. Senior Fulbright research professor, the Netherlands, 1983. *Member:* British Society for the History of Science, Royal Society of Medicine (fellow), Royal Society of

Arts (fellow), Modern Language Association of America, American Society of Eighteenth-Century Studies, History of Science Society, Augustan Reprint Society. *Awards, honors:* Woodrow Wilson fellowship, 1966; American Council of Learned Societies fellowship, 1970; Cambridge University, visiting fellowship, 1979, overseas visiting fellow commoner, Trinity College, 1982.

WRITINGS: (With Marjorie Hope Nicolson) *The Long Disease My Life: Alexander Pope and the Sciences,* Princeton University Press, 1968; (editor and author of introduction) John Hill, *Hypochondriasis,* University of California Press, 1969; (editor) *Twentieth-Century Interpretations of "The Rape of the Lock"* (essay collection), Prentice-Hall, 1969; (editor and contributor) *The Augustan Milieu: Essays Presented to Louis A. Landa,* Clarendon Press, 1970; (with Neil Rudenstine) *English Poetic Satire: Wyatt to Byron,* Holt, 1971; (editor) *Organic Form,* Routledge & Kegan Paul, 1972; *Oliver Goldsmith: The Critical Heritage,* Routledge & Kegan Paul, 1974; (with Roy Porter) *The Ferment of Knowledge: Studies in the Historiography of Eighteenth-Century Science,* Cambridge University Press, 1980; *Tobias Smollett: Essays of Two Decades,* T. & T. Clark, 1982; *The Letters and Papers of Sir John Hill,* [New York], 1982.

Contributor of about one hundred articles and reviews to professional journals. Advisory editor, *The Eighteenth Century, Journal of the History of Ideas,* and other journals. Critic for *New York Times Book Review, Times Literary Supplement,* and other journals.

WORK IN PROGRESS: A biography of Sir John Hill, a little-known eighteenth-century medical and scientific figure; a study of the theoretical relations of literature and science in the early modern world.

SIDELIGHTS: George Sebastian Rousseau told *CA:* "I write to know and I want to know because knowledge is the last hope. The whole history of civilization demonstrates that agreement has rarely existed among mankind. For this reason we should not pin our hope for the future on the peg of simple agreement, in persuading everyone of a single point of view. The real hope is education: the ideal that everyone can be as well informed as he possibly can. Even if widespread global education prevails man's future may not be long in geological time; without education man's destiny in geological time will be shaped by the laws of brevity." Rousseau adds that his books about culture in the European Enlightenment "show what happens to societies who crave for knowledge—and thus also for writing—beyond the boundaries of all previous epochs."

BIOGRAPHICAL/CRITICAL SOURCES: Times Literary Supplement, January 22, 1982, June 3, 1983; *London Review of Books,* October 21, 1982.

* * *

ROYALL, Vanessa
See HINKEMEYER, Michael T(homas)

* * *

RUEGE, Klaus 1934-

PERSONAL: Surname is pronounced *Roo*-gy; born April 12, 1934, in Germany; came to the United States in 1952, naturalized in 1955; son of Gerhard (an editor) and Maria (Becker) Ruege; married Marilyn Montgomery, February 23, 1955; children: Michael, Michele, Matthew. *Education:* Spencerian Col-

lege, B.B.A., 1959. *Religion:* Lutheran. *Home:* 4278 North Hazel St., Chicago, Ill. 60613. *Office:* Montgomery Ward Enterprises, Inc., 2020 West Dempster St., Evanston, Ill. 60202.

CAREER: Milway Inc., Milwaukee, Wis., credit manager and assistant treasurer, 1955-62; Bell & Howell, Lincolnwood, Ill., president of Direct Marketing Group, 1962-69; Douglas Dunhill, Inc., Chicago, Ill., president, 1969-74; Verbatim, Northbrook, Ill. president, 1974-81; Montgomery Ward Enterprises, Inc., Evanston, Ill., senior vice-president, 1982—. Founder of Young Sportsmen's Soccer League; president of Illinois Youth Soccer Association. *Military service:* U.S. Military Police Corps, 1954-56. *Member:* International Society of Certified Consumer Credit Executives (charter member).

WRITINGS: Inside Soccer, Regnery, 1976; *Contemporary Soccer,* Contemporary Books, 1978. Contributor to direct marketing magazines in the United States and Europe.

WORK IN PROGRESS: Book on soccer, aimed at the novice coach, to assist in organizing effective practice sessions and in step-by-step application of modern tactics.

* * *

RUIZ, Ramon Eduardo 1921-

PERSONAL: Born September 9, 1921, in Pacific Beach, Calif.; son of Ramon and Dolores (Urueta) Ruiz; married Natalia Marrujo (a teacher), October 14, 1944; children: Olivia Teresa, Maura Natalia. *Education:* San Diego State College (now University), B.A., 1947; Claremont Graduate School, M.A., 1948; University of California, Berkeley, Ph.D., 1954. *Politics:* Independent. *Residence:* Rancho Santa Fe, Calif. *Office:* Department of History, University of California, San Diego, Calif.

CAREER: University of Oregon, Eugene, instructor, 1955-56, assistant professor of history, 1956-57; Southern Methodist University, Dallas, Tex., assistant professor of Spanish, 1957-58; Smith College, Northampton, Mass., assistant professor, 1958-60, associate professor, 1960-63, professor of history, 1963-69; University of California, San Diego, professor of history, 1970—. *Military service:* U.S. Army Air Forces, 1943-46; became second lieutenant. *Member:* American Historical Association, Conference on Latin American History, Phi Beta Kappa. *Awards, honors:* Huntington Library fellow, 1958; American Philosophical Society fellow, 1959; Fulbright scholar in Mexico, 1965-66.

WRITINGS: (Editor) *An American in Maximilian's Mexico,* Huntington Library, 1959; *Mexico, the Challenge of Poverty and Illiteracy,* Huntington Library, 1963; (editor) *The Mexican War—Was It Manifest Destiny?,* Holt, 1963; *Cuba: The Making of a Revolution,* University of Massachusetts Press, 1968; (with John William Tebbel) *South by Southwest: The Mexican-American and His Heritage,* Doubleday, 1969; (with James David Atwater) *Out from Under: Benito Juarez and the Struggle for Mexican Independence,* Doubleday, 1969; (editor) *Interpreting Latin American History,* Holt, 1970; *Labor and the Ambivalent Revolutionaries: Mexico, 1911-1923,* Johns Hopkins Press, 1976; (editor with Robert Detweiler) *Liberation in the Americas,* Campile Press, 1978; *The Great Rebellion: Mexico, 1905-1924,* Norton, 1980.

WORK IN PROGRESS: The Children of Don Porfirio: Sonora, 1885-1910.

SIDELIGHTS: "The prevailing American view of the Mexican Revolution is of an oppressed people rising up against foreign bosses, military dictatorship, and feudalism, recovering national pride, establishing popular rule, . . . and providing justice for the worker; in short, 'the first of the 20th-century social revolutions,''' writes John Womack, Jr. in his *New Republic* review of Ramon Eduardo Ruiz's *The Great Rebellion: Mexico, 1905-1924*. The ''chief merit [of the book],'' Womack says, ''is its central thesis, that far from a 'radical change' of Mexican society the revolution was 'essentially a face-lifting of Mexican capitalism, . . . one of the last bourgeois protests of the 19th century, and not . . . the precursor of the socialist explosions of the 20th century.'''

While the critic finds that Ruiz's ''thesis is not original,'' he states that *The Great Rebellion* ''is the first major statement by an eminent American historian of Mexico that the real revolution was not a triumph of 'the people' at large, but a long, violent, specifically bourgeois reform, which crushed other popular uprisings for the sake of better business.'' And although Womack cites ''several faults'' in the book, including the author's discussion of the difference between ''a rebellion'' and ''a revolution'' and his omission of Mexico's financial history during the conflict, the reviewer ultimately concludes that the work ''deserves wide circulation. More than a reinterpretation of the Mexican Revolution, Ruiz implicitly offers important wisdom on contemporary Mexico.''

BIOGRAPHICAL/CRITICAL SOURCES: New Republic, July 20, 1968, February 14, 1981; *Nation,* July 22, 1968; *Book World,* August 18, 1968; Ramon Eduardo Ruiz, *The Great Rebellion: Mexico, 1905-1924,* Norton, 1980; *New York Times Book Review,* November 16, 1980.

* * *

RUMPLEFORESKIN
See KRASSNER, Paul

* * *

RUNKEL, Philip J(ulian) 1917-

PERSONAL: Born June 25, 1917, in La Crosse, Wis.; son of Kenneth E. and Bernice (Hanan) Runkel; married Margaret West, April 26, 1943. *Education:* Central State Teachers College (now University of Wisconsin—Stevens Point), B.S., 1939; University of Michigan, M.A., 1954, Ph.D., 1956. *Office:* Division of Educational Policy and Management, University of Oregon, Eugene, Ore. 97403.

CAREER: West High School, Madison, Wis., teacher of geometry and general science, 1940-41; engineering draftsman, Panama Canal, Canal Zone, 1941-44, 1946-48; La Boca High School, Canal Zone, supervising teacher, 1948-51; University of Illinois, Urbana, 1955-64, began as research assistant professor, professor of educational psychology and member of Bureau of Educational Research, 1963-64; University of Oregon, Division of Educational Policy and Management, Eugene, professor of psychology and research associate, 1964—, professor of education and psychology, 1980—. *Military service:* U.S. Army, Corps of Engineers, 1944-46.

MEMBER: Certified Consultants International, American Educational Research Association, American Psychological Association (fellow), Society for General Systems Research, National Training Laboratories. *Awards, honors:* Douglas McGregor Memorial Award (shared with R. A. Schmuck and Daniel Langmeyer), 1969, for ''Improving Organizational Problem-Solving in a School Faculty,'' published in *Journal of Applied Behavioral Science*.

WRITINGS: (Editor with wife, Margaret Runkel, and Roger Harrison, and contributor) *The Changing College Classroom,* Jossey-Bass, 1969; (with J. E. McGrath) *Research on Human Behavior: A Systematic Guide to Method,* Holt, 1972; (with S. H. Wyant, W. E. Bell, and M. Runkel) *Organizational Renewal in a School District: Self-Help through a Cadre of Organizational Specialists,* Center for Educational Policy and Management, University of Oregon, 1980.

With R. A. Schmuck: *Organizational Training for a School Faculty,* Center for the Advanced Study of Educational Administration, University of Oregon, 1970; (with S. L. Saturen, R. T. Martell, and C. B. Derr) *Handbook of Organization Development in Schools,* National Press Books, 1972; (with J. H. Arends and R. I. Arends) *Second Handbook of Organization Development in Schools,* Mayfield, 1977; (with J. H. Arends, and R. P. Francisco) *Transforming the School's Capacity for Problem Solving,* Center for Educational Policy and Management, University of Oregon, 1979.

Contributor to academic journals.

WORK IN PROGRESS: Third Handbook of Organization Development in Schools, with R. A. Schmuck, for Mayfield; a book tentatively entitled *Social Research Strategy: Choices and Methods in Studying Human Behavior,* with D. Langmeyer and J. E. McGrath, for Sage.

* * *

RUSS, Joanna 1937-

PERSONAL: Born February 22, 1937, in New York, N.Y.; daughter of Evarett I. (a teacher) and Bertha (a teacher; maiden name, Zinner) Russ. *Education:* Cornell University, B.A., 1957; Yale University, M.F.A., 1960. *Politics:* Feminist. *Religion:* None. *Agent:* Ellen Levine, Curtis Brown Ltd., 60 East 56th St., New York, N.Y. 10022. *Office:* Department of English, University of Washington, Seattle, Wash. 98105.

CAREER: Queensborough Community College, Bayside, N.Y., lecturer in speech, 1966-67; Cornell University, Ithaca, N.Y., instructor, 1967-70, assistant professor of English, 1970-72; State University of New York at Binghamton, assistant professor of English, 1972-75; University of Colorado, Boulder, assistant professor of English, 1975-77; University of Washington, Seattle, associate professor of English, 1977—. Member of New York University Hall of Fame Players, 1964-66.

MEMBER: Modern Language Association of America, Science Fiction Writers of America. *Awards, honors:* Nebula Award, Science Fiction Writers of America, 1972, for short story ''When It Changed''; National Endowment for the Humanities fellow, 1974-75; Hugo Award, World Science Fiction Convention, 1983, and Nebula Award, 1983, both for novella "Souls."

WRITINGS: Picnic on Paradise (also see below), Ace Books, 1968; *And Chaos Died,* Ace Books, 1970; *The Female Man,* Bantam, 1975; (author of introduction) Mary Shelley, *Tales and Stories,* G. K. Hall, 1975; *Alyx* (includes *Picnic on Paradise*), G. K. Hall, 1976; *We Who Are About To . . . ,* Dell, 1977; *The Two of Them,* Berkley, 1978; *Kittatinny: A Tale of Magic,* Daughters Publishing, 1978; *On Strike Against God,* Out & Out, 1979.

Contributor: Robin Scott Wilson, editor, *Clarion,* New American Library, 1971; Wilson, editor, *Clarion 2,* New American Library, 1972; Harlan Ellison, editor, *Again, Dangerous Visions,* Doubleday, 1972; Susan Cornillon, editor, *Images of Women in Fiction: Feminist Perspectives,* Popular Press, 1972; Wilson, editor, *Those Who Can,* New American Library, 1973;

Frank N. Magill, editor, *The Contemporary Literary Scene, 1973*, Salem Press, 1974; Damon Knight, editor, *Turning Points*, Harper, 1977; Honor Moore, editor, *The New Women's Theatre*, Random House, 1977; Robert Silverberg, editor, *Alpha 9*, Berkley, 1978; Pamela Sargent, editor, *The New Women of Wonder*, Vintage Books, 1978.

Recordings: "Joanna Russ Interpreting Her Stories," Alternate World Records, 1977.

Contributor of short stories, articles, and poetry to *Magazine of Fantasy and Science Fiction*, *Ms.*, *Extrapolation*, *Manhattan Review*, *Cimarron Review*, *Science-Fiction Studies*, and other periodicals. Book reviewer, *Magazine of Fantasy and Science Fiction*, 1966-79.

SIDELIGHTS: Joanna Russ combines a feminist perspective with a sophisticated style to write science fiction novels which, Marge Piercy states in the *American Poetry Review*, "are interesting beyond the ordinary. They ask nasty and necessary questions [and] offer a gallery of some of the most interesting female protagonists in current fiction." Gerald Jonas of the *New York Times Book Review* notes that in her early work, "Russ used science fiction as a vehicle for the most intelligent, hard-minded commentary on feminism that you are likely to find anywhere."

The Female Man is perhaps the novel in which Russ's feminist ideas are most completely expressed. The book's four heroines—each from a different time and place—represent different possibilities for women in society. "Each of these fictional realities," writes Barbara Garland in the *Dictionary of Literary Biography*, "makes a statement about the self versus society and about male versus female; and each has a distinctive style." In their book *Science Fiction: History, Science, Vision*, Robert Scholes and Eric S. Rabkin find that in *The Female Man*, Russ "has used the visionary potential of science fiction to convey the contrast between life as it is presently lived by many women and life as it might be. Among other things, Russ has demonstrated the unique potential of science fiction for embodying radically different life styles, which can hardly be conveyed in fiction bound by the customs of present literature."

Not all critics judge *The Female Man* to have successfully presented its feminist ideas. Jonas, for example, thinks that Russ, "with her obvious grasp of the biological givens and her command of so many science-fictional weapons, . . . might have produced a truly provocative study of 'woman's fate.' Unfortunately, she keeps slipping into the easy rhetoric of mainstream feminist tracts." Michael Goodwin of *Mother Jones* claims that *The Female Man* "is not a novel—it's a scream of anger. . . . It's unfair, it's maddening, it's depressing. I hated it. . . . And yet, a year after reading it, *The Female Man* remains perfectly clear in my mind—seductive, disturbing and hateful. I'm not sure whether that makes it a good book or not, but I think it makes it an important one."

In an article for *Extrapolation*, Natalie M. Rosinsky analyzes *The Female Man* as "a model of the ways in which feminist humor can operate within a literary text" and sees Russ concerned primarily with "the ways in which humor has been used as a weapon against women." Although each female character in the novel comes from a different time and place, Rosinsky states, "all live in worlds in which humor is used as a weapon against women. Only Janet, the visitor from the all-female universe of Whileaway, has freely experienced and created a different kind of humor, one that does not wound or function to maintain a hierarchical status quo."

Rosinsky sees this difference in humor as pivotal to an understanding of the novel. "We can transcend and transform our lives," she states, "take what has been male-identified and make it female-identified or gender-free. Redefining what is or is not truly funny is one way to begin. And thus, humor in *The Female Man* is not peripheral to either its themes or structure, but is instead an integral, though often undervalued, component of its composition." Rosinsky calls the book "a classic of feminist polemical literature," while Ellen Morgan of *Radical Teacher* judges it "the truest, most complete account available of what it feels like to be alienated as a woman and a feminist."

BIOGRAPHICAL/CRITICAL SOURCES—Books: Robert Scholes and Eric S. Rabkin, *Science Fiction: History, Science, Vision*, Oxford University Press, 1977; Paul Walker, *Speaking of Science Fiction: The Paul Walker Interviews*, Luna Press, 1978; *Contemporary Literary Criticism*, Volume XV, Gale, 1980; David Cowart and Thomas L. Wymer, editors, *Dictionary of Literary Biography*, Volume VIII: *Twentieth Century American Science Fiction Writers*, Gale, 1980.

Periodicals: *Science Fiction Review*, May, 1975, May, 1978; *New York Times Book Review*, May 4, 1975, September 25, 1977, June 25, 1978; *Algol*, summer, 1975; *Magazine of Fantasy and Science Fiction*, August, 1975, February, 1978, April, 1979; *Mother Jones*, August, 1976; *American Poetry Review*, May-June, 1977; *Booklist*, November 1, 1977; *Radical Teacher*, No. 10, 1978; *Frontiers*, spring, 1979; *Extrapolation*, spring, 1982; *Fantasy Newsletter*, April, 1983.

* * *

RUSSELL, Franklin (Alexander) 1926-

PERSONAL: Born October 9, 1926, in Christchurch, Canterbury, New Zealand; came to United States, 1963; son of Alexander Grant and Vida (McKay) Russell; married Jacqueline Scully, October, 1966; children: Alexander. *Education:* Attended Nelson College, 1942, and Victoria University of Wellington, New Zealand. *Politics:* None. *Religion:* None. *Home:* 27 Spring Close Hwy., East Hampton, N.Y. 11937. *Agent:* John Cushman Associates, Inc., 24 East 38th St., New York, N.Y. 10016.

CAREER: Professional writer. Member of staff of New Zealand newspapers, 1947-49, *Sydney Morning Herald*, Sydney, Australia, 1949-50, Associated Newspapers, Ltd., Sydney, 1950-52; free-lance writer for Fleet Street newspapers, magazines, and British Medical Association, London, England, 1952-54, and for Canadian magazines, 1954-63. *Awards, honors:* Guggenheim fellow, 1964-65; award from National Association of Independent Scholars, 1965; Canada Council fellow, 1966, senior arts fellow, 1976.

WRITINGS: Watchers at the Pond, Knopf, 1961, revised edition, with new introduction by Gerald Darrell, Time-Life, 1966; (self-illustrated) *Argen the Gull*, Knopf, 1964; *The Frightened Hare* (juvenile), Holt, 1965; *Hawk in the Sky* (juvenile), Holt, 1965; (self-illustrated) *The Secret Islands*, Norton, 1966; *The Honeybees* (juvenile), Knopf, 1967; *Searchers at the Gulf*, Norton, 1970; *The Atlantic Coast*, N.S.L. (Toronto), 1971; *Corvus the Crow* (juvenile; also see below), Four Winds Press, 1972; *Lotor the Raccoon* (juvenile; also see below), Four Winds Press, 1972; *Datra the Muskrat* (juvenile; also see below), Four Winds Press, 1972; *At the Pond* (juvenile; contains *Corvus the Crow*, *Lotor the Raccoon*, and *Datra the Muskrat*), Four Winds Press, 1972; (with the editors of Time-Life Books) *The*

Okefenokee Swamp, Time-Life, 1973; *The Sea Has Wings,* Dutton, 1973; *Season on the Plain,* Reader's Digest Press, 1974; *Wild Creatures: A Pageant of the Untamed,* Simon & Schuster, 1975; *The Mountains of America: From Alaska to the Great Smokies,* Abrams, 1975; (with Lorus Milne and Margery Milne) *The Secret Life of Animals: Pioneering Discoveries in Animal Behavior,* Dutton, 1975; (with Les Line) *The Audubon Society Book of Wild Birds,* Abrams, 1976. Contributor of articles and reviews to periodicals.

WORK IN PROGRESS: Studies in animal behavior, the ocean, and history; juvenile books.†

* * *

RUSSELL, Jeffrey Burton 1934-

PERSONAL: Born August 1, 1934, in Fresno, Calif.; son of Lewis Henry (a publishers' representative) and Ieda (Ogborn) Russell; married Diana Mansfield (a teacher of English), June 30, 1956; children: Jennifer, Mark, William, Penelope. *Education:* University of California, Berkeley, A.B., 1955, A.M., 1957; University of Liege, Belgium, graduate study, 1959-60; Emory University, Ph.D., 1960. *Politics:* Democrat. *Religion:* Catholic. *Agent:* Gerard McCauley Agency, P.O. Box AE, Katonah, N.Y. *Office:* Department of History, University of California, Santa Barbara, Calif. 93106.

CAREER: University of New Mexico, Albuquerque, assistant professor of history, 1960-61; Harvard University, Cambridge, Mass., junior fellow, Society of Fellows, 1961-62; University of California, Riverside, assistant professor, 1962-65, associate professor, 1965-69, professor of medieval and religious history, 1969-75; University of Notre Dame, Notre Dame, Ind., Michael P. Grace Professor of Medieval Studies and director of Medieval Institute, 1975-79; University of California, Santa Barbara, professor of medieval and church history, 1979—.

MEMBER: American Historical Association, Mediaeval Academy of America, Medieval Association of the Pacific, American Society of Church History, Catholic Historical Association, Phi Beta Kappa, Sierra Club. *Awards, honors:* Fulbright fellowship, 1959; Guggenheim fellowship, 1968; National Endowment for the Humanities senior fellowship, 1972; grants-in-aid from American Council of Learned Societies and Social Science Research Council.

WRITINGS: Dissent and Reform in the Early Middle Ages, University of California Press, 1965; (contributor) Lynn White, editor, *The Transformation of the Roman World,* University of California Press, 1966; *Medieval Civilization,* Wiley, 1968; *A History of Medieval Christianity: Prophecy and Order,* Crowell, 1968; (editor) *Religious Dissent in the Middle Ages,* Wiley, 1971; *Witchcraft in the Middle Ages,* Cornell University Press, 1972; *The Devil: Perceptions of Evil from Antiquity to Primitive Christianity,* Cornell University Press, 1977; *A History of Witchcraft: Sorcerers, Heretics and Pagans,* Thames & Hudson, 1980; (with Carl T. Berkhout) *Medieval Heresies: A Bibliography 1960-1979,* Pontifical Institute of Mediaeval Studies, 1981; *Satan: The Early Christian Tradition,* Cornell University Press, 1981.

Contributor to *Revue d'Histoire ecclesiastique, Medieval Studies, Church History, Speculum, American Historical Review, Catholic Historical Review,* and other journals of history.

WORK IN PROGRESS: Lucifer: The Devil in the Middle Ages.

SIDELIGHTS: Jeffrey Russell told *CA* that "using the history of evil as an example," he has explored "the ways in which concepts may be most fully understood and accurately defined in terms of their history and sociology." He continued, "I am trying to develop an historical method uniting philosophy and content analysis with traditional historical approaches." He has lived a year each in Britain and Belgium, and has traveled extensively elsewhere in Europe. He is fluent in French, reads and writes German, and reads Italian, Spanish, Latin, Dutch, Greek, and Old English.

AVOCATIONAL INTERESTS: Conservation and preservation of wilderness, numismatics, Baroque music, and British mystery stories.

* * *

RUSSELL, Ken(neth Victor) 1929-

PERSONAL: Born November 11, 1929, in England; son of Arthur Victor and Doris (Cotterill) Russell; married Doreen Mary Stanton (a journalist), October 27, 1956; children: Nicola, Simon Stanton. *Education:* Sheffield College of Education, Teachers' Certificate, 1952; University of Birmingham, Diploma in Religious Education, 1954, Diploma in Education, 1961; University of Leicester, Master in Education, 1967; University of Kent, Ph.D., 1976. *Politics:* Labour. *Religion:* Baptist. *Home:* Cedar House, Leicester Rd., Glenfield, Leicestershire, England. *Office address:* Law School, Leicester Polytechnic, P.O. Box 143, Leicester LE1 9BH, England.

CAREER: Deputy headmaster at schools in Staffordshire, England, 1957-59, and West Bromwich, England, 1961-63; Leicester College of Education, Leicester, England, senior lecturer in education, 1963-76; Leicester Polytechnic, Law School, Leicester, principal lecturer, 1976—. Labour candidate for Parliament for Edgbaston, Birmingham, 1955, and Shrewsbury, 1959. Member of Brierley Hill Urban District Council, 1954-58; secretary, Interprofessional Committee Enquiring into Drug Abuse in Leicester, 1967; Leicester Trades Council, president, 1968-69, financial secretary, 1970-72. *Military service:* Royal Air Force, 1948-50; became leading aircraftsman. *Member:* National Union of Teachers, Connecticut State Association of Chiefs of Police (honorary member), Brierley Hill Labour Club.

WRITINGS: (With Joan Tooke) *Learning to Give,* Pergamon, 1968; (contributor) Tooke, editor, *Religious Studies,* Blond Educational, 1970; *Crime Is Our Business,* Pergamon, 1973; *Projects in Religious Education,* Batsford, 1974; *Complaints against the Police: A Sociological View,* Milltak, 1976. Contributor to British Broadcasting Corporation radio and television scripts; contributor to *Blond's Encyclopaedia of Education:* also contributor to newspapers, including *London Mail, Sunday Times, Sunday Telegraph, Express and Star,* and *Birmingham Post.*

SIDELIGHTS: Ken Russell has made five trips to Yugoslavia, 1956-59, 1961; he has traveled to other countries on the continent almost annually since 1954. He visited Morocco in 1965, the Canary Islands in 1968, China in 1983, and has traveled regularly throughout the United States since 1973.

* * *

RYCROFT, Charles (Frederick) 1914-

PERSONAL: Born September 9, 1914, in Basingstoke, England; son of Sir Richard and Emily (Lowry-Corry) Rycroft; married Chloe Majolier (a physician), 1946 (divorced, 1962);

married Jenny Pearson, 1977; children: (first marriage) Julia, Catherine, Francis. *Education:* Trinity College, Cambridge, B.A. (first class honors), 1936; University College, London, M.B., 1945, B.S., 1945. *Home:* 69 Gloucester Rd., Kew, Surrey, England. *Agent:* A. D. Peters, 10 Buckingham St., London W.C. 2, England. *Office:* 18 Wimpole St., London W.1, England.

CAREER: House physician at Maudsley Hospital, London, England, 1946; psychotherapist and psychoanalyst in private practice, London, 1948—. Part-time consultant in psychotherapy to Tavistock Clinic, London, 1956-68. *Member:* British Psycho-Analytical Society (librarian, 1950-56; scientific secretary, 1956-58).

WRITINGS: (Editor) *Psychoanalysis Observed,* Coward, 1967; (contributor) James Mitchell, editor, *The God I Want,* Constable, 1967; *Anxiety and Neurosis,* Penguin, 1968; *Imagination and Reality,* Hogarth, 1968; *Critical Dictionary of Psychoanalysis,* Basic Books, 1969; *Reich,* Viking, 1971; *The Innocence of Dreams,* Pantheon, 1979.

Contributor of reviews to *Observer, New Society,* and *New York Review of Books.* Assistant editor, *International Journal of Psycho-Analysis,* 1955-58.

SIDELIGHTS: In *The Innocence of Dreams,* Charles Rycroft examines dreams and their meanings from a psychological perspective distinct from that of Sigmund Freud or Carl Jung, the two psychiatrists whose pioneering studies of the dream state are still immensely influential. Rycroft particularly disagrees with Freud, "who saw in dreams the expression of unconscious wishes" and believed, Jean Strouse of *Newsweek* quotes Rycroft, that "artists and writers are neurotic and that dreaming is a universally occurring neurotic symptom." Rycroft explains the dream state as "the sleeping form of creative imagination." Edgar Levenson of the *New York Times Book Review* clarifies Rycroft's idea further: "Rather than maintaining the traditional division of dream into manifest and latent content—what is evident and what is concealed—Dr. Rycroft treats the medium as the message. The dream is what the dream purports to be, 'the form taken by the imagination during sleep,' [not] an 'abnormal psychical phenomenon.'" "Rycroft's book," Levenson believes, "is so lucid, so logically developed, and so deceptively simple, that . . . one is tempted to miss the quantum leap that he . . . is making away from Freud and Jung."

BIOGRAPHICAL/CRITICAL SOURCES: Observer, May 6, 1979; *Spectator,* May 12, 1979; *Listener,* May 24, 1979; *New York Times Book Review,* August 26, 1979; *Newsweek,* September 3, 1979; *Times Literary Supplement,* November 23, 1979.

*   *   *

RYKWERT, Joseph   1926-

PERSONAL: Born April 5, 1926, in Warsaw, Poland; son of Szymon Mieczyslaw (an engineer) and Elizabeth (Melup) Rykwert; married Jane Morton, 1960 (divorced, 1967); married Anne-Marie Sandersley (a lawyer), February 14, 1972; children: Simon Sebastian, Marina Joanna Engel (stepdaughter). *Education:* Attended Bartlett School of Architecture, University of London, 1942-44, and Architectural Association School of Architecture, 1944-47. *Address:* The Savile Club, 69 Brook St., London W1, England. *Office:* Department of Architecture, Cambridge University, 1 Scroope Ter., Cambridge CB2 1PX, England.

CAREER: Architect, E. Maxwell Fry & Jane Drew, 1947; architect, Richard Sheppard & Partners, 1947-48; member of editorial staff, *Chambers Encyclopaedia,* 1948-49; studio master and lecturer in the history of architecture, Hammersmith School of Arts and Crafts, 1952-53; Royal College of Art, London, England, librarian and tutor in the history of architecture, 1961-67; University of Essex, Essex, England, professor of art, 1967-79, chairman of department, 1967-70; Cambridge University, Cambridge, England, Slade Professor of Fine Arts and visiting fellow, Darwin College, 1979-80, lecturer in architecture, 1980—.

Lecturer at numerous institutions, including Delft Polytechnic, University of Louvain, York University, Columbia University, Carnegie-Mellon University, University of Pennsylvania, Cooper Union, Harvard University, Massachusetts Institute of Technology, Cambridge University, University of Naples, and University of Palermo; visiting professor, University of Paris, 1974-76, Princeton University and Cooper Union, 1977, Ecole Polytechnique Federale de Lausanne, 1979-80, Harvard University, 1980, University of Palermo, 1981, University of Louvain and University of Pennsylvania, 1982. Member of commission, Venice Biennale, 1974-77; visiting fellow, Darwin College, Cambridge, 1979-80; member of committee, Comite International des Antiques d'Architecture, 1980—; senior fellow, Center of Advanced Studies in the Visual Arts, National Gallery, Washington, D.C., 1981. Has broadcast on French, German, and British programs.

AWARDS, HONORS: Graham Foundation fellowship at Institute for Architecture and Urban Studies, New York, 1969-71; award from Royal College of Art, 1970; senior fellow of Princeton University's Council of the Humanities, 1971.

WRITINGS: The Golden House (poem), Anthony Froshaug, 1951; (editor) Leone Battista Alberti, *Ten Books on Architecture,* Alec Tiranti, 1955; *Church Building,* Hawthorn, 1966; *On the Early Pictures of Giorgio de Chirico: A Poem,* VERB Editions, 1969; *On Adam's House in Paradise: The Idea of the Primitive Hut in Architectural History,* Museum of Modern Art, 1972, 2nd edition, MIT Press, 1982; (editor) A. Loos, *Parole nel Vuoto,* Adelphi, 1972; *The Idea of a Town: The Anthropology of Urban Form in Rome, Italy, and the Ancient World,* Princeton University Press, 1976; *The First Moderns: Architects of the Eighteenth Century,* MIT Press, 1980; *The Necessity of Artifice,* Academy Editions, 1982.

Contributor: John Heath-Stubbs, editor, *Image of Tomorrow,* S.C.M. Press, 1953. Also contributor to *Ideas,* Grosvenor Press, 1954, and *Art, Artists, and Thinkers,* Longman, 1956. Contributor to *Garzanti Enzyclopaedia.* Contributor of more than sixty poems, articles, and reviews to art and architecture journals, literary magazines, including *Time and Tide, Domus, Casabella,* and *Times Literary Supplement,* and to newspapers. Contributing editor of *Lotus* and *Res.*

WORK IN PROGRESS: Research on the orders of architecture.

SIDELIGHTS: Joseph Rykwert's book *The First Moderns: Architects of the Eighteenth Century* attempts, according to *Times Literary Supplement* reviewer Frances Yates, "to base the history of culture on the history of architecture understood in a very wide sense." Yates also notes that "a leading theme of [the book is] to include Masonic history with the history of architecture. To give one example, [Rykwert] points out that the explosion of architectural publications in the second and third decades of the eighteenth century coincided with the inception of Grand Lodge Masonry. And that the philosophy of

Isaac Newton, the discoverer of laws governing the architecture of the universe, was propagated by noted Masons, James Anderson, author of the *Constitutions,* and John Desaguliers, the Huguenot refugee, prominent in British Masonry.''

''The range of Rykwert's learning is enormous,'' Yates continues. ''History of gardens, Chinese influences, festival architecture, all contribute to the overflowing wealth. Great figures in the history of thought and science—Bacon, Newton, Vico—are seen from new angles.'' And although the critic feels that the expanse of Rykwert's research crowds the book and ''makes for rather difficult reading,'' Yates concludes that the ''reward for perseverance is great. This is no superficial history of styles, no conventional history of ideas. [*The First Moderns*] invigorates both through the attempt at a new kind of history of architecture.''

Rykwert's books have been translated into Italian, Spanish, and German.

BIOGRAPHICAL/CRITICAL SOURCES: Times Literary Supplement, January 16, 1981, October 8, 1982.

S

SABIN, Francene

PERSONAL: Married Louis Sabin (a writer); children: Keith. *Home and office:* 103 Connolly Dr., Milltown, N.J. 08850. *Agent:* Toni Mendez, Inc., 140 East 56th St., New York, N.Y. 10022.

CAREER: Writer. *Member:* American Society of Journalists and Authors, National Press Club.

WRITINGS: Women Who Win, Random House, 1975; *Set Point: the Story of Chris Evert*, Putnam, 1977; *Jimmy Connors: King of the Courts*, Putnam, 1978; *Amazing World of Ants*, Troll, 1981; *The Magic String*, Troll, 1981; *Wonders of the Forest*, Troll, 1981; *Wonders of the Pond*, Troll, 1981; *Courage of Helen Keller*, Troll, 1982; *Elizabeth Blackwell: The First Woman Doctor*, Troll, 1982. Contributor of articles to magazines, including *Exploring, Family Circle, Seventeen, Omni, American Education*, and *Parade*.

With husband, Louis Sabin: *Dogs of America*, Putnam, 1967; *The One, the Only, the Original Jigsaw Puzzle Book*, Regnery, 1977; *Perfect Pets*, Putnam, 1978; *Run Faster, Jump Higher, Throw Farther: How to Win at Track and Field*, McKay, 1980; *The Great Easter Egg Mystery*, Troll, 1981; *The Great Santa Claus Mystery*, Troll, 1981; *Mystery at the Jellybean Fctory*, Troll, 1981; *Secret of the Haunted House*, Troll, 1981; *All About Dogs as Pets*, Messner, 1983.

"Discovering the Seasons" series, with Louis Santrey (pseudonym of husband, L. Sabin); all published by Troll, 1982: *Spring; Summer; Autumn; Winter.*

SIDELIGHTS: Francene Sabin told *CA:* "I write because I love to and because it's what I do best. Almost everything interests me, whether or not I have the opportunity to use it professionally. Beyond that, I am a very private person."

*   *   *

SABIN, Lou
See SABIN, Louis

*   *   *

SABIN, Louis   1930-
(Lou Sabin; pseudonyms: Larry Bains, Keith Brandt, Louis Santrey)

PERSONAL: Born June 25, 1930, in Salt Lake City, Utah; son of Philip and Betty Sabin; married; wife's name, Francene (a writer); children: Keith. *Education:* Brooklyn College (now Brooklyn College of the City University of New York), B.A., 1955; New York University, M.A., 1957. *Home and office:* 103 Connolly Dr., Milltown, N.J. 08850. *Agent:* Toni Mendez, Inc., 140 East 56th St., New York, N.Y. 10022.

CAREER: Editor of various magazines, including *True Detective, Saga,* and *Boys' Life*, 1953-73; full-time free-lance writer, 1973—. Teacher of English at Middlesex County College, 1974. *Military service:* U.S. Air Force, 1947-49. *Member:* American Society of Journalists and Authors.

WRITINGS: Basketball Stars of 1970, Pyramid Books, 1969; *Pele: Soccer Superstar*, Putnam, 1976; *The Fabulous Dr. J.: All Time All Star*, Putnam, 1976; *Basketball's Greatest: Selected All-Star Offensive and Defensive Teams*, Putnam, 1976; *Walt Frazier: No. 1 Guard of the NBA*, Putnam, 1976; *Johnny Bench: King of Catchers*, Putnam, 1977; (under pseudonym Keith Brandt) *Pete Rose: Mr. 300*, Putnam, 1977; *100 Great Moments in Sports*, Putnam, 1978; *Amazing World of Butterflies and Moths*, Troll, 1981; *Birthday Surprise*, Troll, 1981; *Wonders of the Desert*, Troll, 1981; *Wonders of the Sea*, Troll, 1981; (editor and contributor) *Challenger Crossword Puzzle Books*, Simon & Schuster, 1981; *Narcissa Whitman: Brave Pioneer*, Troll, 1982; *Patrick Henry: Voice of American Revolution*, Troll, 1982; *Amazing Dog Stories*, Scholastic Book Services, 1983.

With wife, Francene Sabin: *Dogs of America*, Putnam, 1967; *The One, the Only, the Original Jigsaw Puzzle Book*, Regnery, 1977; *Perfect Pets*, Putnam, 1978; *Run Faster, Jump Higher, Throw Farther: How to Win at Track and Field*, McKay, 1980; *All About Dogs as Pets*, Messner, 1983.

Under name Lou Sabin: (With Dave Sendler) *Stars of Pro Basketball*, Random House, 1970, revised edition, 1973; *Great Teams of Pro Basketball*, Random House, 1971; *Pete Maravich: Basketball Magician*, Scholastic Book Services, 1973; *Record-Breakers of the Major Leagues*, Random House, 1974; *Hot Shots of Pro Basketball*, Random House, 1974.

Under name Lou Sabin; with wife, F. Sabin: *The Great Easter Egg Mystery*, Troll, 1981; *The Great Santa Claus Mystery*, Troll, 1981; *Mystery at the Jellybean Factory*, Troll, 1981; *Secret of the Haunted House*, Troll, 1981.

Under pseudonym Louis Santrey; with wife, F. Sabin; "Discovering the Seasons" series; all published by Troll, 1982: *Spring; Summer; Autumn; Winter*.

Contributor of articles and crossword puzzles to magazines, including *Today's Health, Family Weekly, Seventeen, Soap Opera Digest, Seniority,* and *Ladies' Home Journal*.

* * *

SABOURIN, Leopold 1919-

PERSONAL: Born September 7, 1919, in St.-Jean-Baptiste, Manitoba, Canada; son of Omer (a farmer) and Mathilda (a farmer; maiden name, Clement) Sabourin. *Education:* University of Manitoba, B.A., 1939; University of Montreal, M.A., 1941; Pontifical Biblical Institute, Rome, Licentiate in Scripture, 1956; Jesuit Faculties, Montreal, Doctorate in Theology, 1959. *Home and office:* University of Sudbury, Sudbury, Ontario, Canada P3E 2C6.

CAREER: Ordained Roman Catholic priest of Society of Jesus (S.J.), 1945; University College of Addis Ababa, Addis Ababa, Ethiopia, teacher of philosophy, 1950-53; Theological Seminary, Port-au-Prince, Haiti, teacher of scripture, 1959-64; Biblical Institute, Jerusalem, Israel, teacher of scripture, 1964-67; Pontifical Biblical Institute, Rome, Italy, professor of psalms and synoptic gospels, 1967-78; Aquinas Seminary, Nairobi, Kenya, Scripture professor, 1979-80; University of Calgary, Calgary, Alberta, professor of religious studies, 1980-81; University of Sudbury, Sudbury, Ontario, professor of religious studies, 1981—. *Member:* Catholic Biblical Association of America. *Awards, honors:* Quebec Government award, 1962, for *Redemption sacrificielle*.

WRITINGS: Redemption sacrificielle: Une enquete exegetique, Desclee de Brouwer, 1961, partial translation included as Part 3 of *Sin, Redemption, and Sacrifice: A Biblical and Patristic Study* (with Stanislas Lyonnet), Biblical Institute (Rome), 1970; *Les Noms et les titres de Jesus: Themes de Theologie Biblique,* Desclee de Brouwer, 1963, translation by Maurice Carroll published as *The Names and Titles of Jesus: Themes of Biblical Theology,* Macmillan, 1967; *Un classement litteraire des Psaumes* (title means "Literary Classification of the Psalms"), Desclee de Brouwer, 1964; *The Psalms: Their Origin and Meaning,* Alba House, 1969, 2nd edition, 1974.

Priesthood: A Comparative Study, E. J. Brill, 1973; *Il Vangelo di Matteo,* Edizioni Paoline, 1975, 2nd edition, 1976; *The Divine Miracles Discussed and Defended,* Catholic Book Agency (Rome), 1977; *L'Evangile selon saint Matthieu et ses principaux paralleles,* Biblical Institute Press, 1978; *The Bible and Christ: The Unity of the Two Testaments,* Alba House, 1980; *The Gospel according to Matthew,* two volumes, St. Paul Publications (India), 1983; (contributor) *Supplement au Dictionnaire de la Bible,* Letouzey & Ane (Paris), 1983; *The Gospel according to Luke,* St. Paul Publications, 1984. Editor, *Biblical Theology Bulletin,* 1971-76, and *Religious Studies Bulletin,* 1981—.

WORK IN PROGRESS: A textbook on Christology for college-level students.

SIDELIGHTS: Leopold Sabourin told *CA* that in his writings he "attempts to bridge the gap between specialized scholarship and the increased demand for serious but not too technical exposition in exegesis and biblical theology."

SAFER, Daniel J. 1934-

PERSONAL: Born June 29, 1934, in Milwaukee, Wis.; son of Mendel (a food store manager) and Belle (a social worker; maiden name, Rottman) Safer; married Elaine Berkman (a professor), June 5, 1960; children: Debra L., Alan M., Judith A. *Education:* University of Wisconsin, B.S., 1956, M.D., 1959. *Home:* 301 Radcliffe Dr., Newark, Del. 19711. *Office:* Eastern Community Mental Health Center, Baltimore County Department of Health, 9100 Franklin Square Dr., Baltimore, Md. 21237.

CAREER: Certified by American Board of Psychiatry and Neurology in general psychiatry, 1973, and in child psychiatry, 1982. District of Columbia General Hospital, Washington, D.C., intern, 1959-60; Cleveland Psychiatric Institute, Cleveland, Ohio, psychiatric resident, 1960-63; Institute for Juvenile Research, Chicago, Ill., fellow in child psychiatry, 1963-64; Johns Hopkins Hospital, Baltimore, Md., fellow in child psychiatry, 1968-69; Baltimore County Department of Health, Baltimore, Md., co-director of School Child Mental Health Service, 1969-72, regional director of Child Psychiatry Service, 1972—. Instructor in psychiatry, Northwestern University School of Medicine, 1964-66, and Johns Hopkins Hospital, 1969-70; Johns Hopkins University School of Medicine, assistant professor, 1970-79, associate professor of psychology, 1979—. Assistant attending psychiatrist, Children's Memorial Hospital, Chicago, Ill., 1964-66. Psychiatric consultant to Baltimore City Hospitals, 1966-68, Franklin Square Hospital, Rosedale, Md., 1970-73, and Delaware Guidance Services for Children, 1981-82. *Military service:* U.S. Army, 1966-68; became captain. *Member:* American Psychiatric Association (fellow), American Orthopsychiatric Association, Maryland Psychiatric Society, Baltimore County Medical Society.

WRITINGS: (With Richard P. Allen) *Hyperactive Children: Diagnosis and Management,* University Park Press, 1976; (with others) *School Programs for Disruptive Adolescents,* University Park Press, 1982; (with others) *Teaching Bad Boys: Perspectives on an In-School Program for Disruptive Adolescents* (manual), American Young Co., 1981.

Contributor: (With Allen) Rachel Gittleman-Klein, editor, *Recent Advances in Childhood Psychopharmacology,* Behavioral Publications, 1976; L. L. Iversen, S. D. Iversen, and S. H. Snyder, editors, *Handbook of Psychopharmacology,* Volume XI, Plenum, 1977; L. E. Arnold, editor, *Principles of Parent Guidance for Professionals,* Brunner, 1978; (with Allen) M. Cohen, editor, *Drugs and the Special Child,* Gardner Press, 1979; (with S. Gabel) Gabel, editor, *Behavioral Problems in Childhood,* Grune, 1981; (with G. C. Fernandopulle) L. R. Derogatis, editor, *Psychopharmacology in Clinic Practice,* Addison-Wesley, in press; Jr. R. Field, G. F. Ostrom, and L. Herschberg, editors, *Handbook of Violence and Its Prevention,* Spectrum, in press; D. M. Doleys, T. B. Vaughan, and M. L. Cantrell, editors, *Assessment and Treatment of Developmental Problems,* Spectrum, in press.

Also author of tapes "Hyperactive Children: Treatment Considerations," Behavior Science Tape Library, 1974, "Whose Problem Child?," Forest Hospital Foundation, 1971, and "Behavior Problems: Disruptive Students," Forest Hospital Foundation, 1980. Contributor of articles to professional journals, including *New England Journal of Medicine, Pediatrics,* and *Journal of American Academy of Child Psychiatry*.

SAFFELL, David C(lyde) 1941-

PERSONAL: Born February 10, 1941, in Wheeling, W.Va.; son of Lloyd and Helen (Smith) Saffell; married Ainsley Brye, 1965; children: Paul, Heather. *Education:* Baldwin-Wallace College, B.A., 1963; University of Minnesota, M.A., 1965, Ph.D., 1969. *Religion:* Protestant. *Home:* 502 West North St., Ada, Ohio 45810. *Office:* Department of Political Science, Ohio Northern University, Ada, Ohio 45810.

CAREER: St. Cloud State University, St. Cloud, Minn., assistant professor of political science, 1966-70; Ashland College, Ashland, Ohio, assistant professor of political science, 1970-72; Ohio Northern University, Ada, 1972—, began as associate professor, currently professor of political science. *Member:* American Political Science Association, Midwest Political Science Association.

WRITINGS: Politics of American National Government, Winthrop Publishing, 1973, 4th edition, 1981; *Watergate: Its Effects on the American Political System,* Winthrop Publishing, 1974; *American Government: Reform in the Post-Watergate Era,* Winthrop Publishing, 1976; *State and Local Government,* Addison-Wesley, 1978, 2nd edition, 1982; (editor with others) *Subnational Politics,* Addison-Wesley, 1982; *State Politics,* Addison-Wesley, 1983. Contributor of articles and reviews to *Dictionary of American History* and *Perspective.*

* * *

SAGAN, Carl (Edward) 1934-

PERSONAL: Born November 9, 1934, in New York, N.Y.; son of Samuel (a cloth cutter) and Rachel (Gruber) Sagan; married Lynn Alexander, June 16, 1957 (divorced, 1963); married Linda Salzman (a painter), April 6, 1968 (divorced); married Ann Druyan (a writer); children: (first marriage) Dorian Solomon, Jeremy Ethan; (second marriage) Nicholas; (third marriage) Alexandra. *Education:* University of Chicago, A.B. (with general and special honors), 1954, B.S., 1955, M.A., 1956, Ph.D., 1960. *Office:* Laboratory for Planetary Studies, Space Science Building, Cornell University, Ithaca, N.Y. 14853.

CAREER: University of California, Berkeley, Miller research fellow in astronomy, 1960-62; Harvard University, Cambridge, Mass., 1962-68, began as lecturer, became assistant professor of astronomy; Smithsonian Institution, Astrophysical Observatory, Cambridge, Mass., astrophysicist, 1962-68; Cornell University, Ithaca, N.Y., associate professor, 1968-70, professor of astronomy and space sciences, 1970—, David Duncan Professor of Astronomy and Space Sciences, 1976—, director of Laboratory for Planetary Studies, 1968—, associate director of Center for Radiophysics and Space Research, 1972-81; writer.

Visiting assistant professor of genetics, Stanford University Medical School, 1962-63; National Science Foundation-American Astronomical Society visiting professor at various colleges, 1963-67; Condon Lecturer, University of Oregon and Oregon State University, 1967-68; National Aeronautics and Space Administration (NASA) lecturer in astronaut training program, 1969-72; Holiday Lecturer, American Association for the Advancement of Science, 1970; Vanuxem Lecturer, Princeton University, 1973; Smith Lecturer, Dartmouth University, 1974, 1977; Wagner Lecturer, University of Pennsylvania, 1975; Philips Lecturer, Haverford College, 1975; Jacob

Bronowski Lecturer, University of Toronto, 1975; Anson Clark Memorial Lecturer, University of Texas at Dallas, 1976; Danz Lecturer, University of Washington, 1976; Stahl Lecturer, Bowdoin College, 1977; Christmas Lecturer, Royal Institution, London, 1977; Menninger Memorial Lecturer, American Psychiatric Association, 1978; Carver Memorial Lecturer, Tuskegee Institute, 1981; Feinstone Lecturer, United States Military Academy, 1981; Class day lecturer, Yale University, 1981; George Pal Lecturer, Motion Picture Academy of Arts and Sciences, 1982; Phelps Dodge Lecturer, University of Arizona, 1982; H. L. Welsh Lecturer in Physics, University of Toronto, 1982. Also lecturer at numerous other colleges and universities.

President, Carl Sagan Productions, Inc. (scientific books and supplies), 1981—. Member of Committee to Review Project Blue Book (U.S. Air Force), 1956-66. Experimenter, Mariner mission to Venus, 1962, Mariner and Viking missions to Mars, 1969—, designer of Pioneer 10 and 11 and Voyager 1 and 2 interstellar messages. Member of council, Smithsonian Institution, 1975—; member, American Committee on East-West Accord, 1983—. Judge, National Book Awards, 1976—. Member of various advisory groups of National Aeronautics and Space Administration; member of advisory panel, Civil Space Station Study, Office of Technology Assessment, U.S. Congress, 1982—; consultant to National Academy of Science.

MEMBER: International Astronomical Union (member of organizing committee, Commission of Physical Study of Planets), International Council of Scientific Unions (vice chairman; member of executive council, committee on space research; co-chairman, working group on moon and planets), International Academy of Astronautics, International Society for the Study of the Origin of Life (member of council, 1980—), P.E.N. International, American Astronomical Society (councillor; chairman, division of planetary sciences, 1975-76), American Physical Society, American Geophysical Union (president, planetology section, 1980—), American Association for the Advancement of Science (fellow; chairman, astronomy section, 1975), American Institute of Aeronautics and Astronautics (associate fellow), American Astronautical Society (member of council, 1976), Federation of American Scientists (member of council, 1977), Society for the Study of Evolution, British Interplanetary Society (fellow), Astronomical Society of the Pacific, Genetics Society of America, Authors Guild, Authors League of America, Phi Beta Kappa, Sigma Xi, Explorers Club.

AWARDS, HONORS: National Science Foundation post-doctoral fellowship, 1955-60; Alfred P. Sloan Foundation research fellowship at Harvard University, 1963-67; Smith Prize, Harvard University, 1964; National Aeronautics and Space Administration, Apollo Achievement Award, 1970, medal for exceptional scientific achievement, 1972, medal for distinguished public service, 1977, 1981; Prix Galabert (international astronautics prize), 1973; Klumpke-Roberts Prize, Astronomical Society of the Pacific, 1974; John W. Campbell Memorial Award, World Science Fiction Convention, 1974; Golden Plate Award, American Academy of Achievement, 1975; Joseph Priestly Award, Dickinson College, 1975; D.Sc. from Rensselaer Polytechnic University, 1975, Denison University, 1976, and Clarkson College, 1977; D.H.L., Skidmore College, 1976; Pulitzer Prize for Literature, 1978, for *The Dragons of Eden: Speculations on the Evolution of Human Intelligence;* Washburn Medal, 1978; Rittenhouse Medal, 1980; 75th Anniversary Award, Explorers Club, 1980; *Cosmos* named among best books for young adults, American Library Association, 1980; American Book Award nominations for *Cosmos* (hardcover) and *Broca's Brain: Reflections on the Romance of Science* (paperback), both 1981; Peabody Award, 1981, for "Cosmos"; Seaborg Prize, 1981; Roe Medal, American Society of Mechanical Engineers, 1981; Humanist of the Year Award, American Humanist Association, 1981; Ohio State University annual award for television excellence, 1982, for "Cosmos"; Stony Brook Foundation award, with Frank Press, for distinguished contributions to higher education, 1982; John F. Kennedy Astronautics Award, American Astronautical Society, 1983.

WRITINGS: (With W. W. Kellogg) *The Atmospheres of Mars and Venus*, National Academy of Sciences, 1961; (with I. S. Shklovskii) *Intelligent Life in the Universe*, Holden-Day, 1963, reprinted, 1978; (with Jonathan Leonard) *Planets*, Time-Life Science Library, 1966.

Planetary Exploration: The Condon Lectures, University of Oregon Press, 1970; (editor with T. Owen and H. J. Smith) *Planetary Atmospheres*, D. Reidel, 1971; (editor with K. Y. Kondratyev and M. Ryecroft) *Space Research XI*, two volumes, Akademie Verlag, 1971; (with R. Littauer and others) *The Air War in Indochina*, Center for International Studies, Cornell University, 1971; (editor with T. Page) *UFOs: A Scientific Debate*, Cornell University Press, 1972; (editor) *Communication with Extraterrestrial Intelligence*, MIT Press, 1973; (with Ray Bradbury, Arthur Clarke, Bruce Murray, and Walter Sullivan) *Mars and the Mind of Man*, Harper, 1973; (with R. Berendzen, A. Montagu, P. Morrison, K. Stendhal, and G. Wald) *Life beyond Earth and the Mind of Man*, U.S. Government Printing Office, 1973; (editor) *The Cosmic Connection: An Extraterrestrial Perspective* (selection of several book clubs, including Library of Science Book Club and Natural History Book Club), Doubleday, 1973; *Other Worlds*, Bantam, 1975.

The Dragons of Eden: Speculations on the Evolution of Human Intelligence (Book-of-the-Month Club selection; also selection of other book clubs, including *Psychology Today* Book Club and McGraw-Hill Book Club), Random House, 1977; (with F. D. Drake, A. Druyan, J. Lomberg, and T. Ferris) *Murmurs of Earth: The Voyager Interstellar Record* (Book-of-the-Month Club and other book clubs selection), Random House, 1978; *Broca's Brain: Reflections on the Romance of Science* (Book-of-the-Month Club and other book clubs selection), Random House, 1979; *Cosmos* (also see below; Book-of-the-Month Club and Natural History Book Club main selection; also selection of other book clubs, including Library of World History Book Club and Natural Science Book Club), Random House, 1980. Also contributor to several books on science.

Author of radio and television scripts, including "Cosmos," Public Broadcasting System, 1980, and scripts for Voice of America, American Chemical Society radio series, and British Broadcasting Corp. Contributor to *Encyclopedia Americana*, *Encyclopaedia Britannica*, and *Whole Earth Catalog*, 1971. Contributor of more than 350 papers to scientific journals, and of articles to periodicals, including *National Geographic*, *Saturday Review*, *Discovery*, *Washington Post*, *Natural History*, *Scientific American*, and *New York Times*. *Icarus: International Journal of Solar System Studies*, associate editor, 1962-68, editor-in-chief, 1968-79; member of editorial board, *Origins of Life*, 1974—, *Climatic Change*, 1976—, and *Science*, 1979—.

WORK IN PROGRESS: A novel, *Contact*, for Simon & Schuster; a screen adaptation of *Contact*, for Columbia.

SIDELIGHTS: When Carl Sagan was twelve years old, his grandfather asked him what he wanted to be when he grew up.

"An astronomer," answered Carl, whereupon his grandfather replied, "Yes, but how will you make your living?"

As one of the most widely known and outspoken scientists in America, Carl Sagan has made both his living and a considerable reputation in astronomy, biology, physics, and the emerging science of exobiology, the study of extraterrestrial life. In his bestselling books, such as *The Dragons of Eden: Speculations on the Evolution of Human Intelligence* and *Broca's Brain: Reflections on the Romance of Science*, and in the extremely popular television series "Cosmos" (itself adapted into book form), Sagan, according to Frederic Golden of *Time*, "sends out an exuberant message: science is not only vital for humanity's future well-being, but it is rousing good fun as well."

The Cornell University-based scientist, who published his first research article ("Radiation and the Origin of the Gene") at age twenty-two, grew up in Brooklyn, New York, the son of an American-born mother and a Russian-immigrant father. Sagan describes himself as a science-fiction addict from an early age who became hooked on astronomy after learning that each star in the evening sky represented a distant sun. He tells Golden: "This just blew my mind. Until then the universe had been my neighborhood. Now I tried to imagine how far away I'd have to move the sun to make it as faint as a star. I got my first sense of the immensity of the universe." In a *New Yorker* interview, Sagan tells Henry S.F. Cooper, Jr.: "I didn't make a decision to pursue astronomy; rather, it just grabbed me and I had no thought of escaping. But I didn't know that you could get paid for it. . . . Then, in my sophomore year in high school, my biology teacher . . . told me he was pretty sure Harvard paid [noted astronomer] Harold Shapley a salary. That was a splendid day—when I began to suspect that if I tried hard I could do astronomy full time, not just part time." At sixteen, Sagan entered the University of Chicago on a scholarship. As early as his undergraduate days, the student began earning a reputation as a maverick; according to Golden, Sagan organized a popular campus lecture series and included himself as one of the speakers. At the same time, he shunned traditional courses of study in favor of his own intellectual pursuits.

On leaving the University of Chicago with a Ph.D. in astronomy and astrophysics in 1960, Sagan began research at Harvard University where, with colleague James Pollack, he challenged standard scientific views on the periodic lightening and darkening surface of Mars. Sagan's theory—that the alternating shades of surface light were caused by wind storms—was confirmed several years later with photographs of Mars. Speculations of that type cemented Sagan's image as an iconoclast. However, writes Golden, "even Sagan's scientific friends acknowledge that he does not have the patience or persistence for the slow, painstaking experimentation that is at the heart of the scientific process. Nor has he come close to the kind of breakthrough work that wins Nobel Prizes. But he more than compensates with other significant talents. He has a penchant for asking provocative questions. Sometimes, as Sagan fully concedes, this can rile others. But such prodding can inspire students and colleagues, lead to brilliant new insights, and generally create a mood of intellectual excitement." As one of Sagan's associates tells Cooper in the *New Yorker*: "Carl sees himself as an intellectual gadfly. . . . His talent is speculating, more than data analysis or collection. He works that talent—he theorizes, he gets people to admit things they wouldn't admit earlier. He creates an expansive view of man and the universe. But the fact that he can be quite passionate in his arguments makes people mad."

It is not only his speculations, though, that have made people mad. For instance, one of Sagan's more unusual projects involves interstellar communication. For the explorer ships Pioneer 10 and 11, both slated to leave our solar system, Sagan and Cornell colleague Frank Drake designed plaques to be installed on the crafts. Using illustrations and symbolic language, the plaques depict, according to Cooper's article, "the time of the launch in relation to the history of our galaxy, . . . a sort of return address, in case they fell into the hands (or whatever) of extraterrestrial beings, . . . [and] pictures of those who had launched the craft—delineations of a nude man and woman." Cooper reports that the scientist "still gets letters from people complaining about his sending smut into space."

Sagan's writing career has evolved along with his scientific career. In 1963 he became interested in a Russian book called *Intelligent Life in the Universe* and was given permission to work on its English translation. In the process Sagan added ten new chapters (more than doubling the original length of the book), thus becoming, according to Stuart Bauer in *New York,* "more than 60 per cent responsible for the first comprehensive treatment of the entire panorama of natural evolution, covering the origin of the universe, the evolution of the stars and planets, and the beginning of life on earth." (Bauer credits Sagan's expansion of the Russian original for the fact that *Intelligent Life in the Universe* has since gone into fourteen printings.) The scientist further distinguished himself as an expert in these fields in 1971, when, according to Bauer, "the *Encyclopaedia Britannica* invited [Sagan] to write its definitive 25,000-word essay on 'Life'; in 1973, in a manner of speaking, he took out a patent on it—U.S. Patent 3,756,934 for the production of amino acids from gaseous mixtures."

The Dragons of Eden, Sagan's first popular book to delve outside the study of astronomy, was published in 1977. Essentially an exploration of human intelligence, the work has met with mixed critical reaction. Robert Manning of *Atlantic,* for instance, finds *The Dragons of Eden* "rational, elegant and witty" but warns that reading parts of it is "akin to climbing the Matterhorn without crampons or ice ax. One must pay attention to every crack and cranny." R. J. Herrnstein writes in *Commentary* that although the author is "asking his readers to change their minds about almost nothing," he does so with "grace, humor and style." John Updike finds fault with the author's subject matter. "Versatile though he is," Updike remarks in the *New Yorker,* "[Sagan] is simply not enough saturated in his subject to speculate; what he can do is summarize and, to a limited degree, correlate the results of scattered and tentative modern research on the human brain. . . . [His] speculations, where they are not cheerfully wild, seem tacked on and trivial." *Newsweek*'s Raymond Sokolov also feels that the author "tries to 'speculate' about matters beyond scientific knowledge," but he "manages to get away with such airy inquiries because he is so open about their tentative science-fiction status."

On the other hand, Stephen Toulmin, in a *New York Review of Books* article, praises *The Dragons of Eden* as an "engaging and well written . . . antidote to much of the recent controversy about human evolution." Toulmin cites the author's "briskness and astringency" of style and suggests that the book shows Sagan as "a true 'natural philosopher,' . . . whose real goal is to produce a revised version of the story of human history and destiny, within the boundary conditions set by the ideas of twentieth-century science."

The inspiration for Sagan's next work, *Broca's Brain,* came during a tour of the Musee de l'Homme in Paris, where he came upon a collection of jars containing human brains. Examining one of the jars, he found he was holding the brain of Paul Broca, a distinguished nineteenth-century anatomist. The idea for a book "flashed through his mind," according to Judy Klemsrud of the *New York Times Book Review. Broca's Brain,* a compilation of essays ranging in topic from ancient astronauts to mathematically-gifted horses, became another bestseller, prompting Sagan to tell Klemsrud that he believes "the public is a lot brighter and more interested in science than they're given credit for. . . . They're not numbskulls. Thinking scientifically is as natural as breathing."

As with *The Dragons of Eden, Broca's Brain* has elicited mixed reaction from the critics. While most praise Sagan's scientific expertise, some, like Maureen Bodo in *National Review,* think "Sagan is on less firm ground when speculating on semiphilosophical topics," a view shared by *New York Times Book Review* critic Robert Jastrow. Although Jastrow writes that "the skeptical chapters on pseudoscience . . . are delightful" and that Sagan is "capable of first-class reasoning when disciplined," he adds that the scientist "soars all too often on flights of meaningless fancy." Ultimately, though, Jastrow finds *Broca's Brain* worth reading, as does *Science* magazine's Richard Berendzen. "For the nonspecialist," Berendzen writes, "the book will be frustrating reading, with uneven technical detail, loose connections, and an overabundance of polysyllabic jargon. But if the reader can make it through, this curious volume can answer old questions, raise new ones, open vistas, become unforgettable. In short, Sagan has done it again. The book's title might be *Broca's Brain,* but its subject is Sagan's."

Television has played an important part in Carl Sagan's career. In the early 1970s he appeared on "The Tonight Show" and, as *New York*'s Bauer puts it, "launched into a cosmological crash course for adults. It was one of the great reckless solos of late-night television." After the scientist finished his long monologue on the evolution of the earth, Bauer writes, "one was willing to bet that if a million teenagers had been watching, at least a hundred thousand vowed on the spot to become full-time astronomers like him." Late in 1980, Sagan's involvement with the medium led to the television series "Cosmos," an eight million-dollar Public Broadcasting System production that eventually reached a worldwide audience of 150 million viewers—or, as Sagan prefers to think of it, three per cent of the earth's population. Filmed over a period of three years on forty locations in twelve countries, "Cosmos," introduced and narrated by Sagan, and written by Sagan, Ann Druyan, and Steven Soter, uses elaborate sets and special effects to explain the wide spectrum of the universe, from the expanse of a solar black hole to the intricacies of a living cell.

"Cosmos" is "dazzling" in its theme and presentation, observes Harry F. Waters in *Newsweek;* yet the reviewer feels that "Sagan undermines the show's scientific credibility by lapsing into fanciful speculation. . . . Equally unsettling is Sagan's perpetual expression of awestruck reverence as he beholds the heavens." John S. DeMott, who likewise finds Sagan's presentation "unabashedly awestruck," writes in *Time* that "each segment [of 'Cosmos'] has flair, excellent special effects and a dash of good ethical showmanship" and calls Sagan "a man clearly in love with his subject."

As "Cosmos" became public television's most highly-rated series to date, Sagan's book adaptation, *Cosmos,* proved equally popular, topping the bestseller lists for several months. In a *Christian Science Monitor* review, R. C. Cowan labels the book "as magnificent, challenging, and idiosyncratic as . . .

the TV series.'' James Michener, writing in the *New York Times Book Review*, also finds *Cosmos* ''a cleverly written, imaginatively illustrated summary . . . about our universe.'' Sagan's style, according to Michener, is ''irridescent, with lights flashing upon unexpected juxtapositions of thought.'' The reviewer sums up, ''*Cosmos* is an inviting smorgasbord of nutritious ideas well worth sampling.'' Citing the author's ''personal voice,'' *Washington Post* critic Eliot Marshall feels that Sagan ''lends his work a resonance and coherence it would otherwise lack.'' Marshall concludes that *Cosmos* is ''a little overbearing, but still informative and entertaining.''

Jeffery Marsh, however, takes exception to the book and the television series, emphasizing in *Commentary* the one criticism that has often been leveled against Sagan's theories: ''Most blameworthy of all in this avowedly serious attempt to explain the nature and essence of scientific thinking is Sagan's systematic blurring of the distinction between proof and assertion, and between fact and hypothesis.'' As an example Marsh points out the author's ''flat assertion that 'evolution is a fact, not a theory'. . . . What Sagan should have said is that the concept of evolution is accepted by . . . modern biologists.'' Marsh also contends that ''Sagan's unwillingness to countenance seriously any form of particularism . . . is seen also in his failure to come to grips with the significance of religion, which he basically regards as a malignant force.'' Yet, the critic continues, ''Sagan has no qualms about expounding . . . his personal messianic belief that the receipt of a radio transmission from a superior extraterrestrial intelligence . . . will somehow transform human behavior.''

In recent years, Sagan has devoted much of his time to writing and lecturing about the long-term effects of nuclear warfare. The scientists' vision of the total devastation and widespread death brought on by radiation poisoning has made him a leading spokesman in the nuclear disarmament movement. Representing this cause, Sagan appeared in a panel debate with such figures as William F. Buckley, Jr., Elie Wiesel, and Henry Kissinger, following a broadcast of the highly-publicized television film ''The Day After,'' which dramatized the aftermath of a nuclear attack on Lawrence, Kansas.

Despite the controversies surrounding the speculative nature of his work, Carl Sagan continues to be one of modern science's most popular spokesmen. In his lectures and books, he often tries to establish man's place in relation to the universe. In *Time*, Sagan writes of the significance of man: ''As long as there have been humans we have searched for our place in the cosmos. Where are we? Who are we? . . . We make our world significant by the courage of our questions and by the depth of our answers.''

Several of Sagan's books, including *The Cosmic Connection*, *The Dragons of Eden*, *Broca's Brain*, and *Cosmos*, have been translated into numerous languages, including French, Portuguese, Chinese, Hebrew, Greek, Japanese, Dutch, and Serbo-Croation.

MEDIA ADAPTATIONS: Planets has been adapted into a film.

BIOGRAPHICAL/CRITICAL SOURCES: Time, January 24, 1974, September 29, 1980, October 20, 1980, December 14, 1981; *New York*, September 1, 1975; *New Yorker*, June 21, 1976, June 28, 1976, August 2, 1977; *New York Times*, May 17, 1977; *Chicago Tribune*, May 20, 1977; *Detroit News*, May 27, 1977; *Washington Post Book World*, May 27, 1977, November 17, 1980; *New York Review of Books*, June 9, 1977; *Newsweek*, June 27, 1977, October 6, 1980, November 23,

1981; *Atlantic*, August, 1977; *Commentary*, August, 1977, May, 1981; *New York Times Book Review*, June 10, 1979, July 19, 1979, January 25, 1981; *Science*, July 6, 1979; *National Review*, August 3, 1979; Carl Sagan, *Cosmos*, Random House, 1980; *New Statesman*, April 4, 1980; *Saturday Review*, August, 1980; *Christian Science Monitor*, November 19, 1980; *People*, December 15, 1980; *America*, February 7, 1981; *Humanist*, July-August, 1981; *Science Digest*, March, 1982; *Saturday Evening Post*, July-August, 1982; *Omni*, June, 1983; *Contemporary Issues Criticism*, Volume II, Gale, 1984.

—*Sketch by Susan Salter*

*   *   *

SAGARRA, Eda   1933-

PERSONAL: Born August 15, 1933, in Dublin, Ireland; daughter of Kevin Roantree (a judge) and Cecil (Smiddy) O'Shiel; married Albert Sagarra (a professor of petrochemistry), April 4, 1961; children: Mireia. *Education:* National University of Ireland, B.A. (with first class honors), 1954; University of Freibourg, M.A., 1955; additional graduate study at University of Zurich, 1955-56; University of Vienna, Ph.D., 1958. *Religion:* Roman Catholic. *Politics:* Mild Conservative. *Home:* 30 Garville Ave., Rathgar, Dublin 6, Ireland. *Office:* Department of German, Trinity College, Dublin, Ireland.

CAREER: University of Manchester, Manchester, England, assistant lecturer, 1958-61, lecturer in German, 1961-68, lecturer in German history, 1968-75; Trinity College, Dublin, Ireland, professor of German, 1975—, dean of visiting students, 1979—, registrar, 1981—. *Member:* Association of German Teachers, Association of University Teachers, Irish Federation of University Teachers, Philological Club (University of Manchester).

WRITINGS: (Translator) *Zen Buddhism*, Ryder & Co., 1961; (translator) *Pain*, Hutchinson, 1963; *Tradition and Revolution: German Literature and Society, 1830-1890*, Basic Books, 1971; *A Social History of Germany, 1648-1918*, Methuen, 1977; *Germany in the Nineteenth Century*, Longman, 1980; (editor with J. Thunecke) *Formen der realistischen Erzaehlkunst*, Sherwood, 1980; (editor with C. J. Carr) *Tradition und Gegenwart: Oesterreichische Literatur*, [Dublin], 1983. Also author of *Bibliography of Women's Autobiographical Writings, 1740-1918*, 1984. Translator of book by M. Rodoreda, 1965. Contributor of articles and reviews to language and history journals.

WORK IN PROGRESS: Friendship in German Letters, 1700-1914.

SIDELIGHTS: Eda Sagarra writes: ''I had planned to be a writer since I was six and read a heavy history tome ostentatiously in front of visitors. No one was prepared to publish my work [except for translations], however, until the arrival of our daughter forced me to be much more disciplined. The only time I had to write then was between 5:30 and 7 a.m., and I've stuck to that timetable ever since—apart from Christmas Day. I recommend it as the best advice I ever got in my writing career.

''In my work I try to discover for myself—and others maybe—life as it was lived in the past and as it seemed to people living at the time, in order to remind people that the world isn't going from bad to worse. Some things are much better, others worse, and it will always be like that to the end of time.

''There are two more books I would like to write. One is a history of friendship—social and economic rather than literary.

The other, a memoir of my own family, half Cork, small farming people, half Tyrone, holding on to a bit of hilly land to which they were transplanted in the seventeenth century when only a few Catholics managed to hold on to a notion of land through their friendship with the Protestant gentry. The family tradition of good neighbourliness was perpetuated down to my grandfather, who was the only Catholic solicitor in Northern Ireland (practising for nearly seventy years) and who had at least as many non-Catholic as Catholic clients.''

* * *

SAHGAL, Nayantara (Pandit) 1927-

PERSONAL: Born May 10, 1927, in Allahabad, Uttar Pradesh, India; daughter of Ranjit Sitaram (a Sanskrit scholar; in law and politics) and Vijaya Lakshmi (Nehru) Pandit; married Gautam Sahgal (in industry), January 2, 1949 (divorced March 2, 1967); married E. N. Mangat Rai, September, 1979; children: (first marriage) Nonika, Ranjit, Gita. *Education:* Attended schools in India; Wellesley College, B.A., 1947. *Religion:* Hindu. *Residence:* Dehra Dun, Uttar Pradesh, India.

CAREER: Novelist and free-lance political journalist. Lecturer on U.S. tours, 1962, 1963; scholar-in-residence at Southern Methodist University, 1973, 1977; research scholar at Radcliffe Institute, Harvard University, 1976; lecturer for ''Semester-at-Sea'' program, Colorado University, 1979. Member of Indian delegation to United Nations General Assembly, 1978. *Member:* National Council of People's Union of Civil Liberties. *Awards, honors:* Woodrow Wilson International Center for Scholars fellow, 1981-82; National Humanities Center fellow, 1983-84.

WRITINGS: Prison and Chocolate Cake (autobiography), Knopf, 1954; *A Time to Be Happy* (novel; Book Society selection), Knopf, 1958; *From Fear Set Free* (autobiography), Gollancz, 1962, Norton, 1963; *This Time of Morning* (novel), Gollancz, 1965, Norton, 1966; *Storm in Chandigarh* (novel), Norton, 1969; *The Freedom Movement in India,* National Council of Educational Research and Training (India), 1970; (editor) *Sunlight Surround You,* [New Delhi], 1970; *A Situation in New Delhi* (novel), London Magazine Editions, 1977; *A Voice for Freedom,* Hind Pocket Books (New Delhi), 1977; *Indira Gandhi's Emergence and Style,* Carolina Academic Press, 1978; *Indira Gandhi: Her Road to Power,* Ungar, 1982. Contributor to newspapers and magazines in India and abroad.

WORK IN PROGRESS: Two novels, *Rich Like Us* and *A Man-Size Cloud.*

AVOCATIONAL INTERESTS: Cross-country walks, European and Indian classical music, theatre, good contemporary novels.

BIOGRAPHICAL/CRITICAL SOURCES: Village Voice, May 15, 1969; *Times Literary Supplement,* June 26, 1969.

* * *

SAKOL, Jeannie 1928-

PERSONAL: Born September 26, 1928, in New York, N.Y.; daughter of Henry and Helen (Abrahams) Sakol. *Politics:* Democrat. *Religion:* Jewish. *Home:* 230 East 48th St., New York, N.Y. 10017.

WRITINGS: What About Teen-Age Marriage?, Messner, 1961; *Young People in the White House,* Messner, 1966; *The Inept Seducer; or, Bad Intentions Are Not Enough; Being an Alarming Report on the Dumb Things Men Do, Plus a Heartfelt Plea*

to All Males: Please Pay Attention!, Price, Stern, 1967; *Gumdrop, Gumdrop, Let Down Your Hair,* Prentice-Hall, 1969; *I Was Never the Princess: A Novel,* Collins & World, 1971; (with Lucianne Goldberg) *Purr, Baby, Purr,* Hawthorn, 1971; *New Year's Eve: A Novel,* Lippincott, 1974; *Promise Me Romance,* Nordon, 1979; *The Wonderful World of Country Music,* Grosset, 1979; *Hot Thirty,* Delacorte, 1980; *Mothers and Lovers,* Nordon, 1980; *Maiden Voyage,* Leisure Books, 1981. Also author of *Flora Sweet,* 1977, and *All Day, All Night, All Woman,* 1978.†

* * *

SALSBURY, Stephen 1931-

PERSONAL: Born October 12, 1931, in Oakland, Calif.; son of Ralph Thomas (a mining engineer) and Roma E. (Connor) Salsbury. *Education:* Occidental College, A.B., 1953; Harvard University, A.M., 1957, Ph.D., 1961. *Home:* 28 Wahroonga Ave., Wahroonga, New South Wales 2076, Australia. *Office:* Department of Economic History, University of Sydney, Sydney, New South Wales 2006, Australia.

CAREER: Harvard University, Graduate School of Business Administration, Boston, Mass., research associate, 1961-62; University of Delaware, Newark, assistant professor, 1963-68, associate professor, 1968-70, professor of history, 1970-77, chairman of department, 1974-77; University of Sydney, Sydney, Australia, professor of economic history and head of department, 1977—, dean, faculty of economics, 1980—. Visiting assistant professor of history, Johns Hopkins University, 1967-68. *Military service:* U.S. Air Force, 1955-57, 1962-63; became first lieutenant; received Commendation Medal for service in Turkey, 1963. *Member:* American Historical Association, Organization of American Historians, Economic History Association, Economic History Association of Australia and New Zealand, Agricultural History Society, Railway and Locomotive Historical Society, Historical Society of Delaware.

WRITINGS: The State, the Investor, and the Railroad, Harvard University Press, 1967; (with Alfred D. Chandler, Jr.) *Pierre S. duPont and the Making of the Modern Corporation,* Harper, 1971; *Essays on the History of the American West,* Dryden, 1975; *No Way to Run a Railroad,* McGraw, 1982.

WORK IN PROGRESS: The History of the Sydney Stock Exchange.

AVOCATIONAL INTERESTS: Railroads; Australian history, natural resources, and flora.

* * *

SALZMAN, Jack 1937-

PERSONAL: Born December 8, 1937, in Cologne, Germany; naturalized U.S. citizen; son of David and Mimi (Wehrman) Salzman; married Cecily Falkenstein (a teacher), 1959; children: Ellen, Linda. *Education:* Brooklyn College (now Brooklyn College of the City University of New York), B.A., 1958; New York University, M.A., 1960, Ph.D., 1966. *Home:* 20 Carey Rd., Great Neck, N.Y. 11021. *Office:* Department of English, Hofstra University, Hempstead, N.Y. 11550.

CAREER: Brooklyn College (now Brooklyn College of the City University of New York), Brooklyn, N.Y., lecturer in English, 1959-64; Michigan State University, East Lansing, instructor in English, 1964-65; Brooklyn Center of Long Island University, Brooklyn, assistant professor, 1966-71, associate professor of English, 1971-77; Hofstra University, Hempstead, N.Y., John Crawford Adams Professor of English, 1975-77, professor of English, 1977—. Fulbright lecturer in American literature at Turku University, Turku, Finland, 1967-68, and Rikkyo University, Tokyo, Japan, 1972.

WRITINGS—Editor, except as indicated: *Years of Protest* (collection of American writing of the 1930s), Pegasus, 1967; *The Survival Years* (collection of American writing of the 1940s), Pegasus, 1969; (author of introduction to reprint of 1901 edition) Theodore Dreiser, *Sister Carrie*, Johnson Reprint, 1969; (and author of introduction) Theodore Dreiser, *Sister Carrie*, Bobbs-Merrill, 1969.

Theodore Dreiser: The Critical Reception, David Lewis, 1972; *Social Poetry of the 1930s*, B. Franklin, 1978; (author) *Albert Maltz*, Twayne, 1978; *The Jack Conroy Reader*, B. Franklin, 1979; *Sherwood Anderson: The Writer and His Craft*, Appel, 1979. Contributor to professional journals. Editor, *Prospects: An Annual Journal of American Cultural Studies*.

WORK IN PROGRESS: A cultural history of the 1930s, for Random House.

BIOGRAPHICAL/CRITICAL SOURCES: Nation, February 12, 1968; *Washington Post*, July 25, 1969.

*   *   *

SAMPEDRO, Jose Luis   1917-

PERSONAL: Born February 1, 1917, in Barcelona, Spain; son of Luis and Matilde (Saez) Sampedro; married Isabel Pellicer, July 10, 1944; children: Isabel. *Education:* University of Madrid, Dr.Econ. (with highest honors), 1950. *Home:* Reina, 31, Madrid 4, Spain. *Office:* Fundacion Banco Exterior, Victor Hugo, 4, Madrid 4, Spain.

CAREER: Spanish Ministry of Finance, Madrid, civil officer, 1935-48; University of Madrid, Faculty of Political and Economic Sciences, Madrid, Spain, assistant lecturer, 1949-55, professor of economic structure, 1955-72; Direccion General de Aduanas, Madrid, head of technical cabinet, 1972—. Adviser to Spanish Ministry of Commerce, 1951-57, and Ministry of Finance, 1957-62; representative of Ministry of Finance at Organisation Europeenne de Cooperation Economique-Organisation de Cooperation et de Developpement Economiques in Paris, 1958-62. *Military service:* Spanish Army, 1936-39. *Member:* Colegio Nacion de Economistas, Sociedad de Autores de Espana. *Awards, honors:* Calderon de la Barca (national prize for Spanish playwrights), 1950.

WRITINGS: Congreso en Estocolmo (novel), Aguilar, 1952; *Principios Practicos de Localizacion Industrial*, Aguilar, 1952; *Efectos de la Unidad Economica Europea*, Espasa-Calpe, 1957; *Realidad Economica y Analisis Estructural*, Aguilar, 1958; *El Futuro Europeo de Espana*, Espasa-Calpe, 1960; *El Rio que nos Lleva* (novel), Aguilar, 1961; *Perfiles Economicos de las Regiones Espanolas*, Sociedad de Estudios y Publicaciones del Banco Urquijo, 1964; *Las Fuerzas Economicas de Nuestro Tiempo*, Guadarrama, 1967, translation by S. E. Nodder published as *Decisive Forces in World Economics*, McGraw, 1967.

El Caballo Desnudo (novel), Planeta, 1970; *Conciencia del Subdesarrallo*, Salvat, 1972; *La Inflacion en Version Completa*, Planeta, 1976; *Octubre, Octubre* (novel), Alfaguara, 1981. Also author of plays "La Paloma de Carton," 1950, and "Un Sitio para Vivir," 1956.

WORK IN PROGRESS: A novel, *The Archduchess;* research on economic structuralism applied to development theory.

SIDELIGHTS: "Main interest is understanding life," Jose Luis Sampedro writes, "and expressing my insights about [it]. Main pleasure is to try to reconcile several ways for this understanding: (a) a logical and scientific way (hence my interest in formal structuralism as a general theory); (b) intuitive and artistic visions (hence my literary work; science is not enough); (c) comprehensive, quasi-physical attempts to wholeness in an 'Oriental Wisdom' style (very much interested by Tao, I-Ching Book, and dialectics). I am a NIP (non-important person)." Sampedro speaks or reads six languages, including English and German.

*   *   *

SANCHA, Sheila   1924-

PERSONAL: Born November 27, 1924, in Grimsby, England; daughter of Neal (a businessman) and Phylis (Middleton) Green; married Carlos Luis Sancha (a portrait painter), August 14, 1948; children: Anita Luisa (Mrs. Douglas Lear), Jeremy Christian, Nicholas Simon. *Education:* Attended Byam Shaw School of Drawing and Painting. *Politics:* None. *Religion:* "None (nothing orthodox)." *Home:* 8 Melbury Rd., Flat 5, London W14 8LR, England.

CAREER: Shell-B.P. News, London, England, illustrator, 1957-67; writer and illustrator, 1970—. *Military service:* Women's Royal Naval Service, transport driver, 1943-46. *Member:* Royal Archaeological Institute, Society of Authors.

WRITINGS—All juveniles; all self-illustrated: *Knight After Knight*, Collins, 1974; *The Castle Story*, Kestrel Books, 1979; *The Luttrell Village*, Collins, 1982.

Also illustrator of Barbara Kerr Wilson's *A Story to Tell*, Garnet Miller, 1964. Contributor of drawings to magazines, including *Past and Future* and *Puffin Post*.

WORK IN PROGRESS: Researching the towns of Stamford and Lincoln (both in Lincolnshire, England) for a book about a medieval town.

SIDELIGHTS: Sheila Sancha writes: "When my contributions to the *Shell-B.P. News* ended in 1967, I felt I needed a change of direction. I had been drawing the adventures of a knight called 'Sir Bastion' for the historical magazine *Past and Future* and I decided to enlarge on this and write a book about knights. I soon realized that I was ignorant of the architecture and conditions under which these knights lived and, before I knew what had happened, I was up to my neck in history and archaeology.

"*Knight after Knight*, and particularly *The Castle Story* and *The Luttrell Village*, are firmly based on research. Illustrations that include people start with a good look at medieval manuscript drawings, sculptures and brasses; the cut and cloth of their clothes are analysed; and they can then be put into the settings of existing buildings—or buildings that have been destroyed but feature in archaeological reports.

"I lead a busy life because I also act as my husband's secretary, and he is always painting interesting people. Writing and illustrating is a solitary profession, and I enjoy putting down my pen and serving cups of coffee and occasional lunches to his visitors, many of whom are at the top of their profession and in a position to alter the course of modern life. Talking to them emphasises the fact that history is a continuing process."

In a review of Sancha's *The Castle Story* in the *Washington Post Book World*, Alice Digilio calls the work "a definitive yet accessible book on castles. . . . For any child fascinated by the romance of chivalry and castle-storming, it makes absorbing reading.'' And reviewing *The Luttrell Village* for the same newspaper, Digilio writes: ''In all her books, Sancha conveys an enormous amount of information in relatively little space, often through detailed illustration. . . . Children at about the age of 9 often develop an almost insatiable appetite for detail—which perhaps explains their fixation with stamp collections, Dungeons and Dragons, J.R.R. Tolkien, and the fine points of medieval lore. *The Luttrell Village* should satisfy that craving in a most agreeable way.''

BIOGRAPHICAL/CRITICAL SOURCES: Washington Post Book World, March 14, 1982, March 13, 1983.

* * *

SANDBERG, (Karin) Inger 1930-

PERSONAL: Born August 2, 1930, in Karlstad, Sweden; daughter of Johan and Hanna (a teacher; maiden name, Carlstedt) Erikson; married Lasse Sandberg (an artist), April 27, 1950; children: Lena, Niklas, Mathias. *Education:* Swedish Training College for Teachers, teacher's certificate, 1954. *Home:* Vaestra Raden 16, 65227 Karlstad, Sweden; and Alusbacka, Sweden (summer).

CAREER: Teacher in Karlstad, Sweden public schools, 1957-63; writer of books and of television and radio productions for children, 1963—. *Member:* Swedish Union of Writers, Swedish P.E.N. Club, Zonta International. *Awards, honors:* Swedish Author's Fund award, 1963; Karlstad culture prize, 1965; Hans Christian Andersen honorable mention and International Board on Books for Young People (IBBY) honorable mention, both 1966, and Leipzig International Book Exhibit award, 1971, all for *Niklas roeda dag;* Heffaklump award from *Expressen* newspaper (Sweden), 1969, for *Pappa, kom ut!;* Nils Holgersson Medal, 1973; Astrid Lindgren Prize, 1974; Varmlands Lanslandstings Kulturstipendium, 1976.

WRITINGS—All illustrated by husband, Lasse Sandberg: *Faaret Ullrik Faar medalj* (title means ''Woolrik the Sheep Gets a Medal''), Eklund, 1953; *Jag maalar en . . .* (title means ''I Paint a . . .''), Eklund, 1955; *Jonas bilen och aeventyret* (title means ''Jonas the Car and the Adventure''), Geber, 1959.

Godnattsagor paa rullgardinen (title means ''Bedtime Stories on the Blind''), Geber, 1960; *Filuren paa aeventyr* (title means ''The Adventure of the Little Filur''), Geber, 1961; *Hemma hos mej* (title means ''At My Place''), Geber, 1962; *Lena beraettar*, Geber, 1963, 3rd edition, 1971, translation by Patricia Crampton published as *Here's Lena*, Methuen, 1970; *Trollen i Lill-Skogen* (title means ''The Trolls in the Little Wood''), Karlstad Town, 1963; *Niklas roeda dag*, Geber, 1964, 2nd edition, 1967, translation published as *Nicholas' Red Day*, Delacorte, 1967; *Barnens bildordlista* (title means ''Children's Wordbook''), Skrivrit, 1965; *Den musikaliska myran* (title means ''The Musical Ant''), Geber, 1965, 2nd edition, 1970; *En morgon i varuhuset* (title means ''One Morning in the Department Store''), [Stockholm], 1965.

Published by Raben & Sjoegren, except as indicated: *Johan*, 1965, 3rd edition, 1970, translation by Patricia Crampton published as *Johan's Year*, Methuen, 1971; *Pojken med de Hundra bilarna*, 1966, translation published as *The Boy with 100 Cars*, Delacorte, 1967; *Tomtens stadsresa* (title means ''The Tomten Goes to Town''), General Post Office (Sweden), 1966; *En konstig foersta maj*, 1967; *Niklas oenskedjur*, 1967, translation by R. Sadler published as *Nicholas' Ideal Pet*, Sadler & Brown,

1968, published as *Nicholas' Favorite Pet*, Delacorte, 1969; *Pojken med de maanga husen*, 1968, translation published as *The Boy with Many Houses*, Delacorte, 1969; *Vi passar oss sjaelva* (title means ''We Look after Ourselves''), Geber, 1968; *Pappa, kom ut!*, 1969, translation published as *Daddy Come Out!*, Sadler & Brown, 1970, published as *Come On Out, Daddy*, Delacorte, 1971; *Johan i2:an*, 1969, 2nd edition, 1970, translation by Patricia Crampton published as *Johan at School*, Methuen, 1972; *Filurstjaernan* (title means ''The Filurstar''), Geber, 1969.

Buffalo Bengt och indianerna, 1970, translation published as *Buffalo Bengt and the Indians*, Sadler & Brown, 1971; *Lena staar i koe* (title means ''Lena Lines Up''), Geber, 1970; *Stora Tokboken* (title means ''The Big Crazybook''), Geber, 1970; *Vad aer det som ryker?*, 1971, translation by Merloyd Lawrence published as *Where Does All That Smoke Come From?*, Delacorte, 1972; *Fred Strid krymper* (title means ''Mr. Fred Strid Shrinks''), 1972; *Vi leker oeken, Froeken*, 1973, translation published as *Let's Play Desert*, Delacorte, 1974 (published in England as *The Desert Game*, Methuen, 1974); *Hej, vaelkommen till mej!*, 1974, translation published as *Let's Be Friends*, Methuen, 1975; *Perry och osynlige Wrolf* (title means ''Perry and the Invisible Wrolf''), 1975; *Var aer laanga farbrorns hatt?* (title means ''Where's Tall Uncle's Hat?''), 1976; *Var aer Langa Farbrorns hatt?*, 1976; *Tummens resa*, 1978.

Tummen tittar pa natten, 1980; *Tummen far en vaen*, 1980; *Tummens mamma slutar roeka*, 1980; *En fin dag foer Johan*, 1981; *Tummen och Tossingarna*, 1982; *Titta daer, sa Pulvret*, 1983; *Hjaelpa till, sa Pulvret*, 1983.

''Little Anna'' series; published by Raben & Sjoegren, except as indicated: *Vad Anna fick se*, 1964, 4th edition, 1974, translation published as *What Anna Saw*, Lothrop, 1964; *Lilla Anna och trollerihatten*, 1965, 4th edition, 1976, translation published as *Little Anna and the Magic Hat*, Lothrop, 1965 (published in England as *Anna and the Magic Hat*, Sadler & Brown, 1965); *Vad lilla Anna sparade paa*, 1965, 4th edition, 1974, translation published as *What Little Anna Saved*, Lothrop, 1965 (published in England as *What Anna Saved*, Sadler & Brown, 1965); *Lilla Annas mamma fyller aar*, 1966, 4th edition, 1974, translation published as *Little Anna's Mama Has a Birthday*, Sadler & Brown, 1965, Lothrop, 1966; *Naer lilla Anna var foerkyld*, 1966, 4th edition, 1974, translation published as *When Little Anna Had a Cold*, Lothrop, 1966 (published in England as *When Anna Had a Cold*, Sadler & Brown, 1966).

Lilla Anna och Laanga Farbrorn paa havet, 1971, translation published as *Little Anna and the Tall Uncle*, Methuen, 1973; *Var aer lilla Annas hund?*, 1972, translation published as *Where Is Little Anna's Dog?*, Methuen, 1974; *Lilla Annas julklapp*, 1972, 3rd edition, 1974, translation published as *Kate's Christmas Present*, A. & C. Black, 1974; *Lilla Anna flyttar saker*, 1972, 3rd edition, 1974, translation published as *Kate's Upside Down Day*, A. & C. Black, 1974; *Lilla Anna leker med bollar*, 1973, translation published as *Kate's Bouncy Ball*, A. & C. Black, 1974; *Lilla Anna kom och hjaelp!*, 1972, 2nd edition, 1974, translation published as *Kate, Kate Come and Help!*, A. & C. Black, 1974; *Lilla Anna i glada skolan* (title means ''Little Anna in the Happy School''), 1975; *Lilla Anna och de mystiska froena*, 1979; *Lilla Anna reser till Landet Mittemot*, 1982.

''Little Spook'' series; published by Raben & Sjoegren, except as indicated: *Lilla spoeket Laban*, Geber, 1965, 3rd edition, 1976, translation by Nancy S. Leupold published as *Little Ghost Godfrey*, Delacorte, 1968, translation by Kertsi French published as *Little Spook,* Methuen, 1969; *Lilla spoeket Laban far en lillasyster,* 1977, translation published as *Little Spook's Baby Sister,* Methuen, 1978; *Labolinas Lina,* 1977, translation published as *Tiny Spook's Tugging Game,* Methuen, 1978; *Labolinas snubbeldag,* 1977, translation published as *Tiny Spook's Tumbles,* Methuen, 1978; *Gissa vem jag aer idag? sa Labolina,* 1977, translation published as *Tiny Spook's Guessing Game,* Methuen, 1978; *Kommer snart, sa Laban och Labolina,* 1977, translation published as *Little Spook's Grubby Day,* Methuen, 1978; *Pappa aer sjuk, sa lilla spoeket Laban,* 1977, translation published as *Little Spook Haunts Again,* Methuen, 1978; *Var aer Labolinas Millimina?,* translation published as *Little Spook and the Lost Doll,* Methuen, 1980.

Mathias series; published by Raben & Sjoegren, except as indicated: *Mathias bakar kakor,* 1968, 3rd edition, 1974, translation published as *Daniel and the Coconut Cakes,* A. & C. Black, 1973; *Mathias och trollet,* 1968, translation published as *Daniel's Mysterious Monster,* A. & C. Black, 1973; *Mathias maalar en . . . ,* 1969, translation published as *Daniel Paints a Picture,* A. & C. Black, 1973; *Mathias hjaelper till,* 1969, 2nd edition, 1974, translation published as *Daniel's Helping Hand,* A. & C. Black, 1973.

Writer, with husband, of over 180 children's television and radio programs broadcast in Sweden. Contributor to Swedish journals and magazines.

WORK IN PROGRESS: Two books about Pulvret; five television programs about Pulvret for Swedish and Norwegian television; ten television programs about Tummen for Swedish television.

SIDELIGHTS: "The big challenge," Inger Sandberg told *CA,* "is to write books which make tiny little ones, from one year of age, happy and make them laugh and also expand their emotions and artistic and linguistic ability. One must *know* a lot about children, and above all, one must know what one wants and where one's loyalties are.

"The environment, the life of the modern city, means a lot to our work, both in the fifties when we lived in a tall block of flats, and now when we live in a modern terrace house. What we see and experience, we use, just like other writers use their own special environment. [Ours] is an environment where the big and the small play together and work together; an environment in which the little ones are rightful citizens with rights and responsibilities. We want to be on the side of the children in what we are doing, in our books about and for people living in the world today.

"I don't think that any book for children can explain our complex, mad world to a child—hopefully the *good* book can explain a bit of what's going on—and make the world—the everyday life—more understandable."

*   *   *

SANTREY, Louis
See SABIN, Louis

*   *   *

SarDESAI, D(amodar) R.   1931-

PERSONAL: Born January 5, 1931, in Goa, India; son of Ramaji H. and Sunderabai (Salker) SarDesai; married Bhanu D. Gandhi (a librarian), July 26, 1960; children: Vandana, Archana (daughters). *Education:* University of Bombay, B.A.

(with honors), 1952, M.A., 1955; University of California, Los Angeles, Ph.D., 1965. *Home:* 3952 Bledsoe Ave., Los Angeles, Calif. 90066. *Office:* Department of History, University of California, Los Angeles, Calif. 90024.

CAREER: University of Bombay, Siddharth College, Bombay, India, lecturer in history, 1955-61; California State College (now University), Los Angeles, assistant professor of history, 1965-66; University of California, Los Angeles, assistant professor, 1966-70, associate professor of Southeast Asian history, 1970-77, professor of history, 1977—, vice-chairman of department, 1979-80, chairman of Asian Colloquium, 1969-71, member of executive committee, College of Letters and Science, 1975-77. Visiting professor of history and chairman of department, University of Bombay, 1972-73. Member of Maharashtra Government Board of Archives and of Indian Historical Records Commission, and chairman of board of studies, University of Bombay, 1972-73; member of Asian Studies Committee, Indian Council of Social Science Research, 1972-74. Consultant to National Endowment for the Humanities, Social Science Research Council, and Ohio State University; also consultant to several university presses and to a number of television stations in the Los Angeles area.

MEMBER: International Congress of Orientalists, International Conference on Asian History, Association for Asian Studies, Conference on Asian History, Royal Historical Society (London; fellow), Indian Council of World Affairs, Asiatic Society of Bombay. *Awards, honors:* William Wedderburn prize, University of Bombay, 1955; Watumull Foundation scholarship, American Historical Association, 1962; American Institute of Indian Studies fellowship, 1963-64; Ford Foundation fellowship and University of California Institute of Humanities grant, 1968-69; University of California Regents' fellowship, 1975-76; American Institute of Indian Studies senior fellowship, 1980-81.

WRITINGS: (With B. K. Gokhale) *A Survey of World History,* Kitab Mahal, 1958; (with K. C. Vyas and S. R. Nayak) *India through the Ages,* Allied Publishers, 1960, 6th edition, 1976; *Indian Foreign Policy in Cambodia, Laos, and Vietnam, 1947-1964,* University of California Press, 1968; *Trade and Empire in Malaya and Singapore, 1869-1874,* Southeast Asia Program, Ohio University, 1970; (editor with wife, Bhanu D. SarDesai) *Theses and Dissertations on Southeast Asia: An International Bibliography in Social Sciences, Education, and Fine Arts,* International Documentation Conference (Leiden), 1970; (contributor) S. Chawla and others, editors, *Southeast Asia under the New Balance of Power,* Praeger, 1974; (contributor) B. R. Nanda, editor, *Indian Foreign Policy: The Nehru Years,* East-West Center Press, 1976; *British Trade and Expansion in Southeast Asia, 1830-1914,* Allied Publishers, 1977; (with Chawla) *Changing Patterns of Security and Stability in Asia,* Praeger, 1980; *Southeast Asia, Past and Present,* Vikas (New Delhi), 1981, 2nd edition, 1983.

General editor of "The World Around Us" series, twenty-six volumes on Asia and Africa, Somaiya Publications (Bombay). Contributor of articles and reviews to professional journals, including *Journal of Southeast Asian History, China Report, Choice, American Historical Review,* and *Pacific Historical Review.* Editor of Southeast Asia bibliography section of *American Historical Review,* 1967-80; member of editorial board, *China Report,* 1964—, *Southeast Asia Quarterly,* 1968-69, *United Asia,* 1968—, *Journal of the Asiatic Society of Bombay,* 1972-73, and *Indian Review,* 1978—.

WORK IN PROGRESS: India's Relations with Southeast Asia, 1947-1981; Trade and Society in Western India in the Sixteenth Century.

SIDELIGHTS: D. R. SarDesai reads, writes, and speaks French, Portuguese, Hindi, Marathi, and Konkani; he reads Sanskrit and Gujarati.

*   *   *

SATTERFIELD, Charles
    See POHL, Frederik

*   *   *

SAUVAGEAU, Juan 1917-

PERSONAL: Born December 26, 1917, in Sorel, Quebec, Canada; son of Charles (a ship builder) and Jeannette (Pro) Sauvageau; married Margarita Gonzalez Trevino (a university professor), December 28, 1971; children: Roger. *Education:* Attended University of Ottawa, 1937-41; Tulane University, M.A., 1963, Ph.D., 1967; Our Lady of the Lake College, M.Ed., 1970; St. Mary's University, M.A., 1972. *Home:* 10769 Longrifle, Boise, Idaho 83709. *Agent:* Publishing-Oasis Services, 1287 Lawrence Station, Sunnyvale, Calif. 94807. *Office:* Department of Foreign Languages, Boise State University, Boise, Idaho 83707.

CAREER: Pan American University, Edinburg, Tex., assistant professor, 1961-68; Our Lady of the Lake College, San Antonio, Tex., assistant professor of French and Spanish, 1968-71; Incarnate Word College, San Antonio, Tex., visiting professor, 1970-71; San Antonio Junior College, San Antonio, Tex., member of staff of Spanish department, 1971—; Texas A & I University, Kingsville, associate professor of French and Spanish, 1971-81; Boise State University, Boise, Idaho, associate professor of French and Spanish, 1981—.

MEMBER: Modern Language Association of America, American Association of University Professors, Association of Professors of French, Association of Professors of Spanish, Texas Association of College Teachers. *Awards, honors:* First prize in Sigma Delti Pi poetry contest, 1975.

WRITINGS—Folklore studies, except as indicated: *Le Portrait du pretre dans "La Comedie Humaine" de Balzac* (criticism), Fournier, 1967; *Stories That Must Not Die,* Oasis Press, Volume I, 1975, Volume II, 1975, Volume III, 1976; *Cuentos de ayer para ninos de hoy* (title means "Tales of Yesterday for Today's Children"), two volumes, Twin Palms Editorial, 1975; *A pesar del rio—In Spite of the River* (bilingual novel), Twin Palms Editorial, 1979; *Spanish for You and Me,* Boise State University Press, 1983. Also author of a fourth volume of *Stories That Must Not Die,* and of *Fabulas para siempre—Fables Are Forever* (bilingual) for Twin Palms Editorial. Contributor to *Le Samedi Litteraire.*

SIDELIGHTS: Juan Sauvageau writes that his three books of folkloric studies are the result of a lifetime interest in the folklore of the region.

*   *   *

SCHEFFER, Victor B(lanchard) 1906-

PERSONAL: Born November 27, 1906, in Manhattan, Kan.; son of Theophilus (a biologist) and Celia E. (Blanchard) Scheffer; married Beth MacInnes, October 12, 1935; children: Brian M., Susan E. (Mrs. Robert Irvine), Ann B. (Mrs. William

Carlstrom). *Education:* University of Washington, Seattle, B.S., 1930, M.S., 1932, Ph.D., 1936. *Home:* 14806 Southeast 54th St., Bellevue, Wash. 98006.

CAREER: U.S. Fish and Wildlife Service, biologist in Olympia and Seattle, Wash., and Fort Collins, Colo., 1937-69. Lecturer at University of Washington, 1966, 1967, 1968, 1971, and 1972. Chairman, Marine Mammal Commission, 1973-76. *Member:* American Society of Mammalogists, Wildlife Society, Wilderness Society, Nature Conservancy, National Wildlife Foundation, National Audubon Society. *Awards, honors:* John Burroughs Medal, 1970, for *The Year of the Whale;* Joseph Wood Krutch Medal, 1975, for *A Voice for Wildlife.*

WRITINGS—Published by Scribner, except as indicated: *Seals, Sea Lions, and Walruses,* Stanford University Press, 1958; *The Year of the Whale,* 1969; *The Year of the Seal,* 1970; *The Little Calf,* 1970; *The Seeing Eye,* 1971; *A Voice for Wildlife,* 1974; *A Natural History of Marine Mammals,* 1976; *Adventures of a Zoologist,* 1980; *The Amazing Sea Otter,* 1981; *Spires of Form,* University of Washington Press, 1983.

BIOGRAPHICAL/CRITICAL SOURCES: Time, August 15, 1969; *Best Sellers,* September 1, 1969; *New Yorker,* September 20, 1969; *New York Times,* November 5, 1970.

*   *   *

SCHEIBE, Karl E(dward) 1937-

PERSONAL: Born March 5, 1937, in Belleville, Ill.; son of John Henry and Esther (Friesen) Scheibe; married Elizabeth Mixter (an admissions officer), September 10, 1961; children: David Sawyer, Robert Daniel. *Education:* Trinity College, Hartford, Conn., B.S., 1959; University of California, Berkeley, Ph.D., 1963. *Home:* 11 Long Lane, Middletown, Conn. 06457. *Office:* Department of Psychology, Wesleyan University, Middletown, Conn. 06457.

CAREER: Wesleyan University, Middletown, Conn., assistant professor, 1963-67, associate professor, 1967-73, professor of psychology, 1973—. Visiting professor, University of Brasilia, 1968; Fulbright fellow, Catholic University, Sao Paulo, 1972-73. Member of board of trustees, 1977-83, and board of fellows, Trinity College, Hartford, Conn. *Member:* American Psychological Association, American Association for the Advancement of Science, American Association of University Professors, Sociedade Interamericana de Psicologia, Eastern Psychological Association, New England Psychological Association, Phi Beta Kappa. *Awards, honors:* Woodrow Wilson fellowship.

WRITINGS: Beliefs and Values, Holt, 1970; *Mirrors, Masks, Lies and Secrets,* Praeger, 1979; (editor with Vernon Allen) *The Social Context of Conduct,* Praeger, 1982; (editor with Theodore R. Sarbin) *Studies in Social Identity,* Praeger, 1983.

WORK IN PROGRESS: Study of games, gambling, and the maintenance of human identity.

*   *   *

SCHERMAN, Katharine 1915-

PERSONAL: Born October 7, 1915, in New York, N.Y.; daughter of Harry and Bernardine (Kielty) Scherman; married Axel G. Rosin (associated with Book-of-the-Month Club), April 10, 1943; children: Karen, Susanna. *Education:* Swarthmore College, B.A., 1938. *Residence:* New York, N.Y. *Agent:* Harold Ober Associates, 40 East 49th St., New York, N.Y. 10017.

CAREER: Saturday Review of Literature, New York City, secretary, 1938-40; J. B. Lippincott Co., New York City, editor, 1940-41; *Life,* New York City, researcher and writer, 1941-44; Book-of-the-Month Club, New York City, writer and editor, 1944-49.

WRITINGS: The Slave Who Freed Haiti: The Story of Toussaint Louverture (juvenile), Random House, 1954; *Spring on an Arctic Island,* Little, Brown, 1956; *Catherine the Great* (juvenile), Random House, 1957; *The Sword of Siegfried* (juvenile), Random House, 1959; *William Tell* (juvenile), Random House, 1961; *The Long White Night,* Little, Brown, 1964; *Two Islands: Grand Manan and Sanibel,* Little, Brown, 1971; *Daughter of Fire: A Portrait of Iceland,* Little, Brown, 1976; *The Flowering of Ireland,* Little, Brown, 1981.

SIDELIGHTS: In an *Atlantic* review of Katharine Scherman's book *Daughter of Fire: A Portrait of Iceland,* P. L. Adams explains that the reader is introduced to a country that is "strange and beautiful" with "a violent past, a volcanically dangerous present, [and] a superb literature." And a reviewer for *Choice* comments: "Here is a travel book in the old style: readable, leisurely, detailed, and intelligent. . . . Scherman's account evokes the atmosphere of Iceland in a uniquely imaginative way."

Another of Scherman's books *The Flowering of Ireland* recounts the history of Ireland between the 5th and 12th centuries, before that country's conversion to Christianity. Michiko Kakutani writes in *New York Times* that Scherman's *The Flowering of Ireland* is a "fine and decorous portrait of a country and its faith." R. E. Dunbar explains in the *Christian Science Monitor* that while researching this book Scherman "visited many, if not all, of the places about which she has written, and her vivid, firsthand accounts make her readers feel they are right beside her."

AVOCATIONAL INTERESTS: Ornithology, mountainclimbing, and music (plays both piano and cello in chamber music ensembles).

BIOGRAPHICAL/CRITICAL SOURCES: Library Journal, March 15, 1976, May 15, 1981; *Atlantic,* April, 1976; *Choice,* June, 1976; *New York Times,* July 21, 1980; *Christian Science Monitor,* September 2, 1981.†

*   *   *

SCHIEFELBUSCH, Richard L. 1918-

PERSONAL: Born July 23, 1918, in Osawatomie, Kan.; son of Edward F. and Emma (Martie) Schiefelbusch; married Ruth Magee, September 15, 1942; children: Lary, Carol, Jean. *Education:* Kansas State Teachers College (now Emporia State University), B.S., 1940; University of Kansas, M.A., 1947; Northwestern University, Ph.D., 1951. *Office:* Bureau of Child Research, 223 Haworth, University of Kansas, Lawrence, Kan. 66044.

CAREER: University of Kansas, Lawrence, instructor, 1947-48, assistant professor, 1949-53, associate professor, 1953-59, professor of speech pathology and audiology in the university and at the Medical Center, 1959—, university distinguished professor, 1969—, director of Bureau of Child Research, 1956—, director of Kansas Center for Research in Mental Retardation and Human Development, 1966—. Lecturer or conductor of workshops at University of Michigan, Boston University, Indiana University, University of Hawaii, and other universities. Consultant to U.S. Public Health Service, 1965—; special con-

sultant to National Institute of Mental Health, 1963-65, U.S. Office of Education, 1964—, National Institute of Child Health and Human Development, 1964-67, and National Institute of Neurological Diseases and Blindness, 1965-69.

MEMBER: American Speech and Hearing Association (fellow), Society for Research in Child Development (fellow), American Association on Mental Deficiency (fellow), Council for Exceptional Children. *Awards, honors:* Grants, as director of research projects, from U.S. Public Health Service, National Institute of Mental Health, and National Institute of Neurological Diseases and Blindness; special award from American Association on Mental Deficiency, 1975.

WRITINGS: (Contributor) S. Kirk and Bluma Weiner, editors, *Behavioral Research on Exceptional Children,* Council for Exceptional Children, 1963; (with J. Dodd) *Our Underachieving Children,* Bureau of Child Research, University of Kansas, 1963; (editor with R. H. Copeland and J. O. Smith) *Language and Mental Retardation: Empirical and Conceptual Considerations,* Holt, 1967; (editor with Norris G. Haring) *Methods in Special Education,* McGraw, 1967.

(Contributor) M. Marge and J. Irwin, editors, *Language Disabilities in Children,* Appleton-Century-Crofts, 1972; (editor) *The Language of the Mentally Retarded,* University Park Press, 1972; (with J. E. McLean and D. E. Yoder) *Language Intervention with the Retarded: Developing Strategies,* University Park Press, 1972; (editor with L. L. Lloyd) *Language Perspectives: Acquisition, Retardation and Intervention,* University Park Press, 1974; (editor with N. G. Haring) *Teaching Special Children,* McGraw, 1976; (editor) *Bases of Language Intervention,* University Park Press, 1978; (editor) *Language Intervention Strategies,* University Park Press, 1978; (with K. E. Allen and V. A. Holm) *Early Language: A Team Approach,* University Park Press, 1978; (with J. H. Hollis) *Language Intervention from Ape to Child,* University Park Press, 1979.

(Editor) *Nonspeech Language and Communication, Analysis and Intervention,* University Park Press, 1980; (with D. Bricker) *Early Language: Acquisition and Intention,* University Park Press, 1981; (with Yoder and J. Miller) *Language Intervention,* American Speech and Hearing Association, 1982.

Contributor of many articles to medical, speech, and education journals. Associate editor, *ASHA* (journal of American Speech and Hearing Association), 1962-64, and *International Review of Research in Mental Retardation,* 1965—.

*   *   *

SCHLUETER, Paul (George) 1933-

PERSONAL: Surname pronounced "Shlooter"; born May 10, 1933, in Chicago, Ill.; son of Paul George and Ruby (Browning) Schlueter; married Rosetta Van Diggelen, July 14, 1956 (divorced, 1971); married June Mayer (a college professor of English), November 9, 1974; children: (first marriage) Paul George III, Greta Renee, Laurie Ann. *Education:* Attended Bethel College, 1954-57; University of Minnesota, B.A., 1958; University of Denver, M.A., 1963; Southern Illinois University, Ph.D., 1968. *Home:* McCartney St. Easton, Pa. 18042.

CAREER: College of St. Thomas, St. Paul, Minn., lecturer in English, 1959-60; Moorhead State College (now University), Moorhead, Minn., instructor in English and director of public relations, 1960-62; University of Denver, Denver, Colo., teaching assistant in English, 1962-63; Southern Illinois University, Carbondale, instructor in English, 1963-66; Adrian

College, Adrian, Mich., assistant professor of English, 1966-68; University of Evansville, Evansville, Ind., assistant professor of English, 1968-72; Kean College of New Jersey, Union, assistant professor of English, 1973-76, director of composition, 1974-76; independent scholar, researcher and consultant, 1976—. Visiting professor, Midwestern University, summer, 1964; guest professor, University of Hamburg, 1973, and University of Giessen and University of Kassel, 1978-79, all West Germany; speaker at colleges and universities in United States and West Germany. Director, Bicentennial Conference on New Jersey's Literary Heritage, 1975-76; member of selection committee, German Academic Exchange Service (DAAD), 1979. Participant, panelist, speaker, and seminar leader at professional conferences.

MEMBER: Doris Lessing Society (member of executive council), Modern Language Association of America (Religious Approaches to Literature Division, member of executive committee, 1975-78, chairman, 1977-78), College English Association, Conference on Christianity and Literature (secretary, 1971-73), North East Modern Language Association, Midwest Modern Language Association, Pennsylvania College English Association (member of executive board), Canadian Studies Conference of New Jersey (member of executive committee, 1975-77), Lambda Iota Tau (secretary, 1966-68), Phi Delta Epsilon (honorary member).

WRITINGS: (Contributor) Harry T. Moore, editor, *Contemporary American Novelists,* Southern Illinois University Press, 1964; (contributor) Charles Shapiro, editor, *Contemporary British Novelists,* Southern Illinois University Press, 1965; (contributor of check list) Alister Kershaw and F. J. Temple, editors, *Richard Aldington: An Intimate Portrait,* Southern Illinois University Press, 1965; (contributor) Wolfgang B. Fleischmann, editor, *Encyclopedia of World Literature,* Ungar, Volume I, 1967.

(Editor) *Literature and Religion: Thorton Wilder's "The Eighth Day,"* Modern Language Association, 1970; (editor) *The Fiction of Doris Lessing,* Modern Language Association, 1971; *The Novels of Doris Lessing,* Southern Illinois University Press, 1973; (editor) *The Small Personal Voice: Essays, Reviews, Interviews by Doris Lessing,* Knopf, 1974.

Shirley Ann Grau, Twayne, 1981; (editor with wife, June Schlueter) *The English Novel: Twentieth Century Criticism,* Volume II, Ohio University Press, 1982; (editor with Joseph Grau) *Shirley Ann Grau: An Annotated Bibliography,* Garland, 1983; (editor with J. Schlueter) *Modern American Literature: Supplement Two,* Ungar, 1983; (contributor) *Dictionary of Literary Biography,* Volume XV: *British Novelists, 1930-1959,* edited by Bernard Oldsey, Gale, 1983; (editor) *Names and American Literature,* Irvington, in press.

Editor of *Proceedings of the Sixteenth National Conference on the Administration of Research,* Denver Research Institute, 1963. Contributor of articles on twentieth-century authors to *Encyclopedia of World Literature in the Twentieth Century,* 1967, revised edition, 1981-83, and to the *Micopaedia* volumes of *Encyclopaedia Britannica,* 1974; also contributor of more than 1,500 book reviews to newspapers and magazines, including *Chicago Daily News, Chicago Sun-Times, Denver Post, St. Louis Post-Dispatch, Milwaukee Journal, Louisville Courier-Journal, Philadelphia Bulletin, Cleveland Plain-Dealer, Baltimore Sun, Kansas City Star, Studies in Short Fiction, Motive, Christianity and Literature, Studies in American Fiction, Christian Century, Journal of Religion, Saturday Review, Focus/Midwest, Choice, Best Sellers,* and *Harper's Bookletter.*

Editor, *Lambda Iota Tau Newsletter,* 1966-68; *Christianity and Literature,* editor, 1971-72, "Personalia" editor, 1975-77; member of advisory board, *Virginia Woolf Quarterly,* 1976-79; *Doris Lessing Newsletter,* member of advisory board, 1978—, editor, 1980-82, associate editor, 1982—; co-editor, *Pennsylvania English,* 1981—.

WORK IN PROGRESS: An article in *Dictionary of Literary Biography: British Poets since World War II;* a study of twentieth-century women writers.

SIDELIGHTS: Paul Schlueter told *CA,* "[I am] particularly interested in relationships between the arts (especially literature) and religious faith (especially Christianity)."

BIOGRAPHICAL/CRITICAL SOURCES: Modern Fiction Studies 19, 1973; *Christian Century,* May 9, 1973; *Psychology Today,* August, 1973; *Books Abroad,* winter, 1974; *Christianity and Literature,* summer, 1974; *Research in African Literatures,* fall, 1974; *Journal of Modern Literature,* November, 1974.

*   *   *

SCHREIBER, Flora Rheta   1918-

PERSONAL: Born April 24, 1918, in New York, N.Y.; daughter of William Leonard (a librarian) and Esther (a librarian; maiden name, Aaronson) Schreiber. *Education:* Columbia University, B.S., 1938, M.A., 1939; Central School of Speech Training and Dramatic Art, London, certificate, 1938; attended New York University, 1941-42. *Politics:* Independent. *Religion:* "Free thinker." *Home:* 32 Gramercy Park S., New York, N.Y. 10003. *Agent:* Patricia Myrer, McIntosh & Otis, Inc., 475 Fifth Ave., New York, N.Y. 10017. *Office:* John Jay College of Criminal Justice, City University of New York, 444 West 56th St., New York, N.Y. 10019.

CAREER: Instructor at Exeter College, University of the Southwest, England, 1937; Brooklyn College (now Brooklyn College of the City University of New York), Brooklyn, N.Y., instructor in speech and dramatic art, and creator and producer of radio forum, 1944-46; Adelphi College (now University), Garden City, Long Island, N.Y., assistant professor of speech and dramatic arts, 1947-53, director of radio and television division in Center for Creative Arts, 1948-51; City University of New York, New York, N.Y., lecturer, 1952—, John Jay College of Criminal Justice, member of faculty, 1964—, professor of English and speech, 1974—, director of public relations, director of publications, and assistant to president, 1964—. Lecturer in writing, New School for Social Research, 1952-76; lecturer at colleges and universities, including Brown University, Boston University, St. John's College, and Northern Illinois University. Has appeared on numerous local and national television and radio programs; producer of community theatre forum for NBC Radio, 1949. Consultant to National Broadcasting Company production of "Sybil"; consultant to Batten, Barton, Durstine, & Osborn, Inc., and other organizations.

MEMBER: Overseas Press Club, P.E.N., American Association of University Professors, Speech Communications Association, Speech Association of America, American National Theater and Academy, American Association of University Women, Society of Magazine Writers (secretary, 1963; vice-president, 1973-74), Authors League of America, American Society of Journalists and Authors (vice-president for three terms, concluding 1976), Speech Association of Eastern States. *Awards, honors:* Family Service Association of America award, 1960, for magazine article, "The Tragedy of Emotional Divorce''; certificate of merit from Dictionary of International Biology, 1969; American Medical Writers award for distinguished service in medical book writing, for *Sybil.*

WRITINGS: (With Vincent Persichetti) *William Schuman* (biography), G. Schirmer, 1954; *Your Child's Speech: A Practical Guide for Parents for the First Five Years,* Putnam, 1956, revised edition published as *Your Child's Speech,* Ballantine, 1973; *A Job with a Future in Law Enforcement and Related Fields,* Grosset, 1970; *Sybil,* Regnery, 1973; *The Shoemaker: Anatomy of a Psychotic,* Simon & Schuster, 1983.

Author of three-act play, ''Bending Sickle.'' Also author of short stories, opera libretti, and additional plays. Monthly columnist, *Science Digest;* columnist for Belle-McClure and United Feature Syndicate, Inc.; drama critic for *Players' Magazine,* 1941-46; author of syndicated articles for New York Times Special Features. Contributor of numerous articles to magazines and journals, including *Cosmopolitan, Redbook, Ladies' Home Journal, Quarterly Journal of Speech, Poet Lore,* and *Quarterly of Film, Radio and Television.* Psychiatry editor, *Science Digest,* 1962-67.

WORK IN PROGRESS: A ''psycho-historical-biographical'' book about recent U.S. presidents, particularly Kennedy, Johnson, and Nixon; *The Nazi Aftermath,* recollections of concentration camps.

SIDELIGHTS: Flora Rheta Schreiber is ''a writer of stature in the field of psychiatry,'' according to Connie Lauerman in the *Chicago Tribune.* Schreiber told *CA* that in her two psychological portraits, *Sybil* and *The Shoemaker,* she attempts ''to distill reality so as to emerge with the genre of the nonfiction novel.'' The nonfiction novel is a biography written in a novelistic structure and style.

Schreiber spent six years researching *The Shoemaker,* a novelistic recreation of the life and criminal activity of Joseph Kallinger, an abused child who, as an adult, was eventually convicted of murder. Before writing the book, she spoke with Kallinger, his family, neighbors, and children's teachers, as well as with prosecutors, defense lawyers, and prison and hospital psychiatrists. Schreiber first met Kallinger in a New Jersey jail where he was being held for the murder of a nurse, and, after his conviction, she continued interviewing him in jail and at state institutions in Pennsylvania. During those conversations, he also confessed to murdering one of his sons and a Puerto Rican youth. After publication of his confessions in *The Shoemaker,* he was arrested for those crimes. *Psychology Today* reviewer Paul Robinson writes that ''Schreiber unfolds these and other horrors with all the skill of a novelist,'' while Lauerman describes the time the author spent with Kallinger as ''an intense, chilling total immersion into the Gothic labyrinth of his psychosis.''

Kallinger grew up in Philadelphia, the adopted son of a cobbler and his wife who wanted Kallinger to learn the family business and provide them with a source of income after they retired. They abused him physically and psychologically. ''It is so heartbreaking,'' Schreiber remarked to Lauerman about Kallinger's victimization. ''He's a man with a lot of potentiality. But he was squelched from the moment of conception.'' It is Schreiber's thesis that Kallinger's psychosis originated in childhood. His illness was characterized by delusions and hallucinations that caused him to abuse his own children and set his house on fire four times and eventually led him to robbery, burglary, attempted rape, brutalization, and murder. According to Schreiber, writes Lauerman, Kallinger's ''childhood was as

deadly as it can be and became the incubator of his illness, and the crimes are identical with the illness. He went from fetus to felon. Actually, you could read *The Shoemaker* as a primer for proper child rearing—if you read it in reverse. If you want to prevent psychosis and prevent crimes stemming from psychosis, do the opposite.'' Robinson contends that the book ''manages to survive . . . its mechanistic psychology because it gives such a richly detailed account of Kallinger's illness.''

Schreiber's earlier study of another abused child, *Sybil,* tells the story of Sybil Isabel Dorsett, the pseudonym of a woman who, before psychoanalysis, was possessed by sixteen different personalities. In the *American Journal of Psychiatry,* Dominick A. Barbara describes the best-selling work as ''a brilliant and powerful portrait'' that ''is destined to stand as a significant landmark both in psychiatry and literature.'' Florence Rome of the *Chicago Tribune Book World* agrees, writing that Sybil's ''unique psychoanalysis . . . involved tracing down all the clues which led to such spectacular splintering off into all those other 'selves' that Sybil became. Flora Rheta Schreiber has painstakingly assembled the clues and set them down in a sometimes tragic, sometimes exhilarating narrative.''

Schreiber was first introduced to Sybil in the 1960s after Dr. Cornelia Wilbur, Sybil's psychiatrist, contacted Schreiber about the possibility of writing a book about her story. As psychiatry editor of *Science Digest* and a writer who specializes in psychological subjects, Schreiber had previously written articles about some of Wilbur's cases. Sybil was still in treatment when she met the author, and as Schreiber commented in an interview with Helen Dudar of the *New York Post,* ''I think the doctor felt Sybil's involvement in the book might be a good part of her therapy.'' That therapy included hypnosis, and at one session, the doctor introduced Schreiber to Sybil's other selves. Schreiber told Dudar that she was ''really shaken'' by the experience. ''There was no question in my mind that these were individual people.''

These other selves first began to manifest themselves during Sybil's childhood as a defensive response to an abusive, schizophrenic mother and a passive, non-intervening father. ''By the age of three and a half,'' Schreiber commented in a *Houston Post* interview with Charlotte Phelan, ''Sybil had to break away. She was too little to run away and too strong to surrender completely, so she took refuge in a multiple personality, a proliferating personality, which was strictly a defensive maneuver.'' Thus, according to Dudar, Sybil's story is ''a celebration of the hidden resources which allowed one frail girl to survive intolerable physical and psychic abuse. Sybil's mother was a split and fragmented personality; but the diverse personalities born in Sybil's unconscious were whole, autonomous personalities that gave her emotional refuge and escape.''

These other personalities developed independently, with Sybil totally unaware of their existence. They were able to draw from Sybil's storehouse of knowledge, but any skills or memories acquired by her other selves were lost to Sybil, since she experienced blackouts during the periods in which they were dominant. These blackouts and other nervous symptoms eventually forced Sybil to seek the help of Dr. Wilbur. Using a combination of techniques, Wilbur slowly revealed Sybil's past to her. After eleven years of psychoanalysis, at the age of forty-two, Sybil was integrated into one new personality, the sum of her parts, with memories and skills that had previously been lost to her.

Schreiber began the biography *Sybil* after the integration was complete. "I was interested in the book from a literary point of view and from a psychiatric point of view," explained Schreiber to Phelan. "The commercial possibilities never once occurred to me." To research the book, she sifted through Wilbur's notes and tapes, Sybil's diaries and letters, and hospital and family records; she also studied medical literature about multiple personality, classified as a psychoneurosis. Included in the book is research indicating that the different selves of a multiple personality display vastly different reactions to psychological and neurological tests.

Although *Sybil* contains medical information, it is essentially a nonfictional dramatization of Sybil's life, written in novelistic style. As Phoebe Adams notes in the *Atlantic,* the style leaves the reader "very uncertain where fact ends and ornamental liberties begin." D. W. Harding in *New York Review of Books* is of a similar opinion, writing that "a straightforward technical report in which [the treatment] might have become clearer would to me have been more fascinating and no less moving, but the premise of this book is that the reading public pays the publisher and calls the tune." And Roy H. Hart in *Medical Counterpoint* comments that "as much as I admire and respect Prof. Schreiber's considerable skills as a writer and unquestioned integrity at reportage, from a scientific point of view the case remains incomplete until we have read Dr. Wilbur's own psychiatric report on Sybil."

According to Schreiber, however, Dr. Wilbur believes "it was not sufficient . . . to present this history-making case in a medical journal, because in addition to great medical significance, the case had broad psychological and philosophical implications for the general public." Concludes Barbara: "By combining science with art, this book . . . is sensitizing the general public not only to multiple personality but also to psychiatry as a whole."

MEDIA ADAPTATIONS: The film version of *Sybil* was produced for television by the National Broadcasting Company in 1976 and has been shown in more than twenty-five foreign countries.

CA INTERVIEW

CA interviewed Flora Schreiber by phone September 13, 1983, at her home in New York City.

CA: Your interests and work have been quite varied. What were your original plans for a career?

SCHREIBER: To be a writer, but also to get into the theater. For my elementary school yearbook I was asked, "What do you want to be?" I said "Author and teacher." That's when I was about twelve or thirteen. Then later, when I was at Columbia as an undergraduate, I won the Cornelia Otis Skinner Fellowship for acting. I went to the Central School of Speech Training and Dramatic Art in London, where I studied with Elsie Fogerty, who was the teacher of such actors as Sir John Gielgud, Lord Olivier, and Dame Peggy Ashcroft. Dame Elsie said that I had acting genius, and she broke her lifetime rule of not arranging for auditions; she wrote a letter to Margaret Webster in New York asking her to give me an audition. Margaret Webster did. I stood on the stage of St. James's Theatre with my little piece well learned, and instead of performing, I walked down to the apron of the stage and said, "Miss Webster, I'm afraid there's been a mistake. I don't want to be an actress. I want to be a writer." Exit. I was nineteen. To

this day, I do not know whether that was a sense of calling or just plain stage fright. However, I did not pursue an acting career. I became a professor of speech and English at John Jay College of Criminal Justice, City University of New York. I taught speech for many years concurrently with everything else I was doing and I've been active in college plays. But the question of acting or writing had been a conflict to begin with. I had said "writer" in that elementary school yearbook, and I had started to "write" before I *could* write. I would dictate letters to my father when I was two years old, before I knew the alphabet and had penmanship.

CA: You are best known to the public for the book Sybil, *the story of a woman who had sixteen separate personalities. Was it difficult to become Sybil's friend?*

SCHREIBER: That's an interesting question. It involved lots of complexities. She was a constant house guest here in my apartment. For the last three weeks of her residency in New York, she lived here with my mother and me. She was integrated by then. We went through the very early integration when the personalities we had met in the past were blended in a total personality, and we could see the manifestations of them in her new, integrated personality. It was fascinating.

CA: Was it difficult for her to warm up to you?

SCHREIBER: No, actually it was her idea and her psychiatrist's idea that a book be written. Dr. Cornelia B. Wilbur, the psychiatrist, approached me about it, and I said at that time that I didn't know whether there was a book, because a book has to have a beginning, a middle, and an end. Sybil was not integrated at that point, therefore there was no ending. So I told Dr. Wilbur that I didn't want to do anything about it at that stage, we would wait and see what happened; but she was very persistent. She said, "Well, wouldn't you like to meet her anyway?" I said, "Who wouldn't?" The three of us met at Longchamps, a restaurant at Madison Avenue and 79th Street in New York City. Sybil and I were drawn to each other because we had similar interests. I had written a psychograph of the poetry of Emily Dickinson, and Sybil was a Dickinson fan. We had lots in common. I invited her to my home and she developed a very strong feeling for my mother, who acted as an antidote to Sybil's abusive mother. Sybil was here at least once a week for dinner. We became very good friends long before I had made the decision to write the book. The integration took place about three years after we had met, and even then I wanted to wait to see if the integration really held before I presented this to a publisher. So it was a natural development, I think, as far as the friendship was concerned.

CA: Have you gotten much mail from readers of the book who felt they might have related problems?

SCHREIBER: Oh, have I ever! It hasn't stopped yet. The mail still comes in, and this is eight years after the hardcover was published, and seven since the paperback. There's been a very large foreign publication—it was published in sixteen foreign countries. There is some mail from other countries, although it's nowhere as extensive as the mail here.

CA: Now it appears that cases of multiple personalities are not so rare as was once believed. Have you continued to read on the subject?

SCHREIBER: Yes, but the point is that cases were never really that rare; it was a failure to diagnose them that made them seem so. Most psychiatrists really don't recognize the phenomenon. First of all, they have no knowledge of it, and second, they're suspicious of it. There are more diagnoses now than there used to be. But I don't think multiple personality was ever as rare as was reported. Yet it remains relatively uncommon. It isn't like measles.

CA: Are you still in contact with Sybil?

SCHREIBER: Oh yes, I talked to her about a month ago. She's completely integrated and there has been absolutely no recurrence. There *wouldn't* be a recurrence; it's over. She's integrated. She is *one*. She may have problems like you and me, but she's not going to have *that* problem again.

CA: The criticism has been made that Dr. Wilbur didn't present Sybil's case in medical literature. Has she done that since?

SCHREIBER: She has not.

CA: Were you pleased with the NBC television production of Sybil?

SCHREIBER: No.

CA: Did you act as consultant for the production?

SCHREIBER: In the earliest stage, yes, I was a script consultant. I had the power of comment, but not of acceptance or rejection. But that isn't the point. There are certain basic things I disliked about the script and the whole production. The trivial took the place of the serious. The introduction of a lover and his son, who were never part of Sybil's life, was phony. The ending, in which little girls, who were supposed to be symbolic of Sybil's other selves, came trippingly out of the woods to be reunited with Sybil, was corny. The lover's son's saying, "I always knew Sybil was just stuffed with people," was ludicrous and just plain silly. These inventions, meant as dramatic devices, were both unfortunate and psychiatrically untrue: they weakened—at least for me—the psychological impact of the story and turned a complex case into a simplistic cinematic misrepresentation of my book.

CA: You encourage women to utilize their talents and abilities to the fullest. Do you think many women are able to do this successfully and be wives and mothers as well?

SCHREIBER: I don't know. I think probably theoretically it's getting easier, but whether it is in actuality I rather doubt. Domesticity and creativity present *very* different worlds. I don't think the combination comes too easily. This is not to say that the combination isn't desirable. But desirable as it is, there are obstacles to achieving it. I don't think that all women who have important careers should sacrifice their personal lives, but on the other hand I think there are terrible pressures for a woman who is asked to perform the traditional role and also to perform the other roles. She has many more problems than the man who is building a career. *Every* career is difficult for a man or a woman, there are so many problems along the way. But a woman has the extra complication.

CA: Have you done any work in psychodrama?

SCHREIBER: Not directly, no. I've written about it.

CA: Do you think it's helpful to a great many people?

SCHREIBER: I think it's very valuable.

CA: Have you written about or studied the use of art and writing as therapy?

SCHREIBER: Yes. They are also very valuable.

CA: As professor of speech and English at John Jay College of Criminal Justice, what kind of students do you have?

SCHREIBER: They are primarily students who are interested in criminal justice, because John Jay College of Criminal Justice is what its name implies. It's a special interest and liberal arts college at the same time. Some of the students are already with law enforcement agencies, and some of them are hoping to become lawyers or FBI agents, policemen, teachers of criminal justice, and so on. They are primarily interested in criminal justice. The course I introduced, developed, and have been teaching for a number of years is on the impact of the mass media on the administration of justice. This is my major course. In class, we wrestle with lots of problems that grow out of the First Amendment. My students are very good. This is a vital, mature group.

CA: Are you still public relations director for the college?

SCHREIBER: Yes, officially, though I've been very busy lately promoting my new book, *The Shoemaker: Anatomy of a Psychotic.* I'm a full professor and assistant to the president of the college.

CA: Let's talk about the book. How did you get interested in doing this one?

SCHREIBER: Actually, it's not as simple as *Sybil.* No one asked me to write this new book. But I read about the case because I read this kind of data for my class on the impact of the mass media. As I read the newspaper account, I thought of the piece on family psychotherapy that I had written for *Cosmopolitan.* My feeling was that the Kallinger family, like those I had been writing about, was a sick family. So from the very beginning I was interested in Joseph Kallinger from a psychological point of view rather than from a criminologial point of view, though I certainly couldn't have written or researched this book without dealing with both levels. I like to think of the book as the story of an abused child who became a murderer. One of the interesting aspects of this case is that it is one of those rare cases in which the crime grew out of a psychosis. This psychosis itself was caused by specific incidents of abuse in childhood in a milieu of total emotional deprivation. The integration between what happened in childhood and the criminal act is most astonishing.

CA: Are you becoming more convinced that child abuse is a major factor in the formation of the psychotic criminal personality?

SCHREIBER: Not all abused children become criminals, but many criminals were abused children. This certainly was so in Kallinger's case. He was abandoned by his mother when he was four weeks old. He was adopted by a very rigid couple who abused him both physically and psychologically. They belittled him, they denied him his sense of worth. There was no overt sexual abuse, but when he came home after a hernia operation, his adoptive parents told him that the doctor had operated not only on the hernia but also on his "little bird," which was a family euphemism for the penis. Joseph was also told that a demon had been removed from the "bird," and that the penis would never grow and would never become hard, that he would always be a good boy and a good man. By creating a castration complex, the parents sowed the seeds of the schizophrenia from which Joseph's sexual offenses and murders stemmed. It's absolutely ghastly.

CA: Did you find the research for the book more difficult than the research for Sybil?

SCHREIBER: It was more extensive. For *Sybil,* I talked with Sybil, Dr. Wilbur, other psychiatrists, and read extensively in the medical literature. Then I went to Sybil's hometown, where I talked to a few people. I also talked with Sybil's friends in New York. But in the case of the Kallinger book, I had trials to attend, trial transcripts to read, prison authorities, lawyers, psychiatrists, the members of Joseph's family—he has seven children—to consult. And of course my interviewing of Joseph Kallinger himself breaks all records. It was the most intense, in-depth daily interviewing, spanning over six years and many, many *thousands* of hours. I talked to him two and a half hours a day on the telephone, and we had many months of face-to-face visits in the Bergen County jail, the Camden County jail, The State Correctional Institution at Huntingdon, Pennsylvania, and at Farview State Hospital in Waymart, Pennsylvania. Face-to-face interviews ran from four to eight hours at a time. The extent was staggering.

CA: Was there a lot of legal evidence that you had to go through?

SCHREIBER: Yes, even though the point of view of the book is psychological rather than legal. Never in history as far as I know has any writer had as close contact with somebody who is convicted of murder as I've had.

CA: Have you ever felt a conflict between jobs in your multifaceted career?

SCHREIBER: What I really should be doing, what I would like best to be doing rather than what I am doing currently? Yes, I've had that conflict from time to time very strongly. Every now and then I've found myself saying, "I should have been an actress. Why did I walk off that stage when I was nineteen?"

BIOGRAPHICAL/CRITICAL SOURCES: Flora Rheta Schreiber, *Sybil,* Regnery, 1973; *New York Post,* May 2, 1973; *Chicago Tribune Book World,* May 20, 1973; *Atlantic,* June, 1973; *Philadelphia Sunday Bulletin,* June 10, 1973; *New York Review of Books,* June 14, 1973; *New York Times Book Review,* June 17, 1973, May 12, 1974; *Houston Post,* September 16, 1973; *Globe and Mail,* June 24, 1974; *Toronto Star,* June 25, 1974; *Best Sellers,* August, 1974; *American Journal of Psychiatry,* August, 1974; *Times Literary Supplement,* September 27, 1974; *Medical Counterpoint,* December, 1974; *American Journal of Psychoanalysis,* Volume XXXIV, Number 2, 1974; *Psychology Today,* July, 1983; *Detroit Free Press,* July 24, 1983; *Los Angeles Times,* August 2, 1983; *Chicago Tribune,* August 14, 1983.

—*Sketch by Candace Cloutier*
—*Interview by Jean W. Ross*

*   *   *

SCHWARTZ, Sheila (Ruth)   1929-

PERSONAL: Born March 15, 1929, in New York, N.Y.; daughter of Mark (a lawyer) and Sylvia (Schwartz) Frackman; divorced; children: Nancy (deceased), Jonathan, Elizabeth. *Education:* Adelphi University, B.A., 1946; Columbia University, M.A., 1948; New York University, Ed.D., 1964. *Home:* 5 Spies Rd., New Paltz, N.Y. 12561. *Office:* Department of Education, State University of New York College, New Paltz, N.Y. 12561.

CAREER: Instructor at Hofstra University, Hempstead, N.Y., 1958-60, and City College of the City University of New York, New York, N.Y., 1962-63; State University of New York College at New Paltz, professor of English education, 1963—. Part-time professor of English in Associate in Arts Program, New York University, 1963—; Fulbright fellow in Ireland, 1977. *Member:* P.E.N., Authors League of America, National Council of Teachers of English, New York State English Council (former president), National Association for Humanities Education (former president, Northeast branch). *Awards, honors:* Awards from New York State English Council, 1979, for excellence in teaching and excellence in letters; award from Adolescent Literature Association, 1980, for contributions to adolescent literature.

WRITINGS: (With Gabriel Reuben) *How People Lived in Ancient Greece and Rome,* Benefic, 1967; (with daughter, Nancy Lynn Schwartz) *How People Live in Mexico,* Benefic, 1969; *Readings in the Humanities,* Macmillan, 1970; (compiler) *Teaching the Humanities: Selected Readings,* Macmillan, 1970; *Introduction to Science Fiction,* Dell, 1974; *Science Fiction for the Secondary School,* Dell, 1974; (co-author) *The Creative Approach to Teaching English,* Macmillan, 1975; *Earth in Transit,* Dell, 1976; *Teaching Reading through Adolescent Literature,* Prentice-Hall, 1978; *Growing up Guilty* (young adult novel), Pantheon, 1978; *Like Mother, Like Me,* Pantheon, 1978; *Teaching Adolescent Literature,* Hayden, 1979; *The Solid Gold Circle* (novel), Crown, 1981; *One Day You'll Go,* Scholastic Book Services, 1982; (with N. L. Schwartz) *The Hollywood Writers' Wars,* Knopf, 1982; *Jealousy,* Scholastic Book Services, 1983. Contributor of more than one hundred twenty-five articles and reviews to periodicals, including *New York Times Book Review* and *Psychology Today.*

WORK IN PROGRESS: Elegy for Nancy, a biography of Nancy Lynn Schwartz; *Elegant Panther,* a novel; *College President,* a novel; *Greg's Father,* a young adult novel; *History of Women Screen Writers,* a research project.

SIDELIGHTS: Sheila Schwartz told *CA:* "The world of books has always been my favorite; reading and writing my favorite activities. I can still remember being praised in elementary school for my writing and trudging from room to room to read my work, at my teacher's behest, to other classes. I do not ever remember playing with dolls. Whenever I was asked what I wanted for birthdays, it was always books, books, and more books. I used to spend much of my free time in our small local library, and the first part-time job I got was working there. I was fired soon after, though, for getting lost in the stacks. I could not resist picking up a book that excited my imagination and beginning to read it right there on the spot.

"But life came between me and my writing. I got married, had three children, taught school, and began to work on my doctorate. I wrote articles, did book reviews, and began to publish small non-fiction books as the children got older. One of my proudest literary achievements at that time was the fact that my daughter Nancy wrote *How People Live in Mexico* with me when she was only seventeen.

"The years passed. I obtained my doctorate, became a college teacher, and still I was not writing fiction. Nancy went out to Hollywood to work as a screenwriter, the other two children went to college, my marriage broke up, and in 1976, I had a big empty house and a big empty heart. Finally there was room for fiction. My first young adult novel was *Growing up Guilty,* about a fat, homely girl in Brooklyn at the onset of World War II. Was the girl me? Emotionally yes, but in actuality no.

"My next novel was *Like Mother, Like Me,* which dealt with the relationship between a teenage girl and her recently separated mother. Nancy liked this book so much that she wrote the screenplay for it, and it was presented on CBS and starred Kristy McNichol and Linda Lavin. But Nancy did not live to see it on television. Suddenly, out of nowhere, this beautiful, brilliant girl complained of headaches. The CAT scan revealed a brain tumor, and she died two weeks later in 1978. . . . I not only lost my beloved daughter; I lost my dearest friend, my literary collaborator.

"At the time of her death, Nancy had been working on *The Hollywood Writers' Wars,* a history of the blacklist in Hollywood. The day after her death I was at work to complete the book, so there would be one book in libraries with her name on it.

"I have two other children, and it is their love plus my writing work that have enabled me to survive. I work every day, . . . and feel fortunate that life has given me work and love."

MEDIA ADAPTATIONS: Like Mother Like Me was adapted for CBS-TV by Sheila Schwartz's daughter, Nancy.

*   *   *

SCOTT, Anthony Dalton   1923-

PERSONAL: Born August 2, 1923, in Vancouver, British Columbia, Canada; son of Sydney Dunn and Edith Evelyn Scott; married, December 13, 1952; children: two. *Education:* University of British Columbia, B.Comm., 1946, B.A., 1947; Harvard University, M.A., 1949; London School of Economics and Political Science, Ph.D., 1953. *Office:* Department of Economics, University of British Columbia, Vancouver, British Columbia, Canada V6T 1W5.

CAREER: University of British Columbia, Vancouver, lecturer in economics, summer, 1949; Cambridge University, Cambridge, England, junior research worker in applied economics, 1949-50; University of London, London School of Economics and Political Science, London, England, assistant lecturer in economics, 1950-53; University of British Columbia, lecturer, 1953-54, instructor, 1954, assistant professor, 1954-57, associate professor, 1957-61, professor of economics, 1961—. Member of International Joint Commission, 1963; executive of British Columbia Natural Resources Conference, 1963-68; member of National Advisory Council on Water Resources, 1966-71; delegate to environmental directorate of Organization for Economic Cooperation and Development, 1971-75.

MEMBER: Social Science Research Council of Canada, Canadian Political Science Association (member of executive committee, 1956-57; president, 1966-67), Royal Society of Canada (fellow, 1969—; president of Academy II, 1979-80), Canadian Economics Association, Law of the Sea Institute (member of executive board, 1978-79), American Economic Association (member of executive committee, 1966-70), American Association for Environmental Economics (member of board of officers, 1975-78; vice president, 1978-80).

AWARDS, HONORS: Canada Council senior research fellow, 1959-60, 1971-72, Killam fellow, 1972, Killam senior research fellow, 1973-74; Lilly faculty fellow at University of Chicago, 1964-65; grants from Energy, Mines, and Resources Development and Environmental and Provincial Institute for Policy Analysis, Development and Environmental Fisheries, Canada Council, and Donner Foundation.

WRITINGS: (With William C. Hood) *Output: Labour and Capital in the Canadian Economy,* [Ottawa], 1958; (with T. N. Brewis, H. E. English, and Pauline Jewett) *Canadian Economic Policy,* Macmillan, 1961, revised edition, 1965; (with W.R.D. Sewell, John Davis, and D. W. Ross) *Guide to Benefit-Cost Analysis,* Queen's Printer, 1962; (with F. T. Christy, Jr.) *The Common Wealth in Ocean Fisheries,* Johns Hopkins Press, 1966, 2nd edition, 1973; (editor) Paul A. Samuelson, *Economics* (Canadian edition), McGraw, 1966, 5th edition, 1980; (editor with J. D. Rae) Stefan Stykolt, *Efficiency in the Open Economy: Collected Writings on Canadian Economic Problems and Policies,* Oxford University Press, 1969.

(Editor and contributor) *Economics of Fisheries Management: A Symposium,* Institute of Animal Resource Ecology, University of British Columbia, 1970; *Government Policy and Self Sufficiency,* University of Calgary Press, 1976; (editor and contributor) *Natural Resource Revenues: A Test of Federalism,* University of British Columbia Press, 1976; (with H. G. Grubel) *The Brain Drain: Determinants, Measurement and Welfare Effects,* Sir Wilfred Laurier University Press, 1977; (with Albert Breton) *The Economic Constitution of Federal States,* University of Toronto Press, 1978; (with P. A. Neher) *The Public Regulation of Commercial Fisheries in Canada,* Supply and Services, 1981.

Contributor: *Natural Resources: The Economics of Conservation,* University of Toronto Press, 1955, revised edition, McClelland & Stewart, 1973; Ralph Turvey and Jack Wiseman, editors, *The Economics of Fisheries,* FAO (Rome), 1958; R. Goldsmith and C. Saunders, editors, *Income and Wealth,* Bowes & Bowes, 1959.

Wesley Ballaine, editor, *Taxation and Conservation of Privately Owned Timber,* Bureau of Business Research, University of Oregon, 1960; R. M. Clark, editor, *Canadian Issues: Essays in Honour of Henry F. Angus,* University of Toronto Press, 1961; R. Hamlisch, editor, *Economic and Biologic Aspects of Fishery Regulation,* United Nations Food and Agriculture Organization, 1962; Marion Clawson, editor, *Natural Resources and International Development,* Johns Hopkins Press, 1964; D. B. Turner, editor, *Inventory of the Natural Resources of British Columbia,* Queen's Printer, 1964; Mason Gaffney, editor, *Extractive Resources and Taxation,* University of Wisconsin Press, 1967; M. Blaug, editor, *Economics of Education,* Penguin, 1969.

William J. McNeil, editor, *Marine Aquiculture,* Oregon State University Press, 1970; W. Lee Hansen, editor, *Education, Income, and Human Capital: Studies in Income and Wealth,* Columbia University Press, 1970; Charles Kindleberger and Andrew Shonfield, editors, *North American and Western European Economic Policies,* Macmillan, 1971; *Problems of Environmental Economics,* Organization for Economic Cooperation and Development (Paris), 1972; D. A. Auld, editor, *Economic Thinking and Pollution Problems,* University of Toronto Press, 1972; P. J. Crabbe and I. M. Spry, editors, *Natural Resource Development in Canada: A Multi-Disciplinary Seminar,* University of Ottawa Press, 1973; *Problems in Transfrontier Pollution,* Organization for Economic Cooperation and

Development, 1973; P. H. Pearse, editor, *The Mackenzie Pipeline,* McClelland & Stewart, 1974.

Ingo Walter, editor, *Studies in International Environmental Economics,* Wiley, 1976; Annette B. Fox, A. O. Hero, and J. S. Nye, editors, *Canada and the United States: Transnational and Transgovernmental Relations,* Columbia University Press, 1976; Emilio Gerelli and others, editors, *Economics of Transfrontier Pollution,* Organization for Economic Cooperation and Development, 1976; Neil Swainson, editor, *Managing the Water Environment,* University of British Columbia Press, 1976; Walter, editor, *Studies in International Environmental Economics,* New York University Press, 1976; Michael Crommelin, editor, *Minerals Leasing,* Institute for Economic Policy, University of British Columbia, 1976; William McKillup and Walter Mead, editors, *Timber Policy Issues in British Columbia,* University of British Columbia Press, 1976; D. Hartle and Geoffrey Young, editors, *Intergovernmental Relations,* Ontario Economic Council, 1977; (with Breton) M. S. Feldstein and R. P. Inman, editors, *The Economics of Public Services,* Macmillan, 1977; S. D. Berkowitz, editor, *Canada's Third Option,* Macmillan, 1978; Horst Siebert, Walter, and Klaus Zimmerman, editors, *Regional Environmental Policy: The Economic Issues,* New York University Press, 1979.

Todd Sandler, editor, *Theories and Structures of International Political Economy,* Westview, 1980; (with David Le-Marquand) O. Dwivedi, editor, *Resources and the Environment,* McClelland & Stewart, 1980; (with Harry F. Campbell) P. Nemetz, editor, *Resource Policy: International Implications,* Institute for Research on Public Policy, 1980; (with G. Rosenbluth) D. M. Nowland and R. Bellaire, editors, *Financing Canadian Universities,* Institute for Public Policy, University of Toronto, 1981.

Contributor to *Encyclopedia Americana* and *International Encyclopedia of the Social Sciences;* contributor to proceedings; contributor of articles and reviews to numerous professional journals. Member of board of editors of *Western Economic Journal,* 1968-71, *Land Economics,* 1969-75, and *Journal of Environmental Economics and Management,* 1973—; special editor of *British Columbia Studies,* 1972; *Canadian Public Policy,* member of board of editors, 1980-82, editor, 1982—.

*   *   *

SCOTT, Kenneth 1900-

PERSONAL: Born May 4, 1900, in Waterbury, Conn.; son of John Linus (a manufacturer) and Julie (Cooke) Scott; married Aurelia Grether (a professor of English), June 17, 1926; children: Jean Helen, Kenneth John. *Education:* Williams College, A.B., 1921; attended American School of Classical Studies, Athens, Greece, 1921-22; University of Wisconsin—Madison, M.A., 1923, Ph.D., 1925. *Politics:* Republican. *Religion:* Episcopalian. *Home:* 42-05 243 St., Douglaston, N.Y. 11363.

CAREER: University of Wisconsin—Madison, instructor in Latin, 1923-24, assistant professor of classics, 1925-27; Yale University, New Haven, Conn., assistant professor of Latin, 1927-29; Western Reserve University (now Case Western Reserve University), Cleveland, Ohio, professor of classics, 1929-42; master of classics and modern languages at private school in Concord, N.H., 1942-47, and of modern languages at a private school in Simsbury, Conn., 1947-48; Upsala College, East Orange, N.J., professor of classical languages, 1948-49; Wagner College, Staten Island, N.Y., professor of modern languages, 1949-59, chairman of department, 1950-59;

Queensborough Community College of the City University of New York, Bayside, N.Y., assistant professor, 1960-61, associate professor, 1961-62, professor of foreign languages and chairman of department, 1962-65; Queens College of the City University of New York, Flushing, N.Y., professor of history, 1965-70, professor emeritus, 1970—.

MEMBER: American Society of Genealogists (fellow), American Philological Association, National Genealogical Society (fellow), New York Historical Society, New York Genealogical and Biographical Society, Holland Society of New York (fellow). *Awards, honors:* Markham traveling fellowship, University of Berlin, 1926-27; Guggenheim fellowship, 1934; commander of the Order of St. Agatha (San Marino), 1937; knight of the Order of the Crown (Italy), 1938.

WRITINGS: (With Karl P. Harrington) *Selections from Latin Prose and Poetry,* Ginn, 1933; (with R. S. Rogers and Margaret Ward) *Caesaris Augusti Res Gestae et Fragmenta* (title means "Deeds and Fragments of Caesar Augustus"), Heath, 1935; *The Imperial Cult under the Flavians,* W. Kohlhammer Verlag, 1936; *Notes on the Bowman, Harter, and Sauer Families,* Warner Press, 1948.

Counterfeiting in Colonial New York, American Numismatic Society, 1953; *Counterfeiting in Colonial Pennsylvania,* American Numismatic Society, 1955; *Counterfeiting in Colonial America,* Oxford University Press, 1957; *Counterfeiting in Colonial Connecticut,* American Numismatic Society, 1957.

Counterfeiting in Colonial Rhode Island, Rhode Island Historical Society, 1960; (with Julius Bloch, Leo Hershkowitz, and Constance Sherman) *An Account of Her Majesty's Revenue in the Province of New York, 1701-1709,* Gregg, 1967; *Genealogical Data from New York Administration Bonds, 1753-1799,* New York Genealogical and Biographical Society, 1969; *Jasper Danckaert's Diary of Our Second Trip from Holland to New Netherlands,* Gregg, 1969.

Genealogical Data from the New York Post-Boy, 1743-1773, National Geographical Society, 1970; *The Voyages and Travels of Francis Goelet, 1746-1758,* Gregg, 1970; (with James Owre) *Genealogical Data from Inventories of New York Estates, 1666-1825,* New York Genealogical Society, 1970; *Genealogical Data from Further New York Administration Bonds,* New York Genealogical and Biographical Society, 1971; *Genealogical Data from the Pennsylvania Chronicle, 1767-1774,* National Genealogical Society, 1971; *Records of the Chancery Court of New York—Guardianships, 1691-1815,* Holland Society of New York, 1971.

Calendar of New York Colonial Commissions Book, Volume IV: 1770-1776, National Society of Colonial Dames in the State of New York, 1972; *Genealogical Data from Administration Papers from the New York State Court of Appeals in Albany,* National Society of Colonial Dames in the State of New York, 1972; *The Slave Insurrection in New York in 1712,* Bobbs-Merrill, 1972; *New York Marriage Bonds, 1753-1783,* St. Nicholas Society in the City of New York, 1972; *Rivington's New York Newspaper: Excerpts from a Loyalist Press, 1773-1783,* New York Historical Society, 1973; *Genealogical Abstracts from the American Weekly Mercury, 1719-1746,* Genealogical Publishing, 1974.

Abstracts from Ben Franklin's Pennsylvania Gazette, 1728-1748, Genealogical Publishing, 1975; *New York: State Census of Albany County Towns in 1790,* Genealogical Publishing, 1975; (with Kenn Stryker-Rodda) *Denizations, Naturalizations and Oaths of Allegiance in Colonial New York,* Genealogical

Publishing, 1975; (with Kristin L. Gibbons) *The New York Magazine: Marriages and Deaths, 1790-1797*, Polyanthos, 1975; (with Susan E. Klaffky) *A History of the Joseph Lloyd Manor House*, Society for the Preservation of Long Island Antiquities, 1976; (editor with Stryker-Rodda) E. B. O'Callaghan, *The Minutes of the Orphanmasters of New Amsterdam, 1663-1668*, Genealogical Publishing, 1976; *Abstracts (Mainly Deaths) from the Pennsylvania Gazette, 1775-1783*, Genealogical Publishing, 1976; *Joseph Gavit's American Deaths and Marriages, 1784-1829: An Index to Non-Principal Names*, Polyanthos, 1976.

(Editor with Stryker-Rodda) O'Callaghan, translator, *The Register of Solomon Lachaire: Notary Public of New Amsterdam, 1661-1662*, Genealogical Publishing, 1977; *Genealogical Data from Colonial New York Newspapers*, Genealogical Publishing, 1977; (with Stryker-Rodda) *Varied Genealogical Data: A Complete List of Addressed Letters Left in the Post Offices of Philadelphia, Lancaster, Chester, Trenton and Wilmington between 1748-1780*, Genealogical Publishing, 1977; (with Janet R. Clarke) *Abstracts from the Pennsylvania Gazette, 1748-1755*, Genealogical Publishing, 1977; (editor with Rosanne K. Conway) *Abstracts from Colonial Connecticut Newspapers: New Haven, 1755-1775*, Genealogical Publishing, 1977; (with Rosanne Conway) *New York Alien Residents, 1825-1848*, Genealogical Publishing, 1978; *British Aliens in the United States during the War of 1812*, Genealogical Publishing, 1979.

Early New York Naturalizations, Genealogical Publishing, 1981; *New York City Court Records, 1684-1760*, National Genealogical Society, 1982; *Minutes of the Mayors Court of New York, 1674-1675*, Genealogical Publishing, 1983; *New York City Court Records, 1760-1797*, National Genealogical Society, 1983. Contributing editor of *National Genealogical Society Quarterly*.

SIDELIGHTS: Kenneth Scott reads Latin and Greek and speaks Italian, French, German, Spanish, modern Greek, Danish, and Turkish.

*   *   *

SCOTT, William G(eorge) 1926-

PERSONAL: Born October 19, 1926, in Chicago, Ill.; son of George E. (an architect) and Esther (Mooney) Scott; married Julia Eigelsbach, September 3, 1955; children: Therese, William, Gerard, Andrea, Mary. *Education:* DePaul University, A.B., 1950; Loyola University, Chicago, Ill., M.S.I.R., 1952; Indiana University, D.B.A., 1957. *Office:* Department of Management, University of Washington, Seattle, Wash. 98105.

CAREER: Loyola University, Chicago, Ill., instructor in labor relations, 1952-53; Indiana University at Bloomington, lecturer in management, 1954-56; Georgia State College (now Georgia State University), Atlanta, associate professor of management, 1956-59; DePaul University, Chicago, associate professor, 1959-62, professor of management, 1962-66, chairman of department, 1959-62; University of Washington, Seattle, professor of management, 1966—. Visiting professor, Willamette University. Consultant to U.S. Internal Revenue Service, Field Educational Enterprises, and Battelle Memorial Institute. *Military service:* U.S. Army, Medical Corps, 1946-47. *Member:* Academy of Management (fellow).

WRITINGS: Social Ethic in Management Literature, Georgia State College, 1959; *Human Relations in Management*, Irwin, 1962; (editor with Keith Davis) *Readings in Human Relations*, McGraw, 1963, 3rd edition published as *Human Relations and*

Organizational Behavior: Readings and Comments, 1969; *Management of Conflict*, Irwin, 1965; *Organization Theory: A Structural and Behavioral Analysis*, Irwin, 1967, 4th edition (with Terence Mitchell and Philip Burnbaum), 1980; (compiler) *Organization Concepts and Analysis*, Dickenson, 1969.

(With Theo Haimann) *Management in the Modern Organization*, Houghton, 1970, 4th edition (with Haimann and Patrick E. Connor), 1982; (with David K. Hart) *Organizational America*, Houghton, 1979. Former associate editor, *Academy of Management Journal*.

SIDELIGHTS: Organizational America by William G. Scott and David K. Hart examines the role of the corporation in American society and how it has changed American beliefs about individual freedom. The corporation, writes Clarence Peterson of the *Chicago Tribune Book World*, "has refined its techniques for managerial and technological control, and has thus fostered values inconsistent with the individualistic values that gave rise to the organization in the first place. In this, the authors . . . see a drift toward a thinly veiled totalitarianism." H. George Frederickson of the *Public Administration Review* sees *Organizational America* as "the quintessential statement of our condition."

BIOGRAPHICAL/CRITICAL SOURCES: Public Administration Review, January, 1980; *Harvard Business Review*, July, 1980; *Chicago Tribune Book World*, October 19, 1980.

*   *   *

SCOUTEN, Arthur Hawley 1910-

PERSONAL: Born February 15, 1910, in Baton Rouge, La.; son of Oren Miller (a clergyman) and Margaret (Frasier) Scouten; married Josephine Rebecca Bradshaw; children: Margaret, Ellen Bradshaw, Robert Edward Lee. *Education:* Louisiana State University, B.A., 1935, M.A., 1938, Ph.D., 1942. *Politics:* Democrat. *Religion:* Baptist. *Home:* 3 rue Vivaldi, St. Germaine-en-Laye 78100, France.

CAREER: University of Texas, Austin, instructor in English, 1943-46; Auburn University, Auburn, Ala., assistant professor of English, 1946-47; University of Pennsylvania, Philadelphia, associate professor, 1950-60, professor of English, 1960-80. Visiting professor of English literature, University of South Florida, 1972; visiting professor, University of Warwick, 1973-74; distinguished visiting professor, University of Delaware, 1981. *Member:* Academy for Literary Studies, Modern Humanities Research Association, Society for Theatre Research, Modern Language Association of America, American Association of University Professors. *Awards, honors:* Fellow, Folger Shakespeare Library, 1952; Ford Foundation fellow, 1953-54; Guggenheim fellow, 1954-55; National Endowment for the Humanities fellow, 1980-82.

WRITINGS: (Editor, with Leo Hughes) *Ten English Farces*, University of Texas Press, 1948, reprinted, Books for Libraries, 1970; (contributor of Part 3) *The London Stage*, two volumes, Southern Illinois University Press, 1961; (editor) Herman Teerink, *A Bibliography of The Writings of Jonathan Swift*, 2nd edition (Scouten was not associated with original edition), University of Pennsylvania Press, 1963; (contributor of Part 1, with Emmett L. Avery and William B. VanLennep) *The London Stage*, one volume, Southern Illinois University Press, 1965; (with Avery) *London Stage, 1660-1700: A Critical Introduction*, Southern Illinois University Press, 1968; (editor with Robert E. Hume) Robert Howard and George Villiers, *The Country Gentleman: A ''Lost'' Play and Its Background*,

University of Pennsylvania Press, 1976; (co-author) *Revels History of Drama in English,* Volume V, Methuen, 1976. Contributor of about forty articles on Jonathan Swift, Daniel Defoe, and on London theaters to learned journals.

WORK IN PROGRESS: Stage history of London theaters in the eighteenth century, for Southern Illinois University Press.

AVOCATIONAL INTERESTS: American Civil War.

* * *

SCULLY, James 1937-

PERSONAL: Born February 23, 1937, in New Haven, Conn.; son of James (a glass grinder) and Hazel (Donovan) Scully; married Arlene Steeves, September 10, 1960; children: John Grandin, Aaron Patrick (deceased), Deirdre. *Education:* Southern Connecticut State College, student, 1955-57; University of Connecticut, B.A., 1959, Ph.D., 1964. *Politics:* Marxist. *Religion:* None. *Home:* Warrenville Rd., Mansfield Center, Conn. 06250. *Office:* Department of English, University of Connecticut, Storrs, Conn. 06268.

CAREER: Rutgers University, New Brunswick, N.J., instructor in English, 1963-64; University of Connecticut, Storrs, assistant professor, 1965-67, associate professor, 1968-74, professor of English, 1975—. Teacher, Hartford Street Academy, 1969; visiting writer, University of Massachusetts, 1973. *Member:* Phi Beta Kappa, Phi Kappa Phi.

AWARDS, HONORS: Ingram Merrill Foundation fellowship, 1962-63; *The Marches* was the Lamont Poetry Selection of Academy of American Poets, 1967 (the award is in the form of purchase of one thousand copies for distribution to membership of Academy of American Poets); Guggenheim fellowship, 1973-74; Islands and Continents translation award, 1979, for *De Repente/ All of a Sudden.*

WRITINGS: Modern Poetics, McGraw, 1965, revised edition published as *Modern Poets on Modern Poetry,* Collins, 1966; *The Marches* (poems), Holt, 1967.

Avenue of the Americas (poems), University of Massachusetts Press, 1971; *Santiago Poems,* Curbstone Press, 1975; (translator with C. J. Herington) Aeschylus, *Prometheus Bound,* edited by William Arrowsmith, Oxford University Press, 1975; (translator with Marie A. Proser) *Quechua Peoples Poetry,* Curbstone Press, 1976; *Scrap Book* (poems), Ziesing Brothers, 1977; (translator with Proser and wife, Arlene Scully) Theresa de Jesus, *De Repente/ All of a Sudden,* Curbstone Press, 1979.

May Day (poems), Minnesota Review Press, 1980; (editor and translator with A. Scully) Roque Dalton, *Poetry and Militancy in Latin America,* Curbstone Press, 1981; *Apollo Helmet* (poems), Curbstone Press, 1983. General editor of "Art on the Line" series for Curbstone Press.

SIDELIGHTS: James Scully spent almost a year in Europe, 1962-63, mostly in Rome; he lived in Santiago, Chile in 1973-74.

BIOGRAPHICAL/CRITICAL SOURCES: Christian Science Monitor, November 9, 1967; *Poetry,* December, 1967.

* * *

SEIBEL, Hans Dieter 1941-

PERSONAL: Born February 1, 1941, in Muelheim, Germany; son of Peter (an administrative director) and Anna (Gross)

Seibel; married Helga Renate Wolf (a sociologist), November 11, 1963; children: Saskia Tatjana, Tjark Errit. *Education:* University of Freiburg, Dr.phil., 1966; University of Muenster, Dr.phil.habil., 1972; also attended University of London and University of Ibadan. *Home:* Bergelchenort 14, 4600 Dortmund 16, Germany. *Office:* University of Cologne, Gronewaldstrasse 2, 5000 Koeln 41, Germany.

CAREER: Arnold-Bergstraesser Institute, Freiburg, Germany, chairman of Africa department, 1966-67; University of Liberia, Monrovia, associate professor of sociology and chairman of department of sociology and anthropology, 1967-69; Princeton University, Princeton, N.J., visiting lecturer, 1969-72; Manhattanville College, Purchase, N.Y., associate professor of sociology and chairman of department, 1972-75; Paedagogische Hochschule Ruhr, Dortmund, Germany, professor of sociology, 1975-80; University of Cologne, Koeln, Germany, professor of sociology, 1980—. Visiting professor, University of Muenster, 1971-72. *Member:* American Sociological Association, Nigerian Economic Society, Deutsche Gesellschaft fuer Soziologie.

AWARDS, HONORS: German Academic Exchange Service fellowship, 1967-69; Tubman Center of African Culture grant, 1967-68; German Research Council grant, 1968-69, 1969-71; Thyssen Foundation grant, 1968-69; Princeton University and Kraus-Thomson Organization grant, 1973; Volkswagen Foundation grant, 1974-75; Minister fuer Wissenschaft und Forschung NW grant, 1978-80.

WRITINGS: Industriearbeit und Kulturwandel in Nigeria (title means "Industrial Labor and Cultural Change in Nigeria"), Westdeutscher Verlag, 1968; (contributor) Robert A. Scott and Jack D. Douglas, editors, *Theoretical Perspectives on Deviance,* Basic Books, 1972; *The Dynamics of Achievement: A Radical Perspective,* Bobbs-Merrill, 1974; (with Andreas Massing) *Traditional Organizations and Economic Development: Studies of Indigenous Cooperatives in Liberia,* Praeger, 1974; (with Guenter Schroeder) *Ethnographic Survey of Southeastern Liberia: The Liberian Kran and the Sapo,* Liberian Studies Association in America (Newark, Del.), 1974; *Struktur und Entwicklung der Gesellschaft* (title means "Structure and Development of Society"), Kohlhammer Verlag, 1980.

Published by Bertelsmann Universitaetsverlag: (Contributor) Dieter Oberndoerfer, editor, *Africana Collecta,* Volume I: *Beitraege zum Studium von Politik, Gesellschaft und Wirtschaft afrikanischer Laender,* 1968, Volume II: *Beitraege zu Geschichte, Gesellschaft, Politik und Wirtschaft afrikanischer Laender,* 1971; (with Michael Koll) *Einheimische Genossenschaften in Afrika: Formen wirtschaftlicher Zusammenarbeit bei westafrikanischen Staemmen* (title means "Indigenous Cooperatives in Africa: Types of Economic Cooperation among West African Tribes"), 1968; *Gesellschaft im Leistungskonflikt* (title means "The Dilemma of the Achieving Society"), 1973.

With Ukandi G. Damachi: (Editor and contributor) *Social Change and Economic Development in Nigeria,* Praeger, 1973; (editor with Lester Trachtman) *Industrial Relations in Africa,* Macmillan, 1979; *Self-Management in Yugoslavia and the Developing World,* Macmillan, 1982; *Self-Help Organizations: Guidelines and Case Studies for Development Planners and Field Workers—A Participative Approach,* Friedrich-Ebert-Stiftung Bonn, 1982.

Contributor of articles and book reviews to journals, including *American Journal of Sociology, Nigerian Journal of Social and Economic Research, Soziale Welt, Internationales Afrika-*

forum, Koelner Zeitschrift fuer Soziologie und Sozialpsychologie, and *Zeitschrift fuer Soziologie.*

WORK IN PROGRESS: Work and Mental Health.

AVOCATIONAL INTERESTS: International travel, wind-surfing, tennis, and skiing.

* * *

SELLERS, Charles Coleman   1903-1980

PERSONAL: Born March 16, 1903, in Overbrook, Pa.; died January 31, 1980, in Sydney, Australia; son of Horace Wells (an architect) and Cora (Wells) Sellers; married Helen Earle Gilbert, October 6, 1932 (died February, 1951); married Barbara Stow Roberts, June 12, 1952; children: (first marriage) Horace Wells, Susan Pendleton Siemanoski. *Education:* Haverford College, B.A., 1925; Harvard University, M.A., 1926. *Politics:* Democrat. *Religion:* Episcopalian. *Home:* 161 West Louther St., Carlisle, Pa. 17013.

CAREER: In antiquarian book business, 1932-35; Wesleyan University, Middletown, Conn., bibliographical librarian, 1935-49; Dickinson College, Carlisle, Pa., member of library staff and teacher of American art, 1949-56, librarian, 1956-68, librarian emeritus, 1968-80, curator of Dickinsoniana. Writer and researcher, 1927-80. Research associate, American Philosophical Society, 1947-51; librarian, Waldron Phoenix Belknap, Jr. Research Library of American Painting, Wintherthur, Del., 1956-59.

MEMBER: American Association of University Professors (chapter president, 1961-62), College Art Association. *Awards, honors:* Litt.D., Temple University, 1957; Bancroft Prize, Columbia University, 1970, for *Charles Willson Peale.*

WRITINGS: Lorenzo Dow: Bearer of the Word, Minton, Balch, 1928; *Benedict Arnold: The Proud Warrior,* Minton, Balch, 1930, new edition, 1932; *Theophilus, the Battle-axe: A History of the Lives and Adventures of Theophilus Ransom Gates and the Battle-axes,* privately printed, 1930; *The Artist of the Revolution: The Early Life of Charles Willson Peale* (also see below), Feather & Good, 1939; *Charles Willson Peale* (also see below), two volumes (first volume includes *The Artist of the Revolution: The Early Life of Charles Willson Peale),* American Philosophical Society, 1947; *Portraits and Miniatures by Charles Willson Peale,* American Philosophical Society, 1952, supplement published as *Charles Willson Peale with Patron and Populace,* 1969; (editor) Waldron Phoenix Belknap, *American Colonial Painting,* Belknap Press, 1959.

(Editor) Waldron P. Belknap, Jr., *American Colonial Painting: Material for a History,* Harvard University Press, 1960; *Benjamin Franklin in Portraiture,* Yale University Press, 1962; *Descendants of Samuel Sellers: Materials for Use in the Compilation of a Family History,* Ardmore, 1962; *Charles Willson Peale* (based on earlier publication with same title), Scribner, 1969; (compiler with Martha Calvert Slotten) *Archives and Manuscript Collections of Dickinson College: A Guide,* Friends of Dickinson College Library, 1972; *Dickinson College: A History,* Wesleyan University Press, 1973; *Patience Wright: American Artist and Spy in George III's London,* Weslyan University Press, 1976; *Mr. Peale's Museum: Charles Willson Peale and the First Popular Museum of Natural Science and Art,* Norton, 1980.

Also author of a biography of James K. Polk. Contributor to *Britannica Encyclopedia of American Art,* and of articles on art history to periodicals.

SIDELIGHTS: Charles Coleman Sellers was the great-great-grandson of his favorite subject, Charles Willson Peale, the early American painter and naturalist who established the first popular museum of natural history in 1786. In his third and final book on Peale, *Mr. Peale's Museum: Charles Willson Peale and the First Popular Museum of Natural Science and Art,* published one month after his death, Sellers examined the birth and history of the museum his ancestor established with the support of George Washington, Thomas Jefferson, Benjamin Franklin, Alexander Hamilton, and other friends. Although noting that *Mr. Peale's Museum* covered some of the same information as Sellers's earlier works on Peale, *New York Times Book Review* contributing critic Jospeh Kastner commented that Sellers "did not lose his eye for the enlivening fact, his astonishment at Peale's efforts and accomplishments. And the book does bring out what historians too often overlook: the pervasive influence of natural history on the culture of the early republic, the way it fed the eagerness for knowledge and deepened the fresh, almost innocent patriotism of Americans who saw in the natural beauties and wonders around them new reasons to glorify the nation they had created."

BIOGRAPHICAL/CRITICAL SOURCES: New York Times Book Review, March 2, 1980; *Science,* May 16, 1980; *Natural History,* June, 1980.

OBITUARIES: New York Times, February 7, 1980.†

* * *

SENDAK, Maurice (Bernard)   1928-

PERSONAL: Born June 10, 1928, in Brooklyn, N.Y.; son of Philip and Sarah (Schindler) Sendak. *Education:* Attended Art Students' League, New York, N.Y., 1949-51. *Home:* 200 Chestnut Hill Rd., Ridgefield, Conn. 06877.

CAREER: Writer and illustrator of children's books, 1951—. Worked for comic book syndicate All American Comics part time during high school, adapting the "Mutt and Jeff" newspaper strip for comic books; Timely Service (window display house), New York City, window display artist, 1946; F.A.O. Schwartz, New York City, display artist, 1948-51. Illustrations have been displayed in one-man shows at School of Visual Arts, New York City, 1964, Rosenbach Foundation, Philadelphia, Pa., 1970 and 1975, Galerie Daniel Keel, Zurich, Switzerland, 1974, Ashmolean Museum, Oxford University, 1975, American Cultural Center, Paris, France, 1978, and Pierpont Morgan Library, New York City, 1981. Set and costume designer for a number of opera productions in the United States and Great Britain, including Wolfgang Amadeus Mozart's "The Magic Flute," for Houston Grand Opera, 1980, Leos Janacek's "The Cunning Little Vixen," for New York City Opera, 1981, and Serge Prokofiev's "Love for Three Oranges," for Glyndebourne Opera, 1982. *Member:* Authors League of America.

AWARDS, HONORS: Recipient of eighteen *New York Times* awards for illustrations, 1952-76; Caldecott Medal, American Library Association, 1964, for *Where the Wild Things Are,* runner-up for his illustrations in *A Very Special House, Little Bear's Visit, The Moon Jumpers, Mr. Rabbit and the Lovely Present,* and *What Do You Say, Dear?;* Hans Christian Andersen International Medal (first American to receive this award), 1970, for the entire body of his work; L.H.D., Boston University, 1977; American Book Award nomination, 1980, for *Higglety Pigglety Pop!; or, There Must Be More to Life;* American Book Award, 1982, for *Outside Over There;* Laura Ingalls Wilder Award, Association for Library Service to Children,

1983, for "a substantial and lasting contribution to children's literature."

WRITINGS—All children's books; self-illustrated, except as indicated; published by Harper, except as indicated: *Kenny's Window*, 1956; *Very Far Away*, 1957; *The Sign on Rosie's Door*, 1960; *Chicken Soup with Rice* (also see below), 1962; *One Was Johnny* (also see below), 1962; *Alligators All Around* (also see below), 1962; *Pierre* (also see below), 1962; *Nutshell Library* (contains *Chicken Soup with Rice, One Was Johnny, Alligators All Around,* and *Pierre*), 1962; *Where the Wild Things Are*, 1963, reprinted, Penguin, 1979; *Hector Protector* [and] *As I Went Over the Water*, 1965; *Higglety Pigglety Pop!; or, There Must Be More to Life*, 1967.

In the Night Kitchen, 1970; *Ten Little Rabbits: A Counting Book with Mino the Magician*, Philip H. Rosenbach, 1970; *Fantasy Sketches* (published in conjunction with one-man show at Rosenbach Foundation), Philip H. Rosenbach, 1970; *Pictures by Maurice Sendak*, 1971; *Maurice Sendak's Really Rosie* (based on the television program of the same title; also see below), 1975; (author of appreciation) *The Publishing Archive of Lothar Meggendorfer*, Schiller, 1975; (with Matthew Margolis) *Some Swell Pup; or, Are You Sure You Want a Dog?*, Farrar, Straus, 1976; (editor) *The Disney Poster Book*, illustrated by Walt Disney Studios, 1977; *Seven Little Monsters*, 1977; *Outside Over There*, 1981.

Illustrator; children's books, except as indicated; published by Harper, except as indicated: M. L. Eidinoff and H. Ruchlis, *Atomics for the Millions* (adult book), McGraw, 1947; Robert Garvey, *Good Shabbos, Everybody!*, United Synagogue Commission on Jewish Education, 1951; Marcel Ayme, *The Wonderful Farm*, 1951; Ruth Krauss, *A Hole Is to Dig*, 1952; Ruth Sawyer, *Maggie Rose: Her Birthday Christmas*, 1952; Beatrice S. de Regniers, *The Giant Story*, 1953; Meindert De Jong, *Hurry Home, Candy*, 1953; De Jong, *Shadrach*, 1953; Krauss, *A Very Special House*, 1953; Hyman Chanover, *Happy Hanukkah, Everybody*, United Synagogue Commission on Jewish Education, 1954; Krauss, *I'll Be You and You Be Me*, 1954; Edward Tripp, *The Tin Fiddle*, Oxford University Press, 1954; Ayme, *Magic Pictures*, 1954; Betty MacDonald, *Mrs. Piggle-Wiggle's Farm*, Lippincott, 1954; De Jong, *The Wheel on the School*, 1954.

Krauss, *Charlotte and the White Horse*, 1955; De Jong, *The Little Cow and the Turtle*, 1955; Jean Ritchie, *Singing Family of the Cumberlands*, Oxford University Press, 1955; de Regniers, *What Can You Do with a Shoe?*, 1955; Jack Sendak (brother), *Happy Rain*, 1956; De Jong, *The House of Sixty Fathers*, 1956; Krauss, *I Want to Paint My Bathroom Blue*, 1956; Krauss, *Birthday Party*, 1957; J. Sendak, *Circus Girl*, 1957; Ogden Nash, *You Can't Get There from Here*, Little, Brown, 1957; Else Minarik, *Little Bear*, 1957; De Jong, *Along Came a Dog*, 1958; Minarik, *No Fighting, No Biting!*, 1958; Krauss, *Somebody Else's Nut Tree*, 1958; Sesyle Joslyn, *What Do You Say, Dear?*, W. R. Scott, 1958; Minarik, *Father Bear Comes Home*, 1959; Janice Udry, *The Moon Jumpers*, 1959; Hans Christian Andersen, *Seven Tales*, 1959.

Wilhelm Hauff, *Dwarf Long-Nose*, Random House, 1960; Minarik, *Little Bear's Friend*, 1960; Krauss, *Open House for Butterflies*, 1960; Udrey, *Let's Be Enemies*, 1961; Clemens Brentano, *The Tale of Gockel, Hinkel & Gackeliah*, Random House, 1961; Minarik, *Little Bear's Visit*, 1961; Joslyn, *What Do You Do, Dear?*, Young Scott Books, 1961; Brentano, *Schoolmaster Whackwell's Wonderful Sons*, Random House, 1962; Charlotte Zolotow, *Mr. Rabbit and the Lovely Present*,

1962; De Jong, *The Singing Hill*, 1962; Leo Tolstoy, *Nikolenka's Childhood*, 1963; Robert Keeshan, *She Loves Me, She Loves Me Not*, 1963; Randall Jarrell, *The Bat-Poet*, Collier, 1964; Amos Vogel, *How Little Lori Visited Times Square*, 1964; Jan Wahl, *Pleasant Fieldmouse*, 1964.

William Engvick, editor, *Lullabies and Night Songs*, Pantheon, 1965; Jarrell, *The Animal Family*, Pantheon, 1965; Isaac Bashevis Singer, *Zlateh the Goat and Other Stories*, 1966; George Macdonald, *The Golden Key*, 1967; Robert Graves, *The Big Green Book*, Crowell, 1968; Frank Stockton, *Griffin and the Minor Canon*, Collins, 1968; Minarik, *A Kiss for Little Bear*, 1968; Macdonald, *The Light Princess*, Bodley Head, 1969.

Stockton, *The Bee-Man of Orn*, Holt, 1971; Doris Orgel, *Sarah's Room*, Bodley Head, 1971; Jakob Grimm and Wilhelm Grimm, *The Juniper Tree, and Other Tales from Grimm*, Farrar, Straus, 1973; Marie Catherine Jumelle de Berneville Aulnoy, *Fortunia: A Tale by Mme. D'Aulnoy*, translation by Richard Schaubeck, Frank Hallman, 1974; Jarrell, *Fly by Night*, Farrar, Straus, 1976; J. Grimm and W. Grimm, *King Grisley-Beard*, 1978.

Other works: (Author, director, and lyricist) *Really Rosie* (thirty-minute animated television special; based on characters from *The Nutshell Library* and *Sign on Rosie's Door* [also see below]; produced on Columbia Broadcasting System, 1975), music composed and performed by Carol King, Harper, 1975; (lyricist and set designer) "Really Rosie" (musical play; based on television special of the same title), music by King, first produced Off-Broadway, October, 1980; (lyricist, set designer, and costume designer) "Where the Wild Things Are" (opera; based on his book of the same title), music by Oliver Knussen, first produced in Belgium by Brussels Opera, November, 1980.

Many of Sendak's book have been translated into foreign languages. Contributor of illustrations to *McCall's* and *Ladies' Home Journal*, 1964.

WORK IN PROGRESS: Designing sets and costumes and writing the libretto for the opera version of *Higglety, Pigglety, Pop!*, to be performed by the Glyndebourne Opera in England, October, 1984; designing sets and costumes for "The Abduction from the Seraglio" to be performed by the New York City Opera in 1984; designing sets and costumes for two one-act operas by Ravel to be performed by the Glyndebourne Opera in 1986; writing the libretto for a three-act fantasy opera to be composed by Oliver Knussen and scheduled to be performed in 1988; illustrating the recently discovered manuscript of a previously unpublished Grimm fairy tale.

SIDELIGHTS: In the fall of 1963, Maurice Sendak published a picture book that would prove to be as popular as it is controversial—*Where the Wild Things Are*. Not only did the book (a 1964 Caldecott Medal winner) launch Sendak's international reputation as an author-illustrator, it also launched a philosophical argument about the nature of children's literature that has yet to be resolved. Because the graphically illustrated text depicts a small child's rage at his mother, some psychologists and librarians consider it unsuitable for children. These critics advocate a prescriptive form of children's literature that depicts what a child *ought* to be, not what he is. "To this tradition," reports Saul Braun in the *New York Times Magazine*, "Maurice Sendak appears as a virtual one-man revolution or counterculture. Sendak shouts a resounding 'No!' to the idea that there is something inherently good about a tidy, obedient child." According to *Newsweek*'s Walter Clemons, "Sendak belongs, not with sensible, sociologically oriented concocters of edifying kiddie books, with audience age ('5 to 8') coded on the jacket, but with the great eccentric visionaries like Lewis Carroll and George Macdonald who simply wrote books they had to write.''

Sendak, the only American ever to be awarded the Hans Christian Andersen International Medal for the body of his illustration, shares this view of his work: ''I don't write for children specifically,'' he told Virginia Haviland in a conversation reprinted in the *Quarterly Journal of the Library of Congress.* ''I certainly am not conscious of sitting down and writing a book for children. I think it would be fatal if one did. So I write *books*, and I hope that they are books anybody can read.''

Enjoyed by readers of all ages, Sendak's books are nonetheless inspired by elements of childhood—elements, Sendak told Selma Lanes, that come from his deepest self. Later in that *New York Times Book Review* article, Sendak explains how the artist ''draws on a peculiar vein of childhood that is always open and alive. That is his particular gift. The artist understands that children know a lot more than people give them credit for. Children are willing to deal with many dubious subjects that grownups think they shouldn't know about. But children are small courageous people who have to deal every day with a multitude of problems, just as we adults do.'' The majority of critics applaud his insight. Writing in the *Washington Post Book World,* for example, Jonathan Cott commends Sendak's ''uncanny ability to make us, as adults, reexperience the way a child experiences his or her earliest emotions.'' And Saul Braun expresses a similar view: ''To Sendak, the truth of childhood lies in his recollected emotions, and truth is what he wants most of all in his books. The passionate involvement of his boys and girls is Sendak's own.''

In his quest for truth and excellence, Sendak may well have opened new doors in the world of children's literature. Lanes credits him with elevating the ''American children's picture book to a high art form,'' while Farrar, Straus & Giroux editor Michael di Capua told Braun that Sendak has ''turned the entire tide of what is acceptable . . . to put in a children's book illustration. There is nobody to compare with Maurice.''

The youngest of three children born to Jewish immigrants, Maurice was a sickly baby who spent most of his early years indoors. ''I was miserable as a kid, I couldn't make friends. I couldn't play stoopball terrific, I couldn't skate great. I stayed home and drew pictures,'' he told an interviewer from *Rolling Stone.* ''You *know* what they all thought of me: sissy Maurice Sendak. When I wanted to go out and do something, my father would say: 'You'll catch a cold.' And I did. . . . I did whatever he told me.''

To pass the time, young Sendak spent many hours gazing out his apartment window or listening with his brother and sister to the tales his father would often tell. In *The Art of Maurice Sendak,* Selma Lanes suggests that these elaborate stories—spun of fantasy and Jewish folklore—''constituted the first important source from which his work developed. One tale that he remembers vividly was about a child taking a walk with his parents. 'Somehow he becomes separated from them, and snow begins to fall. The child shivers in the cold and huddles under a tree, sobbing in terror. Then, an enormous, angelic figure hovers over him and says, as he draws the boy up, ''I am Abraham, your father.'' His fear gone, the child looks up and also sees Sarah. When his mother and father find him, he is dead.''''

Such melancholy tales coupled with his own frail health to color Sendak's vision. So, too, did the succession of lower-middle-class Brooklyn neighborhoods in which he lived. ''My mother, for some reason, could not bear the smell of paint,'' he told *Washington Post* reporter Paul Richard. ''So every three years, rather than repaint the walls, we would change apartments. She liked to move. I hated it.'' Occasionally, Maurice would take trips with his family into Manhattan. His memories of the city, with its bright lights and tall buildings, its elegant theatres and fashionable restaurants, would later figure in his work.

Another significant childhood recollection concerns the day his sister brought him *The Prince and the Pauper,* which he describes as ''my first book. . . . A ritual began with that book which I recall very clearly,'' he told Virginia Haviland in the *Quarterly Journal of the Library of Congress.* ''The first thing was to set it up on the table and stare at it for a long time. Not because I was impressed with Mark Twain; it was just such a beautiful object. Then came the smelling of it. I think the smelling of books began with *The Prince and the Pauper,* because it was printed on particularly fine paper, unlike the Disney books I had gotten previous to that, which were printed on very poor paper and smelled poor. *The Prince and the Pauper*—smelled good and it also had a shiny cover. I flipped over that. And it was very solid. I mean, it was bound very tightly. I remember trying to bite into it, which I don't imagine is what my sister intended when she bought the book for me. But the last thing I did . . . was to read it. It was all right. But I think it started then, a passion for books and bookmaking.''

Throughout his youth and adolescence, Sendak was an apathetic student, but his enthusiasm and talent got him an illustrating job when he was still in high school. Working for All American Comics, Sendak adapted the popular ''Mutt and Jeff'' newspaper strip for comic books. After graduation, he took a job at a window-display house in lower Manhattan, where he helped create life-size storybook characters from papier-mache. He left the job in 1948 when a promotion took him away from the work he enjoyed.

That summer he and his brother Jack set up a home workshop and built elaborate mechanical toys based on eighteenth-century German models. Jack engineered the moveable parts and Maurice did the carving and painting. When they took their collection to F.A.O. Schwarz, they were told that their beautifully crafted pieces were much too expensive to mass produce. But the window-dresser was so impressed with the craftsmanship that he offered Maurice a job.

The store featured an excellent children's book department, which served both to educate and to inspire the young artist. One day, when some of his sketches were on display throughout the building, his co-workers arranged to have children's editor Ursula Nordstrom drop by. ''He was very young when I met him,'' Nordstrom recalled in a conversation with Braun. ''Very shy. . . . He didn't project his personality.'' Nonetheless, she was sufficiently impressed with his drawings to invite him to illustrate *The Wonderful Farm* (1951).

Some time later, Nordstrom asked to review Sendak's personal sketchbook, and what she saw convinced her that Maurice was the right choice for an exciting project. ''We had already turned down a number of illustrators for the new Ruth Krauss book, *A Hole Is to Dig.* We needed something very special, and Maurice's sketchbook made me think he would be perfect for it,'' she told Braun.

A series of definitions made up by children, the book is now considered a modern classic. Its publication in 1952 not only established Sendak's career as an illustrator, it also prompted a rash of imitations. But, of these competitors, Nordstrom observed: "None of them have Maurice's vision. He has a tremendous number of imitators, but nobody has his emotional equipment."

With book-illustration offers pouring in, Sendak was able to quit his F.A.O. Schwarz job and become a free-lance illustrator. In just a few years, he was writing books of his own, the first of which, *Kenny's Window,* he completed in 1955. "Looked at today," Selma Lanes writes in *The Art of Maurice Sendak,* *"Kenny's Window* is a dreamlike and tentative evocation of the new kind of hero and heroine Sendak would introduce to young children's books. Though the story is overlong and overwritten, it is a treasure trove of the themes, situations, and psychological excursions that would become the core of Sendak's mature work."

Sendak considers not only *Kenny's Window,* but all his early works to be illustrated books, i.e., books in which the pictures are secondary to the text. But in the early 1960s Sendak was ready to attempt a project in which the illustrations would carry as much weight as the story; in other words, a picture book. As it turned out, his first endeavor would be his most successful, for the picture book he created was *Where the Wild Things Are.*

The brief 338-word text tells the story of a little boy named Max who dresses up in a wolf suit and behaves mischievously. When his mother calls him a "Wild Thing" and sends him to bed without supper, he says, "I'll eat you up." Once in his room, Max watches as trees grow from his bedposts and a magical forest springs up all around, carrying him to a land where the wild things are. After taming them, Max becomes their king and he leads them on an uninhibited romp through the wild. Soon, however, Max tires of the game and, growing lonely, longs to be "where someone loves him best of all." Retracing his steps, Max finds himself back in his own bedroom, where his supper is waiting—"and it was still hot."

Though Max's adventure is a fantasy, his journey is motivated by actual events. "In *Where the Wild Things Are,*" notes Lanes, "the hero's adventure among the wild things is preceded by the real-life fact of his rage against his mother—which is precipitated by another fact: he has been sent to bed without any supper." Lanes believes that these factors lend the book its underlying strength. Complimenting Sendak's understanding of young children, Constantine Georgiou writes in *Children and Their Literature,* that the book "offers the momentary escape that most children need. It vicariously provides wild adventure and a refreshed return to a relatively calmer reality. This need for release or escape is common to humankind and to children particularly, on whom so many social limits for conformity are imposed."

But child psychologist Bruno Bettelheim attacks the book in the *Ladies' Home Journal,* stating that "the author was obviously captivated by an adult psychological understanding of how to deal with destructive fantasies in the child. What he failed to understand is the incredible fear it evokes in the child to be sent to bed without supper, and this by the first and foremost giver of food and security—his mother." Bettelheim also notes that his objections were based strictly on principle—he had not actually read the book. *Saturday Review* contributing critic Alice Dalgliesh argues that the "book has disturbing possibilities for the child who does not need this catharsis," and concludes that "how children feel about the whole book remains to be seen."

If sales figures are any indication, children feel very good about the book indeed. *Where the Wild Things Are* has sold over 700,000 hardback copies and been translated into thirteen foreign languages. An additional 1,800,000 paperback copies of the book have been sold in the school market alone. "Those adults who were apprehensive about the possibility of the wild things . . . frightening children seem to have been mistaken," conclude May Hill Arbuthnot and Zena Sutherland in *Children and Books.* "The pictures amuse and delight small children, and many Sendak fans have sent him their own pictures of wild things. . . . And children see the reassurance in Max's return home from his fantasy land when he 'wanted to be where someone loved him best of all.'"

Sendak has said that the book marked an important stage in his development. "I feel that I am at the end of a long apprenticeship," he remarked on accepting the Caldecott Medal. "By that I mean all my previous work now seems to have been an elaborate preparation for it. I believe [*Where the Wild Things Are*] is an immense step forward for me, a critical stage in my work."

Despite his professional success, Sendak experienced personal hardships during the next few years. His mother was afflicted with cancer, he suffered a heart attack, and the dog he had cherished for fourteen years, a Sealyham named Jennie, had to be put to sleep. The turmoil of this period is reflected in a book he dedicated to Jennie in 1967—*Higglety, Pigglety, Pop!; or, There Must Be More to Life.* ("Somehow it was easier to work up an anxiety about the dog's dying than about my mother," Sendak explained to Lanes in *The Art of Maurice Sendak,* "because that was just too much to go for.")

In the story, Jennie, a pampered pet with "two pillows, two bowls, a red wool sweater, eyedrops, eardrops, two different bottles of pills" and a master who loves her, decides "there must be more to life than having everything" and runs away from home. "What she wants, of course," says Eliot Fremont-Smith in the *New York Times,* "is an identifying experience; she is Everyman in the guise of Everydog, and will risk even death to have her day." Jennie's search takes her to a house where she is welcomed as a new nurse for Baby. Only Baby, apparently abandoned by her parents, has already had six nurses, all of whom have been fed to the downstairs lion when they couldn't get Baby to eat. Jennie fares no better, gobbling up the baby's food herself. But, the dog redeems herself by putting her head into the lion's mouth to protect Baby and is herself saved by a piece of luck. Her reward for this experience is a leading role in the World Mother Goose Theatre production of "Higglety, Pigglety, Pop."

The book has been widely reviewed by critics, many of whom feel that it is equally appealing to children and adults. "A triumph," proclaims Fremont-Smith, "and outside of genre. A children's book, of course, but one could just as well call it a mind-expanding novel, an anthropomorphic *Pilgrim's Progress,* a psycholanalytic revision of Mother Goose or anything else. Names don't matter; it's a delight, which should be exciting enough."

Other critics focus on the skillful intermingling of real and fantastic elements that characterizes not only this, but so much of Sendak's work. "For those who have followed Sendak's development from the dark night when the Wild Things danced, it becomes increasingly clear that his sensibility is engaged in a continuing dialogue between the real and the fantastic," writes Barbara Novak O'Doherty in the *New York Times Book Review.* And the *National Observer* critic suggests that what the author makes of Mother Goose's simple rhyme is "unmistakably Sendak, a surreal excursion worthy of Lewis Carroll."

Although it features a different style of illustration, *In the Night Kitchen* (1970) also recounts a fantastic voyage. A little boy named Mickey (in honor of Mickey Mouse, one of Sendak's childhood heroes) is awakened from slumber, falls through the dark, out of his pajamas (much to the dismay of conservative librarians), and into the night kitchen where buildings are shaped like bottles, salt shakers, and jelly jars. Here three bakers, each the image of Oliver Hardy, mistake him for the milk they need and bake him into a cake. Mickey escapes by fashioning an airplane from the dough and flies up to the Milky Way to fetch the real ingredient from a giant milk bottle. Mission accomplished, he slides back down, returning home "cakefree and dried."

Unlike the somber undercurrents which run through *Higglety Pigglety Pop!*, the fantasy in the night kitchen is a happy one which "poses few problems for its hero and asks nothing of its audience beyond the willingness to surrender to its own irrepressible dream logic," Lanes says. Here, according to Margot Hentoff in the *New York Review of Books*, "the elevated trains still run, and the dark starry sky is the one which, in the imagination of a Thirties child, appeared nightly over Radio City Music Hall." Sendak himself has acknowledged to Virginia Haviland in the *Quarterly Journal of the Library of Congress*, that the book "is a kind of homage to New York City, the city I loved so much and still love. . . . It also is homage to the things that really affected me esthetically. I did not get to museums, I did not see art books. I was really quite rough in the sense of what was going on artistically. 'Fantasia' was perhaps the most esthetic experience of my childhood, and that's a very dubious experience. But mainly there were the comic books and there was Walt Disney."

With its full-color illustrations and balloons of conversation, the book is indeed reminiscent of certain comics, but according to George A. Woods in the *New York Times Book Review*, it also possesses "a newness as if Sendak were picking up where comic books went wrong and pointing a new direction. Where other illustrators remain static in development as colorists, collagists, cartoonists, his talent grows."

One reason for his continued growth is Sendak's experimentation with various techniques of illustration. "To get trapped in a style," he told Haviland, "is to lose all flexibility. And I have worked very hard not to get trapped that way. . . . I worked up a very elaborate pen and ink style in *Higglety*, which is very finely cross-hatched. But I can abandon that for a magic marker as I did in *Night Kitchen* and just go back to very simple, outlined, broad drawings with flat, or flatter, colors. Each book obviously demands an individual stylistic approach. If you have one style, then you're going to do the same book over and over, which is, of course, pretty dull."

In 1981, Sendak completed *Outside Over There*, a book that is stylistically as different from *In the Night Kitchen* as *In the Night Kitchen* is different from his first picture book *Where the Wild Things Are*. And yet, as Sendak explains to Lanes, the three "are all variations on the same theme: how children master various feelings—anger, boredom, fear, frustration, jealousy—and manage to come to grips with the realities of their lives." For this reason, Sendak views the books as a trilogy.

In *Outside Over There*—as in all his storybooks—Sendak completed the text before he conceived the pictures. "Not many

of the artist's admirers are aware of how seriously he takes the texts of his own tales," says Lanes. "*Outside Over There*, a story with only 359 words, took almost a year and a half—and more than one hundred drafts—to complete. 'I have a hostility towards books which are not well written,' Sendak says."

Set in a rural eighteenth-century landscape that was sketched while Sendak listened to Mozart, *Outside Over There* dramatizes what *Newsweek* reviewer Walter Clemons calls "fears, rages, and appetites that adults would prefer to believe children don't experience. But *Outside Over There* . . . deals with the more complex feelings of an older child." As the story opens, nine-year-old Ida, whose father is away at sea and whose mother is in the arbor, sits absentmindedly watching her baby sister and playing her Magic Horn. When goblins come and steal the baby away, replacing it with a figure of ice, Ida doesn't even notice. But once the ice melts and she realizes what has happened, she dons an enormous yellow rain cloak and sets off to rescue the babe. "Unlike Max and Mickey, who rampage unhindered in fantasy worlds of their own," notes Clemons, "Ida is discovered in a difficult relation with others—a ruminative, preoccupied mother, an absent father whose approval Ida wants . . . and a heavy baby she dutifully tends but never directly looks at until the story's climactic moment."

John Gardner calls it, "a book for children that treats the child-reader as a serious, intelligent, troubled and vulnerable human being. Another writer might have softened the tale's effect by humor," he continues in the *New York Times Book Review*, "Mr. Sendak does something better: By the lyricism and gentle irony of his words and pictures, he transmutes guilt and insecurity—the dual bane of every child's existence—the things one can muse on without undue fear and escape triumphant. More specifically, he examines, with great accuracy and tenderness, the archetypal older girl-child's longing-filled love for her father and her jealousy toward her mother and younger sibling, and he shows how the father's love and respect are won."

"Like most great fairy tales," notes *Washington Post Book World* contributing reviewer Jonathan Cott, *Outside Over There* "has the simplicity of an elemental story and at the same time the mysteriousness, the depth, and the multiplicity of meanings of a dream . . . as we, like Ida, enter the underworld of the goblins' cave, where what is outer becomes inner, and where what is lost is found."

The complexity of its theme has led several reviewers to conclude that *Outside Over There* may not be a "children's book" at all. Walter Clemons expresses this opinion, and so does Christopher Lehmann-Haupt when he writes in the *New York Times* that the child within him is "bewildered" by much of the book. "There is a grandeur and complexity about the pictures that intimidate . . . They have a quality of nightmare. That is not necessarily a bad thing in a book such as this. In fact, it may be a very good thing. But, so far, my child isn't absolutely certain."

Sendak told *Publishers Weekly* that "the book is a release of something that has long pressured my internal self. It sounds hyperbolic but it's true; it's like profound salvation. If for only once in my life, I have touched the place where I wanted to go and, when Ida goes home, I go home. No other work of art has given me this inner peace and happiness. I have caught the thing that has eluded me for so long, so critical to living; and knowing that means everything, regardless of what anyone else says about the book. I'm not a happy man. I'm notorious for that. *Outside Over There* made me happy.''

MEDIA ADAPTATIONS: Where the Wild Things Are was made into a filmstrip by Western Woods in 1968; *Maurice Sendak's Really Rosie* was filmed as ''Really Rosie Starring the Nutshell Kids,'' by Western Woods in 1976; *Pierre, Chicken Soup with Rice, Alligators All Around,* and *One Was Johnny* were made into filmstrips with cassettes, all by Western Woods, all 1976.

CA INTERVIEW

CA interviewed Maurice Sendak by phone on August 25, 1982, at his home in Ridgefield, Connecticut.

CA: You've just done the sets and costumes for The Love for Three Oranges *at the Glyndebourne Opera House, in England, another coup in the latest facet of your career. Are you enjoying your work in opera?*

SENDAK: Yes, I am. Aside from the normal liabilities in dealing with human beings, it's quite wonderful.

CA: Does it put you under very different kinds of pressures from those involved in writing and illustrating books?

SENDAK: Entirely, entirely. And part of the problem is that, having been in a profession for nearly thirty years in which I could make my own way, allot and control my own time, I'm moderately spoiled in that sense. Now that freedom in dealing with time is taken away from me. Other people pull at me and demand certain things, and I have to fit myself into their time problems. The other concern is travel, which is really something I do not enjoy. I don't mean *being* in a different place; I do enjoy that. But getting there is what I loathe—the whole business of airplanes, schedules, sudden gettings up to make trips, the unexpected. I'm a very pedantic and slow person. I really like to know precisely what everything is going to be like for the whole coming week or month or year, if possible. Those are the two aspects of working in opera that I am having difficulty adjusting to. But I'm determined to adjust, because the work is worth it.

CA: The Glyndebourne production doesn't seem to have been reviewed in the United States.

SENDAK: No. It was not, and to our dismay, because it had the most incredible reviews in England. I mean both controversial and glowing. It was one of the most remarkable events that Glyndebourne has had, and I got this from their own lips, but none of it came to America. Later I spoke to Beverly Sills and told her how disappointed we were. She was very wry. She said, ''If you had hired a press agent, it would have been in the paper.'' And, you know, at my advanced age it dawned on me that these things are not spontaneous; they are all prearranged, and they have to be thought of in advance. And once I knew that, I didn't give a damn, because I wouldn't have done that on pain of death anyway.

CA: But it should have been covered because it was news.

SENDAK: And I'm shocked, frankly, that it wasn't, but so far as I'm concerned the important people know, the music people. Like publishing, music is a small world and everybody knows what your reviews are. So within a very short time I was getting congratulations from people in the States who knew exactly

what had happened in Glyndebourne. It just wasn't written anywhere for the general public. There's no question that it was disappointing. Frank Corsaro, who directed it, and I were the first Americans ever asked to do a production in Glyndebourne, and to have come off with such flying colors, well, one would have thought that was sufficient reason to write it up, but apparently it wasn't.

CA: Let's go back a bit and talk about your books. They've been translated into at least thirteen languages. Do you get mail from kids all over the world?

SENDAK: Yes. Not lots, but I do get some. The letters usually come in packets.

CA: More from any one country particularly?

SENDAK: Outside the United States, probably more from England. I've had Japanese children write to me, and occasionally German. But I cannot think of French children or Italian children having written, though they must have. My memory says mostly English. I've had some wonderful Australian letters, hilarious letters. Those kids are really original, very abandoned.

CA: Do you hear from more children than adults?

SENDAK: I would say an equal mixture of children and adolescents, with a smaller percentage of adults.

CA: I read that you were happy to find out that your work was being used successfully to reach autistic children.

SENDAK: Yes. Well, the only specific book I know that that's been done with is *Wild Things*. I don't know that others have been experimented with.

CA: Have you found it less difficult to illustrate other writers' work than your own?

SENDAK: Without question. Though maybe I shouldn't say less difficult; the problems are different and not as complicated as those one faces in illustrating one's own book. You choose other writers because they have facets of your own personality or similar quirks, or there's some instinctual thing that draws you to their work. But it's a particular current or a particular emotion that attracted you.

In your own books you're dealing with a vast range of emotions, and so the task is much more complicated. Also, doing anything with yourself is much more difficult. It is easier to work *with* somebody, especially if it's a unique, wonderfully talented person—a Randall Jarrell, for example. Then there's a tremendous learning excitement that takes over and a great wish to become a part of that person's book and support in every conceivable way the writing of that book. My life as a collaborator on books has probably dwindled to almost nothing at this point. It was once a great ambition, which it no longer is, honestly.

CA: You've noted the influence of several other artists on your own work—especially the nineteenth-century English illustrators, beginning with Blake. Do you continue to study the work of other artists?

SENDAK: Not in a conscientious, theoretical way, no. It's more random, what I happen to see at a given point, going through museums or to new exhibitions and finding someone I didn't know or getting excited over a picture in a book. I don't go out and seek it.

CA: Your own work has had two fine shows recently, one at the Pierpont Morgan Library last fall and a show currently at the Rosenbach Museum and Library.

SENDAK: Yes. The current show is of what I call the trilogy: *Where the Wild Things Are, In the Night Kitchen,* and *Outside Over There.* The exhibition at the Morgan was *The Magic Flute* and *Outside Over There,* with a sprinkling of *The Juniper Tree.* The secret god in all of this was Mozart, so the exhibition was basically arranged about the tremendous influence of Mozart in my life and its obvious manifestation in sets and costumes for one of his last operas, also some of the great influence he had on me during the writing and illustrating of *Outside Over There* and his presence earlier on in *The Juniper Tree.*

CA: When did music become important to you?

SENDAK: Almost instantly, as early as I can recollect. I know for a fact that I was an insomniac child as I am an insomniac adult, and one way that my mother could obliterate my yakking and crying and carrying on was to put the record player on. It was an old gramophone that I guess she had to wind up; it must have been very primitive, because we're talking about the late '20s. Perhaps that's not the best way to deal with a child who is sleepless, but nevertheless it may have been the beginning of my music appreciation. I still remember tunes from that early period. They were not Mozart, just whatever songs were popular back then. I think music is the most basic art in existence and I think it makes an impact on all of us. It is a spiritual language that is eminently available to all of us, much more available than reading or art or painting, because music is a language you don't have to be afraid of.

CA: Do you play an instrument at all?

SENDAK: I did when I was a young man. I played the easiest possible instrument, the recorder. Never well; I had great difficulty reading music. I played with a small amateur group of friends. We played Handel's sonatas for piano, flute, recorder, and cello, and Telemann sonatas. I never got past Handel or Telemann, although those were wonderful occasions nevertheless. I really did not play well, and I am not saying that out of modesty; I played only decently.

In fact the gift I would have most wished for, could I have been in a fairy tale and made a wish from my cradle, would have been the gift of musical talent so that I might have been a composer, or if not a composer, at least an instrumentalist, a pianist, a Gieseking or a Schnabel. I can't tell you how I envy someone who just casually sits down at a piano and begins to play Mozart. To me they have a secret that unlocks things which I can only sit and hear. I can only listen to records, and it's a great frustration that I have no musical gift that brings me closer.

That is why the operas are so important, because by costuming and setting them I have come as close to the music as I ever have in my life. I'm now literally on the stage, and I'm coloring Mozart, illustrating him in the way I used to illustrate people's stories.

CA: Are there colors that you particularly favor working with, or colors that are difficult?

SENDAK: No. It's all instinctual. I have no preconceptions, none. I make no preliminary studies; I always jump off the diving board. That means I do an awful lot of lousy drawings, that's all, but something in me refuses to prepare. I prepare up in my head; I do lots of sketches and preparation layouts, and I'm very meticulous about that, but when it comes to the painting of a picture, I do not prepare. I believe up to that point you should have done all your rehearsing backstage, meaning you've thought about it, you've done your homework, you've done layouts, dummies, sketches, you've done everything to prepare for onstage. (I'm full of theatrical similes at this point!) Doing your full-color paintings is when you come onstage. You've got to depend on your instincts at that moment and that includes the choice of color, which is a purely instinctual thing.

CA: Is it true, as I've read, that you don't like working for television?

SENDAK: I don't. I hate to, and it's infuriating because it's a wonderful medium. What I really mean is, I'd *love* to, but because of its present standards, and because of my experience with it, and because of the idiotic people I've had to contend with, it simply isn't worth it. It's a profession so hopelessly ruled by money. Publishing is almost as hopelessly ruled by money. It's getting closer and closer each year to being like television. Soon they'll be undifferentiated. In the past one heard that television was the Whore of Babylon and one ran back to the safety of publishing. But now you don't know where the Whore of Babylon lives.

I think—to bring us back again to music—the great beauty of what I'm doing now is that there is very little money. Opera is a grandiose antique; it's a prehistoric creature. Everybody groans because there isn't enough to pay for anything. Everybody is underpaid. So whatever we do, we do out of passion, because there is no financial gain. I don't mean to sound like Shirley Temple, to say that if you make no money then everything automatically has to be good. That's not true. But because there's a lack of financial aggression—and this is what you find in publishing and television—there is a different attitude. There are people who work hard sewing costumes and painting sets who get paid very little, but they choose to do it anyway. That makes for a different personality, it makes for a different atmosphere, and it makes for a different form entirely. It's much more honest and there's something going on that's more integrated with art and less with greed.

It's a long-winded answer to your question. It's a very frustrating question because television has always been beckoning. What artist wouldn't want to use a medium that would affect so many more children than you ever could attract with an expensive picture book? But at this point they won't let you do what you want. That's the long and the short of it.

CA: You read and collect books—Melville, Dostoevski, Henry James, Mark Twain, and Kafka, among others. Do you read any contemporary fiction?

SENDAK: Very little, to be honest. I do sometimes when friends urge and insist because they think I am so hokeypokey in reading only nineteenth-century stuff. *I* have felt that I am hokeypokey, and I have tried to read contemporary things, but with exceedingly few exceptions I can't stand the stuff. That's a terrible thing to say, and I'm generalizing horribly because I have read very few modern books. But it's an effort, just as it's an effort to hear very contemporary twentieth-century music. It bores the hell out of me; I can't pretend otherwise. And I accept the fact that I probably have a tin ear. My nephew and niece gave me up years ago because I wouldn't listen to rock and roll, which they thought was as real as what I love. I grant that it might well be, but I just can't bear it.

And then, you approach your glorious mid-fifties and you suddenly realize you don't *have* to like it, and you don't *care* if you're hokeypokey; so I've thrown everything out the window and gone back to the eighteenth and nineteenth centuries and I'm going to stay put until I kick the bucket and that's the way it is. You can finally say to yourself, I'm not a well-rounded, cultivated person. I *can't* be a well-rounded, cultivated person, so why fight it?

One of the great emancipations of my life came at the San Francisco Opera some years ago at a performance of *Die Meistersinger* by Wagner. That's an opera I loved as a young man. It made me uneasy through my middle thirties and my forties, and it only dawned on me when I was about fifty that I hated this work with a passion. The knowledge of that hatred had taken that long to reach the surface of my consciousness, but once it had, I could stand up at the end of the first act, turn to my friend, and say, "You know, I'm going home. I never want to hear this again and happily I never have to!" And that was the end of that. It gave me such a sense of freedom and joy that I would never have to listen to *Die Meistersinger* again as long as I lived, that I was no longer in thrall to a long-winded opera that pays such groveling homage to middle-class values.

CA: Are you doing any teaching now at all?

SENDAK: No, I'm not because there simply isn't any time. I would like to teach again, and there are some prospects on the horizon, but it won't be for a while. I can't see my way to doing it now.

CA: Although Where the Wild Things Are *and* In the Night Kitchen *also had great critical success, only* Outside Over There *seems to have made you truly happy.*

SENDAK: Yes. I think it's the best thing I've done in my life, and that's a lot to say; it sounds very egocentric. And a lot of people don't agree. But that doesn't concern me. *I* know what it is and that's why I'm resting now, that's why I'm doing other things. It's the book I searched for and scratched for, and the search was very hard and very cruel; and I finally got it. I got it as best I *could* get it—I didn't get it to the extent one always wishes one could. What I got was as close to the realization of vision as I've ever experienced in my creative life, so it does give me an immense sense of accomplishment and personal joy, and that finally is why we do this work. That really is the primary reason. It's a personal salvation and recovery of vision, and that's what it was for me. To an extent, some of my books have done that in varying degrees, but none to the depth and power of *Outside Over There*. I know because the suffering it caused me was unique in my life, and then the kind of pleasure that came from it afterwards was like a royal gift.

CA: If you had to go back and start over, would you do anything differently?

SENDAK: I'd slit my wrists.

CA: You've really suffered, obviously, in the creation of everything you've done.

SENDAK: Yes, I have—in everything that was important. But a lot of things that I do are unimportant. Some of them I really look away from with disgust. Of the whole packet of things I have done there is a handful (a largish handful, I would say; I'm lucky) that I'm quite proud of. And of those there are some very few that I'm *immensely* proud of. But in a large body of work, you have to do some junk. I began very early, before I was twenty. I grew up in the business, you see. I learned to be an artist and a human being all at the same time, and I used the form of the book to do that. So it would have been incredible had I done less than wreck many books unwittingly.

CA: Do you have specific plans for future books?

SENDAK: No. My hopes for the future are very unformed, but I have a great confidence in my talent. I really do. I've had people say to me, as they will, ad nauseum, "How are you going to top that one?" or "What are you going to do now?" which is the American artist's nightmare. As if you're going to blow your brains out because you can't possibly do something better than you just did. Happily that is something I have never troubled myself about. I am not a religious person at all; I'm an atheist, if you have to put a name to what I am. But when it comes to the creative process, I'm an ardent priest. I have total belief in whatever this thing is. If I don't believe in the mysteries of religion and the Heavenly Father, then I do believe in the mysteries of art, which are just as mysterious.

So I see that in the future something else will happen. I have no idea what it is, but I know I will write another book, unless I die before I can do it, and that's something you just have to accept the possibility of. It will not be a picture book. I will not do a picture book again. I've heard people insist that I'm being dramatic when I say I'm done. They don't realize what I mean. I did every picture book in order to find *Outside Over There*. Having found *Outside Over There*, I no longer have any interest whatsoever in that particular form, the picture book. I might illustrate somebody else's picture book; that's always possible. I can contradict myself because if something came up that was wonderful, I would do it. But I will not write one.

That doesn't mean, however, that I don't want to write a book. I will write a different kind of book probably, more like *Higglety Pigglety Pop!*, which is perhaps my next favorite after *Outside Over There*. To go to another form, a lengthier work, a textual work, is something I suspect will happen to me, but it probably won't happen for another five to ten years. In the interim I will be doing operas.

CA: What operas are definitely in the future?

SENDAK: There's an opera version of *Wild Things* which was performed in Brussels in 1980 in a rough form. That is now going to be performed at the National Theatre in London on New Year's Eve 1983, morning of '84, with the score revised and the sets and costumes redone by me and my libretto polished—everything under the imprimatur of Glyndebourne at the National. I'm about to begin work on a ballet, the *Nutcracker*, with the Seattle Ballet, to open Christmas 1983. And in the fall of 1984 an opera that I'll be working on shortly with the composer of *Wild Things*, Oliver Knussen. We have been commissioned to do an opera based on *Higglety Pigglety Pop!* The two one-act operas, *Higglety* and *Wild Things*, will open at Glyndebourne in the fall of '84. This is a great coup for us because these are commissioned by the English; that is a rare thing to happen in any country, and I'm very pleased and happy about it.

Also in 1984 I'll be designing sets and costumes for *The Abduction from the Seraglio* for the New York City Opera. Then in 1986 two one-act operas by Ravel at Glyndebourne again. And for 1988, if one can think so far ahead, I've been commissioned to create an original work with Oliver, a three-act fantasy opera based on any subject—I don't have the subject yet. I'll write the libretto for that. So between now and my dotage or senility or whatever, I will have accomplished, I hope, many things.

BIOGRAPHICAL/CRITICAL SOURCES—Books: Maurice Sendak, *Where the Wild Things Are*, Harper, 1963; Sendak, *Higglety, Pigglety, Pop!; or, There Must Be More to Life*, Harper, 1967; Constantine Georgiou, *Children and Their Literature*, Prentice-Hall, 1969; Lee Bennett Hopkins, *Books Are by People*, Citation Press, 1969; Sendak, *In the Night Kitchen*, Harper, 1970; May Hill Arbuthnot and Zena Sutherland, *Children and Books*, 4th edition, Scott, Foresman, 1972; Jeffrey Jon Smith, *A Conversation with Maurice Sendak*, Smith (Illinois), 1974; *Children's Literature Review*, Volume I, Gale, 1976; Selma G. Lanes, *The Art of Maurice Sendak*, Abrams, 1980.

Periodicals: *Saturday Review*, December 14, 1963; *New Yorker*, January 22, 1966; *New York Times Book Review*, October 22, 1967, November 1, 1970, April 29, 1979, April 26, 1981; *New York Times*, November 1, 1967, December 9, 1970, October 15, 1980, April 11, 1981, June 1, 1981, November 30, 1981; *National Observer*, November 27, 1967; *Ladies Home Journal*, March, 1969; *Books and Bookmen*, June, 1969; *New York Times Magazine*, June 7, 1970; *School Library Journal*, December, 1970; *New York Review of Books*, December 17, 1970; *Times Literary Supplement*, July 2, 1971; *Quarterly Journal of the Library of Congress*, Volume XXVIII, number 4, 1971; *Rolling Stone*, December 30, 1976; *Washington Post*, November 1, 1978, November 20, 1981; *Chicago Tribune*, July 17, 1980; *Los Angeles Times*, February 6, 1981, December 10, 1982; *Publishers Weekly*, April 10, 1981; *Chicago Tribune Book World*, May 3, 1981; *Washington Post Book World*, May 10, 1981; *Newsweek*, May 18, 1981; *Time*, July 6, 1981.

—*Sketch by Donna Olendorf*

—*Interview by Jean W. Ross*

*   *   *

SERVADIO, Gaia   1938-

PERSONAL: Surname is pronounced Ser-va-*dee-o;* born September 13, 1938, in Padua, Italy; daughter of Luxardo Massimo (an industrial chemist) and Bianca Maria (Prinzi) Servadio; married William Mostyn-Owen (a British art historian), September 28, 1961; children: Owen William Luxardo Mozart, Allegra Gemma Aglaja, Orlando Parsifal. *Education:* Received primary and secondary education at government schools in Italy; Camberwell School of Art, Camberwell, London, degree in graphic design, 1961; also studied at St. Martin's School of Art, London. *Politics:* "Cynical." *Religion:* Agnostic. *Home:* 31 Bloomfield Ter., London SW1W 8PQ, England; and Woodhouse Hall, West Felton, Oswestry, Shropshire, England. *Agent:* Ed Victor, Ed Victor Ltd., 162 Wardour St., London W1V 4AB, England.

CAREER: Journalist in England for Italian newspapers, 1958—, as correspondent for *Il Mondo*, Rome, 1960-63, feature writer for *L'Espresso*, Rome, 1963-64, and *La Stampa*, Turin, 1965—.

Art correspondent for British Broadcasting Corp. and Italian television, 1964-67; feature writer for *Evening Standard*, London, 1967-68; also political writer for *Times*, London, 1973-75. Lecturer for Associazione Culturale Italiana, 1968. Member of executive committee, London Symphony Orchestra, 1979—. Has acted in experimental films and exhibited her paintings in Rome. *Member:* Accademia degli Informi (Rome; honorary member), Foreign Press Association (vice-president, 1974-77).

WRITINGS: Tanto gentile e tanto onesta (novel), Feltrinelli (Milan), 1967, translation by L. K. Conrad published as *Melinda*, Farrar, Straus, 1968; *Don Giovanni: Il dissoluto punito* [and] *L'Azione consiste*, Feltrinelli, 1968, translation by Conrad published as *Don Giovanni: Notes for a Revised Opera* [and] *Salome: Notes for a New Novel*, Farrar, Straus, 1969; *Il Metodo* (novel), Feltrinelli, 1970; *A Siberian Encounter*, Weidenfeld & Nicolson, 1971, Farrar, Straus, 1972; *Angelo le Barbera: The Profile of a Mafia Boss*, translation from the Italian manuscript by Gwyn Morris, edited by Michael Bygrave, Quartet, 1974.

(Author of introduction) *76 Valpreda Papers*, Gollancz, 1975; *Mafioso: A History of the Mafia from Its Origins to the Present Day*, Stein & Day, 1976; *To a Different World*, Hamish Hamilton, 1979; *Insider Outsider*, Weidenfeld & Nicolson, 1979; *Luchino Visconti*, Weidenfeld & Nicolson, 1983.

WORK IN PROGRESS: A novel.

SIDELIGHTS: Melinda, the protagonist of Gaia Servadio's novel of the same name, "is a comic book heroine, . . . a mixture of Modesty Blaise and James Bond," remarks Marian Engel in *New York Times Book Review*. Throughout the book, Melinda dashes from country to country, adventure to adventure, man to man. "Melinda, like the Lorelei of 'Gentlemen Prefer Blondes,' is a tireless ambassadress of pleasure," says Charles Poore in the *New York Times*. "Operating from a British base, she happily stalks men everywhere."

The furious pace of *Melinda*—the book borrows from films, operas, Greek tragedies, comic books, and novels as its heroine finds herself involved in incest, orgies, marriages, a sperm-donor clinic for rich women, murder, a spy-ring (although Melinda doesn't know for which side), the British Parliament, and the Great Train Robbery, among other adventures—prompts Poore to call Servadio's style "a collage of script-teasing. I don't think you'll find a more blithely entertaining new conte drolatique." Engel recounts that she "found it easy to cast myself as a reader in an Antonioni film" as she read the book.

"It's a totally absurd book, really," Servadio told Jim Hicks in a *Life* magazine interview. "It is meant Voltairean, laughing, condemning, using satire. . . . Of course, I exaggerate by far. . . . But a bit of Melinda is like people today. This terror of boredom. And this hurry for experiences. They want to get in everything. She is not totally bad. She is just that way. I wanted to write sex on a ridiculous side and totally unromantic side. Because sex can be terribly ridiculous." According to a *Time* reviewer, *Melinda* "is a catchy packaging job of the familiar semi-exaggerations about how the super-rich and super-famous flit mindlessly from pleasure to pleasure in ever-tightening circles that lead to self-destruction. . . . Because she is not a character, but the author's representation of nascent id, Melinda cannot suffer hell or damnation."

While Engel, Poore, and the *Time* critic consider *Melinda* a spoof and therefore forgive some of its failings, other critics make a harsher judgment. "Gaia Servadio's book is really no more than a lengthy synopsis with a few good jokes," writes a *Times Literary Supplement* reviewer. "There are the makings of any number of interesting situations in this outline of Melinda Publishing's short and pappy life; but—unlike Melinda—they are seldom actually made. . . . *Melinda* is the fruit of some industrious fantasizing, and offers a reader plenty of stimulus or complementary labours . . . ; but scarcely anything resembling novelist's work intervenes to help the process on its way." Jack Richardson, contributing critic to *New York Review of Books,* also finds *Melinda* sketchily written. "That is Miss Servadio's literary style," Richardson notes. "She tells us that things are happening in *Melinda* which are scandalous, witty, and amusing, supposing that as good ladies and gentlemen we will believe her." On the other hand, Poore believes that "with so many lights playing on Melinda, Miss Servadio can be forgiven, I think, for fudging occasionally from the news of the day and the cutting-room floor. Old scripts never die—they just become fade-ins, ostensibly parodic, like as not, for other works in progress."

The madcap satire and fantasy that is the essence of *Melinda* is disagreeable to Richardson. Upon reading the novel's first sentence ("At the age of thirteen, after having seduced her father, Melinda was placed under the care of the best analyst in the world, Professor Hochtensteil."), Richardson reports that his "heart sank. . . . With such a beginning one knows that either a most extraordinary *tour-de-force* is at hand or else some disastrous pretentiousness. Miss Servadio has not written a *tour-de-force.* . . . [I became] so numb from the long catalogue of the heroine's outrageous adventures—adventures that had lain on the pages frantically winking for attention—that I had to let her continue alone." Engel delivers a different judgment: "This isn't the sort of wish-fulfillment book written by frumps. . . . Dreams come expensive these days, and books as untainted by high seriousness or morality as Melinda herself are hard to come by, too. One wonders whether she'll be played by Monica Vitti or Mary Quant—and if they'll hate her in England."

BIOGRAPHICAL/CRITICAL SOURCES: New York Times, May 15, 1968; *New Yorker,* May 18, 1968, April 1, 1972; *Life,* June 7, 1968; *New York Times Book Review,* June 9, 1968, July 16, 1969, September 21, 1969; *Times Literary Supplement,* June 13, 1968, February 25, 1972; *Observer,* June 16, 1968, November 2, 1969, December 5, 1971, September 5, 1976, February 4, 1979; *Spectator,* June 21, 1968, September 11, 1976, September 23, 1978; *Time,* June 21, 1968; *Punch,* June 26, 1968; *Books and Bookmen,* August, 1968, July, 1969, January, 1977; *New York Review of Books,* August 1, 1968, February 17, 1977; *Hudson Review,* autumn, 1968; *Listener,* November 25, 1971, October 26, 1978; *Economist,* January 15, 1972, January 27, 1979; *Book World,* April 9, 1972; *New Statesman,* October 20, 1978.

*   *   *

SETON-WATSON, Christopher   1918-

PERSONAL: Born August 6, 1918, in London, England; son of Robert William (a professor) and Marion (Stack) Seton-Watson. *Education:* Attended New College, Oxford, 1937-39. *Home:* 73 Thornton Rd., London SW 12, England.

CAREER: Oxford University, Oxford, England, fellow of Oriel College, 1946-83, lecturer in politics, 1950-83. Chairman of United Kingdom council, World University Service, 1964-69, and Czechoslovak Student Scholarship Fund, 1968-72. *Military service:* British Army, Royal Horse Artillery, 1939-45;

became major; received Military Cross, 1941, and bar, 1945. *Member:* Royal Historical Society (fellow), Association for the Study of Modern Italy (chairman, 1982—), Istituto per la Storia del Risorgimento Italiano (honorary member).

WRITINGS: Italy from Liberalism to Fascism: 1870-1925, Methuen, 1967; (contributor) S. J. Woolf, editor, *European Fascism,* Weidenfeld & Nicolson, 1968, revised edition published as *Fascism in Europe,* Methuen, 1981; (with brother, Hugh Seton-Watson) *The Making of a New Europe: R. W. Seton-Watson and the Last Years of Austria-Hungary,* Methuen, 1981; (contributor) R. Kindersley, editor, *In Search of Eurocommunism,* Macmillan, 1981; (contributor) *Ricasoli e il suo tempo: Atti del congresso internazionale di studi ricasoliani,* Olschki, 1981; (contributor) D. Butler and V. Bogdanor, editors, *Democracy and Elections,* Cambridge University Press, 1983; (contributor) L. Kettenhauer and W. J. Mommsen, editors, *The Fascist Challenge and the Policy of Appeasement,* Allen & Unwin, 1983. Also contributor to *Atti del XLIX Congresso di Storia del Risorgimento Italiano,* 1979.

WORK IN PROGRESS: A political history of Italy since 1943; research in twentieth century European history and international relations, with special reference to British-Italian relations.

SIDELIGHTS: A reviewer of *Italy from Liberalism to Fascism* in the *Observer Review* calls the book "impressive in the sanity of its judgments and the clarity of its narrative." Denis Mack Smith, in the *New York Review of Books,* writes that Christopher Seton-Watson "has written a thorough and even meticulous political history with plentiful footnotes and a useful bibliography. . . . Not even in Italian does there exist a comparable survey which covers the years 1870-1925 in such detail."

BIOGRAPHICAL/CRITICAL SOURCES: Observer Review, December 10, 1967; *New York Review of Books,* October 24, 1968.

*   *   *

SHAO, Stephen P(inyee)   1924-

PERSONAL: Born January 24, 1924, in I-hsing, Kiangsu, China; came to United States in 1948, naturalized in 1956; son of Chu Tang (an educator) and Shawyuen (Wang) Shao; married Betty Lucille Outen, June 18, 1953 (deceased); married Priscilla Griffin, September 1, 1969; children: (first marriage) Stephen Pinyee, Jr., Dale Hilton, Lawrence Peter, Alan Terence; (second marriage) Patricia Sue, Christina Lynn, Aron Eastwood, David Zachary. *Education:* National Hunan University of China, B.B.A., 1946; Baylor University, M.A., 1949; University of Texas, Ph.D., 1956. *Religion:* Baptist. *Home:* 5161 Lake Shore Rd., Virginia Beach, Va. 23455. *Office:* Old Dominion University, Hampton Blvd., Norfolk, Va. 23508.

CAREER: Board for Texas State Hospitals and Special Schools, Austin, chief accountant, 1952-54; Bluefield College, Bluefield, Va., head of department of business administration, 1954-56; College of William and Mary, Norfolk, Va., assistant professor, 1956-57, associate professor, 1957-58, professor of management and statistics, 1958-62; Old Dominion University, Norfolk, Va., professor of quantitative sciences and chairman of business and economics department, 1962-77, eminent professor of management information systems, 1978—. Visiting professor, National Chengchi University and National Taiwan University, 1977-78. Lecturer at universities in Taiwan and Hong Kong, summer, 1961, and in Peking and Harbin,

1980. Senior statistics consultant, Norfolk Naval Supply Center, 1962-68.

MEMBER: American Statistical Association, American Economic Association, American Accounting Association, American Institute for Decision Sciences, Southern Management Association, Alpha Kappa Psi.

WRITINGS: Mathematics of Finance, South-Western, 1962, 2nd edition published as *Mathematics for Management and Finance, with Basic and Modern Algebra,* 1969, 4th edition, 1980; *Statistics for Business and Economics,* C. E. Merrill, 1967, 3rd edition, 1976; *Workbook for Statistics,* C. E. Merrill, 1973; *Mathematics and Quantitative Methods for Business and Economics,* South-Western, 1976; *Essentials of Business Statistics,* C. E. Merrill, 1977.

WORK IN PROGRESS: Business Mathematics.

SIDELIGHTS: Stephen Shao told *CA:* "I moved to Virginia for the purpose of fishing, swimming, and playing tennis. However, I have fished only twice in the nearby ocean after having lived in Virginia Beach almost 20 years. I have spent most of my time on 'land,' writing my books and teaching college students."

*   *   *

SHAULL, (Millard) Richard 1919-

PERSONAL: Born November 24, 1919, in Felton, Pa.; son of Millard (a welfare worker) and Anna (Brenneman) Shaull; married Mildred Miller (a teacher), May 17, 1941 (divorced, 1973); children: Madelyn, Wendy. *Education:* Elizabethtown College, B.A., 1938; Princeton Theological Seminary, Th.B., 1941, Th.D., 1959. *Politics:* Democrat. *Home:* 156 Maplewood St., Philadelphia, Pa. 19144.

CAREER: Presbyterian missionary in Colombia, 1942-50; Campinas Theological Seminary, Campinas, Brazil, professor of church history, 1952-59; Mackenzie Institute, Sao Paulo, Brazil, vice-president, 1960-62; Princeton Theological Seminary, Princeton, N.J., professor of ecumenics, 1962-82, professor emeritus, 1982—; Instituto Pastoral Hispano, New York, N.Y., academic director, 1982—. Brazilian Student Christian Movement, general secretary, 1956-58, and participant in World Student Christian Federation programs and consultations in Japan, Korea, India, Germany, France, and throughout Latin America. Chairman of board of directors, North American Congress on Latin America, 1966—; chairman, World Student Christian Federation, 1968-73. *Awards, honors:* Guggenheim fellowship for study of Latin American political ideologies, 1965.

WRITINGS: Encounter with Revolution, Association Press, 1955; (with Carl Oglesby) *Containment and Change,* Macmillan, 1967; *Befreiung durch veraenderung,* Kaiser, 1970; (with Gustavo Gutierrez) *Liberation and Change,* John Knox, 1977.

WORK IN PROGRESS: A study of the Latin American theology of liberation.

*   *   *

SHEEHAN, James J(ohn) 1937-

PERSONAL: Born May 31, 1937, in San Francisco, Calif.; son of James B. (a businessman) and Sally (Walsh) Sheehan; married Elena Masharov (a teacher), June 12, 1960. *Education:* Stanford University, A.B., 1958; University of California.

Berkeley, M.A., 1959, Ph.D., 1964. *Office:* Department of History, Stanford University, Stanford, Calif. 94305.

CAREER: Stanford University, Stanford, Calif., instructor in history, 1962-64; Northwestern University, Evanston, Ill., assistant professor, 1964-67, associate professor, 1967-71, professor of history, 1971-79; Stanford University, professor of history, 1979—. Visiting fellow, Institute for Advanced Studies, 1973-74, and Wolfson College, Oxford University, 1981. *Member:* American Historical Association. *Awards, honors:* Fellowships from National Endowment for the Humanities, 1972, and American Council of Learned Societies, 1981-82.

WRITINGS: (Contributor) Stephen Baxter and others, editors, *Major Crises in Western Civilization,* Harcourt, 1965; (editor) *Industrialization and Industrial Labor in Nineteenth-Century Europe,* Wiley, 1973; (editor and author of introduction) *Imperial Germany,* New Viewpoints, 1976; *German Liberalism in the Nineteenth Century,* University of Chicago Press, 1978. Contributor of articles and reviews to journals.

BIOGRAPHICAL/CRITICAL SOURCES: Times Literary Supplement, March 9, 1967.†

*   *   *

SHELTON, William Roy 1919-

PERSONAL: Born April 9, 1919, in Rutherfordton, N.D.; son of William R. (a minister and lawyer) and Virginia H. Shelton; married Helene Lea Wells, November 7, 1943 (died, 1968); children: Dana. *Education:* Attended University of North Carolina, 1937-40; Rollins College, B.A., 1948; University of Iowa, additional study, 1950. *Address:* The Children's Home, P.O. Box 993, Winston-Salem, N.C. 27102.

CAREER: Rollins College, Winter Park, Fla., assistant professor of English, 1950-54; *Time,* Miami, Fla., and Chicago, Ill., bureau chief and correspondent, 1956-62; *Saturday Evening Post,* New York N.Y., contributing editor, 1962-63; free-lance author. Writer and producer of documentary and educational films. Space affairs consultant to CBS News and IBM. *Military service:* U.S. Army Air Forces, B-25 pilot, World War II; became captain; awarded Air Medal with eight oak leaf clusters. *Member:* Society of Authors and Journalists. *Awards, honors: Atlantic Monthly* "First" Award for short story "The Snow Girl," 1947; O. Henry Prize Stories Award, 1948; Eugene F. Saxton fellowship, 1950; Rollins College Medal of Honor, 1962.

WRITINGS: Land of the Everglades, Florida Department of Agriculture, 1958; *Countdown: The Story of Cape Canaveral,* Little, Brown, 1960; *Flights of the Astronauts,* Little, Brown, 1963; *American Space Exploration: The First Decade,* Little, Brown, 1967; *Man's Conquest of Space,* National Geographic, 1968, 4th edition, 1975; *Soviet Space Exploration: The First Decade,* Washington Square Press, 1968.

Winning the Moon, Little, Brown, 1970; *Stowaway to the Moon* (novel; also see below), Doubleday, 1973; *New Hope for the Dead* (poetry), Wings Press, 1977; *Houston: Superiority of the Southwest,* Doubleday, 1978.

Also author, with Sidney Carroll, of script for a television movie, "Stowaway to the Moon" (based on novel of same title), produced by Twentieth Century-Fox. Contributor of short stories and articles to periodicals including *Atlantic, Fortune, Saturday Evening Post,* and *Life.*

SIDELIGHTS: William Roy Shelton explained to *CA* his purpose in writing books about America's venture into space. "I first got the idea for writing books for young readers in 1958 when I drove three boys from Winter Park (Florida) Junior High School to old Cape Canaveral to watch the launch of a Thor rocket. The boys were amateur rocket builders and I was so impressed with their enthusiasm and knowledge of rocketry that I decided to write books for young Americans who did not have the opportunity we had of watching the dawn of the age of space. I resigned my teaching job and have been writing about space ever since.''

Shelton informed *CA* that he has witnessed and reported on over fifty-seven U.S. rocket launches and that he was the first writer of a national publication to cover Cape Canaveral.

Many reviewers point to Shelton's many years as a seasoned reporter covering America's exploration of space as reason for his effectiveness as a writer. One such reviewer, Henry Hubbard, writes of *Countdown* in the *New York Times Book Review* that ''it is refreshing to read the personal account of an experienced observer.'' In a review of *American Space Exploration*, R. S. Potts remarks in *Library Journal* that Shelton ''has given his book the 'personal touch' and the reader has the feeling of being on the inside.'' And Ethna Sheehan states in *America* that in *Winning the Moon* ''the human interest angle is paramount, but a great deal of excellent primary scientific source material is included, with many direct quotations from statements made at memorable stages.''

BIOGRAPHICAL/CRITICAL SOURCES: New York Times Book Review, November 20, 1960, January 17, 1971; *Christian Science Monitor*, May 9, 1963; *America*, June 1, 1963, December 5, 1970; *Library Journal*, September 1, 1967, April 15, 1971; *Best Sellers*, November 15, 1970; *Authors in the News*, Volume I, Gale, 1976.†

*   *   *

SHEPHARD, Roy J(esse) 1929-

PERSONAL: Born May 8, 1929, in London, England; son of Jesse (a civil servant) and Esther Rose (Cummins) Shephard; married Muriel Neve Cullum, August 18, 1956; children: Sarah Elizabeth, Rachel Judith. *Education:* University of London, Guy's Hospital Medical School, B.Sc. (with first class honors), 1949, M.B.B.S. (with honors), 1952, Ph.D., 1954, M.D., 1959. *Politics:* Liberal. *Religion:* United Church of Canada. *Home:* 42 Tollerton Ave., Willowdale, Ontario, Canada M2K 2H3. *Office:* University of Toronto, 320 Huron St., Toronto, Ontario, Canada M5S 1A1.

CAREER: University of Cincinnati, Cincinnati, Ohio, assistant professor of applied physiology, 1956-58; United Kingdom Ministry of Defence, Chemical Defence Experimental Establishment, Porton Down, Wiltshire, England, principal scientific officer, 1958-64; University of Toronto, Toronto, Ontario, professor of applied physiology, 1964—, director, School of Physical and Health Education, 1979—. Consultant, Toronto Rehabilitation Centre, Gage Research Institute (Toronto), and Universite du Quebec a Trois Rivieres. *Military service:* Royal Air Force, 1954-56; became flight lieutenant.

MEMBER: Canadian Physiological Society, Canadian Association for Health, Physical Education, and Recreation, Canadian Association of Sports Sciences (president, 1970-71), American Physiological Society, American Association for Health, Physical Education, and Recreation, American College of Sports Medicine (fellow; board member, 1970—; president, 1975-76), United Kingdom Physiological Society, British Medical Association, British Association for Sports Medicine

(honorary member), Belgian Association for Sports Medicine (honorary member), Ergonomics Research Society, Medical Research Society. *Awards, honors:* University of London postgraduate fellowship, 1952-53; Fulbright research fellowship, 1956-58; Phillip Noel Baker prize, UNESCO; fitness citation, province of Ontario.

WRITINGS: Endurance Fitness, University of Toronto Press, 1969, 2nd edition, 1976; (editor) *Frontiers of Fitness*, C. C Thomas, 1971; (with others) *Fundamentals of Exercise Testing*, World Health Organization, 1971; *Alive Man: Physiology of Physical Activity*, C. C Thomas, 1972; *Men at Work: Applications of Ergonomics to Performance and Design*, C. C Thomas, 1974; (editor with S. Itoh) *Circumpolar Health*, University of Toronto Press, 1976; *Fit Athlete*, Oxford University Press, 1978; *Physical Activity and Aging*, Croom Helm, 1978; *Human Physiological Work Capacity*, Cambridge University Press, 1978; (with H. Lavallee) *Physical Fitness Assessment*, C. C Thomas, 1978.

(With J. L. Anderson and others) *Year Book of Sport Medicine*, Year Book Medical Publishers, 1980-83; *Ischaemic Heart Disease and Physical Activity*, Croom Helm, 1981; *Textbook of Exercise Physiology and Biochemistry*, Praeger, 1982; *Physical Activity and Growth*, Year Book Medical Publishers, 1982; *Risks of Passive Smoking*, Croom Helm, 1982; *Carbon Monoxide: The Silent Killer*, C. C Thomas, 1983; *Exercise Biochemistry*, C. C Thomas, 1983.

Also author of more than five hundred technical papers, including more than forty for the United Kingdom Chemical Defence Experimental Establishment, twelve for the Flying Personnel Research Committee of the Royal Air Force, and more than three hundred reviews and lectures for various medical and physiological societies, conferences, and international symposia. Editor of *Proceedings* of International Symposium on Physical Activity and Cardiovascular Disease, Canadian Medical Association, 1967.

Contributor: Dorothy S. Dittmer and R. M. Grebe, editors, *Handbook of Respiration*, American Physiological Society, 1958; Dittmer and Grebe, editors, *Handbook of Circulation*, American Physiological Society, 1959; C. N. Davies, editor, *Inhaled Particles and Vapours*, Pergamon, 1961; Davies, editor, *Ergonomics of the Respirator*, Pergamon, 1961; P. L. Altman and Dittmer, editors, *Handbook of Environmental Biology*, Federation of American Societies for Experimental Biology, 1965; R. Goddard, editor, *The Effects of Altitude on Physical Performance* (proceedings of international symposium), Athletic Institute, 1967. Contributor to *Encyclopaedia of Sports Medicine*, edited by L. Larson.

Also contributor of several hundred scientific articles to more than fifty medical journals, including *British Heart Journal*, *Ergonomics*, *Journal of Physiology*, *Thorax*, *Archives of Environmental Health* (A.M.A.), *Canadian Medical Association Journal*, *British Journal of Industrial Medicine*, *Arbeitsphysiologie*, *International Journal of Air Pollution*, *Journal of Aerospace Medicine*, *Poumon Coeur*, *Malattie Cardiovasculari*, *South African Medical Journal*, *Journal of Sports Medicine and Fitness* (Italy), *Research Quarterly*, and *Internationale Zeitschrift fuer angewandte Physiologie*.

WORK IN PROGRESS: Employee Fitness, for Year Book Medical Publishers; *Economics of Fitness*, for Croom Helm; *Child Health*, for Pelican (Quebec City); and *The Fit Athlete* for Oxford University Press; research on exercise, cardio-respiratory health, and aging.

SIDELIGHTS: Roy J. Shephard told *CA* that he has "visited many parts of the world to study inter-relations of physical activity, health and environment and present the results of his research to international conferences; one of the most fascinating of these excursions was to study the fitness of Eskimos in the northern Arctic."

*　　*　　*

SHERMAN, Charlotte A.
　See SHERMAN, Jory (Tecumseh)

*　　*　　*

SHERMAN, Jory (Tecumseh) 1932-
　(Frank Anvic, Walt Denver, Cort Martin, Hank
　Mitchum, Charlotte A. Sherman, Wilma Tarrant)

PERSONAL: Born October 20, 1932, in St. Paul, Minn.; son of Keith Edward (a franchise consultant) and Mercedes (a stenographer; maiden name, Sheplee) Sherman; married Remy Montes Roxas, June 10, 1951 (deceased); married wife Felicia, August 15, 1958 (divorced December, 1967); married Charlotte Balcom (a writer), March 2, 1968; children: Francis Antonio, Jory Vittorio, Forrest Redmond, Gina Felice, Misty April, Marcus Tecumseh; (stepchildren) Gerald LeRoy Wilhite, David Dean Wilhite, Janet Lynn Wilhite. *Education:* Attended San Francisco State College (now University) and University of Minnesota. *Politics:* Democrat. *Home address:* P.O. Box 1069, Branson, Mo. 65616. *Agent:* Eleanor Langdon, 457 Oakdale Ave., Chicago, Ill. 60657.

CAREER: Denver Dry Goods, Denver, Colo., advertising copywriter, 1949-50; American President Lines, San Francisco, Calif., computer programmer, 1953-54; Great Plays Co., Lethbridge, Alberta, actor, 1954-55; *San Francisco Examiner,* San Francisco, editor, 1960-61; American Art Enterprise, North Hollywood, Calif., magazine editor, 1961-65; free-lance editor, 1965-67; newspaper columnist, 1965—. San Bernardino County press chairperson for Gerald Brown; press chairperson for John Tunney and Jesse Unruh. Teacher of creative writing for adults. President, MicroDramas Co., Rialto, Calif., 1969-71. Editor, Academy Press, Chatsworth, Calif., 1971-72. *Military service:* U.S. Navy, 1950-53. *Member:* Writers Guild of America, Authors Guild, Western Writers of America, Ozark Writers League (vice-president), Twin Counties Press Club (member of board of directors, 1966-70), Desert-Mountain Press Club, Baja California Writers Association. *Awards, honors:* Best newspaper column award from Twin Counties Press Club, 1970; best radio station public service program award from Twin Counties Press Club, 1970 and 1971.

WRITINGS: So Many Rooms, Galley Sail Publications, 1960; *My Face in Wax,* Windfall Press, 1965; *Lust on Canvas,* Anchor Publications, 1965; *The October Scarf,* Challenge Books, 1966; *The Sculptor,* Private Edition Books, 1966; *The Fires of Autumn,* All Star Books, 1967; *Nightsong,* All Star Books, 1968; *Blood Jungle,* Triumph News, 1968.

The Love Rain, Tecumseh Press, 1971; *There Are Ways of Making Love to You,* Tecumseh Press, 1974; *Gun for Hire,* Major Books, 1975; *Ride Hard, Ride Fast,* Major Books, 1976; *Buzzard Bait,* Major Books, 1977; *Hellfire Trail,* Leisure Books, 1979; *The Reincarnation of Jenny James,* Carlyle Books, 1979; *The Fugitive Gun,* Leisure Books, 1980; *Bukowski: Friendship, Fame, and Bestial Myth,* Blue Horse Publications, 1981; *My Heart Is in the Ozarks,* First Ozark Press, 1982.

Published by Pinnacle: *Satan's Seed,* 1978; *Chill,* 1978; *The Bamboo Demons,* 1979; *Vegas Vampire,* 1980; *The Phoenix Man,* 1980; *House of Scorpions,* 1980; *Shadows,* 1980; *Gunman's Curse,* 1983.

Published by Zebra Books: *Dawn of Revenge,* 1980; *Mexican Showdown,* 1980; *Death's Head Trail,* 1980; *Blood Justice,* 1980; *Winter Hell,* 1980; *Duel in Purgatory,* 1981; *Law of the Rope,* 1981; *Apache Arrows,* 1981; *Boothill Bounty,* 1981; *Hard Bullets,* 1981; *Trial by Sixgun,* 1981; *The Widow Maker,* 1982; *Arizona Hardcase,* 1982; *The Buff Runners,* 1982; *Drygulched,* 1983; *Wyoming Wanton,* 1983; *Tucson Twosome,* 1983; *Blood Warriors,* 1983; *Death Valley,* 1984; *Red Tomahawk,* 1984; *Ironheart,* 1984; *Blood Trail South,* 1984.

Under pseudonym Frank Anvic: *The All Girl Crew,* Barclay, 1973; *The Hard Riders,* Barclay, 1973; *We Have Your Daughter,* Brandon Books, 1974; *Bride of Satan,* Brandon Books, 1974.

Under pseudonym Walt Denver: *Pistolero,* Zebra Books, 1983.

Under pseudonym Cort Martin: *The Star,* Dominion, 1968; *Quest,* Powell Publications, 1969; *The Edge of Passion,* Saber Books, 1969; *First Blood,* Zebra Books, 1981.

Under pseudonym Hank Mitchum: *Stagecoach Station 8: Fort Yuma,* Bantam, 1983.

Under pseudonym Charlotte A. Sherman: *The Shuttered Room,* Major Books, 1975.

Under pseudonym Wilma Tarrant: *Her Strange Needs,* Carlyle Communications, 1976; *Trying Out Tricia,* Carlyle Communications, 1976.

Author of columns, "View on Living," *Grand Terrace Living,* 1966-67, "Ensenada at Bay," *Ensenada Hello,* 1966-67, "The New Notebook," *San Bernardino Independent,* 1970-71, "Baja Notebook," *Fiesta,* 1972-75, "Bear with Me," *Big Bear News,* 1972-75, and a column in *San Bernardino Mountain Highlander,* 1975-76.

Author of two series of educational tapes for radio, "Youth and Drugs" and "Youth and Alcohol," distributed by Classroom World Productions. Contributor of poetry to literary journals. West Coast editor, *Outsider;* advisory editor, *Black Cat Review.*

WORK IN PROGRESS: Three books in "The Saga of the Santa Fe Trails" series, for Zebra Books; two books about the Ozarks for First Ozark Press; "The Genesis Chronicles" series; four more books for Zebra.

SIDELIGHTS: Jory Sherman told *CA:* "Now, at age fifty, life gets sweeter, the writing gets harder, more interesting. I have more plans now than I ever did, more books contracted for than ever before. I use computers now and enjoy them immensely, but there are still not enough hours in the day, not enough days in a week, to do all that I want to do. Still, the best times are when I write something about the Ozark hills, when there's no money on the line, no deadline, no publisher in mind. This writing is for me and if it sees print, that's fine, too. But that is not the important thing. What is important is that creative juices are flowing, that I can still see and feel and touch a secret part of myself and paint a picture in words with the colors I have in hand."

AVOCATIONAL INTERESTS: Black powder guns, hunting, fishing, computer programming, local and western history.

BIOGRAPHICAL/CRITICAL SOURCES: Listen, April, 1971.

SHETH, Jagdish N(anchand) 1938-

PERSONAL: Born September 3, 1938, in Rangoon, Burma; son of Nanchand J. (a businessman) and Diwaliben (Mehta) Sheth; married Madhu Shah, December 22, 1962; children: Reshma J., Raju J. *Education:* Madras University, B.Com. (with honors), 1960; University of Pittsburgh, M.B.A., 1962, Ph.D., 1966. *Home:* 414 Brookens Dr., Urbana, Ill. 61801. *Office:* Department of Business Administration, University of Illinois, 146 Commerce W., Urbana, Ill. 61801.

CAREER: Columbia University, New York, N.Y., research associate in business, 1963-65; Massachusetts Institute of Technology, Cambridge, assistant professor of business administration, 1965-66; Columbia University, assistant professor of business, 1966-69; University of Illinois at Urbana-Champaign, associate professor, 1969-71, research professor, 1971—, Illinois Business Associates Distinguished Professor of Business, 1973-79, Walter H. Stellner Distinguished Professor of Marketing, 1979—, head of department, 1970-72, 1978, member and chairman of numerous department, college, and university committees.

Visiting professor, Indian Institute of Management, spring, 1968; visiting lecturer, International Marketing Institute, Harvard University, summer, 1969; visiting professor, Columbia University, summer, 1970; Albert Frey Visiting Professor of Marketing, University of Pittsburgh, 1973; guest lecturer, University of Ottawa, Copenhagen School of Economics and Business, and Norwegian School of Business and Economics, 1977, and University of Southern California, 1978; guest speaker, Louisiana State University, 1981. Distinguished speaker, University of Minnesota, 1972; distinguished lecturer, Washington State University, 1973; Root & Kelly Distinguished Lecturer, Louisiana State University, 1975; distinguished speaker, University of Kansas, 1975; distinguished lecturer, University of Kansas, 1978; Kellogg Distinguished Lecturer, Alabama State University, 1980. Visiting scholar, State University of New York at Buffalo, 1974; distinguished visitor, Virginia Polytechnic Institute, 1979. Director, Office of International Consumer Behavior Studies. Has conducted more than four hundred seminars in twenty countries and presented papers and lectures at conferences and workshops. Advisory editor, Harper & Row Publishers, Inc., 1970—. Member of advisory council, Institute for Social Research, University of Illinois, 1978—, and University of Michigan. Consultant to General Motors, American Telephone & Telegraph, B. F. Goodrich, and more than fifty other companies and government agencies in fifteen countries.

MEMBER: Association for International Business, Association for Consumer Research, American Institute for Decision Sciences, American Statistical Association, American Marketing Association (director of Central Illinois chapter, 1972-73), American Psychological Association (fellow), Academy of Marketing Science, Southern Marketing Association.

AWARDS, HONORS: Outstanding Teacher of the Year award, College of Commerce, 1975; Texas Instruments Award nominee, University of Illinois, 1978-79; Viktor Matajal Medal, Austrian Research Society, 1979; Outstanding Teaching Award in Continuing Education, 1981.

WRITINGS: (With John A. Howard) *The Theory of Buyer Behavior,* Wiley, 1969; (editor with S. P. Sethi and contributor) *Multinational Business Operations: Advanced Readings,*

Goodyear Publishing, 1973, Volume I: *Environmental Aspects of Operating Abroad,* Volume II: *Long-Range Planning, Organization, and Management,* Volume III: *Marketing Management,* Volume IV: *Financial Management;* (editor and contributor) *Models of Buyer Behavior: Conceptual, Quantitative, and Empirical,* Harper, 1974; (editor with Peter Wright and contributor) *Marketing Analysis for Societal Problems,* Bureau of Economics and Business Research, University of Illinois, 1974.

(Editor and contributor) *Multivariate Methods for Market and Survey Research,* American Marketing Association, 1977; (editor with Arch G. Woodside and Peter Bennett and contributor) *Consumer and Industrial Buying Behavior,* American Elsevier, 1977; (editor with Hans-Martin Schoenfeld and contributor) *Export Marketing: Lessons from Europe,* Bureau of Economics and Business Research, University of Illinois, 1981.

Contributor: Reed Moyer, editor, *Changing Marketing Systems,* American Marketing Association, 1967; J. B. Kernan and M. S. Sommers, editors, *Perspectives in Marketing Theory,* Appleton, 1968; Johan Arndt, editor, *Insights into Consumer Behavior,* Allyn & Bacon, 1968; R. L. King, editor, *Marketing and the New Science of Planning,* American Marketing Association, 1968.

P. R. McDonald, editor, *Marketing Involvement in Society and the Economy,* American Marketing Association, 1970; Paul Pellemans, editor, *Insights in Consumer and Market Behavior,* Namur University, 1971; *Segmentation and Typology,* European Society for Opinion Surveys and Market Research, 1972; *Consumer Psychology and Motivation Research,* European Society for Opinion Surveys and Market Research, 1972; Richard Holton and Sethi, editors, *Management of the Multinationals,* Free Press, 1974; Robert Ferber, editor, *Handbook of Marketing Research,* McGraw, 1974.

Beverly Anderson, editor, *Advances in Consumer Research,* Volume III, Association for Consumer Research, 1976; Andreasen and Sudman, *Public Policy and Marketing Thought,* American Marketing Association, 1976; *Marketing for Today and Tomorrow,* [Amsterdam], 1976; James Leigh and Claude R. Martin, Jr., editors, *Current Issues and Research in Advertising: 1978,* Graduate School of Business, University of Michigan, 1978; (with Robert Redinger) R. L. Bittell, editor, *Professional Encyclopedia of Management,* McGraw, 1978; (with P. S. Raju) H. Meffert, H. Steffenhagen, and H. Freter, editors, *Konsumentenverhalten und Information,* Gabler, 1979; W. R. King and G. Zaltman, editors, *Marketing Scientific and Technical Information,* Westview, 1979.

R. W. Stampfl and E. C. Hirschman, editors, *Theory in Retailing: Traditional and Nontraditional Sources,* American Marketing Association, 1981; Leigh McAlister, editor, *Choice Models for Buyer Behavior,* Jai Press, 1982; P. H. Reingen and Woodside, editors, *Buyer-Seller Interactions: Empirical Research and Normative Issues,* American Marketing Association, 1982; William Darden and Robert Lusch, editors, *Patronage Behavior and Retail Management,* Elsevier-North Holland, 1982; (with David Gardner) *Marketing Theory,* American Marketing Association, 1982.

Also contributor to *Advances in Consumer Research,* Volume II, published by Association for Consumer Research. Editor of "Research in Marketing" series, Jai Press, 1978—. Contributor to *Encyclopedie du Marketing,* Volume IV, 1976; contributor to numerous seminar publications and proceedings of professional organizations. Reviewer for *Journal of the Acad-*

emy of Marketing Science, 1978—, and other periodicals; ad hoc reviewer, *Journal of Consumer Research, Decision Sciences, Journal of Business,* and *Journal of Applied Psychology;* review member, *Journal of Applied Psychology,* 1976-79; contributor of more than fifty articles and book reviews to business and advertising journals. *Journal of Marketing,* editor of marketing theory section, 1981—, and buyer behavior section, 1982—. Member of editorial boards, *Journal of Marketing,* 1971—, *Quarterly Review of Economics and Business,* and *Journal of the Academy of Marketing Science.*

* * *

SHOSTECK, Robert 1910-1979

PERSONAL: Born April 25, 1910, in Newark, N.J.; died March 18, 1979, in Bethesda, Md.; married Dora G. Rabinovitz (died, 1969); married Ruth Okrent (a social worker), December 19, 1970; children: Herschel, Sara Shosteck Williams. *Education:* George Washington University, A.B., 1939, B.A., 1953. *Politics:* Democrat. *Religion:* Jewish. *Home:* 5100 Alta Vista Rd., Bethesda, Md. 20014.

CAREER: National Roster of Scientific and Specialized Personnel, Washington, D.C., assistant director of placement, 1940-45; B'nai B'rith Vocational Service, Washington, D.C., director of research, 1945-56; B'nai B'rith Museum, Washington, D.C., curator, 1957-75, curator-consultant, 1975-79. Lecturer at Montgomery College and Smithsonian Institution. Regular guest on local edition of national television program, "PM Magazine." Consultant to National Park Service, 1975-79. *Member:* Jewish Historical Society of Washington (president, 1961).

WRITINGS: Potomac Trail Book, Potomac Books, 1967, revised edition, 1973; *Weekender's Guide: Places of Historic, Scenic, Cultural and Recreational Interest within 200 Miles of the Washington-Baltimore Area,* Potomac Books, 1969, 7th revised edition, 1979, published as *Weekender's Guide to the Four Seasons: Sports and Recreation, Scenic, Historic and Cultural Places and Activities within 200 Miles of Washington, Baltimore and Richmond,* 1982; *Flowers and Plants: An International Lexicon,* Quadrangle, 1974; (co-author) *Washington Guide,* Washingtonian Magazine, 1975; *Rock Creek Watershed Habitat Survey and Inventory of Fauna and Flora,* Maryland-National Capital Park and Planning Commission, Montgomery County Planning Board, 1977; *Camper's Park Guide: Where to Camp, What to Do in 888 Parks, Forests, and Other Recreation Areas from Maine to Florida,* EPM Publications, 1978.

OBITUARIES: Washington Post, March 20, 1979.†

* * *

SHYER, Marlene Fanta

PERSONAL: Born in Czechoslovakia; daughter of Eric G. and Gertrude Fanta; married Robert M. Shyer (an optical manufacturing executive), June 3, 1954; children: Kirby, Christopher, Alison. *Education:* University of Bridgeport, B.S. *Religion:* Unitarian. *Residence:* Larchmont, N.Y. *Agent:* Julie Fallowfield, McIntosh & Otis, Inc., 475 Fifth Ave., New York, N.Y. 10017.

CAREER: Writer. Elementary school teacher in Portchester, N.Y., public schools, 1955-57. *Member:* P.E.N., Writers Guild, Authors League of America. *Awards, honors:* Children's Book

of the Year Award from Child Study Association of America, 1969, for *Tino.*

WRITINGS: Tino (juvenile), Random House, 1969; *Local Talent* (novel), Bobbs-Merrill, 1974; *Blood in the Snow* (juvenile), Houghton, 1975; *Welcome Home Jellybean* (juvenile), Scribner, 1978; *Never Trust a Handsome Man* (novel), Coward, 1979; *My Brother, the Thief,* Scribner, 1980; *Adorable Sunday,* Scribner, 1983. Also author of several television scripts. Contributor of numerous short stories and articles to popular magazines and other periodicals, including *Writer, Redbook, McCall's, Good Housekeeping,* and *Ladies Home Journal.*

SIDELIGHTS: Marlene Fanta Shyer explains in an article for *Writer:* "I'm not one of the people who can sit down and write out an outline of the story I will then flesh out, the writer who incredibly seems to know at the beginning how the story will end at the end. Although I do think it's important to know ahead the climax of the plot (like aiming at the bull's-eye), I seem to have only vague inklings about the rest of the story, which constantly gets overhauled as I go along. I'm a sloppy soul, untidy to the marrow. I have the closets, drawers and first drafts to prove it.''

Known for her short stories in popular magazines as well as for novels aimed at both adults and young readers, Shyer covers a wide variety of themes and styles in her work. The children's book *Welcome Home Jellybean,* for instance, examines the trials and triumphs of a brain-damaged girl and her apartment-dwelling family, while the adult novel *Local Talent* traces the comic action as several housewives try to establish a brothel in their suburban neighborhood. *Blood in the Snow,* set in the harsh and often cruel world of rural Vermont, focuses on fear, violence, compassion, and individual bravery as it tells the story of its young hero, Max Murphy, and a silver fox cub.

Whatever her subject, maintains the author, the plot must be probable, not merely possible. "Truth is stranger than fiction, but fiction should be less strange than truth.'' Concludes Shyer in another *Writer* article, "Actually, the best story ideas are at the A&P and in the chiropodist's waiting room if I'm listening, which I am, all the time.''

BIOGRAPHICAL/CRITICAL SOURCES: Writer, May, 1970, April, 1972; *New York Times Book Review,* October 20, 1974, February 1, 1976, April 30, 1978, March 25, 1979.

* * *

SILVER, Nathan 1936-

PERSONAL: Born March 11, 1936, in New York, N.Y.; son of Isaac (an architect) and Libby (Nachimowsky) Silver; married Caroline Green (a writer; divorced); married Helen McNeil (a university lecturer; divorced); children: Liberty, Gabriel. *Education:* Cooper Union Art School, student, 1952-55; Columbia University, B.Arch., 1958; Cambridge University, M.A., 1966. *Home:* 6 Westchester House, Seymour St., London W2 2JG, England. *Office:* School of Architecture, Northeast London Polytechnic, Holbrook Centre, Holbrook Rd., London E15 3EA, England.

CAREER: Registered architect, New York State. Columbia University, School of Architecture, New York, N.Y., assistant professor of architecture, 1961-65; Cambridge University, School of Architecture, Cambridge, England, lecturer in architecture, 1965-68; architect, Partner, Silver, Penney, 1967-68, Nathan Silver, London, England, 1969-72, Feilden & Mawson Architects, London, 1973-77; Northeast London Polytechnic,

London, head of School of Architecture, 1979—. *Military service:* Army National Guard. *Member:* Royal Institute of British Architects, National Council of Architectural Registration Boards.

AWARDS, HONORS: Guggenheim fellowship, 1968; certificate of merit, Municipal Art Society, 1968; National Book Award nomination from National Book Committee, 1968, for *Lost New York;* National Endowment for the Arts grant, 1970.

WRITINGS: Lost New York, Houghton, 1967; (with Charles Jencks) *Adhocism: The Case for Improvisation,* Doubleday, 1973; (co-editor) *Why Is British Architecture So Lousy?,* Newman, 1980. Contributor to *New Statesman* and architectural journals. Architectural critic, *New Statesman,* 1966-74.

WORK IN PROGRESS: The Making of Beaubourg; Fairy Darkness.

*   *   *

SILVER, Samuel M.   1912-

PERSONAL: Born June 7, 1912, in Wilmington, Del.; son of Adolph D. (a tailor) and Adela (Hacker) Silver; married Elaine Shapiro (a concert pianist), February 8, 1954; children: Leon, Joshua, Barry, Noah, Daniel. *Education:* University of Delaware, B.A., 1933; Hebrew Union College—Jewish Institute of Religion, Rabbi and M.H.L., 1940. *Politics:* Independent. *Home:* 2005 Northwest Ninth St., Delray Beach, Fla. 33445. *Office:* Temple Sinai, 188 South Swinton Ave., Delray Beach, Fla.

CAREER: Rabbi. University of Maryland, College Park, director of Hillel Foundation, 1940-42; assistant rabbi of congregation in Cleveland, Ohio, 1946-52; Union of American Hebrew Congregations, New York, N.Y., editor of *American Judaism,* 1952-59; Temple Sinai, Stamford, Conn., rabbi, 1959-77, rabbi emeritus, 1977—; Reform Jewish Congregation, Cape Coral, Fla., rabbi, 1977-80; Temple Sinai, Delray Beach, Fla., rabbi, 1980—. Philosophy teacher at various schools and junior colleges, including New Dimensions Institute of Palm Beach Junior College, 1982. *Military service:* U.S. Army, 98th Infantry Division, chaplain, 1942-46; served in Hawaii and Philippines.

MEMBER: Fellowship in Prayer (vice-president), Central Conference of American Rabbis, Association of Jewish Chaplains (president, 1963-64), Rabbinic Association of South Palm Beach County, Fla., Delray Beach Clergy Association (president). *Awards, honors:* D.H.L. from Hebrew Union College—Jewish Institute of Religion, 1965.

WRITINGS: How to Enjoy This Moment, Trident, 1967; (editor) *The Quotable American Rabbis,* Droke, 1967; (with Libbie L. Braverman) *The Six Day Warriors,* Bloch, 1969; *Explaining Judaism to Jews and Christians,* privately printed, 1971, Arco, 1973; *Mixed Marriage between Jew and Christian,* Arco, 1977. Also author of *When You Talk English You're Often Speaking Hebrew,* 1974. Author of weekly columns, "Digest of Yiddish Press" in *National Jewish Post & Opinion,* and "Silver Linings" for Seven Arts Feature Syndicate of the Jewish Telegraphic Agency.

BIOGRAPHICAL/CRITICAL SOURCES: Evening Times (West Palm Beach, Fla.), April 1, 1982.

*   *   *

SILVERMAN, Hillel E.   1924-

PERSONAL: Born February 24, 1924, in Hartford, Conn.; son

of Morris (a rabbi) and Althea (a writer; maiden name, Osber) Silverman; married Devora Halaban, January 8, 1950; children: Gail, Sharon, Jonathan. *Education:* Yale University, B.A. (with highest honors), 1944; graduate study at Hebrew University of Jerusalem, 1947; Jewish Theological Seminary of America, Rabbi and M.A., 1949, Ph.D., 1951. *Office:* Temple Shalom, 300 East Putnam Ave., Greenwich, Conn. 06830.

CAREER: Congregation Shearith Israel, Dallas, Tex., rabbi, 1954-64; Sinai Temple, Los Angeles, Calif., rabbi, 1964-80; Temple Shalom, Greenwich, Conn., rabbi, 1980—. Member of board of a number of Los Angeles civic, religious, and philanthropic organizations, including Community Relations Council and Jewish Family Service. *Military service:* U.S. Navy, Chaplain Corps, 1951-54; served overseas in Mediterranean Theater. U.S. Naval Reserve, 1954—; present rank, commander. *Member:* Jewish Historical Society (member of board of directors), United Jewish Appeal (member of national board of directors of rabbinical advisory council), Rabbinical Assembly of America (member of national cabinet), Zionist Organization of America (past regional president).

WRITINGS: (With father, Morris Silverman) *Selihot Prayers for Forgiveness,* Prayer Book Press, 1954; (with M. Silverman) *Prayer Book for Summer Camps,* Prayer Book Press, 1954; (with M. Silverman) *Tishah B'av Eve Service,* Prayer Book Press, 1955; *Judaism Looks at Life,* Jonathan David, 1967; *Judaism Meets the Challenge,* Jonathan David, 1973; *From Week to Week,* Hartmore, 1975; *From Heart to Heart,* Ktav, 1979. Sermons anthologized in *Best Sermons of 1961, Best Sermons of 1963,* and *Best Sermons of 1967.* Contributor to magazines and journals, including *Jewish Spectator, Jewish Digest,* and *Congress Weekly.*

*   *   *

SIMON, Seymour   1931-

PERSONAL: Born August 9, 1931, in New York, N.Y.; son of David and Clara (Liftin) Simon; married Joyce Shanock (a travel agent), December 25, 1953; children: Robert Paul, Michael Alan. *Education:* City College (now City College of the City University of New York), B.A., 1953, graduate study, 1955-60. *Home:* 4 Sheffield Rd., Great Neck, N.Y. 11021.

CAREER: Writer. New York City public schools, science teacher, 1955-79. *Military service:* U.S. Army, 1953-55. *Member:* United Federation of Teachers, National Science Teachers Association, Authors Guild, Authors League of America. *Awards, honors:* Children's Book Showcase award, Children's Book Council, 1972, for *The Paper Airplane Book;* awards from National Science Teachers Association and Children's Book Council, 1972-83, for outstanding science books for children.

WRITINGS—Youth books: *Animals in Field and Laboratory: Projects in Animal Behavior,* McGraw, 1968; *The Look-It-Up Book of the Earth,* Random House, 1968; *Motion,* Coward, 1968; *Soap Bubbles,* Hawthorn, 1969; *Weather and Climate,* Random House, 1969; *Exploring with a Microscope,* Random House, 1969.

Handful of Soil, Hawthorn, 1970; *Science in a Vacant Lot,* Viking, 1970; *Science at Work: Easy Models You Can Make,* F. Watts, 1971; *Chemistry in the Kitchen,* Viking, 1971; *The Paper Airplane Book,* Viking, 1971; *Science at Work: Projects in Space Science,* F. Watts, 1971; *Science Projects in Ecology,* Holiday House, 1972; *Science Projects in Pollution,* Holiday House, 1972; *Science at Work: Projects in Oceanography,* F. Watts, 1972; *From Shore to Ocean Floor: How Life Survives in the Sea,* F. Watts, 1973; *The Rock-Hounds' Book,* Viking, 1973; *A Tree on Your Street,* Holiday House, 1973; *A Building on Your Street,* Holiday House, 1973; *Projects with Plants,* F. Watts, 1973; *Birds on Your Street,* Holiday House, 1974; *Life in the Dark: How Animals Survive at Night,* F. Watts, 1974.

Projects with Air, F. Watts, 1975; *Pets in a Jar: Collecting and Caring for Small Wild Animals,* Viking, 1975; *Everything Moves,* Walker & Co., 1976; *The Optical Illusion Book,* Four Winds Press, 1976; *Life on Ice,* F. Watts, 1976; *Ghosts,* Lippincott, 1976; *Life and Death in Nature,* McGraw, 1976; *Animals in Your Neighborhood,* Walker & Co., 1976; *The Saltwater Tropical Aquarium Book: How to Set Them Up and Keep Them Going,* Viking, 1976; *What Do You Want To Know about Guppies?,* Four Winds Press, 1977; *Beneath Your Feet,* Walker & Co., 1977; *Space Monsters,* Lippincott, 1977; *Look to the Night Sky,* Viking, 1977; *Exploring Fields and Lots,* Garrard, 1978; *Killer Whales,* Lippincott, 1978; *About Your Lungs,* McGraw, 1978; *Animal Fact/Animal Fable,* Crown, 1979; *Danger from Below,* Four Winds Press, 1979; *The Secret Clocks,* Viking, 1979; *Meet the Giant Snakes,* Walker & Co., 1979; *Creatures from Lost Worlds,* Lippincott, 1979; *The Long View into Space,* Crown, 1979; *Deadly Ants,* Four Winds Press, 1979; *About the Foods You Eat,* McGraw, 1979.

Meet Baby Animals, Random House, 1980; *Animals Nobody Loves,* Random House, 1980; *Strange Mysteries,* Four Winds Press, 1980; *Goony Birds, Bush Babies, and Devil Rays,* Random House, 1980; *Mirror Magic,* Lothrop, 1980; *Silly Animal Jokes and Riddles,* McGraw, 1980; *Poisonous Snakes,* Four Winds Press, 1981; *Mad Scientists, Weird Doctors, and Time Travelers,* Lippincott, 1981; *About Your Brain,* McGraw, 1981; *Strange Creatures,* Four Winds Press, 1981; *Body Sense, Body Nonsense,* Lippincott, 1981; *The Smallest Dinosaurs,* Crown, 1982; *How to Be a Space Scientist in Your Own Home,* Lippincott, 1982; *The Long Journey from Space,* Crown, 1982; *Little Giants,* Morrow, 1983; *Hidden Worlds: Pictures of the Invisible,* Morrow, in press.

"Discovering" series; published by McGraw: *Discovering What Earthworms Do,* 1969; . . . *What Frogs Do,* 1969; . . . *What Goldfish Do,* 1970; . . . *What Gerbils Do,* 1971; . . . *What Crickets Do,* 1973; . . . *What Garter Snakes Do,* 1975; . . . *What Puppies Do,* 1977.

"Let's Try It Out" series; published by McGraw: *Let's Try It Out: Wet and Dry,* 1969; . . . *Light and Dark,* 1970; . . . *Finding Out with Your Senses,* 1971; . . . *Hot and Cold,* 1972; . . . *About Your Heart,* 1974.

"Einstein Anderson" series, published by Viking: *Einstein Anderson, Science Sleuth,* 1980; . . . *Shocks His Friends,* 1980; . . . *Makes Up for Lost Time,* 1981; . . . *Tells a Comet's Tale,* 1981; . . . *Goes to Bat,* 1982; . . . *Lights Up the Sky,* 1982; . . . *Sees through the Invisible Man,* in press.

WORK IN PROGRESS: An introduction to computers; a new fiction series involving computers; an introductory series of books on space; a television adaptation of *Einstein Anderson.*

SIDELIGHTS: Seymour Simon writes: "To me, science is a way of finding out about the world. It's easy enough to read what an authority says about a particular subject, but it's so much more satisfying and rewarding to find out the answer to a question by working at it yourself. Many of the books I write are really in the nature of guidebooks to unknown territories. Each territory has to be discovered again by a child venturing into it for the first time."

AVOCATIONAL INTERESTS: Reading, collecting books and art, playing chess and tennis, listening to music, traveling, computers.

* * *

SIMPSON, Myrtle L(illias)   1931-
(M. L. Emslie)

PERSONAL: Born July 5, 1931, in Great Britain; daughter of Hamish and Kathleen (Calvert) Emslie; married Hugh W. Simpson (a pathologist and explorer), March 21, 1959; children: Robin, Bruce, Rona, Rory. *Education:* Educated in United Kingdom and India. *Politics:* "Tory, with overtones of Scottish Nationalist." *Religion:* Presbyterian. *Home:* Farletter, Insh, Kingussie, Inverness-shire, Scotland. *Agent:* Towers Winant Ltd., Clerkenwell House, 45-47 Clerkenwell Green, London EC1R 0HT, England.

CAREER: Mountaineer and explorer; first woman to cross the Greenland ice cap. Trained as a radiographer in Edinburgh, Scotland, qualifying in 1953; went to New Zealand that same year, looking for higher hills to climb than those in the Scottish highlands; moved on to Australia, 1956, and spent two years traveling the continent, working at a variety of jobs "when out of pocket," including pearl diving and cooking for alligator hunters in the Northern Territory; returned to Scotland to help organize the Edinburgh Andean expedition in 1958; climbed the highest mountain in Peru and five other summits over 22,000 feet (married an expedition scientist the following year); member of the Scottish Spitsbergen expedition, 1960, two expeditions to Iceland, 1961 and 1962, and the Scottish Surinam expedition in South America, 1963; with her husband and two other men crossed the Greenland ice cap on skis, 1965; reached most northerly latitude achieved by a woman in 1968, on *Daily Telegraph* North Pole expedition; returned to Greenland with British Broadcasting Corp. to film Eskimo way of life, 1970-73; member of the British Ladies Himalayan expedition, 1974. Guide on tourist ship *Lindblad Explorer.* Lecturer and broadcaster.

MEMBER: Society of Authors, P.E.N., Scottish Ski Club (president). *Awards, honors: Daily Telegraph* travel award, December 1967, for a Greenland trip the Simpsons made with their children the previous summer; Mungo Park medal for exploration, 1971.

WRITINGS—Published by Gollancz, except as indicated: *Home Is a Tent* (autobiographical), 1964; *White Horizons* (autobiographical), 1967; *Due North!,* 1970; *Simpson, the Obstetrician: A Biography,* foreword by Ian Donald, 1972; *Greenland Summer: Based on a True Expedition,* 1973; *Armadillo Stew,* Blackie & Son, 1975; *Vikings, Scots, and Scraelings,* 1977; *Skisters: The Story of Scottish Skiing,* Landmark Press, 1982.

Under name M. L. Emslie; "Far and Near Readers" series on travel; published by W. & R. Chambers, 1960: *Journey to Amazon; Black Fellows and Buffaloes; Lapland Journey; Spitsbergen Adventure; Three in the Andes.*

Contributor to periodicals, including *National Geographic, Woman's Own, Sunday Express* (London), *She,* and *Guardian.*

WORK IN PROGRESS: A book on Himalayan journey; a biography of Lady Franklin; a biography of Simpson's aunt, Lady I. Emslie Hutton.

SIDELIGHTS: Believers in keeping the family together and exposing children to the simple primitive life, explorers Myrtle L. and Hugh W. Simpson took their firstborn son, Robin, then an infant, on the Spitzbergen expedition, a four-month sojourn six hundred miles from the North Pole. When Bruce was born in 1961 and Rona in 1962, they, too, accompanied their parents on the 1963 Surinam expedition to South America, living for a time in a Wai Ana Indian village deep in the rain forest. The three children were left behind on the crossing of the Greenland ice cap, but flew to join their parents at Stromfjord and spent the summer living in an Eskimo encampment. Sportswoman Simpson told *CA* she is "very involved in ski training of Scottish juniors to competition standard."

BIOGRAPHICAL/CRITICAL SOURCES: Myrtle L. Simpson, *Home Is a Tent,* Gollancz, 1964; Simpson, *White Horizons,* Gollancz, 1967.

* * *

SINCLAIR, Olga   1923-
(Ellen Clare)

PERSONAL: Born January 23, 1923, in Watton, England; daughter of Daniel Robert and Betty (Sapey) Waters; married Stanley George Sinclair (a headmaster), April 1, 1945; children: Michael, Alistair, Jeremy. *Education:* Educated in Norfolk, England. *Religion:* None. *Home and office:* Dove House Farm, Potter Heigham, Norfolk NR29 5LJ, England.

CAREER: Writer. Bank clerk, 1940-42; justice of the peace in county of Norfolk, England, 1966—; district councillor. *Wartime service:* Auxiliary Territorial Service, payclerk, 1942-45. *Member:* Society of Authors, Society of Women Writers and Journalists, Romantic Novelists Association. *Awards, honors:* Margaret Rhonda Award from Society of Authors, 1972, for research on Lithuanian immigrants.

WRITINGS—Novels, except as indicated: *Children's Games* (children's nonfiction), Basil Blackwell, 1961; *Gypsies* (children's nonfiction), Basil Blackwell, 1967; *Night of the Black Tower,* Lancer Books, 1968; *Man of the River,* R. Hale, 1968; *Dancing in Britain,* Basil Blackwell, 1970; *The Man at the Manor,* Dell, 1972; *Bitter Sweet Summer,* Simon & Schuster, 1972; *Wild Dreams,* R. Hale, 1973; *Toys and Toymaking* (children's nonfiction), Basil Blackwell, 1975; *My Dear Fugitive,* R. Hale, 1976; *Never Fall in Love,* R. Hale, 1977; *Master of Melthorpe,* R. Hale, 1979; *Gypsy Girl,* Collins, 1981; (under pseudonym Ellen Clare) *Ripening Vine Mills,* Mills & Boon, 1981.

WORK IN PROGRESS: Brides of Gretna Green.

SIDELIGHTS: Olga Sinclair writes *CA:* "[My] novel *Bitter Sweet Summer* was based on a camping holiday with my family in the summer of 1968, through East Germany to Czechoslovakia, that fateful summer when Czechoslovakia was invaded. Whilst in Prague the sound of machine gun fire in Wenceslas Square made us hasten for the Austrian border." She continues: "[My] continuing interest in the Romany race has resulted in another children's book *Gypsy Girl.* Based on fact, this highlights the problems and pleasures of these fascinating nomadic people."

* * *

SINOR, John   1930-

PERSONAL: Surname is pronounced *Sigh*-ner; born December 24, 1930, in Elk City, Okla.; son of J. D. (a chef) and Orvia (a sales manager; maiden name, Mitchell) Sinor; married Charlene Hodge, August 23, 1950 (divorced, 1968); married Diane

Faulk (a teacher and actress), January 19, 1970; children: Michael, Mark, Matthew, Madeline, Michelle; (six stepchildren). *Education:* Attended Modesto Junior College, 1953-59, and San Jose State University. *Politics:* Democrat. *Religion:* "Retired Catholic." *Residence:* San Diego, Calif. *Office: San Diego Tribune,* San Diego, Calif. 92112.

CAREER: Free-lance journalist, 1948—. Copley News Service, San Diego, Calif., author of weekly column, "John Sinor Column," syndicated to six hundred newspapers, and of daily column. Also author of daily column in *San Diego Tribune;* member of teaching staff at San Diego State University Extension. *Military service:* U.S. Air Force.

MEMBER: San Diego Press Club, Sigma Delta Chi. *Awards, honors:* National Headliners Award for best local column; California-Arizona Associated Press award for best feature; annual award for best feature story from Copley News Service, 1964; medal of honor from Freedoms Foundation, 1967.

*WRITINGS—*Published by Joyce Press, except as indicated: *Eleven Albatrosses in My Bluebird Tree,* 1976; *Finsterhall of San Pasqual,* 1976; *Ghosts of Cabrillo Lighthouse,* 1977; *Finsterhall Goes over the Wall,* 1978; *Some Ladies in My Life,* 1979; *Best of San Diego,* Rosebud Books, 1982.

SIDELIGHTS: John Sinor writes that he is "presently working on screenwriting and a desired growth in craft. I intend to write more books and screenplays and hope to do considerable more travel. Interest in daily newspapering is waning, but I intend to keep writing as long as I can."

MEDIA ADAPTATIONS: Finsterhall of San Pasqual was made into a film by Walt Disney Studios.

AVOCATIONAL INTERESTS: "I've tried all of them. Archery, fishing, hunting, golf, skin diving, photography. . . . Still do some of them occasionally."

* * *

SIRE, James W(alter)   1933-

PERSONAL: Born October 17, 1933, in Inman, Neb.; son of Walter Guy and Elsie (Mulford) Sire; married Marjorie Ruth Wanner (a laboratory technician), June 14, 1955; children: Carol, Eugene, Richard, Ann. *Education:* University of Nebraska, B.A., 1955; Washington State University, M.A., 1958; University of Missouri—Columbia, Ph.D., 1964. *Religion:* Christian. *Office:* Inter-Varsity Press, 5206 Main, Downers Grove, Ill. 60515.

CAREER: University of Missouri—Columbia, instructor in English, 1958-64; Nebraska Wesleyan University, Lincoln, assistant professor, 1964-66, associate professor of English, 1966-68; Inter-Varsity Press, Downers Grove, Ill., editor, 1968—. Part-time associate professor at Northern Illinois University, 1969-70, and Trinity College, Deerfield, Ill., 1971-75; visiting summer professor at University of Nebraska, 1966, University of Missouri, 1967, Regent College, 1977, and New College, Berkeley, 1983. *Military service:* U.S. Army, Ordnance, 1955-57; became first lieutenant. *Member:* Conference on Christianity and Literature, Milton Society, American Scientific Affiliation.

*WRITINGS—*Published by Inter-Varsity Press, except as indicated: (With Robert Beum) *Papers on Literature: Models and Methods,* Holt, 1970; *Program for a New Man,* 1973; *Jeremiah, Meet the Twentieth Century,* 1975; *The Universe Next Door,* 1976; *How to Read Slowly,* 1978; *Scripture Twisting,* 1980; *Beginning with God,* 1981.

SIDELIGHTS: James W. Sire told *CA:* ''Though I have written since 1976 a number of books, articles and reviews, *The Universe Next Door* remains my own favorite and, apparently, a favorite among readers. While the book concentrates on outlining seven basic worldviews, including Christian theism, naturalism, pantheism and the new consciousness, it does so from a uniquely Christian perspective. I have been pleased to see that over seventy colleges and universities, both state and private, have used this book as a text in a wide variety of courses from philosophy and religion, on the one hand, to English and history on the other. I left the university teaching world over ten years ago, but am pleased to see that my books have continued to keep me on campus. I have also been pleased that the Christian perspective in these books has been getting a hearing even on secular campuses.''

*   *   *

SKIDELSKY, Robert 1939-

PERSONAL: Surname is pronounced Ski-*del*-ski; born April 25, 1939, in Harbin, Manchuria; son of Boris J. and Galia (Sapelkin) Skidelsky. *Education:* Jesus College, Oxford, B.A., 1961; Nuffield College, Oxford, Ph.D., 1965. *Religion:* Church of England. *Home:* 54 Colebrooke Row, London N1, England. *Agent:* A. D. Peters & Co. Ltd., 10 Buckingham St., London WC2N 6BU, England. *Office:* Department of International Studies, University of Warwick, Coventry CV4 7AL, England.

CAREER: Oxford University, Nuffield College, Oxford, England, research fellow, 1965-68; British Academy, London, England, research fellow, 1968-70; Johns Hopkins University, School of Advanced International Studies, Washington, D.C., visiting and associate professor, 1970-76; Polytechnic of North London, London, head of department of history and philosophy, 1976-78; University of Warwick, Coventry, England, professor of international studies, 1978—. Visiting professor, Columbia University, 1973.

WRITINGS: Politicians and the Slump: The Labour Government of 1929-1931, Macmillan, 1967; (contributor) S. J. Woolf, editor, *European Fascism,* Weidenfeld & Nicolson, 1968, Random House, 1969, new edition, Weidenfeld & Nicolson, 1981; *English Progressive Schools,* Penguin, 1969; (editor with Vernon Bogdanor) *The Age of Affluence, 1951-1964,* Macmillan, 1970; *Oswald Mosley,* Holt, 1975; (contributor) Milo Keynes, editor, *Essays on John Maynard Keynes,* Cambridge University Press, 1975; (editor) *The End of the Keynesian Era,* Macmillan, 1977; (editor with Michael Holroyd) William Gerhardie, *God's Fifth Column: A Biography of the Age, 1890-1940,* Simon & Schuster, 1981; *John Maynard Keynes,* Macmillan, Volume I: *Hopes Betrayed, 1883-1920,* 1983. Contributor to *Times, Times Literary Supplement, New Society, Encounter, Spectator,* and other journals and newspapers.

WORK IN PROGRESS: Volume II of *John Maynard Keynes.*

AVOCATIONAL INTERESTS: Music, especially opera and piano; tennis and table tennis.

BIOGRAPHICAL/CRITICAL SOURCES: Listener, November 30, 1967; *Times Literary Supplement,* December 14, 1967, April 16, 1970; April 4, 1975, April 3, 1981; *Spectator,* December 20, 1969; *Books,* January, 1970; *New Statesman,* March 21, 1975; *Financial Times,* April 3, 1975; *London Times,* April 3, 1975; *New Society,* April 3, 1975; *New York Times Book Review,* May 11, 1975; *Encounter,* June, 1975; *Time,* June 9, 1975.

SLOBIN, Dan Isaac 1939-

PERSONAL: Born May 7, 1939, in Detroit, Mich.; son of Norval L. (a high school teacher) and Judith (a teacher; maiden name, Liepah) Slobin; married Ellen Wyzanski Holmes, December 23, 1962 (divorced, 1969); married Kathleen Gail Overin (a painter), May 23, 1969 (divorced); children: (second marriage) Heida Quisno Gordon (stepdaughter), Shem Alexander. *Education:* University of Michigan, B.A. (with honors), 1960; Harvard University, M.A., 1962, Ph.D., 1964. *Home:* 2323 Rose St., Berkeley, Calif. 94708. *Office:* Department of Psychology, University of California, Berkeley, Calif. 94720.

CAREER: Language Research, Inc., Cambridge, Mass., psycholinguistic consultant, 1961-62; Educational Services, Inc., Watertown, Mass., psychologist, 1962; University of California, Berkeley, assistant professor, 1963-67, associate professor, 1967-72, professor of psychology, 1972—, assistant research psychologist at Institute of Human Learning, 1963-67, associate research psychologist, 1967-72, research psychologist, 1972—.

MEMBER: International Association for the Study of Child Language (vice-president), International Association for Cross-Cultural Psychology, American Association for the Advancement of Science (fellow), Linguistic Society of America, Society for Research in Child Development, American Psychological Association, Society for the Psychological Study of Social Issues.

AWARDS, HONORS: U.S. Office of Education fellowship, 1966-67; grants from Ford Foundation, 1968-69, National Institute of Mental Health, 1969-76, Grant Foundation, 1972-75, Social Science Research Council, 1974-75, National Science Foundation, 1979-84, and United States-Israel Binational Science Foundation, 1982-85.

WRITINGS: (Editor and contributor) *A Field Manual for Cross-Cultural Study of the Acquisition of Communicative Competence,* Associated Students of the University of California Bookstore, University of California, 1967; (editor and contributor) *The Ontogenesis of Grammar: A Theoretical Symposium,* Academic Press, 1971; *Psycholinguistics,* Scott, Foresman, 1971, 2nd edition, 1979; *Leopold's Bibliography of Child Language: Revised and Augmented Edition,* University of Indiana Press, 1972; (editor with Josef Brozek) *Fifty Years of Soviet Psychology: An Historical Perspective,* International Arts and Sciences Press, 1972; (editor with Charles A. Ferguson, and contributor) *Studies of Child Language Development,* Holt, 1973; (editor with A. A. Aksu) *The Cross-linguistic Study of Language Acquisition,* Lawrence Earlbaum Associates, in press.

Contributor: Neil O'Connor, editor, *Present-Day Russian Psychology: A Symposium by Seven Authors,* Pergamon, 1966; F. Smith and G. A. Miller, editors, *The Genesis of Language: A Psycholinguistic Approach,* M.I.T Press, 1966; N. S. Endler, L. R. Boulter, and H. Osser, editors, *Contemporary Issues in Developmental Psychology,* Holt, 1968.

Giovanni B. Flores d'Arcais and Wilhelm J. M. Levelt, editors, *Advances in Psycholinguistics,* North-Holland Publishing, 1970; Celia B. Lavatelli, editor, *Language Training in Early Childhood Education,* University of Illinois Press, 1971; William O. Dingwall, editor, *A Survey of Linguistic Science,* Linguistics Program, University of Maryland, 1971; A. Bar-Adon and W. F. Leopold, editors, *Child Language: A Book of Readings,*

Prentice-Hall, 1971; T. Slama-Cazacu, editor, *La Psycholin-guistique: Lectures,* Klincksieck (Paris), 1972; Peter C. Dod-well, editor, *New Horizons in Psychology II,* Penguin, 1972; Serge Moscovici, editor, *The Psychosociology of Language,* Markham, 1972; David Krech, Richard S. Crutchfield, and Norman Livson, editors, *Elements of Psychology,* Knopf, 3rd edition (Slobin was not associated with earlier editions), 1974; Helen Leuninger, Max H. Miller, and Frank Mueller, editors, *Linguistik und Psychologie: Ein Reader,* Volume II: *Zur Psychologie der Sprachentwicklung,* Athenaeum, 1974; M. Jocic and S. Savic, editors, *Modeli u sintaksi decjeg govora,* Institut za Lingvistiku (Novi Sad, Yugoslavia), 1974.

Developmental Psychology Today, Random House, 2nd edition (Slobin was not associated with 1st edition), 1975; Eric H. Lenneberg and Elizabeth Lenneberg, editors, *Foundations of Language Development: A Multi-Disciplinary Approach,* Academic Press, 1975; John Macnamara, editor, *Language Learning and Thought,* Academic Press, 1977; Charles Schaefer, editor, *The Therapeutic Use of Child's Play,* Jason Aronson, 1977; Vladimir Honsa and M. J. Hardman-de-Bautista, editors, *Papers on Linguistics and Child Language: Ruth Hirsch Memorial Volume,* Mouton & Co., 1978; Lois Bloom, editor, *Selected Readings in Language Development,* Wiley, 1978; A. Sinclair, R. Jarvella, and Levelt, editors, *The Child's Conception of Language,* Springer-Verlag, 1978.

G. W. Shugar and M. Smoczynska, editors, *Bandania nad rozwojem jezyka dziecka: Wybor prac,* Panstwowe Wydawnictwo Naukowe, 1980; U. Bellugi and M. Studdert-Kennedy, editors, *Signed and Spoken Language: Biological Constraints on Linguistic Form,* Verlag Chemie, 1980; W. Deutsch, editor, *The Child's Construction of Language,* Academic Press, 1981; P. J. Hopper and S. A. Thompson, editors, *Syntax and Semantics,* Volume XV: *Studies in Transitivity,* Academic Press, 1982; L. R. Gleitman and E. Wanner, editors, *Language Acquisition: State of the Art,* Cambridge University Press, 1982.

P. Mussen, J. Conger, and J. Kagan, editors, *Readings in Child and Adolescent Psychology,* Harper, in press; Ross D. Parke and E. Mavis Heatherington, editors, *Child Psychology: Contemporary Readings,* 2nd edition, McGraw, in press; R. W. Andersen, editor, *The Relationship between Pidginization, Creolization, and Language Acquisition,* Newbury House, in press; Hopper, editor, *Tense and Aspect: Between Semantics and Pragmatics,* John Benjamins, in press; (author of preface) M. Beveridge, editor, *Children Thinking through Language,* Edward Arnold, in press; W. Chafe and J. Nichols, editors, *Evidentiality in Language,* Ablex Publishing, in press; H. Ahlqvist, editor, *Papers Presented at the Fifth International Conference on Historical Linguistics,* John Benjamins, in press.

Contributor of articles and reviews to language and psychology journals. Founding editor of *Soviet Psychology,* 1962-69; member of editorial board of *Cognition, Journal of Child Language, International Journal of Psycholinguistics, International Review of Slavic Linguistics, Journal of Verbal Learning and Verbal Behavior,* "Language, Thought, and Culture," a series, for Academic Press, and "Amsterdam Studies in the Theory and History of Linguistic Science."

WORK IN PROGRESS: Research on cross-linguistic investigation of early language and cognitive development, with a monograph expected to result; *Studies in Turkish Linguistics,* with K. Zimmer, for John Benjamins.

SIDELIGHTS: Dan Isaac Slobin's books and articles have been widely translated. He writes: "My basic interest is in the growth

of the human mind, specifically in the child's ability to reconstruct on his own the structure of his language and culture. This has involved me in widespread cross-cultural research on early language and cognitive development (United States, Soviet Union, Yugoslavia, Italy, Turkey, Israel, Spain). . . . I have also spent much time in interpreting Soviet psychological research for American audiences. . . . I addressed the International Congress of Psychology in Russian, in Moscow in 1966. . . . I have spent several years doing research in Turkey, at the same time becoming deeply involved in ethnomusicology (learning to play a Turkish stringed instrument, the saz) and Byzantine and Islamic art history. My current interests are in the representation of time and temporal experiences, the role of cognition in language universals, and the relations between child language development and historical language change."

*   *   *

SMALL, Ernest
    See LENT, Blair

*   *   *

SMEDES, Lewis B. 1921-

PERSONAL: Born August 20, 1921, in Michigan; son of Mele (a smith) and Rena (Benedict) Smedes; married Doris Dekker (a librarian), August 5, 1950; children: Catherine, Charles, John. *Education:* Calvin College, A.B., 1947; Calvin Theological Seminary, M.Div., 1950; Free University of Amsterdam, Ph.D., 1953. *Politics:* Democrat. *Religion:* Christian Reformed. *Home:* 475 Fairview, Sierra Madre, Calif. 91024. *Office:* Fuller Theological Seminary, 135 North Oakland, Pasadena, Calif. 91101.

CAREER: Calvin College, Grand Rapids, Mich., associate professor, 1957-60, professor of religion, 1960-68; Fuller Theological Seminary, Pasadena, Calif., professor of theology and ethics, 1968—. Guest professor at Free University of Amsterdam, 1976. President of Urban League of Grand Rapids, 1960-65. *Member:* American Society of Christian Ethics. *Awards, honors:* Award for editorial of the year from Church Press Association, 1976, for "The Case of Karen Quinlan."

WRITINGS—Published by Eerdmans, except as indicated: *The Incarnation,* KOK, 1954; *All Things Made New,* 1967; *Sex for Christians,* 1976; (editor) *God and the Good,* 1977; *Love within Limits,* 1979; *How Can It Be All Right When Everything Is All Wrong,* Harper, 1982; *Mere Morality: What God Expects of Ordinary People,* 1983. Co-editor of and contributor to *Reformed Journal.*

WORK IN PROGRESS: A book on the dynamics, the ethics, and the possibility of forgiveness.

*   *   *

SMITH, Bert Kruger 1915-

PERSONAL: Born November 18, 1915, in Wichita Falls, Tex.; daughter of Sam and Fania (a poet; maiden name, Feldman) Kruger; married Sidney S. Smith (a realtor), January 19, 1936; children: Sheldon Stuart, Jared Burt (deceased), Sarann (Mrs. John Campbell Huke). *Education:* University of Missouri, B.J., 1936; University of Texas, M.A., 1949. *Religion:* Jewish. *Home address:* P.O. Box 9116, Northwest Station, Austin, Tex. 78731. *Office address:* Hogg Foundation for Mental Health, P.O. Box 7998, University Station, Austin, Tex. 78712. *Agent:* c/o Beacon Press, 25 Beacon St., Boston, Mass. 02108.

CAREER: Former newspaperwoman in Wichita Falls, Tex.; *Coleman Daily Democratic Voice,* Coleman, Tex., associate publisher, 1951-52; University of Texas at Austin, associate editor of *Junior College Journal,* 1952-55, Hogg Foundation for Mental Health, beginning 1952, head of mental health education, 1955-81; writer. Texas and national delegate, 1981 White House Conference on Aging. Associate producer, "How to Be Human" television series, KLRN-TV, 1967. Member and past member of numerous councils and boards, including medical-professional committee, United Cerebral Palsy Association of Texas, 1973-74, Texas Commission on Organizations for the Handicapped, 1973-74, and planning committee, Texas Commission on Alcoholism. Chairman, Professional Information Committee, Texas Association for Children with Learning Disabilities. Consultant to school boards, churches, and government agencies.

MEMBER: National Association of Science Writers, Women in Communications, Texas Psychological Association (member of Professional Standards Review Committee), Authors Guild, Authors League of America, Delta Kappa Gamma (honorary member). *Awards, honors:* Winner of *Atlantic Monthly* Essay Contest, 1935; Southwest Writers Conference Novel Award, 1951, for manuscript, "Far from the Tree"; Theta Sigma Phi, Writer's Round-Up Authors Award, 1965, 1968, National Headliner, 1966; *Austin-American Statesman*'s Outstanding Career Woman Award, 1966; "Women Doers" Award, White House, 1968; Golden Key Award, Texas Association for Children with Learning Disabilities, 1970; 25th Annual Texas Writer's Round-Up Award, Women in Communications, 1974, for *Aging in America;* Texas Association of Homes for the Aging Distinguished Service Award, 1974; Texas Association for Retarded Citizens Recognition Award, 1975; Commissioner's Award for Volunteer Service, Texas Department of Mental Health and Mental Retardation, 1976; Church Women United Award as one of Austin's "Valiant Women," 1976; Most Outstanding Alumna, Alpha Epsilon Phi, 1977; National Conference of Christians and Jews Distinguished Service Award, 1978; "Outstanding Women in Texas" Award, American Association of University Women, 1979; Texas Psychological Association Award for contribution to psychology in Texas, 1979.

WRITINGS: (With Robert L. Sutherland, Wayne H. Holtzman, and Earl A. Koile) *Personality Factors on the College Campus,* Hogg Foundation for Mental Health (Austin), 1962; *No Language But a Cry,* Beacon Press, 1964; (editor) *And the Winds Blew,* Hogg Foundation for Mental Health, 1964; (with Sutherland) *Understanding Mental Health,* Van Nostrand, 1965; (editor) *Wilderness Road,* Hogg Foundation for Mental Health, 1965; *Your Non-Learning Child: His World Upside Down,* Beacon Press, 1968; *A Teaspoon of Honey* (fiction), Aurora Publishing, 1970; *Insights for Uptights,* American Universal Artforms, 1973; *Aging in America,* Beacon Press, 1973; *The Pursuit of Dignity: Some Living Alternatives for the Elderly,* Beacon Press, 1977.

Also author and editor of numerous pamphlets and booklets, most published by Hogg Foundation for Mental Health. Author of filmscripts, "In a Strange Land," produced by Hogg Foundation for Mental Health in cooperation with Texas Junior Chamber of Commerce, 1956, "Peace of Mind," 1976, and "Portraits of Aging," 1978, both Fred Miller Productions; interviewer, "The Human Condition" radio series, KUT-FM. Contributor of articles to numerous publications, including *International Journal of Religious Education, Single Parent Magazine, Texas Journal on Alcoholism, Presbyterian Theo-* logical *Seminary Bulletin, American Education,* and *Mental Hospitals.*

*   *   *

SMITH, Datus C(lifford), Jr.   1907-

PERSONAL: Born May 3, 1907, in Jackson, Mich.; son of Datus C. and Marion (Houston) Smith; married Dorothy Hunt, August 29, 1931 (died, 1973); children: Sandra (Mrs. Leonard E. Opdycke), Karen. *Education:* Princeton University, B.S., 1929. *Home:* 29 Wilson Rd., Princeton, N.J. 08540.

CAREER: Princeton University, Princeton, N.J., graduate manager of student employment, 1929-30, assistant editor, *Princeton Alumni Weekly,* 1930-31, editor, 1931-40, assistant managing editor, *Public Opinion Quarterly,* 1937-39, associate professor, 1943-47, professor, 1947-53; Princeton University Press, Princeton, assistant editor, 1940-41, editor, 1941-53, director, 1943-53; Franklin Book Programs, New York City, president, 1952-67, chairman, 1975-79. Vice-president and associate, John D. Rockefeller III Fund, Inc., 1967-73; coordinator of Japan philanthropy project, Council on Foundations, 1974-75; president of U.S. Committee for UNICEF, 1978-80, and U.S. Board on Books for Young People, 1980-83. Lecturer on book publishing, Radcliffe College and New York University. Member of U.S. National Commission for UNESCO, 1964-70; member of executive council, Center for the Book, Library of Congress. Trustee of Japan Center for International Exchange, United Board for Christian Higher Education in Asia, Haskins Laboratory, National Council for Children and Television, UNICEF, Asia Society, International School Service, and Center for Applied Linguistics. Consultant to numerous organizations, foundations, and institutions.

MEMBER: Association of American University Presses (president, 1947-48), Publishers Lunch Club (president, 1956-57), American Book Publishers Council (board of directors, 1948-51), National Book Committee, Princeton Club. *Awards, honors:* M.A., Princeton University, 1958; distinguished service award, Association of American University Presses, 1975.

WRITINGS: American Books in the Non-Western World: Some Moral Issues, New York Public Library, 1958; *The Land and People of Indonesia,* Lippincott, 1961, 3rd edition, 1983; (compiler with William E. Spaulding) *Books in West Africa,* Franklin Book, 1963; (with others) *A Guide to Book-Publishing,* Bowker, 1966; *The Economics of Book Publishing in Developing Countries,* UNESCO, 1977. Contributor to *Atlantic Monthly, Saturday Review, Foreign Affairs,* and numerous other periodicals.

SIDELIGHTS: Datus C. Smith writes *CA:* "One of the most valuable contributions of an author, I think, is to help the reader get a feeling of how other people live—whether in different walks of life in one's own country or in other lands and other cultures far away. I was lucky enough to have visited Indonesia often, and to have many Indonesian friends. So I felt it was a high privilege to write about that country and help my fellow Americans know something about that fascinating country on the other side of the world."

*   *   *

SMITH, Doris Buchanan   1934-

PERSONAL: Born June 1, 1934, in Washington, D.C.; daughter of Charles A. (a business executive) and Flora (an executive secretary; maiden name, Robinson) Buchanan; married R. Carroll Smith (a building contractor), December 18, 1954 (divorced, 1977); children: Robb, Willie, Randy, Susan, Matthew. *Education:* Attended South Georgia College. *Politics:* Independent. *Religion:* None. *Home and office address:* P.O. Box 1142, Brunswick, Ga. 31520. *Agent:* Paul R. Reynolds, Inc., 12 East 41st St., New York, N.Y. 10017.

CAREER: Writer, 1971—. *Awards, honors:* American Library Association notable book award and Child Study Association book of the year award, both 1973, Georgia children's book author of the year and Georgia general author of the year award, both from Dixie Council of Authors and Journalists, 1974, Georgia Children's Book Award, 1975, and Sue Hafner Award and Kinderbook Award, both 1977, all for *A Taste of Blackberries;* Georgia children's book author of the year award from Dixie Council of Authors and Journalists and notable children's book award from National Council for Social Studies, both 1975, for *Kelly's Creek;* Breadloaf fellowship, 1975; Georgia children's book author of the year award from Dixie Council of Authors and Journalists and best book of the year award from *School Library Journal*, both 1982, for *Last Was Lloyd.*

WRITINGS—For children: *A Taste of Blackberries,* Crowell, 1973; *Kick a Stone Home,* Crowell, 1974; *Tough Chauncey,* Morrow, 1974; *Kelly's Creek,* Crowell, 1975; *Up and Over,* Morrow, 1976; *Dreams and Drummers,* Crowell, 1978; *Salted Lemons,* Four Winds, 1980; *Last Was Lloyd,* Viking, 1981; *Moonshadow of Cherry Mountain,* Four Winds, 1982; *My First Hard Times,* Viking, 1983; *Karate Dancer,* Four Winds, in press.

WORK IN PROGRESS: The Christmas Witch, for Viking.

SIDELIGHTS: Doris Buchanan Smith told *CA:* "Currently I live half the year in that writer's dream—a cabin in the woods. The writing produced the cabin, however, not vice versa.

"Occasionally someone will speak of another writer as my 'competition' and I always blink in surprise. Other writers are my fellows, laboring and laughing over this mysterious thing of making life on paper. My only competition is myself, to do my own best at what I do best and to do a number of other things with a marvelously mad mediocrity.

"My main pursuit is my life, to live it richly and fully enough so there will be something to spill over onto the page. I love people with verve, who are thrilled both by a rafting trip or a slow walk in the woods, who are equally excited over a planned observation such as a moonshot or the unexpected one such as the crack of the first autumn acorn on the roof.

"Gaining the discipline to do my work and accepting the fact that the Muse works only in proportion to my endeavors was the hardest thing I've ever done in my life and also the best. To do work that one loves and to make it work is such a kick, and with the vision to see a direction and the discipline and effort to follow it, I think we can all have that kick. Mine happens to be writing and I happen to be doing it."

AVOCATIONAL INTERESTS: Reading, walking, canoeing, bicycling, the woods (especially the mountains), pottery, ceramic sculpture, and music.

*　　*　　*

SMITH, Hedrick (Laurence) 1933-

PERSONAL: Born July 9, 1933, in Kilmacolm, Scotland; son of American citizens, Sterling L. (in management) and Phebe (an artist; maiden name, Hedrick) Smith; married Ann Bickford (an educator), June 29, 1957; children: Laurel, Jennifer, Scott, Lesley. *Education:* Williams College, B.A., 1955; graduate study at Balliol College, Oxford, 1955-56, and Harvard University, 1969-70. *Home:* 2208 Washington Ave., Apt. 101, Silver Springs, Md. 20910. *Agent:* Julian Bach Literary Agency, Inc., 747 Third Ave., New York, N.Y. 10017. *Office: New York Times,* 1717 K St. N.W., Washington, D.C. 20036.

CAREER: United Press International, New York City, reporter in Tennessee, 1959-61, Georgia, 1961-62, and at Cape Canaveral, 1962; *New York Times,* New York City, reporter in Washington, D.C., 1962-63, Saigon (now Ho Chi Minh City), South Vietnam, 1963-64, Cairo, Egypt, 1964-66, diplomatic correspondent in Washington, D.C., 1966-71, bureau chief in Moscow, U.S.S.R., 1971-74, deputy national editor in New York City, 1975-76, bureau chief, 1976-79, and chief correspondent, 1979—, in Washington, D.C. *Military service:* U.S. Air Force, 1956-59. *Member:* White House Correspondents Club, Gridiron Club. *Awards, honors:* Fulbright scholar, 1955-56; Nieman Fellow at Harvard University, 1969-70; member of Pulitzer Prize winning reporting team, 1972; Pulitzer Prize for International Reporting, 1974; Litt.D. from Williams College, 1975; Overseas Press Club Book Award, 1976, for *The Russians.*

WRITINGS: (With Neil Sheehan, E. W. Kenworthy, and others) *The Pentagon Papers,* Quadrangle, 1971; (contributor) Eugene Fodor, *Fodor's Soviet Union, 1974-1975: A Definitive Handbook of the U.S.S.R. for Foreign Visitors,* McKay, 1974; *The Russians,* New York Times Co., 1976, revised edition, 1983; (with Leonard Silk, Adam Clymer, Richard Burt, and Robert Lindsey) *Reagan: The Man, the President,* Macmillan, 1980; (contributor) *Counterattack: The U.S. Response to Japan,* Times Books, 1983. Contributor to magazines, including *Atlantic, Saturday Review,* and *Reader's Digest.*

SIDELIGHTS: During his years as Moscow bureau chief for the *New York Times,* Hedrick Smith lived as close to the Russians as his position allowed. Determined to explore the lives of Soviet citizens, he enrolled his children in Russian schools, shopped where average families bought their limited supplies of goods and produce, and actively sought both Russians' and Westerners' reactions to events and conditions in the U.S.S.R. "I can testify that getting Smith to sit down at his own dinner table in Moscow was a most difficult challenge," reports fellow American writer Allen H. Kassof in *New Republic.* "When he finally did quit work to put in an appearance after dessert, he would give his guests an inquisitorial grilling through the small hours of the morning on life and times in the U.S.S.R." Smith relates his experiences and findings in *The Russians,* a book written, he says, "to convey . . . the human quotient, the texture and fabric of the personal lives of the Russian people."

Smith's tone as he views the country through the activities and concerns of its populace is personal rather than strictly documentary. This focus, several reviewers feel, adds a vitality to the work that similar Western accounts of the Soviet Union lack. "Smith's greatest appeal is his ability to weave together a colorful and persuasive portrait of Russians as people, rich in detail and sensitive to nuance," Kassoff claims, adding that "his warm and sympathetic accounts of family life, of love and friendship in an imposing social and political environment, and of patience and endurance in the face of perennial shortages and mismanagement are among the best I have seen." Commenting in *Newsweek,* Paul D. Zimmerman agrees that the author writes "vividly and with a greater feel for the texture of everyday life" than other commentators on contemporary

Russia. For instance, not only does Smith "describe the inevitable shortfalls of consumer goods in the Kremlin's planned economy, but [he] also jams the reader into the labyrinth of lines at a local Soviet supermarket, coaching him on how to play nine queues at once."

Dividing the book into sections on "The People," "The System," and "The Issues," Smith presents a varied compendium of information and ideas. Most critics approve of the breadth of his endeavor and note that he includes numerous minor, but revealing, details. "He has an unerring reporter's eye and ear for small but significant nuances of social and political behavior," writes Adam B. Ulum in *Saturday Review*. "Smith digs out and makes the most of the skimpiest news item he can get his hands on." In the *New York Times Book Review*, Philip Knightley agrees that the author has "a card-index mind: nothing that happened in his presence in the U.S.S.R. escaped his notice or his notebook." While Smith's detailed "news" items provide "the pleasures of armchair tourism—trips to communal baths, factories, restaurants, racetracks . . . [and] resorts," as Zimmerman points out, the author also explores "the liberal mores at the universities, the primitive state of contraception . . . and the drastic effects of limited family-living space." He approaches these and other potentially political topics—including the status of women, Jews, and dissidents—as familiarly as he discusses lighter subjects and, as V. S. Pritchett writes in the *New Yorker*, "enlivens his analysis with portraits of people he has known." Adds Christopher Lehmann-Haupt of the *New York Times*, "Though Mr. Smith is not after the big story, we begin to glimpse a big picture—a picture of what makes the Soviet Union tick in these days of post-Stalinist repression, a picture of what is likely to happen in the future."

Smith's nonacademic manner, however, is considered a weakness by several reviewers who feel that "the personal and anecdotal method provides much information; but the frightening implications of the experiences . . . often remain obscure," as Gennady Shmakov and John Malmstad claim in *New York Review of Books*. Similarly, in a *Harpers* magazine review George Feifer comments that the book covers a wide range of material but feels that its analysis is "not deep enough." Implying that this diffuseness might result from Smith's "passionate attachment to the human qualities of existence" in Russia, Kassof points out that *The Russians* is not intended to offer in-depth political or psychological analysis. He believes that, given Smith's attachment to the country's people, it is all the more significant that the author "in fact produced a very gloomy book, and his time in the Soviet Union made him more, not less, pessimistic about prospects for the future."

Despite their reservations, Shmakow and Malmstad declare the book to be "full of solidly documented reporting on life in Russia and much information which no tourist can ever hope to learn. Anyone interested in Russia," they summarize," can read [it] with profit." States Lehmann-Haupt, "The result of [Smith's] accretion of detail is not only highly entertaining and readable, but instructive as well." Echoing these sentiments, several other reviewers note that the author offers both a lively narrative and a sound knowledge of Soviet studies in the West. This combination, many believe, creates a book of value to both the uninitiated and scholars of Russian society. Yet critics remain divided on what they feel is, in the final analysis, the book's main strength. Some, like Feifer, believe the author's greatest achievement "is to have de-enigmatized Russia, vividly, sensibly and comprehensively." Others emphasize Smith's sensitivity to "the human quotient" and commend his exploration of the average Russian's life. Concludes Knightley, "For

the first time, I now know something about today's Russians as a people."

AVOCATIONAL INTERESTS: Foreign travel, skiing, sailing, tennis, wine.

BIOGRAPHICAL/CRITICAL SOURCES: Hedrick Smith, *The Russians*, New York Times Co., 1976; *New York Times*, January 8, 1976, January 9, 1976, July 30, 1976; *Newsweek*, January 19, 1976; *Wall Street Journal*, January 19, 1976, December 8, 1976; *New York Times Book Review*, January 25, 1976; *Christian Science Monitor*, January 28, 1976; *Saturday Review*, February 7, 1976; *Harpers*, March, 1976; *New York Review of Books*, April 1, 1976; *New Yorker*, April 26, 1976; *New Review*, May 1, 1976; *Time*, May 10, 1976; *Virginia Quarterly Review*, summer, 1976; *Spectator*, June 5, 1976; *America*, June 12, 1976, January 29, 1977; *Commonweal*, June 18, 1976; *New Statesman*, December 9, 1977.

—*Sketch by Nancy Hebb*

*   *   *

SMITH, Marion Jaques 1899-

PERSONAL: Born November 16, 1899, in Haverhill, Mass.; daughter of Frank Waterman (a contractor and carpenter) and Edna Lee (Parks) Jaques; married H. Kenneth Smith (a marine electrician), November 9, 1935; children: Lucy Lee (Mrs. Robert S. Trial, Jr.). *Education:* University of Maine, B.S., 1932; also attended Gorham Normal School, Clark University, Boston University, and Harvard University. *Politics:* Conservative Republican. *Religion:* Episcopal. *Home:* 893 High St., Bath, Me. 04530.

CAREER: Rural teacher in Maine, 1920-21, helping teacher, 1923; elementary school teacher in West Bath, Me., 1925-26, social studies teacher in Bath, Me., 1926-30, elementary school teacher in Bath, 1931-39; Bath Junior High School, Bath, social studies teacher, 1954-63; writer, 1963—. Member of local citizens' advisory committee. *Member:* National Federation of Business and Professional Women's Clubs (honorary member), National Teachers Association, Maine Teachers Association, Bath-Brunswick Business and Professional Women's Club (vice-regent), Bath Retired Teachers Association, Brunswick Retired Teachers Association, Daughters of the American Revolution (vice-regent of local chapter), Daughters of American Colonists.

WRITINGS: A History of Maine: From Wilderness to Statehood, Falmouth Publishing House, 1949, 2nd edition, Bond Wheelwright, 1960; *On the Way North: A Mother Bear's Troubled Trip* (self-illustrated juvenile), Bond Wheelwright, 1967, 2nd edition, 1976; *Pokey and Timothy of Stonehouse Farm* (self-illustrated juvenile), Bond Wheelwright, 1973; *William King*, Down East, 1980; *A Short History of Grace Episcopal Church*, [Bath, Maine], 1983.

Also author of *Maine and the Revolution*, written for Maine's Bicentennial Committee, 1976.

SIDELIGHTS: Marion Jaques Smith grew up in Bath, Maine, and still lives there. She spent her childhood and young adult years living on her parents' farm or at the home of a great aunt and uncle, who refreshed her knowledge of local history. She began writing her own history of Maine when she found that standard elementary texts were "old and dull," and eventually for younger children made several stories, handprinted and illustrated in pen and ink, that taught history through the eyes of a little black bear. These stories have been collected and published as *On the Way North.*

*   *   *

SMITH, Michael (Townsend) 1935-

PERSONAL: Born October 5, 1935, in Kansas City, Mo.; son of Lewis Motter (a merchant) and Dorothy Jane (Pew) Smith. *Education:* Yale University, student, 1953-56. *Home:* 23 Cross St., Westerly, R.I. 02891. *Office address:* Zuckermann Harpsichords, Inc., Box 121, Stonington, Conn. 06378.

CAREER: Village Voice (newspaper), New York City, theatre critic, 1959-74, associate editor, 1962-65, Obie award judge, 1962-68, 1972-74; Bobbs-Merrill Co. Inc., New York City, director of Theatre Genesis, beginning 1971; Zuckermann Harpsichords, Inc., instrument maker, 1974-77, 1979—.

Manager and co-director, Sundance Festival Theatre, Upper Black Eddy, Pa., 1966-68; producer and co-director, Caffe Cino (cafe theatre), New York City, 1968. Director of plays (produced in New York City, except as indicated), including: "I Like It," 1963; Gertrude Stein, "Three Sisters Who Are Not Sisters," 1964; Sam Shepard, "Icarus' Mother," 1965; Soren Agenoux, "Charles Dickens' 'Christmas Carol,'" 1967; "Vorspeil nach Marienstein," 1967; H. M. Kontoukas, "With Creatures Make My Way," 1967; Ronald Tavel, "The Life of Juanita Castro," Denver, 1968; Maria Irene Fornes, "Dr. Kheal," Denver, 1968; Emanuel Peluso, "Hurricane of the Eye," 1969; "Captain Jack's Revenge," 1970; "Peas," Denver, 1971; Jean-Claude van Itallie, "Eat Cake," Denver, 1971; "Country Music," 1971; Tavel, "Bigfoot," 1972; Fornes, "Tango Palace," 1973; Samuel Becket, "Krapp's Last Tape," Taos, 1977; Edward Albee, "The Zoo Story," Taos, 1977; Arthur Laurents, "West Side Story," Taos, 1978. Instructor at New School for Social Research, 1964-65, Project Radius, 1972, and Hunter College of the City University of New York, 1972.

AWARDS, HONORS: Brandeis University creative arts citation, 1965; *Village Voice* Off-Broadway (Obie) award, 1972, for direction of "Country Music"; Rockefeller Foundation award in playwriting, 1976.

WRITINGS: (Editor with Nick Orzel, and author of introduction) *Eight Plays from Off-Off Broadway,* Bobbs-Merrill, 1966; *Theatre Trip,* Bobbs-Merrill, 1968; *Theatre Journal, Winter 1967,* University of Missouri Press, 1968; (editor) *The Best of Off-Off Broadway,* Dutton, 1969; *More Plays from Off-Off Broadway,* Bobbs-Merrill, 1972; (contributor) *American Dreams: The Imagination of Sam Shepard,* Performing Arts Journal Publications, 1981; *American Baby* (poem), Fast Books, 1983.

Plays: "I Like It" (first produced in New York City, 1963), published in *Kulchur,* 1963; "The Next Thing" (first produced in New York City, 1966), published in *The Best of Off-Off Broadway,* edited by the author, Dutton, 1969; (with Johnny Dodd and Remy Charlip) "More! More! I Want More!," first produced in New York City, 1966; (with Dodd and Ondine) "Vorspiel nach Marienstein," first produced in New York City, 1967.

"Captain Jack's Revenge" (first produced Off-Off Broadway at Cafe La Mama, March, 1970, produced on the West End at Royal Court Theatre, January 22, 1971), published in *New American Plays 4,* edited by William M. Hoffmann, Hill & Wang, 1971; "A Dog's Love" (opera; music by John Herbert

McDowell), first produced in New York City, 1971; "Tony," first produced in New York City, 1971; "Peas," first produced in Denver, 1971; "Country Music" (first produced in New York City, 1971), published in *The Off-Off Broadway Book,* edited by Albert Poland and Bruce Mailman, Bobbs-Merrill, 1972; "Double Solitaire," first produced in Denver, 1973; "Prussian Suite," first produced in New York City, 1974; "A Wedding Party," first produced in Denver, 1974; "Cowgirl Ecstasy," first produced in Denver, 1976; "Life Is Dream" (translation of Calderon de la Barca's "La Vida es Sueno"), first produced in Taos, 1979.

Also author of plays "Heavy Pockets," 1981, "Turnip Family Secrets," 1982, and "One Hundred Thousand Songs." Music critic for the *Day,* New London, Conn., 1982—.

Occasional contributor to *New York Times, Drama Review, Plays and Players,* and other periodicals. Art editor, *Taos News,* 1978-79.

WORK IN PROGRESS: "Agatha," translation of a play by Marguerite Duras.

SIDELIGHTS: Michael Smith told *CA:* "I wanted to be a writer because I wanted a writer's life: to be able to work anywhere, to play and work in the same gesture, to travel, to be able to use many interests, to live on the freedom of imagination. I've had quite a number of plays produced, but not in a context of commercial or popular success. I've written novels which haven't been published. Criticism is what I get the most reinforcement for, because it's useful to other people. The main theme of my writing is individual consciousness in the context of the family and of historical circumstance.

"As a theatre critic, I went to the theatre several times a week for fifteen years. I went often to Europe in the sixties, seeing theatre everywhere I went. I spent two months in India and Southeast Asia in 1970 seeing traditional theatre.

"My major area of interest as a critic has been contemporary experimental theatre, originally from a more or less literary point of view, then from the vantage of a theatre worker (I have worked extensively in stage lighting and production and have directed plays by myself and other contemporary dramatists). A major part of my life is music: Since 1974 I have made my livelihood as an instrument maker, building harpsichords and forte pianos and producing instrument kits . . . for Zuckermann Harpsichords, Inc. . . . . My family and job are demanding and rewarding. But writing defines me."

*   *   *

SMITH, Ray 1915-

PERSONAL: Born May 1, 1915, Minneapolis, Minn.; son of Walter R. and Emily (Lundin) Smith. *Education:* Hamline University, B.A., 1937; University of Minnesota, M.A. in American Studies, 1947, M.A.L.S., 1957. *Home address:* Route 1, Box 216A, Vashon, Wash. 98070.

CAREER: University of Minnesota (now University of Minnesota-Twin Cities), Minneapolis, instructor in English, 1946-52; truck farmer, graduate student, creative writing teacher, Minneapolis, Minnesota, 1953-56; Mason City Public Library, Mason City, Iowa, librarian, 1957-66; Mason City Community College, Mason City, Iowa, member of adult education advisory board, 1964-66; Dakota-Scott Library System, West St. Paul, Minn., director, 1966-68; Immaculate Heart College, Los Angeles, Calif., associate professor, 1968-71; Superior Public Library, Superior, Wis., director, 1971-75; University of Minnesota-Duluth, visiting lecturer in English, 1975-83. Lecturer at University of Chicago, Chicago, Ill., graduate library school, August, 1962, University of Minnesota Library School, Minneapolis, summer sessions, 1963, 1964, and University of Iowa, Iowa City, library workshop, 1965. Member of writing panel, Wisconsin Arts Board, 1980-82; poetry consultant, *Wisconsin Academy Review,* 1981-83. *Military service:* U.S. Army, 1941-45; became first lieutenant; awarded Silver Star.

MEMBER: American Library Association (member of Notable Books Council, 1964-68), Iowa Library Association (chairman of Intellectual Freedom Committee, 1959-60; vice president and director of district meetings, 1962-63; president, 1963-64). *Awards, honors:* Guarantors Prize, *Poetry* magazine, 1945; Wisconsin Arts Board fellowship in poetry, 1976 and 1978.

WRITINGS: No Eclipse (poems), Prometheus Press, 1945; (contributor) Helmut Olles, editor, *Lexicon of Contemporary Literature,* Verlag Herder (Freiburg), 1960; (contributor) Carnovky and Winger, editors, *The Medium-Sized Public Library: Its Status and Future,* University of Chicago Press, 1963; (contributor) Olles, editor, *Kleines Lexikon,* Verlag Herder, 1964; (contributor) Walter Lowenfels, editor, *Poets of Today,* International Publishers, 1964; *The Greening Tree* (poems), James D. Thueson (Minneapolis), 1965; *October Rain* (poems), Mary Bauer, 1969.

The Deer on the Freeway (poems), Dakota Press, 1973; *Permanent Fires: Review of Poetry, 1958-1973,* Scarecrow, 1975; *The Yellow Lamp* (poems), Uzzano, 1978; (translator with Mara Smith) *Some Yellow Flowers,* Kirk Press, 1978; *The Second Pond,* Kirk Press, 1979; *Weathering* (poems), Uzzano, 1980.

Work represented in anthologies, including *From the Belly of the Shark,* edited by Walter Lowenfels, Random House, 1973, and *For Neruda/For Chile,* edited by Lowenfels, Beacon Press, 1975. Reviewer, *Library Journal,* 1958-69. Poetry editor, *North Country Anvil* (Minnesota bimonthly magazine). Contributor to *Library Quarterly, Wilson Library Bulletin, Poetry, Epoch,* and other periodicals.

WORK IN PROGRESS: The Breathless Aisle, a collection of poems.

AVOCATIONAL INTERESTS: Fishing, camping.

*   *   *

SMITH, Ruth Schluchter 1917-

PERSONAL: Born October 18, 1917, in Detroit, Mich.; daughter of Clayton John and Gertrude (Kastler) Schluchter; married Thomas Guilford Smith (a manufacturers' representative and engineer), September 28, 1946; children: Pemberton III. *Education:* Wayne University (now Wayne State University), A.B., 1939; University of Michigan, A.B. in L.S., 1942. *Politics:* Republican. *Religion:* Methodist. *Home:* 5304 Glenwood Rd., Bethesda, Md. 20014. *Office:* National Technical Information Service, 5285 Port Royal Rd., Springfield, Va. 22161.

CAREER: Detroit Public Library, Detroit, Mich., junior librarian, 1936-43; University of Pennsylvania, Moore School of Electrical Engineering, Philadelphia, research assistant, 1946-47; Bethesda Methodist Church Library, Bethesda, Md., librarian, 1955-61; Institute for Defense Analyses, Arlington, Va., reference librarian and chief of reader services, 1961-65, chief of unclassified library section, 1965-67, head librarian, 1967-75, manager of technical information services, 1975-81; National Technical Information Service, Springfield, Va., chief

of office of customer services, 1981—. *Military service:* U.S. Naval Reserve, Women Accepted for Volunteer Emergency Service (WAVES), 1943-46; became lieutenant, junior grade. *Member:* Church and Synagogue Library Association (founding member and president, 1967-68; member of executive board, 1967-77), Special Libraries Association (chairman of aerospace division, 1975-76, library management division, 1978-79, and division cabinet, 1980-81; member of board of directors, 1981-83), American Society for Information Science. *Awards, honors:* John Cotton Dana Award, School Library Association, 1979.

WRITINGS: Outline for Building Vitality in Your Church Library, Church Library Council, 1961; (with Robert Collins) *Lasers* (bibliography), Institute for Defense Analyses, 1963; (with Jay Schwartz, J. Kaiser, and Joseph Aein) *Multiple Access to a Common Radio Repeater* (bibliography), Institute for Defense Analyses, 1964; *Publicity for a Church Library,* Zondervan, 1966; (contributor) Allen Kent and Harold Lancour, editors, *Encyclopedia of Library and Information Science,* Volume IV, Dekker, 1970; *Workshop Planning,* Church and Synagogue Library Association, 1972; *Getting the Books off the Shelves,* Hawthorn, 1975; (with Claudia Hannaford) *Promotion Planning,* Church and Synagogue Library Association, 1975; *Cataloging Books Step-by-Step,* Church and Synagogue Library Association, 1977; *Cataloging Made Easy,* Seabury, 1978; *Running a Library,* Seabury, 1982.

Author of scripts for video presentations. Contributor to *Special Libraries, Library Journal, New Christian Advocate,* and other periodicals.

SIDELIGHTS: Ruth Schluchter Smith told *CA:* "A life long enthusiasm for libraries, seasoned by an early interest in journalism, just naturally gave birth to writing—most of it interpretive reporting based on experience in the library field. As an administrator of a scientific research library, I have dealt with the problems of coping with federal government information sources and services, organizing user feedback groups, and participating in cooperative library networks. As the chairman of a church library committee and formerly a church librarian, I have described the challenges of organizing and administering a church library ministry, promoting and publicizing its services, and inspiring or training volunteer workers through workshops and interfaith library fellowship activities."

*   *   *

SMITH, Sally Liberman 1929-

PERSONAL: Born May 7, 1929, in New York, N.Y.; daughter of I. (a businessman) and Bertha B. Liberman; married Robert Solwin Smith, March 12, 1953 (divorced); children: Randall Alan, Nicholas Lee, Gary Gordon. *Education:* Bennington College, B.A., 1950; New York University, M.A., 1955. *Politics:* Democrat. *Home:* 3216 Cleveland Ave. N.W., Washington, D.C. 20008. *Office:* Lab School of Washington, 4759 Reservoir Rd. N.W., Washington, D.C. 20007; and School of Education, American University, Washington, D.C. 20016.

CAREER: Lab School, Washington, D.C., founder and director, 1967—; American University, School of Education, Washington, D.C., associate professor, 1976-82, professor of special education, 1982—, director of learning disabilities program, 1976—. Free-lance writer and lecturer in field of social and psychological problems and elementary education. Designer of experimental projects using the arts as the route to teaching elementary school children, including the Potomac summer project, 1966, and the Friends-Morgan Project, 1967. Member of board, National Child Research Center, 1964-67; member of congressional task force on the definition of developmental disabilities, 1976-77; member of national advisory board, Maryland State Department of Education, 1979—; member of professional advisory board, National Association of Children with Learning Disabilities, 1983—. *Member:* Pan-Pacific Southeast Asia Women's Group (program chairman, 1963-65).

AWARDS, HONORS: Named one of ten outstanding young women of the year by *Mademoiselle* (magazine), 1955, for work in mental health field; National Endowment for the Arts grant, 1977; Bennington Award, 1980, for outstanding contributions to education; Arts for the Handicapped award, 1980; Council for Exceptional Children award, 1981, for outstanding achievement; named Washingtonian of the Year by *Washingtonian* (magazine), 1982; Jefferson Award finalist, American Institute of Public Service, 1982.

WRITINGS: A Child's Guide to a Parent's Mind, Schuman, 1951; *Nobody Said It's Easy,* Macmillan, 1965; (contributor) Rachel Cohn, *L'Apprentissage precoce de la lecture,* Presses Universitaires de France, 1977; *No Easy Answers: The Learning Disabled Child* (monograph), U.S. Government Printing Office, 1978, revised and expanded textbook edition published as *No Easy Answers: Teaching the Learning Disabled Child,* Winthrop Publishing, 1979, revised and expanded mass market edition published as *No Easy Answers: The Learning Disabled Child at Home and at School,* Bantam, 1981; (contributor) Ann M. Shaw and C. J. Stevens, editors, *Drama, Theatre, and the Handicapped,* American Theatre Association, 1979; (author of foreword) M. Behr, A. Snyder, and A. Clopton, *Drama Integrates Basic Skills: Lesson Plans for the Learning Disabled,* C. C Thomas, 1979.

Also author and producer of films documenting work at the Lab School. Contributor of articles to popular and professional publications.

WORK IN PROGRESS: A book on educating children with learning disabilities in unorthodox ways.

SIDELIGHTS: In the spring of 1967, Sally Liberman Smith was faced with the task of finding help for her son Gary, a seven-year-old first-grader with learning disabilities so severe his teachers predicted he would never be able to read. She began her search by inquiring at several alternative schools in the Washington, D.C., area. To her dismay, Smith soon discovered that although there were programs designed for mentally retarded and emotionally disturbed children, none existed for those children who, like her son, were of average or above average intelligence but had difficulty organizing and processing information received from the senses.

Among the places Smith visited during her search was the Kingsbury Center, a Washington-based institution devoted to the diagnosis and treatment of children's and adults' academic problems. Officials at the center understood Smith's frustration but could offer little assistance; they had neither the money nor the space to establish the type of program Gary Smith and other learning-disabled children needed. Several months after her visit there, however, Smith received a call from Kingsbury's director informing her that the center had been offered use of a townhouse that was roomy enough to accommodate a small school. Would she be interested in making arrangements for some classes for learning-disabled students? Smith hesitated at first, wondering how she, a nonprofessional, could possibly hope to run such a program. But when she realized

that her son's future might very well depend on her decision, she agreed to try. "It was an act of a desperate mother," Smith recalled in an interview with *People*'s Gary Clifford.

Smith's first priority as director of the new Lab School of the Kingsbury Center was to develop a curriculum that would benefit the greatest number of learning-disabled children, many of whom suffer from a variety of conditions. Despite their individual differences, most of these children exhibit a basic inability to distinguish between relevant and irrelevant information. "The child is literally consumed by disorder," Smith explained to Clifford. "His brain gets overloaded easily. We tend to think of distractedness as not paying attention. But [these children] are paying attention to too many things at once." As a result, she notes in a *New York Times* article by Fred M. Hechinger, "teaching the learning-disabled child the approach to a task is as important as teaching the task itself."

To this end, Smith has made the arts—music, dance, drama, wood-working, and even film-making—central to her philosophy of education because they require children to coordinate hand and eye movements, think in terms of sequences, pay close attention to detail, and associate certain sounds and symbols. Once these skills are mastered, they can then be transferred to academic situations to assist the child in learning to read, write, and do arithmetic. Students at the Lab School spend about half of their day in art programs and the other half in the classroom.

Another unusual feature of the Lab School curriculum is the concept of the "academic club." Since many learning-disabled children have trouble relating the abstract to the concrete, Smith reasoned that they could be taught about history, social organization, art, and other subjects while pretending to be cave dwellers, Egyptians, Greek and Roman gods, and people of the Middle Ages or the Renaissance. Club members do all the necessary research, then act out the appropriate roles, progressing from one type of club to another as they grow older. An added benefit of the system, Smith is quick to point out, is the sense of belonging the children experience; for many of them, it is the first time they have not felt like outsiders.

Since its opening in September, 1967, the Lab School (which became independent from the Kingsbury Center in July, 1982) has helped over ninety percent of its more than 650 students return to regular classrooms, where they have managed to keep up with their peers and graduate from high school. Many of them are now in college or are college-bound, and some have gone on to graduate school. Though initially somewhat skeptical, parents and educators are now convinced that Smith personifies the kind of dedication, determination, and innovativeness it takes to help a learning-disabled child. Her attitude may, at times, seem unsympathetic; as she told Hechinger, "when parents recognize that their child has learning disabilities, they have the same choices as the child: to pity themselves or to do the best with what he has and work hard at it." But she is well aware of the anger and despair these parents feel as they watch their children struggle—and fail—to learn as most other children do. After all, Smith explained to Earl and Miriam Selby in a *Reader's Digest* article, "I have already been where they are."

AVOCATIONAL INTERESTS: Theater, dance, world affairs, jazz, movies.

BIOGRAPHICAL/CRITICAL SOURCES: New York Times, July 31, 1979; *People,* July 28, 1980; *Reader's Digest,* December, 1981; *Washington Post,* December 18, 1982, September 8, 1983.

SMITH, Samuel 1904-

PERSONAL: Born December 24, 1904, in Meretz, Lithuania; came to the United States in 1906, naturalized in 1914; son of Louis (a merchant) and Lillian (Samuelson) Smith. *Education:* Attended Harvard University, 1921-24; New York University, B.S., M.A., Ph.D., 1933. *Politics:* Democrat. *Religion:* Hebrew. *Home address:* R.D. 1, Box 220, Monroe, N.Y. 10950.

CAREER: A. Smith & Bros. (importers), New York City, partner, 1924-30; music teacher in New York, 1934-35; research assistant for New York State Board Regents Inquiry, 1937-38; Acorn Publishing Co., New York City, research director, 1939-41; superintendent, National Education Programs, 1941-43; Dryden Press, New York City, editor, 1944; Hinds, Hayden & Eldredge, New York City, editor, 1945-49; Barnes & Noble, Inc., New York City, editor-in-chief, 1950-69. *Member:* Phi Delta Kappa, Masons.

WRITINGS: (With Robert K. Speer) *Supervision in the Elementary School,* Dryden, 1938; (with Speer and George R. Cressman) *Education and Society: An Introduction to Education for a Democracy,* Dryden, 1942; *Ideas of the Great Educators,* Harper, 1979; *Ideas of the Great Psychologists,* Harper, 1983.

Published by Barnes & Noble: (Editor with others) *An Outline of Educational Psychology,* 1934, 6th edition, 1970; (with Arthur W. Littlefield and others) *Best Methods of Study: A Practical Guide for the Student,* 1938, 2nd edition published as *An Outline of Best Methods of Study,* 1951, 4th edition published under original title, 1970; (contributor with Robert E. Park and others) *Principles of Sociology,* 1939, 3rd edition, 1969; (editor with Bernard Joseph Stern) *Understanding the Russians: A Study of Soviet Life and Culture,* 1947; (contributor) *The Constitution of the United States,* 1956; (with others) *Atlas of Human Anatomy,* 5th edition, edited by M. F. Ashley Montagu, 1959, 6th edition, 1961; (contributor) *American Government,* 1962; *Read It Right and Remember What You Read,* 1970.

Research director and co-author of National Achievement Tests, 1939—; general editor of "College Outline" series and "Everyday Handbook" series, 1956—. Also editor of a series of biographies of educators published by Twayne.

WORK IN PROGRESS: An autobiography, *Recollections and Reflections of a Book Editor, 1904-1984.*

*   *   *

SMYTH, John (George) 1893-1983

PERSONAL: Born October 24, 1893, in Teignmouth, England; died April 26, 1983; son of W. J. Smyth (in Indian civil service); married Margaret Dundas, 1920 (divorced, 1940); married Frances Read Chambers, 1940; children: (first marriage) three sons (two deceased), one daughter. *Education:* Educated at Sandhurst Royal Military College. *Home:* 807 Nelson House, Dolphin Sq., London SW1V 3PA, England.

CAREER: British Army, regular officer, 1912-42, retired as colonel, named honorary brigadier, 1943; correspondent for Kelmsley newspapers, 1943-44, and *Daily Sketch* and *Sunday Times,* 1945-46; lawn tennis correspondent for *Sunday Times,* 1946-51, and *News of the World,* 1956-57; member of Parliament for Norwood Division of Lambeth, 1950-66; writer. Served in both World Wars and in seven campaigns in the Middle East

and India, 1914-35; instructor at Camberley Staff College, 1931-34; commander of infantry brigade in France and Belgium, 1940-41; commanded 17th Division in Burma at time of Japanese invasion. Parliamentary secretary in Ministry of Pensions, 1951-53, and in Ministry of Pensions and National Insurance, 1953-55, Member, Royal Institute of International Affairs. Director, Creative Journals Ltd., 1957-63. Commentator, British Broadcasting Corp. television. Governor, Gypsy Road Secondary Schools, 1947-49, West Norwood Secondary Schools, 1947-51, Strand Secondary Schools, 1949-51, St. Martin's High School for Girls, 1950-52, Dragon School, 1953-66, and Queen Mary's Hospital, Roehampton, 1956-62; comptroller, Royal Alexandra and Albert School, 1948-63; trustee, Far East Prisoners of War and Internee Fund, 1959-61.

MEMBER: International Lawn Tennis Club of Great Britain (vice-president, 1966), International Lawn Tennis Club of the United States, International Lawn Tennis Club of France, Returned British Prisoners of War Association (executive, 1946-51; honorary vice-president, 1960), Far Eastern Prisoners of War Federation (honorary vice-president, 1960), Victoria Cross and George Cross Association (founder; first chairman, 1956-71; life president, 1966-83), Not Forgotten Association (vice-president, 1956), Burma Star Association (president of South London branch, beginning 1957), Distinguished Conduct Medal League (vice-president, 1957; president, 1958-70), Freeman of City of London in Worshipful Company of Farriers, Dunkirk Veterans Association (vice-president, beginning 1963), Old Reptonian Society (president, 1960-61), All England Lawn Tennis Club. *Awards, honors:* Victoria Cross, 1915; Russian Order of St. George; Military Cross, 1920; created first baronet, 1955; appointed privy councillor, 1962.

WRITINGS: Defence Is Our Business, Hutchinson, 1945; (editor and author of introduction) *The Western Defences,* Allan Wingate, 1951; *Lawn Tennis,* Batsford, 1953; *The Game's the Same: Lawn Tennis in the World of Sport,* Cassell, 1956, Philosophical Library, 1957; *Before the Dawn: A Story of Two Historic Retreats,* Cassell, 1957, 2nd edition, 1957; *Paradise Island* (juvenile), Max Parrish, 1958; *The Only Enemy: An Autobiography,* Hutchinson, 1959; *Trouble in Paradise: The Further Adventures of Ann Sheldon* (juvenile), Max Parrish, 1959.

Ann Goes Hunting (juvenile), Max Parrish, 1960; *Sandhurst: The History of the Royal Military Academy, Woolwich, the Royal Military College, Sandhurst, and the Royal Military Academy, Sandhurst, 1741-1961,* Weidenfeld & Nicholson, 1961; *The Story of the Victoria Cross, 1856-1963,* Muller, 1962, abridged edition, 1965; *Beloved Cats,* Muller, 1963, Citadel, 1965; *Blue Magnolia,* Muller, 1964; (with Archibald Duncan Campbell Macauley) *Behind the Scenes at Wimbledon,* Collins, 1965, St. Martin's, 1966; *Ming: The Story of a Cat Family,* Muller, 1966; *The Rebellious Rani,* Muller, 1966; *Bolo Whistler: The Life of General Sir Lashmer Whistler,* Muller, 1967; *The Story of the George Cross,* Arthur Barker, 1968; *In This Sign Conquer: The Story of the Army Chaplains,* Mowbray, 1968.

The Valiant, Mowbray, 1970; *The Will to Live: The Story of Dame Margot Turner,* Cassell, 1970; *Percival and the Tragedy of Singapore,* Macdonald & Co., 1971; *Leadership in War, 1939-1945: The Generals in Victory and Defeat,* St. Martin's, 1974; *Jean Borotra, the Bounding Basque: His Life of Work and Play,* Stanley Paul, 1974; *Leadership in Battle, 1914-1918,* David & Charles, 1975, Hippocrene, 1976; *Great Stories of the Victoria Cross,* Arthur Barker, 1977; *Milestones* (memoir), Sidgwick & Jackson, 1979.

Also author, with Ian Hays, of two plays, "Burma Road," produced, 1945, revised television version produced as "Until the Morning," 1951, and "The Commissioner's Bungalow." Contributor of articles to Wimbledon Programmes, 1947-73; regular contributor to *Lawn Tennis and Badminton* and *British Lawn Tennis.*

BIOGRAPHICAL/CRITICAL SOURCES: John Smyth, *The Only Enemy: An Autobiography,* Hutchinson, 1959; Smyth, *Milestones,* Sidgwick & Jackson, 1979.

OBITUARIES: London Times, April 27, 1983.

*   *   *

SOELLE, Dorothee 1929-

PERSONAL: Born September 30, 1929, in Cologne, Germany; daughter of Hans C. Nipperdey (a professor); married Dietrich Soelle, June 3, 1954 (divorced, 1963); married Fulbert Steffensky (a professor), October 24, 1969; children: Martin, Michaela, Caroline, Mirjiam. *Education:* Attended University of Cologne and University of Freiburg; University of Goettingen, degree of philosophy, 1954. *Religion:* Evangelical Church of Germany. *Home:* 99 Claremont Ave., New York, N.Y. 10027; and 2000 Hamburg 52, Roosens Weg 7, Federal Republic of Germany.

CAREER: Instructor in German and religion in West German high schools, 1954-60; Technical University of Aachen, Philosophical Institute, Aachen, Germany, research assistant, 1962-64; University of Cologne, Institute for Germanistick, Cologne, Germany, teacher, 1964-67, lecturer in German literature, 1971-75; University of Mainz, Mainz, Germany, lecturer, 1972-75; Union Theological Seminary, New York, N.Y., visiting lecturer in systematic theology, 1975-77, Harry Emerson Fosdick Visiting Professor, 1977—. *Member:* Royal Scientific Academy of Utrecht, P.E.N. *Awards, honors:* Grant, German Society for Research, 1967; Theodore Heuss Medal, 1974; honorary doctorate, Protestant Faculty, Paris, France; Droste Award for Poetry, Meersburg, 1982.

WRITINGS: Stellvertretung: Ein Kapitel Theologie nach dem Tode Gottes, [Stuttgart], 1965, translation published as *Christ the Representative,* Fortress, 1967; *Die Wahrheit ist konkret,* [Olten], 1967, translation by Dinah Livingstone published as *The Truth Is Concrete,* Herder, 1969; *Atheistisch an Gott glauben* (title means "Atheistically Believing in God"), [Olten], 1968; *Meditationen und Gebrauchstexte* (title means "Meditations and Usable Texts"), Wolfgang-Fietkau Verlag, 1969; (editor with husband, Fulbert Steffensky) *Politisches Nachtgebet in Koeln* (title means "Political Evening Prayer"), [Stuttgart], Volume I, 1969, Volume II, 1970.

Phantasie und Gehorsam: Ueberlegungen zu einer kuenftigen christlichen Ethick, [Stuttgart], translation by Lawrence W. Denef published as *Beyond Mere Obedience,* Augsburg, 1970; *Das Recht, ein anderer zu werden: Theologische Texte* (title means "The Right to Become Another"), [Neuwied], 1971; *Politische Theologie: Auseinandersetzung mit Rudolph Bultmann,* [Stuttgart], 1971, translation by John Shelley published as *Political Theology,* Fortress, 1974; *Realisation: Studien zum Verhaeltnis von Theologie und Dichtung nach der Aufklaerung* (title means "Realization: Studies Toward the Relation of Theology and Literature After the Enlightenment"), [Neuwied], 1973; *Leiden: Thesen der Theologie,* [Stuttgart], 1973, translation by Everett Kalin published as *Suffering,* Fortress, 1975; *Die revolutionaere Geduld: Gedichte,* Wolfgang-Fietkau Ver-

lag, 1974, translation by Bob Kimber and Rita Kimber published as *Revolutionary Patience,* Orbis, 1977.

Die Hinreise: Zur Religioesen Erfahrung—Teste und Ueberlegvngen, [Stuttgart], 1976, translation published as *Death by Bread Alone,* Fortress, 1976; *Sympathie, Theologisch-politische Traktate,* [Stuttgart], 1980; *Fliegen lernen Gedichte,* Wolfgang-Fietkau Verlag, 1980; *Waehlt das Leben,* [Stuttgart], 1981, translation by Margaret Kohl published as *Choosing Life,* Fortress, 1982; *Im Hause des Menschenfressers,* Texte zum Frieden Rowohlt, 1981, translation by B. Kimber and R. Kimber published as *Of War and Love,* Orbis Press, 1983; *Aufruestung toetet auch ohne Krieg,* [Stuttgart], 1982, translation by Gerhard Elston published as *The Arms Race Kills Even without a War,* Fortress, 1983; *Spiel doch von Brot und Rosen,* Wolfgang-Fietkau Verlag, 1982; (with F. Steffensky) *Nicht nur Ja und Amen: Von Christen im Widerstand,* [Hamburg], 1983, Fortress, 1984; (with Shirley Cloyes) *To Work and to Love: A Theology of Creation,* Fortress, 1984.

Also author of *Truth Within Us,* published by Burns & Oates.

SIDELIGHTS: Dorothee Soelle and her husband Fulbert Steffensky founded the ecumenical group "Political Evening Prayer." She described it as a movement of "theological-political reflection and action, with aims at an understanding of and feeling for the crucified Christ today, and how Christians need to respond."

*   *   *

SPALDING, Henry D(aniel) 1915-
(Dan Sping)

PERSONAL: Born February 2, 1915, in New York, N.Y.; son of Charles (an artist and teacher) and Mary (Berson) Spalding; married Louvenia Alberta Cathey (a music publisher), July 4, 1973; children: (previous marriage) Henry D., Jr., Randolph Page, Susan Dexter Perea, Laurie Lewis. *Education:* Quit school in the eighth grade. "Continued informal education through correspondence courses and voluminous reading." *Politics:* Republican. *Home and office:* 9023 Lindley Ave., Northridge, Calif. 91325.

CAREER: Writer. After dropping out of school, shined shoes, sold papers, and danced in New York streets to his own harmonica accompaniment; while in his early teens, delivered the *New York Graphic* to newsstands; worked as copy boy for the *New York Journal* and cub reporter for *New York Daily Mirror;* joined the Civilian Conservation Corps during the Depression, and then had a civil service job with the Treasury Department in Washington, D.C.; in his early twenties, began writing for magazines and continued writing while operating his own export-import firm in Washington, D.C.; wandered across the country, ending his "Skid Row interlude" in Los Angeles, where he washed dishes in a restaurant; editor of *Disk* (popular music periodical), Hollywood, Calif., 1949-52; wrote "Inside Congress," a column syndicated by Washington Trade Press, Washington, D.C., 1952-55; editor of *Deejay* (television-radio trade magazine), Hollywood, 1955-57; editor of *Hollywood Talent News* (show business trade journal), Hollywood, 1957-71; garden columnist for San Fernando Valley *Daily News,* Van Nuys, Calif., 1978—. Co-founder and director of publicity, Draft Eisenhower for President League, 1946-49, and originator of slogan, "I Like Ike." *Member:* Authors Guild, Authors League of America, Garden Writers Association of America, American Folklore Society, Texas Folklore Society, California Folklore Society, Hollywood Press Club.

WRITINGS—Published by Jonathan David, except as indicated: *The Yellow Press*, Newsstand Library, 1957; *A Quill to Survive* (autobiography), Newsstand Library, 1958; *Encyclopedia of Jewish Humor: From Biblical Times to the Modern Age*, 1969; *Encyclopedia of Black Humor and Folklore*, 1972; *The Nixon Nobody Knows*, 1972; *The Treasure Trove of American Jewish Humor*, 1976; *Lilt of the Irish*, 1977; *Joys of Italian Humor and Folklore*, 1980; *Jewish Laffs*, 1982; *Irish Laffs*, 1982.

WORK IN PROGRESS: *Naughty-Shmaughty: A Compendium of Jewish Party Jokes and Anecdotes; The Ninth Note*, a fantasy poem written in narrative prose.

SIDELIGHTS: Henry D. Spalding writes: "I have little more than a nodding acquaintance with academia. My formal education ended at Public School 6 in the Bronx. That eighth-grade grammar-school education imparted an inchoate awareness of the riddles of life—and few answers. So I asked questions. Oh, how that boy I was asked questions!

"As a youngster I lived on Manhattan's east side, a down-at-the-heels section of New York City where the tenements, even then in the early 1920s, leaned on each other to support themselves against the imminent prospect of collapsing from old age and exhaustion. The denizens of the area—Jewish, Italian, Irish—were, for the most part, recently arrived immigrants. They were my 'teachers,' and my questions were many. Some of their answers were poignant, stories of hunger, privation, and persecution. But others were humorous, and it was those that filled my youthful heart with delight. . . . I began to write them down on whatever slips of paper were conveniently handy, quoting the story-teller as closely as I could recall in an effort to preserve their authenticity, accent and all. As my collection of quips and anecdotes grew through the years and I started to classify them under specific categories (i.e. courtship, marriage, children, working), I gradually became aware of their correlationship with history: anecdotes rich in irony and satire, told by peoples who dared not voice their convictions openly in the oppressive societies in which they had formerly lived.

"Folklore, especially as revealed in folk humor, is a *social* documentation of a people, as opposed to orthodox history. My books, based on my lifelong collection of authentic folk humor, demonstrate that humor is not necessarily a laughing matter; sometimes they evoke a sigh. But educational though some of my books may be when the tales, jokes, songs and even poems revolve around known historical events, their primary objective is entertainment. Should they stimulate a desire in the reader to learn more of his people's culture and history through further study, then I am doubly gratified.

"Nowadays it is considered boorish to relate a story using a Jewish accent, an Irish brogue, an Italian dialect, or a black 'plantation' drawl. But the denouement of a story often depends on the use of an accent, usually a misunderstanding of English. For example: Mrs. Epstein, unable to sleep, consults a psychiatrist. After a number of questions, the psychiatrist asks, 'What do you think of sex?' Mrs. Epstein replies enthusiastically, 'I love it. It's the finest store on Fift Evnoo.'

"True enough, the use of accented English has often been employed as a cloak for bigotry, but authentic folk humor does not disparage. That is how the immigrants and blacks spoke in days past; they did not converse in Harvard accents. To be true to himself and to his readers, the folklorist, whether the subject matter is funny or not, must tell it like it is—and like it *was*. I have tried to do just that, and my works have met with modest success in the United States and in other lands. Agreed, I have had my moments of despair, but in retrospect, having attained my allotted three-score-and-ten, I am as happy as any man who ever danced the Charleston atop Mount Parnassus."

BIOGRAPHICAL/CRITICAL SOURCES: Henry D. Spalding, *A Quill to Survive*, Newsstand Library, 1958; *Talent News*, January, 1968.

*   *   *

SPANOS, William V(aios)   1925-

PERSONAL: Born January 1, 1925, in Newport, N.H.; son of Vaios and Mary (Stassos) Spanos; married Margaret Prince (a college instructor), June 10, 1954 (divorced); married Susan Strehle (an associate professor of English); children: (first marriage) Maria, Stephania, Aristides; (second marriage) Adam. *Education:* Wesleyan University, Middletown, Conn., A.B., 1950; Columbia University, M.A., 1954; University of Wisconsin, Ph.D., 1964. *Home:* 43 Matthew St., Binghamton, N.Y. *Office:* State University of New York, Binghamton, N.Y. 13901.

CAREER: Mount Hermon School, Mount Hermon, Mass., teacher of English, 1951-53; *Encyclopedia Americana*, editor and writer, 1953-55; University of Kentucky, Lexington, instructor in English, 1960-62; Knox College, Galesburg, Ill., assistant professor of English, 1962-66; State University of New York at Binghamton, 1966—, began as assistant professor, currently professor of English. Fulbright professor, National University of Athens, 1969-70. *Military service:* U.S. Army, Infantry, 1943-45; received European Theater Medal with two battle stars, Combat Infantry Badge, Purple Heart. *Member:* Modern Language Association of America, American Association of University Professors, Phi Beta Kappa.

WRITINGS: (Editor) *A Casebook on Existentialism*, Crowell, 1966; *The Christian Tradition in Modern British Verse Drama: The Poetics of Sacramental Time*, Rutgers University Press, 1967; (editor) *A Casebook on Existentialism 2*, Crowell, 1976; (editor) *Martin Heidegger and the Question of Literature: Towards a Postmodern Hermeneutics*, Indiana University Press, 1980; (editor with Paul Bove and Daniel O'Hara) *The Question of Textuality: Strategies of Reading in Contemporary American Criticism*, Indiana University Press, 1981. Contributor of articles, reviews, and monographs to scholarly journals. Founder and co-editor, *boundary 2: A Journal of Postmodern Literature*, 1972—.

WORK IN PROGRESS: *Icon and Time: Towards a Postmodern Hermeneutics;* a book on postmodern literature; a book examining humanistic education in the academy.

SIDELIGHTS: William Spanos told *CA*: "The teaching and study of literature in America is done *sub specie aeternitatis* in an age that demands of the teacher and the critic a recognition of our finiteness. Our *raison d'etre* is not that we are authoritative centers elsewhere and thus judges, but decentered beings-in-the-world whose purpose is to *explore* our occasional condition. What this means is that it is our task as teachers and critics to undermine the very *logos* that has traditionally sanctioned our progression. Our measure should be the 'measure of our occasion,' as the poet Robert Creeley has put it. This should make the progression of literary studies as solitary as that of the poet. Indeed, as subversive."

SPERGEL, Irving A.   1924-

PERSONAL: Surname is pronounced Spur-gull; born January 17, 1924, in New York, N.Y.; son of Julius and Frieda (Mann) Spergel; married Bertha Jampel (a reading specialist), September 1, 1949; children: Barry, Mark, Daniel. *Education:* Attended University of Birmingham, 1945; City College (now City College of the City University of New York), B.S.S. (cum laude), 1946; Columbia University, M.A., 1947, D.S.W., 1960; University of Strasbourg, graduate study in literature and languages, 1948; University of Illinois, M.S.W., 1952. *Religion:* Hebrew. *Home:* 5729 South Maryland, Chicago, Ill. 60637. *Office:* School of Social Service Administration, University of Chicago, 969 East 60th St., Chicago, Ill. 60637.

CAREER: Young Men's-Young Women's Hebrew Association, Wilmington, Del., program assistant, 1948-49; Good Neighbor Federation, New York City, group worker, 1950; New York City Youth Board, New York City, street gang worker, supervisor, court representative, and consultant, 1952-54, 1958-60; Lenox Hill Neighborhood Association, Neighbors United Street Club Project, New York City, director of street gang project, 1954-57; New York University, School of Social Work, New York City, lecturer in social research, 1959-60; Columbia University, New York City, research associate, 1960; University of Chicago, School of Social Service Administration, Chicago, Ill., professor, 1960—, Center for Social Organization, professor and fellow, 1967—.

Member of numerous committees and boards, University of Chicago, 1965—. Social worker, Fountain House Foundation, 1953-55, and William Alanson White Psychiatric Institute, 1958-60. United Nations advisor on youth work to Hong Kong (on leave from University of Chicago), 1970-71; referee in social work, University of Hong Kong, 1974-75; external examiner in social work, Chung Chi College, Chinese University, 1978-81. Consultant or advisor to numerous organizations and government agencies, including B'nai Brith Youth Organization, 1955-56, U.S. Justice Department, 1965-79, U.S. Labor Department, 1966-68, U.S. State Department, 1971-74, American Social Health Association, 1971-74, and Illinois Department of Corrections, 1979-80. *Military service:* U.S. Army, 1943-46. *Member:* National Association of Social Workers, Council on Social Work Education.

AWARDS, HONORS: Research awards from numerous organizations and agencies, including National Institute of Mental Health, Ford Foundation, President's Committee on Juvenile Delinquency and Youth Development, Office of Economic Opportunity, Youth Development and Delinquency Prevention Administration, Law Enforcement Assistance Administration, U.S. Department of Justice, and Illinois Law Enforcement Commission.

WRITINGS: (With Richard E. Mundy) *East Woodlawn: Problems, Programs, Proposals,* School of Social Service Administration, University of Chicago, 1963; *Racketville, Slumtown, Haulberg,* University of Chicago Press, 1964; *Street Gang Work,* Addison-Wesley, 1966; (with Castellano Turner, John Pleas, and Patricia Brown) *Youth Manpower: What Happened in Woodlawn,* School of Social Service Administration, University of Chicago, 1969; *Community Problem Solving: The Delinquency Example,* University of Chicago Press, 1969; *Mission as Advisor in Youth Work,* Hong Kong Government, 1971; (editor) *Community Organizations: Studies in Constraints,* Sage Publications, 1972; *Planning for Youth Development: The Hong*

Kong Experience, United Nations Assoc., 1973; *Social Innovation: Politics, Program, Evaluation,* School of Social Service Administration, University of Chicago, 1982.

Contributor: Dale B. Harris and John A. Sample, editors, *Violence in Contemporary American Society,* Pennsylvania State University Press, 1961; Rose Giallombardo, editor, *Juvenile Delinquency,* Wiley, 1966; Malcolm W. Klein, editor, *Juvenile Gangs in Context,* Prentice-Hall, 1967; Louis Masotti and Don Bowen, editors, *Riots and Rebellion: Civil Violence in the Urban Community,* Sage Publications, 1968; Donald Cressey and David Ward, editors, *Delinquency, Crime, and Social Process,* Harper, 1969.

Robert W. Klenck and Robert M. Ryan, editors, *The Practice of Social Work,* Wadsworth, 1970; *Evaluation Research: Strategies and Methods,* American Institutes for Research, 1970; Paul Lerman, editor, *Delinquency and Social Policy,* Praeger, 1971; (with Darrel Vorwaller and Elaine Switzer) Lawrence Witmer, editor, *Issues in Community Organization,* Center for the Scientific Study of Religion, 1972; Cox, Erlich, Rothman, and Tropman, editors, *Strategies of Community Organization,* F. E. Peacock, 1974; Kramer and Specht, editors, *Readings in Community Organization Practice,* Prentice-Hall, 1975; *Introduction to the Juvenile Justice System,* West Publishing, 1975; Larry F. Moore, editor, *Volunteer Administration: Readings for the Practitioner,* Taft Corp., 1975; J. Monahan, editor, *Community Mental Health and the Criminal Justice System,* Pergamon, 1976; Klein, editor, *The Juvenile Justice System,* Sage Publications, 1976; Simon Slavin, editor, *Social Work Administration—The Management of the Social Services,* 2nd edition, Hayworth Press, 1977; Peter J. Fick and Brenda Bradshaus, editors, *New Directions for Corrections,* Institute for Urban Studies, University of Houston, 1977.

Daniel Sanders, editor, *The Development Perspective in Social Work,* Council on Social Work Education, 1980; Robert Rubel, editor, *Delinquency Prevention: Emerging Perspectives of the 1980s,* Volume I, Institute of Criminal Justice Studies, Southwest Texas State University, 1980.

Also author of more than ten organizational publications and research reports. Contributor of articles on social services to professional journals.

WORK IN PROGRESS: Violent Gangs in Chicago.

AVOCATIONAL INTERESTS: Handball, swimming, jogging.

*   *   *

SPING, Dan
See SPALDING, Henry D(aniel)

*   *   *

SPOTO, Donald   1941-

PERSONAL: Born June 28, 1941, in New Rochelle, N.Y.; son of Michael G. (an executive) and Anne (a public relations aide; maiden name, Werden) Spoto. *Education:* Iona College, B.A. (summa cum laude), 1963; Fordham University, M.A., 1966, Ph.D., 1970. *Religion:* Roman Catholic. *Agent:* Elaine Markson Literary Agency, Inc., 44 Greenwich Ave., New York, N.Y. 10011. *Office:* New School for Social Research, 66 West 12th St., New York, N.Y. 10011.

CAREER: Fairfield University, Fairfield, Conn., assistant professor of theology and humanities, 1966-68; College of New Rochelle, New Rochelle, N.Y., assistant professor of religious studies, 1968-74; City University of New York, New York City, assistant professor of classics, 1974-75; New School for Social Research, New York City, professor of humanities, 1975—. *Member:* Authors Guild, Authors League of America, P.E.N.

WRITINGS: Stanley Kramer, Film Maker, Putnam, 1978; *Camerado: Hollywood and the American Man,* New American Library, 1978; *The Art of Alfred Hitchcock,* Doubleday, 1979; *The Dark Side of Genius: The Life of Alfred Hitchcock,* Little, Brown, 1983.

WORK IN PROGRESS: A major critical biography of Tennessee Williams, for Little, Brown.

SIDELIGHTS: Of the several books Donald Spoto has written about films and filmmakers, his critical biography *The Dark Side of Genius: The Life of Alfred Hitchcock* is perhaps the most notable to date. The work "digs deeper than any previous book-length study of Hitchcock," says Christoper Lehmann-Haupt of the *New York Times.* "It is not a heroic portrait of [the director] that Donald Spoto has presented here. It is instead the picture of a severely repressed, even twisted, Victorian gentleman."

Indeed, Spoto describes his subject as a cold, insensitive man who was often silently obsessed with the leading ladies of his films—the famous "Hitchcock blondes" characterized by Ingrid Bergman, Grace Kelly, and Kim Novak. His passion for Tippi Hedren—the former model he hand-picked to star in "The Birds" and "Marnie"—culminated in a sexual proposition to her. When she refused him, Hitchcock threatened to destroy the acting career he had launched for her. At the same time, the famed director was a practical joker of sometimes cruel proportions: After betting a stagehand that the man couldn't spend the night manacled to a camera in an empty studio, Hitchcock gave him some brandy to help him through the night—not telling the unfortunate man that the liqueur was laced with a powerful laxative.

"And so, yes, certainly Alfred Hitchcock had his dark side," concedes *Washington Post Book World* critic Bruce Cook, "but was he a genius? This is taken for granted by Donald Spoto, as it has been proclaimed for years by the French auterists Francois Truffaut, Claude Chabrol, and Eric Rohmer, and [by American critic] Andrew Sarris." Yet, Cook continues, their mentor, Andre Bazin, was content merely to call Hitchcock "'a technician and story teller of considerable distinction.' To put it bluntly, can a filmmaker who was so absorbed by the technical aspect of his craft and so indifferent to its humane side truly be considered a genius?" "For those who [do] consider Hitchcock a dark genius, Mr. Spoto's book is absolutely compulsory reading," writes Richard Grenier. In a *New York Times Book Review* article Grenier comments: "The Hitchcock that emerges from these pages is a figure of uncommon loathesomeness, a cruel, ungenerous, cowardly man, unable to thank or praise, filled with hate and fear. He had no friends. . . . [The author] dutifully records all the meanness and malignity of Hitchcock's character—such as the strong signs of a sadistic attitude toward women—but, since he worships Hitchcock's art, he goes to sometimes desperate lengths to show how all these character failings 'enrich' his work." Grenier notes Spoto's parallel between Alfred Hitchcock and the fifteenth-century Dutch surrealist Hieronymus Bosch: "Both were craftsmen steeped in personal guilt. . . . Both perceived life as an effort to avoid the always imminent calamity and accident that was sure to befall the unwary."

Finally, *Time* reviewer John Skow suggests that Spoto "is too shrewd to imagine . . . that an artist is the sum of his quirks. Hitchcock's brilliance was entangled with his personal grotesqueries, but it was real brilliance. . . . His final obsession was secretiveness, but he has been well served by a knowledgeable and revealing biography."

Donald Spoto told *CA:* "The writer's vocation is extraordinarily simple, and simply extraordinary—and at the same time a positive horror. It is nothing less than the constant attempt to make order out of chaos, first within himself, then with words, for the healing of the world."

BIOGRAPHICAL/CRITICAL SOURCES: Film Quarterly, spring, 1977, summer, 1979; *Nation,* January 6, 1978; *New York Times Book Review,* November 11, 1979, March 6, 1983; Donald Spoto, *The Dark Side of Genius: The Life of Alfred Hitchcock,* Little, Brown, 1983; *New York Times,* March 15, 1983; *Newsweek,* April 11, 1983; *Washington Post Book World,* April 17, 1983; *Time,* May 9, 1983; *London Times,* May 19, 1983; *Village Voice,* October 18, 1983.

*   *   *

STANLEY, Dave
    See DACHS, David

*   *   *

STARR, Roger 1918-

PERSONAL: Born April 16, 1918, in New York, N.Y.; son of Frederick and Lillie (Bernhard) Starr; married Manya (Fifi) Garbat (a screen and television writer), December 2, 1945 (divorced, May, 1978); married Joanne Elizabeth Ward Green, May 24, 1978; children: Adam, Barnaby. *Education:* Yale University, B.A., 1939. *Politics:* Democrat. *Religion:* Jewish (Reform). *Home:* 300 East 40th St., New York, N.Y. 10016. *Agent:* Julian S. Bach, Jr., 3 East 48th St., New York, N.Y. 10017. *Office: New York Times,* 229 West 43rd St., New York, N.Y. 10036.

CAREER: Frederick Starr Contracting Co., New York City, president, 1945-73; Citizens' Housing and Planning Council of New York, Inc., New York City, executive director, 1958-73; Housing and Development Administration, New York City, administrator and commissioner, beginning 1974; *New York Times,* New York City, member of editorial board, 1977—; writer. Lecturer, Pratt Institute, 1960—, New School for Social Research, 1964—; adjunct professor, City College of the City University of New York, 1970—. Member of board of directors, American Society of Planning Officials, National Housing Conference and United Neighborhood Houses of New York; chairman, Rent Guidelines Board, 1969-73. *Military service:* U.S. Army, Office of Strategic Services, 1943-45; served in Burma and China; became first lieutenant.

WRITINGS: The Living End, Coward, 1966; *Urban Choices,* Penguin, 1968; *Housing and the Money Market,* Basic Books, 1975; *America's Housing Challenge,* Farrar, Straus, 1978.

Contributor of articles on housing and related subjects to *Horizon, Journal of Housing, Fordham Law Review, New Leader, Village Voice, Public Interest, Commentary, New York Times Sunday Magazine, American Heritage, New York Affairs, New Republic, New York,* and *National Review.*

*   *   *

STEELMAN, Robert J(ames) 1914-

PERSONAL: Born March 7, 1914, in Columbus, Ohio; son of

Charles William and Nell (Blair) Steelman; married Janet Eyler, August 23, 1941; children: Karen (Mrs. Gene Berson), Michael. *Education:* Ohio State University, B.S., 1938. *Politics:* "Unaffiliated." *Religion:* Presbyterian. *Home and office:* 875 Amiford Dr., San Diego, Calif. 92107. *Agent:* Robert P. Mills Ltd., 333 Fifth Ave., New York, N.Y. 10016.

CAREER: U.S. Army, Signal Corps, civilian electronics engineer, 1939-46; U.S. Navy, civilian electronics engineer, 1946-69.

WRITINGS: Stages South, Ace Books, 1956; *Apache Wells,* Ballantine, 1959; *Winter of the Sioux,* Ballantine, 1959; *Call of the Arctic* (Arctic adventure novel), Coward, 1960; *Ambush at Three Rivers,* Ballantine, 1964; *Dakota Territory,* Ballantine, 1974; *White Medicine Man,* Ace Books, 1979; *The Santee Massacre,* Dell, 1982.

All published by Doubleday: *Cheyenne Vengeance,* 1974; *The Fox Dancer,* 1975; *Sun Boy,* 1975; *Portrait of a Sioux,* 1976; *Lord Apache,* 1977; *The Galvanized Reb,* 1977; *Surgeon to the Sioux,* 1979; *The Great Yellowstone Steamboat Race,* 1980; *The Man They Hanged,* 1980; *The Prairie Baroness,* 1981.

Contributor to Western magazines, including *Ranch Romances,* and to men's adventure magazines.

WORK IN PROGRESS: Continuing research on the frontier West.

SIDELIGHTS: "My writing is largely of the Old West," Robert J. Steelman told *CA.* "I try hard to make my books authoritative and true to the times. Perhaps my principal aim is to do what I can to elevate the 'western' to some literary significance, rather than see it condemned to a second-rate genre status."

BIOGRAPHICAL/CRITICAL SOURCES: Roundup, July, 1957.

*   *   *

STEINMETZ, Lawrence L(eo)   1938-

PERSONAL: Born September 26, 1938, in Newburg, Mo.; son of Leo Ewald (a photogrammetric engineer) and Sadie (Kriete) Steinmetz; married Sally Wismer, December 27, 1958; children: Susan Diane, James Bradley, Marcy Marie. *Education:* University of Missouri, B.S., 1959, M.S., 1960; University of Michigan, Ph.D., 1964. *Politics:* Republican. *Home:* 245 Fair Place, Boulder, Colo. 80302. *Office:* High Yield Management, Inc., 3333 Iris Ave., Boulder, Colo. 80301.

CAREER: The Kroger Company, Little Rock, Ark., management training, 1959-61; Henry Ford Community College, Dearborn, Mich., lecturer, 1961-63; University of Colorado, Boulder, assistant professor, 1964-66, associate professor, 1966-69, professor of management, 1969-77, head of Management and Organization Division, 1971-74; High Yield Management, Inc., Boulder, president, 1968—. Consultant to IBM, TRW, General Dynamics, and other corporations. *Military service:* U.S. Army, 1960-61; became first lieutenant. *Member:* Academy of Management, Colorado Society of Personnel Administrators, Sigma Iota Epsilon, Beta Gamma Sigma, Delta Sigma Pi.

WRITINGS: Grass Roots Approach to Industrial Peace, Bureau of Industrial Relations, University of Michigan, 1966; (with A. Dale Allen and Robert J. Johnson) *Labor Law,* Media Masters, 1967; (with others) *Managing the Small Business,* Irwin, 1968, 3rd edition, 1982; *Managing the Marginal and Unsatisfactory Performer,* Addison-Wesley, 1969; *Interviewing Skills*

for Supervisors, Addison-Wesley, 1971; *First Line Management,* Business Publications, 1975, 3rd edition, 1983; *Art and Skill of Delegation,* Addison-Wesley, 1976; *Human Relations: People and Work,* Harper, 1979.

*   *   *

STEVENS, Edward   1928-

PERSONAL: Born November 28, 1928, in Boston, Mass.; son of Edward (an accountant) and Alice (Murphy) Stevens; married Pheme Perkins, 1978. *Education:* Woodstock College, A.B., 1952, S.T.L., 1960; Fordham University, M.A., 1955; St. Louis University, Ph.D., 1965. *Office:* Department of Religious Studies, Regis College, Weston, Mass.

CAREER: Teacher at Brooklyn Preparatory School, Brooklyn, N.Y., 1953-54, and Xavier High School, New York, N.Y., 1954-56; St. Louis University, St. Louis, Mo., part-time instructor in philosophy, 1963-65; Canisius College, Buffalo, N.Y., beginning 1965, began as assistant professor, became associate professor of philosophy; Regis College, Weston, Mass., currently professor of philosophy and chairman of religious studies department. *Member:* American Philosophical Association, Council for the Study of Religion, Society for the Study of Christian Ethics, American Management Association.

WRITINGS—All published by Paulist/Newman: *Making Moral Decisions,* 1969, revised edition, 1982; *Oriental Mysticism,* 1972; *The Morals Game,* 1974; *The Religion Game: American Style,* 1976; *Business Ethics,* 1979. Contributor to sociology, education, and religious periodicals.

WORK IN PROGRESS: A book on practical techniques for directing inner consciousness.

*   *   *

STEVENS, R. L.
See HOCH, Edward D(entinger)

*   *   *

STIMMEL, Barry   1939-

PERSONAL: Born October 8, 1939, in Brooklyn, N.Y.; son of Abraham and Mabel (Bovit) Stimmel; married Barbara Barovick (a psychoanalyst); children: Alexander, Matthew. *Education:* Brooklyn College (now Brooklyn College of the City University of New York), B.S., 1960; State University of New York Downstate Medical Center, M.D., 1964. *Residence:* New York, N.Y. *Office:* Mt. Sinai School of Medicine, City University of New York, 100th St. and 5th Ave., New York, N.Y. 10029.

CAREER: Internist, 1969—; cardiologist, 1970—. Mt. Sinai School of Medicine of City University of New York, associate dean, 1971-81, dean for academic affairs, admissions, and student affairs, 1981—, associate professor of medicine, 1975—, chairman of department of medical education, 1979—. Executive director, Narcotic Rehabilitation Center, 1975—. Member of committee on planning, priorities, and evaluations of New York Metropolitan Regional Medical Program, 1971-73. Member of advisory committee of National Center for Urban Problems at City University of New York, 1970-71, and of New York State Office of Drug Abuse Services, 1976—; member of scientific advisory board of National Council on Drug Abuse, 1976—. *Military service:* U.S. Navy, physician, 1965-67; became lieutenant senior grade.

MEMBER: American Federation for Clinical Research, Research Society on Alcoholism, American Medical Society on Alcoholism, Association for Medical Education and Research in Substance Abuse, American Public Health Association, American Council on Science and Health, American Society of Law and Medicine, American Heart Association, National Association for the Prevention of Addiction to Narcotics, American Association for Higher Education, Society for the Study of Addiction to Alcohol, American Society of Internal Medicine, American Association of University Professors, American College of Cardiology, American Board of Internal Medicine, National Board of Medical Examiners, American Association of Physician Assistants (member of advisory board, 1972-73), New York Heart Association, New York Academy of Medicine, New York Academy of Science.

WRITINGS: Heroin Dependency: Medical, Social, and Economic Aspects, Stratton Intercontinental Medical Book Corp., 1975; *Mood Altering Drugs and the Cardiovascular System,* Raven Press, 1979; *Pain Analgesia and Addiction: The Pharmacologic Treatment of Pain,* Raven Press, 1983; *Ambulatory Medicine,* Raven Press, 1984.

Contributor: E. Donoso, editor, *Drugs in Cardiology,* Stratton Intercontinental Medical Book Corp., 1975; S. Rahimtolla, editor, *Infective Endocarditis,* Grune, 1978; A. Schecter and S. Mule, editors, *Rehabilitation and Treatment Aspects of Drug Dependence,* CRC Press, 1978; J. Niebyl and F. Zuspan, editors, *Current Drug Use in Pregnancy,* Lea & Febiger, 1982; N. Kase, S. Cherry, and R. Berkowitz, editors, *Medical, Surgical, and Gynecologic Complications of Pregnancy,* Williams & Wilkins, in press; R. E. Rakel, editor, *Conn's Current Therapy,* Saunders, in press.

Contributor of about one hundred articles to professional journals. Editor, *Advances in Alcoholism and Substance Abuse;* associate editor, *American Journal of Drug and Alcohol Abuse.*

WORK IN PROGRESS: Research on medical education, drug dependency, and cardiology.

SIDELIGHTS: Barry Stimmel told *CA:* "Dissemination of knowledge to all interested in learning has been a prime motivating factor in my writing. All too often one's thoughts developed from completely erroneous concepts become prejudices which are extremely difficult to overcome. My book on heroin dependency attempts to objectively assess the various aspects of heroin addiction from a social and psychological as well as medical standpoint to provide any interested reader with the opportunity to learn more about this disabling illness. My other books address common clinical problems of concern to both physicians and patients in an attempt to provide a rationale for effective management and patient care."

*   *   *

STOREY, R(obin) L(indsay)   1927-

PERSONAL: Born July 25, 1927, in Newcastle upon Tyne, England; son of George Frederick and Jean Wright (Brough) Storey; married Sheila Bredon Challenger, June 16, 1956; children: Hugh James, Rachel Alison. *Education:* New College, Oxford, B.A., 1951, M.A., 1955; University of Durham, Ph.D., 1954. *Home:* 19 Elm Ave., Beeston, Nottinghamshire, England. *Office:* History Department, University of Nottingham, Nottinghamshire, England.

CAREER: Public Record Office, London, England, assistant keeper, 1953-62; University of Nottingham, Nottinghamshire,

England, lecturer, 1962-64, senior lecturer, 1964-66, reader in history, 1966-73, professor of English history, 1973—, dean of Faculty of Arts, 1979-82. *Member:* Royal Historical Society (fellow; vice-president, 1981—), Canterbury and York Society (honorary treasurer, 1958-65; member of council, 1965-68, 1979—; honorary general editor, 1968-79), Thornton Society of Nottinghamshire (honorary general editor of Record Section, 1966-79).

WRITINGS: The Register of Thomas Langley, Volumes I-VI, Surtees Society, 1956-70; *Thomas Langley and the Bishopric of Durham,* S.P.C.K., 1961; *The End of the House of Lancaster,* Barrie & Rockliff, 1966, Stein & Day, 1967; *The Reign of Henry VII,* Blandford, 1968; (editor with Donald A. Bullough) *The Study of Medieval Records: Essays in Honour of Kathleen Major,* Oxford University Press, 1971; *Diocesan Administration in Fifteenth-Century England,* 2nd revised edition, St. Anthony's Press, 1972; *Chronology of the Medieval World 800-1491,* Barrie & Jenkins, 1973. Also author of *Progression, Vocation and Culture in Later Medieval England,* edited by Ctt. Clough, 1982; contributor to *New College, Oxford, 1379-1979,* edited by J. Buxton and P. Williams, 1979. Contributor of articles and reviews to history journals.

WORK IN PROGRESS: History of pre-Reformation church in England.

*   *   *

STORY, Ronald (D.)   1946-

PERSONAL: Born February 12, 1946, in Joplin, Mo.; son of Raymond Christopher (a carpenter) and Willa (a licensed practical nurse; maiden name, Johnson) Story; married Rita Lynn Motherway, October 30, 1969; children: Brenda Ann, Brian Alan. *Education:* University of Arizona, B.A. (with honors), 1970. *Politics:* Independent. *Religion:* Nondenominational. *Home:* 4739 East Waverly St., Tucson, Ariz. 85712. *Agent:* Felicia Eth, Writers House, Inc., 21 West 26th St., New York, N.Y. 10010. *Office address:* Hughes Aircraft Co., P.O. Box 11337, Tucson, Ariz. 85734.

CAREER: Assistant manager of retail stores in Santa Maria, Calif., and Tucson, Ariz., 1970-72; Tucson Gas and Electric Co., Tucson, Ariz., buyer of electrical equipment, 1972-78; free-lance writer and editor, 1978-80; Hughes Aircraft Co., Tucson, Ariz., buyer of electronic test equipment, 1980-82, technical editor, 1982—. Consultant to CBS-TV News, National Geographic Society, and other organizations. *Military service:* U.S. Navy, 1963-69; served in Vietnam. *Member:* Society of Southwestern Authors.

WRITINGS: The Space Gods Revealed: A Close Look at the Theories of Erich von Daniken, Harper, 1976; *Guardians of the Universe?,* St. Martin's, 1980; (editor) *The Encyclopedia of UFOs,* Doubleday, 1980; *UFOs and the Limits of Science,* Morrow, 1981; (contributor) Kendrick Frazier, editor, *Paranormal Borderlands of Science,* Prometheus Books, 1981. Contributor to periodicals. Consultant to *Frontiers of Science* and *Reader's Digest.*

WORK IN PROGRESS: A revised edition of *The Encyclopedia of UFOs.*

SIDELIGHTS: Ronald Story's first book, *The Space Gods Revealed: A Close Look at the Theories of Erich von Daniken,* is a scientific rebuttal of the widely discussed theory that extraterrestrials visited the earth in the distant past and left their marks in our archaeological record. "I was outraged [that] so many publications, movies, and TV shows came out with such blatant inaccuracies,'' says Story. *The Space Gods Revealed* begins with a discussion of the topic in general and then, in detail, examines the speculative arguments of von Daniken—the best selling author of *The Chariots of the Gods* who has popularized the theory that ancient visitors from space are responsible for artifacts such as the massive statues on Easter Island and the ''landing strip'' formations on the Peruvian coast. Story claims every important scientist he talked to rejected von Daniken's arguments, ''however, most of our anthropologists, archaeologists, astronomers, theologians, and philosophers have remained [publicly] silent on the issue.''

According to Walter V. Addiego in the *San Francisco Examiner,* Story says that because von Daniken's works ''have been largely ignored by scientists and academicians,'' they have gained an unwarranted public following. In the foreword to Story's work, Carl Sagan maintains that von Daniken's idea implies ''our ancestors were too stupid to create the most impressive surviving ancient architectural and artistic works.'' ''*The Space Gods Revealed* is a coherent and much-needed refutation,'' comments R. Z. Sheppard in *Time.* Sheppard, who calls the author's ''attack'' on *Chariots of the Gods* ''a series of bull's-eyes scored at 3 ft.,'' adds, ''Story easily demonstrates that von Daniken's use of details and . . . imaginings are on a par with those of children seeing camels and puppies in cloud formations.'' Concludes a *Publishers Weekly* writer: ''Many won't appreciate Story's yanking away of the lollipop, but somebody had to do it.''

Story followed his initial publishing success with another debunking book entitled *Guardians of the Universe?* ''Here,'' says Jill Schensul in the *Arizona Daily Star,* ''Story takes up where he left off [in his examination of von Daniken] . . . and also scrutinizes the theories of other space-god proponents,'' including Robert Charroux, Morris Jessup, and Robert Temple. The book, which a *Choice* reviewer calls ''popular literature that has been well researched and presented clearly,'' systematically examines the evidence von Daniken and others use to support their claims. Story attempts to clarify the facts and define legitimate questions to which, he insists, the answers remain uncertain. In his introduction the author explains that, where UFOs and other unexplained phenomenon are concerned, his own viewpoint ''may be summarized as follows: objectivity and open-mindedness should reign supreme, but with a high degree of prudence based on the body of hard-won scientific knowledge that we already possess. Shoddy evidence and apparent deceptions should be weeded out, wherever found, and not confused with reasonable thinking on unorthodox subjects.'' Story adds, ''Despite what many readers are bound to think, I am not out to 'crucify' von Daniken as a person; but rather, it is the particular brand of irrationality which he represents that I feel is potentially dangerous.''

To combat ''irrational'' claims about UFOs and present to the public a broad range of ideas on the subject, Story compiled *The Encyclopedia of UFOs.* Organized in an A-through-Z format with more than three hundred entries by one hundred contributors with differing opinions, the work covers evidence, hypotheses, prominent people in the field, government projects, and reports of one hundred significant UFO sightings. ''Story . . . dives into the existing material on alleged extraterrestrial influences with a level head and a skeptical eye,'' Schensul reports. ''It is this objectivity that makes *The Encyclopedia of UFOs . . .* the valid reference book it was meant to be.'' Richard Hall, former assistant director of the National Investigations Committee of Aerial Phenomena, states in *Fron-*

tiers of Science: ''This volume brings together under one cover more than thirty years of UFO history, providing a wealth of information for anyone interested in some part—or all—of the continuing UFO mystery. The selection of material is outstanding, accurately reflecting the current state-of-the-art of ufology.'' While he finds that the book's ''cover claim that the volume includes 'every bit of important information . . . to date' must be understood as a typical publisher's exaggeration,'' Hall nonetheless labels it ''a peerless reference book.''

Moving from a comprehensive presentation of the subject to a study of specific, select incidents, Story next produced *UFOs and the Limits of Science.* A *Kirkus Reviews* critic calls the volume ''a much crisper piece of analysis [than *The Encyclopedia of UFOs*] that's engrossing beyond [Story's] stated premise, . . . that our science, in its present state, is not capable of illuminating the phenomenon.'' The author examines what he calls the ''ten best cases'' of UFO sightings—those with multiple witnesses acting or reporting independently of each other, having better-than-average documentation, and with no other apparent explanation. Story studies both the theories of UFO proponents and official rationalizations concerning sightings that occurred around the globe between 1952 and 1978. As he points out, none of these encounters provides the concrete evidence necessary to make scientific fact of what he sees as a physical, psychological, and sociological enigma which should be approached using the resources of every branch of science.

Story told *CA:* ''I believe in the power of three virtues: reason, honesty, and compassion, to solve human problems. I do not believe in blatant exploitation of human ignorance and gullibility. This is why I want to expose the pseudo-sciences by attempting to bring to light some of the many little-known facts in certain scientific areas. My principal goal is to seek the truth while attempting to make academic science interesting to the general public.''

BIOGRAPHICAL/CRITICAL SOURCES—Books: Ronald Story, *The Space Gods Revealed: A Close Look at the Theories of Erich Von Daniken,* Harper, 1976; Randall Fitzgerald, *The Complete Book of Extraterrestrial Encounters,* P. Collier, 1979; Story, *Guardians of the Universe?,* St. Martin's, 1980.

Periodicals: *Kirkus Reviews,* May 15, 1976, January 15, 1981; *Publishers Weekly,* May 31, 1976, May 2, 1980, January 23, 1981; *Atlantic,* August, 1976; *Time,* August 2, 1976; *New York Times,* August 6, 1976; *Arizona Daily Star,* August 15, 1976, November 30, 1976, August 10, 1980; *Booklist,* September 15, 1976, June 1, 1980; *San Francisco Examiner,* October 13, 1976; *Science Digest,* December, 1976; *Playboy,* July, 1978; *Chicago Tribune,* May 11, 1980; *Frontiers of Science,* July/August, 1980, May/June, 1981; *Los Angeles Times,* March 29, 1981.

*   *   *

STRAKER, J(ohn) F(oster) 1904-
(Ian Rosse)

PERSONAL: Born March 26, 1904, in Farnborough, Kent, England; son of Leonard Herbert (an engineer) and Elizabeth (Foster) Straker; married Margaret Brydon, January 24, 1935; children: Ian Christopher. *Education:* Attended Framlingham College. *Politics:* Conservative. *Religion:* Church of England. *Home:* Lincoln Cottage, Horsted Keynes, Sussex, England.

CAREER: Kingsland Grange School, Shrewsbury, Shropshire, England, mathematics master, 1926-34; Blackheath Preparatory School, London, England, joint headmaster, 1936-38;

Cumnor House School, Danehill, Sussex, England, mathematics master, 1944-79. *Military service:* British Army, 1939-45; served as staff officer in Middle East; became major.

WRITINGS—Published by Harrap: *Postman's Knock*, 1954; *Pick up the Pieces*, 1955; *The Ginger Horse*, 1956; *A Gun to Play With*, 1956; *Goodbye, Aunt Charlotte!*, 1958; *Hell Is Empty*, 1958; *Death of a Good Woman*, 1961; *Murder for Missemily*, 1961; *A Coil of Rope*, 1962; *Final Witness*, 1963; *The Shape of Murder*, 1964; *Ricochet*, 1965; *Miscarriage of Murder*, 1967; *Sin and Johnny Inch*, 1968; *A Man Who Cannot Kill*, 1969; *Tight Circle*, 1970; *A Letter For Obi*, 1971; *The Goat*, 1972.

Published by R. Hale: *Arthur's Night*, 1976; *Swallow Them Up*, 1977; *Death on a Sunday Morning*, 1978; *A Pity It Wasn't George*, 1979; *Countersnatch*, 1980; *Another Man's Poison*, 1983; *A Choice of Victims*, 1984.

Other books: (Under pseudonym Ian Rosse) *The Droop*, New English Library, 1972; *Going Places, Southeast England*, Royal Automobile Club, 1981.

Contributor of short stories to *Evening Standard, Evening News*.

SIDELIGHTS: Dust jackets of J. F. Straker's books have been designed by his son, a commercial artist. Many of Straker's publications have been translated into foreign languages, including German, Dutch, Swedish, Norwegian, Spanish, Italian, and Danish. *Media adaptations: Hell Is Empty* was made into a motion picture.

AVOCATIONAL INTERESTS: Travel, music, carpentry, gardening, all games and sports (now as a spectator).

BIOGRAPHICAL/CRITICAL SOURCES: Smith's Trade News, April 14, 1956; *Books and Bookmen*, September 22, 1958; *Evening Dispatch*, May 19, 1973.

*   *   *

STREETEN, Paul Patrick   1917-

PERSONAL: Born July 18, 1917, in Vienna, Austria; married Ann Hilary Higgins, June 9, 1951; children: Patricia Doria, Judith Andrea; stepchildren: Jay D. Palmer. *Education:* University of Aberdeen, M.A., 1940; Balliol College, Oxford, B.A. (with first class honors), 1947, M.A., 1952; attended Nuffield College, Oxford, 1947-48. *Home:* 21 Penniman Rd., Brookline, Mass. 02146. *Office:* World Development Institute, Boston University, 264 Bay State Rd., Boston, Mass. 02215.

CAREER: Oxford University, Oxford, England, fellow of Balliol College, 1948-66 and 1968-78, university lecturer and associate of Institute of Economics and Statistics, 1960-64, director of Institute of Commonwealth Studies and warden of Queen Elizabeth House, 1968-78; Ministry of Overseas Development, London, England, deputy director-general of economic planning staff, 1964-66; University of Sussex, Institute of Development Studies, Stanmer, Brighton, England, professor of economics, acting director, and fellow, 1966-68, member and vice-chairman of governing body; currently director, World Development Institute, Boston University, Boston, Mass. Visiting professor, Stanford University, 1956, and University of Buenos Aires, 1963; visiting lecturer, Economic Development Institute of the World Bank. Research fellow, Johns Hopkins University, 1955-56; fellow, Center for Advanced Studies, Wesleyan University, 1962.

Member of council, Walloon Institute of Economic Development; member of provisional council, University of Mauritius,

1965; UNESCO, member of United Kingdom National Commission, 1966, and vice-chairman of Advisory Committee on Social Sciences; member of the board, Commonwealth Development Corp., 1967-72; member of council, Dominion Students Trust, London; member of Africa Publications Trust. Member of Royal Commission on Environmental Pollution, 1974-76. Special advisor to the World Bank, 1976-80; member of advisory committee, Arab Planning Institute, Kuwait. *Military service:* British Army and Royal Marine Commandos, Hampshire Regiment, 1941-43; became sergeant; wounded in Sicily.

MEMBER: Society for International Development (president of United Kingdom chapter), Royal Economic Society, American Economic Association, United Oxford and Cambridge Club. *Awards, honors:* Rockefeller fellow in United States, 1950-51; D.Litt., University of Aberdeen, 1980; honorary fellow, Institute of Development Studies, University of Sussex.

WRITINGS: (Editor and translator) Gunnar Myrdal, *The Political Element in the Development of Economic Theory*, Routledge & Kegan Paul, 1953; (reviser, editor, and contributor) *The Great Economists*, Eyre & Spottiswoode, 1955; (editor and author of foreword) Myrdal, *Value in Social Theory*, Routledge & Kegan Paul, 1958; *Economic Integration: Aspects and Problems*, Sijthoff, 1961, 2nd edition, 1963; (editor with M. Lipton) *The Crisis of Indian Planning*, Oxford University Press, 1968; (member of international team of six assistants) Myrdal, *Asian Drama: An Inquiry into the Poverty of Nations*, three volumes, Twentieth Century Fund, 1968.

(Editor) *Unfashionable Economics: Essays in Honor of Lord Balogh*, Weidenfeld & Nicolson, 1970; (editor with Hugh Corbet) *Commonwealth Policy in a Global Context*, Cass, 1971; (with Diane Elson) *Diversification and Development: The Case of Coffee*, Praeger, 1971; *Aid to Africa*, Praeger, 1972; *The Frontiers of Development Studies*, Macmillan, 1972; *Trade Strategies for Development*, Macmillan, 1973; *The Limits of Development Research*, Pergamon, 1974; *Foreign Investment, Transnationals and the Developing Countries*, Macmillan, 1977; *Development Perspectives*, Macmillan, 1981; *First Things First*, Oxford University Press, 1981; (editor with Richard Jolly) *Recent Issues in World Development*, Pergamon, 1982.

Contributor: *Vollbeschaeftigung*, Bund Verlag (Cologne), 1950; K. Kurihara, editor, *Post-Keynesian Economics*, Allen & Unwin, 1954; *Studi in Memoria di Benevenuto Griziotti*, Editore A. Guiffre, 1959; *Theorie et Politique de l'expansion regionale*, Librairie Encyclopedique (Brussels), 1961; G.D.N. Worswick and P. H. Ady, editors, *The British Economy in the Nineteen-Fifties*, Clarendon Press, 1962; von Beckerath and Giersch, editors, *Probleme der normativen Oekonomik und der wirtschaftspolitischen Beratung*, [Berlin], 1963; *Bergedorfer Protokolle: Economic Aid—A Way to Growth or Decline?*, Decker Verlag, 1964.

P. D. Henderson, editor, *Economic Growth in Great Britain*, Humanities, 1966; Kurt Martin and John Knapp, editors, *The Teaching of Development Economics*, Cass, 1967; Hans K. Schneider, editor, *Grundsatzprobleme wirtschaftspolitscher Beratung*, Duncker & Humblot (Berlin), 1968; Klaus Hufner and Jens Naumann, editors, *Economics of Education in Transition*, Ernst Klett Verlag (Stuttgart), 1969; *SEANZA Lectures*, Central Bank of Ceylon, 1969; A. N. Agarwala and S. P. Singh, editors, *Accelerating Investment in Developing Countries*, Oxford University Press, 1969; John Harry Dunning, editor, *The Multinational Enterprise*, Praeger, 1972; Dunning, editor, *Economic Analysis and the Multinational Enterprise*,

Allen & Unwin, 1974. Also contributor to *Basic Needs in Danger,* 1983.

Former secretary and member of editorial board, "Oxford Economic Papers." Contributor to *UNESCO Dictionary of Political and Social Terms* and *Collier's Encyclopedia;* contributor of about 100 articles to journals in England, Germany, France, Belgium, Italy, Canada, and India. Editor of *World Development* and Oxford University Institute of Economics and Statistics *Bulletin,* 1961-64.

WORK IN PROGRESS: Research on private overseas investment, aid, basic needs, and food pricing policies.

* * *

STROH, Thomas F.   1924-

PERSONAL: Born November 2, 1924, in Freeport, N.Y.; son of August F. (a certified public accountant) and Florence Stroh; married Audrey Merrit, September 19, 1946. *Education:* Colgate University, B.A., 1948; Columbia University, M.A., 1963, professional diploma, 1965, Ed.D., 1968. *Office:* Department of Marketing, Florida Atlantic University, 500 Northwest 20th St., Boca Raton, Fla. 33431; and Intercollegiate Video Clearing House, Miami, Fla. 33133.

CAREER: Dun & Bradstreet, New York City, reporter, 1948-52; Shaw Walker, New York City, salesman, 1952-57, sales manager, 1957-64; West Virginia Pulp & Paper Co., New York City, supervisor of marketing training, 1964-66; private business education consultant, 1966—; Florida Atlantic University, Boca Raton, member of department of marketing faculty, 1968—; Intercollegiate Video Clearing House, Miami, Fla., editor and trustee, 1974—. *Military service:* U.S. Marine Corps, 1942-46; participated in three invasions; wounded twice. *Member:* Phi Kappa Psi, Delta Pi Epsilon. *Awards, honors:* Landis Annual Film Competition first prize, Industrial Management Society, 1974, for "Eastern Air Lines Marketing Case History."

WRITINGS: Salesmanship: Personal Communication and Persuasion in Marketing, Irwin, 1966; *Techniques of Practical Selling,* Dow Jones-Irwin, 1966; *The Uses of Video Tape in Training and Development,* American Management Association, 1969; *Managing the New Generation in Business,* McGraw, 1972; *Training and Developing the Professional Salesman,* American Management Association, 1973; *Effective Psychology for Sales Managers,* Prentice-Hall, 1974.

The Purchasing Agent's Guide to the Naked Salesman, Cahners, 1975; *Managing the Sales Function,* McGraw, 1978; *How to Start and Succeed in Your Own Small Business,* Clemprint, 1980; (contributor) Stuart H. Britt and Norman Guess, editors, *Marketing Manager's Handbook,* Dartnell, 1983. Author and producer of more than thirty educational films and videocassettes, with teaching notes, for Intercollegiate Video Clearing House, Florida Atlantic University, ABC-Radio, Bantam Books, Inc., and other companies, 1968—. Editor of "Video Library Listings" series for Intercollegiate Video Clearing House, 1974—. Contributor of monthly articles to *Marketing News Letter.*

WORK IN PROGRESS: If You Ever Get to Heaven's Scenes, a novel about the Fourth Marine Division in World War II.

SIDELIGHTS: In the early 1970s, Thomas F. Stroh's monthly articles in *Marketing News Letter* were translated into Spanish and Portuguese for publication in South America. "Because of translation problems," the author told *CA,* "I learned to simplify my writing by talking to the reader and [giving] many examples. . . . Now, writing for video, I have learned to *show* the viewer while [I talk] to him—truly a new dimension for me." Most of Stroh's books have been published in Spanish and Japanese, and his videocassettes have been used in Japan, Hong Kong, New Zealand, Australia, Saudi Arabia, South Africa, Belgium, England, and Canada, as well as throughout the United States.

* * *

STROTHER, Elsie (Frances Warmoth Weitzel) 1912-

PERSONAL: Born June 15, 1912, in New York, N.Y.; daughter of Frank S. (a sugar planter) and Phyllis S. (Aitken) Warmoth; married George J. Weitzel, March 22, 1935 (died, 1959); married Dean C. Strother (a general in the U.S. Air Force), December 29, 1964; children: (first marriage) Carroll (Mrs. G.L.B. Rivers), Sallie (Mrs. Jamie Gough). *Education:* Attended New York School of Design, Grand Central Fine Arts School, and St. James Ecole in Paris, France. *Home:* 8 Polo Dr., Colorado Springs, Colo. 80906.

CAREER: Art teacher in private schools in Aiken, S.C., 1950-59, and in Charleston, S.C., 1959-62. Painter, especially of animals. *Member:* National League of American Pen Women (vice-president of local branch), Authors Guild, Authors League of America.

WRITINGS—All novels for young adults; published by Avalon, except as indicated: *The Royal Cheetah and the Untouchables,* Westminster, 1974; *Rendezvous at Live Oaks,* 1975; *Island of Terror,* 1976; *Follow Through to Love,* 1977; *A Kiss to Remember,* 1980; *Safari into Danger,* Elgen Publishing, 1981; *A Time for Deceit,* 1981; *That Special Kiss,* 1982.

Also author of *Love's Sweet Treasure,* published by Avalon. Author of column, "The Children's Nook," in *Aiken Standard and Review,* beginning 1951. Contributor of stories and articles to children's magazines.

WORK IN PROGRESS: A historical novel set in nineteenth-century Haiti.

SIDELIGHTS: Elsie Strother told *CA* that she was "brought up in the West Indies with education acquired through governesses, tutors, and voluminous reading. I have traveled and lived all over the world and have painted and written about most of it." *Avocational interests:* Golf, music.

* * *

SUBOND, Valerie
See GRAYLAND, Valerie (Merle Spanner)

* * *

SUCHOFF, Benjamin   1918-

PERSONAL: Born January 19, 1918, in New York, N.Y.; son of Aaron (a manufacturer) and Sadie (Leishin) Suchoff; married Eleanor Rosen; children: Michael Alan, Susan Carol, Deborah Ann. *Education:* Cornell University, B.S., 1940; New York University, M.A., 1949, Ed.D., 1956. *Home:* 2 Tulip St., Cedarhurst, N.Y. 11516. *Office:* Center for Contemporary Arts and Letters, State University of New York, Stony Brook, N.Y.

CAREER: Hewlett-Woodmere Public Schools, Hewlett, N.Y., district director of music, 1950-78. New York Bartok Archive, curator, 1953-67, director, 1968-82, trustee of estate of Bela Bartok, 1968-82. Adjunct professor at Center for Contemporary Arts and Letters, State University of New York at Stony Brook, 1973—. Diplomate of the Hungarian Peoples Republic, 1981. *Military service:* U.S. Army, 1941-45.

MEMBER: International Folk Music Council, International Musicological Society, American Society of Composers, Authors and Publishers, American Musicological Society, Society for Ethnomusicology, College Music Society, Music Educators National Conference, New York State School Music Association, Composer's Laboratory of New York (fellow). *Awards, honors:* New York University Founders Day Award, 1957; American Council of Learned Societies grant, 1966.

WRITINGS: (Editor) *Bartok: Rumanian Folk Music,* five volumes, Nijhoff, 1967-75; *Guide to Bartok's Mikrokosmos,* Boosey & Hawkes, 1970, 3rd edition, Da Capo Press, 1983; *Electronic Music Techniques,* Multivox Corp., 1975; (editor) *Bartok: Turkish Folk Music from Asia Minor,* Princeton University Press, 1976; (editor) *Bela Bartok Essays,* St. Martin's, 1976; (editor) *Bartok: Yugoslav Folk Music,* four volumes, State University of New York Press, 1978; (editor) *Bartok: The Hungarian Folk Song,* State University of New York Press, 1981; (editor) *The Bartok Archive Edition,* two volumes, Dover, 1981. Also author of liner notes for album "Bela Bartok: A Celebration," 1981.

Composer of more than 200 musical works and arrangements for chorus, piano, band, and instrumental ensemble.

WORK IN PROGRESS: Editing *Bartok: Slovak Folk Music,* three volumes, for State University of New York Press; writing a guide to Bartok's recently discovered system of musical composition.

* * *

SUMMERS, Robert S(amuel) 1933-

PERSONAL: Born September 19, 1933, in Halfway, Ore.; son of Orson (a farmer) and Estella (a farmer; maiden name, Robertson) Summers; married Dorothy Kopp, 1955; children: Brent, William, Thomas, Elizabeth Anne, Robert. *Education:* University of Oregon, B.S., 1955; Harvard University, LL.B., 1959; further graduate study at Oxford University, 1964-65, 1974-75. *Office:* School of Law, Myron Taylor Hall, Cornell University, Ithaca, N.Y. 14853.

CAREER: Admitted to Oregon State Bar, 1959, and to New York State Bar, 1974; King, Miller, Anderson, Nash & Yerke, Portland, Ore., associate, 1959-60; University of Oregon, Eugene, assistant professor of law, 1960-63; Stanford University, Stanford, Calif., visiting associate professor of law, 1963-64; University of Oregon, associate professor, 1964-68, professor of law, 1968-69; Cornell University, Ithaca, N.Y., professor of law, 1969-76, McRoberts Professor of Law, 1976—. Visiting professor (summers) at Indiana University, 1969, University of Michigan, 1974, University of Warwick, 1975, University of Miami, 1976-80, University of Sydney, 1977, University of Oregon, 1980, and Emory University, 1981-83. Visiting research fellow, Merton College, Oxford University, 1981-82.

MEMBER: International Association of Philosophers of Law, American Law Institute, American Society for Political and Legal Philosophy, Association of American Law Schools, Phi Beta Kappa. *Awards, honors:* Fulbright fellowship, University of Southampton, 1954-55; Social Science Research Council fellowship, Oxford University, 1964-65.

WRITINGS: (Contributor) Dennis Lloyd, editor, *Introduction to Jurisprudence,* Praeger, 1959, 3rd edition, 1972; (with Charles Howard) *Law, Its Nature, Functions, and Limits,* Prentice-Hall, 1965, 2nd edition, 1972; (editor and author of introduction) *Essays in Legal Philosophy,* University of California Press, 1968; (contributor) Graham Hughes, editor, *Law, Reason and Justice,* New York University Press, 1969; (with Richard Speidel and James White) *Teaching Materials on Commercial Transactions,* West Publishing, 1969; (with Speidel and White) *Teaching Materials on Commercial and Consumer Law,* West Publishing, 1969, 3rd edition, 1981.

(Editor and author of introduction) *More Essays in Legal Philosophy,* University of California Press, 1971; (with White) *The Uniform Commercial Code.* West Publishing, 1972, 2nd edition, 1980; (with Gail Hubbard and A. Bruce Campbell) *Justice and Order through Law* (high school text), Ginn, 1973; (with Campbell and John Bozzone) *The American Legal System* (junior high school text), Ginn, 1973; (contributor) Joseph Raz and Peter Hacker, editors, *Festschrift for H.L.A. Hart,* Oxford University Press, 1977; *Instrumentalism and American Legal Theory,* Cornell University Press, 1982; *Lon L. Fuller—Life and Work,* Stanford University Press, in press.

Contributor to law journals, including *Oregon Law Review, Virginia Law Review, Journal of Legal Education,* and *Ottawa Law Review.* Editor of *Cornell Law Forum,* 1973-81.

* * *

**SUTPHEN, Dick
See SUTPHEN, Richard Charles**

* * *

**SUTPHEN, Richard Charles 1937-
(Dick Sutphen; Todd Richards, a pseudonym)**

PERSONAL: Surname pronounced Sut-fen; born April 3, 1937, in Omaha, Neb.; son of Earle Charles (a salesman) and Jennie E. (a secretary, maiden name, Roberts) Sutphen; married second wife, Judith Ann, July 5, 1969 (divorced); married Trenna Laraine (a writer, psychic, and seminar trainer); children: (second marriage) Scott, Todd, Steven, Jessi; (third marriage) Travis. *Education:* Attended Art Center School, Los Angeles, Calif., 1956-57. *Politics:* Republican. *Religion:* "Metaphysics." *Address:* P.O. Box 38, Malibu, Calif. 90265.

CAREER: Art director for advertising firms in Omaha, Neb., 1955, 1958-59; *Better Homes and Gardens,* Des Moines, Iowa, designer, 1959-60; Knox Reeves Advertising, Minneapolis, Minn., art director, 1961-64; MacManus, John & Adams, Inc., Minneapolis, art director, 1964-65; Dick Sutphen Studio, Inc., Minneapolis, and Scottsdale, Ariz., operator of advertising design and illustration services and publisher of books for the advertising market, 1965-76; Sutphen Corp./Valley of the Sun Publishing, Malibu, Calif., owner, 1976—. Conductor of Sutphen Seminars, 1976—. Designer of contemporary (studio) cards for Hallmark, and creator of a line of Arizona-oriented studio cards and framed prints; producer of more than 300 hypnosis and self-help cassette tape programs.

*WRITINGS—*Under name Dick Sutphen, except as indicated: *The Mad Old Ads,* McGraw, 1967; *Studio Cards,* Famous American Studios, 1968; *You Were Born Again to Be Together,* Simon & Schuster, 1976; *The Pen and Ink and Cross Hatch Styles of the Early Illustrators,* Art Direction Book, 1976; *Attention-Getting Old Engravings,* Art Direction Book, 1976;

Past Lives, Future Loves, Simon & Schuster, 1978; *Unseen Influences,* Simon & Schuster, 1980.

Published by Dick Sutphen Studios: (Editor) *Old Engravings and Illustrations,* two volumes, 1965; (editor) *Uncensored Situations,* 1966; (editor) *The Wildest Old Engravings and Illustrations,* 1966; (editor) *Designy Devices,* 1967; *Antiques, Filigree and Rococo,* 1967.

Published by Valley of the Sun Publishing: (Editor) *The Encyclopedia of Small Spot Engravings,* 1969; *Sometimes the Words of Love Have No Words,* 1969; *A Deep Breath of Yesterday,* 1970; *I Love to Have You Touch Me,* 1971; *Sex, Liquor, Tobacco, and Candy Are Bad for You,* 1972; *Know Thy Higher Self,* 1972; (under pseudonym Todd Richards) *Your Voice Makes My Knees Tickle!* (verse), 1972; *Burying Pompeii,* 1973; *Open Hand Love* (poems), 1975; *Past Life Hypnotic Regression Course,* 1977; *The Dick Sutphen Assertiveness Training Course,* 1978; (with wife, Trenna Sutphen) *The Master of Life Manual,* 1980; (with T. Sutphen) *Bushido SST Graduate Manual,* 1981. Also author of *Past Life Therapy in Action.*

Illustrator: Billi Haeberle, *Radio and Television,* Dillon, 1970; Betty Kane, *Dentistry,* Dillon, 1972; Jo Nelson, *Home Economics,* 2nd edition, Dillon, 1974; Peter Treuenfels, *Computers,* 2nd edition, Dillon, 1975.

AVOCATIONAL INTERESTS: Zen, Eastern philosophy, martial arts, running.

BIOGRAPHICAL/CRITICAL SOURCES: American Artist, June, 1967; Alan Weisman, *We, Immortals,* Pocket Books, 1979.

* * *

SWEETING, George 1924-

PERSONAL: Born October 1, 1924, in Haledon, N.J.; son of William and Mary Sweeting; married Hilda Schnell, 1947; children: George, James, Donald, Robert. *Education:* Moody Bible Institute, Diploma, 1945; Gordon College, B.A., 1948; Gordon-Conwell Divinity School, D.D., 1970. *Home:* 38213 North Bolton Pl., Antioch, Ill. 60002. *Office:* Moody Bible Institute, 820 North LaSalle St., Chicago, Ill. 60610.

CAREER: Pastor in Clifton, N.J., 1950-52; evangelist in South America, North America, and Europe, 1951-61; pastor in Paterson, N.J., 1961-66, and Chicago, Ill., 1966-71; Moody Bible Institute, Chicago, Ill., president, 1971—. *Awards, honors:* D.Hum., Azusa Pacific College, 1971; LL.D., Tennessee Temple College, 1971; LL.D., John Brown University, 1983.

WRITINGS: How to Be a Chalk Artist, Zondervan, 1953; *The Jack Wyrtzen Story: The Personal Story of the Man, His Message, and His Ministry,* Zondervan, 1960; *And the Greatest of These: The Power of Christian Love,* Revell, 1968, revised edition published as *Love Is the Greatest,* Moody, 1974, 2nd revised edition published as *Catch the Spirit of Love,* Victor Books, 1983; *Living Stones: Guidelines for New Christians,* Baker Book, 1970.

Published by Moody: *The City: A Matter of Conscience, and Other Messages,* 1972; *How to Solve Conflicts,* 1973; *Living in a Dying World,* 1974; *How to Witness Successfully,* 1978; *Talking It Over,* 1979; *Special Sermons for Special Days,* 1979; *Special Sermons on Special Issues,* 1981; *Special Sermons on the Family,* 1981; *Special Sermons on Major Bible Doctrines,* 1981; *Special Sermons for Evangelism,* 1982.

Also author of *Discovering the Will of God,* 1974, and *How to Begin the Christian Life,* 1975. Editor-in-chief of *Moody Monthly,* 1971—.

SWIGART, Rob 1941-

PERSONAL: Surname is pronounced with a long "i"; born January 7, 1941, in Chicago, Ill.; son of Eugene (a businessman) and Ruth (an actress and theatrical producer; maiden name, Robison) Swigart; married Jane Bugas (a psychotherapist), March 26, 1969; children: Saramanda Nell. *Education:* Princeton University, B.A., 1962; State University of New York at Buffalo, Ph.D., 1972. *Politics:* "Buddhist." *Religion:* Zen. *Home:* 255 Cerrito Ave., Redwood City, Calif. 94061. *Agent:* Ellen Levine, Curtis Brown Ltd., 575 Madison Ave., New York, N.Y. 10022. *Office:* Department of English, San Jose State University, San Jose, Calif. 95114.

CAREER: Cincinnati Enquirer, Cincinnati, Ohio, reporter, 1963; Harper & Row Publishers, Inc., New York, N.Y., salesman, 1965-69; San Jose State University, San Jose, Calif., assistant professor of English, 1972—. Owner, producer, cameraman, editor, and sound recordist for Marley & Swigart Films, 1973—. *Military service:* U.S. Army, 1964-65. U.S. Army Reserve, 1965-70. *Member:* Authors Guild, Authors League of America, American Association for the Advancement of Science, Science Fiction Writers of America, Planetary Society, California Academy of Sciences.

WRITINGS: Still Lives (poems), No Dead Lines, 1976; *Little America* (novel), Houghton, 1977; *A.K.A.: A Cosmic Fable* (novel), Houghton, 1978; *The Time Trip* (novel), Houghton, 1979; *The Book of Revelations* (novel), Dutton, 1981; (contributor and translator) *Women Poets of the World,* Macmillan, 1983. Author of documentary film scripts "Inishmaan: Beyond the Pale," "Firstborn," and "Little America" (based on his novel of the same title), and documentary videotape "The Clean-Room Environment"; also author of technical articles on computers and other topics for Apple Computer, Inc., and other firms. Contributor of articles and poems to periodicals, including *Poetry, Atlantic Monthly, New York Quarterly, Choice, Poetry Northwest,* and *Antaeus.*

WORK IN PROGRESS: Two novels, *Moby Pig* and *Final Vector;* a nonfiction book about "visionary vision," entitled *Persistence of Vision.*

SIDELIGHTS: To read the novels of Rob Swigart is to enter the realm of the fantastic, faddish, and mythological. Steven Kosek, writing in the *Chicago Tribune Book World,* remarks that Swigart's novels "are best described as weird word-cartoons in the style of Kurt Vonnegut and Tom Robbins. They fall into that small genre, the cosmic fable." Dealing with such subjects as time travel and reincarnation, Swigart's works have explored both man's technological future and his ancient past. Describing his approach to fiction, Swigart told *CA:* "I am . . . concerned with the ethics of science and the nature of vision and how it can be created or recreated."

In reviews of Swigart's work, critics have commented on both his concern with themes of time, technology, and the cosmos, and on his style. Discussing *The Book of Revelations* in the *Los Angeles Times,* Robert Gish calls Swigart's use of current, popular issues and ideas "more than just allusive, trendy talk by another post-contemporary author. . . . Swigart's novel pays plenty of attention to the futuristic 'fads' of our moment— concerns incipient in the 1980s as good bets to change from science fiction to science" in the future. These include UFOs, aphrodisiacs, computers, and communication with animals. Offering a somewhat different assessment of Swigart's use of "futuristic fads," Kosek refers to the same novel as "an anachronistic cartoon whose subject is terribly out of fashion."

A similar divergence of opinion exists concerning Swigart's style, with critics speaking both favorably and unfavorably about the influence of Kurt Vonnegut on Swigart's prose. Kosek feels that *The Book of Revelations* "lacks some important quality of narration. . . . Swigart has managed to mimic the bits and pieces of Vonnegut and Robbins, but has altogether missed the spirit of their novels." On the other hand, Jerome Klinkowitz, in his *Chicago Tribune Book World* review, states that "Rob Swigart cut his teeth on Kurt Vonnegut, and the lessons of *Slaughter House Five* have been well learned in the *Time Trip*. . . . It presents a nice smooth narrative line with no real complications." And Gish, who calls Swigart a "worker in the vineyards of Vonnegut," declares that "for fanciful description and believeable make-believe, Swigart's *Book* proves there's still hope . . . for . . . the resurrection of the novel as a literary form."

AVOCATIONAL INTERESTS: Aikido (black belt, 1982), cello, and flying (pilot).

BIOGRAPHICAL/CRITICAL SOURCES: Chicago Tribune Book World, April 22, 1979, November 1, 1981; *Los Angeles Times,* September 25, 1981; *New York Times Book Review,* November 1, 1981.

* * *

SZANTON, Peter L(oeb) 1930-

PERSONAL: Born November 7, 1930, in New York, N.Y.; son of Jules G. (a businessman) and Carolyn (a teacher; maiden name, Loeb) Szanton; married Eleanor Stokes (a consultant), June 22, 1957; children: Nathan Stokes, Andrew Emlew, Sarah Loeb. *Education:* Harvard University, A.B., 1952, A.M., 1955, LL.B., 1958. *Home:* 3458 Macomb St. N.W., Washington, D.C. 20016. *Office:* 11 Dupont Circle N.W., Suite 803, Washington, D.C. 20036.

CAREER: U.S. District Court, San Francisco, Calif., law clerk, 1958-59; attorney in New York City, 1959-62; member of policy planning staff of Assistant Secretary of Defense for International Security Affairs in Washington, D.C., 1962-65;

Bureau of the Budget, Washington, D.C., deputy director of program evaluation staff, 1965-67; Rand Corp., New York City, president of New York City-Rand Institute, 1967-71; Harvard University, Cambridge, Mass., fellow of Institute of Politics, 1971-72; Rand Corp., senior staff member, 1972-73; Commission on Organization of the Government for the Conduct of Foreign Policy (Murphy Commission), Washington, D.C., research director, 1973-75; independent researcher and writer, 1975-77; Office of Management and Budget, Washington, D.C., associate director, 1977-79; Hamilton, Rabinovitz & Szanton, Inc., Washington, D.C., partner, 1979—. Instructor at Harvard University, 1957-58. Consultant to National Science Foundation, Organization for Economic Cooperation and Development, Ford Foundation, Executive Office of the President, and Civil Service Institute of Israel. *Military service:* U.S. Army, 1952-54; served in Korea.

WRITINGS: (Contributor) *The Engineer and the City,* National Academy of Engineering, 1969; (contributor) A. W. Drake and other editors, *Analysis of Public Systems,* M.I.T. Press, 1972; (contributor) Henry Owen and Charles Schultze, editors, *Setting National Priorities,* Brookings Institution, 1976; (with Graham Allison) *Remaking Foreign Policy: The Organizational Connection,* Basic Books, 1976; *Not Well Advised,* Russell Sage & Ford Foundations, 1981; (editor) *Federal Reorganization,* Chatham House, 1981; (contributor) *Politics and the Oval Office,* Institute for Contemporary Studies, 1981.

Contributor to law journals and to *Operations Research* and *Foreign Policy.*

WORK IN PROGRESS: A study of the potential value and feasibility of various forms of civilian national service.

SIDELIGHTS: Peter L. Szanton writes: "Interest in public affairs took me from law practice to government. Experience in government made me interested in why government works so poorly, and what might realistically be done about it. That is the theme of most of my writing."

BIOGRAPHICAL/CRITICAL SOURCES: Paul Dickson, *Think Tanks,* Atheneum, 1971; Martin Greenberger and others, editors, *Models in the Policy Process,* Russell Sage, 1976.

T

TABARD, Peter
See BLAKE, L(eslie) J(ames)

* * *

TANSELLE, G(eorge) Thomas 1934-

PERSONAL: Surname is pronounced *Tan*-sell; born January 29, 1934, in Lebanon, Ind.; son of K. Edwin and Madge (Miller) Tanselle. *Education:* Yale University, B.A. (magna cum laude), 1955; Northwestern University, M.A., 1956, Ph.D., 1959. *Office:* John Simon Guggenheim Memorial Foundation, 90 Park Ave., New York, N.Y. 10016.

CAREER: Chicago City Junior College, Chicago, Ill., instructor in English, 1958-60; University of Wisconsin—Madison, instructor, 1960-61, assistant professor, 1961-63, associate professor, 1963-68, professor of English, 1968-78; John Simon Guggenheim Memorial Foundation, New York, N.Y., vice-president, 1978—. Adjunct professor of English, Columbia University, 1980—. Director, Literary Classics of the United States, 1979—. Member of Planning Institute of Commission on English, Ann Arbor, summer, 1961, Center for Editions of American Authors, 1970-73, Kennedy Center Advisory Committee for Drama for the Bicentennial, 1974-75, Soviet-American symposium on editing, Indiana University, 1976, executive committee, Center for Scholarly Editions, 1976—, and North American Committee for 18th-century short title catalog, 1978—. Also member of national advisory board, Center for Books, Library of Congress, 1978—, and advisory committee, North American imprints program, 1980—.

MEMBER: Modern Language Association of America, Modern Humanities Research Association, National Council of Teachers of English, Society for Textual Scholarship, Renaissance Society of America, American Society for Eighteenth-Century Studies, Society for Bibliography of Natural History, American Printing Historical Association, Printing Historical Society, Private Libraries Association, Manuscript Society (member of board of directors, 1974-79), Typophiles, Guild Book Workers, Fellows Morgan Library, American Antiquarian Society (council member, 1974—), Bibliographical Society of America (member of council, 1970), Bibliographical Society (London), Edinburgh Bibliographical Society, Oxford Bibliographical Society, Cambridge Bibliographical Society, Bibliographical Society of the University of Virginia, Wisconsin Academy of Sciences, Arts, and Letters, Indiana Research Libraries Association, Book Club of California, Yale Club, Century Club, Grolier Club, Caxton Club, Phi Beta Kappa.

AWARDS, HONORS: Kiekhofer Teaching Award, University of Wisconsin, 1963; Guggenheim fellowship, 1969-70; Jenkins Prize for Bibliography, Union College, 1973; American Council of Learned Societies fellowship, 1973-74; National Endowment for the Humanities fellowship, 1977-78.

WRITINGS: Royall Tyler, Harvard University Press, 1967; *Guide to the Study of United States Imprints,* Belknap, 1971; *A Checklist of Editions of Moby Dick,* Northwestern University Press and Newberry Library, 1976; *Selected Studies in Bibliography,* University Press of Virginia, 1979; (editor) *Herman Melville: Typee, Omoo, Mardi,* Library of America, 1982.

Contributor to books and to scholarly journals, including *Studies in Bibliography, Book Collector, Library, Shakespeare Quarterly, Gutenberg Jahrbuch, Modern Language Review, American Literature,* and *PMLA.* Member of board of editors, *Contemporary Literature,* 1962—, *Abstracts of English Studies,* 1964-78, *Resources for American Literary Study,* 1971—, *Analytical and Enumerative Bibliography,* 1977—, *Review,* 1978—, and *American Literature,* 1979-82; member of advisory board of *Burton's Anatomy of Melancholy,* 1978—, and *Publishing and Printing History, A Guide to Manuscript Resources in the U.S.,* 1980—.

WORK IN PROGRESS: Essays on the theory and techniques of analytical and descriptive bibliography; a descriptive bibliography of Herman Melville; a study of the publishing career of B. W. Huebsch; research in the history of American publishing and printing.

SIDELIGHTS: G. Thomas Tanselle's edition of *Herman Melville: Typee, Omoo, Mardi* is one of the first volumes published by the Library of America in its effort to keep classic works of American literature in print and available to the reading public in durable, yet reasonably priced, volumes. Writing in the *New York Times Book Review,* Malcolm Cowley calls the book ''an induction to what will be a complete Melville, the first set of his works offered to general readers in this country.''

AVOCATIONAL INTERESTS: Collecting books pertaining to the development of literary publishing in the United States; collecting bibliography.

BIOGRAPHICAL/CRITICAL SOURCES: Times Literary Supplement, November 24, 1972; New York Times Book Review, April 25, 1982; Washington Post Book World, May 2, 1982.

*   *   *

TARRANT, Wilma
See SHERMAN, Jory (Tecumseh)

*   *   *

TAYLOR, Andrew (McDonald)   1940-

PERSONAL: Born March 19, 1940, in Warrnambool, Victoria, Australia; son of John McDonald (a lawyer) and Margaret (Fraser) Taylor; married Jill Burriss, January 31, 1965 (separated, 1975); children: Travis. Education: University of Melbourne, B.A. (with first class honors), 1961, M.A. (with first class honors), 1970; State University of New York at Buffalo, additional graduate study, 1970-71. Politics: "Unattached Left." Home: 334 Halifax St., Adelaide, South Australia 5000, Australia. Office: Department of English, University of Adelaide, Adelaide, South Australia 5001, Australia.

CAREER: British Institute, Rome, Italy, English teacher, 1964-65; University of Melbourne, Melbourne, Australia, Lockie Fellow in Australia Literature, 1965-69; University of Adelaide, Adelaide, Australia, lecturer, 1971-74, senior lecturer in English, 1974—. Member of the literature board of the Australian Council, 1978-81. Helped to organize Adelaide's "Friendly Street" poetry readings; chairman of writers' week committee of Adelaide Festival of Arts, 1980 and 1982. Consultant to Australian Broadcasting Commission. Member: Australian and New Zealand American Studies Association, Association for the Study of Australian Literature (member of executive section), Teachers Association of South Australia. Awards, honors: American Council of Learned Societies fellowship, 1970-71.

WRITINGS: (Editor) Byron, Selected Poems, Cassell, 1971; The Cool Change (poems), University of Queensland Press, 1971; Ice Fishing (poems), University of Queensland Press, 1973; The Invention of Fire (poems), University of Queensland Press, 1976; The Cat's Chin and Ears, A Bestiary, Angus & Robertson, 1976; Parabolas: Prose Poems, Makar Press, 1976; The Crystal Absences, the Trout (poems), Island Press, 1978; (editor) Number Two Friendly Street, Adelaide University Union Press, 1978; Selected Poems, University of Queensland Press, 1982. Author of radio scripts on poetry for Australian Broadcasting Commission. Contributor to magazines and newspapers.

WORK IN PROGRESS: A book of poems; stories; prose poems and "experiments in prose."

SIDELIGHTS: Andrew Taylor writes: "Several years living in Europe and several in the U.S.A., Canada, and Mexico have counteracted Australia's isolation (my involvement with Adelaide Festival of Arts is another attempt at this). But I also like watching plants grow slowly and resolutely in one place. . . ." He adds that his interests are in "modern psychology and phenomenology, in origins (my own rather than my country's)."

AVOCATIONAL INTERESTS: Travel, gardening, animals, children.

*   *   *

TAYLOR, Charles   1931-

PERSONAL: Born November 5, 1931, in Montreal, Quebec, Canada; son of Walter Margrave (an industrialist) and Simone (a fashion designer; maiden name, Beaubien) Taylor; married Alba Romer (an artist), April 2, 1956; children: Karen, Miriam, Wanda, Gabriella, Gretta. Education: McGill University, B.A., 1952; Oxford University, B.A., 1955, M.A., 1960, D.Phil., 1961. Politics: New Democratic Party (social democrat). Religion: Roman Catholic. Home: 344 Metcalfe Ave., Montreal, Quebec, Canada H3Z 2T3. Office: Department of Philosophy, McGill University, Box 6070, Station A, Montreal, Quebec, Canada H3C 3G1.

CAREER: McGill University, Montreal, Quebec, 1961—, began as assistant professor, currently professor of philosophy and political science. Professor of philosophy, University of Montreal, 1962-71. Chichele Professor of Social and Political Theory, Oxford University, 1976—. Vice-president of New Democrat Party of Canada, 1965-73. Member: Canadian Philosophical Association, Canadian Political Science Association, Royal Society of Canada, Ligue des Droits de l'Homme.

WRITINGS: The Explanation of Behaviour, Humanities, 1964; Pattern of Politics, McClelland & Stewart, 1970; Hegel, Cambridge University Press, 1975; Erklaerung und Interpretation in den Wissenschaften vom Menschen, Suhrkamp, 1975; Hegel and Modern Society, Cambridge University Press, 1979.

Contributor of articles to political and philosophical journals. Founder and former editor, New Left Review.

WORK IN PROGRESS: "Working on philosophy of language, nature of subjectivity, social philosophy, and the problem of growth."

SIDELIGHTS: Charles Taylor wrote CA: "I am interested in philosophical anthropology, the theory of human nature; I am dissatisfied with widespread mechanistic accounts, more drawn to views defended in other philosophical traditions, e.g., Hegel, Humboldt, Heidegger; but believe these must be reformulated. No one philosophical school has the resources for this reformulation alone.

"I am very interested in French and German, as well as Anglo-Saxon philosophy. Being from Montreal, I grew up bi-lingual; and have since also learned German, Spanish, some Italian and Polish, and of course, Latin and Greek."

*   *   *

TAYLOR, L(ester) B(arbour), Jr.   1932-

PERSONAL: Born November 9, 1932, in Lynchburg, Va.; son of Lester B. (a salesman) and Ruth (Hanna) Taylor; married Norma Billings, September 6, 1958; children: Cynthia, Chris, Tony. Education: Florida State University, B.S., 1955. Home: 114 Little John Rd., Williamsburg, Va. 23185. Office: Badische Corp., Route 60, Williamsburg, Va. 23185.

CAREER: Pan-American Airlines, Kennedy Space Center, Cape Kennedy, Fla., public relations representative, 1957-62; Radio Corporation of America (now RCA Corp.), Kennedy Space Center, writer and editor, 1963-64; Ling, Temco, Vought (LTV), Kennedy Space Center, writer and editor, 1964-66; National Aeronautics and Space Administration, Kennedy Space Center, public information officer, 1966-68; Rockwell International, Pittsburgh, Pa., manager of publications, 1968-74; Badische Corp., Williamsburg, Va., public relations director, 1974—. Military service: U.S. Army, 1955-57. Member: Public Relations Society of America. Awards, honors: Special citation from Aviation and Space Writers Association, 1975, for For

All Mankind: America's Space Programs of the Seventies and Beyond.

WRITINGS—All young adult books: *Pieces of Eight: Recovering the Riches of a Lost Spanish Treasure Fleet,* Dutton, 1966; *That Others Might Live: The Aerospace Rescue and Recovery Service,* Dutton, 1967; *Liftoff: The Story of America's Spaceport,* Dutton, 1968; *For All Mankind: America's Space Programs of the Seventies and Beyond,* Dutton, 1974; *Gifts from Space: How Space Technology Is Improving Life on Earth* (Junior Literary Guild selection), Crowell, 1977; *Space Shuttle,* Crowell, 1980; *Teenage Idols,* Simon & Schuster, 1982.

Published by F. Watts: *Chemistry Careers,* 1978; *Rescue: True Stories of Heroism,* 1979; *Emergency Squads,* 1979; *Shoplifting,* 1979; *The Draft: A Necessary Evil?,* 1981; *Southeast Africa,* 1981; *The New Right,* 1981; *The Nuclear Arms Race,* 1982; *The Military in Space,* 1982.

Contributor of more than three hundred articles to national magazines, including *Ladies' Home Journal, Reader's Digest, Saturday Evening Post, True, Parade,* and *Family Weekly.*

WORK IN PROGRESS: *Haunted Houses,* for Simon & Schuster.

SIDELIGHTS: L. B. Taylor, Jr. told *CA:* "I enjoy writing books and magazine articles because it exposes me to such a variety of intriguing subject matter and introduces me to so many interesting people. My book topics, for example, have included treasure hunting, the space shuttle, teenage heroes, haunted houses, and such celebrities as Scott Baio and John Schneider. I view writing, or at least my type of writing, as a craft at which you must work hard to master. The rewards from such effort can be very self-satisfying."

AVOCATIONAL INTERESTS: More writing, golf, gin rummy.

*   *   *

TEICHER, Morton I(rving) 1920-

PERSONAL: Born March 10, 1920, in New York, N.Y.; son of Sam (a waiter) and Celia (Roth) Teicher; married Mildred Adler (a social worker), October 4, 1941; children: Phyllis (Mrs. Alvin Goldman), Oren. *Education:* City College of New York (now City College of the City University of New York), B.S.S., 1940; University of Pennsylvania, M.S.W., 1942; University of Toronto, Ph.D., 1956. *Politics:* Democrat. *Religion:* Jewish. *Home:* 720 Shadylawn Rd., Chapel Hill, N.C. 27514. *Office:* School of Social Work, University of North Carolina, Chapel Hill, N.C. 27514.

CAREER: U.S. Veterans Administration, Boston, Mass., chief social worker, 1946-48; University of Toronto, Toronto, Ontario, assistant professor of social work, 1948-56; Yeshiva University, New York, N.Y., dean and professor of social work, 1956-72; University of North Carolina, Chapel Hill, professor of social work, 1972—, dean of social work, 1972-82.

Visiting scholar, University of Michigan, 1966. Council on Social Work Education, chairman, deans' meeting, 1962, 1971, member of commission on international social work, beginning 1967, member of publications committee, 1967-70, delegate to House of Delegates; International Council on Social Welfare, member, nominating committee, U.S. committee, 1967-70, chairman, nominating committee, U.S. committee, beginning 1971, member, U.S. committee, beginning, 1971. Board member and workshop co-ordinator, International Conference of

Jewish Communal Service; executive secretary, National Conference of Jewish Communal Service, 1968-70. Participant in and study tour leader of various international conferences on social welfare and mental health. Has done anthropological field work on Eskimos and Iroquois in Canada. External examiner, University of Zambia, 1968, 1969, and Institute of Local Government Administrators of Zambia, 1969, 1970. Consultant, Oppenheimer College, Lusaka, Zambia, 1962-63, 1965, 1968, 1969, and Bar Ilan University, Israel, 1965-70. *Military service:* U.S. Army, 1942-46, became first lieutenant; served in China, Burma, and India.

MEMBER: American Anthropological Association (fellow), Society for Applied Anthropology (fellow), National Association of Social Workers (chairman, Westchester chapter, 1960-62; member, commission on social work ethics, 1964-67), American Association for the Advancement of Science, American Association of University Professors, Gerontological Society, Otto Rank Society. *Awards, honors:* Certificate of Appreciation from Westchester County, N.Y., 1967.

WRITINGS: *Planning Implications of Study of Coordination of Health Services for Patients with Long-Term Illness,* Council of Jewish Federations and Welfare Funds, 1960; *Windigo Psychosis: A Study of a Relationship between Belief and Behavior among the Indians of Northeastern Canada,* University of Washington Press, 1960; (contributor) Myron A. Coler, editor, *Essays on Creativity in the Sciences,* New York University Press, 1963; (editor and contributor) *Values in Social Work: A Re-examination,* National Association of Social Workers, 1966; (editor with others) *Reaching the Aged: Social Services in Forty-four Countries,* Sage Publications, 1979; (co-editor) *Data-Based Planning in the Field of Aging,* University Press of Florida, 1982.

Author of foreword: Charles S. Levy, *Education for Social Group Work Practice,* Yeshiva University, 1959; Levy, *From Education to Practice in Social Group Work,* Yeshiva University, 1960; Harold B. Werner, *A National Approach to Social Casework,* Associated Press, 1965.

Contributor to Federation of Jewish Philanthropies conference proceedings, December, 1964. Also contributor of articles and book reviews to various professional journals, including *Social Service Review, American Journal of Psychiatry,* and *Social Work Journal.* Book review editor, *Journal of Jewish Communal Service,* 1960-68; member of editorial board, *Human Organization,* 1963-68; book reviewer, *Jewish Floridian,* 1982—.

SIDELIGHTS: Morton I. Teicher has travelled throughout Africa, Europe, and the Middle East.

*   *   *

TENN, Ada N(ina) 1915-

PERSONAL: Born August 28, 1915, in Nyack, N.Y.; daughter of Nigel (a ferry captain) and Oona (Bloom) Noonan; married Karl J. Tenn (a psychoanalyst), July 20, 1937; children: Sigmund F., Joyce B., Sonya. *Education:* Haverstraw Normal College of Education, B.A., 1936; additional study at L'Institute Cheval, Belgium. *Home:* 221 Lewiston Rd., Grosse Pointe Farms, Mich. 48236.

CAREER: Teacher of foreign languages in elementary schools in New York and Michigan, 1936-66; playwright, 1966—. Member of panel, Conference of General Knowledge, 1971. *Member:* Avant League (eastern region), Cercle des Ecrivains

Contemporains pour les Enfants, Daughters of American Waterways. *Awards, honors:* Leafy Glade fellowship in juvenile writing, 1963; Grand Cercle Award of Cercle des Ecrivains Contemporains, 1965, for *The Little Red Couch.*

WRITINGS: Singing and Speaking French: Grades One through Three, Harvey Press, 1942, 3rd edition, 1973; *Chantons, mes enfants!,* Harvey Press, 1950; *Let's Ride on the Ferry,* Mapledale Press, 1955; *Why I Teach and Write for Children,* Mapledale Press, 1962; *The Little Red Couch,* Adler-Young, 1965; *Young Sigmund* (juvenile biography), Adler-Young, 1968; *Idiot Savant!* (juvenile fiction), Garfetta, 1972; *It Might Have Been Verse* (poetry), Garfetta, 1976; (with husband, Karl J. Tenn) *Analysis of Passion,* Garfetta, 1982.

Plays: "To Yonkers and Back," first produced Off-Off-Broadway at Take Six Workshop, March, 1967; "Michigannianna," first produced Off-Off-Broadway at Mid Sight Theater, May, 1968; "Grand Chou, Petit Chou," first produced in Detroit, Mich., at Grand Avenue Theater, December, 1970.

WORK IN PROGRESS: A stage musical version of *The Little Red Couch.*

SIDELIGHTS: Ada N. Tenn told *CA* that she can "ask where the bathroom is" in German, French, Spanish, and Welsh. *Avocational interests:* European travel, etymology, fine wines and beers.

BIOGRAPHICAL/CRITICAL SOURCES: Juvenile Writers, May, 1965, March, 1969; *New Plays,* April, 1967; *Histrionics Monthly,* June, 1970.

*   *   *

TERPSTRA, Vern   1927-

PERSONAL: Born August 20, 1927, in Wayland, Mich.; son of Benjamin and Lucy (Jonker) Terpstra; married Bonnie Lou Fuller, September 18, 1950; children: Benjamin, Mark, Kathryn Ann, James Richard. *Education:* University of Michigan, B.B.A., 1950, M.B.A., 1951, Ph.D., 1965; University of Brussels, graduate study, 1952-53. *Religion:* Presbyterian. *Home:* 750 Lans Way, Ann Arbor, Mich. *Office:* Graduate School of Business, University of Michigan, Ann Arbor, Mich. 48109.

CAREER: Church Missionary Society, director of education for the Congo, and director of a Congo normal school, 1953-61; Marketing Science Institute, Philadelphia, Pa., resident fellow, 1963-64; University of Pennsylvania, Wharton School, Philadelphia, assistant professor of marketing, 1964-66; University of Michigan, Graduate School of Business, Ann Arbor, associate professor, 1966-70, professor of international business, 1970—. Consultant in international studies, Marketing Science Institute, 1964-66; consulting editor on international business, Holt, Rinehart & Winston, 1971—. *Military service:* U.S. Navy, 1945-46. *Member:* Academy of International Business (president, 1971-72), American Economic Association, American Marketing Association.

WRITINGS: (With Liander and Sherbini) *Marketing Development in the European Economic Community,* McGraw, 1964; (editor with Alderson and Shapiro) *Patents and Progress: Sources and Impact of Changing Technology,* Irwin, 1965; (with Sherbini, Yoshino, and Liander) *Comparative Analysis for International Marketing,* Allyn & Bacon, 1967; *American Marketing in the Common Market,* Praeger, 1967; *University Education for International Business,* Academy of International Business, 1969.

International Marketing, Holt, 1972, 3rd edition, Dryden, 1983; *The Cultural Environment of International Business,* Southwestern Co., 1978; *The International Dimensions of Marketing,* Kent State University Press, 1982.

WORK IN PROGRESS: Research in international marketing by multinational firms.

*   *   *

TeSELLE, Sallie McFague
See McFAGUE, Sallie

*   *   *

THACHER, Alida McKay   1951-

PERSONAL: Born January 7, 1951, in Bloomington, Ind.; daughter of Henry C., Jr. (a professor of computer science) and Ann (a writer; maiden name, Peters) Thacher. *Education:* University of Wisconsin—Madison, B.A. (with honors), 1972, M.S. in education, 1978. *Home:* 2466 24th Ave. E., Seattle, Wash. 98112.

CAREER: Western Publishing Co., Racine, Wis., editor, 1972-74; free-lance writer and designer of audio-visual instructional materials, 1974-80; Northwest Film Study Center, Portland, Ore., instructor in television production, Artists in the Schools program, 1981-83; Cablesystems Pacific Television, Portland, producer of weekly show "Get Movin'," 1982-83; Clark County Government Channel 48, Vancouver, Wash., television producer, 1983—. Instructor, Portland Community College and Southwest Senior Center, beginning 1983. *Awards, honors:* Home Town Video USA Award for narrowcasting from National Federation of Local Cable Programmers, 1983, for "Get Movin'."

WRITINGS—For children; published by Raintree, except as indicated: *Golden Shoe Book,* Western Publishing, 1974; *Elephant on Wheels,* Western Publishing, 1974; *Raising a Racket: Rosie Casals,* 1976; *In the Center: Kareem Abdul-Jabbar,* 1976; *Games for All Seasons,* 1978; *Fastest Woman on Earth,* 1980; *Perilous Journey to the Top,* 1980. Also author of television scripts.

SIDELIGHTS: Alida McKay Thacher told *CA:* "After writing children's books for about eight years, I finally decided that the work is just too hard for me, at least for now. Sitting alone at my typewriter and trying to put something down on a blank sheet of paper is excruciatingly painful to me. I like people too much for all the solitude that requires; I want to be talking on the phone or visiting. And I think there are a lot of people who just are better at writing books than I am. I also am too hyperactive to sit still for that long.

"So, for the past couple of years I have been producing television programs for cable TV. That's work that requires a lot of gabbing with people and a lot of running around: perfect for me. I'm still writing scripts, but I'm also collecting props; going out on location and shooting the scripts; finding talented, interesting people to be on the shows; and working with sound and visual images as well as words.

"I've also started teaching other people to write. I've been teaching a class where older people are writing their life stories, and it's one of the most interesting, exciting things I've ever done. If you ever want to hear a good story, I suggest you ask an older adult to tell you about her or his life. I hope to keep working in cable TV, and I also hope to keep teaching writing classes."

THELIN, John R(obert) 1947-

PERSONAL: Born October 15, 1947, in Newton, Mass.; son of George Willard (an engineer and designer) and Rozalija (Komarec) Thelin; married A. Sharon Blackburn, June 24, 1978. *Education:* Brown University, A.B. (cum laude), 1969; University of California, Berkeley, M.A., 1972, Ph.D., 1973. *Home:* 421 Scotland St., No. 6, Williamsburg, Va. 23185.

CAREER: University of California, Berkeley, editor and lecturer in sociology of education and history, 1973-74; University of Kentucky, Lexington, assistant professor of history of education, 1974-77; Marquandia Society, Los Angeles, Calif., curator, 1977; The Claremont Colleges, Pomona College, Claremont, Calif., assistant dean of admissions, 1977-79; assistant director and research director, Association of Independent California Colleges and Universities, 1979-81; College of William and Mary, Williamsburg, Va., associate professor of American studies, 1981—, co-director of higher education doctoral program. Visiting professor and lecturer, Claremont Graduate School, 1977-79. *Member:* History of Education Society, American Educational Studies Association, Association for the Study of Higher Education, Marquandia Society, California Historical Society, Amherst Historical Society, Phi Beta Kappa.

WRITINGS: The Cultivation of Ivy: A Saga of the College in America, Schenkman, 1976; *Higher Education and Its Useful Past,* Schenkman, 1983. Contributor to history and education journals, and to *Down River, Berkshire Review,* and *Runner's World.* Member of editorial board, *Educational Studies;* essay review editor, *Review of Higher Education.*

WORK IN PROGRESS: Research on regional and institutional history, especially on colleges and universities in the 19th and 20th centuries; analyzing social and educational policies, especially in higher education; studying the works of such novelists as Raymond Chandler and John P. Marquand to understand Los Angeles and Boston in the late 19th and early 20th centuries.

SIDELIGHTS: John R. Thelin told *CA* that his aim is to write history for non-historians. His main interest "is in the use of historical methods for understanding the recent past"; he uses unorthodox sources, artifacts, documents, and icons; he studies mass culture and institutions, commercial art, and architectural forms. Of his book, *Higher Education and Its Useful Past,* the *Change* reviewer wrote, "This is a lively, refreshing, wholesomely skeptical book. It seeks to wean educational administrators and researchers away from such fashionable approaches as those of business-oriented management training, system analysis, futurology, and quantitative model-building."

AVOCATIONAL INTERESTS: Long-distance running, historic preservation.

BIOGRAPHICAL/CRITICAL SOURCES: Change, April-May, 1983.

*   *   *

THEOCHARIS, Reghinos D(emetrios) 1929-

PERSONAL: Born February 10, 1929, in Nicosia, Cyprus; son of Demetrios (an advocate) and Florentia (Mylona) Theocharis; married Madeleine Loumbou, June 6, 1954; children: Charis, Eleni. *Education:* Athens School of Economics and Commercial Science (now Athens School of Economics and Business),

Diploma in Economics, 1949; University of Aberdeen, Certificate in Economics, 1952; Garnett College, Teacher's Certificate, 1953; London School of Economics and Political Science, London, Ph.D., 1958. *Religion:* Greek Orthodox. *Home:* Raidestou 2, Athens 510, Greece. *Office:* Athens School of Economics and Business, Patission 76, Athens 104, Greece.

CAREER: Inspector of secondary schools and secondary teacher of economics and commerce in Cyprus, 1949-51, 1953-56; Bank of Greece, Athens, Greece, research department, 1958-59; Minister of Finance, Cyprus, 1959-62; Bank of Cyprus Ltd., Nicosia, Cyprus, governor, 1962-75; Athens School of Economics and Business, Athens, professor of economics, 1975—. Scientific director general of Center of Planning and Economic Research, 1978-81. Honorary fellow, London School of Economics and Political Science. *Member:* Royal Economic Society (fellow).

WRITINGS: The Dynamic Stability of Equilibrium (in Greek), [Athens], 1959; *Early Developments in Mathematical Economics,* Macmillan, 1961, revised edition, Porcupine Press, 1981; *History of Economic Analysis,* Papazissis, Volume I, 1979, Volume II, 1980. Contributor to economics journals.

SIDELIGHTS: Reghinos D. Theocharis speaks English, French, and German. *Avocational interests:* Reading and chess.

*   *   *

THIELICKE, Helmut 1908-

PERSONAL: Born December 4, 1908, in Wueppertal-Barmen, Germany; son of Reinhard and Laura (Koehler) Thielicke; married Marie-Luise Herrmann, September 28, 1937; children: Wolfram, Berthold, Elisabeth, Rainer. *Education:* Attended University of Greifswald, University of Marburg, and University of Bonn; University of Erlangen, Dr.Phil., 1932, Dr.Theol., 1934. *Religion:* Lutheran. *Home:* Barkenkoppel 2, 2000 Hamburg 65, West Germany. *Office:* Sedanstrasse 19, 2000 Hamburg 13, West Germany.

CAREER: University of Heidelberg, Heidelberg, Germany, professor, 1936-40; ordained priest in Lutheran Church, 1941; parish priest in Ravensburg, Germany, 1941-42; head of Theological Office of Wuerttemberg Church, 1943-45; University of Tuebingen, Tuebingen, Germany, professor of systematic theology, 1945-54, rector of the university, 1951; University of Hamburg, Hamburg, Germany, professor of systematic theology, 1954—, rector of the university, 1960. President of Conference of University Rectors of West Germany, 1951. *Awards, honors:* Great cross of order of merit (West Germany); Dr. Theol., University of Heidelberg, 1946; D.D., University of Glasgow, 1956; LL.D., University of Waterloo (Canada), 1974; Litt.D., Lenoir Rhyne College, 1975.

WRITINGS—Books appearing only in English translation: Christ and the Meaning of Life: A Book of Sermons and Meditations, translation by John W. Doberstein, Harper, 1962; *The Silence of God,* translation by Geoffrey Bromiley, Eerdmans, 1962; *The Freedom of the Christian Man: A Christian Confrontation with the Secular Gods,* Harper, 1963; *The Prayer That Spans the World,* translation by Doberstein, Attic Press, 1978; *The Waiting Father,* translation by Doberstein, Attic Press, 1978; *Being a Christian When the Chips Are Down,* translation by H. George Anderson, Fortress Press, 1979; *A Thielicke Trilogy,* translation by C. C. Barber and Bromiley, Baker Book, 1980.

German books in English translation: (First published anonymously) *Fragen des Christentums an die moderne Welt: Eine christliche Kulturkritik*, Editions Oikumene (Geneva), 1944, published under real name as *Fragen des Christentums an die moderne Welt: Untersuchungen zur geistigen und religioesen Krise des Abendlandes*, Mohr (Tuebingen), 1947, translation of chapter 12 by Doberstein published in *Man in God's World*, Harper, 1963; *Tod und Leben: Studien zur christlichen Anthropologie*, Editions Oikumene, c. 1944, translation by Edward Schroeder published as *Death and Life*, Fortress Press, 1970; *Jesus Christus am Scheidewege*, Furche-Verlag (Berlin), 1938, published as *Zwischen Gott und Satan, eine biblische Besinnung*, Furche-Verlag (Tuebingen), 1946, translation by C. C. Barber published as *Between God and Satan*, Eerdmans, 1958.

Der Nihilismus, Reichel (Tuebingen), 1950, translation by Doberstein published as *Nihilism, Its Origin and Nature, with a Christian Answer*, Harper, 1961; *Theologische Ethik*, Mohr, Volume I: *Prinzipienlehre: Dogmatische, philosophische und kontroverstheologische Grundlegung*, c. 1951, 5th edition, 1981, Volume II: *Ethik des Politischen*, 1958, 3rd edition, 1974, Volume III: *Ethik des Besellschaft, des Rechtes, der Sexualitaet, und der Kunst*, c. 1951, 2nd edition, 1958, translation of abridgment of Volumes I and II by William Lazareth published as *Theological Ethics*, Fortress Press, Volume I: *Foundations*, 1966, Volume II: *Politics*, 1966, translation of chapter of Volume III by Doberstein published as *The Ethics of Sex*, Harper, 1964; *Das Gebet, das die Welt umspannt: Reden veber das Vaterunser*, Quell-Verlag (Stuttgart), 1953, 13th edition, 1973, translation by Doberstein published as *Our Heavenly Father: Sermons on the Lord's Prayer*, Harper, 1960; *Die Lebensangst und ihre Ueberwindung*, Bertelsmann (Guetersloh), 1954, translation by Bromiley published as *Out of the Depths*, Eerdmans, 1962.

Das Leben kann noch einmal beginnen: Ein Gang durch die Bergpredigt, Quell-Verlag, 1956, 8th edition, 1965, translation by Doberstein published as *Life Can Begin Again: Sermons on the Sermon on the Mount*, Fortress Press, 1963; *Das Bilderbuch Gottes: Reden ueber die Gleichnisse Jesu*, Quell-Verlag, 1958, 3rd edition, 1962, translation by Doberstein published as *The Waiting Father: Sermons on the Parables of Jesus*, Harper, 1959, excerpt from translation published as *The Five Brothers of the Rich Man*, Church Pastoral-Aid Society (London), 1962; *Der Glaube der Christenheit: Unser Welt vor Jesus Christus*, Vendenhoeck & Ruprecht (Goettingen), 1958, 5th edition, 1965, translation of chapters 18-32 by Doberstein published in *Man in God's World*, Harper, 1963; *Vom Schiff ans gesehen: Tagebuch einer Ostasienreise*, Guetersloher Verlagshaus, 1959, translation by Doberstein published as *Voyage to the Far East*, Muhlenberg Press, 1962.

Wie die Welt begann: Der Mensch in der Urgeschichte der Bibel, Quell-Verlag, 1960, translation by Doberstein published as *How the World Began: Man in the First Chapters of the Bible*, Muhlenberg Press, 1961; *Vom geistlichen Reden: Begegnung mit Spurgeon*, Quell-Verlag, 1961, translation by Doberstein published as *Encounter with Spurgeon*, Fortress Press, 1963; *Gespraeche ueber Himmel und Erde: Begegnungen in Amerika*, Quell-Verlag, 1964, 2nd edition, 1965, translation by Doberstein published as *Between Heaven and Earth: Conversations with American Christians*, Harper, 1965.

Leiden an der Kirche: Ein persoenliches Wort, Furche-Verlag, 1965, translation by Doberstein published as *The Trouble with the Church: A Call for Renewal*, Harper, 1965; *Ich glaube: Das Bekanntnis der Christen*, Quell-Verlag, 1965, translation by H. George Anderson and Doberstein published as *I Believe:*

The Christian's Creed, Fortress Press, 1968; *Wie modern darf die Theologie sein?*, Quell-Verlag, 1967, published as *Theologisches Denken und verunsicherter Glaube: Eine Hinfuehrung zur "modernen" Theologie*, Herder (Freiburg), 1974, translation by Anderson published as *How Modern Should Theology Be?*, Fortress Press, 1969; *Der evangelische Glaube: Grundzuege der Dogmatik*, three volumes, Mohr, 1968-?, translation by Bromiley published as *The Evangelical Faith*, Eerdmans, 1974-82, Volume I: *Prolegomena: The Relation of Theology to Modern Thought Forms*, Volume II: *Theology and Christology*, Volume III: *Theology of Spirit*.

Und wenn Gott waere: Reden ueber die Frage nach Gott, Quell-Verlag, 1970, translation by Anderson published as *How to Believe Again*, Fortress Press, 1972; *Wer darf leben? Ethische Probleme den modernen Medizin*, Goldmann (Munich), 1970, translation published as *The Doctor as Judge of Who Shall Live and Who Shall Die*, Fortress Press, 1976; *So sah ich Afrika; Tagebuch einer Schiffsreise*, Mohr, 1971, translation published as *African Diary: My Search for Understanding*, Word Books (Waco, Tex.), 1974; *Leben mit dem Tod*, Mohr, 1980, translation by Bromiley published as *Living with Death*, Eerdmans, 1983.

In English: *Our Heavenly Father*, Baker Book, 1974; *The Faith Letters*, Word Books, 1978.

Other work: *Das Verhaeltnis zwischen dem Ethischen und dem Aesthelischen, eine systematische Untersuchung*, Meiner (Leipzig), 1932; *Geschichte und Existenz: Grundlegung einer evangelichen Geschichtstheologie*, Berteismann, 1935, 2nd edition, Mohr, 1964; *Vernunft und Offenbarung: Eine Studie euber die Religionsphilosophie Lessings*, Bertelsmann, 1936, 3rd edition published as *Offenbarung, Vernunft und Existenz: Studien zur Religionsphilosophie Lessings*, 1957, 5th edition, Mohr, 1957.

Wo ist Gott? Aus einem Briefwechsel, Vandenhoeck & Ruprecht, 1940; *Gottes Wort*, Oekumenische Kommission fuer die Pastoration der Kriegsgefangenen, 1944; *Die Grundgedanken des christlichen Glaubens*, Oekumenische Kommission fuer die Pastoration der Kriegsgefangenen, c. 1944.

Die evangelische Kirche und die Politik: Ethisch-politischer Traktat ueber einige Zietfragen, Evangelisches Verlagswerk (Stuttgart), 1953; (with Kurt Pentzlin) *Mensch und Arbeit im technischen Zeitalter*, Mohr, 1954; *In Amerika ist alles anders: Begegnungen und Beobachtungen*, Furche-Verlag, 1956, revised and enlarged edition published in *Auf Kanzel und Katheder: Aufzeichnungen aus Arbeit und Leben*, 1965; *Mensch zwischen Konstruktionen* (excerpts from *Theologische Ethik*), Cranach (Munich), 1956; *Christliche Verantwortung im Atomzeitalter: Ethisch-politischer Traktat uever einige Zeitfragen*, Evangelisches Verlagswerk, 1957; *Begegnungen*, Furche-Verlag, 1957, revised and enlarged edition published in *Auf Kanzel und Katheder: Aufzeichnungen aus Arbeit und Leben*, 1965; *Die Atomwaffe als Frage an die christliche Ethik*, Mohr, 1958; *Die Angst vor der Welt: Zur Begegnung mit dem Nihilismus*, Jugenddienst-Verlag (Wuppertal-Barmen), 1956; *Ethik des Politischen* (excerpt from *Theologische Ethik*), Mohr, 1958.

Brauchen wir Leitbilder? Ein Wort an die Jugend ueber Grosse und Elend der Ideale, Furche-Verlag, 1961; *Das Amt des Beters: Eine Besinnung auf das Wesen des Gebetes*, Schriftenmissions-Verlag (Gladbeck), 1961; *Das Schweigen Gottes: Fragen von heute an des Evangelium*, Furche-Verlag, 1962; *Unser Leben mit Gott*, Diefel (Wuppertal-Barmen), 1962; *Die Chance, der Freiheit nuetzen*, Bundesdruckerei (Bonn), 1962;

Einfuehrung in die christliche Ethik, Piper (Munich), 1963; *Der Einzelne und der Apparat: Von der Freiheit des Menschen im technischen Zeitalter,* Furche-Verlag, 1964; (with Ekkehard Othmer) *Deutschland: Demokratie oder Vaterland,* Wunderlich (Tuebingen), 1964.

Was ist Wahrheit?, edited by Hans Mueller-Schwefe, Vandenhoeck & Ruprecht, 1965; *Das Schweigen Gottes: Fragen von heute an das Evangelium,* Furche-Verlag, 1965; *Theologie und Zeitgenossenschaft: Gesammelte Aufsaetze,* Wunderlich (Tuebingen), 1967; *Ueber die Angst des heutigen Theologiestudenten vor dem geistlichen Amt,* Mohr, 1967; *Wer darf leben? Der Arzt als Richter,* Wunderlich, 1968; *Kulturkritik der studentischen Rebellion,* Mohr, 1969.

Thielicke-Brevier: Meditationen fuer jeden Tag, compiled and edited by Wolfgang Erk and Heinrich Kuhfuss, Steinkopf (Stuttgart), 1972; *Die geheime Frage nach Gott: Hintergruende unserer geistigen Situation,* Herder, 1972; *Notwendigkeit und Begrenzung des politischen Auftrags der Kirche,* Mohr, 1974; *Das Lachen der Heiligen und Narren: Nachdenklichen ueber Witz und Humor,* Herder, 1974; *Mensch sein, Mensch werden: Entwurf einer christlichen Anthropologie,* Piper, 1976, translation by Bromiley, Doubleday, 1984. Also author of *Glauben und Denken in der Neuzeit—Die grossen Systeme der Theologie und Religionsphilosophie,* 1983.

AVOCATIONAL INTERESTS: Photography.

* * *

THOGER, Marie   1923-

PERSONAL: Born July 25, 1923, in Lindum, Denmark; daughter of Jens (a farmer) and Karen Thoger. *Education:* Attended Ranum Seminary, 1941-46. *Home:* Kielshoj 48, 3520 Farum, Denmark. *Office:* Ulrikkenborg School, Kongens Lyngby, Denmark.

CAREER: Ulrikkenborg School, Kongens Lyngby, Denmark, teacher, 1951—, librarian, 1978—. Educational specialist for UNESCO, working on adult literacy in India, 1952-53, and in East Pakistan, 1965-66.

WRITINGS: Inderdrengen Ranga, Gyldendal, 1957; *Indien pa vej,* Gyldendal, 1961; *Shanta* (juvenile), Gyldendal, 1961, translation by Eileen Amos published under same title, University of London Press, 1966, Follett, 1968; *Kibbutznik,* Gyldendal, 1967; *God rejse,* Munksgard, 1975; *Didi and Puspa,* Gyldendal, 1981; *Kamla,* Special paedagogisk forlag i Herning, 1982; *Enken Kamla,* Special paedagogisk forlag i Herning, in press.

SIDELIGHTS: "My first book was written after I had worked in India from November, 1952 to December, 1953," Marie Thoger told *CA.* "A colleague in the school asked me to tell the Danish children about my experience in the East.

"I decided to use the fiction form and try to make a novel, reasonably exciting and easy to read, but at the same time giving absolutely realistic facts about living conditions for the children in this vast country of India. I had the hope that my book would add a little to understanding and toleration in the world.

"Now I feel that bookwriting is my way of working for peace. For the last ten years, I have been involved in villages, working among women in a far-off valley in the northern part of India— Kumaon in Himalaya. Since then I have concentrated more and more on giving a true picture of those hill women's daily life. At the same time, I have tried to develop a skill of telling the story in few and simple words, so that untrained readers can get the messages without too much trouble.''

Inderdrengen Ranga has been translated into Polish and several Scandinavian languages.

* * *

THORNE, Christopher   1934-

PERSONAL: Born May 17, 1934, in Surrey, England; married; children: two daughters. *Education:* Attended St. Edmund Hall, Oxford, 1955-58. *Office:* University of Sussex, Sussex, England.

CAREER: Charterhouse, Godalming, Surrey, England, senior history master, 1951-56; British Broadcasting Corp., Radio, London, England, head of further education, 1966-68; University of Sussex, Sussex, England, 1968—, began as lecturer, currently professor of international relations. *Military service:* Royal Navy, 1953-55; became lieutenant.

AWARDS, HONORS: Elected fellow of the British Academy; Bancroft Prize, 1979, for *Allies of a Kind.*

WRITINGS: Ideology and Power, Macmillan, 1965; *Chartism,* Macmillan, 1966; (editor) *The Approach of War, 1938-39,* St. Martin's, 1967; (editor) A. J. Nicholls, *Weimar and the Rise of Hitler,* St. Martin's, 1969; *The Limits of Foreign Policy,* Hamish Hamilton, 1972, Putnam, 1973; *Allies of a Kind: The United States, Britain, and the War against Japan, 1941-1945,* Oxford University Press, 1978; *Racial Aspects of the Far Eastern War, 1941-1945,* British Academy, 1982. Reviewer for various periodicals, including *Times Literary Supplement.*

WORK IN PROGRESS: A thematic and comparative study of the Far Eastern War of 1941-1945.

SIDELIGHTS: In his award-winning book, *Allies of a Kind: The United States, Britain, and the War against Japan, 1941-1945,* historian Christopher Thorne explores the relationship between the U.S. and Great Britain in their struggle against Japan. "His main aim and his main achievement is to illuminate the character of Anglo-American relations," observes Paul Addison in the *New Statesman.* Despite their united purpose in Europe, "east of the Suez the two nations were competitors as well as allies. The Americans made no secret of the fact that they intended to inherit not only the white man's burden but his trade and investments." And Britain, aware that her status as a world power was dwindling, wanted to maneuver the U.S. in such a way that England's continued participation in world commerce was assured. Thorne sums up their positions this way: "On the American side [there were] suspicions of the British and an assumption of conflicting interests; on the part of the British, a belief in mutual long-term Anglo-American interests and hopes for close collaboration." According to Thorne, both nations were guilty of imperialism and white supremacy.

Unlike historians who draw their accounts from records of formal transactions between nations, Thorne focuses much of his study on the men who shaped such policies—in this case, Franklin Delano Roosevelt and Winston Churchill. "Great care is taken to be scrupulously fair to both parties," reports Richard Storry in the *Times Literary Supplement,* "although Thorne in no way conceals his own dislike of Churchill's political opinions. He refers more than once to Churchill's 'racism,' describing this as 'ignorant, ugly and at times vicious.' He clearly regards Churchill as hopelessly reactionary. Yet he concedes that Churchill had 'the strength of genuineness,' that he was temperamentally unsuited to intrigue. . . . By contrast, Roosevelt, his style 'a combination of halo-polishing and hard politics,' emerges as much the smaller man.''

In summary of Thorne's treatment, Addison observes that Thorne ''combines the cold qualities of control and the warm qualities of passion and imagination which flow together in the making of a first-class history. As a writer he is cool, patient and judicious, never reaching a verdict without a meticulous reckoning of the pros and cons. Yet the overall effect is far-reaching: the most searching, the most imaginative, and the most radical analysis we have yet had of the relations between John Bull and Uncle Sam in the 20th century.''

AVOCATIONAL INTERESTS: Singing, sports (played cricket for England Schools team and for British Navy).

BIOGRAPHICAL/CRITICAL SOURCES: Times Literary Supplement, February 2, 1973, June 2, 1978; *New York Review of Books,* May 17, 1973; Christopher Thorne, *Allies of a Kind: The United States, Britain, and the War against Japan, 1941-1945,* Oxford University Press, 1978; *New Statesman,* March 24, 1978; *Listener,* June 8, 1978.

* * *

TIBBETTS, Orlando L(ailer), Jr.   1919-

PERSONAL: Born April 9, 1919, in Portland, Me.; son of Orlando Lailer and Ruby (Wilkinson) Tibbetts; married Phyllis Jones, June 25, 1941; children: Roger, Douglas, Faith (Mrs. Dexter Benedict), Judith (Mrs. Dwight Foster). *Education:* Gordon College, A.B., 1940; Andover Newton Theological School, B.D., 1943, S.T.M., 1952, D.Min., 1973. *Home address:* P.O. Box 1601, Manchester, Conn. 06040. *Office:* First Baptist Church in America, 75 North Main St., Providence, R.I. 02906.

CAREER: Ordained to ministry of Baptist Church, 1943; Baptist Seminary, Mexico City, Mexico, founder, and president, 1947-53; pastor of Baptist churches in Ohio, 1953-63; Boston Baptist City Mission Society, Boston, Mass., executive minister, 1963-68; Massachusetts Council of Churches, Boston, executive minister of Metropolitan Boston Commission, 1968-70; American Baptist Churches of Connecticut, Hartford, executive minister, 1971-81; Eastern Baptist Theological Seminary, Philadelphia, Pa., adjunct professor, beginning 1982; First Baptist Church in America, Providence, R.I., senior minister, 1983—. Chaplain, Home for Unwed Mothers, Boston; treasurer, Boston Industrial Mission; member of board of directors, North Conway Institute.

MEMBER: American Protestant Hospital Association, National Council of Churches, Association of Council Secretaries, Massachusetts Conference on Social Welfare, Iona Community (Scotland; associate member). *Awards, honors:* D.D. from Rio Grande College, Rio Grande, Ohio; Best seller award, Judson Press, 1981, for *The Work of the Church Trustee.*

WRITINGS—All published by Judson: *The Reconciling Community,* 1969; *Sidewalk Prayers,* 1971; *More Sidewalk Prayers,* 1973; *The Work of the Church Trustee,* 1979; *How to Keep Useful Church Records,* 1983.

AVOCATIONAL INTERESTS: Music (plays a number of instruments), painting in oils.

TINDALL, Gillian   1938-

PERSONAL: Born May 4, 1938, in London, England; married R. G. Lansdown (a psychologist); children: Harry. *Education:* Oxford University, M.A. (with first class honors), 1959. *Politics:* None. *Religion:* None. *Agent:* Curtis Brown Group Ltd., 162-168 Regent St., London W1R 5TA, England.

CAREER: Writer. *Awards, honors:* Somerset Maugham Award for *Fly Away Home.*

WRITINGS: No Name in the Street, Cassell, 1959, published as *When We Had Other Names,* Morrow, 1960; *The Water and the Sound,* Cassell, 1961, Morrow, 1962; *The Edge of the Paper,* Cassell, 1963; *The Israeli Twins,* J. Cape, 1963; *A Handbook on Witches,* Arthur Barker, 1965, Atheneum, 1966.

The Youngest, Secker & Warburg, 1967, Walker & Co., 1968; *Someone Else,* Walker & Co., 1969; *Fly Away Home,* Walker & Co., 1971; *Dances of Death* (short stories), Walker & Co., 1973; *The Born Exile: George Gissing* (biography), Harcourt, 1974; *The Traveller and His Child,* Hodder & Stoughton, 1975.

The Fields Beneath: The History of One London Village (urban history), Temple Smith, 1977; *The Intruder,* Hodder & Stoughton, 1979; *The China Egg* (short stories), Hodder & Stoughton, 1981; *City of Gold: The Biography of Bombay* (urban history), Temple Smith, 1982; *Looking Forward,* Hodder & Stoughton, 1983.

Regular contributor to *Times* (London), *Sunday Times,* and *New Society.*

SIDELIGHTS: Though she is best known for her fiction, the versatile British writer Gillian Tindall has also turned her hand to urban history and literary biography. About all her subjects, she is ''insatiably curious,'' according to Dilip Hiro, who writes in the *New Statesman* that ''Gillian Tindall does not rest until she gets to the origins of whatever interests her.''

One of her novels, the award-winning *Fly Away Home,* is written as the diary of an unhappy young Englishwoman trying to come to terms with her life. Aware that she has not matured since her boarding school days, the protagonist Antonia Boileau turns to her journal in an effort to rid herself of ''the sudden, sickly attraction toward tragedy and drama, toward the artificially violent situation'' that troubles her. She reflects upon her flight from home at eighteen, her decision to have children instead of going to college, and her seemingly aimless existence as a Frenchman's wife. Compared to an old friend in London, Antonia feels rootless and uncommitted, feelings that are exacerbated by her husband Marc's refusal to acknowledge his Jewishness—even after the eruption of the 1967 Six-Day War. It takes a trip back to Israel, where she revisits an old lover, and a series of personal tragedies to convince Antonia that the past as she remembers it no longer exists. Having come full circle, she returns home to Marc.

''All this adds up to a serious, valid and occasionally moving attempt to reproduce the texture of a life,'' writes Clive Jordan in the *New Statesman.* ''Yet,'' he continues, ''often life escapes. Mainly I think, it's a question of style. Measured, flat, undemonstrative, analytic, the language takes off so rarely into metaphor that when it does the diarist herself remarks upon the fact.''

At least one reviewer attributes this stylistic quality to the journalist in Tindall, striving to chart an interior personal crisis against exterior public events, such as the Six-Day War. While this approach has drawbacks, it has some advantages as well. "Perhaps Antonia is not quite spontaneous enough in her unceasing self-absorption, her conformity more apparent, maybe, than Miss Tindall is aware," notes the *Times Literary Supplement* reviewer. "But the critical intelligence that is allowed to appear provides some sparkling comment on the external events that colour her diary."

Tindall's more recent novels include *The Traveller and His Child*, a study of a divorced father grieving for the effective loss of his son, and *The Intruder*, which is set in wartime France and charts the experiences of a young Englishwoman who finds herself caught there under the occupation with her schoolboy son. A critical success in the United Kingdom, *The Intruder* was described by a *Listener* critic as "a marvelous account of what survival is like, as well as being an authentic evocation of French rural life." Tindall's 1983 novel, *Looking Forward*, has had a more mixed reception but has nowhere been dismissed as unimportant. It depicts the life of a woman doctor, born in 1902, showing her personal development against the background of her times. Regarded by some as over-documentary, to the *Sunday Telegraph* critic it appeared an "ultimately moving comment . . . not just on its characters' lives but on all our hopes and fears."

While *Looking Forward* garnered mixed reviews, Tindall's first biography, *The Born Exile: George Gissing,* was well-received. The *New Yorker* characterizes Tindall's study of this minor Victorian novelist as "intelligent and sensitive," and Peter Stansky suggests that any renewed interest in Gissing's books may well be traced to this "excellent" work. "One could not ask for a better, or better written, introduction to Gissing than *The Born Exile*," Stansky observes in the *New York Times Book Review*. "It is intelligent, provocative and informed, in touch with current scholarship and the latest biographical 'finds,' firmly based in its knowledge of its subject's works—Miss Tindall seems to have read and thought about them all—as well as his life, his psychology, and the world in which he lived."

Largely remembered for his classic account of nineteenth-century professional writing (*New Grub Street*), Gissing was a sad and self-destructive figure. He was a brilliant student, on scholarship and destined for an academic career, when he was caught stealing money from the school cloakroom. The money was not for him, but his mistress Nell—a prostitute whom he hoped to save from the streets. Unmoved by his altruistic motives, officials expelled him from the school, and he was sentenced to a month in prison. Freed, he fled to America in total disgrace, but he kept in touch with Nell and eventually returned to England to marry her. She drank heavily, occasionally returning to prostitution and making Gissing's life miserable. "He was 22," Stansky observes, "and already he was creating that ambience of moral and physical squalor that was to torment him for much of his life; it was to prove essential to him as a writer—the material he reproduced in so many of his novels." Whatever his reasons, after Nell's death, Gissing married another working-class girl. She went crazy.

In her study, Tindall proposes that "as a writer Gissing needed such relationships as these, and half-consciously sought them out," explains the *Times Literary Supplement* reviewer. "There were—although she does not put it in quite this way—two Gissings. One of them looked back to the academic career of which he had been deprived. . . . The other Gissing makes sure, through the wretched marriages, of what Mrs. Tindall

calls 'the escape downwards.' He involves himself in a way of life which he says he loathes, but which in fact he need not have endured for more than a few years from a purely financial point of view."

Despite her exploration of the parallels between Gissing's life and his writing, Tindall does not consider his novels autobiographical. Instead, as V. S. Pritchett observes in the *New Statesman*, "she looks at the interrelation between the two people—often with 'irreconcilable needs'—the writer and the man, noting that Gissing set about experimenting with a personal dilemma in his writings and then went clean against his own judgment in his life." The *Times Literary Supplement* reviewer says that while "the idea of Gissing's need for escape downwards must be conjectural . . . , it is documented by Mrs. Tindall in convincing detail and with great sympathy." For these reasons, he deems it "by far the best critical study of Gissing yet written."

In addition to biography, Tindall has also branched into urban history, and she told *CA* that her "recent nonfiction has been particularly concerned with the development of cities." In *The Fields Beneath: The History of One London Village*, Tindall explores the heritage of Kentish Town, an ancient inner suburb that became little more than a thoroughfare to the north with the advent of the railways. "Not the most glamorous area, indeed: rather seedy and down-at-heel, heir to the drab legacy of mid-nineteenth-century exploitation of once rural estates," is how Mary Cosh, writing in the London *Times*, describes the area. In her book, Tindall, herself a long-time resident of the district, traces its roots back to the Norman Conquest and helps it recover a sense of itself as a place to live. Her study is not "blighted by sociology," according to the *New Statesman's* V. S. Pritchett. "It is felt, original and vivid, and her research is thorough and concerned. The book is indeed a model for future writers who feel the new desire of city dwellers to know where they live and what the meaning of a sense of livable place is."

BIOGRAPHICAL/CRITICAL SOURCES: Gillian Tindall, *Fly Away Home*, Walker & Co., 1971; *New Statesman*, July 2, 1971, February 1, 1974, September 16, 1977, September 14, 1979, April 16, 1982; *Spectator*, July 10, 1971; *Times Literary Supplement*, July 16, 1971, February 22, 1974, June 20, 1975, November 23, 1979, March 27, 1981, April 16, 1982; *New York Times Book Review*, December 19, 1971, November 25, 1973, September 8, 1974; *New Yorker*, September 2, 1974; *New York Review of Books*, October 31, 1974; *Contemporary Literary Criticism*, Volume VII, Gale, 1977; *Listener*, September 13, 1979; *Times* (London), March 1, 1980; *Sunday Telegraph*, October 16, 1983.

—*Sketch by Donna Olendorf*

*   *   *

TOMPERT, Ann 1918-

PERSONAL: Born January 11, 1918, in Detroit, Mich.; daughter of Joseph (a farmer) and Florence (Pollitt) Bakeman; married Robert S. Tompert (a social service employee), March 31, 1951. *Education:* Siena Heights College, B.A. (summa cum laude); Wayne State University, graduate study. *Politics:* "Independent with Republican leanings." *Religion:* Christian. *Home:* 141 Loretta Rd., Marine City, Mich. 48039.

CAREER: Teacher in elementary and junior and senior high schools of St. Clair Shores, East Detroit, Grosse Pointe, Marine City, and other cities in Michigan, 1939-59; writer, 1959—.

Member: Society of Children's Book Writers, River District Hospital Auxiliary (life member; St. Clair, Mich.). *Awards, honors: Little Fox Goes to the End of the World* was named notable children's book by American Library Association, 1976, and by *School Library Journal,* and was cited for honors by Chicago Children's Reading Round Table, 1979; *Little Otter Remembers* was cited as a classroom choice by the International Reading Association, 1978; *Charlotte and Charles* was named an Irma Simonton Black award honor book, 1980; Woodward Park School annual book award.

WRITINGS—Children's books, except as indicated: *What Makes My Cat Purr?,* Whitman Publishing, 1965; *The Big Whistle,* Whitman Publishing, 1968; *When Rooster Crowed,* Whitman Publishing, 1968; *Maybe a Dog Will Come,* Follett, 1968; *A Horse for Charlie,* Whitman Publishing, 1969.

The Crow, the Kite, and the Golden Umbrella, Abelard, 1971; *Fun for Ozzie,* Steck, 1971; *Hyacinth, the Reluctant Duck,* Steck, 1972; *It May Come in Handy Someday,* McGraw, 1975; *Little Fox Goes to the End of the World* (Junior Literary Guild selection), Crown, 1976; (editor) *The Way Things Were* (adult autobiography of Marine City, Mich., pioneer, Emily Ward), privately printed, 1976; *Little Otter Remembers,* Crown, 1977; *The Clever Princess,* Lollipop Power, Inc., 1977; *Badger on His Own,* Crown, 1978; *Three Foolish Tales,* Crown, 1979; *Charlotte and Charles,* Crown, 1979.

Contributor: Dorothy Haas, editor, *The Real Books of First Stories,* Rand McNally, 1973; Ira E. Aaron, editor, *Sea Treasures,* Scott, Foresman, 1981. Also contributor to children's magazines, including *Jack and Jill, Wee Wisdom,* and *Friend.*

WORK IN PROGRESS: A Dollhouse for Lisa, for Rand McNally; *Just a Little Bit,* for Four Winds Press; *Nothing Sticks Like a Shadow,* for Houghton.

SIDELIGHTS: The schools Ann Tompert has taught in range from a two-room country schoolhouse in the thumb area of Michigan to the large metropolitan schools of suburban Detroit. In addition, she worked part time in an antique shop and in a local vegetable and flower nursery.

She told *CA:* "I was reared on a small farm on the outskirts of Detroit where my father raised vegetables which were sold at a roadside stand in front of our house; and I have never forgotten my 'roots.' I suppose we were what today would be called 'underprivileged,' but we weren't aware of it. We had few toys so we made our fun. . . . But books were the most important things in my life.

"Because my life has been so influenced by what I read as a child (for example: I knew I wanted to be a writer like Jo Marsh when I read *Little Women*), I am very committed to the idea of fostering positive values in my books for children.

"We as a nation are so dedicated to preserving our physical environment and our quality of life (making ourselves safe from all harm—auto safety, cancer research, pure food laws, etc.); yet, when it comes to dealing with our minds, anything and everything is permissible. I find this very disturbing, to say the least."

Little Fox Goes to the End of the World and *Little Otter Remembers* have been translated into Japanese.

AVOCATIONAL INTERESTS: Reading new writers, collecting paperweights and milkglass, working in her wildflower garden, caning chairs, refinishing furniture, sewing, and needlework.

TRABASSO, Tom 1935-

PERSONAL: Born May 25, 1935, in Poughkeepsie, N.Y.; son of Anthony J. and Viola (Opitz) Trabasso; married Susan Schwerdtle, June 28, 1958; married Nancy Stein, August 15, 1982. *Education:* Union College, Schenectady, N.Y., B.S., 1957; Michigan State University, M.A., 1959, Ph.D., 1961. *Office:* Department of Education and Behavioral Sciences, University of Chicago, 5835 South Kimbark, Chicago, Ill. 60637.

CAREER: University of California, Los Angeles, associate professor of psychology, 1963-69; Princeton University, Princeton, N.J., professor of psychology, 1969-76; University of Minnesota, Institute of Child Development, Minneapolis, professor, 1976-79; University of Chicago, Chicago, Ill., professor of education and behavioral sciences, 1979—.

WRITINGS: (With Gordon H. Bower) *Attention in Learning: Theory and Research,* Wiley, 1968; (with Deborah Harrison) *Black English: A Seminar,* Lawrence Erlbaum Associates, 1976; (with Heinz Mandl and wife, Nancy Stein) *Comprehension and Learning of Text,* Lawrence Erlbaum Associates, 1983. Contributor of articles to professional journals.

WORK IN PROGRESS: Research in human cognition, thinking and language comprehension, and cognitive development.

*   *   *

TREFETHEN, James B(yron, Jr.) 1916-1976

PERSONAL: Surname is accented on second syllable, Tre-*feth*-en; born June 3, 1916, in Brockton, Mass.; died December 30, 1976, in Washington, D.C.; son of James Byron (a contractor) and Mabel (Churchill) Trefethen; married Julia Edes, August 30, 1941; children: James Edes, Ann (Mrs. William Kerr), Frances (Mrs. Glenn Hopkins), Clinton David, Holly (Mrs. Donald Snide). *Education:* Northeastern University, B.A., 1940; University of Massachusetts, M.S., 1948. *Office:* 1000 Vermont Ave. N.W., Washington, D.C. 20005.

CAREER: Retail Credit Co., Boston, Mass., insurance investigator, 1941-43; Wildlife Management Institute, Washington, D.C., editor of *Outdoor News Bulletin,* 1948-52, director of publications, 1952-76. Assistant editor, Executive News Service, Natural Resources Council of America, 1971-75. Chairman of Conservation Roundtable, Washington, D.C., 1974-75; lecturer on wildlife topics. *Military service:* U.S. Army, 1943-45; served in northern France campaigns, including Battle of Normandy.

MEMBER: International Association of Game, Fish, and Conservation Commissioners, Wildlife Society (vice-president of Nation's Capital chapter, 1973; president, 1974), National Rifle Association (life member), Outdoor Writers Association of America, Forest History Society, Boone and Crockett Club (New York City). *Awards, honors:* Jade of Chiefs Award, Outdoor Writers Association of America, 1975; Conservation Education Award, Wildlife Society, 1976, for *An American Crusade for Wildlife.*

WRITINGS: Crusade for Wildlife, Stackpole, 1961; *Wildlife Management and Conservation,* Heath, 1963; (editor with Leonard Miracle) *Hunters Encyclopedia,* Stackpole, 1966; *Americans and Their Guns,* Stackpole, 1967; (editor with Clarence Cottam) *Whitewings: The Life History, Status, and Management of the White-winged Dove,* Van Nostrand, 1968.

(Editor) *A Forty-Year Cumulative Index of the Transactions of the North American Wildlife and Natural Resources Conferences, Volumes I-XXXIV, and the Proceedings of the American Game Conference, Volumes XV-XXI,* Wildlife Management Institute, 1970; *The Wild Sheep in Modern North America,* Winchester Press, 1975; *An American Crusade for Wildlife,* Winchester Press, 1975; *The American Landscape, 1776-1976: Two Centuries of Change,* Wildlife Management Institute, 1976. Editor, *Transactions* of the North American Wildlife and Natural Resources Conference, 1953-75, and *Proceedings* of the National Watershed Congress, 1954-74. Contributor of numerous articles to periodicals, including *American Heritage, Audubon,* and *Sports Illustrated.*

AVOCATIONAL INTERESTS: Outdoor sports, including shooting.

OBITUARIES: Washington Post, January 1, 1977.†

*   *   *

TRUBO, Richard 1946-

PERSONAL: Born April 2, 1946, in Los Angeles, Calif.; son of William and Ida (Singer) Trubo; married Donna Grodin (a teacher), June 24, 1973; children: Melissa Suzanne. *Education:* University of California, Los Angeles, B.A., 1967, M.A., 1968.

CAREER: KOST Radio, Los Angeles, Calif., producer-writer, 1968-71; free-lance writer, 1971—. *Member:* American Society of Journalists and Authors, Authors Guild.

WRITINGS: An Act of Mercy, Nash Publishing, 1973; (with Richard Guarino) *The Great American Insurance Hoax,* Nash Publishing, 1974; (with Guarino) *Your Insurance Handbook,* Doubleday, 1975; *How to Get a Good Night's Sleep,* Little, Brown, 1978; *The Consumer's Book of Hints and Tips,* Jonathan David, 1978; (with David E. Bresler) *Free Yourself from Pain,* Simon & Schuster, 1979; (with Barry Behrstock) *The Parents' When-Not-to-Worry Book: Straight Talk About All Those Myths You've Learned from Your Parents, Friends—and Even Doctors,* Harper, 1981.

Contributor to popular magazines, including *Holiday, True, Coronet, TV Guide, Parade,* and *Family Weekly;* contributor to newspapers, including *Detroit News, San Francisco Chronicle, Chicago Sun-Times, Chicago Tribune,* and *Los Angeles Times.*

WORK IN PROGRESS: A documentary motion picture about emotionally-disturbed teenage girls.†

*   *   *

TUCKER, Helen 1926-

PERSONAL: Born November 1, 1926, in Raleigh, N.C.; daughter of William Blair and Helen (Welch) Tucker; married William Thad Beckwith, January 9, 1971. *Education:* Wake Forest University, B.A., 1946; graduate study at Columbia University, 1957-58. *Religion:* Episcopalian. *Home:* 2930 Hostetler St., Raleigh, N.C. 27609. *Agent:* Curtis Brown, Ltd., 575 Madison Ave., New York, N.Y. 10022.

CAREER: Reporter on newspapers in Burlington, N.C., 1946-47, Twin Falls, Idaho, 1948-49, and Boise, Idaho, 1950-51; KDYL Radio, Salt Lake City, Utah, copywriter, 1951-52; WPTF Radio Co., Raleigh, N.C., copy supervisor, 1953-55; *Raleigh Times,* Raleigh, reporter, 1955-57; Columbia University Press,

New York, N.Y., editorial assistant, 1959-60; North Carolina Museum of Art, Raleigh, director of publicity, 1967-70. *Awards, honors:* Distinguished Alumni award, Wake Forest University, 1971.

WRITINGS—Published by Stein & Day: *The Sound of Summer Voices* (novel), 1969; *The Guilt of August Fielding,* 1971; *No Need of Glory,* 1972; *The Virgin of Lontano,* 1973.

Published by Fawcett: *A Strange and Ill-Starred Marriage,* 1978; *A Reason for Rivalry,* 1979; *A Mistress to the Regent,* 1980; *An Infamous Attachment,* 1980; *The Halverton Scandal,* 1980; *A Wedding Day Deception,* 1981; *The Double Dealers,* 1982; *Season of Dishonor,* 1982.

Published by Pocket Books: *Ardent Vows,* 1983.

BIOGRAPHICAL/CRITICAL SOURCES: Best Sellers, November 15, 1969; *Book World,* May 12, 1970.

*   *   *

TUCKER, Nicholas 1936-

PERSONAL: Born November 13, 1936, in London, England; son of Archie (a professor) and Betty (Hills) Tucker; married Jacqueline Elizabeth Anthony (a teacher), 1964; children: Matthew, Emma, Lucy. *Education:* King's College, Cambridge, B.A., 1958. *Politics:* Socialist. *Religion:* Atheist. *Home:* 56 Prince Edwards Rd., Lewes, Sussex BN7 1BH, England. *Office:* University of Sussex, Falmer, Brighton, Sussex BN1 9QX, England.

CAREER: University of Sussex, Falmer, Brighton, England, lecturer in developmental psychology, 1969—.

WRITINGS: Understanding the Mass Media, Cambridge University Press, 1964; (editor) *One Hundred of the Best "Times Educational Supplement" Cartoons,* Penguin, 1968; (editor) *Mother Goose Lost,* Crowell, 1971; (editor) *Mother Goose Abroad,* Crowell, 1975; *The Look Book,* Penguin, 1975; (editor) *Suitable for Children: Controversies in Children's Literature,* University of California Press, 1976; *What Is a Child?,* Open Books, 1977; *A Skeleton in the Cupboard,* Puffin, 1979; *The Child and the Book: A Psychological and Literary Exploration,* Cambridge University Press, 1981.

WORK IN PROGRESS: Progressive Schoolboy: Memoirs of an Unorthodox Education, for Cambridge University Press.

SIDELIGHTS: "I have always been interested in writing either about or for children," Nicholas Tucker told *CA.* "Where this interest comes from I'm not sure: being a member of a large family helps, I suspect, since at the time there were moments when one has to become an expert child-watcher in order to survive at all! The 1939-1945 war was also an extraordinary time to be a child; for a time one was almost on a basis of equality with adults, sharing most of their fears and fantasies about 'the enemy.' The ending of early childhood coinciding with the ending of the war served to make both happenings something of extra fascination for me ever since.

"Since I was also an exceptionally well-loved child, I have always felt especially for children who are not so lucky, hence my other career as a child psychologist. In all my work, however, I am always anxious to get adults to think and feel about children in a more informed, sensitive way than often seems to be the case. One particular reason I am so interested in children's literature in general is precisely because children's novelists often seem much better than anyone else at describing what exactly it can be like to be a child."

BIOGRAPHICAL/CRITICAL SOURCES: Times Literary Supplement, July 24, 1981.

* * *

TUCKMAN, Bruce W(ayne) 1938-

PERSONAL: Born November 24, 1938, in New York, N.Y.; son of Jack S. (an accountant) and Sophie (Goldberg) Tuckman; married second wife, Darby Godwin, July 24, 1980; children: (first marriage) Blair Zoe, Bret Ashley. *Education:* Rensselaer Polytechnic Institute, B.S., 1960; Princeton University, M.A., 1962, Ph.D., 1963. *Home:* 2068 West Forest Dr., Tallahassee, Fla. 32303. *Office:* Florida State University, Tallahassee, Fla. 32306.

CAREER: Naval Medical Research Institute, Bethesda, Md., research psychologist, 1963-65; Rutgers University, New Brunswick, N.J., associate professor, 1965-70, professor of education, 1970-78, director of research, 1975-78; Bernard M. Baruch College of the City University of New York, New York City, dean of education, 1978-82; Graduate School and University Center of the City University of New York, New York City, senior research fellow, 1982-83; Florida State University, Tallahassee, dean of education, 1983—. Curriculum developer, American Association for the Advancement of Science, 1965-67. *Member:* American Psychological Association (fellow), American Educational Research Association, National Council on Measurement in Education, Phi Delta Kappa.

WRITINGS: (Editor with J. L. O'Brian) *Preparing to Teach the Disadvantaged,* Free Press, 1969; *Conducting Educational Research,* Harcourt, 1972, 2nd edition, 1978; *Measuring Educational Outcomes: Fundamentals of Testing,* Harcourt, 1975; *Evaluating Instructional Outcomes,* Allyn & Bacon, 1979; *Analyzing and Designing Educational Research,* Harcourt, 1979. Contributor to psychological and educational research journals.

WORK IN PROGRESS: Books and research on sports psychology.

* * *

TURNER, Darwin T(heodore) 1931-

PERSONAL: Born May 7, 1931, in Cincinnati, Ohio; son of Darwin Romanes (a pharmacist) and Laura (a teacher; maiden name, Knight) Turner; married Edna Bonner, June 1, 1949 (divorced August, 1961); married Maggie Jean Lewis (a teacher), February 29, 1968; children: Pamela (Mrs. Robert Welch), Darwin Keith, Rachon. *Education:* University of Cincinnati, B.A., 1947, M.A., 1949; University of Chicago, Ph.D., 1956. *Home:* 5 Washington Pl., Iowa City, Iowa 52240. *Office:* University of Iowa, 303 English-Philosophy Bldg., Iowa City, Iowa 55242.

CAREER: Clark College, Atlanta, Ga., instructor in English, 1949-51; Morgan State College (now Morgan State University), Baltimore, Md., assistant professor of English, 1952-57; Florida A & M University, Tallahassee, professor of English and chairman of department, 1957-59; North Carolina Agricultural and Technical State University, Greensboro, professor of English, 1959-70, chairman of English department, 1959-66, dean of Graduate School, 1966-70; University of Michigan, Ann Arbor, professor of English, 1970-71; University of Iowa, Iowa City, visiting professor, 1971-72, professor, 1972-81, University of Iowa Foundation Distinguished Professor of English, 1981—, chairman of Afro-American studies, 1972—.

Workshop director, Institute for Teachers of English in Colleges, Indiana University, 1965; visiting professor at University of Wisconsin—Madison, 1969, and University of Hawaii, summer, 1971. State chair for Iowa, Second International Festival of Black and African Culture, 1975-77; delegate to American Studies African Regional Conference, 1976, and to Second International Festival of Black and African Arts, 1977. Member of Wellesley Conference on Pre-College Programs for Southern Negro Students, 1964, advisory committee to U.S. Office of Education, 1965, Graduate Record Examination Board, 1970-73, board of directors, National Council of Black Studies, 1976-79, Rockefeller Commission on the Humanities, 1978-80, and board of trustees, National Humanities Center, 1978—. Consultant to National Endowment for the Humanities programs in ethnic studies and humanities, 1973—, American Council of Learned Societies, 1979-81, and to Rockefeller Foundation, 1980-83.

MEMBER: Modern Language Association of America, National Council of Teachers of English (director, beginning 1971, director of commission on literature, 1982—), American Association for the Advancement of the Humanities, College Language Association (president, 1963-65), Conference on College Composition and Communication (member of executive committee, 1965-67), College English Association (member of board of directors, 1971-74), Association for the Study of Afro-American Life and History, National Association for the Advancement of Colored People, Midwest Modern Language Association, South Atlantic Modern Language Association, North Carolina-Virginia College English Association, North Carolina Teachers Association, Phi Beta Kappa, Alpha Phi Alpha, Theta Alpha Phi, Lambda Iota Tau.

AWARDS, HONORS: American Council of Learned Societies research grant, 1965; Duke University-University of North Carolina Cooperative Program in Humanities fellowship, 1965-66; Creative Scholarship Award, College Language Association, 1970; Rockefeller Foundation research grant, 1971; Professional Achievement Award, University of Chicago Alumni Association, 1972; Carter G. Woodson Award, 1974; National Endowment for the Humanities grants for work and research in Afro-American studies, 1974-78; Distinguished Alumnus Award, University of Cincinnati Alumni Association, 1982; Doctor of Letters, University of Cincinnati, 1983.

WRITINGS: Katharsis, Wellesley Press, 1964; *Nathaniel Hawthorne's "The Scarlet Letter,"* Dell, 1967; *In a Minor Chord: Three Afro-American Writers and Their Search for Identity,* Southern Illinois University Press, 1971; (co-author) *The Teaching of Literature by Afro-American Writers: Theory and Practice,* National Council of Teachers of English, 1972.

Editor: (With Jean M. Bright) *Images of the Negro in America,* Heath, 1965; *Black American Literature: Essays,* C. E. Merrill, 1969; *Black American Literature: Fiction,* C. E. Merrill, 1969; *Black American Literature: Poetry,* C. E. Merrill, 1969; (and compiler) *Afro-American Writers,* Appleton, 1970; *Black American Literature: Essays, Poetry, Fiction, Drama,* C. E. Merrill, 1970; (and author of introduction) *Black Drama in America: An Anthology,* Fawcett, 1971; *Voices from the Black Experience: African and Afro-American Literature,* Ginn, 1972; *Responding: Five,* Ginn, 1973; *The Wayward and the Seeking: A Collection of Writings by Jean Toomer,* Howard University Press, 1980; (with John Sekora) *The Art of the Slave Narrative: Original Essays in Criticism and Theory,* Western Illinois University Press, 1982.

Author of introduction: Paul Laurence Dunbar, *The Strength of Gideon*, Arno, 1969; Charles W. Chesnutt, *The House behind the Cedars*, Collier, 1969; Dunbar, *The Sport of the Gods*, Arno, 1969; Dunbar, *Lyrics of Lowly Life*, Arno, 1969; Zora Neale Hurston, *Mules and Men*, Harper, 1970; Countee Cullen, *Color*, Arno, 1970; Cullen, *One Way to Heaven*, Lorrimer, 1972; Hurston, editor, *Dust Tracks on a Road*, Arno, 1970; Jean Toomer, *Cane*, Liveright, 1975.

Contributor: Lindsay Patterson, editor, *Anthology of the American Negro in the Theatre*, Association for the Study of Negro Life and History, 1967; Louis Rubin, editor, *A Biographical Guide to Southern Literature*, University of North Carolina Press, 1969; R. Hemenway, editor, *The Black Novelist*, C. E. Merrill, 1970; N. Wright, Jr., editor, *What Black Educators Are Saying*, Hawthorn, 1970; (and author of introduction) William Brasmer and Dominick Consolo, editors, *Black Drama: An Anthology*, C. E. Merrill, 1970; A. Gayle, editor, *The Black Aesthetic*, Doubleday, 1971; John Blassingame, editor, *New Perspectives on Black Studies*, University of Illinois Press, 1971; Ruth Miller, editor, *Backgrounds to Black American Literature*, Chandler, 1971; Therman B. O'Daniel, editor, *Langston Hughes, Black Genius: A Critical Evaluation*, Morrow, 1971; Jay Martin, editor, *A Singer in the Dawn: Reinterpretations of Paul Laurence Dunbar*, Dodd, 1975.

Roy Browne and others, editors, *Dimensions of Detective Fiction*, Bowling Green University Popular Press, 1976; T. B. O'Daniel, editor, *James Baldwin: A Critical Evaluation*, Howard University Press, 1977; Evans Harrington and Ann L. Abadie, editors, *The South and Faulkner's Yoknapatawpha: The Actual and the Apocryphal*, University Press of Mississippi, 1977; James Nagel, editor, *American Fiction*, Twayne, 1977; W. Zyla and W. Aycock, editors, *Ethnic Literatures since 1776: The Many Voices of America*, Texas Tech University Press, 1978.

Louis Budd and others, editors, *Toward a New American Literary History*, Duke University Press, 1980; Errol Hill, editor, *The Theater of Black America*, Volume I, Prentice Hall, 1980; Joseph Harris, editor, *Global Perspectives*, Howard University Press, 1983.

Author of afterword: Haki R. Madhubuti, *Earthquakes and Sun Rise Missions*, Third World Press, 1983.

Poetry represented in many anthologies, including *A Rock against the Wind*, edited by Lindsay Patterson, Dodd, 1974, and *When the Mode of the Music Changes: A Short Course in Song Lyrics and Poems*, Ginn, 1975.

Contributor to *Encyclopaedia Britannica, Encyclopedia International, Dictionary of American Biography, Contemporary Dramatists*, and *Encyclopedia of World Literature in the Twentieth Century*. Also contributor of articles, book reviews, and poetry to English, history, and sociology journals. Advisory editor, College Language Association *Journal*, 1960—, *Bulletin of Black Books*, 1971—, *Obsidian*, 1974—, and *American Literature*, 1976-78.

SIDELIGHTS: Darwin T. Turner told *CA:* "I write poetry to purge myself of particular emotions and ideas. I write articles because I've been asked or because I have something which I believe other people should know or may want to know. No single writer has been a major influence." *Avocational interests:* Chess, bridge.

BIOGRAPHICAL/CRITICAL SOURCES: Cincinnati Post, June 6, 1944, September 25, 1944; *Baltimore Afro-American*, May 10, 1947; *Chicago Defender*, May 24, 1947; *Cincinnati Post and Times Star*, June 12, 1964; *Negro Digest*, January, 1969; *Washington Post Book World*, July 13, 1980; *New York Times Book Review*, July 13, 1980.

*   *   *

TURNER, Philip   1925-
(Stephen Chance)

PERSONAL: Born December 3, 1925, in Rossland, British Columbia, Canada; son of Christopher Edward (a clergyman) and Emma (Johnston) Turner; married Margaret Diana Samson, September 23, 1950; children: Simon, Stephen, Jane. *Education:* Worcester College, Oxford, B.A., 1950, M.A., 1962. *Address:* St. Francis, 1 West Malvern Rd., Malvern, Worcestershire, England. *Agent:* Watson, Little Ltd., Suite 8, 26 Charing Cross Rd., London WC2H 0DG, England.

CAREER: Ordained priest of Church of England, 1951; curate in Leeds, 1951-56; priest-in-charge, Crawley, Sussex, 1956-62; vicar of St. Matthews, Northampton, 1962-66; British Broadcasting Corp., Midland Region, Birmingham, religious broadcasting organizer, 1966-70; Briar Mill High School, Droitwich, England, teacher of English and divinity, 1971-73; Eton College, Windsor, England, chaplain, 1973-75; writer. Part-time instructor of history, Malvern College, beginning 1975. *Military service:* Royal Naval Volunteer Reserve, 1943-46; became sub-lieutenant. *Member:* Society of Authors. *Awards, honors:* Carnegie Medal for best children's book published in United Kingdom, Library Association, 1965, for *The Grange at High Force*.

WRITINGS—Children's books: *Colonel Sheperton's Clock*, Oxford University Press, 1964, World Publishing, 1966; *The Grange at High Force*, Oxford University Press, 1965, World Publishing, 1967; *Sea Peril*, Oxford University Press, 1966, World Publishing, 1968; *Steam on the Line*, Oxford University Press, 1966, World Publishing, 1968; *The Bible Story*, Oxford University Press, 1968; (author of text) *Brian Wildsmith's Illustrated Bible Stories*, F. Watts, 1969; *War on the Darnel*, World Publishing, 1969; *Wigwig and Homer*, Oxford University Press, 1969, World Publishing, 1970.

Devil's Nob, Hamish Hamilton, 1970, Thomas Nelson, 1973; *Powder Quay*, Hamish Hamilton, 1971; *Dunkirk Summer*, Hamish Hamilton, 1973; *Skull Island*, Dent, 1977; *Decision in the Dark* (short stories), Dent, 1978; *Rookoo and Bree*, Dent, 1979.

Under pseudonym Stephen Chance: *Septimus and the Danedyke Mystery*, Bodley Head, 1971, Thomas Nelson, 1973; *Septimus and the Minster Ghost*, Bodley Head, 1972, published as *Septimus and the Minster Ghost Mystery*, Thomas Nelson, 1974; *Septimus and the Stone of Offering*, Bodley Head, 1976; *Captain Septimus and the Black Box*, Bodley Head, 1979.

Plays; under name Philip Turner: *Christ in the Concrete City*, S.P.C.K., 1956; *Tell It with Trumpets*, S.P.C.K., 1959; *Cry Dawn in Dark Babylon*, S.P.C.K., 1959; *This Is the Word in "Word Made Flesh,"* S.P.C.K., 1962; *Casey*, S.P.C.K., 1962; *Men in Stone* (also see below), Baker Plays, 1966; *Sex Morality: Two Plays—So Long at the Fair, and Men in Stone*, Joint Board of Christian Education of Australia and New Zealand, 1966; *Cantata for Derelicts*, United Church Publishing House (Canada), 1967; *Madonna in Concrete*, S.P.C.K., 1971.

SIDELIGHTS: Philip Turner told *CA:* "I think my motivation—both in plays and children's books—has been ultimately religious. Not in an ecclesiastical sense, but as part of the unending search for the truth about Man's condition. Sounds extraordinarily pompous, but it is as near the truth as I can get. I am also moved by a strong sense of 'place,' and by the comedy of being human at all. As I get older, I find myself more and more preoccupied by the sheer wonder of creation, its preciousness and fragility.''

Several of Turner's books have been translated into foreign languages, including German and Japanese.

BIOGRAPHICAL/CRITICAL SOURCES: Books and Bookmen, May, 1968.

*　　*　　*

TUTTLE, William M., Jr.   1937-

PERSONAL: Born October 7, 1937, in Detroit, Mich.; son of William M. (a surgeon) and Geneva (Duvall) Tuttle; married Linda Stumpp, December 12, 1959 (divorced); married Mary Erickson, January 1, 1981; children: (first marriage) William M. III, Catharine Terry, Andrew Sanford. *Education:* Denison University, B.A., 1959; University of Wisconsin, M.A., 1964, Ph.D., 1967. *Politics:* Democrat. *Religion:* Unitarian Universalist. *Home:* 21 Winona Ave., Lawrence, Kan. 66044. *Office:* Department of History, University of Kansas, Lawrence, Kan. 66045.

CAREER: Historian for recent U.S. history, Study of American Education, Princeton, N.J., 1965-67; University of Kansas, Lawrence, assistant professor, 1967-70, associate professor, 1970-75, professor of American history, 1975—, intra-university professor, 1982-83. Senior fellow in Southern and Negro history, Johns Hopkins University, Baltimore, Md., 1969-70; research fellow, Warren Center, Harvard University, 1972-73; associate fellow, Stanford Humanities Center, Stanford University, 1983-84. *Military service:* U.S. Air Force, 1959-62; became first lieutenant; received Air Force Commendation Medal. *Member:* Society of American Historians, American Historical Association, Organization of American Historians, Association for the Study of Afro-American Life and History.

AWARDS, HONORS: Harry S. Truman Library Institute research grant, 1968; Award of Merit for State History, Illinois State Historical Society, 1971; American Council of Learned Societies grant-in-aid, 1972; Younger Humanist fellowship, National Endowment for the Humanities, 1972-73; Award of Merit, American Association of State and Local History, 1972; grants-in-aid, Lilly Endowment, 1975, 1976; Tom L. Evans grant, Harry S. Truman Library Institute, 1975-76; John Simon Guggenheim Memorial fellowship, 1975-76; Albert J. Beveridge grant, American Historical Association, 1982; independent study and research fellowship, National Endowment for the Humanities, 1983-84.

WRITINGS: Race Riot: Chicago in the Red Summer of 1919, Atheneum, 1970; *W.E.B. DuBois,* Prentice-Hall, 1973; (with David M. Katzman) *Plain Folk: The Life Stories of Undistinguished Americans,* University of Illinois, 1982; (with Mary Beth Norton and others) *A People and a Nation,* Houghton, 1982.

Contributor: Richard Resh, editor, *Black America: Confrontation and Accommodation in the Twentieth Century,* Heath, 1969; Thomas R. Frazier, editor, *Afro-American History: Primary Sources,* Harcourt, 1970; Milton Cantor, editor, *Black Labor in America,* Negro Universities Press, 1970; John Bracey and others, editors, *Black Workers and Organized Labor,*

Wadsworth, 1971; Kenneth Jackson and Stanley Schultz, editors, *American History: Urban Perspective,* Knopf, 1971; Norman Cohen, editor, *Civil Strife in America,* Dryden, 1972; Herbert Gutman and G. S. Kealey, editors, *Many Pasts,* Prentice-Hall, 1973; Thomas R. Frazier, editor, *The Underside of American History,* Harcourt, 1978. Also contributor to *Annual Editions: Readings in American History,* Dushkin, 1972, 1973, 1975, 1978, 1980, and 1982, and to history journals.

WORK IN PROGRESS: A history of American children on the home front during the Second World War.

*　　*　　*

TWISLETON-WYKEHAM-FIENNES, Richard Nathaniel   1909-
(Richard Fiennes)

PERSONAL: Born November 26, 1909, in London, England; son of Gerard Yorke and Gwendolen (Gisborne) Twisleton-Wykeham-Fiennes; married Alice Isobel Cowie, 1946; children: Frances Elizabeth, Richard George. *Education:* Royal (Dick) Veterinary College, Edinburgh, Scotland, M.R.C.V.S., 1934; Cambridge University, B.A., 1935. *Politics:* "Agin the Government!" *Religion:* Church of England. *Address:* c/o Zoological Society, Regents Park, London N.W.1, England.

CAREER: British Colonial Veterinary Service, 1935-53, serving successively as veterinary officer, veterinary research officer, and dean of Veterinary School in Uganda, and senior veterinary research officer in Kabete, Kenya; University of Ghana, Legon, Accra, senior lecturer in veterinary science, 1953-56; London Zoo, London, England, resident veterinary pathologist, 1956-75; Nuffield Institute of Comparative Medicine, London, England, head of pathology department, 1964-75. Member of chemotherapy panel and of tsetse and trypanosomiasis committee, British Ministry of Overseas Development. Councillor, Richmond Borough Council, 1961-64. *Military service:* Uganda Defence Force, World War II. *Member:* Royal Society of Medicine (secretary of comparative medicine section).

WRITINGS—Under name Richard Fiennes: *Man, Nature, and Disease,* Weidenfeld & Nicolson, 1964, New American Library, 1965; (editor) *Some Recent Developments in Comparative Medicine,* Academic Press, 1966; *Zoonoses of Primates: The Epidemiology and Ecology of Simian Diseases in Relation to Man,* Cornell University Press, 1967; (with wife, Alice Twisleton-Wykeham-Fiennes) *Natural History of the Dog,* Weidenfeld & Nicolson, 1968, published as *The Natural History of Dogs,* Natural History Press, 1970.

(Editor) *Biology of Nutrition: the Evolution and Nature of Living Systems,* Pergamon, 1972; (editor) *Pathology of Simian Primates,* Karger, Volume I: *General Pathology,* 1972, Volume II: *Infectious and Parasitic Diseases,* 1972; *Know about Apes and Monkeys,* Thomas Nelson, 1975; *The Order of Wolves,* Bobbs-Merrill, 1976; *Ecology and Earth History,* Croom Helm, 1976; *The Environment of Man,* Croom Helm, 1978; *Zoonoses and the Origins and Ecology of Human Disease,* Academic Press, 1978.

Infectious Cancers of Animals and Man, Academic Press, 1982.

WORK IN PROGRESS: Animal Survival: Zoos and Game Parks in Conservation; Horse and Man; Must We Die of Cancer?

SIDELIGHTS: In 1983, Richard Nathaniel Twisleton-Wykeham-Fiennes told *CA* that he has been "retired these eight years and living close to Kew Botanical Gardens. Writings appear to be diverse, but all incorporate the central theme of animal/man relationships.'' *Avocational interests:* Botanizing, fishing, photography, travel.

BIOGRAPHICAL/CRITICAL SOURCES: New York Times Book Review, June 26, 1977.

*   *   *

TYLER, Anne   1941-

PERSONAL: Born October 25, 1941, in Minneapolis, Minn.; daughter of Lloyd Parry (a chemist) and Phyllis (Mahon) Tyler; married Taghi Modarressi (a psychiatrist), May 3, 1963; children: Tezh, Mitra. *Education:* Duke University, B.A., 1961; graduate study at Columbia University, 1961-62. *Religion:* Quaker. *Home:* 222 Tunbridge Rd., Baltimore, Md. 21212. *Agent:* Russell & Volkening, 551 Fifth Ave., New York, N.Y. 10017.

CAREER: Writer. Duke University Library, Durham, N.C., Russian bibliographer, 1962-63; McGill University Law Library, Montreal, Quebec, Canada, assistant to the librarian, 1964-65. *Member:* P.E.N., Authors Guild, Authors League of America, American Academy and Institute of Arts and Letters, Phi Beta Kappa. *Awards, honors: Mademoiselle* award for writing, 1966; Award for Literature, American Academy and Institute of Arts and Letters, 1977; National Book Critics Circle fiction award nomination, 1980, Janet Heidinger Kafka prize, 1981, and American Book Award nomination in paperback fiction, 1982, all for *Morgan's Passing;* National Book Critics Circle fiction award nomination, 1982, and American Book Award nomination in fiction, P.E.N./Faulkner Award for fiction, and Pulitzer Prize nomination for fiction, all 1983, all for *Dinner at the Homesick Restaurant.*

WRITINGS—Novels, all published by Knopf: *If Morning Ever Comes,* 1964; *The Tin Can Tree;* 1965; *A Slipping-Down Life,* 1970; *The Clock Winder,* 1972; *Celestial Navigation,* 1974; *Searching for Caleb,* 1976; *Earthly Possessions,* 1977; *Morgan's Passing,* 1980; *Dinner at the Homesick Restaurant,* 1982.

Editor: (With Shannon Ravenel, and author of introduction) *Best American Short Stories 1983,* Houghton, 1983.

Contributor of short stories to *Saturday Evening Post, New Yorker, Seventeen, Critic, Antioch Review,* and *Southern Review.*

SIDELIGHTS: Despite her status as a bestselling novelist, Anne Tyler remains a private person who rarely lets public demands interfere with family life. She shuns most interviewers, avoids talk show appearances, and prefers Baltimore—where she lives with her husband and two daughters—to New York. Nonetheless she is a well-established writer, having earned what former *Detroit News* reporter Bruce Cook calls ''a solid *literary* reputation . . . that is based solely on the quality of her books.'' Tyler's work has always been critically well-received, but reviews of her early novels were generally relegated to the back pages of the book sections. Not until the publication of *Celestial Navigation* (1974), when she captured the attention of novelist Gail Godwin, and *Searching for Caleb* (1976), when John Updike recommended her to readers, did she gain widespread acclaim. ''Now,'' says Cook, ''her books are reviewed in the *front* of the literary journals—and that means she is somebody to reckon with. No longer one of America's best unknown writers, she is now recognized as one of America's best writers. Period.''

Born in Minnesota, Tyler lived in various Quaker communes throughout the midwest and south before settling in the mountains of North Carolina for five years. She attended high school in Raleigh, and at sixteen, entered Duke University where she fell under the influence of Reynolds Price, then a promising young novelist who had attended her high school. It was Price who encouraged the young Russian major to pursue her writing, and she did—but it remained a secondary pursuit until 1967, the year she and her husband settled in Baltimore.

In an interview with Bruce Cook, published in the *Saturday Review,* Tyler describes the city as ''wonderful territory for a writer—so many different things to poke around in.'' And the longer she stays there, the more prominently Baltimore figures in her books, lending them an ambience both citified and southern and leading Reynolds Price to proclaim her ''the nearest thing we have to an urban Southern novelist.'' Writing in the *New Yorker,* John Updike compares her to Flannery O'Connor, Carson McCullers, and Eudora Welty, noting: ''Anne Tyler, in her gifts both of dreaming and of realizing, evokes comparison with these writers, and in her tone and subject matter seems deliberately to seek association with the Southern ambience that, in less cosmopolitan times, they naturally and inevitably breathed. Even their aura of regional isolation is imitated by Miss Tyler as she holds fast, in her imagination and in her person, to a Baltimore with only Southern exits; her characters when they flee, never flee north. Yet she is a citizen of the world, born in Minneapolis, a graduate student of Russian at Columbia, and now married to a psychiatrist from Iran. The brand names, the fads, the bastardized vistas of our great homogenized nation glint out at us from her fiction with a cheerful authority.''

Other reviewers, such as Katha Pollitt, find Tyler's novels more difficult to classify. ''They are Southern in their sure sense of family and place,'' she writes in the *New York Times Book Review,* ''but lack the taste for violence and the Gothic that often characterizes self-consciously Southern literature. They are modern in their fictional techniques, yet utterly unconcerned with the contemporary moment as a subject, so that, with only minor dislocations, her stories could just as well have taken place in the twenties or thirties. The current school of feminist-influenced novels seems to have passed her by completely: her women are strong, often stronger than the men in their lives, but solidly grounded in traditional roles.''

The key to Tyler's writing may well lie in the homage she pays to Eudora Welty, her favorite writer and one to whom she is repeatedly compared. ''Reading her taught me there were stories to be written about the mundane life around me,'' she told Cook. Or as Tyler phrased it to Marguerite Michaels in the *New York Times Book Review,* ''Reading Eudora Welty when I was growing up showed me that very small things are often really larger than the large things.'' Thomas M. Disch is one of several critics who believes that Tyler's insight into the lives of ordinary people is her special gift. Writing in the *Washington Post Book World,* he calls it an ''uncommon accomplishment that she can make such characters interesting and amusing without violating their limitations.''

Despite their resemblances to people we meet in real life, Tyler's characters are totally fictitious. ''None of the people I write about are people I know,'' she told Marguerite Michaels. ''That would be no fun. And it would be very boring to write about me. Even if I led an exciting life, why live it again on paper? I want to live other lives. I've never quite believed that one chance is all I get. Writing is my way of making other chances.'' She perceives the ''real heroes'' of her books as ''first the ones who manage to endure and second the ones who are somehow able to grant other people the privacy of the space around them and yet still produce some warmth.''

Her major theme, according to Mary Ellen Brooks in the *Dictionary of Literary Biography,* ''is the obstinate endurance of the human spirit, reflected in every character's acceptance or rejection of his fate and in how that attitude affects his day to day life. She uses the family unit as a vehicle for portraying 'how people manage to endure together—how they grate against each other, adjust, intrude and protect themselves from intrusions, give up, and start all over again in the morning.''' Frequently her characters respond to stress by running away, but their flight, Brook continues, ''proves to be only a temporary and ineffectual means of dealing with reality.''

Because the action of her novels is so often circular—ending exactly where it begins—Tyler's fiction has been criticized for lack of development. This is especially true of her early novels where the narratives are straightforward and the pacing slow. In fact, what impressed reviewers most about Tyler's first book, *If Morning Ever Comes,* was not the story itself but the promise it seemed to hold for future fictions. ''The trouble with this competently put-together book is that the hero is hardly better defined at the end than he is at the beginning,'' observes Julian Gloag in the *Saturday Review.* ''Writing about a dull and totally humorless character, Miss Tyler has inevitably produced a totally humorless and mainly dull novel. . . . Anne Tyler is only twenty-two, and in the light of this . . . her refusal to take risks is a bit puzzling. I'd like to see what she could do if she stopped narrowing her own eyes and let herself go. It might be very good.'' The *Times Literary Supplement* reviewer echoes these sentiments: ''It will be surprising if a writer so young . . . does not outgrow her hesitant efforts to produce big answers to emotional muddles and her sometimes over-literary sentences, and let her considerable gift for dialogue and comedy produce a very good novel indeed.''

For her part, Tyler reportedly now hates her first book—and also her second, which received similar criticism. Written largely to pass the time while she was looking for a job, *The Tin Can Tree* concerns the inhabitants of a three-family house on the edge of a North Carolina tobacco field and their reactions to the accidental death of the six-year-old girl who lives there. Though the family is initially devastated by the tragedy, their emotional balance is restored in the end, and, for this reason, some critics find the novel static. Millicent Bell, for example, writes in the *New York Times Book Review:* ''Life, this young writer seems to be saying, achieves its once-and-for-all shape and then the camera clicks. This view, which brings her characters back on the last page to where they started, does not make for that sense of development which is the true novel's motive force. Because of it, I think, her book remains a sketch, a description, a snapshot. But as such, it still has a certain dry clarity. And the hand that has clicked its shutter has selected a moment of truth.''

Perhaps the most salient feature of Tyler's next novel *A Slipping-Down Life* (which was misclassified as young adult literature and thus not widely reviewed) is its genesis. In discussing her craft with Marguerite Michaels, Tyler said: ''Sometimes a book will start with a picture that pops into my mind and I ask myself questions about it and if I put all the answers together, I've got a novel. A real picture would be the old newspaper clipping about the Texas girl who slashed 'Elvis' in her forehead.'' In the novel, this incident is trans-

formed into an episode in the life of Evie Decker, a fictive teenager grappling for her identity. ''I believe this is the best thing I've ever done,'' Evie says of her self-mutilation. ''Something out of character. Definite.'' In the *Dictionary of Literary Biography,* Mary Ellen Brooks describes the novel as ''an accurate description of loneliness, failure to communicate, and regrets over decisions that are irreversible—problems with which any age group can identify. Tyler, who describes *A Slipping-Down Life* as one of her most bizarre works, believes that the novel 'is flawed, but represents, for me, a certain brave stepping forth.'''

So, too, does Tyler's fifth novel, *Celestial Navigation,* a book that the author wrote while ''fighting the urge to remain in retreat even though the children had started school.'' In the character of Jeremy Paulding, an agoraphobic artist who is afraid to leave his Baltimore block, Tyler sees much of herself. While her characters are not usually autobiographical, Tyler told Brooks that creating Jeremy was a way of investigating her own ''tendency to turn more and more inward.''

The story opens with the death of Jeremy's mother and moves quickly to an exploration of the relationship he establishes with the woman who will take her place—a self-sufficient boarder named Mary Tell. Attracted by her sunny self-confidence, Jeremy proposes marriage and soon Mary has stepped in as Jeremy's intermediary to the outside world. As years pass, he comes to feel dwarfed by Mary's competence—she does not even alert him when she leaves for the hospital to have his fifth child because she knows he dreads the trip. Suffocated by her over-protectiveness, the disoriented artist withdraws even further into the private world of his studio where he fashions collages from scraps of other people's lives. Eventually Mary and the children abandon him, and Jeremy does venture out to find them. But the price he pays for conquering his fear is that he loses them for good. At the novel's end, Mary and Jeremy each remain in a separate existence, each still dominated by what Brooks calls ''his innate driving characteristic. Jeremy returns to his life as a reclusive artist in a crumbling dark house while Mary prepares for winter in a run-down shack, knowing that another man will eventually provide for her.''

Told from the viewpoints of six different characters, *Celestial Navigation* is far more intricate than Tyler's earlier novels, and most critics consider it a breakthrough. Katha Pollitt finds the work ''extraordinarily moving and beautiful,'' while Doris Grumbach proclaims Tyler's ''ability to enmesh the reader in what is a simple, uneventful story . . . a notable achievement.'' In her *New York Times Book Review* article, Gail Godwin explains how ''Tyler is especially gifted at the art of freeing her characters and then keeping track of them as they move in their unique and often solitary orbits. Her fiction is filled with displaced persons who persist stubbornly in their own destinies. They are 'oddballs,' visionaries, lonely souls, but she has a way of transcribing their peculiarities with such loving wholeness that when we examine them we keep finding more and more pieces of ourselves.''

In her eighth novel, *Morgan's Passing,* Tyler turns from an exploration of the ''oddball'' as introvert to the ''oddball'' as extrovert in the creation of Morgan Gower—a 42-year-old hardware store manager with a knack for assuming other roles. Simply put, Morgan is an imposter, a man who changes identities every time he changes clothes. ''You're walking down the street with him and this total stranger asks him when the International Brotherhood of Magicians is meeting next,'' his wife Bonny explains. "You're listening to a politician's speech and suddenly you notice Morgan on the platform, sitting beside a senator's wife with a carnation in his buttonhole. You're waiting for your crabs at Lexington Market and who's behind the counter but Morgan in a rubber apron, telling the other customers where he caught such fine oysters." These fantasies contrast sharply with the dullness of Morgan's actual life. At home, in the brick colonial house acquired with his wife's money, he feels overwhelmed by the clutter of his wife, their seven daughters, his adult sister, and his feeble-minded mother.

The novel opens with one of Morgan's escapades. During the performance of a puppet show, the puppeteer, Leon Meredith, emerges from behind the curtains to request a doctor's assistance: his wife Emily has gone into labor. Morgan steps forward and, posing as a doctor, delivers the baby in the back seat of his car. In the process he becomes fascinated by what he perceives to be the simple existence of the Merediths. Emily, in particular, becomes "an emblem for Morgan of that spartan order he longs to bring to his over-furnished life," says Thomas M. Disch in the *Washington Post Book World*. But neither Emily nor Leon are as blithe as they seem, and by juxtaposing the reality of these characters with Morgan's fantasies of them, Tyler creates her drama, critics say.

Though *Morgan's Passing* was nominated for a National Book Critics Circle Award in hardback and an American Book Award in paperback fiction, critics are sharply divided in their assessment of the work. Those who like it praise Tyler's handling of character and her artful mingling of comedy and seriousness. "Though she allows her tale to veer toward farce, Tyler always checks it in time with the tug of an emotion, a twitch of regret," writes *Time*'s Paul Gray. He concludes: "*Morgan's Passing* is not another novel about a mid-life crisis, it is a buoyant story about a struggle unto death." Tyler acknowledged in her *Detroit News* interview with Bruce Cook that her "big worry in doing the book was that people would be morally offended by [Morgan]." But critic Marilyn Murray Willison sings his praises. "In spite of his inability to restore order to his life, his nicotine-stained hands and teeth, his silly wardrobe, his refusal to accept reality, Morgan emerges from Tyler's book a true hero," she writes in the *Los Angeles Times Book Review*.

Other critics, however, dislike the character and consider the book a disappointment. "For all its many felicities of observation and incident, *Morgan's Passing* does not come up to the high standard of Anne Tyler's other recent work. There is a self-indulgence in the portraiture of Morgan himself, whose numerous identity assumptions became for me merely tiresome," Paul Binding writes in the *New Statesman*. And *New York Review of Books* contributing critic James Wolcott dismisses *Morgan's Passing* as "a book of small compass, pent-up energy. Long before Morgan and Emily link arms, the reader has connected the dots separating them, so there's no suspense, no surprise. Instead, the book is stuffed with accounts of weddings, crowded dinners, cute squabbles, . . . and symbolic-as-all-get-out puppet shows. . . . Sentence by sentence, the book is engaging, but there's nothing beneath the jokes and tussles to propel the reader through these cluttered lives. It's a book with an idle motor." Writing in the *New Yorker*, John Updike explains his disappointment: "Anne Tyler continues to look close, and to fabricate, out of the cardboard and Magic Markers available to the festive imagination, images of the illusory lives we lead. More than that it would be unkind to ask, did we not imagine, for the scope of the gift displayed, that something of that gift is still being withheld."

With *Dinner at the Homesick Restaurant,* her ninth and, some say, finest novel, Tyler redeems herself in many critics' eyes. Updike, for instance, maintains that this book achieves "a new level of power and gives us a lucid and delightful yet complex and sombre improvisation on her favorite theme, family life." Writing in the *Chicago Tribune Book World*, Larry McMurtry echoes these sentiments: "She recognizes and conveys beautifully the alternations of tragedy and farce in family life, and never more beautifully than in *Dinner at the Homesick Restaurant*." Benjamin Demott is even more impressed. "Funny, heart-hammering, wise, [the novel] edges deep into truth that's simultaneously (and interdependently) psychological, moral and formal—deeper than many living novelists of serious reputation have penetrated, deeper than Miss Tyler herself has gone before. It is a border crossing," he writes in the *New York Times Book Review*.

The story's plot is a simple one—"deceptively simple," Sarah English notes in the *Dictionary of Literary Biography Yearbook*. Eighty-five-year-old Pearl Tull—who married late in life and bore three children before being deserted by her traveling salesman husband—is lying on her deathbed recollecting the past. She reconstructs the moment, thirty-five years before when Beck Tull announced he was leaving, the years of struggle that ensued as she single-handedly (and sometimes heartlessly) raised her children, and the scars which Cody, Jenny, and Ezra still bear. "Something," Pearl thought, "was wrong with all her children. They were so frustrating—attractive, likeable people, the three of them, but closed off from her in some perverse way . . . . She wondered if her children blamed her for something. Sitting close at family gatherings . . . they tended to recall only poverty and loneliness. . . . [They] referred continually to Pearl's short temper, displaying it against a background of stunned, childish faces so sad and bewildered that Pearl herself hardly recognized them. Honestly, she thought, wasn't there some statute of limitations here?"

In this darkest of Tyler's novels, the answer is no. "None of the three Tull children manages to cut loose from the family past," explains Demott. "Each is, to a degree, stunted; each turns for help to Pearl Tull in an hour of desperate adult need; and Pearl's conviction that something is wrong with each of them never recedes from the reader's consciousness."

The novel unfolds in a series of self-contained chapters, each, in Updike's words, "rounded like a short story," and each reflecting a different family member's point of view. This narrative technique, as Sarah English notes, "allows [Tyler] to juxtapose past and present and thus to convey the vision— that she has always had—of the past not as a continuum but as layer of still, vivid memories. The wealth of points of view also allows Tyler to show more fully than ever the essential subjectivity of the past. Cody and Jenny remember Pearl as a witch; Ezra remembers her as a source of strength and security. . . . Every character's vision of the past is different."

Larry McMurtry believes that the book "amply demonstrates the tenacity of familial involvement," while *Los Angeles Times* reporter Carolyn See says Tyler shows how a family "is alive with needs of its own; it never relaxes its hold. Even when you are far away (especially when you're far away), it immobilizes you in its grip, which can—in another way—be looked at as a caress."

This portrait of family entanglements is too somber for some critics' tastes, including Cynthia Propper Seton's. "What may be the trouble with *Dinner at the Homesick Restaurant*," she writes in the *Washington Post Book World*, "is that the Tull family is not marginal enough, its members are too grave a proposition for a mind so full of mischief as Anne Tyler's. They depressed her.'' In her *Detroit News* review, however, Cynthia King maintains that ''despite the joyless atmosphere, the author's humor bubbles through—in Pearl's tackiness, in Jenny's self-protective flippancy. And more than a few times— awful as Pearl is, warped and doomed as her children are— what keeps us turning pages is the suspicion that there may be a bit of each of them in each of us.''

Concludes Benjamin Demott: ''What one wants to do on finishing such a work as *Dinner at the Homesick Restaurant* is maintain balance, keep things intact for a stretch, stay under the spell as long as possible. The before and after are immaterial; nothing counts except the knowledge, solid and serene, that's all at once breathing in the room. We're speaking obviously, about an extremely beautiful book.''

BIOGRAPHICAL/CRITICAL SOURCES—Books: *Contemporary Literary Criticism*, Gale, Volume VII, 1977, Volume XI, 1979, Volume XVIII, 1981; *Dictionary of Literary Biography*, Gale, Volume VI: *American Novelists since World War II, Second Series*, 1980, *Yearbook: 1982*, 1983.

Periodicals: *New York Times Book Review*, November 22, 1964, November 21, 1965, March 15, 1970, May 21, 1972, April 28, 1974, January 18, 1976, May 8, 1977, March 14, 1982; *Saturday Review*, December 26, 1964, November 20, 1965, June 17, 1972, March 6, 1976, September 4, 1976, March 15, 1980; *Times Literary Supplement*, July 15, 1965, May 23, 1975, December 9, 1977, October 31, 1980, October 29, 1982; *New Republic*, May 13, 1972, May 28, 1977, March 22, 1980; *New Statesman*, April 4, 1975, December 5, 1980; *Atlantic Monthly*, March, 1976; *New Yorker*, March 29, 1976, June 6, 1977, June 23, 1980, April 5, 1982; *New York Times*, May 3, 1977, March 17, 1980, March 22, 1982; *Time*, May 9, 1977, March 17, 1980, April 5, 1982; *National Observer*, May 30, 1977; *Ms.*, August, 1977; *Washington Post Book World*, March 16, 1980, April 4, 1982; *Chicago Tribune Book World*, March 23, 1980, March 21, 1982; *Los Angeles Times Book Review*, March 30, 1980; *New York Review of Books*, April 3, 1980; *Detroit News*, April 6, 1980, April 18, 1982; *Los Angeles Times*, March 30, 1982, September 14, 1983; *Newsweek*, April 5, 1982.

—Sketch by Donna Olendorf

U

UNDERDOWN, David (Edward) 1925-

PERSONAL: Born August 19, 1925, in Wells, Somerset, England; son of John Percival and Ethel (Gell) Underdown; married Mary Ebba Ingholt, 1954; children: Harold D., Peter C., Philip J. *Education:* Exeter College, Oxford, B.A., 1950, M.A., 1951, B.Litt., 1953; Yale University, M.A., 1952. *Office:* Department of History, Brown University, Providence, R.I. 02912.

CAREER: Royal Holloway College, London, England, tutorial fellow, 1952-53; University of the South, Sewanee, Tenn., assistant professor, 1953-58, associate professor of history, 1958-62; University of Virginia, Charlottesville, associate professor of history, 1962-68; Brown University, Providence, R.I., professor of history, 1968—. Member of editorial board, Yale Center for Parliamentary History. *Military service:* Royal Air Force, 1944-47; became sergeant. *Member:* American Historical Association, Conference on British Studies, Royal Historical Society (fellow). *Awards, honors:* Guggenheim fellow, 1964-65; American Council of Learned Societies fellow, 1973-74; National Endowment for the Humanities fellow, 1980-81; D.Litt., University of the South, 1981.

WRITINGS: Royalist Conspiracy in England, 1649-1660, Yale University Press, 1960; *Pride's Purge: Politics in the Puritan Revolution,* Oxford University Press, 1971; *Somerset in the Civil War and Interregnum,* Shoe String, 1973. Contributor of articles and reviews to professional journals.

*   *   *

UPHOFF, Norman T(homas) 1940-

PERSONAL: Born July 22, 1940, in Madison, Wis.; son of Walter Henry (a professor) and Mary Jo (Weiler) Uphoff; married Marguerite Helen McKay (a physician); children: Elisabeth, Jonathan. *Education:* Attended University of Cologne, 1958-59; University of Minnesota, B.A., 1963; Princeton University, M.P.A., 1966; University of California, Berkeley, Ph.D., 1970. *Religion:* Society of Friends (Quaker). *Home:*

16 Cedar Lane, Ithaca, N.Y. 14850. *Office:* Department of Government, Cornell University, Ithaca, N.Y. 14850.

CAREER: University of California, Berkeley, research political scientist, Institute of International Studies, working on Ghana aid project, 1967-69; Cornell University, Department of Government and Center for International Studies, Ithaca, N.Y., professor of government, 1970—, chairman of rural development committee, 1971-78, 1982—. Chairman, development administration panel, Southeast Asia Development Advisory Group, 1972-74; director, project on rural development participation, Cornell University, 1977-82; member, South Asia committee, Social Science Research Council, 1982—. Visiting research fellow, Agrarian Research and Training Institute, Sri Lanka, 1978-79. Consultant on development to numerous organizations, including Nigeria project, Education and World Affairs, New York, 1966, Ford Foundation, Centre for Economic Development and Administration, Nepal, 1972-73, World Bank, 1979-80, and Agrarian Research and Training Institute, 1980-83. Member of advisory committees, United States Agency for International Development, 1982—, and Overseas Development Council, 1983—. *Member:* American Political Science Association, Phi Beta Kappa.

WRITINGS: (With Warren Ilchman) *The Political Economy of Change,* University of California Press, 1969; *Ghana's Experience in Using External Aid for Development, 1957-1966,* Institute of International Studies, University of California, 1970; *The Political Economy of Development: Theoretical and Empirical Contributions,* University of California Press, 1972; (with Raphael Littauer) *The Air War in Indochina,* Beacon Press, 1972; *The Student Internationals,* Scarecrow, 1973; *Small Farmer Credit,* Center for International Studies, Cornell University, 1973; (with Milton Esman) *Local Organization for Rural Development: Analysis of Asian Experience,* Center for International Studies, Cornell University, 1974; (with John M. Cohen) *Rural Development Participation: Concepts and Measures for Project Design Implementation and Evaluation,* Center for International Studies, Cornell University, 1977; (editor) *Rural Development and Local Organization in Asia,* three volumes, Macmillan (New Delhi), 1982-83; (with Esman) *Local Organizations: Intermediaries in Rural Development,* Cornell University Press, 1984.

WORK IN PROGRESS: The Roots of Self-Reliance: Village-Level Successes and Failures in Sri Lanka, book based on research in 1978-79 and follow-up study in 1984; with Michael Cernea, *Social Methodologies for Building Local Development Capacity,* case studies of strengthening bottom-up development initiative; *Farmer Participation and Bureaucratic Reorientation: Assessment of a Strategy for Water Management Improvement in Sri Lanka,* an analysis of a program to institutionalize farmer organizations in Sri Lanka.

V

van BUREN, Paul (Matthews) 1924-

PERSONAL: Born April 20, 1924, in Norfolk, Va.; son of Harold Sheffield and Charlotte (Matthews) van Buren; married Anne Hagopian, February 7, 1948; children: Alice, Eleanor, Philip, Thomas. *Education:* Harvard University, B.A., 1948; Episcopal Theological School, B.D., 1951; University of Basel, Th.D., 1957. *Home:* 134 Chestnut St., Boston, Mass. 02108. *Office:* Department of Religion, Temple University, Philadelphia, Pa. 19122.

CAREER: Ordained to the ministry of the Episcopal Church, 1951; minister in Detroit, Mich., 1954-57; Episcopal Theological Seminary of the Southwest, Austin, Tex., assistant professor, 1957-60, associate professor of theology, 1960-64; Temple University, Philadelphia, Pa., associate professor, 1964-66, professor of religion, 1966—, chairman of department, 1974-76. Visiting professor of theology, Harvard Divinity School, 1981. Consultant to Detroit Industrial Mission, 1956-66; Jeffrey Lecturer, Goucher College, 1966; Fulbright senior lecturer, Oxford University, 1967-68. *Military service:* U.S. Coast Guard Reserve, 1943; U.S. Naval Reserve, 1943-45.

MEMBER: Society for Values in Higher Education (fellow), American Academy of Religion, National Association for the Advancement of Colored People (NAACP), American Association of University Professors, American Civil Liberties Union. *Awards, honors:* Guggenheim fellowship, 1967-68; National Endowment for the Humanities fellowship, 1982-83.

WRITINGS: Christ in Our Place: The Substitutionary Character of Calvin's Doctrine of Reconciliation, Oliver & Boyd, 1957; *The Secular Meaning of the Gospel: Based on an Analysis of Its Language,* Macmillan, 1963; *Theological Explorations,* Macmillan, 1968; (contributor) Peter Vorkink, compiler, *Bonhoeffer in a World Come of Age: Essays by Paul M. van Buren and Others,* Fortress, 1968; *The Edges of Language: An Essay in the Logic of a Religion,* Macmillan, 1972; *The Burden of Freedom: Americans and the God of Israel,* Seabury, 1976; *Discerning the Way: A Theology of the Jewish-Christian Reality,* Seabury, 1980; *A Theology of the Jewish-Christian Reality, Part II: A Christian Theology of the People Israel,* Seabury, 1983.

Contributor of articles to scholarly journals, including *Religion in Life, Religious Studies, Journal of Ecumenical Studies,* and *Journal of the American Academy of Religion.*

SIDELIGHTS: Paul van Buren told *CA:* "Let no humanist or word-crafter be too 'high-minded' to shift to a word-processor. I am finding the computer an incredible aid in the art of crafting clear sentences and well-constructed paragraphs. I recommend it to all."

*   *   *

Van LEEUWEN, Jean 1937-

PERSONAL: Surname is pronounced Van *Loo*-en; born December 26, 1937, in Glen Ridge, N.J.; daughter of Cornelius (a clergyman) and Dorothy (Charlton) Van Leeuwen; married Bruce David Gavril (a digital computer systems designer), July 7, 1968; children: David Andrew, Elizabeth Eva. *Education:* Syracuse University, B.A., 1959. *Home:* 7 Colony Row, Chappaqua, N.Y. 10514.

CAREER: Random House, Inc., New York City, began as assistant editor, became associate editor of juvenile books, 1963-68; Viking Press, Inc., New York City, associate editor of juvenile books, 1968-70; Dial Press, New York City, senior editor of juvenile books, 1971-73; currently a full-time writer. *Awards, honors:* William Allen White Award, 1978, and 1978-79 South Carolina Children's Book Award, both for *The Great Christmas Kidnaping Caper; Seems Like This Road Goes on Forever* was named one of the best books of 1979 by Young Adult Services Division of American Library Association; Massachusetts Honor Book Award, 1981, for *The Great Cheese Conspiracy.*

WRITINGS—Juveniles; published by Dial, except as indicated: (Editor) *A Time of Growing,* Random House, 1967; *Timothy's Flower,* Random House, 1967; *One Day in Summer,* Random House, 1969; *The Great Cheese Conspiracy,* Random House, 1969; *I Was a Ninety-Eight-Pound Duckling,* 1972; *Too Hot for Ice Cream,* 1974; *The Great Christmas Kidnaping Caper,* 1975; *Seems Like This Road Goes on Forever,* 1979; *Tales of Oliver Pig,* 1979; *More Tales of Oliver Pig,* 1981; *The Great Rescue Operation,* 1982; *Amanda Pig and Her Big Brother Oliver,* 1982; *Benjy and the Power of Zingies,* 1982; *Tales of Amanda Pig,* 1983; *Benjy in Business,* 1983.

SIDELIGHTS: Jean Van Leeuwen told *CA:* "Trying to find some common denominator in my writing, I guess I would say that more and more I am trying to do two things—to use humor to put across something serious that I want to say, and to recreate certain remembered turning points in my own life in terms that will be meaningful to readers of today. My only comment about my way of working is that it is slow—achingly, frustratingly, agonizingly slow.''

AVOCATIONAL INTERESTS: Photography, reading, travel, music.

BIOGRAPHICAL/CRITICAL SOURCES: New York Times Book Review, November 5, 1967.

* * *

Van RIPER, Francis A(lbert) 1946-
(Frank Van Riper)

PERSONAL: Born September 4, 1946, in New York, N.Y.; son of Albert (a note teller) and Mildred (a bookkeeper; maiden name, Casullo) Van Riper; married Christine Rossi (a management consultant), October 18, 1970 (divorced, 1980); married Judith Goodman (a photographer), 1983. *Education:* City College of the City University of New York, B.A., 1967. *Religion:* Roman Catholic. *Home:* 3502 Quesada St. N.W., Washington, D.C. 20015. *Office: New York Daily News,* 2101 L St. N.W., Suite 407, Washington, D.C. 20037.

CAREER: New York Herald Tribune, New York City, stringer and news clerk, 1967; *New York Post,* New York City, assistant to night city editor, 1965-67; *New York Daily News,* New York City, Washington bureau correspondent, 1967—, White House correspondent, 1975-80, national political correspondent, 1980—. Notable assignments include U.S. presidential campaigns since 1968, Vietnam antiwar movement, Senate Watergate hearings, House Judiciary Committee Impeachment proceedings, the Nixon resignation, and the Iran hostage crisis. Lecturer. *Member:* White House Correspondents Association, National Press Club, Holland Society of New York, Sigma Delta Chi. *Awards, honors:* Nieman fellow, Harvard University, 1979; Merriman Smith Memorial Award, 1980.

*WRITINGS—*Under name Frank Van Riper: *Glenn: The Astronaut Who Would Be President,* Empire Books, 1983.

WORK IN PROGRESS: Articles, commentary, and reviews on contemporary politics and government.

SIDELIGHTS: Frank Van Riper told *CA* he ''broke many of the major Watergate exclusives, along with James Wieghart: prospective John N. Mitchell coverup indictment, contents of sealed grand jury report on Nixon's Watergate involvement, running exclusives on grand jury and special prosecutor investigations, major series of exclusives on secret evidence presented to House impeachment hearings.'' Van Riper also ''broke copyrighted series of stories on the F.B.I. and National Security Agency interception of international cable traffic, prompting hearings and investigations by Senate Intelligence Committee and House Individual Liberties Subcommittee.''

CA asked Van Riper his opinion of the 1977 David Frost/Richard Nixon interviews. ''The Nixon/Frost interviews were useful,'' he responded, ''if only as a vehicle for Frost to express indignation for all of us over the things Nixon did, or condoned.

''Much as I wanted to denigrate Frost, he did an overall excellent job. He did his homework and knew enough to let Nixon do himself in with his own words, particularly as they related to his perverted perception of a President's right to violate the law.''

On writing the biography of John Glenn, Van Riper told *CA:* ''Chronicling the career of a war hero, astronaut, and presidential candidate required the cooperation and patience of scores of people, including former astronauts, politicians, journalists, military men, historians, and one octogenarian correspondent from Ohio who volunteered his written recollections of Glenn's formidable mother, Clara.

''Glenn himself was very cooperative, doubtless realizing that it would be in his interest to be so, even if it meant taking important time from his campaign for the 1984 Democratic presidental nomination to submit to hours of taped interviews. In all, 68 people were interviewed, countless documents and articles scanned and more than 130,000 words written. The deadline pressure was intense. The book was finished in six months, though I calculate that the 12-hour days and seven-day weeks were the equivalent of more than fourteen months' work.''

AVOCATIONAL INTERESTS: Photography, travel, cooking, wine, squash, racquetball.

* * *

Van RIPER, Frank
See Van RIPER, Francis A(lbert)

* * *

Van WOERKOM, Dorothy (O'Brien) 1924-

PERSONAL: Born June 26, 1924, in Buffalo, N.Y.; daughter of Peter S. (a refinery superintendent) and Helen (Miller) O'Brien; married John W. Van Woerkom (an administrator at Rice University), February 22, 1961. *Education:* Attended Mount Mercy Academy and Bryant and Stratton Business College. *Politics:* ''To me the candidate, not the party, matters.'' *Religion:* Roman Catholic. *Home and office:* 8826 McAvoy Dr., Houston, Tex. 77074.

CAREER: Free-lance writer. U.S. Army Corps of Engineers, Buffalo, N.Y., secretary, 1943-47; elementary school teacher in the parochial schools of Buffalo, N.Y., 1947-51; U.S. Army Corps of Engineers, Buffalo, secretary, 1951-61. *Member:* Association of Childhood Education International, Associated Authors of Children's Literature, Society of Children's Book Writers, American Library Association, Children's Literature Association, National Wilderness Society, National Audubon Society. *Awards, honors: Stepka and the Magic Fire* was named best religious children's book of 1974 by Catholic Press Association; *Harry and Shellburt* was named a notable book by American Library Association in 1977.

*WRITINGS—*All juveniles: *The Queen Who Couldn't Bake Gingerbread* (Junior Literary Guild selection), Knopf, 1975; *Becky and the Bear* (Junior Literary Guild selection), Putnam, 1975; *Sea Frog, City Frog,* Macmillan, 1975; *Abu Ali: Three Tales of the Middle East,* Macmillan, 1976; *The Rat, the Ox, and the Zodiac,* Crown, 1976; *Meat Pies and Sausages,* Greenwillow, 1976; *Tit for Tat,* Greenwillow, 1977; *Harry and Shellburt,* Macmillan, 1977; *Donkey Ysabel,* Macmillan, 1978; *Alexandra the Rock-Eater,* Knopf, 1978; *Friends of Abu Ali: Three More Tales of the Middle East,* Macmillan, 1978; *Hidden Messages,* Crown, 1979; *Pearl in the Egg,* Crowell, 1980; *Try Again, Mendelssohn!,* Crown, 1980; *A Mascot for the Team,* Garrard, 1980; *Something to Crow About,* Whitman Publishing, 1982.

Published by Concordia: *Stepka and the Magic Fire*, 1974; *Journeys to Bethlehem*, 1974; *The Dove and the Messiah*, 1975; *Let Us Go to Bethlehem!*, 1976; *Wake Up and Listen*, 1976; *A Hundred Angels Singing*, 1976; *When All the World Was Waiting*, 1979; *Lands of Fire and Ice*, 1980; (with Mary Blount Christian) *Bible Heroes, Kings and Prophets*, 1981.

WORK IN PROGRESS: Several books for beginning readers; an historical novel for middle readers.

SIDELIGHTS: Dorothy Van Woerkom's book *Pearl in the Egg* is the story of an eleven-year-old serf girl who becomes a minstrel at the court of King Edward I. "What is truly memorable" about *Pearl in the Egg*, writes Jean Fritz in the *New York Times Book Review*, "is the thirteenth century, . . . which springs to life on the first page and never languishes. . . . [It] takes skill and grace, as well as scholarship, to re-create that time with such apparent ease—in language, detail, texture and color."

AVOCATIONAL INTERESTS: Needlework, travel to historic places.

BIOGRAPHICAL/CRITICAL SOURCES: New York Times Book Review, January 11, 1982.

*   *   *

VEATCH, Robert M(arlin)   1939-

PERSONAL: Born January 22, 1939, in Utica, N.Y.; son of Cecil R. (a pharmacist) and Regina (Braddock) Veatch; married Laurelyn Lovett (a sociologist), June 17, 1961; children: Paul Martin, Carlton Elliot. *Education:* Purdue University, B.S. (summa cum laude), 1961; University of California, San Francisco, M.S., 1962; Harvard University, B.D. (magna cum laude), 1964, M.A., 1970, Ph.D., 1971. *Home:* 98 Interpromontory Rd., Great Falls, Va. 22066. *Office:* Kennedy Institute of Ethics, Georgetown University, Washington, D.C. 20057.

CAREER: University of Ife, Ibadan, Nigeria, assistant lecturer in pharmacology, 1963; high school teacher of biology in Ogbomosho, Nigeria, 1963-64; Hastings Center, Institute of Society, Ethics and the Life Sciences, Hastings-on-Hudson, N.Y., senior associate and staff director of research group on death and dying, 1970-79; Georgetown University, Kennedy Institute of Ethics, Washington, D.C., professor of medical ethics, 1979—. Visiting faculty member at Brown University, Vassar College, Manhattanville College, and Dartmouth College. Research associate at Columbia University, 1971-72. *Member:* American Association for the Advancement of Science, American Population Association, American Sociological Association, Society of Christian Ethics, Society for the Scientific Study of Religion.

WRITINGS: Death, Dying, and the Biological Revolution, Yale University Press, 1976; *Value-Freedom in Science and Technology*, Scholars' Press, 1976; *Case Studies in Medical Ethics*, Harvard University Press, 1977; *A Theory of Medical Ethics*, Basic Books, 1981.

Editor: (With Sharmon Sollitto) *Bibliography of Society, Ethics and the Life Sciences*, Hastings Center, 1973, 4th edition, 1976; (with Willard Gaylin and Councilman Morgan) *The Teaching of Medical Ethics*, Hastings Center, 1973; (with Peter Steinfels) *Death Inside Out*, Harper, 1975; (with Roy Branson) *Ethics and Health Policy*, Ballinger, 1976; *Population Policy and Ethics: The American Experience*, Irvington Books, 1976; *Teaching of Bioethics: Report of the Commission on the Teach-*

ing of Bioethics, Hastings Center, 1976; (with Carol Levine) *Cases in Bioethics from the Hastings Center Report*, Hastings Center, 1982.

Contributor of about one hundred articles to learned journals. Associate editor of *Encyclopedia of Bioethics* and *IRB: A Review of Human Subjects Research;* contributing editor of *Hospital Physician;* member of editorial board of *Journal of the American Medical Association, Harvard Theological Review*, and *Journal of Medicine and Philosophy.*

WORK IN PROGRESS: Research on medical ethics, the relation of science to public policy, death and dying, and experimentation on human subjects.

SIDELIGHTS: In *A Theory of Medical Ethics*, Robert M. Veatch argues that existent medical codes such as the Hippocratic Oath are narrowly focused and lacking in universal foundations. "Worst of all," reports Jack Geiger in the *New York Times Book Review*, "most of the existing medical codes are professionally ethnocentric, doctor-focused, when the vast majority of medical decisions, in fact, have always been made and continue to be made by ordinary people, like the patients who decide whether or not to seek treatment." The solution to this problem, Veatch argues in his book, "is to abandon the idea that an ethic for medicine can be based on a professionally articulated code. Medical ethics can no longer be seen as a set of principles or commitments generated from within a profession and transmitted to new members during their socialization into it."

In place of this outmoded system, Veatch proposes a "covenant" theory of medical ethics, which contributing *America* reviewer Lisa Sowle Cahill calls "a version of the 'social contract' in the tradition of Locke, Hobbes, and Rousseau." Describing the book as "carefully crafted," Cahill concludes that "it will be stimulating both for those who seek a cogent theoretical perspective on the complexities of medical practice and research and for those intrigued by the difficulties and challenges of applying recent contract theory to concrete moral issues."

BIOGRAPHICAL/CRITICAL SOURCES: Robert M. Veatch, *A Theory of Medical Ethics*, Basic Books, 1981; *New York Times Book Review*, January 31, 1982; *America*, April 24, 1982.

*   *   *

VERGHESE, T. Paul
See GREGORIOS, Paulos Mar

*   *   *

VICKERS, Douglas   1924-

PERSONAL: Born July 13, 1924, in Rockhampton, Australia; son of John William and Vera (Turner) Vickers; married Miriam Betts, October 12, 1946; children: Paul. *Education:* University of Queensland, B.Com., 1949; University of London, B.Sc., 1952, Ph.D., 1956. *Office:* Department of Economics, University of Massachusetts, Amherst, Mass. 01003.

CAREER: Affiliated with National Bank of Australasia, London, England, 1949-55, and Vauxhall Motors Ltd., England, 1955-57; University of Pennsylvania, Philadelphia, assistant professor, 1957-61, associate professor, 1961-67, professor of finance, 1967-72, chairman of department, 1969-72; University of Western Australia, Nedlands, professor of economics,

1972-77; University of Massachusetts—Amherst, professor of economics, 1978—. *Military service:* Royal Australian Air Force, 1942-46. *Member:* Royal Economic Society, American Economic Association, American Finance Association, Academy of Social Sciences (Australia; fellow). *Awards, honors:* Ford Foundation faculty research fellow, 1964-65.

WRITINGS: Studies in the Theory of Money 1690-1776, Chilton, 1959; (with Irwin Friend, F. E. Brown, and E. S. Herman) *A Study of Mutual Funds,* U.S. Government Printing Office, 1962; *The Theory of the Firm: Production, Capital and Finance,* McGraw, 1968; *Man in the Maelstrom of Modern Thought: An Essay in Theological Perspective,* Presbyterian & Reformed, 1975; *Economics and Man: Prelude to a Christian Critique,* Craig Press, 1976; (contributor) T. Wilson and A. Skinner, editors, *Essays on Adam Smith,* Clarendon Press, 1976; (contributor) Sidney Weintraub, editor, *Modern Economic Thought,* University of Pennsylvania Press, 1977; *Financial Markets in the Capitalist Process,* University of Pennsylvania Press, 1978; *A Christian Approach to Economics and the Cultural Condition,* Exposition Press, 1982; *Now that You Have Believed,* Exposition Press, 1982. Contributor to economics, accounting, and finance journals.

*   *   *

VOGEL, David 1947-

PERSONAL: Born April 14, 1947, in New York, N.Y.; son of Harry (an optician) and Charlotte (Rab) Vogel; married Virginia Glicker; children: Philip, Barbara. *Education:* Queens College of the City University of New York, B.A., 1967; Princeton University, Ph.D., 1974. *Religion:* Jewish. *Office:* School of Business Administration, University of California, Berkeley, Calif. 94720.

CAREER: University of California, Berkeley, associate professor in School of Business Administration, 1973—. *Member:* American Political Science Association.

WRITINGS: (With Leonard Silk) *Ethics and Profits: The Crisis of Confidence in American Business,* Simon & Schuster, 1976; *Lobbying the Corporation: Citizen Challenges to Business Authority,* Basic Books, 1978; (editor with Thornton Bradshaw) *Corporations and Their Critics: Issues and Answers on the Problems of Corporate Social Responsibilities,* McGraw, 1981.

Contributor to popular and scholarly journals, including *Nation, Polity, New Republic, Daedalus, New York Review of Books, New York Times,* and *Wall Street Journal.* Editor of *California Management Review,* 1982—.

WORK IN PROGRESS: Two books, tentatively entitled *Comparing Government Regulation,* for Cornell University Press, and *The Fall and Rise of Corporate Power in America,* for Basic Books.

SIDELIGHTS: David Vogel's *Lobbying the Corporation: Citizen Challenges to Business Authority* chronicles the successes and failures of past attempts to influence corporate practices. Described by David Kusnet in *New Republic* as a "comprehensive, well researched, and clearly written study," the book tells the story of various groups that have pressured such companies as Dow Chemical, General Motors, and Eastman Kodak to change their policies on social and environmental issues. The book covers some of the better-known consumer advocate groups and, notes Kusnet, is also valuable for including a "detailed history of the largely unheralded work of [research] organizations . . . which have scrutinized the operations of major corporations and revealed much about their ownership, their profitability and the impact of their policies upon society."

In the *New York Times Book Review,* Andrew Hacker comments that "we are told slightly more than we need to know" about some of the groups mentioned. He adds that since few had large or stable memberships, "to style these organizations a 'movement'—as Mr. Vogel tends to do—begs some important questions." Kusnet concludes, however, that the "bottom line of this study of anti-corporate campaigning is: there's still no substitute for organizing. You could learn this lesson without reading this book, but—if only for its impressive assemblage of easily accessible facts about recent challenges to the corporations—anyone interested in challenging the corporations should read *Lobbying the Corporation.*"

BIOGRAPHICAL/CRITICAL SOURCES: New York Times Book Review, January 14, 1979; *New Republic,* February 10, 1979.

*   *   *

VOIGT, Ellen Bryant 1943-

PERSONAL: Born May 9, 1943, in Danville, Va.; daughter of Lloyd (a farmer) and Zue (an elementary school teacher; maiden name, Yeatts) Bryant; married Francis George Wilhelm Voigt (a college dean), September 5, 1965; children: Jula Dudley, William Bryant. *Education:* Converse College, B.A., 1964; University of Iowa, M.F.A., 1966. *Home address:* P.O. Box 16, Marshfield, Vt. 05658.

CAREER: Iowa Wesleyan College, Mount Pleasant, instructor in English, 1966-69; Goddard College, Plainfield, Vt., teacher of literature and writing, 1970-78, director of writing program, 1975-78; Massachusetts Institute of Technology, Cambridge, associate professor of creative writing, 1979-82; Warren Wilson College, M.F.A. program for writers, Swannanoa, N.C., visiting faculty member, 1981—. Professional pianist. Member of board of directors of Associated Writing Programs; has given poetry readings at schools and colleges, and served as judge of poetry contests. *Awards, honors:* Grants from Vermont Council on the Arts, 1974-75, National Endowment for the Arts, 1976-77, and the Guggenheim Foundation, 1978-79.

WRITINGS: Claiming Kin (poems), Wesleyan University Press, 1976; *The Forces of Plenty* (poems), Norton, 1983.

Anthologized in *Poetry in Public Places,* American International Sculptors Symposium, 1977, and *Ardis Anthology of New American Poetry,* edited by David Rigsby, Ardis, 1977.

Contributor to *Nation, New Yorker, Atlantic,* and *New Republic,* and to literary journals, including *Shenandoah, Sewanee Review, American Poetry Review, Southern Review, Antaeus, Ploughshares,* and *Poetry.* Advisory editor of *Arion's Dolphin,* 1971-75.

WORK IN PROGRESS: Poetry.

SIDELIGHTS: In her first book of poems, *Claiming Kin,* Ellen Bryant Voigt reveals "a Southerner's devotion to family and a naturalist's devotion to the physical world," Edward Hirsch observes in his *Nation* review. The title poem of the collection reflects both impulses, for in addressing her early life in her mother's house, Voigt compares herself to a barren plant: "Mother, this poem is from your middle / child who, like your private second self / rising at night to wander the dark / house, / grew in the shady places: / a green plant in a brass pot, / rootbound, without blossoms."

What Peter Schjeldahl finds interesting about Voigt's poems, he writes in the *New York Times Book Review,* "is evidence of a pretty ferocious sensibility: powerful sexual yearnings and repulsions, fascinations with physical rot and murderous impulses." And Hirsch alludes to "a sort of Plathean intensity, a bleak energy of mourning" permeating her work. "As a book," Hirsch concludes, "*Claiming Kin* is restless, sometimes violent, always physical. Its poems stand on both sides of a barren winter. But in the end, through the magical, saving grace of language, Ellen Bryant Voigt's poems resist and transcend their seasons of hard weather. *Claiming Kin* is a stunning first collection."

BIOGRAPHICAL/CRITICAL SOURCES: New York Times Book Review, May 1, 1977, July 17, 1983; *American Poetry Review,* July, 1977; *Nation,* August 6, 1977.

W

WAHLKE, John C(harles) 1917-

PERSONAL: Born October 29, 1917, in Cincinnati, Ohio; son of Albert B.C. and Clara (Ernst) Wahlke; married Virginia Joan Higgins, December 1, 1943; children: Janet, Dale. *Education:* Harvard University, B.A., 1939, M.A., 1947, Ph.D., 1952. *Home:* 5462 North Entrada Catorce, Tucson, Ariz. 85718. *Office:* Department of Political Science, University of Arizona, Tucson, Ariz. 85721.

CAREER: Traffic clerk for industrial firms, 1939-42; Amherst College, Amherst, Mass., instructor, 1944-51, assistant professor of political science, 1951-53; Vanderbilt University, Nashville, Tenn., assistant professor, 1953-55, associate professor, 1955-61, professor of political science, 1961-63; State University of New York at Buffalo, professor of political science, 1963-66, chairman of department, 1965-66; University of Iowa, Iowa City, professor of political science, 1966-71; State University of New York at Stony Brook, professor of political science, 1971-73; University of Iowa, professor of political science, 1973-79; University of Arizona, Tucson, professor of political science, 1979—. Visiting professor at University of Massachusetts, 1951-52, and University of California, Berkeley, 1958-59. *Military service:* U.S. Army, observation pilot, Field Artillery, 1942-45; became captain; received Air Medal with two oak leaf clusters.

MEMBER: American Political Science Association (member of executive committee, 1964-65; member of council, 1964-66; president, 1977-78), International Political Science Association, American Association of University Professors, Midwest Political Science Association (president, 1970-71), Southern Political Science Association, Phi Beta Kappa. *Awards, honors:* Social Science Research Council faculty grant, 1955.

WRITINGS: (Editor) *The Causes of the American Revolution,* Heath, 1950, 3rd edition, 1973; (editor) *Loyalty in a Democratic State,* Heath, 1952, 3rd edition, 1973; (editor with Heinz Eulau) *Legislative Behavior,* Free Press of Glencoe, 1959; (with Eulau, W. Buchanan, and L. Ferguson) *The Legislative System,* Wiley, 1962; (co-editor and co-author) *Government and Politics,* Random House, 1966, 2nd edition, 1971; (editor with Bernard E. Brown) *The American Political System,* Dorsey, 1967, revised edition, 1973; (editor with Samuel C. Patterson) *Comparative Legislative Behavior,* Wiley, 1972; (with Eulau) *The Politics of Representation,* Sage, 1978.

WORK IN PROGRESS: Biobehavioral bases of political behavior.

* * *

WALKER, Edward L(ewis) 1914-

PERSONAL: Born June 18, 1914, in Connersville, Ind.; son of Earl Lewis (a restaurateur) and Norma (Cloud) Walker; married Alice Elizabeth Johnson, June 21, 1939 (deceased); married Kathryn Sage, April 18, 1976; children: (first marriage) Bruce Edward (deceased); (second marriage) William Clark Sage, Robert Douglas Sage. *Education:* Indiana University, A.B., 1938, M.A., 1940; University of Iowa, graduate study, 1941-42; Stanford University, Ph.D., 1947. *Politics:* Independent. *Religion:* None. *Home and office:* 3041 Lopez, Pebble Beach, Calif. 93953.

CAREER: *Connersville News-Examiner,* Connersville, Ind., 1932-34, began as reporter, became acting city editor; junior clinical psychologist, Indiana Department of Public Welfare, Department of Corrections, 1938-41; University of Michigan, Ann Arbor, instructor, 1947-48, assistant professor, 1948-50, associate professor, 1950-56, professor of psychology, 1956-77, professor emeritus, 1978—; Hedgehog Press, Pebble Beach, Calif., publisher, 1982—. Visiting associate professor of psychology, Stanford University, 1951. National Institute of Mental Health, member of research scientist developmental review committee, 1968-72, chairman, 1970-72. Consultant to U.S. Veterans Administration, 1948-55, and Human Resources Research Office, George Washington University, 1952-62. *Military service:* U.S. Naval Reserve, Medical Corps, active duty, 1943-46; became lieutenant.

MEMBER: American Psychological Association (fellow; chairman of evaluation committee, 1966-67), American Association for the Advancement of Science (fellow), Eastern Psychological Association, Midwestern Psychological Association (secretary-treasurer, 1966-68; president, 1968-69), Sigma Xi. *Awards, honors:* National Institutes of Health research career award, 1964; Center for Advanced Study in the Behavioral Sciences fellow, 1972-73.

WRITINGS: (With Robert W. Heyns) *An Anatomy for Conformity,* Prentice-Hall, 1962; (with B. E. Boothe and Anne H. Rosenfeld) *Toward a Science of Psychiatry: The Impact of the*

Research Development Program of the Institute of Mental Health, Brooks/Cole, 1974; *Psychological Complexity and Preference: A Hedgehog Theory of Behavior,* Brooks/Cole, 1980; *Hot Bread, Crawdads and Other Ana,* Hedgehog Press, 1982.

"Beginning Course in Psychology" series, editor of sixteen books and demonstration kit, Brooks/Cole, 1966-72, and author of the following books in the series: (With D. J. Weintraub) *Perception,* 1966; (with W. J. McKeachie) *Teaching the Beginning Course in Psychology,* 1967; *Conditioning and Instrumental Learning,* 1967; *Psychology as a Natural and Social Science,* 1970; (with Weintraub) *Perception Demonstration Kit,* 1972.

Contributor: J. W. Atkinson, editor, *Motives in Fantasy, Action and Society,* Van Nostrand, 1958; McKeachie and J. E. Milholland, editors, *The Underground Curriculum in Psychology,* Scott, Foresman, 1961; *The Teaching of Architecture,* Cranbrook Press, 1964; *Nebraska Symposium on Motivation,* University of Nebraska Press, 1964; D. P. Kimble, editor, *The Organization of Recall,* New York Academy of Science, 1967; J. T. Tapp, editor, *Reinforcement and Behavior,* Academic Press, 1969; D. E. Berlyne, editor, *Pleasure, Reward, Preference,* Academic Press, 1973; H. I. Day, editor, *Implications of Intrinsic Motivation Theory,* Plenum, 1981; *Documentary Report of the Ann Arbor Symposium: Applications of Psychology to the Teaching and Learning of Music,* Music Educators Conference, 1981.

Also author of eight psychological reports for the U.S. Navy, 1943-46. Also contributor to *International Encyclopedia of Psychiatry, Psychology, Psychoanalysis, and Neurology,* Aesculapius Publishers, 1980. Contributor of papers to symposia; contributor of more than sixty articles, reports, and reviews to professional journals, including *Journal of General Psychology, Psychological Record, American Journal of Psychology, Current Issues in Higher Education, Journal of Experimental Psychology,* and *Journal of Consulting Psychology.* Consulting editor, *Motivation and Emotion.*

SIDELIGHTS: Edward L. Walker told *CA:* "Nearly a third of a century was spent preparing to be an academic, and another third writing academic material. The next third of a century offers the opportunity to write for pleasure—my own and I hope that of others."

*   *   *

WALLACE, Barbara Brooks

PERSONAL: Born in Soochow, China; daughter of Otis Frank (a businessman) and Nicia E. Brooks; married James Wallace, Jr. (in U.S. Air Force), February 27, 1954; children: James. *Education:* Attended schools in Hankow, Tientsin, and Shanghai, China, Baguio, Philippines, and Claremont, Calif.; attended Pomona College, 1940-41; University of California, Los Angeles, B.A., 1945. *Religion:* Episcopalian. *Home:* 2708 George Mason Pl., Alexandria, Va. 22305.

MEMBER: National League of American Pen Women, Children's Book Guild of Washington, D.C., Alpha Phi. *Awards, honors:* National League of American Pen Women juvenile book award, 1970, for *Claudia,* and 1974, for *The Secret Summer of L.E.B.;* William Allen White award, 1983, for *Peppermints in the Parlor.*

WRITINGS—All juveniles; published by Follett, except as indicated: *Claudia,* 1969; *Andrew the Big Deal,* 1971; *Trouble with Miss Switch,* Abingdon, 1971; *Victoria,* 1972; *Can Do,*

Missy Charlie, 1974; *The Secret Summer of L.E.B.,* 1974; *Julia and the Third Bad Thing,* 1975; *Palmer Patch,* 1976; *Hawkins,* Abington, 1977; *Peppermints in the Parlor,* Atheneum, 1980; *The Contest Kid Strikes Again,* Abingdon, 1980; *Hawkins and the Soccer Solution,* Abingdon, 1981; *Miss Switch to the Rescue,* Abingdon, 1981; *Hello, Claudia!,* Modern Curriculum Press, 1982; *Claudia and Duffy,* Modern Curriculum Press, 1982.

WORK IN PROGRESS: A fantasy for young readers.

*   *   *

WALLACH, Michael A(rthur)   1933-

PERSONAL: Born April 8, 1933, in New York, N.Y.; son of Max and Wilma (Cheiker) Wallach; married Lise Wertheimer (a psychologist), July 26, 1959; children: Rachel Paula. *Education:* Swarthmore College, B.A. (with highest honors), 1954; Harvard University, Ph.D., 1958; Cambridge University, Westengard traveling fellow from Harvard, 1955-56. *Office:* Department of Psychology, Duke University, Durham, N.C. 27706.

CAREER: Harvard University, Cambridge, Mass., instructor in social psychology, 1958-59; Massachusetts Institute of Technology, Cambridge, assistant professor of psychology, 1959-62; Duke University, Durham, N.C., associate professor, 1962-66; professor of psychology, 1966-72; University of Chicago, Chicago, Ill., William S. Gray Professor of Education, 1972-73; Duke University, professor of psychology, 1973—. Principal or co-principal investigator in research projects for National Institute of Mental Health, 1958-61, U.S. Office of Education, 1961-65, and National Science Foundation, 1961-63, 1964-67. *Awards, honors:* Social Science Research Council research grant, 1962.

WRITINGS: (With Kogan) *Risk Taking: A Study in Cognition and Personality,* Holt, 1964; (with Kogan) *Modes of Thinking in Young Children: A Study of the Creativity-Intelligence Distinction,* Holt, 1965; (with C. W. Wing, Jr.) *The Talented Student: A Validation of the Creativity-Intelligence Distinction,* Holt, 1969; (with Wing) *College Admission and the Psychology of Talent,* Holt, 1971; *The Intelligence/Creativity Distinction,* General Learning Press, 1971; (with wife Lise Wallach) *Teaching All Children to Read,* University of Chicago Press, 1976; (with L. Wallach) *The Teaching All Children to Read Kit,* University of Chicago Press, 1976; *Letter Tracing and Drawing Spirit Masters,* University of Chicago Press, 1976.

Contributor: P. H. Hoch and J. Zubin, editors, *Psychopathology of Aging,* Grune, 1961; L. C. Crow and A. Crow, editors, *Readings in Child and Adolescent Psychology,* Longmans, Green, 1961; S. Messick and J. Ross, editors, *Measurement in Personality and Cognition,* Wiley, 1962; H. W. Stevenson, editor, *Child Psychology: The Sixty-Second Yearbook of the National Society for the Study of Education,* University of Chicago Press, 1963; R.J.C. Harper, C. C. Anderson, C. M. Christensen, and S. M. Hunka, editors, *The Cognitive Processes: Readings,* Prentice-Hall, 1964.

M. Kornrich, editor, *Underachievement,* C. C Thomas, 1965; M. Schwebel, editor, *Behavioral Science and Human Survival,* Science and Behavior Books, 1965; A. H. Rubenstein and C. J. Haberstroh, editors, *Some Theories of Organization,* Dorsey, 1966; R. Jessor and S. Feshbach, editors, *Cognition, Personality, and Clinical Psychology,* Jossey-Bass, 1967; J. Hagan, editor, *Creativity and Learning,* Houghton, 1967; *New Directions in Psychology III,* Holt, 1967; D. Cartwright and A.

Zander, editors, *Group Dynamics: Research and Theory,* 3rd edition, Harper, 1968; B. L. Neugarten, editor, *Middle Ages and Aging: A Reader in Social Psychology,* University of Chicago Press, 1968; C. C. Spielberger, R. Fox, and B. Masterton, editors, *Contributions to General Psychology,* Ronald, 1968; R. K. Parker, editor, *Readings in Educational Psychology,* Allyn & Bacon, 1968; Rogers, editor, *Readings in Child Psychology,* Brooks/Cole, 1969.

J. C. Mancuso, editor, *Readings for a Cognitive Theory of Personality,* Holt, 1970; M. Wertheimer, editor, *Confrontation: Psychology and the Problems of Today,* Scott, Foresman, 1970; P. H. Mussen, editor, *Carmichael's Manual of Child Psychology,* 3rd edition, Wiley, 1970; R. D. Strom, editor, *Teachers and the Learning Process,* Prentice-Hall, 1971; J. L. Freedman, J. M. Carlsmith, and D. O. Sears, editors, *Readings in Social Psychology,* Prentice-Hall, 1971; M. Berbaum and G. Stricker, editors, *Search for Human Understanding,* Holt, 1971; J. J. Eysenck, editor, *Readings in Extraversion-Introversion,* Halsted, Volume II: *Fields of Application,* 1971, Volume III: *Bearings on Basic Psychological Processes,* 1971; R. A. Baron and R. M. Liebert, editors, *Human Social Behavior,* Dorsey, 1971; J. McV. Hunt, editor, *Human Intelligence,* Transaction Books, 1972; C. A. Insko and J. Schople, editors, *Experimental Social Psychology: Text with Illustrative Readings,* Academic Press, 1972; A. R. Binter and S. H. Frey, editors, *The Psychology of the Elementary School Child,* Rand McNally, 1972; R. J. Ofshe, editor, *Interpersonal Behavior in Small Groups,* Prentice-Hall, 1973; M. Bloomberg, editor, *Creativity: Theory and Research,* College & University Press, 1973; H. Z. Lopata, editor, *Marriages and Families,* Van Nostrand, 1973.

Eysenck, editor, *The Measurement of Personality,* University Park Press, 1976; A. Rothenberg and C. R. Hausman, editors, *The Creativity Question,* Duke University Press, 1976; N. S. Endler and D. Magnusson, editors, *Interactional Psychology and Personality,* Halsted, 1976; Messick and others, editors, *Individuality in Learning: Implications of Cognitive Styles and Creativity for Human Development,* Jossey-Bass, 1976; I. L. Janis, editor, *Current Trends in Psychology: Readings from American Scientists,* William Kaufmann, 1977; Wertheimer and L. Rappoport, editors, *Psychology and the Problems of Today,* Scott, Foresman, 1978; L. B. Resnick and P. A. Weaver, editors, *Theory and Practice of Early Reading,* Lawrence Erlbaum Associates, 1979; F. R. Connors, editor, *Developmental Reading Handbook,* McGraw-Hill, in press.

Contributor of numerous articles to various journals, including *Journal of Abnormal and Social Psychology, American Journal of Psychology, Psychological Reports, Journal of Consulting Psychology,* and *Journal of Aesthetics and Art Criticism.* Editor of *Journal of Personality,* 1963-72.

* * *

WALLENSTEIN, Barry J(ay)   1940-

PERSONAL: Born February 13, 1940, in New York, N.Y.; son of Maxwell (a businessman) and Pearl (Squires) Wallenstein; married second wife, Lorna Harbus, March, 1978; children: Daniel. *Education:* New York University, B.A., 1962, M.A., 1963, Ph.D., 1972. *Religion:* Jewish. *Home:* 890 West End Ave., New York, N.Y. 10025. *Office:* Department of English, City College of the City University of New York, 138 St. and Convent Ave., New York, N.Y. 10031.

CAREER: Yeshiva University, Stern College, New York City, instructor in English, 1963-65; City College of the City Uni-

versity of New York, New York City, 1965—, began as assistant professor, currently associate professor of English. Exchange professor at the University of Paris, 1981-82. Lecturer at Cooper Union Adult Forum, 1965—. *Member:* Modern Language Association of America, Poetry Society of America, Poets & Writers, Inc.

WRITINGS: (With Jack Salzman) *Years of Protest,* Pegasus, 1967; *Visions and Revisions: An Approach to Poetry,* Crowell, 1970; *Beast Is a Wolf with Brown Fire* (poetry), BOA Editions, 1977; *Roller Coaster Kid* (poetry), Crowell, 1982. Contributor of criticism to professional journals.

WORK IN PROGRESS: A third volume of poetry; critical essays on modern American poetry.

SIDELIGHTS: Barry J. Wallenstein performs his poetry to jazz accompaniment. In 1978, AK-BA Records released a recording of his work.

* * *

WALSH, William   1916-

PERSONAL: Born February 23, 1916, in London, England; son of William and Elizabeth (Kennedy) Walsh; married Toosey May Watson, 1945; children: Margaret, Timothy. *Education:* Cambridge University, M.A., 1945; University of London, M.A., 1951. *Religion:* Church of England. *Home:* 27 Moor Dr., Headingley, Leeds, West Yorkshire LS6 4BY, England. *Office:* Office of the Vice-Chancellor, University of Leeds, Leeds, West Yorkshire LS2 9JT, England.

CAREER: Schoolmaster in England, 1943-51; University College of North Staffordshire, North Staffordshire, England, lecturer in education, 1951-53; University of Edinburgh, Edinburgh, Scotland, lecturer in education, 1953-57; University of Leeds, Leeds, England, professor of education and head of department, 1957-72, professor of Commonwealth literature, 1972-81, acting vice-chancellor, 1981—, chairman of board of Combined Faculties of Arts, Economics, Social Studies, and Law, 1964-66, pro-vice-chancellor, 1965-67, chairman of board of adult education, 1966-77, chairman of School of Education, 1969-72. Director of Yorkshire Television, 1967—. Member of Independent Broadcasting Authority's Adult Education Committee, 1974-76, and Education Advisory Committee, 1976-81. *Member:* Royal Society of Arts (fellow). *Awards, honors:* Australian Commonwealth visiting fellow, 1970.

WRITINGS: Use of Imagination, Chatto & Windus, 1959; *A Human Idiom,* Chatto & Windus, 1965; *Coleridge: The Work and the Relevance,* Chatto & Windus, 1967; *A Manifold Voice: Studies in Commonwealth Literature,* Barnes & Noble, 1970; *V. S. Naipaul,* Barnes & Noble, 1973; *Commonwealth Literature,* Oxford University Press, 1973; (editor) *Readings in Commonwealth Literature,* Clarendon Press, 1973; *D. J. Enright: Poet of Humanism,* Cambridge University Press, 1974; *Patrick White: "Voss,"* Edward Arnold, 1976; *Patrick White's Fiction,* Rowman & Littlefield, 1977; *F. R. Leavis,* Indiana University Press, 1980; *Introduction to Keats,* Methuen, 1981; *R. K. Narayan: A Critical Appreciation,* University of Chicago Press, 1982. Also author of *Monarch Notes on Shakespeare's "Antony & Cleopatra,"* Monarch Press.

Contributor: A. F. Scott, editor, *Speaking of the Famous,* Macmillan, 1962; *The Teaching of English Literature Overseas,* Methuen, 1963; J. Lawlor, editor, *Higher Education: Patterns of Change in the 1970s,* Routledge & Kegan Paul, 1972; Bruce

Alvin King, editor, *Literatures of the World in English*, Routledge & Kegan Paul, 1974; Meenakshi Mukherjee, editor, *Considerations*, Allied Publications (Bombay), 1977; C. D. Narasimhaiah, editor, *Awakened Conscience: Studies in Commonwealth Literature*, Humanities, 1978. Also contributor to *From Blake to Byron*, 1957, *Young Writers, Young Readers*, 1960, *F. R. Leavis: Some Aspects of His Work*, 1963, *Indo-English Literature*, 1977, *Perspectives on Mulk Raj Anand*, 1978, and *The Study of Education*, Volume I, 1980. Contributor to periodicals, including *Encounter, Spectator, New Statesman, New Review, Listener, Notes and Queries,* and *Sewanee Review.*

WORK IN PROGRESS: Work on the Romantics and on higher education.

BIOGRAPHICAL/CRITICAL SOURCES: Times Literary Supplement, November 21, 1980, March 5, 1982, March 4, 1983.

* * *

WARNER, Francis (Robert le Plastrier) 1937-

PERSONAL: Born October 21, 1937, in Bishopthorpe, Yorkshire, England; son of Hugh Compton (an Anglican priest) and Nancy le Plastrier (Owen) Warner; married Mary Hall, August 8, 1958; children: Georgina Claire, Lucy Robine. *Education:* Attended Christ's Hospital and London College of Music; St. Catharine's College, Cambridge, B.A., 1958, M.A., 1965. *Religion:* Church of England. *Agent:* Patricia Macnaughton, P. L. Representation, 33 Sloane St., London S.W.1, England. *Office:* St. Peter's College, Oxford University, Oxford, England.

CAREER: Cambridge University, St. Catharine's College, Cambridge, England, teacher, 1958-65; Oxford University, Oxford, England, fellow and tutor in English literature at St. Peter's College and university lecturer, 1965—. Founder of Pilgrim's Way Players, 1954; founder of Cambridge University Elgar Centenary Choir and Orchestra, 1957; director of first James Joyce Symposium in Dublin, 1967; assistant director of Yeats International Summer School, 1961-67; founder of Samuel Beckett Theatre, 1967. *Member:* Athenaeum Club. *Awards, honors:* Messing International Award, 1972, for distinguished contributions to literature.

WRITINGS: (Compiler) *Garland: A Little Anthology of Poetry and Engravings*, Golden Head Press, 1968; (contributor) R. O. Driscoll, editor, *Theatre and Nationalism in Twentieth Century Ireland*, University of Toronto Press, 1971; *Francis Warner: Poet and Dramatist*, edited by Tim Prentki, Sceptre Press, 1977.

Poems: *Perennia*, Golden Head Press, 1962; *Early Poems*, Fortune Press, 1964; *Experimental Sonnets*, Fortune Press, 1965; *Madrigals*, Fortune Press, 1967; *Poetry of Francis Warner*, Pilgrim Press, 1970; *Lucca Quartet: For Lorraine*, Omphalos Press, 1975; *Poetry*, Smythe, 1978.

Plays: *Maquettes* (a trilogy of one-act plays; contains "Troat," "Emblem," and "Lumen"; first produced in Oxford at The Playhouse, July 27, 1970), Oxford Theatre Texts, 1972; *Lying Figures* (one act; first produced in Oxford at Jennetta Cochrane Theatre, April 10, 1972), Oxford Theatre Texts, 1972; *Meeting Ends* (one act), Oxford Theatre Texts, 1974; *Killing Time* (one-act), Oxford Theatre Texts, 1976; *A Conception of Love*, Smythe, 1978; *Light Shadows*, Smythe, 1979; *Requiem* (trilogy; contains "Lying Figures," "Killing Time," and "Meeting Ends"), Smythe, 1981.

BIOGRAPHICAL/CRITICAL SOURCES: Stage, August 6, 1970, April 20, 1972; *Choice*, July, 1971, April, 1975, June, 1977; *Times Literary Supplement*, March 30, 1973; *Drama*, winter, 1976; *Contemporary Literary Criticism*, Volume XIV, Gale, 1980.†

* * *

WARNER, Lucille Schulberg

PERSONAL: Born in Mount Vernon, N.Y.; daughter of Sol and Emma (Zeeman) Schulberg; married Henry Goldsmith Warner (a certified public accountant and money manager), January 12, 1971; stepchildren: Alison, Marc. *Education:* Attended Carnegie Institute of Technology (now Carnegie-Mellon University). *Home:* 50 Sutton Place S., New York, N.Y. 10022. *Agent:* Charlotte Sheedy Literary Agency, 145 West 86th St., New York, N.Y. 10024.

CAREER: American National Red Cross, public relations correspondent in France and Germany, 1945-47; Young & Rubicam, New York City, advertising copywriter, 1952-59; Compton Advertising Agencies, New York City, advertising copywriter, 1959-62; Time-Life Books, New York City, staff writer, 1962-69; free-lance writer, 1969—. Fellow of MacDowell Colony. *Member:* Authors Guild, Authors League of America, American Society of Journalists and Authors, Writers Room. *Awards, honors: Boston Globe-Hornbook* Award for *From Slave to Abolitionist: The Life of William Wells Brown.*

WRITINGS—All juveniles; published by Scholastic Book Services, except as indicated: *Historic India*, Time-Life, 1968; (adapter) *From Slave to Abolitionist: The Life of William Wells Brown*, Dial, 1976; (with Ann Reit) *Your A to Z Super Personality Quiz*, 1977; *Your A to Z Super Problem Solver*, 1978; *Your A to Z Super Guide to the Opposite Sex*, 1979; *Love Comes to Anne*, 1979; *Goodbye, Pretty One*, 1982; *You're No Friend of Mine*, 1983. Also author of *Teen Talk.*

WORK IN PROGRESS: An historical novel.

* * *

WATSON, Pauline 1925-
(POLA)

PERSONAL: Born July 24, 1925, in New Iberia, La.; daughter of Luke and Rosalie (Catalano) Bennett; married Jimmy T. Watson, October 19, 1947; children: Cindy (Mrs. Scott Walling), Jim, Duke, Vicki, Mike. *Education:* Palmer Institute of Authorship, graduate, 1951. *Home:* 24420 Stuebner Airline, Tomball, Tex. 77375.

CAREER: Accountant and office manager for an automobile dealership in New Iberia, La., 1942-47; writer, 1950—. *Member:* Houston Writer's Workshop (president, 1970—), Associated Authors of Children's Literature, Houston (president, 1975—), International Toastmistress Club (secretary and publicity chairman of Houston's Noonday branch, 1968—), Federated Woman's Club (Beaumont, Tex.).

WRITINGS—Juveniles: *A Surprise for Mother*, Prentice-Hall, 1976; *Curley Cat Baby-Sits*, Harcourt, 1977; *Days with Daddy*, Prentice-Hall, 1977; (with the editors of *Cricket* magazine) *Cricket's Cookery*, Random House, 1977; *Wriggles: The Little Wishing Pig*, Seabury, 1978; *What Would You Do?*, Prentice-Hall, 1979; *The Walking Coat*, Walker & Co., 1980; *My Turn, Your Turn*, Prentice-Hall, in press.

Work anthologized in *Cricket's Choice*, edited by Clifton Fadiman and Marianne Carus, 1975. Author of weekly column, "Post Oak Patter," in *Bellaire Texan*, 1969, and of monthly columns, "Kitchen Klatter," 1972-79, and, under pseudonym POLA, "Washboard Wisdom," 1974-79, both syndicated by Features Unlimited. Contributor of stories, articles, and poems to periodicals, including *My Weekly Reader, Cricket, Woman's Day, Southern Living, Reader's Digest, Highlights, Tempo,* and *Parents' Magazine.*

WORK IN PROGRESS: "There is always a story or an article or a poem in my typewriter."

SIDELIGHTS: Pauline Watson sold her first story in 1950 while taking a home-study course in creative writing. She told *CA* that she tries "to learn something new everyday and to have a long range plan of study toward goals that I have privately set for myself." Though her articles, poems, and stories have appeared in numerous publications for both adults and children, she considers writing for children more rewarding because it keeps her feeling young. "An added joy in writing for children," she says, "is the fun of getting to speak to hundreds of them about writing and books, and how poems can be found hiding inside each of us. [One] summer I discovered Polly Popcorn inside of me when I became the story lady at our local library. I enjoyed being this character so much [that] I will surely use her again, somewhere, in my writing."

BIOGRAPHICAL/CRITICAL SOURCES: Woodlands Sun, July 20, 1977.

*   *   *

WATTS, A. J.
See WATTS, Anthony J(ohn)

*   *   *

WATTS, Anthony J(ohn)   1942-
(A. J. Watts)

PERSONAL: Born April 3, 1942, in Frome, Somersetshire, England; son of Harold (a company secretary) and Dorothy (Smith) Watts; married Mary Elizabeth Cartwright (a social worker for the blind), October 14, 1967. *Education:* Attended country grammar school in Cornwall, 1953-61; studied music privately in London, becoming associate of London College of Music. *Home and office:* Hunters Moon, Hogspudding Lane, Newdigate, Surrey, England.

CAREER: British Broadcasting Corp., London, England, engineer, 1961-65, program operations assistant, 1965-78; editor, *Navy International*, 1978—. Free-lance naval publishing consultant. *Member:* U.S. Naval Institute (associate member), Warship Record Club.

WRITINGS: Japanese Warships of World War II, Ian Allan, 1966, revised edition, Doubleday, 1968; (under name A. J. Watts) *The Loss of the "Schornhorst,"* Ian Allan, 1970; *Pictorial History of the Royal Navy*, Ian Allan, Volume I: *1816-1880*, 1970, Volume II: *1880-1914*, 1971; (with B. G. Gordon) *Imperial Japanese Navy, 1872-1945*, Doubleday, 1971 (with Adrian English) *Battle for the Falklands (2) Naval Forces*, Osprey Publishing, 1982.

Published by Ward, Lock: *A Source Book of Submarines and Submersibles*, 1976; *A Source Book of Naval Aircraft and Aircraft Carriers*, 1977, revised edition, 1980; *A Source Book of*

Hydrofoils and Hovercraft, 1978; *A Source Book of Helicopters and Vertical Take-off Aircraft*, 1982.

Published by Macdonald & Jane's: *The U-Boat Hunters*, 1976; *Axis Submarines*, 1977; *Allied Submarines of World War II*, 1977; *Battleships*, 1978; *Axis Cruisers*, 1979; *Allied Cruisers*, 1979.

Editor: *Warships and Navies*, Ian Allan, 1972; Friedrich Ruge, *Scapa Flow 1919: The End of the German Fleet*, translation by Derek Masters, Ian Allan, 1973; Juergen Rohwher and Gerhard Huemmelchen, *Chronology of the War at Sea*, Volume II: *1943-1945*, translation by D. Masters, Ian Allan, 1974; *Warships and Navies Review*, Ian Allan, 1974.

Author of radio documentary, "Ship of the Line," broadcast by British Broadcasting Corp.

WORK IN PROGRESS: A book for Macdonald & Jane's, *The Imperial Soviet Navy.*

SIDELIGHTS: Anthony J. Watts has always lived by the sea near naval ports and air stations. He began studying warships as a young boy. *Avocational interests:* Singing, music, and all aspects of history and natural history.

*   *   *

WAYNE, David
See BALSIGER, David W(ayne)

*   *   *

WEIGLE, Marta   1944-

PERSONAL: Original name, Mary Martha; born July 3, 1944, in Janesville, Wis.; daughter of Richard Daniel (a college president) and Mary (Day) Weigle. *Education:* Attended St. John's College, Annapolis, Md., 1961-62; Radcliffe College, A.B., 1965; University of Pennsylvania, M.A., 1968, Ph.D., 1971. *Office:* Department of Anthropology, University of New Mexico, Albuquerque, N.M. 87131.

CAREER: University of New Mexico, Albuquerque, assistant professor, 1972-77, associate professor of folklore, 1977-83, professor of anthropology, English, and American studies, 1983—. President and editor of Ancient City Press, 1981—. *Member:* American Folklore Society, New Mexico Folklore Society, Texas Folklore Society. *Awards, honors:* Award of honor from New Mexico Cultural Properties Review Committee, 1976; Zia Award from New Mexico Press Women, 1977.

WRITINGS: Follow My Fancy: The Book of Jacks and Jack Games, Dover, 1970; *The Penitentes of the Southwest*, Ancient City Press, 1970; *Brothers of Light, Brothers of Blood: The Penitentes of the Southwest*, University of New Mexico Press, 1976; (with Kyle Fiore) *Santa Fe and Taos: The Writer's Era, 1916-1941*, Ancient City Press, 1982; *Spiders & Spinsters: Women and Mythology*, University of New Mexico Press, 1982.

Editor: Lorenzo de Cordova, *Echoes of the Flute*, Ancient City Press, 1972; *Hispanic Villages of Northern New Mexico*, Lightning Tree, 1975; *The Lightning Tree Bicentennial Southwestern Reader for 1976: An Anthology of Folklore with Weekly Calendar*, Lightning Tree, 1975; *The Annual Lightning Tree Southwestern Reader with Weekly Calendar for 1977*, Lightning Tree, 1976; *A Penitente Bibliography*, University of New Mexico Press, 1976; *Hispano Folklife of New Mexico*, University of New Mexico Press, 1978; *Hispanic Arts and Eth-nohistory in the Southwest,* Ancient City Press, 1983.

Author of "Lightning Tree Southwestern Calendar," 1974-75. Contributor to history, anthropology, and folklore journals.

WORK IN PROGRESS: A book on New Mexico folklore.

SIDELIGHTS: Marta Weigle told *CA* that she is "working on women and oral tradition and various aspects of the Southwest, especially tourism and Hispanic folk culture there."

BIOGRAPHICAL/CRITICAL SOURCES: Los Angeles Times Book Review, October 3, 1982.

*   *   *

WEISS, Ann E(dwards)   1943-

PERSONAL: Born March 21, 1943, in Newton, Mass.; daughter of Donald Loring (a teacher) and Dorothy (a teacher; maiden name, Poole) Charlton; married Malcolm E. Weiss (a writer), January 31, 1966; children: Margot Elizabeth, Rebecca Bates. *Education:* Brown University, A.B., 1965. *Home address:* R.D.1, Box 415, North Whitefield, Me. 04353.

CAREER: Scholastic Magazines, Inc., New York, N.Y., writer and assistant editor, 1965-69, associate editor, 1969-72; free-lance writer, 1972—. *Awards, honors:* Christopher Award, 1974, for *Save the Mustangs; Save the Mustangs, The School on Madison Avenue,* and *God and Government* were named notable children's trade books by the National Council for the Social Studies Children's Book Council for 1974, 1978, and 1982, respectively; Outstanding Science Trade Book for Children Award, National Science Teachers Association, 1976, for *The Vitamin Puzzle,* and 1981, for *The Nuclear Question.*

WRITINGS—Children's books; published by Messner, except as indicated: *Five Roads to the White House,* 1970; *We Will Be Heard: Dissent in the United States,* 1972; *Save the Mustangs: How a Federal Law Is Passed,* 1974; (with husband, Malcolm E. Weiss) *The Vitamin Puzzle,* 1976; *The American Presidency,* 1976; *The American Congress,* 1977; *News or Not?,* Dutton, 1977; *Polls and Surveys: A Look at Public Opinion Research,* F. Watts, 1979; *The School on Madison Avenue: Advertising and What It Teaches* (Junior Literary Guild selection), Dutton, 1979.

What's That You Said?, Harcourt, 1980; *Party Politics, Party Problems,* Harper, 1980; *The Nuclear Question,* Harcourt, 1981; *Tune In, Tune Out: Broadcasting Regulation in the United States,* Houghton, 1981; *God and Government: The Separation of Church and State,* Houghton, 1982; *The Nuclear Arms Race: Can We Survive It?,* Houghton, 1983; *Over-the-Counter Drugs,* F. Watts, 1984.

WORK IN PROGRESS: Biofeedback: Fact or Fad?; a book for junior high on bioethics.

*   *   *

WEISS, Elizabeth S(chwartz)   1944-

PERSONAL: Born January 14, 1944, in Rochester, N.Y.; daughter of Raymond (a lawyer) and Josephine (a guidance counselor) Schwartz; married Stanley E. Weiss (an internist and nephrologist), November 22, 1970; children: Mark William, Gregory Scott. *Education:* Skidmore College, B.A., 1965; Boston University, M.A., 1966. *Home:* 1160 Park Ave., New York, N.Y. 10028.

CAREER: Writer. Scholastic Book Services, New York City, associate editor, 1967-68; Doubleday & Co., Inc., New York City, associate editor, 1968-71.

WRITINGS: (With Rita Wolfson) *The Gourmet's Low Cholesterol Cookbook,* Regnery, 1973; (with Wolfson) *The Cholesterol Counter,* Pyramid Publications, 1973; (with Joan Lasky) *Cookmates* (juvenile cookbook), Macrae, 1973; (with Wolfson) *Protein Planner,* Pyramid Publications, 1974; *The Female Breast,* Bantam, 1975; *Female Fatigue,* Zebra Books, 1976; *From Female Depression to Contented Womanhood,* Zebra Books, 1977; *Recovering from the Heart Attack Experience: Emotional Feelings, Medical Facts,* Macmillan, 1980. Contributor to *New Woman.*

*   *   *

WEISS, Malcolm E.   1928-

PERSONAL: Born January 22, 1928, in Philadelphia, Pa.; son of Amos and Doris (Tractenberg) Weiss; married Ann Edwards Charlton (a writer), December 31, 1966; children: Margot Elizabeth, Rebecca Bates. *Education:* University of Chicago, B.A. equivalent by examination, and graduate study, 1949-50; evening study, City College (now City College of the City University of New York), 1954-56. *Home and office address:* R.D. 1, Box 415, North Whitefield, Me. 04353.

CAREER: Scholastic Magazines, New York, N.Y., science editor for Elementary Division, 1964-69; free-lance writer, 1969—. Part-time science consultant to Scholastic Magazines, 1969—. *Awards, honors:* Outstanding Science Trade Book for Children Award, National Science Teachers Association, 1969, for *Man Explores the Sea,* 1973, for *Storms: From the Inside Out,* and 1976, for *The Vitamin Puzzle* and *Seeing through the Dark;* Distinguished Achievement Award, Educational Press Association, 1972; *One Sea, One Law?: The Fight for a Law of the Sea* was cited as a notable children's trade book in the field of social studies, 1982.

WRITINGS—Juveniles: *Clues to the Riddle of Life,* Hawthorn, 1968; *Man Explores the Sea,* Messner, 1969; *Storms: From the Inside Out,* Messner, 1973; *The World within the Brain,* Messner, 1974; *Lands Adrift: The Story of Continental Drift,* Parents' Magazine Press, 1975.

666 Jellybeans! All That?: An Introduction to Algebra, Crowell, 1976; (with wife, Ann E. Weiss) *The Vitamin Puzzle,* Messner, 1976; *Seeing through the Dark: Blind and Sighted, The Vision We Share,* Harcourt, 1976; *Why Glass Breaks, Rubber Bends, and Glue Sticks,* Harcourt, 1977; *What's Happening to Our Climate?,* Messner, 1978; *A First Book of Blindness,* F. Watts, 1980; *Gods, Stars, and Computers,* Doubleday, 1980; *Sky Watchers of Ages Past,* Houghton, 1982; *One Sea, One Law?: The Fight for a Law of the Sea,* Harcourt, 1982; *Far Out Factories: Manufacturing in Space,* Lodestar, 1984.

Contributor to poetry journals, including *Poetry Digest,* 1959—; author of monthly science supplement for *News Time,* Scholastic's sixth-grade magazine. Associate editor, *Science World* (weekly high school science magazine).

WORK IN PROGRESS: Hazardous Wastes, for F. Watts.

SIDELIGHTS: Malcolm E. Weiss writes to *CA:* "Children are curious. Children are doubters. These are also outstanding qualities of the creative scientist. One thing any good children's science book should do is to enable its readers to participate in the working out of these shared qualities. . . . For example, any beginning book for stargazers can hardly avoid interweaving myth and fact. Nor should it. Myths and legends are not necessarily fairy tales without basis in reality. And science is not eternal Truth descended out of heaven to replace the vain fancies of earlier ages, although in elementary school it is often taught that way. . . . Through the course of history, myth-making and poetry, art and science, tend to merge into one another.

''Almost certainly no one children's book can contain this theme. But any good elementary science book ought to illuminate some aspect of it. Hopefully even a few textbooks will get around to doing so before the millenium.''

''Under continual attack by some humanists, scientists are apt to complain that one of their number is likely to know more about literature and the arts than the average humanist knows about any branch of science. I think the complaint is valid. I also happen to think I'm one of the exceptions. But to prove that, I have to try to redress the balance.''

Of his *Sky Watchers of Ages Past,* Jane Langton observes in the *Washington Post Book World:* ''Weiss writes clearly, and the drawings are helpful. His examples are well chosen, revealing how universal was the fascination with the sky, and how widespread were the attempts to understand the relation of sun, moon and stars to the passage of time and the changing of the seasons.''

BIOGRAPHICAL/CRITICAL SOURCES: Washington Post Book World, July 11, 1982.

*   *   *

WEISSMAN, Stephen R(ichard)   1941-
(Steve Weissman)

PERSONAL: Born April 10, 1941, in New York, N.Y.; son of Herman B. (a businessman) and Beatrice (a secretary; maiden name, Siegel) Weissman; married Nancy Schaff (a social worker), March 10, 1967; children: Daniel. *Education:* Cornell University, B.A. (with honors), 1961; graduate study at Princeton University, 1962-63; University of Chicago, A.M., 1965, Ph.D., 1969.

CAREER: New York City Welfare Department, New York, N.Y., caseworker, 1961-62; Fordham University, Bronx, N.Y., instructor, 1966-69, assistant professor of political science (on leave), 1969-71; Jersey City State College, Jersey City, N.J., assistant professor of political science, 1971-72; former editor for Ramparts Press, Palo Alto, Calif. Faculty consultant to New York City Urban Corps Educational Program, 1967; associate professor at Free University of the Congo, 1969-71; Stanford University Community Development Study, research associate, 1972-73, consultant, beginning 1973. *Member:* American Political Science Association, Phi Beta Kappa, Phi Kappa Phi.

WRITINGS: American Foreign Policy in the Congo: 1960-1964, Cornell University Press, 1974; (contributor) J. Sneed and S. A. Waldhorn, editors, *Restructuring the Federal System: Approaches to Accountability,* Crane, Russak, 1975.

Under name Steve Weissman: (Compiler) *Big Brother and the Holding Company: The World behind Watergate,* introduction by Noam Chomsky, Ramparts, 1974; (with members of the Pacific Studies Center and the North American Congress on Latin America) *The Trojan Horse: A Radical Look at Foreign Aid,* Ramparts, 1974, revised edition, 1975; (with Herbert

Krosney) *The Islamic Bomb: The Nuclear Threat to Israel and the Middle East,* Times Books, 1981.

Contributor of articles to *Journal of Modern African Studies, Polity, Nation, New Leader,* and *Commonweal.*

WORK IN PROGRESS: Research on the urban policy system, especially the areas of manpower, housing, education and day care in San Francisco, and on a quantitative and qualitative comparison of the ''community controlled'' Model Cities manpower system and the Department of Labor's Concentrated Employment Program.

SIDELIGHTS: In *The Islamic Bomb: The Nuclear Threat to Israel and the Middle East,* Steve Weissman and Herbert Krosney discuss the danger of nuclear proliferation in the Middle East, noting that there are larger implications. ''If it is true, as they argue, that the proliferation treaty [of 1968] has failed,'' writes Edwin M. Yoder, Jr. in the *Washington Post Book World,* ''it remains imperative to find legal and direct diplomatic ways to restrain proliferation. For if diplomacy fails, the prospect is that those directly threatened by regional bombs will turn to terrorism, sabotage and even open attack as a remedy.'' Yoder calls *The Islamic Bomb* ''an important book,'' adding that it ''is a goldmine of information, apparently factual, about what is or should be our number one worry.''

BIOGRAPHICAL/CRITICAL SOURCES: Washington Post Book World, January 24, 1982; *New York Times Book Review,* March 7, 1982.†

*   *   *

WEISSMAN, Steve
See WEISSMAN, Stephen R(ichard)

*   *   *

WERE, Gideon S(aulo)   1934-

PERSONAL: Born October 27, 1934, in Kenya; son of Saulo (a teacher) and Abisage Wanzetse Omukofu; married Naomi Asoka (an education officer), September, 1964; children: Saulo, Abisage, Evaline, Masakha, Peres, Walter. *Education:* Royal Technical College of East Africa, G.C.E., 1959; London School of Oriental and African Studies, London, 1963-65; University of Wales, B.A. (with honors), 1963, Ph.D., 1966. *Religion:* Anglican. *Home:* Westlands, Nairobi, Kenya. *Office:* Department of History, University of Nairobi, P.O. Box 30197, Nairobi, Kenya.

CAREER: University of Nairobi, Nairobi, Kenya, special lecturer, 1966-67, lecturer, 1967-70, senior lecturer, 1970-73, associate professor of history, 1973-78, acting chairman of department, 1973-74, dean of Faculty of Arts, 1974-78. Member of Kenya Secondary School History Panel and Public Archives Advisory Council. *Member:* Historical Association of Kenya.

WRITINGS: A History of the Abaluyia of Western Kenya, circa 1500-1930, East African Publishing House, 1967; *Western Kenya Historical Texts,* East African Literature Bureau, 1967; *The Survivors,* Equatorial Publishers, 1968, new edition, 1978; (with Derek A. Wilson) *East Africa through a Thousand Years,* Evans Brothers, 1968, revised edition, 1972; (contributor) B. A. Ogot and J. A. Kieran, editors, *Zamani,* Longmans, Green, 1968, revised edition, 1973; (author of introduction) S. G. Ayany, *A History of Zanzibar,* East African Literature Bureau, 1970; *A History of South Africa,* Evans Brothers, 1974, new edition, 1982; *History, Public Morality and Nation-Building: A Survey of Africa since Independence*, University of Nairobi, 1981; *Leadership and Underdevelopment in Africa*, privately printed, 1983; *Circumcision Rites among the Bamasaba*, Acta Musicologia et Linguistica, in press. Also author of *Essays in African Religion in Western Kenya*, East African Literature Bureau, and, with M. A. Ogutu, *Essays in the History of South-Central Africa*, East African Literature Bureau. Contributor to academic journals. Editor, *Journal of Eastern African Research and Development* and *Transafrican Journal of History*.

WORK IN PROGRESS: A *History of Kenya*, for Evans Brothers; "The Wanga Kingdom," to be included in *East African Kingdoms during the Nineteenth Century*, edited by M.S.M. Kiwanuka; research on the pre-colonial history of Bugisu and the role of religion in society.

*   *   *

WESLEY, James
See RIGONI, Orlando (Joseph)

*   *   *

WESSEL, Helen (Strain)   1924-

PERSONAL: Born January 9, 1924, in San Anselmo, Calif.; daughter of John Albert and Laura (Hammerli) Strain; married Walter W. Wessel (a Baptist minister), June 22, 1945; children: Margaret, Sharyl, Deborah, Dorothy, Daniel, Donald. *Education:* Sioux Falls College, B.A., 1960; additional study at University of Minnesota. *Religion:* Christian. *Home:* 5365 Aztec Dr., Apt. 42, La Mesa, Calif. 92041. *Office address:* Bookmates International, Inc., P.O. Box 9883, Fresno, Calif. 93795.

CAREER: Author and publisher. President, Bookmates International, Inc., Fresno, Calif. Founder, Apple Tree Family Life Seminars. *Member:* International Childbirth Education Association (president, 1964-66).

WRITINGS: Natural Childbirth and the Christian Family, Harper, 1963, revised edition published as *Natural Childbirth and the Family*, 1973, 2nd revised edition published as *The Joy of Natural Childbirth*, 1976; (editor with Harlan F. Ellis) Grantly Dick-Read, *Childbirth without Fear*, 4th edition, Harper, 1972; (editor) Charles G. Finney, *The Autobiography of Charles G. Finney*, Bethany Press, 1977; (with Hermon Pettit) *Jubilee!: The Autobiography of Hermon Pettit*, Bookmates, 1979; (with Pettit) *Hebrews: Handbook for World Revival*, Bookmates, 1979; *Under the Apple Tree: Marrying, Birthing, Parenting*, Bookmates, 1981.

WORK IN PROGRESS: Several book manuscripts.

SIDELIGHTS: Helen Wessel wrote *CA:* "I write because I long to share with others what is in my heart. My love for people, all kinds of people, motivates me to put down in print those things I have learned from them that may help bring happiness in the lives of many others. Faith in God is the wellspring of my life and is the source of many of my thoughts. My children and grandchildren also teach me nuances of life I would miss without them. For these reasons, my writings focus around themes that improve the quality of personal, inward life, and relationships with others.

"Writers develop through reading. I have always been a voracious reader, preferring biographies and the classics. Among my favorites are Glenn Clark, Agnes Sanford and [Aleksandr] Solzhenitsyn."

WESTERGAARD, John (Harald)   1927-

PERSONAL: Born October 13, 1927, in London, England; son of Otto (a civil engineer) and Inger (a textile buyer; maiden name, Nyrop) Westergaard; married Inge Soerensen, August, 1950 (divorced); married Hanne Larsen (a potter), January, 1975; children: (first marriage) Susan, Michael; (second marriage) Camilla. *Education:* London School of Economics and Political Science, B.Sc., 1951. *Politics:* "Left-wing socialist." *Religion:* None. *Home:* 39 Rutland Park, Sheffield S.10, England. *Office:* Department of Sociological Studies, University of Sheffield, Sheffield S10 2TN, England.

CAREER: Held research posts at University College, University of London, and University of Nottingham, 1951-56; University of London, London School of Economics and Political Science, London, England, assistant lecturer, 1956-59, lecturer, 1959-66, senior lecturer, 1966-70, reader in sociology, 1970-75, research associate and deputy director of Centre for Urban Studies, 1960-75; University of Sheffield, Sheffield, England, professor of sociology and head of department, 1975—. Visiting lecturer at Brown University, 1963-64. Co-director of study "After Redundancy" in Sheffield, England. Committee member of Britain's Social Science Research Council, Council for National Academic Awards, and Council for Academic Freedom and Democracy. *Member:* Centre for Urban Studies.

WRITINGS: (With Ruth Glass) *London's Housing Needs*, Centre for Urban Studies, University of London, 1965; *Scandinavian Urbanism*, Institute for Organization and Industrial Sociology (Copenhagen), 1968; (with Glass) *Housing in Camden*, London Borough of Camden, 1969; (with Anne Weyman and Paul Wiles) *Modern British Society: A Bibliography*, Frances Pinter, 1974, revised edition, 1977; (with Henrietta Resler) *Class in a Capitalist Society: A Study of Contemporary Britain*, Basic Books, 1975.

Contributor: *London: Aspects of Change*, MacGibbon & Kee, 1964; Perry Anderson and Robin Blackburn, editors, *Towards Socialism*, Cornell University Press, 1965; *Social Objectives in Educational Planning*, Organisation for Economic Cooperation and Development, 1967; R. Miliband and J. Saville, editors, *The Socialist Register 1970*, Merlin Press (London), 1970; M. Craft, editor, *Family, Class, and Education*, Longman, 1970; R. Blackburn, editor, *Ideology in Social Science*, Fontana, 1973; J. Rex, editor, *Approaches to Sociology*, Routledge & Kegan Paul, 1974.

M. Bulmer, editor, *Working Class Images of Society*, Routledge & Kegan Paul, 1975; A. Blowers and G. Thompson, editors, *Inequalities, Conflict, and Change*, Open University Press, 1976; James Curran and others, editors, *Mass Communication and Society*, Edward Arnold, 1977; A. Hunt, editor, *Class and Class Structure*, Lawrence and Wishart, 1977; P. Worsley, editor, *Problems of Modern Society*, 2nd edition (Westergaard was not associated with earlier edition), Penguin Books, 1978; Miliband and Saville, editors, *The Socialist Register 1978*, Merlin Press, 1978; D. Coates and G. Johnston, editors, *Socialist Arguments*, Martin Robertson, 1983; P. Bean and S. MacPherson, editors, *Approaches to Welfare*, Routledge & Kegan Paul, 1983. Contributor to professional journals.

WORK IN PROGRESS: Continuing research on various aspects of contemporary class structure, and public policy relevant to inequality.

WESTHUES, Kenneth 1944-

PERSONAL: Born July 26, 1944, in Glasgow, Mo.; son of John (a farmer) and Olive (Conran) Westhues; *Education:* Immaculate Conception Seminary, Conception, Mo., B.A., 1966; Vanderbilt University, M.A., 1968, Ph.D., 1969. *Office:* Department of Sociology, University of Waterloo, Waterloo, Ontario, Canada N2L 3G1.

CAREER: Fordham University, New York, N.Y., assistant professor of sociology, 1969-70; University of Guelph, Guelph, Ontario, assistant professor of sociology, 1970-72; University of Western Ontario, London, professor of sociology, 1972-75; University of Waterloo, Waterloo, Ontario, professor of sociology, 1975—, chairman of department, 1975-78. Visiting professor at Memorial University of Newfoundland, 1982-83. *Member:* Canadian Association for Sociology and Anthropology, American Sociological Association, and numerous other associations.

WRITINGS: The Dream of Thirteen Men, Glasgow Lions Club (Glasgow, Mo.), 1966; *The Religious Community and the Secular State*, Lippincott, 1968; *Society's Shadow: Studies in the Sociology of Countercultures*, McGraw, 1972; (with P. R. Sinclair) *Village in Crisis*, Holt, 1974; *First Sociology*, McGraw, 1982.

WORK IN PROGRESS: A book on the lessons of Newfoundland.

*   *   *

WHEELER, Leslie A. 1945-

PERSONAL: Born August 21, 1945, in Pasadena, Calif.; daughter of John Leonard (a lawyer) and Helene (an interior decorator; maiden name, Albright) Wheeler; married Philip Lief (a book producer), October 2, 1976. *Education:* Stanford University, B.A., 1967; University of California, Berkeley, M.A., 1969. *Politics:* Liberal Democrat. *Home address:* Cagney Rd., Southfield, Mass. 01259.

CAREER: Free-lance writer. New York City Adult Training Center, New York, N.Y., teacher, 1969-71; Barron's Educational Series, Inc., Woodbury, N.Y., writer and editor, 1971-73. *Member:* Authors Guild, Authors League of America, National Women's Studies Association, Phi Beta Kappa. *Awards, honors: Loving Warriors: Selected Letters of Lucy Stone and Henry B. Blackwell, 1853-1893* was designated "Ambassador of Honor" by English Speaking Union of the United States for "its outstanding contribution to interpreting the life and culture of the United States to the people of other countries."

WRITINGS: Jimmy Who?, Barron's, 1976; (editor and author of introduction) *Loving Warriors: Selected Letters of Lucy Stone and Henry B. Blackwell, 1853-1893*, Dial, 1981; (contributor) Dale Spender, editor, *Feminist Theorists*, The Women's Press, 1983, Pantheon, in press. Contributor to *American History Illustrated* and *Montana: The Magazine of Western History*.

WORK IN PROGRESS: Sisters of the Heart, a novel about three women in mid-nineteenth-century America.

SIDELIGHTS: In her review of *Loving Warriors: Selected Letters of Lucy Stone and Henry B. Blackwell, 1853-1893*, Martha Saxton writes in the *Washington Post Book World* that "Leslie Wheeler's sensitive selection of letters between abolitionist-feminist Lucy Stone and her husband, Henry Blackwell, is a vivid introduction to this odd pair of nineteenth-century reformers. The letters are eminently readable and Wheeler has provided a series of solid essays filling in the gaps." Wheeler, according to Saxton, "has used a biographer's eye in selecting these letters and they can be read with the same pleasure as a good biography. . . . This [is] a touching and immediate book."

Similarly, Elaine Kendall writes in the *Los Angeles Times Book Review* that, taken alone, Lucy Stone's letters "would be no more than an accurate but dreary record of small triumphs and large disappointments in the nascent movement for women's rights; but read in conjunction with Henry's, they form a dual chronicle of emotional and intellectual growth."

Wheeler told *CA* of the motivation behind her historical literary endeavors: "The novel I am currently working on, [*Sisters of the Heart,*] is an outgrowth of research I did about nineteenth-century American women's history in connection with editing the Stone-Blackwell letters. It combines two strong and long-time interests—one in American history and the other in the Victorian novel—and enables me to explore through fiction the options facing women at the middle of the last century.

"I can't imagine living without writing; it's such an essential activity for me that on those days I don't write anything—whether it's only a short note—I feel that something vital is lacking. I can't say that writing comes easily for me, but there is nothing quite as exhilarating as constructing a sentence or paragraph that really works.

"Like Joan Didion, I write to find out what I'm thinking, and now that I'm writing fiction, I'm frankly fascinated by the process that's involved. When I started my historical novel, I thought that the characters and situations were far removed from my own life, but the more I write and reflect on what I've written, the more I'm aware that this simply isn't the case; that although I'm writing about three women who live in another century and are to a certain extent based on real-life figures I've read about, I'm also writing about myself, about my own deeply-felt experiences and concerns. So my book has become for me a kind of 'distant mirror' in which I see reflected both the past of others and my own present."

Jimmy Who? has been translated into French, Spanish, and Japanese.

BIOGRAPHICAL/CRITICAL SOURCES: Los Angeles Times Book Review, July 2, 1981; *Newsday*, July 19, 1981; *Philadelphia Inquirer*, July 19, 1981; *Washington Post Book World*, August 23, 1981.

*   *   *

WHETTEN, Lawrence L. 1932-

PERSONAL: Born June 12, 1932, in Provo, Utah. *Education:* Brigham Young University, B.A., 1954, M.A., 1955; Rutgers University, graduate study, 1955-56; New York University, Ph.D. (with honors), 1963. *Address:* Widenmayerstrasse 41, 8000 Munich 22, West Germany.

CAREER: U.S. Air Force, operations intelligence officer, 10th Tactical Reconnaisance Wing, Europe, 1960-63, senior political analyst, Headquarters USAF Europe, Wiesbaden, Germany, 1963-70; University of Oklahoma European Program, Munich, Germany, guest professor of political science, 1970-71; University of Southern California Graduate Program in International Relations, Munich, Germany, resident professor and director of program, 1971—. Part-time guest professor,

University of Maryland European Programs, Heidelberg, various periods between 1963-71. Staff consultant, Foreign Policy Research Institute, Philadelphia, 1969-70, 1971-72; consultant to Stiftung fuer Wissenschaft und Politik, 1976-79, and Research and Development Associates, 1977-79.

MEMBER: International Institute for Strategic Studies, United States Strategic Institute, American Academy of Political and Social Science, American Association for the Advancement of Soviet Studies, Royal Institute of International Affairs (London), International Institute for Strategic Studies. *Awards, honors:* Research grants from Foreign Policy Research Institute, 1969, 1970, Royal Institute for International Affairs, 1970, Ford Foundation, 1970, University of Southern California, 1975, 1976, Stiftung fuer Wissenschaft und Politik, 1975, 1977, 1978, Thyssen Foundation, 1979-82, and Volkswagen Foundation, 1980-82.

WRITINGS: Germany's Ostpolitik: Relations between the Federal Republic and the Warsaw Pact Countries, Oxford University Press for Royal Institute of International Affairs, 1971; *The Soviet Presence in the Middle East* (monograph), National Strategy Information Agency, 1971; *Contemporary American Foreign Policy: Minimal Diplomacy, Defensive Strategy and Detente Management,* Heath, 1974; *The Canal War: Four Power Conflict in the Middle East,* M.I.T. Press, 1974.

(Editor and contributor) *The Future of Soviet Military Power,* Crane, Russak, 1976; *Current Research in Comparative Communism: An Analysis and Bibliographic Guide to the Soviet System,* Praeger, 1976; (editor and contributor) *Political Implications of Soviet Military Power,* Crane, Russak, 1976; *Great Power Behavior in the Arab-Israeli Conflict,* International Institute for Strategic Studies, 1976; *The Political Implications of Nuclear Terrorism in Europe,* Research and Development Associates, 1977; *Management of Soviet Scientific Research and Technological Development: Some Military Aspects,* Stiftung Wissenschaft und Politik, 1977.

Germany East and West: Conflicts, Collaboration and Confrontation, New York University Press, 1981; *Scientific Establishment in Relation to the Soviet Military-Industrial Complex,* Delft University, 1981; *New International Communism: The Foreign and Defense Policies of Latin European Communist Parties,* Lexington Books, 1982; (editor) *Future Courses in International Communism,* Lexington Books, 1982; (with Sabri Sayari) *Analysis of Turkish Foreign Policy and Its Domestic Origins,* Lexington Books, 1982.

Contributor: William Kinter, editor, *European Security for the 1970s,* Foreign Policy Research Institute, 1971; Robert Pfaltzgraff, editor, *Alliance Problems in the 1970s,* Foreign Policy Research Institute, 1972; Phillip A. Richardson, editor, *American Strategy at the Crossroads,* U.S. Government Printing Office, 1973; Robert R. King and Robert W. Dean, editors, *East European Perspectives on European Security and Cooperation,* Praeger, 1974; *Strategic Appraisals of the Middle East,* Air War College, 1976; Se-Jin Kim, editor, *International Peace and Inter-System Relations in Divided Countries,* Research Center for Peace and Unification (Seoul), 1977; P. E. Haley and Lewis Snider, editors, *In the Lion's Bed: The Lebanese War and the Limits of Conflict and Power in the Middle East,* Syracuse University Press, 1978; Arlene McCown, editor, *The Future of NATO and the Warsaw Pact,* Westview, 1982.

Also editor of *Detente and Security Matters within the Warsaw Pact,* M.I.T. Press. Contributor of numerous articles to inter-

national relations and military journals in the United States, Switzerland, England, and Argentina. Member of editorial board, *Studies in Comparative Communism* and *Afro-Asian Studies.*

*   *   *

WHITE, James P(atrick)   1940-

PERSONAL: Born September 28, 1940, in Wichita Falls, Tex.; son of Joseph and Minnie (Mann) White; married Janice Lou Turner, September 11, 1961; children: Christopher Jules. *Education:* University of Texas, B.A. (with honors), 1961; Vanderbilt University, M.A. (history), 1967; graduate study at Texas Christian University, 1969-71; Brown University, M.A. (creative writing), 1973. *Home:* 1814 Elder Dr., Arlington, Tex. 76010. *Agent:* Julie Fallowfield, McIntosh & Otis, Inc., 475 Fifth Ave., New York, N.Y. 10017. *Office:* Department of Creative Writing, University of South Alabama, Mobile, Ala. 36688.

CAREER: Blue Mountain College, Blue Mountain, Miss., associate professor of history, 1964-66; free-lance writer in Europe and the United States, 1967-70; University of Texas of the Permian Basin, Odessa, assistant professor, 1973-74, associate professor of creative writing and chairman of department, 1974-76; Texas Center for Writers, Dallas, Tex., founder and director, 1976-77; University of Texas at Dallas, visiting professor, 1977-78; University of Southern California, Los Angeles, director of master of arts program in professional writing, 1979-83; University of South Alabama, Mobile, director of creative writing, 1983—. Member of state executive committee, Texas Joint English Committee for Schools and Colleges, 1973-74; chairman of advisory board, Down Center Stage, Dallas Theater Center, 1978-79.

MEMBER: American Literary Translators Association (member of international editorial board, 1978—), Associated Writing Programs (member of national editorial board, 1973-75), Conference of College Teachers of English (state chairman of creative writing section, 1975-76), Modern Language Association of America (South Central section), Texas Association of Creative Writers (founding president, 1973-74), Theta Xi, Phi Delta Phi, Phi Alpha Theta, Phi Eta Sigma. *Awards, honors:* Marston fellow, 1971.

WRITINGS: (Editor) *Bicentennial Collection of Texas Short Stories,* Texas Center for Writers Press, 1974; (editor) *New and Experimental Literature,* Texas Center for Writers Press, 1975; *Birdsong* (novel), Copper Beech Press, 1977, 2nd edition, 1978; (with Anne Reed Rooth) *The Ninth Car* (novel), Putnam, 1978; (with wife, Janice L. White) *Clarity: A Text on Writing,* Paul Hanson, 1981; *The Persian Oven* (novella), Imperial Press, 1983.

Plays: "Broadside" (three-act), first produced in Cleveland, Ohio, at Muse Theatre, 1969; "Family Circle" (three-act), first produced in Providence, R.I., at Brown University, 1973.

Also editor of *King's S.W.,* 1975, and author of *Poems,* 1978; co-editor with W. McDonald of *Texas Stories and Poems,* 1978, and with J. White of *Poetry Dallas,* 1978. Contributor of articles, poems, and short stories to over twenty periodicals, including *Kansas Quarterly, Quartet, Texas Quarterly, Arizona Quarterly, Arts and Letters, Mundus Artium, Contemporary Literary Scene, Journal of African History, Markham Review,* and *New Writers.* Editor, *Texas Writer's Newsletter,* 1973-76, and *Sand,* 1976—; co-editor and publisher, *Texas Books in Review,* 1975-78.

SIDELIGHTS: "I think that the most important thing about writing," James P. White told *CA*, "is obviously the work itself—enjoying, developing, and caring about it and the writing of others. I've been involved in a lot of literary activities and have run several writing programs. What matters is a person's work. I particularly admire Christopher Isherwood and Thomas Williams and Susan Fromberg Schaeffer. Building a literary career is difficult; much of it adds up to nothing. But what really matters is continuing to learn about writing and caring about writing well."

*　　*　　*

WHITMAN, John 1944-

PERSONAL: Born November 26, 1944, in Norwalk, Conn.; son of Albert R. (in advertising) and Edith (Whitridge) Whitman. *Education:* Attended Princeton University, 1962-65; College of St. Thomas, M.A.T., 1970; graduate study at University of Grenoble and University of Bordeaux.

CAREER: Translator for newsmen during the Olympic Games at Grenoble, France; French teacher at Highcroft Country Day School, 1966-67; researcher for Simplified Travel, Inc., 1972; *Twin Cities Magazine*, Minneapolis, Minn., restaurant editor, 1978-79, travel editor, beginning 1980.

WRITINGS: The Special Guide to Europe, New American Library, 1972; *The Psychic Power of Plants*, New American Library, 1974; *Whitman's Off Season Travel Guide to Europe*, St. Martin's, 1975; *Starting from Scratch*, Quadrangle, 1976; *Whitman's Restaurant Guide to Minnesota*, Nodin, 1976; *Whitman's Travel Guide to Minnesota*, Nodin, 1977; *The Uncommon Guide to Europe*, St. Martin's, 1978; *Whitman's Twin Cities Shopping Guide*, Whitman Press, 1978; *Whitman's Best European Travel Tips*, Meadowbrook, 1980.

"The Best Free Attractions" series, published by Meadowbrook, 1981: *The Best Free Attractions in the Eastern States; . . .in the Western States; . . . in the Midwestern States; . . . in the Southern States.* Contributing editor to travel magazines and newsletters.

WORK IN PROGRESS: Writing a film script for a full-length wilderness adventure aimed at the younger market, for Markle Productions, Inc.

SIDELIGHTS: John Whitman is competent in French, Italian, Spanish, Portuguese, and Swedish. He has traveled almost a million miles in the past ten years and has traveled through Europe and North Africa on a motorcycle.

BIOGRAPHICAL/CRITICAL SOURCES: Los Angeles Times Book Review, May 16, 1982.

*　　*　　*

WIERSMA, Stanley M(arvin) 1930-
(Sietze Buning)

PERSONAL: Born July 15, 1930, in Orange City, Iowa; son of Samuel (a farmer) and Hermina (Peters) Wiersma; married Irene Hanenburg, July 11, 1955; children: Samuel Christian, Robert Mouw. *Education:* Calvin College, A.B., 1951; University of Wisconsin, M.Sc., 1956, Ph.D., 1961. *Politics:* Democrat. *Religion:* Christian Reformed Church. *Home:* 1330 Logan S.E., Grand Rapids, Mich. 49506. *Office:* Department of English, Calvin College, Grand Rapids, Mich. 49506.

CAREER: High school English teacher in Hull, Iowa, 1951-52; Calvin College, Grand Rapids, Mich., instructor, 1959-

61, assistant professor, 1961-63, associate professor, 1963-67, professor of English, 1967—. Fulbright lecturer, Free University of Amsterdam, 1968-69. Summer lecturer at Grand Valley State College, 1963-65, University of Idaho, 1968. *Military service:* U.S. Army, 1953-54. *Member:* Modern Language Association of America, Conference on Christianity and Literature. *Awards, honors:* National Endowment for the Humanities fellowship in linguistics, 1978.

WRITINGS: Christopher Fry, Eerdmans, 1970; (with Merle Meeter) *Contrasting Christian Approaches to Teaching Literature* (monograph), Calvin College, 1970; (translator) Gerrit Achterberg, *A Tourist Does Golgotha and Other Poems*, Being Press, 1972; (under pseudonym Sietz Buning) *Purpaleanie and Other Permutations*, Middleburg Press, 1978; (translator; under pseudonym Sietze Buning) Hans Bouma, *With an Eye on Israel*, Middleburg Press, 1979; (under pseudonym Sietze Buning) *Style and Class*, Middleburg Press, 1982; *More Than the Ear Discovers: God in the Plays of Christopher Fry*, Loyola University Press, 1983.

WORK IN PROGRESS: Catching the Dove in Flight: An Exercise in Literary Criticism; Karl Mannheim, translation of a Dutch biography and criticism by Henk Woldring; as Sietze Buning, an autobiographical novel.

SIDELIGHTS: "My pseudonym has nothing to do with secrecy and everything to do with freedom," Stanley M. Wiersma told *CA.* "My given name is also the name I try to hatch into academic reputation; on it I hang my academic degree and my professional rank. The degrees and the rank inhibit me when I try to write poems and stories, especially about my Dutch ethnic past; the whole academic and literary tradition seems to sit in judgment on every line. As Sietze Buning I can shed temporarily all the inhibiting accoutrements of the great tradition and become free enough to be the farm kid who needs to express himself as much as anybody."

*　　*　　*

WILBUR, C. Keith 1923-

PERSONAL: Born June 21, 1923, in Providence, R.I.; son of Clifford Keith (a chemist) and Ruth (Williams) Wilbur; married Ruth Elizabeth Asker, June 29, 1946; children: David Williams, Carol Ann, Bruce Alan, Jody Elizabeth. *Education:* Bates College, B.S., 1948; University of Vermont, M.D., 1952. *Religion:* Congregational (United Church of Christ). *Home and office:* 397 Prospect St., Northampton, Mass. 01060.

CAREER: Intern and resident at Salem Hospital, Salem, Mass., 1952-53; family practice of medicine in Northampton, Mass., 1953—. Staff member of Cooley Dickinson Hospital and Smith College infirmary. Chairman, Northampton Historical Fair, 1969; member, Northampton Bicentennial Committee. *Military service:* U.S. Navy, 1942-46; commanded submarine chaser; became lieutenant junior grade. *Member:* American Academy of Family Practice (fellow), National Tree Farmers Association, National Wood Carvers Association, Company of Military Historians (fellow), Massachusetts Medical Society, Massachusetts Archeological Society, Hampshire County Medical Society, Northampton Historical Society, Northampton Historical Commission (chairman), Sixth Massachusetts Continentals, Old Deerfield Pocumtuck Society, College Club (Bates College). *Awards, honors:* Heritage Foundation Award, 1963, for pageant "Rebels and Redcoats."

WRITINGS: Picture Book of the Continental Soldier, Stackpole, 1969; *Picture Book of the Revolution's Privateers*, Stackpole, 1973; *Medical Crisis in Washington's Army*, Bristol Pharmaceutical Co., 1976; *The New England Indians*, Globe Pequot, 1978; *Revolutionary Medicine, 1700-1800*, Globe Pequot, 1980; (with wife, Ruth E. Wilbur) *Bid Us God Speed: The History of the Edwards Church, Northampton, Massachusetts, 1833-1983*, Phoenix Publishing, 1983. Also author of *New England Indian Handcrafts* and of historical pageant "Rebels and Redcoats."

WORK IN PROGRESS: Editing *Ranger Handbook*, the book on instruction for Roger's Rangers, 1755-1760; *Medical Americana*, an illustrated history of medical and surgical instruments in America.

SIDELIGHTS: Interest in America's military past prompted C. Keith Wilbur to organize the Sixth Massachusetts Continentals, a group that drills and fires colonial weapons. He collects colonial military pieces, scuba-dives for relics, and does archaeological work.

* * *

WILDE, W(illiam) H(enry) 1923-

PERSONAL: Born November 19, 1923, in Tamworth, New South Wales, Australia; son of William Henry and Ivy May (Corbett) Wilde; married Ena Fay McKeough, December 20, 1948; children: William Ross, Margaret Ruth (Mrs. Terrence William Conn). *Education:* University of Sydney, B.A., 1946, diploma in education, 1947, M.A., 1964. *Home:* 12 Verco St., Hackett, Canberra, Australian Capital Territory 2602, Australia. *Office:* Department of English Faculty of Military Studies, University of New South Wales, Duntroon, Canberra, Australian Capital Territory, Australia.

CAREER: Royal Australian Naval College, Jervis Bay, Australia, master on civil professorial staff, 1953-58, senior master, 1958-63; Royal Military College, Canberra, Australia, senior lecturer, 1965-68; University of New South Wales, Canberra, senior lecturer, 1968-76, associate professor of English, 1977—. *Member:* Australian College of Education.

WRITINGS: Three Radicals, Oxford University Press, 1969; *Adam Lindsay Gordon*, Oxford University Press, 1973; *Henry Kendall*, Twayne, 1976; (with B. G. Andrews) *Australian Literature to 1900*, Gale, 1980; (with T. Inglis Moore) *Letters of Mary Gilmore*, Melbourne University Press, 1980; (with Andrews and Joy Hooton) *The Oxford Companion to Australian Literature*, Oxford University Press, in press. Contributor to *Meanjin* and *National Times*.

WORK IN PROGRESS: The Biography of Dame Mary Gilmore, for Melbourne University Press.

SIDELIGHTS: W. H. Wilde told *CA* that *The Oxford Companion to Australian Literature* is the result of over four years of work and contains nearly three-quarters of a million words.

* * *

WILDER-SMITH, A(rthur) E(rnest) 1915-

PERSONAL: Born December 22, 1915, in Reading, England; son of Arthur William (a farmer) and Elfrida Minne (Wilder) Smith; married Beate Gottwaldt, September 17, 1950; children: Oliver, Petra, Clive, Einar. *Education:* University of Reading, B.Sc. (general), 1937, B.Sc. (chemistry; with honors), 1938, Ph.D., 1941; Geneva University, P.D., 1955, Dr. es sciences, 1964; Eidgenoessische Technische Hochschule Zuerich, D.Sc.,

1964. *Politics:* None. *Religion:* Evangelical (Anglican). *Home and office:* Roggern, Einigen CH 3646, Switzerland.

CAREER: Imperial Chemical Industries, Billingham, England, technical assistant on senior staff, 1940-45; University of London, British Empire Cancer Campaign, London, England, Countess of Lisburne Memorial Fellow in Cancer Research, 1945-49; Geistlich Soehne Ltd. (pharmaceuticals firm), Lucerne, Switzerland, chief of research, 1951-55; University of Geneva, Ecole de Medecine, Geneva, Switzerland, privat docent, 1956-64; University of Illinois, Medical Center, Chicago, professor of pharmacology and member of College of Nursing faculty, 1964-71; lecturer at university seminars throughout Europe and North America, 1971—. Visiting assistant professor, University of Illinois, 1957-58; visiting professor, University of Bergen, 1960-62, Hacetepe University, 1969-71. Has appeared on television shows. Consultant to North Atlantic Treaty Organization (NATO) on drug abuse, 1969-74, and to European and U.S. pharmaceutical firms.

MEMBER: Chemical Society (London), Royal Institute of Chemistry (fellow), Sigma Psi, Rho Chi. *Awards, honors:* Ridley research fellow, 1939-40; University of Illinois, senior class instructor of the year, 1966, 1967, 1968, and 1969, Golden Apple award, 1966, 1967, and 1969.

WRITINGS—Published by Haenssler, except as indicated: (With wife, Beate Wilder-Smith) *Die Ehe* (title means "Marriage"), 1957; *Why Does God Allow It? and Other Essays*, Victory Press, 1960, reprinted, C.L.P. Master Books (San Diego), 1981, original German edition published as *Warum laesst Gott es zu?*, Haenssler, 1973; *Herkunft und Zukunft des Menschen: Ein kritischer Ueberblick der dem Darwinismus und Christentum zugrunde liegenden naturwissenschaftlichen und geistlichen Prinzipien*, Brunnen (Basel), 1966, translation published as *Man's Origin, Man's Destiny: A Critical Survey of the Principles of Evolution and Christianity*, H. Shaw, 1968; *The Drug Users: The Psychopharmacology of Turning On*, H. Shaw, 1969.

Die Erschaffung das Lebens, 1970, translation published as *The Creation of Life: A Cybernetic Approach to Evolution*, H. Shaw, 1970; *The Paradox of Pain*, H. Shaw, 1971; *Ist das ein Gott der Liebe?* (title means "Is This a God of Love?"), 1971; *Tauferkenntnis und Liebe zu Jesus Christus* (title means "Baptismal Doctrine and Christian Devotion"), 1973; *Gott: Sein oder Nichtsein?*, 1973, translation published as *God: To Be Or Not To Be?*, 1975; *Grundlage zu einer neuen Biologie*, 1974, translation published as *A Basis for a New Biology*, 1975; *Ursache und Behandlung der Drogenepidemie*, 1974, translation published as *Causes and Cures of the Drug Epidemic*, 1974.

Ergriffen? Ergreife! (title means "Won? Then Win!"), 1975; *A Basis for a New Biology*, 1976; *Die Demission des wissenschaftlichen Materialismus*, 1976; *Der Mensch im Stress* (title means "Man under Stress"), 1977; (with B. Wilder-Smith) *Kunst und Wissenschaft der Ehe*, 1977; *Die Zuverlaessigheit der Bibel und christliche Vollmacht*, Schulte & Gerth (Germany), 1978; *Greift der Christ zur Waffe*, Schulte & Gerth, 1978; *Die Naturwissenschaften Kennen Keine Evolution*, Schwabe-Verlag, 1978, translation by Petra Wilder-Smith published as *The Natural Sciences Know Nothing of Evolution*, C.L.P. Master Books, 1981; *Der Mensch-ein sprechender Computer*, Schulte & Gerth, 1979.

Terrorismus: Das kriminelle Gehirn, Schulte & Gerth, 1980; *Wer denkt, muss glauben*, 1980, translation published as *He*

Who Thinks Has to Believe, C.L.P. Master Books, 1981; *Alternative zur Evolutionstheorie: Taxogenese,* Schwabe-Verlag, 1982, translation published as *Alternative to NeoDarwinian Evolutionary Theory: Taxogenesis,* C.L.P. Master Books, 1982.

Also author of *Christsein: Warum une Wie* and *Allversoehung: Ausweg oder Irrweg,* both Prodromos-Serie. Author of video film scripts, all produced by Evangelische Omroep, including "How the World Came to Be" (seven-part television series), 1980-81, "Drug Abuse" (film), 1981, and "Dimension Theory, Black Holes, and Flatland," 1981. Contributor to journals in his field.

WORK IN PROGRESS: Inflation: Its Origin and Treatment and *The Origin of the Elements,* each in both English and German; an educational series of videocassettes for schools and universities.

SIDELIGHTS: A. E. Wilder-Smith told *CA:* "In my writings it has been and still is my aim to try to correct some of the ravages of scientific materialism in the personal lives of my readers. A few years ago anything appearing under the title of science was automatically regarded as sancrosanct. In recent years this form of 'scientism' is being corrected, though we have a long way to go.

"Some of my works are concerned with the direct consequences of scientific materialism on the 'man in the street.' A poll taken recently in some main cities in Germany asked two questions: 1) Do you believe in a personal God? and 2) If not, why? 52% of the questioned answered with 'no,' they were atheists. Of these 52% some 85% justified their 'no' with, 'Because Evolution has proved that there is no God, Chance did it all.' The clearest proof that Evolution has never delivered such a proof, lies in the nature of the genetic code itself, which can be considered as containing three separate aspects: a) The reduced entropy system used as a carrier for the genetic information, b) The language or code system which rides on the reduced entropy system and which is very nearly universal for all types of biology, c) The bytes of genetic information which ride on a) and b). Neither a), b), nor c) can, according to recent developments in information theory, ever be considered for a moment to be products of chance or random molecular movements. They are all results of programming, and if programming arises by pure NeoDarwinian randomness, then all information theory becomes valueless. But all programmes always demand a programmer somewhere down the line.

"The first part of my writings deals with this aspect of modern science and the arisal of creation as we know it. The second part deals with the more philosophical aspects of the problems of life. If a good Programmer programmed the elements and biology, why did He allow all the terrible things which happen daily in the world around us to happen with impunity? In fact, 'Why does God allow it?' This title has been on sale for some three years in Germany, Austria, and Switzerland (German-speaking) and deals with a very live issue in these countries indeed. Europe has seen war as America has not, so that this question is by no means academic. My book dealing with this question of 'Warum laesst Gott es zu?' ('Why does God allow it?') has been sold on the German-speaking market to the tune of some 600,000 copies in the past three or four years. It has just appeared on the U.S. market as *Why Does God Allow It* in C.L.P. Master Books, San Diego, California.

"Europe, and particularly German-speaking Europe, prides itself on being philosophically minded. They boast, rightly, of their Goethes and their Immanuel Kants. Many of these phil-osophically proud people think that if they use their brains and thought processes they cannot be so naive as to believe in a Creator, be He good or bad or indifferent. With this audience in mind I wrote the short book entitled *Wer denkt, muss glauben (He Who Thinks Has to Believe),* which has in a few months sold in the German-speaking world to the tune of some 40,000 [copies]. The small book has just appeared on the U.S. market. The question is whether the American approaches his problems as does the European. I somehow think that in his heart of hearts he does."

Wilder-Smith's work has been translated into English, French, Norwegian, Finnish, Rumanian, Czechoslovakian, Dutch, Russian, and Hebrew.

*   *   *

WILKINSON, Winifred
See HAUSMANN, Winifred

*   *   *

WILLIAMS, Ioan Miles   1941-

PERSONAL: Born September 10, 1941, in Tredegar, Monmouthshire, Wales; son of William Evan (a headmaster) and Myfanwy (Williams) Williams; married Margaret Jacob (a teacher), January 14, 1964; children: Ema Miles, Anwen Miles, Rhannon Miles, Myfanwy Miles, Ejan Miles. *Education:* St. Catherine's College, Oxford, B.A. (with first class honors), 1963, B.Litt., 1965, M.A., 1968; graduate study at University College of Wales, 1976-80. *Politics:* Plaid Cymru. *Religion:* Christian. *Home:* Y Gwyndy, Llerod, Dyfed, Wales.

CAREER: University of Exeter, Exeter, England, assistant lecturer in English, 1964-66; University of Warwick, Coventry, England, 1967-76, began as lecturer, became senior lecturer in English; currently lecturer in drama in department of Welsh, University College of Wales, Aberystwyth.

WRITINGS: Robert Browning, Evans Brothers, 1967; *William Thackeray,* Evans Brothers, 1968; *Sir Walter Scott on Novelists and Fiction,* Barnes & Noble, 1968; *Novel and Romance, 1700-1800: A Documentary Record,* Barnes & Noble, 1969; *The Literary and Social Criticism of Henry Fielding,* Barnes & Noble, 1970; *George Meredith,* Routledge & Kegan Paul, 1971; *The Realist Novel in England: A Study in Development,* Macmillan, 1974; *The Idea of the Novel in Europe, 1600-1800,* New York University Press, 1979; *Emyr Humphreys,* University of Wales Press, 1980; *Y Noju,* Gwasg Gomer, 1983; *Kitchenes Davis,* Gwasg Gwynedd, in press.

*   *   *

WILLIAMS, Philip W(alter)   1941-

PERSONAL: Born January 19, 1941, in Niagara Falls, N.Y.; son of Walter E. (a clergyman) and Ruth (Schultz) Williams; married Nancy Arlene Mellish, June 13, 1965; children: Jason Philip, Jenna Jill. *Education:* Capital University, B.A., 1963; Lutheran Theological Seminary, B.D., 1967; Andover Newton Theological Seminary, S.T.M., 1970. *Residence:* South Bend, Ind. *Office:* Memorial Hospital, 615 Michigan, South Bend, Ind. 46601.

CAREER: Ordained American Lutheran minister, 1967; assistant pastor of Lutheran church in Baltimore, Md., 1967-69; Wausau Hospitals, Wausau, Wis., director of pastoral care, 1971-83; Memorial Hospital, South Bend, Ind., associate director of clinical pastoral education, 1983—. *Member:* Association for Clinical Pastoral Education, American Protestant Hospital Association (College of Chaplains), Association of Mental Health Clergy.

WRITINGS: When a Loved One Dies, Augsburg, 1976; *When Death Draws Near,* Augsburg, 1979.

WORK IN PROGRESS: A book on reflective meditation.

SIDELIGHTS: Philip W. Williams comments: "Writing is a creative avocation; my object is to write about areas of the human experience in non-technical language for 'common consumption.' My publisher believes I have a basic, simple style of writing which can communicate to the so-called 'average person' who wants and needs education and inspiration, but is put off by technical works."

AVOCATIONAL INTERESTS: Athletics, gardening, camping, photography.

*   *   *

WILSON, Dirk
   See POHL, Frederik

*   *   *

WILSON, (Leslie) Granville   1912-

PERSONAL: Born February 10, 1912, in Castleford, West Yorkshire, England; son of Smith (a carpenter) and Mary Ann (Shackleton) Wilson; married Irene Dunn, July 27, 1935; children: Joan (Mrs. Maurice Gray), Arnold Ley. *Education:* Attended Castleford and Normantown Technical College, Castleford, England, 1928-30. *Home:* 6 Rosemoor Close, Hunmanby, Filey, North Yorkshire YO14 0NB, England. *Agent:* D. P. King, 5125 North Cumberland Blvd., Whitefish Bay, Wis. 53217.

CAREER: Journalist. *Wakefield Express* newspapers, reporter and feature writer in Pontefract, Castleford, Wakefield, and Yorkshire, England, 1929-42; *Yorkshire Post,* reporter, feature writer, book reviewer, and industrial correspondent in Leeds and Yorkshire, England, 1942-53; *Westminster Press,* London, England, industrial correspondent, 1953-54; *Evening Gazette,* Middlesbrough, England, chief editorial writer, feature writer, sub-editor, 1954-67. *Member:* Society of Authors, Crime Writers Association.

WRITINGS—For children, except as indicated: *The Silver Cup and Other Tales,* Kangaroo Books, 1946; *The Gateway to Journalism,* Oceana, 1946; *Murder Goes Underground* (adult), Fiction House, 1949; *Jonathan Enters Journalism,* Chatto & Windus, 1956; *Formula for Murder* (adult), Brown, Watson, 1960; *A First Look at Newspapers,* F. Watts, 1974; *A First Look at the Police,* F. Watts, 1976; *War of the Computers,* Granada, 1981; *The Terror Cubes,* Granada, 1982.

Author of television play "Death of an Editor," broadcast in Holland, 1970, and radio comedy "Hot Stuff," broadcast in 1980. Contributor to anthologies. Contributor of numerous articles and short stories to newspapers and magazines in twenty-two countries.

SIDELIGHTS: Granville Wilson told *CA:* "A lifelong motivation has been the search for independence to write freely." He describes himself as "a compulsive reader. Could read before I was aged five. Began collecting books when I was

nine; still at it." He considers reading the most durable of pleasures and feels that borrowing books is not enough; one should own them.

*   *   *

WILSON, John Stuart Gladstone   1916-

PERSONAL: Born August 18, 1916, in St. Kilda, Victoria, Australia; son of Herbert Gladstone and Mary Buchanan (Wylie) Wilson; married Beryl Margaret Gibson, July, 1943. *Education:* University of Western Australia, Diploma in Commerce, 1939, B.A. (with honors), 1941, M.A., 1948. *Office:* Department of Economics and Commerce, University of Hull, Hull, North Humberside HU6 7RX, England.

CAREER: Affiliated with the Commonwealth Bank of Australia, 1935-41; lecturer in economics at University of Tasmania, Hobart, Australia, 1941-43, University of Sydney, Sydney, Australia, 1944-45, University College, Canberra, 1946-47; University of London, London, England, lecturer in economics at London School of Economics and Political Science, 1948-49, university reader in economics, 1950-59; University of Hull, Hull, England, professor of economics and commerce, 1959-82, professor emeritus, 1982—, head of department, 1959-71, 1974-77, dean of Faculty of Social Sciences and Law, 1962-65, director of Centre for Joint Study of Economics, Politics and Sociology, 1980-82. Made comparative studies of banking and financial institutions in Europe, 1950-59, 1981, in India and Pakistan, 1950, 1968-69, 1973-74, 1980, United States and Canada, 1955-56, 1962, 1969, 1974, 1979, Australia, New Zealand, New Guinea, and Southeast Asia, 1967, 1970, 1978, Mexico, 1978, and South America and Sri Lanka, 1980. Conducted economic surveys of New Hebrides for British Colonial Office, 1958-59, and 1963-66. Chairman of Centre for South East Asian Studies, 1963-66; Institute of Commonwealth Studies, member of management commmittee, 1960-77, honorary life member, 1980—. Governor of School of Oriental and African Studies, University of London.

MEMBER: Royal Economic Society, American Economic Association, Economics Society of Australia. *Awards, honors:* Houblon-Norman Award, 1950, 1951-55, 1960, 1973; Leverhulme Research Award to visit United States and Canada, 1955; Social Sciences Research Council Award, 1977-82; British Academy Award, 1980; Leverhulme emeritus fellowship, 1983-84.

WRITINGS: (Contributor) R. S. Sayers, editor, *Banking in the British Commonwealth,* Oxford University Press, 1952; *French Banking Structure and Credit Policy,* Bell, for London School of Economics, 1957.

(Contributor) Sayers, editor, *Banking in Western Europe,* Oxford University Press, 1962; (contributor) W. B. Hamilton, K. Robinson, and C.D.W. Goodwin, editors, *A Decade of the Commonwealth, 1955-1965,* Duke University Press, 1966; *Economic Survey of the New Hebrides,* H.M.S.O., 1966; *Monetary Policy and the Development of Money Markets,* Allen & Unwin, 1966; (editor with C. R. Whittlesey) *Essays in Money and Banking,* Clarendon Press, 1968.

Availability of Capital and Credit to United Kingdom Agriculture, H.M.S.O., 1973; (editor with C. F. Scheffer) *Multinational Enterprises: Financial and Monetary Aspects,* Sijthoff, 1974; *Credit to Agriculture: United Kingdom,* European Economic Commission, 1975; *The London Money Markets,* Societe Universitaire Europeene de Recherches Financieres,

1976; (editor with J. E. Wadsworth and H. Fournier) *The Development of Financial Institutions in Europe, 1956-1976,* Sijthoff, 1977; *Industrial Banking: A Comparative Survey,* Societe Universitaire Europeene de Recherches Financieres, 1978.

Also author of *Economic Environment and Development Programmes,* 1960. Contributor to *International Encyclopaedia of the Social Sciences* and *Encyclopaedia Britannica;* also contributor to numerous periodicals, including *Economic Journal, Journal of Political Economy,* and *Economic Record.* Editor of *Yorkshire Bulletin of Economic and Social Research,* 1964-67; member of editorial board of *Modern Asian Studies,* 1966—.

WORK IN PROGRESS: Assets and Liabilities Management in OECD Countries; Studies in Money Markets; Banking Policy and Structure: A Comparative Analysis.

AVOCATIONAL INTERESTS: Gardening, photography, the theater, and art.

*　　*　　*

WILTGEN, Ralph M(ichael)   1921-

PERSONAL: Born December 17, 1921, in Chicago, Ill.; son of Michael and Martha (Clesen) Wiltgen. *Education:* Studied at Quigley Preparatory Seminary, Chicago, at Divine Word seminaries in East Troy, Wis., Girard, Pa., and Techny, Ill., and at Pontifical Institute for Oriental Studies, Rome; Pontifical Gregorian University, Rome, Doctorate in Missiology, 1953. *Home:* Collegio del Verbo Divino, Cas. Post. 5080, Rome, Italy.

CAREER: Society of the Divine Word (S.V.D.) missionary, ordained Roman Catholic priest in 1950; publicity director for Divine Word Missionaries in Techny, Ill., 1953-58, and Madang, Papua, New Guinea, 1958-60; Society of the Divine Word, Rome, Italy, international publicity director, 1960-63, founder, director, and editor of Divine Word Mission News Service, 1960-63, and of Divine Word Council News Service, established to cover the Second Vatican Council, 1962-65; interpreter for conferences, interpreting from German or Italian into English, beginning 1965; Theological Library Network, Rome, founder, 1981—. Professor of missiology at Divine Word Major Seminary, 1954-57; member of Divine Word Missiological Institute, St. Augustin, West Germany. *Member:* Societe des Oceanistes. *Awards, honors:* Bene Merenti Medal bestowed by Pope Pius XII, 1953.

WRITINGS: Gold Coast Mission History, 1471-1880, Divine Word Publications, 1956; *The Death of Bishop Loerks and His Companions,* Collegio del Verbo Divino, 1965; *The Rhine Flows into the Tiber: The Unknown Council,* Hawthorn, 1967; *The Religious Life Defined,* Divine Word Publications, 1970; *The Founding of the Roman Catholic Church in Oceania: 1825-1850,* Australian National University Press, 1979; *Online Union Catalog of Periodicals of the Theological Library Network,* Collegio del Verbo Divino, 1982; *How to Use a Computer in Ten Easy Lessons,* Collegio del Verbo Divino, 1983.

Contributor: Norman Ruffing, editor, *The Word in the World,* Divine Word Publications, 1969; *The History of Melanesia,* Research School of Pacific Studies, Australian National University, 1969; Josef Metzler, editor, *Compendio di Storia della Sacra Congregazione par l'Evangelizzazione dei Popoli o "De Propaganda Fide,"* 1622-1972, Pontifical Urban University, 1974; *Sacrae Congregationis de Propaganda Fide Memoria Rerum: Three Hundred Fifty Years in the Service of the Missions,* Herder, 1976; *Riccio's Terra Australis, 1676,* Central

Mapping Authority of New South Wales, 1982. Contributor to *New Catholic Encyclopedia,* 1967, and of reviews and articles to periodicals, including *Verbum* (Rome), *Nouvelle Revue de Science Missionnaire, Regnum Die-Collectanea Theatina, World Mission, Australian Author,* and *Hemisphere.*

WORK IN PROGRESS: The Founding of the Roman Catholic Church in Melanesia and Micronesia, 1850-1884.

SIDELIGHTS: Ralph M. Wiltgen's New Guinea research, begun in the years 1958-60, was interrupted for six years by an assignment to direct the six-language Divine Word news services in Rome. During his two years in New Guinea, he interviewed missionary survivors of World War II (122 of 230 missionaries lost their lives in the war and most archival material in northwest New Guinea was destroyed). Then, to obtain the hardship perspective of early missionaries, he made a ten-day trip on foot from the coast near Madang to the top of 15,400-foot Mount Wilhelm in the interior.

Wiltgen, who has varying degrees of proficiency in Latin, German, Italian, French, Spanish, Portuguese, and pidgin English, told *CA* that the "archive material for *The Founding of the Roman Catholic Church in Oceania, 1825-1850* is in foreign languages. Sources for the first chapter were in French (letters from France to Rome), and in Latin (minutes of meetings in Rome), and I wrote the manuscript in English. Two bookshelves contain 15,000 pages of notes made over the years, [and] also the chronological file card index of them." Hugh Laracy, writing in the *Catholic Historical Review,* calls Wiltgen's study of the Church in Oceania "a magnificent scholarly achievement. It is exhaustively detailed, yet written clearly and with a light touch."

Wiltgen offers this advice to aspiring writers: "The most important parts of your book are the first sentence, the first paragraph, the first page. The writing on the first page must flow smoothly, be interesting, and make your readers turn to page two. If you work as hard on page two as you did on page one, and as hard on all other pages after that, your book will be read to the very end. And if that happens, you will be recognized as a good writer and you will have no difficulty in finding a publisher."

BIOGRAPHICAL/CRITICAL SOURCES: Religious Studies Review, January, 1981; *Missiology,* April, 1981; *Worldmission,* summer, 1981; *Catholic Historical Review,* October, 1981.

*　　*　　*

WINDHAM, Kathryn T(ucker)   1918-

PERSONAL: Born June 2, 1918, in Selma, Ala.; daughter of James Wilson (a banker) and Helen (an insurance agent; maiden name, Tabb) Tucker; married Amasa Benjamin Windham, February 10, 1946 (deceased); children: Kathryn Tabb, Amasa Benjamin, Jr., Helen Ann. *Education:* Huntingdon College, A.B., 1939. *Politics:* Democrat. *Religion:* United Methodist. *Home:* 2004 Royal St., Selma, Ala. 36701.

CAREER: Alabama Journal, Montgomery, police reporter, 1940-42; U.S. Treasury Department, Birmingham, Ala., statewide promoter of war bonds, 1942-44; *Birmingham News,* Birmingham, state editor, general reporter, and photographer, 1944-46; *Selma Times-Journal,* Selma, Ala., 1960-73, worked as reporter, city editor, state editor, associate editor; Area Agency on Aging, Camden, Ala., community service planner, 1973-77; writer, 1977—. Member of board of directors of Southern Women's Archives; member of board of advisers of Alabama

State Historical Commission; member of Selma School Board, 1960-72. *Member:* National Association for the Preservation and Perpetuation of Storytelling (former member of board of directors). *Awards, honors:* Best nonfiction award, Alabama Library Association, 1975, for *Alabama: One Big Front Porch;* journalism awards from Associated Press and Alabama Press Association, for photography, features, and spot news.

WRITINGS—All published by Strode: *Treasured Alabama Recipes,* 1964; (with Margaret Gillis Figh) *Thirteen Alabama Ghosts and Jeffrey,* 1969; *Exploring Alabama,* 1969; *Jeffrey Introduces Thirteen More Southern Ghosts,* 1971; *Treasured Tennessee Recipes,* 1972; *Thirteen Georgia Ghosts and Jeffrey,* 1973; *Treasured Georgia Recipes,* 1973; *Thirteen Mississippi Ghosts and Jeffrey,* 1974; *Alabama: One Big Front Porch,* 1975; *Thirteen Tennessee Ghosts and Jeffrey,* 1976; *Southern Cooking to Remember,* 1978; *Count Those Buzzards! Stamp Those Grey Mules,* 1979; *Jeffrey's Latest Thirteen: More Alabama Ghosts,* 1982.

WORK IN PROGRESS: Collecting Southern ghost tales, games, folklore, and songs; photographing the changing South; a one-woman show on the life of Julia S. Tutwiler.

SIDELIGHTS: Kathryn T. Windham writes: "My desire is to preserve our Southern ghost tales—the true ones—before they are lost. I use a newspaper reporter's training to check the stories, verify dates, names, places, etc. The sites of all the stories can be visited—but I make no promise that the ghosts can be seen! Jeffrey is the 'something' that lives in our house."

BIOGRAPHICAL/CRITICAL SOURCES: Chicago Tribune, October 31, 1978.

*   *   *

WOLCOTT, Leonard Thompson

PERSONAL: Born in Buenos Aires, Argentina; son of Maynard (a minister) and Edna (Thompson) Wolcott; married Carolyn Muller, September 31, 1951; children: Joy (Mrs. Bruce Vaughan). *Education:* Asbury College, B.A.; Hartford Seminary Foundation, M.A.; Drew University, M.Div.; Oxford University, D.Phil. *Home:* 3372 Mimosa Dr., Nashville, Tenn. 37211.

CAREER: Methodist minister. Methodist Church, church worker in Bihar, India, 1945-50; Scarritt College for Christian Workers, Nashville, Tenn., Mabel K. Howell Professor of Missions, 1953-80; affiliated with Institut Superieur de Theologie, Mulungwishi, Zaire, 1980-81. Lecturer at universities and colleges in India, and lecturer throughout America. Ford Foundation Southern Regional Scholar in Indian Studies. Consultant at Sat Tal Ashram, India, 1974. *Member:* Association of Professors of Missions (secretary-treasurer, 1960-62), American Oriental Society, Society of Biblical Literature, American Association of University Professors, American Society of Missiology, North American Academy of Ecumenists, Midwest Fellowship of Professors of Missions (president, 1973-74). *Awards, honors:* Grant from Dr. William's Trust (British) for research.

WRITINGS: Twelve Modern Disciples, Upper Room, 1964; *Meditations on Ephesians,* Abingdon, 1965; (with wife, Carolyn Wolcott) *Religions Around the World,* Abingdon, 1967; *La Iglesia en El Mundo,* Centro de Estudios Teologicos, 1972; (with C. Wolcott) *Through the Moongate,* Friendship Press, 1978; *New Testament Odyssey,* Kerr, 1979. Also author of *Reflexions du Nouveau Testament,* 1982. Contributor to *Sri Candra Manu Gupta Abhindudan Granth,* a festschrift. Also

author of study-guide books and curriculum materials for church schools. Regular columnist, *Indian Witness* (Lucknow); contributor to *Journal of Asian Studies,* and to *International Review of Missions* and other church magazines.

SIDELIGHTS: Leonard Thompson Wolcott told *CA*: "A delight in the artistry of words came to me from my grandfather whom I never saw. An editor, book-reviewer, aspiring journalist, he died at age 29, but left a library of literary classics which I read when I was a boy. And it came to me from my mother who never tired of writing poetry, short stories, and novels.

"My own writing started with poetry published in my teen years in magazines and anthologies. Rhythm and sound combinations are what interest me in poetry. These and atmosphere. My first full-length manuscript—a play—was accepted by a drama publisher when I was a university student. It was a play of college students, war, and peace. Afterwards I took time away from my writing by living in the drama of the world, among a variety of cultures, in many environments, speaking in different languages, even writing in three of them besides English.

"Most of my writing has been by assignment: curricula for church school, articles for church magazines, exegetical studies, book reviews, biographies, studies in Bible, in world religions, in ideological movements. The assignments continue. The most difficult (and exclusive) medium to break into, and the least remunerative, is that of scholarly journalism. I have enjoyed contributing to these journals, too.

"At last I am free from a teaching profession, free to write what I please. It will take another hundred years to do all I have in mind!

"Life is inexhaustible in its variety of wonders and beauties, of magic and meanings, of joys even through tears, and of possibilities even despite cruelties. Writing (like acting and painting) is for me the most satisfying way creatively to respond to this life. So I must write, whether for money or not, whether for readers or not (but both are welcomed)!

"For the arts and for literature this is a Hellenistic type of age: an age that has inherited the products, but has lacked the creativity, of an earlier classic period. Much of today's literature, therefore, tends to be arty, smarty, using a limited vocabulary of thought, repeating a stylized jargon. Nevertheless, out of the welter of modern mass communication occasional writers are appearing who are uniquely themselves, who escape the cliches, who climb out of the rut of existential dreariness, and who do not need the props of shock and ribaldry. There are writers who observe all of life closely and react to it sensitively. They have something to say. May they be read by many for long."

Wolcott spent a sabbatical in 1963 researching in rural and industrial India and, while on sabbatical in 1971 wrote for the Centro de Estudios Teologicos in Ecuador. Wolcott has lived at other periods in England, Germany, and Zaire, and has travelled widely in Europe, Asia, Africa, and South America. He is competent in Hindi, French, German, and Spanish.

AVOCATIONAL INTERESTS: Folk dancing, bird study, drama, violin, Sanskrit, and Greek.

*   *   *

WOLFE, Gerard R(aymond) 1926-

PERSONAL: Born April 2, 1926, in New York, N.Y.; son of

Samuel (a controller) and Anna Wolfe. *Education:* City College (now of the City University of New York), B.B.A., 1948; New York University, A.M., 1949; Sorbonne, University of Paris, certificat, 1954; Union for Experimenting Colleges and Universities/Union Graduate School, Ph.D., 1978; also attended Middlebury College and University of Mexico. *Home:* 7-13 Washington Sq. N., New York, N.Y. 10003. *Office:* Foreign Language Program, New York University, 332 Shimkin Hall, New York, N.Y. 10003.

CAREER: High school French and Spanish teacher in New York City, 1949-51, and Floral Park, N.Y., 1951-58; New York University, New York City, lecturer in Spanish and French, 1958-66, associate professor, 1966-76, professor of continuing education, 1976—, director of Peace Corps training program for Turkey, 1966, chairman of university senate educational policies committee, 1974-76, former director of foreign language program. Guest lecturer at Jewish Museum, 1969—; lecturer at Hofstra University, 1973-80; academic coordinator, Skidmore College; director of University without Walls Program in New York City, 1981—. Researcher for American Museum of Natural History, 1959-64; consultant, New York City Landmarks Preservation Committee, 1969—. Guest on radio and television programs. *Military service:* U.S. Army, 1944-46; served in Germany; became technical sergeant; received one combat star.

MEMBER: Modern Language Association of America, National University Continuing Education Association, National Trust for Historic Preservation, American Council of Teachers of Foreign Languages, American Jewish Historical Society, American Scandinavian Foundation, Smithsonian Institution, New York Historical Society, Long Island Historical Society. *Awards, honors:* Winifred Fisher Award for Creative Programming, Adult Education Council of New York, 1976; two National Bicentennial awards for creative programming, 1976; Twenty-Five-Year Service Award, New York University, 1983.

WRITINGS: How to Pass Spanish, Yes Books, 1959; *How to Study,* Yes Books, 1960; (editor) W. H. Starr and A. G. Pellegrino, *New Functional French,* American Book Co., 1960; (editor) M. T. Brunetti, *Read, Write, Speak French,* Bantam, 1960; (editor) *Les du Pont* (title means "The Du Ponts"), American Book Co., 1966; *The Peace Corps in Turkey* (training manual), School of Continuing Education, New York University, 1966; *New York: A Guide to the Metropolis,* New York University Press, 1975, revised edition, McGraw, 1983; *The Synagogues of New York's Lower East Side,* illustrated with photographs by Jo Renee Fine, New York University Press, 1977; *The House of Appleton: The History of a Publishing House and Its Relationship to the Cultural, Social, and Political Events That Helped Shape the Destiny of New York City,* Scarecrow, 1981; *New York University's Midtown Center,* New York University, 1982. Contributor to travel section of *New York Times.*

WORK IN PROGRESS: Research on New York City's architectural history and on the decline of New York's Lower East Side.

SIDELIGHTS: Gerard R. Wolfe's work for the American Museum of Natural History included twelve summers in Mexico and Latin America conducting photographic research, and additional time photographing the interior regions of Iceland and Greenland. A speaker of Spanish, French, Dutch, and Portuguese, he has also conducted study tours of Mexico and Guatemala. Wolfe is best known, however, for his work on the

architecture and history of New York City. In addition to teaching, he has for years conducted architectural and historical walking tours of New York for preservation courses and groups. His tours of the synagogues on the Lower East Side "have represented for many a return to 'the world of our fathers,'" writes Richard F. Shepard in the *New York Times.* Shepard calls Wolfe's book on the subject, *The Synagogues of New York's Lower East Side,* "an absorbing account to anyone interested in New York history."

AVOCATIONAL INTERESTS: Playing piano and flute, photography, antiques, Southwestern and Maya archaeology, Hopi and Navajo culture.

BIOGRAPHICAL/CRITICAL SOURCES: New York Times, March 10, 1978, September 9, 1983.

*   *   *

WOLMAN, Benjamin B. 1908-

PERSONAL: Born October 27, 1908, in Warsaw, Poland; son of Jehuda Leib (a playwright) and Hinda Leah (Cukier) Wolman; married; children: Danielle. *Education:* University of Warsaw, M.A., 1932, Ph.D., 1935. *Religion:* Jewish. *Office:* 10 West 66th St., New York, N.Y. 10023.

CAREER: Director of mental health clinic, Tel-Aviv, Palestine, 1935-42; Columbia University, New York City, staff member, 1949-53; psychologist-psychoanalyst in private practice, New York City, 1952—; Adelphi University, Garden City, N.Y., clinical professor of psychology, 1963-65; Institute of Applied Psychoanalysis, New York City, dean of faculty, 1965-72; Long Island University, Brooklyn, N.Y., professor of psychology, 1965-78, professor emeritus, 1978—. *Member:* International Organization for the Study of Group Tensions (president), American Psychological Association (fellow), Association for Advancement of Psychotherapy (fellow), Association for Applied Psychoanalysis (co-chairman of committee on faculty). *Awards, honors:* Outstanding Educators of America Award, 1973; Dartmouth Medal, American Library Association, 1977, for *International Encyclopedia of Psychiatry, Psychology, Psychoanalysis, and Neurology;* American Psychological Association distinguished contribution award, 1978.

WRITINGS: Contemporary Theories and Systems in Psychology, Harper, 1960, 2nd edition (with Susan Knapp), Plenum, 1981; (editor with E. Nagel) *Scientific Psychology,* Basic Books, 1965; (editor) *Handbook of Clinical Psychology,* McGraw, 1965; *Vectoriasis Praecox or the Group Schizophrenias,* C. C Thomas, 1966; (editor) *Historical Roots of Contemporary Psychology,* Harper, 1966; (with others) *Psychoanalytic Techniques: A Handbook for the Practicing Psychoanalyst,* Basic Books, 1967; *The Unconscious Mind: The Meaning of Freudian Psychology,* Prentice-Hall, 1968; (with others) *Psychoanalysis as Art and Science,* Wayne University Press, 1968.

Children without Childhood: A Study of Childhood Schizophrenia, Grune, 1970; (with others) *Psychoanalytic Interpretation of History,* Basic Books, 1971; (editor) *Manual of Child Psychopathology,* McGraw, 1972; (editor and contributor) *Success and Failure in Psychoanalysis and Psychotherapy,* Macmillan, 1972; (with others) *Handbook of Child Psychoanalysis,* Van Nostrand, 1972; *Call No Man Normal,* International Universities Press, 1973; (editor and contributor) *Handbook of General Psychology,* Prentice-Hall, 1973; *Victims of Success,* Quadrangle Books, 1973; (editor and contributor) *Dictionary of Behavioral Science,* Van Nostrand, 1973; *The Therapist*

Handbook: Treatment of Mental Disorders, Van Nostrand, 1976; (editor) *International Encyclopedia of Psychiatry, Psychology, Psychoanalysis, and Neurology,* Aesculapius Publications (New York), 1977; (editor) *Handbook of Treatment of Mental Disorders in Childhood and Adolescence,* Prentice-Hall, 1978; (editor) *Clinical Diagnosis of Mental Disorders: A Handbook,* Plenum, 1978; (editor) *Handbook of Dreams: Research, Theories, and Applications,* Van Nostrand, 1979; *The International Directory of Psychology,* Plenum, 1979; *Children's Fears,* New American Library, 1979.

(With John Money) *Handbook of Human Sexuality,* Prentice-Hall, 1980; *Psychological Aspects of Obesity: A Handbook,* Van Nostrand, 1981; (editor with others) *Handbook of Parapsychology,* Van Nostrand, 1981; (editor) *Handbook of Developmental Psychology,* Prentice-Hall, 1982. Editor, *International Journal of Group Tensions.*

SIDELIGHTS: Several of Benjamin B. Wolman's books have been translated for publication in Europe, Asia, and South America.

*   *   *

WONDERS, Anne
See PASSEL, Anne W(onders)

*   *   *

WOOD, Kenneth 1922-

PERSONAL: Born September 13, 1922, in Sheffield, England; son of Thomas Pashley and Mary Winifred (Horsfield) Wood; married Patricia O'Donnell, April 29, 1962; children: John Michael, Julia. *Education:* University of Sheffield, B.A., 1948, diploma in education, 1949, M.A., 1950. *Politics:* "Inconsistent." *Home:* 7 Church Howle Crescent, Marske-by-the-Sea, Redcar, Cleveland, England. *Agent:* David Higham Associates Ltd., 5-8 Lower John St., London W1R 4HA, England.

CAREER: Teacher in Blackpool, England, 1951-52, Briancon, France, 1952-53, Manchester, England, 1953-55, and Middlesbrough, England, 1955—.

WRITINGS—Juvenile fiction, except as indicated: *Gulls,* Dobson, 1974; *A Period of Violence,* Dobson, 1977; *Shadows,* Dobson, 1979; *Shining Armour,* Julia MacRae, 1982.

Author of "The Wheel" (radio play), British Broadcasting Corp., 1971.

WORK IN PROGRESS: Search.

SIDELIGHTS: "I spent the first ten years of my life in a small village near Sheffield, England," writes Kenneth Wood, "and I think this fact has coloured my outlook: I am by nature inclined to be introverted, disliking large social gatherings and prefering to have a few close friends. I did a great deal of reading as a child, but I have no recollection of attempting to write fiction. I was middle-aged when I began to write. I regret this: I have many things I would like to say which will probably never be said. As a writer, I try to express something real and meaningful in language that would really be used by the people involved. I am concerned about the plight of individuals trapped in systems—teenagers in large, impersonal schools, for example. I think education offered in schools often fails to meet the needs of today's young people.

"My writing is always hard work, as I seek precision of expression. . . . I fuss interminably over details of dialogue. The characters about which I write appear very real to me. I once did a radio interview about my writing, and found that I could remember the names of the fictional characters but forgot that of the man to whom I was speaking!"

AVOCATIONAL INTERESTS: Ornithology, games, walks by the sea and in the countryside.

BIOGRAPHICAL/CRITICAL SOURCES: Times Literary Supplement, March 26, 1982.

*   *   *

WOODS, John (Hayden) 1937-

PERSONAL: Born March 16, 1937, in Barrie, Ontario, Canada; son of John Frederick and Gertrude Mary (Hayden) Woods; married Carol Arnold (an educator), June 13, 1957; children: Catherine Lynn, Kelly Ann, Michael John. *Education:* University of Toronto, B.A., 1958, M.A., 1959; University of Michigan, Ph.D., 1965. *Home:* 1410 20th Ave. S., Lethbridge, Alberta, Canada T1K 1E9. *Office:* Office of the President, University of Lethbridge, Lethbridge, Alberta, Canada T1K 3M4.

CAREER: University of Michigan, Ann Arbor, instructor in philosophy, 1961-62; University of Toronto, Toronto, Ontario, lecturer, 1962-64, assistant professor, 1964-66, associate professor of linguistic studies, 1966-71, associate professor of philosophy, 1966-71; University of Victoria, Victoria, British Columbia, associate professor, 1971-72, professor of philosophy, 1972-76, acting chairman of department, 1974-75, associate dean of arts and sciences and dean of humanities, 1975-76; University of Calgary, Calgary, Alberta, dean of humanities, 1976-79; University of Lethbridge, Lethbridge, Alberta, president, vice-chancellor, and professor of philosophy, 1979—. Assistant professor at University of Calgary, summer, 1965; associate professor at University of Michigan, summer, 1967; Stanford University, visiting scholar, 1968-69, visiting professor, summer, 1971. Chairman of the board and chief executive officer, The Berczy Group, 1980—.

MEMBER: Canadian Philosophical Association, Association for Symbolic Logic, Philosophy of Science Association, American Philosophical Association (member of executive committee, 1971-74), Society for Exact Philosophy, Humanities Research Council of Canada, Canadian Federation for the Humanities (member of executive committee, 1978—; vice-president, 1980-81; president, 1981-82), Humanities Association of Canada, Canadian Association of University Teachers, Renaissance Society of America, Universities Coordinating Council (Alberta), Phi Beta Kappa, Chinook Club, University Club (Toronto).

AWARDS, HONORS: Horace H. Rackham fellow, 1961; grants from Canada Council for research on quantified modal logic at Stanford University, 1968-69, and for research on the identity relation at Stanford University, 1971; Humanities Research Council of Canada grant, 1974.

WRITINGS: (Editor with L. W. Sumner) *Necessary Truth,* Random House, 1969; (contributor) M. K. Munitz, editor, *Identity and Individuation,* New York University Press, 1971; (contributor) R. S. Peters, editor, *The Philosophy of Education,* Oxford University Press, 1974; *Logic of Fiction: A Philosophical Sounding of Deviant Logics,* Mouton, 1974; *Proof and Truth: Mathematical Logic for Non-Mathematicians,* Peter

Martin Associates, 1974; *Engineered Death: Abortion, Suicide, Euthanasia, Senecide,* University of Ottawa Press, 1978; (editor with Harold G. Coward) *Humanities in the Present Day,* Wilfred Laurier University Press, 1979.

Also author of *Identity and Modality* (monograph), 1975, co-editor of *Literature and Formal Semantic,* 1979, and co-author of *Argument: The Logic of the Fallacies,* 1981. Contributor of over seventy articles to philosophy and language journals. Co-editor of *Proceedings of the Victorial Conference in Formal Ontology,* 1974; editor of *Dialogue: Canadian Philosophical Review,* 1974-81; member of editorial board of *Philosophical Research Archives* and *Canadian Semantic Research.*

SIDELIGHTS: John Woods writes: "I have long deplored the Canadian characteristic of cultural self-abasement. Determined that something should be done about it, I have taken the not entirely modest corrective of resisting the temptation and opportunity to be Elsewhere. . . . It is no longer true that the best Canadians are expatriate Canadians, and there is now some reason to think that writers in this country can regularly find their way into print without the corporate intervention of New York, London, Bombay, Caracas, or Tierra del Fuego. Still, Canadians must not exchange vapidity for jingoism. There is precious little gain in being insufferable."

AVOCATIONAL INTERESTS: Alpine hiking, cross-country skiing.

*   *   *

WORMSER, Rene A(lbert)   1896-1981

PERSONAL: Born July 17, 1896, in Santa Barbara, Calif.; died July 14, 1981, in Greenwich, Conn.; son of David (a merchant) and Angeline (Boeseke) Wormser; married Ella Madge Ward, August 7, 1945; children: Angele Boeseke, Elissa Ward. *Education:* Columbia University, B.S., 1917, LL.B., 1920. *Politics:* Republican. *Home:* 1 Ginkgo Lane, Greenwich, Conn. 06830.

CAREER: Admitted to Bar of New York State, 1920; attorney in New York City with Hornblower, Miller, Garrison & Potter, 1920-22, Bate, Boyd & Swinnerton, 1923, and in private practice, 1924-30; partner in New York City law firms Wormser & Kemp, 1930-35, Wormser, Morris & Kemp, 1935-37, Folger, Rockwood, Wormser & Kemp, 1937-39, Delaney, Myles & Wormser, 1939-40, Haggerty, Myles & Wormser, 1941-50, Myles, Wormser & Koch, 1950-60, and Wormser, Koch, Kiely & Alessandroni, 1960-71; Wormser, Kiely, Alessandroni, Mahoney & McCann, New York City, senior partner, 1971-81. New York University, member of faculty and planning committee of Federal Tax Institute, 1945-55, lecturer on estate planning, 1948-55; chairman of advanced estate planning panels, Practising Law Institute, 1956-68; University of Miami, chairman of advisory committee, Estate Planning Institute, 1967-81, visiting adjunct professor, Law School, 1973-81. General counsel, U.S. House of Representatives Special Committee to Investigate Tax Exempt Foundations, 1953-54; member of advisory committee on tax exempt organizations, Commissioner of Internal Revenue, 1970-71. Lecturer to bar associations. *Military service:* U.S. Navy, World War I.

MEMBER: American Bar Association, New York State Bar Association, Association of the Bar of the City of New York, Delta Upsilon, University Club and Union League Club (both New York), Belle Haven Club (Greenwich). *Awards, honors:* LL.D., Valparaiso University, 1964, and University of Miami, 1976.

WRITINGS: Your Will and What Not to Do about It, Simon & Schuster, 1937; *Personal Estate Planning in a Changing World,* Simon & Schuster, 1942, 8th revised edition, 1955; *Collection of International War Damage Claims: A Practical Guide for Laymen and Lawyers to the Kinds of War Damage Claims That May Be Brought, the Rules Which Govern Their Allowance, the Methods of Presentation, Proof and Determination, with Particular Regard to the Treatment of Claims after World War II,* Alexander, 1944; *The Theory and Practice of Estate Planning,* Callaghan, 1946, 2nd edition, 1948; *The Law: The Story of Lawmakers and the Law We Have Lived by, from the Earliest Times to the Present Day,* Simon & Schuster, 1949, revised edition published as *The Story of the Law and the Men Who Made It, from the Earliest Times to the Present,* 1962.

The Myth of the Good and Bad Nations, foreword by Raymond Moley, Regnery, 1954; *Foundations: Their Power and Influence,* Devin-Adair, 1958; *Guide to Estate Planning,* Prentice-Hall, 1958; (editor) *The Planning and Administration of Estates,* Practising Law Institute, 1961, 2nd revised edition, 1966; *The Story of Family Estate Planning and How to Apply It to Your Own Personal Problems,* Boston Safe Deposit & Trust Co., 1963.

Wills That Made History, Newkirk Associates, 1973; *Conservatively Speaking: A Review and Analysis of Some of the Major Errors Committed by U.S. Leaders in Shaping the Political and Economic Policies of the U.S. over the Past Six Decades,* Dorland, 1979. Also author of *Family Estate Planning,* 1953, and of brochures on taxes and estate planning. Contributor of articles to periodicals.

WORK IN PROGRESS: Journal articles.

AVOCATIONAL INTERESTS: Painting and wood carving.

OBITUARIES: New York Times, July 15, 1981.†

*   *   *

WORONOFF, Jon   1938-

PERSONAL: Born January 19, 1938, in New York, N.Y.; son of Jules and Sophie (Tabor) Woronoff. *Education:* New York University, B.A., 1959; University of Geneva, Diploma of Interpreters School, 1962, License in Political Science of Graduate Institute of International Studies, 1966. *Home:* 340 East 64th St., New York, N.Y. 10021.

CAREER: Free-lance interpreter and translator for United Nations and other organizations working in Europe, Africa, Asia, and United States, 1962-73; managing director, Interlingua Language Services Ltd., 1973-78; free-lance journalist based in Tokyo, Japan.

WRITINGS: Organizing African Unity, Scarecrow, 1970; *West African Wager,* Scarecrow, 1972; *Japan: The Coming Economic Crisis,* Lotus Press, 1979; *Hong Kong: Capitalist Paradise,* Heinemann, 1980; *Japan: The Coming Social Crisis,* Lotus Press, 1980; *Inside Japan, Inc.,* Lotus Press, 1982; *Japan's Wasted Workers,* Rowman & Allenheld, 1983; *World Trade War,* Praeger, 1983; *Korea's Economy, Man-Made Miracle,* Si-sa-yong-o-sa Publishers, 1983; *Japan's Commercial Empire,* Lotus Press, 1984. Regular contributor to periodicals, including *Asian Business, Modern Asia, Oriental Economist, Japan Economic Journal, South China Morning Post,* and *Mainichi Daily News.*

WORK IN PROGRESS: Studies of the newly industrialized countries of East Asia; studies of the Confucian ethic; comparisons between Asian and American economies and business practices.

* * *

WOSMEK, Frances 1917-
(Frances Brailsford)

PERSONAL: Born December 16, 1917, in Popple, Minn.; daughter of Frank J. (a farmer) and Rebecca (Fenton) Wosmek; married Paul Brailsford, November 18, 1949 (divorced); children: Brian, Robin. *Education:* Attended Wadena Teachers Training College, Wadena, Minn., and Meinzinger's Art School, Detroit, Mich. *Religion:* "Somewhere outside the limitations of any special creed." *Home:* 44 Lexington Ave., Magnolia, Mass. 01930.

CAREER: School teacher in rural Minnesota; designer of greeting cards; also has done layout and advertising art; presently free-lance designer and writer. Teacher of writing classes. *Awards, honors:* Three first prizes for adult short stories; special Edgar Allen Poe Award, Mystery Writers of America, for *Mystery of the Eagle's Claw.*

WRITINGS—Self-illustrated juveniles: Sky High, John Martin's House, 1949; *Twinkle Tot Tales,* Lowe, 1949; *Cuddles and His Friends,* Lowe, 1949; *A Bowl of Sun,* Children's Press, 1976; *The ABC of Ecology,* md Books, 1982; *It's Nice to Be Nice,* Kiddie Products, 1983.

Juveniles: *Little Dog, Little Dog,* Rand McNally, 1963; (under name Frances Brailsford) *In the Space of a Wink,* illustrations by Ati Forberg, Follet, 1969; *Never Mind Murder,* Westminster, 1977; *Mystery of the Eagle's Claw,* Westminster, 1979; *Let's Make Music,* Houghton, 1981.

Illustrator: Edith May Lowe, *Throughout the Day,* John Martin's House, 1949; Rosemary Smith Fitzgerald, *Bobby and Buttons,* Garden City Books, 1949; Josephine Van Dolzen Pease, *One, Two, Cock-a-doodle-do,* Rand McNally, 1950; Helen Earle Gilbert, *Go to Sleep Book,* Rand McNally, 1969.

Has contributed poems to *Christian Science Monitor* and *North Shore Examiner.*

WORK IN PROGRESS: Children's books; designing children's toys and products.

SIDELIGHTS: "My career has been an attempt to be as true to who I am in as honest an expression as I am able," Frances Wosmek told *CA.* "It has not always been easy. Our society believes itself to be a practical one and is impatient with the 'frills.' However, some of us remain convinced that forms of reality are produced and supported from within by the same living spirit that is the source of an artist's inspiration. Science seems about ready to confirm that 'poetry' and pattern are, in the final count, the real reality."

* * *

WRIGHT, J(ohn) Stafford 1905-

PERSONAL: Born February 15, 1905, in Matlock, Derbyshire, England; son of Walter Herbert (a dentist) and Grace (Jackson) Wright; married Sylvia Beatrice Mary Lewis, July 22, 1931; children: Richard Vernon Stafford, Christopher Stafford, John Robert Stafford, Paul Stafford. *Education:* Sidney Sussex College, Cambridge, M.A., 1927. *Politics:* Conservative. *Religion:* Church of England. *Home:* 6 Kensington Pl., Bristol BS8 3AH, England.

CAREER: Ordained clergyman of Church of England, 1928. Tyndale Hall, Bristol, England, tutor, 1930-45, vice-principal, 1930-45; Oak Hill College, London, England, tutor, 1945-51; Tyndale Hall, principal, 1951-69. *Member:* Society for Psychical Research, Victoria Institute, Lundy Field Society. *Awards, honors:* Honorary canon of Bristol Cathedral, 1967.

WRITINGS: The Date of Ezra's Coming to Jerusalem, Tyndale Press, 1946; (with W. S. Hooton) *The First Twenty-Five Years of the Bible Churchmen's Missionary Society,* Bible Churchmen's Missionary Society, 1947; *What Is Man?,* Paternoster Press, 1955, revised edition published as *Mind, Man, and the Spirit,* Zondervan, 1971; (with Oswald Sanders) *Some Modern Religions,* Tyndale Press, 1956; *Building of the Second Temple,* Tyndale Press, 1958.

(Reviser) Alfred Taylor Schofield, *Christian Sanity,* Marshall, Morgan & Scott, 1965; (contributor) C. A. Joyce, editor, *My Call to the Ministry,* Marshall, Morgan & Scott, 1968; *Ezra, Nehemiah, Esther, Job,* Eerdmans, 1968; *Lamentations, Ezekiel, Daniel,* Eerdmans, 1970; (contributor) *Bible Characters and Doctrines,* Eerdmans, 1972; *Christianity and the Occult,* Scripture Union, 1972, revised edition published as *Understanding the Supernatural,* 1977; (with Maurice Burrell) *Some Modern Faiths,* Tyndale Press, 1974; (translator) James S. Gilchrist, *La Mente y lo Desconocido,* Edit Caribe, 1976; (with Burrell) *Whom Then Can We Believe?,* Moody, 1976; *Dictionary of Bible People,* Scripture Union, 1978, published as *Revell's Dictionary of Bible People,* Revell, 1978.

Also author of monographs on the Old Testament, Zen, and spiritualism. Contributor to *Bible Dictionary* and *Bible Commentaries;* contributor of articles and reviews to theological journals.

WORK IN PROGRESS: The Incarnation; children's books.

SIDELIGHTS: J. Stafford Wright told *CA,* "My Christian experience has been basic to my writing in interpreting the Bible." *Avocational interests:* Psychical research, children's books.

BIOGRAPHICAL/CRITICAL SOURCES; C. A. Joyce, editor, *My Call to the Ministry,* Marshall, Morgan & Scott, 1968.

* * *

WRIGHT, Linda Raney 1945-

PERSONAL: Born April 10, 1945, in San Diego, Calif.; daughter of Ralph D. (in U.S. Air Force) and Laura (a nurse; maiden name, Powell) Raney; married Russell Sims Wright (a college lecturer), May 24, 1975. *Education:* University of California, Berkeley, A.B., 1976. *Residence:* Crestline, Calif.

CAREER: Writer and public speaker, 1972—.

WRITINGS: Raising Children, Tyndale, 1975; *Dynamic Sex,* Here's Life Publications, 1979; *Success Helper,* Tyndale, 1980; *How to Unlock the Secret to Love, Sex and Marriage,* Harvest House, 1981. Also author of *Staying on Top When Things Go Wrong,* 1983. Contributor to popular magazines, including *Ladies' Home Journal* and *Decision,* and to religious magazines.

WORK IN PROGRESS: A book on block by block evangelism and one on knowing God.

SIDELIGHTS: Linda Raney Wright comments, "I believe the general public needs to see God's viewpoint on subjects from the Scriptures."

WRIGHTSMAN, Lawrence S(amuel), Jr. 1931-

PERSONAL: Born October 31, 1931, in Houston, Tex.; son of Lawrence Samuel (an engineer) and Vivian (Grove) Wrightsman; married Shirley Fish (a researcher), October 21, 1955 (divorced, March 31, 1977); married Lois Stephenson Niehaus (a social worker), January 1, 1981; children: Allan Jefferson. *Education:* Southern Methodist University, B.A., 1953, M.A., 1954; University of Minnesota, Ph.D., 1959. *Home:* 1625 St. Andrews, Lawrence, Kan. 66044. *Office:* Department of Psychology, University of Kansas, Lawrence, Kan. 66045.

CAREER: Instructor in psychology at University of Minnesota, Minneapolis, 1955-58, and at Hamline University, St. Paul, Minn., 1956; George Peabody College for Teachers, Nashville, Tenn., assistant professor, 1958-61, associate professor, 1961-66, professor of psychology, 1966-76; University of Kansas, Lawrence, professor of psychology, 1976—, chairman of department, 1976-81. Visiting associate professor of psychology, University of Hawaii, 1965-66. *Member:* American Psychological Association, American Association for the Advancement of Science, Society for the Psychological Study of Social Issues.

WRITINGS—All published by Brooks/Cole: (Editor) *Contemporary Issues in Social Psychology,* 1968, 2nd edition (with J. C. Brigham), 1973; (with F. H. Sanford) *Psychology: A Scientific Study of Man,* 3rd edition (Wrightsman was not associated with earlier editions), 1970, 4th edition, 1975; (editor with J. O'Connor and N. J. Baker) *Cooperation and Competition: Readings in Mixed Motive Games,* 1972; *Social Psychology in the Seventies,* 1972, 2nd edition, 1976; *Assumptions about Human Nature: A Social Psychological Analysis,* 1974; (with Kay Deaux) *Social Psychology in the Eighties,* 1981. Contributor to professional journals.

* * *

WYATT, B. D.
See ROBINSON, Spider

Y

YOINGCO, Angel Q. 1921-

PERSONAL: Born September 14, 1921, in Butuan City, Agusan, Philippines; son of Calixto (a businessman) and Alejandra (Quintana) Yoingco; married Fe Torrente (a bank official), December 29, 1943; children: Angel, Jr., Estrella, Ramon, Manuel, David Ricardo. *Education:* Philippine College of Commerce, graduate, 1942; University of the East, B.B.A. (summa cum laude), 1950, M.A. (economics), 1954; Syracuse University, M.A. (public administration), 1953; Centro Escolar University, D.P.A., 1976. *Home:* 171 Don Manuel, Quezon City, Philippines. *Office:* National Tax Research Center, Fourth Floor, BF Condominium, Aduana, Intramuros, Manila, Philippines.

CAREER: University of the East, Manila, Philippines, instructor, 1950-53, assistant professor, 1953-54, associate professor of economics, 1955-64; Lyceum of the Philippines, Manila, Andres Soriano Professor of Economics, 1965—. Executive director of Joint Legislative-Executive Tax Commission, Manila, 1960-72, and National Tax Research Center, 1972—; member of Philippine panel in final negotiation of Philippine-U.S. Tax Treaty, 1964. Lecturer on urban economics and taxation sponsored by Land Reform Training Institute, Taiwan, 1977—, and German Foundation for International Development, 1981—; professor, Asian Tax Program, University of the Philippines, 1980—. Member of board of trustees and consultant to the Graduate School, Lyceum of the Philippines, 1978—; governor and founding member, Asian-Pacific Tax and Investment Research Centre, Singapore, 1982. Delegate (representing the Philippines) and adviser at tax and economic conferences. *Member:* National Research Council of the Philippines, Philippine Statistical Association (founding member), International Institute of Public Finance, Philippine Economic Society, International Fiscal Association.

AWARDS, HONORS: Named most distinguished alumnus by Philippine College of Commerce, 1961, and most distinguished alumnus in government by University of the East, 1962, 1968; Syracuse University distinguished award in public service, 1975; award for outstanding achievement in Philippine taxation, Polytechnic University of the Philippines, 1981; achievement award in research, National Research Council of the Philippines, 1982.

WRITINGS: (With Jose V. Gragasin and Eliodoro G. Robles) *Economic Analysis,* GIC Enterprises (Manila), 1966; (with Ruben F. Trinidad) *Fiscal Systems and Practices in Selected Asian Countries,* Praeger, 1968; (with Eduardo Z. Romualdez and Antonio O. Casem) *Philippine Tax System,* GIC Enterprises, 1970; *Philippine Tax System under the New Society,* GIC Enterprises, 1979; (with Sutadi Sukarya) *A Brief History of the Study Group on Asian Tax Administration and Research,* [Manila], 1980. Also author of *New Individual Income Tax in the Philippines* and *Philippine Agrarian Reform and the New Taxation.* Contributor to periodicals. Managing editor, *Economic Research Journal,* 1954-64; editor, *Lyceum Research Journal,* 1979—.

WORK IN PROGRESS: The New Philippine Public Finance.

SIDELIGHTS: Angel Q. Yoingco describes himself as "a terrible 'workaholic' [who] is most at home when he is searching for ideas that can be developed into tax research studies." For over twenty years he has been director of the agency that studies tax policies of the Philippine government, and his books are products of his experience in tax formulation. In writing them, he aims "to capture in printed form the conflicts, intricacies, and processes in drawing up tax measures."

*   *   *

YOLA, Yerima
See KIRK-GREENE, Anthony (Hamilton Millard)

*   *   *

YOLEN, Jane (Hyatt) 1939-

PERSONAL: Born February 11, 1939, in New York, N.Y.; daughter of Will Hyatt (a public relations man) and Isabelle (Berlin) Yolen; married David W. Stemple (a computer expert), September 2, 1962; children: Heidi Elisabet, Adam Douglas, Jason Frederic. *Education:* Smith College, B.A., 1960; University of Massachusetts, M.Ed., 1976; College of Our Lady of the Elms, Doctor of Laws, 1980. *Politics:* Liberal Democrat. *Religion:* Jewish/Quaker. *Home:* Phoenix Farm, 31 School St., Box 27, Hatfield, Mass. 01038. *Agent:* Marilyn Marlow, Curtis Brown Ltd., 575 Madison Ave., New York, N.Y. 10022.

CAREER: *Saturday Review* (magazine), New York City, production assistant, 1960-61; Gold Medal Books (publishers), New York City, assistant editor, 1961-62; Rutledge Books (publishers), New York City, associate editor, 1962-63; Alfred A. Knopf, Inc. (publishers), New York City, assistant juvenile editor, 1963-65; full-time professional writer, 1965—. Lecturer, Smith College; chairman of board of library trustees, Hatfield, Mass., 1976-83; member of arts council, Hatfield, Mass.

MEMBER: Society of Childrens Book Writers (member of board of directors), Childrens Literature Association, Science Fiction Writers of America, Science Fiction Poetry Association, National Association for the Preservation and Perpetuation of Storytelling, Bay State Writers Guild. *Awards, honors:* Boys Clubs of America award, 1968; *The Emperor and the Kite* was named an American Library Association Notable Book, was chosen as one of the best books of the year by the *New York Times,* and was a Caldecott Honor Book, 1968; Lewis Carroll Shelf Award, 1973, for *The Girl Who Loved the Wind;* Gold Kite Award, Society of Childrens Book Writers, 1974, for *The Girl Who Cried Flowers and Other Tales,* 1975, for *The Transfigured Hart,* and 1976, for *Moon Ribbon and Other Tales; The Girl Who Cried Flowers and Other Tales* was a National Book Award nominee; Christopher Award, 1977, for *The Seeing Stick;* Garden State Children's Book Award for *Commander Toad in Space.*

WRITINGS—Juveniles: *See This Little Line?,* McKay, 1963; *Pirates in Petticoats,* McKay, 1963; *The Witch Who Wasn't,* Macmillan, 1964; *Gwinellen, The Princess Who Could Not Sleep,* Macmillan, 1965; (with Anne Huston) *Trust a City Kid,* Lothrop, 1966; ''Robin Hood'' (play), first produced in Boston, Mass., 1967; *The Emperor and the Kite,* World Publishing, 1967; *The Minstrel and the Mountain,* World Publishing, 1967; *Isabel's Noel,* Funk, 1967; *World on a String: The Story of Kites,* World Publishing, 1968; *Greyling,* World Publishing, 1968; *The Longest Name on the Block,* Funk, 1968; *The Inway Investigators; or, The Mystery at McCracken's Place,* Seabury, 1969; *The Wizard of Washington Square,* World Publishing, 1969; *It All Depends,* Funk, 1969.

The Seventh Mandarin, Seabury, 1970; *Hobo Toad and the Motorcycle Gang,* World Publishing, 1970; *The Bird of Time,* Crowell, 1971; *The Girl Who Loved the Wind,* Crowell, 1972; *Friend: The Story of George Fox and the Quakers,* Seabury, 1972; (editor) *The Fireside Song Book of Birds and Beasts,* Simon & Schuster, 1972; *The Wizard Islands,* Crowell, 1973; (editor) *Zoo 2000: Twelve Stories of Science Fiction and Fantasy Beasts,* Seabury, 1973; *The Adventures of Eeka Mouse,* Xerox Education Publications, 1974; *The Girl Who Cried Flowers and Other Tales,* Crowell, 1974; *The Rainbow Rider,* Crowell, 1974; *The Boy Who Had Wings,* Crowell, 1974; *The Magic Three of Solatia,* Crowell, 1974; *The Little Spotted Fish,* Seabury, 1975; *Ring Out!: A Book of Bells,* Seabury, 1975; *The Transfigured Hart,* Crowell, 1975.

Moon Ribbon and Other Tales, Crowell, 1976; *Milkweed Days,* Crowell, 1976; *Simple Gifts: The Story of the Shakers,* Viking, 1976; (editor) *Shape Shifters: Fantasy and Science Fiction Tales about Humans Who Can Change Their Shapes,* Seabury, 1976; *The Sultan's Perfect Tree,* Parents' Magazine Press, 1977; *The Seeing Stick,* Crowell, 1977; *The Hundredth Dove and Other Tales,* Crowell, 1977; *The Giants' Farm,* Seabury, 1977; *Hannah Dreaming,* Springfield Museum of Art, 1977; (editor) *Rounds about Rounds,* F. Watts, 1977; *An Invitation to the Butterfly Ball,* Parents' Magazine Press, 1977; *The Mer-*

maid's Three Wisdoms, Collins, 1979; *All in the Woodland Early,* Collins, 1979; *Spider Jane,* Coward, 1979; *The Giants Go Camping,* Seabury, 1979; *Dream Weaver,* Philomel, 1979.

No Bath Tonight, Crowell, 1980; *How Beastly!: A Menagerie of Nonsense,* Collins, 1980; *Spider Jane on the Move,* Coward, 1980; *Commander Toad in Space,* Coward, 1980; *Mice on Ice,* Dutton, 1980; *The Robot and Rebecca: The Mystery of the Code-Carrying Kids,* Knopf, 1980; *Dragon Night and Other Lullabies,* Methuen, 1980; *Shirlick Holmes and the Case of the Wandering Wardrobe,* Coward, 1981; *The Gift of Sarah Baker,* Viking, 1981; *The Boy Who Spoke Chimp,* Knopf, 1981; *The Robot and Rebecca: The Missing Owser,* Knopf, 1981; *The Acorn Quest,* Harper, 1981; *Brothers of the Wind,* Philomel, 1981; *Sleeping Ugly,* Coward, 1981; *Uncle Lemon's Spring,* Dutton, 1981; *Commander Toad and the Planet of the Grapes,* Coward, 1982; *Dragon's Blood,* Delacorte, 1982; *Neptune Rising: Songs and Tales of the Undersea Folk,* Putnam, 1982; *Commander Toad and the Big Black Hole,* Coward, 1983; *Children of the Wolf,* Viking, 1984; *Heart's Blood,* Delacorte, 1984.

Adult: *Writing Books for Children,* Writer, Inc., 1973, revised edition, 1982; *Touch Magic: Fantasy, Faerie, and Folklore in the Literature of Childhood,* Philomel, 1981; *Tales of Wonder,* Schocken, 1983.

Contributor: Orson Scott Card, editor, *Dragons of Light,* Ace Books, 1981; Terri Windling and Mark Alan Arnold, editors, *Elsewhere, Volume I,* Ace Books, 1981; Windling and Arnold, editors, *Elsewhere, Volume II,* Ace Books, 1982; Susan Schwartz, editor, *Hecate's Cauldron,* Daw Books, 1982; Jessica Amanda Salmonson, editor, *Heroic Visions,* Ace Books, 1983.

Author of column ''Children's Bookfare,'' *Daily Hampshire Gazette.* Contributor of articles, reviews, poems, and short stories to *Writer, Parabola, New York Times, Horn Book, Magazine of Fantasy and Science Fiction, Isaac Asimov's Science Fiction Magazine, Language Arts,* and other periodicals. Member of editorial board, *Advocate* and *Yarnspinner.*

SIDELIGHTS: Jane Yolen's books for children are usually fantasies involving the familiar characters and situations of fables and folklore, while being told in a gentle, almost musical style which owes much to the oral storytelling tradition. Yolen's books, Jane Langton of the *New York Times Book Review* believes, ''are told with sober strength and native wit. They are simple and perfect, with not a word too much.'' A critic for *Publishers Weekly* sees the hallmarks of Yolen's work as ''deep insights, unhampered imagination, and graceful telling.''

The importance of traditional folklore to Yolen's work lies partly in her conscious desire to rework folklore motifs into contemporary stories. Yolen, writes Selma G. Lanes of the *New York Times Book Review,* ''is uncommonly skilled at using elements from other storytellers and folklorists, transforming them into new and different tales.'' Her story collection *Dream Weaver,* for example, borrows its plots from Greek mythology and the Grimm brothers, although the book, according to Violet H. Harada of *Children's Book Review Service,* ''combines threads of classic folklore with modern strains of psychological insight into a rich tapestry of fantasy.''

Yolen's emphasis on how her stories sound—on whether they can be read aloud successfully—is also related to her interest in folklore and its tradition of oral storytelling. Yolen told *CA:*

"Each word, each sentence, each paragraph in a picture book must be polished. I write a sentence and then read it out loud before going on to the next. Then the paragraph is read aloud. Finally, the entire book is read and reread to the walls, to the bathtub, to the blank television, to my long-suffering husband." The success of this method is attested to by M. R. Singer of *Library Journal*, who finds that *The Girl Who Loved the Wind* has "the polish that usually comes from centuries of telling."

In her book *Touch Magic: Fantasy, Faerie, and Folklore in the Literature of Childhood*, Yolen explores the relationship between traditional folk tales and contemporary children's literature: "Folklore is . . . the perfect guidebook to the human psyche; it leads us to the understanding of the deepest longings and most daring visions of humankind. . . . So when the modern mythmaker, the writer of literary fairy tales, dares to touch the old magic and try to make it work in new ways, it must be done with the surest of touches. . . . Unless the image, character, or situation borrowed speaks to the author's condition, as cryptically and oracularly as a dream, folklore is best left untapped."

BIOGRAPHICAL/CRITICAL SOURCES: Children's Book News, January-February, 1970; *Library Journal*, March 15, 1973; *New York Times Book Review*, May 5, 1974, September 19, 1976, November 20, 1977, January 1, 1978, February 18, 1979, October 28, 1979, May 23, 1982; *Publishers Weekly*, May 7, 1979; *Children's Book Review Service*, September, 1979; *Washington Post Book World*, February 8, 1981; *Children's Literature Review*, Volume IV, Gale, 1982; *Language Arts*, May, 1982; *Chicago Tribune Book World*, November 7, 1982; *Fantasy Newsletter*, September, 1983.

*   *   *

YOUNG, Ian (George) 1945-

PERSONAL: Born January 5, 1945, in London, England; son of George Roland and Joan (Morris) Young. *Education:* Attended Malvern Collegiate Institute, 1957-63, and University of Toronto, 1964-67, 1970-71. *Politics:* Libertarian. *Home and office:* 315 Blantyre Ave., Scarborough, Ontario, Canada M1N 2S6.

CAREER: Writer and publisher. Director of Catalyst Press, 1969-81. *Member:* League of Canadian Poets, Libertarians for Gay Rights. *Awards, honors:* Canada Council awards, 1969, 1972, 1974, 1976; Ontario Arts Council awards, 1970, 1975.

WRITINGS—Poetry collections, except as indicated: *White Garland: 9 Poems for Richard*, Cyclops, 1969; *Year of the Quiet Sun*, Anansi, 1969.

Double Exposure, New Books, 1970, new edition, Crossing Press, 1974; (with Richard Phelan) *Cool Fire: 10 Poems by Ian Young and Richard Phelan*, Catalyst, 1970; (translator) Count Jacques d'Adelsward Fersen, *Curieux d'Amour*, Timothy d'Arch Smith, 1970; (with Phelan) *Lions in the Stream*, Catalyst, 1971; *Some Green Moths*, Catalyst, 1972; (editor) *The Male Muse: A Gay Anthology*, Crossing Press, 1973; *Autumn Angels*, Village Book Store, 1973; *Yuletide Story*, Catalyst, 1973; *Don*, Catalyst, 1973; *Invisible Words*, Missing Link, 1974; *The Male Homosexual in Literature* (bibliography), Scarecrow, 1975, 2nd edition, 1982; *Common-Or-Garden Gods*, Catalyst, 1976; *Alamo*, Dreadnaught Co-operative, 1976; *Whatever Turns You On in the New Year*, Catalyst, 1976.

(Editor) *On the Line: New Gay Fiction*, Crossing Press, 1981; (editor) *Overlooked and Underrated* (essays), Little Caesar Press, 1982; (editor) *The Son of the Male Muse*, Crossing Press, 1983; *Gay Resistance: Homosexuals in the Anti-Nazi Underground* (essays), Crossing Press, 1984.

Work represented in anthologies: *T.O. Now: The Young Toronto Poets*, Anansi, 1968; *Poets of Canada 1969*, Rae-Art, 1969; *Fifteen Winds*, edited by Alred W. Purdy, Ryerson, 1969; *Notes for a Native Land: A New Encounter with Canada*, edited by Andy Wainwright, Oberon Press, 1969.

Printed Matter: An Anthology of Black Moss, edited by Robert Hawkins, Sun Parlor Advertising, 1970; *Storm Warning*, edited by Al Purdy, McClelland & Stewart, 1971; *The Book Cellar Anthology*, edited by Randall Ware, Peter Martin, 1971; *New American and Canadian Poetry*, edited by John Gill, Beacon Press, 1971; *Contemporaries: Twenty-Eight New American Poets*, edited by Jean Malley and Hale Tokay, Viking, 1972; *Voice and Vision*, edited by Jack Hodgins and William H. New, McClelland & Stewart, 1972; *The Speaking Earth*, edited by John Metcalf, Van Nostrand, 1973; *Angels of the Lyre*, edited by Winston Leyland, Panjandrum Books/Gay Sunshine, 1975; *Mirrors*, edited by Jon Pearce, Gage, 1975.

This Is My Best, Coach House, 1976; *Orgasms of Light*, edited by Leyland, Gay Sunshine, 1977; *End of the World Speshul*, edited by bill bissett, blewointmentpress, 1977; *Larkspur and Lad's Love*, edited by Clare MacCulloch, Brandstead Press, 1977; *Gay Source: A Catalog for Men*, edited by Dennis Sanders, Coward, 1977; *The Poets of Canada*, edited by John Robert Colombo, Hurtig, 1978; *Lavender Culture*, edited by Karla Jay and Allen Young, Jove, 1978; *Fire*, edited by Peter Carver, Peter Martin, 1978; *Tributaries*, edited by Barry Dempster, Mosaic Press/Valley Editions, 1978; *To Say the Least: Canadian Poets from A to Z*, edited by P. K. Page, Press Porcepic, 1979; *The New Gay Liberation Book*, edited by Len Richmond and Gary Noguera, Ramparts Press, 1979.

A True Likeness: Lesbian and Gay Writing Today, edited by Felice Picano, Sea Horse Press, 1980; *Flaunting It!: A Decade of Gay Journalism from the Body Politic*, edited by Ed Jackson and Stan Persky, New Star Books/Pink Triangle Press, 1982; *Structure and Meaning*, Houghton, 1983; *The World of the Novel: The Stone Angel*, edited by Lillian Perigoe and Beverley Copping, Prentice-Hall, 1983; *The Penguin Book of Homosexual Verse*, edited by Stephen Coote, Penguin, 1983.

Contributor to *Body Politic*, *Gay News*, *Magasin Gai* (Sweden), and other publications.

WORK IN PROGRESS: Sex/Magick, a collection of poems; two nonfiction books.

SIDELIGHTS: Ian Young once told *CA:* "I write what I call an objectivist poetry (that is, poetry which has as its prime reference an objective reality, an object or event in the material world). What is often referred to as 'irony' in this sort of writing is in fact an unexpected but appropriate and revealing relationship or juxtaposition of things, images, events or states of being, in a taut and meaningful way to illuminate, to bring a subtle and perhaps hidden aspect of a situation or condition, into awareness. This is why I write: to bring into consciousness, to make connections, and thus to gain better control of my reality and to help others gain better control of theirs. When someone tells me a poem of mine has brought something into focus or shown him something that he *almost* knew but couldn't quite 'put his finger on,' I know the poem has been successful for that person: it has caused that personal metamorphosis which art should create.

"Much of my writing and publishing activity has reflected my involvement in the gay liberation and libertarian/anarchist movements. My book publishing company, Catalyst, is especially interested in the work of gay writers and Canadian writers, and we are eager to read manuscripts of all sorts, particularly fiction and poetry."

BIOGRAPHICAL/CRITICAL SOURCES: Vancouver Province, February 7, 1969; *Saturday Night,* February, 1970; *Carleton,* February 6, 1970; *Varsity,* February 6, 1970; *Gay Sunshine,* January/February, 1973; *Advocate,* April 25, 1973; *Margins,* March, 1976; *Books in Canada,* May, 1976; *Quill & Quire,* July, 1976; *Christopher Street,* Volume 1, Number 6, 1976; *Ian Young: A Bibliography, 1962-1980,* Canadian Gay Archives, 1981; *Gay News,* September 3-16, 1982; *Gay Books Bulletin,* fall/winter, 1982.

Z

ZAWODNY, J(anusz) K(azimierz)   1921-

PERSONAL: Born December 11, 1921, in Warsaw, Poland; naturalized American citizen; married La Rae Koppit; children: Roman Janusz. *Education:* London School of Foreign Trade, diploma, 1948; University of Iowa, B.S., 1950, M.A., 1951; Stanford University, Ph.D., 1955, post-doctoral study in psychology, 1958-59. *Home:* 23703 Northeast Margaret Rd., Brush Prairie, Wash. 98606.

CAREER: Princeton University, Princeton, N.J., instructor, 1955-57, assistant professor, 1957-58; University of Pennsylvania, Philadelphia, associate professor of political science, 1962-63; Washington University, St. Louis, Mo., professor, 1963-65; University of Pennsylvania, Wharton School of Finance and Commerce, professor of international relations, 1965-75; Claremont Graduate School and Pomona College, Claremont, Calif., Avery Professor of International Relations, 1975-82. Research associate, Center for International Affairs, Harvard University, 1968; senior associate, St. Antony's College, Oxford University, 1968-69; member of Institute for Advanced Study, Princeton University, 1971-72; member of National Security Council staff, 1979—. Consultant to Office of the President. *Military service:* Polish Underground Forces, 1940-44; became second lieutenant. Second Polish Corps, attached to Eighth British Army, 1945-58; became lieutenant. *Member:* Medicus Association of Doctors of Medicine (life member).

AWARDS, HONORS—Military: Holds orders of Virtuti Militari and Krzyz Walecznych; Grand Officer, Polona Restituta. Civilian: Social Science Research Council fellow, 1953-54; Center for Advanced Study in the Behavioral Sciences fellow, 1962-63; Gold Medal, Medicus Association of Doctors of Medicine, 1980; Jurzykowski Foundation Award and Citation, 1982.

WRITINGS: Death in the Forest: The Story of the Katyn Forest Massacre, University of Notre Dame Press, 1962, reprinted, 1980; *Guide to the Study of International Relations,* Chandler Publishing, 1966; (editor and contributor) *Man and International Relations: Contributions of the Social Sciences to the Study of Conflict and Integration,* two volumes, Chandler Publishing, 1967; *Nothing but Honour: The Story of the Warsaw Uprising, 1944,* Hoover Institution, 1978.

Contributor to *International Encyclopedia of Social Sciences,* and to scholarly journals, including *Annals of American Acad-*emy of Political and Social Science, American Scholar, Soviet Studies,* and *Industrial and Labor Relations Review.*

WORK IN PROGRESS: Cross-cultural study on urban violence.

SIDELIGHTS: A member of the Polish Underground Forces during World War II, J. K. Zawodny has produced what several critics consider to be the definitive accounts of the Katyn Forest Massacre and the Warsaw Uprising of 1944. *Death in the Forest* investigates the mysterious murder and burial of several thousand Polish prisoners (chiefly officers) in the forest of Katyn, near Smolensk. The incident made world headlines in 1943, when the Nazis announced that their troops had discovered the bodies and that the Russians were responsible for the mass slaughter; the Soviets, however, claimed it was the work of the Germans. "While numerous studies have been made of this subject, including an extensive inquiry by the U.S. House of Representatives," writes H. L. Roberts in the *New York Times Book Review,* "Zawodny has done a laudable job of tracking down the considerable but scattered evidence . . . , evaluating it, and presenting with remarkable restraint and balance the conclusions he has drawn."

Reviewing *Death in the Forest* in *Annals of American Academy of Political and Social Science,* Simon Wolin points out that Zawodny realizes, "as have earlier students of the case, that both Germany and the Soviet Union might have been prompted by the same motive: the desire to exterminate Polish intellectuals, who constituted the majority of the officer corps and were the potential leaders of a Polish fight for independence." Nevertheless, Wolin believes Zawodny's presentation and analysis of the material "proves Soviet guilt," and H. C. Wolfe concurs in *Saturday Review:* "Scrupulously sifting every shred of available evidence from far-flung sources, interviewing numerous survivors of Polish prison camps in Russia, and weaving a tortuous way through tangled wartime politics and propaganda, Dr. Zawodny pieced together a mosaic of facts that shaped themselves into a finger of accusation." Wolfe concludes that *Death in the Forest* will remain the definitive work on the subject "unless additional information is revealed some day from Moscow's secret files."

Nothing but Honour deals with the attempt by the Polish Home Army (Armia Krajowa) in August, 1944 to capture Warsaw from the Nazis before the advancing Soviet troops could take control. The insurrection, in which Zawodny participated as a platoon commander, was aimed militarily against the Germans and politically against the Soviets and Polish Communists, who wished to ally postwar Poland with Moscow. The Polish Home Army gambled that a free Warsaw would provide an opportunity for the establishment of an administration loyal to the exiled government in London, thereby forcing Stalin to risk alienating Anglo-American opinion by setting up a puppet regime. The Uprising failed miserably, however, for lack of Russo-Polish military cooperation and substantial air support from the West. Over 200,000 of the city's inhabitants were killed, 800,000 were exiled, and Warsaw itself was reduced to rubble.

A *Choice* reviewer remarks that in *Nothing but Honour,* "Zawodny has once again written the definitive account of a crucial event in World War II. Many studies of the uprising have appeared; Zawodny's . . . encompasses them all." An *Economist* critic says Zawodny tells the story "with scrupulous care to be just to everybody. He tells it as fairly as it can be told by anyone who was himself a platoon commander in the rising and who is now a professor in the United States."

In the *Times Literary Supplement,* Jan M. Ciechanowski singles out those parts of the book where Zawodny "writes not only as an historian but also as a veteran. . . . He knows well from his personal experiences what efforts and sacrifices were needed from the badly armed insurgents to withstand constant German attacks for more than sixty days. He knows a great deal about the ordeal of civilians, who suffered even more than the soldiers." Ciechanowski, however sees one weakness in the book: "The examination of political and ideological background which Zawodny has regrettably decided to eschew would not only have helped to illuminate the initial call to insurrection but would have continued to throw fuller light on the decision taken during the rising's course. His account does not make it clear that the authors of the insurrection were guided in all that they did by the doctrine of two enemies." Nonetheless, Ciechanowski believes Zawodny "has produced a useful contribution for students of [the Uprising's] history, by giving us a clear account of its actual course."

BIOGRAPHICAL/CRITICAL SOURCES: New York Times Book Review, November 18, 1962; *Saturday Review,* November 24, 1962; *Annals of American Academy of Political and Social Science,* September, 1963; *Economist,* April 22, 1978; *Times Literary Supplement,* July 28, 1978; *Choice,* November, 1978.